LAND LAW

LAND LAW

Text, Cases, and Materials

FOURTH EDITION

Ben McFarlane, Nicholas Hopkins,
and Sarah Nield

OXFORD

UNIVERSITY PRESS

OXFORD
UNIVERSITY PRESS

Great Clarendon Street, Oxford, OX2 6DP,
United Kingdom

Oxford University Press is a department of the University of Oxford.
It furthers the University's objective of excellence in research, scholarship,
and education by publishing worldwide. Oxford is a registered trade mark of
Oxford University Press in the UK and in certain other countries

First edition 2009
Second edition 2012
Third edition 2015
Impression: 2

Published in the United States of America by Oxford University Press
198 Madison Avenue, New York, NY 10016, United States of America

British Library Cataloguing in Publication Data
Data available

Library of Congress Control Number: 2018932227

ISBN 978–0–19–880606–6

Printed in Great Britain by
Bell & Bain Ltd., Glasgow

PREFACE TO THE FOURTH EDITION

We are pleased that our book has received such a positive reception from land law students and teachers alike. This new edition has provided an opportunity to incorporate their feedback as well as changes in the key areas of land law. These changes demonstrate that land law continues to be a vibrant subject that must deal with the constant challenges presented by our relationship to land as a unique form of property.

The third edition included a reorganized treatment of Land Registration, and we have been able to use that structure to consider not only important judicial developments in the law, such as the Court of Appeal's decision in *Swift 1st Ltd v Chief Land Registrar*, but also the suggestions made by the Law Commission in its 2016 Consultation Paper on Updating the Land Registration Act 2002, examined in a re-written Chapter 18. As for the structure of this new edition, we have benefitted greatly from the experience of producing a new *Core Text* in Land Law. First, we have moved our treatment of licences to Chapter 7, where they are examined as the key example of a personal right relating to land. Second, we have incorporated discussion of the doctrine of anticipation in Chapter 8, as part of the wider discussion of the stages of a conveyance of a legal estate, and have moved the discussion of overreaching to Chapter 17, so it now takes its place in Part E, which focusses on priorities and the defences question. Third, the chapters on Priorities in Unregistered Land and on Successive Ownership, updated of course to take account of any relevant new material, are now available only online. We have also switched the order of Chapters 26 and 27 so that our consideration of Lender's Rights and Remedies precedes the Protection of the Borrower. Overall, this means that the book, whilst of course functioning as a stand-alone text in itself, can also easily be used alongside the *Core Text*. Moreover, it means that we have been able to reduce the overall length of the published book whilst still providing full coverage of key developments.

Those key developments incorporated in this edition include, in Chapter 9, the Court of Appeal's decision in *Best v Chief Land Registrar* (and the ensuing related decision of the First Tier Tribunal) on the impact on adverse possession of the criminalization of squatting in a residential building; in Chapters 5, 8, 16, and 17, the difficult case of *Baker v Craggs*, which raises a number of issues relating to the definition of a legal estate, the 'registration gap', and overreaching (at time of writing, an appeal from that first instance decision was pending, and updates will be provided as part of the book's online resources); and in Chapters 11 and 12, the Privy Council's decision in *Marr v Collie*, which is the latest judicial attempt in the ongoing quest to understand the nature and scope of trusts of the family home. Chapter 4 also considers the important decision of *McDonald v McDonald* on horizontal effect of human rights in the private rental context, although for the time being we have retained in individual chapters our thoughts of the possibly horizontal impact of human rights in other areas. Court of Appeal decisions in *Davies v Davies* (proprietary estoppel), *Mortgage Express v Lambert* (overreaching), and *Regency Villas Title Ltd v Diamond Resorts Ltd* (recreational easements) are discussed in Chapters 10, 17, and 22 respectively. The controversial view of that court as to priorities in *Wishart v Credit and Mercantile plc* is considered in Chapter 15. This is to name just a few examples of the new cases considered. Of course, developments in the law do not come just from the cases, and in Chapter 20, for example, we note the potential significance of the Renting Homes (Wales) Act 2016. Chapter 24 on Flat Ownership may also become more prominent in the light of current proposals to revive and possibly reform commonhold. As in the past three editions, we have also strived to include some of the excellent academic commentary that has accompanied these developments, to show how issues in land law can generate differing opinions and arguments.

Whilst all three of us were closely involved in the planning and structuring of the new edition, Nick Hopkins has taken a break from writing this book in order to focus on his work as Law Commissioner. As will be clear from the book, Nick's work still forms the basis of many of the chapters, but the revision and updating work has been divided between Ben and Sarah, with Ben responsible for Chapters 1–3, 5–11, 15–16, and 18–20, and Sarah for Chapters 4, 12–14, 17, and 21–27.

All three of us remain enormously grateful to colleagues, friends, and the staff at OUP who have guided us in the writing and publication of each edition and particularly this fourth edition. The comments of anonymous referees have been invaluable in shaping the content and focus of each edition. We wish again to pay tribute to Professor John Mee, Amy Goymour, Professor David Clarke, and Peter Smith whose comments on previous editions continue to be influential as the book evolves. The value of Rupert Seal's and Ruth Hudson's development of the online resources has been significant and enduring. Sarah is grateful for the invaluable comments of Dr Nick Roberts on Chapter 24: Flat Ownership, and Ben thanks Orestis Sherman, who assisted in collecting materials and also provided helpful comments on draft chapters. A special thank you must go to key people within OUP and particularly our Publishing and Production Editors, Felicity Boughton and Alec Swann respectively. They have worked tirelessly to support us in the writing of this edition and to ensure that its production has been seamless.

Ben McFarlane; Nicholas Hopkins; Sarah Nield
January 2018

Nick Hopkins is the Property, Family and Trusts Law Commissioner for England and Wales, but nothing in this work should be taken as representing the views of the Law Commission.

LATE NEWS

At a number of points in the book, we consider issues arising from the first instance decision in *Baker v Craggs* [2016] EWHC 3250 (Ch) and note that an appeal from Newey J's somewhat controversial decision is in progress. The facts of the case are summarized in Chapter 8, section 6.5.1. In a judgment handed down on 18 May 2018, just before this book went to press, the Court of Appeal reversed the finding of Newey J on the specific point of what the term 'legal estate in land' means when used, by s 2 of the Law of Property Act 1925 (LPA 1925), to set the scope of the overreaching defence. This meant that the Bakers, who had been granted a legal easement over particular land by the Charltons, could not use the overreaching defence against the pre-existing equitable interest that Mr Craggs had in that same land. That was because the Court of Appeal, reversing Newey J, held that a legal easement does not count, for the purposes of s 2, as a 'legal estate in land'.

The Court of Appeal's decision is therefore relevant to the discussion in Chapter 5, section 6.2, of the distinction between a legal estate and a legal interest. We note there that s 1(4) of the LPA 1925 (reflected also in the general definitions in section 205(1)(x)) states that the 'estates, interests and charges' that can exist at law are referred to in the LPA 1925 as 'legal estates': this means that there must be at least some sections of the LPA 1925 where the term 'legal estate' is used in such a way as to include a legal interest such as an easement. The point made by the Court of Appeal, however, is that s 2 of the LPA 1925 limits the scope of overreaching to cases where a party acquires a 'legal estate in land'; and s 1(1) of the LPA 1925 makes clear that only a freehold or a lease can count as a 'legal estate in land'. So as the Bakers had acquired a legal easement, they could not use the overreaching defence: whilst an easement can count as a 'legal estate' for the purposes of s 1(4), it cannot count as a 'legal estate *in land*' for the purposes of s 2. This is a very good example of the point that, in land law, statutes are important and must be interpreted very carefully! The fact that s 1(4) includes both the legal estates in land set out in s 1(1) and the legal interests and charges, included easements, set out in s 1(2) within the term 'legal estates' for the purposes of the statute does not alter the fundamental framework found in ss 1(1) and 1(2). It merely reflects a convenient drafting shorthand. The Court of Appeal in giving its reasons also referred to the challenge, presented by the High Court's decision, to the concept of overreaching as a compensatory device to shift the beneficial interest to the proceeds of sale (if any).

The Court of Appeal's decision is therefore also relevant to the discussion in Chapter 17, section 2.3, of overreaching. We note there that it was quite a surprise that Newey J's decision allowed the grant of a legal easement to have an overreaching effect. The Court of Appeal confirms that, for overreaching to occur, a party must acquire a legal freehold, a legal lease, or a legal charge. The first of those two rights are defined as legal estates in land by s 1(1) of the LPA 1925 (see Chapter 5, section 3) and a legal charge suffices because of section 87 of the LPA 1925. As we note in Chapter 25, section 4.2, s 87 confers on a legal chargee all the same protections as if they held a mortgage created by way of sub-demise: that is by the creation of a lease.

We also consider the first instance decision in *Baker v Craggs* at various points in Chapter 8 (section 4.3, on the definition of an 'estate contract'; section 5.1 on the effect of completion of a contract for the sale of land; and section 6.5.1 on the registration gap). Newey J's views on those points did not need to be considered by the Court of Appeal, given its view on the interpretation of s 2 of the LPA 1925. The Court of Appeal's decision that the Bakers could not use the overreaching defence meant that the 'registration gap' did not in fact cause a problem to Craggs on the facts of the case; but as noted in Chapter 8, section 6.5.1, the gap may cause a problem where a different defence can be used against a pre-existing equitable interest.

The key paragraphs from the judgment of Henderson LJ, with whom Flax and Patten LJJ agreed, are set out here.

Baker v Craggs [2018] EWCA Civ 1126

Henderson LJ

[5]

Since the judge below was a very experienced Chancery judge (Newey J, now Newey LJ), the argument clearly merits careful consideration, although it was only one of several issues of fact and law which he had to determine (and no appeal is brought by either side in relation to any of those other issues). Nevertheless, with the greatest respect to the judge I have to say that his conclusion on this one point was in my view unsustainable. That is so for a number of reasons, of which the simplest is that section 2(1) of LPA 1925 applies only upon a conveyance to a purchaser 'of a legal estate in land', and although an easement is capable of being a 'legal estate' in the nomenclature of LPA 1925, it is not 'a legal estate in land'. By virtue of section 1(1) of LPA 1925, indeed the opening subsection of the entire Act:

'The only estates in land which are capable of subsisting or of being conveyed or created at law are —

(a) An estate in fee simple absolute in possession;

(b) A term of years absolute.'

[25]–[32]

... By virtue of section 1(4), the two estates in land referred to in subsection (1), and the interests or charges in or over land which are itemised in subsection (2), are together defined as 'legal estates', and that definition is reflected in section 205(1)(x) [of the LPA 1925]. By contrast, all other estates, interests, and charges in or over land take effect as equitable interests: see section 1(3), and (again) section 205(1)(x).

This is the carefully constructed conceptual framework within which the overreaching provisions in section 2(1) of LPA 1925 have to be placed. The opening words of the section confine its operation to cases where there is '[a] conveyance to a purchaser of a legal estate in land'. Section 1(1) has just taught us that the only legal estates in land which are capable of subsisting, or of being conveyed or created, are an estate in fee simple absolute in possession and a term of years absolute. Accordingly, it would seem to follow that the doctrine of overreaching can only apply where such an estate in land is conveyed to a purchaser. The grant of an easement to a purchaser of land is not a conveyance of a legal estate in land within the meaning of section 1(1). Rather, it is the grant of an interest over land which, if it is granted for an interest equivalent to an estate in fee simple absolute in possession or a term of years absolute, is the grant of a 'legal estate' within the meaning of subsections (2) and (4) . . ..

The reference to a conveyance to a purchaser 'of a legal estate in land', in section 2(1), is naturally read as a reference to a conveyance of one of the two types of estate in land which section 1(1) has just told us are capable of being conveyed at law. If the draftsman (Sir Benjamin Cherry) had intended section 2 to extend to the grant of a legal easement, he would surely have made this clear. . . .

For these short reasons, therefore, I am satisfied that the judge was wrong to conclude that the grant of the easement over the yard by the Charltons to the Bakers was capable of engaging the overreaching provisions in section 2(1), because it was not a conveyance to a purchaser of 'a legal estate in land' within the meaning of the section. This conclusion is in my view reinforced by some of the conceptual difficulties to which the judge's analysis would give rise. On the assumption that section 2(1) did apply, its effect would be to overreach 'any equitable interest . . . affecting that estate', which would have to mean an equitable interest in the legal estate conveyed to the purchaser, namely the easement itself. But the easement had no prior existence before it was granted by the Charltons, and the equitable interest which Mr Craggs had was his beneficial interest in the servient tenement under the bare trust arising on completion of his purchase, not an equitable interest of any description in or over the land sold to the Bakers.

This leads me on to what I would regard as the second main objection to the judge's analysis, namely the conceptual impossibility of identifying any part of the proceeds of sale of the land sold to the Bakers to which Mr Craggs' equitable interest could somehow have attached once it had been overreached. Overreaching occurs where the relevant proceeds of sale or capital money are paid to at least two individual trustees or a trust corporation, typically in accordance with the requirements of section 27 of LPA 1925 (quoted above). But in the present case, as I have explained, Mr Craggs had no prior equitable interest in the subject matter of the relevant conveyance, namely the grant of the easement itself to the Bakers, he was not a party to the sale to the Bakers, nor was there any apportionment of the proceeds of sale paid by the Bakers to the Charltons. To my mind, Mr Talbot-Ponsonby had no remotely convincing answer to the problem of how Mr Craggs' equitable interest in the yard as part of the servient tenement could somehow be translated into an interest in part of the purchase price of the different land (the dominant tenement) sold by the Charltons to the Bakers. This point was not explored at all by the judge in his judgment, but in my view it provides another convincing reason for holding that his approach was flawed.

ACKNOWLEDGEMENTS

Grateful acknowledgement is made to all the authors and publishers of copyright material which appears in this book, and in particular to the following for permission to reprint material from the sources indicated:

Crown copyright material is reproduced under Class Licence Number C2006010631 with the permission of the Controller of OPSI and the Queen's Printer for Scotland. Parliamentary copyright material is reproduced with the permission of the Controller of Her Majesty's Stationery Office on behalf of Parliament.

Bloomsbury Publishing Plc: for extracts from Hart Publishing (an imprint of Bloomsbury Publishing Plc.): S Bright: *Landlord and Tenant Law in Context* (Hart, 2007); Gardener & MacKenzie: *An Introduction to Land Law* (Hart, 2015); McFarlane: *The Structure of Property Law* (Hart, 2008); and from *Modern Studies of Property Law*: S Nield: 'Proportionality and the Vindication of Property Rights' (Volume 9, 2017) and P O'Connor: 'Registration of Title in England and Australia' (Volume 2, 2003).

Cambridge University Press and the authors: for extracts from A Clarke and P Kohler: *Property Law: Commentary and Materials* (CUP, 2005); extracts from *Cambridge Law Journal*: S Bright: 'Avoiding Tenancy Legislation: Sham and Contracting Out Revisited', CLJ 146 (2002); Lord D Neuberger of Abbotsbury: 'The Stuffing of Minerva's Owl? Taxonomy and Taxidermy in Equity' Vol. 68, No. 3 CLJ 537 (2009); and extracts from Legal Studies: J Hill: 'Intention and the Creation of Proprietary Rights: Are Leases Different?' Vol. 16, No. 2 LS (1996); B Sloan: 'Keeping up with the Jones case: Establishing constructive trusts in "sole legal owner" scenarios' Vol. 35, No. 2 LS (2015) Reproduced with permission.

Financial Conduct Authority: for an extract from the FSA Handbook.

Incorporated Council of Law Reporting: for extracts from the Law Reports: *Appeal Cases* (AC), *Chancery Division* (Ch), *Family Division* (Fam), *King's Bench Division* (KB), *Law Reports* (LR App Cas), *Queen's Bench Division* (QB), and *Weekly Law Reports* (WLR).

Jeffrey Hackney: for extract from J Hackney: *Understanding Equity and Trusts* (Fontana Press, 1987).

RELX (UK) Limited, trading as LexisNexis: for extracts from *All England Law Reports* (All ER) and *Family Law Reports* (FLR). Reproduced by permission of RELX (UK) Limited, trading as LexisNexis

Oxford University Press: for extracts from P Birks: 'Before We Begin: Five Keys to Land Law' in Bright and Dewar (eds) *Land Law: Themes and Perspectives* (OUP, 1998); Gray & Gray: *Elements of Land Law*, 5th edition (OUP, 2009); B McFarlane and E Simpson: 'Tackling Avoidance' in J. Getzler (ed) *Rationalizing Property, Equity and Trusts: Essays in Honour of Edward Burn* (OUP, 2003); Harris: *Property and Justice* (OUP, 1996); and for extracts from *Oxford Journal of Legal Studies*: A Burrows: 'We do this at Common Law but that in Equity' 22 OJLS 1 (2002). By permission of Oxford University Press.

Palgrave Macmilllan: for extracts from D Cowan, L Fox O'Mahony, and N Cobb: *Great Debates in Property Law*, 1st edition (Palgrave, 2012). Reproduced with permission of Palgrave Macmillan.

Reed Business Information: for an extract from case reports published in *Estates Gazette* and *Estates Gazette Law Reports* (http://www.egi.co.uk).

Sweet & Maxwell: for extracts from *Law Quarterly Review*: S Bright: 'Leases, Exclusive Possession and Estates' 116 LQR 7 (2000) and S Gardner: 'The Remedial Discretion in Proprietary Estoppel—Again' 122 LQR 492 (2006); for extracts from *The Conveyancer and Property Lawyer*: B McFarlane: 'Identifying Property Rights: A Reply to Mr Watt' Conv 473, 475 (2003); K Loi: 'Receiver's Power of Sale and Duty of Care' Cov 369 (2010); A Robertson: 'The Reliance Basis of Proprietary Estoppel Remedies' Conv 295, 300–3 (2008); and L Tee: 'Severance Revisited' Conv 105–6, 110–13 (1995); extracts from *Property, Planning and Compensation Reports* (P & CR) and extracts from *European Human Rights Reports* (EHRR). All Sweet & Maxwell publications reproduced with permission of the Licensor through PLSclear.

Taylor & Francis Books UK: for extracts from S Bridge: 'Leases: Contract, Property and Status'; K Gray: 'Land Law and Human Rights'; and R Smith: 'The Role of Registration in Modern Land Law' all in L Tee (ed): *Land Law: Issues, Debates, Policy* (Willan, 2002). Reproduced by permission of Taylor & Francis Books UK.

Thomson Reuters: for extract from L Smith: 'Fusion and Tradition' in S Degeling and J Edelman (eds): *Equity in Commercial Law* (Lawbook Co, 2005). Reproduced with permission of Thomson Reuters (Professional) Australia Limited, www.thomsonreuters.com.au.

Every effort has been made to trace and contact copyright holders prior to publication but this has not been possible in every case. If notified, the publisher will undertake to rectify any errors or omissions at the earliest opportunity.

GUIDE TO USING THE ONLINE RESOURCES

This book is accompanied by online resources on an open-access website designed to support the book. The website can be found at: www.oup.com/uk/mcfarlane4e/

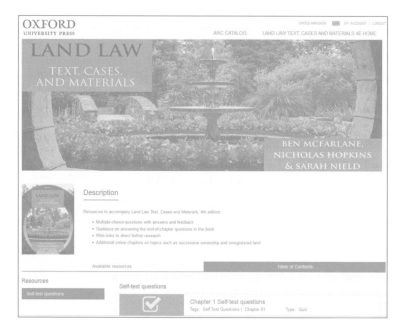

The online resources that accompany this book provides students with ready-to-use learning materials. These materials are free of charge and are designed to maximize your learning experience.

Guidance on answering the end-of-chapter questions

Each chapter of the book contains self-test questions to help you test your knowledge and practise your written assessment skills. Prepare your own answer, and then read the authors' advice on what an exemplary answer should include.

Multiple-choice questions

Use these questions to test your knowledge of the law covered within each chapter of the textbook. Immediate feedback on your answers makes it easy for you to assess your level of understanding.

Additional materials

The authors include extra coverage on adverse possession, successive ownership, and unregistered land to help you gain a more rounded understanding.

Web links

The author has carefully selected web links to direct you to the most useful and reliable online information, allowing you to be focused and efficient with your research.

Updates

Regular legal updates provide easy access to changes in the law so that your study is as timely and relevant as possible.

OUTLINE CONTENTS

PART A INTRODUCTION

  1 What's Special about Land?   2

  2 What is Land?   25

  3 Registration   58

PART B THE CONTENT QUESTION

  4 Human Rights and Land   87

  5 Legal Estates and Legal Interests   154

  6 Equitable Interests   179

  7 Personal Rights: Licences   204

PART C THE ACQUISITION QUESTION

  8 Formal Methods of Acquisition: Contracts, Deeds, and Registration   259

  9 Adverse Possession   309

  10 Proprietary Estoppel   359

  11 Trusts   417

PART D THE SHARED HOME

  12 Interests in the Home: The Acquisition Question   454

  13 Regulating Co-ownership: The Content Question   503

  14 Co-ownership and Third Parties: Applications for Sale   549

PART E PRIORITY—THE DEFENCES QUESTION AND LAND REGISTRATION

  15 The Priority Triangle   578

  16 Priorities in Registered Land   607

  17 Co-ownership and Priorities: The Defences Question   648

  18 Reform of the Land Registration Act 2002   693

PART F LEASES

19 Leases   728

20 Regulating Leases and Protecting Occupiers   806

21 Leasehold Covenants   832

PART G NEIGHBOURS AND NEIGHBOURHOODS

22 Easements   885

23 Freehold Covenants   957

24 Flat Ownership: Long Leases and Commonhold   1008

PART H SECURITY RIGHTS

25 Security Interests in Land   1032

26 Lender's Rights and Remedies   1064

27 Protection of the Borrower   1116

CONTENTS

Table of Cases	*xxxi*
Table of Statutes	*li*
List of Abbreviations	*lix*

PART A   INTRODUCTION

1   WHAT'S SPECIAL ABOUT LAND?   2

1 The Importance of Land	2
2 The Scope of this Book	3
3 Three Underlying Questions	6
4 The Special Features of Land	7
5 Land Law in Practice: An Example	11
5.1 The Facts of the Case and the Dilemma	11
5.2 Two Possible Approaches	13
5.3 The Court of Appeal's Approach in *Ainsworth*	14
5.4 The House of Lords' Approach in *Ainsworth*	17
5.5 Comparing the Approaches of the Court of Appeal and the House of Lords	19
5.6 Developments after *Ainsworth*: Rights of Occupation	20
5.7 Developments after *Ainsworth*: Property Rights in the Family Home	21
6 Conclusion	22

2   WHAT IS LAND?   25

1 Land as a Form of Private Property	25
2 The Meaning of 'Land'	30
2.1 The Physical Reach of Land	30
2.2 What Objects does the Land Include?	38

3   REGISTRATION   58

1 The Distinction between Registered and Unregistered Land	59
2 Registration Systems and Land Law	60
2.1 Registration Systems: General Aims	60
2.2 Registration and Land Law	61

2.3 Registration of Title and Purchaser Protection   62
2.4 The Choices to be made by a Registration System   64
2.5 Three Basic Principles   66

3 The Basic Scheme of the LRA 2002   67
3.1 The Aims of the LRA 2002   67
3.2 The Protection of Registered Parties   70
3.3 Looking Outside the Registration System   79

PART B: THE CONTENT QUESTION

4 HUMAN RIGHTS AND LAND   87

1 Introduction   88

2 Adjudication under the Human Rights Act 1998   89
2.1 The Court's Duties under the HRA 1998   90
2.2 Qualified Rights and the Justification Formula   92
2.3 Vertical Effect   101
2.4 Horizontal Effect   106

3 Article 1 of the First Protocol to the ECHR   113
3.1 When is Article 1 Engaged?   115
3.2 When is an Interference Justified?   120

4 Article 8: The Right to Respect for Private and Family Life and the Home   127
4.1 When is Article 8(1) Engaged?   127
4.2 When is an Interference Justified under Article 8(2)?   131

5 The Impact of Human Rights   150

5 LEGAL ESTATES AND LEGAL INTERESTS   154

1 The Concept of a Property Right   155

2 The Concept of a Legal Estate in Land   160

3 Legal Estates in Land: The *Content* Question   163
3.1 The Content of a Legal Freehold   165
3.2 The Content of a Legal Lease   167
3.3 Why Only Two Legal Estates in Land?   167

4 Legal Estates in Land: The *Acquisition* Question   169

5 The Concept of a Legal Interest in Land   169

6 Legal Interests in Land: The *Content* Question   170
6.1 The *Numerus Clausus* Principle   170
6.2 A Reminder: The Effect of Section 1(4) of the LPA 1925   173

7   Legal Interests in Land: The *Acquisition* Question   175

8   Conclusion   176

6 EQUITABLE INTERESTS   179

1   Equity and Equitable Property Rights   180
    1.1   The Function of Equity   180
    1.2   The Development of Equitable Property Rights   181

2   The Concept of an Equitable Interest in Land   184

3   Rights under Trusts: The *Content* Question   185

4   Rights under Trusts: The *Acquisition* Question   188

5   Other Equitable Interests: The *Content* Question   189
    5.1   A Longer List of Property Rights   189
    5.2   The List of Equitable Interests   189
    5.3   Limiting the Content of Equitable Interests   191

6   Other Equitable Interests: The *Acquisition* Question   193

7   The Relationship between Common Law and Equity   194

7 PERSONAL RIGHTS: LICENCES   204

1   The Concept of a Personal Right and the Nature of a Licence   205
    1.1   The Distinction between Property Rights and Personal Rights   205
    1.2   Two Warnings   205
    1.3   The Concept of a Licence   207

2   Bare Licences   209
    2.1   B's Rights Against A   209
    2.2   B's Rights Against X   210
    2.3   B's Rights Against C   210

3   Contractual Licences   211
    3.1   B's Rights Against A   213
    3.2   B's Rights Against X   218
    3.3   B's Rights Against C   222

4   Estoppel Licences   245
    4.1   B's Rights Against A   246
    4.2   B's Rights Against X   247
    4.3   B's Rights Against C   248

5   Statutory Licences   250
    5.1   B's Rights Against A   251
    5.2   B's Rights Against X   252
    5.3   B's Rights Against C   252

6   Licences Coupled with an Interest   253

    6.1   B's Rights Against A   254

    6.2   B's Rights Against X   255

    6.3   B's Rights Against C   256

PART C   THE ACQUISITION QUESTION

8   FORMAL METHODS OF ACQUISITION: CONTRACTS, DEEDS, AND REGISTRATION   259

1   Introduction   260

2   Formality Requirements for the Creation or Transfer of Legal Estates and Interests   262

3   Contract   263

    3.1   Section 2 of the 1989 Act   263

    3.2   When Does Section 2 Apply?   266

    3.3   The Concept of an Exchange   268

    3.4   The Requirement of a Signature   269

    3.5   Executed Contracts   271

    3.6   Collateral Contracts   272

    3.7   Rectification of a Contractual Document   275

    3.8   Proprietary Estoppel and Constructive Trusts   277

4   The Effect of a Contract   284

    4.1   The Requirements of the Doctrine of Anticipation   284

    4.2   The Nature of B's Interest   286

    4.3   Estate Contracts   287

    4.4   Does B have a Power to Create Property Rights in Others?   288

5   Completion: Disposition by Transfer or Grant   289

    5.1   The Effect of Completion   290

    5.2   The Requirements of a Deed   293

6   Registration of Title   295

    6.1   Registration and the Acquisition Question   295

    6.2   First Registration: Dealings with Unregistered Land   295

    6.3   Grades of Title   297

    6.4   Dealings with Registered Land   297

    6.5   The Registration Gap   298

    6.6   The Effect of Registration   306

    6.7   Outline of a Registered Title   306

9 ADVERSE POSSESSION 309

1 Introduction 310

2 Is Adverse Possession Justified? 311

3 An Outline of the Operation of Adverse Possession 313

4 The Inception of Adverse Possession 314
  4.1 'Adverse' Possession Defined 316
  4.2 'Possession' Defined 319
  4.3 Termination of Adverse Possession 326

5 The Effect of Adverse Possession 333
  5.1 Unregistered Land 333
  5.2 Registered Land: Land Registration Act 1925 334
  5.3 Registered Land: Land Registration Act 2002 336

6 Adverse Possession and the Criminalization of Residential Squatting 344
  6.1 The Offence of Squatting in a Residential Building 345
  6.2 The Impact of the Offence on Adverse Possession 346
  6.3 The Outcome in the *Best* Litigation 349
  6.4 Evaluating the Outcome in the *Best* Litigation 351

7 Human Rights and Adverse Possession 352

8 Conclusion 356

10 PROPRIETARY ESTOPPEL 359

1 Introduction: The Nature of Proprietary Estoppel 360
  1.1 Proprietary Estoppel in Practice 360
  1.2 Forms of Proprietary Estoppel 365

2 The Requirements of Proprietary Estoppel 369
  2.1 An Assurance by A 370
  2.2 Reliance by B 382
  2.3 The Prospect of Detriment to B 386
  2.4 The Role of Unconscionability 389

3 The Extent of A's Liability to B: Remedying a Proprietary Estoppel 395
  3.1 The Current Position 395
  3.2 The First Approach: B's Expectation as a Starting Point 404
  3.3 The Second Approach: Detriment as the Key Factor 406
  3.4 A Further Approach: Proportionality to Both Expectation and Detriment 409

4 The Effect of Proprietary Estoppel on a Third Party: Priority and the Defences Question 410
  4.1 Introduction 410
  4.2 B's Position *After* a Court Order in His or Her Favour 411
  4.3 B's Position *Before* a Court Order in His or Her Favour 411

11 TRUSTS 417

1 Introduction 418

2 Express Trusts 420

3 Resulting Trusts 421
   3.1 The Purchase Money Resulting Trust 423
   3.2 The Scope of the Purchase Money Resulting Trust 429

4 Constructive Trusts 434
   4.1 Institutional and Remedial Constructive Trusts 435
   4.2 Constructive Trusts of Land 436

5 The Doctrine in *Rochefoucauld v Boustead* 437
   5.1 The Two-Party Case 438
   5.2 The Three-Party Case 441

6 The *Pallant v Morgan* Constructive Trust 443
   6.1 The Elements of the *Pallant v Morgan* Constructive Trust 443
   6.2 The Nature of the Unconscionability 446
   6.3 The Basis of the *Pallant v Morgan* Constructive Trust 447

7 Towards a Rationalization of the Constructive Trusts 448

PART D THE SHARED HOME

12 INTERESTS IN THE HOME: THE ACQUISITION QUESTION 454

1 Introduction 455

2 Trusts and the Home 457
   2.1 Joint Legal Owners 461
   2.2 Quantification of Beneficial Interests under a Constructive Trust 463
   2.3 Sole Legal Owner 475
   2.4 A Critique of the Common Intention 492

3 Occupation Rights 494

4 Recommendations for Reform 495

13 REGULATING CO-OWNERSHIP: THE CONTENT QUESTION 503

1 Introduction 503

2 Joint Tenants and Tenants in Common 504
   2.1 Identifying Joint Tenants and Tenants in Common 506

2.2 Survivorship 509

2.3 Severance 510

3 Termination of Co-ownership 529

4 Is the Beneficial Joint Tenancy Desirable? 530

5 Trusts and Co-ownership 531

5.1 Scope of the Trust of Land 533

5.2 Trustees' Powers 533

5.3 Beneficiaries' Rights 535

5.4 Applications to Court 540

5.5 Regulation of Co-ownership Outside of the Trusts of Land and
Appointment of Trustees Act 1996 545

14 CO-OWNERSHIP AND THIRD PARTIES: APPLICATIONS FOR SALE 549

1 Introduction 549

2 Policy Considerations 551

3 Applications by Creditors 553

3.1 Applications for Sale by Creditors Post-*Shaire* 558

3.2 Applications by Creditors: The Human Rights Dimension 562

3.3 Has s 15 of the Trusts of Land and Appointment of Trustees Act 1996
Changed the Law? 563

3.4 Applications for Sale and the Family Law Act 1996 564

4 Applications by Trustees in Bankruptcy 565

4.1 The Courts' General Approach to Defining 'Exceptional Circumstances' 568

4.2 Exceptional Circumstances: The Human Rights Dimension 571

4.3 A 'Fresh Start' for Bankrupts 573

PART E   PRIORITY—THE DEFENCES QUESTION AND LAND REGISTRATION

15 THE PRIORITY TRIANGLE 578

1 Introduction: The Priority Triangle in Practice 579

2 The Basic Rule 580

3 The *Timing* Question 581

3.1 Whose Right is First in Time? Charges 582

3.2 Whose Right is First in Time? Subrogation 590

3.3 Whose Right is First in Time? Independently Acquired Rights 591

4   Exceptions to the Basic Rule: The *Defences* Question   591

    4.1   The Possibility of a Defence   591

    4.2   Registered Land and the Lack of Registration Defence   592

    4.3   Overreaching   594

    4.4   Defences Based on B's Consent   596

    4.5   Defences Based on the Lapse of Time   602

    4.6   Defences and the Distinction between Legal and Equitable Property Rights   604

5   Conclusion   605

16   PRIORITIES IN REGISTERED LAND   607

1   Introduction   608

2   An Overview: The Lack of Registration Defence   608

    2.1   The Effect of the Lack of Registration Defence   610

3   Entry of a Notice   611

    3.1   Nature and Effect   611

    3.2   Scope   612

    3.3   Applying for Entry of a Notice   613

4   Overriding Interests   615

    4.1   Nature and Effect   615

    4.2   Schedule 3, Para 2: Property Rights Held by Persons in Occupation   616

    4.3   Schedule 3, Para 1: Legal Leases of Seven Years or Less   637

    4.4   Schedule 3, Para 3: Legal Easements and *Profits à Prendre*   637

5   Restrictions on Owner's Powers   638

    5.1   Nature and Effect of a Restriction   639

    5.2   Applying for a Restriction   641

6   The Effect of Fraud   641

    6.1   C's Fraud and the Lack of Registration Defence   641

    6.2   C's Fraud and New, Direct Rights   643

7   Conclusion   645

17   CO-OWNERSHIP AND PRIORITIES: THE DEFENCES QUESTION   648

1   Introduction   649

2   Overreaching   649

    2.1   The Scope of Overreaching   651

    2.2   Interests Capable of being Overreached   652

    2.3   Transactions with Overreaching Effect   662

3 Co-ownership, Overreaching, and Occupying Beneficiaries 669

4 Overreaching and Breach of Trust 674
    4.1 Trustees' Ability, Authority, and Duties 674
    4.2 Protection of Purchasers 677
    4.3 Summary 679

5 Is Overreaching Justified? 680

6 The Future of Overreaching 682
    6.1 Qualifying and Restricting the Scope of Overreaching 682
    6.2 Human Rights and Overreaching 683
    6.3 Alternative Causes of Action 685

7 Priority Rules where Overreaching Does Not Take Place 688

18 REFORM OF THE LAND REGISTRATION ACT 2002   693

1 Aims and Rhetoric 694
    1.1 The Law Commission's 2001 Report 694
    1.2 The Law Commission's 2016 Consultation Paper 695

2 The Impact of the Land Registration Act 2002: An Overview 697
    2.1 The *Content* Question 698
    2.2 The *Acquisition* Question 698
    2.3 The *Defences* Question 700
    2.4 Summary 701

3 The Scope of Rectification 702
    3.1 The Meaning of 'Mistake' 702
    3.2 Limits to Rectification 712
    3.3 Rectification: Summary 716

4 Overriding Interests 717
    4.1 The Rationale of Overriding Interests 717
    4.2 Can a Right to Rectify be an Overriding Interest under Sch 3, Para 2? 719
    4.3 Overriding Interests and Indemnities 722

5 Conclusion: Balancing the Needs of B and C 724

PART F   LEASES

19 LEASES   728

1 Introduction: The Importance of the Lease 729
    1.1 The Practical Importance and Diversity of Leases 729

	1.2 The Effect of a Lease	731
	1.3 The Landlord–Tenant Relationship	740
2	The *Content* Question	741
	2.1 Where A does not Intend to Grant B Lease	741
	2.2 Intention to Create Legal Relations	745
	2.3 A Right to Exclusive Possession: General Position	746
	2.4 A Right to Exclusive Possession: Shams and Pretences	749
	2.5 A Right to Exclusive Possession: Multiple Occupancy	759
	2.6 A Proprietary Right to Exclusive Possession	763
	2.7 A Right to Exclusive Possession for a Limited Period	764
	2.8 Exceptions?	783
	2.9 Summary	785
3	The *Acquisition* Question	785
	3.1 Legal Leases	785
	3.2 Equitable Leases	792
	3.3 Methods by which a Lease may End	794
4	The *Defences* Question	800
	4.1 Legal Leases	800
	4.2 Equitable Leases	801
5	The Contractual Aspect of a Lease	801

20 REGULATING LEASES AND PROTECTING OCCUPIERS — 806

1	Introduction	807
2	The *Status-conferring* Aspect of a Lease: Background	808
3	The *Status-conferring* Aspect of a Lease: Practice	811
4	The *Status-conferring* Aspect of a Lease: Its Impact on the Definition of the Lease	815
	4.1 *Bruton v London & Quadrant Housing Trust*	816
5	The *Status-conferring* Aspect of a Lease: Reform?	826

21 LEASEHOLD COVENANTS — 832

1	Introduction	833
	1.1 Leasehold Covenant Terminology	833
	1.2 Contract and Estate-based Liability	834
2	The Original Parties (LO and TO) and Contractual Enforceability	836
	2.1 Pre-1996 Law	836
	2.2 Post-1995 Law	839

3 Assignees (LA and TA) and Estate-based Liability   842
  3.1 Pre-1996 Law   842
  3.2 Post-1995 Leases   847

4 The Continuing Liability for Breaches of Covenant   851
  4.1 Continuing Rights to Enforce Breaches of Covenant   852

5 Sub-lessees   854

6 Remedies for Breach of Leasehold Covenants   856
  6.1 Damages   856
  6.2 Specific Performance   857
  6.3 Distress and Taking Control of the Tenant's Goods   857
  6.4 Forfeiture   858

PART G   NEIGHBOURS AND NEIGHBOURHOODS

22 EASEMENTS   885

1 Introduction   885
  1.1 What are Easements?   885
  1.2 The Utility Balance   887

2 The *Content* Question   888
  2.1 'There Must be a Dominant Tenement and a Servient Tenement'   888
  2.2 The Dominant and Servient Tenements must be in Separate Ownership and Occupation   896
  2.3 An Easement must Accommodate the Dominant Land   897
  2.4 The Right must be Capable of Being the Subject Matter of a Grant   902

3 The *Acquisition* Question   910
  3.1 Express Grant   910
  3.2 Implied Grant   911
  3.3 Presumed Grant: Prescription   935

4 Easements: The *Defences* Question   951

5 Excessive User   953

6 Extinguishment of Easements   954

23 FREEHOLD COVENANTS   957

1 Introduction   957
  1.1 The Role of Land Covenants   958
  1.2 The Structure and Terminology of Land Covenants   959

2 The Burden: Who Can be Sued? 961
  2.1 The Covenant must Relate to Land 962
  2.2 Benefit to Dominant Land 963
  2.3 Negativity 968
  2.4 Indirect Enforcement of Positive Covenants 971
  2.5 The Acquisition and Priority of Restrictive Covenants 975

3 The Benefit: Who Can Sue? 977
  3.1 Assignment 978
  3.2 Annexation 979
  3.3 Building Scheme 988

4 Enforcement, Discharge, and Modification of Covenants 995
  4.1 Enforcement 995
  4.2 Extinction and Modification of Covenants 999

5 Reform 1003

24 FLAT OWNERSHIP: LONG LEASES AND COMMONHOLD 1008

1 Introduction 1009

2 Long Leases of Flats 1011
  2.1 Who is the Landlord? 1012
  2.2 The Leasehold Term, and Rights to Enfranchisement and Extension 1013
  2.3 Maintenance and Repair 1014
  2.4 Communal Living 1016
  2.5 Variation 1017
  2.6 Forfeiture 1017

3 Commonhold 1018
  3.1 The Structure of Commonhold 1018
  3.2 Creation of Commonhold 1019
  3.3 Commonhold Land Ownership 1020
  3.4 The Commonhold Association 1021
  3.5 Commonhold Community Statement 1023
  3.6 The Management of Commonhold 1025
  3.7 Dispute Resolution 1028

4 Conclusion 1028

PART H   SECURITY RIGHTS

25   SECURITY INTERESTS IN LAND   1032

1   Introduction   1032

2   The Role and Importance of Security   1033

3   General Forms of Security   1037
3.1   The Pledge   1038
3.2   The Lien   1038
3.3   The Mortgage   1039
3.4   The Charge   1040

4   Forms of Security over Land: Mortgages and Charges   1042
4.1   Development of Mortgages of Land   1042
4.2   The Legal Charge by Way of Mortgage   1043
4.3   Equitable Mortgages and Equitable Charges of Land   1046
4.4   Charging Orders   1050

5   Equity of Redemption   1055
5.1   Development of the Equity of Redemption   1055
5.2   Equity of Redemption and the Legal Charge   1056

6   Modern Developments on Mortgage Forms   1059
6.1   Islamic Mortgages or Home Purchase Plans   1059
6.2   Low Cost Home Ownership   1060
6.3   Equity Release or Home Reversion Plans   1061
6.4   The Eurohypothec   1061

26   LENDER'S RIGHTS AND REMEDIES   1064

1   Introduction   1064
1.1   Source of the Lender's Rights and Remedies   1065
1.2   Regulation of the Lender's Rights and Remedies   1067

2   Possession   1071
2.1   The Starting Point: An Immediate Right to Possession   1071
2.2   The Equitable Duty to Account   1072
2.3   The Purpose of Taking Possession   1073
2.4   Procedural Safeguards   1074
2.5   Dwelling Houses and s 36 of the Administration of Justice Act 1970
       (as Amended)   1075
2.6   Home Repossession and Human Rights   1090

3   Sale   1091
    3.1 Mechanics of Sale   1091
    3.2 Duties of the Mortgagee in the Conduct of the Sale   1095

4   Appointment of a Receiver   1108
    4.1 Functions and Powers of a Receiver   1108
    4.2 Receiver as Agent for the Borrower   1109
    4.3 Duties of a Receiver   1111

5   A Final Word about the Covenant to Repay   1114

27 PROTECTION OF THE BORROWER   1116

1   Introduction   1116

2   Market Regulation   1118
    2.1 Financial Services and Markets Act 2000, and Regulated
         Mortgage Contracts   1120
    2.2 Consumer Credit Act 1974 (CCA)   1126
    2.3 Financial Ombudsman Service   1128

3   Creation of the Mortgage   1129
    3.1 Factors Governing Procedural Fairness   1129
    3.2 The Conceptual Underpinnings   1135
    3.3 Undue Influence and Mortgages   1136

4   Control of Mortgage Terms   1149
    4.1 Sources of Control   1150
    4.2 Particular Mortgage Terms: Redemption   1156
    4.3 Particular Mortgage Terms: Collateral Advantages   1161
    4.4 Particular Mortgage Terms: Interest Rates   1164

Index   1171

TABLE OF CASES

88 Berkeley Road, Re [1971] 1 All ER
254 . . . 515, 517

89 Holland Park (Management) Ltd v Hicks
[2013] EWHC 391 . . . 984

A Child, Re [2008] UKHL 66 . . . 106

AG Securities v Vaughan: Antioniades v Villiers
[1988] UKHL 8, [1990] 1 AC 417 . . . 735,
749–53, 759, 762

A Ketley Ltd v Scott [1980] CCLR 37 . . . 1127

Abbey National v Cann [1991] 1 AC 56,
HL . . . 292, 299, 582–7, 596–8, 617

Abbey National plc v Moss [1994] 2 FCR
587 . . . 555

Abbey National Bank plc v Stringer [2006]
EWCA Civ 338 . . . 1143

Abbey National Building Society v Maybeech
[1985] Ch 190 . . . 880

Abbott v Abbott [2007] UKPC 53, [2007] 2 All
ER 432 . . . 430, 485, 486

Ackroyd v Smith (1850) 10 CB 164 . . . 157

Adealon International Corp Pty Ltd v Merton
LBC [2007] EWCA Civ 362; [2007] 1 WLR
1898 . . . 914

Ahmed v Kendrick [1988] 2 FLR 22 . . . 1049

Akerman v Richmond on Thames LBC [2017]
EWHC 84 . . . 128

Akerman-Livingstone v Aster Communities
Ltd [2015] UKSC 15 . . . 135

Akers v Samba Financial Group [2017] AC
424 . . . 199

Akici v LR Butlin Ltd [2006] 1 WLR 201,
CA . . . 865–6, 869–71

Akita Holdings Ltd v Attorney General of
the Turks and Caicos Island [2017] AC
590 . . . 686

Albany Home Loans Ltd v Massey (1997) 37
P & CR 509 . . . 1074

Alec Lobb Garages Ltd v Total Oil (GB) Ltd
[1885] 1 WLR 173, CA . . . 1134, 1163

Alexander v West Bromwich Mortgage Co Ltd
[2016] EWCA Civ 496 . . . 1164

Alford v Hannaford [2011] EWCA Civ
1099 . . . 929

Allan v Liverpool Overseers (1874) LR 9 QB
180 . . . 734, 738

Allcard v Skinner (1887) 36 Ch D
145 . . . 1131, 1143

Allen v England (1862) 3 F & F 49 . . . 328

Alliance and Leicester plc v Slayford (2001) 33
HLR 66 . . . 563

Alliance Perpetual Building Society v Belrum
Investments Ltd [1957] 1 WLR 720 . . . 1071

Alpstream AG v PK Airfinance Sarl [2015]
EWCA Civ 1318 . . . 1098–9, 1103, 1105, 1106

Amalgamated Investment & Property Co. Ltd
v Texas Commerce International Bank Ltd
[1982] QB 84 . . . 385

Amsprop Trading Ltd v Harris Distribution Ltd
[1997] 1 WLR 1025 . . . 855

Amstrong v Shappard & Shroff [1959] 2 QB
384 . . . 954

Anchor Brewhouse Developments Ltd v Berkley
House [1987] 2 EGLR 173 . . . 33

Anderson Antiques (UK) Ltd v Anderson
Wharf (Hull) Ltd [2007] EWHC 2086 . . . 78

Angus v Dalton (1877) LR 3 QBD 85 . . . 940

Anneveld v Robinson [2005] WL 3142400
(county court), judgment 12 August
2005 . . . 542

Antoniades v UK (App No 15434/89) . . . 116

Antoniades v Villiers [1990] 1 AC 417 . . . 753–5,
758, 825

Argyle Building Society v Hammond (1984) 49
P & CR 148 . . . 705, 706

Arif v Anwar [2015] EWHC 124 (Fam); [2016] 1
FLR 359 . . . 372, 408

Armory v Delamirie (1722) 5 Stra
505 . . . 47, 49, 51

Arnold v Britton [2015] AC 1619 . . . 1016

Arrondelle v UK (1983) 5 EHRR 118 . . . 130

Arthur v Attorney General of the Turks and
Caicos Islands [2012] UKPC 30 . . . 686

Ashburn Anstalt v Arnold [1989] Ch 1,
CA . . . 227–9, 234–7, 242, 645, 746, 765,
766, 800

Asher v Whitlock (1865) LR 1 QB 1 . . . 602, 738

Ashley Guarantee v Zacaria [1993] 1 WLR
62 . . . 1072

Aslan v Murphy [1989] EWCA Civ
2 . . . 756, 758

Aspden v Elvy [2012] EWHC 1387
(Ch) . . . 474, 488

Associated Provincial Picture Houses
Ltd v Wednesbury Corp [1948] 1 KB
223 . . . 106

Astley v Reynolds (1731) 2 Str 915 . . . 1130

Aston Cantlow and Wilmcote with Billesley
Parochial Church Council v Wallbank [2003]
UKHL 37, [2004] 1 AC 546 . . . 102, 117, 355

Atkinson v Atkinson, unreported, Judgment 30
June 2010 (Leeds County Court) . . . 529

Attorney-General for Hong Kong v Blake [2001] 1 AC 268 ... 213, 999

Attorney-General for Hong Kong v Fairfax Ltd [1997] 1 WLR 149 ... 999

Attorney-General of Hong Kong v Humphrey's Estate [1987] 2 All ER 387 ... 379

Attorney-General for Scotland v Taylor [2003] SLT 1340 ... 126

Attorney-General for Southern Nigeria v John Holt & Co (Liverpool) Ltd [1915] AC 599 ... 906

Austerberry v Oldham Corp (1885) 29 Ch D 750 ... 961

Azfar's Application, Re (2002) 1 P & CR 215 ... 1001

Aziz v Caixa d'Estalvis de Catalunya, Tarragona i Manresa [2013] 3 CMLR 5 ... 1071, 1154–5

B Johnson & Co (Builders) Ltd, Re [1955] Ch 634 ... 1110

BCCI v Aboody [1990] 1 QB 923 ... 1140, 1144

BHP Petroleum Great Britain Ltd v Chesterfield Properties Ltd [2002] 2 Ch 195, CA ... 839

BP Properties Ltd v Buckler (1988) 55 P & CR 337, CA ... 316–18

Bagum v Hafz [2016] Ch 241 ... 540

Bainbrigge v Browne (1881) 18 Ch D 188 ... 1137

Baker v Baker (1993) 25 HLR 408 ... 216, 408

Baker v Craggs [2016] EWHC 3250 (Ch); [2017] Ch 295 ... 174, 175, 177, 185, 188, 287, 292, 301–4, 620, 631–3, 653, 662–4, 717

Bakewell Management Ltd v Brandwood [2004] 2 AC 519, HL ... 946–7

Bakrania v Lloyds Bank [2017] UKFTT 0364 (Property Chamber) ... 704

Ballards Conveyance, Re [1937] Ch 473 ... 967, 980

Banco Exterior Internacional SA v Thomas [1997] 1 WLR 221 ... 1138

Baner v Sweden (1989) 60 DR 128 ... 118, 124

Banfield v Leeds Building Society [2007] EWCA Civ 1369 ... 1083

Bank of Credit & Commerce International (Overseas) Ltd v Akindele [2001] Ch 437 ... 392

Bank of Ireland Home Mortgages Ltd v Bell [2001] 2 FLR 809 ... 550, 558–60

Bank Mellat v HM Treasury (No2) [2014] AC 700 ... 97

Bank of Scotland v Brogan [2012] NICH 21 ... 488

Bank of Scotland v Grimes [1986] QB1179 ... 1080

Bank of Scotland v Hill [2002] EWCA Civ 1081 ... 1148

Bank of Scotland v Miller [2001] EWCA Civ 344; [2002] QB 255 ... 1076

Bank of Scotland plc v Rea, McGeady, Laverty [2014] NI Master 11 ... 1086, 1164

Bank of Scotland v Waugh [2014] EWHC 2117 (Ch) ... 1047

Bank of Scotland Plc v Zinda [2012] 1 WLR 728 ... 1086–8

Banner Homes Group plc v Luff Developments Ltd [2000] Ch 372 ... 443–7

Bannister v Bannister [1948] 2 All ER 133, CA ... 230, 237, 439–40

Banque Financière de la Cité v Parc (Battersea) Ltd ... 590, 591

Barca v Mears [2004] EWHC 2170, HC ... 571–3

Barclays Bank plc v Guy [2008] EWCA Civ 452 ... 696, 703, 722

Barclays Bank plc v O'Brien [1994] 1 AC 180, HL ... 1132–3, 1135–7, 1140, 1145, 1146

Barclays Bank v Coleman [2002] 2 AC 773 [1985] AC 686 ... 1142

Barkshire v Grubb (1881) 18 Ch D 816 ... 914

Barnes v Phillips [2015] EWCA Civ 1056 ... 477

Barons Finance Ltd v Olubisi, unreported, 26 April 2010 ... 1166

Barrett v Morgan [2000] 2 AC 264 ... 799

Barton v Armstrong [1976] AC 104 ... 1130

Basham, Re [1987] 1 All ER 405 ... 370

Batchelor v Marlow [2001] EWCA Civ 1051, [2003] 1 WLR 764 ... 906

Batt v Adams [2001] 32 EG 90 ... 323

Battersea Property Co v London Borough of Wandsworth [2001] 19 EG 148 ... 323

Baxter v Four Oaks Properties Ltd [1965] Ch 816 ... 989, 992

Baxter v Mannion [2011] EWCA Civ 120; [2011] 2 All ER 574 ... 73, 339, 697, 702

Baynes Clarke v Corless [2010] EWCA 338 ... 446

Begley v Taylor [2014] EWHC 1180 ... 907

Belchikova v Russia (App No 2408/06) ... 148

Belfast CC v Miss Behavin' Ltd [2007] UKHL 19 ... 106

Bellcourt Estates Ltd v Adesina [2005] EWCA Civ 208 ... 799

Bendal v McWhirter [1952] 2 QB 466 (CA) ... 17

Benn v Hardinge (1993) 66 P & CR 246 ... 954

Berger-Krall v Slovenia (App No 14717/04) ... 118, 122

Berkley v Poulett (1977) EGLR 86 ... 289

Bernstein of Leigh (Baron) v Skyviews & General Ltd [1978] QB 479 ... 31–2, 36, 37

Berrisford v Mexfield Housing Co-operative Ltd [2011] UKSC 52; [2012] 1 AC 955 ... 20, 767–78, 780–2

Best v Chief Land Registrar [2014] EWHC 1370 (Admin); [2015] EWCA Civ 17, [2016] QB 23 . . . 347–9, 428

Best v Curtis [2016] EWLandRA 2015_0130 (11 April 2016) . . . 349–50

Betterment Properties (Weymouth) Ltd v Dorset CC [2012] EWCA Civ 250 . . . 945

Biggs v Hodinott [1898] 2 Ch 307 . . . 1161

Billson v Residential Apartments Ltd [1992] 1 AC 494, HL . . . 859–60, 873, 874, 876–8

Billson v Residential Apartments (No 2) [1993] EGCS 155 . . . 875

Binions v Evans [1972] Ch 359, CA . . . 207, 225, 226, 230, 231, 437

Binns v First Plus Financial groups Plc [2013] EWHC 2436 . . . 1129

Bird v Syme-Thomson [1979] 1 WLR 440, HC . . . 625

Birdlip v Hunter [2016] EWCA Civ 603 . . . 990–2

Birmingham Citizens Permanent Building Society v Caunt [1962] Ch 883, HC . . . 1071–2

Birmingham City Council v Doherty [2008] 3 WLR 636, HL . . . 92, 105, 111, 137

Birmingham City Council v Frisby [2011] 2 AC 186 . . . 813

Birmingham CC v Lloyd [2012] HLR 44 . . . 139

Birmingham Midshires Mortgage Services Ltd v Sabherwal (2000) 80 P & CR 256, CA . . . 652, 658–61, 673, 681

Birmingham, Dudley and District Banking Co v Ross (1887) 38 Ch D 295 . . . 911

Bishop v Bonham [1988] 1 WLR 742 . . . 1102

Bitto v Slovakia (App No 30255/09) . . . 118, 122

Bjedov v Croatia (App no. 42150/09) . . . 132

Blacklocks v JB Developments Ltd [1982] Ch 183 . . . 720

Bland v Ingram's Estates Ltd [2001] EWCA Civ 1088 . . . 875, 879

Bland v Ingram's Estates Ltd (No 2) [2002] Ch 177 . . . 878

Bligh v Martin [1968] 1 WLR 804 . . . 329

Bofinger v Kingsway Group Ltd (2009) 239 CLR 269 (High Court of Australia) . . . 590

Booker v Palmer [1942] 2 All ER 674, CA . . . 745, 784

Borman v Griffith [1930] 1 Ch 493 . . . 923, 924

Botham and ors v TSB Bank plc [1996] EWCA Civ 549, CA . . . 43–6

Botta v Italy (1998) 26 EHRR 241 . . . 109

Boyer v Warbey [1953] 1 QB 234, CA . . . 847

Bradbury v Taylor [2012] EWCA Civ 1208 . . . 371

Bradford & Bingley plc v Ross [2005] EWCA Civ 394 . . . 1105

Bradley v Governor of Bank of Ireland (unreported) . . . 1146

Bradley v Carritt [1903] AC 25 . . . 1161

Breams Property Investment co Ltd v Strougler [1948] 2 KB 1 . . . 773

Bremner, Re [1999] 1 FLR 912 . . . 569, 570

Brezec v Croatia [2014] HLR 3 . . . 132, 148

Bridges v Hawkesworth (1821) 21 LJ (QB) 75 . . . 47, 48, 50

Briggs v Gleeds [2014] EWHC 1178 (Ch) . . . 294

Brighton & Hove CC v Audus [2009] EWHC 340 . . . 1157

Brikom Investments Ltd v Carr [1979] 2 All ER 753 . . . 382

Bristol & West Building Society v Ellis (1997) 73 P & CR 158, CA . . . 1084–5

Bristol & West Building Society v Henning [1985] 1 WLR 778 . . . 597

Bristol & West Building Society v Mothew [1998] Ch 1 . . . 190

Bristol Airport plc v Powdrill [1990] Ch 744, CA . . . 234, 1033

Britannia Building Society v Earl [1990] 1 WLR 422 . . . 1079

British Anzani (Felixstowe) Ltd v International Marine Management (UK) Ltd [1980] QB 137 . . . 857

British Petroleum Pension Trust Ltd v Behrendt (1985) 52 P & CR 117 . . . 869

British Railways Board v Glass [1965] Ch 538 . . . 953

Brocklesby v Temperance Building Society [1895] AC 173 . . . 598, 599, 601

Brown & Root Technology Ltd v Sun Alliance and London Assurance Co Ltd [2001] Ch 733, CA . . . 301

Brown v Raindle (1796) 3 Ves 296, (1796) 30 ER 998 . . . 518

Browne v Pritchard [1975] 1 WLR 1366 . . . 544

Brunner v Greenslade [1971] Ch 993 . . . 856, 994

Bruton v London & Quadrant Housing Trust Ltd [2000] 1 AC 406; [1988] QB 834, CA . . . 736, 764, 785, 802, 816–26

Buchanan-Wollaston's Conveyance, Re [1939] Ch 738 . . . 541

Buckingham County Council v Moran [1990] Ch 623 . . . 310, 322, 324, 357

Buckland v UK (2013) 56 EHRR 16 . . . 139, 149

Buckley v UK (1997) 23 EHRR 101 . . . 95, 96, 128, 129, 131

Bunney v Burns Andersen Plc [2007] EWHC 1240 . . . 1129

Burbank Securities Ltd v Wong [2008] EWHC 552 . . . 1145, 1146

Burgess v Rawnsley [1975] Ch 429, CA . . . 512, 518, 523–5

Burke v Burke [1974] 1 WLR 1063 . . . 544

Burnip v Birmingham CC [2012] EWCA Civ 629 . . . 112

Burns v Burns [1984] Ch 317 . . . 485

Busuioc v Moldova (App No 61382/09) . . . 130

Butler v Rice [1910] 2 Ch 277 . . . 590

Byford dec'd, Re [2004] 1 FLR 56 . . . 537

C Putnam & Sons v Taylor [2009] EWHC 317 (Ch) . . . 521, 553, 562

CIBC Mortgages plc v Pitt [1994] 1 AC 200 . . . 1132, 1146

Cable v Bryant [1908] 1 Ch 259 . . . 911

Cadogan v Dimovic [1984] 1 WLR 609 . . . 879

Caern Motor Services Ltd v Texaco Ltd [1994] 1 WLR 1249 . . . 845, 846

Camden London Borough v Shortlife Community Housing (1992) 25 HLR 330 . . . 783

Campbell v Banks [2011] EWCA Civ 61 . . . 929

Campbell v Holyland (1877) 7 Ch D 166 . . . 1065

Canas Property Co Ltd v KL Television Services Ltd [1970] 2 QB 433 . . . 860

Cantrell v Wycombe DC [2008] EWCA Civ 866 . . . 965

Capethorn v Harris [2015] EWCA Civ 955 . . . 489

Cardiothoracic Institute v Shrewdcrest Ltd [1986] 1 WLR 36 . . . 790

Cardwell v Walker [2003] EWHC 3117 . . . 845, 846

Carey v HSBC Plc [2009] EWHC 3417 . . . 1127

Carlton v Goodman [2002] 2 FLR 259, CA . . . 458

Casborne v Scarfe (1738) 1 Atk 603, 26 ER 377 . . . 1056

Catt v Tourle (1869) LR 4 Ch 654 . . . 963

Cave v Cave (1880) 15 Ch D 639 . . . 687

Celsteel Ltd v Alton House Holdings Ltd [1985] 1 WLR 204 . . . 638, 951

Central Estates (Belgravia) Ltd v Woolgar (No 2) [1972] 1 WLR 1048 . . . 862, 869, 878

Central London Commercial Estates Ltd v Kato Kagaku Co Ltd [1998] EWHC 314 . . . 336

Central London Property Trust Ltd v High Trees House [1947] KB 130 . . . 360, 598

Central Midlands Estates Ltd v Leicester Dyers Ltd [2003] 2 P & CR D1 . . . 906

Centrax Trustees v Ross [1979] 2 All ER 952 . . . 1080

Centrovincial Estates plc v Bulk Storage Ltd (1983) 46 P & CR 393 . . . 837

Chadwick v Collinson [2014] EWHC 3055 (Ch) . . . 525

Chaffe v Kingsley (2000) 79 P & CR 404 . . . 919

Chahal v UK (1997) 23 EHRR 413 . . . 92

Chan v Leung, unreported 30 November 2001, HC . . . 546, 547

Chan v Leung [2003] 1 FLR 23 . . . 546

Chapman v UK (2001) 33 EHRR 318 . . . 96

Chartered Trust plc v Davies [1997] 2 EGLR 83 . . . 799, 804

Chase Manhattan Bank NA v Israel-British Bank (London) Ltd [1981] Ch 105 . . . 423

Chassagnou v France (App Nos 25088/94, 28331/95, & 28443/95) (2000) 29 EHRR 615 . . . 118

Chaudhary v Yavuz [2013] Ch 249 . . . 7, 78, 80, 206, 228, 413, 593, 610, 619, 626, 627, 645, 700

Chater v Mortgage Services Agency Number Two Ltd [2003] EWCA Civ 490 . . . 1143, 1146

Chatham Empire Theatres (1955) Ltd v Ultrans Ltd [1961] 1 WLR 817 . . . 879

Chatsworth Estates Co v Fewell [1931] 1 Ch 224 . . . 999

Chattey v Farndale Holdings Inc [1997] 1 EGLR 153 . . . 231

Cheltenham & Gloucester Building Society v Grant (1994) 26 HLR 703 . . . 1084

Cheltenham & Gloucester Building Society v Norgan [1996] 1 WLR 343, CA . . . 1080–2

Cheltenham & Gloucester Plc v Booker (1997) 73 P & CR 412, CA . . . 1085

Cheltenham & Gloucester plc v Krausz [1997] 1 WLR 1558, CA . . . 1089

Chester v Buckingham Travel Ltd [1981] 1 WLR 96 . . . 858

Chesterfield v BC v Bailey (2011) unreported . . . 141

Cheval Bridging Finance Ltd v Bhasin [2008] EWCA Civ 1613 . . . 1078

China and South Seas Bank Ltd v Tan [1990] 1 AC 536, PC . . . 1100–1

China Field Ltd v Appeal Tribunal (Buildings) [2009] HKCU 1650 . . . 950

Chhokar v Chhokar [1984] FLR 313 . . . 634

Chowood's Registered Land, Re [1933] Ch 574 . . . 78, 81, 615, 719

Christine Goodwin v United Kingdom (2002) 35 EHRR 18 . . . 95

Chubb & Bruce v Dean [2014] EWHC 1282 . . . 1166

Churchhill v Temple [2010] EWHC 3369 . . . 984

Citibank Trust Ltd v Ayivor [1987] 1 WLR 1157 . . . 1072

Citro, Re [1991] Ch 142, CA . . . 554, 556, 563, 568, 569, 572

City and Metropolitan Properties Ltd v Greycroft Ltd [1987] 1 WLR 1085, HC . . . 853–4

City of London Building Society v Flegg [1986] Ch 605; [1988] AC 54, HL . . . 536, 595, 615, 650, 668, 670–3, 676, 677, 680, 701

City of London Corp v Fell [1994] 1 AC 458, HL ...835–7

City Permanent Building Society v Miller [1952] Ch 840, CA ...637, 801

Cityland & Property (Holdings) Ltd v Dabrah [1968] Ch 166 ...1161, 1166

Clarke v In Focus Asset Management & Tax Solutions Ltd [2014] 1 WLR 2502 ...1129

Clarke v Meadus [2010] EWHC 3117 (Ch) ...386

Claughton v Charalambous [1999] 1 FLR 740 ...569

Cleveland Petroleum Ltd v Dartstone Ltd [1969] 1 WLR 116 ...1163

Clore v Theatrical Properties Ltd [1936] 3 All ER 483 ...232, 244

Close Invoice Finance Ltd v Pile [2008] EWHC 1580; [2009] 1 FLR 873 ...553

Cobb v Lane [1952] 1 All ER 1199; [1952] 1 TLR 1037 ...241, 745

Cobbe v Yeoman's Row Management Ltd [2008] UKHL 55, [2008] 1 WLR 1752 ...180, 278, 371, 372, 375–80, 389, 392–5, 401

Colin Dawson Windows Ltd v King's Lynn, West Norfolk [2005] EWCA Civ 9; [2005] 2 P & CR 19 ...319

Collins Application, Re (1974) 30 P & CR 527 ...1002

Collins v Collins [2016] P & CR 6 ...919

Commission for the New Towns v Cooper [1995] Ch 259, CA ...268, 275

Commission for the New Towns v Gallagher [2002] EWHC 2668, (2003) 2 P & CR 24 ...927

Commissioner for Railways v Valuer-General [1974] AC 325 ...35

Commissioner of Stamp Duties (Queensland) v Livingstone [1964] 3 AC 694 (PC) ...349

Commonwealth Bank of Australia Ltd v Amadio (1983) 151 CLR 447 ...1134

Commonwealth v Verwayen (1990) 117 CLR 394, 413 (High Court of Australia) ...407

Connaught Restaurants Ltd v Indoor Leisure Ltd [1994] 1 WLR 501 ...857

Connors v UK (2005) 40 EHRR 9 ...94–6, 109, 111, 130, 131, 137

Consolidated Finance Ltd v Collins [2013] EWCA Civ 475 ...1127

Cook v The Mortgage Business [2012] EWCA Civ 17 ...588

Cooke v Chilcott (1876) 3 Ch D 694 ...968

Co-operative Bank Plc v Phillips [2014] EWHC 2862 ...1074

Copeland v Greenhalf [1952] Ch 488, HC ...905–6

Corbett v Halifax Building Society [2002] EWCA Civ 1849; [2003] 1 WLR 964 ...1102, 1106–7

Cornillie v Saha (1996) 72 P & CR 147 ...862

Coronation Street Industrial Properties Ltd v Ignall Industries Ltd [1989] 1 WLR 304 ...845

Corporation of London v Riggs (1880) 13 Ch D 798 ...914

Cosic v Croatia (App No 28261/06) (2011) 52 EHRR 39 ...130, 132

Cosslett Contractors Ltd, Re [1998] Ch 495 ...1038, 1040

Costello v Chief Constable of Derbyshire [2001] EWCA Civ 381; [2001] 3 All ER 150 ...49, 56

County Leasing Ltd v East [2007] EWHC 2907 ...1168

Coventry (t/a RDC Promotions) v Lawrence [2014] AC 822 ...903, 942, 995–9

Cowcher v Cowcher [1972] 1 WLR 425 ...506

Cox v Bishop (1857) 8 De GM & G 815 ...847

Cox v Jones [2004] EWHC 1476 ...448

Crabb v Arun DC [1976] Ch 179, CA ...278, 360, 362, 371, 374–5, 377, 380, 381, 395, 398, 406, 411, 439, 911

Crago v Julian [1992] 1 WLR 372 ...290, 791

Credit and Mercantile plc v Kaymuu Ltd [2014] EWHC 1746 (Ch) ...599

Credit and Mercantile plc v Marks [2004] EWCA Civ 568 ...1071

Credit Lyonnais v Burch [1997] 1 All ER 144 ...1143

Crest Nicholson Residential (South) Ltd v McAllister [2004] 1 WLR 2409, CA ...984–7

Crossco No 4 Unlimited v Jolan Ltd [2011] EWHC 803 (Ch); [2011] EWCA Civ 1619 ...380, 445, 447

Cryer v Scott Brothers (Sudbury) Ltd (1988) 55 P & CR 183 ...967

Cuckmere Brick Co v Mutual Finance [1971] Ch 949, CA ...1096–7

Cukurova Finance International Ltd v Alfa Telecom Turkey Ltd [2009] UKPC 19; [2013] UKPC 2; [2013] UKPC 20 ...1065, 1074

Cumberland Court (Brighton) Ltd v Taylor [1964] Ch 29 ...1045

Cundy v Lindsay (1878) 3 App Cas 459, HL ...12

DHN Food Distributors Ltd v London Borough of Tower Hamlets [1976] 3 All ER 462, CA ...236–7, 241

DKLR Holding Co (No 2) Ltd v Commissioner of Stamp Duties (1982) 149 CLR 431 (High Court of Australia) ...186

D Pride & Partners v Institute for Animal Health [2009] EWHC 685 (QB) ...165

DSDN Subsea Ltd v Petroleum Geo-services ASA [2000] BLR 530 ...1130

Dalton v Angus & Co (1881) 6 LR App Cas 740 ...939, 948

Daniel v Drew [2005] EWCA Civ 507 . . . 1131

Dann v Spurrier (1802) 7 Ves 231 . . . 373

Das v Linden Mews [2002] EWCA Civ 590, [2003] 2 P & CR 4 . . . 891, 892

Davies v Bramwell [2007] EWCA Civ 821 . . . 916

Davies v Davies [2016] EWCA Civ 463 . . . 371, 386, 400–4, 408, 409

Davies v Direct Loans [1986] 1 WLR 823 . . . 1127

Davies v Jones [2010] 1 P & CR 22 . . . 974

Davis v Jackson [2017] EWHC 698 . . . 537

Davis v Smith, unreported, judgment 23 November 2011 . . . 522

de Bruyne v de Bruyne [2010] EWCA Civ 519 . . . 441, 442

De Freitas v Permanent Secretary of Ministry of Agriculture, Fisheries, Lands and Housing [1999]1 AC 69 . . . 97

Delaforce v Simpson-Cook (2010) 78 NSWLR 483 . . . 404

Dempster v Cleghorn (1813) 2 Dow 40 . . . 900

Dennis, Re [1996] Ch 80 . . . 521, 522

Dillwyn v Llewellyn (1862) 4 De G F & J 517 . . . 246

Di Palma v UK (1986) 10 EHRR 149 . . . 148, 1017

Director General of Fair Trading v First National Bank plc [2001] UKHL 52; [2002] 1 AC 481, HL . . . 1153–6, 1166

Doe d. Aslin v Summersett (1830) 1 B & Ad 135 . . . 796, 797

Doherty v Allman (1878) 3 App Cas 709 . . . 998

Doherty v Birmingham CC [2008] UKHL 57; [2009] 1 AC 367 . . . 130, 133, 134, 140, 798

Dolphin's Conveyance, Re [1970] Ch 654 . . . 988, 989, 991–4

Domb v Isoz [1980] Ch. 548 . . . 269

Donaldson v Smith [2006] All ER (D) 293 . . . 921

Donohoe v Ingram [2006] EWHC 282 . . . 569

Downsview Nominees Ltd v First City Corp [1993] AC 295 . . . 1074, 1097, 1105, 1111

Drake v Whipp [1996] 1 FLR 826 . . . 464

Draper's Conveyance, Re [1969] 1 Ch 486 . . . 512–13

Driscoll v Church Commissioners [1957] Ch 70 . . . 861

Duffield v Gandy [2008] EWCA Civ 379 . . . 1001

Duffy v Lamb (1998) 75 P & CR 364 . . . 903

Duke of Beaufort v Patrick (1853) 17 Beav 60 . . . 412

Duke of Bedford v British Museum Trustees (1822) 2 My & K 552 . . . 999

Duke of Westminster v Guild [1985] QB 688 . . . 903

Duke v Robson [1973] 1 WLR 267 . . . 1078

Duke v Wynne [1990] 1 WLR 766 . . . 756

Dunbar v Plant [1998] Ch 412 . . . 525

Dunraven Securities Ltd v Hollaway [1982] 2 EGLR 47 . . . 869

Dwyer v Westminster CC [2014] 2 P & CR 7 . . . 954

Dyce v Lady James Hay (1852) 1 Macq 305 . . . 900, 904

Dyer v Dyer (1788) 2 Cox 92 . . . 423

EMI Group Ltd v O&H Q1Ltd [2016] Ch 529 . . . 840

E R Ives Investment Ltd v High [1967] 2 QB 379; [1967] 1 All ER 504 . . . 190, 248, 412, 658

Earl of Leicester v Wells-next-the-Sea UDC [1973] Ch 110 . . . 967

Earl of Worcester v Finch (1600) 4 Co Inst 85 . . . 201

Eastland Homes Partnership Ltd v Whyte [2010] EWHC 695 . . . 104

Eccles v Bryant and Pollock [1948] Ch 93 . . . 269

Ecclesiastical Commissioners for England v Kino (1880) 14 Ch D 213 . . . 954

Edwardes v Barrington (1901) 85 LT 650 . . . 235

Edwards v Kumarasamy [2016] AC 1334 . . . 175

Edwards v Lee's Administrator 96 SW 2d 1028 (1936, Court of Appeals of Kentucky) . . . 31

Edwards v Lloyds TSB [2004] EWHC 1745 . . . 558, 560–3

Edwards v Malta (App No 17647/04) . . . 118

Egerton v Esplanade Hotel, London Ltd [1947] 2 All ER 88 . . . 869

Elitestone Ltd v Morris [1997] 1 WLR 687, HL . . . 38–42

Ellenborough Park, Re [1956] Ch 131, CA . . . 888, 898–900, 904, 906

Ellison v Cleghorn [2013] EWHC 5 (Ch) . . . 529

Elliston v Reacher [1908] 2 Ch 374 . . . 989, 992, 993

Elwood v Goodman [2014] 2 WLR 967 . . . 974, 977

Embassy Court Residents Association v Lipman (1984) 271 EG 545, . . . 1016

Emile Elias & Co Ltd v Pine Groves Ltd [1993] 1 WLR 305 . . . 992

Emmanuel College v Evans (1625) 1 Ch Rep 18 . . . 1055

Emptage v Financial Services Compensation Scheme Ltd [2013] EWCA Civ 729 . . . 1123

Entick v Carrington (1765) 2 Wils KB 274, Common Pleas . . . 26–30

Equity & Law Home Loans Ltd v Prestidge [1992] 1 WLR 137 . . . 597

Erimus Housing Ltd v Barclays Wealth Trustees (Jersey) Ltd [2014] EWCA Civ 303 ... 790

Errington v Errington & Woods [1952] 1 KB 290, CA ... 232–4, 241, 242, 245

Escalus Properties Ltd v Robinson [1996] QB 231 ... 874, 879

Esso Petroleum Co Ltd v Harpers Garage (Stourport) Ltd [1968] AC 269 ... 1163

Esso Petroleum Co Ltd v Kingswood Motors Ltd and ors [1974] QB 142 ... 223, 224

Evans v Cherry Tree Finance Ltd [2008] EWCA Civ 331 ... 1160

Everitt v Budhram [2009] EWHC 1219 (Ch) ... 566

Evers' Trust, Re [1980] 1 WLR 1327 ... 544

Eves v Eves [1975] 1 WLR 1338 ... 479, 480

Ewart v Fryer [1901] 1 Ch 499 ... 879

Expert Clothing Service & Sales Ltd v Hillgate House Ltd [1986] Ch 340, CA ... 867–8, 872–3

FHR European Ventures LLP v Mankarious [2014] 3 WLR 535 ... 448

FOS v Heather Moor & Edgecombe Ltd [2008] EWCA Civ 643 ... 1128

Fairclough v Swan Brewery Co [1912] AC 565 ... 1158

Fairweather v St Marylebone Property Co Ltd [1963] AC 510, HL ... 333, 336

Falco Finance Ltd v Gough [1999] CCLR 16 ... 1160, 1166, 1168

Family Housing Association v Jones [1990] 1 WLR 779 ... 818

Farah Constructions Pty Ltd v Say-Dee Pty Ltd [2007] HCA 222 ... 686

Farrars v Farrars Ltd (1889) 40 Ch D 395 ... 1105

Federated Homes Ltd v Mill Lodge Properties Ltd [1980] 1 WLR 594, CA ... 981–3, 987

Ferris v Weaven [1952] 2 All ER 233 ... 17, 165, 166

Ferrishurst Ltd v Wallcite Ltd [1999] Ch 353 ... 617, 618

Ffrench's Estate (1887) 21 LR (Ir) 283 ... 687

Figgins Holdings Pty Ltd v SEAA Enterpises Ltd (1999) 196 CLR 245 ... 1057

Figurasin v Central Capital Ltd [2014] EWCA Civ 504 ... 1123

Finch v Hall [2013] EWHC 4360 (Ch) ... 541

Finchbourne Ltd v Rodrigues [1976] 3 All ER 581 ... 1016

First Middlesbrough Trading and Mortgage Co. Ltd v Cunningham (1974) 28 P & CR 69 ... 1081

First National Bank plc v Achampong [2003] EWCA 487 ... 550, 558, 563, 564

First National Securities Ltd v Hegerty [1985] QB 850 ... 519, 1049

Firstpost Homes Ltd v Johnson [1995] 1 WLR 1567, CA ... 263, 269, 270

Fitzkriston LLP v Panayi [2008] EWCA Civ 283 ... 788

Fitzwilliam v Richall Holding Services Ltd [2013] EWHC 86 (Ch); [2013] 1 P & CR 19 ... 69, 81

Flack v National Crime Authority (1998) 156 ALR 501 ... 53

Fletcher v Chief Constable of Leicestershire [2013] EWHC 3357 (Admin) ... 49

Flight v Bentley (1835) 7 Sim 149 ... 853

Foenander v Allan [2006] BPIR 1392 ... 569, 570

Ford v Alexander [2012] EWHC 266 (Ch) ... 573

Former King of Greece v Greece (App No 25701/94) ... 123

Forrester Ketley & Co v Brent [2009] EWHC 2441 (Ch) ... 553, 563

Foskett v McKeown [2001] AC 102 ... 687

Foster v Warblington Urban District Council [1906] 1 KB 648 ... 737, 739

Four-Maids Ltd v Dudley Marshall (Properties) Ltd [1957] Ch 317, HC ... 1071

Fowler v Barron [2008] EWCA 377 ... 462, 466

Fred Perry Holdings v Genis [2015] 1 P & CR DG5 ... 564

Freifeld v West Kensington Court Ltd [2015] EWCA Civ 80 ... 878

French v Barcham [2009] 1 WLR 1124 ... 537

Frencher Ltd (in liq) v Bank of East Asia [1995] 2 HKC 263 ... 1065

Friends Provident Life Office v British Railways Board (1997) 73 P & CR 9 ... 837

Friends Provident Life Office, Re [1999] 1 All ER (Comm.) ... 821

G & K Kreglinger v New Patagonia Meat and Cold Storage Co Ltd [1914] AC 25, HL ... 1150–1, 1157, 1161–3

GS Fashions Ltd v B&Q plc [1995] 1 WLR 1088 ... 861

Gadds Land Transfer, Re [1966] Ch 56 ... 966

Gafford v Graham (1999) 77 P & CR 73 ... 998, 999

Gallarotti v Sebastinelli [2012] 2 FLR 1231 ... 492

Gan Insurance case [2001] EWCA Civ 1047 ... 1165

Gaskell v Gosling [1896] 1 QB 669 ... 1175

Geary v Rankine [2012] EWCA Civ 555 ... 487

Generator Developments Ltd v Lidl UK GmbH [2016] EWHC 814 (Ch) ... 447

George Inglefield Ltd, Re [1933] Ch 1 ... 755

George Wimpey Bristol Ltd v Gloucester Housing Association Ltd [2011] UKUT 91 ... 1002

George Wimpey UK Ltd v VI Construction Ltd [2005] EWCA Civ 77 ... 275

Germanotta v Germanotta [2012] QSC 116 ... 394, 409

Ghaidan v Godin-Mendoza [2004] UKHL 30, [2004] 2 AC 557 ... 91, 107, 112

Giles v Tarry [2012] 2 P & CR 15 ... 895

Gill v Lewis [1956] 2 QB 1, CA ... 875

Gillett v Holt [2001] Ch 210, CA ... 369, 386–8, 391, 401, 404

Gillow v UK (1989) 11 EHRR 335 ... 95, 118, 127–9

Gissing v Gissing [1971] AC 886 ... 426, 458, 467, 469, 473, 477–9

Gladysheva v Russia (App no 7097/10) ... 132

Glass v Kencakes [1966] 1 QB 611 ... 869

Gold Harp Properties Ltd v Macleod [2014] EWCA Civ 1084; [2015] 1 WLR 124 ... 73, 84, 699, 704–8, 711, 716

Goldberg v Edwards [1950] Ch 247 ... 923, 928, 933–5

Gomba Holdings UK Ltd v Homan [1986] 1 WLR 1301 ... 1110

Good Harvest Partnership LLP v Centaur Services Ltd [2010] EWHC 330 (Ch), [2010] Ch 426 ... 840

Goodman v Gallant [1986] 2 WLR 236; [1986] Fam 106 ... 420, 510

Gore v Naheed [2017] EWCA Civ 639 ... 891, 892

Gould v Vaggelas (1984) 157 CLR 215 ... 383

Gow v Grant [2012] UKSC 29 ... 500

Grace v Black Horse Ltd [2014] EWCA Civ 1413 ... 1127

Grand Junction Co Ltd v Bates [1954] 2 QB 160 ... 878, 1045

Grant v Baker [2017] 2 FLR 646 ... 569

Grant v Edwards [1986] Ch 638 ... 467, 469, 479–82, 492, 658

Gray v Taylor [1998] 4 All ER 17 ... 784

Greasley v Cooke [1980] 1 WLR 1306; [1980] 3 All ER 710, CA ... 382–3, 388

Green v Ashco Horticulturist Ltd [1966] 1 WLR 889 ... 927, 934, 935

Green v Ireland [2011] EWHC 1305 (Ch) ... 268, 270

Green v Royal Bank of Scotland [2013] EWCA Civ 1197 ... 1123

Greenwood Reversions Ltd v World Environment Foundations Ltd [2008] EWCA Civ 47 [2008] HLR 31 ... 862, 878

Greig v Watson (1881) 7 VR 79 ... 1059

Grindal v Hooper, unreported, judgment 6 December 1999 ... 690

Grossman v Hooper [2001] EWCA Civ 615, CA ... 272–3

Grundt v Great Boulder Pty Gold Mines Ltd (1938) 59 CLR 641 ... 386

Guardian Ocean Cargors Ltd v Banco Brasil SA (No 3) [1992] 2 Lloyds Rep 193 ... 1166

Guerra v Italy (1998) 26 EHRR 357 ... 130

Gustovarac v Croatia (App No 60223/09) ... 138

H Waites Ltd v Hambledon Court Ltd [2014] EWHC 651 (Ch) ... 30, 1012

Habib Bank Ltd v Tailor [1982] 1 WLR 1218 ... 1080

Hair v Gillman (2000) 80 P & CR 108 ... 906, 927

Halifax Building Society v Clark [1973] Ch 307 ... 1079

Halifax plc v Curry Popeck [2008] EWHC 1692 (Ch) ... 414, 581, 604, 611

Hall v Erwin (1887) 37 Ch D 74 ... 855, 963

Halsall v Brizell [1957] Ch 169 ... 971

Hammersmith and Fulham LBC v Alexander-David [2010] Ch 272 ... 419

Hammersmith & Fulham LBC v Monk [1992] 1 AC 478, HL ... 794–7, 802

Hammond v Mitchell [1991] 1 WLR 1127, HC ... 479

Hang Seng Bank v Mee Ching Development Ltd [1970] HKLR 94 ... 1065

Hannah v Peel [1945] 1 KB 509 ... 46–50, 51, 53, 55

Hansford v Jargo [1921] 1 Ch 322 ... 923

Harman v Glencross [1986] Fam 81, CA ... 1052–3

Harris v De Pinna (1886) 33 Ch D 238 ... 903

Harris v Flower (1904) 74 LJ Ch 127 ... 890–1, 894

Harris v Goddard [1983] 3 All ER 242, CA ... 513–14

Harrison v Harrison [2013] VSCA 170 ... 404

Harrow LBC v Qazi [2004] 1 AC 983, HL ... 128, 130, 133, 814

Hart v O'Connor [1985] AC 1000 ... 1133

Harwood v Harwood [1991] 2 FLR 274 ... 507

Hatton v UK (App No 36022/97) (2002) 34 EHRR 1; (2003) 37 EHRR 28 ... 95, 130, 131

Hayward v Brunswick Permanent Benefit Building Society (1881) 8 QBD 403 ... 968, 969

Heather Moor & Edgecomb Ltd v UK (2011) 53 EHRR SE18 ... 1128

Helby v Matthews [1895] AC 471 ... 755

Helden v Strathmore Ltd [2011] EWCA Civ 542 ... 1122

Hemingway Securities Ltd v Dunraven Ltd (1996) 71 P & CR 30, HC ... 855

Henderson v Merrett Syndicates Ltd [1995] 2 AC 145 ... 1113

Henry v Henry [2010] 1 All ER 988 ... 388–9, 401, 413, 414

Hentrich v France (1994) 18 EHRR 440 ... 120, 126

Herbert v Doyle [2010] EWCA Civ 1095 ... 279, 380

Hewett v First Plus Financial Group Plc [2010] 2 P & CR 22 ... 1133, 1144

Hill v Griffin [1987] 1 EGLR 81 ... 879

Hill v Tupper (1863) 2 H & C 122 ... 157–8, 170, 176, 221

Hindcastle Ltd v Barbara Attenborough & Associates Ltd [1997] AC 70, HL ... 836–7

Hitch v Stone [2001] STC 214 ... 753

Hodgson v Marks [1971] Ch 892, CA ... 622

Hoffman v Fineberg [1949] Ch 245 ... 869

Hoggett v Hoggett (1980) 39 P & CR 121 (CA) ... 636

Holiday Inns v Broadhead (1974) 232 EG 951 ... 380

Holland v Hodgson (1872) LR 7 CP 328 ... 40

Holliday, Re [1981] Ch 405 ... 563, 569, 572

Holman v Howes [2007] EWCA 877 ... 486

Holmes v Goring (1824) 2 Bing 76 ... 914

Holmes v Westminster CC [2011] EWHC 2857 ... 141

Holwell Securities Ltd v Hughes [1973] 2 All ER 476 ... 517

Holy Monasteries v Greece (1995) 20 EHRR 1 ... 123

Hong Kong Fir v Kawasaki [1962] 1 All ER 474 ... 799

Hopgood v Brown [1955] 1 WLR 213 ... 371

Horrocks v Forray [1976] 1 WLR 230 ... 213

Horsefall v Mather (1815) Holt NP 7 ... 732

Horsey Estate Ltd v Steiger [1899] 2 QB 79, CA ... 864, 873

Horsham Properties Group Ltd v Clark [2008] EWHC 2327 ... 653, 1057, 1067, 1078, 1092–5

Hosking v Michaelides [2004] All ER (D) 147 ... 568

Hounslow LBC v Powell [2011] UKSC 8; [2011] 2 WLR 287; [2011] 2 AC 186 ... 129, 130, 132, 136, 137, 146, 239, 240, 813, 1090

Hounslow LBC v Twickenham GD Ltd [1971] Ch 233 ... 216, 218

Housden v Conservators of Wimbledon and Putney Commons [2008] EWCA Civ 200 [2008] 1 WLR 1172 ... 938

Howard E Perry v British Railway Board [1980] 1 WLR 1375 ... 255

Howard v Fanshawe [1895] 2 Ch 581 ... 874

Howard v UK (1987) 9 EHRR CD116 ... 118, 129

Hoyl Group Ltd v Cromer Town Council [2015] EWCA Civ 782 ... 368, 371

HSBC Plc v Brown [2015] EWHC 359 ... 1148

HSBC Bank plc v Dyche [2009] EWHC 2954 (Ch) ... 676, 677, 687

HSBC v Kloeckner [1990] 2 QB 514 ... 857

Hua Chiao Commercial Bank Ltd v Chiap Hua Industries Ltd [1987] AC 99 ... 846

Huang v Secretray of State for the Home Department [2007] UKHL 11, [2007] 2 AC 167 ... 97, 100, 106

Huckvale v Aegean Hotels Ltd (1989) 58 P & CR 163 ... 914

Hughes v Waite [1957] 1 WLR 713 ... 1071

Hunter and ors v Canary Wharf Ltd [1997] AC 665, HL ... 9, 219, 736–9, 794, 903, 941–2

Hunter v Babbage (1995) 69 P & CR 548 ... 524, 525

Huntingford v Hobbs [1993] 1 FLR 736 ... 464, 507

Hunts Refuse Disposals Ltd v Norfolk Environmental Waste Services Ltd [1997] 1 EGLR 16, CA ... 747

Hurst v Picture Theatres Ltd [1915] 1 KB 1, CA ... 216–17, 255

Hussain's Application, Re [2016] UKUT 297 ... 1002

Hussein v Mehlman [1992] 2 EGLR 87 (County Court) ... 798, 799, 780, 809

Hutten-Czapska v Poland (2007) 45 EHRR 4 ... 118, 121–3

Huyton SA v Peter Cremer & Co [1999] CLC 230 ... 1130

Hydeshire Ltd's Application, Re (1994) 67 P & CR 93 ... 1001

Hypo Mortgage Services Ltd v Robinson [1997] 2 FLR 71 ... 625

IAM Group plc v Chowdrey [2012] EWCA Civ 505; [2012] P & CR 13 ... 341, 342

IDC Group Ltd v Clark [1992] 1 EGLR 187; (1992) 65 P & CR 179 ... 744

Immobiliare Saffi v Italy (2000) 30 EHRR 756 ... 95

Ingram v IRC [1997] 4 All ER 395 ... 584, 802

International Tea Stores Co v Hobbs [1903] 2 Ch 165 ... 925

Inwards v Baker [1965] 2 QB 29, CA ... 245–6, 248, 371, 412

Irish Life and Permanent plc v Dunne [2015] IESC 46 ... 1075

Ivanova & Cherkezov v Bulgaria (App No 46577/15) ... 149

Ivory Gate Ltd v Spetale (1999) 77 P & CR 141 ... 861

J Pereira Fernandes SA v Mehta [2006] 1 WLR
1543 . . . 270

J Sainsbury plc v Enfield LBC [1989] 1 WLR
590 . . . 981

J Willis & Sons v Willis 1986] 1 EGLR
62 . . . 399

JA Pye (Oxford) Ltd v Graham [2001] EWCA
Civ 117; [2002] UKHL 30; [2003] 1 AC
419 . . . 107, 311, 315–16, 318, 320–5, 332,
352, 357

JA Pye (Oxford) Ltd v UK (App No 44302/02)
(2006) 43 EHRR 3; [2008] 1 EHRLR 132;
(2008) 46 EHRR 45, Grand Chamber . . . 117,
119–20, 124, 125, 311, 352–5

J&O Operations Ltd v Kingston & St Andrew
Corp [2012] UKPC 7 . . . 914

Jaggard v Sawyer [1995] 1 WLR 269,
CA . . . 998, 999

Jamaica Mutual Life Assurance Society v
Hillsborough Ltd [1989] 1 WLR 1101 . . . 992

James Jones & Sons Ltd v Earl of Tankerville
[1909] 2 Ch 440 . . . 254–6

James v Thomas [2008] 1 FLR 1598 . . . 487

James v UK (1986) 8 EHRR 123 . . . 94, 112, 115,
118, 121, 124, 809

Javins v First National Realty (1970) 428 F
2d 1071 (District of Columbia Court of
Appeals) . . . 732

Jennings v Rice [2002] EWCA Civ 159; [2003]
1 P & CR 100 . . . 246, 278, 396–9, 401, 403,
406, 407, 410, 411, 413, 482

Jerome v Kelly [2004] UKHL 25, [2004] 1 WLR
1409 . . . 286

Jervis v Harris [1996] 1 ALL ER 303 . . . 857

Jeune v Queen's Cross Properties Ltd [1974] Ch
97 . . . 857

Jobson v Record [1998] 1 EGLR 113 . . . 893

Jones v Canal & River Trust [2017] EWCA Civ
135 . . . 128, 136

Jones v Challenger [1960] 2 WLR 695 . . . 543

Jones v Kernott [2010] EWCA Civ 578; [2010]
1 WLR 2401; [2011] 3 WLR 1121 . . . 430–1,
457–63, 468–74, 476, 477, 485–92, 495, 507–9,
525, 526

Jones v Morgan [2001] EWCA Civ 995 . . . 1130,
1151, 1157

Jones v Price [1965] 2 QB 618 . . . 904

Jorden v Money (1854) 5 HL Cas 185 . . . 368

Josceleyne v Nissen [1970] 2 QB 86 . . . 275

K, Re [1985] Ch 85 . . . 525

K/S Victoria St. v House of Fraser (Stores
Management) Ltd [2011] EWCA Civ 904;
[2011] 2 P & CR 15 . . . 840

Kammins Ballrooms Co Ltd v Zenith
Investments (Torquay) Ltd [1971] AC
850 . . . 366

Karl Construction Ltd v Palisade Properties Ltd
[2002] SLT 312 . . . 126

Kateb v Howard de Walden Estates Ltd [2017] 1
WLR 1761 . . . 121

Kaur v Gill [1988] Fam 110 . . . 21

Kay v Lambeth LBC [2006] UKHL 10, [2006]
2 AC 465 . . . 90, 100, 130, 140, 142, 239, 764,
799, 800, 820

Kay v UK [2011] HLR 2 . . . 96, 130, 132, 133

Kearns Brothers Ltd v Hova Developments Ltd
[2012] EWHC 2968 (Ch) . . . 445

Keay v Morris Homes (West Midlands) Ltd
[2012] 1 WLR 2855 . . . 271–5

Keegan v UK (2007) 44 EHRR 33 . . . 129

Kennet Properties Ltd Application, Re (1996) 72
P & CR 353 . . . 1000–2

Kent v Kavanagh [2006] EWCA Civ 162, [2007]
Ch 1 . . . 928, 929

Keppell v Bailey (1834) 2 My & K 517 . . . 170–1,
176, 224, 242, 645, 976

Ker v Optima Community Housing Association
[2013] EWCA Civ 579 . . . 116

Kettel v Bloomfold Ltd [2012] EWHC 1442 . . . 1013

Kettel v Bloomfold Ltd [2012] L&TR 30 . . . 907

Khatun v UK (1998) 26 EHRR CD
212 . . . 130, 131

Khorasandijan v Bush [1993] QB 727 . . . 737

Khurshid Mustafa v Sweden (App No 23883/
06) . . . 148

Khursid Musafa & TarziBachi v Sweden (2011)
52 EHRR 24 . . . 1017

Kilcarne Holdings Ltd v Targetfellow
(Birmingham) Ltd [2005] EWCA
1355 . . . 271, 445

Kilgour v Gaddes [1904] 1 KB 457 . . . 896, 950

Kinane v Mackie-Conteh [2005] EWCA Civ 45,
CA . . . 279, 280, 283, 447, 1048

Kinch v Bullard [1999] 1 WLR 423, HC . . . 515–17

King v David Allen & Sons, Billposting Ltd
[1916] 2 AC 54, HL . . . 224, 231–2, 235,
237, 244

King, Re [1963] Ch 459, CA . . . 854

Kingsnorth Finance Co Ltd v Tizard [1986] 1
WLR 783, HC . . . 688

Knightsbridge Estates Trust Ltd v Byrne [1939]
Ch 441, CA . . . 1158–60

Kremen v Agrest [2013] 2 FLR 187 . . . 1053–4

Kryvitska & Kryvitskyy v Ukraine (App No
30856/03) . . . 93, 132

Kumar v Dunning [1989] QB 193 . . . 846, 988

Kuwait Airways v Iraqi Airways (Nos 4 & 5)
[2002] 2 AC 883 . . . 255

Lace v Chantler [1944] KB 368 . . . 772

Ladup Ltd v William & Glyns Bank plc [1985] 1
WLR 851 . . . 874

Lancashire CC v Taylor [2005] 1 P & CR 2 ... 118

Laskar v Laskar [2008] 1 WLR 2695 ... 426, 431, 459

Lawntown Ltd v Kamenzuli [2007] EWCA Civ 949 ... 1002

Lawrence v South County Freeholds Ltd [1939] Ch 656 ... 988

Lee Parker v Izzet [1971] 1 WLR 1688 ... 857

Lee's Application, Re (1996) 72 P & CR 439 ... 1002

Leeds CC v Price [2006] 2 AC 465 ... 129, 799, 800

Leeds City Council v Hall [2011] 2 AC 186 ... 813

Leigh & Sillivan Ltd v Aliakmon Shipping Co Ltd (The Aliakmon) [1986] AC 785 ... 200, 201

Leigh v Jack (1879) 5 Ex D 264 ... 325

Leigh v Taylor ... 40

Lemo & others v Croatia (App nos. 3925/10, 3955/10, 3974/10, 4009/10, 4054/10, 4128/10, 4132/10–4133/10) ... 132, 136, 148

Lester v Woodgate [2010] EWCA Civ 199 ... 955

Lewis v Averay [1972] 1 QB 198, CA ... 12

Lewis v Frank Love [1961] 1 WLR 261 ... 1157

Lewis v Metropolitan Properties Realisations Ltd [2010] Ch 148 ... 574–5

Liden v Burton [2016] EWCA Civ 275 ... 372

Lindheim v Norway (App Nos 13221/08 & 2139/10) ... 118, 122

Link Lending Ltd v Bustard [2010] EWCA Civ 424 ... 619, 628, 630, 633, 634, 636

Lithgow v UK (1986) 8 EHRR 329 ... 94, 118, 120

Littledale v Liverpool College [1990] 1 Ch 19 ... 323

Liverpool City Council v Irwin [1977] AC 239 ... 803, 904

Llewellyn v Lorey [2011] EWCA Civ 37 ... 950

Lloyd v Dugdale [2001] EWCA Civ 1754; [2002] 2 P & CR 13, CA ... 79, 229, 645, 793

Lloyds and Lloyds Application, Re (1993) 66 P & CR 112 ... 1002

Lloyds Bank v Byrne [1993] 1 FLR 369 ... 553, 554, 556

Lloyds Bank v Carrick [1996] 4 All ER 630; [1996] 2 FLR 600; (1997) 73 P & CR 314 ... 288, 660

Lloyds Bank v Rosset [1989] Ch 350; [1991] 1 AC 107, [1990] 1 All ER 1111 ... 281, 283, 475–7, 488, 622, 626, 630, 659

Lloyds TSB Bank Plc v Holdgate [2002] EWCA Civ 1543; [2003] HLR 25 ... 1148

Lohia v Lohia (2000) 13 ITELR 11 ... 424

London & Blenheim Estates Ltd v Ladbroke Retail Parks Ltd [1992] 1 WLR 1278; [1994] 1 WLR 31, CA ... 890, 906, 907

London Borough of Lambeth v Rumbelow, unreported, judgment 25 January 2001 ... 319

London & County (A&D) Ltd v Wilfred Sportsman Ltd [1971] Ch 764 ... 853

London & Regional Investments Ltd v TBI plc [2002] EWCA 355 ... 445

London and South West Railway v Gomm (1882) 20 Ch D 562 ... 968

London CC v Allen [1914] 3 KB 642, CA ... 964–5

London Development Agency v Nidai [2009] EWHC 1730 (Ch) ... 238

London Diocesan Fund v Phithwa [2005] 1 WLR 3956; [2005] UKHL 70 ... 840–2

London North Securities Ltd v Meadows [2005] EWCA Civ 956 ... 1127

London Quadrant Housing Trust v Weaver [2009] EWCA Civ 587, [2010] 1 WLR 363 ... 104

London Scottish Finance Ltd (in Administration), Re [2014] Bus LR 424 ... 1075, 1127

London Tara Hotel Ltd v Kensington Close Hotel Ltd [2010] EWHC 2749 ... 948

Long v Gowlett [1923] 2 Ch 177, HC ... 928, 929

Long v Tower Hamlets LBC [1998] Ch 197 ... 290, 788–90

Longman v Viscount Chelsea (1989) 58 P & CR 189, CA ... 294

Lopez Ostra v Spain (1995) 20 EHRR 277 ... 130

Lord Advocate v Lord Blantyre (1878–79) LR 4 All Cas 770 ... 322

Lord Compton's Case (1586) 3 Leo 196 ... 201

Lordsvale Finance Ltd v Bank of Zambia [1996] QB 752 ... 1168

Louth v Diprose (1992) 175 CLR 621 ... 1133

Lovelock v Margo [1963] 2 QB 786 ... 874

Lovett v Fairclough (1991) 61 P & CR 385 ... 310

Luker v Dennis (1877) 7 Ch D 227 ... 963

Lumley v Gye (1853) 2 E & B 216 ... 223

Lund v Taylor (1975) 31 P & CR 16 ... 992

Lysaght v Edwards (1876) 2 Ch D 499 ... 263, 286

Lyus v Prowsa Development Ltd [1982] 1 WLR 1044 ... 79, 206, 227, 437, 644

MCC Proceeds Inc v Lehman Bros [1998] 4 All ER 675 ... 201

MRA Engineering Ltd v Trimster (1988) 50 P & CR 1 ... 914

McAdams Homes Ltd v Robinson [2005] 1 P & CR 30, CA ... 953–4

McCann v UK (2008) 47 EHRR 40 ... 96, 130, 131, 137, 798

McCausland v Duncan Lawrie Ltd [1997] 1
WLR 38 . . . 266

McDonald v McDonald [2014] EWCA Civ 1049;
[2015] 2 WLR 567; [2016] UKSC 28 . . . 91,
107, 143–7, 149, 239, 573, 685, 1091

Macepark (Whittlebury) Ltd v Sargeant (No
2) [2003] 1 WLR 2284, HC . . . 892–5

McHugh v Union Bank of Canada [1913] AC
299 . . . 1101

McKerrell, Re [1912] 2 Ch 648 . . . 763

McLaughlin v Duffill [2010] Ch 1 . . . 266

Mcleod v UK (1999) 27 EHRR 493 . . . 129

McMorris v Brown [1999] 1 AC
142 . . . 1000, 1002

McMullon v Secure the Bridge Ltd
(unreported) . . . 1128

McPhail v Persons Unknown [1973] Ch
447 . . . 138, 147

Mago v Bosnia & Herzogovina (App nos 12959/
05, 19724/05, 47860/06, 8367/08, 9872/09 &
11706/09) . . . 123

Magrath v Parkside Hotels Ltd [2011] EWHC
143 . . . 903

Maguire v Itoh [2004] SLT (Sheriff Ct)
120 . . . 126

Maira, The [1990] 1 AC 637 . . . 1166

Makdessi v Cavendish Square Holdings
BV: ParkingEye Ltd v Bevis [2016] AC
1172 . . . 1151

Maklin v Dowsett [2004] EWCA Civ
904 . . . 1143

Malayan Credit v Jack Chia [1986] AC 549,
PC . . . 507

Malik v Fassenfelt [2013] EWCA Civ 798 . . . 88,
138, 152

Malory Enterprises Ltd v Cheshire Homes (UK)
Ltd [2002] Ch 216 . . . 80–3, 619, 632, 719–22

Manchester Airport plc v Dutton and ors
[2000] QB 133, CA . . . 210, 219, 221, 222

Manchester CC v Pinnock [2010] UKSC 45;
[2010] 3 WLR 1441; [2011] 2 AC 104 . . . 90,
98, 105, 109, 130, 132–7, 139–42, 146, 148,
239, 240, 573, 812, 813, 1090

Manchester Ship Canal Developments v
Persons Unknown [2014] EWHC 645 . . . 129

Manjang v Drammeh (1991) 61 P & CR 194,
PC . . . 914

Mann v Stephens (1846) 15 Sim 377 . . . 961

Marchant v Charters [1977] 1 WLR 1181 . . . 241

Marckx v Belgium (1979) 2 EHRR 330 . . . 116

Marcroft Wagons v Smith [1951] 2 KB
496 . . . 241, 745

Margerison v Bates [2008] EWHC 1211 . . . 984

Marquess of Zetland v Driver [1939] Ch 1,
CA . . . 967, 979–80

Marr v Collie [2017] UKPC 17, [2017] 3 WLR
1507 . . . 431–4, 459–63, 490, 492, 509

Marsden v Edward Heyes [1927] 2 KB 1 . . . 732

Marten v Flight Refueling Ltd [1962] 1 Ch
115 . . . 965, 967

Martin-Sklan v White [2007] BPIR 76 . . . 570

Maryland Estate v Joseph [1991] 1 WLR
83 . . . 861

Marzari v Italy (2000) 30 EHRR CD218 . . . 109

Mascall v Mascall (1985) 50 P & CR 19 . . . 292

Massey v Boulden [2003] 1 WLR 1792 . . . 892

Matchmove Ltd v Dowding [2017] 1 WLR
749 . . . 277, 283, 447

Matos E Silva Lda v Portugal (1997) 24 EHRR
573 . . . 116

Matthew v TH Sutton [1949] 4 All ER
793 . . . 1038

Matthews v Smallwood [1910] 1 Ch 777 . . . 862

Mayo, Re [1943] 1 Ch 302 . . . 543

Mayor of London v Hall and others [2010]
EWCA Civ 817 . . . 222

Meadows v Clerical Medical & General
Life Assurance Society [1981] Ch 70,
HC . . . 861–2

Medforth v Blake [1999] 3 All ER 97; [2000] Ch
86, CA . . . 1072, 1112–13

Mellacher v Austria (A/169) (1990) 12 EHRR
391 . . . 95

Mellor v Watkins (1874) LR 9 QB 400 . . . 800

Melville v Grapelodge Developments Ltd (1978)
39 P & CR 179 . . . 857

Menelaou v Bank of Cyprus UK Ltd [2014] 1
WLR 854 . . . 590

Meretz Investment NV v ACP Ltd [2007]
EWCA Civ 303; [2008] Ch 244 . . . 1105

Metropolitan Railway Co v Fowler [1892] 1 QB
165 . . . 896

Mew v Tristmire Ltd [2011] EWCA Civ
912 . . . 41

Michael v Miller [2004] 2 EGLR 151,
CA . . . 1103–4

Michael v Phillips [2017] EWHC 614
(QB) . . . 445

Midland Bank plc v Cooke [1995] 4 All ER
562 . . . 429, 464, 485, 508

Midland Railway Co's Agreement, Re [1971] Ch
725 . . . 766, 775

Mikeover v Brady [1989] 3 All ER 618,
CA . . . 760–3

Miles v Bull [1969] 1 QB 258 . . . 167

Miles v Easter [1933] Ch 611, CA . . . 978–9

Mileva v Bulgaria (App Nos 43449/02 & 21475/
04) . . . 130

Miller Smith v Miller Smith [2010] 1 FLR
1402 . . . 543, 546–7

Miller v Emcer Products [1956] Ch 304 . . . 906

Millman v Ellis (1995) 71 P & CR 158 . . . 923

Mills v Silver [1991] Ch 271 . . . 938

Milmo v Carreras [1946] KB 306 . . . 821

Mitchell v Mosley [1914] 1 Ch 438 . . . 35, 37

Mobil Oil Co Ltd v Rawlinson (1982) 43 P & CR 221 . . . 1072

Mohammadzadeh v Joseph [2006] EWHC 1040 . . . 986

Moldovan v Romania (2007) 44 EHRR 16 . . . 119

Moncrieff v Jamieson [2007] UKHL 42; [2007] 1 WLR 2620 . . . 170, 906–10

Montrose Court Holdings Ltd v Shamash [2006] All ER D 272 . . . 906

Moody v Steggles (1879) 12 Ch D 261 . . . 897, 899

Moore v SS for Home Department [2016] EWHC 2736 (Admin) . . . 116

Moreno Gomez v Spain (App No 4143/02) . . . 130

Morland v Cook (1868) LR 6 Eq 252 . . . 968, 969

Morrells of Oxford Ltd v Oxford United Football Club Ltd [2001] Ch 459 . . . 962

Morris v Morris [2008] EWCA Civ 257 . . . 487

Mortgage Business plc v Green [2013] EWHC 4243 . . . 1146

Mortgage Corporation v Shaire [2001] 4 All ER 364, HC . . . 544, 550, 554–6, 563

Mortgage Express Ltd v Lambert [2017] Ch 93 . . . 190, 424, 615, 619, 622–3, 657, 660, 661, 709

Mortgage Express Ltd v McDonnell [2001] EWCA Civ 887 . . . 590

Mortgage Express v Mardner [2004] EWCA Civ 1859 . . . 1105

Motivate Publishing FZ LLC v Hello Ltd [2015] EWHC 1554 (Ch) . . . 370, 372

Moule v Garrett (1872) LR 7 EX 101 . . . 837

Mountney v Treharne [2003] Ch 135 . . . 284

Muhammad v ARY Properties Ltd [2016] EWHC 1698 (Ch) . . . 279

Multiservice Bookbinding Ltd v Marden [1979] Ch 84, HC . . . 1134, 1164, 1166–8

Murphy v Gooch [2007] 3 FLR 934 . . . 537

Murray Bull & Co v Murray [1953] 1 QB 211 . . . 241

NRAM Ltd v Evans [2017] EWCA Civ 1013 . . . 708–11

Nash v Eads (1880) 25 SJ 95 . . . 1095

National & Provincial Building Society v Ahmed [1995] 2 EGLR 127 . . . 1078

National Carriers Ltd v Panalpina (Northern) Ltd [1981] AC 675 . . . 798, 799, 803

National Commercial Bank (Jamaica) Ltd v Hew [2003] UKPC 51 . . . 1143

National Crime Agency v Dong [2017] EWHC 3116 (Ch) . . . 425

National Provincial Bank v Ainsworth (sub nom National Provincial Bank v Hastings Car Mart and ors) [1964] Ch 665 (CA); [1965] AC 1175, HL . . . 12–23, 159, 165, 176, 184, 191, 193, 195, 199, 205–7, 210, 211, 235, 238, 251–3, 285, 580, 594, 739

National Trust v White [1987] 1 WLR 907 . . . 892

National Westminster Bank plc v Malhan [2004] EWHC 847 . . . 683, 684

National Westminster Bank plc v Morgan [1985] AC 686 . . . 1143

National Westminster Bank plc v Rushmer [2010] EWHC 554 (Ch); [2010] 2 FLR 362 . . . 553

National Westminster Bank plc v Skelton [1993] 1 WLR 72 . . . 1072

Nationwide Building Society v Wright [2009] EWCA Civ 811; [2010] Ch 318 . . . 1052

Neale v Willis (1968) 19 P & CR 836, CA . . . 441–2, 450

Nelmes v Nram plc [2016] EWCA Civ 941 . . . 1128

New Pinehurst Residents Association (Cambridge) v Silow [1988] 1 EGLR 227 . . . 1016

Newham LBC v Khatun [2004] EWCA Civ 55; [2005] QB 37 . . . 1152

Newton Abbott Co-operative Society v Williamson & Treadgold Ltd [1952] 1 Ch 286 . . . 962, 966–7

Nexis Property Ltd v Royal Bank of Scotland [2013] EWHC 3167 . . . 1123

Nicholls v Lan [2007] 1 FLR 744 . . . 571, 573

Nickerson v Barraclough [1981] Ch 426, CA . . . 914–15

Nielson-Jones v Fedden [1975] Ch 222 . . . 512, 514, 525

Nisbet & Potts Contract, Re [1906] 1 Ch 386, CA . . . 199, 334, 976–7

Noakes v Rice [1902] AC 24 . . . 1161

Nocton v Lord Ashburton [1914] AC 932 . . . 439

North Eastern Properties Ltd v Coleman [2010] 1 WLR 2715 . . . 273, 274

North Sydney Printing Pty Ltd v Sabemo Investment Corporation Pty Ltd [1971] 2 NSWLR 150 . . . 915

Norwich City College of Further and Higher Education v McQuillin [2009] EWHC 1496 . . . 984

Nynehead Developments Ltd v RH Fibreboard Containers Ltd [1991] 1 EGLR 7 . . . 799

OBG Ltd v Allan [2007] 2 WLR 920; [2008] 1 AC 1 . . . 223

O'Neill v Ulster Bank Ltd [2016] BPIR 126 . . . 1146

O'Rourke v UK (App No 39022/97) . . . 129

Oceanic Village Ltd v United Attractions Ltd [2000] Ch 234 . . . 856

Odessa, The [1916] 1 AC 145 . . . 1038

Odogwu v Vastguide Ltd [2009] EWHC 3565 (Ch) . . . 704

Office of Fair Trading v Abbey National plc [2008] EWHC 875 . . . 1156

Official Custodian for Charities v Parway Estates Development Ltd [1984] 3 WLR 525 . . . 880

Ofulue v Bossert [2008] EWCA Civ 7; [2009] 1 AC 990; [2009] Ch 1 . . . 94, 107, 330–2, 355–6

Old Grovebury Manor Farm Ltd v W Seymour Plant Sales and Hire Ltd (No 2) [1979] 1 WLR 1397 . . . 91

Oluic v Croatia (App N 61260/08) . . . 130

Onslow v Corriw (1817) 2 Madd 330 . . . 851

Orlic v Croatia (App No. 48833/07) . . . 132

Ottey v Grundy [2003] EWCA Civ 1176 . . . 409

Oun v Ahmad [2008] EWHC 545 . . . 276–7

Oxley v Hiscock [2004] EWCA Civ 546; [2005] Fam 211 . . . 283, 464–7, 470, 493

P&A Swift Investments v Combined English Stores Group plc [1989] AC 632 . . . 846

P&S Platt Ltd v Crouch [2003] EWCA Civ 1110; [2004] 1 P & CR 18 . . . 906, 924

Padden v Bevan Ashford [2012] 1 WLR 1759 . . . 1148

Paddington BC v Mendelsohn (1985) 50 P & CR 244 . . . 597

Page's Application, Re (1996) 71 P & CR 440 . . . 1001

Palk v Mortgage Service Funding plc [1993] Ch 330, CA . . . 1067–8, 1088

Pallant v Morgan [1953] 1 Ch 43 . . . 278, 380, 417, 418, 437, 443–8

Parker v Parker [2003] EWHC 1846 (Ch) . . . 408, 413

Parker v Taswell (1858) 2 De G & J 559 . . . 793

Palmer, Re [1994] Ch 316 . . . 521, 522

Pankhania v Chandegra [2013] 3 FCR 16 . . . 457, 506

Pao On v Lau Yiu Long [1980] AC 614 . . . 1130

Paragon Finance plc v DB Thakerar & Co [1999] 1 All ER 400 . . . 435

Paragon Finance plc v Nash [2002] 1 WLR 685, CA . . . 1127, 1164–5

Paragon Finance v Pender [2005] EWCA Civ 760 . . . 1164

Parker v British Airways Board [1982] QB 1004, CA . . . 49–53, 784

Parker v Taswell (1858) 2 De G & J 559 . . . 793

Parker-Tweedale v Dunbar Bank (No 1) [1991] Ch 12, CA . . . 1099–1100

Parshall v Hackney [2013] EWCA Civ 240 . . . 313, 314, 319, 712, 714

Pascoe v Turner [1979] 1 WLR 431 . . . 399

Patel v Ali [1984] Ch 283 . . . 285

Patel v K&J Restaurants Ltd [2010] EWCA Civ 1211 . . . 878

Patel v Mirza [2017] AC 467 . . . 348, 427–9

Pathania v Adedeji [2010] EWHC 3085 . . . 1144

Paulic v Croatia (App No 3572/06) . . . 132, 139

Payne v Cardiff RDC [1932] 1 KB 241 . . . 1091

Pchelintseva v Russia (App nos 47724/ 07, 58677/11, 2920/13, 3127/13 & 15320/ 13) . . . 123

Peacock v Custins [2002] 1 WLR 1815, CA . . . 891–2

Peckham v Ellison (2000) 79 P & CR 276 . . . 919

Peel Land and Property (Ports No 3) Ltd v TS Sheerness Steel Ltd [2014] 2 P & CR 8, CA . . . 42

Peffer v Rigg [1977] 1 WLR 285, HC . . . 79, 81, 642

Peires v Bickerton's Aerodromes Ltd [2017] EWCA Civ 273, [2017] 1 WLR 2865 . . . 32

Pelipenko v Russia (App No 69037/10) . . . 92, 109, 132

Pennine Raceways Ltd v Kirklees MBC [1983] QB 382 . . . 237

Pennycook v Shaws (EAL) Ltd [2004] Ch 296 . . . 116

Penton v Barnett [1898] 1 QB 276 . . . 862

Perry v Rolfe [1848] VLR 297 . . . 1059

Pettitt v Pettitt [1969] 2 All ER 385; [1970] AC 777, HL . . . 425–6, 458, 467, 479, 482, 491

Pettkus v Becker (1980) 117 DLR (3d) 257 . . . 492

Phillips v Mobil Oil Co Ltd [1989] 1 WLR 888 . . . 846

Phillips v Phillips' (2002) 118 LQR 296 . . . 190

Phipps v Pears [1965] 1 QB 76, CA . . . 904–5, 934

Phoenix Recoveries (UK) Ltd v Kotecha [2011] EWCA Civ 105 . . . 1127

Pickard v Sears (1837) 6 Ad & El 469 . . . 360

Pickering v Rudd (1815) 4 Camp 219 . . . 32

Pine Valley Developments Ltd v Ireland (1992) 14 EHRR 319 . . . 116, 118

Pinewood Estates, Re [1958] Ch 280 . . . 988

Pinnock v Manchester City Council [2011] 2 AC 104 . . . 798

Piskor's Case [1954] Ch 553 . . . 586

Pitt v PHH Asset Management Ltd [1994] 1 WLR 327 . . . 266

Plevin v Paragon Personal Finance Ltd [2014] UKSC 61 . . . 1128

Plimmer v Wellington Corpn (1884) 9 App Cas 699 (PC) . . . 246

Polly Peck International (No 2), Re [1998] 3 All ER 812 . . . 436

Ponyayyeva v Russia (App No 63508/11) . . . 123

Poplar Housing and Regeneration Community Association v Donoghue [2001] EWCA Civ 595, [2002] QB 48 . . . 102

Pountney v Clayton (1883) 11 QBD 820 . . . 35

Powell and Rayner v UK (1990) 12 EHRR 355 . . . 130, 131

Powell v McFarlane (1979) 38 P & CR 452 . . . 315, 320–4

Preedy v Dunne [2015] EWHC 2713 (Ch) . . . 250

Prest v Petrodel Resources Ltd [2013] 2 AC 415 . . . 425

Pritchard v Briggs [1980] Ch 338 . . . 697

Proctor v Bennis (1887) 36 Ch D 740, CA . . . 367

Proctor v Hodgson (1855) 10 Exch 824 . . . 914

Prokopovich v Russia (App No 58255/00) . . . 92

Property and Bloodstock Ltd v Emerton [1968] Ch 94 . . . 1107

Prudential Assurance Ltd v London Residuary Body [1992] 2 AC 386, HL . . . 764–7, 770, 773, 777, 781, 783, 790, 794

Pugh v Savage [1970] 2 QB 373 . . . 950

Purbrick v London Borough of Hackney [2003] EWHC 1871 . . . 324

Purchase v Lichfield Brewery Co [1915] 1 KB 184 . . . 847

Pwllbach Colliery Co Ltd v Woodman [1915] AC 634 . . . 916

Pye v Stodday Land Ltd [2016] EWHC 2454 (Ch), [2016] 4 WLR 168 . . . 72, 300–1, 303, 638

Pye v UK (2006) 43 EHRR 3; (2008) 46 EHRR 45 . . . 352, 355

Quaffers Ltd, Re (1988) 56 P & CR 142 . . . 1000

Quennell v Maltby [1979] 1 WLR 318, CA . . . 1073–4, 1105

Quigley v Masterson [2011] EWHC 2529 (Ch) . . . 514

RHP Ltd v Mirror Group Newspapers and Mirror Group Holdings (1992) 65 P & CR 252 . . . 837

R v Ahmad [2014] 3 WLR 23 . . . 118

R v Hardcastle [2009] UKSC 14 . . . 90

R v May [2008] 1 AC 1028 . . . 118

R v Muzafar and Qurban Unreported, Judgment 10 June 2014, Leeds CC . . . 492

R v Oxfordshire CC, ex p Sunningwell Parish Council [2000] 1 AC 335 . . . 936–8

R v Tower Hamlets, ex p van Goetz [1999] 2 WLR 582 . . . 793

R v Waya [2013] 1 AC 294 . . . 118, 122, 588

R (Barkas) v North Yorkshire CC [2014] 2 WLR 1360 . . . 948–9

R (Beresford) v Sunderland CC [2003] UKHL 60 [2004] 1 AC 889 . . . 936, 948

R (Hooper) v Secretary of State for Work and Pensions . . . 105

R (Lewis) v Redcar & Cleveland Borough Council [2010] UKSC 11; [2010] 2 AC 70 . . . 936, 943–5

R (MA) v SSWP [2013] EWHC 2213 . . . 112

R (Ullah) v Special Adjudicator . . . 90

R (on the application of Barkas) v North Yorkshire County Council [2014] UKSC 31; [2014] 2 WLR 1360 . . . 319, 936

R (on the application of Begum) v Denbigh High School Governors [2006] UKHL 15 . . . 106

R (on the application of British Bankers Association) v FSA [2011] EWHC 999 . . . 1124, 1128

R (on the application of Carmichael & others) v SSWP [2016] UKSC 58; [2016] 1 WLR. 455 . . . 112

R (on the application of Daly) v SS for the Home Department [2001] UKHL 26 . . . 106

R (on the application of IFG Financial Services Ltd v FSO [2005] EWHC 1153 . . . 1128

R (on the application of Macleod) v Peabody Trust Governors [2016] EWHC 737 . . . 102

R(on the application of Mott) v Environment Agency [2016] 1 WLR 4338 . . . 116, 119, 125

R (on the application of N) v Lewisham LBC:R (on the application of H) v Newham LBC [2014] 3 WLR 1548 . . . 92, 136, 140–1

R (on the application of Williams v FOS [2008] EWHC 2142 . . . 1129

R & L, SRO & Others v The Czech Republic (App Nos. 37926/05, 25784/09, 36002/09, 44410/09 & 65546/09) . . . 92, 120

Rabiu v Marlbray Ltd [2016] EWCA Civ 476, [2016] 1 WLR 5147 . . . 270

Rainbow Estates Ltd v Tokenhold Ltd 1999] Ch 64 . . . 857

Rains v Buxton (1880) 14 Ch D 537 . . . 106

Raja v Austin Gray [2003] 1 EGLR 91 . . . 1098, 1110

Ramroop (Sampson) v Ishmael and Heerasingh [2010] UKPC 14 . . . 322

Ramsden v Dyson (1866) LR 1 HL 129 . . . 246, 365–8, 373, 377, 391

Rance v Elvin (1985) 50 P & CR 9 . . . 903

Randall v Stevens (1853) 2 E & B 641 . . . 329

Rees Investment Ltd v Groves [2002] 1 P & CR DG 9 . . . 1080

Rees v Sherrett [2001] EWCA Civ 760; [2001] 1 WLR 1541 . . . 904

Reeve v Lisle [1902] AC 461 . . . 1157

Regan v Paul Properties Ltd [2006] EWCA Civ 1391, [2007] Ch 135 . . . 995

Regency Villas Title Ltd v Diamond Resorts (Europe) Ltd [2017] EWCA Civ 238 . . . 901–2

Regent Oil Co Ltd v JA Gregory (Hatch End) Ltd [1966] Ch 402 . . . 1045

Reichman v Beveridge [2006] EWCA Civ 1659 . . . 856

Reid v Bickerstaff [1909] 2 Ch 305 . . . 989

Renals v Cowlishaw (1878) 8 Ch D 125 . . . 979, 989

Rexhaven Ltd v Nurse (1995) 28 HLR 241 . . . 880

Rhone v Stephens [1994] 2 AC 310 . . . 191–3, 961, 969–70, 972–3

Richard Clarke & Co Ltd v Widnall [1976] 1 WLR 845 . . . 859

Ricketts v Scothorn 77 NW 365 (1898) . . . 370

Ridgewood Properties Group Ltd v Valero Energy Ltd [2013] EWHC 98 . . . 849

Rimmer v Rimmer [1953] 1 QB 63 . . . 491

Roake v Chadha [1984] 1 WLR 40, HC . . . 983–4, 988

Robert Leonard Developments v Wright [1994] NPC 49 . . . 275

Roberts v Bank of Scotland [2014] EWCA Civ 882 . . . 1074

Roberts v Lawton [2017] 1 P & CR 3 . . . 1044

Roberts v Swangrove Estates Ltd [2007] 2 P & CR 17 . . . 322

Roberts Petroleum Ltd v Bernard Kenny Ltd [1983] 2 AC 192 . . . 1052

Robertson v Fraser (1870–71) LR 6 Ch App 696 . . . 507

Rochefoucauld v Boustead [1897] 1 Ch 196 . . . 226, 278, 417, 418, 420, 437–42, 448, 450

Rodway v Landy [2001] Ch 703, CA . . . 538–9, 542

Roe v Siddons (1889) 22 QBD 224 . . . 896

Rogers v Hosegood [1900] 2 Ch 388 . . . 979

Rollerteam Ltd v Riley [2016] EWCA Civ 1291 . . . 265, 266

Ropaigealach v Barclays Bank plc [2000] QB 263, CA . . . 1092

Ropemaker Properties Ltd v Noonhaven Ltd [1989] 2 EGLR 50 . . . 878

Rose, Re [1949] Ch 78 . . . 292

Rose, Re; Rose v IRC [1952] Ch 499 . . . 292, 295

Rose v Hyman [1912] AC 623 . . . 878

Rousk v Sweden (App No. 27183/04) . . . 96

Rowland v Environment Agency [2003] EWCA Civ 1885 . . . 116

Royal Bank of Scotland Plc v Chandra [2011] EWCA Civ 192; [2010] 1 Lloyds Rep 677 . . . 1133, 1144

Royal Bank of Scotland v Etridge (No 2) [2001] UKHL 44; [2002] 2 AC 773 . . . 550, 590, 1131, 1132, 1136, 1138–48

Royal Trust Co of Canada v Markham [1975] 1 WLR 1416 . . . 1076

Royal Victoria Pavilion, Ramsgate, Re [1961] Ch 58 . . . 962

Rugby School (Governors) v Tannahill [1935] 1 KB 87 . . . 866, 869

SEDAC Investments Ltd v Tanner [1982] 1 WLR 1342 . . . 857

Saadi v Italy [2009] 49 EHRR 30 . . . 92

Saeed v Plustrade Ltd [2001] EWCA Civ 2011, [2002] 2 P & CR 19 . . . 906

Samuel Keller Holdings Ltd v Martins Bank Ltd [1971] 1 WLR 43 . . . 1072

Samuel v Jarrah Timber & Wood Paving Corporation Ltd [1904] AC 323, HL . . . 1157

Saunders v Anglia Building Society, sub nom Gallie v Lee [1971] AC 1004 . . . 1130

Saunders v Vautier (1841) 4 Beav 115 . . . 529

Saville v Central Capital Ltd [2014] EWCA 337 . . . 1123

Savmots v Investments Ltd v Secretary of State for the Environment [1979] AC 145 . . . 923

Savva v Hussein (1997) 73 P & CR 150, CA . . . 867

Sayers v Collyer (1885) 28 Ch D 103 . . . 999

Scala House & District Property Co Ltd v Forbes [1974] QB 575 . . . 869, 873

Schwann v Cotton [1916] 2 Ch 120; [1916] 2 Ch 459 . . . 903, 921

Scott (Rosemary) v Southern Pacific Mortgages Ltd [2014] UKSC 52; [2015] AC 385 . . . 11, 23, 83, 284, 288, 290, 292, 298, 299, 302, 584–91, 641, 697, 724

Scott v UK (App No 10741/84) . . . 116, 1002

Seddon v Smith (1877) 36 LT 168 . . . 324

Segal Securities Ltd v Thoseby [1963] 1 QB 887, HC . . . 863–4

Selby DC v Samuel Smith Old Brewery (Tadcaster) Ltd (2000) 80 P & CR 466 . . . 924

Selous Street Properties Ltd v Oronel Fabrics Ltd (1984) 270 EG 643 . . . 837

Semiahmoo Indian Band v Canada (1997) 148 DLR (4th) 523 . . . 439

Seymour Road (Southampton) Ltd v Williams [2010] EWHC 111 . . . 981

Shadwell v Shadwell (1860) 142 ER 62 (CCP) . . . 370

Shah v Forsters LLP [2017] EWHC 2433 . . . 510

Shah v Shah [2002] QB 35 . . . 294

Shami v Shami [2012] EWHC 664 (Ch) . . . 668

Sharpe, Re [1980] 1 WLR 219 . . . 237

Shaw v Applegate [1977] 1 WLR 970 . . . 998

Sheffield CC v Smart [2002] HLR 34 . . . 118

Shelfer v City of London Electric Lighting Co [1895] 1 Ch 287 . . . 995

Shell UK Ltd & ors v Total UK Ltd & ors [2010] EWCA Civ 180, [2011] QB 86 ... 199–202, 739

Shelwith (Leisure) Ltd v Armstrong [2016] 2 WLR 144 ... 1067

Shepherd Homes Ltd v Sandham [1971] Ch 340 ... 998

Sheppard v Turner [2006] 2 P & CR 28 ... 1001

Shiloh Spinners Ltd v Harding [1973] AC 691 ... 658, 880

Shipman v Shipman [1924] 2 Ch 140 ... 15

Shropshire CC v Edwards (1982) 46 P & CR 270 ... 987

Sidhu v van Dyke [2014] HCA 19 ... 383, 404

Sidnell v Wilson [1966] 2 QB 67 ... 1017

Siew Soon Wah alias Siew Pooi Tong v Yong Tong Hong [1973] AC 836 ... 237

Silven Properties Ltd v Royal Bank of Scotland plc [2004] 1 WLR 997, CA ... 1097–8, 1101–2, 1109–10, 1113

Simmons v Dobson [1991] 1 WLR 720 ... 950

Sims v Dacorum BC [2013] 3 WLR 1006 ... 118, 131, 137, 138, 797

Site Developments (Ferndown) Ltd v Barrett Homes Ltd [2007] EWHC 415 .... 998, 1002

Skelwith (Leisure) Ltd v Armstrong [2015] EWHC 2830, [2016] Ch 345 .... 84, 1047

Skilleter v Charles [1992] 13 EG 113 ... 1016

Skrtic v Croatia (App no. 64982/12) ... 132

Small v Oliver & Saunders [2006] EWHC 1293 981

Smart v Lambeth LBC [2013] EWCA Civ 1375; [2014] HLR 7 ... 319

Smith v Bottomley [2014] 1 FLR 626 ... 476

Smith v Brudenell-Bruce [2002] 2 P & CR 51, HC ... 945

Smith v Chadwick (1884) 9 App Cas 187 ... 383

Smith v Molyneaux [2016] UKPC 35, [2017] 1 P & CR 7 ... 317

Smith and Snipes Hall Farm Ltd v River Douglas Catchment Board [1949] 2 KB 500 ... 978

Snaith and Dolding's Application, Re (1995) 67 P & CR 93 ... 1001

Snook v London and West Ridings Investments Ltd [1967] 2 QB 786, CA ... 754–5

Sobey v Sainsbury [1913] 2 Ch 513 ... 999

Southend-on-Sea BC v Armour [2014] HLR 23 ... 141, 813

South Pacific Mortgages Ltd v V [2015] EWMisc B42 ... 113

Southward Housing Co-operative Ltd v Walker [2016] Ch 443 ... 102, 112, 777–81

Southwark Roman Catholic Diocesan Corp v South London Church Fund and Southwark Diocesan Board of Finance [2009] EWHC 3368 ... 981

Southwell v Blackburn [2014] EWCA Civ 1347 ... 372, 388, 409

Sovmots Investment Ltd v Secretary of State for the Environment [1979] AC 144 ... 922, 929

Spectrum Plus Ltd, Re [2005] 2 AC 680, HL ... 1041

Spencer's Case (1583) 5 Co Rep 16a ... 242, 845–6

Spielplatz Ltd v Pearson [2015] EWCA Civ 804 ... 41

Spicer v Martin (1888) 14 App Cas 12 ... 989

Spiro v Glencrown Properties Ltd [1991] Ch 537, HC ... 267

Sporrong and Lonnroth v Sweden (1982) 8 EHRR 123; (1983) 5 EHRR 35 ... 115, 116, 119, 120

Springette v Defoe [1992] 2 FLR 388; (1993) 65 P & CR 1 ... 456, 464

Squarrey v Harris Smith (1981) 42 P & CR 118 ... 923

Stack v Dowden [2007] 2 AC 432 ... 20, 283, 426, 429–33, 457–68, 475–8, 485–92, 495–7, 507, 509, 525, 526, 537

Stafford v Lee (1993) 63 P & CR 172, CA ... 917–18

Statileo v Croatia (App No 12027/10) ... 118

Standard Chartered Bank Ltd v Walker [1982] 1 WLR 1410 ... 1097

Stanhope v Haworth (1886) 3 TLR 34 ... 875

Stannard v Issa [1987] AC 175 ... 1001

Star Energy Weald Basin Ltd and another v Bocardo SA [2009] 3 WLR 1010; [2010] Ch 100; [2010] UKSC 35, [2010] 3 WLR 654 ... 35, 37

State Bank of India v Sood [1997] Ch 276, CA ... 665–8

Steadman v Steadman [1974] 2 All ER 977; [1976] AC 536 ... 265

Steria Ltd v Hutchison [2007] ICR 445 ... 383

Stewart v Lancashire Mortgage Corporation Ltd [2010] EWLandRA 2009/86 ... 703

Stockholm Finance Ltd v Garden Holdings Inc [1984] FLR 313 ... 634

Stocks v Whitgift Homes Ltd [2001] EWCA Civ 1732 ... 987

Stokes v Anderson [1991] 1 FLR 391 ... 464

Stonham v Ramrattan [2011] 1 WLR 1617 ... 574

Strand Securities Ltd v Caswell [1965] Ch 958, CA ... 626

Street v Denham [1954] 1 WLR 624 ... 17

Street v Mountford [1985] AC 809 ... 167, 208, 240, 732–5, 739–46, 749, 752, 783–5, 811, 815, 825, 826

Street v Mountford (1996) 16 LS 200 ... 758

Stretch v UK (2004) 38 EHRR 12 ... 116

Sturges v Bridgman (1879) LR 11 Ch D 852 ... 942–3

Stynes v Western Power (East Midlands) plc [2013] UKUT 214 (LC) . . . 33

Sugarman v Porter [2006] EWHC 331 . . . 988

Suggitt v Suggitt [2012] EWCA Civ 1140 . . . 404

Surrey County Council v Bredero Homes Ltd [1993] 1 WLR 1361 . . . 999

Swallow Securities Ltd v Brand (1981) 45 P & CR 328 . . . 857

Swift Advances plc v Okokenu [2015] CTLC 30 . . . 1128

Swift 1st Ltd v Chief Land Registrar [2015] EWCA Civ 330; [2015] Ch 602 (CA) . . . 69, 73, 82–4, 615, 699, 702, 708, 720, 724

Swift 1st Ltd v Colin [2011] EWHC 2410 . . . 1047

Swiss Bank Group v Lloyds Bank Ltd [1979] 1 Ch 548; [1982] AC 584, HL . . . 243, 1039

Swynson Ltd v Lowick Rose LLP [2017] UKSC 32 . . . 590

TSB plc v Marshall [1998] 2 FLR 769 . . . 556

Tanner v Tanner [1975] 1 WLR 1346, CA . . . 210–14

Taylor v Central Bedfordshire Council [2009] EWCA Civ 613 . . . 106

Taylor v Dickens [1998] 1 FLR 806 . . . 401

Taylor Fashions Ltd v Liverpool Victoria Trustees Co Ltd [1982] QB 133 . . . 368, 390–2

Tehidy Minerals Ltd v Norman [1971] 2 QB 518 . . . 938, 942, 954

Telchadder v Wickland Holdings Ltd [2014] UKSC 57 . . . 871–2

Texaco Antilles v Kernochan [1973] AC 609 . . . 994

Texaco v Mulberry Filling Station [1972] 1 WLR 814 . . . 1163

Thakker v Northern Rock Plc [2014] EWHC 2017 . . . 1075

Thames Guaranty Ltd v Campbell [1985] QB 210 . . . 1049

Thamesmead Town Ltd v Allotey (2000) 79 P & CR 557, CA . . . 973–4

Thomas v Clydesdale Bank [2010] EWHC 2755; [2010] NPC 107, QB . . . 627, 633, 634, 636

Thomas v Hayward (1869) LR 4 Ex 311 . . . 846

Thomas v Sorrell (1673) Vaugh 330, Exchequer Chamber . . . 207

Thompson v Foy [2010] 1 P & CR 16 . . . 598–600, 602, 620, 622, 627, 631, 636

Thompson v Hurst [2014] 1 FLR 238 . . . 461, 474

Thompson v Park [1944] KB 408 . . . 215–16, 218, 732

Thorner v Major [2009] UKHL 18, [2009] 1 WLR 776; [2009] 3 All ER 945 . . . 292, 360–6, 369–74, 379–82, 386, 394, 402, 404, 410, 411, 436, 1048

Tichborne v Weir (1892) 67 LTR 735 . . . 333

Tijardovic v Croatia (App No. 38906/13) . . . 132

Tindall Cobham 1 Ltd v Adda Hotels [2014] EWCA Civ 1215 . . . 840

Tinsley v Milligan [1994] 1 AC 340, HL . . . 427, 428

Titchmarsh v Royston Water Co Ltd (1899) 81 LT 673 . . . 914

Tito v Wadell (No 2) [1977] 1 Ch 106 . . . 972

Tomina v Russia App Nos 20578/08, 21159/08, 22903/08, 24519/08, 24728/08, 25084/08, 25558/08, 25559/08, 27555/08, 27568/08, 28031/08, 30511/08, 31038/08, 45120/08, 45124/08, 45131/08, 45133/08, 45141/08, 45167/08 & 45173/08 . . . 123

Tomlin v Luce (1889) 43 ChD 191 . . . 1098

Tootal Clothing Ltd v Guinea Property Management Ltd (1992) 64 P & CR 452, CA . . . 271, 272

Tophams Ltd v Earl of Sefton [1967] 1 AC 50 . . . 962

Topplan Estates Ltd v Townley [2004] EWCA 1369 . . . 324, 334

Tower Hamlets LBC v Bromley LBC [2015] EWHC 1954 (Ch) . . . 41

Tribe v Tribe [1996] Ch 107 . . . 427

Truman Hanbury Buxton & Co Ltd's Application, Re [1956] 1 QB 261 . . . 1000

Tse Kwong Lam v Wong Chit Sen [1983] 1 WLR 1349 . . . 1103, 1105, 1106

Tulk v Moxhay (1848) 2 Ph 774 . . . 192, 242, 243, 961–2, 964, 968, 969, 975, 1016

Turkey v Awadh [2005] 2 FCR 7 . . . 1143

Twentieth Century Banking Corp v Wilkinson [1977] Ch 99 . . . 1091

Twinsectra Ltd v Hynes [(1995) 71 P & CR 145 . . . 861

UBC Corporate Services Ltd v Williams [2002] EWCA Civ 555 . . . 1144

UK Housing Alliance (North West) Ltd v Francis [2010] EWCA Civ 117 . . . 1154

US v Causby 328 US 256 (1946) . . . 37

Uglow v Uglow [2004] EWCA Civ 987 . . . 394, 409

Ulrich v Ulrich and Felton [1968] 1 WLR 180 . . . 491

Union Lighterage Co v London Graving Dock Co [1902] 2 Ch 557, CA . . . 947, 948

United Bank of Kuwait plc v Sahib [1996] 3 WLR 472; [1997] Ch 107, CA . . . 265, 1047–8

United Dominions Trust Ltd v Shellpoint Trustees Ltd [1993] 4 All ER 310 . . . 874

Universe Sentinel, The [1983] 1 AC 366, HL . . . 1131

Van Haarlam v Kasner (1992) 64 P & CR 214 . . . 869, 878

Vandepitte v Preferred Insurance Corp of
   New York [1933] AC 70 ... 158
Vandervell's Trusts (No 2), Re [1974] Ch
   269 ... 421, 429
Vernon v Bethell (1761) 2 Eden 113 ... 1149
Verrall v Great Yarmouth Borough Council
   [1981] QB 202, CA ... 216, 732
Verrin v Welcome Financial Services Ltd [2017]
   ECC 7 ... 1128
Vincent v Premo Enterprises (Voucher Sales)
   Ltd [1969] 2 QB 609, CA ... 294
Virdi v Chana [2008] EWHC 2901 ... 907
Voyce v Voyce (1991) 62 P & CR 290 ... 412

Wakeham v Wood (1982) 43 P & CR 40 ... 998
Walby v Walby [2012] EWHC 3089 ... 914
Walker v Burton [2013] EWCA Civ 1228; [2014]
   1 P & CR 9 ... 74
Walker v Hall [1984] 1 FLR 126 ... 464
Wall v Collins [2007] EWCA Civ 444; [2007] Ch
   390 ... 896
Wallingford v Mutual Society (1880) 5 App Cas
   685 ... 1168
Wallis's Cayton Bay Holiday Camp Ltd
   v Shell-Mex and BP Ltd [1975] QB 94,
   CA ... 318, 325
Walsh v Lonsdale (1882) 21 Ch D 9 ... 193, 194,
   263, 284, 792
Walton v Walton, unreported, 14 Apr 1994,
   CA ... 362, 372–3, 399
Waltons Stores v Maher (1988) 164 CLR
   387 ... 370
Wandsworth Board of Works v United
   Telephone Co. Ltd (1884) 13 QBD 904 ... 32
Ward v Kirkland [1967] Ch 194 ... 922
Waring v London and Manchester Assurance
   Co Ltd [1935] Ch 310 ... 1107
Warnborough Ltd v Garmite Ltd [2003] EWCA
   Civ 1544, CA ... 1158
Waterside Finance Ltd v Karim [2013] 1 P & CR
   21 ... 1127
Watts v Stewart [2017] 2 WLR 1107 ... 735, 739,
   745, 747, 783, 814
Waverley Borough Council v Fletcher [1996]
   QB 334, CA ... 54–6
Wayling v Jones (1993) 69 P & CR 170,
   CA ... 383–6, 484
Webb v Frank Bevis Ltd [1940] 1 All ER
   247 ... 42
Webb v Pollmount [1966] Ch 584 ... 617
Webb's Lease, Re [1951] Ch 808, CA ... 918–20
Weg Motors Ltd v Hales [1962] Ch 49 ... 1045
West Bromwich Building Society v Crammer
   [2002] EWHC 2618 ... 1093
West Bromwich Building Society v Wilkinson
   [2005] UKHL 44 ... 1114

West Kent Housing Association Ltd v Haycroft
   [2011] EWHC 2857 ... 141
West London Commercial Bank v Reliance
   Permanent Building Society (1885) 29 Ch D
   954 ... 1093
West Sussex Constabulary's Widows, Children
   and Benevolent (1930) Fund Trusts, Re [1971]
   Ch 1 ... 421
Westdeutsche Landesbank Gorozentrale v
   Islington LBC [1996] AC 669 ... 421, 422,
   426, 427, 429, 435–6, 1166
Western Bank Ltd v Schindler [1977] Ch
   1 ... 1074
Westminster City Council v Clarke [1992] 2 AC
   288, HL ... 747–9
Whale v Viasystems [2002] EWCA Civ
   480 ... 589
Whatman v Gibson (1839) 2 My & K 517 ... 961
Wheeldon v Burrows (1879) 12 LR Ch D
   31 ... 885, 911, 913, 920–2, 928, 933
Wheeler v Saunders [1996] Ch 19 ... 923
White Rose Cottage, Re [1965] Ch 940 ... 1066
White v City of London Brewery (1889) 42 Ch D
   237 ... 1072
White v Jones [1995] 2 AC 207 ... 201
White v White [2003] EWCA 924, CA ... 553
White v White [2004] 2 FLR 321 ... 541–3,
   547, 548
Whittaker v Kinnear [2011] EWHC 1479
   (QB) ... 279
William Old International Ltd v Arya [2009]
   EWHC 599 ... 903
Williams & Glyn's Bank v Boland [1979]
   Ch 312; [1981] AC 487, HL ... 183, 186, 456,
   536, 581, 582, 594, 595, 618, 622–5, 628–9,
   670, 689
Williams v Hensman (1861) J&H 546, (1861) 70
   ER 862 ... 510–11, 518, 522, 524, 527, 528
Williams v Kiley (t/a CK Supermarkets Ltd)
   (No 1) [2003] L & TR 20 ... 856
Williams v Sandy Lane (Chester) Ltd [2006]
   EWCA Civ 1738 ... 950, 954
Williams v Staite [1979] Ch 291, CA ... 247, 249
Williams v Williams [1976] 3 WLR 494 ... 544
Willmott v Barber (1880) 15 Ch D 96 ... 391
Wilson v First County Council Trust Ltd (No 2)
   [2003] UKHL 40, [2004] 1 AC 816 ... 99–101,
   117, 1127
Wilson v Secretary of State for Trade &
   Industry [2003] UKHL 40 ... 683
Wimbledon and Putney Commons [2008]
   EWCA Civ 200; [2008] 1 WLR 1172 ... 938
Winter Garden Theatre (London) Ltd v
   Millennium Productions Ltd [1948] AC 173,
   HL ... 210, 213, 214, 216, 233, 999
Winter v Traditional & Contemporary
   Contracts [2007] EWCA Civ 1088 ... 999

Winterburn v Bennett [2016] EWCA Civ
482 . . . 936, 945–6

Winterstein v France [2013] (App
no. 27013/07) . . . 109, 138

Wishart v Credit & Mercantile plc; Credit
and Mercantile plc v Kaymuu Ltd [2015]
EWCA Civ 655; [2015] 2 P & CR 15 . . . 11,
598–602, 615

Wodzicki v Wodzicki [2017] EWCA Civ
95 . . . 459

Wong v Beaumont Property Trust Ltd [1965] 1
QB 173 . . . 916

Wood v Leadbitter (1845) 13 M & W
838 . . . 209, 217, 233, 255

Wood v Manley (1839) 11 Ad & E 34 . . . 254

Wood v UK (1997) 24 EHRR CD 69 . . . 1090

Wood v Waddington [2014] EWHC
1358 . . . 929–32

Woodall v Clifton [1905] 2 Ch 257, 279 . . . 846

Woolwich Building Society v Brown [1996]
CLC 625 . . . 1083

Worcester (Earl of) v Finch (1600) 4 Co Inst
85 . . . 201

Wright v Macadam [1949] 2 KB 744,
CA . . . 906, 925–7

Wrotham Park Estate Co Ltd v Parkside Homes
Ltd [1974] 1 WLR 798, HC . . . 968, 998, 999

YL v Birmingham CC [2008] 1 AC 95, . . . 102

Yanner v Eaton (1999) 201 CLR 351 (High
Court of Australia) . . . 27, 28

Yaxley v Gotts [2000] 1 Ch 162,
CA . . . 279–84, 447

Yeoman's Row Management Ltd v Cobbe
[2008] UKHL 55; [2008] 1 WLR 1752 . . . 434,
445, 1048

Yordanova v Bulgaria (App No 25446/
06) . . . 138

Yorkshire Bank Plc v Hall [1999] 1 WLR
1713 . . . 1111

Yorkshire Railway Co v Maclure (1882) 21 Ch D
309 . . . 755

Z, Re (A Minor) (Identification: Restrictions on
Publication) [1997] Fam 1, 33 . . . 470

Zabor v Poland (App no 33690/06) . . . 129

Zarb v Parry [2012] 1 WLR 1240 . . . 326–9, 341

Zehentner v Austria [2011] 52 EHRR 22 . . . 111,
126, 132, 148

Zrilic v Croatia (App No 46726/11) . . . 148

TABLE OF STATUTES

The European Convention on Human Rights is tabled under Sch 1 of the Human Rights Act

Access to Neighbouring Land Act 1992 ... 910
Administration of Estates Act 1925, s
   9(1) ... 350
Administration of Justice Act 1970
   s 36 ... 1064, 1075, 1078, 1079, 1091
   s 36(1) ... 1085
   s 36(2) ... 1186
   s 36(3) ... 1186
   s 39(1) ... 1078
Administration of Justice Act 1973,
   s 8 ... 1079
Anti-social Behaviour Act 2003 ... 813

Banking (Special Provisions) Act 2008 ... 13
Bankruptcy Act 1914 ... 521

Charging Orders Act 1979
   s 1(1) ... 1051
   s 1(5) ... 1052
   s 1(7) ... 1052
   s 1(8) ... 1052
   s 2(1)(a)(i) ... 1051
   s 3(4) ... 1051
   s 3(5) ... 1053
Children Act 1989 ... 140, 547
   s 15 ... 140
   Sch 1 ... 213
Civil Aviation Act 1949, s 40 ... 32
Civil Aviation Act 1982, s 76(1) ... 32
Civil Partnership Act 2004
   s 82 ... 20, 251
   Sch 5, para 2 ... 456
   Sch 9 ... 20, 251
Commonhold and Leasehold Reform Act
   2002 ... 1008
   s 3(1)(b) ... 1019
   s 7 ... 1019
   s 7(3) ... 1020
   s 8 ... 1020
   s 9 ... 1019
   s 9(3)(f) ... 1020
   s 10 ... 1020
   s 14 ... 1025
   s 15 ... 1021
   s 16 ... 1024

   s 17 ... 1021
   s 17(5) ... 1021
   s 20 ... 1021
   s 21 ... 1021
   s 22 ... 1021
   s 23 ... 1020
   s 24 ... 1020
   s 26 ... 1025
   ss 27–29 ... 1021
   s 30 ... 1020
   s 31 ... 1023
   s 35 ... 1027
   s 35(3)(b) ... 1028
   s 38 ... 1026
   s 39 ... 1026
   s 39(4) ... 1025
   s 42 ... 1028
   s 119 ... 1013
   s 120 ... 1013
   s 156 ... 1016
   s 162 ... 1016
   s 167 ... 1017
   s 168 ... 1017
   Sch 1 ... 1019, 1021
   Sch 2 ... 1019, 1021
   Sch 3 ... 1023, 1028
Common Law Procedure Act 1852 ... 879
   s 210 ... 874
   s 212 ... 874
Commons Registration Act 1965 ... 298, 637
Consumer Credit Act 1974 (CCA 1974) ... 99,
   1116, 1118, 1126–8
   s 8 ... 1126
   s 15 ... 117
   s 55 ... 1127
   s 55C ... 1127
   s 58 ... 1127
   ss 60–64 ... 1127
   ss 61A–64 ... 1127
   s 65 ... 1127
   s 76 ... 1127
   ss 77–78A ... 1127
   s 105 ... 1127
   s 106 ... 1127
   ss 107–111 ... 1127

s 126 ... 1074, 1076, 1127
s 127 ... 1127
s 127(3) ... 99
s 129 ... 1076, 1127
s 130 ... 1076
s 135 ... 1127
s 136 ... 1076, 1127
ss 137–140 ... 1127
s 140A(5) ... 1128
ss 140A–140C ... 1128
s 140B(1) ... 1128
s 189 ... 1126
Consumer Credit Act 2006 (CCA
  2006) ... 1118
s 15 ... 99
Consumer Rights Act 2015 (CRA
  2015) ... 1070, 1152
s 62 ... 1152–3
s 62(5) ... 810, 1154
s 63 ... 1153
s 64 ... 1153
s 64(1) ... 1155
s 64(2)–(4) ... 1156
s 70 ... 1152
Sch 1 ... 1156
Sch 2 ... 1153, 1164, 1168
Contracts (Rights of Third Parties) Act 1999
s 1 ... 228, 994, 995
s 1(b) ... 855
s 2 ... 225
s 2(1) ... 225
Conveyancing Act 1881 ... 843
s 6 ... 924
Conveyancing Act 1911 ... 843
Countryside and Rights of Way Act
  2000 ... 886
County Court Act 1984 ... 879
s 138(2)–(4) ... 874
s 138(9A) ... 874
s 139(2) ... 874
Criminal Justice Act 2003, s 281(5) ... 345
Criminal Law Act 1977
s 6 ... 3, 240, 345
s 7 ... 345
s 12(3)–(5) ... 345
s 12A ... 345

Defective Premises Act 1972 ... 857

Electricity Act 1989, Sch 4 ... 33, 886
Enterprise Act 2002 ... 1037
Environmental Protection Act 1990,
  ss 79–82 ... 809

Equality Act 2010 ... 111, 113, 426
s 15(1)(a)–(b) ... 113
s 20 ... 113
s 21 ... 113
s 35(1)(b) ... 113

Family Law Act 1996 (FLA 1996) ... 252,
  455, 613
s 30 ... 251, 253
s 30(1) ... 494–5
s 30(2) ... 251
s 30(8) ... 251
s 30(9) ... 494–5
ss 30–33 ... 20
s 31 ... 252–3
s 31(2) ... 253
s 31(10) ... 253, 698
s 33 ... 21, 545
s 33(1) ... 545
s 33(6) ... 564
s 34(2) ... 564
s 35 ... 495
s 36 ... 495
s 55(2) ... 1078
s 56 ... 1078
s 62(3) ... 545
Family Law (Scotland) Act 2006 ... 500
Financial Services Act 2010 ... 1125
Financial Services Act 2012 ... 1119
Financial Services (Banking Reform) Act
  2013 ... 1119
Financial Services and Markets Act 2000
  (FSMA 2000) ... 264, 1068, 1116
s 1B(2) ... 1121
s 1B(3) ... 1122
ss 1C–1E ... 1122
s 1M ... 1123
ss 1M–1R ... 1122
s 3S ... 1125
s 19 ... 1122, 1127
s 20 ... 1127
s 23 ... 1122, 1127
s 26 ... 1122
s 26A ... 1122, 1127
ss 26–28A ... 1122
s 27 ... 1127
s 28A ... 1127
s 29 ... 1129
ss 56–58 ... 1122
ss 59–59B ... 1122
s 71 ... 1122
s 150 ... 1123
s 228 ... 1128

s 230A ... 1129
s 231 ... 1128
Sch 17, para 8 ... 1128
Forfeiture Act 1982 ... 525

Gas Act 1986 ... 886
Grantee of Reversions Act 1540 ... 843
Greater London Authority Act 1999
s 384 ... 222
s 385 ... 222

Habeas Corpus Act 1679 ... 254
Housing Act 1974 ... 1015
Housing Act 1980 ... 811, 1015
s 89 ... 139, 143, 146
Housing Act 1985 ... 736, 797
Pt IV ... 747
s 79 ... 811
s 79(3) ... 812
s 80(1) ... 812
s 84 ... 137
s 84(2) ... 812
s 609 ... 965
Housing Act 1988
s 21 ... 145
Housing Act 1996 ... 1015
s 81 ... 1017
s 127 ... 137
s 143D ... 137
s 153A ... 813
s 153B ... 813
s 188 ... 140
s 190 ... 140
Housing Act 2004, Pt 6 ... 1060
Housing Finance Act 1971 ... 1015
Housing and Planning Act 2016 ... 829
Human Rights Act 1998 (HRA 1998)
s 2 ... 90, 94, 109, 148
s 3 ... 87, 91, 98, 105, 107, 137, 572, 683
s 3(1) ... 91
s 4 ... 91, 98
s 6 ... 87, 91, 101, 102, 105, 107–8, 137, 143
s 6(1) ... 104, 108
s 6(2) ... 104–5
s 6(2)(b) ... 105
s 6(3) ... 91, 102
s 6(3)(b) ... 107
s 7 ... 101, 105, 106
s 10 ... 91, 148
ECHR ... 88
Sch 1 ... 137
Art 1 ... 99

Art 3 ... 92, 562
Art 6 ... 87, 99, 109, 1128
Art 8 ... 87–9, 91–3, 95, 96, 98, 100, 107–11,
    114, 127–52, 239, 240, 549, 562, 563, 571–3,
    683–5, 798, 809, 814
Art 8(1) ... 128–30
Art 8(2) ... 128, 130, 131
Art 10 ... 87
Art 11 ... 87
Art 14 ... 87, 111, 112, 573, 684
Protocol 1, Art 1 ... 87, 89, 92–6, 98, 100, 107,
    110, 112–26, 150, 352, 549, 562, 683–5, 798,
    809, 914, 1094, 1095
Protocol 12 ... 111

Inheritance (Provision for Family and
    Dependants) Act 1975 ... 385
Insolvency Act 1986
s 51 ... 1022
s 122 ... 1022
s 124 ... 1022
s 283A ... 573, 574
s 283A(3)(b) ... 575
s 306 ... 521
s 313A ... 573
s 335A ... 551, 553, 554, 565–74
s 335A(3) ... 566
s 336 ... 569
s 337 ... 574
s 339 ... 574
s 421A ... 522
Sch B1 ... 1037
Insolvency Act 2000 ... 522
Insolvency Act 2006, s 72A ... 1108
Interpretation Act 1978, s 6 ... 657

Judicature Acts 1873–75 ... 793

Land Charges Act 1925 ... 288
Land Charges Act 1972 ... 848, 986, 1004
s 3(5) ... 987
s 6(1)(a) ... 1051
Land Registration Act 1925 (LRA 1925) ... 58,
    60, 119
s 3 ... 80
s 20 ... 80, 82
s 50(1) ... 987
s 59 ... 80
s 69 ... 80
s 70(1)(a) ... 638
s 70(1)(f) ... 78
s 70(1)(g) ... 594, 628, 633
s 75 ... 334–6

s 75(1) ... 335, 336
s 75(2) ... 335, 336
s 75(3) ... 336
s 82(2) ... 706
s 114 ... 82
Land Registration Act 2002 (LRA 2002) ... 6,
    58–84, 310, 693–725, 786, 887
s 2 ... 295, 296
s 2(1) ... 302
s 3 ... 60
s 3(3) ... 296
s 4 ... 296–7, 306, 786, 952
s 4(1) ... 698
s 4(1)(d)–(f) ... 787
s 4(1)(g) ... 1044
s 4(2)(a) ... 295
s 4(8) ... 297
s 7(1) ... 296
s 11(3)–(7) ... 297
s 12 ... 297
s 12(4) ... 297
s 12(7) ... 297
s 23 ... 71, 72, 84, 299, 673, 678–9, 696,
    703, 1044
s 24 ... 71, 72, 703
s 24(b) ... 299, 300
s 26 ... 673, 678, 679, 684
s 27 ... 70, 174, 290, 298, 300, 303, 306, 786,
    910, 951
s 27(1) ... 297, 299, 687
s 27(2)(a) ... 295
s 27(2)(b) ... 614
s 27(2)(b)(ii)–(v) ... 787
s 27(2)(d) ... 298, 614
s 27(2)(e) ... 637
s 27(2)(f) ... 298
s 27(7) ... 925
s 28 ... 581, 592, 608
s 28(1) ... 592
s 29 ... 76–80, 206, 253, 291, 302, 413, 581,
    592–4, 601, 604, 608–11, 616, 641, 686,
    700, 793
s 29(2)(a) ... 951
s 29(2)(a)(i) ... 593, 613
s 29(2)(a)(ii) ... 593
s 29(4) ... 77, 593, 609, 794
s 30 ... 76, 253, 581, 592, 604, 608, 609, 616
s 32 ... 611
ss 32–34 ... 1051
ss 32–39 ... 610
s 33 ... 612, 639
s 33(a) ... 688
s 33(a)(i) ... 77, 613

s 33(a)(ii) ... 613
s 33(a)–(c) ... 612
s 33(b) ... 613
s 33(c) ... 613
s 34 ... 613
s 34(3) ... 614
s 35 ... 614
s 36 ... 614
s 37 ... 613, 614
s 38 ... 614
s 40 ... 639
ss 40–47 ... 307
s 41 ... 639
s 42 ... 641
s 42(1) ... 1051
s 42(4) ... 1051
s 43 ... 641
s 43(1)(a)–(c) ... 641
s 44(1) ... 640, 641
s 51 ... 1044
s 52 ... 678, 786, 1107, 1108
s 58 ... 70–2, 77, 165, 612, 638, 696, 699,
    703, 787
s 58(1) ... 70, 71, 306
s 72(2) ... 299
s 73 ... 614
s 74 ... 299
s 93 ... 304, 700
s 93(2) ... 305
s 93(4) ... 244
s 96 ... 337, 603, 604
s 115 ... 698
s 115(b) ... 190
s 116 ... 190, 238, 249, 412, 698
s 116(a) ... 249, 250, 413–15
s 116(b) ... 238, 249, 619, 634
s 131 ... 713, 714
s 132(1) ... 71, 164, 610
Sch 1 ... 616
Sch 1, para 1 ... 800
Sch 1, para 2 ... 801
Sch 3 ... 77, 302, 610, 616, 952
Sch 3, para 1 ... 604, 613, 619, 637, 701, 800
Sch 3, para 2 ... 77, 79, 299, 594, 616–26, 637,
    688, 717, 719, 801
Sch 3, para 2(b) ... 624
Sch 3, para 2(c) ... 621, 622
Sch 3, para 2(c)(i) ... 621
Sch 3, para 3 ... 604, 637–8, 701, 722, 911, 952
Sch 4 ... 72
Sch 4, para 1 ... 73, 74
Sch 4, para 2 ... 708

Sch 4, para 2(1)(a) ... 696, 708, 709, 716
Sch 4, para 2(1)(b) ... 708
Sch 4, para 3 ... 74
Sch 4, para 3(3) ... 702, 708
Sch 4, para 5(a) ... 716
Sch 4, para 6 ... 498
Sch 4, para 6(2) ... 74, 712
Sch 4, para 6(3) ... 702
Sch 4, para 8 ... 708
Sch 6 ... 73, 338, 339, 347, 354
Sch 6, para 1 ... 336
Sch 6, para 3(2) ... 349
Sch 6, para 5(1)–(4) ... 340, 349
Sch 6, para 5(4) ... 342
Sch 6, para 9 ... 344
Sch 6, para 11 ... 314, 338
Sch 6, para 12 ... 349, 350
Sch 8 ... 75
Sch 8, para 1(1)(a) ... 75, 76
Sch 8, para 1(1)(b) ... 76
Sch 8, para 1(2)(b) ... 720, 721
Sch 8, para 5 ... 708, 719
Sch 12, para 9 ... 951
Sch 12, para 18 ... 336
Sch 12, para 20 ... 837
Land Registry Act 1862 ... 63
Land Transfer Act 1897 ... 60
Landlord and Tenant Act 1927, s 18 ... 856
Landlord and Tenant Act 1954,
    Pt II ... 736, 790
Landlord and Tenant Act 1985 ... 736
    s 11 ... 816, 817, 823
    s 17 ... 857
    ss 18 ... 1015
    s 19 ... 1015
    s 20 ... 1016
    s 20ZA ... 1016
    s 21 ... 1016
    s 21A ... 1016
    s 21B ... 1016
    s 22 ... 1016
    s 27A ... 1016
    s 30A ... 1016
    s 32 ... 857
    Sch 1, para 9 ... 1016
Landlord and Tenant Act 1987
    s 35 ... 1017
    s 37 ... 1017
    s 42 ... 1016
Landlord and Tenant (Covenants) Act
    1995 ... 613, 834
    s 2 ... 849

s 3 ... 848
s 3(2) ... 847
s 3(3) ... 847
s 3(5) ... 856
s 4 ... 847
s 5 ... 839, 840, 851
s 6 ... 40, 851
s 16 ... 839
s 17 ... 838
s 18 ... 838
s 19 ... 839
s 23 ... 839, 851, 852, 854
s 24 ... 839, 840
s 25 ... 840
s 27 ... 838
s 28(1) ... 849
Law of Property Act 1922
    3(2)(ii) ... 666
    s 96(3) ... 985
    s 145 ... 770
Law of Property Act 1925 (LPA 1925)
    s 1 ... 154, 163, 164, 188, 232, 741, 747, 764
    s 1(1) ... 163, 185, 662, 663, 765
    s 1(1)(e) ... 858
    s 1(2) ... 163, 173, 185, 192, 663
    s 1(3) ... 173, 185, 1017
    s 1(4) ... 71, 164, 173–6, 287, 663
    s 1(5) ... 1017
    s 1(6) ... 505, 506, 759
    s 2 ... 174, 188, 287, 288, 651–2, 657, 658, 674,
        675, 677, 680
    s 2(1) ... 604, 652, 653, 662
    s 2(1)(i) ... 664
    s 2(1)(i)–(iv) ... 662
    s 2(1)(ii) ... 657, 662
    s 2(1)(iii) ... 1093
    s 2(2) ... 287, 653, 661
    s 2(3) ... 287, 652
    s 2(3)(iv) ... 287
    s 4 ... 242
    s 4(1) ... 192, 193, 232
    s 14 ... 670
    s 27 ... 595, 657, 661, 662
    s 27(1) ... 653, 654, 675
    s 27(2) ... 664, 668, 669
    s 28 ... 675, 677
    s 28(1) ... 592
    s 30 ... 532, 543, 553, 555, 557, 563
    s 34(2) ... 506, 759
    s 36 ... 513
    s 36(2) ... 505, 510–15, 518, 525
    s 40 ... 263–70, 523

s 40(1) ... 265
s 52 ... 289, 290, 663, 1057
s 52(1) ... 173–5
s 52(2) ... 310
s 52(2)(c) ... 799
s 53 ... 194, 266, 438
s 53(1) ... 194
s 53(1)(a) ... 187, 194, 793, 975, 1049
s 53(1)(b) ... 187, 420, 421, 439, 442
s 53(1)(c) ... 526
s 53(2) ... 194, 421, 457, 526
s 54 ... 289–90
s 54(1B) ... 1002
s 54(2) ... 290, 699, 787–9, 791
s 56 ... 855, 994
s 56(1) ... 994
s 60 ... 424
s 60(3) ... 424, 425
s 62 ... 794, 911, 913, 924, 925–35, 952
s 62(1) ... 924
s 62(4) ... 924
s 77(1)(c) ... 837
s 78 ... 977, 981–6
s 79 ... 962, 963, 983
s 79(1) ... 962
s 84 ... 957, 999, 1002, 1005
s 84(1) ... 1000, 1002
s 84(1A) ... 1001
s 84(1B) ... 1001
s 84(3) ... 1000
s 84(7) ... 1000
s 85(1) ... 1043
s 85(2) ... 1043
s 86 ... 1043
s 87(1) ... 147, 1044, 1057, 1071
s 88 ... 1066
s 88(1) ... 1078, 1093
s 88(2) ... 1065
s 88(6) ... 1047
s 89(1) ... 1078, 1093
s 89(2) ... 1065
s 91 ... 1088, 1089
s 91(2) ... 1065
s 93 ... 1059
s 101 ... 1066
s 101(1) ... 1066
s 101(1)(i) ... 1091, 1094, 1108
s 101(1)(iii) ... 1064, 1108
s 101(3)–(4) ... 1067
s 103 ... 1092
s 104 ... 1094, 1106
s 104(2) ... 1107

s 105 ... 1093–5
s 106 ... 1067
s 107(1) ... 1094
s 109 ... 1109
s 115 ... 1057
s 141 ... 843–6, 852, 853
s 142 ... 843, 845, 846, 853
s 142(1) ... 843
s 146 ... 857, 866, 867
s 146(1) ... 865, 867, 876
s 146(1)(b) ... 866
s 146(2) ... 873, 875, 876, 878, 879
s 146(4) ... 878–9
s 146(5) ... 879
s 146(5)(b) ... 879
s 146(7) ... 859
s 146(9) ... 865
s 146(10) ... 865
s 149(6) ... 767, 769, 777
s 184 ... 510
s 185 ... 800
s 193 ... 886
s 193(4) ... 946
s 196(3) ... 515, 517
s 196(4) ... 515
s 205 ... 677
s 205(1)(xxi) ... 668
s 205(1)(xxvii) ... 733, 746
Law of Property (Amendment) Act 1926
    s 7 ... 688
    Sch ... 688
Law of Property (Joint Tenants) Act 1964,
    s 1 ... 688–9
Law of Property (Miscellaneous Provisions)
    Act 1989 (LP(MP)A 1989) ... 3, 365
    s 1 ... 293–4
    s 1(3)(a)(i) ... 294
    s 2 ... 194, 225, 263–85, 294, 304, 376, 381,
        786, 793
    s 2(1) ... 117, 225, 267, 270, 273, 277, 278, 280,
        523, 1047
    s 2(4) ... 275
    s 2(5) ... 278, 280, 281, 283
Leasehold Property (Repairs) Act 1938 ... 856
Leasehold Reform Act 1967 ... 94, 809, 1013
    s 8 ... 928
    s 10 ... 928
Leasehold Reform Housing and Urban
    Development Act 1993 ... 1013
    s 87 ... 1015
Legal Aid, Sentencing and Punishment of
    Offenders Act (LASPOA) 2012 ... 347
    s 144 ... 3, 345–52

Limitation Act 1623 ... 936
Limitation Act 1980
   s 3(2) ... 41, 603
   s 4 ... 42, 603
   s 15 ... 119, 313, 332, 333
   s 15(1) ... 314, 602, 603
   s 17 ... 119, 313, 602, 603
   s 18 ... 603
   s 20(1) ... 1114
   s 20(5) ... 1114
   s 28 ... 334
   s 29 ... 330–2
   s 30 ... 330–2
   s 32 ... 334
   Sch 1, para 1 ... 315, 316
   Sch 1, para 5 ... 788
   Sch 1, para 5(2) ... 332
   Sch 1, para 8 ... 315
   Sch 1, para 8(4) ... 318, 325
   Sch 1, para 9 ... 334
   Sch 1, para 10 ... 334
   Sch 1, para 11 ... 334
Localism Act 2011
   Pt 7 ... 814
   s 160 ... 814
   s 166 ... 816
Lord Cairns Act 1858 ... 995, 999

Married Woman's Property Act 1882,
   s 17 ... 512, 546
Matrimonial Causes Act 1973 ... 513
   s 23 ... 456
Matrimonial Homes Act 1967 ... 21, 251
Mines (Working Facilities and Support) Act
   1966 ... 34
Mobile Homes Act 1983, Sch 1 ... 137
Moneylenders Act 1900 ... 1166
Mortgage Repossession (Protection of Tenants
   etc) Act 2010 ... 1079

Occupiers Liability Act 1984 ... 904

Party Walls Act 1996 ... 910
Petroleum Production Act 1934 ... 34
Petroleum Act 1998 ... 34
Prescription Act 1832 ... 938
Proceeds of Crime Act 2002, s 298(2)(b) ... 49
Protection from Eviction Act 1977 ... 140,
   143, 798, 809
   s 1 ... 3, 9
   s 1(2) ... 240
   s 1(3) ... 1074
   s 2 ... 146

   s 3 ... 146
   s 3A ... 239
   s 5(1A) ... 239
Protection from Harassment Act 1997 ... 737

Rent Act 1977 ... 38, 735, 810
Rentcharges Act 1977 ... 173, 732, 733
   s 2(1) ... 975
   s 2(2) ... 975
   s 2(3)(c) ... 975
   s 2(4)(b) ... 975
   s 2(5) ... 975
Renting Homes (Wales) Act 2016 ... 759
   s 7 ... 829
   s 7(4) ... 829
   ss 31–41 ... 830
   ss 43–47 ... 830
   s 52 ... 830
   s 69(2) ... 792
   s 72(2) ... 792
   ss 73–83 ... 830
   ss 111–112 ... 830
   ss 130–131 ... 830
   s 236 ... 792

Settled Land Act 1925
   s 1(7) ... 533
   s 72 ... 653
Statute of Frauds 1677 ... 261, 270, 438
Statute of Gloucester 1278 ... 733
Statute Law Revision (No. 2) Act 1888 ... 937
Statute of Merton 1235 ... 936
Statute of Westminster I 1275 ... 936
Supreme Court of Judicature Act 1873, s 11 ... 195

Telecommunications Act 1984 ... 886
Torts (Interference with Goods) Act 1977,
   s 3 ... 255
Town and Country Planning Act 1990,
   s 106 ... 965
Treasure Act 1996 ... 54
Tribunals, Courts and Enforcement Act 2007
   Pt 3 ... 857
   s 71 ... 857
   ss 72–80 ... 857
Trustee Act 1925
   s 17 ... 675
   s 34(2) ... 505, 506
Trustee Act 2000
   s 1 ... 675
Trusts of Land and Appointment of Trustees
   Act 1996 (TOLATA 1996) ... 455, 762
   s 1 ... 533

s 1(2)(a) . . . 419
s 1(3) . . . 533
s 3 . . . 654
s 4 . . . 535
s 5 . . . 673
s 6 . . . 533, 534, 656, 661, 673, 675
s 6(1) . . . 185, 675, 676
s 6(5) . . . 535, 675
s 6(6) . . . 185, 535, 536, 675, 676
s 6(8) . . . 535
s 7 . . . 529, 538
s 7(1)–(5) . . . 529
s 8 . . . 534, 535, 676
s 11 . . . 676
s 11(1)(a) . . . 535
s 11(1)(b) . . . 535
s 11(2)(a) . . . 535
s 12 . . . 494, 536, 537, 673
s 12(1) . . . 536, 539
s 12(2) . . . 536, 539
s 13 . . . 537, 543, 545, 673
s 13(3) . . . 536
s 13(4) . . . 537
s 13(5) . . . 536
s 13(6) . . . 537
s 14 . . . 456, 529, 539, 540, 545, 546, 550, 556, 558, 562, 1054, 1079
s 15 . . . 539, 540, 543, 544, 550–64, 570, 571, 1079
s 15(1) . . . 556
s 15(1)(a) . . . 541, 542, 556, 565
s 15(1)(b) . . . 541, 556, 559, 565
s 15(1)(c) . . . 541–3, 561, 562
s 15(1)(d) . . . 541, 554
s 15(2) . . . 543
s 15(3) . . . 556
s 15(4) . . . 551, 554

s 16 . . . 673, 676–8
Sch 1, para 1(1) . . . 419
Sch 3, para 2 . . . 673

Unfair Contract Terms Act 1977 . . . 758
Usury Laws Repeal Act 1854 . . . 1042

Water Industry Act 1991 . . . 886
Wills Act 1837, s 24 . . . 362

Statutory Instruments

Assured Tenancies (Amendment) (England) Order 2010 (SI 2010/908) . . . 813

Civil Procedure Rules 1998 (SI 1998/3132), Pt 55 . . . 1078
Consumer Protection from Unfair Practices Regulations 2008 (SI 2008/1277) . . . 1152

Financial Collateral Arrangements (No 2) Regulations 2003 (SI 2003/3226) . . . 1065
Financial Services and Markets Act 2000 (Regulated Activities) Order 2001 (SI 2001/544), art 61(3) . . . 1121

Land Registration Rules 2003 (SI 2003/1417)
  r 74 . . . 952
  r 86(3) . . . 614
  r 189 . . . 339
  r 194 . . . 350

Mortgage Credit Directive Order 2015 SI 2015/910 . . . 1119
  art 4(2) . . . 1121

Unfair Terms in Consumer Contracts Regulations 1999 (SI 1999/2083) . . . 1152

LIST OF ABBREVIATIONS

AALR	Anglo-American Law Review
APR	annual percentage rate
BERR	Department of Business Enterprise and Regulatory Reform
CA	Court of Appeal
CBLJ	Canadian Business Law Journal
CCA 1974	Consumer Credit Act 1974
CCA 2006	Consumer Credit Act 2006
CCLR	Carbon & Climate Law Review
CLJ	Cambridge Law Journal
CLR	Commonwealth Law Reports
ECHR	European Convention on Human Rights
EGLR	Estates Gazette Law Reports
EHRR	European Human Rights Reports
EWCA	England and Wales Court of Appeal
EWHC	High Court of England and Wales
FCA	Financial Conduct Authority
FLA 1996	Family Law Act 1996
FSA	Financial Services Authority
FSMA 2000	Financial Services and Markets Act 2000
FSO	Financial Services Ombudsman
HRA 1998	Human Rights Act 1998
LCA 1925	Land Charges Act 1925
LCA 1972	Land Charges Act 1972
LPA 1925	Law of Property Act 1925
LPA 1969	Law of Property Act 1969
LP(MP)A 1989	Law of Property (Miscellaneous Provisions) Act 1989
LQR	Law Quarterly Review
LRA 1925	Land Registration Act 1925
LRA 2002	Land Registration Act 2002
LS	Legal Studies
MCOB	Mortgage Conduct of Business Sourcebook
MLR	Modern Law Review
OFT	Office of Fair Trading
P & CR	Property and Compensation Reports
TOLATA 1996	Trusts of Land and Appointment of Trustees Act 1996
WLR	Weekly Law Reports

PART A

INTRODUCTION

1 What's Special about Land? 2

2 What is Land? 25

3 Registration 58

WHAT'S SPECIAL ABOUT LAND?

CENTRAL ISSUES

1. This introductory chapter aims to show the importance of land, and hence of land law. It focusses on the features that make land special and the distinctive legal rules produced by those features. By considering a specific example, it also shows how and why land law can give rise to very difficult questions of both doctrine and policy.

2. This chapter thus helps to answer an important question: why is it worth studying land law? Firstly, the special features of land mean that rules regulating the use of land are very important *in practice*. Secondly, those special features mean that the rules are *analytically* interesting: they try to perform the very difficult job of balancing the interests of a number of deserving parties. Thirdly, although many land law rules are rooted in tradition, the practical importance of land law means that the rules must change in response to new social and economic conditions. This means that land law can be a *topical* and *lively* subject.

3. In this chapter, our focus is on what makes land (and thus land law) special. As we will see, however, land law is part of the broader subject of property law. This gives us a further important reason for studying land law: it is a very useful way in which to learn about core concepts that apply not only where land is concerned, but in many other situations as well.

4. In this chapter, we will look at a particular situation that shows the sharp debates and difficult questions that can arise in land law. In later chapters, we will return to that situation in more detail and closely examine the relevant legal rules. Our purpose here, however, is to see what can be discerned about the special concerns of land law.

1 THE IMPORTANCE OF LAND

No one needs to be told that land is important. In fact, in the United Kingdom, land is something of a national obsession. We would not necessarily think it odd if a friend were to spend the morning on some do-it-yourself jobs in her house, stop to look in the windows of a local estate agency whilst out for lunch, come back to do some gardening in the afternoon, and then spend the evening watching a television programme about the property market, and playing a board game based on buying land and renting out houses in London. And that is only at the weekend, when she is not out at work earning money to make her mortgage payments. And, of course, land can be even more important for those who are not fortunate enough to own a home: a tenant may worry that his landlord will fail to make the necessary repairs to his roof or is about to raise his rent, while someone with nowhere at all to live will face the more urgent task of finding shelter for the night.

So, whilst we may sometimes take it for granted, land is always there: under our noses, beneath our feet, and perhaps even in our souls. As a result, land looms large in much of the law. For example, in the law of torts, occupiers' liability forms a discrete area due to the special responsibilities placed on those with control of land. Conversely, the criminal law gives special protection to a residential occupier of land: if another party uses force or the threat of force to come onto land despite the objections of the occupier, that party can be guilty of a special criminal offence.[1] In the law of contract, special rules regulate agreements relating to land: the importance of land is recognized by the requirement that contracts to sell land must be made in writing, signed by both vendor and purchaser.[2] In administrative and public law, special responsibilities are placed on local authorities, in certain circumstances, to provide accommodation to those with nowhere to live.

2 THE SCOPE OF THIS BOOK

This book cannot focus on all of the varied areas of law in which land is important. Its focus instead is on the special rules that govern *private rights to use land*. By 'private' rights, we mean the rights that, in theory, *any* of us might acquire. For example, the government or a local authority may have a statutory power to acquire land for particular purposes: for example, the London Development Agency, by means of compulsory purchase orders approved by the Secretary of State for Trade and Industry in 2005, was permitted to buy land needed for use in connection with the 2012 Olympics, even if the current owners of that land did not agree to sell. Such special powers to use land are *not* considered in this book.

Similarly, we will not examine the various tort claims that may arise against an occupier of land: if you are injured at a friend's house and claim damages from her, you claim a right to be paid money, not a right to use her land. Nor will we look at all the special crimes that may apply where land is concerned:[3] to be seen as criminal, a party's conduct must be deserving of public sanction; it is not enough for that conduct simply to interfere with another party's rights. And we will not look directly at the special statutory responsibilities placed on local authorities: those duties do not necessarily respond to any individual's private right. Equally, we will not examine the special public limits that may be placed on private rights. For example, if you own a house, you may wish to convert it into a block of flats: to do so,

---

[1] See Criminal Law Act 1977, s 6. To commit the crime, the party must know of the occupier's presence on the land and of his objection to that party's entry. The crime is not committed if the party entering is a 'displaced residential occupier'—that is, someone who was himself earlier removed from the land. See also the Protection from Eviction Act 1977, s 1, for a further example of a crime protecting the use of land and note that the Legal Aid, Sentencing and Punishment of Offenders Act 2012, s 144 introduced the criminal offence of squatting in a residential building, which can be committed where a party, having entered a residential building as a trespasser, lives in that building or intends to live there for any period: see the discussion in Chapter 9, section 6.

[2] See Law of Property (Miscellaneous Provisions) Act 1989, discussed in Chapter 8, section 3.

[3] See Chapter 9, section 6 for discussion of the criminal offence of squatting in a residential building.

you will need planning permission, because your private rights, as an owner of the land, are limited by the need for the approval of a public body.

This is not to suggest that the areas outside this book are unimportant, or lacking in interest. In fact, to have a full picture of how the law regulates the use of land, it is vital to be aware of the relevant parts of the law of torts, of criminal law and of public law. But no book can sensibly examine *all* of the legal rules that can regulate the use of land; rather, this book focusses on a set of rules that are joined together not only by the *context* in which they apply, but also by the *concepts* that underlie them. In this way, the book fits with the meaning of 'land law', as set out in the following extract.[4]

Birks, 'Before We Begin: Five Keys to Land Law' in *Land Law: Themes and Perspectives* (eds Bright and Dewar, 1998, pp 457–60)

The name 'land law' suggests a simple contextual category: all the law about land. The law does use many such categories, ordered only by the alphabet: all the law about aviation, banks, commerce, dogs, education and so on. They take as their subject some aspect of life, just as a non-lawyer would identify it. But in this case things are not quite so straightforward. By the end of this section we will have formulated a more complex proposition: land law, as generally understood, is a contextual subset of a legal-conceptual category.

The socio-historical context

It will help to start with some background. The role of land, and hence of land law, has changed dramatically since the Industrial Revolution and the rise of the limited liability company. The paragraphs which follow sketch in that change and two others.

The managed fund

For institutions and individuals with serious wealth, land has lost its central role. The managed fund has displaced the rolling acres. Land used to be the pre-eminent form of wealth. Landed property was the focus of dynastic ambition. Land opened the door to high social status and political power. A landed family had by that fact alone a stake in governmental power. Keeping land in the family mattered. That has changed. Land, important as it is, has lost its pride of place. For the mega-wealthy, land has become just one species of investment, much as agriculture has become just one more industry. Pension funds and wealthy institutions hold mixed portfolios. They hold some land, some works of art, and many shares in many companies. Rich individuals do the same. The dynastic urge has been translated, with one eye constantly on the tax man, into trust funds and private companies [. . .]

The fragility of the environment

The notion of land as scarce and fragile is relatively new. The Industrial Revolution created a few black spots. Blake's dark, satanic mills were terrible to behold, but local. It is only relatively recently that we have realized that our transport systems, our power stations, our industrial processes, and our intensive agricultural methods have the potential utterly

---

4 As is the case with all such extracts in this book, footnotes, numbering, and cross-references have been omitted unless essential to understanding the extract.

to destroy this green and pleasant land. The private law of nuisance, the historic role of which was to control annoying activities as between one neighbour and another, cannot sufficiently express the social interest in the safety of this scarce resource. Protection of the environment means more social control of land use. There will have to be more planning control, more conservation legislation, more anti-pollution legislation [. . .]

Public-sector housing

Local government is nowadays a powerful force in the provision of housing, adding a public law dimension new to land law as it been historically determined. During the Thatcher era the public sector experienced an upheaval, partly from shortage of money, partly from being opened to the private market through the right-to-buy legislation [. . .] The public sector ultimately rests on concepts identical to those of the private sector, overlaid by principles of public law and a mass of highly technical legislation. It is in every way a part of land law, but, because of the mass of detail, it has become a specialism. As a lawyer you have at some stage to decide whether to make yourself an expert in that field. The same is largely true of the statutory regime controlling the relations of landlord and tenant in the private sector.

The core of land law

A target has a centre. Taking land law as a simple contextual category, we can identify at least five topics, all of which have already figured in the discussion. Four of these must on reflection be located in the second or third circles, just outside the bull's-eye at which we are aiming. They matter, but they do not relieve us of the intellectual necessity of mastering the core. Two belong largely in public law. One of these comprises the social control essential if the environment is to be protected. The other is the housing law which applies to local government tenancies. Within private law, a third unit lies in the law of civil wrongs and deals with the duties imposed by the law for regulating the behaviours of neighbours towards each other, especially through the torts of nuisance and trespass to land. Fourthly, there is the structuring of mega-wealth, the mission of the old Lincoln's Inn conveyancers. That is breaking away, not specifically land law any longer but wealth management. Its principal vehicle is the trust, often enough off-shore, in which land becomes just one kind of asset in a rolling fund. Fifthly and last of all, there is the unit at the very centre of the target. When lawyers speak of land law, it is usually to this core that they refer.

Every business needs premises, every factory needs a site. For most of us as private individuals our home is the centre of our lives. Functionally, this core of land law has the task of providing the structure within which people and businesses can safely acquire and exploit land for daily use, to live and to work. To discharge that function, it has to have its own conceptual apparatus. The proper content of this fifth unit thus becomes the nature, creation and protection of interests in land. Those interests and their implications are the conceptual apparatus of our land law.

The word 'interests' is slightly evasive. The law recognizes different kinds of rights, among them property rights. By 'interest' we mean 'property right'. The category of all property rights (or, in other words and more simply, 'the law of property') is a legal-conceptual category. It differs from, say, the law of dogs in that its subject is a legal concept, the concept of a proprietary right. The core of land law is the subset formed when the conceptual category of 'property right' is confined to one context: the law relating to property rights in land. To focus on that core is neither to downgrade the importance of the units in the next circles nor to forget that in real life all the units which we have identified, and others, cohere together.

3 THREE UNDERLYING QUESTIONS

As Birks suggests, the focus of land law, and hence of this book, is on private *property rights* to use land. We will examine the concept of a property right in Chapters 5 and 6. Birks suggests that land law examines the '*nature, creation and protection*' of property rights relating to land. Certainly, at a very general level, the questions that we will examine in this book can be organized into three broad groups: firstly, there are questions about the *content* of rights to use land; secondly, there are questions about the *acquisition* of rights to use land; thirdly, there are questions about the *defences* available to one party where another party has a right to use land. In Part B of this book, we will look in detail at the different content of particular rights to use land. In Part C, and in Chapter 12, we will look at how a person can acquire such rights. And in Part E when considering how the law establishes the priority of competing rights to use land, we will look at the defences that may be available to a person against another's right to use land. In the remaining parts of the book, we will look in more detail at specific contexts in which these questions about content, acquisition and defences may arise.

To take a simple example, imagine that you are interested in buying a house advertised in the window of a local estate agency. It is important to know whether the house is advertised as 'freehold' or 'leasehold'. The point is that the vendor is not simply selling a house: she is selling her *right to use the land*. If you go ahead and buy her house, you will acquire a particular private right to use land. As Birks suggests, land law deals with the nature of that right. In particular, it is vital for you to know the *content* of the right: if you acquire the right, how will you be able to use the land? As we will see in Chapter 5, a freehold will give you ownership of the land for an unlimited period; a leasehold also gives you ownership, but only for a limited period.

Let us say that you have established that the vendor is selling a freehold, and that you have decided to go ahead and make an offer. Your focus will then shift to the *acquisition* question: what has to be done in order for you to acquire the vendor's freehold? In Birks' terms, land law deals with the creation of your right to use the land. There will generally be two stages to the process, often known as 'contract' and 'conveyance'. At the first stage, you need to know (or, at least, your solicitor or conveyancer needs to know) what has to be done in order to reach a legally binding agreement with the vendor. As noted above, there are special rules that regulate contracts to transfer a right such as a freehold. We will examine those rules in this book (see Chapter 8, section 3), because they are crucial in defining how a party can acquire a private right to use land.

At the second stage, you need to know (or, at least, your solicitor or conveyancer needs to know) what has to be done in order for you actually to acquire the vendor's freehold: we will also examine those rules in Chapter 8. As we will see, *registration* forms a crucial part of the process: even if you pay the vendor and even if you move into her house, you do not actually acquire her freehold unless and until you are recorded on the central register as holding that right. Indeed, the registration system under the Land Registration Act 2002 plays a crucial role in modern land law, and so we will also examine that system throughout the book, and particularly in Chapters 3, 16, and 18.

If all goes well and you are now registered as holding a freehold, it might seem that you are home and dry. But let us say that one of your new neighbours, when walking to his house from the road, regularly takes a short cut across your new front garden. You (very politely) object to this and he (equally politely) claims that a former owner of your land granted him a right of way over your land. This is the first that you have heard of such a right: in fact, when acquiring your freehold, you checked on the central register and there was no mention of the land being subject to a right of way. If your neighbour was indeed given a right of way over your land, it will be necessary to establish which of the two competing rights (your freehold on the one hand and his right of way on the other) is to be given priority. At this point, the *defences* question is crucial. Even if your neighbour can show that he was given a right of way over your land, it may well be that you have a defence to his right and so do not need to let him walk across your land. In our example, that defence may come from the facts that: (i) you paid for, and registered, your freehold; and (ii) your neighbour failed to have his right of way noted on the register.[5] This is just one example of how land law, to use Birks' words, deals with the protection of rights: it may be that your neighbour should have protected his right by having it noted on the register.[6]

What if your neighbour instead claims that there is a *public* right of way, such as a public footpath, running over your land? If that is the case, then any member of the public will be able to walk over your front garden. We will not examine such public rights in this book, because our focus is on *private* rights: rights that can be held by an individual as an individual, not as a member of the public.

4 THE SPECIAL FEATURES OF LAND

Birks suggests that land law is a 'contextual subset' of property law. This raises the question of why we should gather together the legal rules relating to private rights to use land. We could equally, for example, study private rights to use chairs. Yet, whilst there are lots of books and courses dealing with 'land law', very few deal with 'chair law'. One reason, of course, is the practical importance of land—but then chairs are pretty useful too. A linked, but better, reason is that land has certain features that make it a unique resource, fundamentally different from other types of physical thing. The legal rules relating to rights to use chairs are essentially identical to those relating to rights to use tables, bikes, or cauliflowers. So, those rules can be found in books or courses dealing with 'personal property law'. In fact, personal property law deals with private rights to use just about any physical thing *other* than land. Land is separated out for special treatment because, due to its fundamentally different physical characteristics, rights to use land are regulated by fundamentally different legal rules.

The following extract discusses those special features and the special legal rules to which they give rise.

McFarlane, *The Structure of Property Law* (2008, pp 7–11)

Permanence

Subject to the rarest of exceptions, land is permanent. Whereas other objects that can be physically located (e.g. bikes) wear out, the usefulness of land endures. This special feature of land is reflected by a special feature of the land law system: ownership of land can be split up over time. For example, A, an owner of land, can give B a Lease: B then has ownership

---

[5] See further Chapter 3, section 3, Chapter 15, section 4.2, and Chapter 16, sections 2–4.

[6] For an example of a party losing out through failing to protect a right of way by means of a notice on the register, see *Chaudhary v Yavuz* [2013] Ch 249, esp *per* Lloyd LJ at [9].

of that land for a limited period. In contrast, if A is an owner of a bike, A *cannot* give B ownership of that bike for a limited period.

Uniqueness

"Location, location, location": a crucial feature of any piece of land is its physical location. That physical location can never be shared by another piece of land. In this significant sense, all pieces of land are unique. This special feature of land explains two special rules of land law.

Recovery of the thing itself from X or C?

First, let us say that: (i) B owns a thing, such as a bike; and (ii) X takes physical control of that thing without B's consent or other lawful authority. B can assert his right, as an owner of the thing, against X: by interfering with B's right, X commits a wrong against B. However, there is no guarantee that a court will order X to return the bike to B: rather than getting his thing back, B may well have to settle for receiving money from X [. . .]

In contrast, if: (i) B has ownership of some land; and (ii) X takes physical control of that land without B's consent or other lawful authority; then (iii) a court *will* make an order (a "possession order") allowing B to remove X and to take physical control of the land. This difference between land and other things thus relates to the remedies question: the question of how a court will protect B's right. It explains why land is sometimes known as "real property". "Real" comes from the Latin for "thing" (*res*); when used in the phrase "real property" it indicates that B can recover the *thing itself* if wrongfully deprived of it by X or C.

Forcing A to transfer the thing itself to B?

Second, let's say A owns a bike and makes a contractual promise to transfer his ownership to B. A then changes his mind and refuses to go ahead with the transfer. B can assert his right against A: by breaching his contractual duty to B, A commits a wrong against B. However, it is unlikely that the court will order A to transfer the bike itself to B; B will, almost always, have to settle for receiving money from A. The aim of remedies for breach of contract is to put B in the position he would have been in had A kept his promise: B's right is adequately protected if A gives B any money necessary to allow B to buy a similar bike elsewhere.

However, where A promises to transfer a *unique thing* to B, the position is different. To put B in the position he would have been had A kept his promise, A must give B the *thing itself*. So, in the rare case where A promises to transfer a unique bike to B, A may be ordered to keep his promise. In contrast, if A promises to transfer land to B, the standard position is that a court will order A to keep his promise and to transfer his right to the land to B: after all, each piece of land is unique. Again, this difference between land and other things relates to the remedies question: the question of how a court will protect B's right. Where B's contractual right is to acquire a right to land, it is, in general, specifically protected; where B's contractual right is to acquire a right to a thing other than land, B usually has to settle for receiving money.

Capacity for multiple simultaneous use

The same piece of land can be used in many different ways, by many different people, at the same time. For example, let's say:

1. A buys No.32 Acacia Gardens from A0.

2. A0 owns a local shop and makes A promise, when buying No.32, that neither A nor future owners of No.32 will use it as a shop.

3. A acquires No.32 with a "mortgage" loan: in return for a loan from C Bank, A gives C Bank a security right. C Bank thus has a right, if A fails to pay back the loan, to: (i) remove A and other occupiers from the land; (ii) sell the land; and (iii) use the proceeds to pay off A's debt.

4. In return for payment from E, a neighbour, A gives E a right to reach E's house by using a path crossing the garden of No.32.

5. A then moves away. He decides to keep the land and use it as an investment by renting it to B. So, in return for paying money to A, B is permitted to occupy the land. B uses the land as his home and allows his lover, D, to live with him.

Each of A0, A, B, C, D and E has a right to make some use (or at least to prevent a particular use) of the land. Things other than land are also capable of multiple, simultaneous use. If A owns a bike, A can: (i) give B permission to ride the bike; and (ii) offer his bike as security for a loan from C. The difference between land and other things is therefore one of *degree*. However, the difference remains important as it poses a significant question for the land law system: can it reconcile the competing desires of all those who simultaneously want to use the same piece of land? It certainly helps to explain another special feature of the land law system: the longer list of property rights in land.

Social importance

Land is uniquely capable of meeting important social needs. B can only acquire the sense of security and identity that comes with establishing a home *if* he has some sort of right in relation to land. Similarly, it is very difficult to establish business premises without a right to use land. As a result, an interference with B's use of land can have dramatic consequences. For example, eviction from a settled home can cause great stress and disruption; eviction from business premises can cause grave commercial harm.

This special feature of land is reflected in a number of special rules. For example, if: (i) B occupies land as his home; and (ii) C unlawfully prevents B occupying that land *or* with the intention of causing B to leave the land, interferes with the "peace or comfort" of B or members of B's household, then (iii) C commits a criminal offence.[7] Further, if B has ownership of some land, the rest of the world is under a *prima facie* duty not to unreasonably interfere with B's use and enjoyment of that land. So, if C's pig farm, next to B's land, produces nauseating smells, C breaches that duty and thus commits the wrong of nuisance against B. However, C commits no such wrong if he interferes, in a similar way, with B's enjoyment of a thing other than land.[8] Further, in some circumstances, A and B's private agreement can be regulated by mandatory rules protecting B's use of land. So, if A gives B a Lease of land for one year, B may have a statutory right to remain even after the year has expired.

This special feature of land also means that certain human rights may be of particular relevance in land law. For example, Article 8 of the European Convention of Human Rights states that: "Everyone has the right to respect for his private and family life, his home and his correspondence." [. . .] [T]his right is of course subject to qualifications; but the social importance of land means that the right *may* have a role in shaping the rules of the land law system.

[7] [Under the Protection from Eviction Act 1977, s 1.]

[8] [To bring a claim in nuisance, B must have a property right in land: see *Hunter v Canary Wharf* [1997] AC 655.]

Limited availability

It is impossible to make more land. This special feature of land has a number of consequences. First, coupled with the many valuable uses to which land can be put, it ensures that land is an *expensive commodity*. For most, acquiring ownership of land is impossible unless a lender, such as C Bank, is willing to provide a substantial loan. In return, C Bank will demand a security right over the land. Second, the limited availability of land intensifies the need for the stock of land to be *freely marketable*. As a result, it is particularly undesirable for an owner to remove land from the market by placing permanent restrictions on its use.

The limited availability of land, coupled with its importance and uniqueness, can lead to special limits being placed on an owner of land. For example, the need to promote the marketability of land has led the land law system to give protection to certain parties [e.g. C] who acquire rights relating to land. As we will see, registration rules, particularly prominent in land law, are one means of giving C such protection. Equally, the rules of the land law system have long tried to promote marketability by preventing an owner from limiting the use of land after his death. Further, legislation commonly allows public bodies compulsory purchase powers: powers to acquire land from an owner in order to use it for a specific purpose, such as the building of a motorway.

More startling is the doctrine of *adverse possession*: a means by which an owner of land can lose his right without receiving any compensation. Due to changes in the registered land system, the doctrine of adverse possession now has much less of an impact. However, where it applies, its effect is dramatic. If: (i) X occupies B's land without B's consent; and (ii) B fails, over a long period, to take steps to remove X; then (iii) B's right to the land can be extinguished. The doctrine only applies if X has been acting as an owner of the land: it protects X's claimed ownership, exercised over the long period, by extinguishing B's prior ownership. It can protect X even if X is fully aware that the land initially belongs to B. In this way, the doctrine recognises X's claim (established by his long use) and removes the right of B, who has failed to make use of his land.

The doctrine of adverse possession applies only to land. If: (i) X takes physical control of B's bike without B's consent or other authority; and (ii) B fails, over a long period, to assert his ownership against X; then (iii) there is *no* general rule that the passage of time, by itself, can lead to B losing his ownership of the bike. The limited availability of land supports the idea that land is too scarce a commodity to remain under the ownership of a party who fails, over a long period, to assert his right. As seen above, it also heightens the need for land to be freely marketable. The doctrine of adverse possession certainly promotes that goal: the extinction of B's right not only protects X, but also anyone later acquiring a right from X.

As demonstrated by the extract, the special *physical* features of land lead to special *legal* rules that regulate private rights to use land. Those rules can be organized into three general groups: some regulate the *content* of those rights; other rules regulate the means by which those rights can be *acquired*; and further rules, determine the *priority* of competing private rights to use land by setting out the *defences* that may be used against such rights

One of the most distinctive features of land law is that the *content* of property rights can be more varied than the content of property rights relating to, say, chairs. This is because many of the property rights that we will examine in later chapters can exist *only* in relation to land: this is the case, for example, with the lease (see Chapters 19 and 20), easement (see Chapter 22), and restrictive covenant (see Chapter 23). Due to the social importance of land, there may also be special means by which a party can *acquire* a right to use land. For example, if you set up home with your partner, then, even if your partner is registered as the sole owner of the home, you may nonetheless be able to rely on special rules, developed by the courts, to show that you have acquired a property right: we will examine those rules in detail in Chapter 12. In contrast, the limited availability of land may make it easier for you to lose a property right relating to land: there may be special *defences* that someone can use against your right to use the land. For example, the extract above refers to the doctrine of adverse possession: if you own land, but fail, over a long period, to assert your right to that land, a squatter may then gain a defence to your property right. We will examine adverse possession in detail in Chapter 9.

5 LAND LAW IN PRACTICE: AN EXAMPLE

There is no doubt that land law is a difficult subject. In defining and regulating private rights to use land, land law has some very tough choices to make. The best way to see this is by considering an example. In this section, we will consider the facts and result of an important land law case involving a dispute between an occupier of land and a bank. We will return to the case in later chapters, when we will examine the relevant principles in greater detail.[9] Our purpose here is simply to use the case, focussing on one specific aspect of land law, to highlight some of the difficult questions raised by the subject as well as some of the different approaches to tackling those questions. The case also exemplifies a type of dispute that often arises in land law, and can be seen in many important decisions: between, on the one hand, a party who wants to continue occupying land as his or her home and, on the other hand, a lender who has provided finance and now wishes to recover at least some of the money owed to it by selling the property.[10]

When examining the case, as well as the other cases included in this book, we will necessarily look at how the rules of land law are used to solve disputes about the use of land. It is important, however, to bear in mind that those rules, as well as solving disputes, affect parties' future conduct. In particular, the rules form the background against which an owner of land can arrange his affairs. It is therefore important to remember that land law is not only about resolving disputes; it also aims to create a settled legal background against which parties can plan their future use of land.

5.1 THE FACTS OF THE CASE AND THE DILEMMA

Mr and Mrs Ainsworth lived together in Milward Road, Hastings, Sussex. Mr Ainsworth was registered as owner of the home. In 1957, Mr Ainsworth moved out. In 1958, he borrowed £1,000 from the National Provincial Bank.[11] The money was borrowed as part of a mortgage deal: to secure his duty to repay that sum, plus interest, Mr Ainsworth gave the bank a particular right (a charge) over his home.[12] This meant that, if Mr Ainsworth were

---

[9] See e.g. Chapter 6, sections 2 and 5.4 and Chapter 7, sections 2.2 and 3.3.2.

[10] For a more recent example in which the courts have considered such disputes, see e.g. *Scott v Southern Pacific Mortgages Ltd* [2014] UKSC 52, [2015] AC 385. In *Wishart v Credit & Mercantile plc* [2015] EWCA Civ 655, the dispute was very similar, but the home had already been sold and the question was whether Mr Wishart had a claim to part of the proceeds of sale.

[11] Formerly one of the largest banks in England and Wales, the National Provincial Bank became part of the National Westminster Bank in 1970.

[12] In fact, before borrowing the money and giving the bank the charge, Mr Ainsworth had transferred his title to the home to a company: that company then granted the bank its charge. In separate

to fall behind in his repayments, the bank would have a power to sell the land and use the proceeds to meet his debt. By 1962, Mr Ainsworth had fallen behind on his repayments to the bank. The bank wished to sell the land. To get a good price, the bank knew that it had to sell the home with vacant possession. Because Mrs Ainsworth refused to leave, the bank applied for an order for possession of the home. Mrs Ainsworth resisted that application, and the case eventually reached the House of Lords, where it was reported as *National Provincial Bank v Ainsworth*.[13]

The majority of the Court of Appeal, led by Lord Denning MR, had found that Mrs Ainsworth had a right to occupy the land that bound the bank.[14] On that basis, the bank's claim for possession would fail. But the House of Lords reversed the finding of the Court of Appeal: Mrs Ainsworth had to leave the land. As we will see in Chapter 6, section 5.4, the House of Lords' decision depended in part on the *content* question: in contrast to the Court of Appeal, it found that Mrs Ainsworth's right did *not* count as a property right and so was not capable of binding the bank. The House of Lords also found that Mrs Ainsworth had no direct right against the bank: there was nothing in the bank's own conduct that placed it under a duty to allow Mrs Ainsworth to remain in her home.

The House of Lords, like the Court of Appeal, had a tough choice to make. Mrs Ainsworth and the bank can each be seen as victims, in different ways, of Mr Ainsworth—he gave the bank a charge over the home without telling his wife; equally, her claim came as a surprise to the bank, as Mr Ainsworth, when giving the bank that charge, had not informed the bank that he had deserted his wife. The court was thus forced to choose between two parties who can each be seen as 'innocent'.

This type of dilemma is common in property law. For example, consider a case in which the claimant owns property and sells that property to a fraudster, who then fails to pay for the goods. Before the fraud is discovered, the rogue sells the goods on to the defendant, who pays the usual market price for them. Of course, each of the claimant and the defendant has a good claim against the fraudster; in practice, however, such a claim is likely to be rendered useless by the fraudster's disappearance or hopeless insolvency. A crucial question, then, is who has the better right to the goods: the claimant or the defendant? If it is the claimant, then the innocent defendant will lose out, as he or she will have to pay the value of the goods to the claimant. If the defendant has the better right, in contrast, the innocent claimant will lose out, as he or she will have parted with their goods without receiving any payment in return.[15]

As the following extract shows, when the dilemma arises in relation to land rather than goods, the special features of land sharpen the court's dilemma. To translate the passage to the case, Mr Ainsworth equates to the party referred to as 'A'; Mrs Ainsworth to 'B'; and the bank takes the role of 'C Bank'.

proceedings against her husband, however, Mrs Ainsworth succeeded in having the transfer to the company set aside, so the later litigation between the bank and Mrs Ainsworth proceeded on the basis that the company had not been involved, and that Mr Ainsworth had retained title to the home, and given the bank its charge directly.

13 [1965] AC 1175, HL.

14 The Court of Appeal's decision was reported as *National Provincial Bank v Hastings Car Mart* [1964] Ch 665 (CA).

15 For an example in which the claimant, the initial owner of the goods, prevailed, see *Cundy v Lindsay* (1878) 3 App Cas 459 (HL); for an example in which the defendant, the later purchaser of the goods, was the winner, see *Lewis v Averay* [1972] 1 QB 198 (CA).

McFarlane, *The Structure of Property Law* (2008, pp 11–12)

On the one hand, B can point to the social importance of land: [she] is currently using the land as a home and uprooting that home will cause severe disruption. B can also point to the uniqueness of land: even if B is able to find a home elsewhere, it will be in a different location and so B may be forced to change many aspects of [her] life. So it might seem that the social importance and uniqueness of land should cause the rules of the land law system to lean in favour of someone, such as B, who is currently occupying or otherwise making use of land.

However, C Bank can make a powerful counter-argument. It may well have made a substantial loan to A: the limited availability of land, along with its social importance, ensures that land has a high value. So, if C Bank is unable to sell the land, it is likely to be left substantially out of pocket. It is also important to think about the wider consequences of finding in favour of B. First, whilst it is easy to have sympathy with B rather than with a faceless bank, it should be remembered that if banks have systematic problems in recovering loans, this can have repercussions not just for the bank's customers but for the wider economy.[16] Second, if C Bank is unable to sell the land, we need to consider the effect of such a decision on lenders' future practice. Will lenders have to carry out extensive and expensive checks to ensure that there are no other users of the home who may later thwart a lender's attempt to sell the land? After all, as land is capable of multiple, simultaneous use, there may be many potential rights that a lender will need to watch out for. The costs incurred by lenders would then be passed on to borrowers. As land is already very expensive, this will make it harder still for would-be homeowners to enter the market. And, given its limited availability, it would be unfortunate if land became very difficult to trade in. Given we can't produce new land, we should be particularly careful to make sure the land we do have does not become permanently burdened and thus difficult to buy or sell.

[. . . T]he dispute between B and C Bank could be characterised as part of a wider clash between commerce and market forces on the one hand and the need for social protection and the maintenance of a home on the other. The fact that the dispute involves land, a special kind of thing, does *not* help us resolve this conflict; instead, it *heightens the tension*. The dispute between market forces and social protection thus draws out the ambivalent nature of land itself. On the one hand, it is of limited availability and constitutes an important financial investment: we therefore do not want the process of buying land to be unduly difficult. Yet on the other hand, it is unique and socially important: we therefore do not want to give insufficient protection to those who use and, in particular, occupy land.

5.2 TWO POSSIBLE APPROACHES

Before we examine the reasoning of the courts in *National Provincial Bank v Ainsworth*, it is worth asking how a court *should* approach the dispute between the occupier and the bank. In the following extract, Harris contrasts two broad types of possible approach. He opens with a quotation from Max Weber, the political economist and sociologist.

---

[16] The importance to the wider economy of such banks was dramatically emphasized by the UK government's nationalization of Northern Rock plc using powers under the Banking (Special Provisions) Act 2008. The problems faced by that bank, a major 'mortgage' lender, were *not* caused by difficulties faced by the bank in recovering loans, but the highly unusual steps taken by the government nonetheless demonstrate the importance of such banks to the wider economy.

Harris, 'Legal Doctrine and Interests in Land' in *Oxford Essays in Jurisprudence* (3rd series, eds Eekelaar and Bell, 1987, pp 168–9)

'The expectations of the parties are oriented towards the economic and utilitarian meaning of a legal proposition. However, from the point of view of legal logic, this meaning is an "irrational one" [. . .] a "lawyers' law" has never been and never will be brought into conformity with lay expectation unless it totally renounce that formal character which is immanent in it. This is just as true of the English law which we glorify so much to-day, as it has been of the ancient Roman jurists or of the methods of modern continental legal thought.'[17]

So wrote Max Weber some seventy years ago. It constitutes one of his leading conclusions about the nature of lawyers' law. It points to a contrast between formal-doctrinal (and hence circumscribed) reasoning which, he claimed, was intrinsic to professional legal thinking, and open-ended consequentialist controversy over the interpretation of legal propositions. If there are rival views as to the meaning of a legal rule, the layman expects the choice to be made according to which version will have the best outcome, all things considered. The professional lawyer, however, will settle the issue by reference to doctrinal arguments based upon existing legal materials.

I propose to examine this alleged contrast in the context of current issues concerning interests in land in English law. I shall argue that the dichotomy exists, but not in the stark Weberian form. Consequentialist interpretation is not, from the point of view of legal logic, 'irrational'. On the contrary, it constitutes the basis of one professionally accepted style of reasoning—what I call the 'utility model of rationality'. However, the 'doctrine model of rationality'—along with two other models—also plays a crucial role in the development of the law. To the extent that 'policy' can never totally displace doctrine, so long as our legal institutions retain anything like their present character, Weber was correct [. . .] if we want to ditch doctrine, we need to invent new institutions, new lawyers, and a new conception of 'law' itself.

Harris thus identifies two prominent, but contrasting, models that may inform a court's approach when dealing with cases such as *Ainsworth*. The 'utility model of rationality' is based on what Weber sees as a non-specialist's expectation of how the dispute should be decided: it essentially consists of weighing up, on one side, the practical advantages of favouring the occupier and, on the other, the practical advantages of finding for the bank. The 'doctrinal model of rationality' is based on what Weber calls 'lawyers' law': the dispute is resolved by the application of specific legal rules, not by a general weighing of the consequences of finding in favour of the occupier or the bank.

Was either of those models important in the decisions in *Ainsworth*? To test this, we can examine an extract from each of the Court of Appeal and House of Lords decisions.

5.3 THE COURT OF APPEAL'S APPROACH IN *AINSWORTH*

Although Russell LJ dissented, the majority of the Court of Appeal (Lord Denning MR and Donovan LJ) found in favour of Mrs Ainsworth. The case was the culmination of a series of decisions in which the Court of Appeal, under Lord Denning's direction, had first created

---

[17] Weber, *Law in Economy and Society* (ed Rheinstein, 1954) pp 307–8.

and then developed a right that protected a party such as Mrs Ainsworth: the 'deserted wife's equity'. In the extract below, Lord Denning relies on those decisions to find that Mrs Ainsworth's 'deserted wife's equity' protected her not only against her husband, but also against the bank.

National Provincial Bank v Ainsworth (sub nom National Provincial Bank v Hastings Car Mart and ors)
[1964] Ch 665 (CA)

Lord Denning MR

At 683–5

Since the war there have been many cases in this court which have established that a wife, who has been deserted by her husband, has a right to remain in occupation of the matrimonial home unless and until the court orders her to go. The development can be easily traced. Prior to the war it was recognised that, where the husband owns the matrimonial home and is living there himself, he cannot turn his wife out. He cannot treat her as a stranger. He cannot exclude her from the house without good cause.[18] Now suppose he deserts his wife and goes off, leaving her in the matrimonial home with the children. Is he to be in any better position because he has deserted her? Can he turn her out as if she was a stranger? Clearly not. He cannot take advantage of his own wrong—of his own desertion—and use it as a ground for ejecting her. The reason is simply this: it is the husband's duty to provide the wife with a roof over her head; and, by providing the matrimonial home, he gives her an authority to be there. It is an authority which he cannot revoke, so long as it remains the matrimonial home. He certainly cannot revoke it on his desertion. Just as in olden days a deserted wife had an irrevocable authority to pledge his credit for necessaries, so in these days she has an irrevocable authority to remain in the matrimonial home [. . .]

But the question here is: what is the position of successors in title? Suppose the husband, after deserting his wife, sells the house over her head, or mortgages it without her knowledge. Can the purchaser or mortgagee turn her out? [. . .]

It seems to me that, if the cases I have mentioned were correctly decided,[19] as I believe them to be, it can only be on the footing that the wife *has a right* to remain in the matrimonial home—and a right which is enforceable against the successors of the husband—save, of course, a purchaser for value without notice [. . .]

At 690–1

It is said that this will put an undue burden on purchasers and mortgagees, but I do not see this. If the husband, on deserting his wife, had granted the wife a tenancy (as he might well have done) they would be bound by it if they made no inquiry of her. So, in order to be safe, they should make inquiry at the house. I do not see why it should be in the least embarrassing. All they need say is: 'As we are buying (or lending money on) the house, we wish to verify the occupation of it.' She may say: 'I live here with my husband,' or 'I am a

---

[18] See *Shipman v Shipman* [1924] 2 Ch 140, 146, *per* Atkin LJ.

[19] [The cases discussed by Lord Denning MR had given a holder of a 'deserted wife's equity' protection against: (i) the trustee in bankruptcy of the husband; and (ii) a third party (such as a company controlled by the husband) to whom the husband had transferred the land so that the third party could then try to remove the wife from the property.]

tenant,' or 'My husband has left me.' The husband may deny it, but his denial would not affect her right, if she was a tenant. Nor should it, if she has been deserted . . .

The question remains: what order should be made? When should the wife go? It is a matter for the discretion of the court. On the one hand there is the bank who desire to recoup themselves all that is owing to them. On the other hand there is the wife with four children, receiving nothing from her husband, and on National Assistance. Of all the creditors of the husband, she has the most crying claim of all. It is a case where I would fain temper justice with mercy. Justice to the bank, with mercy to the wife.

[Further evidence was then filed, as to the sums owing to the bank and to the value of the house. After hearing that evidence, Lord Denning MR formulated the court's order: Mrs Ainsworth was permitted to stay in the house, with her children, for 12 months, but, after one month, she would have to pay £3 a week to the bank, to cover interest due to the bank on the money owed to it by Mr Ainsworth, and repairs required to keep the property in good condition. Either party would be at liberty to apply to the court during or at the end of the 12 months.]

In analysing Lord Denning's approach, we can use both of the models of legal reasoning identified by Harris: the 'utility model' and the 'doctrinal model'. In one way, Lord Denning appeals to the doctrinal model: he argues that protecting a deserted wife against a bank involves only a logical, incremental extension of the existing case law. In another, more significant way, however, his Lordship's approach is motivated by the utility model: by the desire to find what Harris calls the 'best outcome, all things considered'. Firstly, consider Lord Denning's analysis of the facts of the case: he emphasizes the vulnerability of Mrs Ainsworth and her children and contrasts their innocence not only with the adultery of Mr Ainsworth but also with the laxity of the bank, who failed to make its own inspection of the house before acquiring a charge over the land. Secondly, and most importantly, Lord Denning's conclusion ensures that the court has a very wide discretion to reach whatever result it considers just. To find that Mrs Ainsworth's deserted wife's equity binds the bank does *not* mean that the bank is necessarily denied a possession order. For the effect of that equity can only be determined by a court, considering all the facts (including the parties' respective financial positions) and combining '[j]ustice to the bank, with mercy to the wife'. On this approach, then, the ultimate resolution of the case depends entirely on the judges' view of what is 'the best outcome, all things considered'. As we will see in the next extract, however, the House of Lords decisively rejected this view.

To understand Lord Denning's approach, it is important to be aware of the social and economic context in which the courts developed the concept of the 'deserted wife's equity'. This context is discussed in the following extract.

Dunn, *'National Provincial Bank v Ainsworth* (1965)' in *Landmark Cases in Equity* (eds Mitchell and Mitchell, 2012, pp 577–78)

In a decade leading up to legislative reform on equal pay and sex discrimination, concern with the economic vulnerability of women had become a worldwide issue. The legal, social and fiscal vulnerability of the abandoned spouse will be evident in any age, but for the wife was particularly acute in the 1950s and 1960s. In an age which saw the beginnings of an erosion of traditionalist values and attitudes towards the family, rising divorce rates and ultimately a liberalisation of divorce laws, this was a period in which wives tended not to be in circumstances which would allow them to establish financial independence or housing security. Whilst there was a rise in numbers of women going out to work and earning a separate income, wage rates in this period were insufficient to afford independent housing. The post-war housing shortage also meant that there was a dearth of affordable housing, and for a deserted wife (and her children) the possibility of homelessness was a real one. Against this background, wives' vulnerability was addressed directly by Lord Denning within the case law as a process of welfare-based discretionary justice to prevent a husband from 'taking advantage of his own wrong'.[20]

5.4 THE HOUSE OF LORDS' APPROACH IN *AINSWORTH*

A unanimous House of Lords differed from the majority of the Court of Appeal as to the answer to be given to the crucial *content* question: did Mrs Ainsworth's 'deserted wife's equity' count as a property right, capable of binding not only Mr Ainsworth but also a third party such as the bank? The House of Lords thus rejected Lord Denning's analysis, not only allowing the bank's appeal but also overruling the previous Court of Appeal and first instance decisions, relied on by Lord Denning, that had allowed a 'deserted wife's equity' to bind a party other than the relevant husband.[21]

National Provincial Bank v Ainsworth
[1965] AC 1175, HL

Lord Upjohn

At 1233–4

In this case your Lordships are dealing with essentially conveyancing matters. It has been the policy of the law for over a hundred years to simplify and facilitate transactions in real property. It is of great importance that persons should be able freely and easily to raise money on the security of their property. [Lord Upjohn then considered what would happen if, before making such a secured loan, the bank were to check the husband's property and ask the deserted wife what rights she had in that land.] The answer 'I am a deserted wife' (if given) only gives notice of a right so imprecise, so incapable of definition, so impossible of measurement in legal phraseology or terms of money that if [it] is to be safe the [bank] will refuse to do business and much unnecessary harm will be done [. . .] It does not seem to me that an inquiry as to the marital status of a woman in occupation of property is one which the law can reasonably require to be made; it is not reasonable for a third party to be compelled by law to make inquiries into the delicate and possibly uncertain and fluctuating state

---

[20] *National Provincial Bank v Ainsworth* (sub nom *National Provincial Bank v Hastings Car Mart* [1964] Ch 665 (CA) 683 (Lord Denning MR). Also accepted was the emotional cruelty which could occur in permitting a husband to sell the matrimonial home to his new partner over the head of his wife, as occurred for example in *Street v Denham* [1954] 1 WLR 624.

[21] See the House of Lords decision: [1965] AC 1175 at [1252], *per* Lord Wilberforce. The decisions in *Bendal v McWhirter* [1952] 2 QB 466 and *Street v Denham* [1954] 1 WLR 624 were overruled, and the decision in *Ferris v Weaven* [1952] 2 All ER 233 was explained on a different basis—for that explanation, see Chapter 5, section 3.1.

of affairs between a couple whose marriage is going wrong. Still less can it be reasonable to make an inquiry if the answer to be expected will probably lead to no conclusion which can inform the inquirer with any certainty as to the rights of the occupant. These considerations give strong support to the opinion I have already expressed that the rights of the wife must be regarded as purely personal between herself and her husband.

Lord Wilberforce

At 1241–3

My Lords, the doctrine of the 'deserted wife's equity' has been evolved by the courts during the past 13 years in an attempt to mitigate some effects of the housing shortage which has persisted since the 1939–45 war. To a woman, whose husband has left her, especially if she has children, it is of little use to receive periodical payments for her maintenance (even if these are in fact punctually made) if she is left without a home. Once possession of a house has been lost, the process of acquiring another place to live in may be painful and prolonged. So, even though, as is normally the case, the home is in law the property of the husband, the courts have intervened to prevent him from using his right of property to remove his deserted wife from it and they have correspondingly recognised that she has a right, or 'equity' as it has come to be called, which the law will protect, to remain there.

This case relates to one aspect, and one aspect only, of [the deserted wife's equity]. No question arises here as to any claim which a deserted wife may have against her husband: all that we are concerned with is the right of a deserted wife to remain in possession as against a third party, claiming, in good faith, under the husband. And the issue is even narrower than that: it relates only to the position of a third party whose title arises subsequently to the desertion [. . .]

The issue is thus a narrow one, affecting a small proportion only of those deserted wives who are left in occupation of their husband's house. Nevertheless as to them, as to [Mrs Ainsworth], issues of importance, and probably of hardship, are involved. The ultimate question must be whether such persons can be given the protection which social considerations of humanity evidently indicate without injustice to third parties and a radical departure from sound principles of real property law [. . .]

The appeal raises two questions, one of general, the other of more limited scope.[22] The general question is whether the respondent Mrs. Ainsworth as the deserted wife of her husband, the owner of the house, has any interest in or right over it which is capable of binding the bank as the proprietor of a legal interest in the land. This is a general question of real property law [. . .]

I turn to the first and more general question: what is the nature of the deserted wife's interest, or right? [Lord Wilberforce then analysed the duties imposed on Mr Ainsworth by the deserted wife's equity: his conclusion is set out below.]

At 1247–8

The position then, at the present time, is this. The wife has no specific right against her husband to be provided with any particular house, nor to remain in any particular house. She has a right to cohabitation and support. But, in considering whether the husband should be given possession of property of his, the court will have regard to the duty of the spouses

---

22 [The second question was the *defences* question: even if Mrs Ainsworth's right counted as a property right and was thus capable of binding a third party, did the bank have a defence to that right? We will consider the particular defence raised by the bank, referred to in this book as the '*lack of registration defence*' in Chapter 3, section 3, Chapter 15, section 4.2, and Chapter 16, sections 2–4.]

to each other, and the decision it reaches will be based on a consideration of what may be called the matrimonial circumstances. These include such matters as whether the husband can provide alternative accommodation and if so whether such accommodation is suitable having regard to the estate and condition of the spouses; whether the husband's conduct amounts to desertion, whether the conduct of the wife has been such as to deprive her of any of her rights against the husband. And the order to be made must be fashioned accordingly: it may be that the wife should leave immediately or after a certain period: it may be subject to revision on a change of circumstances.

The conclusion emerges to my mind very clearly from this that the wife's rights, as regards the occupation of her husband's property, are essentially of a personal kind: personal in the sense that a decision can only be reached on the basis of considerations essentially dependent on the mutual claims of husband and wife as spouses and as the result of a broad weighing of circumstances and merit. Moreover, these rights are at no time definitive, they are provisional and subject to review at any time according as changes take place in the material circumstances and conduct of the parties.

On any division, then, which is to be made between property rights on the one hand, and personal rights on the other hand, however broad or penumbral the separating band between these two kinds of rights may be, there can be little doubt where the wife's rights fall. Before a right or an interest can be admitted into the category of property, or of a right affecting property, it must be definable, identifiable by third parties, capable in its nature of assumption by third parties, and have some degree of permanence or stability. The wife's right has none of these qualities, it is characterised by the reverse of them.

5.5 COMPARING THE APPROACHES OF THE COURT OF APPEAL AND THE HOUSE OF LORDS

It would be over-simplistic to say that the difference in the results reached by the Court of Appeal and the House of Lords depended entirely on the former's adoption of the 'utility model' of reasoning, whereas the latter favoured the 'doctrinal model'. Firstly, as noted above, Lord Denning did at least pay lip-service to the doctrinal model, by claiming that the Court of Appeal's decision was a logical extension of the pre-existing case law as to the effect of a deserted wife's equity. Secondly, we can see the influence of the utility model in the extract, set out above, from Lord Upjohn's speech. The divergence from Lord Denning's approach is that Lord Upjohn attaches greater significance to the practical disadvantages of making it harder for banks to take an unencumbered security over land. Thirdly, in the first paragraph of the extract set out above, Lord Wilberforce acknowledges the social and economic factors that may well have motivated the Court of Appeal's decision.

It thus seems that the approaches of each of Lord Denning, Lord Upjohn, and Lord Wilberforce can be seen as combining, in different proportions, elements of each of the utility model and the doctrinal model. This should be no surprise; we should not expect any judge deciding a difficult case wholly to ignore either the wider policy questions or the technical legal rules. It does seem, nonetheless, that in Lord Wilberforce's speech, the doctrinal model is more prominent: in particular, there is a concern to avoid '*a radical departure from sound principles of real property law.*'[23] In other words, a decision in favour of

---

[23] This point is noted by Harris: see 'Legal Doctrine and Interests in Land' in *Oxford Essays in Jurisprudence* (3rd series, eds Eekelaar and Bell, Oxford: OUP, 1987, n 60). See too Chapter 12, section 3.1.3.

Mrs Ainsworth can be made only if it can be reconciled with the doctrinal, technical rules of land law. And, according to Lord Wilberforce, those rules meant that Mrs Ainsworth's right could count as a property right (a right capable of binding the bank) only if it was *'definable, identifiable by third parties, capable in its nature of assumption by third parties, and ha[d] some degree of permanence or stability'*.[24] Because Mrs Ainsworth's right did not have those features, the *content* question was decided against her and the bank was therefore free to remove her from her home.

It should be noted that, whilst the House of Lords was unanimous in its decision, each of Lord Cohen[25] and Lord Upjohn[26] called upon Parliament to consider legislative reform of the law, to improve the protection afforded to a deserted wife against third parties. In contrast, Lord Denning clearly felt that such protection could be developed by judicial means. This demonstrates an important point: a judge's view as to the constitutional limits on judges' freedom to create and develop the law may have an important influence on his or her approach. If, for example, a judge takes a fairly strict view as to those limits, the doctrinal model may be more appealing. As Harris noted, concerns about the 'separation of powers' and the 'rule of law' may be used to limit reliance on the utility model: *'If judges resolve an uncertain question about the present law by an assessment and balancing of social consequences, are they not trespassing on the functions of the legislature?'*.[27]

Certainly, at a number of points in this book, we will come across land law rules that are subject to disapproval, not only by commentators but also by the judges themselves. At such points, it is important to consider not only *if* the rules should be changed, but also *how* they should be changed. For example, in Chapter 12, section 2, we will examine a Supreme Court decision concerning the application of the acquisition question to interests in the family home;[28] and in Chapter 19, section 2.7, we will examine a Supreme Court decision concerning the application of the content question to leases.[29] Each case raised the question of whether it would be better to reform existing land law rules through judicial intervention or, instead, by legislation.

5.6 DEVELOPMENTS AFTER *AINSWORTH*: RIGHTS OF OCCUPATION

Parliament did not ignore Lord Cohen and Lord Upjohn's call for legislation to protect a party such as Mrs Ainsworth. The Matrimonial Homes Act 1967 established: (i) that a spouse has a (qualified) statutory right to occupy a home owned by his or her partner; and (ii) that the statutory right to occupy is capable of binding a third party, such as a bank, *if* and *only if* the spouse registers the right of occupation before the third party acquires its right. The 'spouse's right to occupy' thus replaces the 'deserted wife's equity': the statutory right is extended to husbands, and is not limited to spouses who have been deserted. Indeed the statutory right to occupy, now found in the Family Law Act 1996,[30] was extended to civil partners by the Civil Partnership Act 2004.[31]

---

24 [1965] AC 1175, [1248].   25 Ibid, 1228.   26 Ibid, 1241.

27 Harris, 'Legal Doctrine and Interests in Land' in *Oxford Essays in Jurisprudence* (3rd series, eds Eekelaar and Bell, Oxford: OUP, 1987), p 171.

28 *Stack v Dowden* [2007] 2 AC 432.   29 *Berrisford v Mexfield* [2012] 1 AC 955.

30 Family Law Act 1996, ss 30–33: see Chapter 7, section 5 and Chapter 12, section 3.

31 Civil Partnership Act 2004, s 82, Sch 9.

Parliament thus reformed the law by coming up with a specific, tailored solution that it believed formed the best compromise between the need to protect an occupying spouse and the need to protect a third party such as a bank.[32] That compromise could not have been reached by purely judicial reform, as it avoids the doctrinal question of whether the right to occupy counts as a property right; instead, the right is allowed to bind a third party, such as a bank, *only* if it is registered. This is a way of addressing Lord Upjohn's concern, expressed in the extract above, that a bank should not have to undertake exhaustive or delicate enquiries: instead, the bank need only check the relevant register. If the spouse's right is not registered, then, even if the spouse is in occupation of the home when the bank acquires its right, the bank will not be bound. And, even if the right is registered, a court still has the discretion to allow a third party to remove the occupying spouse.[33]

5.7 DEVELOPMENTS AFTER *AINSWORTH*: PROPERTY RIGHTS IN THE FAMILY HOME

Whilst the Matrimonial Homes Act 1967 eventually settled the specific dilemma arising in *National Provincial Bank v Ainsworth*, the wider issues raised by that case have certainly not gone away. First, the issue of women's rights in relation to family homes remains prominent, and the courts continue to be confronted by the question of whether the existing land law rules respond adequately to changing social and economic factors. Indeed, as we will see in Chapter 12, the question now relates not just to the rights of wives, but also to those of unmarried partners, and the focus has now shifted from the content question to the acquisition question. In other words, the question is not whether a 'deserted wife's equity', based on a wife's right to maintenance from her husband, can count as a property right and so bind a third party. Rather, the question now is how can a partner (married or unmarried) acquire a recognized property right: a share of ownership of the family home? Indeed, as the following extract indicates, this question was already an important one, even at the time of the *Ainsworth* litigation.

Kahn-Freund, 'Recent Legislation on Matrimonial Property' (1970) 33 MLR 601

At 606–7

The acquisition for family use of durable assets, immovable [i.e. land] and movable, is one of the dominant features of economic life in the Western world [. . .] Very often such acquisition is made possible through much improved facilities for married women to participate in gainful employment, owing to the state of the labour market, owing to family planning, and also owing to that mechanisation of the household which is in its turn the result of the ability of the family to use part of its current income towards the acquisition of durable assets [. . .] Mrs X may, by her thrift as a housewife, contribute as much to the acquisition of the matrimonial home or of the family car or the television set as her neighbour Mrs Y does by working in a factory or in an office. The maintenance obligation which the law imposes on the husband

---

[32] Lord Denning, it is interesting to note, regarded Parliament's reforms as a 'good result': see Denning, *The Due Process of Law* (London: Butterworths, 1980), p 222.

[33] See Family Law Act 1996, s 33: *Kaur v Gill* [1988] Fam 110 provides an example of the court exercising that discretion in favour of a third party.

used to be considered as an answer to the question raised by the economic dependence of wives upon husbands which results from the arrangements of nature rather than those of society. As a housewife and as a mother the wife was 'rewarded' in this way. This approach to the problem had a certain plausibility as long as the large majority of married couples were compelled to spend their income on current needs of food, clothing and shelter for themselves and their children. The link between the law of matrimonial property and the law of matrimonial maintenance is as close today as ever it was, but how can one seriously assert that supply by the husband of the means to cover these elementary needs can be an equivalent to the wife's economic contribution (in whatever form) where a large part of the contribution is destined for the acquisition of durable goods, and especially of a home for the family?

[. . .] Today the problem of sharing between the spouses and of the protection of the non-earning housewife (which is part of it) can no longer be solved through the law of maintenance. It must comprise her share in what has been called 'household property' or 'family assets'. Much the most important of these is the family home, whether it be freehold or rented property.

Kahn-Freund's analysis must now, of course, be extended to unmarried cohabiting partners. His central point is that, even by the middle of the 1960's, the 'deserted wife's equity' was an anachronism. The equity was an elaboration of a husband's historic duty to maintain his wife: Lord Denning drew an explicit link between the equity and the wife's power 'in olden days' to pay for necessaries (such as food) by using her husband's credit.[34] This raises a real difficulty for Lord Denning's idea that the equity could bind a third party such as the bank—if the wife's right is ultimately based on a husband's duty to maintain his wife, how can the right also bind a third party, such as a bank? After all, the bank has no such duty to maintain Mrs Ainsworth. This difficulty, of course, was exposed when the case reached the House of Lords.

As Kahn-Freund suggests, a focus on maintenance is outdated: the real issue is as to the ownership of property acquired by cohabiting partners. And land, chiefly the home in which the partners live, is by far the most valuable and significant piece of such property. It may be, for example, that the land is registered in the name of only one of the partners; but, as Kahn-Freund suggests, there may be strong arguments that the other partner should nonetheless have a share of the benefit of the property. It is therefore no surprise that, as we will see in Chapter 12, the modern focus of the law is on whether a partner has *acquired* a recognized property right in the family home. As we will see, however, the general issues raised by the *Ainsworth* litigation remain important. The dilemma faced by judges and Parliament is as acute as ever, and the tension between the utility model and the doctrinal model remains unresolved.

6 CONCLUSION

Although the *Ainsworth* litigation focussed on one particular corner of land law, it teaches us a number of general lessons. Firstly, as we noted in section 1, land law is clearly very important in practice: the outcome of the litigation had significant practical consequences

---

[34] *National Provincial Bank v Ainsworth* (sub nom *National Provincial Bank v Hastings Car Mart* [1964] Ch 665 (CA) 683.

not only for Mrs Ainsworth and the National Provincial Bank, but also for thousands of other occupiers and mortgage lenders sharing their positions.

Secondly, the case focussed on whether the occupier had a *private right* to use land that she could assert against the bank: did Mrs Ainsworth have an interest in land (i.e. a property right) that could bind the bank? That question can usefully be broken down into three further questions: the *content*, *acquisition*, and *defences* questions. The *content* question considers the nature of a party's right and, in particular, asks if that right counts as a property right. The *acquisition* question concerns the means by which a party can acquire a private right to use land and, in particular, how a property right can be acquired. The *defences* question asks whether a party later acquiring a private right to use land may have a defence to a pre-existing property right held by another party and thus allows us to ascertain which of two or more competing property rights has *priority*. The *Ainsworth* litigation concerned the first of those questions; as suggested in section 5.7, its modern day equivalents, to be examined in Chapter 12, focus on the second of those questions.

The simple facts of *Ainsworth* demonstrate a tension that runs throughout land law: the tension between two parties who each claim competing rights to use the land. At a more abstract level, the judges' differing approaches to the case show a further tension: between a 'utility model' (in which a court should make the decision having what it regards as the best practical consequences) and a 'doctrinal model' (in which a court should make the decision that best accords with the existing legal rules). That tension continues to be evident in more recent land law decisions, many of which have also dealt with the very difficult issue of resolving a dispute between an occupier who wishes to stay in his or her home and a lender who wishes to sell the home to recoup at least some of a debt owed to it.[35]

This leads us to perhaps the most important lesson of *Ainsworth*. Imagine that you are employed to act as a lawyer for one of the parties in the case. If acting for Mrs Ainsworth, you may want to emphasize the social importance of land and the need to allow her and her children to continue living in their home. If you are instead acting for the bank, you may want to focus on the need to keep the cost of mortgages down by ensuring that banks do not need to make time-consuming enquiries before making a mortgage loan. Either way, however, it will not be enough simply to go to court and make those general points. If you want to do the best job for your client, it is vital to understand, and to be confident in using, the doctrinal rules that make up land law.

This should not be taken to mean that the 'utility model' is irrelevant or that there is no need to consider the practical merits or wider justice of the doctrinal rules of land law. On the contrary, the social importance of land law means that it is vital not only to understand land law rules, but also to evaluate them. After all, as we noted in sections 5.6 and 5.7, and as we will see throughout this book, land law, like other areas of law, necessarily changes over time; the crucial question is whether those changes are for the better.

QUESTIONS

1. In what ways does land differ from other physical things? What consequences do those differences have for land law?

2. What is 'land law'? Does it involve all legal rules related to the use of land?

---

[35] See e.g. *Scott v Southern Pacific Mortgages Ltd* [2014] UKSC 52, [2015] AC 385.

3. Harris suggests that the 'utility model' and the 'doctrinal model' may be useful in understanding particular approaches to land law. What are the differences between the two models?

4. Why did the Court of Appeal and House of Lords reach differing results in *National Provincial Bank v Ainsworth*? In your view, what should the result be in such a case?

5. Land law has a reputation as a subject that is full of technical rules. Even if that reputation is true, is it necessarily a bad thing?

 For guidance on how to answer these questions visit the online resources at www.oup.com/uk/mcfarlane4e/.

FURTHER READING

Birks, 'Five Keys to Land Law' in *Land Law: Themes and Perspectives* (eds Bright and Dewar, Oxford: OUP, 1998)

Dunn, '*National Provincial Bank v Ainsworth* (1965)' in *Landmark Cases in Equity* (eds Mitchell and Mitchell, Oxford: Hart, 2012)

Harris, 'Legal Doctrine and Interests in Land' in *Oxford Essays in Jurisprudence* (3rd series, eds Eekelaar and Bell, Oxford: OUP, 1987)

Kahn-Freund, 'Recent Legislation on Matrimonial Property' (1970) 33 MLR 601

Law Commission Report No 307, *Cohabitation: The Financial Consequences of Relationship Breakdown* (2007, Pts I and II)

McFarlane, *The Structure of Property Law* (Oxford: Hart, 2008, Pt A)

2

WHAT IS LAND?

CENTRAL ISSUES

1. In Chapter 1, we looked at the special features of land and saw that land law is a special part of property law. In this chapter, we will look more closely at the legal meaning of land.

2. Firstly, in section 1 of this Chapter, we will look at the fundamental question of what it means to say that land is a form of property. We will see that it is important to focus not on the land itself, but rather on the relationship between a person and the land. That relationship can take the form of a right: so, a party claiming that he or she owns particular land is claiming that he or she has a property right in that land.

3. Secondly, in section 2 of this Chapter, we will look in more detail at what it means to say that someone owns 'land'. We will see that an 'owner' of

   land has a particular type of property right in that land: a freehold or a lease. The rights of such an owner of land are not limited to the physical surface of the land: they extend both downwards and upwards from that surface. We will also consider the extent to which an owner's right to exclusive control of land entails a right to exclusive control of objects attached to that land, or found in or on that land.

4. We noted in Chapter 1 that the focus of land law, as a distinct subject, is on property rights to use land. In this Chapter, we will begin to see some of the questions with which the courts have to deal in deciding on the nature and extent of parties' property rights. We will look at these questions in more detail in Chapters 5 and 6.

1 LAND AS A FORM OF PRIVATE PROPERTY

In Chapter 1, section 1, we noted that rules relating to land can be seen throughout the law, not only in land law. The following extract, taken from a seminal constitutional law case, provides an example of this. It is important to note that the case does not only concern the protection of land; the claimant also complained of the theft of some of his papers. Those two aspects of the case are not separated out by the court: as we will see, the case depends not on the special features of land, but rather on the protection given to *any* property right.

Entick v Carrington
(1765) 2 Wils KB 274, Common Pleas

Facts: Carrington and three others (messengers to the King) entered the house of Entick without his consent, searched it, and removed various papers. They were acting under a warrant issued by the Earl of Halifax, one of the King's Secretaries of State. The warrant authorized them to search for papers at the house of Entick, because he was '*the author of, or one concerned in the writing of, several weekly very seditious papers, entitled* The Monitor *or* British Freeholder *containing gross and scandalous reflections and invectives upon His Majesty's Government, and upon both Houses of Parliament*'.

Lord Camden, Lord Chief Justice, considered whether the warrant could authorize the actions of Carrington and the other messengers.

Lord Camden, LCJ

At 291–2

The warrant in our case was an execution in the first instance, without any previous summons, examination, hearing, or proof that he [Entick] was author of the supposed libels; a power claimed by no other magistrate whatsoever; [. . .] it was left to the discretion of these defendants to execute the warrant in the absence or presence of [Entick], when he might have no witness present to see what they did; for they were to seize all papers, bank bills, or any other valuable papers they might take away if they were so disposed; there might be nobody to detect them.

[W]e were told by one of these messengers that he was obliged by his oath to sweep away all papers whatsoever; if this is law it would be found in our books, but no such law ever existed in this country; our law holds the property of every man so sacred, that no man can set his foot upon his neighbour's close without leave; if he does he is a trespasser, though he does no damage at all; if he will tread upon his neighbour's ground he must justify it by law.

The defendants have no right to avail themselves of the usage of these warrants since the Revolution [. . .] we can safely say there is no law in this country to justify the defendants in what they have done; if there was, it would destroy all the comforts of society; for papers are often the dearest property a man can have [. . .]

We shall now consider the usage of these warrants since the Revolution; if it began then, it is too modern to be law; the common law did not begin with the Revolution; the ancient constitution which had almost been overthrown and destroyed was then repaired and revived; the Revolution added a new buttress to the ancient venerable edifice: the Kings Bench lately said that no objection had ever been taken to general warrants, they have passed *sub silentio*:[1] this is the first instance of an attempt to prove a modern practice of a private office to make and execute warrants to enter a man's house, search for and take way all his books and papers in the first instance, to be law, which is not to be found in our books. It must have been the guilt or poverty of those upon whom such warrants have been executed, that deterred or hindered them from contending against the power of the Secretary of State, or such warrants could never have passed for lawful till this time [. . .]

Our law is wise and merciful, and supposes every man accused to be innocent before he is tried by his peers: upon the whole, we are all of opinion that this warrant is wholly illegal

---

1 [Under silence; without comment].

and void. One word more for ourselves; we are no advocates for libels, all Governments must set their faces against them, and whenever they come before us and a jury we shall set our faces against them; and if juries do not prevent them they may prove fatal to liberty, destroy Government and introduce anarchy; but tyranny is better than anarchy, and the worst Government better than none at all.

When analysing *Entick v Carrington*,[2] it is useful to bear in mind the Fourth Amendment to the Constitution of the United States:

The right of the people to be secure in their persons, houses, papers, and effects, against unreasonable searches and seizures, shall not be violated, and no warrants shall issue, but upon probable cause, supported by oath or affirmation, and particularly describing the place to be searched, and the persons or things to be seized.

That constitutional guarantee was passed, in large part, to prevent an abuse of governmental power that had occurred in the 1760s, when tax collectors had been given a very wide power to enter and search private homes. It is worth noting that, in *Entick*, the reasoning of Lord Camden was not based on a *special* limit on governmental power, such as that later established by the Fourth Amendment, but rather on the *general* rules of property law. More precisely, because Entick had a property right in relation to both his house and papers, *no one* could interfere with those things without showing some lawful authority to do so. So, even without an explicit constitutional guarantee, Entick's land, like his papers, could be seen as private property, safe from unjustified interference.

In a case such as *Entick*, it is tempting to say that the land and papers were each 'Entick's property'. As the following extract shows, however, that general description may not, in fact, be an accurate picture of the legal position.

Gray and Gray, *Elements of Land Law* (5th edn, 2009, pp 86–8)

Few concepts are quite so fragile, so elusive and so frequently misused as the notion of property. There is a pervasive element of shared deception in our normal property talk: property is not theft, but *fraud*. We commonly speak of property as if its meaning were entirely clear and logical, but property is a conceptual mirage which slips tantalisingly from view just when it seems most solidly attainable. Amongst the misperceptions which dominate the conventional analysis of both lay persons and lawyers is the lazy myth that property is a 'monolithic notion of standard content and invariable intensity'.[3] Our daily references to property therefore tend to comprise a mutual conspiracy of unsophisticated semantic allusions and confusions, which we tolerate—frequently, indeed, do not notice—largely because our linguistic shorthand commands a certain low-level communicative efficiency [. . .]

---

[2] For full discussion of the decision and its many implications, see Tomkins and Scott (eds) *Entick v Carrington: 250 Years of the Rule of Law* (2015), in particular Chapter 5, by Scott, '*Entick v Carrington* and the Legal Protection of Property', which argues that the decision shows '*many of the key themes of the common law's attempts to protect property*'.

[3] See *Yanner v Eaton* (1999) 201 CLR 351 (High Court of Australia) at [19], *per* Gleeson CJ, and Gaudron, Kirby, and Hayne JJ.

It remains painfully true that most of our everyday references to property are unreflective, naive and relatively meaningless. In our crude way we are seldom concerned to look behind the immediately practical or functional sense in which we employ the term 'property' in relation to land. What does it really mean to say that Julian Bishop 'owns' 25 Mountfield Gardens or that these premises are his 'property'? [. . .]

The mistaken reification of property[4]

As the High Court of Australia acknowledged in *Yanner v Eaton*,[5] much of our false thinking about property 'stems from the residual perception that "property" is itself a thing or resource rather than a legally endorsed concentration of power over things and resources.' The root of the difficulty lies in the fact that non-lawyers (and often lawyers) tend to speak rather loosely of 'property' as the *thing* which is owned (e.g. 'that book/car/house is my property'). Whilst this reification of property is harmless enough in casual conversation, it has the effect of obscuring important features of property as a legal and social institution.

Property is not a thing but a power relationship

Deep at the heart of the phenomenon of property is the semantic reality that 'property' is not a thing, but rather the condition of being 'proper' to a particular person (e.g. 'That book/car/house is *proper* to me'). For serious students of property, the beginning of truth is the recognition that property is not a thing but a *power relationship*—a relationship of social and legal legitimacy existing between a person and a valued resource (whether tangible or intangible). To claim 'property' in a resource is, in effect, to assert a significant degree of control over that resource. Moreover, as Karl Renner once said, '[p]ower over matter begets personal power'.[6] 'Property' ultimately articulates a political relationship between persons. Land—the physical substratum of all human interaction—becomes a vital component of all social and economic engineering.

All property talk is value-laden

All property references are, at some level, a statement about the social legitimacy attaching to the claim in question. The etymological links between terms such as 'property', 'proper', 'appropriate', and 'propriety' underscore the value-laden complexity of inter-relating nuances of property talk. Genuine property discourse thinly conceals a subtext of social propriety. The law of property incorporates a series of critical value judgments, reflecting the cultural norms, the social ethics and the political economy prevalent in any given community. It is inevitable that property law should serve in this way as a vehicle for ideology, for 'property' has commonly been the epithet used to identify that which people most greatly value. The terminology of 'property' also points more subtly to relationships of dependence, for dependence is the inescapable outcome of unequal distributions of that which is valued. The terms 'property' and 'dependence' are merely positive and negative descriptions of existing distributions of control over socially valued resources.

---

4 [Reification means 'turning into a thing'—the argument here is that it is a mistake to equate 'property' as a concept or organizing idea with physical things, such as land or cars.]

5 [(1999) 201 CLR 351 at [18], *per* Gleeson CJ, and Gaudron, Kirby and Hayne JJ.]

6 *The Institutions of Private Law and Their Social Functions* (ed O Kahn-Freund, 1949) p 107.

Gray and Gray make a number of important points: some of them can assist us to understand, internally, how land law works; others can help us to stand outside land law and evaluate the system. The first crucial point is that, to understand property as it is used in legal contexts, we cannot equate it with physical things: so, in *Entick v Carrington*, it is not enough simply to say that the land or papers were Mr Entick's property; instead, we need to make clear that there is something *in between* Mr Entick and those physical things. Gray and Gray develop this point by focussing on property as a 'power relationship' between, say, Mr Entick and his land or papers. A different way of developing the point (linking it into our discussion of the scope of land law in Chapter 1, section 2) is to say that what stands between Mr Entick and his land or papers is a *right*. In defining the *content* of that right, we can build on Gray and Gray's definition of the content of the 'power relationship': it is a right to a '*significant degree of control over that resource*'.

So, the first vital lesson to take from Gray and Gray's analysis is that we cannot always equate 'property' with 'things'. If we say that the house broken into by Mr Carrington was Mr Entick's property, what we really mean is that Mr Entick had a particular type of *right* in relation to that land—a right that gave him a significant degree of control over that land. We can describe Mr Entick's right as a *property right* in relation to that land. We can therefore say that land (like papers) counts as a form of private property in the sense that land is a resource in relation to which a private individual (such as Mr Entick) can have a property right. This means that, in thinking about the notion of property in land law, we really need to focus on the concept of a *property right*. We will examine the nature of a property right in land in more detail in Chapters 5 and 6. A key feature of such a right is that it imposes a prima facie duty on the rest of the world. In *Entick*, the King's messengers, along with everyone else in the world, were thus under a duty to Mr Entick, and that duty arose because Mr Entick had a property right in relation to both the land and papers.

In the extract above, Gray and Gray also point out the assumptions that we may make when saying, for example, that the land and papers are Mr Entick's property. That formulation implies that the land and papers are *proper to* Mr Entick—that is, they are due to, or appropriate to, him. That point is made clearer if, instead of describing the land and papers as his property, we say that Mr Entick has a property right in relation to them. The terminology of 'rights' is also, to use Gray and Gray's term, 'value-laden' because it implies something about the legitimacy of Mr Entick's claim.

At this point, it is very useful to distinguish between two different kinds of legitimacy. In *Entick* itself, Mr Entick was not concerned to show that, for moral, social, or economic reasons, it was appropriate for him to have a significant degree of control over the land or papers; his only concern was to show that his claim to that control was *legally* legitimate—that is, to show that he had a right that the courts were prepared to protect and enforce. His focus was therefore on showing that the rules of property law gave him a property right in relation to both the land and the papers. When considering his claim from that internal perspective, we can therefore limit ourselves to looking at the land law rules and seeing if they do, indeed, give him a property right in relation to the land in question. We can, however, say that Mr Entick does have such a property right and still consider whether, for moral, social, or economic (or other) reasons, Mr Entick *should* have that degree of control over the land or papers. It is at this point that the '*critical value judgments*' referred to by Gray and Gray play a very important role.

Of course, it would be naive to think that these two kinds of legitimacy can, or should, be kept firmly separate. After all, as judges or legislators develop the law, they have to keep in mind the wider (moral, social, economic, etc.) effects of the legal rules. In fact, the contrast between two kinds of legitimacy links in to the contrast between the two approaches that we examined in Chapter 1, section 5.2—that is, what Harris called the 'doctrinal model' and the 'utility model'. The first question in *Entick* is whether Mr Entick's claim to a property right in the land and papers is legally legitimate: does it accord with the doctrinal rules of property law? The second question, is whether, taking into account a broad range of considerations (e.g. moral, social, economic, etc.), it would be better or worse to recognize that Mr Entick has such a right: does recognizing such a right have better consequences than not recognizing it? And, as we saw in the previous chapter, the 'utility model' can play a role not only when Parliament decides how to reform the law for the future, but also when judges decide on the current state of the law.

2 THE MEANING OF 'LAND'

2.1 THE PHYSICAL REACH OF LAND

In the extract set out above, Gray and Gray raise a fundamental question: '*What does it really mean to say that Julian Bishop "owns" 25 Mountfield Gardens or that these premises are his "property"?*' As we have seen, the first step is to understand that statement as simply shorthand for the more accurate analysis: Julian Bishop has a property right in relation to that land. After all, as we noted in Chapter 1, section 3, if Julian Bishop puts 25 Mountfield Gardens up for sale and you decide to put a bid in, then you are not bidding for the land as such; instead, you are bidding for his property right in that land—either a freehold or a lease. Gray and Gray's question therefore boils down to a question about the *content* of a freehold or a lease: if you acquire such a right, what rights to use the land will you get? We will examine that question in Chapter 5, section 3, when we focus on the nature of the freehold and the lease.

There is also a more practical side to the content of your freehold or lease. It will give you rights to use the land—but what do we mean by 'the land'? You might think of yourself as buying 'a house', but, clearly, if you get Julian Bishop's freehold or lease, you get more than the house. After all, if the house were to burn down, you would still have your freehold or lease. Indeed, the decision of McNair J in *Kelsen v Imperial Tobacco Co*[7] shows that a party with a property right in land also has rights in relation to the sky.

Mr Kelsen had a lease of a tobacconist's shop in City Road, Islington, London. The Imperial Tobacco Co maintained a large advertising sign that projected into the air above that shop. Initially, Mr Kelsen made no complaint, but he later demanded that the sign be removed. The company refused, arguing that, because its sign did not substantially interfere with Mr Kelsen's enjoyment of his land, the tort of nuisance was not made out. McNair J, however, ordered the sign to be removed: Mr Kelsen's lease gave him a right to exclusive control not only of the shop itself, but also of the air above it. As a result, the tobacco company, like the rest of the world, had a prima facie duty not to encroach on that space without Mr Kelsen's consent. An injunction could therefore be granted to prevent the company's ongoing act of trespass.[8]

---

7 [1957] 2 QB 334.
8 See too *H Waites Ltd v Hambledon Court Ltd* [2014] EWHC 651 (Ch): Morgan J held that the grant of a 999 year lease of a garage also gave the lessee a right to the airspace above the garage. Of course, as noted there at [49], if a lease is granted of part of a building which is horizontally divided (such as a flat in a block of flats), the definition of the premises leased will almost certainly make clear the horizontal limits on the rights of the lessee.

Whilst the *Kelsen* decision deals with a landowner's rights above the ground, an American case, *Edwards v Lee's Administrator*,[9] provides a memorable example of a landowner's rights below the ground. Mr and Mrs Edwards owned land in Kentucky, near the famous Mammoth Cave. They discovered a spectacular cave under their own land: they dubbed it the 'Great Onyx Cave', charged tourists for entry, and built a hotel on their land. The only entrance to the cave was on the Edwards' land, but a third of the cave was in fact situated beneath the land of Lee, one of the Edwards' neighbours. As Lee had not given permission for visitors to enter the part of the cave below his land, he claimed that the Edwards had committed the tort of trespass and should be made to pay him a share of their profits. The Kentucky Court of Appeals upheld an order that the tort of trespass had been committed and that the Edwards should pay Lee a third of their net profits. In doing so, the court found that Lee's rights extended below the surface of his land, and it referred to an important maxim, or brocard: *cujus est solum, ejus est usque ad cœlum et ad infernos* (to whomsoever the soil belongs, he owns also to the sky and to the depths). Like most maxims, however— particularly those in Latin—the expression *cujus est solum, ejus est usque ad cœlum et ad infernos* can be misleading, as the next extract shows.

Bernstein of Leigh (Baron) v Skyviews & General Ltd
[1978] QB 479

Facts: Skyviews took aerial photographs of houses and then offered to sell copies of the photographs to residents of the houses. On receiving an offer to buy such a photograph of his country house in Leigh, Kent, Lord Bernstein took exception, not only turning down the offer, but also complaining of an invasion of his privacy and requesting the destruction of any negatives or prints of his house. Unfortunately, his letter of complaint was answered by an 18-year-old who had just joined Skyviews. She replied by offering to sell Lord Bernstein the negative of his house. This led to another letter of complaint, in the absence of an answer to which, Lord Bernstein began legal proceedings. The chief part of his claim was that Skyviews had committed the wrong of trespass by flying over his land without permission. Griffiths J, however, dismissed the claim, finding that Skyviews had not interfered with Lord Bernstein's property right.

Griffiths J

At 485–8

I therefore find that on August 3, 1974, [Skyviews] flew over [Lord Bernstein's] land for the purpose of photographing his house and did so without his permission.

I turn now to the law. [Lord Bernstein] claims that as owner of the land he is also owner of the air space above the land, or at least has the right to exclude any entry into the air space above his land. He relies upon the old Latin maxim, *cujus est solum ejus est usque ad coelum et ad inferos*, a colourful phrase often upon the lips of lawyers since it was first coined by Accursius in Bologna in the 13th century.[10] There are a number of cases in which the maxim

---

[9] 96 SW 2d 1028 (1936, Court of Appeals of Kentucky).

[10] [Franciscus Accursius was a professor of law at the University of Bologna. By compiling the 'Great Gloss' of the Roman law under Justinian, he played a pivotal role in the spread of Roman law thinking in the European medieval world and beyond.]

has been used by English judges, but an examination of those cases shows that they have all been concerned with structures attached to the adjoining land, such as overhanging buildings, signs or telegraph wires, and for their solution it has not been necessary for the judge to cast his eyes towards the heavens; he has been concerned with the rights of the owner in the air space immediately adjacent to the surface of the land.

That an owner has certain rights in the air space above his land is well established by authority. He has the right to lop the branches of trees that may overhang his boundary, although this right seems to be founded in nuisance rather than trespass: see *Lemmon v. Webb*.[11] In *Wandsworth Board of Works v. United Telephone Co. Ltd.*,[12] the Court of Appeal did not doubt that the owner of land would have the right to cut a wire placed over his land [. . .]

It may be a sound and practical rule to regard any incursion into the air space at a height which may interfere with the ordinary user of the land as a trespass rather than a nuisance. Adjoining owners then know where they stand; they have no right to erect structures overhanging or passing over their neighbours' land and there is no room for argument whether they are thereby causing damage or annoyance to their neighbours about which there may be much room for argument and uncertainty. But wholly different considerations arise when considering the passage of aircraft at a height which in no way affects the user of the land.

There is no direct authority on this question, but as long ago as 1815 Lord Ellenborough in *Pickering v. Rudd*[13] expressed the view that it would not be a trespass to pass over a man's land in a balloon [. . .]

I can find no support in authority for the view that a landowner's rights in the air space above his property extend to an unlimited height. In *Wandsworth Board of Works v. United Telephone Co. Ltd.*[14] Bowen L.J. described the maxim, *usque ad coelum*, as a fanciful phrase, to which I would add that if applied literally it is a fanciful notion leading to the absurdity of a trespass at common law being committed by a satellite every time it passes over a suburban garden. The academic writers speak with one voice in rejecting the uncritical and literal application of the maxim [. . .]

The problem is to balance the rights of an owner to enjoy the use of his land against the rights of the general public to take advantage of all that science now offers in the use of air space. This balance is in my judgment best struck in our present society by restricting the rights of an owner in the air space above his land to such height as is necessary for the ordinary use and enjoyment of his land and the structures upon it, and declaring that above that height he has no greater rights in the air space than any other member of the public.

Applying this test to the facts of this case, I find that [Skyviews'] aircraft did not infringe any rights in [Lord Bernstein's] air space, and thus no trespass was committed. It was on any view of the evidence flying many hundreds of feet above the ground and it is not suggested that by its mere presence in the air space it caused any interference with any use to which [Lord Bernstein] put or might wish to put his land. [Lord Bernstein's] complaint is not that the aircraft interfered with the use of his land but that a photograph was taken from it. There is, however, no law against taking a photograph, and the mere taking of a photograph cannot turn an act which is not a trespass into the plaintiff's air space into one that is a trespass.

Section 40 of the Civil Aviation Act 1949 made clear that simply flying at a reasonable height above another's land does not constitute a wrong against that landowner.[15] Griffiths

---

11 [1894] 3 Ch 1.   12 (1884) 13 QBD 904.   13 (1815) 4 Camp 219.   14 (1884) 13 QBD 904.
15 See now Civil Aviation Act 1982, s 76(1). As made clear by the Court of Appeal in *Peires v Bickerton's Aerodromes Ltd* [2017] EWCA Civ 273, [2017] 1 WLR 2865, the protection provided by the statute does not depend on showing that the flight was, in all senses, reasonable—the reasonableness requirement applies

J decided that, in any case, there is an inherent limit on a landowner's property right. So, whilst a property right unquestionably allows its holder to assert a significant degree of control over a resource, that control must be limited—in some circumstances, at least—in order to take account of the needs of others.[16]

Some care must be taken, however, in formulating the precise nature and content of the limit on a landowner's rights to the airspace above the surface of the land. In *Anchor Brewhouse Developments Ltd v Berkley House*,[17] the court found that the tort of trespass had been committed when a crane on the defendant's land swung over the claimant's neighbouring land. The defendant's argument, based on the approach of Griffiths J in *Bernstein*, was that the court had to balance the rights of the claimant and the defendant. Scott J rejected that contention, stating that: '*it would be an incorrect use of authority to extract Griffiths J's approach to the difficult question of overflying aircraft and seek to apply that approach to the invasion of air space in general... If an adjoining owner places a structure on his land that overhangs the neighbour's land, he thereby takes into his possession air space to which his neighbour is entitled. That, in my judgment, is trespass. It does not depend on any balancing of rights.*' Scott J went on to say that: '*One of the characteristics of the common law of trespass is, or ought to be, certainty. The extent of proprietary rights enjoyed by landowners ought to be clear.*'

As a matter of authority, it is possible to reconcile the decisions in *Bernstein* and *Anchor Brewhouse*: the balancing approach advocated in the former can be regarded as applying only where the claimed trespass comes from the movement of something through the air space above land, rather than from the invasion of an object standing on neighbouring land. At a more abstract level, however, there is clearly a tension between, on the one hand, the preference for weighing up the competing merits of the parties' position (which perhaps may be based on the 'utility model' of reasoning we discussed in Chapter 1, section 5.2) and, on the other hand, a desire for certainty and hard-edged property rights (which is closer to the 'doctrinal model' of reasoning set out in Chapter 1, section 5.2).

In the next extract, the Supreme Court considered the usefulness of the *cujus est solum ejus est usque ad cœlum et ad infernos* brocard to establishing the reach of a landowner's rights below the surface of the land: its preference, like that of Scott J in *Anchor Brewhouse*, was not to extend the balancing approach adopted in *Bernstein*.

Star Energy Weald Basin Ltd and another v Bocardo SA
[2010] UKSC 35, [2010] 3 WLR 654

Facts: The case concerned an oil field in the unlikely location of Surrey. The apex of the Palmers Wood Oil Field, located near Caterham, lies beneath a plot of land, the freehold of which was held by Bocardo, the claimant. The defendant, Star Energy, had drilled

---

only to the *height* of the flight. The protection was applied in that case as a defence to a nuisance claim brought by a landowner against the defendant's nearby aerodrome.

[16] For example, under the provisions of Sch 4 to the Electricity Act 1989, the Secretary of State for Energy and Climate Change may grant a wayleave permitting the running of electricity lines over an individual's land, even though the running of such lines would otherwise constitute a trespass: see, for example, *Stynes v Western Power (East Midlands) plc* [2013] UKUT 214 (LC) at [37]–[47]. In such a case, the relevant power company must then pay compensation to the landowner.

[17] [1987] 2 EGLR 173.

diagonally from the surface of neighbouring land in order to extract oil from the apex of the field. When, in 2006, Bocardo discovered this, it sought damages from Star Energy.

Bocardo did not claim that it owned the oil beneath its land, or even that it had a right to search or drill for such oil. By statute (formerly the Petroleum Production Act 1934, now the Petroleum Act 1998), those rights were vested in the relevant licence holder: in this case, Star Energy. Bocardo did, however, claim that, by extracting oil from beneath the surface of its land without its permission, Star Energy had committed a trespass to Bocardo's land.

At first instance, Peter Smith J found in favour of Bocardo. This finding was upheld by the Court of Appeal and Star Energy appealed to the Supreme Court. The Supreme Court unanimously held that a trespass had occurred. There was also a cross-appeal by Bocardo as to the extent of the damages awarded to it. The question of damages in such a case is regulated by the Mines (Working Facilities and Support) Act 1966. The view of the Court of Appeal, upheld by a majority of the Supreme Court, was that, in light of the 1966 Act, Bocardo's damages were limited to £1,000.

Lord Hope

At [5]–[31]

(a) Trespass

[. . .] The question which this issue raises is whether an oil company which has been granted a licence to search, bore for and get petroleum in the licensed area which is beneath land belonging to another, and drills wells at depth beneath that land in order to recover petroleum from within the licensed area without obtaining the landholder's agreement or an ancillary right under the Mines (Working Facilities and Support) Act 1966 to do so, is committing a trespass [. . .]

It is common ground that a trespass occurs when there is an unjustified intrusion by one party upon land which is in the possession of another [. . .]

The question whether the drilling of the three wells under Bocardo's land, and the continued presence of the well casing and tubing within them, was an actionable trespass raises the following issues: (1) whether Bocardo's title to the land extends down to the strata below the surface through which the three wells and their casing and tubing pass; (2) whether possession or a right to possession is a pre-condition for bringing a claim for trespass and, if so, whether Bocardo has or is entitled to possession of the subsurface strata through which these facilities pass; (3) whether [Star Energy] have a right under the 1934 Act (and subsequently the 1998 Act) to drill and use the three wells and their casing and tubing to extract petroleum from beneath Bocardo's land which gives them a defence to a claim in trespass.

Ownership: how far below the surface?

There is, of course, nothing new in one person carrying out works under land whose surface is in the ownership or the possession of another. Operations of that kind have been familiar since at least Roman times. They ranged from great public works such as catacombs on the one hand to modest cellars for the storage of wine or other commodities on the other. What is new is the depth at which the operations that are said to constitute a trespass in this case have been carried out. The advance of modern technology has led to the discovery of things below the surface, and the desire to obtain access to and remove them, that were

unimaginable when the depths to which people could go were limited by what manual labour could achieve.

Bocardo's case is that it is trite law that a conveyance of land includes the surface and
everything below it, unless there have been exceptions from the grant such as commonly
occurs in the case of minerals. [Star Energy] do not dispute this proposition as a general rule
that applies where the rights of the surface owner are interfered with. But they maintain that
it does not extend to the depth at which the operations were and are being carried out in this
case. The minimum depth was 800 feet, while for the most part the depths were greatly
in excess of this. [Counsel for Star Energy] said that he accepted that in law the surface
owner owned the substrata to some depth, but not that far. He submitted that the wells and
their tubes and casing did not interfere with or enter upon "land" in any meaningful way at
all. Moreover the right to search, bore for and get the petroleum was vested in the Crown.
Bocardo did not own, and had no right to possess, the petroleum.

It has often been said that prima facie the owner of the surface is entitled to the surface itself
and everything below it down to the centre of the earth . . . Plainly, the source for these remarks
was the well-known Latin brocard *cuius est solum, eius est usque ad coelum et ad inferos* [. . .]

As Lord Wilberforce pointed out,[18] the maxim only has authority at common law in so far
as it has been adopted by decisions, or equivalent authority. I am inclined to think that the
observations by the Court of Appeal in *Mitchell v Mosley*,[19] seen against the background of
various dicta in the 19th Century cases including *Pountney v Clayton*,[20] measure up to that
requirement. In the present context, therefore, I believe that the brocard does have something to offer us.

The particular relevance of the brocard to the dispute in this case is that, taken literally, it
answers [counsel for Star Energy's] point that the wells in question were too deep for the
landowner's interest in his land to be affected. If the brocard is accepted as a sound guide to
what the law is, there is no stopping point. This makes it unnecessary to speculate as to how
it can be applied in practice as one gets close to the earth's centre. The depths to which the
wells in question were drilled in this case do not get anywhere near to approaching the point
of absurdity. The fact that there were substances at that depth which can be reached and
got by human activity is sufficient to raise the question as to who, if anybody, is the owner of
the strata where they are to be found. The Crown has asserted ownership of the petroleum,
but it does not assert ownership of the strata that surround it. The only plausible candidate
is the registered owner of the land above, which is exactly what the brocard itself indicates.
[Counsel for Star Energy] was unable to point to any contrary authority. [. . .]

I think that it is significant that the glossator [Accursius of Bologna, who coined the *ad
coelum* maxim] took as his starting point the rule that applied to the underlying strata and
then applied it to what took place above the surface. The context for the annotation was the
proposition that, while the owner may erect structures as high as he likes on the solum of
land in his ownership, his freedom to do so is restricted by the praedial servitude *non altius
tollendi* which protects his neighbour's right to light and prospect. The owner of the dominant
tenement is entitled to insist that there should be no interference with the sky over his land.
The assumption appears to have been that it was generally understood that the ownership
of land carried with it the right to everything that lay below the surface. The point that the
glossator was making, as an explanation for the praedial servitude, was that the existing rule
as to what lay below (*cuius est solum*) should be (*debet esse*) applied to the air-space above
it. The rule that applied to the underlying strata appears to have been of greater antiquity.

[18] [In *Commissioner for Railways v Valuer-General* [1974] AC 328, 351.]
[19] [[1914] 1 Ch 438, 450.]   [20] [(1883) 11 QBD 820, 838.]

The problems that a rule in these terms might give rise to as man's understanding of the earth's structure improved, airspace began to be used for the passage of aircraft and means were developed to penetrate deep below the surface were not, of course, obvious in the 13th century. But the simple notion that each landowner is the proprietor of a column or cylinder of land that stretches down to the centre of the earth and upwards indefinitely into outer space is plainly no longer tenable. The earth is not flat, as the glossator may have supposed. A greater understanding of geology has taught us that most of the earth's interior, due to extremes of pressure and temperature, is a complex and inhospitable structure that is beyond man's capacity to enter or make use of. It has been observed that anything that is drilled below a depth of about 8.7 miles or 14 kilometres would be crushed by the earth's pressure of 50,000 pounds per square inch and vaporised by a temperature of 1,000 degrees Fahrenheit.[21] [P]roductive human activity is possible only within the shallowest portion of the earth's crust, and humans have never penetrated below it.[22] As for that portion of it, the development of heat mining and carbon capture, storage and sequestration technologies to reduce greenhouse gas emissions[23] would be difficult to achieve if the subsurface within which it is sought to carry out these activities in the public interest were to be broken up into columns of rock owned by the surface owners.

As for the position above the surface, the development of powered flight has made it impossible to apply the brocard *usque ad coelum* literally. In *Bernstein of Leigh (Baron) v Skyviews & General Ltd*[24] Baron Bernstein failed in his claim that the defendants, who had flown over his land to take an aerial photograph of his property which they then offered to sell to him, were guilty of trespass [...] Griffiths J was willing to accept, as a sound and practical rule, that any incursion into air space at a height which may interfere with the ordinary user of land was a trespass. But he said that wholly different considerations arise when considering the passage of aircraft at a height which in no way affects the user of the land. In his judgment,[25] the balance was best struck by restricting the rights of the owner to such height as necessary for the ordinary use and enjoyment of his land and the structures upon it, and declaring that above that height he has no greater rights in the air space than any other member of the public.

[Star Energy] say that this analysis should be applied to subsurface ownership too. They submit that a sensible and pragmatic solution would be for each surface owner to own directly down beneath the boundaries of his land as far down as is necessary for the use and enjoyment of the surface, the buildings on the surface and any minerals which have not been excluded from his ownership by conveyance, common law or statute which lie beneath it. [Counsel for Star Energy] was unable to point to any English authority that provided direct support for this approach to the position beneath the surface. But there is some support for it in the United States [...]

Sprankling[26] points out however that most modern US legal texts continue to endorse the centre of the earth theory and that almost all modern cases continue to embrace it too [...] Addressing himself to the question, how far below the earth's surface do property rights extend, he asserts that the surface owner should certainly hold property rights to a portion of the subsurface.[27] [...]

Coming closer to home, Dr Jean Howell[28] acknowledges that it might be argued that the same test as that which Griffiths J applied in *Bernstein of Leigh (Baron) v Skyviews &*

---

21 Sprankling, 'Owning the Center of the Earth' (2008) 55 UCLA L Rev 979, 993, fn 84.
22 Ibid, 994.   23 Ibid, 1030–2.   24 [1978] QB 479.   25 [1978] QB 479, [488].
26 'Owning the Center of the Earth' (2008) 55 UCLA L Rev 979, 991–2.   27 Ibid, 1033.
28 'Subterranean Land Law: Rights below the Surface of Land' (2002) 53 Northern Ireland Legal Quarterly 268, 270.

General Ltd should be used for land below the surface. But, as she also notes, it was implicit in that case that even above the notional height at which the land owner's usable rights stop, there is not a free for all in the airspace above. To characterise the surface owner's rights as following technological advances as to the depth at which land can be exploited, she says, would offend against all notions of "property" whose defining quality in land is certainty. She concludes[29] that any intrusion into land which is not sanctioned by some countervailing property right will be a trespass and that, although the surface owner will not usually wish to or be able to utilise the ground below the surface, he has rights in the land which could be valuable.

In my opinion the brocard still has value in English law as encapsulating, in simple language, a proposition of law which has commanded general acceptance. It is an imperfect guide, as it has ceased to apply to the use of airspace above a height which may interfere with the ordinary user of land: *Bernstein of Leigh (Baron) v Skyviews & General Ltd* [. . .] But I think that the reasons for holding that the brocard has no place in the modern world as regards what goes on below the surface, even in England, are not by any means as compelling as they are in relation to the use of airspace. In *US v Causby*[30] the US Supreme Court regarded the airspace as a public highway to which only the public had a just claim. The same cannot be said of the strata below the surface. As Aikens LJ said in the Court of Appeal, it is not helpful to try to make analogies between the rights of an owner of land with regard to the airspace above it and his rights with regard to the strata beneath the surface.[31] Although modern technology has found new ways of making use of it in the public interest, there is no question of it having become a public highway [. . .]

The better view, as the Court of Appeal recognised[32] is to hold that the owner of the surface is the owner of the strata beneath it, including the minerals that are to be found there, unless there has been an alienation of them by a conveyance, at common law or by statute to someone else. That was the view which the Court of Appeal took in *Mitchell v Mosley*.[33] Much has happened since then, as the use of technology has penetrated deeper and deeper into the earth's surface. But I see no reason why its view should not still be regarded as good law. There must obviously be some stopping point, as one reaches the point at which physical features such as pressure and temperature render the concept of the strata belonging to anybody so absurd as to be not worth arguing about. But the wells that are at issue in this case, extending from about 800 feet to 2,800 feet below the surface, are far from being so deep as to reach the point of absurdity. Indeed the fact that the strata can be worked upon at those depths points to the opposite conclusion.

I would hold therefore that [Bocardo's] title extends down to the strata through which the three wells and their casing and tubing pass.

Lord Hope went on to find that, if possession was required for a trespass claim, Bocardo could be said to be in possession of the strata used by Star Energy, as it had registered title to the land, and no other party claimed to be in actual possession of the strata. It was further held that the relevant legislation gave Star Energy no defence to a trespass claim.

For our purposes, the importance of *Star Energy v Bocardo* lies in the Supreme Court's refusal to extend the reasoning in *Bernstein v Skyviews* to the question of how far *below* ground the rights of a freehold owner extend. This has two consequences. First, a freehold owner's rights are better protected below ground than above it. In Lord Hope's view, this reflects the historical development of the *cujus est solum* maxim: that an owner's right to the

---

29 Ibid, 285.   30 328 US 256 (1946).   31 [2009] 3 WLR 1010, [2010] Ch 100, [61].
32 [2009] 3 WLR 1010, [2010] Ch 100, [59].   33 [1914] 1 Ch 438.

strata beneath his or her land was recognized first, and only then extended by analogy to the area above his land. After all, a balance must be struck between protecting the position of an owner of land and preserving the freedom of those who do not own the land; in Roman times as today, the activities of such non-owners are more likely to take place above the land than below it. It is worth noting, however, that the boundaries of the maxim, like the extent of the statutory limits imposed on the rights of an owner of land, may well have to respond to technological developments.[34] Second, as in *Anchor Brewhouse*, the demands of certainty had an important effect on the court's reasoning, and led it to reject the idea that any general balancing of the merits of each party's claim was necessary.

2.2 WHAT OBJECTS DOES THE LAND INCLUDE?

2.2.1 Things attached to, or part and parcel of, the land

On 23 May 2002, the BBC News website reported on a decision from the Colchester county court. Mr Bennis had a property right in a large detached house. He sold that right to Mr and Mrs McMahon. When the McMahons moved in, they were disappointed to find that Mr Bennis had removed a number of items from the house (including a towel rail attached to the central heating system, and signs with the name and number of the house), as well as taking paving stones from the garden. Mr Bennis believed that he was entitled to remove those things: it seems that the contract between him and the McMahons did not specifically list those items as part of the sale. Nonetheless, the county court found in favour of the McMahons and Mr Bennis was ordered to pay them £1,166. The point is that Mr Bennis had clearly agreed to transfer his property right in the land—and that property right includes not only the house and the surface of the land, but also any items that are viewed as part of that land.

How, then, can we tell if a particular object is included within the scope of a property right in land? The relevant principles are considered in the following extract.

Elitestone Ltd v Morris
[1997] 1 WLR 687, HL

Facts: Elitestone Ltd had a property right in land in Murton, Swansea. Mr Morris (along with Ms Sked) lived in a wooden bungalow on that land and paid an annual fee to Elitestone Ltd. Elitestone Ltd wished to redevelop the land and brought proceedings to remove Mr Morris from the land. Mr Morris claimed that, under the provisions of the Rent Act 1977, he had a protected tenancy. If that claim were correct, the grounds on which Elitestone Ltd could apply for possession of the land were limited by statute and none of those grounds was available to them. Both sides accepted that, to have a protected tenancy, Mr Morris had to show that he had a property right in land (a lease). Elitestone Ltd argued that Mr Morris could not have a property right in land because, instead, he simply owned a wooden bungalow—that is, a separate object not forming

---

[34] It has been suggested, for example, that the potential public good deriving from storing carbon dioxide underground may justify legislation giving ownership of at least some subterranean space to the Crown: Morgan, 'Digging Deep: Property Rights in Subterranean Space and the Challenge of Carbon Capture and Storage' (2013) 62 ICLQ 813.

part of any land. The Court of Appeal accepted that argument and Mr Morris appealed to the House of Lords, which allowed his appeal.

Lord Lloyd

At 689–93

The assistant recorder held, correctly, at the end of what was necessarily a very lengthy judgment that the question in Mr. Morris's case turned on whether or not the bungalow formed part of the realty.[35] [. . .]

Having visited the site, the assistant recorder had this to say:

'While the house rested on the concrete pillars which were themselves attached to the ground, it seems to me clear that at least by 1985 and probably before, it would have been clear to anybody that this was a structure that was not meant to be enjoyed as a chattel to be picked up and moved in due course but that it should be a long-term feature of the realty albeit that, because of its construction, it would plainly need more regular maintenance.'

The Court of Appeal disagreed[36] [. . .] Aldous L.J., who gave the leading judgment, was much influenced by the fact that the bungalow was resting by its own weight on concrete pillars, without any attachment. He was also influenced by the uncertainty of Mr. Morris's tenure. Although Mr. Morris had been in occupation since 1971, he was required to obtain an annual "licence." At first the licence fee was £3 a year. It rose to £10 in 1984, then to £52 in 1985, and finally to £85 in 1989. In 1990 the plaintiffs required a licence fee of £1,000: but Mr. Morris, and the other occupiers declined to pay. [. . .]

Unlike the judge, the Court of Appeal did not have the advantage of having seen the bungalow. Nor were they shown any of the photographs, some of which were put before your Lordships. These photographs were taken only very recently. Like all photographs they can be deceptive. But if the Court of Appeal had seen the photographs, it is at least possible that they would have taken a different view. For the photographs show very clearly what the bungalow is, and especially what it is not. It is *not* like a Portakabin, or mobile home. The nature of the structure is such that it could not be taken down and re-erected elsewhere. It could only be removed by a process of demolition. This, as will appear later, is a factor of great importance in the present case. If a structure can only be enjoyed *in situ*, and is such that it cannot be removed in whole or in sections to another site, there is at least a strong inference that the purpose of placing the structure on the original site was that it should form part of the realty at that site, and therefore cease to be a chattel [. . .]

It will be noticed that in framing the issue for decision I have avoided the use of the word 'fixture.' There are two reasons for this. The first is that 'fixture,' though a hallowed term in this branch of the law, does not always bear the same meaning in law as it does in everyday life. In ordinary language one thinks of a fixture as being something fixed to a building. One would not ordinarily think of the building itself as a fixture [. . .] There is another reason. The term fixture is apt to be a source of misunderstanding owing to the existence of the category of so called 'tenants' fixtures' (a term used to cover both trade fixtures and ornamental fixtures), which are fixtures in the full sense of the word (and therefore part of the realty) but which may nevertheless be removed by the tenant in the course of or at the end of his tenancy. Such fixtures are sometimes confused with chattels which have never become fixtures at all. Indeed the confusion arose in this very case [. . .]

---

[35] ['[T]he realty' here refers to the land in relation to which Elitestone Ltd had a property right.]
[36] Court of Appeal (Civil Division) Transcript No. 1025 of 1995 (unreported, 28 July 1995).

For my part I find it better in the present case to avoid the traditional twofold distinction between chattels and fixtures, and to adopt the three-fold classification set out in *Woodfall, Landlord and Tenant*:

'An object which is brought onto land may be classified under one of three broad heads. It may be (a) a chattel; (b) a fixture; or (c) part and parcel of the land itself. Objects in categories (b) and (c) are treated as being part of the land.'

So the question in the present appeal is whether, when the bungalow was built, it became part and parcel of the land itself. The materials out of which the bungalow was constructed, that is to say, the timber frame walls, the feather boarding, the suspended timber floors, the chipboard ceilings, and so on, were all, of course, chattels when they were brought onto the site. Did they cease to be chattels when they were built into the composite structure? The answer to the question, as Blackburn J. pointed out in *Holland v. Hodgson*,[37] depends on the circumstances of each case, but mainly on two factors, the degree of annexation to the land, and the object of the annexation.

Degree of annexation

The importance of the degree of annexation will vary from object to object. In the case of a large object, such as a house, the question does not often arise. Annexation goes without saying [. . .]

Purpose of annexation

Many different tests have been suggested, such as whether the object which has been fixed to the property has been so fixed for the better enjoyment of the object as a chattel, or whether it has been fixed with a view to effecting a permanent improvement of the freehold. This and similar tests are useful when one is considering an object such as a tapestry, which may or may not be fixed to a house so as to become part of the freehold: see *Leigh v. Taylor*.[38] These tests are less useful when one is considering the house itself. In the case of the house the answer is as much a matter of common sense as precise analysis. A house which is constructed in such a way so as to be removable, whether as a unit, or in sections, may well remain a chattel, even though it is connected temporarily to mains services such as water and electricity. But a house which is constructed in such a way that it cannot be removed at all, save by destruction, cannot have been intended to remain as a chattel. It must have been intended to form part of the realty. I know of no better analogy than the example given by Blackburn J. in *Holland v. Hodgson*:[39]

'Thus blocks of stone placed one on the top of another without any mortar or cement for the purpose of forming a dry stone wall would become part of the land, though the same stones, if deposited in a builder's yard and for convenience sake stacked on the top of each other in the form of a wall, would remain chattels.'

Applying that analogy to the present case, I do not doubt that when Mr. Morris's bungalow was built, and as each of the timber frame walls were placed in position, they all became part of the structure, which was itself part and parcel of the land. The object of bringing the individual bits of wood onto the site seems to be so clear that the absence of any attachment to the soil (save by gravity) becomes an irrelevance.

---

[37] (1872) LR 7 CP 328.   [38] [1902] AC 157.   [39] (1872) LR 7 CP 328, [335].

Lord Clyde

At 698

It is important to observe that intention in this context is to be assessed objectively and not subjectively. Indeed it may be that the use of the word intention is misleading. It is the purpose which the object is serving which has to be regarded, not the purpose of the person who put it there. The question is whether the object is designed for the use or enjoyment of the land or for the more complete or convenient use or enjoyment of the thing itself.

The other members of the House of Lords agreed with both Lord Clyde and Lord Lloyd. Mr Morris's bungalow was therefore regarded as part of the land in relation to which Elitestone Ltd had a property right. As a result, Mr Morris had a lease (another property right in relation to that same land) and resulting statutory protection that allowed him to resist Elitestone Ltd's claim for possession.[40] In *Spielplatz Ltd v Pearson*[41] the Court of Appeal, applying the approach in *Elitestone*, reached a similar result, finding that a chalet which had been erected on a plot within a 'woodland naturist resort' near St Albans was part and parcel of the land: '*assessed objectively, a house built in such a way that it could not be removed except by destruction could not have been intended to remain a chattel and must have been intended to form part of the realty*'.[42] Lord Clyde's point about the difference between subjective and objective tests for intention was important, as the Pearsons, the current occupiers of the chalet, had all along regarded the chalet as separate from the land; this was not decisive, however, as the purpose of annexation had to be assessed objectively.

The decision of Norris J in *Tower Hamlets LBC v Bromley LBC*[43] provides a useful contrast: the test in *Elitestone* was again applied, but it led to a different result.[44] The case concerned a battle over a Henry Moore sculpture, 'Draped Seated Woman' (more commonly known as 'Old Flo'), which had been situated for 35 years near three tower blocks on a housing estate in Stepney, East London. In 1997, when the housing estate was demolished, the sculpture was moved to the Yorkshire Sculpture Park. In 2012, Tower Hamlets, who owned the land on which the housing estate stood, wished to sell the sculpture and so claimed that, prior to 1997, it had become part and parcel of their land. Norris J rejected that particular contention, noting that: '*The sculpture is an entire object in itself. It rested by its own weight upon the ground and could be (and was) removed without damage and without diminishing its inherent beauty. It might adorn or beautify a location, but it was not in any real sense dependent upon that location.*' The sculpture therefore remained an independent piece of property, distinct from the land; however, Tower Hamlets was able to succeed on other grounds. Since at least 1997, it had honestly believed that it had good title to the sculpture, and had acted as its owner: as a result, under s 3(2) of the Limitation Act 1980, the prior ownership

---

[40] See Chapter 20 for discussion of some of the statutory protection given to parties who occupy their home under a lease.

[41] [2015] EWCA Civ 804.   [42] [2015] EWCA Civ 804, [17].

[43] [2015] EWHC 1954 (Ch). For a helpful discussion of the case, see M Iljadica, 'Is Sculpture Land?' [2016] Conv 242, which raises the question of whether a court should also take into account the public good in having a particular object, perhaps integral to the design of a particular space, remain in that space.

[44] See too *Mew v Tristmire Ltd* [2011] EWCA Civ 912: houseboats which were not attached to the land but (like the bungalow in *Elitestone*) rested on supports were found not to be part of the land: they could, initially at least, have been removed from the land without destruction and they '*fall into a category of items such as caravans which, as designed, are movable*' (ibid, [42]).

right of Bromley had been extinguished, and so it had no grounds for preventing Tower Hamlets from selling the sculpture.[45] The story, nonetheless, has a happy ending: Tower Hamlets, responding to a public outcry,[46] decided not to sell the sculpture, and it instead remained on display at the Yorkshire Sculpture Park until October 2017, when it was returned to East London. It can now be seen at Cabot Square in Canary Wharf.

Lord Lloyd's reasoning in *Elitestone* also shows the potentially confusing nature of the term 'fixture'. For example, it used to be said that an object (such as the towel rail and paving stones in the McMahon's case, or the bungalow in Mr Morris's case) had to be *either* a chattel (something independent of the land and so not covered by a property right in that land) *or* a fixture (something attached to the land and so covered by a property right in that land). As Lord Lloyd points out, however, it would be odd to think of a building, such as a house, as merely attached to land: it is covered by a property right in the land not because of its attachment, but rather because it is part and parcel of the land itself.

Lord Lloyd's second reason for treating the word 'fixture' with care is that it has a special meaning when used to refer to 'tenant's fixtures' or 'landlord's fixtures'. Those terms are used to solve a related, but different problem. Imagine that an owner of land gives you a lease of business premises. When the lease ends, you can clearly take your office furniture with you; equally clearly, you cannot rip out the toilets and take those with you. But what if you have installed a special shed in which to store your stock? That shed may have become attached to, or be part and parcel of, the land, because you may have attached it with iron straps to a concrete floor. But, as the Court of Appeal confirmed in *Webb v Frank Bevis Ltd*,[47] you may nonetheless be allowed to remove the shed at the end of the lease. The term 'tenant's fixtures' is used to refer to objects attached to the land or forming part and parcel of the land that the tenant is, at common law, allowed to remove at the end of the lease (such as the shed);[48] the term 'landlord's fixtures' is used to refer to such objects (such as the toilets) that the tenant cannot remove.

Once any confusion over the concept of 'fixtures' is dealt with, we are left with the position that a property right in land covers: (i) the surface of the land itself; (ii) anything that is part and parcel of that land (e.g. a house built on the land); and (iii) anything that is sufficiently attached to that land (e.g. a towel rail connected to the central heating system). Of course, in practice, it may not be obvious whether a particular object falls into either of (ii) or (iii); in such cases, as shown by Lord Lloyd's approach in *Elitestone Ltd v Morris*, a court has to look at both the degree of attachment to the land and the purpose of such attachment.

The following extract provides a useful practical example of the results that a court may reach.

---

[45] The result of the case shows how a form of 'adverse possession' can apply even in relation to chattels; but note that, under s 4 of the 1980 Act, a special rule applies in case of theft, so if Tower Hamlets had dishonestly asserted ownership of the sculpture, it would not have been able to take advantage of any limitation period against Bromley.

[46] Which included, but was not limited to, an open letter signed by, inter alia, Henry Moore's daughter, the director of the Tate Gallery, and Danny Boyle, the film director.

[47] [1940] 1 All ER 247.

[48] It is important to note that the tenant's prima facie common law right to remove such tenant's fixtures may be excluded by the particular terms of the lease: see, for example, *Peel Land and Property (Ports No 3) Ltd v TS Sheerness Steel Ltd* [2014] 2 P & CR 8 (CA). As noted there by Vos LJ at [44], if the relevant terms of the lease are ambiguous, the court when interpreting those terms 'will take into account the policy of the law to the effect that tenants should generally be permitted to remove their trade fixtures in order to encourage commercial investment.' If, however, as was held to be the case by the Court of Appeal in *Peel Land* itself, the only possible meaning of the term is that the tenant cannot remove such fixtures, then the court must give effect to that meaning.

Botham and ors v TSB Bank plc
[1996] EWCA Civ 549, CA

Facts: Mr Botham owned a luxury flat at 90 Cheyne Walk, Chelsea, London. He borrowed money from TSB Bank and, in return, granted TSB a mortgage over his flat. TSB thus acquired a property right (technically, a charge by way of legal mortgage—see Chapter 5, section 6) in the land. Mr Botham failed to repay TSB as agreed; TSB therefore acquired a power to sell the flat and use the proceeds towards meeting Mr Botham's debt. A dispute arose as to the scope of TSB's property right in the land: did it give TSB a power to sell (and use the proceeds) of particular objects within the flat, such as the fitted carpets, light fittings, the dishwasher in the fitted kitchen, etc.? Mr Botham claimed that such items were *not* covered by TSB's property right, because they were not fixtures and therefore not part of the land.

The first instance judge split the various objects in dispute into nine groups. Table 2.1 sets out the groups, along with the related decision of the first instance judge and then of the Court of Appeal.

The first instance judge, by examining the degree and purpose of annexation, thus found that almost all of the disputed objects (including the kitchen sink) were fixtures, and therefore that TSB did have the power to sell those objects and use the proceeds of sale towards meeting Mr Botham's debt.

The Court of Appeal applied the same basic test, but reached different conclusions. (See Table 2.1.)

Table 2.1 Items considered in *Botham and ors v TSB Bank plc*

	First instance judge	Court of Appeal
1. Fitted carpets	Fixtures: part of the land	*Not fixtures*
2. Light fittings fixed to a wall or ceiling	Fixtures: part of the land	*Not fixtures*[1]
3. Four decorative gas flame-effect fires of the mock coal type	Fixtures: part of the land	*Not fixtures*
4. Curtains and blinds	Fixtures: part of the land	*Not fixtures*
5. Bathroom fittings A (towel rails, soap dishes, and lavatory roll holders)	Fixtures: part of the land	Fixtures: part of the land
6. Bathroom fittings B (fittings on baths and basins—namely, the taps, plugs, and shower heads)	Fixtures: part of the land	Fixtures: part of the land
7. Bathroom fittings C (mirrors and marble panels on the walls)	Conceded by Mr Botham as fixtures: part of the land	Conceded by Mr Botham as fixtures: part of the land
8. Kitchen units and work surfaces (including a fitted sink)	Fixtures: part of the land	Fixtures: part of the land
9. White goods in the kitchen (the oven, the dishwasher, the extractor, the hob, the fridge, and the freezer)	Fixtures: part of the land	*Not fixtures*

[1] [Under silence; without comment.]

Lord Justice Roch

The tests, in the case of an item which has been attached to the building in some way other than simply by its own weight, seem to be the purpose of the item and the purpose of the link between the item and the building. If the item viewed objectively is intended to be permanent and to afford a lasting improvement to the building, the thing will have become a fixture. If the attachment is temporary and is no more than is necessary for the item to be used and enjoyed, then it will remain a chattel. Some indicators can be identified. For example, if the item is ornamental and the attachment is simply to enable the item to be displayed and en- joyed as an adornment that will often indicate that this item is a chattel. Obvious examples are pictures. But this will not be the result in every case; for example ornamental tiles on the walls of kitchens and bathrooms. The ability to remove an item or its attachment from the building without damaging the fabric of the building is another indicator. The same item may in some areas be a chattel and in others a fixture. For example a cooker will, if free standing and connected to the building only by an electric flex, be a chattel. But it may be otherwise if the cooker is a split level cooker with the hob set into a work surface and the oven forming part of one of the cabinets in the kitchen. It must be remembered that in many cases the item being considered may be one that has been bought by the mortgagor on hire purchase, where the ownership of the item remains in the supplier until the instalments have been paid. Holding such items to be fixtures simply because they are housed in a fitted cupboard and linked to the building by an electric cable, and, in cases of washing machines, by the necessary plumbing would cause difficulties and such findings should only be made where the intent to effect a permanent improvement in the building is incontrovertible. The type of person who installs or attaches the item to the land can be a further indicator. Thus items installed by a builder, eg the wall tiles will probably be fixtures, whereas items installed by eg a carpet contractor or curtain supplier or by the occupier of the building himself or herself may well not be [. . .]

I have no hesitation in agreeing with the judge that Groups 5 and 6, the bathroom fittings namely the taps, plugs and showerhead together with the towel rails, soap dishes and lav- atory roll holders which are all the items listed under the heading "Ironmongery" in the schedule of disputed items helpfully prepared by Mr Chapman, the Bank's counsel for the purpose of this appeal, are fixtures.

Those items are attached to the building in such a way as to demonstrate a significant connection with the building, and are of a type consistent with the bathroom fittings such as the basins, baths, bidets and lavatories, as to demonstrate an intention to effect a permanent improvement to the flat. They are items necessary for a room which is used as a bathroom. They are not there, on the evidence which was before the judge and which is before us, to be enjoyed for themselves, but they are there as accessories which enable the room to be used and enjoyed as a bathroom. Viewed objectively, they were intended to be permanent and to afford a lasting improvement to the property.

The third group about which I have no doubt is Group 8, the kitchen units, including the sink [. . .] Again in my judgment the degree of annexation, the fact that between the working sur- faces and the underside of the wall cupboards of the wall units there is tiling, demonstrates both a degree of annexation and an intention to effect a permanent improvement to the kit- chen of the flat so as to make those units fixtures. Further, as a matter of common sense, those units could not be removed without damaging the fabric of the flat, even if the damage is no more that the leaving of a pattern of tiling which is unlikely to be of use if different units had to be installed.

The seventh group of items, the marble panels and mirrors in the principal bathroom were conceded by Mr Botham's counsel before the judge to be fixtures and [counsel for Mr Botham] in this appeal, accepts that that concession was rightly made [. . .]

I would allow the appeal with regard to the fitted carpets and the curtains and blinds i.e., Groups 1 and 4. These items, although made or cut to fit the particular floor or window concerned, are attached to the building in an insubstantial manner. Carpets can easily be lifted off gripper rods and removed and can be used again elsewhere. In my judgment neither the degree of annexation nor the surrounding circumstances indicate an intention to effect a permanent improvement in the building [...]

With regard to Group 2, the light fittings, [counsel for Mr Botham] conceded that two of the light fittings recessed into the ceilings shown in photographs 129 and 138 were fixtures. I would hold that [TSB Bank] on the admissible evidence have failed to show that the other lighting items were fixtures. There is no admissible evidence as to the method of attachment of these items to the walls and ceilings other than that the photographs show that they must be attached in some manner. [Counsel for Mr Botham] submitted that their removal cannot be too difficult because in many cases the fitting would have to be removed in order to replace a bulb or connection that had failed. In my judgment, these light fittings, in the absence of evidence other than the photographs of them, remain chattels as would lamp shades or ornamental light fittings or chandeliers suspended from a ceiling rose.

Group 3 were the gas fires. In their case the only connection between them and the building was a gas pipe. In the gas pipes, shortly before the pipes enter these gas fires, gas taps are to be seen in the photographs. Apart from that link, which is essential if they are to be used as gas fires, nothing secures the gas fires, on the evidence, other than their own weight [...] I am of the view that electric fires and heaters which are simply plugged into the electricity supply of a house are not fixtures and I do not see any sensible distinction between such electric fires and these four gas fires on the evidence which was available to the judge and is available to us [...]

Many of [the items in Groups 8 & 9] were made by a single manufacturer, Neff. The judge said that whilst the kitchen units and sink were manifestly fixtures, the white goods he had found to be the most difficult items he had had to decide. He found that they were manufactured to standard sizes, they were fitted into standard sized holes and that they were removable. They were very probably expensive items, although he had no direct evidence of their value [...] Clearly all of these items are items one would not be surprised to find in a kitchen, but then so is an electric kettle, a food mixer and a microwave oven, which are all normally 'plugged in'. No one, I venture to suggest would look on these as fixtures. Here the judge should have reminded himself that the degree of annexation was slight: no more than that which was needed for these items to be used for their normal purposes. In fact these items remain in position by their own weight and not by virtue of the links between them and the building. All these items can be bought separately, and are often acquired on an instalment payment basis, when ownership does not pass to the householder immediately. Many of these items are designed to last for a limited period of time and will require replacing after a relatively short number of years. The degree of annexation is therefore slight. Disconnection can be done without damage to the fabric of the building and normally without difficulty. The purpose of such links as there were to the building was to enable these machines to be used to wash clothes or dishes or preserve or cook food. Absent any evidence other than the photographs, it was not open to the judge, in my opinion, to infer that these items were installed with the intention that they were to be a permanent or lasting improvement to the building. This is not a case where the intent to effect a permanent improvement in the building by installing these machines so that they became part of the realty was incontrovertible, as the judge's doubts illustrated.

The Court of Appeal's decision in *Botham v TSB Bank* is useful not only because it shows how the fixtures test can be applied in practice, but also because it shows that the test is *not* based on reasonable expectations or common practice as to what B, a party buying or renting land from A, would expect to find when moving in. It might be unusual, as noted by the first instance judge, for A to remove gas fires previously connected to pipes, or an oven fitted and installed into a particular slot in the kitchen. Nonetheless, this does not mean that such items necessarily count as part of the land. If B wants to ensure that, as well as acquiring a property right in the land, she also acquires the right to have or use those items, she needs to ensure that A makes a contractual promise to give B such rights.

2.2.2 Things found on, or in, the land

We have seen that if a party (B) has a property right in land, he also has a right to control of: (i) (within limits) the area above and below the surface of the land; (ii) anything that is part and parcel of the land (such as a house); and (iii) anything that is sufficiently attached to the land (such as a towel rail attached to the central heating system). Of course, this does not mean that B's property right in the land gives him a right to control of *everything* that may be in or on his land. As can be seen from the following extract, the basic rule is that if an object is not part and parcel of B's land, then the mere fact that the object was found on B's land does *not* give B any special rights to that object.

Hannah v Peel
[1945] 1 KB 509

Facts: In 1938, Major Peel bought Gwernhaylod House, Overton-on-Dee, Shropshire, and thereby acquired a property right in that land: a freehold. He did not move in immediately and the house remained empty, apart from periods during which it was requisitioned by the government and used by the armed forces. In August 1940, during one of those periods of requisition, Mr Hannah, a lance corporal stationed at the house, dislodged a brooch that had been in a crevice by a window frame. He later handed it to the police. No one came forward to claim the brooch and it was given by the police to Major Peel. He offered Mr Hannah a reward for having found the brooch, but Mr Hannah refused to accept the reward: he claimed that, because he found the brooch, he had a property right to it and that Major Peel was under a duty not to interfere with that property right. Major Peel, however, kept and then sold the brooch. Mr Hannah claimed that Major Peel thereby committed a tort: he had interfered with Mr Hannah's property right and so should pay damages as a result. Major Peel claimed that he was, in fact, entitled to the brooch because it had been found on his land. Birkett J found in favour of Mr Hannah.

Birkett J

At 513–15

As to the issue in law, the rival claims of the parties can be stated in this way: [Mr Hannah] says: "I claim the brooch as its finder and I have a good title against all the world, save only the true owner." [Major Peel] says: "My claim is superior to yours inasmuch as I am the freeholder. The brooch was found on my property, although I was never in occupation, and my title, therefore, ousts yours and in the absence of the true owner I am entitled to the brooch or its value." Unhappily the law on this issue is in a very uncertain state and there is need of an authoritative decision of a higher court [. . .]

In the famous case of *Armory v. Delamirie*,[49] the plaintiff, who was a chimney sweeper's boy, found a jewel and carried it to the defendant's shop, who was a goldsmith, in order to know what it was, and he delivered it into the hands of the apprentice in the goldsmith's shop, who made a pretence of weighing it and took out the stones and called to the master to let him know that it came to three-halfpence. The master offered the boy the money who refused to take it and insisted on having the jewel again. Whereupon the apprentice handed him back the socket of the jewel without the stones, and an action was brought in trover against the master [i.e. the boy claimed that the master committed a tort by interfering with the boy's property right in the jewel], and it was ruled "that the finder of a jewel, though he does not by such finding acquire an absolute property or ownership, yet he has such a property as will enable him to keep it against all but the rightful owner, and consequently may maintain trover [i.e. sue in tort]." The case of *Bridges v. Hawkesworth*[50] is in process of becoming almost equally as famous because of the disputation which has raged around it. The headnote in the Jurist is as follows: "The place in which a lost article is found does not constitute any exception to the general rule of law, that the finder is entitled to it as against all persons except the owner."

The case was in fact an appeal against a decision of the county court judge at Westminster. The facts appear to have been that in the year 1847 the plaintiff, who was a commercial traveller, called on a firm named Byfield & Hawkesworth on business, as he was in the habit of doing, and as he was leaving the shop he picked up a small parcel which was lying on the floor. He immediately showed it to the shopman, and opened it in his presence, when it was found to consist of a quantity of Bank of England notes, to the amount of £65. The defendant, who was a partner in the firm of Byfield & Hawkesworth, was then called, and the plaintiff told him he had found the notes, and asked the defendant to keep them until the owner appeared to claim them. Then various advertisements were put in the papers asking for the owner, but the true owner was never found. No person having appeared to claim them, and three years having elapsed since they were found, the plaintiff applied to the defendant to have the notes returned to him, and offered to pay the expenses of the advertisements, and to give an indemnity. The defendant refused to deliver them up to the plaintiff, and an action was brought in the county court of Westminster in consequence of that refusal. The county court judge decided that the defendant, the shopkeeper, was entitled to the custody of the notes as against the plaintiff, and gave judgment for the defendant. Thereupon the appeal was brought which came before the court composed of Patteson J. and Wightman J. Patteson J. said:

"The notes which are the subject of this action were incidentally dropped, by mere accident, in the shop of the defendant, by the owner of them. The facts do not warrant the supposition that they had been deposited there intentionally, nor has the case been put at all upon that ground. The plaintiff found them on the floor, they being manifestly lost by someone. The general right of the finder to any article which has been lost, as against all the world, except the true owner, was established in the case of *Armory v. Delamirie* which has never been disputed. This right would clearly have accrued to the plaintiff had the notes been picked up by him outside the shop of the defendant and if he once had the right, the case finds that he did

[49] (1722) 5 Stra 505.   [50] (1821) 21 LJ (QB) 75.

not intend, by delivering the notes to the defendant, to waive the title (if any) which he had to them, but they were handed to the defendant merely for the purpose of delivering them to the owner should he appear."

Then a little later:

"The case, therefore, resolves itself into the single point on which it appears that the learned judge decided it, namely, whether the circumstance of the notes being found inside the defendant's shop gives him, the defendant, the right to have them as against the plaintiff, who found them."

After discussing the cases, and the argument, the learned judge said:

"If the discovery had never been communicated to the defendant, could the real owner have had any cause of action against him because they were found in his house? Certainly not. The notes never were in the custody of the defendant, nor within the protection of his house, before they were found, as they would have been had they been intentionally deposited there; and the defendant has come under no responsibility, except from the communication made to him by the plaintiff, the finder, and the steps taken by way of advertisement [. . .] We find, therefore, no circumstances in this case to take it out of the general rule of law, that the finder of a lost article is entitled to it as against all persons except the real owner, and we think that that rule must prevail, and that the learned judge was mistaken in holding that the place in which they were found makes any legal difference. Our judgment, therefore, is that the plaintiff is entitled to these notes as against the defendant."

It is to be observed that in *Bridges v. Hawkesworth* which has been the subject of immense disputation, neither counsel put forward any argument on the fact that the notes were found in a shop. Counsel for the appellant assumed throughout that the position was the same as if the parcel had been found in a private house, and the learned judge spoke of "the protection of his (the shopkeeper's) house." The case for the appellant was that the shopkeeper never knew of the notes. Again, what is curious is that there was no suggestion that the place where the notes were found was in any way material; indeed, the judge in giving the judgment of the court expressly repudiates this and said in terms "The learned judge was mistaken in holding that the place in which they were found makes any legal difference." [. . .]

At 521

There is no doubt that in this case the brooch was lost in the ordinary meaning of that term, and I should imagine it had been lost for a very considerable time. Indeed, from this correspondence it appears that at one time the predecessors in title of the defendant were considering making some claim. But the moment the plaintiff discovered that the brooch might be of some value, he took the advice of his commanding officer and handed it to the police. His conduct was commendable and meritorious. The defendant was never physically in possession of these premises at any time. It is clear that the brooch was never his, in the ordinary acceptation of the term, in that he had the prior possession. He had no knowledge of it, until it was brought to his notice by the finder. A discussion of the merits does not seem to help, but it is clear on the facts that the brooch was "lost" in the ordinary meaning of that word; that it was "found" by the plaintiff in the ordinary meaning of that word, that its true owner has never been found, that the defendant was the owner of the premises and had his notice drawn to this matter by the plaintiff, who found the brooch. In those circumstances I propose to follow the decision in *Bridges v. Hawkesworth*, and to give judgment in this case for [Mr Hannah] for £66.

The first point to take from this decision is the important general principle that if a party takes possession of an object (e.g. by finding it),[51] he acquires a property right in that object.[52] This is a fundamental principle of property law. Indeed, even a thief can benefit from that principle: even though he has dishonestly taken physical control of an object, he still acquires a property right in it.[53] Of course, this does not mean that the finder or thief has the *best* property right: the party who lost the thing, or from whom it was stolen, also has a property right. And the general rule is that he or she can assert that property right against the finder or thief, because his or her property right arose *before* that of the finder or thief.[54] As we will see in Chapter 15, section 3, timing is absolutely crucial when considering the priority of conflicting property rights: the general rule is that the party with the *earliest* property right will win.

So, in *Hannah v Peel*, Mr Hannah clearly had a property right in the brooch: he acquired that right simply by taking physical control of the brooch, just as the chimney sweep's boy in *Armory v Delamrie* acquired a property right by taking physical control of the jewel. Equally clearly, the party who lost the brooch had an earlier property right in the brooch: so, *if* that party were to have come forward, she would have been able to bring a claim against Mr Hannah. But that party did *not* come forward: the dispute was between Mr Hannah (who clearly had a property right in the brooch) and Major Peel. So, Major Peel had to show that: (i) he, too, had a property right in the brooch; *and* (ii) he acquired that property right *before* Mr Hannah found the brooch.

How could Major Peel, the owner of the land, show that he had such a property right? Clearly, he never had physical control of the brooch itself; indeed, he had not even gone into occupation of his land. In theory, he could try to claim that his property right in the land also covered the brooch. But, as we saw in section 2.2.1 above, he could only make that argument if the brooch, when lost, had become part and parcel of his land, or was sufficiently attached to his land. Given that the brooch was easily dislodged from the crevice, it clearly was not part and parcel of, or sufficiently attached to, Major Peel's land. Further, if that argument were accepted, then the party who lost the brooch, even were she to come forward, would not be able to claim the brooch: her property right would have disappeared when the brooch became part of Major Peel's land.

---

[51] The principle is a general one, and there are exceptions: for example, if an employee takes physical control of an object in the course of her employment, this can be regarded as giving possession, and hence a property right, to her employer: see e.g. *Parker v British Airways Board* [1982] QB 1004, 1017. For discussion of this point, see Hickey, *Property and the Law of Finders* (Oxford: Hart Publishing, 2010) 135–9.

[52] Although note that it is possible to argue that the courts instead simply *treat* such a person as having a property right when deciding a dispute between such a person and a party who cannot show a pre-existing property right: see L Rostill, 'Relative Title and Deemed Ownership in English Personal Property Law' (2014) 14 OJLS 1.

[53] See *Costello v Chief Constable of Derbyshire* [2001] EWCA Civ 381, [2001] 3 All ER 150. For discussion see, for example, Hickey, 'Possession Taken by Theft and the Original Acquisition of Personal Property Rights' in *Modern Studies in Property Law Vol 7* (ed Hopkins, Oxford: Hart Publishing, 2013) 401.

[54] Note too that a finder, like any other holder of a property right, may lose his or her right as a result of the operation of a relevant statute. In *Fletcher v Chief Constable of Leicestershire* [2013] EWHC 3357 (Admin), for example, Mr Fletcher was renovating an unoccupied flat when he found a hidden metal box containing £17, 940 in £20 notes. He took the box to the police, who applied to the magistrates' court for an order that the money be forfeited under the Proceeds of Crime Act 2002, s 298(2)(b), as 'intended by any person for use in unlawful conduct', on the assumption that the box had been hidden by a criminal who had intended to recover it. The order was made, and confirmed by Lewis J, even though it deprived Fletcher of any property right he had as a finder.

So, Major Peel tried a different argument, proposing that he automatically acquired a property right in *anything* found on his land. Birkett J rejected that argument. As shown by the earlier decision in *Bridges v Hawkesworth*, the mere fact that something was lost or found on a party's land does not give that party a property right in the thing. After all, as was the case in *Hannah v Peel*, the party with the property right in the land may not even know that the thing is on his land.

It may therefore seem that the position is fairly simple: a party with a property right in land has no special rights in relation to anything lost or found on his land. The following extract, however, is from a case that (perhaps unnecessarily) introduced some complications.

Parker v British Airways Board
[1982] QB 1004, CA

Facts: In November 1978, Mr Parker was waiting for a flight in an executive lounge at Heathrow Terminal One. He spotted a gold bracelet on the floor that had been dropped by an unknown passenger. He handed the bracelet to British Airways staff in case that unknown passenger should come forward to claim it; he also gave the staff his contact details and said that the bracelet should be returned to him if no one came forward to claim it. By June 1979, no one had come forward. Although Mr Parker had requested that it be sent to him, British Airways sold the bracelet for £850. Mr Parker claimed that, by finding and taking control of the bracelet, he had a property right in the bracelet and that, by refusing to give it to him, British Airways had committed the tort of conversion. The first instance judge accepted Mr Parker's arguments and ordered British Airways to pay him £850 plus interest. The Court of Appeal dismissed British Airways' appeal.

Donaldson LJ

On November 15, 1978, the plaintiff, Alan George Parker, had a date with fate—and perhaps with legal immortality. He found himself in the international executive lounge at terminal one, Heathrow Airport. And that was not all that he found. He also found a gold bracelet lying on the floor.

We know very little about the plaintiff, and it would be nice to know more. He was lawfully in the lounge and, as events showed, he was an honest man. Clearly he had not forgotten the schoolboy maxim 'Finders keepers.' But, equally clearly, he was well aware of the adult qualification 'unless the true owner claims the article.' He had had to clear customs and security to reach the lounge. He was almost certainly an outgoing passenger because the defendants, British Airways Board, as lessees of the lounge from the British Airports Authority and its occupiers, limit its use to passengers who hold first class tickets or boarding passes or who are members of their Executive Club which is a passengers' 'club.' Perhaps the plaintiff's flight had just been called and he was pressed for time. Perhaps the only officials in sight were employees of the defendants. Whatever the reason, he gave the bracelet to an anonymous official of the defendants instead of to the police. He also gave the official a note of his name and address and asked for the bracelet to be returned to him if it was not claimed by the owner. The official handed the bracelet to the lost property department of the defendants. Although the owner never claimed the bracelet, the defendants did not return it to the plaintiff. Instead they sold it and kept the proceeds which amounted to £850. The plaintiff discovered what had happened and was more than a little annoyed. I can understand his annoyance. He sued the defendants in the Brentford County Court and was awarded £850 as damages and £50 as interest. The defendants now appeal.

It is astonishing that there should be any doubt as to who is right. But there is. Indeed, it seems that the academics have been debating this problem for years. In 1971 the Law Reform Committee reported that it was by no means clear who had the better claim to lost property when the protagonists were the finder and the occupier of the premises where the property was found. Whatever else may be in doubt, the committee was abundantly right in this conclusion. The committee recommended legislative action but, as is not uncommon, nothing has been done. The rights of the parties thus depend upon the common law.

As a matter of legal theory, the common law has a ready made solution for every problem and it is only for the judges, as legal technicians, to find it. The reality is somewhat different. Take the present case. The conflicting rights of finder and occupier have indeed been considered by various courts in the past. But under the rules of English jurisprudence, none of their decisions binds this court. We therefore have both the right and the duty to extend and adapt the common law in the light of established principles and the current needs of the community. This is not to say that we start with a clean sheet. In doing so, we should draw from the experience of the past as revealed by the previous decisions of the courts.

Neither the plaintiff nor the defendants lay any claim to the bracelet either as owner of it or as one who derives title from that owner. The plaintiff's claim is founded upon the ancient common law rule that the act of finding a chattel which has been lost and taking control of it gives the finder rights with respect to that chattel. The defendants' claim has a different basis. They cannot and do not claim to have found the bracelet when it was handed to them by the plaintiff. At that stage it was no longer lost and they received and accepted the bracelet from the plaintiff on terms that it would be returned to him if the owner could not be found. They must and do claim on the basis that they had rights in relation to the bracelet immediately *before* the plaintiff found it and that these rights are superior to the plaintiff's. The defendants' claim is based upon the proposition that at common law an occupier of land has such rights over all lost chattels which are on that land, whether or not the occupier knows of their existence.

The common law right asserted by the plaintiff has been recognised for centuries. [Donaldson LJ here referred to *Armory v Delamrie*,[55] which is considered in the extract above from *Hannah v Peel*] [. . .] Some qualification has also to be made in the case of the trespassing finder. The person vis à vis whom he is a trespasser has a better title. The fundamental basis of this is clearly public policy. Wrongdoers should not benefit from their wrongdoing. This requirement would be met if the trespassing finder acquired no rights. That would, however, produce [a] free-for-all situation [. . .], in that anyone could take the article from the trespassing finder. Accordingly, the common law has been obliged to give rights to someone else, the owner *ex hypothesi* being unknown. The obvious candidate is the occupier of the property upon which the finder was trespassing.

Curiously enough, it is difficult to find any case in which the rule is stated in this simple form, but I have no doubt that this is the law [. . .] One might have expected there to be decisions clearly qualifying the general rule where the circumstances are that someone finds a chattel and thereupon forms the dishonest intention of keeping it regardless of the rights of the true owner or of anyone else. But that is not the case [. . .]

[55] (1722) 2 Stra 505.

[Donaldson LJ then surveyed previous cases and set out the following five propositions as to the rights and duties of a finder:]

1. The finder of a chattel acquires no rights over it unless (a) it has been abandoned or lost and (b) he takes it into his care and control.

2. The finder of a chattel acquires very limited rights over it if he takes it into his care and control with dishonest intent or in the course of trespassing.

3. Subject to the foregoing and to point 4 below, a finder of a chattel, whilst not acquiring any absolute property or ownership in the chattel, acquires a right to keep it against all but the true owner or those in a position to claim through the true owner or one who can assert a prior right to keep the chattel which was subsisting at the time when the finder took the chattel into his care and control.

4. Unless otherwise agreed, any servant or agent who finds a chattel in the course of his employment or agency and not wholly incidentally or collaterally thereto and who takes it into his care and control does so on behalf of his employer or principal who acquires a finder's rights to the exclusion of those of the actual finder.

5. A person having a finder's rights has an obligation to take such measures as in all the circumstances are reasonable to acquaint the true owner of the finding and present whereabouts of the chattel and to care for it meanwhile.

[Donaldson LJ also set out the following four propositions as to the rights and duties of an occupier of land on which a thing is found:]

6. An occupier of land has rights superior to those of a finder over chattels in or attached to that land and an occupier of a building has similar rights in respect of chattels attached to that building, whether in either case the occupier is aware of the presence of the chattel.

7. An occupier of a building has rights superior to those of a finder over chattels upon or in, but not attached to, that building if, but only if, before the chattel is found, he has manifested an intention to exercise control over the building and the things which may be upon it or in it.

8. An occupier who manifests an intention to exercise control over a building and the things which may be upon or in it so as to acquire rights superior to those of a finder is under an obligation to take such measures as in all the circumstances are reasonable to ensure that lost chattels are found and, upon their being found, whether by him or by a third party, to acquaint the true owner of the finding and to care for the chattels meanwhile. The manifestation of intention may be express or implied from the circumstances including, in particular, the circumstance that the occupier manifestly accepts or is obliged by law to accept liability for chattels lost upon his "premises," e.g. an innkeeper or carrier's liability.

9. An 'occupier' of a chattel, e.g. a ship, motor car, caravan or aircraft, is to be treated as if he were the occupier of a building for the purposes of the foregoing rules [. . .]

The plaintiff was not a trespasser in the executive lounge and, in taking the bracelet into his care and control, he was acting with obvious honesty. Prima facie, therefore, he had a full finder's rights and obligations. He in fact discharged those obligations by handing the bracelet to an official of the defendants' although he could equally have done so by handing the bracelet to the police or in other ways such as informing the police of the find and himself caring for the bracelet.

The plaintiff's prima facie entitlement to a finder's rights was not displaced in favour of an employer or principal. There is no evidence that he was in the executive lounge in the course of any employment or agency and, if he was, the finding of the bracelet was quite clearly collateral thereto. The position would have been otherwise in the case of most or perhaps all the defendants' employees.

The defendants, for their part, cannot assert any title to the bracelet based upon the rights of an occupier over chattels attached to a building. The bracelet was lying loose on the floor. Their claim must, on my view of the law, be based upon a manifest intention to exercise control over the lounge and all things which might be in it. The evidence is that they claimed the right to decide who should and who should not be permitted to enter and use the lounge, but their control was in general exercised upon the basis of classes or categories of user and the availability of the lounge in the light of the need to clean and maintain it. I do not doubt that they also claimed the right to exclude individual undesirables, such as drunks, and specific types of chattels such as guns and bombs. But this control has no real relevance to a manifest intention to assert custody and control over lost articles. There was no evidence that they searched for such articles regularly or at all.

On the evidence available, there was no sufficient manifestation of any intention to exercise control over lost property before it was found such as would give the defendants a right superior to that of the plaintiff or indeed any right over the bracelet. As the true owner has never come forward, it is a case of 'finders keepers.'

On the one hand, the *result* in *Parker v British Airways Board* is consistent with the simple position adopted in *Hannah v Peel*: British Airways did not acquire a property right in the bracelet simply because it was lost and found on its land. On the other, the *reasoning* of Donaldson LJ introduces a complication: it means that B, a party with a property right in land, can acquire a property right in a thing lost and found on its land *if* it can show a '*manifest intention to exercise control over the* [land] *and all things which might be in it*'. If that is correct, it means that B can acquire a property right over an object even before B is aware of that object.[56] In *Parker*, British Airways was found not to have manifested such an intention, but the position is likely to be different where an object is found in a private house occupied by B,[57] rather than in an area to which there is (at least some) general public access. It is not immediately obvious, however, why a landowner's *intention* to control such things should give it a property right: why change the general rule that, to acquire a property right in relation to a lost or found thing, a party needs to take actual physical control of the thing?

Despite this problem, the reasoning of Donaldson LJ was relied on by the Court of Appeal in the following case.

---

[56] Note that there is no need to apply the same test when asking if a defendant has 'possession' of goods such as to be guilty of a criminal offence: see e.g. the discussion in *Warner v Metropolitan Police Commissioner* [1969] 2 AC 256.

[57] See *Flack v National Crime Authority* (1998) 156 ALR 501 (a decision of the Full Federal Court of Australia), where it was held that a briefcase full of cash (amounting to $433,000), found in a cupboard by police carrying out a search of the premises, had to be returned to Mrs Flack, the owner of the premises, even though she had been entirely unaware of its presence in the house. It was held that Mrs Flack had a general intention to exercise control over objects in her house, and so it could be said she had manifested an intention to exercise control over the briefcase. Note that, in *Hannah v Peel*, at the point when the brooch was found by Mr Hannah, Major Peel had not yet moved into occupation of the land.

Waverley Borough Council v Fletcher
[1996] QB 334, CA

Facts: Waverley Borough Council had a property right (a freehold) in Farnham Park, Farnham, Surrey. The park was open to the public for recreational use. In August 1992, Mr Fletcher visited the park with a metal detector and, after some digging, uncovered a medieval gold brooch about nine inches below the surface of the ground. Mr Fletcher thus took physical control of the brooch. Under the terms of the Treasure Act 1996, the Crown acquires a property right to any 'treasure' as soon as it is found. It was determined, however, that the brooch did not count as treasure and that the Crown consequently had no claim to it. The Council, however, claimed that, because it had been lost and found on its land, it had a prior property right in the brooch. The first instance judge found in favour of Mr Fletcher; the Court of Appeal allowed the Council's appeal.

Auld LJ

At 341–2

[Auld LJ, adding his own emphasis, referred to the following passage from Pollock and Wright, *Possession in the Common Law* (1888) at p 41, dealing with objects attached to or in land]:

> 'The possession of land carries with it in general, by our law, possession of everything which is *attached to or under* that land, and, in the absence of a better title elsewhere, the right to possess it also. And it makes no difference that the possessor is not aware of the thing's existence. So it was lately held concerning a prehistoric boat imbedded in the soil. It is free to any one who requires a specific intention as part of de facto possession to treat this as a positive rule of law. But it seems preferable to say that the legal possession rests on a real de facto possession, constituted by the occupier's general power and intent to exclude unauthorized interference.'

[. . .] The test of possession, in its most abstract form, may have a constant meaning whether applied to objects in or unattached and on land. But it is clear from Pollock and Wright's statement [. . .] that they regarded its application to objects in land to be free from the uncertainties inherent in disputes about entitlement to unattached objects found on land. Their proposition was that in practice possession of land should generally be taken as carrying with it an intent to possession of objects in or attached to it [. . .]

At 345–6

[Counsel for Mr Fletcher] argued that it is against commonsense that it should make all the difference whether an object is just under or on the surface. That was also the view of the [first instance] judge. He said that he could see no reason in common sense why the better possessory claim should depend upon whether an object was found on or in ground. [Counsel for Mr Fletcher] gave as one of a number of examples in support of his argument, a lost watch on a muddy path which might within a day or two become covered by a thin coating of mud. Why, he asked, should the landowner's claim be different and stronger when the watch finally, but only just, disappears from sight?

In my view, the authorities reveal a number of sound and practical reasons for the distinction.

First, as Donaldson L.J. said in *Parker v. British Airways Board*,[58] an object in land "is to be treated as an integral part of the realty as against all but the true owner" or that the finder in detaching the object would, in the absence of licence to do so, become a trespasser. [Counsel for Mr Fletcher] suggested that this is wrong because if an object is treated as part of the realty the true owner cannot have priority. However, the English law of ownership and possession, unlike that of Roman Law, is not a system of identifying absolute entitlement but of priority of entitlement, and Donaldson L.J.'s rationale is consistent with that [. . .]

Second, removal of an object in or attached to land would normally involve interference with the land and may damage it [. . .]

Third, putting aside the borderline case of a recently lost article which has worked its way just under the surface, in the case of an object in the ground its original owner is unlikely in most cases to be there to claim it. The law, therefore, looks for a substitute owner, the owner or possessor of the land in which it is lodged. Whereas in the case of an unattached object on the surface, it is likely in most cases to have been recently lost, and the true owner may well claim it. In the meantime, there is no compelling reason why it should pass into the possession of the landowner as against a finder unless he, the landowner, has manifested an intention to possess it. As to borderline cases of the sort mentioned by [counsel for Mr Fletcher], potential absurdities can always be found at the margins in the application of any sound principle. It is for the trial judge to determine as a matter of fact and degree on which side of the line, on or in the land, an object is found [. . .]

In my view, the two main principles established by the authorities, and for good practical reasons, are as stated by Donaldson L.J. in *Parker v. British Airways Board*. I venture to re-state them with particular reference to objects found on or in land, for he was concerned primarily with an object found in a building. (1) Where an article is found in or attached to land, as between the owner or lawful possessor of the land and the finder of the article, the owner or lawful possessor of the land has the better title. (2) Where an article is found unattached on land, as between the two, the owner or lawful possessor of the land has a better title only if he exercised such manifest control over the land as to indicate an intention to control the land and anything that might be found on it [. . .]

At 350

Accordingly, I can see no basis for not applying the general rule that an owner or lawful possessor of land has a better title to an object found in or attached to his land than the finder, or for modifying it in some way to produce a different result in the circumstances of this case. Mr. Fletcher did not derive a superior right to the brooch simply because he was entitled as a member of the public to engage in recreational pursuits in the park. Metal detecting was not a recreation of the sort permitted under the terms under which the council held the land on behalf of the general public. In any event, digging and removal of property in the land were not such a permitted use, and were acts of trespass. And the council was entitled to exercise its civil remedy for protection of its property regardless of the absence of any applicable byelaw.

According to the reasoning of Auld LJ, the crucial point in *Waverley BC v Fletcher*, which distinguishes that case from *Hannah v Peel*, is that the brooch was found *in* the land rather than *on* the land.

---

[58] [1982] QB 1004, [1010].

In summary then, there seem to be three refinements to the basic rule that B, an owner of land does not, by mere fact of that ownership, gain a property right in an object lost and found on that land:

(i) if B occupies a building on the land, and, before the object was lost, B had manifested an intention to exercise control over the building and things which may be in it, then B has a property right superior to that of the finder of the object;[59]

(ii) if the finder was a trespasser on B's land, then, as a matter of 'public policy', B will have a property right superior to that of the finder;[60]

(iii) if the object was found in rather than on the land, B will have a property right superior to the finder.[61]

We have seen, however, that the first of those refinements can be challenged. The second is also somewhat dubious: as the courts have accepted that even a thief of an object acquires a property right when taking possession of it,[62] it is hard to see that *public policy* requires limiting the rights of a mere trespasser. The third refinement can also be queried, as in the following extract.

McFarlane, *The Structure of Property Law* (2008, pp 157–8)

The Court of Appeal's reasoning in *Waverley BC* is flawed. First, it was said that once the brooch was submerged, it became part and parcel of [the Council's] land, so that [the Council], as an owner of the land, also had Ownership of the brooch. It is true that if one thing loses its physical identity and becomes subsumed into another thing, the first thing ceases to have an independent existence [. . .] However, if this had occurred in *Waverley BC* then *all*—pre-existing property rights in the brooch would have ceased to exist. On that view, the person who originally lost the brooch (A) would lose his Ownership of the brooch and so would be unable to assert a right against either [Mr Fletcher] or [the Council]. However, the Court of Appeal's view was that A *retained* Ownership and so, if he came forward, could assert his right against each of [Mr Fletcher] and [the Council].[63] But a court cannot have it both ways: *either* (i) the brooch lost its identity and became part of the land, so that A's pre-existing property right is destroyed; *or* (ii) the brooch did not lose its identity and A still has a property right he can assert against each of [Mr Fletcher] and [the Council]. On that second view, the brooch does not count as part of [the Council's] land: so [the Council's] position as an owner of the land does *not* give [it] Ownership of the brooch.

The puzzling statement of Donaldson LJ in *Parker v British Airways Board*,[64] relied on in *Waverley BC*, that a thing can become an "integral part of the realty [i.e. the land] as against all but the true owner" must be rejected. Either the brooch lost its identity and became part of the land or it did not. The better view must be that it did not. The brooch did not become part of [the Council's] land simply by being submerged by the top soil. The brooch remained a distinct physical object: after all, once he found the brooch, [Mr Fletcher] was easily able to remove it from [the Council's] land.

---

[59] *Parker v British Airways Board* [1982] QB 1004, 1018.   [60] Ibid, 1017.

[61] Ibid, 1018 and *Waverley BC v Fletcher* [1996] QB 334, 346.

[62] See, as noted earlier, *Costello v Chief Constable of Derbyshire* [2001] 3 All ER 150.

[63] See *per* Auld LJ at [345].   [64] [1984] QB 1004, [1010].

QUESTIONS

1. In *Entick v Carrington*, what rights did Mr Entick assert against the King's messengers?

2. What does it mean if we say that 25 Mountfield Gardens is 'B's property'?

3. '*To whomsoever the soil belongs, he owns also to the sky and to the depths.*' Is that an accurate statement of English law?

4. Why might it matter whether or not a particular thing counts as part of a plot of land?

5. Whilst on B's land, A finds a gold ring. What factors are relevant to deciding which of A or B has a better claim to the ring?

For guidance on how to answer these questions visit the online resources at www.oup.com/uk/mcfarlane4e/.

FURTHER READING

Goodhart, 'Three Cases on Possession' [1929] CLJ 195

Gray, 'Property in Thin Air' [1991] CLJ 252

Gray and Gray, *Elements of Land Law* (5th edn, Oxford: OUP, 2009, Part 1.5)

Hickey, *Property and the Law of Finders* (Oxford: Hart Publishing, 2010, ch 2)

Howell, 'Subterranean Land Law: Rights Below the Surface of Land' (2002) 53 NILQ 268

Morgan, 'Digging Deep: Property Rights in Subterranean Space and the Challenge of Carbon Capture and Storage' (2013) 62 ICLQ 813

Scott, '*Entick v Carrington* and the Legal Protection of Property' in Tomkins and Scott (ed), *Entick v Carrington: 250 Years of the Rule of Law* (London: Hart, 2015).

3

REGISTRATION

CENTRAL ISSUES

1. Registration is a key concept in land law. The question of whether or not a right appears on the register maintained by the Land Registry can have an important effect on the *acquisition* and *defences* question. As a result, throughout this book, we will need to consider the provisions of the Land Registration Act 2002 (the LRA 2002). We will examine the detailed operation of specific provisions of the LRA 2002 in later chapters, when focussing on the acquisition and defences question. The purpose of this chapter is simply to provide a relatively brief introduction to the idea of registration of title and to the key concepts employed by the LRA 2002.

2. In order to understand the specific scheme implemented by the LRA 2002, it is necessary first to stand back and consider the relevance of registration schemes, in general, to land law. In section 2 of this chapter, we will see how the special features of land can explain the prominence of registration systems in land law.

3. We will also see in section 2 that a registration system can give C, a party planning to acquire a right in land, very useful protection against the risk that the party with whom C is dealing

does not in fact have the power to give C a valid right to the land, or to give C a right that will have priority over competing claims to the land. This does not mean, however, that all registration systems are the same, or that the success of such a system is to be judged solely by the extent of the protection it affords to C.

4. In section 3, we will look at the basic scheme imposed by the LRA 2002. The Act was the product of work by the Law Commission and we will consider its aims when proposing the reform of the previous regime under the Land Registration Act 1925 (the LRA 1925), as well as the key concepts employed by the LRA 2002. We will see that the LRA 2002 scheme, whilst primarily intended to increase the protection of C, also allows for the recognition and protection of a prior property right of B, even if that right was not evident on the register when C acquired C's right in the land.

5. We will see in section 3 that there has been some uncertainty and controversy as to how the courts should interpret the LRA 2002. In particular, there is a sharp debate as to the extent to which general principles of property law can continue to have a role to

play within the registration scheme. As a result, the Law Commission are currently considering how to amend and improve the LRA 2002. We will consider the details of this debate, and the proposed reforms, in later parts of the book, in particular in Chapter 18. The debate is a useful reminder of the fact that choices have to be made when implementing a registration scheme. Certainly, the existence of a registration system cannot provide an instant solution to the very difficult task faced by land law in resolving conflicts over competing claims to private rights to use land. The possibility of reform of the LRA 2002 underlines the point that it is important to be aware of the policy questions that underlie both the design of a registration system and the interpretation of the LRA 2002.

1 THE DISTINCTION BETWEEN REGISTERED AND UNREGISTERED LAND

In Chapter 1, section 3, we noted that, if you are interested in buying a particular home, you need to know if the right offered by the vendor is a freehold or a leasehold. As we will see in Chapter 5, the content of each right is different: a freehold gives you ownership of the land without limit of time; a leasehold gives you ownership, but only for a limited period. It is also important for you to know whether the right held by the vendor is registered or not: if the vendor's freehold or leasehold (or, as it is often said, his or her *title* to the land) is registered, then the provisions of the Land Registration Act 2002 (LRA 2002) will determine what you must do to acquire the vendor's title, and which, if any, pre-existing property rights in the land will be binding on you.

If you have seen a particular property advertised for sale in an estate agency window, the overwhelming likelihood is that the title being offered will be registered. Nearly 25 million titles are recorded in the Land Register, and those titles relate to almost 85 per cent of the land mass of England and Wales.[1] When people refer to 'registered land', they mean land the title to which is registered in the records administered and maintained by the Land Registry.[2] More than one registered title may subsist in relation to the same piece of land: for example, A may have a freehold of land whilst B simultaneously has a ninety-nine-year lease of that same land. The provisions of the LRA 2002 are also relevant when considering dealings with unregistered title: section 4 of that Act sets out certain dealings with unregistered title that must be completed by registration (see Chapter 8, section 6.2). So, for example, if A holds an unregistered legal freehold, and wants to sell that right, or transfer it by gift to B, the transfer to B can be completed only if B registers his or her title. In this way, the title will be brought on to the register for the first time. Unregistered land is, therefore, usually land

---

[1] HM Land Registry, Annual Report and Accounts 2016–17 p 6.

[2] The institution, officially entitled 'Her Majesty's Land Registry' now refers to itself simply as 'Land Registry', without any definite article. As that sounds a little silly, however, we will refer to it in this book as 'the Land Registry'.

that is infrequently transferred: perhaps, for example, a large rural estate that has remained in a family trust. In fact, even if A, a holder of an unregistered title, does not plan to transfer that land, A can choose simply to register his or her title[3]—as we will see in Chapter 9, one incentive for A to do so is that a registered title has far stronger protection against the risk of loss through adverse possession.

As a result, then, land law in practice is very much focussed on dealings in registered title. Those dealings bring in income for the Land Registry, as it charges fees for its services, for example in updating the register when there is a sale of a registered title.[4] In historical terms, the shift to the primacy of registration has occurred fairly rapidly.[5] Even at the time of the 1925 property legislation, which included the Land Registration Act 1925 (LRA 1925), registration of title was still seen as experimental.[6] Although no formal decision on the matter was ever taken, the system of registration was gradually extended. Indeed, the Law Commission report that led to the LRA 2002 (which replaced the LRA 1925) claimed that: *'unregistered land has had its day. In the comparatively near future, it will be necessary to take steps to bring what is left of it on to the register.'* [7] Whilst 'total registration' was therefore identified as a worthwhile goal,[8] the LRA 2002 did not in the end include a mechanism for achieving that aim, as the Law Commission decided it would be best first to assess the impact of the LRA 2002, and also had understandable doubts about the political acceptability of requiring registration of a landowner who had no immediate plans to deal with his or her land.[9] Nonetheless, the Land Registry currently aims to *'achieve comprehensive registration by 2030'.*[10]

2 REGISTRATION SYSTEMS AND LAND LAW

2.1 REGISTRATION SYSTEMS: GENERAL AIMS

When considering the possible aims of a registration system, it is important to bear in mind that the usefulness of registration is not confined to land law. The following extract refers to two examples in which rights unrelated to land may be registered. The first concerns the registration of company shares; the second, the registration of security interests over company assets.

---

[3] Such voluntary registration is possible under s 3 of the LRA 2002, and the fee payable for such registration is lower than that payable for a standard compulsory registration (although a bigger discount is available where electronic means are used to deliver title details of a compulsory registration): see Land Registry, *Registration Services Fees* (March 2016, as updated).

[4] In 2016–17, the total income of the Land Registry was £311.4m: HM Land Registry, Annual Report and Accounts 2016–17 p 95. The fee charged in 2017 to transfer registered title of land worth more than £200,000 but no more than £500,000, where the application is made electronically, is £135.

[5] A form of registration of title was provided by the Land Transfer Act 1875, following recommendations made by a Royal Commission on Registration of Title in 1857.

[6] See Dixon et al, *Ruoff and Roper: Registered Conveyancing* (London: Sweet and Maxwell, 2018), [1–008]: when the 1925 legislation came into force, registration was compulsory only in the County of London and the County Borough of Eastbourne.

[7] Law Com No 271 (2001) [1.6].   [8] Law Com No 271 (2001) [2.13].

[9] Law Com No 271 (2001) [2.10]–[2.12].

[10] HM Land Registry, Annual Report and Accounts 2016–17 p 4.

McFarlane, *The Structure of Property Law* (2008, pp 82–3)

The central purpose of any register is to provide *publicity*. For example, a register of births, marriages and deaths gives interested parties the opportunity to discover important information about a community. The publicity provided by a register of rights may be useful to a number of different groups: for example, it may provide the State with information it can use when making tax assessments [. . .]

Registration can thus be particularly useful to C [a party acquiring a right from A], both in disputes about the use of a thing and in disputes about the use of a right. A registration system can protect C against the two chief risks he faces when attempting to acquire a right:

1. A, the party C deals with, may in fact lack the power to give C the right. This is the risk from which a register of rights, such as a register of company share-holders, aims to protect C.

2. Even if A does have the power to give C the right, B may have a pre-existing right that he can assert against C and that will thus reduce the value of C's right. This is the risk from which a register of pre-existing powers or rights, such as a register of floating charges against a company's rights,[11] aims to protect C.

[. . .] The publicity provided by a register of rights can never provide C with full protection: in practice, no such register can ever be completely accurate. In Example 1, a register may record A as the holder of some shares, but can C be sure that the register is correct? In Example 2, a register may make no mention of a pre-existing floating charge but, again, can C be sure that the register is correct? Of course, if the register is not complete, C may have to make his own enquiries as to whether A is indeed a holder of the shares; or whether there is a floating charge against A Co's assets. The usefulness of having a register will then be reduced: C will have to spend time and money on his own investigations; as a result the possible deal between A and C will be delayed, or perhaps even called off.

Ideally, C would like to have a *guarantee*. In Example 1, he wants a guarantee that: (i) if A is recorded as the holder of the shares, then (ii) A does indeed hold those shares. In Example 2, he wants a guarantee that: (i) if there is no floating charge recorded on the register; then (ii) no-one will be able to assert such a power against him. Such a guarantee can only be provided if *legal consequences* are attached to the fact that a right is, or is not, recorded on a register. Once those legal consequences exist, registration no longer operates neutrally, as a simple record. Rather, registration begins to operate as a legal concept. This introduction of legal consequences allows registration systems to affect the basic structure of property law and hence to have a greater impact on resolving the basic tension [i.e. the tension between the wishes of B, on the one hand, and of C, on the other].

2.2 REGISTRATION AND LAND LAW

The extract above noted that a registration system may help to protect C, a party aiming to acquire a property right, against two, linked risks: (i) the risk that the party with whom he or she deals (A) may not have the power to give C such a right; *and* (ii) the risk that, even if A does have that power, another party (B) may have a pre-existing property right in the

---

[11] [As we will see in Chapter 25, section 3.4, a floating charge is a particular form of security interest:, for example, it can be used by a company to give a lender security over that company's current and future assets.]

land that binds C. As the next extract notes, it is clear that both of those risks may be faced by C, a purchaser of a freehold or leasehold of land. As the extract suggests, the prominence of registration can perhaps be explained by the special features of land (as examined in the extract from the same author set out in Chapter 1, section 4).[12]

McFarlane, *The Structure of Property Law* (2008, pp 86–7)

Registration is particularly prominent in land law. We can explain this by looking at the special features of land [. . .]

1. Due to its fixed location, each piece of land is easy to identify. As a result, if a register exists, it is easy to look up a particular piece of land in that register.

2. Due to its capacity for multiple, simultaneous use, as well as its social importance, the list of [property rights in land] is longer than the list of such rights in things other than land. So, if C acquires a right in land from A, there is an increased risk to C of being bound by a pre-existing right of B.

3. Due to its permanence, there is an increased risk of a pre-existing [property right] existing in relation to a particular piece of land. So, if C acquires a right in land from A, there is an increased risk to C of being bound by a pre-existing right of B.

4. Due to its limited availability, land is already very expensive. As a result, there is a particularly strong desire to limit the time and cost C must expend in acquiring a right in land. The more expensive the process of buying land becomes, the more difficult it becomes for those of even average wealth to acquire the land they need to set up a home or run a business.

So, the special features of land both: (i) make a registration system possible; and (ii) justify the extra protection such a system can provide to C. However, this leaves open the question of *how* a land registration system should operate. The basic tension [between B and C] will govern not only *whether* the concept of registration applies, but also *how* it applies.

2.3 REGISTRATION OF TITLE AND PURCHASER PROTECTION

The discussion so far has suggested that the chief advantage of a system of registration of title to land lies in its ability to provide valuable protection to C, a party aiming to acquire a property right in particular land, for example by the purchase of a freehold or a leasehold. In 1857, for example, a Royal Commission identified such a system as a means of allowing '*owners to deal with land in as simple and easy a manner, as far as the title is concerned, and the difference in the nature and the subject matter may allow, as they now*

---

[12] Given that the special features of land are the same the world over, it is no surprise to find registration systems in many different jurisdictions and across many different times. For a useful survey of the position in other European jurisdictions, see Cooke, *The New Law of Land Registration* (2003) ch 9. In ch 1, Cooke notes, at p 2, that '*the ancient Egyptians, for example, kept a record of ownership in documentary form, so that land could be allocated accurately when it became accessible following the annual flooding of the Nile*'. She also notes that images of such papyrus can be seen online, via the Duke (University) Papyrus Library: see <https://library.duke.edu/rubenstein/scriptorium/papyrus/> (accessed 19 January 2018).

can deal with movable chattels or stock'.[13] As the next extract notes, this 'conveyancing' perspective, which focusses on the specific transaction between A and C, can be complemented, and broadened, by a consideration of the possible economic advantages[14] of a registration of title scheme.[15]

O'Connor, 'Registration of Title in England and Australia' in *Modern Studies in Property Law: Vol 2* (ed Cooke, 2003, pp 84–5)

While lawyers tend to view registration of title as a law reform project to overcome problems in common law conveyancing, governments and economists regard it as a market-supporting mechanism operated as a government program. The system is, as Mapp said, 'overwhelmingly administrative in operation',[16] with economic objects, namely, to improve security of title and to facilitate the transfer of interests in land. These two objects are found in the preamble to the very first English registration of title statute, the Land Registry Act 1862, which began: 'Whereas it is expedient to give certainty to the title to real estates and to facilitate the proof thereof and also to render the dealing with land more simple and economical'.

Economists have long recognised that secure property rights are a precondition for investment and economic growth. Puzzled by the difficulty of replicating the economic success of Western capitalism in the Third World, economists have in the past decade turned their attention to examining the nature of the legal institutions and property laws that underpin capitalism in developed countries. The new 'institutional economics' has rediscovered a long-overlooked connection between property laws and prosperity. Laws that ensure the security and transferability of property establish the framework of incentives that enable the creation of new wealth from existing assets.

Secure titles have been found to contribute to economic growth in a multiplicity of ways. They provide owners with an incentive to invest in improving and developing their land, for they are assured of reaping the benefits for themselves. Owners who wish to invest are better able to obtain the development capital they need on favourable terms if they can offer a good title as collateral for a loan. If purchasers can easily satisfy themselves that the title they are acquiring is clear, the costs of transacting in land will fall. Lower transaction costs assist the market to allocate land assets to their most productive uses, by allowing them to pass to those who value them most highly.

---

[13] Royal Commission, *Registration of Title* (1857) 23–4.

[14] For an ambitious statement of possible advantages, both economic and non-economic, of a land registration system, see the view of John Manthorpe, a former Chief Land Registrar, as expressed in *The Guardian* (4 April 2016): '*The ever-changing legal relationship of land and people is constantly and instantly reflected in a public place, through the registry. What would otherwise be hidden is synthesised into a common, guaranteed and public record open to all. Security, confidence, transparency, choice – all these become possible. Individually, land rights protect the interests of the registered owner; together they constitute the underwritten record of the collective wealth of the country. Across the world, a trusted system of land registration is central to social stability and economic success.*'

[15] The analysis of O'Connor draws on that of the developmental economist Hernando de Soto. His work was also referred to in a piece on the BBC News website on 6 November 2017, asking if the adoption of formal land registration systems in developing economies could help the 'world's poor unlock trillions': <http://www.bbc.co.uk/news/business-41650606>, accessed 18 November 2017.

[16] Mapp, *Torrens' Elusive Title: Basic Principles of an Efficient Torrens System* (Edmonton: University of Alberta, 1978) p 63.

2.4 THE CHOICES TO BE MADE BY A REGISTRATION SYSTEM

We have seen that the protection provided to C, a party planning to acquire a property right in land, is the key advantage of a system of registration of title. It would, however, be a mistake then to think that such a system must simply aim to do all it can to protect C, or to think that all registration systems are the same. It is not enough simply to state that having *a* registration of title system can be useful in land law; we also have to ask what *sort* of registration of title system should apply. In particular, as the following extract explores, we need to ask how our registration of title system should balance the needs of a prior user of land (such as A or B) with those of a party later acquiring a right in relation to the land (such as C).

O'Connor, 'Registration of Title in England and Australia' in *Modern Studies in Property Law: Vol 2* (ed Cooke, 2003, pp 85–6)

A title to land is secure if it is at no risk, or no significant risk, of being found to be defective or subordinate to another interest. While economists assume that security of title is a good that property laws can bestow, it is, as Mapp said 'an elusive ideal',[17] for it incorporates contradictory elements. There are two competing aspects of security of title, that Demogue called 'static' and 'dynamic' security.[18]

Static security

The law of private conveyancing was based on the principle of static security, which protects the rights of existing owners at the expense, if necessary, of purchasers. This was achieved through rules such as *nemo dat quod non habet*,[19] the preference of both law and equity for the interest first in time when adjudicating the priority of competing interests, and the doctrines of notice and equitable fraud. Equity's preference for the 'bona fide purchaser for value without notice' was an attempt to balance static security against the reasonable expectations of purchasers in good faith, but the standard of inquiry required of purchasers under the extended doctrine was onerous.

Conveyancing rules based on static security suited a society emerging from feudalism, where land ownership was confined to the privileged few, and was rarely traded. By the mid nineteenth century, England and Australia were developing market economies, in which value is captured through exchange. The old conveyancing rules inhibited exchange of land by imposing high transaction costs upon purchasers, and exposing them to the risk of acquiring defective or subordinate titles.

Dynamic security

The enactment of registration of title legislation in mid-nineteenth century England and Australia decisively shifted the conveyancing law towards the opposing principle of dynamic security. Dynamic security is provided by legal rules that protect the reasonable expectations of those who purchase in good faith. It facilitates exchange by reducing or eliminating

---

[17] Ibid, p 63.   [18] Demogue, 'Security' in *Modern French Legal Philosophy* (eds Fouillee et al, 1916).
[19] One many not grant a better title than one has.

the risk that the purchaser's title will be subject to unknown prior claims and title defects. This lowers transaction costs by limiting the inquiries that purchasers need to make. By relieving against risk, it also restores value to clouded titles [. . .]

The shift to dynamic security in the law of real and personal transactions was an essential condition for the operation of market capitalism. De Soto explains that, while the law in Western countries seeks to promote both types of security, dynamic security is favoured because of its greater economic importance:

'Although they are established to protect both the security of ownership and that of transactions, it is obvious that Western systems emphasize the latter. Security is principally focussed on producing trust in transactions so that people can more easily make their assets lead a parallel life as capital.'[20]

It is natural to equate dynamic security with protection for purchasers, but this is too simple. While dynamic security reduces purchasers' costs and risks in transactions, it also benefits owners. Without it, owners' titles can be disturbed years after purchase if a defect in their title or a prior interest comes to light within the relevant limitation period.

The 'security of title' object of registration refers to both static and dynamic security. The dilemma for the law is that the two stand in an inverse relationship. Measures that improve dynamic security tend to diminish static security to some extent, and vice versa. The law must determine how to balance dynamic and static security in the formulation of the rules, taking into account a range of policy considerations. Different evaluation of the considerations accounts for much of the variation and instability in the rules of registration of title systems.

2.4.1 The role of indemnity payments

It is important to note that, in attempting to find a balance between the claims of dynamic and static security or, in a particular case, between the claims of B and of C, a land registration system has an important advantage. It need not adopt a purely binary approach, in which either, B wins and C is left empty-handed, or vice versa. At least one further possibility is added if the system incorporates the idea of an indemnity payment. If, as is the case under the LRA 2002, parties registering as the holder of freehold or leasehold title must pay for such registration, those payments can then support an indemnity fund that can be used to offer compensation to either B or C.

For example, consider a case in which B holds a registered freehold of land that is unoccupied—perhaps it is a plot that B plans to develop. X, by means of fraud and forgery, procures his own registration in place of B. X then offers to sell his registered freehold to C, who is wholly innocent of X's fraud. C checks the register, which confirms X's title. C therefore pays her fee to the Land Registry and is registered as the new holder of freehold title. B then discovers the fraud. In the ensuing dispute between B and C, only one of the two parties can be recognized as having the better property right, and so only one of our two innocent parties will be able to enjoy good title to the land. The other party, however, could be protected by means of an indemnity payment, designed to compensate them for the loss they have suffered as a result of the mistaken registration of X. By opening up this additional

---

[20] De Soto, *The Mystery of Capital* (London: Basic Books, 2000) p 61.

means of resolving the tension between B and C, the possibility of an indemnity can play an important role in a registration system.[21]

2.5 THREE BASIC PRINCIPLES

The introduction of registration of title into English law matched a parallel development in Australia, in the introduction to New South Wales of the Torrens system of registration, pioneered by Sir Robert Torrens. The following extract is from a seminal work that identified three basic principles underlying systems of registered title.

Ruoff, *An Englishman Looks at the Torrens System* (1957, pp 7–14)

The essential features of every system of registered title are that the State authoritatively establishes title by declaring, under a guarantee of indemnity, that it is vested in a named person or persons, subject to specified incumbrances and qualifications. Anterior defects of title are cured, and thenceforth all investigation of the history of how the named owner came to be entitled is ruled out for ever and all future transactions are carried out by simple forms and simple machinery. No transaction is effective until it has been entered on the official record kept by the State, but once this has happened it cannot (apart from fraud) be upset—that is the broad theory.

It remains for me to indicate what I believe to be the merits or faults of this system. I suggest that in each particular country or state it succeeds or fails according to the degree with which the local law and the local administration accord, or do not accord, with certain fundamental principles. I will call these:

1. The mirror principle.
2. The curtain principle.
3. The insurance principle.

The mirror principle involves the proposition that the register of title is a mirror which reflects accurately and completely and beyond all argument the current facts that are material to a man's title [. . .]

The curtain principle is one which provides that the register is the sole source of information for proposing purchasers, who need not and, indeed, must not concern themselves with trusts and equities which lie behind the curtain [. . .]

The true [insurance] principle is this, that the mirror that is the register is deemed to give an absolutely correct reflection of title but if, through human frailty, a flaw appears, anyone who thereby suffers loss must be put in the same position, so far as money can do it, as if the reflection were a true one. A lost right is converted into hard cash.

It is helpful to bear in mind the three principles identified by Ruoff when examining a particular system of registration of title, such as that operating under the LRA 2002. It would, however, be a mistake to think that the success or failure of a registration system depends on the extent to which it gives effect to each of these three principles. There is, for example, a

---

[21] In 2016–17, the Land Registry paid out £6.9m in indemnity payments, as against its total revenue for the same period of £311.4m. Its operating surplus in 2016–17 was £69.4m.

tension between the mirror and insurance principles: if the register really were an accurate reflection of property rights held in relation to land at any one time, there would be no need for indemnity payments or insurance. Indeed, Ruoff acknowledged that *'in this imperfect world the mirror does not invariably give a completely reliable reflection'*.[22]

As in the example we considered in section 2.4.1, the fraud of X is one instance of 'human frailty' through which a flaw may appear. There is also cause to question whether it can ever be reasonable to expect the registration of all property rights held in relation to land. As we will see at various points in the book, it is sometimes possible for such rights to be acquired informally, and it might be somewhat contradictory for a land law system both to allow B to acquire a property right without the use of any writing or other formality, and at the same time to require B to register that right if it is to have any chance of affecting C, a party later acquiring a right in the land. Similarly, we will see that such informal property rights of B may arise under a trust, and if those rights are then allowed to bind C even without their inclusion on the register, the curtain principle will be departed from; but this may be necessary in order to achieve a fair balance between B and C.

3 THE BASIC SCHEME OF THE LRA 2002

So far, we have seen that: (i) there are good reasons why registration is particularly important in land law; (ii) those advantages of registration are maximized if registration of title is required; but (iii) nonetheless, a question remains as to precisely how a land registration system should operate. We can now focus on the LRA 2002 and its specific aims.

3.1 THE AIMS OF THE LRA 2002

The 2002 Act resulted from the Law Commission's work: in the following extract, the Law Commission[23] sets out its aims in producing the draft Bill that led to the Act.

Law Commission Report No 271, *Land Registration for the Twenty-First Century: A Conveyancing Revolution* (2001, [1.5]–[1.10])

The fundamental objective of the Bill is that, under the system of electronic dealing with land that it seeks to create, the register should be a complete and accurate reflection of the state of the title of the land at any given time, so that it is possible to investigate title to land on line, with the absolute minimum of additional enquiries and inspections.

Although that ultimate objective may seem an obvious one, its implications are considerable, and virtually all the changes that the Bill makes to the present law flow directly from it. The Bill is necessarily limited in its scope to registered land or to dealings with unregistered land in England and Wales that will trigger first registration. Although the great majority of titles are in fact now registered, there are still substantial amounts of land (particularly in rural areas) that are unregistered. However, as we explain in Part II, unregistered land has had its

---

[22] Ruoff, *An Englishman Looks at the Torrens System* (Sydney: The Lawbook Co, 1957) p 9.

[23] The 2001 Law Commission Report was a product of joint work between the Law Commission and HM Land Registry, but will be referred to here, for convenience, as the Law Commission's 2001 Report.

day. In the comparatively near future, it will be necessary to take steps to bring what is left of it on to the register.

The process of registration of title is conducted by the State through the agency of HM Land Registry. Indeed, the State guarantees the title to registered land. If, therefore, any person suffers loss as a result of some mistake or omission in the register of title, he or she is entitled to be indemnified for that loss. At present, there is no requirement that a disposition of registered land has to be entered in the register if it is to be effective. Even without registration, dispositions are valid not only between the parties to them, but as against many but not necessarily all third parties who subsequently acquire an interest in the same registered land. This is a necessity under the present law because there is a hiatus—called the "registration gap"[24]—between the making of any disposition and its subsequent registration. The transfer or grant has to be submitted to the Land Registry for registration, which inevitably takes some time. It would be wholly unacceptable for the transfer or grant to have no legal effect in that interim period. It should be noted that there are some interests in registered land, presently known as overriding interests, which are not protected in the register at all but which nonetheless bind *any* person who subsequently acquires an interest in the land affected. This is so whether or not that person knew of, or could readily have discovered, the existence of these interests.

If it is to be possible to achieve the fundamental objective of the Bill mentioned [above]—

1. all express dispositions of registered land will have to be appropriately protected on the register unless there are very good reasons for not doing so;

2. the categories of overriding interests will have to be very significantly reduced in scope; and

3. dispositions of registered land will have to be registered simultaneously, so that it becomes impossible to make most dispositions of registered land except by registering them.

The aim stated in (3) will be possible only if conveyancing practitioners are authorised to initiate the process of registration when dispositions of registered land are made by their clients. This is a very significant departure from present practice.

To achieve the goals stated [above] will also require a change in attitude.

There is a widely-held perception that it is unreasonable to expect people to register their rights over land. We find this puzzling given the overwhelming prevalence of registered title. Furthermore, the law has long required compliance with certain formal requirements for the transfer of interests in land and for contracts to sell or dispose of such interests. The wisdom of these requirements is not seriously questioned. We cannot see why the further step of registration should be regarded as so onerous. In any event, under the system of electronic conveyancing that we envisage (and for which the Bill makes provision), not only will the process of registration become very much easier, but the execution of the transaction in electronic form and its simultaneous registration will be inextricably linked.

These changes will necessarily alter the perception of title to land. It will be the fact of registration and registration alone that confers title. This is entirely in accordance with the fundamental principle of a conclusive register which underpins the Bill.

In order to understand the LRA 2002, it is crucial to understand its basic aims, as stated by the Law Commission in the extract above. It is possible to extract perhaps six basic points from the statement above, and we will examine four of those in this chapter. The fifth, the importance of e-conveyancing, will be discussed in Chapter 8, section 6.5.3, as well as in

---

[24] [The concept of the 'registration gap' is discussed in Chapter 8, section 6.5.]

Chapter 18, sections 1 and 2. Linked to this is a sixth idea, the elimination of the 'registration gap', which will be examined in Chapter 8, section 6.5.

Firstly, the Act clearly aims to prioritize dynamic security: to protect a third party (C) attempting to acquire a legal property right in land from the risk of being bound by a pre-existing, but hidden, property right. So, in the example given in section 2.4.1 above (where X fraudulently registers as the new holder of B's freehold and then transfers that freehold to C), we might expect the Act to protect C rather than B. Indeed, if it is truly 'the fact of registration and registration alone that confers title', we might expect C to win even if C knew about X's fraud. The application of the LRA 2002 to such a case will be examined in detail in Chapter 18, section 3. In section 3.2 below, we will examine the basic means used by the LRA 2002 to give such protection to C and will also consider a closely related case:[25] where X does not register as holding a right but X's fraud nonetheless results in C, without B's consent or knowledge, either replacing B as registered proprietor,[26] or acquiring a registered charge over B's land.[27]

Secondly, however, it seems that the prioritization of dynamic security is not absolute. the Law Commission's statement recognizes, as Ruoff did in the extract set out at section 2.5 above, that the register can never be complete and accurate: the mirror will never be perfect. Indeed, there is a tension inherent even in the single sentence that: 'the register should be a complete and accurate reflection of the state of the title of the land at any given time, so that it is possible to investigate title to land on line, with the absolute minimum of additional enquiries and inspections.' Of course, if the register really were complete and accurate, there would be no need for *any* further investigation of title: such enquiries would be eliminated, rather than minimized. Certainly, it would be dangerous for C to think that he or she can rely on the register with complete confidence and will *always* be fully protected from an unregistered, but pre-existing, property right of B. As noted in the extract above, for example, an overriding interest is a pre-existing property right of B that is capable of binding C even if it does not appear on the register, and, as we will see in section 3.2.2 below, the LRA 2002 certainly does not abolish such rights.

Thirdly, the extract above makes reference to the possibility of indemnity payments: 'the State guarantees the title to registered land. If, therefore, any person suffers loss as a result of some mistake or omission in the register of title, he or she is entitled to be indemnified for that loss.' As noted in section 2.4.1 above, such payments can play an important role in achieving a balance between B and C, and they are certainly a feature of the scheme under the LRA 2002. Again, however, the need for such payments underlines the point that C cannot expect the register to be complete and accurate: there may be a 'mistake or omission'. We will consider the role of indemnity payments under the LRA 2002 in section 3.2.1 below.

Fourthly, the Law Commission emphasize the need for a 'change in attitude'. The primary focus here is perhaps on the attitude of parties, such as B, who hold a property right in land and may previously have expected that right to be capable of binding C even without its being noted on the register. As we have already noted, the possibility of B's right being an overriding interest still exists under the LRA 2002, and so it would be wrong to think that

---

[25] This form of case can be called a 'two party' case, to contrast with the 'three party' case where X fraudulently registers and then deals with C. The Law Commission, in its 2016 Consultation Paper, *Updating the Land Registration Act 2002*, refers to the two party case as the 'AB scenario' and the three party case as the 'ABC scenario': see Chapter 18, section 3.1.1.

[26] As in e.g. *Fitzwilliam v Richall Holding Services Ltd* [2013] EWHC 86 (Ch).

[27] As in e.g. *Swift 1st Ltd v Chief Land Registrar* [2015] Ch 602 (CA): see section 3.3.2.

such registration is always required of B. The secondary focus may be on the views of the judges applying the provisions of the LRA 2002. As we will see in section 3.3, the approach taken by judges when interpreting the LRA 2002 has to be considered to see how the Act, in practice, balances the claims of B and C. There is also a more fundamental question, to be considered in section 3.4 below, of the extent to which general principles of property law, not expressly barred by the LRA 2002, may still operate in relation to registered land. Is the system to be seen as wholly self-contained, or can judges modify its effects by relying on well-established concepts that were features of English land law long before any system of registration of title was introduced?

3.2 THE PROTECTION OF REGISTERED PARTIES

We noted in section 2.2 above that a registration system may help to protect C, a party aiming to acquire a property right, against two, linked risks: (i) the risk that the party with whom he or she deals (A) may not have the power to give C such a right; *and* (ii) the risk that, even if A does have that power, another party (B) may have a pre-existing property right in the land that binds C. We can see how the LRA 2002 protects C against each of those two risks by the attribution of legal consequences to C's registration, or to B's failure to have a right noted on the register.

3.2.1 Acquisition of title: basic position

If A is registered as holding a legal freehold or leasehold in land, the fact of A's registration operates in a *positive* sense, and has an impact on the acquisition question: simply by virtue of A's registration, A is deemed to hold the registered right.[28] This result is produced by s 58 of the LRA 2002.[29]

Land Registration Act 2002, s 58

Conclusiveness

(1) If, on the entry of a person in the register as the proprietor of a legal estate, the legal estate would not otherwise be vested in him, it shall be deemed to be vested in him as a result of the registration.

(2) Subsection (1) does not apply where the entry is made in pursuance of a registrable disposition in relation to which some other registration requirement remains to be met.

Where s 58(1) operates, registration can be seen as substantive, or constitutive: it is the fact of registration that gives A the right and which also, of course, gives C the right after a registered transfer. Such registration rules can thus protect C against the risk that A may not have the power to give C good title. The constitutive operation of s 58(1) is therefore crucial to a key

---

[28] If, in contrast, A attempts to transfer A's registered freehold or lease to B, but B is *not* registered as the new holder of the estate, then B does *not* acquire that legal estate, which remains with A: see LRA 2002, s 27, discussed in Chapter 8, section 6.4. In that sense, the registration scheme can operate negatively: a failure to register can prevent a party acquiring a legal property right.

[29] See too Chapter 8, section 6.6.

idea of the LRA 2002: that it is a system of *title by registration* rather than of registration of title:[30] in other words, the act of registration creates title, and does not merely record it.

Not all rights can be registered in this way. Section 58(1) operates only where A has a *legal estate*: for the purposes of the Act,[31] that term includes not only a legal freehold and a legal leasehold, but also a legal interest in land (such as a charge held by a bank or building society): we will examine such rights in Chapter 5. However, it clearly does not include equitable interests: so, if B, for example, has only an equitable interest in land (such rights will be considered in Chapter 6) B will never be able to show an entitlement to that right simply as a result of registering it. Moreover, not all legal estates can be registered in this way: in general, for example, a leasehold of seven years or less cannot be registered. If a party has an interest that cannot be registered in its own right so as to gain protection under s 58, it may well still be possible for that party to have that right noted on the register by a notice, or by a restriction. So, for example, where A holds a registered freehold, and B claims an equitable lease in the land, B might have a notice entered on the register: in that sense, B might be said to have registered his or her right. However, the entry of a notice does *not* give B the protection of s 58, and so the existence of the notice, by itself, does not give any reassurance to a party who might wish to buy B's equitable lease. The role of the notice is different, as we will see in section 3.2.2.

If A has a registered freehold or lease, the protection given to C by means of s 58 is buttressed by the provisions of ss 23 and 24 of the LRA 2002. Section 24 confirms that, by virtue of his or her registration, A is able to '*exercise owner's powers*' in relation to that legal estate.

Land Registration Act 2002, s 24

A person is entitled to exercise owner's powers in relation to a registered estate or charge if he is—

(a) the registered proprietor, or

(b) entitled to be registered as the proprietor.

The definition of '*owner's powers*' is found in s 23:

Land Registration Act 2002, s 23

(1) Owner's powers in relation to a registered estate consist of—

    (a) power to make a disposition of any kind permitted by the general law in relation to an interest of that description, other than a mortgage by demise or sub-demise, and

    (b) power to charge the estate at law with the payment of money.

(2) Owner's powers in relation to a registered charge consist of—

    (a) power to make a disposition of any kind permitted by the general law in relation to an interest of that description, other than a legal sub-mortgage, and

    (b) power to charge at law with the payment of money indebtedness secured by the registered charge.

---

[30] See Law Com No 271 (2001) 1.10.
[31] LRA 2002, s 132(1), adopting the same meaning for the term 'legal estate' as used under LPA 1925, s 1(4). See further Chapter 5, section 3.

The combined effect of ss 58, 23, and 24 is to provide reassurance for C when entering into a transaction with A, a party with a registered right. For example, if A is registered with freehold title, C can assume that A has the power to grant C a valid charge over the land. As Norris J put it in *Pye v Stodday Land Ltd*,[32] the effect of s 24, is that: '*Shortly put, subject to the limitations provided in s 23 and any other specific limitations,*[33] *the registered proprietor of the estate has power to make an effective disposition of any kind permitted by the general law, and has all the general powers of dealing of a natural person who holds an interest of that kind in unregistered land.*'

3.2.2 Acquisition of title: C's protection is not absolute

It should not be thought that the protection given to C under ss 58, 23, and 24 is absolute. The LRA 2002 was never intended to ensure that C, a party acquiring for value a registered estate, was absolutely secure: it rather set up a system of '*qualified indefeasibility*'.[34] It therefore allows for the possibility that the register may be changed to remove C's right.

Land Registration Act 2002, Schedule 4

Alteration of the Register

1. In this Schedule, references to rectification, in relation to alteration of the register, are to alteration which—

    (a) involves the correction of a mistake, and

    (b) prejudicially affects the title of a registered proprietor.

2.—(1) The court[35] may make an order for alteration of the register for the purpose of—

    (a) correcting a mistake, and

    (b) bringing the register up to date, or

    (c) giving effect to any estate, right or interest excepted from the effect of registration.

    [...]

3.—(1) This paragraph applies to the power under paragraph 2, so far as relating to rectification.

    (2) If alteration affects the title of the proprietor of a registered estate in land, no order may be made under paragraph 2 without the proprietor's consent in relation to land in his possession unless –

    (a) he has by fraud or lack of proper care caused or substantially contributed to the mistake, or

    (b) it would for any other reason be unjust for the alteration not to be made.

    (3) If in any proceedings the court has power to make an order under paragraph 2, it must do so, unless there are exceptional circumstances which justify its not doing so.

As far as the protection afforded to C is concerned, the key provision is clearly Sch 4, para 2(1)(a), which allows for the register to be changed for the purpose of correcting a

---

[32] [2016] EWHC 2454 (Ch), [2016] 4 WLR 168 at [33].

[33] [Note that s 26 of the LRA 2002 allows C to assume that A's owner's powers are free from any limitations, except those which appear in an entry on the register. Such limitations are entered on the register by means of a restriction: see Chapter 16, section 5.]

[34] Law Com No 254 (1998), [8.47].

[35] [Substantially the same powers to alter the register are given to the registrar in Sch 4, para 5.]

mistake. Where this is done and C's title is prejudicially affected, the change is known, in the terminology of Sch 4, para 1, as a '*rectification*'. This demonstrates that C's title is not absolutely secure. An example is provided by *Baxter v Mannion*.[36]

Mr Mannion was the registered proprietor of land, and Mr Baxter claimed to have been in adverse possession of that land for over ten years. As we will see in Chapter 9, Sch 6 of the LRA 2002 provides a mechanism for an adverse possessor in such a case to apply to be registered as proprietor of the land. Mr Baxter made such an application, and Mr Mannion did not object within the time limit imposed by Sch 6. As a result, Mr Baxter was registered as the new proprietor. When Mr Mannion applied for the register to be changed, it was found that, on the facts, Mr Baxter had not been in adverse possession of the land for the minimum ten-year period required by Sch 6, and the register could therefore be changed, as Mr Baxter's registration was a 'mistake'. Mr Baxter appealed on the basis that his registration was not mistaken, as the procedure under Sch 6 had been followed. The Court of Appeal roundly rejected that argument, and Jacob LJ stated that there was no reason to give a '*special, limited meaning*' to the term 'mistake', and that: '*[a] registration obtained by a person not entitled to apply for it would be mistaken*'.[37] It was noted that Mr Baxter was in possession of the land at the time of the application for the register to be changed, and so Sch 4, para 3(2), as set out above, applied to place a further hurdle in the way of a change to the register. On the facts, however, the Court of Appeal found that it would be unjust not to change the register; it was true that Mr Mannion had failed to meet the deadline for objecting to the registration of Mr Baxter, but Jacob LJ poetically stated that: '*Mere failure to operate bureaucratic machinery is as thistledown to Mr Mannion losing his land and Mr Baxter getting it when he had never been in adverse possession.*'[38]

Similarly, consider a case in which C Bank attempts to assert a registered legal charge against A, the initial registered proprietor, only for A to point out that her signature had been forged on the document purporting to create the charge: as a result of the fraud, the register can be changed so as to remove C's registered charge.[39] A more difficult situation arises where the fraudster, X, who has had no dealings with A themselves, acquires registered title, then grants a charge to C Bank. X's registration is of course a mistake, but C might argue that, as X was in fact the registered proprietor at the time when he or she granted the charge to C, the registration of the charge is *not* a mistake. The courts initially had some difficulties in deciding whether or not C's registration, in such a case,[40] can be seen as a mistake, and we will consider the point in more detail in Chapter 18, section 3.1.2. It will be seen there that the position has now been clarified and that, in such a case, C's registration *is* seen as mistaken, and so the register can be changed not only to remove the X's registered title, but also to remove C's charge.[41] In general,[42] the removal of C's right is clearly a *rectification*, as

---

[36] [2011] EWCA Civ 120, [2011] 2 All ER 574.

[37] [2011] EWCA Civ 120, [2011] 2 All ER 574, [33].

[38] [2011] EWCA Civ 120, [2011] 2 All ER 574, [42].

[39] This was the background to *Swift 1st Ltd v Chief Land Registrar* [2015] Ch 602, discussed in section 3.3.2.

[40] As noted at n 25, such a case can be referred to as a 'three party case'; it differs from a 'two party' case such as *Baxter v Mannion* as C, the party resisting rectification, did acquire a right with the consent of the party (the fraudster) who was, at the time of the disposition to C, the registered proprietor.

[41] See e.g. *Gold Harp Properties Ltd v Macleod* [2015] 1 WLR 1249; Law Com CP No 227, [13.29].

[42] The qualification is necessary as, in the case where B happens to have been in actual occupation of the land at the time of the disposition from X to C, it can be argued that B has an overriding interest (see section 3.2.4) that binds C, and so the change to remove C's charge does not cause loss to C, as it simply updates the

set out in in the Sch 4, para (1)(a), rather than an alteration, as it clearly does prejudicially affect C's title.

Whilst the possibility of rectification must be borne in mind, two points mean that the protection provided to C by s 58, and ss 23 and 24, is still very important.

Limits on rectification where C is in possession

If C is in possession of the land to which his or her registered title relates then, even if the registration can be shown to be the result of a mistake, rectification will be granted only if C:[43] '*has, by fraud or lack of proper care caused or substantially contributed to the mistake*' or if '*it would for any other reason be unjust for the alteration not to be made*'. This restriction on rectification is discussed in Chapter 18, section 3.2.1.

In *Baxter v Mannion*, as discussed earlier, this additional protection did not in fact assist Mr Baxter, as the Court of Appeal held that, given his failure to establish adverse possession for the minimum period, it would clearly be unjust to allow him to retain, for free, the title initially held by Mr Mannion. However, it should not be thought that the mere fact of a mistaken registration necessarily means that it would be unjust not to alter the registration; if that were the case, after all, the additional protection in Sch 4, para 3(2) would be completely toothless.

The decision of the Court of Appeal in *Walker v Burton*[44] provides an unusual, but memorable, example of the practical protection provided by the LRA 2002. The dispute was between 'irate villagers in Ireby (Lancashire) and the Burtons, who are more recent newcomers to the village'. It concerned a moorland fell to the north of the village. After buying a farmhouse, the Burtons had registered their claimed Lordship of the Manor. As part of that lordship, they claimed title to Ireby Fell and were registered as its proprietors. The villagers objected, and they showed that the supposed Lordship had long since ceased to exist. Although the basis of the Burtons' claim to the Fell thus disappeared, the fact of their registration ensured that they nonetheless had good title to the Fell. The Burtons' right would therefore continue to be valid unless and until the register was changed, and their title removed. The Court of Appeal, however, confirmed the decision of a Deputy Adjudicator[45] that the villagers' application for such rectification should not succeed.[46] The Burtons were in possession of the land; they had not been fraudulent, nor had they failed to take proper care;[47] and the villagers had not shown that it would be unjust not to rectify. The villagers were not claiming that they had title to the Fell; indeed, no one other than the Burtons had come forward to claim such title,[48] and it was

---

register to reflect the fact that C is bound by B's overriding interest. This difficult point (often referred to as the '*Malory 2* argument': see e.g. Law Com CP No 227 (2016) [13.60]-[13.76]) is explored in Chapter 18, section 4.2.

[43] LRA 2002, Sch 4, para 6(2).   [44] [2013] EWCA Civ 1228; [2014] 1 P & CR 9.

[45] Such Land Registry Adjudicators had powers to rectify the register under Sch 4 of the 2002 Act. As from 1 July 2013, their role is now performed by the Land Registration division of the Property Chamber (First-tier Tribunal).

[46] The decision had already been upheld by a Deputy Judge: the appeal to the Court of Appeal was a second appeal.

[47] The Burtons honestly believed that they were entitled to the Lordship and, with it, the Fell: that belief derived from a document of 1836 and it was '*unreasonable to expect [Mr Burton] to go back beyond that in order to research the earlier origins of the Lordship*': [2013] EWCA Civ 1228; [2014] 1 P & CR, [98] (Mummery LJ).

[48] The villagers' argument was that the Fell was vested in the Crown, but the Crown had not been joined as a party and, whilst it was aware of the proceedings, had chosen not to intervene: see [2013] EWCA Civ 1228; [2014] 1 P & CR 9 [17]–[20] and [90]–[93]. Mummery LJ described the Crown's caution as '*understandable. It is usually unwise to intervene in other peoples' litigation, especially if it is about property to which you make no claim. The ownership of the Fell has been uncertain for many years.*'

a 'relevant consideration that the Fell should be owned by someone rather than left in limbo with continuing uncertainty about title to it'.[49] Moreover, the Burtons had invested 'time, effort and money on improving the Fell and its management, had discouraged harmful practices, such as tipping waste and use of motorised vehicles, had used the property as an amenity and had entered into commitments on which they and others relied'.[50]

Indemnity payments

Even if rectification does occur, C will generally qualify for an indemnity payment, compensating C for loss caused by such a change to the register.

Land Registration Act 2002, Schedule 8

Indemnities

1. (1) A person is entitled to be indemnified by the registrar if he suffers loss by reason of—
    (a) rectification of the register,
    (b) a mistake whose correction would involve rectification of the register,
    [...]
    (2) For the purposes of sub-paragaph 1(a)—
    (a) [...]
    (b) the proprietor of a registered estate or charge claiming in good faith under a forged disposition is, where the register is rectified, to be regarded as having suffered loss by reason of such rectification as if the disposition had not been forged.
    [...]
(5)—(1) No indemnity is payable under this Schedule on account of any loss suffered by a claimant—
    (a) wholly or partly as a result of his own fraud, or
    (b) wholly as a result of his own lack of proper care.
    (2) Where any loss is suffered by a claimant partly as a result of his own lack of proper care, any indemnity payable to him is to be reduced to such extent as is fair having regard to his share in the responsibility for the loss.
    (3) For the purposes of this paragraph any fraud or lack of care on the part of a person from whom the claimant derives title (otherwise than under a disposition for valuable consideration which is registered or protected by an entry in the register) is to be treated as if it were fraud or lack of care on the part of the claimant.

The basic effect of Sch 8 is that, in the case of rectification, an indemnity will be paid to C unless the loss was suffered by C wholly or partly as a result of C's fraud, or wholly as a result of C's lack of proper care.[51] As we noted in section 2.4.1, the possibility of such indemnity plays an important role in balancing the interests of C with those of other parties, and

---

[49] [2013] EWCA Civ 1228; [2014] 1 P & CR 9, [102] (Mummery LJ).
[50] [2013] EWCA Civ 1228; [2014] 1 P & CR 9, [105] (Mummery LJ).
[51] In a case where, e.g., C acquires his or her right as a gift from X, and so not for valuable consideration, then X's fraud or lack of proper care is attributed to C: Sch 8, para 5(3).

it also gives effect to the insurance principle discussed in section 2.5, as C's protection will sometimes come in the way of money, by way of indemnity, rather than by a continuing entitlement to the land itself. Consider our example where B is the initial registered proprietor, and X, a fraudster, is then registered in place of B (without having dealt with B at all) and grants a charge to C Bank. If the register is rectified to restore B's right and remove C Bank's charge then, assuming it used proper care, C Bank will receive a full indemnity under Sch 8, para 1(1)(a) to compensate it for loss caused by the rectification. In contrast, if rectification is not granted, but it is recognized that C Bank's registration was a mistake, then B will receive a full indemnity under Sch 8, para 1(1)(b), assuming again that B used proper care. It is worth noting that the value of C's indemnity will depend on the value of its right immediately before the register is rectified, whereas B's indemnity, as the law currently stands,[52] depends on the value of its right at the time *'when the mistake which caused the loss was made':*[53] this will be an earlier point, when the value of the land may have been different.

3.2.3 A defence against pre-existing non-registered rights: basic position

If C plans to acquire for value a right from A, who has a registered estate, the LRA 2002 also gives C protection against the risk that, whilst A has the power to transfer title, another party (B) may have a hidden, pre-existing property right in the land that binds C. If B's right is noted on the register, then of course it will be a simple matter for C to discover it. If, B's right is not so noted, then C's protection comes from the *defences* question: C can take priority over B's pre-existing right by relying on s 29 of the LRA 2002.[54]

Land Registration Act 2002, s 29

Effect of registered dispositions: estates

(1) If a registrable disposition of a registered estate is made for valuable consideration, completion of the disposition by registration has the effect of postponing to the interest under the disposition any interest affecting the estate immediately before the disposition whose priority is not protected at the time of registration.

(2) For the purposes of subsection (1), the priority of an interest is protected –

    (a) in any case, if the interest –

        (i)   is a registered charge or the subject of a notice in the register.

        (ii) falls within any of the paragraphs of Schedule 3, or

        (iii) appears from the register to be excepted from the effect of registration, and

    (b) in the case of a disposition of a leasehold estate, if the burden of the interest is incident to the estate.

---

[52] The Law Commission has recently proposed a change to this position: Law Com CP No 227 (2016) [14.159]; see Chapter 18, section 3.2.1.

[53] LRA 2002, Sch 8, para 6(b).

[54] If C instead deals with A, the registered proprietor of a charge, then C's protection (which is essentially the same) derives instead from s 30 of the LRA 2002.

> (3) Subsection 2(a)(ii) does not apply to an interest which has been the subject of a notice in the register at any time since the coming into force of this section.
>
> (4) Where the grant of a leasehold estate in land out of a registered estate does not involve a registrable disposition, this section has effect as if –
>
> (a) the grant involved such a disposition; and
>
> (b) the disposition was registered at the time of the grant.

The wording of s 29 is necessarily technical, and we will return to consider it in more detail in Chapter 16, section 2, but its basic effect can be simply summarized. If A has a registered freehold or lease, and C acquires for value from A, and registers, a legal estate, then C will have priority over any pre-existing property right of B that was not noted on the register *unless* B's right falls within the list of rights set out in the paragraphs of Sch 3.

One way of understanding s 29 is to see it as giving a particular defence to C against a pre-existing property right of B. Two crucial requirements of that defence are C's registration,[55] and B's failure to have his or her right noted on the register. We can now see why, in a case where B does not have a legal estate or interest that can be registered substantively, or constitutively, so as to gain the protection of s 58, it is still wise for B to have a notice entered on the register. In our example in 3.2.1, where A has a registered freehold and B has an equitable lease, if B has a notice entered on the register, then that will ensure that if A later sells the freehold to C, C will not be able to use the s 29 defence against B's right. The entry of such a notice does not mean that B is deemed to have the right, so it does not operate positively; but it does operate negatively in the sense that, by protecting the priority of B's right, it prevents C later using the s 29 defence.

Not all rights can be protected by an entry of a notice on the register: as we will see in Chapter 16, section 5, if B's equitable interest arises under a trust, for example, B's only option is to have a restriction entered on the register.[56] This does not, however, protect the priority of B's right and, in practice, the restriction will simply alert C to the possibility of using a different defence (the overreaching defence)[57] against B's right. This treatment of rights under trusts is consistent with the curtain principle, discussed in section 2.5. It does not mean, however, that C will always be able to use the s 29 defence against B's right under a trust: if B's right is not overreached, then like any property right, it may still be capable of binding C if B is in actual occupation of the land at the relevant time.[58] This is because of the protection afforded by Schedule 3 to particular types of pre-existing right, which we will now examine.

3.2.4 A defence against pre-existing non-registered rights: C's protection is not absolute

In a case where B's pre-existing right does fall within the list of rights set out in Schedule 3, it can be called an *'overriding interest'*: as we saw in the extract set out in section 3.1, such a right is capable of binding C even if not noted on the register. It is therefore clear that, even

---

[55] LRA 2002, s 29(4) extends the s 29 defence to C where C acquires a legal lease that, because of its short length, cannot be constitutively registered under s 58.

[56] LRA 2002, s 33(a)(i).   [57] See Chapter 17.

[58] LRA 2002, Sch 3, para 2: see Chapter 16, section 4.21.

if C meets the threshold criteria under s 29, by registering a right acquired for valuable consideration, C's protection against a pre-existing non-registered right of B is not absolute.

We saw earlier that the possibility of rectification weakens the protection given to C against the risk of A's not having the power to transfer good title to C. Similarly, the possibility of an overriding interest—a pre-existing property right that can bind C even if it has not been noted on the register—reduces C's protection against the risk of being bound by a property right of B. Indeed, the reduction is greater, as it is a core rule of the LRA 2002 (as it was under the LRA 1925)[59] that if the register is changed simply to give effect to an overriding interest, no indemnity is payable to C.[60]

The effect of overriding interests notwithstanding, s 29 of the LRA 2002 gives C very useful protection against the risk of being bound by a hidden property right of B. First, the LRA 2002 did, as indicated in the extract set out in section 3.1 above, reduce the list of overriding interests.[61] We will examine the contents of that list in Chapter 16, section 4. Second, if B's pre-existing property right has not been noted on the register, and is not an overriding interest, then s 29 can give C a defence, even if C knew, or could easily have discovered, B's right.

The decision of the Court of Appeal in *Chaudhary v Yavuz*[62] provides a good demonstration of the protection given to C—and also of the truth, universally acknowledged by devotees of television soap operas that, in the East of London, it may be risky to rely on an informal agreement with one's neighbour.[63] B (Chaudhary) relied on a staircase on the land of A (Chaudhary's neighbour, Vijay) as a means of access, via an attached balcony, to the upper floors of B's property. The staircase and the balcony it led to had been built under an informal agreement with A, and B paid the costs of construction. It was found by the first instance judge, and accepted in the Court of Appeal, that the dealings between A and B, although they were never formalized, gave B an equitable interest in A's land, arising as a result of proprietary estoppel.[64] A later sold his registered title to Yavuz (C) who then essentially dismantled the staircase. B argued that such action by C was inconsistent with B's equitable interest, which gave B a right, binding on C, to use the staircase. Lloyd LJ pointed out that if B, before A's sale to C, had ensured that a notice of his claimed property right was entered on the register, then C '*would have taken subject to the rights to which the notice related: see s 29(2)(a)(i) [of the LRA 2002]*'.[65]

As B had, however, failed to have such a notice entered on the register C invoked the defence under s 29: C had paid for, and was now registered as holding, a legal estate in the land and B had not protected the priority of his right. A crucial question, then, was whether B's right was overriding: was it included in any of the paragraphs of Sch 3? Certain property rights qualify as overriding because of their content;[66] B's right was however an equitable interest and such rights are overriding only if B was in actual occupation of the relevant

---

[59] See *re Chowood's Registered Land* [1933] Ch 574.

[60] Arguments for amending the legislation so as to change that position are considered in Chapter 18, section 4.3.

[61] For example, rights 'acquired or in the course of being acquired' through adverse possession were overriding under s 70(1)(f) of the LRA 1925, but are not protected under Sch 3 of the LRA 2002.

[62] [2013] Ch 249.

[63] See McFarlane, 'Eastenders, Neighbours, and Upstairs, Downstairs' [2013] Conv 74.

[64] See Chapter 10 for a general discussion of proprietary estoppel, and Chapter 10, section 4.3 for specific discussion of how rights arising under the doctrine may bind a third party.

[65] [2013] Ch 249 at [9].

[66] See, for example, Sch 3, para 1 (certain types of legal lease: see Chapter 19, section 4.1) and Sch 3, para 3 (certain types of legal easement: see Chapter 22, section 4.1).

land at the time when C committed to acquiring his right in that land.[67] The first instance judge had found that B had been in actual occupation of the staircase/balcony structure, principally because of the frequent use that B's tenants had made of the staircase when going to and from the upper floor flats on B's land. The Court of Appeal disagreed, with Lloyd LJ making the point that use is not the same as occupation and there was no need to assume that *someone* must have been in occupation of the staircase. As a result, C was able to use the s 29 defence against B's pre-existing property right. That was the case even though B had a strong argument that his right, even if not noted on the register, was easily discoverable: the staircase/balcony structure was an obvious feature of A's land, and was clearly a means of access to B's neighbouring property. Lloyd LJ emphasized that, to take advantage of the s 29 defence, C does not need to be in 'good faith' or to show that he was unaware of B's right.[68] He cited with approval the following analysis of Sir Christopher Slade in an earlier case, decided under the LRA 1925:[69] '*There is no general principle which renders it unconscionable for a purchaser of land to rely on want of registration of a claim against registered land, even though he took with express notice of it. A decision to the contrary would defeat the purpose of the legislature in introducing the system of registration embodied in the 1925 Act.*' Indeed, Lloyd LJ took the view that such an approach '*is even more amply justified under the 2002 Act than it was before.*'[70] As the LRA 2002 was intended by the Law Commission to strengthen the protection available to C (see section 3.1 above) its scheme would be undermined by introducing a good faith, or absence of notice, requirement into the operation of the s 29 defence.

3.3 LOOKING OUTSIDE THE REGISTRATION SYSTEM

We have set out so far the basic scheme of the LRA 2002, looking at both the ways in which it provides protection to C, thus promoting dynamic security, and also the limits on that protection. A crucial further question, however, is the extent to which judges might allow more general principles of property law to modify the operation of that basic scheme. We noted in section 3.1 above that the Law Commission Report which led to the LRA 2002 called for a '*change in attitude*'. This can be seen as a call for the judges interpreting and applying the rules to enhance the protection available to C, by applying the rules strictly and by thus minimizing the role of the general principles of property law that apply outside the registration system. Certainly, there was some evidence that judges had *not* adopted such an approach under the LRA 1925.

3.3.1 Looking outside the LRA 1925

In *Peffer v Rigg,*[71] the court had to apply the provisions of the LRA 1925 in a case where B had a pre-existing equitable interest in land owned by A. A then transferred the registered title to C, who knew about B's equitable interest. B's interest had not, however, been noted on the

---

[67] See Sch 3, para 2: examined in detail in Chapter 16, section 4.2.

[68] In some circumstances, C's conduct may be such as to give B a new, direct right against C: see, for example, *Lyus v Prowsa Developments Ltd* [1982] 1 WLR 1044, and the discussion in *Lloyd v Dugdale* [2002] 2 P & CR 13. Mere knowledge or notice by C does not suffice, however: in *Lyus*, the key point was that C was regarded as '*reneging on a positive stipulation in favour of [B] in the bargain under which [C] acquired the land*': [1982] 1 WLR 1044 *per* Dillon J at 1054-5. For the circumstances in which such a promise by C can give rise to a direct right for B, see Chapter 7, section 3.3.

[69] *Lloyd v Dugdale* [2002] 2 P & CR 13 at [50], cited [2013] Ch 249 at [67].

[70] [2013] Ch 249 at [68].   [71] [1977] 1 WLR 285.

register; and it did not count as an overriding interest, as B was not in actual occupation of the land at the time of A's disposition to C. It therefore seemed that, under s 20 of the LRA 1925, which performed the function now carried out by s 29 of the LRA 2002, C had a good defence to B's pre-existing equitable interest, and so would not be bound by it. Indeed, s 59 of the 1925 Act stated that, overriding interests aside, a purchaser such as C was not to be concerned with rights not on the register, '*whether he has or has not notice thereof*'.

Under the general law of property, however, the position would be different: the general rule is that a pre-existing equitable interest does bind a purchaser who buys with knowledge of that interest. As a result, Graham J, relying on s 3 of the LRA 1925, which defined a purchaser as a '*purchaser in good faith for valuable consideration*', held that C's knowledge of B's equitable interest meant that B was not in good faith, did not count as a purchaser, and so could not take advantage of the lack of registration defence provided by s 20 of the LRA 1925. The reasoning of the judge was rightly criticized: the reference to 'good faith' came in s 3 of the Act, which set out some general definitions, to be applied only '*unless the context otherwise requires*', and s 59 of the Act made clear that notice of B's earlier equitable interest should not prevent C from using the lack of registration defence.

Certainly, the LRA 2002 makes *very* clear that C's knowledge of B's equitable interest will *not* prevent C from relying on the lack of registration defence in s 29 of the LRA 2002: as we saw in section 3.2.2, that point was confirmed by the Court of Appeal in *Chaudhary v Yavuz*.[72] *Peffer* was not, however, the only example of a court taking into account general property law principles in order to limit the effect of the registration scheme imposed by the LRA 1925. In *Malory Enterprises Ltd v Cheshire Homes (UK) Ltd*,[73] the Court of Appeal had to consider the following situation. Malory Enterprises Ltd (B), a British Virgin Islands company, was the registered proprietor of a derelict development site in Manchester. A different company (X), also called Malory Enterprises, was dishonestly set up and registered in the UK. As a result of the deception, X succeeded in obtaining a land certificate in its name for that same land, and then purported to sell the land to Cheshire Homes (C), which registered as the new holder of the estate, in place of B. When B discovered this, it asked for its registered title to be reinstated, and also claimed damages from C, on the basis that, by taking possession of the land without B's permission, C had committed the tort of trespass. As a matter of general principle, it seems clear that there should at least be a possibility of rectification, as C's registration was the result of a mistake; and that, assuming C was neither fraudulent nor careless, if rectification were ordered, C would then qualify for an indemnity. The scheme of the LRA 1925, like that of the LRA 2002, certainly allows for that result.

As part of its consideration of B's claim for damages for trespass, however, the Court of Appeal noted that there was another means of protecting B, which did *not* depend on rectification. Arden LJ noted that s 69 of the LRA 1925—which deemed the registered proprietor to have the legal estate in the land vested in him[74]— '*deals only with the legal estate*.'[75] This meant that, whilst s 69 ensured that, despite the fraud of X, C had to be regarded as holding a legal freehold, B could rely on general property law principles to argue that, as a victim of fraud, and as a party who never even attempted to transfer its title to X, B had kept an *equitable* interest

---

[72] [2013] Ch 249 at [67]. The lack of registration defence provided by LRA 2002 s 29 makes no reference to good faith: see too Law Com No 254 (1998) [3.46] and Law Com No 271 (2001) [5.16].

[73] [2002] Ch 216.

[74] Thus, fulfilling a similar function to s 58 of the LRA 2002: see section 3.2.1 above.

[75] [2002] Ch 216 at 232.

in the land.[76] That analysis, often now referred to as the '*Malory* 1' argument,[77] causes some problems for a party such as C. In particular, it means that, if B was in actual occupation of the land at the relevant time, B's equitable interest would be an overriding interest and so C could not use the lack of registration defence against it. This would mean that, even if the register were changed so as to remove C, C would not get an indemnity, as C was all along bound by B's overriding interest, and so would not suffer any loss as a result of the change to the register. [78]

The Court of Appeal's decision in *Malory* thus provides further evidence that, under the LRA 1925, at least, some judges were prepared to rely on general principles of property law when interpreting the provisions of the registration system. The decision attracted criticism for precisely that reason.[79] For example, Harpum—the Law Commissioner chiefly responsible for the work that led to the LRA 2002—regarded the approach in *Malory*, with its recognition of an equitable interest of B that existed even after B's loss of registered title, as providing a means by which '*the scheme laid down in the LRA 1925 for dealing with mistakes in the register by means of rectification and indemnity will be circumvented. The system of rectification and indemnity goes to the root of the system of registered conveyancing, and there would be grave hardship if it could be side-stepped in this way.*' [80] Indeed, as we will see in section 3.3.2, the Court of Appeal has since ruled that the '*Malory* 1 argument' is incorrect, even as a matter of interpreting the LRA 1925, and the decision in *Malory* on that point was given *per incuriam*.

3.3.2 Looking outside the LRA 2002

We noted earlier, the LRA 2002 leaves no room for the view, taken in *Peffer v Rigg*, that C's knowledge of B's pre-existing equitable interest will prevent C from using the lack of registration defence against B's right. The decision in *Malory*, however, was made only four days before the LRA 2002 received its Royal Assent. If the decision had come out earlier, it might well have been the case that the LRA 2002 could have been drafted so as to make clear that such an approach should not be taken under the new Act. It seems to be the case, however, that those concerned with drafting the LRA 2002 had not considered that such an interpretation could be given to the words of the 1925 Act, and so did not perceive a need to significantly alter the relevant wording. Indeed, the relevant provisions of the LRA 2002 have essentially the same wording as their equivalents in the LRA 1925:[81] s 58 of the 2002 Act, in setting out the conclusive effect of registration, refers only to the position as regards the *legal* estate, so it might still be argued by B that, where X's forgery leads to a mistaken registration, B has retained an equitable interest in the land. In the following extract, however, the Court of Appeal rejected that argument; not by distinguishing between the effect of the 2002 Act and the 1925 Act, but rather by taking the dramatic step of finding that the

---

[76] We will examine equitable interests, and the distinction between such rights and legal property rights, in Chapter 6.

[77] Law Com CP No 227 (2016), [13.43]–[13.59].

[78] For the position under the LRA 1925, see e.g. *re Chowood's Registered Land* [1933] Ch 574: no indemnity payable if C is bound by an overriding interest of B.

[79] Further criticisms of *Malory* are noted by Newey J in *Fitzwilliam v Richall Holding Services Ltd* [2013] EWHC 86 (Ch) at [75]: see the extract in section 3.3.2 below.

[80] Harpum, 'Registered Land: A Law Unto Itself?' in *Rationalizing Property, Equity and Trusts: Essays for Edward Burn* (ed Getzler, Oxford: OUP, 2002) pp 198–9.

[81] A point confirmed by Newey J in *Fitzwilliam v Richall Holding Services Ltd* [2013] EWHC 86 (Ch), [2013] 1 P & CR 19.

decision in *Malory* was wrong as to the effect of a forged transfer on B, as it had overlooked both a relevant authority and relevant parts of the LRA 1925. The '*Malory* 1' argument was thus incorrect as an interpretation of the LRA 1925, and so necessarily also incorrect as an interpretation of the essentially identical provisions retained in the LRA 2002.

Swift 1ˢᵗ Ltd v Chief Land Registrar
[2015] EWCA Civ 330, [2015] Ch 602

Rani (B) was the registered proprietor of her home in Essex. Using a forged document, X purported to grant a charge over the land to Swift 1ˢᵗ Ltd (C), as security for money advanced by C to X. When X failed to pay, C sought possession of the land from B. B successfully opposed those proceedings and it was agreed by C that, given the forgery, the charge should be removed from the register. C, naturally enough, then wished to obtain an indemnity payment from the Land Registry: after all, it would seem a clear case for the application of the insurance principle discussed in section 2.5. The Registrar, however, refused to make such a payment. The Registrar's main argument was that the change to the register simply gave effect to B's pre-existing equitable interest; it did not, in itself, cause any loss to C, and so no indemnity needed to be paid. Such an analysis is obviously unattractive, but it does flow from the acceptance of the '*Malory* 1' argument in *Malory Homes*. To reject it, the Court of Appeal therefore had to show why its earlier decision on that point could be departed from.

Patten LJ (with whom Tomlinson and Moore-Bick JJ agreed)

At [39]–[45]

We are, of course, bound by the decision in *Malory* on the beneficial ownership issue [i.e. the point that, notwithstanding the change in the register, B retained an equitable interest in the land] unless it can be said that the question was decided *per incuriam*. Two matters have been drawn to our attention on this point. The first is that Arden LJ makes no reference in her judgment to the earlier decision of the Court of Appeal in *Argyle Building Society v Hammond*[82] where Slade LJ, giving the judgment of the court, refers to the statutory magic of s 69(1) which has the effect of vesting title by registration even when the transfer has been a forgery [. . .]

   The second, and perhaps more important point is that the court's attention was not drawn to s 114 of the 1925 Act which provided that: '*Subject to the provisions in this Act contained with respect to indemnity and to registered dispositions for valuable consideration, any disposition of land or of a charge, which if unregistered would be fraudulent and void, shall, notwithstanding registration, be fraudulent and void in like manner.*' An important, perhaps even critical, part of Arden LJ's reasoning in [65] of her judgment in *Malory* was that s 20 of the 1925 Act had no application to a forged disposition. But s 114 makes clear that, although a registered disposition which would be fraudulent and void if unregistered remains fraudulent and void even if registered, this takes effect subject to the provisions of the 1925 Act with respect to registered dispositions for valuable consideration one of which is, of course, s 20. It is therefore not possible to construe s 20 as having no application to a fraudulent transfer for valuable consideration that is registered.

---

[82] (1985) 49 P & CR 148.

> Although hesitating before differing from Arden LJ and the other members of the court in *Malory* on this point, I am satisfied that the beneficial ownership issue was decided *per incuriam* for the reasons I have given and is wrong.

The decision of the Court of Appeal in *Swift 1st* of course has some important practical effects, and we will consider the scope of rectification in more detail in Chapter 18, section 3. For example, where X's forgery has led to the removal of B's registered right and the registration of C, B can no longer argue that he or she retained an equitable title to the land that is capable of binding C as an overriding interest. This is important as we saw earlier that, if C is bound by an overriding interest of B, then the removal of C's right from the register will be an alteration, simply updating the position applying in any case under the LRA scheme, and not a rectification, and so no indemnity will be payable to C when C's right is removed.[83]

3.3.3 A tension between two approaches: revolution or adaptation?

For our present purposes, however, the important aspect of the contrast between *Malory* on the one hand, and *Swift 1st* on the other, is that the two cases show how different judges may take a different view of when, if ever, it is appropriate to look outside the specific rules of a land registration system, and invoke instead more general rules of property law. For example, in *Swift 1st*, Patten LJ stated that the reasoning in *Malory* '*runs contrary to the general principle . . . that the register is a complete record of all enforceable estates and interests except for overriding interests and that it is registration rather than transfer which confers title.*'[84] Such a view fits with the approach urged by the Law Commission in the Report which led to the LRA 2002: as we saw in section 3.1, its aim was that the '*the register should be a complete and accurate reflection of the state of the title of the land*'. Indeed, that was a central part of what the Law Commission described in the title of that report as a '*conveyancing revolution*'.

The contrasting approach is one in which the rules of a registration system are seen by a judge as subject to wider principles of property law, such as the simple idea that if B has an interest in property, then it should not usually be possible for B to lose that right through the forgery of X. As academics have noted,[85] there is some evidence that judges, even when applying the LRA 2002, have preferred such an approach, which could be said to regard the registration scheme as adapting general property rules, rather than fundamentally breaking away from them. Indeed, in *Scott v Southern Pacific Mortgages Ltd*,[86] Lady Hale stated that:

> It is important to bear in mind that the system of land registration is merely conveyancing machinery. The underlying law relating to the creation of estates and interests in land remains the same. It is therefore logical to start with what proprietary interests are recognised by the

---

[83] In *Malory*, however, the Court of Appeal also suggested a second means by which B, in such a case, can assert a pre-existing equitable interest against C: B can argue that his or her right to rectify the register (following the fraudulent transfer) is an equitable interest that may be overriding. That suggestion (referred to by the Law Commission as the '*Malory 2*' argument (Law Com CP No 227 (2016) [13.60])) was *not* rejected by the Court of Appeal in *Swift 1st* and will be considered further at Chapter 18, section 4.2.

[84] [2015] EWCA Civ 330, [2015] Ch 602 at [41].

[85] See e.g. Nair, 'Morality and the Mirror: The Normative Limits of the "Principles of Land Registration"' in *Modern Studies in Property Law Vol 6* (ed Bright, Oxford: Hart Publishing, 2011); Goymour, 'Mistaken Registration of Land: Exploding the Myth of "Title by Registration"' [2013] CLJ 617.

[86] [2014] UKSC 52, [2015] AC 385, [96]. We will examine the case in detail in Chapter 8, section 4.4 and Chapter 15, section 3.1.3.

> law and then to ask whether the conveyancing machinery has given effect to them and what
> the consequences are if it has not. Otherwise we are in danger of letting the land registration
> tail wag the land ownership dog.

It is difficult to accept Lady Hale's statement as a literal truth: as we have seen in this chapter, the rules imposed by the LRA 2002 have a significant impact on the acquisition and defences questions, and are, therefore, part and parcel of the rules that govern private rights to use land.[87] To regard them as mere machinery would be to overlook the important policy aims that the rules seek to achieve, and the substantive effect that they have in deciding how to resolve competing claims to make use of land. Nonetheless, Lady Hale's view reflects the important idea, clear, for example, in the approach courts have now adopted in considering when an order can be made for the rectification of the register on grounds of mistake,[88] that a registration system need not always favour a registered party at the expense of an unregistered one. Certainly, it would be a mistake to think that the rules of the LRA 2002 entirely exclude general principles of property law as applied in unregistered land: for example, the definition of 'owner's powers' given by s 23 of the Act gives the registered party *'powers to make a disposition of any kind permitted by the general law in relation to an interest of that description'* and so expressly draws on the general law.[89]

There is, therefore, a clear tension between two contrasting approaches to the role of land registration in English law. It is that tension which explains why the courts have not always been entirely consistent in their interpretation of land registration provisions. It also explains why the Law Commission, in its 2016 Consultation Paper, has emphasized that the law on land registration must serve different policy needs, of which the provision of certainty to C is only one, and so needs *'some in-built flexibility to ensure that the land should pass to or remain in the ownership of the person who most needs it or values it'.*[90] We will examine the case law and the Law Commission's 2016 proposals in detail in Chapter 18, but it is important at this stage to emphasize the need for *balance*. The registration rules seek to provide a balance between the claims of B and C and, just as it would be a mistake to think that a registration system must always favour a registered party at the expense of an unregistered one, it would equally be an error to think that the presence or absence of registration is unimportant. As we saw in Chapter 1, there is always room for disagreement about the appropriate way to resolve competing claims to make use of land.

QUESTIONS

1. What risks does C, a party planning to acquire a right in land, face when acquiring such a right? How might a registration system protect C against such risks?

2. What is the difference between 'dynamic security' and 'static security'?

---

[87] For discussion of the dangers of seeing land registration rules as merely machinery, see e.g. Hopkins, 'Priorities and Sale and Lease Back: A Wrong Question, Much Ado About Nothing and a Story of Tails and Dogs' [2015] Conv 245, 252–3.

[88] See Chapter 18, section 3.1.2, discussing e.g. *Gold Harp Properties Ltd v Macleod* [2014] EWCA Civ 1084, [2015] 1 WLR 1249.

[89] That point was important in e.g. *Skelwith (Leisure) Ltd v Armstrong* [2015] EWHC 2830, [2016] Ch 345 at [57]–[58].

[90] Law Com CP No 227 (2016), *Updating the Land Registration Act 2002*, [13.15].

3. Is it accurate to regard the LRA 2002 as implementing a system of 'title by registration' rather than one of 'registration of title'?

4. What is the effect of entering a notice on the register recording B's interest in the registered land?

5. Does the result in *Walker v Burton* show that too much protection is given by the LRA 2002 to a registered proprietor in possession?

6. What is the '*Malory* 1' argument? Why did the Court of Appeal in the *Swift 1st* case reject that analysis?

7. Lady Hale, in *Scott v Southern Pacific Mortgages Ltd*, referred to the system of land registration as '*merely conveyancing machinery*'. Do you agree with that view? Do you think the Law Commission intended the LRA 2002 to be seen in such a light?

For guidance on how to answer these questions visit the online resources at www.oup.com/uk/mcfarlane4e/.

FURTHER READING

Cooper, 'Resolving Title Conflicts in Registered Land' (2015) 131 LQR 108

Dixon, 'Updating the Land Registration Act 2002: Title Guarantee, Rectification and Indefeasibility' [2016] Conv 423

Gardner, 'Alteration of the Register: An Alternative View' [2013] Conv 530

Goymour, 'Mistaken Registration of Land: Exploding the Myth of "Title by Registration"' [2013] CLJ 617

Hopkins, 'Priorities and Sale and Lease Back: A Wrong Question, Much Ado About Nothing and a Story of Tails and Dogs' [2015] Conv 245

Law Commission Report No 271, *Land Registration for the Twenty-First Century: A Conveyancing Revolution* (2001)

Law Commission Consultation Paper No 227, *Updating the Land Registration Act 2002* (2016), chs 1, 2, and 13

Lees, 'Registration, Make-Believe and Forgery' (2015) 131 LQR 515

O'Connor, 'Registration of Title in England and Australia' in *Modern Studies in Property Law: vol 2* (ed Cooke, London: Hart Publishing, 2003)

PART B

THE CONTENT QUESTION

4 Human Rights and Land 87
5 Legal Estates and Legal Interests 154
6 Equitable Interests 179
7 Personal Rights: Licences 204

4

HUMAN RIGHTS AND LAND

CENTRAL ISSUES

1. The Human Rights Act 1998 (HRA 1998) prospectively incorporates the European Convention on Human Rights (ECHR) into domestic law by placing a number of duties upon our domestic courts. Article 1 of the First Protocol and Art 8 have particular relevance to land law.

2. These Articles of the ECHR confer qualified protections and infringements may be justified. The government enjoys a wide margin of appreciation in identifying and implementing a legitimate purpose, but nevertheless must act proportionately.

3. The HRA 1998 has vertical effect: under s 6, public authorities must act in accordance with the ECHR.

4. The ECHR, as a consequence of States' positive duties, as well as the HRA 1998 may also have limited horizontal effect (i.e. between private individuals) as a result of s 3, which requires legislation to be interpreted in accordance with the ECHR, and s 6, which requires the courts (as public authorities) to act in accordance with the ECHR.

5. Article 1 of the First Protocol guarantees the peaceful enjoyment of possessions. It provides that a person is not to be deprived of, or subject to controls over, their possessions except in the public or general interest.

6. Article 8 guarantees respect for the home, the enjoyment of which may only be infringed so far as is necessary in a democratic society: for example, in the national economic interest or to protect the rights of others.

7. Other Articles may also impact upon land, for instance Art 6 ensures the right to a fair trial in the determination of property rights, Arts 10 and 11 ensure freedom of speech and assembly and association which may impinge upon the use of land for these purposes,[1] and Art 14 provides that individuals should not be discriminated against in the enjoyment of their ECHR rights.

8. Although it is clear that property lawyers must understand the effect of the HRA 1998 on property law, to date the impact of human rights norms has been marginal.

---

[1] See Lees, 'Actions for Possession in the Context of Political Protest: The Role of Article 1 Protocol 1 and Horizontal Effect' [2013] Conv 211.

1 INTRODUCTION

The Human Rights Act 1998 (HRA 1998) incorporates the European Convention on Human Rights (ECHR) into the domestic law of England and Wales. As such, it is said to bring human rights home by permitting an infringement of the ECHR to be raised and considered in the domestic courts.[2] Previously, a claimant had to bring his or her case against the United Kingdom before the European Court of Human Rights in Strasbourg (the Strasbourg Court) once he or she had exhausted any redress under English law in the domestic courts.[3]

The ECHR is a product of post-war Europe. In the face of the cold war, its object was to set out the freedoms that are considered central to human life in a civilized and democratic society. The majority of these rights were agreed and incorporated into the original form of the ECHR, to which the United Kingdom became a signatory in 1951, but the right to property proved more controversial and was not agreed until 1954. It is thus contained in a separate Protocol.

Although the ECHR was only incorporated into domestic law by the HRA 1998, the rights that it espouses are not a radical departure from the traditional principles upon which property law has been founded for centuries. As Gray explains, the principle that no one should be arbitrarily deprived of their property found in Art 1 of the First Protocol has found expression in national laws for centuries.

Gray, 'Land Law and Human Rights' in *Land Law Issues, Debates, Policy* (ed Tee, 2002, p 216)

The safeguards provided by the Convention are, in their way, mirrored across the expanse of European history during the past millennium. The human right to protection from arbitrary dispossession by the state is born of a deep impulse which views lawless seizure of property as a particularly violating kind of molestation—a form of proprietary rape. An instinct against arbitrary dissessin of freehold is at least as old as the Magna Carta and went on to animate the great eighteenth century declarations of social and civil liberties. For Blackstone, writing in 1765, it was inconceivable that 'sacred and inviolable rights to private property' should be postponed to 'public necessity' without 'a full indemnification and equivalent for the injury thereby sustained'. As Blackstone explained in strikingly modern parlance, the state cannot act 'even for the general good of the community [. . .] by simply stripping the subject of his property in an arbitrary manner'. Blackstone's premise was adopted, quickly and in virtually identical terms, in the French Declaration of the Rights of Man and of the Citizen and has since inspired a vast range of national and international prohibitions on the taking of property by the state except for justifiable purposes and on payment of a fair value.

The sanctity of the home that forms the basis of Art 8 also reflects the fundamental sentiment that the home is a personal inviolable space reflected in the time-honoured phrase that 'an Englishman's home is his castle'.[4]

---

[2] *Rights Brought Home* CM 3782.

[3] In 1966, the UK adopted the optional clauses that enabled an individual claimant to bring a case before the Strasbourg Court. See Harpum, 'Property Law: The Human Rights Dimension—Part 1' [2000] L&T Rev 4, for details of the pre-HRA effect of the ECHR.

[4] See *Malik v Fassenfelt* [2013] EWCA Civ 798 at [1].

However, the HRA 1998 may have a more far reaching impact upon our property law by requiring us to rethink concepts of ownership, as a result of a new form of property protection based upon the human rights enshrined in the ECHR, as Bright suggests in the following extract concerning a leading case on Art 8.

'Bright, Manchester City Council v Pinnock (2010): Shifting Ideas of Ownership of Law' in *Landmark Cases in Land Law* (ed Gravels, 2013, p 274)

It does, however, also have a wider significance in terms of the idea of ownership and the right to possess [. . .] The right to recover possession of land that is occupied as a home by someone with no lawful right to occupy can no longer be seen as automatic, no longer a foregone conclusion that flows from a simple application of a traditional understanding of the hierarchy of rights in land [. . .] Article 8 requires a new way of thinking about the right to recover possession. When Article 8 is engaged, and raised as defence, the owner will not be entitled to an order for possession merely by showing that the occupier has no lawful right to occupy; it will be necessary to show that the recovery of possession is justified by the pursuit of a legitimate aim [. . .] The proportionality question does require a shift towards a contextualised, non-hierarchical way of thinking, in which factors extraneous to property doctrine come into play [. . .] This is a different way of thinking about ownership.

In this chapter, we will look firstly at how the HRA 1998 brings human rights home; we will then go on to examine the two principal Articles of the ECHR that are of direct importance to property lawyers—namely, Art 1 of the First Protocol (protection of possessions) and Art 8 (respect for the home). We will refer to the remaining relevant Articles where appropriate. The chapter will conclude with an assessment of the impact of the HRA 1998 on property law to date and in particular the emergence of a new human rights based protection of property. Throughout the remaining chapters we will point out where human rights issues have been, or possibly may be, raised to question established property doctrine.

2 ADJUDICATION UNDER THE HUMAN RIGHTS ACT 1998

As Goymour has explained, to rely on breach of a Convention right within domestic property law 'there are two hurdles for a litigant to clear'.[5] First a State's liability must be engaged because the law is incompatible with the ECHR, and secondly the HRA 1998 must provide a route by which that breach can be relied upon in the domestic courts. We address the first hurdle in section 2.2. In order to consider the second hurdle we need to briefly remind ourselves of the salient provisions of the HRA 1998.

---

[5] 'Property and Housing' in *The Impact of the UK Human Rights Act on Private Law* (ed Hoffman, Cambridge: CUP, 2011) p 260.

2.1 THE COURT'S DUTIES UNDER THE HRA 1998

As readers will know from their study of public law, the HRA 1998 has triggered considerable debate concerning its impact upon our constitutional framework by imposing duties and powers upon our courts. First, by section 2 the courts 'must take account' of Strasbourg jurisprudence in their interpretation of rights enshrined in the ECHR.

> ### 2. —Interpretation of Convention rights.
>
> 1. A court or tribunal determining a question which has arisen in connection with a Convention right must take into account any—
>
>   a. judgment, decision, declaration or advisory opinion of the European Court of Human Rights,
>
>   b. opinion of the Commission given in a report adopted under Article 31 of the Convention,
>
>   c. decision of the Commission in connection with Article 26 or 27(2) of the Convention, or
>
>   d. decision of the Committee of Ministers taken under Article 46 of the Convention,
>
>   whenever made or given, so far as, in the opinion of the court or tribunal, it is relevant to the proceedings in which that question has arisen.

The difficulty lies in working out what 'taking account' requires. It is clear that our domestic courts are not required to follow the Strasbourg Court's rulings as a matter of strict precedent '[but] it is ordinarily the clear duty of our domestic courts, save where and so far as constrained by the primary domestic legislation, to give practical recognition to the principles laid down by the Strasbourg court.'[6] On occasions the courts have struggled to accept the opinions of the Strasbourg Court. In *R v Hardcastle*[7] it was suggested that the Supreme Court should enjoy a degree of latitude where they believe that the Strasbourg Court does not appreciate the domestic context. A dissatisfied victim may then appeal to the Strasbourg Court resulting in a dialogue, through the judgments of the two courts, to hopefully resolve any misunderstanding. Nevertheless, no such dialogue is appropriate where there is a clear and consistent line of authority from the Strasbourg Court.[8]

There was an expectation that Strasbourg jurisprudence would operate as a floor below which domestic law would not fall, but in fact judges have shown reluctance in building upon the foundations laid by Strasbourg particularly in property disputes. In the much quoted words of Lord Bingham in *R (Ullah) v Special Adjudicator* '[t]he duty of national courts is to keep pace with the Strasbourg jurisprudence as it evolves over time: no more, but certainly no less.'[9] Thus, Strasbourg Court decisions have tended to operate as a ceiling on the development of our domestic human rights.[10]

---

[6] *Kay v Lambeth LBC; Leeds CC v Price* [2006] 2 AC 465 *per* Lord Bingham at [28]. It should be noted that, where a Strasbourg ruling is at odds with a domestic authority of the higher court, the lower courts will continue to be bound until this inconsistent domestic decision is overruled by the Supreme Court or Court of Appeal as appropriate see Lord Bingham ibid at [40]–[45].

[7] *R v Hardcastle* [2009] UKSC 14 *per* Lord Phillips at [11].

[8] *Manchester CC v Pinnock* [2011] 2 AC 104, [48], *per* Lord Neuberger.   [9] [2004] 2 AC 323 at [20].

[10] Masterman, 'Aspiration or Foundation? The Status of Strasbourg Jurisprudence and "Convention Rights" under Domestic Law' in *Judicial reasoning under the Human Rights Act* (eds Fenwick, Phillipson,

Secondly, s 3 requires all bodies, including the courts, to give effect to legislation, whether enacted before or after the coming into force of the HRA 1998, in a manner that is compatible with the ECHR. Where a court finds that it cannot do so, it may issue a declaration of incompatibility under s 4, whereupon the government may amend the offending legislation using the fast-track procedure set out in s 10.[11] In this manner, parliamentary sovereignty is respected, whilst ensuring that Parliament itself does not infringe the ECHR.

Human Rights Act 1998, s 3(1)

Interpretation of legislation

So far as it is possible to do so, primary legislation and subordinate legislation must be read and given effect in a way which is compatible with the Convention rights.

The width of the court's power of statutory interpretation under s 3 has proved controversial. This question was considered by the House of Lords in the leading case of *Ghaidan v Godin-Mendoza*.[12] Their Lordship decided that the phrased 'So far as it is possible to do so' conferred upon the courts extensive powers of interpretation, which went beyond resolving ambiguities in legislation, to enable the court to depart from the stated legislative intention of Parliament. Thus, a court could modify the meaning of legislation to achieve compatibility, for instance by reading in words. However, the courts could not encroach upon Parliamentary sovereignty by adopting a meaning that was inconsistent with the fundamental thrust of the legislation.[13] We will see examples of the court's powers under s 3 when considering the compatibility with Art 8 of mandatory grounds for possession in section 4.2.2, when it seems evident that the courts will be more inclined to utilize their powers of statutory interpretation under s 3 in the public, rather than the private, context.[14]

Lastly s 6(3) of the HRA 1998, (extracted at section 2.3 below), defines a court as a public authority. All public authorities are by s 6 required to act in a manner that is compatible with the ECHR, thus the courts in their work should have human rights firmly in mind. It is this duty that has sparked considerable debate to the extent that s 6 may have horizontal effect upon the relations between private parties. This difficult issue will be considered at section 2.4 below. Suffice it to say at this point that the court's duty under s 6 may impose upon the courts a duty to apply and develop the common law in a manner that is compatible with Convention rights. Although property law is increasingly regulated by legislation, much is still reliant upon common law. It has been pointed out that it is both arbitrary and difficult to draw a distinction between statute and the common law when it is 'largely a matter of chance'[15] whether a particular area of property law is regulated by legislation or the common law. Furthermore, the common law inevitably provides the backdrop against

---

and Masterman, Cambridge, CUP: 2007) ch 3 and Lewis, *The European Ceiling on Human Rights* [2007] PL 720.

[11] The county court cannot issue a declaration of incompatibility and, thus, proceedings will have to be adjourned to enable the higher courts to deal with the matter of incompatibility: see s 4(5) HRA, and *Kay v Lambeth LBC* [2006] 2 AC 465, *per* Lord Hope at [110].

[12] [2004] 2 AC 557.   [13] See, for instance, ibid at [27]–[33] *per* Lord Nicholls.

[14] See *McDonald v McDonald* [2016] UKSC 28 at [61]–[70] *per* Lord Neuberger.

[15] Howell, 'The Human Rights Act 1998: Land, Private Citizens, and the Common Law' (2007) 123 LQR 618 at [627].

which legislation is framed much 'like a patch of grass in the middle of a motorway junction', thus 'it would be unrealistic, and productive of error, not to look at the whole picture'.[16]

2.2 QUALIFIED RIGHTS AND THE JUSTIFICATION FORMULA

The nature of the Articles contained in the ECHR differs. Some provide an absolute protection: for example, no circumstances can justify a departure from the absolute prohibition against torture contained in Art 3.[17] Art 1 Protocol 1 and Art 8 are both clearly qualified by the acknowledgement that an interference with the protections that they enshrine may be justified in prescribed circumstances. Thus, once it is established that a qualified right is infringed, a human rights challenge will focus upon whether or not the infringement is justified.

In considering whether or not an interference is justified, the Strasbourg Court has developed a tried-and-tested formula which is also followed by the domestic courts.[18] An interference will be justified if it is in *accordance with the law* and in pursuit of a *legitimate aim*, within the qualifications set out in the appropriate Article, as well as *proportionate* in striking a 'fair balance' between the legitimate aim and the interference with the individual's human rights. States enjoy a wide *margin of appreciation* in identifying a legitimate aim and the means to achieve that aim. We need to examine each of these elements.

2.2.1 In accordance with the law

The interference must be in accordance with the law of the particular State.[19] Although it is for States to articulate that law, the Strasbourg Court is concerned that the law also meets a minimum qualitative threshold in terms of clarity and rationale application.

R & L, SRO & Others v The Czech Republic
App Nos 37926/05, 25784/09, 36002/09, 44410/09, and 65546/09

At 113–16

The rule of law, one of the fundamental principles of a democratic society, is a notion inherent in all the Articles of the Convention [. . .] However, the existence of a legal basis in the domestic law does not suffice, in itself, to satisfy the principle of lawfulness. In addition, the legal basis must have a certain quality, namely it must be compatible with the rule of law and must provide guarantees against arbitrariness. In this connection it should be pointed out that when speaking of "law", Article 1 of Protocol No. 1 alludes to the very same concept as that to which the Convention refers elsewhere when using that term. It follows that, in addition to being in accordance with the domestic law of the Contracting State, including its Constitution, the legal norms upon which the deprivation of property is based should be sufficiently accessible, precise and foreseeable in their application [. . .]

---

[16] *Birmingham CC v Doherty* [2009] 1 AC 367 *per* Lord Walker at [100].

[17] See *Chahal v UK* (1997) 23 EHRR 413; *Saadi v Italy* [2009] 49 EHRR 30.

[18] See, for instance, *R (on the application of N) v Lewisham LBC; R (on the application of H) v Newham LBC* [2014] 3 WLR 1548 at [62].

[19] *Prokopovich v Russia* App No 58255/00 and *Pelipenko v Russia* App No 69037/10.

Further, the Court observes that it has always understood the term "law" in its "substantive" sense, not its "formal" one; it has included both "written law", encompassing enactments of lower ranking statutes and regulatory measures taken by professional regulatory bodies under independent rule-making powers delegated to them by Parliament, and unwritten law. "Law" must be understood to include both statutory law and judge-made "law". In sum, the "law" is the provision in force as the competent courts have interpreted it [. . .]

For the purposes of its examination of lawfulness, the Court reiterates that it is primarily for the national authorities, notably the courts, to interpret and apply domestic law and to decide on issues of constitutionality [. . .]

It can be seen from the above extract that law has a wide meaning and includes case law. The following case makes clear that judge-made law should also be supported by clear and rational reasoning.

Kryvitska and Kryvitskyy v Ukraine App No 30856/03

At 43–4

While the Court is not in a position to substitute its own judgment for that of the national courts and its power to review compliance with domestic law is limited [. . .], it is the Court's function to review the reasoning adduced by domestic judicial authorities from the point of view of the Convention [. . .] To protect a person against arbitrariness it is not sufficient to provide a formal possibility of bringing adversarial proceedings to contest the application of a legal provision to his or her case. Where a resulting judicial decision lacks reasoning or an evidentiary basis, ensuing interference with a Convention right may become unforeseeable and consequently fall short of the lawfulness requirement.

[. . .] Lack of reasoning in a judicial decision as to the grounds of application of a statute may, even where the formal requirements have been complied with, be taken into account among other factors in determining whether the measure complained of struck a fair balance.

2.2.2 Legitimate aim

An interference must be made for a legitimate purpose that serves the appropriate qualification. The legitimate aims are set out in general terms in the Articles themselves. Thus, for example, an interference with Art 1 of the First Protocol must be in the public or general interest; an interference with Art 8 must be necessary in a democratic society to address a pressing social need, because, for example, it is for the economic well-being of the country, or because it protects the rights and freedoms of others.

2.2.3 Margin of appreciation

A State is afforded a margin of appreciation, or discretion, in determining the legitimate aim and the means of achieving that aim, because a State is generally in a better position to assess the society's needs and the best means of achieving those needs within its own country. The Strasbourg Court explained the concept in the context of a challenge to the compatibility with Art 1 of the First Protocol of legislation entitling a tenant to purchase his landlord's reversion.

James v UK
(1986) 8 EHRR 123

Facts: The Duke of Westminster, whose estate comprised a significant number of houses in London let on long leases, unsuccessfully questioned the compatibility with Art 1 of the First Protocol of the Leasehold Reform Act 1967. The Act entitled the tenants of the houses to require him to transfer the freehold reversion to them for sums (as defined by the legislation) that were less than their market value.

At 46

Because of their direct knowledge of their society and its needs, the national authorities are in principle better placed than the international judge to appreciate what is "in the public interest." Under the system of protection established by the Convention, it is thus for the national authorities to make the initial assessment both of the existence of the problem of public concern warranting measures of deprivation of property and of the remedial action to be taken [. . .] Here as in other fields to which the safeguards of the Convention extend, the national authorities accordingly enjoy a certain margin of appreciation.

   Furthermore, the notion of "public interest" is necessarily extensive, in particular, as the Commission noted, the decision to enact laws expropriating property will commonly involve consideration of political, economic and social issues on which opinions within a democratic society may reasonably differ widely. The Court finding it natural that the margin of appreciation available to the legislature in implementing social and economic policies should be a wide one, will respect the legislature's judgment as to what is "in the public interest" unless that judgment be manifestly without reasonable foundation [. . .]

Thus, a State's actions taken in the public interest under Art 1 Protocol will be respected unless they are 'manifestly without reasonable foundation', in the sense that no reasonable government would have come to a similar decision in the circumstances.[20] It should be noted that in pursuance of their obligations under s 2 of the HRA 1998, the domestic courts, save in exceptional circumstances, will accept the compatibility of a law which the Strasbourg Court has held to be within the United Kingdom's margin of appreciation.[21]

   A State's margin of appreciation, however, will depend on, and may vary according to, the Article and context in which it is exercised.

Connors v UK
(2005) 40 EHRR 9

Facts: The Connors were gypsies. The family occupied the same local authority site under a licence for over thirteen years, but, after their daughter married and their sons grew up, it was alleged that their pitch was a 'magnet for trouble'. As a result, the local authority terminated their licence to occupy and summarily evicted them from the site, but without citing any reasons. The local authority chose not to rely upon the

---

[20] See, also, *Lithgow v UK* (1986) 8 EHRR 329, which concerned the compensation to be paid for nationalization of certain areas of the ship and aircraft-building business.
[21] See in the context of adverse possession *Ofulue v Bossert* [2009] Ch 1, CA, [37] and [52].

Connors' alleged 'antisocial' behaviour. The Connor family successfully claimed that their summary eviction breached their rights to respect for their home and way of life as gypsies under Art 8.

At 82

In this regard, a margin of appreciation must, inevitably, be left to the national authorities, who by reason of their direct and continuous contact with the vital forces of their countries are in principle better placed than an international court to evaluate local needs and conditions. This margin will vary according to the nature of the Convention right in issue, its importance for the individual and the nature of the activities restricted, as well as the nature of the aim pursued by the restrictions. The margin will tend to be narrower where the right at stake is crucial to the individual's effective enjoyment of intimate or key rights. [. . .] On the other hand, in spheres involving the application of social or economic policies, there is authority that the margin of appreciation is wide, as in the planning context where the Court has found that: "[i]n so far as the exercise of discretion involving a multitude of local factors is inherent in the choice and implementation of planning policies, the national authorities in principle enjoy a wide margin of appreciation". *Buckley v United Kingdom* (1997) 23 E.H.R.R. 101 at [75].

The Court has also stated that in spheres such as housing, which play a central role in the welfare and economic policies of modern societies, it will respect the legislature's judgment as to what is in the general interest unless that judgment is manifestly without reasonable foundation. See *Mellacher v Austria* (A/169) (1990) 12 E.H.R.R. 391 at [45]; *Immobiliare Saffi v Italy* (2000) 30 E.H.R.R. 756 at [49]. It may be noted however that this was in the context of Art.1 of Protocol No.1, not Art.8 which concerns rights of central importance to the individual's identity, self-determination, physical and moral integrity, maintenance of relationships with others and a settled and secure place in the community. See, *Gillow v United Kingdom* at [55]; *Pretty v United Kingdom* (2002) 35 E.C.H.R. 1; *Christine Goodwin v United Kingdom* (2002) 35 E.H.R.R. 18 at [90]. Where general social and economic policy considerations have arisen in the context of Art.8 itself, the scope of the margin of appreciation depends on the context of the case, with particular significance attaching to the extent of the intrusion into the personal sphere of the applicant. *Hatton v United Kingdom* (2002) 34 E.H.R.R. 1 at [103] and [123].

The justification of public interest found in Art 1 Protocol 1 is generally taken to be a wider test than the demands of necessity to meet a pressing social need which defines the justification under Art 8. The margin of appreciation may, thus, be narrower under Art 8, particularly where the nature of the interference is severe.

The existence and adequacy of procedural safeguards, that enable the court to assess the proportionality of the interference, are crucial in determining whether or not a State has remained within its margin of appreciation.[22] In the following case, concerning Art 8, the court underlined the need for adequate procedural safeguards, particularly where the interference with the Convention right is severe.

---

[22] See Hickman, *Public Law after the Human Rights Act* (Oxford: Hart Publishing, 2010) pp 118–19.

Kay v UK
(2012) 54 EHRR 30

At 67

it is clear from the case law of the Court that the requirement under art.8(2) that the interference be "necessary in a democratic society" raises a question of procedure as well as one of substance. (*Connors v UK, McCann v UK*). The procedural safeguards available to the individual will be especially material in determining whether the respondent State has, when fixing the regulatory framework, remained within its margin of appreciation. In particular, the Court must examine whether the decision-making process leading to measures of interference was fair and such as to afford due respect to the interests safeguarded to the individual by Article 8 (*Buckley v UK, Chapman v UK*, and *Connors v UK*).

The interaction between the substantive law, which gives effect to a given social or economic policy, and the procedural safeguards, which attend the implementation of that policy, are difficult to separate, as Nield observes in the following extract.

Nield, 'Clash of the Titan: Article 8, Occupiers and Respect for their Home'
in *Modern Studies in Property Law* (ed S Bright, 2011, pp 100–29)

It would be tempting to conclude that whilst on matters of the substantive content of the law implementing a particular social or economic policy, where a party is granted a right to possession against another, the State's margin of appreciation remains wide; but as a matter of the procedural operation of that policy, where the consequences dictate repossession of an individual's home, the margin is narrow. But this distinction is too simplistic. The two issues are intimately entwined because the substantive law will define the circumstances when the occupier may be heard before the court [. . .] As Loveland has succinctly put the issue [referring to *McCann v UK*]; 'it is not what the council had done but what the court could not do'.

2.2.4 Proportionality or fair balance

Although States enjoy a wide margin of appreciation, there must nevertheless be a fair balance, or proportionality, between the means employed to address the legitimate aim and the interference with an individual's human rights that results. The principle is that no single individual should be expected to bear an excessive burden in meeting the particular community or social object of the legitimate aim. If it is possible to achieve that aim without interfering unduly with an individual's rights, then that route should be adopted in preference to other solutions that do so trespass. A clear example is found in the case of *Rousk v Sweden*.[23] Mr Rousk's home was sold for Euro 186,000 pursuant to enforcement proceedings to recover taxes he owed. Initially the sum he owed was Euro 27,000 but by the time of the sale this debt had been reduced to about Euro 800. The Strasbourg Court found that the sale was a disproportionate response, under both Art 1 Protocol 1 and Art 8, to the recovery of Mr Rousk's unpaid taxes.

[23] App No 27183/04.

As explained in the following extract, the courts are slowly developing an analytical approach to proportionality which comprises four limbs and is similar to the approach in other common law jurisdictions.[24]

Nield, 'Proportionality and the Vindication of Property Rights' in *Modern Studies in Property Law Vol 9* (ed E Conway and R Hickey, 2017, ch 3, footnotes omitted)

This approach to proportionality comprises four limbs.

(i) *The First Limb: The Legitimate Objective*

This limb raises the question of whether the public interest is of sufficient importance to justify limiting a right. Such public interests may be many and various. In the context of repossession cases, centre stage will be the vindication of property rights namely: the right to exclude for instance by landowner or creditor. Other legitimate objectives are also evident in domestic and ECtHR case law including the control of antisocial behaviour, the management of housing resources, planning and environmental conservation, and public health.

(ii) *The Second Limb: Suitability*

Repossession, as a measure designed to meet the objective, must be rationally connected to that objective in the sense that it is capable of meeting it. Repossession is invariably connected to the vindication of a property right, thus this stage rarely presents any difficulty. The physicality of the subject matter provides the connection and repossession with a powerful incentive to meet a given objective.

(iii) *Stage 3: Minimal Impairment*

This stage raises the question of whether repossession goes no further than is necessary to achieve the legitimate aim. It thus presses beyond suitability to look at the functionality of the right to exclude in the context of the circumstances at issue. It raises the question of balancing means and ends. Where the right to possession is determining relative claims to possession of the land arising from the vindication of ownership, the connection between means and ends is relatively straightforward; where the right to repossess pursues some other function, however, the connection may be less clear cut. Rights granted by way of security are a case in point. For instance, in *Zehentner v Austria* the ECtHR, though accepting that the sale of the victim's property was a suitable means to meet creditors' claims, did not believe, particularly in the light of Ms Zehentner's incapacity, that it was an appropriate route to recover a relatively small judgment debt. Similar concerns are reflected in the criticisms levelled at the use of charging orders in this jurisdiction to recover relatively small debts.

(iv) *Stage 4: Overall Balance (Proportionality Stricto Sensu)*

The last stage requires a fair balance to be struck between the right of the individual and the public interest. Inherent within this balancing is a contextual consideration of the individual's circumstances, since no individual should bear an excessive burden in pursuit of the public

---

[24] See *De Freitas v Permanent Secretary of Ministry of Agriculture, Fisheries, Lands and Housing* [1999]1 AC 69; *Huang v Secretary of State for the Home Department* [2007] 2 AC 167; and *Bank Mellat v HM Treasury (No2)* [2014] AC 700.

interest. Balancing thus dictates that the independent tribunal charged with assessing proportionality has sufficient discretion to consider all relevant factors.

It is important to recognise that proportionality can be employed at different levels. For instance, under the HRA 1998, proportionality has a role in assessing the compatibility of legislation with human rights ('legislative review') and also when the decision making of public authorities is challenged for falling short of human rights standards ('applied review'). For example, various Supreme Court Article 8 decisions have considered both proportionality of the legislative scheme granting a right to possession of the home and the compatibility of the local housing authority' s exercise of that right. The relationship between these two levels of decision making is critical. Indeed, it is this relationship that was at issue in the well-known dialogue between the ECtHR and our highest court which resulted in the final acknowledgement in *Manchester CC v Pinnock* (*Pinnock*) that statutory processes by which a public authority can repossess a home must admit applied review by which the proportionality of the repossession can be tested.

This extract also highlights that proportionality operates at two levels of intensity.[25] First, there is the fair balance that must be struck between individual Convention rights and the general interest of the public or society; here it is the law itself that is under scrutiny and the balance it strikes between the legitimate aim and the severity of the infringement resulting from the means employed to achieve that aim. Here proportionality operates at a macro-level or as in the extract 'legislative review'. Secondly, there is the proportionality of the impact of that law as applied to an individual victim in their particular circumstances. Here proportionality operates at the micro-level or as in the extract as 'applied review'. In order to conduct this latter review there should be an adequate process to determine proportionality at this micro-level. Although there may be macro-proportionality between the legitimate aim and the interference, there may still be a breach of the relevant Article where the victim is afforded no, or an inadequate, opportunity to question its impact upon their particular rights.

It is the lack of procedural safeguards that has often triggered incompatibility under both Art 1 Protocol 1 and Art 8, which we will consider in more detail when considering these Articles in sections 3 and 4. Importantly, we will see in the housing context of Art 8 that the Supreme Court has not adopted the structured approach to proportionality outlined above but has developed a more restrictive approach.

2.2.5 The domestic context and 'deference' or 'weight'

The concept of a State's margin of appreciation does not really fit the domestic context when the courts are called upon to consider the compatibility of a public authority's actions pursuant to s 6 or the compatibility of the law in accordance with their duties under ss 3 and 6. Lord Nicholls described the court's new role under s 3 in the following case. In so doing he refers to the familiar concepts of legitimate aim and proportionality but not the margin of appreciation.

---

[25] See Lord Neuberger's judgment in *Manchester CC v Pinnock* [2011] 2 AC 104, which demonstrates these two levels. Bright refers to these levels as the 'justification limb' and the 'impact limb', see 'Manchester City Council v Pinnock (2010): Shifting Ideas of Ownership' in *Landmark Cases in Land Law* (ed Gravells, Oxford: Hart Publishing, 2013) p 269.

Wilson v First County Trust Ltd (No 2)
[2004] 1 AC 816, HL

Facts: Mrs Wilson entered into a consumer credit agreement with First County in January 1999. The agreement was unenforceable, because it breached the Consumer Credit Act 1974 by failing to state accurately the total amount of credit.[26] First County argued that the statutory provision was incompatible with Arts 1 and 6, but the House of Lords declined to determine the questions, because the HRA 1998 did not have retrospective effect.

Lord Nicholls

At 61–3

The Human Rights Act 1998 requires the court to exercise a new role in respect of primary legislation. This new role is fundamentally different from interpreting and applying legislation. The courts are now required to evaluate the effect of primary legislation in terms of Convention rights and, where appropriate, make a formal declaration of incompatibility. In carrying out this evaluation the court has to compare the effect of the legislation with the Convention right. If the legislation impinges upon a Convention right the court must then compare the policy objective of the legislation with the policy objective which under the Convention may justify a prima facie infringement of the Convention right. When making these two comparisons the court will look primarily at the legislation, but not exclusively so. Convention rights are concerned with practicalities. When identifying the practical effect of an impugned statutory provision the court may need to look outside the statute in order to see the complete picture [. . .] What is relevant is the underlying social purpose sought to be achieved by the statutory provision. Frequently that purpose will be self-evident, but this will not always be so.

The legislation must not only have a legitimate policy objective. It must also satisfy a "proportionality" test. The court must decide whether the means employed by the statute to achieve the policy objective is appropriate and not disproportionate in its adverse effect. This involves a "value judgment" by the court, made by reference to the circumstances prevailing when the issue has to be decided. It is the current effect and impact of the legislation which matter, not the position when the legislation was enacted or came into force [. . .]

Nevertheless, a similar concept to the margin of appreciation is evident in the domestic context. Here the appropriate consideration is the proper constitutional balance between Parliament, the administration, and the courts given the courts' new role under the HRA 1998 as adjudicators of Convention compatibility. Unsurprisingly, the fundamental question of the extent to which the courts should pay heed to the policy choices of Parliament or the administrative decisions of public authorities has attracted considerable academic attention.[27] Commentators have described this domestic concept

---

[26] See s 127(3), which has since been amended by the Consumer Credit Act 2006, s 15.

[27] See e.g. Jowell, 'Judicial deference' [2003] PL 592, Allan, 'Human Rights and Judicial Review: A Critique of Due Deference' (2006) 65 CLJ 671, King, 'Institutional Approaches to Judicial Restraint' (2008) 28 OJLS 409, and Kavanagh, 'Defending deference in public law and constitutional theory' (2010) 126 LQR 222.

as deference, although the courts prefer to use the term 'weight', to acknowledge the respect to be given to the opinion of those[28] who are in a better position to make an evaluation, either because of their superior knowledge and experience or their democratic legitimacy.

In areas of property and housing law, the courts have given considerable weight to the legislative design of Parliament when conducting legislative review and, in the case of social housing, the decisions of social housing providers when considering applied review. We will see this weight when we consider in more detail the impact of Art 1 Protocol 1 and Art 8. For the time being it is instructive to provide an example by Baroness Hale, who was considering the compatibility of social housing policy from the case of *Kay v Lambeth LBC*.[29]

Baroness Hale

At 185–7

This is an area of the law much trampled over by the legislature as it has tried to respond to shifting and conflicting social and economic pressures. If there were enough suitable and affordable housing to share amongst those who needed it there would be no problem. But there is not, so priorities have to be established, either by Parliament or by the public sector landlord, who has to allocate this scarce resource in accordance with the priorities set by Parliament.

The balance has changed over time in accordance with what were perceived to be the needs of the time. Once upon a time, it was thought necessary to control the freedom of private landlords to let for such terms and on such rents as the market allowed. Public sector landlords, on the other hand, could be left to manage the public housing stock in a responsible manner. Then things changed. Controls over private landlords were progressively relaxed, although never abandoned, with a view to expanding the supply of privately rented homes. Controls over public sector landlords, on the other hand, were increased and public sector tenants were given the security which previously only private sector tenants had enjoyed. This and other measures reduced the supply of public sector rented homes. These were all intensely political judgments. The extent to which, and the terms on which, public authorities should be engaged in providing housing for those who for whatever reason cannot or will not buy it on the private market was one of the most politically controversial issues of the 20th century.

To the extent that a court insists that a public authority does not rely upon its right to evict an occupier, it is obliging that public authority to continue to supply that person with a home in circumstances where Parliament has not obliged (and may not even have empowered) it to do so. In this politically contentious area of social and economic policy, any court should think long and hard before intervening in the balance currently struck by the elected legislature. There may be more scope for argument in a case not covered by statute [. . .]

Nevertheless, the courts would be failing in their role under the HRA 1998 if they merely assumed that the existing law, or a decision of a public authority, is compatible.[30]

---

[28] *Huang v Secretary of State for the Home Department* [2007] 2 AC 167, *per* Lord Nicholls at [16].
[29] [2006] 2 AC 465.
[30] See also Lees 'Article 8, Proportionality and Horizontal Effect' (2017) 133 LQR 31.

Nield, 'Clash of the Titans: Occupiers Article 8 and their Home' in *Modern Studies in Property Law Vol 6* (ed S Bright, 2011, ch 5)

In assessing the proper extent of judicial deference, context is everything. Qazi demonstrates an extreme degree of deference in which proprietary rights to possession are not to be questioned at all—they were in fact nonjusticiable! In *Kay* the House of Lords has shown, in both the views of the majority and minority, that in relation to the regulation of housing they will show exceptional deference to the policy choices of Parliament. This is not surprising given both the degree of Parliamentary scrutiny of housing policy and the public funding underpinning that policy. Similar substantial deference is to be expected in relation to proprietary rules governing possession where certainty and due balancing of the rights of third parties is necessary. However, it should not mean that the ECHR compatibility of proprietary rules should be non-justiciable or even that substantial deference should be automatic. Judicial deference should be assessed on a case-by-case (or rule-by-rule) basis.

2.3 VERTICAL EFFECT

The HRA 1998 not only affects the work of the court but also places a direct duty upon all public authorities to act in a manner that is compatible with the EHCR.

Human Rights Act 1998, s 6

Acts of public authorities

1. It is unlawful for a public authority to act in a way which is incompatible with a Convention right.

2. [. . . see section 2.2.3 below]

3. In this section "public authority" includes—

   (a) a court or tribunal, and

   (b) any person certain of whose functions are functions of a public nature, but does not include either House of Parliament or a person exercising functions in connection with proceedings in Parliament.

4. In subsection (3) "Parliament" does not include the House of Lords in its judicial capacity.

5. In relation to a particular act, a person is not a public authority by virtue only of subsection (3)(b) if the nature of the act is private.

6. "An act" includes a failure to act but does not include a failure to—

   (a) introduce in, or lay before, Parliament a proposal for legislation; or

   (b) make any primary legislation or remedial order.

This duty is known as the vertical effect of the HRA 1998 because s 7 of the HRA 1998 confers upon a victim of an infringement of his or her human rights by a public authority a direct cause of action so that he or she may bring proceedings against, or defend proceedings brought by, that authority. A 'victim' is a person who is directly affected by the act or omission of the public authority.[31] Where the court finds that a public authority has failed to act as required by s 6, the court may grant such remedy as it deems to be 'just and appropriate', including the award of damages.[32]

2.3.1 Public authorities

Central to vertical effect is what we mean by a 'public authority'. A distinction must be drawn between *core* public authorities and *hybrid* public authorities, which may not appear to be public in nature, but which may nevertheless carry out some public functions. The House of Lords made this functional distinction in *Aston Cantlow and Wilmcote with Billesley Parochial Church Council v Wallbank*.[33]

A core public authority is required to comply with the ECHR in the performance of all of its functions because it is a public authority 'through and through'.[34] The identification of a core public authority should be relatively straightforward: for example, a local authority is a public authority and thus must observe the ECHR when exercising all of its functions, including when acting as a landlord of local authority housing.

A hybrid public authority is only required to comply with the ECHR when exercising those functions that are of a public nature.[35] It is not so constrained when performing a private function. Whether or not a particular body is subject to s 6 as a hybrid public authority thus requires 'a two-fold assessment':[36] firstly, a consideration of whether some of its functions have a public character, so that it qualifies as a hybrid public authority; and secondly, whether the particular function in question was a public function and thus subject to scrutiny. The tests are not always easy to divine.[37] Howell has complained that '*unfortunately the cases reveal at best a lack of consistency and, at worst an apparent lack of awareness of the importance of the question, or at least a disinclination to deal with it directly*'.[38] Yet, given the privatization of a range of public services, the distinction is vital. For instance, the provision of social housing by registered providers, utilizing public funding and subject to statutorily regulated management responsibilities, raises these two key questions.[39]

The Court of Appeal has provided some guidance in *London Quadrant Housing Trust v Weaver*.[40] As a registered provider, London Quadrant entered into private tenancy agreements directly with its tenants, some of whom were nominated by local authorities to meet their statutory housing responsibilities to the homeless. Mrs Weaver was one such tenant. However, she fell into rental arrears and was evicted by London Quadrant. The issue to be determined was whether in terminating Mrs Weaver's tenancy London Quadrant was subject to s 6 of the HRA 1998 because it was a hybrid public authority which was acting

---

[31] Section 7(7) HRA 1998, and Art 34 of the ECHR.   [32] Section 8.   [33] [2004] 1 AC 546.

[34] *Per* Lord Hope at [35].   [35] See s 6(3).

[36] See *Aston Cantlow and Wilmcote with Billesley Parochial Church Council v Wallbank* [2004] 1 AC 546, *per* Lord Hobhouse at [85].

[37] The House of Lords was divided in *Aston Cantlow*, with Lord Scott deciding that the parochial church council, whilst not a core public authority, was exercising a public function as a hybrid public authority. See, also, *YL v Birmingham CC* [2008] 1 AC 95. The restricted scope of the definition has been criticized: see Clayton, 'The Human Rights Act Six Years On: Where Are We Now?' [2007] EHRLR 11.

[38] 'The Human Rights Act 1998: Land, Private Citizens, and the Common Law' (2007) 123 LQR 618.

[39] In the absence of some element of public funding and only a limited level of statutory regulation, a body is unlikely to be classed as a hybrid public authority, see *R (on the application of Macleod) v Peabody Trust Governors* [2016] EWHC 737 and *Southwark Housing Co-operative Ltd v Walker* [2016] Ch 443.

[40] [2010] 1 WLR 363. See also the previous decision in *Poplar Housing and Regeneration Community Association v Donoghue* [2002] QB 48.

in a public, rather than a private, capacity. London Quadrant conceded that it was a hybrid public authority but maintained that in terminating Mrs Weaver's tenancy they were acting as a private landlord. The majority of the Court of Appeal disagreed. In determining whether the act of terminating Mrs Weaver's tenancy was a private act they looked also to the public functions of London Quadrant as a hybrid public authority. They thus treated the two issues as intertwined and provided an insight into how to recognize a hybrid public authority.

Elias LJ

At 66–81

The essential question is whether the act of terminating the tenancy is a private act. When considering how to characterise the nature of the act, it is in my view important to focus on the context in which the act occurs; the act cannot be considered in isolation simply asking whether it involves the exercise of a private law power or not. As Lord Mance observed in YL, both the source and nature of the activities need to be considered when deciding whether a function is public or not, and in my view the same approach is required when determining whether an act is a private act or not within the meaning of section 6(5). Indeed, the difficulty of distinguishing between acts and functions reinforces that conclusion.

In this case there are a number of features which in my judgment bring the act of terminating a social tenancy within the purview of the Human Rights Act.

A useful starting point is to analyse the Trust's function of allocating and managing housing with respect to the four criteria identified by Lord Nicholls in paragraph 12 in the Aston Cantlow case [. . .] First, there is a significant reliance on public finance; there is a substantial public subsidy which enables the Trust to achieve its objectives. This does not involve, as in YL, the payment of money by reference to specific services provided but significant capital payments designed to enable the Trust to meet its publicly desirable objectives.

Second, although not directly taking the place of local government, the Trust in its allocation of social housing operates in very close harmony with it, assisting it to achieve the authority's statutory duties and objectives. In this context the allocation agreements play a particularly important role and in practice severely circumscribe the freedom of the Trust to allocate properties. This is not simply the exercise of choice by the RSL but is the result of a statutory duty to co-operate. That link is reinforced by the extent to which there has been a voluntary transfer of housing stock from local authorities to RSLs.

Third, the provision of subsidised housing, as opposed to the provision of housing itself, is, in my opinion a function which can properly be described as governmental. Almost by definition it is the antithesis of a private commercial activity. The provision of subsidy to meet the needs of the poorer section of the community is typically, although not necessarily, a function which government provides. The Trust, as one of the larger RSLs, makes a valuable contribution to achieving the government's objectives of providing subsidised housing. For similar reasons it seems to me that it can properly be described as providing a public service of a nature described in the Lord Nicholls' fourth factor.

Furthermore, these factors, which point in favour of treating its housing functions as public functions, are reinforced by the following considerations. First, the Trust is acting in the public interest and has charitable objectives. I agree with the Divisional Court that this at least places it outside the traditional area of private commercial activity. Second, the regulation to which it is subjected is not designed simply to render its activities more transparent, or to ensure proper standards of performance in the public interest. Rather the regulations over such matters as rent and eviction are designed, at least in part, to ensure that the objectives of government policy with respect to this vulnerable group in society are achieved and that low cost housing is effectively provided to those in need of it. Moreover, it is intrusive regulation on various aspects of allocation and management, and even restricts the power to dispose of land and property.

None of these factors taken in isolation would suffice to make the functions of the provision of housing public functions, but I am satisfied that when considered cumulatively, they establish sufficient public flavour to bring the provision of social housing by this particular RSL within that concept. That is particularly so given that their Lordships have emphasised the need to give a broad and generous construction to the concept of a hybrid authority.

Is termination of a tenancy a private act?

That still leaves the central question whether the act of termination itself can nonetheless be treated as a private act. Can it be said that since it involves the exercise of a contractual power, it is therefore to be characterised solely as a private act? [. . .]

In my judgment, the act of termination is so bound up with the provision of social housing that once the latter is seen, in the context of this particular body, as the exercise of a public function, then acts which are necessarily involved in the regulation of the function must also be public acts. The grant of a tenancy and its subsequent termination are part and parcel of determining who should be allowed to take advantage of this public benefit. This is not an act which is purely incidental or supplementary to the principal function, such as contracting out the cleaning of the windows of the Trust's properties. That could readily be seen as a private function of a kind carried on by both public and private bodies. No doubt the termination of such a contract would be a private act (unless the body were a core public authority).

In my opinion, if an act were necessarily a private act because it involved the exercise of rights conferred by private law, that would significantly undermine the protection which Parliament intended to afford to potential victims of hybrid authorities. Public bodies necessarily fulfil their functions by entering into contractual arrangements. It would severely limit the significance of identifying certain bodies as hybrid authorities if the fact that the act under consideration was a contractual act meant that it was a private act falling within section 6(5)[. . .]

It follows that in my view the act of terminating the tenancy of Mrs Weaver did not constitute an act of a private nature, and was in principle subject to human rights considerations [. . .]

Rix LJ, however, delivered a dissenting judgment. He was strongly of the view that in terminating a tenancy a social landlord was exercising a private right conferred by a private tenancy agreement.[41] An appeal to the Supreme Court was refused in *Weaver*, although given the importance of the issue, it may well be that another case will be the subject of an appeal.[42]

2.3.2 Section 6(2): defences

The duty imposed by s 6(1) upon public authorities to act in a manner that is compliant with the ECHR is subject to the defences set out in s 6(2).

---

[41] At [147]–[159]. He furthermore expressed doubts about the concession made by London Quadrant that it was a hybrid public authority at [160].

[42] See also *Eastland Homes Partnership Ltd v Whyte* [2010] EWHC 695 where Eastland accepted they were bound by *Weaver* but reserved their position in the event of an appeal.

Human Rights Act 1998, s 6(2)

(2) Subsection (1) does not apply to an act if—

   (a) as the result of one or more provisions of primary legislation, the authority could not have acted differently; or

   (b) in the case of one or more provisions of, or made under, primary legislation which cannot be read or given effect in a way which is compatible with the Convention rights, the authority was acting so as to give effect to or enforce those provisions.

Until an incompatible law is brought into line with the ECHR, public authorities must still go about their work, which may involve applying an incompatible law. Section 6(2) provides a defence to public authorities if they find themselves in this unenviable position.

Section 6(2)(a) provides a defence where a public authority is under a duty to apply an incompatible provision because it 'could not have acted differently'; s 6(2)(b) provides a defence where a public authority has a power, which it may or may not exercise, conferred by an incompatible, but still current, statute. It should be noted that the s 6(2) defences have no application where a public authority is acting under a statutory power which can be interpreted compatibly with the ECHR pursuant to s 3 of the HRA 1998.[43]

The operation of s 6(2)(b) raises several difficult questions. The fundamental issue is whether the subsection enables a public authority to exercise a power or discretion in a way that infringes Convention rights when it could have acted differently. The answer is not yet clear. Lord Hope in *Birmingham CC v Doherty*,[44] in the context of a decision to take possession proceedings pursuant to a statutory scheme, was of the view that s 6(2)(b) should provide a defence in these circumstances. But Lord Mance was of the view that the subsection should not do so[45] and it is with Lord Mance's views that Lord Neuberger in *Manchester CC v Pinnock* expressed agreement.[46] Their Lordships were of the opinion that in taking the decision to recover possession, a public authority would not be acting 'to give effect to' incompatible primary legislation because the public authority would be merely exercising its general powers of management. Its decision was not dictated by the legislation in question and thus the public authority was still under a s 6 duty to act in accordance with Convention values.

A further gloss lies in determining the scope of powers arising under non-compliant primary legislation. As we have noted, statute and the common law are often entwined. Their Lordships in *Doherty* also expressed divergent views as to whether a s 6(2) defence could encompass common law rules, which operate within a statutory framework. Lord Hope was of the view that a defence was available in these circumstances,[47] but Lord Mance disagreed.[48]

2.3.3 The interface with judicial review

As we have noted, s 7 of the HRA 1998 provides a direct cause of action where a public authority has breached its s 6 duty to act in a Convention compliant manner. In addition

---

[43] *Manchester CC v Pinnock* [2011] 2 AC 104 *per* Lord Neuberger, [93]–[103].

[44] [2009] 1 AC 367 at [38]–[40] following his views expressed in *R (Hooper) v Secretary of State for Work and Pensions* [2005] 1 WLR 1681, with which Lord Hoffman agreed.

[45] Ibid at [153]–[159]. Lord Walker also expressed reservations at [113].

[46] [2011] 2 AC 104, [93]–[103].   [47] [2008] 2 WLR 636, [38]–[40].   [48] Ibid [153]–[159].

a public authority's administrative decisions can be questioned through judicial review traditionally based upon the need to meet the requisite procedural standards and the well-known *Wednesbury* reasonableness standard.[49] The enactment of the HRA 1998 has raised two fundamental and controversial issues. First, what is the appropriate standard to be applied where judicial review is founded upon a public authority's failure to comply with human rights standards, and secondly, what is the interface between a s 7 direct human rights cause of action and a public law action by judicial review?

In addressing the first question it is apparent from a series of cases that the courts look beyond the conventional *Wednesbury* test to a standard of proportionality within judicial review proceedings raising a failure to act compatibly with human rights standards.[50] Given this emerging wider basis of judicial review, it has been suggested in answer to the second question that there is little difference between a direct s 7 HRA 1998 challenge and judicial review.[51] But it is important to recognize that the court is engaged in distinct roles. For instance, Hickman has described these roles as the adjudication of standards of review and standards of legality.[52] Judicial review empowers the courts to intervene to question a public authority's decision but no overt duty is placed upon the public authority itself. Whereas standards of legality, whether derived from the rules of natural justice or the HRA 1998, impose duties upon public authorities that the courts, as adjudicators, decide whether or not have been met. Standards of legality, thus, look to *what* the public authority is lawfully able to do and standards of review can question *how* they do so.

These distinctions are reflected in the procedural and remedial frameworks of the two remedies. In judicial review it is for the complainant to demonstrate that the public authority's decision making fell short of the required standard, whereas a challenge under the HRA 1998 requires the public authority to demonstrate that they have acted in a human rights compatible manner. In judicial review it is the validity of the decision that is impugned, whereas a victim of a public authority's failure to meet its duties under the HRA 1998 may obtain personal redress in the form of damages.[53]

2.4 HORIZONTAL EFFECT

The extent to which human rights can operate in a dispute between private individuals is a much debated and complex issue but is particularly significant for land lawyers. It should be noted at the outset that, in contrast to vertical effect, horizontal effect operates not by conferring a cause of action between individual litigants—an individual cannot thus directly claim that his or her human rights have been infringed by another individual. Instead it can operate by permitting a breach of human rights to be claimed in the context

---

[49] *Associated Provincial Picture Houses Ltd v Wednesbury Corp* [1948] 1 KB 223.

[50] *R (on the application of Daly) v SS for the Home Department* [2001] UKHL 26, *R (on the application of Begum) v Denbigh High School Governors* [2006] UKHL 15, *Huang v SS for the Home Department* [2007] UKHL 11, *Belfast CC v Miss Behavin' Ltd* [2007] UKHL 19, *Re (A Child)* [2008] UKHL 66, and *R (on the application of Nasseri) v SS for the Home Department* [2009] UKHL 23.

[51] See, for instance, comments of Walker LJ in *Taylor v Central Bedfordshire Council* [2009] EWCA Civ 613, [38] that the distinction 'has, very largely, become academic'.

[52] Hickman, *Public Law after the HRA* (Oxford: Hart, 2010) ch 4. See also I Leigh, 'Taking Rights Proportionately: Judicial Review, the Human Rights Act and Strasbourg' (2002) PL 265.

[53] Section 8 HRA 1998.

of other proceedings: for instance, by questioning the human rights compatibility of the law governing the dispute.

To engage with this challenging debate, we need to understand the different ways in which horizontality can operate[54] which Leigh has conveniently categorized to identify six possible routes.[55] When we come to consider Art 1 Protocol 1 and Art 8, we can then appreciate their possible horizontal effect. In this regard we will have to consider both the important Supreme Court decision of *McDonald v McDonald*[56] on Art 8 horizontality as well as try to divine the Strasbourg Courts' position.[57]

2.4.1 Direct statutory horizontality—section 3

The obligation of the courts to interpret legislation in a human rights compatible manner has been applied to disputes between private individuals. Indeed the leading s 3 case of *Ghaidan v Godin-Mendoza*[58] involved a dispute between private individuals. Likewise, we shall see in Chapter 9 that courts have considered the human rights compatibility of the law on adverse possession, even though the protagonists were private individuals, because the law is statute-based.[59]

2.4.2 Public liability horizontality—section 6

When considering vertical effect in section 2.3 we saw that a private body may be classified as a hybrid public authority by virtue of s 6(3)(b) and thus required to act in a human rights compliant manner when carrying out functions of a public nature.[60]

2.4.3 The courts and remedial and procedural horizontality—section 6

We noted in section 2.1 the courts' duty, as a public authority, under s 6 to act in a human rights compatible manner. Thus, in adjudicating a dispute between private parties the question arises as to the extent of the courts duties to protect and observe the rights enshrined in the ECHR for instance when exercising any discretion or in the grant of remedial relief.

2.4.4 The courts and indirect and direct horizontality—section 6

The next two forms of horizontality identified by Leigh are also derived from the courts' duties to act in a human rights compatible manner under s 6. They are perhaps the most controversial as they relate to the nature of the courts' duties in the development of the

---

[54] For a most useful explanation see Young, 'Mapping Horizontal Effect' in *The Impact of the UK Human Rights Act on Private Law* (ed Hoffman, Cambridge: CUP, 2011) ch 2.

[55] Leigh, 'Horizontal Rights, the Human Rights Act and Privacy: lessons from the Commonwealth?' (1999) 48 ICLQ 57 at [74]–[85].

[56] [2016] UKSC 28.   [57] See sections 4.2.4 and 4.2.5.   [58] [2004] 2 AC 557.

[59] *Ofulue v Bossert* [2008] EWCA Civ 7. In *JA Pye (Oxford) Ltd v Graham* [2001] EWCA Civ 117, the Court of Appeal considered briefly the application of the HRA 1998. The House of Lords ([2003] 1 AC 419) decided that the HRA 1998 was not applicable, because it did not have retrospective effect, not because it did not have horizontal application.

[60] Section 6(5) HRA 1998.

common law through case law.[61] It has been suggested that the courts as public authorities are required, pursuant to s 6, to comply with human rights norms when performing this role. In the context of land law we have already noted that it can be difficult to treat statute and common law differently because the two sources can be so intimately intertwined. In these instances we can perhaps expect a greater willingness from the courts to pay regard to such norms.

Advocates of this s 6 duty point to the development of the tort of misuse of private information as evidence of the court's acknowledgement of their obligations in this regard.[62] However, there is a divergence of views in the extent and nature of this duty.[63] At one end of this debate are those who suggest that the courts are under a direct duty to develop appropriate common law rights and remedies that permit private parties to take direct action to protect their Convention rights.[64] At the other end of the debate are those who suggest that the courts are only under an indirect obligation in interpreting the common law governing the relations of private parties. Supporters of indirect horizontal effect are divided between those who believe that in this task s 6 merely requires the court to give weight to Convention values (referred to as weak indirect horizontal effect)[65] and those who believe that this obligation imposes a stronger duty upon the courts (referred to as strong indirect horizontal effect).[66]

2.4.5 Intermediate horizontality—section 6 and ECHR

There are occasions when a public authority by reason of their duties under s 6(1) are obliged to ensure that a private individual or body also acts in a human rights compliant manner. Thus, for instance, a public authority may be required to ensure that a non-State actor complies with planning or environmental standards in order to pay due respect a private individual's home and private life under Art 8.

However, our attention is also directed at the higher level of States' duties to observe and protect Convention rights under the ECHR. It is accepted that States are not just subject to a negative obligation not to breach the Convention. They also can owe positive duties to 'protect individual persons from threats to their Convention rights or to assist them to achieve full enjoyment of those rights' by ensuring that non-State actors

---

[61] See Wright, 'A Damp Squib? The Impact of Section 6 HRA on the Common Law: Horizontal Effect and Beyond' [2014] PL 289 for a critique of these arguments.

[62] Phillipson, 'The Common Law, Privacy and the Convention' in *Judicial Reasoning under the Human Rights Act* (eds Fenwick, Phillipson, and Masterman, Cambridge: CUP, 2007) p 9 and Bennett, 'Horizontality's New Horizon's—Re-Examining Horizontal Effect: Privacy Defamation and the Human Rights Act' (2010) 21 Ent LR 96.

[63] See for a summary of the debate Phillipson, 'Clarity Postponed: Horizontal Effect after Campbell' in *Judicial Reasoning under the Human Rights Act* p 215 and Bennett, ibid.

[64] Professor Wade has argued for direct horizontal effect: see 'Horizons of Horizontality' (2000) 116 LQR 217. His views have some support: see Morgan 'Questioning the True Effect of the HRA' (2002) 2 LS 259, Beyleveld and Pattison 'Horizontal Application and Horizontal Effect' (2002) 118 LQR 623, and Bennett, 'Horizontality's New Horizons—Re-Examining Horizontal Effect: Privacy Defamation and the Human Rights Act' (2010) 21 Ent LR 96 and 145.

[65] See Phillipson, 'The Human Rights Act, "Horizontal Effect" and the Common Law: A Bang or a Whimper' (1999) 62 MLR 824 and Phillipson and Alexander, 'Horizontal Effect and the Constitutional Constraint' (2011) 74 MLR 878.

[66] The case for a strong indirect effect is made by Hunt, 'The Horizontal Effect of the Human Rights Act' [1998] PL 423, Lester and Pannick, 'The Impact of the Human Rights Act on Private Law: The Knights Move' (2000) 116 LQR 380, and Beatson and Grosz, 'Horizontality: A Footnote' (2000) 116 LQR 385.

observe Convention norms.[67] The domestic courts need to pay heed to these positive duties through their responsibility to take account of Strasbourg jurisprudence under s 2 of the HRA 1998. These positive duties primarily relate to a State ensuring adequate procedural safeguards in disputes between private parties and that vulnerable victims are adequately protected.[68]

We have already noted in section 2.2.3 the importance that the Strasbourg courts attach to procedural safeguards, to ensure that a state has fallen within its margin of appreciation. Such procedural safeguards are important to ensure that a body, independent of the State, for instance a court or other tribunal, has been able to assess the proportionality of an infringement of a convention right. In particular the independent tribunal should be able to assess whether a fair balance has been struck between the legitimate aim and the impact upon the individual victim, taking into consideration that victim's personal circumstances. The significance of procedural safeguards becomes all the more important where the infringement is extreme. In section 4.2 we look in more detail at adequate procedural safeguards in the context of the important case law concerning the compatibility with Art 8 of rights to possession of a home.

For the time being it is important to note that these procedural safeguards are distinct from the right to a fair trial assured by Art 6 of the ECHR. Article 6 demands due process in the determination of civil rights and obligations including property rights through a timely, fair, and public hearing before an independent tribunal as well as timely execution of any judgment made at that hearing.[69] There are a number of traditional self-help remedies which fall short of these demands, for example, where the landlord is able to exercise a right of re-entry, or right to seize the tenant's possessions by way of distress for unpaid rent without seeking the assistance of the court.[70] The entire course of proceedings, including any right of appeal or to question a decision via judicial review, will be considered when assessing compliance with Art 6.[71] Thus, the fact that a body, that is neither independent nor impartial, initially decides a matter will not necessarily be fatal where there is an adequate right of appeal to a court that is independent and impartial.

Protective positive duties are particularly important where a victim is vulnerable—for instance because of ill health (both physical and mental), age (both young and old),[72] or because they are from a cultural or ethnic background which has traditionally suffered from discrimination (for example Roma or gypsies).[73] The following case illustrates the strength of States' positive duties to protect vulnerable victims even where important property-based consideration such as the enforcement of private contractual obligations, certainty, and the protection of bona fide purchasers are at stake. It also illustrates the importance of procedural safeguards.

---

[67] See, for instance, Kenna, 'Housing Rights: Positive Duties and Enforceable Rights at the European Court of Human Rights' (2008) 2 EHRLR 193, [199].

[68] See Peroni and Timmer, 'Vulnerable Groups: The Promising of an Emerging Concept in European Human Rights Convention Law' (2013) 11 International Journal of Constitutional Law 1056.

[69] *Pelipenko v Russia* [2013] App No 69037/10.   [70] See Chapter 21.

[71] *Manchester CC v Pinnock* [2011] 2 AC 104 at [45].

[72] *Bjedov v Croatia* Application No 42150/09.

[73] For instance gypsies e.g. *Moldovan v Romania* (2007) 44 EHRR 16, *Connors v UK* (2005) 40 EHRR 9, *Yordanova v Bulgaria* Application No 25446/06, *Winterstein v France* Application No 27013/07; and the physically disabled e.g. *Botta v Italy* (1998) 26 EHRR 241 and *Marzari v Italy* (2000) 30 EHRR CD218.

Zehentner v Austria
[2011] 52 EHRR 22

Facts: Ms Zehentner had repairs carried out to her flat but unfortunately suffered from mental illness and had left her flat to receive treatment before she could pay for the repairs. Her workmen obtained judgment for the cost of these repairs which they enforced by obtaining the Austrian equivalent of a charging order. The flat was subsequently sold when the strict time limits for payment of the now secured judgment debt had expired. Because of her illness Ms Zehentner was unaware of the enforcement proceedings and the sale of her flat. However, when she recovered sufficiently to learn of what had happened she successfully claimed that she had been unjustifiably deprived of her possessions under Art 1 Protocol 1 and the right to respect for her home under Art 8 had been violated.

At 61–5

The Court notes at the outset that the judicial sale of the applicant's apartment was authorised on the basis of a payment order which had been issued in summary proceedings. While this may be in the interest of efficient enforcement proceedings, the Court has doubts as to whether the debtor's interests are adequately taken into account where such a payment order, moreover for a comparatively minor sum, can be the basis for the judicial sale of a debtor's "home" within the meaning of Article 8. While the Court does not have to examine this system in the abstract, it notes that in the circumstances of the present case it was particularly detrimental to the applicant. It appears from the expert opinion provided in the guardianship proceedings that by the time the judicial sale of her apartment took place she had lacked legal capacity for years. As a result she had not been in a position either to object to the payment order underlying the decision authorising the judicial sale or to make use of the remedies available to the debtor under the Enforcement Act.

It is true, as the Government pointed out, that the courts were not and could not have been aware of the applicant's lack of legal capacity when conducting the proceedings at issue. However, the Court attaches weight to the fact that once the applicant's lack of legal capacity had been established and a guardian had been appointed for her, she was left without any means of obtaining a review of her case due to the absolute nature of the time-limit for appealing against a judicial sale laid down in section 187 § 1 of the Enforcement Act.

The Court notes the Supreme Court's and the Government's arguments that the said time-limit served to protect the *bona fide* purchaser and the general interests of an efficient administration of justice and of preserving legal certainty. Nevertheless, persons who lack legal capacity are particularly vulnerable and States may thus have a positive obligation under Article 8 to provide them with specific protection by the law (see, *mutatis mutandis, Connors*). While generally there may be good reasons for having an absolute time-limit for lodging an appeal against a judicial sale of real estate, specific justification would be required where a person lacking legal capacity is concerned. The Court notes that the Supreme Court has not given any such justification and has not carried out any weighing of the conflicting interests at stake, namely the interests of the *bona fide* purchaser on the one hand and the debtor lacking legal capacity on the other hand [. . .]

In the present case, neither the protection of the *bona fide* purchaser nor the general interest of preserving legal certainty are sufficient to outweigh the consideration that the applicant, who lacked legal capacity, was dispossessed of her home without being able to participate effectively in the proceedings and without having any possibility to have the proportionality of the measure determined by the courts. It follows that, because of the lack of procedural safeguards, there has been a violation of Article 8 of the Convention in the instant case.

At 73–8

The Court does not overlook the fact that the present case concerned proceedings between private parties, namely the applicant and her creditors on the one hand and the applicant and the purchaser of the apartment on the other hand. However, even in cases involving private litigation the State is under an obligation to afford the parties to the dispute judicial procedures which offer the necessary procedural guarantees and therefore enable the domestic courts and tribunals to adjudicate effectively and fairly in the light of the applicable law (see [. . .] *J.A. Pye*).

In *Zehentner* the source of the State's positive duties lay in providing adequate procedural safeguards to protect Ms Zehentner's vulnerability as a mentally disabled person facing enforcement proceedings in which she lost her home and her property because of the non-payment of relatively small unsecured debts. In the context of Art 8 we will consider other cases where vulnerability has played a key role.

2.4.6 Other protections for the vulnerable—Article 14 and the Equality Act 2010

Vulnerability may also be addressed by invoking Art 14 which prevents discrimination in the enjoyment of Convention rights or by relying on the Equality Act 2010.

European Convention on Human Rights, Art 14

The enjoyment of the rights and freedoms set forth in this Convention shall be secured without discrimination on any ground such as sex, race, colour, language, religion, political or other opinion, national or social origin, association with a national minority, property birth or other status.

Article 14 does not provide a free-standing protection against discrimination.[74] Its operation is directed against discrimination in the enjoyment of the other rights protected by the ECHR. It is said to be parasitic in nature. It is thus necessary for another Article (the 'host Article') to be engaged before Art 14 can be considered. If the breach of the host Article is proved, the court will often not progress to consider whether or not Art 14 has been infringed.[75] But if there is no breach of the host Article, the court may go on to consider whether or not there has been a breach of Art 14: for example, because the justification for

---

[74] The Twelfth Protocol of the ECHR includes a free-standing right against discrimination, but the Protocol has not been signed or ratified by the United Kingdom.

[75] See *Connors v UK* (2005) 40 EHRR 9, although the House of Lords in *Doherty* noted the discriminatory treatment of occupiers evicted from local authority and privately owned travellers' sites—a distinction that has now been removed from the legislation.

infringement of the host Article is itself discriminatory because of one or more of the characteristics protected by Art 14. In this sense, Art 14 is said to be autonomous and can provide an effective weapon that belies its parasitic nature.

Baroness Hale, in the following case, outlined the issues to be established under Art 14.

Ghaidan v Godin-Mendoza [2004] 2 AC 557, HL

Baroness Hale

At 133 and 134

It is common ground that five questions arise in an article 14 inquiry [. . .] The original four questions were: (i) Do the facts fall within the ambit of one or more of the Convention rights? (ii) Was there a difference in treatment in respect of that right between the complainant and others put forward for comparison? (iii) Were those others in an analogous situation? (iv) Was the difference in treatment objectively justifiable? i.e. did it have a legitimate aim and bear a reasonable relationship of proportionality to that aim?

The additional question is whether the difference in treatment is based on one or more of the grounds proscribed—whether expressly or by inference—in article 14. The appellant argued that that question should be asked after question (iv), the respondent that it should be asked after question (ii). In my view, the [. . .] questions are a useful tool of analysis but there is a considerable overlap between them: in particular between whether the situations to be compared were truly analogous, whether the difference in treatment was based on a proscribed ground and whether it had an objective justification. If the situations were not truly analogous it may be easier to conclude that the difference was based on something other than a proscribed ground. The reasons why their situations are analogous but their treatment different will be relevant to whether the treatment is objectively justified. A rigidly formulaic approach is to be avoided.

The victim must thus establish that he or she was treated differently from another person who is in an analogous position because of a proscribed ground—a non-exhaustive list is set out in the Article itself largely based upon innate and immutable characteristics.[76] For example, Mr Godin-Mendoza was able to prove that, as a homosexual, he would be treated differently from a heterosexual partner. The victim must then prove that his or her discriminatory treatment was not reasonably and objectively justifiable: not only must the discrimination be based upon unacceptable grounds but it must also be unjustified.[77] The discriminatory effects of the controversial bedroom tax upon disabled persons, requiring additional space to cope with their disability, have been successfully challenged under Art 14 and Art 1 Protocol 1.[78] By contrast, an Art 14 challenge based upon the difference in the treatment of tenants of a mutual housing association and other residential tenants has been rejected.[79]

---

[76] See discussion in *Southward Housing Co-operative Ltd v Walker* [2016] Ch 443 at [174]–[190] *per* Hildyard J.

[77] See *James v UK* (1986) 8 EHRR 123 and *Chassagnou v France* (2000) 29 EHRR 615.

[78] See *Burnip v Birmingham CC* [2012] EWCA Civ 629, *R(MA) v SSWP* [2013] EWHC 2213 and *R (on the application of Carmichael & others) v SSWP* [2016] UKSC 58; [2016] 1 WLR 4550.

[79] *Southward Housing Co-operative Ltd v Walker* [2016] Ch 443.

The Equality Act 2010 is a free-standing prohibition against discrimination, for instance, in the provision of services (including financial services)[80] or in relation to premises,[81] based on what are known as protected characteristics including race, physical and mental disability, gender, and religion. It is overtly rights-based legislation—it even uses the concept of proportionality. It has vertical and horizontal application because it places duties on both public authorities and private individuals not to discriminate either directly or indirectly.[82] Thus, for instance, no landlord, public or private, can evict an individual because of a protected characteristic, nor can they indirectly discriminate by evicting an individual unless they can prove that their actions or inactions are proportionate.[83] Additionally, in relation to disability the Act imposes both a negative duty not to treat a disabled person less favourably because of their disability unless such treatment may be justified as proportionate in achieving a legitimate aim[84] and a positive duty to make reasonable adjustments to address that disability.[85]

2.4.7 Balancing Convention rights

The horizontal application of the ECHR to property law, whilst beguiling, is problematic. The most significant problem of applying human rights between private individuals is the possibility that the assertion of one party's human rights may lead to the infringement of another's human rights. For instance, in possession proceedings the issue would be where the balance should come to rest between the occupier's Art 8 right to respect for their home and the Art 1 Protocol 1 rights of the owner asserting the right to possession. The issue of competing human rights is beginning to emerge in the balance to be struck between the competing rights under Art 1 Protocol 1 and the freedom of expression under Art 10 where protestors have occupied land.[86] The issue is not confined to competing rights under different Articles but is also important to competing rights under the same Article, for instance, the conflict might be between individuals both claiming interference with their Art 1 Protocol 1 rights.

3 ARTICLE 1 OF THE FIRST PROTOCOL TO THE ECHR

European Convention on Human Rights, First Protocol, Art 1

Protection of property

Every natural or legal person is entitled to the peaceful enjoyment of his possessions. No one shall be deprived of his possessions except in the public interest and subject to the conditions provided for by law and by the general principles of international law.

---

[80] See, for instance, *South Pacific Mortgages Ltd v V* [2015] EWMisc B42.
[81] See Part 4 and particularly s 35(1)(b).
[82] Public authorities are under an additional positive duty to promote equality, see s 149.
[83] *Akerman-Livingstone v Aster Communities Ltd* [2015] UKSC 15.   [84] Section 15(1)(a)–(b).
[85] Sections 20 and 21.
[86] See Lees, 'Actions for Possession in the Context of Political Protest: The Role of Article 1 Protocol 1 and Horizontal Effect' [2014] Conv 211.

The preceding provisions shall not, however, in any way impair the right of a State to enforce such laws as it deems necessary to control the use of property in accordance with the general interest or to secure the payment of taxes or other contributions or penalties.

Article 1 provides a right *of* property and not *to* property. Its object is thus to protect existing property that a person holds by both positively guaranteeing that a person is entitled to the peaceful enjoyment of his or her property, and by providing supporting negative prohibitions upon a person being deprived of his or her possession or being subject to controls over his or her enjoyment of those possessions, unless such incursions can be justified in the public or general interest. In the following extract Gray highlights the fundamental dilemma this balancing creates in defining the nature and social obligations inherent in land ownership.[87]

Gray, 'Land Law and Human Rights' in *Land Law Issues, Debates, Policy* (ed Tee, 2002) 211

At 221

In most areas of property law there exists a tension between two philosophical starting points, which may perhaps be characterised as the perspectives of the *property absolutist* and the *property relativist*. Most lay persons tend, by natural disposition, to be property absolutists – in that they believe passionately and instinctively that ownership of an estate in land confers inviolable and exclusive rights of enjoyment and exploitation. By contrast the property relativist pictures property in terms, not of absolute rights, but rather of qualified entitlements based on social accommodation, community-directed obligation and notions of reasonable user. The dominant modern juristic perception of property is, without much doubt, that of the relativist, partly because the pressures of crowded urban coexistence have forced a fresh recognition of the heavily interdependent nature of our social and economic arrangements. There remain today few true property absolutists, although those who tend towards this view maintain that all regulatory interference with land use necessarily constitutes a compensable 'taking' of property. In its most unqualified form, the absolutist approach castigates uncompensated regulation as environmental fascism and insists that if the community wants environmental welfare, it must purchase it fairly rather than simply dump the unalleviated cost on isolated owners of real estate.

At 241

What *is* certain is that all modern jurisdictions are actively and inevitably engaged in defining (and redefining) the social boundaries of the institution of property. The overall goal is the formulation of a new 'land ethic', replicating in perhaps more contemporary terms Aldo Leopold's noble vision of the propriety of property. And, in exploring in this chapter the social ethics of land ownership, we too have been reaching out towards the elaboration of a new civic morality in the field of property relationships.

---

[87] Walsh points to a similar dilemma in Art 8, see Walsh, 'Stability and Predictability in English Property Law: The Impact of Article 8 of the European Convention on Human Rights Reassessed' (2015) LQR 585.

3.1 WHEN IS ARTICLE 1 ENGAGED?

The first step to consider is whether Art 1 has been engaged, because there has been an interference with possessions under one of the three elements of the Article identified by the Strasbourg Court, in the following case.

Sporrong and Lonnroth v Sweden
(1983) 5 EHRR 35

At 61

The first rule, which is of a general nature, announces the principle of peaceful enjoyment of property; it is set out in the first sentence of the first paragraph. The second rule covers deprivation of possessions and subjects it to certain conditions; it appears in the second sentence of the same paragraph. The third rule recognizes that the States are entitled, amongst other things, to control the use of property in accordance with the general interest, by enforcing such laws as they deem necessary for the purpose; it is contained in the second paragraph.

The rules may be distinct, but it is clear that they are also interrelated, as the Strasbourg Court stated in the following case.

James v UK
[1986] 8 EHRR 123

At 37

The three rules are not however "distinct" in the sense of being unconnected. The second and third rules are concerned with particular instances of interference with the right to peaceful enjoyment of property and should therefore be construed in the light of the general principle enunciated in the first rule.

Thus, the second and third rules need to be considered in the light of the overarching nature of the first rule. An interference that is justified under these rules by their limiting conditions will also satisfy the first rule. This point was also made in *James*.

James v UK
[1986] 8 EHRR 123

At 71

The rule (in the second sentence) subjects deprivation of possessions to certain conditions concerns a particular category, indeed of the most radical kind, of interference with the right to peaceful enjoyment of property [. . .]; the second sentence supplements and qualifies the general principle enunciated in the first sentence. This being so, it is inconceivable that application of the general principle to the present case should lead to any conclusion different from that already arrived at by the court in the application of the second sentence.

The courts will look to see whether the last two rules are applicable before considering whether the first rule has been infringed.[88] This analysis and approach has been adopted in subsequent cases.

3.1.1 The meaning of 'possessions'

'Possessions' bears what is known as an autonomous meaning in Strasbourg jurisprudence.[89] This means that the Strasbourg Court develops its own interpretation of a term. In so doing, it will look to, but will not be bound by, the meaning of the term within the appropriate domestic jurisdiction.[90] In fact, the Strasbourg Court has adopted a wide interpretation of 'possessions', and there is no doubt that our established notions of estates and interests in land fall within its meaning. The term also covers other accepted categories of property rights that fall outside the scope of this book, such as personal and intellectual property, as well as rights that may arise from contractual relations, a tortious claim, or statute.[91] But an expectation that you may receive property in the future—for example, by inheritance—is not a possession for the purposes of Art 1.[92] This raises the question of whether an inchoate equity—for example, arising by estoppel (see Chapter 10)—constitutes a possession for the purpose of Art 1. Case law before the Strasbourg Courts and our domestic courts raises the distinct possibility, at least where a public authority raises a legitimate expectation of entitlement.[93]

Land may have the benefit of certain rights: for example, an easement (see Chapter 22), or the benefit of a covenant (see Chapter 23), or, in the case of a leasehold reversion, a right to receive rent and to re-enter for breach of the tenant's covenants (see Chapter 21). These benefits do not constitute separate possessions for the purposes of Art 1; rather, they are encompassed within the property to which they are attached.[94] Likewise, land may be subject to an encumbrance in favour of a third person: for example, an easement or restrictive covenant in favour of a neighbouring owner. The possession that is vested in the landowner is the appropriate estate in the land, as burdened by the encumbrance. In other words, if you acquire land that is already subject to a burden, the burden does not engage Art 1.

The House of Lords confirmed this approach in the following case. The encumbrance in question was a liability to pay for chancel repairs to the local church: an unusual liability that can be difficult to discover, but which Lord Hope described as follows.

---

[88] See *Sporrong and Lonnroth v Sweden* (1983) 5 EHRR 35, [61].

[89] Allen, 'The Autonomous Meaning of "Possessions" under the European Convention on Human Rights' in *Modern Studies in Property Law Vol 2* (ed Cooke, 2003) p 58.

[90] See *Matos E Silva Lda v Portugal* (1997) 24 EHRR 573. Although see comments of Patten LJ in *Ker v Optima Community Housing Association* [2013] EWCA Civ 579 at [36], criticized in Bright, Hopkins, and Macklam, 'Possession Proceedings and Human Rights: Something More Required' [2013] Conv 422.

[91] E.g. a statutory right to apply for a new tenancy, see *Pennycook v Shaws (EAL) Ltd* [2004] Ch 296, to fishing quotas *R(on the application of Mott) v Environment Agency* [2016] 1 WLR 4338, or to an allotment *Moore v SS for Home Department* [2016] EWHC 2736 (Admin).

[92] *Marckx v Belgium* (1979) 2 EHRR 330.

[93] *Stretch v UK* (2004) 38 EHRR 12. See also *Pine Valley Developments Ltd v Ireland* (1992) 14 EHRR 319. The principle has been applied by the domestic courts in *Rowland v Environment Agency* [2003] EWCA Civ 1885 but see *Ker v Optima Community Association* [2013] EWCA Civ 579. See Elliott, 'Legitimate Expectations and Unlawful Representations' (2004) 63 CLJ 261.

[94] *Antoniades v UK* (App No 15434/89) and *Scott v UK* (App No 10741/84).

Aston Cantlow and Wilmcote with Billesley Parochial Church Council v Wallbank
[2004] 1 AC 546, HL

Lord Hope

At 71

[. . .] just like any other burden which runs with the land which is, and has been at all times within the scope of the property right which [was] acquired and among other factors to be taken into account in determining its value [. . .] The enforcement of the liability under the general law is an incident of the property right which is now vested jointly in Mr and Mrs Wallbank. It is not [. . .] an outside intervention by way of a form of tax.

The creation of a new encumbrance or burden may, however, engage Art 1. In most cases, the owner will have consensually created that encumbrance and so can hardly complain that his or her rights have been infringed. It is where that encumbrance has arisen, or is deemed to have arisen, by operation of external legal rules that Art 1 may be engaged.[95]

A further difficult question is whether or not a contract that is void under the terms of a statute is capable of comprising a possession within the terms of the Article. The House of Lords considered this issue in *Wilson v First County Trust Ltd*,[96] although they did not speak with one voice. In *Wilson*, the credit agreement was void for failing to comply with necessary statutory requirements.[97] Lords Hope and Scott decided that no agreement had been created in the first place, and thus there was no possession of which First County could be deprived. Lord Nicholls disagreed. He believed that a statutory provision that robbed an agreement of its force should not escape review under the HRA 1998, otherwise '[a] *Convention right guaranteeing a right to property would have nothing to say*'.

A similar, although slightly different, question is whether a possession is also inherently limited by the operation of the legal rules to which it is subject and therefore cannot be infringed by the operation of those rules. Here, the law regulates the possession, rather than dictates its creation. The answer to this question is clear: the operation of such rules may engage Art 1.[98] Goymour explains why.

Goymour, 'Proprietary Claims and Human Rights: A "Reservoir of Entitlement"?' (2006) 65 CLJ 696, p 711

At 711

However this argument, whilst technically compelling, would largely strip Article 1 of any sensible meaning. Indeed, one type of conduct which Article 1 Protocol 1 typically regulates is arbitrary compulsory acquisition of private property by the State. If one were to say that

---

[95] E.g. an easement arising by implication or by prescription: see, further, Chapter 22.

[96] [2004] 1 AC 816, although their comments are dicta.

[97] The offending s 127 has been amended by the Consumer Credit Act 2006, s 15. However, similar concerns may arise with a contract for the sale of land that is void under s 2(1), Law of Property (Miscellaneous Provisions) Act 1989.

[98] *JA Pye (Oxford) Ltd v UK* (2008) 46 EHRR 45. See also (2006) 43 EHRR 3.

all property is inherently liable to compulsory acquisition, Article 1 Protocol 1 would rarely, if ever, bite. The Convention is supposed to guard against interference with property rights. To say Article 1, Protocol 1 fails to be engaged because property rights are inherently vulnerable is logical but circular.

3.1.2 Deprivation of possessions: the second limb

The second limb of Art 1 is concerned with the deprivation of possessions. A 'deprivation' is generally defined by a transfer or shift in ownership: examples include the compulsory purchase of land,[99] the nationalization of a business by the government,[100] or the confiscation of the proceeds of crime.[101] The transfer need not be to the government, or other public authority; it may be to another private individual, where the State has sanctioned that transfer by legislation.[102]

By contrast, what might at first sight appear to be deprivation, on closer examination is a consequence of the delineation of the possession itself. Most obviously, the determination of a lease (whether by the expiry of the term, by a notice to quit, or by a right of forfeiture) does not deprive the tenant of his or her possessions, because the lease is defined by these means of termination from the outset.[103] For instance, in *Sims v Dacorum BC*,[104] the Supreme Court held that the exercise of a contractual right to terminate a joint lease by one joint tenant did not constitute a deprivation of possession, it was a feature of the lease itself. More difficult are questions of whether a power of trustees or a mortgagee to sell and overreach the beneficiaries' or mortgagor's possession is an inherent characteristic of those possessions. Goymour suggests that the question may turn on whether the power is taken to be expressly conferred, and thus defines the possession, or is a consequence of statutory imposition.[105]

3.1.3 Controls over possessions: the third limb

A government may enact laws that control the use of land, the most obvious example being planning controls.[106] Rent controls and limitations upon a landlord's right to recover their property from a tenant are further examples of controls over possessions.[107] More unusual examples include controls over fishing,[108] and hunting rights over land,[109] or controls over who can actually use the land.[110]

---

[99] *Howard v UK* (1987) 9 EHRR CD 116.   [100] *Lithgow v UK* (1986) 8 EHRR 329.

[101] *R v May* [2008] 1 AC 1028, *R v Waya* [2013] 1 AC 294, and *R v Ahmad* [2014] 3 WLR 23.

[102] *James v UK* (1986) 8 EHRR 123.

[103] *Sheffield CC v Smart* [2002] HLR 34 at [46] and *Lancashire CC v Taylor* [2005] 1 P & CR 2 at [57].

[104] [2013] 3 WLR 1006 at [14].

[105] 'Property and Housing' in *The Impact of the UK Human Rights Act on Private Law*, (ed Hoffman, Cambridge: CUP, 2011) ch 12, pp 281–4.

[106] *Pine Valley Development Ltd v Ireland* (1992) 14 EHRR 319.

[107] *Hutten-Czapska v Poland* (2007) 45 EHRR 4, *Lindheim v Norway* App No 13221/08 and 2139/10, *Edwards v Malta* App No 17647/04, *Bitto v Slovakia* App No 30255/09, *Statileo v Croatia* App No 12027/10, and *Berger-Krall v Slovenia* App No 14717/04.

[108] *Baner v Sweden* (App No 11763/85).

[109] *Chassagnou v France* (App Nos 25088/94, 28331/95, and 28443/95).

[110] *Gillow v UK* (1989) 11 EHRR 335.

3.1.4 Deprivation or control?

Whether or not an interference constitutes a deprivation or control of property is not always as clear-cut as the above examples.[111] The distinction is significant when it comes to considering whether or not the interference is proportionate and in particular the payment of compensation. An extensive control over a possession may amount to a de facto expropriation where the victim is deprived of all meaningful use of their property.[112] For instance in *R (on the application of Mott) v Environment Agency*,[113] controls over a lease granting a right to fish salmon in the Severn estuary which reduced the catch by 95 per cent was held to be closer to a deprivation than a control and in any event called for the payment of compensation.

It might initially be thought that the extinction of the paper owner's title by the operation of adverse possession is a clear example of a deprivation of property.[114] The Grand Chamber of the Strasbourg Court decided, however, that the effect of the limitation periods for the recovery of possession of land and their consequent effect on the paper owner's title was a control of property. In effect, the Court viewed the extinction of the paper owner's title more as an administrative step that brought the legal evidence of ownership into line with the de facto position when the squatter could no longer be evicted.

JA Pye (Oxford) Ltd v UK
(2008) 46 EHRR 45, Grand Chamber

Facts: Pye owned land that it intended to develop. In the meantime, it licensed the land to a neighbouring farmer, Mr Graham. When the licence expired, Mr Graham continued in adverse possession of the land for a period in excess of the limitation period of twelve years. When Pye eventually tried to evict Mr Graham, the House of Lords dismissed its claim and held that Mr Graham was entitled to be registered as the owner. Pye unsuccessfully claimed that it had been deprived of its ownership in breach of Art 1 of the First Protocol.

At 65

The applicant companies did not lose their land because of a legislative provision which permitted the State to transfer ownership in particular circumstances (as in the cases of *AGOSI, Air Canada, Gasus*), or because of a social policy of transfer of ownership (as in the case of *James*), but rather as the result of the operation of the generally applicable rules on limitation periods for actions for recovery of land.

At 66

The statutory provisions which resulted in the applicant companies' loss of beneficial ownership were thus not intended to deprive paper owners of their ownership, but rather to regulate questions of title in a system in which, historically, 12 years' adverse possession was

---

[111] See discussion in Bright, Hopkins, and Macklam, 'Owning Part but Losing All' in *Modern Studies in Property Law Vol 7* (ed Hopkins, Oxford: Hart Publishing, 2013) pp 24–9.
[112] *Sporrong v Sweden* (1982) 5 EHRR 35 at [63] and *Fredin v Sweden* (1991) 13 EHRR 784 at [41].
[113] [2016] 1 WLR 4336.
[114] See ss 15 and 17 Limitation Act 1980, s 75 Land Registration Act 1925, and Chapter 9.

sufficient to extinguish the former owner's right to re-enter or to recover possession, and the new title depended on the principle that unchallenged lengthy possession gave a title. The provisions of the 1925 and 1980 Acts which were applied to the applicant companies were part of the general land law, and were concerned to regulate, amongst other things, limitation periods in the context of the use and ownership of land as between individuals. The applicant companies were therefore affected, not by a "deprivation of possessions" within the meaning of the second sentence of the first paragraph of Article 1, but rather by a "control of use" of land within the meaning of the second paragraph of the provision.

3.1.5 Peaceful enjoyment: the first limb

An interference that does not fall within the second or third limb may nevertheless be an interference with the peaceful enjoyment of possession under the residual category provided by the first limb. *Sporrong and Lonnroth v Sweden*[115] provides an example. The complainants owed land in Stockholm that was earmarked for development and the authorities issued expropriation notices.[116] Although the notices were never implemented, the complainants' ability to deal with their land was blighted. The Court found that there was no deprivation or control under the second and third limbs, but did find that there was an infringement of the first rule.

3.2 WHEN IS AN INTERFERENCE JUSTIFIED?

Here, we must apply the justification formula which we considered in section 2.2. Under Art 1 of the First Protocol, a deprivation of possession may be justified if it is '*in the public interest and subject to the conditions provided for by law and by the general principles of international law*', whilst a control of possessions may be justified if it is made pursuant to '*laws as* [the State] *deems necessary* [. . .] *in accordance with the general interest or to secure the payment of taxes or other contributions or penalties*'.

3.2.1 Subject to the law

The interference must be in accordance with domestic law.[117] Furthermore, that domestic law must satisfy the fundamental requirements of the rule of law. It must not operate arbitrarily, it must be certain and accessible, and it must provide adequate procedural safeguards.[118]

3.2.2 The public and general interest

It is not thought that there is a distinction between the public and general interest. These expressions define the legitimate interest in respect of which a deprivation or control may

---

[115] (1983) 5 EHRR 35.

[116] Prohibition notices prohibiting building were also issued, but these had lapsed.

[117] *R & L, SRO & others v The Czech Republic* App Nos 37926/05, 25784/09, 36002/09, 44410/09, and 65546/09.

[118] In contrast to *Lithgow v UK* (1986) 8 EHRR 329, *James v UK* (1986) 8 EHRR 329, the Court in *Hentrich v France* (1994) 18 EHRR 440 found that the domestic law failed to satisfy the rule of law. It operated arbitrarily and did not provide adequate procedural safeguards.

be justified. States enjoy a wide margin of appreciation in both identifying what is in the public interest and in formulating the appropriate measures to address that interest. The width of a State's margin of appreciation is evident from *James v UK*.[119]

James v UK
(1986) 8 EHRR 123

At 43

In the Court's opinion, even if there could be a difference between the concepts of "public interest" and "general interest" in Article 1 (P-1), on the point under consideration no fundamental distinction of the kind contended for by the applicants can be drawn between them [. . .]

At 47

The aim of the 1967 Act as spelt out in the 1966 White Paper, was to right the injustice which was felt to be caused to occupying tenants by the operation of the long leasehold system of tenure (see para 18 above). The Act was designed to reform the existing law, said to be inequitable to the leaseholder," and to give effect to what was described as the occupying tenant's "moral entitlement" to the ownership of the house.

Eliminating what are judged to be social injustices is an example of the functions of a democratic legislature. More especially, modern societies consider housing of the population to be a prime social need, the regulation of which cannot entirely be left to the play of market forces. The margin of appreciation is wide enough to cover legislation aimed at securing greater social justice in the sphere of people's homes, even where such legislation interferes with the existing contractual relations between private parties and confers no direct benefit on the State or the community at large. In principle therefore the aim pursued by the leasehold reform legislation is a legitimate one.

The transition of Eastern European countries from communist regimes to democratic States has necessitated a reform of their property laws, in particular reforms to residential tenancies. These reforms have spawned a number of Art 1 Protocol 1 challenges in which the Grand Chamber have acknowledged the difficulty of this transition, which they found fell within the State's margin of appreciation.

Hutten-Czapska v Poland
(2007) 45 EHRR 4

At 166

The notion of "public" or "general" interest is necessarily extensive. In particular, spheres such as housing of the population, which modern societies consider a prime social need and which plays a central role in the welfare and economic policies of contracting states, may often call for some form of regulation by the state. In that sphere decisions as to whether, and if so when, it may fully be left to the play of free market forces or whether it should be

---

[119] See also *Kateb v Howard de Walden Estates Ltd* [2017] 1 WLR 1761.

subject to state control, as well as the choice of measures for securing the housing needs of the community and of the timing for their implementation, necessarily involve consideration of complex social, economic and political issues.

Finding it natural that the margin of appreciation available to the legislature in implementing social and economic policies should be a wide one, the Court has on many occasions declared that it will respect the legislature's judgment as to what is in the "public" or "general" interest unless that judgment is manifestly without reasonable foundation. These principles apply equally, if not a fortiori, to the measures adopted in the course of the fundamental reform of the country's political, legal and economic system in the transition from a totalitarian regime to a democratic state.

The real focus of the courts' review is thus on the proportionality of the interference in meeting the public interest.[120] In assessing proportionality, the courts will need to determine whether a fair balance has been struck between the public interest to be addressed and the individual's right to the protection of his or her possessions. A number of factors may need to be considered, depending on the circumstances of the particular case, but two factors are particularly prominent: firstly, the availability of compensation; and secondly, the adequacy of the process to challenge the interference.

The reform of housing policy in Eastern Europe, already referred to, demonstrates the delicate tightrope that may need to be negotiated to find this fair balance. Challenges have been asserted primarily by landlords chaffing against rent and security of tenure controls[121] but also by tenants bemoaning the loss of protection.[122] Although the Grand Chamber in *Hutten-Czapska* found that the impugned legislation was within the Polish State's margin of appreciation, they decided that it failed to achieve the necessary fair balance because landlords were expected to bear a disproportionate burden. Thus, there had been a breach of Art 1 Protocol 1.

Hutten-Czapska v Poland
(2007) 45 EHRR 4

At 224–5

[The Grand Chamber explicitly agreed with the opinion of The Chamber]

In this regard the Court would once again refer to its case law confirming that in many cases involving limitations on the rights of landlords – which were and are common in countries facing housing shortages – the limitations applied have been found to be justified and proportionate to the aims pursued by the State in the general interest (see Spadea and Scalabrino, cited above, § 18, and Mellacher and Others, cited above, §§ 27 and 55). However, in none of those cases had the authorities restricted the applicants' rights to such a considerable extent as in the present case [. . .]

---

[120] In the domestic context see the acknowledgement of the need for proportionality in the confiscation of crime proceeds in *R v Waya* [2013] 1 AC 294.

[121] See also *Bitto v Slovakia* App No 30255/09 and *Statileo v Croatia* App No 12027/10. Such controls imposed as a matter of housing policy in other States have also been subject to scrutiny, see *Lindheim v Norway* App No 13221/08 and 2139/10, *Edwards v Malta* App No 17647/04.

[122] *Berger-Krall v Slovenia* App No 14717/04.

It is true that, as stated in the Chamber judgment, the Polish State, which inherited from the communist regime the acute shortage of flats available for lease at an affordable level of rent, had to balance the exceptionally difficult and socially sensitive issues involved in reconciling the conflicting interests of landlords and tenants. It had, on the one hand, to secure the protection of the property rights of the former and, on the other, to respect the social rights of the latter, often vulnerable individuals (see paragraphs 12–19 and 176 above). Nevertheless, the legitimate interests of the community in such situations call for a fair distribution of the social and financial burden involved in the transformation and reform of the country's housing supply. This burden cannot, as in the present case, be placed on one particular social group, however important the interests of the other group or the community as a whole.

In the light of the foregoing, and having regard to the effects of the operation of the rent-control legislation during the whole period under consideration on the rights of the applicant and other persons in a similar situation, the Court considers that the Polish State has failed to strike the requisite fair balance between the general interests of the community and the protection of the right of property.

There has accordingly been a violation of Article 1 of Protocol No. 1.

A further interesting question on striking a fair balance arises in a number of Strasbourg cases (all against Russia) dealing with the responsibility for the loss of ownership of a victim's land (usually their home) where fraud has been uncovered in the chain of their registered title.[123] The Strasbourg Court held the State liable in these cases where the relevant registration regime provided no compensation to the victim. There was, however, a strong dissenting voice which suggested that the risk should lie with the victims because they should have investigated their title more carefully in the light of the traditional caveat emptor or 'buyer beware' principle. Fortunately, the Land Registration Act 2002 does provide for the possibility of compensation in such circumstances—see Chapter 18.

3.2.3 Compensation

Many constitutional guarantees of property rights include an express right to compensation upon the compulsory acquisition of property by the State. Article 1 does not expressly do so,[124] but the Strasbourg Court has made clear that where the second limb of the Article is engaged (i.e. where there is a deprivation of property), compensation is to be expected, although that compensation may be less than market value.[125]

---

[123] *Ponyayyeva v Russia* App No 63508/11, *Pchelintseva v Russia* App nos 47724/07, 58677/11, 2920/13, 3127/13 and 15320/13. See also *Tomina v Russia* App Nos 20578/08, 21159/08, 22903/08, 24519/08, 24728/08, 25084/08, 25558/08, 25559/08, 27555/08, 27568/08, 28031/08, 30511/08, 31038/08, 45120/08, 45124/08, 45131/08, 45133/08, 45141/08, 45167/08 ,and 45173/08).

[124] Allen explains that this omission was because the right to compensation was controversial in, 'Liberalism, social democracy and the value of property under the European Convention on Human Rights' (2010) 59 ICLQ 1055.

[125] See also *Holy Monasteries v Greece* (1995) 20 EHRR 51 and *The Former King of Greece v Greece* (App No 25701/94) and *Mago v Bosnia & Herzogovina* Application Nos 12959/05, 19724/05, 47860/06, 8367/08, 9872/09 and 11706/09. Allen ibid questions Strasbourg's approach to the calculation of compensation.

James v UK
(1986) 8 EHRR 123

At 54

The taking of property in the public interest without payment of compensation is treated as justifiable only in exceptional circumstances [. . .] As far as Article 1 (P1–1) is concerned, the protection of the right to property it affords would be largely illusory and ineffective in the absence of any equivalent principle. Clearly compensation terms are material to the assessment whether the contested legislation respects a fair balance between the various interests at stake and, notably, it does not impose a disproportionate burden on the applicants [. . .]

The Court further accepts the Commission's conclusion as to the standard of compensation: the taking of property without payment of an amount reasonably related to the value would normally constitute a disproportionate interference which could not be considered justifiable under Article 1 (P1–1). Article 1 (P1–1) does not, however guarantee a right to full compensation in all circumstances. Legitimate objectives of "public interest" such as pursued in measures of economic reform or measures designed to achieve greater social justice may call for less than reimbursement of the full market value. Furthermore, the Court's power of review is limited to ascertaining whether the choice of compensation terms falls outside the State's wide margin of appreciation in this domain.

The requirement for compensation is not so strong where the interference is a control over property under the third limb.[126] For example, the Grand Chamber in *Pye*, having decided that the interference was a control rather than a deprivation of possession, went on to hold that a lack of compensation to the paper owner whose title is extinguished could be justified.

JA Pye (Oxford) Ltd v UK
(2008) 46 EHRR 45

At 79

The Chamber and the applicant companies emphasised the absence of compensation for what they both perceived as a deprivation of the applicant's companies' possessions. The Court has found the interference with the applicant's companies' possession was a control of use, rather than a deprivation of possession, such that the case law on compensation for deprivations is not directly applicable. Further, in the cases in which a situation was analysed as a control of use even though the application lost possessions (*AGOSI*, and *Air Canada* [. . .]), no mention was made of a right to compensation. The Court would note, in agreement with the Government, that a requirement of compensation for the situation brought about by a party failing to observe a limitation period would sit uneasily alongside the very concept of limitation periods, whose aim is to further legal certainty by preventing a party from pursuing action after a certain date. The Court would also add that, even under the provisions of the Land Registration Act 2002, which the applicant companies use as confirmation that the provisions of earlier legislation were not compatible with the Convention, no compensation is payable by a person who is ultimately registered as a new owner of registered land on expiry of the limitation period.

[126] *Baner v Sweden* (1989) 60 DR 128; *Chassagnou v France* (2000) 29 EHRR 615.

Nevertheless Gray, in the context of environmental regulation, points out the difficult dividing line between extensive regulatory control and deprivation and its consequences in terms of who should bear the cost. Indeed in *R (on the application of Mott) v Environment Agency*,[127] the Court of Appeal accepted the possibility that an extensive environmental control might call for the payment of compensation to achieve a fair balance.

Gray, 'Land Law and Human Rights' in *Land Law Issues, Debates, Policy* (ed Tee, 2002) 211

At 218

The pertinent difficulty is that much modern governmental activity involves, not the outright acquisition of a freehold or leasehold estate in land, but rather the imposition of substantial community-oriented restrictions upon the *free enjoyment* of estate ownership. In such cases the landowner suffers not expropriation, but a form of 'injurious affection'. We live in an age of unprecedented regulation [. . .] with the consequence that the landowner's user rights are potentially cut back by a plethora of regulatory controls which, without any divesting of his formal proprietary title, severely limit the landowner's ability to exploit his land in precisely the way he may wish. Such constraints range from urban planning legislation to nature conservation measures; from negative controls which restrict the scope of future development to positive impositions which require that the landowner cede various rights of user over his land or even reinstate the land to prescribed environmental standards. It is particularly significant, in this context, that increasing emphasis is nowadays placed on the importance of enhanced public access to recreational land and leisure opportunities as a necessary precondition of improved community health and the promotion of 'social equity' [. . .] In the present context the critical question is not about the statutory competence of relevant forms of regulation. By and large we all agree, at least at the level of abstract principle, that important features of environmental value require protection. The central question relates instead to the allocation of the *cost* of the environmental protection which we all profess to desire; and this cost may be measured in terms of forgone development value or lost amenity or sheer cash outlay. It remains a contingent fact of life that the promotion of environmental welfare comes at a price which must be paid either by the general community or by some subset of it. Should the individual landowner be left to bear the cost of a regulatory intervention which enures to the wider benefit of the whole community?

The question of whether or not compensation is required is thus likely to call for a closer examination of the legitimate aim, as well as the financial impact of the control or disturbance upon the complainant. The minority in *Pye* also drew a connection between the need for compensation and the procedural safeguards available:[128] '[. . .] *the fact that the landowner received no compensation made the loss of beneficial ownership the more serious and required, in our view, particularly strong measures of protection of the registered owner's property rights if a fair balance was to be preserved*'.

---

[127] [2016]1 WLR 4338 at [87].   [128] At [16].

3.2.4 Procedural safeguards

The process by which a person is deprived of their possessions, or by which controls are imposed upon their possessions, is an important aspect of proportionality. The fair balance may be upset if the individual has no opportunity to question the interference.[129] The importance of procedural safeguards under Art 1 Protocol 1 is illustrated by the case of *Zehentner v Austria*, which we first looked at in section 2.4.3. The Strasbourg Court held that in respect of Art 1 Protocol 1 the judicial sale of the victim's property was a disproportionate interference with the victim's property, given the relatively small debts involved, and because the process took no account of the victim's incapacity. Furthermore, the procedural possibility of challenging the debts themselves on the grounds of the victim's lack of capacity did not constitute a viable alternative.

Zehentner v Austria
(2011) 52 EHRR 22

At 73–8

The present case raises an issue regarding the applicant's procedural protection in the proceedings at issue.

In that respect, the Court [. . .] has doubts as to whether the debtor's interests are adequately taken into account where a payment order for a comparatively minor sum issued in summary proceedings can serve as a basis for the judicial sale of real estate of considerable value [. . .]

However, under Article 1 of Protocol No. 1 the Court is examining the judicial sale of the applicant's apartment not from the point of view that it was the applicant's "home" but from the point of view of property rights. In that context the Government's argument that the applicant had alternative means to protect her pecuniary interests needs to be examined. The Government pointed out that the applicant, represented by her guardian, had obtained a finding that the payment orders underlying the judicial sale were not enforceable due to her lack of legal capacity. Subsequently, she would be able to obtain a review of the proceedings on the merits and, if they resulted in her creditor's claims being dismissed, she could claim reimbursement of the amounts which had been paid to them from the proceeds of the judicial sale.

However, the Court is not convinced that this procedural mechanism, which requires conducting a number of consecutive sets of proceedings against each of the applicant's creditors, offers adequate protection to a person lacking legal capacity. It therefore refers to its above considerations dismissing the Government's argument that the strict time-limit for appealing against a judicial sale was justified in the interests of protecting the *bona fide* purchaser and in the general interests of an efficient administration of justice and of preserving legal certainty. In sum the Court does not find any reasons to come to a different conclusion under Article 1 of Protocol No. 1.

The Chamber's decision in *Pye*[130] was also largely premised on the lack of procedural safeguards afforded to the paper owner, whose registered title was automatically extinguished

---

[129] *Hentrich v France* (1994) 18 EHRR 440. See also the Scottish decisions of *Karl Construction Ltd v Palisade Properties Ltd* [2002] SLT 312; *AG for Scotland v Taylor* [2003] SLT 1340; *Maguire v Itoh* [2004] SLT (Sheriff Ct) 120.
[130] (2006) 43 EHRR 3.

(without notification) on the expiration of the twelve-year limitation period.[131] On appeal, the majority of the Grand Chamber, however, was satisfied that adequate procedural safeguards did exist.[132]

4 ARTICLE 8: THE RIGHT TO RESPECT FOR PRIVATE AND FAMILY LIFE AND THE HOME

European Convention on Human Rights, Art 8

1. Everyone has the right to respect for his private and family life, his home and his correspondence.

2. There shall be no interference by a public authority with the exercise of this right except such as is in accordance with the law and is necessary in a democratic society in the interests of national security, public safety or the economic well-being of the country, for the prevention of disorder or crime, for the protection of health or morals, or for the protection of the rights and freedoms of others.

The inspiration for Art 8 is drawn from rights to privacy commonly found in other international human rights instruments,[133] although it does not refer explicitly to a right to privacy, but rather to a right to respect. Our discussion of Art 8 will concentrate on the respect that it affords to the home. At the outset, it should be noted that the Article does not confer a right to a home, nor does it place upon the government an obligation to meet an individual's housing needs.[134] The focus is upon the protection afforded to an individual's existing home. In this context, there are clear interactions between the home and a person's private and family life, which is also protected under Art 8.

4.1 WHEN IS ARTICLE 8(1) ENGAGED?

4.1.1 Meaning of 'home'

'Home' has an autonomous meaning, being a place of residence with which the individual has '*sufficient and continuing links*', and is not dependent upon that person having a legal right of occupation. This test was developed by the Strasbourg Court in the case of *Gillow v UK*,[135] and has been consistently applied in subsequent cases by the Strasbourg Court, the House of Lords, and the Supreme Court.

---

[131] See ss 15 and 17 Limitation Act 1980, and s 75 of the Land Registration Act 1925. The same lack of notification also affects unregistered land.

[132] (2008) 46 EHRR 45. See Chapter 9.

[133] E.g. Art 17 of the International Covenant on Civil and Political Rights provides that: '*No one shall be subjected to arbitrary or unlawful interference with his privacy, family and home or correspondence, nor to unlawful attacks on his honour and reputation. Everyone has the right to the protection of the law against such interference or attacks.*' Art 12 of the Universal Declaration of Human Rights is identical, but is contained in a single paragraph.

[134] *Chapman v UK* (2001) 33 EHRR 318, [99].   [135] (1989) 11 EHRR 335.

Harrow LBC v Qazi
[2004] 1 AC 983, HL

Lord Bingham

At 8–10

Not surprisingly, the need for some protection of the home was recognised in the Convention, since few things are more central to the enjoyment of human life than having somewhere to live. On a straightforward reading of the Convention, its use of the expression "home" appears to invite a down-to-earth and pragmatic consideration whether [. . .] the place in question is that where a person "lives and to which he returns and which forms the centre of his existence", since "home" is not a legal term of art and article 8 is not directed to the protection of property interests or contractual rights.

[. . .] this has been the approach of the Strasbourg institutions also. In *Gillow v United Kingdom* (1986) 11 EHRR 335, para 46, the court held that the house in question was the applicants' home because although they had been absent from Guernsey for many years they had not established any other home elsewhere in the United Kingdom and had retained "sufficient continuing links" with the house for it to be considered their home for the purposes of article 8. This test was repeated and elaborated by the commission in *Buckley v United Kingdom* (1996) 23 EHRR 101, 115, para 63:

> " 'Home' is an autonomous concept which does not depend on classification under domestic law. Whether or not a particular habitation constitutes a 'home' which attracts the protection of article 8(1) will depend on the factual circumstances, namely, the existence of sufficient and continuous links. The factor of 'unlawfulness' is relevant rather to considerations under paragraph 2 of that provision of 'in accordance with law' and to the balancing exercise undertaken between the interests of the community and those of the individual in assessing the necessity of any interference." [. . .]

The general approach of the Strasbourg institutions has however been to apply a simple, factual and untechnical test, taking full account of the factual circumstances but very little of legal niceties.

Although the test of 'sufficient and continuing links' is well established, the nature of these links is not easy to pin down.[136] It is clear that the links are not forged by property interests. Thus, even though an occupier's legal right to remain in possession may have ceased, or indeed never arisen, their residence may still qualify as their home for the purposes of Art 8(1).[137] The legality of their occupation is relevant only to the justification balance under Art 8(2). Looking beyond property rights raises the possibility that Art 8 may offer a new measure of human rights based protection of the home—see section 7.

Physical occupation of the property as a residence[138] for a period will be the norm to forge the emotional connection that a person forms with their home and

---

[136] Busye, 'Strings Attached: the concept of home in the case law of the ECHR' (2006) 3 EHRLR 294.

[137] Nield and Hopkins suggest that accordingly the Art 8 rights of family members with no property interest, for example, children should be considered, see 'Human Rights and Mortgage Repossessions: Beyong Property Law Using Article 8' (2013) 33 LS 431.

[138] Including a house boat, see *Akerman v Richmond on Thames LBC* [2017] EWHC 84 and *Jones v Canal & River Trust* [2017] EWCA Civ 135.

neighbourhood.[139] In the following extract, Nield explains these aspects of home referring to the contribution of academic commentators.

Nield, 'Article 8 Respect for the Home: A Human Property Right?' (2013) 24 KLJ p 149

The challenge is to gain a clearer idea of what are 'sufficient and continuing links' that define home. There must be a physical space within which such links may be forged, but home encompasses more than the physicality of a shelter. The Article 8 concept of home is concerned also with the social and psychological connections that a person develops with a particular dwelling. For instance, in *Connors v UK* the ECtHR described 'rights of central importance to the individual's identity, self determination, physical and mental integrity, maintenance of relationships and a settled and secure place in the community', and Baroness Hale in *R (Countryside Alliance) v AG* referred to 'the inviolability of a different kind of space, the personal and psychological space within which each individual develops his or her sense of self and relationships with other people'. These more abstract functions of home find a synergy with the work of Lorna Fox on the concept of home and the X factor values she describes beyond home as 'shelter' and 'investment' to home as 'identity', home as 'territory' and home as 'a social and cultural expression'.

Although the meaning of home is not easy to pin down, the home test of 'sufficient and continuing links' has generally not been difficult for a victim to pass unless their temporal connection with their home has been brief.[140] For instance, in *Leeds CC v Price*,[141] occupation of a traveller's site for just a few days was insufficient.[142]

4.1.2 The implications of respect

Respect has both negative and positive connotations that can encompass a wide variety of actions. Negative protection of the home encompasses protection from government interference, from (for example) police powers of entry and search,[143] or the regulation of land use through compulsory purchase,[144] and planning or residency controls.[145] Article 8(2) suggests that the interference must be by a public authority, but a public authority will be taken to have engaged Art 8(1) where it is responsible for the conditions that allow a private body to disturb an individual's enjoyment of his or her home. For instance, we have noted in section 2.4 when considering horizontality that a State is responsible for the legal framework which governs the relations of non-State actors and may owe positive duties

---

[139] Although see *Gillow v UK* referred to in Lord Bingham's extracted judgment. However, note *Zabor v Poland* App no 33690/06, where an absence of thirty years severed any continuing and sufficient links.

[140] *Hounslow LBC v Powell* [2011] 2 AC 186 [33], *Manchester Ship Canal Developments v Persons Unknown* [2014] EWHC 645.

[141] [2006] 2 AC 465.

[142] See also *O'Rourke v UK* App No 39022/97 where occupation of a hotel room for less than a month was inadequate.

[143] *McLeod v UK* (1999) 27 EHRR 493 and *Keegan v UK* (2007) 44 EHRR 33.

[144] *Howard v UK* (1987) 9 EHRR CD116.

[145] *Gillow v UK* (1989) 11 EHRR 335 and *Buckley v United Kingdom* (1997) 23 EHRR 101.

to protect human rights norms from unjustified infringement by private individuals or bodies.

An example of this positive duty is evident from cases that have challenged anti-social behaviour,[146] domestic violence,[147] and environmental pollution.[148] For example, in *Lopez Ostra v Spain*,[149] a waste treatment plant and its operation without the requisite licence presented a health risk to the applicant that breached Art 8. The Spanish government was responsible, because it had authorized the construction of the plant close to the applicant's home and had failed to take steps to ensure that its operation did not cause a nuisance to neighbouring occupiers. Similar challenges to environmental pollution, caused by Heathrow and Gatwick Airports,[150] and road construction in the East End of London,[151] have also interfered with the respect that Art 8(1) affords the home—although, in each case, the interference was justified under Art 8(2).

Although respect under Art 8 is a nuanced concept recognizing degrees of interference, we will concentrate our attention upon repossession as an interference with respect for the home because repossession presents the clearest interface between human rights and property rights. The exercise of a right to possession, for instance by a landlord or a creditor, is the most serious interference with the respect due to the home under Art 8(1) even though sanctioned by domestic law and thus must be justified as legitimate and proportionate under Art 8(2).[152]

McCann v UK
(2008) 47 EHRR 40

At 50

The loss of one's home is the most extreme form of interference with the right to respect for the home. Any person at risk of an interference of this magnitude should in principle be able to have the proportionality of the measure determined by an independent tribunal in the light of the relevant principles under art 8 of the Convention, notwithstanding that, under domestic law, his right of occupation has come to an end.

The threat of eviction from the institution of possession proceedings is sufficient to constitute the interference.[153] However, it appears that the termination of the right to occupy,

---

[146] *Mileva v Bulgaria* App Nos 43449/02 and 21475/04; *Moreno Gomez v Spain* App No 4143/02; *Oluic v Croatia* App No 61260/08.

[147] *Busuioc v Moldova* App No 61382/09.

[148] *Arrondelle v UK* (1983) 5 EHRR 118; *Hatton v UK* (2003) 37 EHRR 28; *Powell and Ryaner v UK* (1990) 12 EHRR 355; *Khatun v UK* (1998) 26 EHRR CD 212; *Lopez Ostra v Spain* (1995) 20 EHRR 277; *Guerra v Italy* (1998) 26 EHRR 357. A positive duty may also arise to protect a particularly vulnerable group: see *Connors v UK* (2005) 40 EHRR 9.

[149] Ibid.

[150] *Hatton v UK* (2003) 37 EHRR 28 and *Powell and Ryaner v UK* (1990) 12 EHRR 355.

[151] *Khatun v UK* (1998) 26 EHRR CD 212.

[152] The House of Lords had tried to limit this conclusion in *Harrow LBC v Qazi* [2004] 1 AC 983, *Kay v Lambeth LBC* [2006] 2 AC 465, and *Doherty v Birmingham CC* [2009] 1 AC 367 but the Supreme Court in *Manchester CC v Pinnock* [2011] 2 AC 104 and *Hounslow LBC v Powell* [2011] 2 AC 186 finally acknowledged this clear and consistent message from the Strasbourg Courts; see also *Kay v UK* (2012) 54 EHRR 30.

[153] *McCann v UK* (2008) 47 EHRR 40 at [47] and *Cosic v Croatia* (2011) 52 EHRR 39 at [18].

for instance by the service of a notice to quit, may not amount to a sufficient threat to engage Art 8.[154]

4.2 WHEN IS AN INTERFERENCE JUSTIFIED UNDER ARTICLE 8(2)?

Article 8(2) sets out the grounds upon which an interference with the home may be justified. These grounds set out the legitimate aims. They are comprehensive and, in many instances, an interference will be justified under one or more grounds. The most common grounds for our purposes are measures that are designed to promote the economic well-being of the country, to protect public safety, or to protect the rights and freedom of others. For example, planning controls and powers of compulsory purchase will often be justified on all three grounds,[155] environmental pollution may be justified to attain national economic goals.[156]

Rights to possession, which have been the subject of considerable case law both before the Strasbourg Courts and our domestic courts, may be vindicated on all three grounds but clearly the superior property rights of others will feature prominently. This case law has drawn a sharp distinction between the vertical application of Art 8, where a public authority is seeking possession of a home, and the horizontal application of Art 8, where a private individual or body is doing so. In our consideration of this important issue we will consider the vertical application of Art 8 before looking at whether Art 8 can have horizontal application.

4.2.1 Vertical application: proportionality in possession proceedings by a public authority

The measures taken to achieve one or more of the legitimate aims identified in Art 8(2) must be necessary in a democratic society in order to address a pressing social need. Furthermore, they must be a proportionate response to that need, which strikes a fair balance between the respect due to an individual's home and the necessary social objective. A pressing social need is, without doubt, the provision of adequate housing, in which social landlords play a vital and prominent role. It is thus not surprising that possession proceedings by social landlords have come under scrutiny on human rights grounds. Indeed this scrutiny sparked 'a dialogue' between the Strasbourg Court and our highest courts.[157] The Strasbourg Courts' position was formulated in the cases of *Connors v UK*,[158] and *McCann v UK*[159] and is summarized in the following extract from

---

[154] *Sims v Dacorum BC* [2014] 3 WLR 1600.

[155] See *Buckley v United Kingdom* (1997) 23 EHRR 101.

[156] See *Hatton v UK* (2003) 37 EHRR 28; *Powell and Rayner v UK* (1990) 12 EHRR 355; *Khatun v UK* (1998) 26 EHRR CD 212.

[157] For details of this dialogue see Nield, 'Clash of the Titans: Article 8, Occupiers and their Home' in *Modern Studies in Property Law Vol 6* (ed S Bright, Oxford: Hart Publishing, 2011) ch 5, Goymour, 'Property and Housing' in *The Impact of the UK Human Rights Act on Private Law* (ed Hoffman, Cambridge: CUP, 2011) ch 12, and Bright, 'Manchester City Council v Pinnock (2010): Shifting Ideas of Ownership' in *Landmark Cases in Land Law* (ed Gravells, Oxford: Hart Publishing, 2013) ch 11.

[158] (2009) 40 EHRR 189.   [159] (2008) 47 EHRR 913.

Kay v UK. This approach has been consistently applied by the Strasbourg Court in subsequent cases.[160]

Kay v UK
(2012) 54 EHRR 30

At 65–8

In making their initial assessment of the necessity of the measure, the national authorities enjoy a margin of appreciation in recognition of the fact that they are better placed than an international court to evaluate local needs and conditions. The margin afforded to national authorities will vary depending on the Convention right in issue and its importance to the individual in question. The Court set out the approach in *Connors*:

> "The margin will tend to be narrower where the right at stake is crucial to the individual's effective enjoyment of intimate key rights [. . .] The Court has [. . .] stated that in spheres such as housing, which play a central role in the welfare and economic policies of modern societies, it will respect the legislature's judgment as to what is in the general interest unless that judgment is without reasonable foundation. It may be noted however that this was in the context of Article 1 Protocol 1, not Article 8 which concerns rights of central importance to the individual's identity, self-determination, physical and moral integrity, maintenance of relationships with others and a settled a secure place in the community. Where general social and economic conditions have arisen in the context of Article 8 itself the scope of the margin of appreciation depends on the context of the case, with particular significance attaching to the extent of the intrusion into the personal sphere of the applicant."

Further it is clear from the case law of the Court that the requirement under Article 8(2) that the interference must be necessary in a democratic society raises questions of procedure as well as one of substance. The procedural safeguards available to the individual will be especially material in determining whether the respondent State has, when fixing the regulatory framework, remained within its margin of appreciation. In particular the Court must examine whether the decision making process leading to measures of interference was fair and such as to afford due respect to the interests safeguarded to the individual by Article 8.

As the Court has emphasised in *McCann* the loss of one's home is the most extreme form of interference with the right to respect for the home. Any person at risk of an interference of this magnitude should in principle be able to have the proportionality of the measure determined by an independent tribunal in the light of the relevant principles under Article 8 of the Convention notwithstanding that, under domestic law, his right to occupation has come to an end.

The Supreme Court finally acknowledged this clear and consistent jurisprudence in *Manchester CC v Pinnock*, which was closely followed by their decision in *Hounslow LBC v Powell*.[161]

---

[160] See *Cosic v Croatia* (2011) 52 EHRR 39, *Paulic v Croatia* App No 3572/06, *Zehentner v Austria* (2011) 52 EHRR 22, *Kryvitska & Kryvitskyy v Ukraine* App No 30856/03, *Orlic v Croatia* App No 48833/07, *Gladysheva v Russia* App No 7097/10, *Bjedov v Croatia* App No 42150/09, *Brezec v Croatia* App No 7177/10, *Pelipenko v Russia* App No 69037/10, *Skrtic v Croatia* App No 64982/12, *Tijardovic v Croatia* App No 38906/13, and *Lemo & others v Croatia*, App Nos 3925/10, 3955/10, 3974/10, 4009/10, 4054/10, 4128/10, 4132/10, and 4133/10.

[161] [2011] 2 AC 186.

Manchester CC v Pinnock
[2011] 2 AC 104

Lord Neuberger

At 45 and 49

[. . .] it is clear that the following propositions are now well established in the jurisprudence of the European court: (a) Any person at risk of being dispossessed of his home at the suit of a local authority should in principle have the right to raise the question of the proportionality of the measure, and to have it determined by an independent tribunal in the light of article 8, even if his right of occupation under domestic law has come to an end [. . .] (b) A judicial procedure which is limited to addressing the proportionality of the measure through the medium of traditional judicial review (i e, one which does not permit the court to make its own assessment of the facts in an appropriate case) is inadequate as it is not appropriate for resolving sensitive factual issues [. . .] (c) Where the measure includes proceedings involving more than one stage, it is the proceedings as a whole which must be considered in order to see if article 8 has been complied with [. . .] (d) If the court concludes that it would be disproportionate to evict a person from his home notwithstanding the fact that he has no domestic right to remain there, it would be unlawful to evict him so long as the conclusion obtains—for example, for a specified period, or until a specified event occurs, or a particular condition is satisfied. Although it cannot be described as a point of principle, it seems that the European court has also franked the view that it will only be in exceptional cases that article 8 proportionality would even arguably give a right to continued possession where the applicant has no right under domestic law to remain [. . .]

We have referred in a little detail to the European court jurisprudence. This is because it is important for the court to emphasise what is now the unambiguous and consistent approach of the European court, when we have to consider whether it is appropriate for this court to depart from the three decisions of the House of Lords [. . .]

In the present case there is no question of the jurisprudence of the European court failing to take into account some principle or cutting across our domestic substantive or procedural law in some fundamental way. That is clear from the minority opinions in Harrow London Borough Council v Qazi [2004] 1 AC 983 and Kay v Lambeth London Borough Council [2006] 2 AC 465, and also from the fact that our domestic law was already moving in the direction of the European jurisprudence in Doherty v Birmingham City Council [2009] AC 367. Even before the decision in Kay v United Kingdom [. . .], we would, in any event, have been of the opinion that this court should now accept and apply the minority view of the House of Lords in those cases. In the light of Kay v United Kingdom that is clearly the right conclusion. Therefore, if our law is to be compatible with article 8, where a court is asked to make an order for possession of a person's home at the suit of a local authority, the court must have the power to assess the proportionality of making the order, and, in making that assessment, to resolve any relevant dispute of fact.

It is clear, however, that, although an occupier is entitled to question the proportionality of the eviction from his or her home by a public authority, a finding that his or her eviction is disproportionate and a thus a breach of Art 8 will be rare. The word 'exceptional' has been used to describe the likelihood of a disproportionate result but Lord Neuberger, in *Pinnock*, criticized its use and tried to articulate a more useful guide. In so doing he suggests that the vindication of a social landlord's property rights and their duties of housing management in almost all cases will provide the necessary pressing social need to demonstrate proportionality.

Lord Neuberger

At 51–4

It is necessary to address the proposition that it will only be in "very highly exceptional cases" that it will be appropriate for the court to consider a proportionality argument. Such a proposition undoubtedly derives support from the views expressed by Lord Bingham, and has been referred to with apparent approval by the European court in more than one case. Nevertheless, it seems to us to be both unsafe and unhelpful to invoke exceptionality as a guide. It is unhelpful because, as Baroness Hale of Richmond JSC pointed out in argument, exceptionality is an outcome and not a guide. It is unsafe because, as Lord Walker observed in Doherty v Birmingham City Council [2009] AC 367, para 122, there may be more cases than the European court or Lord Bingham supposed where article 8 could reasonably be invoked by a residential tenant.

We would prefer to express the position slightly differently. The question is always whether the eviction is a proportionate means of achieving a legitimate aim. Where a person has no right in domestic law to remain in occupation of his home, the proportionality of making an order for possession at the suit of the local authority will be supported not merely by the fact that it would serve to vindicate the authority's ownership rights. It will also, at least normally, be supported by the fact that it would enable the authority to comply with its duties in relation to the distribution and management of its housing stock, including, for example, the fair allocation of its housing, the redevelopment of the site, the refurbishing of sub-standard accommodation, the need to move people who are in accommodation that now exceeds their needs, and the need to move vulnerable people into sheltered or warden-assisted housing. Furthermore, in many cases (such as this appeal) other cogent reasons, such as the need to remove a source of nuisance to neighbours, may support the proportionality of dispossessing the occupiers.

In this connection, it is right to refer to a point raised by the Secretary of State. He submitted that a local authority's aim in wanting possession should be a "given", which does not have to be explained or justified in court, so that the court will only be concerned with the occupiers' personal circumstances. In our view, there is indeed force in the point, which finds support in Lord Bingham's comment in Kay v Lambeth London Borough Council [2006] 2 AC 465, 491, para 29, that to require the local authority routinely, from the outset, to plead and prove that the possession order sought is justified would, in the overwhelming majority of cases, be burdensome and futile. In other words, the fact that the authority is entitled to possession and should, in the absence of cogent evidence to the contrary, be assumed to be acting in accordance with its duties, will be a strong factor in support of the proportionality of making an order for possession. But, in a particular case, the authority may have what it believes to be particularly strong or unusual reasons for wanting possession—for example, that the property is the only occupied part of a site intended for immediate development for community housing. The authority could rely on that factor, but would have to plead it and adduce evidence to support it.

Unencumbered property rights, even where they are enjoyed by a public body such as a local authority, are of real weight when it comes to proportionality. So, too, is the right—indeed the obligation—of a local authority to decide who should occupy its residential property. As Lord Bingham said in Harrow London Borough Council v Qazi [2004] 1 AC 983, 997, para 25: "the administration of public housing under various statutory schemes is entrusted to local housing authorities. It is not for the court to second-guess allocation decisions. The Strasbourg authorities have adopted a very pragmatic and realistic approach to the issue of justification."

Therefore, in virtually every case where a residential occupier has no contractual or statutory protection, and the local authority is entitled to possession as a matter of domestic law, there will be a very strong case for saying that making an order for possession would be proportionate. However, in some cases there may be factors which would tell the other way.

Lord Neuberger's views regarding the legitimate aim of the interference presented by possession proceedings were repeated in *Powell*, where Lord Hope emphasized that in the case of social landlords the vindication of their property rights was by itself insufficient.[162] He also went onto reject the need for a more structured approach to proportionality, which would look to the particular policy of the ground for possession under scrutiny.[163] Before turning to look at the consequences of these decisions, we should note the concerns of our domestic courts in their reluctance to heed the message from Strasbourg.

First, there is a concern not to upset the social housing regime articulated through detailed statutory schemes emanating from Parliament. Here we have an example of judicial deference to Parliament in a key area of socio-economic policy that attracts significant state funding. The judiciary is keen to acknowledge the democratic mandate of the legislature in determining housing policy and the expertise of those responsible for the articulation and administration of those policy choices (section 2.2.5).

Secondly, there is, as dictated by Strasbourg jurisprudence, the importance attached to procedural safeguards which we will consider in more detail later.

Lastly, the decisions highlight the Supreme Court's concern with the practicalities of possession proceedings which occupy much of the business of our County Courts. It is the County Courts which must apply those rules fairly yet efficiently. The following extract is from *Pinnock* but similar views are repeated by Lord Hope in *Powell*.[164]

Lord Neuberger

At 60–4

Nevertheless, certain general points can be made, even at this stage.

First, it is only where a person's "home" is under threat that article 8 comes into play, and there may be cases where it is open to argument whether the premises involved are the defendant's home (eg where very short-term accommodation has been provided). Secondly, as a general rule, article 8 need only be considered by the court if it is raised in the proceedings by or on behalf of the residential occupier. Thirdly, if an article 8 point is raised, the court should initially consider it summarily, and if, as will no doubt often be the case, the court is satisfied that, even if the facts relied on are made out, the point would not succeed, it should be dismissed. Only if the court is satisfied that it could affect the order that the court might make should the point be further entertained.

---

[162] [2011] 2 AC 186 at [35]–[37].

[163] Ibid at [41]. See by way of contrast the structured approach to proportionality for the purposes of the Equality Act 2010 in *Akerman-Livingstone v Aster Communities Ltd* [2015] UKSC 15.

[164] [2011] 2 AC 186 at [34].

Fourthly, if domestic law justifies an outright order for possession, the effect of article 8 may, albeit in exceptional cases, justify (in ascending order of effect) granting an extended period for possession, suspending the order for possession on the happening of an event, or even refusing an order altogether.

Fifthly, the conclusion that the court must have the ability to assess the article 8 proportionality of making a possession order in respect of a person's home may require certain statutory and procedural provisions to be revisited [. . .] we say no more on the point, since these aspects were not canvassed on the present appeal to any significant extent, save in relation to the legislation on demoted tenancies which we are about to discuss under the third issue.

Sixthly, the suggestions put forward on behalf of the Equality and Human Rights Commission, that proportionality is more likely to be a relevant issue "in respect of occupants who are vulnerable as a result of mental illness, physical or learning disability, poor health or frailty", and that "the issue may also require the local authority to explain why they are not securing alternative accommodation in such cases" seem to us well made.

Thus, the Supreme Court is at pains to keep human rights challenges to social housing possession proceedings within strict bounds and in *Powell* they rejected a structured approach to proportionality, instead compatibility is presumed and it is for the occupier to raise an Art 8 defence.[165] Accordingly, an occupier should be informed at an early stage of the reasons for the possession proceedings so they can consider the possibility of raising a defence.[166] Nevertheless, successful challenges have proved rare. It is the last two matters that Lord Neuberger identifies in the above extract, namely the adequacy of the process to assess proportionality and the disproportionate consequences of repossession resulting from a particular occupier's vulnerability, that have proved the most common focus of subsequent challenges. We noted the importance of these factors but it is useful to see how they play out in the context of Art 8.

4.2.2 Proportionality and procedural safeguards

The importance of procedural safeguards within the justification process arises from the need not just to assess the human rights compatibility of the legal rules that govern rights to possession (legislative review or macro-compatibility) but also the impact of those rules upon the respect due to the home of the particular victim (applied review or micro-compatibility). There must thus be both an adequate process and adequate judicial discretion within that process to assess proportionality, including its impact on the individual occupier.

Section 3 of the Protection from Eviction Act ensures that proceedings for possession of dwelling-houses are subject to court proceedings.[167] The grounds upon which possession proceedings may be brought can be mandatory, in the sense that the court must order

---

[165] The Strasbourg Court appears to have approved this approach, see for instance *Lemo & others v Croatia* App Nos 3925/10, 3955/10, 3974/10, 4009/10, 4054/10, 4128/10, 4132/10, and 4133/10. This presumption of compatibility appears to rest on the institutional competence of the public authority in question see *Jones v Canal & River Trust* [2017] EWCA Civ 136.

[166] See *Powell* [2011] 2 AC 186 at [115]–[117] *per* Lord Phillips.

[167] See *R (on the application of N) v Lewisham LBC: R (on the application of H) v Newham LBC* [2014] 3 WLR 1548 for the definition of a dwelling-house.

possession on proof of the relevant facts, or the grounds can confer a discretion on the court. Possession proceedings against public authority secure tenants do not generally present a problem because the court has a statutory discretion to assess the reasonableness (and thus proportionality) of the order for possession.[168] But mandatory grounds for possession are problematic. Here the victim will have no defence to the claim for possession and the court no, or very limited, discretion to refuse or delay an order for possession.

Mandatory grounds for possession fall into three broad groups.[169] First, certain rights to possession are determined by the court itself in their decision that grounds exist for the tenancy to be brought to an end. Demoted and introductory tenancies (to address anti-social behaviour) and non-secure tenancies for the homeless provide examples. The compatibility of the termination of a demoted tenancy[170] was in issue in *Pinnock* and the compatibility of introductory tenancies[171] and non-secure tenancies[172] was examined in *Powell*.[173] In order to ensure compatibility of each of these regimes, the Supreme Court interpreted the relevant statutory provisions, in accordance with their duties under s 3 of the HRA 1998, to confer a discretion to assess proportionality.[174]

The second group of mandatory possession proceedings comprises situations where domestic property rules have already brought to an end the home-occupier's right to possession (leaving them a trespasser) so that the court's jurisdiction is confined to confirming the operation of those rules to the facts and regulating the possession order they are bound to make. Examples of this group include the operation of the rule in *Hammersmith LBC v Monk*,[175] pursuant to which one joint tenant can terminate a joint tenancy by giving notice. The termination of licences of mobile home sites did fall within this group but legislation has largely addressed previous compatibility issues[176] by conferring a discretion on the court to consider the proportionality of eviction.[177]

The grant of a possession order after a tenancy had been terminated by the operation of *Monk* was found incompatible in *McCann v UK*[178] because the court had no discretion to consider the proportionality of the possession order against Mr McCann who by then was a trespasser. However, in *Sims v Dacorum BC*,[179] in similar circumstances to *McCann*, compatibility was achieved by the court considering proportionality when deciding whether or not to make the possession order. Following *Pinnock* and *Powell*, and presumably in pursuance of their duty to act compatibly under s 6 of the HRA 1998, the court felt bound to consider the proportionality of the possession order. However, they found, in exercise of that discretion, that the possession order was proportionate in Mr Sims' particular circumstances.

Whilst, in this second group, the courts have admitted within their conduct of possession proceedings sufficient discretion to consider a claim by the occupier that his or her eviction

---

[168] See Housing Act 1985, s 84.

[169] See Nield, 'Strasbourg Triggers Another Article 8 Dialogue' [2013] Conv 148.

[170] See s 143D Housing Act 1996.   [171] See s 127 Housing Act 1996.

[172] See Part VII Housing Act 1996.

[173] Also Ground 8, by which rent arrears provide a ground for termination.

[174] See *Pinnock* at [75] and *Powell* at [55]–[56]. The eviction of Mr Pinnock and the introductory tenants in *Powell* was nevertheless found proportionate. The non-secure tenant in *Powell* was offered alternative accommodation.

[175] See Chapter 22, section 3.3.1.

[176] Raised by *Connors v UK* (2005) 40 EHRR 9 and *Birmingham CC v Doherty* [2009] 1 AC 367.

[177] See Sch1 Mobile Homes Act 1983 but note *Buckland v UK* (2013) 56 EHRR 16.

[178] (2008) 47 EHRR 40.   [179] [2014] 3 WLR 1600.

would be disproportionate, in *Sims* they would not track back to hold that the rule in *Monk* was itself incompatible with Art 8. It was only when possession proceedings were brought to evict the now trespassing former tenant that Art 8 was engaged.

Lastly, there are those mandatory possession cases where the home occupier never had a right to occupy but by the operation of statutory rules may acquire such a right. Squatters and occupiers who enjoy a right to succeed to a tenancy fall into this third category. Here the threat of eviction is ever present until a court rules that the home occupier has acquired a right to possession.

In *Yordanova v Bulgaria*,[180] the Strasbourg Court found a breach of Art 8 when Roma gypsies were threatened with eviction from land that had been their home since the 1960s. It is thus evident that the lawfulness or otherwise of the basis for the occupation of land as a home is neither a bar to the engagement of Art 8 nor an automatic justification for possession proceedings. It must still be established that the possession proceedings are proportionate.[181] Factors affecting the proportionality of an eviction where occupation is unlawfully established are evident in the following opinion of the Strasbourg Court in the similar case of *Winterstein v France*. They include the steps taken to secure alternative accommodation, the impact on the local community, and positive duties to support a minority group.

Winterstein v France
[2013] App No 27013/07

At 76

When considering whether an eviction measure is proportionate, the following considerations should be taken into account in particular. If the home was lawfully established, this factor would weigh against the legitimacy of requiring the individual to move. Conversely, if the establishment of the home was unlawful, the position of the individual concerned would be less strong. If no alternative accommodation is available the interference is more serious than where such accommodation is available. The evaluation of the suitability of alternative accommodation will involve a consideration of, on the one hand, the particular needs of the person concerned and, on the other, the rights of the local community to environmental protection [. . .]

Lastly, the vulnerable position of Roma and travellers as a minority means that some special consideration should be given to their needs and their different lifestyle both in the relevant regulatory planning framework and in reaching decisions in particular cases [. . .] to this extent, there is thus a positive obligation imposed on the Contracting States by virtue of Article 8 to facilitate the way of life of the Roma and travellers [. . .]

These decisions throw into question the human rights compatibility of the rule in *McPhail v Persons Unknown*.[182] The rule provides a summary and mandatory route to repossession against squatters which excludes a consideration of proportionality. Sir Alan Ward, in *Malik v Fassenfelt*,[183] believed that the rule was thus incompatible; but his opinion is obiter and his fellow judges declined to express an opinion. Nevertheless, even if procedurally a proportionality assessment is necessary, a squatter would have only a very slim chance of a successful Art 8 defence.

---

[180] App No 25446/06.   [181] Although see *Gustovarac v Croatia* App No 60223/09.
[182] [1973] Ch 447.   [183] See [2013] EWCA Civ 798.

Birmingham CC v Lloyd
[2012] HLR 44, CA

Lord Neuberger

At 18

It would, I accept, be wrong to say that it could never be right for the court to permit a person, who had never been more than a trespasser, to invoke art.8 as a defence against an order for possession. But such a person seeking to raise an art.8 argument would face a very uphill task indeed, and, while exceptionality is rarely a helpful test, it seems to me that it would be require the most extraordinarily exceptional circumstances.

The question remains as to what sort of process is sufficient to provide adequate procedural safeguards. In *Paulic v Croatia*,[184] the Strasbourg Court indicated that enforcement proceedings, as opposed to the possession proceedings themselves, are inadequate. In their opinion these proceedings 'which by their nature are non-contentious and whose primary purpose is to secure the effective execution of the judgment debts are unlike regular civil proceedings neither designated nor properly equipped with procedural tools and safeguards for the thorough and adversarial examination of such complex legal issues'.[185] This view is reinforced in *Buckland v UK*, where the court's ability to suspend the execution of the possession order was inadequate process.[186]

Buckland v UK
(2013) 56 EHRR 16

At 68

However, the fact remains that the applicant was not able to argue that no possession order ought to have been made at all. The possibility of suspension for up to twelve months of the possession order is inadequate, by itself, to provide the necessary procedural guarantees under art.8. Although further suspensions may be granted, suspension merely delays, and does [not] remove, the threat of eviction. The Court cannot accept that the fact that an individual may effectively be able to remain in her home in the long-term by making repeated applications to extend suspension of a possession order removes any incompatibility of the procedure with art.8. It is further significant that in the present case the county court judge considered the applicant's personal circumstances to be such that suspension was justified and he granted a suspension for the full period sought. In the circumstances it is not possible for the Court to predict what decision he might have reached on the granting of the possession order had he considered it open to him to refuse the grant on the basis of personal circumstances.

---

184 App No 3572/06.   185 Ibid, at [44].
186 Lord Neuberger in *Pinnock* at [63] questioned the compatibility of s 89 Housing Act 1980, which restricts the courts discretion to postpone the execution of certain possession orders. However, the Supreme Court in *Powell* held that the section was compatible, see [57]–[60].

It is clear that the whole process of repossession can be considered when looking at the adequacy of procedural safeguards. It is not unusual for a housing authority's decision to evict to be subject to an internal review by the housing authority. In addition, their decisions may be questioned by judicial review. However, judicial review, on its own, has proved problematic as an adequate process, both in the extent to which human rights compatibility can be examined within the grounds of judicial review and in the ability of the court within such proceedings to resolve disputed facts which are particularly pertinent in assessing the impact of the eviction upon the occupier's personal circumstances.[187] Nevertheless, judicial review may contribute to the compatibility of the whole process of repossession, the adequacy of which may depend upon the strength and nature of the continuing links of the victim to their home.[188]

R (on the application of N) v Lewisham LBC: R (on the application of H) v Newham LBC
[2014] 3 WLR 1548, SC

Facts: In each case the homeless single mother of a child had been provided with emergency accommodation whilst the council considered they obligations to provide more permanent housing. The accommodation was provided under a licence that allowed the council to terminate the arrangement on a day's notice and without the need for a court order. In each case the council concluded that the mothers had become intentionally homeless and thus they had no statutory duty to provide accommodation. In seeking to evict the mothers and their children, they claimed that no court order was needed. In each case judicial review proceedings were brought to question the council's decision.

Held: No court order was required under the Protection from Eviction Act 1977 because the accommodation provided did not constitute a dwelling (Lord Neuberger and Baroness Hale strongly dissented). Although Art 8 was engaged, the statutory review processes and the availability of judicial review provided the appropriate procedural safeguards to assess proportionality.

Lord Hodge

At 64–74

In my view, when one looks at the procedures as a whole, the procedural safeguards contained in the 1996 Act, the procedures available under the Children Act 1989 and the possibility of judicial review of the authority's section 202 decision by a court with enhanced powers are sufficient to comply with article 8 of ECHR in this context. See paras 70–71 below. Article 8's procedural guarantee does not require further involvement of the court in granting an order for possession. The interim accommodation which an authority provides under section 188 of the 1996 Act is but transient accommodation, a stop gap pending the completion of inquiries and a decision on the scope of the authority's duties

---

[187] See in particular *Kay v Lambeth LBC* [2006] 2 AC 465 and *Doherty v Birmingham CC* [2009] 1 AC 367 and *Kay v UK* (2012) 54 EHRR 30.
[188] See also *Manchester CC v Pinnock* [2011] 2 AC 104 at [72]–[74] and [81] *per* Lord Neuberger.

towards a homeless person. As I have set out above, domestic law requires less formal procedures at the final stage of the recovery of possession in such circumstances than when the occupier has a more substantial and long term connection with the accommodation [. . .]

There are also safeguards in the decision-making process that allow the occupant to be involved in the process and, through an appeal to the county court or by judicial review in the Administrative Court, give an opportunity for him or her to raise the question of proportionality before an independent tribunal. There is no need for an additional procedural hurdle which would impose costs on an authority without any significant benefit to the applicant.

[Lord Hodge then considered the relevant safeguards]

Having regard to the proceedings as a whole, there are several opportunities for the applicant to involve himself or herself in the decision-making process and also procedures by which an independent tribunal can assess the proportionality of the decision to re-possess the accommodation and determine relevant factual disputes. In my view there are sufficient procedural safeguards to satisfy the applicant's article 8 rights. The article 8 challenge therefore fails.

4.2.3 Proportionality and vulnerability

The difficulty is in identifying those very few cases where repossession may be disproportionate. There may be the odd case where the court is persuaded that a public authority's use of repossession is a disproportionate exercise of their housing management functions.[189] For instance, in *Southend-on-Sea BC v Armour*,[190] the local authority sought to terminate an introductory tenancy and regain possession due to the anti-social behaviour of the tenant. However, by the time the proceedings came before the court the tenant had mended his ways for almost a year. As a result the judge at first instance found it would be disproportionate to evict the tenant in the light of his improved behaviour; a judgment that the Court of Appeal refused to overturn.

Alternatively there may be the rare case where an immediate eviction will impact too severely upon a particular occupier because that occupier suffers from some vulnerability, for instance old age, disability, ill health (whether physical or mental), or is from a cultural minority (for instance as a Gypsy or traveller) which will be exacerbated by the eviction. Lord Neuberger, in *Pinnock*, acknowledged that the particular vulnerability of the individual occupier may tip the balance.[191] In the following extract Nield refers to examples of the type of vulnerability that may do so.[192]

---

[189] See also *Chesterfield v BC v Bailey* (2011) unreported, the Court, although they refused possession on other grounds, observed the use of the rule in *Hammersmith v Monk* in the circumstances of the case would be disproportionate. Mrs Bailey had been a previously secure tenant but had been persuaded by her local authority landlord to move properties and enter into a joint tenancy with her husband. Upon the failure of their marriage her husband served a notice terminating the tenancy and the local authority took advantage of his act to evict Mrs Bailey although she was blameless of any misconduct.

[190] [2014] HLR 23.

[191] At [64].

[192] See also *Holmes v Westminster CC* [2011] EWHC 2857 and *West Kent Housing Association Ltd v Haycroft* [2012] EWHC 276.

Nield, 'Article 8 Respect for the Home: A Human Property Right?'
(2013) 24 KLJ p 163

The occupier will undoubtedly need to present some particular vulnerability, such as illness, age or mental incapacity. For instance Ms Zehentner was mentally incapable and could not respond adequately to the enforcement process in which she found herself embroiled. In *Bedjov v Croatia*, age and ill health contributed to a disproportion eviction, with the offer of alterative accommodation being too little too late. But in *Thurrock BC v West* the Court of Appeal threw cold water on the sufficient vulnerability of a young couple with a young child and limited means to overturn the proportionality of the local authority's decision to evict them from accommodation they never had a right to occupy and which exceeded their needs. Vulnerability must be seen in the context of the eviction, in the sense that the vulnerability will be exacerbated by the eviction. In Bjedov there was evidence that the health of 78 year old Mrs Bjedov would have been seriously affected by her eviction. By contrast in *Corby v Scott* a murderous assault on the occupier was discounted because it was unconnected with the eviction.

Indeed our higher courts have been reluctant to be too specific. Lord Bingham in *Kay v Lambeth LBC*[193] was of the view that County Court judges should be able to spot those rare cases and furthermore that the eviction needs to be seen in the context of other services that may address, or at least alleviate, the occupier's vulnerability.

Lord Bingham

At 38

I do not think it possible or desirable to attempt to define what facts or circumstances might rank as highly exceptional. The practical experience of county court judges is likely to prove the surest guide, provided always that the stringency of the test is borne in mind. They are well used to exercising their judgment under existing statutory schemes and will recognise a highly exceptional case when they see it. I do not, however, consider that problems and afflictions of a personal nature should avail the occupier where there are public services available to address and alleviate those problems, and if under the relevant social legislation the occupier is specifically disentitled from eligibility for relief it will be necessary to consider the democratic judgment reflected in that provision. Nor can article 8 avail a tenant, otherwise perhaps than for a very brief period, if he can be appropriately accommodated elsewhere (whether publicly or privately). Where, as notably in the case of gipsies, scarcity of land adversely affects many members of the class, an article 8(2) defence could only, I think, succeed if advanced by a member of the class who had grounds for complaint substantially stronger than members of the class in general.

4.2.4 Horizontal application: repossession by a private landowner?

In *Pinnock* the Supreme Court decline to pass comment on the application of Art 8 to repossession of a tenancy between private parties. However, in the following case they had to answer the question head on in respect of the almost universal short-term tenancy of

[193] [2006] 2 AC 465.

residential property—the assured shorthold tenancy. Whilst they accepted that the most common means of terminating an assured shorthold tenancy by a two-month notice to quit by the landlord did engage Art 8, they rejected the right of the tenant to question the proportionality of the order for possession that the court was bound to make.

McDonald v McDonald
[2015] 2 WLR 567

Facts: The McDonalds wished to buy a house for their mentally troubled daughter, Fiona. They raised the money by obtaining a mortgage from Capital Homes Ltd. They rented the house to Fiona on an assured shorthold tenancy and used the rent funded by Fiona's housing benefit, to meet the mortgage repayments. However, the McDonalds were unable to keep up their mortgage repayments and Capital Homes appointed a receiver, who, acting as an agent for the McDonalds, terminated Fiona's tenancy by serving a two months notice to quit and claimed possession. Fiona argued that this mandatory ground upon which the receiver claimed possession infringed her Art 8 rights to respect for their home because it provided no opportunity for the court, pursuant to the court's obligations as a public authority under s6 of the HRA 1998, to consider the proportionality of her eviction.

Lord Neuberger and Lady Hale

At [40]–[46]

In the absence of any clear and authoritative guidance from the Strasbourg court to the contrary, we would take the view that, although it may well be that article 8 is engaged when a judge makes an order for possession of a tenant's home at the suit of a private sector landlord, it is not open to the tenant to contend that article 8 could justify a different order from that which is mandated by the contractual relationship between the parties, at least where, as here, there are legislative provisions which the democratically elected legislature has decided properly balance the competing interests of private sector landlords and residential tenants. In effect the provisions of the Protection from Eviction Act 1977, section 89 of the Housing Act 1980 and Chapters I and IV of the 1988 Act, as amended from time to time, reflect the state's assessment of where to strike the balance between the article 8 rights of residential tenants and the A1P1 rights of private sector landlords when their tenancy contract has ended. (It is true that the balance was initially struck in statutes enacted before the 1998 Act came into force in 2000. However, the effect of those statutes has not only been considered and approved in government reports since 2000, as mentioned in para 19 above, but they have been effectively confirmed on a number of occasions by Parliament, when approving amendments to those statutes since 2000).

To hold otherwise would involve the Convention effectively being directly enforceable as between private citizens so as to alter their contractual rights and obligations, whereas the purpose of the Convention is, as we have mentioned, to protect citizens from having their rights infringed by the state. To hold otherwise would also mean that the Convention could be invoked to interfere with the A1P1 rights of the landlord, and in a way which was unpredictable. Indeed, if article 8 permitted the court to postpone the execution of an order for possession for a significant period, it could well result in financial loss without compensation — for instance if the landlord wished, or even needed, to sell the property with vacant possession (which notoriously commands a higher price than if the property is occupied).

The contrary view would also mean that article 8 could only be invoked in cases where a private sector landowner, or other private sector entity entitled to possession in domestic law, was either required by law, or voluntarily chose, to enforce its rights through the court, as opposed to taking the law into its own hands — eg by changing the locks when the residential occupier was absent. There are a number of types of residential occupiers who are not protected by the Protection from Eviction Act 1977, and who can therefore be physically (albeit peaceably) evicted, such as trespassers, bare licensees, sharers with the landlord and some temporary occupiers, as well, it appears, as mortgagors — see Ropaigealach v Barclays Bank plc [2000] 1 QB 263. The risk of otherwise facing an article 8 defence seems a somewhat perverse incentive for a private sector landowner to take the unattractive course of locking out the occupier rather than the more civilised course of seeking possession through the courts.

More broadly, it would be unsatisfactory if a domestic legislature could not impose a general set of rules protecting residential tenants in the private sector without thereby forcing the state to accept a super-added requirement of addressing the issue of proportionality in each case where possession is sought. In the field of proprietary rights between parties neither of whom is a public authority, the state should be allowed to lay down rules which are of general application, with a view to ensuring consistency of application and certainty of outcome. Those are two essential ingredients of the rule of law, and accepting the appellant's argument in this case would involve diluting those rules in relation to possession actions in the private rented sector.

It is, of course, true that a court, which is a public authority for the purposes of the 1998 Act (and is regarded as part of the state by the Strasbourg court), actually makes the order for possession which deprives the tenant of his home — and indeed puts an end to the AST. However, as Lord Millett explained in *Harrow London Borough Council v Qazi [2004] 1 AC 983*, paras 108-109, the court is "merely the forum for the determination of the civil right in dispute between the parties" and "once it concludes that the landlord is entitled to an order for possession, there is nothing further to investigate".

This conclusion does not mean that a tenant could not contend that the provisions of the 1988 Act did not, for some reason, properly protect the article 8 rights of assured shorthold tenants: that would involve arguing that the legislature had not carried out its obligations under the Convention. However, quite rightly, no such argument was advanced on behalf of the appellant in this case. As the summary in paras 11-19 above shows, the Government's approach to the private rented sector in England has been designed to confer a measure of protection on residential occupiers, without conferring so much protection as to deter private individuals and companies from making residential properties available for letting. The extent of the protection afforded to tenants under ASTs is significant, if limited, and it enables both landlords and tenants to know exactly where they stand. While there will of course occasionally be hard cases, it does not seem to us that they justify the conclusion that in every case where a private sector landlord seeks possession, a residential tenant should be entitled to require the court to consider the proportionality of the order for possession which she has agreed should be made, subject to what the legislature considers appropriate.

Of course, there are many cases where the court can be required to balance conflicting Convention rights of two parties, eg where a person is seeking to rely on her article 8 rights to restrain a newspaper from publishing an article which breaches her privacy, and where the newspaper relies on article 10. But such disputes arise not from contractual arrangements made between two private parties, but from tortious or quasi-tortious relationships, where the legislature has expressly, impliedly or through inaction, left it to the courts to carry out

> the balancing exercise. It is in sharp contrast to the present type of case where the parties are in a contractual relationship in respect of which the legislature has prescribed how their respective Convention rights are to be respected.

A number of points emerge from this extract. First, to note is that the basis of Fiona's challenge was the court's duty under s 6 in making an order for possession, i.e. remedial horizontality. Her counsel argued that the court was not 'merely the forum' for the resolution of disputes' but, pursuant to its duty to act in a human rights compatible manner, was required to look beyond contract and statute to consider, if called upon by a victim, the proportionality of the possession order. This was a change of tactics from the argument presented to the Court of Appeal which challenged the compatibility of the relevant legislation[194] granting the landlord a mandatory right to terminate the tenancy, i.e. legislative horizontality. The Court of Appeal had held that this mandatory right was compatible and the Supreme Court indicated their obiter agreement.[195]

Secondly, there is the emphasis placed on the private consensual nature of the tenancy agreement in contrast to liability that might arise between private parties in tort where the court has been willing to intervene on human rights grounds. However, the consensual nature of assured shorthold tenancies within the private rental sector has been questioned given that it is often the only leasehold tenure on offer.

Nield, 'Shutting the Door on Horizontal Effect: McDonald v McDonald' (2017) 81 Conv 47

At 53

The Supreme Court also emphasised the contractual relationship of the parties under an AST as that relationship is shaped by legislative regulation. But they failed to note that the contractual freedom of tenants in the private rental housing market is illusory. If only ASTs are on offer that is all that private tenants can enter into. The very weak security of tenure afforded to AST tenants may work for those that have the few ties and the resources, both financial and personal, to cope with the frequent changes of home that may result. But not all who have to resort to the private rental market value this flexibility—families with children wishing to maintain local ties are an obvious example. The physically or mentally vulnerable, like Fiona, may also need greater security of tenure on health grounds.

Although the Supreme Court noted that the policy shaping ASTs has not waivered since the Housing Act 1988, it is undeniable that the housing market, and with it housing policy, has moved on. The significance of the private rental sector, and with it ASTs, has grown considerably and now forms an important element of the housing market. The private rental sector in England almost doubled in size between 2000 and 2012 mostly at the expense of the public rented sector. Accordingly, there is growing disquiet at the limited protection it affords the diversity of AST tenants. Admittedly these are policy issues but they are issues which are integral to respect for the home under art.8 which the HRA 1998 calls upon the courts to adjudicate.

---

194 Housing Act 1988, s 21(4).   195 At [45].

Thirdly, the Supreme Court demonstrated again deference to the legislative function of Parliament in balancing the Art 8 rights of the tenant to respect for their home and the landlord's rights to the protection of their possessions under Art 1 Protocol 1. In their judgment they reviewed the evolution of the legislation governing the private rental sector, but they did not question its human rights compatibility. The following extract suggests that by doing so the Supreme Court overlooked its responsibilities under the HRA 1998 particularly as they acknowledged that Art 8 was engaged.

Lees, 'Article 8, Proportionality and Horizontal Effect' (2017) 133 LQR 31

At 32–34

At the heart of the court's conclusion is the view that where the rights and obligations of private parties are determined by statute and/or contract, it is not the role of the court to interfere with that balance (at [40]–[46]). That reasoning is strange. First, the potentially relevant statutory provisions must, on any view, include the impact of the Human Rights Act 1998 since this is precisely what the interpretation obligation in the HRA is intended to achieve. This must be true even where "the effect of those statutes has ... been effectively confirmed on a number of occasions by Parliament" (at [40]) since all of these "confirmations" took place against the background of the 1998 Act. This argument is not conclusive as to outcome, but it does mean that we ought not to assume that Parliament "intends" the balance between the rights of the occupier and the landlord to be governed by the Housing Act 1988 *alone*, but possibly by that Act modified by controls which provide for human rights protection where appropriate [...]

Furthermore, although the court acknowledged that art.8 is engaged (since an individual was deprived of their home, at [50]), their Lordships held that no proportionality test should be carried out. However, art.8 itself requires a proportionality assessment to determine whether the rights it embodies have been breached. This is not a matter of judicial precedent, but interpretation of the articles within the Convention as mandated by the HRA [...]

These reasons do not therefore support the Supreme Court's conclusion. The recognition that art.8 is engaged, the jurisprudence of the ECtHR and the Supreme Court in relation to public authorities, and of the wording of art.8 itself, as incorporated into national law by the HRA, mandate that a proportionality assessment be carried out. The court's concerns about the proper judicial role and the balance struck between occupier and landlord should filter into this proportionality test under the concept of the margin of appreciation or deference. They do not justify no assessment being carried out.

The decision in *McDonald* creates a clear dividing line between the protection afforded by Art 8 to tenants of a private and a public or quasi-public landlord. Given the restrictive approach to proportionality developed in *Pinnock* and *Powell*, this difference may not have a significant practical impact but it does leave the respect due to a private tenant's home in the event of repossession of little meaning. The Supreme Court in the extracted judgment above suggest that a private tenant does enjoy quite significant protection—a court order is required[196] and the court has discretion to afford tenants a short time before the possession order that the court is bound to make is executed by the arrival of the bailiff.[197]

---

[196] Protection from Eviction Act 1977, ss 2–3.   [197] Housing Act 1980, s 89.

These 'protections' may be of little comfort to a vulnerable tenant, who may need a little longer to find suitable alternative accommodation, or a tenant faced with a retaliatory eviction following a reasonable complaint about their tenancy. The following extract voices these concerns.

Nield, 'Shutting the Door on Horizontal Effect: McDonald v McDonald' (2017) 81 Conv 47

At 70

Effectively, we now have a two tier protection between tenants within the public and private sectors. This is increasingly significant given the growth of less secure tenancies in the public sector. Tenants of a public or quasi-public authority may raise a proportionality defence but private tenants cannot. The distinction is further muddied by measures such as a local authority's ability to discharge its homelessness duties by resort to the private sector. Exactly where the line is drawn between quasi public and private landlords is thus critical. Even if the import of this public/private divide is to some extent ameliorated by the narrow application of proportionality in public or quasi-public authority possession proceedings laid down in *Pinnock* and *Powell*. Yet the test to determine a quasi-public authority is not without controversy. Many housing associations will be quasi-public authorities [. . .] [h]owever their status as quasi-public authorities can raise difficult and functionally fact sensitive questions.

The rejection of remedial horizontality, through the court's duties under the HRA 1998 s.6, reflects the general concern that has been expressed on the impact of human rights on private law in compromising personal autonomy and the constitutional importance of separation of powers. The Supreme Court's judgment is shot through with statements that these principles must be preserved. They reiterate that any compromise to that autonomy through the balancing of private parties' respective human rights is a matter for Parliament in their proper constitutional role.

As such the judgment reflects the traditional property law values of clarity and certainty. However, in so doing it empties art.8 of little meaning in the context of possession proceedings brought by private landlords. It is only where the law itself can be challenged as incompatible or where a State is found to be under a positive duty under the ECHR, for instance to protect vulnerability, that human rights may play a role. Whether the Strasbourg Court agrees with this restrictive application of the balance between art.1 Protocol 1 and art.8 to home repossession remains to be seen.

McDonald rejects horizontality between a private landlord and tenant under an assured shorthold tenancy but its impact is likely to be wider in rejecting horizontal effect in relation to other mandatory rights to possession of a home, whether exercised by a private landlord against a tenant,[198] a mortgagee against a mortgagor,[199] or a private landowner against a squatter.[200] Nevertheless, it is suggested that Art 8 should, as a minimum, require a court order to repossess a home—as the above extract from *McDonald* indicates, there are still

---

[198] E.g. on the basis of rent arrears under Ground 8 Housing Act 198 or the operation of the rule in *Hammersmith v Monk*.

[199] See s 87(1) Law of Property Act 1925, considered further in Chapter 26.

[200] *McPhail v Persons Unknown* [1973] Ch 447.

some instances in English law where this is not the case. In addition, Art 8 should require some latitude for a court to consider legislative review of rights to possession conferred by the common law or legislation, at least where such rights have not been subject to recent consideration by Parliament. There also remains the possibility that the Strasbourg Courts may interpret respect for the home as dictating, at least in some contexts, a consideration of proportionality through applied review when a home is repossessed. We now turn to consider the state of Strasbourg jurisprudence on this issue.

4.2.5 Strasbourg and the horizontal effect of Article 8

The Supreme Court in *McDonald* drew attention to the fact that the Strasbourg Court has yet to provide definitive guidance on the possibility of horizontal effect of Art 8 in home possession proceedings.[201] The Supreme Court has tended to approach their obligations under s 2 of the HRA 1998 to take account of Strasbourg decisions as a ceiling rather than a floor[202] and thus only to follow the Strasbourg Courts where 'there is a clear and consistent line' of decisions.[203] Their review of the Strasbourg case law led them to conclude that compatibility did not demand that a victim had the right to question the proportionality of a repossession of their home. But what can we learn about the divergent opinions found in the Strasbourg case law?

Strasbourg's traditional approach is found in *Di Palma v UK*,[204] where an attempt to claim that the exercise of contractual agreed right to forfeit a lease by a private landlord was a breach of Art 8 was robustly rejected as 'manifestly ill founded'.[205] However, a rather different attitude is evident in the more recent forfeiture case of *Khurshid Mustafa v Sweden*,[206] where the Strasbourg Court held that a repossession by a private landlord, based upon the breach of the tenant's covenant not to erect a satellite dish on the exterior of a block of flats, was admissible and indeed a breach of Art 10 (freedom of expression).[207] It made the following general statement demanding human rights compatibility of domestic courts (as a State body) even though the dispute before them is private.

> **At 33**
>
> Admittedly, the [Strasbourg] Court is not in theory required to settle disputes of a purely private nature. That being said, in exercising the European supervision incumbent on it, it cannot remain passive where a national court's interpretation of a legal act, be it a testamentary disposition, a private contract, a public document, a statutory provision or an administrative practice appears unreasonable, arbitrary, discriminatory or, more broadly, inconsistent with the principles underlying the Convention.

The case of *Zehentner v Austria* that we have already considered is also an important decision in which the positive duties of a State to provide adequate procedural safeguards was

---

[201] There are some cases involving private parties where a breach of Art 8 has been found but each can to a greater or lesser extent be distinguished; see *Zrilic v Croatia* App No 46726/11, *Brezec v Croatia* [2014] HLR 3 *Lemo v Coratia* App No 3925/10, and *Belchikova v Russsia* App No 2408/06.

[202] See Lewis, 'The European Ceiling on Human Rights' [2007] PL 720.

[203] See *Manchester CC v Pinnock* [2011] 2 AC 104 at [48].   [204] (1996) 10 EHRR 149.

[205] At 211.   [206] App No 23883/06.

[207] A breach of Art 8 was also alleged but, in view of the breach of Art 10, the court did not go on to consider this alleged violation.

central to the finding of incompatibility with Art 8 even though the parties to the under-lying dispute were private.

But doubts persist—most significantly in comments made by Judge de Gaetano in his sep-arate opinion in *Buckland v UK*.[208]

> My only reservation in this case is with the principle as set out in the second sentence of [65]. This sentence is a verbatim reproduction of what is found at [50] of *McCann* and at [68] of *Kay*. However, all the cases quoted in support of the principle as thus formulated are cases where the landlord was either the Government or a local authority. None were cases where the landlord was a private individual. In my view while it is perfectly reasonable to require that an eviction or repossession notice issued by the Government or by a local authority—both of which are normally under a public law obligation to provide accommo-dation for people within their jurisdiction—or possibly even by a private entity in receipt of public funds, should be capable of being challenged on the grounds of proportionality, when the landlord is a private individual the tenant's right should in principle be limited to challenging whether the occupation—tenancy, lease, encroachment concession, etc.—has in fact come to an end according to law. In this latter case the proportionality of the evic-tion or repossession in light of the relevant principles under art.8 should not come into the equation. This is not to say, of course, that the Government may not, by legislation, impose restrictions on the use of the property by the landlord upon or after the termination of the occupancy, from which restrictions the last tenant or occupant might even benefit; but this is a totally different issue from what is being proposed in the second sentence at [65].

Unfortunately Strasbourg cases decided subsequent to *McDonald* do not speak with one voice. In *Vrzic v Croatia*,[209] the court rejected the need to consider proportionality in judi-cial sale proceedings brought by a mortgagee wishing to recover mortgage arrears. The court emphasized the private contractual nature of the mortgage under which the mortgagor ac-cepted the risk that they could lose their home if they failed to repay. Yet in *Ivanova & Cherkezov v Bulgaria*,[210] in proceedings concerning the demolition of a home built in contra-vention of planning laws, the court embarked upon their clearest and strongest reassertion of a victim's right to question the proportionality of their eviction, in terms which suggest their comments were not restricted to repossession by a public authority—indeed they re-ferred to cases involving private parties including *Zehentner*.[211] The reason for demanding proportionality in home repossession is clearly stated in the following extract from *Ivanova*.

> **At 54**
>
> But given that the right to respect for one's home under article 8 […] touches upon issues of central importance to the individual's physical and moral integrity, maintenance of rela-tionships with others and a settled and secured place in the community, the balancing ex-ercise under that provision in cases where the interference consist in the loss of a person's only home is of a different order, with particular significance attaching to the extent of the intrusion into the personal sphere of those concerned […] this can normally only be exam-ined case by case.

---

[208] (2013) 56 EHRR 16.   [209] App No 43777/13.   [210] App No 46577/15.
[211] At [52]–[53].

Ultimately it seems that there is no black-and-white answer to horizontal effect. The question is far more nuanced. Not only are there different categories of horizontality (see section 2.4), but much depends on two key questions. First, the nature of the private parties' relationship—just how private and consensual is it in striking a balancing between their respective Convention rights? And secondly there is the courts' role—are they a mere forum for the resolution of disputes in accordance with domestic law or are they, as a State body, arbiters and upholders of Convention values?

5 THE IMPACT OF HUMAN RIGHTS

The crucial question is to what extent the HRA 1998 will impact on proprietary rights. The House of Lords, and now the Supreme Court, has been tussling with these issues for quite sometime.

Allen has suggested two possibilities: either there will be little change, because human rights values are already embedded in our fundamental proprietary principles, or there will be a greater impact through the influence of an alternative process of balancing competing proprietary interests, and also a further basis on which to claim rights affecting property.

Allen, *Property and The Human Rights Act 1998* (2005, p 250)

This leaves the central question open: what are the values that may affect the development of substantive principles of the private law of property? In the discussion on the applicability of P1(1) [Art 1 of the First Protocol] and other Convention rights, it was said that human autonomy and dignity are values in both human rights law and private law, Similarly, both human rights and private law often require a balance to be struck between competing interests. However, if the values only take effect at a very high level of generality, alongside other private law values such as certainty, fairness and the like, the effect of human rights law is unlikely to be significant. It may add a new rhetorical dimension to the reasoning in private law cases, but without changing the outcome. But once values are identified at a high level of generality, it should be possible to move to two more specific aspects relating to the development of private law doctrines where human rights law may prove significant (and is already proving significant). The first relates to the nature of the balancing process, and the second to the interest which private law seeks to protect.

The alternative balancing process to which Allen refers is found in the elements that we have examined in the justification formula and, in particular, the fair balance upon which proportionality depends. Fox has described the human rights framework as offering 'a useful lens',[212] whilst Gray and Gray have offered the analogy of a 'prism'[213] through which compliant legislation must pass. Although the ECHR is a product of traditional property values, it does seek to articulate those values in a manner that affords greater clarity and legitimacy to the balancing process. Nevertheless, we have seen, through our consideration of Art 1 Protocol 1 and Art 8, that the courts are reluctant to overturn establish property rules or to question the social and economic ramifications of housing policy.

[212] Fox, *Conceptualising Home: Theories, Law, and Policies* (Oxford: Hart, 2007) p 512.
[213] Gray and Gray, *Land Law* (5th edn, Oxford: OUP, 2009), [1.6.17].

The implementation of policy through the law reform process is, however, not always logical and seamless. Anomalies and lacunae do occur—particularly in land law, in which, throughout its long history, prospective and piecemeal evolution predominates. It is in these circumstances that the new balancing process may have most to contribute and we will, in the remainder of this book, try to identify those areas in which we think that a human rights challenge might make a difference.

Allen notes that Art 1 of the First Protocol '*is a very conservative element in the protection of human rights*',[214] and indeed Goymour (writing in 2011) noted that there has been no case in this jurisdiction when an Art 1 Protocol challenge had been upheld.[215]

By contrast, Art 8 has attracted attention as a possible foundation for a new human rights based protection of the home, although following *McDonald* this protection is currently only available to occupiers of social housing.[216] This protection springs from a victim's particular status—it is a *human* not a property right—which will be more potent where the victim is viewed as vulnerable and the State thus under a positive duty to protect. It is also now clear that the proportionality balance under Art 8 looks both to the fair balance of the substantive law and to the impact of that interference upon the personal circumstances of the victim. In order to address this latter demand of proportionality, there must be a process by which an independent tribunal can make that assessment which demands both adequate legal proceedings and adequate judicial discretion within those proceedings.

These developments mark shifts in the traditional emphasis of land law. First, there is a shift from repossession as a positive vindication of property rights towards the characterization of repossession as a violation of the respect due to the home under Art 8. Secondly, there is a shift from the primacy of a property owner's right to exclude towards an acknowledgement of context and the need to temper this 'absolute' right given the personal circumstances of the victim. Thirdly, there is the demand for procedural safeguards by which this tempering can be measured through proportionality which calls for judicial discretion in place of the bald application of possessory rights. Nevertheless as Walsh notes in the following extract, the courts have worked hard to maintain the traditional stability and efficiency of property rules to ensure that these shifts are kept to the margins of our property law.

Walsh, 'Stability and Predictability in English Property Law – The Impact of Article 8 of the European Convention on Human Rights Reassessed' (2015) 131 LQR 585

At 600–603

Article 8 has increased the complexity of English property law by introducing scope for contextual considerations without undue loss of efficiency. Thus far, the decisions indicate that the courts favour simplicity and predictability, and with it, the protection of owner's exclusionary rights. Article 8 is confined to the periphery of property law through the enforcement of a threshold requirement that rules out balancing in all but very complex and exceptional

---

[214] Allen, 'The Autonomous Meaning of "Possessions" under the European Convention of Human Rights' in *Modern Studies in Property Law Vol 2* (ed Cooke, Oxford: Hart, 2003) p 57.

[215] 'Property & Housing' in *The Impact of the UK Human Rights Act on Private Law* (ed Hoffman, Cambridge: CUP, 2011) ch 12, p 286.

[216] See, for instance, Nield, 'Article 8 Respect for the Home: A Human Property Right' (2103) 24 KLJ 147.

cases [...] However, the application of a proportionality analysis in the context of seriously arguable art. 8 defences can be understood as marking the incorporation of a new set of governance rules into the periphery of English property law. The shift towards the governance end of the spectrum has been slight, with threshold requirements employed to ensure that proportionality analysis is not required in standard possession disputes. This structure for dealing with art.8 in the context of possession disputes is welcome – the courts have responded to the need to secure the efficient administration of public housing and the efficiency of property law generally, without excluding the potential relevance of art. 8 in hard cases [...]

However, English property law's exclusionary rhetoric is no longer absolutist – as Ward LJ pointed out in Malik v Fassenfelt, the "castle" has been replaced by balancing. This shift should ensure greater alignment between the rhetoric and reality of property law in relation to exclusion, since [...] the intuitive image of the owner's absolute freedom in relation to his or her property is not reflected in social practice. Moreover it opens up valuable new space for debate about the appropriate balance between securing efficiency and other social and individual values in property law and raises the possibility of developing property law in a way that ground property rights at in part in the interest of communities, rather than solely in the interest of individuals.

QUESTIONS

1. How is an interference with the qualified human rights found in Art 1 Protocol 1 and Art 8 justified?

2. To what extent does the European Convention on Human Rights affect relations between private landowners?

3. How does Art 1 of the First Protocol define a possession?

4. Why are mandatory rights to possession problematic in the context of Art 8?

5. Is there such a concept as a human property right?

6. How may human rights based courses of action protect those in society who may be classified as vulnerable?

7. To what extent is it appropriate for the courts to consider government policy in determining the compliance of property rules with the ECHR?

8. How useful is the human rights 'prism' through which the law governing property rights must now pass?

 For guidance on how to answer these questions visit the online resources at www.oup.com/uk/mcfarlane4e/.

FURTHER READING

Allen, *Property and The Human Rights Act 1998* (Oxford: Hart Publishing, 2005)

Bright, '*Manchester City Council v Pinnock* (2010)' in *Landmark Cases in Land Law* (ed Gravells, Oxford: Hart Publishing, 2013, ch 11)

Cowan, O'Mahony, and Cobb, *Great Debates in Property Law* (Basingstoke: Palgrave Macmillan, 2012, ch 8)

Gray, 'Land Law and Human Rights' in *Land Law: Issues, Debates, Policy* (ed Tee, Devon: Willan, 2002, ch 7)

Goymour, 'Property & Housing' in *The Impact of the UK Human Rights Act on Private Law* (ed Hoffman, Cambridge: CUP, 2011, ch 12)

Howell, 'The Human Rights Act 1998: Land, Private Citizens, and the Common Law' (2007) 123 LQR 618

Lees, 'Article 8, Proportionality and Horizontal Effect' (2017) 133 LQR 31

Nield, 'Shutting the Door on Horizontal Effect' (2017) 81 Conv 47

Nield, 'Article 8 Respect for the Home: A Human Property Right?' (2013) 24 KLJ 147

Walsh, 'Stability and Predictability in English Property Law—The Impact of Article 8 of the European Convention on Human Rights Reassessed' (2015) 131 LQR 585

5

LEGAL ESTATES AND LEGAL INTERESTS

CENTRAL ISSUES

1. In Chapter 4, we considered how human rights may be relevant to the use of land. In the next three chapters, we will look at other forms of right that are relevant to the use of land.

2. In this chapter, we will look at one of the key building blocks of land law: legal property rights in land. As we noted in Chapter 1, section 3, it is useful to ask three questions when looking at property rights in land: the *content* question; the *acquisition* question; and the *defences* question.

3. In this chapter, we will look at the content of legal property rights in land. Our question is a simple one: what types of right can count as a legal property right in land? In Chapters 8 and 9, we will look in detail at how legal property rights in land are acquired; and in Chapters 15 and 16, we will look at the defences that may be available against such rights. Before we can examine those questions, however, we need to know what rights count as legal property rights in land.

4. We will see that, when considering the content question, the *numerus clausus* (or 'closed list') principle is of crucial importance. It ensures that there is a limited list of legal property rights in land. It means that individual parties, such as A and B, cannot simply decide that a right given to B is to count as a legal property right in land: the right can only have that effect if its content matches that of one of the rights on the list. The list of legal property rights in land is a statutory one: it is provided by s 1 of the Law of Property Act 1925.

5. The Law of Property Act 1925 makes a general distinction between two classes of legal property rights in land: legal estates and legal interests. We will see that the content of a legal estate can be defined by reference to the concept of ownership: if B has a legal estate in land, he has a right to exclusive possession of that land, and so can be said to be its owner, either forever or for a limited period. In contrast, legal interests in land are those property rights in land with a limited content: a party with a legal interest does not have any ownership of the land. In some specific contexts, however, this general definition is departed from, and certain legal interests are treated, for the purpose of applying particular statutory rules, as legal estates.

6. Whilst there are, thus, differences between legal estates and legal interests, each is a form of legal property right in land. As a result, each has the crucial feature of imposing a *prima facie* duty on the rest of the world. So, even if B acquires a legal property right from A, B's right is capable of binding not only A but also anyone else who may attempt to use or interfere with the land. In this way, a legal property right in land is more powerful than a personal right against A, as such a personal right can be asserted only against A.

7. It is important to bear in mind that even if B cannot show he has a legal estate or legal interest in land, it may still be possible for B to show that he has an *equitable* interest in land. If B's right is not on the list of legal estates and legal interests, it may nonetheless count as an equitable interest. The content of equitable interests, therefore, differs from the content of legal estates and legal interests. We will examine the content of equitable interests in Chapter 6. One important point to bear in mind is that certain equitable interests may be related to certain legal property rights. For example, an easement can count as a legal property right in land, but it is also possible for B to have an *equitable* easement. In Chapter 6, we will consider how the effect of such an equitable property right may differ from the effect of a legal property right.

1 THE CONCEPT OF A PROPERTY RIGHT

In Chapter 2, we saw that land is a form of private property. To understand the law relating to private property, it is crucial to understand the concept of a 'property right'. A number of different terms can be used to describe such a right: for example, a property right can also be referred to as a 'right *in rem*' (from the Latin, this literally means a right against a thing), or, on the same basis, as 'a real right'. As we saw in Chapter 2, land is sometimes referred to as 'real property', but, as the following extract notes, it is important to realize that property rights can exist not only in relation to land, but also in relation to other things, such as books.

Lawson and Rudden, *The Law of Property* (3rd edn, 2002, p 14)

Real, or property rights. At this juncture, however, a further complication of terminology needs to be explained. *'Real property'* means land. But the expression *'real right'* can be used with regard to *any* type of property (movable or immovable). It is used to describe those interests which, broadly speaking, (a) can be alienated; (b) die when their object perishes or is lost without trace; (c) until then can be asserted against an indefinite number of people; (d) if the holder of the thing itself is bankrupt, enable the holder of the real right to take out of the bankruptcy the interest protected by the real right.

This apparently complicated statement can be illustrated quite simply. If you own this book you have a real right. As to point (a), you can give away or sell both the book and ownership of the book. As to point (b) if the book is destroyed in a fire, it is no longer yours and you bear the loss. As to (c) if you lend the book to a friend, of course you can claim it (or its value) back from him or her. But if your friend lends it to someone else you can claim it from them; indeed, in English law, you can claim it from someone to whom your friend sells it—your right is enforceable against an indefinite number of persons. Finally, as to (d), if your friend goes bankrupt while reading the book, you do not have to prove as a creditor in the bankruptcy proceedings. The book does not vest in the trustee in bankruptcy, since your friend cannot pay off his or her creditors with your book.

Other ways of referring to these features of a 'real right' are to speak of 'a *property* right' or '*proprietary* right'.

The term 'property right' is often used to distinguish a particular right from a 'personal right'. Again, the term 'personal right' is often referred to using Latin, as a 'right *in personam*' (i.e. a right against a person). To understand the concept of a property right, it can therefore be useful to see how it differs from a personal right. And because the distinction flows from Roman law, it is helpful to consider the following extract.

Nicholas, *An Introduction to Roman Law* (1962, pp 99–100)

Property and obligations—actions and rights in rem and in personam. A man's assets are either property or obligations. The difference between the two is the difference between owning and being owed something. Thus a man's assets may be his house and his furniture, which he owns, his bank balance which, however much one may speak of 'having money in the bank', is a debt owed by the bank, and his right to his unpaid salary, which is likewise a debt. His assets will often, of course, be more complicated than this, but they will still fall into one of the two categories. For example, if he is a shopkeeper he will own, we may suppose, his shop and his stock-in-trade; he may have ordered, but not received, further supplies from a wholesaler, and these will, from the Roman point of view, be still owned by the wholesalers but will be owed to him (and if he has not yet paid for them he will correspondingly owe the price); he will have supplied goods on credit to his customers, and here again there is obviously a debt. He may have acquired the goodwill of the business of a former competitor, and this constitutes once more a debt—the debtor's duty being not, as in the previous cases, to pay a sum of money or to supply goods, but to refrain from soliciting his former customers.

This difference between owning and being owed is expressed by the Roman lawyer in the distinction between actions *in rem* and actions *in personam*. Any claim is either *in rem* or *in personam*, and there is an unbridgeable division between them. An action *in rem* asserts a relationship between a person and a thing, an action *in personam* a relationship between persons [. . .] The Romans think in terms of actions not of rights, but in substance one action asserts a right over a thing, the other a right against a person, and hence comes the modern dichotomy between rights *in rem* and rights *in personam*. Obviously there cannot be a dispute between a person and a thing, and therefore even in an action *in rem* there must be a defendant, but he is there not because he is alleged to be under a duty to the plaintiff but because by some act he is denying the alleged right of the plaintiff.

Of course, it may be thought that, in the modern world, this distinction between 'owning' (property rights) and 'owing' (personal rights) is too simplistic. Certainly, there is no obvious reason why a distinction derived from Roman law should help us to classify concepts such as intellectual property rights. Indeed, as we will see in Chapter 6, it is not obvious that the Roman distinction can be applied to equitable property rights. But modern-day land law still retains the key distinction between a personal right (which can be asserted only against a specific person) and a legal property right (a right relating to land that is capable of binding the whole world). That distinction was particularly important in the following case.

Hill v Tupper
(1863) 2 H & C 122, Exchequer Chamber

Facts: The Company of Proprietors of the Basingstoke Canal Navigation owned the Basingstoke Canal. It made a contractual promise to Mr Hill that he would have the exclusive right to put pleasure boats on the canal and to hire out those boats to paying customers. Mr Tupper was the landlord of an inn at Aldershot, which adjoined the canal. He also started to hire out pleasure boats on the canal. Mr Hill objected, claiming that Mr Tupper was interfering with Mr Hill's exclusive right and was thus committing a tort against Mr Hill. The Exchequer Chamber rejected Mr Hill's claim.

Pollock CB

At 127–8

After the very full argument which has taken place, I do not think it necessary to assign any other reason for our decision, than that the case of *Ackroyd v Smith*[1] expressly decided that it is not competent to create rights unconnected with the use and enjoyment of land, and annex them to it so as to constitute a property in the grantee.[2] This grant merely operates as a licence or covenant on the part of the grantors, and is binding on them as between themselves and [Mr Hill], but gives [Mr Hill] no right of action in his own name for any infringement of the supposed exclusive right. It is argued that, as the owner of an estate may grant a right to cut turves, or to fish or hunt,[3] there is no reason why he may not grant such a right as is now claimed by [Mr Hill]. The answer is, that the law will not allow it. So the law will not permit the owner of an estate to grant it alternately to his heirs male and heirs female. A new species of incorporeal hereditament[4] cannot be created at the will and pleasure of the owner of property, but he must be content to accept the estate and the right to dispose of it subject to the law as settled by decisions or controlled by acts of parliament. A grantor may bind himself by covenant to allow any right he pleases over his property, but he cannot annex it to a new incident, so as to enable the grantee to sue in his own name for an infringement of such a limited right as that now claimed.

---

[1] (1850) 10 CB 164.

[2] [On the fact of *Hill v Tupper*, the canal company is the *grantor* (because it gave Mr Hill a right) and Mr Hill is the *grantee* (because he was given a right by the canal company).]

[3] [Such rights are example of profits, a recognized legal property right in land: see section 6 below. A right to cut turves is a right to remove turf or peat from another's land to use as fuel: it is more commonly called a 'right of turbary'.]

[4] [As used in this particular context, that term is synonymous with 'a legal property right'. Technically, a 'hereditament' is a right that can count as 'real property' and so, for example, will be included in the scope of a term in a will *leaving all my real property to X*. Land (including fixtures) can be seen as a 'corporeal hereditament', because it has a physical form; an easement (a right capable of counting as a legal property right in land, for example, a right of way over another's land) is an 'incorporeal hereditament', because it has no physical form.]

Martin B

At 128

I am of the same opinion. This grant is perfectly valid as between [Mr Hill] and the canal Company, but in order to support this action, [Mr Hill] must establish that such an estate or interest vested in him that the act of [Mr Tupper] amounted to an eviction. None of the cases cited are at all analogous to this, and some authority must be produced before we can hold that such a right can be created. To admit the right would lead to the creation of an infinite variety of interests in land, and an indefinite increase of possible estates. The only consequence is that, as between [Mr Hill] and the canal Company, he has a perfect right to enjoy the advantage of the covenant or contract; and, if he has been disturbed in the enjoyment of it, he must obtain the permission of the canal Company to sue in their name.

Hill v Tupper is an important case for a number of reasons. One reason, which we will examine in section 6 below, concerns the approach of the Exchequer Chamber in deciding whether Mr Hill's right counted as a legal property right in land. For our present purposes, the case is significant because it is a very good example of a key difference between a legal property right in land and a personal right. The Exchequer Chamber found that the canal company's contractual promise to Mr Hill gave him only a personal right against the company. So, if a third party, such as Mr Tupper, also puts out boats on the canal, Mr Hill's only option is to assert his right against the company. He can ask for an injunction, forcing the company, as owner of the canal, to take action against Mr Tupper;[5] he can also ask for an order that the company pay him damages, to compensate him for any loss that he has suffered as a result of Mr Tupper's action. Mr Hill's only recourse, however, is against the canal company: he has no claim against Mr Tupper.[6] If his contract with the company had instead given Mr Hill a *legal property right*, things would be very different. Mr Hill's exclusive right to put boats on the canal would then be capable of binding not only the party who granted that right (in this case, the canal company), but also *any other party* who interferes with that right (such as Mr Tupper).

In the following extract, Birks explains both this fundamental difference between a personal right and a property right, and also its importance to land law.[7]

---

[5] It has been suggested by Han, 'Licensee v Trespasser: *Hill v Tupper* Resuscitated' (2016) 6 Property Law Review 87, that Mr Hill could have taken advantage of a particular procedure (known as the *Vandepitte* procedure, from *Vandepitte v Preferred Insurance Corp of New York* [1933] AC 70) to combine in one proceedings, with both the company and Mr Tupper as defendants, a claim (based on his contract with the company) to force the company to sue Mr Tupper *and* the company's claim against Mr Tupper. Such a procedure can be used, for example, by a beneficiary under a trust who wishes to force a trustee to assert a right the trustee has against a third party; there is no authority, however, as to whether it is also available where the claimant has only a personal right, such as a licence.

[6] Note that even if, as discussed in the previous footnote, the *Vandepitte* procedure were to be available, it would still be the company's claim that is asserted against Mr Tupper, even if that claim is adjudicated along with Mr Hill's claim to force the company to sue Mr Tupper.

[7] The usefulness of the distinction between personal rights and property rights has been challenged (see, for example, Worthington, 'The Disappearing Divide between Property and Obligation: The Impact of Aligning Legal Analysis and Commercial Expectation' in *Equity in Commercial Law* (eds Degeling and Edelman, Sydney: Law Book Co. of Australasia, 2005)). Such challenges have, however, tended to focus on the application of the distinction to commercial dealings with intangible wealth, rather than on its usefulness in land law.

Birks, 'Five Keys to Land Law' in *Land Law: Themes and Perspectives* (eds Bright and Dewar, 1998, pp 472–3)

Real rights and personal rights

We move now to the kind of 'reality' or 'thing-relatedness' which matters in the modern law. The key proposition is that land law is, centrally, the law of real rights in land [. . .] 'Real' and 'personal' here anglicize the Latin labels *in rem* and *in personam*. Many people prefer to use the Latin labels. The Latin tells us that a right *in rem* is a right in or against a thing, while a right *in personam* is a right in or against a person.

One can change to different language. A right *in personam* can be called an obligation. A right *in personam* and an obligation are one and the same thing, but looked at from different ends. I have an overdraft. I owe my bank £1,000. The bank has a right *in personam*, the person here being me. I have an obligation to pay. The relationship can be named from either end, and in practice we usually name it from the liability end. Here we very frequently speak, not of the law of personal rights or of rights *in personam*, but of obligations. As for rights *in rem*, if we drop both the Latin and the latinate English, they usually become 'property rights' or 'proprietary rights'.

We sometimes use 'property' loosely to mean 'wealth'. In that loose sense 'property' wobbles. Sometimes 'my property' evokes and is intended to evoke more specific things, such as cars and clothes and cottages. Sometimes, and rather more technically, 'my property' denoted mere rights vested in me, such as a fee simple, a lease, ownership, or the obligations of my debtors. Whichever the focus, the loose notion of property as wealth is too broad to be useful in analysis. To think clearly the law has to draw a bright line between two classes of right, both of which can fall within the loose notion of wealth.

The bright line distinguishes between property and obligations. When that line is drawn, property clearly has a narrower and much more technical sense. Within wealth, taken as including all assets, the law of obligations is the law of rights *in personam* and the law of property is the law of rights *in rem*. Hence a 'property right' or 'proprietary right' is a real right, is a right *in rem*. The law of property is the law of all known real rights, and land law is the law of real rights in land.

What is the difference? The practical difference bears on this question. Against whom can the right be demanded? 'Demandability' is intelligible but not really English. But another word for 'to demand' is 'to exact', which gives us 'exigible' and 'exigibility'. A right *in rem* is a right the exigibility of which is defined by the location of a thing. The exigibility of a right *in personam* is defined by the location of the person. Where I have a right *in personam* the notional chain in my hand is tied round that person's neck. Where I have a right *in rem*, the notional chain in my hand is tied around a thing. Between me and the car which I own there is such a chain.

So, if B has a personal right against A, it is only possible for him to assert that right against A. If B has a property right in a piece of land, then B's right is *capable* of binding the rest of the world. The word 'capable' is important: it is possible for a particular third party to have a *defence* to B's property right. But this does not undermine the importance of the distinction between personal rights and property rights. For example, the distinction was crucial in *National Provincial Bank v Ainsworth*,[8] a case we examined in Chapter 1. The House of Lords decided that Mrs Ainsworth's 'deserted wife's equity' was only a personal right

---

[8] [1965] AC 1175.

against her husband and, as a result, she could not assert it against the bank, who wished to remove her from the land.[9]

2 THE CONCEPT OF A LEGAL ESTATE IN LAND

The extracts in section 1 all use ownership as the core example of a property right; indeed, Nicholas portrays the distinction between a property right and a personal right as the difference between owning and being owed. In Chapter 2, we saw how it is possible to identify a particular person (B) as an owner of land. Technically speaking, however, it is true to say that, in English law, no one owns land. Even if you buy a house and think of yourself as owning that land, you technically have an estate in that land: either a freehold or a lease. This raises an important question: is the concept of ownership irrelevant to English land law?

In the following extract, Harris: (i) outlines the historical reasons why English law has a doctrine of estates in land; (ii) notes the argument that, as a result, ownership is irrelevant to English land law; but (iii) argues that ownership *is* nonetheless crucial to understanding English land law, because it enables us to understand the very concept of an estate in land.

Harris, *Property and Justice* (1996, pp 68–9)

The significance of ownership interests as an every-day organizing idea is commonly obscured for lawyers in common law systems, and for theorists who seek to build upon the insights of the common law, by the doctrine of estates in land. Land-transfer transactions in common law systems convey or create estates, freehold or leasehold, never *dominium* or ownership. This is a consequence of the feudal origins of English real property law.

In Early English feudal law, that interest which was to develop into the fee simple estate was a grant of seisin by a superior lord to be held by the grantee and his heirs subject to one or other variant of free tenure. It seems that the consent of both the lord and the heir were necessary before the grantee could alienate his land. Free alienability *inter vivos* of this estate evolved at common law, and free testamentary disposition of it was conferred by statute in the sixteenth century. There were as well lesser estates of freehold: estates for life; estates *pur autre vie*;[10] and the estate tail which emerged as the result of judicial interpretation of the Statute *de donis conditionalibus* of 1285.[11] There were also a variety of copyhold estates, the outcome of the progressive emancipation of land held on non-free tenure.

The leasehold estate was unknown to feudal law, but evolved from the end of the Middle Ages as common law actions were adapted to confer trespassory protection on a leaseholder, eventually, against all-comers to the land. Like the fee simple, the leasehold estate became freely transmissible *inter vivos* or on death. A covenant in a lease may prohibit assignment of the estate. Its effect is not, technically, to make the estate inalienable but to give rise to a ground for forfeiture should the estate be assigned in breach of covenant.

---

[9] See the extract from the speech of Lord Wilberforce, set out in Chapter 1, section 5.4.

[10] [For the life of another:, for example, A could give B a right to land for the duration of X's life.]

[11] [*De donis conditionalibus* means 'relating to conditional gifts'. So, if A leaves land in his will to B1 for B1's life, then to B2 provided that B2 is married, B2's right to the land is conditional on both his marriage and the death of B1.]

The terminology and conceptual structures elaborated in works on English real property law have reflected the technical concerns of conveyancers. Since what is conveyed is always an estate in the land, it has been widely assumed that 'ownership' of land, as such, is not a conception internal to English land law. A. D. Hargreaves gave robust expression to this view:

> 'English land law has made no contribution to the legal theory of ownership more striking, more brilliant and of more permanent value than the separation of the land from the estate in the land [. . .] By distinguishing the land from the estate, English land law has shown conclusively that even within a society as individualistic and as legalistic as England in the nineteenth century, ownership is not a necessary legal concept. The problem of ownership remains, but it is not a legal problem; it is the concern of the politician, the economist, the sociologist, the moralist, the psychologist—of any and every specialist who can contribute his grain to the common heap. Ultimately the philosopher will try to unify this shifting mass into a coherent whole.'[12]

The story of the evolution of the doctrine of estates is one of complex elaboration based on the writ system, ancient statutes, and the conveyancing cunning of legal practitioners. If asked what was the content of the interests which came thus to be freely disposable by their holders, the traditional real property lawyer will answer that it consisted of a right to seisin or possession of the land. But if a man was the beneficiary of seisin or possession, what use-privileges over the land did that entail, and what powers to control uses by others? No general answer to that question is usually to be found in land law textbooks, although the case law on nuisance summarized in works on tort is replete with partial answers to it.

The answer to the general question about the normative content of a right to seisin or a right to possession is glaringly obvious. Perhaps it is so manifest as to be trite, and so beneath the notice of a technical lawyer who seeks to expound only that which is obscure and arcane. The truth is that ownership interests in land, of varying magnitudes, are and always have been incidents of legal estates in land. The jurist of the early medieval period took it for granted that the tenant who holds land in demesne is as much *dominus rei* as is the owner of a chattel.[13] As Pollock and Maitland point out, Bracton and contemporaries (rightly in their view) 'ascribed to the tenant in demesne ownership and nothing less than ownership'[14] [. . .]

This truth, however trite, makes claims such as those contained in the above citation from Hargreaves patently absurd. Ownership of land is not a conveyancer's problem, but it is a conception—or rather a battery of conceptions—internal to the law. An indefinitely large set of use-privileges and control-powers over the land follow from the fact that, as an incident to the estate, a person has an ownership interest over the land itself.

Harris' argument may seem complicated, but it can be summed up quite shortly. Although it is *technically* true to say that B can never own land itself, it is also true to say that, if B has an estate in land, he has ownership rights over that land. So, if we want to know what, in practice, the holder of a freehold can do with his land, we need to consider, as we did in Chapter 2, what 'ownership' means. If this is right, we may well wonder why English law developed the doctrine of estates: it seems strange to have a system in which, whilst B cannot own the land itself, he can hold an estate that gives him ownership rights.

The following extract tackles this point.

---

[12] Hargreaves, 'Modern Real Property' (1956) 19 MLR 14, [17].
[13] [Demesne is pronounced 'demean'. A tenant holding in demesne acquired rights in relation to the land under a grant from a feudal lord.]
[14] Pollock and Maitland, *History of English Law* (1911) pp ii, 2–6.

Birks, 'Five Keys to Land Law' in *Land Law: Themes and Perspectives* (eds Bright and Dewar, 1998, pp 462–3)

Although bits do occasionally wash away or slip into the sea, land is in general permanent. For most human purposes we have to regard it as lasting for ever. There is a powerful urge to deal in slices of time. It is not confined to land. The institution of the trust makes it relatively easy to turn all kinds of wealth into an enduring fund, and that facility in turn excites and to a degree gratifies the urge to deal in slices of time. However, it is the natural permanence of land which makes slices of time a dominant feature of land law.

Two motivations

Why do people want to deal in slices of time? It is an urge which has been fed from at least two sources. One is essentially commercial, the other not.

The commercial motivation

Commercial motivation means, in plain words, the desire to get money out of land. There are all sorts of ways of getting money out of land. For instance, one can farm the land and sell the produce. The most extreme method of all is to sell one's whole interest in the land. This means selling the whole slice of time over which one has control. The largest interest in land—the greatest slice of time—is "for ever". In everyday conversation I tend to say 'my house' or 'the house I own'. In all probability, what I actually have is my house 'for ever', a slice of time measured by the length of time the land will last. There is no harm in calling that ownership. That is in effect what it is. But in the technical language of the law that huge slice of time measured by the life of the land itself is called a fee simple. The fee simple in the land on which my house stands is worth about £200,000. I could mortgage it or sell it. But there is another possibility. I could keep 'for ever' and deal instead in a shorter slice of time.

The commercial motivation for dealing in lesser slices of time is to realize in money some of the value of the land without giving up one's whole interest. The lease is the proprietary interest which most obviously facilitates this. I might let my land for a fixed number of years, say for ten years. If I go for that option, I have further choices. I could take a single capital sum, or I might prefer a flow of income in the form of an annual rent, or a mixture of both, say £20,000 now and £5,000 per annum by way of rent. Whichever I choose, the fee simple remains mine, though occluded by the lease. When the ten years have passed, the shadow occluding my interest will vanish, and my fee simple will once again be unencumbered. The reversion has value even during the ten years during which I am out of possession. If I choose to, I can sell it even while the ten years are running.

The family motivation

The primary non-commercial motivation for dealing in slices of time is concern for one's family. In obsolescent aristocratic terms this might be restated as a dynastic motivation. The idea of benefiting the different generations of one's family is perfectly natural. The desire to keep land permanently in the family or part of the family has been a routine temptation.

As Birks notes, it is useful to see an estate in land as a 'slice of time'. We noted in Chapter 1, section 4, that permanence is one of the distinctive features of land. This means that, where land is concerned, it is very useful for an owner of land to be able to divide up his owner-ship over time. The doctrine of estates allows this to happen. As Birks notes, an owner of a thing other than land (eg a painting) can divide up the benefit of that thing by setting up a trust: for example, if A owns a painting, he can transfer it to T to hold on trust for B1 for ten years, then for B2. B2 can thus acquire an equitable property right. It is impossible, however, for A to give B1 a *legal* property right amounting to ownership of the painting for ten years. A special feature of land, then, is that, by creating a lease, an owner of land can give B own-ership rights over that land *for a limited period*.

3 LEGAL ESTATES IN LAND: THE *CONTENT* QUESTION

When examining if B has a legal estate in land, the first question to ask is the *content* ques-tion: does the right claimed by B count as a legal estate in land? As a result of s 1 of the Law of Property Act 1925 (LPA 1925), that question is relatively easy: there are now only two permissible legal estates in land.

Law of Property Act 1925, s 1

(1) The only estates in land which are capable of subsisting or of being conveyed or created at law are—

    (a) An estate in fee simple absolute in possession;

    (b) A term of years absolute.

'*An estate in fee simple absolute in possession*' is more commonly referred to as a 'fee simple'[15] or, as we will call it in this book, a *freehold*. And '*a term of years absolute*' is more commonly referred to as a 'leasehold' or, as we will call it in this book, a *lease*. So, for ex-ample, if you are buying a house, you are, in fact, buying either a freehold or a lease. In this section, we will examine the content of a freehold and of a lease, before asking the important question of *why* the LPA 1925 imposed this limit on the types of permissible legal estate in land.

The other forms of permissible legal property rights in land are then set out in s 1(2) of the LPA 1925 (see section 6 below), where they are referred to as '*interests or charges*'. For con-venience, when dealing in this book with this category of those legal property rights that do not fall within s 1(1), we will refer to that category as '*legal interests*'.

In principle, then, there is a clear distinction between legal estates (the freehold and the lease) and legal interests (all other legal property rights in land). As we will see, that dis-tinction can be defended as the legal freehold and the legal lease share a feature lacked by all other legal property rights: they confer rights of ownership. The prohibition on other legal estates in land means that no other legal property rights conferring ownership can be created: following the LPA 1925, for example, it is no longer possible to have a legal property right to own land for life, or a legal property right to own land only from some point in the future. Such life estates and future estates could exist as legal property rights

---

[15] As in the extract by Birks given in section 2 above.

before the LPA 1925, and can still be created in some jurisdictions which have never had a similar reform.[16]

Nonetheless, care must be taken in using the terminology of estates and interests, given the following provision:

Law of Property Act 1925, s 1

[…]

(4) The estates, interests, and charges which under this section are authorised to subsist or to be conveyed or created at law are (when subsisting or conveyed or created at law) in this Act referred to as "legal estates", and have the same incidents as legal estates subsisting at the commencement of this Act; and the owner of a legal estate is referred to as "an estate owner" and his legal estate is referred to as his estate.

The key point of s 1(4) is that, *for the purpose of interpreting subsequent rules contained in the LPA 1925*, the term 'legal estate' is taken to include not only the freehold and the lease (which might be seen as the 'true' legal estates under s 1(1)), but also all other legal property rights in land. This provision made life easier for the drafters of the Act as when setting out rules later in the Act which apply to all legal property rights in land, there would be no need to refer to 'legal estates, interests and charges' as a simple reference to 'legal estate' will suffice. It is, however, a potential source of confusion, as we need to keep in mind both the general point of principle that, as legal estates, the freehold and the lease have a special content not shared by other legal property rights in land; and the specific point of statutory interpretation that, when the LPA 1925 uses the term 'legal estate' to set the scope of a particular rule, that rule will apply not only to the freehold and the lease, but also to other legal property rights in land. We will see a practical application of this point in section 6 below, and in Chapter 17, section 2.3.

It is also worth noting the following provision of another key statutory provision: the Land Registration Act 2002.

Land Registration Act 2002, s 132

General Interpretation

(1) In this Act—

[...]

"legal estate" has the same meaning as in the Law of Property Act 1925;

[...]

This means that, given s 1(4), the term 'legal estate' when used in the LRA 2002 also includes a legal interest, such as a legal easement, or a legal charge. For example, in

---

[16] Legal life estates and legal future estates are a feature, for example, of the law in many jurisdictions in the United States.

Chapter 3, section 3.2.1, we saw that s 58 of the LRA 2002 ensures that '*on the entry of [B] in the register as the proprietor of a legal estate*', that legal estate is deemed to be vested in B. As a result, it seems that s 58 applies not only where B is registered as holding a legal freehold or lease, but also where B is registered as holding a legal easement[17] or legal charge.

3.1 THE CONTENT OF A LEGAL FREEHOLD

A freehold can be described as 'ownership of land for an unlimited period' as, if B has a freehold, he has a right to exclusive possession forever of a piece of land. This right correlates to the *prima facie* duties owed to B, by the rest of the world, not to interfere with B's land.[18] In practice, there is usually very little doubt as to whether B's right counts as a freehold: in particular, if A has a freehold of land and simply transfers that right to B, it is clear that B now has a freehold. There are, however, some contexts in which we do have to test to see if B really does have a freehold. The following extract provides an example.

Miles v Bull
[1969] 1 QB 258

Facts: Mr Bull and his brother had a freehold of a farmhouse and adjacent land. Mr Bull occupied the land with his wife until 1965, when he left the home. Under the Matrimonial Homes Act 1967, Mrs Bull had a statutory right to remain in occupation of the home.[19] As a result, Mr Bull and his brother could not remove her from the land. In 1968, Mr Bull and his brother sold their freehold to Mr Miles for £10,000. Mr Miles wished to remove Mrs Bull from the land. Mrs Bull could not assert her statutory right to remain in occupation against Mr Miles, because she had not properly registered that right. Mr Miles therefore applied for summary judgment in his favour. Mrs Bull claimed, however, that she deserved to have the chance to argue her case at a full trial because: (i) the supposed transfer of the freehold to Mr Miles was, in fact, a sham; so (ii) the freehold was still held by Mr Bull and his brother; and therefore (iii) Mr Miles had no right to remove her from the land. In considering that argument, Megarry J had to consider the decision of Jones J in *Ferris v Weaven*,[20] in which it had been held that a purported transfer of a freehold was, in fact, a sham.

---

[17] In the case of an easement, a notice will be entered in the register of the title affected by the easement (the servient tenement: see Chapter 22, section 2.1), and, where the easement is for the benefit of another registered estate, the proprietor of that estate will also be registered as the proprietor of the easement: LRA 2002, Sch 2, para 7.

[18] It is easy to think of a freehold owner as having a 'right to use' the land, but this can be misleading, as it is not true to say that third parties have a general duty not to interfere with a freehold owner's use of the land: see, for example, *D Pride & Partners v Institute for Animal Health* [2009] EWHC 685 (QB) and the discussion by S Douglas, 'The Content of a Freehold' in *Modern Studies in Property Law: vol 7* (ed N Hopkins, Oxford: Hart Publishing, 2013) p 359.

[19] As discussed in Chapter 1, section 5.6, this statutory right of occupation was introduced in response to the House of Lords' decision in *NPB v Ainsworth* [1965] AC 1175.

[20] [1952] 2 All ER 233.

Megarry J

At 262–5

Accordingly, it seems to me that there is a strong preponderance of high authority for the view that the decision in *Ferris v. Weaven* can be supported on the basis that the transaction there was a sham, and that although a genuine purchaser will take free from the rights of a deserted wife, a sham purchaser will not. It is therefore necessary to examine the facts of *Ferris v. Weaven* with some care [. . .]

In that case the husband deserted his wife in 1941, leaving her in occupation of his house; he continued to pay the building society instalments and the rates on it. He wrote to her telling her that he would "carry on paying on the house providing you do not annoy me." This state of affairs continued for some 10 years. Then:

> 'In June, 1951, wishing to obtain possession of the house so that he could dispose of it, the husband sold it for £30 to his brother-in-law, Herbert James Ferris, the plaintiff. The £30 was not, in fact, paid to the husband, the plaintiff entering into the transaction only to oblige the husband and enable him to obtain possession of the house from the wife. He did not exercise any act of ownership in respect of it, and the husband continued to pay the rates and the mortgage instalments, the amount of which due at the time of the sale was £1,600.'[21]

[. . .] In his judgment, dismissing the plaintiff's claim for possession against the wife, Jones J. said of the plaintiff:

> 'I find that he bought the house by agreement with the husband, not because he wanted to buy it, but simply to enable the husband to defeat a right which the husband believed the wife possessed as a result of the arrangement which the husband had made with her in 1941.'[22]

[. . .] The essential features of the so-called sale in that case were thus that the price was £30; that the purchaser neither paid it nor exercised any act of ownership over the house, even though it was conveyed to him; that the husband continued paying the rates and mortgage instalments as he had done before entering into the transaction; and that the object of both the husband and the purchaser was to obtain possession of the house for the husband so that he could dispose of it. The purchaser (who was the husband's brother-in-law) entered into the transaction with the object of obliging the husband. I can readily see how such a transaction could properly be described as a 'sham' for; although in outward show the ownership was vested in the purchaser, in substance and reality it was still vested in the husband. The documents lied; they made false representations, concealing what was and asserting what was not. The purchaser could not evict the wife, for the ownership of the property upon which he based his claim to possession was a mere pretence.

On the other hand, a transaction is no sham merely because it is carried out with a particular purpose or object. If what is done is genuinely done, it does not remain undone merely because there was an ulterior purpose in doing it. If in *Ferris v. Weaven* the purchaser had sought to exercise acts of ownership, and the husband had ceased to do them, and there had been no common objective of enabling the husband (as distinct from the purchaser) to dispose of the property, it would, in my judgment, be very difficult to contend that the low price and the failure to pay it made the transaction a sham. After all, some genuine transactions

---

[21] [1952] 2 All ER 233, [234].   [22] Ibid, 237.

within the family are carried out at low prices; and some genuine purchasers fail to discharge their obligation to pay the full purchase price, if the vendor is incautious enough to make this possible. Mere circumstances of suspicion do not by themselves establish a transaction as a sham; it must be shown that the outward and visible form does not coincide with the inward and substantial truth.

In the end, Megarry J decided that summary judgment in Mr Miles' favour should *not* be given: Mrs Bull's argument that there had, in fact, been no transfer of the freehold deserved to be evaluated at a full trial.

For our purposes, the important point about Megarry J's analysis is his use of the concept of ownership. On his Lordship's analysis, the simple fact that the supposed transfer in *Ferris v Weaven* was carried out with the motive of removing Mrs Weaven did not make that transfer a sham. Instead, it was a sham because the documents lied. They said that Mr Ferris had a freehold, but *'although in outward show the ownership was vested in the purchaser, in substance and reality it was still vested in the husband'*. This confirms the analysis given by Harris (see the extract in section 2 above): the concept of ownership is vital to understanding the content of a freehold.[23]

3.2 THE CONTENT OF A LEGAL LEASE

We will examine the content of a lease in detail in Chapter 19. Three general points are, however, worth noting here. Firstly, as Harris has argued, the content of a lease, like the content of a freehold, can be understood by using the concept of ownership. In fact, in a seminal case on the content of a lease, *Street v Mountford*,[24] Lord Templeman referred to a tenant (a party holding a lease) as someone *'able to exercise the rights of an owner of land which is in the real sense his land, albeit temporarily and subject to certain restrictions'*.

Secondly, as Lord Templeman's statement makes clear, the difference between a freehold and a lease is that the latter consists of ownership *for a limited period*. This is why s 1 of the LPA 1925 describes the lease as a *'term of years absolute'*. 'Term', here, comes from the same root as 'terminal' or 'terminus', and means that a lease must come to an end—that is, that it must be for a limited period (see Chapter 19, section 2.7).

Thirdly, as we will see in Chapter 6, it is possible for B to have an *equitable lease*. In such a case, B does not have a legal property right in land, nor, according to the terminology of the LPA 1925, does he have an estate in land; instead, B has an equitable interest in land. In Chapter 6, we will consider how the effect of an equitable interest may differ from that of a legal estate or interest; in Chapter 19, section 4.2, we will specifically see why it may be better for B to show that he has a legal lease rather than an equitable lease.

3.3 WHY ONLY TWO LEGAL ESTATES IN LAND?

It may seem puzzling that the LPA 1925 imposes a limit on the types of legal estate. After all, in the final extract given in section 2 above, Birks set out some of the advantages, to an

---

[23] Harris, therefore, refers to *Miles v Bull* to support his analysis: see *Property and Justice*, p 71.
[24] [1985] AC 809, 816. See further Chapter 19, section 1.1.

owner of land, of being able to divide his ownership into slices of time and then distribute those slices to others. An owner may well want to give another a legal estate that is neither a freehold nor a lease: for example, he may want to give his eldest child ownership of the land for her life, then give ownership for the future, taking effect on the eldest child's death, to his eldest grandchild, and so on. So why has English law limited an owner's ability to create those different sorts of legal estate in land?

Birks, 'Five Keys to Land Law' in *Land Law: Themes and Perspectives* (eds Bright and Dewar, 1998, p 464)

Carried to extremes, the dynastic temptation might have led to an infinite series of life estates: to A, my eldest son, for life, then to A's eldest son for life, then to the eldest son of A's eldest son, and so on. The effect would have been to give each successive son only the slice of time measured by the thread of his life. He could deal in that slice, but no buyer would ever get, or pay for, more than an estate *pur autre vie*.[25] [Some of the bad effects of such an arrangement are instantly appreciable. Nobody would ever have a marketable slice of time. No money could be raised to invest in the land. It is in nobody's interest to produce an impoverished class of landowners. If such arrangements prevailed, the value of land would be locked up and sterilized.

At page 463

[. . .] The law now does everything it can to ensure that land is freely alienable and that any future interests granted to descendants are detached from the land and transferred to the fund represented by the money for which it is sold. Since the great reforms of 1925, anyone wanting to deal in slices of time other than leases, and less than for ever, has had to do it in equity, behind the curtain of a trust. In other words, in front of the curtain there are now only two slices of time known to the law, 'for ever' and the lease for whatever time is agreed. All other slices of time once recognized directly by the common law have been abolished.

As Birks notes, it is no longer possible for A to give B1 a *legal* property right consisting of ownership of land for his life, or to give B2 a *legal* property right consisting of ownership from the time of B1's death. The closest that A can come to dividing up his ownership in that way is to set up a trust, under which B1 and B2 each acquire an *equitable* property right. These types of trust, allowing for successive interests, are considered in detail in a separate chapter, available with the online resources. Two basic points can be noted here. Firstly, A's ability to set up such a trust is not limited to land and so does not depend on the doctrine of estates: for example, A can set up an identical trust in relation to his ownership of a painting. Secondly, under such a trust, it is very important that B1 and B2 each have an *equitable*, and not a *legal*, property right. In particular, as we will see in Chapter 17, it means that there may well be situations in which B1 and B2 cannot assert that right against a later purchaser of the land. This may be bad news for B1 and B2, but, by protecting the purchaser, it promotes the goal of allowing land to be 'freely alienable'—that is, to be transferred free from pre-existing rights of parties such as B1 and B2.

---

[25] That is, an estate terminating on the death of another.

4 LEGAL ESTATES IN LAND: THE *ACQUISITION* QUESTION

To show that he has a legal estate in land, B needs to show not only that his claimed right counts as a freehold or lease, but also that he has, in fact, acquired that right. The obvious way for B to acquire a freehold or lease is through a *dependent acquisition*—that is, by showing that A, an owner of the land, has given B that legal estate. So, if B claims that A has transferred his freehold to B, or that A has granted him a lease, B relies on a dependent acquisition. We will examine the rules applying to a dependent acquisition of a legal estate in Chapter 8, although it is worth noting that, as we saw in Chapter 3, section 3, the transfer of A's legal freehold to B, or the grant by A to B of a lease of over seven years, will be completed only by B's registration as the holder of that estate.

It is also possible for B to acquire a legal freehold by means of an *independent acquisition*.[26] In such a case, B does not claim that A has given him a legal estate; instead, B acquires that right through his own, unilateral conduct. For example, if B simply goes onto A's land and takes physical control of it, B acquires a legal freehold of that land, even if he acts without A's permission.[27] We will examine this point in detail in Chapter 9.

5 THE CONCEPT OF A LEGAL INTEREST IN LAND

A legal interest in land is a legal property right in land that does not give its holder a right to exclusive possession, and so does not confer ownership of that land. In the following extract, Lawson and Rudden discuss one example of a legal interest in land: a legal easement.

Lawson and Rudden, *The Law of Property* (3rd edn, 2002, pp 14–15)

We have used the simple example of ownership, but as we shall see later there is a limited number of other interests which can be described as 'real' or 'proprietary'. This can be illustrated by considering your right to leave your car in next door's yard. Probably at the moment you have no such right. If your neighbour lets you, you can park but you have no right to stay. If you pay for parking, say by the month, you have a contractual right to leave your car, enforceable by an action for damages and possibly an injunction, but enforceable against your neighbour only.[28] If, however, you have an easement—a recognized real right—your claim to park will prevail against whoever owns next door. But before the common law will recognize it as a property interest, the right to park must comply with certain requirements both of substance and form; you must own the freehold or leasehold of your house; the parking must not be a claim to possession of your neighbour's entire yard; it must be intended to add to the value of the house and not just to confer a personal benefit on you; and it must be created by deed and entered on the Land Register, or else have been acquired by over twenty years open user.

---

[26] As to whether a legal lease can be acquired independently, see Chapter 19, section 3.1.

[27] It has been suggested that, in such a case, B acquires only an *equitable* freehold. That view is, however, difficult to support: see Chapter 9, section 3.

[28] [Such a right is an example of a *contractual licence*, which is a type of right that we will examine in Chapter 21, section 3.]

The key *positive* feature of a legal interest in land, such as an easement, is thus that it counts as a legal property right in land. As a result, it is capable of binding not only A (the party giving B the right), but also the rest of the world (including, for example, any later owners of A's land). For example, in *Hill v Tupper*,[29] which we examined in section 1 above, Mr Hill was unable to show that the right he acquired from the canal company counted as an easement, or as any other form of legal interest in land. As a result, Mr Hill could not assert that right against Mr Tupper. In contrast, if Mr Hill *had* been able to show that he had a legal interest in land, that right would have been *prima facie* binding not only on the canal company, but also on the rest of the world—including, of course, Mr Tupper.

The key *negative* feature of a legal interest in land, such as an easement, is that it does *not* give its holder ownership, as it does not consist of a right to exclusive possession of land. As we will see in Chapter 22, section 2.4.4, that point can be important when considering B's claim to an easement. B's right cannot count as an easement if it amounts to a claim of ownership of a particular piece of land.[30] If B wants to claim such a right, he must show that he has an estate in land—that is, a freehold or a lease.

It is worth noting that the concept of a property right that does not involve ownership may well be unique to land law. Certainly, it is impossible, for example, to have an easement over property other than land. It seems that the special features of land that we examined in Chapter 1, section 4 (in particular, its capacity for multiple, simultaneous use) may justify the recognition of special forms of property right that can exist only in relation to land.

6 LEGAL INTERESTS IN LAND: THE *CONTENT* QUESTION

6.1 THE *NUMERUS CLAUSUS* PRINCIPLE

In *Hill v Tupper*,[31] which we examined in section 1 above, Mr Hill tried to argue that his exclusive right to put boats on the canal should be regarded by the court as a new form of legal interest in land. The Exchequer Chamber made very clear, however, that individuals, such as Mr Hill and the canal company, cannot simply choose to create new forms of legal interest in land. That important point is confirmed by the following extract.

Keppell v Bailey
(1834) 2 My & K 517

Facts: Edward and John Kendall were the proprietors of an ironworks in Monmouthshire. They set up a joint stock company, along with a number of other parties, to build the Trevill railroad. The Kendalls made a binding promise to the other stockholders that the limestone used in their ironworks would come only from the Trevill quarry (and so would be carried on the Trevill railroad, thus earning money for the joint stock company). Following the deaths of the Kendalls, the ironworks was passed on, and was eventually bought by Joseph and Crayshaw Bailey. The Baileys planned to use limestone from a different quarry and to build a new railroad to carry that limestone to

---

[29] (1863) 2 H & C 122.
[30] See e.g. *per* Lord Scott in *Moncrieff v Jamieson* [2007] 1 WLR 2620 (HL) [55].   [31] Ibid.

the ironworks. Stockholders in the joint stock company (including Mr Keppell) applied for an injunction preventing the Baileys from using any limestone not taken from the Trevill quarry. They argued: (i) that the promise made by the Kendalls bound not only themselves, but also any later owners of the ironworks, such as the Baileys; and, alternatively, that (ii) even if the promise made by the Kendalls did not create a property right, it should bind the Baileys, because they acquired the ironworks knowing of that earlier promise. The High Court of Chancery rejected both of those arguments.

We will examine that second argument in Chapter 6, section 2.6; our focus here is on the first argument.

Lord Brougham LC

At 535

There are certain known incidents to property and its enjoyment; among others, certain burdens wherewith it may be affected, or rights which may be created and may be enjoyed over it by parties other than the owner; all which incidents are recognised by the law [. . .] All these kinds of property, however, all these holdings, are well known to the law and familiarly dealt with by its principles. But it must not therefore be supposed that incidents of a novel kind can be devised and attached to property at the fancy or caprice of any owner. It is clearly inconvenient both to the science of the law and to the public weal that such a latitude should be given. There can be no harm in allowing the fullest latitude to men in binding themselves and their representatives, that is, their assets real and personal, to answer in damages for breach of their obligations. This tends to no mischief, and is a reasonable liberty to bestow; but great detriment would arise and much confusion of rights if parties were allowed to invent new modes of holding and enjoying real property, and to impress upon their lands and tenements a peculiar character, which should follow them into all hands, however remote. Every close, every messuage,[32] might thus be held in a several fashion; and it would hardly be possible to know what rights the acquisition of any parcel conferred, or what obligations it imposed. The right of way or of common is of a public as well as of a simple nature, and no one who sees the premises can be ignorant of what the vicinage[33] knows. But if one man may bind his messuage and land to take lime from a particular kiln, another may bind his to take coals from a certain pit, while a third may load his property with further obligations to employ one blacksmith's forge, or the members of one corporate body, in various operations upon the premises, besides many other restraints as infinite in variety as the imagination can make them; for there can be no reason whatever to support the covenant in question, which would not extend to every covenant that can be devised.

Lord Brougham LC thus set out some of the dangers that would come from allowing individuals to create new legal interests in land. The central point is that a third party, such as someone later acquiring a right in that land, would then find it very difficult to know what burdens he may have to bear. We can also make the separate point that if new types of burden are imposed on land, the value of that land may be severely reduced. These fears have resulted in the adoption of the *numerus clausus* ('closed list') principle: there is a set list

---

[32] [That is, every piece of land: 'messuage' means a piece of land on which a house stands.]

[33] ['Vicinage' here means the neighbourhood or, more specifically, other neighbours who are entitled to exercise rights of common over a piece of land.]

of legal property rights in relation to land and if B's right is not on that list, it simply cannot count as a legal property right in land.

Doubts have been expressed about the true usefulness of the principle. For example, whilst noting that the principle seems to exist in all non-feudal legal systems, Rudden[34] also argues that it may not be efficient: if A and B are unable to create a desired property right, they may well resort to complicated legal mechanisms in an effort to achieve, as far as possible, the same effect. As Rudden puts it:

> all that the law of many countries does is to prevent an owner from simply and cheaply creating fancy property interests; he can almost always achieve his aims at some cost by the use of devices [. . .] which, when one stands back and contemplates them calmly, appear largely mumbo-jumbo.

As we will see in Chapter 23, section 2.4, when examining the law relating to positive covenants, there is some truth in that observation.[35]

It can also be argued that the *numerus clausus* principle allows judges to evade their responsibility to explain precisely why particular rights count as legal interests in land, whilst others do not. Gray and Gray have made this criticism forcefully.[36]

Gray and Gray, *Elements of Land Law* (5th edn, 2009, pp 96–7)

Nowhere, perhaps, is the imperfect logic of English land law more clearly apparent than in its attempt to demarcate proprietary rights from merely personal rights in land. The outcome is a philosophical shambles, but English law has never been overly concerned with philosophical propriety. Although the way in which the law identifies the categories of proprietary right is deeply unsatisfactory, the difficulties (albeit irksome) should not be over-estimated. Somehow English law blunders its way towards roughly the correct conclusions and there is usually little doubt, except perhaps at the perimeters of the field, as to whether a particular entitlement is or is not proprietary in the relevant conveyancing sense [. . .]

The difficulty with this orthodox understanding of proprietary quality is, of course, that it is riddled with circularity: the definition of proprietary character becomes entirely self-fulfilling. If naively we ask which entitlements are 'proprietary', we are told that they are those rights which are assignable to and enforceable against third parties. When we then ask which rights these may be, we are told that they comprise, of course, the entitlements which are traditionally identified as 'proprietary'. It is radical and obscurantist nonsense to formulate a test of proprietary quality in this way.

Nonetheless, as the following extract shows, the *numerus clausus* principle, as far as legal interests in land is concerned, has been given statutory confirmation.

---

[34] 'Economic Theory v Property Law' in *Oxford Essays in Jurisprudence* (3rd series, eds Eekelaar and Bell, Oxford: Clarendon Press, 1987).

[35] It is also worth noting, however, that various commentators have attempted to meet Rudden's challenge by putting forward economic justifications for the *numerus clausus* rule: see, for example, Merrill and Smith, 'Optimal Standardization in the Law of Property: The Numerus Clausus Principle' (2001) 110 Yale LJ 1.

[36] See, also, Gray and Gray, 'The Rhetoric of Realty' in *Rationalizing Property, Equity and Trusts: Essays in Honour of Edward Burn* (ed Getzler, Oxford: OUP, 2003).

Law of Property Act 1925, s 1(2) and (3)

(2) The only interests or charges in or over land which are capable of subsisting or of being conveyed or created at law are—

(a) An easement, right or privilege in or over land for an interest equivalent to an estate in fee simple absolute in possession or a term of years absolute;

(b) A rentcharge in possession issuing out of or charged on land being either perpetual or for a term of years absolute;

(c) A charge by way of legal mortgage;

(d) Any other similar charge on land which is not created by an instrument;

(e) Rights of entry exercisable over or in respect of a legal term of years absolute, or annexed, for any purpose, to a legal rentcharge.

(3) All other estates, interests, and charges in or over land take effect as equitable interests.

So, just as s 1(1) of the LPA 1925 limits the number of possible legal estates in land, s 1(2) of the same Act limits the numbers of possible legal interests in land. Essentially, there are five types of permissible legal interest: an easement; a profit; a charge; a rentcharge; and a right of entry. If B's right does not match the content of one of those five rights, it cannot count as a legal interest in land.

In Chapter 22, we will examine the content of the easement in detail; we will do the same for the charge in Chapter 25. Profits, rentcharges, and rights of entry are of less practical importance, and will not be examined in detail. A profit is a right to take something from A's land (e.g. turf, timber, fish, or wild animals);[37] a rentcharge is a right to receive money from a freehold owner of land.[38] A right of entry may arise as part of a lease, where a landlord reserves a right to enter the land if, for example, the tenant fails to pay rent as agreed; it may also arise as part of a rentcharge to allow the party holding the rentcharge to enter the freeholder's land if that charge is not paid.

The list imposed by s 1(2) of the 1925 Act is not necessarily fixed forever. For example, as we will see in Chapter 23, the Law Commission has recently suggested an addition: the 'land obligation'. It does mean, however, that any change to the list can be made only by Parliament, and by amending s 1(2).

6.2 A REMINDER: THE EFFECT OF SECTION 1(4) OF THE LPA 1925

We noted at the start of section 3 the effect of s 1(4) of the LPA 1925: a legal property right that is not a legal estate in land under s 1(1) of the LPA 1925, must however be regarded as a 'legal estate' when it comes to interpreting that phrase in the context of rules set out by the rest of the LPA 1925. This means, for example, that a right such as a legal easement may be deemed to be a 'legal estate' when interpreting a provision such as s 52(1) of the LPA 1925, which states the following general rule.

---

[37] For more detail, see Law Commission Consultation Paper No 186 (2008, Part 6).

[38] For more detail, see Rentcharges Act 1977; Gray and Gray, *Elements of Land Law* (5th edn, Oxford: OUP, 2009, Part 6.6).

Law of Property Act 1925, s 52

(1) All conveyances of land or of any interest therein are void for the purpose of conveying or creating a legal estate unless made by deed.

A 'legal estate', by virtue of s 1(4) LPA 1925, refers to *any* legal property right in land; an attempt by A to give B a legal easement or legal charge in or over A's land will therefore fail unless a deed is used. We will examine the scope and requirements of s 52 in Chapter 8, section 5, when looking at the formal acquisition of legal property rights.

The importance of s 1(4) LPA was made clear in *Baker v Craggs*.[39] There was a dispute between the Craggs (B) and the Bakers (C) as to the use of particular land:[40] the Charltons (A1 and A2)[41] had initially sold land to B, and had then purported to grant C an easement (in this case, a right of way) over part of that land. At the time of the transaction between A1 and A2 and C, B had not yet succeeded in being registered as holding the land sold to it by A1 and A2. This meant that, at that point, B had not acquired A1 and A2's legal freehold in the land:[42] it was one of those situations, as already noted in section 4, where registration is required in order for B to acquire A1 and A2's legal estate in the land. As a result of the contract between A1 and A2 and B, however, B did have, at the time when C acquired the easement, an equitable interest in the land.[43] This meant that, when C acquired its right in the land, B had a pre-existing property right in that land.

As one might expect, given the general rule that the property right arising first in time prevails,[44] B's pre-existing property right was prima facie binding on C. C, however, argued that it had a *defence* to B's right. One of the defences C invoked was the overreaching defence, which we will examine in detail in Chapter 17. In this context, that defence is regulated by s 2 of the LPA 1925, which begins in the following way.

Law of Property Act 1925, s 2

(1) A conveyance to a purchaser of a legal estate in land shall overreach any equitable interest or power affecting that estate, whether or not he has notice thereof, if [...]

B's right, as we have seen, was an equitable interest, but it might appear that, as C had acquired only an easement over the land (and not a freehold or lease), there had been no conveyance to C of a legal estate. After all, as Lord Neuberger noted: *'as a matter of property law, a right of way over land constitutes an interest in that land, although it does not constitute an*

---

[39] [2017] Ch 295.

[40] It is unfortunate for our purposes that the parties first acquiring a right (the Craggs) had a surname beginning with C, and the parties later acquiring a right (the Bakers) had a surname beginning with B; but they are referred to here as B and C respectively to keep to the scheme introduced in Chapter 1 and generally used elsewhere in the book when considering such priority disputes.

[41] As will be seen in Chapter 17, section 2.3, it was also significant in *Baker* that C acquired the right from *two* parties, which is why the Charltons are referred to here as A1 and A2.

[42] Land Registration Act 2002, s 27: see Chapter 8, section 6.4.

[43] See Chapter 6, section 4 and Chapter 8, section 4.3.

[44] See Chapter 2, section 2.2.2 and, for a more detailed discussion, Chapter 15, section 3.

estate in that land.[45] That is of course correct as a matter of general property law principle; but this is where s 1(4) is crucial, as explained by the judge in *Baker v Craggs*.

Baker v Craggs [2016] EWHC 3250 (Ch), [2017] Ch 295

The facts of the case are set out in Chapter 8, section 6.5.1.

Newey J

[27] The term 'legal estate', which features more than once in section 2 of the LPA, is explained in section 1. While section 1(1) states that an 'estate in fee simple absolute in possession' and a 'term of years absolute' are the 'only estates which are capable of subsisting or of being conveyed or created at law', section 1(4) explains that the 'estates, interests, and charges' authorised to subsist or be conveyed or created at law by the section are referred to in the Act as 'legal estates'. The definition thus extends to the various interests 'capable of subsisting or of being conveyed or created at law' specified in section 1(2). These include an 'easement, right, or privilege in or over land for an interest equivalent to an estate in fee simple absolute in possession or a term of years absolute': section 1(2)(a).

The effect of s 1(4), then, was that the grant by A1 and A2 to C of a legal easement allowed C to meet one of the requirements of the overreaching defence, as set out in s 2, and show that there had been a conveyance to C of a 'legal estate' in land. As we will see in Chapter 17, section 2.3, there has been some criticism of allowing overreaching to operate in C's favour in such a case,[46] and, at the time of writing, an appeal is pending in *Baker v Craggs*.[47] Nonetheless, on the specific point as to the interpretation of s 1(4), the view of Newey J seems hard to fault.

7 LEGAL INTERESTS IN LAND: THE *ACQUISITION* QUESTION

The obvious way for B to acquire a legal interest in land is through a *dependent acquisition*— that is, by showing that A has given B that right. In Chapter 8, we will look at the general rules applying to the dependent acquisition of a legal interest in land. As seen in section 6, the effect of s 52(1) of the LPA 1925 is that a deed is required for the creation of a legal easement or a legal charge. Further, as is the case in relation to the acquisition of legal estates, it is again worth noting, as we saw in Chapter 3, section 3, that registration of B's right is generally required if A's attempted grant of a legal interest to B is to succeed. In Chapter 22, section 3, and Chapter 25, section 4, we will examine the specific rules applying to a dependent acquisition of, respectively, a legal easement and a legal charge.

---

[45] *Edwards v Kumarasamy* [2016] AC 1334, [23]. The relevant statutory rules there were not part of the LPA 1925; s 1(4) of the LPA 1925 had no application.

[46] See e.g. Dixon, 'The Registration Gap and Overreaching' [2017] Conv 1; Owen, 'Priorities and Registered Land During the Registration Gap' [2017] Conv 230.

[47] For updates, see the online resources.

As for independent acquisition, we will see in Chapter 22, section 3.3, that it is also possible for B to acquire an easement simply by exercising a right over a long period. In such a case, B's easement is said to arise 'through prescription' and there is no need for B to show that he has registered that right, or that A used a deed (or even any writing) to give B that right. Where B relies on prescription to acquire an easement, it may well seem that he is relying on an independent acquisition—that is, he is claiming a right as a result of his own, unilateral conduct, just as occurs where B acquires a freehold by taking physical control of land. As we will see in Chapter 22, section 3.3, however, the courts have not adopted this view.

8 CONCLUSION

The facts of *Hill v Tupper*[48] (see section 1 above) and *Keppell v Bailey*[49] (see section 6 above) provide particular examples of a more general question that land law has to tackle: if A owns land and B then acquires a right that relates to A's land, can B also assert that right against C, a third party? That was, of course, the same foundational question that we examined in Chapter 1, section 5, when looking at *National Provincial Bank v Ainsworth*.[50] To answer that question, we need to be aware of the crucial distinction between: (i) a legal property right in land; and (ii) a personal right.[51] If, as in *Hill* and *Keppell*,[52] B's right is simply a personal right against A, then it is impossible for B to assert that right against C. However, if B can instead show that his right is a legal property right in land, that right is capable of binding the rest of the world, including C.

Legal property rights in land can be divided into two types: legal estates and legal interests. The difference is that the former category, unlike the latter, give their holder ownership rights over a piece of land. The LPA 1925 carefully restricts the number of legal estates and legal interests in land: there are only two permissible legal estates (freehold and lease), and, for our purposes, there are only two significant legal interests (easement and charge).[53] If B claims to have a legal estate or legal interest, he must pass both the *content* test and the *acquisition* test. To pass the *content* test, B needs to show that the right he claims counts as a legal estate or legal interest. To pass the *acquisition* test, B needs to show that he has, in fact, acquired that right: as we will see in Chapter 7, it is generally the case that, to do so, B needs to show that he is registered as holding that right and/or that A has used a particular form (such as a deed) to give him that right.

Clearly, legal estates and interests form a crucial part of land law. But to avoid overstating their importance, we need to bear four points in mind. Firstly, even if B has no legal or equitable property right in land, there may be some cases in which B can nonetheless rely on a *human right* as protection against both A and C. We discussed the impact of human rights on land law in Chapter 4.

---

[48] (1863) 2 H & C 122.   [49] (1834) 2 My & K 517.   [50] [1965] AC 1175.

[51] It is important to note that if B has an equitable property right, such a right can also bind C: we will consider such rights in Chapter 6.

[52] And, on the view of the House of Lords, *National Provincial Bank v Ainsworth* too.

[53] As we saw in section 6.2, as a result of s 1(4) of the LPA 1925, a legal easement and a legal charge each fall within the scope of the term 'legal estate' as it is used in rules laid down in the remainder of the 1925 Act.

Secondly, if B fails to show that he has a legal property right in land, this does not necessarily mean that B has only a personal right against A. Instead, as we will see in Chapter 6, it is still possible for B to have an *equitable* property right. And such a right may give B precisely the protection that he needs: not only against A, but also against a third party later acquiring a right in A's land.

Thirdly, even if B *does* have a legal property right in land, there may, in theory, be circumstances in which he cannot assert that right against a particular third party: as we saw in Chapter 3, section 3.2.2, it may be possible for C to have a *defence* against B's legal property right.

Finally, if B wants protection simply against a specific third party (rather than any third party later acquiring a right in A's land), it is not always necessary for B to show that he has either a legal or equitable property right. Instead, B may be protected by showing he has a *direct right* against that particular third party, arising as a result of the conduct of that party. We will consider some examples of such direct rights in Chapter 7, section 3.3.

QUESTIONS

1. What is the difference between a 'personal' right and a 'property' right?

2. How might the result in *Hill v Tupper* have been different if Mr Hill's right had counted as a property right?

3. What role, if any, does the concept of ownership play in English land law?

4. Why did the Law of Property Act 1925 limit the number of possible legal estates in land?

5. What is the difference between dependent and independent acquisition?

6. What is the *numerus clausus* principle? Is it an unjustified limit on the ability of an owner of land to create new property rights in that land?

7. What is the significance of s 1(4) of the LPA 1925 in a case such as *Baker v Craggs*?

For guidance on how to answer these questions visit the online resources at www.oup.com/uk/mcfarlane4e/.

FURTHER READING

Birks, 'Five Keys to *Land Law*' in *Land Law: Themes and Perspectives* (eds Bright and Dewar, Oxford: OUP, 1998)

Bright, 'Of Estates and Interests: A Tale of Ownership and Property Rights' in *Land Law: Themes and Perspectives* (eds Bright and Dewar, Oxford: OUP, 1998)

Douglas, 'The Content of a Freehold: A 'Right to Use' Land?' in *Modern Studies in Property Law vol 7* (ed Hopkins, Oxford: Hart Publishing, 2013)

Harris, 'Legal Doctrine and Interests in Land' in *Oxford Essays in Jurisprudence* (3rd series, eds Eekelaar and Bell, Oxford: OUP, 1987)

Merrill and Smith, 'Optimal Standardization in the Law of Property: The Numerus *Clausus Principle*' (2000) 110 Yale LJ 1

Rudden, 'Economic Theory v Property Law' in *Oxford Essays in Jurisprudence* (3rd series, eds Eekelaar and Bell, Oxford: OUP, 1987)

6

EQUITABLE INTERESTS

CENTRAL ISSUES

1. It is generally said that there are two sorts of property right in land: legal property rights and equitable property rights. We examined the content of legal property rights in Chapter 5; we will examine the content of equitable property rights in this chapter.

2. We saw in Chapter 5 that legal property rights in land can be split into two groups: legal estates and legal interests. In contrast, under the scheme of the Law of Property Act 1925, there is no such thing as an equitable estate in land. All equitable property rights in land are equitable *interests*. Equitable interests in land can usefully be split into two groups: equitable interests arising under a trust; and other equitable interests.

3. As we also saw in Chapter 5, there is a limited number of legal estates and legal interests in land. The list of possible equitable interests in land is also limited, but is longer than the list of legal interests. In particular, a right under a trust counts as an equitable interest—and rights under a trust can have very varied content. This means that whilst the content of B's right may prevent it from being a legal interest in land, it may still count as an equitable interest in land.

4. Equitable interests in land share a key feature of legal estates and legal interests: they are capable of being asserted against third parties. For example, consider a case where A has a legal estate in land and B, through his dealings with A, acquires an equitable interest in A's land. B's right will then be *prima facie* binding on C, a party who later acquires a right from A. In this way, equitable interests in land have a power lacked by personal rights.

5. It is clear that the *content* and *acquisition* questions are answered differently depending on whether B claims a legal or equitable property right. In section 7 of this chapter, we will consider whether these differences can be justified. One important point is that if B has an equitable property right rather than a legal property right, it will generally be easier for a third party to show that he has a defence to B's right. We will focus on the *defences* question in Chapters 15, 16, and 17. It may also be the case that equitable interests are conceptually, as well as historically, distinct from legal property rights.

1 EQUITY AND EQUITABLE PROPERTY RIGHTS

1.1 THE FUNCTION OF EQUITY

In land law, as in many other areas of law, it is possible to distinguish between common law rules and equitable rules. Historically, the distinction is a simple one: common law rules were developed by the common law courts, equitable rules were developed by courts of equity. As a result of procedural reform in the late nineteenth century, there are no longer separate common law courts and equitable courts; rather, all courts must consider any relevant common law rules and equitable rules.

As Hackney has put it, the arrangement of having two separate sets of courts, often with overlapping and competing jurisdictions was 'ludicrous'.[1] Nonetheless, this arrangement, now abolished, left a very valuable legacy, not least in land law. As we will see in this chapter, and throughout the book, equitable interests in land are a crucial part of the land law system and the means of acquiring such rights give vital flexibility and often offer invaluable protection to parties who would otherwise be denied any redress. In Chapter 10, for example, we will examine in detail the equitable doctrine of proprietary estoppel, which can provide protection to B where B has relied to his or her detriment on A's promise to give B a right in A's land. That protection is available even if A has made no formal grant of a right to A, even if B has not registered any right, and even if there is no written agreement between the parties. From one perspective, the equitable rules thus seem to undermine the formality and strict requirements imposed by the common law and by statute for the acquisition of a legal property right, or for the formation of a contract for the sale or other disposition of an interest in land. It can be argued that the equitable rules undermine the certainty of clear legal rules and thus can even be said to depart from a core value of the rule of law. From another perspective, explored in the following extract, the equitable rules instead provide a vital 'safety valve' by giving the courts a means to prevent a party such as A from exploiting those strict legal rules. By performing this function, the equitable rules can, in exceptional cases, mitigate the potential harshness of those common law rules and thus reconcile the parties' rights with general moral understandings by preventing behaviour which would 'shock the conscience of the court'.[2] Indeed, it can be argued that, if there were no such safety valve, it would be impossible to justify the strictness of the common law and statutory rules.

H Smith, 'Property, Equity and the Rule of Law' in *Private Law and the Rule of Law* (eds Austin and Klimchuk, 2014, pp 232–3)

One limit to formalism is its vulnerability to evasion by opportunists. This is one reason to allow for equitable intervention.

The simple structures of the law are open to exploitation by opportunists [. . .] Traditionally, equity concerned itself with 'near fraud', which is behaviour that is close to the line of fraud

---

[1] Hackney, *Understanding Equity and Trusts* (London: Fontana, 1987) ch 1.
[2] The phrase used as a threshold for equitable intervention, through proprietary estoppel, by Lord Walker in *Cobbe v Yeoman's Row Management Ltd* [2008] 1 WLR 1752 at [92].

or may well be fraud but cannot be proved as such. Picking up on this notion, I have defined opportunism as such:

'Behaviour that is undesirable but that cannot be cost-effectively captured – defined, detected, and deterred – by explicit ex ante rulemaking [. . .] It often consists of behaviour that is technically legal but is done with a view to securing unintended benefits from the system, and these benefits are usually smaller than the costs they impose on others.'

[. . .] a major theme of traditional equity was to counteract opportunism. To do so equity needs to go beyond *ex ante* bright line rules, because it is difficult to anticipate all the avenues of evasion. Plugging nine out of ten loopholes is hopeless if all the evaders can rush through the tenth. Equity employs *ex post* standards, emphasizes good faith and notice, couches its reasoning in terms of morals, and is sometimes vague rather than bright line. To cabin such a powerful tool, equity courts were only supposed to act in personam and not in rem, and the substantive doctrines of equity counselled caution in undermining the law. Equity was not designed to root out every last bit of opportunism and courts recognized that equitable doctrines and remedies, not least injunctions, themselves could be exploited by opportunistic litigants unless courts were on their guard and were willing to stay the hand of equity.

Smith's argument is a very interesting one, as it suggests that 'doing without any equitable safety valve will be very difficult'[3] as the rule of law itself demands that judges have some means of dealing with those whose actions, by exploiting the strict common law and statutory rules in ways widely regarded as unfair or immoral, can reduce people's respect for, and willingness to follow, such rules. Smith also notes, however, that equity cannot be wholly discretionary, and is at its most effective when it prevents conduct which would be widely regarded as exploitative or otherwise immoral. This tension will be evident throughout the book when we examine equitable doctrines such as proprietary estoppel (in Chapter 10) or common intention constructive trusts (in Chapter 12). As far as land law is concerned, it is important to note that equity has clearly moved beyond any traditional limit of acting only 'in personam': it is clear that, if B has an equitable interest in land, that right is capable of binding not only A, but also later parties, such as C, acquiring a right in A's land. This creates a further reason why care must be taken before allowing B equitable protection: an equitable right acquired by B, if it counts as an equitable interest in land, will also be capable of binding C-a party who, unlike A, may not have behaved opportunistically. The nature and development of equitable interests is considered in the next section.

1.2 THE DEVELOPMENT OF EQUITABLE PROPERTY RIGHTS

In land law, one of the lasting contributions of those equitable rules is the concept of an *equitable property right*. In Chapter 5, section 1, we considered the fundamental distinction between a personal right and a property right: whereas a personal right can be asserted only against a specific person, a property right has a wider range of application. An equitable property right shares a very important feature with a legal property right: it does more than simply bind a specific person. For example, if A has a freehold or lease of land and then gives B an equitable property right, B has a right that is capable of binding not only A, *but also C*, a party who later acquires A's land.

---

[3] Smith, 'Property, Equity, and the Rule of Law' in *Private Law and the Rule of Law* (eds Austin and Klimchuk, Oxford: OUP, 2014) p 246.

In the following extract, Lionel Smith discusses the development of equitable property rights. He makes the important point that these rights, unlike the legal property rights that we examined in Chapter 5, are necessarily based on A's being under a *duty* to B.

L Smith, 'Fusion and Tradition' in *Equity in Commercial Law* (eds Degeling and Edelman, 2005, pp 32–3)

I would argue that there are at least two examples of norms that are enforced routinely by Equity, but only sporadically by the common law, and that it is here that the true distinctiveness of Equity may lie. In other words, leaving aside the mass of detailed doctrine in both traditions, these are examples of situations in which Equity enforces a norm or value which the common law generally does not.

Respect for other people's obligations

This section can be introduced with a simple normative problem. Imagine that John owns a boat. He lends it to Mary, promising her that she can keep it for one month. After one week, Eleanor offers to buy the boat from John. John accepts her offer and Eleanor becomes the owner of the boat. Is she required to allow Mary to retain possession during the rest of the one-month period? Reasonable people could differ. Many people would say that it depends upon whether Eleanor was aware of the arrangements between John and Mary, and some might think it was relevant whether Mary had paid for her one month of use, or whether it was in the nature of a gift.

In the Romanist tradition, the most fundamental distinction in private law is the one between obligations and property rights. A right of ownership binds everyone. Obligations bind only the parties to the obligation: the debtor is bound to the creditor. The common law, in the narrow sense that excludes Equity, basically follows this line. Both modern civil law and the common law in the narrow sense admit the possibility that someone can commit a wrongful act by interfering with the fulfilment of another person's obligation. But short of that fault-based wrong, obligations do not have effects except on the debtor and the creditor. Equity takes a different view. Some obligations systematically have third-party effects, without recourse to the law of wrongs. These are obligations that relate to the benefit of particular property, or an interest therein.

This approach is seen in a crucial technique of legal reasoning that underlies much of the original jurisdiction of Equity. At the risk of leaving out much doctrinal detail, it can be stated in this way. If a person is under an obligation, and the obligation relates to the benefit of particular property or an interest therein, then another person who comes into possession or control of that particular property—even though he does so without any personal culpability—is not allowed to get in the way of the fulfilment of the obligation. The defendant can free himself of this constraint only by affirmative proof that he gave value in good faith without notice of the obligation, and that the interest he acquired was a common law interest and not an Equitable one only [. . .] The representative of creditors is also caught, although he represents persons who are in good faith and who, for the most part, gave value.

This principle is not totally alien to the common law. First, as we have noted, the common law recognises that one person should not deliberately interfere in another person's performance of his obligations. But in this tort context, it looks for a level of cognition on the part of the defendant that allows us to understand the defendant as having committed a genuinely wrongful act. In that setting, of course, it is irrelevant whether the obligation relates to specific property or not. More interestingly, in one crucial context, the common law did exactly what Equity does routinely: it said that if the obligation does relate to specific property, then a recipient of that property must allow the obligation to be performed, even though the recipient does not owe the obligation, and without any finding that the recipient acted wrongfully. That context is the lease of land. The lessee's rights were enforceable against a transferee from the lessor, and later against all the world, first in damages only, but later by specific recovery.

In Equity, however, this principle is ubiquitous, and routinely turns an obligation relating to a particular asset into a kind of property right, held by the beneficiary or creditor of the obligation, in the particular asset. Effectively, people are bound by other people's obligations—not bound to perform them, but bound not to interfere with them.

In the following extract, Hackney also discusses how equitable property rights developed from an initial duty of A to B. In doing so, he uses the trust as an example. As we will see in this chapter, the trust is a classic example of a situation in which B has an equitable property right. A trust arises where A (the trustee) has a right (the trust property) and is under a duty to use that right for the benefit of B (or B and others, known as the 'beneficiaries'), as well as a duty not to use that right for A's own benefit.[4] If another party has specifically set up the trust, that party is often referred to as the 'settlor'.

Hackney, *Understanding Equity and Trusts* (1987, pp 20–2)

In the course of the mid seventeenth to early nineteenth centuries, Equity[5] was turned into a systematic body of principles as refined, rigorous and ultimately unyielding as anything produced by the common law [. . .]

One consequence of the 'regularisation' of Equity was the creation of a law of property. The Chancellor had originally intervened by imposing personal obligations on particular defendants. So the early trustee of land would be under a personal obligation to administer the property for his beneficiary, but the trustee might still be seen as the owner of the land. The particular novelty of the trust is that the beneficiary need not have been a party to a transaction establishing the trust, yet he is still able to enforce it, and what is more, the person who does set up the transaction finds he has no standing to intervene to see that it is honoured. By the end of this period the beneficiary of the trust is perceived as having an equitable proprietary interest in the asset, not just rights enforceable only against the trustee. He can enforce his rights against total strangers, from whom he can demand the asset. This 'exigibility'—demandability—is one of the characteristics of property. He can also alienate and pass a good equitable title. For some of the beneficiary's protection his trustee will have to use the mechanism of the common law courts, and the beneficiary of the trust may have to invoke the assistance of the Chancellor to drive a reluctant trustee to take the necessary

---

[4] It is possible for there to be trusts in which A, as well as being a trustee, is also a beneficiary of the trust: see for example *Williams & Glyn's Bank v Boland* [1981] AC 813, HL, which we will discuss in section 2 of this Chapter. In such a case, A is permitted to use the trust property for his own benefit (but only to the extent that he is a beneficiary).

[5] [The author uses Equity with a capital E to refer to the body of specific rules developed by courts of equity and to distinguish those rules from the general concept of 'equity' with its broader sense of what is fair.]

steps. But it is important to see that the trustee is no longer exercising rights. His common law ownership was made up of a set of rights, powers and duties. The Chancellor's intervention has overridden or destroyed the rights, which the trustee can no longer exercise at his own election and for his own benefit, and has converted them into equitable duties, to be performed for the sole benefit of the beneficiary. No principle seems more central to the law of trusts than that the trustee may not derive a profit from the trust. There is today no sensible usage of 'owner' which can apply to the trustee, and every sensible usage which can apply to the beneficiary. The trustee has a legal title and access to common law courts and remedies, but he is a driven vehicle for the superior rights of his beneficiary. He litigates at common law in response to his equitable duties, and not to his common law rights, which have been subordinated. The trustee is now a manager in an institution which is a hybrid between the creation of an agency and the disposition of property.

2 THE CONCEPT OF AN EQUITABLE INTEREST IN LAND

In Chapter 1, we considered the decision of the House of Lords in *National Provincial Bank v Ainsworth*.[6] It was held that Mrs Ainsworth's right, her 'deserted wife's equity', whilst clearly a product of equitable rules, did not count as an equitable interest in land. Instead, it was simply an equitable personal right against her husband. As a result, Mrs Ainsworth could not assert that right against the bank, who had acquired a right in the land from her husband. That decision can be contrasted with the decision of the House of Lords in *Williams & Glyn's Bank v Boland*.[7] Mr Boland was registered as holding a freehold of a home in Ridge Park, Beddington, Surrey. Mr Boland and his brother were directors of a building company. To support the business, Mr Boland borrowed money from the Williams & Glyn's Bank. The money was borrowed as part of a mortgage deal: to secure his duty to repay that sum, plus interest, Mr Boland gave the bank a legal charge over his home. When Mr Boland failed to repay the loan, the bank wished to sell the land. To get a good price, the bank knew that it had to sell the home with vacant possession. Because Mrs Boland refused to leave, the bank applied for an order for possession of the home.

The facts of *Boland* thus have much in common with those of *Ainsworth*. The crucial difference between the two cases was as to the *content* of the wife's right. Mrs Boland did not attempt to assert a 'deserted wife's equity' against the bank. Rather, because Mr Boland had acquired his freehold of the land with Mrs Boland's financial assistance, he was under a duty to use that freehold not for his own sole benefit, but for the benefit of both himself and his wife.[8] Mr Boland thus held his freehold on trust, and both he and his wife were beneficiaries of that trust. A beneficiary of a trust has an equitable interest, and so Mrs Boland, unlike Mrs Ainsworth, had more than a mere personal right against her husband. As confirmed by the House of Lords, Mrs Boland had an equitable interest in the land: a right capable of binding a third party, such as the bank, later acquiring a right from Mr Boland.

It is important to note that the House of Lords considered whether the bank had a defence to Mrs Boland's pre-existing equitable property right. The fact that an equitable

---

[6] [1965] AC 1175.   [7] [1981] AC 813.
[8] We will consider the circumstances in which such trusts can arise in Chapter 12.

interest in land is *capable* of binding a party other than A does not mean that such a right will *always* bind such parties. We noted in Chapter 5, section 1, that it is possible for a third party to have a defence to a pre-existing legal estate or legal interest; it is also possible for a third party to have a defence to a pre-existing *equitable* interest. In fact, if B has an equitable property right rather than a legal property right, it will generally be easier for a third party, C, to show that he or she has a defence to B's right. For example, in Chapter 5, section 6.2, we touched on the overreaching defence made available under s 2 of the LPA 1925:[9] that defence may protect C against '*any equitable interest or power*'. The fact that B has an equitable interest rather than a legal property right may thus be crucial in allowing C to invoke a particular defence against that pre-existing right of B.[10] We will consider defences in detail in Part E of this book.

3   RIGHTS UNDER TRUSTS: THE *CONTENT* QUESTION

Let us say that S, who has a freehold, wants to divide up his ownership of land by making B1 owner of the land for B1's life, with B2 becoming owner on the death of B1. We know that S cannot achieve his aims by giving either of B1 or B2 a *legal* estate in land. This is because, as we saw in Chapter 5, section 3, the Law of Property Act 1925 allows for only two forms of legal estate in land: the freehold and the lease. S can, however, set up a trust, by transferring his freehold to A1 and A2 subject to a duty to use that freehold: (i) for the benefit of B1 during B1's life; then (ii) for the benefit of B2 forever. In such a case, A1 and A2 clearly have a legal estate: a freehold. But, as noted in the Hackney extract set out in section 1 above, the trust imposed on A1 and A2 means that they cannot use their ownership rights for their own benefit: instead, they must use their freehold for the benefit of B1, then for the benefit of B2. So, whilst A1 and A2 have ownership, they are under equitable duties to B1 and B2; and those duties ensure that it is B1 and B2 who take the benefit of A1 and A2's ownership.

This structure is made clear in the Trusts of Land and Appointment of Trustees Act 1996 (TOLATA 1996).

Trusts of Land and Appointment of Trustees Act 1996, s 6(1) and (6)

(1) For the purpose of exercising their functions as trustee, the trustees of land have in relation to the land subject to the trust all the powers of an absolute owner.

[. . .]

(6) The powers conferred by this section shall not be exercised in contravention of, or of any order made in pursuance of, any other enactment or any rule of law or equity.

In our example, each of B1 and B2 has an equitable property right that allows her to take the benefits, for a slice of time, of ownership of land. Nonetheless, it would be inaccurate to say that either of B1 or B2 has an 'equitable estate'. Firstly, the Law of Property Act 1925 (LPA 1925) does not use that term. As we saw in Chapter 5, s 1(1) of the Act sets out permissible legal estates and s 1(2) sets out permissible legal interests. Section 1(3) then states that: '*All*

---

[9] For full discussion of the overreaching defence, see Chapter 17.
[10] That was the case in *Baker v Craggs* [2017] Ch 295, discussed in Chapter 5, section 6.2.

other estates, interests, and charges in or over land take effect as equitable interests.' So, if we are to follow that terminology, we should treat all equitable property rights as equitable interests.

Secondly, and more importantly, in Chapter 5, section 2, we defined an estate as a property right giving its holder ownership rights. In our example in which A1 and A2 hold a freehold on trust for B1 and B2, it is not accurate to say that B1 and B2 have ownership rights; rather, A1 and A2 have ownership, and A1 and A2 are under a duty to use that ownership for the benefit of each of B1 and B2. As Maitland once put it, if a trust exists, *equity does not say that the beneficiaries are the owners of the land, it rather says that the trustees are the owners, but adds that the trustees are bound to hold the land for the benefit of the beneficiaries.*[11] As a result, each of B1 and B2 can, in practice, enjoy the *benefit* of A1 and A2's ownership. For example, if the land consists of commercial premises rented out to a business, the rent will be paid to A1 and A2, but A1 and A2 will be under a duty (depending on the exact terms of the trust) to pay that rental income to B1 during B1's life.

It is therefore important to distinguish two cases. In the first case, A, a freehold owner of land, grants B a lease of that land. In the second case, A, a freehold owner of land, transfers that freehold to A1 and A2 to hold on trust for B1 and B2. In the first case, A can be seen as splitting, or carving up, A's right to exclusive possession of the land: that right goes to B for the duration of the lease, before returning to A. In the second case, there is no such splitting or carving up. Rather, A's freehold is transferred intact to A1 and A2, who acquire A's right to exclusive possession of the land forever. In the second case, the rights of B1 and B2 therefore derive not from any splitting or carving up of A's freehold, but rather from A's imposition of a *duty* on A1 and A2. As an Australian judge once put it: '*An equitable interest is not carved out of a legal estate but impressed upon it.*'[12] In the second case, the equitable interest is impressed upon the freehold of A1 and A2 because of the duty imposed on A1 and A2. That duty, owed to each of B1 and B2, relates to the freehold held by A1 and A2, as it limits the uses that A1 and A2 can make of the freehold. It ensures, in particular, that A1 and A2 must use the freehold not for their own benefit, but rather for the benefit of each of B1 and B2.

As far as the content question is concerned, that is the key feature of the trust: A must hold a right, and also be under a duty to B not to use that right for A's own benefit, unless and to the extent that A is also a beneficiary of the trust. We saw that, in *Williams & Glyn's Bank v Boland*,[13] for example, Mr Boland held his freehold on trust for each of himself and his wife. As a result, Mr Boland was permitted, to a certain extent, to use his freehold to his own benefit: if the freehold was sold, for example, Mr Boland would be entitled to retain a proportion of the proceeds of sale for his own benefit. The presence of the trust, however, means that, in such a case, he would be under a duty to pay a proportion of those proceeds to Mrs Boland; and also that, when deciding whether to sell his freehold, he would be under a duty to take into account the wishes of his wife.

---

[11] Maitland, *Equity – A Course of Lectures* (2nd edn, Cambridge: CUP, 1936) p 17.

[12] *Per* Brennan J in *DKLR Holding Co (No 2) Ltd v Commissioner of Stamp Duties* (1982) 149 CLR 431 (High Court of Australia). See Swadling, 'Property' in Burrows (ed) *English Private Law* (Oxford: OUP, 3rd edn, 2013) 4.145–4.150. This view also fits with the historical development of the trust: see N Jones 'Trusts in England after the Statute of Uses: A View from the Sixteenth Century' in *Itinera Fiduciae: Trust and Treuhand in Historical Perspective* (eds R Helmholz and R Zimmerman, Berlin: Duncker & Humblot, 1998) p 190: '*The interest of* [a beneficiary of a trust] *depends upon the interest of the trustee: the creation of a trust is a process of cumulation, and not division*'.

[13] [1981] AC 813, HL (the facts of the case are discussed in section 2 of this chapter).

In analysing equitable interests in land, it is important to distinguish rights under trusts from other forms of equitable interest in land. Firstly, as we will see in Chapter 13,[14] a special statutory regime regulates trusts of land, but does not apply to other equitable interests in land; secondly, as we will see in Chapter 11, section 2, a special formality rule applies to the acquisition of rights under trusts of land.[15]

To make this distinction between rights under trusts and other forms of equitable interest in land, we need to focus on the content of A's duty. In a trust, A is under a duty in relation to the whole of a particular right held by A, such as A's freehold or A's lease. In contrast, if B has a different form of equitable interest, it seems that A is under a narrower, more specific duty: for example, if B has an equitable easement, A's duty is simply to grant B an easement and A is otherwise free to use A's freehold or lease for A's own benefit.

It is important to remember that a trust will often have more than one beneficiary. We have already discussed the example where A1 and A2 hold a freehold on trust for B1 and B2, with a duty to use the freehold for B1's benefit during B1's life, and then for the benefit of B2. This example demonstrates one of the great advantages of the trust: it can be used to divide up the benefits of a right in almost any way.[16] The next extract considers examples that do not involve land, but, as shown by our examples above, the flexibility of the trust also applies where the right held on trust is a freehold or lease of land.

Worthington, *Equity* (2nd edn, 2006, pp 73–7)

Now that the idea of a trust is clearer, with its ingenious splitting of the ownership 'bundle of rights' into legal and Equitable ownership, it is possible to explore some of the enormous practical advantages of the trust [. . .]

[. . . T]rusts enable proprietary interests to be divided along a time line. A trustee can hold a Rembrandt painting on trust 'for A for life, then B for life, remainder to C' (and death need not be the only marker along the time line). This arrangement gives each party (the trustee, A, B and C) some immediate proprietary interest in the painting, with all the protection this entails, even though B and C have to wait some time before they are entitled to possession of the painting. A contract could achieve a similar result, but again without the important protections that proprietary interests afford [. . .]

[. . . T]rusts are enormously flexible in slicing up property rights in ways that would be inconceivable without the trust. Consider company shares. A shareholder who wishes to deal with his shares can only transfer full ownership or a security interest in the entire bundle of rights associated with the share. He cannot sell part of a share; he certainly cannot parcel out the different benefits inherent in shareholding to different transferees, giving one the right to dividends, another the right to vote and yet another the right to capital gains. Under the umbrella of a trust, however, all of this is possible. The owner (as settlor) simply has to specify the beneficiaries' rights under the trust in the appropriate way.

In the chapter dealing with successive interests, available with the online resources, we will look more closely at the ways in which a trust can be used to divide up the benefits of ownership over time (as in our first example). One question is, however, worth asking

---

[14] See also the chapter, available with the online resources, on successive interests.

[15] That rule is set out in s 53(1)(b) of the Law of Property Act 1925; it differs from the general formality rule applying to the acquisition of equitable interests in land, set out in s 53(1)(a) of the same Act.

[16] One of the limits is imposed by the rule against perpetuities: see section 3.1 of the online chapter on successive interests.

here: does the possibility of creating diverse equitable interests in land undermine the aim of s 1 of the LPA 1925? After all, as we saw in Chapter 5, section 3.3, part of the purpose of that provision is to protect third parties against the risk of being bound by complicated and unusual property rights. So, for example, it is impossible for B1 to have a legal life estate, or for B2 to have a legal estate giving B2 ownership of the land after B1's death. Yet in our example above, in which A1 and A2 hold a freehold on trust for B1 for B1's life, and then for B2, each of B1 and B2 has an *equitable* property right, capable of binding a third party who, for example, acquires the freehold of A1 and A2. So there may seem to be little point limiting the content of legal estates and interests in land if those limits can be evaded by simply setting up a trust.

The key point, however, is that where a party has an equitable interest, it is far easier for C (a third party later acquiring a right from A1 and A2) to have a *defence* to that pre-existing right. Indeed, in our example, if C acquires the freehold of A1 and A2, he may well be able to take free from the equitable interests of B1 and B2, even if C knows about those rights, and even if B1 or B2 is in actual occupation of the land when C acquires his right. This is because C may well be able to rely on the overreaching defence, as made available by s 2 of the LPA 1925. We saw an example of this defence in Chapter 5, section 6.2,[17] and will explore it in detail in Chapter 17: it gives C valuable protection against the risk of being bound by a pre-existing equitable interest arising under a trust. It thus seems that, as far as the protection of third parties is concerned, the LPA 1925 has a clear, logical structure:

- in order to protect third parties such as C, s 1 limits the list of legal estates and interests in land;

- this means that particular arrangements (such as giving B1 a right to benefit from the land for B1's life, with the right to benefit thereafter going to B2) have to take effect behind a trust, with each of B1 and B2 having only an equitable interest;

- s 2 then recognizes that C can use a special overreaching defence against a pre-existing *equitable* property right arising under a trust.

4 RIGHTS UNDER TRUSTS: THE *ACQUISITION* QUESTION

As we noted in section 1, any equitable property right depends on A being under an initial duty to B. So, the first step for B in showing that he has a right under a trust is to show that A is under a duty to him. In Chapter 5, section 4, we saw that it may be possible for B to acquire a legal estate in land by an *independent acquisition*—that is, through relying simply on his own, unilateral conduct. In contrast, it is *impossible* for B to acquire a right under a trust by relying on an independent acquisition. This is because B can acquire an equitable property right only when A is under a duty to B; and A cannot come under a duty to B simply as a result of B's own, unilateral conduct.

In practice, however, the need to show that A is under a duty to B *increases* B's chances of showing that he has acquired a right under a trust. This is because there are many different

---

[17] When considering *Baker v Craggs* [2017] Ch 295.

means by which A can come under a duty to B.[18] We will discuss these means in Chapters 10–12. For example, if A makes a contractual promise to transfer his freehold to B, that contract, by itself, does not transfer A's freehold: as we will see in Chapter 8, sections 5 and 6, further formalities must be completed before B acquires A's freehold. The contract between A and B, however, imposes a duty on A: a duty in relation to A's freehold. As a result, as we will see in Chapter 8, section 4 the contract itself may suffice to give B a right under a trust of A's freehold.

5 OTHER EQUITABLE INTERESTS: THE *CONTENT* QUESTION

5.1 A LONGER LIST OF PROPERTY RIGHTS

In the following extract, Swadling considers one of the contributions of equity to property law: the recognition of a longer list of property rights.

Swadling, 'The Law of Property' in *English Private Law* (ed Burrows, 3rd edn, 2013, [4.26])

A longer list

All rights recognized as property rights at common law are also recognized as such by equity. So, it is possible to have an easement, for example a right of way over land, both at common law and in equity. But there are also some rights recognized in equity as propri-etary which at common law either do not exist at all or, if they do, are only recognized as personal rights. An example of the latter is the restrictive covenant over land. Others are contracts and options to purchase certain types of legal property rights. The mortgagor's equity of redemption is an example of equity creating a property right where no corres-ponding personal right exists at law.

5.2 THE LIST OF EQUITABLE INTERESTS

It is possible to come up with a list of rights that, in addition to rights under a trust, count as equitable interests in land. Building on Swadling's approach in the extract above, that list can be usefully split into two categories. In the first category are those rights that do not correspond to any legal estate or legal interest in land. Examples of such rights are: (i) the restrictive covenant (which we will examine in Chapter 23); and (ii) the mortgagor's equity of redemption (see Chapter 25, section 5). Where registered land is concerned, we can also include: (i) an 'equity by estoppel' (see Chapter 10, section 4.3); and (ii) a 'mere equity'.[19]

---

[18] This point is noted by Smith, 'Fusion and Tradition' in *Equity and Commercial Law* (eds Degeling and Edelman, 2005) p 34. See, also, Chambers, 'Constructive Trusts in Canada' (1999) 37 Alberta Law Rev 173.

[19] For a very helpful discussion of such rights, see Cooper and Lees, 'Interests, Powers and Mere Equities in Modern Land Law' (2017) 37 OJLS 435, 452–3. One example of a 'mere equity' is an equitable power to rescind a transfer of a right. Such a power to rescind may arise where e.g. the transfer was the

Under s 116 of the Land Registration Act 2002 (LRA 2002), those rights are expressly said to be capable of binding a third party acquiring a right in relation to registered land.

In the second category are equitable interests that do correspond to a legal estate or legal interest in land. Clear examples of such rights are: (i) equitable leases (see Chapter 19, section 3.2); (ii) equitable easements (as noted by Swadling in the extract above, and see further Chapter 22); and (iii) equitable charges (see Chapter 25, section 4.3). In each of those cases, B's equitable interest arises because A is under a duty to grant B a recognized legal property right in land. The content of the equitable property right thus reflects the content of the legal estate or interest in question.[20] The crucial difference is that A has not yet granted B the relevant legal estate or legal interest; rather, A is under a duty to do so.

In this category, we can also include what Swadling refers to as '*contracts and options to purchase certain types of legal property rights*'. Such equitable property rights can be broken down into: (i) estate contracts (see Chapter 8, section 4.3); and (ii) options to purchase. Where registered land is concerned, we can add a further right: (iii) the right of pre-emption. Under s 115(b) of the LRA 2002, that right is expressly said to be capable of binding a third party acquiring a right in relation to registered land. As we will see in section 6 below, equity's contribution here again relates to the *acquisition* question, not the *content* question. To show that he has an estate contract, option to purchase, or right of pre-emption, B always needs to show that A has a legal estate. To show that he has an estate contract, B also needs to show that A is under an existing contractual duty to transfer that estate to B. To show that he has an option to purchase, B need only show that B has the option to impose a contractual duty on A to transfer A's estate to B. And to show that he has a right of pre-emption, B only needs to show that, if A chooses to sell A's estate, B has the option to impose a contractual duty on A to transfer that estate to B.

It is, therefore, possible to come up with the set of equitable interests in land illustrated in Table 6.1.

Table 6.1 Equitable interests in land

Group A	Rights under trusts
Group B	Rights with a content not corresponding to a legal estate or legal interest General: (i) restrictive covenant; (ii) mortgagor's equity of redemption In relation to registered land: (i) equity by estoppel; (ii) mere equity
Group C	Rights with a content corresponding to a legal estate or legal interest General: (i) equitable lease; (ii) equitable easement; (iii) equitable charge; (iv) estate contract; (v) option to purchase In relation to registered land: (i) right of pre-emption

result of an innocent misrepresentation made by the transferee (see *Bristol & West Building Society v Mothew* [1998] Ch 1, 22–3) or it was the result of an unconscionable bargain (see *Mortgage Express Ltd v Lambert* [2017] Ch 93, [16]–[18]). In such a case, when the transferor exercises his power to rescind, he or she acquires a full equitable interest; but, before then, he or she has only a 'mere equity': a power to acquire an equitable interest: see McFarlane, *The Structure of Property Law* (2008) pp 224–7; O'Sullivan, 'The Rule in *Phillips v Phillips*' (2002) 118 LQR 296.

[20] There can, however, be a slight difference. To count as a legal interest in land, an easement or charge must last forever (like a freehold) or for a certain, limited period (like a lease). As a result, if A gives B a right of way that is due to last only for B's life, that right, even if passes the content test for an easement (see Chapter 22, section 2), cannot count as a legal easement. Nonetheless, it can count as an equitable easement: see *ER Ives Investments Ltd v High* [1967] 2 QB 379, 395, *per* Lord Denning MR.

5.3 LIMITING THE CONTENT OF EQUITABLE INTERESTS

Whilst all equitable interests depend on A being under a duty to B, it is clear that B does not have an equitable interest in all cases where A is under a duty to B. For example, as we noted in section 2 above, the House of Lords held in *National Provincial Bank v Ainsworth* that, whilst Mr Ainsworth was under an equitable duty to Mrs Ainsworth, his 'deserted wife', that duty did not give Mrs Ainsworth an equitable interest.[21]

Equally, the content of those rights that do count as equitable interests is carefully controlled by the courts. This can be shown by the following extract, in which Lord Templeman considers the content of the restrictive covenant. As we will see in Chapter 23, section 2.3, it is possible to take issue with Lord Templeman's reasoning, but, for our present purposes, it is important to note one key point. We saw in section 1 above that equitable property rights arose because of equity's willingness to allow an obligation owed by A to B to affect a third party, C (see Table 6.1); as the following extract demonstrates, it is clear that equity does not allow *all* obligations to have that effect.

Rhone v Stephens
[1994] 2 AC 310, HL

Facts: Walford House in Combwich, Somerset, was divided by its owner into a house and a cottage. The roof of the house overhung the cottage. In 1960, the former owner then sold a freehold of the cottage. When doing so, he promised the purchasers of the cottage '*for himself and his successors in title* [. . .] *to maintain* [. . .] *such part of the roof of Walford House* [. . .] *as lies above the property conveyed in wind and watertight condition*'. After that, both the house and the cottage were sold on. By 1991, the freehold of the house was held by Ms Stephens, and the freehold of the cottage was held by Mr and Mrs Rhone. Mr and Mrs Rhone claimed that Ms Stephens was under a duty to repair the roof of the house, as a result of the covenant entered into by the former owner of the house in 1960. On that basis, they claimed compensation from Ms Stephens for damage that they had suffered as a result of the state of the roof and also asked for an order forcing Ms Stephens to ensure that the necessary repairs were done. The first instance judge found in favour of Mr and Mrs Rhone; but the Court of Appeal reversed that finding, holding that the promise made in 1960 did not give rise to an equitable property right, because it imposed a *positive* burden (a duty to do repairs) and so did not count as a *restrictive* covenant. The House of Lords upheld that finding.

Lord Templeman

At 317–18

My Lords, equity supplements but does not contradict the common law. When freehold land is conveyed without restriction, the conveyance confers on the purchaser the right to do with the land as he pleases provided that he does not interfere with the rights of others or infringe statutory restrictions. The conveyance may however impose restrictions which, in favour of the covenantee, deprive the purchaser of some of the rights inherent in the

---

21 [1965] AC 1175. See the discussion of the case in Chapter 1.

ownership of unrestricted land. In *Tulk v. Moxhay* (1848) 2 Ph. 774 a purchaser of land covenanted that no buildings would be erected on Leicester Square. A subsequent purchaser of Leicester Square was restrained from building. The conveyance to the original purchaser deprived him and every subsequent purchaser taking with notice of the covenant of the right, otherwise part and parcel of the freehold, to develop the square by the construction of buildings. Equity does not contradict the common law by enforcing a restrictive covenant against a successor in title of the covenantor but prevents the successor from exercising a right which he never acquired [. . .]

Equity can thus prevent or punish the breach of a negative covenant which restricts the user of land or the exercise of other rights in connection with land. Restrictive covenants deprive an owner of a right which he could otherwise exercise. Equity cannot compel an owner to comply with a positive covenant entered into by his predecessors in title without flatly contradicting the common law rule that a person cannot be made liable upon a contract unless he was a party to it. Enforcement of a positive covenant lies in contract; a positive covenant compels an owner to exercise his rights. Enforcement of a negative covenant lies in property; a negative covenant deprives the owner of a right over property.

In the extract above, Lord Templeman could have supported his analysis by referring to the following statutory provision (emphasis added), which makes clear that there is a limit to the content of equitable interests.

Law of Property Act 1925, s 4(1)

Creation and disposition of equitable interests

(1) Interests in land validly created or arising after the commencement of this Act, which are not capable of subsisting as legal estates, shall take effect as equitable interests, and, save as otherwise expressly provided by statute, interests in land which under the Statute of Uses or otherwise could before the commencement of this Act have been created as legal interests, shall be capable of being created as equitable interests:

Provided that, after the commencement of this Act (and save as hereinafter expressly enacted) an equitable interest in land shall only be capable of being validly created in any case in which an equivalent equitable interest in property real or personal could have been validly created before such commencement.

It thus seems that, whilst s 1(2) of the Act limits the content of legal interests, s 4(1) does the same job for the content of equitable interests. Rather than setting out the permissible equitable interests, s 4(1) instead imposes a freeze on the development of new equitable interests, as noted by Briggs:

Briggs, 'Contractual Licences: A Reply' [1983] Conv 285, 290

'[Section 4(1)] seems clear enough [. . .] If [particular rights] are to bind purchasers of land as proprietary interests, then they must be shown to have existed in pre-1926 land law [. . .]'

It is certainly the case that the courts have developed no new equitable interests since 1926. Perhaps surprisingly, however, the courts have not supported that approach by relying on s 4(1). For example, we saw in Chapter 1 that, when finding in *National Provincial Bank v Ainsworth*[22] that a 'deserted wife's equity' did not count as an equitable interest, Lord Wilberforce did not refer to s 4(1), but instead explained that the content of the 'deserted wife's equity' meant that it was unsuited to binding anyone other than the husband. In an important passage, he stated that:

National Provincial Bank v Ainsworth
[1965] AC 1175, 1248

Lord Wilberforce

Before a right or an interest can be admitted into the category of property, or of a right affecting property, it must be definable, identifiable by third parties, capable in its nature of assumption by third parties, and have some degree of permanence or stability. The wife's right has none of these qualities, it is characterised by the reverse of them.

Once it had been decided that Mr Ainsworth was not under a duty to allow Mrs Ainsworth to live in *her current house*, but instead simply had a duty to provide her with *some* accommodation, Mrs Ainsworth's claim to an equitable property right was doomed to fail: she could not show that her husband's duty to her related to his freehold. But Lord Wilberforce went further and set out criteria that can be used to analyse a claim that B has an equitable property right. To count as such a right, B's right must be:

- definable;
- identifiable by third parties;
- capable in its nature of assumption by third parties; and
- (to some degree) permanent and stable.

It is important to realize, however, that a right will not count as an equitable property right *simply* because it meets Lord Wilberforce's criteria. For example, a positive covenant, such as that considered by Lord Templeman in *Rhone v Stephens*[23] (see section 5.3), gives its holder a right that has all of the characteristics specified by Lord Wilberforce, but does not count as an equitable property right. So whilst these characteristics may be *necessary* if B's right is to count as an equitable property right, they are clearly not *sufficient*.

6 OTHER EQUITABLE INTERESTS: THE *ACQUISITION* QUESTION

In section 4, we noted that, to acquire a right under a trust, B must show that A is under a duty to B. The same is true when B claims any form of equitable interest. For example, in *Walsh v Lonsdale*,[24] which we will examine in Chapter 8, section 4.1 and Chapter 19, section

---

[22] [1965] AC 1175.   [23] [1994] 2 AC 310, HL.   [24] (1882) LR 21 Ch D 9, CA.

3.2, Lonsdale had made a contractual agreement to grant Walsh a seven-year lease. Walsh did not acquire a legal lease because no grant was made. Nonetheless, the Court of Appeal held that Walsh had an *equitable* lease, arising as a result of Lonsdale's contractual duty to grant Walsh the promised legal lease.

In Chapter 8, section 4.1, we will examine the general doctrine exemplified by *Walsh v Lonsdale*, referred to in this book as the doctrine of anticipation. In Chapter 10, we will examine another general means by which B may acquire an equitable interest: the doctrine of proprietary estoppel. In other chapters, we will consider the acquisition of specific equitable interests: for example, in Chapter 19, section 3.2, we will consider the acquisition of an equitable lease; in Chapter 23, sections 2.5 and 3, we will consider the acquisition of a restrictive covenant. It is important to bear in mind that formality rules may regulate the acquisition of an equitable interest: for example, we will see in Chapter 8, section 3 that a contract for the grant of a seven-year lease (such as was relied on in *Walsh v Lonsdale*) is only valid if it complies with the formality rule imposed by s 2 of the Law of Property (Miscellaneous Provisions) Act 1989. The general formality rule applying to the acquisition of an equitable interest in land is set out by section 53(1)(a) of the Law of Property Act 1925:

Law of Property Act 1925, s 53

Instruments required to be in writing

(1) Subject to the provision hereinafter contained with respect to the creation of interests in land by parol—

    (a) no interest in land can be created or disposed of except by writing signed by the person creating or conveying the same, or by his agent thereunto lawfully authorised in writing, or by will, or by operation of law.

    (b) [. . .]

    (c) [. . .]

(2) This section does not affect the creation or operation of resulting, implied or constructive trusts.

In Chapters 10, 11, and 12, we will examine a number of means by which B can acquire an equitable interest even in the absence of any writing. Chapter 10 is concerned with proprietary estoppel and Chapter 12 closely examines common intention constructive trusts: we will consider the reasons why those doctrines do not require formality in Chapter 8, section 3.9, and in Chapter 10, section 2.4. In Chapter 11, sections 3 and 4, we will consider resulting and constructive trusts, which fall within the exception permitted by s 53(2).

7 THE RELATIONSHIP BETWEEN COMMON LAW AND EQUITY

Many land law cases share a basic form: A, an owner of land, has some dealings with B; as a result, B acquires a right to make a particular use of A's land. A then gives C a right in relation to the land: for example, by selling his freehold or lease to C, or by granting C a legal charge over the land. B wishes to carry on using the land, but C wants to prevent B from using the land in that way. For example, in *National Provincial Bank v Ainsworth*[25] (see Chapter 1 as well as section 5.4 above), the bank (C) wanted to prevent Mrs Ainsworth (B) from continuing to occupy the home owned by Mr Ainsworth (A).

In such cases, it is important to ask if B's right, acquired from A, counts as a property right. If it does, it is capable of binding C. If it does not, and is simply a personal right against A, B cannot assert that right against C (although, as we will see in Chapter 7, section 2.3, it may still be possible for B to assert a *new*, direct right against C, arising as a result of C's conduct). To see if B's right counts as a property right, we need to look at both the *content* question and the *acquisition* question. But in the past two chapters, we have seen that, as far as the content question is concerned, there are two sets of answers: one set is provided by the common law rules; another set, by the equitable rules. For example, a restrictive covenant does not count as a legal estate or interest in land, but it can count as an equitable interest (see section 5.3 above). As pointed out in the following extract, these differences raise an awkward question: does it make sense for common law and equity to give different answers to the same question?

Burrows, 'We Do This at Common Law But That in Equity' (2002) 22 OJLS 1

[T]he fusion of law and equity is a topic that provokes strong reactions. But the question remains of what, exactly, is meant by fusion. One way of answering this is to give a short description of the essence of first, the anti-fusion school of thought; and second, the fusion school of thought.

According to the anti-fusion school of thought, the Supreme Court of Judicature Acts 1873–5 fused the administration of the courts but did not fuse the substantive law. Common law and equity sit alongside one another. Moreover, they can happily sit alongside one another. Clashes or conflicts or inconsistencies between them are very rare. Where they exist, and in so far as they are not resolved by the more specific provisions of the 1873–5 Acts, they are resolved by the general provision in section 11 of the 1873 Act which lays down that 'equity shall prevail'. This is not to say that common law or equity is frozen in the position it was in before 1873. Rather common law and equity can independently develop incrementally. But one should not develop the law by reasoning from common law to equity or vice versa. To do so would cut across the historical underpinnings of the two areas; and a harmonized rule or principle that has features of both common law and equity but cannot be said clearly to be one or the other, would be unacceptable.

In contrast, the fusion school of thought argues that the fusion of the administration of the courts brought about by the 1873–5 Acts, whilst not dictating the fusion of the substantive law, rendered this, for the first time, a realistic possibility. While there are areas where common law and equity can happily sit alongside one another, there are many examples of inconsistencies between them. It is important to remove the inconsistencies thereby producing a coherent or harmonized law. In developing the law it is legitimate for the courts to reason from common law to equity and vice versa. A harmonized rule or principle that has features of both common law and equity is at the very least acceptable and, depending on the rule or principle in question, may represent the best way for the law to develop.

It is submitted that the latter view is to be strongly preferred. There are numerous instances of inconsistencies between common law and equity; and to support fusion seems

---

[25] [1965] AC 1175.

self-evident, resting, as it does, on not being slaves to history and on recognizing the importance of coherence in the law and of 'like cases being treated alike' [. . .]

[Burrows goes on to suggest that cases in which common law and equitable rules do differ
can be placed into one of three categories:]

The first category is where common law and equity co-exist coherently and where the historical labels of common law and equity remain the best or, at least, useful terminology [. . .]

The second category is where common law and equity co-exist coherently but, in contrast
to the first category, there is nothing to be gained by adherence to those historical labels.
If we are to take fusion seriously, the labels common law and equity in the areas of the law
covered by this category should be abandoned at a stroke [. . .]

The third category is more complex. It comprises probably most of our civil law. In this
category, in contrast to both of the first two categories, common law and equity do not exist
co-exist coherently. If we are to take fusion seriously, what is needed is a change in the law,
albeit often only a small change, so as to produce a principled product which may combine
elements of law and equity.

As Burrows notes, the 'fusion' debate provokes strong reactions. Certainly, his preference
for what he calls the 'fusion approach' is not universally shared: for a robustly-expressed
alternative view, see, for example, *Meagher, Gummow and Lehane's Equity: Doctrines
and Remedies*.[26] Nonetheless, the central point raised by Burrows seems to be a valid
one: where there is a difference between common law rules and equitable rules, we need
to ask whether that difference can be justified. After all, history can explain why we *have*
two different sets of rules, but, by itself, history cannot justify why we should *keep* them.
If we apply that same approach to the law of property rights, we need to be able to justify
the special rules, noted in this chapter, that apply to equitable property rights but not to
their legal counterparts.

It seems that these differences can be justified if we focus on the different *effects* of legal
and equitable property rights. The list of legal property rights is shorter, and such rights are,
in general, harder to acquire—but, if B has a legal property right, then he receives better
protection. Firstly, as noted at the start of section 2, it is far harder for C to have a defence
to a pre-existing *legal* property right in land; where B has a pre-existing *equitable* interest, a
number of additional defences may be available to C.

Secondly, as we saw in Chapter 4, section 1, a key feature of a legal property right is that it
imposes a *prima facie* duty on the rest of the world. As noted in the following extracts, however, that does not seem to be the case with all equitable interests.

Swadling, 'The Law of Property' in *English Private Law* (ed Burrows,
3rd edn, 2013, [4.23])

[E]quitable rights which might be seen as 'proprietary' behave in a slightly different fashion
to those at common law. At common law, as we have seen, the right is exigible directly
against anyone interfering with it. Thus, the holder of a common law easement can sue for
damages and an injunction against any third party, be it a successor in title of the original

---

[26] Heydon, Leeming, and Turner *Equity: Doctrine and Remedies* (5th edn, London: Butterworths,
2015) ch 2.

grantor or even a complete stranger, who interferes with his right. This is not generally true for equitable property rights. Take, for example, the case of an option to purchase a fee simple estate in land [. . .] such a right will generally bind transferees of the fee simple in question from its grantor, and so is classed as a property right. But it will not bind other third parties, such as squatters. Although a squatter will be bound by easements granted by the person he has dispossessed, he will not be bound by an option to purchase. Indeed, he could not be bound by any such right, for the burden of such a right entails a duty to convey the right contracted to be sold, and the squatter does not have that right. The only exception would seem to be the restrictive covenant, which has been held to bind persons other than a successor in title of the grantor.

Penner, 'Duty and Liability in Respect of Funds' in *Commercial Law: Perspectives and Practice* (eds Lowry and Mistelis, 2006, pp 214–16)

[I]t is necessary to make a distinction between two version of the notion of rights *in rem*, both of which operate in law but which are often not clearly distinguished. The best way to see the distinction is not to focus on the right, but on the corresponding duties or liabilities. Under the first, 'trespassory' version of rights *in rem*, a right is protected by duties *in rem* that everyone owes to the right holder, which bind everyone unconditionally all the time. The best example is the case of the ownership of a chattel: all persons presently have a right not to interfere with your chattels. Of course there may be factual contingency here—I may be in no position to interfere with your Rolls-Royce at the minute because it is in the shop in Guildford, but that doesn't mean I have no duty not to interfere with it in law. This notion of rights/duties *in rem* is the one normally spoken of by philosophers when they speak of rights of property binding all the world.

The second, 'successor' version is distinct but equally often encountered in the law. Such a right *in rem* is one which *in principle, may* bind all others, not because of the fact that each of us all presently owe a duty to the rightholder, but because of the fact that in principle all persons may become a successor in title or possession to property which is bound by the right-holder's right. Here, the right-holder's right is *in rem*, binds all the world, because it binds successors in title or possession to another distinct property, and the right holder's interest runs with that property, and anyone, in principle, might be a successor in title or— possession to it [. . .]

I will now look at the liability of third party recipients of trust property [. . . i]n doing so I will rely upon the distinction just drawn. It is one of the features of the particular property interest that exists in a trust fund that the trust reveals the distinction between the trespassory and successor versions of the right *in rem* in the following way: in so far as their proprietary rights are concerned, the trust divides the rights of the trustee and the rights of the beneficiary such that the trustee has all the trespassory rights *in rem* to the trust property, while the beneficiaries' rights are purely successor rights *in rem*—rights to enforce the trust against successors in title to the trustee of any property which can be seen to constitute an asset of the [trust] fund.

It may, therefore, be the case that legal property rights and equitable property rights are conceptually, as well as historically, different. Each type of right differs from a personal right, as each is capable of binding a third party. If B has an legal estate or legal interest in land, we know that B's right is then capable of binding *any* third party, as the rest of the world is under a *prima facie* duty to B not to interfere with the land. In contrast, if B has an equitable interest, all we can say for sure is that B's right is capable of binding A and parties later acquiring a right from A: in other words, successors to A are *prima facie* bound, but we cannot say that the rest of the world as a whole is under a *prima facie* duty to B.

This possible difference in the effect of legal and equitable property rights can be related to the different content of each type of right. In particular, we have seen in this Chapter that an equitable interest in land depends on A's coming under a duty to B. In the following extract, it is suggested that the difference between equitable property rights on the one hand, and personal rights on the other, is that in the former case, A's duty to B relates to a specific right held by A. As a result, B is permitted to assert a right not only against A, but also against third parties who later acquire A's right, or a right that depends on A's right. B, however, is not permitted to assert a right against X, a third party who does not acquire any right from A, as, in such a case, it is not possible for B to trace A's right into X's hands.

McFarlane and Stevens, 'The Nature of Equitable Property' (2010, 4 Journal of Equity 1, pp 1–2)

This article proposes three principal theses about the nature of equitable property rights. The first is that such rights are fundamentally different not only from personal rights but also from the property rights recognised by common law. An equitable property right is neither a right against a person nor a right against a thing. Rather, it is a right against a right [. . .]

The second thesis is that, whenever a party (B) has a right against a right of another (A), B's right is *prima facie* binding on anyone who acquires a right that derives from A's right [. . .] Nonetheless, there remains a difference between a right against a thing and a right against a right. The key attribute of a right against a thing is its universal exigibility: if B has a right against a thing, B's right is *prima facie* binding on the rest of the world. The key attribute of a right against a right can be labelled persistence: if B has a right against A's right, B's right is *prima facie* binding on anyone who acquires a right that derives from A's right.

The third thesis is that B will acquire such a persistent right *whenever* A is under a duty to hold a specific claim-right or power, in a particular way, for B [. . .]

[The approach taken in this article] it rejects a very common, not to say orthodox, view of the nature of equitable property rights. On that view, such rights are, in effect, a weaker, more vulnerable version of the property rights recognised at common law. Both types of right give their holder the power to exclude others from making use of a thing, but the equitable variety is weaker than its common law counterpart as it is generally vulnerable to the bona fide purchaser defence. That view, however, overlooks the genius of equity. That genius consists in its willingness to transcend, not to duplicate, the classic division between rights against things and rights against people. This has resulted in the concept of a right against a right. By recognising the distinctiveness of that concept, it is possible to avoid the orthodox, but unattractive, view that English law contains two competing laws of property.

In many cases, this possible difference between the effect of legal and equitable property rights is often hidden. In most cases, B's reason for claiming a property right is to assert that right against C, a party who later acquired a right from A. This helps to explain why, in such cases, judges often confidently assert that equitable property rights are rights *in rem*, without considering the possible difference between rights that *prima facie* bind the rest of the world and rights that *prima facie* bind only successors in title to A.[27] So, in *National Provincial Bank v Ainsworth*,[28] for example, Mrs Ainsworth wished to show that a right she held against Mr Ainsworth could also bind the bank: a party later acquiring a right from Mr Ainsworth. In such a case, Mrs Ainsworth would be happy either with a right in the land itself (a right against a thing) or a right against Mr Ainsworth's right: each type of right would be *prima facie* binding on the bank.

McFarlane and Stevens do acknowledge in their article that one particular equitable property right, the restrictive covenant, has departed from the 'right against a right' model as it has been allowed to bind C, even if C has not acquired a right from A.[29] This occurred in a case where B was allowed to assert a restrictive covenant against a squatter:[30] a third party who had not acquired his title to the land from A, but who had rather acquired that right independently,[31] through his action in taking possession of the land. They argue, however, that the restrictive covenant has been allowed to operate in this anomalous way for particular policy reasons: to use the terms we discussed in Chapter 1, section 5.2, this is an example of courts giving more weight to the 'utility model' rather than the 'doctrinal model'. A different argument has been made by Gardner, who accepts the key distinction between those property rights which impose a *prima facie* duty on the rest of the world and those which instead bind only A and successors of A, but points to the restrictive covenant in arguing that there is no reason why equitable interests should necessarily fall into the latter class of property rights.[32]

In the following case, B's right was not a restrictive covenant; it was rather an equitable interest arising under a trust. On the facts of the case, it was important to know if B's right was a right in a thing (*prima facie* binding on anyone interfering with the thing) or a right against A's right (*prima facie* binding only on those later acquiring a right that derives from A's right).

Shell UK Ltd & ors v Total UK Ltd & ors
[2010] EWCA Civ 180, [2011] QB 86

Facts: The largest peace-time explosion in Britain occurred in the early morning of 11 December 2005 at the Buncefield oil storage terminal in Hertfordshire. The explosion was caused by the careless overfilling of a fuel storage tank, for which the

---

[27] See e.g. *Akers v Samba Financial Group* [2017] AC 424, [83], where Lord Sumption stated that: '*The proprietary character of an equitable interest in property has sometimes been doubted, but in English law the position must be regarded as settled. An equitable interest possesses the essential hallmark of any right in rem, namely that it is good against third parties into whose hands the property or its traceable proceeds may have come, subject to [a possible defence for the third party].*' This equation of '*in rem*' status with binding successors in title seems to overlook the different, and more orthodox, definition of a right '*in rem*' as one which is *prima facie* binding on *all* third parties, whether or not they are parties '*into whose hands the property or its traceable proceeds may have come.*'

[28] [1965] AC 1175.   [29] (2010) 4 Journal of Equity 1, 13–14.

[30] *Re Nisbet & Potts Contract* [1906] 1 Ch 386 (see Chapter 26, section 2.5.2).

[31] The distinction between dependent and independent acquisition is discussed in Chapter 5, section 4. See Chapter 8 for further discussion of adverse possession.

[32] See Gardner, ' "Persistent Rights" Appraised' in *Modern Studies in Property Law Vol 7* (ed Hopkins, Oxford: Hart Publishing, 2013) 321, at 345–7 and 354–7. For different criticisms of the argument of McFarlane and Stevens, focussing instead on the nature of an equitable interest under a trust, see Penner, 'The (True) Nature of a Beneficiary's Equitable Proprietary Interest under a Trust' (2014) 27 Canadian Journal of Law and Jurisprudence 473.

defendants were responsible. The destruction and damage extended to fuel storage and pipeline facilities used by Shell. As a result, Shell suffered serious loss through its temporary inability to supply fuel to customers in the South East of England. Shell sought to recover compensation from the defendants. The defendants conceded that their negligence had caused Shell to suffer economic loss, but argued that they owed no duty of care to Shell. This argument was based on the fact that Shell did not hold legal title to the damaged facilities, nor to the land on which those facilities stood. The legal title to the land and facilities was held by two service companies on trust for four beneficiaries, including Shell. The defendants' argument succeeded at first instance, where David Steel J held that the general rule that there is no duty to avoid carelessly causing economic loss applied: Shell's equitable interest in the damaged property did not prevent the application of that rule. Particular reliance was placed on the decision of the House of Lords in *Leigh & Sillivan Ltd v Aliakmon Shipping Co Ltd (The Aliakmon)*,[33] in which Lord Brandon found that a beneficiary of a trust of goods could not bring a claim against a party who had carelessly damaged those goods, stating that: '*in order to enable a person to claim in negligence for loss caused to him by reason of loss or damage to property, he must have had either the legal ownership of or a possessory title to the property concerned at the time when the loss or damage occurred*'.[34] The Court of Appeal, however, upheld Shell's appeal. Waller LJ delivered a judgment of the court, to which its other members (Longmore and Richards LJJ) also contributed. It was held at [128]–[131] that *The Aliakmon* was not decisive, as it did not consider the possibility that the beneficiary of the trust [B] could be allowed to sue the party damaging the property [X] if, as was the case here, the legal owner of the property [A] had been joined to the claim by B against X, so that all three parties could be before the court.

At [132]–[136]

In the absence of any directly applicable authority, it is necessary to look in a little more detail at the exclusionary rule [i.e. the rule that if X carelessly damages property belonging to A, and B suffers economic loss as a result, B in general has no claim against X] and the rationale for it. The rule is set out in *Clerk & Lindsell on Torts*[35]

> "no duty is owed by a defendant who negligently damages property belonging to a third party, to a claimant who suffers loss because of a dependence upon that property or its owner."

So on the facts of this case Total, who has admittedly damaged the pipelines owned by [the service companies], submits that it owes no duty to Shell who has a contractual right to have its fuel loaded into, carried and discharged from the pipelines. If Shell were a complete stranger to the transaction that would be understandable but Shell is not a complete stranger. It is the (co-) beneficial owner of the pipelines and the contract to use the pipeline is only an incident of its beneficial ownership (albeit a necessary incident, since it is a co-owner of the pipelines with others who also wish to use it). On the face of things, it is legalistic to deny Shell a right to recovery by reference to the exclusionary rule. It is, after all, Shell who is (along with BP, Total and Chevron) the "real" owner, the "legal" owner being little more than a bare trustee of the pipelines [. . .]

---

33 [1986] AC 785.   34 Ibid, 809.   35 (London: Sweet & Maxwell, 19th edn, 2006), [8.115].

The editors of *Clerk & Lindsell on Torts*, summarise the position by saying:[36]

"To allow all claims for such economic loss would lead to unacceptable indeterminacy because of the ripple effects caused by contracts and expectations. Proximity requires some
special relationship between the defendant and the person suffering relational economic loss,
one which goes beyond mere contractual or non-contractual dependence on the damaged
property."

Beneficial ownership of the damaged property goes well beyond contractual or non-
contractual dependence on the damaged property and does indeed constitute a special relationship of the kind required by the editors. It is, in fact, a closer relationship in many ways
than that of a bare trustee having no more than the legal title.

At [143]–[144]

We must confess to being somewhat influenced [. . .] by what Lord Goff of Chieveley in
White v Jones called "the impulse to do practical justice".[37] It should not be legally relevant that the co-owners of the relevant pipelines, for reasons that seemed good to them,
decided to vest the legal title to the pipelines in their service companies and enjoy the
beneficial ownership rather than the formal legal title. Differing views about the wisdom
of the exclusionary rule are widely held but however much one may think that, in general,
there should be no duty to mere contracting parties who suffer economic loss as a result of
damage to a third party's property, it would be a triumph of form over substance to deny a
remedy to the beneficial owner of that property when the legal owner is a bare trustee for
that beneficial owner.

The judge understandably relied on *The Aliakmon* to dismiss Shell's claim but, for the
reasons given, *The Aliakmon* does not conclude the argument about equitable ownership
once the legal owner has been joined [. . .] It leaves the question open for this court to determine and we would reverse the judge on this aspect of this case and hold that Shell can
recover for its provable loss or, if formality is necessary, that [the service companies holding
the land on trust] can recover the amount which Shell has lost but will hold the sums so recovered as trustees for Shell.

The reasoning of the Court of Appeal in *Shell UK v Total UK* is, perhaps, rather surprising.[38]
A number of previous decisions, not only *The Aliakmon*, seemed to establish that if A holds
a property right on trust for B, and the property is taken or damaged by X, then, assuming B
did not have possession of the property, only A can bring a claim against X.[39] On this model,
any damages recovered by A will then be held on trust for B, but A's claim against X is based
on X's breach of a duty owed to A. This means that if, as in *Shell UK v Total UK*, B suffers
consequential loss as a result of X's breach of duty, that loss is *not* recoverable from X. After
all, if A has a property right, A can in theory declare that he holds that right on trust for an
unlimited number of people; can all of those people then recover their consequential loss
from X if X has the misfortune carelessly to damage A's property?

---

[36] Ibid, [8.116].

[37] [1995] 2 AC 207, 259–60.

[38] For discussion of the decision, and of its departure from previously accepted rules as to the operation
of equitable interests under a trust, see, for example, Edelman, 'Two Fundamental Questions for the Law of
Trusts' (2013) 129 LQR 66, 67–72.

[39] See *Lord Compton's Case* (1586) 3 Leo 196; *Earl of Worcester v Finch* (1600) 4 Co Inst 85; *MCC Proceeds
Inc v Lehman Bros* [1998] 4 All ER 675.

The defendants were given permission to appeal to the Supreme Court, but the case was settled before any such appeal was heard. There may have been a number of alternative bases on which Shell's claim could have been allowed. First, it was accepted by the first instance judge that, if Shell could show that it had suffered loss which was 'particular, substantial and direct' as a result of the explosion, a claim in public nuisance would be available.[40] Such a claim can be made in respect of purely economic loss and does not depend on the claimant having any legal, or even equitable, property right. Second, it may have been possible for Shell to argue that it had a legal property right by virtue of its possession of the land and facilities, such possession arising because the service companies were acting as agents for Shell and the other beneficiaries, and their possession was thus attributable to Shell and the other beneficiaries.

The *result* reached by the Court of Appeal may therefore not be too surprising; but its reasoning has attracted a great deal of criticism.[41] It is the first and thus far only decision in which, in effect, B's interest under a trust has been held binding against a stranger, rather than against a third party later acquiring a right from A. The difficulty is that the court equated the position of a beneficiary of a trust of land with that of an owner of land, stating that it would be '*legalistic*' to deny Shell's claim simply because it had an equitable interest in the land rather than a legal estate or legal interest. To use the language of McFarlane & Stevens in the extract set out above, that analysis seems to adopt the '*very common, not to say orthodox, view*' that the only difference in the effect of legal and equitable property rights is that the latter are subject to a greater range of defences. It overlooks the argument, developed in the extracts set out in this section, that at least some equitable property rights are conceptually different from legal property rights, as such rights can bind only A and A's successors, whereas legal property rights can bind the whole world. Moreover, the reasoning of the Court of Appeal in the *Shell* case is internally inconsistent. The result is explained as depending on an exception to the exclusionary rule. Such an exception is needed only if the rule is *prima facie* applicable, which is only the case if the defendant has not damaged the claimant's own property. Therefore, in finding an exception to the exclusionary rule, the Court of Appeal is characterizing Shell's loss as pure economic loss, i.e. as loss that flows from damage to property that does *not* belong to Shell. It is then inconsistent to justify the exception by saying that Shell is, after all, in some 'real' (i.e. non-legal) sense, the owner of the property.

It is true that the Court of Appeal did impose a condition on Shell's claim: the service companies, as trustees, had to be joined to the claim against Total. This requirement preserves a formal difference between legal and equitable property rights. The surprise in *Shell UK v Total UK*, however, is that Total could be made to pay not only for the value of the destroyed or damaged property but also for the consequential loss suffered by Shell, but not by the service companies.

QUESTIONS

1. How did equitable property rights develop?
2. Why might the term 'equitable estate in land' be misleading?

---

[40] [2009] EWHC 540 (Comm) at 434.

[41] In addition to Edelman, 'Two Fundamental Questions for the Law of Trusts' (2013) 129 LQR 66, 67–72, see also Turner, 'Consequential Loss and the Trust Beneficiary' [2010] CLJ 445; Low, 'Equitable Title and Economic Loss' (2010) 126 LQR 507; Rushworth and Scott, 'Total Chaos' [2010] LMCLQ 536.

3. Why might a party with a freehold or lease decide to set up a trust of that right?

4. Is the limit on the number of permissible legal estates in land, imposed by s 1 of the Law of Property Act 1925, undermined by the variety of different rights which may be enjoyed by a beneficiary of a trust of land?

5. The criteria for proprietary status set out by Lord Wilberforce in *National Provincial Bank v Ainsworth* have been described as 'riddled with circularity'.[42] Do you agree?

6. In what ways do equitable property rights have a different effect from that of legal property rights?

For guidance on how to answer these questions visit the online resources at www.oup.com/uk/mcfarlane4e/.

FURTHER READING

Bright, 'Of Estates and Interests: A Tale of Ownership and Property Rights' in *Land Law: Themes and Perspectives* (eds Bright and Dewar, Oxford: OUP, 1998)

Edelman, 'Two Fundamental Questions for the Law of Trusts' (2013) 129 LQR 66

Gardner, '"Persistent Rights" Appraised' in *Modern Studies in Property Law Vol 7* (ed Hopkins, Oxford: Hart Publishing, 2013)

Hackney, *Understanding Equity and Trusts* (London: Fontana, 1987, ch 1)

Harris, 'Legal Doctrine and Interests in Land' in *Oxford Essays in Jurisprudence* (3rd series, eds Eekelaar and Bell, Oxford: OUP, 1987)

Jaffey, 'Explaining the Trust' (2015) 131 LQR 377

McFarlane, *The Structure of Property Law* (Oxford: Hart Publishing, 2008, Parts B & C1)

McFarlane and Stevens, 'The Nature of Equitable Property' (2010) 4 Journal of Equity 1

Smith, 'Fusion and Tradition' in *Equity in Commercial Law* (eds Degeling and Edelman, Sydney: Lawbook Co, 2005)

Worthington, *Equity* (2nd edn, Oxford: OUP, 2006, ch 3)

---

[42] See Gray and Gray, *Elements of Land Law* (5th edn, 2009) p 97.

7

PERSONAL RIGHTS: LICENCES

CENTRAL ISSUES

1. Having examined property rights in each of Chapters 5 and 6, we now turn to look at personal rights. After a reminder of the crucial distinction between personal rights and property rights, we focus on the most prominent example of a personal right in land law: the licence.

2. A licence exists where one party (B) has a liberty to use land belonging to another (A). In considering licences, we need to examine: the rights that B has against A; the rights that B has against X, a stranger who interferes with B's use of A's land; and the rights that B has against C, a party who acquires a right from A and then interferes with B's use of the land.

3. Licences can be grouped into a number of categories. A bare licence exists where B has *only* a liberty to use A's land. The law governing such a licence is straightforward. It can be revoked by A, and B cannot assert it against X or C.

4. A contractual licence exists where B has a liberty to use A's land *and* A is under a contractual duty to B not to revoke that liberty. A's contractual duty is clearly important when considering what rights B has against A. The crucial question is whether the existence of this contract can also affect B's rights

against X and C. This has been a controversial question.

5. In considering what rights B, a party with a contractual licence, may have against X or C, we need to keep in mind two different ways in which it may be possible for B to assert a right against such a party. Firstly, B may be able to assert a new, direct right against X or C, arising as a result of X or C's conduct. Such a right may arise under a 'constructive trust'— but controversy surrounds both the source and nature of this trust.

6. Secondly, if B is unable to assert a direct right against X or C, he or she will have to argue that his or her contractual licence counts as a legal or equitable property right in land. The current position is that a contractual licence does *not* count as such a right—but this is another controversial area. A number of arguments have been made in favour of the view that at least some types of contractual licence should count as an equitable interest in land. One of these arguments involves a comparison with a third type of licence: an estoppel licence.

7. When examining licences to use land, we also need to consider statutory licences and licences coupled with an interest. We will see, however, that the latter category is of dubious value.

1 THE CONCEPT OF A PERSONAL RIGHT AND THE NATURE OF A LICENCE

1.1 THE DISTINCTION BETWEEN PROPERTY RIGHTS AND PERSONAL RIGHTS

In Chapter 5, section 1, we considered the concept of a property right, and noted the key distinction between a property right and a personal right. If B has a personal right against A, that right, by itself, binds only A. A personal right is a right against a specific person. If B instead has a property right, that right is capable of binding not only A, but also third parties, such as C. That is because a property right is not simply a right against a specific person, but is a right that relates to something independent of a specific person, such as some land.

The case of *National Provincial Bank v Ainsworth*,[1] discussed in Chapter 1, section 5, provides an excellent example of the distinction. The Court of Appeal found that Mrs Ainsworth's right—a 'deserted wife's equity'—was an equitable property right in land and therefore capable of binding not only Mr Ainsworth but also a third party, such as the bank, which had acquired its charge over the land from Mr Ainsworth. In contrast, the House of Lords held that her right was only a personal right—a right specifically against her husband. This was critical to the outcome in the case, as it meant that, whilst Mrs Ainsworth could enforce her right against Mr Ainsworth, she could not assert it against anyone else, and so could do nothing to prevent the bank from enforcing its charge by removing her from the land and then selling it with vacant possession. The case shows how personal rights are necessarily precarious: B may be protected against A, but that personal right against A will be of no assistance if B's use of the land conflicts with that of a third party.

1.2 TWO WARNINGS

The facts of *NPB v Ainsworth* provide just one example of a scenario often seen in land law: B has some dealings with A, an owner of land, and C later acquires a right in the land from A.

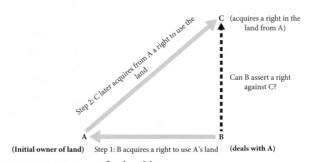

Figure 7.1 A common structure for land law cases

---

[1] [1964] Ch 665 (CA), [1965] AC 1175 (HL).

In such a case, as in *NPB v Ainsworth*, the critical question is whether B can assert a right against C. It would be easy to think that, if B's dealings with A gave B a property right (i.e. a legal estate, legal interest, or equitable interest) in the land, then B will win;[2] whereas if those dealings gave B only a personal right, or indeed no right at all, against A, then C will win. Such a view would be mistaken for two reasons, set out below.

1.2.1 The possibility of a defence for C

If B did have a property right in the land when C acquired C's right, that does not mean that B will necessarily prevail against C. We have seen that there is still the possibility of C's having a defence to B's pre-existing property right:[3] we will examine such defences in detail in Chapters 15–17. In Chapter 3, section 3.2.3, for example, we noted the powerful protection that s 29 of the Land Registration Act 2002 may give to C against a pre-existing property right that has not been entered on the register.

1.2.2 The possibility of a new, direct right for B

If B had only a personal right against A (or no right at all) when C acquired C's right, that does not mean that B will necessarily lose against C. It is possible that B may be able to assert a *different* right against C, acquired directly against C as a result of C's conduct. In such a case, B does not rely on any initial personal right against A, but rather on a *new* right. In some cases, the existence of an initial personal right of B against A may be one of the conditions of B acquiring that new, direct right against C;[4] but in all such cases, C is bound by that new, direct right of B, rather than any initial personal right that B had against A. A very simple case would be where C, before buying land from A, makes a contract with B allowing B to make a particular use of the land for the next year. Even if B had no initial right at all, either against A or in relation to the land, B's contract with C clearly gives B a direct right against C. Depending on its content, that right may be either a personal right against C, or a property right in the land; it would be crucial to know which if C, within the next year, sells the land to C2, and B then tries to assert that right, acquired from C, against C2.[5]

It is worth noting that the Land Registration Act 2002 contains no special limit on the operation of such new, direct rights and, in principle at least, such a right might assist B in a case where B *did* have a property right prior to C's acquisition of a right, and C had a defence to that right.[6] Although such a case might arise only rarely, it is possible for B to have a new, direct right against C in such a case, as the facts giving C a defence to the pre-existing property right may not be inconsistent with the facts on which a new, direct right of B arises.[7]

In any case, when acquiring land from A, it is unlikely that C would willingly act in such a way as to give B a new, direct right, and so it is only in rare cases that such rights are relevant.

---

[2] Note that if the third party, X, does not acquire a right in the land from A, but simply interferes with the property directly, then there is an argument that X can be bound only by a pre-existing *legal* property right of B, and not by a pre-existing equitable property right: see Chapter 6, section 7.

[3] See e.g. Chapter 1, section 3; Chapter 5, section 6.2; Chapter 6, section 2.

[4] See e.g. the tort of procuring a breach of contract, discussed in section 3.3.1, which of course depends on there being an initial contract between A and B, under which B has a personal right against A.

[5] See the discussion of this point in the final paragraph of section 3.3.1.

[6] See Chapter 16, section 6.2.

[7] For an example, see *Lyus v Prowsa Developments Ltd* [1982] 1 WLR 1044, although note the cautious treatment of that case by Lloyd LJ in *Chaudhary v Yavuz* [2013] Ch 249.

In *NPB v Ainsworth*, for example, as in many land law cases, there was nothing at all in the conduct of the bank on which Mrs Ainsworth could base a claim to a new, direct right. Nonetheless, it is important not to overlook new, direct rights entirely, and we will see some examples of such rights in this chapter.[8]

1.3 THE CONCEPT OF A LICENCE

In this chapter, we will explore the general idea of personal rights by focussing on the most prominent example of a personal right in land law: the licence. Let us say that A, a freehold owner of land, invites B to her house for dinner. When B is on A's land, B is described as having a licence. The word 'licence' simply means *permission*. Because A has a legal estate in the land, B, like the rest of the world, is under a *prima facie* duty not to make any use of A's land (see Chapter 5, section 1). If, however, A gives B permission to make a particular use of A's land, B's duty disappears: an act that would otherwise be wrongful (coming onto A's land) becomes permissible.

Thomas v Sorrell
(1673) Vaugh 330, Exchequer Chamber

Facts: Mr Thomas, acting on behalf of the Crown, demanded payment from Mr Sorrell on the basis that Mr Sorrell had sold wine in the parish of Stepney without a licence. Mr Sorrell claimed that he had a licence to sell wine in his capacity of a member of the '*Masters, Warden, Freemen, and Commonality of the Mystery of Vintners of the City of London*'. Vaughan CJ considered the meaning of the term 'licence'.

Vaughan CJ

At 351

A dispensation or licence properly passeth no interest, nor alters or transfers property in any thing, but only makes an action lawful which, without it, had been unlawful. As a licence to go beyond the seas, to hunt in a man's park, to come into his house, are only actions, which without licence, had been unlawful.

The limited consequences of the licence mean that, even when B is enjoying his dinner at A's home, we need to be careful in saying that B has a 'right' to be on A's land.

The great American jurist Hohfeld noted that we use the word 'right' to cover many different situations.[9] For example, if we say that B has a right that A must not poison B's food, we mean that A is under a *duty to B* not to poison B's food. In such a case, in Hohfeld's terms, B has a particular form of right: a *claim right*. In contrast, if we say that B has a right to be on A's land, we mean something different. In our example, after all, A is not under a duty to allow B to stay on A's land. So, if B makes a controversial comment over dinner, A is free to ask B to leave without any dessert. So, when we say that B has a right to be on A's land,

---

[8] See e.g. the discussion of *Binions v Evans* [1972] Ch 359 in section 3.3.1.

[9] See Hohfeld, *Fundamental Legal Conceptions as Applied in Judicial Reasoning* (1920; based on (1913) 23 Yale LJ 16 and (1917) 26 Yale LJ 710).

what we really mean is that, at least until A revokes the permission, B is *not under a duty to A not to be on A's land*. In such a case, in Hohfeld's terms, B has a particular form of right: a *privilege* or *liberty*.

Hohfeld, 'Faulty Analysis in Easement and License Cases'[10] (1917) Yale LJ 66, 94

Suppose that A says to B, "I give you permission to walk across my land, Longacre." This language in and of itself purports merely to create in B the privilege, or more strictly, series of privileges, of walking across A's land. In correlative terms, A's right that B stay off the land is extinguished, and no-rights substituted. The important point is that the permission constitutes a *grant* to *B* of privileges alone: B is not granted any accompanying rights (or claims) that A or other persons shall not interfere with B's entering on the land, Longacre, and walking across. If, therefore, B succeeds in entering on the land, no rights (or claims) of A are violated; but if on the other hand, A closes the gate in the high stone wall, or bars the one and only path midway, no rights (or claims) of B are violated; and so also if some third party locks the gate or bars the path halfway across Longacre.

All licences thus involve a *liberty* of B to make some use of A's land.[11] There are, however, situations in which B has a liberty to use A's land and is not treated as having a licence. We can modify Hohfeld's example so that A, instead of simply giving B permission to walk across the land, grants B a legal easement that allows B to walk across A's land. If B has a legal easement, he has a liberty to make some use of A's land, *and* A is under a duty not to interfere with B's liberty, *and* the rest of the world is also under a duty not to interfere with B's liberty. These duties are imposed on A and the rest of the world because, as we saw in Chapter 5, sections 5 and 6, B's easement counts as a legal interest in land. In such a case, we would not say that B has a licence. The term 'licence' is thus reserved for cases in which B has a liberty to make some use of A's land, *and* that liberty is not part of a legal or equitable property right held by B.

So, in *Street v Mountford*,[12] a case that we will examine in Chapter 19, section 1.2.1, the House of Lords considered a situation in which, in return for payment from B, A made a contractual promise to allow B to occupy A's land for a limited period. The contract described B's right as a 'licence'—but the House of Lords held that, because B had a right to exclusive possession of the land for a limited period, A had instead given B a *lease*. This meant that B had more than permission to make some use of A's land: she had a legal property right in A's land. So, during the period fixed by the contract, A and the rest of the world had a duty not to interfere with B's occupation of the land.

Strictly speaking, then, to define a 'licence', we also need to define property rights such as an 'easement' or a 'lease'. We outlined the content of those rights in Chapter 5, and will

---

[10] 'License' is the American English spelling for the noun. In British English usage, 'licence' is the noun and 'license' the verb (hence 'licensor' for a party granting a licence and 'licensee' for a party with the benefit of a licence).

[11] Hohfeld preferred the term 'privilege' to refer to the right of a party, such as B in the extract above, who has a *special* liberty not held by others. On this view, almost all licences give B a privilege. But the term 'liberty' is used in this chapter, because it can also encompass cases in which B has a licence not because of his special position, or any dealings with A, but because of a general rule permitting a particular use of A's land.

[12] [1985] AC 809.

consider those definitions in more detail in Chapters 22 (the easement) and 19 (the lease). In the meantime, we can define a licence as follows.

B has a licence where he has:

- a liberty to make some use of A's land; *and*
- that liberty is *not* part of a property right held by B.

Within that general definition, we can then identify different forms of licence. There are five main varieties: bare licences; contractual licences; estoppel licences; statutory licences; and licences coupled with an interest. We will examine each form of licence by looking at its effect firstly on A, the party against whom the licence arises; then on X, a stranger who interferes with the land without A's consent; then on C, a third party who acquires a right in the land from A. The distinction between X and C is based on the distinction between 'trespassory' and 'successor' liability discussed in Chapter 6, section 7.[13]

2 BARE LICENCES

A bare licence is the simplest form of licence. It exists where B has a liberty to make some use of A's land *and* A is free to revoke that liberty—that is, A is not under a duty to B not to revoke B's permission to use A's land. When A invites B to A's house for dinner, B has a bare licence. As we have seen, A is free to revoke B's liberty and may do so either before B arrives or during B's visit. As the key effect of the licence is simply to authorize otherwise wrongful action of B, it seems a bare licence can arise simply through the unilateral fact of A's permission, without any action of B.[14] A bare licence may also be implied: for example, although not expressly invited by A, a collector for a charity, unless expressly warned otherwise,[15] has a bare licence to come onto A's land and knock on A's door to pursue his lawful business.

2.1 B'S RIGHTS AGAINST A

The key feature of a bare licence is that A is under no duty to B not to revoke the licence: as Alderson B put it in *Wood v Leadbitter*:[16] '*[A] mere licence is revocable.*' So, if A invites B around for dinner, A can change his mind and revoke the invitation. If B decides to come anyway, B commits the tort of trespass: he breaches his duty to A not to interfere with A's land.[17] If B is *already* on A's land when A revokes his invitation, there is a problem with saying that B immediately becomes a trespasser. If that were the case, A would immediately be able to use reasonable force to remove B from the land. It would, of course, be unfair on

---

[13] For the use of those terms, see the extract in Chapter 6, section 7 from Penner, 'Duty and Liability in Respect of Funds' in *Commercial Law: Perspectives and Practice* (eds Lowry and Mistelis, 2006) 214–16.

[14] As we will see in Chapter 9, section 4.1, this can cause some problems to B in a case where B wishes to establish adverse possession of the land, as the existence of the licence means that B's possession is no longer adverse to A.

[15] For example, if A puts up a notice expressly denying permission to such callers to enter A's land, no licence can be implied.

[16] (1845) 13 M & W 838, 844.

[17] That is the case even if B is unaware that A has revoked the invitation and so honestly believes that he is entitled to come onto A's land.

B if A could use such force before giving B a reasonable time in which to leave A's land. So, given A's initial invitation and B's reliance on that invitation by coming onto A's land, the law does not allow A's revocation of the licence to turn B immediately into a trespasser.[18] Whilst the courts have not been entirely consistent in the means used to reach that conclusion, the simplest rationale, as noted by Hill,[19] is that the law aims '*to ensure that the licensee is given a reasonable period in which to make alternative arrangements (where necessary). The packing-up period provides the mechanism whereby the law can achieve an appropriate balance between the licensor's interest in determining the licence and the licensee's interest in not suffering excessive disruption.*'

2.2 B'S RIGHTS AGAINST X

If B has a bare licence, then, as Hohfeld noted, in the extract above, that licence does not impose any duty on X, a stranger, not to interfere with B's use of A's land. In some cases, however, B can acquire a property right *in addition* to his bare licence; that property right will then impose a duty on X. For example, let us say that A goes on holiday for a week and asks B to 'house-sit'. A and B's arrangement is that B is under no duty to do so, and that, if he does choose to house-sit, A will not pay him. If B does go onto and occupy A's land for that week, X is under a duty not to interfere with B's occupation of the land. This is confirmed by Lord Upjohn's analysis, in *National Provincial Bank v Ainsworth*,[20] of the position of Mrs Ainsworth *after* Mr Ainsworth moved out of the family home (see Chapter 1, section 5.1, and Chapter 6, section 5.3, for discussion of this case). His Lordship stated that '*in this case in truth and in fact the wife at all material times was and is in exclusive occupation of the home. Until her husband returns she has dominion over the house and she could clearly bring proceedings against trespassers*'.[21]

In such a case, however, X's duty does not arise because of B's licence; instead, it arises because B, as a result of having possession of A's land, has a legal estate in land—that is, a freehold. That right is acquired *independently* of A: B acquires the right simply by taking possession of the land (see Chapter 5, section 4, for discussion of the concept of independent acquisition and Chapter 9, section 3). This means that B acquires such a right even if he takes possession of the land *without* A's permission and therefore has no licence. Where B does have A's permission then, of course, B will not be in *adverse* possession of the land (see Chapter 9, section 4.1), and so B's occupation will not lead to A's title being lost; but B will nonetheless have a property right in the land, capable of binding X, simply as a result of B's sole possession of the land.

2.3 B'S RIGHTS AGAINST C

As noted in section 1.2, there are two ways in which B *may* have a right against C: firstly, it may be that C has acted in such a way as to give B a *new, direct right* against C; secondly, it may be that B has a *pre-existing property right* that he can assert against C.

---

[18] See, for example, *Winter Garden Theatre (London) Ltd v Millennium Productions Ltd* [1948] AC 173 (HL), *per* Viscount Simon at 188–9 and *per* Lord Macdermott at 204.

[19] Hill, 'The Termination of Bare Licences' [2001] CLJ 87, 107.   [20] [1965] AC 1175, [1232].

[21] That view was confirmed by the Court of Appeal in *Manchester Airport plc v Dutton* [2000] QB 133.

2.3.1 Direct rights

There are many different ways in which B may acquire a direct right against C. All of these methods depend on C's conduct: there must be something in the way that C behaves that justifies B's acquisition of a new, direct right against C. In practice, if B simply has a bare licence, there is no reason why A, when transferring the land to C, would take steps to ensure that C gives B a new, direct right, and there is no obvious reason why C would, on his or her own initiative, act in such a way as to give B such a right.

2.3.2 A pre-existing property right?

If B's bare licence counts as a property right, then it will be *prima facie* binding on C. It is clear, however, that a bare licence does *not* count as a property right. Firstly, as we saw in Chapter 5, section 6, and Chapter 6, section 5.3, there is a *closed* list of legal and equitable property rights in land. As confirmed by the House of Lords in *National Provincial Bank v Ainsworth*, licences do not form part of this list. Further, it is very unlikely that a bare licence will ever be admitted into the list of property rights: it cannot meet the criteria laid down by Lord Wilberforce in the following extract.

National Provincial Bank v Ainsworth
[1965] AC 1175, HL

Lord Wilberforce

At 1247–8

Before a right or interest can be admitted into the category of property, or of a right affecting property, it must be definable, identifiable by third parties, capable in its nature of assumption by third parties, and have some degree of permanence or stability.

If B simply has a bare licence, his right clearly lacks that quality of 'permanence and stability'; after all, as we have seen, it can simply be revoked by A.

3 CONTRACTUAL LICENCES

A contractual licence exists where B has a liberty to make some use of A's land *and* A is under a contractual duty to B in relation to A's power to revoke that liberty. This means that—in some circumstances, at least—A is under a contractual duty to B not to revoke B's licence. For example, let us say A and B make an agreement that B, in return for paying A £500 up front, can share occupation of A's house for three months. As we will see in Chapter 19, section 1.2.1, such an arrangement will not give B a lease: because he can only share occupation of A's house, B does not have a right to exclusive possession of any land. B does, however, have more than a bare licence: A is also under a contractual duty not to revoke B's permission to occupy during the next three months. Of course, A's duty is not absolute: even if they have not expressly agreed it, A will have an implied power to revoke B's permission in certain circumstances—for example, if he discovers that B is stealing from him.

The distinction between a bare licence and a contractual licence thus turns on the question of whether A is under a contractual duty to B. Contractual duties can be implied as well as expressed and, in some cases, the courts have been very creative in finding such a contract.

Tanner v Tanner
[1975] 1 WLR 1346, CA

Facts: Mr Tanner (described by Lord Denning MR as a '*milkman by day and a croupier by night*') entered into an extramarital relationship with Miss Macdermott. She later gave birth to twins fathered by Mr Tanner and changed her name to 'Mrs Tanner'—but the two never married. Mr Tanner bought a house in which Mrs Tanner and the twins were to live. To move into this house, Mrs Tanner gave up her rent-controlled tenancy on the basis that she and the twins would be allowed to remain in the new house, at least until the twins left school. Mr Tanner and his first wife divorced, but Mr Tanner then married another woman and decided to remove Mrs Tanner from the house. He offered her £4,000 to leave, but she refused. Mr Tanner (A) brought proceedings to remove Mrs Tanner (B). A succeeded at first instance and B (with the children) moved into local authority accommodation. B appealed, arguing that A was under a contractual duty to allow B to remain, at least until the twins left school. B did not, however, ask the Court of Appeal for an order forcing A to let her back into occupation. The Court of Appeal found that, in removing B and the twins, A had breached his contractual duty to B and so should pay B damages of £2,000.

Lord Denning MR

At 1350

It is said that [B and the twins] were only licensees—bare licensees—under a licence revocable at will; and that [A] was entitled in law to turn her and the twins out on a moment's notice. I cannot believe that this is the law [. . .] I think he had a legal duty towards them. Not only towards the babies but also towards their mother. She was looking after them and bringing them up. In order to fulfil his duty towards the babies, he was under a duty to provide for the mother too. She had given up her flat where she was protected by the Rent Acts [. . .] at his instance so as to be able the better to bring up the children. It is impossible to suppose that in that situation she and the babies were bare licensees whom he could turn out at a moment's notice. He recognised this when he offered to pay her £4,000 to get her out.

What then was their legal position? She herself said in evidence: 'The house was supposed to be ours until the children left school.' It seems to me [. . .] that in all the circumstances it is to be implied that she had a licence—a contractual licence—to have accommodation in the house for herself and the children so long as they were of school age and the accommodation was reasonably required for her and the children. There was, it is true, no express contract to that effect, but the circumstances are such that the court should imply a contract by him [. . .] whereby they were entitled to have the use of the house as their home until the girls had finished school. It may be that if circumstances changed—so that the accommodation was not reasonably required—the licence might be determinable. But it was not determinable in the circumstances in which he sought to determine it, namely to turn her out with the children

> and to bring in his new wife with her family. It was a contractual licence of the kind which is specifically enforceable on her behalf, and which he can be restrained from breaking; and he could not sell the house over her head so as to get her out in that way.
>
> If therefore the lady had sought an injunction restraining him from determining the licence, it should have been granted [. . .]

It is important to note that a contemporary court is unlikely to adopt the very creative approach to finding a contractual licence taken by Lord Denning MR in *Tanner v Tanner*.[22] In that case, the contractual licence seems to have been imposed as a means to the end of imposing a duty on Mr Tanner to provide some form of financial assistance to Mrs Tanner and the twins (in the case itself, Mrs Tanner's only claim was for damages). Nowadays, because Parliament has recognized that particular policy need, there are statutory means by which a party such as Mr Tanner can come under a duty to make financial provision for his children.[23] As a result, there is no longer a need to bend doctrinal rules, as in *Tanner v Tanner*, in order to find a contractual licence. Indeed, under the Children Act 1989, s 15 and Sch 1, it is possible to impose a duty on a party such as Mr Tanner to allow his children (and their mother) to remain in occupation of a particular home until leaving school. As a result, there is no longer a need to stretch the concept of a contractual licence.

3.1 B'S RIGHTS AGAINST A

The Court of Appeal's decision in *Tanner v Tanner* provides a good example of the protection available to B if she has a contractual licence. Lord Denning MR indicated that, *if* B had applied to court in time, a court would have prevented A from breaching his contractual duty not to revoke B's liberty to occupy A's land. In *Tanner* itself, it was too late for the court to protect B in that way. As a result, A was ordered to pay B damages; those damages had the aim of putting B, as far as possible, in the position in which she would have been had A kept his contractual promise.[24]

In assessing B's position against A, there are two key questions: firstly, is A's actual or threatened action a breach of his contractual duty to B? Secondly, if it is, or would be, a breach, how will a court respond?

3.1.1 Is A's actual or threatened conduct a breach of contract?

Of course, this will depend on the precise terms of the contract between A and B. It is vital to note that, in most cases, it may be possible, in certain circumstances, for A to revoke B's liberty to use A's land *without* breaching his contract with B. For example, in *Winter Garden Theatre (London) Ltd v Millennium Productions Ltd*,[25] the contract between A and B for B's use of A's theatre was not for a fixed period, but it was clear that the parties did

---

[22] Indeed, in *Horrocks v Forray* [1976] 1 WLR 230, a differently constituted Court of Appeal, faced with a similar case, distinguished *Tanner v Tanner*.

[23] See Children Act 1989, Sch 1.

[24] In very rare cases, as a result of A's breach of contract, B can obtain damages based on the gain that A has made by the breach: see *A-G v Blake* [2001] 1 AC 268.

[25] [1948] AC 173.

not intend it to be perpetual, so the House of Lords held that A had a contractual power to revoke the licence by giving reasonable notice to B.[26]

3.1.2 If A's conduct is a breach, how will a court respond?

We have already seen that, in *Tanner v Tanner*, Lord Denning MR stated that, if approached in time, a court would have issued an injunction to prevent A's breach of B's contractual licence. As Lord Uthwatt noted in the *Winter Garden* case: '*The settled practice of the courts of equity is to do what they can by an injunction to preserve the sanctity of a bargain. To my mind, as at present advised, a licensee who has refused to accept the wrongful repudiation of the bargain which is involved in an unauthorised revocation of the licence is as much entitled to the protection of an injunction as a licensee who has not received any notice of revocation.*'[27]

This preference for specifically protecting B's contractual licence (rather than allowing A to breach it and leaving B to claim money from A) can also be seen in cases in which, in contrast to *Tanner* and *Winter Garden*, B has not yet started to make use of A's land.

Verrall v Great Yarmouth Borough Council
[1981] QB 202, CA

Facts: Great Yarmouth Borough Council owned a hall (the Wellington Pier Pavilion) in that seaside town. It made a contractual promise in April 1979 to allow the National Front to use the hall for its two-day national conference in October. Following a change in its political control, the council (A) attempted, in May, to revoke the National Front's licence. Mr Verrall (B), suing on his own behalf and representing all members of that organization, applied for an order forcing A to perform its contractual promise. Such an order was granted. The council appealed unsuccessfully to the Court of Appeal.

Lord Denning MR

At 216

Since the *Winter Garden* case, it is clear that once a man has entered under his contract of licence, he cannot be turned out. An injunction can be obtained against the licensor to prevent his being turned out. On principle it is the same if it happens before he enters. If he has a contractual right to enter, and the licensor refuses to let him come in, then he can come to the court and in a proper case get an order for specific performance to allow him to come in. An illustration was taken in the course of the argument. Supposing one of the great political parties—say, the Conservative Party—had booked its hall at Brighton for its conference in September of this year: it had made all its arrangements accordingly: it had all its delegates coming: it had booked its hotels, and so on. Would it be open to the local council to repudiate that agreement, and say that the Conservative Party could not go there? Would the only remedy be damages? Clearly not. The court would order the council in such a case to perform its contract. It would be the same in the case of the Labour

---

[26] On the facts of the case, it was held that the one month's notice given by A to B was reasonable.
[27] [1948] AC 173 at [202].

Party, or whoever it may be. When arrangements are made for a licence of this kind of such importance and magnitude affecting many people, the licensors cannot be allowed to repudiate it and simply pay damages. It must be open to the court to grant specific performance in such cases.

It should not be assumed, however, that a court will *always* specifically protect B's contractual licence. After all, a court has a discretion as to whether to give B an equitable remedy such as specific performance or an injunction. And, in some circumstances, it may be inappropriate to prevent A from revoking B's contractual licence.

Thompson v Park
[1944] KB 408, CA

Facts: Mr Thompson and Mr Park each owned a school. The schools were amalgamated and the new school was set up on the site of Mr Thompson's school, Broughton Hall, near Eccleshall, Staffordshire. Mr Thompson gave Mr Park, and twenty-five of Mr Park's pupils, permission to join the school. The working relationship between Mr Thompson and Mr Park broke down, and Mr Thompson attempted to revoke the licence of Mr Park and his pupils to remain at the school. Having initially left, Mr Park forced his way back onto the premises and refused to leave. Mr Thompson (A) brought proceedings for an injunction ordering Mr Park (B) to leave. A also asked for an interim injunction ordering B to leave before the court determined A's application for an injunction. The Court of Appeal granted the interim injunction.

Goddard LJ

At 409–10

If [B] thought that he had a grievance which could be lawfully asserted the courts were open to him. I am not saying what the result of any application by him would have been, for though this is not the sort of agreement which any court could specifically enforce—for the court cannot specifically enforce an agreement for two people to live peaceably under the same roof—yet, of course, if the contract is broken, [B] has got a common law remedy in damages, which, if he is right, might be heavy. [B], however did not seek the intervention of the court, but took the law into his own hands and remedied the grievances under which he felt he was suffering in a manner which seems to me to have been wholly deplorable, all the more so when one considers that he is in charge of small boys at a preparatory school and ought to be inculcating into them a respect for authority and discipline. It appears to me that on his own showing he has been guilty at least of riot, affray, wilful damage, forcible entry and, perhaps, conspiracy [. . .]

The strength of the argument which was put forward on [B]'s behalf was that, assuming that there had been a breach of contract on the part of [A], [B] had a right to be where he was. That is an entire misconception of the legal position, which was that the defendant was a licensee on the premises. That licence has been withdrawn. Whether it has been rightly withdrawn or wrongly withdrawn matters nothing for this purpose. The licensee, once his licence is withdrawn, has no right to re-enter on the land. If he does, he is a common trespasser.

It is important to separate out two questions, both discussed by Goddard LJ in *Thompson v Park*. The first is whether, if B had applied to court *after* leaving A's land, a court would order A to perform his contractual promise to share occupation with B. Goddard LJ's statement is surely correct: '*the court cannot specifically enforce an agreement for two people to live peaceably under the same roof.*'[28] It would be unduly onerous on A to force him to live with B, given the breakdown in their relationship. And B would not receive the full value of his promise: sharing occupation with A, after the two have fallen out, is clearly different from sharing occupation when A and B are on good terms. So, whilst A's action in revoking the licence may well be a breach of contract, B may have to settle for receiving money from A.

The second question is whether, if A revokes his licence in breach of contract, B can then insist on remaining on A's land. Goddard LJ thought not—but it is not clear that this is consistent with the decision in *Verall v Great Yarmouth BC*.[29] The point is that, even if a court would not order specific performance of A's contractual promise, once A has made such a promise, B does have a *legal right* to be on A's land for the duration of his contractual licence. In other words, even if the contract is not specifically enforced, A is under a contractual *duty* to B to allow B to use the land as promised. As can be seen in the next extract, this point has important consequences.

Hurst v Picture Theatres Ltd
[1915] 1 KB 1, CA

Facts: On 17 March 1913, a film of Lake Garda[30] was shown at a cinema in High Street Kensington, London, owned by Picture Theatres Ltd. Mr Hurst bought a ticket. He did not misbehave, but was forced to leave by the manager of the cinema, who mistakenly believed that B had not paid for his seat. Mr Hurst (B) claimed that Picture Theatres Ltd (A), through the actions of its employee, had committed the tort of trespass to the person: it had breached its duty not to interfere with B's physical integrity. A argued that, once it had exercised its power to revoke B's licence, B became a trespasser and so A was permitted to use reasonable force to remove B from the land. A argued that even if its action in revoking the licence was a breach of contract, that did not change the fact that, once the licence was revoked, B was a trespasser on A's land and so reasonable force could be used to remove him. The Court of Appeal

---

[28] That statement was also approved by Megarry V-C in *Hounslow LBC v Twickenham GD Ltd* [1971] Ch 233, [250]. The same concern is also clear in proprietary estoppel cases: when considering how to respond to a successful estoppel claim, a court will not make an order that forces parties who have since fallen out to live together: see *Baker v Baker* (1993) 25 HLR 408.

[29] [1981] 1 QB 202, [216]. Note also the reasoning of Viscount Simon in *Winter Garden (Theatre) Ltd v Millennium Productions Ltd* [1948] AC 173 at [189], stating that where a ticket is sold to B to watch a particular event: 'the implication of the arrangement, however it may be classified in law, plainly is that the ticket entitles the purchaser to enter and, if he behaves himself, to remain on the premises until the end of the event which he has paid his money to witness.'

[30] It is likely to have been a Kinemacolor film produced in 1910 (entitled *Lake Garda, Italy*), currently held by the Nederlands Filmmuseum and shown at the British Film Institute's Conservation Centre in February 2008.

rejected that argument, affirming the decision of Channell J that B was entitled to substantial damages.

Buckley LJ

At 7

[B] in the present action paid his money to enjoy the sight of a particular spectacle. He was anxious to go into a picture theatre to see a series of views or pictures during, I suppose, an hour or a couple of hours. That which was granted to him was the right to enjoy looking at a spectacle, to attend a performance from its beginning to its end. That which was called the licence, the right to go upon the premises, was only something granted to him for the purpose of enabling him to have that which had been granted him, namely, the right to see. He could not see the performance unless he went into the building. His right to go into the building was something given to him in order to enable him to have the benefit of that which had been granted to him, namely, the right to hear the opera, or see the theatrical performance, or see the moving pictures as was the case here.

At 11

[A] had, I think, for value contracted that [B] should see a certain spectacle from its commencement to its termination. They broke that contract and it was a tort on their part to remove him. They committed an assault upon him in law. It was not of a violent kind, because, like a wise man, [B] gave way to superior force and left the theatre. They sought to justify the assault by saying that they were entitled to remove him because he had not paid. He had paid, the jury have so found. Failing on that question of fact, they say that they were entitled to remove him because his licence was revocable. In my opinion, it was not. There was, I think, no justification for the assault here committed. Under the circumstances it was for the jury to give him such a sum as was right for the assault which was committed upon him, and for the serious indignity to a gentleman of being seized and treated in this way in a place of public resort. The jury have found that he was originally in the theatre as a spectator, that the assault was committed upon him, and that it was a wrongful act.

An earlier decision, *Wood v Leadbitter*,[31] had held to the contrary on the basis that, because a contractual licence does not count as a property right in land, A remains free to revoke it. That approach is, however, impossible to defend; the decision in *Hurst* is clearly correct. A contractual licence is different from a bare licence: B has a liberty to use A's land *and* A is under a contractual duty to B not to revoke that liberty. So, even if A does attempt to revoke the licence by removing B, B's *right* (in Hohfeld's terms, a 'claim right') to be on the land remains. So A's attempt to revoke the licence does *not* turn B into a trespasser. That means that A is *not* allowed to use reasonable force to remove B from the land.

It is important to note that this analysis applies whether or not a court would grant an order of specific performance to protect B's contractual right. That point was made in the following case.

---

[31] (1845) 13 M & W 838.

Hounslow LBC v Twickenham GD Ltd
[1971] 1 Ch 233

Megarry V-C

At 254–5

I have said nothing about an ejected licensee's right to claim damages for assault, for such issues do not arise in this case. All that I need say, in order to avoid possible misunderstanding, is that in light of the *Winter Garden* case I find it difficult to see how a contractual licensee can be treated as a trespasser so long as his contract entitles him to be on the land; and this is so whether or not his contract is specifically enforceable. I do not think that the licence can be detached from the contract, as it were, and separately revoked; the licensee is on the land by contractual right and is not as a trespasser. I may add that I say nothing about the rights of licensees against third parties.

It, therefore, seems clear that even if B's contractual licence would not be protected by an order for specific performance, B nonetheless has a right against A to be on A's land for the duration of his contractual licence. This suggests that the decision in *Hurst v Picture Theatres Ltd* should be the same *whether or not* A's contractual duty to B is specifically enforceable. This means that in a case like *Thompson v Park*, in which B's contractual licence allows him to share occupation of A's land with A, the following position applies if A and B fall out during the period of the contractual licence.

- If A attempts to revoke B's licence in breach of contract and B remains on the land, B does not become a trespasser—so A cannot use reasonable force to remove B from the land. Instead, A needs to apply to court for an order that B must leave. Because A's contractual duty is not specifically enforceable, a court is likely to grant such an order (although A will, of course, have to pay B damages for revoking B's licence in breach of contract).

- If A attempts to revoke B's licence in breach of contract and B is *not* on the land, B cannot force his way back onto the land. Instead, B needs to apply to court for an order that A must allow him back onto the land—but because A's contractual duty is not specifically enforceable, a court is unlikely to grant such an order and B will have to settle for damages.

3.2 B'S RIGHTS AGAINST X

In the passage from *Hounslow LBC v Twickenham GD Ltd* set out above, Megarry V-C concludes his survey of B's rights against A by stating that: '*I may add that I say nothing about the rights of licensees against third parties.*' It is indeed very important to draw this distinction. For example, if we say that B has a right to be on A's land for the duration of his contractual licence, this means that B has a right *against A* to be on A's land. A thus has a duty not to interfere with B's use of the land. That does *not* mean that a third party, such as X, has a duty to B: after all, A's duty arises as a result of his contractual promise to B, and X has made no such promise.

This means that there is an important difference between a licence, even a contractual licence, and a legal lease. If B has a legal lease then the rest of the world is under a duty to B: for example, we will see in Chapter 19, section 1.2.2, that if X interferes with B's reasonable enjoyment of the land, X commits the tort of nuisance against B. As the House of Lords confirmed in *Hunter v Canary Wharf*,[32] however, the tort of nuisance does not protect B if he or she has only a licence.

We noted in section 2.2 that, even if B only has a bare licence, X will be under a duty to B *if* B acquires a property right by taking physical control of A's land. Clearly, the same is true if B has a contractual licence; in such a case it is not the licence itself that binds X, but rather the property right that B acquires by taking physical control of A's land. The following decision of the Court of Appeal goes further: it assumes that, if A gives B a contractual licence permitting B to take physical control of A's land, X can be under a duty to B even *before* B goes onto A's land.

Manchester Airport plc v Dutton and ors
[1999] EWCA Civ 844, [2000] QB 133, CA

Facts: The National Trust owned some land adjacent to Manchester Airport. Manchester Airport plc was building a new runway. It needed to ensure that trees on the National Trust's land were cut down to prevent interference with flight paths to and from the new runway. The National Trust (A) gave Manchester Airport plc (B) and its authorized subcontractors permission to go onto the National Trust land to do the necessary work. Before B or its subcontractors entered the land, Mr Dutton (one of a number of environmental protestors) occupied the land with the intention of interfering with the planned work. Manchester Airport plc (B) applied for an order against Mr Dutton (X) for possession of the land, using the special summary procedure provided by Order 113 of the Rules of the Supreme Court.

Laws LJ (with whom Kennedy LJ agreed)

Now, I think it is clear that if [B] had been in actual occupation under the licence and the trespassers had then entered on the site, [B] could have obtained an order for possession; at least if it was in effective control of the land. Clause 1 of the licence confers a right to occupy the whole of the area edged red on the plan. The places where the trespassers have gone lie within that area. [B's] claim for possession would not, were it in occupation, fall in my judgment to be defeated by the circumstance that it enjoys no title or estate in the land, nor any right of exclusive possession as against [A] [. . .]

But if [B], were it in actual occupation and control of the site, could obtain an order for possession against the trespassers, why may it not obtain such an order *before* it enters into occupation, so as to evict the trespassers and enjoy the licence granted to it? As I understand it, the principal objection to the grant of such relief is that it would amount to an ejectment, and ejectment is a remedy available only to a party with title to or estate in the land; which as a mere licensee [B] plainly lacks [. . .]

---

[32] [1997] AC 665. See further Chapter 19, section 1.2.2.

But I think there is a logical mistake in the notion that because ejectment was only available to estate owners, possession cannot be available to licensees who do not enjoy de facto occupation. The mistake inheres in this: if the action for ejectment was by definition concerned *only* with the rights of estate owners, it is necessarily silent upon the question, what relief might be available to a licensee. The limited and specific nature of ejectment means only that it was not available to a licensee; it does not imply the further proposition that *no* remedy by way of possession can now be granted to a licensee not in occupation. Nowadays there is no distinct remedy of ejectment; a plaintiff sues for an order of possession, whether he is himself in occupation or not. The proposition that a plaintiff not in occupation may only obtain the remedy if he is an estate owner assumes that he must bring himself within the old law of ejectment. I think it is a false assumption.

I would hold that the court today has ample power to grant a remedy to a licensee which will protect but not exceed his legal rights granted by the licence. If, as here, that requires an order for possession, the spectre of history (which, in the true tradition of the common law, ought to be a friendly ghost) does not stand in the way. The law of ejectment has no voice in the question; it cannot speak beyond its own limits.

In my judgment the true principle is that a licensee not in occupation may claim possession against a trespasser if that is a necessary remedy to vindicate and give effect to such rights of occupation as by contract with his licensor he enjoys. This is the same principle as allows a licensee who is in de facto possession to evict a trespasser. There is no respectable distinction, in law or logic, between the two situations. An estate owner may seek an order whether he is in possession or not. So, in my judgment, may a licensee, if other things are equal. In both cases, the plaintiff's remedy is strictly limited to what is required to make good his legal right. The principle applies although the licensee has no right to exclude the licensor himself. Elementarily he cannot exclude any occupier who, by contract or estate, has a claim to possession equal or superior to his own. Obviously, however, that will not avail a bare trespasser.

Chadwick LJ (dissenting)

There was no material, in the present case, on which the judge could reach the conclusion that [B] was in de facto possession of the relevant part of [A's land]; and, for my part, I do not think that she did reach that conclusion. She treated the question as one which turned on the construction of the licence. In my view the judge was in error when she held, in a passage in her judgment to which I have already referred, that:

> 'The licence gives the right of possession and this is, I am satisfied, a right of possession which does not give absolute title, but it does nevertheless give a power against trespassers.'

She did not make the distinction, essential in cases of this nature, between a plaintiff who is in possession and who seeks protection from those who interfere with that possession, and a plaintiff who has not gone into possession but who seeks to evict those who are already on the land. In the latter case (which is this case) the plaintiff must succeed by the strength of his title, not on the weakness (or lack) of any title in the defendant.

All three members of the Court of Appeal thus agreed that if X interfered with B's use of A's land *after* B had gone into occupation of the land, B would be able to bring a claim for possession against X. That is certainly the case: it is simply an application of the point made in section 2.2 above—that is, whenever B takes possession of land, whether with the consent of an owner or not, he acquires a legal property right in that land and so the rest of the world comes under a *prima facie* duty to B not to interfere with B's use of the land. We will examine this point in Chapter 9, section 3.

But Chadwick LJ and the majority disagreed about the answer in a situation in which, as in *Manchester Airport* itself, X interfered with B's use of A's land *before* B had gone into occupation. There is a strong argument in favour of Chadwick LJ's analysis. The crucial point is that, once B takes physical control of A's land—whether under a licence or not—B acquires a legal property right in A's land. Before that point, B has only a contractual right against A: there is no reason why A's contract with B should impose a duty on X.

Swadling makes this point in the following extract.

Swadling, 'Opening the *Numerus Clausus*' (2000) 116 LQ Rev 358

[. . .] In *Manchester Airport v Dutton* Laws LJ asserted] that no logical distinction can be drawn between a licensee in and a licensee out of possession, so that if the former can bring trespass against third parties, so can the latter. With respect, it would have been appropriate at this point to consider why a licensee in possession is able to bring trespass; the reason is in fact one which cannot apply in the case of a licensee out of possession. The reason why a licensee in possession can bring an action for possession is that he has a right of possession which is completely independent of the licence under which he occupies the land.

Take the deserted wife in *Ainsworth's case* [*National Provincial Bank v Ainsworth*[33]—see the discussion in section 2.2 above]. She is, we are told, entitled to sue those who interfere with her possession of the matrimonial home, from which it follows that she has a right to the possession of that matrimonial home. But from where does her right to possession spring? Not from her licence to be on the premises, for that is a right which the House of Lords held bound the husband alone. It must therefore be some other event which creates this right of possession [. . .] and this other event is her unilateral act of taking possession of the house. In other words, her right of possession arises from the fact of her possession [. . .]

The error into which, with respect, Laws L.J. falls is in failing to notice that a contractual licensee in occupation of land has rights derived from two separate sources, some from the contract, some from the fact of possession. Those derived from the contract prevent the licensor from denying him possession of the land. But those rights, because of the doctrine of privity, and notwithstanding the recent reform of that doctrine, bind the licensor alone. It is the rights derived from the second source, from the fact of possession, which bind third parties [. . .] There is, therefore, a distinction which does still need to be drawn between a plaintiff whose right to occupy the land in question arises from title and one whose right arises from the contract alone.

It is thus possible to disapprove of the decision of the Court of Appeal in *Manchester Airport plc v Dutton*. Indeed, it is interesting to compare it to the decision of in *Hill v Tupper*,[34] which we examined in Chapter 5, section 1. In that case, the Basingstoke Canal Company (A) gave Mr Hill (B) an 'exclusive' contractual licence to hire boats out on the canal. The Exchequer Chamber made clear that A's contract with B did *not* give B a legal property right and so did not impose a duty to B on Mr Tupper (X), who had also hired out boats on the canal. So, if Mr Hill wanted to stop Mr Tupper from hiring out boats, he had to ask or force the Canal Company, as owner of the canal, to assert its property right against Mr Tupper.

---

[33] [1965] AC 1175. [34] (1863) 2 H & C 122.

The same analysis should apply in *Manchester Airport plc v Dutton*: the airport should use its contract with the National Trust to ask or force the National Trust to use its property right, as owner of the land, against Mr Dutton and the other protestors. The interesting point, of course, is that at least some members of the National Trust may have refused to support such an action against the protestors.[35]

In *Mayor of London v Hall and others*,[36] the Mayor of London sought an order for possession of Parliament Square Gardens in London; the defendants had set up a camp there and named it 'Democracy Village'. One of the arguments made by the defendants was that, as legal title to the Gardens vested in the Crown, the Mayor had no property right on which he could base a claim for possession. In the end, the Court of Appeal upheld the possession order granted to the Mayor on the basis that ss 384 and 385 of the Greater London Authority Act 1999 gave the Mayor a statutory right to seek possession of the land. In an *obiter* part of the court's judgment, Lord Neuberger MR also considered the defendant's argument that the reasoning of the majority in *Dutton* could not be relied on by the Mayor, as authorities such as *Hill v Tupper*[37] had not been cited to the court in *Dutton*. Lord Neuberger MR noted that '*if the law governing the right to claim possession is governed by the same principles as those that governed the right to maintain a claim in ejectment, the [defendant's] argument seems very powerful.*'[38] However, his Lordship went on to say that '*there is obvious force in the point that the modern law relating to possession claims should not be shackled by arcane and archaic rules relating to ejectment, and, in particular, that it should develop and adapt to accommodate a claim by anyone entitled to use and control, effectively amounting to possession, of the land in question [. . .]*'.[39] Lord Neuberger MR thus granted his approval to the basic, but conceptually controversial, approach in *Dutton*: that if B has a right to use and occupy land, B should be able to remove a trespasser from that land, even if B's right is not a property right.[40]

The decision in *Manchester Airport plc v Dutton* could also be seen as part of a deliberate move to increase the protection given to a contractual licensee against third parties. Swadling criticizes the decision for blurring the divide between personal rights and property rights, but others see the decision as taking a welcome step towards allowing (at least some) contractual licences to count as property rights.[41] To that extent, one's view of the *Manchester Airport* decision depends on one's view as to the crucial question, to be examined in section 3.3.2 below, as to whether a contractual licence should count as a property right in land.

3.3 B'S RIGHTS AGAINST C

As noted in section 2.3, in relation to bare licences, there are two ways in which B *may* have a right against C: firstly, it may be that C has acted in such a way as to give B a *new, direct right* against C; secondly, it may be that B has a *pre-existing property right* that he can assert against C.

---

[35] See McFarlane, *The Structure of Property Law* (2008) p 345, fn 22.   [36] [2010] EWCA Civ 817.
[37] (1863) 2 H & C 122.   [38] [2010] EWCA Civ 817, [26].   [39] Ibid, [27].
[40] For criticism of Lord Neuberger MR's approach in *Mayor of London v Hall*, see Lochery, 'Pushing the Boundaries of *Dutton*?' [2011] Conv 74.
[41] See Gray and Gray, *Elements of Land Law* (5th edn, 2009), [10.5.13]–[10.5.15].

3.3.1 Direct rights

There are a number of different means by which, in theory, B can acquire a new, direct right against C.[42] In this section, we will look at the principles most likely to be relevant where, prior to his dealings with C, A has given B a contractual licence.

The tort of procuring a breach by A of A's contract with B

The existence of a contract between A and B imposes a duty on the rest of the world not to procure a breach by A of A's contractual duty to B.[43] For example, if A has a contract to perform at B's theatre, and C, knowing about that contract, persuades A to breach it and to perform at C's theatre instead, C commits a wrong against B.[44] There is a very difficult question as to whether C commits this tort if he simply knows about A's contractual licence with B, and, despite that, goes ahead and acquires a right from A with the intention of *not* allowing B to continue using A's land. Megaw LJ noted the possibility, in passing, in *Binions v Evans*.[45] But his Lordship went on to note that: '*However, it may be that there are special technical considerations in the law relating to land that would require to be reviewed before one could confidently assert that the ordinary principles as to the protection of known contractual rights would apply.*'

Certainly, as Roger Smith has pointed out,[46] there is a fear that allowing the tort to apply would make it far too easy for B to assert a direct right against C, and would thus undermine the protection due to a party acquiring a right in land. Indeed, Smith suggests that '*where real property principles accord priority to a contract or conveyance over an earlier contract, it should not be open to the earlier contracting party to rely on tort*'.[47]

On that view, the tort should *not* be able to provide any protection to B's contractual licence, because such a right does not currently count as a property right in land. There is, however, at least one case in which the tort was applied to a case involving land in relation to which B did not have a property right. In *Esso Petroleum Co Ltd v Kingswood Motors Ltd and ors*,[48] Kingswood Motors Ltd (A) operated a petrol station. Esso Petroleum Co Ltd (B) supplied petrol to A. A was under a contractual duty to B: (i) to notify B before selling the petrol station; and (ii) to ensure that any purchaser also entered into an agreement to use only fuel supplied by B. A breached this duty by selling to Impact Motor Ltd (C) without taking those steps. It was held that, because C knew about B's contract with A, C had committed the tort of procuring a breach of contract. In fact, Bridge J ordered C to transfer the petrol station back to B, so that A could continue to assert its contractual rights against B.

The decision is discussed in the following extract, which makes clear that *Esso v Kingswood* is not a standard contractual licence case.

---

[42] Note that the Land Registration Act 2002 does not exclude the possibility of such new, direct rights arising: see Chapter 16, section 6.2.

[43] See *OBG Ltd v Allan* [2008] 1 AC 1.   [44] See *Lumley v Gye* (1853) 2 E & B 216.

[45] [1972] Ch 359, 371.

[46] 'The Economic Torts: Their Impact on Real Property' (1977) 41 Conv 318.   [47] Ibid, 329.

[48] [1974] QB 142.

McFarlane, *The Structure of Property Law* (2008, p 438)

[T]he courts *are* willing to apply the wrong [of procuring a breach of contract] even where land is concerned. This is demonstrated by *Esso Petroleum Co Ltd v Kingswood Motors Ltd* [. . .] This willingness to apply the wrong even where land is concerned seems correct. The purpose of the wrong is to protect B's contractual right against A: it should therefore apply *whenever* B has a contractual right against A. It seems that the wrong is based on the need for the rest of the world to respect B's contractual relationship with A. There is no obvious reason why contractual rights relating to the use of land should attract less protection. For example, let's say that A, a cinema owner, makes a contractual promise to allow B to run a confectionary stall from part of that land for five years. That promise gives B a contractual licence: a personal right against A. However, if C, a competitor of B, pays A money to persuade A to breach the contract by removing B from the land, C commits the wrong of procuring a breach of the contract.

However, this does *not* mean that C will necessarily commit the wrong if, in [a standard contractual licence case] he goes ahead and buys A's Freehold and then seeks to remove B from the land. There is an important difference between [a standard contractual licence case] and the situation in *Kingswood Motors*. In the latter case, A was under an explicit contractual duty *not to transfer his Freehold to C* unless certain conditions were met. A therefore breached his contractual duty to B *as soon as* he transferred that right to C: that is, as soon as A sold the land to C. C, by participating in a sale that he knew to breach those conditions, was actively facilitating A's breach of contract. In [a standard contractual licence case], however [. . .] A has *not* made a contractual promise not to transfer his Freehold unless certain conditions are met. As a result, the sale to C, *by itself*, does *not* breach A's contractual duty to B: that duty is breached only at a later stage: when C asserts his right and prevents B from using the land.

This analysis *may* provide a way in which to justify the courts' apparent reluctance to apply the tort of procuring a breach of contract in a standard contractual licence case. Certainly, the courts have been careful to ensure that the means by which B can acquire a direct right are not expanded to the point at which C can be bound simply as a result of his knowledge of B's pre-existing personal right against A.[49]

The Contract (Rights of Third Parties) Act 1999

The presence of a contractual licence between A and B may have a different, more significant impact on B's chances of acquiring a direct right against C. If B has a bare licence, it is very unlikely that he will acquire such a right: C simply has no incentive to act in such a way as to give B such a right. But things may be different where B has a contractual licence. For example, let us say that A makes a contractual promise to B to allow B to make a particular use of A's land for five years. Two years later, A plans to sell the land to C. A knows that if he sells the land to C and C stops B from using the land, A will be in breach of his contractual promise to B. A will therefore have to pay money to B to put B in the position in which he would have been had A kept his promise to allow B to use the land for the full five years.[50]

---

[49] See, for example, *Keppell v Bailey* (1834) 2 My & K 517, *per* Lord Brougham LC at 546–8.

[50] See *King v David Allen & Sons Billposting Ltd* [1916] 2 AC 54, HL.

This gives A a reason to insist that C, when buying the land, makes a promise to allow B to continue using the land until the five years are up.

The Contract (Rights of Third Parties) Act 1999 allows B, in certain circumstances, to acquire a direct right against C as a result of a contractual promise made by C to A. If C makes a contractual promise to A to allow B to continue to use the land for the remainder of the five years, that promise clearly 'purports to confer a benefit' on B. Section 1(1)(b) of the 1999 Act can therefore operate to give B a direct right against C *even though*: (i) C's promise to allow B to use the land is made to A not B; and (ii) consideration for the promise is provided by A not B. Section 1(5) of the 1999 Act means that the remedies available to B as against C can then be determined by applying the principles (examined in section 3.1 above) that govern the remedies available to B against A. It is true that, under s 2 of the 1999 Act, A and C may have a power to vary C's contractual promise and hence to weaken or remove B's right against C.[51] In our example, however, there is no reason for A to wish to do so: A's aim is to give B a right against C that will absolve A from having to pay damages for breach of contract to B.

For the 1999 Act to apply, C must make a *contractual* promise to A. If, as in our example, C's promise is made as part of the contractual deal in which A promises to transfer his land to C, C's promise only counts as a contractual promise if the formality rule set out by section 2 of the Law of Property (Miscellaneous Provisions) Act 1989 (LP(MP)A 1989) is satisfied. We will examine that rule in detail in Chapter 8, section 4. For present purposes, it suffices to note that if, when acquiring his right from A, C makes an *oral* promise A to allow B to continue using A's land, that promise will *not* be contractually binding on C.[52] If so, B will be unable to rely on the 1999 Act to acquire a direct right against C—but B may be able to rely on a different means of enforcing C's promise.

The 'constructive trust' principle in Binions v Evans

In some decisions made before the Contract (Rights of Third Parties) Act 1999, B acquired a direct right against C as a result of C's promise to A. One such case was *Binions v Evans*. Lord Denning MR took the view that, even if Mrs Evans (B) had no legal or equitable property right that she could assert against Mr and Mrs Binions (C), the Binions could still be prevented from removing Mrs Evans from the cottage. That reasoning was based on the fact that, when acquiring a freehold of the cottage from the trustees of the Tredegar Estate (A), the Binions had made a promise to allow Mrs Evans to remain in the cottage for the rest of her life.

Binions v Evans
[1972] Ch 359, CA

Facts: Mrs Evans lived with her husband in a cottage in Cardiff Road, Newport. The cottage was owned by the husband's employers, the trustees of the Tredegar Estate. After her husband died, Mrs Evans entered into an agreement with the trustees, under which

---

[51] There are limits to that power—for example, it is lost if B has 'communicated his assent' to C's promise to C; if C is aware that B has relied on C's promise; or if B has relied on the promise and C could reasonably be expected to have foreseen such reliance: see s 2(1) of the 1999 Act.

[52] C's oral promise may be contractually binding if it seen as separate from the contract dealing with C's acquisition of a right from A and so counts as a 'collateral contract', however, the courts are generally reluctant to view such promises as collateral to the main contract between A and : see Chapter 8, section 3.6.

she was allowed to remain in the cottage for the rest of her life. The trustees then sold some land, including the cottage, to Mr and Mrs Binions.

The trustees warned them that Mrs Evans was entitled to remain in the cottage for the rest of her life and sold the land 'subject to' her right; as a result, Mr and Mrs Binions bought the land for a reduced price. They then brought proceedings to remove Mrs Evans from the cottage. Mrs Evans claimed that: (i) her agreement with the trustees gave her a pre-existing property right that was binding on Mr and Mrs Binions; and, in any case, (ii) the term included in the sale to Mr and Mrs Binions gave her a direct right against them.

Lord Denning MR

At 367

[The trustees] stipulated with [Mr and Mrs Binions] that they were to take the house 'subject to' [Mrs Evans'] rights under the agreement. They supplied [Mr and Mrs Binions] with a copy of the contract: and [Mr and Mrs Binions] paid less because of her right to stay there. In these circumstances, this court will impose on [Mr and Mrs Binions] a constructive trust for [Mrs Evans'] benefit: for the simple reason that it would be utterly inequitable for Mr and Mrs Binions to turn Mrs Evans out contrary to the stipulation subject to which they took the premises. That seems to me clear from the important decision of *Bannister v Bannister*,[53] which was applied by the judge and which I gladly follow.

It is worth noting that there are a number of other possible explanations for the result in *Binions v Evans*. Firstly, the majority of the Court of Appeal (Megaw and Stephenson LJJ) found that B's initial agreement with A gave B more than a contractual licence: she had an equitable life interest in the land and that equitable interest was capable of binding C. On that analysis, the case has nothing to do with contractual licences.

Secondly, Lord Denning MR also contended that B's contractual licence counted, by itself, as an equitable interest in land. We will examine that argument in the next section. As we will see, it is, to say the least, somewhat controversial: it is therefore no surprise that Lord Denning MR also considered whether B had a new, direct right against C.

It is that suggestion on which we will focus here: the idea that B acquired a direct right against C, because, given that C acquired the land on the basis of allowing B to remain in occupation, it would be 'utterly inequitable' if C were now free to go back on that promise. That suggestion is consistent with a number of cases in which B acquires a direct right against C where:

- C acquires a property right in land from A; *and*

- prior to that, C made a promise to A to give B a right to make some use of that land; *and*

- as a result of that promise, A allowed C to acquire the property right in the land, or allowed C to acquire that right for a lower price.

The precise basis of the principle applied in these cases has been contested.[54] Nonetheless, the following extract, from a Court of Appeal decision, confirms that this principle may be used in a case in which B initially has a contractual licence from A.

---

[53] [1948] 2 All ER 133.

[54] On one view, the principle is the same as that underlying the *Rochefoucauld v Bousted* and *Pallant v Morgan* constructive trusts, discussed in Chapter 11, sections 5 and 6: see e.g. McFarlane, 'Constructive

Ashburn Anstalt v Arnold
[1989] Ch 1, CA

Facts: Mr Arnold had a headlease of business premises. Arnold & Co went into possession of the land under a sublease from Mr Arnold. Cavendish Land Co Ltd then acquired the freehold of the land subject to Mr Arnold's headlease. Mr Arnold contracted to sell his headlease to Matlodge Ltd, who also contracted to buy Arnold & Co's sublease. As part of that sale, Matlodge made a contractual promise to Arnold & Co that it could remain in occupation of the land until it was needed for redevelopment. Cavendish Land Co Ltd then acquired the benefit of Matlodge's rights to both the headlease and the sublease, also taking on Matlodge's contractual duties to Arnold & Co. As a result, Cavendish now held the freehold free from the headlease and sublease, whilst Arnold & Co remained in occupation of the land. Cavendish was later taken over by Legal & General Assurance Society Ltd, which also took on the contractual duties to Arnold & Co. Legal & General (A) then sold its freehold to Ashburn Anstalt (C). Under the terms of the sale contract, C took its freehold 'subject to' the contractual rights of Arnold & Co (B) against A, arising as a result of the original agreement with Matlodge. C had no plans to redevelop the land, but sought possession from B. B's first argument was that its initial agreement with A gave B a property right (a lease) that was binding on C. As we will see in Chapter 19, section 2.2, the Court of Appeal accepted that argument and found in B's favour. The Court of Appeal also went on to consider B's argument that, even if its agreement with A gave it only a contractual licence, B could assert that contractual licence against C. As we will see in section 3.3.2, the Court of Appeal rejected that argument. It was pointed out, however, that, in some circumstances, a party with a contractual licence can acquire a right against C as a result of a promise made by C to A.

Fox LJ

At 25–6

It is said that when a person sells land and stipulates that the sale should be 'subject to' a contractual licence, the court will impose a constructive trust upon the purchaser to give effect to the licence [. . .]

We do not feel able to accept that as a general proposition. We agree with the observations of Dillon J. in *Lyus v. Prowsa Developments Ltd* [1982] 1 W.L.R. 1044, 1051:

> 'By contrast, there are many cases in which land is expressly conveyed subject to possible incumbrances when there is no thought at all of conferring any fresh rights on third parties who may be entitled to the benefit of the incumbrances. The land is expressed to be sold subject to incumbrances to satisfy the vendor's duty to disclose all possible incumbrances known to him, and to protect the vendor against any possible claim by the purchaser [. . .] So, for instance, land may be contracted to be sold and may be expressed to be conveyed subject to the restrictive covenants contained in a conveyance some 60 or 90 years old. No one would suggest that by accepting such a form of contract or conveyance a purchaser is assuming a new liability in favour of third parties to observe the covenants if there was for any reason

Trusts Arising on Receipt of Property *Sub Conditione*' (2004) 120 LQR 667. As we will see in Chapter 11, however, the principle applying in such cases is itself a matter of debate.

> before the contract or conveyance no one who could make out a title as against the purchaser to the benefit of the covenants.'

> The court will not impose a constructive trust unless it is satisfied that the conscience of the estate owner is affected. The mere fact that that land is expressed to be conveyed 'subject to' a contract does not necessarily imply that the grantee is to be under an obligation, not otherwise existing, to give effect to the provisions of the contract. The fact that the conveyance is expressed to be subject to the contract may often, for the reasons indicated by Dillon J., be at least as consistent with an intention merely to protect the grantor against claims by the grantee as an intention to impose an obligation on the grantee. The words 'subject to' will, of course, impose notice. But notice is not enough to impose on somebody an obligation to give effect to a contract into which he did not enter. Thus, mere notice of a restrictive covenant is not enough to impose upon the estate owner an obligation or equity to give effect to it [. . .]

> [. . .] In matters relating to the title to land, certainty is of prime importance. We do not think it desirable that constructive trusts of land should be imposed in reliance on inferences from slender materials. In our opinion the available evidence in the present case is insufficient. The deputy judge, while he did not have to decide the matter, was not disposed to infer a constructive trust, and we agree with him.

> So far as [A and B's initial agreement] is concerned, it created either a lease or some form of licence. If it created a lease, there was no need to impose any obligation upon [C] [. . .] If, on the other hand, the agreement created some form of licence and [A] was insisting that [C] assume an obligation to give effect to [A and B's initial agreement], it seems to us highly unlikely that it would have relied upon such vague words as 'subject to' without the addition of an express obligation. Thus, if [A] was concerned about the possibility of claims against either [A's predecessor] or itself, we would have expected a clearly expressed obligation imposed on [C] [. . .] [but] we see no indication in the 1973 agreement that [A] was concerned with the protection of [B] [. . .]

> In general, we should emphasise that it is important not to lose sight of the question: 'Whose conscience are we considering?' It is [C's], and the issue is whether [C] has acted in such a way that, as a matter of justice, a trust must be imposed. For the reasons which we have indicated, we are not satisfied that it should be.

This discussion makes the important point that B will not acquire a direct right against C *simply* because C acquires his land 'subject to' any rights that B may have against A. The key point of C's promise must be to give B a right against C, not to protect A from a claim by C.

The provisions of the 1999 Act make the same distinction: under s 1, B acquires a right against C only if C's promise to A 'purports to confer a benefit' on B. So, the crucial question is whether C, when acquiring his land, made an express or implied promise to give B a *new* right.

Sir Christopher Slade summed up the crucial question when giving the judgment of the Court of Appeal in the following case.[55]

---

[55] See also *Chaudhary v Yavuz* [2013] Ch 249, where the Court of Appeal confirmed that a term in the contract of sale between A and C, stating that the property is sold subject to incumbrances 'discoverable by inspection of the property before the contract' did not, in itself, suffice to show that C had undertaken a new obligation to give effect to any such discoverable right of B.

Lloyd v Dugdale
[2001] EWCA Civ 1754, [2002] 2 P & CR 13

Sir Christopher Slade

At [52]

In deciding whether or not the conscience of the new estate owner is affected in such circumstances, the crucially important question is whether he has undertaken a new obligation, not otherwise existing, to give effect to the relevant incumbrance or prior interest. If, but only if, he has undertaken such a new obligation will a constructive trust be imposed.

There are two key questions about this principle. The first is whether it makes sense for B to acquire a direct right against C in these cases. We will consider that question in more detail in Chapter 11, sections 5 and 6 when looking at other cases that involve C acquiring land after making a promise relating to that land. Here, it is perhaps enough to note an argument made by Bright.

Bright, 'The Third Party's Conscience in Land Law' [2000] Conv 398, 417

There are situations in which [B] ought, as a minimum, to be able to prevent [C] from suing in breach of the promise made to A. To allow [C] to succeed would effectively mean that the courts are sanctioning [C] to do the very thing that he promised not to do. This does not seem proper, nor does it seem just.

The second key question is whether it makes sense for B to acquire a right against C *under a constructive trust*. It was assumed by Lord Denning MR in *Binions* itself, and by the Court of Appeal in *Ashburn Anstalt v Arnold*, that, if the principle applies, B's right arises under such a trust. We will examine constructive trusts in more detail in Chapter 11, sections 4–6. As we saw in Chapter 6, sections 1 and 3, to say that C holds 'on trust' for B means that C (the trustee) has a right (the trust property or subject matter of the trust) and is under a duty to use that right for the benefit of B (or for B and others—that is, for the beneficiaries), as well as a duty not to use that right for C's own benefit.[56] In cases such as *Binions*, it is very difficult to see how the facts fit with that basic pattern.

Swadling, 'Property' in *English Private Law* (3rd edn, ed Burrows, 2013, [4.126])

[I]t is not clear what might have been the subject matter of this constructive trust [i.e. the constructive trust in *Binions*]. The subject matter can hardly have been the title to the cottage for, were that to be so, it would have given [B] far more than she was ever intended to have. And it could not have been the benefit of the licence either, for that was already

---

[56] It is possible for there to be trusts in which C, as well as being a trustee, is also a beneficiary of the trust. In such a case, C is permitted to use the trust property for his own benefit (to the extent that he is a beneficiary).

vested in her, and it was [C] who we are told [is] the trustee. It might be argued that the subject matter of the trust was the benefit of the covenant in the conveyance of the fee simple title under which [C] promised [A] that [it] would respect [B's] rights, and, further, that [C's] liability for breach of this covenant could be enforced by [B] by compelling [A] to sue on it. But this analysis does not work either, for the benefit of the promise was in the hands of [A], not [C].

Why, then, does Lord Denning MR describe B's right in *Binions* as arising under a constructive trust? One explanation is that, as is evident from the passage from *Binions* set out above, his Lordship relied on the decision of the Court of Appeal in *Bannister v Bannister*.[57] In that case, C, when buying a freehold from A, had promised to hold that freehold *on trust* for A (only two parties were involved). So, when forcing C to keep that promise, the Court of Appeal found that C held his land on constructive trust for A. It makes sense to say that a trust arose in that case: after all, the court simply enforced C's promise, and C's promise was to hold his freehold on trust. In *Binions*, however, C had *not* promised to hold any rights on trust; he had simply promised to allow B to remain in occupation of the land. So, as confirmed in the following extracts, there should be no trust in a case such as *Binions*.

Bright, 'The Third Party's Conscience in Land Law' [2000] Conv 398, 402

[T]he *Binions* [. . .] use of the constructive trust raises conceptual difficulties which do not occur with the true *Bannister* constructive trust. With trusts, the legal and equitable titles are owned by different persons, and the trustee owes fiduciary duties. This is the model found in *Bannister* [. . .] where [C] holds the legal title subject to a (proprietary) beneficial interest for [A]. But if we look at *Binions*, [C] held the ownership interest, which was not split between legal and equitable title, and what was held on trust was [B's] 'right to remain'.

McFarlane, 'Constructive Trusts Arising on a Receipt of Property Sub Conditione' (2004) 118 LQR 667, 691

[T]he fact that B can acquire a right against C will not always justify the imposition of a constructive trust. In cases where C's undertaking is to recognise that B has a beneficial interest in the property [. . .] then a constructive trust of the property will be appropriate [. . .] Where C's undertaking is to confer a personal right on B, then a constructive trust of the property C has received will not be appropriate, as it will give B a property right. Rather, B's personal right should be enforced directly.

On this analysis, we have to assess the nature of C's promise. If C promises to hold his freehold on trust, as in *Bannister*, it is appropriate for C to hold subject to a constructive trust and B thus acquires an equitable interest in C's land. If C instead simply promises to allow B to remain on the land, as in *Binions*, C comes under a duty to honour B's licence. In such a

---

[57] [1948] 2 All ER 133.

case, there is no need for a trust. After all, when A makes a promise to B to allow B to use A's land, there is no trust; there is simply a licence.

In a case such as *Binions*, the use of the 'constructive trust' label can cause confusion. In particular, it may be very important if C, having promised to honour B's licence, then transfers his land to C2.[58] It is then very important to know if the direct right that B acquired against C is a personal right or, instead, a legal or equitable property right. *If* C held the land subject to a constructive trust in B's favour, as *Binions* suggests, then B's direct right against C is an equitable property right and is therefore *prima facie* binding on C2. But the answer suggested by the extracts above is that, if C promised simply to honour B's licence, there should be no constructive trust. On that view, B will only be protected against C2 if he can show that he has a *second* direct right, arising because of *C2's* conduct.[59]

3.3.2 A pre-existing property right?

The starting point

We saw, in section 2.2, that a bare licence does not count as a property right—but does it make a difference if A is under a contractual duty to B not to revoke B's licence?

King v David Allen & Sons, Billposting Ltd
[1916] 2 AC 54, HL

Facts: Mr King owned land in Madras Place, Dublin.[60] He planned to build a cinema on the land and made a contractual promise to the David Allen & Sons billposting company allowing it to display posters on the wall of the cinema, when built. Mr King then gave a 40-year lease of the site to the Phibsboro' Picture House company. The cinema was completed in May 1914. In June 1924, David Allen & Sons (B) attempted to display its posters on its wall, but the Phibsboro' Picture House company (C) prevented B from doing so. B brought a claim for breach of contract against Mr King (A). A claimed that its action had caused B no loss, because B could simply assert its contractual licence against C. A decision in favour of B was affirmed by the Court of Appeal in Ireland. A appealed unsuccessfully to the House of Lords.

Lord Buckmaster LC

At 61

There is a contract between [A] and [B] which creates nothing but a personal obligation. It is a licence given for good and valuable consideration and to endure for a certain time [. . .] [T] he sole right is to fix bills against a flank wall, and it is unreasonable to attempt to construct the relationship of landlord and tenant or grantor and grantee of an easement out of such a transaction, and I find it difficult to see how it can be reasonably urged that anything beyond

---

58 Such a situation was inconclusively considered by the Court of Appeal in *Chattey v Farndale Holdings Inc* [1997] 1 EGLR 153.

59 For further discussion, see McFarlane, *The Structure of Property Law* (2008) pp 434–5.

60 Madras Place was the base of Antoni Rabaiotti, whose ice-cream car is mentioned in Joyce's *Ulysses* (1922) ch 10. Joyce himself was a driving force behind *The Volta*, Dublin's first permanent cinema, which opened in 1909 and closed in 1910.

personal rights was ever contemplated by the parties. Those rights have undoubtedly been taken away by the action on the part of [C], who has been enabled to prevent [B] from exercising [its] rights owing to the lease granted by [A], and [A] is accordingly liable in damages, although it was certainly not with his will, and indeed against his own express desire, that [C] has declined to honour his agreement.

Earl Loreburn

At 62

But we must look at the [agreement between A and B], and it seems to me that it does not create any interest in land at all; it merely amounts to a promise on the part of [A] that he would allow the other party to the contract to use the wall for advertising purposes, and there was an implied undertaking that he would not disable himself from carrying out his contract. Now [A] has altered his legal position in respect of his control of this land. Those to whom he granted the lease have disregarded his wishes and refused to allow his bargain to be carried out, and they have been practically enabled to do so by reason of the demise that he executed. In these circumstances it seems to me that there has been a breach in law of the contract of July 1, and [A] has disabled himself from giving effect to it as intended by parting with his right to present possession.

In *King*, the House of Lords thus made clear that the contractual licence is *not* on the list of property rights in land. As a result, the contractual licence given to B by A was *not* capable of binding C, a successor in title to A. Section 1 of the Law of Property Act 1925 sets out the list of legal property rights in land; the contractual licence is not included; as we saw in Chapter 6, section 5.3, s 4(1) of the Act appears to state that a court cannot add to the list of equitable interests in land recognized at the time of the 1925 Act. So, because the contractual licence was not recognized as an equitable property right in land before the passing of the 1925 Act, it seems clear that it cannot be recognized as such after that Act. This point is forcefully made by Briggs:[61] '*If contractual licences are to bind purchasers as proprietary interests, then they must be shown so to have existed in pre-1926 land law (and* King v David Allen *makes that impossible) or section 4 must be conjured out of existence.*'

Lord Denning's first attempt to change the position

This orthodox position continued to operate—it was, for example, confirmed by the Court of Appeal in *Clore v Theatrical Properties Ltd*[62]—until the judgment of Denning LJ in the following case.

Errington v Errington & Woods
[1952] 1 KB 290, CA

Facts: Mr Errington bought a house in Milvain Avenue, Newcastle, as a home for his son and daughter-in-law. Mr Errington paid £250 and the remaining £500 of the purchase price was financed by a mortgage loan. The mortgage instalments were paid by the son

---

[61] 'Contractual Licences: A Reply' [1983] Conv 285, 290–1.   [62] [1936] 3 All ER 483, CA.

and daughter-in-law, who occupied the land. Mr Errington (A) promised the son (B1) and daughter-in-law (B2) that they could remain in occupation as long as they paid the mortgage instalments. He also promised them that, when all of the instalments were paid, the land would be theirs. A died and B1 left the home, moving in with A's widow, his mother. B2 remained in occupation. A's widow sought possession of the house from B2. The county court judge dismissed that claim for possession. A's widow unsuccessfully appealed to the Court of Appeal.

Denning LJ

At 295

Ample content is given to the whole arrangement by holding that [A] promised that the house should belong to the couple as soon as they paid off the mortgage. The parties did not discuss what was to happen if the couple failed to pay the instalments to the building society, but I should have thought it clear that, if they did fail to pay the instalments, [A] would not be bound to transfer the house to them. [A's] promise was a unilateral contract—a promise of the house in return for their act of paying the instalments. It could not be revoked by him once the couple entered on performance of the act, but it would cease to bind him if they left it incomplete and unperformed, which they have not done. If that was the position during [A's] lifetime, so it must be after his death. If [B2] continues to pay all the building society instalments, [B1 and B2] will be entitled to have the property transferred to them as soon as the mortgage is paid off; but if [B2] does not do so, then the building society will claim the instalments from [A's] estate and the estate will have to pay them. I cannot think that in those circumstances [A's] estate would be bound to transfer the house to them, any more than the [A] himself would have been.

At 298–9

[I]t seems to me that, although the couple had exclusive possession of the house, there was clearly no relationship of landlord and tenant. They were not tenants at will but licensees. They had a mere personal privilege to remain there, with no right to assign or sub-let. They were, however, not bare licensees. They were licensees with a contractual right to remain. As such they have no right at law to remain, but only in equity, and equitable rights now prevail. I confess, however, that it has taken the courts some time to reach this position. At common law a licence was always revocable at will, notwithstanding a contract to the contrary: *Wood v Leadbitter*.[63] The remedy for a breach of the contract was only in damages. That was the view generally held until a few years ago [. . .] The rule has, however, been altered owing to the interposition of equity.

   Law and equity have been fused for nearly 80 years, and since 1948 it has been clear that, as a result of the fusion, a licensor will not be permitted to eject a licensee in breach of a contract to allow him to remain: see *Winter Garden Theatre v. Millennium Productions Ltd*,[64] *per* Lord Greene, and in the House of Lords *per* Lord Simon [. . .] This infusion of equity means that contractual licences now have a force and validity of their own and cannot be revoked in breach of the contract. Neither the licensor nor anyone who claims through him can disregard the contract except a purchaser for value without notice [. . .]

---

[63] (1845) 13 M & W 838.   [64] [1948] AC 173, [191].

The actual decision in *Errington* can be justified on a number of different grounds.[65] For example, A had made a contractual promise to transfer his land to B1 and B2. As we noted in Chapter 6, section 5.2, such a promise is acknowledged to give rise to an equitable property right, often known as an 'estate contract' (see Chapter 8, section 4.3 for more details). So there was no need for B2 to rely only on her contractual licence. Nonetheless, the reasoning of Denning LJ is important, because it constitutes one attempt to turn the contractual licence into an equitable property right. His Lordship's reasoning is based on the fact that a court will often protect B's contractual licence by ordering A not to revoke that licence in breach of his contract with B. Lord Denning assumes that B therefore has a right to use A's land for the duration of his contract, and so B has a right not only against A, but also in relation to A's land.

Whilst it has found some academic[66] and judicial[67] support, there is, however, a clear flaw in Denning LJ's argument.

McFarlane, 'Identifying Property Rights: A Reply to Mr Watt' [2003] Conv 473, 475

[Denning LJ's argument] misunderstands the true effect of the availability of specific performance on the proprietary status of a right: it treats something which is at most a *necessary* condition of a right to use property's being proprietary as a *sufficient* condition of that consequence. When deciding if specific performance is available against A, a court is simply deciding on the most appropriate remedy to give in response to B's clear contractual right against A. In so doing, the court will have to balance the various interests of A and B and will consider, for example, any practical difficulties which may prevent specific performance of the contract and the adequacy of damages as a means to protect B's interests. If, in general, specific performance is not granted in cases where B has a particular type of right to use property, that right is unlikely to be viewed as proprietary—if B's enjoyment of the property itself does not merit protection as against A, the party who made a contractual promise to B, then there seems to be little reason why B's right to use the property should be capable of enduring against C. However, the mere fact that specific performance is available against A does not prove that B's right *must* be proprietary. The question of whether to confer proprietary status on a right involves considerations additional to those addressed when deciding that specific performance is available against A. The needs of B must be balanced not just against those of A but also against those of actual and potential third parties. Most obviously, B must show why he should be protected as against a party who, unlike A, has made no contractual promise to him. Further, B's needs must be strong enough to overcome the disadvantages inherent in allowing the contract between A and B to impose a burden on the property and hence to restrict the ease of its transfer. This is not to say that no initially contractual right can ever gain proprietary status, but rather that the concerns to be addressed before allowing such a shift are additional to, and more serious than, those to be overcome before awarding B specific performance against his contractual partner. Hence, the mere fact that B can gain specific performance against A does not demonstrate that B's right has the proprietary status it needs to be protected from interference by C.

---

[65] As noted by Fox LJ in *Ashburn Anstalt v Arnold* [1989] Ch 1, 17.
[66] See Watt, 'The Proprietary Effect of a Chattel Lease' [2003] Conv 61.
[67] See *per* Browne-Wilkinson V-C in *Bristol Airport v Powdrill* [1990] Ch 744, [759].

Lord Wilberforce also pointed out this flaw in Denning LJ's argument.

National Provincial Bank v Ainsworth
[1965] AC 1175, HL

Lord Wilberforce

At 1253

[T]he fact that a contractual right can be specifically performed, or its breach prevented by injunction, does not mean that the right is any the less of a personal character or that a purchaser with notice is bound by it: what is relevant is the nature of the right, not the remedy which exists for its enforcement.

As we will see in Chapter 8, section 4.1 there is a principle (it can be called the 'doctrine of anticipation') that allows B to acquire an equitable interest in land if A is under a specifically enforceable contractual duty to give B a legal estate or interest in land. But that principle cannot apply if A's contractual duty is simply not to revoke a licence: in such a case, there is no eventual grant of a legal property right for equity to anticipate.[68] It is therefore no surprise that, in the following case, the Court of Appeal rejected B's attempt to rely on *Errington* in order to show that a contractual licence could bind a third party.

Ashburn Anstalt v Arnold
[1989] Ch 1, CA

Fox LJ

At 21–2

But there must be very real doubts whether *Errington* can be reconciled with the earlier decisions of the House of Lords in *Edwardes v. Barrington*[69] and *King v. David Allen and Sons (Billposting) Ltd.* It would seem that we must follow those cases or choose between the two lines of authority. It is not, however, necessary to consider those alternative courses in detail, since in our judgment the House of Lords cases, whether or not as a matter of strict precedent they conclude this question, state the correct principle which we should follow.

Our reasons for reaching this conclusion are based upon essentially the same reasons as those given by Russell L.J. in the *Hastings Car Mart* case[70] and by Professor Wade in the article, 'Licences and Third Parties'[71] to which Russell L.J. refers. Before *Errington* the law appears to have been clear and well understood. It rested on an important and intelligible distinction between contractual obligations which gave rise to no estate or interest in the

---

68 This point is also made by Wade (1952) 68 LQR 337, 338–9, and Swadling, 'Property' in *English Private Law* (3rd edn, ed Burrows, 2013), [4.33].

69 (1901) 85 LT 650.

70 The name given to *NPB v Ainsworth* in the Court of Appeal: [1964] Ch 665, [697].

71 (1952) 68 LQR 337.

land and proprietary rights which, by definition, did. The far-reaching statement of principle in *Errington* was not supported by authority, not necessary for the decision of the case and *per incuriam* in the sense that it was made without reference to authorities which, if they would not have compelled, would surely have persuaded the court to adopt a different ratio. Of course, the law must be free to develop. But as a response to problems which had arisen, the *Errington* rule (without more) was neither practically necessary nor theoretically convincing.

Denning LJ's bold reasoning in *Errington* is therefore not an accurate reflection of the current law.

Lord Denning's second attempt to change the position

Lord Denning later adopted a different technique for reaching his desired conclusion that a contractual licence can count as a property right. That technique built on the idea in *Binions v Evans*[72] that a constructive trust can be used to protect a party with a contractual licence.

DHN Food Distributors Ltd v London Borough of Tower Hamlets
[1976] 3 All ER 462, CA

Facts: Bronze Ltd, a wholly owned subsidiary company of DHN Food Distributors Ltd, owned a warehouse and cash-and-carry in Malmesbury Road, Bow, London. DHN (B) ran its fruit distribution business from the premises; it occupied the land under a contractual agreement with Bronze (A). The Tower Hamlets London Borough Council made a compulsory purchase order relating to the land; it planned to demolish the warehouse and build housing. The council paid A for the land. The council argued that it had no statutory duty to pay A compensation for disturbance of its business, because A was not carrying out any business on the land. B was carrying out a business, but the relevant statute stated that B qualified for compensation for disturbance only if it had an 'interest' in the land. The council argued that B had no such right, because it simply had a contractual licence, and so had no legal or equitable interest in the land. The Lands Tribunal accepted the council's argument. B (along with a third associated company in the same position as B) successfully appealed to the Court of Appeal.

Lord Denning MR

At 466–7

The directors of [A] could not turn out themselves as directors of [B] [. . .] In the circumstances, I think the licence was virtually an irrevocable licence. [B was] the parent company holding all the shares in [A]. In those circumstances, [B was] in a position to carry on their business on these premises unless and until, in their own interests, B no longer wished to continue to stay there. It was equivalent to a contract between the two companies whereby A granted an irrevocable licence to B to carry on [its] business on the premises. In this situation counsel for the claimants cited to us *Binions v Evans*, to which I would add *Bannister*

---

[72] [1972] Ch 359.

v Bannister and *Siew Soon Wah alias Siew Pooi Tong v Yong Tong Hong* [1973] AC 836.
Those cases show that a contractual licence (under which a person has the right to occupy
premises indefinitely) gives rise to a constructive trust, under which the legal owner is not
allowed to turn out the licensee. So here. This irrevocable licence gave to [B] a sufficient
interest in the land to qualify them for compensation for disturbance.

The decision in *DHN*, like that in *Errington*, can be justified on other grounds. For example,
both Goff and Shaw LJJ found that, as a result of various transactions between A and B,
A held its right to the land on trust for B. B therefore had a recognized equitable interest and
could claim compensation on that basis. Further, it can be argued that the term 'interest',
when used in a statute setting rules for compensation for disturbance caused by a compulsory purchase order, is not necessarily confined to legal or equitable property rights in
land.[73] Moreover, it could even be argued that, when interpreting such a statute, a court can
'pierce the corporate veil' and treat constituent companies within a group, such as Bronze
Ltd and DHN Ltd, as one entity.

Lord Denning's specific reasoning in *DHN*, like that in *Errington*, is, however, impossible to defend. His Lordship's argument is that, *as soon as* A comes under a duty to B not
to revoke B's licence, a constructive trust arises in B's favour. This means that, if A were
later to transfer his freehold to C, C would *prima facie* be bound by B's licence.[74] *Bannister v
Bannister* and *Binions v Evans* are cited in favour of that proposition—but the constructive
trusts in those cases did *not* arise as soon as A made a contractual promise to B; rather, the
constructive trusts arose as a result of *C's* later promise to A, made when acquiring his right
from A.

Certainly, in the following case, the Court or Appeal rejected the *DHN* analysis.

Ashburn Anstalt v Arnold
[1989] Ch 1, CA

Fox LJ

At 24

For the reasons which we have already indicated, we prefer the line of authorities which
determine that a contractual licence does not create a property interest. We do not
think that the argument is assisted by the bare assertion that the interest arises under a
constructive trust.

It is clear, then, that Lord Denning MR in *DHN* used the constructive trust not as a
means for B to acquire a new, direct right against C, but rather as a vehicle to turn
all contractual licences into immediate equitable property rights. That approach, of
course, is illegitimate as a matter of precedent: the House of Lords in *King v David Allen*

---

73 See *Pennine Raceways Ltd v Kirklees MBC* [1983] QB 382.
74 Of course, *DHN v Tower Hamlets* itself did not involve a third party. In *Re Sharpe* [1980] 1 WLR 219,
however, Browne-Wilkinson J (somewhat reluctantly) applied the reasoning in *DHN* to allow a licence between A and B to bind C, A's trustee in bankruptcy.

and *National Provincial Bank v Ainsworth* had already made clear that a contractual licence does *not* count as an equitable interest in land. Parliament may be able to change the law and turn a contractual licence into an equitable interest, but Lord Denning MR had no power to do so.

It is, therefore, clear that a contractual licence given by A to B is not *prima facie* binding on C, a party who later acquires A's land.[75] The interesting question is, of course, whether Parliament *should* make a change to that position. Before looking at that question, we need briefly to consider an argument that Parliament may already (and inadvertently) have allowed a contractual licence to bind a third party.

The impact of the Land Registration Act 2002, s 116

Land Registration Act 2002, s 116

It is hereby declared for the avoidance of doubt that, in relation to registered land, each of the following:

(a) an equity by estoppel, and

(b) a mere equity

has effect from the time the equity arises as an interest capable of binding successors in title (subject to the rules about the effect of dispositions on priority).

If B has a contractual licence, B may try to argue that he or she has a 'mere equity' and thus that, under s 116(b), that right is capable of binding C. Certainly, B has an 'equity' in the sense that, as we saw in section 3.1.2, a court may well protect B's contract with A through the equitable remedies of specific performance or an injunction. It is clear, however, that, when proposing the clause that became s 116(b), the Law Commission did not intend to change the status of a contractual licence.[76] Instead, the term 'mere equity', as discussed in Chapter 6, section 5.2, is intended to refer to situations in which B has a power to obtain an equitable property right by, for example, having a document rectified or setting aside a transfer of a right to A.[77] Certainly, it would be very odd if a section of the Land Registration Act 2002 (LRA 2002)—an Act primarily intended to protect a third party acquiring a right in registered land—were to *increase* the burdens on such a third party by allowing a contractual licence to function as an equitable interest.

Future reform?

It is thus clear that, as the law stands, a contractual licence does *not* count as a property right. A number of arguments have, however, been made in favour of changing the law.

---

[75] This point was conceded by B in *London Development Agency v Nidai* [2009] EWHC 1730 (Ch) at [11].

[76] See Law Com No 271, [5.32]–[5.37].

[77] For further discussion of mere equities, see McFarlane, *The Structure of Property Law* (2008) pp 226–7; *Snell's Equity* (33rd edn, eds McGhee et al., 2015), [2–006]; Cooper and Lees, 'Interests, Powers and Mere Equities in Modern Land Law' (2017) 37 OJLS 435.

European Convention on Human Rights, Art 8

(1) Everyone has the right to respect for his private and family life, his home and his correspondence.

(2) There shall be no interference by a public authority with the exercise of this right except such as is in accordance with the law and is necessary in a democratic society in the interests of national security, public safety or the economic well-being of the country, for the prevention of disorder or crime, for the protection of health or morals, or for the protection of the rights and freedoms of others.

In some cases, B's only right to his 'home' may come from a contractual licence with A. B may then argue that if C, a party to whom A has sold his land, is able to remove B from the land, B's right to respect for his home is interfered with.[78]

In Chapter 4, we looked in detail at how such human rights arguments can have an impact in land law. In particular, we saw that, following the decision of the Supreme Court in *McDonald v McDonald*,[79] it is unlikely that such an argument can, by itself, assist B in a case that purely involves private parties with no connection to the state. Two further points are particularly worth noting here. First, we need to consider the approach adopted by the Supreme Court in *Manchester CC v Pinnock*[80] and *Hounslow LBC v Powell*,[81] and discussed in Chapter 4, section 4.2.1. In the presumably rare case where C is a public authority and attempts to evict B, who occupied land as his or her home under a contractual licence from A, there must be a means for B to question the proportionality of C's decision to evict B. As noted by Lord Neuberger in *Pinnock*, the fact that C, under general principles of property law, is not bound by B's contractual licence will be highly relevant to an assessment of proportionality: *'the fact that the authority is entitled to possession and should, in the absence of cogent evidence to the contrary, be assumed to be acting in accordance with its duties, will be a strong factor in support of the proportionality of making an order for possession . . . Unencumbered property rights, even where they are enjoyed by a public body such as a local authority, are of real weight when it comes to proportionality.'*[82] In assessing proportionality, it is also important to note that there are other forms of protection for B's right to his home. If C removes B from the land before the end of the period of B's contractual licence with A, B will be able to claim damages for breach of contract from A. This right to receive money provides B with some protection for his Art 8 right.[83] Further, the law also protects B by allowing B, in certain situations, to acquire a new, direct right against C (see section 3.3.1 above). And, even if C is allowed to remove B, the Protection from Eviction Act 1977 may ensure that C has to give B four weeks' notice before insisting that B move out.[84] Indeed, that

---

[78] As we saw in Chapter 4, section 4.1.1, particular land can count as B's home even if B has no recognized legal or equitable property right in relation to that land.

[79] [2016] UKSC 28, [2017] AC 273.   [80] [2011] 2 AC 104.   [81] [2011] 2 AC 186.

[82] [2011] 2 AC 104 at [53]–[54]. See also *Kay v Lambeth LBC* [2006] 2 AC 465.

[83] A contractual right, such as a contractual licence, can also count as a 'possession' for the purposes of Art 1 of the First Protocol to the ECHR: see Chapter 4, section 3. Clearly, B's right to peaceful enjoyment of that possession does not mean that B must be able to assert his contractual right against a third party such as C; instead, B must rely on his remedies against A, including a claim for damages for A's breach of contract.

[84] Section 5(1A) applies where B has a *'periodic licence to occupy premises as a dwelling'*—for example, where B pays A £50 a week to occupy A's land. Some contractual licences are excluded from the 1977 Act: see s 3A. The Act does not apply, for example, if the licence involves B sharing accommodation with A or a

Act provides strong protection for B: s 1(2) means that C commits a criminal offence if it attempts to remove B without giving the requisite notice.[85]

Secondly, it is important to note that the approach adopted in *Pinnock* and *Powell* shows that Art 8 can be acknowledged to have some impact even if a contractual licence to occupy a home is not to be regarded as a new type of interest in land. If such licences were given such status, then they would always be *prima facie* binding on C, even if C were not a public body. The current approach seems to be a more nuanced and direct way of giving effect to the human rights concerns. Moreover, as we will see in the next section, if B occupies under a contract that gives B a right to exclusive possession of the land for a set period then, even if B's right is described in the contract as a licence, it is almost certain to be a lease, and so will in any case count as a property right.[86]

Contractual licences and exclusive possession

In the following extract, Maudsley draws a distinction between contractual licences that give B a right to exclusive possession of A's land, and other contractual licences. He argues that the former, but not the latter, should count as equitable property rights in land.

Maudsley, 'Licences to Remain on Land (Other than a Wife's Licence)'
(1956) 20 Conv 281

At 285

For, while it is consistent with principle, authority and policy to protect licensees in certain cases where they have exclusive possession of land, the protection of contractual licensees having something less than exclusive possession would cause far more problems than it would solve. For it would mean that every lodger would be entitled to remain in his room after a sale to anyone except a purchaser of the legal estate for value without notice;[87] and this would have a serious effect on land sales.

At 288–9

In most cases, of course, in which one party goes into possession of land in consideration of payment to the owner, he will be a tenant; but that is not invariably the case [. . .]

The present practice of holding certain persons who are in exclusive possession to be licensees and not tenants is of importance only in the opposite type of case, where the object is to help the landlord; the result of it is that in certain cases where the landlord, who would be unable to evict a tenant because of the tenant's statutory protection (by the Rent

---

member of A's family, or if, immediately before giving B the licence, A occupied the land as his only or principal home.

[85] C does not commit the offence if he deprives B of occupation whilst reasonably believing that B had, in any case, moved out: see s 1(2). Under the Criminal Law Act 1977, s 6, it is also a criminal offence to use or threaten violence in an attempt to gain possession of residential premises occupied by B.

[86] See *Street v Mountford* [1985] AC 809, discussed in Chapter 19, sections 1.2.1 and 2.1.

[87] [Note that the reference here to the 'bona fide purchaser' defence is now outdated. In registered land, a registered purchaser for value is protected against a pre-existing equitable interest unless: (i) that interest is protected by a notice on the register; or (ii) the holder of the interest is in actual occupation of the land at the relevant time—see Chapter 3, section 3.2.3, and Chapter 16, sections 2-4.]

Acts[88] or the Limitation Acts)[89] is able to do so if the court can be persuaded that the party in occupation is not a tenant but only a licensee [. . .] It is submitted therefore that cases in which one party goes into exclusive possession in consideration of making periodic payments to the owners will be held to create tenancies unless the court, in order to deprive an undeserving tenant of the statutory protection, can do justice between the parties by construing the tenancy, according to the intentions of the parties, as a licence.

Maudsley's argument is important, because it reveals the context in which Lord Denning made his attempts (in cases such as *Errington v Errington*[90] and *DHN v Tower Hamlets*)[91] to establish a contractual licence as an equitable property right. As we will see in Chapter 19, section 2, the standard position today is that if the contract between A and B gives B a right, for a limited period, to exclusive possession of A's land, B has a lease. A lease counts as property right and B therefore has a right that is capable of binding C.

But from the 1950s until the mid-1980s, the Court of Appeal, again led by Lord Denning, adopted a much narrower definition of a lease. Under that definition, A could give B a right to exclusive possession of A's land for a fixed period and still deny B a lease: A simply needed to make clear that he did not intend to give B a 'stake in the land'. As Lord Denning MR put it in *Errington v Errington & Woods*:[92] '*The result of all these cases is that, although a person who is let into exclusive possession is, prima facie, to be considered to be a tenant, nevertheless he will not be held to be so if the circumstances negative any intention to create a tenancy.*'

The chief reason for this narrow definition of a lease, it seems, was to allow A to avoid the statutes that gave extra rights to a party with a lease:[93] for example, if he had a lease, B might gain a statutory right to remain in occupation of A's land even after the end of the agreed contractual period (we will consider the question of statutory protection for residential tenants in Chapter 20). But the courts' narrow definition of a lease meant that, in some cases in which B would nowadays be regarded as having a lease—that is, where B had a contractual right to exclusive possession of A's land for a limited period—B was instead regarded as having only a contractual licence. Maudsley's argument recognizes that, in such cases, B should have a property right. The law *has* now adopted that argument—but by recognizing that, in such cases, B has a lease.[94] This means that much of the pressure for allowing contractual licences to count as property rights has now disappeared.

An analogy with the development of restrictive covenants?

In the following article, Cheshire discusses and defends the reasoning of Denning LJ in *Errington v Errington*.

Cheshire, 'A New Equitable Interest in Land' (1953) 16 MLR 1, 9

[I]s the equity to specific performance enforceable against the successor in title to the licensor? Does the licensee acquire a proprietary, not a merely contractual right? [. . .] At

---

88 *Marcroft Wagons v Smith* [1951] 2 KB 496; *Murray Bull & Co v Murray* [1953] 1 QB 211.
89 *Cobb v Lane* [1952] 1 All ER 1199.   90 [1952] 1 KB 290.   91 [1976] 3 All ER 462.
92 [1952] KB 290, [298].   93 See *Marchant v Charters* [1977] 1 WLR 1181, [1185].
94 See *Street v Mountford* [1985] AC 809, discussed in Chapter 19, sections 1.2.1 and 2.1.

least one learned writer in the Law Quarterly Review, Mr HWR Wade, holds it to be unjustifiable on several counts. 'It is,' he says, 'revolutionary to hold that a contract for a licence, (not being a contract for sale or lease, or a restrictive covenant) can be enforced against a person not a party to it.'[95] Perhaps, however, it may be suggested with respect that the recent decisions illustrate a peaceful penetration, not a revolution. The doctrine of privity was penetrated by the common law courts themselves in *Spencer's Case*[96] and by the Court of Chancery in *Tulk v Moxhay*,[97] and there seems no reason that what was possible and beneficial in an earlier age should become outmoded by the mere passage of time.

Another criticism made by Mr Wade is that the list of equitable proprietary interests in land should be regarded as closed and that this invention of a new type will unsettle the law of real property for many years. Similar warnings have been uttered in the past, but they have failed to impede the living growth of English law. For example, in 1834, Lord Brougham, in holding that a covenant does not run with land at law and cannot be made to run with it in equity, adorned his judgment with the following homily:

'Great detriment would arise and much confusion of rights if parties were allowed to invent new modes of holding and enjoying real property, and to impress upon their lands and tenements a peculiar character which should follow them into all hands, no matter how remote.'[98]

Yet, only fourteen years later, *Tulk v Moxhay* invented the restrictive covenant, a new interest of remarkable virility that nobody then or since has regretted.

Although Cheshire takes issue with it, Wade's article was referred to with approval by the Court of Appeal in *Ashburn Anstalt v Arnold*.[99] And, as we saw when considering the decision in *Errington v Errington*, Wade is right to emphasize the difference between cases in which A makes a contractual promise to give B a recognized property right and those in which A simply promises to allow B to make a particular use of A's land. Cheshire's reply therefore focusses on the restrictive covenant: as we will see in Chapter 23, it is a recognized equitable property right that can arise as a result of a contractual promise by A to B, even though A's promise is *not* a promise give B, in the future, a property right.

The restrictive covenant is a very important point of comparison: it is the most recent example of the courts developing a new form of equitable property right in land. As Cheshire notes, it shows that the list of property rights *can* be added to. Two points are, however, worth noting. Firstly, the restrictive covenant was recognized as a property right *before* 1925 (see Chapter 6, section 5). In contrast, as we have seen, s 4 of the LPA 1925 now prevents the courts from developing the contractual licence as a new form of property right; any such change would have to come from Parliament.

Secondly, when the restrictive covenant was recognized as an equitable property right, the courts imposed important restrictions on precisely what type of promise by A to B could give rise to such a property right. Such restrictions would also have to be imposed by Parliament if it were to allow any contractual licences to count as property rights. Certainly, the debate is not as to whether *all* contractual licences should become property rights; rather, it is as to whether *particular sorts* of contractual licence should do so.

Thirdly, it is important to note *how* restrictive covenants came to be regarded as property rights. Cheshire cites *Tulk v Moxhay* as a key decision but that case, in fact, seems to have

---

[95] (1952) 68 LQR 337, 338–9.   [96] (1583) 5 Co Rep 16a.   [97] (1848) 2 Ph 774.
[98] *Keppell v Bailey* (1834) 2 My & K 517, 536.   [99] [1989] Ch 1, 22.

involved B acquiring a new, direct right against C.[100] This raises the question of whether a gradual extension of the circumstances in which B can acquire such a right could, over time, prompt Parliament to elevate some forms of contractual licence to the status of an equitable interest in land.

McFarlane, 'Identifying Property Rights: A Reply to Mr Watt' [2003] Conv 473

At 482

[The passage to proprietary status of restrictive covenants] depended on an initial recognition that a covenantee could be protected against a third party by means of a new, direct right. This can be seen from a consideration of *Tulk v Moxhay*. That decision did not in itself establish the proprietary status of a restrictive covenant, as is clear from Lord Cottenham L.C.'s judgment:

> 'the question is, not whether the covenant runs with the land, but whether a party shall be permitted to use the land in a manner inconsistent with the contract entered into by his vendor, and with notice of which he purchased.'

B's protection in *Tulk v Moxhay* therefore seems to depend on a new right which arises as a result of C's conduct in purchasing the property with notice of the covenant. However, from this starting point, the restrictive covenant began a journey which culminated in the acquisition of proprietary status.

At 485–6

[The] history [of restrictive covenants] demonstrates that a right is generally only allowed to become proprietary on certain terms. In *Tulk v Moxhay* itself, no distinction is made between positive and negative covenants; nor does it seem necessary for the covenantee to have land for the benefit of which the covenant was taken. As the judgment in that case focuses on the culpability of C's conduct, these requirements, relating to the nature of B's original right, may well seem out of place. However, as the analysis shifts and that original right comes to be regarded as proprietary, it is inevitable that the courts will consider such restrictions. For a recognition that a particular right is proprietary must be based on a decision that the right is, by its nature, sufficiently important to warrant protection even if the property to which it relates changes hands. Therefore it is scarcely surprising that the courts will think carefully about the precise nature of the right in question before allowing it to have proprietary status. For example, given the burdens which will be placed on C's property as a result, it may well make sense to restrict proprietary status to those rights that confer a compensating benefit on another piece of property. Further, the particular disadvantage of allowing a right to be proprietary, that it can bind third parties without their consent, may be thought too great when dealing with certain types of right, such as those that impose positive obligations. Hence it may be thought unlikely that English law will ever accept that *all* [. . .] licences of land have proprietary status. As a result, it can be concluded not only that a general category consisting of all [. . .] licences of land is currently absent from the list of property rights recognised by English law, but also that it may well always remain so.

---

[100] See, for example, (1848) 2 Ph 774 at 777–8 *per* Lord Cottenham LC: '*the question is, not whether the covenant runs with the land, but whether a party shall be permitted to use the land in a manner inconsistent with the contract entered into by his vendor, and with notice of which he purchased.*' See too *per* Browne-Wilkinson V-C in *Swiss Bank v Lloyds Bank* [1979] 1 Ch 548 at [571].

A final argument in favour of the proprietary status of contractual licences is made by Moriarty in the following extract. It rests on an unusual definition of a contractual licence.

Moriarty, 'Licences and Land Law: Legal Principles and Public Policies' (1984) 100 LQR 376

At 376

The device of the licence, it will be argued, is no more than a mechanism by which the law sanctions the informal creation of proprietary rights in land.

At 397

The point, then is that we have to make a distinction between two different kinds of rule in land law. There are, first, the substantive rules of the subject which govern and define what kinds of right the law will accept as having the potential to bind third parties, as property rights, in the first place. And then there are the procedural rules of the subject which, important as they are, merely regulate the method by which they are created. *King* [*v David Allen Ltd*] and *Clore* [*v Theatrical Properties Ltd*], it is suggested, authoritatively rule out the possibility of the contractual licence being used to subvert the former, and more fundamental, rules of the subject. But they leave untouched the use of the contractual licence as a means of supplementing the procedural rules for creation. It is in this latter context that the contractual licence is most commonly found; and it is in this latter context that the device shares so much in common with the estoppel licence. In such a context, therefore, there can be no objection to contractual licences binding third parties, unless it is an objection to all licences binding third parties.

The distinction made by Moriarty between the 'substantive' and 'procedural' rules of land law seems to match the distinction between the *content* question and the *acquisition* question. Moriarty's argument is thus slightly surprising. The issue that we are currently considering relates to the *content* question: should a particular type of right (a contractual licence) be regarded as an equitable interest in land? Yet Moriarty sees the issue as instead related to the *acquisition* question: given our list of equitable interests in land, by what means should B be able to acquire such a right? It is therefore important to note that Moriarty's argument does *not* involve reversing the results in cases such as *King v David Allen*[101] and *Clore v Theatrical Properties Ltd*;[102] rather, his argument is that, in a case such as *Errington v Errington*,[103] B2 had, in fact, acquired, through an informal means, a recognized equitable property right. That analysis seems to be correct: it was noted above that *Errington* could be analysed as a case in which, as a result of A's informal promise to transfer his land to them, B1 and B2 had acquired an estate contract. Crucially, then, Moriarty's analysis does *not* involve promoting the contractual licence to a property right; instead, it can be used to defend the status quo, by re-analysing some (but not all) contractual licence cases as cases in which, in fact, B acquired not only a licence, but also a recognized equitable property right.

In his article, Moriarty also draws a link between the contractual licence and the estoppel licence. He notes, firstly, that the courts have regularly held that an estoppel licence can bind

---

[101] [1916] 2 AC 54.   [102] [1936] 3 All ER 483.   [103] [1952] 1 KB 290.

a third party, and, secondly, that estoppel licences and contractual licences are very similar. We will consider estoppel licences, and their effect on third parties, in the next section.

4 ESTOPPEL LICENCES

An estoppel licence exists where B has a liberty to make some use of A's land *and* A is under a duty to B, arising as a result of the doctrine of proprietary estoppel. This means that—in some circumstances, at least—A is under a duty to B not to revoke B's licence. An estoppel licence is thus similar to a contractual licence. The key difference is the *source* of A's duty to B: in this case, the duty arises not because of a contract, but, instead, under the doctrine of proprietary estoppel. We will examine that doctrine in detail in Chapter 10. It allows B to acquire a right against A where B has reasonably relied on a commitment made by A to allow B a right relating to land, and B would, as a result of that reliance, suffer a detriment if A were wholly free to go back on the commitment. As the following extract demonstrates, the doctrine can thus impose a duty on A even if A has made no contractual bargain with B.

Inwards v Baker
[1965] 2 QB 29, CA

Facts: Mr Baker owned land at Dunsmore, near Wendover, in Buckinghamshire. In 1931, Mr Baker (A) invited his son, John (B), to build a bungalow on the land. B accepted the invitation. He moved into the bungalow and lived there in the belief that he could remain, if he wished, for the rest of his life. A died in 1951 and, under his will, made in 1922, his land passed to trustees who were to hold the land for the benefit of parties other than B. The trustees attempted to remove B from the land. The judge at the Aylesbury county court found in favour of the trustees, but B successfully appealed to the Court of Appeal.

Lord Denning MR

At 36–7

The trustees say that at the most [B] had a licence to be in the bungalow but that it had been revoked and he had no right to stay. The judge has held in their favour. He was referred to *Errington v. Errington and Woods,* but the judge held that that decision only protected a contractual licensee. He thought that, in order to be protected, the licensee must have a contract or promise by which he is entitled to be there. The judge said:

'I can find no promise made by the father to the son that he should remain in the property at all—no contractual arrangement between them. True the father said that the son could live in the property, expressly or impliedly, but there is no evidence that this was arrived at as the result of a contract or promise—merely an arrangement made casually because of the relationship which existed and knowledge that the son wished to erect a bungalow for residence.'

Thereupon, the judge, with much reluctance, thought the case was not within *Errington's* case, and said the son must go.

The son appeals to this court. We have had the advantage of cases which were not cited to the county court judge[104] [. . .] It is quite plain from those authorities that if the owner of land requests another, or indeed allows another, to expend money on the land under an expectation created or encouraged by the landlord that he will be able to remain there, that raises an equity in the licensee such as to entitle him to stay. He has a licence coupled with an equity.

So in this case, even though there is no binding contract to grant any particular interest to the licensee, nevertheless the court can look at the circumstances and see whether there is an equity arising out of the expenditure of money. All that is necessary is that the licensee should, at the request or with the encouragement of the landlord, have spent the money in the expectation of being allowed to stay there. If so, the court will not allow that expectation to be defeated where it would be inequitable so to do. In this case it is quite plain that the father allowed an expectation to be created in the son's mind that this bungalow was to be his home. It was to be his home for his life or, at all events, his home as long as he wished it to remain his home. It seems to me, in the light of that equity, that the father could not in 1932 have turned to his son and said: 'You are to go. It is my land and my house.' Nor could he at any time thereafter so long as the son wanted it as his home.

4.1 B'S RIGHTS AGAINST A

The nature of B's rights against A depends on the nature of A's duty to B. The key point is that the doctrine of proprietary estoppel may have a number of different effects. For example, in *Jennings v Rice*,[105] B had been staying for a number of nights each week on A's land, in order to care for A. A had promised B that she would leave her land to B in her will; A did not do so. The Court of Appeal confirmed the finding of the trial judge: the doctrine of proprietary estoppel imposed a duty on A (and now on A's estate) to pay B £200,000. In that case, it seems, A was *not* under a duty not to revoke B's licence: A would have been able to remove B from the land. As a result of failing to honour her promise to leave her land to B, however, A was instead under a duty to pay B a sum of money.

In some cases, the doctrine of proprietary estoppel may impose a duty on A not to revoke B's licence. For example, in the passage from *Inwards v Baker* quoted above, Lord Denning MR confirms that, at least once B had built and moved into his bungalow, A was under a duty not to remove B from the land. In such a case, it seems, the discussion set out in section 3.1 above will apply: firstly, in general, a court will specifically enforce, by means of an injunction, A's duty not to revoke B's licence; secondly, for as long as A's duty lasts and B remains on A's land, B will not become a trespasser, even if A attempts to revoke B's licence.

It might be thought that where A's duty not to revoke a licence arises under the equitable doctrine of proprietary estoppel, B's right to remain on the land is dependent on factors such as B's behaviour and is thus more fragile than in a case in which B has a contractual licence. As the following extract shows, however, that does not seem to be the case.

---

[104] [The cases mentioned are classic proprietary estoppel cases: *Dillwyn v Llewellyn* (1862) 4 De G F & J 517; *Plimmer v Wellington Corpn* (1884) 9 App Cas 699 (PC); *Ramsden v Dyson* (1866) LR 1 HL 129.]
[105] [2003] 1 P & CR 100.

Williams v Staite
[1979] Ch 291, CA

Facts: Mrs Moore (A) owned two neighbouring cottages in Llangibby, Gwent. Her daughter married Mr Staite. A then invited the Staites to move into one of the cottages. A promised them that they could remain in that cottage for as long as they wished. Mr Staite lived in a cottage provided with his job, but, following A's promise, he gave up that accommodation to move into A's cottage. After moving in, the Staites spent money improving the cottage; they also cared for A and her husband, who lived next door. A died and her land was eventually sold to C. C then attempted to remove the Staites (B1 and B2) from the cottage. The judge found in favour of B1 and B2, holding that their licence was binding on C. C did not appeal against that finding—but C later claimed that, due to the bad behaviour of B1 and B2, he was entitled to remove them from the cottage. The judge in the Pontypool and Abergavenny county court found in C's favour. B1 and B2 then successfully appealed to the Court of Appeal.

Lord Denning MR

At 297–8

[B1 and B2] had an equitable licence under which they were entitled to live in [the cottage] for their lives or for as long as they wished it to be their home. It may in some circumstances be revoked, but I do not think it can be revoked in such circumstances as are found in the present case. I know that the judge took a poor view of the conduct of [B1 and B2]—and I am not sure he was altogether fair to them—[. . .] but to my mind their conduct, however reprehensible, was not such as to justify revocation of their licence to occupy the cottage as their home.

Goff LJ

At 300

Excessive user or bad behaviour towards the legal owner cannot bring the equity to an end or forfeit it. It may give rise to an action for damages for trespass or nuisance or to injunctions to restrain such behaviour, but I see no ground on which the equity, once established, can be forfeited. Of course, the court might have held, and might hold in any proper case, that the equity is in its nature for a limited period only or determinable upon a condition certain. In such a case the court must then see whether, in the events which have happened, it has determined or it has expired or been determined by the happening of that condition.

It is important to note that C did not appeal against the initial holding that the estoppel licence of B1 and B2 was capable of binding C. We will consider that question in detail in section 4.3 below.

4.2 B'S RIGHTS AGAINST X

If the doctrine of proprietary estoppel simply imposes a duty on A not to revoke B's licence, B's position against X should be exactly the same as if he had a contractual licence. In such a case, the discussion in section 3.2 above should apply.

4.3 B'S RIGHTS AGAINST C

4.3.1 Direct rights

The discussion of direct rights in section 3.3.1 above applies equally where B has an estoppel licence. Certainly, if the doctrine of proprietary estoppel imposes a duty on A not to revoke B's licence, A will have the same incentive, when transferring his land to C, to ask C to promise to respect B's licence.

4.3.2 A pre-existing property right?

Inwards v Baker
[1965] 2 QB 29, CA

Facts: See above.

Lord Denning MR

At 37

[C's counsel] put the case of a purchaser. He suggested that the father could sell the land to a purchaser who could get the son out. But I think that any purchaser who took with notice would clearly be bound by the equity. So here, too, the present plaintiffs, the successors in title of the father, are clearly themselves bound by this equity. It is an equity well recognised in law. It arises from the expenditure of money by a person in actual occupation of land when he is led to believe that, as the result of that expenditure, he will be allowed to remain there. It is for the court to say in what way the equity can be satisfied. I am quite clear in this case it can be satisfied by holding that the defendant can remain there as long as he desires to as his home.

Lord Denning MR's view is thus that, on the facts of *Inwards v Baker*, B had a right that was capable of binding C. That conclusion seems correct. In a case such as *Inwards*, as Lord Denning noted, it would be inequitable for B's expectation of a home for life to be defeated. It can therefore be argued that the doctrine of proprietary estoppel imposed a duty on A to allow B to exclusive possession of the bungalow for B's life (at least). If that is correct, B has a recognized equitable property right: an equitable life interest arising under a trust. It can be argued that it is B's equitable interest, rather than any licence, that is capable of binding C.

A number of cases in which an estoppel licence is said to be capable of binding C can be explained in this way. For example, in *ER Ives Investment Ltd v High*,[106] A agreed that, in return for A being able to place foundations on part of B's land, B would have a right of way across A's land. The Court of Appeal held that B had a right that was capable of binding C, a later owner of A's land. There are a number of possible explanations for this decision.[107] One explanation is that B had a licence to use A's land *and* the doctrine of proprietary estoppel

---

[106] [1967] 2 QB 379.
[107] See Battersby [1995] MLR 637; Swadling, 'Property' in *English Private Law* (3rd edn, ed Burrows, 2013), [4.128].

imposed a duty on A to give B the promised right of way: an easement. On that view, A was under a duty to give B a recognized property right and so B acquired an equitable easement. It is that easement, rather than B's licence, that is capable of binding C.

There are, however, some cases in which the doctrine of proprietary estoppel has simply imposed a duty on A not to revoke B's licence. *Williams v Staite*,[108] discussed above, is one example. In that case, as we have seen, it had earlier been held, by the county court judge, that a pre-existing estoppel licence was binding on C. That assumption does seem to create an inconsistency with the law relating to contractual licences. A contractual licence, like the estoppel licence in *Williams v Staite*, consists of B having a liberty to use A's land and A's being under a duty to B not to revoke that liberty. As a number of commentators have suggested,[109] B's right should not be treated differently only because A's duty arises under proprietary estoppel rather than due to a contract.

On this view, either *both* estoppel licences and contractual licences can count as equitable property rights, or *neither* can. We saw in section 3.3.2 above that no contractual licences are currently viewed as equitable property rights. This means that no estoppel licences should be viewed as equitable property rights. But this does not mean that the assumption made in *Williams v Staite* was a surprising one: after all, *at the time*, the Court of Appeal, led by Lord Denning MR, regarded the contractual licence as an equitable property right. It is therefore no surprise that B's estoppel licence was also viewed as such a right. Now that it is clear that a contractual licence is *not* an equitable property right, however, the same must also be true of an estoppel licence.

The impact of the Land Registration Act 2002, s 116

Land Registration Act 2002, s 116

It is hereby declared for the avoidance of doubt that, in relation to registered land, each of the following:

(a) an equity by estoppel, and

(b) a mere equity

has effect from the time the equity arises as an interest capable of binding successors in title (subject to the rules about the effect of dispositions on priority).

We looked at the possible effect of s 116(b) of the LRA 2002 on contractual licences in section 3.3.2 above. It seems that s 116(a) may have an important effect on estoppel licences. As we will see in Chapter 10, section 4.3, an 'equity by estoppel' is said to arise *whenever* A is under a duty to B arising as a result of the doctrine of proprietary estoppel. The 'equity' is the right that B has in the period *after* the estoppel has arisen and *before* a court makes an order in B's favour. So, even in a case in which A's only duty is a duty not to revoke B's licence, B initially has an 'equity by estoppel'—and the effect of s 116(a), on its natural reading, is to allow that 'equity by estoppel' to be capable of binding C, and thus to function as an equitable property

---

[108] [1979] Ch 291.
[109] See Thompson [1983] Conv 57; Moriarty, 'Informal Transactions in Land: Estoppel and Registration' (1984) 100 LQR 376.

right. That result does seem to have been intended by the Law Commission, as can be seen in the report that led to the LRA 2002.[110] As the following extract points out, however, it also seems to lead to an inconsistency in the law.

McFarlane, 'Proprietary Estoppel and Third Parties After the Land Registration Act 2002' [2003] CLJ 661, 690

Although they view s.116(a) as solving one of the most persistent debates relating to estoppel, the Law Commission's interpretation of that section re-awakens another such debate which might have been thought settled. As a result of s.116(a), a licence arising through proprietary estoppel would operate differently to a contractual licence: the former could bind C, provided the land was transferred to him before a court order granting B the licence. It could be argued in such a case that it is not the licence itself which binds C, but rather the independent 'equity' that arose as a result of the estoppel before the licence was awarded by the court. Yet why does no such 'equity' arise in the case of a contractual licence: surely a contractual licensee also has the right to [go to court: see further Chapter 10, section 4.3]? Once again, unconvincing distinctions arise as a result of separating estoppel from other means of acquiring rights. Indeed, it seems that the position under s.116(a) could be even less satisfactory than that favoured by Lord Denning [. . .] at least his Lordship intended that contractual and estoppel licences should be treated consistently.

We will expand on this point in Chapter 10, section 4.3: it can be argued that s 116(a) should *not* be interpreted so as to mean that B acquires a right that is capable of binding C *whenever* the doctrine of proprietary estoppel imposes a duty on A to B. On that view, B's right should only be capable of binding C if, at the point when C acquired C's right in the land, B's proprietary estoppel claim would have been satisfied by ordering A to give B a recognized property right in the land. That would mean, of course, that if A would only have been ordered not to revoke a licence of B, then B's right, like a contractual licence, would not bind C. That view requires giving a limited interpretation to 'equity by estoppel', so that it does not extent to *all* proprietary estoppel claims. Under the interpretation intended by the Law Commission, however, 'equity by estoppel' does have that broad meaning, so the holder of an estoppel licence, at least in the period before a court order is made in his or her favour, has a right that is capable of binding C.[111]

5   STATUTORY LICENCES

We can use the term 'statutory licence' to refer to situations in which B has a liberty to make some use of A's land *and* A is under a statutory duty to B not to revoke B's licence. A statutory

---

[110] Law Commission Report No 271, *Land Registration for the Twenty-First Century* (2001), [5.29]–[5.32]. Note that, in *Preedy v Dunne* [2015] EWHC 2713 (Ch), Master Matthews suggested at [54] that a proprietary estoppel equity claimed by B would also be capable of binding a purchaser of the land from A, even though B's right was also described as a licence. Such a view is consistent with the Law Commission's intended interpretation of s 116(a).

[111] It is very unlikely that B will have protected his or her right by entering a notice on the register and so, if B is not in actual occupation of the registered land, C may well have be able to use the lack of registration defence to B's 'equity by estoppel': see Chapter 3, section 3.3.2, and Chapter 16, section 2.

licence is thus similar to a contractual licence or an estoppel licence. The key difference again is the *source* of A's duty to B. When considering the effect of a statutory licence on A, X, and C, it is difficult to set out general principles: the statute in question will generally specify the effect of B's right. In this section, we will consider, in outline only, one particularly important form of statutory licence: the licence of one spouse[112] to occupy land owned by another.[113]

Family Law Act 1996, s 30

(1) This section applies if—

   (a) one spouse is entitled to occupy a dwelling-house by virtue of

      (i) a beneficial estate or interest or contract; or

      (ii) any enactment giving that spouse the right to remain in occupation; and

   (b) the other spouse is not so entitled.

(2) Subject to the provisions of this Part, the spouse not so entitled has the following rights ("matrimonial home rights")—

   (a) if in occupation, a right not to be evicted or excluded from the dwelling-house or any part of it by the other spouse except with the leave of the court given by an order under s.33;

   (b) if not in occupation, a right with the leave of the court so given to enter into and occupy the dwelling-house.

5.1 B'S RIGHTS AGAINST A

The statutory predecessors of s 30 of the Family Law Act 1996 (FLA 1996) were, in part, a reaction to the House of Lords' decision in *National Provincial Bank v Ainsworth*[114] (see Chapter 1, section 5, and Chapter 6, section 5.3). In that case, Mrs Ainsworth's right to occupy the matrimonial home was said to depend on a 'deserted wife's equity'. This right, essentially improvised by the courts, arose only after Mr Ainsworth left the home. And it was of a very uncertain nature: in particular, it would not always be clear if the home-owning spouse (A) was under a duty to allow the non-owning spouse (B) to remain in occupation of the current home. Parliament intervened, first through the Matrimonial Homes Act 1967, in the hope of making B's position clearer and more secure (see Chapter 1, section 5.7).

Whilst B's basic right to occupy A's land is set out in s 30, s 33 gives a court wide powers to exclude or restrict B's right. Section 33(6) directs a court exercising those powers to take into account a number of factors, including: (i) the housing needs and resources of A and B, and of any 'relevant child'; (ii) the financial resources of A and B; (iii) the likely effect of any order on the health, safety, or well-being of A and B, and of any relevant child; and (iv) the conduct of A and B in relation to each other and otherwise. Under s 33(7), special rules apply

---

[112] The statutory licence arising under the Family Law Act 1996, s 30, now also applies to parties in a registered civil partnership: see Civil Partnership Act 2004, s 82 and Sch 9, para 1, amending the 1996 Act.

[113] We will also consider that right when looking specifically at rights in the family home in Chapter 12: see Chapter 12, section 3.

[114] [1965] AC 1175.

where there is a likelihood of one of the parties or a relevant child suffering '*significant harm attributable to conduct*' of the other party.

It is thus clear that, in order to balance the various needs of the spouses and any relevant children, the court has a wide discretion to exclude or restrict B's right against A.

5.2 B'S RIGHTS AGAINST X

The provisions of the FLA 1996 are not too important in regulating B's position against X. In *National Provincial Bank v Ainsworth* itself, Lord Upjohn noted that, if B is in sole occupation of A's land, strangers such as X are under a duty not to interfere with B's possession of that land.[115] As noted in section 2.2 above, B's right, in such a case, does not arise from any licence, but rather from the fact of B's physical control of the land.

5.3 B'S RIGHTS AGAINST C

5.3.1 Direct rights

Where B has a statutory licence under the FLA 1996, it is, of course, possible for B to acquire a direct right against C. Such a right can only arise, however, if C's conduct falls into one of the means, such as those examined in section 3.3.1 above, by which B can acquire a direct right against C.

5.3.2 A pre-existing property right?

Family Law Act 1996, s 31

(1) Subsections (2) and (3) apply if, at any time during a marriage, one spouse is entitled to occupy a dwelling-house by virtue of a beneficial estate or interest.

(2) The other spouse's matrimonial home rights are a charge on the estate or interest.

(3) The charge created by subsection (2) has the same priority as if it were an equitable interest created at whichever is the latest of the following dates—

    (a) the date on which the spouse so entitled acquires the estate or interest;

    (b) the date of the marriage; and

    (c) 1st January 1968 (the commencement date of the Matrimonial Homes Act 1967)
    [. . .]

(8) Even though a spouse's matrimonial home rights are a charge on an estate or interest in the dwelling-house, those rights are brought to an end by—

    (a) the death of the other spouse, or

    (b) the termination (otherwise than by death) of the marriage, unless the court directs under s.33(5)
    [. . .]

---

[115] [1965] AC 1175, 1232.

(10) If the title to the legal estate by virtue of which a spouse is entitled to occupy a dwelling-house [. . .] is registered under the Land Registration Act 2002 or any enactment replaced by that Act—

(a) registration of a land charge affecting the dwelling-house by virtue of this Part is to be effected by registering a notice under the Act; and

(b) a spouse's matrimonial home rights are not to be capable of falling within paragraph 2 of Schedule 1 or 3 of that Act.

In *National Provincial Bank v Ainsworth*, the House of Lords held that B's right to occupy A's land, arising under a 'deserted wife's equity', did *not* count as a property right in land and so was not capable of binding C. Section 31(2) of the FLA 1996 clearly adopts a different position: B's statutory right to occupy is capable of binding C.

It is important to note, however, that B's statutory right does not operate in quite the same way as a standard interest in land. For example, consider the case in which B has a standard equitable interest in relation to registered land. If B fails to protect that right by entering a notice on the register, then, as we have seen, it may be possible for C to use the lack of registration defence against it (see Chapter 3, section 3.2.3). But if B is in *actual occupation* of the registered land at the relevant time, C cannot use that lack of registration defence against B (see further Chapter 16, section 4.1).

In contrast, if B does not have a standard equitable interest, and instead has only a statutory right under s 30 of the FLA 1996, B's failure to protect that right by entering a notice on the register *prevents* B from asserting that right against C. B's actual occupation makes no difference: s 31(10) ensures that B's right remains subject to the lack of registration defence. This means that, in most cases,[116] B can only assert his or her right against C if, before C registers C's right, B protects his or her statutory right by entering a notice on the register.

6 LICENCES COUPLED WITH AN INTEREST

A licence coupled with an interest arises where B has a liberty to make some use of A's land *and* that liberty protects, or arises as part of, a property right held by B. It is very doubtful, however, that 'licences coupled with an interest' are a useful concept. After all, as we saw in section 1 above, the general definition of a licence excludes situations where B's liberty to use A's land arises as part of a property right held by B: for example, if B has a lease of A's land, it is true that B has permission to be on A's land, but B's rights as against A, X, and C do not depend on this licence. Where B has a 'licence coupled with an interest' then, as against A, we would expect B's position to depend on: (i) the terms of the contract between A and B, if any; and (ii) the nature of B's property right. As against X and C, we would expect B's position simply to depend on the nature of B's property right. This does, indeed, seem to be the case; it is therefore of little use to speak of B as *also* having a licence coupled to his property right. In fact, as we will see in section 6.1, the concept of a 'licence coupled with an interest' has chiefly been used by the courts as a way in which to develop the remedies available to B

---

[116] If C does not acquire his right for value, C cannot rely on B's failure to register as a defence to B's statutory right to occupy: the protection given to C by ss 29 and 30 of the Land Registration Act 2002 applies only if C acquires his right 'for valuable consideration'.

when he has a contractual licence, whilst at the same time *technically* respecting past (but outdated) decisions that limited those remedies.

6.1 B'S RIGHTS AGAINST A

James Jones & Sons Ltd v Earl of Tankerville
[1909] 2 Ch 440

Facts: The Earl of Tankerville (A) owned the Chillingham estate in Northumberland.[117] He made a contractual promise to James Jones & Sons Ltd (B) allowing them to come onto A's land, cut down timber on that land, set up a sawmill on A's land, and then remove the timber from A's land. A breached the agreement and forcibly removed B's employees from the land. B applied for an injunction to restrain A from acting in that way. Parker J granted the injunction.

Parker J

At 442

A contract for the sale of specific timber growing on the vendor's property, on the terms that such timber is cut and carried away by the purchaser, certainly confers on the purchaser a licence to enter and cut the timber sold, and, at any rate as soon as the purchaser has severed the timber, the legal property in the severed trees vests in him. A licence to enter a man's property is prima facie revocable, but is irrevocable even at law if coupled with or granted in aid of a legal interest conferred on the purchaser, and the interest so conferred may be a purely chattel interest or an interest in realty. If A sells to B felled timber lying on A's land on the terms that B may enter and carry it away, the licence conferred is an irrevocable licence coupled with and granted in aid of the legal property in the timber which the contract for sale confers on B: *Wood v. Manley*.[118] [. . .] Even, therefore, if no interest at law passes by a contract for the sale of specific growing timber to be cut by the purchaser, it is difficult to see why on principle equity should not restrain the vendor from revoking the licence conferred by such a contract, though it might be unable to compel the purchaser to cut the timber if he refused to do so. When once the purchaser has cut any part of the timber, the legal property in the timber so cut is certainly in the purchaser, and the licence so far as that timber is concerned is irrevocable even at law, and a Court of Equity in granting an injunction would only be restraining the violation of a legal right. An injunction restraining the revocation of the licence, when it is revocable at law, may in a sense be called relief by way of specific performance, but it is not specific performance in the sense of compelling the vendor to do anything. It merely prevents him from breaking his contract [. . .]

---

[117] Lord Grey succeeded to the estate in 1675 and was made Earl of Tankerville in 1695, and later Lord Privy Seal. He is said to have played a pivotal role in the passage of the Habeas Corpus Act 1679, by deliberately miscounting the number of Lords voting for the bill when acting as a teller in the House of Lords, the other teller supposedly being too drunk to notice (see WD Christie, *Life of the First Earl of Shaftesbury, vol ii* (1871) pp 335–6). I am grateful to Jamie Glister for bringing this fact to my attention. The estate, including Chillingham Castle, remained with the family until the death of the ninth Earl in 1980. The twelfth-century castle (claimed to be one of the most haunted places in Britain) is now open to the public. The estate remains home to a rare breed of white cattle, said to be the only wild cattle in the world.

[118] (1839) 11 Ad & E 34.

It is important to note the date of this judgment. When it was given, there was some doubt as to whether a court could order specific performance of a standard contractual licence: *Hurst v Picture Theatres Ltd*[119] (see section 3.1.2 above) had not yet been decided. It was therefore helpful for the judge to distinguish past cases[120] in which it had been assumed that a standard contractual licence could not be protected by specific performance, by saying that B had a 'licence coupled with an interest'.[121] Nowadays, as we saw in section 3.1.2 above, there is no such difficulty in ordering A to perform a contractual duty not to revoke B's licence. It seems, then, that, in a case such as *James Jones*, B's rights against A—as far as his liberty to use A's land is concerned—should be governed simply by A's contractual agreement with B and the principles discussed in section 3.1.2 above.

The concept of a 'licence coupled with an interest' may be more important in a case in which A is *not* under a contractual duty to B. For example, let us say that property belonging to B finds its way onto A's land. It may be that B's car is stolen and then parked on A's land. In such a case, A may refuse B permission to come onto A's land and retrieve the car.

There are two ways in which the law could respond. Firstly, it could be said that B has a 'licence coupled with an interest': B's ownership of the car imposes a duty on A *either* to deliver the car to B *or* to allow B to come onto the land to collect it. The question then would be whether a court would grant an order forcing A to comply with that duty, or would instead order A to pay damages to B.

Secondly, it could be said that, by refusing to allow B to collect the car, A is interfering with B's ownership of the car and so is committing a wrong: the tort of conversion.[122] If A commits such a tort, B can ask the court to order A to 'deliver up' the car to B,[123] but the court does not have to make such an order. In fact, the usual response of the court is to order A to pay B damages.

6.2 B'S RIGHTS AGAINST X

Where B has a licence coupled with an interest, B also has a property right. If X interferes with that property right, he commits a wrong against B. For example, in *James Jones*, if X were to trespass onto A's land and take away some of B's timber, X would commit the tort of conversion against B. It is also possible for B's licence to be coupled with a property right in A's land. For example, as we will see in Chapter 22, section 1.1, there is a particular form of property right in land, akin to an easement, known as a 'profit' or '*profit à prendre*'. It is a property right that allows B to come onto A's land and remove something that would otherwise be owned by A—for example, turf or trees growing on A's land. If B has such a right, X is under a duty not to interfere with B's right to come onto A's land and remove the thing in question. But X's duty does not arise because B has a licence; rather, it arises because B has a profit—that is, a property right in A's land. In *James Jones*, it is unclear whether B had such

---

[119] [1915] 1 KB 1.   [120] Such as *Wood v Leadbitter* (1845) 13 M & W 838.

[121] Indeed, in *Hurst* itself, the chief argument of Mr Hurst's counsel was that Mr Hurst, on buying the cinema ticket, had a licence coupled with an interest. And both judges in the majority, do refer to that argument at points in their judgments (see Buckley LJ, 5–6 and Kennedy LJ, 13–14).

[122] For a discussion of the requirements of the tort, see *Kuwait Airways v Iraqi Airways (Nos 4 & 5)* [2002] 2 AC 883. *Howard E Perry v British Railway Board* [1980] 1 WLR 1375 provides an example in which the defendant committed the tort of conversion simply by refusing to return goods, currently controlled by the defendant, to the claimant.

[123] See Torts (Interference with Goods) Act 1977, s 3.

a property right: it seems that, because A had not used a deed to give B his right, B could not claim a legal *profit à prendre*—but B may have had an equitable *profit à prendre*.

6.3 B'S RIGHTS AGAINST C

6.3.1 Direct rights

If, as in *James Jones*, A is under a contractual duty to allow B to make a particular use of A's land, the discussion of direct rights in section 3.3.1 above is applicable. Certainly, A will have the same incentive, when transferring his land to C, to ask C to promise to respect B's licence.

6.3.2 A pre-existing property right?

We have seen that, in general, the fact that A is under a duty not to revoke B's licence does *not*, by itself, give B a property right in A's land. But where B has a licence coupled with an interest, the interest is, in itself, a property right. So, if the interest is a property right in A's land, such as a *profit à prendre*, it is capable of binding C. If the interest is instead a property right in a thing on A's land, that property right is also capable of binding C, just as it is capable of binding X. So, if, in *James Jones*, A were to sell his land to C, the timber already cut down by B and stored on A's land would continue to belong to B. C would therefore commit the tort of conversion if he were to refuse to allow B to collect that timber.

> **QUESTIONS**
>
> 1. What is the key difference between a personal right and a property right? Is it true to say that, if B has a pre-existing property right, that right will always bind C; whereas if B has only a personal right, then B will never have a claim against C?
>
> 2. What is the key feature of a licence? Does Hohfeld's distinction between a 'privilege', or 'liberty' on the one hand and a 'claim right' on the other help in understanding the position of a licensee?
>
> 3. What are the different forms of licence? Given their variety, is it useful to think of licences as a single category?
>
> 4. In what circumstances might a court refuse to order specific performance of A's duty not to revoke B's contractual licence?
>
> 5. When can B rely on a 'constructive trust' to assert a right against C? Does such a constructive trust arise as soon as A gives B a contractual licence, or does it only arise at a later point?
>
> 6. Do you think that particular forms of contractual licence may one day be recognized as property rights?
>
> 7. Are cases in which 'estoppel licences' bind third parties in fact better seen as cases in which B has more than a licence, and instead has a recognized equitable interest, arising as a result of proprietary estoppel?

 For guidance on how to answer these questions visit the online resources at www.oup.com/uk/mcfarlane4e/.

FURTHER READING

Battersby, 'Informally Created Interests' in *Land Law: Themes and Perspectives* (eds Bright and Dewar, Oxford: OUP, 1998)

Bright, 'The Third Party's Conscience in Land Law' [2000] Conv 398

Hohfeld, 'Faulty Analysis in Easement and License Cases' (1917) Yale LJ 66

Lochery, 'Pushing the Boundaries of *Dutton*?' [2011] Conv 74

McFarlane, 'Identifying Property Rights: A Reply to Mr Watt' [2003] Conv 473

Moriarty, 'Licences and Land Law: Legal Principles and Public Policies' (1984) 100 LQR 376

Smith, 'The Economic Torts: Their Impact on Real Property' (1977) 41 Conv 318

Swadling, 'Property' in *English Private Law* (3rd edn, ed Burrows, Oxford: OUP, 2013, [4.114]–[4.128])

Wade, 'Licences and Third Parties' (1952) 68 LQR 337

PART C

THE ACQUISITION QUESTION

8 Formal Methods of Acquisition: Contracts, Deeds, and Registration 259

9 Adverse Possession 309

10 Proprietary Estoppel 359

11 Trusts 417

8

FORMAL METHODS OF ACQUISITION: CONTRACTS, DEEDS, AND REGISTRATION

CENTRAL ISSUES

1. The creation and transfer of legal rights is heavily regulated by statutory formality requirements. Land is more complex to deal with than other property—a position that is considered desirable because of the uniqueness of land.

2. Specific formality requirements must be met to enter a contract for sale or other disposition of an interest in land and to create or transfer legal rights. The creation and transfer of legal estates is generally subject to a further requirement of registration.

3. The requirements for a contract for sale or other disposition of land are provided in the Law of Property (Miscellaneous Provisions) Act 1989. The effect of non-compliance is that no contract exists, although devices of rectification and collateral contracts may be used to save invalid agreements.

4. In the absence of a contract, rights may also arise through the doctrine of proprietary estoppel. This is just one possible application of a much broader doctrine (which is discussed fully in Chapter 10) and its application in the context of a failed contract remains highly controversial.

5. The creation or transfer of legal rights generally requires a deed. In the absence of a deed, legal rights will not be created. Equitable rights may, however, be obtained through the doctrine of anticipation if the parties have entered a valid contract.

6. In registered land, the importance of registration when considering the acquisition question can be simply stated: in most cases, the formal transfer or creation of a legal estate or interest in land is only complete when registered. Registered land is now governed by the Land Registration Act 2002, which repealed and replaced the Land Registration Act 1925. The underlying objective of the Act was to facilitate the introduction of e-conveyancing, but work towards this has now been placed on hold.

1 INTRODUCTION

In Chapter 5 section 4, we saw that legal estates and interests in land can be acquired *dependently*, where they are granted by a person with property rights in land, and *independently*, by the unilateral conduct of the person acquiring the right. In most cases, dependent acquisition of a legal right requires compliance with statutory formality requirements.

In this chapter, we consider the formality requirements that must be complied with for the creation or transfer of legal estates and interests in land. We also consider the consequences where the parties do not comply with these requirements, and the possibility that, even if a party does not require the desired legal estate or interest in land, an equitable interest may instead arise. The statutory formality requirements are generally based on the need for the transaction to be in signed writing, usually witnessed, and sometimes require the written document to take the specific form of a deed. For the creation and transfer of legal estates (except for short leases), there is an overarching requirement of registration. In the introduction to this chapter, we will explore two issues: what are formality requirements and why do we have them in relation to land?

Critchley considers a legal definition of 'formality'.[1]

Critchley, 'Taking Formalities Seriously' in *Land Law: Themes and Perspectives* (eds Bright and Dewar, 1998, p 508)

One good starting point might be the common legal distinction between matters of 'substance' and 'form'. This suggests a definition of formality as something which is external or *added* to the transaction, rather than a constituent, substantive part of it. In legal usage, formality is generally also seen as a *requirement*, rather than a mere habit or convention, so it would be helpful for our definition to express the notion that formality is something mandatory. Further, it is typical (though not essential), where a legal formality is imposed, to have some sort of *sanction* for breach of the rule: some legal disbenefit, or some failure to obtain a legal benefit. The sanction is frequently the invalidation of a non-complying transaction, but there are other possibilities: for example, there might be procedural disadvantages (limiting the type of evidence which may be used to prove the transaction in legal proceedings); or the transaction might be valid as regards the original parties to it, but invalid against third parties. Whatever the sanction is, it would clearly also be useful to have a definition which would cover a formality rule with a sanction attached. Putting all of this together, then, we reach the following definition: 'in law, a formality is a requirement that matters of substance must be put into a particular form (in order to have a specified legal effect).'

The effect of formality requirements is undoubtedly that land is more complex to deal with than other forms of property. Why, then, are they considered desirable? Ultimately, it is for all of the reasons relating to the uniqueness of land that we have outlined in Chapter 1, section 4. This is reflected, too, in the following extract, in which Birks highlights the particular need for formality requirements in light of the nature of rights in land.

---

[1] See further Fuller, 'Consideration and Form' (1941) 41 CL Rev 799.

Birks, 'Before We Begin: Five Keys to Land Law' in *Land Law: Themes and Perspectives* (eds Bright and Dewar, 1998, p 483)

There is an extra reason [for formality requirements] too. It derives from the invisibility of real rights. Just as one cannot see a fee simple, so one cannot see an easement or a restrictive covenant. A neighbour's right to pass over a field does not reveal itself in a pink line, nor will even an infra-red camera disclose his right to restrict or forbid building. If one is buying a fee simple from a company, and a firm of solicitors is in daily occupation of the premises doing the business of soliciting, one might reasonably infer that the firm holds a lease. But still a lease is not visible, nor a pyramid of sub-leases. Real rights have to be made apparent through documents. Acquiring land would otherwise be a nightmare unless the law made really massive erosions of the principle of *nemo dat*.

In addition, however, formality requirements serve functional roles. Immediately prior to the comment extracted above, Birks acknowledges, for example, their role in encouraging people to think about the job in hand, and in preventing doubt and argument.

In making recommendations relating to one aspect of formality requirements (those concerning contracts for the sale of land), the Law Commission highlighted the practical functions served by the requirements in issue. These can fairly be carried over to all formality requirements.

Law Commission Report No 164, *Transfer of Land Formalities for Contracts for Sale etc of Land* (1987, [2.7]–[2.13])

One principal justification for perpetuating formalities for contracts dealing with land is the need for certainty. The existence and terms of oral contracts are always difficult to establish and the resulting confusion [. . .] would, we anticipate, lead to increased litigation. To minimise disputes, reliable uncontrovertible evidence of the existence and terms of a transaction needs to be available for later reference. In the light of this, the value of the evidential function of writing cannot be doubted.

The evidential function of writing is also valuable in assisting the prevention of fraud. The requirement goes some way to ensuring that parties are not bound in the absence of actual agreement. In fact, the prevention of fraud was the rationale of the original Act, the Statute of Frauds 1677 [. . .]

A related argument in favour of formalities for contracts for the sale of land is based upon consumer protection. Whilst it has been suggested that laymen appreciate the significance of entering into a contract for the sale of land, we still consider that some form of protection imposed from outside is necessary. The consumer should be warned about the gravity of the transaction into which he is about to enter. He needs time to reflect and, if necessary, to seek legal advice. This is especially important in the case of contracts dealing with land because they often involve acceptance of a complexity of rights and duties. A formal requirement of writing is, in our view, suited to this cautionary role. At least, it prevents a person from becoming bound without realizing it, since most people nowadays are aware that signature of a written document imports some binding effect. The need for consumer protection is particularly strong in the case of the sale or purchase of a dwelling, house or flat. The majority of people, at some time in their life, will enter into such a transaction, and it will involve them in major financial commitments and general upheaval. In such circumstances, it appears vital that a consumer takes all reasonable precautions and is fully protected [. . .]

The cautionary role of formalities is not confined to the consumer protection context. It is equally important for all types of contract dealing with land, whether in domestic or commercial conveyancing, because it prevents the parties from being bound inadvertently or prematurely. Without formalities, it may be difficult to ascertain the exact time when a contract is created, and this would lead to confusion. As a result, pre-contract negotiations would be unnecessarily uncertain and hazardous.

Another recognised function performed by formalities is the "channelling" function. This describes the way in which formalities mark off transactions from one another and create a standardised form of transaction. As a result, the identification and classification of certain types of transaction are facilitated, enabling them to be dealt with routinely. Such a function contributes to certainty by making clear the effect of non-compliance with formalities [. . .]

The general uniqueness of land constitutes another argument for requiring formalities for contracts relating to it: each particular piece of land is regarded as unique from which it follows that interests in or rights over it should not be created or disposed of casually [. . .] It has also been argued that land is different from other property because there can exist simultaneously several interests, whether corporeal or incorporeal, in or over the same piece of land. Therefore, so the argument goes, writing is desirable to avoid so far as possible confusion about who owns what. As was said in the working paper, this argument may be found persuasive but not totally compelling, because third party interests can also be created in other forms of property.

Finally [. . .] most other legal jurisdictions require more formality for contracts relating to land.

2 FORMALITY REQUIREMENTS FOR THE CREATION OR TRANSFER OF LEGAL ESTATES AND INTERESTS

The process of creating and transferring legal estates or interests can be divided into three stages: contract; completion; and registration. These stages are most apparent in a typical conveyance, or sale, of a home.

1. *Contract* The vendor and purchaser enter a contract for sale of the legal estate (whether freehold or leasehold). The purchaser usually pays a deposit.

2. *Completion* The contract is executed by the vendor making the disposition: in our example, by transferring title. This stage is commonly referred to as 'completion', and is the stage at which the purchase money is paid (less the deposit) and the purchaser takes possession of the land.

3. *Registration* The purchaser applies to be registered as proprietor of the estate. Legal title does not vest in the purchaser until registration.

Although legal title does not vest in the purchaser until registration, equitable rights arise from the moment at which the parties have entered a specifically enforceable contract. The principle under which such equitable rights arise will be referred to in this book as the 'doctrine of anticipation' and is associated with cases such as *Lysaght v Edwards*[2] and *Walsh v Lonsdale*.[3] Under that doctrine, discussed in more detail in section 4.1, the purchaser acquires an equitable interest (under an 'estate contract') as soon as the contract is concluded.

It might then be thought that the two key stages are the conclusion of the contract (at which point the purchaser can acquire an equitable interest) and registration of the disposition (at which point the purchaser acquires legal title). It is, however, still vital to distinguish between, on the one hand, the position after the contract but before completion, and, on the other hand, the position after completion but before registration. By performing the contract, and thus making the promised disposition,[4] the vendor completes his or her part in the transaction and, as we will see in section 5, this can make a significant difference to the position of the parties.

The same three-stage process may be followed whether the conveyance of land involves the transfer of an existing legal estate or interest (for example, the transfer of a freehold or assignment of the existing term of a lease) or the creation of a new one (such as the grant of a new lease). Not every transaction in which a legal right is created or transferred will follow each stage of this process. For example, a gift of land necessarily does not involve a contract between the parties. Further, the requirement of registration only arises in relation to specified legal rights. And, as we will see in section 4 (and discuss further in Chapter 19, section 3.1), it remains possible to create certain short leases without the need to comply with any formality requirements.

3 CONTRACT

3.1 SECTION 2 OF THE 1989 ACT

The requirements for a valid contract for the sale or other disposition of an interest in land are provided by s 2 of the Law of Property (Miscellaneous Provisions) Act 1989 (LP(MP)A 1989). That Act is the product of work of the Law Commission[5] and replaced the previous formality requirement contained in s 40 of the Law of Property Act 1925 (LPA 1925). The 1989 Act has been considered to mark a change in philosophy from previous legislation, focussing attention on the written contract. As a result, case law under the previous legislation may no longer be authoritative.[6]

As will be apparent from the following analysis, the 1989 Act has proved controversial in a number of respects. Writing extra-judicially Lord Neuberger offered the damning indictment, *"[n]ow that the Law Commission, by needlessly meddling, Parliament, with misconceived drafting, and the courts, through inconsistent decisions, have had their wicked ways with section 2, we are worse off than we ever were with section 40"*.[7] Section 2 has increased the formality requirements for contracts and made more severe the consequences

---

[2] (1876) 2 Ch D 499 (CA).   [3] (1882) 21 Ch D 9 (CA).

[4] The making of the contract, whilst it can give rise to an equitable interest in the purchaser, is not in itself a disposition of an equitable interest.

[5] Law Commission Report No 164, *Transfer of Land: Formalities for Contracts for Sale etc of Land* (1987).

[6] These comments were made in *Firstpost Homes Ltd v Johnson* [1995] 1 WLR 1567 in relation to the requirement of a signature under the 1989 Act, but are clearly of more general application.

[7] Neuberger, 'The Stuffing of Minerva's Owl? Taxonomy and Taxidermy in Equity' (2009) 68 CLJ 537, 545.

of non-compliance. Recurring concerns have been that the report and the legislation (which differs from the draft Bill annexed to the Law Commission's report) failed to consider the consequences of the changes, and failed to make adequate express provision to protect B where B has acted in good faith in the belief that he or she has a binding contract with A, when in fact a failure to comply with s 2 means that there is, on the facts, no such contract.

Law of Property (Miscellaneous Provisions) Act 1989, s 2

(1) A contract for the sale or other disposition of an interest in land can only be made in writing and only by incorporating all the terms which the parties have expressly agreed in one document or, where contracts are exchanged, in each.

(2) The terms may be incorporated in a document either by being set out in it or by reference to some other document.

(3) The document incorporating the terms or, where contracts are exchanged, one of the documents incorporating them (but not necessarily the same one) must be signed by or on behalf of each party to the contract.

(4) Where a contract for the sale or other disposition of an interest in land satisfies the conditions of this section by reason only of the rectification of one or more documents in pursuance of an order of a court, the contract shall come into being, or be deemed to have come into being, at such time as may be specified in the order.

(5) This section does not apply in relation to—

    (a) a contract to grant such a lease as is mentioned in section 54(2) of the Law of Property Act 1925 (short leases);

    (b) a contract made in the course of a public auction; or

    (c) a contract regulated under the Financial Services and Markets Act 2000, other than a regulated mortgage contract, a regulated home reversion plan, a regulated home purchase plan or a regulated sale and rent back agreement;

and nothing in this section affects the creation or operation of resulting, implied or constructive trusts.

(6) In this section—

"disposition" has the same meaning as in the Law of Property Act 1925;

"interest in land" means any estate, interest or charge in or over land;

"regulated mortgage contract"[,"regulated home reversion plan","regulated home purchase plan" and "regulated sale and rent back agreement"] must be read with

    (a) section 22 of the Financial Services and Markets Act 2000,

    (b) any relevant order under that section, and

    (c) Schedule 2 to that Act.

(7) Nothing in this section shall apply in relation to contracts made before this section comes into force.

(8) Section 40 of the Law of Property Act 1925 (which is superseded by this section) shall cease to have effect.

Section 2 governs all contracts entered into on or after the 27 September 1989. It differs from s 40 of the LPA 1925 both as regards the formality requirements specified and the consequences of non-compliance.[8] As regards the formality requirements, under s 40, there was no requirement for a contract to be in writing; it was necessary only for it to be *evidenced* in writing. In contrast, s 2 of the LP(MP)A 1989 requires the contract to be in writing. This difference has a direct effect on the consequence of non-compliance. Under s 40 of the 1925 Act, a contract that was not evidenced in writing remained valid, but was not enforceable by action. Under s 2 of the 1989 Act, no contract exists unless and until formality requirements are fulfilled. There is no concept of a contract being valid, but unenforceable.

The principal significance of this difference is the abolition by s 2 of the doctrine of part performance.[9] That doctrine enabled the court to order specific performance of an oral contract if there was a sufficient act of part performance by the claimant.[10] Essential to the application of the doctrine was the fact that, under s 40 of the LPA 1925, an oral contract was valid. Without a valid contract, there is nothing in relation to which specific performance can be ordered. The uncertainty created by the doctrine of part performance was identified by the Law Commission as one of the key defects in the operation of s 40.[11] Its effect was that *'an oral contract for sale can readily and unilaterally be rendered enforceable and the provisions of section 40 left to beat the air'*.[12] It was considered a *'blunt instrument for doing justice'*[13] where formality requirements have not been complied with. Its abolition was therefore a key recommendation in the Law Commission's report. Although nothing in the terms of s 2 of the LP(MP)A 1989 expressly abolishes the doctrine, no such provision is necessary. Its abolition was recognized by the Law Commission as inherent in the requirement for a contract to be in writing.[14] As noted by Peter Gibson LJ in the following statement, frequently cited in the courts:[15]

Firstpost Homes Ltd v Johnson
[1995] 1 WLR 1567 (CA), 1571

Section 2 brought about a markedly different regime from that which obtained hitherto. Whereas under section 40 contracts which did not comply with its requirements were not void but were merely unenforceable by action, contracts which do not comply with section 2 are ineffective: a contract for the sale of an interest in land can only be made in writing and in conformity with the other provisions of section 2 [...] oral contracts are now of no effect at all and contracts must be signed by or on behalf of all the parties.

Under s 2, the written contract may take one of two forms: a single document signed by both parties; or separate documents each signed by one of the parties and exchanged. The

---

[8] Law of Property Act 1925, s 40(1), provided as follows: *'No action may be brought upon any contract for the sale or other disposition of land or any interest in land, unless the agreement upon which such action is brought, or some memorandum or note thereof, is in writing, and signed by the party to be charged or by some other person thereunto by him lawfully authorised.'*

[9] The application of part performance was expressly provided for by the Law of Property Act 1925, s 40(2).

[10] For an example of the operation of part performance, see *Steadman v Steadman* [1976] AC 536.

[11] Law Commission Report No 164 (1987, [1.9]).   [12] Ibid.   [13] Ibid.

[14] Law Commission Report No 164 (1987, [4.13]). The abolition of the doctrine has been given effect to by the courts: see e.g. *United Bank of Kuwait v Sahib* [1997] Ch 107, where it was acknowledged that the abolition of part performance prevented the practice of creating a mortgage by the deposit of title deeds. The doctrine has nonetheless attracted some academic support: see e.g. Griffiths, 'Part Performance: Still Trying to Replace the Irreplaceable' [2002] Conv 216.

[15] See e.g. *Rollerteam Ltd v Riley* [2016] EWCA Civ 1291, [28].

document—or each document, in the case of an exchange—must contain all of the terms expressly agreed by the parties. The terms may be contained in the signed document—or documents, in the case of exchange—or be contained in a separate document that is incorporated by reference. Four main issues arise for discussion: the circumstances in which s 2 applies; the possibility of contracts by correspondence; the concept of an exchange; and the requirement of a signature.

3.2   WHEN DOES SECTION 2 APPLY?

Section 2 of the LP(MP)A 1989 applies to all contracts for the creation or transfer of an interest in land.[16] In *McCausland v Duncan Lawrie Ltd*,[17] it was held that s 2 also applies to the variation of such a contract. As a result, unless the variation complies with s 2, the terms of the contract as originally agreed remain enforceable. In that case, an attempt to vary the completion date in a contract failed for non-compliance with s 2, with the effect that the vendor's attempt to rescind the contract was premature.[18]

In this chapter, our focus is on the acquisition of legal rights, but it should be noted that s 2 applies equally to equitable interests, and so would apply, for example, to a contract for the transfer of an existing equitable interest in land.[19] Moreover, if a party invoking the doctrine of anticipation claims to have acquired an equitable interest because of the conclusion of a contract for the creation or transfer of an interest in land, then they will of course have to show that s 2 has been complied with.

Section 2 applies only to contracts *for* the sale or other disposition of an interest in land. This has two important consequences. Firstly, it does not apply to contracts that do not have a disposing purpose, even if that is the effect of the contract. Hence, in *Pitt v PHH Asset Management Ltd*,[20] it was held that s 2 did not apply to a 'lock-out' agreement, through which a vendor agreed not to negotiate with anyone other than the purchaser for a fixed period of time. In *Yeates v Line*[21] s 2 was held not to apply to a compromise agreement reached in a boundary dispute. The agreement had the effect of disposing of land, but this was not its purpose. Secondly, s 2 does not apply to a contract that *itself* disposes of an interest in land and thus effects an immediate disposition, as such a contract is not a promise to make a disposition in the future. Hence, in *Rollerteam Ltd v Riley*,[22] it was held that s 2 did not apply to an agreement which involved immediate declarations of trust over particular plots of land. Such actual dispositions are subject to the different formality requirements governing the creation of equitable interests, as set out in s 53 of the LPA 1925.[23] A distinction must therefore be drawn between '*a contract* of *disposition, as opposed to an executory contract* for *disposition*':[24] s 2 applies only to the latter. A specific issue has arisen as regards the application of s 2 to an option to purchase. An option to purchase land consists of two stages: in the first stage, the option is granted; in the second,

---

[16] Law Commission Report No 164 (1987, [4.3]).   [17] [1997] 1 WLR 38.

[18] The case is further discussed by Thompson, 'Mere Formalities' [1996] Conv 366.

[19.] See Law Commission Report No 164 (1987, [4.4]).   [20] [1994] 1 WLR 327.

[21] [2013] Ch 363.   [22] [2016] EWCA Civ 1291.

[23] The same distinction was important in *McLaughlin v Duffill* [2000] Ch 1, where it was held that a contract for the sale of a legal estate was a promise to make a disposition in the future, and was not itself a disposition of any equitable interest: it was therefore governed by s 2 of the 1989 Act rather than by s 53 of the LPA 1925.

[24] *Rollerteam Ltd v Riley* [2016] EWCA Civ 1291, [39] (Henderson LJ).

the option is exercised by the grantee. Before the 1989 Act, it had always been clear that the contract by which the option is created must comply with the relevant formality rule, but it had been assumed that the exercise of the option itself need not. Adams, however, suggested that the exercise of the option by the grantee would need to comply with s 2:[25] an outcome that would run counter to commercial practice[26] and that, Stark suggested, would give the provision 'seismic effect' by leaving the exercise of options to 'the whim of the vendor'.[27] The issue soon arose for decision in the following case, which arose from an option granted a matter of weeks after s 2 came into force.

Spiro v Glencrown Properties Ltd
[1991] Ch 537

Facts: The vendor granted the purchaser an option to purchase land, exercisable the same day by notice in writing. The grant of the option complied with s 2(1), but was exercisable by unilateral notice by the purchaser. The purchaser exercised the option, but failed to complete and the vendor had been awarded damages for breach of contract. In an action for judgment against the purchaser's guarantor, the question arose whether the exercise of the option was required to comply with s 2(1).

Hoffmann J

At 541

Apart from authority, it seems to me plain enough that section 2 was intended to apply to the agreement which created the option and not to the notice by which it was exercised. Section 2, which replaced section 40 of the Law of Property Act 1925, was intended to prevent disputes over whether the parties had entered into a binding agreement or over what terms they had agreed. It prescribes the formalities for recording their mutual consent. But only the grant of the option depends upon consent. The exercise of the option is a unilateral act. It would destroy the very purpose of the option if the purchaser had to obtain the vendor's countersignature to the notice by which it was exercised. The only way in which the concept of an option to buy land could survive section 2 would be if the purchaser ensured that the vendor not only signed the agreement by which the option was granted but also at the same time provided him with a countersigned form to use if he decided to exercise it. There seems no conceivable reason why the legislature should have required this additional formality.

The language of section 2 places no obstacle in the way of construing the grant of the option as the relevant contract. An option to buy land can properly be described as a contract for the sale of that land conditional on the exercise of the option. A number of eminent judges have so described it.

Following a review of authorities, Hoffmann J concluded that nothing prevented him from interpreting s 2 in that way. Hence, while the grant of an option must comply

---

[25] Adams, 'You've No Option: More Consequences of Section 2 of the Law of Property (Miscellaneous Provisions) Act 1989' [1990] Conv 9.
[26] Ibid.   [27] Stark, 'The Option to Purchase: A Legal Chameleon' [1992] JBL 296, 296.

with s 2, the exercise of the option is a unilateral act by the purchaser and need not comply with s 2.

The decision has been welcomed as regards the practical operation of options under s 2, although the 'conditional contract' analysis of options taken by Hoffmann J to achieve this may be more problematic in other contexts.[28]

Under s 40 it was possible for a contract for sale of land to come into existence though correspondence between the parties—the correspondence providing the written evidence of the contract required by s 40 of the LPA 1925. Parties could prevent their correspondence from being interpreted this way by indorsing it 'subject to contract'. In its report, the Law Commission anticipated that contracts by correspondence would remain possible.[29] In *Commission for the New Towns v Cooper*[30] the Court of Appeal considered that Parliament had gone further than the Law Commission had anticipated and that contracts by correspondence were not possible under s 2. It is clear that correspondence would not meet the requirements for an 'exchange' given in that case (and discussed below). However, correspondence may produce a contract where it results in the creation of a single document signed by both parties.[31] Hence, in *Green v Ireland* the court accepted in principle that a 'string' of e-mails which contains the (typed) signatures of both parties could create a contract under s 2, although the claim failed on the facts.[32]

3.3 THE CONCEPT OF AN EXCHANGE

The concept of an exchange was considered in *Commission for the New Towns v Cooper*.

Commission for the New Towns v Cooper
[1995] Ch 259, CA

Stuart-Smith LJ

At 285

In my opinion, the authorities show that, even if the expression "exchange of contracts" is not a term of art, it is a well-recognised concept understood both by lawyers and laymen which has the following features.

1. Each party draws up or is given a document which incorporates all the terms which they have agreed, and which is intended to record their proposed contract. The terms that have been agreed may have been agreed either orally or in writing or partly orally or partly in writing.

2. The documents are referred to as "contracts" or "parts of contract," although they need not be so entitled. They are intended to take effect as formal documents of title and must be capable on their face of being fairly described as contracts having that effect.

---

[28] Ibid; Smith, 'Options to Purchase: A Nasty Twist' [1991] Conv 140, 144.
[29] Law Commission Report No 164 (1987, [4.15]).   [30] [1995] Ch 259, 287.
[31] Oakley, 'Conveyancing Contracts by Exchange of Letters' [1995] CLJ 502.
[32] [2011] EWHC 1305 (Ch) [43]–[48].

3. Each party signs his part in the expectation that the other party has also executed or will execute a corresponding part incorporating the same terms.

4. At the time of execution neither party is bound by the terms of the document which he has executed, it being their mutual intention that neither will be bound until the executed parts are exchanged.

5. The act of exchange is a formal delivery by each party of its part into the actual or constructive possession of the other with the intention that the parties will become actually bound when exchange occurs, but not before.

6. The manner of exchange may be agreed and determined by the parties. The traditional method was by mutual exchange across the table, both parties or their solicitors being present. It also commonly takes place by post, especially where the parties or their solicitors are at a distance. In such a case exchange is sequential and does not take place until the second document to be dispatched has been received or posted.[33] Exchange can also take place by telephone, in which case it will be simultaneous.[34]

It is notable, therefore, that the concept of an exchange is a formal one, characterized by the parties' mutual intentions as regards the documents and a 'formal delivery'.

3.4 THE REQUIREMENT OF A SIGNATURE

To constitute a contract within s 2 of the LP(MP)A 1989, the 'document' or 'documents' in the case of an exchange must be 'signed'. In *Firstpost Homes v Johnson* the court had to consider what constitutes both the 'document' and a signature for s 2. There, an Ordnance Survey plan was attached to a letter that purported to record an agreement for the sale of land.[35] The vendor signed the letter and the plan, but the director acting for the purchaser had signed only the plan. It was held that the 'document' requiring signature for s 2 was the letter alone, the plan being a separate document incorporated into the letter by reference. Peter Gibson LJ acknowledged that the identification of the document was '*largely one of first impression*', but, on the facts, the 'natural' interpretation was to treat the letter alone as the document.[36] In the absence of the purchaser's handwritten signature on the letter, the question arose whether the requirement of a signature was met by the appearance of his printed or typed name. The purchaser had prepared the letter for the vendor and so had placed its Director's name on the letter as the intended addressee (in the format 'Dear Geoff'). In deciding that this did not suffice to meet the requirement, Peter Gibson LJ indicated that s 2 marked a clean-break with a liberal approach that had been taken to the definition of signature under previous legislation.

---

[33] *Eccles v. Bryant and Pollock* [1948] Ch. 93, 97–98 (Lord Greene MR).
[34] *Domb v. Isoz* [1980] Ch. 548, 558 (Buckley LJ).
[35] In fact, it was held that the letter did not constitute a contract, because it failed to contain an obligation to buy: [1995] 1 WLR 1567.
[36] [1995] 1 WLR 1567, 1573.

Firstpost Homes Ltd v Johnson
[1995] 1 WLR 1567, CA

Peter Gibson LJ

At 1575–6

In my judgment, it is an artificial use of language to describe the printing or the typing of the name of an addressee in the letter as the signature by the addressee when he has printed or typed that document. Ordinary language does not, it seems to me, extend so far [. . .]

In any event, I do not accept that authorities on what was a sufficient signature for the purposes of the Statute of Frauds 1677 and section 40 of the Act of 1925 should continue to govern the interpretation of the word "signed" in section 2 of the Act of 1989. Prior to the Act of 1989 the courts viewed with some disfavour those who made oral contracts but did not abide by them. The courts were prepared to interpret the statutory requirements generously to enable contracts to be enforced and in relation to the question whether there was a sufficient memorandum evidencing an agreement extrinsic evidence was admissible [. . .]

The Act of 1989 seems to me to have a new and different philosophy from that which the Statute of Frauds 1677 and section 40 of the Act of 1925 had. Oral contracts are no longer permitted. To my mind it is clear that Parliament intended that questions as to whether there was a contract, and what were the terms of the contract, should be readily ascertained by looking at the single document said to constitute the contract [. . .]

For my part, I do not see why it is right to encumber the new Act with so much ancient baggage, particularly when it does not leave the "signed" with a meaning which the ordinary man would understand it to have. This decision is of course limited to a case where the party whose signature is said to appear on a contract is only named as the addressee of a letter prepared by him. No doubt other considerations will apply in other circumstances. I therefore do not accept Mr. Seymour's contention that a signature of the purchaser appears on the letter.

Peter Gibson LJ's clear limitation of his judgment leaves the matter open to discussion in other circumstances. In *Green v Ireland*,[37] the court accepted that a typed name at the end of an e-mail constitutes a signature for the purposes of s 2(1). In *J Pereira Fernandes SA v Mehta*,[38] outside the context of s 2, the court held that the name of the sender of an e-mail, which is automatically inserted into the header, was not a signature as it had not been inserted to give the document authenticity.

Further, the courts will be reluctant to allow a party to rely on an overly technical reading of s 2 as a means to avoid a contractual duty. In *Rabiu v Marlbray Ltd*,[39] for example, the contract for sale stated that a husband and wife were to be joint purchasers, but the contract was not signed by the wife: the husband had purported to sign on her behalf, but had no authority to do so. It was held that there was a valid contract between the vendor and the husband, and that s 2 did not mean that the wife, as a supposed party, also had to sign. Gloster LJ stated that:[40] *'It is of course the case that section 2 introduced a stricter regime than that which previously prevailed under section 40 of the LPA 1925 [. . .] However, there is nothing in any of the cases [cited by the husband's counsel][. . .] which suggests that, in circumstances such*

---

[37] [2011] EWHC 1305 (Ch).　　[38] [2006] 1 WLR 1543, [27].

[39] [2016] EWCA Civ 476, [2016] 1 WLR 5147: for discussion see Strauss, 'Principal's Lack of Authority to Contract for Co-Principal' [2016] LMCLQ 470.

[40] [2016] EWCA Civ 476, [2016] 1 WLR 5147, [72].

as the present, section 2 has to be construed in the artificial way which she [i.e the husband's counsel] suggests, to enable the [husband] to escape from his liabilities under the several contract.[41] Thus, the fact that the contract placed the vendor under a duty to make a transfer to the husband and wife jointly did not mean that s 2 also required the signature of the wife, as the contract could still be regarded as one solely between the vendor and the husband.

3.5 EXECUTED CONTRACTS

In *Tootal Clothing Ltd v Guinea Property Management Ltd* the Court of Appeal held that the question of compliance with s 2 could not be raised once a contract has been executed. Scott LJ explained:[42]

> section 2 is of relevance only to executory contracts. It has no relevance to contracts which have been completed. If parties choose to complete an oral land contract or a land contract that does not in some respect or other comply with section 2, they are at liberty to do so. Once they have done so, it becomes irrelevant that the contract they have completed may not have been in accordance with section 2.

The effect of *Tootal Clothing* has, however, proved to be contentious. There, the parties had entered into two agreements: first an agreement for the grant of a twenty-five-year lease of commercial premises to Tootal Clothing; and secondly a 'supplemental agreement' that the landlord (Guinea) would pay Tootal Clothing £30,000 on completion of work to fit the premises for use as a shop. The Court of Appeal held that once the lease had been granted, Guinea could not raise non-compliance with s 2 to challenge the enforceability of its agreement to pay Tootal for the works. In *Kilcarne Holdings Ltd v Targetfellow (Birmingham) Ltd*, Lewison J interpreted *Tootal Clothing* to mean that '*once all the land elements of an alleged contract have been performed, the remaining parts of the alleged contract can be examined without reference to section 2*'.[43] This interpretation was rejected by the Court of Appeal in the following case.

Keay v Morris Homes (West Midlands) Ltd
[2012] 1 WLR 2855

Facts: The Keays had transferred development land to Morris Homes pursuant to a contract for sale. After the contract had been made, the parties entered a written supplemental agreement to reduce the purchase price and vary instalment payments. The Keays alleged that on the same day the parties had entered an oral 'works obligation' requiring Morris Homes to make prompt progress on the construction of a medical centre which was to be leased back to the Keays on a 125 year lease. The transfer of land to Morris Homes had been completed, but prompt progress was not made on the medical centre. The Keays commenced proceedings claiming approximately £2.7m damages for breach of the works obligation. Morris Homes argued that the supplemental agreement was void for non-compliance with s 2. In response, the Keays contended—relying

---

[41] The 'several contract' refers to the distinct contract between vendor and husband under which he is severally (i.e. individually) liable.

[42] (1992) 64 P & CR 452.   [43] [2005] 2 P & CR 105, [198].

on Tootal Clothing—that the question of compatibility could not be raised as the land had been transferred.

Rimer LJ

At 46–7

I anyway find it impossible to derive from what Scott LJ said [in *Tootal Clothing*] that he was subscribing to a principle that, in a case in which a purported land contract is void for want of compliance with section 2 of the 1989 Act, the practical completion of the land elements of the void contract will thereupon cause the hitherto void, non-land, terms of the purported contract to become enforceable. Whilst I regard the *Tootal* case as a difficult one, I do not regard it as authority for any such proposition. Whatever it did decide, it did not decide that, and neither Scott nor Parker LJJ came even close to the express adoption of any such principle.

I conclude, therefore, *Tootal Clothing Ltd v Guinea Properties Management Ltd* 64 P & CR 452 is not authority for the principle attributed to it by Lewison J in *Kilcarne Holdings Ltd v Targetfollow (Birmingham) Ltd* [2005] 2 P & CR 105. The proposition that a void contract can, by acts in the nature of part performance, mature into a valid one is contrary to principle and wrong.

The Court of Appeal concluded that the omission of the works obligation from the supplemental agreement rendered the agreement null under s 2 and no action for breach of the obligation could, therefore, be brought by the Keays. The nullity of the supplemental agreement meant that the parties were bound by the terms of the original contract—including the original sales price.[44] The correctness of the decision in *Tootal Clothing* was not doubted by the court. Rimer LJ suggested that the case could have been decided on the basis that the supplemental agreement was compliant with s 2, although he acknowledged that this is not the basis of the decision in the case.[45]

Hence the effect of *Tootal Clothing* is that, once land has been transferred, the court will not permit the validity of the transfer to be challenged for non-compliance of the contract with s 2. However, non-compliance with s 2 will still prevent the enforcement of any aspects of the parties' agreement that remain executory.

3.6 COLLATERAL CONTRACTS

Section 2 of the LP(MP)A 1989 requires a contract for sale of land to contain all of the terms agreed by the parties. Hence, if a term is omitted, there is no contract, even where there is a written and signed document (or documents, in the case of exchange). However, s 2 does not prevent parties from entering a composite transaction, consisting of a contract for sale of land and other, separate or collateral, agreements. The challenge for the courts lies in distinguishing between those cases where the parties have entered a composite transaction from those in which an omitted term is part of the bargain for the transfer of land. If parties are permitted to 'hive off' parts of their bargain into separate contracts, then the purpose of s 2 is undermined.[46] However, s 2 is also open to abuse by parties who '*look around for expressly agreed terms which have not found their way into the final form of land contract*' in

---

[44] [2012] 1 WLR 2855, [18]. The application of s 2 to variations of a contract is explained in section 3.1 of this chapter above.

[45] Ibid.

[46] Cf: the discussion by Sir Christopher Staughton in *Grossman v Hooper* [2001] EWCA Civ 615, [31]–[36].

order to escape from a bargain following a change of mind.[47] Whether a term is part of a contract for sale of land is a question of fact.[48] In *Keay v Morris Homes*,[49] Rimer LJ explained:

> [t]he question to which section 2(1) requires an answer is whether the written document the parties have signed as recording the terms of the sale or other disposition of an interest in land includes *all* the terms of such sale or disposition that they have expressly agreed.

A collateral contract was imposed in *Grossman v Hooper* and its use in that case has subsequently been approved.[50] There, the Court of Appeal held that an agreement by Miss Hooper to repay a loan to a third party was collateral to a contract for Mr Grossman to transfer legal title to the parties' former home to her on the breakdown of their relationship. In the course of his judgment, Chadwick LJ offered the following example.

Grossman v Hooper
[2001] EWCA Civ 615, CA

Chadwick LJ

At 21

[. . .] Suppose that A wishes to purchase a house from B; and wishes, also, to purchase the carpets and curtains that are in the house. Before anything is put in writing A and B negotiate a price for the house, say £500,000, and a separate price for the carpets and curtains, say £50,000. But the negotiation for the sale of the house is made subject to contract; and it is implicit neither A nor B intends to become bound to a purchase and sale of the carpets and curtains (if at all) until after the terms for the sale of the house have been put in writing and signed. A contract for the sale of the house at a price of £500,000 is drawn up and is signed by both A and B. The document contains no reference to the sale of carpets or curtains. The question, in such a case, in the context of section 2(1) of the 1989 Act, is whether it was a term of the contract for the sale of the house that A would purchase and B would sell the carpets and curtains. That is a question of fact in each case. It would have been open to A and B to agree that the sale of the house was independent of any sale of the carpets and curtains; so that A was to buy the house whether or not he bought the carpets and curtains as well. It would, equally, have been open to A and B to agree that the sale of the house was conditional upon a sale of the carpets and curtains; so that A would not be obliged to buy the house, nor B to sell it, unless the carpets and curtains were sold also. In the first case, the requirements of section 2(1) of the 1989 Act would be satisfied; in the second case those requirements would not be satisfied. The requirements would not be satisfied in the second case because, upon a true understanding of the bargain between the parties, it was a term of the contract for the sale of the house that A would purchase and B would sell the carpets and curtains; and that term was not incorporated in the document signed by the parties.

---

[47] *North Eastern Properties Ltd v Coleman* [2010] 1 WLR 2715, [43] per Briggs J.

[48] *Grossman v Hooper* [2001] EWCA Civ 615; approved in *Keay v Morris Homes (West Midlands) Ltd* [2012] 1 WLR 2855, [27].

[49] Ibid, [27] (emphasis in the original).

[50] *North Eastern Properties v Coleman* [2010] 1 WLR 2715; *Keay v Morris Homes (West Midlands) Ltd* [2012] 1 WLR 2855.

In *North Eastern Properties Ltd v Coleman*, Briggs J referred to Chadwick LJ's example in setting out a number of points of principle to explain the circumstances in which a collateral contract will be found. Briggs J's explanation was subsequently cited with approval by the Court of Appeal in *Keay v Morris Homes*.[51]

North Eastern Properties Ltd v Coleman
[2010] EWCA Civ 277, [2010] 1 WLR 2715

Briggs J

At [54]

(i) Nothing in section 2 of the 1989 Act is designed to prevent parties to a composite transaction which includes a land contract from structuring their bargain so that the land contract is genuinely separated from the rest of the transaction in the sense that its performance is not made conditional upon the performance of some other expressly agreed part of the bargain. Thus, in Chadwick LJ's example in *Grossman v Hooper [2001] 2 EGLR 82*, parties may agree to the sale and purchase both of a house and of its curtains and carpets in a single composite transaction. None the less it is open to them to agree either (a) that completion of the purchase of the house is dependent upon the sale of the carpets and curtains or (b) that it is not. They are free to separate the terms of a transaction of type (b) into two separate documents (one for the house and the other for the carpets and curtains) without falling foul of section 2. They may also agree to structure a transaction which includes the sale of two or more parcels of land by way of separate contracts for each, so that none of the land contracts is conditional upon the performance of any of the others.

(ii) By contrast, the parties to a composite transaction are not free to separate into a separate document expressly agreed terms, for example as to the sale of chattels or the provision of services, if upon the true construction of the whole of the agreement, performance of the land sale is conditional upon the chattel sale or service provision. That would, albeit for reasons which seem to me to frustrate rather than serve the purposes for which the 1989 Act was passed, fall foul of section 2(1), however purposively construed. So would a series of separate contracts for the sale of separate parcels of land, if each was conditional upon the performance of the other.

(iii) Since the splitting into separate contracts of parts of a composite transaction is inherently likely to give rise to uncertainties as to whether performance of the one is conditional upon performance of the other, the parties are free, and in my opinion should positively be encouraged, to make plain by express terms whether or not that conditionality exists. To do so serves rather than evades or frustrates the purposes of section 2, an important part of which is to encourage clarity rather than uncertainty in land transactions.

There, the court held that an agreement for payment of a 'finder's fee' on exchange was not part of a number of contracts entered into between the parties for the sale of flats in a development (each one of eleven contracts between the parties relating to a separate flat). Instead, the parties had entered into a composite transaction consisting of the purchase of the flats

---

[51] *Keay v Morris Homes (West Midland) Ltd* [2012] 1 WLR 2855, [28].

and the payment of the fee. Performance of the land contract was not considered to be conditional upon performance of the finder's fee agreement.[52] Further, the court noted that there were sound commercial reasons why the agreements had been structured so that the finder's fee was not part of the contracts for sale of land.[53]

In *Keay v Morris Homes* the Keays sought damages from Morris Homes for breach of a 'works obligation' that required the developers to make prompt progress with the construction of a medical centre following a transfer of land to them from the Keays. The works obligation was an oral agreement that the Keays contended had been entered alongside a supplemental agreement that reduced the sale price of the land. In section 3.5 above we saw that the Keays unsuccessfully argued that Morris Homes could not raise the question of compliance with s 2 as the transfer of land had been executed. As an alternative, the Keays argued that the works obligation was a collateral contract: it was a separate promise that Morris Homes had agreed to '*if* the Keays entered into the supplemental agreement'.[54] On this basis, the supplemental agreement provided consideration for the works obligation. The court accepted that if the Keays' analysis was correct, then the works obligation was collateral. However, the evidence available to the court equally suggested that the works obligation was an express term of the supplemental agreement.[55] The court, therefore, held that the matter could not be determined in the current proceedings, which were an application for summary judgment.[56]

3.7 RECTIFICATION OF A CONTRACTUAL DOCUMENT

Where the parties have reached an agreement, but the terms are not all recorded in the document (or documents, in the case of exchange), or are recorded wrongly, the court may order rectification, with the result that the document then satisfies s 2 of the LP(MP)A 1989. The possibility of rectification is specifically referred to in s 2(4), which confers on the court discretion to determine the time at which the contract comes into being. This is to enable the court to take into account the possible effect of rectification on third parties who enter a transaction between the date of the original 'contract' (void at the time for non-compliance with s 2) and the court's decision to rectify the agreement.[57]

It is established as a matter of contract law that rectification may be awarded where there is a prior agreement or common intention to contract on specified terms, and convincing proof[58] that the written agreement does not reflect those terms.[59] More controversially, rectification may also be available in cases of unilateral mistake, but only where the party not mistaken has acted unconscionably.[60] To date, there is little authority on the use of rectification in relation to contracts for sale of land. The remedy was adopted in *Robert Leonard Developments Ltd v Wright*.[61] In that case, a purchaser had agreed to

---

[52] [2010] 1 WLR 2715, [58].   [53] Ibid [66].

[54] [2012] 1 WLR 2855, [32] (emphasis in the original).   [55] Ibid.   [56] Ibid, [33].

[57] Law Commission Report No 164 (1987, [5.6]).

[58] See Thompson, 'Blowing Hot and Cold' [1995] Conv 484. He suggests that this may be diluted to a test based on the balance of probabilities.

[59] *Josceleyne v Nissen* [1970] 2 QB 86.

[60] For example, through estoppel, fraud, undue influence, breach of fiduciary duty, or though actual knowledge of the mistake. In *Commission for the New Towns v Cooper* [1995] Ch 259, 277–82, it was suggested, obiter, that it would also be sufficient if one party merely suspects the other to be mistaken and intends them to be so, without proof of inducement. See further on unilateral mistakes *George Wimpey UK Ltd v VI Construction Ltd* [2005] EWCA Civ 77.

[61] [1994] NPC 49.

buy a show flat, the price of which was to include carpets and furnishings. This term was not included in both written contracts on exchange and the vendor removed the furniture. The contract was executed by the transfer of the lease of the flat and therefore the validity of the contract could no longer be questioned—but the purchaser sought damages for breach of contract. The Court of Appeal considered that there was no separate or collateral contract for the sale of the furnishings; it was part of one package for the sale of the flat. Instead, the Court held that the contract should be rectified to include the omitted term.

In the following case, the court refused rectification where a term had been deliberately omitted from the parties' agreement.

Oun v Ahmad
[2008] EWHC 545

Facts: Mr Ahmad and Mr Oun signed an agreement (referred to in the judgment as the 'first document') for the sale of premises comprising of a residential flat and an off-licence. The sale was never completed and the question arose as to whether a valid contract for sale had been entered. The agreement signed by the parties did not refer to an apportionment of the purchase price between the building, fixtures, and fittings, and the business goodwill. This matter was instead recorded by the parties in a second document. Mr Oun, the proposed purchaser, argued that the parties' agreement should be rectified to include this term.

Morgan J

At [41]–[43]

Because of the arguments addressed to me, it is necessary to consider the possibility of rectification in more detail. I will distinguish between two types of case.

In the first type of case, the written document does not incorporate all the terms expressly agreed, by reason of a mistake in the recording of the agreement. In such a case, the court can rectify the written document so as to incorporate all the terms expressly agreed and then the document as rectified complies with section 2.

The second (rather more unusual) type of case is as follows. Say the parties expressly agree upon five terms of their agreement. They agree to record four of them in a written document and they do so. They agree that the fifth term shall remain unrecorded in writing. The result is that the written document does not comply with section 2 and is of no effect. Can one party seek an order for rectification to the effect that the fifth term should be incorporated into the written document so that the written document will then comply with section 2? Will the position be different if the court finds that the parties believed that they had made a binding contract and that it was unnecessary for them to record the fifth term in writing? [. . .]

At [48]

It appears from the above formulation that the court can order rectification where the relevant mistake is as to the meaning or effect of the words used in the instrument and, indeed, as to the legal effect of the instrument as a whole [. . .]

At [51]

But rectification is not available where the parties have executed the document they intended to execute and the mistake is as to the legal consequences of that document. In *Allnutt v Wilding*, the parties had created a discretionary trust. They believed that the creation of a discretionary trust would be a potentially exempt transfer for the purposes of inheritance tax. It was not. If they had appreciated that legal consequence, their claim was that they would have created an interest in possession trust. It was held that a change in the document from one which created a discretionary trust into one which created an interest in possession trust was outside the ambit of rectification [. . .]

At [55]

In my judgment, this express agreement to omit the term means that there is no defect or mistake in the recording of, or the expression of, the arrangement and it is beyond the ambit of rectification to write into the written agreement a term which the parties expressly agreed should not be so recorded. I reach this conclusion applying what I understand to be conventional principles as to the availability of rectification and not some special set of rules as to rectification for the purposes of section 2(4) of the 1989 Act. In my judgment, this approach serves the legislative objective of section 2 of the 1989 Act [. . .]

On the facts, Morgan J considered that the parties had agreed on the apportionment of the purchase price at the time that the first document was signed and had further agreed that this should not be included in the document. Both parties had mistakenly considered that, notwithstanding the absence of the term, the document would still be a valid contract. This mistake was beyond the scope of rectification and therefore there was no contract for sale of the premises.

3.8 PROPRIETARY ESTOPPEL AND CONSTRUCTIVE TRUSTS

As noted in section 3.1, the effect of non-compliance with s 2 of the LP(MP)A 1989 is that there is no contract. The Law Commission, in the Report which led to the Act, acknowledged however that: '*While it is important not to undermine the general rule that the formalities should be observed, it is equally important that the law should not be so inflexible as to cause unacceptable hardship in cases of non-compliance.*'[62]

There are three possible ways to mitigate such hardship. Firstly, we have seen in section 3.6 and 3.7 that, where the parties have written and signed a document—or documents, in the case of exchange—but the terms are absent or wrong, rectification or the finding of a collateral contract may be invoked to create a contract that complies with s 2.[63] Secondly, it may be possible to rely on an express exception to the basic s 2(1) formality requirement: s 2(5), for example, states that the operation of a constructive trust is not to be affected by that requirement. If, therefore, a party can base a claim on a constructive trust, such as the common intention constructive trust (to be discussed in Chapter 12),[64] or the constructive

---

[62] Law Commission Report No 164 (1987), [5.1].

[63] The possibility of each claim was recognized by the Law Commission: Law Commission Report No 164 (1987, [5.6]–[5.8]).

[64] For an example, see *Matchmove Ltd v Dowding* [2017] 1 WLR 749, [28].

trust arising under the doctrines of either *Rochefoucauld v Boustead* or *Pallant v Morgan* (to be discussed in Chapter 11), then that party can acquire an equitable interest in land even if there is no valid contract.

Thirdly, even in a case where an express exception such as s 2(5) does not apply, it may still be possible to seek a non-contractual remedy. The Law Commission specifically anticipated the doctrine of proprietary estoppel playing a role in this regard.[65] The doctrine can give B a claim against A if three basic requirements are met: firstly, a promise or representation by A that B has or will acquire a right in A's land; secondly, reliance by B on that promise or representation; thirdly, the prospect of detriment to B if A were wholly free to go back on that promise or representation. If B is able to establish such a claim, a court will provide a remedy to B, but it is not the case that A's promise or representation will necessarily be enforced; in some cases, for example, the claim will be satisfied if A simply pays a sum of money to B.[66]

We will examine the requirements of proprietary estoppel in Chapter 10: the question to be considered here is the specific one of whether, assuming those basic requirements have been met, s 2 of the 1989 Act presents any obstacle to an estoppel claim. It is clear that, in practice, proprietary estoppel *has* been allowed to operate in cases where s 2 has not been satisfied,[67] but there are differing views as to how that result can be justified.

3.8.1 VIEW 1: PROPRIETARY ESTOPPEL CAN BE USED ONLY IF IT GIVES RISE TO A CONSTRUCTIVE TRUST

Section 2(5) makes clear that the s 2(1) formality rule does not affect the operation of constructive trusts. In some cases, the operation of proprietary estoppel can give rise to such a trust, and so it is clear that, in such cases, an estoppel claim can succeed even if it is based on a purely oral promise or bargain. In some cases, however, a proprietary estoppel claim does *not* give rise to a constructive trust, but instead gives the claimant a different right (such as, for example, a right to receive money from the defendant). On View 1, then, in such cases, s 2 may operate to defeat the proprietary estoppel claim. In an *obiter* consideration of the point, in *Cobbe v Yeoman's Row Management Ltd*,[68] Lord Scott commented:

> My present view, however, is that proprietary estoppel cannot be prayed in aid in order to render enforceable an agreement that statute has declared to be void. The proposition that an owner of land can be estopped from asserting that an agreement is void for want of compliance with the requirements of section 2 is, in my opinion, unacceptable. The assertion is no more than the statute provides. Equity can surely not contradict the statute.[69]

That view has attracted some (again *obiter*) judicial support.[70] There is, however, a difficulty with Lord Scott's reasoning: it assumes that s 2 operates to render an *agreement* void, so that the agreement can have no legal consequences. However, the wording of s 2 simply means that a non-complying agreement does not have *contractual* effect; that is not inconsistent with allowing the

---

[65] Law Commission Report No 164 (1987), [5.4]–[5.5].

[66] See e.g. *Jennings v Rice* [2002] EWCA Civ 159, [2003] 1 P & CR 8.

[67] Certainly, it has never been suggested that any promise by A to give B a right in land in the future must always be in writing if B is to have a proprietary estoppel claim: that would be inconsistent with the results in such seminal cases as *Crabb v Arun DC* [1976] Ch 179 (CA) and *Thorner v Major* [2009] 1 WLR 1776.

[68] [2008] 1 WLR 1752. The case is discussed in Chapter 10, section 2.1.4.   [69] Ibid, [29].

[70] See e.g. *Anderson Antiques (UK) Ltd v Anderson Wharf (Hull) Ltd* [2007] EWHC 2086, [33].

agreement to be used as part of a different, non-contractual claim, such as a proprietary estoppel claim. It is therefore not surprising that some judges have refused to follow Lord Scott's analysis.[71]

3.8.2 VIEW 2: PROPRIETARY ESTOPPEL CAN BE USED WHETHER OR NOT IT GIVES RISE TO A CONSTRUCTIVE TRUST

This view gives proprietary estoppel freer rein to operate in cases where s 2 is not complied with, thus allowing the doctrine to fulfil the Law Commission's aim of alleviating hardship in at least some cases where there is no contract between the parties. On this view, there is no need to consider the express exception for constructive trusts, as the general s 2 formality rule applies only to contracts, and so is not engaged in the first place: s 2(5) is a 'red herring, because proprietary estoppel is not about enforcing a contract at all.'[72] This view has a good deal of academic support,[73] as well as extra-judicial backing from Lord Neuberger:

Lord Neuberger of Abbotsbury 'The Stuffing of Minerva's Owl: Taxonomy and Taxidermy in Equity' (2009) 68 CLJ 537, 545–46

If Lord Scott's approach [see section 3.8.1] is right, there are two possibilities. First, as section 2 would prevent the claimant from mounting a claim in contract, every proprietary estoppel claim must fail, as the statutory formalities were not complied with. Alternatively, section 2 presents no problem where the statement or indication is so imprecise that we are not near contractual territory. Either alternative is unpalatable. The first would mean that any proprietary estoppel claim based on an indication or promise that the claimant will get an interest in land will fall foul of section 2, unless the claimant happens to be able to erect a constructive trust out of the arrangement [...] The second would mean that the clearer and more precise the defendant's indication or promise, and therefore the stronger the claimant's case in principle, the more likely it is that section 2 will scotch any proprietary estoppel claim [...]

However, it is only fair to acknowledge that Lord Scott's approach was consistent with a number of previous Court of Appeal decisions, including two to which Lord Walker and I were parties—*Yaxley* v. *Gotts*[74] and *Kinane* v. *Mackie-Conteh*.[75] However, in agreement with the Court of Appeal and Etherton J. in *Cobbe*,[76] I suggest that section 2 has nothing to do with the matter [...] the estoppel rests on the finding that it would be inequitable for the defendant to insist on his strict legal rights. So the fact that, if there was a contract, it would be void is irrelevant: indeed the very reason for mounting the proprietary estoppel claim is that there is no enforceable contract. I accept of course that it is not open to a claimant to

---

[71] See e.g. *Whittaker v Kinnear* [2011] EWHC 1479 (QB), where Bean J refused to follow Lord Scott's view, stating at [30] that: '*notwithstanding Lord Scott's dicta in* Cobbe, *proprietary estoppel in a case involving the sale of land has survived the enactment of s 2 of the 1989 Act.*' See too *Herbert v Doyle* [2008] EWHC 1950 (Ch) [15].

[72] Master Matthews in *Muhammad v ARY Properties Ltd* [2016] EWHC 1698 (Ch) at [49].

[73] See e.g. McFarlane, *The Law of Proprietary Estoppel* (2014) [6.10].   [74] [2000] 1 Ch 162.

[75] [2005] EWCA Civ 45, [2005] WTLR 345.

[76] [The citation for the decision of Etherton J is [2005] EWHC 1755 (Ch); that for the Court of Appeal is [2006] 1 WLR 2964.]

take the unvarnished point that it is inequitable for a defendant to rely on the argument that an apparent contract is void for not complying with the requirements of section 2. But where there is the superadded fact that the claimant, with the conscious encouragement of the defendant, has acted in the belief that there is a valid contract, I suggest that section 2 offers no bar to a claim based in equity.

3.8.3 THE CASE LAW

In the extract in section 3.8.2, Lord Neuberger refers to two Court of Appeal cases in which a party who had acted in reliance on an agreement that did not satisfy the requirements of s 2 was nonetheless allowed to acquire an interest in land: *Yaxley v Gotts* and *Kinane v Mackie-Conteh*. In each case, the result is consistent with each of View 1 and View 2, as a proprietary estoppel claim was allowed, but the court also found that a constructive trust had arisen, and thus the s 2(5) exception was also available.

The decision in *Yaxley* has had an important influence on the development of the law, and is therefore extracted below. As will be seen, there are some differences in the approaches of Robert Walker LJ and Beldam LJ, with Robert Walker LJ's approach seeming to correspond with View 1, whereas Beldam LJ's approach, which gives more weight to the views of the Law Commission in the report that led to the 1989 Act, is closer to View 2. Clarke LJ then states agreement with both of those judgments.

Yaxley v Gotts
[2000] 1 Ch 162, CA

Facts: Mr Yaxley, a builder, found a property ripe for redevelopment. He entered an oral agreement, described as a 'gentleman's agreement', with his friend, Mr Brownie Gotts. The terms of the agreement were that Brownie would purchase the property, and that Mr Yaxley would undertake the redevelopment and manage the building, in return for which he would be given the two ground-floor flats. The property was, in fact, purchased in the name of Brownie's son, Mr Alan Gotts. Mr Yaxley carried out the works, but, following a falling out between the friends, Alan refused to transfer the flats to Mr Yaxley. At first instance, the judge had found that Mr Yaxley could invoke proprietary estoppel and ordered a long lease of the flats to be granted to him. On appeal, the Gotts argued that the agreement with Mr Yaxley was void for non-compliance with s 2(1) of the LP(MP)A 1989 and estoppel could not be invoked to give effect to the void agreement.

Robert Walker LJ

At 174–80

Parliament's requirement that any contract for the disposition of an interest in land must be made in a particular documentary form, and will otherwise be void, does not have such an obviously social aim as statutory provisions relating to contracts by or with moneylenders, infants, or protected tenants. Nevertheless it can be seen as embodying

Parliament's conclusion, in the general public interest, that the need for certainty as to the formation of contracts of this type must in general outweigh the disappointment of those who make informal bargains in ignorance of the statutory requirement. If an estoppel would have the effect of enforcing a void contract and subverting Parliament's purpose it may have to yield to the statutory law which confronts it, except so far as the statute's saving for a constructive trust provides a means of reconciliation of the apparent conflict.

None of the recent authorities referred to by counsel is determinative of this appeal [. . .] Nor can anything in the Law Commission's report (or its earlier working paper) be decisive. The report and the working paper are invaluable guides to the old law and to the problems which constituted the "mischief" at which section 2 of the Act of 1989 is directed, but they cannot be conclusive as to how section 2, as enacted, is to be construed and applied.

Proprietary estoppel and constructive trusts

At a high level of generality, there is much common ground between the doctrines of proprietary estoppel and the constructive trust, just as there is between proprietary estoppel and part performance. All are concerned with equity's intervention to provide relief against unconscionable conduct, whether as between neighbouring landowners, or vendor and purchaser, or relatives who make informal arrangements for sharing a home, or a fiduciary and the beneficiary or client to whom he owes a fiduciary obligation ...

In this case the judge did not make any finding as to the existence of a constructive trust. He was not asked to do so, because it was not then seen as an issue in the case. But on the findings of fact which the judge did make it was not disputed that a proprietary estoppel arose, and that the appropriate remedy was the grant to Mr. Yaxley, in satisfaction of his equitable entitlement, of a long leasehold interest, rent free, of the ground floor of the property. Those findings do in my judgment equally provide the basis for the conclusion that Mr. Yaxley was entitled to such an interest under a constructive trust. The oral bargain which the judge found to have been made between Mr. Yaxley and Mr. Brownie Gotts, and to have been adopted by Mr. Alan Gotts, was definite enough to meet the test stated by Lord Bridge in *Lloyds Bank Plc. v. Rosset* [1991] 1 A.C. 107, 132.

[. . .] To give [section 2(5)] what I take to be its natural meaning [. . .] would not create a huge and unexpected gap in section 2. It would allow a limited exception, expressly contemplated by Parliament, for those cases in which a supposed bargain has been so fully performed by one side, and the general circumstances of the matter are such, that it would be inequitable to disregard the claimant's expectations, and insufficient to grant him no more than a restitutionary remedy.

Beldam LJ

At 190

In the present case the policy behind the Commission's proposals was as clearly stated as its intention that the proposal should not affect the power of the court to give effect in equity to the principles of proprietary estoppel and constructive trusts. Even if the use to be made of the Commission's report is to be confined to identifying the defect in the law which the proposals were intended to correct, in a case such as the present it is unrealistic to divorce the defect in the law from the policy adopted to correct it. The Commission's report makes it clear that in proposing legislation to exclude the uncertainty and complexities introduced into unregistered conveyancing by the doctrine of part performance, it did not intend to affect the availability of the equitable remedies to which it referred.

[. . .]

There are circumstances in which it is not possible to infer any agreement, arrangement or understanding that the property is to be shared beneficially but in which nevertheless equity has been prepared to hold that the conduct of an owner in allowing a claimant to expend money or act otherwise to his detriment will be precluded from denying that the claimant has a proprietary interest in the property. In such a case it could not be said that to give effect to a proprietary estoppel was contrary to the policy of section 2(1) of the Act of 1989. Yet it would be a strange policy which denied similar relief to a claimant who had acted on a clear promise or representation that he should have an interest in the property. Moreover claims based on proprietary estoppel are more likely to arise where the claimant has acted after an informal promise has been made to him [. . .]

For my part I cannot see that there is any reason to qualify the plain words of section 2(5). They were included to preserve the equitable remedies to which the Commission had referred. I do not think it inherent in a social policy of simplifying conveyancing by requiring the certainty of a written document that unconscionable conduct or equitable fraud should be allowed to prevail.

In my view the provision that nothing in section 2 of the Act of 1989 is to affect the creation or operation of resulting, implied or constructive trusts effectively excludes from the operation of the section cases in which an interest in land might equally well be claimed by relying on constructive trust or proprietary estoppel.

That, to my mind, is the case here. There was on the judge's findings, as I interpret them, a clear promise made by Brownie Gotts to the plaintiff that he would have a beneficial interest in the ground floor of the premises. That promise was known to Alan Gotts when he acquired the property and he permitted the plaintiff to carry out the whole of the work needed to the property and to convert the ground floor in the belief that he had such an interest. It would be unconscionable to allow either Alan or Brownie Gotts to resile from the representations made by Brownie Gotts and adopted by Alan Gotts. For my part I would hold that the plaintiff established facts on which a court of equity would find that Alan Gotts held the property subject to a constructive trust in favour of the plaintiff for an interest in the ground floor and that that interest should be satisfied by the grant of a 99-year lease. I consider the judge was entitled to reach the same conclusion by finding a proprietary estoppel in favour of the plaintiff [. . .]

Clarke LJ

At 181–2

It seems to me that in considering whether a particular estoppel relied upon would offend the public policy behind a statute it is necessary to consider the mischief at which the statute is directed. Where a statute has been enacted as a result of the recommendations of the Law Commission, it is, as I see it, both appropriate and permissible for the court to consider those recommendations in order to help to identify both the mischief which the Act is designed to cure and the public policy underlying it. Indeed, although I agree with Robert Walker L.J. that they cannot be conclusive as to how a particular provision should be construed, I entirely agree with Beldam L.J. that the policy behind section 2 of the Act of 1989 can clearly be seen from the Law Commission Report to which he refers. In my opinion the contents of that report will be of the greatest assistance in deciding whether or not the principles of particular types of estoppel should be held to be contrary to the public policy underlying the Act.

The first instance judge had ordered that Mr Gotts should pay Mr Yaxley the value of the promised 99-year lease of the ground-floor flats, or grant him such a lease, and Mr Gotts' appeal against that ruling failed.

The result in *Yaxley* does not assist in deciding as between View 1 and View 2, as, on the facts, the court was willing to find that a constructive trust had arisen. The same can be said of the Court of Appeal's decision in *Kinane v Mackie-Conteh*.[77] Mr Mackie-Conteh (A) had agreed in a letter to grant a charge over his home as security for a loan from Mr Kinane (B). B provided the loan money, but A refused to grant the charge. A argued that he was under no contractual duty to do so, as the letter had been signed only by him, and not by B, and so the requirements of s 2 had not been met. B therefore argued that A was under a duty to him as a result of proprietary estoppel, or a constructive trust. The Court of Appeal found that the requirements of proprietary estoppel had been met, and also those of a common intention constructive trust. Again, the result is consistent with either View 1 or View 2, although the reasoning of the court, like that of Robert Walker LJ in *Yaxley*, is perhaps closer to View 1: Arden LJ asked whether Mr Kinane could demonstrate an estoppel 'overlapping' with a constructive trust,[78] and Neuberger LJ proceeded on the basis that Mr Kinane's claim would fail under s 2 if he could only establish an estoppel, but not a constructive trust.[79] The courts' hesitation to adopt View 2 can also be seen in *Matchmove Ltd v Dowding*.[80] The first instance finding in favour of the claimants was based on both proprietary estoppel and a common intention constructive trust, but the Court of Appeal's decision was based solely on the second of those doctrines, as then the express s 2(5) exception could be employed.

It has been pointed out, however,[81] that there are some difficulties with the courts' current approach, which seems in practice to give effect to View 2 (permitting proprietary estoppel claims to succeed in the absence of the formalities required by s 2), whilst formally following View 1 (as the successful claims are said to arise under constructive trusts). Firstly, it is not apparent, for example, that the agreement in *Yaxley* (to grant a lease) or that in *Kinane* (to grant a charge) can be explained on the basis of a constructive trust:[82] for such a trust to arise, there must be an intention to share the beneficial *ownership* of the property.[83] Secondly, forcing a claim into the constructive trust category may also distort the test applied to such a claim. Where a proprietary estoppel arises, it is clear that a promise on which the claimant has relied will not always be enforced (see Chapter 10, section 3): sometimes the claimant will have to settle for a lesser remedy. In contrast, the common intention constructive trust doctrine is based on the intentions of the parties and so it seems that, where it is based on a specific promise made by A to B, such a promise will be enforced.[84] There is therefore a risk that, by using a constructive trust analysis to bring s 2(5) into play, a court may also allow a claimant access to an unjustifiably generous remedy.[85]

---

[77] [2005] EWCA Civ 45, [2005] WTLR 345.   [78] [2005] EWCA Civ 45, [2005] WTLR 345, [31].

[79] [2005] EWCA Civ 45, [2005] WTLR 345, [45]. Note that, judging from the extract set out in section 3.8.2 from the Cambridge Law Journal, Lord Neuberger since changed his mind on that point.

[80] [2017] 1 WLR 749.

[81] See e.g. Smith, 'Oral Contracts for Sale of Land: Estoppels and Constructive Trusts' (2000) 116 LQR 11. McFarlane, 'Proprietary Estoppel and Failed Contractual Negotiations' [2005] Conv 501, Owen and Rees, 'Section 2(5) of the Law of Property (Miscellaneous Provisions) Act 1989: A Misconceived Approach?' [2011] Conv 495.

[82] Smith, 'Oral Contracts for Sale of Land: Estoppels and Constructive Trusts' (2000) 116 LQR 11.

[83] *Lloyds Bank plc v Rosset* [1991] 1 AC 107.

[84] See e.g. *Oxley v Hiscock* [2004] EWCA Civ 546, [2005] Fam 211, [69] (Chadwick LJ) and Lord Walker in *Stack v Dowden* [2007] 2 AC 432, [37].

[85] A point made by e.g. Boncey and Ng, '"Common Intention" Constructive Trusts Arising from Informal Agreements to Dispose of Land' [2017] Conv 146.

It is therefore significant that, since *Yaxley*, there are signs of a change in the courts' general attitude to the relationship between proprietary estoppel and constructive trusts. Indeed, Robert Walker LJ himself later retreated from his view, expressed in *Yaxley*, of the close relationship between the doctrines, and, as Lord Walker, instead emphasized the differences between them.[86] Once the doctrines are separated, accepting View 2 is the only way of ensuring that proprietary estoppel, as intended by the Law Commission, can fulfil its aim of avoiding the harsh results that may occur where B relies on an agreement with A but cannot bring a contractual claim. It is perhaps unfortunate, therefore, that the 1989 Act does not expressly state that proprietary estoppel claims are unaffected by s 2, as this would have made the position absolutely clear, and prevented the courts from feeling the need to force proprietary estoppel claims where a defendant invokes s 2 into the often ill-fitting guise of a constructive trust.

4 THE EFFECT OF A CONTRACT

The conclusion of a contract between A and B for the transfer or grant of a legal estate or interest is of course different from the actual transfer or grant of that interest. If, for example, A makes a contract to transfer a registered estate to B, further steps need to be taken before B can acquire legal title: the transfer must be completed (see section 5 below) and B must also be registered as proprietor (see section 6 below). Nonetheless, the entry into a contract is a significant step, and not only as concerns the rights and duties of A and B: this is because, from the moment that A comes under a duty to give B an estate or interest in land, B acquires an equitable interest in A's land. This interest can be seen as dependent on an equitable principle that we will refer to as the 'doctrine of anticipation'.

4.1 THE REQUIREMENTS OF THE DOCTRINE OF ANTICIPATION

The doctrine, which is associated with the traditional equitable maxim that 'equity regards as done what ought to be done', applies where A is under a duty to give B a recognized property right, but has not yet done so. Equity anticipates the grant of that right by conferring on B an immediate equitable interest that mirrors the right that A is under a duty to give B. A classic example is provided by *Walsh v Lonsdale*,[87] which we will examine in Chapter 19, section 3.2: as A (Lonsdale) was under a contractual duty to grant a lease to B (Walsh), B acquired an immediate equitable interest in the land. That interest, an equitable lease, mirrored the lease that A had promised to grant, and so the terms of the promised lease were decisive in working out the parties' rights and duties against each other. Similarly, where A makes a contract of sale of land with B, then, as recognized by the Supreme Court in *Scott v Southern Pacific*,[88] there is a '*long line of authorities*' which show that B acquires an immediate equitable interest in A's land.

The doctrine can apply whenever A is under a duty to give B a property right, whether or not A's duty arose under a contract. So if, for example, a court orders A to transfer an estate to B, B acquires an equitable interest from the moment of the court order.[89] If, however, B

---

[86] *Stack v Dowden* [2007] 2 AC 432, [37].   [87] (1882) LR 21 Ch D 9 (CA).
[88] [2015] AC 385, [57] and [65] (Lord Collins).   [89] *Mountney v Treharne* [2003] Ch 135.

wishes to show that A is under a *contractual* duty to B to give B an interest in land, then B must show that all the requirements for such a contract, including compliance with s 2 of the 1989 Act, have been met: the doctrine can regulate the effect of a contract, but it does not allow the requirements for such a contract to be avoided. Moreover, the doctrine can apply only if the contract does impose a duty to give B a *recognized* property right: if the contract simply obliges A, for example, to share occupation with B, then, as noted in Chapter 7, section 3.1, B will have only a personal right: a contractual licence.

It is also generally said to be the case that, where the doctrine is based on a contractual duty owed by A to B, it can apply only where the contract is capable of specific performance. It should be emphasized that, on this view, the availability of specific performance is an additional requirement, and is not a substitute for the point that A's duty must be one to give B a recognized property right.[90] As noted in Chapter 1, section 4, the unique nature of land means that damages will be seen as an inadequate remedy if A were to breach a contract to give B a recognized property right in land. In our standard case, then, this specific enforceability requirement causes no obstacle to B's acquisition of an equitable interest. In some cases, however, particular facts may mean that B would be unsuccessful if asking a court for an order for specific performance: the courts have discretion in awarding such an equitable remedy, and facts occurring after entry into the contract may be relevant to the exercise of that discretion. If, for example, such facts would mean that A would now suffer personal hardship were specific performance to be granted, a court may refuse to order specific performance.[91] This has led some to argue that it must be a mistake to think that the question of whether or not B has acquired an equitable interest, capable of binding a third party, can depend on the availability of specific performance.[92]

A possible solution is suggested by Turner in the following extract, and is based on a distinction between two senses of 'specific performance'. His analysis is focussed on the particular situation where A's contractual duty is to transfer an estate in land to B, and so A is the vendor and B the purchaser, but it also applies more generally.

Turner, 'Understanding the Constructive Trust Between Vendor and Purchaser'
(2012) 128 LQR 582, 590–1

For the purchaser to acquire an interest in land, the contract must be 'specifically enforceable'. But fewer facts need to be proved than to establish 'specific enforceability' in the second sense, of being entitled to an order for immediate performance of the contract. All that the purchaser need prove is that:

(i)   formation and performance of the contract are legal;

(ii) the contract is for valuable consideration; and

(iii) the subject matter of the contract is 'unique'.

---

[90] See Chapter 7, section 3.1, referring to Lord Wilberforce's statement in *National Provincial Bank v Ainsworth* [1965] AC 1175.

[91] See e.g. *Patel v Ali* [1984] Ch 283.

[92] See e.g. Gardner, 'Equity, Estate Contracts and the Judicature Acts: *Walsh v Lonsdale* Revisited' (1987) 7 OJLS 60, 74.

Because he would have to prove these facts if he sought a specific performance decree, these two senses of 'specific enforceability' are not mutually exclusive. Yet they are radically different […] for the purpose of answering [the question of whether or not B has an equitable interest as soon as the contract is made], facts that could prompt a court otherwise minded to decree specific performance to refuse a decree in its discretion are also ignored. The time for deciding whether to exercise that discretion is the time of judgment. Earlier, when the contract is formed, it is assumed that no facts in this category will be proved in any later suit for specific performance of the contract. If they are proved at that later stage, then the interest created in the purchaser when the contract was formed will, again, prove to be of no further use.

4.2 THE NATURE OF B'S INTEREST

Where the doctrine of anticipation operates, B acquires an equitable interest in A's land, and so B's right is capable of binding a third party, such as C, later acquiring a right in the land, and is also protected on A's insolvency. The doctrine thus provides important protection to B and, as noted by Turner, it *'operate[s] to fulfil the parties' intentions'* by assisting B to acquire a right in the land itself, as promised by A.[93] The specific type of equitable interest acquired under the doctrine of anticipation is dependent on the content of A's duty to B. Where it is a duty to grant B a lease, or an interest in land, B obtains the equitable equivalent of the intended right: an agreement for a lease gives rise to an equitable lease, an agreement for an easement gives rise to an equitable easement, etc. Where the duty is for A to transfer A's legal estate to B, as in our standard case of a sale of land, A holds that estate on trust for B, as explained by Lord Jessel MR in *Lysaght v Edwards*:[94]

The moment you have a valid contract for sale the vendor becomes in equity a trustee for the purchaser of the estate sold, and the beneficial ownership passes to the purchaser, the vendor having a right to the purchase-money, a charge or lien on the estate for the security of that purchase-money, and a right to retain possession of the estate until the purchase-money is paid, in the absence of express contract as to the time of delivering possession.

As is evident from Lord Jessel MR's description, this vendor–purchaser trust is somewhat unusual: although A holds on trust, he or she is entitled still to make some use of the property for his or her own benefit, at least until the purchase price is paid.[95] As Lord Walker explained in *Jerome v Kelly*:[96]

It would therefore be wrong to treat an uncompleted contract for the sale of land as equivalent to an immediate, irrevocable declaration of trust (or assignment of beneficial interest)

---

[93] Turner, 'Understanding the Constructive Trust between Vendor and Purchaser' (2012) 128 LQR 582, 605. Of course, the doctrine of anticipation does not give B the very interest that B is due to acquire under the contract, only an equitable equivalent. However, Turner's point is that, by giving B a right that can bind a third party, the doctrine gives B a chance still to acquire the promised right even if, for example, A sells the land to C before completing the contract with B.

[94] (1876) 2 Ch D 499, 506.

[95] The usual position, applying as a default for example in an express trust, is that A, as trustee, is under a duty to B not to use the property for A's own benefit.

[96] [2004] UKHL 25, [2004] 1 WLR 1409, [32].

> in the land. Neither the seller nor the buyer has unqualified beneficial ownership. Beneficial
> ownership of the land is in a sense split between the seller and the buyer on the provisional
> assumptions that specific performance is available and that the contract will in due course
> be completed, if necessary by the court ordering specific performance. In the meantime, the
> seller is entitled to enjoyment of the land or its rental income. The provisional assumptions
> may be falsified by events, such as rescission of the contract (either under a contractual term
> or on breach). If the contract proceeds to completion the equitable interest can be viewed
> as passing to the buyer in stages, as title is made and accepted and as the purchase price is
> paid in full.

Lord Walker's analysis has been developed by Turner, who concludes that:[97] '*The vendor-purchaser trust is not a single equitable "response" to a single "event". It comprises several equities that can be seen as plural "responses" to plural "events". These "events" are sets of facts that differ as the contract matures from formation onwards.*'

4.3 ESTATE CONTRACTS

Where B acquires an equitable interest as a result of A's contractual duty to transfer or grant a legal property right in land, that interest can also be said to arise under an 'estate contract'. Under s 2(3)(iv) of the LPA 1925, an estate contract is defined as: '*any contract to convey or create a legal estate, including a contract conferring either expressly or by statutory implication a valid option to purchase, a right of pre-emption, or any other like right.*'[98] The benefit of such a contract is listed in s 2(3) as one of the equitable interests that cannot be overreached under s 2(2) of the Act. As we noted in Chapter 6, section 3, overreaching is a particular defence that can be used by C against a pre-existing interest of B: we will examine the defence in detail in Chapter 17.

It seems, therefore, that, in our standard case of a contract of sale of land from A to B,[99] the equitable interest immediately acquired by B can be seen as both an estate contract and as a (limited) beneficial interest under a trust. If C then attempts to use the overreaching defence to take priority to B's equitable interest, B will argue that B's right is immune from that defence by the operation of s 2(3)(iv) of the LPA 1925. Characterization of B's right as an estate contract can therefore assist B. As we noted in Chapter 5, section 6.2, and as we will see in section 5.1 below, it was, however, held in *Baker v Craggs*[100] that, once the contract between A and B has been completed by A's execution of a deed transferring A's estate to B, B can no longer be regarded as having an estate contract. Prior to the introduction of registration statutes, B would, at that point, have acquired A's legal estate; now, however, it is very likely

---

[97] Turner, 'Understanding the Constructive Trust between Vendor and Purchaser' (2012) 128 LQR 582, 605.

[98] Note that, as a result of s 1(4) of the LPA 1925 (see Chapter 5, section 3), the reference in s 2(3)(iv) to a 'legal estate' includes within its scope any legal estate, easement or charge. As a result, for example, A's contract to grant B an easement gives rise to an estate contract.

[99] In *Baker v Craggs* [2017] Ch 295, [32], Newey J stated that, '*for the purposes of s 2 of the LPA, "legal estate" is defined in such a way as to include an easement.*' The significance of this point (which is based on s 1(4) of the LPA 1925) was that the acquisition of a legal estate by C is a requirement for C to invoke the overreaching defence: see Chapter 17, section 2.3. If the point is correct, it would presumably also mean that a contract to grant an easement would count as an estate contract.

[100] [2017] Ch 295, [40].

that B will need to register and so will acquire legal title only when the disposition from A to B is registered. In such a case, in the period after completion and before registration, B has only a (full) beneficial interest under a trust. Such a right, unlike an estate contract, *is* subject to the overreaching defence under s 2 of the LPA 1925. This means that, as far as exposure to the overreaching defence is concerned, B is therefore in a worse position if C acquires a right in the land *after* completion of A and B's contract, rather than before completion of that contract. This may seem counter-intuitive and, indeed, the decision in *Baker* is currently under appeal; but, as will be discussed in section 5.1, it may be possible to defend this interpretation of the term 'estate contract'.

In contrast, under the priority rules applying to unregistered land under the Land Charges Act 1925,[101] an estate contract that has not been registered as a land charge will be void against C, a third party later acquiring a property right in the land for value. This means that, in a priority dispute with C in unregistered land, B may instead wish to argue that he or she does *not* have an estate contract, but rather a different form of equitable interest, which does not need to be registered as a land charge. In *Lloyds Bank v Carrick*,[102] however, the Court of Appeal rejected such an argument: B claimed an equitable interest arising under a bare trust (which would not require registration as a land charge), but as that trust was necessarily based on A's contractual promise to sell his lease to B, it was held that B had no interest that was separate and distinct from the estate contract. The decision in *Baker* might seem to be inconsistent with that analysis, but Newey J distinguished *Carrick* on the basis that, in that earlier case: '*no conveyance or transfer had been executed*'.[103] Although B had paid the purchase price to A in *Carrick*, A had not yet made the transfer to B, and so B's right could still be seen as dependent on A's contractual promise to B, and thus as an estate contract. On this view, the significance of completion of the contract is that A has performed his or her duty under the contract, so B's equitable interest can no longer be seen as arising under an 'estate contract' and becomes instead a full beneficial interest under a trust.

4.4 DOES B HAVE A POWER TO CREATE PROPERTY RIGHTS IN OTHERS?

We have seen that, in our standard case of a contract of sale of land from A to B, B acquires an equitable interest, both under an estate contract and as a (limited) beneficial interest, as soon as the contract is made. As an equitable interest, B's right is capable of binding a third party, such as C, later acquiring a right in the land, and is also protected on A's insolvency. In *Scott v Southern Pacific Mortgages Ltd*,[104] the facts of which are set out in full in Chapter 15, section 3.1.3, the Supreme Court considered the question of whether the equitable interest held by B under a contract for sale allowed B, before completion of the contract of sale, to create property rights in others. The question arose because Mrs Scott wished to show that, as a result of a proprietary estoppel operating against the purchaser (B), she had acquired an equitable interest, derived from B's interest, that was capable of binding a mortgagee, C. To bind C, Mrs Scott had to show that she acquired a proprietary right *before* the sale to B was completed.[105]

---

[101] Those rules are considered in a specific additional chapter available with the online resources.
[102] [1996] 4 All ER 630 (CA).   [103] [2017] Ch 295, [40].   [104] [2015] AC 385.
[105] On the facts of *Scott*, Mrs Scott was in fact also the vendor of the property (A), as she was selling her home to B. For present purposes, nothing turns on that point, although it may be important for other questions decided in the *Scott* case (see the view of Calnan as set out in Chapter 15, section 3.1.3).

She therefore argued that her proprietary right in the land arose as soon as B acquired an equitable interest under the contract of sale to B. The Supreme Court unanimously held that Mrs Scott had not acquired such an equitable interest: her claim against B could give her an equitable interest only at the later point when the sale contract between A and B was completed. For example, Lord Collins stated that:[106] *'where the proprietary right is claimed to be derived from the rights of a person who does not have the legal estate, then the right needs to be "fed" by the acquisition of the legal estate before it can be asserted otherwise than personally.'*[107]

There is, however, at least one instance where it appears that B can create immediate property rights in others: where there is a sub-sale in which B contracts to sell the title to a third party prior to the transfer of title to B.[108] The sub-sale is itself an estate contract and gives rise to a sub-trust, whereby B's own (limited) beneficial interest in A's land is held by B on sub-trust for the sub-purchaser. It is possible, however, that such a sub-trust may be distinguished from a claim, such as that in *Scott*, to a property right that is different in type to the interest held by B.

5 COMPLETION: DISPOSITION BY TRANSFER OR GRANT

Once a contract for the sale or other disposition of an interest in land is created by A and B, it is then completed by each side performing his or her duties under the contract. Where A has promised to transfer a legal estate or interest to B, or to grant B a legal estate or interest, A must therefore take steps to make that disposition to B. As seen in section 3.5, once the contract is executed, no question of compliance with s 2 of the LP(MP)A 1989 can be raised. The basic formality requirements necessary for the creation or transfer of the legal right, and their exceptions, are provided by ss 52 and 54 of the LPA 1925.

Law of Property Act 1925, ss 52 and 54

52 (1) All conveyances of land or of any interest therein are void for the purpose of conveying or creating a legal estate unless made by deed.

   (2) This section does not apply to— [. . .]

     (d) leases or tenancies or other assurances not required by law to be made in writing; [. . .]

     (g) conveyances taking effect by operation of law.

54 (1) All interests in land created by parol and not put in writing and signed by the persons so creating the same, or by their agents thereunto lawfully authorised in writing, have, notwithstanding any consideration having been given for the same, the force and effect of interests at will only.

---

[106] [2015] AC 385, [71].

[107] It seems here that, when referring to *'acquisition of the legal estate'*, Lord Collins does not mean to refer to the point when B is registered as proprietor, but rather to the earlier point when the contract is completed (see the discussion of this point in section 5).

[108] For example, *Berkley v Poulett* (1977) EGLR 86.

> (2) Nothing in the foregoing provisions of this Part of this Act shall affect the creation by parol of leases taking effect in possession for a term not exceeding three years (whether or not the lessee is given power to extend the term) at the best rent which can be reasonably obtained without taking a fine.

Hence, save in exceptional cases, the creation or transfer of a legal right requires the execution of a deed. The most notable exception to the need for a deed is that contained in s 54(2) for short leases. This is limited by the terms of the provision to a lease that meets all of the following criteria: it is for three years or less; involves payment of a market rent, without a premium; and takes effect in possession. It has been held that the right to possession must be immediate and so arise as soon as the oral grant is made.[109] We will examine those requirements in Chapter 19, section 3.1, but two points are worth noting here. Firstly, even if a legal lease was *created* orally as it met the requirements of s 54(2), the *transfer* of that lease will require the use of a deed.[110] Secondly, whilst the creation of a legal lease meeting the requirements of s 54(2) does not require the use of a deed, if, at the same time, an easement is expressly granted to the tenant, such an easement must be created by a deed if it is to take effect as a legal property right.[111]

5.1 THE EFFECT OF COMPLETION

If A has made a contract to grant or transfer a legal estate or interest to B, the effect of non-compliance with s 52 is that legal title does not pass and that the contract is not performed. As discussed in section 4, B may still have an equitable interest, arising as a result of the contract under the doctrine of anticipation.[112] If s 52 is complied with, the mere fact of completion does not, however, ensure that B has acquired a legal interest: in many cases, registration will be required (see section 6). So, whilst it is commonly said that, on completion, A has made the transfer or grant to B, it is important to remember that it will very often also be necessary for B to take the additional step of registration before B can acquire a legal estate or interest. To take the example of contract of sale of A's registered estate to B, we can say the contract is completed, or that a transfer is made by A, when A executes the necessary documents,[113] but we must remember that B acquires the legal estate only on registration, and that A retains the legal estate until that point. To use the language of s 27 of the LRA 2002, completion means that a disposition of the registered estate has occurred, but that

---

[109] *Long v Tower Hamlets LBC* [1998] Ch 197. The implications of the decision are considered by Bright, 'Beware the Informal Lease: The (Very) Narrow Scope of S.54(2) Law of Property Act 1925' [1998] Conv 229.

[110] *Crago v Julian* [1992] 1 WLR 372 (CA).

[111] See Law Com CP No 227 (2016) [16.17], noting that neither s 52 nor s 54 of the LPA 1925 contains an exception for such easements, and so the general rule in s 52(1) applies. Where an easement arises by implied, rather than express, grant, and is implied into a short oral lease which, thanks to s 54(2), creates a legal lease, the position is less clear: again, there is no express exception from the s 52(1) rule, but there is this time an argument that, as the easement is implied into the grant of a legal lease, it must itself be legal. The position is described by the Law Commission as 'equivocal': Law Com CP No 227 (2016) [16.20].

[112] See e.g. *Scott v Southern Pacific Morgages Ltd* [2015] AC 385, [113] (Lady Hale): '*There is a gap between any transaction and its registration ... Until registration, the purchaser (and indeed the mortgagee) have only equitable interests.*'

[113] The language of transfer is used in relation to completion, for example, by each of Lord Collins and Lady Hale in *Scott v Southern Pacific Morgages Ltd* [2015] AC 385, [79] and [115].

disposition will not operate at law, and so will not give B a legal estate, unless and until it is registered.

Nonetheless, completion of the contract still has some significant effects.

Firstly, we noted in Chapter 3, section 3.2.3 that, if B does go on to register as the new holder of A's estate, B may be able to take priority over pre-existing property rights in the land by using the lack of registration defence. As we will see in Chapter 16, section 4, that defence may operate, under s 29 of the LRA 2002, to give B protection against an interest affecting A's estate immediately before the '*disposition*' to B. The timing of the disposition (i.e. of completion) can therefore be important. Moreover, if a party with a prior interest that has not been protected by an entry of a notice on the register wishes to claim that the right is an overriding interest, owing to his or her actual occupation of the land, then such actual occupation must be present at the time of the *disposition* to B.[114]

Secondly, it seems that the *nature* of B's equitable interest changes on completion. Lord Walker in *Jerome v Kelly*,[115] stated that: '*the equitable interest can be viewed as passing to the buyer in stages, as title is made and accepted and as the purchase price is paid in full*'. After the contract is concluded, but before completion, B has an estate contract (see section 4) as well as an interest under a trust. On completion, however, it seems that B can no longer be regarded as having an estate contract, and has instead a full beneficial interest under a trust. In *Baker v Craggs*,[116] Newey J explained that:

> A contract for the sale of unregistered land normally merges in the conveyance when it is executed, and the better view appears to me to be that a contract for the sale of registered land likewise merges in a transfer [. . .] the original contract will generally be spent or, in other words, the purchaser will no longer have the benefit of an 'estate contract'.

That consequence of completion may seem a very technical one but, as we noted in Chapter 5, section 6.2, and as we will see in Chapter 17, section 2.2, it had an important consequence in *Craggs*: there, land was sold to B by A1 and A2, and a third party, C, had acquired a right in the land from A1 and A2 after completion of the transfer from A1 and A2 to B, but before B had registered that disposition. C wanted to take priority over B's pre-existing equitable interest by using the overreaching defence, but that defence cannot be used against an estate contract. By finding that B's right, after completion, was no longer an estate contract, but instead a beneficial interest under a trust, Newey J gave C the chance to rely on the overreaching defence to take priority over B's right. An appeal is pending against that decision, and Newey J's analysis of the effect of completion is controversial, chiefly because it might seem to be too ready to carry over the unregistered analysis into the different registered land scheme.[117] Certainly, there is a difference between unregistered and registered land as to when B acquires a legal estate. It can still be argued, however, that there is a logical basis to Newey J's analysis: once the contract has been executed by the use of a deed, and A has done all that is required of him or her under the contract, it seems odd still to regard B's right as arising under an 'estate contract'.

---

[114] See Chapter 16, section 4.2.6. As will be discussed there, it has been suggested, somewhat controversially, that such actual occupation must also be present at the time of B's registration.

[115] [2004] 1 WLR 1409, [32].   [116] [2017] Ch 295.

[117] As noted by Dixon, 'The Registration Gap and Overreaching' [2017] Conv 1, 3, the point as to the effect of completion on B's right is 'novel and difficult'; it is similarly described by Owen, 'Priorities and Registered Land During the Registration Gap' [2017] Conv 230, 241, as 'fraught with difficulty'.

Newey J's analysis is also consistent with an equitable principle, distinct from the doctrine of anticipation, that can operate where A seeks to make a gift of a registered estate to B. If a deed is used,[118] so that A has now done all that A can to ensure that the gift is completed, but B has failed to register, it may be possible for B to show that he or she has a beneficial interest in the estate under the principle, identified with the case of *re Rose*,[119] that where A has done all that he or she can to make a voluntary transfer of a right to B, A then holds that right on constructive trust for B. That principle, of course, can operate only after the deed has been used, and A's mere statement or promise to make such a transfer does not, of itself, give B any rights.[120] The principle has been applied in relation to registered land,[121] and it has been suggested that it might also be applicable in a case such as *Craggs*, and could thus provide an explanation for B's holding an equitable interest, on completion, that does not arise under an estate contract.[122]

Thirdly, we noted in section 4.4 that, before completion, B's equitable interest is not such as to give B a general power to create property rights in others. In *Scott v Southern Pacific Mortgages Ltd*,[123] however, each of Lord Collins and Lady Hale stated that a party who had dealt with B could acquire a property right when B's contract of sale with A was completed by a transfer from A to B.[124] Lord Collins did at one point refer to the party acquiring a property right from B only when B acquired a legal estate;[125] strictly speaking, of course, B acquires a legal estate only on registration, but the context makes reasonably clear that it is completion rather than registration that was regarded by Lord Collins as the decisive moment.[126]

Finally, if, as is often the case, B finances his or her acquisition of the registered estate by means of a mortgage, and a priority dispute arises between the mortgagee and a third party claiming a right in relation to the land, then the mortgagee's right will be regarded, for the purposes of such a dispute, as having arisen on completion of the transfer, even if that transfer has not yet been registered. We will consider this point in more detail in Chapter 15, section 3.1. We will see there that, in *Scott v Southern Pacific*,[127] a majority of the Supreme Court refused to extend that approach and say that the mortgagee's right could be regarded as arising at the moment when the contract between A and B was made. This means there is a further practical difference between the entry into a contract and completion: if a third party has a property right at the time of the entry into a contract of sale between A and B,

---

[118] Indeed, as noted in section 5.2, the usual procedure is for the deed to consist of the very TR1 form that B needs to provide to the registry when applying for registration of his or her estate.

[119] *Re Rose, Rose v IRC* [1952] 1 Ch 499 (CA).

[120] If B relies on a promise to make a voluntary transfer, a proprietary estoppel claim may arise: see e.g. *Thorner v Major* [2009] 1 WLR 776 (discussed in Chapter 10, section 1.1).

[121] See e.g. *Mascall v Mascall* (1985) 50 P & CR 19.

[122] Simoncelli-Allan, '*Baker v Craggs*: Trusts during the Registration Gap in Registered Land' (2017) 23 Trusts & Trustees 958.

[123] [2015] AC 385.

[124] See e.g. [2015] AC 385, [95] (Lady Hale): '*the purchaser was not in a position either at the date of exchange or at any time up until completion of the purchase to confer equitable proprietary, as opposed to merely personal, rights*'.

[125] [2015] AC 385, [71] (as set out in section 4.4).

[126] [2015] AC 385, [79] where Lord Collins refers to Mrs Scott's rights becoming proprietary when '*fed by the purchasers' acquisition of the legal estate on completion*' and also refers to *Abbey National v Cann* [1991] 1 AC 56, where the rights of B's mortgagee were regarded as arising on completion rather than at the later point when B registered. See too Lady Hale at [113], referring to registration as a means to make the transfer (i.e. completion) 'operate at law'.

[127] [2015] AC 385.

then that property right is capable of binding B's mortgagee; if the third party's property right arises only on completion of the sale to B, then that property right is not capable of binding B's mortgagee.

5.2 THE REQUIREMENTS OF A DEED

The requirements of a deed are provided in s 1 of the LP(MP)A 1989.

Law of Property (Miscellaneous Provisions) Act 1989, s 1

Deeds and their execution

(1) Any rule of law which—

    (a) restricts the substances on which a deed may be written;

    (b) requires a seal for the valid execution of an instrument as a deed by an individual; or

    (c) requires authority by one person to another to deliver an instrument as a deed on his behalf to be given by deed,

    is abolished.

(2) An instrument shall not be a deed unless—

    (a) it makes it clear on its face that it is intended to be a deed by the person making it or, as the case may be, by the parties to it (whether by describing itself as a deed or expressing itself to be executed or signed as a deed or otherwise); and

    (b) it is validly executed as a deed—

        (i) by that person or a person authorised to execute it in the name or on behalf of that person, or

        (ii) by one or more of those parties or a person authorised to execute it in the name or on behalf of one or more of those parties.

(2A) For the purposes of subsection (2)(a) above, an instrument shall not be taken to make it clear on its face that it is intended to be a deed merely because it is executed under seal.

(3) An instrument is validly executed as a deed by an individual if, and only if—

    (a) it is signed—

        (i) by him in the presence of a witness who attests the signature; or

        (ii) at his direction and in his presence and the presence of two witnesses who each attest the signature; and

    (b) it is delivered as a deed.

(4) In subsections (2) and (3) above "sign", in relation to an instrument, includes

    (a) an individual signing the name of the person or party on whose behalf he executes the instrument; and

    (b) making one's mark on the instrument,

    and "signature" is to be construed accordingly.

(4A) Subsection (3) above applies in the case of an instrument executed by an individual in the name or on behalf of another person whether or not that person is also an individual.

In our example, where A sells a registered estate to B, A completes by executing a TR1 form: this counts as a deed and is also the form required to allow B to apply to be registered as proprietor. In such standard cases, therefore, the requirement of a deed is met simply as part of the registration process.

Like s 2 of the 1989 Act, s 1 implements recommendations by the Law Commission.[128] It represents a modernization of the requirements for a deed. Under the provision, the key requirements for a document to be a deed are that it is signed and attested, and that it specifies on its face that it is a deed. The specific need for attestation, explained in s 1(3)(a)(i), is that the document is signed '*in the presence of a witness*', who then signs the deed him or herself.[129] This requirement is not met, for example, if a witness was not present when the party executing the deed signed it. Where a deed appears on its face to comply with the requirement of attestation, the party executing the deed will be estopped from seeking to invalidate it on the basis that attestation did not in fact take place.[130] However, estoppel will not apply where non-compliance is apparent on the face of the document; for example, where there is no space for attestation.[131]

A deed takes effect when it is 'delivered as a deed'.[132] This will be immediate if the document specifies that it is 'signed and delivered' as a deed; in other cases, there will need to be a subsequent delivery. Delivery originally denoted a physical act, but the requirement has evolved to relate to an intention to be bound.[133] This means that the continued use of the term 'delivery' can cause confusion.[134] Moreover, delivery in this sense can occur even if the transaction is not intended to have immediate effect, as explained in the following extract:

Longman v Viscount Chelsea
(1989) 58 P & CR 189, CA

Nourse LJ

At 195

A writing cannot become a deed unless it is signed, [. . .] and delivered as a deed. Having reached that stage, it is correctly described as having been "executed" as a deed. Having been signed [. . .], it may be delivered in one of three ways. First, it may be delivered as an unconditional deed, being irrevocable and taking immediate effect. Secondly, it may be delivered as an escrow, being irrevocable but not taking effect unless and until the condition or conditions of the escrow are fulfilled. Thirdly, it may be handed to an agent of the maker with instructions to deal with it in a certain way in a certain event, being revocable and of no effect unless and until it is so dealt with, whereupon it is delivered and takes effect [. . .]

---

[128] Law Commission Report No 163, *Deeds and Escrows* (1987).
[129] For discussion of the requirement, see M Dray, 'Deeds Speak Louder than Words. Attesting Time for Deeds?' [2013] Conv 298.
[130] *Shah v Shah* [2002] QB 35.
[131] For example, *Briggs v Gleeds* [2014] EWHC 1178 (Ch); *Bank of Scotland v Waugh* [2014] EWHC 2117 (Ch).
[132] Section 1(3)(b) of the 1989 Act.
[133] See e.g. *Vincent v Premo Enterprises (Voucher Sales) Ltd* [1969] 2 QB 609 (CA), 619 (Lord Denning MR): '*Delivery in this connection does not mean "handed over" to the other side. It means delivered in the old legal sense, namely, an act done so as to evince an intention to be bound.*'
[134] As noted by e.g. Yale, 'The Delivery of a Deed' [1970] CLJ 52, 73–4.

Whether a deed is within the second or third category is dependent on the intention of the party executing the deed. In that case, Mrs Longman, who held a long lease of a residential property, had negotiated with her landlord, the Cadogan Estate, for the surrender of her existing lease and the grant of a new one with an extended term. Each part of the transaction required a deed and both parties had signed deeds in preparation for completion. The Estate then withdrew and made a fresh offer for a new lease at a vastly increased cost. Mrs Longman argued that the Estate could not withdraw as the deed granting the new lease had been delivered as an escrow and that the remaining conditions had been, or could be, fulfilled. Her claim failed, because there was no intent on the part of the landlord to deliver the deed. This was evident by the fact that the parties' negotiations had been expressly conducted subject to the formal execution of the deeds. The Court was critical of the conduct of the landlord, which was considered 'deplorable',[135] but conscious that, in everyday conveyancing, it is usual for deeds to be signed in advance of completion without being intended to be irrevocable.

6 REGISTRATION OF TITLE

6.1 REGISTRATION AND THE ACQUISITION QUESTION

We saw in Chapter 3 that registration plays a very important role in land law. In this section, we will consider the specific provisions of the LRA 2002 that have an impact on the acquisition of property rights in land. In Chapter 16, we will look at how the Act also affects the defences question, by determining the priority of competing property rights. We will also provide an overview of the impact of the LRA 2002 in Chapter 18, section 2.

The importance of registration when considering the acquisition question can be simply stated: in most cases, if A wishes to transfer to, or grant, B a legal estate or interest in land, that legal estate or interest will only be acquired by B on registration.[136] When considering the transfer of a legal freehold, for example, either the legal title being transferred will already be subject to registration,[137] or the transfer in question will trigger compulsory first registration.[138] Where registration is required, failure to do so carries the consequence that legal title will not be transferred. Title remains with the transferor, although, in the case of a sale, the transferee will have an equitable interest under the doctrine of anticipation, as discussed in section 4.1.[139]

6.2 FIRST REGISTRATION: DEALINGS WITH UNREGISTERED LAND

The scope of registration of title is outlined in s 2 of the LRA 2002.

---

[135] (1989) 58 P & CR 189, [199], *per* Taylor LJ.

[136] The scope of registration is discussed below. The principle exception relates to the grant or transfer of leases of seven years' duration or less.

[137] LRA 2002, s 27(2)(a).   [138] LRA 2002, s 4(2)(a).

[139] The doctrine of anticipation will not operate if A has simply attempted to make a gift to B, although B may acquire an equitable interest in such a case if e.g. the rule in *re Rose* [1952] 1 Ch 499 (CA) is met (see section 5.1) or if B has a proprietary estoppel claim (see Chapter 10).

Land Registration Act 2002, s 2

This Act makes provision about the registration of title to—

(a) unregistered legal estates which are interests of any of the following kinds—

    (i) an estate in land,

    (ii) a rentcharge,

    (iii) a franchise,

    (iv) a profit à prendre in gross, and

    (v) any other interest or charge which subsists for the benefit of, or is a charge on, an interest the title to which is registered; and

(b) interests capable of subsisting at law which are created by a disposition of an interest the title to which is registered.

The legal property rights with which we are concerned in this book—the freehold, lease, easement, and charge—are therefore all within the scope of registration of title. Section 3 concerns voluntary registration, enabling the proprietor of a freehold and of a lease with more than seven years left to run to apply to have the title registered. It is not possible to apply to be registered as proprietor of a lease of seven years or less.[140] Section 4 then identifies the events that trigger compulsory registration: in such a case, if registration does not occur, then B, the party attempting to acquire a right, cannot acquire any legal property right in the land.[141]

Land Registration Act 2002, s 4

(1) The requirement of registration applies on the occurrence of any of the following events—

    (a) the transfer of a qualifying estate—

        (i) for valuable or other consideration, by way of gift or in pursuance of an order of any court, or

        (ii) by means of an assent (including a vesting assent);

        [. . .]

    (c) the grant out of a qualifying estate of an estate in land—

        (i) for a term of years absolute of more than seven years from the date of the grant, and

        (ii) for valuable or other consideration, by way of gift or in pursuance of an order of any court;

    (d) the grant out of a qualifying estate of an estate in land for a term of years absolute to take effect in possession after the end of the period of three months beginning with the date of the grant; [. . .]

---

[140] LRA 2002, s 3(3): there is an exception in s 3(4) for a discontinuous lease: e.g. a lease which gives B a right to possess property only for particular weeks of the year. For discussion of such leases and registration, see Law Com CP No 227 (2016) [3.68]–[3.79].

[141] LRA 2002, s 7(1).

(f) the grant of a lease out of an unregistered legal estate in land in such circumstances as are mentioned in paragraph (b);

(g) the creation of a protected first legal mortgage of a qualifying estate.

(2) For the purposes of subsection (1), a qualifying estate is an unregistered legal estate which is—

(a) a freehold estate in land, or

(b) a leasehold estate in land for a term which, at the time of the transfer, grant or creation, has more than seven years to run.

Hence, registration is required for the transfer of freehold titles and of leases with more than seven years to run, and for the creation of new leases of more than seven years' duration, as well as for the creation of a protected first legal mortgage.[142]

6.3 GRADES OF TITLE

On first registration, a freehold estate is registered with absolute, qualified, or possessory title. 'Absolute' title is the usual expectation, and vests the estate in the proprietor subject principally to burdens on the register and overriding interests.[143] 'Qualified' or 'possessory' title may be awarded (respectively) where there is a possible defect in the applicant's title or insufficient documentary proof. Registration is additionally subject to estates, rights, or interests that are excepted from registration (in the case of qualified title), or are subsisting or capable of arising at the date of registration (in the case of possessory title).[144]

A fourfold scheme applies to leasehold title.[145] Absolute, qualified, and possessory leasehold titles have analogous effect to those grades of freehold title, with additional provision that they are subject to covenants, obligations, and liabilities in the lease.[146] Absolute leasehold is only available, however, where the freehold is also registered or proved to the satisfaction of the Registrar. Where this is not the case, good leasehold title is granted, leaving open a possible challenge against the estate out of which the lease was granted.[147]

6.4 DEALINGS WITH REGISTERED LAND

It is essential that the register is kept up to date. Hence, once a title has been brought onto the register through voluntary or compulsory first registration, subsequent dealings must be completed by registration. If A and B attempt such dealings, and B's right is not registered, then s 27(1) of the LRA 2002 makes clear that the disposition from A to B cannot create a legal property right.

---

[142] As defined by LRA 2002, s 4(8).   [143] LRA 2002, s 11(3)–(5).
[144] LRA 2002, s 11(6)–(7).   [145] LRA 2002, s 12.   [146] LRA 2002, s 12(4).
[147] LRA 2002, s 12(7).

Land Registration Act 2002, s 27

(1) If a disposition of a registered estate or registered charge is required to be completed by registration, it does not operate at law until the relevant registration requirements are met.

(2) In the case of a registered estate, the following are the dispositions which are required to be completed by registration—

(a) a transfer,

(b) where the registered estate is an estate in land, the grant of a term of years absolute—

    (i) for a term of more than seven years from the date of the grant,

    (ii) to take effect in possession after the end of the period of three months beginning with the date of the grant,

    (iii) under which the right to possession is discontinuous,

    (iv) in pursuance of Part 5 of the Housing Act 1985 (c. 68) (the right to buy), or

    (v) in circumstances where section 171A of that Act applies (disposal by landlord which leads to a person no longer being a secure tenant),

(c) where the registered estate is a franchise or manor, the grant of a lease,

(d) the express grant or reservation of an interest of a kind falling within section 1(2)(a) of the Law of Property Act 1925 (c. 20), other than one which is capable of being registered under the Commons Registration Act 1965 (c. 64),

(e) the express grant or reservation of an interest of a kind falling within section 1(2)(b) or (e) of the Law of Property Act 1925, and

(f) the grant of a legal charge.

There is a logical symmetry between the scope of registered dispositions and events triggering compulsory first registration. Hence, the transfer of a registered freehold or leasehold title, and the creation of a lease or more than seven years' duration, are all included in the list of registrable dispositions. The express grant of a legal easement (s 27(2)(d)) and the grant of a legal charge (s 27(2)(f)) also require registration.

It should be noted that the transfer of a registered lease requires registration even if there is less than seven years of the term left to run. It should also be noted that, whilst the creation of a lease of seven years or less does not require completion by registration, if, at the same time, any express easements are granted to the tenant, such an easement *does* require registration if it is to take effect as a legal property right. This can cause a trap, and the Law Commission have proposed that the law should be changed so that:[148] '*where the grant of a lease is not a registrable disposition, easements which benefit the lease and which are created within the lease itself should not be required to be completed by registration in order to operate at law.*'

6.5 THE REGISTRATION GAP

6.5.1 The problem

In *Scott v Southern Pacific Mortgages Ltd*,[149] Lady Hale noted that: '*There is a gap between any transaction and its registration […] Until registration, the purchaser (and indeed the*

---

[148] Law Com CP No 227 (2016) [16.32].   [149] [2015] AC 385, [113].

mortgagee) have only equitable interests.' Inherent within s 27(1) of the LRA 2002 is the existence of a 'registration gap'—that is, a period between completion of a transfer by execution of a deed and the vesting of legal title by registration. So if, for example, A sells his or her registered estate to B, and A completes the transfer by executing the relevant document, A has completed his or her contractual duties to B, but (in contrast to the position in unregistered land), A retains the registered estate. As noted by Lady Hale, and already discussed in section 4, B has an equitable interest, but the fact that legal title remains with A may cause problems for B.

Some aspects of the scheme under the LRA 2002 reduce the risks to B of the registration gap. Firstly, prior to completion, B can make a priority search of the register. As well as checking the state of the register at that point, such a search also gives B a priority period of 30 business days: if B then applies for the registration of the transfer of the registered estate from A to B within that priority period, then *'any entry made in the register during the priority period relating to the application is postponed to any entry made in pursuance of it'.*[150] Secondly, if B's application for registration is successful, it will be backdated to the date when the application was received by the Land Registry.[151] Thirdly, under s 24(b) of the Act, the *'owner's powers'* set out by s 23 are available not only to a registered proprietor, but also to a person *'entitled to be registered as proprietor'.* This allows B to make at least some valid dealings with the land during the registration gap; we will see, however, when looking at *Pye v Stodday Land Ltd*,[152] that this provision does not mean that B has *all* the powers that go with holding legal title: there are still some powers that can be acquired only on registration.

Fourthly, a property right of a person in actual occupation of registered land counts as an overriding interest, and so, as we noted in Chapter 3, section 3.2.4, is capable of binding a registered purchaser of land even if that property right has not been protected by an entry on the register. It might then be thought that B could be bound by such an overriding interest if a party with a pre-existing property right goes into occupation of the land after completion but before registration. That would be a problem for B as checks made by B as to the physical condition of the land, which include seeing if there is any third party in occupation of the land, naturally take place only before completion. The problem does not arise, however, as the House of Lords in *Abbey National v Cann*,[153] when interpreting the actual occupation provision under the LRA 1925, held that B can only be bound by such a right if the third party is in actual occupation at the time of completion, not at the later point when B registers. That is now confirmed by the wording of the relevant provision of the LRA 2002: Sch 3, para 2, which states that the overriding interest must belong *'at the time of disposition to a person in actual occupation.'*[154] Disposition, as used there, is the same as completion.

Finally, if before B's registration, A deals with the property in a way adverse to B, A is very likely to be in breach of a duty to B and so will come under a personal liability to B if such dealings cause B loss. The usefulness to B of such a claim will depend on the practical chances of locating A, and on A's ability to pay, but it may provide some disincentive for A: of course, in the standard case, once completion has occurred, A has little motivation to deal with the property.

---

[150] LRA 2002, s 72(2). As noted by the Law Com CP No 227 (2016) [6.64], in practice the registrar will in any case defer dealing with any other application for registration until B's priority period has expired.

[151] LRA 2002, s 74.   [152] [2016] EWHC 2454 (Ch), [2016] 4 WLR 168.

[153] [1991] 1 AC 56.

[154] See Lord Collins in *Scott v Southern Pacific* [2015] AC 385, [47]. For discussion, see Chapter 16, section 4.

Nonetheless, the registration gap can still cause some problems for B, as shown by the following two recent cases.

Pye v Stodday Land Ltd
[2016] EWHC 2454 (Ch), [2016] 4 WLR 168 (Ch D)

Facts: By a contract completed on 19 June 2013, Stodday Land Ltd sold part of its farm-land to Ripway Properties Ltd. Ripway became the registered proprietors of that land on 16 July 2013. Pye held an agricultural tenancy of land which included both the part of the farmland sold to Ripway and farmland retained by Stodday. On 1 July 2013, Ripway served a notice to quit on Pye, seeking possession of its land. On the same day, Stodday served a similar notice to quit to Pye in relation to its retained land. Pye argued that Ripway's notice to quit was not valid, as it was given before Ripway had registered, and thus before Ripway had acquired its legal estate in the land. If that argument was correct, it also meant that Stodday's notice was invalid, as notice to quit has to be given in relation to all the land included in an agricultural tenancy.

Norris J accepted Pye's argument: Ripway's notice to quit was not valid, as, when it was given, Ripway had not yet acquired a legal estate in the land.

Norris J

[25]

There is a well-established and coherent body of law in support of the proposition that where a legal right to bring a tenancy to an end by notice to the tenant is being exercised, then it is the person in whom the reversionary estate[155] is vested who must give the notice. On this appeal, counsel for Stodday and Ripway submits that this analysis [...] has been overtaken by developments in the law, and does not in any event recognise the serious problem posed by the 'registration gap'.

[32]

The right to serve the notice to quit arose from the nature of the estate granted and held: and the relevant relationship is 'privity of estate' not 'privity of contract'. The notice to quit could only be served by the legal owner of the reversion, not the equitable owner. The legal owner of the reversion was Stodday, not Ripway.

[37]–[41]

[Stodday and Ripway also argued that s 24(b) of the LRA 2002 authorized Ripway to give the notice to quit as it allows a person *'entitled to be registered as the proprietor'* to exercise *'owner's powers'* in relation to a registered estate]

I do not consider that [there is] authority for the proposition that someone entitled to be registered as proprietor is enabled by section 24 to undertake transactions that will be effective at law even before he is registered. To read the section in that way would deprive s 27 of the 2002 Act of any real effect. Rather, as is pointed out in *Ruoff & Roper: Registered*

---

155 [i.e. the estate held by the landlord.]

Conveyancing: 'A person's right to exercise owner's powers, by virtue of being entitled to be registered as proprietor, does not mean that he has unlimited powers of disposition. The fact that he has acquired such a right under a registrable disposition which has not yet been completed by registration, and which therefore takes effect in equity only until registered, of itself means that his powers of disposition under the general law are limited.'

The giving of a notice to quit is one of the instances in which, under the general law, the ownership of the equitable title does not suffice for the service of an effective notice, and where subsequent acquisition of the legal estate cannot validate the notice retrospectively. [. . .]

As a concluding remark I do not accept the submission of counsel for Stodday and Ripway that this is an overly formalistic approach which magnifies the risk arising from the 'registration gap'. The same problem exists in unregistered conveyancing. It is not difficult to address it. The time will come when every completion pack for the sale of a reversion includes a document in appropriate form constituting the transferee the agent of the transferor in respect of all matters concerning the estate transferred pending registration, a copy of which will be provided by the landlord to the tenant along with notice of the assignment.

The result in *Pye* is consistent with the approach taken under the LRA 1925. In *Brown & Root Technology Ltd v Sun Alliance and London Assurance Co Ltd*,[156] an assignment of a lease from A to B had not been registered and, as a result, A, as the party continuing to hold legal title to the lease, was able to exercise a break clause and terminate the lease. In that case, A was in fact a company owned by B, and the exercise of the break clause enabled B to escape an unwanted lease; B's non-registration therefore operated to its advantage. In *Pye*, the failed attempt by Ripway to serve the notice to quit, in contrast, was a source of frustration to Ripway, but the problem was of its own making, as it could have waited until registration before serving the notice. The next case, in contrast, shows how the registration gap can cause a difficulty beyond B's control.

***

Baker v Craggs
[2016] EWHC 3250 (Ch), [2017] Ch 295

The Charltons (A1 and A2) sold some fields, a barn and yard to Mr Craggs (B). The sale was completed on 17 January 2012, and the transfer was lodged for registration on 10 February. There was, however, a problem with the plan of the land provided by B in the application to register and, as a result of a delay in amending the application, the application had to be withdrawn, and a fresh application submitted. The second application was submitted on 16 May. Meanwhile, on 9 February, A1 and A2 had contracted to sell some neighbouring land to Mr and Mrs Baker (C) and that sale was completed on 20 February. As part of completion, A1 and A2 purported to include the grant of a right of way to C over the yard that had been sold to B. It seems that none of A1, A2, C, or their lawyers had realised that the yard had already been sold to B. The transfer to C was registered on 14 March.

B's second application for registration was successful, and so B was registered as proprietor of the land, including the yard, with the effect of the registration backdated to

---

[156] [2001] Ch 733 (CA).

the date of that second application, 16 May. The Land Registry recorded B's title as being subject to the right of way over the yard registered by C on 14 March. The question for the court was whether C's right of way was indeed binding on B. B argued that, from the time of B's contract with A1 and A2 (entered into before January 2012) he had an equitable interest in the yard, and that right was binding on C. C argued that, whilst B's equitable interest arose before C's acquisition of the easement, C nonetheless had a defence to that pre-existing interest and so took priority over it.[157] The two defences relied on by C were the lack of registration defence and the overreaching defence. We will consider each defence in more detail elsewhere,[158] but our focus here is simply on the issue of the registration gap.

Newey J

[10]

Points on which [counsel for B and C] agreed can be summarised as follows:

(i)   When [A1 and A2] transferred land to [B] on 17 January 2012,[159] he at once became its beneficial owner [...] Legal ownership did not pass, however, until he was entered on the register as the proprietor of the property: see section 2(1) of the Land Registration Act 2002 [...] In the meantime, [A1 and A2] retained legal ownership as the registered proprietors.

(ii) Had [B's] initial application for registration of the transfer to him been in order, the grant to [C] of a right of way over the yard comprised in the transfer would have been ineffective. The property of which [B] would have become registered proprietor would not have been bound by the purported right of way.

(iii) In the event, however, [B's] first application for registration was cancelled. He is therefore taken to have had no more than an equitable interest when [C] applied for the transfer [to C] to be registered.

(iv) Under section 29 of the Land Registration Act 2002 [...] [B's] interest in the property transferred to him cannot prevail over the grant of the right of way [to C] unless it was 'protected' when the transfer of the [land to C] was registered and, on the facts, that could be so only if the interest fell within a paragraph of Schedule 3 to the 2002 Act.[160]

(v)   The relevant paragraph of Schedule 3 to the 2002 Act for present purposes is paragraph 2 [...]

(vii) It follows that [B's] land must be bound by the right of way granted to [C] unless (a) [B] was in 'actual occupation' of the relevant land (as he contends, but [C] denies) and (b) his interest was not (as [C] contends but [B] denies) overreached.

Newey J found that B, who had been carrying out work on the land to which C's easement related, was in actual occupation of that land when the easement was granted to C, and so C could not use the lack of registration defence against B's pre-existing equitable interest.

---

[157] For the concept of a defence to a pre-existing property right, see e.g. Chapter 1, section 3 and Chapter 15.

[158] See Chapter 16, section 4 and Chapter 17.

[159] [Note that, as in *Scott v Southern Pacific Mortgages Ltd* [2015] AC 385, [79] and [113], the term 'transfer' is here used to refer to completion, not the later point when B, by registration, acquires the legal estate formerly registered in A1 and A2's names.]

[160] [In other words, B's right could bind C only if it was an overriding interest.]

However, C was able to invoke the overreaching defence: it had been granted the easement, a legal interest, by A1 and A2, as part of a transaction in which the purchase money was paid to A1 and A2. The decision is currently on appeal[161] and, as we will see in Chapter 17, section 2, the finding as to overreaching is controversial for a number of reasons.

For present purposes, however, the key point to take from *Craggs* is the vulnerability of B during the 'registration gap'. The facts of the case are unusual, as, following the failure to resolve the initial problem with the application, B had to make a second application for registration, and so the backdating of B's registration was only to the time of that second application, and C's registration also then fell outside the relevant priority period for B's registration. As A1 and A2 retained legal title to the land sold to B, it was still possible for A1 and A2 to grant a legal right to C, and for C to be registered as holding that right. Whilst B does have an equitable interest during the gap between completion and registration, as shown by *Craggs*, it may well be possible for C to take priority over B's right by showing that C has a defence to B's pre-existing equitable interest. As noted in Chapter 6, it is fundamental to the structure of land law that equitable interests are subject to more defences than legal estates or interests. It is therefore an inevitable effect of s 27 of the LRA 2002 that, in the period before B has registered any right, and so has no legal estate or interest, B is more vulnerable to a defence. The decision that C could rely on overreaching in *Craggs* was controversial, but if B had not been in actual occupation of the land, it seems quite clear that C would then have been able to use the lack of registration defence to take free from B's interest.

6.5.2 Solutions?

It is therefore clear that the registration gap can cause some problems for B. In its 2016 Consultation Paper, the Law Commission considered possible solutions.[162] One suggestion, which would have dealt with the problem arising in *Stodday Land*, was to extend the powers of a person entitled to be registered as proprietor so as to include all the powers that go with legal title;[163] another suggestion, which would have dealt with the problem arising in *Craggs*, was to strip A of any powers to deal with the land as soon as completion occurs;[164] a third, which also would have protected B in *Craggs*, was to vest legal title in B as soon as an application for registration is received by the Land Registry.[165] The Law Commission concluded however that the problems:[166] '*are practical problems, caused by operational limitations – resources within Land Registry – rather than legal ones. In our view a legal solution is not appropriate.*'

The Law Commission's Consultation Paper was published before the decisions in either *Stodday Land* or *Craggs*. It is unlikely that the first of those decisions would have made a difference to the Law Commision's discussion, which is in any case focussed on issues in relation to leases and notes the same practical solution referred to by Norris J in *Stodday Land*:[167] '*One [practical solution] is for the seller to grant a power of attorney in favour of the*

---

[161] Please see the online resources for updates on the appeal.

[162] Law Com CP No 227, *Updating the Land Registration Act* [5.79]–[5.82].

[163] Ripway would then have had the power to issue the notice to quit.

[164] It would then have been impossible for A1 and A2 to grant a legal easement to C, or to enter into any transaction with C that could overreach B's equitable interest under the contract of sale to B.

[165] B would then have had a legal estate, rather than an equitable interest arising under a trust, and that legal right would not have been vulnerable to overreaching.

[166] Law Com CP No 227, *Updating the Land Registration Act* [5.74].

[167] Law Com Co No 227, [5.84].

buyer, so that the buyer can serve notices and take other steps in the seller's name. A buyer can also seek obligations from the seller not to exercise rights under occupational leases, to pass on any notices that are received to the buyer, and to take action at the direction of the buyer.' The decision in *Craggs*, however, may well be significant, as it shows a particular consequence of the registration gap, arising outside the context of giving notices under leases, which seems to go beyond the purely practical problems that had been reported to the Law Commission. As noted earlier, the facts of *Craggs* (with the lapse of B's first application for registration) are somewhat unusual, and the decision on the applicability of overreaching is controversial, but it does certainly strengthen the case for some legal reform of the registration gap, even if not changing the difficulties of such reform as noted by the Law Commission.[168]

6.5.3 E-conveyancing?

In the 2001 Report that led to the 2002 Act, the Law Commission had envisaged that the registration gap would ultimately be removed by the introduction of electronic conveyancing.[169] It was intended that, once a system of e-conveyancing was in place, changes could be made to the formality rules considered in this chapter. The statutory power to introduce such rules is conferred by the following provision:

Land Registration Act 2002, s 93

Power to require simultaneous registration

(1) This section applies to a disposition of—
   (a) a registered estate or charge, or
   (b) an interest which is the subject of a notice in the register, where the disposition is of a description specified by rules.

(2) A disposition to which this section applies, or a contract to make such a disposition, only has effect if it is made by means of a document in electronic form and if, when the document purports to take effect—
   (a) it is electronically communicated to the registrar, and
   (b) the relevant registration requirements are met.

[...]

(5) Before making rules under this section the Lord Chancellor must consult such persons as he considers appropriate.

As can be seen from s 93, the intention was that rules could be introduced to mean that completion could occur only by the use of an electronic document communicated to the registrar. The consequence would be that the registration gap that currently exists between completion and an application to register would be removed. The initial entry into a contract could remain a separate stage, but the requirements of s 2 of the 1989 Act would be changed

---

[168] Law Com Co No 227, [5.78]–[5.85]. See Law Com No 254 (1998), [11.26]–[11.29] and Law Com No 271 (2001), [1.20].
[169] Law Com No 271, [13.79].

to mean that an electronic document, and communication to the registrar, would also be required for the contract to be valid.

The introduction of e-conveyancing, and the making of rules under s 93(2), would thus have eliminated the registration gap, by making completion and registration simultaneous. This has not, however, occurred. First, owing in part to practical difficulties in developing the technology required for a secure system, a full e-conveyancing system has not yet been introduced and, in 2011, work on the project was placed 'on hold'.[170]

Second, in its 2016 Consultation Paper, the Law Commission concluded that '*simultaneous completion and registration does not provide a practical way forward at this time*'.[171] It is therefore no longer proposed that an e-conveyancing system would necessarily, in the first instance at least, remove the registration gap. The Law Commission gives its reasons for that conclusion in the following extract:

Law Commission Consultation Paper No 227 (2016), *Updating the Land Registration Act 2002* [20.16]–[20.20]

We consider that simultaneous completion and registration should remain the goal of electronic conveyancing. We have concluded, however, that it is not practical to move directly from a paper-based system to a model of electronic conveyancing based on simultaneous completion and registration. Stakeholders have identified a number of issues with the policy.

First, the policy in our 2001 Report assumed that technology would develop in a way that has not yet occurred. Simultaneous completion and registration, in the context of a chain of transactions, requires coordination between the dispositions. A particular challenge has been the development of a system that is broadly acceptable to the market.

Secondly, at the current time, a number of practical barriers stand to block implementation of simultaneous completion and registration[172] [...]

Thirdly there remain, at this time, questions as to the desirability of simultaneous transactions. Commercially, the freedom for parties to structure their dealings so that they are completed at a time that suits their interests could be limited by a requirement for simultaneous registration. This is because notional registers would need to be devised and approved prior to registration. Registration would also depend on the state of other dealings that fall within the same transactional chain. Separately, there remain concerns about how the courts would treat incidences of non-compliance; for example where an attempt was made to create or deal with a property right outside the electronic conveyancing system. Those who suffer hardship in the wake of non-compliance may attract great judicial sympathy. Professor Martin Dixon has predicted that this sympathy may result in a 'boom' in proprietary estoppel claims.[173] As we noted in our 1998 Consultation Paper, proprietary

---

[170] Land Registry E-conveyancing: Consultation, Secondary Legislation Part 3, [5.2]. For the reasons given by the Land Registry for this decision, see Land Registry Report on Responses to E-Conveyancing Secondary Legislation Part 3, [5.1].

[171] Law Com Co No 227, [20.23].

[172] [A specific issue mentioned here by the Law Commission is coordination with the process for producing a certificate showing that Stamp Duty Land Tax has been paid.]

[173] Dixon, 'Proprietary Estoppel and Formalities in Land Law and the Land Registration Act 2002: A Theory of Unconscionability' in *Modern Studies in Property Law: vol 2* (ed Cooke, Oxford: Hart Publishing, 2003) 165.

> estoppel can provide a legitimate safety net. An expansive approach to the application of the doctrine could, however, have the effect of circumventing the simultaneous completion and registration requirement and therefore operate contrary to the aim of a complete and accurate register.
>
> In light of these concerns, simultaneous completion and registration does not provide a practical way forward at this time. We feel that for electronic conveyancing to become a reality it is necessary to step back from the goal. We consider that doing so opens up the avenues along which electronic conveyancing could develop.

On the Law Commission's current view, therefore, simultaneous completion and registration remains the *'ultimate, if long term, goal'*,[174] but, for the foreseeable future, there will still be a registration gap.

6.6 THE EFFECT OF REGISTRATION

We have seen that, as a result of ss 4 and 27 of the LRA 2002, a failure to register the transfer or grant of a legal estate may prevent a party from acquiring that legal estate. As noted in Chapter 3, section 3, this can be seen as an example of the negative operation of registration. We also noted there, however, that if a party does register his or her legal estate, as required, then registration also operates positively: s 58(1) states that *'If, on the entry of a person in the register as the proprietor of a legal estate, the legal estate would not otherwise be vested in him, it shall be deemed to be vested in him as a result of the registration.'* Similarly, ss 23 and 24 ensure that, if a party is registered as the holder of a legal estate, he or she has *'owner's powers'*.

We also saw in Chapter 3, section 3.2, however, that the protection of a registered party is not absolute. The possibility of rectification means that a change may be made to the register— for example, for the purpose of *'correcting a mistake'*—even if such a change causes the registered party to suffer a loss; for example, by the removal of his or her right from the register. In such cases, an indemnity may be payable to the registered party who has suffered such loss. Clearly then, the definition of the term *'correcting a mistake'* is crucial to understanding the effect of the registration of a legal estate. There has, however, been a great deal of uncertainty as to the meaning of the term, and we will consider the debate in detail in Chapter 18, section 3.

6.7 OUTLINE OF A REGISTERED TITLE

A sample registered title, with helpful annotations, is provide by the Land Registry online.[175] Each registered title is given a unique title number. The information recorded is divided into three parts.

- The *property register* identifies the title as freehold or leasehold, and, in the case of a lease, provides brief details of its terms. It identifies the land by a description, usually

---

[174] Law Com CP No 227, [20.24].

[175] Source: https://eservices.landregistry.gov.uk/www/wps/QDMPS-Portlet/resources/example_register. pdf (accessed 28 December 2017).

the address, and by reference to the official plan. It also lists rights that benefit the title, such as the benefit of an easement.

- The *proprietorship register* gives the name and address of the registered proprietor(s) and any restrictions on their ability to deal with the land.[176] It may also state the price paid for the title.

- The *charges register* contains information on registered mortgages and other secured interests, and any other burdens affecting the title: for example, leases, easements, and covenants to which the land is subject.

QUESTION

1. Are formality requirements necessary?

2. Assess the role of rectification, collateral contracts, and proprietary estoppel under s 2 of the Law of Property (Miscellaneous Provisions) Act 1989.

3. Compare and contrast a deed, a 'non-deed', and an escrow.

4. How do the rights of a purchaser on completion vary from their rights at the point of entry into a contract of sale? How do the rights of a purchaser on registration vary from their rights at the point of completion?

5. What is the 'registration gap' and how did it arise on the facts of *Baker v Craggs*?

6. What is the best way to solve problems caused by the registration gap?

For guidance on how to answer these questions visit the online resources at www.oup.com/uk/mcfarlane4e/.

FURTHER READING

Cooke, *The New Law of Land Registration* (Oxford: Hart Publishing, 2003)

Critchley, 'Taking Formalities Seriously' in *Land Law: Themes and Perspectives* (eds Bright and Dewar, Oxford: OUP, 1998)

Dixon, 'Confining and Defining Proprietary Estoppel: The Role of Unconscionability' (2010) 30 LS 408

Grinlinton (ed), *Torrens in the Twenty-First Century* (Wellington: LexisNexis, 2003)

Law Commission Report No 164, *Transfer of Land Formalities for Contracts for Sale etc of Land* (1987)

Law Commission Report No 271, *Land Registration for the Twenty-First Century: A Conveyancing Revolution* (2001)

McFarlane, *The Law of Proprietary Estoppel* (Oxford: OUP, 2014), ch 6, 6.04–6.120

Nair, 'Morality and the Mirror: The Normative Limits of the "Principles of Land Registration"' in *Modern Studies in Property Law Vol 6* (ed Bright, Oxford: Hart (2011)

---

[176] The entry and removal of restrictions is governed by the 2002 Act, ss 40–47. Restrictions are considered in Chapter 16, section 5.

Neuberger 'The Stuffing of Minerva's Owl: Taxonomy and Taxidermy in Equity' (2009) 68 CLJ 537

O'Connor, 'Registration of Title in England and Australia: A Theoretical and Comparative Analysis' in *Modern Studies in Property Law Vol 2* (ed Cooke, Oxford: Hart Publishing, 2003)

O'Connor, 'The Top 10 Legal Questions for Registered Title Systems' in *Property and Security: Selected Essays* (eds Bennett Moses, Edgeworth, and Sherry, Sydney: The Lawbook Co, 2010)

Owen, 'Priorities and Registered Land During the Registration Gap' [2017] Conv 230

9

ADVERSE POSSESSION

CENTRAL ISSUES

1. Adverse possession enables the informal acquisition of a legal estate in land. Adverse possession, as a form of possession that fulfils specific criteria, can be contrasted with squatting, as that term carries a wider meaning.

2. An adverse possession claim has two stages. The first stage—establishing 'adverse possession'—has rules that are common to registered and unregistered land. The second—the consequences of adverse possession—operates differently in relation to registered and unregistered land.

3. Adverse possession has its roots in the concepts of title by possession and relativity of title, combined with the operation of rules on limitation of actions. Its operation reflects ideas underlying unregistered titles. As a result, its operation has been modified in registered land. The Land Registration Act 1925 sought to minimize the differences between the operation of adverse possession in registered land and in unregistered land, but the Land Registration Act 2002 departed from this approach.

4. Under the 2002 Act, it is not possible to acquire title automatically by adverse possession; instead, a claimant has access to a procedure, the outcome of which may be the award of title by registration. The scheme is, however, heavily weighted against claims, except in limited circumstances in which adverse possession is considered still to play a legitimate role.

5. Adverse possession necessarily involves trespass—a civil wrong—and in some circumstances constitutes a criminal offence. The relationship between criminal acts and adverse possession has been considered by the courts, and it is established that, at least in some circumstances, the fact that a criminal offence may have been committed does not prevent a claim to adverse possession.

6. Adverse possession rules have been challenged on the basis that they interfere with the human rights of a party who loses his or her title to land, but such rules have been held to be human rights compliant.

1 INTRODUCTION

In Chapter 5, we saw that legal estates and interests in land can be acquired *dependently*, where they are granted by a person with property rights in land, and *independently*, by the unilateral conduct of the person acquiring the right. In Chapter 8, we considered the formality requirements that govern the dependent acquisition of legal estates and interests. We have seen that the creation of some legal rights is exempt from the statutory formality requirements: in particular, the grant of a lease for a term of three years or less may be exempt from the requirement of a deed.[1] Apart from these specific exemptions, however, legal estates and interests cannot be created though informal *dependent* acquisition. Generally, informal dependent acquisition is the provenance of equitable intervention. We consider the acquisition of equitable interests in land in Chapters 10–12.

Legal rights may, however, be acquired informally through *independent* acquisition. There are two means through which such rights may arise: firstly, the rules of adverse possession, which provide a means of acquiring a legal estate; secondly, a number of doctrines enable the informal acquisition of a legal easement. The basis for the acquisition of a legal estate by adverse possession is *long use*. This basis is shared by *prescription*, which is one of the sources of an informally acquired easement. If a claimant uses land, or exercises a right with the characteristics of an easement over land, for a period of time, then he or she may obtain legal title, or a legal easement, by virtue of that use.

The similarity between adverse possession and prescription begins and ends with their common foundation in long use.[2] The doctrines differ in how long use is analysed as conferring rights. On the one hand, adverse possession has historically viewed long use as having a *negative* effect—of extinguishing previous titles. This remains the case in relation to unregistered land, although, as we will see, the Land Registration Act 2002 (LRA 2002) adopts a different approach to the effect of adverse possession. Prescription, on the other hand, views long use as having a *positive* effect—of implying the grant of a legal easement.

In *Buckinghamshire County Council v Moran*,[3] Nourse LJ explained the essential difference between the claims as being that prescription requires possession 'as of right', while adverse possession concerns possession 'as of wrong'. This, in turn, means that, in prescription, the intention of the grantor may be significant, while, as will be seen, in adverse possession, the focus is on the intention of the claimant.[4] For the remainder of this chapter, our discussion is confined to adverse possession. Prescription and the other doctrines enabling the informal acquisition of legal easements are considered in Chapter 22.[5]

Adverse possession is a legal term of art used to describe a claim to title to land founded on possession. It is the technical language of property statutes. Property legislation tends to eschew references to squatters and squatting, which is used in criminal justice legislation. Adverse possession and squatting are not, however, synonymous. Adverse possessors may be described as squatters (perhaps most appropriately where the adverse possession involves residing in the property, though it is used more generally). But the term squatter is also used

---

[1] Law of Property Act 1925, s 52(2).

[2] A point made judicially in *Lovett v Fairclough* (1991) 61 P & CR 385, 398, *per* Mummery J.

[3] [1990] Ch 623, [644].   [4] Ibid.

[5] A conjoined discussion of the doctrines is provided by Hopkins, *The Informal Acquisition of Rights in Land* (London: Sweet & Maxwell, 2000) ch 10. For a general discussion of long use and proprietary rights, see Goymour, 'The Acquisition of Rights in Property by the Effluxion of Time' in *Modern Studies in Property Law Vol 4* (ed Cooke, Oxford: Hart Publishing, 2007).

more widely and applied to those in unauthorized occupation of land whose occupation is not such as to support a claim to title; for example, demonstrators and protestors whose occupation does not fulfil the technical requirements of adverse possession that are explained in this chapter.

The English law of adverse possession came under close scrutiny in the *Pye* litigation, which plays a central role in this chapter. The first case, the House of Lords' decision in *JA Pye (Oxford) Ltd v Graham*,[6] concerned a successful claim to adverse possession by Mr and Mrs Graham to valuable development land of which Pye was the registered proprietor. Following the loss of its land, Pye brought an action against the UK before the European Court of Human Rights. It argued that the English law on adverse possession was contrary to the European Convention on Human Rights (ECHR) and that, as a result, it should receive financial compensation for the loss of its land. The Grand Chamber of the European Court of Human Rights rejected Pye's claim.[7] The decision of that Court has been discussed in Chapter 4, but it is necessary to return to the decision in this chapter in order to place it in the context of the substantive laws challenged by *Pye* and how those laws have been changed by the LRA 2002.

2 IS ADVERSE POSSESSION JUSTIFIED?

We have noted that the basis on which rights are acquired by adverse possession is long use. As Howard and Hill explain, this is not an obvious basis for conferring rights on a claimant.

Howard and Hill, 'The Informal Creation of Interests in Land' (1995)
15 LS 356, 372–3

> The fact that a claimant has enjoyed a gratuitous benefit for a period in excess [of the statutory requirements] is not in itself a justification for allowing the claimant to continue to enjoy that benefit. If, for example, a newsagent does not object when each week a stranger comes into his shop and takes a Sunday newspaper without paying for it, does the passage of time enable the stranger to assert a right to a Sunday newspaper when the newsagent's good-nature is finally exhausted?

Why, then, is long use seen as sufficient to confer a legal right in land?

Holmes[8] suggested that what lies at the heart of justifications is *'the deepest instincts of man'*. He explained: *'A thing which you have enjoyed and used as your own for a long time [. . .] takes root in your being and cannot be torn away without your resenting the act and trying to defend yourself, however you came by it.'*[9] Holmes emphasized the need to look at limitation rules from the position of the person who gains a right, not that of the 'loser'. In this respect, long use has a 'curative' effect[10] through which the courts clothe fact with right.

Dockray[11] discussed four reasons why adverse possession is needed. Adverse possession forms part of the general law of limitation of actions—that is, rules that place a long stop on

---

[6] [2003] 1 AC 419.   [7] *JA Pye (Oxford) Ltd v UK* (App No 44302/02) [2008] 1 EHRLR 132.
[8] 'The Path of the Law' (1897) 10 Harv LR 457, 477.   [9] Ibid.
[10] Goodman, 'Adverse Possession of Land: Morality and Motive' (1970) 33 MLR 281.
[11] 'Why Do We Need Adverse Possession?' [1985] Conv 272.

the time during which a claimant may commence proceedings to assert his or her rights. Therefore, Dockray took as a starting point the general justifications for the operation of limitation periods, drawn from the Law Reform Committee.

Law Reform Committee 21st Report, *Final Report on Limitation of Actions* (1977, Cmnd 6923, [1.7])

[...]

1. to protect defendants from stale claims

2. to encourage plaintiffs not to sleep on their rights; and

3. to ensure that a person may feel confident, after the lapse of a given period of time, that an incident which might have led to a claim against him is finally closed.

Dockray concluded that these objectives themselves, while relevant, do not fully explain the limitation of actions to recover land. The rules of adverse possession do not operate in a manner that is wholly consistent with any of the three objectives, while, in relation to the third, there is also insufficient evidence that it has influenced the development of the law. Dockray suggested that a fourth objective is at work, which he identified as facilitating the investigation of title to unregistered land.[12]

Dockray, 'Why do we Need Adverse Possession?' [1985] Conv 272, 277–8

To outline the policy, it is necessary to start by recalling that a vendor of unregistered land is obliged nowadays (subject to contrary agreement) to prove his title over a period of at least 15 years starting from a good root. However, as Professor J.T. Farrand points out in *Contract and Conveyance*, this does not require the vendor to give anything like a complete history, the account may not be of ownership at all, some third party being the true owner all the time.

But if this is possible why, it might be asked, does the legislation only require (and why are purchasers generally content only to require) a vendor to prove his title over a minimum period of 15 years. The answer, according to the theory on which the Statute of Limitations is based, is that this is because it is reasonably safe to do so, And it is reasonably safe to do so, according to the same theory, because the Statute was designed to and does provide a kind of qualified guarantee that any outstanding claims to ownership by third parties are time-barred.

The Law Commission considered this to be the 'strongest justification' for adverse possession.[13] The identification of this objective is significant, because, if the justification is rooted in the operation of unregistered land, an obvious question arises as to its applicability in registered land. As we will see, the incompatibility of adverse possession with principles of registered land resulted in significant reforms in the LRA 2002.

---

[12] See also Goodman (1970, 282–3).

[13] Law Commission Report No 254, *Land Registration for the Twenty-First Century: A Consultative Document* (1998), [10.9]–[10.10].

3 AN OUTLINE OF THE OPERATION OF ADVERSE POSSESSION

Adverse possession has its roots in the concept of relativity of title[14] and the operation of limitation periods. The paradigm case, on which the following explanation is based, is adverse possession by the claimant (C) in unregistered land, of which the title, traced through the title deeds, belongs to the paper owner (PO). In English law, there is no concept of absolute title: title is relative and is based on possession. In a dispute between two parties, the court determines which party has the stronger claim to possession. As soon as C enters into adverse possession, he or she obtains a legal freehold title to the land.[15] C's right to possession is stronger than that of any subsequent possessor, but is vulnerable to earlier claims. Hence, PO can bring an action against C to recover the land, relying on its earlier claim to possession evidenced by the paper title. In other words, in a dispute between the parties, PO has the relatively stronger title. But s 15 of the Limitation Act 1980 provides a twelve-year limitation period for actions to recover land. If PO does not take action within that time, then its claim is time-barred. Section 17 of the Limitation Act 1980 provides that, once time-barred, PO's title is extinguished. There is no transfer of PO's title to C. Once the limitation period has expired, however, the title that C obtained by the inception of adverse possession becomes unimpeachable by PO (and anyone claiming through PO's title).

The basis of adverse possession in the concept of relativity of title led to the rejection of a claim in *Parshall v Hackney*.[16] The case concerned a small strip of land, described as being under two metres at its widest point and four metres long, that adjoined two properties (numbers 29 and 31). It was first registered, in 1904, as part of the registered title to number 29. In 1980, however, the strip was mistakenly included in the registered title to number 31, and the owners of number 31 began to use the strip, putting up a chain link fence around it in 1988. In 2000, the strip was then mistakenly removed from the registered title to number 29. In 2008, having discovered the mistake, the registered proprietor of number 29 applied to have the register changed, so that the strip would be included in the title to number 29. Although the strip was small, it was in Chelsea, where its utility as a parking space gave it a value disproportionate to its size. One of the grounds on which the registered proprietors of number 31 argued against a change to the register, restoring the title to number 29, was that they had obtained title to the land by adverse possession. The court, however, perceived a difficulty in using such an argument in such a case of double registration. Mummery LJ explained, '*[t]his is a case of equality of registered titles, rather than the normal case of relativity of titles. The two registered titles co-exist on the register unless and until corrected by rectification*'.[17] However, the concept of 'equal' titles is conceptually problematic in English law. As Lees argues in the following extract, even two registered titles can be analysed in relative terms.

---

[14] For a general analysis of this concept in property law, see Fox, 'Relativity of Title at Law and in Equity' (2006) 65 CLJ 330.

[15] The classification of the title as legal is not beyond doubt. The different views are summarized by Cooke, 'Adverse Possession: Problems of Title in Registered Land' (1994) 14 LS 1, 4–5.

[16] [2013] EWCA Civ 240. See too section 4 below and Chapter 18, section 3.2.

[17] [2013] EWCA Civ 240, [89] (emphasis in the original). The outcome in *Parshall* was that the register was changed, so as to include the disputed strip in the registered title to number 29. As discussed in Chapter 18, section 3.2, the result would be different under the reforms to the operation of rectification suggested by the Law Commission: Law Com CP No 227 (2016) [13.135]–[13.138].

Lees, *'Parshall v Hackney*: A Tale of Two Titles' [2013] Conv 222, 230

[W]hilst the two titles may enjoy an "equality" nonetheless they also have a relativity. The appellant's title [appurtenant to number 29] was prior and clear from any defects. By contrast, the respondent's title [appurtenant to number 31] was created later, in error, and subject to an inherent defect that it was always susceptible to rectification. The statutory magic cannot in reality make these titles equal. There may well be two separate and distinct titles, but they do not exist in isolation of each other. All the statutory magic can do is to result in both parties enjoying absolute freehold titles to the same parcel of land. There is no reason in principle or authority for this affecting the court's (necessary) ability to examine, *as between themselves,* who has the better *right to immediate possession.*

The acquisition of title by adverse possession consists of two distinct stages: firstly, the inception of adverse possession; and secondly, the operation of limitation rules at the end of the requisite period of adverse possession. The principles applying to the inception of adverse possession apply uniformly to registered and unregistered land. Differences emerge, however, in the operation of limitation rules. The concept of title being acquired by possession and extinguished at the end of the limitation period makes no sense in the context of registered land. In registered land, as we have seen in Chapter 8, section 6, titles are acquired by registration. A registered title cannot be 'extinguished' unless and until a change is made to the register. The Land Registration Act 1925 (LRA 1925) sought to align registered land with the operation of adverse possession in unregistered land. Hence, it enabled title to be acquired automatically in registered land by adverse possession, using the device of a trust to reconcile the extinguishment of a title with registered land principles. The LRA 2002 provides a significant departure from the previous law. There is no concept of title being acquired by adverse possession, or of a limitation period at the end of which the assertion of title is automatically time-barred. Instead, adverse possession provides access to a procedure though which the claimant may acquire title by registration.

In the next section of this chapter, we consider the rules governing the inception of adverse possession; these rules remain applicable to all claims. We will then consider the effect of adverse possession: by the operation of limitation rules in unregistered land and registered land under the LRA 1925, and the new scheme provided for registered land by the LRA 2002. Having explained the general operation of adverse possession the chapter then addresses two specific issues; the criminalization of squatting in residential premises and the human rights challenge to adverse possession.

4 THE INCEPTION OF ADVERSE POSSESSION

The key date to identify is the date at which a cause of action accrues against the paper owner. In unregistered land (and registered land under the LRA 1925), that is the date from which the limitation period begins to run.[18] In registered land, under the LRA 2002, that is the date from which a person is treated as being in adverse possession.[19] The events that trigger the accrual of a right of action are provided by the Limitation Act 1980.

---

[18] Limitation Act 1980, s 15(1).   [19] Land Registration Act 2002, Sch 6, para 11.

Limitation Act 1980, Sch 1, paras 1 and 8

1 Where the person bringing an action to recover land, or some person through whom he claims, has been in possession of the land, and has while entitled to the land been dispossessed or discontinued his possession, the right of action shall be treated as having accrued on the date of the dispossession or discontinuance.

8 (1) No right of action to recover land shall be treated as accruing unless the land is in the possession of some person in whose favour the period of limitation can run (referred to below in this paragraph as 'adverse possession'); and where under the preceding provisions of this Schedule any such right of action is treated as accruing on a certain date and no person is in adverse possession on that date, the right of action shall not be treated as accruing unless and until adverse possession is taken of the land.

Hence the inception of adverse possession is dependent on demonstrating either dispossession of the paper owner or its discontinuance in possession. In the latter case, it will be necessary to show separately that the claimant has moved into adverse possession. In relation to the former, as will be seen, the commencement of adverse possession by the claimant is inherent in the definition of dispossession.

Discontinuance arises where '*the person in possession abandons possession and another then takes it*'.[20] Discontinuance in *possession* is not demonstrated by discontinuance in physical *occupation*; rather, it is analogous to abandonment of land. In *Powell v McFarlane*,[21] Slade J noted that '*merely very slight acts by an owner in relation to the land are sufficient to negative discontinuance*'. Dispossession arises by '*a person coming in and putting another out of possession*'.[22]

The meaning of dispossession was considered by the House of Lords in the following case, the facts of which it is useful to set out at this stage. In this case, whether the Grahams had dispossessed Pye was identified as one of two key issues that determined the outcome of the case.[23]

JA Pye (Oxford) Ltd v Graham
[2002] UKHL 30, [2003] 1 AC 419, HL

Facts: Pye was the registered proprietor of development land that adjoined the Graham's farm. The land was enclosed by hedges, except for a gate, to which the Grahams held the only key, and a public footpath and highway. Pye had initially granted the Grahams a short grazing agreement to use the land. On the expiry of the agreement, Pye refused a request for renewal, because it was concerned that the existence of an agreement could adversely affect its application for planning permission. The Grahams continued to use the land for their farm, including uses that went beyond the original agreement. Initially, the Grahams continued to seek a renewal of the licence, but their requests went unanswered. Pye did nothing in relation to the land and the Grahams argued that they had acquired title by adverse possession. The House of Lords considered that the claim depended on whether the Grahams had

---

[20] *Powell v McFarlane* (1979) 38 P & CR 452, 468, *per* Slade J.   [21] Ibid.   [22] Ibid.
[23] [2003] 1 AC 491, [27]–[28].

dispossessed Pye (there being no suggestion that Pye had discontinued in possession) and, if so, whether the Grahams had remained in possession for the requisite limitation period.

Lord Browne-Wilkinson

At [36]

[. . .] The question is simply whether the defendant squatter has dispossessed the paper owner by going into ordinary possession of the land for the requisite period without the consent of the owner [. . .]

At [38]

It is sometimes said that ouster by the squatter is necessary to constitute dispossession: see for example *Rains v Buxton* (1880) 14 Ch D 537, 539 *per* Fry J. The word "ouster" is derived from the old law of adverse possession and has overtones of confrontational, knowing removal of the true owner from possession. Such an approach is quite incorrect. There will be a "dispossession" of the paper owner in any case where (there being no discontinuance of possession by the paper owner) a squatter assumes possession in the ordinary sense of the word. Except in the case of joint possessors, possession is single and exclusive. Therefore if the squatter is in possession the paper owner cannot be. If the paper owner was at one stage in possession of the land but the squatter's subsequent occupation of it in law constitutes possession the squatter must have "dispossessed" the true owner for the purposes of Schedule 1, paragraph 1 [. . .]

Hence, in a case of dispossession, the right of action accrues at the date at which the claimant commences possession. Therefore, the answer to the question of whether the Grahams had dispossessed Pye lay in determining whether the Grahams could establish that they were in possession of the land.

Before considering the meaning of 'possession', it is useful to consider the definition of 'adverse'.

4.1 'ADVERSE' POSSESSION DEFINED

A claimant's possession is not adverse if he or she is present with the licence of the paper owner. In the following case, a claim to adverse possession failed, because the paper owner had unilaterally granted a licence.

BP Properties Ltd v Buckler
(1988) 55 P & CR 337, CA

Facts: The appellant's parents had been in adverse possession of their home by remaining in occupation at the end of their lease. An order of possession was obtained within the limitation period, but was not enforced. BP Properties then purchased the freehold and wrote to Mrs Buckler, informing her that she could remain in the property rent-free for her life. Mrs Buckler neither accepted nor rejected the terms of the letter. Following her death, the appellant sought to establish that his parents had obtained title by adverse possession.

Dillon LJ

At 346–7

The claim that a unilateral licence can stop time running is a new one. It may be of some general importance in that it would enable a person who is not prepared to incur the obloquy of bringing proceedings for possession, or of enforcing a possession order, to keep his title alive for very many years until it suits him to evict. It might be thought that for title to be kept alive in this way was contrary to the policy of the statute as exemplified by section 13 of the 1939 Act which reproduced earlier statutory provision to the same effect and prevented any right of action to recover land being preserved by formal entry or continual claim.

So far as the facts are concerned, it would in my judgment be artificial to say that Mrs. Buckler "accepted" the terms set out in the two letters; B.P. Properties Ltd. neither sought nor waited for her acceptance. It would be equally artificial to say that there was any consideration in law for those terms.

It may be that the result would have been different if Mrs. Buckler had, as soon as she learned of the letters, plainly told B.P. Properties Ltd. that she did not accept the letters, and maintained her claims to be already the owner of the property; she did not however do that. She accepted her solicitors' advice that as the warrant for possession had been withdrawn, she should do nothing while the 12-year period from the date of the possession order of December 11, 1962 expired. In essence she was not asserting during the time from the receipt of the letters until after December 11, 1974—or indeed thereafter—any claim to ownership of the farmhouse and garden, or any intention to exclude the owner of the paper title.

Whether B.P. Properties Ltd. could or could not in law, in the absence of consideration have sought to determine in her lifetime the licence granted to Mrs. Buckler by the two letters, they did not in fact seek to do so. Had they sought to do so, they would in the absence of any repudiation of the letters by Mrs. Buckler have had to give Mrs. Buckler a reasonable time to quit as with any licensee.

The nature of Mrs. Buckler's possession after receipt of the letters cannot be decided just by looking at what was locked up in her own mind. It must depend even more, on this aspect of the case, on the position as seen from the standpoint of the person with the paper title. What could that person have done? The rule that possession is not adverse if it can be referred to a lawful title applies even if the person in possession did not know of the lawful title; the lawful title would still preclude the person with the paper title from evicting the person in possession. So far as Mrs. Buckler was concerned, even though she did not "accept" the terms of the letters, B.P. Properties Ltd. would, in the absence of any repudiation by her of the two letters, have been bound to treat her as in possession as licensee on the terms of the letters. They could not have evicted her (if they could have done so at all) without determining the licence.

I can see no escape therefore from the conclusion that, whether she liked it or not, from the time of her receipt of the letters, Mrs. Buckler was in possession of the farmhouse and garden by the licence of B.P. Properties Ltd., and her possession was no longer adverse within the meaning of s 10 of the 1939 Act.

As noted by the Privy Council in *Smith v Molyneaux*,[24] the key point in *BP v Buckler* is that, to prevent possession being adverse, '*it is sufficient that permission is given unilaterally*'. In the *Smith* case, the parties and court accepted that the principle was correct, but it has

---

[24] [2016] UKPC 35, [2017] 1 P & CR 7, [28].

attracted criticism.[25] Hickey, for example, has argued that the principle is inconsistent with the approach of the House of Lords in *Pye v Graham*:

Hickey, 'The Effect of Supervening Permission on Adverse Possession' [2017] Conv 223, 223, 228–9

[I]t is argued that *Buckler* is not safe authority [. . .] it cannot and should not withstand *Pye* because (i) it risks reintroducing the 'heresy' that the intentions of a paper/registered title holder are relevant to the question whether adverse possession exists on the facts; and (ii) it is insensitive to a plausible distinction between the effects of initial and supervening permission in the context of adverse possession, and following *Pye*'s rationalisation of the law there is reason to treat such a distinction seriously.

[. . .] If a possessor enters land with express permission, it is clear that her possession is not adverse. That was the case in *Pye* itself, where the early periods of possession were referable to a grazing agreement, and the very question at stake was whether acts which amounted to subsequent non-permissive continuation of this lawful possession could amount to 'adverse' possession. The trite effect of the licence in such a situation is to render lawful that which would otherwise be unlawful, such that adverse possession can only begin at a date following expiry of the initial permission. However, it simply does not follow that supervening permission operates to inhibit adverse possession in the same way. In circumstances where adverse possession is established, the position of the possessor under the law is qualitatively different. The orthodox view is that she acquires a fee simple estate from the inception of her possession, albeit one relatively inferior to the continuing title of the paper owner. Accordingly, to accept the argument that supervening permission, unilaterally granted, operates to bring adverse possession to an end, we must accept the proposition that the grant of such a licence is sufficient to divest the possessor of her common law fee simple. This proposition is not self-evident [. . .]

These matters need to be considered fully and carefully, and it is regrettable the Board did not take the occasion afforded by *Smith* to do so.

In considering the robustness or otherwise of the approach in the *Buckler* case to the impact of later express permission from the paper owner (PO), it is worth noting the fate of a previous attempt to limit adverse possession by means of finding an implied permission. In *Wallis's Cayton Bay Holiday Camp Ltd v Shell-Mex and BP Ltd*,[26] Lord Denning MR held that if the possessor's conduct was not inconsistent with the PO's plans for the land, it would not amount to adverse possession, as the PO could be said to have impliedly given permission to the possessor. This is no longer the law, however: not only was the reasoning behind it expressly rejected as '*wrong*' in *Pye*,[27] the specific point had, by then, already been also reversed by legislation.[28] This does not mean, of course, that an implied licence can never be found; rather that such implication can occur only if there is: '*some overt act*

---

[25] See e.g. Law Com No 271 [14.56].   [26] [1975] QB 974 (CA). See too section 4.2.3.
[27] [2003] 1 AC 419 at [32].
[28] Limitation Act 1980, Sch 1, para 8(4): '*For the purpose of determining whether a person occupying any land is in adverse possession of the land it shall not be assumed by implication of law that his occupation is by permission of the person entitled to the land merely by virtue of the fact that his occupation is not inconsistent with the latter's present or future enjoyment of the land.*'

by the landowner or some demonstrable circumstance from which the consent can be implied'.[29] For example,[30] in *Smart v Lambeth LBC*[31] a local authority had placed occupation of properties on a permissive footing by agreeing a licence scheme administered through a housing association and a co-operative consisting of the occupiers. The authority had given residents permission to occupy during the negotiations. The claimant to adverse possession argued that his occupation was adverse as neither he nor his predecessors had been granted a licence in the form required by the agreement reached with the local authority. The claim to adverse possession failed. Floyd LJ explained that *'once it is conceded as it is that [the claimant's predecessors] were permitted by Lambeth to occupy the property during the period of negotiation, it would be a surprising result if the* successful *conclusion of those negotiations was to make them trespassers'.*[32] The successful completion of negotiations kept the residents' possession on a permissive footing despite the fact they had not been given consent in a specified form.

In section 3 of this chapter we have seen that in *Parshall v Hackney* a claim to adverse possession failed where the disputed triangle of land had mistakenly been registered under two separate titles. In examining the elements of adverse possession, the court concluded that in view of the registered title held by the claimant to adverse possession, their possession was 'lawful' and as such it could not be adverse. The claimants were not in possession with the licence of the PO. The decision, therefore, suggests that possession is not adverse if it is either based on a licence or is otherwise lawful. It is difficult to imagine circumstances beyond the mistaken dual registration of title where possession will be lawful but not permissive. However, as Xu comments, the practical consequence of the court's interpretation could be to render registered titles vulnerable to claims by a PO where mistakes come to light decades later.[33] Further, the decision has the curious effect that the claimants to adverse possession, who may have reasonably supposed that the land was theirs, are in a worse position than if they had parked their car on land that they knew did not belong to them. As Xu explains, 'if they [the claimants to adverse possession] parked their car and set up those bollards anywhere else in London for so many years, they would have acquired the land'.[34] The distinction between permissive and non-permissive but lawful use is one that has caused difficulties for the courts in other instances where claims to rights over land are based on long use.[35]

4.2 'POSSESSION' DEFINED

As has been noted, in *Pye v Graham*, the House of Lords considered that the Grahams would establish that they had dispossessed Pye by demonstrating that they had entered into possession of the land. This, in turn, raised the question of the meaning of 'possession'.

---

[29] *Smart v Lambeth LBC* [2013] EWCA Civ 1375; [2014] HLR 7, [35] citing *London Borough of Lambeth v Rumbelow*, unreported, judgment 25 January 2001.

[30] See too *Colin Dawson Windows Ltd v King's Lynn, West Norfolk* [2005] EWCA Civ 9, [2005] 2 P & CR 19.

[31] [2013] EWCA Civ 1375; [2014] HLR 7.   [32] Ibid, [51] (emphasis in the original).

[33] L. Xu, 'What do we Protect in Land Registration?' (2013) 129 LQR 477, 480. Although note that this concern can be solved by other means, such as introducing a 'long-stop' provision to limit rectification on the basis of a mistake that occurred a number of years earlier: see the proposal in Law Com CP No 227 (2016) [13.135]–[13.138], discussed in Chapter 18, section 3.2.

[34] Xu, 'What do we Protect in Land Registration?' (2013) 129 LQR 477, 480.

[35] For example, in connection with registration of land as a town or village green. See *R (on the application of Barkas) v North Yorkshire County Council* [2014] UKSC 31; [2014] 2 WLR 1360.

Defining this term forms the bedrock of case law on adverse possession. Although the term is being defined for a particular purpose, Green argues that the courts are influenced by, and construct, a particular concept of landowner.

Green, 'Citizens and Squatters' in *Land Law: Themes and Perspectives*
(eds Bright and Dewar, 1998, p 230)

In each case of adverse possession, the judges have to decide whether what the claimant did to the land amounts to possession of it. In making these decisions, they are, little by little, fleshing out the character and activities of 'the landowner', while at the same time his pre-existing mythical figure is affecting their decisions. This is because such mythical figures as 'the landowner' 'resonate across space and over time' to anchor a philosophy of having and being 'which can influence events, behaviour and perception'. The judges are thus stabilizing and making transparent the boundaries not only on the surface of the land but also in the ideology of ownership.

In *Pye v Graham*, the House of Lords confirmed that 'possession' is to be understood in the *'ordinary sense of the word'*.[36] The House of Lords defined it in a manner closely following an analysis by Slade J in *Powell v McFarlane*.[37]

JA Pye (Oxford) Ltd v Graham
[2002] UKHL 30, [2003] 1 AC 419, HL

Lord Browne-Wilkinson

At [40]

[There] are two elements necessary for legal possession: (1) a sufficient degree of physical custody and control ("factual possession"); (2) an intention to exercise such custody and control on one's own behalf and for one's own benefit ("intention to possess"). What is crucial is to understand that, without the requisite intention, in law there can be no possession [. . .] [There] has always, both in Roman law and in common law, been a requirement to show an intention to possess in addition to objective acts of physical possession. Such intention may be, and frequently is, deduced from the physical acts themselves. But there is no doubt in my judgment that there are two separate elements in legal possession. So far as English law is concerned intention as a separate element is obviously necessary. Suppose a case where A is found to be in occupation of a locked house. He may be there as a squatter, as an overnight trespasser, or as a friend looking after the house of the paper owner during his absence on holiday. The acts done by A in any given period do not tell you whether there is legal possession. If A is there as a squatter he intends to stay as long as he can for his own benefit: his intention is an intention to possess. But if he only intends to trespass for the night or has expressly agreed to look after the house for his friend he does not have possession. It is not the nature of the acts which A does but the intention with which he does them which determines whether or not he is in possession.

---

[36] [2003] 1 AC 419, [36]–[39].   [37] (1979) 38 P & CR 452, 470.

It is necessary to address each of these elements separately—that is the approach taken by the courts in determining claims to adverse possession—but it should be borne in mind at the outset that the two are closely interconnected. As we will see, ultimately, a claimant's acts provide the strongest evidence of his or her intent. Indeed, such is the connection between them that there is some doubt as to whether intent, in fact, exists as a free-standing element.

4.2.1 Factual possession

In *Pye v Graham*, the House of Lords approved a definition of factual possession given by Slade J in the following case.

Powell v McFarlane
(1979) 38 P & CR 452, HC

Facts: The claimant, Mr Powell, lived on a farm with his grandparents. As a 14-year-old boy, he had started to use neighbouring land for purposes connected with the farm. In particular, he cut hay and made 'rough and ready' repairs to the boundary fence, so that the land could be used to graze the family's cow. The paper owner, Mr McFarlane, was working overseas and, on his return, Mr Powell argued that he had obtained title to the land by adverse possession.

Slade J

At 470–1

Factual possession signifies an appropriate degree of physical control. It must be a single and [exclusive] possession, though there can be a single possession exercised by or on behalf of several persons jointly. Thus an owner of land and a person intruding on that land without his consent cannot both be in possession of the land at the same time. The question what acts constitute a sufficient degree of exclusive physical control must depend on the circumstances, in particular the nature of the land and the manner in which land of that nature is commonly used or enjoyed. In the case of open land, absolute physical control is normally impracticable, if only because it is generally impossible to secure every part of a boundary so as to prevent intrusion [. . .] Everything must depend on the particular circumstances, but broadly, I think what must be shown as constituting factual possession is that the alleged possessor has been dealing with the land in question as an occupying owner might have been expected to deal with it and that no-one else has done so.

Mr Powell's claim to adverse possession failed on the basis that he could not demonstrate an intention to possess (that aspect of the case is considered in section 4.2.2 below). No specific findings were made in relation to factual possession. In *Pye v Graham*, it was held that the Grahams were in occupation of the land with exclusive physical control. Pye was physically excluded by the hedges and by the lack of a key to the only gate.[38] Therefore, factual possession was established.

---

[38] [2003] 1 AC 419, [41].

The geographical scope of a claim to adverse possession is not necessarily limited to the extent of the land over which the acts that constitute factual possession have been exercised. In *Roberts v Swangrove Estates Ltd*, Lindsay J explained that the question of the scope of a claim is '*necessarily one of fact and degree*'.[39] He suggested, for example, that '*a squatter [who] has occupied a terraced house, has lived in it and has denied access through its doors other than to his visitors, he would, no doubt, be taken to have had possession of the whole house notwithstanding that he failed to prove he had occupied a back room on the top floor. Conversely a squatter who created for himself a small kitchen garden in a corner of a 40 acre field might find, on claiming title as to the whole 40 acres, that all he acquired by adverse possession was a fee simple in the kitchen garden part*'.[40] Possession of part will also constitute possession of the whole where such an inference is reasonably drawn from a '*common character of locality*'.[41]

The claimant's acts of possession must be open, but in the absence of deliberate concealment it is not necessary for the paper owner to be aware of them.[42] If the paper owner credibly denies knowledge, the test is an objective one, '*whether a reasonable owner of the plot, paying that due regard to his interests as owner of it which was to be expected of him, would have acquired notice of them and would thereby have clearly appreciated that the squatter concerned was seeking to dispossess him*'.[43]

The requirement of exclusive possession has raised a specific question whether it is possible to claim adverse possession of part of a building; for example, a room in a house or one flat in a block. In *Ramroop (Sampson) v Ishmael and Heerasingh*,[44] the Privy Council noted that there is '*surprisingly little authority*'[45] on the point, but accepted that such claims follow logically from the fact that land can be held horizontally. It must be shown, however, that '*part of the building was capable of being possessed by the claimant to the exclusion of others*'.[46] The Privy Council noted that this '*might be relatively easy to plead and prove if the property in question was a self-contained residential flat in a purpose-built block. It might be much more difficult in a building which had slipped into informal multiple occupation with shared facilities*'.[47] On the facts, the claim failed. The claimant argued that she was in adverse possession of the downstairs of a house, but had not provided sufficient evidence of the extent of her claim or of the layout of the house in question.

4.2.2 Intention to possess

In *Pye v Graham*, the House of Lords approved the decision in *Buckinghamshire County Council v Moran*,[48] in which an intention to possess had been distinguished from an intention to 'own'.[49] Adopting the formulation of the judge at first instance, the Court of Appeal in *Moran* held that what is required is '*not an intention to own or even an intention to acquire ownership but an intention to possess*'.[50] The distinction had been significant on the facts of

---

[39] *Roberts v Swangrove Estates Ltd* [2007] 2 P & CR 17, [54].   [40] Ibid.
[41] *Lord Advocate v Lord Blantyre* (1878–79) LR 4 All Cas 770, 791 *per* Lord Blackburn.
[42] *Powell v McFarlane* (1979) 38 P & CR 452, 480.
[43] *Roberts v Swangrove Estates Ltd* [2007] 2 P & CR 17, [43] *per* Lindsay J.   [44] [2010] UKPC 14.
[45] Ibid, [23].   [46] Ibid, [25].   [47] Ibid.   [48] [1990] Ch 623.
[49] This formulation was rejected by Tee, who argued that an intention to own should be required: 'Adverse Possession and the Intention to Possess' [2000] Conv 113. Her argument is countered by Harpum and Radley-Gardner, 'Adverse Possession and the Intention to Possess: A Reply' [2001] Conv 155.
[50] [1990] Ch 623, [643].

that case. The council had acquired the disputed land for future use as part of a road. The land adjoined the claimant's garden and he used the land as an extension of his garden. The only access to the land was through the claimant's garden, or by a gate, which the claimant had locked. The claimant had conceded that he would have been obliged to leave the land if it was required for the road. This may have defeated an intention to 'own' the land, but it did not preclude the claimant demonstrating that he intended to possess the land, for the time being, to the exclusion of all others.[51]

Similarly, in *Pye v Graham*, the Grahams' willingness to enter into another agreement with Pye and to pay for the use of the land may have defeated an intention to own, but did not preclude an intention to possess. Lord Browne-Wilkinson explained: '*[An] admission of title by the squatter is not inconsistent with the squatter being in possession in the meantime.*'[52]

It is necessary to show an intention to exclude the world at large, including the paper owner.[53] For the duration of the limitation period, however, the claimant remains vulnerable to the paper owner's assertion of its stronger title. With this in mind, the requirement of intention was reformulated in *Powell v McFarlane*, in a manner approved by the House of Lords in *Pye v Graham*.[54]

Powell v McFarlane
(1979) 38 P & CR 452, HC

Slade J
At 471–2

What is really meant, in my judgment, is that, the *animus possidendi* involves the intention, in one's own name and on one's own behalf, to exclude the world at large, including the owner with the paper title [. . .] so far as is reasonably practicable and so far as the processes of the law will allow.

As has been noted, in *Powell v McFarlane*, the claim to adverse possession failed on the basis of intention. Slade J considered Mr Powell's acts to be equivocal, in the sense that they were open to interpretation as demonstrating intent merely to use the land for so long as the paper owner took no steps to prevent the use, without intending to appropriate the land.[55] The claimant's age at the time that his acts began appeared to be a significant consideration in this regard.[56] Subsequently, Mr Powell had erected signs on the land and parked lorries on it in connection with his business. Slade J acknowledged that, at that later stage, the claimant may have established an intention to possess, but these acts occurred within the limitation period.

In *Pye v Graham*, the House of Lords held that the Grahams could establish an intention to possess. In continuing to use the land at the expiry of the original grazing agreement,

---

[51] Ibid, [642]–[643].   [52] [2003] 1 AC 419, [46].

[53] *Littledale v Liverpool College* [1990] 1 Ch 19, 23. For examples of cases that have failed on this point, see *Battersea Property Co v London Borough of Wandsworth* [2001] 19 EG 148 (no intention to exclude the world where the claimant provided access to the land to holders of allotments) and *Batt v Adams* [2001] 32 EG 90 (claimant did not intend to exclude the person that he wrongly believed to be the paper owner).

[54] [2003] 1 AC 419, [43].   [55] (1979) 38 P & CR 452, 478.   [56] Ibid, 480.

they had acted in a way that they knew to be contrary to the wishes of Pye. They had made such use of the land as they had wished, including for purposes beyond the scope of the original grazing agreement. In essence, the Grahams had used the land '*for all practical purposes* [. . .] *as their own and in a way normal for an owner to use it*'.[57]

How to prove intent, and the relationship between intent and factual possession, remains unclear. In *Powell*, as has been seen, the failure of intent related directly to the nature of the claimant's acts: his acts were not sufficient, in qualitative terms, to establish intent. Further, it appears that the only way in which Mr Powell could have established intent would have been to show that he had done more. Slade LJ indicated that little weight would be afforded to self-serving declarations by a claimant as to his or her intent.[58] Similarly, in *Pye v Graham*, the claimants succeeded in establishing intent because their acts were qualitatively strong: they had used the land as an owner would.

In *Pye v Graham*,[59] Lord Browne-Wilkinson acknowledged that intent may be deduced by the claimant's physical acts. Lord Hutton suggested that where the claimant makes full use of the land as if he or she were the owner, the claimant's conduct is sufficient to establish intent. The burden then shifts to the paper owner to provide evidence that points to the contrary.[60] In *Powell v McFarlane*, Slade J suggested that 'unequivocal' acts by the claimant established intent, unless the paper owner could demonstrate otherwise. Such acts include enclosure, which has been described as the strongest evidence of intent,[61] the cultivation of agricultural land, placing and enforcing 'keep out' notices, and locking or blocking the only means of access.[62] Where the claimant's acts are equivocal (as they were considered to be in that case), the claimant will need to adduce additional evidence to demonstrate his or her intent.[63]

On the face of it, this suggests that, in some cases, intent will be determined by reference to the claimant's acts, while in others, the claimant will be invited positively to prove his or her intent. Given the courts' (understandable) reticence to give weight to self-serving statements by claimants as to their intent, however, it is difficult to know what evidence, other than the claimant's acts, could be adduced. It has even been doubted whether intent is, in fact, a free-standing requirement,[64] though the weight of the authorities practically puts the matter beyond doubt.

In *Purbrick v London Borough of Hackney*,[65] Neuberger J emphasized the need to assess the claim on the basis of what the claimant has done. The fact that the claimant could have done more does not defeat a claim if what he or she has done is sufficient to demonstrate factual possession and an intention to possess. Similarly, in *Topplan Estates v Townley*,[66] the claimant's acts were sufficient to establish intent even though his use of the land did not change following the expiry of a previous grazing agreement, which, on its terms, purported not to grant possession. The acts fell to be assessed on their own merits and were not 'diluted or denatured' by reference to the parties' previous dealings.[67]

---

[57] [2003] 1 AC 419, [61], *per* Lord Browne-Wilkinson.   [58] (1979) 38 P & CR 452, 476.

[59] [2003] 1 AC 419, [40] (extracted in section 4.2 above).   [60] [2003] 1 AC 419, [75]–[76].

[61] *Seddon v Smith* (1877) 36 LT 168. See further the discussion of enclosure in *Buckinghamshire County Council v Moran* [1990] Ch 623 and *Powell v McFarlane* (1979) 38 P & CR 452.

[62] (1979) 38 P & CR 452, 478.   [63] Ibid, *Pye v Graham* [2003] 1 AC 419, [76].

[64] Radley-Gardner, 'Civilized Squatting' (2005) 25 OJLS 727.

[65] [2003] EWHC 1871, [20]–[23].   [66] [2004] EWCA 1369.

[67] Ibid, [79], *per* Jonathan Parker LJ.

4.2.3 The rule in *Leigh v Jack*

We have seen that, in the *Wallis's* case, the Court of Appeal held that a licence would be implied where a person enters into possession, but does not act in a manner inconsistent with the holder of the paper title, although that decision has since been reversed by Sch 1, para 8(4), of the Limitation Act 1980. The *Wallis's* case was based on a more specific doctrine derived from *Leigh v Jack*.[68] In that case, it was held that there is no 'dispossession' of the paper owner by a claimant whose acts are not inconsistent with the paper owner's future use of the land. On the facts, the claimant's use of land for storage connected with his business was held not to constitute a dispossession of the paper owner, because the acts were not inconsistent with the paper owner's intention to dedicate the land to the public as a road. Doubt has been expressed about whether this rule is reversed by Sch 1, para 8(4), of the Limitation Act 1980,[69] but it has been held, in any event, to be wrong as a matter of law.[70]

The underlying difficulty with the rule is that the sufficiency of the claimant's acts is made dependent upon the paper owner's intent. In this way, the rule focusses on the intention of the paper owner and not the intention of the adverse possessor. In *Pye v Graham*, Lord Browne-Wilkinson commented that '*the suggestion that the sufficiency of the possession can depend on the intention not of the squatter but of the true owner is heretical and wrong*'.[71] This is not to say, however, that the paper owner's intended use of the land is invariably irrelevant.

JA Pye (Oxford) Ltd v Graham
[2002] UKHL 30, [2003] 1 AC 419, HL

Lord Browne-Wilkinson

At [45]

The highest it can be put is that, if the squatter is aware of a special purpose for which the paper owner uses or intends to use the land and the use made by the squatter does not conflict with that use, that may provide some support for a finding as a question of fact that the squatter had no intention to possess the land in the ordinary sense but only an intention to occupy it until needed by the paper owner. For myself I think there will be few occasions in which such inference could be properly drawn in cases where the true owner has been physically excluded from the land. But it remains a possible, if improbable, inference in some cases.

In this way, Lord Browne-Wilkinson refocussed *Leigh v Jack* on the intention of the claimant: the paper owner's intended use of the land may be relevant, but only to the extent that it sheds light on the intention of the claimant. The decision on the facts of *Leigh v Jack* is generally considered to have been correct. It has been suggested that either the paper owner was not dispossessed, because he had continued to carry out repairs to a fence,[72] or that the adverse possessor, who was aware of the intended use of the land, thereby fell short of demonstrating factual possession or an intention to possess.[73]

---

[68] (1879) 5 Ex D 264.   [69] Dockray, 'Adverse Possession and Intention II' [1982] Conv 345.
[70] *Pye v Graham* [2003] 1 AC 419, [45].   [71] Ibid.   [72] Ibid.
[73] *Buckinghamshire County Council v Moran* [1990] Ch 623, [639]–[40].

4.3 TERMINATION OF ADVERSE POSSESSION

Once a period of adverse possession has commenced it is terminated if the claimant moves out of adverse possession, whether on his or her own accord or by the execution of a judgment for possession obtained by the PO. There are, however, other circumstances in which an existing period of adverse possession will come to an end and a fresh period will immediately begin. Such is the effect of an interruption of the claimant's adverse possession by the PO or of an acknowledgement by the claimant of the PO's title.

4.3.1 Interruption of adverse possession by the PO

If a claimant's adverse possession is interrupted by the PO, the period of adverse possession comes to an end. If the claimant remains in adverse possession after the interruption, then a fresh right of action is accrued. What constitutes a sufficient interruption to bring a period of adverse possession to an end was considered by the Court of Appeal in the following case.

Zarb v Parry
[2011] EWCA Civ 1306, [2012] 1 WLR 1240

Facts: The Zarbs and the Parrys were in dispute over ownership of a strip of land that physically formed part of the Parrys' garden. The Parry's land had once been in common ownership with the Zarbs' land and had been sold by the Zarbs' predecessor in title to the Parrys' predecessor in title, the Ceens. The Ceens had always treated the boundary as being marked by a hedge, while the Zarbs contended that the boundary was 12 feet north of the hedge. A dispute between the Zarbs and the Ceens appeared to have been resolved in 2002 when the Parrys purchased the land, but erupted again in 2007. The Zarbs had entered the disputed strip (apparently in the belief the Parrys were away), cut down a tree and uprooted a fence post. A confrontation ensued in which the Zarbs initially refused to leave, insisting the land belonged to them, and started marking a boundary with surveyors' tape. The incident lasted for around 20 minutes, and ended when the Parrys threatened to call the police. In subsequent proceedings commenced by the Zarbs it was established that they had paper title to the strip of land, but that the Parrys had obtained title through adverse possession. One of the grounds on which the Zarbs challenged the Parry's claim was that the confrontation in 2007 constituted an interruption of the Parry's adverse possession. This argument had been rejected by the judge at first instance, whose decision was confirmed by the Court of Appeal.

Arden LJ:

At [35], [38–40], [43–44]

So the question on this issue is whether the acts of the Zarbs were sufficient to bring the Parrys' possession of the strip to an end. The primary evidence on this point is important. The Zarbs did not retake exclusive possession of the strip as they intended to do by banging in posts and starting to erect a wire fence. They decided to withdraw part way through that exercise, because of the protests from the Parrys. The mere erection of a surveyor's tape is not sufficient to enclose the land where it is laid out merely for the temporary purpose of measuring the line at which a fence is to go. However, it was clear that the Zarbs intended that they should recover possession. That intention was made clear through words and deed. They were the paper title owners. Assuming for this purpose that they can meet the defence raised against them based on paragraph 5(4) [of the LRA 2002], they had a better right to possession of the land than the Parrys. The strip was not a home or building. It can, therefore, forcefully be said that the law ought to look favourably on a paper title owner who intends to make a peaceable re-entry of land of this nature and makes manifest that intention by incontrovertible words. It can also be said that it should not matter that the paper title owner's statement of intention was accompanied by only preliminary acts.

[38] [. . .] an adverse possessor has to show he has exclusive possession in the sense of exclusive physical control. If he loses exclusive physical control, his adverse possession is interrupted and comes to an end. Time begins to run again. In this case, the Zarbs had banged fence posts into the ground so that it might be said that the Parrys lost exclusive control of the limited area affected by those posts. However, the area occupied by each post would have been small and could not justify a conclusion that adverse possession of the whole of the strip had been interrupted.

The paper title owner has the advantage in law that, to effect repossession of property, it is sufficient to show that possession has been resumed for a short period of time. This was established in *Randall v Stevens* (1853) 2 E & B 641 where a landlord evicted a tenant who had failed to pay any rent for 20 years. Statute provided that a house could not be repossessed simply by exercising a right of entry. Lord Campbell CJ, giving the judgment of the Court of Queen's Bench on appeal from a judgment given at assizes, held at p 652 that entry could be made "by stepping on any corner of the land in the night time and pronouncing a few words, without any attempt or intention or wish to take possession". However, where possession was taken with an intention to possess, then "whether possession was retained by the landlord an hour or a week must for this purpose [ie taking possession other than by mere entry] be immaterial".

The adverse possessor is, therefore, at risk of losing possession for a brief period of time, perhaps while he is out taking a walk or doing some shopping. The fact that the paper title owner can interrupt his possession in this way lends support to the view that the act of interruption should be effective to bring the adverse possessor's exclusive possession to an end. It would potentially be unfair if a paper title owner could interrupt adverse possession by the simple act of erecting a notice on the property saying, for example, "Private Property—Keep Out", so that the period of adverse possession will start all over again.

[43] [. . .] In my judgment, however, the principle on which *Bligh v Martin* was decided, namely that the factual possession of the adverse possessor must be brought to an end, is clearly correct and determines the result on this issue. The principle achieves a simple test for ascertaining whether the period of adverse possession has been brought to an end. Interruption will be overt and so it can be more easily proved or disproved if the question has to be litigated many years later. Furthermore, if the paper title owner did something less than exclude the adverse possessor, such as plant a flag, put up a notice or make an oral declaration of ownership, the adverse possessor would continue to have factual possession in the sense defined in the *Pye* case [2003] 1 AC 419. A person might, therefore, continue to have the intent to possess and factual possession throughout the period of any interruption of his adverse possession by symbolic acts such as I have mentioned. It would, in my judgment, be inconsistent with the *Pye* case if an adverse possessor could at one and the same time fulfil the requirements for adverse possession but yet have his possession effectively interrupted by the paper title owner. Finally, there is no need for the paper title owner to know that he is bringing the adverse possession to an end or to say that he is doing so: it is the quality of the acts which matters and not any oral declarations.

For all the reasons given above, the Zarbs clearly did not, in my judgment, retake possession in any meaningful sense. It was not enough that the Zarbs planted stakes or took other steps symbolic of taking possession of the whole of the strip. In my judgment, the judge was entitled to come to the conclusion that he did. I would thus dismiss the appeal in so far as it is based on this issue.

Lord Neuberger MR

At [68]–[76]

[. . .] Although the Zarbs were present on the strip for less than an hour, they carried out acts which may be said to be to be (i) inherently redolent of ownership, and/or (ii) signalling the retaking of possession. Chopping down the elderflower tree is in category (i). Category (ii) includes Mr Zarb marking off the paper boundary with a tape, stating that he was taking back the strip as it belonged to him, and refusing to vacate until threatened with the police being called. Into both categories are uprooting the Parrys' fence and banging in posts to mark the paper boundary.

The fact that the Zarbs were present on the strip for less than an hour does not prevent their actions when on the strip from being a retaking of possession—see *Randall v Stevens* (1853) 2 E & B 641, per Lord Campbell CJ. In that case, it was held that possession had been retaken, but the facts were stronger than in this case in that the paper title holder physically evicted the occupier, his family and all his furniture, albeit only for an hour, from the property in question, which was a house. Accordingly, there is no doubt that the person claiming adverse possession was physically completely excluded from the property, which remained, albeit for a short period, in the exclusive occupation and control of the paper title owner.

The judgment of Erle CJ in *Allen v England* (1862) 3 F & F 49, 52 at any rate at first sight, gives some support for the Zarbs' case in that it includes the proposition that "every time [the paper title owner] put his foot on the land, it [is] … in his possession". However, that apparently rather extreme view is in my judgment explained by reference to the particular facts of the case, which involved "permissive user of a garden", as Pennycuick J put it in *Bligh v Martin* [1968] 1 WLR 804, 812. In that later case, it was found that, although he had occupied and made use of the land in question, the paper title owner had never retaken possession of it. However, just as the facts in *Randall v Stevens*, and indeed in *Allen v England*, were more strongly in favour of the paper title owner than those of this case, so it seems to me clear that the facts in *Bligh v Martin* were weaker from the point of view of the paper title owner than those in the present case.

However, the decision in *Bligh v Martin* is valuable for present purposes in that Pennycuick J gave some guidance of general application, when he said at p 812 that "in the ordinary case of adverse possession … one must find that the [paper title] owner took possession in the ordinary sense of that word, to the exclusion of the [person claiming adverse possession]". Given the fact-specific and nebulous nature of possession, I consider that, in so far as general guidance can be given in relation to the task of deciding whether, on particular facts, the paper title owner has retaken possession at any time during the period of alleged adverse possession, that is probably as good as it can get.

In the present case, applying that general guidance, I have reached the conclusion that the Zarbs did not retake possession of the strip on the occasion in July 2007 described in para 7 above, and that the judge was entitled to reach that conclusion (which he did in very brief terms). What the Zarbs did, in my opinion, was to prepare to take possession, but they never completed the exercise. When they knew the Parrys were away from their property on a shopping expedition, the Zarbs took preliminary steps with a view to excluding the Parrys from the strip, by removing some of the Parrys' fence, and starting to erect their own fence (presumably on the paper boundary), but they got no further than taking preliminary steps.

When the confrontation with the Parrys occurred, the strip had not been fenced off from the Parrys' property by the Zarbs, and, although the Zarbs initially threatened to exclude the Parrys when challenged and asked to vacate, the Zarbs ultimately backed down, and departed from the strip, leaving the Parrys in control.

In other words, while the Zarbs embarked on an enterprise which, if it had been completed, would have involved their retaking possession of the strip, they were interrupted by the Parrys before the enterprise had been completed, and, in the ensuing confrontation, they abandoned the enterprise. Accordingly, rather than retaking possession of the strip, it seems to me that, although they got some way towards achieving that aim, the Zarbs were thwarted in their attempt to do so, and had not completed it before the Parrys appeared, and, thereafter, when challenged, the Zarbs backed down pretty promptly (and, most people would I think say, properly).

Unlike the adverse possessors of the house in *Randall v Stevens* 2 E & B 641, the Parrys never lost control or possession of the strip to the paper title owners, although it may have been a pretty close run thing: if they had stayed out shopping for another hour, the Zarbs may have completed the execution of their plan. However, as Pennycuick J pointed out in *Bligh v Martin* [1968] 1 WLR 804, 812, in order to succeed in their argument, the Zarbs would have to have taken possession "to the exclusion of the [Parrys]".

It is true that the Zarbs also did things which may arguably be characterised as acts of ownership in the form of chopping down a tree and pulling up a fence, and they must be taken into account as part of the totality of the facts of that rather fraught hour on 29 July 2007. However, even taking them into account, I do not consider that the Zarbs did enough to be able to say that they effectively excluded the Parrys from the strip. The pulling up of the fence was part of the preparatory work done in order to retake possession, but, as I have said, that work never reached fruition. As for the tree-chopping, it seems to have been little more than a rather spiteful act involving an elder, which many people would characterise as a shrub rather than a tree. Further, although the Zarbs' case cannot fail simply because of the fact that they are relying on events which took place over a very short period, I do consider that, when assessing whether the Parrys were excluded, the fact that the Zarbs rely on events which occurred over a very short length of time is a relevant factor.

I must admit to having found the Zarbs's second point much more difficult to resolve than I think Arden LJ has done. However, in the end, for the reasons which I have attempted to give, I consider that the judge was entitled to reject it, and if, as is probably the case, it is a point which this court has to decide on a binary, right or wrong, basis, I have concluded that the judge was right.

Jackson LJ expressed agreement with both judgments, preferring that of Arden LJ 'in so far as there is any difference of emphasis' between them.[74]

4.3.2 Acknowledgement of title

A right of action that has accrued to the paper owner on the inception of adverse possession is brought to an end and replaced with a fresh right of action if the adverse possessor acknowledges the paper owner's title. The date of the acknowledgement of title, therefore, replaces the date of adverse possession as the time from which the limitation period begins to run in unregistered land or the adverse possession is treated as having commenced in

---

[74] [2011] EWCA Civ 1306; [2012] 1 WLR 1240, [60].

registered land. However, only a formal acknowledgement, made in writing and signed by the person making it, is effective. The relevant provisions are found in ss 29 and 30 of the Limitation Act 1980.

Limitation Act 1980, ss 29 and 30

29(1) Subsections (2) [. . .] below apply where any right of action (including a foreshore action) to recover land [. . .] has accrued.

(2) If the person in possession of the land [. . .] in question acknowledges the title of the person to whom the right of action has accrued –

(a) the right shall be treated as having accrued on and not before the date of the acknowledgment [. . .]

(7) [. . .] a current period of limitation may be repeatedly extended under this section by further acknowledgements [. . .], but a right of action, once barred by this Act, shall not be revived by by any subsequent acknowledgement [. . .]

30(1) To be effective for the purposes of section 29 of this Act, an acknowledgment must be in writing and signed by the person making it.

(2) For the purposes of section 29, any acknowledgment [. . .] –

(a) may be sent by the agent of the person by whom it is required to be made under that section; and

(b) shall be made to the person, or to an agent of the person, whose title or claim is being acknowledged [. . .]

The operation of these provisions was scrutinized by the House of Lords in the following case.

Ofulue v Bossert
[2009] UKHL 16, [2009] 1 AC 990

Facts: Mr and Mrs Ofulue were registered proprietors of a property which they had let to tenants when they went to live abroad. Since 1981 or 1982 the property had been occupied by Ms Bossert who had been given possession, together with her father (who was now deceased), by the previous tenant. Possession proceedings had initially been commenced against Ms Bossert and her father in 1987, but these had been struck out in 2002. The current proceedings had then been launched in 2003. The initial proceedings had commenced well within the limitation period and so adverse possession had not been raised. When Ms Bossert claimed adverse possession in response to the current proceedings, the Ofulues argued that two events related to the initial proceedings constituted an acknowledgment of title under s 29. One event was an offer to buy the property which the Bosserts had made in correspondence with the Ofulues in 1992. The House of Lords agreed with the Court of Appeal that an offer to buy constituted an acknowledgement of title, but the difficulty faced by the Ofulues was that the correspondence was labelled 'without prejudice'. The majority of their Lordships (Lord Scott dissenting) concluded that the correspondence fell within the scope of a general rule of evidence which prohibited 'without prejudice' correspondence from being relied upon in court. This aspect of the case, which concerns the operation of rules of evidence rather than adverse possession, is not further discussed. The second event relied upon, while sub-sidiary to the Ofulues' claim, raised more substantive issues on the interpretation of s 29 of the Limitation Act 1980. In their defence to the initial proceedings, the Bosserts had counter-claimed for a lease, which Ms Bossert's father argued he had been promised by the Ofulues in return for repairs and improvements to the property. This gave rise to two questions. First, whether an acknowledgement of title is sufficient if it does not admit an immediate right to possession on the part of the claimants. Secondly, if there was an acknowledgement of title, whether it was confined to the date the defence was issued in 1990, or continued to operate until the proceedings were struck out in 2002. This was significant as an acknowledgement confined to the date the defence was issued would no longer assist the Ofulues. Under the limitation rules that applied to registered land at the time of the claim (which are discussed in section 5.2 of this chapter) their title would still be defeated as the Bosserts had remained in occupation for 12 years since that date.

Lord Neuberger

At [74]–[75] and [78]–[81]

The Court of Appeal concluded that the admission in the defence in the first proceedings did not amount to an acknowledgement within section 29, because it was only an acknow-ledgement of the Ofulues' title to the freehold, and not an admission of their right to im-mediate possession [. . .] But the conclusion that section 29 requires an acknowledgement of a right to immediate possession, as opposed to an acknowledgement of title, is, in my judgment, wrong for two separate reasons, which may be shortly stated

First, the conclusion reached by the Court if Appeal is inconsistent with the wording of section 29(2), which refers in clear terms to acknowledging "the title" of the person whose claim is said to be time-barred. Secondly, in any event, the concept of "possession" is more subtle than the reasoning of the Court of Appeal appears to have assumed. The effect of the defence in the earlier proceedings was to acknowledge the Ofulues' right to possession, albeit subject to the Bosserts' rights as tenants (in law or equity). This analysis also accords with common sense. The current dispute is whether the Ofulues effectively lost the freehold interest in the property to Ms Bossert, so it would be strange if a plain acknowledgement by Ms Bossert of their ownership of that very interest was not a sufficient acknowledgement for the purposes of section 29. It would also be strange if the Bosserts' contention that they held, or were entitled to the grant of, an interest in premises from the Ofulues did not operate as an acknowledgement by them of the Ofulees's title.

The admission of title in the defence as a continuing acknowledgement

[78] Mr Richard Wilson QC, on behalf of Mrs Ofulue, contended that the admission in the defence constituted an effective acknowledgement which prevented time running for the period up to the time the proceedings in which it was served were dismissed. The principal basis for this contention was that, by maintaining her case in the defence from the date it was served until the first proceedings were dismissed in 2002, Ms Bossert was affirming her acknowledgement of the Ofulues' title to the property for the purpose of section 29(2).

I can see no reason why a statement in a pleading or statement of case, or in any other court document, cannot amount to an acknowledgement for the purposes of section 29. Accordingly, the admission in the defence in this case, as I see it, operated as such as an acknowledgement of the Ofulues' title as at 18 July 1990, the date on which it was served.

Indeed, although the point was in issue below, the contrary was not argued by Mr Peter Crampin QC, for Ms Bossert.

However, in my opinion, the argument that the admission continued to operate as such an acknowledgement beyond 18 July 1990 was rightly rejected by the Court of Appeal. It is inconsistent both with the language of the relevant provisions, and with the policy, of the 1980 Act. Conceptually and as a matter of language, I accept that an "acknowledgement" could cover a continuing state of affairs. However, particularly where it has to be embodied in a signed document, the more natural meaning of the word would suggest that it arises as at the date of the document—most naturally the date on which the document is provided to the person to whom the acknowledgement is made. The requirement in section 30(1) that an acknowledgement must be in writing and signed was no doubt intended to minimise the room for argument as to whether and when it was made.

The effect of section 15 of the 1980 Act is that a formal record, such as a conveyance or entry on the register, which appears to establish the paper title owner's title against the world, cannot be relied on after 12 years of adverse possession have passed. In those circumstances, it would seem very odd if an informal written acknowledgement could be relied on under section 29 of the same Act, where the adverse possession has thereafter continued for a longer period. If Mr Wilson's argument were correct, an offer to purchase, which remained open for acceptance, because it was not time-limited and not rejected, would presumably continue to operate as an acknowledgement for a potentially indefinite period. That appears surprising, inconvenient, and inconsistent with the purpose of the 1980 Act. Further, it seems clear that an act which could be said to refer to the future, namely a payment of rent in advance, will only stop time running up to the date it actually occurs: see paragraph 5(2) of Schedule 1 to the 1980 Act [. . .]

Ms Bossert's claim to adverse possession therefore succeeded. Although the Bosserts had acknowledged the Ofulues' title on two occasions, on the facts neither operated to prevent their claim under s 29 of the Limitation Act 1980.

The acceptance of the Bosserts' acknowledgement of the Ofulues' freehold title as sufficient under s 29 leads to a curious juxtaposition with the requirement of intention in establishing the existence of adverse possession, which serves to highlight the significance of the formality requirement in s 30. As we have seen in section 4.2.2 of this chapter, in order to establish adverse possession a claimant must demonstrate only an intention to possess not an intention to own. Hence, we have noted that in *Pye v Graham*, the Grahams' willingness to enter into a new licence did not defeat their claim to adverse possession. Their willingness to do so was conceded in evidence, but there was no written acknowledgement within ss 29 and 30. Similarly, the Bosserts' claim to be tenants was held by the Court of Appeal not to prevent their ability to demonstrate an intention to possess for the purpose of establishing their adverse possession.[75]

It is possible that s 29 does not apply to claims to adverse possession arising under the LRA 2002 and discussed in section 5.3 of this chapter.[76] While the matter remains unresolved, such a conclusion would be a surprising and apparently unexpected consequence of the disapplication of s 15 of the Limitation Act 1980 in the new scheme of limitations provided by the LRA 2002.

---

[75] For further discussion when a claimant may be considered to have provided written acknowledgement of title, see Jourdan and Radley-Gardner, *Adverse Possession* (2nd edn, 2011), [16–65]–[16–80].

[76] Jourdan and Radley-Gardner, ibid, [22–40]–[22–41].

5 THE EFFECT OF ADVERSE POSSESSION

As has been noted, the effect of adverse possession differs between unregistered land, registered land claims governed by the LRA 1925, and registered land claims governed by the LRA 2002.

5.1 UNREGISTERED LAND

Unregistered land displays the purity and simplicity of the operation of adverse possession in a system of relative titles. The general limitation period of twelve years is provided in s 15 of the Limitation Act 1980. Once adverse possession has continued for the twelve-year limitation period, the paper owner's title is extinguished by the operation of limitation of actions.

Limitation Act 1980, s 17

[. . .] at the expiration of the period prescribed by this Act for any person to bring an action to recover land (including a redemption action) the title of that person to the land shall be extinguished.

The twelve-year period may be completed by a single adverse possessor, or by two or more adverse possessors in succession: for example, where one adverse possessor is him or herself dispossessed by another before the expiry of the twelve-year period. At this stage, the adverse possessor's title is relatively superior to that of the paper owner, or persons claiming title through the paper owner.[77] There is no 'statutory conveyance' of the paper owner's title to the adverse possessor.[78] The effect of the statute is entirely negative.

Fairweather v St Marylebone Property Co Ltd
[1963] AC 510, HL

Lord Radcliffe

At 535

It is necessary to start, I think, by recalling the principle that defines a squatter's rights. He is not at any stage of his possession a successor to the title of the man he has dispossessed. He comes in and remains in always by right of possession, which in due course becomes incapable of disturbance as time exhausts the one or more periods allowed by statute for successful intervention. His title, therefore, is never derived through but arises always in spite of the dispossessed owner.

---

[77] In a case of successive adverse possessors, where C1 is dispossessed by C2, C1's title remains superior to that of C2 for 12 years from the date of dispossession. This is a consequence of relativity of title, discussed in section 3 of this chapter.

[78] *Tichborne v Weir* (1892) 67 LTR 735, 737.

The adverse possessor acquires an independent freehold title from the time at which he or she commenced adverse possession. The effect of the limitation rules, combined with relativity of title, is that the adverse possessor's title becomes inviolable by the paper owner. But the adverse possessor is not a purchaser for value of the land and therefore will be bound by pre-existing property rights affecting the paper owner's title: for example, the adverse possessor is bound by any easements or restrictive covenants affecting use of the land.[79]

Exceptions to the operation of the twelve-year limitation period are provided in a number of special cases, including: the mental incapacity of the paper owner;[80] fraud and concealment on the part of the adverse possessor and cases of mistake;[81] acts between parties to a trust of land;[82] Crown lands and the foreshore.[83]

5.2 REGISTERED LAND: LAND REGISTRATION ACT 1925

As has been noted, the LRA 1925 sought to align registered land with the operation of adverse possession in unregistered land. Registered land was subject to the same limitation rules, except the extinguishment of title was replaced by s 75 of the Act.

Land Registration Act 1925, s 75

(1) The Limitation Acts shall apply to registered land in the same manner and to the same extent as those Acts apply to land not registered, except that where, if the land were not registered, the estate of the person registered would be extinguished, such estate shall not be extinguished but shall be deemed to be held by the proprietor for the time being in trust for the person who, by virtue of the said Acts, has acquired title against any proprietor, but without prejudice to the estates and interests of any other person interested in the land whose estate or interest is not extinguished by those Acts.

(2) Any person claiming to have acquired a title under the Limitation Acts to a registered estate in the land may apply to be registered as proprietor thereof.

(3) The registrar shall, on being satisfied as to the applicant's title, enter the applicant as proprietor either with absolute, good leasehold, qualified or possessory title, as the case may require, but without prejudice to any estate or interest protected by any entry on the register which may not have been extinguished under the Limitation Acts, and such registration shall, subject as aforesaid, have the same effect as the

---

[79] *Re Nisbet and Potts Contract* [1906] 1 Ch 386.

[80] Limitation Act 1980, s 28. A paper owner who is under a disability when the right of action accrues and regains capacity after the 12-year limitation period had expired has six years from the time at which he or she regains capacity to bring an action. This is subject to a long stop of thirty years from the date at which the right of action accrued.

[81] Limitation Act 1980, s 32. The limitation period commences from the date at which the claimant discovers the fraud, concealment, or mistake, or could have done so through reasonable diligence. Beyond concealment, there is no obligation on the part of the adverse possessor to bring its acts to the attention of the paper owner. See *Topplan Estates Ltd v Townley* [2004] EWCA 1369, [85]–[86].

[82] Limitation Act 1980, Sch 1, para 9, prevents a right of action accruing in favour of one beneficiary or a trustee against another beneficiary.

[83] Limitation Act 1980, Sch 1, para 10, provides for a thirty-year limitation period for adverse possession against the Crown and para 11 provides for a sixty-year period in relation to the foreshore.

registration of a first proprietor; but the proprietor or the applicant or any other person interested may apply to the court for the determination of any question arising under this section.

At first sight, the imposition of a trust appears to be an expedient means of reconciling the idea of title being extinguished with registered land principles. As Cooke notes:[84] '[A] trust is the English lawyer's natural response to a situation where true ownership and paper title diverge.' In fact, however, the Law Commission noted that a trust was not necessary. All that was required was provision for the adverse possessor to apply for registration.[85]

The imposition of a trust was a source of confusion. It had the potential to confer a windfall on the adverse possessor, by providing a choice of enforcing his or her rights against the land, or enforcing personal liability against the dispossessed registered proprietor as trustee.[86] Further, the consequential imposition of fiduciary duties on the registered proprietor towards the adverse possessor appeared inappropriate.[87]

A separate issue arising from the imposition of the trust is the nature of the interest acquired by the adverse possessor. In registered land, as in unregistered land, the claimant obtains a freehold title from the inception of the adverse possession. This title is independent from the title held by the registered proprietor. Once the trust is imposed by s 75(1) of the LRA 1925, however, the adverse possessor necessarily has a beneficial interest in the registered proprietor's estate. Therefore, the adverse possessor of registered land appears to have two distinct interests in the land: the independently acquired freehold title, and a beneficial interest in the registered proprietor's estate.[88]

As Cooke explains, this has consequences for understanding the nature of the right with which the adverse possessor should be registered if he or she applies under s 75(2) of the LRA 1925.

Cooke, 'Adverse Possession: Problems of Title in Registered Land' (1994) 14 LS 1, 5–6

Once the limitation period has expired, the well-advised squatter will apply to be registered as proprietor. As we have seen, under s 75(2) 'any person claiming to have acquired a title under the Limitation Acts to a registered estate in the land may apply to be registered as proprietor thereof.'

Does 'thereof' mean 'of the land' or 'of the registered estate to which he claims to have acquired title'? In either case, does it mean that X is to be registered as proprietor 'of the fee simple arising by adverse possession' or 'of X's already registered estate, to which he has the equitable title by virtue of the trust imposed by s 75'?

In unregistered land, there is no question of the squatter's acquiring the dispossessed owner's estate by a 'parliamentary conveyance.' The fact that it is land registry practice to give [the squatter] a new title number indicates that [the squatter] is getting something new, and that he is being registered with title to his own independent fee simple so as to mirror his position in unregistered land. This is of course what the position should be.

---

84 *The New Law of Land Registration* (2003) p 136.
85 Law Commission Report No 254 (1998), [10.27].   86 Ibid, [10.30].
87 Cooke, 'Adverse Possession: Problems of Title in Registered Land' (1994) 14 LS 3–4.
88 Cooke, 'Adverse Possession: Problems of Title in Registered Land' (1994) 14 LS 1, 5.

It is debatable whether the 1925 Act provided for a parliamentary conveyance. The opening of a new title by the Land Registry suggests that this is not the case. Under the LRA 1925 (as in unregistered land cases), the adverse possessor obtained an independent freehold title, although he or she remained bound by property rights affecting the previous registered title.[89] The final closing of the registered proprietor's title produced a result analogous to the extinction of an unregistered title.

Notwithstanding, in *Fairweather v St Marylebone Property Co Ltd*,[90] a case involving unregistered land, Lord Radcliffe suggested obiter that s 75 of the LRA 1925 achieved a parliamentary conveyance. This analysis was subsequently taken in a first instance decision involving registered land.[91] But both of those cases concerned adverse possession against a leasehold estate. Specific difficulties arise in that context, which are explored in the online resources at www.oup.com/uk/mcfarlane4e/.

The LRA 2002 preserves the rights of adverse possessors acquired under the 1925 Act, but removes the s 75 trust. That section is repealed (without any saving) and transitional provisions are provided in Sch 12 of the 2002 Act.

Land Registration Act 2002, Sch 12, para 18

(1) Where a registered estate in land is held in trust for a person by virtue of section 75(1) of the Land Registration Act 1925 immediately before the coming into force of section 97, he is entitled to be registered as the proprietor of the estate.

(2) A person has a defence to any action for the possession of land (in addition to any other defence he may have) if he is entitled under this paragraph to be registered as the proprietor of an estate in the land.

The LRA 2002 came into force on 13 October 2003. As a result of Sch 12, para 18(1), the rights of a claimant who had completed twelve years of adverse possession (so that the s 75(1) trust had come into existence) on or before 12 October 2003 are preserved. The trust is removed by the repeal of s 75 of the 1925 Act, but the adverse possessor retains the right (originally conferred by s 75(2)) to be registered as proprietor. The entitlement to be registered as proprietor 'of the estate' confirms that a statutory transfer takes place.

5.3 REGISTERED LAND: LAND REGISTRATION ACT 2002

The LRA 2002 provides a new scheme of adverse possession. The scheme applies to adverse possessors in registered land who had not completed twelve years of adverse possession on or before the 12 October 2003.[92] It marks a clean break from attempting to transplant the operation of adverse possession in unregistered land into registered land. Instead, it

---

[89] Land Registration Act 1925, s 75(3), extracted above.   [90] [1963] AC 510, 542.

[91] *Central London Commercial Estates Ltd v Kato Kagaku Co Ltd* [1998] EWHC 314.

[92] It is not necessary that the title was registered throughout the period of adverse possession: Land Registration Act 2002, Sch 6, para 1(4). Hence the scheme will apply where a claimant enters into possession of unregistered land, but the title is registered before being extinguished by the expiry of the limitation period.

takes as its starting point the underlying principle that, in registered land, registration alone confers title, and seeks to provide a more appropriate balance between the registered proprietor and adverse possessor.[93]

The Law Commission explains the aims of the scheme.

Law Commission Report No 271, *Land Registration for the Twenty-First Century: A Conveyancing Revolution* (2001, [14.6])

The aims of the scheme are as follows.

1. Registration should of itself provide a means of protection against adverse possession, though it should not be unlimited protection. Title to registered land is not possession-based as is title to unregistered land. It is registration that vests the legal estate in the owner and that person's ownership is apparent from the register. The registered pro-prietor and other interested persons, such as the proprietor of a registered charge, are therefore given the opportunity to oppose an application by a squatter to be registered as proprietor.

2. If the application is not opposed, however, whether because the registered proprietor has disappeared or is unwilling to take steps to evict the squatter, the squatter will be registered as proprietor instead. This ensures that land which has (say) been abandoned by the proprietor, or which he or she does not consider to be worth the price of posses-sion proceedings, will remain in commerce.

3. If the registered proprietor (or other interested person) opposes the registration, then it is incumbent on him or her to ensure that the squatter is either evicted or his or her position regularised within two years. If the squatter remains in adverse possession for two years after such objection has been made, he or she will be entitled to apply once again to be registered, and this time the registered proprietor will not be able to object. In other words, the scheme provides a registered proprietor with one chance, but only one chance, to prevent a squatter from acquiring title to his or her land. The proprietor who fails to take appropriate action following his or her objection will lose the land to the squatter.

4. Consistently with the approach set out above, a registered proprietor who takes pos-session proceedings against a squatter will succeed, unless the squatter can bring him or herself within some very limited exceptions.

It will be apparent from this summary that one of the essential features of the scheme is that it must produce a decisive result. Either the squatter is evicted or otherwise ceases to be in *adverse* possession, or he or she is registered as proprietor of the land.

Under the 2002 Act, there is no concept of title being acquired by adverse possession or of a limitation period barring the assertion of a registered proprietor's title. Sections 15 and 17 of the Limitation Act 1980, which provide the twelve-year limitation period for an action to recover land, and 'extinguish' title at the end of that period, are disap-plied in relation to registered land.[94] Instead, the completion of a minimum of ten years'

---

[93] Law Commission Report No 254 (1998), [10.43]; Law Commission Report No 271, *Land Registration for the Twenty-First Century: A Conveyancing Revolution* (2001), [14.4].

[94] Land Registration Act 2002, s 96.

adverse possession[95] enables the claimant to access a procedure that will result in one of two outcomes: either with the claimant acquiring title to the land *by registration* (not by adverse possession itself); or with the assertion of title by the registered proprietor. Where the adverse possessor acquires title, there is a 'statutory transfer' of the registered proprietor's estate.

Sch 6 of the LRA 2002 provides the scheme. We will first outline the operation of the procedure and then assess the impact of the 2002 Act on adverse possession.

5.3.1 The new scheme of adverse possession

Land Registration Act 2002, Sch 6, paras 1–4

1(1) A person may apply to the registrar to be registered as the proprietor of a registered estate in land if he has been in adverse possession of the estate for the period of ten years ending on the date of the application. [. . .]

2(1) The registrar must give notice of an application under paragraph 1 to—

  (a) the proprietor of the estate to which the application relates,

  (b) the proprietor of any registered charge on the estate,

  (c) where the estate is leasehold, the proprietor of any superior registered estate,

  (d) any person who is registered in accordance with rules as a person to be notified under this paragraph, and

  (e) such other persons as rules may provide.

 (2) Notice under this paragraph shall include notice of the effect of paragraph 4.

3(1) A person given notice under paragraph 2 may require that the application to which the notice relates be dealt with under paragraph 5.

 (2) The right under this paragraph is exercisable by notice to the registrar given before the end of such period as rules may provide.

4 If an application under paragraph 1 is not required to be dealt with under paragraph 5, the applicant is entitled to be entered in the register as the new proprietor of the estate.

By virtue of Sch 6, adverse possession has no effect unless or until an application for registration is made. Adverse possession must have been maintained for at least ten years immediately prior to the application. Further, the applicant must generally have completed the adverse possession; successive periods of adverse possession by different squatters cannot be added together.[96] This ensures that if the adverse possessor succeeds in obtaining registration, his or her title is not vulnerable to challenge by a prior possessor. Security of the

---

[95] Ibid, Sch 6, para 1, extracted in section 5.3.1. The adoption of ten years as the requisite period reflects separate recommendations made by the Law Commission for reform of limitation of actions: Law Commission Report No 271 (2001), [14.19].

[96] This is in contrast to the position in unregistered land explained in section 5.1 above. Successive periods of adverse possession were also possible in registered land under the 1925 Act. Limited exceptions to the bar on successive periods of adverse possession are provided by the 2002 Act, Sch 6, para 11(2). This includes where the applicant is the successor in title to a previous adverse possessor. For further discussion of these, see Law Commission Report No 271 (2001), [14.20]–[14.21].

adverse possessor's title is preferred over the continued recognition of relativity of title, consistent with the underlying acceptance that title is based on registration, not possession. The general period of ten years provided in para 1(1) is subject to exceptions: in particular, an application cannot be made against a registered proprietor who is incapacitated by mental disability.[97] Applications relating to Crown foreshore land can be made only after a period of sixty years' adverse possession.[98]

Once an application for registration is made, the registered proprietor (and the other persons specified in para 2) are notified of the application by the Registrar. The onus then shifts to the registered proprietor to take steps to assert his or her title by issuing a counter-notice requiring the application to be dealt with under para 5. The period that has been provided in which the registered proprietor can do so under para 3(2) is 65 business days from the date of issue of the notification.[99] If the proprietor fails to issue a counter-notice within that period, then, by para 4, a statutory transfer of the estate is affected to the adverse possessor. The adverse possessor thereby acquires title to the land by registration.

If a counter-notice is issued, then (save in three exceptional cases in para 5, discussed in section 5.3.2. below) the application for registration is rejected. Under para 6, the registered proprietor has two years in which to commence proceedings for possession of the land. If no such proceedings are commenced within that period, then the adverse possessor may make a further application for registration.[100] This application does not instigate a new system of notifications. On making this application, the adverse possessor is immediately entitled to be registered as proprietor of the estate.[101]

We have seen that, in unregistered land, and in registered land under the LRA 1925, even though the adverse possessor acquires an independent freehold title, the title is subject to burdens affecting the old title. The position is clearer in the LRA 2002 where there is a statutory transfer of the exiting title. Sch 6, para 9, confirms that the registration of the adverse possessor does not affect the priority of interests affecting the estate. An exception is, however, made as regards registered charges. A registered chargee is notified by the Registrar of the adverse possessor's application for registration, and has the same opportunity as the registered proprietor to issue a counter-notice and bring proceedings for possession against the adverse possessor.[102] If a chargee fails to do so, then there is no justification for enabling him or her to enforce his or her charge against an adverse possessor who obtains registration.

While Sch 6 confers on a successful applicant an entitlement to be registered, that entitlement presupposes the existence of the underlying claim to adverse possession. The existence of adverse possession is a pre-condition to the right to make an application under Sch 6 and of the entitlement to obtain registration if that claim is successful. In *Baxter v Mannion*,[103] Mr Baxter obtained registration of title to a field under Sch 6 when the registered proprietor, Mr Mannion, failed to issue a counter-notice on receiving notice of his application for registration. Mr Mannion successfully argued that the registration of Mr Baxter had been a 'mistake' and obtained rectification of the register under the procedure in Sch 4 of the LRA 2002 (discussed in Chapter 18, section 3.1). It had been established on the facts that Mr Baxter's use of the land did not in fact constitute adverse possession and, therefore, he

---

[97] Land Registration Act 2002, Sch 6, para 8(2). Other exceptions are provided for registered proprietors who are enemies or are detained in enemy territory.

[98] Ibid, Sch 6, para 13.   [99] Land Registration Rules 2003 (SI 2003/1417), r 189.

[100] Land Registration Act 2002, Sch 6, para 6(1).   [101] Ibid, para 7.   [102] Ibid, [14.74].

[103] [2011] 1 WLR 1594. See too Chapter 3, section 3.2.2.

was not entitled to have been registered under Sch 6. The Court of Appeal refused to allow the '*bureaucratic machinery*' of Sch 6 to '*[trump] reality*'.[104]

5.3.2 Exceptional circumstances

In three exceptional cases, an adverse possessor's application will be successful despite a counter-notice being issued under Sch 6 para 3(1).

Land Registration Act 2002, Sch 6, para 5(1)–(4)

(1) If an application under paragraph 1 is required to be dealt with under this paragraph, the applicant is only entitled to be registered as the new proprietor of the estate if any of the following conditions is met.

(2) The first condition is that—

    (a) it would be unconscionable because of an equity by estoppel for the registered proprietor to seek to dispossess the applicant, and

    (b) the circumstances are such that the applicant ought to be registered as the proprietor.

(3) The second condition is that the applicant is for some other reason entitled to be registered as the proprietor of the estate.

(4) The third condition is that—

    (a) the land to which the application relates is adjacent to land belonging to the applicant,

    (b) the exact line of the boundary between the two has not been determined under rules under section 60,

    (c) for at least ten years of the period of adverse possession ending on the date of the application, the applicant (or any predecessor in title) reasonably believed that the land to which the application relates belonged to him, and

    (d) the estate to which the application relates was registered more than one year prior to the date of the application.

The third of these is the only true exception. In each of the other situations, the underlying assumption is that the adverse possessor, in fact, has a separate claim to the land.[105] As a result, the Law Commission in a 2016 Consultation Paper has asked for evidence as to the use of the first and second conditions, and has suggested that if they are removed, claims under Sch 6 can be focussed on cases where the claim depends on adverse possession, rather than some distinct principle, such as proprietary estoppel.[106]

---

[104] Ibid, para 1 *per* Jacob LJ.

[105] The relationship between estoppel and adverse possession is considered by Nield, 'Adverse Possession and Estoppel' [2004] Conv 123. As Cooke notes in *The New Law of Land Registration* (Oxford: Hart Publishing, 2003) p 142, the utility of combining estoppel with adverse possession is unclear. The Law Commission Report No 271 (2001, [14.43]) suggested that the second exception could apply where the adverse possessor is entitled to the land under the will or intestacy of the registered proprietor, or where a sale of land had not been formally completed, but purchase money has been paid, so that the registered proprietor, in fact, holds the land on trust for the adverse possessor.

[106] Law Com CP No 227, *Updating the Land Registration Act 2002*, [17.32].

The third exception reflects what the Law Commission, in 2001, acknowledged to be a legitimate conveyancing justification for adverse possession in registered land.[107] The register is not conclusive as to boundaries and, therefore, there is no conflict with the concept of title by registration to enable adverse possession to be used to settle genuine boundary disputes.

Two key points of interpretation arise from the third exception: first, at what point must the adverse possessor have held a reasonable belief that the land is theirs for ten years; and secondly, what constitutes a reasonable belief? As regards the timing of the claimant's belief, Milne suggests that although on its terms para 4(c) appears open to two interpretations, in *Zarb v Parry*[108] the Court of Appeal adopted a third.[109] On its terms, para 4(c) could require the belief to be held for at least ten years and persist at the date of application, or be held for ten years at any time during the adverse possession (even if it has ended any time before the date of application).[110] In *Zarb v Parry*, as we have seen in section 4.3.1 above, a dispute had arisen over the ownership of a strip of land that formed part of the Parrys' garden. The Court of Appeal held that while paper title to the strip was held by the Zarbs, the Parrys had established adverse possession. The final question for the court to consider was whether the case fell within para 5(4) so that the Parrys should be registered as proprietors, despite the paper owner's objection. Arden LJ explained the effect of the requirement of ten years' belief in the following terms:[111]

> The necessary effect of the way that paragraph 5(4) is expressed is to make the unreasonable belief of the adverse possessor in the last ten years of his possession prior to the application for registration a potentially disqualifying factor even though his belief started out as reasonable but became unreasonable as a result of circumstances after the completion by him and/or his predecessor in title of a ten-year period of possession. The consequence of that is that the paper title owner will have a last chance to recover the land if the adverse possessor did not have a reasonable belief during the last ten years. The moral is that, as soon as the adverse possessor learns facts which might make his belief in his own ownership unreasonable, he should take steps to secure registration as proprietor.

As Milne suggests, Arden LJ's statement indicates that *'the 10-year mistaken belief does not have to endure up to the date of the application, but it cannot end more than a short time before then'*.[112] In its 2016 Consultation Paper, the Law Commission states that:[113] such an interpretation is *'consistent with the policy reflected in the third condition. It ensures that once a person's reasonable belief comes to an end, ownership is determined through the schedule 6 procedure. It also reflects the fact that for so long as the reasonable belief is held the claimant would have no reason to make an application under schedule 6.'* As the Commission recognizes, this means there is some uncertainty as to how much time can pass

---

[107] Law Commission Report No 271 (2001), [14.3].

[108] [2011] EWCA Civ 1240; [2012] 1 WLR 1240.

[109] Milne, 'Mistaken Belief and Adverse Possession–Mistaken Interpretation? *IAM Group plc v Chowdrey* [2012] Conv 343.

[110] Milne suggests that the latter interpretation is implicitly supported by the Law Commission: ibid, pp 344–5.

[111] [2011] EWCA Civ 1240; [2012] 1 WLR 1240, at [17].   [112] Milne [2012] Conv 343 346.

[113] Law Com CP No 227, *Updating the Land Registration Act*, [17.42].

between the reasonable belief coming to an end and an application being made under Sch 6. The Commission has therefore suggested that statute should fix a period, so that, when a claimant relies on the condition in Sch 6, para 5(4), his or her reasonable belief must not have ended more than six months from the date of the application.[114]

The second question of interpretation is what constitutes reasonable belief on the part of the adverse possessor. Establishing the requisite belief did not appear to present difficulties for the Parrys and the Court of Appeal confirmed the judge's decision that they should be registered with title to the disputed strip under the exception in para 5(4). At the time the Parrys purchased their home, a dispute as to title between the Zarbs and the Parrys' vendors appeared to be settled and problems did not arise for a further five years. After the Zarbs' attempt to retake possession (discussed in section 4.3.1. above) the parties had instructed a surveyor who had concluded that the boundary lay where the Parrys' had believed. Indeed, in view of the surveyor's opinion (and other findings by the judge) Lord Neuberger MR considered it 'impossible to maintain [. . .] that the belief of the Parrys to the same effect was unreasonable'.[115]

The nature of the adverse possessor's reasonable belief came under further scrutiny by the Court of Appeal in *IAM Group plc v Chowdrey*.[116] Mr Chowdrey had purchased the freehold title to commercial premises, No 26A, that he had previously rented. Throughout his tenancy, Mr Chowdrey had used two floors of neighbouring premises, No 26, which were only accessible through No 26A. He continued to use the two floors following his purchase of the freehold. In fact, the two floors were in the paper title to No 26, which was now held by IAM Group, who commenced proceedings for possession. The Court of Appeal held that the requisite knowledge for para 5(4) is that of the adverse possessor. The relevant question is whether the adverse possessor '*was reasonable in holding the belief that he or she did in all the circumstances*'.[117] In answering this question, it is relevant for the court to consider whether the adverse possessor '*should have made inquiries*' as to what fell within his paper title.[118] However, the court rejected IAM Group's argument that Mr Chowdrey should be imputed with knowledge held by his solicitor. On the facts, there was no basis for placing Mr Chowdrey on notice of a need to make inquiries. He had used the two floors whilst a tenant and had continued to use them having purchased the freehold. His use had been unchallenged for eighteen years. Against the background of Mr Chowdrey's use, letters that had been sent to him by IAM Group asserting their title were not considered to render his belief unreasonable.

5.3.3 Assessment of the Land Registration Act 2002

As we have noted, one of the Law Commission's aims in its recommendations for adverse possession is to provide a more appropriate balance between adverse possessors and the registered proprietor. In fact, the new system is heavily weighted in favour of the registered proprietor. The LRA 2002 has been described as the 'emasculation' of adverse possession[119] and as making registered land 'virtually squatter proof'.[120] The role of adverse possession is reduced to settling boundary disputes and ensuring the marketability of abandoned land.[121]

---

114 Law Com CP No 227, [17.46].   115 [2011] EWCA Civ 1240; [2012] 1 WLR 1240, at [80].
116 [2012] EWCA Civ 505; [2012] P & CR 13.   117 Ibid, at [27] *per* Etherton LJ.   118 Ibid.
119 Dixon, 'The Reform of Property Law and the Land Registration Act 2002: A Risk Assessment' [2003] Conv 136, 150.
120 Cooke (2003) p 139.   121 Ibid, p 133.

This is a deliberate policy choice to make registered land more secure and, in so doing, encourage voluntary registration.[122]

While the Act favours the registered proprietor, there is an underlying obligation of personal responsibility. To benefit from the protection afforded by Sch 6, registered proprietors must act on receipt of a notification by the Registrar and, in order to do so, must have systems in place to manage their land. This may pose few difficulties for the individual homeowner, but presents more of a challenge to large landowners, including some local authorities that have failed to protect their interests under the LRA 1925.[123]

Bogusz argues that the approach taken by the 2002 Act is to be welcomed.

Bogusz, 'Bringing Land Registration into the Twenty-First Century: The Land Registration Act 2002' (2002) 65 MLR 556, 563

From a legal perspective, the Act reflects the true position that the basis of title to registered land is the fact of registration and is not based (as is the case in unregistered land) on the concept of possession. The Act intends to ensure an accurate register and restricting adverse possession in this way is necessary to achieve this. Adverse possession is therefore difficult to validate in the way it perhaps was in 1925. Arguments justifying adverse possession such as preventing the neglect of land or that there was a social need for wider land ownership are not so relevant today in a property owning democracy. Land ownership is not limited to a small proportion of the population, who, as was progressively becoming the case, did not have the resources to maintain the quality and value of their land. Adverse possession had a role to play when feudal landowners could no longer manage the estates they owned and when there was a need for some form of land redistribution.

Adverse possession with this egalitarian dimension is difficult to justify, at least in its present form, within a jurisdiction where land prices are high and the commercial market in land is particularly buoyant. The concept of alienability of land, which went to the heart of 1925 legislation, is very much a reality today. The economic reality of land being an important commercial commodity, that is freely and widely traded, makes adverse possession appear to be a very outdated concept. In this sense the LRA 2002 has very much lived up to the objectives of the Law Commission's Consultation Document of 1998 and as far as adverse possession is concerned, brought land registration into the twenty-first century.

Bogusz suggests that the reforms are equally welcome from a moral perspective.

Dixon, meanwhile, emphasizes that the approach taken by the LRA 2002 is not an inevitable one, but represents a policy choice.

Dixon, 'The Reform of Property Law and the Land Registration Act 2002: A Risk Assessment' [2003] Conv 136, 151–2

[The reform of adverse possession] is also a reflection of a political philosophy that sees adverse possession as "land theft" and as inherently inconsistent with a registration

---

[122] Law Commission Report No 271 (2001), [2.10].
[123] Cobb and Fox, 'Living Outside the System? The (Im)morality of Urban Squatting after the Land Registration Act 2002' (2007) 27 LS 236, 239. The authors suggest that the Law Commission's proposals were 'heavily influenced' by media criticism of the loss of local authority housing by adverse possession.

> system. Of course, there is merit in both these views: modern expositions of the law on adverse possession appear to have favoured the rights of possessors over the rights of paper owners and the existence of an off-register mechanism for destroying titles seems to make a mockery of the state guarantee of title. On the other hand, the social and economic justifications for principles of adverse possession have been well documented and instead of "land theft", adverse possession can be seen as encouraging "productive land use". Again, there is nothing inherently contradictory in having principles of adverse possession operate in registered land, at least if those principles are seen positively as a method of transferring title from one person to another instead of a method of unfairly snatching it from them. It is a matter of perception, not of incontrovertible logic. Consequently, given that the Act has chosen to emasculate adverse possession—and so favours one policy perspective—we must be alive to the possibility that there will be some creative interpretation of the relevant provisions by a differently minded judiciary [. . .]

We have noted that the LRA 2002 seeks to provide a scheme of adverse possession that is consistent with the underlying principle of title by registration. Cooke[124] notes that, under the Act, '*proof of title has been divorced from proof of possession*' and that relativity of title, a concept central to unregistered land, is no longer important.[125] These concepts have not been removed from registered land. The adverse possessor still relies on the inception of possession as the foundation of his or her claim. It is still recognized that adverse possession confers an independent freehold title from the moment at which possession begins. Hence, Sch 6, para 9 of the 2002 Act provides that this title (in contradistinction to that of the registered proprietor) is 'extinguished' when the adverse possessor becomes registered proprietor of the estate. Of course, given the difficulties of resisting an objection to an adverse possessor's application for registration, there may be many adverse possessors who decide not to make an application for registration.[126] Such a party may still then deal with his or her freehold, without applying for registration. This may create a '*dark market in possessory titles outside the registered land system*',[127] but it means that the traditional unregistered land concepts retain only a shadowy existence, as the overarching principle is that the adverse possessor remains vulnerable to the assertion of the registered title unless and until that title is acquired by the adverse possessor by registration.

6 ADVERSE POSSESSION AND THE CRIMINALIZATION OF RESIDENTIAL SQUATTING

Adverse possession necessarily involves trespass to land and, therefore, constitutes a civil wrong. The focus of criminal law has been on squatters whose conduct—as explained in section 1 of this chapter—may or may not constitute adverse possession. Until relatively

---

[124] Cooke, *Land Law* (Oxford: OUP, 2006) p 211.   [125] Ibid, p 203.

[126] As noted by Law Com CP No 227 (2016) [17.66]. See too the survey of advice given by solicitors in Pawlowski and Brown, 'Adverse Possession and the Transmissibility of Possessory Rights – The Dark Side of Land Registration?' [2017] Conv 116.

[127] Pawlowski and Brown, ibid, 128.

recently, the main criminal offences were those contained in ss 6 and 7 of the Criminal Law Act 1977. Under s 6, an offence is committed (in certain specified circumstances) where a person 'without lawful authority, uses or threatens violence for the purpose of gaining entry into any premises'. A defence is provided where the attempt to gain entry is a 'self-help' remedy being exercised by a displaced residential occupier[128] or a protected intending occupier.[129] By s 7 a person commits an offence if he or she fails to leave premises in which he or she is trespassing on being required to do so by or on behalf of a displaced residential occupier or a protected intended occupier.

6.1 THE OFFENCE OF SQUATTING IN A RESIDENTIAL BUILDING

The use of criminal law as a response to squatting was extended significantly by the introduction in 2012 of a new offence of squatting in residential premises.

Legal Aid, Sentencing and Punishment of Offenders Act 2012, s 144(1)–(7)

144 Offence of squatting in a residential building

(1) A person commits an offence if—

  (a) the person is in a residential building as a trespasser having entered it as a trespasser,

  (b) the person knows or ought to know that he or she is a trespasser, and

  (c) the person is living in the building or intends to live there for any period.

(2) The offence is not committed by a person holding over after the end of a lease or licence (even if the person leaves and re-enters the building).

(3) For the purposes of this section—

  (a) *"building"* includes any structure or part of a structure (including a temporary or moveable structure), and

  (b) a building is "residential" if it is designed or adapted, before the time of entry, for use as a place to live.

(4) For the purposes of this section the fact that a person derives title from a trespasser, or has the permission of a trespasser, does not prevent the person from being a trespasser.

(5) A person convicted of an offence under this section is liable on summary conviction to imprisonment for a term not exceeding 51 weeks or a fine not exceeding level 5 on the standard scale (or both).

(6) In relation to an offence committed before the commencement of section 281(5) of the Criminal Justice Act 2003, the reference in subsection (5) to 51 weeks is to be read as a reference to 6 months.

(7) For the purposes of subsection (1)(a) it is irrelevant whether the person entered the building as a trespasser before or after the commencement of this section.

---

[128] Defined in the Criminal Law Act 1977, s 12(3)–(5).
[129] Defined in the Criminal Law Act 1977, s 12A.

Hence, the offence is committed where a person is living in, or intends to live in, a residential building, which he or she entered as a trespasser. No exemption is provided for those who entered the building as a trespasser before the section came into force (on 1 September 2012). However, the offence does not extend to those who remain in premises at the end of a lease or licence.

The offence was introduced as a means of enhancing the rights of property owners, but its necessity has been doubted.[130] As the following extract illustrates, criminalization has provoked criticism for tackling a symptom rather than the underlying disease.

Cowan, Fox-O'Mahony, and Cobb, *Great Debates: Property Law*, p 112–13

The move to criminalization has been shaped by wider constructions of squatting and the squatter within popular discourse. The validity of the criminal law depends on conceptions of individual wrongdoing and blame, and media representations of squatting are replete with stories that present squatting as no more than a lifestyle choice, and construct squatters as irresponsible, feckless and the source of crime and anti-social behaviour. There is, however, a counterpoint to this rhetoric of moral indignation and culpability. Research has shown that for many squatting is not a lifestyle choice but a necessity brought about by the lack of decent and affordable housing, particularly in areas such as London with high demand and limited supplies of low-cost privately rented homes as well as social housing. These squatters have been described as part of the 'hidden homeless', and it has been noted that squatting attracts some of the most vulnerable, with often the greatest housing need as well as ancillary needs (mental illness, drug or alcohol dependency, recent release from prison) which can make it especially difficult for them to access mainstream housing support.

Recognizing the role of housing need and homelessness in decisions to squat adds a new layer of complexity to the debates around the criminalization of squatters. Several questions might usefully be asked about the urge to criminalize in light of this alternative conception of the squatter's motivation. Is the use of criminal law an inappropriately severe response to what is sometimes a response grounded in necessity rather than mere choice or lifestyle? Is it acceptable to label and stigmatize as criminals those who are some of the most vulnerable in society? And does the individualized conception of the problem of squatting draw our attention away from (and allow the state to ignore its own responsibilities for) the structural problems with the current housing market which have created the conditions that have encouraged squatting to take root?

6.2 THE IMPACT OF THE OFFENCE ON ADVERSE POSSESSION

The effect of the criminalization of squatting in a residential building on a claim to adverse possession arose for decision in the following case.

---

[130] Letter to the Editor, 'Media and Politicians are Misleading About Law on Squatters', *The Guardian*, Sunday September 25, 2011 signed by 160 practitioners and academics: see <http://www.theguardian.com/society/2011/sep/25/squatting-law-media-politicians> (accessed 22 December 2017).

Best v Chief Land Registrar
[2015] EWCA Civ 17, [2016] QB 23

Facts: Mr Best, a builder, had noticed an empty and abandoned house in 1997 and, having learnt that the owner had died and her son had not been seen for around a year, he began to repair and renovate the house in 2000, with the intention of making it his home. He moved in to the house in January 2012 and in November 2012 he applied under LRA 2002, Sch 6 to become registered proprietor. Mr Best's application for registration was refused by the Land Registry on the basis that, since the coming into force of s 144 of the Legal Aid, Sentencing and Punishment of Offenders Act 2012 (LASPOA) on 1 September 2012, his occupation had been a criminal offence. The Chief Land Registrar took the view that a period of adverse possession that constituted a criminal offence could not be used to establish the basis for an application under the LRA 2002. Mr Best successfully sought judicial review of the Registrar's decision, and the Court of Appeal upheld Ouseley J's decision that the Chief Land Registrar could not refuse registration simply on the basis that Mr Best's occupation had been a criminal offence.

In the Court of Appeal, counsel for Mr Best put forward a 'wide' and a 'narrow' argument as to the effect of illegality on the operation of Sch 6. On a wide view, the illegality had no impact; on a narrow view, some qualification could be made for illegality in some cases, but the balance of public policy favoured allowing the claim to succeed if the only illegality was an offence under s 144 of LASPOA.

Sales LJ (with whom McCombe LJ agreed)

At [67]–[77]

The difficulty with [counsel for B's] wider submission is that it covers such an extensive and protean category of conduct that it might be said to be difficult to say, in advance, of every conceivable form of criminally unlawful action bearing upon acquisition of title to registered land by adverse possession that Parliament intended it should have no impact at all upon the operation of the LRA. For example, I would wish to reserve my opinion regarding a case in which a trespasser in occupation of a residential building bribed a police officer not to expel him in reliance on s 144 of LASPOA, thus procuring or participating in an offence of corruption in a public office to gain the benefit of being registered as the proprietor with the title to the land; or a case in which a trespasser murdered the true owner in order to prevent him from claiming possession of the property.

Adoption of the approach in line with [counsel for B's] narrower submission appears to me to be in accordance with an appropriate general principle which it is reasonable to infer Parliament intended should apply by implication in the operation of the LRA. This approach allows for a properly modulated and focused weighing of the competing public policies which might come into play, whether considering legislation passed prior to the LRA or enacted after it.

Following this approach, I accept [counsel for B's] submission that the relevant balance of public policy considerations shows clearly that the fact that a relevant period of adverse possession for the purposes of the LRA included times during which the possessor's actions constituted a criminal offence under s 144 of LASPOA does not prevent his conduct throughout from qualifying as relevant adverse possession for the purposes of the LRA.

[. . .] The stated objective of s 144 was to provide deterrence and practical, on the ground assistance for home-owners in removing squatters from their property. Disruption of the law of adverse possession was not mentioned [in the consultation paper that preceded the Act] as an intended effect of the provision, nor was it suggested that it was being introduced to try to re-balance the rights of property owners as against those of adverse possessors with respect to the entitlement to be treated as title-holder in relation to property.

[. . .] Acceptance of the Registrar's arguments would have a profoundly disruptive effect in relation to what has been the long established effect of the law of adverse possession for the purposes of acquiring title for both registered and unregistered land. It is not plausible to suppose that Parliament would have been silent about the impact of a provision like s 144 on the delicate and comprehensive balance of interests set out in the Limitation Act 1980 and in Schedule 6 to the LRA, had it truly intended that s 144 should have any impact at all on those regimes.

[. . .] The Registrar's argument, if correct, would mean that for registered land no-one could be sure that the title entered on the register as a result of adverse possession was in fact a true title; someone (e.g. the former owner) might come forward at any later date and raise a case that part of the period of adverse possession was in fact affected by a violation of s 144, so that the register ought to be rectified by reason of a mistake of the Registrar in accepting the application for registration of that title. The effect of the argument would also include disruption to the operation of the defence of adverse possession to a claim for possession of land as set out in s 98 of the LRA, opening up what on the face of it is a relatively simple factual inquiry whether a requisite period of adverse possession has been established, into an investigation into the quality of the adverse possession and whether the acts included any violations of s 144. The effect of the argument would be even more disruptive in relation to title to unregistered land [. . .]

[. . .] [The Registrar's argument] would involve a capricious distinction between the rules of adverse possession affecting residential buildings and the rules affecting other forms of real property, with no good justification for such distinction. It would involve potentially wholly disproportionate and arbitrary impact for even very limited periods of breach of s 144 (perhaps lasting only a matter of days) upon periods of adverse possession lasting many years, or even decades [. . .] A person can be in possession of a property, and hence build up a period of adverse possession asserting his rights against the world, without living or intending to live in the property or even being in the property. Erection and maintenance of a fence around a property might be sufficient to constitute taking possession of it. The facts of the present case demonstrate the point: it was only because Mr Best moved into the house as his home in January 2012, at the end of a long period of adverse possession without living in the house, that he fell foul of the impact of s 144. There seems to be no justification for saying that s 144 should prevent his adverse possession from having effect under the LRA [. . .]

Sales LJ therefore concluded that Parliament, when passing s 144 of LASPOA:[131] 'is not lightly to be taken to have legislated with the intention of producing such capricious and arbitrary effects upon a carefully crafted and comprehensive statutory regime such as that contained in the LRA'. This conclusion as to parliamentary intention was shared by Arden LJ,[132] who gave a separate concurring judgment, without adopting quite the same approach, of balancing factors, as Sales LJ. Nonetheless, Sales LJ's analysis is very persuasive and provides an excellent example of the general approach, as confirmed by a majority of the Supreme Court in *Patel v Mirza*[133] (see Chapter 11, section 3.1.3), which a court should take to the question of the impact of illegality on a cause of action. Rather than taking an absolute line that prevents

---

131 [2015] EWCA Civ 17, [2016] QB 23, [80].   132 Ibid, [108].   133 [2017] AC 467.

a claimant from relying on any unlawful act as part of the basis of the claim, the courts need instead to consider a range of factors, including the policy behind the rule making the conduct unlawful, the particular conduct of the claimant, and whether denying the claim would have a disproportionate impact on the claimant.[134] The Court of Appeal's analysis recognizes, as Dixon[135] noted in relation to the decision of Ouseley J at first instance, '*the policy value in accepting some claims to title based on adverse possession; a value that is strong enough to require explicit Parliamentary authority before the delicate compromise found in the LRA 2002 can be unbalanced*'. That policy value must be balanced against the policy behind s 144 in order to understand their interaction and, as found by the Court of Appeal, to find that s 144 simply eliminates any adverse possession claim that involves any breach of s 144 would be a blunt resolution that would lead to practical absurdities.

6.3 THE OUTCOME IN THE *BEST* LITIGATION

The Court of Appeal therefore upheld Ouseley J's order to quash the decision of the Land Registrar not to proceed with Mr Best's application for registration. As a result of that earlier order, the standard procedure had been followed: in May 2014, a notice was sent to the registered proprietor, Mrs Doris Curtis. She had died in 1998 without leaving a will and her son, Mr Curtis, who was entitled to her estate, had taken no steps until 2014 to administer the estate, or become registered as proprietor in her place. However, as a result of the publicity relating to the judicial review application, Mr Curtis was now aware of Mr Best's claim, and had contacted the Land Registry. When sending out the notice to the registered proprietor in May 2014, therefore, the Registrar also informed Mr Curtis.[136] The question then was whether Mr Curtis could give a counter-notice under Sch 6, para 3(2) (see section 5.3.1), which would mean that Mr Best's application would then have to be dealt with under para 5. If Mr Curtis could give the counter-notice, Mr Best's application would fail, as none of the three conditions set out in para 5(2)–(4) (see section 5.3.2) applied on the facts. It was also argued for Mr Curtis that Mr Best's application should fail as, following the death of Mrs Curtis and the lack of administration of her estate, the land was held on trust, with no beneficiary of the trust having an interest in possession of the land, and Sch 6, para 12 stipulates that: '*A person is not to be regarded as being in adverse possession of an estate for the purposes of this Schedule at any time when the estate is subject to a trust, unless the interest of each of the beneficiaries in the estate is an interest in possession.*'

Those questions were decided by HH Judge Cooke in the Property Chamber of the First-Tier Tribunal.[137] On the trust question, it was held that, where a deceased's estate is being administered, legal title is held by personal representatives, but they are not strictly trustees, as, until administration of the estate is complete, they do not hold any specific property on trust for any specific beneficiaries.[138] Further, on the facts of the case, there

---

[134] The application of the *Patel v Mirza* approach is also consistent with the result in *Bakewell Management Ltd v Brandwood* [2004] 2 AC 519 (see Chapter 22, section 3.3.2), given the limited nature of the illegal conduct and the disproportionate impact of denying that the claimant had acquired an easement by prescription.

[135] Dixon, 'Criminal Squatting and Adverse Possession: The Best Solution?' [2014] JHL 94, 97.

[136] Rule 17 of the Land Registration Rules 2003 gives the registrar power to '*refuse to complete or proceed with an application*' until relevant '*documents, evidence or notices*' have been supplied.

[137] *Best v Curtis* [2016] EWLAndRA 0130 (11 April 2016).

[138] Ibid, [23], relying on *Commissioner of Stamp Duties (Queensland) v Livingstone* [1964] 3 AC 694 (PC).

was no personal representative at the relevant time as Mr Curtis had not taken any steps to administer the estate until late in 2014. As noted by HHJ Cooke: *'Throughout the period of adverse possession therefore the estate was vested in the Public Trustee'*[139] who by statute does not hold subject to any duties in respect of the property, and so the estate was not held 'subject to a trust' in the sense used by Sch 6, para 12. HHJ Cooke noted that this finding ensured that Sch 6, para 12 did not interfere with an important policy concern of the adverse possession regime:[140]

> [Counsel for Mr Best] points out the present situation was actually anticipated by the Law Commission and Land Registry in the consultation paper that preceded the drafting of the bill that became the 2002 Act. In *Land Registration for the Twenty-First Century – A Consultative Document*,[141] they said:
>
> > 'It sometimes happens that a registered proprietor abandons his or her land, or dies in circumstances in which no steps are taken to wind up his or her estate. A squatter then takes possession of the land. Here adverse possession fulfils a useful role ... [T]he doctrine of adverse possession does at least ensure that in such cases land remains in commerce and is not rendered sterile.'
>
> Mr Best has done a great deal of work on property that Mr Curtis abandoned for more than a quarter of a century. If property in these circumstances is protected by para 12, then no adverse possession is possible in precisely the situation where those who designed and drafted the statute thought that it should be possible.

It should be noted that this point provides further force to the policy analysis of Sales LJ in the Court of Appeal: if s 144 were to prevent a claim for adverse possession being made in relation to abandoned land, this could interfere with an important aim of the scheme under Schedule 6, as envisaged by those who designed it.

On the question of whether Mr Curtis could give a counter-notice requiring that the application proceed under para 5, the interpretation of Sch 6, para 3 was crucial: it refers to such an objection being made by *'A person given notice under para 2'*. It was held that Mr Curtis was not such a person, with HHJ Cooke stating that: *'Nowhere is there any mention in paragraph 2 of the personal representative of a deceased proprietor (let alone of anyone who might be entitled to take out letters of administration but has not yet done so, which was [Mr Curtis's situation] when notice was given under para 2 on 6 June 2014).'* Where the registered proprietor dies, there is a procedure by which *'any person who can satisfy the registrar that he has an interest in a registered estate in land [. . .] which would be prejudiced by the registration of any other person as proprietor of that estate under Schedule 6 to the Act'* can apply to be registered as a person to be notified under para 2,[142] but of course Mr Curtis had not followed that procedure. So, whilst the Registrar had informed Mr Curtis of Mr Best's application in June 2014, using its power to seek further evidence as to an application, it had not, and could not have, served notice on Mr Curtis *under para 2*, which meant that Mr Curtis could not then give a counter-notice under para 3. As a result, the Chief Land Registrar was

---

[139] By virtue of Administration of Estates Act 1925, s 9(1).

[140] [2016] EWLAndRA 0130 (11 April 2016), [28]–[29].   [141] Law Com No 254 (1998), [10.13].

[142] Land Registration Rules 2003, Rule 194.

directed by the court to give effect to Mr Best's application as if Mr Curtis's objection had not been made.

6.4 EVALUATING THE OUTCOME IN THE *BEST* LITIGATION

It has been suggested that various reforms in relation to adverse possession have been informed, at least in part, by negative media portrayals of the effects of the doctrine: certainly, some media responses to the *Best* litigation have taken a particular view of the merits of the case, emphasizing the criminality of Mr Best's conduct and the links of Mr Curtis to his former family home. As Hickey has noted,[143] the broad arguments made in such coverage contrast markedly with the careful legal reasoning seen in the decision of the Property Chamber. He gives as an example the view expressed in a *Daily Mail* article that the decision 'epitomises the old saying that law and justice are not the same', and that Mr Curtis's objection was dismissed on a 'technicality'.[144] Certainly, the operation of adverse possession can be met with some emotive responses. It is useful to keep in mind the distinction between the 'utility' and 'doctrinal' models of rationality in legal reasoning, as discussed in Chapter 1, section 5.2: the decision of the Property Chamber, and indeed that of the Court of Appeal, in the *Best* litigation, can certainly be seen as examples of 'lawyers' law', but it would be a mistake to see either as purely technical. Just as policy concerns against wrongful possession have influenced both the restrictions placed on adverse possession by the LRA 2002, and the criminalization of residential squatting under LASPOA 2012, so have the competing policy concerns, such as the desirability of giving a means for the position on the ground to be reflected in the register, and to keep land available for use and transfer, informed the detail of the scheme as set out in Sch 6.

Whilst Mr Best was, therefore, ultimately successful, the litigation is unlikely to be the final word on the interplay of adverse possession and the offence under s 144 of LASPOA, and, as noted in the following extract, there is room for further discussion, on the levels of both policy and doctrine.

Hickey, 'The *Best* Outcome: The Application of Schedule 6 and the Reinforcement of Adverse Possession Policy under the Land Registration Act 2002' [2017] Conv 53, 60

The potentially criminal nature of Mr Best's presence in residential premises has not at all affected the outcome of this case, but then the criminal provision was not in force at the beginning of this story. We do not know whether this will continue, or if in time s 144 will act as a deterrent to would be possessors. For now, it seems at least strange for law on the one hand to recognise the potential for adverse possessors to become registered proprietors and on the other to posit a criminal offence likely to catch anyone adversely possessing residential premises. Either adverse possession has productive social value or it does not. The judgment here can be taken to suggest that it does, at least insofar as it expressly confirms

---

[143] Hickey, 'The *Best* Outcome: The Application of Schedule 6 and the Reinforcement of Adverse Possession Policy under the Land Registration Act 2002' [2017] Conv 53, 58.

[144] 'How the squatter who 'stole' a pensioners' three-bedroom house with the blessing of the law cost YOU £250,000' *Daily Mail*, 22 May 2016 <http://www.dailymail.co.uk/news/article-3601741/Squatter-stole-pensioner-s-three-bedroom-house-blessing-law-cost-250-000.html)> (accessed 31 December 2017).

the policy stance adopted in LRA 2002 which recognises that in very limited circumstances the adverse possessor of a registered estate deserves to be registered as proprietor. If this view is to stand, then at some stage we will need to address again the relationship between these provisions and the criminal offence in LASPOA 2012 s 144.

Human rights challenges provide another means by which these broader policy arguments can be considered, as we will now see.

7 HUMAN RIGHTS AND ADVERSE POSSESSION

Following the decision in *Pye v Graham*, Pye commenced proceedings in the European Court of Human Rights. It argued that the loss of its land was an infringement of its right of property under Art 1 of the First Protocol to the ECHR, for which it was entitled to compensation from the government. The Human Rights Act 1998 (HRA 1998), which incorporates the ECHR into domestic law, was not applicable to *Pye v Graham*, because the cause of action arose before that Act came into force.[145] Hence a direct action in the Strasbourg Court was the only means through which the human rights argument could be raised. The financial stakes were high, with Pye assessing its loss at £10m (a sum disputed by the government). The legal stakes were higher, with the legitimacy of rules of adverse possession called into question. The case focussed on the operation of limitation periods under the LRA 1925, the scheme applied in *Pye v Graham*, although raised more generally the justification for adverse possession claims in a system of registered title.

In *Pye v UK*, the Grand Chamber of the European Court of Human Rights ultimately rejected Pye's claim by ten votes to seven.[146] This decision reversed that of the ordinary Chamber, in which Pye had succeeded by the narrowest of margins (four to three votes).[147] We have seen, in Chapter 4, the different stages of a claim under Art 1 of the First Protocol. Firstly, it must be established that the provision of the ECHR is engaged, and secondly, if it is, the possibility of justification must be considered. As we have seen in Chapter 4, the Grand Chamber agreed that Art 1 was engaged, and considered the operation of limitation rules to be concerned with the control of possessions, rather than with deprivation. The Court then turned its attention to the possibility of justification, considering, firstly, whether the limitation period serves a legitimate aim.

JA Pye (Oxford) Ltd v UK **(App No 44302/02)** [2008] 1 EHRLR 132,
Grand Chamber

At [74]

It is a characteristic of property that different countries regulate its use and transfer in a variety of ways. The relevant rules reflect social policies against the background of the local conception of the importance and role of property. Even where title to real property is registered, it must be open to the legislature to attach more weight to lengthy, unchallenged

---

[145] See Chapter 4.   [146] (App No 44302/02) [2008] 1 EHRLR 132.
[147] (App No 44302/02) (2006) 43 EHRR 3.

possession than to the formal fact of registration. The Court accepts that to extinguish title where the former owner is prevented, as a consequence of the application of the law, from recovering possession of land cannot be said to be manifestly without reasonable foundation. There existed therefore a general interest in both the limitation period itself and the extinguishment of title at the end of the period.

Applying its justification formula,[148] the Court held that the rules struck a fair balance between the general interest and the interest of the individuals. The absence of provision for compensation in domestic law was not considered significant in the context of limitation rules, while adequate procedural protection was available to Pye to enforce its rights. The Court was not swayed in its conclusions by the extent of Pye's loss and the corresponding gain enjoyed by the Grahams.

JA Pye (Oxford) Ltd v UK **(App No 44302/02)** [2008] 1 EHRLR 132, Grand Chamber

At [83]–[4]

The applicant companies contended that their loss was so great, and the windfall to the Grahams so significant, that the fair balance required by Article 1 of Protocol No. 1 was upset. The Court would first note that, in the case of *James*, the Court found that the view taken by Parliament as to the tenant's "moral entitlement" to ownership of the houses at issue fell within the State's margin of appreciation. In the present case, too, whilst it would be strained to talk of the "acquired rights" of an adverse possessor during the currency of the limitation period, it must be recalled that the registered land regime in the United Kingdom is a reflection of a long-established system in which a term of years' possession gave sufficient title to sell. Such arrangements fall within the State's margin of appreciation, unless they give rise to results which are so anomalous as to render the legislation unacceptable. The acquisition of unassailable rights by the adverse possessor must go hand in hand with a corresponding loss of property rights for the former owner. In *James and Others*, the possibility of "undeserving" tenants being able to make "windfall profits" did not affect the overall assessment of the proportionality of the legislation and any windfall for the Grahams must be regarded in the same light in the present case.

As to the loss for the applicant companies, it is not disputed that the land lost by them, especially those parts with development potential, will have been worth a substantial sum of money. However, limitation periods, if they are to fulfil their purpose (see paragraphs 67–74 above), must apply regardless of the size of the claim. The value of the land cannot therefore be of any consequence to the outcome of the present case.

It was on the issue of a fair balance that five of the seven dissenting judges disagreed with the majority.[149] In this respect, they highlighted the difference between unregistered and registered land.

[148] See Chapter 4.

[149] The other two dissenting judges considered that the application of the limitation rules in the context of registered land did not serve a legitimate function. They further considered that even if a legitimate function was served, the rules provided by the 1925 Act were disproportionate.

JA Pye (Oxford) Ltd v UK (App No 44302/02) [2008] 1 EHRLR 132,
Grand Chamber

At [10]–[11] of the first dissenting judgment

In the case of unregistered land, title was made out by establishing a number of years' possession. Title deeds served only as evidence in support of possession, and could be defeated by a person who could prove actual (adverse) possession for the requisite number of years. In such a system, the extinguishment of title at the end of the limitation period could be seen as a coherent element in the rules on acquisition of title [. . .]

In the case of registered land, however, title depends not on possession, but on registration as the proprietor. A potential purchaser of land can ascertain the owner of the land by searching the register, and there is no need for a potential vendor to establish title by proving possession. As pointed out by the Law Commission, the traditional reasons advanced to justify a law of adverse possession which resulted in the extinguishment of title on expiry of the limitation period had lost much of their cogency. This view was shared in the circumstances of the present case both by Lord Bingham and by Neuberger J., who found that the uncertainties which sometimes arose in relation to the ownership of land were very unlikely to arise in the context of a system of land ownership where the owner of the land was readily identifiable by inspecting the proprietorship register.

In the view of these dissenting judges, the absence of compensation carried a requirement of strong measures of protection for registered proprietors, which were not provided by the LRA 1925. In this respect, they contrasted the 1925 Act with the new safeguards provided by the LRA 2002 through the Sch 6 notification procedure.

Although based on the 1925 Act, it is implicit in the judgment of the Grand Chamber that the operation of adverse possession in unregistered land, and in registered land under the 2002 Act, is also human rights compliant.[150] The Grand Chamber accepted the legitimacy of limitation rules and hence the crucial issue is that of fair balance. The holder of unregistered land enjoys the same level of procedural protection as his LRA 1925 counterpart. The acceptance of the scheme under the 1925 Act necessarily means that the LRA 2002, with its additional protection for registered proprietors, would satisfy this test. This is implicit even in the joint judgment of five of the seven dissenting judges.

Jones argues further that the Grand Chamber was wrong to consider that Art 1 of the First Protocol was engaged.

Jones, 'Out with the Owners! The Eurasian Sequels to *JA Pye (Oxford) Ltd v United Kingdom*' (2008) 27 CJQ 260, 265–6

This [the conclusion that Article 1, Protocol 1 is engaged] is mistaken. The key term in Art.1 is "possessions". Article 1 is ultimately bound by its ordinary meaning, i.e. things which a person holds, according to the circumstances in which they were acquired. Thus, Art.1 merely confers a right to retain property in manner in which it has come to be held. The provision cannot be used to broaden the original scope of ownership. For this would have it

---

[150] Jones, 'Out with the Owners! The Eurasian Sequels to *JA Pye (Oxford) Ltd v United Kingdom*' (2008) 27 Civil Justice Quarterly 260.

confer a right, not to retention, but to acquisition of property, on more generous terms that did not, on the facts, emerge. As the Grand Chamber itself stated, "[i]t does not [. . .] guarantee the right to acquire property".

Paradoxically, this is precisely what the Grand Chamber's conclusion allows. As it indicated, the applicants' title to the Berkshire land was, "necessarily limited by the various rules of statute and common law applicable to real estate", including "the various rules on adverse possession". Thus, when "the applicant companies lost the beneficial ownership of [the land]", title had simply lapsed according to the terms on which it was acquired. The process was no more objectionable than the expiration of a lease by the effluxion of time. It could not attract the protection of Art.1, without suggesting that the provision guarantees the right to acquire title free from the possibility of adverse possession. As indicated, the provision does not go this far. In short, it was anything but "inescapable [. . .] that Article 1 of Protocol No 1 is applicable".

Jones' point is that once the issue goes to the matter of a fair balance, the division of opinion in the Grand Chamber (and, previously, in the ordinary Chamber judgment) shows that there is an element of subjectivity.

His argument has resonance with the approach of the House of Lords in a different context in *Aston Cantlow Parochial Church Council v Wallbank*.[151] In that case, as we have seen in Chapter 4, it was held that liability for chancel repairs did not engage Art 1, because it was an encumbrance that defined the nature of the possession. There is, however, an analytical difference between an encumbrance, as a right held by a third party affecting ownership, and the possibility of losing ownership through limitation of actions.

The Grand Chamber decision in *Pye v UK* is not technically binding on English courts, but it has since been followed by the Court of Appeal in the following case.[152] The Court rejected an argument that the justification for the operation of adverse possession is a matter that arises for reconsideration where a claim is distinguishable on the facts from *Pye v Graham*.

Ofulue v Bossert
[2008] EWCA Civ 7, CA

Facts: The facts of the case are outlined above in part 4.3.2 where the House of Lords decision is discussed. In the Court of Appeal, the Ofulues argued that the loss of their title through adverse possession was a violation of Art 1 Protocol 1. This issue was not raised again in the House of Lords.

Arden LJ

At [52]–[3]

The written submissions of the Ofulues proceed on the basis that it is open to this court to distinguish the decision in *Pye* on its facts or by reference to the applicability of the policy reasons for adverse possession identified by the Law Commission. In my judgment, this approach fundamentally misunderstands the purpose of the doctrine of the margin of

---

151 [2003] UKHL 37, [2004] 1 AC 546.
152 See also Dixon, 'Human Rights and Adverse Possession: The Final Nail' [2008] Conv 160.

appreciation. The Strasbourg Court accepted that the national authorities could in general determine the rules for the extinction of title as a result of the occupation of the land by a person who was not the true owner. That determination applies to all decisions on adverse possession and it is not open to this court not to follow that determination because the case is distinguishable on its facts. For the doctrine of the margin of appreciation to be inapplicable, the results would have to be so anomalous as to render the legislation unacceptable (see [83] of the judgment of the Strasbourg Court), and in my judgment that has not been demonstrated in this case.

The Ofulues' submissions additionally proceed on the basis that this court must apply the test of legitimate aim and proportionality to each different case of adverse possession which arises. Again, in my judgment this fundamentally misunderstands the function of this court. The Strasbourg Court considered the compatibility with the Convention of the limitation period in the case of adverse possession with Art.1 of Protocol No.1 and assessed its legitimate aim and proportionality as a general rule and not simply in the context of the specific facts of the *Pye* case. It would not therefore be appropriate for this court to proceed to examine the questions of legitimate aim and proportionality simply from the perspective of the facts of this case and the relationship between them and the policy considerations in the Law Commission's Consultation Paper.

8 CONCLUSION

The LRA 2002 brings the modern law of adverse possession in line with principles of registration of title. In so doing, its practical impact is to reduce the role of adverse possession and reduce the significance of concepts that have long underlined English land law: title by possession and relativity of title.

At the outset of our discussion of possession, we noted Green's suggestion that, in defining this concept, the case law is influenced by, and constructs, the concept of an ideal landowner. Green identifies the characteristics of that individual.

Green, 'Citizens and Squatters' in *Land Law: Themes and Perspectives* (eds Bright and Dewar, 1998, p 241)

The ideal landowner constructed by the laws of adverse possession is clearly no threat to civilised society. On the contrary, he is settled and stable, and honours both man-made and natural laws. His cultivation involves hard work. The sturdy figure of the ideal English landowner as reflected and maintained in adverse possession law invests his physical, intellectual, and emotional energies in the ground: he has entirely committed himself, through his engagement with the earth, to his plot of land. He wants to be a fixture in the landscape. He fences his land and locks his gates in order to exclude those who might detract from his hard labour—addressing the world outside as well as the land within his boundaries.

Green draws comparisons between the ideal landowner and the ideal citizen. She notes that, by drawing an ideal, the law also has an exclusionary effect. Green highlights that the most successful adverse possessors are those who already own land (and, therefore, are already included) and are trying to extend their boundaries. The successful claimants in the leading cases of *Pye v Graham* and *Moran* clearly fit within this category. The least successful (on Green's analysis) are the 'have nots' who want to join the 'haves'. The unsuccessful claimant in *Powell* may be so described: he is presented in the court's judgment as a strong-willed rebellious teenager, acting despite (rather than in pursuance of) the wishes of his elderly, landowning grandparents.

Cobb and Fox further highlight the exclusionary effect of adverse possession.[153] They argue that, by setting the odds against claims, the LRA 2002 encourages urban squatters to lie low and not draw attention to their actions by applying for registration—that is, in this way, to live 'outside the system'.

While the practical role of adverse possession may therefore have been reduced and re-formed by the 2002 Act, this is an area of law that continues to have resonance with important issues for land law and law in general: issues of ownership and use of land, and of inclusion and exclusion.

Where an adverse possessor moves into possession of land which is subject to a lease, additional questions arise as regards the relationship between the adverse possessor, the leaseholder, and the freeholder. We explore these issues in the online resources.

QUESTIONS

1. What do you understand by the concepts of 'title by possession', 'relativity of title', and the 'extinguishment' of a title by limitations?

2. To what extent are the concepts in the above question compatible with registration of title? Consider how any differences that you identify are reflected in the operation of adverse possession in registered land.

3. How is adverse possession established? To what extent is this dependent on the intention of the adverse possessor and the paper owner/registered proprietor?

4. Should it be possible to obtain a legal title to land when the occupation of the land is a criminal offence?

For guidance on how to answer these questions visit the online resources at www.oup.com/uk/mcfarlane4e/.

FURTHER READING

Cobb and Fox, 'Living Outside the System? The (Im)morality of Urban Squatting after the Land Registration Act 2002' (2007) 27 LS 236

Conway and Stannard, 'The Emotional Paradoxes of Adverse Possession' (2013) 64 NILQ 75

Cooke, *The New Law of Land Registration* (Oxford: Hart Publishing, 2003) ch 7

Cowan, Fox O'Mahony, and Cobb, *Great Debates: Property Law* (Basingstoke: Palgrave Macmillan, 2012) ch 6

---

[153] Cobb and Fox, 'Living Outside the System? The (Im)morality of Urban Squatting after the Land Registration Act 2002' (2007) 27 LS 236.

Dockray, 'Why do we Need Adverse Possession?' [1985] Conv 272

Fox O'Mahony and Cobb, 'Taxonomies of Squatting: Unlawful Occupation in a New Legal Order' (2008) 71 MLR 878

Green, 'Citizens and Squatters' in *Land Law: Themes and Perspectives* (eds Bright and Dewar, Oxford: OUP, 1998)

Hickey, 'The *Best* Outcome: The Application of Schedule 6 and the Reinforcement of Adverse Possession Policy under the Land Registration Act 2002' [2017] Conv 53

Hickey, 'The Effect of Supervening Permission on Adverse Possession' [2017] Conv 223

Jones, 'Out with the Owners! The Eurasian Sequels to *JA Pye (Oxford) Ltd v United Kingdom*' (2008) 27 CJQ 260

Jourdan and Radley-Gardner, *Adverse Possession* (2nd edn, Haywards Heath: Bloomsbury Professional, 2011)

Radley-Gardner, 'Civilized Squatting' (2005) 25 OJLS 727

10

PROPRIETARY ESTOPPEL

CENTRAL ISSUES

1. Proprietary estoppel is a means, originally developed by courts of equity, by which a party (B) can gain some protection against an owner of land (A), even if he or she has no contract with A and even if A has not formally given B a property right in relation to A's land. That protection consists of A coming under a duty to B. This means that, in some cases at least, proprietary estoppel is a means by which B can acquire a property right in land.

2. It is important to distinguish proprietary estoppel from other forms of estoppel. As we will see in the first section of this chapter, proprietary estoppel is not merely a means by which B can prevent A from asserting a right against B, or by which B can prevent A from denying that B already has a right. Rather, proprietary estoppel is an independent means by which B can acquire a right against A: it can be used not only as a 'shield' to defend B from A, but also as a 'sword' to impose a duty on A to B.

3. It is often said that there are three key requirements for a successful proprietary estoppel claim. First, A assured B that B already has a right in relation to A's land, or that B will get such a right in the future. Second, B reasonably relied on A's assurance. Third, B would now suffer a detriment if A were not under a duty to B. We will examine each of these requirements in the second section, having noted though that there are three distinct strands to proprietary estoppel, each with differing requirements. We will also consider the suggestion that there is a further, fourth requirement: that A must be shown to have acted unconscionably.

4. If B makes a successful proprietary estoppel claim, a question then arises as to the *extent of the right* acquired by B. In other words, what is the content of A's duty to B? For example, will A necessarily be under a duty to honour the assurance made to B? We will examine this question below, in section 3.

5. Having established the content of A's duty to B, we then need to work out the *effect of B's right on third parties*. For example, if B successfully claims a proprietary estoppel against A, will it ever be possible for B to rely on that same claim against C, a party who later acquires A's land? And, to answer that question, do we simply apply the content question, as outlined in Chapter 6, and ask if the content of A's duty to B is such that B has a recognized equitable interest in A's land? Or are there special rules that apply only to cases of proprietary estoppel? We will examine these questions in section 4 of this chapter.

1 INTRODUCTION: THE NATURE OF PROPRIETARY ESTOPPEL

1.1 PROPRIETARY ESTOPPEL IN PRACTICE

The term 'estoppel' can be confusing. In law, there are many different forms of estoppel but, in general, the term is used to refer to situations in which a party is *prevented*—that is, stopped or, in old French, *estopped*—from denying the truth of a particular matter of fact or law. In general, then, we would not expect an estoppel, by itself, to give B a right against A; at most, it could assist B in acquiring a right, by preventing A from denying one of the matters of fact or law that B may have to establish to acquire a right. This is certainly true of two important forms of estoppel: estoppel by representation (which prevents A, sometimes only temporarily, from denying the truth of a representation of existing fact or law made to B, where B has relied on that representation);[1] and promissory estoppel (which prevents A from enforcing an existing right against B, where A has promised not to do so and where B would suffer a detriment if A were allowed to enforce his right).[2]

There is, however, a fundamental difference between proprietary estoppel and each of estoppel by representation and promissory estoppel. The difference is that, unlike the other two forms of estoppel, proprietary estoppel *can*, by itself, give B a right against A. As Lord Denning MR once put it: '*there are estoppels and estoppels. Some do give rise to a cause of action. Some do not. In the species of estoppel called proprietary estoppel, it does give rise to a cause of action … The new rights and interests, so created by estoppel, in or over land, will be protected by the courts and in this way give rise to a cause of action.*'[3] In other words, proprietary estoppel, unlike the other two forms of estoppel, is relevant to the acquisition question.

This special feature of proprietary estoppel was recently confirmed by the House of Lords, as can be seen in the following extract.

Thorner v Major
[2009] UKHL 18, [2009] 1 WLR 776

Facts: Peter Thorner owned Steart Farm, by the village of Cheddar in Somerset. David Thorner, whose father was a cousin of Peter, worked on that farm, for Peter, for 30 years. David was not paid for that work. He also worked on his parents' farm, and his parents gave him accommodation and pocket money. As a result of working for both his parents and Peter, David worked very long hours. David believed that, on Peter's death, he would inherit Steart Farm. There was no explicit promise or assurance by Peter to David, but David's belief developed over a period of 15 years and was encouraged by Peter's conduct. For example, in 1990, Peter gave David a bonus notice relating to two assurance policies on Peter's life, saying 'That's for my death duties'. As a result of his belief that he would inherit the farm, David continued to work for Peter and did

---

[1] See *Pickard v Sears* (1837) 6 Ad & El 469.
[2] See *Central London Property Trust Ltd v High Trees House* [1947] KB 130.
[3] *Crabb v Arun DC* [1976] Ch 179, [187].

not pursue other opportunities. Peter did in fact make a will leaving the farm to David. However, that will also gave specific sums of money to other individuals; when Peter later fell out with some of those individuals, he destroyed his will. Unfortunately, Peter died without making a new will and so his property, including the farm, passed not to David but to the closer relatives of Peter who, by statute, received his estate on the event of his intestacy.

David made a claim against Peter's estate, claiming that, when Peter died, he was under a duty, arising as a result of proprietary estoppel, to leave the farm to David. The first instance judge found in favour of David and ordered that Peter (and so now Peter's estate) was under a duty to transfer Steart Farm to David. For these purposes the farm included the land and buildings, worth around £2.4 million, as well as other farm assets (e.g. machinery and live stock), worth an additional £650,000 or so, plus whatever limited amount of working capital was credited to the farm's trading accounts at the time of Peter's death.

The Court of Appeal, however, held that David had no proprietary estoppel claim. Before the House of Lords, the argument centred on two issues. First, had Peter made an assurance that was capable of giving rise to a proprietary estoppel? Second, if such an assurance was made, was the land to which it related adequately identified? Each of these issues was decided in David's favour, and the House of Lords thus restored the order of the first instance judge that Peter's estate was under a duty to transfer Steart Farm to David.

Lord Walker

At [29]–[30]

This appeal is concerned with proprietary estoppel [. . .] most scholars agree that the doctrine is based on three main elements, although they express them in slightly different terms: a representation or assurance made to the claimant; reliance on it by the claimant; and detriment to the claimant in consequence of his (reasonable) reliance.[4]

This appeal raises two issues. The first and main issue concerns the character or quality of the representation or assurance made to the claimant. The other (which could be regarded as a subsidiary part of the main issue, but was argued before your Lordships as a separate point) is whether, if the other elements for proprietary estoppel are established, the claimant must fail if the land to which the assurance relates has been inadequately identified, or has undergone a change (in its situation or extent) during the period between the giving of the assurance and its eventual repudiation.

At [55]–[57]

I would prefer to say (while conscious that it is a thoroughly question-begging formulation) that to establish a proprietary estoppel the relevant assurance must be clear enough. What amounts to sufficient clarity, in a case of this sort, is hugely dependent on context. I respectfully concur in the way Hoffmann LJ put it in *Walton v Walton* (in which the

---

[4] [The books quoted by Lord Walker were Harpum et al (eds) *Megarry & Wade's Law of Real Property* (London: Sweet & Maxwell, 7th edn, 2008) para 16–001; Gray and Gray, *Elements of Land Law* (5th edn, Oxford: OUP, 2009) para 9.2.8; McGhee et al (eds), *Snell's Equity* (31st edn, 2005) paras 10–16 and 10–19; and Gardner, *An Introduction to Land Law* (Oxford: Hart Publishing, 2007) para 7.1.1.]

mother's 'stock phrase' to her son, who had worked for low wages on her farm since he left school at fifteen, was 'You can't have more money and a farm one day'). Hoffmann LJ stated:[5]

> 'The promise must be unambiguous and must appear to have been intended to be taken seriously. Taken in its context, it must have been a promise which one might reasonably expect to be relied upon by the person to whom it was made.'[6]

At [60]–[66]

I respectfully consider that the Court of Appeal did not give sufficient weight to the advantage that the trial judge had in seeing and hearing the witnesses. They concentrated too much, I think, on the 1990 incident of the bonus notice. That was certainly an important part of the narrative. For David it marked the transition from hope to expectation. But it did not stand alone. The evidence showed a continuing pattern of conduct by Peter for the remaining 15 years of his life and it would not be helpful to try to break down that pattern into discrete elements (and then treat each as being, on its own, insignificant). To my mind the deputy judge did find that Peter's assurances, objectively assessed, were intended to be taken seriously and to be relied on.[7] In the end it is a short point; I do not think that there was sufficient reason for the Court of Appeal to reverse the trial judge's careful findings and conclusion. I do not share the Court of Appeal's apparent apprehension that floodgates might be opened, because cases like this are fairly rare, and trial judges realise the need to subject the evidence (whether as to assurances, as to reliance or as to detriment) to careful, and sometimes sceptical, scrutiny [. . .]

The identity of the farm

In my opinion it is a necessary element of proprietary estoppel that the assurances given to the claimant (expressly or impliedly, or, in standing-by cases, tacitly) should relate to identified property owned (or, perhaps, about to be owned) by the defendant. That is one of the main distinguishing features between the two varieties of equitable estoppel, that is promissory estoppel and proprietary estoppel. The former must be based on an existing legal *relationship* (usually a contract, but not necessarily a contract relating to land). The latter need not be based on an existing legal relationship, but it must relate to *identified property* (usually land) owned (or, perhaps, about to be owned) by the defendant. It is the relation to identified land of the defendant that has enabled proprietary estoppel to develop as a sword, and not merely a shield: see Lord Denning MR in *Crabb v Arun DC*.

In this case the deputy judge made a clear finding of an assurance by Peter that David would become entitled to Steart Farm ... There is no reason to doubt that their common understanding was that Peter's assurance related to whatever the farm consisted of at Peter's death (as it would have done, barring any restrictive language, under s 24 of the Wills Act 1837, had Peter made a specific devise of Steart Farm). This fits in with the retrospective aspect of proprietary estoppel noted in *Walton v Walton*.[8]

---

[5] 14 April 1994 (unreported), [16].

[6] At [57], Lord Walker approved of a further quotation from Hoffmann LJ's judgment in *Walton v Walton*: this paragraph is set out in section 2.1.3 below.

[7] [2007] EWHC 2422 (Ch) at [94], [98].   [8] 14 April 1994, unreported.

Lord Neuberger

At [77]–[78]

In my judgment, those findings clearly indicate that the deputy judge was of the opinion, contrary to the view expressed by the Court of Appeal, that the statements he found to have been made by Peter were reasonably understood by David to indicate that Peter was committing himself to leaving the farm to David, and were reasonably relied on by David as having that effect. Such a reading is strongly supported by the deputy judge's observations that, if it was necessary to make such a finding, he would have regarded Peter's statement in 1990 as 'tantamount to an assurance to David', and that he did 'not accept' that it was 'ambiguous'.[9]

[. . .] It may be that there could be exceptional cases where, even though a person reasonably relied on a statement, it might be wrong to conclude that the statement-maker was estopped, because he could not reasonably have expected the person so to rely. However, such cases would be rare, and, in the light of the facts found by the deputy judge, it has not been, and could not be, suggested that this was such a case.

At [95]

In this case, the extent of the farm might change, but, on the deputy judge's analysis, there is, as I see it, no doubt as to what was the subject of the assurance, namely the farm as it existed from time to time. Accordingly, the nature of the interest to be received by David was clear: it was the farm as it existed on Peter's death. As in the case of a very different equitable concept, namely a floating charge, the property the subject of the equity could be conceptually identified from the moment the equity came into existence, but its precise extent fell to be determined when the equity crystallised, namely on Peter's death.

Lord Hoffmann

At [1]–[9]

My Lords, the appellant David Thorner is a Somerset farmer who, for nearly 30 years, did substantial work without pay on the farm of his father's cousin Peter Thorner. The judge found that from 1990 until his death in 2005 Peter encouraged David to believe that he would inherit the farm and that David acted in reliance upon this assurance. In the event, however, Peter left no will. In these proceedings, David claims that by reason of the assurance and reliance, Peter's estate is estopped from denying that he has acquired the beneficial interest in the farm [. . .]

Such a claim, under the principle known as proprietary estoppel, requires the claimant to prove a promise or assurance that he will acquire a proprietary interest in specified property. A distinctive feature of this case, as Lloyd LJ remarked in the Court of Appeal, was that the representation was never made expressly but was 'a matter of implication and inference from indirect statements and conduct'.[10] It consisted of such matters as handing over to David in 1990 an insurance policy bonus notice with the words 'that's for my death duties' and other oblique remarks on subsequent occasions which indicated that Peter intended David to inherit the farm. As Lloyd LJ observed such conduct and language might have been consistent with a current intention rather than a definite assurance.[11] But the judge found as

---

[9] [2007] EWHC 2422 (Ch), [125].   [10] [2008] EWCA Civ 732, [65].   [11] Ibid, [67].

a fact that these words and acts were reasonably understood by David as an assurance that he would inherit the farm and that Peter intended them to be so understood.

The Court of Appeal said, correctly, that the fact that Peter had actually intended David to inherit the farm was irrelevant. The question was whether his words and acts would reasonably have conveyed to David an assurance that he would do so. But Lloyd LJ accepted that the finding as to what Peter would reasonably have been understood to mean by his words and acts was a finding of fact which was not open to challenge.[12] That must be right. The fact that he spoke in oblique and allusive terms does not matter if it was reasonable for David, given his knowledge of Peter and the background circumstances, to have understood him to mean not merely that his present intention was to leave David the farm but that he definitely would do so.

However, the Court of Appeal allowed the appeal on the ground that the judge had not found that the assurance was intended to be relied upon and that there was no material upon which he could have made such a finding. The judge had found that David had relied upon the assurance by not pursuing other opportunities but not, said Lloyd LJ, that Peter had known about these opportunities or intended to discourage David from pursuing them.

At that point, it seems to me, the Court of Appeal departed from their previously objective examination of the meaning which Peter's words and acts would reasonably have conveyed and required proof of his subjective understanding of the effect which those words would have upon David. In my opinion it did not matter whether Peter knew of any specific alternatives which David might be contemplating. It was enough that the meaning he conveyed would reasonably have been understood as intended to be taken seriously as an assurance which could be relied upon. If David did then rely upon it to his detriment, the necessary element of the estoppel is in my opinion established. It is not necessary that Peter should have known or foreseen the particular act of reliance.

The judge found not only that it was reasonable for David to have understood Peter's words and acts to mean that 'he would be Peter's successor to [the farm]' but that it was reasonable for him to rely upon them.[13] These findings of fact were in my opinion sufficient to support the judge's decision [. . .]

I do not think that the judge was trying to pinpoint the date at which the assurance became unequivocal and I think it would be unrealistic in a case like this to try to do so. There was a close and ongoing daily relationship between the parties. Past events provide context and background for the interpretation of subsequent events and subsequent events throw retrospective light upon the meaning of past events. The owl of Minerva spreads its wings only with the falling of the dusk.[14] The finding was that David reasonably relied upon the assurance from 1990, even if it required later events to confirm that it was reasonable for him to have done so.

The second ground of objection is that the farm when Peter died in 2005 was not the same as it was in 1990. In between, he had sold some land and bought other land. I agree with my noble and learned friends Lord Walker of Gestingthorpe and Lord Neuberger of Abbotsbury that changes in the character or extent of the property in question are relevant to the relief which equity will provide but do not exclude such a remedy when there is still an identifiable

---

[12] Ibid, [66].   [13] [2007] EWHC 2422 (Ch), [98].

[14] [This aphorism was coined by Hegel, writing in 1820, at the end of the Preface to his *Philosophy of Right* (see Knox (trs) *Hegel's Philosophy of Right*, 1967). Minerva was the Roman goddess of, amongst other things, wisdom. The idea behind the aphorism is that, in some contexts at least, the truth is known only after the event. Hegel used it to make the point that philosophy should not be expected to lay down how one ought to behave in the future. As we will see in section 2.1.3 of this chapter, Lord Hoffmann uses the aphorism to capture an important difference between proprietary estoppel and contractual claims.]

property. In the present case, I see no reason to question the judge's decision that David was entitled to the beneficial interest in the farm and the farming business as they were at Peter's death.

The decision of the House of Lords in *Thorner v Major* provides a graphic demonstration of the power of proprietary estoppel. Peter did not make a testamentary gift to David, as he died without a valid will. Nor could David show that Peter was under any contractual duty to give him the farm: certainly, as we saw in Chapter 8, section 3, the Law of Property (Miscellaneous Provisions) Act 1989 ensures that any such contract would have required a formal, written agreement. Nonetheless, thanks to proprietary estoppel, Peter was, at the time of his death, under a duty to transfer the farm land and business assets, worth over £3 million, to David. As Lord Hoffmann put it, David was '*entitled to the beneficial interest in the farm and farming business as they were at Peter's death*'. This beneficial interest can be seen to arise as a result of the doctrine of anticipation, discussed in Chapter 8, section 4.1: as Peter was under a duty to transfer the farm land to David, David acquired an immediate equitable interest in that land.

1.2 FORMS OF PROPRIETARY ESTOPPEL

One of the very few House of Lords' decisions considering what would now be called proprietary estoppel is *Ramsden v Dyson*. In that case, as shown in the following extract, each of Lord Cranworth and Lord Wensleydale identified an equitable principle which could operate so as to allow B to bring a claim against A.

Ramsden v Dyson
(1866) LR 1 HL 129

Lord Cranworth

At 140–1

If a stranger begins to build on my land supposing it to be his own, and I, perceiving his mistake, abstain from setting him right, and leave him to persevere in his error, a Court of equity will not allow me afterwards to assert my title to the land on which he had expended money on the supposition that the land was his own. It considers that, when I saw the mistake into which he had fallen, it was my duty to be active and to state my adverse title; and that it would be dishonest in me to remain wilfully passive on such an occasion, in order afterwards to profit by the mistake which I might have prevented.

But it will be observed that to raise such an equity two things are required, first, that the person expending the money supposes himself to be building on his own land; and, secondly, that the real owner at the time of the expenditure knows that the land belongs to him and not to the person expending the money in the belief that he is the owner. For if a stranger builds on my land knowing it to be mine, there is no principle of equity which would prevent my claiming the land with the benefit of all the expenditure made on it. There would be nothing in my conduct, active or passive, making it inequitable in me to assert my legal rights.

Lord Wensleydale

At 168

If a stranger build on my land, supposing it to be his own, and I, knowing it to be mine, do not interfere, but leave him to go on, equity considers it to be dishonest in me to remain passive and afterwards to interfere and take the profit. But if a stranger build knowingly upon my land, there is no principle of equity which prevents me from insisting on having back my land, with all the additional value which the occupier has imprudently added to it.

The principle identified by Lord Cranworth and Lord Wensleydale can be seen as based on A's 'acquiescence' in B's mistaken belief that B currently has a particular right in land. It is now seen as an example of proprietary estoppel. As Lord Neuberger has put it: '*The classic example of proprietary estoppel, standing by whilst one's neighbour builds on one's land believing it be his property, can be characterised as acquiescence*.'[15]

The acquiescence principle seems to have quite specific requirements. For example, each of Lord Cranworth and Lord Wensleydale emphasized that A must know of B's mistake. Further, on the facts of *Ramsden* itself, each of those judges regarded the principle as inapplicable as B did not rely on a mistaken belief that B *currently* had a right in relation to A's land, but instead relied only on the expectation that A would grant B such a right in the future. These and other requirements of the acquiescence principle were set out by Fry J in *Willmott v Barber*[16] and one commentator has summarized them as follows: '*[the principle] applies where B adopts a particular course of conduct in reliance on a mistaken belief as to B's current rights and A, knowing both of B's belief and of the existence of A's own, inconsistent right, fails to assert that right against B*.'[17]

It is important to note that the requirements of the acquiescence principle were not met in *Thorner v Major*. David did not act in reliance on the belief that he already had a right in Peter's land; rather, he relied on Peter's promise that he would, in the future, give David a right in that land. Nonetheless, as we have seen, David's proprietary estoppel claim was successful. The best way to explain this, it has been suggested,[18] is to regard the overall doctrine of proprietary estoppel as comprised of more than one distinct strand, each of which may have differing requirements. For example, if we were instead to try to come up with a unified test for all forms of proprietary estoppel, we might have to say that, in the case where A stands by and acquiesces in B's mistaken belief, A's silence is just a different means of A making a promise or assurance to B. That analysis, however, seems artificial, particularly in a case where B may be entirely unaware of A, and so is not responding to any conduct of A. As noted in the following extract, the acquiescence principle as recognized in *Ramsden v Dyson* seems to be playing a different role to the promise-based principle as applied in *Thorner v Major*.[19]

[15] *Fisher v Brooker* [2009] 1 WLR 1764 at [62].

[16] (1880) 15 Ch D 96 at 105. The test applied to the acquiescence principle in *Willmott* was approved by Lord Diplock in *Kammins Ballrooms Co Ltd v Zenith Investments (Torquay) Ltd* [1971] AC 850 at [884].

[17] McFarlane, *The Law of Proprietary Estoppel* (Oxford: OUP, 2014) para 1.06.

[18] See, for example, Low, 'Nonfeasance in Equity' (2012) 128 LQR 63; Mee 'Proprietary Estoppel, Promises and Mistaken Belief' in *Modern Studies in Property Law Vol 6* (Oxford: Hart Publishing, 2011); McFarlane, *The Law of Proprietary Estoppel* (Oxford: OUP, 2014) ch 1.

[19] For consideration of possible justifications for the acquiescence principle, see Low, 'Nonfeasance in Equity' (2012) 128 LQR 63 and Samet, 'Proprietary Estoppel and Responsibility for Omissions' (2015) 78 MLR 85.

Mee, 'Proprietary Estoppel, Promises and Mistaken Belief' in *Modern Studies in Property Law Vol 6* (ed Bright, 2011, p 182)

The acquiescence scenario is clearly covered by the fundamental statements of principle by the majority in *Ramsden v Dyson*.[20] This category, which the older cases also refer to in terms of 'lying by', has also been recognised in cases arising outside the context of disputes over land.[21] In the view of the current author, the tendency to treat [A]'s failure to speak as a representation by silence due to the fact that he was under a duty to speak [. . .] serves only to confuse the matter. In principle, nothing which can be construed as a representation needs to be communicated from [A] to [B], so that the principle can apply in a case where [B] was unaware that [A] was observing events and [B] could not, therefore, have read anything into [A's] failure to intervene. The reason for equitable intervention is not the fact that [A] has led [B] to act to his detriment by means of a representation or promise but rather that [A] has failed to act when he was aware that [B] was acting to [B's] detriment on the basis of a mistake concerning [B's] rights (although the precise scope of the principle is in need of further analysis).

Mee's suggestion of identifying different strands has been applied in a recent analysis of proprietary estoppel, which, as shown by the following extract, organizes the doctrine into three strands.

McFarlane, *The Law of Proprietary Estoppel* (2014) 1.03–1.05

In setting out the law of proprietary estoppel, one of the principal aims of this book is to provide a more precise account of the principle applied in *Thorner v Major*. In order to do so, it is necessary to identify, and distinguish between, three distinct stands of proprietary estoppel, each of which has different requirements. The first of these is based on A's acquiescence in B's mistaken belief as to B's current rights; the second on a representation of an existing state of affairs made by A to B; the third, applied in *Thorner*, is based on A's promise to B.

At an abstract level, it can be said that the three distinct strands have a common aim: each operates to ensure that A does not act in such a way as to leave B to suffer a detriment as a result of B's reasonable reliance on A. It is therefore possible to provide a general formulation of the modern law of proprietary estoppel that is broad enough to encompass all three strands of the doctrine. In *Thorner*, for example, Lord Walker noted the scholarly consensus that proprietary estoppel: 'is based on three main elements ... a representation or assurance made to the claimant; reliance on it by the claimant; and detriment to the claimant in consequence of his (reasonable) reliance.'

This general formulation, however, cannot be, nor was intended to serve as, a test that can be applied to determine the practical operation of proprietary estoppel to a particular set of facts. The main point made in this book is that the specific principles established in

---

[20] [These statements of Lord Cranworth and Lord Wensleydale are set out in the extract above. Lord Cranworth noted ((1866) LR 1 HL 129, 162) that Lord Brougham, who was present at the hearing but unable to attend the House of Lords when the speeches were delivered, concurred with Lord Cranworth. Lord Kingsdown dissented.]

[21] See *Proctor v Bennis* (1887) 36 Ch D 740 (CA), 759–61 (Cotton LJ); 761–2 (Bowen LJ); 765–66 (Fry LJ).

the cases can be understood only if the three separate, irreducibly dissimilar, strands of the doctrine are carefully distinguished. In particular, principles developed in relation to each of the longer-established acquiescence and representation-based strands may well be ill-suited to the more recently developed, but more practically important, promise-based strand applied in cases such as *Thorner v Major*.

There is, however, a tension between a desire to organize proprietary estoppel into distinct strands and a reluctance, often displayed by judges, to limit the flexibility of the doctrine. In *Hoyl Group Ltd v Cromer Town Council*,[22] for example, Floyd LJ stated that: 'A proprietary estoppel does not have to fit neatly into the pure acquiescence-based pigeon hole or the assurance one.' In the *Hoyl Group* case itself, the point may simply have been that, on the facts of that case, it was possible to say that A *both* made an implied assurance to B, and also failed to prevent B from acting under a mistaken belief as to B's rights in A's land. However, Floyd LJ also referred to earlier authorities which emphasized the utility of proprietary estoppel as a means to respond to unconscionable conduct,[23] and so the comment also shows a more general reluctance to pin down the requirements of the doctrine. The difficulty with such a stance is that the discretion it gives to the courts necessarily causes uncertainty, particularly for third parties who, as we will see in section 4 below, may be bound by a right arising as a result of B's proprietary estoppel claim against A.

In any case, the key development in proprietary estoppel, occurring over the last fifty years or so, is the emergence of claims, such as that in *Thorner v Major*, based on A's assurance not as to B's current rights, but rather as to rights that B will acquire in the future in A's land. Those are the claims we will focus on in this Chapter, and will refer to as promise-based claims. Crucially, unlike either the acquiescence or representation-based strands,[24] a promise-based claim can assist B where B relies on a belief that A will give B a right in the future.[25] It is worth noting that this form of proprietary estoppel operates quite differently from a standard estoppel by representation: it is not simply an evidential doctrine that prevents A from denying a particular matter of fact, or of B's current rights. As a result, the term 'estoppel', when applied to a principle such as that operating in *Thorner v Major*, has the potential to mislead,[26] and it would be dangerous to attach much significance to the name of the doctrine when attempting to understand its nature and operation.

---

[22] [2015] EWCA Civ 782, [72].

[23] See e.g. *Taylors Fashions Ltd v Liverpool Victoria Trustees Co Ltd* [1982] QB 133, 151–2 (see too section 2.4 below).

[24] For an example of the representation-based strand see the analysis of Lord Evershed MR in *Hopgood v Brown* [1955] 1 WLR 213, esp at [223] where claims based on a representation by A as to B's rights are distinguished from those based solely on A's acquiescence: the test set out in *Willmott v Barber* was said to be 'addressed to and limited to cases where the party is alleged to be estopped by acquiescence, and it is not intended to be a comprehensive formulation of the necessary requisites of any case of estoppel by representation.'

[25] It has been recognized that a representation-based doctrine can apply only where A makes a statement as to a matter of existing fact, or of current rights: see, for example, *Jorden v Money* (1854) 5 HL Cas 185.

[26] See, for example, McFarlane, 'Understanding Equitable Estoppel: From Metaphors to Better Laws' (2013) 66 CLP 267 and 271–7.

2 THE REQUIREMENTS OF PROPRIETARY ESTOPPEL

In section 1, we considered the nature of proprietary estoppel and saw that it can be used, in some cases at least, as a means by which B can acquire an equitable interest in A's land. We also saw that, in *Thorner v Major*, Lord Walker noted that there are generally said to be three elements of the doctrine.[27] Writing extra-judicially, Lord Neuberger has also summarized proprietary estoppel as consisting of three requirements.

Lord Neuberger, 'The Stuffing of Minerva's Owl? Taxonomy and Taxidermy in Equity' [2009] CLJ 537

At 538

In very summary terms, the ingredients of proprietary estoppel are the following:

1. a statement or action (which can include silence or inaction) by the defendant, who ought to appreciate the claimant will rely on it;

2. an act by the claimant in the reasonable belief that he has or will get an interest in land, induced by that statement or action;

3. consequent detriment to the claimant if the defendant is entitled to resile from his statement or action.

We will now examine each of those three elements, basing our terminology on that used by Lord Walker in *Thorner v Major*. We will focus on the operation of the promise-based strand of proprietary estoppel, but will need to bear in mind the point made in section 1.2 that the acquiescence and representation-based strands may have different requirements. It is also important to keep in mind the point made in the following extract.

Gillett v Holt
[2000] EWCA Civ 66, [2001] Ch 210, CA

Walker LJ

At 225

[A]lthough the judgment is, for convenience, divided into several sections with headings which give a rough indication of the subject matter, it is important to note at the outset that the doctrine of proprietary estoppel cannot be treated as subdivided into three or four watertight compartments. Both sides are agreed on that, and in the course of the oral argument in this court it repeatedly became apparent that the quality of the relevant assurances may influence the issue of reliance, that reliance and detriment are often intertwined [. . .] Moreover the fundamental principle that equity is concerned to prevent unconscionable conduct permeates all the elements of the doctrine. In the end the court must look at the matter in the round.

---

[27] [2009] 1 WLR 776, [29] (set out in the extract in section 1.1 above).

This passage also raises the question of what role the concept of unconscionability plays in proprietary estoppel: we will examine that issue in section 2.4 below, after looking at each of the three elements of assurance, reliance, and detriment.

2.1 AN ASSURANCE BY A

2.1.1 The content of A's assurance

A's assurance must be that B already has, or will receive in the future, a right that relates to A's land.[28] In other common law jurisdictions, including those in the United States[29] and in Australia,[30] B's reliance on A's assurance is capable of giving B a right against A even if A's assurance does not relate to land. In England, however, this does not seem to be the case: proprietary estoppel has developed specifically to deal with situations in which B has relied on an assurance relating to land. This limitation does seem to be rather difficult to justify, and it can be argued that, if it is possible for a cause of action to arise as a result of detrimental reliance on A's assurance, then there is no good reason to limit such a cause of action to assurances of an interest in land.[31] One explanation for the current position may be that, in cases not related to land, English courts have been more willing to find that, where B has relied on A's assurance, B has provided consideration for that assurance, and so A is under a contractual duty to B.[32] In contrast, where land is concerned, that contractual route has generally been blocked by the formality rules applying to contracts to dispose of an interest in land.[33]

This does not mean, however, that any duty imposed on A by proprietary estoppel is limited to A's land. As we saw in *Thorner v Major*, if A's assurance relates, at least in part, to land, then the duty imposed on A may extend beyond A's land and also encompass A's personal property (such as farm machinery and livestock) and personal rights of A (such as the farm's trading account: a personal right against a bank).[34]

2.1.2 Finding an assurance

It is important here to distinguish between the three different forms of proprietary estoppel identified in section 1.2. In an acquiescence case, there is no need for A to have made a genuine promise or representation to B: it is A's conduct in standing by in silence, knowing

---

[28] See *Thorner v Major* [2009] 1 WLR 776 at [61] per Lord Walker: proprietary estoppel '*must relate to identified property (usually land) owned (or, perhaps, about to be owned) by [A]*.'

[29] See Restatement (Second) of Contracts, s 90.

[30] See *Waltons Stores v Maher* (1988) 164 CLR 387.

[31] See e.g. McFarlane and Sales, 'Promises, Liability, and Detriment: Lessons from Proprietary Estoppel' (2015) 131 LQR 610. Note that in *Motivate Publishing FZ LLC v Hello Ltd* [2015] EWHC 1554 (Ch), [61], Birss J did not rule out a proprietary estoppel claim simply because it was based on an alleged assurance that B would have a licence to use intellectual property rights, rather than a licence to use land. For discussion, see Shaw-Mellors, 'Proprietary Estoppel and the Enforcement of Promises' [2015] Conv 529.

[32] See *Shadwell v Shadwell* (1860) 142 ER 62 (CCP): B's marriage, following A's promise to pay B a yearly sum during B's life, was found to constitute consideration for A's promise. Compare *Ricketts v Scothorn* 77 NW 365 (1898), in which the Supreme Court of Nebraska, in a similar case, based its enforcement of A's promise on the grounds of promissory estoppel.

[33] We examined those rules in Chapter 8, section 3.

[34] See too *Re Basham* [1987] 1 All ER 405.

of B's mistaken belief and of A's inconsistent right, that *'serves as the element of assurance.'*[35] In a representation case, it suffices if A makes a sufficiently clear representation as to a matter of fact, or mixed fact and law (e.g. a representation as to the location of a boundary between A's land and B's land), when it is reasonable for B to believe that A intended, or at least foresaw, that B would rely on that representation.[36] Where B instead relies simply on a belief as to A's future action, as in *Thorner*, then it is clear that a mere representation by A *cannot* be used as the basis of a proprietary estoppel claim, as if A simply tells B that A's plan is to leave his or her land to B, then this statement, by itself, does not amount to an assurance that A will, in the end, stick to that plan.[37] An assurance can only be found if A can be seen as making some form of commitment that B will acquire a right in relation to A's land. As Lord Hoffmann put it in *Thorner v Major*, the question is whether *'the meaning [A] conveyed would reasonably have been understood as intended to be taken seriously as an assurance which could be relied upon'.*[38]

There is no need, however, for A to have made an express assurance to B. As demonstrated by the House of Lords' analysis in *Thorner*, the question is whether A's conduct, taken as a whole, and viewed objectively, provides grounds for finding an express or implied assurance.[39] The discussion in section 2.1.4 of *Thorner* and *Cobbe v Yeoman's Row Management Ltd*[40] suggests that such an assurance is equivalent to a promise by A to B, and, in this chapter, the word 'promise' is used to refer to an assurance as to B's future rights that is capable of supporting a proprietary estoppel claim. It should be noted, however, that there are some judicial statements to the effect that such a claim can arise without a promise, as long as A can be said to have 'encouraged' B to believe that B will acquire a right in A's land.[41] In *Hoyl Group Ltd v Cromer Town Council*, for example, Floyd LJ expressly asked if A could be said to have 'encouraged' B,[42] and so seemingly rejected A's submission that a promise is required in a case where B relies on a belief as to B's future rights in A's land. The distance between that view and the view that a promise is necessary is reduced, however, by the possibility of finding an implied promise.[43] Moreover, care must be taken in asserting that encouragement is sufficient: in section 2.1.4, we will see an example of a case in which A clearly

---

[35] Lord Walker in *Thorner v Major* [2009] 1 WLR 776 at [55].

[36] See, for example, *Hopgood v Brown* [1955] 1 WLR 213 *per* Lord Evershed MR at [223]–[224].

[37] See e.g. *Davies v Davies* [2016] EWCA Civ 463, [47], noting that, where A showed B a draft will leaving A's property to B, this was not an assurance but merely an indication of A's intention at that time.

[38] [2009] 1 WLR 776, [5].

[39] In *Bradbury v Taylor* [2012] EWCA Civ 1208, the required commitment was found by the court even though it was likely that A had sent a letter to B1 and B2 stating that there was to be no contract between the parties, only a 'friendly arrangement'. Whilst this finding can be criticized (see e.g. Mee [2013] Conv 280), it may perhaps be justified on the basis that B1 and B2 were making a very significant decision, moving with young children from Cornwall to Sheffield, and the first instance judge had found that A had 'wished to do enough to entice them to come and live [with him].' In those circumstances, it may well have been reasonable for B1 and B2 to interpret A's conduct as, overall, amounting to a commitment.

[40] [2008] 1 WLR 1752 (HL).

[41] See e.g. *Inwards v Baker* [1965] 2 QB 29 (although note there that B was not seeking to establish a cause of action, but only to resist an application for possession, and so the result can be explained as resting on principles of waiver, rather than on the promise-based strand of proprietary estoppel: see McFarlane, *The Law of Proprietary Estoppel* (Oxford: OUP, 2014) para 2.107; *Crabb v Arun District Council* [1976] Ch 179, 188 (Lord Denning MR): note that in *Cobbe*, Lord Walker described *Crabb* as a *'difficult case'*: the difficulty, it is submitted, is in finding any express or implied promise by A.

[42] [2015] EWCA Civ 782, [65]–[75].

[43] It can be argued, for example, that an implied promise by A could have been found on the facts of the *Hoyl Group* case.

encouraged B, yet was found by the House of Lords not to have acted in such a way as to give B a possible proprietary estoppel claim.[44]

2.1.3 The certainty of A's assurance

In cases of estoppel by representation, or of promissory estoppel, it is often said that A's representation or promise must be 'clear and unequivocal': is this also the case in proprietary estoppel? As we saw in the extract set out in section 1 above, this question was considered by the House of Lords in *Thorner v Major*. Lord Walker clearly wished to avoid any overrefinement of the test, stating that: '*to establish a proprietary estoppel the relevant assurance must be clear enough. What amounts to sufficient clarity, in a case of this sort, is hugely dependent on context.*'[45] Certainly, judges have distinguished between the degree of certainty expected in a domestic as opposed to a commercial context.[46] Perhaps more importantly, it is also necessary to distinguish between the certainty required for a contractual claim as opposed to a proprietary estoppel claim. In *Thorner*, for example, Lord Walker went on to quote with approval a passage from the judgment of Hoffmann LJ in *Walton v Walton* which raises this point, and part of which is set out below.

Walton v Walton
(14 Apr 1994, CA, unrep)

Hoffmann LJ

At [19]–[21]

In many cases of promises made in a family or social context, there is no intention to create an immediately binding contract. There are several reasons why the law is reluctant to assume that there was. One which is relevant in this case is that such promises are often subject to unspoken and ill-defined qualifications. Take for example the promise in this case. When it was first made, Mrs Walton did not know what the future might hold. Anything might happen which could make it inappropriate for the farm to go to the plaintiff.

But a contract, subject to the narrow doctrine of frustration, must be performed come what may. This is why [counsel for the plaintiff] has always accepted that Mrs Walton's promise could not have been intended to become a contract.

But none of this reasoning applies to equitable estoppel, because it does not look forward into the future and guess what might happen. It looks backwards from the moment when the promise falls due to be performed and asks whether, in the circumstances which have actually happened, it would be unconscionable for the promise not to be kept.

---

44 *Cobbe v Yeoman's Row Management Ltd* [2008] 1 WLR 1752 (HL). See too *Motivate Publishing FZ LLC v Hello Ltd* [2015] EWHC 1554 (Ch), [72], where it was found that no assurance had been made, even though A's conduct clearly did provide some encouragement to B.

45 [2009] 1 WLR 776 at [56]. See too *Liden v Burton* [2016] EWCA Civ 275, [24].

46 See e.g. *Ely v Robson* [2016] EWCA Civ 774, [41]. Note too *Arif v Anwar* [2015] EWHC 124 (Fam), [2016] 1 FLR 359: in a domestic context, a proprietary estoppel claim succeeded where the parties' agreement was found at [69] to be one that B should acquire '*some sort of interest to be sorted out later*'. In *Southwell v Blackburn* [2014] EWCA Civ 1347, [2015] 2 FLR 1240, again in the context of cohabiting partners, an assurance that B would have a secure home with A sufficed for a proprietary estoppel claim (whereas it would not support a common intention constructive trust claim, as there was no common intention that beneficial ownership of the home would be shared by A and B).

The analysis of Hoffmann LJ in *Walton v Walton* makes an important distinction between the requirements of a contract and of proprietary estoppel. It demonstrates that, even if A's assurance is not certain enough to be contractually binding, it may nonetheless form the basis of a proprietary estoppel claim. The justification given for this in *Walton v Walton* was, perhaps not surprisingly, affirmed by Lord Hoffmann in *Thorner v Major*, when stating that: '*Past events provide context and background for the interpretation of subsequent events and subsequent events throw retrospective light upon the meaning of past events. The owl of Minerva spreads its wings only with the falling of dusk.*'[47] The point seems to be that, because a contract imposes an immediate duty to perform a promise, the terms of that promise must be clear from the outset. In contrast, proprietary estoppel does not impose such an immediate duty: instead, a court can ask whether, in the light not only of A's assurance, but also of subsequent events (such as B's reliance), A came under some form of liability to B. As we will see in section 4 below, even if B's proprietary estoppel succeeds, A will not necessarily be ordered to honour A's promise to B. It seems then that, when Lord Walker stated that '*[w]hat amounts to sufficient clarity, in a case of this sort, depends hugely on context*', that context can include events occurring after the moment of any initial assurance of A.

It thus seems that, in practice, it is not necessary for B to prove that A's assurance was 'clear and unequivocal'. In *Thorner v Major*, Lord Neuberger was reluctant to depart from that test; but, as we can see in the extract now set out, the qualifications he permits deprive the test of much of its practical impact.

Thorner v Major
[2009] UKHL 18, [2009] 1 WLR 776

Lord Neuberger

At [84]–[86]

It should be emphasised that I am not seeking to cast doubt on the proposition, heavily relied on by the Court of Appeal,[48] that there must be some sort of an assurance which is 'clear and unequivocal' before it can be relied on to found an estoppel. However, that proposition must be read as subject to three qualifications. First, it does not detract from the normal principle, so well articulated in this case by Lord Walker, that the effect of words or actions must be assessed in their context. Just as a sentence can have one meaning in one context and a very different meaning in another context, so can a sentence, which would be ambiguous or unclear in one context, be a clear and unambiguous assurance in another context. Indeed, as Lord Walker says, the point is underlined by the fact that perhaps the classic example of proprietary estoppel is based on silence and inaction, rather than any statement or action.[49]

Secondly, it would be quite wrong to be unrealistically rigorous when applying the 'clear and unambiguous' test. The court should not search for ambiguity or uncertainty, but should assess the question of clarity and certainty practically and sensibly, as well as contextually. Again, this point is underlined by the authorities [. . .] which support the proposition that, at

---

[47] At [8]. For an explanation of the 'owl of Minerva' metaphor, see fn 14 above.
[48] See [2008] 2 FCR 435, [71], [74].
[49] See *per* Lord Eldon LC ('knowingly, though but passively') in *Dann v Spurrier* (1802) 7 Ves 231, 235–6 and *per* Lord Kingsdown ('with the knowledge [. . .] and without objection') in *Ramsden v Dyson* (1866) LR 1 HL 129, 170.

least normally, it is sufficient for the person invoking the estoppel to establish that he reasonably understood the statement or action to be an assurance on which he could rely.

Thirdly, as pointed out in argument by my noble and learned friend Lord Rodger of Earlsferry, there may be cases where the statement relied on to found an estoppel could amount to an assurance which could reasonably be understood as having more than one possible meaning. In such a case, if the facts otherwise satisfy all the requirements of an estoppel, it seems to me that, at least normally, the ambiguity should not deprive a person who reasonably relied on the assurance of all relief: it may well be right, however, that he should be accorded relief on the basis of the interpretation least beneficial to him.

2.1.4 Pre-contractual negotiations

In *Thorner v Major*, Lord Walker emphasized that, in deciding if A has made a sufficiently certain assurance to B, much will depend on context. This context can include not only later events (such as B's reliance), but also whether the assurance is made in a commercial or domestic setting. In particular, in a case where A and B have begun contractual negotiations, but have not yet concluded a formal contract, it may be difficult for B to show that A has made the required assurance. It is helpful to contrast two cases. In the first, as will be seen in the extract below, B's proprietary estoppel claim succeeded; in the second, it did not.

Crabb v Arun District Council
[1976] Ch 179, CA

Facts: The council (A) and Mr Crabb (B) owned neighbouring plots of land. They entered negotiations concerning the potential grant to Mr Crabb of a right of way over the council's land. An agreement in principle was reached, and a particular access point ('point B') for Mr Crabb was identified, but no formal contract was concluded. When the council later put up a fence to separate its land from Mr Crabb's land, a gap was left at the planned access point for Mr Crabb, and a gate was later installed there. Confident that he had, or would get, a right of way over the council's land, Mr Crabb then sold off part of his land without reserving a right of way over that land. Unfortunately for Mr Crabb, the council then took down the gate, built a wall over the gap, and refused to grant him a right of way over its land. Mr Crabb had no other means of access to his retained land, and claimed that the council were estopped from denying him access to its land. The Court of Appeal held that proprietary estoppel imposed a duty on the council to allow Mr Crabb access to its land.

Lord Denning MR

At 188

The question then is: were the circumstances here such as to raise an equity in favour of the plaintiff? [. . .] The judge found that there was 'no definite assurance' by the defendants' representative, and 'no firm commitment,' but only an 'agreement in principle,' meaning I suppose that, as Mr. Alford [counsel for the council] said, there were 'some further processes' to be gone through before it would become binding. But if there were any such processes in the mind of the parties, the subsequent conduct of the defendants was such as to dispense with them. The defendants actually put up the gates at point B at considerable expense.

That certainly led the plaintiff to believe that they agreed that he should have the right of access through point B without more ado.

Scarman LJ

At 193

[. . .] I can conceive of cases in which it would be absolutely appropriate for a defendant to say: 'But you should not have acted to your detriment until you had had a word with me and I could have put you right.' But there are cases in which it is far too late for a defendant to get himself out of his pickle by putting upon the plaintiff that sort of duty; and this, in my judgment, is one of those cases.

In *Crabb v Arun DC*, then, A's express communication to B (in the negotiations over the planned right of way) and other, non-verbal conduct of A (in leaving the gap in the fence and later installing a gate there) was found to amount to the required assurance. Indeed, as already noted in section 2.1.2, Lord Denning MR went as far as to suggest that B's claim could succeed even in the absence of an express or implied promise from A.[50] That position is, however, difficult to square with the analysis in *Thorner v Major* and also with the decision of the House of Lords in the following case.

Cobbe v Yeoman's Row Management Ltd
[2008] UKHL 55, [2008] 1 WLR 1752, HL

Facts: Yeoman's Row Management Limited (YRML) held the registered freehold of land in Knightsbridge. Mr and Mrs Lisle-Mainwaring controlled the company. A building on the land contained thirteen flats. Mrs Lisle-Mainwaring hoped to redevelop the land: if planning permission could be obtained, six houses could be built, thereby greatly increasing the value of the land. Mrs Lisle-Mainwaring, acting on behalf of YRML, entered into lengthy negotiations with Mr Cobbe, a property developer. They came to an oral agreement, with the following key points: (i) Mr Cobbe, at his own expense, would apply for planning permission to demolish the existing block of flats and to erect, in its place, a terrace of six houses; (ii) upon the grant of planning permission and the obtaining of vacant possession, YRML would sell its freehold to Mr Cobbe (or to a company nominated by him) for an up-front price of £12m; (iii) Mr Cobbe (or his nominee company) would develop the property in accordance with the planning permission; and (iv) Mr Cobbe (or his nominee company) would sell the six houses and pay to YRML 50 *per* cent of the amount, if any, by which the gross proceeds of sale exceeded £24m.[51]

The basics of the deal were thus clear: if Mr Cobbe were to fail to obtain planning permission, he would be paid nothing. But, if he were to succeed in getting planning permission, he and YRML would be able to share in the profits made from the redevelopment of the land. Mr Cobbe and Mrs Lisle-Mainwaring were both experienced business people: they both knew that the oral agreement was not legally binding and that a later, signed contract would have to be concluded, dealing with further issues not covered by the oral agreement. Nonetheless, Mr Cobbe, with the encouragement of Mrs Lisle-Mainwaring, spent considerable time and effort and incurred considerable

---

50 [1976] Ch 179 at [188].   51 [2008] 1 WLR 1752, [6].

expense, between late 2002 and March 2004, in applying for planning permission. By late 2003, Mrs Lisle-Mainwaring had formed an intention not to comply with the oral agreement, deciding instead to ask for more than £12m up-front before selling the freehold—but she hid her plan from Mr Cobbe, deliberately giving him the impression that, if planning permission were obtained, she would enter into a binding contract based on the oral agreement.

In March 2004, as a result of Mr Cobbe's efforts, planning permission was granted. As a result, before any redevelopment work had been started, it seems that YRML's freehold increased in value by around £4m. Mrs Lisle-Mainwaring then informed Mr Cobbe that she would only sell the land if he paid £20m up-front (as well as the agreed share of the proceeds should Mr Cobbe sell on for over £24m). Mr Cobbe objected and brought a claim against YRML. At first, he alleged a breach of contract—a claim that was doomed to fail, because no final agreement had been reached, and there was, in any case, no signed, written agreement between the parties complying with s 2 of the Law of Property (Miscellaneous Provisions) Act 1989 (LP(MP)A 1989) (see Chapter 7, section 3). Mr Cobbe then amended his pleadings to seek relief on the basis of proprietary estoppel, a constructive trust, or unjust enrichment.

At first instance, Etherton J found that Mr Cobbe did have a good proprietary estoppel claim; as a result, he ordered YRML to pay Mr Cobbe a sum equal to half of the increase in value of YRML's freehold caused by the grant of planning permission (as it turned out, this meant that YRML had to pay Mr Cobbe £2m). The Court of Appeal upheld that decision. The House of Lords, however, found that Mr Cobbe had *no* proprietary estoppel claim. It also found that he had not acquired a right under a constructive trust. The House of Lords did decide that he had a claim based on YRML's unjust enrichment, because YRML had received the benefit of his services without paying for them; but that claim allowed him to recover only his expenses in applying for planning permission, plus a reasonable fee to cover his professional services. As a result, Mr Cobbe was therefore limited to receiving only around £150,000—far less than the £2m awarded to him by Etherton J.

Our focus here is on the House of Lords' reasoning in rejecting Mr Cobbe's proprietary estoppel claim.

Lord Walker

At [68]–[72]

[. . .] In the commercial context, the claimant is typically a business person with access to legal advice and what he or she is expecting to get is a *contract*. In the domestic or family context, the typical claimant is not a business person and is not receiving legal advice. What he or she wants and expects to get is an *interest* in immovable property, often for long-term occupation as a home. The focus is not on intangible legal rights but on the tangible property which he or she expects to get. The typical domestic claimant does not stop to reflect (until disappointed expectations lead to litigation) whether some further legal transaction (such as a grant by deed, or the making of a will or codicil) is necessary to complete the promised title [. . .]

So the judge found that Mr Cobbe believed that Mrs Lisle-Mainwaring was, and regarded herself as, bound in honour to enter into a formal written contract if planning permission was granted; and that Mr Cobbe regarded himself as similarly bound. It is implicit—in my view necessarily and deliberately implicit—in the judge's carefully chosen language that neither Mrs Lisle-Mainwaring nor Mr Cobbe regarded herself or himself as legally bound. They were both very experienced in property matters and they knew perfectly well that that was not the position.

Another unusual feature of this case is the judge's finding that Mr Cobbe believed that he would be reimbursed his reasonable expenditure if Mrs Lisle-Mainwaring decided to withdraw from the arrangement before planning permission was granted. This emphasis on the actual grant of planning permission as the crucial condition produces a strange result: would it be conscionable for Mrs Lisle-Mainwaring to withdraw (subject only to reimbursement) at a stage when 99% of the work necessary to obtain planning permission had been done, and success was virtually certain, but unconscionable to do so once success had actually been achieved? This feature of the arrangement emphasises the risk which Mr Cobbe was undertaking, in deciding to rely on Mrs Lisle-Mainwaring's sense of honour.

At [79]–[91]

Crabb v Arun District Council,[52] the facts of which are well known, is a difficult case, not least because of different views taken by different members of the Court [. . .] The situation was that of a commercial negotiation in which both sides expected formal legal documents to be agreed and executed. The case is best explained, I think, by recognising that the Council's erection of the two sets of gates was an act so unequivocal that it led to Mr Crabb irretrievably altering his position, putting the matter beyond the stage at which it was open to negotiation [. . .]

[. . .] In my opinion none of these cases casts any doubt on the general principle laid down by this House in *Ramsden v Dyson*,[53] that conscious reliance on honour alone will not give rise to an estoppel. Nor do they cast doubt on the general principle that the court should be very slow to introduce uncertainty into commercial transactions by over-ready use of equitable concepts such as fiduciary obligations and equitable estoppel. That applies to commercial negotiations whether or not they are expressly stated to be subject to contract.

[. . .] The informal bargain made in this case was unusually complex, as both courts below acknowledged. When a claim based on equitable estoppel is made in a domestic setting the informal bargain or understanding is typically on the following lines: if you live here as my carer/companion/lover you will have a home for life. The expectation is of acquiring and keeping an interest in an identified property. In this case, by contrast, Mr Cobbe was expecting to get a contract. Under that contract he (or much more probably a company controlled by him) would have been entitled to acquire the property for a down-payment of £12m, but only as part of a deal under which the block of flats on the site was to be demolished, the site cleared, and six very expensive townhouses were to be erected instead, and sold for the best prices that they would fetch [. . .]

[. . .] Mr Cobbe's case seems to me to fail on the simple but fundamental point that, as persons experienced in the property world, both parties knew that there was no legally binding contract, and that either was therefore free to discontinue the negotiations without legal liability—that is liability in equity as well as at law [. . .] Mr Cobbe was therefore running a risk, but he stood to make a handsome profit if the deal went ahead, and the market stayed favourable. He may have thought that any attempt to get Mrs Lisle-Mainwaring to enter into a written contract before the grant of planning permission would be counter-productive. Whatever his reasons for doing so, the fact is that he ran a commercial risk, with his eyes open, and the outcome has proved unfortunate for him. It is true that he did not expressly state, at the time, that he was relying solely on Mrs Lisle-Mainwaring's sense of honour, but to draw that sort of distinction in a commercial context would be as unrealistic, in my opinion, as to draw a firm distinction depending on whether the formula "subject to contract" had or had not actually been used.

---

[52] [1976] Ch 179.   [53] (1866) LR 1 HL 129.

Lord Scott

At [14]–[16]

An "estoppel" bars the object of it from asserting some fact or facts, or, sometimes, something that is a mixture of fact and law, that stands in the way of some right claimed by the person entitled to the benefit of the estoppel. The estoppel becomes a "proprietary" estoppel—a subspecies of a "promissory" estoppel—if the right claimed is a proprietary right, usually a right to or over land but, in principle, equally available in relation to chattels or choses in action. So, what is the fact or facts, or the matter of mixed fact and law, that, in the present case, [YRML] is said to be barred from asserting? And what is the proprietary right claimed by Mr Cobbe that the facts and matters [YRML] is barred from asserting might otherwise defeat? [. . .]

My Lords, unconscionability of conduct may well lead to a remedy but, in my opinion, proprietary estoppel cannot be the route to it unless the ingredients for a proprietary estoppel are present. These ingredients should include, in principle, a proprietary claim made by a claimant and an answer to that claim based on some fact, or some point of mixed fact and law, that the person against whom the claim is made can be estopped from asserting. To treat a "proprietary estoppel equity" as requiring neither a proprietary claim by the claimant nor an estoppel against the defendant but simply unconscionable behaviour is, in my respectful opinion, a recipe for confusion.

At [20]

[. . .] The problem (for Mr Cobbe's proprietary estoppel claim) is that when he made the planning application his expectation was, for proprietary estoppel purposes, the wrong sort of expectation. It was not an expectation that he would, if the planning application succeeded, become entitled to "a certain interest in land". His expectation was that he and Mrs Lisle-Mainwaring, or their respective legal advisers, would sit down and agree the outstanding contractual terms to be incorporated into the formal written agreement, which he justifiably believed would include the already agreed core financial terms, and that his purchase, and subsequently his development of the property, in accordance with that written agreement would follow.

At [27]–[28]

[. . .] It would be an unusually unsophisticated negotiator who was not well aware that oral agreements relating to [the transfer of estates in land] are by statute unenforceable and that no express reservation to make them so is needed. Mr Cobbe was an experienced property developer and Mrs Lisle-Mainwaring gives every impression of knowing her way around the negotiating table. Mr Cobbe did not spend his money and time on the planning application in the mistaken belief that the agreement was legally enforceable. He spent his money and time well aware that it was not. Mrs Lisle-Mainwaring did not encourage in him a belief that the second agreement was enforceable. She encouraged in him a belief that she would abide by it although it was not. Mr Cobbe's belief, or expectation, was always speculative. He knew she was not legally bound. He regarded her as bound "in honour" but that is an acknowledgement that she was not legally bound.

The reality of this case, in my opinion, is that Etherton J and the Court of Appeal regarded their finding that Mrs Lisle-Mainwaring's behaviour in repudiating, and seeking an improvement on, the core financial terms of the second agreement was unconscionable, an evaluation from which I do not in the least dissent, as sufficient to justify the creation of a "proprietary estoppel equity". As Mummery LJ said,[54] she took unconscionable advantage

---

[54] [2006] 1 WLR 2964, [123].

of Mr Cobbe. The advantage taken was the benefit of his services, his time and his money, in obtaining planning permission for the property. The advantage was unconscionable because immediately following the grant of planning permission, she repudiated the financial terms on which Mr Cobbe had been expecting to be able to purchase the property. But to leap from there to a conclusion that a proprietary estoppel case was made out was not, in my opinion, justified.

Although the House of Lords overturned the decisions of Etherton J and the Court of Appeal, the result in *Cobbe* is not too surprising. Lord Scott, as in *Thorner v Major*, viewed proprietary estoppel as simply a form of estoppel by representation or promissory estoppel. As we saw in section 1 above, however, this view is difficult to support and it is impliedly rejected by all the members of the House of Lords (other than Lord Scott) in *Thorner v Major*. Yet Lord Scott's analysis, like that of Lord Walker, rests on the finding that Mr Cobbe, by undertaking work when he knew that there was no contract between him and YRML, was running a risk: the risk that, even if he did obtain planning permission, Mrs Lisle-Mainwaring (on behalf of YRML) might pull out of the planned contract. The House of Lords' assessment of the facts seems to be that: (i) it was perhaps dishonourable or immoral for Mrs Lisle-Mainwaring to lead on Mr Cobbe and then pull out of the planned agreement; but (ii) Mr Cobbe, an experienced property developer, should have been aware that business people do not always do the right thing.

Attorney-General of Hong Kong v Humphrey's Estate is an example of a similar case.[55] B started work on some land in the belief that A would sell that land to B. A and B had made a preliminary agreement for a sale, but that agreement was expressly 'subject to contract'. A thus made clear to B that, until a final contract was signed, A was not bound to transfer its ownership of the land to B. As a result, A could not be said to have made the necessary assurance: B acted at his own risk when undertaking the work and so proprietary estoppel did *not* impose a duty on A to B.

Equally, there are clear differences between the facts of *Thorner v Major* and those of *Cobbe*. This can be seen in Lord Neuberger's comparison of the two cases, set out in the next extract.

Thorner v Major
[2009] UKHL 18, [2009] 1 WLR 776

Lord Neuberger

At [93]–[98]

There are two fundamental differences between [*Cobbe*] and this case. First, the nature of the uncertainty in the two cases is entirely different [. . .] In [*Cobbe*], there was no doubt about the physical identity of the property. However, there was total uncertainty as to the nature or terms of any benefit (property interest, contractual right, or money), and, if a property interest, as to the nature of that interest (freehold, leasehold, or charge), to be accorded to Mr Cobbe.

---

[55] [1987] 2 All ER 387.

In this case, the extent of the farm might change, but, on the deputy judge's analysis, there is, as I see it, no doubt as to what was the subject of the assurance, namely the farm as it existed from time to time. Accordingly, the nature of the interest to be received by David was clear: it was the farm as it existed on Peter's death. As in the case of a very different equitable concept, namely a floating charge,[56] the property the subject of the equity could be conceptually identified from the moment the equity came into existence, but its precise extent fell to be determined when the equity crystallised, namely on Peter's death.

Secondly, the analysis of the law in *Cobbe*'s case was against the background of very different facts. The relationship between the parties in that case was entirely arm's length and commercial, and the person raising the estoppel was a highly experienced businessman. The circumstances were such that the parties could well have been expected to enter into a contract, however, although they discussed contractual terms, they had consciously chosen not to do so. They had intentionally left their legal relationship to be negotiated, and each of them knew that neither of them was legally bound [. . .]

In this case, by contrast, the relationship between Peter and David was familial and personal, and neither of them, least of all David, had much commercial experience. Further, at no time had either of them even started to contemplate entering into a formal contract as to the ownership of the farm after Peter's death. Nor could such a contract have been reasonably expected even to be discussed between them. On the deputy judge's findings, it was a relatively straightforward case: Peter made what were, in the circumstances, clear and unambiguous assurances that he would leave his farm to David, and David reasonably relied on, and reasonably acted to his detriment on the basis of, those assurances, over a long period.

In these circumstances, I see nothing in the reasoning of Lord Scott in *Cobbe*'s case which assists the respondents in this case. It would represent a regrettable and substantial emasculation of the beneficial principle of proprietary estoppel if it were artificially fettered so as to require the precise extent of the property the subject of the alleged estoppel to be strictly defined in every case. Concentrating on the perceived morality of the parties' behaviour can lead to an unacceptable degree of uncertainty of outcome, and hence I welcome the decision in *Cobbe*'s case. However, it is equally true that focussing on technicalities can lead to a degree of strictness inconsistent with the fundamental aims of equity.

The distinction made by Lord Neuberger between domestic and commercial cases was also made by Lord Walker in *Cobbe* itself, as we saw in the extract set out above. The crucial distinction, however, may be between those cases, such as *Cobbe*, in which the parties have been involved in pre-contractual negotiations and other cases, such as *Thorner*, where no contract has been discussed. In the former class of cases, as Lord Walker explained in *Cobbe*, B faces the difficulty of showing that A's assurance is that B will acquire a particular right in A's land, and is not merely an assurance that A will negotiate in good faith with B, or that *some sort* of contract will be concluded, which may or may not give B a right in specific land of A. Indeed, the approach in *Cobbe* may cast doubt on previous decisions, such as *Crabb v Arun DC*,[57] in which a proprietary estoppel was said to arise against the context of pre-contractual negotiations: as one judge has put it, there is a question as to the '*Cobbe-compliance*' of such decisions.[58] In *Cobbe*, for example, Lord Walker referred to *Crabb* as a

---

[56] [We will look briefly at floating charges in Chapter 25, section 3.4].

[57] See also *Holiday Inns v Broadhead* (1974) 232 EG 951 and *Yaxley v Gotts* [2000] Ch 162.

[58] *Per* Arden LJ in *Herbert v Doyle* [2010] EWCA Civ 1095, [6]. In *Cobbe v Yeoman's Row* [2008] 1 WLR 1752, [24] and [31], Lord Scott suggested that, in a case where B knows that there is no legally binding agreement with A, it may still be possible for B to show that a constructive trust has arisen under the principle in *Pallant v Morgan* [1953] 1 Ch 43 (the same suggestion was made by Morgan J in *Crossco No 4*

'difficult case', and the difficulty seems to come from the fact that it is hard to spell out a clear implied promise from A's conduct: by leaving a gap in the fence, for example, A may simply have been making it easier for itself to give B a right of way *if* A chose to do so in the future.

The standing of *Crabb v Arun DC* after the decision in *Cobbe*, as well as the significance of the distinction between domestic and commercial cases, has been discussed by Lord Neuberger in an extra-judicial contribution.[59]

Lord Neuberger, 'The Stuffing of Minerva's Owl? Taxonomy and Taxidermy in Equity' [2009] CLJ 537

At 541–2

Both parties [in *Cobbe*] knew there was no contractual arrangement: indeed, they intended it. They both appreciated that there was an arrangement binding in honour only. The message from the House of Lords is that it is simply not for the courts to go galumphing in, wielding some Denningesque sword of justice, to rescue a miscalculating, improvident or optimistic property developer from the commercially unattractive, or even ruthless, actions of a property owner, which are lawful at common law.

[. . .] I suggest that, before he can establish a proprietary estoppel claim, a claimant must show that he has acted in the belief that he has something which can be characterized as a legal right—at least in a commercial arm's length context.

I add that qualification, because it is perhaps in this connection that the difference between commercial and domestic cases (which Lord Walker discussed in *Cobbe* at [66]–[68], and which I also touched on in *Thorner v Major* at [96]–[97]) comes into focus. The notion that a claimant takes his chance, where he knows that he has no legally enforceable right, is easier to accept in the context of a commercial and arm's length relationship than in a domestic or familial context. In a commercial situation, the absence of a contractual relationship normally arises from the parties, with easy access to legal advice, considering themselves better off, or at least choosing to take a risk, rather than being bound. Maybe Mr Cobbe wanted to be free to walk away, rather than being committed to paying £12m and developing the property, if the market went the wrong way. Maybe he thought that he might be able to negotiate a better deal once planning permission was obtained. But, whatever his reason for not having a contract, he faced no emotional or social impediment to insisting on some form of legally binding protection before he went ahead with seeking planning permission. Why should equity assist him, when YRML decided to negotiate a better deal?

But it is much easier to see why David Thorner should have been able to invoke proprietary estoppel. His older, gruff and taciturn cousin led him to believe that, if he continued to provide work and companionship, he would inherit the farm. The notion that David could or should have asked for a commitment in writing, in the context of an informal family relationship, seems somewhat unreal. It would have risked harming the relationship with Peter, and the only solicitor he knew would no doubt have been advising Peter. Unlike in *Cobbe*, formal contractual rights and obligations were simply not the stuff of the relationship between Peter and David Thorner [. . .]

Unlimited v Jolan Ltd [2011] EWHC 803 (Ch), [279]). For discussion of that form of constructive trust, see Chapter 11, section 5.

[59] In the same article, Lord Neuberger also set out his view that s 2 of the Law of Property (Miscellaneous Provisions) Act 1989 has no impact on a proprietary estoppel claim (see the extract from the article in Chapter 8, section 3.9.) The same view is taken by McFarlane, 'Proprietary Estoppel and Failed Contractual Negotiations' [2005] Conv 501.

It may very well be that proprietary estoppel will not often assist a claimant in the commercial context, but that is probably all to the good: in the business world, certainty and clarity are particularly important, and judges should be slow to encourage the introduction of uncertainties based on their views of the ethical acceptability of the behaviour of one of the parties.

[. . .] If Mr Crabb believed, to the Council's knowledge, that he had been promised the grant of a right of way, and sold off his field in that belief, there is no reason to doubt that his claim in proprietary estoppel was rightly accepted by the Court of Appeal. But if his claim was simply based on a 'subject to contract' agreement (whether or not those words were used) or on moral indignation, then it may well be that it does not survive *Cobbe*.

2.2 RELIANCE BY B

To bring a proprietary estoppel claim, B must show that he has relied on A's assurance that B has, or will acquire, a right in relation to A's land. This requirement of reliance is a feature not only of the promise-based strand of the doctrine, but also of the acquiescence and representation-based strands. As the facts of the next two cases demonstrate, it might seem that, particularly in domestic or family cases, reliance will be difficult to prove. Nonetheless, in each case, the Court of Appeal held that reliance had occurred.

Greasley v Cooke
[1980] 1 WLR 1306, CA

Facts: Ms Cooke lived in a home owned by Kenneth and Hedley Greasley. She was Kenneth's partner and also cared for Clarice, another member of the Greasley family. Both Kenneth and Hedley had assured Ms Cooke that she would have 'a home for life', but Kenneth died without giving her any right to remain on the land and the current owners of the land wished to remove her. Ms Cooke's proprietary estoppel claim was based on the fact that, because of the assurances that she would have a 'home for life', she had remained there and cared for Clarice, rather than leaving to find paid work. It might seem difficult for her to prove such reliance: after all, because she was, in any case, 'one of the family', she may well have cared for Clarice even if she had not been given any assurances about remaining in the home. Nonetheless, the Court of Appeal held that reliance had occurred.

Lord Denning MR

At 713

The first point is on the burden of proof. [In *Brikom Investments Ltd v Carr* [1979] 2 All ER 753 at 759] I said that, when a person makes a representation intending that another should act on it—

'It is no answer for the maker to say: "You would have gone on with the transaction anyway." That must be mere speculation. No one can be sure what he would, or would not, have done in a hypothetical state of affairs which never took place [. . .] Once it is shown that a representation was calculated to influence the judgment of a reasonable man, the presumption is that he was so influenced.'

> So here. These statements to [Ms Cooke] were calculated to influence her, so as to put her mind at rest, so that she should not worry about being turned out. No one can say what she would have done if Kenneth and Hedley had not made those statements. It is quite possible that she would have said to herself: 'I am not married to Kenneth. I am on my own. What will happen to me if anything happens to him? I had better look out for another job now rather than stay here where I have no security.' So, instead of looking for another job, she stayed on in the house looking after Kenneth and Clarice. There is a presumption that she did so relying on the assurances given to her by Kenneth and Hedley. The burden is not on her but on them to prove that she did not rely on their assurances. They did not prove it, neither did their representatives.

The decision in *Greasley v Cooke* is often said to support a 'presumption of reliance' in proprietary estoppel. Care must be taken, however. On the one hand, if A has made a representation or promise that is likely, objectively speaking, to cause B to act in a particular way, and B does so act, then this may well allow a court to infer, as a matter of fact, that A did indeed rely on that representation or promise. Lord Denning MR seems to go further, however, and to suggest that, in all cases, the burden is on A to disprove reliance. The Court of Appeal has rejected that approach in relation to other forms of estoppel,[60] and the High Court of Australia has rejected it in the specific context of proprietary estoppel,[61] rightly pointing out that high authority in both England[62] and Australia[63] supports the basic proposition that it is for the claimant to prove all the elements of his or her case. It would, therefore, be surprising if a future court were to allow a proprietary estoppel claim to succeed in a case where it could not be inferred, on the balance of probabilities from the factual evidence, that A had indeed relied on B's representation or promise or (in an acquiescence case) on B's mistaken belief as to B's rights.

The next case seems to provide a further example of the Court of Appeal departing from a generally accepted test in order to allow B's proprietary estoppel claim.

Wayling v Jones
(1993) 69 P & CR 170, CA

Facts: Mr Wayling first met Mr Jones in 1967. In 1971, they began a homosexual relationship and started to live together. At that time, Mr Wayling, a chef, was 21 years of age, while Mr Jones was aged 56. Over the following years, as well as living with Mr Jones, Mr Wayling worked in a number of Mr Jones' businesses. Mr Wayling received 'pocket money' and expenses, but was never given a standard salary for his work. Mr Jones made a will in which Mr Wayling was given a particular hotel

---

[60] *Steria Ltd v Hutchison* [2007] ICR 445: see esp *per* Neuberger LJ at [129]: '*I very much doubt whether it could be right to hold that in every case where a representation is established, the onus must always be on the representor to show that it was not acted on. As a matter of normal principle it seems to me that, as a matter of law, the onus must be on the person alleging the estoppel to establish unconscionability, or, to put it another way, to establish, in the case of estoppel by representation, the three essential ingredients of representation, reliance and detriment.*' The discussion in *Steria* concerned estoppel by representation, estoppel by convention, and promissory estoppel, but the same analysis seems to be applicable to proprietary estoppel.

[61] *Sidhu v van Dyke* [2014] HCA 19.   [62] See *Smith v Chadwick* (1884) 9 App Cas 187, 196.

[63] See *Gould v Vaggelas* (1984) 157 CLR 215.

(the Glen-y-Mor Hotel) owned by Mr Jones. That hotel was later sold and a different hotel bought (the Royal Hotel), but the will was never updated. So, when Mr Jones died in 1987, his will did not succeed in giving anything to Mr Wayling. Mr Wayling claimed that Mr Jones was under a duty (now binding on Mr Jones' executors), arising under the doctrine of proprietary estoppel, to give Mr Wayling ownership of the Royal Hotel.

Mr Jones had made a number of promises to Mr Wayling as to what would happen on Mr Jones's death: he promised that ownership of the Glen-y-Mor Hotel, and then the Royal Hotel, would go to Mr Wayling. The following exchange took place when Mr Wayling was cross-examined in court by counsel for Mr Jones' executors:

'Q: If he had not made that promise to you, would you still have stayed with him?
A: Yes [. . .]
Q: The promises were not the reason why you remained with the deceased?
A: No, we got on very well together. He always wanted to reward me.'

The judge at first instance took this to mean that, because Mr Wayling would have acted in the same way even if he had never been promised Mr Jones' hotel, he could not show that he had relied on Mr Jones' assurances. But the Court of Appeal upheld Mr Wayling's appeal.

Balcombe LJ

At 1030

I am satisfied that [Mr Wayling's] conduct in helping [Mr Jones] run the café in Hastings Street and the Glen-y-Mor Hotel and managing the Royal Hotel for what was at best little more than pocket money [. . .] was conduct from which his reliance on [Mr Jones's] clear promises could be inferred. The question is whether [Mr Jones' executors] have established that [Mr Wayling] did not rely on these promises.

In his affidavit evidence [Mr Wayling] stated that he relied on [Mr Jones'] promises. In his oral evidence-in-chief he said:

'Q: One question, Mr Wayling. Assuming you were in the Royal Hotel bar before [Mr Jones's] death and [Mr Jones] was there, if [Mr Jones] had told you that he was not going to give the Royal Hotel to you but to somebody else after his death, what would you have done?
   A: I would have left.'

[. . .] I am satisfied that [Mr Wayling's] answers in cross-examination do not relate to the only question that mattered: "What would you have done if [Mr Jones] had told you that he was no longer prepared to implement his promises?".

   [. . .] I am satisfied:

(a) that the promises were made;

(b) that [Mr Wayling's] conduct was of such a nature that inducement may be inferred;

(c) that [Mr Jones' executors] have not discharged the burden upon them of establishing that the plaintiff did not rely on the promises.

Mr Wayling was a deserving claimant because: (i) only a technical mistake (Mr Jones' failure to update his will) prevented him from acquiring the hotel as expected; and (ii) he had lived with, and worked for, Mr Jones as part of a long-term relationship—he had made sacrifices as a result of that relationship and was, to an extent, dependent on Mr Jones. Nowadays, as well as bringing a proprietary estoppel claim, a party in Mr Wayling's position can also bring a claim under the Inheritance (Provision for Family and Dependants) Act 1975. That Act gives the court a power to award a share of A's estate to B, an adult dependant of A, where adequate provision for B has not been made in A's will. When *Wayling v Jones* was decided, however, the Act did not give the court a power to make an order in favour of A's homosexual partner. So, proprietary estoppel was Mr Wayling's only recourse.

It is therefore, unsurprising, that the Court of Appeal wished to allow B's claim. The difficulty is that, because Mr Wayling had *admitted* that he would have worked for low pay even if he had not been promised the hotel, it would seem that the executors had met the burden recognized in *Greasley v Cooke*: they had proved that, in fact, Mr Wayling had not relied on Mr Jones's promises. Yet the Court of Appeal nonetheless allowed Mr Wayling's proprietary estoppel claim. As explained by Cooke in the following extract, this was done by applying an unusual test: to prove that Mr Wayling had not relied, the executors had to show that Mr Wayling would have continued to work for low pay *even if* he had been told by Mr Jones that Mr Jones intended to break his promise to leave the hotel to him.

Cooke, 'Reliance and Estoppel' [1995] 111 LQR 389, 391

That this is an unusual interpretation of reliance is best seen by comparing a case where it was held that there was no reliance. In *Coombes v. Smith*[64] the plaintiff left her husband, moved into the defendant's house and bore his child. She claimed an interest in the property on the basis of proprietary estoppel. She failed for a number of reasons, among them the fact that she acted as she did, not in reliance upon the defendant's assurance that he would provide for her, but simply because she wanted to. Imagine her reaction if she had heard her partner say that he was not going to provide for her, in spite of his promise. Surely she would have left, because that would have undermined her relationship with him. She would thus have met the *Wayling* test. But it was held that she did not rely upon the assurance, because the giving of that assurance, and her expectation of an entitlement to the property, did not influence her actions.

Reliance is an aspect of causation. When we say that someone acted in reliance upon a promise we generally mean that he would not have so acted *but for* the making of the promise. We cannot say that of Wayling. Alternatively, it seems that reliance in the context of estoppel can mean that the plaintiff would not have acted as he did *but for* a belief, which was then encouraged by the promise.[65] Wayling could not meet that test either, since he did not set up home with Jones in the belief that the latter would leave his property to him. He did so, and he stayed, because of his relationship with the defendant; because, as he put it, "he needed me". Obviously, if he had discovered that Jones was not going to change his will, the relationship would have been undermined, and he would have left. But any broken promise could have had the same effect.

---

[64] [1986] 1 W.L.R. 809.

[65] As envisaged by Robert Goff J., as he then was, in *Amalgamated Investment & Property Co. Ltd. v. Texas Commerce International Bank Ltd.* [1982] Q.B. 84, 104–105.

The treatment of reliance in *Wayling v. Jones* is thus unusually generous. Despite the obvious justice of the result, the means of reaching it was inconsistent with earlier estoppel cases.

It may well be that in *Wayling v Jones*, the Court of Appeal modified the general rule in order to give full effect to the nature of the relationship between A and B. As we will see in Chapter 16, a similar relaxation of the general rules is in evidence when B claims shared ownership of a family home. In section 2.1.4 above, we saw that, in applying the first requirement of proprietary estoppel (the need for an assurance by A), there seems to be an important difference between domestic and commercial cases. As a result of *Wayling v Jones*, that distinction also seems to be significant when considering the requirement of reliance by B. Certainly, it is very unlikely that the same test of reliance, with its generosity to B, would be applied in a commercial case.

2.3 THE PROSPECT OF DETRIMENT TO B

The third element of proprietary estoppel is often referred to as detriment, but it is important to note that B's reliance, in itself, does not need to be detrimental; rather, the key question is whether, given B's reliance, he *would* suffer a detriment if he had no proprietary estoppel claim against A.[66] In addition: '*The issue of detriment must be judged at the moment when the person who has given the assurance seeks to go back on it.*'[67] This supports the point made by Lord Hoffmann in *Thorner v Major*, when invoking the owl of Minerva, which flies only at dusk. In a bilateral contract, for example, A's promise coincides with B's provision of consideration to create an immediate duty on A; in contrast, in proprietary estoppel, detriment is judged not at the time of A's assurance, but at a later point.

Gillett v Holt
[2000] EWCA Civ 66, [2001] Ch 210, CA

Facts: Geoffrey Gillett first met Mr Holt at Woodhall Spa golf club in 1952. Geoffrey was then aged 12 and Mr Holt was a gentleman farmer aged 38. Geoffrey became Mr Holt's regular caddie and a friendship developed between them. In 1956, Geoffrey left school to start working on Mr Holt's farm (The Limes). He continued working for Mr Holt, taking on extra responsibilities, for over thirty-eight years. In 1971, Mr Gillett and his wife moved into a farmhouse (The Beeches), newly acquired by a company (KAHL) controlled by Mr Holt. In 1995, Mr Holt attempted to sack Mr Gillett and to remove him from The Beeches. Mr Holt also altered his will so that Mr Gillett was no longer the principal beneficiary.[68]

---

[66] This point is made most clearly in an influential passage from the judgment of Dixon J in *Grundt v Great Boulder Pty Gold Mines Ltd* (1938) 59 CLR 641, 674–5. That passage was quoted with approval by Robert Walker LJ in *Gillett v Holt* [2001] Ch 210, [232]–[233].

[67] *Davies v Davies* [2016] EWCA Civ 463, [38] (Lewison LJ). See too *Clarke v Meadus* [2010] EWHC 3117 (Ch), [65].

[68] The principal beneficiary instead was a Mr Wood, whom Mr Holt had met in 1992. According to the first instance judge in *Gillett v Holt*, '*Mr Holt's relationship with Mr Wood developed into something of an obsession, which was of concern to his family and other friends*': see [2001] Ch 210, 222.

Mr Gillett claimed that Mr Holt was under a duty, arising as a result of proprietary estoppel: (i) not to remove him and his wife from The Beeches; and (ii) to transfer to him at least some of the The Limes. Mr Gillett claimed that, during the period from 1964 to 1989, Mr Holt gave seven 'specific assurances' that 'one day, he (Mr Gillett) would own the farm'. It was claimed that these assurances reflected a general understanding between Mr Gillett and Mr Holt, and were usually at significant events: for example, after Mr Gillett brought in his first harvest (1964) and at the christening of Mr Gillett's first child (1971).

Robert Walker LJ

[. . .] [I]n this case Mr Holt's assurances were repeated over a long period, usually before the assembled company on special family occasions, and some of them (such as "it was all going to be ours anyway" [in 1975]) were completely unambiguous [. . .] Plainly the assurances given on this occasion were intended to be relied on, and were in fact relied on.
[. . .]
It is therefore necessary to go on to consider detriment [. . .] It is understandable that the judge devoted most attention to the issue of Mr Gillett being underpaid because that was the issue (affecting detriment) on which most time was spent in cross-examination [. . .] The judge said that he was not persuaded, on the evidence, that Mr Gillett did in fact receive less than a reasonable wage for his services as a manager, or that he did so as part of an understanding related to his expectations, and that conclusion has not been seriously challenged in this court.

Both sides agree that the element of detriment is an essential ingredient of proprietary estoppel [. . .] The overwhelming weight of authority shows that detriment is required. But the authorities also show that it is not a narrow or technical concept. The detriment need not consist of the expenditure of money or other quantifiable financial detriment, so long as it is something substantial. The requirement must be approached as part of a broad inquiry as to whether repudiation of an assurance is or is not unconscionable in all the circumstances.

[. . .] There must be sufficient causal link between the assurance relied on and the detriment asserted. The issue of detriment must be judged at the moment when the person who has given the assurance seeks to go back on it. Whether the detriment is sufficiently substantial is to be tested by whether it would be unjust or inequitable to allow the assurance to be disregarded—that is, again, the essential test of unconscionability. The detriment alleged must be pleaded and proved [. . .]

The matters which Mr Gillett pleaded as detriment, and on which he adduced evidence of detriment, included, apart from the level of his remuneration, (i) his continuing in Mr Holt's employment (through KAHL) and not seeking or accepting offers of employment elsewhere, or going into business on his own account; (ii) carrying out tasks and spending time beyond the normal scope of an employee's duty; (iii) taking no substantial steps to secure his future wealth, either by larger pension contributions or otherwise; and (iv) expenditure on improving The Beeches farmhouse which was, Mr Gillett said, barely habitable when it was first acquired by KAHL in 1971. That company paid for some structural work, with a local authority improvement grant, but Mr Gillett paid for new fittings and materials and carried out a good deal of the work himself [. . .]

[. . .] After listening to lengthy submissions about the judgment, and after reading much of Mr Gillett's evidence both in his witness statement and under cross-examination, I am left with the feeling that the judge, despite his very clear and careful judgment, did not stand back and look at the matter in the round. Had he done so I think he would have recognised that

> Mr Gillett's case on detriment (on the facts found by the judge, and on Mr Gillett's uncontra-dicted evidence) was an unusually compelling one.
>
> [Having decided that the requirements of proprietary estoppel had been met, Robert Walker LJ went on to consider how to 'satisfy the equity'—that is, how to decide on the extent of Mr Gillett's right. It was held that Mr Holt and KAHL were under a duty to: (i) transfer to Mr Gillett the freehold of The Beeches (including the farmhouse and 42 hectares of attached land); and (ii) pay Mr Gillett £100,000 as compensation for not receiving any of The Limes.]

The Court of Appeal thus rejected the argument that detriment should be interpreted in a narrow, purely financial way. As Lord Denning MR had earlier put it in *Greasley v Cooke:*[69] '*It so happens that in many of these cases there has been expenditure of money. But that is not a necessary element* [. . .] *It is sufficient if the party, to whom the assurance is given, acts on the faith of it in such circumstances that it would be unjust and inequitable for the party making the assurance to go back on it* [. . .]'.

The decision in *Gillett v Holt* also shows that B's action in reliance on A's assurance does not need to be wholly detrimental to B. For example, in *Gillett*, it could be said that Geoffrey benefitted from being allowed to live, with his wife, in The Beeches. Such countervailing benefits are important, as they must be taken into account in working out the overall extent of B's detriment; as is the case with detriment, non-financial benefits must be taken into account too.[70] As the Privy Council explained in the following case, however, the crucial question in relation to detriment is whether such benefits outweigh the prejudice that B would suffer if A were wholly free to go back on A's assurance to B.

Henry v Henry
[2010] UKPC 3, [2010] 1 All ER 988

Facts: Calixtus Henry claimed to be entitled to an undivided half share in a plot of rural land on a hillside in Jalousie, St Lucia; Theresa Henry was the registered proprietor of that half-share, having purchased it in 1999 from Geraldine Pierre, just two months before Geraldine's death. During her life, Geraldine had told her relatives that they could possess the land if they remained to work the land and care for her. Calixtus was the only person to accept this offer; other relatives left St Lucia and moved to St Croix, in the US Virgin Islands, for an easier life. By the time of Geraldine's death, Calixtus had lived on the land for more than 30 years, cultivating it and caring for Geraldine, who had made further promises to Calixtus that she would then leave her share in the plot to him. The trial judge dismissed Calixtus' proprietary estoppel claim. One of his grounds for doing so was that Calixtus had not suffered a detriment: whilst he had cared for Geraldine and cultivated the land, he had also received the countervailing advantages of rent-free accommodation and the benefit of any produce of the land not personally needed by Geraldine. The Court of Appeal of the Eastern Caribbean Supreme Court allowed Calixtus's appeal, declaring that he was the true owner of the half share registered in Theresa's name. The Privy Council considered various points, both on appeal on cross-appeal. One of these points was as to whether the correct test had been applied on the question of detriment.

---

69 [1980] 3 All ER 710, CA (see section 2.2 above).
70 *Southwell v Blackburn* [2014] EWCA Civ 1347, [2015] 2 FLR 1240.

Sir Jonathan Parker (giving the advice of the Board)

At [51]–[53]

In the judgment of the Board, the [trial] judge clearly misdirected himself in his approach to the issue of detriment. He said [. . .] that Calixtus Henry could not say that he had acted to his detriment and that, far from having suffered detriment because of his reliance on the deceased's promises, he positively benefited. But he did not attempt to weigh the disadvantages suffered by Calixtus Henry by reason of his reliance on Geraldine Pierre's promises against the countervailing advantages which he enjoyed as a consequence of that reliance. That is a process which, on principle, he should have undertaken [. . .]

[. . .] Had he done so, he would have brought into account on, as it were, the debit side of the account [. . .] the fact that other members of the family had not responded to Geraldine's offer of 'an opportunity to possess land on the mountain … if they would work the land and cared for her in her own country as she did not want to leave St Lucia to live abroad or to live in St Croix', but instead had moved to St Croix where they were able to live more comfortably.

As well as establishing *if* a detriment would occur if A were free to renege on his or her assurance to B, a court will usually also have to take a view on the *extent* of B's detriment. This is because, as we will see in section 3 below, the nature of A's duty to B may well depend, at least in part, on the degree of detriment to which B is exposed by A's failure to honour his or her assurance.

2.4 THE ROLE OF UNCONSCIONABILITY

There is a debate as to the precise role of unconscionability within the doctrine of proprietary estoppel. It is clear that B cannot bypass the three requirements set out above and acquire a right by simply showing that A has behaved unconscionably. For example, Lord Scott in *Cobbe v Yeoman's Row* stated that '*unconscionability of conduct may well lead to a remedy but, in my opinion, proprietary estoppel cannot be the route to it unless the ingredients for a proprietary estoppel are present.*'[71] And, writing extra-judicially, Lord Neuberger has opined that: '*equity is not a sort of moral US fifth cavalry riding to the rescue every time a claimant is left worse off than he anticipated as a result of the defendants behaving badly, and the common law affords him no remedy.*'[72] It is equally clear that the concept of unconscionability has played some role in the fashioning of the requirements of proprietary estoppel, and of the judges' interpretation of those requirements. As Robert Walker LJ put it in *Gillett v Holt*:

the fundamental principle that equity is concerned to prevent unconscionable conduct permeates all the elements of the doctrine. In the end the court must look at the matter in the round.[73]

---

[71] [2008] 1 WLR 1752, [16].

[72] 'The Stuffing of Minerva's Owl? Taxonomy and Taxidermy in Equity' (2009) 68 CLJ 537, 540.

[73] [2001] Ch 210 (CA), 225. See too *Davies v Davies* [2016] EWCA Civ 463, [38] (Lewison LJ): '*The question is whether (and if so to what extent) it would be unjust or inequitable to allow the person who has given the assurance to go back on it. The essential test is that of unconscionability.*'

The difficulty of establishing the exact role of unconscionability is well demonstrated by the Court of Appeal's decision in the following case.

Taylors Fashions v Liverpool Victoria Trustees; Old & Campbell v Liverpool Victoria Friendly Society
[1982] QB 133, CA

Facts: Each of Taylors Fashions (Taylors) and Old & Campbell (Olds) made a separate claim that it had a right to renew a lease of business premises. The landlord, Liverpool Victoria, denied that either Taylors or Olds had such a right. All of the parties had acted on the basis that both Taylors and Olds *did* have a right to renew the lease: they all assumed that an earlier lease that contained such a right bound Liverpool Victoria. As a result, Taylors and Olds had, for example, spent money on improving the premises. But that general assumption was mistaken: Liverpool Victoria was not bound by the earlier lease. Taylors and Olds, because each had acted in reliance on the mistaken belief that it had a right to renew, argued that Liverpool Victoria was now estopped from denying the existence of the right to renew. Liverpool Victoria argued that proprietary estoppel could not apply, because it had not acted unconscionably, nor had it tried to deceive Taylors or Olds: it, too, had genuinely believed that it was bound by the earlier lease.

Oliver J

At 144

This is the principal point upon which the parties divide. [Counsel for Taylors and Olds] contend that what the court has to look at in relation to the party alleged to be estopped is only his conduct and its result, and not—or, at any rate, not necessarily—his state of mind. It then has to ask whether what that party is now seeking to do is unconscionable. [Counsel for Liverpool Victoria] contends that it is an essential feature of this particular equitable doctrine that the party alleged to be estopped must, before the assertion of his strict rights can be considered unconscionable, be aware both of what his strict rights were and of the fact that the other party is acting in the belief that they will not be enforced against him [That contention of counsel was supported by the decision of Fry J in *Willmott v Barber*.[74] In that case, Fry J set out five criteria or 'probanda' for proprietary estoppel, one of which is that A, when making a representation to B that B has a particular right in relation to A's land, must be aware of his true rights against B.]

Now, convenient and attractive as I find [counsel for Liverpool Victoria's] submissions as a matter of argument, I am not at all sure that so orderly and tidy a theory is really deducible from the authorities—certainly from the more recent authorities, which seem to me to support a much wider equitable jurisdiction to interfere in cases where the assertion of strict legal rights is found by the court to be unconscionable. It may well be (although I think that this must now be considered open to doubt) that the strict *Willmott v. Barber* probanda are applicable as necessary requirements in those cases where all that has happened is that the party alleged to be estopped has stood by without protest while his rights have been infringed [. . .] in a case of mere passivity, it is readily intelligible that there must be shown a

---

[74] (1880) 15 Ch D 96.

duty to speak, protest or interfere which cannot normally arise in the absence of knowledge or at least a suspicion of the true position.

[Oliver J then examined a number of authorities, before continuing as follows.]

[. . .] the more recent cases indicate, in my judgment, that the application of the *Ramsden v Dyson*[75] principle—whether you call it proprietary estoppel, estoppel by acquiescence or estoppel by encouragement is really immaterial—requires a very much broader approach which is directed rather at ascertaining whether, in particular individual circumstances, it would be unconscionable for a party to be permitted to deny that which knowingly, or unknowingly, he has allowed or encouraged another to assume to his detriment than to inquiring whether the circumstances can be fitted within the confines of some preconceived formula serving as a universal yardstick for every form of unconscionable behaviour.

So regarded, knowledge of the true position by the party alleged to be estopped becomes merely one of the relevant factors—it may even be a determining factor in certain cases—in the overall inquiry [. . .]

The inquiry which I have to make therefore, as it seems to me, is simply whether, in all the circumstances of this case, it was unconscionable for the defendants to seek to take advantage of the mistake which, at the material time, everybody shared, and, in approaching that, I must consider the cases of the two plaintiffs separately because it may be that quite different considerations apply to each.

Oliver J's conclusion was that Taylors' claim failed, but Olds' claim succeeded. The difficulties for Taylors were: (i) Liverpool Victoria had not encouraged Taylors to believe that it had a right to renew the lease; but instead, both parties had *assumed* that such a right existed; and (ii) it was not clear that the improvements made to the premises by Taylors were carried out in reliance on its belief that it had a right to renew the lease, because Taylors, in any case, benefited from those improvements by continuing to use the premises up to the end of its existing lease. In contrast, Olds had been encouraged by Liverpool Victoria to spend a 'very large sum' on improving the premises precisely because of the belief that it would be able, at the end of the existing lease, to renew that lease and continue using the premises. As a result, Liverpool Victoria was ordered to allow Olds to renew its lease.

The decision in *Taylors Fashions* has been hailed as allowing an important relaxation in the requirements of proprietary estoppel: indeed, it has been called a '*watershed in the development of proprietary estoppel*'.[76] Certainly, Oliver J made clear that B can acquire a right through proprietary estoppel even if the five strict requirements laid down by *Willmott v Barber* have not all been fulfilled. And, in reaching that conclusion, Oliver J emphasized that proprietary estoppel, a doctrine developed by courts of equity, ultimately depends on the notion of unconscionability.

However, we need to be careful. First, as the *Willmott* requirements are best seen as regulating the acquiescence-based strand of proprietary estoppel, it is no surprise that cases developing the promise-based strand of the doctrine have rejected those criteria.[77] Second,

---

[75] (1866) LR 1 HL 129 (see section 2.1.2).

[76] See Robert Walker LJ in *Gillett v Holt* [2001] Ch 210, [225], quoting from Gray and Gray, *Elements of Land Law* (2nd edn, 1993, p 324). See now *Elements of Land Law* (5th edn, 2009, [9.2.36]). For a detailed analysis of the decision in *Taylors Fashions*, see Dixon, 'Stitching Together Modern Estoppel' in *Landmark Cases in Land Law* (ed Gravells, Oxford: Hart Publishing, 2013).

[77] Indeed, there is a strong argument that the *Willmott* criteria remain applicable where B's claim is based purely on A's acquiescence, and not on any representation or promise by A: see, for example, McFarlane, *The Law of Proprietary Estoppel* (Oxford: OUP, 2014) para 2.08–2.13.

it was counsel for the defendants, Liverpool Victoria, who emphasized the importance of unconscionability. This is because Liverpool Victoria had *not* acted deceitfully or led anyone 'up the garden path': when leading Olds to believe that Olds had a right to renew its lease, Liverpool Victoria had honestly (but mistakenly) believed that Olds did have such a right. The actual decision in *Taylors Fashions* thus demonstrates that a proprietary estoppel claim can succeed even if A has not deceived B by leading B to believe something that A knows to be false. In other words, the decision could be said to stand for the fact that, if the three elements of proprietary estoppel are satisfied, it does not matter whether or not A's behaviour can be said, in a general sense, to be unconscionable.

Taylors Fashions, then, cannot provide us with a clear answer as to the role of unconscionability. The question was also considered by Lord Walker in *Cobbe*.

Cobbe v Yeoman's Row Management Limited
[2008] UKHL 55, [2008] 1 WLR 1752, HL

Lord Walker

At [92]

[Counsel for Mrs Lisle-Mainwaring] devoted a separate section of his printed case to arguing that even if the elements for an estoppel were in other respects present, it would not in any event be unconscionable for Mrs Lisle-Mainwaring to insist on her legal rights. That argument raises the question whether "unconscionability" is a separate element in making out a case of estoppel, or whether to regard it as a separate element would be what Professor Peter Birks once called "a fifth wheel on the coach".[78] But Birks was there criticising the use of "unconscionable" to describe a state of mind.[79] Here it is being used (as in my opinion it should always be used) as an objective value judgment on behaviour (regardless of the state of mind of the individual in question). As such it does in my opinion play a very important part in the doctrine of equitable estoppel, in unifying and confirming, as it were, the other elements. If the other elements appear to be present but the result does not shock the conscience of the court, the analysis needs to be looked at again. In this case Mrs Lisle-Mainwaring's conduct was unattractive. She chose to stand on her rights rather than respecting her non-binding assurances, while Mr Cobbe continued to spend time and effort, between Christmas 2003 and March 2004, in obtaining planning permission. But Mr Cobbe knew that she was bound in honour only, and so in the eyes of equity her conduct, although unattractive, was not unconscionable.

Lord Walker thus seems to suggest that unconscionability may have a role to play in the test for proprietary estoppel: not as a separate requirement, but rather as a concept to be borne in mind when interpreting the specific criteria of the doctrine. This point is developed in the following extract, which also notes that Lord Walker's view of the role of unconscionability may have shifted since his discussion of it in *Gillett v Holt*.[80]

---

[78] [See Birks in *Breach of Trust* (eds Birks and Pretto, Oxford: Hart Publishing, 2002) p 226.]

[79] [The specific use of the term discussed by Birks comes from *Bank of Credit and Commerce International (Overseas) Ltd v Akindele* [2001] Ch 437, [455], *per* Nourse LJ. That case did not concern estoppel, but rather the question of whether a third party receiving a right held on trust can be liable, due to his 'knowing receipt' of the right, to account to the beneficiary of the trust.]

[80] [2001] Ch 210, CA: see section 2.3 above.

Hopkins, 'Proprietary Estoppel: A Functional Analysis' (2010) 4 Journal
of Equity 201

At 212–13

Robert Walker LJ [in *Gillett v Holt*] appeared to envisage two distinct roles for
unconscionability. First as feeding into the assessment of whether the other elements of
the claim were fulfilled: hence in *Gillett*, conduct that had been considered insufficient to
constitute detriment at first instance when viewed in isolation, was considered by the Court
of Appeal to be 'unusually compelling' when judged as a question of whether the claimant
had so conducted himself that it would now be unconscionable for the representor to renege on the assurance. Second, the concept appeared to provide a mechanism through
which the court would assess claims 'in the round.' The consequence of this second role appeared to be that even where an assurance, reliance and detriment were found, a successful
claim was subject to the court being satisfied, on a holistic assessment, that at the time the
representor reneged it was unconscionable for him or her to do so [. . .]

[Given] Lord Walker's own previous enthusiasm for the concept, the relative lack of discussion of unconscionability in *Cobbe* and *Thorner* appears both significant and surprising. It
will be suggested that while no uniform picture emerges, there is evidence of an attempt by
Lord Walker to shift the focus of unconscionability further towards the other elements of an
estoppel claim. In this way, unconscionability continues to play a central role in the informal
acquisition of rights in land through proprietary estoppels [. . .]

At 217–18

In Lord Walker's view in *Cobbe* [. . .] the other elements [i.e. assurance, reliance, and det-
riment] cannot be fulfilled unless the result 'shocks the conscience'. The other elements
may only *appear* to be fulfilled. Hence, having found that the other elements were not
present, Lord Walker could not concur with the classification of Mrs Lisle-Mainwaring's
conduct as unconscionable. In his judgment, unconscionability has no role independent
from the other elements. Implicitly, this means that those other elements should be
assessed in the context of determining whether it would be unconscionable for the
representor to renege. Only by doing so can the courts ensure that the elements will
be fulfilled only when the result 'shocks the conscience'. In effect, what seemed to be
two distinct roles for unconscionability outlined by Robert Walker LJ in *Gillett* became
a single role in *Cobbe*. Whether seen as part-and-parcel of the assessment of the other
elements, or as the basis for an 'in the round' evaluation, only two outcomes are possible: a claim will succeed because the three elements of assurance, reliance and detriment are present and this necessarily means that it is unconscionable for the representor
to renege; or a claim will fail because one or more of those requirements has not been
met. It is logically impossible under Lord Walker's judgment [. . .] for a court to find that
an assurance, reliance and detriment are actually present (as opposed to *appearing* to be
present), but for a claim still to fail on the basis that it would not be unconscionable for
the representor to renege.

[. . .] [T]he absence of discussion of unconscionability in *Cobbe* and *Thorner* does not
necessarily make a move away from the significance of the concept in estoppel claims.
Instead, what may emerge from the cases is a greater focus on the connection between
unconscionability and the other elements of an estoppel claim. If maintained, the effect
may be to consolidate the role of unconscionability by preventing the potential misuse of
the concept that can arise when it is seen as not merely having a role independent from

those elements but sufficient on its own to form the basis of a claim [. . .] However, our understanding and interpretation of the detailed rules, and therefore of the informal acquisition of rights in land through estoppel, is inseparable from the underlying concept of unconscionability.

For an example of Hopkins' point, consider how a court might decide a case where, following A's promise to B, and B's reliance, there was a significant change in the circumstances of the parties—perhaps A was compelled to sell part of A's land to pay medical bills.[81] In such a case, although the three main elements of assurance, reliance, and detriment are met, an invocation of unconscionability would provide the court with a means to take into account A's change of circumstances,[82] by either reducing the extent of B's claim, or by denying it completely.[83]

Another suggested function of unconscionability relates to a very significant practical feature of proprietary estoppel: its ability to give rise to a claim even where there have been no formal, written dealings between A and B.[84]

Dixon, 'Proprietary Estoppel and Formalities in Land Law and the Land Registration Act 2002: A Theory of Unconscionability' in *Modern Studies in Property Law Vol 2* (ed Cooke, 2002)

At p 175

The central role that unconscionability plays in the law of estoppel seems, at least to the present writer, to be in inverse proportion to the analysis devoted to it in the cases. All judges are agreed that unconscionability is vital, but few seem willing to share their understanding of the concept [. . .]

At p 180

In so far as the general law requires the creation, transfer or enforcement of proprietary rights to be undertaken in certain forms, estoppel can be used to side-step these requirements only where there is a clear justification. That it would be 'unconscionable' for one of the parties to rely on the absence of the required formality is that justification. This means that unconscionability cannot be merely a function of assurance, reliance and detriment (the factual elements of estoppel) for otherwise it is devoid of meaning [. . .] 'unconscionability' *can* explain why the absence of formality may be ignored—in the sense that a right still ensues for the claimant—if the concept is tied to the formality rules. Hence, it will be unconscionable for a representor to withdraw an assurance, relied on to detriment, if the assurance of the rights carries with it (expressly or impliedly) a further assurance that the right

---

[81] Such a possibility was mooted by Lord Scott in *Thorner v Major*: [2009] 1 WLR 776 [19].

[82] See, for example, the discussion of Mummery LJ in *Uglow v Uglow* [2004] EWCA Civ 987 at [30]. For an Australian example, see *Germanotta v Germanotta* [2012] QSC 116.

[83] For an analysis that reaches a similar conclusion to that of Hopkins, see McFarlane, *The Law of Proprietary Estoppel* (Oxford: OUP, 2014) ch 5.

[84] The extract was written before the decisions in *Cobbe* and *Thorner*, but the author's views on the issue remain essentially the same after those cases: see Dixon, 'Confining and Defining Proprietary Estoppel: the Role of Unconscionability' (2010) 30 LS 408.

will ensue even if the formalities necessary to convey the right are not complied with. It is the withdrawal of the promise of the right after the second assurance (assuming detrimental reliance) that constitutes the unconscionability required for a successful claim in estoppel.

At p 182

Although it is submitted that unconscionability in the narrow sense just discussed must be present before a claim *can* succeed, that does not mean that the claim *must* then succeed ... There still remains the broad equitable jurisdiction either to deny the remedy or modify the remedy because of the background circumstances of the case [. . .] Of course, this is not [an] unfettered and unprincipled discretion ... but it is in keeping with the use of estoppel as a remedy protecting those who cannot rely on formality and who instead must plead the favour of the court.

Dixon's main point is an important one and raises the question we noted in Chapter 8, section 3.9: if a failure to satisfy a formality rule means that A has not granted B a property right, nor made a contractual promise to B, is that formality rule undermined if we recognize that B has acquired a right through proprietary estoppel?[85]

A sensitivity to the formality rules does not mean, however, that the role of proprietary estoppel can be justified *only* by viewing unconscionability as an independent requirement of the doctrine. It rather means that, if we take the view that B's claim arises simply because of A's commitment, B's reliance, and the prospect of B's detriment, we need to explain *why* those factors impose a liability on A to B, and also why that liability can arise in the absence of formality. One possible use of the notion of unconscionability may be to provide a link to one of the underlying aims of equity: the prevention of opportunistic conduct by A.[86] If no claim were available to B in a case such as *Thorner*, for example, A would be free to leave B to suffer the detriment resulting from B's reasonable reliance on A's promise. Such action could be seen as exploitation by A of the formal rules surrounding the acquisition of rights in land, and of an abuse of B's trust: that may be why it would 'shock the conscience of the court' if no redress were available to B.

3   THE EXTENT OF A'S LIABILITY TO B: REMEDYING A PROPRIETARY ESTOPPEL

3.1   THE CURRENT POSITION

If B can show that proprietary estoppel imposes a liability on A, we then need to know the *extent* of that liability. This task is often said to be one of deciding what remedy to give, or how best to 'satisfy the equity' arising,[87] where B has made a successful proprietary estoppel claim.

---

[85] See too Dixon's statement in 'Confining and Defining Proprietary Estoppel: the Role of Unconscionability' (2010) 30 LS 408, 418: '[u]nconscionability is a function of formality, not of assurance, reliance and detriment'.

[86] See the discussion in Chapter 6, section 1.1.

[87] In accordance with the terminology employed in *Crabb v Arun DC* [1976] Ch 179 by Lord Denning MR (at 190) and by Scarman LJ (at 193, 198–9).

In any particular case, there are a number of possible ways in which the extent of A's liability might be determined. For example, it could be that:

- A is under a duty to *honour his commitment to B*—in such a case, the extent of B's right depends on the extent of A's commitment to B; *or*

- A is under a liability to *ensure B suffers no detriment as a result of A's failure to honour his commitment*—in such a case, the extent of B's right depends on the extent of B's potential detriment; *or*

- A is under a liability to *pay B the value of any benefit A has received as a result of B's reliance on A*—in such a case, the extent of B's right is determined by the extent of the benefit that A has received at B's expense; *or*

- A is under a duty to do whatever is necessary to ensure that A does not act unconscionably—in such a case, the extent of B's right depends on what a court determines that A must do to avoid behaving badly.

Of course, there may be other possibilities; equally, one of the four measures could be adopted in a certain set of cases, with other measures used in other cases.[88] Unfortunately, it is not currently possible to describe the courts' approach in a way which is both clear and consistent with the results of the cases.

Jennings v Rice
[2002] EWCA Civ 159, [2003] 1 P & CR 100, CA

Facts: Mrs Royle, a childless widow, lived at Lawn House, Shapwick, in Somerset. She died in 1997. Mr Jennings had started to work for her in 1970 as a part-time gardener. He later began to do other work for her (e.g. running errands, taking her shopping, doing minor maintenance work). In the late 1980s, Mrs Royle stopped paying Mr Jennings for these services, but she provided him with £2,000 towards the purchase of a house. By the mid-1990s, Mr Jennings, at Mrs Royle's request, cared for her and stayed overnight at her house. In return, Mrs Royle assured him that, in her will, she would 'see him right'—but she died without leaving a will.

Mr Jennings claimed that, at her death, Mrs Royle was under a duty to Mr Jennings, arising as a result of proprietary estoppel. The first instance judge held that Mrs Royle (and so now Mr Rice, her personal representative) was under a duty to pay Mr Jennings £200,000. Mr Jennings appealed, claiming that Mr Rice was under a duty to give him the whole of Mrs Royle's estate (valued at £1.285m) or, at least, a sum equal to the value of Mrs Royle's house and its furniture (£435,000). The Court of Appeal upheld the award of the first instance judge: on her death, Mrs Royle was under a duty to pay Mr Jennings £200,000.

Aldous LJ

At [15]–[22]

The [first instance] judge then had to decide what was the appropriate relief [. . .] He concluded that he had a discretion to be exercised judicially in the light of all the relevant circumstances.

---

[88] See the discussion in Gardner, 'The Remedial Discretion in Proprietary Estoppel,' (1999) 115 LQR 438, esp at 440.

He took into account, first that Mr Jennings did not know the extent of Mrs Royle's wealth and second, that the value of her actual estate and even the part known to Mr Jennings was out of all proportion to what Mr Jennings might reasonably have charged for the services he provided free. He then considered whether it would be equitable for Mr Jennings to take the house and the furniture which were the minimum he expected, and also what the judge called the problem of proportionality. The judge reminded himself that the house was valued at £420,000 and was not a suitable house for Mr Jennings to reside in on his own and he took into account that Mrs Royle had no special obligations to her family. He said that to reward an employee on the scale of £420,000 was excessive. He also compared the cost of full-time nursing care, which he estimated at £200,000, with the value of the house. He reasoned that Mr Jennings would probably need £150,000 to buy a house. He concluded:

'I do not think that he could complain that he had been unfairly treated if he had been left £200,000 in Mrs Royle's will. Most people would say that she would, at least, then have performed her promise to see him all right. The quality of her assurance affects not only questions of belief, encouragement, reliance and detriment, but also unconscionability and the extent of the equity.'

At [36]–[38]

There is a clear line of authority from at least *Crabb's* case to the present day which establishes that once the elements of proprietary estoppel are established an equity arises. The value of that equity will depend upon all the circumstances including the expectation and the detriment. The task of the court is to do justice. The most essential requirement is that there must be proportionality between the expectation and the detriment.

Mr Warner warned against the conclusion I have reached. He submitted that it led to uncertainty and that the appropriate course was to satisfy the expectation. I accept that the flexible approach adopted in the past may mean that there is room for what has been referred to as a judicial discretion, but the rigidity of the approach advocated by Mr Warner can lead to injustice which could not form the basis of an equitable result. One only has to alter the facts of this case to illustrate the unsatisfactory nature of Mr Warner's submissions. The expectation was that Mr Jennings would receive the house and furniture valued at £435,000. If he had been left £5 or £50,000 or £200,000 in Mrs Royle's will, or she had died one month, one year or 20 years after making the representation relied on, should the court award the same sum? Yes, said Mr Warner. The result could then have been that Mr Jennings would receive £635,000 made up of the expectation and the legacy of £200,000, or perhaps, £435,000 in total, even when the detriment was say £800.

The judge was right to conclude that the award must be proportionate. He took into account the relevant factors as placed before him, namely the expectation, the detriment, the position of Mr Jennings and the amount available. His conclusion was the result of a judgment to which he was entitled to come. I would not interfere with it and would dismiss the appeal.

Robert Walker LJ

At [41]–[56]

I also agree that this appeal should be dismissed for the reasons given by Aldous LJ. Because of the general interest of this appeal I add some observations of my own.

It cannot be doubted that in this as in every other area of the law, the court must take a principled approach, and cannot exercise a completely unfettered discretion according to the individual judge's notion of what is fair in any particular case [. . .]

The need to search for the right principles cannot be avoided. But it is unlikely to be a short or simple search, because (as appears from both the English and the Australian authorities) proprietary estoppel can apply in a wide variety of factual situations, and any summary formula is likely to prove to be an over-simplification . . .

If the claimant's expectations are uncertain (as will be the case with many honest claimants) then their specific vindication cannot be the appropriate test. A similar problem arises if the court, although satisfied that the claimant has a genuine claim, is not satisfied that the high level of the claimant's expectations is fairly derived from his deceased patron's assurances, which may have justified only a lower level of expectation. In such cases the court may still take the claimant's expectations (or the upper end of any range of expectations) as a starting point, but unless constrained by authority I would regard it as no more than a starting point.

I do not see that approach as being inconsistent with authority. On the contrary, I think it is supported by a substantial body of English authority. Scarman LJ's well-known reference to 'the minimum equity to do justice to the plaintiff'[89] must no doubt be read in the context of the rather unusual facts of that case, but it does not stand alone [. . .] Scarman LJ's reference to the minimum does not require the court to be constitutionally parsimonious, but it does implicitly recognise that the court must also do justice to the defendant.

It is no coincidence that these statements of principle refer to satisfying the equity (rather than satisfying, or vindicating, the claimant's expectations). The equity arises not from the claimant's expectations alone, but from the combination of expectations, detrimental reliance, and the unconscionableness of allowing the benefactor (or the deceased benefactor's estate) to go back on the assurances.

To recapitulate: there is a category of case in which the benefactor and the claimant have reached a mutual understanding which is in reasonably clear terms but does not amount to a contract. I have already referred to the typical case of a carer who has the expectation of coming into the benefactor's house, either outright or for life. In such a case the court's natural response is to fulfil the claimant's expectations. But if the claimant's expectations are uncertain, or extravagant, or out of all proportion to the detriment which the claimant has suffered, the court can and should recognise that the claimant's equity should be satisfied in another (and generally more limited) way.

But that does not mean that the court should in such a case abandon expectations completely, and look to the detriment suffered by the claimant as defining the appropriate measure of relief. Indeed in many cases the detriment may be even more difficult to quantify, in financial terms, than the claimant's expectations. Detriment can be quantified with reasonable precision if it consists solely of expenditure on improvements to another person's house, and in some cases of that sort an equitable charge for the expenditure may be sufficient to satisfy the equity.[90] But the detriment of an ever increasing burden of care for an elderly person, and of having to be subservient to his or her moods and wishes, is very difficult to quantify in money terms. Moreover the claimant may not be motivated solely by reliance on the benefactor's assurances, and may receive some countervailing benefits (such as free bed and board). In such circumstances the court has to exercise a wide judgmental discretion.

It would be unwise to attempt any comprehensive enumeration of the factors relevant to the exercise of the court's discretion, or to suggest any hierarchy of factors. In my view they include, but are not limited to, the factors mentioned in Dr Gardner's third hypothesis[91]

---

[89] *Crabb v Arun DC* [1976] Ch 179, [198].

[90] [Walker LJ here referred to *Snell's Equity* (30th edn, 2000), [39–21] and the authorities mentioned in that paragraph.]

[91] [The reference here is to Gardner 'The Remedial Discretion in Proprietary Estoppel' (1999) 115 LQR 438.]

(misconduct of the claimant as in *J Willis & Sons v Willis*[92] or particularly oppressive conduct on the part of the defendant, as in *Crabb's* case or *Pascoe v Turner*).[93] To these can safely be added: the court's recognition that it cannot compel people who have fallen out to live peaceably together, so that there may be a need for a clean break; alterations in the benefactor's assets and circumstances, especially where the benefactor's assurances have been given, and the claimant's detriment has been suffered, over a long period of years; the likely effect of taxation; and (to a limited degree) the other claims (legal or moral) on the benefactor or his or her estate. No doubt there are many other factors which it may be right for the court to take into account in particular factual situations.

[...] The essence of the doctrine of proprietary estoppel is to do what is necessary to avoid an unconscionable result, and a disproportionate remedy cannot be the right way of going about that.

On the approach adopted by the Court of Appeal in *Jennings*, proprietary estoppel does not always lead to A being under a duty to honour a commitment made to B. This point was emphasized by the Privy Council in *Henry v Henry* (the facts of the case are set out in section 2.3 above).[94] The court below had assumed that, once it had held that Calixtus had made out his proprietary estoppel claim, Geraldine must necessarily have been under a duty to honour her assurance to Calixtus. The Privy Council firmly rejected this approach: as Sir Jonathan Parker put it, the approach of the court below: '*betrays a fundamental misconception as to the nature and purpose of the doctrine of proprietary estoppel* [...] *Proportionality lies at the heart of the doctrine of proprietary estoppel and permeates its every application.*'[95]

Certainly, it would be difficult to defend a rule that, in all cases of proprietary estoppel, A's duty must be to honour his or her assurance to B.[96] After all, in cases such as *Jennings* and *Henry*, A is under no contractual duty to B, not least because of the absence of the signed writing required for a contract to dispose of an interest in land (see further Chapter 8, section 3). We saw in section 2.1.3 above that, in *Walton v Walton*,[97] Hoffmann LJ (as he then was) emphasized the distinction between contractual claims and proprietary estoppel. In the latter case, A's assurance does not impose an immediate duty on A; rather, B's claim arises only if, as a result of B's reliance on A's assurance, B would suffer a detriment if A were wholly free to resile on his or her assurance. If, then, B's claim arises only because of B's reliance on A, and the prospect of B's suffering a detriment, it would be strange if the extent of A's duty were fixed solely by the content of A's assurance to B. In fact, it may seem better to think of A as under a liability to B, with a duty arising only if and when a court order fixes the extent of that liability.

It is therefore clear that a successful proprietary estoppel claim does not always lead to the enforcement of A's assurance. Nonetheless, two difficulties remain. Firstly, in what case will A's assurance be enforced? Secondly, if A's assurance is not enforced, how will a court determine the extent of A's liability? For example, it is clear that the concept of 'proportionality' has an important role to play; but what is that role, and what does proportionality entail?

As can be seen in the following extract, a number of different approaches have been suggested, but none has yet been conclusively adopted.

---

[92] [1986] 1 EGLR 62. [93] [1979] 1 WLR 431. [94] [2010] 1 All ER 988.
[95] Ibid, 1001–2.
[96] See Mee, 'The Role of Expectation in the Determination of Proprietary Estoppel Remedies' in *Modern Studies in Property Law Vol 5* (ed Dixon, Oxford: Hart Publishing, 2009).
[97] 14 April 1994 (unreported), CA.

Davies v Davies
[2016] EWCA Civ 463

Facts: Eirian Davies (B) succeeded in a proprietary estoppel claim, based on assurances made to her by her parents (A)[98] as to rights she would receive in the family farm in Wales. The land was owned by A and the farm business was run until 2002 by a partnership, and then by a company. A number of different assurances had been made to B over the years, starting in 1985 with an assurance that B would inherit the farm from A. That first assurance had been made on the condition that B would work on the farm in return, but B left the farm in 1989. B returned in 1991, and worked on the farm, for which she was paid. There was an assurance in 1998 that B would join the partnership, but that was falsified in 2001, after which B again left the farm. When B returned again to live in a farmhouse on the land, there was an assurance at the end of 2007 that B could continue to live there for the rest of her life; and a promise in 2008 that B would acquire shares in the company through which the farm business was conducted. In 2008, B left a job elsewhere that she had started in 2007 in order to work on the farm, for a salary of £1,500 per month plus payment of rates and the electricity bill for the farmhouse, in which she was already living. In 2009, A showed B draft wills under which B was to be left the land and buildings and a share in the company. In 2010, however, B was shown a new will, in which she did not receive the farm. The relationship between A and B deteriorated and in 2012, B left the farm for the last time. The net value of the farm and farming business at the time of trial was around £3 million, with most of that value being the value of the land.

A argued that B's equity would be satisfied by a payment of £350,000. This was comprised of: (a) £180,000 to enable B to pay off the mortgage on B's own property, thus giving B secure accommodation for life elsewhere than on the farm; (b) £22,000 as profits to which B would have been entitled had she been made a partner in the business in 1998; (c) £120,000 as a half share of the profits made by the company from 2008–12; (d) a further £28,000 to make up for underpayment for the work B had done on the farm in the years before she received a salary. B argued instead that she was entitled to the farm and the business.

At first instance, the judge found that it would not be appropriate for the farm and business itself (still owned and run by A) to be transferred to B, and instead ordered that B be paid £1.3 million, which was 'just over or under one third of the net value of the farm and farming business', considering that to be a 'fair reflection of the expectation and detriment and other factors [identified in the judgment]'. One of those other factors mentioned by the judge was the 'significant role' of A in bringing B's expectation to an end when the parties fell out in 2012.

B now accepted that a money award would be appropriate, but A argued on appeal that the first instance award was too high, pointing out that it was 'equivalent to £65,000 after tax for every year [B] worked on the farm'. The Court of Appeal reduced the award to a sum of £500,000.

---

[98] The claim was against both parents, but as they acted together throughout and their positions were not considered separately in the case, they are referred to for convenience here as simply 'A'.

(i) Working for long hours on the farm without full payment; and

(ii) Had she not worked on the farm she would have been able to work shorter hours in a working environment of her choosing and she would have been free of the difficult working relationship she had with her parents.

[Lewison LJ then analysed A's argument for a payment of £350,000, broken down into four distinct elements and set out above with the facts of the case. On (a), he noted that the freehold value of the farmhouse in which B had been promised accommodation for life was £300,000 and so the value of B's expectation would have to be less than that, *'scaled down to some extent to reflect the difference between a personal entitlement to a home for life and a freehold capital asset'*.[113] On (b)–(d), the judge's view was that they ignored the fact that B had expected to inherit the land, and not just have a share of the business, but that there was no basis for saying that B had been made a definite, sustained promise of inheriting the land, and the sums offered by A in relation to the business represented 85 per cent of the overall current value of the company. He then rejected the judge's point that the conduct of A in the breakdown of the relationship with B could be relevant to the size of the award.]

[62]–[69]

So far as [A's] 'significant role of brining [B's] expectation to an end'[114] is concerned, it is inherent in almost every claim based on proprietary estoppel that the representor or promisor has resiled from the representation or promise that he has made. It is, therefore, always the representor or promisor who has a significant role in bringing the expectation to an end. But there is no warrant (and no authority that we were shown) for increasing a monetary award on that account [. . .]

How then did the judge bridge the gap between [A's] offer of £350,000 and his award of £1.3 million? The only explanation, based on the judge's own reasoning, is that he attributed a value of close to £1 million to the non-financial aspects of the detrimental reliance and/or that (although not expressly mentioned) he ascribed a very large value to the disappointment of [B's] expectation of inheriting the land (as opposed to the business and the herd).

Let me take the last element first [. . .] Accepting that she had an expectation of inheritance, it was in my judgment an expectation which was at a high level and could not fairly be derived from what she was told between 2009 and 2012.[115] It cannot carry much weight in an overall assessment. I am prepared to accept that some award must be made under this head, but in my judgment it will be a relatively modest one.

The non-financial detrimental reliance that the judge identified was that [B] gave up the ability to work shorter hours in a working environment of her choice and freedom from the difficult working relationship she had with her parents. All this is true, but the effect of the rupture is that she is now free to do all that which the judge said that she had given up. He made no finding that any of what she gave up was irretrievable. To the contrary, he found expressly that this was not a case in which [B's] whole life was positioned on the representations [. . .] Again I accept that some award must be made under this head, but in my judgment it will be a relatively modest one.

In some cases it may well be that the impossibility of evaluating the extent of imponderable and speculative non-financial detriment (for example life-changing choices) may lead

---

[113] [58].   [114] This was the phrase used by the judge at first instance.
[115] See *Jennings v Rice* [2002] EWCA Civ 159, [2003] 1 P & CR 8, [47].

the court to decide that relief in specie[116] should be given. But that is not this case, not least because the judge rejected the claim for the transfer of assets in specie.

Neither of these factors is capable of precise valuation, but since it is now common ground that the ultimate award will be a purely monetary one, we must do the best that we can. In different situations, the court is often called upon to award compensation for non-pecuniary losses, and the difficulty of assessment is no bar to an award.

Finally [. . .] to the extent that the offer includes compensation for past expectations (in particular, the partnership element, the company element, and the underpayment element) some additional sum must be allowed to reflect delay in payment and the changes in value of money since those expectations were created. On the other hand, in so far as a monetary award covers future expectations it must be discounted for early payment.

Taking all these factors into account I would increase [A's] offer by a further £150,000 making a total award of £500,000. I would thus allow the appeal and reduce the judge's award from £1.3 million to £500,000.

The extract above demonstrates that, on Lewison LJ's view, the result in *Davies v Davies* would have been the same on each of the three possible general approaches to determining the extent of B's rights. On the first approach, which has fulfilling A's assurance as a starting point, and departs from that only where it would be disproportionate to give B such a right, such a departure was warranted, given the shifting nature of A's assurances and the fact that B's detriment was either capable of being quantified, or only moderate, and was not as extensive as in a case (such as, for example, *Gillett v Holt* or *Thorner v Major*) where B could be said to have positioned his or her whole life on A's assurances. On the second approach, where the immediate and sole focus is on avoiding possible detriment to B, then again the extent and nature of the detriment was such that the judge's award had to be reduced. On the third approach, of reflecting both expectation and detriment, again the somewhat weak expectation and the relatively limited detriment would both argue for a reduction in the judge's award.

Lewison LJ did express some sympathy for the second approach as '*logical*', and the final award in the case does seem to be focussed on the extent of B's detriment, which is of course consistent with that approach. As there remains uncertainty, however, as to the correct approach, we need to look at each of them.

3.2 THE FIRST APPROACH: B'S EXPECTATION AS A STARTING POINT

On this approach, A will not always be under a duty to honour his or her assurance to B, but this should still be the starting point: in other words, B's expectation will be protected *unless* it would be disproportionate to do so. If it is disproportionate the court will then, to use Walker LJ's phrase, decide on A's duty by exercising its 'wide judgmental discretion'.[117] Such an approach may seem appealing and can be supported by the analysis of the Court of Appeal in *Suggitt v Suggitt*.[118] Arden LJ there stated that the need for proportionality:[119]

---

[116] [In this context, 'relief in specie' means enforcement of A's assurance.]

[117] [2002] EWCA Civ 159, [2003] 1 P & CR 8, [51].

[118] [2012] EWCA Civ 1140. There is also support for this approach in the more recent Australian case law on proprietary estoppel: see e.g. *Delaforce v Simpson-Cook* (2010) 78 NSWLR 483, *Harrison v Harrison* [2013] VSCA 170; *Sidhu v van Dyke* [2014] HCA 19, [85]–[86].

[119] [2012] EWCA Civ 1140, [44].

does not mean that there has to be a relationship of proportionality between the level of detriment and the relief awarded. What Walker LJ holds [in Jennings] is that if the expectations are extravagant or 'out of all proportion to the detriment which the claimant has suffered', the court can and should recognise that the claimant's equity should be satisfied in another and generally more limited way. So the question is: was the relief that the judge granted 'out of all proportion to the detriment' suffered.

As the following extract demonstrates, however, such an approach seems to lead to unprincipled results.

Mee, 'The Role of Expectation in the Determination of Proprietary Estoppel Remedies' in *Modern Studies in Property Law: Vol 5* (ed Dixon, 2009, pp 402–4)

The Flaw in the 'Expectation as Starting Point' Approach

Consider a hypothetical case where D has promised to leave C a certain house and where, in reliance on this, C has incurred detriment which is substantial but difficult to quantify. On the approach under discussion, the court should grant an expectation remedy unless this would be disproportionate to the detriment incurred by C. A crucial variable in the hypothetical scenario is, therefore, the value of the house. The argument will proceed by examining the consequences of adjusting the example by increasing the value of the hypothetical house, while holding constant the level of C's detriment and the other features of the case. Let it first be said that the house is worth (say) £100,000 and that, on the facts, it would not be disproportionate for the court to fulfil C's expectation when it is set at this level. In these circumstances, the court would grant the house to C by way of remedy.

Consider next a case where the value of the house is adjusted upwards to the highest level whereby it would still not be disproportionate to fulfil C's expectation. Let it be said that this value of the house is £400,000. In the version of the example where the house has this value, the court will once more fulfil C's expectation and grant him the house worth £400,000 … Consider finally a variation on the example where all the facts are the same except that the house is now worth £1,000,000. In this situation, it would be disproportionate to order that C should receive the house, given the disparity in value between the expectation and C's detriment. Therefore the court must devise a remedy in the exercise of its 'wide judgmental discretion'. Depending on the way in which the relevant factors operate in the particular circumstances of the case, the court might award a monetary remedy valued at (say) £200,000 or £300,000 or £400,000 … Imagine that, in the circumstances of the case, the court exercises its discretion to choose a remedy of £300,000.

Thus, with an expectation valued at £400,000, C received a remedy valued at £400,000 (the fulfilment of the expectation); however, when the expectation was greater, being valued at £1,000,000, the award was only £300,000. That cannot be right. It is not possible to defend a position where, with all the other facts in the scenario being held constant, a *higher* expectation on the part of C can lead to a *lower* remedy … Yet this anomaly is the inevitable consequence of an approach which seeks to privilege the expectation remedy as 'the starting point' in the remedial inquiry, i.e. as the prima facie remedy which will be granted unless it is disproportionate to C's detriment. Either one applies the same approach to determining the remedy in all cases—in which case the expectation remedy loses its status as the prima facie remedy—or else one faces the absurdity that C may be in a stronger position if he can show that the expectation induced in him by D was sufficiently low to count as 'not disproportionate' to his detriment.

3.3 THE SECOND APPROACH: DETRIMENT AS THE KEY FACTOR

A further interpretation of proportionality suggests that the extent of A's liability should be proportionate *solely* to B's detriment: in other words, the right acquired by B should be no more and no less than the right required to prevent B from suffering a detriment as a result of his or her reliance on A's assurance. Such an interpretation is explored in each of the following extracts.

Bright and McFarlane, 'Proprietary Estoppel and Property Rights' [2005]
CLJ 449, 452–4

In order to determine the nature and extent of rights arising through proprietary estoppel it is crucial to ask why proprietary estoppel is recognized as a source of rights. Any account of the underlying purpose of the doctrine must be consistent both with the test for the availability of a proprietary estoppel claim, and with the extent of the rights awarded in response to such a claim. In particular cases proprietary estoppel may have the effect of allowing the informal grant of a property right; of enforcing a promise; or of reversing an unjust enrichment. Yet none of these three aims can constitute the basic purpose of the doctrine as, by itself, each fails to account both for the test for the availability of a claim and for the extent of the rights thereby gained by B.

On this approach, the only satisfactory theory of proprietary estoppel is one which explains proprietary estoppel as generating rights in order to protect B's reliance. Analysis of the case law shows that proprietary estoppel is concerned with reacting to and protecting B's reasonable reliance, where A can be said to be responsible for the expectation on which that reliance was based. This particular form of reliance seems to be the unifying feature which justifies the courts' view of proprietary estoppel as a single doctrine.

Moreover, this aim of protecting B's reliance explains the diverse range of responses to a proprietary estoppel claim. It does not follow that protecting reliance will limit B to recovering the direct financial cost of his reliance. This is no surprise: the reliance B needs to show in order to bring a claim is not limited to financial expenditure; hence the reliance protected by B's consequent right is not so limited. This can be seen in *Crabb v. Arun District Council*. B's reliance in that case consisted of selling part of his land without reserving a right of access to his remaining land. Were A then able to deny B his expected easement over A's land, B would be left without access to that remaining land. That particular reliance could only be protected by allowing B to have the expected easement over A's land. In some cases, protecting B's reliance will require B's receiving a property right through an informal grant; in others it will require the enforcement of a promise by A; in others the reversal of A's unjust enrichment; in others the reimbursement of money spent by B. In each case, however, each response will not be a goal in itself but will rather be a means to the end of protecting B's reliance [. . .]

The use of proportionality in recent English decisions supports the view that the purpose of proprietary estoppel is to protect B's reliance: making a proportionate award, like finding the "minimum equity to do justice to [B]", entails recognizing that B has a right which adequately protects his reliance, but goes no further. The application of this principle in practice can be seen by a consideration of *Jennings v. Rice* [. . .] It is possible to take the [result in *Jennings*] as evidence of the wide discretion a court has when responding to an estoppel claim. Certainly, there is a tendency to equate the move away from the automatic enforcement of expectations with a move towards the courts having discretion to react to a proprietary estoppel as they see fit and even to re-distribute property rights. However [. . .] it is preferable to find specific principles which can be used to regulate that task: even when departing from expectations a court must, as Robert Walker L.J. emphasized in *Jennings v. Rice*, "take a principled approach". Admittedly, protecting B's reliance is a less predictable standard than routinely enforcing B's expectation: there will always be an element of judgement in gauging what is proportionate. The matter will not, however, be left to the unbridled discretion of the court: the crucial point is that the response to the estoppel will be guided by the goal of protecting B's reliance.

Robertson, 'The Reliance Basis of Proprietary Estoppel Remedies' [2008]
Conv 295, 300–3

The outcomes of the English and Australian cases fall into a clear and consistent pattern. In most cases it is found that the claimant's equity can be satisfied only by granting expectation relief, either *in specie* or in monetary form. In a small but significant number of cases it is necessary to grant more limited relief in order to give effect to the minimum equity principle. In a few cases the courts seek to quantify the claimant's reliance loss by reference to a mathematical formula. In a similar number of cases the courts prefer to adopt a broad-brush approach to relief, framing the remedy by reference neither to the value of claimant's expectations nor the extent of his or her reliance loss. Together those two categories of case, the mathematical and the broad-brush, show that the proportionality principle is playing an important role in the determination of relief in proprietary estoppel cases [. . .]

The minimum equity principle requires that, in fashioning a remedy to give effect to proprietary estoppel, the court must go no further than is necessary to prevent detriment. This principle recognises reliance-based harm as the core of the estoppel equity: the touchstone in the determination of relief is the overriding goal of protecting against harm resulting from reliance on inconsistent conduct. The decision in *Jennings v Rice* was based on a rejection of the idea that the purpose of proprietary estoppel is to protect expectations or to enforce promises [. . .] In *Commonwealth v Verwayen*, Mason C.J. said that, in giving effect to an estoppel, "[i]t would be wholly inequitable and unjust to insist upon a disproportionate making good of the relevant assumption".[120] Mason C.J. did not, however, explain why it would be unjust or inequitable to do so. If the expectation of a benefit and harm or potential harm, resulting from reliance, are both essential elements in the establishment of an estoppel, why should the claimant be limited to a remedy which protects his or her reliance interest? Why is it not necessary to protect the expectation interest? The answer is that both expectation loss and reliance loss are essential elements of the equity, and, once either the expectation is fulfilled or reliance loss is prevented, the relying party has no claim in estoppel. This is why it is said in estoppel cases that the relying party has nothing to complain about while the assumption is adhered to. It is also why even proprietary estoppel can, in some situations, have a suspensory effect: if the representor is able to and does give the relying party the opportunity to resume his or her original position, there is no longer an equity arising by way of

---

[120] (1990) 117 CLR 394, 413 (High Court of Australia).

estoppel. If either the expectation loss or the reliance loss is in one way or another avoided or taken away, the reason for the court's intervention comes to an end.

The reason reliance loss rather than expectation loss provides a loose cap on the remedy is simply that, where there is a discernable difference in value between the reliance interest and the expectation interest, the reliance interest is almost always the smaller. It usually makes no sense to expend £100 in the expectation of a benefit worth £50. Since both expectation loss and reliance loss are essential elements of an estoppel claim, the remedy must necessarily be limited by the smaller of the two measures. Once the lesser interest has been satisfied, an essential element of the claim has been removed. When the reliance-based harm has been prevented or compensated, there is no longer any need for the court to intervene. But just as we can say that, where there is no reliance loss, there is no claim, we can equally say that, where there is no expectation loss, there is no claim. For this reason, in the rare situation in which the claimant's reliance interest exceeds the value of the expectation, the expectation interest provides the upper limit of the remedy. *Baker v Baker* stands as authority for this proposition.[121] There, the claimant contributed £33,950 to the purchase of a house by his son's family in the expectation of having the right to occupy a room in the house for the rest of his life. The arrangement came to an end when the relationship between the parties broke down. The trial judge's award of (reliance-based) compensation in the amount of £33,950 was held on appeal to be unjustifiable because it exceeded the value of the expectation. The starting point should have been the value of the expectancy (the right to occupy), since that was less valuable than the reliance loss (the claimant's contribution to the purchase price).

In summary, then, the proportionality principle can be justified on the basis that both reliance loss and expectation loss are necessary to an estoppel claim. Where the lesser interest has been met, the equity is satisfied because an essential element of the claim has been removed. In those rare instances in which the expectation interest is less valuable, it will provide a cap on the claim. Almost invariably, however, the reliance interest is the smaller. That is why the minimum equity principle requires the courts to go no further in granting relief than is necessary to prevent reliance loss.

An approach in which the extent of A's liability to B is determined by the need to prevent B suffering a detriment as a result of his or her reliance on A's assurance is, at least, capable of being stated clearly; it is also consistent with the results in cases such as *Jennings v Rice* and *Davies v Davies*.[122] As we have seen, Lewison LJ in the latter case stated that: '*Logically, there is much to be said for [this] approach. Since the essence of proprietary estoppel is the combination of expectation and detriment, if either is absent, the claim must fail.*'[123] This also explains why the content of A's assurance sets a cap on B's recovery: if, for example, the potential detriment to B were to exceed the value of a right promised to B, B could not recover that full detriment.[124] This is because, if A were now to put B in the position that B would have been in had the assurance been kept, it cannot be said that A has acted unconscionably.

It cannot be said, however, that this approach has been finally adopted by the courts: other factors, such as the need to avoid unconscionable conduct by A, continue to feature

---

[121] (1993) 25 HLR 408.

[122] See too *Arif v Anwar* [2015] EWHC 124 (Fam), [2016] 1 FLR 359, [96], where Norris J considered: '*what relief is right and conscionable to grant so as to ensure that [B] suffers no detriment*'.

[123] [2016] EWCA Civ 463, [39].

[124] See e.g. *Parker v Parker* [2003] EWHC 1846 (Ch) (Lewison J): '*The expectation is the maximum extent of the equity*'.

prominently in the courts' reasoning.[125] For example, in *Ottey v Grundy*,[126] Arden LJ stated that: '*the purpose of proprietary estoppel is not to enforce an obligation that does not amount to a contract nor yet to reverse the detriment which the claimant has suffered but to grant an appropriate remedy in respect of the unconscionable conduct.*' As noted in section 2.4, one reason for allowing unconscionability to play at least a residual role is to allow a court to take into account the impact of changed circumstances on A's liability: there may be cases where, for example due to an unexpected change in A's position, it would not be unconscionable for A to leave B to suffer some detriment as a result of B's reliance on A.[127] On this view, just as in relation to the initial question of whether a proprietary estoppel claim arises at all, unconscionability could not be used to increase A's liability beyond what is necessary to prevent B's detriment, but it could be used in some cases to reduce that liability.[128] This would be consistent with the key point in favour of an approach focussed on detriment: the need to ensure that, whenever A comes under a duty or liability to B, whether because of proprietary estoppel or some other means, the extent of A's duty or liability, and hence of B's right, must depend on the reason, or reasons, for which it has arisen.

3.4 A FURTHER APPROACH: PROPORTIONALITY TO BOTH EXPECTATION AND DETRIMENT

In *Davies v Davies*,[129] Lewison LJ also noted the possibility of an approach in which '*the outcome will reflect both the expectation and the reliance interest and [. . .] will normally be somewhere between the two.*' B's expectation is not treated as a starting point, but it has a definite role in determining the extent of A's liability to B. This is because proportionality is interpreted as demanding that the extent of A's liability be proportionate to *both* B's expectation and B's detriment. Whilst there is some academic support for such an approach,[130] it appears to have some difficulties.

Mee, 'The Role of Expectation in the Determination of Proprietary Estoppel Remedies' in *Modern Studies in Property Law Vol 5* (ed Dixon, 2009, pp 405–6)

Consider the facts of *Jennings*, where the claimant acted to his detriment in the expectation of inheriting a house worth £435,000 and was awarded a remedy of £200,000. If the expectation had been to inherit a house worth £1,000,000, would this have justified an

---

[125] The analysis of McFarlane, *The Law of Proprietary Estoppel* (Oxford: OUP, 2014) ch 7 takes this into account by proposing that, in a promise-based case, the basic test is that A's liability is to do what is required to prevent B's suffering a detriment as a result of B's reasonable reliance on A's promise; but that it may be possible in some cases for A to reduce that liability by showing that it would not, on the facts, be unconscionable for A to leave B to suffer some detriment.

[126] [2003] EWCA Civ 1176, [61].

[127] See e.g. the discussion of Mummery LJ in *Uglow v Uglow* [2004] EWCA Civ 987 at [30]. For an Australian example, see *Germanotta v Germanotta* [2012] QSC 116.

[128] Note that the factor relied on by A must have some link to the elements of the claim itself: in *Southwell v Blackburn* [2014] EWCA Civ 1347, [2015] 2 FLR 1240, Tomlinson LJ at [20] rejected A's argument that the nature of A and B's unmarried relationship meant that it would not be unconscionable for A to go back on an assurance and leave B without a remedy.

[129] [2016] EWCA Civ 463, [39].

[130] Lewison LJ refers to Gardner, 'The Remedial Discretion in Proprietary Estoppel – Again' (2006) 122 LQR 492.

increase in the value of the remedy? In other words, in *Jennings*, the defendant 'promised Mr Jennings the moon and left him nothing';[131] would Jennings have deserved a greater remedy if he had been promised the moon *and* the stars? [. . .] it is difficult to see why, as a matter of principle, the claimant in a case like *Jennings* should receive an ever greater remedy, on the basis of the same detriment, as one increases the extent of the hypothetical expectation [. . .]

A central problem with an approach which gives a role to expectation as a factor in the determination of the remedy is that, unless it is to be an entirely arbitrary process, there must be some principled way of determining the extent to which the expectation impacts upon the remedy. However, no such principled mechanism is available. One must ask how, as a matter of logic, the remedy can be made proportional to two different values, the expectation *and* the detriment?

4 THE EFFECT OF PROPRIETARY ESTOPPEL ON A THIRD PARTY: PRIORITY AND THE DEFENCES QUESTION

4.1 INTRODUCTION

In land law, as we saw in Part A of this book, one of the most fundamental questions is as follows: if B acquires a right from A, when will it be possible for B to assert that right against C, a party later acquiring a right in relation to A's land? For example, we can go back to *Thorner v Major*.[132] In that case, the only question was as to the rights of David Thorner against Peter Thorner: any duties that Peter was under at the time of his death were also binding on Peter's administrators. But what if, before his death, Peter had fallen out with David, and sold the farm to a third party: would David then have had any claim against that third party?

As we have seen, for example in Chapter 1, as well as Chapters 5 and 6, land law provides a clear structure for determining this fundamental question of whether B can assert his or her initial right against C.[133] That structure depends on asking whether B, at the time of the sale to C, had a property right in relation to A's land. This in turn depends on the content and acquisition questions. First, is the right claimed by B capable of counting as legal estate or legal interest, or as an equitable interest? Second, has B in fact acquired that right? If B can show that he or she did have such a right then there is an issue as to the *priority* of B and C's competing rights. As B acquired his or her right before C, the question will be whether C has a defence to B's pre-existing property right.

Where does proprietary estoppel fit into this structure? The obvious answer would be that proprietary estoppel is concerned solely with the *acquisition* question: it is simply a means by which A can come under a duty or liability to B. The mere fact that B's right has arisen through proprietary estoppel should tell us nothing about the content of B's right: that will depend on the content of A's duty or liability to B. It seems, however, that, where proprietary

---

[131] [2003] 1 P & CR 100, [14].   [132] [2009] UKHL 18, [2009] 1 WLR 776.

[133] There is, of course, a separate question as to whether B can assert a new, direct right against C: see, for example, Chapter 7, section 3.3.1. In such a case, B relies on the new, direct right, rather than the right initially acquired from A.

estoppel is concerned, things are more complicated than the obvious answer would suggest. In answering the question as to whether B's right can bind C, the usual approach is to distinguish between two situations: (i) where the sale to C occurs *after* a court has made an order in B's favour; and (ii) where the sale to C occurs *before* such an order.

4.2 B'S POSITION *AFTER* A COURT ORDER IN HIS OR HER FAVOUR

The position here seems to be clear, and it is consistent with the obvious answer set out above. We simply need to examine the content of A's duty to B, as determined by the court order made in B's favour. So if, as *Thorner v Major*,[134] that duty is to transfer A's legal estate to B, then, at the date of the court order, B has an immediate equitable interest in A's land. In *Crabb v Arun DC*,[135] the Court of Appeal ordered that A's duty, arising as a result of proprietary estoppel, was to allow B a right of access over A's land. That right of access, in theory, could have taken the form of either a personal right against A (a licence) or a property right in relation to A's land (an easement). In the former case, B's right would not have been capable of binding C: as we saw in Chapter 7, a licence, even if A is under a duty not to revoke it, does not count as an equitable interest in land.[136] In the latter case, A's duty to grant B a legal easement would give B an immediate equitable easement and such a right would be capable of binding any third party acquiring A's land after the court order in B's favour.[137] It seems that, in *Crabb*, A was under a duty to grant B an easement: the detriment B faced consisted of having no means of access to his land and, to secure such access in the future, B required a right that was capable of binding not only A, but also any party later acquiring A's land.

In some cases, however, the court's order does not recognize that B has a property right. For example, in *Jennings v Rice* (see section 3 above) Mrs Royal (and then her estate) was simply under a duty to pay Mr Jennings a sum of money: £200,000. Because that duty to pay money was not in any way secured on the land,[138] it could only give Mr Jennings a personal right. So it seems that if the land had been sold to C *after* the court order in favour of Mr Jennings, he would have had no legal or equitable property right to assert against C.

4.3 B'S POSITION *BEFORE* A COURT ORDER IN HIS OR HER FAVOUR

The general view is that, before any court order is made in his or her favour, B has only an 'estoppel equity', or 'inchoate equity'—that is, a right to go to court. This is the case even if the test for proprietary estoppel has been clearly satisfied, so that we know that A is under *some* form of liability to B. This means that, if A sells the land to C *after* B has relied to his or her detriment on a commitment made by A, but *before* a court has made any order in B's favour, the crucial question is whether B's 'estoppel equity' counts as a property right.

---

[134] [2009] UKHL 18, [2009] 1 WLR 776.   [135] [1976] Ch 179 (CA).

[136] Although it is true that there have been some complications surrounding the status of an 'estoppel licence': these are discussed in Chapter 7, section 4.

[137] C may of course be able to rely on a defence to take priority over B's equitable easement: see e.g. the use of the lack of registration defence discussed in Chapter 3, section 3.2.3 and Chapter 16, sections 2–4.

[138] The possible forms of security right in relation to land are discussed in Chapter 25.

In relation to registered land, the position has now been clarified by s 116(a) of the Land Registration Act 2002 (LRA 2002).

Land Registration Act 2002, s 116

It is hereby declared for the avoidance of doubt that, in relation to registered land, each of the following:

(a) an equity by estoppel, and

(b) a mere equity

has effect from the time the equity arises as an interest capable of binding successors in title (subject to the rules about the effect of dispositions on priority).

The thinking behind this provision is explained in the following extract from the Law Commission Report that led to the 2002 Act.

Law Commission Report No 271, *Land Registration for the Twenty-First Century: A Conveyancing Revolution* (2001, [5.30])

Our concern was with the status of B's 'inchoate equity' that arises after he or she has acted to his or her detriment but before the court can make an order giving effect to it. Although the point is not finally settled, the weight of authority firmly favours the view that such an equity is a proprietary and not merely a personal right.[139] HM Land Registry treats it as such, permitting the entry of a caution or notice in relation to such equities. It has also been assumed that a person in actual occupation can protect such an equity in relation to land as an overriding interest. We pointed out in the Consultative Document that proprietary estoppel is increasingly important as a mechanism for the informal creation of property rights. To put the matter beyond doubt, we recommended that the proprietary status of an equity arising by estoppel should be confirmed in relation to registered land. It could therefore be protected by the entry of a notice in the register or, where the claimant was in actual occupation of the land in relation to which he or she claimed an equity, as an overriding interest. This recommendation was more contentious than our proposal in relation to rights of pre-emption. It was supported by 55 *per* cent of those who responded to the point (of whom there were not many). Those who opposed it were mainly academics, several of whom were defending their published views. On the other hand members of the legal profession generally supported the proposal. We have therefore decided to take the proposal forward, particularly as we consider that we are merely confirming what is probably the present law.

---

[139] [The report here refers to *Megarry & Wade's Law of Real Property* (eds Harpum et al, 6th edn, 2000, [13–028]–[13–032]). Law Commission Consultation Paper No 254, which first suggested the provision to become s 116(a) of the Land Registration Act 2002, listed the following authorities at [3.35]: *Duke of Beaufort v Patrick* (1853) 17 Beav 60, 78; *Inwards v Baker* [1965] 2 QB 29, [37]; *E R Ives Investment Ltd v High* [1967] 2 QB 379; *Voyce v Voyce* (1991) 62 P & CR 290, 294 and 296.]

It is important to note that s 116(a) does not mean that B's 'equity by estoppel' will *always* bind C. After all, any property right may be subject to defences. In particular, we have seen that, if C pays for and registers his or her right, C will have a defence against B's 'equity by estoppel' *unless*: (i) B has protected his or her equity by entering a notice on the register; (ii) *or* B can show that he or she was in actual occupation of the land at the relevant time.[140] For example, in *Chaudhary v Yavuz*,[141] the first instance judge found that, as a result of his dealings with his former neighbour (A) a proprietary estoppel claim had arisen in favour of Chaudhary (B). The former neighbour had however sold the land to Yavuz (C) before any court order giving effect to that proprietary estoppel claim. As C paid for the land and acquired registered title, he could rely on the Land Registration Act 2002 as a defence to Chaudhary's "equity by estoppel" as it had not been protected by the entry of a notice on the register and, on the view taken by the Court of Appeal, Chaudhary had not been in actual occupation of any part of A's land at the relevant time. The case can be contrasted with *Henry v Henry*,[142] the facts of which are set out in section 2.3 above. Calixtus Henry wished to assert a right not against Geraldine Pierre, who had promised to leave her land to him, but rather against Theresa Henry, to whom Geraldine had sold her land shortly before Geraldine's death. The case was governed by the law of St Lucia, and s 28 of the Land Registration Act (St Lucia) sets out the list of overriding interests: that list, includes, in paragraph (g), 'the rights of a person in actual occupation of land [. . .] save where inquiry is made of such person and the rights are not disclosed'. As a result, the Court of Appeal of the Eastern Caribbean Supreme Court concluded (and this point was not challenged on appeal to the Privy Council) that Calixtus' estoppel equity bound Theresa: as a result of his actual occupation of A's land, his estoppel equity counted as an overriding interest.

4.3.1 Should every 'equity by estoppel' be capable of binding C?

The position seemingly adopted by s 116(a) of the Land Registration Act 2002 is that, in the period before any court order in B's favour, B's proprietary estoppel claim gives B a right capable of binding C, a party later acquiring a right in A's land. This makes good sense in a case such as *Henry v Henry*, where the Privy Council advised that Calixtus was entitled to one half of Theresa's interest in the land. This means that if C had acquired a right in A's land *after* such a court order in B's favour, B's right (a beneficial interest under a trust) would clearly have been capable of binding C. A problem may, however, arise in a case where, had a court order been made in B's favour immediately before C's acquisition of a right, A would only have been ordered to pay money to B,[143] or to allow B a licence.[144] In such a case, B, after the court order, would have only a personal right against A; such a right is not, in itself, capable of binding C. It, therefore, seems strange that B should be in a stronger position simply because no such court order had been made, as B then has an 'equity by estoppel' which, under s 116(a), is capable of binding C.

---

[140] Section 29 LRA 2002: for discussion of this lack of registration defence, see Chapter 3, section 3.2.3 and Chapter 16, sections 2–4.

[141] [2013] Ch 249.   [142] [2010] 1 All ER 988.

[143] As was the case in, for example, *Jennings v Rice* [2003] 1 P & CR 8.

[144] As was the case in, for example, *Parker v Parker* [2003] EWHC 1846 (Ch).

On its most obvious interpretation, therefore,[145] s 116(a) has been criticized as it:[146]

> fails to distinguish between those proprietary estoppel claims in which the right acquired by B is only a personal right (such as a right to receive money from A, or a licence to use A's land) and those in which the right acquired is a recognized equitable interest (as where A's liability is to transfer A's legal estate to B or to grant B a recognized property right, such as a lease or an easement).

That obvious interpretation of s 116(a) was adopted in *Halifax plc v Curry Popeck*,[147] where the parties accepted that, in the words of Norris J, '*a proprietary estoppel, including an inchoate one, is a property interest.*' In that case, however, it seems clear that A's liability, arising under proprietary estoppel, was to grant B a legal charge. The decision in *Halifax plc v Curry Popeck*, like that in *Henry v Henry*, is thus consistent with the view that a right arising through proprietary estoppel should be capable of binding a third party only if it gives rise to a recognized equitable interest.

It has, therefore, been suggested that a different, more limited interpretation should be given to s 116(a).[148] Given that the section was expressly enacted 'for the avoidance of doubt', it can be argued that the term 'equity by estoppel' should be given a limited interpretation, and should refer only to cases in which two requirements are both met: (i) B has a proprietary estoppel claim; and (ii) had that claim been satisfied immediately before the time of C's acquisition of a right, A would have been ordered to grant or allow B a recognized property right.[149] Such an interpretation would of course differ from that intended by the Law Commission, but that is not a decisive objection.[150]

A possible further complication to the operation of s 116(a) was considered by the Privy Council in *Henry v Henry*.[151] Counsel for Theresa Henry, who had bought Geraldine's share in the land, argued that 'the test of unconscionability must be considered afresh in relation to the position of Theresa Henry as purchaser.'[152] That argument was rejected on the technical grounds that it had not been pleaded or pursued at the initial trial of the case, but Sir Jonathan Parker stated that the Privy Council '*does not rule out the possibility that cases may arise in which the particular circumstances surrounding a third party purchase may, notwithstanding the claimant's overriding interest, require the court to reassess the extent of the claimant's equity in the property.*'[153] There is some academic support for that position:[154] its logic is that, where C acquires his or her right before any court order in B's favour, C is bound by B's inchoate estoppel equity. In satisfying that equity, the court then has to consider whether C's action in attempting to deny B a right relating to the land is

---

[145] That interpretation is also consistent with the Law Commission's view, as set out above.

[146] McFarlane, *The Law of Proprietary Estoppel* (Oxford: OUP, 2014) para 8.83.

[147] [2008] EWHC 1692 (Ch).

[148] See McFarlane, 'Proprietary Estoppel and Third Parties After the Land Registration Act 2002' [2003] CLJ 661 and 693–6.

[149] Note that a similarly limited interpretation must be given to the term 'mere equity' in s 116(b) as it cannot be intended to refer to cases in which B has *any* sort of equitable right: see Chapter 21, section 3.3.2.

[150] See, for example, *Yaxley v Gotts* [2000] Ch 162 where Robert Walker LJ noted at 176 that the Law Commission report leading to the enactment of the Law of Property (Miscellaneous Provisions) Act 1989 'cannot be conclusive as to how section 2, as enacted, is to be construed and applied.'

[151] [2010] 1 All ER 988.

[152] This is how the argument was summarized by Sir Jonathan Parker at [46].

[153] [2010] 1 All ER 988, [56].

[154] See Gray & Gray, *Elements of Land Law* (5th edn, 2009) para 9.2.93.

unconscionable. Of course, B will have no independent proprietary estoppel claim against C, as C has made no assurance on which B has relied. So, in determining whether or not C has acted unconscionably, a court will not be able to rely on the three elements of proprietary estoppel but, presumably, must adopt a wider notion of what conscience demands of C. In contrast, if the general land law position were to be adopted, there would be no room for an independent assessment of C's behaviour: if B had an equitable interest before C acquired C's right in the land, and if C has no defence to B's right, B can assert that interest against C. It is difficult to see what, if anything, is to be gained by departing from this general position and making special rules for proprietary estoppel. In particular, it is surprising that s 116(a) of the LRA 2002, part of an Act that was introduced to protect the position of a third party purchaser for value of registered land,[155] seems to have rendered C's position so uncertain.

QUESTIONS

1. In *Thorner v Major*, why was Peter Thorner under a liability to transfer Steart Farm to David Thorner?

2. Is our understanding of how a proprietary estoppel claim differs from a contractual claim aided by Lord Hoffmann's metaphor, in his discussion of proprietary estoppel in *Thorner v Major*, that 'the owl of Minerva spreads its wings only with the falling of the dusk'?

3. In *Cobbe v Yeoman's Row Management Ltd*, should Mr Cobbe have been entitled to at least some of the increase in value of YRML's land, given that his work was crucial in obtaining the planning permission that led to that increase?

4. Can proprietary estoppel apply even if A (the party against whom proprietary estoppel is used) has acted perfectly innocently? How does the decision in *Taylors Fashions v Liverpool Victoria Trustees* affect your answer?

5. What role, if any, should unconscionability play in a proprietary estoppel claim?

6. Do you agree with the results reached by the Court of Appeal in *Jennings v Rice* and in *Davies v Davies*?

7. Does s 116(a) of the Land Registration Act 2002 impose a potentially unfair burden on a third party acquiring land subject to a proprietary estoppel claim?

For guidance on how to answer these questions visit the online resources at www.oup.com/uk/mcfarlane4e/.

FURTHER READING

Bright and McFarlane, 'Proprietary Estoppel and Proprietary Rights' [2005] CLJ 449

Dixon, 'Confining and Defining Proprietary Estoppel: the Role of Unconscionability' (2010) 30 LS 408

Gardner, 'The Remedial Discretion in Proprietary Estoppel—Again' (2006) 122 LQR 492

---

[155] See further Chapter 3, section 3.1, Chapter 18, section 1.1.

Hopkins, 'Proprietary Estoppel: A Functional Analysis' (2010) 4 Journal of Equity 201

McFarlane, 'Proprietary Estoppel and Third Parties After the Land Registration Act 2002' [2003] CLJ 661

McFarlane and Sales, 'Promises, Liability, and Detriment: Lessons from Proprietary Estoppel' (2015) 131 LQR 610

Mee, 'Proprietary Estoppel, Promises and Mistaken Belief' in *Modern Studies in Property Law Vol 6* (ed Bright, Oxford: Hart Publishing, 2011)

Robertson, 'The Reliance Basis of Proprietary Estoppel Remedies' [2008] Conv 295

11

TRUSTS

CENTRAL ISSUES

1. Beneficial interests under a trust of land may be acquired through an express, resulting, or constructive trust.

2. An express trust of land must be evidenced by signed writing to fulfil statutory formality requirements. Resulting and constructive trusts of land are exempt from this requirement.

3. A purchase money resulting trust arises where A purchases or contributes to the purchase of land in the name of B, or where land is purchased in the joint names of A and B, but with no express declaration as to their beneficial shares. The trust confers on the parties beneficial interests in proportion to their contribution.

4. The basis of the resulting trust remains subject to debate. There is also some uncertainty as to the relationship between the purchase money resulting trust and the common intention constructive trust, although it may be that recent developments have reduced the significance of the distinction between the resulting trust and constructive trust approaches.

5. Constructive trusts arise in a number of circumstances in which, through the existence of specific factors, it is considered unconscionable for the legal owner to assert his or her own beneficial ownership, and to deny the beneficial interest of another.

6. There is no exhaustive definition of the circumstances giving rise to a constructive trust. Two types of constructive trust are considered in this chapter: those arising under the doctrine in *Rochefoucauld v Boustead*;[1] and those arising under the *Pallant v Morgan*[2] equity.

7. Constructive trusts arise under the doctrine in *Rochefoucauld v Boustead* where A transfers land to B intending B to hold on trust for A, and where A transfers land to C intending C to hold on trust for B, a third party. If for some reason, such as a failure to comply with formality requirements, no express trust arises, it seems that a constructive trust is necessary to prevent the recipient of the property from reneging on the terms of an agreement with A by claiming the land for him or herself.

8. Constructive trusts arise under the *Pallant v Morgan* equity where one party acquires land pursuant to an informal commercial joint venture and

---

[1] [1897] 1 Ch 196, CA.   [2] [1953] 1 Ch 43.

> reneges on an agreement that another party will have an interest in the land. The non-acquiring party must have relied on the agreement, but it is not necessary that he or she acted to his or her detriment in so doing.

> 9. There is debate as to the basis on which each of the *Rochefoucauld v Boustead* and *Pallant v Morgan* constructive trusts arises, and also as to whether each trust can be seen as depending on a unifying underlying principle.

1 INTRODUCTION

In this chapter, we consider how equitable interests in land are acquired by the creation of a trust. Not all equitable interests take effect under a trust. The difference between equitable interests under a trust and other forms of equitable interests is explained in Chapter 6. There are three principal categories of trust that need to be considered: express, resulting, and constructive. These categories of trust are differentiated by their method of creation and, specifically, by the different role afforded to the settlor's intention in the creation of the trust.[3]

Snell's Equity (33rd edn, ed McGhee, 2014, [21-018]–[21-021])

A classification of trusts in these terms [express, resulting, and constructive] refers to the degree to which the trust arises through the expression of a settlor's actual intention to create it, or by operation of law and irrespective of the settlor's intention. The distinction is often a fine one, and depends on a close analysis of the relevant transaction.

(a) *Express trust*. An express trust is created by the actual intention of the person in whom the property is vested, as where A declares himself a trustee of Whiteacre for B, or conveys it to C on trust for B [. . .]

(b) *Resulting trust*. A resulting trust arises by operation of law, though in response to a legal presumption about the intentions of the person who transfers the property which becomes subject to the trust. If A transfers property to B when it is unclear whether A intends B to have the beneficial interest in it, then B may hold the property on resulting trust for A. The trust arises by operation of law to give effect to a presumption that A did not intend B to take the property beneficially.

(c) *Constructive trust*. A constructive trust is imposed by operation of law, rather than through the express or presumed intention of the owner of the property to create a trust or to retain any beneficial interest for himself. The trust may even arise contrary to the actual intentions of the owner [. . .] In other cases the distinction between constructive and express trusts is less clear. So a constructive trust may be imposed on property to

---

[3] This orthodox understanding of the relationship between express, resulting, and constructive trusts is contested by Swadling. He argues that 'only the express trust is genuine': 'The Fiction of the Constructive Trust' (2011) 64 CLP 399, 400. Swadling, however, includes as express trusts the purchase money resulting trust (discussed in section 3.1 below) and some forms of constructive trust (see 416–19). Other constructive trusts Swadling considers to be 'merely an inappropriate label' to describe particular court orders: 400.

give effect to a person's intention to make a gift to another or to act as an express trustee, but where the formalities necessary to give effect to the gift or the express trust have not been fully complied with.

A fourth and fifth category of trust are also commonly referred to. We note these categories here but they are not further discussed. The fourth category—the 'implied trust'—lacks a clear and consistent usage. It is sometimes used to refer to a trust created by a settlor, but where the settlor's intention is inferred, rather than express. This use of the implied trust has no application in relation to land,[4] where, as we will see, written evidence of intent is required. At other times, the expression 'implied trust' is used simply as an umbrella term for resulting and constructive trusts, in contradistinction to express trusts. The final category is the statutory trust. Trusts are imposed by statute in a disparate range of circumstances. The consequence can be significant for the unwary statutory trustee. One example is a purported conveyance of a legal estate in land to a minor. A minor cannot hold legal title to land[5] and the effect of such a transfer is a statutory trust under which the legal title is held on trust for the minor by the transferor.[6] In *Hammersmith and Fulham LBC v Alexander-David*[7] a local authority purported to grant a legal lease to a 16-year-old homeless girl. The result was that the local authority held the lease on trust for her. This had the practical consequence that the local authority could not terminate the lease using their usual powers as landlord as this would destroy the trust property. As such, it would be a breach of trust.

An alternative means of classifying trusts has been suggested based on the causative event that triggers the imposition of the trust.[8] This development should be seen in the broader context of the taxonomy of private law pioneered by Professor Peter Birks.[9] He demonstrated that obligations arise on the basis of consent, wrongs, unjust enrichment, and through a category of miscellaneous other events. This scheme appeals to a sense of logic and rationalization by aligning the creation of trusts with the creation of obligations in private law—but as the language of the traditional scheme is embedded in statute, and in centuries of judicial usage, a wholesale change appears unlikely.

Once a trust comes into existence, the method of creation and the consequent classification of the trust are of limited significance. Hence, the priority rules determining the enforcement of trusts against third parties (the defences question) operate in the same way, regardless of how the trust came into existence. Equally, express, resulting, and constructive trusts of land are all 'trusts of land' within s 1(2)(a) of the Trusts of Land and Appointment of Trustees Act 1996 (TOLATA 1996). That Act, which is discussed in Chapters 13 and 14, deals with the content question: it sets out the general rights of beneficiaries and duties of the trustees for all trusts of land. The Act draws no distinction between different categories of trust, except that, where a trust is created expressly, the settlor may make specific provision as regards those rights and duties. In some instances, however, differences emerge through specific rules applicable to trusts arising in particular circumstances. For example, as noted in Chapter 8, section 4.2, the constructive trust arising under the doctrine of anticipation where there is a contract for sale of land has some unusual features.

---

[4] *Lewin on Trusts* (19th edn, ed Tucker, Le Poidevin and Brightwell, 2014), [7–04].

[5] LPA 1924, s 1(6).   [6] Trusts of Land and Appointment of Trustees Act 1996, Sch 1, para 1(1).

[7] [2010] Ch 272.

[8] See *Snell's Equity* (33rd edn, ed McGhee, 2014), [21-023]–[21-026] and Swadling, 'Property' in *English Private Law* (3rd edn, ed Burrows, 2013).

[9] See e.g. Birks, *An Introduction to the Law of Restitution* (Oxford: Clarendon Press, 1985).

The classification of a trust therefore seems to be of secondary importance. In the beginning, it is more important to understand when a beneficial interest will arise than whether it is called an 'express', 'resulting', or 'constructive' trust.

Once these rules are understood, however, the issue of classification becomes more significant. The scope of resulting and constructive trusts ultimately lies in the development of doctrine by the courts. Rationalizing the basis on which these trusts come into existence can provide an important benchmark for distinguishing the uses and abuses of these doctrines. As a result, a seemingly sterile debate as to whether a trust should be seen as, for example, 'resulting' or 'constructive' may in fact be a debate about the reason for which the trust arises (or, in Birks' terms, the event giving rise to the trust), and precisely identifying that reason may have important practical consequences: it may, for example, determine the extent of a party's beneficial interest.[10] With this in mind, this chapter considers the application of express, resulting, and constructive trusts to land, and places this discussion in the broader context of current debate concerning the basis on which such trusts arise, and thus the means by which the beneficial interests under such trusts have been acquired.

2   EXPRESS TRUSTS

As we have seen, an express trust is one created by the actual intention of the settlor. The creation of express trusts of land is subject to compliance with formality requirements. These are contained in s 53(1)(b) of the Law of Property Act 1925 (LPA 1925).

Law of Property Act 1925, s 53(1)(b) and (2)

(1) [. . .]

    (b) a declaration of trust respecting any land or any interest therein must be manifested and proved by some writing signed by some person who is able to declare such trust or by his will;

    [. . .]

(2) This section does not affect the creation or operation of resulting, implied or constructive trusts.

An express declaration of trust is conclusive as to the existence of the trust. If the declaration specifies the parties' respective beneficial shares, it is also conclusive in that respect;[11] otherwise, the parties' shares will be determined by the application of resulting and constructive trust principles.[12]

Debate arises as to whether a trust that the settlor intends to create, but which does not comply with s 53(1)(b) of the LPA 1925, should still be classified as 'express'. One instance of this debate is considered below, as regards the classification of the trust arising under the doctrine in *Rochefoucauld v Boustead*. The better view, it is suggested, is that a trust of land

---

[10] As we will see when considering the debate about the boundary between resulting trusts and common intention constructive trusts in section 3.2.

[11] *Goodman v Gallant* [1986] 2 WLR 236.

[12] The quantification of shares in such cases is considered in Chapter 12, section 2.2.2.

should be classified as an express trust only where s 53(1)(b) is complied with. In the absence of compliance, the trust should be classified as resulting or constructive to invoke the exception in s 53(2).

3 RESULTING TRUSTS

As shown in the following extract, resulting trusts are traditionally defined by reference to the circumstances in which they arise:

Westdeutsche Landesbank Girozentrale v Islington LBC
[1996] AC 669, 708

Lord Browne-Wilkinson

Under existing law, a resulting trust arises in two sets of circumstances:

(A) Where A makes a voluntary payment to B or pays (wholly or in part) for the purchase of property which is vested either in B alone or in the joint names of A and B, there is a presumption that A did not intend to make a gift to B: the money or property is held on trust for A (if he is the sole provider of the money) or in the case of a joint purchase by A and B in shares proportionate to their contributions. It is important to stress that this is only a presumption, which presumption is easily rebutted either by the counter-presumption of advancement or by direct evidence of A's intention to make an outright transfer.

(B) Where A transfers property to B on express trusts, but the trusts declared do not exhaust the whole beneficial interest.

The resulting trust arising in the first of those two sets of circumstances is called a 'presumed resulting trust', although there is some debate as to what precisely is presumed in such cases. It can also arise where A makes a voluntary (i.e. gratuitous) transfer of property to B.[13] The orthodox view is that it is a presumption that A intended B to hold on trust for A, although it has instead been argued that the presumption is that a trust was declared in A's favour.[14] The resulting trust arising in the second of those two sets of circumstances is often called an 'automatic resulting trust', on the basis that it arises automatically if the intended express trust fails.[15] In the *Westdeutsche* case, however, Lord Browne-Wilkinson pointed out that the trust is not necessarily automatic in that sense, as: '*if [A] has expressly, or by necessary implication, abandoned any beneficial interest in the trust property, there is in my view no resulting trust: the undisposed-of equitable interest vests in the Crown as bona vacantia.*'[16] It has

---

[13] See e.g. Lord Millett, 'Pension Schemes and the Law of Trusts' (2000) 13 Tru L I 66, 73: '*Resulting trusts arise in three situations: voluntary payment or transfer; purchase in the name of another; and incomplete disposal of the beneficial interest. The first two have been described as "apparent gifts"; the last as "failing trusts".*'

[14] That argument is made by Swadling, 'A New Role for Resulting Trusts?' (1996) 16 LS 110; for the counter-argument in favour of the orthodox view of the presumption see Mee, 'Presumed Resulting Trusts, Intention and Declaration' [2014] CLJ 86, 90–4.

[15] See e.g. *re Vandervell's Trusts (No 2)* [1974] Ch 269, 274 (Megarry J).

[16] [1996] AC 669, 708, citing *re West Sussex Constabulary's Widows, Children and Benevolent (1930) Fund Trusts* [1971] Ch 1.

therefore been suggested that 'gap-filling' might be a better term for such resulting trusts, on the basis that A's intention that B should hold on trust is crucial and, on the failure of the intended trust, is given effect to by identifying A as the beneficiary.

An argument has been made that resulting trusts in fact have a much wider scope. Professors Birks and Chambers[17] have thus argued that a resulting trust arises as a result of A (the transferor or purchaser) lacking intention to benefit B, and the effect of the trust is to provide restitution for unjust enrichment. On this view, for example, the presumption in a presumed resulting trust is simply that A did not intend B to benefit from the property. On this view, there is no good reason to limit the scope of resulting trusts to the two traditional categories of presumed and gap-filling resulting trusts: such trusts are simply examples of a broader principle that aims to ensure B is not unjustly enriched at A's expense.

Chambers, *Resulting Trusts* (1997, p 220)

There are two requirements for every resulting trust: (i) a transfer of property (ii) in circumstances in which the provider of that property did not intend to benefit the recipient. The property may be any interest in any type of property or asset, so long as it is capable of being the subject of the trust. The provider may be the previous owner of the property in question or someone who has contributed to the recipient's acquisition of that property [. . .]

All resulting trusts effect restitution of what would otherwise be the unjust enrichment of the recipient. They are created neither by the consent of the recipient nor by the intention of the provider to create a trust. The resulting trust is not merely the passive preservation of the provider's pre-existing property interest, but is one of equity's active responses to non-voluntary transfer.

This broader view of the resulting trust was rejected by the House of Lords in *Westdeutsche v Landesbank Girozentrale v Islington LBC*.[18] The House of Lords preferred the traditional view as to the scope of the resulting trust, confining the trust to its two categories. Placing the resulting trust in the context of general principles of trust law, however, Lord Browne-Wilkinson added a further restriction, not apparent in the traditional treatment of the resulting trust, as he stated that the trust could not arise until the trustees' conscience is affected by knowledge of the factors giving rise to the trust.[19]

The chief practical differences between the traditional view of the resulting trust, on the one hand, and Birks' and Chambers' view, on the other, is that the former confines the operation of the trust to its two traditional applications. The chief practical difference between the traditional view and Lord Browne-Wilkinson's view, with the added requirement that B's conscience is affected, relates to the timing of the trust: on Lord Browne-Wilkinson's view, the trust does not arise until the trustee has knowledge of the factors that give rise to the trust. This difference in timing can be particularly significant where the recipient

---

[17] See e.g. Birks, 'Restitution and Resulting Trusts' in Goldstein (ed) *Equity and Contemporary Legal Developments* (Jerusalem: Hebrew University); Chambers, *Resulting Trusts* (Oxford: Clarendon Press, 1997). It should be noted that there has also been academic criticism of the Birks/Chambers account: see e.g. Swadling, 'A New Role for Resulting Trusts?' (1996) 16 LS 110, 116–17, Penner, 'Resulting Trusts and Unjust Enrichment: Three Controversies' in Mitchell (ed) *Constructive and Resulting Trusts* (Oxford: Hart, 2009); Mee, 'The Past, Present, and Future of Resulting Trusts' (2017) 70 CLP 189.

[18] [1996] AC 669.   [19] [1996] AC 669, [709].

becomes bankrupt between the date of receipt and the date on which the trustee becomes aware of the relevant facts.[20]

In relation to land, the most significant application of the resulting trust is the purchase money resulting trust, arising where A purchases or contributes to the purchase of land in the name of B. It is that resulting trust that we will focus on in this chapter. In such a case, which general analysis of resulting trusts is adopted may have no practical impact. The trust is within the two traditional categories and, because B will necessarily have knowledge of A's contribution, whichever analysis is taken, the trust will arise at the time of receipt. In view of this, and in line with prevailing judicial preference, the traditional analysis of the resulting trust is followed in the remainder of this chapter.

3.1 THE PURCHASE MONEY RESULTING TRUST

Where A purchases or contributes to the purchase of land in the name of B, a resulting trust arises. A classic exposition of the trust is contained in the following case.

Dyer v Dyer
(1788) 2 Cox 92

Eyre CB

At 93

The clear result of all the cases, without a single exception, is that the trust of a legal estate whether freehold, copyhold, or leasehold, whether taken in the names of the purchaser and others jointly, or in the names of others without that of the purchaser, whether in one name or several, whether jointly or successive, results to the man who advances the purchase money.

The link between the trust and payment of purchase money is reflected in the quantification of shares under the resulting trust. Each party receives a share in proportion to their contribution.

The precise nature of the presumption involved in the trust is contentious. On the Birks and Chambers' analysis the presumption is that A lacked intent to benefit B.[21] Swadling has argued that the presumption is an evidentiary one that an express declaration of trust has been made.[22] Both of these interpretations are rejected by Mee.[23] Through an analysis of case law, Mee argues, '*the presumption of resulting trust is a presumption that the transferor [A] intended the recipient [B] to take as a trustee for the grantor [A]*'.[24] Mee rejects the Birks and Chambers analysis, pointing out, for example, that the law has many different responses to

---

[20] See the discussion of *Chase Manhattan Bank NA v Israel-British Bank (London) Ltd* [1981] Ch 105 in *Westdeutsche v Landesbank Girozentrale v Islington LBC* [1996] AC 669, [714]–[715].

[21] See Chambers (1997) p 21.

[22] Swadling, 'Explaining Resulting Trusts' (2008) 124 LQR 72 and 74. Chambers directly refutes Swadling's views in Chambers, 'Is There a Presumption of Resulting Trust?' in *Resulting and Constructive Trusts* (ed Mitchell, Oxford: Hart Publishing, 2009).

[23] Mee, 'Presumed Resulting Trusts, Intention and Declaration' (2014) 73 CLJ 86.

[24] Ibid, 100.

cases where A makes a transfer to B but does not intend to benefit B, and so there is no principle that a trust must arise in such cases.[25] Mee considers that the case law does not support Swadling's interpretation of a presumed express declaration of trust, which causes specific difficulties in the context of purchase money resulting trusts: A cannot expressly declare a trust of property that he or she does not own, but which is transferred directly from the vendor to B. A can, however, intend B to take from the vendor as trustee for A.

Mee also makes the point that there was once good grounds for the view that a presumed resulting trust depends on a presumption that A intended B to hold on trust for A, as, historically, that was often A's intention when making a voluntary transfer of land to B.[26] Given, however, that the historical reasons for that assumption no longer apply, and also the differences between a voluntary transfer of land and a case where A pays all or part of the purchase price of land put in B's name, Mee questions whether the law should continue to apply the presumption[27] and proposes that the courts should instead try to ascertain directly the intentions of A and B on the receipt of the property by B. On that view A would be protected, where necessary, by finding a common intention constructive trust rather than a presumed resulting trust.[28] We will consider the differences between such trusts in section 3.2.

One important point in relation to the debate about the continued use of presumed resulting trusts in land arises from the following statutory provision:

Law of Property Act 1925, s 60

(1) A conveyance of freehold land to any person without words of limitation, or any equivalent expression, shall pass to the grantee the fee simple or other the whole interest which the grantor had power to convey in such land, unless a contrary intention appears in the conveyance [. . .]

(3) In a voluntary conveyance a resulting trust for the grantor shall not be implied merely by reason that the property is not expressed to be conveyed for the use or benefit of the grantee.

Whereas the presumed resulting trust of land is traditionally said to arise either when A pays for property put in B's name, or when A makes a voluntary transfer of land to B, s 60(3) seems, on a literal reading, to abolish the presumption in the case of the voluntary transfer.[29] This would mean that, in the very situation of a voluntary transfer of land from A to B, the situation that informed the historical basis of the presumption of resulting trust,

---

[25] Mee, 'The Past, Present, and Future of Resulting Trusts' (2017) 70 CLP 189, 208–9. For example, if the transfer to B can be set aside as procured by undue influence, A acquires a 'mere equity' rather than an immediate interest under a trust (compare e.g. *Mortgage Express v Lambert* [2016] EWCA Civ 555, [2017] Ch 93, discussed in Chapter 16, section 4.2.3); in other cases (e.g. where A lacks the mental capacity required to make the gift), the flaw in A's intention may mean that the apparent transfer to B is in fact void.

[26] This was because feudal restrictions that limited A's freedom to deal with legal title to land on A's death could be avoided if A instead dealt with an interest under a use (the forerunner to the trust): see Mee, 'The Past, Present, and Future of Resulting Trusts' (2017) 70 CLP 189, 192.

[27] Mee, ibid, 212.

[28] See too the extra-judicial suggestion of Lord Briggs, that: '*the only underlying principle of law is that a resulting trust will be inferred or implied (where not imposed in express terms) where to do so would give effect to the common intention or understanding of the parties*' (ACTAPS Newsletter 181, December 2014).

[29] As noted by Nicholas Strauss QC in *Lohia v Lohia* (2000) 13 ITELR 117, 129.

the presumption no longer applies. Whilst s 60(3) has no direct application to the case we are focussing on, where A provides all or part of the purchase money of a property put in B's name, this reading of the provision would lend some further weight to the argument that land law can do without the presumed resulting trust. The precise effect of s 60(3), however, remains unclear.[30]

3.1.1 Presumption of advancement

In a limited number of circumstances, due to the relationship between A and B, no presumption of resulting trust is currently drawn; instead, it is presumed that A did, in fact, intend to make a gift of the land to B. These cases are described as involving a 'presumption of advancement', or a 'presumption of gift'. The relationships to which the presumption of advancement applies were established by the early twentieth century and reflect the prevailing views of relationships in which there is a moral obligation for A to provide for B. Hence, the presumption applies to transfers from a husband to his wife (but not from a wife to her husband, or between cohabiting partners), and from a father to his child. In *Laskar v Laskar*,[31] the Court of Appeal assumed that it would also apply to a transfer from a mother to her child although counsel did not argue for its application on the facts.[32]

The values on which the presumption of advancement is based now appear outdated. Its continuing application on a transfer from husband to wife has met with particular criticism. A presumption is no more than a means of proving the existence of a fact. As Lord Diplock explains, this means that a presumption is only as valid as the underlying assumptions upon which it is drawn.

Pettitt v Pettitt
[1970] AC 777, HL

Lord Diplock

At 824

But the most likely inference as to a person's intention in the transactions of his everyday life depends upon the social environment in which he lives and the common habits of thought of those who live in it. The consensus of judicial opinion which gave rise to the presumptions of "advancement" and "resulting trust" in transactions between husband and wife is to be found in cases relating to the propertied classes of the nineteenth century and the first quarter

---

[30] On appeal from the decision of Nicholas Strauss QC, the Court of Appeal did not have to determine what Sir Christopher Slade called the '*knotty question whether the presumption of resulting trust on the voluntary conveyance of land survives the enactment of s 60(3)*'. The section was also not mentioned at all by the Supreme Court in *Prest v Petrodel Resources Ltd* [2013] 2 AC 415, even though it was held there that particular voluntary conveyances of land made on the facts gave rise to presumed resulting trusts. In *National Crime Agency v Dong* [2017] EWHC 3116 (Ch), Chief Master Marsh considered the differing views but proceeded '*on the basis that the presumption remains in being despite what has been described as the literal effect of the words in s 60(3)*'. For academic discussion of the section see Mee, 'Resulting Trusts and Voluntary Conveyances of Land' [2012] Conv 307.

[31] [2008] EWCA 347, [20].

[32] The application of thre presumption in relation to parents is considered by Glister, 'The Presumption of Advancement' in *Resulting and Constructive Trusts* (ed Mitchell, Oxford: Hart Publishing, 2009).

of the twentieth century among whom marriage settlements were common, and it was unusual for the wife to contribute by her earnings to the family income. It was not until after World War II that the courts were required to consider the proprietary rights in family assets of a different social class. The advent of legal aid, the wider employment of married women in industry, commerce and the professions and the emergence of a property-owning, particularly a real-property-mortgaged-to-a-building-society-owning, democracy has compelled the courts to direct their attention to this during the last 20 years. It would, in my view, be an abuse of the legal technique for ascertaining or imputing intention to apply to transactions between the post-war generation of married couples "presumptions" which are based upon inferences of fact which an earlier generation of judges drew as to the most likely intentions of earlier generations of spouses belonging to the propertied classes of a different social era.

Although the presumption of advancement still exists in a transfer from husband and wife, it will readily be rebutted. In *Stack v Dowden*,[33] Lord Neuberger noted: '*[T]he presumption of advancement, as between man and wife, which was so important in the 18th and 19th centuries has now become much weakened, although not quite to the point of disappearance.*'

While the courts have therefore made some attempt at modernizing the operation of the presumption, the underlying discriminatory treatment of transfers by husbands and fathers on the one hand and wives and mothers (subject to the assumption in *Laskar v Laskar*) on the other is impossible to rationalize in a modern context. The Equality Act 2010 contains a provision in section 199 for the abolition of the presumption of advancement. The section is not yet in force and will apply only to transfers undertaken after it comes into effect. Following abolition of the presumption of advancement, the presumption of resulting trust will apply to transfers in its place.

3.1.2 Rebutting the presumptions: general principles

The presumptions of resulting trust and of advancement can be displaced by evidence of the actual intention of A. Where the presumption of resulting trust is rebutted, A does not obtain a beneficial interest in the land despite his or her financial contribution to its purchase. Where the presumption of advancement is rebutted, the land is held on resulting trust for A, who provided the purchase money, just as in a case where the presumption of resulting trust applies.

Debate has centred on the nature of the evidence required to rebut the presumption of resulting trust. Evidence that a gift was, in fact, intended would clearly rebut the presumption of trust. But the presumption may be rebutted by a wider range of evidence, and this is consistent with the traditional view that the presumption drawn is an intention that B hold on trust for A. In *Westdeutsche v Landesbank Girozentrale v Islington LBC*,[34] Lord Browne-Wilkinson cited with approval Swadling's view[35] that (in Lord Browne-Wilkinson's words) '*the presumption of resulting trust is rebutted by evidence of any intention inconsistent with such a trust*'.[36] In doing so, he rejected the view that the presumption is rebutted only by evidence of an intention to make a gift.

---

[33] [2007] 2 AC 432, [101]. See further *Gissing v Gissing* [1971] AC 886, [907], in which Lord Diplock suggested that the presumption would seldom be decisive.

[34] [1996] AC 669, [708].

[35] Swadling, 'A New Role for Resulting Trusts?' (1996) 16 LS 110, 116–117.   [36] Ibid.

Lord Browne-Wilkinson's analysis in *Westdeutsche* is also significant because it emphasizes the importance of the parties' actual intentions. This means that it should only be in very rare cases that a result is determined simply by the operation of a presumption, whether it be of resulting trust or of advancement. This is consistent with Lord Kerr's statement in *Marr v Collie* that: *'save perhaps where there is no evidence from which the parties' intentions can be identified, the answer is not to be provided by the triumph of one presumption over another.'*[37] It is true that the comment was in the specific context of a supposed clash between the presumption of resulting trust and the presumption that, where legal title is in the joint names of A and B, the beneficial interest should also be held jointly by A and B, but it can also be seen as sensibly minimizing the role played by presumptions in the modern law.

3.1.3 Rebutting the presumptions: transfers for an illegal purpose

Until recently, it had been the case that presumptions could be very important in one specific context: where A transfers land to B, or contributes to the purchase of property in B's name, in order to facilitate an illegal activity. The approach taken by the House of Lords in *Tinsley v Milligan*[38] was that A was not to be permitted to bring evidence of his or her own illegal activity. So, if the presumption of resulting trust applied, all was well for A as A could simply rely on the presumption, and need not give evidence as to any actual intentions or scheme. Conversely, if the presumption of advancement applied between A and B (as where A is B's father) then A would face a problem, as rebutting that presumption would require bringing evidence as to A's actual intentions and thus of the illegal scheme.

It is clear, then, that the presumptions could be decisive in cases of illegal activity, and it seemed arbitrary that so much could turn on which presumption applied, especially given that, in general, relatively little evidence is required to displace either presumption. As it happens, in the leading cases, the courts were able to rely on specific facts to reach sensible results, allowing A to claim a beneficial interest proportionate to his or her contribution to the purchase price. In *Tinsley*, the presumption of resulting trust applied and A was able to establish a trust even though the reason for putting the property in B's name had been to allow A to make fraudulent social security claims. In *Tribe v Tribe*,[39] by contrast, the presumption of advancement applied, but the court held that A (B's father) could plead the illegal scheme and so establish a resulting trust, as the scheme had not in the end been carried out.

Nonetheless, the overall position was unsatisfactory. Fortunately, the courts now adopt a quite different approach to the general question of the impact of illegality on a claim, as can be seen from the following extract.

Patel v Mirza
[2016] UKSC 42, [2017] AC 467

The facts are unimportant for present purposes: they were not related to land law, but raised the general question of the impact of illegal activity on a claim.

---

[37] [2017] UKPC 17, [2017] 3 WLR 1507, [54].   [38] [1994] 1 AC 340.
[39] [1996] Ch 107 (CA).

Lord Toulson

[20]

Tinsley v Milligan has been the subject of much criticism in this and other jurisdictions, for its reasoning rather than its result, but this is the first time in this jurisdiction that its reasoning has been directly called into question. Two decades have since passed since the decision and it is right to trace the developments which have occurred in that period.

[Lord Toulson then considered the Law Commission's work on illegality,[40] which had criticized the approach in *Tinsley* and advocated a more flexible approach, allowing a court to balance a range of factors in deciding if, on the facts, illegality should prevent a claim being made. As well as examining the position in other jurisdictions, he also referred to case law since *Tinsley*, which contained some examples of courts taking such a flexible approach. He concluded that the *Tinsley* view should be replaced by such a more flexible approach.]

[101]

One cannot judge whether allowing a claim which is in some way tainted by illegality would be contrary to the public interest, because it would be harmful to the integrity of the legal system, without (a) considering the underlying purpose of the prohibition which has been transgressed, (b) considering conversely any other relevant public policies which may be rendered ineffective or less effective by denial of the claim, and (c) keeping in mind the possibility of overkill unless the law is applied with a due sense of proportionality.

There had been a long-running judicial debate as to the proper approach to illegality and, in *Patel*, Lord Sumption in a dissenting judgment favoured retaining the *Tinsley* approach of simply preventing a claimant from bringing evidence of illegal activity. Nonetheless, the position has now been clarified by *Patel*. The new approach is also consistent with the Court of Appeal's handling of the impact on an adverse possession claim of a statute criminalizing residential squatting.[41] Whatever one's view of the general question, the new approach certainly contributes to minimizing the modern impact of the presumptions of resulting trust and of advancement.

The judgments of the majority also confirm that, under that new approach, the results in *Tinsley* and in *Tribe* would remain unchanged. As to the former case, Lord Toulson stated that:[42] '*even if [A] had not owned up and come to terms with the DSS [the agency she had planned to defraud], it would have been disproportionate to have prevented her from enforcing her equitable interest in the property and conversely to have left Mrs Tinsley unjustly enriched.*' As to the latter case, Lord Neuberger[43] supported the result in *Tribe* as consistent with the general rule that a claim should be permitted where money has been paid '*pursuant to a contract to carry out an illegal activity, and the illegal activity is not in the event proceeded with owing to matters beyond the control of either party.*' Such analyses are broadly consistent with the proposal of the Law Commission that a beneficiary of a trust should be able to retain their interest and enforce a trust despite the illegality, other than in 'exceptional circumstances' where the court may exercise a discretion to deprive the beneficiary of their

---

[40] Law Commission Report No 320, *The Illegality Defence* (2010). The report contained a draft Trusts (Concealment of Interests) Bill.

[41] See the discussion of *Best v Chief Land Registrar* in Chapter 9, section 6.2.

[42] [2016] UKSC 42, [2017] AC 467, [112]. See too Lord Neuberger at [181].

[43] [2016] UKSC 42, [2017] AC 467, [151] and [171], referring to the general rule set out at [145].

interest.[44] Under those proposals, where the discretion is exercised, the court would then decide in whom the property should vest:[45] the approach proposed is (like the current law) one of 'all or nothing'.[46] Either the beneficiary obtains their full share unconditionally,[47] or they are deprived of their entire interest.

3.2 THE SCOPE OF THE PURCHASE MONEY RESULTING TRUST

3.2.1 The impact of the common intention constructive trust

The scope of the purchase money resulting trust is curtailed by its relationship with the common intention constructive trust. Where A purchases or contributes to the purchase of land in B's name, or land is purchased in the joint names of A and B, but there is no express declaration of trust, a constructive trust may be imposed to give effect to the common intention of the parties. We will examine the common intention constructive trust in detail in Chapter 12. The key practical difference between the constructive and resulting trusts relates to the quantification of the parties' respective beneficial shares. In the common intention constructive trust, beneficial shares are determined in accordance with the common intention of the parties, and so A's share need not be determined wholly by the size of A's financial contribution to the purchase price. In *Midland Bank plc v Cooke*,[48] for example, A's financial contribution of less then 7 per cent of the purchase price of a property registered in B's sole name led to the finding of a common intention constructive trust under which A and B each had a 50 per cent beneficial share.[49]

As noted at the beginning of section 3.1, it has been suggested that the presumed resulting trust should have a limited, if any, role in the modern law, and it is certainly possible to detect a judicial trend that favours applying a common intention constructive trust analysis.[50] Indeed, in the *Westdeutsche* case, Lord Browne-Wilkinson stated that resulting trusts are '*traditionally regarded as examples of trusts giving effect to the common intention of the parties*'.[51] It overstates things to say that was traditionally the case,[52] but it would be consistent with a move to focus more directly on the parties' intentions rather than simply on presumptions. On this view, it would be a mistake to say that there is a direct conflict between the purchase money resulting trust and the common intention constructive trust: each could be seen as serving the goal of giving effect to the parties' intentions, with the traditional resulting trust outcome of a share proportionate to the financial contributions being reserved for cases where, on the facts, such were the parties' intentions.[53] A key question then would be as to the quantification of interests

---

[44] Law Commission Report No 320, [2.58]–[2.60].

[45] Law Commission Report No 320, [2.87]–[2.99].

[46] Davies, 'The Illegality Defence: Turning Back the Clock' [2010] Conv 282, 291.

[47] The Law Commission considered but rejected the possibility that the court could impose terms on the beneficiary's retention of the property: Law Commission Report No 320, [2.81]–[2.86].

[48] [1995] 2 FLR 915.

[49] It is possible that A and B in fact initially had a joint beneficial interest, but it was clear on the facts that severance of any such joint interest had occurred: for severance, see Chapter 13, section 2.3.

[50] See nn 27 and 28.   [51] [1996] AC 669, 708.

[52] See e.g. *re Vandervell's Trusts (No 2)* [1974] Ch 269, 274 (Megarry J): the view expressed there that some resulting trusts are 'automatic' and do not depend on the intention of A is of course inconsistent with Lord Browne-Wilkinson's view.

[53] It is notable that whilst Lord Neuberger took a different approach to the other judges in *Stack v Dowden* [2007] 2 AC 432, preferring a resulting trust analysis to a constructive trust approach, he nonetheless reached essentially the same view as the other judges as to the size of the parties' beneficial shares in the property.

under a common intention constructive trust, in a case where an actual express or inferred intention of A and B as to the size of their beneficial interests cannot be found: in such a case, should a court simply find that the interests are determined by the proportionate financial contributions? As we will see in Chapter 12, section 2.2.2, the courts are now willing in such cases to 'impute' a common intention as to the size of the parties' shares and, whilst the size of their respective financial contributions will be a key factor (and, outside the purely domestic context, perhaps the decisive factor) it need not be the only consideration.

3.2.2 A role for the purchase money resulting trust?

There is no doubt that in standard family home cases, where the property in question is a home occupied by A and B as romantic partners, the size of the parties' beneficial shares will *not* be determined simply by their respective financial contributions:

Jones v Kernott
[2011] UKSC 53, [2012] 1 AC 776, [24]–[25]

For the facts and context of the case, see Chapter 12, section 2.2.2.

Lord Walker and Lady Hale

In the context of the acquisition of a family home, the presumption of a resulting trust made a great deal more sense when social and economic conditions were different and when it was tempered by the presumption of advancement. The breadwinner husband who provided the money to buy a house in his wife's name, or in their joint names, was presumed to be making her a gift of it, or of a joint interest in it. That simple assumption—which was itself an exercise in imputing an intention which the parties may never have had—was thought unrealistic in the modern world by three of their Lordships in *Pettitt v Pettitt* [1970] AC 777. It was also discriminatory as between men and women and married and unmarried couples. That problem might have been solved had equity been able to extend the presumption of advancement to unmarried couples and remove the sex discrimination. Instead, the tool which equity has chosen to develop law is the "common intention" constructive trust. Abandoning the presumption of advancement while retaining the presumption of resulting trust would place an even greater emphasis upon who paid for what, an emphasis which most commentators now agree to have been too narrow: hence the general welcome given to the "more promising vehicle" of the constructive trust.[54] The presumption of advancement is to receive its quietus when section 199 of the Equality Act 2010 is brought into force.

The time has come to make it clear, in line with *Stack v Dowden*,[55] that in the case of the purchase of a house or flat in joint names for joint occupation by a married or unmarried couple, where both are responsible for any mortgage, there is no presumption of a resulting trust arising from their having contributed to the deposit (or indeed the rest of the purchase) in unequal shares. The presumption is that the parties intended a joint tenancy both in law and in equity. But that presumption can of course be rebutted by evidence of a contrary intention, which may more readily be shown where the parties did not share their financial resources.

---

[54] See Gardner and Davidson, 'The Future of *Stack v Dowden*' (2011) 127 LQR 13, 16.
[55] [2007] 2 AC 432 [see Chapter 12, section 2.1]. See also *Abbott v Abbott* [2007] UKPC 53, [2007] 2 All ER 432.

Jones v Kernott, like *Stack v Dowden*, was a case where the legal title was held jointly by A and B, but there is no reason to think that the preference for the common intention constructive trust analysis is confined to such situations. In *Abbott v Abbott*, for example, a Privy Council case in which legal title to the home was in the sole name of B, Lady Hale again side-lined the resulting trust, stating that: '*It is now clear that the constructive trust is generally the more appropriate tool of analysis in most matrimonial cases.*'[56]

Does this mean that there is now no role for the purchase money resulting trust in domestic cases? In *Laskar v Laskar*,[57] where a mother and daughter jointly acquired legal title to a house, used by them as an investment and immediately let out to tenants, the Court of Appeal used a traditional resulting trust analysis to determine the size of the parties' beneficial interests. Lord Neuberger stated that:[58] '*it would not be right to apply the reasoning in* Stack v Dowden *to such a case as this, where the parties purchased the property as an investment for rental income and capital appreciation, even where their relationship is a familial one.*' Indeed, in *Stack v Dowden*, Lord Neuberger, whilst agreeing as to the outcome of the case, had expressed doubts about the reasoning of Lord Walker and Lady Hale, which could be seen to entail having to draw a distinction, which will not always be easy to make, between domestic and commercial contexts.[59]

It is significant, therefore, that a decision of the Privy Council, in a panel comprising both Lady Hale and Lord Neuberger, not only examined *Stack v Dowden* and *Laskar v Laskar*, but also set out an approach which does not depend on identifying in advance sets of situations where either the resulting trust approach or the common intention constructive trust approach applies.

Marr v Collie
[2017] UKPC 17, [2017] 3 WLR 1507

Mr Marr and Mr Collie were in a personal relationship with each other between 1991 and 2008. When the relationship ended, a dispute arose as to ownership of property they had acquired during the relationship, including land as well as works of art, a boat, and a truck. Legal title to the land concerned had been acquired in the joint names of Mr Marr and Mr Collie. In general, Mr Marr claimed full beneficial ownership of all the land, on the basis that he had almost entirely funded their purchase, and so argued that a presumed resulting trust analysis should apply as the land, like that in *Laskar v Laskar*, had been purchased for investment purposes. Mr Collie argued instead that the common intention constructive analysis, including the presumption of joint beneficial ownership operating in *Stack v Dowden* and *Jones v Kernott*, should apply, and that on the facts that presumption could not be rebutted. The Court of Appeal of the Bahamas found that, even though the properties were purchased for investment purposes, the parties had a common intention, when purchasing the properties, to share the beneficial interest in them, and so any presumption of resulting trust in Mr Marr's favour was rebutted. Mr Marr appealed to the Privy Council.

---

[56] [2008] 1 FLR 1451, [4].   [57] [2008] 1 WLR 2695.   [58] [2008] 1 WLR 2695, [17].
[59] For similar academic concerns, see Hopkins, 'The Relevance of Context in Property Law: A Case for Judicial Restraint?' (2011) LS 175.

Lord Kerr (giving the decision of the panel)

At [40]–[49]

At [56] in her opinion in *Stack* Lady Hale expressed the fundamental principle in commendably clear and simple terms: 'the starting point where there is joint legal ownership is joint beneficial ownership.' Although the statement was made in a case where the dispute between the parties was in relation to property which was a family home, there is no reason to doubt its possible applicability to property purchased by a couple in an enterprise reflecting their joint commercial, as well as personal, commitment. When Lady Hale said, at [58], that 'at least in the domestic consumer context, a conveyance into joint names indicates both legal and beneficial joint tenancy, unless and until the contrary is proved', it is clear that she did not intend that the principle should be confined exclusively to the domestic setting. Of course, when the conveyance occurs in circumstances where the parties are involved only in a personal relationship, the fact that they have elected to have the property in their joint names may make it easier to infer an intention that they should share the beneficial ownership. But that does not mean that where there is a commercial dimension to the acquisition of the property, the decision to have the legal ownership declared to be jointly shared is bereft of significance. The intention of the parties will still be a crucial factor.

At [59] *et seq*, Lady Hale addressed the question of how the prima facie position (that the legal and beneficial interests should be joint and equal where a domestic property was conveyed into the joint names of cohabitants) could be displaced. She posed the question whether the starting point was the presumption of resulting trust, reflecting the financial contributions made by the respective parties to the acquisition of the property or whether one should look at all the circumstances in order to discern the parties' intention. She pointed out at [60] that the presumption of resulting trust was not a rule of law and concluded that the 'search is to ascertain the parties' shared intentions, actual, inferred or imputed, with respect to the property in light of their whole course of conduct in relation to it.'

[Lord Kerr then set out [68] and [69] from *Stack*, which are extracted in Chapter 12, section 2.2.1. He then went on to consider Lord Neuberger's judgment in *Stack*, which had given a wider role to what Lord Neuberger called the 'resulting trust solution' and had thus differed from that of Lady Hale, even though its application led to the same result on the facts of *Stack*].

Where additional evidence is available in the form of testimony from the parties themselves as to what their intentions were when the property was acquired, even on Lord Neuberger's formulation, this can rebut the presumption of resulting trust. In that event, there should be a direct focus on what the intentions of the parties were. That focus could only be avoided if the decision in *Stack* could properly be regarded as applying only to purely domestic arrangements [. . .] the Board considers that it cannot be so regarded[60] and that the trial judge was wrong to dismiss it on that basis. In doing so, he relied on the decision in *Laskar v Laskar*.

[. . .]

In *Laskar*, of course, the co-funding of the purchase was required because the mother could not have afforded to buy the house herself. This was a joint investment impelled by her circumstances. Although the relationship was familial, the financial venture on which the parties had embarked was not associated with a mutual commitment to each other for the future. The investment could therefore be characterised as a purely financial one, designed to

---

[60] [Reference was made here to [38]–[39] of the judgment in *Marr v Collie*.]

pay dividends to each of the participants but shorn of any aspiration for a future equal sharing of proceeds. Further [. . .] the judge had found that there were no discussions between the parties as to the ownership of the beneficial interest in the property, and it does not appear to have been suggested that the court could or should infer any intention in that connection on the part of the parties.

The Board does not consider, therefore, that *Laskar* is authority for the proposition that the principle in *Stack v Dowden* (that a conveyance into joint names indicates legal and beneficial joint tenancy unless the contrary is proved) applies only in the 'domestic consumer context'. Where a property is bought in the joint names of a cohabiting couple, even if that is as an investment, it does not follow inexorably that the 'resulting trust solution' must provide the inevitable answer as to how its beneficial ownership is to be determined. Lord Neuberger [in *Laskar*] did not intend to draw a strict line of demarcation between, on the one hand, the purchase of a family home and, on the other, the acquisition of a so-called investment property in whatever circumstances that took place. It is entirely conceivable that partners in a relationship would buy, as an investment, property which is conveyed into their joint names with the intention that the beneficial ownership should be shared equally between them, even though they contributed in different shares to the purchase. Where there is evidence to support such a conclusion, it would be both illogical and wrong to impose the resulting trust solution on the subsequent distribution of the property.

At [53]–[56]

If what Lady Hale described as a 'starting point' (that joint legal ownership should signify joint beneficial ownership) is to be regarded as a presumption, is it in conflict with the presumption of a resulting trust where the parties have contributed unequally to the purchase of property in their joint names? A simplistic answer to that question might be that, if the property is purchased in joint names by parties in a domestic relationship the presumption of joint beneficial ownership applies but if bought in a wholly non-domestic situation it does not. In the latter case, it might be said that the resulting trust presumption obtains.

The Board considers that, save perhaps where there is no evidence from which the parties' intentions can be identified, the answer is not to be provided by the triumph of one presumption over another. In this, as in so many areas of law, context counts for, if not everything, a lot. Context here is set by the parties' common intention – or by the lack of it. If it is the unambiguous mutual wish of the parties, contributing in unequal shares to the purchase of property, that the joint beneficial ownership should reflect their joint legal ownership, then effect should be given to that wish. If, on the other hand, that is not their wish, or if they have not formed any intention as to beneficial ownership but had, for instance, accepted advice that the property be acquired in joint names, without considering or being aware of the possible consequences of that, the resulting trust solution may provide the answer.

Of course, the initial intention (or lack of it) at the time of purchase may change. This was the reason that the majority in *Stack v Dowden* emphasised that examination of the course of conduct of the parties over the years in which they dealt with the property is relevant. And it is why an intense examination is warranted of why the properties acquired in this case in 2008 were purchased in joint names. By that time, many of the contributions which, according to Mr Marr, he expected Mr Collie to have made, had not materialised. Why did he continue to agree that the properties should be acquired in joint names?

In this case, each party was relying on common intention, although they could not agree on what it was. Given the intention of the parties is central to the resolution of the issues in this appeal, has it been addressed sufficiently by the trial judge and/or the Court of Appeal?

The Privy Council concluded that neither the trial judge nor the Court of Appeal had properly examined the crucial question of the parties' intentions, and so the dispute was remitted to the Supreme Court of the Bahamas.

On one view, the decision in *Marr v Collie* could be seen as favouring the extension of the common intention constructive trust approach, by confirming that it is not confined to the classic shared home case of romantic partners acquiring a home in which to live together. It may, however, be better to see the approach in the case as limiting the differences between the presumed resulting trust and the common intention constructive trust, by emphasizing the key role played by the parties' intention in each type of trust. Indeed, Lord Kerr does note that, in some cases, the *'resulting trust solution may provide the answer'*,[61] but that will only be the case if a different intention as to beneficial ownership cannot be found on the particular facts of the case (or, presumably, if the facts show the parties did in fact intend that their beneficial ownership should be determined by the size of their financial contributions to the acquisition of the property).[62] The key question, therefore, is not as to the boundary between the resulting trust and the common intention constructive trust, nor as to the general distinction between domestic and commercial contexts, but rather as to the specific factual circumstances of each case, and what can or cannot be established about the parties' intentions in relation to beneficial ownership of the land.

4 CONSTRUCTIVE TRUSTS

Constructive trusts represent the broadest and least clearly defined of the three categories of trust.

Yeoman's Row Management Ltd v Cobbe
[2008] UKHL 55, [2008] 1 WLR 1752

Lord Scott

At 30

It is impossible to prescribe exhaustively the circumstances sufficient to create a constructive trust but it is possible to recognise particular factual circumstances that will do so and also to recognise other factual circumstances that will not.

Judicial attempts at definition have tended to be made at a high level of generality, as in the following case.

---

[61] [2017] UKPC 17, [2017] 3 WLR 1507, [54].

[62] In *Stack v Dowden* [2007] 2 AC 432, [117]–[120], Lord Neuberger considered, without needing to decide, if, for the resulting trust analysis, contributions made to mortgage payments could qualify as contributions to the acquisition of the property, and noted there was a strong argument in favour of including such contributions. If that is right, the gap between the resulting trust solution and the common intention constructive trust narrows still further.

Paragon Finance plc v DB Thakerar & Co
[1999] 1 All ER 400

Millett LJ

At 409

A constructive trust arises by operation of law whenever the circumstances are such that it would be unconscionable for the owner of property [. . .] to assert his own beneficial interest in the property and deny the beneficial interest of another.

The reference in this definition to unconscionability is significant, but of limited utility. In *Westdeutsche*, Lord Browne-Wilkinson considered unconscionability to be the foundation for the whole of the law of trusts. Notwithstanding, the constructive trust is the only category explicitly defined on this basis. The concept of unconscionability provides a common thread that ties together all trusts classified as constructive. The concept is of limited utility, however, because it does not operate at large. Indeed, in so far as it is indicative of a general discretionary jurisdiction to impose constructive trusts, it is entirely misleading. At best, it may be said that the combination of elements required for the imposition of a constructive trust in each particular application of the doctrine collectively establish conduct considered by the courts to be unconscionable.

4.1 INSTITUTIONAL AND REMEDIAL CONSTRUCTIVE TRUSTS

A key division in constructive trust doctrine is that between institutional and remedial versions of the trust.[63] Lord Browne-Wilkinson explained the difference between these in *Westdeutsche*.

Westdeutsche Landesbank Girozentrale v Islington LBC
[1996] AC 669, HL

Lord Browne-Wilkinson

At 714–15

Under an institutional constructive trust, the trust arises by operation of law as from the date of the circumstances which give rise to it: the function of the court is merely to declare that such trust has arisen in the past. The consequences that flow from such trust having arisen (including the possibly unfair consequences to third parties who in the interim have received the trust property) are also determined by rules of law, not under a discretion. A remedial constructive trust, as I understand it, is different. It is a judicial remedy giving rise to an enforceable equitable obligation: the extent to which it operates retrospectively to the prejudice of third parties lies in the discretion of the court.

---

[63] Although see Webb, 'The Myth of the Remedial Constructive Trust' [2016] CLP 353 for the view that the idea of a distinct 'remedial' constructive trust is a distraction from the key question of determining the grounds on which constructive trusts may arise.

This difference can be illustrated as follows. Assume that a claimant has fulfilled the elements of a claim to a constructive trust of land on 31 January 2015, but that a court does not decide the claim until 31 January 2018. If the trust is institutional, then the role of the court, having found the constituent elements of the claim to be established since 31 January 2015, is to declare that the trust arose on that date. Since that date, the claimant has had a proprietary interest in the land. If the defendant has sold the land since that date, or has become bankrupt, then the claimant's interest may bind the purchaser and the claimant will have priority in the bankruptcy against unsecured creditors. If, however, the trust is remedial, then the court has discretion to decide what effect, if any, it should have prior to its decision on 31 January 2018. The court, therefore, has a discretion to determine the claimant's ability to enforce his or her interest against a purchaser who has bought the land since 31 January 2015, and to determine whether the claimant should be treated as a secured creditor in a bankruptcy.

The remedial version of the trust has been embraced in North American jurisdictions, but its place in English law is uncertain. Undoubtedly, there are instances in which English courts impose a constructive trust as a remedy.[64] Nield highlights that a constructive trust imposed as the remedy for proprietary estoppel would be classified in this way.[65] Outside such isolated incidences, however, attempts to develop the remedial constructive trust have faltered.[66] The underlying objection to the remedial constructive trust is captured by Nourse LJ, who explained:[67]

> we must recognise that the remedial constructive trust gives the court a discretion to vary proprietary rights. You cannot grant a property right to A, who has not had one beforehand, without taking some proprietary right away from B. No English court has ever had the power to do that, except with the authority of Parliament.

Beyond isolated incidents of remedial trusts, the constructive trust recognized by English law is the institutional trust.

4.2 CONSTRUCTIVE TRUSTS OF LAND

There are five principal types of constructive trust that are specifically concerned with the acquisition of beneficial interests in land:

- the common intention constructive trust that is used to determine ownership of the home;

---

[64] See Liew, 'Reanalysing Institutional and Remedial Constructive Trusts' [2016] CLJ 528 for an argument that English law has more room for remedial constructive trusts than is commonly thought.

[65] Nield, 'Constructive Trusts and Estoppel' (2003) 23 LS 311, 312.

[66] Most famously, Lord Denning's remedial 'constructive trust of a new model' (*Eves v Eves* [1975] 1 WLR 1338, [1341], which has been supplanted by the institutional common intention constructive trust (discussed in Chapter 12). More recent suggestions that remedial constructive trusts may be a vehicle to provide a proprietary response to unjust enrichment (*Westdeutsche v Islington LBC* [1996] AC 669, [716] *per* Lord Browne-Wilkinson) or are a preferable device than proprietary estoppel to respond to promises of an inheritance (*Thorner v Major* [2009] 1 WLR 776, [19]–[21] *per* Lord Scott) have not found acceptance. The former idea was rejected in *Re Polly Peck International (No 2)* [1998] 3 All ER 812. In respect of the latter, Lord Scott's preference for the trust was not shared by the other members of the House of Lords.

[67] *Re Polly Peck International (No 2)* [1998] 3 All ER 812, [830]–[831].

- constructive trusts imposed on a vendor under a specifically enforceable contract for sale of land;
- constructive trusts arising to give effect to a proprietary estoppel claim;
- constructive trusts imposed under the doctrine in *Rochefoucauld v Boustead*;[68]
- constructive trusts arising under the *Pallant v Morgan*[69] equity.

The common intention constructive trust is considered in Chapter 12, while the trust imposed on a vendor has been considered in Chapter 8, section 4.2, and the operation of proprietary estoppel, which in some cases but not all gives rise to a constructive trust, was considered in Chapter 10. In this chapter, we will consider constructive trusts arising under the doctrine in *Rochefoucauld v Boustead* and the *Pallant v Morgan* equity.

5   THE DOCTRINE IN *ROCHEFOUCAULD V BOUSTEAD*

The doctrine in *Rochefoucauld v Boustead* stems from the maxim that 'equity will not allow a statute to be used as an instrument of fraud'.[70] Where land is transferred on trust, but the statutory requirements for an express trust are not complied with, a constructive trust is imposed to prevent the transferee from reneging on the trust and seeking to retain the property for him or herself. The paradigm case within the doctrine is a two-party case, in which land is transferred from A to B, to hold on trust for A. An extension to this paradigm is a three-party case, in which land is transferred from A to C, to hold on trust for a third party, B. These are illustrated in Figure 11.1.

The doctrine has been further extended to situations in which A transfers land to C expressly 'subject to' rights in favour of B, where the rights intended to be enjoyed by B have either been proprietary rights that do not generally take effect under a trust,[71] or personal rights.[72] In such cases, the courts have, notwithstanding, held that a constructive trust may be imposed to prevent C reneging on the 'subject to' agreement. This extension of the doctrine has been particularly significant in cases in which A has conferred a contractual licence on B (a personal right) and wants to protect B's occupation on a transfer of the land to

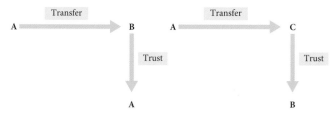

Figure 11.1 *Rochefoucauld v Boustead* in two and three-party cases

---

[68] [1897] 1 Ch 196.   [69] [1953] Ch 43.

[70] The relationship between the 'instrument of fraud' principle and the imposition of the trust is explored by Allan, 'Once a Fraud, Forever a Fraud: The Time Honoured Doctrine of Parol Agreement Trusts' (2014) 34 LS 419, 437–9.

[71] See *Lyus v Prowsa Developments Ltd* [1982] 1 WLR 1044, in which the transfer was made 'subject to' an option to purchase (an estate contract).

[72] See *Binions v Evans* [1972] Ch 359, in which the transfer was 'subject to' a contractual licence.

C. The imposition of a constructive trust pursuant to a 'subject to' transfer was considered in Chapter 7, section 3.3.1 in the context of licences. In this chapter, we consider the imposition of a constructive trust on a transfer of land from A to B on trust for A, or a transfer from A to C on trust for a third party, B.

5.1 THE TWO-PARTY CASE

The two-party case provides the factual context of the decision from which this doctrine takes its name.

Rochefoucauld v Boustead
[1897] 1 Ch 196, CA

Facts: Rochefoucauld owned coffee estates in Ceylon, but had been unable to pay mortgages on the estates. She transferred the estates to Boustead, who had subsequently sold them. Rochefoucauld argued that the estates had been transferred to Boustead on trust for her and that the surplus proceeds of sale (after discharge of sums owed to Boustead) should therefore be paid to her. The Court doubted that there was written evidence of the trust, as was required under the Statute of Frauds 1677—the precursor to s 53 of the LPA 1925.

Lindley LJ

At 206

It is further established by a series of cases, the propriety of which cannot now be questioned, that the Statute of Frauds does not prevent the proof of a fraud; and that it is a fraud on the part of a person to whom land is conveyed as a trustee, and who knows it was so conveyed, to deny the trust and claim the land himself. Consequently, notwithstanding the statute, it is competent for a person claiming land conveyed to another to prove by parol evidence that it was so conveyed upon trust for the claimant, and that the grantee, knowing the facts, is denying the trust and relying upon the form of conveyance and the statute, in order to keep the land himself.

The effect of the fraud was to enable oral evidence to be admitted as to the existence of the trust. On the facts, the Court was satisfied that the evidence established that the land had been transferred on trust in favour of Rochefouaculd.

5.1.1 Elements of the *Rochefoucauld v Boustead* constructive trust

The court's intervention is triggered by B's (the transferee's) denial of the trust pursuant to which the land was transferred. It is necessary only to establish that the land was transferred on trust and that the transferee has reneged on this agreement. In *Rochefoucauld v Boustead*, as we have seen in the extract in section 5.1 above, Lindley LJ described Boustead's conduct as fraudulent. It is important to note that Lindley LJ's reference is to the concept of equitable fraud. In equity, fraud is a broad concept and has no inherent connection to an intention to cheat, or to the tort of deceit. Equitable fraud and unconscionability have been defined by reference to each other, and nothing turns on the classification of the conduct as 'fraudulent' as opposed to 'unconscionable'.[73] Discussing the terminology of fraud and unconscionability in another context (that of proprietary estoppel), Scarman LJ commented: ' *"[F]raud" was a word often in the mouths of those robust judges who adorned the bench in the 19th century. It is less often in the mouths of the more wary judicial spirits today who sit upon the bench.'*[74]

The key difficulty with the concept of fraud in *Rochefoucauld v Boustead* is that the fraud consists in denying the trust, which is the very thing that s 53(1)(b) of the LPA 1925 requires to be evidenced in writing.

Hopkins, *The Informal Acquisition of Rights in Land* (2000, pp 31–2)

Applied broadly, *Rochefoucauld v. Boustead* has the effect that when land is transferred on trust, the trust is enforced as long as it is evidenced: in writing (within section 53(1)(b)); or orally. The effect of such a rule would be to reduce section 53(1)(b) to trusts declared by (current) holders of land. This would be a startling result for a rule purportedly based on the prevention of fraud. The underlying difficulty is in determining why the denial of an informal trust should, in some circumstances, be considered fraudulent [. . .] it may be argued that the fraud lies in the combination of the trustee's wrongdoing and the harm to the transferor [. . .] However, it seems that such a definition does no more than beg the question as to the nature of the underlying wrongdoing and harm, in light of non-compliance with statutory formalities.

Three important points about the operation of the doctrine in *Rochefoucauld v Boustead* are derived from its application in the following case.

Bannister v Bannister
[1948] 2 All ER 133, CA

Facts: The defendant had inherited two cottages, one of which was her home, on the death of her husband. She transferred the cottages to the plaintiff, her brother-in-law, for less than the market value, pursuant to an oral agreement that she would remain living in her home, rent-free, for life. The plaintiff reneged on the agreement and sought possession of the defendant's home.

Scott LJ

At 136

It is, we think, clearly a mistake to suppose that the equitable principle on which a constructive trust is raised against a person who insists on the absolute character of a conveyance to himself for the purpose of defeating a beneficial interest, which, according to the

---

[73] See *Nocton v Lord Ashburton* [1914] AC 932, [954]; *Semiahmoo Indian Band v Canada* (1997) 148 DLR (4th) 523, 551–2. Further discussion of the relationship between these terms is provided by Hopkins, 'Understanding Unconscionability in Proprietary Estoppel' (2004) 20 JCL 210, 212–14.

[74] *Crabb v Arun DC* [1976] 1 Ch 179, [195].

> true bargain, was to belong to another, is confined to cases in which the conveyance itself was fraudulently obtained. The fraud which brings the principle into play arises as soon as the absolute character of the conveyance is set up for the purpose of defeating the beneficial interest, and that is the fraud to cover which the Statute of Frauds or the corresponding provisions of the Law of Property Act, 1925 cannot be called in aid in cases in which no written evidence of the real bargain is available. Nor is it, in our opinion, necessary that the bargain on which the absolute conveyance is made should include any express stipulation that the grantee is in so many words to hold as trustee. It is enough that the bargain should have included a stipulation under which some sufficiently defined beneficial interest in the property was to be taken by another.

It is clear, therefore, that: firstly, the conveyance need not be obtained by fraud; secondly, the transfer need not use the technical language of trust; and thirdly, that no weight was given to the fact that the conveyance was at an undervalue. Intervention was triggered solely by the fraud consisting in the denial of the trust. As we will see below, this is significant in understanding the basis of intervention.

5.1.2. The classification of the trust: express or constructive?

In *Rochefoucauld v Boustead*, the Court classified the trust as an express trust. Without doubt, the trust was one that the parties intended to create. On that basis, Swadling considers that the trust is correctly considered to be express.[75] But the classification of the trust was discussed in the context of the prevailing Statute of Limitations.[76] As McFarlane explains, the classification of a trust for that purpose is not conclusive. (In this extract C is the transferee.)

McFarlane, 'Constructive Trusts Arising on Receipt of Property Sub Conditione'
(2004) 120 LQR 667, p 675

> [The] characterisation of trusts adopted when applying limitation statutes cannot be taken as definitive: to say that a trust is to be treated as an express trust "within the meaning" of a limitation statute is not the same as saying that trust is an express trust for all purposes. As far as the current inquiry is concerned, the critical question is: "what is the event which leads the court to recognise the new right arising on the transfer to C in *Rochefoucauld*?" On this point, there seems to be little controversy. On the constructive trust analysis, the trust does not arise simply because the former owner of the property so intended; rather, the trust arises to prevent C's reneging on the understanding subject to which he received the property. The trust is therefore constructive, and can arise without being manifested and proved by writing. It is thus possible to accept the view in *Rochefoucauld* that the trust is an express one for limitation purposes, as it was one that B (and C) intended to create, without admitting that the trust is an express one in the sense that this intention is by itself sufficient to create the trust.

---

[75] Swadling, 'The Nature of the Trust in *Rochefoucauld v Boustead*' in *Constructive and Resulting Trusts* (ed Mitchell, Oxford: Hart, 2009); Swadling, 'The Fiction of the Constructive Trust' (2011) 64 CLP 399, pp 416–17.

[76] A point discussed by Swadling, 'The Nature of the Trust in *Rochefoucauld v Boustead*' ibid.

While the parties in *Rochefoucauld v Boustead* intended a trust, this was not the basis upon which a trust was imposed: the trust was imposed to prevent Boustead's fraudulent denial of the agreement pursuant to which the land was transferred. As we have noted, nothing turns on the description of the conduct as fraudulent rather than unconscionable. The trust was therefore imposed to prevent unconscionable conduct and contrary to the view maintained by Swadling is correctly classified as a constructive trust.[77] This classification of the trust was adopted by the Court of Appeal (without discussion) in *Bannister v Bannister.*[78]

5.2 THE THREE-PARTY CASE

As we have noted, the three-party case involves a transfer of land from A to C on trust for B. This is only a slight extension from the paradigm two-party case and there is no doubt that the doctrine in *Rochefoucauld v Boustead* applies in this context.[79] The doctrine has been further applied beyond this factual matrix, where the agreement for the trust in favour of B is entered into between C (the transferee) and a party (X) providing finance for the purchase of land (Figure 11.2).

Neale v Willis
(1968) 19 P & CR 836, CA

Facts: A husband obtained a loan from his mother-in-law in connection with the purchase of the house. The loan was made pursuant to an agreement that the house would be bought in the joint names of the husband and wife. The husband reneged on this agreement and bought the house in his sole name. Following the couple's divorce, the question arose as to the beneficial ownership of the house.

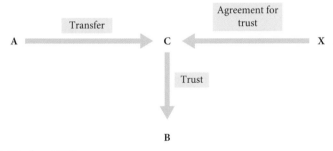

Figure 11.2 *Neale v Willis*

---

[77] Hopkins, 'Conscience, Discretion and the Creation of Property Rights' (2006) 26 LS 475, 480. The classification of the trust as constructive is supported by Allan, 'Once a Fraud, Forever a Fraud: The Time Honoured Doctrine of Parol Agreement Trusts' (2014) 34 LS 419.

[78] [1948] 2 All ER 133.

[79] See Youdan (1984) p 326. See too *de Bruyne v de Bruyne* [2010] EWCA Civ 519, as discussed by Liew, *Rationalising Constructive Trusts* (Oxford: Hart, 2017) 77–8.

Lord Denning MR

At 839

This was a binding contract and a court of equity will not allow the husband to go back on it. It will enforce it by holding that the husband holds the property on a constructive trust for himself and his wife. This follows from *Bannister v Bannister*. That case shows that if a person who takes a conveyance to himself, which is absolute in form, nevertheless has made a bargain that he will give a beneficial interest to another, he will be held to be a constructive trustee for it for the other. He cannot insist on the absolute character of a conveyance to himself for the purpose of defeating a beneficial interest which according to the true bargain is to belong to another. So here we have a husband who is seeking to insist on the absolute character of the conveyance to himself and to him alone. He does it for the purpose of defeating a beneficial interest which according to the true bargain was to belong to his wife. He holds it on a constructive trust to carry out the bargain.

5.2.1 In whose favour does the constructive trust operate?

The key question that has arisen in three-party cases is whether the trust should operate in favour of B, the intended beneficiary, or A, the transferor. The debate has been complicated by the absence of clear authority,[80] and the consequential impact on this issue of competing views as to the nature of the trust in issue and the basis of intervention. Hence, if *Rochefoucauld v Boustead* enforces the parties' express trust, then, in the three-party case, the trust necessarily operates in favour of B. If the doctrine is founded on unjust enrichment, then this necessarily dictates intervention in favour of A, as the party at whose expense C is otherwise unjustly enriched.[81]

It was argued in section 5.1, however, that the doctrine imposes a constructive trust in response to C's fraudulent or unconscionable conduct. The question is then whether C's conduct can best be seen as unconscionable vis-à-vis A or vis-à-vis B. Youdan and Feltham expressed opposing views: Youdan supporting the claim of B,[82] and Feltham, that of A.[83] In favour of a trust for A, the purpose of the doctrine is to prevent C's fraudulent or unconscionable conduct, and intervention should go no further than is necessary to achieve this purpose. B is a volunteer and 'equity does not assist a volunteer'. The imposition of a trust in favour of A provides A with a further opportunity to benefit B. Finally, intervention in favour of A does less violence to the formality requirement in s 53(1)(b) of the LPA 1925.[84] In favour of a trust for B is the point made by Liew that, if C were in fact to honour the agreement to confer a right on B, it is very unlikely that A could complain and claim a trust in A's favour. Why should B's position then depend on whether or not C does honour the agreement?[85] Further, if, as suggested by Lord Denning in the extract from *Neale v Willis* above, C's unconscionable conduct lies in departing from the agreement subject to which the property was transferred to C, an agreement to give a right to B, then the most direct response is to enforce that agreement by recognizing B's interest.

---

[80] Although, as noted by Liew, *Rationalising Constructive Trusts* (Oxford: Hart, 2017) 77–8, the decision in *de Bruyne v de Bruyne* [2010] EWCA Civ 519 provides support for a trust in favour of B, the point was not fully argued in that case.

[81] See the example discussed by Worthington (2006) pp 203–4.

[82] [1984] CLJ 306, [1988] Conv 267.   [83] [1987] Conv 246.

[84] Youdan (1984) p 335; Worthington (2006) p 204.

[85] Liew, *Rationalising Constructive Trusts* (Oxford: Hart, 2017) 75.

It is of course also possible to adopt an intermediate position, arguing that intervention in favour of B is justified only in particular circumstances:

Hopkins, *The Informal Acquisition of Rights in Land* (2000, pp 37–8)

First, there may be exceptional circumstances where intervention in [B's] favour is the only means of preventing fraud. This possibility is illustrated by *Neale v. Willis* [. . .] it would not have been appropriate for the land to be held in favour of the mother-in-law with whom the agreement had been entered. The agreement did not envisage that she, as a lender, should acquire rights in the house.

Secondly, an assumption underlying the reasoning against [B] is that A will have another opportunity to grant rights to [B]. There are circumstances in which no such opportunity in practice arises. The clearest example is where A has died. On a strict view this (unlike the first situation) does not alter the reasoning against [B]. The purpose of the rule, of preventing fraud, is still achieved by vesting the beneficial interest in A's estate. However, a concession in favour of [B] may be justified in terms of giving effect to A's intentions as he has died in the belief the gift was effective.

---

6 THE *PALLANT V MORGAN* CONSTRUCTIVE TRUST

Although taking its name from the decision in *Pallant v Morgan*,[86] the operation of this constructive trust received its most comprehensive judicial analysis and rationalization in *Banner Homes Group plc v Luff Developments Ltd*.[87] As Nield has demonstrated, the origins of the trust ultimately lie in the doctrine of *Rochefoucauld v Boustead*.[88] As with the doctrine in *Rochefoucauld v Boustead*, the trigger for the imposition of the constructive trust lies in the transferee of land reneging on an agreement pursuant to which land is acquired—but the agreement arises in a different factual matrix and the finding of unconscionability is not based solely on the transferee reneging on the agreement.

6.1 THE ELEMENTS OF THE *PALLANT V MORGAN* CONSTRUCTIVE TRUST

The requirements of the claim were enumerated in *Banner Homes*.

Banner Homes Group plc v Luff Developments Ltd
[2000] Ch 372, CA

Facts: Banner Homes (the claimant) and Luff Developments (the defendant) had commenced negotiations for a joint venture for the acquisition of development land. The parties had reached an agreement in principle for the joint venture, but no contract had been concluded, when the land was acquired by S Ltd, a wholly owned subsidiary of

---

[86] [1953] 1 Ch 43.   [87] [2000] Ch 372.
[88] Nield, 'Constructive Trusts and Estoppel' (2003) 23 LS 311, 315.

Luff. Unknown to Banner Homes, Luff had had second thoughts about the suitability of Banner Homes as a joint venture partner. Luff had not informed Banner Homes of this, out of concern that Banner Homes would mount a rival bid for the land. Banner Homes sought to establish entitlement to the land through a constructive trust.

Chadwick LJ

At 397–400

It is important, however, to identify the features which will give rise to a *Pallant v. Morgan* equity and to define its scope; while keeping in mind that it is undesirable to attempt anything in the nature of an exhaustive classification [. . .]

1. A *Pallant v. Morgan* equity may arise where the arrangement or understanding on which it is based precedes the acquisition of the relevant property by one party to that arrangement. It is the pre-acquisition arrangement which colours the subsequent acquisition by the defendant and leads to his being treated as a trustee if he seeks to act inconsistently with it [. . .]

2. It is unnecessary that the arrangement or understanding should be contractually enforceable. Indeed, if there is an agreement which is enforceable as a contract, there is unlikely to be any need to invoke the *Pallant v. Morgan* equity; equity can act through the remedy of specific performance and will recognise the existence of a corresponding trust [. . .]

3. It is necessary that the pre-acquisition arrangement or understanding should contemplate that one party ("the acquiring party") will take steps to acquire the relevant property; and that, if he does so, the other party ("the non-acquiring party") will obtain some interest in that property. Further, it is necessary that (whatever private reservations the acquiring party may have) he has not informed the non-acquiring party before the acquisition (or, perhaps more accurately, before it is too late for the parties to be restored to a position of no advantage/no detriment) that he no longer intends to honour the arrangement or understanding.

4. It is necessary that, in reliance on the arrangement or understanding, the non-acquiring party should do (or omit to do) something which confers an advantage on the acquiring party in relation to the acquisition of the property; or is detrimental to the ability of the non-acquiring party to acquire the property on equal terms. It is the existence of the advantage to the one, or detriment to the other, gained or suffered as a consequence of the arrangement or understanding, which leads to the conclusion that it would be inequitable or unconscionable to allow the acquiring party to retain the property for himself, in a manner inconsistent with the arrangement or understanding which enabled him to acquire it. *Pallant v. Morgan* [1953] Ch. 43 itself provides an illustration of this principle. There was nothing inequitable in allowing the defendant to retain for himself the lot (lot 15) in respect to which the plaintiff's agent had no instructions to bid. In many cases the advantage/detriment will be found in the agreement of the non-acquiring party to keep out of the market. That will usually be both to the advantage of the acquiring party—in that he can bid without competition from the non-acquiring party—and to the detriment of the non-acquiring party—in that he loses the opportunity to acquire the property for himself. But there may be advantage to the one without corresponding detriment to the other. Again, *Pallant v. Morgan* provides an illustration. The plaintiff's agreement (through his agent) to keep out of the bidding gave an advantage to the defendant—in that he was able to obtain the property for a lower price than would otherwise have been possible; but the failure of the plaintiff's agent to bid did not, in fact, cause detriment to the

plaintiff—because, on the facts, the agent's instructions would not have permitted him to outbid the defendant. Nevertheless, the equity was invoked.

5. That leads, I think, to the further conclusions: (i) that although, in many cases, the advantage/detriment will be found in the agreement of the non-acquiring party to keep out of the market, that is not a necessary feature; and (ii) that although there will usually be advantage to the one and correlative disadvantage to the other, the existence of both advantage and detriment is not essential—either will do. What is essential is that the circumstances make it inequitable for the acquiring party to retain the property for himself in a manner inconsistent with the arrangement or understanding on which the non-acquiring party has acted. Those circumstances may arise where the non-acquiring party was never "in the market" for the whole of the property to be acquired; but (on the faith of an arrangement or understanding that he shall have a part of that property) provides support in relation to the acquisition of the whole which is of advantage to the acquiring party. They may arise where the assistance provided to the acquiring party (in pursuance of the arrangement or understanding) involves no detriment to the non-acquiring party; or where the non-acquiring party acts to his detriment (in pursuance of the arrangement or understanding) without the acquiring party obtaining any advantage therefrom.

On the facts of the case, the requirements for the constructive trust were fulfilled. There was a pre-acquisition agreement (falling short of a specifically enforceable contract) that a jointly owned company would acquire the land. Banner Homes had relied on this agreement by treating the site as 'out of play', as a potential acquisition in its own right.[89] This conferred an advantage on Luff of keeping Banner Homes out of the market as a potential competitor. The shares in S Ltd were, therefore, to be held on constructive trust for Banner Homes and Luff equally, charged with the payment by Banner Homes of half the purchase price.

Subsequent case law has cast light on the interpretation of individual elements of a claim. In doing so, courts have indicated that there is little room for manoeuvre around the elements stated by Chadwick LJ. Perhaps as a result, the *Pallant v Morgan* trust has been described as being 'notable for instances of its rejection, rather than its successful application'.[90] In *Yeoman's Row Management Ltd v Cobbe*,[91] the House of Lords held that *Pallant v Morgan* was not applicable, because the land in question was already owned by one of the parties to the joint venture agreement. The Court of Appeal also noted this factor in rejecting a claim in *London & Regional Investments Ltd v TBI plc*.[92] In that case, in any event, the claim failed, because the negotiations between the parties had been conducted expressly 'subject to contract'. In these circumstances, it was not unconscionable for the party to withdraw from discussions following the acquisition of the land.[93] In *Kilcarne Holdings Ltd v Targetfellow (Birmingham) Ltd*,[94] it was suggested that it was not essential for the non-acquiring party to have intended to obtain the land on their own account. The claim failed on the facts, however, because there was no agreement that the property would be acquired for the parties' joint benefit. In *Crossco No 4 Unlimited v Jolan Ltd* the claim to a trust failed because

---

[89] [2000] Ch 372, [400], *per* Chadwick LJ.

[90] Hopkins, 'The *Pallant v Morgan* "Equity" – Again: *Crossco No 4 Unlimited v Jolan Ltd*' [2012] Conv 327, [327]. See too *Michael v Phillips* [2017] EWHC 614 (QB). Successful applications of the doctrine, in addition to *Pallant* and *Banner Homes* include *Cox v Jones* [2004] EWHC 1476 and *Kearns Brothers Ltd v Hova Developments Ltd* [2012] EWHC 2968 (Ch).

[91] [2008] UKHL 55, [33].   [92] [2002] EWCA 355, [48].   [93] Ibid, [42].

[94] [2005] EWCA 1355, [21].

the agreement alleged to have been entered was not an agreement to share the beneficial interest.[95] However, in that case there were other 'insuperable difficulties'[96] to the imposition of a trust, including an expectation that any agreement reached between the parties required a formal contract to be binding. Hence, in substance, if not form, the parties' dealings were 'subject to contract' and a claim to a trust would have failed on that basis.[97]

6.2 THE NATURE OF THE UNCONSCIONABILITY

As we have noted, the unconscionability on which the constructive trust is based does not lie solely in the trustee reneging on the agreement. It must also be demonstrated that the party in whose favour the trust is imposed had relied on the agreement. This is the fourth of the five elements of the trust in Chadwick LJ's judgment (extracted in section 6.1 above). Whether it is unconscionable for the trustee to renege requires an objective assessment of the agreement and the effect that it has had, rather than being concerned with the trustee's subjective state of mind.[98] A requirement of reliance is found in other doctrines through which equitable interests may be acquired: for example, the common intention constructive trust and proprietary estoppel. In those doctrines, however, the requirement is explicitly one of detrimental reliance. The distinctive feature of the *Pallant v Morgan* constructive trust is that it suffices for the reliance to confer an advantage on the acquiring party, with no requirement of a corresponding detriment on the part of the non-acquiring party.

Nield highlights that the focus on the detriment or advantage in *Banner Homes* marks a development from the earlier cases.

Nield, 'Constructive Trusts and Estoppel' (2003) 23 LS 311, 324–5

[. . .] Earlier cases do not focus on this possible detriment or advantage, but upon the unconscionability inherent in the breach of trust and confidence that the non-acquiring party placed in the acquiring party to carry out their arrangements for the acquisition of certain property. This duty may be articulated as an agency, but it does not have to fit neatly within defined categories of fiduciary relationship, provided the central characteristics of a fiduciary relationship can be identified. For instance, commercial enterprises, husband and wife, relatives and neighbours have all been required by equity to adhere to their informal arrangements for the joint acquisition of property because of the trust and confidence placed in them to act not only in their own interests, but also the interests of the non-acquiring party. In this context equity seems to demand remarkably high standards of conduct and perhaps what is surprising about the *Banner Homes* decision is the line drawn between acceptable commercial tactics and a breach of duty justifying the imposition of one of equity's most potent weapons, the constructive trust.

In many cases that fulfil the requirements of the *Pallant v Morgan* trust, there will, in any event, be detrimental reliance. It is significant though that, in *Pallant* itself, no detriment arose as a result of reliance on the defendant. Immediately before the start of an auction, agents acting for the parties agreed that the claimant would refrain from bidding and, if

---

[95] [2011] EWCA Civ 1619, [97].   [96] Ibid, [107].   [97] Ibid, [108].
[98] *Baynes Clarke v Corless* [2010] EWCA 338, [40] and [51].

the defendant succeeded in acquiring the land, part would be sold on to the claimant. The defendant's agent obtained the land with a bid of £1,000, but the defendant then reneged on the agreement. The defendant's agent was authorized to bid up to £3,000, while the claimant's agent was authorized to bid to £2,000. On these facts, it is clear that the claimant suffered no detriment, because the land would not have been acquired by him even in the absence of the agreement—but the defendant obtained an advantage, because the land was acquired for half of the sum that would have been necessary to outbid the claimant. Judgment in the case is not given explicitly in terms of a constructive trust. The Court considered that the defendant's agent had acted for both parties at the auction. The defendant therefore held the land for himself and the claimant jointly, subject to agreement by the parties as to its division (with provision for a resale if no such agreement was reached).

6.3 THE BASIS OF THE *PALLANT V MORGAN* CONSTRUCTIVE TRUST

The jurisprudential basis of the *Pallant v Morgan* trust was addressed by the Court of Appeal in *Crossco No 4 Unlimited v Jalan Limited*.[99] There, the court was presented with competing arguments by counsel that the trust was either a common intention constructive trust or was founded on a breach of fiduciary duty. The majority of the court (McFarlane and Arden LJJ) felt bound by the authority of *Banner Homes* to hold that *Pallant v Morgan* is an example of the common intention constructive trust.[100] We will examine such trusts in detail in Chapter 12, as they play a very important role in the context of disputes as to ownership of a shared home. Nonetheless, it is accepted that such trusts can arise in the commercial context too,[101] at least in cases where there is a sufficiently clear intention that the parties should be in some way bound to each other. In a minority judgment, however, Etherton LJ considered that the link between *Pallant v Morgan* and the common intention constructive trust had become '*untenable*'.[102] He explained that the common intention constructive trust was now '*driven by policy consider-ations and the special facts that normally apply in the dealings between those living in an in-timate relationship*', which made it inappropriate to apply in a commercial context.[103] Etherton LJ considered that cases in which *Pallant v Morgan* has been applied '*can all be explained, and, in my judgment, ought to be explained in wholly conventional terms by the existence and breach of fiduciary duty*'.[104]

There are difficulties with either analysis of the trust. Yip suggests, despite Etherton LJ's concerns, that it is not 'untenable' for a doctrine of common intention constructive trust to be applied in the commercial context.[105] Dixon, further, considers that '[t]here is very little to suggest that the common intention constructive trust is applicable only in family

---

[99] [2011] EWCA Civ 1619.   [100] Ibid, [122] (McFarlane LJ) and [129] (Arden LJ).

[101] See too the Court of Appeal cases discussed in Chapter 8, section 3.9.3: *Yaxley v Gotts* [2000] Ch 162 (CA); *Kinane v Mackie-Conteh* [2005] EWCA Civ 45, [2005] WTLR 345; *Matchmove Ltd v Dowding* [2017] 1 WLR 749.

[102] Ibid, [87].   [103] Ibid, [85]–[86].

[104] Ibid, [88]. Academic support for that view is provided by, for example, Grower 'Explaining the "*Pallant v Morgan*" Equity' [2016] Conv 434, who argues that the equity depends on a breach of a fiduciary duty arising in an agency relationship, and so can apply even in the absence of an agreement that is intended to be binding. The argument focusses on the decision in *Generator Developments Ltd v Lidl UK GmbH* [2016] EWHC 814 (Ch), in which an appeal is pending.

[105] Yip, 'The *Pallant v Morgan* Equity Reconsidered' (2013) 33 LS 549.

cases'.[106] However, accepting the availability of common intention constructive trusts in the commercial context in principle, there are still difficulties in classifying the *Pallant v Morgan* trust in this way. Hopkins has highlighted that the gain-based nature of the *Pallant v Morgan* trust is at odds with the detrimental reliance basis of the common intention constructive trust.[107] In *Cox v Jones*, Mann J described the two doctrines of common intention constructive trust and *Pallant v Morgan* as being 'slightly different, though probably conceptually related'.[108]

If the trust is based on a breach of fiduciary duty, however, then it is unclear to what extent *Pallant v Morgan* is required. Hopkins notes, for example, that if there is a breach of fiduciary duty, then a remedy would be available in the absence of finding that the elements of a *Pallant v Morgan* trust were fulfilled.[109] Lower suggests that the adoption of breach of fiduciary duty as the basis of intervention may enable the court to provide relief otherwise than through a constructive trust in 'exceptional cases' where the trust would not be appropriate.[110] Conversely, it is possible that fulfilling the elements of *Pallant v Morgan* may make a proprietary remedy available when a breach of fiduciary duty would not otherwise give rise to such a remedy. However, as Yip asks, if *Pallant v Morgan* is founded on a breach of fiduciary duty, 'why should cases with such features be set apart from other cases of breach of fiduciary duty'?[111] Through a comprehensive analysis of the alternative basis of the trust, Yip doubts whether *Pallant v Morgan* should be recognized as an independent doctrine. She suggests that in some cases the proprietary award may be justified by principles of agency.[112] A potential link with agency is significant in light of the Supreme Court's judgment in *FHR European Ventures LLP v Mankarious*.[113] There, in another context (that of bribes and secret commissions) the court signalled that 'any benefit acquired by an agent as a result of his agency and in breach of his fiduciary duty is held on trust for the principal'.[114]

7 TOWARDS A RATIONALIZATION OF THE CONSTRUCTIVE TRUSTS

A number of attempts have been made to locate the trusts imposed in *Rochefoucauld v Boustead* and *Pallant v Morgan*, along with some other constructive trusts, within a single principle. McFarlane sees both trusts as examples of what he terms a 'receipt after promise' principle. The scope of McFarlane's idea, which has attracted criticism,[115] is outlined in the following extract.

---

[106] Dixon, [2014] 'Editorial' Conv 279, 281.

[107] Hopkins, 'The *Pallant v Morgan* "Equity?"' [2002] Conv 35, 36.

[108] [2004] EWHC 1486, [45].

[109] Hopkins, 'The *Pallant v Morgan* "equity" – Again: *Crossco No 4 Ltd v Jolan Ltd*' [2012] Conv 327, 330–1.

[110] Lower, 'The *Pallant v Morgan* Equity' [2012] Conv 379, 385–6.

[111] Yip, 'The *Pallant v Morgan* Equity Reconsidered' (2013) 33 LS 549, 564.   [112] Ibid, 565–7.

[113] [2014] 3 WLR 535.   [114] Ibid, [35] *per* Lord Neuberger.

[115] Hopkins, 'Conscience, Discretion and the Creation of Property Rights' (2006) 26 LS 475; Gardner, 'Reliance-Based Constructive Trusts' and Swadling, 'The Nature of the Trust in *Rochefoucauld v Boustead*' in *Resulting and Constructive Trusts* (ed Mitchell, Oxford: Hart, 2009). Swadling rejects any attempt to unify *Rochefoucauld v Boustead* with other types of constructive trust as he considers that the trust is an express trust (a view rejected in part 5.1.2 above), but he also outlines, at pp 106–7 a number of reasons for resisting McFarlane's analysis.

McFarlane, *The Structure of Property Law* (2008, pp 270–1)

[T]he courts seem to apply a clear principle, which can be called the "receipt after a promise" principle [. . .] The principle means that if:

1. C makes a promise to come under a duty to B; *and*

2. C's promise relates to the use of a particular right; *and*

3. C acquires, as a result of that promise, an advantage in relation to the acquisition of that right; *then*

4. C is under a duty to B to keep that promise, as far as it relates to the right advantageously acquired by C.

[. . .] The principle thus allows C's promise, even though it was made to A, to be enforced by B, the party who benefits from the promise. It is important to note that B's right does *not* arise as a result of a contract between B and C. Rather, it is based on the principle that, having received a right on a particular basis (that he will allow B to make some use of that right), C is not then allowed to enjoy that right on a different basis."

Liew has identified a broader distinction which may similarly help to classify constructive trusts.

Liew, *Rationalising Constructive Trusts* (2017, p 15)

There are two distinct and mutually exclusive situations in which constructive trusts arise. The first is where the property in question is at the outset owned *absolutely* by B, the person against whom the trust obligation arises. Here, one of the causative events to which the constructive trust responds is an act of B in relation to *his own* property. The second relates to property which B does not previously own. Here, one of the material events is an act of B in relation to property he has yet to acquire, and the result is that, when B later obtains title to the property in question, a constructive trust arises with the effect that he ever only takes a *qualified* interest in that property.

On that approach, the two constructive trusts considered in detail in this chapter are both examples of 'qualified interest' constructive trusts. As Liew goes on to note,[116] they thus share a similarity with the standard express trusts arising where a settlor transfers property to a trustee to hold for a beneficiary: the obligation constituting the trust arises as soon as the property is received. In contrast, a constructive trust arising in the case of proprietary estoppel is an 'absolute interest' constructive trust: the claimant needs to show why a limit should be placed on the defendant's previous liberty to use his or her property as he or she wishes. If it is accepted that such an absolute interest trust is therefore more difficult to establish than a qualified interest trust, this may help to explain the differing requirements of certain doctrines. It was noted in section 6.2, for example, that the *Pallant v Morgan* equity

---

[116] Liew, *Rationalising Constructive Trusts* (Oxford: Hart, 2017) 16.

does not require *detrimental* reliance by the claimant, whereas that is a requirement of proprietary estoppel.

Gardner offers an alternative means of unifying a number of constructive trusts. He suggests that trusts, including not only the *Rochefoucauld* and *Pallant* constructive trusts, but also those arising in response to proprietary estoppel, are imposed, 'to correct a reliance loss—specifically the loss that someone suffers when, acting in reasonable reliance on another's undertaking, he foregoes his opportunity to achieve the content of the undertaking in some other way'.[117] Reliance is also considered to be an essential element of the trusts by Allan. He considers that the trusts form part of what he calls a 'doctrine of parol agreement trusts … [imposed] to prevent a party from perpetuating a fraud by refusing to give effect to an agreement'.[118]

There are undoubtedly advantages if it could be concluded that apparently separate applications of constructive trusts are in fact linked by a general principle. This would provide greater coherence, assist us in understanding possible developments, and help explain cases that otherwise appear difficult to rationalize: for example, *Neale v Willis*[119] (extracted in section 5.2 above), which, in the absence of a general principle, appears an awkward deviation from the factual matrix of a claim within *Rochefoucauld v Boustead*. In *Crossco No 4 Unlimited v Jolan Limited*, Etherton LJ noted the merit in McFarlane and Gardner's arguments insofar as they are '*put forward as principled explanations for a range of constructive trusts*'.[120] But the sense of unity provided is illusory if it in fact masks genuine differences in the operation of each trust. Further, the correct application of a trust may be stultified by superimposing requirements that have never been required within a particular doctrine. Neither McFarlane nor Gardner's approach was endorsed by Etherton LJ, who noted that it was '*not possible to do full justice in the context of this judgment to the alternative explanations*' whilst reiterating the specific basis on which he considered the *Pallant v Morga*n trust could be rationalized.[121] Commenting on McFarlane's analysis, Hopkins has highlighted the danger of losing sight of the fact that *Rochefoucauld v Boustead* enables the court to intervene solely on the basis of preventing the transferee's fraudulent or unconscionable attempt to renege from the trust and claim the land for him or herself.[122] He suggests that this feature of the trust 'links together the application of *Rochefoucauld v Boustead* in both two- and three-party cases, and distinguishes this instance of unconscionability'.[123] In the present state of the authorities recognition of a unifying principle appears some way off.[124]

QUESTIONS

1. Assess the different role afforded to the settlor's intention in the creation of express, resulting, and constructive trusts.

---

[117] Gardner, Reliance-Based Constructive Trusts' in *Resulting and Constructive Trusts* (ed Mitchell, Oxford: Hart Publishing, 2009) p 63.

[118] Allan, 'Once a Fraud, Forever a Fraud: The Time Honoured Doctrine of Parol Agreement Trusts' (2014) 34 LS 419, 437.

[119] (1968) 19 P & CR 836, 839.   [120] [2011] EWCA Civ 1619, [94].   [121] Ibid.

[122] Hopkins, 'Conscience, Discretion and the Creation of Property Rights (2006) 26 LS 475, 487.

[123] Ibid.

[124] For an ambitious attempt to classify constructive trusts, which recognizes a principle linking the *Rochefoucauld* and *Pallant* constructive trusts, along with further constructive trusts, see Liew, *Rationalising Constructive Trusts* (Oxford: Hart, 2017).

2. Would the following situations, each concerning the purchase of an investment property, give rise to a presumption of resulting trust or a presumption of advancement? Do your answers yield a logical result?

   a. The property is purchased in the joint names of Mr and Mrs X, with the purchase money provided by Mr X.

   b. The property is purchased in the joint names of Mr and Mrs X, with the purchase money provided by Mrs X.

   c. The property is purchased in the joint names of Mr Y and his son, with the purchase money provided by Mr Y.

   d. The property is purchased in the joint names of Mr Y and his son, with the purchase money provided by the son.

3. Does the approach of the Privy Council in *Marr v Collie* lessen the importance of the distinction between the resulting trust and the common intention constructive trust?

4. What is the nature of the unconscionable of fraudulent conduct that triggers the imposition of the constructive trust under the doctrine in *Rochefoucauld v Boustead*? Compare and contrast this with the conduct required for a trust under the *Pallant v Morgan* constructive trust.

5. Is it necessary or appropriate to recognize the *Pallant v Morgan* constructive trust as an independent principle?

For guidance on how to answer these questions visit the online resources at www.oup.com/uk/mcfarlane4e/.

FURTHER READING

Allan, 'Once a Fraud, Forever a Fraud: The Time Honoured Doctrine of Parol Agreement Trusts' (2014) 34 LS 419

Chambers, *Resulting Trusts* (Oxford: Clarendon Press, 1997)

Gardner, Reliance-Based Constructive Trusts' in *Resulting and Constructive Trusts*, (ed Mitchell, Oxford: Hart Publishing, 2009)

Grower, 'Explaining the "*Pallant v Morgan*" Equity' [2016] Conv 434

Hopkins, 'Conscience, Discretion and the Creation of Property Rights' (2006) 26 LS 475

Hopkins, *The Informal Acquisition of Rights in Land* (London: Sweet & Maxwell, 2000), ch 3

Liew, *Rationalising Constructive Trusts* (Oxford: Hart Publishing, 2017)

McFarlane, 'Constructive Trusts Arising on Receipt of Property Sub Conditione' (2004) 120 LQR 667

Mee, 'Presumed Resulting Trusts, Intention and Declaration' (2014) 73 CLJ 86

Mee, 'The Past, Present, and Future of Resulting Trusts' (2017) 70 CLP 189

Turano-Taylor, 'Misplaced Trust: First Principles and the Conveyance of Legal Leases to Minors' in *Modern Studies in Property Law Volume 7* (ed Hopkins, Oxford: Hart Publishing, 2013)

Swadling, 'Explaining Resulting Trusts' (2008) 124 LQR 72

Swadling, 'The Fiction of the Constructive Trust' (2011) 64 CLP 399

Yip, 'The *Pallant v Morgan* Equity Reconsidered' (2013) 33 LS 549

Youdan, 'Formalities for Trusts of Land, and the Doctrine in *Rochefoucauld v. Boustead*' (1984) 43 CLJ 306

PART D

THE SHARED HOME

12 Interests in the Home: The Acquisition Question 454

13 Regulating Co-ownership: The Content Question 503

14 Co-ownership and Third Parties: Applications for Sale 549

12

INTERESTS IN THE HOME:
THE ACQUISITION QUESTION

CENTRAL ISSUES

1. In most situations, ownership of the home falls to be determined by the application of property law principles, particularly the doctrines of resulting and constructive trusts. These trusts differ in relation to how they are created and the means by which the parties' beneficial interests are quantified.

2. Where there is joint legal ownership of the home, but no express declaration of the parties' respective beneficial shares, the initial presumption is of joint and equal beneficial ownership. This presumption will be rebutted only exceptionally and through the common intention constructive trust. In this instance the constructive trust is used only to quantify the parties' beneficial shares.

3. In certain other joint names cases, the presumption of joint and equal beneficial ownership can be rebutted by a presumption of resulting trust where the parties contributed unequally to the purchase so that the beneficiaries receive a share proportionate to their contribution. A constructive trust may, however, be claimed by a party who wishes to establish a disproportionate share.

4. Where there is sole legal ownership of the home, the initial presumption is of sole beneficial ownership. A claimant may use a resulting or constructive trust both to establish the existence of a beneficial interest (the primary acquisition question) and to quantify his or her share (the secondary quantification question).

5. Both the primary acquisition question of the creation of a common intention constructive trust and the secondary question of the quantification of shares are determined on the basis of the 'common intention' of the parties. In relation to the primary question the parties' common intention may be express or inferred. In respect of the secondary question the common intention may also, in limited circumstances, be imputed. The difference between an inferred and imputed intent is that the former is one actually held by the parties, while the latter is one attributed to the parties that they did not in fact hold.

6. The basis on which a common intention may be inferred has developed separately in relation to acquisition and quantification, with more restrictive criteria applying at the acquisition stage. A key question has

arisen—to which there is no definitive answer—whether the courts' approach to inferred intention at the quantification stage now also applies to the acquisition stage. As a result there is significant uncertainty as to the circumstances in which, in a sole legal ownership case, a constructive trust can successfully be claimed.

7. Reliance on property law principles to determine rights in the home has been criticized, particularly in the context of relationship breakdown between cohabitants. Law Commission recommendations, if enacted, will replace the application of the constructive trust (and other property principles) in this narrow category of case with a more flexible regime, where certain eligibility criteria are met.

8. Statutory rights of occupation of the home are conferred both by the Trusts of Land and Appointment of Trustees Act 1996 (which is considered in Chapter 13) and by the Family Law Act 1996.

1 INTRODUCTION

This chapter is concerned with ownership of the home. We consider how a person who does not have property rights in his or her home—for example, as owner of the legal title or a beneficiary under an expressly created trust of land—may acquire rights through the doctrines of resulting and constructive trusts. While our principal concern is with ownership of the home, we also consider the statutory routes through which a person may claim a right to occupy his or her home, whether or not he or she has a property right in the home.

We have considered the general operation of resulting and constructive trusts in Chapter 11. Our discussion of these doctrines in this chapter is focussed on their use in respect of the home. In this context, the specific type of constructive trust that applies is the 'common intention constructive trust'. As a constructive trust, the trust is imposed by operation of law, but it is based on the existence of a common intention between the parties to share the beneficial ownership. References to 'constructive trust' in this chapter are to the 'common intention constructive trust'. In addition to the doctrines of resulting and constructive trusts, interests in a home may also be obtained through a claim to proprietary estoppel, the scope and nature of which was considered in Chapter 10.

There are a number of circumstances under which it becomes necessary to determine ownership of the home. The Law Commission identified four key circumstances in which the issue may arise.

Law Commission Report No 278, *Sharing Homes: A Discussion Paper* (2002, [1.11])

[. . .]

1. The persons (two or more) who share a home cease to do so. Typically, one leaves. It may be that this follows the breakdown of a relationship between the sharers. It may be that

the living arrangement is no longer convenient to the person who leaves, as they have obtained employment elsewhere. The question arises of whether the person who leaves is entitled to receive payment of a capital sum representing their share of the property, or indeed, in the event of no satisfaction being obtained, whether that person can force a sale thereof.

2. One of the persons who has been sharing the home dies. The question arises whether that person had an interest in the property, and, if so, what therefore is now to happen to it.

3. The home is subject to a mortgage securing a loan negotiated by its owner or owners to facilitate the acquisition of the property or to provide funds for other purposes. The borrower defaults on the mortgage, and the mortgagee seeks possession in order to realise its security by sale of the property. The question arises whether any of those living in the home can assert an interest in that property against the mortgagee, and whether they can successfully defend the proceedings for repossession.

4. A creditor whose debt is not secured over the property by way of mortgage seeks to have the property sold so that the demand can be satisfied. The question arises whether any person who has been sharing with the debtor can successfully hold out against the creditor's claim.

In most circumstances in which the issue of ownership arises, it falls to be determined by the application of the property rules discussed in this chapter. The principal exception is the breakdown of a marriage by divorce, or the dissolution of a civil partnership, in which statutory schemes enable the courts to make property adjustment orders between the parties.[1] Significantly, however, no equivalent legislation applies on the breakdown of a relationship between cohabitants who live together without having married or entered a civil partnership. Even in the case of marriage and civil partnerships, the statutory schemes are confined in their application to determining the parties' rights on a relationship breakdown. They do not apply, for example, where the parties' rights fall to be determined in a dispute between a mortgagor or creditor within the third or fourth situations, where property rules must be invoked.[2]

Where the issue of ownership arises as a matter of property law, the question for the court is what each party *actually* owns, not what they *ought* to own. As Dillon LJ commented:[3] '*The court does not as yet sit, as under a palm tree, to exercise a general discretion to do what the man in the street, on a general overview of the case, might regard as fair.*' While English law does not have a special regime for determining rights to family property,[4] there has been an increasing '*familialisation*'[5] of applicable property law doctrines, involving the

---

[1] Matrimonial Causes Act 1973, s 23; Civil Partnership Act 2004, Sch 5, para 2.

[2] In most of the case law discussed in this chapter, the issue of ownership has, in fact, arisen in the context of relationship breakdown (the first situation).The third situation is exemplified by *Williams & Glyn's Bank v Boland* [1981] AC 487, HL, and subsequent case law, which is examined in Chapter 16. The fourth situation would arise on an application for sale under s 14 of the Trusts of Land and Appointment of Trustees Act 1996, the operation of which is considered in Chapter 14.

[3] *Springette v Defoe* (1993) 65 P & CR 1, 6.

[4] Compare Law Commission Report No 278, *Sharing Homes: A Discussion Paper* (2002), [1.18], in which the Law Commission noted that English law does not have a special property regime even in relation to married couples. The major distinction between married couples (and couples with a civil partnership) and others is the applicable regime on the breakdown of the parties' relationship.

[5] An expression coined by Dewar, 'Land, Law and the Family Home' in *Land Law: Themes and Perspectives* (eds Bright and Dewar, Oxford: OUP, 1998). The development of the process is identified by Hayward, ' "Family Property" and the Process of Familialisation of Property Law' (2012) 24 CFLQ 284.

modification of *'general principles of land law or trusts to accommodate the specific needs of family members'*.[6] This development reflects increasing dissatisfaction with the operation of property rules to determine parties' rights in their home combined with frustration at the absence of legislative intervention. But familialization raises questions about whether the doctrines that result can be described as property at all. Commenting on the development of the common intention constructive trust to determine ownership of the home, Dixon suggested *'call it family law, call it an exercise of the court's inherent equitable jurisdiction, but, maybe, do not call it property law'*.[7]

Dissatisfaction with property principles is especially acute where the question of ownership arises following the breakdown of a relationship between cohabitants. In such circumstances the strict application of property rules stands in stark contrast to the property adjustment orders available on a divorce or the dissolution of a civil partnership. The Law Commission has noted[8] that the current law is generally accepted as being *'unduly complex, arbitrary and uncertain in its application. It is ill-suited to determining the property rights of those who, because of the informal nature of their relationship, may not have considered their respective entitlements'*. In response, the Law Commission has recommended a scheme that, if enacted, will replace the determination of the parties' property rights with a more flexible scheme to provide financial relief on the breakdown of a relationship between cohabitants who fulfil certain eligibility criteria. As we will see in section 4 of this chapter, the Law Commission's proposals have not yet been implemented.

2   TRUSTS AND THE HOME

In Chapter 11, the basic rules for the acquisition of rights under a trust of land were outlined. As we saw, an express trust must be evidence by signed writing within s 53(1)(b) of the Law of Property Act 1925 (LPA 1925). But s 53(2) exempts from this requirement *'implied, resulting and constructive trusts'*.

Where an express trust exists, it is generally considered to be conclusive both as to the existence of a trust and (if declared) the extent of the parties' beneficial interests.[9] There is no room for the operation of resulting or constructive trusts. The preponderance of claims to these trusts thus arises through the failure of parties to determine expressly the ownership of their home, despite repeated pleas from the judiciary to legal advisers to encourage parties to do so.

---

[6] Dewar ibid, 328.

[7] Dixon, 'Editor's notebook: the still not ended, never-ending story' [2012] Conv 83, 86. Contrast, Hayward, '*Stack v Dowden; Jones v Kernott*: Finding a Home for "Family Property"' in *Landmark Cases in Land Law* (ed Gravells, Hart Publishing, 2013) pp 251–2.

[8] Law Commission Report No 274, *Eighth Programme of Law Reform* (2001) p 7.

[9] *Goodman v Gallant* [1986] Fam 106, applied in *Pankhania v Chandegra* [2013] 3 FCR 16. But contrast *Clarke v Meadus* [2010] EWHC 3117. The case is discussed by Pawlowski, 'Informal Variation of Express Trusts' [2011] Conv 245. In *Stack v Dowden*, Baroness Hale explained that an express declaration of the parties' beneficial interests is *'conclusive unless varied by subsequent agreement or affected by proprietary estoppel'*: [2007] 2 AC 432 [49].

Carlton v Goodman
[2002] 2 FLR 259, CA

Ward LJ

At 44

I ask in despair how often this court has to remind conveyancers that they would save their clients a great deal of later difficulty if only they would sit the purchasers down, explain the difference between a joint tenancy and a tenancy in common, ascertain what they want and then expressly declare in the conveyance or transfer how the beneficial interest is to be held because that will be conclusive and save all argument. When are conveyancers going to do this as a matter of invariable standard practice? This court has urged that time after time. Perhaps conveyancers do not read the law reports. I will try one more time: ALWAYS TRY TO AGREE ON AND THEN RECORD HOW THE BENEFICIAL INTEREST IS TO BE HELD. It is not very difficult to do.

The application of resulting and constructive trusts in the context of the home must now be understood in light of two significant decisions of the highest appellate court in England and Wales: the House of Lords in *Stack v Dowden*[10] and the Supreme Court in *Jones v Kernott*.[11] In both cases, the question in issue was the quantification of shares in a property that had been purchased in the joint names of a cohabiting couple with no express declaration of their respective beneficial interest. The issue of quantification of shares is secondary to that of the existence or creation of a trust; that primary acquisition question had already been considered by the House of Lords in three previous cases.[12] However, the significance of *Stack v Dowden* and *Jones v Kernott* extends beyond the matter of quantification. In *Stack v Dowden* the majority made a policy decision to treat the home differently to other property when determining ownership.[13] The decision of the majority, led by Baroness Hale, is underpinned with the ethos that '*in law "context is everything" and the domestic context is very different from the commercial world*'.[14] The focus on context provided the key point of departure for Lord Neuberger. He delivered a minority judgment in which he reached the same outcome as the majority on the facts but through different reasoning. Lord Neuberger was unconvinced that the domestic context requires '*a different approach in principle*'.[15] On his view: '*In the absence of statutory provisions to the contrary, the same principles should apply to assess the apportionment of the beneficial interest as between legal co-owners, whether in a sexual, platonic, familial, amicable or commercial relationship.*'[16]

In *Jones v Kernott* the Supreme Court offered clarification of key aspects of the decision in *Stack v Dowden*. The focus of the case is the meaning of 'common intention', which had been adopted in *Stack v Dowden* as the criteria for determining the quantification of the parties' shares (the secondary question) and is also the basis of a claim to the existence or creation of a trust (the primary question). However, the Supreme Court also appeared to define the

---

[10] [2007] 2 AC 432.   [11] [2012] AC 776.

[12] *Pettitt v Pettitt* [1970] AC 777; *Gissing v Gissing* [1971] AC 886; *Lloyds Bank plc v Rosset* [1991] 1 AC 107.

[13] Hopkins, 'Regulating Trusts of the Home: Private Law and Social Policy' (2009) 125 LQR 310, p 333. See also Hopkins, 'The Relevance of Context in Property Law: A Case for Judicial Restraint?' (2011) 31 LS 175, 189–91.

[14] [2007] 2 AC 432, [69], *per* Baroness Hale.   [15] Ibid, [107].   [16] Ibid.

scope of *Stack v Dowden*. Central to *Stack v Dowden* is the rejection of the presumption of resulting trust (discussed further in part 2.3.4) as providing the starting point to determine beneficial ownership of the home. In *Jones v Kernott* the Supreme Court removed the operation of the presumption in respect of homes purchased '*in joint names for joint occupation by a married or unmarried couple, where both are responsible for any mortgage*'.[17] This appears a more restrictive category than the 'domestic context' referred to in *Stack v Dowden*.

However, the relevance of context has been reasserted in the Privy Council case of *Marr v Collie*[18] on appeal from the Bahamas. In *Marr v Collie* several properties were held as legal joint tenants by the parties, who were both domestic and commercial partners, with one party generally providing the money to purchase the houses and the other party intended to 'contribute' his labour to renovate them. There was a return to the language of context and an explicit rejection of the narrow context suggested by *Jones v Kernow*—'*to consign the reasoning in Stack to the purely domestic setting would be wrong*'.[19] The case thus raises the prospect of the wider application of the constructive trust analysis beyond the narrow confines of the home.

To the extent that this Privy Council decision represents the views of the Supreme Court, a clear and simple divide in the application of the constructive and resulting trust analyses between the domestic and commercial setting thus is open to doubt. The constructive trust analysis based upon the parties' ascertainable intentions appears the preferred approach where cohabitees are also connected by investment in a commercial joint venture. It may also be that a constructive trust analysis will be adopted in the context of property bought jointly by family members or friends where it is possible to divine their intentions as to ownership.[20] It is where there is no ascertainable evidence of the parties' common intention that the resulting trust approach based upon the parties' contributions may continue to have a part to play.

Marr v Collie
[2017] UKPC 17 Lord Kerr

At 46

Where additional evidence is available in the form of testimony from the parties themselves as to what their intentions were when the property was acquired, even on Lord Neuberger's formulation, this can rebut the presumption of resulting trust. In that event, there should be a direct focus on what the intentions of the parties were. That focus could only be avoided if the decision in *Stack* could properly be regarded as applying only to purely domestic arrangements. For the reasons given earlier (in paras 38 and 39) the Board considers that it cannot be so regarded and that the trial judge was wrong to dismiss it on that basis.

At 53–55

A clash of presumptions?

If what Lady Hale described as a "starting point" (that joint legal ownership should signify joint beneficial ownership) is to be regarded as a presumption, is it in conflict with the

---

[17] *Jones v Kernott* [2011] 3 WLR 1121, [25] *per* Lord Walker and Baroness Hale.
[18] [2017] UKPC 17.   [19] At [39].
[20] See e.g. *Laskar v Laskar* [2008] EWCA Civ 347 and *Wodzicki v Wodzicki* [2017] EWCA Civ 95.

presumption of a resulting trust where the parties have contributed unequally to the purchase of property in their joint names? A simplistic answer to that question might be that, if
the property is purchased in joint names by parties in a domestic relationship the presumption of joint beneficial ownership applies but if bought in a wholly non-domestic situation
it does not. In the latter case, it might be said that the resulting trust presumption obtains.

The Board considers that, save perhaps where there is no evidence from which the parties' intentions can be identified, the answer is not to be provided by the triumph of one
presumption over another. In this, as in so many areas of law, context counts for, if not everything, a lot. Context here is set by the parties' common intention – or by the lack of it. If it is
the unambiguous mutual wish of the parties, contributing in unequal shares to the purchase
of property, that the joint beneficial ownership should reflect their joint legal ownership, then
effect should be given to that wish. If, on the other hand, that is not their wish, or if they have
not formed any intention as to beneficial ownership but had, for instance, accepted advice
that the property be acquired in joint names, without considering or being aware of the possible consequences of that, the resulting trust solution may provide the answer.

Of course, the initial intention (or lack of it) at the time of purchase may change. This was
the reason that the majority in *Stack v Dowden* emphasised that examination of the course
of conduct of the parties over the years in which they dealt with the property is relevant.
And it is why an intense examination is warranted of why the properties acquired in this case
in 2008 were purchased in joint names. By that time, many of the contributions which, according to Mr Marr, he expected Mr Collie to have made, had not materialised. Why did he
continue to agree that the properties should be acquired in joint names?

The courts have kept distinct two circumstances in which resulting and constructive trusts
may be claimed. The first situation comprises cases of sole legal ownership, in which legal
title is conveyed to one person alone. The second situation concerns joint legal ownership,
in which legal title is conveyed to the claimant and another person (or persons), but there is
no declaration as regards the parties' respective beneficial shares. These situations are kept
separate by the courts as the starting point for legal analysis in each is different, as are the
issues that must be addressed.

In the case of joint legal ownership, following the maxim that equity follows the law the
starting point is that the parties are beneficial joint tenants.[21] The conveyance into joint
names is conclusive as to the existence of a trust, but a resulting or constructive trust may
be claimed to show that the beneficial interest is held in unequal shares. Hence, in joint legal
ownership cases, the application of the trust is concerned only with the secondary matter
of quantification of the parties' shares. The circumstances in which this initial presumption
is displaced, and whether this is through a resulting or constructive trust, lies at the heart
of the decisions in *Stack v Dowden, Jones v Kernott* and *Marr v Colley* and is addressed in
section 2.1.

---

[21] This starting point is unanimously agreed by the House of Lords in *Stack v Dowden* [2007] 2 AC 432.
There at [109]–[110] Lord Neuberger treats the presumption of resulting trust, when it is applied, as rebutting
an initial presumption of joint and equal beneficial ownership. In *Jones v Kernott* [2011] 3 WLR 1121, [23]
Lord Walker and Baroness Hale go further and treat the presumption of joint and equal beneficial ownership in the context of the home as an *alternative* to the presumption of resulting trust and offer a different rationale than the maxim that equity follows the law: see further at [19]–[22]. The approach adopted in this text
is preferred as being consistent with general principle and with the tenor of *Jones v Kernott*. For example, in
providing a summary of the principles applicable in joint names cases, Lord Walker and Baroness Hale note,
[51] '[t]he starting point is that equity follows the law and they are joint tenants both in law and in equity'.

In a case of sole legal ownership the maxim that equity follows the law means the starting point is that the sole legal owner is also the sole beneficial owner. A claimant may use resulting or constructive trusts to establish that he or she is also beneficially entitled. If the trust is successfully established, the claimant's beneficial share must then be quantified. Hence, in sole legal ownership cases, the trust is used both to determine whether the claimant has a beneficial interest (the primary acquisition question), and, if so, to quantify the extent of his or her share (the secondary quantification issue).

The separation between cases of sole and joint beneficial interests is strictly maintained. In *Thompson v Hurst*[22] the Court of Appeal rejected an argument that the starting point in a case of sole legal ownership should be the same as that in a case of joint legal ownership where the parties had wanted to purchase a property in joint names, but it had been purchased in the sole name of one of them in order to secure mortgage finance. Etherton LJ described the proposition that the case should be treated the same as one of joint legal ownership as '*neither consistent with principle nor sound policy*'.[23]

The division between sole and joint legal ownership provides the basis of the structure of this section of the chapter. The chapter continues with a consideration of joint legal ownership and the secondary question of quantification. Sole legal ownership and the primary acquisition question are then addressed. This structure is adopted because current debate in cases of sole legal ownership centres on the extent to which the approach to quantification can be carried over to the primary acquisition question. Therefore, it is necessary to understand the courts' approach to quantification fully to appreciate the issues that now arise in relation to the primary question.

2.1 JOINT LEGAL OWNERS

Where legal title to a home is conveyed into the joint names of the parties, the conveyance is conclusive as to the existence of a trust. If the conveyance identifies the parties' respective shares, then it is generally conclusive as to those shares.[24] This leaves the exceptional case of joint ownership in which, as in *Stack v Dowden, Jones v Kernott* and *Marr v Collie*, a conveyance into joint names is silent as to the parties' respective shares.[25]

As we have seen in section 2 of this chapter, the starting point in cases of joint legal ownership is joint and equal beneficial ownership. The question that arises is when and how this presumption may be displaced. The presumption of joint and equal beneficial ownership can be rebutted through proof of a constructive trust founded on the common intention of the parties. Where the constructive trust is invoked to rebut the presumption of joint and equal beneficial ownership, it is used solely to quantify the claimant's share. The existence of the trust is established by the fact of conveyance into joint names. In other instances of joint legal ownership, where a common intention to support a constructive trust to quantify the beneficial ownership cannot be established, the presumption of resulting trust continues to have a part to play. In these cases the presumption of joint and equal beneficial ownership may be rebutted by a presumption of resulting trust where the parties have not contributed equally so that the parties will obtain beneficial shares in proportion to their contributions.

---

[22] [2014] 1 FLR 238.   [23] Ibid, [20].   [24] See the discussion in section 2 above.
[25] Contrast the view of Sparkes, 'Non-declaration of Beneficial Ownership' [2012] Conv 207. He argues that the assumption there is a 'vacuum' in beneficial entitlement in the absence of an express declaration of shares is incorrect.

As in the case of sole legal ownership discussed in section 2.3 of this chapter, however, a beneficiary who wishes to establish a share, other than in proportion to their direct financial contribution, may do so though a constructive trust.

In *Stack v Dowden*, Baroness Hale warned that the task of rebutting the initial quantification presumption of joint beneficial ownership is not one that should be undertaken lightly by the claimant.

Stack v Dowden
[2007] 2 AC 432, HL

Facts: Mr Stack and Ms Dowden had cohabited for nearly twenty years and had four children. Their home was registered in their joint names but with no express declaration as to their respective beneficial shares. The purchase had been funded from the proceeds of sale of a previous home (held in Ms Dowden's sole name), money from her bank account, and a joint loan. While both parties contributed to the discharge of the loan, Ms Dowden's contributions were higher. Throughout their relationship they had kept their financial affairs separate. On the breakdown of their relationship, Ms Dowden claimed to be entitled to 65 per cent of the beneficial share.

Baroness Hale

At 68

In family disputes, strong feelings are aroused when couples split up. These often lead the parties, honestly but mistakenly, to reinterpret the past in self-exculpatory or vengeful terms. They also lead people to spend far more on the legal battle than is warranted by the sums actually at stake. A full examination of the facts is likely to involve disproportionate costs. In joint names cases it is also unlikely to lead to a different result unless the facts are very unusual.

There is little guidance on the types of factor that would make a case 'unusual' enough to justify a departure from the presumption of joint and equal beneficial ownership. In *Stack v Dowden*, Baroness Hale was satisfied that the facts of the case were sufficiently unusual to depart from the presumption and in doing so she emphasized the fact that throughout their long relationship the couple had kept their financial affairs rigidly separate.[26]

In contrast, in *Fowler v Barron*,[27] the Court of Appeal rejected Mr Barron's claim to depart from the presumption of equal beneficial ownership. In that case, the parties' home had been placed in their joint names, although Mr Barron alone provided the deposit and paid the mortgage instalments. Miss Fowler's income was used to meet day-to-day expenses, and additional expenditure towards such matters as school trips, holidays, and special occasions. Arden LJ considered that this was tantamount to the parties treating their income as *'one pool from which household expenses will be paid'*. There was nothing unusual to justify departing from the presumption.

The presumption of joint and equal beneficial ownership may be rebutted not only at the time of acquisition of the property, but also at a later stage. This feature of the constructive

---

[26] [2007] 2 AC 432, [92].   [27] [2008] EWCA 377, [46].

trust led Lord Hoffmann in argument in *Stack v Dowden* to describe the trust as 'ambulatory'.[28] *Jones v Kernott* involved a post-acquisition alteration of the parties' intention. There, the common intention of the parties was considered to have changed sometime after the breakdown of their relationship when a life insurance policy was cashed in to enable Mr Kernott, who had moved out of the home the parties had shared, to buy a home for himself.[29] In *Stack v Dowden*, Baroness Hale gave as an example a situation where '*one party has financed (or constructed himself) an extension or substantial improvement to the property, so that what they have now is significantly different from what they had [at the time of acquisition]*'.[30]

2.2 QUANTIFICATION OF BENEFICIAL INTERESTS UNDER A CONSTRUCTIVE TRUST

The issue of quantification of a beneficial interest under a constructive trust may arise in three circumstances:

- First, in cases of joint legal ownership within the domestic context (such as *Stack v Dowden* and *Jones v Kernott*) where the presumption of joint and equal beneficial ownership has been rebutted by a claimant who seeks to obtain an unequal share.

- Second, in other cases of joint legal ownership (such as *Marr v Collie*) where a constructive trust has been established by a claimant who seeks to obtain a share otherwise than in proportion to their direct financial contribution.

- Third, in cases of sole legal ownership where a constructive trust has been established.

The approach to take to the quantification of shares under a constructive trust in the first situation was the central question in *Stack v Dowden* and *Jones v Kernott*. In *Abbott v Abbott* the same approach to quantification was applied by the Privy Council in the third situation (sole legal ownership). This position was confirmed by the Supreme Court in *Jones v Kernott* whilst emphasizing the different starting point in cases of sole legal ownership.[31] *Marr v Collie* suggests that the same approach to quantification will be applied in the second situation, as there is no basis to treat the first and second situations differently. Even though the quantification of shares is, therefore, determined by the same rules in all cases, the fact that the starting point is different may still affect the outcome of the application of those rules.[32]

2.2.1 Quantification and *Stack v Dowden*: the shift to common intention

In *Stack v Dowden* the House of Lords noted a curious (and perhaps unintended) distinction that had emerged in previous case law. In sole ownership cases, a flexible approach to quantification of beneficial shares had developed through the application of the constructive

---

[28] As explained in *Stack v Dowden* [2007] 2 AC 432, [62] *per* Baroness Hale. See further *Jones v Kernott* [2012] AC 776, [14].

[29] [2012] AC 776, [48].   [30] [2007] 2 AC 432, [70].   [31] [2012] AC 776, [52].

[32] This is acknowledged in *Stack v Dowden* [2007] 2 AC 432 at [69] where Baroness Hale explains '*[w]here a couple are joint owners of the home and jointly liable for the mortgage, the inferences to be drawn from who pays for what may be very different from the inferences to be drawn when only one is owner of the home*'. The paragraph is extracted in full below.

trust.[33] In joint ownership cases, the courts had appeared to prefer basing decisions on the resulting trust, with its rigid approach to quantification as a proportion of each party's contribution.[34] Baroness Hale noted:[35] '*The approach to quantification in cases where the home is conveyed into joint names should certainly be no stricter than the approach to quantification in cases where it has been conveyed into the name of one only.*' The House of Lords then proceeded to state and develop the basis on which quantification is determined.

Prior to *Stack v Dowden*, the Court of Appeal had comprehensively addressed the issue of quantification in the following case, involving a sole legal owner.

Oxley v Hiscock
[2005] Fam 211, CA

Facts: The parties were cohabitants whose home was in the sole legal ownership of Mr Hiscock. Both parties had provided a cash contribution to the purchase (approximately 28 per cent by Mrs Oxley and 48 per cent by Mr Hiscock), with the remainder raised by a mortgage. Throughout the parties' relationship, they had both contributed to the household expenditure, including the discharge of the mortgage, and to improvements and maintenance. On the breakdown of the relationship, Mrs Oxley claimed 50 per cent of the proceeds of sale. Following a review of the authorities, Chadwick LJ summarized the principles governing quantification. Chadwick LJ referred to this as the 'second question'—arising once the existence of a constructive trust (the first question) has been established.

Chadwick LJ

At 69

In those circumstances, the second question to be answered in cases of this nature is 'what is the extent of the parties' respective beneficial interests in the property?'. Again, in many such cases, the answer will be provided by evidence of what they said and did at the time of the acquisition. But, in a case where there is no evidence of any discussion between them as to the amount of the share which each was to have—and even in a case where the evidence is that there was no discussion on that point—the question still requires an answer. It must now be accepted that (at least in this court and below) the answer is that each is entitled to that share which the court considers fair having regard to the whole course of dealing between them in relation to the property. And, in that context, 'the whole course of dealing between them in relation to the property' includes the arrangements which they make from time to time in order to meet the outgoings (for example, mortgage contributions, council tax and utilities, repairs, insurance and housekeeping) which have to be met if they are to live in the property as their home.

---

[33] See, in particular, *Stokes v Anderson* [1991] 1 FLR 391; *Midland Bank plc v Cooke* [1995] 4 All ER 562; *Drake v Whipp* [1996] 1 FLR 826; *Oxley v Hiscock* [2005] Fam 211.

[34] In this respect, Baroness Hale highlighted the decisions in *Walker v Hall* [1984] 1 FLR 126, *Springette v Defoe* [1992] 2 FLR 388, and *Huntingford v Hobbs* [1993] 1 FLR 736. She held that, to the extent that these decisions hold that a stricter approach to quantification applies in joint ownership cases, they should not be followed: *Stack v Dowden* [2007] 2 AC 432, [65].

[35] Ibid.

On the facts of the case, the Court of Appeal held that Mrs Oxley was entitled to a 40 per cent beneficial share. An equal share was considered disproportionate in light of the difference in the parties' initial cash contributions.

In *Stack v Dowden*, Baroness Hale referred to Chadwick LJ's formula before shifting the emphasis away from 'fairness' towards the parties' common intention.

Stack v Dowden
[2007] 2 AC 432, HL

Baroness Hale

At 61

[. . .] *Oxley v Hiscock* has been hailed by Gray and Gray as 'An important breakthrough' (see p 931 (para 10.138)). The passage quoted is very similar to the view of the Law Commission in *Sharing Homes: A Discussion Paper* (Law Com no 278) p 69 (para 4.27) on the quantification of beneficial entitlement:

> 'If the question really is one of the parties' "common intention", we believe that there is much to be said for adopting what has been called a "holistic approach" to quantification, undertaking a survey of the whole course of dealing between the parties and taking account of all conduct which throws light on the question what shares were intended.'

That may be the preferable way of expressing what is essentially the same thought, for two reasons. First, it emphasises that the search is still for the result which reflects what the parties must, in the light of their conduct, be taken to have intended. Second, therefore, it does not enable the court to abandon that search in favour of the result which the court itself considers fair. For the court to impose its own view of what is fair upon the situation in which the parties find themselves would be to return to the days before *Pettitt v Pettitt* [1969] 2 All ER 385, [1970] AC 777 without even the fig leaf of s 17 of the 1882 Act [. . .]

At 69–70

In law, 'context is everything' and the domestic context is very different from the commercial world. Each case will turn on its own facts. Many more factors than financial contributions may be relevant to divining the parties' true intentions. These include: any advice or discussions at the time of the transfer which cast light upon their intentions then; the reasons why the home was acquired in their joint names; the reasons why (if it be the case) the survivor was authorised to give a receipt for the capital moneys; the purpose for which the home was acquired; the nature of the parties' relationship; whether they had children for whom they both had responsibility to provide a home; how the purchase was financed, both initially and subsequently; how the parties arranged their finances, whether separately or together or a bit of both; how they discharged the outgoings on the property and their other household expenses. When a couple are joint owners of the home and jointly liable for the mortgage, the inferences to be drawn from who pays for what may be very different from the inferences to be drawn when only one is owner of the home. The arithmetical calculation of how much was paid by each is also likely to be less important. It will be easier to draw the inference that they intended that each should contribute as much to the household as they reasonably could and that they would share the eventual benefit or burden equally. The parties' individual characters and personalities may also be a factor in deciding where their true intentions lay. In the cohabitation context, mercenary considerations may be more to the fore than they would be in marriage, but it should not be assumed that they always take pride of place over natural love and affection. At the end of the day, having taken all this into account, cases in which the joint legal owners are to be taken to have intended that their beneficial interests should be different from their legal interests will be very unusual.

This is not, of course, an exhaustive list. There may also be reason to conclude that, whatever the parties' intentions at the outset, these have now changed. An example might be where one party has financed (or constructed himself) an extension or substantial improvement to the property, so that what they have now is significantly different from what they had then.

Baroness Hale's formula represents the view of the majority of the House of Lords.[36] The proposition that emerges from the case is that the issue of quantification is addressed by reference to the '*whole course of dealings between the parties*' (as stated in *Oxley v Hiscock*), but with a view to establishing the common intention of the parties, rather than determining what would constitute a 'fair' share. On the facts of the case, the House of Lords unanimously agreed that Ms Dowden was entitled to the 65 per cent share that she claimed. In *Fowler v Barron*,[37] the Court of Appeal emphasized that the parties' *common* intention alone is relevant. Mr Barron argued that the parties' home had been placed in their joint names to ensure that Miss Fowler (who was considerably younger than him) would benefit on his death, on the assumption that the couple were still together at that time. He had not appreciated that the effect of joint ownership was to confer an immediate beneficial interest on Miss Fowler. This 'secret intention',[38] which was not communicated to Miss Fowler, had no effect on the initial presumption of equal beneficial ownership.

2.2.2 Quantification and *Jones v Kernott*: common intention clarified

Although the common intention basis for rebutting the presumption of joint beneficial ownership is clear, what was left unclear in *Stack v Dowden* is the width of the court's ability to find that common intention given that parties within a close relationship often do not express their intentions in clear and unequivocal terms. Even if they do so, in the light of the ambulatory nature of the constructive trust, the courts may be persuaded to consider whether that intention has changed or should be read in the light of the subsequent course of the parties' joint lives including its ultimate breakdown. For instance, in the unusual case of *Gallarotti v Sebastinelli*[39] there was an express agreement as regards the parties' beneficial interests which was not reflected in an express written trust. Generally the courts will give effect to such an agreement, but on the facts the court considered that the agreement '*did not apply in the events which unfolded*'.[40] The parties were friends with a '*strong, platonic*'[41] relationship who had purchased a home together but in Mr Sebastinelli's sole name. The parties had agreed that they would each have a 50 per cent share, notwithstanding unequal contributions. The parties' friendship came to an end and Mr Gallarotti was excluded from the flat. At first instance, the judge gave effect to the parties' express agreement. The Court of Appeal allowed an appeal and awarded Mr Sebastinelli a 75 per cent beneficial share reflecting his greater contribution. Arden LJ noted that the parties' agreement had anticipated

---

[36] While Lord Neuberger also considered quantification under the constructive trust to be based on the parties' common intention, his approach to quantification otherwise differs in key respects.

[37] [2008] EWCA 377.   [38] Ibid, [36].   [39] [2012] 2 FLR 1231.

[40] Ibid, [24] *per* Arden LJ.   [41] Ibid, [3] *per* Arden LJ.

only a slight imbalance in their contributions, rather than the significant one that had transpired. Judged as a whole *'the only inference that could be drawn was that the parties intended the beneficial ownership should, in substance, reflect their financial contributions'.*[42]

There is no doubt that the court can infer the parties' intentions in determining the quantification of their beneficial entitlement, but the key question is whether a common intention can be imputed as well as inferred. This raised a question as to the interpretation of Baroness Hale's judgment in *Stack v Dowden*, particularly in respect of her comments in para 61 (extracted in section 2.2.1) relating to *Oxley v Hiscock* and the relevance of 'fairness'.[43]

The definition of inferred and imputed intent was considered in *Stack v Dowden* by Lord Neuberger.

Stack v Dowden
[2007] 2 AC 432, HL

Lord Neuberger

At 125–7

While an intention may be inferred as well as express, it may not, at least in my opinion, be imputed. That appears to me to be consistent both with normal principles and with the majority view of this House in *Pettitt v Pettitt*, as accepted by all but Lord Reid in *Gissing v Gissing* (see [1970] 2 All ER 780 at 783, 783–784, 786, 789, [1971] AC 886 at 897, 898, 900, 901, 904), and reiterated by the Court of Appeal in *Grant v Edwards* [1986] 2 All ER 426 at 434–435, [1986] Ch 638 at 651–653. The distinction between inference and imputation may appear a fine one (and in *Gissing v Gissing* [1970] 2 All ER 780 at 787–788, [1971] AC 886 at 902, Lord Pearson, who, on a fair reading I think rejected imputation, seems to have equated it with inference), but it is important.

An inferred intention is one which is objectively deduced to be the subjective actual intention of the parties, in the light of their actions and statements. An imputed intention is one which is attributed to the parties, even though no such actual intention can be deduced from their actions and statements, and even though they had no such intention. Imputation involves concluding what the parties would have intended, whereas inference involves concluding what they did intend.

To impute an intention would not only be wrong in principle and a departure from two decisions of your Lordships' House in this very area, but it also would involve a judge in an exercise which was difficult, subjective and uncertain. (Hence the advantage of the resulting trust presumption.) It would be difficult because the judge would be constructing an intention where none existed at the time, and where the parties may well not have been able to agree. It would be subjective for obvious reasons. It would be uncertain because it is unclear whether one considers a hypothetical negotiation between the actual parties, or what reasonable parties would have agreed. The former is more logical, but would redound to the advantage of an unreasonable party. The latter is more attractive, but is inconsistent with the principle, identified by Baroness Hale (at [61], above), that the court's view of fairness is not the correct yardstick for determining the parties' shares (and see *Pettitt v Pettitt* [1969] 2 All ER 385 at 395, 402, 416, [1970] AC 777 at 801, 809, 826).

---

[42] Ibid, [26] *per* Arden LJ.
[43] On this issue, see Lord Wilson's analysis of Baroness Hale's judgment [2012] AC 776, [85]–[87] with which Lord Walker and Baroness Hale express their disagreement at [13]. These paragraphs are extracted below.

This view was not endorsed by the majority of the House of Lords. Although she did not directly address the distinction between inferred and imputed intent, Baroness Hale emphasized the need to determine the parties' shared intentions 'actual, inferred or *imputed*'.[44]

The meaning of common intention, and in particular the role of imputed intent, was addressed by the Supreme Court in *Jones v Kernott* in a clarification of *Stack v Dowden*. As the extracts that follow show, the Supreme Court unanimously accepted that the parties' common intention can be imputed in limited circumstances but solely in relation to the secondary question of the quantification of beneficial shares. On the facts, the Supreme Court was divided three to two as to whether it was necessary to impute an intention and, indeed, on whether the analysis of particular facts carried practical significance once the legitimacy of imputing an intent was accepted.

Jones v Kernott
[2012] AC 776

Facts: Ms Jones and Mr Kernott were an unmarried couple who had cohabited for a period of ten years. They had initially lived in a property that Ms Jones had bought in her sole name, but they had then acquired the property in question, 39 Badger Hall Avenue, in their joint names and lived there for eight years until the breakdown of their relationship. At that stage, Mr Kernott had left the property while Ms Jones remained with the couple's two children. A deposit for the purchase had been provided by the proceeds of sale of Ms Jones' previous home, while the household expenses had been shared. Once Mr Kernott had moved out, Ms Jones took sole responsibility for the household expenses and had now done so for over 14 years. Shortly after the relationship had broken down, an unsuccessful attempt was made to sell the property. Following this, an endowment policy had been surrendered and the proceeds had been used as a deposit on a home for Mr Kernott, 114 Stanley Road, which was bought in his sole name. The proceedings had been commenced by Mr Kernott to establish his beneficial share in 39 Badger Hall Avenue. At first instance, the judge awarded Ms Jones 90 per cent and Mr Kernott 10 per cent. The Court of Appeal, by a two to one majority allowed an appeal by Mr Kernott and declared that the parties were entitled to equal shares. Ms Jones appealed to the Supreme Court.

Lord Walker and Baroness Hale

At 26–36

Inference or imputation?

In *Stack v Dowden* Lord Neuberger observed (paras 125–126):

"While an intention may be inferred as well as express, it may not, at least in my opinion, be imputed. That appears to me to be consistent both with normal principles and with the majority view of this House in *Pettitt* [1970] AC 777, as accepted by all but Lord Reid in *Gissing v Gissing* [1971] AC 886, 897H, 898B-D, 900E-G, 901B-D, 904E-F, and reiterated by the Court

---

[44] Ibid, [60] (emphasis added).

of Appeal in *Grant v Edwards* [1986] Ch 638 at 651F-653A. The distinction between inference and imputation may appear a fine one (and in *Gissing v Gissing* [1971] AC 886, at 902G-H, Lord Pearson, who, on a fair reading I think rejected imputation, seems to have equated it with inference), but it is important.

An inferred intention is one which is objectively deduced to be the subjective actual intention of the parties, in the light of their actions and statements. An imputed intention is one which is attributed to the parties, even though no such actual intention can be deduced from their actions and statements, and even though they had no such intention. Imputation involves concluding what the parties would have intended, whereas inference involves concluding what they did intend."

Rimer LJ made some similar observations in the Court of Appeal in this case [2010] EWCA Civ 578, [2010] 1 WLR 2401, paras 76–77.

Both observations had been to some extent anticipated as long ago as 1970 by Lord Reid in his speech in *Gissing v Gissing* [1971] AC 886, 897 [. . .]

This sort of constructive intention (or any other constructive state of mind), and the difficulties that they raise, are familiar in many branches of the law. Whenever a judge concludes that an individual "intended, or must be taken to have intended," or "knew, or must be taken to have known," there is an elision between what the judge can find as a fact (usually by inference) on consideration of the admissible evidence, and what the law may supply (to fill the evidential gap) by way of a presumption. The presumption of a resulting trust is a clear example of a rule by which the law *does* impute an intention, the rule being based on a very broad generalisation about human motivation, as Lord Diplock noted in *Pettitt v Pettitt* [1970] AC 777, 824:

"It would, in my view, be an abuse of the legal technique for ascertaining or imputing intention to apply to transactions between the post-war generation of married couples 'presumptions' which are based upon inferences of fact which an earlier generation of judges drew as to the most likely intentions of earlier generations of spouses belonging to the propertied classes of a different social era."

That was 40 years ago and we are now another generation on.

The decision in *Stack v Dowden* produced a division of the net proceeds of sale of the house in shares roughly corresponding to the parties' financial contributions over the years. The majority reached that conclusion by inferring a common intention (see Lady Hale's opinion at para 92, following her detailed analysis of the facts starting at para 86). Only Lord Neuberger reached the same result by applying the classic resulting trust doctrine (which involved, it is to be noted, imputing an intention to the parties).

In deference to the comments of Lord Neuberger and Rimer LJ, we accept that the search is primarily to ascertain the parties' actual shared intentions, whether expressed or to be inferred from their conduct. However, there are at least two exceptions. The first, which is not this case, is where the classic resulting trust presumption applies. Indeed, this would be rare in a domestic context, but might perhaps arise where domestic partners were also business partners: see *Stack v Dowden*, para 32. The second, which for reasons which will appear later is in our view also not this case but will arise much more frequently, is where it is clear that the beneficial interests are to be shared, but it is impossible to divine a common intention as to the proportions in which they are to be shared. In those two situations, the court is driven to impute an intention to the parties which they may never have had.

Lord Diplock, in *Gissing v Gissing* [1971] AC 886, 909, pointed out that, once the court was satisfied that it was the parties' common intention that the beneficial interest was to be shared in some proportion or other, the court might have to give effect to that common intention by determining what in all the circumstances was a fair share. And it is that thought which is picked up in the subsequent cases, culminating in the judgment of Chadwick LJ in *Oxley v Hiscock* [2005] Fam 211, paras 65, 66 and 69, and in particular the passage in para 69 which was given qualified approval in *Stack v Dowden*:

> "the answer is that each is entitled to that share which the court considers fair having regard to the whole course of dealing between them in relation to the property."

Chadwick LJ was not there saying that fairness was the criterion for determining whether or not the property should be shared, but he was saying that the court might have to impute an intention to the parties as to the proportions in which the property would be shared. In deducing what the parties, as reasonable people, would have thought at the relevant time, regard would obviously be had to their whole course of dealing in relation to the property.

However, while the conceptual difference between inferring and imputing is clear, the difference in practice may not be so great. In this area, as in many others, the scope for inference is wide. The law recognizes that a legitimate inference may not correspond to an individual's subjective state of mind. As Lord Diplock also put it in *Gissing v Gissing* [1971] AC 886, 906:

> "As in so many branches of English law in which legal rights and obligations depend upon the intentions of the parties to a transaction, the relevant intention of each party is the intention which was reasonably understood by the other party to be manifested by that party's words or conduct notwithstanding that he did not consciously formulate that intention in his own mind or even acted with some different intention which he did not communicate to the other party."

This point has been developed by Nick Piska, "Intention, Fairness and the Presumption of Resulting Trust after *Stack v Dowden*" (2008) 71 MLR 120. He observes at pp 127–128:

> "Subjective intentions can never be accessed directly, so the court must always direct itself to a consideration of the parties' objective intentions through a careful consideration of the relevant facts. The point is that the imputation/inference distinction may well be a distinction without a difference with regard to the process of determining parties' intentions. It is not that the parties' subjective intentions are irrelevant but rather that a finding as to subjective intention can only be made on an objective basis."

In several parts of the British Commonwealth federal or provincial legislation has given the court a limited jurisdiction to vary or adjust proprietary rights in the home when an unmarried couple split up. Most require a minimum period of two years' cohabitation (or less if there are children) before the jurisdiction is exercisable. In England the Law Commission has made recommendations on similar lines (Law Com No 307, *Cohabitation: The Financial Consequences of Relationship Breakdown*, 2007), but there are no plans to implement them in the near future.

In the meantime there will continue to be many difficult cases in which the court has to reach a conclusion on sparse and conflicting evidence. It is the court's duty to reach a decision on even the most difficult case. As the deputy judge (Mr Nicholas Strauss QC) said in his admirable judgment [2009] EWHC 1713 (Ch), [2010] 1 WLR 2401, para 33 (in the context of a discussion of fairness) "that is what courts are for." That was an echo (conscious or unconscious) of what Sir Thomas Bingham MR said, in a different family law context, in *Re Z (A Minor) (Identification: Restrictions on Publication)* [1997] Fam 1, 33. The trial judge has the onerous task of finding the primary facts and drawing the necessary inferences and conclusions, and appellate courts will be slow to overturn the trial judge's findings.

Lord Collins

At 64–5

I agree, therefore, that authority justifies the conceptual approach of Lord Walker and Lady Hale that, in joint names cases, the common intention to displace the presumption of equality can, in the absence of express agreement, be inferred (rather than imputed: see para 31 of the joint judgment) from their conduct, and where, in such a case, it is not possible to ascertain or infer what share was intended, each will be entitled to a fair share in the light of the whole course of dealing between them in relation to the property.

That said, it is my view that in the present context the difference between inference and imputation will hardly ever matter (as Lord Walker and Lady Hale recognise at para 34), and that what is one person's inference will be another person's imputation. A similar point has arisen in many other contexts, for example, the difference between implied terms which depend on the parties' actual intention, terms based on a rule of law, and implied terms based on an intention imputed to the parties from their actual circumstances: *Luxor (Eastbourne) Ltd v Cooper* [1941] AC 108, 137, per Lord Wright. Or the point under the law prior to the Contracts (Applicable Law) Act 1990 as to whether (in the absence of an express choice) the proper law of the contract depended on an intention to be inferred from the circumstances or on the law which had the closest connection with the contract.

Lord Kerr

At 72–5

It is hardly controversial to suggest that the parties' intention should be given effect to where it can be ascertained and that, although discussions between them will always be the most reliable basis on which to draw an inference as to that intention, these are not the only circumstances in which that exercise will be possible. There is a natural inclination to prefer inferring an intention to imputing one. If the parties' intention can be inferred, the court is not imposing a solution. It is, instead, deciding what the parties must be taken to have intended and where that is possible it is obviously preferable to the court's enforcing a resolution. But the conscientious quest to discover the parties' actual intention should cease when it becomes clear either that this is simply not deducible from the evidence or that no common intention exists. It would be unfortunate if the concept of inferring were to be strained so as to avoid the less immediately attractive option of imputation. In summary, therefore, I believe that the court should anxiously examine the circumstances in order, where possible, to ascertain the parties' intention but it should not be reluctant to recognise, when it is appropriate to do so, that inference of an intention is not possible and that imputation of an intention is the only course to follow [. . .]

The reason that I question the aptness of the notion of imputing an intention is that, in the final analysis, the exercise is wholly unrelated to ascertainment of the parties' views. It involves the court deciding what is fair in light of the whole course of dealing with the property. That decision has nothing to do with what the parties intended, or what might be supposed would have been their intention had they addressed that question. In many ways, it would be preferable to have a stark choice between deciding whether it is possible to deduce what their intention was and, where it is not, deciding what is fair, without elliptical references to what their intention might have—or should have—been. But imputing intention has entered the lexicon of this area of law and it is probably impossible to discard it now.

While the dichotomy between inferring and imputing an intention remains, however, it seems to me that it is necessary that there be a well marked dividing line between the two.

As soon as it is clear that inferring an intention is not possible, the focus of the court's attention should be squarely on what is fair and, as I have said, that is an obviously different examination than is involved in deciding what the parties actually intended.

Lord Wilson

At 85–9

In para 61 of her ground-breaking speech in *Stack v Dowden* Lady Hale quoted, with emphasis, the words of Chadwick LJ in para 69 of *Oxley v Hiscock*, which I have quoted in para 71 above. Then she quoted a passage from a Discussion Paper published by the Law Commission in July 2002 and entitled "Sharing Homes" about the proper approach to identifying the proportions which "were intended". Finally she added four sentences to each of which, in quoting them as follows, I take the liberty of attributing a number:

> "[1.] That may be the preferable way of expressing what is essentially the same thought, for two reasons. [2.] First, it emphasises that the search is still for the result which reflects what the parties must, in the light of their conduct, be taken to have intended. [3.] Second, therefore, it does not enable the court to abandon that search in favour of the result which the court itself considers fair. [4.] For the court to impose its own view of what is fair upon the situation in which the parties find themselves would be to return to the days before *Pettitt v Pettitt* ... without even the fig leaf of section 17 of the 1882 Act."

I leave on one side Lady Hale's first sentence although, whereas Chadwick LJ was identifying the criterion for imputing the common intention, the context of the passage in the Discussion Paper suggests that the Law Commission was postulating a criterion for inferring it. On any view Lady Hale's second sentence is helpful; and, by her reference to what the parties must, in the light of their conduct, be taken to have intended (as opposed to what they did intend), Lady Hale made clear that, by then, she was addressing the power to resort to imputation. Lady Hale's fourth sentence has been neatly explained—by Mr Nicholas Strauss QC, deputy judge of the Chancery Division, who determined the first appeal in these proceedings, at para 30—as being that, in the event that the evidence were to suggest that, whether by expression or by inference, the parties intended that the beneficial interests in the home should be held in certain proportions, equity would not "impose" different proportions upon them; and, at para 47 above, Lord Walker and Lady Hale endorse Mr Strauss's explanation.

The problem has lain in Lady Hale's third sentence. Where equity is driven to impute the common intention, how can it do so other than by search for the result which the court itself considers fair? The sentence was not obiter dictum so rightly, under our system, judges below the level of this court have been unable to ignore it. Even in these proceedings judges in the courts below have wrestled with it. Mr Strauss observed, at para 31, that it was difficult to see how—at that final stage of the inquiry—the process could work without the court's supply of what it considered to be fair. In his judgment on the second appeal Lord Justice Rimer went so far as to suggest, at para 77, that Lady Hale's third sentence must have meant that, contrary to appearances, she had not intended to recognise a power to impute a common intention at all.

I respectfully disagree with Lady Hale's third sentence.

Lord Walker and Lady Hale observe, at para 34 above, that in practice the difference between inferring and imputing a common intention to the parties may not be great. I consider that, as a generalisation, their observation goes too far—at least if the court is to take (as in my view it should) an ordinarily rigorous approach to the task of inference. Indeed in the present case they conclude, at paras 48 and 49, that, in relation to Chadwick LJ's second question the proper inference from the evidence, which, if he did not draw, the trial judge should have drawn, was that the parties came to intend that the proportions of the beneficial interests in the home should be held on a basis which in effect equates to 90% to Ms Jones and to 10% to Mr Kernott (being the proportions in favour of which the judge ruled). As it happens, reflective perhaps of the more rigorous approach to the task of inference which I prefer, I regard it, as did Mr Strauss at [48] and [49] of his judgment, as more realistic, in the light of the evidence before the judge, to conclude that inference is impossible but to proceed to impute to the parties the intention that it should be held on a basis which equates to those proportions. At all events I readily concur in the result which Lord Walker and Lady Hale propose.

The Supreme Court reinstated an order made by the judge at first instance (that had been overturned on appeal) granting Ms Jones a 90 per cent beneficial interest. Lord Walker and Baroness Hale consider the 'logical inference' of the parties' conduct was that Mr Kernott's interest in the parties' shared home crystallized at the point at which an endowment policy was surrendered to enable him to buy his own home and, therefore, that a common intention could be inferred.[45] Lord Collins agreed with this analysis.[46] Lord Kerr and Lord Wilson preferred to base the decision on an imputed intent.[47]

The approach to quantification of beneficial shares in a constructive trust following *Jones v Kernott* is summarized in the following extract.

Jones v Kernott
[2012] AC 776

Lord Walker and Baroness Hale

At 51–2

In summary, therefore, the following are the principles applicable in a case such as this, where a family home is bought in the joint names of a cohabiting couple who are both responsible for any mortgage, but without any express declaration of their beneficial interests.
  (1) The starting point is that equity follows the law and they are joint tenants both in law and in equity. (2) That presumption can be displaced by showing (a) that the parties had a different common intention at the time when they acquired the home, or (b) that they later formed the common intention that their respective shares would change. (3) Their common intention is to be deduced objectively from their conduct: "the relevant intention of each party is the intention which was reasonably understood by the other party to be manifested by that party's words and conduct notwithstanding that he did not consciously formulate that intention in his own mind or even acted with some different intention which he did not communicate to the other party" (Lord Diplock in *Gissing v Gissing* [1971] AC 886, 906). Examples of the sort of evidence which might be relevant to drawing such inferences are given in *Stack v Dowden*, at para 69. (4) In those cases where it is clear either (a) that the parties did not intend joint tenancy at the outset, or (b) had changed their original intention, but it is not possible to ascertain by direct evidence or by inference what their actual intention was as to the shares in which they would own the property, "the answer is that each is entitled to that share which

---

45 [2012] AC 776, [48].   46 Ibid, [55].   47 Ibid, [76]–[77] and [89].

the court considers fair having regard to the whole course of dealing between them in relation to the property": Chadwick LJ in *Oxley v Hiscock* [2005] Fam 211, para 69. In our judgment, "the whole course of dealing [. . .] in relation to the property" should be given a broad
meaning, enabling a similar range of factors to be taken into account as may be relevant to
ascertaining the parties' actual intentions. (5) Each case will turn on its own facts. Financial
contributions are relevant but there are many other factors which may enable the court to
decide what shares were either intended (as in case (3)) or fair (as in case (4)).

   This case is not concerned with a family home that is put into the name of one party only.
The starting point is different. The first issue is whether it was intended that the other party
have any beneficial interest in the property at all. If he does, the second issue is what that
interest is. There is no presumption of joint beneficial ownership. But their common intention has once again to be deduced objectively from their conduct. If the evidence shows a
common intention to share beneficial ownership but does not show what shares were intended, the court will have to proceed as at para 51(4) and (5) above.

Thus the courts will look only to an express or inferred intention to establish the constructive
trust by which the presumption of joint beneficial ownership may in unusual circumstances
be rebutted. However, once that common intention is established the court can look to wider
factors, which may involve imputation, to determine exactly what those shares should be.
It can be tempting to run these two stages together with a loose use of language. This was a
trap into which the first instance judge fell in *Barnes v Phillips*.[48] In dismissing the appeal,
the Court of Appeal reiterated the limited role of imputation and generously re-interpreting
the first instance judge's approach along the correct lines.

   Subsequent to *Jones v Kernott*, an imputed intent was used to determine this second
element of the quantification question in the case of *Aspden v Elvy*.[49] Mr Aspden successfully established an inferred agreement to share the beneficial interest in a property in the
sole legal ownership of Ms Elvy (that aspect of the case is discussed in section 2.3.3 below).
Having established that Mr Aspden was entitled to a share, HHJ Behrens imputed an intention that Mr Aspden should receive a 25 per cent share although he acknowledged that the
figure was '*somewhat arbitrary*'.[50]

   Arbitrariness seems almost inevitable since once the court looks beyond the 'actual' intention of the parties, it is difficult to know precisely how shares will be quantified or the
weight that will be placed on individual factors. Gardner has suggested that the outcome
where resort is made to an imputed intent should depend on whether the parties' relationship is a 'materially communal' one in which there has been a pooling of resources. Where
this is the case, the parties should receive equal shares. In non-materially communal relationships the initial presumption of beneficial ownership should be reversed to the extent
necessary to correct the unjust enrichment of one party by the other's contributions.[51]

---

[48] [2015] EWCA Civ 1056. See Hayward, 'Common Intention Constructive Trusts and the Role of
Imputation in Theory and Practice' [2016] Conv 233.

[49] [2012] EWHC 1387 (Ch). See Lee, '"And the Waters Began to Subside": Imputing Intention under
Jones v Kernott' [2012] Conv 421. See also *Thompson v Hurst* [2014] 1 FLR 238 where a 10 per cent share was
awarded through imputed intent.

[50] Ibid, [128].

[51] Gardner, 'Family Property Today' (2008) 124 LQR 422, 431–3, developed in Gardner and MacKenzie,
An Introduction to Land Law (Oxford: Hart Publishing, 4th edn, 2015) para 9.3.5–9.3.7.

2.3 SOLE LEGAL OWNER

Where there is sole legal ownership the initial presumption is of sole beneficial ownership. If a claimant argues that he or she has a beneficial interest, then a primary acquisition question arises. A claimant may establish a beneficial interest through a constructive or resulting trust. If successful, then the claimant's beneficial share must be quantified.

2.3.1 Constructive trust

The leading case on the elements of a claim to a common intention constructive trust is the House of Lords' decision, prior to *Stack v Dowden*, in *Lloyds Bank plc v Rosset*.[52] In that case, Lord Bridge drew a clear distinction between two distinct forms of the common intention constructive trust.

Lloyds Bank plc v Rosset
[1991] 1 AC 107, HL

Facts: The claimant, Mrs Rosset, sought to establish a beneficial interest in the matrimonial home, which was solely owned by her husband. The house had been purchased in a semi-derelict condition with money from Mr Rosset's family trust and the trustees had insisted on his sole ownership. Mr Rosset had also funded the cost of the renovations. Mrs Rosset had made no financial contribution to the acquisition, or the cost of renovations, but she had assisted in the building works in various respects.

Lord Bridge

At 132–3

The first and fundamental question which must always be resolved is whether, independently of any inference to be drawn from the conduct of the parties in the course of sharing the house as their home and managing their joint affairs, there has at any time prior to acquisition, or exceptionally at some later date, been any agreement, arrangement or understanding reached between them that the property is to be shared beneficially. The finding of an agreement or arrangement to share in this sense can only, I think, be based on evidence of express discussions between the partners, however imperfectly remembered and however imprecise their terms may have been. Once a finding to this effect is made it will only be necessary for the partner asserting a claim to a beneficial interest against the partner entitled to the legal estate to show that he or she has acted to his or her detriment or significantly altered his or her position in reliance on the agreement in order to give rise to a constructive trust or a proprietary estoppel.

In sharp contrast with this situation is the very different one where there is no evidence to support a finding of an agreement or arrangement to share, however reasonable it might have been for the parties to reach such an arrangement if they had applied their minds to the question, and where the court must rely entirely on the conduct of the parties both as the basis from which to infer a common intention to share the property beneficially and as the conduct relied on to give rise to a constructive trust. In this situation direct contributions

---

[52] [1991] 1 AC 107.

> to the purchase price by the partner who is not the legal owner, whether initially or by payment of mortgage instalments, will readily justify the inference necessary to the creation of a constructive trust. But, as I read the authorities, it is at least extremely doubtful whether anything less will do.

Hence, according to *Rosset*, the common intention constructive trust is divided into those founded on an express agreement and those in which the agreement between the parties is inferred by '*direct contributions to the purchase price*'. Where there is an express agreement, the claimant must also show detrimental reliance on the agreement, while in inferred agreement cases, the claimant's contribution serves the dual purpose of providing evidence of the agreement and of detrimental reliance. On the facts of the case, Mrs Rosset's claim failed: there was no express agreement between the parties and Mrs Rosset had not made any direct contribution to the purchase, which Lord Bridge considered necessary for an agreement to be inferred.

For a claim to succeed, the common intention must be established between the claimant and the legal owner of the property. In *Smith v Bottomley*[53] Ms Smith's claim to a beneficial interest in a Barn failed. Her claim was based on promises made by her former cohabitee, Mr Bottomley but the Barn had been acquired by a company which was wholly owned and controlled by him. Sales J explained that no claim that Ms Smith had against Mr Bottomley personally was converted into a claim against the company as a separate legal person.[54]

Lord Bridge's analysis of the acquisition question has met with significant criticism, exemplified by the following extract.

Fox O'Mahony, 'Property Outsiders and the Hidden Politics of Doctrinalism' (2014) 67 CLP 409, 430–1

From the margins, we are reminded that the rules set out in Rosset, protecting financial contributions and expressed intentions, embedded a deeply conservative vision of property, in which claimants are judged for their conduct against normative expectations that favour acquisitive-individualism over family-communitarianism, self-interest over trust, and the 'tidy lives' of consent, private ordering, and capital investment over non-financial contributions and the messy realities of family life. On one level, this can be explained as a necessary consequence of our commitment to 'certainty', to enable solicitors to advise their clients and to support those clients in avoiding litigation. Yet, as a reason not to admit more 'flexible' criteria to the common intention constructive trust, the commitment to certainty inflates the value and significance of legal advice in the conveyancing process. Certainty is also advanced as a necessary value to avoid litigation, and yet this is countered by the argument that litigation is sometimes necessary to ensure that certain types of cases (for example, cases which reveal the existence, or perhaps the extent, of specific injustices) reach a public forum.

Following *Stack v Dowden* and *Jones v Kernott* both the acquisition of a beneficial interest under a constructive trust and the quantification of shares is founded on the common intention of the parties. This alignment of the basis on which beneficial interests are acquired and quantified raises the question whether common intention should be determined the same

---

[53] [2014] 1 FLR 626.   [54] Ibid, [57].

way in both stages of the trust. Two issues must be separated. First, *Rosset* enables a common intention to be express or inferred while, as we have seen, *Jones v Kernott* also provides for a common intention to be imputed. At the present stage, there is no suggestion that a common intention at the primary acquisition stage can be imputed.[55] Secondly, and more significantly, is the issue of whether some or all of the criteria given by Lady Hale in para [69] of her judgment in *Stack v Dowden* (extracted in section 2.2.1) as being relevant to inferring the parties' common intention in respect of quantification can also be used to determine the parties' common intention to share beneficial ownership. Such a development would represent a significant expansion of the grounds on which *Rosset* enables a common intention to be inferred and consign to legal history key debates that have arisen on the interpretation of *Rosset*.

To date there is no definitive guidance on the extent to which, if at all, para [69] can be applied to infer a common intention to share the beneficial interest. In light of the precedential value of *Rosset* as a decision of the House of Lords, such guidance could come only from the Supreme Court in a case involving sole legal ownership. The operation of the constructive trust at the primary acquisition stage in cases of sole legal ownership is currently at a crossroads. As the trust continues to develop two possible futures arise: either the application of para [69] in whole or part to infer a common intention; or the maintenance of the *Rosset* criteria, with some relaxation in respect of the requirement (for an inferred agreement) of direct financial contributions. Therefore, we set out the *Rosset* model of the trust before considering the possible expansion to the acquisition question of the *Stack v Dowden* and *Jones v Kernott* model of inferred agreement.

2.3.2 The *Rosset* model of express and inferred agreement constructive trusts

On Lord Bridge's model, an agreement to share beneficial ownership can be inferred only on the basis of a direct cash contribution to the purchase of property, either initially or by contributions to a mortgage. In *Stack v Dowden*, in the context of a general discussion of the development of the constructive trust, Lord Walker doubted that this aspect of Lord Bridge's judgment took full account of conflicting views in *Gissing v Gissing*[56] and noted that it had attracted 'trenchant criticism' from academic commentators. He suggested that '*the law has moved on*'[57]—a comment that appeared to be endorsed by Baroness Hale.[58] The opposing views expressed in *Gissing v Gissing* are set out in the following extract.

Gissing v Gissing
[1971] AC 886, HL

Lord Reid

At 896

As I understand it, the competing view is that, when the wife makes direct contributions to the purchase by paying something either to the vendor or to the building society which

---

[55] See *Jones v Kernott* [2012] AC 776, [78]–[84] where Lord Wilson carefully limits the operation of imputed intent to quantification. See further Lord Collins at [66] and *Barnes v Phillips* [2015] EWCA Civ 1056.
[56] [1971] AC 886.   [57] [2007] 2 AC 432, [26].   [58] Ibid, [60].

is financing the purchase, she gets a beneficial interest in the house although nothing was ever said or agreed about this at the time: but that, when her contributions are only indirect by way of paying sums which the husband would otherwise have had to pay, she gets nothing unless at the time of the acquisition there was some agreement that she should get a share. I can see no good reason for this distinction and I think that in many cases it would be unworkable. Suppose the spouses have a joint bank account. In accordance with their arrangement she pays in enough money to meet the household bills and so there is enough to pay the purchase price instalments and their bills as well as their personal expenses. They never discuss whose money is to go to pay for the house and whose is to go to pay for other things. How can anyone tell whether she has made a direct or only an indirect contribution to paying for the house? It cannot surely depend on who signs which cheques. Is she to be deprived of a share if she says 'I can pay in enough to pay for the household bills,' but given a share if she says 'I can pay in £10 per week regularly.'

Lord Diplock

At 909

Where the wife has made no initial contribution to the cash deposit and legal charges and no direct contribution to the mortgage instalments nor any adjustment to her contribution to other expenses of the household which it can be inferred was referable to the acquisition of the house, there is in the absence of evidence of an express agreement between the parties no material to justify the court in inferring that it was the common intention of the parties that she should have any beneficial interest in a matrimonial home conveyed into the sole name of the husband, merely because she continued to contribute out of her own earnings or private income to other expenses of the household. For such conduct is no less consistent with a common intention to share the day-to-day expenses of the household, while each spouse retains a separate interest in capital assets acquired with their own moneys or obtained by inheritance or gift. There is nothing here to rebut the prima facie inference that a purchaser of land who pays the purchase price and takes a conveyance and grants a mortgage in his own name intends to acquire the sole beneficial interest as well as the legal estate [. . .]

It is suggested that, as regards indirect financial contributions, it is difficult to disagree with the tenor of Lord Reid's judgment that the determination of rights in the home should not be dependent on the happenstance of how a family's finances are arranged. In light of the divergence in authorities on this point prior to *Lloyds Bank plc v Rosset* (as acknowledged in *Stack v Dowden*), such an extension of the inferred agreement constructive trust would be a modest development.

An express agreement constructive trust will be imposed where there is an agreement to share the beneficial interest, in reliance on which the claimant has acted to his or her detriment. In *Rosset*, Lord Bridge held that the agreement must be based on '*evidence of express discussions between the partners, however imperfectly remembered and however imprecise their terms may have been*'. Further, he suggested that the agreement must be reached prior to acquisition, or only exceptionally at a later date. Applied strictly, this latter requirement would preclude the trust arising where the claimant moves into a home already purchased by the legal owner. In practice, post-acquisition express agreements have been accepted, without reference to a requirement that the case must be 'exceptional'.[59]

The requirement of 'express discussions' appears to be unrealistic in the domestic context. In *Pettitt v Pettitt*, Lord Hodson noted:[60] '*The conception of a normal married couple spending the long winter evenings hammering out agreements about their possessions appears grotesque.*' As the following extract illustrates, there is a sense of artificiality in the courts' detailed examination of the parties' relationship in the search for evidence of an agreement.

Hammond v Mitchell
[1991] 1 WLR 1127, HC

Waite J

At 1139

[The] tenderest exchanges of a common law courtship may assume an unforeseen significance many years later when they are brought under equity's microscope and subjected to an analysis under which many thousands of pounds of value may be liable to turn on fine questions as to whether the relevant words were spoken in earnest or in dalliance and with or without representational intent.

The artificiality of the search for an agreement is highlighted by Lord Bridge's acceptance in *Rosset* of *Eves v Eves*[61] and *Grant v Edwards*[62] as 'outstanding examples' of agreements.[63] In these cases, an agreement was found in the fact that the legal owner had given the claimant an 'excuse' for not placing the property in the parties' joint names: in *Eves v Eves*, the claimant had been told that, but for the fact she was under the age of 21 (the age of majority at the time), the house would have been placed in the parties' joint names; in *Grant v Edwards*, the claimant was told that the house was not put in joint names because this could prejudice her own divorce proceedings. Lord Bridge suggested that such excuses provide evidence of an agreement, because the claimant '*had been clearly led by the [legal owner] to believe, when they set up home together, that the property would belong to them jointly*'.[64] However, the appropriate interpretation of an 'excuse' has proved contentious and has attracted competing academic views.[65]

Where the trust is based on an express agreement, it is necessary to consider whether the claimant has relied on the agreement to his or her detriment. The requirement of detriment is concerned with what acts the claimant has done. It is assessed objectively.[66] The most authoritative judicial discussion of what acts constitute sufficient detriment is contained in *Grant v Edwards*. Nourse LJ gave the leading judgment in the case. While Mustill LJ and Browne-Wilkinson VC indicated their agreement, in fact, there are some differences in each judge's approach to detriment.

---

[59] See *Hammond v Mitchell* [1991] 1 WLR 1127.   [60] [1971] AC 777, [810].
[61] [1975] 1 WLR 1338.   [62] [1986] Ch 638.   [63] [1991] 1 AC 107, [133].   [64] Ibid.
[65] Compare, in particular, the views of Gardner, 'Rethinking Family Property' (1993) 109 LQR 263; Glover and Todd, 'The Myth of Common Intention' (1996) 16 LS 325, 331; Mee, *The Property Rights of Cohabitees* (1999), p 123.
[66] Lawson, 'The Things We Do for Love: Detrimental Reliance in the Family Home' [1996] LS 218, 219.

Grant v Edwards
[1986] Ch 638, CA

Facts: Mrs Grant and Mr Edwards were cohabitants. As we have noted, Mr Edwards had given Mrs Grant an excuse for not conveying their home into their joint names and this constituted an express agreement for the purposes of a constructive trust. Mr Edwards had paid a deposit and the mortgage instalments for the house, while Mrs Grant had made substantial contributions to the general household expenses and to bringing up the parties' children. It was clear from the evidence that Mr Edwards would have been unable to maintain payments on two mortgages secured over the home without Mrs Grant's contributions. The Court of Appeal held that Mrs Grant had acted sufficiently to her detriment (and had done so in reliance on the agreement) for her claim to a constructive trust to succeed.

Nourse LJ

At 649–50

It seems therefore, on the authorities as they stand, that a distinction is to be made between conduct from which the common intention can be inferred on the one hand and conduct which amounts to an acting upon it on the other. There remains this difficult question: what is the quality of conduct required for the latter purpose? The difficulty is caused, I think because although the common intention has been made plain, everything else remains a matter of inference. Let me illustrate it in this way. It would be possible to take the view that the mere moving into the house by the woman amounted to an acting upon the common intention. But that was evidently not the view of the majority in *Eves v. Eves* [1975] 1 W.L.R. 1338. and the reason for that may be that, in the absence of evidence, the law is not so cynical as to infer that a woman will only go to live with a man to whom she is not married if she understands that she is to have an interest in their home. So what sort of conduct is required? In my judgment it must be conduct on which the woman could not reasonably have been expected to embark unless she was to have an interest in the house. If she was not to have such an interest, she could reasonably be expected to go and live with her lover, but not, for example, to wield a 14-lb. sledge hammer in the front garden. In adopting the latter kind of conduct she is seen to act to her detriment on the faith of the common intention [. . .]

In the circumstances, it seems that it may properly be inferred that the plaintiff did make substantial indirect contributions to the instalments payable under both mortgages. This is a point which seems to have escaped the judge, but I think that there is an explanation for that. He was concentrating, as no doubt were counsel, on the plaintiff's claim that she herself had paid all the instalments under the second mortgage. It seems very likely that the indirect consequences of her very substantial contribution to the other expenses were not fully explored.

Was the conduct of the plaintiff in making substantial indirect contributions to the instalments payable under both mortgages conduct upon which she could not reasonably have been expected to embark unless she was to have an interest in the house? I answer that question in the affirmative. I cannot see upon what other basis she could reasonably have been expected to give the defendant such substantial assistance in paying off mortgages on his house. I therefore conclude that the plaintiff did act to her detriment on the faith of the common intention between her and the defendant that she was to have some sort of proprietary interest in the house.

Mustill LJ

At 652–3

(4) For present purposes, the event happening on acquisition may take one of the following shapes. (a) An express bargain whereby the proprietor promises the claimant an interest in the property, in return for an explicit undertaking by the claimant to act in a certain way. (b) An express but incomplete bargain whereby the proprietor promises the claimant an interest in the property, on the basis that the claimant will do something in return. The parties do not themselves make explicit what the claimant is to do. The court therefore has to complete the bargain for them by means of implication, when it comes to decide whether the proprietor's promise has been matched by conduct falling within whatever undertaking the claimant must be taken to have given sub silentio. (c) An explicit promise by the proprietor that the claimant will have an interest in the property, unaccompanied by any express or tacit agreement as to a quid pro quo. (d) A common intention, not made explicit, to the effect that the claimant will have an interest in the property, if she subsequently acts in a particular way [. . .]

The propositions do not touch two questions of general importance [. . .] The second question is closer to the present case: namely, whether a promise by the proprietor to confer an interest, but with no element of mutuality (i.e. situation (c) above) can effectively confer an interest if the claimant relies upon it by acting to her detriment. This question was not directly addressed in *Gissing v. Gissing* [1971] A.C. 886, although the speech of Lord Diplock, at p. 905, supports an affirmative answer. The plaintiff's case was not argued on this footing in the present appeal, and since the appeal can be decided on other grounds, I prefer not to express an opinion on this important point.

Browne-Wilkinson VC

At 656–7

There is little guidance in the authorities on constructive trusts as to what is necessary to prove that the claimant so acted to her detriment. What "link" has to be shown between the common intention and the actions relied on? Does there have to be positive evidence that the claimant did the acts in conscious reliance on the common intention? Does the court have to be satisfied that she would not have done the acts relied on but for the common intention, e.g. would not the claimant have contributed to household expenses out of affection for the legal owner and as part of their joint life together even if she had no interest in the house? Do the acts relied on as a detriment have to be inherently referable to the house, e.g. contribution to the purchase or physical labour on the house?

I do not think it is necessary to express any concluded view on these questions in order to decide this case [. . .]

As at present advised, once it has been shown that there was a common intention that the claimant should have an interest in the house, any act done by her to her detriment relating to the joint lives of the parties is, in my judgment, sufficient detriment to qualify. The acts do not have to be inherently referable to the house.

Mustill LJ's approach is notable as looking for a quid pro quo between the parties. This reflects the basis of the trust in the parties' common intention. While a clear bargain may be unusual, where one exists, it seems legitimate for the court to treat the bargained-for acts as sufficient detriment.[67]

There is a significant difference, however, between the approaches adopted by Nourse LJ and Browne-Wilkinson VC. On Nourse LJ's test, detriment requires conduct on the part of the claimant that he or she could not reasonably be expected to do unless he or she was to have an interest in the house. In contrast, Browne-Wilkinson VC's accepts as detriment all acts done by the claimant as part of the parties' joint lives. Subsequent decisions have favoured Nourse LJ's test, which has required courts to reject conduct that the court considers it 'reasonable' for the claimant to have undertaken by reason of the parties' relationship (unless explicitly done as part of a quid pro quo).

The assumption underlying this test is highlighted by Lawson.

Lawson, 'The Things We Do for Love: Detrimental Reliance in the Family Home' (1996) LS 218, 219–20

Nourse LJ's test rests on the assumption that certain types of behaviour can reasonably be expected of people who believe that they have an interest in their home, but not of people who have no such belief. If the behaviour is of a type that can reasonably be expected of people acting purely out of love and affection or the desire to live in pleasant, comfortable surroundings, it will not normally be considered detrimental. It may be so regarded, however, if it was actually requested by the legal owner as the quid pro quo for the beneficial interest. If conduct of a type judges might ordinarily expect of a claimant motivated by love and affection has been requested by the legal owner, judges will be prepared to assume that, had it not been for the promise of the beneficial interest, the claimant would not have performed the conduct.

Direct contributions to the purchase of property, which would be sufficient for the courts to infer an agreement to share, would necessarily be sufficient to constitute detriment where there is an express agreement between the parties. Indirect financial contributions, as illustrated in *Grant v Edwards*, are also accepted as detriment, regardless of the debate as to whether such contributions should also be a sufficient basis for the courts to infer an agreement. Substantial improvements to property will also suffice,[68] but not redecoration of a more 'ephemeral'[69] nature. Beyond such clear examples, it has been difficult for the courts to assess what conduct the claimant could not reasonably be expected to perform unless he or she was to obtain an interest in the home.

Unfortunately, in making such assessments, courts have tended to draw on outdated stereotypes of what conduct it is reasonable to expect of a man or woman. Because most claimants have been women, the most significant effect of this approach has been the rejection of domestic work and childcare as constituting acts of detriment.

---

[67] Compare *Jennings v Rice* [2002] EWCA Civ 159, [45], in which, in the context of exercising remedial discretion in proprietary estoppel, Robert Walker LJ indicated that where the claimant's expectations and detriment have been defined with reasonable clarity, the consensual character of the case would justify the award of expectations.

[68] *Eves v Eves* [1975] 1 WLR 1338.   [69] *Pettitt v Pettitt* [1970] AC 777, [796], *per* Lord Reid.

A powerful feminist critique of the courts' approach is reflected in the comments of Flynn and Lawson. The examples to which they refer in the following extract draw on case law covering both constructive trusts and proprietary estoppel, which shares the requirements of reliance and detriment.[70]

Flynn and Lawson, 'Gender, Sexuality and the Doctrine of Detrimental Reliance' [1995] Fem Leg Stud 105, 106, 117–18

The status of women in Western, market-economy societies is intimately dependent on their position in the public world of the market and in the private domestic sphere, and on the relationship between those arenas as constructed in opposition to one another. Feminist lawyers now possess a coherent, (almost) canonical account of the relationship between 'separate spheres' ideology and the legitimation of inequality for women in our society. This model sees the legal system participating in the active segregation of the domestic world of the household from the public space of the market and gendering the qualities of each, notwithstanding women's on-going presence in and contributions to both. The domestic arena is anointed as fit and proper for women to occupy, and its defining qualities of care, intimacy and selflessness held out as the binary opposite of the market characterised by self-centred, arms-length bargaining. The household and the feminine qualities which are associated with it in this schema are simultaneously exalted and demeaned. In this ideological framework, the qualities of the domestic sphere are represented as a justification of appropriate female behaviour and treatment and as an explanation of its consequences [. . .]

If a claimant's behaviour is taken by the court to consist of nothing more than normal, everyday actions, then her claim will not succeed because she will not have acted to her detriment. In their construction of normality, the decision of the courts display the tenacious hold of 'separate spheres' ideology. All the behaviour which is placed in the realm of the domestic, no matter how arduous, will not amount to detriment because it can be expected of any woman in an intimate relationship with a man. Behaviour which takes the claimant outside the domestic realm is categorised as abnormal, and, in order to explain it, it must be placed in the context of a market-like transaction giving rise to a property interest. According to the authorities one cannot expect women, out of the love they have for their partners or of the desire to live in a comfortable place, to pay towards mortgage instalments. Nor is it reasonable to expect them to spend small sums on improvements, at least when those small sums represent a quarter or all their worldly wealth and their partner is a relatively rich man. A woman cannot be reasonably expected to wield 14-lb sledge-hammers or work cement mixers out of love or the desire for more pleasant surroundings. Prompted by such motives, however, it is reasonable to expect women to leave their husbands, move in with their lovers, bear their babies, refrain from seeking employment, wallpaper, paint, and generally decorate and design their lovers' houses, and to organize builders working on those same houses, even when this includes the purchase and delivery of the building materials. In order to succeed, female claimants must show that they "did much more than most women would do", or rather that they did more than the judges would expect most women to do. If a claimant's conduct [is] of a type regarded by judges as "the most natural thing in the world for a wife" to have done, she will not succeed. The use of the stereotype as a norm, from which deviation has to be established, is an almost inevitable consequence of the adoption of Nourse L.J.'s test.

---

[70] Although the point is not without controversy, there seems little, if any, distinction between how these requirements are met under the constructive trust and proprietary estoppel. For consideration of this point, see Ferguson, 'Constructive Trusts: A Note of Caution' (1993) 109 LQR 114, 115–20.

While detriment focusses objectively on what acts the claimant has done, the element of reliance focusses subjectively on the claimant's motive in doing those acts.[71] For a constructive trust to arise, there must be a causative link between the common intention and the detriment. The leading authority on how this requirement is fulfilled is the proprietary estoppel case of *Wayling v Jones*, in which Balcombe LJ drew jointly on constructive trust and estoppel cases to summarize how the requirement of reliance is fulfilled.[72]

Wayling v Jones
(1995) 69 P & CR 170, CA

Balcombe LJ

At 173

1. There must be a sufficient link between the promises relied upon and the conduct which constitutes the detriment—see *Eves v. Eves*, in particular *per* Brightman J. *Grant v. Edwards, per* Nourse L.J. and *per* Browne-Wilkinson V.-C. and in particular the passage where he equates the principles applicable in cases of constructive trust to those of proprietary estoppel.

2. The promises relied upon do not have to be the sole inducement for the conduct: it is sufficient if they are an inducement—*Amalgamated Property Co. v. Texas Bank.*

3. Once it has been established that promises were made, and that there has been conduct by the plaintiff of such a nature that inducement may be inferred then the burden of proof shifts to the defendants to establish that he did not rely on the promises—*Greasley v. Cooke; Grant v. Edwards.*

The question that arises from Balcombe LJ's third point is this: once the burden of proof has shifted to the defendant, how can reliance be disproved?

In *Wayling v Jones*, Mr Wayling was held to have acted to his detriment by acting as 'companion and chauffeur' to his partner, and working without full remuneration within his partner's businesses. In his evidence, he acknowledged that he would have acted the same way if no promise of a property right had been made. At first instance, the judge considered this to be fatal to his claim, as demonstrating that he had not acted in reliance on the promise. This decision was overruled on appeal. The Court of Appeal held that it was not sufficient to show that Mr Wayling would have acted the same way if no promise had been made. To discharge the burden of proof, the defendant must show that Mr Wayling would have acted the same way if the promise, once made, had been revoked. Mr Wayling had stated in his evidence that, in such circumstances, he would have left Mr Jones and therefore the burden of disproving reliance had not been discharged.

The test of reliance has not been specifically discussed in the context of a constructive trust claim subsequent to the decision in *Wayling v Jones*. Some restatement is required to apply the test to a constructive trust to reflect the existence of a common intention, rather than a promise. It is suggested that, in a claim to a constructive trust, once the burden shifts

---

[71] Lawson (1996) p 219.
[72] For the relationship between proprietary estoppel and constructive trusts as regards the requirements of detriment and reliance, see fn 80 above.

to the defendant in order to disprove reliance, he or she would have to demonstrate that the claimant would have acted the same way even if informed that the defendant would not comply with the parties' initial common intention.

2.3.3 The *Stack v Dowden* and *Jones v Kernott* model of inferred agreement constructive trust

If it is possible to infer an agreement to share beneficial ownership on the basis of some or all of the criteria in para [69] of *Stack v Dowden*, then two key consequences follow. First, it would reduce the need for the courts to search for evidence of express discussions for an express agreement constructive trust, and hence remove criticism of the artificiality of this exercise that we have seen in the 'excuses' cases. The broader the range of conduct from which a common intention can be inferred, the less need there is to search for an express agreement.[73] Secondly, and most radically, it would mean that domestic conduct that is not currently considered sufficient detriment in reliance on an express agreement would become relevant to determining the existence of an inferred common intention to create a trust. Such a development may be welcomed. As we have seen, the current approach to detriment has been criticized for its denigration of domestic activities. The failed claim in *Burns v Burns*[74] has become a *cause celebre* to highlight the issue.[75] There, the Court of Appeal held that no agreement to share the beneficial interest could be inferred by Mrs Burns' eighteen years of domestic duties or her contributions to household expenses. Mrs Burns had not contributed—directly or indirectly—to the purchase of the home, but had been '*free to do what she liked with her earnings*'.[76] A curious position is thus reached through the courts' divergent approach to common intention at the acquisition and quantification stages. A claimant whose activities are confined to domestic conduct receives no interest, but one who has made a small direct financial contribution (to give rise to an inferred agreement) can have their domestic conduct taken into account to quantify their share.[77]

There are indications at the highest judicial level of a willingness to extend para [69] to the acquisition question. As we have seen, in *Stack v Dowden* Lord Walker considered that 'the law has moved on' from *Rosset*.[78] Although his comment is directed at the approach to indirect financial contributions, the academic literature to which he refers goes beyond this. Shortly after the House of Lords' decision in *Stack v Dowden*, in *Abbott v Abbott*[79] the Privy Council considered disputed ownership of a home in the context of sole legal ownership. The parties in the case were married, but, in the jurisdiction from which the case was referred (Antigua and Barbuda), entitlement fell to be determined as a matter of property law. Three members of the Board (Lords Walker and Neuberger, and Baroness Hale) had also decided *Stack v Dowden* and the Opinion of the Board was delivered by Baroness Hale, who noted that '*the law has indeed moved on*' since *Lloyds Bank plc v Rosset*.[80] As regards determining ownership of the home, Baroness Hale explained:[81] '*The parties' whole course*

---

[73] See Gardner, 'Rethinking Family Property' (1993) 109 LQR 263, 265. He suggests that, in the excuses cases, the courts '*were engaged in the business of inventing agreements on women's behalf*' because, in the absence of a direct financial contribution, this was the only way in which a beneficial interest could be conferred.

[74] [1984] Ch 317.

[75] Cowan, Fox O'Mahony, and Cobb, *Great Debates in Property Law* (Basingstoke: Palgrave Macmillan, 2012) p 211 (though noting that the authors 'take rather different messages from the case').

[76] [1984] Ch 317, [328] per Fox LJ.

[77] See, for example, *Midland Bank plc v Cooke* [1995] 2 FLR 915 where the claimant's 6.47 per cent direct financial contribution to the purchase of the home provided the basis for a constructive trust, under which her share was quantified as 50 per cent.

[78] [2007] 2 AC 432, [26].   [79] [2007] UKPC 53.   [80] Ibid, [20].   [81] Ibid.

of conduct in relation to the property must be taken into account in determining their shared intentions as to its ownership.' As a decision of the Privy Council, however, *Abbott* is not binding on English law. Further, on the facts of the case, Mr Abbott did not dispute that Mrs Abbott should obtain a share of the beneficial interest; the dispute concerned the extent of her share.[82] In *Holman v Howes*,[83] the Court of Appeal suggested that there is not necessarily any difference between cases of joint legal ownership and those of sole legal ownership in which it is not disputed that the claimant is entitled to some share of the beneficial interest. In both cases, the only issue for determination is the quantification of the parties' shares.

In a discussion of the Court of Appeal's decision in *Jones v Kernott*, Gardner and Davidson commented, *'[it] is to be hoped, incidentally, that the Supreme Court will also make clear that constructive trusts of family homes are governed by a single regime, dispelling any impression that different rules apply to "joint names" and "single name" cases, and to the "establishment" and the "quantum" of the constructive trust.'*[84] The Supreme Court did not go that far. In response to Gardner and Davidson, Lord Walker and Baroness Hale emphasized the different starting points in joint and sole name cases while noting that *'[a]t a high level of generality, there is of course a single regime: the law of trusts'.*[85] Notwithstanding, Gardner appears confident that the criteria for an inferred agreement are the same at the acquisition and quantification stage and has suggested that Mrs Burns would succeed before a modern court.[86]

The argument as to whether *Stack v Dowden* and *Jones v Kernott* support the expansion of para [69] to the acquisition question is summarized in the following extract.

Sloan, 'Keeping up with the Jones Case: Establishing Constructive Trusts in "Sole Legal Owner" Scenarios' (2014) LS DOI: 10.1111/lest.12052

On the one hand, admittedly Lord Walker and Lady Hale [in *Stack v Dowden*] did not either repeat or refer to their earlier suggestions in *Stack* that *Rosset* no longer governed the establishment issue, and there is a possibility that the phrase 'once again' related to the ascertainment of the common intention on the quantification of interests rather than their establishment in a 'sole name' case, since the next stage in the analysis is said to be imputation. The two Justices avoided explicitly disapplying Lord Bridge's restrictions as forming part of the method by which the relevant objective deduction on establishment should be performed and, by analogy with the detrimental reliance requirement, it could be argued that those *Rosset* restrictions were so fundamental to the general understanding of this area of the law that a mere omission to cite them in *Jones* (or in any other relevant case) should not be thought significant. Lord Walker and Lady Hale's remarks were clearly obiter as regards sole-owner cases, and the reinforced strength of the presumption that equity follows the law suggests that the legal non-owner still carries a heavy burden even if he is not restricted to the *Rosset* criteria. Moreover, Lord Collins explicitly mentioned sole-owner cases only to point out that the cases pre-dating *Stack* involved different facts, and Lord Kerr did not appear to mention them at all.

---

[82] Ibid, [19].   [83] [2007] EWCA 877, [28].

[84] Gardner and Davidson, 'The Future of *Stack v Dowden*' (2011) 127 LQR 13, 15.

[85] [2012] AC 776, [16].

[86] Gardner, 'Problems in Family Property' (2013) 72 CLJ 301, 307. Gardner's confidence is not shared by Sloan, 'Keeping up with the Jones Case: Establishing Constructive Trusts in "Sole Legal Owner" Scenarios' (2014) LS DOI: 10.1111/lest.12052.

Nevertheless, on the other side of the argument, it remains true that Lord Walker and Lady Hale did not expressly limit the conduct by reference to which the common intention could be inferred to the types stipulated in *Rosset*. Indeed, they did not cite *Rosset* at all, and the only citation of that earlier case came from Lord Collins when discussing the differences between inference and imputation. This failure to cite *Rosset* on the question of establishing an interest coupled with the earlier criticism of it in *Stack* and the implication that it had stopped representing the law before *Stack* was decided suggests that it should no longer be followed. Even if there are difficulties with relying on a mere omission to cite it in *Jones*, the analogy with the omission of the detrimental reliance requirement is not exact since, unlike *Rosset*, detrimental reliance was not mentioned in *Stack* either. In addition, the deliberate repetition of the language of objective deduction from conduct implies that the factors from para 69 of *Stack* are relevant to establishing an interest as well as quantifying it, and that establishing an interest in a 'sole name' cases is equivalent to demonstrating that legal and equitable interests should differ in a 'joint names' case, although it is true that the Justices did not expressly refer back to their earlier use of that language in spite of the fact that they were prepared to make similar cross-references on the approach to quantification. As regards the obiter status of their remarks, it is clear that Lord Walker and Lady Hale set out to provide a coherent framework for both sole- and joint-owner cases, even if the former were not directly relevant on the facts, and Lady Hale expressed the view in *Stack* that Lord Bridge's restrictions in *Rosset* were themselves obiter, presumably because the criteria did not need to be set so onerously in order to decide the case. Finally, while Lord Wilson opined that the question whether *imputation* was permitted in establishing that the legal and equitable interest differed (rather than the quantification of the equitable interest) would 'merit careful thought' in an appropriate case, he did not place any limitations upon the methods by which such an intention could be inferred.

Subsequent to *Jones v Kernott*, in *Geary v Rankine*[87] a claim to an inferred agreement constructive trust based on non-financial contributions was considered by the Court of Appeal. Mrs Geary claimed a beneficial interest in a guesthouse which she had helped her partner, Mr Rankine, to run. The guesthouse was in the sole legal ownership of Mr Rankine and had been purchased by him using his own savings. The parties had cohabited for nineteen years at the time of the breakdown of their relationship. Mrs Geary's claim failed on the facts for two reasons.[88] First, her argument was founded on a common intention that the business would be a joint venture. Lewison LJ explained, '*it is an impermissible leap to go from a common intention that the parties would run a business together to a conclusion that it was their common intention that the property in which the business was run, and which was bought entirely with money provided by one of them, would belong to both of them*'.[89] In any event, it was apparent that there was no *common* intention on the facts. At the time Mrs Geary and Mr Rankine began to cohabit, Mrs Geary was separated from her husband but had not yet divorced. The evidence showed that Mr Rankine had '*refuse[d] to recognise her*' until she was divorced as he was concerned with the possibility of her husband making a claim against the business.[90] When asked directly about the security he would provide for Mrs Geary and her son, Mr Rankine had consistently said that the business would remain in his sole name or had been non-committal.[91] Notwithstanding the failure of the claim, Lees

---

[87] [2012] EWCA Civ 555.

[88] Claims to a beneficial interest founded on support provided for a business also failed in *Morris v Morris* [2008] EWCA Civ 257 and *James v Thomas* [2008] 1 FLR 1598.

[89] [2012] EWCA Civ 555, [21].   [90] Ibid, [22].   [91] Ibid.

argues that the decision '*provides welcome confirmation* [. . .] *that the acquisition stage of sole name cases is equally governed by the* Kernott *principles*'.[92] Lees' suggestion is made on the basis that the claim failed on the facts, rather than as a matter of principle. However, Sloan urges caution in placing too much reliance on the courts' '*mere omission to cite the* [Rosset] *restrictions*'.[93]

In a comprehensive review of the post-*Jones v Kernott* case law, Sloan[94] concludes that the only case in which the outcome of a claim to a beneficial share in a sole ownership case is inconsistent with *Rosset* is the first instance decision in *Aspden v Elvy*.[95] There, Mr Aspden had initially been the sole legal owner of Outlaithe Farm, which included Outlaithe Barn. He transferred title to the Barn to his cohabitee, Ms Elvy, who became the sole legal and beneficial owner of the Barn.[96] At the time of the transfer, the couple had already separated. Mr Aspden subsequently contributed £65–70,000 towards the cost of converting the Barn into a dwelling, in addition to providing his own physical labour. He argued that he had done so on the basis of a common intention the parties would marry or cohabit. Mrs Elvy denied his claim to a beneficial interest and argued that his contributions were by way of gift. HHJ Behrens held that '*the proper inference from the whole course of dealing is that there was a common intention that Mr Aspden should have some interest in Outlaithe Barn as a result of the very substantial contributions made to the conversion works*'.[97] As Sloan explains, while the case involves financial contributions, it moves away from *Rosset* insofar as those contributions were not to the acquisition of the property.[98] However, in this respect it seems at most a modest departure. It is a small step to say that direct financial contributions to the conversion of a property into a dwelling suffice to establish an inferred intent, particularly in light of the recognition in *Stack v Dowden* of the 'ambulatory' nature of the trust.

Outside of this jurisdiction, the decision of the Northern Irish High Court in *Bank of Scotland v Brogan*[99] may also reflect a departure from the *Rosset* criteria. Mrs Brogan successfully claimed a 50 per cent beneficial share in the home that was in the sole legal ownership of her husband. Mr Brogan had made '*light-hearted*' comments to the effect that what was his was hers, but these seemed to fall short of an express agreement.[100] In inferring an intention to share, Deeny J took into account a number of factors including Mrs Brogan's contribution to '*the economic life of the family*'[101] by manual labour on the farm, care that she had provided to her mother-in-law (who lived with them) and the fact the parties were married, which was considered to indicate '*a high degree of commitment*'.[102] Such factors clearly go beyond those recognized as relevant to an inferred intent in *Rosset*. However, as in *Aspen v Elvy*, Mrs Brogan had made a substantial financial contribution to improvements to the home—representing around one third of its value. Deeny J made clear, however, that Mrs Brogan's care of the couple's four children was not a factor that he had taken into account

---

[92] Lees, *Geary v Rankine*: Money isn't Everything' [2012] Conv 412, 417.

[93] Sloan, 'Keeping up with the Jones Case: Establishing Constructive Trusts in "Sole Legal Owner" Scenarios' (2014) LS DOI: 10.1111/lest.12052.

[94] Ibid.   [95] [2012] EWHC 1387 (Ch).   [96] Ibid, [118].   [97] Ibid, [125].

[98] Sloan, 'Keeping up with the Jones Case: Establishing Constructive Trusts in "Sole Legal Owner" Scenarios' (2014) LS DOI: 10.1111/lest.12052 .

[99] [2012] NICH 21.

[100] Ibid, [31]. See Conway, 'Constructive Trusts and the Family Home (Yet Again)' [2013] Conv 538, 542–3.

[101] Ibid, [36].

[102] Ibid, [35]. Deeny J suggested that 'social conditions' in Northern Ireland meant that marriage carried greater weight than may be the case in England: [34].

and that 'a wife who performs the duties of a devoted wife and mother does not thereby automatically obtain an interest in the property'.[103]

What is clear is that the acquisition question cannot be resolved by imputing an intention.
Unsurprisingly, given the approach to imputation in *Jones and Kernow* which we considered
at 2.2.2, no authority goes this far. Indeed in *Capethorn v Harris*[104] the Court of Appeal applied the approach to imputation in joint ownership cases to reject the first instance judges'
reliance on imputation. Mr Harris claimed a share in a property, Sunnyside Farm, in which
he and Mrs Capethorn had lived and ran their business until the break-up of their relationship when Mrs Capethorn moved out. The farm was held in the sole name of Mrs Capethorn
having been bought by her from her mother. The Court of Appeal found that the judge at
first instance had not, as they should have done, kept the acquisition and quantifications
questions separate and as a result had incorrectly imputed a common intention for the farm
to be held by Mrs Capethorn on trust for herself and Mr Harris. The Court, referring to the
two stages of acquisition and quantification, summarized the position.

Sales LJ

At [17]

There is an important difference between the approach applicable at each stage. At the first
stage, an actual agreement has to be found to have been made, which may be inferred from
conduct in an appropriate case. At the second stage, the court is entitled to impute an intention that each person is entitled to the share which the court considers fair having regard to
the whole course of dealing between them in relation to the property. A court is not entitled
to impute an intention to the parties at the first stage in the analysis.

Where a constructive trust is successfully established, the claimant's beneficial share must
then be quantified. The quantification of the share is determined by reference to the principles in *Stack v Dowden* and *Jones v Kernott* outlined in section 2.2 of this chapter.

2.3.4 Resulting trust

Where the claimant has made a direct financial contribution to the purchase of property in
another person's sole name, a purchase money resulting trust may be imposed. The rationale
for the trust is a presumption that the claimant did not intend to make a gift of his or her
contribution. This rationale is reflected in the division of the beneficial interest in proportion to each party's contribution. The presumption of resulting trust is discussed further in
Chapter 11, section 3.

The majority of the House of Lords in *Stack v Dowden* and the Supreme Court in *Jones
v Kernott* doubted the utility of the resulting trust in the context of determining proprietary rights in the home.[105] Although, in his minority judgment in *Stack v Dowden*, Lord
Neuberger supported the application of the resulting trust in both joint and sole ownership

---

[103] Ibid, [35], [38]. Though Mrs Brogan's care of the children was seen as indicating the 'extra effort' involved in her work on the farm and the care provided for her mother-in-law: [38].

[104] [2015] EWCA Civ 955.

[105] For criticism of *Stack v Dowden* [2007] 2 AC 432 in this respect see Swadling, 'The Common Intention
Constructive Trust in the House of Lords: An Opportunity Missed' (2007) 123 LQR 511 and Sparkes, 'How
Beneficial Interests Stack Up' [2011] Conv 156.

cases. On his view, the starting point for a claimant who has made a direct financial contribution to the purchase of property in another's name is that the claimant has a beneficial interest in proportion to his or her contribution through a resulting trust.

In *Stack v Dowden* Lord Walker suggested that it should not generally be used to determine ownership of the home, even in cases of sole legal ownership.[106] Its focus on the parties' financial contributions is considered to be more apt in a commercial context, with the constructive trust preferred in relation to domestic property. As regards domestic property, Lord Walker suggested that the resulting trust '*may still have a useful function in cases where two people have lived and worked together in what has amounted to both an emotional and a commercial relationship*';[107] a comment echoed in *Jones v Kernott*.[108]

However the Privy Council's decision in *Marr v Collie*, which we considered in section 2, suggests that the common intention trust analysis may also be more appropriate even in these circumstances.

Where a resulting trust is imposed, two issues may arise: firstly, the scope of direct financial contributions on which the trust is based—is the trust confined to cash contributions, or does it also take into account contributions to a mortgage? Secondly, how to quantify the claimant's beneficial share where each party's contribution cannot accurately be ascertained. In *Stack v Dowden*, Lord Neuberger discussed these matters.

Stack v Dowden
[2007] 2 AC 432, HL

Lord Neuberger

At 117–21

There are two other aspects of the resulting trust analysis which I should like to mention. First, there is the effect of liability under a mortgage. This will normally be a relevant, often a very important, factor, because, as Lord Walker points out, the overwhelming majority of houses and flats are acquired with the assistance of secured borrowing. There is attraction in the notion that liability under a mortgage should be equivalent to a cash contribution. On that basis, if a property is acquired for £300,000, which is made up of one party's contribution of £100,000, and both parties taking on joint liability for a £200,000 mortgage, the beneficial interest would be two-thirds owned by the party who made the contribution, and one-third by the other. If one party then repays more of the mortgage advance, equitable accounting might be invoked to adjust the beneficial ownerships at least in a suitable case. Such an adjustment would be consistent with the resulting trust analysis, as repayments of mortgage capital may be seen as retrospective contributions towards the cost of acquisition, or as payments which increase the value of the equity of redemption.

However, there is an argument that taking on liability under a mortgage should not be equivalent to a cash payment. The cash contribution is effectively equity, whereas the mortgage liability arises in relation to a secured loan. If the value of the property in the example just given had fallen by 25% when it came to be sold, the party who made the cash contribution would lose £75,000 of his £100,000, whereas the other party would lose nothing (unless he would be liable to pay £25,000 to the former, which seems intuitively improbable).

---

[106] [2007] 2 AC 432, [31].   [107] [2007] 2 AC 432, [32].   [108] [2012] AC 776, [31].

In *Ulrich v Ulrich and Felton* [1968] 1 WLR 180, an engaged couple (who subsequently married) had bought a house, she paying one-sixth of the acquisition cost in cash, and he raising the balance by a mortgage in his name. In passages at pp 186 and 189 (approved in *Pettitt v Pettitt* [1970] AC 777, 816 A), Lord Denning MR and Diplock LJ held it was wrong to treat a mortgage contribution as equivalent to a cash contribution.

Desirable though it is to give as much guidance as possible, this is not an appropriate case in which to express a view as to whether liability under a mortgage should be treated as the equivalent of a cash contribution for the purpose of assessing the shares in which the beneficial interest is held. Certainty, simplicity and first impression suggest a positive answer, perhaps particularly where a home is bought almost exclusively by means of a mortgage. More sophisticated economic and legal analysis may suggest otherwise, especially where the cash contributions are very different and, at least in the case of one party, substantial. The point has not been fully canvassed here, because, however one treats the mortgage, the outcome of the appeal is the same.

The final aspect I wish to deal with in relation to the resulting trust analysis is where the evidence is so unsatisfactory that it is impossible to reach a clear conclusion as to the parties' respective contributions to the purchase price. In many such cases, the evidence may be so hopeless or may suggest contributions of the same sort of order, and equality would be the appropriate outcome (as in *Rimmer v Rimmer* [1953] 1 QB 63, 72, approved in *Pettitt v Pettitt* [1970] AC 777, 804 A–B, 810 H, 815 H). However, in other cases (as here, in my opinion), the court may conclude that, while it is impossible to be precise as to the relative contributions, one party cannot have contributed more (or less) than Y%. In such cases, where Y is clearly below (or above) 50, to decide that the party concerned had more (or less) than Y% of the beneficial interest would be wrong.

As we have seen in section 2.3.2, a direct financial contribution provides evidence of an inferred common intention to share beneficial ownership for the purposes of a claim to a constructive trust, even on the restrictive criteria provided by *Rosset*. As a result, an overlap exists between the resulting trust and inferred agreement constructive trust because both may arise on the basis of a direct financial contribution to the purchase of land. These two trusts are, however, also mutually exclusive, because the basis upon which the claimant's beneficial interest is quantified is different under each: in a resulting trust, the claimant obtains an interest in proportion to his or her contribution; in the constructive trust, the claimant's interest is quantified by reference to the common intention of the parties.

This difference in the method of quantifying the claimant's share reflects a conceptual difference in how the claimant's contribution is analysed under each doctrine. A resulting trust is imposed on the *negative* basis that the claimant did not intend (or is presumed not to have intended) to make a gift of his or her contribution to the legal owner. A constructive trust is imposed on the basis that the claimant's contribution infers a *positive* agreement between the parties to share the beneficial interest. The trust arises because it would be unconscionable for the legal owner to deny the claimant a share.

There are two possible bases for distinguishing the respective scope of operation of the resulting trust and inferred agreement constructive trust. The first, reflected in Lord Neuberger's analysis in *Stack v Dowden*, is to rely on the doctrinal differences between the trusts as a means of distinguishing their scope of application. On this basis, direct financial contributions lead to a constructive trust where a common intention to share beneficial ownership can be inferred between the parties. This leaves the resulting trust to apply where a direct financial contribution has been made but no common intention to share beneficial ownership can be inferred. An alternative approach is to rely on the context of the claim so that a direct financial contribution made in respect of the home is used to infer a common intention for a constructive trust, leaving the resulting trust to apply outside of the home. This approach reflects the view of the majority of the House of Lords in *Stack v Dowden* and the Supreme Court in *Jones v Kernott*, as well as the Privy Council in *Marr v Collie*. The difficulty with this solution is a definitional one in understanding what context favours the constructive trust approach rather than a resulting trust analysis.

It is suggested that where the context of the purchase is purely for investment or commercial purposes the resulting trust analysis is more likely to find favour, but where the parties' relationship is both emotional and commercial the court's will prefer the greater flexibility afforded by the constructive trust approach. As well as *Marr v Collie*, illustrations can be found in post-*Stack v Dowden* case law. In *R v Muzafar and Qurban*[109] a father purchased property in the names of two of his sons in order to provide a home for his daughter. In finding a resulting trust in favour of the father HHJ Behrens commented that '*[t]his was plainly not the ordinary domestic context*' anticipated by *Stack v Dowden* insofar as the sons had neither occupied nor received any rents from the property.[110] Conversely a constructive trust was preferred in *Gallarotti v Sebastianelli*[111] where two friends had purchased a property in the sole name of one of them. The Court of Appeal agreed with the judge at first instance that the case was '*more in the domestic than the commercial context*' and was appropriately decided by reference to the common intention constructive trust.[112] Arden LJ explained that the constructive trust is '*more appropriate [than a resulting trust] where the parties have incurred expenditure on the strength of their personal relationship and without expectation of having to account, or to call for an account, of every item as they would have to do in the case of a true legal partnership*'.[113] Ultimately, the two bases for distinguishing the respective scope of the trusts may not be far apart. A common intention to share beneficial ownership other than in proportion to direct financial contributions is more likely to be inferred in relation to a home, and (though more arguably) is perhaps more likely to arise between parties in an intimate relationship than in respect of other co-owned homes.

2.4 A CRITIQUE OF THE COMMON INTENTION

Following *Stack v Dowden*, the parties' common intention now provides the basis of both the creation of a constructive trust and the quantification of shares under the trust. Academic opinion has been divided on whether the parties' common intention provides an appropriate rationale for the constructive trust.[114] The common intention has been variously described as a myth[115] and a phantom.[116] The endorsement of imputed intent by the Supreme Court in *Jones v Kernott*, albeit confined to the issue of quantification, further confirms its fallacy. An imputed intent, as has been seen, is one acknowledged not to have been held by the parties. In endorsing imputed intent, the Supreme Court acknowledges the close link between this

---

[109] Unreported, Judgment 10 June 2014, Leeds CC.   [110] Ibid, [31].
[111] [2012] 2 FLR 1231.   [112] Ibid, [6].   [113] Ibid, [5].
[114] See the contrasting views on *Grant v Edwards* [1986] Ch 638 by Montgomery, 'A Question of Intention' [1987] Conv 16 (supporting common intention) and Eekelaar, 'A Woman's Place: A Conflict between Law and Social Values' [1987] Conv 93 (against common intention).
[115] Glover and Todd, 'The Myth of Common Intention' (1996) LS 325.
[116] See *Pettkus v Becker* (1980) 117 DLR (3d) 257, *per* Dixon J.

concept and fairness;[117] the criterion rejected in *Stack v Dowden* as providing the basis for the quantification of shares. There are, however, differences in emphasis between the justices of the Supreme Court. In the judgment of Lord Walker and Baroness Hale, Chadwick LJ's comment in *Oxley v Hiscock* that '*each is entitled to that share which the court considers fair having regard to the whole course of dealing between them in relation to the property*' is conflated with imputed intent.[118] Lord Wilson asks the rhetorical question '[w]*here equity is driven to impute the common intention, how can it do so other than by search for the result which the court itself considers fair?*'[119] Lord Kerr appears prepared to go further and favours a '*stark choice*' between an inferred intent (actually held) and fairness, but accepts that the language of imputation is now embedded.[120] The question raised by these views is why, despite recognizing the link with fairness, the Supreme Court still clothes the exercise being undertaken with common intent? It seems that the concept has a power or legitimizing effect, at least as a justificatory tool for intervention, that remains compelling to the court.

While academic commentators have suggested alternative bases for intervention no clear consensus has developed.[121] Alternative schemes may simply raise different concerns. The Law Commission abandoned its own attempt to replace the parties' common intention as the basis of determining property rights in the home,[122] noting that its '*uncompromising rejection of intention was ultimately impossible to justify*' and could prejudice many of those who would obtain an interest under the current law.[123]

Bottomley, who had previously argued that the requirement of a common intention led to discrimination against female claimants,[124] became an unlikely proponent for this approach. This support comes from a specific understanding of what is involved in finding a common intention.

Bottomley, 'Women and Trust(s): Portraying the Family in the Gallery of the Law' in *Land Law: Themes and Perspectives* (eds Bright and Dewar, 1998, pp 206, 227–8)

"I would contend that neither the Courts of Law nor the Courts of Criticism could continue to function if we really let go of the notion of an intended meaning."[125]

Gombrich, in accepting that a work of art may 'hold' many readings, recognizes a more complex picture of the artist/author than one which assumes that authorial knowledge or control is absolute. Value may be given to a work in a series of readings which 'mean' more than the artist/author might have intended or foreseen. However he is holding, as a historian, to a basic need to attempt to draw a distinction between drawing a meaning from a work of art

---

[117] Then link between fairness and imputed intent is identified by Piska, 'Intention, Fairness and the Presumption of Resulting Trust after *Stack v Dowden*' (2008) 71 MLR 120, 128.
[118] [2011] 3 WLR 1121, [51] extracted above.   [119] Ibid, [87].   [120] Ibid, [74].
[121] See Gardner, 'Rethinking Family Property' (1993) 109 LQR 263 (relationship-based approach) and Barlow and Lind, 'A Matter of Trust: The Allocation of Rights in the Family Home' (1999) 19 LS 468 (a form of community property).
[122] Law Commission Report No 278, *Sharing Homes: A Discussion Paper* (2006), [1.11].
[123] Ibid, [3.76]–[3.78].
[124] Bottomley, 'Self and Subjectivities: Languages of Claim in Property Law' in *Feminist Theory and Legal Strategy* (eds Bottomley and Conaghan, 1993).
[125] [Gombrich, *Gombrich on The Renaissance* (3rd edn, London, Phaidon, 1984) p ii.]

and attributing that meaning to the creator. In a sense it is a recovery of the artist, but with a clear recognition that this is only one mode of analysis, of normative and functional value, rather than a simple reality to be asserted (imposed) to the exclusion of all else [. . .]

The value of intention returns us to the value of 'intended meaning'. It focuses on a need to try and attribute to actors a purpose to their actions which was within their own foresight. As policy in law, this gives credence to individuals and also, as a broader statement, encourages in individuals the need to take responsibility for their actions [. . .]

The importance of holding to the idea of 'intended meaning' seems, to me, to be crucial both for women and for feminists when faced with the alternatives of being rewarded (protected) on the basis of status or arguments based on economic exchange or presumed mutuality. It ascribes to us the freedom we seek to make our own decisions; what the law must act to mitigate are those situations which circumscribe our freedom through the power relations emanating from, and creating, economic or emotional dependency.

Much, therefore, may lie on how the requirement of common intention is understood. The acceptance of imputed intent means that a common intention can now be found even where there is no suggestion of an actual agreement between the parties (and therefore, no need artificially to construct one). This chimes with the understanding of an intention on which Bottomley's conversion is based.

3 OCCUPATION RIGHTS

A right to occupy a home may be claimed in two ways. Firstly, it may be claimed by virtue of holding a property right of a type that confers a right to occupy. In this respect, where the home is held on trust (whether an express trust or a trust arising under the principles discussed in this chapter), the trust will be a trust of land within the Trusts of Land and Appointment of Trustees Act 1996 (TOLATA 1996). Section 12 of that Act confers a right to occupy on beneficiaries as long as specified preconditions are met. The scope of this right to occupy is considered in Chapter 13. The trustees regulate exercise of the right, in the first instance, with an application to the court under ss 14–15 of that Act in the event of any dispute.

Secondly, a statutory right to occupy is conferred on certain categories of person under the Family Law Act 1996 (FLA 1996), irrespective of holding a property right. In some instances, the right arises automatically; in others, it is dependent on an application to the court. Rights to occupy derived from the FLA 1996 are regulated by applications to the court under that Act.

The FLA 1996 confers an automatic right to occupy (referred to as 'home rights') on a spouse or civil partner in circumstances outlined in s 30. No equivalent rights are conferred on cohabitants.

Family Law Act 1996, s 30(1) and (9)

(1) This section applies if—

    (a) one spouse or civil partner ("A") is entitled to occupy a dwelling-house by virtue of—

        (i)   a beneficial estate or interest or contract; or

        (ii) any enactment giving A the right to remain in occupation; and

(b) the other spouse or civil partner ("B") is not so entitled.

[...]

(9) It is hereby declared that [a person]—

(a) who has an equitable interest in a dwelling-house or in its proceeds of sale, but

(b) is not [a person] in whom there is vested (whether solely or as joint tenant) a legal estate in fee simple or a legal term of years absolute in the dwelling-house,

is to be treated, only for the purpose of determining whether he has home rights, as not being entitled to occupy the dwelling-house by virtue of that interest.

Hence, B obtains a right to occupy in two circumstances: firstly, where B has no proprietary, statutory, or contractual right to occupy outside of the Act (and B's spouse or civil partner does enjoy such rights); secondly, where B's only proprietary right is as a beneficiary and B does not also hold legal title. In this instance, B may also have a right to occupy under the TOLATA 1996 by virtue of holding a beneficial interest. The scope of the rights conferred by each statute is, however, different. The 'home rights' conferred by the FLA 1996 are confined to the right, if in occupation, not be evicted by his or her spouse or civil partner and, if not in occupation, to enter and occupy with the leave of the court.[126] They are generally limited in duration to the subsistence of the marriage or civil partnership and the continuance of A's own right to occupy.[127]

A right to occupy may be obtained on application to the court by a former spouse or civil partner (s 35) or a former cohabitant (s 36). As with the automatic home rights conferred on spouses and civil partners, applications are confined to parties who cannot claim a right to occupy outside of the Act, or whose only claim is as a beneficiary.[128] The rights are further limited to houses that were occupied, or intended by the parties to be occupied, as their home.[129] Any right to occupy obtained by an application under ss 35 or 36 is temporary, with an absolute maximum duration of one year.[130]

4 RECOMMENDATIONS FOR REFORM

The decisions in *Stack v Dowden* and *Jones v Kernott* were prompted by the absence of legislative intervention determining the property rights of cohabitees.[131] As Baroness Hale explained in *Stack v Dowden*, this is an area in which law reform has not kept pace with social and economic developments.[132] She highlighted the social significance of rules applicable on the breakdown of a relationship between cohabitants, and the clear divergence between how property rights are *actually* resolved and how many people *believe* that such issues are resolved.

---

[126] Family Law Act 1996, s 30(2).

[127] Ibid, s 30(8). The rights may be extended by the court under s 33(5).

[128] Ibid, ss 35(1) and (11), and 36(1) and (11).   [129] Ibid, ss 35(1)(c) and 36(1)(c).

[130] Ibid, ss 35(10) and 36(10). The maximum length of a court order is six months, with the possibility of extension on one further application for another maximum of six months.

[131] *Stack v Dowden* [2007] 2 AC 432, [40]–[48]; *Jones v Kernott* [2012] AC 776, [35].   [132] Ibid.

Stack v Dowden
[2007] 2 AC 432, HL

Baroness Hale

At 41–2

[. . .] The first development is, of course, the huge expansion in home ownership which has taken place since the Second World War and was given a further boost by the 'right to buy' legislation of the 1980s. Coupled with this has been continuing house price inflation, albeit with occasional interruptions such as occurred at the end of the 1980s. This has meant that it is almost always more advantageous for someone who has contributed to the acquisition of the home to claim a share in its ownership rather than the return of the money contributed, even with interest.

Another development has been the recognition in the courts that, to put it at its lowest, the interpretation to be put on the behaviour of people living together in an intimate relationship may be different from the interpretation to be put upon similar behaviour between commercial men. To put it at its highest, an outcome which might seem just in a purely commercial transaction may appear highly unjust in a transaction between husband and wife or cohabitant and cohabitant [. . .]

At 44–5

Inter vivos disputes between unmarried cohabiting couples are still governed by the ordinary law. These disputes have become increasingly visible in recent years as more and more couples live together without marrying. The full picture has recently been painted by the Law Commission in *Cohabitation: The Financial Consequences of Relationship Breakdown—A Consultation Paper* (Law Com Consultation Paper no 179) (2006) Pt 2, and its Overview paper, paras 2.3 to 2.11. For example, the 2001 census recorded over 10 million married couples in England and Wales, with over 7 5 million dependent children; but it also recorded over two million cohabiting couples, with over one-and-a-quarter million children dependent upon them. This was a 67% increase in cohabitation over the previous ten years and a doubling of the numbers of such households with dependent children. The Government Actuaries Department predicts that the proportion of couples cohabiting will continue to grow, from the present one in six of all couples to one in four by 2031.

Cohabitation comes in many different shapes and sizes. People embarking on their first serious relationship more commonly cohabit than marry. Many of these relationships may be quite short lived and childless. But most people these days cohabit before marriage—in 2003, 78.7% of spouses gave identical addresses before marriage, and the figures are even higher for second marriages. So many couples are cohabiting with a view to marriage at some later date—as long ago as 1998 the British Household Panel Survey found that 75% of current cohabitants expected to marry, although only a third had firm plans (see J Ermisch 'Personal Relationships and Marriage Expectations: Evidence from the 1998 British Household Panel' (2000) Working Papers of the Institute of Social and Economic Research: Paper 2000-27). Cohabitation is much more likely to end in separation than is marriage, and cohabitations which end in separation tend to last for a shorter time than marriages which end in divorce. But increasing numbers of couples cohabit for long periods without marrying and their reasons for doing so vary from conscious rejection of marriage as a legal institution to regarding themselves 'as good as married' anyway (see Law Com Consultation Paper no 179, Pt 2, p 39 (para 2.45)). There is evidence of a wide-spread myth of the 'common law marriage' in which unmarried couples acquire the same rights as married after a period of cohabitation (see A Barlow et al 'Just a Piece of Paper? Marriage and Cohabitation', in A Park et al *British Social Attitudes: Public policy, social ties. The 18th Report* (2001), pp 29–57). There is also evidence that 'the legal implications of marriage are a long way down the list of most couples' considerations when deciding whether to marry' (see Law Com Consultation Paper no 179, Pt 5, p 96 (para 5.10)).

In the absence of legislative reform, the onus has fallen on the courts to expand and develop equity's principles. Whilst acknowledging the need for an active role on the part of the courts, Hopkins has questioned whether in *Stack v Dowden* the House of Lords provided sufficient justification for a policy decision to treat the home differently. Drawing an analogy with the debate in public law on judicial deference, he notes that whether specific rules should be provided in respect of the home *'raises questions of social policy that have not received a consistent approach in those areas where legislation has been enacted. The issue may be described as polycentric*[133] *given that the ramifications of the decision reach far beyond the resolution of the dispute before the court'.*[134] Reporting on the results of empirical research, Douglas, Pearce, and Woodward have suggested that the need for reform extends beyond a legislative scheme for determining the property rights of cohabitees and requires *'a reappraisal of the law and practice of homebuying'.*[135]

The Law Commission first indicated that it was considering the property rights of home sharers in 1995.[136] The intervening period has seen a significant shift in the focus of the Law Commission's work. Its initial aim was to provide a scheme to determine the property rights of all those who share their home, including married and unmarried couples, and others who share homes as friends, relatives, or for companionship or support.[137] The Law Commission explored the possibility of developing a single scheme to determine ownership of the home in all circumstances in which the issue arose[138] (except cases of relationship breakdown covered by existing statutory schemes), and to the exclusion of claims based on the doctrines of trust (discussed in this chapter) and estoppel (examined in Chapter 10). The Law Commission published its conclusions on this work in *Sharing Homes: A Discussion Paper*.[139] The Law Commission concluded that such a scheme simply is not possible:[140] the diversity of situations in which people share homes precludes a uniform approach to determining their property rights.

Subsequently, the focus of the Law Commission's work shifted. It narrowed the scope of its work to consider only the position of cohabitants *'living as a couple in a joint household'*[141]

---

[133] Polycentric issues are those comprised of 'a large and complicated web of interdependent relationships, such that a change to one factor produces an incalculable series of changes to other factors': King, 'The Pervasiveness of Polycentricity' [2008] PL 101, 101.

[134] Hopkins, 'The Relevance of Context in Property Law: A Case for Judicial Restraint?' (2011) 31 LS 175, 196.

[135] Douglas, Pearce and Woodward, 'Cohabitants, Property and the Law: A Study of Injustice' (2009) 72 MLR 24, 47.

[136] Law Commission Report No 234, *Sixth Programme of Law Reform* (1995) item 8.

[137] Law Commission Report No 278, *Sharing Homes: A Discussion Paper* (2006) p vi.

[138] That is, the four circumstances outlined by the Law Commission in the extract in section 1 above.

[139] Law Commission Report No 278 (2006).

[140] Ibid, [15] of the Executive Summary and Pt VI of the Discussion Paper.

[141] Law Commission Report No 307, *Cohabitation: The Financial Consequence of Relationship Breakdown* (2007), [3.13]. This expression is intended, *in substance*, to denote parties living together as though they were

(who have not married or entered a civil partnership) and principally in the context of relationship breakdown.[142] Within this narrow context, however, the Law Commission's work has moved outside the confines of determining property ownership to consider more broadly the financial consequences of relationship breakdown. Its recommendations were published in *Cohabitation: The Financial Consequences of Relationship Breakdown*.[143]

In its report the Law Commission recommended a scheme to provide financial relief to cohabitants on the breakdown of their relationship. The proposed scheme will provide a more flexible approach than the property rules discussed in this chapter, but is intentionally not modelled on existing schemes applicable to divorce or the dissolution of a civil partnership.[144] The scheme will apply where cohabitants meet specified eligibility criteria. These are that *either* the cohabitants have a child together, *or* they have cohabited for a minimum duration, which the Law Commission recommends is set between two and five years. It will be possible for cohabitants to opt out of the scheme.[145] This must be achieved through a signed agreement between the parties, which '*makes clear the parties' intention to disapply the statute*'.[146] Notably, an express declaration of trust will not, without more, constitute such an opt-out. The proposed scheme will still apply unless the parties have also made it clear that they intend to disapply the new scheme.[147]

The Law Commission explains, in the following extract, the basis on which relief is determined and the form that the relief may take.

Law Commission Report No 307, *Cohabitation: The Financial Consequences of Relationship Breakdown* (2007, [4.32]–[4.41])

We recommend that financial relief on separation should be granted in accordance with a statutory scheme based upon the economic impact of cohabitation, to the following effect.

An eligible cohabitant applying for relief following separation ("the applicant") must prove that:

1. the respondent has a retained benefit; or

2. the applicant has an economic disadvantage;

as a result of qualifying contributions the applicant has made.

A qualifying contribution is any contribution arising from the cohabiting relationship which is made to the parties' shared lives or to the welfare of members of their families. Contributions are not limited to financial contributions, and include future contributions, in particular to the care of the parties' children following separation.

A retained benefit may take the form of capital, income or earning capacity that has been acquired, retained or enhanced.

---

married or in a civil partnership, whilst deliberately avoiding the *language* of relationships 'analogous' to marriage or a civil partnership.

[142] Consequential changes are also proposed to the Inheritance (Provision for Family and Dependents) Act 1975 where a relationship ends through the death of a cohabitant.

[143] Law Commission Report No 307 (2007). The report was preceded by Law Commission Consultation Paper No 179, *Cohabitation: The Financial Consequences of Relationship Breakdown* (2006).

[144] Law Commission Report No 307 (2007), [1.2].   [145] Ibid, Pt 5.   [146] Ibid, [5.56].

[147] Ibid, [5.64].

An economic disadvantage is a present or future loss. It may include a diminution in current savings as a result of expenditure or of earnings lost during the relationship, lost future earnings, or the future cost of paid childcare.

The court may make an order to adjust the retained benefit, if any, by reversing it in so far as that is reasonable and practicable having regard to the discretionary factors listed below. If, after the reversal of any retained benefit, the applicant would still bear an economic disadvantage, the court may make an order sharing that loss equally between the parties, in so far as it is reasonable and practicable to do so, having regard to the discretionary factors:

The discretionary factors are:

1. the welfare while a minor of any child of both parties who has not attained the age of eighteen;

2. the financial needs and obligations of both parties;

3. the extent and nature of the financial resources which each party has or is likely to have in the foreseeable future;

4. the welfare of any children who live with, or might reasonably be expected to live with, either party; and

5. the conduct of each party, defined restrictively but so as to include cases where a qualifying contribution can be shown to have been made despite the express disagreement of the other party.

Of these discretionary factors, item (1) above shall be the court's first consideration.

In making an order to share economic disadvantage, the court shall not place the applicant, for the foreseeable future, in a stronger economic position than the respondent.

The following range of orders should be available to the court:

1. lump sums, including payment by instalment, secured lump sums, lump sums paid by way of pensions attachment, and interim payments;

2. property transfers;

3. property settlements;

4. orders for sale; and

5. pension sharing.

Unlike on divorce, periodical payments should not generally be available.

In so far as the scheme is engaged, it should apply between the parties to the exclusion of the general law of implied trusts, estoppel and contract.

It should be emphasized that the proposed scheme moves the enquiry away from determining the parties' ownership of property. Where the scheme applies, issues of ownership become otiose. It is consistent with this that the scheme will operate to the exclusion of claims based on the property principles discussed in this chapter. If adopted, there will be a clear demarcation between circumstances in which the scheme applies and circumstances in which the parties' ownership of their home will need to be determined under the property rules discussed in this chapter (see Table 12.1). The departure from the parties' property rights at the point of relationship breakdown has led Gardner to suggest that the proposed scheme may violate A1P1 of the European Convention on Human Rights.[148]

---

[148] Gardner, 'Problems in Family Property' (2013) 72 CLJ 301.

Table 12.1 Scope of the Law Commission's Proposals

When the Law Commission's scheme will apply (if implemented)	When ownership will continue to be determined using property law principles discussed in this chapter
(i) Cohabitants have been living as a couple in a joint household; and (ii) the eligibility criteria are met; and (iii) the parties have not executed a valid opt out; and (iv) an application for financial relief is made by one of the parties following the breakdown of their relationship.	(i) The parties are not cohabitants living as a couple in a joint household. This will include relatives and friends who share a home, and those who live together to provide care or companionship; or (ii) cohabitants have lived together as a couple in a joint household, but do not meet the eligibility criteria; or (iii) the parties have executed a valid opt-out; or (iv) in all cases in which the parties' rights need to be determined in circumstances other than relationship breakdown.

On 6 September 2011, the government announced that it did not intend to implement the Law Commission's recommendations at least for the time being.[149] Following this announcement pressure for reform has continued. The Law Commission expressed a hope that implementation '*will not be delayed beyond the early days of the next Parliament, in view of the hardship and injustice caused by the current law*'.[150] In *Gow v Grant*,[151] delivering the Opinion of the Privy Council on the interpretation of the Family Law (Scotland) Act 2006, which enables the provision of financial compensation on the breakdown of a relationship between cohabitees, Lady Hale called for reform of English law. She suggested, '*[t]here is some reason to think that a family law remedy such as that proposed by the Law Commission would be less costly and more productive of settlements as well as achieving fairer results than the present law*.'[152] A private member's bill promising reform was introduced in the 2014/15 parliamentary session but the government did not back the proposed legislation and it consequently faltered due to lack of parliamentary time. It remains to be seen if continued pressure will ultimately bear fruit in much-needed reform.[153]

QUESTIONS

1. Compare and contrast resulting and constructive trusts. Why do you think constructive trusts are preferred as a means of determining rights in the home?

---

[149] Written Ministerial Statement by Jonathan Djanogly, Parliamentary Under-Secretary of State, Ministry of Justice, 6 September 2011, Hansard HL, cols WS18–19.

[150] <http://www.justice.gov.uk/lawcommission/docs/20110906_Statement_on_Govt_response.pdf> (accessed 4 January 2012).

[151] [2012] UKSC 29. See, Miles, 'Cohabitation: Lessons for the South from North of the Border?' (2012) 72 CLJ 492.

[152] Ibid, [47].

[153] The Bill was also designed to implement the Law Commission's proposals on intestacy and cohabitation, contained in Part 8 of a separate Report: Law Commission Report No 331, *Intestacy and Family Provision Claims on Death* (2011).

2. Are the problems of gender stereotypes that have been encountered in ascertaining the existence of detriment inherent in the adoption of the test provided by Nourse LJ in *Grant v Edwards*? Is Browne-Wilkinson VC's test (in the same case) preferable?

3. Compare and contrast an inferred and an imputed intent. What role does each currently play as regards (a) the creation of a constructive trust and (b) the quantification of beneficial shares under a constructive trust?

4. Following *Stack v Dowden, Jones v Kernott*, and *Marr v Collie* what reforms (if any) do you consider desirable to the current law concerning the creation of a common intention constructive trust?

5. What are the advantages and disadvantages of determining ownership of the home through the application of property law principles? Is the Law Commission justified in singling out relationship breakdown between cohabitants as a situation to be dealt with outside property law principles?

For guidance on how to answer these questions visit the online resources at www.oup.com/uk/mcfarlane4e/.

FURTHER READING

Bottomley, 'Women and Trust(s): Portraying the Family in the Gallery of the Law' in *Land Law: Themes and Perspectives* (eds Bright and Dewar, Oxford: OUP, 1998)

Cowan, Fox O'Mahony, and Cobb, *Great Debates in Property Law* (Basingstoke: Palgrave Macmillan, 2012) ch 11

Douglas, Pearce, and Woodward, 'Cohabitants, Property and the Law: A Study of Injustice' (2009) MLR 24

Fox O'Mahony, 'Property Outsiders and the Hidden Politics of Doctrinalism' (2014) 67 CLP 409

Hayward, '"Family Property" and the Process of "Familialisation" of Property Law' (2012) 24 CFLQ 284

Hayward, '*Stack v Dowden* (2007); *Jones v Kernott* (2009): Finding a Home for "Family Property"' in *Landmark Cases in Land Law* (ed Gravells, Oxford: Hart Publsihing, 2013)

Hopkins, 'Regulating Trusts of the Home: Private Law and Social Policy' (2009) 125 LQR 310

Hopkins, 'The Relevance of Context in Property Law: A Case for Judicial Restraint?' (2011) 31 LS 175

Law Commission Report No 307, *Cohabitation: The Financial Consequence of Relationship Breakdown* (2007)

Mee, *The Property Rights of Cohabitees* (Oxford: Hart Publishing, 1999)

Miles, 'Property Law v Family Law: Resolving the Problems of Family Property' (2003) LS 624

Piska, 'Constructive Trusts and Constructing Intention' in Dixon (ed), *Modern Studies in Property Law Vol 5* (Oxford: Hart Publishing, 2009)

Probert, 'Equality in the Family Home?' (2007) 15 FLS 341

Sloan, 'Keeping up with the Jones Case: Establishing Constructive Trusts in "Sole Legal Owner" Scenarios' (2014) LS DOI: 10.1111/lest.12052

13

REGULATING CO-OWNERSHIP:
THE CONTENT QUESTION

CENTRAL ISSUES

1. Through the existence of express and implied trusts (particularly constructive trusts arising under the principles discussed in Chapter 12), it is common for the home to be co-owned.

2. English law has two forms of co-ownership: the *joint tenancy* and the *tenancy in common*. The legal position of the co-owners as between themselves differs under each form.

3. The distinguishing feature of the joint tenancy is the operation of survivorship on the death of a joint tenant.

4. A joint tenant can become a tenant in common through severance of the joint tenancy. This may occur unilaterally, by the individual act of one or more joint tenants, or mutually, by all of the joint tenants.

5. In both forms of co-ownership, the rights and duties of the co-owners are regulated through the imposition of a trust of land, governed by the Trusts of Land and Appointment of Trustees Act 1996.

6. The 1996 Act confers powers on the trustees in relation to the management of the land and rights on the beneficiaries. In particular, it confers on certain beneficiaries a right to occupy the land.

7. The 1996 Act provides a procedure through which disputes between the co-owners are resolved by an application to court.

1 INTRODUCTION

Co-ownership describes the situation in which two or more people are concurrently entitled to legal and/or beneficial title to an estate in land. Co-ownership may arise either in relation to a freehold or leasehold estate, and is of particular relevance in understanding the legal regulation of the home. The home may be co-owned either through the existence of an express trust, or through a successful claim to ownership of the home being made under the constructive or resulting trust discussed in Chapter 12. The defining characteristic of co-ownership is that the parties have 'unity of possession'—that is, they are each entitled to possession of the whole of the land. It is unity of possession that distinguishes co-ownership from successive ownership,[1] in which possession is enjoyed consecutively, and from separate ownership of neighbouring plots of land.

The presence of co-ownership gives rise both to internal issues, in relation to the relationship between the co-owners themselves, and external issues, as regards the relationship between the co-owners and third parties. The purpose of this chapter is to consider the internal regulation of co-ownership. It is concerned with the *content* question: the relationship between the co-owners themselves, including their rights and duties in relation to each other, and whether one co-owner can insist on a sale of the land against the wishes of another. External issues with third parties are considered in Chapters 14 and 17. Chapter 14, looks at applications for sale of co-owned land by third parties, whilst Chapter 17 considers priority between the co-owners and third-party purchasers of the land through the concept of overreaching.

The internal regulation of co-ownership is dominated by two features of English law: firstly, the recognition of two distinct types of co-ownership—the *joint tenancy* and the *tenancy in common*; and secondly, the imposition of a trust in all cases of co-ownership. When considering the internal regulation of co-ownership, the trust is best seen as a device through which the powers of management and disposition of the land are separated from the enjoyment of the land, whether 'enjoyment' takes the form of occupation, or receipt of profits and the proceeds of sale. Through the imposition of the trust, the powers of management and disposition are vested in the legal owner or co-owners as trustee(s), while enjoyment of the land vests in the beneficial or equitable owners. Even when the same people are both trustees and beneficiaries, it is important to differentiate the capacity in which a person is exercising his or her rights and duties in relation to the land.

2 JOINT TENANTS AND TENANTS IN COMMON

Co-ownership may take the form of a joint tenancy or a tenancy in common. The essence of a *joint tenancy* is that each joint tenant is wholly entitled to the land when acting collectively, but that, individually, no single joint tenant has any 'share' in the land with which he or she can separately deal. This is reflected in Coke's[2] description of the joint tenancy: '*[E]ach joint tenant holds the whole and holds nothing, that is, he holds the whole jointly and nothing separately.*' The practical consequence of each joint tenant holding 'the whole' is that, when one dies, there is no 'share' to pass by will or intestacy. Title simply 'survives' in the remaining joint tenants through the process of survivorship: there is no passing or vesting of title in the remaining joint tenants, because they were already 'wholly entitled' themselves. The operation of survivorship is the key practical difference between the joint tenancy and the tenancy in common.

Tenants in common hold what are described as 'undivided shares' in the land. Lawson and Rudden explain this concept using the analogy of a company.

---

[1] See online resources.   [2] *Coke upon Littleton* (19th edn, 1832) p 186a.

Lawson and Rudden, *The Law of Property* (3rd edn, 2002, p 93)

The simplest way to grasp the idea [of tenants in common] is to think of shares in a company. The shareholders each have a separate thing which they can alienate or leave to pass on their death, but none of them can go to the company's head office, point at a particular room and say 'I claim my share'. So if there are two owners in common of a house each has a separate, though intangible, asset: it is the house which is not divided into distinct 'shares'.

Each tenant in common may deal with his or her share individually during his or her lifetime (for example, by selling the share to another co-owner, or to a third party). On the death of a tenant in common, his or her share passes through his or her will or under the rules of intestacy. In sum, it may be said that while joint tenants can act only *collectively* and their acts necessarily affect the whole of the co-owned estate, tenants in common can also act *individually* in relation to their own undivided shares in the estate.

Where co-owners start out as joint tenants, one or more of the co-owners may subsequently become a tenant in common through the process of severance. Co-ownership of a legal estate is, however, subject to a particular statutory framework that, through a series of provisions, confines the creation of legal co-ownership to a joint tenancy, precludes any subsequent severance of that joint tenancy, and imposes a maximum number of four joint legal owners.

Law of Property Act 1925, s 1(6)

(6) A legal estate is not capable of subsisting or of being created in an undivided share in land [. . .]

Law of Property Act 1925, s 36(2)

(2) No severance of a joint tenancy of a legal estate, so as to create a tenancy in common in land, shall be permissible, whether by operation of law or otherwise, but this subsection does not affect the right of a joint tenant to release his interest to the other joint tenants, or the right to server a joint tenancy in an equitable interest whether or not the legal estate is vested in the joint tenants [. . .]

Trustee Act 1925, s 34(2)

(2) In the case of settlements and dispositions [creating trusts of land] made or coming into operation after the commencement of this Act—

(a) the number of trustees thereof shall not in any case exceed four, and where more than four persons are named as such trustees, the four first named (who are able and willing to act) shall alone be the trustees, and the other persons named shall not be trustees unless appointed on the occurrence of a vacancy;

(b) the number of the trustees shall not be increased beyond four.

Hence, s 1(6) of the Law of Property Act 1925 (LPA 1925) prohibits legal tenancies in common ('undivided shares'), while s 34(2) of the Trustee Act 1925 imposes a limit of four trustees or owners of the legal title. The effect of these provisions is to create a single and indivisible legal title, held by (and registered in the names of) a maximum of four co-owners. The prohibition of severance—a logical consequence of s 1(6) of the LPA 1925—is put beyond doubt by s 36(2) of that Act. Because legal title cannot be fragmented through severance, purchasers can deal confidently with the legal owners as collective managers of the sole legal title. The certainty provided to purchasers does not come at the expense of flexibility for the co-owners: flexibility is ensured through the fact that co-ownership necessarily arises under a trust.

These provisions affect only the legal title held by the trustees. Beneficial co-owners remain free to choose between the joint tenancy and tenancy in common, with no limitation on their number.

So what happens if, contrary to these provisions, land is purported to be transferred as a legal tenancy in common? This possibility is dealt with by s 34(2) of the LPA 1925.

Law of Property Act 1925, s 34(2)

(2) Where, after the commencement of this Act, land is expressed to be conveyed to any persons in undivided shares and those persons are of full age, the conveyance shall (notwithstanding anything to the contrary in this Act) operate as if the land had been expressed to be conveyed to the grantees, or, if there are more than four grantees, to the four first named in the conveyance, as joint tenants in trust for the persons interested in the land [. . .]

2.1 IDENTIFYING JOINT TENANTS AND TENANTS IN COMMON

While legal title must be held as a joint tenancy, in equity, the beneficiaries may be either joint tenants or tenants in common. So how do we know whether co-owners are joint tenants or tenants in common?

Three factors may determine this. Firstly, the joint tenancy is characterized by four 'unities', which must be present for the beneficiaries to be joint tenants. In addition to unity of *possession*, these are unity of *interest* (the joint tenants have the same interest in the land), unity of *title* (the joint tenants must derive their title from the same act, for example, of adverse possession, or document), and unity of *time* (joint tenants derive their title at the same time). But while the presence of all four unities is a prerequisite for a joint tenancy, it is not determinative. A tenancy in common may still be found where the unities are present.[3]

Secondly, in an express trust, the parties may declare the capacity in which beneficial entitlement is held. In *Goodman v Gallant*,[4] the court held that such a declaration is conclusive. In *Cowcher v Cowcher*,[5] Bagnell J considered that '*A trust for A and B without further definition creates an equitable joint interest*'. In registered land, joint transferees have the opportunity to state whether equitable title is to be held as a joint tenancy[6]—but there

---

[3] Smith, *Plural Ownership* (2005) p 27.
[4] [1986] Fam 106. See also *Pankhania v Chandegra* [2013] 1 P&CR 16.
[5] [1972] 1 WLR 425, [430].
[6] Either on form TR1 (transfer of registered property) or separately on form JO (joint ownership).

is no requirement to do so and, therefore, issues of interpretation will continue to arise as to whether the terms of a trust are sufficient to declare a joint tenancy.[7] In *Robertson v Fraser*,[8] Lord Hatherley LC noted: '*I cannot doubt, having regard to the authorities respecting the effect of such words as amongst and respectively that anything which in the slightest degree indicates an intention to divide the property must be held to abrogate the idea of a joint tenancy, and to create a tenancy in common.*' A declaration that a survivor can give a valid receipt for capital moneys has been held insufficient to establish an express joint tenancy.[9]

Thirdly, in the absence of an express declaration by the parties, it is necessary to try and determine the intention of the parties. This is a question that we have already explored in Chapter 12. It will be recalled that in this enquiry the law employs presumptions. The general presumption is that equity follows the law. As the parties are necessarily joint tenants in law, they will be joint tenants in equity. Prior to *Stack v Dowden*[10] the initial presumption of a joint tenancy was considered to be readily rebutted where parties contributed to the purchase of land in unequal shares. In such circumstances it was considered that equity favoured the tenancy in common as crediting parties with a share reflecting their actual contribution and avoiding the capricious effect of survivorship that the longest survivor gains all. This approach was preferred by Lord Neuberger in his minority judgment in the case.[11] The majority in *Stack* considered that it was significant to look at the context in which the parties had purchased the property. In the 'domestic consumer context' the presumption of joint tenancy will only be rebutted where the contrary is proved through a common intention constructive trust. Further, it was considered that cases in which the presumption would be rebutted in this way would be 'very unusual'.[12]

This approach was endorsed by the Supreme Court in *Jones v Kernott*,[13] but with useful clarification as to the type of case to which *Stack v Dowden* applies and as to the reasons underpinning the presumption in the cases where a couple purchase a home for their joint occupation. In the following extract, they explain the reasoning for the operation of the presumption.

Jones v Kernott
[2011] 3 WLR 1121

Lord Walker and Baroness Hale

At 19–22

The presumption of a beneficial joint tenancy is not based on a mantra as to "equity following the law" (though many non-lawyers would find it hard to understand the notion that equity might do anything else). There are two much more substantial reasons (which

---

[7] *Stack v Dowden* [2007] UKHL 17, [52]–[53]. See further Powlowski and Brown, 'Joint Purchasers and the Presumption of Joint Beneficial Ownership—A Matter of Informed Choice?' (2013) 27 Tru LI 3, 9–11.

[8] (1870–71) LR 6 Ch App 696.

[9] *Stack v Dowden* [2007] 2 AC 432, [51], approving the Court of Appeal decisions in this respect in *Harwood v Harwood* [1991] 2 FLR 274 and *Huntingford v Hobbs* [1993] 1 FLR 736.

[10] [2007] 2 AC 432, [58] *per* Baroness Hale.

[11] Ibid, [109]–[110]. The presumption of a tenancy in common where parties contribute unequally remains intact in commercial cases. See, e.g., *Malayan Credit v Jack Chia* [1986] AC 549, PC.

[12] [2007] 2 AC 432, [68], *per* Baroness Hale.   [13] [2011] UKSC 53, [25] and [68].

overlap) why a challenge to the presumption of beneficial joint tenancy is not to be lightly embarked on. The first is implicit in the nature of the enterprise. If a couple in an intimate relationship (whether married or unmarried) decide to buy a house or flat in which to live together, almost always with the help of a mortgage for which they are jointly and severally liable, that is on the face of things a strong indication of emotional and economic commitment to a joint enterprise. That is so even if the parties, for whatever reason, fail to make that clear by any overt declaration or agreement. The court has often drawn attention to this. Jacob LJ did so in his dissenting judgment in this case: [2010] EWCA Civ 578, [2010] 1 WLR 2401, para 90.

One of the most striking expressions of this approach is in the judgment of Waite LJ in *Midland Bank plc v Cooke* [1995] 4 All ER 562, 575. It is worth quoting it at some length, even though the case was a single-name case and the couple were married (the husband was 19, and the wife a little older, at the time of the marriage):

> Equity has traditionally been a system which matches established principle to the demands of social change. The mass diffusion of home ownership has been one of the most striking social changes of our own time. The present case is typical of hundreds, perhaps even thousands, of others. When people, especially young people, agree to share their lives in joint homes they do so on a basis of mutual trust and in the expectation that their relationship will endure. Despite the efforts that have been made by many responsible bodies to counsel prospective cohabitants as to the risks of taking shared interests in property without legal advice, it is unrealistic to expect that advice to be followed on a universal scale. For a couple embarking on a serious relationship, discussion of the terms to apply at parting is almost a contradiction of the shared hopes that have brought them together. There will inevitably be numerous couples, married or unmarried, who have no discussion about ownership and who, perhaps advisedly, make no agreement about it. It would be anomalous, against that background, to create a range of home-buyers who were beyond the pale of equity's assistance in formulating a fair presumed basis for the sharing of beneficial title, simply because they had been honest enough to admit that they never gave ownership a thought or reached any agreement about it.

Gardner and Davidson make the same point at (2011) 127 LQR 13, 15–16:

> The context under discussion is one in which people will not normally formulate agreements, but (this is crucial) the very reason for this—the parties' familial trust in one another—also warrants the law's intervention nonetheless. Unless the law reacts to such trust as much as to more individualistic forms of interaction, those who put their faith in the former rather than the latter will find their interests thereby exposed.

Gardner has termed this "a materially communal relationship: ie one in which, in practical terms, they pool their material resources (including money, other assets, and labour)": *An Introduction to Land Law*, 2nd ed (2009) para 8.3.7.

The notion that in a trusting personal relationship the parties do not hold each other to account financially is underpinned by the practical difficulty, in many cases, of taking any such account, perhaps after 20 years or more of the ups and downs of living together as an unmarried couple. That is the second reason for caution before going to law in order to displace the presumption of beneficial joint tenancy. Lady Hale pointed this out in *Stack v Dowden* at para 68 (see para 12 above), as did Lord Walker at para 33:

> In the ordinary domestic case where there are joint legal owners there will be a heavy burden in establishing to the court's satisfaction that an intention to keep a sort of balance-sheet of contributions actually existed, or should be inferred, or imputed to the parties. The presumption will be that equity follows the law. In such cases the court should not readily embark on the sort of detailed examination of the parties' relationship and finances that was attempted (with limited success) in this case.

Subsequently, the Privy Council in the case of *Marr v Collie*[14] have reiterated the importance of context and the centrality of determining the parties' intention if necessary by imposing a common intention constructive trust, rather than merely relying on legal presumptions. Given that the parties have not expressly declared a trust, those intentions might be evidenced from any oral discussions or inferred from the context and circumstance of the parties' relations. In *Marr* the parties were in a close emotional relationship and had purchased a home and several investment properties in their joint names so that the context produced a clash between the presumptions of a joint tenancy in the domestic context and the presumption of a tenancy in common in the investment or commercial context of their relationship. The Privy Council thus returned the case to the lower courts to determine (if possible) the parties' intention. To the extent that *Marr v Collie* reflects the views of the Supreme Court, the starting point now seems to be to try to establish the parties' intention, if necessary by use of a common intention constructive trust, and resort to the legal presumptions only when that enquiry has failed.

In respect of homes bought in joint names by parties who are not in an intimate relationship (for example, those bought jointly by parents and children, siblings, or friends), *Stack v Dowden* and *Jones v Kernow* suggested that there will still be an initial presumption of joint tenancy based on the '*mantra*' that equity follows the law. However, that initial presumption would be more readily replaced with a presumption of resulting trust where the parties contributed unequally so that the beneficial shares reflect their contributions which, if unequal, dictates that they will necessarily be tenants in common. However, *Marr v Collie* suggests that before employing any presumption it is necessary to see if there is any evidence of the parties' common intention.

In *Stack v Dowden* and *Jones v Kernott* the status of the co-owners as joint tenants or tenants in common was addressed only in relation to cases of joint legal ownership. The decisions do not indicate the status of parties in a case of sole legal ownership where another party (or parties) establish a beneficial interest through a resulting or constructive trust. Prior to *Stack v Dowden*, as with cases of joint legal ownership, the status of the parties would be dependent on whether they contributed equally or unequally: equal contributions were considered to be consistent with a joint tenancy; unequal contributions with a tenancy in common. In cases of sole legal ownership, there is no initial presumption of co-ownership; the initial presumption is of sole beneficial ownership. This may be sufficient to differentiate such cases and leave the existing presumptions intact. But *Stack v Dowden* and *Marr v Collie* moves the ethos in determining co-ownership rights, particularly when acquired by married and unmarried cohabitees, away from contributions (and the resulting trust) to the parties' common intention through the constructive trust. It is consistent with this to suggest that, in sole legal ownership cases, parties should be joint tenants despite contributing unequally to the purchase where, on a constructive trust analysis, there is a common intention to share beneficial ownership equally.

2.2 SURVIVORSHIP

As has been noted, survivorship operates in a joint tenancy, with the effect that, on the death of one co-owner, title simply remains in the survivors. Through this process, the longest surviving co-owner becomes the sole owner. Practical difficulties that would arise where the

---

[14] [2017] UKPC 17.

co-owners die in circumstances where it cannot be determined who died first are precluded by an arbitrary rule in s 184 of the LPA 1925.

Law of Property Act 1925, s 184

In all cases where, after the commencement of this Act, two or more persons have died in circumstances rendering it uncertain which of them survived the other or others, such deaths shall (subject to any order of the court), for all purposes affecting the title to property, be presumed to have occurred in order of seniority, and accordingly the younger shall be deemed to have survived the elder.

The effect of this provision is that, in the event of simultaneous deaths of joint tenants, the land passes wholly under the terms of the will (or rules of intestacy) of the youngest co-owner.

2.3 SEVERANCE

Severance is the process through which a beneficial joint tenant may become a tenant in common. By doing so, the severing joint tenant obtains an undivided share in the land that can be separately dealt with and which, on his or her death, will pass under the terms of their will or through statutory rules applicable to intestacy. The severing joint tenant is no longer affected by survivorship, which continues to operate as between any remaining joint tenants. Severance is irreversible. Because survivorship operates immediately upon the joint tenants' death, severance must take place during their lifetime. In particular, this carries the consequence that severance cannot take place by will.[15] The severing joint tenant is invariably credited with an equal share.[16]

Four methods of severance exist. One is provided by statute in s 36(2) of the LPA 1925. That subsection also preserves the operation of other methods of severance. Three other methods have developed through case law and were summarized in the following case.

Williams v Hensman
(1861) 1 J&H 546

Page-Wood VC

At 557

A joint-tenancy may be severed in three ways: in the first place, an act of any one of the persons interested operating upon his own share may create a severance as to that share. The right of each joint-tenant is a right by survivorship only in the event of no severance having taken place of the share which is claimed under the *jus accrescendi*. Each one is at liberty to dispose of his own interest in such manner as to sever it from the joint fund—losing, of

---

[15] See *Shah v Forsters LLP* [2017] EWHC 2433 for an example of the implications of this rule.
[16] *Goodman v Gallant* [1986] Fam 106.

course, at the same time, his own right of survivorship. Secondly, a joint-tenancy may be severed by mutual agreement. And, in the third pace, there may be a severance by any course of dealing sufficient to intimate that the interests of all were mutually treated as constituting a tenancy in common. When the severance depends on an inference of this kind without any express act of severance, it will not suffice to rely on an intention, with respect to the particular share, declared only behind the backs of the other persons interested. You must find in this class of cases a course of dealing by which the shares of all the parties to the context have been effected [. . .]

The methods identified by Page-Wood VC may be referred to, respectively, as an act of a joint tenant operating on his or her share, mutual agreement, and severance by a course of dealing. Of these four methods, a joint tenant may use the first two (statutory severance and an act operating on a share) unilaterally. For so long as there are two or more joint tenants, their joint tenancy remains intact between them and exists side by side with the severed tenant in common. The effect of such unilateral severance is illustrated in Figure 13.1.

The other two methods (mutual agreement and course of dealing) necessarily involve the participation of all of the joint tenants and, if applied, bring the joint tenancy to an end by turning all of the beneficiaries into tenants in common. These methods of severance cannot be used, for example, by two of four joint tenants to sever their joint tenancy, but leave the joint tenancy intact as between the others.

In addition to these methods, severance may also arise as a consequence of the unlawful killing of one joint tenant by another.

2.3.1 Statutory severance

The statutory method of severance is found in the proviso to s 36(2) of the LPA 1925.

Law of Property Act 1925, s 36(2)

(2) Provided that, where a legal estate (not being settled land) is vested in joint tenants beneficially, and any tenant desires to sever the joint tenancy in equity, he shall give to the other joint tenants a notice in writing of such desire or do such other acts or things as would, in the case of personal estate, have been effectual to sever the tenancy in equity, and thereupon [the land shall be held in trust on terms] which would have been requisite for giving effect to the beneficial interests if there had been an actual severance.

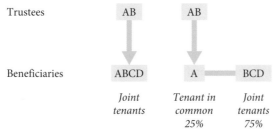

Figure 13.1 Unilateral severance by one joint tenant (A)

It is important to note that, to be effective, written notice must be served on all of the joint tenants. Written notice that is not served on all of the joint tenants will not constitute severance under this provision.

Two key issues have arisen in the application of s 36(2): firstly, what constitutes written notice; and secondly, how to identify the point in time at which notice is validly served.

What constitutes written notice?

While there is no particular form that the notice must take,[17] it must express an immediate severance and must relate to the ownership of the land or proceeds of sale in a manner inconsistent with a joint tenancy. In this respect it is important to bear in mind that a joint tenancy continues to subsist as the property held on trust is exchanged: for example, a joint tenancy of a house continues into the proceeds of sale. The need for a notice to relate to ownership is highlighted by *Nielson-Jones v Fedden*.[18] In that case, severance was held not to have taken place, because the written notice dealt with use, rather than ownership, of the proceeds of sale. The notice, which took the form of a memorandum agreed between the parties, directed the husband to '*use his entire discretion and free will*' to decide whether to sell the parties' former matrimonial home in order to purchase a home for himself. Walton J noted that the memorandum was 'wholly ambiguous' as to ownership of the proceeds of sale.[19] It gave the husband use of the whole of the proceeds of sale, but this did not imply that he was entitled to half absolutely. It is entirely consistent with the unity of possession that is characteristic of co-ownership for one joint tenant to have use of the whole property.

In *Burgess v Rawnsley*,[20] Lord Denning MR suggested that the decision in *Nielson-Jones v Fedden* was wrong. He did not, however, discuss the specific issue regarding a declaration of use.

The need for the notice to express an immediate severance is illustrated by contrasting the two following cases.

Re Draper's Conveyance
[1969] 1 Ch 486, HC

Facts: A husband and wife were joint tenants of their matrimonial home. Following their divorce, the wife issued a summons under s 17 of the Married Woman's Property Act 1882 for an order that the house be sold, and the proceeds distributed equally between her and her husband—a request reflected in an affidavit sworn by her in support of her application. An order for possession and sale, and equal division of the proceeds, was made, but the husband remained in possession until his death. The question then arose as to whether severance had occurred.

Plowman J

At 492–4

The summons, coupled with the affidavit in support of it, clearly evinced an intention on the part of the plaintiff that she wished the property to be sold and the proceeds distributed, a

---

[17] There is no requirement that the notice is signed: *Re Draper's Conveyance* [1969] 1 Ch 486, [492].
[18] [1975] Ch 222.   [19] Ibid, 229.
[20] [1975] Ch 429. See further Prichard, 'Joint Tenancies: Severance' [1975] CLJ 28, 30–1.

half to her and a half to the deceased. It seems to me that that is wholly inconsistent with the notion that a beneficial joint tenancy in that property is to continue, and therefore, apart from these objections to which I will refer in a moment, I feel little doubt that in one way or the other this joint tenancy was severed in equity before the end of February, 1966, as a result of the summons which was served on the plaintiff's then husband and as a result of what the plaintiff stated in her affidavit in support of the summons of Feb. 11, 1966 [. . .]

Counsel for the plaintiff took another point. Counsel for the defendants, in argument, having indicated that he relied not only on the summons as operating to sever the joint tenancy but on the orders as well, counsel for the plaintiff submitted on the authority of *Bedson v. Bedson* that there was no power in the court by an order made under the Married Women's Property Act, 1882, to sever a beneficial joint tenancy. He submitted that the power of the court was to declare what the rights of the parties were and not to alter those rights. That may well be so—for the purposes of my judgment I am prepared to assume that counsel for the plaintiff is right about that—but the view which I take is that the question does not arise here. The severance, in my judgment, is effected by the summons and the affidavit, not by any order that was made. Accordingly, in my judgment, the beneficial joint tenancy was severed by the plaintiff in the lifetime of the deceased husband, and I propose to declare that on the true construction of the above-mentioned conveyance and s. 36 of the Law of Property Act, 1925, and in the events which have happened, the plaintiff, as trustee, holds the beneficial interest in any proceeds of sale of the property after discharge of incumbrances and costs for herself and the estate of the deceased as tenants in common in equal shares.

Harris v Goddard
[1983] 3 All ER 242, CA

Facts: As in *Re Draper's Conveyance*, a husband and wife were joint tenants of their matrimonial home. Following the breakdown of the relationship, the wife petitioned for divorce and requested, under the Matrimonial Causes Act 1973, '*That such order may be made by way of transfer of property and/or settlement in respect of the former matrimonial home [. . .] and otherwise as may be just*'. The husband was subsequently killed in an accident and the question arose whether this petition had acted to sever the joint tenancy.

Lawton LJ

At 246

When a notice in writing of a desire to sever is served pursuant to s. 36(2) it takes effect forthwith. It follows that a desire to sever must evince an intention to bring about the wanted result immediately. A notice in writing which expresses a desire to bring about the wanted result as some time in the future is not, in my judgment, a notice in writing within s. 36(2). Further, the notice must be one which shows an intent to bring about the consequences set out in s. 36(2), namely that the net proceeds of the statutory trust for sale "[. . .] shall be held upon the trust which would have been requisite for giving effect to the beneficial interests if there had been an actual severance". I am unable to accept Mr Berry's submission that a notice in writing which shows no more than a desire to bring the existing interest to an end is a good notice. It must be a desire to sever which is intended to have the statutory consequences. Paragraph 3 of the prayer to the petition does no more than invite the court to consider at some future time whether to exercise its jurisdiction under s. 24 of the 1973 Act or, if it does, to do so in one or more of three different ways. Orders under s. 24(1)(a) and (b) could bring co-ownership to an end by ways other than by severance. It follows, in my judgment, that para. 3 of the prayer of the petition did not operate as a notice in writing to sever the joint tenancy in equity. This tenancy had not been severed when Mr Harris died with the consequence that Mrs Harris is entitled to the whole of the fund held by the first and second defendants as trustees. I wish to stress that all I am saying is that para. 3 in the petition under consideration in this case did not operate as a notice of severance.

The key difference between the cases is that that the petition in *Harris v Goddard* did not evince an *immediate* desire to sever. It should be emphasized that, in *Re Draper's Conveyance*, the court acknowledged that severance was caused by the summons and affidavit, not the order of the court. Hence, where the application constitutes written notice, severance occurs regardless of whether the application is heard or, if it is, regardless of the outcome. The courts' reliance on the summons and affidavit in *Re Draper's Conveyance* caused doubt to be cast on the decision. In *Nielson-Jones v Fedden*,[21] Walton J noted that, until a court order is made, proceedings can be withdrawn. He considered that notice under s 36(2) of the LPA 1925 must be irrevocable, and therefore doubted that a summons and affidavit could suffice. This doubt was cast aside in *Harris v Goddard*.[22] Lawton LJ noted that the revocable nature of court proceedings is simply a factor for the court to consider in all of the circumstances when determining whether, on the facts of the case, notice has been served within s 36(2).

Whether it is necessary for the notice to be irrevocable appears to remain unsettled. Notably, in responding to Walton J's judgment, Lawton LJ does not explicitly reject such a requirement. But Smith suggests that the endorsement of *Re Draper's Conveyance* by the Court of Appeal, both in *Harris v Goddard* and in a further decision,[23] suffices to dispel the need to show that notice is irrevocable.[24]

Re Draper's Conveyance was applied in the context of different judicial proceedings in *Quigley v Masterson*.[25] There, the judge was satisfied that an application to the Court of Protection in which one joint tenant sought authority to sell a house and divide the proceeds between herself and the other joint tenant, her former partner, constituted notice.

When is notice of severance validly served?

Whether notice of severance has been validly served is a matter of importance, as it is from that moment that the joint tenancy is irreversibly severed, the severing joint tenant becomes a tenant in common and, as such, is no longer subject to survivorship. In most cases, this issue does not cause difficulties: written notice is sent and received, and the matter is beyond doubt. Where the notice is connected to judicial proceedings it will be served in the context of those proceedings.[26] But understanding when notice is validly served may be crucial

---

[21] [1975] Ch 222, [236].   [22] [1983] 1 WLR 1203, [1210]–[1211].
[23] *Burgess v Rawnsley* [1975] Ch 429.   [24] Smith (2005) p 51.   [25] [2011] EWHC 2529 (Ch).
[26] Cf: *Quigley v Masterson* [2011] EWHC 2529 (Ch). There, the joint tenant on whom notice needed to be served was not a party to proceedings which related to an application to the Court of Protection to appoint a Deputy to act on his behalf. The notice was treated as having been served on his Deputy from the time that she was appointed by the court to act on his behalf.

where a death occurs in close proximity of time or a joint tenant, having issued notice, seeks to intercept it following a change of mind.

The requirement in s 36(2) of the LPA 1925 is that the notice is 'given' to the joint tenants. General guidelines on service of a notice are provided in s 196 of the Act. These have been applied to s 36(2), 'given' and 'served' being considered in this context to be synonymous.[27]

Law of Property Act 1925, s 196(3) and (4)

(3) Any notice required or authorised by this Act to be served shall be sufficiently served if it is left at the last-known place of abode or business in the United Kingdom of the lessee, lessor, mortgagee, mortgagor, or other person to be served, or, in case of a notice required or authorised to be served on a lessee or mortgagor, is affixed or left for him on the land or any house or building comprised in the lease or mortgage, or, in case of a mining lease, is left for the lessee at the office or counting-house of the mine.

(4) Any notice required or authorised by this Act to be served shall also be sufficiently served, if it is sent by post in a registered letter addressed to the lessee, lessor, mortgagee, mortgagor, or other person to be served, by name, at the aforesaid place of abode or business, office, or counting-house, and if that letter is not returned [by the postal operator (within the meaning of the Postal Services Act 2000) concerned] undelivered; and that service shall be deemed to be made at the time at which the registered letter would in the ordinary course be delivered.

It should be noted that there is no requirement that the notice is actually *received* or seen by the intended recipient. It is sufficient that it reaches (or is deemed to have reached) the joint tenant's last known address. Where notice is sent by ordinary post, it is served within s 196(3) when the postman delivers the letter, because this constitutes leaving the notice at the '*last known place of abode*'.

This was held in the following case, which contains the most thorough judicial analysis of when written notice is served. As Neuberger J highlights, the seemingly unending possible factual permutations justify a clear rule.

Kinch v Bullard
[1999] 1 WLR 423, HC

Facts: Mr and Mrs Johnson were beneficial joint tenants of their matrimonial home. The parties were divorcing and Mrs Johnson, who was terminally ill, sent a notice of severance to Mr Johnson by ordinary first-class post. The letter was duly delivered, but, before seeing it, Mr Johnson suffered a serious heart attack. Realizing that she was now likely to outlive her husband, Mrs Johnson destroyed the letter. Mr Johnson died a couple of weeks later, followed, in a matter of months, by Mrs Johnson. An action was brought by the parties' respective executors to determine whether the notice—delivered, but then destroyed—had operated to sever the joint tenancy. If it had, then each party had

---

[27] *Re 88 Berkeley Road* [1971] 1 All ER 254.

a 50 per cent share to pass under the terms of their respective wills; if not, survivorship would have operated on Mr Johnson's death, leaving the entire property to pass under Mrs Johnson's will.

Neuberger J

At 427–30

Section 196(4) deems service on the premises to have taken place if the requirements of sending by registered post and non-return by the Post Office are satisfied, even if it can be shown that physical service did not in fact take place on those premises. Section 196(3), on the other hand, requires it to be established that physical service did in fact take place on the appropriate premises, before any deemed service can arise. It appears to me that the natural meaning of s 196(3) is that if a notice can be shown to have been left at the last known abode or place of business of the addressee, then that constitutes good service, even if the addressee does not actually receive it [. . .]

Thirdly, it was contended on behalf of the defendants that the fact that Mrs Johnson changed her mind and no longer '(desired) to sever the joint tenancy' by the time that the notice might otherwise have been said to have been 'given' (ie by the time that the notice arrived at the property) meant that the notice was ineffective to effect such severance. This argument is based on the language of s 36(2). Assuming that the notice was validly 'given' pursuant to s 196(3), the giving of the notice only occurred when it was actually delivered to the property, and at that time Mrs Johnson no longer 'desire[d] to sever the joint tenancy'. Accordingly, it is said that the statutory precondition for the giving of a valid notice was not, at the date it was given, satisfied, because at that date Mrs Johnson did not have the necessary 'desire'.

In my judgment, this argument is not correct. The function of the relevant part of s 36(2) is to instruct any joint tenant who desires to sever the joint tenancy how to do it: he is to give the appropriate notice (or do such other things as are prescribed by the section). Clear words would be required, in my judgment, before a provision such as s 36(2) could be construed as requiring the court to inquire into the state of mind of the sender of the notice. Once the sender has served the requisite notice, the deed is done and cannot be undone. The position is the same as with a contractual right to determine a lease, which normally entitles either or both parties to serve notice to determine the lease if it desires to put an end to the term. Once the procedure has been set in train, and the relevant notice has been served, it is not open to the giver of the notice to withdraw the notice, and I have never heard it suggested that a change of mind before the notice is given would render it ineffective.

I reach this conclusion based on the proper construction of s 36(2). However, it appears to me that it is also correct as a matter of policy. If it were possible for a notice of severance or any other notice to be ineffective because, between the sender putting it in the post and the addressee receiving it, the sender changed his mind, it would be inconvenient and potentially unfair. The addressee would not be able to rely confidently upon a notice after it had been received, because he might subsequently be faced with the argument that the sender had changed his mind after sending it and before its receipt. Further, as I have already mentioned, it is scarcely realistic to think that the legislature intended that the court could be required to inquire into the state of mind of the sender of the notice in order to decide whether the notice was valid.

I am inclined to think that the position would be different if, before the notice was 'given', the sender had informed the addressee that he wished to revoke it. In such a case, it appears to me that the notice would have been withdrawn before it had been 'given'. After all, as is clear from the reasoning at first instance and in the Court of Appeal in *Holwell Securities Ltd v Hughes* [1973] 2 All ER 476 at 481, [1973] 1 WLR 757 at 761–762; [1974] 1 All ER 161 at 164, 166–167, [1974] 1 WLR 155 at 158–159, 160–162, a notice sent by post is not 'served' in accordance with s 196(3) until it arrives at the premises to which it has been addressed. Accordingly, it seems to me that, while the notice is still in the post, it has not been given, and, until it is given, the sender has in effect a locus poenitentiae whereby he can withdraw the notice, but only provided his withdrawal is communicated to the addressee before the notice is given to, or served on, the addressee. I should emphasise, however, that this is no more than a tentative view.

Fourthly, it is said that, in the present case, the notice was not 'left' at the property within the meaning of s 196(3). Assuming that, before the notice was actually posted through the letter box, Mrs Johnson had decided that she would pick it up and destroy it, and bearing in mind that she was the person whose notice it was, it is said that the notice was never really 'left' for Mr Johnson at the property. In my judgment, that argument is wrong as a matter of principle, and would be inconvenient to apply in practice.

So far as the principle is concerned, it seems to me that, by putting the notice in the post, Mrs Johnson effectively left it to the Post Office to serve the notice on her behalf. One therefore has to ask oneself whether the person who was, in effect, appointed by Mrs Johnson to serve the notice, acted in accordance with the test propounded by Russell LJ in Lord Newborough's case. In my judgment, by posting the envelope containing the notice, and addressed to Mr Johnson at the property, through the letter box of the property, the postman served the notice in accordance with that test. I do not think that it is right to test the matter by reference to what Mrs Johnson thought or intended, because, she left it to the Post Office to serve the notice. Accordingly, subject to any other arguments, once the notice was posted through the letter box, it had been 'served' in accordance with s 196(3), and therefore 'given' in accordance with s 36(2), and, as I have mentioned, such a notice cannot be 'un-served' or 'un-given'.

So far as convenience is concerned, I consider that, if s 196(3) is satisfied once it is shown that the relevant document was bona fide delivered to the last-known place of abode or business of the addressee, then, although it might lead to an unfair result in an exceptional case, the law is at least simple and clear. On the other hand, if the court starts implying exceptions into the clear and simple statutory procedure, confusion and uncertainty could result. Thus, if, by picking up the notice after it was posted through the front door of the property, Mrs Johnson might have prevented the notice being 'served', problems could arise. Would there be a maximum time within which Mrs Johnson would have to pick up the notice before it would be held to be validly served? Would it make any difference if Mr Johnson had seen the envelope containing the notice on the mat? What if Mrs Johnson had picked up the notice and had kept it but not destroyed it? What if she had picked up the notice intending to destroy it but had changed her mind? What if she had picked up the notice and tried to destroy it, but Mr Johnson had seen her doing it, or had seen and read the imperfectly burnt notice?

Hence, notice was served at the time that the letter was delivered. Once this had occurred, it was too late for Mrs Johnson to seek to change her mind.

Similarly, in the earlier case of *Re 88 Berkeley Road*,[28] severance was held to have occurred when written notice was sent by registered post and signed for on delivery by the sender without, it seems, ever being passed on to the other joint tenant.

---

[28] [1971] 1 All ER 254.

2.3.2 An act of a joint tenant operating on his or her share

An act of a joint tenant severs the joint tenancy by destroying one or more of the unities of title, time, and interest.[29] This first head of severance, identified in *Williams v Hensman*,[30] runs into the immediate logical difficulty that joint tenants do not have 'shares': on what basis can a joint tenant 'act' upon a share that he or she does not have? Logical difficulties are sidestepped by treating the act itself as causing severance and so freeing up the share as the subject matter of the act in question.[31]

In *Williams v Hensman*, Page-Wood VC referred to an act of disposition. The disposition may be voluntary—for example, through the sale of a share—or involuntary—as where a joint tenant's bankruptcy causes his or her share to vest in their trustee in bankruptcy. Despite the terms of Page-Wood VC's judgment, an actual disposition appears unnecessary. Joint tenants have also been held to have acted on their share by, for example, entering a contract for sale,[32] or simply through acquiring a greater share than other joint tenants.[33]

The position is more complex if one joint tenant buys out the share of another. In such a case, the purchasing joint tenant is a tenant in common as regards the newly acquired share, but remains a joint tenant in relation to his or her original interest. Hence, just as the joint tenancy and tenancy in common can subsist side by side, the same beneficiary may be a joint tenant in relation to his or her initial interest and a tenant in common as regards a subsequently acquired interest (see Figure 13.2).

The ultimate limit on the scope of this head of severance is that there must be *an act* operating on the share. A unilateral declaration of intent to sever by a joint tenant is not effective. In the absence of an act operating on his or her share, the joint tenant must follow the requirements of s 36(2) of the LPA 1925 and serve written notice in order to affect severance. In *Nielson-Jones v Fedden*,[34] Walton J considered there to be 'no conceivable ground' for suggesting that a unilateral declaration can ever be effective to sever.

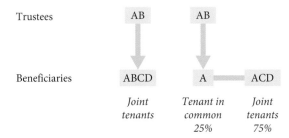

Figure 13.2 Severance by one joint tenant (B) selling his or her share to another joint tenant (A)

---

[29] Prichard (1975, p 29) (referring specifically to destruction of unity of title).

[30] (1861) J&H 546, (1861) 70 ER 862.

[31] Crown, 'Severance of Joint Tenancy by Partial Alienation' (2001) 117 LQR 477, 478.

[32] *Brown v Raindle* (1796) 3 Ves 296, (1796) 30 ER 998.

[33] *Megarry and Wade: The Law of Real Property* (7th edn, eds Harpum et al, 2008), [13–041].

[34] [1975] Ch 222, [230]. Previous judicial acceptance to the contrary is criticized by Baker (1968) 84 LQR 462. See further, *Burgess v Rawnsley* [1975] Ch 429, 448, where, in a summary of principles, Sir John Pennycuick noted: '*An uncommunicated declaration by one party to the other or indeed a mere verbal notice by one party to another clearly cannot operate as a severance.*'

Voluntary acts

An outright transfer of a share by a joint tenant by sale or gift, whether to another joint tenant or a third party, is the clearest example of an act operating on a share. More contentious is the effect of a partial alienation, where the transferring joint tenant retains an interest and the transfer itself may have only temporal effect.[35]

The most significant practical example of partial alienation is a mortgage or charge of an equitable share. The beneficiary-mortgagor retains an interest in property and (subject to an action for default) the mortgage will eventually be discharged. Such mortgages may be unlikely to be granted expressly, because the security of a beneficial share may not be commercially attractive, but they arise, not infrequently, as the result of a failed attempt by a single joint tenant to mortgage the legal title through, for example, forgery or undue influence committed against the other co-owners.[36] Such a mortgage has no effect on the legal title, but operates as a mortgage of the joint tenant's beneficial interest: does such a mortgage affect a severance? The issue is of importance, because, if severance does not take place, the mortgagee '*joins the survivorship wheel of fortune*', with his or her security interest over the property lost on the death of the mortgagor.[37]

In *First National Security v Hegerty*,[38] a husband forged his wife's signature on a legal charge to use the property as security for a loan. Bingham J considered this to constitute a disposition of the husband's beneficial share, which severed the beneficial joint tenancy and created a valid equitable charge over the husband's share. While this remains the current position, the matter was not argued in the case (it being unclear whether the parties were joint tenants or tenants in common) and academic doubt has since been cast on the issue.

Nield suggests that the distinction between a mortgage and a charge may be crucial in this context. A mortgage of an equitable interest necessarily takes effect as an assignment of the interest and therefore involves a disposition.[39] In contrast, she argues that the inherent nature of a charge means that an equitable charge should not affect severance.

Nield, 'To Sever or Not to Sever: The Effect of a Mortgage by One Joint Tenant'
[2001] Conv 462, 469–70

However the historical and comparative evidence against severance by equitable charge is strong. At common law, although alienation was preferred over survivorship, survivorship was preferred over the creation of a mere encumbrance. It has long been asserted that easements and rentcharges do not effect a severance. They are encumbrances and as such are said not to be inconsistent with the nature of a joint tenancy, even though they may create a distinction between the interests of the joint tenants. For instance, it has been suggested that a rentcharge would not disturb the joint tenancy for it could be paid out of the joint tenant's portion of the income from the land, even though re-entry might follow if payments were not made. An easement granted by one joint tenant will only effect the interest held by that joint tenant and the right granted thus must be exercised in common with the rights of the other joint tenant.

---

[35] Crown (2001) pp 479–80.
[36] Nield, 'To Sever or not to Sever: The Effect of a Mortgage by One Joint Tenant' [2001] Conv 462, 462–3.
[37] Ibid, p 463. The debt remains and will need to be met from the mortgagor's estate.
[38] [1965] 1 QB 850.   [39] Nield (2001) p 467.

Equitable charges are mere encumbrances that give no right to possession. The chargee may apply to court for an order for sale or the appointment of a receiver over the charged property. It is accepted that an equitable charge creates some sort of interest that is proprietary in nature but there is considerable hesitation in acknowledging this interest as an interest in the land itself. There are thus even weaker grounds for claiming that an equitable charge should effect a severance, because it destroys the unities, than in the case of a rentcharge or easement, which are clearly interests in land.

In contrast, Crown considers that the issue of severance should not be left to technical questions as to whether alienation occurs. He suggests the matter should be addressed by considering whether there are policy reasons for preferring one approach to the other.

Crown, 'Severance of a Joint Tenancy of Land by Partial Alienation' (2001) 117 LQR 477, 483

One can easily imagine a situation where A and B are joint tenants in law and equity of land. A grants an equitable mortgage of his "share". If the approach of *Re Sharer* is adopted, this severs the joint tenancy in equity, but B may know nothing about it. Suppose A repays the loan with the result that the mortgage is discharged, and subsequently B dies. B's personal representatives will have no way of finding out about the creation of the mortgage and the result will be that A will succeed to the entire estate by virtue of the doctrine of survivorship. If A were to die first, however, a different result might well occur. A's personal representatives may well find documentary evidence of the creation of the mortgage while going through his papers. They will then be able to argue successfully that the joint tenancy was severed with the result that they will succeed to half the estate. Policy considerations therefore point strongly towards adopting the view that the grant of an equitable mortgage will not sever a joint tenancy.

Underlying Crown's concern is the risk of a mortgage of an equitable interest causing severance without the knowledge of other joint tenants. While the example he gives is not an attractive outcome, however, it is acknowledged as a unique feature of this head of severance that it enables a joint tenant to sever in secret, without the participation of, or giving of notice to, the other joint tenants.[40]

A novel approach to severance has been suggested in relation to a different example of partial alienation: the unilateral grant of a lease by one joint tenant. As with a mortgage, the joint tenant retains an interest in the land and the status quo is returned to at the end of the lease. As will be seen in Chapter 19, the essential characteristic of a lease is exclusive possession. The effect of a single joint tenant granting a lease is therefore to confer on the tenant of the lease exclusive possession against all persons other than those joint tenants who did not take part in the grant.[41] There is no clear authority determining whether the grant of a lease by one joint tenant constitutes an act of severance.[42] One possibility in such a case is

---

[40] Smith (2005) p 58.   [41] Crown (2001) p 484.
[42] Ibid, pp 485–90. He notes that while sixteenth-century cases indicate that the grant of a lease by one joint tenant of a leasehold estate affects a severance, there is no authority dealing with the grant of a lease by one joint tenant of a freehold estate. Courts in other jurisdictions have reached different conclusions on the matter.

that the joint tenancy is suspended for the duration of the lease, but is resurrected when the lease expires.[43] The suspension of the joint tenancy ensures that if the grantor of the lease dies during its duration, survivorship does not operate, which ensures that the tenant's lease is unaffected by the death.

If accepted, could the same solution be adopted to the more practically important case of a mortgage? Crown highlights that leases are different from mortgages, because a lease must come to an end, while a mortgage only carries the risk that the security will be enforced. He suggests that this may explain the different effect each has on severance.[44] Nield, however considers the suspension of the joint tenancy (or some other means of modifying survivorship) to '*provide tantalising compromises to balance the interests of the mortgagee and joint tenants and deserve serious consideration*'.[45]

A final example of partial alienation is a declaration by a joint tenant of a trust of his or her share. In this instance, severance seems likely to arise by analogy with the effect of a contract to sell the share outright. Such a contract gives rise to a constructive trust through the maxim 'equity looks on as done that which ought to be done'. If a constructive trust effects severance, it necessarily follows that an express trust must also do so.[46]

Involuntary acts

An involuntary act operating on a share is most likely to arise through the interception of a debt affecting one of the joint tenants. Bankruptcy has provided the focus of attention, although the grant of a charging order also operates to sever a joint tenancy as the debt becomes secured against the debtor's share.[47] While bankruptcy undoubtedly causes severance, debate continues as to the time at which severance occurs. This can be significant where the bankrupt (or another joint tenant) dies during the course of the bankruptcy. If death pre-dates the time of severance, then survivorship operates, taking the beneficial interest beyond the reach of the creditors.

There are three possible dates from which severance may take effect: the date of the act of bankruptcy; the date on which the joint tenant is declared bankrupt; and the date of appointment of the trustee in bankruptcy.

The date of the act of bankruptcy was favoured by the common law and was applied under the Bankruptcy Act 1914 in *Re Dennis*.[48] In that case, the bankrupt and his wife were joint tenants of their home. Between the date of the act of bankruptcy (by failing to comply with a bankruptcy notice) and the declaration of bankruptcy, the wife died. The court held that severance occurred at the date of the act of bankruptcy. This meant that, on her death, the wife was a tenant in common of a 50 per cent share, which passed to the couple's children. If the date of the declaration of bankruptcy had been chosen, survivorship would have operated on the wife's death, leaving the bankrupt as sole owner and the entire house therefore available to his creditors.

In *Re Palmer*,[49] which was decided under the Insolvency Act 1986, a different analysis was taken. Under s 306 of that Act, the bankrupt's estate vests in the trustee in bankruptcy immediately upon appointment; from the time of the declaration of bankruptcy, however,

---

[43] For discussion see Crown ibid and Fox, 'Unilateral Demise by a Joint Tenant: Does it Effect a Severance?' [2000] Conv 208.

[44] Crown (2001) p 484.   [45] Nield (2001) p 474.

[46] Smith (2005) pp 59–60; Crown (2001) pp 490–2.

[47] See C *Putnam & Sons v Taylor* [2009] EWHC 317 (Ch), [20].   [48] [1996] Ch 80.

[49] [1994] Ch 316.

the Official Receiver holds the estate in trust. The court held that severance therefore occurs at the time of the declaration of bankruptcy. In that case, Mr Palmer was declared bankrupt after his death. In such a case, the declaration dates back to the day of death, so the bankrupt's estate on that day vests in the trustee in bankruptcy. The court held, however, that this did not include a joint tenancy that the bankrupt had at the start of the day, but which ceased to exist at the moment of his death through survivorship. Through survivorship, Mr Palmer's wife became solely entitled to the home, which was protected from the effect of the bankruptcy.

Both decisions produce results that are sympathetic to the bankrupt's family. The courts' choice as to the date of severance conflicts and, while factually distinct, there is no logical reason for treating the date of severance as different, according to whether bankruptcy occurs during the bankrupt's lifetime, or after his or her death. The analysis in *Re Palmer* should now be followed in all cases, because it applies the current legislation. If applied to the facts of *Re Dennis*, it would appear to reverse the decision in that case.

Subsequent to the decision in *Re Palmer*, the Insolvency Act 2000 inserted s 421A into the Insolvency Act 1986. The effect of that provision is that where a joint tenant is declared bankrupt after his or her death (so that survivorship operates in favour of the remaining joint tenants), the survivors may be required by the court, on an application by the trustee in bankruptcy, to compensate the bankrupt's estate by payment of a sum not exceeding the value lost through survivorship. Hence, while the operation of severance remains governed by *Re Palmer*, the financial consequences of the decision may be reversed by an application under s 421A.

2.3.3 Severance through mutual agreement

The scope of the second category of severance identified by Page-Wood VC in *Williams v Hensman* is difficult to pinpoint in the abstract: it is sandwiched between the stricter requirement of an 'act' and the more liberal third category of a course of dealings. Collectively, mutual agreement and a course of dealings differ from statutory severance and an act operating on a share, because they only enable severance by all of the joint tenants. They differ from the other common law methods of severance as regards the rationale for severance. As we have noted, an act operating on a share effects severance by the destruction of one or more of the unities of title, time, and interest.[50] In cases of mutual agreement and a course of dealings, the rationale for severance is the common intention of the parties. For example, in *Davis v Smith*[51] the Court of Appeal held severance to have taken place where correspondence between the joint tenants evidenced a common intention that a house should be sold and the proceeds divided equally. Destruction of a unity is the result of the severance, not the cause of it.[52]

The Court of Appeal applied severance by mutual agreement in the following case. Browne LJ's judgment demonstrates both the similarities and differences between this method and the other two recognized in *Williams v Hensman*.

---

[50] See section 2.3.2.

[51] Unreported, judgment 23 November 2011 (CA).   [52] Prichard (1975) pp 29–30.

Burgess v Rawnsley
[1975] Ch 429, CA

Facts: Mr Honick and Mrs Rawnsley were joint tenants of a house occupied by Mr Honick alone. The property had been purchased in the expectation that the parties would both live there, but while Mr Honick anticipated marriage, Mrs Rawnsley intended to live alone in the upstairs flat. The parties' mismatched expectations came to light after the purchase. Mrs Rawnsley did not move in, but reached an oral agreement to sell her share to Mr Honick for £750. She then changed her mind and sought a higher price. Matters stood this way at Mr Honick's death, whereupon the house was sold and Mrs Burgess, his administratrix, sought to establish that severance had occurred, leaving his estate entitled to 50 per cent of the proceeds of sale.

Browne LJ

At 443–4

Counsel for Mrs Rawnsley conceded, as is clearly right, that if there had been an enforceable agreement by Mrs Rawnsley to sell her share to Mr Honick, that would produce a severance of the joint tenancy; but he says that an oral agreement, unenforceable because of s 40 of the Law of Property Act 1925, is not enough. Section 40 merely makes a contract for the disposition of an interest in land unenforceable by action in the absence of writing. It does not make it void. But here Mrs Burgess is not seeking to enforce by action the agreement by Mrs Rawnsley to sell her share to Mr Honick. She relies on it as effecting the severance in equity of the joint tenancy. An agreement to sever can be inferred from a course of dealing (see Lefroy B in *Wilson v Bell* and Stirling J in *Re Wilks*) and there would in such a case ex hypothesi be no express agreement but only an inferred, tacit agreement, in respect of which there would seldom if ever be writing sufficient to satisfy s 40. It seems to me that the point is that the agreement establishes that the parties no longer intended the tenancy to operate as a joint tenancy and that automatically effects a severance. I think the reference in *Megarry and Wade* to specifically enforceable contracts only applies where the suggestion is that the joint tenancy has been severed by an alienation by one joint tenant to a third party, and does not apply to severance by agreement between joint tenants. I agree with counsel for Mrs Burgess that s 40 ought to have been pleaded, but I should be very reluctant to decide this case on a pleading point.

The result is that I would uphold the county court judge's judgment on his second ground, namely, that the joint tenancy was severed by an agreement between Mrs Rawnsley and Mr Honick that she would sell her share to him for £750. In my view her subsequent repudiation of that agreement makes no difference. I would dismiss the appeal on this ground.

Section 40 of the LPA 1925 has since between replaced by s 2(1) of the Law of Property (Miscellaneous Provisions) Act 1989 (LP(MP)A 1989), under which an oral contract for sale of land is void. This change does not, however, alter the decision in the case. Browne LJ's judgment demonstrates that there was no act operating on a share in the absence of a specifically enforceable contract; there was, instead, an informal agreement, drawn from the parties' course of dealing. It is emphasized, however, that severance was based on mutual agreement, not on the course of dealings itself. The Court of Appeal was unanimous that severance had occurred under this method, while, as will be seen, the judges were divided on the possible application of course of dealings as an alternative basis for severance. Browne LJ's judgment leaves that method of severance to apply where the course of dealings falls short of even an informal agreement.

In *Hunter v Babbage*,[53] although an informal agreement was found on the facts, the court suggested that such an agreement is not necessary for this method of severance. Drawing on comments in the judgment of *Williams v Hensman*, Deputy Judge John McDonnell QC considered that it would be sufficient if it could be inferred that the parties had mutually treated their interests as a tenancy in common.[54]

2.3.4 Severance through a course of dealings

Actions between parties falling short of establishing a mutual agreement will still sever if there is a sufficient course of dealings to intimate that the parties regarded themselves as tenants in common. The exact demarcation of this method with mutual agreement may be difficult to identify with certainty, particularly if, as has been suggested, mutual agreement can include cases falling short of an actual agreement. Practically, nothing may turn on any overlap between the categories. It is more important to note, as was emphasized by Pennycuick LJ in *Burgess v Rawnsley*,[55] that this method of severance is distinct from mutual agreement, not merely a subheading of that category.

In that case, the judges were divided on whether a course of dealings provided an alternative means of severance on the facts.

Burgess v Rawnsley
[1975] Ch 429, CA

Lord Denning MR

At 440

Even if there was not any firm agreement but only a course of dealing, it clearly evinced an intention by both parties that the property should henceforth be held in common and not jointly.

Pennycuick LJ

At 447

I do not doubt myself that where one tenant negotiates with another for some rearrangement of interest, it may be possible to infer from the particular facts a common intention to sever even though the negotiations break down. Whether such an inference can be drawn must I think depend on the particular facts. In the present case the negotiations between Mr Honick and Mrs Rawnsley, if they can be properly described as negotiations at all, fall, it seems to me, far short of warranting an inference. One could not ascribe to joint tenants an intention to sever merely because one offers to buy out the other for £X and the other makes a counter-offer of £Y.

Browne LJ expressed no final opinion on the matter. The key issue appears to be when negotiations falling short of an agreement are sufficient to effect severance. Lord Denning

---

[53] (1995) 69 P & CR 548.   [54] Ibid, 554.   [55] [1975] Ch 429, [447].

MR appears to take a broad view of this issue, reflected both in his decision in *Burgess v Rawnsley* and in his discussion, in his judgment in that case, of *Nielson-Jones v Fedden*.[56] In that case, as has been seen,[57] a memorandum granting the husband discretion to sell the house was considered insufficient to sever under s 36(2) of the LPA 1925 on the basis that it dealt with use, rather than ownership of the proceeds of sale. At the time of the husband's death, a contract for sale had been entered and a deposit paid by the purchaser. It was argued, as an alternative to s 36(2), that the parties' discussions, as regards their financial arrangements and the distribution of part of the deposit, constituted severance. Walton J rejected this argument, on the basis that no agreement could be drawn from the parties' ongoing negotiations.

We have seen that Lord Denning MR considered the decision to be wrong in relation to s 36(2). He further suggested that severance had occurred through a course of dealings:[58] '*The husband and wife entered on a course of dealing sufficient to sever the joint tenancy. They entered into negotiations that the property should be sold. Each received £200 out of the deposit paid by the purchaser. That was sufficient.*' To the extent that reliance is placed on negotiations, these should be accepted only where the agreement, if reached, would have been sufficient to sever within the category of mutual conduct. If the agreement would have been insufficient to affect severance, it necessarily follows that negotiations for the agreement cannot do so.[59]

2.3.5 Severance through unlawful killing

Public policy prevents a person responsible for the unlawful death of another from benefiting from their death. Such benefit could arise through the operation of survivorship where one joint tenant is responsible for the death of another. The public policy rule is achieved through forfeiture under the Forfeiture Act 1982, with the possibility of relief.

In *Re K*,[60] Vinelott J accepted the view of counsel that '*the forfeiture rule unless modified under the Act of 1982 applies in effect to sever the joint tenancy in the proceeds of sale and in the rents and profits until sale*'. This implies that, where relief is awarded, the correct analysis is that severance does not occur, leaving survivorship to operate. Hence, it is the availability of relief that determines whether severance occurs.[61] In *Re K*, relief was awarded where a battered wife, who had unintentionally shot and killed her husband (her intention had been merely to threaten him), had been convicted of manslaughter.

The culpability of the defendant has since been confirmed as the principal factor in determining relief.[62]

2.3.6 Severance and the common intention constructive trust: unresolved issues

In section 2.1 of this chapter we have seen that the effect of the decisions in *Stack v Dowden*[63] and *Jones v Kernott*[64] is to impose a presumption of joint tenancy in respect of particular

---

[56] [1975] Ch 222.   [57] See section 2.3.1.   [58] *Burgess v Rawnsley* [1975] Ch 429, [440].
[59] *Hunter v Babbage* (1995) 69 P & CR 548, 560.   [60] [1985] Ch 85, [100].
[61] The practical focus on the availability of relief is noted by Bridge, 'Assisting Suicide Rendered Financially Painless' [1998] CLJ 31, 32.
[62] *Dunbar v Plant* [1998] Ch 412 (relief from forfeiture awarded); *Chadwick v Collinson* [2014] EWHC 3055 (Ch) (relief declined).
[63] [2007] 2 AC 432.   [64] [2011] 3 WLR 1121.

properties that are purchased as homes. The presumption can be rebutted through a common intention constructive trust. We have seen in Chapter 12, section 2.2 that that type of trust is 'ambulatory' meaning that the parties' intentions (and, therefore, their beneficial shares) can change over time. In *Stack* and *Jones* the parties' shares were ultimately quantified as being unequal: respectively 65/35 per cent, and 90/10 per cent. There are unresolved doctrinal issues as to how the outcome in these cases can be rationalized with the rules of severance. If parties begin (as they did in those cases) as equitable joint tenants, but end with unequal shares, then severance must have taken place. But on what basis? Further, as we have seen in section 2.3, severance credits the parties with equal shares. Hence it appears that severance alone cannot explain the outcome in the cases. If the parties severed in equal shares and a transfer of a beneficial interest was then made to leave the parties with the correct proportions, that transfer appears to constitute a disposition of an equitable interest—which s 51(1)(c) of the Law of Property Act 1925 requires to be in writing.

A number of analyses of the operation of constructive trusts have been proffered,[65] but the doctrinal explanation for the outcome in the cases remains unresolved. The ambulatory nature of the trust has been relied upon to explain both the severance and alteration of the parties' beneficial shares.[66] But it remains unclear which head of severance—if any—would thereby apply. A change in the parties' common intention could constitute severance through mutual agreement (discussed in section 2.3.3). Alternatively, there could be an act operating on a share (as discussed in section 2.3.2).[67] Mee suggests that s 53(1)(c) does not apply 'because each new division of the beneficial ownership occurs under a new, or (to put it s different way) newly refreshed, constructive trusts'.[68] The creation and operation of constructive trusts is exempt from the formality requirement by s 53(2). Powlowski and Brown suggest that s 53(2) applies to exempt the (notional) transfer if that transfer takes place under the *existing* constructive trust. If each new common intention gives rise to a *new* trust, then the authors suggest that there is no reason in principle why the parties should not be able to agree to sever in unequal shares.[69] On that basis, no question of the application of s 53(1)(c) arises.

2.3.7 Are the current severance rules satisfactory?

In 1985, in its Working Paper on *Trusts of Land*, the Law Commission considered two radical reforms of severance: firstly, limiting severance to the statutory method of written notice; secondly, enabling severance by will.[70] Reform of severance was not carried over into the subsequent final report on *Trusts of Land*, on the basis that the issue is also relevant to personal property; instead, the Law Commission indicated that the matter would form the basis of a separate, future report.[71] The Law Commission has, in fact, carried out no further work in this respect.

---

[65] For discussion of the issues, see Briggs, 'Co-Ownership and an Equitable Non-Sequitur' (2012) 128 LQR 183; Dixon, Editor's Notebook [2012] Conv 83; Mee, 'Ambulation, Severance and the Common Intention Constructive Trust (2012) 128 LQR 500; Powlowski and Brown, 'Co-Ownership and Severance after *Stack*' (2013) 27 Tru LI 59; Powlowski and Brown, 'Co-Owners and Severance – Determining Beneficial Entitlement after *Stack*' (2013) 27 Tru LI 172.

[66] In particular by Mee (2012) 128 LQR 500.   [67] Powlowski and Brown (2013) 27 Tru LI 59.

[68] Mee (2012) 128 LQR 500, 501.   [69] (2013) 27 Tru LI 172, 175 and 178.

[70] Law Commission Working Paper No 94, *Trusts of Land* (1985), [16.11]–[16.14].

[71] Law Commission Report No 181, *Transfer of Land: Trusts of Land* (1989), [1.3].

The limitation of severance to written notice necessarily carries the consequence of the abolition of the *Williams v Hensman* methods of severance. We have seen that these methods of severance do cause difficulties in interpretation and application. The underlying question, therefore, is whether these difficulties are sufficient to support the extreme response of abolition—a question addressed by Tee, together with the other reform discussed by the Law Commission: the introduction of severance by will.

Tee, 'Severance Revisited' [1995] Conv 105, 110–13

The abolition of severance by acting upon one's share has a certain attraction in logic—there has always been an intellectual sleight of hand which allows the alienation both to transform and transfer the interest, but it would effectively prevent a joint tenant from dealing with his equitable interest in any way.... An absolute requirement of written notice would complicate an already difficult area of the law and could result in unfairness to creditors where the bankrupt held property as a beneficial joint tenant.

The abolition of severance by mutual agreement or by mutual conduct would have fewer legal repercussions. It is arguable that severance on such grounds has been found so rarely by the courts over the last 50 years that the abolition of these methods would not in practice amount to a serious limitation, and would produce much needed certainty. When personal representatives feel obliged to go to court to discover the beneficial entitlement to a home after the death of an erstwhile joint tenant, land law is shown in a poor light; the stress of any litigation is self-evident, and the timing, shortly after a death, and the subject matter, a home, must only compound the unhappiness for the parties involved.

What is uncertain, however, is how often severance on one of these grounds has been recognised and accepted by practitioners without resort to court. The Working Paper suggests that "if either has behaved as though the joint tenancy does not exist and treated the property as his own, it seems right that the law should accept that [. . .]" If indeed people often act in this way, then the abolition of informal methods of severance could result in widespread unfairness. The advantage of permitting informal methods, in terms of fairness to lay people, has to be weighed against the disadvantage of the uncertainty engendered by the possibility of informal severance having taken place.

(c) The introduction of severance by will

This is a radical suggestion, which runs counter to the whole concept of joint tenancy with its right of survivorship. This right is its distinctive feature, and is why equity in general favours the less capricious tenancy in common. Thus the arguments in favour of introducing severance by will must be carefully examined. The Working Paper mentions that in a matrimonial breakdown a spouse may be anxious to sever but unwilling to serve a notice and thereby aggravate negotiations over, for example, access to the children. The argument has a certain force, but the period during which such considerations hold sway should be quite short. In any relationship breakdown negotiations over children and property may be delicate and fraught, but they still need to be pursued and any property arrangement would be incomplete without an explicit decision as to the beneficial ownership of the home.

A more persuasive argument is that severance by will would prevent undesired devolution of property. There must be many cases where a beneficial joint tenant leaves his property by will, fondly (and not unreasonably) imagining that thereby the "half share" in the house will go to his children, his new loved one or whomever. No doubt the testator was told about the right of survivorship and the methods of severance when he originally bought the house, but that could have been many years ago. Presumably, the deceased testator is never aware that his wishes have been frustrated. The cases do not come to court because the law is clear: one cannot bequeath a beneficial joint tenancy. Although the problem would not occur if a testator took proper legal advice before making a will, this frequently does not happen.

The counter argument is two-fold: first, it would be unfair to allow severance by will and second, difficult questions of construction would arise. The first argument is that a "rogue" beneficial joint tenant could secretly sever by will and then enjoy the possibility of the right of survivorship without any risk to his estate. If he survived his co-tenant, he would take all, and if he pre-deceased, his chosen beneficiaries would inherit his share. Thus he could both "have his cake and eat it". His co-tenant, meanwhile, would not know of his severance by will, and would assume that the right of survivorship was going to operate. By the time she discovered her mistake (after the rogue's death), it would be too late for her to rearrange her affairs. Or she might die first, never knowing that she had been duped. It is possible to riposte that she must have been content that the rogue should take the house or she, too, would have made a will to the contrary, or would previously have severed inter vivos. ...But still one's immediate reaction is that the law should not facilitate such apparently unscrupulous behaviour, or permit a joint tenant to break faith with his co-tenants with impunity. A sophisticated argument that the unfairness is more apparent than real is not the basis upon which to apply legislative reform, especially one which directly affects so many people.

The other difficulty with severance by will is a practical one—the construction of the will. The Working Paper states that severance by will should be specified and explicit: "Severance should not be implied by a gift, for example, of all the residue to a charity, but a gift of 'my halfshare of Blackacre' should be sufficiently explicit to sever". Those examples seem clear enough, but the gift of all the residue to the testator's children, or indeed of "all to mother", would be far more problematic. At present, it is sometimes uncertain whether inter vivos severance has taken place; the additional possibility of severance by will would no doubt result in still more uncertainty for the survivors and a succession of applications to the court. The question to be decided is whether the real problem of undesired property devolution is sufficiently serious to warrant a reform which will in turn produce problems both of principle and practice.

While both reforms discussed by the Law Commission are drawn from dissatisfaction with the operation of the current rules, they provide polarized responses that strengthen or weaken the role of survivorship. Abolition of the *Williams v Hensman* methods of severance would inevitably appear to increase the incidence of survivorship; in contrast, the introduction of severance by will would enable joint tenants to undermine the very essence of the joint tenancy as a gamble on survivorship. Because survivorship is the key difference between the two forms of co-ownership, perhaps the underlying issue is the desirability of the beneficial joint tenancy. The scope and purpose of any reform must logically reflect a policy decision as to the desirability of the joint tenancy. Without this, there is a danger of focussing on the symptoms, whilst ignoring the disease.

We return to this issue in section 4 of this chapter, after first noting the methods through which co-ownership is brought to an end.

3 TERMINATION OF CO-OWNERSHIP

Co-ownership comes to an end once there is a sole legal and equitable owner. Where the same person is entitled in law and equity, this also marks the end of the trust. Where the legal and equitable owners are different (for example, if *T* is the sole legal owner and *B* the sole beneficial owner), a bare trust remains.

Termination of co-ownership in this way may arise through a variety of circumstances. In a joint tenancy, the longest surviving co-owner will become solely entitled through survivorship. A sole beneficiary who is of full age and capacity may insist that legal co-owners transfer legal title to him or her through the rule in *Saunders v Vautier*.[72] It should be noted, however, that where co-owned land is sold to a single purchaser, even assuming that the beneficial interests do not bind the purchaser under the priority rules discussed in Chapter 17, co-ownership is not terminated. While the purchaser solely owns the land, the co-owner's interests (whether as joint tenants or tenants in common) shift from the land into the proceeds of sale.

Co-ownership may also be brought to an end through the process of partition. Section 7 of TOLATA 1996 provides for partition by the trustees, though it may also be ordered by the court in the exercise of its powers under s 14[73] (the courts powers under that section are discussed in section 5.7 of this chapter). Partition is a process through which the trustees may physically divide the land and transfer separate plots into the sole ownership of the beneficiaries. The beneficiaries thus cease to be co-owners, with unity of possession over the land, and become sole owners of their separate parcels of land.

Trusts of Land and Appointment of Trustees Act 1996, s 7(1)–(5)

(1) The trustees of land may, where beneficiaries of full age are absolutely entitled in undivided shares to land subject to the trust, partition the land, or any part of it, and provide (by way of mortgage or otherwise) for the payment of any equality money.

(2) The trustees shall give effect to any such partition by conveying the partitioned land in severalty (whether or not subject to any legal mortgage created for raising equality money), either absolutely or in trust, in accordance with the rights of those beneficiaries.

(3) Before exercising their powers under subsection (2) the trustees shall obtain the consent of each of those beneficiaries.

(4) Where a share in the land is affected by an incumbrance, the trustees may either give effect to it or provide for its discharge from the property allotted to that share as they think fit.

(5) If a share in the land is absolutely vested in a minor, subsections (1) to (4) apply as if he were of full age, except that the trustees may act on his behalf and retain land or other property representing his share in trust for him.

It should be noted that partition is limited to circumstances in which the beneficiaries are tenants in common. This precludes the trustees from interfering with the consequences of survivorship while joint tenants remain. The joint tenancy would thus need to sever before

---

[72] (1841) 4 Beav 115.

[73] *Atkinson v Atkinson*, unreported judgment 30 June 2010 (Leeds County Court); *Ellison v Cleghorn* [2013] EWHC 5 (Ch).

partition is possible. While it is also initially restricted to trusts in which the beneficiaries are of full age (subs (1)), subs (5) enables the trustees to partition even where there are minor beneficiaries—in which case, the minor's land is held on trust by the trustees.

4 IS THE BENEFICIAL JOINT TENANCY DESIRABLE?

The operation of survivorship is the key practical difference between the joint tenancy and the tenancy in common. As has been noted, the two reforms of the severance rules discussed by the Law Commission would strengthen or weaken the role of survivorship. It was suggested, therefore, that the reforms raise an underlying issue of the desirability of the beneficial joint tenancy. Difficulties and uncertainties in the application of severance rules would be removed at a stroke by confining equitable ownership to the tenancy in common. But because this would come at the expense of the loss of survivorship, is this a price worth paying?

The operation of survivorship is most obviously consistent with the likely intentions of parties embarking on what they anticipate will be a lifelong relationship. Smith notes that relationship breakdown, where survivorship ceases to match the parties' intentions, now provides the factual context for the 'great majority' of severance cases[74]—but he also notes that the abolition of the joint tenancy will not resolve problems.

Smith, *Plural Ownership* (2005, pp 87–8)

We now need to investigate the broken down relationship in more details. This context is the major source of concern as far as the operation of the joint tenancy is concerned. How well would the law operate if there were no joint tenancy? Obviously, if the parties never wanted survivorship, then the tenancy in common works well. However, in most relationships the parties are likely to want the survivor to get the property. We have just seen that this can cause problems if one dies during the relationship without making a will. The tenancy in common demands that wills be made in order to that the parties' intentions are fulfilled. What happens if a will has been made and then the relationship breaks down? In theory, the answer is simple: a new will should be made. In practice, the obvious danger is that this will be overlooked (as with joint tenancies, unexpected deaths pose the greatest problems) so that on death the property passes to the estranged spouse or partner. This is exactly the same outcome as with an unsevered joint tenancy. The lawyer who sees the problem is as likely to sever a joint tenancy as to urge the making of a new will. In other words, the problems will be just as severe whether a joint tenancy or tenancy in common is employed. Any legal structure which provides for property to go a particular person is apt to malfunction if the relationship with that person has broken down. It is difficult to avoid the conclusion that positive steps must be taken to change the destination of the property and that those steps are in fact not taken in many cases. Indeed, one may argue that joint tenancy is much more likely to produce the correct result because of the court's ability to find a suitable agreement or course of dealing to achieve severance; implying terms into wills is far more difficult [. . .]

The main advantages of joint tenancies lie in fulfilling the wishes of co-owners when one dies during the relationship. Both joint tenancy and tenancy in common can cause inappropriate results once the relationship breaks down. It seems likely that breakdown of relationships has become more common. This is reflected in the growth of divorce rates and is likely

---

[74] Smith (2005) p 85.

to be related to greater numbers living together outside marriage. These changes tend to reduce the advantages of the joint tenancy.

As this extract shows, the underlying problem is not with the joint tenancy itself, but with the failure of the parties to utilize legal devices to ensure that their intentions are met. While the joint tenancy remains apt to give effect to the parties' intentions where the relationship continues at the time of death, the tenancy in common places the onus on the parties, in all cases, to ensure that their intentions are reflected in an up-to-date will. The arguments for and against abolition of the beneficial joint tenancy appear finely balanced and dependent on many variables. Smith suggests that the case for abolition has not been made out,[75] but he acknowledges that evidence as to the true intentions of purchasers, the incidence of relationship breakdown, and the use of wills may all affect our perception of where the balance currently lies.[76]

5 TRUSTS AND CO-OWNERSHIP

Whenever land is co-owned, whether co-ownership arises in relation to the legal title, the beneficial interests, or both, the land is held on trust. As was noted in section 1, the imposition of a trust in all cases is a dominant feature of the regulation of co-ownership in English law. All co-ownership trusts now constitute 'trusts of land' and are governed by the TOLATA 1996—an Act that originated in Law Commission recommendations.[77] Of its time, and in terms of its effect on the conceptual scheme of land law, the Act was described as '*the most significant measure of property law reform since the legislation of 1925*'.[78] Prior to the 1996 Act, co-ownership trusts were almost invariably classified as 'trusts for sale'—a form of trust regulated by the LPA 1925. To understand the significance of the TOLATA 1996, it is therefore necessary to consider how the trust of land differs from this previous form of regulation.

The Law Commission succinctly highlighted the key differences, both in substance and ethos in its report.

Law Commission Report No 181, *Transfer of Land: Trusts of Land* (1989, [3.1]–[3.5])

Part II

The Trust of Land

Concurrent interests

At present, most concurrent interests fall under a trust for sale, either expressly or by implication. The defining feature of the trust for sale, at least as it was originally designed, is that

---

[75] Ibid, p 89.   [76] Ibid.
[77] Law Commission No 181 (1989). For general discussions of the Act, see Oakley, 'Towards a Law of Trusts for the Twenty-First Century' [1996] Conv 401; Hopkins, 'The Trusts of Land and Appointment of Trustees Act 1996' [1996] Conv 411; Clements, 'The Changing Face of Trusts: The Trusts of Land and Appointment of Trustees Act 1996' (1998) 61 MLR 56.
[78] Harpum, 'The Law Commission and Land Law' in *Land Law Themes and Perspectives* (eds Bright and Dewar, 1998) p 169.

the trustees are under a duty to sell the trust land. Implicit in this is the notion that this land should be held primarily as an investment asset rather than as a 'use' asset.

This formulation may well have been suitable or convenient for the purposes which it was designed to serve. However, since the passing of the 1925 property legislation, social conditions have altered to such an extent that the invariable imposition of a duty to sell now seems wholly artificial. This is largely because the incidence of owner-occupation has, over the last sixty-three years, risen to such a level that most dwellings are now owner-occupied. Most of these are occupied by joint owners. One consequence of this is that the imposition of a duty to sell seems clearly inconsistent with the interests and intentions of the majority of those who acquire land as co-owners. In such cases the intention will rarely be that the land should be held pending a sale; it is much more probable that it will be retained primarily for occupation. In other words, the property will not be held simply as an investment asset, but rather as a 'use' asset.

The courts have sought to neutralise this artificiality by developing the principle that, where the 'collateral purpose' of the trust is, for example, to provide a family of matrimonial home, and where that purpose still subsists, the court may, in the exercise of its discretion under section 30 of the Law of Property Act 1925, refuse to order a sale. In that a single trustee is no longer able to force a sale (as against occupiers' interests) the 'use' value of the property is given recognition. It is, however, somewhat illogical that the courts should be required to develop and maintain a doctrine which takes as its foundation the artificiality of the trust for sale.

As a corollary of the duty to sell, and in accordance with the doctrine of conversion, any interest held under a trust for sale is an interest in the proceeds of the sale of the land. Consequently, the beneficiaries are deemed not to have an interest in the land as such. Once again, the courts have intervened to mitigate the artificiality of the position. This intervention has, however, resulted in an unsatisfactory division between those circumstances in which an interest under a trust for sale will be held to be an interest in land and certain others in which it will not, or might not.

Our proposals in relation to concurrent interests are focussed upon two features of the trust for sale. Our principal recommendations are, firstly, that all land which previously would have been held under an implied trust for sale should now be held under the new system by trustees with a power to retain and a power to sell, and, secondly, that the doctrine of conversion should cease to apply. Thus, the main purpose of the trust will no longer be the realisation of the capital value of the land. Although this purpose is often seen as a merely notional one, judicial interpretation has not been so consistent as to exclude the occasional reappearance of the 'old' approach. The new system will be more readily intelligible to non-lawyers than the trust for sale. The point here is not simply that it should be easier for practitioners to explain the law to their clients, but also that co-ownership should take a form which non-lawyers can make sense of for themselves.

Section 30 of the LPA 1925 concerning the powers of the court under a trust for sale, referred to in this extract, has been repealed by the TOLATA 1996, and replaced by ss 14 and 15 of that Act.

Hence, as a matter of policy, the trust of land represents a shift to a form of regulation that is more suited to the use of land as a home, reflecting modern trends of home ownership. This shift is marked, in particular, by the removal of the duty to sell—the defining characteristic of the trust for sale—together with the abolition, in this context,[79] of the doctrine of

---

[79] Ibid, p 173. He notes that the sidenote to the Trusts of Land and Appointment of Trustees Act 1996, s 3, which reads '*Abolition of doctrine of conversion*' has '*excited some attention amongst academic commentators*'. In fact, the Act only purports to abolish the doctrine in the specific context of its application to trusts for sale.

conversion (which is further discussed in section 5.3 below). Against this background, the key provisions of the 1996 Act can be considered.

5.1 SCOPE OF THE TRUST OF LAND

While we are considering trusts of land in the context of co-ownership trusts, it is important to note that the trust of land itself is broader in scope. One of the principal objectives of the Law Commission was to replace the prevailing tripartite scheme with a single form of regulation for all trusts of land.[80] Prior to the TOLATA 1996, in addition to the trust for sale governing (principally) co-ownership trusts, trusts under which the beneficiaries are entitled in succession were usually regulated by the Settled Land Act 1925.[81] Bare trusts, in which there is one adult beneficiary, fell outside both of these schemes of regulation.

The scope of the trust of land is defined in s 1 of the TOLATA 1996.

Trusts of Land and Appointment of Trustees Act 1996, s 1

(1) In this Act—

    (a) "trust of land" means (subject to subsection (3)) any trust of property which consists of or includes land; and

    (b) "trustees of land" means trustees of a trust of land.

(2) The reference in subsection (1)(a) to a trust—

    (a) is to any description of trust (whether express, implied, resulting or constructive), including a trust for sale and a bare trust, and

    (b) includes a trust created, or arising, before the commencement of this Act.

(3) The reference to land in subsection (1)(a) does not include land which (despite section 2) is settled land or which is land to which the Universities and College Estates Act 1925 applies.

Through this section, all trusts that consist of or include land are brought within the scope of the 1996 Act, whether express or created, for example, through the doctrines of resulting and constructive trust considered in Chapters 11 and 12. The application of the Act was extended to trusts in existence at the date of its commencement (1 January 1997). All trusts for sale and bare trusts in existence at that date were turned into trusts of land. But by s 1(3), existing successive interest trusts governed by the Settled Land Act 1925 remain unaffected.

5.2 TRUSTEES' POWERS

The powers of trustees of land are set out in broad terms in s 6 of the TOLATA 1996.

---

[80] Law Commission No 181 (1989), [8.1].

[81] Settled Land Act 1925, s 1(7), precluded the application of that Act to trusts for sale, enabling successive interest trusts to be expressly created as trusts for sale.

Trusts of Land and Appointment of Trustees Act 1996, s 6

(1) For the purpose of exercising their functions as trustees, the trustees of land have in relation to the land subject to the trust all the powers of an absolute owner.

[...]

(3) The trustees of land have power to acquire land under the power conferred by section 8 of the Trustee Act 2000.

[...]

(5) In exercising the powers conferred by this section trustees shall have regard to the rights of the beneficiaries.

(6) The powers conferred by this section shall not be exercised in contravention of, or of any order made in pursuance of, any other enactment or any rule of law or equity.

(7) The reference in subsection (6) to an order includes an order of any court or of the [Charity Commission]

(8) Where any enactment other than this section confers on trustees authority to act subject to any restriction, limitation or condition, trustees of land may not exercise the powers conferred by this section to do any act which they are prevented from doing under the other enactment by reason of the restriction, limitation or condition.

(9) The duty of care under section 1 of the Trustee Act 2000 applies to trustees of land when exercising the powers conferred by this section.

The Law Commission acknowledged that many trustees, particularly of a co-owned home, considered themselves to be 'owners'. Hence, s 6 represents an attempt to reflect this, while ensuring that general equitable duties imposed on trustees are respected.[82] The trustees have the same powers as an absolute owner, but these are conferred on them specifically in their capacity as trustees of the land, not as absolute owners entitled to enjoy the land (by occupation or receipt or profits) themselves.[83] Hence, the powers are to be exercised with regard to the rights of the beneficiaries[84] and in a manner consistent with any other enactment or rule of law or equity.

Section 8 of the TOLATA 1996 enables further limitations to be imposed on the trustees' powers where the trust is expressly created.[85] Under that section, the settlor of the trust may remove or restrict the trustees' powers, or make their exercise subject to obtaining consent.

Section 6 has the effect of removing the duty to sell imposed under a trust for sale: the powers of an owner include the power to sell or to retain the land.[86] While these are equally weighted, the Act is, in fact, biased against sale,[87] reflecting the recognition that land is commonly held on trust for use as a home, rather than as an investment. Section 8 conceivably

---

[82] Law Commission No 181 (1989), [10.4].   [83] Hopkins (1996) p 413.

[84] On the interpretation of s 6(5) see Ferris and Bramley, 'The Construction of Sub-section 6(5) of the Trusts of Land and Appointment of Trustees Act 1996: When is a "Right" not a "Right"?' [2009] Conv 39.

[85] Trusts of Land and Appointment of Trustees Act 1996, s 8, applies to trusts 'created by a disposition'. This may not, in fact, cover all express trusts. As Clements notes (1998, p 58), the need for a 'disposition' may exclude the situation in which a settlor declares him or herself to be holding on trust. The section would then be confined to express trusts created where the settlor transfers the land to trustees on trust. There is, however, no logical reason for drawing such a distinction.

[86] Law Commission No 181 (1989), [10.6].   [87] Hopkins (1996) p 414.

enables the settlor of a trust to exclude the power of sale and, by so doing, make land inalienable. In contrast, a settlor cannot compel trustees to sell. While a duty to sell can be expressly imposed, in any such trust, s 4 of the Act provides the trustees with a power to postpone the sale and indefinite protection against liability for so doing.[88]

The limitations on the trustees' powers—both general, within s 6, and any expressly imposed by the terms of the trust, through s 8—have a limited impact on purchasers of the land. In this respect, a clear distinction is drawn between the internal regulation of the trust and its effect on third parties. Trustees who act contrary to limitations on their powers may be held personally liable to the beneficiaries for breach of trust. As regards purchasers, s 16 provides specific protection in the context of unregistered land. Purchasers are not concerned with whether s 6(5) has been complied with, and are protected against a conveyance carried out in contravention of ss 6(6) and (8) or contrary to limitations on the trustees' powers imposed through s 8, unless they have actual notice of the contravention or limitation. Section 16 does not apply to registered land where, under the general operation of the Land Registration Act 2002 (LRA 2002), a purchaser would be affected only by a limitation on the trustees' powers entered as a restriction on the register.[89]

5.3 BENEFICIARIES' RIGHTS

The TOLATA 1996 confers two key rights on beneficiaries. Firstly, it confers a right to be consulted by the trustees, who are directed in s 11(1)(b) to give effect to the wishes of the majority (in terms of the parties' beneficial shares) '*so far as consistent with the general interest of the trust*'. By s 11(1)(a), this right is enjoyed by all adult co-owners. It is of practical significance to a beneficiary who is not also a legal owner and who does not therefore play a direct role in the management of the trust: for example, where A holds the parties' home on trust for A and B, s 11(1)(a) requires A to consult B in the exercise of his or her powers as trustee. The right to be consulted may be excluded in express trusts.[90] It does not apply to all trusts that were in existence at the commencement of the 1996 Act.[91]

Secondly, the most important right conferred on beneficiaries is the right to occupy the land. Where co-owners hold their home on trust, it seems remarkable to have to question whether, as beneficiaries, they have a right to occupy—but the imposition of a trust *for sale* brought the beneficiaries' right to occupy into question. As the Law Commission noted in [3.4] of its report (extracted above), the doctrine of conversion had the effect that beneficiaries under a trust for sale had an interest in the proceeds of sale, not in the land. The application of the doctrine arose through a combination of the trustees' duty to sell and equity's maxim 'equity looks upon as done that which ought to be done'. Because the trustees *ought* to sell, equity treated the parties as though sale had already taken place. So if the beneficiaries had no interest in the land, on what basis could they claim a right to occupy?

---

[88] Ibid.

[89] Full discussion of the purchaser protection provisions is provided in Chapter 16, section 4.2.

[90] As with the Trusts of Land and Appointment of Trustees Act 1996, s 8, s 11(2)(a) applies where a trust is 'created by a disposition'. Whether this includes all express trusts is dependent on the same comment made in relation to the previous provision above fn 83.

[91] Trusts of Land and Appointment of Trustees Act 1996, s 11(2)(b) and (3), excludes the requirement of consultation from express trusts (with provision for the settlors of those trusts to opt in to the new arrangements) and will trusts created prior to the commencement of the Act. This ensures that settlors who relied on the previous law (where a duty to consult would not be imposed unless expressly provided) are respected.

In practice, the courts did not invariably apply the doctrine of conversion.[92] It was clear that trustees for sale, in the exercise of their powers of management, could allow the beneficiaries to occupy. Further, a right to occupy was acknowledged to exist in leading case law,[93] although the basis of the right was uncertain. In particular, it remained unresolved as to whether occupation was a right enjoyed by all beneficial co-owners, or only in circumstances in which the trust had been created for the purpose of his or her occupation.[94] The abolition of the doctrine of conversion, and the shift to a scheme of regulation focussed on the use of trust land as a home, paved the way for the introduction of a statutory right to occupy. This is provided for in s 12 of the TOLATA 1996.

Trusts of Land and Appointment of Trustees Act 1996, s 12

(1) A beneficiary who is beneficially entitled to an interest in possession in land subject to a trust of land is entitled by reason of his interest to occupy the land at any time if at that time—

(a) the purposes of the trust include making the land available for his occupation (or for the occupation of beneficiaries of a class of which he is a member or of beneficiaries in general), or

(b) the land is held by the trustees so as to be so available.

(2) Subsection (1) does not confer on a beneficiary a right to occupy land if it is either unavailable or unsuitable for occupation by him.

(3) This section is subject to section 13.

Hence, the existence of a right to occupy is dependent on the criteria in s 12(1) and (2) being fulfilled. As regards the interpretation of these criteria, the purpose of the trust may be derived from the declaration of an express trust, or be ascertained by the circumstances. The alternative criterion of availability enables the right to be claimed where the land is available for occupation, even if this is not within the purposes of the trust. For the trustees to make land available for occupation contrary to the express wishes of the settlor would, however, constitute a breach of trust and therefore would be outside the trustees' powers within s 6(6).[95] The additional requirement, in all cases, that the land is 'suitable' for occupation enables the subjective characteristics of the beneficiaries to be taken into account: for example, no right to occupy will arise if the land is a farm and the beneficiary is not a farmer.[96] Sections 13(3) and (5) enable the trustees to impose 'reasonable conditions' on beneficiaries

---

[92] For example, in *Williams v Glyn's Bank v Boland* [1981] AC 487, the House of Lords held that Mrs Boland's beneficial interest under a trust for sale was an 'interest in land' protected as an overriding interest through her occupation.

[93] The existence of the right was acknowledged by the House of Lords in *Williams v Glyn's Bank v Boland* [1981] AC 487 and *City of London Building Society v Flegg* [1988] AC 54.

[94] Ross Martyn, 'Co-owners and their Entitlement to Occupy their Land Before and After the Trusts of Land and Appointment of Trustees Act 1996: Theoretical Doubts are Replaced by Practical Difficulties' [1997] Conv 254.

[95] Hopkins (1996, p 421); Pascoe, 'Right to Occupy Under a Trust of Land: Muddled Legislative Logic' [2006] Conv 54, 59.

[96] This has been a popular example in highlighting the interpretation of the right since first raised by Smith 'Trusts of Land Reform' [1989] Conv 12, 19. See further Pascoe (2006) p 62.

in occupation by virtue of their entitlement under s 12. The conditions may include paying outgoings or expenses in respect of the land.

Where two or more beneficiaries are entitled to occupy, s 13 of the 1996 Act enables the trustees to exclude or restrict one or more of those entitled, but at least one qualifying beneficiary must be allowed to occupy. Where a beneficiary's occupation has been excluded or restricted by the trustees, the beneficiary or beneficiaries in occupation may be required by the trustees under s 13(6) to pay compensation to those excluded from occupation. Gardner suggests that the general jurisdiction in s 13(3) may also be used to require payments to be made to non-occupying beneficiaries in situations where the non-occupying beneficiary has not been excluded by the trustees (and, therefore, falls outside s 13(6)), but he notes that the jurisdiction under s 13(3) remains under-explored.[97] Prior to the enactment of the TOLATA, the only route to payment of an occupation rent was the general doctrine of equitable accounting. Equitable accounting was initially confined to cases of exclusion or ouster of one joint tenant, but it has developed to apply, '*in any case where [an occupation rent] is necessary to do broad justice or equity between the parties*'.[98] The relationship between the statute and the general law was initially unclear, but it has now been established that s 13 operates to the exclusion of equitable accounting in respect of cases within its scope where the parties enjoy a statutory right of occupation under s 12,[99] leaving equitable accounting available for those outside. For instance, the trustee in bankruptcy of one co-owner will be beyond the scope of s 13 because they are most unlikely to enjoy a statutory right to occupy under s 12; the property being unsuitable for them to occupy.[100] In these instances equitable accounting has a role to play conferring a broad jurisdiction upon the court to do justice between the parties which may or may not justify the payment of an occupational rent by the occupying co-owner to the trustee in bankruptcy.[101]

As Bright explains, the quantum of liability under s 13 is potentially higher than that available through equitable accounting.[102] Equitable accounting is generally confined to the rental value of the property. In contrast, under s 13(4) trustees are directed to have regard to a number of '*wider-non-property concerns*',[103] including the intentions of the settlor(s), the purposes for which the land is held, and the circumstances and wishes of beneficiaries who have a right to occupy.[104] This difference in quantum is explained by Bright as a shift from '*property to welfare*'.[105] Nevertheless, rental value remains attractive to the court as it is '*a relatively objective value on which evidence can easily be supplied*'.[106] An alternative and equally objective basis on which compensation may be quantified is the cost incurred by an excluded beneficiary in obtaining alternative accommodation.[107]

A novel question on the application of s 13 arose in the following case: does the section enable trustees to restrict each beneficiary to occupying part of the trust land?

---

[97] Ibid, 102–4.   [98] *Murphy v Gooch* [2007] 2 FLR 934, [10], *per* Lightman J.

[99] In *Stack v Dowden* [2007] 2 AC 432 at [94] Baroness Hale noted that, '*[t]hese statutory powers replaced the old doctrines of equitable accounting under which a beneficiary who remained in occupation might be required to pay an occupation rent to a beneficiary who was excluded from the property.*' See also *Murphy v Gooch* [2007] 3 FLR 934. See Bright 'Occupation Rents and the Trusts of Land and Appointment of Trustees Act 1996: from Property to Welfare' [2009] Conv 378, 386.

[100] See *French v Barcham* [2009] 1 WLR 1124, *Re Byford dec'd* [2004] 1 FLR 56, and *Davis v Jackson* [2017] EWHC 698.

[101] *Re Pavlou* [1993] 1 WLR 1046, *Re Byford dec'd*, *French v Barcham*, and *Davis v Jackson* ibid.

[102] Ibid. Bright's analysis is based on s 13(6) but the same factors would be relevant if payments were ordered under the general jurisdiction in s 13(3).

[103] Bright [2009] Conv 378, 390.   [104] TOLATA, s 13(4).   [105] Bright [2009] Conv 378.

[106] Ibid, 394.   [107] *Stack v Dowden* [2007] 2 AC 432, [157].

Rodway v Landy
[2001] Ch 703, CA

Facts: Drs Rodway and Landy held the premises of their surgery on trust for themselves in equal shares. In proceedings following the termination of their business partnership, Dr Landy suggested that each of the parties should be given exclusive occupation of part of the surgery.

Peter Gibson LJ

At 712–13

I accept that the limitation on the power to exclude or restrict is expressed as a limitation on the number of beneficiaries who may be excluded or restricted. Plainly it would make no sense if there was no beneficiary left entitled to occupy land subject to a trust of land as a result of the exercise of the power under section 13. That is the force of the words "(but not all)". But if an estate consisting of adjoining properties, Blackacre and Whiteacre, was held subject to a trust of land and A and B were entitled to occupy the estate, it would be very surprising if the trustees were not able under section 13 to exclude or restrict B's entitlement to occupy Blackacre and at the same time to exclude or restrict A's entitlement to occupy Whiteacre, thereby leaving A alone entitled to occupy Blackacre and B Whiteacre. So also I do not see why, in relation to a single building which lends itself to physical partition, the trustees could not exclude or restrict one beneficiary's entitlement to occupy one part and at the same time exclude or restrict the other beneficiary's entitlement to occupy the other part. Each part is land subject to a trust of land and the beneficiaries are entitled to occupy that part until the entitlement of a beneficiary is excluded or restricted by the exercise of the power under section 13. So construed section 13(1) seems to me to make good sense and to provide a useful power which trustees might well wish to exercise in appropriate circumstances so as to be even-handed between beneficiaries. In contrast, I can see no good reason why Parliament should want to confine the trustees to the all or nothing approach [. . .]

The Court ordered that the premises should be divided to provide each of the doctors with a self-contained surgery.[108]

Section 12 remains controversial, both as regards the interpretation of its terms and, more broadly, whether a statutory right of occupation was, in fact, necessary.[109] Pascoe considers the value of the introduction of this right, in its broader context.

Pascoe, 'Right to Occupy Under a Trust of Land: Muddled Legislative Logic'
[2006] Conv 54, 55–7

The introduction of a statutory right may be viewed as mirroring social, cultural and economic developments in society, reflecting a contemporary concern with the maximisation

---

[108] The outcome in this case may be contrasted with partition of the land under the Trusts of Land and Appointment of Trustees Act 1996, s 7. Partition would have involved the physical subdivision of the surgery into two separate properties, each with its own legal title, with the parties receiving legal title to their part of the property. The trust would therefore come to an end.

[109] Barnsley, 'Co-owners' Rights to Occupy Trust Land' (1998) 57 CLJ 123. He argues that, in fact, a broader right to occupy was available under the previous law (as not subject to the conditions imposed by s 12) and that beneficiaries' may still seek to invoke non-statutory rights of occupation.

of material welfare. The significance of the imperative of an increasingly secular and materialistic age is revealingly, if unconsciously, reflected in the very language of the post-war European Convention on Human Rights, which guarantees the entitlement of every natural or legal person to the "peaceful enjoyment of his possessions". The emphasis is thus on the "use" value of property rather than the "exchange" or capital value and the changing social consensus on the importance of residential utility and residential security has led to the materialisation of this statutory right. Property law is the basic legal expression of the nature of economic life in all its aspects and this development has to be understood in relation to the social context in which it gains its significance as a mode of regulating behaviour [. . .]

The right to occupy represents part of a shift in power from trustees to beneficiaries. With the abolition of conversion, this right emphasises that beneficiaries under trusts of land have rights in the land. Gray and Gray term this the democratisation of the trust. Where the doctrine of conversion prevailed under trusts for sale, consistency dictated that the trustees would remain the prime decision-makers, but with increasing judicial emphasis on the "use" value of property, the emancipation of beneficiaries inevitably followed as a logical consequence of this progression.

As Pascoe illustrates, in so far as the right to occupy shifts power from the trustees to the beneficiaries, it is logically consistent with the ethos of the trust of land as emphasizing the use value, rather than the investment value, of land. But Pascoe convincingly demonstrates the absence of doctrinal cohesiveness underlying the new right. This arises largely as a result of the preconditions of the right provided in s 12(1) and (2): that either the purposes of the trust include occupation, or the land is held by the trustees to be available for occupation, and, in all cases, that it is suitable for occupation.

Pascoe, 'Right to Occupy Under a Trust of Land: Muddled Legislative Logic'
[2006] Conv 54, 63

Section 12 represents an amalgam and jumble of principles derived from the old law intermingled with explicitly new concepts of availability and suitability to constitute a qualified right, which may be the subject of great uncertainty and thus litigation due to the impreciseness of drafting of the section. The merits of such a hotchpotch of concepts challenges the sagacity and utility of instituting a new right which displays three conflicting characteristics: beneficiary autonomy, trustee authoritarianism and settlor interposition.

As was noted earlier, under the trust for sale, uncertainty remained as to whether a right to occupy was conferred on all beneficiaries, or only those for whom the purposes of the trust anticipated occupation. TOLATA 1996 continues to send conflicting messages. The right to occupy is conferred by s 12(1) on a beneficiary '*by reason of his interest*', but this is immediately made conditional on an assessment of the purpose of the trust, or the availability of the land for occupation, and its suitability for occupation by the beneficiaries. Practically the position of beneficiaries in respect of occupation may be no more secure than under the trust for sale. They have a right to occupy subject to meeting criteria that will be assessed, in the first instance, by the trustees, with disputes resolved by the court under ss 14 and 15 of TOLATA 1996.

5.4 APPLICATIONS TO COURT

Section 14 of the TOLATA 1996 enables an application to be made to the court by a trustee or a person with an interest in the trust property '*relating to the exercise by the trustees of any of their functions*'. Section 15 then provides guidance to the court of the factors for the court to take into account when making decisions.

Trusts of Land and Appointment of Trustees Act 1996, s 15

(1) The matters to which the court is to have regard in determining an application for an order under section 14 include—

  (a) the intentions of the person or persons (if any) who created the trust,

  (b) the purposes for which the property subject to the trust is held,

  (c) the welfare of any minor who occupies or might reasonably be expected to occupy any land subject to the trust as his home, and

  (d) the interests of any secured creditor of any beneficiary.

(2) In the case of an application relating to the exercise in relation to any land of the powers conferred on the trustees by section 13 the matters to which the court is to have regard also include the circumstances and wishes of each of the beneficiaries who is (or apart from any previous exercise by the trustees of those powers would be) entitled to occupy the land under section 12.

(3) In the case of any other application, other than one relating to the exercise of the power mentioned in section 6(2), the matters to which the court is to have regard also include the circumstances and wishes of any beneficiaries of full age and entitled to an interest in possession in property subject to the trust or (in case of dispute) of the majority (according to the value of their combined interests).

(4) This section does not apply to an application if section 335A of the Insolvency Act 1986 (which is inserted by Schedule 3 and relates to applications by a trustee of a bankrupt) applies to it.

A wide range of matters may be referred to the court under s 14. [110] In *Bagum v Hafiz* Briggs LJ stated that the purpose of the court's power were '*to enable the property to be dealt with justly and effectively when that basis of [the beneficiaries'] consent breaks down*'.[111] It was on the basis of s 14, for example, that the court resolved the issue of the beneficiaries' occupation in *Rodway v Landy*. In particular, however, s 14 is the basis on which the courts will consider disputes as to whether the land should be sold. In Chapter 14, we consider applications for sale brought by third parties to the trust: in particular, creditors and trustees in bankruptcy of the beneficiaries. In this chapter, however, we are concerned with how disputed sales are determined when the parties to the trust refer the matter to the court themselves. This may arise, for example, when co-owners are unable to agree on

---

[110] Although in *Bagum v Hafiz* [2016] Ch 241 the court acknowledged that they had no power to direct or order a beneficiary to sell or transfer their interest to another beneficiary because it was not an exercise of a trustee's function to directly deal with the beneficial interests. By contrast, and to much the same result, the trustees themselves may sell the property to one of the beneficiaries, see *Bagum v Hafiz* ibid.

[111] Ibid at [25].

the sale of property held as an investment. In *Finch v Hall*[112] a property was inherited by four siblings following their parents' deaths. After a period of renting the property, the parties marketed it for sale on an express agreement that a sale required their unanimous agreement. An offer was made which three of the four co-owners wished to accept. On an application under s 14 the court refused to set aside the parties' express agreement and, therefore, declined to order sale.[113]

However, the most complex disputes between co-owners in respect of sale arise where A and B are co-owners of their home, and, following a breakdown of the parties' relationship, A wishes to remain in the home (either alone or with children), while B wants the house to be sold. Such cases raise directly the tension between the house as a home and as an investment. Ultimately, in the example outlined, the question that arises is in what circumstances A's desire to remain in the home takes precedence over B's wish to realize his or her capital investment and 'move on'.[114] To answer this question, it is necessary first to consider the general principles and then to address specifically situations in which the welfare of minor children need to be taken into account through s 15(1)(c). We will then consider the extent to which s 15 represents a change in the law from the position under the trust for sale. This is a matter to which is addressed in Chapter 14, where we consider whether s 15 has changed the law from the position under the trust for sale if the application for sale is made by a third party, such as a creditor, rather than by one of the beneficiaries themselves.

5.4.1 General principles

In all applications, s 15 of the TOLATA 1996 directs the court to have regard to the intentions of the persons who created the trust (s 15(1)(a)), the purposes for which the property is held (s 15(1)(b)), and the interests of secured creditors (s 15(1)(d)).

Arden LJ considered the interpretation of the first two of these factors, and the difference between them, in the following case.

White v White
[2004] 2 FLR 321

Facts: Mr and Mrs White were co-owners of their home. Following the breakdown of their relationship, Mr White remained in occupation of the home with the couple's young daughters. Mrs White sought an application for sale of the home. The welfare of the children fell to be considered under s 15(1)(c) and this aspect of the decision is considered below. In this extract, Arden LJ considers whether the provision of a home for the children constituted the intentions of the Whites within s 15(1)(a), or the purposes for which they held the home within s 15(1)(b). The home had been purchased before the children were born.

---

[112] [2013] EWHC 4360 (Ch).
[113] The court applied *Re Buchanan-Wollaston's Conveyance* [1939] Ch 738 where beneficiaries under a trust for sale had covenanted to act unanimously.
[114] Gardner, 'Material Relief between Ex-Cohabitants 1: Liquidating Beneficial Interests Otherwise than by Sale' [2014] Conv 95.

Arden LJ

At 22–4

[Arden LJ cited s 15 and continued] [. . .] Where more than one person created the trust, the intention for the purposes of section 15(1)(a) must, as I see it, be the intention of all the persons who created the trust and be an intention which they had in common. This is because the subsection speaks of "the intentions of the person or persons [. . .] who created the trust". This may be contrasted with the reference in section 15(1)(c) to the welfare of "any minor". The use of the definite article and the word "person" or "persons" in subsection (1)(a) to my mind make it clear that the intention referred to in section 15(1)(a) must be the intention of the persons who created the trust if more than one in common.

The question then remains whether the intention could include intention subsequently come to, as Mr Routley submits. I do not myself consider that this is the correct construction. Parliament has used the word "intention" which speaks naturally to the intentions of persons prior to the creation of the trust. If that were not its meaning, then it is not clear whether the court should be looking at the parties' intention at the date of the hearing or at some other antecedent point in time and, if so, what date. If Parliament meant the present intention, it would have used some such word as "wishes" rather than the word "intention" which implies some statement or opinion as to the future. In all the circumstances, I consider that the appellant's submissions on the point of law on this point are not correct.

I turn now to what I have termed the third point of law, and it was put in this way. It is that the judge had failed to deal with a submission by the father that there was an additional purpose come to after the property was purchased and the parties had been living there. This was based primarily on paragraph 11 of the father's statement of 22nd February 2001, in which he stated that the trust was entered into to provide a home for the mother and himself but subsequently there arose an additional purpose, namely to provide a home for the children. I would accept that, for the purposes of section 15(1)(b), purposes could have been formulated informally, but they must be the purposes subject to which the property is held. The purpose established at the outset of the trust which, on the judge's finding, did not include the provision of a home for children, could only change if both parties agreed. There was no evidence from which the judge could find that the mother agreed to the additional purpose spoken to by the father. Nor was the assertion that there was such a purpose ever put to the mother. Notwithstanding Mr Routley's submission, I would not accept the argument that the judge's omission to deal with the additional purpose undermines his decision.

Hence, while the 'intentions' of the persons who created the trust are fixed and determined at the time of creation, the purposes can change by agreement of the parties. In *Rodway v Landy*, the Court of Appeal noted that the relevant purposes are those in existence at the time that the application is considered.[115] As we will see below, the interests of the children in *White v White* were still taken into account by the Court through the specific reference to the welfare of children in s 15(1)(c).

As regards the interests of secured creditors, it is important to note that these are relevant even in applications brought by the parties to the trust. In *Anneveld v Robinson*,[116] the practical impossibility of a large mortgage being paid by one of the parties, if allowed to remain in occupation, was a significant factor in the court's order of sale on the breakdown of their relationship.

---

[115] [2001] Ch 703, [711].   [116] [2005] WL 3142400 (county court), judgment 12 August 2005.

Although the '*circumstances and wishes of the beneficiaries*' are referred to in s 15(2) only in respect of the trustees' exercise of powers under s 13 (right to occupy) they may implicitly be relevant in the context of sale. This is because to be effective an order of sale requires vacant possession, which necessarily impacts on the beneficiaries' right to occupy.[117]

In addition to the factors mentioned in s 15, the court should have regard to any other relevant matter; the matters referred to in s 15 are non-exhaustive. In *White v White*, for example, the Court had regard to Mrs White's circumstances and her wish to raise money to provide a home for herself. Arden LJ explained that there is no weighting of the factors within s 15:[118] the responsibility lies with judges to determine how much weight to afford to all relevant factors, including those not specifically referred to in s 15.

5.4.2 Disputed sales and child welfare

Section 15(1)(c) specifically directs the court to have regard to the welfare of minor children who are in occupation of the home, or may be expected to be so. This ensures that the needs of such children are taken into account even where, as in *White v White*, the provision of a home for them was not the intention of the parties and is not an agreed, current purpose of the trust. Section 15(1)(c) is significant in so far as it ensures that the welfare of children is considered. It is consistent with the underlying ethos of the TOLATA 1996 as providing a scheme of regulation for trusts that reflects the fact that much co-owned land is the parties' home.

As we have noted, however, the factors for the court to be take into account in determining applications are not weighted. Other factors may favour sale despite the occupation of children. In *White v White*, the Court of Appeal confirmed an order of sale by the judge at first instance. The Court noted that the judge had correctly taken into account both the interests of the children in remaining in their home and Mrs White's need to realize her only capital asset. In that case, the judge was also satisfied that, following the sale, cheaper suitable accommodation would be available.

5.4.3 Has s 15 changed the law?

Prior to the TOLATA 1996, under the trust for sale, disputes as to sale were considered by the court under s 30 of the LPA 1925. Against the background of the duty to sell, the starting point for the courts was that sale should be ordered unless the trustees unanimously agreed to exercise their power to postpone sale.[119] This was, however, significantly qualified by the courts' recognition that trusts for sale were often created for a purpose other than sale (often referred to as the 'secondary', or 'collateral', purpose of the trust, but, in fact, representing its *primary* purpose). As a general principle, sale would not be ordered for so long as a collateral purpose could still be achieved.[120] Hence, the key issues for the courts in settling disputes was the identification of the purposes of the trust and an assessment of whether any of those purposes could still be achieved. Where children were present, a particularly contentious issue was whether the provision of a home for children formed part of the purposes of the trust or whether their interests were '*only incidentally to be taken into consideration* [. . .]

---

[117] *Miller Smith v Miller Smith* [2010] 1 FLR 1402, [17].   [118] [2004] 2 FLR 321, [26].
[119] *Re Mayo* [1943] 1 Ch 302.   [120] *Jones v Challenger* [1960] 2 WLR 695.

so far as they affect the matter between the two persons entitled to the beneficial interests'.[121] Both views could claim support from conflicting Court of Appeal judgments.[122] The balance of the authorities suggested that, where a house was occupied by one of the beneficiaries with minor children, sale would not be ordered unless alternative (cheaper) accommodation could then be provided.[123]

In its recommendations that led to s 15, the Law Commission considered the relationship between the new provision and the secondary purpose case law.

Law Commission Report No 181, *Transfer of Land: Trusts of Land* (1989, [12.9])

As regards the exercise of these powers [i.e., the powers conferred by s 14 of the Trusts of Land and Appointment of Trustees Act 1996], it is our view that the court's discretion should be developed along the same lines as the current 'primary purpose' doctrine. This approach was moulded to practical requirements, and we consider that it gets the balance more or less right. Nevertheless, we recommend that [s 15] should set out some guidelines for the exercise of the court's discretion, the aim being to consolidate and rationalise the current approach. The criteria which the courts have evolved for settling disputes over trusts for sale are ones which will continue to have validity in the context of the new system. One function of the guidelines will be to put these criteria on a statutory footing [. . .]

In *Mortgage Corporation v Shaire*,[124] in an application for sale brought by a creditor, the court concluded that s 15 of the TOLATA 1996 had changed the law (the case is discussed in Chapter 14, section 3). It is certainly true to say that s 15 has changed the focus of judgments. The court is no longer constrained by a presumption of sale and a need artificially to treat every other purpose as secondary to sale. The purpose or purposes of the trust have become one of a number of factors to which the court is to have regard. Importantly, s 15 has also resolved the issue of the relevance of the welfare of children. It is more difficult to assess the extent to which these changes translate into different outcomes of cases as opposed to the reasoning for those outcomes. There remains relatively little case law concerning disputes between co-owners and as a result it is difficult to draw conclusions.[125] Following a review of the case law, Dixon suggests that there are, however, '*indications of a general approach*', which he summarizes in the following extract.[126]

---

[121] *Burke v Burke* [1974] 1 WLR 1063, [1067], *per* Buckley LJ.

[122] In *Browne v Pritchard* [1975] 1 WLR 1366, *Williams v Williams* [1976] 3 WLR 494, and *Re Evers' Trust* [1980] 1 WLR 1327, sale was refused where, following the breakdown of the parties' relationship, a home was occupied by one beneficiary and children. *Burke v Burke* [1974] 1 WLR 1063 stands alone as a case in which sale was ordered in such circumstances. This approach was also supported in *Re Holliday* [1981] Ch 405, although the case itself concerned an application by a trustee in bankruptcy, rather than by one of the parties to the trust.

[123] *Williams v Williams* [1976] 3 WLR 494, [499].　　[124] [2001] Ch 743.

[125] Hopkins 'Regulating Trusts of the Home: Private Law and Social Policy' (2009) 125 LQR 310, p 325; Dixon, 'To Sell or Not to Sell: That is the Question. The Irony of the Trusts of Land and Appointment of Trustees Act 1996' (2011) 70 CLJ 579, 586.

[126] Ibid, p 586.

Dixon, 'To Sell or Not to Sell: That is the Question. The Irony of the Trusts of Land and Appointment of Trustees Act 1996' (2011) 70 CLJ 579, p 589

An assessment of the relatively modest case law available suggests that the courts adopt a highly flexible, circumstance dependent approach to two-party disputes when acting under section 14 Trusts of Land and Appointment of Trustees Act 1996. The court clearly looks at the factors listed in section 15 as an aid to the exercise of its discretion, but is not prevented from considering other matters. There is no evidence to suggest that the default position of sale as pertained under section 30 Law of Property Act 1925 now carries any force [. . .] The intention of the parties still carries sway, as does the majority interest holding, but neither appears decisive [. . .] The parties stand level in law and it is the court's task to weigh the factors within section [15] and such additional factors as may be relevant.

5.5 REGULATION OF CO-OWNERSHIP OUTSIDE OF THE TRUSTS OF LAND AND APPOINTMENT OF TRUSTEES ACT 1996

This chapter has focussed on the regulation of co-ownership as a matter of property law through the TOLATA 1996. The rights of co-owners may also fall to be regulated by other legislation: for example, within the regime of family law. Where this is the case, questions arise as to the resolution of overlaps between the jurisdictions. These have been addressed by the court in the context of rights to occupy and applications for sale.

In relation to occupation, in addition to the right conferred by s 13 of the TOLATA considered in section 5.3 of this chapter, we have seen in Chapter 12 that rights to occupy a home may be derived from the Family Law Act 1996 (FLA 1996). There is an overlap between the FLA 1996 and the TOLATA 1996 in two respects. First (as noted in Chapter 12, a spouse or civil partner who is a beneficiary, but does not own legal title, may be entitled to a right to occupy ('*home rights*') under the FLA 1996. Secondly, s 33 of the FLA 1996 enables the court to regulate occupation of a house that is, or has been, or was intended to be, the home of the applicant and '*another person with whom he is associated*'. This expression covers a wide range of people, including existing (and former) married couples, civil partners and cohabitants, and others who have shared a home otherwise than through a commercial relationship.[127]

An application may be made to the court under s 33 by (amongst others) a person entitled to occupy as a beneficiary or through holding '*home rights*' conferred by the FLA 1996.[128] Hence, a beneficiary who is entitled to occupy a home under the TOLATA 1996 may apply to the court for an order regulating occupation under the FLA 1996. An overlap in jurisdictions arises because occupation by beneficiaries is also subject to regulation by the court under ss 13 and 14 of the TOLATA 1996.

The range of orders that can be made by the court, and the factors that the court is directed to take into account, differ under each statute. The resolution of this overlap was considered in the following case.

---

[127] Family Law Act 1996, s 62(3).   [128] Ibid, s 33(1).

Chan v Leung, unreported
30 November 2001, HC

Facts: The case arose following the breakdown of a relationship between Miss Chan and Mr Leung, in the course of which, for a period of time, they had lived together in a house that was the subject of the action. Miss Chan had remained in the house and was pursuing university studies. The court held that Miss Chan had a beneficial interest in the house and then considered what order should be made in relation to occupation. The issue arose of whether this matter should be dealt with under TOLATA or the Family Law Act 1996.

HH Judge McGonigal

Where a court is addressing the question of occupation of a house subject to a trust or the alternative of sale, in my view the court should approach it primarily in the context of s 33 of the Family Law Act 1996. It is in this Act that Parliament addresses the question of occupation of the home in most detail. The court is required by s 33(6) to have regard to all the circumstances. These will include the fact that it is a trust property, so that ss 14 and 15 apply to it. Accordingly, the matters specifically referred to in s 15 of the Trusts of Land and Appointment of Trustees Act 1996 and any other relevant consideration arising from the fact that it is a trust property, including the terms of the trust, should be taken into account by the court when considering the question of continued occupation or sale.

Hence, where the jurisdictions overlap, precedence is afforded to the FLA 1996—but the matters that the court would be required to refer to under the TOLATA 1996 are taken into account as part of the circumstances of the case. On the facts, the court issued an order enabling Miss Chan to continue to occupy, to the exclusion of Mr Leung, for the duration of her current studies, following which the house would be sold. The judge's order was affirmed on appeal, although without discussion by the Court of Appeal of the overlap between the jurisdictions.[129]

In Miller Smith v Miller Smith the Court of Appeal considered how an application for sale brought by a beneficiary under s 14 should be treated where divorce proceedings were pending. In addition to an application for sale under the TOLATA, the applicant had sought to obtain sale under s 17 of the Married Woman's Property Act 1882 and an order under s 33 of the Family Law Act 1996 prohibiting his wife from occupying the property.

Miller Smith v Miller Smith
[2010] 1 FLR 1402

Wilson LJ

At 18

I am clear that, confronted with an application under TOLATA between separated spouses, the court should embark upon the discretionary exercise by asking itself whether the issue raised by the application can reasonably be left to be resolved within an application for

---

[129] *Chan v Leung* [2003] 1 FLR 23.

ancillary relief following divorce. It is in principle much more desirable that an issue, as here, about sale of the home should be resolved within an application for ancillary relief. For there the court will undertake a holistic examination of all aspects of the parties' finances, needs, contributions etc; will devise the fairest set of arrangements for the future housing and finances of each of them; and, to that end, will provide for the transfer of capital, as well perhaps as for payment of future income, from one to the other. By an order under TOLATA, on the other hand, the court lays down only one piece of the jigsaw, namely that the home be sold, without its being able to survey the whole picture by laying down the others. So at this threshold stage of the enquiry into an application under TOLATA between spouses the court will, in particular, have regard to the question whether, within a time-frame tolerable in all the circumstances, the parties will become able to apply for ancillary relief. Furthermore if, at first sight, there appears to the court to be any measurable chance that, on an application for ancillary relief made within that time-frame, the respondent to the application for an order for sale under TOLATA will be able to preserve her or his occupation of the home by securing an outright transfer of ownership of it or a variation of the trust, it is hard to conceive that an order for sale would reflect a proper exercise of discretion.

On the facts, Wilson LJ was satisfied that the application should be dealt with under the TOLATA. Mrs Miller Smith contested the divorce and it was unlikely that an application for ancillary relief would be held within a year. In the meantime, Mr Miller Smith remained liable for a £7 million mortgage secured against the property, which appeared to be his only substantial asset. Further, there was 'no measureable chance' that the outcome of ancillary relief would enable Mrs Miller Smith to continue in occupation.[130] Wilson LJ explained that the same factors were also likely to be determinative of the application.[131]

In *Chan v Leung*,[132] we have seen that in determining a right of occupation under the Family Law Act 1996 the court considered that the factors referred to in TOLATA would be taken into account as part of the circumstances of the case. In *Miller Smith v Miller Smith*, without reference to that case, it was argued that in determining the application for sale, the court was required to consider whether an occupation order would be obtained against Mrs Miller Smith under the Family Law Act 1996. While this argument was rejected by the Court of Appeal, Wilson LJ noted that '*it would be surprising if an order that in effect a spouse should give vacant possession of a matrimonial home under TOLATA were to be made in circumstances in which the applicant could not have secured an occupation order*'.[133] He appeared to consider that the breadth of discretion conferred by s 15 was sufficient to ensure adequate protection without a specific requirement for the judge to cross-refer to s 33 of the Family Law Act 1996.

Where different jurisdictions are involved, the outcome of the decision in one may also impact on the application of the TOLATA. This is illustrated by *White v White*.[134] In that case, as has been seen in section 5.4.1, the court ordered sale of a home on an application by Mrs White despite the fact that the house remained occupied by Mr White and the couple's young daughters. Mr White had applied under the Children Act 1989 for a transfer of Mrs White's beneficial interest during their daughters' minority. That application had been suspended pending the outcome of Mrs White's case under the TOLATA 1996.[135] The

---

[130] [2010] 1 FLR 1402, [19].   [131] Ibid, [20].   [132] Unreported, 30 November 2001, HC.
[133] *Miller Smith v Miller Smith* [2010] 1 FLR 1402, [23].
[134] [2004] 2 FLR 321.   [135] Ibid, [5].

consequence of the order for sale was to resurrect Mr White's application. If successful, it would necessarily appear to override the order for sale, because Mrs White would no longer hold the beneficial interest that provided the linchpin of her claim.

QUESTIONS

1. What do you consider to be the main advantages and disadvantages of the joint tenancy and tenancy in common as forms of co-ownership? What factors would you take into account in advising co-owners whether to hold their home as beneficial joint tenants or tenants in common?

2. Assess the methods by which a joint tenancy may be severed: (i) unilaterally, by one joint tenant; and (ii) mutually, by all of the joint tenants. What changes, if any, do you consider desirable to simplify the current law?

3. How does the underlying ethos of the trust of land differ from that of the trust for sale? To what extent is this change in ethos reflected in the rights of the beneficiaries?

4. In what circumstances is the court likely to order sale of a home on an application by one co-owner?

For guidance on how to answer these questions visit the online resources at www.oup.com/uk/mcfarlane4e/.

FURTHER READING

Bright 'Occupation Rents and the Trusts of Land and Appointment of Trustees Act 1996: from Property to Welfare' [2009] Conv 378

Clements, 'The Changing Face of Trusts: The Trusts of Land and Appointment of Trustees Act 1996' (1998) 61 MLR 56

Cooke, *Land Law* (Oxford: OUP, 2nd edn 2012) ch 5

Dixon, 'To Sell or Not to Sell: That is the Question. The Irony of the Trusts of Land and Appointment of Trustees Act 1996' (2011) 70 CLJ 579.

Gardner, 'Material Relief between Ex-Cohabitants 1: Liquidating Beneficial Interests Otherwise than by Sale' [2014] Conv 95

Hopkins 'Regulating Trusts of the Home: Private Law and Social Policy' (2009) 125 LQR 310

Hopkins, 'The Trusts of Land and Appointment of Trustees Act 1996' [1996] Conv 411

Law Commission Report No 181, *Transfer of Land: Trusts of Land* (1989)

Oakley, 'Towards a Law of Trusts for the Twenty-First Century' [1996] Conv 401

Powlowski and Brown, 'Joint Purchasers and the Presumption of Joint Beneficial Ownership—A Matter of Informed Choice?' (2013) 27 Tru LI 3

Smith, *Plural Ownership* (Oxford: OUP, 2005) chs 3–8

14

CO-OWNERSHIP AND THIRD PARTIES: APPLICATIONS FOR SALE

CENTRAL ISSUES

1. Third parties may make an application for sale of co-owned land. The most likely third parties to do so are creditors and trustees in bankruptcy of one of the beneficiaries.

2. Since the Trusts of Land and Appointment of Trustees Act 1996, applications made by creditors are considered under the general provisions of that Act, while those by trustees in bankruptcy are considered under the Insolvency Act 1986.

3. As regards applications by creditors, there has been judicial acknowledgment that the 1996 Act has changed the law from the previous practice, which was heavily weighted in favour of sale. The outcome of cases, however, casts doubt on the extent of any such change.

4. In relation to trustees in bankruptcy, under the Insolvency Act 1986, there is a presumption in favour of sale after an initial one-year adjustment period. Sale may be postponed if there are exceptional circumstances, although this criterion has been narrowly construed.

5. In determining applications for sale of a home the court must have regard to the rights of those affected by the sale under Art 8 ECHR. Where the application is by a creditor it must also be borne in mind that they have a right of property under Article 1 Protocol 1.

6. Where sale is discretionary, the courts have the opportunity to undertake a proportionality balance required to ensure compatibility of the sale with the ECHR. This leaves vulnerable to challenge applications by trustees in bankruptcy under s 335A of the Insolvency Act 1986 where the need to demonstrate exceptional circumstances is a precondition to the existence of discretion.

1 INTRODUCTION

In Chapter 13, we considered how the courts determine applications for the sale of co-owned land where the application is brought by one of the co-owners. It may be recalled that applications for sale (like all other applications relating to the exercise of their functions by trustees of land) are made to the court under s 14 of the Trusts of Land and Appointment of Trustees Act 1996 (TOLATA 1996). Section 15 provides a non-exhaustive list of factors for the court to take into account. In this chapter, we consider applications for sale that are brought by third parties to the trust. Any person with '*an interest in property subject to a trust of land*' may bring an application under s 14. Other than the co-owners themselves, the most likely persons to have an interest in the property are creditors and trustees in bankruptcy of one of the co-owners. As regards creditors, only those whose debt is secured over a beneficial share have '*an interest*' in the property. A creditor may have had a security interest from the outset. Alternatively, the creditor may initially be unsecured, but obtain a charging order over the debtor's land. The effect of a charging order is to turn an unsecured debt into a secured one. Charging orders are discussed in Chapter 25, section 4, where we note that during times of recession their use tends to increase. In these economic conditions, the circumstances in which such creditors can force sale become correspondingly more significant.

On an application for sale by a creditor or trustee in bankruptcy, the court must decide whether the beneficiary should be able to remain in the home, or whether the home should be sold to enable debts to be paid. The resulting case law raises interesting policy questions as to the relative weight that should be given to the desire to remain in the home and the purely financial interests of creditor. An appropriate balance between these interests is all the more difficult to determine given the factual context in which disputes typically arise. The beneficiary resisting sale and the applicant for sale may both be 'victims' of another co-owner's fraud or may be suffering the fallout caused by that co-owner's financial crisis which on occasions can be triggered by economic recession.

As far as creditors with a security interest from the outset are concerned, it is possible for a beneficial tenant in common to grant an equitable charge (or mortgage) over his or her share, but such arrangements are not necessarily commercially attractive to lenders. As will be seen in the case law in this chapter, such interests are more likely to arise because a purported grant of a legal mortgage over the entire estate fails: for example, because one co-owner (A) has exerted undue influence over the other (B),[1] or has forged B's signature to procure a mortgage.[2] The result of the undue influence or forgery is that the charge takes effect only against A's beneficial share. Where a creditor succeeds in obtaining an application for sale, the proceeds of sale are divided proportionately between the beneficiaries in accordance with their respective beneficial shares. Only those proceeds representing the debtor's share are used to discharge the debt.[3] If the co-owners were joint tenants, then the creation of the equitable charge by one co-owner, or the grant of a charging order, constitutes an act operating on the joint tenant's share to sever the joint tenancy (as discussed in Chapter 13).

---

[1] For example, *First National Bank plc v Achampong* [2003] EWCA 487, in which a presumption of undue influence was drawn under the tests provided in *Royal Bank of Scotland plc v Etridge (No 2)* [2001] UKHL 44.

[2] For example, *Mortgage Corporation v Shaire* [2001] 4 All ER 364.

[3] An exceptional decision is *Bank of Ireland Home Mortgages Ltd v Bell* [2001] 2 FLR 908. In that case, an equitable charge arising as the result of Mr Bell's forgery of his wife's signature was, notwithstanding, held to have priority over both parties' beneficial shares. This meant that, on a sale of the home, the debt would be paid out of the full proceeds, not only the part representing Mr Bell's beneficial interest. The Court of Appeal doubted the decision of the first instance judge in this respect, but that aspect of his decision was not subject to appeal.

Where a co-owner becomes bankrupt, all of his or her property vests in the trustee in bankruptcy, who is under a statutory duty to realize the assets. As is the case with creditors, on a sale, only the proceeds of sale representing the bankrupt's share are used to discharge his or her debts. Where the beneficiary is a joint tenant, we have seen in Chapter 13 that bankruptcy also severs the joint tenancy as an (involuntary) act operating on the joint tenant's share.

The starting point in determining an application by a third party is s 15 of the TOLATA 1996.

Trusts of Land and Appointment of Trustees Act 1996, s 15

(1) The matters to which the court is to have regard in determining an application for an order under section 14 include—

   (a) the intentions of the person or persons (if any) who created the trust,

   (b) the purposes for which the property subject to the trust is held,

   (c) the welfare of any minor who occupies or might reasonably be expected to occupy any land subject to the trust as his home, and

   (d) the interests of any secured creditor of any beneficiary.

[...]

(3) In the case of any other application, other than one relating to the exercise of the power mentioned in section 6(2), the matters to which the court is to have regard also include the circumstances and wishes of any beneficiaries of full age and entitled to an interest in possession in property subject to the trust or (in case of dispute) of the majority (according to the value of their combined interests).

(4) This section does not apply to an application if section 335A of the Insolvency Act 1986 (which is inserted by Schedule 3 and relates to applications by a trustee of a bankrupt) applies to it.

The effect of s 15 is that applications by creditors and trustees in bankruptcy are treated differently. The court deals with applications by creditors under s 15. By virtue of s 15(4), however, applications by a trustee in bankruptcy fall to be decided under s 335A of the Insolvency Act 1986. Therefore, each type of application must be considered separately.

To an extent, however, applications by creditors and trustees in bankruptcy raise the same policy considerations. It is useful to highlight these before analysing the case law concerning the different applicants for sale.

2 POLICY CONSIDERATIONS

In Chapter 13, we noted that the policy underlying the TOLATA 1996 was to provide a form of regulation for trusts of land more suited than the trust for sale to the use of land as a home. We noted that where a dispute as to sale arises between the co-owners, this raises the tension between one party's wish to maintain his or her 'home' and the other's desire to realize his or her investment. The tension between the 'use' and 'investment' functions of a home are all the more apparent when the application for sale is brought by a creditor or trustee in bankruptcy of a co-owner, for whom the property has only ever represented a commercial investment.[4]

Fox highlights the opposing concerns of creditors, on the one hand, and of co-owners, on the other, and is critical of the law's track record in protecting the home.

Fox, *Conceptualising Home: Theories, Laws and Policies* (2007, pp 14–15, 23–5)

The concerns of the creditor

It is a truism that, in disputes between creditors and occupiers, the creditor almost invariably wins. Legislative and judicial policy makers have routinely favoured the interests of creditors over those of occupiers, thus demonstrating the greater weight attributed to the concerns of creditors over those of occupiers. It is not difficult to understand why this has been the case. For one thing, the creditor has a legitimate expectation, when he lends money against the security of real property, that the debt will be satisfied or the security honoured. Furthermore, there are a series of policy arguments to bolster the creditor's case, for example, the potentially adverse consequences of diminishing the legal protection of creditors; interests on the availability of credit secured against domestic property, either for acquisition of the property itself or as business capital. By contrast, the occupier's interest in the property which a creditor is seeking to realise as a home is not only inconvenient—operating as it could to subjugate the claims of creditors, whose economic clout weights heavily on the balancing scales—but also difficult to ascertain or represent, relative to the creditor's interest. While the creditor's concerns, which essentially revolve around their economic claim on the property as capital, are relatively straightforward, the occupier's interest in retaining the home for use and occupation is much more complex, and, with its many dimensions—financial, practical, emotional, psychological, social and so on—more difficult to quantify [. . .]

The concerns of the occupier

While the creditor's concerns are relatively straightforward, the home interests of occupiers are much more complex and difficult to quantify [. . .] By drawing upon understandings of the meaning of 'home' as they have developed in other disciplines, legal scholars can begin to appreciate that an occupier's desire to retain the property for use and occupation as a home is not merely sentimental but may also encompass multi-emotional, psychological, social and cultural matters. These meanings can operate to intensify the occupier's attachment to their home, and to exacerbate the experience of losing the home through actions at the hands of a creditor.

However, attempts to argue 'home' interests in law, particularly when positioned against financial interests, are beset by difficulties. Although interdisciplinary research has established the authenticity of home meanings, the relationship between an occupier and his or her home—inherently intangible and difficult to define—is not readily comprehensible to lawyers. For one thing, as home scholars in other disciplines have recognised, an occupier's interest in his or her home is:

> a relative concept, not an absolute one that can be defined in a dictionary or by a linguist. Given that it transcends quantitative, measurable dimensions and includes qualitative subjective ones, it is a complex, ambiguous concept that generates confusion.

---

[4] For further discussion see Hopkins, 'Regulating Trusts of the Home: Private Law and Social Policy' (2009) 125 LQR 310REFO:JART.

It is often difficult to verbalise ideas about home, since they are highly personal, and this adds to the analytical obstacles. Perhaps even more significantly, particularly in the legal domain, the idea of personal attachment to one's home can be portrayed as sentimental and emotional, and as a consequence can become trivialised, particularly when measured against the objective and quantifiable claims of creditors to the capital value of the property. These characteristics provide a ready argument against attempts to develop a coherent legal concept of home. Nevertheless, even setting aside our instinctive appreciation of the importance of home, the proposition that home is a meaningful site and the authenticity of the attachment of occupiers to their homes have been firmly established in other disciplines. In light of this scholarship and the centrality of home to legal discourse, the idea that the subject of 'home' is too difficult for law to comprehend is indefensible.

While Fox refers to creditors, the concerns of the parties are the same whether the application for sale is brought by the creditors themselves or by a trustee in bankruptcy. As we will see, however, under the applicable statutory schemes, the ability of the court to take into account the concerns of the occupier is greater in a dispute with a creditor. Where a creditor has obtained a charging order over one co-owner's beneficial share, a further policy dimension is added to the claim: should the beneficiary resisting the sale (whose interest is not affected by the charging order) lose their home to enable the repayment of debts that were initially *unsecured*? While the initial status of the debt is a point acknowledged by the courts, in practice it does not appear to have had an impact on the courts decisions.[5]

3   APPLICATIONS BY CREDITORS

Applications for sale by a creditor are considered under s 15 of the TOLATA 1996. In applying that section, the responsibility lies with the judge to determine how much weight to afford to each of the factors listed in the provision and all other relevant matters.[6]

Prior to the 1996 Act, applications for sale by creditors and trustees in bankruptcy were considered by courts under s 30 of the Law of Property Act 1925 (LPA 1925). In applying that provision, it was held that no distinction should be made between the applications. It had been established, in *Re Citro*,[7] that, on an application by a trustee in bankruptcy, sale would be ordered unless the circumstances were exceptional (a criterion that is discussed at sections 4.1 and 4.2 of this chapter). In *Lloyds Bank plc v Byrne*,[8] the Court of Appeal considered that the same rule should apply in relation to creditors.

The 1996 Act distinguishes between these applications, because those by creditors are considered under s 15 of that Act, while applications for sale by trustees in bankruptcy are now dealt with under s 335A of the Insolvency Act 1986. Against this background, Neuberger J considered in the following case whether s 15 of the TOLATA 1996 had changed the law.

---

[5] See *Close Invoice Finance Ltd v Pile* [2008] EWHC 1580; [2009] 1 FLR 873; *Forrester Ketley & Co v Brent* [2009] EWHC 2441 (Ch); *C Putnam & Sons v Taylor* [2009] EWHC 317 (Ch); *National Westminster Bank plc v Rushmer* [2010] EWHC 554 (Ch); [2010] 2 FLR 362.

[6] *White v White* [2003] EWCA 924, [26]. See further the discussion in Chapter 13, section 5.4.1.

[7] [1991] Ch 142.   [8] [1993] 1 FLR 369.

Mortgage Corporation v Shaire
[2001] 4 All ER 364, HC

Facts: Mrs Shaire and Mr Fox were joint legal owners of their home. Unknown to Mrs Shaire, Mr Fox had forged her signature to secure mortgages over the house. As a result of the forgery, these took effect only against his beneficial share, which the court assessed as being 25 per cent. Following Mr Fox's death, the mortgagee sought sale of the house.

Neuberger J

At 378–80

To my mind, for a number of reasons, Mr Asif is correct in his submission, on behalf of Mrs Shaire, that s 15 has changed the law.

First, there is the rather trite point that if there was no intention to change the law, it is hard to see why Parliament has set out in s 15(2) and, indeed, on one view, s 15(3), the factors which have to be taken into account specifically, albeit not exclusively, when the court is asked to exercise its jurisdiction to order a sale.

Secondly, it is hard to reconcile the contention that Parliament intended to confirm the law as laid down in *Byrne's case* with the fact that, while the interest of a chargee is one of the four specified factors to be taken into account in s 15(1)(d), there is no suggestion that it is to be given any more importance than the interests of the children residing in the house (see s 15(1)(c)). As is clear from the passage I have quoted from the judgment of Nourse LJ in *Re Citro* as applied to a case such as this in light of *Byrne's case*, that would appear to represent a change in the law.

Thirdly, the very name 'trust for sale' and the law as it has been developed by the courts suggests that under the old law, in the absence of a strong reason to the contrary, the court should order sale. Nothing in the language of the new code as found in the 1996 Act supports that approach.

Fourthly, it is clear from the reasons in *Byrne's case* and indeed the later two first instance cases to which I have referred, that the law, as developed under s 30 of the Law of Property Act 1925, was that the court should adopt precisely the same approach in a case where one of the co-owners was bankrupt (*Re Citro*) and a case where one of the co-owners had charged his interest (*Byrne's case*). It is quite clear that Parliament now considers that a different approach is appropriate in the two cases-compare ss 15(2) and 15(3) of the 1996 Act with s 15(4) and the new s 335A of the Insolvency Act 1986.

Fifthly, an indication from the Court of Appeal that the 1996 Act was intended to change the law is to be found in (an albeit plainly obiter) sentence in the judgment of Peter Gibson LJ in *Banker's Trust Co v Namdar* [1997] CA Transcript 349. Having come to the conclusion that the wife's appeal against an order for sale had to be refused in light of the reasoning in *Re Citro* and *Byrne's case*, Peter Gibson LJ said:

'It is unfortunate for Mrs Namdar, that the very recent Trusts of Land and Appointment of Trustees Act 1996 was not in force at the relevant time [i.e. at the time of the hearing at first instance] [. . .]'

Of course it would be dangerous to build too much on that observation, but it is an indication from the Court of Appeal and indeed from a former chairman of the Law Commission, as to the perceived effect of the 1996 Act.

Sixthly, the leading textbooks support the view that I have reached. In *Megarry & Wade on the Law of Real Property* p 510 (para 9–064) one finds this:

'Although the authorities on the law prior to 1997 will therefore continue to provide guidance, the outcome will not in all cases be the same as it would have been under the previous law. This is because the legislature was much more specific as to the matters which a court is required to take into account.'

Emmet on Title (19th edn, January 1999 release) para 22–035, contains this:

'Cases decided on pre-1997 law may be disregarded as of little, if any, assistance [. . .] because the starting point [. . .] was necessarily a trust for sale implied or expressed as a conveyancing device enabling the convenient co-ownership of the property [. . .]'

Seventhly, the Law Commission report which gave rise to the 1996 Act, *Transfer of Land, Trusts of Land* (Law Com No 181, 8 June 1989), tends to support this view as well. It is fair to say that the Law Commission did not propose a new section in a new Act such as s 15 of the 1996 Act, but a new s 30 of the Law of Property Act 1925. It is also fair to say that the terms of the proposed new s 30 were slightly different from those of s 15. However, in my judgment, the way in which the terms of the 1996 Act, and in particular s 15, have been drafted suggests that the Law Commission's proposals were very much in the mind of, and were substantially adopted by, the legislature. In para 12.9 of the report, the Law Commission describe the aim as being to 'consolidate *and rationalise*' (my emphasis) the current approach. When commenting on the proposed equivalents of what are now s 15(2) and (3), the Law Commission said (note 143):

'Clearly, the terms of these guidelines may influence the exercise of the discretion in some way. For example, it may be that the courts' approach to creditors' interests will be altered by the framing of the guideline as to the welfare of children. If the welfare of children is seen as a factor to be considered independently of the beneficiaries' holdings, the court may be less ready to order the sale of the home than they are at present.'

Finally, the Law Commission said (para 13.6):

'Within the new system, beneficiaries will be in a comparatively better position than beneficiaries of current trusts of land. For example, given that the terms governing applications under section 30 will be less restrictive than they are at present, beneficiaries will have greater scope to challenge the decisions of the trustees and generally influence the management of the trust land.'

Eighthly, to put it at its lowest, it does not seem to me unlikely that the legislature intended to relax the fetters on the way in which the court exercised its discretion in cases such as *Re Citro* and *Byrne's case*, and so as to tip the balance somewhat more in favour of families and against banks and other chargees. Although the law under s 30 was clear following *Re Citro* and *Byrne's case*, there were indications of judicial dissatisfaction with the state of the law at that time. Although Bingham LJ agreed with Nourse LJ in *Re Citro*, he expressed unhappiness with the result ([1990] 3 All ER 952 at 965, [1991] Ch 142 at 161), and Sir George Waller's dissatisfaction went so far as led him to dissent ([1990] 3 All ER 952 at 965–966, [1991] Ch 142 at 161–163). Furthermore, there is a decision of the Court of Appeal in *Abbey National plc v Moss* [1994] 2 FCR 587, which suggests a desire for a new approach.

All these factors, to my mind, when taken together point very strongly to the conclusion that s 15 has changed the law. As a result of s 15, the court has greater flexibility than heretofore, as to how it exercises its jurisdiction on an application for an order for sale on facts such as those in *Re Citro* and *Byrne's case*. There are certain factors which must be taken into account (see s 15(1) and, subject to the next point, s 15(3)). There may be other factors in a particular case which the court can, indeed should, take into account. Once the relevant factors to be taken into account have been identified, it is a matter for the court as to what weight to give to each factor in a particular case.

The only indication the other way is a decision of Judge Wroath in the Newport, Isle of Wight, County Court in *TSB plc v Marshall* [1998] 2 FLR 769 at 771–772, where he said this, having referred to *Byrne's, Moss'*, and *Hendricks'* cases:

'Those three cases were all decided where the applications to the court were under s 30 of the Law of Property Act. However, it has been submitted that the principles established are applicable to an application under s 14, and I accept that submission.'

It does not appear clear to what extent the matter was argued before him, or, indeed, whether it was argued before him. With all due respect to Judge Wroath, I disagree with his conclusion.

A difficult question, having arrived at this conclusion, is the extent to which the old authorities are of assistance, and it is no surprise to find differing views expressed in the two textbooks from which I have quoted. On the one hand, to throw over all the wealth of learning and thought given by so many eminent judges to the problem which is raised on an application for sale of a house where competing interests exist seems somewhat arrogant and possibly rash. On the other hand, where one has concluded that the law has changed in a significant respect so that the court's discretion is significantly less fettered than it was, there are obvious dangers in relying on authorities which proceeded on the basis that the court's discretion was more fettered than it now is. I think it would be wrong to throw over all the earlier cases without paying them any regard. However, they have to be treated with caution, in light of the change in the law, and in many cases they are unlikely to be of great, let alone decisive, assistance.

Applying s 15 of the 1996 Act, Neuberger J noted that the intentions of Mrs Shaire and Mr Fox when the house was acquired (within s 15(1)(a)) were to provide a home for themselves and for Mrs Shaire's son from a previous relationship. The property was now held (within s 15(1)(b)) both as a home and an asset for Mrs Shaire, with 75 per cent of the beneficial interest, and as security for the loan as regards Mr Fox's 25 per cent share. The interest of the creditor fell to be considered under s 15(1)(d), while Mrs Fox's son was now an adult and therefore his position could not be taken into account. Under s 15(3), it was also relevant that Mrs Shaire had the majority of the beneficial interest.

Weighing up these factors, Neuberger J noted,[9] on the one hand, that for Mrs Shaire to leave her home of nearly twenty-five years '*would be a real and significant hardship, but not an enormous one*'; on the other hand, for the mortgagee to be '*locked into a quarter of the equity of a property would be a significant disadvantage unless they had a proper return and a proper protection as far as insurance and repair is concerned*'. He therefore proposed a solution under which the mortgage would be converted into a loan, on which Mrs Shaire would pay interest pending any future sale. Failing agreement on this (or Mrs Shaire's ability to pay), sale would be ordered.

[9] [2001] 4 All ER 364, [383].

The careful balancing act conducted by Neuberger J stands in contrast to how applications for sale by creditors were considered prior to the TOLATA 1996 under s 30 of the LPA 1925. There is no doubt that the facts of the case do not demonstrate 'exceptional circumstances' such as would have prevented sale under s 30.

Pascoe is critical of Neuberger J's decision. The Law Commission had envisaged that s 15 of the 1996 Act would consolidate and rationalize the approach developed by the courts under s 30 of the 1925 Act.[10] Against this background, Pascoe considers that Neuberger J's conclusion that s 15 has changed the law is likely to be read with '*some surprise and bewilderment*'.[11] Her concern lies with the consequences of the decision for secured creditors and, in particular, whether these consequences have been fully considered.

Pascoe, 'Section 15 of the Trusts of Land and Appointment of Trustees Act 1996: A Change in the Law' [2000] Conv 315, 327–8

Neuberger J.'s approach is radical: it recognises more rights for beneficiaries and their children in relation to the land which is arguably a more accurate reflection of the ideals and purposes behind modern home ownership. In his view, section 15 has done more than to codify judicial practice which had been working in the restrictive framework of the 1925 legislation. The new trust of land will therefore better reflect and protect the different expectations which have arisen with the change in our perception of the social role of land. Neuberger J's approach is not one of consolidation and rationalisation; rather he is wiping the slate clean and starting afresh with secured creditors the likely casualties of the new approach. It will be a welcome change in the law for spouses, partners and children living in the property, but an inexpedient, prejudicial and financially detrimental development if one is a secured creditor. Secured creditors must be asking whether the guidelines in section 15 were enacted with proper consideration and deliberation. It must be questionable whether section 15 has abdicated too much responsibility to the judiciary. Perhaps policy should have been formulated by Parliament, rather than relying on ad hoc developments in case law. This will inevitably have commercial and financial repercussions as creditors absorb the effects of the change. Only time will tell if judges are prepared to implement the consequences of Neuberger J.'s judgment and let a fresh wind blow away the remnants of the harshness for families of section 30 of the Law of Property Act 1925 when faced with applications by secured creditors.

Has s 15 of the TOLATA 1996 changed the law? Neuberger J's arguments may appear persuasive, although Pascoe raises legitimate concerns. To the extent that *Shaire* indicates a more sympathetic approach to beneficiaries in actions by creditors, the decision may have been a false dawn. Despite Mrs Shaire's 75 per cent beneficial interest and long-term occupation of the house as her home, sale would only be prevented if the mortgagee's interest could satisfactorily be protected.

---

[10] Law Commission Report No 181, *Transfer of Land: Trusts of Land* (1989), [12.9] (the paragraph is extracted in Chapter 13, section 5.4.3).

[11] Pascoe, 'Section 15 of the Trusts of Land and Appointment of Trustees Act 1996: A Change in the Law' [2000] Conv 315, 316.

3.1 APPLICATIONS FOR SALE BY CREDITORS POST-*SHAIRE*

It is useful to consider the contrasting outcomes in the subsequent cases of *First National Bank plc v Achampong*[12] and *Bank of Ireland Home Mortgages Ltd v Bell*,[13] on the one hand, and *Edwards v Lloyds TSB*,[14] on the other. The following extracts from these decisions show how the courts have exercised their discretion under s 15 of the TOLATA 1996. Analysed together with *Shaire*, the significance attached by the courts to the interest of the secured creditor in determining applications for sale becomes apparent.

First National Bank plc v Achampong
[2003] EWCA 487, CA

Facts: Mrs and Mrs Achampong were co-owners of their home. The parties had granted a mortgage over their home, but Mrs Achampong successfully argued that her agreement had been obtained through the presumed undue influence of her husband. As a result, the mortgage took effect only against his 50 per cent beneficial share. Mr Achampong had returned to Ghana, leaving Mrs Achampong in occupation of the home, with two of the parties' adult children (one of whom was mentally disabled) and three infant grandchildren. Blackburne J considered whether sale should be ordered under s 14 of the 1996 Act.

Blackburne J

At 65

[. . .] I regard it as plain that an order for sale should be made. Prominent among the considerations which lead to that conclusion is that, unless an order for sale is made, the bank will be kept waiting indefinitely for any payment out of what is, for all practical purposes, its own share of the property. While it is relevant to consider the interests of the infant grandchildren in occupation of the property, it is difficult to attach much if any weight to their position in the absence of any evidence as to how their welfare may be adversely affected if an order for sale is now made. It is for the person who resists an order for sale in reliance on section 15(1)(c) to adduce the relevant evidence. Insofar as the Achampongs' intention in creating the trust of the property was to provide themselves with a matrimonial home, and insofar as that was the purpose for which the property was held on trust, that consideration is now spent. Given the many years' absence of contact between Mr and Mrs Achampong, the fact that there has not yet been a divorce cannot disguise the reality that theirs is a marriage which has effectively come to an end. The possibility, therefore, that the property may yet serve again as the matrimonial home can be ignored. Insofar as the purpose of the trust—and the intention of the Achampongs in creating it—was to provide a family home and insofar as that is a purpose which goes wider than simply the provision of a matrimonial home, I am unpersuaded that it is a consideration to which much if any weight should be attached. The children of the marriage have long since reached adulthood. One of them is no longer in occupation. It is true that the elder daughter, Rosemary, is a person under mental disability and remains in occupation but to what extent that fact is material to her continued occupation of the property and therefore to the exercise of any discretion under section 14 is not apparent.

---

12 [2003] EWCA 487.   13 [2001] 2 FLR 809.   14 [2004] EWHC 1745.

Bank of Ireland Home Mortgages v Bell
[2001] 2 FLR 809, CA

Facts: Mr and Mrs Bell were co-owners of their home with, respectively, a 90 per cent and 10 per cent beneficial share. Mr Bell forged Mrs Bell's signature to obtain a mortgage. He had subsequently left the property and the parties had divorced. Mrs Bell, who was in poor health, remained in occupation, with the parties' son. At first instance, the judge had refused an order of sale. This was overturned on appeal.

Peter Gibson LJ

At 26–31

Further, the judge does not mention the fact that the debt was at the time of the trial some £300,000, and increasing daily, no payment of either capital or interest having been received from Mr Bell (or Mrs Bell for that matter) since June 1992. Mrs Bell's beneficial interest is only about 10 per cent at the very most, as Mr De la Rosa conceded, and there is no equity in the property which would be realised for her on a sale of the property. In effect, therefore, the bank would take all the proceeds on a sale. That is a most material consideration to which the judge should have given great weight.

Second, the judge referred to the property being purchased as a family home. Let me accept that as a finding of fact, although Mr Jackson was able to point to other inconsistent evidence from Mrs Bell as to why the property was purchased. Let me assume that the judge thereby had regard to section 15(1)(a), the intentions of the persons creating the trust. But that purpose ceased to be operative once Mr Bell left the family, either in 1991 or at any rate by 1992 when possession proceedings started. Mrs Bell is now divorced from Mr Bell. Therefore that purpose is not a matter to which the judge could properly have regard.

Third, the judge referred to the occupation of the property by Mrs Bell and her son. Let me assume that thereby the judge was referring to section 15(1)(b), the purposes for which the property is held. But that is not an operative purpose of the trust since the departure of Mr Bell. The reference to the son may also be a reflection of section 15(1)(c), the welfare of a minor occupying the property. But the son at the time of the trial was not far short of 18 and therefore that should only have been a very slight consideration.

Fourth, the judge referred to Mrs Bell's poor health. At the time of the trial she was facing an operation. I accept that the judge could properly have regard to this, but it would provide a reason for postponing a sale rather than refusing sale.

Fifth, the judge referred to Lloyds Bank as second chargee. But in my judgment that was not a relevant consideration. There was no obligation to give notice to a subsequent encumbrancer. Nor has it ever been the practice of the court when giving effect to a mortgagee's request for an order for sale to hear the views of subsequent encumbrancers. In theory a subsequent encumbrancer might wish to redeem the prior encumbrance, but in practice there was no possibility of that in the circumstances of the present case given the size of the debt.

Prior to the 1996 Act the courts under section 30 of the Law of Property Act 1925 would order the sale of a matrimonial home at the request of the trustee in bankruptcy of a spouse or at the request of the creditor chargee of a spouse, considering that the creditors' interest should prevail over that of the other spouse and the spouse's family save in exceptional circumstances. The 1996 Act, by requiring the court to have regard to the particular matters specified in section 15, appears to me to have given scope for some change in the court's practice. Nevertheless, a powerful consideration is and ought to be whether the creditor is receiving proper recompense for being kept out of his money, repayment of which is overdue (see *The Mortgage Corporation v Shaire*, a decision of Neuberger J on 25th February 2000). In the present case it is plain that by refusing sale the judge has condemned the bank to go on waiting for its money with no prospect of recovery from Mr and Mrs Bell and with the debt increasing all the time, that debt already exceeding what could be realised on a sale. That seems to me to be very unfair to the bank.

Edwards v Lloyds TSB
[2004] EWHC 1745

Facts: Mr and Mrs Edwards were co-owners of their home. Following the parties' separation, Mrs Edwards remained in occupation of the home, with the couple's children (now aged 15 and 13). Mr Edwards had forged his wife's signature on a mortgage of the property, which therefore took effect only against his 50 per cent share. Mr Edwards could no longer be traced. The bank sought an application for sale. Park J held that sale should be postponed for five years, until the youngest child reached the age of 18.

Park J

At 31–3

In this case the bank has applied for an order for sale, and Mrs Edwards has opposed the application. I must weigh up the various factors which are relevant and do the best I can to reach a balanced conclusion. I mention now two particular points on the facts of this case which were (I believe) not present in any of the three cases to which I was referred. First, if the house was sold now it is hard to see how Mrs Edwards could find the money to buy another smaller one. In the other cases it appears to have been different. For example in *The Mortgage Corporation v Shaire* (supra) Neuberger J said that if the house was sold Mrs Shaire would still have a substantial sum which she could put towards a smaller home. In the present case, in contrast, the house is a two-bedroom house in which Mrs Edwards already has to share a bedroom with her daughter. The house is obviously at the lower end of the range of prices for houses in the area where she lives. If there was a sale and the husband's debt to the bank was taken out of half of the net proceeds before the balance was available to Mrs Edwards, I very much doubt that she would be able to find another house which she could afford to buy and which would be adequate to accommodate her and her children.

Second, whereas in the other three cases it appears that the debt owed to the bank already exceeded the value of the interest over which the bank had an equitable charge, in the present case that is not so. On the figures which I gave in paragraph 12 above the value of the bank's security (a 50% interest in the house) would be (if the entirety were sold) about £70,000. The husband's debt to the bank (£15,000 plus interest plus costs) is unlikely at present to be more than £40,000. It is true that interest is not currently being paid to the bank on the debt owed to it, but interest continues to accrue on the debt, and now and for some time to come the security will be sufficient to cover the increasing amount of the debt.

> In the circumstances I do not want to order an immediate sale, because I believe that that would be unacceptably severe in its consequences upon Mrs Edwards and her children. But equally I believe that I should make some order which, admittedly later rather than sooner, should enable the bank to recover its debt with accrued interest upon it.

Two points are notable about these decisions. The first point to note is the courts' differing approach to the purposes of the trusts. In *Achampong*, Blackburne J was not prepared to afford weight to any subsisting purposes of the trust of providing a 'family' home following the effective termination of the marriage by Mr Achampong's return to Ghana. Similarly, in *Bell*, the departure of Mr Bell was considered to have ended the purpose of the trust. In contrast, in *Edwards*, Park J was satisfied that, following Mr Edwards' departure, '*in part the purpose still survives, because the house is still the home for Mrs Edwards and the two children*'.[15] These differing attitudes to the purpose are significant, because the continuing purpose of the trust is the factor that enables the occupying beneficiary to have his or her interests weighed against those of the creditors under s 15 of the 1996 Act. Where the purpose is considered to have come to an end, the likelihood of sale being postponed appears remote, unless there are children present whose interests fall for consideration under s 15(1)(c).

Probert considered the consequences of the narrow approach to the purpose of the trust in *Achampong* and *Bell* in a discussion of the latter case.

Probert, 'Creditors and Section 15 of the Trusts of Land and Appointment of Trustees Act 1996: First Among Equals' [2002] Conv 61, 66–7

The danger in the reasoning lies in the way that it downgrades the purpose of providing a family home as against the interests of the creditors. If the purpose of providing a family home comes to an end upon the departure of one of the parties and only the original purposes are to be taken into account, then where one party has left the property and there are no children, the only relevant factor remaining is the interests of the creditors. Even where there are children the dispute is reduced to a straightforward contest between the welfare of any minors who might wish to occupy the property and the interests of the creditors. If these two factors are given equal weight then it is possible that either may prevail in the short term. In the long term, the minors will grow up and their interests will cease to be a relevant concern. Moreover, if the interests of those nearing 18 are "only a very slight consideration" then the creditors' interests may prevail even before the former reach adulthood. If the statement that the creditors interests are a "powerful consideration" indicates that more weight is given to this factor than any other, then there is the risk that the interests of creditors will trump the rights of even very young children, once the factors listed in (a) and (b) are negated. If this interpretation of section 15 prevails then the wind has changed and blown us back to where we started.

Does the wider approach to the purpose of the trust adopted in *Edwards* ensure that the interests of the occupying beneficiary (in addition to the welfare of children) are weighed against those of the creditor? The difficulty with the decision lies in understanding when the

---

[15] *Edwards v Lloyds TSB* [2004] EWHC 1745, [29].

wider approach to the purpose will be taken. Objectively, the only difference between the three cases as regards the courts' identification of the purpose is the continuing occupation, in *Edwards*, of the couple's young children. It seems likely that this affected the courts' attitude towards the purpose of the trust, despite the fact that the welfare of children should be taken into account independently through s 15(1)(c) of the TOLATA 1996. Even under *Edwards* it remains unlikely that the purpose of providing a family home will be considered to continue where one beneficiary remains in occupation without children. In such cases, as Probert notes, the only remaining factor under s 15 is the interests of the creditors. However, it is important to recall that the factors listed in s 15 are non-exhaustive. On appropriate facts a factor not specifically referred to in s 15 may justify postponing sale.

The second notable point about the decisions is the differing position of the creditors in each case, as highlighted by Park J in *Edwards*. In *Shaire*, as we have seen, the decision not to order sale was dependent on an arrangement being reached under which the creditor would not be prejudiced; in *Edwards*, it was clear that this criterion was also met. In contrast, in *Achampong*, the debt had reached a level of £180,000. It was enforceable against only a 50 per cent share of the home, which, at the time of the judgment, had a full value of only £195,000; similarly, in *Bell*, as we have noted, the debt already exceeded the value of the house. The cases illustrate a consistent approach by the courts that while the interests of creditors is only one factor for the court to take into account, it will be difficult to resist sale unless the creditor will not be prejudiced. Hence, in *C Putnam & Sons v Taylor*, the judge ordering sale noted that if he refused to do so, '*I would be condemning the [creditor] to go on waiting for its money with no prospect of recovery from any other source and with the debt increasing all the time*'.[16]

3.2 APPLICATIONS BY CREDITORS: THE HUMAN RIGHTS DIMENSION

An application by a creditor for sale of a home under s 14 engages Art 8 of the ECHR (the right to respect for private and family life) in respect of those who will be affected by the sale through the duty of the court to interpret legislation in a human rights compatible manner.[17] 'Home' has an autonomous meaning within Art 8 and all those with 'sufficient and continuing' links to the home must be taken into account, not only those with property rights.[18] Hence, for example, any children in occupation have a right under Art 8 as well as the debtor's co-owner. Against this, however, must be balanced the secured creditor's right of property under Art 1 Protocol 1 of the ECHR, which may be infringed by refusing to enable the creditor to realize their interest. We have examined these human rights in Chapter 4. There we have seen that these rights are not absolute, although any interference must be for a legitimate aim and must be proportionate to that aim. In *National Westminster Bank plc v Rushmer*, Arnold J noted that as a result of the discretion conferred on the court by s 15 the proportionality of the application with Art 8 can undoubtedly be considered. In his view, the balance would necessarily be drawn by taking into account the factors referred to the court under s 15. He explained, '*[I]n my judgment, it will ordinarily be sufficient [. . .] for the court to give due consideration to the factors specified in section 15 of TOLATA. That will ordinarily enable the court to balance the creditor's rights, which include its rights under Article 1 of the First Protocol, with the Article 8 rights of those affected by an*

---

[16] [2009] EWHC 317 (Ch), [34].   [17] HRA 1998, s 3.   [18] See Chapter 4, section 4.1.1.

order for sale. I would not rule out the possibility that there may be circumstances in which it is necessary for the court explicitly to consider whether an order for sale is a proportionate interference with the Article 8 rights of those affected, but I do not consider that this will always be necessary'.[19] There, a creditor had obtained a charging order against Mr Rushmer and had subsequently successfully applied for sale of a home that he jointly owned with his wife. Arnold J rejected a claim that the order should be set aside because there had been no explicit discussion of the rights of Mrs Rushmer and of the couple's children under Art. 8. By weighing all the factors required under s 15, due regard had necessarily been given to the family's Art 8 rights.[20]

3.3 HAS S 15 OF THE TRUSTS OF LAND AND APPOINTMENT OF TRUSTEES ACT 1996 CHANGED THE LAW?

On the basis of the analysis in section 3.1 of applications for sale by creditors post-*Shaire*, we can assess Neuberger J's conclusion that s 15 of the TOLATA 1996 has 'changed the law' from the courts' previous practice under s 30 of the LPA 1925. The decisions in these cases may cast doubt on the extent of any such change. As we have noted, in applications for sale by a creditor under s 30 of the 1925 Act, *Re Citro* established that sale would be ordered unless the circumstances were exceptional. As we will see in part 4.1, at the time of that decision, the only reported case in which this criterion was met was one in which a postponement of sale would not prejudice the interest of the creditor.[21] In view of this, it seems that the decisions in *Achampong, Bell*, and *Edwards* are entirely consistent with the courts' previous practice. In considering applications for sale, courts have continued to stress the discretionary nature of the jurisdiction under s 15.[22] But despite Neuberger J's conclusion in *Shaire*, the decision in that case may stand alone as one in which the 1996 Act has made a practical difference to the outcome.[23]

Two factors may account for the pattern of decisions since *Shaire*. Firstly, the utility of developing a flexible approach under s 15 of the 1996 Act is dependent on creditors bringing their applications under that provision. It was predicted at the time of the Act that s 15 would operate as an incentive for creditors to obtain an order of bankruptcy, enabling them to rely on the more favourable provision in s 335A of the Insolvency Act 1986.[24] Radley-Gardner[25] notes that, by the time of the decision in *Achampong*, the ability of mortgagors to circumvent s 15 by making the defaulting beneficiary bankrupt had become apparent. This is illustrated by *Alliance and Leicester plc v Slayford*,[26] in which a

---

[19] [2010] EWHC 554 (Ch); [2010] 2 FLR 362, [50].

[20] Ibid, [51]. There is no reported case in which sale on an application by a creditor under the TOLATA, s 14 has been considered a disproportionate interference with art 8.

[21] *Re Holliday* [1981] Ch 405.

[22] See *Forrester Ketley & Co v Brent* [2009] EWHC 3442 (Ch), [52].

[23] The decision in *Edwards v Lloyds TSB* [2004] EWHC 1745 may be contentious in this regard. The case shares some analogies with *Re Citro* [1991] Ch 142 (in which sale was ordered under s 30) in so far as the application was made despite the continuing purpose of the trust, but the fact the creditors in *Edwards* would not be prejudiced may have been sufficient, in light of *Re Holliday* [1981] Ch 405, to distinguish the cases even under s 30: see Hopkins, 'Regulating Trusts of the Home: Private Law and Social Policy' (2009) 125 LQR 310, 331.

[24] Hopkins, 'The Trusts of Land and Appointment of Trustees Act 1996' [1996] Conv 411, 425.

[25] Radley-Gardner, 'Section 15 of TOLATA, or, the Importance of Being Earners' [2003] 5 Web JCLI.

[26] (2001) 33 HLR 66.

wife's beneficial interest was binding against a mortgagee, because she had entered into a transaction through her husband's undue influence. The court held that it was not an abuse of process for the mortgagee to sue the husband on his personal covenant to pay the debt, with a view to bankrupting him and bringing an application for sale under the Insolvency Act 1986. Hence, as Radley-Gardner explains: '[E]*ven if a more flexible approach had emerged under section 15, it would have been a paper tiger, easily undercut by recourse to the insolvency regime.*'

Secondly, the decisions in the cases echo Fox's comment, in the extract above, of the difficulty in balancing the qualitative and emotional concerns of occupiers against the quantitative and financial interests of the creditor. In the balancing exercise under s 15, creditors have nothing to prove: their interest in obtaining sale is unarguable. Pitted against this are the more nebulous concepts of the intentions and purposes of the trust, the 'welfare' of children, and a host of matters that may be pleaded to supplement the specific factors listed in s 15. In *Achampong*, little weight was attached to the occupying grandchildren in the absence of evidence as to *how* their welfare would be affected by sale. In *Fred Perry Holdings v Genis*,[27] Master Price noted that while *Shaire* suggested '*a different approach in favour of families might be appropriate following on the reform of the law by [TOLATA]*'[28] the cases showed that '*the upshot has been to give precedence to commercial interests rather than to the residential security of the family. Whilst it may be argued that precedence to such commercial interest fails to take adequate account of the public interest in maintaining a stable family unit, bearing in mind the attendant social costs of eviction and family breakup, this does not seem to be the current state of the authorities in relation to sections 14 and 15 of [TOLATA]*'.[29]

3.4 APPLICATIONS FOR SALE AND THE FAMILY LAW ACT 1996

In section 3 of Chapter 12 we have seen that beneficiaries under a trust of land may, additionally, have 'home rights' under the Family Law Act 1996 (FLA). In section 5.5 of Chapter 13 we have considered how the courts have dealt with the overlapping jurisdiction between TOLATA and the FLA on applications for sale made by a beneficiary. The relationship between the two jurisdictions on an application for sale by a creditor arose in *Fred Perry Holdings v Genis*.[30] There, Mrs Genis had registered her home rights (through entry of a Land Registry notice) at the time her husband's creditors brought an application for sale under s 14 TOLATA. The court noted that under s 15 the balance was in favour of sale. However, the (different) factors the court was required to take into account under the FLA before restricting or terminating Mrs Genis's 'home rights' in favour of the creditors were balanced in her favour.[31] Having identified the apparent tension between the jurisdictions the court ordered sale. Master Price explained that '*to give precedence to [Mrs Genis's] home rights would create an anomaly which cannot be justified*'[32] by affording favourable treatment to a

---

27 Unreported, Judgment 1 August 2014, [2015] 1 P & CR DG5.
28 Ibid, [8].   29 Ibid.   30 Ibid.
31 Under FLA 1996, s 34(2) an application in favour of the creditors could be made if the court was satisfied that 'in all the circumstances it is just and reasonable to do so'. However the court is required to take into account specific factors listed in s 33(6).
32 Ibid, [13].

party who has registered their home rights. The court noted that to do so would be contrary to the apparent policy of the law (in respect of which Master Price expressed some criticism) of affording primacy to commercial interests.[33] Master Price agreed, however, to postpone sale for one year in order to reduce the disruption to the family.

4   APPLICATIONS BY TRUSTEES IN BANKRUPTCY

Where there is a trust of land, applications for sale by a trustee in bankruptcy are considered by the court under s 335A of the Insolvency Act 1986.

Insolvency Act 1986, s 335A

(1) Any application by a trustee of a bankrupt's estate under section 14 of the Trusts of Land and Appointment of Trustees Act 1996 powers of court in relation to trusts of land) for an order under that section for the sale of land shall be made to the court having jurisdiction in relation to the bankruptcy.

(2) On such an application the court shall make such order as it thinks just and reasonable having regard to—
   (a) the interests of the bankrupt's creditors,
   (b) where the application is made in respect of land which includes a dwelling house which is or has been the home of the bankrupt or the bankrupt's spouse or civil partner or former spouse or former civil partner—
      (i) the conduct of the [spouse, civil partner, former spouse, or former civil partner], so far as contributing to the bankruptcy,
      (ii) the needs and financial resources of the [spouse, civil partner, former spouse, or former civil partner], and
      (iii) the needs of any children; and
   (c) all the circumstances of the case other than the needs of the bankrupt.

(3) Where such an application is made after the end of the period of one year beginning with the first vesting under Chapter IV of this Part of the bankrupt's estate in a trustee, the court shall assume, unless the circumstances of the case are exceptional, that the interests of the bankrupt's creditors outweigh all other considerations.

(4) The powers conferred on the court by this section are exercisable on an application whether it is made before or after the commencement of this section.

The circumstances to be taken into account under s 335A of the 1986 Act therefore differ from those under s 15 of the TOLATA 1996. In particular, the intentions of the settlors and the purposes for which the land is held (the criteria contained in s 15(1)(a) and (b) of the 1996 Act) cease to be relevant on bankruptcy. In the following extract, Henderson J considered how the references in s 335A to the 'needs' of various parties should be interpreted.

---

[33] Ibid.

Everitt v Budhram
[2009] EWHC 1219 (Ch)

Facts: Mr and Mrs Budhram had both been declared bankrupt. Both parties suffered from chronic medical conditions. An application for sale of their co-owned home was brought against Mrs Budhram (proceedings against her husband had been stayed through his lack of capacity until legal representation was appointed). Under s 335A the court is directed to disregard the 'needs' of the bankrupt (Mrs Budhram) but take into account those of the bankrupt's spouse (Mr Budhram).

Henderson J

At 36–7

Counsel for the trustee submits that the reference to the "needs of the bankrupt" must be broadly construed and refer to needs of every kind, including not only financial needs but also medical needs and needs of any other description, such as emotional, psychological or mental needs. He submits that this wide construction must be what Parliament intended because, immediately before that, there is a reference to "the needs of any children" as one of the matters that the court should have regard to. He submits, in my view correctly, that the needs of children must be given a very broad interpretation and refer to needs of any kind, and is certainly not confined to needs of a financial nature. Further support for that approach is found in the preceding sub-paragraph, with its reference to "the needs and financial resources of the spouse" of the bankrupt. Again, he submits, and again I would agree, that "needs" should there be given a wide interpretation, and appears to be at least potentially distinct from financial needs or resources, which are the subject of separate express mention. It is true that the reference is to "financial resources" rather than financial needs, but nevertheless the point is still one of some force.

Curiously enough, there seems to be no authority, so far as the researches of counsel have been able to uncover, on the meaning of the word "needs" in this subsection. However, I consider that counsel for the trustee is substantially correct in his submission and that the needs of the bankrupt in paragraph (c) should be broadly interpreted, just as the same word should be broadly interpreted in sub-paragraphs (b)(ii)(iii). Accordingly, the court must disregard not only the financial needs of the bankrupt but also, relevantly for present purposes, the medical and psychological needs of the bankrupt.

On the facts this meant that neither the financial nor medical needs of Mrs Budhram could be taken into account. It is also worth noting that as Mr and Mrs Budhram had both been made bankrupt, if proceedings had continued against both of them, neither of their needs could have been considered. On the facts, however, as Mr Budhram was not a party to the proceedings a broad approach could be taken to interpreting his needs as the bankrupt's spouse. The allowance made by the judge in respect of Mr Budhram's needs is considered in section 4.1.

Through s 335A(3) of the Insolvency Act 1986, as long as the application for sale is brought at least a year after the bankruptcy, the interests of the creditors prevail and sale is therefore ordered unless the circumstances are exceptional. Only if exceptional circumstances are present is the court required to balance the factors listed in the provision.[34]

---

[34] Compare the approach to interpretation of s 335A suggested by Dixon, 'Trusts of Land, Bankruptcy and Human Rights' [2005] Conv 161, 164.

Although s 335A was inserted into the Insolvency Act 1986 by the TOLATA 1996, it is an extension of a provision contained in the original Act, the origins of which lie with the Cork Report. The discussion of the family home in that report remains instructive in understanding the policy represented by s 335A.

Insolvency Law and Practice: Report of the Review Committee (The Cork Report) (Cmnd 8558, 1982, [1118], [1120]–[1123])

The family home

It would be clearly wrong to allow a debtor or his family to continue to live in lavish style at the expense of the debtor's creditors for an extended period. Nevertheless considerable personal hardship can be caused to the debtor's family by a sudden or premature eviction, and we believe it to be consonant with present social attitudes to alleviate the personal hardships of those who are dependent on the debtor but not responsible for his insolvency, if this can be achieved by delaying for an acceptable time the sale of the family home. We propose therefore to delay, but not to cancel, enforcement of the creditors' rights.

[. . .]

Nevertheless we consider that any new Insolvency Act should confer on the Court a specific power to postpone a trustee's rights of possession and sale of the family home. In exercising this power the Court should have particular regard to the welfare of any children of the family and of any adult members of the family who are ailing or elderly [. . .] Giving this power to the Court will, we hope and expect, serve to support the natural inclination of the usually sympathetic [trustee in bankruptcy], and to protect the debtor's family in those cases where lack of sympathy with, or anger at, the debtor produces unfortunate and undeserved consequences for his family.

Where there are dependents, the Court should not order an immediate sale unless satisfied that no avoidable hardship to them will be caused by the sale of the family home. That is not to say that application need be made to the Court in every case; once the correct principles have been established, we believe that in only a very small minority of cases will the Court be concerned.

When an application does come before the Court, we consider that the Court must have wide discretion to enable it to make whatever order may be just and equitable in the great variety of circumstances that may arise. While the Court will first consider the dependants—and the greater their vulnerability the greater will be the protection needed—creditors' rights should be postponed only in order to prevent injury to the welfare of those dependants; not to preserve for them any particular standard of life.

No two cases will be alike; the Court must therefore have complete discretion to do what seems to it to be appropriate. Such guidelines as can be given must of necessity be in the most general terms and, indeed, little more than an indication of the factors for consideration. While some of us have considered that there should be a statutory limit on the length of time for which a postponement could be ordered, all of us are agreed that, in practice, any very lengthy postponement should be rare. The majority of us have concluded that the Court's powers should not be limited in duration. In the reported cases, both under the matrimonial legislation and (more rarely) under the bankruptcy law, much importance has been attached to the ages, welfare and educational prospects of the children.

The report undoubtedly envisages a less prescriptive regime than that provided for in s 335A,[35] while acknowledging the strength of the creditors' claims following bankruptcy. But s 335A does reflect the underlying idea in this extract of alleviating the hardship of a sudden eviction. The effect of s 335A is to provide the bankrupt (and his or her family) with an initial one-year adjustment period, following which the financial claim of the creditors becomes paramount.

The key issue of interpretation arising from s 335A is the meaning of 'exceptional circumstances', which may result in the postponement of sale after the initial year. We will first consider the courts' general approach to defining 'exceptional circumstances' and then address an argument that human rights considerations may require the courts to extend this general interpretation.

4.1 THE COURTS' GENERAL APPROACH TO DEFINING 'EXCEPTIONAL CIRCUMSTANCES'

The test of exceptional circumstances has its origins in the courts' case law under s 30 of the LPA 1925. In applications under that section, *Re Citro* established the general principle that, on an application by a trustee in bankruptcy, sale would be ordered unless there are exceptional circumstances. In doing so, Nourse LJ offered the following definition.

Re Citro
[1991] Ch 142, CA

Nourse LJ

At 157

What then are exceptional circumstances? As the cases show, it is not uncommon for a wife with young children to be faced with eviction in circumstances where the realisation of her beneficial interest will not produce enough to buy a comparable home in the same neighbourhood, or indeed elsewhere. And, if she has to move elsewhere, there may be problems over schooling and so forth. Such circumstances, while engendering a natural sympathy in all who hear of them, cannot be described as exceptional. They are the melancholy consequences of debt and improvidence with which every civilised society has been familiar. It was only in *re Holliday* [1981] Ch. 405 that they helped the wife's voice to prevail, and then only, as I believe, because of one special feature of that case. One of the reasons for the decision given by Sir David Cairns was that it was highly unlikely that postponement of payment of the debts would cause any great hardship to any of the creditors, a matter of which Buckley L.J. no doubt took account as well.

Implicit in Nourse LJ's definition is that 'exceptional' requires something '*out of the ordinary course, or unusual, or special, or uncommon*'.[36]

---

[35] Compare, for example, the '*wide discretion*' and the '*complete discretion to do what seems* [. . .] *appropriate*' in the extract with the actual provision in the Insolvency Act 1986, s 335A. Further, as is noted by Omar, 'Security Over Co-Owned Property and the Creditor's Paramount Status in Recovery Proceedings' [2006] Conv 157, 168, some of the factors the Cork Committee specifically envisaged being taken into account were held in *Re Citro* [1991] Ch 142 not to constitute exceptional circumstances.

[36] *Hosking v Michaelides* [2004] All ER (D) 147, *per* Judge Morgan QC.

In the following case, Judge Sumption QC explained further.

Re Bremner
[1999] 1 FLR 912

Judge Sumption QC

At 915

The test is whether the problems which would result from an eviction are within the broad range of problems, necessarily distressing, which can be expected to arise from the process of bankruptcy and the resultant realisation of the bankrupt's assets, or whether they lie wholly outside that range.

The clearest example of exceptional circumstances is chronic ill health on the part of the bankrupt, or the bankrupt's spouse or partner. In *Claughton v Charalambous*,[37] the bankrupt and his wife were beneficial co-owners of their home. Mrs Charalambous was in poor health, with consequential mobility problems that the couples' home had been altered to accommodate. She had a reduced life expectancy. The judge considered these circumstances to be exceptional and postponed sale for so long as Mrs Charalambous continued to live in the property.[38] In *Re Bremner*, the bankrupt himself was elderly and terminally ill with inoperable cancer. This case raised a specific issue because, under s 335A, the interests of the bankrupt are not themselves a relevant consideration.[39] But the court accepted that the bankrupt's wife, who was also his carer, had a distinct need to continue to provide that care in their home. Sale was postponed until three months after the bankrupt's death. In *Grant v Baker*,[40] the bankrupt's daughter remained living at home as she had the mental age of an 8- or 9-year-old child and furthermore had mobility problems and obsessive compulsive disorder. The court was satisfied that these circumstances were exceptional although not sufficiently so to warrant the indefinite postponement of a sale whilst the daughter remained at home. The sale was postponed for 12 months to allow suitable alternative accommodation to be found.

In the extract from *Re Citro* (above), Nourse LJ notes that, in *Re Holliday*[41] (the only reported case at the time in which exceptional circumstances had been found), the creditors would not be prejudiced by the postponement of sale. In that case, sale was postponed for five years until the bankrupt's children reached 17 years of age, at which point the proceeds of sale represented by the bankrupt's beneficial share would still be sufficient to pay his debts with interest. An immediate sale, however, would leave his former wife with insufficient funds to obtain alternative accommodation.

The fact that creditors will not be prejudiced by a sale is not, in itself, an exceptional circumstance enabling courts to postpone sale.[42] Where exceptional circumstances are

---

[37] [1999] 1 FLR 740.

[38] Contrast *Foenander v Allan* [2006] BPIR 1392. The bankrupt co-owned his home with his brother, who was suffering from progressive dementia. The brother's medical condition was not considered sufficient to postpone sale, although sale was postponed on other grounds.

[39] There was no co-ownership trust in this case, because Mr Bremner was the sole owner of the home. The case was decided under the Insolvency Act 1986, s 336, which is identical in all relevant respects to s 335A.

[40] [2017] 2 FLR 646.   [41] [1981] Ch 40.   [42] *Donohoe v Ingram* [2006] EWHC 282.

present, however, the impact of any delay on the creditors remains a significant factor in the courts' willingness to postpone sale under s 335A. A review of case law under s 335A suggests that the protection of creditors is a point of synergy between applications under that provision and those by creditors under s 15 of the TOLATA 1996.

In *Re Bremner*, the court noted that sale would not necessarily have been delayed if the bankrupt had been younger, or less ill, or had a longer life expectancy. The expected short period of the delay meant that any prejudice to creditors was likely to be modest.[43] In *Everitt v Budhram*,[44] the judge considered that the mental and physical needs of Mr Budhram, including those related to a stroke and diabetes, constituted exceptional circumstances, which he would take into account '*to a limited extent*'.[45] Sale was postponed for a year, or until three months after a possession order was obtained against Mr Budhram (who had also been made bankrupt). In the context of a history of non-co-operation with the trustee in bankruptcy, Henderson J noted that '*[i]f I am too generous, there is a risk that the matter will continue to drag along without anyone taking any serious steps to deal with it. Equally, if I am too severe, I will not give sufficient recognition to the exceptional circumstances which I have found to exist*'.[46] In *Grant v Baker*,[47] the court clearly felt that the indefinite period of postponement of the sale granted by the judge at first instance failed to pay due account to the interests of the creditors' interests as a whole. Although there was clear evidence of the distress the move would cause, the court felt that a move at some point was inevitable and that suitable long-term alternative accommodation should be available in the private rental sector. The reluctance of the court to sanction an indefinite period of delay is also illustrated by *Pickard v Constable*,[48] which, in addition, considered the role of statutory duties to provide accommodation. In *Pickard* Mrs Constable was adjudged bankrupt but her husband was in ill health and unable to walk without a 'zimmer' frame. Furthermore, he was unable to afford alternative accommodation, for instance by renting suitable accommodation in the private sector. Although the district judge considered these circumstances exceptional and warranted an indefinite suspension of sale, his decision was overturned on appeal by the High Court. In the light of the creditors' paramount interests an indefinite period was inappropriate. The stay was reduced to 12 months which Mr Constable could apply to extend. The court also observed that Mr Constable could look to the local authority's statutory duty to provide accommodation. Unfortunately, the reality is that this duty is frequently discharged by the use of temporary accommodation unsuitable to the needs of those with health problems.

In *Foenander v Allan*[49] and *Martin-Sklan v White*,[50] a postponement of sale in light of exceptional circumstances was not expected to prejudice creditors, because the sum realized on sale would still be sufficient to repay the outstanding debt. In *Martin-Sklan*, the postponement maintained the 'web of support' provided to the bankrupt's partner, an alcoholic; *Foenander* is an unusual case in which the exceptional circumstances were financial, rather than personal. In that case, an immediate sale would raise sufficient proceeds to repay creditors with a modest surplus. Sale was postponed on condition that an insurance claim for subsidence was likely to be met in a reasonable period. This would significantly increase the

---

[43] The eventual sale of the house would still provide sufficient proceeds with which to pay the secured creditors the sum due, plus interest, and pay unsecured creditors, with the loss of statutory interest.
[44] [2010] Ch 170.   [45] Ibid, [57].   [46] Ibid, [59].   [47] [2017] 2 FLR 646 at [46]–[50].
[48] [2017] EWHC 2475. It is understood that this decision is to be appealed.
[49] [2006] BPIR 1392.   [50] [2007] BPIR 76.

value of the home, enhancing the surplus available to the bankrupt and his brother, with whom the house was co-owned.

In *Nicholls v Lan*,[51] sale was delayed for a minimum of eighteen months to give the bankrupt's wife, a chronic schizophrenic, an opportunity to raise funds by the sale of another property, which would enable her to buy out the bankrupt's share. Her medical circumstances meant that a forced sale could have specific psychiatric effects. The case is notable in so far as the sale was postponed despite the fact that the proceeds realized by sale would be insufficient to pay the outstanding debts.

4.2 EXCEPTIONAL CIRCUMSTANCES: THE HUMAN RIGHTS DIMENSION

In section 3.2 we have seen that the wide discretion conferred on the courts by s 15 of the TOLATA ensures that due regard is given to the Art 8 ECHR rights of those affected by the sale. Where the application is made by a trustee in bankruptcy more than a year after the bankruptcy the courts do not necessarily have discretion. Under s 335A of the Insolvency Act 1986, a presumption in favour of the creditors arises after one year, unless there are exceptional circumstances. Only if such circumstances are present does the court have discretion whether to order sale. Further, the courts have defined exceptional circumstances narrowly, as meaning circumstances outside those expected to arise on a bankruptcy. Even before the compatibility of s 15 of TOLATA with Art 8 had been raised, in *Barca v Mears* the argument was advanced that the absence of any ability by the court to undertake a proper balancing of interests under s 335A constituted an infringement of Art 8. This argument attracted support by the court, although, on the facts, it was not sufficient to prevent sale.

Barca v Mears
[2004] EWHC 2170, HC

Judge Strauss QC

At 39–42

Clearly, in many or perhaps most cases, the sale of a bankrupt's property in accordance with bankruptcy law will be justifiable on the basis that it is necessary to protect the rights of others, namely the creditors, and will not be a breach of the Convention. Nevertheless, it does seem to me to be questionable whether the narrow approach as to what may be 'exceptional circumstances' adopted in *Re Citro (Domenico) (a Bankrupt)* [1991] Ch 142, is consistent with the Convention. It requires the court to adopt an almost universal rule, which prefers the property rights of the bankrupt's creditors to the property and/or personal rights of third parties, members of his family, who owe the creditors nothing. I think that there is considerable force in what is said by Ms Deborah Rook in *Property Law and Human Rights* (Blackstone Press, 2001), at pp 203–205 to which Mr Gibbon very fairly referred me:

"It is arguable that, in some circumstances, [s 335A(3)] may result in an infringement of Article 8. The mortgagor's partner and children have the right to respect their home and family life under Article 8 even though they may have no proprietary interest in the house [. . .] therefore it

---

[51] [2007] 1 FLR 744.

is possible that the presumption of sale in s 335A and the way that the courts have interpreted it, so that in the majority of cases an innocent partner and the children are evicted from the home, violates Convention rights [. . .]"

The eviction of the family from their home, an event that naturally ensues from the operation of the presumption of sale in s 335A, could be considered to be an infringement of the right to respect of the home and family life under Article 8 if the presumption is given absolute priority without sufficient consideration being given to the Convention rights of the affected family. Allen [Mr T Allen in "The Human Rights Act (UK) and Property Law" in *Property and the Constitution* (Hart Publishing, 1999), at p 163] observes that:

'As the law currently stands, the right to respect for family life and the home receives almost no consideration after the one year period. Whether such a strict limitation is compatible with the Convention is doubtful.'

[. . .] it may be that the courts, in applying s 335A [. . .] will need to adopt a more sympathetic approach to defining what constitutes "exceptional circumstances". If an immediate sale of the property would violate the family's rights under Article 8, the court may be required in compliance with its duty under s 3 of the HRA 1988 to adopt a broad interpretation of "exceptional circumstances" [. . .] to ensure the compatibility of this legislation with Convention rights."

In particular, it may be incompatible with Convention rights to follow the approach taken by the majority in *Re Citro (Domenico) (a Bankrupt)* [1991] Ch 142, in drawing a distinction between what is exceptional, in the sense of being unusual, and what Nourse LJ refers to as the 'usual melancholy consequences' of a bankruptcy. This approach leads to the conclusion that, however disastrous the consequences may be to family life, if they are of the usual kind then they cannot be relied on under s 335A; they will qualify as 'exceptional' only if they are of an unusual kind, for example where a terminal illness is involved.

It seems to me that a shift in emphasis in the interpretation of the statute may be necessary to achieve compatibility with the Convention. There is nothing in the wording of s 335A, or the corresponding wording of ss 336 and 337, to require an interpretation which excludes from the ambit of 'exceptional circumstances' cases in which the consequences of the bankruptcy are of the usual kind, but exceptionally severe. Nor is there anything in the wording to require a court to say that a case may not be exceptional, if it is one of the rare cases in which, on the facts, relatively slight loss which the creditors will suffer as a result of the postponement of the sale would be outweighed by disruption, even if of the usual kind, which will be caused in the lives of the bankrupt and his family. Indeed, on one view, this is what the Court of Appeal decided in *Re Holliday (a Bankrupt) ex parte Trustee of the Property of the Bankrupt v Holliday and Another* [1981] Ch 405.

Thus it may be that, on a reconsideration of the sections in the light of the Convention, they are to be regarded as merely recognising that, in the general run of cases, the creditors' interests will outweigh all other interests, but leaving it open to a court to find that, on a proper consideration of the facts of a particular case, it is one of the exceptional cases in which this proposition is not true. So interpreted, and without the possibly undue bias in favour of the creditors' property interests embodied in the pre-1998 case law, these sections would be compatible with the Convention.

The objection raised to s 335A in *Barca v Mears* is procedural. The possible incompatibility with Art 8 arises where the court is unable to balance the bankrupt's interests against those of the creditors because of the absence of exceptional circumstances. In *Nicholls v Lan*,[52] in which exceptional circumstances were present, Judge Morgan suggested that the balancing exercise that he was therefore required to undertake under s 335A *'precisely captures what is required'* by Art 8. In view of this, while the objection raised is *procedural*, the solution may lie in a *substantive* alteration of the definition of exceptional circumstances. By extending the definition of exceptional circumstances the court gains access to the discretion conferred by s 335A of the Insolvency Act 1986 and is therefore able to undertake the balancing exercise required by Art 8 of the ECHR. Where, even on a wide interpretation of the term, there are no exceptional circumstances, it may be presumed that sale is a proportionate interference with Art 8 rights. In this respect, the existence of the one-year adjustment period before the creditor's interests prevail may be significant. Even in such cases, however, the absence of discretion remains problematic as it excludes any consideration of Art 8. Further, the difference in treatment between applications by creditors on the one hand and trustees in bankruptcy on the other may raise a question of compliance with Art 14 (non-discrimination) unless the difference in treatment can be justified.

Despite these concerns, *Barca v Mears* has had little, if any, impact. Indeed, there is no reported case in which the wide interpretation of exceptional circumstances advocated by Judge Strauss QC has led to sale being postponed to protect an occupier's Art 8 rights. Baker suggests that the subsequent case law *'evidences only a variety of alluring yet ultimately unpersuasive defences of the status quo, intended to keep the* Barca *objection at bay'*.[53]

While *Barca v Mears* focusses on a procedural objection to the jurisdiction in s 335A, in *Ford v Alexander*[54] a substantive challenge was made to the compatibility of the section with Article 8. In Chapter 4 we have seen that in *Manchester City Council v Pinnock*,[55] in the context of possession proceedings by a local authority landlord against a tenant, the Supreme Court held that Art 8 required the proportionality of the eviction to be considered, although *McDonald v McDonald*[56] rejected a similar need for proportionality where an eviction is triggered by a private landlord. In *Ford v Alexander*, it was argued that a proportionality test should, therefore, be read into s 335A, so that exceptional circumstances were present whenever sale would be disproportionate. The argument was rejected by Peter Smith J. He considered that s 335A, as enacted, provides *'a necessary balance as between the rights of creditors and the respect for privacy and the home of the debtor'*. As Cowan and Hunter explain, Peter Smith J considered proportionality and exceptionality to be 'coterminous'.[57]

4.3 A 'FRESH START' FOR BANKRUPTS

Section 335A of the Insolvency Act 1986 must now be read in conjunction with ss 283A and 313A. These provisions were introduced into the Act by the Enterprise Act 2002 and reflect the policy of that Act of providing a 'fresh start' for bankrupts. Under s 313A, sale will not be ordered where the value of the bankrupt's share is below a prescribed level and, therefore, of marginal benefit to the creditors.[58] Under s 283A of the 1986 Act, the beneficiary's share in his or her home is returned to him or her after three years unless the trustee 'realises' the

---

[52] Ibid, [43].
[53] Baker, 'The Judicial Approach to "Exceptional Circumstances" in Bankruptcy: The Impact of the Human Rights Act' [2010] Conv 352, 366.
[54] [2012] EWHC 266 (Ch).   [55] [2011] 2 AC 104.   [56] [2017] AC 273.
[57] Cowan and Hunter, ' "Yeah but, no but", or just "no"? Life after *Pinnock* and *Powell*' [2012] JHL 58, 61.
[58] Ibid, 169–70.

interest by, for example, applying for sale. The section applies in relation to a dwelling-house which, at the time of the bankruptcy, was the sole or principle home of the bankrupt and/ or his or her current or former spouse or civil partner.[59] It has been held to apply only where the bankrupt's interest was vested in him or her at the commencement of the bankruptcy,[60] rather than recovered by the trustee in bankruptcy in the exercise of their powers under the Insolvency Act.[61]

As we have seen in section 4, under s 335A where an application for sale is made by a trustee in bankruptcy more than a year after the bankruptcy, sale is ordered unless there are exceptional circumstances. This gives the bankrupt a one-year adjustment period. Read together, the practical effect of ss 283A and 335A is that the trustee in bankruptcy has a two-year period during which sale will be ordered in the absence of exceptional circumstances. The meaning of 'realises' was considered by the Court of Appeal in the following case.

Lewis v Metropolitan Properties Realisations Ltd
[2010] Ch 148

Facts: Mr and Mrs Lewis were joint tenants of their home. Mr Lewis had become bankrupt. On the day before the third anniversary of his bankruptcy the trustee assigned Mr Lewis's beneficial interest in the home to the respondent for £1 and 25 per cent of the proceeds of any eventual sale. The Court of Appeal was asked whether the trustee had thereby realized the interest to prevent it from revesting in Mr Lewis.

Laws LJ
At 10–11, 22, 24, 27, and 29

All words which require construction or interpreting have to be placed in their proper context. The same is true of "realise" in subsection (3)(a) of the 1986 Act. The question that we have to consider is whether, in its context, it is capable of covering a transaction where there is a deferred monetary consideration during the period before that consideration comes in. None the less, it is an ordinary English word and it is appropriate to start with a consideration of what the normal English meaning of the word is.

The *Oxford English Dictionary* definition of "realise" is: "convert into cash or money". That is a good starting point for the Lewises' case. Alternative definitions are recorded by the judge as being "sell out" and "fetch as a price", which she described as being more general, but we still think that they import the general impression of a completed transaction as opposed to one where the price is still outstanding.

If one pulls these strands together the scheme of section 283A begins to emerge. It is as follows. We assume for the purposes of this paragraph a jointly owned home, and put on one side for the moment the possibility of a sale of the interest at a deferred consideration. (i) The section only applies to that part of the bankrupt's estate comprising his or his spouse/ civil partner's dwelling house. It does not apply to other property. (ii) The trustee has three years to decide what to do where the estate has such an interest. (iii) If he does nothing, then (subject to the provisions of subsection (6), which presumably allow for special cases which we do not consider further) the estate loses the property interest. (iv) If the interest

---

[59] Insolvency Act 1986, s 283A(1).   [60] *Stonham v Ramrattan* [2011] 1 WLR 1617.
[61] For example, under Insolvency Act 1986, s 339 (gifts and other transfers at an undervalue).

is of low value (within the meaning of the 1986 Act) the trustee, while technically owning the interest, will in practice have no enforcement mechanism available to him. If he does nothing, the interest reverts to the bankrupt under section 283A. If he starts proceedings (whether for an order for sale or a charging order), that will technically keep his interest alive while the proceedings are pending (section 283A(3)(b)(d)) but the interest will revest when the proceedings are dismissed under section 313A, as amended: see section 283A(4). (v) If the interest is of significant value, the trustee can do the following. (a) Apply for an order for sale. This keeps the interest out of the scope of section 283A while the proceedings are alive and gives the co-owner the opportunity to buy the trustee out *at the then value*. Alternatively the property will be ordered to be sold and the trustee gets *the then value*. (b) Apply for a charging order (if the conditions of section 313 are fulfilled). This secures *the then value* to the trustee, with future increases going to the bankrupt. (c) Reach an agreement with the bankrupt under section 283A(3)(e)—in effect, sell to the bankrupt. That will obviously reflect *the then value* and secure future increases for the bankrupt. (vi) Sell the interest to someone other than the bankrupt or the civil partner/spouse at a price payable and paid on sale. It is accepted by the Lewises that this would be a realisation. It would be a sale *at the then value*, with future increases accruing to the purchaser. (vii) It should not be forgotten that he might agree with the co-owner to sell, or the co-owner might want to sell anyway, in which case the trustee gets the estate's interest *at its then value*.

There may be some other permutations, but that is the basic scheme which emerges from a consideration of the section. The central feature which emerges is that which appears in the underlined words—the trustee, if he can achieve anything worthwhile at all, gets the equivalent of the then value of the property and is not allowed to hang on for ever as a co-owner, waiting to see property values rise. The provisions also achieve a reasonable degree of certainty for the bankrupt and the co-owner in that by the end of the third year (or the end of litigation commenced within three years) they will by and large know whether the property has to be sold, how much the trustee will get out of the property, that the trustee will no longer be a co-owner, and that the opportunity to make money out of a rising market will not remain with the trustee (giving him an incentive to hang on for some considerable time) but will enure to the benefit of the bankrupt, the co-owner or some other assignee.

Against that background it is now necessary to consider whether a sale of the beneficial interest in exchange for a future price, or a partially future price, would fit into that apparent background. Can it have been intended that such a transaction is a realisation within subsection (3)(a)? It seems to us that it cannot, for the following reasons. (i) For the reasons given above, it would extend the meaning of "realises" beyond its normal English sense. (ii) It would be an unusual transaction for Parliament to have contemplated in these circumstances. Section 283A is designed to deal with a real world problem, operating in a world of real, not fanciful, commercial transactions. A sale of a beneficial interest to an outsider is unusual enough. A sale with fixed monetary consideration left outstanding would be even more unusual. It is hard to imagine who would do such a thing. (iii) A sale with a contingent monetary consideration left outstanding is more conceivable, particularly if the consideration is dependent on a future sale of the property and is otherwise not payable, as the present case demonstrates. But the contingency of the obligation makes it look even less like a "realisation" in everyday terms (pending the fulfilment of the contingency), and it seems to create the very uncertainty that the rest of the scheme seems, by and large, to seek to remove. While the scheme is not spelled out and has to be inferred, and while it is not perfect, this sort of transaction sticks out like a sore thumb against the background of the rest of the section.

We therefore conclude that "realises" in the subsection involves getting in the full cash consideration for the deal.

QUESTIONS

1. Compare and contrast the rules applicable to applications for sale made by creditors and those made by trustees in bankruptcy. Do you consider differences between the applications to be justified by the status of the applicants?

2. In considering applications for sale by creditors, have the courts paid sufficient regard to the interests of beneficiaries who wish to prevent sale of their home? In what circumstances do you consider beneficiaries to be most vulnerable to a sale of their home being ordered?

3. Assess the view that arguments founded on human rights have had little practical impact on the courts' jurisdiction to order sale of the home on an application by a creditor or trustee in bankruptcy.

For guidance on how to answer these questions visit the online resources at www.oup.com/uk/mcfarlane4e/.

FURTHER READING

Baker, 'The Judicial Approach to "Exceptional Circumstances" in Bankruptcy: The Impact of the Human Rights Act 1998' [2010] Conv 352

Dixon, 'To Sell or Not to Sell: That is the Question. The Irony of the Trusts of Land and Appointment of Trustees Act 1996' (2011) 70 CLJ 579

Fox, *Conceptualising Home: Theories, Laws and Policies* (Oxford: Hart Publishing, 2007)

Fox, 'Creditors and the Concept of a "Family Home": A Functional Analysis' (2005) 25 LS 201

Hopkins, 'Regulating Trusts of the Home: Private Law and Social Policy' (2009) 125 LQR 310

Omar, 'Equitable Interests and the Secured Creditor: Determining Priorities' [2006] Conv 509

Omar, 'Security Over Co-Owned Property and the Creditor's Paramount Status in Recovery Proceedings' [2006] Conv 157

PART E

PRIORITY—
THE DEFENCES
QUESTION AND LAND
REGISTRATION

15 The Priority Triangle 578
16 Priorities in Registered Land 607
17 Co-Ownership and Priorities: The Defences Question 648
18 Reform of the Land Registration Act 2002 693

15

THE PRIORITY TRIANGLE

CENTRAL ISSUES

1. Many land law cases share a basic form: a dispute arises between B and C, each of whom wants to make an inconsistent use of the land.

2. The law has adopted a very clear structure to deal with these difficult disputes. Firstly, does B have a pre-existing (legal or equitable) property right that he or she can assert against C? Secondly, if B does have such a property right, does C have a defence to it? Thirdly, does B have a direct right against C?

3. In Chapters 5 and 6, we examined an aspect of the first question—whether the right claimed by B counts as a (legal or equitable) property right. In Chapters 8–11, we looked at another aspect of the first question—whether B can show that he or she has, in fact, acquired a claimed legal or equitable property right. In this chapter, our focus is on the question of when C can have a *defence* to B's pre-existing property right. This question can be thought of as the *priority* question: does B's property right have priority over C's right? In considering this question, we will make frequent use of examples arising in the context of the shared home, and which are thus related to the topics discussed in Chapters 12–14.

4. The question of priority is one of the most important, and most difficult, in land law. In a case where each of B and C has a (legal or equitable) property right in relation to land, it may be very difficult, in the abstract, to decide which of B or C should be free to use the land as he or she wishes. After all, it may well be that each of B and C has paid for his or her right; and that each of B and C is entirely innocent. In such cases, however, the law must try to provide a relatively simple set of rules to establish which right will take priority: B's right or C's right.

5. We will examine the priority question throughout Part E. The aim of this introductory chapter is to set out the *basic principles* that apply when answering the priority question. In Chapter 16, our focus will be on the *detail* of the *specific* statutory rules imposed by the Land Registration Act 2002. The priority question also comes up, of course, in unregistered land—but, given that the vast majority of titles to land in England and Wales are registered, our discussion of the unregistered land rules is now available as part of the online resources accompanying the book. In Chapter 17, we will consider the operation of overreaching, focussing on its possible use as a defence where C

acquires a right in relation to a shared home. In Chapter 18, we will consider the operation of the 2002 Act in cases where a party seeks rectification of the register, and will look at the difficult problems that may arise, for example, where there have been fraudulent dealings in registered land. Such third party fraud very often gives rise to the type of dilemma with which priority rules deal: how best to assess the competing claims of two innocent parties.

1 INTRODUCTION: THE PRIORITY TRIANGLE IN PRACTICE

The cases that we will examine in this chapter share a basic set of facts:

1. A is an owner of some land (i.e. A has a freehold or lease of some land); *and*

2. B then acquires a right to make some use of that land; *and*

3. C then acquires a right in relation to A's land (e.g. C buys A's freehold or lease, or A gives C a charge over A's land).

If C is content for B to continue using the land, there will be no problem for B. In practice, however, C may want to prevent B from continuing to use the land. For example, it may be that A, who has a freehold or lease, has allowed B to occupy all or part of A's land. If C then buys A's freehold or lease, it is likely that C will want to remove B. In such a case, we need to ask if B has a right that he or she can assert against C. This question is sometimes put in the following terms: does B's right to use the land *take priority* over C's right? Or, instead, does C's right *take priority* over B's right? As Figure 15.1 shows, we can consequently think of a *priority triangle* involving A, B, and C.

For example, in Chapter 1, section 5, and Chapter 6, section 5.3, we examined the decision of the House of Lords in *National Provincial Bank v Ainsworth*.[1] The facts of the case provide a good example of the priority triangle in practice. A (Mr Ainsworth) held a freehold. B (Mrs Ainsworth) had a right to use A's land ('a deserted wife's equity').[2] C (National Provincial

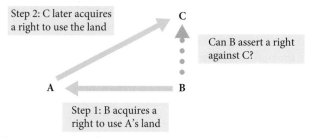

Figure 15.1 The priority triangle

---

[1] [1965] AC 1175.

[2] As we saw in Chapter 1, section 5, a 'deserted wife's equity' was the name given to the right held by a wife as a result of a duty imposed on a husband, having moved out of the matrimonial home, to provide her with financial support and, perhaps, accommodation.

Bank) then acquired a charge over A's land. That charge gave it the power, if A failed to repay a loan as agreed, to sell A's freehold and use the proceeds towards meeting the debt owed to C. As long as A (or someone acting on A's behalf) continued to repay the debt, there was no problem for B. But when A defaulted on the debt, C wanted to recover the sums due to it by selling A's freehold. And, of course, to get a reasonable price for A's freehold, C needed to sell the land with vacant possession (i.e. without B remaining in occupation). So the question was whether B had a right that she could assert against C—or, in other words, who had priority: B or C?

To determine the *priority* question, we have to do more than simply ask whose right came first in time. For example, in *National Provincial Bank v Ainsworth*, Mrs Ainsworth's 'deserted wife's equity' arose *before* the bank received its charge, and yet, as we saw in Chapter 6, section 5.3, Mrs Ainsworth had *no* right that she could assert against the bank: the bank was free to remove Mrs Ainsworth from the land. The crucial point was that the House of Lords saw the 'deserted wife's equity' as giving Mrs Ainsworth only a *personal right* against Mr Ainsworth. As we saw in Chapter 7, section 1, a personal right, by itself, cannot be asserted against a third party. So, in answering the priority question, we first need to ask the following fundamental question:

> Immediately before C acquired C's right, did B already have a (legal or equitable) property right in relation to the land?

As demonstrated by Chapters 5 and 6, the question of whether B had a pre-existing property right can, in turn, be split into two questions:

(a) The *content* question: does the type of right claimed by B count as a property right in relation to land?

(b) The *acquisition* question: on the facts of the case, had B, in fact, acquired that right, so that B had the right immediately before C acquired C's right?

National Provincial Bank v Ainsworth provides a good example of the *content* question in practice. There was no doubt that, when Mr Ainsworth moved out of the matrimonial home, Mrs Ainsworth acquired a right: a 'deserted wife's equity'. And there was no doubt that Mrs Ainsworth had that right *before* the bank acquired its right in the land. But Mrs Ainsworth's right could not bind the bank, because, according to the House of Lords, it did not count as a property right in land: it thus failed the content test. In one sense, then, *National Provincial Bank v Ainsworth* was a relatively straightforward case: the priority question was decided in C's favour as, whilst B had acquired a right before C, B's right was only a personal right. As we will see in this chapter, the priority question can be trickier to solve if, instead, the answer to the fun damental question set out above is Yes. For if B did have a legal or equitable property right in the land immediately before C acquired C's right in the land, then we have a situation where *each of* B and C has a competing (legal or equitable) property right in relation to the land. We will now consider, in section 2, the basic rule that applies in such a case.

2 THE BASIC RULE

When considering the priority triangle, the most difficult cases are those in which *each of* B and C has a property right in relation to the same piece of land. In such a case, the starting point is that *the first in time prevails*. So, if (i) A has a freehold or lease, and (ii) B then acquires a property right in relation to A's land, and (iii) A then transfers his freehold or lease to C, the starting point, in relation to both registered and unregistered land, is as follows:

> **The basic rule:** B's pre-existing (legal or equitable) property right will take priority over C's later property right.

As far as registered land is concerned, that basic rule is now enshrined by statute:

Land Registration Act 2002, s 28

(1) Except as provided by sections 29 and 30, the priority of an interest affecting a registered estate or charge is not affected by a disposition of the estate or charge.

(2) It makes no difference for the purposes of this section whether the interest or disposition is registered.

Of course, in relation to registered land, the exceptions provided by ss 29 and 30 are often more important than the basic rule, as we will see in section 3 of this chapter. Nonetheless, it is important to bear the basic rule in mind: if C does not have a defence to B's pre-existing legal or equitable property right, then B's right will bind C, even if B's right has not been entered on the register.[3]

3 THE *TIMING* QUESTION

To apply the basic rule, we must, of course, know whether or not B's property right arose *before* C's property right. In most cases, it will be very easy to work out the order of the parties' rights. For example, in *Williams & Glyn's Bank v Boland*[4] (a case we discussed in Chapter 6, section 2), Mr and Mrs Boland bought a home together. The registered title to the land was in Mr Boland's sole name, but he held his right to the land on trust for both himself and his wife, as Mrs Boland had contributed to the purchase price of the home. Some years later, Mr Boland borrowed money from the bank to support his business, and this loan, unbeknownst to Mrs Boland, was secured by a charge over the home. So, each of Mrs Boland and the bank had a property right in relation to the home: Mrs Boland had an equitable interest under a trust; the bank had a legal charge. It is, therefore, clear that the basic 'first in time' rule favoured Mrs Boland, and so the onus was on the bank to displace that rule, by showing that it had a defence to Mrs Boland's right.

In other cases, however, it can be more difficult to establish which of two property rights is the first in time.

---

[3] For an example of the application of the general 'first in time' rule in registered land, see *Halifax plc v Curry Popeck* [2008] EWHC 1692 (Ch).

[4] [1981] 1 AC 487.

3.1 WHOSE RIGHT IS FIRST IN TIME? CHARGES

3.1.1 The traditional view: the *scintilla temporis*

In *Boland*, the loan secured by the bank's charge was used to support Mr Boland's business: it was not used to acquire the land itself. It was, therefore, clear that Mrs Boland's equitable interest in the land had arisen before the bank's legal charge. A particular problem can arise, however, in the very common case of an 'acquisition mortgage'. This is where: (i) A borrows money from C *in order to buy* a freehold or lease; and (ii) in return, C acquires a charge over the land to secure A's duty to repay the loan. In such a case, when does C acquire its right? The traditional view was a technical one: C acquires its charge from A, and A can only give C a right in relation to the land if A *already* has a freehold or lease. On that view, A must acquire a property right *before* C: logically, there must be a *scintilla temporis*—that is, a tiny spark of time during which A holds his or her right free from C's charge.

3.1.2 The new view: *Abbey National v Cann*

The traditional view outlined above, whilst logical, may seem unrealistic: after all, if A needs to borrow money from C in order to acquire his or her freehold or lease, why should A's property right take priority to C's charge? In the following case, the House of Lords considered the problem and decided to depart from the traditional view.

Abbey National v Cann
[1991] 1 AC 56, HL

Facts: George Cann lived with his mother, Daisy, in Island Road, Mitcham, South West London, in a home that was registered in George's sole name. Because Daisy had contributed to the purchase price of that home, George held his estate on trust for both himself and Daisy. George and Daisy decided to move to a smaller home in South Lodge Avenue, also in Mitcham. They paid for that home by means of: (i) the proceeds of sale of their previous home in Island Road; and (ii) a loan from the Abbey National Building Society, secured by a charge over their new South Lodge Avenue home. The new home was registered in George's sole name and Daisy was not a party to the loan from the Abbey National. Daisy had known that a mortgage loan was necessary, because the new South Lodge Avenue home cost £4,000 more than the proceeds of sale of the Island Road home. Acting without Daisy's knowledge, however, George had taken out a loan of £25,000 from the Abbey National. When George failed to repay that loan as agreed, the building society attempted to remove Daisy (along with her new husband) from the home so that it could sell the home with vacant possession and use the proceeds to meet George's outstanding debt.

It was accepted that Daisy had an equitable property right: George held his estate in the South Lodge Avenue home on trust for himself and Daisy, because she had contributed to the purchase price by allowing all of the proceeds of sale of Island Road to be used in buying the new home. It was also clear that the Abbey National had a legal property right: the charge that it had acquired from George and then registered. The Abbey National argued that its property right arose *before* Daisy's property right. The Court of Appeal had rejected that argument, but found in favour of the Abbey National on other grounds. The House of Lords, whilst also supporting those other grounds (see below), also accepted Abbey National's argument that its charge arose before Daisy's equitable property right.

Lord Oliver

At 92–3

Of course, as a matter of legal theory, a person cannot charge a legal estate that he does not have, so that there is an attractive legal logic in the ratio in *Piskor's Case* [a decision of the Court of Appeal applying the traditional *scintilla tempors* view].[5] Nevertheless, I cannot help feeling that it flies in the face of reality. The reality is that, in the vast majority of cases, the acquisition of the legal estate and the charge are not only precisely simultaneous but indissolubly bound together. The acquisition of the legal estate is entirely dependent upon the provision of funds which will have been provided before the conveyance can take effect and which are provided only against an agreement that the estate will be charged to secure them. Indeed, in many, if not most, cases of building society mortgages, there will have been, as there was in this case, a formal offer and acceptance of an advance which will ripen into a specifically enforceable agreement immediately the funds are advanced which will normally be a day or more before completion. In many, if not most, cases, the charge itself will have been executed before the execution, let alone the exchange, of the conveyance or transfer of the property. This is given particular point in the case of registered land where the vesting of the estate is made to depend upon registration, for it may well be that the transfer and the charge will be lodged for registration on different days so that the charge, when registered, may actually take effect from a date prior in time to the date from which the registration of the transfer takes effect [. . .] The reality is that the purchaser of land who relies upon a building society or bank loan for the completion of his purchase never in fact acquires anything but an equity of redemption [a concept we will examine in Chapter 28, section 5], for the land is, from the very inception, charged with the amount of the loan without which it could never have been transferred at all and it was never intended that it should be otherwise. The "scintilla temporis" is no more than a legal artifice and, for my part, I would adopt the reasoning of the Court of Appeal in *In re Connolly Brothers Ltd. (No. 2)*[6] and of Harman J. in *Coventry Permanent Economic Building Society v. Jones*[7] and hold that *Piskor's Case* was wrongly decided.

Lord Jauncey

At 101–2

It is of course correct as a matter of strict legal analysis that a purchaser of property cannot grant a mortgage over it until the legal estate has vested in him. The question however is whether having borrowed money in order to complete the purchase against an undertaking to grant security for the loan over the property the purchaser is, for a moment of time, in a position to deal with the legal estate as though the mortgagee had no interest therein [. . .] In my view a purchaser who can only complete the transaction by borrowing money for the security of which he is contractually bound to grant a mortgage to the lender [simultaneously] with the execution of the conveyance in his favour cannot in reality ever be said to have acquired even for a scintilla temporis the unencumbered fee simple or leasehold interest in land whereby he could grant interests having priority over the mortgage [. . .] Since no

---

[5] [1954] Ch 553.   [6] [1912] 2 Ch 25.   [7] [1951] 1 All ER 901.

one can grant what he does not have it follows that such a purchaser could never grant an interest which was not subject to the limitations on his own interest. In so far as *Piskor* decided that such a purchaser could be vested for a moment of time in the unencumbered freehold or leasehold estate with the consequences to which I have just referred, I consider that it was wrongly decided.

The decision in *Cann* certainly has an important effect: it means that, if A takes out a mortgage to assist in acquiring a freehold or lease, then C (the mortgagee: i.e. bank or building society providing the loan) will take priority over B (a party also providing money towards the purchase of the freehold or lease).

The approach adopted in *Cann* has since received further support: for example, in *Ingram v IRC*,[8] Lord Hoffmann stated that: '*For my part, I do not think that a theory based upon the notion of the scintilla temporis can have a very powerful grasp on reality.*' But its operation in a case such as *Cann* itself seems somewhat harsh.[9] Firstly, whilst it may be true to say that George could not have acquired his estate in the South Lodge Avenue home without the mortgage loan, it is equally true to say that George could not have acquired that right without Daisy's financial contribution. Secondly, whilst Daisy knew that a mortgage of around £4,000 was necessary to complete the purchase, George went well beyond that in borrowing £25,000.[10]

3.1.3 The new view confirmed: *Scott v Southern Pacific Mortgages Ltd*

The facts of the *Scott* case are set out below. We examined one aspect of the decision in Chapter 8, section 4.4. For present purposes, the important points are, firstly, that the Supreme Court in *Scott* confirmed the basic point made in *Cann*. At least where the mortgage loan is required for the purchase,[11] and where the charge to the lender is granted at or around the time of the transfer of the legal title to the purchaser,[12] the lender will have priority over any property right acquired by a third party only on the purchaser's acquisition of the legal estate. That is the case even if that third party is, like Mrs Scott, already in occupation of the land, and is in fact the vendor of the land. The court's treatment of this first point can be seen in the following extracts.

Scott v Southern Pacific Mortgages Limited
[2014] UKSC 52, [2015] AC 385

Facts: The dispute concerned a 'mortgage rescue' scheme. Mrs Scott owned a property but was having difficulty meeting her mortgage payments. It was proposed that she should enter into a sale and leaseback arrangement with North East Property Buyers (NEPB). She was assured by NEPB that, if she sold the property to it at a discount on its market price, she would then be allowed to remain in occupation of the home as a tenant, paying a reduced rent, for the rest of her life. Unknown to Mrs Scott, the purchase was being funded by a 'buy to let' mortgage loan given to NEPB by Southern Pacific Mortgages Ltd.

---

[8] [2000] 1 AC 293, [303].
[9] For criticism, see Beaumont [1990] Law Society Gazette, 23 May, p 25, and 25 July, p 27.
[10] See the criticism of *Cann* made by Smith (1990) 109 LQR 545. For further disapproval of this aspect of the decision in *Cann*, see Thompson [1992] Conv 206; Dixon [1992] CLJ 223.
[11] This point was made by Lady Hale [2014] UKSC 52, [2015] AC 385 at [109] and [114].
[12] See Lady Hale's judgment at [114].

B decided to enter into the sale and leaseback arrangement, and so contracted to sell her estate in the land to A, a nominee of NEPB. When the sale to A was completed, A granted a lease to Mrs Scott (B). A funded its purchase with a 'buy-to-let' mortgage provided by Southern Pacific (C), and then defaulted on that mortgage, and so Southern Pacific (C) wished to remove Mrs Scott (B) from her home and sell the land with vacant possession. B argued that she was not bound by the rights of C, as she had a pre-existing property right that bound C.

In its decision, the Supreme Court unanimously confirmed the specific holding in *Cann*: where C's charge secures a loan made to allow A to buy property, then, in a priority dispute with B, C's charge is regarded as arising before completion of the sale to A. That meant that C could not be bound by any property right acquired by B at, or after, completion of the sale to A.

To avoid that effect of *Cann*, B therefore argued that: (i) she had acquired a property right *before* completion of her sale of the land to A; and (ii) C had no defence to that right. She argued that her property right arose through proprietary estoppel, as she had been promised by NEPB, and its nominee (A), that she would be able to remain in occupation of the property; she had relied on that promise by selling the land at a discount; as a result of that reliance, she would suffer a detriment were A wholly free to go back on that promise. She argued that her proprietary estoppel claim took effect as soon as A acquired any interest in the land, and that moment occurred when it contracted to buy the land from her, as it acquired an equitable interest in the land at that point (under the doctrine of anticipation: see Chapter 8, section 4.1).

As we saw in Chapter 8, section 4.2, however, the Supreme Court rejected that argument and found that, although A had acquired an equitable interest at the time of the contract of sale, A was not then in a position to give property rights in the land to other parties by means of proprietary estoppel. This meant that B's claim failed, as she had not passed the acquisition test: her dealings with NEPB and A did *not* give her a property right that existed before the sale to A was completed. That finding was sufficient to decide the case in favour of C.

However, the Supreme Court did consider another argument made by C: that, even if B did have a property right at the time when the contract of sale was entered into between B and A, C's charge should *still* be regarded as having arisen before B's right. That argument was based on extending the logic of *Cann*: the House of Lords held there that, where C's charge secures a loan made to allow A to buy property, then, in a priority dispute with B, C's charge is regarded as arising before completion of the sale to A. Southern Pacific argued that, in such a case, C's charge should also be regarded as arising before the contract of sale between the vendor (in this case, B) and A. Lady Hale (with whom Lord Wilson and Lord Reed agreed) rejected that argument; Lord Collins (with whom Lord Sumption agreed) accepted it.

Lady Hale

At [95]

I am reluctantly driven to agree that this appeal must fail for the reason given by Lord Collins: the purchaser was not in a position either at the date of the exchange of contracts or at any time up until completion of the purchase to confer equitable proprietary, as opposed to merely personal, rights on the vendor. But this produces such a harsh result that I would like to add a few additional words of explanation.

At [114]–[120]

[. . .] It has not been argued in this case that *Cann* was wrongly decided. It has been accepted that, at least in the standard case where completion and mortgage take place virtually simultaneously and the mortgage is granted to secure borrowings without which the purchase would not have taken place, completion and mortgage are one indivisible transaction and there is no scintilla temporis between them [. . .]

[. . .] Whatever one's view of the decision in *Cann* (and Lord Oliver acknowledged that the contrary view had "an attractive … logic" to it)[13] it does make sense. The conveyance vests the legal estate in the purchaser who instantly mortgages it to the lender. All the purchaser ever acquires is the equity of redemption. But that may not be true if the mortgage takes place sometime after the conveyance: there may be a period during which the purchaser owns the land without encumbrances. Not all conveyances and mortgages are indivisible: it depends upon the facts [. . .]

The lender is not a party to the contract to sell the land to the purchaser. This is an entirely separate matter between vendor and purchaser in which the lender is not involved. These days it may well take place on the same day as the conveyance and mortgage but it often takes place days, weeks or even months beforehand. In the olden days, it was common for vendor and purchaser to instruct the same solicitor. But that is no longer permitted, as it is recognised that they may well have a conflict of interest. The vendor may not know, and certainly has no right to know, how the purchaser proposes to fund the purchase and whether or not it is planned to mortgage the property immediately on completion. Indeed, the purchaser, perhaps particularly a corporate purchaser, may not know precisely where the money is coming from at the time when the contract is made. There may be a variety of options available and the choice between them not yet made [. . .]

Thus in no sense is this a "tripartite" transaction, to which vendor, purchaser and lender are all party. Lord Walker and Hughes LJ cannot have meant that it was when they referred to the "tripartite contractual arrangements between vendor, purchaser and mortgage lender" in *R v Waya*.[14] *Waya* was in any event concerned with the true construction of the arrangements between the purchasing borrower and the lender for the purpose of defining the benefit which the borrower had obtained from the lender having made a false statement in his mortgage application form. The contract between vendor and purchaser did not come into it.

I am afraid that I cannot see how it is implicit in the rejection of *Piskor* by the House of Lords in *Cann* that the contract of sale was part of the indivisible transaction. I understand, of course, that the ratio of *Cann* is limited to those cases where the purchaser requires the loan in order to complete his purchase. In that sense, the contract of sale is a necessary precursor to the conveyance and mortgage. But that does not explain why they are indivisible, nor does it explain what is meant by indivisibility in this context. If what is meant is that the purchaser only ever acquires an equity of redemption, out of which she is not able at completion to carve proprietary interests which are inconsistent with the terms of the mortgage, then to talk of the indivisibility of the contract adds nothing to the *Cann* analysis. It is still necessary to decide whether the purchaser can confer proprietary rights before completion. If what is meant is that the purchaser cannot do so, then it adds nothing to the analysis of the first question rehearsed earlier. The risk is that to talk of an indivisible transaction will not only fly in the face of the facts but also create confusion.

---

[13] [1991] 1 AC 56 at [92].   [14] [2013] 1 AC 294 at [53].

Lord Collins

At [74]

[. . .] the conclusion that a purchaser of property cannot grant a proprietary right is strongly supported by the approach of Lord Oliver and Lord Jauncey [in *Cann*]. Lord Oliver said[15] that prior to completion Mrs Cann had no interest in 7 Hillview, because she was not a party to the contract for the purchase of that property and if she had been led to believe that she would have an interest in and the right to occupy that property when George acquired it, at the stage prior to its acquisition she had no more than a personal right against him. Lord Jauncey said[16] that Mrs Cann could not have acquired an equitable interest in 7 Hillview prior to completion because her rights derived from George and she was not a party to the contract of sale [. . .]

At [77]–[89]

The vendors say that the substance of the matter is that they did not sell their homes outright to the purchasers, but simply sold them subject to the rights to the leases which they had been promised, and that *Cann* should be distinguished on the basis that in a sale and leaseback transaction the purchaser in reality has no more than a reversionary interest subject to that leaseback [. . .] [but] I agree with Etherton LJ that the true nature of the transaction was that of a sale and lease back […] In the case of Mrs Scott, for example, the contract provided that the property was to be transferred with "full title guarantee" and "vacant possession" and a transfer in the normal form was executed.

Consequently, in my judgment, the appeal should be dismissed on the principal ground that the vendors acquired no more than personal rights against the purchasers when they agreed to sell their properties on the basis of the purchasers' promises that they would be entitled to remain in occupation. Those rights would only become proprietary and capable of taking priority over a mortgage when they were fed by the purchasers' acquisition of the legal estate on completion, and then *Cann* would apply, with the effect that the acquisition of the legal estate and the grant of the charge would be one indivisible transaction, and the vendors would not be able to assert against the lenders their interests arising only on completion.

An indivisible transaction?

It follows that the question whether the decision in *Cann* that conveyance and mortgage are one transaction also extends to include a case where the equitable interest is said to arise at the time of the contract of sale does not arise. If I am right on the main point, it is not easy to see how this question could arise in any future case, but I propose to express my view on it because it was the main question canvassed in the courts below and on this appeal.

The vendors say that *Cann* did not decide whether the indivisible transaction analysis applies where the equitable interest of the occupier arises on exchange of contracts, and that the answer is that the analysis does not apply. The lenders say that, even if an equitable interest arose on exchange of contracts, in any event the House of Lords has already decided that not only were the conveyance and the charge part of one indivisible transaction, but also that the contract (which had been exchanged some weeks before), conveyance and charge were indivisible [. . .]

The contract of sale does, of course, have separate legal effects, but it would be wholly unrealistic to treat the contract for present purposes as a divisible element in this process.

---

15 [1991] 1 AC 56, 89.   16 [1991] 1 AC 56, 95.

That is why in *R v Waya*[17] this court adopted the reasoning in *Cann* to hold that where the same solicitor acts for a borrower and a mortgage lender, and the mortgage advance is paid to the solicitor to be held in the solicitor's client account, until completion, to the order of the mortgage lender; and on completion the solicitor transfers the advance to the vendor's solicitor against an executed transfer: "In the eyes of the law all these events occurred simultaneously".[18] The purchaser never acquired more than an equity of redemption[19] and "under the tripartite contractual arrangements between vendor, purchaser and mortgage lender, [the purchaser] obtained property in the form of a thing in action which was an indivisible bundle of rights and liabilities".[20]

It would follow that, even if (contrary to my view) the vendors had had equitable rights of a proprietary nature against the purchasers arising on exchange of contracts, the mortgages would have taken priority.

On the extended view of *Cann*, supported by Lord Collins and Lord Sumption in *Southern Pacific*, the making of the contract between vendor and purchaser, completion of the contract of sale, and the grant of a legal charge by the purchaser to a lender can *all* be seen as part of the same transaction, so that the lender's legal charge can be regarded as arising before any rights arising under, or as a result of, the contract of sale. For the majority of the judges in the Supreme Court in *Southern Pacific*, however, the vendor–purchaser contract is instead a separate transaction, distinct in time from completion. This is consistent with our analysis in Chapter 8, section 4, where it is pointed out that there are a number of significant ways in which the rights of the parties after completion differ from the rights at the time of entry into the contract.[21]

A further question arising from *Scott* is whether the approach of looking to the substance rather than technicalities of a transaction should be applied beyond the *Cann* context of a charge. In particular, what would be the result of applying that same substance-based approach to the sale and lease back transaction entered into by Mrs Scott and the purchasing firm? As we saw in the extract above, Lord Collins agreed with the view of Etherton LJ, in the Court of Appeal, that 'the true nature of the transaction was that of a sale and lease back'.[22] On this view, the transaction has two separate stages. At the conclusion of the first stage, the sale to the firm, Mrs Scott loses her rights to the property, and so any right she then claims must be a new right arising as a result of her dealings with the firm. The alternative view, supported in the following extract, is that the transaction between Mrs Scott and the firm was, in substance, a single transaction, in which the firm only ever acquired its legal estate subject to the right of Mrs Scott to remain in occupation.

The argument in the extract was made in response to the Court of Appeal's decision in the litigation (reported under the name *Cook v The Mortgage Business*)[23] that went to the Supreme Court in *Scott*, but the central criticism can also be leveled against the Supreme Court's decision.

---

17 [2013] 1 AC 294.   18 [2013] 1 AC 294 *per* Lord Walker and Hughes LJ at [50].
19 [2013] 1 AC 294 at [53].   20 [2013] 1 AC 294 at [54].
21 This is also the basis on which Hopkins, 'Priorities and Sale and Leaseback: A Wrong Question, Much Ado about Nothing and a Story of Tails and Dogs' [2015] Conv 245, 251–2, supports the analysis of the majority on this point.
22 [2014] UKSC 52 at [78].   23 [2012] EWCA Civ 17.

R Calnan, 'A Question of Priority: Substance or Form?' (2012) BJIBFL 225, 226–7

What the House of Lords was doing in *Cann* was discarding a formalistic approach to a priority question in favour of a substantive approach. The facts of the case involved a purchase and a mortgage, but the logic of the principle espoused by the House of Lords extends to any priority dispute where a series of individual steps can be seen as being part of a single transaction.

The utility of this principle can be tested by looking again at the facts of [*Scott*]. The reality of the situation in that case was that the vendor, as owner of the property, had effectively reserved to [herself] a tenancy for life. It was never intended that the purchaser should obtain the unencumbered legal and beneficial title to the property. It was always intended to be subject to the vendor's interest and, as a result, the mortgagee from the purchaser could obtain no better right.

One of the key factors in the decision[24] was that the transaction documents were drafted not as a sale to the purchaser subject to a condition, but as a sale with vacant possession and a lease-back to the vendor. But it is suggested that this approach is exactly what was rejected by the House of Lords in *Cann*[. . .] What is important is the substance of the transaction, not the form in which it is expressed.[25]

It is worth noting that in *Scott*, Lord Collins, expressing agreement with a point made by Lady Hale in the course of argument, insisted that: '*the court's duty is to apply the law irrespective of an unexpected impact on conveyancing practice and an adverse effect on the risks of secured lending*.'[26] This takes us back to the contrast between the 'doctrinal' and 'utility' models discussed in Chapter 1, section 5. Lord Collins' statement gives a preference to doctrine, stating that it should apply even if the practical results are unwelcome. Similarly, Lady Hale felt compelled by the doctrinal rules to find for the lender, even though expressing reluctance at reaching '*such a harsh result*'.[27] Their possibly different view of the overall merits may, however, come through in their differing views as to the question (not in the end crucial in *Scott* itself) of timing: should a charge granted to a lender be viewed as having priority to an equitable interest arising at the time of the exchange of contracts between vendor and purchaser? Once it has been accepted that the 'logic' of the traditional, *scintilla temporis* view no longer applies, and the judges ask instead if particular elements are 'in substance' or 'in practice' part of the same transaction, it becomes very difficult to apply a clear test: determining the practical substance of arrangements is really a question of judgement and impression, rather than of legal analysis. This is, indeed, a potential danger of the step taken in *Cann*: whilst the prior approach, based on the *scintilla temporis*, was certainly technical, it did, as noted by Lord Oliver in *Cann*[28] and Lady Hale in *Scott*,[29] at least have a sound logical basis.

---

[24] Calnan's article here refers to the Court of Appeal's decision, but the same point can be made about the later Supreme Court decision: see, for example, [2014] UKSC 52 at [77].

[25] [In support of his argument that the substance is important outside the context of a charge, Calnan cites *Whale v Viasystems* [2002] All ER (D) 457, where the Court of Appeal decided that a transaction involving the grant of a headlease to A, followed by A's grant of a sublease for the same period less three days, was in substance one single transaction, so that A only ever acquired a three-day reversionary interest, and at no point had an unencumbered lease. That decision was not discussed by the Supreme Court in *Scott*.]

[26] [2014] UKSC 52 at [88].   [27] [2014] UKSC 52 at [95].   [28] [1991] 1 AC 56 at [92].

[29] [2014] UKSC 52 at [115].

3.2 WHOSE RIGHT IS FIRST IN TIME? SUBROGATION

We saw in section 3.1 that, when taking into consideration the timing question, some care must be taken when considering the position of a party with a charge. If the lender is providing funds necessary for the purchase of land, the charge will take priority over any third party rights that arise when the borrower acquires his or her legal estate in the land. The principles of subrogation may also assist a party, whose money is used to discharge a secured debt, to take priority over third party rights. For example, consider a case such as *Scott* in which a first lender, providing acquisition funds to the purchasing borrower, has priority over any property rights of an occupier such as Mrs Scott. What if the purchaser then borrows money from a second lender and uses that money to pay off the mortgage loan owed to the first lender? It is very likely that the second lender will insist on the grant of a charge having priority over any property rights of an occupier such as Mrs Scott. In some cases, however, such an express arrangement will fail[30]—as may be the case, for example, if the consent of the occupier is procured by the borrower's undue influence.[31] If so, it might then seem clear that any property right acquired by the second lender must arise after that of a third party, such as Mrs Scott, who acquired a right at an earlier time: when the borrower received legal title.

The doctrine of subrogation, however, assists that second lender: as the money provided by it was used to discharge the first loan, the second lender is allowed, in effect, to step into the shoes of the first lender, and so, just as the charge held by the first lender had priority over the third party rights, so will the second lender enjoy the same priority.[32] The term 'subrogation' is applied as it captures the idea of a substitution: the second lender, broadly speaking,[33] takes the place of the first lender, and has the same priority. That outcome applies by operation of law, and so can assist the second lender even if the express arrangement, intended to give that lender priority, fails.[34]

Differing explanations have been put forward for this principle,[35] but the one first accepted by the House of Lords in *Banque Financière de la Cité v Parc (Battersea) Ltd*,[36] and confirmed more recently by the Supreme Court in *Menelaou v Bank of Cyprus*,[37] is that such subrogation operates to prevent unjust enrichment.[38] First, if the borrower were allowed to use money provided by the second lender to get the benefit of removing the charge of the first

---

[30] See, for example, *Menelaou v Bank of Cyprus UK Ltd* [2014] 1 WLR 854, where the lender relied on subrogation after it transpired that the charge it had apparently been given by B had been forged and so did not bind B.

[31] For discussion of when the undue influence exerted by the borrower can allow the third party to set aside consent given to the lender, see *Royal Bank of Scotland plc v Etridge (No 2)* [2002] 2 AC 773, examined in Chapter 27, section 3.3.

[32] See, for example, *Mortgage Express Ltd v McDonnell* [2001] EWCA Civ 887.

[33] Broadly speaking, because the second lender acquires a new, equitable right which will, therefore, not precisely match a pre-existing legal interest held by the first lender: see, for example, *Banque Financière de la Cité v Parc (Battersea) Ltd* [1999] 1 AC 221 per Lord Hoffmann at [236].

[34] Subrogation can, therefore, also assist a party if, for example, its money is used without its permission to pay off a secured debt.

[35] For an analysis based on the presumed intention of the second lender, see, for example, *Butler v Rice* [1910] 2 Ch 277. For a different analysis, based on distinct equitable principles separate from unjust enrichment, see *Bofinger v Kingsway Group Ltd* (2009) 239 CLR 269 (High Court of Australia), discussed by Leeming, 'Subrogation, Equity and Unjust Enrichment' in *Fault Lines in Equity* (eds Glister and Ridge, Oxford: Hart Publishing, 2012).

[36] [1999] 1 AC 221.

[37] [2016] AC 176, e.g. at [50]. See too *Swynson Ltd v Lowick Rose LLP* [2017] UKSC 32 at [31].

[38] See too the discussion in *Goff & Jones: The Law of Unjust Enrichment* (9th edn, ed Mitchell et al, London: Sweet & Maxwell, 2016) ch 39.

lender then, assuming that the second lender did not consent to this, the borrower would benefit unjustly at the expense of the second lender. Second, if the charge of the first lender were simply removed, a third party such as Mrs Scott would also benefit at the expense of the second lender, as her right would no longer be subject to the charge of the first lender: she would gain the windfall of better priority at the expense of the second lender, which thought that it was gaining such priority. It should, therefore, be the case that this form of subrogation does not cause any additional problems to a third party, such as Mrs Scott, whose rights were already subject to those of the first lender. Indeed, it has been recognized that, when granting remedies based on subrogation, a court may be able to tailor relief so as to do no more than is necessary to prevent the unjust enrichment of a third party such as Mrs Scott, and can thus prevent such a third party suffering a detriment as a result of the operation of subrogation.[39]

3.3 WHOSE RIGHT IS FIRST IN TIME? INDEPENDENTLY ACQUIRED RIGHTS

We saw in Chapter 5, section 4 that, where A has an estate in land, it is possible for B *independently* to acquire a property right in that land. For example, if B takes physical control of A's land, even without A's consent, B acquires a freehold of that land. But because A's property right arose before B's freehold, the basic rule tells us that A's pre-existing property right takes priority to that of B. So, A is free to remove B from the land, either by using reasonable force or by seeking a possession order from a court. Initially then, B's freehold may give him or her useful protection against X (a party who later interferes with the land), but it does not protect him or her against A.

Similarly, if A then gives C a property right in the land (for example, by transferring his or her estate to C), C is also free to remove B from the land. From a technical point of view, it may seem that B's pre-existing property right should take priority: after all, B had that right before C acquired his or her right. But the point is that C, by acquiring a property right *from* A, is essentially basing his or her claim on A's property right, which arose before B's property right. In a case in which A gives a property right to B, and then to C, this 'backdating' process cannot assist C because *each of* B and C can backdate his or her right to A's right. Where B acquires his or her right independently, however, he or she does not base the claim on A's right: in such a case, C alone can rely on backdating to take priority to B's right.

It is important to note that if either A or C delays in exercising his or her right to remove B from the land, it may then be possible for B to take priority: the lapse of time, either by itself or coupled with other factors, may give B a defence to the pre-existing property right of A, or to C's backdated property right. We will examine this point in section 3.5 below.

4 EXCEPTIONS TO THE BASIC RULE: THE *DEFENCES* QUESTION

4.1 THE POSSIBILITY OF A DEFENCE

There are exceptions to the basic rule that B's property right, where it arises before C's property right, will take priority. As we noted in Chapters 5 and 6, we have to bear in mind that,

---

[39] *Banque Financière de la Cité v Parc (Battersea) Ltd* [1999] 1 AC 221 *per* Lord Hoffmann at [236]–[237].

even if B has a pre-existing property right relating to land, it may be possible for C to have a *defence* to that right. In such a case, C can use that defence to take priority to B's property right. There is thus a very important qualification to the basic rule that we set out in section 2:

> **The basic rule:** B's pre-existing (legal or equitable) property right will take priority over C's later property right.

> **The qualification**: It may be possible for C to have a defence, which allows C to take priority over B's pre-existing property right.

There are a number of different defences that may be available to C. We will outline them in the remainder of this chapter, and consider some of them in more detail later in the book. When analysing any defence, it is useful to ask two key questions:

(a) What does C have to do to take advantage of the defence?

(b) When will B's pre-existing property right be vulnerable to that defence?

4.2 REGISTERED LAND AND THE LACK OF REGISTRATION DEFENCE

4.2.1 The basic defence

We saw in Chapter 3, section 3.2.3 that the lack of registration defence forms a very important part of the registered land system. As we saw in section 2, s 28 of the Land Registration Act 2002 (LRA 2002) ensures that, where dealings with registered land are concerned, the basic rule applies: B's pre-existing property right will take priority over a later property right of C. But as s 28(1) makes clear, that basic rule is subject to the exceptions provided by ss 29 and 30 of the same Act. Those sections ensure that, in relation to registered land, it may be possible for C to take priority over a pre-existing property right of B that is not recorded on the register. Section 29 is set out below: it governs the position in which A has a registered freehold or lease (a 'registered estate'), and then gives C a property right in the land by means of a 'registrable disposition' (e.g. by transferring his freehold or lease to C, by granting C a new lease of more than seven years' duration, or by giving C a charge). Section 30 is not set out below: it is very similar in effect, and applies only where A has a registered charge.

Land Registration Act 2002, s 29

(1) If a registrable disposition of a registered estate is made for valuable consideration, completion of the disposition by registration has the effect of postponing to the interest under the disposition any interest affecting the estate immediately before the disposition whose priority is not protected at the time of registration.

(2) For the purposes of subsection (1), the priority of an interest is protected—

    (a) in any case, if the interest—

        (i) is a registered charge or the subject of a notice in the register;

        (ii) falls within any of the paragraphs of Schedule 3, or

        (iii) appears from the register to be excepted from the effect of registration, and

(b) in the case of a disposition of a leasehold estate, if the burden of the interest is incident to the estate.

(3) Subsection 2(a)(ii) does not apply to an interest which has been the subject of a notice in the register at any time since the coming into force of this section

(4) Where the grant of a leasehold estate in land out of a registered estate does not involve a registered disposition, this section has effect as if—

(a) the grant involved such a disposition; and

(b) the disposition was registered at the time of the grant.

In Chapter 16, we will examine the lack of registration defence provided by the LRA 2002 in more detail.[40] It is worth noting here how the two key questions set out above can be answered in relation to the lack of registration defence.

When considering what C must do to take advantage of the lack of registration defence, we can see that C must meet certain requirements in order to invoke the defence. Firstly, there must be a *'registrable disposition of a registered estate'* in favour of C. In Chapters 8 and 16, the meaning of 'registrable disposition' is discussed in more detail. As noted in Chapter 5, it includes almost all situations in which A, a holder of a registered freehold or lease, might attempt to give C a *legal* property right. An important exception occurs if A gives C a lease of seven years or less: in general, that does not count as a 'registrable disposition'. But in such a case, s 29(4) comes to C's rescue: it means that C may nonetheless qualify for the lack of registration defence because, for the purposes of s 29, he will be regarded as having acquired his property right by means of a 'registrable disposition'.

Secondly, the disposition in C's favour must be made for 'valuable consideration'. This is an important qualification. It means, for example, that if C acquires his property right by means of a gift from A, or in A's will, then C *cannot* use the lack of registration defence against a pre-existing property right of B.

Thirdly, to qualify for the defence, the *'completion of the disposition by registration'* is necessary: so C must register his newly acquired property right. Again, s 29(4) means that C is viewed as having met that requirement if he acquires a legal lease that, due to its length, cannot be registered.

When applying the second question, and asking when B's pre-existing property right will be vulnerable to the defence, it is of course clear that B's right will *not* be vulnerable to the defence if it has been protected by means of a notice on the register: see further Chapter 16, section 3. In such a case, s 29 (2)(a)(i) applies: the priority of B's right is protected by means of the notice in the register. Crucially, B's right will also be immune from the lack of registration defence if it is within s 29 (2)(a)(ii): if it falls within any of the paragraphs of Schedule 3 to the 2002 Act. Such rights are known as overriding interests.

4.2.2 Overriding interests

If C does qualify for the lack of registration defence, we need to ask if B's pre-existing property right is vulnerable to that defence. The starting point, under both ss 29 and 30 of the LRA 2002, is that B's pre-existing property right, if not appearing on the register, *will* be

---

[40] For an example of the application of the defence in practice, see the discussion in Chapter 3, section 3.2.4 of *Chaudhury v Yavuz* [2013] Ch 249.

vulnerable to the lack of registration defence. There are, however, exceptions. Those pre-existing property rights of B that are *not* vulnerable to the lack of registration defence are known as overriding interests. We noted the existence of such rights in Chapter 3, section 3.2.2 when considering s 29 of the Land Registration Act 2002 and will examine them in detail in Chapter 16, section 5.

It is worth noting here how the priority triangle is resolved in a case where B's property right is not on the register, but nonetheless counts as an overriding interest.

1. The basic rule is that B's pre-existing property right takes priority over the later property right of C.

2. C then attempts to displace that basic rule by using the lack of registration defence.

3. That attempt fails: because B's right counts as an overriding interest, it is immune from the lack of registration defence. The basic rule therefore applies, and B's pre-existing property right takes priority over C's later property right.

This analysis applied in *Williams & Glyn's Bank v Boland*,[41] the case we discussed at the start of section 2 of this chapter. The bank in that case was unable to use the lack of registration defence against Mrs Boland's pre-existing equitable interest, as Mrs Boland's equitable interest counted as an overriding interest. That was because of the fact that Mrs Boland was in actual occupation of the land when the bank acquired its charge. The general rule, now contained in para 2 of Sch 3 of the 2002 Act,[42] is that the property right of a party in actual occupation of the registered land at the relevant time is an overriding interest. It is important to remember, however, that the actual occupation of Mrs Boland was important only because she had a pre-existing *property right*. For example, in *National Provincial Bank v Ainsworth* (see Chapter 1, section 5 and Chapter 6, section 5.4), Mrs Ainsworth lived in the home throughout—but her actual occupation was irrelevant, because she had no pre-existing property right that she could assert against the bank. So, without the support of a pre-existing property right, actual occupation is irrelevant.

Similarly, as we will see in the next extract, there may also be cases in which C takes priority even though B: (i) has a pre-existing property right; *and* (ii) is in actual occupation of the land at the relevant time. This is because B's actual occupation simply means that his or her pre-existing property right is not vulnerable to the lack of registration defence; B's actual occupation does not prevent C from taking priority by using a *different* defence to B's property right. We will consider such different defences in the remainder of section 4 of this chapter. In relation to each defence, we will ask the same two questions: (a) what does C have to do to take advantage of the defence; and (b) when will B's pre-existing property right be vulnerable to that defence?

4.3 OVERREACHING

Overreaching is a general defence that can be used by C whenever A has a *power* to give C a right free from B's pre-existing property right.[43] It is particularly important where

---

[41] [1981] 1 AC 487.

[42] In *Boland* itself, the Land Registration Act 1925 applied, and the relevant provision was s 70(1)(g).

[43] See Harpum, 'Overreaching, Trustees' Powers and the Reform of the 1925 Legislation' [1990] CLJ 277.

trusts are concerned: it may be that, if A holds on trust for B, the terms of the trust give A a power to give C a right free from B's pre-existing equitable interest. And it is particularly important where trusts of land are concerned, because the trustee or trustees will then have a default *statutory* power to give C a right free from B's pre-existing equitable interest.

For example, in *City of London Building Society v Flegg*,[44] Mr and Mrs Flegg had contributed to the purchase price of a house, legal title to which was in the names of their daughter and her husband (Mr and Mrs Maxwell Brown). The Maxwell-Browns, therefore, held their legal freehold on trust for themselves and for Mr and Mrs Flegg, and all four lived in the home together. The Maxwell-Browns later granted a legal charge over the land to the building society, who wished to enforce that charge by removing Mr and Mrs Flegg and selling the land. As in *Williams & Glyn's Bank v Boland*,[45] Mr and Mrs Flegg's right arose before that of the lender; and, as in *Boland*, their pre-existing equitable interests counted as overriding interests, as they were coupled with actual occupation of the land. Nonetheless, the building society in *Flegg* was able to take priority, as it had a defence to Mr and Mrs Flegg's right: the overreaching defence.

We can analyse a case such as *Flegg* by considering the two key questions for defences (see section 4.1). First, C (the building society) was able to take advantage of the defence as: (i) C had given value for its right, by making the mortgage loan; and (ii) the money C had paid by way of the mortgage loan was paid to two trustees: the Maxwell-Browns. Second, the rights of B (the Fleggs) were vulnerable to the defence, as they were rights arising under a trust, and the trustees had a power to create a charge over the land in favour of C.

The requirements and operation of the overreaching defence will be examined in detail in Chapter 17, where we will focus on its application in a case, such as *Flegg*, where B has a beneficial interest in a shared home. We will see there that the decision in *Flegg* provoked a good deal of controversy. Here, our concern is with what *Flegg* can tell us about how the courts deal with the priority triangle. The first point concerns the role of actual occupation. It is wrong to think that if B has a pre-existing property right and is in actual occupation of registered land, B will *always* take priority over C. B's actual occupation may prevent C from using the lack of registration defence against B, but it does *not* prevent C from relying on a different defence, such as overreaching.

The second point demonstrated by *Flegg* is that the availability of a defence may turn on very fine, and seemingly arbitrary, distinctions. In *Flegg*, overreaching was available as C had paid the loan money to *two* trustees.[46] This is why, in *Williams & Glyn's Bank v Boland*, the bank was *not* able to rely on the statutory overreaching defence: in that case, there was only one trustee (Mr Boland) and so the bank did not meet the requirement, imposed by the LPA 1925, that the loan money be paid to at least two trustees. It may seem hard to justify the differing results; but note that it is even more difficult to work out from first principles the best way to balance the competing needs of a prior user of the land, such as B, and a party who later acquires rights in the land, such as C.

---

[44] [1988] AC 54, HL.   [45] [1981] AC 487, HL: see section 2 above.

[46] Section 2(1)(ii) limits overreaching in a case such as *Flegg* to situations in which 'the statutory requirements respecting the payment of capital money arising under the settlement are complied with'. Section 27 of the Law of Property Act 1925 then imposes such a requirement: *if* C pays money in return for its property right, that money must be paid to at least two trustees or to a trust corporation (see Chapter 17, section 2.3).

4.4 DEFENCES BASED ON B'S CONSENT

4.4.1 Where B expressly consents to C taking priority

Imagine a case in which A holds a freehold on trust for both A and B, who share occupation of the home. That freehold was acquired without a mortgage loan. A and B then decide to raise some money by taking out a mortgage loan. A approaches C Bank and informs C Bank that B has a pre-existing equitable property right. If C Bank deals with A alone, it can acquire a charge over the land, because A is a sole registered proprietor. But C Bank is aware that, B's beneficial interest, coupled with B's actual occupation of the land, gives B an overriding interest (see section 4.2.2). As a result, C Bank requires B to give his consent to C Bank's later charge taking priority over B's right. Clearly, if B gives that consent, C Bank's later charge will take priority: B's consent gives C Bank a defence to B's pre-existing equitable property right.

Where B expressly consents to C taking priority, each of the two key questions for defences (see section 4.1) can be easily answered. Firstly, C can take advantage of the defence simply because of the fact of B's consent. Secondly, where such consent is given, C can take priority over *any* pre-existing property right of B.

Problems can, however, arise if B later claims that his consent was not freely given: for example, it may be that A pressured B into giving the consent, or that A lied to B about the terms of the loan. In that case, two questions arise: firstly, was there really any flaw in B's consent—for example, did A use undue influence or make a misrepresentation in order to convince B to give that consent? Secondly, if so, should that flaw in B's consent affect C Bank: after all, if it was A who used the undue influence or made the misrepresentation, why should C Bank lose out?

We will examine the special principles developed to deal with this difficult question in Chapter 27, section 3.3. For the moment, we simply need to note that, *in some circumstances*, a flaw in B's consent, even if procured by A, *can* prevent C Bank from taking priority.

4.4.2 Where B impliedly consents to C taking priority

We saw above that, in *Abbey National v Cann*, Daisy Cann did not give her express consent to the Abbey National taking priority. The Abbey National did not have the chance to ask for such consent, because it was unaware that Daisy had any pre-existing property right: when George Cann applied for the mortgage loan, he lied to the building society and said that he did not plan to share occupation of the home. Daisy did, however, know that a loan would be necessary to provide the extra £4,000 that she and George needed to buy that land. The Court of Appeal therefore decided that Daisy had *impliedly* consented to a mortgage lender, such as the Abbey National, taking priority. We have seen that the House of Lords held that, in any case, there was no need for such consent: the Abbey National did not need a defence to Daisy's equitable property right, because its charge was regarded as arising *before* Daisy acquired that right (see section 3.1.2).

Nonetheless, in the following extracts from the House of Lords' decision, Lord Oliver (with whom Lords Bridge, Ackner, and Griffiths agreed)[47] supported the Court of Appeal's reasoning.

---

[47] Lord Jauncey's reasoning is also consistent with that of Lord Oliver, but at 102–3, Lord Jauncey noted that, in finding that the Abbey National's charge arose before Daisy Cann's equitable property right, '*it is unnecessary to consider whether or not Mrs Cann was aware that George Cann would require to borrow money in order to finance the purchase of [the new home]*'.

Abbey National Building Society v Cann
[1991] 1 AC 56, HL

Facts: See section 3.1.2.

Lord Oliver

At 94

The view that I have formed renders it strictly unnecessary to consider the ground upon which Mrs. Cann's claim failed in the Court of Appeal. What was said was that, despite her initial evidence (in her affidavit) that she did not know of her son's intention to raise any of the money required for the purchase on mortgage, nevertheless her oral evidence before the judge disclosed that she was well aware that there was a shortfall which would have to be met from somewhere. Her own account of the matter was that his reason for selling was that he was in financial difficulties, so that she must have known that he was not going to be able to meet it out of his own resources. Dillon L.J. (with whom, on this point, the other two members of the court agreed) inferred that "she left it to George Cann to raise the balance"[48] from which he further inferred that George Cann had authority to raise that sum from the society. There was no finding to this effect by the judge, but I think, for my part, that it is a necessary conclusion once it is accepted, as it has to be, that she knew that there was a shortfall of some £4,000 apart from conveyancing costs, that George Cann was going to raise it, and that he was in financial difficulties. It is said that there was no evidence that he was going to raise it on the security of this property. There might, for instance, be other property available to him. He might obtain an unsecured loan. In the circumstances of his known lack of resources, however, this is fanciful and in my judgment the court was entitled to draw the inference that it did draw. If that is right, it follows that George Cann was permitted by her to raise money on the security of the property without any limitation on his authority being communicated to the society. She is not, therefore, in a position to complain, as against the lender, that too much was raised and even if, contrary to the view which I have formed, she had been able to establish an interest in the property which would otherwise prevail against the society, the circumstances to which I have alluded would preclude her from relying upon it as prevailing over the society's interest for the reasons given in the judgment of Dillon L.J. in the Court of Appeal. For all these reasons, I would accordingly dismiss the appeal.

The idea that B can be taken to have *impliedly* consented to giving priority to C did not originate in *Cann*,[49] and it has been applied since the House of Lords' decision in that case.[50] Nonetheless, it is somewhat controversial.[51] Firstly, there is a practical question: in *Cann* itself, was it really true to say that Daisy 'must have known' that George would take out a mortgage? After all, it may have been possible to raise the £4,000 by other means.[52]

---

[48] [1989] 2 FLR 265, [276].

[49] It was also applied in *Bristol & West BS v Henning* [1985] 1 WLR 778 and *Paddington BC v Mendelsohn* (1985) 50 P & CR 244.

[50] See *Equity & Law Home Loans Ltd v Prestidge* [1992] 1 WLR 137.

[51] See Smith (1990) 109 LQR 545.

[52] This point is noted by Sawyer, 'A World Safe for Mortgagees? Registering a Scintilla of Doubt' in *Modern Studies in Propety Law: Vol 1* (ed Cooke, 2001, p 209).

Secondly, even if Daisy did know that a mortgage would be necessary, there is a conceptual problem. There is a general doctrine, often referred to as 'promissory estoppel', which can be used to give C a defence against a right of B.[53] For that defence to operate, however, it is usually necessary:

(i) for B to make some form of promise to C (e.g. a promise not to enforce his right against C); and

(ii) for C to rely on that promise.

The difficulty in a case such as *Cann* is that Daisy Cann did not make any promise to the Abbey National; indeed, the cause of the problem was that the Abbey National was entirely unaware of her.[54] Nonetheless, in *Thompson v Foy*, Lewison J formulated the principle in such a way that it does *not* require a third party such as the Abbey National to know of the existence of the party, such as Daisy Cann, who has the pre-existing property right:

Thompson v Foy
[2009] EWHC 1076 (Ch)

Lewison J

At [142]

This [i.e. the view of Lord Oliver in *Cann*, set out in the extract above], as it seems to me is a much broader principle, akin to an estoppel. In the course of his reasoning in the Court of Appeal [in *Cann*] (which Lord Oliver approved) Dillon LJ applied the principle in *Brocklesby v Temperance Permanent Building Society*[55] which was referred to and applied by Farwell J in *Rimmer v Webster*[56] [. . .] Shortly stated [by Farwell J][57] the principle is that when:

> 'the owner is found to have given the vendor or borrower the means of representing himself as the beneficial owner, the case forms one of actual authority apparently equivalent to absolute ownership, and involving the right to deal with the property as owner, and any limitations on this generality must be proved to have been brought to the knowledge of the purchaser or mortgagee.'

It is important to work out if there is such a '*broader principle*' in the law that C may be able to use as a defence and, if so, to establish the limits of that principle. To do so, we need to look at two cases: firstly, the *Brocklesby* case referred to by Lewison J; and secondly, the more recent decision of the Court of Appeal in *Wishart v Credit and Mercantile plc*.

In *Brocklesby v Temperance Building Society*,[58] a father held title to certain land, and gave his son express authority to borrow £2,250 on behalf of the father and to grant charges over that land to secure repayment of the loans. The son, however, granted charges over the land to secure borrowings from the building society of £3,600. The father argued that the charges should be removed if he paid the building society £2,250: the sum he had expressly authorized the son to borrow on his behalf. The House of Lords rejected that argument: whilst the

---

[53] See *Central London Property Trust Ltd v High Trees House* [1947] KB 130.

[54] For discussion of this point, see, for example, McFarlane, *The Structure of Property Law* (Oxford: Hart Publishing, 2009) p 823.

[55] [1895] AC 173.   [56] [1902] 2 Ch 163.   [57] [1902] 2 Ch 163, 173.   [58] [1895] AC 173.

son's express, or actual, authority was limited to borrowing £2,250, the building society did not know about that limit, and there was nothing to suggest to it that the son's authority was limited in that way. By authorizing the son to borrow money on his behalf, and to grant charges over the land, the father had held out the son as having a general authority to borrow, and so the father (and not the building society) had to take the risk of the son going beyond the limits imposed by the father.

On one view, the *Brocklesby* case is simply an application of a general rule of the law of agency: the principle of ostensible, or apparent, authority. The law of agency allows acts of an agent to have a binding legal effect on a principal: this of course provides a very useful facility to principals, as it means they do not always have to act personally when entering transactions. So, for example, where B has an agent who has express authority from B to give consent to C's taking priority over B's right, consent given by that agent can be regarded by the law as consent given by B, thus allowing C to invoke the consent defence outlined in section 4.4.1. However, the use of agents create a risk for C, as it may be difficult for C to know the precise limit on the express authority given to B's agent by B. That risk is reduced by the doctrine of ostensible, or apparent, authority: even if the agent does not have express authority from B to act in a particular way, if B can be said to have 'held out' the agent as having such authority, so that it would be reasonable for a third party to believe that the agent *does* have such express authority, the agent's act can give the third party a right against B, and thus protect C.

If the *Brocklesby* case is seen as turning on the idea of apparent authority, then it does not seem to apply the same principle as applied in *Cann*. For example, it is not clear that George Cann, the son, could be said to be the agent of his mother, Daisy. Certainly, in contrast to the *Brocklesby* case, Daisy did not expressly authorize George to act on her behalf in borrowing money and granting a charge over the land. On this view, then, it is possible to disagree with Lewison J's analysis in *Thompson v Foy* (set out earlier in this section) that the *Brocklesby* case and the idea of implied consent in *Cann* can be combined into a broader principle. Nonetheless, support for Lewison J's analysis is provided by the approach of the Court of Appeal in the following case.

Wishart v Credit and Mercantile plc (also reported as *Credit and Mercantile plc v Kaymuu Ltd*)
[2015] EWCA Civ 655, [2015] 2 P & CR 15

Facts: Mr Wishart was a close friend and business associate of Mr Muduroglu (referred to in the judgment as Sami). Their business dealings were complex, and it was arranged between them that a company, Kaymuu Ltd, wholly owned and controlled by Sami, would use money to which Mr Wishart was entitled to acquire registered title to certain land. As a result, that registered freehold was held by the company on trust for Mr Wishart, who thus had an equitable interest in the land. Mr Wishart moved in to Dalhanna, the house on the land, very soon after it was purchased. A month or so later, acting without the knowledge or permission of Mr Wishart, Kaymuu borrowed a large sum of money from Credit and Mercantile (C&M), and granted it a charge over the land. When the loan was not repaid, C&M sought possession of the land. Mr Wishart agreed to leave Dalhanna, and the land was sold. C&M claimed that it was entitled to use the proceeds of sale to meet the debt owed to it by Kaymuu; Mr Wishart instead claimed that he was entitled to the proceeds of sale, as his pre-existing equitable interest in the land took priority to the charge that Kaymuu had granted to C&M.

The Court of Appeal, however, found in favour of C&M, holding that it had priority over Mr Wishart's pre-existing equitable interest. In justifying that decision, Sales LJ made reference both to the implied consent principle discussed in *Cann* and also to the *Brocklesby* case. Following the analysis of Lewison J in *Thompson v Foy* (see the extract set out earlier in this section), Sales LJ stated that those cases provide evidence for a wider rule, which can also apply where a beneficiary of a trust (such as Mr Wishart) allows a trustee (such as Kaymuu) freedom in practice to deal with the trust property.

Sales LJ

At [52]–[58]

The *Brocklesby* principle is not based on actual authority given to the agent, but rather on a combination of factors: actual authority given by the owner of an asset to a person authorised to deal with it in some way on his behalf; where the owner has furnished the agent with the means of holding himself out to a purchaser or lender as the owner of the asset or as having full authority of the owner to deal with it; together with an omission by the owner to bring to the attention of a person dealing with the agent any limitation that exists as to the extent of the actual authority of the agent. This combination of factors creates a situation in which it is fair, as between the owner of the asset and the innocent purchaser or lender, that the owner should bear the risk of fraud on the part of the agent whom he has set in motion and provided (albeit unwittingly) with the means of perpetrating the fraud. The same principle applies where the dishonest vendor or mortgagor of the asset, who by the sale or mortgage raises money from an innocent third party, has been vested with legal title as a trustee: *Rimmer v Webster*.[59]

[. . .]

In *Abbey National v Cann* [. . .] [the Court of Appeal] held that even if Mrs Cann had been in occupation of the house at the relevant time, her interest did not override the security rights of the building society, which could be enforced to the full extent of the borrowing by George to which the mortgage related.[60] The basis for this ruling was the application of the *Brocklesby* principle.[61] In the House of Lords, Mrs Cann's appeal was dismissed on the grounds that she could not show that she was in actual occupation of the house at the relevant time. However, in the leading speech, Lord Oliver (with whom the other members of the Appellate Committee agreed) also approved, *obiter*, the reasoning of the Court of Appeal.[62]

In my view, this leaves this court in the position that it is formally bound by the reasoning in *Cann* in the Court of Appeal, which forms the *ratio decidendi* at this level and was not disapproved when the case went to the House of Lords; but in any event, it is reasoning expressly endorsed by the House of Lords and should be followed in an equivalent case. The *Brocklesby* principle has been recognised in a number of cases since *Cann: Skipton Building Society v Clayton*,[63] *Thompson v Foy*,[64] and *Bank of Scotland v Hussain*.[65] [. . .]

In our case, as the judge found, Mr Wishart left the acquisition of Dalhanna completely in the hands of Sami. Mr Wishart gave Sami authority to make whatever arrangement he saw fit

---

[59] [1902] 2 Ch 163, 173.   [60] (1989) 57 P & CR 381.
[61] (1989) 57 P & CR 381 at 392, 394, and 395 *per* Dillon LJ, Ralph Gibson LJ, and Woolf LJ respectively.
[62] [1991] 1 AC 56, 94B–G.   [63] (1993) 66 P & CR 16, CA.   [64] [2009] EWHC 1076 (Ch).
[65] [2010] EWHC 2812 (Ch).

to acquire Dalhanna, so long as the net result was that Mr Wishart would have the beneficial ownership of it free of any mortgage. As the judge said, Mr Wishart gave Sami 'free rein' to make the arrangements for the acquisition. Clearly, Sami acted outside the limits of his authority by arranging for the grant of a mortgage over Dalhanna to C&M, but C&M was not on notice of any such restriction on his authority. Mr Wishart exercised no supervisory function whatever in relation to what Sami might do to effect the transaction to acquire Dalhanna [. . .] In this way, in practical terms, Mr Wishart furnished Sami with the means to hold himself out as the true beneficial purchaser of Dalhanna, and hence as the legal and beneficial owner of the property for the purposes of borrowing money from C&M against the mortgage in its favour [. . .]

[. . .] I consider that on the facts as found by the judge, he was right to hold that Mr Wishart was precluded by operation of the *Brocklesby* principle from maintaining that he had a beneficial interest in relation to Dalhanna with potential to have priority over the security interest of C&M, and hence was right to hold that Mr Wishart could not claim to have an overriding interest as against C&M.

As noted by Sales LJ, the result reached by the Court of Appeal in the *Wishart* case can be seen as flowing from the decision in *Brocklesby*. That is true even if we take a limited view of the *Brocklesby* principle, and regard it simply as an application of the general agency principle of apparent authority. The point is that Mr Wishart and Sami, as well as being friends, took part in commercial ventures together, and it is reasonable on the facts to see Mr Wishart as having authorized Sami to act as his agent when using proceeds from a business venture to purchase the land.[66] As is the case with Lewison J's view in *Thompson v Foy*, the controversial aspect of the judgment in *Wishart* is the suggestion that a third party may be able to invoke such a defence in a standard family home case, such as *Abbey National v Cann*.

As Dixon has noted,[67] this raises the possibility that we may even have to re-consider the result in a seminal case such as *Williams & Glyn's Bank v Boland*.[68] In that case, of course, Mrs Boland (B) had a beneficial interest in land registered in the sole name of her husband, who later gave the bank (C) a charge over the land. As the charge was not used to fund the acquisition of the land, and as B was in actual occupation when the charge was granted, C was bound by B's pre-existing equitable interest. There was no form of agency relationship between B and her husband, but on the broader *Brocklesby* principle identified in *Thompson v Foy* and *Wishart*, C might argue that B, as beneficiary under the trust, did nothing to interfere with the impression that her husband, as sole legal owner of the land, was free to deal with it as he wished. As Dixon has argued,[69] that conclusion would be very surprising: the usual view is that, where B has a property right in A's land and is in actual occupation of the land, it is C who needs to make inquiries to see if B has a right; B's actual occupation alone

---

[66] Although there is still a possible objection: *Brocklesby* was of course decided before the LRA 2002 came into force, whereas *Wishart* was not, and Televantos, 'Trusteeship, Ostensible Authority, and Land Registration: The Category Error in *Wishart*' [2016] Conv 181 at 190–1, suggests that s 29 of the LRA 2002 may prevent C from relying on the apparent authority of A, even in a case of genuine agency, as *'a key purpose of the LRA 2002 is to make the issue of what a purchaser knew or ought to have known irrelevant in relation to priority disputes concerning registered land'*.

[67] [2015] Conv 285.   [68] [1981] AC 487.

[69] [2015] Conv 285. See too Televantos [2016] Conv 181.

should provide C with enough warning that there may be some limit on A's powers to deal with the land.

It is understandable that, in *Thompson v Foy* and in *Wishart*, the courts have tried to find a principled explanation for the position in *Cann* that B's implied consent can give C a defence to B's pre-existing property right, and so give C priority. It is also correct to say that there are analogies between such a defence and ideas such as estoppel or apparent authority. It may be dangerous, however, to go beyond mere analogies and say that in fact the *same* principle is being applied in *Cann* as in such cases. For example, as Televantos has argued,[70] the law usually distinguishes carefully between an agency relationship on one hand, and a trust relationship on the other. Certainly, the mere fact that A holds property on trust for B does not mean that A is regarded as B's agent and so can, for example, enter contracts on B's behalf. As far as the implied consent defence is concerned, then, and notwithstanding the suggestion in *Thompson v Foy* and *Wishart*, it may still be best to distinguish cases such as *Brocklesby* and *Wishart* where there is a genuine agency relationship between A and B from cases, such as *Boland*, where A simply holds property on trust for B. That may still leave us with the puzzle of how best to explain the notion of implied consent applied in *Cann*,[71] but that is perhaps a price worth paying to preserve the priority of a party such as Mrs Boland, who has a pre-existing beneficial interest in land and is in actual occupation of that land when a charge is granted to C.

4.5 DEFENCES BASED ON THE LAPSE OF TIME

4.5.1 Unregistered land

Just as it is possible for B to acquire a title to an object simply by taking possession of it,[72] so can B acquire a legal property right (a freehold) simply by taking physical control of a piece of land.[73] That is the case even if B acts with full knowledge that A has a pre-existing property right in the same land. For example, if A has a freehold of a holiday home, and B moves into that home whilst A is away and starts to use the house as his own, B acquires his own freehold. But because A's freehold arose before B's freehold, the basic rule tells us that A's pre-existing property right takes priority to that of B. So, A is free to remove B from the land, either by using reasonable force or by seeking a possession order from a court. Initially, then, B's freehold may give him useful protection against X (a party who later tries to move into the home), but it does not protect him against A.

If B continues to act as an owner of the home over a long period, however, the lapse of time can give B a defence to A's pre-existing property right. Where unregistered land is concerned, the basic rules are set out by ss 15(1) and 17 of the Limitation Act 1980.

---

[70] [2016] Conv 181, 193–6.

[71] The point seems to be that B's knowledge that a mortgage is necessary to fund the acquisition of the land means that B is regarded as having consented to C's charge taking priority; although this does leave open the question of why, in a case such as *Cann*, the charge should take priority in relation to the whole sum borrowed, if B knew that only a smaller sum was needed. The suggestion of Televantos ([2016] Conv 181, 190) is that as B can be said to have given implied actual consent to A's creating a charge with priority over B's right, A can also be said to have apparent authority to raise any sum by way of mortgage.

[72] See Chapter 2, section 2.2.2.

[73] See e.g. *Asher v Whitlock* [1865] 1 QB 1; Law Com CP No 227 (2016) [17.63].

Limitation Act 1980, ss 15(1) and 17

15 Time limit for actions to recover land

(1) No action shall be brought by any person to recover any land after the expiration of twelve years from the date on which the right of action accrued to him or, if it first accrued to some person through whom he claims, to that person [. . .]

17 Extinction of title to land after expiration of time limit

Subject to section 18 of this Act, at the expiration of the period prescribed by this Act for any person to recover land (including a redemption action) the title of that person to the land shall be extinguished.

Section 15(1) allows the lapse of time (twelve years) to give B a defence against A's pre-existing property right. Section 17 goes further: it means that, once twelve years has elapsed, A loses that pre-existing right. This means that not only is B protected from A's previous right, but also that any later users of the land are safe from a claim by A. As a result, B's acquisition of a freehold (which occurs as soon as B takes physical control of the land), coupled with the lapse of time, means that B may be able to acquire, in practice, the best right to the land. In such a case, B's protection is said to depend on the doctrine of *adverse possession*.

We examined the detail of that doctrine in Chapter 9; as far as the priority triangle is concerned, two points are worth noting here. Firstly—in relation to unregistered land, at least—the lapse of time can operate to give a later property right priority to an earlier property right, even if the holder of the later property right has deliberately acted inconsistently with that earlier right.

Secondly, the defence provided by s 15(1) of the Limitation Act 1980 has an unusual effect: it not only protects an adverse possessor from a pre-existing property right; it also *extinguishes* that pre-existing right.[74]

4.5.2 Registered land

Land Registration Act 2002, s 96

(1) No period of limitation under section 15 of the Limitation Act 1980 (time limits in relation to recovery of land) shall run against any person, other than a chargee, in relation to an estate in land or rentcharge the title to which is registered.

(2) [. . .]

(3) Accordingly, section 17 of that Act (extinction of title on expiry of time limit) does not operate to extinguish the title of any person where, by virtue of this section, a period of limitation does not run against him.

---

[74] The limitation defence has the same effect in relation to goods: if B tortiously interferes with A's goods, and A fails to act before the limitation period expires, then s 3(2) of the Limitation Act 1980 operates to extinguish A's pre-existing property right in the goods. In contrast to the position in relation to land, however, the limitation period does not begin to run in favour of B if B dishonestly takes possession: see s 4 of the 1980 Act.

Section 96 of the LRA 2002 thus makes clear that, if A has a registered freehold or lease, the lapse of time, by itself, can *never* give B a defence against A's pre-existing property right. Instead, the 2002 Act provides a new set of rules to deal with cases in which B takes physical control of land covered by a freehold or lease registered in A's name.

We examined the detail of those rules in Chapter 9. One important point to note here is that the 2002 Act enacted a deliberate policy of giving greater protection to A where he or she has a registered freehold or lease. Indeed, if A has a freehold or lease of unregistered land and has no current plans to sell that land, the extra protection given against an adverse possessor provides perhaps the best incentive for A to register his or her property right.

4.6 DEFENCES AND THE DISTINCTION BETWEEN LEGAL AND EQUITABLE PROPERTY RIGHTS

If B has a pre-existing *legal* property right, it is possible for C's later property right to take priority: C may have a defence to B's legal property right. For example, B's express consent can clearly give C such a defence, and we have seen that—in unregistered land, at least—the lapse of time can also give a party a defence against a legal freehold or lease. It is, however, far easier for C to have a defence against a pre-existing *equitable* property right. It is therefore crucial, when considering the defences question, to ask if B's pre-existing property right is legal or equitable: as noted in Chapter 6, section 7, this is one of the main reasons why it is so important to distinguish between legal and equitable property rights.

Similarly, when considering the defences question, it is also very important to know if *C's* property right is legal or equitable. For example, in relation to registered land, if C has only an equitable property right, then it is not possible for C to take advantage of the lack of registration defence set out in ss 29 and 30 of the LRA 2002; instead, the basic rule in s 28 of that Act will apply.[75] Equally, if C acquires only an equitable property right, C will not be able to rely on the statutory overreaching defence discussed in section 3.3 above.[76]

The differences between legal and equitable property rights are particularly clear when we look at the lack of registration defence. Under the LRA 2002, it is almost impossible for C to use the lack of registration defence against a pre-existing *legal* property right. This is for two reasons: firstly, in order to acquire such a legal property right in the first place, B will often need to register it, as we saw in Chapter 8, section 5; in such a case, the lack of registration defence is irrelevant. Secondly, if the LRA 2002 does allow B to acquire a legal property right without registering it, that right will almost always count as an overriding interest; as a result, it will be immune to the lack of registration defence (see section 3.2.2). We will examine the detail of overriding interests in Chapter 16, section 4, and will see there, for example, that, when there is a disposition of registered land, a legal lease[77] or a legal easement[78] may be an overriding interest in its own right, whereas an equitable lease or equitable easement can be overriding *only* if B happens to be in actual occupation of the land at the relevant time.

---

[75] See *Halifax plc v Curry Popeck (a firm)* [2008] EWHC 1692 (Ch), [25], *per* Norris J.

[76] Under s 2(1) of the Law of Property Act 1925, overreaching can occur only if there is a 'conveyance to a purchaser of a legal estate in land'.

[77] LRA 2002, Sch 3, para 1.   [78] LRA 2002, Sch 3, para 3.

5 CONCLUSION

Many disputes about the use of land have the same basic form: (i) B acquires a right to make some use of land from A, who has an estate in that land; (ii) C then acquires a similar right from A; and (iii) B and C want to use that land in mutually inconsistent ways. In such a case, the first question to ask is whether B acquired a legal or equitable property right: as we saw in Chapters 5 and 6, we can break that question down into the *content* and *acquisition* questions. It may be the case that C also acquired a legal or equitable property right from A. If so, there is a *priority triangle*: we need to ask whether B or C's property right is to take priority.

The basic rule is clear: B's property right will take priority because it is *first in time*—that is, it arose before C's property right. As we saw in section 3 above, however, there are some cases in which we need to take care in working out the order in which the property rights arose. And, even if it is clear that B's property right arose before C's property right, it may still be possible for C to take priority: to do so, C needs to show he has a *defence* to B's pre-existing right. In section 4 above, we saw a number of examples of such a defence. In later chapters, we will return to examine some of those defences in more detail: for example, Chapter 16 will focus on the lack of registration defence in registered land, and Chapter 17 will explore overreaching. In relation to each defence, it is helpful to ask two questions:

(a) What does C have to do to take advantage of the defence?

(b) When will B's pre-existing property right be vulnerable to that defence?

QUESTIONS

1. In *National Provincial Bank v Ainsworth*, Mrs Ainsworth acquired her 'deserted wife's equity' before National Provincial Bank acquired its charge. So why was her claim to remain in occupation of the land unsuccessful?

2. Do you agree with the approach to the *scintilla temporis* question adopted by the House of Lords in *Abbey National v Cann*? Should that approach be limited to cases in which a mortgage loan is necessary in order to enable the borrower to buy the land in question? Should the Supreme Court in *Scott v Southern Pacific Mortgages* have been willing to regard Mrs Scott's interest as, in substance, arising prior to that of the purchasing firm, and, therefore, prior to that of the lender?

3. What is an 'overriding interest'? Can you explain why Mrs Boland had such a right in *Williams and Glyn's Bank v Boland*, but Mrs Ainsworth did not in *National Provincial Bank v Ainsworth*?

4. In a case such as *Abbey National Building Society v Cann*, does it make sense to say that Mrs Cann impliedly consented to the building society taking priority?

5. What is the '*Brocklesby* principle'? Should it have been applied to give priority to the bank in *Williams and Glyn's Bank v Boland*?

For guidance on how to answer these questions visit the online resources at www.oup.com/uk/mcfarlane4e/.

FURTHER READING

Calnan, 'A Question of Priority: Substance or Form' (2012) BJIBFL 225

Dixon, 'The *Boland* Requiem' [2015] Conv 284

Hopkins, 'Priorities and Sale and Leaseback: A Wrong Question, Much Ado about Nothing and a Story of Tails and Dogs' [2015] Conv 245

Law Commission Report No 271, *Land Registration for the 21st Century* (2001, Parts I, II, and V)

McFarlane, *The Structure of Property Law* (Oxford: Hart Publishing, 2008, Parts B5, E1.3, E2.3, and G4.4)

Smith, 'Mortgagees and Trust Beneficiaries' (1990) 109 LQR 545

Televantos, 'Trusteeship, Ostensible Authority, and Land Registration: The Category Error in *Wishart*' [2016] Conv 181

16

PRIORITIES IN REGISTERED LAND

CENTRAL ISSUES

1. Where A transfers land to C, priority questions arise as to whether B, who has a pre-existing property right, can enforce that right against C. Property rights are capable of binding all third parties who acquire a right from A, therefore this issue is conceptualized as the *defences* question: does C have a defence against the enforcement of B's pre-existing property right?

2. Priority rules differ between unregistered and registered land. The overreaching mechanism (discussed in Chapter 17) is common to both systems. This chapter considers the priority rules of registered land. As the vast majority of titles to land are now registered, the rules relating to unregistered land are discussed in a separate chapter, available online.

3. The Land Registration Act 2002 provides a distinct set of priority rules for one category of transaction: a registrable disposition of a registered estate for valuable consideration. This category incorporates the most common dealings with land, including an ordinary sale or mortgage.

4. In this category of transactions, C is provided with a defence (referred to here as the 'lack of registration' defence) to B's pre-existing interest where: the disposition complies with any limitations on A's owner's powers that have been entered on the register; B's interest is not entered on the register; and B's interest is not within a category of overriding interests. These are interests that do not appear on the register, but which are, notwithstanding, capable of binding C.

5. The category of overriding interests includes property rights held by persons in actual occupation of the land at the time of the disposition. The meaning of 'occupation' for this purpose has been the subject of debate and the 2002 Act introduced a reasonable inspection qualification to the operation of this category.

6. Where the disposition to C involves fraud or other wrongdoing (but not such as to invalidate the transaction), the policy of the 2002 Act is to enable C still to invoke a defence against B's property right, but to rely on the general law to create new rights that are enforceable against C (new direct rights). This may involve C being held personally liable to B or the creation of new property rights in B's favour.

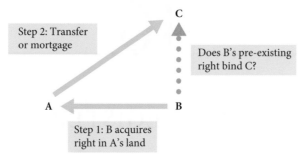

Figure 16.1 The priority triangle

1 INTRODUCTION

In this chapter, we are concerned with how questions of priorities are answered in registered land. The priority triangle was introduced in Chapter 15. For example, where A transfers land to C, or creates a mortgage in favour of C, the priority question asks whether C is bound by a property right held by a third party, B. This is illustrated in Figure 16.1.

It is important to emphasize that we are concerned here only with a pre-existing *property right* of B. Such a right is *prima facie* binding against all third parties who later acquire a right from A, and so the key question, as we saw in Chapter 15, is the *defences* question: does C have a defence against the enforcement of B's pre-existing property right? We considered some examples of possible defences in Chapter 15: as far as priorities in registered land are concerned, the key defence can be called the 'lack of registration' defence.

2 AN OVERVIEW: THE LACK OF REGISTRATION DEFENCE

The starting point in understanding the approach of registered land to priorities is s 28 of the Land Registration Act 2002 (LRA 2002).

Land Registration Act 2002, s 28

(1) Except as provided by sections 29 and 30, the priority of an interest affecting a registered estate or charge is not affected by a disposition of the estate or charge.

(2) It makes no difference for the purposes of this section whether the interest or disposition is registered.

The starting point therefore is that the 2002 Act does not alter how questions of priority are determined under the general law. The **basic rule** that we saw in Chapter 15, section 2 applies: B's pre-existing property right will *prima facie* take priority over C's later right. The exception contained in ss 29 and 30 is, however, highly significant. Those sections give C the chance of a defence to B's right, by identifying a category of transactions that are elevated out of the general law and provided with distinct priority rules. The defence will be referred to here as the 'lack of registration' defence as it can apply only if B's property right does not feature on the register. We will focus here on s 29, as it applies more broadly, whereas s 30 applies only where A holds and deals with a registered charge.

We saw in Chapter 15, section 4.1, that there are two important questions when considering a defence:

(a) What does C have to do to take advantage of the defence?

(b) When will B's pre-existing property right be vulnerable to that defence?

In relation to the lack of registration defence, the first of those questions is answered by s 29 of the LRA 2002.

Land Registration Act 2002, s 29

(1) If a registrable disposition of a registered estate is made for valuable consideration, completion of the disposition by registration has the effect of postponing to the interest under the disposition any interest affecting the estate immediately before the disposition whose priority is not protected at the time of registration.

(2) For the purposes of subsection (1), the priority of an interest is protected—

    (a) in any case, if the interest—

        (i)   is a registered charge or the subject of a notice in the register,

        (ii) falls within any of the paragraphs of Schedule 3, or

        (iii) appears from the register to be excepted from the effect of registration, and

    (b) in the case of a disposition of a leasehold estate, if the burden of the interest is incident to the estate.

(3) Subsection (2)(a)(ii) does not apply to an interest which has been the subject of a notice in the register at any time since the coming into force of this section.

(4) Where the grant of a leasehold estate in land out of a registered estate does not involve a registrable disposition, this section has effect as if—

    (a) the grant involved such a disposition, and

    (b) the disposition were registered at the time of the grant.

Section 29 thus applies to 'registrable dispositions' of registered estates[1] made for 'valuable consideration' and thus regulates dealings with a registered freehold or registered lease. A 'registrable disposition' of a registered estate includes the transfer of a registered estate, the creation out of a registered estate of a new lease of more than seven years' duration, and the creation of a legal mortgage or legal easement. In those cases, of course, C must register in order to acquire his or her legal estate or interest. The creation of a lease of seven years or less is *not* a registrable disposition, but s 29(4) ensures that C may nonetheless be able to take advantage of the lack of registration defence if C is granted such a lease.

---

[1] Land Registration Act 2002, s 30 applies matching rules to registrable dispositions of registered charges.

The requirement of 'valuable consideration' excludes from the scope of the lack of registration defence cases where C acquires a right by way of gift, for nominal consideration,[2] or through adverse possession.[3] The type of transactions to which the distinct scheme of priorities contained in s 29 applies therefore includes the ordinary sale or mortgage of registered land.[4]

This means that the first question (what does C have to do to take advantage of the lack of registration defence?) can be answered as follows: C needs to acquire, for valuable consideration from A, a legal property right. That is not, of course, enough for the lack of registration defence to apply: we also need to ask when will B's pre-existing right be subject to the defence. The answer, again, is provided by s 29: B's right will be vulnerable to the lack of registration defence *unless* (i) B's right is protected by entry on the register; *or* (ii) B's right is an overriding interest within Sch 3 of the LRA 2002.[5] As to (i), the means by which B protects his or her right by entry on the register is the entry of a 'notice'.[6] We will examine notices in section 3 of this chapter and overriding interests in section 4.

2.1 THE EFFECT OF THE LACK OF REGISTRATION DEFENCE

It is first useful to consider the practical effect of the defence afforded by s 29 of the LRA 2002. If acquiring, for example, A's estate in registered land, C will have to conduct both a search of the register and a physical inspection of the land. The search of the register will reveal any notices on the register protecting a pre-existing property right claimed by B;[7] the physical inspection is directed at discovering the existence of overriding interests. The lack of registration defence means that C need only be concerned by rights of B that are either on the register, or overriding interests.

If C proceeds to acquire A's estate then, as seen in Chapter 8, section 5, completion of the disposition from A to C will occur before the time of C's registration. Such registration is, in general,[8] needed before C can invoke the lack of registration defence but, if it occurs, C's basic protection under s 29 is good against any right of B that existed at the time of completion.[9]

It is worth noting a debate about the meaning of s 29 as to the effect of the lack of registration defence. Where C is able to invoke the defence against B's pre-existing property right, it is clear that C will take priority over that right of B. We saw an example of this in Chapter 3, section 3.2.2, when considering *Chaudhury v Yavuz*.[10] A sold A's registered title to C, and C took priority over B's pre-existing equitable interest: that interest had not been protected by

---

[2] Valuable consideration is defined in s 132(1) of the 2002 Act.

[3] The scheme of priorities for registration following a successful application based on adverse possession is provided in the 2002 Act, Sch 6, para 9.

[4] The approach adopted by the 2002 Act to priorities is not intended to make major changes to the position under the Land Registration Act 1925, but to place prevailing rules on a statutory footing. A full explanation is provided in Law Commission Report No 271, *Land Registration for the Twenty-First Century: A Conveyancing Revolution* (2001), Pt V.

[5] Section 29 applies only where B's right affects A's estate '*immediately before the disposition*' to C: this raises the timing question examined in Chapter 14, section 3.

[6] Ibid, ss 32–9.

[7] It will also reveal any restrictions on A's powers as owner: see section 5 in this chapter.

[8] The exception provided by s 29(4) for short legal leases is discussed in section 2.1.

[9] This is because s 29 has the effect of postponing to C's right '*any interest affecting the estate immediately before the disposition*'. See Chapter 8, section 5.1.

[10] [2013] Ch 249.

the entry of a notice on the register, and it was not on the list of overriding interests set out in Sch 3. Some aspects of the effect of s 29 remain unclear, however. In *Halifax plc v Curry Popeck (a firm)*, for example, Norris J endorsed the view advanced in argument that s 29 operates to '*destroy the subsistence of those interests as interests in land, leaving them capable of enforcement as personal rights*'.[11] On this view, C's ability to invoke s 29 means that B has, for all purposes and against all possible defendants, lost his or her property right. Whilst advocating that approach, Dixon has nonetheless highlighted that s 29 is open to an alternative analysis.[12] After all, the section explicitly merely 'postpones' B's interest to that of C, and so it could be argued that, whilst it does not bind C, B's right does remain as an interest in land and so might be able to take priority against any rights that are not derived from the disposition to C.

3 ENTRY OF A NOTICE

The entry of a *notice* on the register tells C about a property right claimed by B. It informs C of a right that—if, in fact, it exists—will be enforceable against him or her. Where B has a property right, and that right is capable of being protected by the entry of a notice, the ability to have a notice entered provides B with a means of ensuring that his or her right will *not* be vulnerable to the lack of registration defence.

   Entry of a notice in registered land must not be confused with the *doctrine* of notice in unregistered land. The doctrine of notice (as part of the 'bona fide purchaser' defence) governs the enforceability of certain equitable property rights against a purchaser of unregistered land. It is concerned with the whole process of the investigation of an unregistered title. Entry of a notice in registered land is used to secure the enforcement of legal and equitable property rights against C. It relates solely to the entry of a notice on the register. Sparkes avoids terminological confusion by referring to entry of a notice in registered land as a 'Land Registry notice'.[13]

3.1 NATURE AND EFFECT

The nature and effect of a notice is provided by s 32 of the LRA 2002.

Land Registration Act 2002, s 32

(1) A notice is an entry in the register in respect of the burden of an interest affecting a registered estate or charge.

(2) The entry of a notice is to be made in relation to the registered estate or charge affected by the interest concerned.

(3) The fact that an interest is the subject of a notice does not necessarily mean that the interest is valid, but does mean that the priority of the interest, if valid, is protected for the purposes of sections 29 and 30.

---

[11] [2008] EWHC 1692 (Ch), [49]. See generally the discussion at [48]–[53].
[12] Dixon, 'Priorities Under the Land Registration Act 2002' (2009) 125 LQR 401.
[13] Sparkes, *A New Land Law* (2nd edn, 2003), [20.02].

Two points are notable in relation to this provision. Firstly, the description of a notice as entry of a 'burden' encapsulates the idea that the entry informs C of B's property right, subject to which he or she will take title to the land. This has a direct impact on the types of right in respect of which it is appropriate to enter a notice. Entry of a notice is confined to property rights that it is anticipated will bind C.[14]

Secondly, entry of a notice does not guarantee the validity of the property right claimed. This is in contrast to the effect of registration of title. As we saw in Chapter 3, section 3.2.1, registration of A as proprietor of a legal estate operates to vest A with legal title. Entry of a notice by B to the effect (for example) that B has a restrictive covenant over A's land does not vest B with a restrictive covenant; instead, it ensures only that *if B in fact has a restrictive covenant*, that restrictive covenant will be enforceable against C.

Cooke suggests terminology to reflect this difference. She describes the entry of a notice as 'recording' an interest, in contradistinction to 'registration' of title.[15] Another way of thinking about the distinction is to regard registration of title as having, under s 58 of the LRA 2002, a positive effect: the fact of registration vests legal title in the registered party. In contrast, the entry of a notice is more negative: it stops C using the lack of registration defence against B's right, but does not guarantee that B's right exists.

3.2 SCOPE

As has already been noted at the beginning of section 3, the entry of a notice is confined to property rights held by B. The LRA 2002 does not attempt to provide an exhaustive list of property interests in respect of which entry of a notice is possible; instead, the Act defines interests that cannot be protected by the entry of a notice. The position, therefore, is that, if B has a legal or equitable property right then it can be protected by the entry of a notice unless: (i) B's right is one that must be registered in its own right (for example, it is a freehold or lease of over seven years); or (ii) B's right is on the list of rights that cannot be protected by an entry of notice. The most important of those exclusions are contained in s 33(a)–(c) of the 2002 Act.[16]

Land Registration Act 2002, s 33

No notice may be entered in the register in respect of any of the following—

(a) an interest under—

　(i)　a trust of land, or

　(ii)　a settlement under the Settled Land Act 1925 (c. 18),

(b) a leasehold estate in land which—

　(i)　is granted for a term of years of three years or less from the date of the grant, and

　(ii)　is not required to be registered,

(c) a restrictive covenant made between a lessor and lessee, so far as relating to the demised premises,

---

[14] Law Commission Report No 271 (2001), [6.9].

[15] Cooke, *The New Law of Land Registration* (Oxford: Hart Publishing, 2003) pp 4 and 72.

[16] An explanation of all property rights excluded from entry of a notice is provided in Law Commission Report No 271 (2001), [6.8]–[6.16].

The rationale for each of these exclusions is different. As for s 33(a)(i) and (ii), the prohibition on entering a notice in respect of an equitable interest under a trust is consistent with the *curtain principle*. As we saw in Chapter 3, section 2.5, that principle, in Ruoff's words, states that: *'the register is the sole source of information for proposing purchasers, who need not and, indeed, must not concern themselves with trusts and equities which lie behind the curtain'*. In other words, a key part of the statutory scheme is that interests under trusts are kept off the register, and so B is not given the chance to use a notice as a mechanism to protect such a right. Where land is held on trust, it is possible for a *restriction* to be entered on the register, noting the fact of the trust and any limits on the powers of the trustee or trustees to deal with the legal title to the land; but, as we will see in section 5, a restriction has a quite different effect from a notice.

The curtain principle does not, however, mean that C will always have a defence against an interest under a trust. After all, we have seen that, in *Williams & Glyn's Bank v Boland*,[17] C, when acquiring its registered charge, *was* bound by B's pre-existing interest under a trust. There was no notice protecting B's right, but C could not rely on the lack of registration defence as B had an overriding interest: as B had been in actual occupation of the land when C acquired its right, B's interest under the trust counted as an overriding interest. How then is C protected against such pre-existing rights under trusts? The answer lies in the quite separate defence of overreaching, which we noted in Chapter 15, section 4.3 and will examine in more detail in Chapter 17.

As for s 33(b), short legal leases are also incapable of being protected by the entry of a notice; this prevents the register becoming 'cluttered' with such short-term rights, and B's short legal lease will bind C in any case as an overriding interest.[18] Finally, as for s 33(c), leasehold covenants are excluded, because their enforcement is subject to a separate statutory scheme.[19]

With these exclusions in mind, the category of interests in respect of which a notice may be entered is broad. It is an appropriate means of protection for any property right that is not specifically excluded. This includes, for example, equitable mortgages, restrictive covenants, legal and equitable easements, legal leases of more than three years (to a maximum of seven years),[20] estate contracts, rights to occupy conferred by the Family Law Act 1996 (FLA 1996),[21] and an inchoate equity arising from a claim to proprietary estoppel. In *Chaudhury v Yavuz*,[22] for example (where, as we have seen, C was able to use the lack of registration defence against B's pre-existing right, an equitable easement arising through proprietary estoppel), Lloyd LJ pointed out that B's error was in failing to ensure that, before any sale from A to C, his right was protected by the entry of a notice on the register.[23]

3.3 APPLYING FOR ENTRY OF A NOTICE

An application for entry of a notice may be made by the registered proprietor or a person claiming an interest in the land.[24] The Registrar may also enter a notice.[25] Notices are

17 [1981] AC 487.   18 Land Registration Act 2002, Sch 3, para 1.
19 Contained in the Landlord and Tenant (Covenants) Act 1995. This Act is discussed in Chapter 24.
20 Leases of more than seven years are registrable estates.
21 These rights of occupation are explained in Chapter 16.   22 [2013] Ch 249.
23 [2013] Ch 249 at [9]: *'What [B] could then have done, but did not do, was to cause to be registered a unilateral notice under s 34 of the 2002 Act. If that had been done before [A's] sale of [the land], [C] would have taken subject to the rights to which the notice related: see s 29(2)(a)(i).'*
24 Land Registration Act 2002, s 34.   25 Ibid, s 37.

subdivided into 'agreed' and 'unilateral'. Each type of notice serves the same function: each ensures that B's property right binds C on a registrable disposition. A unilateral notice is entered where the registered proprietor has not given consent and the Registrar is not satisfied as to the validity of B's claim.[26] The Registrar will then notify the registered proprietor (A) of the entry.[27] A may apply to have a unilateral notice cancelled.[28] If so, B is informed of the application and given a limited timeframe in which to respond.[29] If no response is received, then the notice is cancelled.[30] If notice is received and agreement cannot be reached, the matter is referred to the First-tier Tribunal.[31] If B's claim to a property right is made out, then an appropriate entry will be made.[32] A unilateral notice may also be cancelled by B.[33]

As the Law Commission has recently noted,[34] the procedure relating to a unilateral notice can cause some problems for A: B need produce no evidence to have the notice initially entered, and A may then have to become involved in litigation to remove the notice.[35] The Commission has therefore suggested that B should be required to produce some evidence of his or her right at an earlier stage.[36] Whilst preferring to keep two distinct types of notice, the Commission has also proposed that the terminology be changed, so that the current unilateral and agreed notice be referred to as a 'summary notice' and a 'full notice' respectively. This change would reflect the current position that an agreed notice can be entered even without the consent of A. This may occur, for example, as the Registrar has the power to enter a notice in respect of a number of interests that would be enforceable against C as overriding interests on first registration of title.[37] This power brings those property rights (against which C has no defence) onto the register. The Registrar has a duty to enter a notice on the estate that has the burden of an interest created by various dispositions.[38] For example, on the registration of a legal lease, the Registrar enters a notice of the lease on the freehold title out of which the lease has been created;[39] on the registration of a legal easement, the Registrar will enter a notice on the estate with the burden of the easement.[40]

---

[26] Ibid, s 34(3). [27] Ibid, s 35. [28] Ibid, s 36. [29] Ibid, 36(2).

[30] Ibid, s 36(3). Permitted time frames are given in the Land Registration Rules 2003 (SI 2003/1417), r 86(3).

[31] Land Registration Act 2002, s 73.

[32] Law Commission Report No 271 (2001), [6.31]. This may take the form, e.g. of the entry of an agreed notice or of a restriction.

[33] Land Registration Act 2002, s 35(3).

[34] Law Com CP No 227, *Updating the Land Registration Act 2002* (2016) 9.36–9.40.

[35] These problems were highlighted by the removal of manorial rights and chancel repair liabilities from the list of overriding interests in October 2013: as such rights now require protection by the entry of a notice, a large number of applications were made under the unilateral notice procedure in respect of such right: see Law Com CP No 227, 9.41–9.47.

[36] Law Com CP No 227, 9.98–9.99. The suggestion is that, when making the initial application for a summary notice, B need provide only basic details of the interest claimed: this is to preserve B's confidentiality (see 9.70 and 9.81); but, in contrast to the present system, where B need only provide full evidence if the case comes to the First-tier Tribunal, B will have to provide evidence to the Land Registry if A makes an objection to the summary notice.

[37] Ibid, s 37. The interests in relation to which this power is exercisable are listed ibid, Sch 1.

[38] Ibid, s 38. [39] Ibid, s 27(2)(b). [40] Ibid, s 27(2)(d).

4 OVERRIDING INTERESTS

4.1 NATURE AND EFFECT

As we have noted, overriding interests[41] are property rights that do not appear on the register, but which are immune from the lack of registration defence. As the Law Commission put it in their 2016 Consultation Paper:[42] '*Overriding interests are problematic from a land registration perspective. They bind a purchaser notwithstanding the fact that they do not appear on the register. They therefore undermine the "mirror principle" that the register should be a complete and accurate record of the title.*' Similar points were made by the Commission in the Report that led to the LRA 2002: it is therefore no surprise that the Act reduced the number of overriding interests. Nonetheless, the remaining overriding interests still constitute an important category. The rationale given in the Report that led to the LRA 2002 was that there are circumstances in which it is unreasonable to expect B to register his or her property right to secure its enforcement.[43] Its view was therefore that '*interests should only have overriding status where protection against buyers was needed, but where it was neither reasonable to expect nor sensible to require any entry on the register*'.[44] As we will see, however, the list of overriding interests, even under the 2002 Act, does include some rights that do not meet that test.[45]

As to the effect of overriding interests, two points are worth remembering. Firstly, it is important to remember that an overriding interest is simply a property right that is immune from the lack of registration defence: it does not mean that, if B has such an interest, it will always bind C. After all, C may be able to rely on a *different* defence to take priority over B's right: we saw an example of this in Chapter 15, section 4.3 when considering the operation of the overreaching defence in *City of London Building Society v Flegg*.[46] In some such cases, where C is able to rely on a defence other than the lack of registration defence, the courts have said that the presence of that other defence prevents B's right being an overriding interest.[47] Nothing in practice turns on adopting such language instead of saying, as we do in this chapter, that B does have an overriding interest, but C nonetheless has priority as C can rely on a different defence.

Secondly, if C does not have any other defence, and so is bound by B's overriding interest, that will mean that C is bound by a right that was not on the register. C may therefore argue that the register has not done its job of securing his or her title, and that C should receive an indemnity payment as a result. As noted in Chapter 3, section 3.2.2, the clear position, however, is that C will *not* be able to receive an indemnity as a result of being bound by B's overriding interest. That is the case even if the register is changed in order to reflect B's overriding interest, and even if that change means that C's right is removed from the register. That position was established in *re Chowood's Registered Land*,[48] which considered the LRA 1925, but the principle has been maintained by the LRA 2002.[49] It means that where, for

---

[41] Ibid, Sch 3, refers to this category as '*interests which override registered dispositions*'. The expression 'overriding interests' is not used in the Act, but is the terminology of the Land Registration Act 1925 and remains a useful form of reference.

[42] Law Com CP No 227, *Updating the Land Registration Act 2002* (2016) 11.2.

[43] Law Commission Report No 254, *Land Registration for the Twenty-First Century: A Consultative Document* (1998), [4.4]. For further discussion of this rationale, see Chapter 15.

[44] Law Commission Report No 271 (2001), [8.6].

[45] See the discussion in section 4.2.1 of estate contracts and options to purchase.

[46] [1988] AC 54, HL.

[47] See e.g. *Wishart v Credit and Mercantile plc* [2015] EWCA Civ 655, [47] (Sales LJ) and *Mortgage Express v Lambert* [2017] Ch 93, [21] and [39] (Lewison LJ).

[48] [1933] Ch 574.   [49] See e.g. *Swift 1st Ltd v Chief Land Registrar* [2015] Ch 602 at [20] and [29].

example, each of B and C claims to be entitled to the land, if B has an overriding interest and C has no other defence, then B gets the land and C gets nothing.[50] This is an important factor to consider when assessing whether or not B's right should be regarded as an overriding interest. It also calls into question the supposed rationale of overriding interests. If, as the Law Commission suggested, such rights exist only because there are situations in which B cannot reasonably be expected to register a right, why should C pay the price for this by being denied an indemnity? If, in contrast, at least some rights are overriding because, notwithstanding B's lack of registration, C should in any case have discovered B's property right, then the lack of indemnity is easier to explain: C could and should have taken steps for his or her own protection.

The LRA 2002 provides two distinct lists of overriding interests: those overriding at first registration (listed in Sch 1); and those overriding on a disposition of a registered estate (listed in Sch 3). First registration is treated separately, because the intention is to reflect the state of the title at that time. Whether C is bound by any overriding interests will have been determined prior to registration.[51] Our discussion focusses on interests overriding on a disposition of a registered estate—that is, those transfers that are subject to the distinct priority rules contained in ss 29 and 30 of the LRA 2002.

The full list of these overriding interests is contained in Sch 3 of the 2002 Act. Our discussion is confined to those contained in paras 1–3 of the Schedule, legal leases of seven years or less, property rights held by those in actual occupation, and legal easements and profits à prendre.

We begin with the most important and notorious[52] category.

4.2 SCHEDULE 3, PARA 2: PROPERTY RIGHTS HELD BY PERSONS IN OCCUPATION

Property rights held by persons in actual occupation are given the status of overriding interests in Sch 3, para 2. This category is different in its scope from all other categories. Those categories confer the status of overriding interest on a particular property right. This paragraph, instead, confers the status of overriding interest on *any* property right held by a person in occupation. Its focus is therefore on the factual position of the holder of the right, not on the type of property right held.[53]

Land Registration Act 2002, Sch 3, para 2

An interest belonging at the time of the disposition to a person in actual occupation, so far as relating to land of which he is in actual occupation, except for—

(a) an interest under a settlement under the Settled Land Act 1925 (c. 18);

(b) an interest of a person of whom inquiry was made before the disposition and who failed to disclose the right when he could reasonably have been expected to do so;

---

[50] As noted by Law Com CP No 227, 13.63.

[51] For further discussion, see Law Commission Report No 271 (2001), [8.3]–[8.5]; Harpum. and Bignell, *Registered Land: The New Law* (2002), [2.47].

[52] Law Commission No 254 (1998), [5.56].   [53] Cooke (2003) p 79.

> (c) an interest—
>> (i) which belongs to a person whose occupation would not have been obvious on a reasonably careful inspection of the land at the time of the disposition, and
>> (ii) of which the person to whom the disposition is made does not have actual knowledge at that time;
> (d) a leasehold estate in land granted to take effect in possession after the end of the period of three months beginning with the date of the grant and which has not taken effect in possession at the time of the disposition.

In applying Sch 3, para 2, it is of course crucial to know when B will be regarded as being in actual occupation of the land. We will look in detail at that question in sections 4.2.7, 4.2.8, and 4.2.9. Firstly, however, some other issues as to the operation of Sch 3, para 2 need to be considered.

4.2.1 What property rights can be protected by actual occupation?

Schedule 3, para 2 makes clear that actual occupation can make B's property right overriding only where B has that right '*at the time of the disposition*' to C. This means that if B acquires such a right only after the completion of a transfer from A to C, but before C is registered, that right cannot be protected under Sch 3, para 2.[54] We will consider in section 4.2.6 the separate question of at what point in time B needs to be in actual occupation of the land.

It should be noted that occupation is the trigger for protection, but not the subject of protection. The subject of protection is B's property right. If B is in occupation, but is not entitled to any property rights (e.g. where B is a licensee), then B has nothing capable of binding C under Sch 3, para 2. This is why, for example, it made no difference in *NPB v Ainsworth* that Mrs Ainsworth was in actual occupation of her home at the time when Mr Ainsworth granted a charge to the bank: as she had only a personal right against her husband, and no property right, she had no overriding interest. After all, an overriding interest is simply a right that is not vulnerable to the lack of registration defence and, if B has no pre-existing property right, C has no need to rely on any defence.

Conversely, if B does have a property right, and is in actual occupation, then that right is an overriding interest even if the content of the right itself is unrelated to the occupation of the land. It is the right that is protected, not the occupation. So if, for example, B occupies land as a tenant or sub-tenant of A, and B also has an option to purchase A's freehold (such an option is an equitable interest in land), then that option to purchase counts as an overriding interest, even though it itself gives B no right to occupy the land.[55] This may of course create a trap for C, who may assume that B simply has a lease, and no option to purchase, and proceed to acquire A's land on that basis. When seeing that B is in actual occupation of A's land, then, C must take care to ask B what rights B claims in the land, and not make

---

[54] For the concept of completion, see Chapter 8, section 5. This seems to differ from the position under the Land Registration Act 1925 as, in *Abbey National Building Society v Cann* [1991] 1 AC 56, the House of Lords stated that B's interests at the time of *registration* were protected as long as B was in occupation at the time of the disposition.

[55] See *Webb v Pollmount* [1966] Ch 584 and *Ferrishurst Ltd v Wallcite Ltd* [1999] Ch 355, in which a tenant's option to purchase the freehold reversion was protected as an overriding interest.

assumptions as to B's rights. As we will see, the 2002 Act does protect C if B then fails to disclose a property right when B could reasonably have been expected to do so.[56]

The only qualification to the idea that it is the underlying right, rather than occupation, that is protected occurs where B is in actual occupation of only part of the land to which B's right relates. In such a case, protection is confined to the geographical extent of B's occupation.[57] This reverses the decision under the Land Registration Act 1925 (LRA 1925) in *Ferrishurst Ltd v Wallcite Ltd*,[58] in which a property right (an option to purchase) extending over offices and a garage was protected even though B was in occupation of the offices only.

Estate contracts and options to purchase

As seen in Chapter 8, section 4.3, an estate contract arises where A is under a contractual duty to sell, and B is under a contractual duty to buy, A's estate in the land: in such a case, B acquires an immediate equitable interest in A's land. An option to purchase is also a form of equitable interest, and arises where B has a power, but not a duty, to buy A's land. Such rights will almost always be formally created, often with the assistance of lawyers. The current position is that, if accompanied by actual occupation, such a right can be an overriding interest. Nonetheless, such a right lies outside the rationale for overriding interests given by the Law Commission in the Report that led to the 2002 Act: it is very difficult to say that it was unreasonable to expect B to have registered the right. This is a consequence of the fact that Sch 3, para 2 looks to the factual position of B, not to the content of B's right, or the way in which that right was acquired. Of course, as in a case like *Williams & Glyn's Bank v Boland*,[59] B's property right will sometimes be one which arose informally and of which it would therefore be unreasonable to require registration. As shown with the case of an estate contract or option to purchase, however, it will not always be the case that the property right protected by actual occupation is one of which it would be unreasonable to expect registration.

In its recent Consultation Paper on updating the LRA 2002, the Law Commission considered the fact that Sch 3, para 2 can protect a right which was formally created, and which does not itself give B a right of occupation. Its preference is to allow such rights to continue to be overriding interests. It noted, for example, that such protection might be useful where, for example, A has sold registered land to B, and B has applied for registration and gone into occupation of the land, but for some administrative reason there is a delay in B's registration.[60] If, during that time, A were to take advantage of his or her position as registered owner and grant a right to C, it would seem wrong for C to be able to rely on the lack of registration defence. The reason for this, it is submitted, is simply that, when acquiring a right from A, C should check to see if anyone other than A is in occupation of the land and, on finding such a person, should then ask that person what rights, if any, they claim in the land.

Mere equities

We noted in Chapter 6, section 5.2, that there is a category of rights, which can be called 'mere equities' that are more than mere personal rights, as they are capable of binding a third party, but which lack some of the general characteristics of a standard equitable interest in land. Such rights include, for example, a right to have a transaction set aside where it has been procured by

---

[56] LRA 2002, Sch 3, para 2(b): see section 4.2.3.

[57] This is clear from the wording of Sch 3, para 2, which makes a right overriding '*so far as relating to land of which he is in actual occupation*'.

[58] [1999] Ch 353.   [59] [1981] AC 487.   [60] Law Com CP No 227, 11.26.

undue influence, or amounts to an unconscionable bargain. It can be said that, if B has such a right, B does not have an immediate equitable interest, but rather has a power to acquire such an interest by, for example, choosing to set a transaction aside.[61] To avoid any uncertainty as to whether, in registered land, such rights can bind C, s 116(b) of the LRA 2002 confirms that a mere equity *'has effect from the time the equity arises as an interest capable of binding successors in title (subject to the rules about the effect of dispositions on priority)'.* This means that such a right, if coupled with actual occupation, can count as an overriding interest.[62] Under s 116(a), the same is true of an *'equity by estoppel'*: the impact of that provision was discussed in Chapter 10, section 4.

Rights to rectify the register

As noted in Chapter 3, section 3.2.2, if C is registered as holding a particular right, it is possible for B to apply to have the register changed. One of the grounds for doing so is for the purpose of *'correcting a mistake'* and, where such a correction causes loss to C, it is known as a rectification. The general position is that, if such rectification occurs then, assuming that the mistake was not caused wholly by C's lack of proper care, or wholly or in part by C's fraud, an indemnity will be payable to C. It has generally been assumed that, where such a mistake has occurred, and B has the chance to apply for rectification, B's right to rectify is, like a mere equity, capable of binding a third party[63] and so can be an overriding interest if B is in actual occupation of the registered land.[64] This conclusion, however, appears to lead to some practical problems. The general position is that, if C is bound by an overriding interest, no indemnity is payable to C, and so if B's right to rectify can count as an overriding interest, C may be faced with the prospect of losing his or her registered property right without receiving any indemnity payment. The Law Commission has therefore proposed, in its 2016 Consultation Paper, that the LRA 2002 should be amended, so as to provide that a right to have the register changed, even if held by a party in actual occupation of land, cannot be an overriding interest. That argument can only properly be evaluated as part of a more general consideration of the Law Commission's proposals on rectification, and so will be examined in detail in Chapter 18, section 3.

Easements

A specific question arises with regard to occupation in respect of easements.[65] It should first be noted that the question is only of practical importance in relation to equitable easements. For if B has a legal easement, it will almost always qualify as an overriding interest in its own right under Sch 3, para 1[66] and so there will be no need for B to argue that it is overriding under Sch 3, para 2. In *Chaudhary v Yavuz*,[67] for example, Mr Chaudhary argued that he was

---

[61] See e.g. Cooper and Lees, 'Interests, Powers and Mere Equities in Modern Land Law' (2017) 37 OJLS 435, 439–41.

[62] This was confirmed in *Mortgage Express v Lambert* [2017] Ch 93 (CA), [24], dealing with an equity to set aside an unconscionable bargain, and *Link Lending v Bustard* [2010] EWCA Civ 424, dealing with an equity to set aside a transfer where B lacked capacity.

[63] For full discussion, see e.g. Cooper and Lees, 'Interests, Powers and Mere Equities in Modern Land Law' (2017) 37 OJLS 435, 452–3.

[64] See e.g. *Malory v Cheshire Homes* [2002] Ch 216, [68]–[69] and Law Com CP No 227, [13.60]–[13.74].

[65] Note that if B has a legal easement, such a right will almost always be an overriding interest in its own right, under Sch 3, para 1, and so there is no need to consider if it can be an overriding interest under Sch 3, para 2.

[66] See section 4.4.   [67] [2013] Ch. 249.

in actual occupation of land over which he had an equitable easement. Lloyd LJ suggested that '[at] first sight it seems counter-intuitive, to say the least, to assert that the owner of dominant land [. . .] is in occupation of other land [. . .] over which he asserts an easement'.[68] On the facts Mr Chaudhary's claim failed as he was unable to establish actual occupation (this aspect of the case is discussed in sections 4.2.5 and 4.2.8). However, whilst it is true to say that mere use of land does not, by itself, amount to actual occupation of that land,[69] it might be dangerous to assume that it is never possible for an equitable easement to be protected by actual occupation. McFarlane has suggested that while an easement cannot constitute exclusive possession, its exercise could constitute occupation; for example, by the storage of goods or the parking of a car.[70] Possession and occupation are not synonymous and there is no reason in principle why an equitable easement should not be protected under Sch 3, para 2 if B in fact had actual occupation of the servient land at the relevant time. After all, as we noted in section 4.1, a property right can be an overriding interest if coupled with actual occupation, even if the content of the right itself does not involve occupation.

4.2.2 The qualification in Sch 3, para 2(c): 'Occupation not obvious on a reasonably careful inspection'

The LRA 2002 added a new form of protection for C: Sch 3, para 2(c)(i), of the LRA 2002 protects C against overriding interests claimed by B, by virtue of actual occupation, if *both* of two conditions are met: firstly, B's occupation is not obvious on a reasonably careful inspection; secondly, C did not actually know of the existence of B's property right at the time of the disposition.[71] When proposing that qualification, the Law Commission was careful to state that it does not mean that actual occupation should be seen as depending on the doctrine of notice.

Law Commission Report No 254, *Land Registration for the Twenty-First Century: A Consultative Document* (1998, [5.71]–[5.72])

[. . .] Any requirement that [occupation should have to be apparent] it was said, would introduce into land registration the doctrine of notice [. . .] While we entirely agree that the doctrine of notice should not be introduced into registered land, we do not agree that limiting actual occupation to cases where it is apparent would have that effect.

[. . .] The test is whether the right is apparent on a reasonable inspection of the land, not whether the right would have been discovered if the purchaser had made all the enquiries which ought reasonably to have been made.

While it is no doubt anticipated that an actual inspection will take place, in *Thompson v Foy* Lewison J noted that the paragraph '*does not require an actual inspection*'.[72] Rather, the first question is simply *would* the occupation have been obvious on a reasonably careful

---

68 Ibid, [28].

69 As noted by Newey J in *Baker v Craggs* [2016] EWHC 3250 (Ch) , [2017] Ch 295 at [12].

70 McFarlane, 'Eastenders, Neighbours and Upstairs Downstairs' [2013] Conv 74, 81.

71 Note that the second condition refers to C's knowledge of B's *right*, rather than to C's knowledge of B's *occupation*.

72 *Thompson v Foy* [2010] 1 P & CR 16, [132].

inspection. Where C does in fact conduct a reasonable inspection and this does not reveal B's occupation, it may be expected that this will be considered conclusive in showing that Sch 3, para 2(c)(i) applies. Where C does not inspect, or C's inspection falls short of being reasonable, then the court may address the qualification by asking the hypothetical question, '*whether [B's] occupation would have been obvious on a reasonably careful inspection*'.[73] If it would not have been, then C's failure to inspect will not deprive C of invoking the qualification in Sch 3, para 2(c)(i).

Two chief questions arise in relation to the 'reasonable inspection' proviso in Sch 3, para 2 (c). Firstly, will the proviso, in practice, give C any additional protection? In the following extract, Jackson argues that it will not.

Jackson, 'Title by Registration and Concealed Overriding Interests: The Cause and Effect of Antipathy to Documentary Proof' (2003) 119 LQR 660, 665–7

Contrary to the reasoning of the Law Commission, it is submitted that a reasonable inspection defence will not limit the impact of occupational overriding interests upon the purchaser's registered estate. There are two arguments that support this view. First, there are other important observations that may be drawn from the differences in method of proof of title. A reasonable inspection requirement has no normative content [. . .] the resurrection of the reasonable inspection defence provides no meaningful guidance to purchasers as to the fact or extent of the inspection required of them. In effect, such a defence will not preclude the concealed overriding interest. Although the Law Commission indicates the type of conduct that may amount to "actual occupation", in order to discover an adverse occupational right, a purchaser would require a type of knowledge that was neither based in law nor in fact. The normative guidance of the 2002 Act emphasises the conclusiveness of the register and online inspections. Thus, a purchaser may end up by being bound by an interest that was objectively apparent to the legally minded officious bystander but which was undiscoverable to the purchaser if only because he did not know what he was looking for.

Secondly, there is an implied premise behind the methodology employed by the 2002 Act to reduce the circumstances in which occupational interests will take effect as overriding the estate of a registered proprietor. This premise is the connection of ideas that a purchaser, under s.70(1)(g), risked taking his title subject to a concealed overriding interest because there was no reasonable inspection defence. This is a logically flawed connection. The Law Commission assumes that the absence of an apparency requirement within s.70(1)(g) resulted in the extension of overriding protection to the interests of undiscoverable occupants. It is undeniable that some constructions of the paragraph impose onerous duties of inspection on purchasers. However, these duties resulted from wide interpretations of the type of occupation that could be considered to be apparent and were not the consequence of the absence of such a requirement. This mistaken orthodoxy exists in both registered and unregistered conveyancing.

The underlying issue in the debate as to the correct scope of protection afforded to occupiers lies in the tension between the desire for a conclusive register and the acknowledgment that there are circumstances in which a requirement of registration would be unreasonable.

[73] Ibid, *per* Lewison J.

Jackson concludes that the reasonable inspection qualification does not make the register any more definitive.[74]

The second, broader question is as to the impact of Sch 3, para 2(c) on the courts' general approach to the meaning of 'actual occupation'. On one view, it could be said that, now that C is given such protection, the courts are more free to adopt a natural meaning of actual occupation, as in *Boland* (see section 4.2.7), as there is no longer a need to twist the meaning of that term in order to protect C from the risk of being bound by an undiscoverable right. On an opposing view, it could be said that the desire of the legislature to protect C shown by Sch 3, para 2(c) provides support to a court, like the Court of Appeal in *Rosset* (see section 4.2.7), which instead wishes to interpret the term 'actual occupation' so as to be consistent with the basic idea that C should be bound by a right only if C could reasonably have discovered that right. We will consider the application of those different views when looking at the courts' current approach to assessing if B is in actual occupation in sections 4.2.8 and 4.2.9.

4.2.3 The qualification in Sch 3, para 2(b): B's failure to disclose the property right

If B is in actual occupation, but fails to disclose his or her property right when asked by C, then, as long as B could reasonably have been expected to disclose that right, it will not count as an overriding interest. This can be seen as akin to an estoppel:[75] if C goes ahead and acquires a right in the land on the basis that B has no pre-existing property right, then B can be barred from later asserting such a right against C.[76] Certainly, if C wishes to rely on this qualification, inquiry must be made *of B*: if, for example, C simply asks A about B's rights, then A's failure to disclose B's property right will not prevent B's right being an overriding interest.[77] Further, the provision has no application where inquiries have not in fact been made of B, regardless of whether such inquiries would have revealed the existence of B's interest.[78]

Mortgage Express Ltd v Lambert
[2016] EWCA Civ 555, [2017] Ch 93

Facts: Ms Lambert (B) was the registered owner of a leasehold flat, subject to a mortgage. She was struggling to keep up with mortgage repayments, and agreed to sell her lease (worth around £120,000) to two purchasers (A1 and A2) as part of a 'mortgage rescue' scheme. A1 and A2 promised, as part of that deal, to give B a lease so as to allow her to continue living in the flat indefinitely in exchange for payment of rent. Contracts were exchanged between B and A1 and A2, and they contained the usual condition that B would give A1 and A2 vacant possession of the flat: there was no reference to B having any continuing right to live there. In practice, however, B did remain in occupation. A1 and A2 financed their purchase of the flat with a mortgage, and granted a charge to Mortgage Express (C). When A1 and A2 failed to make repayments under

---

[74] Jackson, 'Title by Registration and Concealed Overriding Interests: The Cause and Effect of Antipathy to Documentary Proof' (2003) 119 LQR 660, 675.

[75] This is the basis on which then operation of the provision is explained in Law Commission Report No 271 (2001), [8.60].

[76] See too Chapter 15, section 4.4.2 and *Mortgage Express Ltd v Lambert* [2017] Ch 93, [41].

[77] This was also the position under the LRA 1925: see e.g. *Hodgson v Marks* [1971] Ch 892.

[78] *Thompson v Foy* [2010] 1 P & CR 16, [132].

that mortgage, C sought possession of the flat. B claimed that her transfer of the lease to A1 and A2 should be set aside as an unconscionable bargain, and she therefore had an interest in the flat, a mere equity, that was capable of binding a third party such as C. B argued that C could not rely on the lack of registration defence as B's interest was overriding under Sch 3, para 2 as a result of her continued occupation of the flat as her home.

As we will see in Chapter 17, section 2.2.5, the Court of Appeal found that, whilst B's mere equity was capable of binding C, C was able to rely on the overreaching defence to gain priority over B's pre-existing right. As a result, the point about overriding interests was irrelevant, as C could in any case use the overreaching defence. Nonetheless, as the point had been fully argued, it was considered by the Court of Appeal. One of the arguments made by C was that, although B had been in actual occupation, C could invoke the proviso in Sch 3, para 2(b), as B had failed to disclose her interest when inquiry was made by C. The Court of Appeal accepted that argument.

Lewison LJ

At [40]–[43]

There is no doubt, on the facts, that inquiry was made of Ms Lambert [B] before the disposition (ie before the grant of the mortgage to Mortgage Express [C]) and that she did not disclose the right that she now asserts. [B's counsel] argued that before exchange of contracts there was no right to disclose, because the bargain had not been made. In that submission I think he is right. However, after exchange of contracts and before completion of the TR1 the requisitions on title confirmed that there had been no change in the information previously provided. In addition the contract provided for vacant possession to be given on completion and [B] gave a full title guarantee in the TR1. This title guarantee includes a presumption that she was disposing of the whole of her interest; that she had the right to dispose of the property as she purported to do and that she would do all she reasonably could to give the person to whom the disposal was made the title she purported to give.

While I would accept that [B] could not reasonably have been expected to have attached the label 'unconscionable bargain' to the right she now claims, I agree with [C's counsel] that it would have been reasonable for her to have disclosed that she was not in fact giving vacant possession; and that the lease would be encumbered in the hands of the purchasers [A1 and A2] by the tenancy that she had agreed to take. As the joint report of the Law Commission and HM Land Registry explains this exception from the class of overriding interests 'operates in the form of an estoppel'.[79] If the occupier does not reveal her rights she cannot thereafter assert them. [B's counsel] argued that [C] could not rely on [B's] failure to disclose the true arrangement between her and [A1 and A2] because [C] had notice of the undervalue [of B's sale to A1 and A2] as a result of the letter informing them that the purchase price was only £30,000; and should have been put on inquiry that something mischievous was going on. I reject that submission. Para 2 of Sch 3 does not mention notice, and the philosophy underlying the Land Registration Act 2002 is that notice is irrelevant. In the context of the rights of persons in occupation of land whose title is registered, that proposition was authoritatively decided by the House of Lords in *Williams & Glyn's Bank v Boland*.[80] [. . .]

The allegation that [C] had notice of [B's] right was the sole reason advanced for disabling it from relying upon her failure to disclose the true arrangement. Since in my judgment that reason is not a good one, it follows that [B] did not have an overriding interest.

---

[79] Law Com No 271, [8.60].   [80] [1981] AC 487.

The judgment makes clear that, if B has failed to disclose his or her right when it would be reasonable to expect B to do so, then B cannot establish an overriding interest through actual occupation. That is the case even if C knew, or ought to have known, of B's right. This is clear from the wording of Sch 3, para 2(b)—in contrast to the qualification in Sch 3, para 2(c), there is nothing in the wording of Sch 3, para 2(b) to prevent its applying where C has actual knowledge of B's right. As noted by Lewison LJ, that conclusion is also consistent with the idea that questions of C's knowledge or notice are, in general, excluded from the LRA scheme.

The judgment also considers an innovation of the LRA 2002: the provision in Sch 3, para 2(b) that B's failure to disclose his or her right on inquiry is relevant only if B could reasonably have been expected to make such disclosure.

It is often the case, that, where it applies, Sch 3 para 2 protects parties whose property rights have arisen informally: for example, under a common intention constructive trust.[81] As such rights may arise on the basis of the parties' intention and conduct during the course of their relationship, it is possible that B may be unaware of the existence of a claim until the relationship is subjected to legal analysis at a time of crisis—including a priority dispute with C. This means that, at the time when C initially acquires its right from A, B may not yet know that he or she has a property right. In such a case, it seems that B's non-disclosure would *not* allow C to take advantage of the qualification in Sch 3, para 2(b), as B could argue that, in the circumstances of the case, B could not reasonably have been expected to disclose the right. In the *Lambert* case, however, it was considered that, even if she could not have been expected to know of her right to have her sale of the property set aside, Mrs Lambert could have told the lender that she was expecting, under the mortgage rescue scheme, to have a right to remain on the property. On that view, it seems that the question is not whether it would have been reasonable for B to disclose the very right he or she now asserts as an overriding interest; it is rather whether B could reasonably have been expected to disclose that he or she had *some sort of right* that might bind C. Such an interpretation goes against the literal wording of Sch 3, para 2(b), which refers only to the case where B fails to disclose '*the right*' (i.e. the right now asserted as an overriding interest), but could be seen as consistent with the broader estoppel idea referred to by Lewison LJ: having failed to take the chance to ring an alarm bell when asked by C, B is now prevented from asserting any overriding interest based on actual occupation.

Even on a literal interpretation, the reference to what B could '*reasonably have been expected to disclose*' does cause some uncertainty, as noted by Dixon.

Dixon, 'The Reform of Property Law and the Land Registration Act 2002: A Risk Assessment' [2003] Conv 136, 146–7

Thus, the right holder loses overriding status (after failure to disclose) only if disclosure could reasonably be expected to be made. Such disclosure might not be reasonably expected where, say, the right holder did not know, and could not reasonably be expected to know, that they actually had a right (e.g. in cases of uncrystallised estoppel). While this is a welcome reform, there are uncertainties. For example, is it "reasonable" to expect disclosure when the right holder knows that the consequences of disclosure will be the loss of the family

---

[81] See e.g. *Williams & Glyn's Bank v Boland* [1981] AC 417.

home because the purchaser will take steps to acquire the property free from the right? Presumably it is, because otherwise it will always be permitted to withhold disclosure if that would result in the loss of a property right and that would defeat the point of the provision. However, the circumstances in which a person may be asked about their rights are many and varied, and the introduction of a reasonableness criterion must introduce uncertainty that can only be settled by litigation.

Indeed, there is some cause to question whether the provision, as enacted by Parliament, was in fact intended by the Law Commission. In its work leading to the 2002 Act, the Law Commission's discussion of reasonableness is not focussed on B's disclosure, but rather on the inquiries made by C. A limitation based on reasonable disclosure by B is substantively different from one based on reasonable inquiries by C. On the other hand, it could be said that the protection of B in cases where it is not reasonable to expect B to disclose his or her right is consistent with the general rationale identified by the Law Commission for overriding interests: if B's failure to protect a right through registration can be excused where it is not reasonable to expect B to have registered,[82] then B's failure to disclose a right should similarly be excused where it is not reasonable to expect B to have disclosed.

4.2.4 Where B is a minor child

The qualification in Sch 3, para 2(b) makes clear the general effect of allowing property rights of those in actual occupation to qualify as overriding interests: on inspecting the land, and encountering someone other than A in occupation, C should first make inquiry of that person to see if he or she has any property right in relation to the land. Under the LRA 1925, it was argued by C that, in some cases, however, the presence of B on the land did not ring any 'alarm bells' for C, as B's occupation could be explained simply by B's relationship with A. In *Bird v Syme-Thomson*,[83] for example, that argument was accepted by the court, with Templeman J stating that: '*if [A] is in actual occupation of the matrimonial home, it cannot be said that his wife also is in actual occupation. I hasten to add that, equally, if [A] is the wife and the house is occupied as the matrimonial home, then it is the wife who is in actual occupation and not the husband.*' This idea, sometimes referred to as the 'shadow doctrine' on the basis that B's occupation is seen merely as a shadow of A's right, has its origins in unregistered land. In cases where the doctrine of notice applied: it might be said that B's presence did not give C any notice of B's equitable interest, if B was simply occupying the matrimonial home. The idea was, however, conclusively rejected by the House of Lords in *Williams & Glyn's Bank v Boland*.[84] As we will see in the extract in section 4.2.7, Lord Wilberforce rejected the analogy between the registration scheme and the notice principle, stating that: '*Occupation, existing as a fact, may protect rights if the person in occupation has rights [. . .] I have no difficulty in concluding that a spouse, living in a house, has an actual occupation capable of conferring protection, as an overriding interest, upon rights of that spouse.*'

Lord Wilberforce's reasoning is clear, and also applies under the LRA 2002, as the provision also depends on the basic idea of actual occupation, which can be seen as simply a matter of fact, free from any of the complications that arose under the doctrine of notice. Nonetheless, the shadow doctrine was applied in relation to minor children in *Hypo Mortgage Services Ltd*

---

[82] Law Com 271, (2001), [8.6]: see section 4.1.   [83] [1979] 1 WLR 440 (HC).
[84] [1981] AC 487 (HL), 504-6.

v Robinson.[85] Nourse LJ considered it 'axiomatic' that such children are not in actual occupation for the purposes of statutory provisions governing overriding interests, but are present '*as shadows of occupation of their parent*'.[86] Nourse LJ justified the application of the doctrine by difficulties of making inquiries of children. This certainly provides a means of distinguishing the position of spouses or partners from those of minor children, and is consistent with the idea that the general effect of actual occupation is to alert C to the need to make inquiries. It would also mean that the limit on minor children having an overriding interest through actual occupation applies even in the unlikely case where the child is in sole occupation. It has been argued, however, that other means of circumventing this difficulty are available.[87] Ultimately, however, the likelihood of minor children having property rights is probably too slim to justify changes to the current position and the conveyancing practice based on it.

4.2.5 Who must be in actual occupation?

The answer to this question is, on the face of it, clear: it is B, the party with the relevant pre-existing property right, who must be in actual occupation if Sch 3, para 2 is to apply. Some care must be taken, however. Firstly, it may be that B is present on the property, but is there on behalf of another, and so it is that other, rather than B, who is regarded as in 'actual occupation' for the purposes of Sch 3, para 2. That was found to be the case in *Lloyd v Dugdale*:[88] Mr Dugdale had a pre-existing interest in land, and was present on that land, but the land was business premises and he was considered to be in occupation solely on behalf of the company that operated from the premises. As a result, the property right that he had acquired in his personal capacity was not binding as an overriding interest when the premises were sold. Secondly, it is possible for B to be in actual occupation through another even if B is not personally present. In *Lloyds Bank plc v Rosset*,[89] the Court of Appeal accepted that the presence of builders working on the land for Mrs Rosset was a means by which Mrs Rosset could be regarded as being in actual occupation. Nicholls LJ suggested that whether occupation by an employee or agent sufficed depended on the '*function which the employee or agent is discharging*'. So, B's resident housekeeper occupies on B's behalf, while B's licensee or tenant[90] does not.[91] This may of course create some difficulty for C, as the evidence of occupation in each case may be indistinguishable.

It is unclear what impact the reasonable inspection qualification may have on cases involving occupation by proxy. Is it necessary to consider, in each case, whether occupation by *B* is reasonably obvious on an inspection of the land that reveals the physical presence of an agent or employee, or does the fact that the presence of the agent or employee is reasonably obvious prevent C from invoking the qualification? *Thomas v Clydesdale Bank plc* may

---

85 [1997] 2 FLR 71.   86 Ibid, 72.

87 See Cooke, 'Children and Real Property: Trusts, Interests and Considerations' [1998] Fam Law 349. She suggests that inquiries could be made of a person with parental responsibility.

88 [2002] 2 P & CR 13. See esp [42]–[49].   89 [1989] Ch 350, [377].

90 In *Chaudhary v Yavuz* [2013] Ch 249, the Court of Appeal left open the question whether tenants were in occupation as proxies of their landlord. The point did not arise for consideration as it was held that the tenants' use fell short of occupation (see section 4.2.1). But it appears likely that the tenants' use was on their own behalf: [35] and McFarlane, 'Eastenders, Neighbours and Upstairs Downstairs' [2013] Conv 74, 77.

91 Compare the examples discussed by Nicholls LJ in *Lloyds Bank plc v Rosset* [1989] Ch 350, 377, and *Strand Securities v Caswell* [1965] Ch 958.

suggest the latter;[92] but the case concerned a preliminary application on a point of law, not a final determination on the facts, and so this specific question was not considered.

There is a separate question as to whether actual occupation can be established even if *no one is physically present on the land*. In *Chaudhary v Yavuz*, Lloyd LJ suggested that '*[o]ccupation must be, or be referable to, personal physical activity by some one or more individuals*'.[93] This comment suggests that the presence of B's possessions alone would not constitute occupation. However, Lloyd LJ's consideration of the point is obiter and, as we will see in section 4.2.9, there are cases in which the courts used the fact that B's possessions remained on the land to support a finding of actual occupation. In *Yavuz* (the facts of which are outlined in Chapter 3, section 3.2.2), Mr Chaudhary argued that he was in occupation of land through the presence on the land of a metal staircase and balcony. Rejecting this argument, Lloyd LJ explained, '*[t]he metal structure became part of the land on any basis, regardless of whether any part of it, as a chattel, belonged [to Mr Chaudhary] [. . .] It thus became part of what could be used or occupied*'.[94] This leaves open the position where occupation is claimed on the basis of the presence of chattels which are not part of the land in respect of which a person seeks to establish occupation.

4.2.6 Timing

Schedule 3, para 2 refers to '*An interest belonging at the time of disposition to a person in actual occupation [. . .]*': this makes clear that B's property right must exist at the time of the '*disposition*' to C, and also that B must be in actual occupation at that point.[95] As discussed in Chapter 8, section 5, the time of disposition will be earlier than the point where C registers its right. The importance of overriding interests, of course, lies in the fact that they are immune to the lack of registration defence, and that defence operates, under s 29 of the LRA 2002, at the time of C's registration. This led Lewison J, in *Thompson v Foy*, to suggest that Sch 3 para 2 can apply only if B is in occupation at the time of registration *as well as* the time of disposition.[96] He suggested that if B needs to be in occupation only at the time of the disposition to C, then the opening phrase of Sch 3, para 2 should read: '*An interest belonging to a person in actual occupation at the time of the disposition*.'[97] Lewison J's comments are obiter and, he acknowledged, against the prevailing commentary.[98] The question of whether B needs to be in actual occupation at the time of C's registration, as well as at the time of the disposition to C, must therefore be considered to remain open.[99]

4.2.7 Approaches to actual occupation

Having cleared a lot of ground in the previous six sections, we can now look at the key question of how the courts determine, in a particular case, if B is in actual occupation. Firstly, it is useful to look at possible approaches that a judge might adopt to the question. Like

---

[92] *Thomas v Clydesdale Bank plc* [2010] NPC 107, [38].   [93] [2013] Ch 249, [32].   [94] Ibid.

[95] Under the LRA 1925, it was also true that B had to be in actual occupation at the time of the disposition to C (see *Abbey National v Cann* [1991] 1 AC 56), but the House of Lords in *Cann* also stated that, as long as B was in actual occupation at that point, a property right held by B at the time of C's *registration*, would also be overriding: that is not the case under the LRA 2002.

[96] [2010] 1 P & CR 16, [122]–[126].   [97] Ibid, [124].   [98] Ibid, [126].

[99] Note that the question would of course disappear if, in a world of e-conveyancing, completion and registration could only occur simultaneously. As noted in Chapter 8, section 6.5.3, however, such a world is a long way off.

its 2002 successor, the LRA 1925 (in s 70(1)(g)) included property rights of those in actual occupation on the list of overriding interests. As a result, the general principles developed to defining actual occupation under the LRA 1925 remain authoritative.[100] In considering those principles, Hayton identified two differing approaches to the interpretation of the actual occupation requirement.

Hayton, *Registered Land* (3rd edn, 1981, p 87)

On the absolutist view [. . .] a person is absolutely bound by the rights of every person in actual occupation of the land [. . .] It matters not that it is unreasonably difficult to ascertain the actual occupier [. . .]; it matters not that it is unreasonable to expect someone to discover certain unusual rights of the occupier [. . .] Any traditional doctrine of notice is excluded from the self-contained paragraph.

The constitutionalist view of those accustomed to traditional conveyancing is that a person is only bound by the rights of every person in actual occupation [. . .] so far as such rights are binding according to traditional conveyancing principles (concerned with legal interests, equitable interests and the doctrine of notice, express, constructive and imputed) except as expressly limited or extended by statute.

Evidence of each approach can be found in cases dealing with actual occupation and so it cannot be said that the courts have conclusively adopted one approach rather than the other. For example, in the following case, the House of Lords preferred the absolutist approach.

Williams & Glyn's Bank v Boland
[1981] AC 487, HL

Facts: Mr Boland was the sole registered proprietor of the home in which he lived together with his wife. He used the home as security for a loan from the bank and subsequently defaulted on the payments. Mrs Boland, in fact, had a beneficial interest in the home as a result of contributions that she had made to its purchase. She argued that, because she was in occupation of the home, her interest bound the bank as an overriding interest. The first question that arose was whether she was in actual occupation. (The case was a consolidated action arising from claims by the bank against Mrs Boland and, in the other case, a Mrs Brown.)

Lord Wilberforce

At 504–6

Were the wives here in "actual occupation"? These words are ordinary words of plain English, and should, in my opinion, be interpreted as such [. . .]

Then, were the wives in actual occupation? I ask: why not? There was physical presence, with all the rights that occupiers have, including the right to exclude all others except

---

[100] *Link Lending Ltd v Bustard* [2010] EWCA Civ 424, [27].

those having similar rights. The house was a matrimonial home, intended to be occupied, and in fact occupied by both spouses, both of whom have an interest in it: it would require some special doctrine of law to avoid the result that each is in occupation. Three arguments were used for a contrary conclusion. First, it was said that if the vendor (I use this word to include a mortgagor) is in occupation, that is enough to prevent the application of the paragraph. This seems to be a proposition of general application, not limited to the case of husbands, and no doubt, if correct, would be very convenient for purchasers and intending mortgagees. But the presence of the vendor, with occupation, does not exclude the possibility of occupation of others. There are observations which suggest the contrary in the unregistered land case of *Caunce v. Caunce* [1969] 1 W.L.R. 286, but I agree with the disapproval of these, and with the assertion of the proposition I have just stated by Russell L.J. in *Hodgson v. Marks* [1971] Ch. 892, 934. Then it was suggested that the wife's occupation was nothing but the shadow of the husband's—a version I suppose of the doctrine of unity of husband and wife. This expression and the argument flowing from it was used by Templeman J. in *Bird v. Syme-Thomson* [1979] 1 W.L.R. 440, 444, a decision preceding and which he followed in the present case. The argument was also inherent in the judgment in *Caunce v. Caunce* [1969] 1 W.L.R. 286 which influenced the decisions of Templeman J. It somewhat faded from the arguments in the present case and appears to me to be heavily obsolete. The appellant's main and final position became in the end this: that, to come within the paragraph, the occupation in question must be apparently inconsistent with the title of the vendor. This, it was suggested, would exclude the wife of a husband-vendor because her apparent occupation would be satisfactorily accounted for by his. But, apart from the rewriting of the paragraph which this would involve, the suggestion is unacceptable. Consistency, or inconsistency, involves the absence, or presence, of an independent right to occupy, though I must observe that "inconsistency" in this context is an inappropriate word. But how can either quality be predicated of a wife, simply qua wife? A wife may, and everyone knows this, have rights of her own, particularly, many wives have a share in a matrimonial home. How can it be said that the presence of a wife in the house, as occupier, is consistent or inconsistent with the husband's rights until one knows what rights she has? and if she has rights, why, just because she is a wife (or in the converse case, just because an occupier is the husband), should these rights be denied protection under the paragraph? If one looks beyond the case or husband and wife, the difficulty of all these arguments stands out if one considers the case of a man living with a mistress, or of a man and a woman—or for that matter two persons of the same sex—living in a house in separate or partially shared rooms. Are these cases of apparently consistent occupation, so that the rights of the other person (other than the vendor) can be disregarded? The only solution which is consistent with the Act (section 70 (1) (g)) and with common sense is to read the paragraph for what it says. Occupation, existing as a fact, may protect rights if the person in occupation has rights. On this part of the case I have no difficulty in concluding that a spouse, living in a house, has an actual occupation capable of conferring protection, as an overriding interest, upon rights of that spouse.

The House of Lords held that Mrs Boland's beneficial interest was therefore enforceable against the bank as an overriding interest. The decision was controversial at the time, because it brought to light the previously unanticipated vulnerability of purchasers and mortgagees to beneficial interests being enforceable as overriding interests.

Notwithstanding the decision in *Boland*, it is still possible to find support for the constitutionalist view of actual occupation, as in the Court of Appeal's decision in the following case.

Lloyds Bank plc v Rosset
[1989] Ch 350, CA

Facts: Mr Rosset was the sole registered proprietor of a semi-derelict house that he and his wife were renovating and into which they were to move as their home. Builders were undertaking work on the house and Mrs Rosset was there almost daily, assisting in the decorating. Mr Rosset mortgaged the house and defaulted on the repayments. Mrs Rosset argued that she had a beneficial interest in the house that was enforceable against the bank as an overriding interest. In the Court of Appeal, Mrs Rosset's claim to a beneficial interest under a constructive trust was successful. The Court therefore considered whether she was in actual occupation.

Purchas LJ

At 403–4

The application of the words "in actual occupation" in section 70(1)(g) is the aspect of this appeal that has given me the most concern. The provisions of the section clearly were intended to import into the law relating to registered land the equitable concept of constructive notice. Thus, a purchaser or a chargee acquiring the title to or an interest in the land where the vendor was not in actual possession in order to protect his interest had to make appropriate inquiries if he found someone else in occupation of the property [. . .]

In order for the wife's interest in the property to qualify as an overriding interest under section 70(1)(g) two things must be established: (a) was she in actual occupation? and (b) would appropriate inquiries made by the bank have elicited the fact of her interest?

The majority of the Court of Appeal held that Mrs Rosset was in occupation and had a beneficial interest enforceable against the bank. The case went on appeal to the House of Lords, where it was held that Mrs Rosset did not, in fact, have a beneficial interest.[101] She therefore did not have any property right capable of protection as an overriding interest and the issue of occupation did not arise for decision.

Hence, under s 70(1)(g) the absolutist and constitutionalist constructions had both attracted judicial support. Which approach is taken is of practical significance in cases where it is unclear whether or not B's connection to the land amounts to actual occupation. As we will see in section 4.2.9, a new twist to the debate has been added by some recent decisions[102] allowing B's intentions and personal circumstances to be taken into account when determining actual occupation. This has led Bogusz to suggest that the approach developed by the courts under the LRA 2002 has in fact marked the adoption of a 'third way':[103]

---

[101] This aspect of the case is considered in Chapter 12, section 2.3.1.
[102] See e.g. *Link Lending v Bustard* [2010] EWCA Civ 424.
[103] As we will see in section 4.2.9, Bevan, 'Overriding and Over-extended? Actual Occupation: A Call to Orthodoxy' [2016] Conv 104, argues that this 'third way' approach is unwelcome, but accepts that there is evidence for it in recent case law.

Bogusz, 'The Relevance of "Intentions and Wishes" to Determine Actual Occupation: A Sea Change in Judicial Thinking?' [2014] Conv 27, 28

The academic analysis has led to the categorisation of actual occupation as either an "absolutist" or "constitutional" construction, and while these may have been helpful in the past, it is at least questionable whether a "constitutional" construction of actual occupation continues to be valid to the same extent it may have been under s.70(1)(g) LRA 1925. Unlike the absolutist construction, which arises principally from the direct factual analysis of actual occupation and remains broadly valid under Sch.3 para.2 of the LRA 2002, the constitutionalist interpretation, which favours a contextual analysis, would appear to have been more recently usurped by a judicial willingness to consider the relevance of extraneous factors in addition to the factual position and create a "third way" of determining actual occupation. The primary effect of this "third way" is that it has "softened" the impact of the absolutist construction by lifting the curtain and apportioning increased significance to what can be most appropriately described as "all the circumstances" of the case. While this hybrid approach may offer improved protection for a person claiming actual occupation, this form of analysis may require the judiciary to resort to supposition and imply occupation on the basis of a person's beliefs or intentions, both of which are difficult to independently corroborate.

4.2.8 Assessing actual occupation: the relevant principles

In *Baker v Craggs*, a case we mentioned in Chapter 5, section 6.2, examined in Chapter 8, section 6.5, and will return to in Chapter 17, section 2.3, one of the more straightforward points considered by Newey J related to actual occupation: by virtue of visiting a barn more or less daily in order to carry out work there, had Mr Craggs been in actual occupation of that land at the point when the Bakers were granted an easement over that land? In deciding that question in favour of Mr Craggs, Newey J first summarized some key legal propositions as to the meaning of actual occupation.[104]

Baker v Craggs
[2016] EWHC 3250 (Ch), [2017] Ch 295

Newey J

At [12]

The authorities seem to me to support the following propositions as regards 'actual occupation'.

(i) The word 'actual' in 'actual occupation' emphasises that what is required is physical presence, not some entitlement in law: *Boland*.[105]

---

[104] An appeal is pending against the decision of Newey J (for updates see the online resources) but the more controversial parts of his judgment are those discussed in Chapters 8 and 17. The summary of the principles relevant to actual occupation closely follows similar summaries given in previous cases, such as that of Lewison J in *Thompson v Foy* [2009] EWHC 1076 (Ch).

[105] [1981] AC 487, 505.

(ii) The nature of the relevant property can matter. 'Occupation', Lord Oliver explained in *Cann*,[106] is a 'concept which may have different connotations according to the nature and purpose of the property which is claimed to be occupied'. In a similar vein, Arden LJ observed in *Malory Enterprises Ltd v Cheshire Homes (UK) Ltd*,[107] 'What constitutes actual occupation of property depends on the nature and state of the property in question.'

(iii) 'Occupation' involves 'some degree of permanence and continuity which would rule out mere fleeting presence' (to quote again from Lord Oliver in *Cann*).[108] Lord Oliver went on to say:[109]

> *'A prospective tenant or purchaser who is allowed, as a matter of indulgence, to go into property in order to plan decorations or measure for furnishings would not, in ordinary parlance, be said to be occupying it, even though he might be there for hours at a time.'*

On the other hand, *'regular and repeated absence'* can be consistent with 'actual occupation': see *Kingsnorth Finance v Tizard*.[110]

(iv) 'Occupation' does 'not necessarily ... involve the personal presence of the personal claiming to occupy': Lord Oliver in *Cann*.[111] Lord Oliver expressed the view that a 'caretaker or the representative of a company can occupy ... on behalf of his employer.'[112] In *Lloyds Bank v Rosset*, Nicholls LJ (in the Court of Appeal)[113] considered that 'the presence of a builder engaged by a householder to do work for him in a house is to be regarded as the presence of the owner when considering whether or not the owner is in actual occupation.' In *Kling v Keston Properties*,[114] Vinelott J considered the plaintiff to have been in 'actual occupation' of a garage in which his wife's car had been confined because the door was blocked and thought that the result would probably have been the same even if the car had not been trapped: the plaintiff, Vinelott J suggested:

> *'should be treated as being in continuous occupation of the garage while he was using it in the ordinary course for the purpose for which the licence was granted, that is, for garaging a car as and when it was convenient to do so.'*

(v) In contrast, 'actual occupation' by a licensee on his own behalf does not represent 'actual occupation' by the licensor: see *Strand Securities Ltd v Caswell*[115] and *Lloyd v Dugdale*.[116] Nor does receipt of rents and profits now suffice to give protection. Section 70(1)(g) of the LRA 1925, the predecessor of para 2 of Sch 3 to the 2002 Act, referred to the rights of a person 'in actual occupation of the land *or in receipt of the rents and profits thereof.*' Nothing comparable to the italicised words is to be found in the 2002 Act.

(vi) Even in the case of a house, 'occupation' need not involve residence. In *Rosset*, Nicholls LJ[117] said that he could '*see no reason, in principle or in practice, why a semi-derelict house ... should not be capable of actual occupation whilst the works proceed and before anyone has started to live in the building.*' See too *Thomas v Clydesdale Bank plc*.[118]

(vii) Occupation needs to be distinguished from mere use. In *Chaudhary v Yavuz*,[119] use of a metal staircase and landing for the purpose of passing and repassing between some flats and the street was held not to amount to 'actual occupation'. Such activity, Lloyd LJ said, is *'use, not occupation.'*

---

[106] [1991] 1 AC 56, 93. [107] [2002] Ch 216, [80]. [108] [1991] 1 AC 56, 93.
[109] [1991] 1 AC 56, 93. [110] [1986] 1 WLR 783, 788. [111] [1991] 1 AC 56, 93.
[112] [1991] 1 AC 56, 93. [113] [1989] Ch 350, 378. [114] (1983) 49 P & CR 212, 219.
[115] [1965] Ch 958, 980–1, 984. [116] [2002] 2 P & CR 13, [45]. [117] [1989] Ch 350, 377.
[118] [2010] EWHC 2755 (QB). [119] [2013] Ch 249.

(viii) As Mummery LJ observed in *Link Lending v Bustard*,[120] when determining whether a person is in 'actual occupation':

> 'The degree of permanence and continuity of presence of the person concerned, the intentions and wishes of that person, the length of absence from the property and the reason for it and the nature of the property and personal circumstances of the person are among the relevant factors.'

(ix) An interest belonging to a person in 'actual occupation' will be protected only if and so far as it relates to land of which he is in actual occupation. This is evident from the wording of para 2 of Sch 3 of the 2002 Act, which in this respect differs significantly from that of section 70(1)(g) of the LRA 1925.

(x) The date on which a person must be in 'actual occupation' to rely on para 2 of Sch 3 to the 2002 Act is the date of disposition, ie completion.

In applying those principles to the facts of the case, Newey J held that Craggs had been in actual occupation of the barn at the relevant time: whilst he had not been sleeping there, that could not be expected of a barn that was being converted into stables, and his almost daily presence there to carry out the conversion work meant that he certainly maintained more than a mere fleeting presence. It was true that, at the time of the disposition to the Bakers, that work had been finished, but Newey J held at [22] that:

> On balance, however, it seems to me that Mr Craggs was still in 'actual occupation' of the yard on 20 February 2012. He had finished the work in the Craggs barn only very recently: probably, in fact, just the previous day. While, moreover, he happened not to visit the farm on 20 February, he continued to go there frequently, albeit often in connection with activities (fencing, for example) in parts of the farm other than the Craggs barn.

4.2.9 Assessing actual occupation: applying the relevant principles

It is notable that, in setting out the principles relevant to actual occupation, Newey J in *Baker v Craggs* did not state a simple general test. Indeed, as noted by Mummery LJ in *Link Lending v Bustard*: '*The trend of the cases shows that the courts are reluctant to lay down, or even suggest, a single legal test for determining whether a person is in actual occupation.*'

This means that, in applying the relevant principles to a specific factual situation, it is often useful to look for analogies between that situation and past cases. For example, in *Baker*, Newey J drew on *Lloyds Bank v Rosset*, where the Court of Appeal had found that, by her regular visits to supervise ongoing building work, Mrs Rosset had been in actual occupation, and also **Thomas v Clydesdale Bank** where, on a preliminary application, the court considered there was an arguable case that Ms Thomas's occupation was established by her almost daily presence while the property was being renovated. In *Link Lending*, Ms Bustard had been absent from the property for over a year as she had been sectioned under the Mental Health Act and admitted to hospital. Her furniture and personal possessions remained at the property and she made brief but regular supervised visits. She had continued to discharge the outgoings and always intended to return home. Indeed, the dispute with the

---

120 [2010] EWCA Civ 424, [27].

lender arose only because she had been tricked into transferring the property to X, who had then used the property as security for the loan from Link Lending. Mrs Bustard thus had an equity to set the transfer aside: a recognized pre-existing equitable interest in land[121] that would bind Link Lending unless it could invoke the lack of registration defence.

The judge at first instance had held that Ms Bustard had remained in actual occupation; this was confirmed by the Court of Appeal. A relevant authority (albeit one not referred to by the court) was *Chhokar v Chhokar*:[122] a wife was absent from the family home as she had gone into hospital to have a baby, but was considered to remain in actual occupation despite her physical absence, as her possessions evidenced her occupation. In *Link Lending*, Mummery LJ distinguished the facts from those of *Stockholm Finance Ltd v Garden Holdings Inc*. There, the court was asked whether a Saudi princess had remained in actual occupation of her London home, in which she had not 'set foot' for a year. Robert Walker J (as he then was) answered in the negative:[123]

> Whether a person's intermittent presence at a house which is fully furnished, and ready for almost immediate use, should be seen as continuous occupation marked (but not inter-rupted) by occasional absences, or whether it should be seen as a pattern of alternating periods of presence and absence, is a matter of perception which defies deep analysis. Not only the length of any absence, but also the reason for it, may be material (a holiday or a business trip may be easier to reconcile with continuing and unbroken occupation than a move to a second home, even though the duration is the same in each case). But there must come a point at which a person's absence from his house is so prolonged that the notion of his continuing to be in actual occupation of it becomes insupportable; and in my judgment that point must have been reached in this case, long before Mr Dawkins visited the house on 4 January 1990 (and still more so, long before 20 February 1990). By then Princess Madawi had not set foot in the property for over a year: she had for over a year been living with her mother in the Islamic household at Riyadh.

The reason for B's absence provides an important difference between *Stockholm Finance* and *Link Lending*: as noted by Mummery LJ in the latter case, B's residence elsewhere was 'invol-untary'. Mummery LJ went further when stating that, in assessing actual occupation: '*The degree of permanence and continuity of presence of the person concerned, the intentions and wishes of that person, the length of absence from the property and the reason for it and the nature of the property and personal circumstances of the person are among the relevant factors.*'

The extent to which B's intentions and wishes should be used to determine whether he or she is in occupation is, however, contentious. It finds support not only in Mummery LJ's statement, but also from the decision in *Thomas v Clydesdale Bank*, where Ramsey J took into account the '*intention and wishes*' of Ms Thomas and her partner to reside in the property once renovations were complete.[124] Taking into account intent as well as physical acts has resonance with how 'possession' is understood—for example, in a claim to adverse possession discussed in Chapter 9. The analogy is not, however, a perfect one: occupation and possession are not synonyms. Further, in the priority context, reference to B's intent is problematic as it is not something that C can discover through an inspection of the land. In

---

[121] This is confirmed, in relation to registered land, by LRA 2002, s 116(b). See section 4.2.1.
[122] [1984] FLR 313.   [123] [1995] NPC 162.   [124] [2010] EWHC 2755 QB, [32].

the following extract, Bogusz suggests that despite the difficulties, B's intentions and wishes are being relied upon by the court both increasingly and strategically.

Bogusz, 'The Relevance of "Intentions and Wishes" to Determine Actual Occupation: A Sea Change in Judicial Thinking?' [2014] Conv 27, 32

The positioning of the "intention and wishes" of the person within the rubric devised by Mummery L.J. cannot be dismissed as merely imprecise judicial language. It is arguably used strategically as the second factor for consideration by the courts, following on from "the degree of permanence and continuity of presence"; and the two component parts would appear to be interdependent upon each other. The latter is determined to some extent by use of a straightforward objective factual assessment of the time periods indicating occupation, and further complemented by an examination of the circumstances which elaborate on the reason for the person's temporary absence. By reference to the intentions and wishes of a party in his statement, Mummery L.J. has formally acknowledged these as relevant factors that the courts should take into consideration. In some sense this should not be such a surprise, since this potentially reflects the reality and logic of what the courts take into account when determining actual occupation; in short this can be considered to form part of the internal logic that arises from assessing factual and contextual occupation. However, the use of intentions and wishes is not without difficulty, not least because the effect of the court employing these imprecise intentions in its reasoning may result in what can be termed "occupation creep". That is to say, the existence of actual occupation may be extended to a person in circumstances where the facts alone are vague with regard to whether Sch.3 para.2 is satisfied. The latent result of confirming the existence of actual occupation by reference to a person's intentions is that it could have a significant and unexpected impact upon the rights of legal owners or third parties, for example mortgagees, who are bound by an interest which, factually, may not have been unequivocally established nor anticipated.

The danger of 'occupation creep', noted by Bogusz, is expanded on by Bevan in the following extract, where he argues that the court should instead adopt a more limited approach, focussed on objective facts observable by C. He regards such a limited approach as fitting better with the overall aim of the LRA 2002 to simplify conveyancing by protecting C against pre-existing interests not recorded on the register, and also as more 'orthodox', as it accords with statements in the House of Lords in *Boland* and *Cann* to the effect that actual occupation is '*essentially a question of fact*'.

Bevan, 'Overriding and Over-extended? Actual Occupation: A Call to Orthodoxy' [2016] Conv 104

108

[The] traditional, objective assessment of actual occupation finds express support in a close reading of the statutory provisions on actual occupation in Sch 3, para 2, for example in the clear objective test of 'obviousness' under para 2(c)(i). Yet this traditional, objective approach to actual occupation has been challenged in recent jurisprudence. A series of contemporary court decisions[125] [. . .] reflects an apparent break from the past and a shift from the hitherto more objective, traditional, fact-led analysis towards a more expansive, more subjective approach that engages notions of party intentions, wishes and feelings.

112

It is contended here that the current approach as seen in the recent case-law can be criticised on four principal grounds: first, for its inconsistency vis-à-vis the clear direction of travel within modern land law towards a narrowing, reduced role for overriding interests as evidenced by both the Law Commission's work and the statutory language of the 2002 Act itself; secondly, for its apparent results-orientated focus and its failure to articulate precisely how such subjective notions are to be discerned and employed as part of an actual occupation analysis. Thirdly, the current, more subjective approach is challenged as resting on shaky foundations stemming from landlord and tenant law rather than rooted in principles of land registration;[126] and, finally, for permitting policy arguments to trump principle in determinations of actual occupation.

114

One might seek to justify the current expansive approach to actual occupation on the grounds that a broader assessment of the circumstances of the case including intentions and feelings affords greater protection to 'vulnerable' claimants (such as Mrs Bustard) who are faced, for example, with losing their home through no apparent fault of their own [. . .] Whilst such a policy aim may be entirely laudable, it must still be underpinned by the statutory language and the legislative history [. . .] There must be a very real risk that the current approach to actual occupation could lead to an unmerited drift in the scope of actual occupation resulting in a burdening of legal owners and third parties, such as mortgagees, with the interests of those in actual occupation in circumstances that display no apparent, physical occupation at all. If such an expansive analysis is materialising, this must require a more robust, democratic legislative underpinning than apparent judicial activism.

In Chapter 18, section 4, we will consider further different approaches to determining the extent of overriding interests. It is interesting to analyse Bevan's argument in light of the tension between the 'doctrinal' and 'utility' models discussed in Chapter 1, section 5.2. As noted there, those models can lead to different conceptions of the proper judicial role: on the former, a judge's function may be seen as more limited, whereas on the latter it may be justifiable for a judge to develop the law in order to reach desired outcomes in specific cases. Bevan's argument can thus be seen as preferring the 'doctrinal' model, even if, on the facts of specific cases such as *Link Lending*, it might lead to seemingly harsh results.

---

[125] [Reference is made here to *Link Lending* [2010] EWCA Civ 424 and *Thomas v Clydesdale Bank* [2010] EWHC 2755 (QB), as well as to *Thompson v Foy* [2009] EWHC 1076 (Ch).]

[126] [Bevan's point here is that Lewison J in *Thompson v Foy* [2009] EWHC 1076 (Ch), one of the cases relied on by Mummery LJ in *Link Lending*, in turn relies on *Hoggett v Hoggett* (1980) 39 P & CR 121 (CA) to show the importance of an intention to return to the property, even though the point in *Hoggett* arose not in the context of overriding interests, but rather in relation to a specific point of landlord and tenant law.]

4.3 SCHEDULE 3, PARA 1: LEGAL LEASES OF SEVEN YEARS OR LESS

As evident from the length of the discussion in section 4.2, the most significant category of overriding interests consists of property rights of those in actual occupation of registered land. It is important, however, to remember that Sch 3, para 2 is not the only provision that allows rights to be overriding. Sch 3, para 1 ensures that, with some exceptions,[127] legal leases created for seven years or less are overriding interests within Sch 3, para 1, of the LRA 2002. This provision therefore covers legal leases that fall below the duration at which a lease becomes a registered estate. The combined effect of this paragraph and s 33 of the Act (concerned with entry of a notice) is to give a dual means of protection to legal leases of more than three years, but not greater than seven years. These leases may be protected by entry of a notice and are overriding interests in the absence of such an entry. Legal leases of three years' duration or less are protected only as overriding interests. Equitable leases fall outside the scope of Sch 3, para 1 (which is confined to 'leases *granted*').[128] An equitable lease that is not protected by entry of notice may be an overriding interest under Sch 3, para 2, where the tenant is in actual occupation.

4.4 SCHEDULE 3, PARA 3: LEGAL EASEMENTS AND *PROFITS À PRENDRE*

Legal easements and profits are overriding interests under Sch 3, para 3, of the LRA 2002.

Land Registration Act 2002, Sch 3, para 3

(1) A legal easement or profit a prendre, except for an easement, or a profit a prendre which is not registered under the Commons Registration Act 1965 (c. 64), which at the time of the disposition—

   (a) is not within the actual knowledge of the person to whom the disposition is made, and

   (b) would not have been obvious on a reasonably careful inspection of the land over which the easement or profit is exercisable.

(2) The exception in sub-paragraph (1) does not apply if the person entitled to the easement or profit proves that it has been exercised in the period of one year ending with the day of the disposition.

The scope of this paragraph needs to be understood in light of the general treatment of easements within the 2002 Act. The express grant of a legal easement is a registered disposition and such easements necessarily appear on the register.[129] Paragraph 3 is therefore directed at legal easements that arise from an implied grant.[130] The limitation of the provision to legal easements is significant: the equivalent provision in the LRA 1925 had controversially been

---

[127] Listed in the 2002 Act, Sch 3, para 1(a) and (b).
[128] See *City Permanent Building Society v Miller* [1952] Ch 840 (CA).   [129] Ibid, s 27(2)(e).
[130] The rules governing the implied grant of easements are considered in Chapter 25.

interpreted as including some equitable easements.[131] Equitable easements will now bind B only if protected by entry on the register or as overriding interests under sch 3, para 2 where actual occupation is established.[132] This is consistent with Sch 3, para 1, which protects short legal leases, but does not apply to equitable leases.

The scope of Sch 3, para 3 appears abstruse, but, unpackaged, it provides as follows: a legal easement arising from an implied grant is overriding if C has actual knowledge of its existence, *or* it is obvious on a reasonably careful inspection of the land, *or* it has been exercised in the year preceding the disposition. The latter is designed to ensure the protection of practically important, but 'invisible', easements, including drainage in an underground pipe.[133] The practical effect of the provision, therefore, is that B's implied legal easement is very likely to be an overriding interest.

The provision has been tightly drawn and is intended to dovetail with inquiries made by C. The underlying goal is that C should become aware of binding easements prior to completion of the disposition.

Law Commission Report No 271, *Land Registration for the Twenty-First Century: A Conveyancing Revolution* (2001, [8.71])

What we wish to encourage is the creation of a straightforward system of standard inquiries as to easements and profits which will prompt sellers to disclose what they can reasonably be expected to know. This in turn will ensure that such rights are then registered. We anticipate that, prior to contract, a seller would be expected to disclose any unregistered easements or profits affecting his or her property of which he or she was aware, at least to the extent that they were not obvious on a reasonably careful inspection of the land. In particular, he or she would be asked to disclose any easements or profits that had been exercised in the year preceding the inquiry. The result of such inquiries is likely to be that the buyer will have actual knowledge of any unregistered legal easements and profits long before the transaction is completed.

5 RESTRICTIONS ON OWNER'S POWERS

In Chapter 3, section 3.2.1, we noted the importance of ss 23 and 24 of the LRA 2002, which set out the '*owner's powers*' held by A, a party registered as holding an estate or charge. Those provisions, along with s 58 of the LRA 2002,[134] give C reassurance that A does indeed have the power to make a disposition in favour of C.[135] In particular cases, however, A's powers may be limited. That would be the case if, for example, A is a trust company holding its estate on trust for B, and the terms of the trust specify that any dealings with the land can be

---

[131] Land Registration Act 1925, s 70(1)(a), as interpreted in *Celsteel Ltd v Alton House Holdings Ltd* [1985] 1 WLR 204.

[132] See further the discussion in section 5.1 above.

[133] Law Commission No 271 (2001), [8.70].

[134] Also discussed in Chapter 3, section 3.2.1.

[135] See e.g. *Pye v Stodday Land Ltd* [2016] EWHC 2454 (Ch), [2016] 4 WLR 168, [33].

made only with the consent of B. How then can B be sure that C is made aware of that special limit on A's powers? As we noted in section 3.2, s 33 of the LRA 2002 makes clear that B cannot enter a notice to protect his or her right under a trust of land. Rather, B can enter a *restriction*: a restriction is the means by which limits on A's owner's powers are recorded on the register.

5.1 NATURE AND EFFECT OF A RESTRICTION

The nature and effect of a restriction is explained in ss 40 and 41 of the LRA 2002.

Land Registration Act 2002, s 40

(1) A restriction is an entry in the register regulating the circumstances in which a disposition of a registered estate or charge may be the subject of an entry in the register.

(2) A restriction may, in particular—

    (a) prohibit the making of an entry in respect of any disposition, or a disposition of a kind specified in the restriction;

    (b) prohibit the making of an entry—

        (i) indefinitely,

        (ii) for a period specified in the restriction, or

        (iii) until the occurrence of an event so specified.

(3) Without prejudice to the generality of subsection (2)(b)(iii), the events which may be specified include—

    (a) the giving of notice,

    (b) the obtaining of consent, and

    (c) the making of an order by the court or registrar.

(4) The entry of a restriction is to be made in relation to the registered estate or charge to which it relates.

Land Registration Act 2002, s 41

(1) Where a restriction is entered in the register, no entry in respect of a disposition to which the restriction applies may be made in the register otherwise than in accordance with the terms of the restriction, subject to any order under subsection (2).

(2) The registrar may by order—

    (a) disapply a restriction in relation to a disposition specified in the order or dispositions of a kind so specified, or

    (b) provide that a restriction has effect, in relation to a disposition specified in the order or dispositions of a kind so specified, with modifications so specified.

(3) The power under subsection (2) is exercisable only on the application of a person who appears to the registrar to have a sufficient interest in the restriction.

So, in our example where A, a trust company, holds its registered estate on trust for B, and the terms of the trust state that A can only dispose of the land with B's consent, a restriction can be entered on the register to ensure that no disposition is recorded on the register unless B's consent has been obtained.[136] We noted in section 3.1 that the entry of a restriction has a quite different effect to the entry of a notice on the register. Whereas a notice can preserve B's priority by preventing C from relying on the lack of registration defence, a restriction aims instead to prevent C acquiring a registered right at all if the limit on A's powers has been exceeded.[137]

As far as priorities are concerned, the most significant use of a restriction is in relation to cases, such as our example, in which B has a beneficial interest (i.e. an interest under a trust). As we noted in Chapter 15, section 4.3, in such cases, C may be able to rely on the overreaching defence in order to gain priority over B's pre-existing beneficial interest. If that defence applies, C will have priority even if B was in actual occupation of the land at the time of the disposition to C. We will examine the overreaching defence in more detail in Chapter 17, but, where the disposition to C involves the payment of purchase money by C, the defence can operate only where C pays that money to a minimum of two trustees, or to a trust corporation. Where land is held on trust, therefore, a restriction should be entered on the register to ensure that the payment condition is met.[138] Indeed, where there are two or more registered proprietors of an estate, the Registrar is obliged to enter a restriction to this effect.

Land Registration Act 2002, s 44(1)

If the registrar enters two or more persons in the register as the proprietor of a registered estate in land, he must also enter in the register such restrictions as rules may provide for the purpose of securing that interests which are capable of being overreached on a disposition of the estate are overreached.

In such a case, it would be very unwise for C to fail to comply with the restriction:[139] the disposition to C could not then be registered, and so C would not gain any legal estate, nor would C be able to rely on the lack of registration defence, nor could C rely on the overreaching defence. In practice, however, the entry of the restriction of course assists C, by ensuring that overreaching takes place. So, whereas the entry of a notice is a means by which B can protect the priority of his or her right, a restriction very often simply ensures that C will be able to take priority, by utilizing the overreaching defence. Restrictions thus support the curtain principle, discussed in Chapter 3, section 2.5, by ensuring that C need not be concerned with the details of any trust affecting the registered estate: C simply needs to pay any purchase money to two trustees or a trust corporation in order to gain priority over any

---

[136] Law Com CP No 227, [10.34].

[137] See Law Com CP No 227, [10.2]. It is also noted at [10.8] that the *'function of restrictions is broader than simply the protection of property rights'* as it is possible to enter a restriction to prevent a disposition which would be a breach by A of a purely personal duty owed to B. There is, of course, no priority issue in such a case, as B's right is only a personal right against A. The use of restrictions in such cases has caused some difficulties in practice and the Law Commission have raised the question of whether there are particular types of purely personal duty that should not be capable of protection by a restriction: Law Com CP No 227, [10.29].

[138] Law Com CP No 227, [10.32].

[139] See e.g. Cooke, *The New Law of Land Registration* (Oxford: Hart Publishing, 2003) at 53, describing a restriction as a *'trip-wire to prevent the making of an* entry *of a disposition; it does not actually prevent the making of the disposition itself'*.

pre-existing beneficial interests. That is why the Law Commission in its 2016 Consultation Paper, having examined the use of restrictions where B has a pre-existing beneficial interest, stated that:[140] *'We conclude that, given the curtain principle [. . .] (a purchaser of land should not be concerned with beneficial interests provided that they are overreached), the existing mechanisms for the protection of beneficial interests under trusts are sufficient and that no further protection is appropriate.'*

5.2 APPLYING FOR A RESTRICTION

We have seen in section 5.1 that, under s 44(1) of the LRA 2002, there is a case in which a restriction *must* be entered by the registrar. In other cases, under s 42, the Registrar has a power to enter a restriction. It is also possible for a person to apply to the registrar for such an entry to be made: under s 43, A may do so (as registered proprietor);[141] a party with A's consent may do so;[142] as may anyone (such as B) who has *'a sufficient interest in the making of an entry'*.[143]

6 THE EFFECT OF FRAUD

We noted in Chapter 3, and will also examine in Chapter 18, the possibility that C (who has acted entirely innocently) may acquire registered title as a result of a fraud by A, or by X. Such cases raise a very difficult issue, canvassed by the Law Commission in its 2016 Consultation Paper,[144] as to the effect of another's fraud on the indefeasibility of C's registered title. What if, however, it is C who is involved in fraud or wrongdoing: can that conduct prevent C from taking advantage of the priority rules put in place by the LRA 2002, in particular the lack of registration defence provided by s 29?[145] Few would argue that C's conduct should be left unchecked,[146] but it is harder to find agreement as to the appropriate response.

6.1 C'S FRAUD AND THE LACK OF REGISTRATION DEFENCE

Torrens systems of registration of title[147] have a two-pronged response to transactions that would on their face enable C to invoke a defence against B's pre-existing property right but in fact involve some fraud or wrongdoing by C.[148] Where the transaction is considered to constitute fraud (a term defined specifically for this purpose), C is denied statutory protection and is bound by B's pre-existing property rights. C's fraud thus prevents C from

---

[140] Law Com CP No 227, [10.47].

[141] LRA 2002, s 43(1)(a), which also allows an application by a person entitled to be registered as proprietor.

[142] LRA 2002, s 43(1)(b): the consent of a person entitled to be registered as proprietor also suffices.

[143] LRA 2002, s 43(1)(c).

[144] Law Com CP No 227 (2016) Chapter 13.

[145] This of course raises a different issue from the effect of another's fraud on the indefeasibility of C's title. The distinction between the two issues is highlighted by Cooke and O'Connor, 'Purchaser Liability to Third Parties in the English Land Registration System: A Comparative Perspective' (2004) 120 LQR 640, 640–3.

[146] See e.g. *Scott v Southern Pacific Mortgages Ltd* [2014] UKSC 52, [122] (Lady Hale).

[147] Torrens systems are those based on the scheme introduced into South Australia by Sir Robert Torrens in 1858 (see Chapter 3, section 2.5) and include the registration systems in e.g. Victoria, New South Wales, and New Zealand.

[148] This summary of the Torrens approach is based on the account provided ibid.

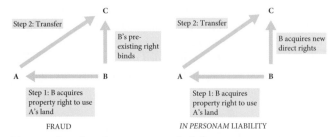

Figure 16.2 Torrens fraud and *in personam* liability

invoking the lack of registration defence. Where C's wrongdoing falls short of fraud, then C can still invoke the lack of registration defence, and will thus have priority over B's pre-existing property right. However, in such a case, B may be able to show that, as a result of C's conduct, B has acquired a *new, direct* right against C. We discussed some examples of such new, direct rights in Chapter 7, section 3.3. The difference between these solutions is illustrated in Figure 16.2.

We saw there that a new direct right may be either a personal right, binding only C, or a property right. It is therefore somewhat unfortunate that, in Torrens systems, cases where C has a defence to B's pre-existing property right, but is instead caught by a new, direct right arising as a result of C's own conduct, are often said to depend on an '*in personam* liability' of C.

The English land registration system is distinct from Torrens systems, and it has never explicitly adopted the same approach to cases of wrongdoing by C. Under the LRA 1925, it was possible to find examples of cases in which C's knowledge of B's pre-existing property right was used as a reason to prevent C from relying on the lack of registration defence.[149] The enforcement of B's pre-existing property rights where B has actual knowledge has attracted some academic support for introducing an ethical element into registration.[150] The LRA 2002, however, contains nothing similar to the Torrens fraud exception to the lack of registration defence, as the Law Commission was very keen to ensure that questions of C's knowledge should not interfere with the simple basic scheme under which B's right can affect C only if it is entered on the register or is overriding.[151]

Law Commission Report No 254, *Land Registration for the Twenty-First Century: A Consultative Document* (1998, [3.46])

[. . .] We have concluded—as the Law Commission has done on two previous occasions—that there should in general be no place for concepts of knowledge or notice in registered land. We have reached this conclusion for the following reasons—

1. It was intended that the system of registration under the Land Registration Act 1925 should displace the doctrine of notice.

---

[149] See e.g. *Peffer v Rigg* [1977] 1 WLR 285.

[150] Battersby, 'Informal Transactions in Land, Estoppel and Registration' (1995) 58 MLR 637, 655–6. The issue is discussed in Law Commission No 254 (1998), [3.44]–[3.46].

[151] The recommendation endorsed in the paragraph extracted here was adopted in Law Commission No 271 (2001), [5.16].

2. There is little evidence of which we are aware that the absence of the doctrine of notice in dealings with registered land has been a cause of injustice in the seventy-two years in which the present system has been operative.

3. The ethical argument is weaker than at first sight it appears to be if the issue is considered in relation to those principles which should in our view, guide the development of land registration. Registration should be regarded as an integral part of the process of creating or transferring interests in registered land, closely akin to the formal requirement of using a deed (or in some cases, writing) in unregistered conveyancing. Just as a deed is required to convey or create a legal estate or interest in unregistered conveyancing, a disposition of registered land must be completed by registration if it is to confer a legal estate or interest. When electronic registration is introduced, it seems probable that many rights will be incapable of being created *except* by registering them.

4. In practice, if it were provided that unregistered rights in or over registered land were binding because a purchaser had *actual* knowledge of them, it would be very difficult to prevent the introduction by judicial interpretation of doctrines of *constructive* notice. If actual knowledge sufficed, the question would inevitably be asked: why not wilful blindness as well? In reality the boundary between actual knowledge and constructive notice is unclear and is, in our view, incapable of precise definition.

5. The mere fact that a purchaser *could* be bound if he or she had actual knowledge of an unregistered right or interest would inevitably weaken the security of title that registered land at present provides. Disappointed third parties, who found their rights apparently defeated by a purchaser, would threaten litigation. Because of the nuisance value of such threats, purchasers would often settle out of court.

Cooke and O'Connor argue that in focussing on notice-based liability the Law Commission lost sight of the possible role that could be played by a requirement of good faith, where a finding of bad faith requires something more than mere notice.

Cooke and O'Connor, 'Purchaser Liability to Third Parties in the English Land Registration System: A Comparative Perspective' (2004) 120 LQR 640, 657–8

Thus, a useful baby (purchaser-liability for Torrens fraud because of the absence of good faith) has been thrown out with the bathwater (purchaser-liability for notice). And all the argument is directed at the bathwater; arguments against imposing liability on the purchaser for Torrens fraud, or against requiring good faith on the purchaser's part, are simply not given.

Nonetheless, the current position is clear: the fact that C has not acted in good faith, and has knowledge of B's pre-existing property right, does not, by itself, prevent C from invoking the lack of registration defence under s 29 of the LRA 2002. English law thus does not contain an equivalent of the Torrens fraud exception.

6.2 C'S FRAUD AND NEW, DIRECT RIGHTS

In emphasizing that C's knowledge of B's pre-existing property right should not, by itself, prevent C from invoking the lack of registration defence, the Law Commission emphasized the possibility that C's conduct might nonetheless allow B to acquire a new, direct right.

Law Commission Report No 254, *Land Registration for the Twenty-First Century: A Consultative Document* (1998, [3.48]–[3.49])

Furthermore, [. . .] the law provides a wide range of *personal* remedies against those who in some way behave improperly. The operation of these personal remedies can be demonstrated by four examples.

1. If A transfers trust property to [C] in breach of trust and [C] knows or (perhaps) has notice of this, [C] is liable as constructive trustee for "knowing receipt" of trust property. Liability is personal and not proprietary and the obligation is to make restitution for the loss suffered by the trust. It has been assumed that this form of liability may apply where the trust property transferred is registered land and the rights of the beneficiaries have not been protected, so that as a matter of property law, the transferee takes the land free of the trust

2. If property is transferred by A to [C] expressly subject to some right of [B's] which will not in fact bind [C], a constructive trust may be imposed upon [C] if he refuses to give effect to [B's] right in circumstances in which that refusal is unconscionable. [C] can in this way be compelled to give effect to [B's] rights [. . .]

3. There may be circumstances where tortious liability is imposed because A conspires with [C] to defeat [B's] proprietary rights.

4. If [C] induces A by misrepresentation or undue influence to charge his or her property to [B] to secure [C's] debts, A will be able to set the charge aside if [B] has notice of [C's] misconduct.

In each of these cases, a purchaser may acquire the registered land free from the rights of the third party, yet find himself personally liable for the loss suffered by that third party or subject to some personal equity, which enables the transaction to be set aside [. . .]

Although described by the Law Commission as 'personal remedies', this, just like the term '*in personam* liability' as used in Torrens systems, is a misnomer. It is apparent from the examples given that the Law Commission, in fact, is referring to new direct rights that may either be personal (as in examples 1, 3, and 4 in the extract above) or proprietary (as in example 2).

Land law does not exist in a vacuum and the possibility of new direct rights arising on a transfer is beyond doubt[152]—but reliance on other principles is not without controversy or difficulty. When C's position is no longer dependent on the registration statutes, there is a risk that liability will be imposed in circumstances that run contrary to the principles of the registration scheme. This raises the question of whether the general rules regulating the acquisition of new, direct rights should be modified in a case where C has acquired, for valuable consideration, a registered right. In *Chaudhary v Yavuz*, for example, Lloyd LJ suggested that such a modification may be suitable where B has failed to take the chance to

---

[152] For an example of B's successfully claiming a new, direct right in a case where C had a defence to B's pre-existing property right, see *Lyus v Prowsa Developments Ltd* [1982] 1 WLR 1044.

protect his or her pre-existing right by entering a notice on the register, and the contract between A and C makes no specific reference to B's right. In such a case, the registration system would be relevant, as C '*may be thought to be entitled to rely on [a party such as B] protecting themselves in the manner provided for under the legislation*'.[153]

The better view, it is submitted, is that there is no such need to modify the general rules. It is true that if, for example, a new direct right were to arise simply on the basis that C ought to have discovered B's pre-existing property right, that would undermine the whole purpose of a registration scheme in limiting the inquiries C has to make when acquiring a right in land. As we saw in Chapter 7, section 3.3, however, the need to limit the grounds on which B can acquire a new, direct right is not unique to registration schemes. Where B's initial right is only a personal right, if the courts were too ready to protect B against C by finding a new, direct right, this would formally respect the fact that B's initial right does not bind C, but would in practice undermine the whole purpose of distinguishing between personal and proprietary rights: the need to protect third parties such as C. That is why it has long been clear, in relation to land, that C's knowledge of B's personal right cannot, by itself, give B a new, direct right against C.[154] It is also why, in *Yavuz* itself, an application of the general rules, unmodified by any concerns specific to registration, ensured that B acquired no new, direct right against C.

Certainly, the English courts' current approach, as seen in Chapter 7, section 3.3, is to be very cautious as to when such new, direct rights can arise and to ensure that they are not recognized, for example, on the basis of '*inferences from slender materials*',[155] or on the mere fact that C knew, or ought to have known, of a pre-existing property right of B. As Sir Christopher Slade LJ stated in *Lloyd v Dugdale*:[156] '*There is no general principle which renders it unconscionable for a purchaser of land to rely on a want of registration of a claim against registered land, even though he took with express notice of it. A decision to the contrary would defeat the purpose of the legislature in introducing the system of registration embodied in the [LRA 1925].*' As noted by Lloyd LJ in *Chaudhary v Yavuz*:[157] '*that approach is even more amply justified under the 2002 Act than it was before. It does not exclude the possibility that the court may find an obligation binding on the registered proprietor personally, by way of, for example, a constructive trust, as a result of which an obligation which is not protected on the register is nevertheless effective.*' In that case, the Court of Appeal refused to find that B can acquire a new, direct right against C whenever B's right (although neither registered nor overriding) would have been obvious for C to spot on inspecting the land. That is perfectly consistent with the position applying generally, even where C does not acquire a registered right: for B to acquire a new, direct right against C, more than mere knowledge is required. C would, for example, have to agree specifically to '*undertake a new obligation, not otherwise existing, to give effect to [B's] prior interest*'.[158]

7 CONCLUSION

The LRA 2002 provides a distinct scheme of priority rules for a category of transactions (registrable dispositions of registered estates for valuable consideration) that incorporates

---

[153] [2013] Ch 249, [62].   [154] See *Keppell v Bailey* (1834) 2 My & K 517.

[155] *Ashburn Anstalt v Arnold* [1989] Ch 1, 26 (*per* Fox LJ).

[156] [2002] 2 P & CR 13, [50].   [157] [2013] Ch 149, [68].

[158] See *Lloyd v Dugdale* [2001] EWCA Civ 1754, [2002] 2 P & CR 13, [52] and *Chaudhary v Yavuz* [2013] Ch 249, [59].

the most common dealings with land. C has a defence (the lack of registration defence) against the enforcement of B's pre-existing property rights, except those that are entered on the register by a notice or binding as an overriding interest. The disposition must also comply with any limitations on A's owner's powers recorded on the register by entry of a restriction.

There is a need to find a satisfactory reconciliation between the operation of these statutory defences, and ensuring that fraud and wrongful conduct by C does not go unchecked. The policy of the 2002 Act is to rely on the creation of new direct rights arising under the general law. This may involve the imposition on C of personal liability to B, or the creation of a new proprietary right for B.

QUESTIONS

1. What do you understand to be meant by a 'registrable disposition of a registered estate for valuable consideration'? What is the significance of this category of transaction for determining questions of priority in registered land?

2. To what extent do the priority rules in registered land implement the 'mirror' and 'curtain' principles?

3. Compare and contrast the scope and effect of entry of a restriction and entry of a notice.

4. How useful are the constitutionalist and absolutist views of the meaning of 'actual occupation' in determining the scope of Sch 3, para 2, of the Land Registration Act 2002?

5. Assess the advantages and disadvantages of responding to fraud or other wrongdoing in a disposition of land to B by: (i) preventing B from invoking statutory defences against C's property rights; and (ii) relying on the creation of new direct rights.

6. What action should the holder of the following property rights in registered land take? In what circumstances will a purchaser of the land have a defence against the enforcement of these rights?

   a. A beneficial interest under a trust.

   b. A legal lease created for five years.

   c. A legal easement arising from an implied grant.

   d. An equitable easement.

   e. A restrictive covenant.

 For guidance on how to answer these questions visit the online resources at www.oup.com/uk/mcfarlane4e/.

FURTHER READING

Bevan, 'Overriding and Over-Extended? Actual Occupation: A Call to Orthodoxy' [2016] Conv 104

Bogusz, 'Defining the Scope of Actual Occupation Under the Land Registration Act 2002: Some Recent Judicial Clarification' [2011] Conv 268

Bogusz, 'The Relevance of "Intentions and Wishes" to Determining Actual Occupation: A Sea Change in Judicial Thinking?' [2014] Conv 27

Cooke and O'Connor, 'Purchaser Liability to Third Parties in the English Land Registration System: A Comparative Perspective' (2004) 120 LQR 640

Dixon, 'The Reform of Property Law and the Land Registration Act 2002: A Risk Assessment' [2003] Conv 136

Jackson, 'Title by Registration and Concealed Overriding Interests: The Cause and Effect of Antipathy to Documentary Proof' (2003) 119 LQR 660

Law Commission Report No 254, *Land Registration for the Twenty-First Century: A Consultative Document* (1998, Parts IV–VII)

Law Commission Report No 271, *Land Registration for the Twenty-First Century: A Conveyancing Revolution* (2001, Parts V, VI, and VIII)

Law Commission Consultation Paper No 227, *Updating the Land Registration Act 2002* (2016, Part III)

Smith, '*Williams and Glyn's Bank Ltd v Boland* (1980): The Development of a System of Title by Registration' in *Landmark Cases in Land Law* (ed Gravells, Oxford: Hart Publishing, 2013)

17

CO-OWNERSHIP AND PRIORITIES: THE DEFENCES QUESTION

CENTRAL ISSUES

1. Where co-owned land is sold or mortgaged, a question of priority may arise between a beneficiary who is not a party to the transaction and the purchaser. In co-owned land, priority is determined primarily by the mechanism of overreaching.

2. This mechanism, which applies to registered and unregistered land, enables the purchaser to take free from beneficial interests as long as certain conditions are met. As such, it operates as a defence to a pre-existing equitable interest in land. The beneficiaries' interests are removed from the land and attach to the proceeds of sale.

3. Where overreaching does not occur, priority between the beneficiary and purchaser is determined using the separate rules of registered and unregistered land.

4. The preconditions for overreaching include a requirement that any purchase money is paid to a minimum of two trustees. As a result, a practical distinction is drawn between one and two trustee trusts. In two-trustee trusts,

priority is determined by overreaching, while in one-trustee trusts, the separate priority rules of unregistered and registered land are applied.

5. The prevailing view is that the basis of overreaching lies in the trustees' powers of disposition and its operation is therefore dependent on the trustees acting within their powers.

6. Purchasers and mortgagees may often benefit from statutory protection even where trustees have acted ultra vires, although the level of protection differs between registered and unregistered land.

7. The operation of overreaching against beneficiaries in occupation continues to be contentious and may remain vulnerable to challenge under the Human Rights Act 1998.

8. Overreaching does not operate in a legal vacuum and new direct rights (proprietary and personal) may arise between beneficiaries and purchasers of trust land through alternative causes of action.

1 INTRODUCTION

This chapter is concerned with the priority rules applicable on the disposition, usually by way of sale or mortgage, of co-owned land. It considers the circumstances in which the beneficial interests of those who are not party to the sale or mortgage as legal owners are binding against the purchaser or mortgagee. In this book, we have conceptualized priority rules as part of the *defences* question (see Chapter 15). In that respect, this chapter is concerned with when a purchaser or mortgagee has a defence against the enforcement of pre-existing beneficial interests.

The priority between beneficiaries and third parties is determined primarily by the mechanism of *overreaching*. Overreaching is a mechanism enabling purchasers to take title free from certain property interests, particularly beneficial interests under a trust. In other words it provides the purchaser or mortgagee with a defence against the enforcement of those interests. The interests are removed from the land and attached instead to the proceeds of sale.

Overreaching applies in relation to both personal property and land, although we are concerned only with its application to land. It applies as long as two conditions are met: firstly, the interest must be capable of being overreached; and secondly, the transaction must be one that has overreaching effect. Where these conditions are met, overreaching applies to the exclusion of other priority rules. Importantly, it applies both to registered and unregistered land. Only where one of the conditions is not met is the enforcement of the beneficial interest against the purchaser determined by the separate priority rules that have been examined in Chapter 16. The priority rules discussed in that chapter are therefore wholly subsidiary to the overreaching mechanism.

In this chapter, we will focus on the particular form of overreaching that applies where a purchaser or mortgagee deals with land held on trust: although we will note other recent examples of overreaching. In such cases, a key element of the requirement that a transaction has overreaching effect is that any capital money is paid to a minimum of two trustees. The practical effect of overreaching is thus to draw a division between transactions undertaken by a single trustee and those executed by two or more trustees. Where there are two or more trustees, issues of priority between a purchaser and beneficiary are determined by overreaching. Where there is a single trustee, priority between a purchaser and the beneficiaries generally falls to be considered under the separate priority rules governing registered and unregistered land.

This chapter focusses on the operation of the overreaching mechanism. The final part of the chapter, section 7, then briefly notes how issues of priority are determined where overreaching does not take place and addresses a specific issue that arises on a sale by a sole surviving legal joint tenant.

2 OVERREACHING

The effect of overreaching is explained in Wolstenholme and Cherry in the following terms.

Wolstenholme and Cherry's Conveyancing Statutes Vol I (12th edn, ed Farrand, 1972, p 51)

In such cases [where overreaching operates] the purchaser is not concerned with the title to the equitable interest or power, or to obtain the concurrence of the owner thereof. On the other hand, the equitable interest or power is not defeated or destroyed by the disposition, but is shifted so as to become a corresponding interest or power in or over the proceeds [. . .] The conveyance to the purchaser is then said to 'overreach' the equitable interest or power [. . .] An overreaching conveyance must be distinguished from one which wholly destroys some interest or right.

The key aspect of this explanation lies in the idea that overreaching operates to *shift* the interest from an interest in land to an interest in the proceeds of the conveyance. The purchaser or mortgagee thus obtains title to the land unencumbered by the interest. The holder of the overreached interest no longer has any proprietary claim in the land, but a beneficial interest in the moneys received by the trustees. His or her interest has shifted from an interest in land to an interest in money. In this way, overreaching draws a clear distinction between the beneficiaries' rights against purchasers, on the one hand, and their rights against their trustees, on the other.

Overreaching operates within a complex statutory framework and implements fundamental principles of the trust curtain and security of transactions, both for purchasers and, more particularly (in the leading cases), mortgage lenders. Because the application of the mechanism has been stretched to (and, some would argue, beyond) its legitimate limits, its continuing fitness for purpose is being called into question, together with its compliance with the Human Rights Act 1998 (HRA 1998).

So why do we have overreaching? In the following case, it was considered that the consequences of not giving full effect to overreaching would be as follows.

City of London Building Society v Flegg [1988] 1 AC 54

Lord Oliver

At 76–7

[To reverse, by judicial decision] the legislative policy of the 1925 legislation of keeping the interests of beneficiaries behind the curtain and confining the investigation of title to the devolution of the legal estate [. . .] financial institutions advancing money on the security of land will face hitherto unsuspected hazards, whether they are dealing with registered or unregistered land.

This comment reflects the twin objectives of implementing the trust curtain and ensuring security of transactions.

In this chapter, we first consider the general scope of overreaching, and then address the operation of overreaching in two particular circumstances: where the beneficiaries are in occupation of the land, and where the transaction is executed ultra vires (outside) the trustees' powers or in breach of trust. Following an assessment of whether overreaching remains fit for its purpose, we consider the future of the mechanism.

2.1 THE SCOPE OF OVERREACHING

For overreaching to take place, two conditions must be met: firstly, the interest must be capable of being overreached; secondly the transaction must be one that has overreaching effect. Both of these requirements are apparent from the terms of s 2 of the Law of Property Act 1925 (LPA 1925).

Law of Property Act 1925, s 2

(1) A conveyance to a purchaser of a legal estate in land shall overreach any equitable interest or power affecting that estate, whether or not he has notice thereof, if—

  (i) the conveyance is made under the powers conferred by the Settled Land Act, 1925, or any additional powers conferred by a settlement, and the equitable interest or power is capable of being overreached thereby, and the statutory requirements respecting the payment of capital money arising under the settlement are complied with;

  (ii) the conveyance is made by trustees of land and the equitable interest or power is at the date of the conveyance capable of being overreached by such trustees under the provisions of subsection (2) of this section or independently of that subsection, and the requirements of section 27 of this Act respecting the payment of capital money arising on such a conveyance are complied with;

  (iii) the conveyance is made by a mortgagee or personal representative in the exercise of his paramount powers, and the equitable interest or power is capable of being overreached by such conveyance, and any capital money arising from the transaction is paid to the mortgagee or personal representative;

  (iv) the conveyance is made under an order of the court and the equitable interest or power is bound by such order, and any capital money arising from the transaction is paid into, or in accordance with the order of, the court.

(1A) An equitable interest in land subject to a trust of land which remains in, or is to revert to, the settlor shall (subject to any contrary intention) be overreached by the conveyance if it would be so overreached were it an interest under the trust.

(2) Where the legal estate affected is subject to [a trust of land], then if at the date of a conveyance made after the commencement of this Act by the trustees, the trustees (whether original or substituted) are either—

  (a) two or more individuals approved or appointed by the court or the successors in office of the individuals so approved or appointed; or

  (b) a trust corporation,

any equitable interest or power having priority to the trust shall, notwithstanding any stipulation to the contrary, be overreached by the conveyance, and shall, according to its priority, take effect as if created or arising by means of a primary trust affecting the proceeds of sale and the income of the land until sale.

(3) The following equitable interests and powers are excepted from the operation of subsection (2) of this section, namely—

  (i) Any equitable interest protected by a deposit of documents relating to the legal estate affected;

(ii) The benefit of any covenant or agreement restrictive of the user of land;

(iii) Any easement, liberty, or privilege over or affecting land and being merely an equitable interest (in this Act referred to as an "equitable easement");

(iv) The benefit of any contract (in this Act referred to as an "estate contract") to convey or create a legal estate, including a contract conferring either expressly or by statutory implication a valid option to purchase, a right of pre-emption, or any other like right;

(v) Any equitable interest protected by registration under the Land Charges Act, 1925, other than—

(a) an annuity within the meaning of Part II, of that Act;

(b) a limited owner's charge or a general equitable charge within the meaning of that Act.

(4) Subject to the protection afforded by this section to the purchaser of a legal estate, nothing contained in this section shall deprive a person entitled to an equitable charge of any of his rights or remedies for enforcing the same.

(5) So far as regards the following interests, created before the commencement of this Act (which accordingly are not within the provisions of the Land Charges Act, 1925), namely—

(a) the benefit of any covenant or agreement restrictive of the user of the land;

(b) any equitable easement;

(c) the interest under a puisne mortgage within the meaning of the Land Charges Act, 1925, unless and until acquired under a transfer made after the commencement of this Act;

(d) the benefit of an estate contract, unless and until the same is acquired under a conveyance made after the commencement of this Act;

a purchaser of a legal estate shall only take subject thereto if he has notice thereof, and the same are not overreached under the provisions contained or in the manner referred to in this section.

2.2 INTERESTS CAPABLE OF BEING OVERREACHED

The remainder of the section substantially curtails the initially broad statement in s 2(1) of the LPA 1925. Firstly, subs (3) excludes certain equitable interests from the scope of overreaching. The general effect of this subsection is to remove from the operation of overreaching most equitable interests that do not take effect under a trust: of particular import are equitable easements, restrictive covenants, and estate contracts. Discussing the scope of overreaching in *Birmingham Midshires Mortgage Services Ltd v Sabherwal*,[1] Robert Walker LJ endorsed a distinction drawn by Megarry and Wade[2] between 'commercial' and 'family' interests. Family interests, such as beneficial interests under a trust, can readily be represented by money; in contrast, commercial interests (which Robert Walker LJ considered to be exemplified by equitable easements and rights of entry) '*cannot sensibly shift from the land*'. They are logically inseparable from the land over which they are intended

---

[1] (2000) 80 P & CR 256, 28.

[2] Citing from *Megarry and Wade: The Law of Real Property* (5th edn, ed Harpum, 1984) p 409.

to be exercised. In this respect, the effect of subs (3) is to exclude such commercial interests from the initially broad wording of s 2(1).

In respect of estate contracts, the case of *Baker v Craggs*[3] has decided, not without controversy, that an estate contract merges with a transfer that had not yet been registered so as to fall outside the subs (3) exclusion and thus was capable of being overreached. We explore this case further in section 2.3.

The second respect in which the broad statement in s 2(1) of the 1925 Act is curtailed is that an interest must be '*capable of being overreached*' through the particular transactions listed in s 2(1)(i)–(iii).[4] Hence, it is necessary to identify which interests are '*capable of being overreached*' by each type of transaction mentioned. Paragraphs (i) and (iii) can be dealt with briefly in this regard. As regards para (i), the interests capable of being overreached by a conveyance made under the Settled Land Act 1925 are identified by s 72 of that Act. This includes (but is not limited to) the beneficial interests under the settlement. It is not discussed further, because the Settled Land Act 1925 is in the process of being phased out.[5]

As regards para (iii), in relation to mortgages, this provision ensures that an exercise of the power of sale overreaches the mortgagor's equity of redemption and any subsequent mortgages.[6] Its operation is further discussed in Chapter 26, section 3.1.2.[7]

Of much greater significance is para (ii), which provides for overreaching on a conveyance by trustees of land. Beneficial interests under a trust of land are '*capable of being overreached*' on a conveyance by the trustees where overreaching is provided for by s 2(2) or '*independently of that subsection*'. Section 2(2) provides for overreaching of interests already in existence at the time the trust was created. This is a concept of extended overreaching that may be invoked only by a trust corporation, or by trustees approved or appointed by the court for the purpose. Section 2(2) does not, however, provide for overreaching of the beneficial interests under the trust: the most common and practically significant use of the mechanism, and the use with which we are particularly concerned in this chapter. The basis for overreaching beneficial interests under a trust of land must therefore be found outside the terms of s 2.

On what basis are the beneficial interests under a trust of land '*capable of being overreached*'? Four theories have been advanced, three of which are consistent with the view that overreaching has the same basis and scope in registered and unregistered land. These three theories are:

- that overreaching is provided for by s 27(1) of the LPA 1925;
- that it is based on the doctrine of conversion; or
- that overreaching is inherent in the trustees' powers of disposition.

It will be seen that only the last of these provides a convincing basis for overreaching of the beneficial interests under a trust of land.

---

[3] [2017] Ch 295.

[4] The analogous requirement in para (iv) is found in the requirement that the interest is 'bound by' the court order.

[5] A full discussion of the scope of the Settled Land Act, s 72, is provided in *Megarry and Wade: The Law of Real Property* (7th edn, eds Harpum et al, 2008) [A-093]–[A-100].

[6] Personal representatives have the same functions as trustees of land (by virtue of the Administration of Estates Act 1925, s 9(1)(ii)) and therefore the interests capable of being overreached on an exercise of these powers are the same as those overreached on a sale by trustees of land.

[7] The effect of such overreaching is considered in *Horsham Properties Group Ltd v Clark* [2008] EWHC 2327, [50]–[51].

The fourth theory is that, while the trustees' powers of disposition provide the basis of overreaching in unregistered land, the Land Registration Act 1925 (LRA 1925) provided—and the Land Registration Act 2002 (LRA 2002) now provides—its own basis for the operation of the mechanism in registered land. On this fourth view, the basis of overreaching and, as a consequence, its scope differs between registered and unregistered land.

2.2.1 Overreaching and s 27(1) of the Law of Property Act 1925

The first theory is that s 27(1) of the LPA 1925 provides the basis of overreaching.

Law of Property Act 1925, s 27(1)

(1) A purchaser of a legal estate from trustees of land shall not be concerned with the trusts affecting the land, the net income of the land or the proceeds of sale of the land whether or not those trusts are declared by the same instrument as that by which the trust of land is created.

From Harpum's seminal analysis of overreaching[8] (parts of which are extracted in section 2.2.2), it is apparent that there are at least two difficulties with using s 27(1) as the basis of the mechanism. Firstly, while we are concerned only with the operation of overreaching in relation to land, the same mechanism is applied to trusts of personal property. Therefore, it cannot have its basis in legislation, such as s 27(1), which is applicable only to land. Secondly, overreaching itself pre-dates the 1925 legislation and therefore its basis must be found outside that legislation.[9]

What, then, is the effect of s 27(1)? It appears to serve two purposes. Firstly, it seems likely that it was intended merely as a declaration of the existing law.[10] It provides a statement of the effect of a conveyance that complies with the conditions of overreaching, but it does not provide the basis for the mechanism itself, nor does it negate the need to show that those conditions have been complied with.[11] Secondly, it absolves the purchasers from any need to ensure that the trustees apply the purchase money in accordance with the terms of the trust.

2.2.2 Overreaching and the doctrine of conversion

The second theory is that the basis of overreaching lies in the doctrine of conversion. That doctrine, which applied to trusts for sale, had the effect that, from the inception of the trust, the beneficiaries were considered to have an interest in the proceeds of sale of the land, rather than the land itself.[12] The doctrine was abolished by s 3 of the Trusts of Land and Appointment of Trustees Act 1996 (TOLATA 1996).

---

[8] Harpum, 'Overreaching, Trusteees' Powers and the Reform of the 1925 Legislation' (1990) 49 CLJ 277.
[9] Ibid, 278.
[10] Explained in the annotation of the section provided by Wolstenholme and Cherry, *Conveyancing Statutes* (11th edn, 1932).
[11] Hopkins, 'Overreaching and the Trusts of Land and Appointment of Trustees Act 1996' [1997] Conv 81, 82.
[12] The doctrine is further explained in Chapter 13, section 5.3.

If the doctrine of conversion provided the basis of overreaching of beneficial interests under a trust for sale, then overreaching should not be possible where trustees hold land under a trust of land, rather than under a trust for sale. This would mean that the 1996 Act, in removing the statutory trust for sale formerly imposed in cases of co-ownership of land, would have dramatically limited the applicability of overreaching. Such a consequence would be wholly unintended. In its report that led to the 1996 Act, the Law Commission specifically envisaged the application of overreaching to trusts of land.[13]

On an initial analysis, there appears to be a logical connection between the doctrine of conversion, providing that beneficiaries have only an interest in proceeds of sale from the inception of the trust, and overreaching, which leaves beneficiaries with a claim against the proceeds on sale. But despite this apparent connection between conversion and overreaching, it seems that conversion did not, in fact, provide the basis on which overreaching took place within a trust for sale. Indeed, Harpum dismissed any suggestion of a connection between the doctrines as a misconception.

Harpum, 'Overreaching, Trustees' Powers and the Reform of the 1925 Legislation' (1990) 49 CLJ 277, 278–9

The second misconception is that overreaching is connected with the doctrine of conversion, at least in relation to trusts for sale. Because of that doctrine, it is said that the interests of the beneficiaries are from the inception of the trust in the proceeds of sale. Such a view is untenable as an explanation of overreaching. First, a disposition under a mere *power* of sale will overreach just as much as a disposition under a trust for sale, and this is so even though the doctrine of conversion has no application to powers of sale. Secondly, the doctrine of conversion is usually relevant to determine whether beneficial interests are in land or in personalty. Overreaching applies as much to trusts for sale of personalty as to trusts of realty. Thirdly, overreaching is concerned to transfer trusts from the original subject-matter of the trust to the *actual* proceeds *after* sale. The beneficial interests of those entitled under a trust for sale, by reason of the doctrine of conversion, are regarded for certain purposes as interests in the *notional* proceeds of sale *from the date of the creation of the trust*. There is no inevitability about the application of the doctrine of conversion to trusts for sale, and indeed the doctrine suffers from inherent logical flaws. The correct approach in every case is, it is suggested, to ask whether, as a matter of policy and for the particular purpose in issue, the interests of the beneficiaries should be regarded as interests in the subject matter of the trust or in the proceeds. It is not easy to predict whether the doctrine of conversion will ever again be used to explain overreaching. Lord Oliver, who in analysing the interests of tenants in common in *City of London Building Society v. Flegg*, favoured a strict application of the doctrine of conversion, certainly assumed that overreaching occurred on sale, but at the same time cited with approval the statement that "[t]he whole purpose of the trust for sale is to make sure, by shifting the equitable interests away from the land and into the proceeds of sale, that a purchaser of the land takes free from the equitable interests".

---

[13] Law Commission Report No 181, *Transfer of Land: Trusts of Land* (1989) [6.1].

2.2.3 Overreaching and trustees' powers of disposition

The third theory is that the basis of overreaching of beneficial interests under a trust is the trustees' powers of disposition. Harpum, who describes overreaching as a 'necessary concomitant' of such powers, favours this theory.[14] In relation to trusts of land, this means that the basis of overreaching of beneficial interests under such trusts is the powers of disposition conferred on trustees by s 6 of the TOLATA 1996.

Locating the basis of overreaching in the trustees' powers has now attracted a significant degree of acceptance.[15] Ultimately, in view of the shortfalls identified in the other two theories, this view provides the most satisfactory explanation of the basis of overreaching of beneficial interests under a trust of land that can be applied to both registered and unregistered land. The theory is not, however, without its own difficulties. For example, as Sparkes notes,[16] there is nothing in the 1996 Act to say that trustees, having exercised a power of sale, hold the proceeds on trust for the beneficiaries. There is no doubt that such a trust exists, because the trustees cannot take the proceeds themselves, but because the trust is the necessary consequence of overreaching, this omission appears odd if the exercise of powers conferred by the 1996 Act provides the basis through which the mechanism operates.[17]

Further, using the trustees' powers as the basis of overreaching has also given rise to one of the key remaining issues on the scope of the mechanism. If the basis of overreaching lies in the trustees' powers, it follows that overreaching can take place only when the trustees are acting *within* those powers. We consider in section 4 the different arguments that have been raised as regards dispositions by trustees that are ultra vires their powers of disposition.

2.2.4 Overreaching in registered land

The final theory to consider is that the LRA 1925 provided its own basis of overreaching for registered land, which has been carried over into the LRA 2002.

Jackson has advanced this argument.[18]

Jackson, 'Overreaching in Registered Land Law' (2006) 69 MLR 214, 227–8

Any purchaser from a trustee also takes a title under section 20 [of the Land Registration Act 1925], *whether he has notice* of adverse equities or not: 'and the disposition shall operate in like manner as if the registered transferor or grantor were [. . .] entitled to the registered land

---

[14] Harpum (1990) p 277.

[15] See *Snell's Equity* (32nd edn, ed McGhee, 2010), [4.013]; Smith, *Plural Ownership* (2005) pp 184–5, Fox, 'Overreaching' in *Breach of Trust* (ed Birks and Pretto, 2002) ch 4; McFarlane, *The Structure of Property Law* (2008) pp 394–404.

[16] Sparkes, *A New Land Law* (2nd edn, 2003), [13.51]. He notes the contrast with the trust for sale, where a trust of the proceeds was express within the terms of the trust.

[17] Although see the explanation provided by McFarlane (2008) pp 400–1.

[18] This argument is not without support in previous literature. For example, see the discussion of the Land Registration Act 1925, s 18, by Harpum (1990) p 308. His comments on s 18 were, however, rejected by Ferris and Battersby, 'The Impact of the Trusts of Land and Appointment of Trustees Act 1996 on Purchasers of Registered Land' (1998) Conv 168, 180–4, further developed in their subsequent work 'Overreaching and the Trusts of Land and Appointment of Trustees Act 1996: A Reply to Mr Dixon' [2001] Conv 221 and 'General Principles of Overreaching and the Reforms of the 1925 Legislation' (2002) 118 LQR 270, 281–2.

in fee simple in possession for his own benefit'. Benjamin Cherry, in his evidence to the *Royal Commission on the Land Transfer Acts*, describes this as the 'overreaching' effect of registration. Apart from restrictions, which prevented registration of a transfer that did not comply with their terms, trusts were kept off the face of title. Section 94(1) of the Land Registration Act 1925 provided that trustees are registered as proprietors, not as trustees. There was also a direction in section 74 to keep trusts, as far as possible, off the face of the register [. . .]

The effect of sections 20, 74 and 94 is to bring about a substantive alteration in the nature of the beneficial interest from a proprietary claim to a claim solely against the substitute property or proceeds of sale in the hands of the trustee(s). Some minor interests could become burdens on the land by registration against the title. Other matters could not be protected against a purchaser in this way, such as interests under a trust for sale or settlements. Such interests could be protected by entries on the register that restricted the registered owner's freedom to deal with the land. The intention behind these restrictions was to ensure that the land was dealt with in accordance with the terms of the trust or settlement. The nature of the beneficiary's interest changed from a proprietary right to a mere restriction or 'restraint on alienation'. But the default position was that trustee proprietors would be able to deal with the land as any ordinary proprietor could.

In essence, Jackson's argument is that, in registered land, overreaching arises through the process of registration itself. It is the cumulative effect of provisions aimed at keeping trusts off the register and those protecting purchasers from matters that have not been entered on the register as a restriction on how land can be dealt with. While the statutory provisions upon which Jackson's argument is based have changed in the LRA 2002, she suggests that the same scheme of overreaching has been maintained.[19]

If Jackson is correct, a chasm has been created between the operation of overreaching in registered and unregistered land. The basis and scope of overreaching in each would need to be separated. Two significant practical consequences follow. Firstly, if overreaching is not based on the trustees' powers of disposition, then it arises regardless of whether the trustees are acting within their powers.[20] The discussion of this matter (in section 4) would be an issue only for unregistered land.

Secondly, a disposition by a single trustee in registered land would overreach beneficial interests. The need for any capital money to be paid to two trustees would not apply to registered land unless, again, entered as a restriction on the register. The discussion (in section 2.3) of this requirement would also be confined to unregistered land.[21]

Jackson's theory, as she acknowledges, is against the 'universally unquestioned' view that ss 2 and 27 of the LPA 1925 apply equally to registered and unregistered land.[22] To date, courts have not differentiated the operation of overreaching in each scheme of land, although the Court of Appeal has made some suggestions that the LRA 2002 does have a part to play in overreaching, which we explore in section 2.2.5.[23] To do so now (with the practical

---

[19] Jackson, 'Overreaching in Registered Land Law' (2006) 69 MLR 214, 241, fn 183.

[20] A consequence confirmed by Jackson, 'Overreaching and Unauthorised Disposition of Registered Land' [2007] Conv 120. She says, at 129: '*I contend that an unauthorised disposition by trustees of registered land would always overreach.*'

[21] In this respect, it should be noted that while the Law of Property Act 1925, s 2(1)(ii), refers to a conveyance by 'trustees of land' in the plural, this is no bar to an argument for overreaching by a single trustee. The Interpretation Act 1978, s 6(c), provides '*words in the singular include the plural and words in the plural include the singular*'.

[22] Jackson (2007) p 229.   [23] See *Mortgage Express v Lambert* [2017] Ch 93.

consequences that would follow) would require a fundamental reversal of current under-standing. It is notable that Jackson's argument is developed around the LRA 1925. If that Act was intended to provide a self-contained scheme of overreaching the LRA 2002 provided an opportunity to reassess the position. In the absence of any clarification provided by that Act it is suggested that the better view remains that, for both registered and unregistered land, the basis of overreaching lies in the trustees' powers of disposition.

2.2.5 Other interests capable of being overreached

In addition to the interests for which overreaching is provided in s 2 of the LPA 1925, it has been accepted that some interests claimed under proprietary estoppel must also be capable of being overreached.

Birmingham Midshires Mortgage Services Ltd v Sabherwal
(2000) 80 P & CR 256, CA

Facts: Mrs Sabherwal lived in a house with her two sons and their families. Legal title to the house was vested in the sons who had defaulted on charges granted to BMMS to raise money to support their business ventures. Mrs Sabherwal sought to establish that she had a proprietary interest in the house binding against BMMS. One argument made was that she had an interest through proprietary estoppel, which, in contrast to a bene-ficial interest under a trust of land, was not capable of being overreached.

Robert Walker LJ

At 24–32

On the facts of this case, Mrs Sabherwal plainly made a substantial financial contribution to all the properties successively owned by the family. She could rely on a resulting trust and had no need to rely on proprietary estoppel (if and so far as the two are, in the context of the family home, distinct doctrines: see the observations of Sir Nicolas Browne-Wilkinson V-C in *Grant v Edwards* [1986] 1 Ch 638, [1986] 2 All ER 426 at 656 of the former report). If she had made no financial contribution, but had nevertheless acted to her detriment in reliance on her sons promises, she might have obtained (through the medium of estoppel rather than through the medium of a trust) equitable rights of a proprietary nature. Her actual occupation of the house would then have promoted those rights into an overriding interest. That, I think, is not conceded by counsel for the respondents but I assume that to be the case. On that basis, it would have been a remarkable result if those more precarious rights were incapable of being overreached, on a sale by trustees, under s 2(1)(ii) of the Law of Property Act 1925.

Mr Beaumont has however contended for that result, citing what Lord Wilberforce said in *Shiloh Spinners v Harding* [1973] AC 691, [1973] 1 All ER 90 at 721 of the former report:

"All this seems to show that there may well be rights, of an equitable character, outside the provisions as to registration and which are incapable of being overreached."

Lord Wilberforce had just before referred to *ER Ives Investment Ltd v High* [1967] 2 QB 379, [1967] 1 All ER 504. In that case a boundary dispute between neighbours had been settled by an informal agreement including the grant of a right of way. The agreement about the right of way was never completed by a deed of grant, and was never registered. The Court of Appeal held that it was binding despite the lack of registration. Similarly, *Shiloh Spinners v Harding* was concerned with an equitable right of entry for enforcement of a covenant arising in what Lord Wilberforce called a dispute [. . .] of a commonplace character between neighbours.

Equitable interests of that character ought not to be overreached, since they are rights which an adjoining owner enjoys over the land itself, regardless of its ownership from time to time. The principle is in my view correctly stated in Megarry and Wade, *The Law of Real Property* 5th ed p 409:

> "In fact the only examples of such equities likely to occur are commercial (as opposed to family) interests, which it is absurd to speak of overreaching. Two instances are an equitable right of way which is yet not an equitable easement, and an equitable right of entry to secure performance of a covenant, and there are probably others. To overreach such interests is to destroy them [. . .]"

The footnotes to this passage refer to *ER Ives Investment Ltd v High* and *Shiloh Spinners v Harding* (cases which were cited to the House of Lords in *Flegg*—see especially counsels argument at p 63—but are not referred to in any of the speeches of their Lordships). The essential distinction is, as the authors of Megarry and Wade note, between commercial and family interests. An equitable easement or an equitable right of entry cannot sensibly shift from the land affected by it to the proceeds of sale. An equitable interest as a tenant in common can do so, even if accompanied by the promise of a home for life, since the proceeds of sale can be used to acquire another home.

Mr Beaumont has also argued that, although in *Grant v Edwards* the Vice-Chancellor regarded interests in the family home created by equitable estoppel or by a constructive trust as closely similar, if not interchangeable, his remarks do not apply to a resulting trust arising from a monetary contribution. This is an area of the law in which the terminology is unfortunately far from uniform, but I do not accept that the Vice-Chancellors remarks were limited in that way. On the contrary, immediately after his reference to proprietary estoppel he said (see [1986] Ch 657, H-658A):

> "Identifiable contributions to the purchase [price] of the house will of course be an important factor in many cases."

Similarly, in *Lloyds Bank v Rosset* [1991] 1 AC 107, [1990] 1 All ER 1111 Lord Bridge (in a very well-known passage at pp 132–3 of the former report) referred to direct contributions to the purchase price by [a party] who is not the legal owner, as readily justifying the creation of a constructive trust. Such a trust, however labelled, does not then leave room for a separate interest by way of equitable estoppel: compare the remarks of Morritt LJ in *Lloyds Bank v Carrick* [1996] 4 All ER 630, [1996] 2 FLR 600 at p 639C-E of the former report. To do so would cause vast confusion in an area which is already quite difficult enough. The confusion is avoided if what Lord Wilberforce said in *Shiloh Spinners v Harding* is limited, as in my judgment it must be, to some unusual types of equitable interest arising in commercial situations. In this type of family situation, the concepts of trust and equitable estoppel are almost interchangeable, and both are affected in the same way by the statutory mechanism of overreaching, the substance of which is not affected by the 1996 Act.

In these circumstances I do not find it necessary to consider how far the judges findings in this area (which were largely limited to a general acceptance of Mrs Sabherwal's evidence) would establish the necessary conditions for proprietary estoppel. I assume in favour of Mrs Sabherwal that they would do so.

On the basis of this decision, family interests under a proprietary estoppel are capable of being overreached, while commercial interests are not. To have held otherwise would have created a significant lacuna in the operation of overreaching: the mechanism could be avoided simply by claiming an interest through proprietary estoppel rather than constructive trust. To that extent, the decision seems correct—but questions may still arise as to its scope and therefore to the extent to which interests claimed through proprietary estoppel can be overreached. It is unclear whether the category of 'family' interests to which overreaching is extended is limited to those circumstances, exemplified by the facts of *Sabherwal*, in which claims to estoppel and constructive trusts coincide, or could apply to other circumstances in which estoppel claims arise in relation to a home. Robert Walker LJ's definition of a family interest is sufficiently broad to cover such cases.

Harpum considered the scope of the judgment. Although generally adopting a restrictive approach, his comment implies that the case is not limited to situations in which trusts and estoppel coincide.

Harpum, 'Overreaching, Trusts of Land and Proprietary Estoppel' (2000) 116 LQR 341, 344–5

Thus in determining whether an inchoate equity arising by estoppel is overreached by a disposition to two or more owners, it is necessary to consider the manner in which the court might have given effect to that equity. Robert Walker L.J. considered that the essential difference was between "commercial and family interests". The latter but not the former were overreachable. That may, however, be an oversimplification. If effect would be given to the equity by the creation or transfer of a legal estate in land or by the grant of a legal or equitable right over land, then the equity should be incapable of being overreached. However, if the appropriate way of giving effect to the equity was by means of an interest that could properly be converted into money on sale, such as an interest under a trust of land or a lien, the equity should be overreachable.

The scope of *Sabherwal* must be considered to remain uncertain. Overreaching of interests claimed through estoppel where a constructive trust would not also be available appears to be outside the ratio of the decision. Because the basis of overreaching is the trustees' powers of disposition, there is a difficulty in extending the operation of the mechanism to situations in which no trust could be claimed. On that view, there is simply no basis on which an equitable interest not arising under a trust can be overreached. Indeed, even if overreaching is limited in that way, it is not necessary to extend overreaching to interests under estoppel. The same result can be achieved by reliance on the suggestion in *Lloyds Bank plc v Carrick*[24] (referred to in the judgment extracted above and discussed in Chapter 10, section 5.8) that the existence of a constructive (or resulting) trust precludes any further claim to an interest through estoppel.

Further difficulties in divining what interests are capable of being overreached are raised by the case of *Mortgage Express v Lambert*,[25] in which a mere equity was held to be

---

[24] [1996] 4 All ER 630.   [25] [2017] Ch 93.

capable of being overreached. The mere equity in question was Ms Lambert's right to set aside the sale of her flat as an unconscionable bargain. She had been persuaded to enter into this sale at a considerable undervalue as part of a so-called mortgage 'rescue' scheme which involved the sale of her flat (worth £120,000) for a mere £30,000 upon the promise by the two purchasers that they would lease the flat back to her. The sale was completed with the help of bridging finance but the purchasers subsequently mortgaged the flat to Mortgage Express who began possession proceedings when the mortgage fell into arrears. Although the Court of Appeal accepted that Ms Lambert's right to set aside was an overriding interest, they held it had been overreached. Relying on the wording of s 2(1) and *Sabherwal*, the Court rejected the notion that overreaching was limited to equitable interests held under a trust and held that Ms Lambert's mere equity fell within the meaning of equitable interest for the purposes of s 2(1) and accordingly had been overreached—the mortgage had been granted by the purchasers, as trustees of the legal estate, and the money paid to them in compliance with s 27.

The decision has been met with academic surprise and criticism. Televantos points out that the facts fall within the ambit of s 2(2) LPA 1925 as an example of extended overreaching of a prior equitable interest, yet the terms of that section had not been met—the purchasers were not a trust corporation or appointed by the court.[26] Ms Lambert's equity to set aside arose as a result of the unconscionable bargain which predated Mortgage Express's mortgage which had only been entered after completion of the sale.[27]

Looking at the basis of overreaching which we considered in sections 2.2.1–2.2.4, there is also confusion found in the judgment between the accepted view that overreaching is based upon the trustee's powers as conferred by s 6 TOLATA and Jackson's more controversial view that overreaching springs from the land registration legislation. The Court seems to rely on both rationales, although, as already explained, they are inherently inconsistent.

Lees, although accepting that the literal terms of section 2(1) may have been met, points to the troubling consequences of equating mere equities with equitable interests for the purposes of the section. Dixon expresses similar concerns.[28]

Lees, 'Overreaching Mere Equities: Mortgage Express v Lambert [2017]' *Conv* 72

However, the conclusion that mere equities can be overreached is troubling, in practical terms. First, mere equities are not akin to trusts such that the two main justifications for allowing overreaching to occur do not apply. Mere equities do not give rise to fiduciary duties so that the right-holder is not entitled to the additional layer of protection which the trust relationship engenders. Secondly, the relationship between the beneficiary of a mere equity and the proceeds of the overreaching transaction is not entirely satisfactory or clear. The conclusion that mere equities are capable of being overreached is not without its difficulties.

[26] Televantos, 'Unconscionable Bargains, Overreaching and Overriding Interests' (2016) 75 CLJ 458.
[27] The court held that Ms Lambert's mere equity arose at the time of exchange of contracts see [16] *per* Lewison LJ.
[28] Dixon, 'Priority, Overreaching and Surprises under the Land Registration Act 2002' 133 (2017) LQR 173.

2.3 TRANSACTIONS WITH OVERREACHING EFFECT

Once it is established that an interest is capable of being overreached, overreaching will take place only if the transaction is one that has such effect. Three requirements must be met. Firstly, there is an overarching requirement, reflecting the fact that overreaching has its basis within the trustees' powers, that the transaction is one that is within the powers of the trustees. We consider in section 4 the effect of transactions that do not fulfil this requirement.

The second and third requirements are drawn from the LPA 1925. The second requirement is that the transaction must be one of those listed in s 2(1)(i)–(iv) of the Act (extracted in section 2.1) as having overreaching effect. Section 2(1) calls for that transaction to be '*[a] conveyance to a purchaser of a legal estate in land*'. This has been assumed to be a legal estate as defined by s 1(1) LPA 1925: namely the conveyance (including a mortgage) of a fee simple absolute or a terms of years absolute (i.e. a lease). However, in the following case the court held that a conveyance of a legal estate also included the grant of an easement.

Baker v Craggs
[2016] EWHC 3250 (Ch)

Facts: The Charltons sold some fields, a barn, and yard to Mr Craggs and granted him a right of way leading from the yard. Unfortunately, the registration of this sale was delayed because of some inconsistency in the plans. In the intervening registration gap the Charltons also sold other land to the Bakers together with a right of way over the yard that they had previously sold to Mr Craggs. Mr Craggs objected to the Bakers exercising this right of way claiming that it was not binding on him given his prior purchase.

Held: The Court held that Mr Craggs' equitable ownership, prior to completion of the registration process, had been overreached by the grant of the easement to the Bakers by the Charltons. The grant of the easement was construed as a conveyance of the legal estate for the purposes of s 2(1) LPA 1925.

Newey J

At [27]–[32]

The term "legal estate", which features more than once in section 2 of the LPA, is explained in section 1. While section 1(1) states that an "estate in fee simple absolute in possession" and a "term of years absolute" are the "only estates in land which are capable of subsisting or of being conveyed or created at law", section 1(4) explains that the "estates, interests, and charges" authorised to subsist or to be conveyed or created at law by the section are referred to in the Act as "legal estates". The definition thus extends to the various interests "capable of subsisting or of being conveyed or created at law" specified in section 1(2). These include an "easement, right, or privilege in or over land for an interest equivalent to an estate in fee simple absolute in possession or a term of years absolute"(ection 1(2)(a)).

The word "conveyance", which is also used in section 2 of the LPA, is defined in section 205(1)(ii) of the Act. This states that "conveyance" includes "a mortgage, charge, lease, assent, vesting declaration, vesting instrument, disclaimer, release and every other assurance of property or of an interest therein by any instrument, except a will"....

The Bakers contend that the present case is comparable. The argument can be developed on the following lines. Despite executing a transfer of the Farm in favour of Mr Craggs, Mr and Mrs Charlton remained the registered proprietors of the property and, hence, its legal owners until Mr Craggs was entered on the register with effect from 16 May 2012. In the meantime, the Farm, like the Baker Barn (up to the point title passed to the Bakers), was subject to a "trust of land" within the meaning of the Trusts of Land and Appointment of Trustees Act 1996 (albeit that the Charltons presumably held the Baker Barn on trust for themselves while the Farm will have been held on bare trust for Mr Craggs) and the Charltons will therefore have had "all the powers of an absolute owner" as regards the Farm under section 6 of the 1996 Act. When, moreover, they granted the Bakers an easement crossing the farm, the proceeds of sale (as part of the purchase price of the Baker Barn) were paid to two trustees. The requirements of sections 2 and 27 of the LPA were therefore satisfied: there was a "conveyance to a purchaser of a legal estate in land" (for relevant purposes, the easement) "made by trustees of land" (namely, the Charltons) and the proceeds of sale were paid to two trustees (again, the Charltons). Accordingly, Mr Craggs's equitable interest in the Farm will (so it is said) have been overreached and subordinated to the easement.

Mr Paton submitted that Mr Talbot-Ponsonby's contentions to this effect are misconceived. Overreaching, he argued, is the process by which equitable interests under a trust of land are converted to interests in the sale proceeds when *that land* is sold to a third party purchaser for consideration. It has nothing to do, he said, with whether an easement over Mr Craggs's property (the Farm) for the benefit of the Bakers' property (the Baker Barn), created during the "registration gap" after the Farm had been transferred but before title was registered, could bind Mr Craggs when he was registered as the Farm's proprietor.

It has to be remembered, however, that, for the purposes of section 2 of the LPA , "legal estate" is defined in such a way as to include an easement.

This interpretation of 'a conveyance of the legal estate' has drawn criticism and the decision may be appealed.[29] The most significant criticism is the interplay between the well-known classification of legal estates, contained in the very first subsection of the LPA 1925, which is followed by the equally well-known classification of legal interests in s 1(2) LPA 1925 including a legal easement, with the definition of legal estate adopted in s 1(4) LPA 1925 which purports to include both legal estates and legal interests as previously classified. This definition has been somewhat overlooked by commentators but has generally been viewed as a convenient shorthand to refer to legal estates and interests, for instance, in other sections in the LPA 1925.[30] It can be suggested that it does not have substantive effect to open up the classification of legal estate so clearly set out in s 1(1) LPA 1925, but, as discussed in Chapter 5, section 6.2, there are also arguments in support of Newey J's interpretation of s 1(4) LPA 1925.

The decision also strikes at the heart of the scope of overreaching. As we have already observed, this has been taken to be limited to a shifting of the equitable interest from the land to the proceeds of sale with attendant effect on the priority of an equitable interest in

---

[29] See Dixon, 'The Registration Gap and Overreaching' [2017] Conv 1, and Owen, 'Priorities and Registered Land during the Registration Gap [2017] Conv 230.

[30] LPA 1925, s 52 is an example.

the land itself. *Baker v Craggs* suggests a wider view of overreaching to encompass a subordination of competing interests which has little connection with any shifting of entitlement to the proceeds of sale and the next requirement for the payment of the purchase price in compliance with s 27.

The third requirement is that s 2(1)(i) and (ii) provides that, to overreach beneficial interests under a trust, statutory requirements as regards payment of capital money must be complied with. These requirements are contained in s 27(2) of the 1925 Act.

Law of Property Act 1925, s 27(2)

(2) Notwithstanding anything to the contrary in the instrument (if any) creating a trust of land or in any trust affecting the net proceeds of sale of the land if it is sold, the proceeds of sale or other capital money shall not be paid to or applied by the direction of fewer than two persons as [trustees], except where the trustee is a trust corporation, but this subsection does not affect the right of a sole personal representative as such to give valid receipts for, or direct the application of, proceeds of sale or other capital money, nor, except where capital money arises on the transaction, render it necessary to have more than one trustee.

This provision, like s 2, applies equally to registered and unregistered land. In registered land, trustees should enter a restriction on the register preventing a disposition unless s 27(2) is complied with. But (contrary to Jackson's argument, discussed in section 2.2.4) the absence of a restriction does not remove the need for the requirement to be complied with in order for a purchaser to rely on the overreaching mechanism.

Neither ss 2 nor 27 state in their terms that there must be capital money for overreaching to take place. They impose requirements to be met when such money does arise. The fact that capital money will be paid may be thought to be inherent in overreaching as a process of 'shifting' beneficial interests from the land to money: if no money is paid, into what can the beneficial interests shift? In identifying the trustees powers of disposition as the basis of overreaching of the beneficial interests under a trust, however, Harpum indicated that this was not, in fact, the case.

Harpum, 'Overreaching, Trusteees' Powers and the Reform of the 1925 Legislation' (1990) 49 CLJ 277, 282

[T]he interest created or the estate granted by the exercise of the power takes priority over the estates and interests under the settlement. The exercise of a power which does not give rise to any capital monies—such as an exchange of land—overreaches just as much as a transaction which does.

This statement proved prescient when the application of overreaching to a transaction in which no capital money arose came to be decided in the following case. The Court of Appeal cited Harpum's comment with approval in holding that such a transaction still has overreaching effect.

State Bank of India v Sood
[1997] Ch 276, CA

Facts: Mr and Mrs Sood were registered proprietors of their home. They granted a charge over the home for existing and future liabilities of themselves and their business. No capital money was advanced contemporaneously with this disposition, but, over a period of time, Mr and Mrs Sood accrued debts of over £1m and the State Bank of India (to which the benefit of the charge had been assigned by the Punjab National Bank) sought to enforce the charge. The five children of the couple (the third to seventh defendants) argued that they were beneficiaries under a trust of land and that their beneficial interests had not been overreached.

Peter Gibson LJ

At 279–90

The question can be formulated in this way: where two trustees for sale hold registered land for themselves and other beneficiaries and mortgage the land as security for existing and future liabilities of themselves and other persons, are the equitable interests of the beneficiaries overreached, notwithstanding that no money was advanced by the mortgagee to or at the direction of the trustees contemporaneously with the mortgage? The judge in effect answered that question in the negative [. . .]

There is no dispute that the equitable interests of the third to seventh defendants were at the date of the legal charge capable of being overreached. That condition of section 2(1)(ii) was therefore satisfied. Most of the argument has turned on the final condition of that paragraph relating to compliance with the statutory requirements respecting the payment of capital money [. . .]

I accept that a novel and important point of law is raised by this appeal. Lending institutions regularly take security from businessmen in the form of a legal charge on property (which very frequently means that the matrimonial home is charged) to secure existing and future indebtedness, and very commonly that property will be registered land held by two registered proprietors on trust for sale with no restriction registered in respect of their power to transfer or mortgage that property. It was not suggested that it had ever been the practice of mortgagees to make inquiries of occupiers of the property as to any claimed rights. Yet if the third to seventh defendants are right, that is what the mortgagees must do if they are not to take subject to the beneficial interests of the occupiers [. . .]

The crucial issue is the true construction of the final condition of section 2(1)(ii) relating to compliance with statutory requirements respecting the payment of capital money. There is no dispute that if capital money does arise under a conveyance by trustees for sale to a purchaser it must be paid to or applied as section 27(2) dictates. But for overreaching to occur, does capital money have to arise on and contemporaneously with the conveyance?

The judge appears to have assumed that there could be no overreaching if no capital money arose.

He said:

> "we have to look to see whether capital money was paid [to] or applied by the direction of the two trustees. If it was, then the defendants have no defence; if it was not, then the bank cannot overreach and they have an arguable defence on the evidence."

Mr. Havey and Mr. Williams submitted that was indeed the position and they said that the arising of capital money on the conveyance was the assumption on which section 2(1)(ii) was drafted. Mr. Crawford's initial submission accorded with that view, but he sought to escape the consequences by contending that capital money arose whenever the Punjab National Bank advanced money, even if before the legal charge was executed. However, I cannot accept that what was done prior to the legal charge has any relevance to the condition that "the statutory requirements respecting the payment of capital money arising under a disposition upon trust for sale are complied with." Nor can I accept Mr. Crawford's further submission that the debt existing at the date of the legal charge was not materially different from the secured debt which existed at the date of the mortgage in *Flegg* and was discharged in that case out of the money raised. The circumstances are wholly different.

Mr. Crawford however had recourse to a further submission, adopting a point suggested by the court, that the relevant condition in section 2(1)(ii) should be construed as applying only to those cases where there was capital money arising under a disposition upon trust for sale, the statutory requirements of section 27(2) being simply irrelevant to a transaction under which no capital money arises. There are several types of conveyance to a purchaser (within the statutory meanings of those terms) other than a charge to secure existing and future debt which do not give rise to capital money, for example, an exchange or a lease not at a premium. Why should the legislature have intended to exclude such conveyances from having an overreaching effect? It is interesting to note that the precursor of section 2(1), viz. section 3(2)(ii) of the Law of Property Act 1922, used as one of the conditions for overreaching to occur the formula "If any capital money arises from the transaction [. . .] the requirements of this Act respecting the payment of capital money arising under a trust for sale [. . .] are complied with." However the form of section 3(2) differed in a number of respects from section 2(1) of the Act of 1925 and it may not be safe to infer that the later provision was intended to re-enact the substance of the earlier provision. But it points to the relevant condition of section 2(1) being worded in surprisingly oblique fashion if what was intended was that capital money must arise so that the statutory requirements can be complied with. Mr. Havey drew attention to the word "any" in connection with "capital money" in section 2(1)(iii) and (iv) and suggested that its omission from the reference to "capital money" in section 2(1)(i) and (ii) was significant. But the structure of those paragraphs is quite different from section 2(1)(iii) and (iv) and the draftsman could not have achieved the effect of section 3(2) of the Act of 1922 by adding "any" before "capital money" in section 2(1)(i) or (ii).

The relevant condition in section 2(1)(ii) is the same as that in section 2(1)(i). The overreaching powers conferred by the Settled Land Act 1925 include power to convey by an exchange or lease as well as by a mortgage or charge where capital money may not arise (see section 72 of that Act). The statutory requirements governing capital money (to be paid to or applied by the direction of not less than two individuals or a trust corporation: sections 94 and 95 of that Act) can only apply to those conveyances giving rise to capital money. The same interpretation must apply to the condition in section 2(1)(i) as it does to the conveyancing condition in section 2(1)(ii).

A more substantial argument of policy advanced on behalf of the third to seventh defendants is that if overreaching occurs where no capital money arises, the beneficiaries' interests may be reduced by the conveyance leaving nothing to which the interests can attach by way of replacement save the equity of redemption, and that may be or become valueless. I see considerable force in this point, but I am not persuaded that it suffices to defeat what I see to be the policy of the legislation, to allow valid dispositions to overreach equitable interests. In my judgment on its true construction section 2(1)(ii) only requires compliance with the statutory requirements respecting the payment of capital money if capital money arises. Accordingly I would hold that capital money did not have to arise under the conveyance.

The judge further said:

"I consider that overreaching must take place at the time of the execution. I think that the plaintiff does not object to that in principle, but says that the defendants' right simply attaches to the equity of redemption; but I do not think one can have a condition of over-reaching on moneys which may or may not be drawn down later. For overreaching to take effect all parts of section 27(2) must be complied with; it is a two stage process which requires, first, the existence of either proceeds of sale or capital moneys and, secondly, those are either to be paid to the two trustees or applied at their discretion. The plaintiff says it does not matter-because there was a general direction for application in the charge-if it comes into existence or is applied at a subsequent time. I think that is wrong; it is necessary for the moneys to be in existence at the time of the charge so that those moneys can either be received or applied at the trustees' directions."

[. . .]

Both Mr. Havey and Mr. Williams supported the judge's conclusion that some capital money must arise contemporaneously with the conveyance for there to be overreaching. They said that if a conveyance provided only for deferred payment, that would not suffice. They further submitted that provided some capital money arose contemporaneously with the conveyance and section 27(2) was complied with, overreaching would occur even though other money was subsequently advanced under the conveyance. Thus if a £1m facility was secured by a mortgage and in the course of time was fully drawn on but at the time of the mortgage only £100 was advanced, there would nevertheless be overreaching in respect of the whole £1m thereby secured, whereas if the £100 had not been advanced at the time of the mortgage, there would have been no overreaching. I do not believe that the statutory language supports a requirement producing such a surprising and illogical result. Mr. Havey drew our attention to a large number of provisions in the Settled Land Act 1925 which, he said, showed that money arising from a transaction must be received or applied at the same time as the transaction. I cannot agree, though I of course accept that to be paid or applied, capital money must be in hand. If and to the extent that capital money arises after the con-veyance, section 27(2) must be complied with for the mortgagee to obtain a good receipt. If it is not, for example if an advance is made after a mortgage has been executed but under a facility provided for by the mortgage but is not paid to or at the direction of two or more trustees or a trust corporation, that would not affect the overreaching which would have oc-curred on the mortgage.

[. . .]

The correct analysis of the position in the present case is that on the execution of the legal charge, the interests of the third to seventh defendants were overreached and attached to the equity of redemption. The legal estate in the property was by the legal charge made sub-ject to the rights thereunder of the Punjab National Bank which were subsequently assigned to the plaintiff, including the right to sell the property. The value of the equity of redemption on the execution of the legal charge would reflect the then existing liabilities thereby secured. That value would be further reduced as further liabilities arose and were secured under the legal charge. In the light of *City of London Building Society v. Flegg* [1986] Ch. 605; [1988] A.C. 54 it follows from the overreaching that section 70(1)(g) does not avail the third to sev-enth defendants and that their defence on this point cannot succeed and should be struck out. On the assumption that they were not consulted about the legal charge by the first and second defendants, it may be that they have the right to obtain redress against the trustees.

Much though I value the principle of overreaching as having aided the simplification of con-veyancing, I cannot pretend that I regard the resulting position in the present case as entirely satisfactory. The safeguard for beneficiaries under the existing legislation is largely limited to having two trustees or a trust corporation where capital money falls to be received. But that is no safeguard at all, as this case has shown, when no capital money is received on and contemporaneously with the conveyance. Further, even when it is received by two trustees as in *City of London Building Society v. Flegg* [1986] Ch. 605; [1988] A.C. 54, it might be thought that beneficiaries in occupation are insufficiently protected. Hence the recommendation for reform in the Law Commission's report, "Transfer of Land, Overreaching: Beneficiaries in Occupation" (1989) (Law Com. No. 188), that a conveyance should not overreach the interest of a sui juris beneficiary in occupation unless he gives his consent. Mr. Harpum in the article to which reference has been made proposed an alternative reform, limiting the power of trustees to mortgage. Whether the legislature will reform the law remains to be seen. I should add for completeness that we were assured by counsel that the recent Trusts of Land and Appointment of Trustees Act 1996 was of no assistance and we have not considered its effect.

In the absence of capital money, there may still be a shifting of the beneficial interests. In *Sood*, the interests shifted to the equity of redemption. To the extent that this may be valueless, where the debt equals or exceeds the value of the property, the result is no harsher than that in a case, exemplified by *City of London Building Society v Flegg*,[31] in which capital money is paid to the trustees, but is dissipated by them.

In *Sood*, two trustees executed the charge. If s 27(2) applies only to dispositions in which capital money is paid, however, it seems that a sole trustee (in registered and unregistered land) can overreach beneficial interests through dispositions that do not involve payment of capital money.[32] There is no independent statutory requirement that the transaction must be undertaken by at least two trustees.[33] In *Shami v Shami*, a first instance judge assumed without discussion that overreaching within *Sood* could take place by the execution of a charge by a single trustee, but his comment on the point was obiter.[34] It is, however, worth noting that if the third party provides *nothing* in return for the right received from the trustees, overreaching will not occur, because the third party has not acquired a right 'for valuable consideration'.[35]

Commenting on the decision in *Sood*, Thompson suggested that the outcome prevents the need to distinguish between different types of mortgage and thus avoids the 'strange results' that Peter Gibson LJ's judgment highlights would result from drawing such distinctions.[36] But if a single trustee can overreach beneficial interests through mortgages (and other dispositions) that do not involve payment of capital money, then the effect of *Sood* is that it is, in fact, necessary to distinguish between such mortgages. The 'strange results' avoided by the decision in trusts with at least two trustees will arise in sole-trustee trusts. Hence, for example, a mortgage by a sole trustee, with £100 advanced at the outset and debts of £1m subsequently accrued, would not overreach (because the application of s 27(2)

---

[31] [1988] AC 54.   [32] See McFarlane (2008) pp 397–400.

[33] Statutory references to 'trustees', e.g. in the Law of Property Act 1925, s 2, may considered by reference to the Interpretation Act 1978, s 6(3), to include a single trustee.

[34] [2012] EWHC 664 (Ch) [63] and [69]. The point did not arise as the claim to a beneficial interest failed. A subsequent appeal related only to other aspects of the case: [2013] EWCA Civ 227. For further discussion see Dixon, 'Editorial' [2013] Conv 165.

[35] Section 2(1) limits overreaching to cases in which the third party is a *'purchaser of a legal estate in land'* (this includes a mortgagee); s 205(1)(xxi) of the Law of Property Act 1925 states that, unless the context otherwise requires, a 'purchaser' means a purchaser for 'valuable consideration'.

[36] Thompson, 'Overreaching without Payment' [1997] Conv 134.

would be triggered by the initial payment of capital money), while a mortgage in which the level of borrowing reached the same amount, but with no initial advanced payment, *would* overreach, because the absence of capital money precludes the application of s 27(2). While it must be doubted that such results are intended, there is no statutory basis for limiting overreaching to transactions undertaken by at least two trustees unless s 27(2) is applied. The unfortunate result is that transactions in which beneficiaries appear most vulnerable are also those in which they are least protected.

Having outlined the general scope of overreaching, we can now consider its application in the specific context of a home occupied by the beneficiaries under a trust of land.

3 CO-OWNERSHIP, OVERREACHING, AND OCCUPYING BENEFICIARIES

We have seen that one of the interests capable of being overreached is the beneficial interest under a trust of land. Indeed, overreaching of such interests is probably the most common and practically important use of the mechanism. The shifting of beneficial interests from land to money appears neither controversial, nor problematic, where the function of the trust property is to provide an investment fund for the beneficiaries. The physical identity of the trust property itself is, then, not of central concern; what is more important is the wealth that it represents. It is of no particular significance to the beneficiaries whether their interest is in any particular piece of land or other type of property; what is important is that the value of the trust fund is maintained by the profitable sale of the land and the reinvestment of the proceeds in other lucrative investments. The trustees' equitable and statutory duties under the Trustee Act 2000 are defined with that objective in mind.

However, a trust of land will also arise where co-owners hold land with the intention that they will occupy it as their home. In the common situation in which a couple purchase a home in their joint names, they are both the legal and beneficial co-owners, and this trust creates no difficulties. Indeed, the couple is likely to be unaware that they deal with the property as trustees for the benefit of themselves as beneficial co-owners.

By contrast, a very real tension can arise where co-owners hold the legal estate on express or implied trust for themselves and others. This is a situation that can occur, for example, where a home is purchased for an extended family, where individuals within the family take the legal estate on trust for themselves and the remaining family members take as beneficial co-owners. The beneficiaries may be concerned not only with the value of their trust property, but also with its identity as their home. Yet overreaching does not recognize this concern. Their interests are assumed to be adequately protected, firstly, by the continued representation of their proprietary rights in the proceeds of sale by the process of overreaching itself, and secondly, by the requirement that at least two trustees receive those proceeds to guard against a misappropriation of the trust property or other breach of duty. If a misappropriation or other breach of duty does occur, the beneficiaries' proprietary interests are placed in jeopardy against a purchaser by overreaching, but the beneficiaries retain their personal remedies against the trustees to redress any loss in value of the trust fund.

The tension between trust property as a home for beneficiaries and the wealth that it represents came to a head in the following case. The Fleggs' main arguments focussed on the need to afford protection to their occupation of the trust property as their home, by treating investment and occupation trusts differently. They argued, relying on *William &*

Glyn's Bank v Boland,[37] that their beneficial interests bound the mortgagees as an overriding interest, and that an overriding beneficial interest should not be overreached. Further, they suggested that s 14 of the LPA 1925 operated to protect the interests of occupiers. If the land had been unregistered, the Fleggs would have argued that their occupation gave a purchaser constructive notice of their interest, so as to confer priority under the doctrine of notice. The House of Lords rejected these arguments. Overreaching operated, provided that the statutory conditions were satisfied. At that point, the Fleggs' beneficial interest in their home was transferred to the proceeds of sale so that there simply was no interest in the land that their occupation (or, indeed, any entry on the register) could protect.

City of London Building Society v Flegg
[1988] AC 54, HL

Facts: Mr and Mrs Flegg sold their home of 28 years and, in 1982, contributed the £18,000 proceeds to the purchase of Bleak House as a new home for themselves, and their daughter and son-in-law, Mrs and Mrs Maxwell-Brown. The balance of the £34,000 purchase price was funded by a mortgage. Despite their solicitor's advice that Bleak House should be registered in the names of all four parties, it was, in fact, registered in the joint names of Mr and Mrs Maxwell-Brown, who, given the Fleggs' contribution to the purchase price, held the house as joint tenants on resulting trust for themselves and Mr and Mrs Flegg. Bleak House was occupied and became the home of all four parties. The Maxwell-Browns ran into financial difficulties and, without the knowledge or consent of the Flegg's, remortgaged the house to the City of London Building Society to raise £37,500. The Fleggs must have been suspicious and, before the mortgage could be registered, they entered a caution against dealings at the Land Registry. Unfortunately, the Maxwell-Browns were unable to meet the repayments under the mortgage, and the building society sought a declaration that the mortgage bound and could be enforced against the Fleggs' interest, and an order for possession.

Lord Templeman

At 71–4

The respondents resist the claim of the appellants to possession of Bleak House and rely on section 14 of the Law of Property Act 1925. Sections 27 and 28 of that Act which overreach the interests of the respondents under the trust for sale of Bleak House are to be found in Part I of the Act. Section 14 provides:

> "This Part of this Act shall not prejudicially affect the interest of any person in possession or in actual occupation of land to which he may be entitled in right of such possession or occupation." The respondents were in actual occupation of Bleak House at the date of the legal charge. It is argued that their beneficial interests under the trust for sale were not overreached by the legal charge or that the respondents were entitled to remain in occupation after the legal charge and against the appellants despite the overreaching of their interests [. . .]

If the argument for the respondents is correct, a purchaser from trustees for sale must ensure that a beneficiary in actual occupation is not only consulted but consents to the sale.

---

[37] [1981] 1 AC 487.

Section 14 of the Law of Property Act 1925 is not apt to confer on a tenant in common of land held on trust for sale, who happens to be in occupation, rights which are different from and superior to the rights of tenants in common, who are not in occupation on the date when the interests of all tenants in common are overreached by a sale or mortgage by trustees for sale [. . .]

In my view the object of section 70 was to reproduce for registered land the same limitations as section 14 of the Law of Property Act 1925 produced for land whether registered or unregistered. The respondents claim to be entitled to overriding interests because they were in actual occupation of Bleak House on the date of the legal charge. But the interests of the respondents cannot at one and the same time be overreached and overridden and at the same time be overriding interests. The appellants cannot at one and the same time take free from all the interests of the respondents yet at the same time be subject to some of those interests. The right of the respondents to be and remain in actual occupation of Bleak House ceased when the respondents' interests were overreached by the legal charge save in so far as their rights were transferred to the equity of redemption. As persons interested under the trust for sale the respondents had no right to possession as against the appellants and the fact that the respondents were in actual occupation at the date of the legal charge did not create a new right or transfer an old right so as to make the right enforceable against the appellants.

One of the main objects of the legislation of 1925 was to effect a compromise between on the one hand the interests of the public in securing that land held in trust is freely marketable and, on the other hand, the interests of the beneficiaries in preserving their rights under the trusts. By the Settled Land Act 1925 a tenant for life may convey the settled land discharged from all the trusts powers and provisions of the settlement. By the Law of Property Act 1925 trustees for sale may convey land held on trust for sale discharged from the trusts affecting the proceeds of sale and rents and profits until sale. Under both forms of trust the protection and the only protection of the beneficiaries is that capital money must be paid to at least two trustees or a trust corporation. Section 14 of the Law of Property Act 1925 and section 70 of the Land Registration Act 1925 cannot have been intended to frustrate this compromise and to subject the purchaser to some beneficial interests but not others depending on the waywardness of actual occupation. The Court of Appeal took a different view, largely in reliance on the decision of this House in *Williams & Glyn's Bank Ltd. v. Boland* [1981] A.C. 487. In that case the sole proprietor of registered land held the land as sole trustee upon trust for sale and to stand possessed of the net proceeds of sale and rents and profits until sale upon trust for himself and his wife as tenants in common. This House held that the wife's beneficial interest coupled with actual possession by her constituted an overriding interest and that a mortgagee from the husband, despite the concluding words of section 20(1), took subject to the wife's overriding interest. But in that case the interest of the wife was not overreached or overridden because the mortgagee advanced capital moneys to a sole trustee. If the wife's interest had been overreached by the mortgagee advancing capital moneys to two trustees there would have been nothing to justify the wife in remaining in occupation as against the mortgagee. There must be a combination of an interest which justifies continuing occupation plus actual occupation to constitute an overriding interest. Actual occupation is not an interest in itself.

Lord Oliver

At 80–1

My Lords, the ambit of section 14 is a matter which has puzzled conveyancers ever since the Law of Property Act was enacted [. . .] For my part, I think that it is unnecessary for present purposes to seek to resolve the conundrum. What section 14 does not do, on any analysis, is to enlarge or add to whatever interest it is that the occupant has "in right of his occupation" and in my judgment the argument that places reliance upon it in the instant case founds itself upon an assumption about the nature of the occupying co-owners' interest that cannot in fact be substantiated. The section cannot of itself create an interest which survives the execution of the trust under which it arises or answer the logically anterior question of what, if any, interest in the land is conferred by the possession or occupation [. . .] the section cannot, in my judgment, have the effect of preserving, as equitable interests in the land, interests which are overreached by the exercise of the trustees' powers or of bringing onto the title which the purchaser from trustees for sale is required to investigate the equitable interest of every beneficiary who happens to be in occupation of the land. That would be to defeat the manifest purpose of the legislature in enacting the sections to which reference has already been made [. . .]

Considered in the context of a transaction complying with the statutory requirements of the Law of Property Act 1925 the question of the effect of section 70(1)(g) of the Land Registration Act 1925 must, in my judgment, be approached by asking first what are the "rights" of the person in occupation and whether they are, at the material time, subsisting in reference to the land. In the instant case the exercise by the registered proprietors of the powers conferred on trustees for sale by section 28(1) of the Law of Property Act 1925 had the effect of overreaching the interests of the respondents under the statutory trusts upon which depended their right to continue in occupation of the land. The appellants took free from those trusts (section 27) and were not, in any event, concerned to see that the respondents' consent to the transaction was obtained (section 26). If, then, one asks what were the subsisting rights of the respondents referable to their occupation, the answer must, in my judgment, be that they were rights which, vis-à-vis the appellants, were, eo instante with the creation of the charge, overreached and therefore subsisted only in relation to the equity of redemption. I do not, for my part, find in *Boland's case* [1981] A.C. 487 anything which compels a contrary conclusion. Granted that the interest of a co-owner pending the execution of the statutory trust for sale is, despite the equitable doctrine of conversion, an interest subsisting in reference to the land the subject matter of the trust and granted also that Boland's case establishes that such an interest, although falling within the definition of minor interest and so liable to be overriden by a registered disposition, will, so long as it subsists, be elevated to the status of an overriding interest if there exists also the additional element of occupation by the co-owner, I cannot for my part accept that, once what I may call the parent interest, by which alone the occupation can be justified, has been overreached and thus subordinated to a legal estate properly created by the trustees under their statutory powers, it can, in relation to the proprietor of the legal estate so created, be any longer said to be a right "for the time being subsisting." Section 70(1)(g) protects only the rights in reference to the land of the occupier whatever they are at the material time—in the instant case the right to enjoy in specie the rents and profits of the land held in trust for him. Once the beneficiary's rights have been shifted from the land to capital moneys in the hands of the trustees, there is no longer an interest in the land to which the occupation can be referred or which it can protect. If the trustees sell in accordance with the statutory provisions and so overreach the beneficial interests in reference to the land, nothing remains to which a right of occupation can attach and the same result must, in my judgment, follow vis-à-vis a chargee by way of legal mortgage so long as the transaction is carried out in the manner prescribed by the Law of Property Act 1925, overreaching the beneficial interests by subordinating them to the estate of the chargee which is no longer "affected" by them so as to become subject to them on registration pursuant to section 20(1) of the Land Registration Act 1925. In the instant case, therefore, I would, for my part, hold that the charge created in favour of the appellants overreached the beneficial interests of the respondents and that there is nothing in section 70(1)(g) of the Land Registration Act 1925 or in Boland's case which has the effect of preserving against the appellants any rights of the respondents to occupy the land by virtue of their beneficial interests in the equity of redemption which remains vested in the trustees.

Although the decision in *Flegg* remains the leading authority on the application of overreaching against the overriding interests of occupiers, the framework of the law has moved on. The TOLATA 1996 has reformed trusts of land, including co-ownership trusts. The Fleggs would no longer hold a beneficial interest under a trust for sale, but under a trust of land, and their beneficial interests would be clearly in the land, in respect of which they would have a right of occupation.[38]

In *Sabherwal* the Court of Appeal considered that the 1996 Act does not affect the application of overreaching. We will see in section 4.1.1 that the matter is not, however, entirely beyond doubt.

Birmingham Midshires Mortgage Services Ltd v Sabherwal
(2000) 80 P & CR 256, CA

Walker LJ

At 261

The judge gave ten reasons for concluding that the decision in Flegg has not been affected by the 1996 Act. Since that conclusion is not directly challenged in this court, at any rate on the grounds that the judge considered, it is sufficient to mention three of the most cogent of his reasons. First, the overreaching effect of the legal charges took place when they were executed in July 1990, and cannot be ousted by the coming into force of the 1996 Act over six years later. Second, the 1996 Act contains nothing to exclude the essential overreaching provision contained in section 2(1)(ii) of the Law of Property Act 1925. On the contrary, that provision is amended so as to meet the new terminology of the 1996 Act (see section 25(1) and Schedule 3 paragraph 4(1)) and so is in effect confirmed, with that new terminology, by the 1996 Act. Third, the abolition of the doctrine of conversion (by section 3 of the 1996 Act) is irrelevant for reasons stated by Lord Oliver in *Flegg*. However, the abolition of that doctrine does explain the amendment of s.27(1) of the Law of Property Act 1925, on which some reliance has been placed.

The 1996 Act does confer wider implied powers of disposition upon trustees[39] than were conferred by the LPA 1925 and, furthermore, provides protection to the purchasers of unregistered land from the trustees.[40] The LRA 2002 replaces the LRA 1925 and preserves the protection afforded to the interests of occupiers as an overriding interest.[41] It also defines the abilities of the registered owner, including trustees, to dispose of the registered land[42] and provides protection to purchasers dealing with the registered owner, even where the registered owner is a trustee.[43]

---

[38] Trusts of Land and Appointment of Trustees Act 1996, ss 5, 12, and 13. The beneficiaries' right to occupy is considered in Chapter 17, section 5.3.
[39] Ibid, s 6.   [40] Ibid, s 16.   [41] Ibid, Sch 3, para 2.
[42] Land Registration Act 2002, s 23.   [43] Ibid, s 26.

4 OVERREACHING AND BREACH OF TRUST

The interplay between a breach of trust and overreaching has been the subject of considerable academic debate.[44] The fact that overreaching is founded upon the trustees' powers of disposition places in question its operation where the trustees are acting in breach of their powers or the duties to which they are required to adhere when exercising those powers. Almost all of the cases on overreaching have concerned unauthorized mortgages by trustees, which have been entered into to raise finance unconnected with the purchase of the property. Unauthorized sales by trustees tend not to lead to the same problems for occupying beneficiaries, although the danger from overreaching exists. A purchaser of land will generally wish to obtain vacant possession of the land and will conduct enquiries to that end, thus invariably revealing the occupying beneficiaries. The purchaser can then take steps to ensure that the occupying beneficiaries are prepared to vacate the property before proceeding with their purchase.[45]

4.1 TRUSTEES' ABILITY, AUTHORITY, AND DUTIES

Ferris and Battersby[46] make the crucial point that it is important, at the outset, to understand the different ways in which we refer to trustees' powers and the different consequences that result from a misuse of these powers. A reference to the powers of trustees may be used to define the ability of the trustees to undertake a certain disposition. Trustees as holders of the legal estate are able to deal with that estate, but they do not have ability to deal with the beneficiaries' equitable interests unless given authority to do so on behalf of the beneficiaries, either by the terms of the trust instrument or by statute. Thus, when we are talking about trustees' powers, we are usually referring to their authority to affect the beneficiaries' equitable interests rather than their ability to deal with the legal estate.[47]

Harpum demonstrated that it has long been the law that a disposition beyond the trustees' authority (ultra vires) cannot overreach the beneficial interests and nor can the purchaser claim the protection of s 2 of the LPA 1925.[48] Other mechanisms are thus necessary if a purchaser is to be protected against the risk that a trustee is acting ultra vires his or her authority.

Trustees may also act within their authority, but, in so doing, misapply the trust property or otherwise breach their duties as trustees. For example, we have seen that, in *Flegg*, the Maxwell-Browns, although they had authority to mortgage Bleak House, acted in breach of trust in doing so without consulting the Fleggs and with the object of

---

44 The debate is led by a series of articles by Ferris and Battersby: 'The Impact of the Trusts of Land and Appointment of Trustees Act 1996 on Purchasers of Registered Land' (1998) Conv 168; 'Overreaching and the Trusts of Land and Appointment of Trustees Act 1996: A Reply to Mr Dixon' (2001) Conv 221; 'General Principles of Overreaching and the Reforms of the 1925 Legislation' (2002) 118 LQR 270; 'The General Principles of Overreaching and the Modern Legislative Reforms 1996–2002' (2003) 119 LQR 94; and Ferris, 'Making Sense of Section 26 of the Land Registration Act 2002' in *Modern Studies in Property Law: Vol 2* (ed Cooke, 2003) p 101. See also Dixon, 'Overreaching and the Trusts of Land and Appointment of Trustees Act 1996' [2000] Conv 267 and Pascoe, 'Improving Conveyancing by Redrafting Section 16' [2005] Conv 140.
45 Harpum (1990) p 312.   46 Ferris and Battersby (2002) 118 LQR 270, 273–80.
47 Contrast the mortgagee's power of sale, discussed in Chapter 30. Mortgagees must be given both the ability to deal with the legal estate and the authority to deal with the borrower's equity of redemption.
48 Harpum (1990) pp 283–5, 294–6.

discharging their own personal debts, rather than in pursuance of their duty to act for the benefit of the trust.

Trustees may also fail to act in accordance with their statutory duty of care, as defined by s 1 of the Trustee Act 2000, or they may breach their equitable fiduciary duties. For example, the trustees may fail to exercise due care in obtaining the true market value for the property, or they may allow their personal interests to conflict with their fiduciary duty to give undivided loyalty to the beneficiaries' interests by dealing with the land for their own benefit. The TOLATA 1996 underlines both the need for the trustees to act in the interests of the beneficiaries, and in accordance with their legal and equitable duties, by reiterating these duties in s 6(5) and (6). These types of breach of duty are sometimes referred to as 'intra vires' breaches of trust, because they are within the ability and authority of the trustees, but are nevertheless proscribed. Ferris and Battersby[49] suggest that overreaching is unaffected by breaches of trust of this nature, because the purchaser can look to the protection of s 2 of the LPA 1925. Where the trust moneys are misapplied, the protections provided both by s 27(1) of that Act and of s 17 of the Trustee Act 1925 should absolve a purchaser from liability.[50]

Being clear about the ability and authority of the trustees to act, on the one hand, and their duties when acting in exercise of that ability or authority, on the other, underlines the matters upon which we need to concentrate when considering the impact of a breach of duty on overreaching. Firstly, the dispositive powers of the trustees are important in defining their authority to deal with the equitable estate and so overreach the beneficial interests. Secondly, if a purchaser cannot rely on the protection of s 2 of the LPA 1925, because the trustees have acted ultra vires, then we need to look at what other protection is available to them.

4.1.1 The source of trustees' powers of disposition

The trustees' authority is defined by the trust instrument and/or implied by statute. Originally, s 28 of the LPA 1925 granted trustees for sale all of the powers that were conferred upon a tenant for life and trustees under the Settled Land Act 1925, so that the purchaser would not necessarily have to examine the trust instrument in order to determine the width of the trustees' authority.[51]

Section 28 of the LPA 1925 has now been repealed and replaced by s 6 of the TOLATA 1996. As we have seen in Chapter 17, section 5.2, s 6(1) of the 1996 Act confers on the trustees *'all the powers of an absolute owner'*, though these powers must be exercised for the benefit of the trust and in a manner consistent with any other enactment of law or equity. Hence, in contrast to the previous law, rather than limiting the trustee's powers by authorizing only particular transactions, the 1996 Act authorizes all types of transaction. Consequently, at first sight, it might be thought that ultra vires transactions are less likely to result. But s 6(1) does not stand alone: s 8 enables a settlor to limit the width of the authority conferred by s 6(1).

---

[49] Ferris and Battersby (2002) pp 283–94. Smith (2005) p 198 suggests that such protection is unnecessary.

[50] Harpum (1990) p 309.

[51] Ibid, p 290. If the disposition contemplated was outside the s 28 (Law of Property Act 1925) powers, the purchaser could demand to see the trust instrument to check if the disposition was nevertheless within the express authority conferred by the trust deed.

Trusts of Land and Appointment of Trustees Act 1996, s 8

(1) Sections 6 and 7 do not apply in the case of a trust of land created by a disposition in so far as provision to the effect that they do not apply is made by the disposition.

(2) If the disposition creating such a trust makes provision requiring any consent to be obtained to the exercise of any power conferred by section 6 or 7, the power may not be exercised without that consent.

Thus, s 8 enables the settlor to limit the trustees' powers by, for example, providing that the trustees cannot act without the consent of a third party, or even by limiting or entirely excluding the implied statutory powers. Thus, where the statutory powers have been limited pursuant to s 8, a sale or mortgage that exceeds these powers will not overreach the beneficial interests and the purchaser or mortgagee will have to find protection elsewhere.

The changes made to the trustees' powers of disposition by the TOLATA 1996 may have a direct impact on the likelihood of an ultra vires disposition arising in the context of a co-owned home. Where co-ownership arises through the joint purchase of a home, the owners are unlikely to limit their own powers as trustees under s 8. As a result, an ultra vires disposition is unlikely to arise. An *intra* vires breach of duty or the misapplication of trust property, as exemplified by *Flegg*, is more likely to arise in such trusts. This is, however, subject to one further argument advanced by Ferris and Battersby.[52] They argue, although others disagree,[53] that the powers conferred by s 6(1) are also circumscribed by further statutory conditions: in particular, s 6(6), which provides that the powers of the trustees conferred by s 6(1) shall not be exercised in contravention of any rule of law or equity, and s 11, which imposes a duty of consultation upon the trustees. Thus, they suggest, the apparent wide authority conferred by s 6(1) is illusory and there is, in fact, a greater risk of transactions that are ultra vires the trustees' authority and thus unable to overreach the beneficial interests.[54] The argument is an important one because if correct it means that the effect of the 1996 Act is to reverse *Flegg*.[55] This reversal would be confined to registered land since, as we will see in section 4.2.1, purchasers in unregistered land are protected by s 16 of TOLATA. It has gained prescience as a result of the decision in *HSBC Bank plc v Dyche*.[56] There, Mr and Mrs Dyche held title to a house on trust for Mr Collelldevall, Mrs Dyche's father. Upon their divorce, they transferred the property into the sole name of Mrs Dyche who used the property as security for a mortgage in favour of HSBC. The question for the court was whether the transfer overreached Mr Collelldevall's beneficial interest. The transfer to Mrs Dyche and the grant of the mortgage constituted a breach of trust. Judge Purle held that '*[o]n the footing that the [. . .] transfer was unauthorised, it is difficult to see how that could as a matter of general principle overreach Mr Collelldevall's interest*'.[57] Gravells suggests that in so holding, '*the judge seems to adopt, without acknowledgement and without any serious debate, the contentious argument of Ferris and Battersby that, in the context of registered land, the Trusts of Land and Appointment*

---

[52] Ferris and Battersby (2002) pp 283–94. Smith (2005) p 198 suggests that such protection is unnecessary.

[53] Pascoe (2005); Smith (2005) p 196; Dixon (2000).

[54] 'The Impact of the Trusts of Land and Appointment of Trustees Act 1996 on Purchasers of Registered Land' [1998] Conv 168, 169–76, developed further in 'The General Principles of Overreaching and the Modern Legislative Reforms 1996–2002' (2003) LQR 94, 95–108.

[55] Ferris and Battersby [1998] Conv, pp 184–8.   [56] [2009] EWHC 2954 (Ch).

[57] Ibid, [37].

of Trustees Act 1996 has expanded the scope of ultra vires dispositions by trustees that will be ineffective to overreach equitable interests under the trust, (thereby reversing, albeit inadvertently, City of London Building Society v Flegg*)'.*[58] It is extremely doubtful, if the opportunity arises, that such a significant change will be endorsed without full discussion. On the facts, there are other grounds on which overreaching would not have taken place. In particular, as we have seen in section 2.3, overreaching requires capital money to be paid to at least two trustees. Judge Purle noted that this requirement had not been met as the capital money had been paid by one trustee (Mrs Dyche) to the other (Mr Dyche).[59]

4.2 PROTECTION OF PURCHASERS

Prior to the 1925 legislation, purchasers were in a particularly vulnerable position.[60] In order to overreach the beneficial interests, the purchaser had to be satisfied that the sale was intra vires and that the sale moneys were to be properly applied in accordance with the trust. The burden placed on purchasers was indeed onerous, particularly because they could be fixed with constructive notice of a breach of trust that the law considered they should have discovered. The LPA 1925 did not relieve a purchaser of the need to check the trustees' authority to sell, but it did try to ensure that purchasers, once they knew that they were dealing with trustees, could easily satisfy themselves of the trustee's authority by relying on the s 28 powers.

A purchaser could, however, be protected from the more difficult to discover intra vires breaches of trust by sheltering under the protection of s 2, provided that he or she followed the prescribed overreaching machinery by paying any capital moneys to two trustees.[61] The purchaser must also be acting in good faith, as the reference to purchaser in s 2 is subject to the definition contained in s 205 of the LPA 1925.[62] This sophisticated framework came under strain with the increased prevalence of implied trusts (particularly of domestic property) that emerged in the latter half of the twentieth century. Where the trust is implied, purchasers may not know they are dealing with trustees and may thus be unaware that they should satisfy themselves that the trustees are acting within their authority.[63]

Differing statutory provisions, depending upon whether the land is unregistered or registered, have addressed this need for greater purchaser protection.

4.2.1 Unregistered land

The protection of purchasers is governed by s 16 of the TOLATA 1996.

Trusts of Land and Appointment of Trustees Act 1996, s 16

(1) A purchaser of land which is or has been subject to a trust need not be concerned to see that any requirement imposed on the trustees by section 6(5), 7(3) or 11(1) has been complied with.

---

[58] Gravells, '*HSBC Bank plc v Dyche*: Getting Your Priorities Right' [2010] Conv 169, 173.
[59] [2009] EWHC 2954 (Ch), [41].   [60] Harpum (1990) pp 283–7.
[61] Ibid and Ferris and Battersby (2002).
[62] *HSBC Bank plc v Dyche* [2009] EWHC 2954 (Ch), [39]–[40].
[63] Ferris and Battersby (2002) pp 297–301.

(2) Where—

(a) trustees of land who convey land which (immediately before it is conveyed) is subject to the trust contravene section 6(6) or (8) but

(b) the purchaser of the land from the trustees has no actual notice of the contravention, the contravention does not invalidate the conveyance.

(3) Where the powers of trustees of land are limited by virtue of section 8—

(a) the trustees shall take all reasonable steps to bring the limitation to the notice of any purchaser of the land from them, but

(b) the limitation does not invalidate any conveyance by the trustees to a purchaser who has no actual notice of the limitation.

(4) Where trustees of land convey land which (immediately before it is conveyed) is subject to the trust to persons believed by them to be beneficiaries absolutely entitled to the land under the trust and of full age and capacity—

(a) the trustees shall execute a deed declaring that they are discharged from the trust in relation to that land, and

(b) if they fail to do so, the court may make an order requiring them to do so.

(5) A purchaser of land to which a deed under subsection (4) relates is entitled to assume that, as from the date of the deed, the land is not subject to the trust unless he has actual notice that the trustees were mistaken in their belief that the land was conveyed to beneficiaries absolutely entitled to the land under the trust and of full age and capacity.

(6) Subsections (2) and (3) do not apply to land held on charitable, ecclesiastical or public trusts.

(7) This section does not apply to registered land.

Hence, purchasers of unregistered land from trustees are protected by the terms of s 16 provided that they do not have actual knowledge of the trustees' breach of trust. The terms of s 16 have, however, been subject to some criticism and are certainly not framed in the clearest terms.[64]

4.2.2 Registered land

Much of the controversy that has, in the past, surrounded the protection of purchasers of registered land[65] has been sidelined by the enactment of ss 23 and 26 of the LRA 2002.[66]

Land Registration Act 2002, s 23

(1) Owner's powers in relation to a registered estate consist of—

(a) power to make a disposition of any kind permitted by the general law in relation to an interest of that description, other than a mortgage by demise or sub-demise, and

(b) power to charge the estate at law with the payment of money.

---

[64] Ferris and Battersby (2003) pp 108–19; Pascoe (2005); Smith (2005) p 197.
[65] Harpum (1990) pp 304–9; Ferris and Battersby (2002) pp 283–94; Dixon (2000).
[66] Land Registration Act 2002, s 52, which deals with dispositions by a registered chargee, is considered in Chapter 26, section 3.2.6.

(2) Owner's powers in relation to a registered charge consist of—

    (a) power to make a disposition of any kind permitted by the general law in relation to an interest of that description, other than a legal sub-mortgage, and

    (b) power to charge at law with the payment of money indebtedness secured by the registered charge.

(3) In subsection (2)(a), "legal sub-mortgage" means—

    (a) a transfer by way of mortgage,

    (b) a sub-mortgage by sub-demise, and

    (c) a charge by way of legal mortgage.

Land Registration Act 2002, s 26

(1) Subject to subsection (2), a person's right to exercise owner's powers in relation to a registered estate or charge is to be taken to be free from any limitation affecting the validity of a disposition.

(2) Subsection (1) does not apply to a limitation—

    (a) reflected by an entry in the register, or

    (b) imposed by, or under, this Act.

(3) This section has effect only for the purpose of preventing the title of a disponee being questioned (and so does not affect the lawfulness of a disposition).

Hence, s 23 confers upon the registered owner almost unfettered ability to dispose of the registered estate. Section 26 provides that no limitation upon a person's right to exercise an owner's power of disposition, including a trustee's authority to deal with the registered estate, will affect a purchaser unless that limitation is protected by the entry of a restriction on the register. The purchaser is thus no longer concerned with any ultra vires lack of authority that is not revealed by the entry of a restriction.

The wide terms of s 26 have already been noted:[67] in particular, the section provides no saving for overriding interests, nor does it call for the purchaser or other person dealing with the trustees to be registered. The provision does not specify that the purchaser must provide value to be protected and therefore appears to provide volunteers with the same degree of protection as purchasers. But a purchaser must provide value to qualify for overreaching under s 2 of the LPA 1925.[68] Further, the defence of lack of registration (including as regards the entry of a restriction) is conferred by s 29 of the LRA 2002 only in respect of registered dispositions made for valuable consideration. Through these routes, it may, in fact, be confined in its scope to purchasers.

4.3 SUMMARY

The liability of a buyer purchasing, or a lender taking a mortgage, from trustees who are acting ultra vires is no longer dependent upon the trustees' powers of disposition, but upon

---

[67] Ferris (2003) p 101. See also Smith (2005) p 194.   [68] See above, fn 35.

the protection afforded by statute. The nature of that protection differs according to whether the land is registered or unregistered. A person purchasing, or acquiring an interest in, registered land will be protected against an ultra vires breach of trust unless the limitation of the trustees' authority is recorded on the register by the entry of a restriction. Common restrictions call for the purchase money to be paid to two trustees, thus triggering overreaching, or a requirement to obtain the consent of a third party. In the absence of a restriction on the register, overreaching will continue to operate, even though the person dealing with the trustees has knowledge of a limitation upon the trustees' authority. By contrast, a purchaser of unregistered land will only be protected if he or she has no actual notice that the trustees are acting in excess of their authority. Actual notice is unlikely where the trust is implied, because the trustees will enjoy the unlimited powers of disposition enjoyed by an absolute owner conferred by the TOLATA 1996. Even where the trust is express, the purchaser is not required to scrutinize the trust instrument to confirm the nature of the trustees' authority.

Purchasers, but not volunteers, of both registered and unregistered land continue to be protected against intra vires breaches of trust by s 2 of the LPA 1925 provided that any capital moneys are paid to two trustees. It has been suggested (but is not yet established) that s 26 of the LRA 2002 might also provide protection to both purchasers and volunteers against intra vires breaches of trust.[69] Doubt is placed on whether a volunteer would be protected under s 26 by the framework of provisions within which the provision operates.

5   IS OVERREACHING JUSTIFIED?

We have noted that overreaching serves the twin objectives of implementing the trust curtain and ensuring security of transactions. Purchasers need not investigate the existence or terms of any trust affecting land. Title is taken unencumbered from such interests as long as overreaching occurs. We have further seen that where land is held on trust as an investment, the shifting of the beneficial interests from land to money is not problematic. In such cases, the effect of overreaching is entirely consistent with the purpose of the trust, because the beneficiaries' key concern is with the maintenance of the trust fund, rather than any particular item of property.

Overreaching is, however, more contentious when it is applied to land held on trust to be used as a home. Even in this context, the mechanism is problematic only in those cases, such as *Flegg*, in which the home is held on trust for the legal owners and others, and a sale or (typically) mortgage is arranged without the knowledge or consent of all of the beneficiaries. It is in these situations that the effect of overreaching, and the underlying assumption that the beneficiaries' concern lies in the maintenance of a fund, clashes with the purpose of the trust. As Hopkins notes, '*[t]he legacy of* Flegg *is that [. . .] on a sale or mortgage by two or more trustees the "use" value of the home – the "thing as thing" – is invisible to the law*'.[70] Overreaching sees homes only as wealth.

The spread of co-ownership of the home could not have been predicted at the time of the 1925 legislation. Both the trust for sale and the overreaching mechanism reflected the use of land as an investment. The shift from investment trusts to trusts of the home was a key

---

69 Cooke, *The New Law of Land Registration* (2003) p 60.
70 Hopkins, '*City of London Building Society v Flegg* (1987): Homes as Wealth' in *Landmark Cases in Land Law* (ed Gravells, Oxford: Hart, Publishing 2013) p 222.

impetus in the replacement of the trust for sale with the trust of land through the TOLATA 1996.[71] But in making the recommendations that led to that Act, the Law Commission envisaged the continuing operation of overreaching. That view has since been endorsed by the Court of Appeal in *Sabherwal*, although *Dyche* has cast doubt on the effect of the Act in registered land. The Law Commission did, however, identify the need to consider separately the impact of overreaching on beneficiaries in occupation and published these recommendations in a separate report.

Law Commission Report No 188, *Transfer of Land. Overreaching: Beneficiaries in Occupation* (1989, [3.1]–[3.3])

Part III

Need for Reform

Change of circumstances

The 1925 legislation compromise between the need to protect beneficiaries under trusts of land and the demand for certainty and simplicity in conveyancing was satisfactory, and perhaps ideal, in the circumstances in which it was intended to operate. A purchaser from the trustees could ignore the beneficial interests so long as he was careful to observe simple precautions in paying the price. This successfully hid the terms of the settlement "behind the curtain". Buying from trustees became as simple as buying from a single beneficial legal owner which it certainly had not been previously. At the same time, the financial interest of the beneficiary was safeguarded by transferring his claim to the proceeds of sale. So long as the trustees properly conducted the affairs of the settlement, it was not important to the beneficiary by what assets his interest was secured.

Doubts about these provisions arise now because, over the years, the patterns of land ownership and the use of settlements have changed. Although the rules with which we are concerned affect all types of real property, the changes relating to residential property are most significant. Since 1925, both the number of dwellings in England and Wales and the percentage of them which are owner-occupied have jumped dramatically. Couples have increasingly bought owner-occupied housing in their joint names, and this trend was accelerated by the decision in *Williams & Glyn's Bank Ltd v. Boland*, following which lending institutions encouraged borrowers to buy jointly so that they, the institutions, had the advantage of the statutory overreaching rules. These couples are technically trustees for sale, whether they hold on trust only for themselves, as is often the case, or whether there are others with beneficial interests.

For this reason, there is now a very large number of cases in which trust beneficiaries occupy trust property as their homes. Sometimes, also, the trust property is where they carry on business. Generally, the trust is a conveyancing technicality, imposed by the Law of Property Act 1925 as part of the scheme to confine normal conveyancing to legal estates. Most individuals in this position would be surprised to hear themselves referred to as trustees or as beneficiaries; they regard themselves simply as joint owners. The changes in circumstances have exposed the 1925 rules for the device which they are. "If the framers of the property legislation in 1925 had been able to foresee the growth in joint ownership of property which, coupled with the vast increase in the breakdown of marriage, has exposed the artificiality of the statutory trust for sale, they might have made clearer provision for the protection of beneficial interests without widening the enquiries needed to be made by a purchaser".

---

[71] Chapter 13, section 5.

In response to the changing circumstances in which trusts arise, the Law Commission made a simple recommendation:[72]

A conveyance of a legal estate in property should not have the effect of overreaching the interest of anyone of full age and capacity who is entitled to a beneficial interest in the property and who has a right to occupy it and is in actual occupation of it at the date of the conveyance, unless that person consents.

The Law Commission's proposal represents a logical extension of the reasoning underlying the introduction of the TOLATA 1996. In this report, as in its report leading to the Act, the Law Commission sought to provide a scheme of regulation for land held on trust that reflects the likely use of that land as a home. The government announced however, that the recommendations on overreaching would not be implemented.[73]

It must be questioned why there is resistance to this proposal. As Smith highlights,[74] a requirement of obtaining consent is not necessarily onerous. Indeed, making enquiries of occupiers is standard procedure in other aspects of conveyancing practice. It is one of the ways in which a balance is sought between protecting the interests of beneficiaries (and other persons with subsisting property rights) and purchasers. It may be suggested that, where overreaching is concerned, there is a clear imbalance in favour of purchasers. The importance of the trust curtain and security of transactions has, it seems, superseded any concerns at the mismatch between a trust of a home and the investments ideals that underpin overreaching. This is contrary to the ethos that underlies TOLATA and leaves an inconsistency in legislative policy towards the home between TOLATA on the one hand and the overreaching mechanism on the other.[75]

6 THE FUTURE OF OVERREACHING

We conclude this discussion of overreaching by considering possible future developments of overreaching and the rules affecting the broader context in which the mechanism operates. Firstly, we consider how the scope of overreaching could be restricted or qualified; secondly, we highlight recent arguments as to whether overreaching is compliant with the HRA 1998; finally, we consider alternative causes of action that may be available to beneficiaries.

6.1 QUALIFYING AND RESTRICTING THE SCOPE OF OVERREACHING

We have seen that the Law Commission's recommendation to qualify the operation of overreaching in relation to a particular type of beneficiary (those in actual occupation), through the imposition of a requirement of consent, has been rejected. Harpum suggested an alternative means of qualifying the mechanism.[76] If the rationale for overreaching is found in the powers of disposition of the trustees, a more logical means of qualification might lie in restricting those powers. It has already been pointed out, and the cases demonstrate, that the most acute tension between overreaching and the interests of the beneficiaries occurs

---

[72] Law Commission Report No 188, *Transfer of Land. Overreaching: Beneficiaries in Occupation* (1989) [4.3].
[73] (1998) 587 HL Deb WA213.   [74] Smith (2005) p 191.
[75] Hopkins, 'Regulating Trusts of the Home: Private Law and Social Policy' (2009) 125 LQR 310, 318–20.
[76] (1990) 49 CLJ 277.

where the trustees utilize the land, which the beneficiaries occupy as their home, as security for a loan that is applied to discharge personal or business debts, rather than towards the acquisition or improvement of the property. Harpum advocated limiting the trustees' power to mortgage the land to first mortgages to secure the purchase, improvement, or repair of the land.[77] However, since the time that Harpum wrote, both TOLATA and the LRA 2002 have expressed the powers of trustees and registered proprietors broadly. Further, restricting the powers of mortgage is contrary to a general recognition of the utility of being able to draw on equity in the home for a variety of purposes.[78] More recently, Owen has suggested that beneficiaries should be able to register their beneficial interest, with overreaching operating only in those cases where registration has not taken place.[79] Owen acknowledges that, in the case of implied trusts, beneficiaries may not be aware of their interest and, in any event, may not wish to register. However, he argues that the LRA 2002 is being too 'paternalistic' in denying the chance of registration to those who wish to do so.[80] To date, however, as we have seen in section 5 above, English law appears resistant to attempts to curtail the curtain principle through which trusts are kept off the register.

6.2 HUMAN RIGHTS AND OVERREACHING

Given that the policy of overreaching with regard to occupying beneficiaries has raised concerns, it is no surprise that it has attracted attention as potentially incompatible with fundamental human rights contained in Art 8 (respect for the home) and Art 1 of the First Protocol (deprivation of property) of the European Convention on Human Rights.

The compatibility of overreaching with human rights was raised both in *Sabherwal*[81] and in *National Westminster Bank plc v Malhan*,[82] but the substantive merit of the claim has not been addressed. In both cases the courts rejected the submission on the simple ground that the HRA 1998 did not have retrospective effect and thus could not affect either of the mortgages, which were both entered into before the Act came into force.[83] However, in *Malhan*, Morritt VC appeared indisposed to the human rights arguments advanced on behalf of the beneficiary and instead found 'much force' in submissions advanced for the bank.[84]

As we have seen in Chapter 4, a claim based upon a breach of the 1998 Act needs to clear a number of hurdles: firstly, we need to establish the horizontal effect of that Act; secondly, we need to prove that one of the Articles of the ECHR is engaged; and finally, we need to examine whether the interference can be justified by the stated qualifications to the enshrined rights. These lie within the government's margin of appreciation, with a requirement that the interference is proportionate in both its aim and its impact upon the individual, which calls for adequate procedural safeguards.

The horizontal effect of the HRA 1998 is established by the dictates of s 3, which requires the court to interpret legislation in a manner that is compatible with the ECHR '*[s]o far as it is possible to do so*'. Further, s 4 empowers a court to declare a statutory provision incompatible with the ECHR. We have examined a number of statutory provisions upon which

---

[77] Ibid, 330–1. See also Thompson (1997). Smith (2005) p 191 suggests a hybrid approach depending both upon a limitation of the trustees' powers of disposition and the consent of occupiers.

[78] The importance attached by homeowners to the ability to do so is noted, for example, by Smith, Searle, and Cook, 'Rethinking the Risks of Home Ownership' (2009) 38 Journal of Social Policy 83.

[79] Owen [2013] Conv 377, 391–4.   [80] Ibid, 394.   [81] (2000) 80 P & CR 256.

[82] [2004] EWHC 847.

[83] *Wilson v Secretary of State for Trade & Industry* [2003] UKHL 40.   [84] [2004] EWHC 847, [53].

overreaching and its effect on purchasers is dependent. Sections 2 and 27 of the LPA 1925 define the scope of overreaching. In the TOLATA 1996, we find, in s 6, the authority of the trustees to overreach by the exercise of their powers of disposition, and in s 16, the protection of purchasers of unregistered land against the effects of an unauthorized disposition. The protection of the purchasers of registered land against an unauthorized disposition is found in s 26 of the LRA 2002. There is thus considerable scope for the courts to examine the compatibility of overreaching with the ECHR.

Article 8 and Art 1 of the First Protocol are the prime targets for engagement. But the argument in *Malhan* was based upon the discriminatory effect of overreaching where there are two trustees in comparison with the failure of overreaching where there is only one trustee. Article 8 and Art 1 of the First Protocol were thus to be read with Art 14 (prohibition of discrimination). In the past, this difference in treatment has been justified by the protection said to be afforded to beneficiaries by two trustees: firstly, as a guard against the commission of a breach of trust; and secondly, by providing two, rather than one, pockets against which to pursue any personal claim for damages. In reality, this so-called 'protection' has proved illusory. This is the case, for example, where the trust is implied and the trustees are ignorant of their responsibilities. Equally, the protection is illusory where, in the face of financial difficulties, an action for breach against the trustees (who may be family members) is worthless. But we have seen that the need for two trustees has been questioned both in the *Sood* situation, in which there are no capital moneys, and possibly (although less convincingly) where, in the absence of an appropriate restriction, a sole proprietor of a registered title deals with the land. The picture is thus rather more complex than the argument in *Malhan* suggests.

In *Malhan*, counsel was driven to rely on Art 14 because it had conceded that a submission based upon Art 8 or Art 1 of the First Protocol alone would not succeed. But what if this concession had not been made?

Possession proceedings against a beneficiary in occupation by a purchaser or mortgagee claiming the benefit of overreaching will engage Art 8 as the most extreme interference with the respect due to an occupier's home. The appropriate enquiry is whether there is a justification for that interference on the policy grounds either of the economic well-being of the country, in maintaining a well-balanced property and lending market, or the protection of the rights and freedoms of others—namely, purchasers and mortgagees.

The operation of overreaching by shifting the beneficial interest from the land to the capital moneys (if any) might also be capable of engaging Art 1 of the First Protocol although it could be argued that the beneficiary's trust interest as a possession is inherently limited by the disposal powers of the trustees from which overreaching springs and so there is no interference with that possession.[85] Overreaching shifts the beneficiary's interest from the land and accordingly will affect its peaceful enjoyment by controlling the identity of the property in which the beneficial interest vests and against which attendant ownership rights can be asserted. An occupying beneficiary's occupation of his or her home is disturbed, because his or her interest is no longer in the land, but in the capital moneys (if any). If Art 1 of the First Protocol is engaged, then both the operation of overreaching must be justified as being in the public interest: for example, in securing a fair and efficient conveyancing system.

---

[85] See Goymour, 'Proprietary Claims and Human Rights: A Reservoir of Entitlement?' (2006) 65 CLJ 696, 714–15.

Any justification, whether required under Art 8 or Art 1 of the First Protocol, must strike a proportionate balance, within the State's margin of appreciation, between the interests of the beneficiary (particularly the beneficiary in occupation) and the purchaser or mortgagee. In addition, the proportionality of the interference upon the personal circumstances of the individual occupier against the proprietary rights of the purchaser or mortgagee will also need to be considered by an adequate process before an independent tribunal clothed with the necessary discretion to make that judgment. However, it seems unlikely, following *McDonald v McDonald*,[86] that the courts will be inclined to question overreaching as a reflection of the policy choices of Parliament in shaping property law, which has evolved over many centuries and which, in the case of statutory rules, have been considered by Parliament. Both the TOLATA 1996 and the LRA 2002 have enabled a recent appraisal of overreaching both by the Law Commission and Parliament.

6.3 ALTERNATIVE CAUSES OF ACTION

Overreaching does not exist in a legal vacuum. In Chapter 16, in the context of our discussion of the priority rules of registered land, we highlighted the possibility of new direct rights being imposed on a purchaser on a transfer of land. These rights, arising from a myriad of alternative causes of action, include *personal* liability being imposed on the trustees and other parties where the sale constituted a breach of trust, and *proprietary* claims over assets purchased by trustees using the proceeds of sale. Hence, one partial solution to concerns as regards the scope of overreaching is to ensure that these alternatives are developed and used. As we will see, however, each of these actions has its own limitations.

6.3.1 Breach of trust

Trustees who act in breach of trust are personally liable to the beneficiaries. In practice, however, the utility of this form of liability is dependent on the financial circumstances of the trustees. For example, we have noted that, in *Flegg*, the Maxwell-Browns acted in breach of trust towards the Fleggs in mortgaging the parties' joint home—but, as a result of the Maxwell-Brown's financial circumstances, an action against them for this breach was of no practical use.

6.3.2 Knowing receipt and dishonest assistance

A purchaser who takes trust property knowing that it is dealt with in breach of trust, or some other person who dishonestly assists in the breach of trust itself, may find him or herself called upon personally to account for the loss suffered by the trust through the equitable doctrines of knowing receipt and dishonest assistance. The beneficial interests continue to be overreached, but a distinct personal liability is imposed, which requires the purchaser or interfering third party to be held to account as if he or she were the trustee committing the breach of trust.

The interplay between statutory defences against the enforcement of *property* rights in registered land and the imposition of *personal* liability is not beyond doubt. Debate has

---

[86] [2017] AC 273.

centred on the availability of recipient liability.[87] In *Arthur v Attorney General of the Turks and Caicos Islands*,[88] the parties before the Privy Council proceeded on the assumption that if the Islands' Registered Land Ordinance protected Mr Arthur from proprietary liability, it would also preclude the imposition of personal recipient-based liability.[89] In that case (in sharp contrast to the position in English law) it was held that the statute did not in fact protect Mr Arthur from proprietary liability. The case arose from an application by Mr Arthur to strike out the claims against him and the outcome of the Privy Council's decision was that both proprietary and personal claims would proceed to a full hearing. Subsequently, the Privy Council has upheld a similar personal claim for knowing receipt in *Akita Holdings Ltd v Attorney General of the Turks and Caicos Islands*.[90] However, in *Farah Constructions Pty Ltd v Say-Dee Pty Ltd*, the High Court of Australia refused to impose recipient liability against a defendant who had statutory protection against the beneficiaries' equitable interests.[91]

In Chapter 16 we have seen that s 29 of the LRA 2002 provides a registered proprietor who has obtained title through a registered disposition of a registered estate for valuable consideration with a defence against pre-existing property rights held by third parties (subject to statutory exceptions explored in that chapter). The effect of s 29, therefore, is to protect purchasers for value from proprietary liability. Conaglen and Goymour suggest that s 29 simultaneously protects the registered proprietor against personal liability for knowing receipt.[92] The basis of their argument is that this form of personal liability is not based solely on wrongdoing by the recipient proprietor, but instead 'the fundamental purpose of the claim seems to be to vindicate the pre-existing property rights that have been lost as a result of the wrongful disposition'.[93] As the personal claim is 'parasitic'[94] on the property right, they argue that it would be 'inherently inappropriate' to impose personal liability in knowing receipt on a purchaser who takes free from the property interests under s 29.[95]

However, it is far from clear that liability for knowing receipt is based on vindication of title, rather than on wrongdoing. Conaglen and Goymour's own support for vindication as the basis of the claim is tentatively expressed.[96] Hopkins suggests that 'the scales could readily be tipped towards wrongdoing as the basis of liability'.[97] He notes that the centrality of the wrong to the imposition of liability has caused tension in a separate debate—an attempt to recast equitable recipient liability as within the common law principle of unjust enrichment.[98] Hopkins argues that, as a matter of policy, where statute protects a purchaser from proprietary liability, recourse to personal liability becomes even more essential. Hopkins explains:[99]

> To put it the other way, it is difficult to see why a recipient of property with knowledge that it has been transferred in breach of trust or fiduciary duty should be able to use legislative protection from a proprietary claim to shield themselves from alternate [personal] liability. To do so appears tantamount to using statute as a cloak for fraud.

---

[87] This basis for liability is suggested by Dixon (2000) p 270 and although initially disputed by Ferris and Battersby (see [2001] Conv 221, 224), they subsequently acknowledged its availability (see (2003) 119 LQR 94, 122).

[88] [2012] UKPC 30.   [89] Ibid, at [38].   [90] [2017] AC 590.

[91] [2007] HCA 222 at [193]–[198]; McFarlane (2008) p 418.

[92] Conaglen and Goymour, 'Knowing Receipt and Registered Land' in *Resulting and Constructive Trusts* (ed Mitchell, 2009).

[93] Ibid, p 172.   [94] Ibid, p 174.

[95] Ibid. Conaglen and Goymour accept that LRA 2002, s 29 does not shield a purchaser from liability founded on dishonest assistance as such liability is based on wrongdoing: pp 178–81.

[96] Ibid, p 172.

[97] Hopkins, 'Recipient Liability in the Privy Council: *Arthur v Attorney General of the Turks and Caicos Islands*' [2013] Conv 61, 66.

[98] Ibid, 67.   [99] Ibid, 66.

Views on the potential scope of personal liability remain mixed. Smith welcomes Conaglen and Goymour's conclusion that receipt-based liability should not be recognized, whilst acknowledging that the distinction between vindication and wrongdoing may not always be clear.[100] Through a comparison with *in personam* liability in Australia, Owen suggests that receipt-based liability should be imposed only where the purchaser has 'more than mere notice of the trustees' breach'; such as where the purchaser acts contrary to a specific undertaking.[101] He suggests, for example, that personal liability could have been imposed in *HSBC Bank plc v Dyche*.[102] There, as we have seen in section 4.1.1 above, the court held that overreaching did not take place on a transfer of land by the trustees, Mr and Mrs Dyche, to Mrs Dyche alone, as the transfer was in breach of trust. In the absence of overreaching Mrs Dyche's liability was proprietary. When the property had been vested in them, Mr and Mrs Dyche had agreed to (re) transfer the land to the beneficiary (Mrs Dyche's father) on the discharge of a debt. Owen questions the imposition of proprietary liability in the case, but instead suggests that Mrs Dyche's breach of the specific undertaking would justify the imposition of personal receipt-based liability on her.[103]

6.3.3 Tracing

Tracing is the process by which beneficiaries can track their proprietary interest into a substitute asset that the trustees may have acquired with the proceeds of sale, following a disposition by the trustees in breach of trust.[104] Once the beneficiaries have done so, they may be able to claim proprietary interests in those substitute assets.

Tracing may be available to beneficiaries in two situations, although the process will only be of any practical assistance to a beneficiary where there are substitute assets. Furthermore, any claim that the beneficiaries may have in relation to those assets is subject to a significant limitation through the defence of bona fide purchaser.

The first situation in which tracing is available is that in which trustees make a disposition that is an ultra vires breach of trust. An unauthorized disposition will not overreach, but, in light of the protection available to purchasers, a beneficiary is unlikely to be able to assert his or her interest in the property disposed of. A beneficiary may be able to trace the proceeds of sale of an unauthorized disposition received by the trustees into any substitute asset acquired with those proceeds.[105]

Secondly, tracing may also assist the beneficiaries once overreaching has occurred and the trustees hold proceeds of sale on trust. Overreaching shifts the beneficial interests into the proceeds of sale. If the trustees then apply those proceeds in breach of trust, the beneficiaries may be able to trace their proprietary interest into assets acquired through that breach. As we have seen, s 27(1) of the LPA 1925 absolves the purchaser of any liability in this regard.

---

[100] Smith, '*Williams and Glyn's Bank v Boland* (1980): The Development of a System of Title by Registration' in *Landmark Cases in Land Law* (ed Gravells, Oxford: Hart Publishing, 2013) p 152.

[101] Owen, 'A New Paradigm for Overreaching—Some Inspiration from Down Under' [2013] Conv 377, 387.

[102] [2009] EWHC 2954 (Ch).   [103] [2013] Conv 377, 386.

[104] *Foskett v McKeown* [2001] AC 102.

[105] See ibid, *Cave v Cave* (1880) 15 Ch D 639, and *Ffrench's Estate* (1887) 21 LR (Ir) 283, referred to by Fox (2002).

As Fox explains, the effect of tracing looks very similar to overreaching's effect in allowing a beneficiary a claim against the proceeds of sale acquired by the trustees.[106] There are, however, important differences between the mechanisms, particularly as regards their effect on the beneficiaries' title. Where overreaching takes place, the beneficiaries have the same interest in the proceeds of sale as they previously had in the land and that interest vests immediately upon overreaching. Where beneficiaries trace funds into a substitute asset, they have a right to elect between a beneficial interest in the asset (a proportionate share of an asset purchased in part with trust finds) or a lien to enforce their personal claim against the trustees for breach of trust.[107] It will not be until they have made that election that their appropriate interest will vest and, prior to that election, their interest is inchoate.

7 PRIORITY RULES WHERE OVERREACHING DOES NOT TAKE PLACE

Where overreaching does not take place, the rules determining the enforcement of a beneficial interest are dependent on whether the title is registered or unregistered. In unregistered land, enforcement of a beneficial interest is determined by the doctrine of notice. Occupation of the home by the beneficiary may be sufficient to fix the purchaser with constructive notice of the interest.[108] In registered land, the curtain principle precludes entry of a notice of a beneficial interest on the register.[109] A beneficial interest that is not overreached may bind a purchaser as an overriding interest where the beneficiary is in occupation (see Chapter 16, section 5.1).[110]

A specific issue arises where, through the process of survivorship (discussed in Chapter 13, section 2.2), legal title remains in a sole surviving joint tenant. A beneficiary may have severed his or her equitable joint tenancy prior to his or her death. A transfer by the sole trustee will not have overreaching effect, leaving a purchaser vulnerable to a claim that the severed beneficial interest is binding against him or her through notice (in unregistered land) or as overriding interests (in registered land). In unregistered land, a statutory solution is provided.

Law of Property (Joint Tenants) Act 1964, s 1

(1) For the purposes of section 36(2) of the Law of Property Act 1925, as amended by section 7 of and the Schedule to the Law of Property (Amendment) Act 1926, the survivor of two or more joint tenants shall, in favour of a purchaser of the legal estate, be deemed to be solely and beneficially interested if [. . .] the conveyance includes a statement that he is so interested.

Provided that the foregoing provisions of this subsection shall not apply if, at any time before the date of the conveyance by the survivor—

(a) a memorandum of severance (that is to say a note or memorandum signed by the joint tenants or one of them and recording that the joint tenancy was severed in equity on a date therein specified) had been endorsed on or annexed to the conveyance by virtue of which the legal estate was vested in the joint tenants; or

---

106 Fox (2002). See also McFarlane (2008) pp 400–1.   107 Fox (2002) p 102.
108 *Kingsnorth Finance Co v Tizard* [1986] 1 WLR 783.
109 Land Registration Act 2002, s 33(a).   110 Ibid, Sch 3, para 2.

(b) a bankruptcy order made against any of the joint tenants, or a petition for such an order, had been registered under the Land Charges Act 1925, being an order or petition of which the purchaser has notice, by virtue of the registration, on the date of the conveyance by the survivor.

(2) The foregoing provisions of this section shall apply with the necessary modifications in relation to a conveyance by the personal representatives of the survivor of joint tenants as they apply in relation to a conveyance by such a survivor.

Hence, as long as the purchaser falls outside of the provisos to s 1(1), he or she is protected against a priority claim by a beneficiary. Although not so described in the statute, Cooke notes[111] that the effect of the provision is that the beneficial interest is overreached, because the beneficiary would have a claim against the proceeds of sale.

The Law of Property (Joint Tenants) Act 1964 is confined in its application to unregistered land. No equivalent statutory protection is provided to a purchaser of registered land. This may be an oversight, explicable on the basis that the prospect of a beneficial interest binding a purchaser in registered land as an overriding interest became apparent only with the decision in *Williams & Glyn's Bank v Boland*,[112] some years after the enactment of the 1964 Act.

Cooke suggests that the problem is a small one and that the solution is simple.

Cooke, 'Beneficial Joint Tenants and the Protection of Purchasers: An Unsolved Problem' [2004] Conv 41, 48

Obviously a simple extension of the 1964 Act to registered land by repealing s.3 will not work; there is no way of making a memorandum of severance on the conveyance or transfer to the vendor and the deceased joint tenant, nor could the purchaser see that memorandum, since he has access only to the register and not to previous title deeds. All that is needed is a corresponding provision to the effect that the surviving joint tenant vendor will be deemed to be solely and beneficially entitled if:

(a) the transfer states that the vendor is solely and beneficially interested in the land;

(b) the purchaser obtains a clean bankruptcy search, exactly as in the 1964 Act;

(c) there is no restriction on the register preventing a disposition by the survivor of the two trustees.

The requirement of the absence of a memorandum of severance is thus matched by the requirement of the absence of a restriction. Neither is in fact conclusive; in unregistered land, severance could have been effected without the making of a memorandum, just as in registered land there could be a severance without the entry of a restriction. In both cases something inconclusive is deemed, for the protection of a purchaser, to be conclusive.

The application of the Act appears to have been qualified by the following case—the first in which a purchaser sought to rely on the protection provided.

---

[111] Cooke, 'Beneficial Joint Tenants and the Protection of Purchasers: An Unsolved Problem' [2004] Conv 41, 42.

[112] [1981] AC 487.

Grindal v Hooper
(unreported judgment 6 December 1999, HC)

Facts: Two sisters, Vera and Sheila, were legal and beneficial joint tenants of a house occupied by Vera. She severed the beneficial joint tenancy by written notice, and, on her death, left her estate to her brother, Brian and other siblings. Sheila, as sole legal owner through survivorship, sold the house to Brian for £600, the market value being in the region of £70,000. Brian knew of the trust and of the severance, but no memorandum had been placed on the conveyance to Vera and Sheila. Following Brian's death, the question arose whether, under the 1964 Act, he was solely entitled to the house (so that it would pass under the terms of his will), or whether he held title on trust for himself and Vera's estate, each estate now entitled to a 50 per cent share.

Judge Jarvis QC

Mr Charman says that Brian in these circumstances is the purchaser of the legal estate, and in order to be a purchaser who is protected by the assumptions given by law under s.1 of the 1964 Act he must fall within the definition of a purchaser under s.205 of the Law of Property Act 1925. At definition 21 a purchaser is defined to mean:

> "a purchaser in good faith for valuable consideration [. . .] and valuable consideration includes marriage but does not include a nominal consideration in money."

In short, Mr Charman says that Brian had notice of the severance before he entered into the agreement to purchase the property. Notice of severance is in these circumstances a notice of the fact that the property was no longer jointly held and therefore that Sheila held the property on trust as to one half for herself and one half for Vera. In those circumstances, where a person has actual notice of circumstances he cannot be said to take in good faith [. . .]

It seems to me that on the facts of this case Brian had full notice of the fact that Vera's interest was held on trust by Sheila, and that to acquire the property in these circumstances could not satisfy the definition of a purchaser for good faith under the Act. He, without doubt, purchased the property at a gross under value with actual notice of the estate's interest, and the only inference that I can draw is that that was a transaction which would be designed to deprive the estate of its interest in the property. I conclude that in any event Brian's estate could not take this property without being bound by the equitable interest of Vera's estate.

As Gravells notes, it is doubtful whether actual notice alone should deny the purchaser statutory protection.

Gravells, 'Co-ownership, Severance and Purchasers: The Law of Property (Joint Tenants) Act 1964 on Trial' [2000] Conv 461, 470

[It] might be questioned whether actual notice is or should be sufficient in itself to negative good faith. It might be argued that, in so far as the operation of section 1(1) is excluded where there is an endorsement of the notice of severance, the 1964 Act provides a means of protection for a beneficial tenant in common following the severance of the joint tenancy; that such endorsement may be seen as a form of "quasi-registration"; and that, if the beneficial tenant in common fails to take advantage of that protection, a purchaser should not be bound by the beneficial interest on the basis of actual notice without more. The view that a purchaser who has actual notice of a protectable but unprotected interest cannot be in good faith has been severely criticised and rejected in analogous circumstances.

As is apparent from the observation at the end of the extract from Gravells, the question of the relationship between good faith and actual notice is not unique to the Law of Property (Joint Tenants) Act 1964. We have explored the relationship between those concepts further in Chapter 13 in our discussion of *Midland Bank plc v Green*.[113]

QUESTIONS

1. Outline the rules that would be used to determine the enforcement of a beneficial interest against a purchaser where purchase money is paid to: (i) one trustee; and (ii) two trustees.

2. To what extent does the requirement that purchase money must be paid to two trustees for overreaching to take place protect the beneficiaries against dissipation of funds by trustees?

3. Does a disposition by trustees in breach of trust (ultra vires or intra vires) have overreaching effect? What is the position of the purchaser following such a disposition?

4. Assess the arguments for and against enabling overreaching of the interests of beneficiaries in occupation. What advice would you give an occupying beneficiary who is concerned that his or her trustee(s) may sell the land?

5. What are the dangers for a purchaser who buys land from a sole surviving joint tenant? To what extent have these dangers been overcome?

For guidance on how to answer these questions visit the online resources at www.oup.com/uk/mcfarlane4e/.

FURTHER READING

Cooke, *Land Law* (Oxford: OUP, 2006, ch 3)

Conaglen and Goymour, 'Knowing Receipt and Registered Land' in *Resulting and Constructive Trusts* (ed Mitchell, 2009)

Ferris, 'Making Sense of Section 26 of the Land Registration Act 2002' in *Modern Studies in Property Law Vol 2* (ed Cooke, Oxford: Hart Publishing, 2003)

Ferris and Battersby, 'General Principles of Overreaching and the Reforms of the 1925 Legislation' (2002) 118 LQR 270

---

[113] [1981] AC 513. See Chapter 13, section 5.6.

Ferris and Battersby, 'The General Principles of Overreaching and the Modern Legislative Reforms 1996–2002' (2003) 119 LQR 94

Harpum, 'Overreaching, Trusteees' Powers and the Reform of the 1925 Legislation' (1990) 49 CLJ 277

Hopkins, 'City of London Building Society v Flegg (1987): Homes as Wealth' in Landmark Cases in Land Law (ed Gravells, Oxford: Hart Publishing, 2013)

Jackson, 'Overreaching and Unauthorised Disposition of Registered Land' [2007] Conv 120

Jackson, 'Overreaching in Registered Land Law' (2006) 69 MLR 214

Owen, 'A New Model for Overreaching—Some Historical Inspiration' [2015] Conv 226

Owen, 'Overreaching—Getting the Balance Right' [2017] Conv 26

Pascoe, 'Improving Conveyancing by Redrafting Section 16' [2005] Conv 140

18

REFORM OF THE LAND REGISTRATION ACT 2002

CENTRAL ISSUES

1. The provisions of the Land Registration Act 2002 have a profound effect in land law. We have seen in previous chapters that those provisions affect the acquisition of legal estates and interests in land (see especially Chapters 3 and 8), as well as the defences available to a pre-existing legal or equitable property right in land (see Chapter 16).

2. This chapter gives us a chance to stand back and examine the impact of the 2002 Act. Firstly, we will bring together some of the material covered in previous chapters in order to summarize the effect of the Act. Secondly, we will evaluate the Act, by asking both whether the Act has achieved its stated purpose and whether that purpose is, in any case, worthwhile. In doing so, we will consider some important recent developments concerning the circumstances in which it is possible to rectify the register.

3. In considering the effect of the 2002 Act, it is useful to look at the three questions that we considered in Chapter 1, section 3—that is, the *content, acquisition*, and *defences* questions. As we will see, the chief impact of the Act is on the second and third of those questions.

4. In analysing the 2002 Act, we have to be careful to separate out its current and future effects. The Act was designed to facilitate a general system of e-conveyancing. As we saw in Chapter 8, section 6.5.3, that system is not yet in place. So we need to distinguish the current effect of the 2002 Act from the effect that it was intended to have in a world of e-conveyancing.

5. In evaluating the 2002 Act, we need to ask if we approve of the answers that it provides to the *acquisition* and *defences* questions. This is not simply a matter of comparing the provisions of the Act to its predecessor, the Land Registration Act 1925; rather, to evaluate the 2002 Act, we have to compare the results that it produces in particular situations with what we would regard as the best results in those cases. This, of course, raises the very difficult question of how we are to decide, in the abstract, what is the 'best possible result' in any particular case.

6. The Law Commission in 2016 published a Consultation Paper entitled 'Updating the Land Registration Act 2002'. This makes it particularly appropriate for us to evaluate the Act and, in this chapter, we will consider some of the suggestions made by the Law Commission as part of its ongoing review of the operation of the 2002 Act.

1 AIMS AND RHETORIC

1.1 THE LAW COMMISSION'S 2001 REPORT

In Chapter 3, we saw that: (i) there are good reasons why registration is particularly important in land law; (ii) those advantages of registration are maximized if registration of title is required; but (iii) nonetheless, a question remains as to precisely how a land registration system should operate. In Chapter 3, section 3.1, we looked at the specific aims of the LRA 2002, as set out in the Law Commission Report[1] that led to the Act. It was stated there that:

Law Commission Report No 271, *Land Registration for the Twenty-First Century: A Conveyancing Revolution* (2001, [1.5]–[1.10])

The fundamental objective of the Bill is that, under the system of electronic dealing with land that it seeks to create, the register should be a complete and accurate reflection of the state of the title of the land at any given time, so that it is possible to investigate title to land online, with the absolute minimum of additional enquiries and inspections.

Firstly, the Act clearly aims to prioritize dynamic security:[2] to protect a third party (C) attempting to acquire a legal property right in land from the risk of being bound by a pre-existing, but hidden, legal or equitable property right. Secondly, it is clear that the standard use of e-conveyancing (and hence electronic registration) was a fundamental part of the scheme of the LRA 2002. It was viewed as providing an important justification for protecting C against pre-existing, but unregistered, rights: the logic is that, because e-conveyancing makes it simpler for B to register a right, it becomes harder for B to excuse a failure to register, and thus fairer to protect C against any unregistered right of B. It was also envisaged that e-conveyancing could lead to the elimination of the 'registration gap' discussed in Chapter 8, section 6.5, as completion of any disposition from A to B could then occur at the very same time as the application for registration of B's right.

Thirdly, and linked to the previous two points, is the fundamental idea that the registration system exists not to set out rights already acquired by parties such as A, B, and C, but, instead, to *create* those rights. In such a world, the register will *necessarily* meet the Law Commission's aim in 2001 that the register be a '*complete and accurate reflection of the state of the title of the land at any given time*'.[3] Indeed, there will be no external standard by which to check the accuracy of the register: anything on the register will be correct, simply because it *is* on the register.

Finally, it is important to remember that the Law Commission described its fundamental objective of a 'complete and accurate register' as an 'ultimate' objective. Certainly, the LRA 2002 did not aim to achieve its intended effects overnight. The most important outstanding step was the standard use of e-conveyancing. This means that, when evaluating

---

[1] The Report was the product of joint work between the Law Commission and HM Land Registry but will simply be referred to in this chapter as the Law Commission's Report, both for convenience and to allow a direct comparison with the Law Commission's 2016 Consultation Paper, which was produced independently of the Registry, although of course with input from the Registry as an important 'stakeholder': see Law Com CP No 227, [1.26]–[1.28].

[2] See Chapter 3, section 2.4 for the definition of 'dynamic security'.   [3] Law Com CP No 271, [1.5].

the Act, we need to be aware that its full impact cannot be determined unless and until that e-conveyancing system is fully operational. Nonetheless, the 2002 Act did make a number of very significant, immediate changes, taking effect independently of e-conveyancing. Those changes will be summarized in the next section and we will evaluate them in section 3.

Before discussing those changes, it is worth noting an important tension in the fundamental objective of the 2002 Act. This can be seen by considering the single sentence from the Law Commission's 2001 Report, set out above. The tension stems from the notion that: (i) the register should be 'complete and accurate'; so that (ii) C can '*investigate title to land on line, with the absolute minimum of additional enquiries and inspections*'. Of course, if the register really were complete and accurate, there would be no need for *any* further investigation of title: such enquiries would be eliminated, rather than minimized. As we saw in Chapter 16, however, when considering overriding interests, the scheme of the LRA 2002 clearly contemplates that C, when acquiring a right in registered land from A, cannot rely *solely* on the register: a physical check of the land itself is required to see if, for example, anyone other than A is in actual occupation of the land and claims a property right in it, or to discover if anyone may be exercising a legal easement over A's land. The fact that the 2002 Act allows for cases in which an unregistered but pre-existing property right of B suggests that the aim of making the register complete and accurate may not only be very difficult to achieve in practice, but may also be of dubious merit. Certainly, as we will see in the next section, it would be dangerous for C to think that he or she can rely on the register with complete confidence and will *always* be fully protected from an unregistered, but pre-existing, property right of A or B.

1.2 THE LAW COMMISSION'S 2016 CONSULTATION PAPER

As part of its current project of considering the operation of the LRA 2002, the Law Commission in 2016 published a Consultation Paper entitled: '*Updating the Land Registration Act 2002*'. At various points in the book, we have considered some of the suggestions made there by the Commission, and we will also look at its proposals in this chapter.

An important preliminary point is that the rhetoric of the 2016 Consultation Paper (CP) is quite different from that of the 2001 Report. Firstly, the 2016 CP recognizes that the bold ambitions of the 2001 Report for e-conveyancing are not workable:[4] '*We will argue that the goals of electronic conveyancing need to be adjusted in response to the technical limitations that have become clear since the LRA 2002 came into force in order to provide a more realistic framework for a future electronic conveyancing system.*' The problems encountered in attempts to promote electronic conveyancing were discussed in Chapter 8, section 6.5.3. It was noted there that the Law Commission no longer sees e-conveyancing as a means, at least in the foreseeable future, of eliminating the registration gap: contrary to the ambitions in the 2001 Report, there will still be a gap between the completion of a disposition and an application for its registration. Whereas the 2001 Report contemplated that, once e-conveyancing was in place, the rules regulating registered land would be reformed, the 2016 CP takes almost the opposite approach: changes to particular existing rules are suggested as a means to smooth the path to a wider uptake of e-conveyancing.[5]

---

[4] Law Com CP No 227, [20.11].

[5] See Law Com CP No 227, [20.36]–[20.48] proposing changes to the rules regulating overreaching: these are discussed in Chapter 17, section 2.3.

Secondly, the 2016 CP carefully examines difficulties that have arisen under the LRA 2002 in the scope of the rectification provisions, and their operation in the difficult 'three-party cases' where a fraudster (X), without having any dealings with the initially registered party (B), is registered in B's place, and then grants a right to C. As noted in Chapter 3, section 3.2.2, if B seeks to be restored to the register, and to have C's right removed, we need to ask if B can meet the test in Sch 4, para 2(1)(a) and show that a change to the register is necessary '*for the purpose of correcting a mistake.*' The rhetoric of the 2001 Report might lead one to think that, in such a case, rectification is not possible against C as there is no mistake to correct. On this view, whilst the registration of the fraudster, X, was mistaken, there is no mistake in the registration of C, who acquired a right from X. After all, s 58 means that, by virtue of his or her registration X, even if a fraudster, is 'deemed' to have acquired a legal estate, simply as a result of his or her registration. This means that, as s 23 of the Act confirms,[6] X does have the power, for example, to grant C a charge over the land. Conversely, of course, because B is no longer registered, B has lost his or her legal estate. The view that, in such a case, B cannot get rectification against C would certainly fit the aim of the 2001 Report to have a '*complete and accurate*' register. Indeed, some judges adopted such a narrow view of the term 'mistake' as used in Sch 4,[7] even though this can lead to very harsh results for B, who can thus lose his or her registered right without having had any dealings with either X or C.

When examining such cases, the rhetoric of the 2016 CP is clearly different from that of the 2001 Report. Importantly, there is an explicit recognition of the competing policy concerns that arise in such a case, which, as noted in Chapter 3, section 3.2.2, can be seen as raising the question of '*indefeasibility*' (i.e. of how secure C's position should be).

Law Commission Consultation Paper No 227, *Updating the Land Registration Act 2002* (2016, [13.15])

Because there are a number of possible answers to the indefeasibility question, it is useful to look at this topic on a principled level. An assessment of what the law is trying to achieve will enable us to evaluate possible solutions. We take the view that the law relating to indefeasibility should achieve four objectives.

(1) Clarity: it should be possible to determine the answer in a given situation as easily and with as little litigation as possible.

(2) Finality: there must come a point, at some stage in a chain of transactions, when there is no question of a registered proprietor losing his or her title because of a mistake that occurred.

(3) Fact-sensitivity: the rules used to determine who gets the land and who gets an indemnity need some in-built flexibility to ensure that the land should pass to or remain in the ownership of the person who most needs it or values it.

(4) Reliability of the register: to be able to rely on the register means knowing that if title is lost, either because the register transpires to have been wrong, or because something happens to remove a name from the register when it should not have been, then an adequate indemnity will be available. An adequate indemnity is one that fully compensates a person for his or her loss, in the cases where the party who takes an indemnity is not only innocent of fraud but also has taken all proper care.

---

[6] See Chapter 3, section 3.2.1.   [7] See e.g. *Barclays Bank v Guy* [2008] EWCA Civ 452.

It might be objected that these four concerns are all quite anodyne, and by themselves can provide little guidance. That would, however, miss the larger point that the rhetoric of the 2016 CP has moved decisively away from that of the 2001 Report: the need to protect the position of C is not the single driving force, but rather must be balanced against other concerns. Further, the role of an indemnity in providing protection to C is acknowledged: for the register to be reliable, it need not always be the case that C retains a registered right; rather, reliability can, in suitable cases, come from monetary compensation for the loss of that right. We will see the practical impact of such a shift of rhetoric when examining the Law Commission's suggested reforms to the three party fraud case, in section 3.1.4.

This discussion is linked to the point made in Chapter 3, section 3.2.2, when we considered the extent to which courts have room to look outside the scheme of the LRA 2002 when interpreting its provisions. We noted there the contrast between two views of the Act: the view of the Law Commission in 2001 that the Act was part of a conveyancing *revolution* was compared with Lady Hale's quite different opinion in *Scott v Southern Pacific Mortgage Ltd* that:[8] '*the system of land registration is merely conveyancing machinery*' and that there is '*a danger of letting the land registration tail wag the land ownership dog*'. Certainly, the approach of the Commission in its 2016 CP can be seen as acknowledging some of the concerns that would arise if a hard-line approach to land registration and the need for a complete and accurate register were to obscure the merits of at least some claims by unregistered parties.[9]

Before we look at some of the key proposals of the 2016 CP, it is first necessary to summarize the impact of the LRA 2002.

2 THE IMPACT OF THE LAND REGISTRATION ACT 2002: AN OVERVIEW

Firstly, it is important to note that the 2002 Act has *no* impact on the question of whether B can assert a new, direct right against C, arising as a result of C's conduct. This point is made clear in the Law Commission reports that led to the Act.[10] As a result, as we noted in Chapter 16, section 6.1, the possible means by which B can acquire a direct right against C are largely unaffected by the 2002 Act.

The focus of the LRA 2002 is therefore on the different question of whether B can assert a pre-existing legal or equitable property right against C. As we saw in Chapter 1, section 3, we can break that key question down into three specific questions.

1. The *content* question: does the right claimed by B count as a property right?

2. The *acquisition* question: has B, in fact, acquired the right that he or she claims?

3. The *defences* question: if B does have a property right, does C have a defence to it?

---

[8] [2015] AC 385, [96].

[9] See too the approach of Jacob LJ in *Baxter v Mannion* [2011] 2 All ER 574, [35] (see Chapter 3, section 3.2.2), refusing to take a narrow view of mistake where rectification was sought against Mr Baxter, who had not in fact been in adverse possession of the registered land for the required period, but had been registered, as Mr Manning had not objected in time to Mr Baxter's application for registration. Jacob LJ stated that: '*Mere failure to operate bureaucratic machinery is as thistledown to Mr Manning losing his land and Mr Baxter getting it when he had never been in adverse possession.*'

[10] See Law Commission Report No 254, *Land Registration for the Twenty-First Century: A Consultative Document* (1998), [3.38]–[4.9] and Law Commission Report No 271, *Land Registration for the Twenty-First Century: A Conveyancing Revolution* (2001), [4.11] and [7.7].

2.1 THE *CONTENT* QUESTION

Dixon has pointed out that, in theory, we could have a registration system that simply ignores the fundamental divide between property rights and personal rights: it could, for example, stipulate that C can be bound by registered rights that are otherwise regarded as personal rights (e.g. contractual licences).[11] The LRA 2002 does *not* set out to do this: after all, given its chief aim is to give extra protection to C, it would be very surprising if it were systematically to allow personal rights to have an effect on C. But it is worth noting that, with the aim of promoting clarity, the Law Commission took a position on whether particular types of rights, the proprietary status of which is uncertain at best, would be capable of binding C. And, thanks to what are now ss 115 and 116 of the 2002 Act, those rights (such as rights of pre-emption,[12] 'mere equities',[13] and 'equities by estoppel')[14] are now prima facie binding on C.

Of course, even if B has such a right, it may still be possible for C to have a defence against it. Nonetheless, it is perhaps surprising that the Act has resolved these doubts in favour of B, rather than C. The Law Commission's position was not based on a particular policy, but rather on its view as to whether such rights were already recognized as equitable interests in land. As we saw in Chapter 10, section 4.3, however, when considering 'equities by estoppel', it may be that—in some cases, at least—the Law Commission's interpretation of the pre-existing law was overly generous to B.

2.2 THE *ACQUISITION* QUESTION

2.2.1 Legal estates and interests

If a party (B or C) claims that A (a party with a registered freehold or lease) has granted B or C a legal estate or interest, the provisions of the LRA 2002 may be crucial. As we saw in Chapter 8, section 5, s 27 of the 2002 Act creates a category of 'registrable dispositions'—that is, certain dealings with A's registered estate that are not complete unless and until they are registered: for example, a transfer of A's registered estate is only complete if and when the transferee registers as the new holder of A's estate. And if A attempts to grant a legal lease of more than seven years,[15] the recipient of that lease again needs to register in order to

---

[11] Dixon, 'Proprietary and Non-Proprietary Rights in Modern Land Law' in *Land Law: Issues, Debates and Policy* (ed Tee, 2002) pp 26–8. Parliament's response to the House of Lords decision in *National Provincial Bank v Ainsworth* [1965] AC 1175, discussed in Chapter 1, section 5.7, provides a specific example of this type of approach: under what is now s 31(10) of the Family Law Act 1996, a spouse or partner's statutory right of occupation is allowed to bind a third party if, and only if, it is noted on the register.

[12] Such as a right of B to enter a contract with A *if* A chooses to sell his legal estate in land. For discussion of whether such a right counts as an equitable interest, see *Pritchard v Briggs* [1980] Ch 338. For the Law Commission's discussion of whether such a right should be capable of binding C, see Law Commission Report No 271 (2001), [5.26]–[5.28].

[13] Such as a power of B to rescind a transfer of a legal estate to A, where that transfer was procured by an innocent misrepresentation of A. For the Law Commission's discussion of whether such a right should be capable of binding C, see Law Commission Report No 271 (2001), [5.32]–[5.36].

[14] For discussion of the impact of s 116 of the LRA 2002 on 'equities by estoppel' see Chapter 10, section 4.3.

[15] In addition, registration is also necessary in relation to certain exceptional forms of shorter lease: see Land Registration Act 2002, s 4(1)(b), (d), and (e) (cases of first registration) and s 27(2)(b)(ii)–(v) (where a lease is granted by a registered proprietor). See further Chapter 22, section 3.1.2.

acquire a legal estate. In addition, even if A's legal estate is *not* registered, certain dealings with that estate have to be registered before the other party can acquire a legal estate from A: for example, a transfer of an unregistered freehold is not complete until the transferee has registered that freehold. In this way, progress can be made to the Law Commission's goal of reducing the number of unregistered titles to land. Further, if e-conveyancing is to take hold, then it would likely lead to an increase in the category of 'registrable dispositions'.[16] In 2001, for example, the Law Commission envisaged that, when e-conveyancing makes it simpler for B to register, the registration requirement for leases will be extended to any legal lease of more than three years.[17] The likelihood is that leases of three years or less will remain outside the scope of compulsory registration. This is no surprise: s 54(2) of the Law of Property Act 1925 (LPA 1925) permits such leases to be created at law without any formality at all, if certain further conditions are met (see further Chapter 19, section 3.1.2).

Where B or C fails to comply with a registration requirement, registration can be seen to operate in a *negative* sense: if B or C fails to register a claimed legal estate, he or she fails to acquire that right. In some cases, this can, of course, assist C. For example, in a case where C is registered as the new holder of A's freehold, B may claim that he or she has a pre-existing legal estate in the land, because A earlier transferred that freehold to B. But because B failed to register as the new holder of A's freehold, B's claim must fail: B's failure to register means that B failed to acquire A's freehold.

In addition, in these cases, registration can also operate in a *positive*, constitutive sense: if a party does register his or her legal estate, then that right is guaranteed—the fact of registration operates positively to mean that he or she has acquired that right. As noted in Chapter 3, section 3.2.1, this result is produced by s 58 of the LRA 2002. In Chapter 3, section 3.2, we considered the impact of this guarantee of title in cases such as *Swift 1st Ltd v Chief Land Registrar*.[18] In those cases, B initially has a registered right and, as a result of X's fraud and without B's consent or knowledge, C is then registered in B's place, or C acquires a registered right, such as a charge, in relation to B's land. In this chapter, in section 3, we will focus on the impact of the guarantee of title in cases where B initially has a registered right and, as a result of X's fraud, X is registered in B's place, or has B's right removed, and C, by dealing with X, then acquires a registered right in the land.[19]

Before leaving the acquisition of legal estates, it is useful to remember an important effect of the LRA 2002, discussed in Chapter 9, section 5.3. There, we saw that under the Act it is impossible for an adverse possessor to claim that the lapse of time, by itself, has extinguished the legal estate of a registered proprietor. As a result, a registered proprietor is given far more effective protection against an adverse possessor than an unregistered holder of a legal estate. In evaluating the 2002 Act as a whole, it is important to take a view as to whether that particular change was desirable. To a large extent, that depends on a consideration of the merits of the claim of an adverse possessor—a question that we examined in Chapter 9, section 2. It is worth noting that the extra protection given to a registered proprietor against an adverse possessor may promote the goal of extending the number of registered titles: an unregistered holder of a freehold or long lease, even if he or she does not plan to deal with

---

[16] Whilst the 2016 CP states that there is no current prospect of e-conveyancing leading to rules that remove the registration gap (see section 1.2), an extension of the category of registrable dispositions could occur without the need for simultaneous completion and registration.

[17] Law Commission Report No 271, 'Land Registration for the Twenty-First Century' (2001) [3.17].

[18] [2015] Ch 602 (CA).

[19] See the discussion in section 3 below of *Gold Harp Properties Ltd v Macleod* [2014] EWCA Civ 1084, [2015] 1 WLR 1249.

the land in the near future, may consider registering his or her legal estate so as to reduce the (admittedly small) risk of losing that estate due to another's adverse possession.

2.2.2 Equitable interests

As it stands, the LRA 2002 does not affect the acquisition of equitable interests. This means that registration does not operate negatively: if B claims to have acquired an equitable interest from A, it is *never* necessary for B to show that his or her right has been recorded on the register. It also means that registration does not operate positively: B can never claim that he or she has acquired an equitable interest simply by virtue of having entered that right on the register. It does not, however, mean that registration is irrelevant when considering equitable interests: if B fails to enter a notice on the register protecting his or her equitable interest, there is a risk that C, when later acquiring a right from A, will be able to use the lack of registration defence against B's right.[20]

In its 2001 Report, the Law Commission intended that the introduction of e-conveyancing would affect the acquisition of those equitable interests, such as those under estate contracts, that arise where A is under a contractual duty to give a property right in land to B (see Chapter 8, section 4). For s 93 of the LRA 2002 makes provision for rules to be made that require not only particular dispositions of registered land, but also *contracts* for such dispositions, to be made electronically and communicated to the registrar (see Chapter 8, section 6.5.3). So in the standard case of the sale of a registered estate from A to B, if the agreement did not comply with those rules, B would not be able to show that an estate contract existed. In the words of the Law Commission in 2001, the impact of the rules introduced under s 93 would be that:[21] '*a disposition has* no *effect whatever, either at law or in equity, until the registration requirements are met*'.[22] As we have seen, however, in its 2016 CP, the Law Commission has accepted that, as things currently stand, there is no immediate prospect of moving to such a system, even if a system of simultaneous creation and registration of rights remains an '*ultimate, if long term, goal*'.[23]

2.3 THE *DEFENCES* QUESTION

2.3.1 Legal estates and interests

As we have seen in Chapter 3, section 3.2.3 and in Chapter 16, s 29 of the LRA 2002 provides a very important defence: the lack of registration defence. If C acquires a legal estate or interest from A *and* if C provides something in return for that right, C may be able to use that defence against a pre-existing right of B. But it is only in the rarest cases that C can use the defence against a pre-existing *legal* estate or interest of B. Firstly, B generally needs to register in order to *acquire* such a legal property right: in such cases, C clearly cannot use the lack of registration defence, because B's right, by definition, will be recorded on the

---

[20] See e.g. *Chaudhary v Yavuz* [2013] Ch 249.   [21] Law Com CP No 271 (2001), [4.13].

[22] Note though that, whilst there would be no contract between A and B, this would not by itself prevent B acquiring an equitable interest, as B could instead attempt to invoke the doctrine of proprietary estoppel or of constructive trusts (see Chapter 8, section 3.9), as noted e.g. by Dixon, 'Proprietary Estoppel and Formalities in Land Law and the Land Registration Act 2002: A Theory of Unconscionability' in *Modern Studies in Property Law: vol 2* (ed Cooke, Oxford: Hart, 2003) 165.

[23] Law Com CP No 227, [20.24].

register. For example, if B has acquired a legal ten-year lease from A, B must necessarily have registered that right. This means that, as far as legal property rights are concerned, the lack of registration defence is only relevant where B has managed to acquire such a right without registering it.

There are two principal situations in which this can occur: firstly, where B acquires a legal lease with a maximum period of seven years or less; secondly, where B acquires an easement that has not been expressly granted to him by A—it being possible for B to acquire a legal easement by means of an implied grant from A (see Chapter 22, section 3.2) or through the doctrine of prescription (see Chapter 22, section 3.3).

In the first case, in which B acquires a legal lease, B's right counts as an overriding interest under Sch 3, para 1, of the LRA 2002. It is therefore impossible for C to rely on the lack of registration defence against such a right (see Chapter 16, section 4.3).

In the second case, in which B acquires a legal easement, B's right will almost always count as such an overriding interest under Sch 3, para 3, of the 2002 Act (see Chapter 16, section 4.4).[24] In this way, the Act essentially preserves the position applying in unregistered land:[25] if B has a pre-existing *legal* property right, it is almost impossible for C to have a defence against that right.

2.3.2 Equitable interests

Where B has a pre-existing equitable interest, the lack of registration defence comes to the fore: for example, whilst a legal lease will count as an overriding interest, an equitable lease, in itself, does not; whilst a legal easement will almost always count as an overriding interest, an equitable easement, in itself, does not. As we saw in Chapter 16, an equitable interest of B, in itself, can never count as an overriding interest: it will only qualify if it is accompanied by B's actual occupation of the registered land.

2.4 SUMMARY

The overview of the operation of the LRA 2002 in this section reveals the gap between the rhetoric of the Law Commission in its 2001 Report, which sets out the '*fundamental objective*' of a '*complete and accurate register*', and the actual content of the Act itself. We have seen that there are two key situations in which C, a party acquiring a registered right for value, may in fact be bound by a claim of B, an unregistered party: firstly, where the register is rectified; secondly, where B has an overriding interest.[26] We will therefore focus on those two situations in the remainder of this chapter, considering not only the present law but also the proposals made more recently by the Law Commission in its 2016 CP. We will see that, consistently with its more balanced rhetoric (see section 1.2), the 2016 CP gives explicit acknowledgement to the need to have a registration system that recognizes other objectives than simply protecting C.

---

[24] The very rare case in which B's legal easement is not overriding occurs only where that legal easement fails to satisfy *any* of the three criteria set out in para 3.

[25] See the chapter, 'Priorities in Unregistered Land' with the online resources.

[26] As noted in Chapter 16, section 4.1, of course, an overriding interest is simply one that is not subject to the lack of registration defence; such a right will not bind C if C has some other defence, such as the overreaching defence (see e.g. *City of London Building Society v Flegg* [1988] AC 54).

3 THE SCOPE OF RECTIFICATION

In Chapter 3, section 3.2.2, we noted that, where C acquires from A and registers a legal estate or interest, the guarantee of title provided by s 58 of the LRA 2002 is not absolute, as Sch 4 allows for the possibility of a change to the register: in other words, C's title is not absolutely indefeasible. That power can be exercised '*for the purpose of correcting a mistake*' and, where such a change prejudicially affects the title of C, it is known as a rectification. In considering the scope of rectification, then, the first question to consider is the meaning of '*mistake*'. It is important to remember that, if rectification is required for the purpose of correcting a mistake then, if C, the currently registered proprietor, is not in possession of the land, Sch 4, para 3(3) and para 6(3) state that change *must* be made, unless there are exceptional circumstances which justify not doing so. Conversely, if rectification is required to correct a mistake, and C is in possession, then C receives further protection, and rectification can occur only if C by fraud or lack of proper care caused or substantially contributed to the mistake, or if it would be for any other reason unjust not to rectify.[27]

3.1 THE MEANING OF 'MISTAKE'

3.1.1 Two party cases

In Chapter 3, section 3.2.2, we considered some examples of what might be called 'two party cases', where the only parties who ever held relevant registered rights are the initially registered party, B, who now seeks rectification, and C, the party who is now registered and against whom rectification is sought. Such a case can arise, for example, where a fraudster steals the identity of B and forges a transfer to C. Such 'two party' cases are referred to by the Law Commission in its 2016 CP as examples of '*the AB scenario*'. That terminology is used because the Commission uses A to refer to the initially registered party, and B to refer to the party against whom rectification is sought. To remain consistent with terminology used elsewhere in this chapter and book, however, we will always call the party seeking rectification B, and the party against whom rectification is sought C, and we will refer to the '*AB scenario*' as the 'two party case'.

In the two party case, whatever terminology is used, there is no difficulty in finding that the registration of C was a mistake: the initially registered party (B) in fact made no disposition to C, as the supposed disposition was a simple forgery.[28] Similarly, even if there is no fraud, but for some other reason C was not entitled to be registered, it is again simple to find that a mistake has occurred.[29] That does not mean, of course, that rectification will necessarily be granted, as additional protection is given under Sch 4 to C where C is in possession of the registered land, but at least B, the party seeking rectification, has cleared the hurdle of showing a mistake.

---

27 Schedule 4, para 3(2) and para 6(2).

28 See e.g. *Swift 1st v Chief Land Registrar* [2015] Ch 602 (CA), discussed in Chapter 3, section 3.3.2.

29 See e.g. *Baxter v Mannion* [2011] 2 All ER 754, as discussed in Chapter 3, section 3.2.2.

3.1.2 Three party cases

A three party case, referred to by the Law Commission in its 2016 CP as an *'ABC* scenario', is more complicated. The key point in such a case is that the fraudster, X in our terminology, without having any dealings with the initially registered party (B in the scheme used in this book), is registered in B's place, and then grants a right to C. From B's perspective, of course, it seems clear that C's registration is mistaken, as B did not consent to it. As noted in section 1.2, however, an argument can be made that, whilst *X's* registration was a mistake, C's was not, as (in contrast to the two party case) C did acquire a right from the party who was, at the time, the registered proprietor. C can thus point to s 58 of the LRA 2002, with its guarantee of the rights of X, as registered proprietor, and ss 23 and 24 of the Act, which confirm that X therefore had powers to deal with the registered estate. Moreover, the aim of having a *'complete and accurate'* register, and the rhetoric of the Law Commission in its 2001 Report in referring to a conveyancing *'revolution'* seem to support such a narrow interpretation of 'mistake'.

As a result, in some cases, judges held that, in the three party case of fraud, C's registration is not a 'mistake' and so rectification is not possible. In *Barclays Bank plc v Guy*,[30] B's registered title had been transferred to X, and X had then granted a registered charge to C. B argued that the transfer to X had taken place without his authority, and so was void. B claimed that he should be reinstated as proprietor, and C's charge should be removed. C was awarded summary judgment on the basis that, even if the transfer to X had taken place without B's authority, its charge was still valid, thanks to s 58 of the LRA 2002. B asked for permission to appeal but this was not granted by the Court of Appeal. Lloyd LJ essentially accepted the narrow view of mistake, stating that:[31]

> while the scope of the phrase "correcting a mistake" is no doubt something that requires to be explored and discussed and developed in the course of future litigation, which will be decided upon the facts and upon the merits of each case, I cannot see that it is arguable that the registration of the charge can be said to be a mistake, or the result of a mistake, unless, at the least, [B] can show that the bank, the mortgagee, had either actual notice, or what amounts to the same, what is referred to as "Nelsonian" or "blind eye notice" of the defect in the title of [X]. I simply cannot see how it could be argued that if [C] knows nothing of the problem underlying the intermediate owner's title, that the registration of the charge or sale to the ultimate purchaser or charge can be said to be a mistake. That seems to me inconsistent with the structure and terms of the 2002 Act.

The reference to C's notice is a little surprising, as there is no indication in the 2002 Act that notice may be relevant to the definition of 'mistake' and the Law Commission in its 2001 Report was very clear, when considering other important parts of the Act, that a general notion of notice is not to be used to reduce the protection available to a party acquiring a right in registered land.[32] That twist aside, however, the approach taken by Lloyd LJ reflects the narrow approach to mistake.

---

[30] [2008] EWCA Civ 452. See too *Stewart v Lancashire Mortgage Corporation Ltd* [2010] EWLandRA 2009/86.

[31] [2008] EWCA Civ 452 [23].

[32] See Law Com CP No 254, [3.44]; Law Com Report No 271, [5.21]. For a different analysis, in which C's knowledge may have a role to play in deciding upon rectification, see Nair, 'Morality and the Mirror: The

This narrow view of mistake is, however, very problematic, and, whilst it had some supporters,[33] it attracted a good deal of academic criticism. The basic problem is that it operates very harshly on B, who can lose his or her registered right, or be subjected to a burden such as a charge, without having consented to such results. Moreover, if C's registration is not a mistake, then it would seem that B cannot receive any indemnity for loss flowing from C's registration. That is because the only potentially relevant provision of Sch 8, para 1(1), is where the loss is caused to B by a *'mistake whose correction would involve rectification of the register'*, and of course if C's registration is not a mistake then that provision does not apply. As McFarlane noted, this point means that *'courts have a reason to take a reasonably broad view of what counts as a "mistake"'*.[34] Indeed, in the words of Cooper:[35]

> the absence of mistake would equally appear to preclude any claim to indemnity. Thus the original owner's rights would have evaporated without compensation in an entirely unacceptable deprivation of property. The statutory empowerment theory[36] consequently appears to be antithetical to the scheme of compensation. This appears to put the interpreter on the prongs of a Morton's fork—one could either acknowledge that [X's] disposition was validated by the statutory owner's powers and thereby deprive the original owner [B] of both land and compensation, or one could admit indemnity and thereby imply that the owner's powers had no real effect in cleansing a mistake.

Fortunately for B, it now seems clear that the courts have rejected the narrow view of mistake and are prepared to find that, in the three party case, at least where there were no dealings between B and X and X's registration purely results from forgery, then C's registration, as well as B's, can be seen as a mistake.[37] As can be seen from the analysis in the following extract, this is consistent with the position under the Land Registration Act 1925, the predecessor to the 2002 Act. It should be noted that the facts of the case do not correspond precisely to our core example, as they did not involve B's initial registered right being lost, and X then being registered and granting a registered right to C. Rather, B (the claimant teachers) initially held a lease, which was removed, without justification, from the register. X, who already held the freehold interest, then took advantage of the removal of B's lease to grant a lease to C (Gold Harp), who would not of course have paid for such a right if B's lease had remained on the register. The basic question raised by those facts is, however, the same as that arising in our core example.

Normative Limits of the "Principles of Land Registration"' in *Modern Studies in Property Law Vol 6* (ed Bright, Oxford: Hart Publishing, 2011).

[33] See e.g. Cooke, *The New Law of Land Registration* (Oxford: Hart Publishing, 2003) pp 122–9; Harpum, 'Registered Land: A Law Unto Itself?' in *Rationalizing Property, Equity and Trusts: Essays in Honour of Edward Burn* (London: Sweet & Maxwell, 2003).

[34] McFarlane, *The Structure of Property Law* (Oxford: Hart Publishing, 2008) p 481.

[35] Cooper, 'Resolving Title Conflicts in Registered Land' (2015) 131 LQR 108, 111.

[36] [This is Cooper's term for the narrow view of mistake, which is based on the idea that s 58, as well as ss 23 and 24, give X the power to grant a valid charge to C.]

[37] In addition to *Gold Harp Properies Ltd v Macleod*, extracted below, see e.g *Odogwu v Vastguide* [2009] EWHC 3565 (Ch); *Bakrania v Lloyds Bank* [2017] UKFTT 0364 (Property Chamber).

Gold Harp Properties Ltd v Macleod
[2014] EWCA Civ 1084, [2015] 1 WLR 1249

Facts: The claimants held long, registered leases of the roofspace of a house that had been converted into flats. The roofspace was not occupied: the claimants, described as 'unworldly folk', were teachers who worked and lived, for most of the time, in Africa. Ralph wished to develop the top floor and so hatched a plan to terminate the claimants' leases. His son, operating under Ralph's instructions, acquired the freehold to the property and then purported to terminate the leases for non-payment of ground rent. The son then made a statutory declaration that the leases had been determined through re-entry and, on that basis, the Land Registry amended the register so as to remove the claimants' leases. In fact, no re-entry had been made, and the son had no power to terminate the leases as rent had been tendered by agents of the claimants. The son then granted a long lease of the roofspace to a company which registered that lease, before assigning it on to another company, which in turn transferred it to Gold Harp. All those companies were controlled by Ralph. Once it had been established that the son in fact had had no power to terminate the leases, the claimants applied for rectification, asking not only that their leases should be re-instated on the register, but that those leases should also have priority over the registered lease now held by Gold Harp. The judge ordered that such rectification should occur. The primary ground of appeal was that, even if it was permissible to reinstate the claimants' leases, those leases should not have been given priority over the lease of Gold Harp, as para 8 of Sch 4 states that: '*The powers under this Schedule to alter the register, so far as relating to rectification, extend to changing for the future the priority of any interest affecting the registered estate or charge concerned.*' Gold Harp argued that the words 'for the future' meant that rectification could not cause it to lose the priority its lease had enjoyed when initially granted. Linked to that point, it also argued that the only relevant 'mistakes' concerned the removal of the claimants' leases—the registration of Gold Harp's lease was not a mistake as the registered freehold owner clearly had the power to create it.

Underhill LJ

At [40]

The reasoning in *Argyle Building Society v Hammond*[38] makes it clear that under the 1925 Act, where the proprietor of a registered interest had been mistakenly removed from the Register, the power to rectify extended to the removal of a competing interest which had been duly registered at a time when the first interest did not appear on the Register: the building society [C] could have had no notice of Mr Steed's [B's] interest, and yet its charge was liable to be invalidated. In one sense the rectification in such a case can be characterised as retrospective, because the charge was valid when created and is only invalidated by a subsequent order of the Court; and that is the sense in which [counsel for Gold Harp] submits that the order made in the present case was retrospective.

---

[38] (1984) 49 P & CR 148.

At [50]

[. . .] it is authoritatively established by *Argyle Building Society v Hammond* that the effect of s 82(2) of the 1925 Act was that the Court (and the Registrar) had the power to remove from the Register a derivative interest created by a person who at the material time was, albeit as the result of a mistake, the registered proprietor, and in that sense – without prejudice to whether this is a relevant sense – to make a 'retrospective' order.

At [65]

There is nothing in the drafting of the bill [the draft Bill contained in Law Com No 271, which led to the LRA 2002] or its exposition in the 2001 report to suggest any change from the thinking in the 1998 consultation paper as summarised above, namely that the effect of s 82(2) should be preserved but on the basis that any changes should be 'prospective only'. The Commission appears to say that in the relevant respects the bill reflects how s 82(2) had been understood and applied and thus that it was not intended to effect any change in the law [. . .]

[. . .] The decision in *Knights Construction* [see section 3.2.2 above] has been accepted as authoritative by the Land Registry. The *Practical Guide to Land Registry Adjudication*, edited by two Deputy Adjudicators, says, at para 18.6 (example 2):

> '*B owns Whiteacre. A forges a transfer of Whiteacre to himself and is registered as freehold proprietor. The effect of registration is that the freehold is deemed to be vested in him: see LRA 2002, s 58(1). Subsequently, A charges Whiteacre as security for a £1m loan from C Bank Ltd. B applies to alter the register by removing A as proprietor and restoring his name as proprietor. This he can do. But can he remove C Bank Ltd's charge? C Bank Ltd argues that because the freehold was deemed to be vested in A at the time of the charge, there has been no mistake.*
>
> *Land Registry no longer accepts that argument and will now accept an application by B to remove C Bank Ltd's charge on the basis that either:*
>
> (i)   *the registration of the charge directly flows from the original mistake;*
>
> (ii) *the charge needs to be removed in order fully to correct the mistake.*'

At [80]

The [narrow view of mistake, as set out by e.g. Lloyd LJ in *Barclays Bank plc v Guy*] would give rise to two particular anomalies [. . .] One was that if the power to correct did not extend to correcting the registration in favour of [C] it was unclear how, on any natural construction of Sch 8, a defrauded owner would be entitled to an indemnity. That would be inconsistent with the evident policy of the legislation that a party who loses his rights by reason of the scheme of registration and cannot have them restored by rectification should be entitled to an indemnity and might indeed involve a breach of his rights under Article 1 of Protocol 1 to the European Convention of Human Rights. The other anomaly is that [the narrow view of mistake] would create an irrational distinction between the case where the fraudster forges a transfer to a third party and where he forges a transfer to himself and then sells on.

At [91]–[98]

I have concluded that the Judge was entitled to make the order that he did. My reasons are as follows [. . .]

[Gold Harp's] case has to be, and is, that the effect of the words 'for the future' is that if [C's] interest has been registered after the mistake but before the rectification, and thus would otherwise enjoy priority, that priority cannot be altered: an alteration to a priority which already exists cannot be described as an alteration 'for the future'. But if that is right then their effect is to prevent the Court from changing priorities in the very situation which paragraph 8 is intended to address [. . .]

It is worth recalling that Schedule 4 is concerned with 'correcting' mistakes in the Register, and it is established by the decisions to which I have referred that the power to do so extends to correcting the consequences of such mistakes. It should be noted that that power is in some circumstances a duty: see paragraph 3(3). [Gold Harp's] construction would mean that in all cases where derivative interests have been created during the period of mistaken de-registration that correction would be less than complete and that in some cases, such as the present, it would be valueless.

Quite apart from those points, [Gold Harp's] construction does not correspond with the words actually used in the statute. What paragraph 8 permits (for the future) is 'changing the priority' of an interest. What an interest having priority means is that the owner can exercise the rights which he enjoys by virtue of that interest to the exclusion of any inconsistent rights of the owner of the competing interest. The concept of priority thus bites at the moment that those rights are sought to be enjoyed. Once that is appreciated the effect of the words 'for the future' seems to me straightforward. They mean that the beneficiary of the change in priority – that is, the person whose interest has been restored to the Register – can exercise his rights as owner of that interest, to the exclusion of the rights of the owner of the competing interest, as from the moment that the order is made, but that he cannot be treated as having been entitled to do so up to that point. The distinction can be illustrated by the facts of this case. The effect of the Judge's order is that thenceforward [the teachers] were entitled to exercise their rights as leaseholders – primarily, that is, their rights to occupy the roofspace – to the exclusion of Gold Harp. But until that point they had no such right: they could not, for example, claim mesne profits from Gold Harp or its predecessors in respect of any occupation (though in fact there was none) up to that date [. . .]

I draw support from my conclusion from what I might call, by way of shorthand, the survival of *Argyle Building Society v Hammond*, as confirmed in *Knights Construction* [. . .]

I see no difficulty with this construction on policy grounds. It is true that it means that the indefeasibility of the Register is qualified to a greater extent than would be the case on [Gold Harp's] construction. But, as all the Law Commission reports acknowledge, the Act was not intended to provide for absolute indefeasibility. Schedule 4 explicitly recognises that the rectification has the potential to prejudice the interests of third parties who have relied in good faith on the Register. The carefully structured provisions of paragraphs 2 and 3 (and their equivalents in the case of rectification by the Registrar), with the special protection given to a proprietor in possession, allow a fair balance between the competing interests to be struck in any particular case; and Schedule 8 gives the loser a right to an indemnity.

I am naturally concerned that my interpretation of paragraph 8 appears to be contrary to that advanced in *Ruoff & Roper* and *Megarry & Wade* and accepted by the Deputy Adjudicators in *Piper Trust* and *DB* – particularly given the involvement of Mr Harpum in one of those works and one of those decisions [. . .] But I have also to say that the reasoning advanced in support of their conclusions seems to me unconvincing. The essential points relied on are twofold – first, the need to preserve what is referred to in *Megarry & Wade* as the 'integrity of the register'; and secondly, that their preferred construction accords with the authorities on the meaning of the 1925 Act [. . .] As to the first, I have already made the point that the guarantee of title conferred by registration is well understood not to be absolute. As to second [. . .] the editors of *Ruoff & Roper* recognise the difficulty posed by *Argyle Building Society v Hammond* and adopt the dual strategy of (unjustifiably) doubting its authority and submitting that it has no application under the 2002 Act notwithstanding the avowed intention of the Law Commission to re-enact the substance of section 82(2).

Underhill LJ thus decided that the power to order rectification for the purpose of correcting a mistake, as set out in para 2 of Sch 4, allowed not only for the reinstatement of the teachers' leases but also for its taking priority over Gold Harp's lease.[39] As a result, as Gold Harp was not in possession of the land, para 3(3) directs that rectification must be ordered, unless there are 'exceptional circumstances which justify [a court] not doing so.' Underhill LJ considered the facts and decided that there were no such circumstances. The first instance judge's decision was thus upheld and reinstatement of the teachers' leases, taking priority over Gold Harp's lease, was ordered. A separate question, not relevant in the immediate proceedings, would then arise as to whether an indemnity was payable by the Land Registry to Gold Harp. Clearly, the rectification caused it loss. Gold Harp, however, like its predecessor in title, was owned and controlled by Ralph, who had instructed his son to acquire the freehold and apply for the removal of the teachers' leases and so a question would arise as to the applicability of para 5(1) of Sch 8, which states that no indemnity is payable on account of any loss suffered by a party '(a) *wholly or partly as a result of his own fraud, or* (b) *wholly as a result of his own lack of proper care.*'

3.1.3 The distinction between void and voidable transactions

In *NRAM Ltd v Evans*,[40] the Court of Appeal considered the definition of 'mistake' in order to establish the boundary between a change to the register made for the purpose of correcting a mistake under Sch 4, para 2(1)(a), and a change made simply to bring the register up to date under Sch 4, para 2(1)(b). The distinction is important for at least three reasons. Firstly, if the change is for the purpose of correcting a mistake, and it prejudicially affects the title of C, then it counts as a rectification (rather than as a mere alteration),[41] and so an indemnity may be payable to C as a result of the change.[42] Secondly, in such a case, if C is in possession of the registered land, C receives additional protection, and, assuming C does not consent to it, the rectification can be made only if C by fraud or lack of proper care caused or substantially contributed to the mistake, or it would for any other reason be unjust not to rectify. Thirdly, if the change is a rectification, then, under Sch 4, para 8, the court has power to change for the future the priority of any interest affecting the estate,[43] and that power may be used to confer additional protection on B: that power does not arise if the change is made simply to keep the register up to date.[44]

As can be seen, in determining that boundary, the distinction between a void and a voidable transaction is crucial. That distinction, made in the general law, is between an apparent transaction which in fact has no effect (such as a document where B's signature is forged)[45]

---

[39] On this point, the Law Commission subsequently pointed out (see Law Com CP No 227 (2016) [13.192]) that Underhill LJ's interpretation of the policy of the Commission in its 2001 Report was mistaken, as that Report had not in fact supported such 'retrospective' rectification, allowing the reinstated right to take priority over a right created before rectification. Nonetheless, the Law Commission in that 2016 Consultation Paper note the advantages of such retrospective rectification as a means to do justice in a case such as *Gold Harp* and propose that it should continue to be possible: [13.195].

[40] [2017] EWCA Civ 1013.   [41] See Chapter 3, section 3.2.2.

[42] No indemnity is payable if the change is made simply to keep the register up to date: see *NRAM Ltd v Evans* [2017] EWCA Civ 1013, [66].

[43] As discussed in *Gold Harp Properties Ltd v Macleod* [2015] 1 WLR 1249: see the extract in section 3.1.2.

[44] See e.g. *NRAM Ltd v Evans* [2017] EWCA Civ 1013, [65].

[45] As in e.g. *Swift 1st v Chief Land Registrar* [2015] Ch 602 (CA).

and a transaction which is valid, but may be set aside by a party (as where B transfers property pursuant to an unconscionable bargain).[46]

NRAM Ltd v Evans
[2017] EWCA Civ 1013

Facts: In 2004, Mr and Mrs Evans took a loan from NRAM to fund the acquisition of a property, and they granted NRAM a charge over the land as a result. They took a further loan from NRAM in 2005, and it was found that the 2005 loan was treated by the parties as secured by the charge. Due to an administrative error, NRAM later overlooked this fact, and, when the 2004 loan was paid off, it submitted the relevant (electronic form) to the Land Registry (form e-DS1) to have the charge removed from the register. The charge was removed, and when NRAM discovered its error it applied to have the charge reinstated on the register, to secure sums outstanding under the 2005 loan. One of the arguments made by Mr and Mrs Evans was that such a change to the register would be made for the purpose of correcting a mistake, and, as it would affect their registered title and as they were in possession of the land, it would be a rectification and so could only be made if they had caused or substantially contributed to the mistake by fraud or lack of proper care, or if it would be for any other reason unjust not to rectify. NRAM argued instead that the change would simply bring the register up to date, as it would reflect the fact that, under the general law, it had rescinded its earlier, mistaken decision to submit the e-DS1 form. The Chief Land Registrar intervened, and similarly argued that there had been no mistake when the charge was removed from the register, as the e-DS1 form had been validly submitted by NRAM and was not void. The Court of Appeal agreed that the change to the register sought by NRAM was simply to bring the register up to date, and that the initial removal of NRAM's charge was not a mistake in the sense required by Sch 4, para 2(1)(a).

Kitchin LJ

At [48]–[60]

The term 'mistake' is not defined in Schedule 4, although para 11 of Schedule 8 provides that, for the purposes of that schedule, it includes mistaken omissions. It is therefore no surprise that the term is generally understood to have a broad if somewhat uncertain scope and to encompass a wide range of circumstances, including, for example, the accidental registration of particular land in two different titles. I also recognise that, in cases where the correction of a mistake will prejudicially affect the title of a registered proprietor, the LRA 2002 makes provision, in Schedule 8, for an indemnity by the registrar in the circumstances there set out. This mechanism for imposing the risk associated with the validity of a transaction on the registrar may be of great value to a disponee but it necessarily follows that, if the alteration does not amount to a mistake, it will not be available.

Despite the scope and largely undefined nature of the term 'mistake' in this context, the Law Commission noted in its 2016 Consultation Paper[47] that a degree of consensus appeared

---

[46] See e.g. *Mortgage Express v Lambert* [2017] Ch 9 , discussed in Chapter 17, section 2.2.5.
[47] Law Com CP No 227, [13.79]–[13.80].

to be emerging as to its boundaries. In that regard, the Law Commission referred to *Megarry & Wade, The Law of Real Property*[48] whose editors observe that:

"What constitutes a mistake is widely interpreted and is not confined to any particular kind of mistake. It is suggested therefore that there will be a mistake whenever the registrar would have done something different had he known the true facts at the time at which he made or deleted the relevant entry in the register, as by:

(i)   making an entry in the register that he would not have made or would not have made in the form in which it was made; or

(ii) deleting an entry which he would not have deleted; or

(iii) failing to make an entry in the register which he would otherwise have made."

The editors of *Megarry & Wade* go on to provide various examples of mistakes, the first of which is the case where a person has been registered as proprietor pursuant to a void disposition, such as a forged transfer, or where the transfer was of land which the seller had already sold. Interestingly, the editors note there is no mistake where the registrar registers a transfer that is voidable but has not been avoided at the date of the registration [. . .]

It will be noted that both of these formulations[49] focus on the position at the point in time that the entry or deletion is made. That, as it seems to me, must be right. If a change in the register is correct at the time it is made it is very hard to see how it can be called a mistake.

It does mean, however, that, as the editors of *Megarry & Wade* noted, a distinction must be drawn between a void and a voidable disposition. On this analysis, an entry made in the register of an interest acquired under a void disposition should not have been made and the registrar would not have made it had the true facts been known at the time. By contrast, a change made to the register to reflect a transaction which is merely voidable is correct at the time it is made [. . .]

[Kitchin LJ then considered some apparently contrary views.]

Nevertheless, the distinction [between a void and a voidable transaction] is, in my view, principled and correct and it derives further support from the decision of the Court of Appeal in *Norwich and Peterborough Building Society v Steed.*[50] [This was a case concerned with the rectification provisions of the LRA 1925, where it was held that the entry of a voidable transaction on the register was not made under a mistake and so could not be rectified under LRA 1925, s 82(1)(h), which applied where '*by reason of any error or omission in the register, or by reason of any entry made under a mistake, it may be deemed just to rectify the register.*']

[. . .]

In my judgment, the registration of a voidable disposition such as that with which we are concerned before it is rescinded is not a mistake for the purposes of Schedule 4 to the LRA 2002. Such a voidable disposition is valid until it is rescinded and the entry in the register of such a disposition before it is rescinded cannot properly be characterised as a mistake. It may be the case that the disposition was made by mistake but that does not render its entry on the register a mistake, and it is entries on the register with which Schedule 4 is concerned. Nor, it seems to me, can such an entry become a mistake if the disposition is at some later

---

[48] 8th edn, 2012 at [7-133] (footnotes omitted from the extract).

[49] [Kitchin LJ had also considered the formulation in another practitioner work, *Ruoff and Roper, Registered Conveyancing*, looseleaf edition, [46.009], which is very similar to that in *Megarry and Wade* extracted above.]

[50] [1993] Ch 116.

date avoided. Were it otherwise, the policy of the LRA 2002 that the register should be a complete and accurate statement of the position at any given time would be undermined.

The second issue is whether, in a case such as the present, the register can be brought up to date once the voidable disposition has been rescinded. In my judgment, it plainly can. Schedule 4, para 2(1)(b) confers on the court a power to make an order for alteration of the register by bringing it up to date; and para 3(3) provides that if in any proceedings the court has power to make an order under para 2, it must do so, unless there are exceptional circumstances which justify its not doing so [. . .] In the present case, once the judge had rescinded the e-DS1, it was necessary to alter the register by bringing it up to date in such a way as to reflect the rights of the parties as the judge had found them to be [. . .] there are in this case no exceptional circumstances which would justify a decision not to exercise the power to update.

Whilst it is a two party case, the reasoning in *NRAM Ltd* shows acceptance of the 'broad' interpretation of mistake given in *Gold Harp*, and is therefore significant for three party cases too. *NRAM Ltd* also shows, of course, that the meaning of 'mistake' in the context of Sch 4, whilst broad, is not unlimited. If, for example, B transfers registered title to X under a disposition which is part of an unconscionable bargain, but B has not yet invoked the power to rescind that transaction, then it is not a mistake for X to be registered in B's place, nor for C to be registered if X grants a right to C. This limit on mistake does not come from any particular need to adopt special registration rules, or from 'revolutionary' changes made by the LRA 2002: it is simply a part of the general law of property and, as noted in *NRAM Ltd*, was also applied under the LRA 1925. Of course, in many voidable transactions, it could be said that B made a mistake by completing the transfer to X;[51] but that in itself does not suffice for rectification. The point, as stated by Kitchin LJ, is that rectification can occur for the purpose of correcting the *registrar's* mistake, not for the purpose of correcting *B's* mistake.

3.1.4 The 2016 Consultation Paper

In its 2016 CP, the Law Commission notes that, following the decision in *Gold Harp*, the position under the LRA 2002 now corresponds to that under the LRA 1925, which *'authorised rectification (subject to protection for the registered proprietor in possession) in any case where the title was registered in the name of a person who would not have been the owner of the estate had the title been unregistered'*.[52] As noted by Underhill LJ in *Gold Harp*,[53] it is in fact consistent with the statement in the Law Commission's 2001 Report that: *'the existing law and practice in relation to rectification are largely sound, and the main deficiencies lie in the way in which the legislation is drafted. In light of this we make recommendations for reform which are primarily clarificatory rather than substantive.'*[54] As a result, it can be said that there is a relevant mistake not only in a two party case, but also in a three party case.

---

[51] Indeed, one example of a voidable transaction is where B makes a gift to X, but that gift has been caused by a sufficiently grave mistake of fact (such as B's having forgotten an earlier gift to X): for discussion see *Pitt v Holt* [2013] 2 AC 108, [99]–[142].

[52] Law Com CP No 227, [13.29], citing s 82 (1)(g) LRA 1925.

[53] *Gold Harp Properties v Macleod* [2014] EWCA Civ 1084 at [62].

[54] Law Com No 254 at 8.1. See too Law Com No 271 at 2.38 and 10.4. Indeed, an earlier Report had recommended expressly retaining the relevant provision of the LRA 1925: 'Land Registration for the Twenty-First Century: A Consultative Document' at 8.54.

In its 2016 CP, the Law Commission supported that approach to defining mistake, stating that it would be *'unsupportable'* and *'contrary to the intention of the legislation'*[55] if, in a three party case involving fraud by X, there was said to be no mistake and thus no means for B either to get rectification or receive an indemnity. In the three party case, therefore, *'it is essential that C's position is not indefeasible. We conclude that the registration of C must be subject to rectification on the basis that there is a mistake.'*[56] Such a position is consistent with the important point, noted in section 1.2, that the Commission in its 2016 CP explicitly recognized that protection for C is not the only policy that a registration scheme should serve.

3.2 LIMITS TO RECTIFICATION *Berechtigung*

As noted at the start of section 3.1, the fact that C's registration can be said to be a mistake does not necessarily mean that rectification will follow. In considering the limits to rectification, it is useful to distinguish between two positions: first, where C, the party against whom rectification is sought, is in possession of the land; second, where C is not in possession.

3.2.1 Where C is in possession

In a case where, for example, X's fraud has led to C acquiring registered title to B's land without B's consent, C may be in possession of the land at the time of B's application for rectification. If so, unless C consents, rectification can be ordered only if: '(a) *[C] has by fraud or lack of proper care caused or substantially contributed to the mistake; or (b) it would for any other reason be unjust for the alteration not to be made.'*[57] As we saw in Chapter 3, section 3.2.2, this additional protection for C was important in the two party case of *Walker v Burton*:[58] whilst it was shown that C, in fact, had no entitlement to be registered as proprietor of the Fell, an application for rectification was refused, as neither provision of para 3(2) applied. The villagers applying for rectification had no claim to the registered title, whereas the Court of Appeal recognized the *'time, effort and money'* C had spent on improving the Fell.

The additional protection where C is in possession, of course, is not always decisive: *Baxter v Mannion*,[59] discussed in Chapter 3, section 3.2.2, provides an example. There, B could show that it would be unjust not to order rectification: C's registration had been based on a period of adverse possession that had not in fact occurred, and, not having paid for its registered title, C's loss would be limited, whereas if no rectification was made, B would lose its entitlement to the land.[60] Nonetheless, the somewhat unusual facts of *Baxter* aside, the additional protection given to C when in possession is significant. Of course, if a mistake has occurred, but rectification is denied to B as a result of that additional protection to C, B will be entitled to an indemnity as compensation for loss caused to B by the mistake.[61] Under the current scheme, the value of that indemnity where B has lost a right cannot exceed the

---

[55] Law Com CP No 227, [13.72].   [56] Law Com CP No 227, [13.73].

[57] Sch 4, para 3(2) (in the case of the power of the court to change the register) and Sch 4, para 6(2) (in the case of the power of the registrar to make the change). 'Alteration' is a wider concept which refers to any change in the register and thus clearly includes rectification.

[58] [2013] EWCA Civ 1228, [2014] 1 P & CR 9.   [59] [2011] 2 All ER 574.

[60] See too *Parshall v Hackney* [2013] Ch 568, for another example where C was in possession, but it was found that it would be unjust not to rectify, as C had acquired its title at B's expense and for free.

[61] Assuming that such loss was not suffered by B wholly or partly as a result of B's fraud, or wholly as a result of B's own lack of proper care: LRA 2002, Sch 8, para 5(1).

value of B's right '*at the time when the mistake which caused the loss was made*';[62] in a rising property market, that value may be substantially lower than the value of the land at the point when the application for rectification is refused.[63] In its 2016 CP, the Law Commission have therefore proposed a different approach, under which the value of B's right will instead be limited by a calculation based on the '*current value of the land in the condition the land was in at the time of the mistake.*'[64] This is intended to meet the concern that, where there has been a mistake but rectification is not granted, B does not lose out on an increase in the capital value of the land following the mistake.[65]

In its 2016 CP, the Law Commission has recommended that the law should continue to give additional protection to C when C is in possession of the land at the time of the application for rectification.[66] One of the policy goals it identified is:[67] '*fact-sensitivity: the rules used to determine who gets the land and who gets an indemnity need some in-built flexibility to ensure that the land should pass to or remain in the ownership of the person who most needs it or values it*' and it can be said that possession is:[68] '*often at least a proxy indication of where justice, or at least convenience, might lie*'. Of course, it is not always the case that the fact of possession means C needs or values the land more than B, but the courts and registrar retain the possibility of ordering rectification, even against a wholly innocent C in possession, in those exceptional circumstances where it would be unjust not to rectify.

As noted by the Law Commission in its 2016 CP, however, that protection may just possibly be inadequate for C where there is a long period between the mistake on which B's application for rectification is based, and that application. It noted an important consequence of the broad view of mistake, which allows for rectification in a three party case:[69]

Law Commission Consultation Paper No 227 (2016) *Updating the Land Registration Act*, [13.74]

If rectification is available against C, then equally it must be available against subsequent purchasers or mortgagees. The fact that a transfer from [B to X] was void for fraud may come to light not only after [X] has transferred land to C, but after C has transferred to D, who has granted a mortgage to E, and so on. As well as C's title being potentially defeasible on the basis that there is a mistake, so are the titles of D and E.

As seen in the extract in section 1.2, '*finality*' was one of the four policy concerns identified by the Commission. It has therefore proposed introducing a 'long stop' so that, after ten years from the time of the mistake, rectification will be possible against a party in possession

---

[62] LRA 2002, Sch 8 para 6(b).

[63] In contrast, if the application for rectification succeeds, and C thus loses C's registered right, the value of the indemnity to C depends on the value of that right at the time of rectification (such value calculated of course on the assumption that the right was not then vulnerable to rectification): LRA 2002, Sch 8 para 6(a).

[64] Law Com CP No 227, [14.159].

[65] As pointed out in the CP at [14.156], the proposal does not necessarily benefit B as compared to the current law, as of course the value of the property could fall between the time of the mistake and the time of the decision not to rectify.

[66] As under the current law, s 131 of the LRA 2002 would apply to mean that C could be in possession through another.

[67] Law Com CP No 227, [13.15].   [68] Law Com CP No 227, [13.30].

[69] Law Com CP No 227, [13.74].

only if that party caused or contributed to the mistake by fraud or lack of proper care.[70] The lapse of time will not, by itself, prevent B claiming an indemnity, but it will thus give additional protection to C (or a party, such as D or E who has later acquired title from C), by removing the possibility of rectification being granted on the basis that it would be unjust not to rectify.

As result of this addition of a 'long-stop', the Law Commission's proposal where C is in possession is as follows:

Law Commission Consultation Paper No 227 (2016) *Updating the Land Registration Act*, **[13.120]**

We provisionally propose that the register should not be rectified to correct a mistake so as to prejudice the registered proprietor [C] who is in possession of the land without that proprietor's consent, except where:

(1) the registered proprietor caused or contributed to the mistake by fraud or lack of proper care; or

(2) less than ten years have passed since the original mistake[71] and it would be unjust not to rectify the register.

This is a slight variation of the existing law, as the LRA 2002 has no such long-stop.[72] Of course, under the current scheme, the lapse of time would be a factor a court could take into account in deciding if it would be unjust not to rectify. The decision of the Court of Appeal in *Parshall v Hackney*,[73] however, shows that, under the current scheme, the lapse of time is not always decisive. As will be recalled from Chapter 9, section 3, that was a case of double registration of a strip of land. The strip was originally included in B's registered title in 1904; when title to the land of C, B's neighbour, was registered in 1980, the strip was mistakenly included in C's title too. C's predecessors in title made use of the strip as part of their land, putting up a chain-link fence that included it in 1988, and in 2000 the strip was mistakenly removed by the Land Registry from B's title. When, in 2008, B sought rectification, C resisted this on the basis of adverse possession, but the Court of Appeal found the concept to be of no assistance. It held that, even though C was in possession of the land, rectification could be ordered as it would be unjust not to rectify, given that C could be said to be '*seeking to take the benefit of a mistake by the Land Registry, which had occurred through no fault of [B]*'.[74] That decision has been criticized on various grounds, and the Law Commission's proposals would lead to a different result, as C would be able to rely on the long-stop and

---

[70] Law Com CP No 227, [13.100]

[71] [Note that, in a case where B's claim is not to have registered title restored, but is rather to have the priority of a derivative right in the registered land (such as a restrictive covenant over A's land) restored where, as a result of a mistake by the Land Registry, there was no notice of that right recorded at the time of the disposition from A to C, the ten-year period would begin from the time of the disposition from A to C: see Law Com No 227 CP [13.166].]

[72] Law Com No 227 CP [13.112]–[13.113] recommends that, as under the current law, C need not be in possession personally, but can possess through a tenant, mortgagee, licensee, or beneficiary in possession with C's consent (see s 131 LRA 2002). It also recommends that C (or C's predecessor(s) in title) need not have been in possession continuously since the mistake.

[73] [2013] Ch 568 (CA).   [74] [2013] Ch 568, [97] (Mummery LJ).

therefore it would no longer be enough for B to claim it would be unjust not to rectify: rectification could only be permitted if, as was not the case in *Parshall*, C had by fraud or lack of proper care caused or contributed to the initial mistake. The operation of the long-stop would not, of course, prevent B receiving an indemnity.[75]

As shown by its application to the facts of a case such as *Parshall*, the Law Commission's point in its 2016 CP as to the benefits of finality is surely a sensible one,[76] and the provision of a specific long-stop period may also promote another policy goal identified in the 2016 CP: the '*clarity*' which means it '*should be possible to determine the answer in a given situation as easily and with as little litigation as possible*'.

3.2.2 Where C is not in possession

The provisions of the LRA 2002 do not make any reference to whether or not B, the party seeking rectification, is in possession of the land; such possession is relevant only in so far as it means that C is *not* in possession, and so C does not qualify for the additional protection available to a registered proprietor in possession. In all such cases (whether B is in possession, or whether neither B nor C is), if rectification is required for the purposes of correcting a mistake, it must be made unless there are '*exceptional circumstances which justify not making the alteration*'.[77]

The Law Commission in its 2016 CP considered whether, where B is in possession of the land at the time when the application for rectification is made, the law should be changed so that B has an '*absolute*' entitlement to rectification, with no proviso for exceptional circumstances. In line with the policy goal of '*fact-sensitivity*', however, it concluded that such a discretion should be preserved as, for example, '*there have been cases where opportunism bordering on sharp practice put [B] in possession at the time when the matter was litigated. Accordingly, we propose a discretion to enable some flexibility, mirroring that found under the current law*'.[78] It would therefore remain the case that, where B is in possession,[79] and a mistake has been made, B will be restored to the register unless there are exceptional circumstances.[80]

The 2016 CP does propose a change in the case, for which no special provision is made under the current rules, where neither B nor C is in possession. In that case, as in the case where C is in possession, a long-stop will apply:[81]

---

[75] Law Com No 227 CP [13.138].

[76] For a contrary view, see Dixon, 'Updating the Land Registration Act 2002: Title Guarantee, Rectification and Indefeasibility' [2016] Conv 423, 425–6, arguing that the current system provides sufficient protection to C (as an application for rectification based on a long past mistake is very unlikely to succeed), whilst also preserving a discretion to allow rectification which may be useful in very unusual circumstances, so that: '*this proposed reform looks like planning for the worst, the very remote worst. It looks like a solution to a non-problem*'.

[77] Sch 4, para 3(3) (in the case of the power of the court to change the register) and Sch 4, para 6(3) (in the case of the power of the registrar to make the change). 'Alteration' is a wider concept which refers to any change in the register and thus clearly includes rectification.

[78] Law Com CP No 227, [13.108].

[79] B must be in possession at the time the application for rectification is made, but need not have been in possession continuously since the time of the mistake: Law Com CP No 227, [13.113].

[80] Law Com CP No 227, [13.109]. The same position would apply where it is B's successor in title in possession: [13.110].

[81] Note again that the application of the long-stop would not prevent B claiming an indemnity.

Law Commission Consultation Paper No 227 (2016) *Updating the Land Registration Act,* **[13.122]**

Where none of the parties are in possession we think that there should come a point where there is finality. After ten years we consider that the need for finality in the register should take precedence over the sympathy felt for [B], who is not in possession of the land. Hence we suggest that where neither [B] nor [C] is in possession of the land, after ten years the register should not be rectified, subject of course to the exception of fraud or lack of proper care.

3.3 RECTIFICATION: SUMMARY

Clearly, to understand and evaluate the operation of a land registration system, it is crucial to know when a registered party can have its rights taken away by rectification. The most important provisions of the LRA 2002, for those purposes, are para 2(1)(a) and para 5(a) of Sch 4, which state that a court and the registrar may order an alteration in the register for the purpose of 'correcting a mistake'. That key term, however, is neither defined in the Act nor discussed in the Law Commission work which preceded it. This initially produced what Gardner called a *'tragic mess'*[82] as the courts struggled to find the best way to define the term 'mistake'.

This confusion, along with the obvious injustice that can arise if a narrow view of 'mistake' is taken and B, an initially registered party, can then lose his or her right, as a result of a X's fraud, without the possibility of either rectification against C or an indemnity, in part prompted the recent review by the Law Commission. As noted in its 2016 CP, the decision in *Gold Harp* seems to have brought much-needed clarity to the meaning of 'mistake', adopting a broader view which removes the potential source of injustice for B in a three party case. That approach to mistake is consistent with the key point, made in section 1.2, that the land registration provisions should not be seen as cut off from more general principles of property law. As a result, the Law Commission in its 2016 CP was also able to focus on other aspects of the rectification regime, discussed in section 3.2, and has made some sensible recommendations which, as well as maintaining the current law's emphasis on possession, introduce a long-stop period in order to promote finality, whilst at the same time preserving a discretion for a court or the registrar to respond to exceptional circumstances that may arise on particular facts.

The current position, based on the broad view of mistake, therefore now seems secure. However, it took some time to prevail, perhaps because its logic was obscured by the rhetoric surrounding the LRA 2002: maintaining the position under the LRA 1925, no matter how sensible that may be, is hardly a *'revolution'*. Moreover, the focus on the new aspects of the proposed reforms may have led the Law Commission in its 2001 Report to sideline the important issue of rectification. The more balanced proposals of its 2016 CP are consistent with, and perhaps even a product of, its more careful rhetoric, with its explicit identification of policy concerns other than simply protecting C, the currently registered proprietor.

---

[82] Gardner, 'Alteration of the Register: An Alternative View' [2013] Conv 350, 535.

There is, however, one further significant point about the operation of the current rectification rules where a significant change is proposed by the 2016 CP. As it relates to overriding interests, we will consider it in the next section.

4 OVERRIDING INTERESTS

4.1 THE RATIONALE OF OVERRIDING INTERESTS

If the possibility of rectification is one dent in the idea of a 'complete and accurate' register, the concept of an overriding interest is another. As we noted in Chapter 3, section 3.1, the Law Commission's view was that the scope of such interests should be limited and that '*interests should* only *have overriding status where protection against buyers was needed, but where it was neither reasonable to expect nor sensible to require any entry on the register.*'[83]

Has the LRA 2002 achieved this aim of limiting overriding interests to situations in which B (a party with a pre-existing legal or equitable property right) cannot reasonably be expected to register that right? Clearly, it has not. For example, under Sch 3, para 2, the current position is that *any* equitable interest of a party in actual occupation counts as an overriding interest (see Chapter 16, section 4.2.1). And, as McFarlane has pointed out:[84] '*the presence or absence of actual occupation is* irrelevant *to the question of whether B can be expected to register his right*'. So, as noted in section 2.2.3 above, the 2002 Act currently allows B to have an overriding interest if: (i) she has bought land from A, and has failed to register as the new holder of A's legal estate; as long as (ii) B is in actual occupation of that land. In such a case, it is usually perfectly reasonable to expect B to register (she may well have been instructed by her solicitor or conveyancer to do so)—yet this does not prevent B from showing that the estate contract arising as a result of her contract with A is, when coupled with B's actual occupation, an overriding interest.

As we saw in Chapter 16, section 4.2.1, the Law Commission in its 2016 CP acknowledged that Sch 3, para 2 can thus give protection to a right that it is reasonable to expect B to register. It proposed maintaining this position. Firstly, B can be protected when B attempts to register but the application is rejected for an administrative reason:[85] in such a case, '*an overriding interest based on actual occupation plugs a useful "gap" where otherwise the transferee may be vulnerable to a loss of priority, without causing undue prejudice to anyone who deals with the land during that time*'.[86] Secondly, as seen in the following extract, it is not unreasonable to expect C to check the land before acquiring a right.

Law Commission Consultation Paper No 227 (2016) *Updating the Land Registration Act,* **[11.28]–[11.29]**

It seems to us that the issue which we have to consider[87] turns on the extent to which the law should impress upon those taking registrable interests in land a duty to carry out extensive and detailed enquiries of occupiers. The LRA 2002 already contains protection for a

---

[83] Law Com No 271 (2001) [8.6].   [84] *The Structure of Property Law* (2008) p 488.

[85] As occurred in *Baker v Craggs* [2017] Ch 295 (for the facts, see Chapter 8, section 6.5). Note there that B was found to have an overriding interest, but C was in any case protected by the defence of overreaching: see Chapter 17, section 2.3.

[86] Law Com CP No 227, [11.26].

[87] [Of whether it should continue to be possible for an estate contract or option to purchase to be an overriding interest if protected by actual occupation.]

disponee where occupation of the interest holder would not have been obvious on a reasonably careful inspection of the land at the time of the disposition.[88]

We can see that, in the case of large multi-let commercial sites such as shopping centres,
the duty to enquire of occupiers imposed by LRA 2002 may be time-consuming to comply
with. However, provided enquiries are in fact made, a purchaser will be protected. It is difficult to justify removing an existing protection for an occupier of a single-let site on the basis
that it produces an administratively burdensome result where the purchase is not of a single
site, but of a much larger property.

The point made here by the Law Commission demonstrates that the question of whether
B could reasonably have been expected to register his or her right *is* not, and *should* not,
be the only criterion when considering if B's pre-existing property right is overriding and
thus immune from the lack of registration defence. The point is that, just as it is reasonable to expect some things of B, so is it reasonable to expect some things of C, and one
of those things is that C, before acquiring a right in registered land, will check not only
the register but also the land itself. Indeed, as discussed in Chapter 16, section 4.2.1, the
scheme of Sch 3, para 2 is premised on the idea that, if B is in actual occupation, C should
discover that on a reasonably careful inspection of the land, and ask B if B claims any
rights that may bind C. Whilst that is clear from the actual terms of the LRA 2002, it was
obscured by the rhetoric of the Law Commission in its 2001 Report, which prioritized the
goal of a '*complete and accurate*' register and thus downplayed the need for C to check not
only the register but also the land itself. In contrast, as noted in section 1.2 of this chapter,
the 2016 CP instead acknowledges that there are other goals which the land registration
system should serve.

Despite adopting this different approach, the 2016 CP does not suggest major reform of
overriding interests. This is largely as a result of the fact that, notwithstanding the rhetoric
of the 2011 Report, the detail of the 2002 Act shows that the question of whether B could
reasonably have been expected to register is not the only concern when asking if B's right is
overriding. For example, when considering Sch 3, para 3, which deals with legal easements,
we saw in Chapter 16, section 4.4, that such an easement will be overriding if it was known
to C, or would have been obvious to C on a reasonably careful inspection of the land to
which it relates. The need for C to check the land itself is therefore evident.[89] Indeed, even if
neither of those two conditions are met, a legal easement can be overriding simply because
it was exercised at some point in the year before the disposition to C.[90] This shows that the
importance of the right to B is a relevant concern, and, in this case, suffices to make a right
overriding even if it would *not* have been obvious to C. This is linked to the policy concern,
identified in the 2016 CP, of '*fact-sensitivity*',[91] just as possession of the land can operate as
a 'proxy' for that concern in relation to rectification,[92] so use of a legal easement can operate
as a proxy for it when considering overriding interests.

Whilst the 2016 CP does not, therefore, recommend widespread changes to overriding
interests, we need to note one significant reform it proposes (see section 4.2) and also one
potentially important omission (see section 4.3).

---

[88] LRA 2002, Sch 3, para 2(c)(i) [as discussed in Chapter 16, section 4.2.2].   [89] Sch 3, para 3(1).
[90] Sch 3, para 3(2).   [91] Law Com CP No 227, [13.15].   [92] See section 3.2.1.

4.2 CAN A RIGHT TO RECTIFY BE AN OVERRIDING INTEREST UNDER SCH 3, PARA 2?

4.2.1 The problem

We saw in section 3 that, where C's registration is the result of a mistake, B may be able to apply for rectification of the register and, if C is not in possession of the registered land, showing such a mistake means that rectification will be ordered, in the absence of exceptional circumstances. Whilst such rectification may of course be inconvenient for C, an indemnity will be available to compensate C for loss arising from the rectification,[93] unless that loss was suffered by C wholly or partly as a result of C's fraud, or wholly as a result of C's own lack of proper care.[94]

Where, following such a mistake, B has the right to apply for rectification, it has generally been assumed that B's right is, like a mere equity, capable of binding a third party[95] such as C and so can be an overriding interest if B is in actual occupation of the registered land. As noted in Chapter 16, section 4.2.1, however, this can lead to a problem for C. It means that, if B's application is successful, and the register is changed, it can be argued that no indemnity should be payable to C, as there is a general rule that, if C is bound by an overriding interest, C does not receive an indemnity. This rule is often known as the rule in *re Chowood*.[96] Such a result seems very harsh to C, as it means C gets the pain of rectification[97] without the relief of an indemnity.

That result does, however, flow from the reasoning of the Court of Appeal in *Malory Enterprises Ltd v Cheshire Homes (UK) Ltd*.[98] Malory Enterprises Ltd (B), a British Virgin Islands company, was the registered proprietor of a derelict development site in Manchester. A different company (X),[99] also called Malory Enterprises, was dishonestly set up and registered in the UK. As a result of the deception, X succeeded in obtaining a land certificate in its name for that same land, and then purported to sell the land to Cheshire Homes (C), which registered as the new holder of the estate, in place of B. In Chapter 3, section 3.3.1, we considered one aspect of the Court of Appeal's decision: the holding that, notwithstanding the fact that C had acquired title from the registered holder of the estate, B had a pre-existing equitable interest under a trust that, coupled with B's actual occupation of the land, was an overriding interest.[100] We saw there that, in *Swift 1st v Chief Land Registrar*,[101] the Court of Appeal rejected that analysis as depending on a mistaken interpretation of the relevant land registration provisions. It is now clear, therefore, that, in such a case, B does not have an equitable interest under a trust.

---

[93] Sch 8, para 1(1)(a).   [94] Sch 8, para 5(2).

[95] For full discussion, see e.g. Cooper and Lees, 'Interests, Powers and Mere Equities in Modern Land Law' (2017) 37 OJLS 435, 452–3.

[96] *In re Chowood's Registered Land* [1933] Ch 574.

[97] As noted by Law Com CP No 227, [13.61] (extracted below), it can be argued that, as the register is on this view being changed to give effect to an overriding interest which in any case binds C, the change is an alteration and not a rectification. This does not, however, add anything to the central point of the argument which is that, as B's right is overriding, C should receive no indemnity.

[98] [2002] Ch 216.

[99] Not that 'X' did not itself acquire any registered rights in the land. For consideration of the case where the fraudster does acquire such rights, see Chapter 15, section 3.1.

[100] This point is referred to by the Law Commission as the '*Malory* 1 argument': Law Com CP No 227, 13.44–13.59.

[101] [2015] Ch 602.

In *Malory*, however, the court also accepted a second argument in B's favour: that B's right to seek rectification, when coupled with B's actual occupation, was an overriding interest.[102] That second argument is referred to by the Law Commission in its 2016 Consultation Paper as the '*Malory* 2' argument.[103] In contrast to the '*Malory* 1 argument' (i.e. the argument that B had an equitable interest under the trust), the *Malory* 2 argument *was* accepted by the Court of Appeal in *Swift 1st*, and so does still operate to prevent C qualifying for an indemnity if the register is changed in B's favour. This means that the rejection of the *Malory* 1 argument, by itself, provides little practical comfort for C, as C still faces the '*potentially disastrous*'[104] risk that it may lose its legal title without receiving an indemnity. The Law Commission stated the position as follows:

Law Commission Consultation Paper No 227, *Updating the Land Registration Act 2002*, [13.61]–[13.62]

The [*Malory* 2] argument artificially creates a claim to an overriding interest where the legislation does not envisage that there will be one. *Malory* 2 is capable of giving rise to strange consequences because where the register is altered to give effect to an overriding interest no indemnity is paid to the registered proprietor. That was the point decided in *re Chowood* [. . .] Views differ on the exact analysis to take, but both lead to the same conclusion; no indemnity is paid because the register is altered, not rectified. Either the alteration is to bring the register up to date, or it is correcting a mistake, but not in a manner prejudicial to the registered proprietor who always held subject to that interest.

The application of *re Chowood* to the situation is therefore potentially disastrous for someone in the position of [C].

4.2.2 Solutions to the problem?

In *Swift 1st*, to preserve the possibility of an indemnity payment for C, the Court of Appeal resorted to what the Law Commission has called a '*creative interpretation*'[105] of Sch 8, para 1(2)(b) of the LRA 2002. That provision states that: '*the proprietor of a registered estate or charge claiming in good faith under a forged disposition is, where the register is rectified, to be regarded as having suffered loss by reason of such rectification as if the disposition had not been forged.*' In the words of Patten LJ in *Swift 1st*, C's argument was that: '*This statutory hypothesis therefore enables the registered proprietor of a forged charge who acts in good faith to obtain an indemnity notwithstanding that his charge was always liable to be set aside on the application of the registered proprietor of the property.*'

---

[102] See e.g. *Malory* [2002] Ch 216 at [68] and [69]. Law Com CP No 227, 13.84 expresses some doubt on that point, noting that such a right is uncertain, as whether the register will be changed or not may involve the exercise of some discretion. Nonetheless, the same could be said of e.g. the right to have a document rectified in the case of a mutual mistake and, in *Blacklocks v JB Developments Ltd* [1982] Ch 183, such a right was regarded as a proprietary right and hence as an overriding interest when coupled with B's actual occupation.

[103] Law Com CP No 227, 13.60–13.74.

[104] The term used by the Law Commission: Law Com CP No 227, 13.62.

[105] Law Com CP No 227, 13.64.

The Court of Appeal, whilst accepting that the position was not clear, accepted that argument.[106] Nonetheless, there are some difficulties with it.[107] The provision relied on, Sch 8, para 1(2)(b), protects C from the argument that a change to the register causes no loss to C as C's right, depending on an earlier forgery, was in any case worthless; it does not, however, seem to protect C from the different argument that C's 'loss' stems from the effect of an overriding interest, and so does not result from the change to the register itself. Indeed, in *Swift 1st*, Patten LJ noted that the issue was not an easy one, and that it '*deserves to be considered in the forthcoming review by the Law Commission of the workings of the LRA 2002*'.[108]

As part of that review, the Law Commission did indeed consider the problem. Its suggestion is that C can be protected, without needing to invoke para 8, Sch 1(2)(b), by amending the LRA 2002 and providing that a right to have the register changed, even if held by a party in actual occupation of land, cannot be an overriding interest:[109]

Law Commission Consultation Paper No 227, *Updating the Land Registration Act 2002*

[13.76]

(2) [W]e propose that the right to seek rectification of the register should no longer be able to be an overriding interest. That in effect disposes of the *Malory* 2 argument and leaves the way for the law in relation to indefeasibility to be set out clearly in the statute without the use of concepts that were not intended to be employed in this context. Without the need to consider overriding interests, indemnity can no longer be blocked by the principle in *re Chowood's Registered Land*.

This proposal of course forms just one part of the Law Commission's wider proposals for rectification, discussed in section 3. On the specific point as to overriding interests, it could be argued, against the Law Commission's proposal, that if the general logic behind protecting rights of those in actual occupation is simply that C should make enquiry of the holder of the right, there is no reason why that logic cannot apply where B's right is a right to have the register changed. On the assumption, accepted by the Law Commission, that a right to seek rectification is capable of binding a third party,[110] why should it become unique in being the only property right expressly prevented from operating as an overriding interest when coupled with actual occupation?

In fact, a different argument could be made to protect C. The *re Chowood* principle is that no indemnity should be payable where C is bound by B's overriding interest. The first point, which will be discussed in section 4.3, is that the principle itself could be challenged: there may be some cases where an indemnity is nonetheless justifiable. The second point is that, whatever the merits of the wider principle, the right to seek rectification deserves special

---

[106] [2015] Ch 602 at [48]–[51].

[107] See e.g. Cooke, 'Chickens Coming Home to Roost' [2014] Conv 444, 446, stating that C's argument '*resolves the problem in a highly unsatisfactory manner [. . .] because it wrenches the sense of Sch 8, para 1(2) (b) and puts the provision to an unintended use*'.

[108] [2015] Ch 602 at [48].   [109] See too Law Com CP No 227, 13.87.

[110] That assumption is queried by Dixon, 'Fraud, Rectification and Land Registration: A Choice' [2017] Conv 161, 163, but is supported by Cooper and Lees, 'Interests, Powers and Mere Equities in Modern Land Law' (2017) 37 OJLS 435, 447–53.

treatment. The right is itself a product of the LRA 2002 and is part of a scheme under which an indemnity may also be payable to C. The problem with the *Malory* 2 argument is the assumption that the right to seek rectification can bind C without C also getting the protection of another fundamental, and linked, part of the statutory scheme: the right to an indemnity. The mere fact that B's right to have the register changed binds C should not mean that C can then be denied something which is part and parcel of that very mechanism by which the register can be changed.

4.3 OVERRIDING INTERESTS AND INDEMNITIES

As seen in section 1.2, the rhetoric of the 2016 CP is significantly different from that of the 2001 Report that led to the LRA 2002, and acknowledges the competing policy concerns that arise in disputes relating to the use of land. The 2016 CP also recognizes the important role that indemnity payments can play in balancing the tension between the competing claims of B and of C.[111] It did not, however, consider the possibility of re-visiting the *re Chowood* principle, discussed in section 4.2, that no indemnity is payable to C if C is bound by an overriding interest of B. It was not surprising that the 2001 Report did not examine this issue: it condemned overriding interests as '*such an unsatisfactory feature of the system of registered conveyancing*'[112] simply because they provide a means for B to win even without registration, and its focus was therefore on limiting such rights, rather than considering the consequences to C of being bound by such a right.[113] In contrast, the approach of the 2016 CP would seem to be more sympathetic to the possibility of C's receiving an indemnity in at least some cases where C is bound by an overriding interest.

Of course, the argument would not be that an indemnity should always be available to C. If part of the rationale for B's right being overriding is that C could reasonably have discovered B's right (e.g. as where B was in actual occupation of the land at the relevant time), then C has no one to blame but themselves (and their legal advisers). C may, however, be bound by an oral legal lease of B under Sch 3, para 1, when B was not in occupation of the property; or by a legal easement of B under Sch 3, para 3 where C did not know about the easement, nor could have discovered it from a reasonable inspection, but is bound simply because B exercised the easement in the previous year. In such cases, there may be good reasons for protecting B, but, given the crack in the registration 'mirror', there is also a case for protecting C by way of an indemnity. That case was quickly dismissed by the Law Commission as part of its review which led to the 2002 Act,[114] and was not examined by it in its 2016 CP, but has attracted some academic support. Smith, for example, noted that denying indemnity in all cases where C is bound by an overriding interest '*severely limits the extent to which imaginative use is made of registration to guarantee a proprietor's title*'.[115] In his discussion of the issue, Smith considered the very

---

[111] See e.g. Law Com CP No 227, [14.24]–[14.29].   [112] Law Com No 271 (2001), [8.6].

[113] The idea of making indemnity payments available in some cases where C is bound by an overriding interest had, however, been raised by an earlier Report: Law Com No 158 (1987), *Property Law: Third Report on Land Registration*.

[114] See Law Commission No 254 (1998), [4.18]–[4.20].

[115] Smith, 'The Role of Registration in Modern Land Law' in *Land Law: Issues, Debates, Policy* (ed Tee 2002) 52.

small proportion of Land Registry income paid out by way of indemnity. That remains the case: the Land Registry enjoyed a healthy operating surplus of £69.4m in 2016–17, on total revenue for the same period of £311.4m, with only £6.9m paid out by way of indemnity.[116] The total paid out in indemnity claims in the five years up to and including 2016–17 is £46.5m, at an average of £9.3m.

It is notable that, whilst Chapter 14 of the 2016 CP is devoted to indemnity, its focus is very clearly on *limiting* the burden to the Land Registry of indemnity payments. For example,[117] it considers (but does not in the end propose) a possible cap on the sum paid out in any one indemnity claim, where the mistake is not the fault of the Land Registry.[118] It also proposes imposing a statutory duty of care on those dealing with the Land Registry, so that, if such a duty is breached, leading to a mistake in the register, and an indemnity payment is made as a result, the Land Registry can recover at least some of the indemnity payment from the party in breach of the statutory duty of care.[119]

It is true that the Land Registry, like all government-funded bodies, is under financial pressure: offices have been closed,[120] its historic headquarters in Lincoln's Inn Fields in London have been sold, and it is expected to continue to make significant further savings. Indeed, there has been governmental interest, on more than one recent occasion, in privatizing much of the work of the Land Registry.[121] Although there are no current plans for such a move,[122] things may of course change and any private operator would want to be confident that the "business" would be profitable. As the Law Commission notes in its 2016 CP, the '*question of whether Land Registry operations should be moved into the private sector is not a matter that falls within the scope of our project. Our project is confined to updating the LRA 2002.*'[123] Nonetheless, the political context is clearly important in considering the likelihood of any suggested reforms to the LRA 2002 being adopted, and it must be admitted that any proposals to extend indemnity payments, even the very limited one canvassed in this section to allow indemnity where particular types of overriding interest bind C, are unlikely to find favour if the profitability of the Land Registry is to be a key political concern in relation to land registration.

---

[116] Land Registry, *Annual Report and Accounts 2016-7*, pp 39 and 95.

[117] Other measures considered (see [14.19] and [14.52]) are reforms to help prevent identity fraud leading to mistakes ([14.86]–[14.101], and limiting the circumstances in which mortgagees can claim indemnity ([14.102]–[14.124]).

[118] Law Com CP No 227, [14.53]–[14.61].

[119] Law Com CP No 227, [14.62]–[14.85]. The Land Registry does currently have rights of recourse against third parties where indemnity payments have been made, but these are limited in scope and in practice have led to the recovery of only a small proportion of indemnity payments: [14.51].

[120] The Harrow and York offices closed in 2010 and the Stevenage and Tunbridge Wells offices in 2011. For further discussion, see Dixon, 'The Future of the Land Registry' [2011] Conv 1.

[121] Department for Business, Innovation and Skills, *Consultation on Moving Land Registry Operations to the Private Sector* (March 2016). The proposal was first floated in 'Introduction of a Land Registry Service Delivery Company' (Department for Business Innovation & Skills, January 2014). For some powerful objections to the proposal, see, for example, [2014] Conv 189, 189–92. The proposal was dropped by the Government in July 2014, but was taken up again in March 2016 .

[122] Following some strong opposition to the 2016 suggestion of privatization, from e.g. the Competition and Markets Authority and the Law Society (for a summary, see House of Commons Library Briefing Paper, 'Land Registry Privatisation' (Number 07556, 9 Dec 2016)), it was announced in HM Treasury's 2016 Autumn Statement (CM 9362, 23 Nov 2016, [1.66]) that the privatization proposals would not be taken forward.

[123] Law Com CP No 227, [1.29].

5 CONCLUSION: BALANCING THE NEEDS OF B AND C

In Chapter 3, section 3.3.2, we noted a tension between two competing views of land regis-tration systems. The first, seen in the rhetoric of the 2001 Law Commission Report that led to the LRA 2002, is that such a system should aim to be 'revolutionary': to provide a new way to deal with the age-old tension, noted in Chapter 1, between protecting a purchaser of land, C, from defects in the title of the vendor, A, and pre-existing rights of B. That view can be seen, for example, in the ambition stated in the 2001 Report that: *'the register should be a complete and accurate reflection of the state of title of the land'*, and also in the identification by Patten LJ in *Swift 1ˢᵗ v Chief Land Registrar* of a general principle that *'the register is a complete record of all enforceable estates and interests except for overriding interests and that it is registration rather than transfer which confers title'*.[124] On that view, where rectification of the register is possible for the purpose of correcting a mistake, the term 'mistake' should be given a narrow meaning; and it should be possible for B's property right to be overriding only where it would be unreasonable to expect B to protect that right through an entry on the register.

The second view is that, whilst a land registration system can provide useful certainty for C, such a system is not isolated from wider principles of property law. Those wider principles include the idea that it should not usually be possible for B to lose his or her property right as a result of forgery, and that C should be bound by B's pre-existing property right in land if, before buying that land, C fails to make straightforward checks that would have led to the discovery of B's right. As we saw in Chapter 3, section 3.3.2, Lady Hale's comments in *Scott v Southern Pacific Mortgages Ltd* represent a somewhat extreme example of that view, and are inconsistent with the significant role that registration plays in modern land law, as much more than *'merely conveyancing machinery'*.[125] The rhetoric of the Law Commission in its 2016 CP is consistent with a more moderate, and therefore realistic, version of this second view. As noted in section 1.2, the CP recognizes that the aim of protecting the position of C, whilst important, is not the single driving force, and so must be balanced against other concerns.

The 2001 Report, of course, led to the LRA 2002; and the 2016 CP may lead to changes to the same Act. Ironically, however, the substance of the LRA 2002 seems to sit more easily with the rhetoric of the later publication. As we noted in section 2, the actual content of the LRA 2002 does recognize the need to balance the positions of C and of B; for example, the list of overriding interests under Schedule 3 is clearly *not* confined to cases where it would be unreasonable to expect B to register that right.[126] Moreover, it now seems clear that the term 'mistake', as used in Schedule 4 of the Act to regulate rectification, is not to be given a narrow meaning, and so can apply in the three party cases discussed in section 3.1.2, where C acquires a right from the then registered proprietor, if that proprietor was registered as a result of, for example, forging B's signature. It might therefore be said that the problem with the 2002 Act as it stands is not so much the Act itself, but the rhetoric which surrounded it. That revolutionary rhetoric, for example, very likely tempted judges to flirt with adopting a narrow view of mistake, and thus of rectification;[127] it also precluded a clearer analysis of the rationale of overriding interests, and thus prevented a fairer hearing to the possibility

---

124 [2015] EWCA Civ 330, [2015] Ch 602 at [41].   125 [2014] UKSC 52, [2015] AC 385, [96].
126 See e.g. the example of estate contracts, discussed in section 4.1.
127 See e.g. *Barclays Bank v Guy* [2008] EWCA Civ 452, [23].

of allowing indemnity payments in some cases where C is bound by an overriding interest. Whilst the 2016 CP deals carefully with the first of those issues, it too fails to grapple with the second. The current difficulty, however, with arguing for any increased role for indemnity payments is not that it might divert from the revolutionary nature of registration, but rather that it might limit the profit line of the Land Registry.[128]

QUESTIONS

1. What were the aims of the Land Registration Act 2002?

2. Following the enactment of the 2002 Act, is it true to say that the register is now 'complete and accurate'? If not, will it be so once e-conveyancing rules have been introduced?

3. Do you agree with the Law Commission's statement in its 2001 Report that over-riding interests are an inherently 'unsatisfactory' aspect of a registration system?

4. What differences are there in the rhetoric of the Law Commission's 2016 Consultation Paper, as compared to its 2011 Report?

5. What different approaches can be taken to interpreting the term 'mistake' in Sch 4 of the 2002 Act? Which approach is preferable?

6. What is the '*Malory* 2' argument? What problems does it cause? What is the best solution to those problems?

7. Is it possible or desirable for the principles of a land registration system to be wholly separate from the general principles of land law?

For guidance on how to answer these questions visit the online resources at www.oup.com/uk/mcfarlane4e/.

FURTHER READING

Cooper, 'Resolving Title Conflicts in Registered Land' (2015) 131 LQR 108

Cooper and Lees, 'Interests, Powers, and Mere Equities in Modern Land Law' (2017) 37 OJLS 435

Dixon, 'The Reform of Property Law and the Land Registration Act 2002: A Risk Assessment' [2003] Conv 136

Dixon, 'Updating the Land Registration Act 2002: Title Guarantee, Rectification and Indefeasibility' [2016] Conv 423

Goymour, 'Mistaken Registrations of Land: Exploding the Myth of "Title by Registration"' [2013] CLJ 617

Harding and Bryan, 'Responding to Fraud in Title Registration Systems: A Comparative Study' in *Modern Studies in Property Law Vol 5* (ed Dixon, Oxford: Hart Publishing, 2009)

Harpum, 'Registered Land: A Law Unto Itself?' in *Rationalizing Property, Equity and Trusts: Essays for Edward Burn* (ed Getzler, London: Butterworths, 2002)

---

[128] See section 4.3.

Jackson, 'Title by Registration and Concealed Overriding Interests: The Cause and Effect of Antipathy to Documentary Proof' (2003) 119 LQR 660

Law Commission Report No 271, *Land Registration for the Twenty-First Century: A Conveyancing Revolution* (2001)

Law Commission Consultation Paper No 227, *Updating the Land Registration Act 2002* (2016), chs 1, 2, and 13

McFarlane, *The Structure of Property Law* (Oxford: Hart Publishing, 2008, Parts C2 and E5)

Nair, 'Morality and the Mirror: The Normative Limits of the "Principles of Land Registration"' in *Modern Studies in Property Law Vol 6* (ed Bright, Oxford: Hart Publishing, 2011)

O'Connor, 'Ten Key Questions' in *Property and Security* (eds Moses et al, Sydney, 2010)

Smith, 'The Role of Registration' in *Modern Land Law in Land Law: Debates, Issues. Policy* (ed Tee, Devon: Willan, 2002)

PART F

LEASES

19 Leases 728

20 Regulating Leases and Protecting Occupiers 806

21 Leasehold Covenants 832

19

LEASES

CENTRAL ISSUES

1. Over the next three chapters, we will examine the lease in detail. In this chapter, we will concentrate on a key feature of a lease: its ability to count as a property right. This crucial aspect of a lease differentiates it from the licence, which we examined in Chapter 7. In this chapter, therefore, we will look at the three principal questions that apply to any property right: the *content* question (when will B's right count as a lease?); the *acquisition* question (how can B acquire a lease?); and the *defences* question (if B has a lease of A's land, when can C, a party later acquiring a right from A, have a defence to B's lease?). In considering the *content* question, we will see precisely how a lease differs from a licence; in considering the *acquisition* question, we will also consider the ways in which a lease may come to an end.

2. Before examining those questions, we will consider why B may wish to show that he or she has a lease. One important consequence of having a legal or equitable lease, of course, is that such a right is capable of binding C, a third party who later acquires a right from A. In addition, if B can show that he or she has a lease, this may mean that additional duties are imposed on A: in particular, such duties may be imposed by statutes that provide protection to B *if* B has a lease.

3. In Chapter 20, we will consider in more detail the statutory protection potentially available to B if he or she has a lease. We will see there that, in some cases, B can be seen as having a lease (at least, in the sense used by a particular statute) even if B has no property right. This suggests that there are two sorts of leases: a proprietary lease, and a non-proprietary lease. In this chapter, we will concentrate on the former type of lease and will consider how the judges' approach to defining the content of a lease *as a property right* may have been influenced by the presence of such statutory protection.

4. The *content* of a lease can be simply defined: B has a lease if he or she has a right to exclusive possession of land for a limited period. In practice, however, there may be difficulties in applying this simple test: for example, how should we deal with cases in which B1 and B2 occupy land together? And what is the effect of a term inserted by A into an occupation agreement with B with the sole purpose of denying B exclusive possession of land?

5. In considering the *acquisition* and *defences* questions, we will see the impact

of the Land Registration Act 2002 on leases. We considered the general effect of that Act in Chapters 3, 8, 16, and 18. When considering the *acquisition* and *defences* questions, we will also need to bear in mind the possibility of B's having an equitable, rather than a legal, lease.

6. Finally, in section 5 below, we will consider a recurrent debate about the conceptual nature of a lease: should it be seen as primarily a contractual right, or, instead, as primarily a property right? It will be suggested that the debate rests on a misconception: there is no reason why a right

cannot be both contractual—that is, acquired as a result of a contractual agreement between A and B—and also proprietary—that is, having a content that means it can count as a legal property right.

7. A lease, in the sense of a property right, will often arise as part of an agreement imposing a number of duties on both A and B. In some cases, those duties, even if positive, can bind not only A and B, but also parties later acquiring the rights of A and B. We will examine this phenomenon in Chapter 21, by looking at the concept of a leasehold covenant.

1 INTRODUCTION: THE IMPORTANCE OF THE LEASE

1.1 THE PRACTICAL IMPORTANCE AND DIVERSITY OF LEASES

Leases are tremendously important in a number of different practical contexts. There is, of course, the residential sector: for many residents, a lease is the property right they hold in the land they call their home. When considering the residential sector, a number of subdivisions can be made. For example, long residential leases are often isolated as a specific category: certainly, there is a clear practical distinction between, on the one hand, a party with a 999-year lease of a flat who acquired that lease by paying a large up-front price and then pays a very small rent, and, on the other, a party with a weekly, monthly, or yearly tenancy of a flat, who pays a regular market rent. Around 37 per cent of homes in the United Kingdom are leased in this second way.[1] Those shorter leases can be divided into three groups, according to the nature of the landlord: private, local authority, or social (e.g. housing association). As we will see in Chapter 20, the statutory rules applying to private landlords are very different from those applying to public landlords, such as local authorities or housing associations.

But it would be a mistake to focus solely on the residential sector. Leases are also very important in other areas: for example, many businesses hold leases of their premises; and many farmers hold leases of their agricultural land. Again, as we will see in Chapter 20, statute has intervened in those areas to give some extra protection to business and agricultural tenants.

The following extract emphasizes the importance and diversity of leases. As demonstrated by the extract, a number of different terms can be used to describe a party with a lease: 'tenant', 'lessee', and so on; the party granting a lease can be referred to as a 'landlord', or 'lessor'; and the property right retained by the landlord or lessor is referred to as a

---

[1] Wilcox et al (eds) *UK Housing Review 2017*, Table 17d.

'reversion', on the basis that, at the end of the lease, a right to exclusive possession of the land goes back to the landlord.

Bright, *Landlord and Tenant Law in Context* (2007, pp 5–6)

The variety of letting arrangements

There is a wide variety within the landlord and tenant relationship. A lease of a house is likely to be very different from a lease of a department store. A tenant who rents a house in order to let out individual rooms to others has quite a different perspective from a tenant renting the house to provide a home for his family. Some tenancies may be intended to last for only a short period, such as a let of holiday accommodation, and some may be for extremely long periods, such as a 999 year lease. Some may be granted in return for a substantial capital payment (known as a premium) and only a nominal rent, others for no premium but for a market rent. Some landlords are motivated primarily by financial considerations, others by social concerns.

It is important to have an overview of how leases are used in practice as different types of lease raise very different legal issues. The student renting a room for the year would, for example, rightly expect the landlord to be responsible for solving the problem of a leaking roof. In contrast, the commercial tenant with a 125 year lease of an entire building would usually be responsible for the maintenance and repair of the property itself. For the landlord, also, the length of the lease will affect its expectations; with a short lease the freehold (or reversion) has a high capital value and so the landlord may take an active role in managing the property in order to preserve this capital value, but with very long term leases the capital value of the reversion will be minimal, and so the landlord may show less interest in managing the property.

At the risk of over-generalisation, there are three broad categories of lease that can be iden-tified based on the length of the lease. The expectations of landlords and tenants in terms of what the relationship provides will differ according to which category the lease comes within. First, there are tenancies for short term occupation which usually involve the payment of a market rent and will be either periodic (weekly, monthly or annual) or for a fixed term up to five years (commercial) or seven years (residential). The tenant pays for occupation and exclusive possession for the term, while the landlord's reversion retains all, or nearly all, of the capital value of the property. Second, medium term leases are generally used to provide occupation for the tenant for up to, say, 25 years for commercial leases and 21 years for resi-dential leases. Again, these leases will usually be at a market rent, with provision for the rent to be reviewed at regular intervals. A premium (a capital sum) may be paid for the grant of the lease, but this would be unusual. The reversion again continues to have a substantial value. In the last category, long leases, there is a greater divergence between the commercial and residential models. The longer commercial lease, typically, for a term of 125 years, may in-volve the payment of a 'ground rent', that is, a market rent that reflects the value of the land only (the site value). In this arrangement, the lessee will often construct the buildings on the site, and the cost of doing so will be written off over the life of the lease, with the expect-ation that the building's useful life will draw to an end as the lease does. Notwithstanding the length of the lease, the reversion will carry a significant capital value because of the substan-tial and reviewable ground rent. In contrast, the long residential lease is typically granted for terms of 99, 125 or 999 years and a substantial premium will be paid to purchase this interest, similar to the amount that would be paid to buy a freehold interest. Here, it is the lease that will have a significant capital value, rather than the reversion. Indeed, the leaseholder will usually perceive of himself as the 'owner' of the property, as a purchaser rather than a renter or tenant. The lease is primarily being used in this context because it enables covenants, such as obligations to repair and financial commitments to contribute towards the cost of shared facilities, to be enforced against successive owners (English common law does not permit positive covenants to be attached to freehold land).

The rights and responsibilities of the landlord and tenant will be most affected by the type of letting, whether it is short term rented housing, a home purchased on a long lease, commercial property or agricultural land. Within these main divisions, there will be further differentiation according to the status of the landlord.

This passage also sets out some of the reasons why a party may acquire a lease, rather than a freehold. In Chapter 24, section 1, we will examine why a party buying a flat will almost always acquire a long lease of that flat rather than a freehold: as explained by Bright, the key point is that, if a lease is used, the 'owner' of each flat can take the benefit and burden of *positive* duties (such as duties to keep the flat in good repair).[2] In Chapter 24, we will also examine the concept of a *commonhold*—a mechanism introduced with the aim of allowing such duties to bind flat 'owners' without the necessity for each such owner to have a lease of his or her flat.

In other cases, the key attraction of a lease is often that it involves a shorter commitment: for example, if moving to a town to study there for three years, B has no need to incur the extra expense necessary in acquiring a freehold. Similarly, if B is starting up a business and is unsure of its long-term prospects, a freehold is an unattractive option. In some cases, however, B may wish to establish a long-term home, but be unable to find the finance needed to acquire a freehold. In such cases, financial necessity may lead B to acquire a shorter residential lease. There is a risk in such cases that B's need for a home, and relatively weak bargaining position, may give A an opportunity to exploit B. This has led to statutory intervention in B's favour and, importantly, such protection has often been limited to parties with leases, and denied to those with mere licences.

1.2 THE EFFECT OF A LEASE

Imagine a case in which A, who holds a registered legal estate in land, makes a contractual agreement with B. A promises to allow B to occupy A's land for a year; in return, B promises to pay A £200 a week. In such a case, B clearly has a permission to use A's land: he or she has, at the very least, a contractual licence (see Chapter 7, section 3). Why might B want to claim that his or her agreement with A instead gives him or her a lease of A's land?

We can answer this question by considering three different types of situation, matching the different situations that we examined in Chapter 7 when considering the effect of a licence. In the first set of situations, B wants to make a claim against A. In the second set of situations, B wants to make a claim against X, a stranger who has not acquired a right in A's land, but who has, in some way, interfered with B's use of that land. In the third set, B wants to make a claim against C, a third party who has acquired a right in A's land.

---

[2] Note that, as we will see in Chapter 23, section 5, the Law Commission has proposed that the law should be changed to allow for the possibility of attaching some positive covenants to freehold land.

1.2.1 The effect of a lease on A

In Chapter 7, section 3.1, we saw that, even if B has a contractual licence rather than a lease, his or her position as against A is fairly secure. In our example in which A has promised to allow B to occupy A's land for a year, it is quite possible that, if A were to threaten to remove B early, B could obtain a court order preventing A from thus breaching his or her contractual duty to B.[3] Nonetheless, if B can show he or she has acquired a lease, A may come under *extra* duties to B, going beyond the express terms of the parties' agreement.

Firstly, if B has a lease, A and B can be said to be in a 'landlord–tenant relationship'. The common law may then impose particular duties on the parties, even if they did not expressly undertake those duties when making their contractual agreement. These implied duties are, however, very limited:[4] for example, B has a duty not permanently to alter the physical character of the land;[5] and A's implied duties include a duty to allow B 'quiet enjoyment' of the land, meaning that A has a duty not to interfere physically with B's expected use of the land, or to interfere substantially with B's enjoyment of the land.

Secondly, and much more importantly in practice, particular statutes may operate to impose duties on A *if and only if* A has given B a lease. We will look at the scope of this statutory protection in more detail in Chapter 20, but its existence is crucial to understanding the context of a number of cases that we will examine in this chapter.

It is certainly apparent in the case from which the following extract is taken. The extract given below is a long one, but the length of the extract is commensurate with the importance of the decision. Lord Templeman's analysis provides the key starting point for any attempt to define the content of a lease or to distinguish a lease from a contractual licence.

Street v Mountford
[1985] UKHL 4, [1985] AC 809, HL

Facts: Roger Street, a solicitor from Bournemouth, owned No 5, St Clement's Gardens, Boscombe. On 7 March 1983, he entered a signed written agreement with Wendy Mountford, allowing her a right to exclusive occupation of two rooms in that house (Rooms 5 and 6). Under the terms of the agreement, Mrs Mountford was under a duty to pay £37 a week to Mr Street and either party was free to terminate the agreement by giving fourteen days' notice. The agreement described itself throughout as a licence: for example, the £37 payment was described as a 'licence fee'. Under the terms of the Rent Act 1977, if the agreement gave Mrs Mountford a lease, then Mr Street was obliged to accept whatever rent was set as a fair rent by an independent officer or tribunal. Mrs Mountford claimed that the agreement did, indeed, give her a lease and applied for a fair rent to be assessed. Mr Street then applied to the county court for a declaration that Mrs Mountford had only a licence. If it were found that

---

3 See *Verrall v Great Yarmouth Borough Council* [1981] QB 202, although note *Thompson v Park* [1944] KB 408. Both cases are discussed in Chapter 7, section 3.1.2.

4 Judges in other jurisdictions have been more willing to impose duties on A: see *Javins v First National Realty* (1970) 428 F 2d 1071 (District of Columbia Court of Appeals). For a comparison between the English and US approaches, see Bright, *Landlord and Tenant Law in Context* (2007) pp 30–5.

5 See *Marsden v Edward Heyes* [1927] 2 KB 1, applying *Horsefall v Mather* (1815) Holt NP 7.

Mrs Mountford had a lease, the Rent Act 1977 would also limit the grounds on which Mr Street could end her occupation and would thus prevent him bringing her occupation to an end by simply giving fourteen days' notice. The county court judge found that Mrs Mountford did, indeed, have a lease. The Court of Appeal upheld Mr Street's appeal, finding that, as the written agreement made clear that Mr Street did not intend to grant Mrs Mountford a lease, Mrs Mountford had only a contractual licence. But the House of Lords held that, this contrary intention notwithstanding, the agreement between Mr Street and Mrs Mountford *did* give her a lease. Lord Templeman, with whom all of their Lordships agreed, gave the only reasoned speech. In it, the term 'tenancy' is used interchangeably with 'lease'.

Lord Templeman

A tenancy is a term of years absolute. This expression, by section 205(1)(xxvii) of the Law of Property Act 1925, reproducing the common law, includes a term from week to week in possession at a rent and liable to determination by notice or re-entry. Originally a term of years was not an estate in land, the lessee having merely a personal action against his lessor. But a legal estate in leaseholds was created by the Statute of Gloucester 1278 and the Act of 1529 21 Hen. VIII, c. 15. Now by section 1 of the Law of Property Act 1925 a term of years absolute is an estate in land capable of subsisting as a legal estate. In the present case if the agreement dated 7 March 1983 created a tenancy, Mrs. Mountford having entered into possession and made weekly payments acquired a legal estate in land. If the agreement is a tenancy, the occupation of Mrs. Mountford is protected by the Rent Acts.

A licence in connection with land while entitling the licensee to use the land for the purposes authorised by the licence does not create an estate in the land. If the agreement dated 7 March 1983 created a licence for Mrs. Mountford to occupy the premises, she did not acquire any estate in the land. If the agreement is a licence then Mrs. Mountford's right of occupation is not protected by the Rent Acts. Hence the practical importance of distinguishing between a tenancy and a licence.

[...]

On behalf of Mrs. Mountford her counsel, Mr. Hicks Q.C., seeks to reaffirm and re-establish the traditional view that an occupier of land for a term at a rent is a tenant providing the occupier is granted exclusive possession. It is conceded on behalf of Mr. Street that the agreement dated 7 March 1983 granted exclusive possession to Mrs. Mountford. The traditional view that the grant of exclusive possession for a term at a rent creates a tenancy is consistent with the elevation of a tenancy into an estate in land. The tenant possessing exclusive possession is able to exercise the rights of an owner of land, which is in the real sense his land albeit temporarily and subject to certain restrictions. A tenant armed with exclusive possession can keep out strangers and keep out the landlord unless the landlord is exercising limited rights reserved to him by the tenancy agreement to enter and view and repair. A licensee lacking exclusive possession can in no sense call the land his own and cannot be said to own any estate in the land. The licence does not create an estate in the land to which it relates but only makes an act lawful which would otherwise be unlawful.

On behalf of Mr. Street his counsel, Mr. Goodhart Q.C., relies on recent authorities which, he submits, demonstrate that an occupier granted exclusive possession for a term at a rent may nevertheless be a licensee if, in the words of Slade L.J. in the present case:

> 'there is manifested the clear intention of both parties that the rights granted are to be merely those of a personal right of occupation and not those of a tenant.'[6]

My Lords, there is no doubt that the traditional distinction between a tenancy and a licence of land lay in the grant of land for a term at a rent with exclusive possession. In some cases it was not clear at first sight whether exclusive possession was in fact granted. For example, an owner of land could grant a licence to cut and remove standing timber. Alternatively the owner could grant a tenancy of the land with the right to cut and remove standing timber during the term of the tenancy. The grant of rights relating to standing timber therefore required careful consideration in order to decide whether the grant conferred exclusive possession of the land for a term at a rent and was therefore a tenancy or whether it merely conferred a bare licence to remove the timber [. . .]

In the case of residential accommodation there is no difficulty in deciding whether the grant confers exclusive possession. An occupier of residential accommodation at a rent for a term is either a lodger or a tenant. The occupier is a lodger if the landlord provides attendance or services which require the landlord or his servants to exercise unrestricted access to and use of the premises. A lodger is entitled to live in the premises but cannot call the place his own. In *Allan v. Liverpool Overseers* Blackburn J. said:[7]

> 'A lodger in a house, although he has the exclusive use of rooms in the house, in the sense that nobody else is to be there, and though his goods are stowed there, yet he is not in exclusive occupation in that sense, because the landlord is there for the purpose of being able, as landlords commonly do in the case of lodgings, to have his own servants to look after the house and the furniture, and has retained to himself the occupation, though he has agreed to give the exclusive enjoyment of the occupation to the lodger.'

If on the other hand residential accommodation is granted for a term at a rent with exclusive possession, the landlord providing neither attendance nor services, the grant is a tenancy; any express reservation to the landlord of limited rights to enter and view the state of the premises and to repair and maintain the premises only serves to emphasise the fact that the grantee is entitled to exclusive possession and is a tenant. In the present case it is conceded that Mrs. Mountford is entitled to exclusive possession and is not a lodger. Mr. Street provided neither attendance nor services and only reserved the limited rights of inspection and maintenance and the like set forth in clause 3 of the agreement. On the traditional view of the matter, Mrs. Mountford not being a lodger must be a tenant.

There can be no tenancy unless the occupier enjoys exclusive possession; but an occupier who enjoys exclusive possession is not necessarily a tenant. He may be owner in fee simple, a trespasser, a mortgagee in possession, an object of charity or a service occupier. To constitute a tenancy the occupier must be granted exclusive possession for a fixed or periodic term certain in consideration of a premium or periodical payments. The grant may be express, or may be inferred where the owner accepts weekly or other periodical payments from the occupier.

[. . .] My Lords, Mr. Street enjoyed freedom to offer Mrs. Mountford the right to occupy the rooms comprised in the agreement on such lawful terms as Mr. Street pleased. Mrs. Mountford enjoyed freedom to negotiate with Mr. Street to obtain different terms. Both parties enjoyed freedom to contract or not to contract and both parties exercised that freedom by contracting on the terms set forth in the written agreement and on no other terms. But

---

[6] [1985] 49 P & CR 324, 332.   [7] (1874) LR 9 QB 180, 191–2.

the consequences in law of the agreement, once concluded, can only be determined by consideration of the effect of the agreement. If the agreement satisfied all the requirements of a tenancy, then the agreement produced a tenancy and the parties cannot alter the effect of the agreement by insisting that they only created a licence. The manufacture of a five-pronged implement for manual digging results in a fork even if the manufacturer, unfamiliar with the English language, insists that he intended to make and has made a spade.

It was also submitted that in deciding whether the agreement created a tenancy or a licence, the court should ignore the Rent Acts. If Mr. Street has succeeded, where owners have failed these past 70 years, in driving a coach and horses through the Rent Acts, he must be left to enjoy the benefit of his ingenuity unless and until Parliament intervenes. I accept that the Rent Acts are irrelevant to the problem of determining the legal effect of the rights granted by the agreement. Like the professed intention of the parties, the Rent Acts cannot alter the effect of the agreement.

In *Street v Mountford*, Lord Templeman thus set out a seemingly simple test for the existence of a lease: B can only have a lease if he or she has exclusive possession of land for a term (i.e. for a limited period). In the extract above, Lord Templeman does refer to the payment of rent: nothing turned on that in *Street* itself and, as we will see in section 2.2, it is now accepted that B can have a lease even if no rent is paid. We will examine the content of a lease and Lord Templeman's test in more detail in section 2.

Street also raises the important question of whether and, if so, how the courts' approach to defining a lease has been affected by the fact that various forms of statutory protection are, or have been, available *only* in cases in which B has a lease. This question may raise the tension between *doctrine* and *utility* that we considered in Chapter 1, section 5.2: if B, according to the doctrinal rules does (or does not) have a lease, should a court bend those rules in order to deny (or give) B the statutory protection that depends on B's having a lease? In the extract above, Lord Templeman takes the view that such statutory protection is '*irrelevant to the problem of determining the legal effect of the rights granted by the agreement*'; but, as we will see, there do seem to be decisions, even involving Lord Templeman himself, in which the judges' reasoning has been influenced by a desire to make statutory protection available to particular occupiers.[8] Indeed, as we will see in section 2.1, it has even been argued that the decision in *Street* itself can only be justified by the practical need to give statutory protection to Mrs Mountford.[9]

For present purposes, however, the key lesson from *Street* is a simple one: like Mrs Mountford, B may claim that he or she has a lease in order to show that A is under statutory duties to B. As we will see in Chapter 20, the particular statutory duties imposed by the Rent Act 1977 are now of marginal relevance. Nowadays, a private landlord, such as Mr Street, has very little to fear from a lease: he can grant a party, such as Mrs Mountford, an 'assured shorthold tenancy'—that is, a form of lease that gives rise to no fair rent duties and places no substantial limits on Mr Street's ability to remove the tenant at the end of the agreed period.

Nonetheless, even where private landlords are concerned, there are still some statutory duties that apply if and only if B has a lease. For example, as we will see in Chapter 20, s 11

---

[8] One example, which we will discuss in section 2.4, is the House of Lords' decision in *AG Securities v Vaughan, Antioniades v Villiers* [1990] 1 AC 417. See too *Watts v Stewart* [2017] 2 WLR 1107, where the policy behind the extent of statutory protection had to be explicitly considered in addressing a human rights challenge to the exclusion of occupiers of almshouses from security of tenure.

[9] See the extract from Hill, 'Intention and the Creation of Proprietary Rights: Are Leases Different?' [1996] LS 200, set out in section 2.1.

of the Landlord and Tenant Act 1985 can impose a duty on a private landlord (A) to keep in repair the structure and exterior of a dwelling house occupied by B. This particular statutory duty (which cannot be varied by the express terms of a lease) provides the context for another important House of Lords decision, *Bruton v London and Quadrant Housing Trust*,[10] which we will consider in detail in Chapter 20, section 4, as well as in section 2.6 of the present chapter. It is important to note here that, in *Bruton*, the House of Lords held that Mr Bruton had a lease, at least for the purposes of the Landlord and Tenant Act 1985, even though his agreement with A did not give him a property right. The idea that B can have a lease even if he has no property right is a controversial and important one: we will examine it further in Chapter 20, section 4—but we will not consider it in this chapter, because our focus here is on the role of a lease *as a property right in land*.

Statutory protection continues to be important in residential cases not involving private landlords. As we will see in Chapter 20, if B can show that he or she has a lease from a local authority, the Housing Act 1985 will apply to impose extra duties on that local authority. For example, the statute limits the grounds on which B can be removed and thus confers on a tenant (but not a licensee) a form of security of tenure. And if B has a lease of business premises, Pt II of the Landlord and Tenant Act 1954 may impose a statutory duty on A to agree to renew B's lease when it reaches the end of the initially agreed period. In contrast, if B has only a licence, A is under no such statutory duty.

1.2.2 The effect of a lease on X

We have seen that the distinction between a lease and a licence can be crucial in deciding whether additional statutory duties will be imposed on A. There is a further, more fundamental distinction between a lease and a licence: a lease, unlike a licence, can count as a property right in land.

As we saw in Chapters 5 and 6, the key feature of a property right is that it is capable of binding parties other than A. In particular, if B has a *legal* estate or interest (such as a legal lease), then the rest of the world is under a prima facie duty not to interfere with B's use of the land. The consequences of such a duty can be seen in the following extract.

Hunter and ors v Canary Wharf Ltd
[1997] AC 665, HL

Facts: Patricia Hunter lived on the Isle of Dogs, in East London. Along with hundreds of other claimants living in that area, she claimed that her television reception had been affected by the construction, on land belonging to Canary Wharf Ltd, of the Canary Wharf Tower.[11] It was claimed that the interference began in 1989, during the construction of the tower, and continued until a relay transmitter was put up in 1991. It seems that the interference was particularly bad in Poplar, to the north of Canary Wharf, as the tower lay between that area and the BBC's Crystal Palace transmitter. It was claimed that, by causing this interference, Canary Wharf Ltd had committed the tort of nuisance. In a separate action, brought against the London Docklands Development Corporation

---

[10] [2000] 1 AC 406.
[11] Also known by its address, 'One Canada Square', the tower rises 235 m from ground level and was the tallest building in the UK until the completion of the Shard London Bridge (306 m high) in 2012.

(LDDC), Ms Hunter and the other claimants sought compensation for damage caused by the dust produced by the LDDC in building the Limehouse Link Road. That separate action alleged that LDDC had committed the torts of negligence and nuisance.

The claims raised a number of difficult legal issues, which were tried as preliminary issues of law. By the time that the case reached the House of Lords, two issues remained. In the words of Lord Goff of Chieveley, they were: '*(1) whether interference with television reception is capable of constituting an actionable nuisance, and (2) whether it is necessary to have an interest in property to claim in private nuisance and, if so, what interest in property will satisfy this requirement.*'[12] The House of Lords held that: (1) interference with television reception, at least when caused by the construction of a building on the defendant's land, cannot amount to a nuisance;[13] and (2) to sue in nuisance, a claimant must have a property right in land, and that property right must give the claimant exclusive possession of land. The claims made by Ms Hunter and other residents of the Isle of Dogs against Canary Wharf Ltd therefore failed. The claims made against LDDC succeeded, but only in relation to those claimants with a right to exclusive possession of land. As we will see in the extracts below, this meant that if Ms Hunter simply had a *licence* of the land that she occupied as her home, she could not bring a nuisance claim in respect of damage caused by the dust; whereas, if she had a *lease* of that land, she could do so.

Lord Goff

At 687

The basic position is, in my opinion, most clearly expressed in Professor Newark's classic article on *The Boundaries of Nuisance* (1949) 65 L.Q.R. 480 when he stated, at p. 482, that the essence of nuisance was that 'it was a tort to land. Or to be more accurate it was a tort directed against the plaintiff's enjoyment of rights over land [. . .]'

[Lord Goff then examined the relevant authorities, finding that they supported Newark's view.][14]

At 692–4

It follows that, on the authorities as they stand, an action in private nuisance will only lie at the suit of a person who has a right to the land affected. Ordinarily, such a person can only sue if he has the right to exclusive possession of the land, such as a freeholder or tenant in possession, or even a licensee with exclusive possession. Exceptionally however, as *Foster v. Warblington Urban District Council*[15] shows, this category may include a person in actual possession who has no right to be there; and in any event a reversioner [e.g. a landlord] can sue in so far his reversionary interest is affected. But a mere licensee on the land has no right to sue.

---

[12] [1997] AC 665, [684].

[13] [One issue considered by the House of Lords was whether it is possible for a party to have an easement to receive television signals, and, if so, whether such an easement could be acquired over the passage of time through the doctrine of prescription. This point is examined in Chapter 22, section 3.3.]

[14] An exception was *Khorasandijan v Bush* [1993] QB 727, in which the Court of Appeal found that the defendant had committed the tort of nuisance by pestering the claimant with unwelcome telephone calls. In *Hunter v Canary Wharf*, the House of Lords rejected the nuisance analysis, noting that the need to prevent such behaviour can be met through use of the Protection from Harassment Act 1997, or by holding that the defendant commits a tort when intentionally causing distress: see *per* Lord Hoffmann at 707.

[15] [1906] 1 KB 648.

[. . .] [A]ny such departure from the established law on this subject, such as that adopted by the Court of Appeal in the present case, faces the problem of defining the category of persons who would have the right to sue. The Court of Appeal adopted the not easily identifiable category of those who have a 'substantial link' with the land, regarding a person who occupied the premises 'as a home' as having a sufficient link for this purpose. But who is to be included in this category? It was plainly intended to include husbands and wives, or partners, and their children, and even other relatives living with them. But is the category also to include the lodger upstairs, or the au pair girl or resident nurse caring for an invalid who makes her home in the house while she works there? If the latter, it seems strange that the category should not extend to include places where people work as well as places where they live, where nuisances such as noise can be just as unpleasant or distracting. In any event, the extension of the tort in this way would transform it from a tort to land into a tort to the person, in which damages could be recovered in respect of something less serious than personal injury and the criteria for liability were founded not upon negligence but upon striking a balance between the interests of neighbours in the use of their land. This is, in my opinion, not an acceptable way in which to develop the law.

Lord Hoffmann

At 702–3

In the dust action it is not disputed that, in principle, activities which cause dust to be deposited on the plaintiff's property can constitute an actionable nuisance. The question raised by the preliminary issue is: who can sue? In order to answer this question, it is necessary to decide what exactly he is suing for. Since these questions are fundamental to the scope of the tort of nuisance, I shall deal with them first.

Up to about 20 years ago, no one would have had the slightest doubt about who could sue. Nuisance is a tort against land, including interests in land such as easements and profits. A plaintiff must therefore have an interest in the land affected by the nuisance … An example of an action for nuisance by a de facto possessor is *Foster v. Warblington Urban District Council*[16] in which the plaintiff sued the council for discharging sewage so as to pollute his oyster ponds on the foreshore. He had some difficulty in proving any title to the soil but Vaughan Williams L.J. said, at pp. 659–660:

'But, even if title could not be proved, in my judgment there has been such an occupation of these beds for such a length of time—not that the length of time is really material for this purpose—as would entitle the plaintiff as against the defendants, who have no interest in the foreshore, to sustain this action for the injury which is alleged has been done by the sewage to his oysters so kept in those beds.'

Thus even a possession which is wrongful against the true owner can found an action for trespass or nuisance against someone else: *Asher v. Whitlock*.[17] In each case, however, the plaintiff (or joint plaintiffs) must be enjoying or asserting exclusive possession of the land: see *per* Blackburn J. in *Allan v. Liverpool Overseers*.[18] Exclusive possession distinguishes an occupier who may in due course acquire title under the Limitation Act 1980 from a mere trespasser. It distinguishes a tenant holding a leasehold estate from a mere licensee. Exclusive possession de jure or de facto, now or in the future, is the bedrock of English land law.

---

[16] [1906] 1 KB 648.   [17] (1865) LR 1 QB 1.   [18] (1874) LR 9 QB 180.

The decision of the House of Lords in *Hunter v Canary Wharf* reveals a point that we examined in Chapter 5, section 1: the key feature of a legal property right is that it imposes a duty on the rest of the world. So, if B has a legal lease of A's land,[19] the rest of the world is under a prima facie duty to B not to interfere with B's use of that land. As a result, B, if he or she has a legal lease, can, for example, bring a nuisance claim against a third party whose activities interfere with B's reasonable enjoyment of the land. In contrast, if B has only a licence to use A's land (even a contractual licence), then, as we saw in Chapter 7, B does *not* have a right that he or she can assert against a third party later acquiring a right in the land. And, as shown by *Hunter v Canary Wharf*, if B has only a licence, then the rest of the world is not under a duty to B.

One point in Lord Goff's judgment may seem puzzling: his Lordship stated that a 'licensee with exclusive possession' may be able to sue in nuisance. As we saw in section 1.2.1, *Street v Mountford* establishes the presence of exclusive possession as the key test for the presence of a lease. So it may seem odd that a party can both be a licensee (rather than a tenant) *and* have exclusive possession. But this problem disappears when we distinguish between two types of exclusive possession. The first type is the form of exclusive possession that matters when considering the test for a lease: it is a right to exclusive possession for a limited period arising as a result of B's agreement with A. This form of exlusive possession can be referred to as '*legal exclusive possession or a legal right of exclusive possession*'.[20] If B is a licensee, then he or she will not have such a right. There is, however, also a second form of exclusive possession. Consider a case such as *National Provincial Bank v Ainsworth*.[21] A has a freehold of a home and lives there with his partner, B. A then moves out, but B remains in occupation. At each stage, B has a licence: certainly, there is no agreement between A and B giving B a right to exclusive possession of the land. But when A moves out, B occupies alone and so assumes sole *factual* control of the land. This second form of exclusive possession can be described as a '*personal right of exclusive occupation*' and does not, by itself, give B a lease.[22] When B is in sole occupation, however, then B does acquire a right to exclusive possession arising as a result of B's conduct in having sole physical control of land. As we saw in Chapter 7, sections 2.2 and 3.2, B's factual control of the land then means that third parties come under a duty to B. That duty arises because, as we saw in Chapter 9, section 3, the *fact* of B's exclusive physical control gives B a legal estate in land: a freehold.

In such a case, B's freehold is the same type of right as held by the claimant in *Foster v Warblington Urban District Council*[23] (referred to by Lords Goff and Hoffmann in the extract above). It is not given to B by A, but is instead acquired independently (see Chapter 5, section 4, for discussion of the concept of independent acquisition).[24] This means that, once

---

[19] An interesting question arises where B has an *equitable* lease rather than a legal lease. As noted in Chapter 6, section 7, it seems that equitable interests, whilst they can bind a third party who later acquires a right in the affected land, do *not* generally impose a duty on the rest of the world (although note the discussion there of the Court of Appeal's decision in *Shell UK (Ltd) v Total UK (Ltd)* [2011] QB 86). If so, this suggests that a party with an equitable lease *cannot* bring a nuisance claim. In *Hunter v Canary Wharf*, however, Lord Hoffmann does make the contrary (but obiter) suggestion (at 708) that a party with an equitable interest under a trust of a family home can bring a nuisance claim.

[20] *Watts v Stewart* [2017] 2 WLR 1107, [31].

[21] [1965] AC 1175. See Chapter 1, section 5 and Chapter 6, section 5.3.

[22] *Watts v Stewart* [2017] 2 WLR 1107, [31].   [23] [1906] 1 KB 648.

[24] Because B's freehold is independently acquired, it arises *after* A's legal estate and so A (or C, a party later acquiring a right from A) can, of course, remove B from the land (see Chapter 15, section 3.3, for the importance of timing when considering conflicting property rights). Of course, if B has a defence to A or C's prior property right, then B will be protected (such a defence could be based, for example, on B's adverse possession of the land: see Chapter 9).

A leaves and B takes sole physical control of the land, B not only has a licence (arising as a result of A's permission for B to remain on the land), but also a legal freehold (arising as a result of B's physical control of the land). It is in such a case that B, in Lord Goff's words, is a 'licensee with exclusive possession'. B's ability to sue in nuisance thus comes from his or her legal freehold, not from his or her licence, and not as a result of any lease.

1.2.3 The effect of a lease on C

When considering B's position as against C (a party who later acquires a right in relation to A's land), it is again vital to bear in mind the key difference between a lease and a licence—that is, that the licence, unlike the lease, can count as a property right in land. So, as we saw in Chapter 6, section 7, an equitable lease, as well as a legal lease, is capable of binding a third party, such as C, who later acquires a right from A.

1.3 THE LANDLORD–TENANT RELATIONSHIP

As is made clear by the decision of the House of Lords in *Street v Mountford*, an agreement can only count as a lease if it gives B a right to exclusive possession of land for a limited period. As we saw in sections 1.2.2 and 1.2.3, once A has given B that core right, third parties can then also come under a duty, during that period, not to interfere with B's right to exclusive possession. In practice, of course, a standard lease agreement will generally include many other terms, imposing additional duties on A (e.g. duties to undertake major repairs), as well as duties on B (e.g. a duty to pay rent). And, in certain circumstances, those additional duties can also affect third parties: for example, it may be that, if A owns other, neighbouring land, he or she will make a binding promise to B not to use that other land in a particular way (e.g. not to build on that land, not to run a business on that land that will compete with the business B plans to operate from the leased premises, etc.). In such a case, A's promise can give B an equitable interest in A's other land: a restrictive covenant (see Chapter 23). Like any equitable interest, that restrictive covenant will be capable of binding C, a third party who later acquires a right in A's other land.

There is a further, important way in which third parties can be affected by the additional duties assumed by A or B in a lease agreement: if the contractual promise giving rise to the duty counts as a 'leasehold covenant', it can bind other parties who later step into the shoes of A or B, and thereby also enter a landlord–tenant relationship. For example, it may be possible for B to assign (i.e. to transfer) his or her lease to another party (B2). In such a case, B's contractual promise to pay A rent will bind B2. If A then transfers his or her reversion (i.e. A's legal estate) to A2, then B2 will be under a duty to pay rent to A2; and, due to the promise to repair made by A in the initial lease, A2 will be under a duty to B2 to do such repairs. In this way, later parties who step into the landlord–tenant relationship will also take the benefit and burden of at least some of the additional duties originally agreed to by A and B. A key question, of course, is *which* of those additional duties should be seen as part of the landlord–tenant relationship, and thus capable of benefiting and binding later parties. We will consider that question, and others, in Chapter 21, when looking in detail at leasehold covenants.[25]

---

[25] In that chapter, the party here referred to as 'B2' (i.e. the party acquiring B's lease) is referred to as 'TA' (i.e. tenant's assignee). Similarly, 'A2' (i.e. the party acquiring A's estate) is referred to as 'LA' (i.e. landlord's assignee).

2 THE *CONTENT* QUESTION

In this chapter, our focus is on the lease as a property right. Section 1 of the Law of Property Act 1925 (LPA 1925) makes clear that a lease, referred to there as a 'term of years absolute', can count as a legal estate in land. But how do we tell if an agreement made between A and B, under which B has a right to occupy A's land, counts as a lease? The basic test, as we saw in section 1.2.1, was set out by Lord Templeman in *Street v Mountford*:[26] a lease consists of a right to exclusive possession of land for a limited period. There are, however, a number of specific points to consider when applying that general test.

2.1 WHERE A DOES NOT INTEND TO GRANT B LEASE

The first question to ask is whether B's right can count as a lease *even if* A, when making the agreement with B, makes it clear that he or she does not intend to grant B a lease. As we saw in section 1.2.1, that question was answered by the House of Lords in *Street v Mountford*: A's lack of intention to grant B a lease does *not* necessarily prevent B's right from counting as a lease.

As evidenced by the following extract, this result came as a surprise to Mr Street.

Street, 'Coach and Horses Trip Cancelled? Rent Act Avoidance after *Street v Mountford*' [1985] Conv 328, 328–9

The Rent Acts are grossly unfair to landlords. A stranger obtains a weekly tenancy of a house: half a century may pass before the owner can have his property again. In the meantime he can only charge a so-called 'fair' rent which in many cases does little more than cover the cost of keeping the property in repair. As a result of all this the capital value of the property drops to between one-third and one-half of its vacant possession value. Little wonder that over the years landlords and their legal advisers have sought various ways of avoiding the potentially horrendous consequences of being caught by the legislation [. . .]

In *Street v. Mountford* the plaintiff was—in the eyes of some—a double rogue, a landlord and a lawyer. He had studied the Court of Appeal decisions of the late 1970s which appeared to confirm a shift of emphasis from status to contract. The traditional view had been that exclusive possession meant a tenancy had been created (subject to one or two well-recognised exceptions), but the approach in the more recent cases suggested the ultimate test was one of intention. Lord Denning's judgments in particular seemed to show this development very clearly. By 1977 he felt able to say:

'What *is* the test to see whether the occupier of one room in a house is a tenant or a licensee? It does not depend on whether he or she has exclusive possession or not [. . .] [The test is] Was it intended that the occupier should have a stake in the room or did he have only permission for himself personally to *occupy* the room, whether under a contract or not, in which case he is a licensee?'

---

[26] [1985] AC 809.

In 1979 the writer decided to take the Court of Appeal at its word and drafted a document, using the simplest possible terms, expressed to be a personal non-assignable licence. A declaration was appended to underline the fact that it was not the intention of the parties to create a tenancy, which would be protected by the Rent Acts. No attempt was made to avoid granting the licensee exclusive possession, as this was not seen as the dominant factor. The document was to mean what it said, the licensee was to have an exclusive right to occupy a room, but this would be revocable on notice and would be outside the scope of the statutory protection afforded to tenants. The writer employed the document from 1979 to 1983 with no problems arising [. . .]

[When the case came to the Court of Appeal] Slade LJ stated:

'Having regard to the form of the document and the declaration at the foot of it, I do not see how [Mr Street] could have made much clearer his intention that what was being offered to [Mrs Mountford] was a mere licence to occupy and not an interest in the premises as tenant. And I do not see how [Mrs Mountford] could have made clearer her acceptance of that offer than by her two signatures.'

The House of Lords unanimously reversed this decision [. . .] Lord Templeman's judgment, with which Lords Scarman, Keith, Bridge and Brightman concurred, turned the clock back more than a quarter of a century, and in doing so expressly disapproved of a number of decisions in recent years. The ancient wisdom is reinstated: save in exceptional 'special category' cases (e.g. master and service occupier, vendor and purchaser) the grant of exclusive possession for a fixed or periodic term in consideration of periodic payments will create a tenancy.

It is, of course, rare to see an article about a reported decision written by one of the very parties to that decision. There is, of course, a question about the writer's objectivity—but Roger Street is certainly correct in pointing out that, prior to the decision of the House of Lords in *Street*, the Court of Appeal had developed a rule that, if A did not intend to grant B a lease, no lease would arise. The question is whether the House of Lords had good reason to depart from that rule.

As noted in Chapter 1, section 5.2, we can approach this question from the perspective of *doctrine*, or from the perspective of *utility*. The following extract argues that the House of Lords' approach in *Street v Mountford* can be justified only from the latter perspective.

Hill, 'Intention and the Creation of Proprietary Rights: Are Leases Different?'
[1996] LS 200

To what extent can the parties effectively deny proprietary effect to an interest which, in terms of its characteristics and in terms of the rights and obligations of the parties *inter se*, has the appearances of an interest to which the law grants proprietary consequences? To what extent can [A] grant to [B] an interest which has the substance of a proprietary interest but determine that the agreement is purely personal to the parties?

There is a group of authorities which suggest that an interest which has the substantive characteristics of a proprietary interest will, nevertheless, not be binding on a purchaser of the property to which the interest relates if there is a sufficient indication that the parties to the transaction which establishes the interest intended to create only personal rights. Perhaps the clearest authority is *IDC Group v Clark*, which concerns the boundary between easements and contractual licences. In this case [A] and [B] were the owners of adjoining buildings. By means of a formal document [A] granted [B] the right to make an opening in a party wall so as to create a fire escape from B's property. Subsequently C acquired a lease of A's property and B2 acquired the other building from B. When the fire escape was blocked off, B2 sought to enforce against C the right granted to B by A. B2 attempted to rely on the fact that the right being claimed was in the nature of an easement which was binding on A's successors in title. C, however, argued that because in the original transaction between A and B the parties had used the words 'grant licence' the right conferred on B was in the nature of a personal licence, the burden of which did not pass.

Although the right granted by A was capable of being the subject-matter of an easement, the Court of Appeal thought that, in view of the fact that 'the simple expression "grant licence" is not one which would have been used by a conveyancer of any experience as the means of creating an easement', the grantor 'intended to grant a licence properly so called and no more.'[27] the court held that the deed created only a personal licence, the burden of which was not binding on C [. . .]

[Hill then goes on to examine a number of other cases in which A's intention, expressed in an agreement with B, is effective to ensure that B's right, whilst matching the content of a particular legal or equitable property right, takes effect only as a personal right against A.]

The pattern of authorities supports the view that as a general rule the parties to an agreement may render personal rights which, in the normal course of events, would have proprietary consequences. An exception exists, however, with regard to leases. Can the exception be explained or justified?

[Hill then notes that, prior to *Street v Mountford*, the Court of Appeal had developed the rule that A's intention not to grant a lease could prevent B from acquiring a property right, even if the agreement between A and B gave B a right to exclusive possession for a term.]

[. . .] This is not to deny the validity of the courts' intervention in *Street v Mountford* or the desirability of the result achieved. The point is rather that the true rationale underlying the decision is to some extent obscured by Lord Templeman's assertion that 'the Rent Acts must not be allowed to alter or influence the construction of an agreement.'[28]

The context in which the distinction between leases and licences has been most relevant is the private sector of the housing market. In *Street v Mountford* the statement in the agreement between the parties that the occupier was a licensee rather than a tenant was not motivated by any desire to ensure that the occupier's interest would not be binding on any subsequent purchaser of the land; it was an attempt to avoid the statutory controls contained in the Rent Acts. In a market in which there is a severe shortage of residential accommodation for rent, the prospective occupier is in a very weak bargaining position vis-à-vis the owner. It is often the case that the prospective occupiers of residential property are desperate to find somewhere to live and have no knowledge of the scope of the protective legislation [. . .]

[T]he most honest approach to the lease/licence distinction would be for the courts to recognise more explicitly the basis of their intervention. Unless external factors suggest that the parties' expressed wished should be overridden, there is no reason why an agreement which confers exclusive possession for a term at a rent should not take effect as a licence if that is what the parties intend to create. Where a transaction is freely entered into on the basis of commercial considerations there is no justification for the law's disregard of the parties' intentions.

---

[27] *Per* Nourse LJ at 183–4.   [28] [1985] AC 809, [825].

> However, where there is inequality between the parties—as is the case in the private
> sector of the housing market—the law is entitled to look behind the form of the agreement
> [. . .] It is widely recognised that '[f]reedom of contract [. . .] is a particularly inappropriate
> model when dealing with the consumer as a contracting party.' Accordingly, it seems reason-
> able to look at the lease/licence distinction from the consumer law perspective rather than
> purely as an aspect of the law relating to real property.

Hill makes the very important point that, as shown by the decision of the Court of Appeal
in *IDC Group v Clark*,[29] there are other areas of land law in which A *is* permitted to give B a
personal right that matches the content of a recognized property right (such as an easement).
His argument is that the same general, doctrinal approach had been applied to leases by the
Court of Appeal, but that such an approach was inappropriate for dealing with the special
problems caused by residential occupation. So, in *Street v Mountford*, the House of Lords
created a special exception to that general approach, departing from doctrine to uphold a
policy of protecting vulnerable residential occupiers.

The next extract takes a different approach. It argues that there are sound doctrinal
reasons for treating leases as different from other forms of property right, such as easements.
On this view, the decision in *Street v Mountford* can be justified from a doctrinal perspective, as well as from a utility perspective.

McFarlane, The Structure of Property Law (2008, pp 661–2)

If the rights given by A to B entitle B to exclusive control of the land for a limited period then,
providing he satisfies the acquisition question, B will have a Lease. This is the case *even if
A did not intend to give B a Lease*. A's intention is of course crucial when we ask the first
question: what rights does the agreement give to B? However, A's intention is irrelevant
when we ask the second question: do the rights given to B amount to a Lease? There are
two points here. First, it is for the land law system, not A, to define a Lease. That point is
not specific to property law. For example, let's say A makes an oral promise to give B £100
in two weeks' time. A and B both call the promise "a contract" and intend it to be binding.
However, it does *not* give B a contractual right against A: no consideration has been provided by B. As the law's test for a contract has not been satisfied, A and B's intention to have
a contract is irrelevant.

The second point that it is simply not possible for A *both* to (i) give B a right to exclusive
control of a thing; and (ii) to deny that B has a property right. This point is specific to property
law. It shows that (i) *if* A gives B a right to exclusive control of a thing; *then* (ii) A's intention
to give B only a personal right is irrelevant. Of course, this does not mean A is trapped into
giving B a Lease. If A is keen to ensure that B does not acquire a Lease, A simply needs
to ensure that the rights he gives B under agreement do not amount to a right to exclusive
control.

We can draw an analogy with cooking. A can choose his own ingredients when cooking:
his intention is therefore crucial to what he produces. But if A chooses to (i) mix together
flour, eggs, sugar, butter and baking powder; and (ii) put the mixture in a tin and heat it in the
oven; then (iii) whether he likes it or not, A makes a cake. It does not matter that A intended to

---

[29] (1992) 65 P & CR 179.

make a casserole: he is judged by what he produces and he has produced a cake. If A wants to make a casserole, the solution is simple: he needs to choose the right ingredients.

[. . .] [The decision of the House of Lords in *Street v Mountford*] might seem to be an example of a court bending the rules to thwart A's unscrupulous attempt to avoid giving B the statutory protection available under the Rent Acts. However, the decision is perfectly correct as a matter of doctrine: it is conceptually impossible for A to give B a right to exclusive control for a limited period and then to claim that B has only a licence.

On the view taken in this extract, the decision of the House of Lords in *Street* returns to the traditional, doctrinal position that, if A's agreement with B gives B a right to exclusive possession, B can acquire a lease even if A does not intend to give B a property right. Indeed, on this view, it was the Court of Appeal, in cases prior to *Street*, which departed from doctrine in order to uphold a policy: a policy of *allowing* owners of land to escape the onerous statutory duties imposed by giving an occupier a lease.[30]

The decision in *Street* demonstrates that a lease can arise even if A did not intend to give B a property right in the land. Similarly, an agreement between A and B may use language indicating that a lease has been granted (e.g. referring to B as a tenant, and as to payments from B to A as rent), and yet limit the rights of B in such a way as to mean that B does not have a right to exclusive possession of the land; in such a case, notwithstanding the language in the agreement, B will not have a lease.[31]

2.2 INTENTION TO CREATE LEGAL RELATIONS

To have a lease, B must show he or she has been given a *right* to exclusive possession.[32] If A and B make an agreement allowing B to occupy A's land, but that agreement is not intended to be legally binding, then A has not given B such a right. This flows from the general rule of contract law: *'An agreement, though supported by consideration, is not binding as a contract if it was made without any intention of creating relations'.*[33] For example, in *Booker v Palmer*,[34] Mr Palmer agreed with a friend that an evacuee could occupy a cottage owned by Mr Palmer. The Court of Appeal found that the evacuee did not have a lease: the informal agreement, under which Mr Palmer received no rent, was not intended to create legal rights. Lord Greene MR stated:[35] *'There is one golden rule which is of very general application, namely, that the law does not impute intention to enter into legal relationships where the circumstances and the conduct of the parties negative any intention of the kind.'*

This requirement is entirely consistent with doctrine: it is a requirement for the creation of all contractual rights. As has been noted in other contexts, however, there is scope for the courts to manipulate that requirement:[36] so, if a court wishes to hold, for a particular policy reason, that B does not have a lease, it may then be inclined to find, as a matter of fact,

---

[30] Certainly, Lord Denning MR openly admitted that the Court of Appeal's approach was affected by the statutory regime: see *Cobb v Lane* [1952] 1 TLR 1037, [1041]; *Marcroft Wagons v Smith* [1051] 2 KB 496. See also *Marchant v Charters* [1977] 1 WLR 1181, 1184. See also Chapter 7, section 3.3.2.

[31] See e.g *Watts v Stewart* [2017] 2 WLR 1107, [39]–[40].

[32] See e.g *Watts v Stewart* [2017] 2 WLR 1107, [31], distinguishing between cases where B has a legal right of exclusive possession (a question of B's legal rights) and those where B instead has only exclusive occupation (a question of the position in practice).

[33] *Treitel's Law of Contract* (13th edn, ed Peel, 2011), [4–001].   [34] [1942] 2 All ER 674, CA.

[35] Ibid, p 676.   [36] See Hepple, 'Intention to Create Legal Relations' (1970) 28 CLJ 122.

that the agreement between A and B was not intended to create legal relations. Certainly, in *Street v Mountford*, Lord Templeman makes a very flexible use of the concept when attempting to explain the results of past cases in which B was found to have no lease.[37]

It is worth noting here that, provided the parties do intend to create legal relations, a lease can exist even if B has no duty to pay rent to A. As was noted in section 1.1, a long lease may be granted for a premium (a substantial one-off payment); and there seems to be no reason why a lease, like any other form of property right, cannot be granted by A to B for free. It is true that there are points in *Street v Mountford* where Lord Templeman refers to a lease as involving 'the grant of exclusive possession for a term at a rent.'[38] In that case, however, there was no issue as to whether rent was a requirement of a lease. Further, s 205(1)(xxvii) of the LPA 1925, defines a 'term of years absolute' (the phrase used to refer to a lease in s 1 of that Act) as a '*term of years (taking effect in possession or in reversion whether or not at a rent) … *'. As a result, in *Ashburn Anstalt v Arnold*,[39] the Court of Appeal confirmed that B's right may count as a lease even if B is under no duty to pay rent.

2.3 A RIGHT TO EXCLUSIVE POSSESSION: GENERAL POSITION

Where A and B's agreement does create contractual rights, it is necessary to see if its terms give B a right to exclusive possession of the land: in the absence of such a right, B cannot have a lease. As we have seen, in *Street v Mountford*, Lord Templeman was confident that the exclusive possession test would be simple to apply in residential cases.

Street v Mountford
[1985] UKHL 4, [1985] AC 809, HL

Lord Templeman

In the case of residential accommodation there is no difficulty in deciding whether the grant confers exclusive possession. An occupier of residential accommodation at a rent for a term is either a lodger or a tenant. The occupier is a lodger if the landlord provides attendance or services which require the landlord or his servants to exercise unrestricted access to and use of the premises. A lodger is entitled to live in the premises but cannot call the place his own.

As explained by Lord Templeman, a right to exclusive possession is synonymous with ownership for a limited period: at one point in *Street*, his Lordship states: '*The tenant possessing exclusive possession is able to exercise the rights of an owner of land, which is in the real sense his land albeit temporarily and subject to certain restrictions.*'[40]

As we noted in Chapter 5, section 3.2, this analysis supports the view of Harris[41] that the concept of ownership is vital to understanding the content of the two legal estates in

---

[37] For example, Bright, *Landlord and Tenant in Context* (2007) at p 69 notes that: '*In Street v Mountford Lord Templeman explained the finding of no tenancy in Marcroft Wagons [v Smith [1951] 2 KB 496, CA] as being due to the fact that the parties did not intend to contract at all*'.
[38] See [1985] 1 AC 809, [816].   [39] [1989] Ch 1.   [40] [1985] AC 809, [816].
[41] Harris, *Property and Justice* (1996) pp 72–3.

land permitted by s 1 of the LPA 1925: the freehold and the lease. According to Harris, a key aspect of any ownership interest is that it gives its holder an *open-ended* set of use privileges and control powers in relation to a resource.

As the following extract shows, that analysis seems to be reflected in the test for a lease: if the agreement between A and B gives B only a limited set of rights, then B cannot have a lease.[42]

Westminster City Council v Clarke
[1992] UKHL 11, [1992] 2 AC 288, HL

Facts: Westminster City Council owned the Cambridge Street Hostel, Cambridge Street, London. Mr Clarke occupied Room 133E. He was provided with that room under an agreement with the council. The agreement was headed 'Licence to occupy'. It stated that Mr Clarke was permitted '*to occupy in common with the council and any other persons to whom the same right is granted accommodation at the single persons hostel at 131–137, Cambridge Street, S.W.1 in the City of Westminster*'. The first clause of the agreement stated:

This licence does not give you and is not intended to give you any of the rights or to impose upon you any of the obligations of a tenant nor does it give you the right of exclusive occupation of any particular accommodation or room which may be allotted to you or which you may be allowed to use nor does it create the relationship of landlord and tenant. The accommodation allotted to you may be changed from time to time without notice as the council directs and you may be required to share such accommodation with any other person as required by the council.

Following complaints by other residents of the hostel, the council sought to remove Mr Clarke. Mr Clarke argued that his agreement gave him a lease, that he therefore had a secure tenancy under Part IV of the Housing Act 1985, and that the council could therefore only remove him if one of the grounds permitted by the Housing Act applied. Mr Clarke's argument failed at first instance, but was accepted by the Court of Appeal. The council then appealed successfully to the House of Lords, who found that Mr Clarke did not have a lease.

Lord Templeman

[...]

The council own a terrace of houses 131–137, Cambridge Street. The premises are used by the council as a hostel. There are 31 single rooms each with a bed and limited cooking facilities. There was originally a common room which has since been vandalised. The occupiers of the hostel are homeless single men, including men with personality disorders or physical disabilities, sometimes eccentric, sometimes frail, sometimes evicted from domestic accommodation or discharged from hospital or from prison. Experience has shown the possibility that the hostel may have to cope with an occupier who is suicidal or alcoholic or addicted to drugs. There is a warden supported by a resettlement team of social workers. The hope is that after a period of rehabilitation and supervision in the hostel, each occupier will be able to move on to permanent accommodation where he will be independent and

---

[42] See too *Hunts Refuse Disposals Ltd v Norfolk Environmental Waste Services Ltd* [1997] 1 EGLR 16, CA, *Watts v Stewart* [2017] 2 WLR 1107, [39]–[40].

look after himself. In the case of Mr. Clarke, the hostel was designed to be a halfway house for rehabilitation and treatment en route to an independent home.

[...]

The question is whether upon the true construction of the licence to occupy and in the circumstances in which Mr. Clarke was allowed to occupy room E, there was a grant by the council to Mr. Clarke of exclusive possession of room E.

From the point of view of the council the grant of exclusive possession would be inconsistent with the purposes for which the council provided the accommodation at Cambridge Street. It was in the interests of Mr. Clarke and each of the occupiers of the hostel that the council should retain possession of each room. If one room became uninhabitable another room could be shared between two occupiers. If one room became unsuitable for an occupier he could be moved elsewhere. If the occupier of one room became a nuisance he could be compelled to move to another room where his actions might be less troublesome to his neighbours. If the occupier of a room had exclusive possession he could prevent the council from entering the room save for the purpose of protecting the council's interests and not for the purpose of supervising and controlling the conduct of the occupier in his interests. If the occupier of a room had exclusive possession he could not be obliged to comply with the terms and the conditions of occupation. Mr. Clarke could not, for example, be obliged to comply with the directions of the warden or to exclude visitors or to comply with any of the other conditions of occupation which are designed to help Mr. Clarke and the other occupiers of the hostel and to enable the hostel to be conducted in an efficient and harmonious manner. The only remedy of the council for breaches of the conditions of occupation would be the lengthy and uncertain procedure required by the [Housing Act 1985] to be operated for the purpose of obtaining possession from a secure tenant. In the circumstances of the present case I consider that the council legitimately and effectively retained for themselves possession of room E and that Mr. Clarke was only a licensee with rights corresponding to the rights of a lodger. In reaching this conclusion I take into account the object of the council, namely the provision of accommodation for vulnerable homeless persons, the necessity for the council to retain possession of all the rooms in order to make and administer arrangements for the suitable accommodation of all the occupiers and the need for the council to retain possession of every room not only in the interests of the council as the owners of the terrace but also for the purpose of providing for the occupiers supervision and assistance. For many obvious reasons it was highly undesirable for the council to grant to any occupier of a room exclusive possession which obstructed the use by the council of all the rooms of the hostel in the interests of every occupier. By the terms of the licence to occupy Mr. Clarke was not entitled to any particular room, he could be required to share with any other person as required by the council and he was only entitled to "occupy accommodation in common with the council whose representative may enter the accommodation at any time." It is accepted that these provisions of the licence to occupy were inserted to enable the council to discharge its responsibilities to the vulnerable persons accommodated at the Cambridge Street terrace and were not inserted for the purpose of enabling the council to avoid the creation of a secure tenancy. The conditions of occupancy support the view that Mr. Clarke was not in exclusive occupation of room E. He was expressly limited in his enjoyment of any accommodation provided for him. He was forbidden to entertain visitors without the approval of the council staff and was bound to comply with the council's warden or other staff in charge of the hostel. These limitations confirmed that the council retained possession of all the rooms of the hostel in order to supervise and control the activities of the occupiers, including Mr. Clarke. Although Mr. Clarke physically occupied room E he did not enjoy possession exclusively of the council.

> This is a very special case which depends on the peculiar nature of the hostel maintained by the council, the use of the hostel by the council, the totality, immediacy, and objectives of the powers exercisable by the council and the restrictions imposed on Mr. Clarke. The decision in this case will not allow a landlord, private or public, to free himself from the Rent Acts or from the restrictions of a secure tenancy merely by adopting or adapting the language of the licence to occupy. The provisions of the licence to occupy and the circumstances in which that licence was granted and continued lead to the conclusion that Mr. Clarke has never enjoyed that exclusive possession which he claims. I would therefore allow the appeal and restore the order for possession made by the trial judge.

The decision in *Westminster City Council* provides an interesting contrast with that in *Street v Mountford*, not least because, in each case, Lord Templeman provided the only reasoned speech. Again, there is a question of whether the decision is best viewed from the perspective of doctrine or utility. From the latter point of view, there is no doubt that the different context of *Westminster City Council* may have influenced their Lordships: there certainly seems to be more sympathy for the objectives of the council than for those of Mr Street. But there is also an important doctrinal difference between the two cases: in *Street v Mountford*, Mr Street (as he admits in the extract in section 2.1) quite readily gave Mrs Mountford a right to exclusive possession; in contrast, in *Westminster City Council*, the council was careful *not* to give Mr Clarke such a right. The contextual factors identified by Lord Templeman explain *why* the council chose not to give Mr Clarke a right to exclusive possession—but from a doctrinal perspective, the only relevant point is the fact that no such right was granted.

2.4 A RIGHT TO EXCLUSIVE POSSESSION: SHAMS AND PRETENCES

The comparison between *Street v Mountford*, on the one hand, and *Westminster City Council v Clarke*, on the other, gives rise to a further question: if a party such as Mr Street wishes to avoid granting an occupier a lease, can he simply insert a term in the agreement that denies the occupier a right to exclusive possession? The first point to remember, noted in section 1.2.1, is that a private landlord no longer has any real need to avoid granting a lease: he can simply grant an 'assured shorthold tenancy'—that is, a form of lease that gives the tenant only trifling statutory protection.

Under the previous statutory regimes, however, private landlords did, indeed, react to *Street* by inserting terms for the purpose of denying an occupier exclusive possession. As the next extract shows, that tactic was not always successful: in some cases, courts showed themselves to be willing, when asking if the agreement gave B a right to exclusive possession, to disregard particular terms inserted with the purpose of denying B such a right.

AG Securities v Vaughan and ors; Antoniades v Villiers and anor
[1988] UKHL 8, [1990] 1 AC 417, HL

Facts: Two separate appeals were heard together by the House of Lords. In the first case, AG Securities (an unlimited company) had a long lease of a flat: No 25 Linden Mansions, Hornsey Lane, London. That flat had four bedrooms, as well as communal areas, and it was rented out to four occupiers: Nigel Vaughan and three others. The four had not moved in as a group: each moved in as and when a former occupier left and a room became available. Mr Vaughan had arrived in 1982; two of the other occupiers, in 1984; the fourth occupier, in 1985. In May 1985, AG Securities attempted to terminate the occupation of the four. The four claimed that, acting together, they jointly held a lease, arising from the terms of their agreements with AG Securities, and therefore qualified for statutory protection. AG Securities sought a declaration that the occupiers each had an individual licence. The first instance judge granted that declaration, but the Court of Appeal (Sir George Waller dissenting) held that the occupiers, acting jointly, had a lease. The House of Lords upheld AG Securities' appeal, holding that the occupiers were, indeed, licensees.

In the second case, Mr Antoniades had a long lease of the top flat at No 6, Whiteley Road, Upper Norwood, London. That flat had a bedroom, a room described as a bed–sitting room, a kitchen, and a bathroom. It was rented out to two occupiers: Mr Villiers and Miss Bridger. They were a couple and moved in together, signing separate, but identical, agreements with Mr Antoniades on the same day: 9 February 1985. Each agreement contained a term (Clause 16) stating that: '*The licensor shall be entitled at any time to use the rooms together with the licensee and permit other persons to use all of the rooms together with the licensee.*' In 1986, Mr Antoniades claimed possession of the flat. The occupiers claimed that, acting jointly, they had a lease, arising as a result of their agreements with Mr Antoniades. If they were found to have a lease, they would qualify for statutory protection and Mr Antoniades' power to remove them would be limited by statute. The first instance judge found that the occupiers did have a lease, but the Court of Appeal held that they were licensees and so allowed Mr Antoniades' appeal. The House of Lords took a different view, restoring the order of the first instance judge, and holding that Mr Villiers and Miss Bridger, acting together, had a lease.

Lord Templeman

Parties to an agreement cannot contract out of the Rent Acts; if they were able to do so the Acts would be a dead letter because in a state of housing shortage a person seeking residential accommodation may agree to anything to obtain shelter. The Rent Acts protect a tenant but they do not protect a licensee. Since parties to an agreement cannot contract out of the Rent Acts, a document which expresses the intention, genuine or bogus, of both parties or of one party to create a licence will nevertheless create a tenancy if the rights and obligations enjoyed and imposed satisfy the legal requirements of a tenancy. A person seeking residential accommodation may concur in any expression of intention in order to obtain shelter ... Since parties to an agreement cannot contract out of the Rent Acts, the grant of a tenancy to two persons jointly cannot be concealed, accidentally or by design, by the creation of two documents in the form of licences. Two persons seeking residential accommodation may sign any number of documents in order to obtain joint shelter. In considering one or more documents for the purpose of deciding whether a tenancy has been created, the court must consider the surrounding circumstances including any relationship between the prospective occupiers, the course of negotiations and the nature and extent of the accommodation and the intended and actual mode of occupation of the accommodation. If the owner of a one-bedroomed flat granted a licence to a husband to occupy the flat provided he shared the flat with his wife and nobody else and granted a similar licence to the wife provided she shared the flat with the husband and nobody else, the court would be bound to consider the effect of both documents together. If the licence to the husband required him to pay a licence fee of £50 per month and the licence to the wife required her to pay a further licence fee of £50 per month, the two documents read together in the light of the property to be occupied and the obvious intended mode of occupation would confer exclusive occupation on the husband and wife jointly and a tenancy at the rent of £100.

Landlords dislike the Rent Acts and wish to enjoy the benefits of letting property without the burden of the restrictions imposed by the Acts. Landlords believe that the Rent Acts unfairly interfere with freedom of contract and exacerbate the housing shortage. Tenants on the other hand believe that the Acts are a necessary protection against the exploitation of people who do not own the freehold or long leases of their homes. The court lacks the knowledge and the power to form any judgment on these arguments which fall to be considered and determined by Parliament. The duty of the court is to enforce the Acts and in so doing to observe one principle which is inherent in the Acts and has been long recognised, the principle that parties cannot contract out of the Acts [. . .]

Where residential accommodation is occupied by two or more persons the occupiers may be licensees or tenants of the whole or each occupier may be a separate tenant of part. In the present appeals the only question raised is whether the occupiers are licensees or tenants of the whole [. . .]

[In *AG Securities v Vaughan*, the Court of Appeal] concluded that the four [occupiers] were jointly entitled to exclusive occupation of the flat. I am unable to agree. If a landlord who owns a three-bedroom flat enters into three separate independent tenancies with three independent tenants each of whom is entitled to one bedroom and to share the common parts, then the three tenants, if they agree, can exclude anyone else from the flat. But they do not enjoy exclusive occupation of the flat jointly under the terms of their tenancies. In the present case, if the four [occupiers] had been jointly entitled to exclusive occupation of the flat then, on the death of one of [the occupiers], the remaining three would be entitled to joint and exclusive occupation. But, in fact, on the death of one [occupier] the remaining three would not be entitled to joint and exclusive occupation of the flat. They could not exclude a fourth person nominated by the company. I would allow the appeal.

In the first appeal the four agreements were independent of one another. In the second appeal [*Antoniades v Villiers*] the two agreements were interdependent. Both would have been signed or neither. The two agreements must therefore be read together. Mr. Villiers and Miss Bridger applied to rent the flat jointly and sought and enjoyed joint and exclusive occupation of the whole of the flat. They shared the rights and the obligations imposed by the terms of their occupation. They acquired joint and exclusive occupation of the flat in consideration of periodical payments and they therefore acquired a tenancy jointly. Mr. Antoniades required each of them, Mr. Villiers and Miss Bridger, to agree to pay one half of each aggregate periodical payment, but this circumstance cannot convert a tenancy into a licence. A tenancy remains a tenancy even though the landlord may choose to require each of two joint tenants to agree expressly to pay one half of the rent. The tenancy conferred on Mr. Villiers and Miss Bridger the right to occupy the whole flat as their dwelling. Clause 16 reserved to Mr. Antoniades the power at any time to go into occupation of the flat jointly with Mr. Villiers and Miss Bridger. The exercise of that power would at common law put an end to the exclusive occupation of the flat by Mr. Villiers and Miss Bridger, terminate the tenancy of Mr. Villiers and Miss Bridger, and convert Mr. Villiers and Miss Bridges into licensees. But the powers reserved to Mr. Antoniades by clause 16 cannot be lawfully exercised because they are inconsistent with the provisions of the Rent Acts [. . .]

Clause 16 is a reservation to Mr. Antoniades of the right to go into occupation or to nominate others to enjoy occupation of the whole of the flat jointly with Mr. Villiers and Miss

Bridger. Until that power is exercised Mr. Villiers and Miss Bridger are jointly in exclusive occupation of the whole of the flat making periodical payments and they are therefore tenants. The Rent Acts prevent the exercise of a power which would destroy the tenancy of Mr. Villiers and Miss Bridger and would deprive them of the exclusive occupation of the flat which they are now enjoying. Clause 16 is inconsistent with the provisions of the Rent Acts.

There is a separate and alternative reason why clause 16 must be ignored. Clause 16 was not a genuine reservation to Mr. Antoniades of a power to share the flat and a power to authorise other persons to share the flat. Mr. Antoniades did not genuinely intend to exercise the powers save possibly to bring pressure to bear to obtain possession. Clause 16 was only intended to deprive Mr. Villiers and Miss Bridger of the protection of the Rent Acts. Mr. Villiers and Miss Bridger had no choice in the matter.

In the notes of [the first instance judge], Mr. Villiers is reported as saying that: 'He [Mr. Antoniades] kept going on about it being a licence and not in the Rent Act. I didn't know either but was pleased to have a place after three or four months of chasing.' The notes of Miss Bridger's evidence include this passage: 'I didn't understand what was meant by exclusive possession or licence. Signed because so glad to move in. Had been looking for three months.'

In *Street v. Mountford*, I said:

> 'Although the Rent Acts must not be allowed to alter or influence the construction of an agreement, the court should, in my opinion, be astute to detect and frustrate sham devices and artificial transactions whose only object is to disguise the grant of a tenancy and to evade the Rent Acts.'[43]

It would have been more accurate and less liable to give rise to misunderstandings if I had substituted the word 'pretence' for the references to 'sham devices' and 'artificial transactions.' *Street v. Mountford* was not a case which involved a pretence concerning exclusive possession. The agreement did not mention exclusive possession and the owner conceded that the occupier enjoyed exclusive possession. In *Somma v. Hazelhurst*[44] and other cases considered in *Street v. Mountford*, the owner wished to let residential accommodation but to avoid the Rent Acts. The occupiers wished to take a letting of residential accommodation. The owner stipulated for the execution of agreements which pretended that exclusive possession was not to be enjoyed by the occupiers. The occupiers were obliged to acquiesce with this pretence in order to obtain the accommodation. In my opinion the occupiers either did not understand the language of the agreements or assumed, justifiably, that in practice the owner would not violate their privacy. The owner's real intention was to rely on the language of the agreement to escape the Rent Acts. The owner allowed the occupiers to enjoy jointly exclusive occupation and accepted rent. A tenancy was created. *Street v. Mountford* reasserted three principles. First, parties to an agreement cannot contract out of the Rent Acts. Secondly, in the absence of special circumstances, not here relevant, the enjoyment of exclusive occupation for a term in consideration of periodic payments creates a tenancy. Thirdly, where the language of licence contradicts the reality of lease, the facts must prevail. The facts must prevail over the language in order that the parties may not contract out of the Rent Acts. In the present case clause 16 was a pretence.

The fact that clause 16 was a pretence appears from its terms and from the negotiations. Clause 16 in terms conferred on Mr. Antoniades and other persons the right to share the bedroom occupied by Mr. Villiers and Miss Bridger. Clause 16 conferred power on Mr. Antoniades to convert the sitting-room occupied by Mr. Villiers and Miss Bridger into a bedroom which could be jointly occupied by Mr. Villiers, Miss Bridger, Mr. Antoniades and any person or

---

[43] [1985] AC 809, [825].   [44] [1978] 1 WLR 1014.

persons nominated by Mr. Antoniades. The facilities in the flat were not suitable for sharing between strangers. The flat, situated in an attic with a sloping roof, was too small for sharing between strangers. If clause 16 had been genuine there would have been some discussion between Mr. Antoniades, Mr. Villiers and Miss Bridger as to how clause 16 might be operated in practice and in whose favour it was likely to be operated. The addendum imposed on Mr. Villiers and Miss Bridger sought to add plausibility to the pretence of sharing by forfeiting the right of Mr. Villiers and Miss Bridger to continue to occupy the flat if their double-bedded romance blossomed into wedding bells. Finally and significantly, Mr. Antoniades never made any attempt to obtain increased income from the flat by exercising the powers which clause 16 purported to reserve to him. Clause 16 was only designed to disguise the grant of a tenancy and to contract out of the Rent Acts. In this case in the Court of Appeal Bingham L.J. said:

> 'The written agreements cannot possibly be construed as giving the occupants, jointly or severally, exclusive possession of the flat or any part of it. They stipulate with reiterated emphasis that the occupants shall not have exclusive possession.'[45]

My Lords, in *Street v. Mountford*, this House stipulated with reiterated emphasis that an express statement of intention is not decisive and that the court must pay attention to the facts and surrounding circumstances and to what people do as well as to what people say.

My Lords, in each of the cases which were disapproved by this House in *Street v. Mountford* and in the second appeal now under consideration, there was, in my opinion, the grant of a joint tenancy for the following reasons. (1) The applicants for the flat applied to rent the flat jointly and to enjoy exclusive occupation. (2) The landlord allowed the applicants jointly to enjoy exclusive occupation and accepted rent. A tenancy was created. (3) The power reserved to the landlord to deprive the applicants of exclusive occupation was inconsistent with the provisions of the Rent Acts. (4) Moreover in all the circumstances the power which the landlord insisted upon to deprive the applicants of exclusive occupation was a pretence only intended to deprive the applicants of the protection of the Rent Acts.

Each of *AG Securities v Vaughan* and *Antoniades v Villiers* raises questions about how multiple occupiers of land can claim a lease. We will examine that issue in detail in section 2.5. For present purposes, we can focus on the appeal in *Antoniades* and the decision that the agreement created a lease even though the clear effect of Clause 16 was to deny the occupiers a right to exclusive possession.

The decision of the House of Lords can only be justified if it is permissible, when deciding if B (or B1 and B2) has a right to exclusive possession, to *disregard* particular contractual terms. In examining this question, we again have to consider both the doctrinal perspective and the utility approach.

From a doctrinal perspective, it is clear that an apparent contractual term can be disregarded if it is not, in fact, contractually binding. One well-established example occurs if an apparent contractual term is a 'sham' (a term used by Lord Templeman in *Street v Mountford* when referring to 'sham devices').[46] Diplock LJ provided the commonly used definition of a sham, in the contractual context at least, in the following case.[47]

---

45 [1988] 3 WLR 139, [148].   46 [1985] AC 809, [825].

47 The reference to documents cannot mean that either all of a document is sham, or none of it: see *Hitch v Stone* [2001] STC 214. Rather, each apparent term within a document must be seen as a relevant 'act', and will only be valid if accompanied by the necessary intention that the term should genuinely create contractual rights.

Snook v London and West Ridings Investments Ltd
[1967] 2 QB 786, CA

Diplock LJ

At 802

If it has any legal meaning, the term 'sham' means acts done or documents executed by the parties to the 'sham' which are intended by them to give to third parties or to the court the appearance of creating between the parties legal rights and obligations different from the actual legal rights and obligations (if any) which the parties intended to create [. . .] for acts or documents to be a 'sham', with whatever legal consequences follow from this, all the parties thereto must have a common intention that the acts or documents are not to create the legal rights and obligations which they give the appearance of creating. No unexpressed intentions of a 'shammer' affect the rights of a party whom he deceived.

As is made clear by that definition, a term can only be dismissed as a sham if *neither* party intends that the term should create genuine legal rights. One example occurs if A sells a painting to B for £10,000, but, to minimize her tax bill, persuades B to sign a contract of sale recording the price as £100. In such a case, each party intends that B should be under a legal duty to pay £10,000; neither party intends that B's duty is to pay only £100. The written 'contract' is therefore of no legal effect: it is a sham as it is not genuinely intended to create legal rights.

It is clear that this model is of very little use in a case such as *Antoniades v Villiers*. In that case, it was abundantly clear that Mr Antoniades *did* intend for Clause 16 to create genuine legal rights: the whole point of the clause was to ensure that the occupiers did not have a right to exclusive possession. It is therefore no surprise that, in *Antoniades*, Lord Templeman did not base his decision on the sham concept; instead, his Lordship based his decision to disregard the sharing clause (Clause 16) on two separate grounds. As suggested in the extract below, those grounds are not free from difficulty.

McFarlane and Simpson, 'Tackling Avoidance' in *Rationalizing Property, Equity and Trusts: Essays in Honour of Edward Burn* (ed Getzler, 2003)

At 151–2

Lord Templeman provides two grounds for denying effect to the sharing clause. First, it was said that Mr Antoniades could never insert others into occupation as [the Rent Acts prevent him from exercising his power to do so]. This reasoning cannot be supported, as it assumes the very thing it purports to prove. The Rent Acts can only apply if the occupiers are lessees, which will only be the case if they have a right to exclusive possession. As the Rent Acts can therefore only apply if the sharing clause, which seems to deny such a right to exclusive possession, is found to be invalid, those Acts cannot also be the means by which such invalidity is proved [. . .]

Secondly, Lord Templeman held that the clause was [. . .] "a pretence [. . .] only designed to disguise the grant of a tenancy and to contract out of the Rent Acts". This reasoning is crucial as it aims to provide a means, independent of the Rent Acts, to render the sharing clause ineffective. It also seems clear that Lord Templeman contemplates going beyond the sham doctrine, as conventionally understood. First, his Lordship prefers to condemn the clause as a "pretence", rather than as a "sham device or artificial transaction." Whilst the concepts of pretence and sham had been used interchangeably in the past, Lord Templeman's explicit preference for the former term does suggest that it involves the adoption of a new means by which a clause may be rendered ineffective. Certainly, Lord Templeman's application of the concept of pretence in *Villiers* goes beyond [. . .] the orthodox 'sham test'.

At 157–8

[. . .] [A suggested justification for the 'pretence' test is that] terms can be disregarded where they are inserted for the purpose of avoiding the Rent Acts by denying a right to exclusive possession. It is true that, at a number of points in his judgment in *Villiers*, Lord Templeman emphasises that this was the owner's aim in including clause 16 in the written agreement [. . .] Nonetheless, the courts have repeatedly rejected any suggestion that they have a general, non-statutory power to disregard agreed terms simply because those terms have been agreed in order to avoid a particular characterisation of the parties' dealings. Any number of examples can be given.

First, the courts have frequently had to consider situations in which parties have, for various reasons, chosen to set up a hire-purchase transaction rather than a simple loan on the security of goods. As long as the parties have genuinely intended to create the legal rights characteristic of hire-purchase, then, even if the only reason for preferring that mechanism has been the desire to avoid creating a secured loan, the agreement will be taken at face-value by the court.[48] The validity of this approach has been upheld in cases dealing with attempts to avoid the very legislation considered in *Antoniades v Villiers*. In *Kaye v Massbetter*,[49] an owner insisted that a tenancy agreement be made with a company created for that purpose, rather than with the individual who was to occupy the property. The only reason for doing so was to avoid the Rent Acts, which do not protect company tenants, yet this device was upheld by the Court of Appeal.

From a doctrinal perspective, then, it seems that the 'pretence' test, if it amounts to disregarding terms inserted for the *purpose* of denying an occupier exclusive possession, cannot be justified. After all, if A simply decides not to grant B exclusive possession, he is perfectly free to do so. In *Antoniades v Villiers* itself, it may nonetheless be possible to reconcile the decision of the House of Lords with doctrine. It can perhaps be explained on a standard contractual principle: a term is only binding on B if A reasonably believes that B is agreeing to be bound by that term.[50] Usually, of course, B's signature of a written document ensures that it *is* reasonable for A to believe that B is agreeing to be bound by all of the terms set out in the document. But if the surrounding factual circumstances serve to make a term as set out in the document wholly implausible, it may just be possible for B to argue that such a term is not binding.

The difficulty with this attempt to exclude the pretence test, however, is that the Court of Appeal adopted that test in cases following *Antoniades*. One example is provided by the

---

[48] See *Helby v Matthews* [1895] AC 471, [475]; *Re George Inglefield Ltd* [1933] Ch 1, *per* Romer LJ; *Yorkshire Railway Co v Maclure* (1882) 21 Ch D 309, *per* Lindley LJ.

[49] [1991] 2 EGLR 97.

[50] This seems to be the approach adopted by Lord Oliver in *Antoniades v Villiers*: see [1990] 1 AC 417, [469].

combined judgment of the Court of Appeal in the cases of *Aslan v Murphy (Nos 1 & 2)* and *Duke v Wynne*.[51] In each case, occupation of residential premises occurred under an agreement that permitted A to share occupation, or to insert other occupiers. In *Aslan*, the agreement also included a term that '*the licensor licenses the licensee to use (but not exclusively) all the furnished room* [...] *on each day between the hours of midnight and 10.30am and between noon and midnight, but at no other times*'. In *Aslan*, B occupied a small basement room in Redcliffe Gardens, London.

In *Duke*, B1 and B2, a married couple, occupied a three-bedroom house in Dunkeld Road, South Norwood, along with their two young sons. The Court of Appeal found that, in each case, a lease had been granted. Lord Donaldson MR, referring to the concept of a pretence, regarded it as important that, in each case, A had not, in practice, attempted to exercise his rights to share occupation, or, in *Aslan*, to remove B from the land between 10.30 a.m. and noon.

Such decisions can only be seen as doctrinally justified if it is possible to find a rationale for the wider pretence test. One such rationale is proposed in the following extract.

Bright, 'Avoiding Tenancy Legislation: Sham and Contracting Out Revisited' [2002] CLJ 146

At 152–3

In practice, the need for a common intention and for a whole transaction to be a sham limits the usefulness of the doctrine. There could not, for example, have been a sham in this strict sense in *Antoniades v. Villiers* where a couple were asked to sign separate licence agreements containing a provision, clause 16, which stated that the "licensor shall be entitled at any time to use the rooms together with the licensee and permit other persons to use all of the rooms together with the licensee [. . .]" Given the size and layout of the accommodation, and the relationship between the couple, it was obvious that the "licensor" would not exercise this right. In holding the couple to have a tenancy and not separate licences, the House of Lords used a variety of language to explain why clause 16 should not be given its face value. Only Lord Oliver spoke of sham [. . .] In moving away from the language of sham to pretence there is the chance to introduce greater flexibility. Essentially, pretence will be found where there is no genuine intention to implement the agreement as it stands. This can also be said of sham, but there are not the same constraints about the need for a common intention and for the whole document to be a lie. Lord Donaldson M.R. clearly saw the two concepts operating differently in *Aslan*:

'[. . .] parties may succumb to the temptation to agree to pretend to have particular rights and duties which are not in fact any part of the true bargain [. . .] [The] courts would be acting unrealistically if they did not keep a weather eye open for pretences, taking due account of how the parties have acted in performance of their apparent bargain. This identification and exposure of such pretences does not necessarily lead to the conclusion that their agreement is a sham, but only to the conclusion that the terms of the true bargain are not wholly the same as that of the bargain appearing on the face of the agreement.'

Throughout the speeches in *Antoniades* it is clear that the reason why the licences were found to be non-genuine was because there was never any intention to rely on clause 16.

---

[51] [1990] 1 WLR 766.

Had they been applying the *Snook* concept of sham the House of Lords would have had to find a mutuality of intention to mislead, but there is no discussion in the speeches of whether both parties intended for clause 16 not to operate, nor was there a third party that they intended to mislead. Nor did it matter that the focus was on two aspects of the transaction rather than the transaction as a whole. The essence of pretence is that the agreement is a smokescreen. It is not sufficient to strike down a device on the grounds that it was intended or designed for the sole purpose of avoiding protective legislation, even if there is no other purpose served by it. As with sham, motive is irrelevant. It does not matter that the only reason why a particular route, however tortuous, is selected is to avoid statutory provisions: the test is simply one of whether or not the device is seriously intended. The transaction must be taken at face value unless it is shown that it was not genuine in the sense that the parties never intended to rely on that device.

At 157–9

Much of value was lost when the dicta of Diplock L.J. in *Snook* became hardened law and it is clear that in *AG Securities* the House of Lords, and Lord Templeman in particular, was seeking to break away from these confines. Both sham and pretence are to do with the same thing, that is, to enable the true nature of a transaction to be revealed. The case law, although rather thin on this, does support a more sophisticated account of sham than is usually given and which accords better with "legal principle and morality". Whatever it is called, this refined doctrine of sham would be able to subsume within it the doctrine of pretence.

Where it is found that documents entered into give the appearance of creating legal rights and obligations between the parties that are not genuine, in the sense that there is no intention of honouring these obligations or enjoying the rights, then:

1. where there is a common intention to deceive, that document will be void as between those parties. It is this automatic consequence of voidness, and possible impact upon third parties, that accounts for the reluctance of courts to find a sham and the need for very clear evidence that the provisions are not genuine. If an innocent third party has relied upon the form of the document, the parties may be estopped from setting up the invalidity of the documents

2. where only one of the parties intended to deceive or inserted provisions which he had no intention of honouring and the other party was ignorant of this (or did not 'know or care') or simply went along with it through absence of choice, the party with the deceitful (non-genuine) intent:

   (i) will not be allowed to take advantage of the formal appearance of rights to the disadvantage of an 'innocent' party. This means that a person innocent of the sham will be allowed to rely upon external evidence to prove that the formal agreement is a sham/non-genuine. Similarly, when applied to the residential tenancy cases, the occupier is allowed to prove that the 'licensor' never had any intention of relying upon clauses which prevent a tenancy arising, as, for example, with the 'sharing clause' in *AG Securities* or the clause requiring a daily 90 minute departure in *Aslan*. As Lord Donaldson M.R. said in *Aslan*, it 'is the true rather than the apparent bargain which determines the question: tenant or lodger?'

   (ii) will not be allowed to set aside the formal document by proving it is a sham and thereby rely on the real/true agreement if an innocent person has relied upon the formal agreement. *Snook* [is an example] [. . .] the court held that there was no sham because there was no common intention to deceive but the effect was the same as saying that the 'shammer' could not set aside the sham document to the detriment of the innocent party.

Bright's argument here is that the pretence test is *not* a special feature of the law of leases, developed to ensure that statutory protection is available to deserving or vulnerable occupiers. Bright instead argued that the pretence test is a logical corollary of the sham test and, indeed, can be subsumed within it.[52] On this view, cases such as *Antoniades* and *Aslan* are simply applying standard contractual principles. The validity of that view therefore depends on a more general question about contract law: is it the case that, for a term to be contractually binding, the parties must intend *not only* that the term should create legal rights, *but also* that the term will be enforced in practice?[53]

Whatever the answer to that question,[54] it may still be possible to justify the pretence test from the perspective of utility rather than doctrine.[55] For example, in section 2.1, we saw Hill's suggestion that policy, rather than doctrine, can justify the decision in *Street v Mountford* that a lease can be created even when A does not intend to give B a property right. In that article, Hill suggests:[56] '*The drafting of a residential agreement as a licence rather than a lease is analogous to the inclusion of an unfair contractual term in a consumer sale.*' On this view, the pretence doctrine is simply a means to an end: it gives judges the power (usually only given by statutes such as the Unfair Contract Terms Act 1977) to disregard terms that, whilst notionally agreed, have been forced on a reluctant occupier. Certainly, as noted by Hill, Lord Templeman did refer in *Antoniades* to the fact that '*a person seeking residential accommodation may concur in any expression of intention [. . .] [and] may sign a document couched in any language in order to obtain shelter*'.[57]

This analysis raises an important point about the utility approach: one that we encountered in Chapter 1, section 5.2. There, we saw Harris's observation that a choice as to whether the doctrinal or utility approach is to be preferred may depend on one's view as to the proper role of judges. For example, it may be plausible to take the view that whilst it is important, in a case such as *Antoniades*, to protect an occupier and to ensure that the relevant statutory protection applies, it is not for judges to take on the power to disregard terms that, according to the usual doctrinal tests, are contractually binding. On that view, it is for Parliament to

---

[52] Note that Bright, Glover, and Prassl, in 'Tenancy Agreements' in *Sham Transactions* (eds Simpson and Stewart, Oxford: OUP, 2013) ch 6, adopt a different view, arguing at 6.35 that there is a pressing doctrinal problem in using the parties' post-contractual conduct as a relevant factor in the interpretation of their agreement.

[53] For a view that a contractual term may, in general, bind even if the parties did not intend to enforce it in practice, see McFarlane and Simpson, 'Tackling Avoidance' in *Rationalizing Property, Equity and Trusts: Essays in Honour of Edward Burn* (ed Getzler, 2003) pp 160–3 and McFarlane, *The Structure of Property Law* (2008) p 665. Note too that Bright, Glover, and Prassl 'Tenancy Agreements' in *Sham Transactions* (eds Simpson and Stewart) ch 6, at 6.57 conclude, contrary to the argument of Bright in the extract above, that the courts' approach in the pretence cases is inconsistent with standard contractual doctrine.

[54] In *Ker v Optima Community Association* [2013] EWCA Civ 579, the Court of Appeal rejected B's attempt to invoke *Antoniades* as, *per* Patten LJ at [45]–[46]: '*it is impossible to deduce from the terms in which the scheme was promoted any intention on the part of [A] or [B] to contract other than on the terms of the agreements which they entered into [. . .] Even if one makes the assessment by looking at subsequent events, there is nothing to show that the contractual conditions were other than as recorded in the two [written] contracts.*' This approach seems to focus on the question of whether there is any evidence that the terms of the written contract were not in fact intended to represent the actual legal rights of the parties.

[55] For example, as we will see in Chapter 20, section 3, McFarlane and Simpson suggest that the approach in *Antoniades* may be justified as a matter of statutory interpretation, if it can be said that Parliament intended the statutory protection to apply not only to parties with a legal right to exclusive possession, but also to parties who, in practice, enjoyed exclusive possession of land for a term: McFarlane and Simpson, 'Tackling Avoidance' in *Rationalizing Property, Equity and Trusts: Essays in Honour of Edward Burn* (ed Getzler, 2003) pp 175–8.

[56] (1996) 16 LS 200, 217.   [57] [1990] 1 AC 417, [458].

make a change to the law: for example, by extending the statutory protection beyond those with leases to parties who occupy their home under a contractual licence. Indeed, as we will see in Chapter 20, section 5, the Law Commission has suggested just that change, and it has been put into practice in the Renting Homes (Wales) Act 2016: the remaining statutory protection (of course, now much diminished in the private rental sector) should not be limited to tenants, but should also be extended to licensees occupying land as their home.

2.5 A RIGHT TO EXCLUSIVE POSSESSION: MULTIPLE OCCUPANCY

In each of *AG Securities* and *Antoniades*, more than one person occupied land. In such a case, it could, in theory, be possible for each occupier to claim a right to exclusive possession of a *particular part* of the land (e.g. of a particular room in a flat). But the occupiers did not pursue that argument in either case; instead, it was argued (unsuccessfully in *AG Securities*, but successfully in *Antoniades*) that the occupiers, seen as a unit, had a single right to exclusive possession to the whole of the land. This is a claim to co-ownership of the land: a claim that the individual occupiers, acting as a team, held a single legal estate. We examined co-ownership in Chapter 13, in section 2 of which we saw that there are two possible forms of co-ownership: the joint tenancy and the tenancy in common. In each case, there is 'unity of possession' amongst the co-owners: each is prima facie entitled to occupy all of the land. In a tenancy in common, unlike a joint tenancy, each co-owner also has an 'undivided share': a right to a particular, individual share of the benefits of the co-owned land. We also saw there that, due to s 1(6) of the LPA 1925, it is impossible for a legal estate (such as a legal lease) to be held by tenants in common: in such a case, the only permitted form of co-ownership is a joint tenancy. So, what happens if A transfers a freehold to B1 and B2, stating that B1 is to have a 40 per cent share and B2 is to have a 60 per cent share? Despite the parties' intentions, B1 and B2 hold the legal freehold as joint tenants (without an individual share). But, under s 34(2) of the 1925 Act, a trust is imposed: B1 and B2 hold that legal freehold as joint tenants, but each also has an individual share to the benefit of that legal right, arising under a trust.

In *AG Securities*, however, the House of Lords adopted a different approach to the specific question of co-ownership of a lease. It was held that the four occupiers had a lease only if they could show that, acting together, they *genuinely* had a joint tenancy of that lease. The assumption is that, if B1, B2, B3, and B4 had intended to receive a right to exclusive possession as tenants in common, no lease would arise: s 34(2) cannot operate to save the lease by allowing B1, B2, B3, and B4 to hold a legal lease as joint tenants on trust for themselves. This approach causes real problems for joint occupiers. As we saw in Chapter 17, section 2, to establish a tenancy in common, the *only* requirement is 'unity of possession'—that is, that each party is entitled to occupy all of the land. To establish a *genuine* joint tenancy (rather than one imposed by s 34(2)), however, the occupiers also need to show that they have not only unity of possession, but also 'unity of interest, time and title'. This means that they must show that they acquired the lease together: without individual shares, at the same time, and in the same way.

In *AG Securities*, it was impossible for the occupiers to show a genuine joint tenancy: it was clearly not the case that they had acquired a lease together, because they had not moved into the land at the same time; rather, they were part of a 'fluctuating population' of occupiers, each of whom moved in whenever an individual room happened to be vacant. In *Antoniades*, Mr Villiers and Miss Bridger had signed separate agreements with Mr Antoniades.

Nonetheless, they were able to show that they had acquired a lease together: the agreements were identical and signed on the same day, and Mr Villiers and Miss Bridger moved in together, as a couple. The decisions thus reflect an important difference between: (i) cases in which rooms in a house or flat are occupied by individuals who move in and move out at different times; and (ii) cases in which the house or flat itself is occupied together by a couple (or group) who move in together and who would expect to move out together. In particular, the *decision* in *AG Securities* seems correct, because, on the facts, it was not plausible to see the four occupiers as a group, co-operating to claim exclusive possession of the entire property.

The *reasoning* in *AG Securities*, however, with its insistence on a joint tenancy requirement, can cause problems even in a case in which a couple or group *do* move in together and exercise joint exclusive control of the property (and thus have unity of possession). As the following extract shows, the difficulties arise if the occupiers undertake individual and separate duties to pay rent (and thus have no unity of interest).

Mikeover v Brady
[1989] 3 All ER 618, CA

Facts: Mikeover Ltd had a long lease of the top floor flat at 179 Southgate Road, London N1. It advertised the flat as available for occupation by two people. The flat consisted of a front room, which had a cooker and refrigerator in it, and a back room, which had a sink in it. In addition, there was a bathroom and lavatory in the attic. Mr Brady and Miss Guile, a couple, responded to the advert and moved into the flat together. Each signed a separate, but identical, agreement, headed as a licence agreement, allowing each of them to share occupation of the flat for six months, in return for paying a monthly rent of £86.66. Once that initial six months had expired, the occupiers were allowed to remain in the flat, on the same terms as set out in the initial agreements. Early in 1986, Miss Guile moved out of the flat. She informed Mr Ferster (a director of Mikeover Ltd, and the party with whom she and Mr Brady had dealt) of this in April 1986. Mr Brady wished to remain and offered to pay £173.32 as monthly rent. Mr Ferster declined that offer, stating: '*I can't accept it. I'll hold you responsible for your share only.*' Nonetheless, even on the basis that he had to pay only £86.66 a month, Mr Brady fell into arrears on the rent payment and, in early 1987, Mikeover Ltd sought to remove him from the flat. Mr Brady claimed that, as a result of the initial agreements signed by the parties, he and Miss Guile had, acting together, acquired a lease of the flat. If that were correct, Mr Brady would then qualify for statutory protection under the Rent Acts. The first instance judge, however, rejected that argument and held that the initial agreements gave each party only a licence. Mr Brady appealed unsuccessfully to the Court of Appeal.

Slade LJ

At 623–7

[Slade LJ found that the agreements should be interpreted together and against the factual background that 'the layout of the flat was such that it was clearly only suitable for occupation by persons who were personally acceptable to one another'. On that basis:] It follows that, in our judgment, [Mr Brady's] agreement on its true construction conferred on him the right (by cl 1) to exclusive occupation of the flat in common only with Miss Guile during its currency [. . .]

It is, however, well settled that four unities must be present for the creation of a joint tenancy, namely the unities of possession, interest, title and time [. . .] In the present case there is no dispute that the two agreements of 6 June 1984 operated to confer on the defendant and Miss Guile unity of possession and title. Likewise, there was unity of time in that each of their interests arose simultaneously and was expressed to endure for six months. The dispute concerns unity of interest. The general principle, as stated in *Megarry and Wade* is:[58]

> 'The interest of each joint tenant is the same in extent, nature and duration, for in theory of law they hold but one estate.'

'Interest' in this context must, in our judgment, include the bundle of rights and obligations representing that interest. The difficulty, from the defendant's point of view, is that the two agreements, instead of imposing a joint liability on him and Miss Guile to pay a deposit of £80 and monthly payments of £173.32, on their face imposed on each of them individual and separate obligations to pay only a deposit of £40 and monthly payments of only £86.66. On the face of it, the absence of joint obligations of payment is inconsistent with the existence of a joint tenancy.

Counsel for [Mr Brady] sought to meet this difficulty in three ways. First, he contended that the two agreements were, as he put it, 'interdependent' and must be read together. When so read, he submitted, they should be construed as placing on the two parties joint obligations. However, it seems to us quite impossible to rewrite the two agreements in this manner as a matter of construction [. . .] [o]ne cannot add up two several [i.e. separate] obligations to pay £X so as to construct a joint obligation to pay £2X.

Next counsel for [Mr Brady], as we understood him, contended that, in so far as the two agreements purported to render each of the defendant and Miss Guile merely individually liable for the payment of a deposit of £40 and monthly payments of £86·66, they were 'shams'. The true intention of the parties, he submitted, to be inferred from all the circumstances, was that they should be jointly liable to make monthly payments of £173.32 and to pay a deposit of £80 (to the return of which they should be jointly entitled in due course).

In this context, the subsequent conduct of the parties is admissible in evidence, not for the purpose of construing the agreements but on the question whether the documents were or were not genuine documents giving effect to the parties' true intentions [. . .]

However, the onus of proving a sham falls on the defendant and, in our judgment, the parties' subsequent conduct affords no support, or at least no sufficient support, to his case in this respect [. . .] we see no sufficient grounds for disturbing the judge's finding that the receipts of sums by [Mikeover Ltd] from [Mr Brady] after Miss Guile left the flat represented no more than was due from him on the footing that he was liable only for monthly payments of £86.66 [. . .] [Mikeover Ltd's] failure to accept [Mr Brady's] offer to pay the higher monthly sum does not in any way assist [Mr Brady's] contention that the provisions for payment contained in the two agreements were shams.

On these authorities, it appears to us that unity of interest imports the existence of joint rights and joint obligations. We therefore conclude that the provisions for payment contained in these two agreements (which were genuinely intended to impose and did impose on each party an obligation to pay no more than the sums reserved to [Mikeover Ltd] by his or her

---

[58] [The reference in the case is to the 5th edn (1984): see now *Megarry and Wade's Law of Real Property* (8th edn, eds Harpum et al, 2012), [13–006].]

separate agreement) were incapable in law of creating a joint tenancy, because the monetary obligations of the two parties were not joint obligations and there was accordingly no complete unity of interest. It follows that there was no joint tenancy.

Mikeover v Brady nicely illustrates the problem caused to occupiers by the approach adopted in *AG Securities*. In *Mikeover*, the individual rent obligation would *not* have prevented Mr Brady from showing that he and Miss Guile held a lease as tenants in common, each with a 50 per cent share of the lease—but it did prevent him from showing that they held a lease as joint tenants (i.e. only as a team and without any individual share), and, under the *AG Securities* approach, it therefore followed that the occupiers did not have a lease.

As explained in the following extract, it is not obvious why the courts should insist on there being a *genuine* joint tenancy of a lease when, as we have seen, there is no such requirement when parties acquire a freehold together.

Sparkes, 'Co-Tenants, Joint Tenants and Tenants in Common' (1989) 18 AALR 151

At 155

In the light of Lord Templeman's speech [in *AG Securities v Vaughan*], it must be asked whether a tenancy in common can exist in an informal tenancy. The House of Lords simply assumed that this could not be the case. The question is by no means easy to answer in view of the well-known inadequacy of the provisions of the Law of Property Act 1925 concerned with the imposition of a statutory [trust of land] on co-ownership.[59] Before 1926, legal tenants could be either joint tenants or tenants in common. Equally landlords could hold in common, so that for example one landlord could serve a notice to quit that was effectual in respect of his undivided share, while leaving intact the term in respect of the undivided shares of other landlords. An informal tenancy could then have created a legal leasehold estate held by tenants in common. Such a tenancy, if it could exist today, would fall squarely within the definition of a protected tenancy.

After 1925, a legal estate must be held by joint tenants. A statutory [trust of land] arises and the beneficial owners might be either joint tenants or tenants in common beneficially. These rules should apply to any legal estate, whether the estate is freehold or leasehold [. . .]

Business tenancies must often exist as equitable tenancies in common, since such tenancies are frequently held by partnerships. A business lease is likely to contain an express declaration of a beneficial tenancy in common, which is best suited for business partnership. In the absence of an express declaration, equity would presume the intention to create a beneficial tenancy in common. Similar considerations apply to agricultural holdings. The question is therefore whether there is something special about residential tenancies which marks them out as uniquely confined to joint tenancies in the technical sense. The Rent Act 1977 contains no express prohibition; nor does the Housing Act 1988 for the assured tenancy present and future [. . .]

---

[59] [The author here refers to a statutory trust for sale, because the article was written before the Trusts of Land and Appointment of Trustees Act 1996. As to the effect of that Act, see Chapter 13, section 5.]

At 163–4

Nothing is clear in the field of co-ownership of short term leases. The courts have confidently equated a co-ownership joint tenancy and a co-tenancy under the Rent Act 1977. It is tentatively submitted that it is wrong to equate these two separate concepts.

In *AG Securities v. Vaughan* the House of Lords decided that four occupiers who were free to leave independently of each other were licensees and not co-tenants. The main ground relied upon was that the occupiers did not together share exclusive possession. Some dicta rest this decision on a different ground—that is the absence of unity of interest. In the absence of this unity at most a tenancy in common was created. This now forms the ratio decidendi of the Court of Appeal decision, *Mikeover v Brady.*

In both cases, it was important to establish whether or not there was a concurrent interest in the four occupiers. If it was concurrent, whether it was a joint tenancy or a tenancy in common or some other kind of relationship was (until the death of one of the parties)[60] quite irrelevant. For a tenancy in common to exist, only one of the four unities—that is unity of possession—would be necessary. An informal tenancy in common might create a statutory trust [. . .] or it might stand altogether outside conventional property law. There is no need to search for the remaining unities—that is time, title and interest.

The court should look to see whether there has been a joint grant of the right to exclusive occupation of the property, or in shorthand, joint exclusive possession. The opinions delivered in *AG Securities v Vaughan* are quite consistent with the general view that it is the substantive existence of a joint right to exclusive possession that is determinative of the existence of a tenancy.

Sparkes' view is thus that the approach in *Mikeover v Brady* cannot be justified as a matter of doctrine.

There are some challenges to that view: for example, Roger Smith[61] has argued that the structure of the LPA 1925 may support the approach of the courts; McFarlane[62] has argued that if, as in *Mikeover*, the occupiers claim that a contractual agreement has given rise to a lease, then they must claim as joint tenants, because, as a matter of general contract law, it is impossible for a contractual right to be held by tenants in common. Whatever your final view on the doctrinal question, however, it is also important to consider the *AG Securities* approach from the utility perspective. From that point of view, the approach, as exemplified by the decision in *Mikeover v Brady*, certainly contrasts with the more generous stance taken towards occupiers in cases such as *Street v Mountford* and *Antoniades v Villiers.*

2.6 A PROPRIETARY RIGHT TO EXCLUSIVE POSSESSION

If I were to make a contractual promise allowing you exclusive possession of Buckingham Palace for five years, recorded in a deed, could that promise give you a property right in Buckingham Palace? Clearly not. The problem is that, whilst you have a right *against me* to

---

[60] [As we saw in Chapter 13, section 2.2, the doctrine of survivorship means that the death of a joint tenant has consequences differing from those arising on the death of a tenant in common.]

[61] See Smith, *Plural Ownership* (2005) pp 24–6.

[62] McFarlane, *The Structure of Property Law* (2008) pp 714–15. The general rule applying to contractual rights is shown by, for example, Coke, *Commentaries on Littleton* (1628, p 198a) and *Re McKerrell* [1912] 2 Ch 648.

have exclusive possession of the Palace, I am simply not in a position to give you a property right in relation to that land. Nonetheless, the reasoning of the House of Lords in *Bruton v London & Quadrant Housing Trust Ltd*[63] appears to mean that, in such a case, our contractual agreement *does* give you a lease.

Not surprisingly, as we will see when examining *Bruton* in Chapter 20, section 4, that decision has attracted a lot of disapproval. It is, however, very important to note that the House of Lords in *Bruton* made clear that, in our example, the contractual agreement does *not* give you a property right.[64] The controversy excited by the decision is about the very idea that B can have a 'lease' *even though* he or she does not have a property right. In effect, *Bruton* means that there are now two sorts of leases: standard leases, which give their holder (B) a property right in land; and contractual leases, which give their holder (B) only a personal right against A. We will therefore postpone our consideration of *Bruton* to Chapter 20; in this chapter, our focus is on the standard, proprietary lease.

2.7 A RIGHT TO EXCLUSIVE POSSESSION FOR A LIMITED PERIOD

To have a lease, B needs to have a right to exclusive possession *for a limited period*. This requirement is reflected in the very phrase used, in s 1 of the LPA 1925, to define a lease—that is, a 'term of years absolute'. In that context, the word 'term'—like 'terminus', or 'terminal'—indicates an end or a limit. This relatively simple requirement has, however, caused a number of practical problems.

Prudential Assurance Ltd v London Residuary Body
[1991] UKHL 10, [1992] 2 AC 386, HL

Facts: Prior to 1930, Mr. Nathan owned shop premises: Nos 263–5, Walworth Road, Southwark, London. The London City Council (LCC) owned the road itself. LCC planned to widen the road: this would lead to its encroaching on part of the strip of land, owned by Mr Nathan, then separating his shop from the road. So the LCC bought Mr Nathan's freehold of that strip of land, agreeing, however, that Mr Nathan could continue to use it until the road-widening project went ahead. The agreement stated the strip was leased back to Mr Nathan for continued use, with the rest of 263–5 Walworth Road, until required for road widening; in return, Mr Nathan agreed to pay £30 a year in rent. It was clear that both parties intended this to be a temporary arrangement, because both believed that the road-widening project would soon go ahead. So, for example, there was no provision to allow the rent to be increased.

By 1988, however, the road widening had not occurred. The London Residuary Body (LRB), a successor of LCC, now held the freehold of the strip of land, and Nos 263–5 were owned by Prudential Assurance Ltd, which also had the benefit of the 1930 agreement. LRB attempted, by giving notice, to end Prudential's right to use the strip of land. It was agreed by valuers acting for each side that the current commercial rent for the strip of land (valuable because it allowed Nos 263–5 to have a shop frontage) was £10,000

---

[63] [2000] 1 AC 406.
[64] This point was confirmed by Lord Scott in *Kay v Lambeth LBC* [2006] 2 AC 465 [145]–[147], where the *Bruton* lease is described as a 'non-estate tenancy'.

per annum rather than the £30 that Prudential was paying under the 1930 agreement. Prudential, however, argued that LRB could not regain possession of the strip, because the land was not yet needed for road widening. Millett J found in favour of Prudential; LRB[65] appealed directly to the House of Lords.[66]

Lord Templeman

[...]

A demise for years is a contract for the exclusive possession and profit of land for some determinate period [. . .] The Law of Property Act 1925 [. . .] provided, by section 1(1), that:

'The only estates in land which are capable of subsisting or of being conveyed or created at law are—(a) An estate in fee simple absolute in possession; (b) A term of years absolute.'

Section 205(1)(xxvii) was in these terms:

'"Term of years absolute" means a term of years [. . .] either certain or liable to determination by notice, re-entry, operation of law, or by a provision for cesser on redemption, or in any other event (other than the dropping of a life, or the determination of a determinable life interest); [. . .] and in this definition the expression 'term of years' includes a term for less than a year, or for a year or years and a fraction of a year or from year to year; [. . .]'

The term expressed to be granted by the agreement in the present case does not fall within this definition [. . .]

When the agreement in the present case was made, it failed to grant an estate in the land. The tenant however entered into possession and paid the yearly rent of £30 reserved by the agreement.

The tenant entering under a void lease became by virtue of possession and the payment of a yearly rent, a yearly tenant holding on the terms of the agreement so far as those terms were consistent with the yearly tenancy. A yearly tenancy is determinable by the landlord or the tenant at the end of the first or any subsequent year of the tenancy by six months' notice unless the agreement between the parties provides otherwise [. . .]

Now it is said that when in the present case the tenant entered pursuant to the agreement and paid a yearly rent he became a tenant from year to year on the terms of the agreement including clause 6 which prevents the landlord from giving notice to quit until the land is required for road widening. This submission would make a nonsense of the rule that a grant for an uncertain term does not create a lease and would make nonsense of the concept of a tenancy from year to year because it is of the essence of a tenancy from year to year that both the landlord and the tenant shall be entitled to give notice determining the tenancy.

[. . .] [T]he agreement in the present case did not create a lease and that the tenancy from year to year enjoyed by the tenant as a result of entering into possession and paying a yearly rent can be determined by six months' notice by either landlord or tenant. The landlord has admittedly served such a notice [. . .]

---

[65] After giving the notice to quit, LRB sold its freehold, so, technically, the new freehold owners brought the appeal.

[66] Such a 'leapfrog' appeal is permitted where, for example, an appellant wishes to challenge the validity of previous Court of Appeal authority: in this case, *Ashburn Anstalt v Arnold* [1989] Ch 1, where the Court of Appeal had held that it was possible for B to have a lease of land until the land was needed for redevelopment. There is no point appealing first to the Court of Appeal because, unlike the House of Lords, it will simply be bound by that Court of Appeal authority.

A tenancy from year to year is saved from being uncertain because each party has power by notice to determine at the end of any year. The term continues until determined as if both parties made a new agreement at the end of each year for a new term for the ensuing year. A power for nobody to determine or for one party only to be able to determine is inconsistent with the concept of a term from year to year [. . .] principle and precedent dictate that it is beyond the power of the landlord and the tenant to create a term which is uncertain [. . .]

In the present case the Court of Appeal were bound by the decisions in *In re Midland Railway Co.'s Agreement*[67] and *Ashburn's case*.[68] In my opinion both these cases were wrongly decided. A grant for an uncertain term does not create a lease. A grant for an uncertain term which takes the form of a yearly tenancy which cannot be determined by the landlord does not create a lease. I would allow the appeal.

Lord Browne-Wilkinson

[...]

As a result of our decision Mr. Nathan's successor in title will be left with the freehold of the remainder of No. 263–265 which, though retail premises, will have no frontage to a shopping street: the L.C.C.'s successors in title will have the freehold to a strip of land with a road frontage but probably incapable of being used save in conjunction with the land from which it was severed in 1930, i.e. the remainder of No. 263–265.

It is difficult to think of a more unsatisfactory outcome or one further away from what the parties to the 1930 agreement can ever have contemplated. Certainly it was not a result their contract, if given effect to, could ever have produced. If the 1930 agreement had taken effect fully, there could never have come a time when the freehold to the remainder of No. 263–265 would be left without a road frontage.

This bizarre outcome results from the application of an ancient and technical rule of law which requires the maximum duration of a term of years to be ascertainable from the outset. No one has produced any satisfactory rationale for the genesis of this rule. No one has been able to point to any useful purpose that it serves at the present day. If, by overruling the existing authorities, this House were able to change the law for the future only I would have urged your Lordships to do so.

But for this House to depart from a rule relating to land law which has been established for many centuries might upset long established titles. I must therefore confine myself to expressing the hope that the Law Commission might look at the subject to see whether there is in fact any good reason now for maintaining a rule which operates to defeat contractually agreed arrangements between the parties (of which all successors in title are aware) and which is capable of producing such an extraordinary result as that in the present case.

There are a number of points to note about the decision of the House of Lords in *Prudential Assurance*. Firstly, whilst the *contractual agreement* entered into in 1930 did not create a lease, because it did not give Mr Nathan a right to exclusive possession for a limited period, he (and, later, Prudential) nonetheless did acquire a lease. That lease did not arise under the agreement, but instead resulted from Mr Nathan's payment of rent and the LCC's acceptance of that rent. This form of lease is known as an 'implied periodic tenancy': it provides a particular means by which B can acquire a lease and so we will examine it in section 3.1. As

---

[67] [1971] Ch 725.   [68] [1989] Ch 1.

Lord Templeman noted, the important point about the lease held by Prudential was that it could be terminated by the giving of notice by the landlord: because it was not based on the initial contractual agreement between the LCC and Mr Nathan, it did not give Prudential a right to use the land until it was needed for road widening.

Secondly, the dispute in *Prudential* did not involve the initial parties to the 1930 agreement: the LRB had made no express promise to allow Prudential to use the land until it was needed for road-widening. This raises the question of what would have happened if the LCC had tried to remove Mr Nathan from the land before it was needed for road-widening: could Mr Nathan have then asked for an injunction preventing the LCC from breaching its contractual promise? As we will see shortly, this question was later addressed (albeit in *obiter dicta*) by the Supreme Court in *Berrisford v Mexfield*.[69]

Third, whilst the House of Lords in *Prudential Assurance* upheld the traditional rule that a lease must have a maximum duration, Lord Browne-Wilkinson expressed some displeasure with the result: it was a *'bizarre outcome'* caused by an *'ancient and technical rule of law'*. It should be said that it is a straightforward matter for well-advised parties to avoid the effect of the rule: for example, as noted by Lord Templeman in *Prudential Assurance*,[70] there is nothing to prevent A from giving B a lease *'for 999 years, to determine if and when the land is need for road-widening'*—such a lease is for a limited period, because 999 years provides a clear maximum duration for the lease. Indeed, this tactic has been adopted by statute to save certain types of intended lease.

Law of Property Act 1925, s 149(6)

Any lease or underlease, at a rent, or in consideration of a fine, for life or lives or for any term of years determinable with life or lives, or on the marriage of the lessee, or any contract therefor, made before or after the commencement of this Act, or created by virtue of Part V of the Law of Property Act, 1922, shall take effect as a lease, underlease or contract therefor, for a term of ninety years determinable after the death or marriage (as the case may be) of the original lessee, or of the survivor of the original lessees, by at least one month's notice in writing given to determine the same on one of the quarter days applicable to the tenancy, either by the lessor or the persons deriving title under him, to the person entitled to the leasehold interest, or if no such person is in existence by affixing the same to the premises, or by the lessee or other persons in whom the leasehold interest is vested to the lessor or the persons deriving title under him:
    Provided that [. . .]

There are further provisos to s 149(6) of the LPA 1925, but the key point for our purposes is that certain forms of lease (e.g. a lease for B's life) are validated by interpreting the lease as a lease for a fixed term (ninety years), with the landlord having the power to determine the lease following the occurrence of a particular event (e.g. B's death).

It is, therefore, tempting to ask, along with Lord Browne-Wilkinson, whether the traditional rule, requiring a lease to have a maximum duration ascertainable at its outset, should be reformed. Lord Browne-Wilkinson's preference was for statutory reform, but, in the following case, a panel of seven Supreme Courts Justices was given the opportunity to consider judicial reform of the rule. The case involved both of the initial parties to the agreement, so

---

[69] [2011] UKSC 52.   [70] [1992] 2 AC 386, [395].

it also gave the court a chance to look at one of the loose ends from *Prudential Assurance* noted above: if a particular term of the parties' agreement prevents a lease arising, by introducing uncertainty, can it nonetheless be enforced between the initial parties as a matter of contract law?

Berrisford v Mexfield Housing Co-operative Limited
[2011] UKSC 52, [2012] 1 AC 955

Facts: Ms Berrisford owned a property in Barnet, North London. She was having difficulty paying the mortgage. In 1993, as part of a 'mortgage rescue scheme', she sold the property to Mexfield, a fully mutual housing co-operative. Mexfield then agreed to allow Ms Berrisford to continue in occupation of the property, and she became a member of the Mexfield co-operative. The statutory protection available to social tenants does not apply to members of housing co-operatives: Parliament took the view that such protection was unnecessary, as, in a co-operative, the 'interests of landlord and tenants as a whole are in effect indivisible'.[71]

Clause 1 of the occupation agreement stated that:

'[Mexfield] shall let and [Ms Berrisord] shall take the [premises] from 13 December 1993 and thereafter from month to month until determined as provided in this Agreement.'

Clauses 5 and 6 were as follows:

5. 'This Agreement shall be determinable by [Ms Berrisford] giving [Mexfield] one month's notice in writing.'

6. 'This Agreement may be brought to an end by [Mexfield] by the exercise of the right of re-entry specified in this clause but ONLY in the following circumstances:

   a) If the rent reserved hereby or any part thereof shall at any time be in arrear and unpaid for 21 days [. . .]

   b) If [Ms Berrisford] shall at any time fail or neglect to perform or observe any of the [terms of] this Agreement which are to be performed and observed by [her]

   c) If [Ms Berrisford] shall cease to be a member of [Mexfield]

   d) If a resolution is passed under [. . .] [Mexfield's] Rules regarding a proposal to dissolve [Mexfield]

THEN in each case it shall be lawful for [Mexfield] to re-enter upon the premises and peaceably to hold and enjoy the premises thenceforth and so that the rights to occupy the premises shall absolutely end and determine as if this Agreement had not be made [. . .]'

---

[71] See the judgment of Lord Hope at [81], set out later in this extract. For further discussion of this analysis, see Loveland, 'Security of Tenure for Tenants of Fully Mutual Housing Co-operatives' [2010] Conv 461, 464. As discussed by Hunter and Cowan, 'The Future of Housing Co-operatives: *Mexfield* and Beyond' (2012) 15 JHL 26, a private member's Co-operative Housing Tenure Bill was introduced in 2012, which would have created a special regime for such housing, arising outside the standard landlord–tenant relationship. That Bill did not attempt to confer any security of tenure on co-operative members.

Ms Berrisford remained in occupation until 2008, at which point Mexfield attempted to remove her from the property. Mexfield admitted that none of the circumstances set out in Clause 6 applied. Nonetheless, it argued that Clause 6 and, indeed, the entire occupancy agreement, was void—it fell foul of the need for a lease to have a certain term. As a result, Mexfield argued that Ms Berrisford did not occupy under the parties' written agreement, but rather under an implied (weekly or monthly) periodic tenancy, arising from her payment, and Mexfield's acceptance, of rent. On this view, Mexfield was not bound by the limits imposed in Clause 6 and was free to remove Ms Berrisford after refusing to renew the implied periodic tenancy.

In the end, Mexfield entered into a new agreement with Ms Berrisford, allowing her to remain in occupation of the property. The litigation was allowed to continue, however, to determine the status of Ms Berrisford's occupation prior to that new agreement. This is an important issue as the occupation agreement entered into by Mexfield and Ms Berrisford is of a standard form used not only by Mexfield, but also by many other housing co-operatives.

At first instance, His Honour Judge Mitchell refused Mexfield's application for summary judgment. Peter Smith J, on appeal, accepted Mexfield's analysis and made a possession order in its favour; Ms Berrisford then appealed to the Court of Appeal. The appeal was dismissed, but Wilson LJ dissented from the majority position of Aikens and Mummery LJJ. The case then proceeded to the Supreme Court.

The Supreme Court heard the case in a special panel of seven Justices. Ms Berrisford, however, did not directly challenge the traditional rule, affirmed in *Prudential Assurance*, that a lease must have a maximum duration, ascertainable from its outset. As a result, the Supreme Court were not invited to overrule *Prudential Assurance* and to discard that rule. Ms Berrisford thus accepted that the occupation agreement, on its own terms, did not create a lease. Nonetheless, she put forward two key reasons in support of the conclusion that Mexfield could remove her from the property only if one of the events set out in Clause 6 had occurred.

The first (a new argument, introduced only at the Supreme Court stage of the appeal) was that, prior to 1926, the occupation agreement would have been treated as a tenancy for the life of Ms Berrisford, which could be terminated by Mexfield during her life only under Clause 6. If that argument was correct, then s 149(6) of the Law of Property Act 1925 would apply, with the effect that Ms Berrisford had a 90 year lease, which could be terminated by Mexfield only on her death, or if one of the events set out in Clause 6 had occurred.

Ms Berrisford's second argument, accepted by Wilson LJ in his dissent in the Court of Appeal, was that, even if Clause 6 could not form part of a valid lease, it was nonetheless contractually binding on Mexfield and so Mexfield could be prevented from removing her in breach of the terms of Clause 6.[72]

The Supreme Court allowed Ms Berrisford's appeal: it rejected both of Mexfield's arguments, and accepted Ms Berrisford's first argument. It was not, therefore, strictly necessary for the court to consider her second argument, but a number of the Justices did so in any

---

[72] Mexfield also introduced a new argument before the Supreme Court. As well as its principal argument that the terms of the agreement itself could not create a lease, it also argued that the agreement itself gave Mexfield an implied contractual right to determine the lease with one month's notice. This argument was swiftly rejected by the Supreme Court as it involved an implausible interpretation of the parties' contract: see *per* Lord Neuberger at [18]–[23].

case—Lord Clarke took the view (at [108]) that Ms Berrisford's second argument was correct, and Lord Neuberger (at [59]), Lord Hope (at [80]), and Lord Dyson (at [120]) all indicated that they found that second argument convincing. As Ms Berrisford did not ask the court to overrule *Prudential Assurance*, it did not consider doing so; but, as can be seen in the extracts below, some of the Justices expressed their views as to the (lack of) merits of the rule that a lease must have a certain term.

Lord Neuberger

At [23]

Is Such An Arrangement Capable Of Being A Tenancy As A Matter of Law?

I turn to the second issue, namely whether an agreement, which can only come to an end by service of one month's notice by the tenant, or by the landlord invoking a right of determination on one or more of the grounds set out in clause 6, is capable, as a matter of law, of being a tenancy in accordance with its terms. [Counsel for Ms Berrisford] accepts that it is not so capable. His concession is supported both by very old authority and by high modern authority.

[Lord Neuberger then considered cases and commentary, up to and including *Prudential Assurance*, confirming what Lord Templeman in that case referred to as '500 years of judicial acceptance [that] the requirement that a term must be certain applies to all leases and tenancy agreements'].[73]

At [34]–[70]

If we accept that that is indeed the law, then, subject to the point to which I next turn, the Agreement cannot take effect as a tenancy according to its terms. As the judgment of Lady Hale demonstrates (and as indeed the disquiet expressed by Lord Browne-Wilkinson and others in *Prudential* itself shows), the law is not in a satisfactory state. There is no apparent practical justification for holding that an agreement for a term of uncertain duration cannot give rise to a tenancy, or that a fetter of uncertain duration on the right to serve a notice to quit is invalid. There is therefore much to be said for changing the law, and overruling what may be called the certainty requirement, which was affirmed in *Prudential*, on the ground that, in so far as it had any practical justification, that justification has long since gone, and, in so far as it is based on principle, the principle is not fundamental enough for the Supreme Court to be bound by it. It may be added that Lady Hale's Carrollian characterisation of the law on this topic is reinforced by the fact that the common law accepted perpetually renewable leases as valid: they have been converted into 2000-year terms by s 145 of the Law of Property Act 1922.

However, I would not support jettisoning the certainty requirement, at any rate in this case. First, as the discussion earlier in this judgment shows, it does appear that for many centuries it has been regarded as fundamental to the concept of a term of years that it had a certain duration when it was created. It seems logical that the subsequent development of a term from year to year (ie a periodic tenancy) should carry with it a similar requirement, and the case law also seems to support this.

Secondly, the 1925 Act appears to support this conclusion. Having stated in s 1(1) that only two estates can exist in land, a fee simple and a term of years, it then defines a term of years in s 205(1)(xxvii) as meaning "a term of years [. . .] either certain or liable to determination by

---

[73] [1992] 2 AC 386, [394].

notice [or] re-entry"; as Lord Templeman said in *Prudential*,[74] this seems to underwrite the established common law position. The notion that the 1925 Act assumed that the certainty requirement existed appears to be supported by the terms of s 149(6). As explained more fully below, this provision effectively converts a life tenancy into a determinable term of 90 years. A tenancy for life is a term of uncertain duration, and it was a species of freehold estate prior to 1926, but, in the light of s 1 of the 1925 Act, if it was to retain its status as a legal estate, it could only be a term of years after that date. Presumably it was converted into a 90-year term because those responsible for drafting the 1925 Act thought it could not be a term of years otherwise.

Thirdly, the certainty requirement was confirmed only some 20 years ago by the House of Lords. Fourthly, while not a very attractive point, there is the concern expressed by Lord Browne-Wilkinson, namely that to change the law in this field "might upset long established titles".[75] Fifthly, at least where the purported grant is to an individual, as opposed to a company or corporation, the arrangement does in fact give rise to a valid tenancy, as explained below. Finally, it has been no part of either party's case that the Agreement gave rise to a valid tenancy according to its terms (if, as I have concluded, it has the meaning for which [Ms Berrisford's counsel] contends).

Would such a tenancy have been treated as a tenancy for life before 1926?

While [counsel for Ms Berrisford] accepts that the arrangement contained in the Agreement would not be capable of constituting a tenancy in accordance with its terms, he contends that, at any rate before 1926, the arrangement would have been treated by the court as a tenancy for the life of Ms Berrisford, determinable before her death by her under cl 5, or by Mexfield under cl 6.

There is much authority to support the proposition that, before the 1925 Act came into force, an agreement for an uncertain term was treated as a tenancy for the life of the tenant, determinable before the tenant's death according to its terms [. . .] As Lord Dyson's reference to Joshua Williams's 1920 textbook shows, the perceived legal position right up to the time of the 1925 property legislation was that terms of uncertain duration were converted into determinable terms for life.

On this basis, then it seems clear that, at least if the Agreement had been entered into before 1 January 1926 (when the 1925 Act came into force), it would have been treated by the court as being the grant of a tenancy to Ms Berrisford for her life, subject to her right to determine pursuant to cl 5 and Mexfield's right to determine pursuant to cl 6.

[. . .] even if an agreement which creates an uncertain term could only have resulted in a tenancy for the life of the tenant if that was the intention of the parties, I consider that, on a true construction of the Agreement, it was intended that Ms Berrisford enjoy the premises for life - subject, of course, to determination pursuant to clauses 5 and 6. I have in mind in particular cl 6(c), which will apply on Ms Berrisford's death, the fact that her interest is unassignable, and the fact that it was intended to ensure that she could stay in her home.

Is the agreement converted into a 90-year term by s 149(6)?

The next step in [counsel for Ms Berrisford's] argument is that, given that the Agreement would have given rise to a tenancy for life prior to 1926, the effect of s 149(6) of the 1925 Act ("s 149(6)") is that the Agreement is now to be treated as a term of 90 years determinable on the death of Ms Berrisford, subject to the rights of determination in clauses 5 and 6.

[The wording of s 149(6), extracted above, is then set out]

---

[74] [1992] 2 AC 386, [391B].   [75] [1992] 2 AC 386, [397A].

As already mentioned, the 1925 Act began by limiting the number of permissible legal estates in land to two, a fee simple and a term of years. Accordingly, it was necessary for the statute to deal with interests, such as estates for lives, which had previously been, but no longer were, valid legal estates. Hence one of the reasons for s 149(6). However, it is clear from its terms that the section was not merely concerned with preserving life interests which existed prior to 1 January 1926: it also expressly applies to life interests granted thereafter. Therefore, says [counsel for Ms Berrisford], the section converts an arrangement such as the Agreement, which, according to the common law, is a life tenancy into a 90-year term.

The first argument which might be raised against this contention is that the Agreement was not a "lease [. . .] for life", merely a contract which would have been treated by established case law as such a lease. I do not consider that can be right. Apart from not being consistent with the wording of s 149(6), it would mean that an agreement such as that described in Littleton s 382, which existed as a continuing valid determinable life estate on the 1 January 1926, would have lost its status as a legal estate, as it would not have been saved by s 149(6): that cannot have been the legislature's intention.

[Counsel for Mexfield] contends that s 149(6) is concerned with tenancies which automatically end with the tenant's death, not with tenancies which can be determined on the tenant's death, and, in this case, the effect of cl 6(c) is that the tenancy can be determined, not that it automatically determines, on the tenant's death. I accept that s 149(6) only applies to tenancies which automatically determine on death, and I am prepared to assume that cl 6(c) can only be invoked by service of a notice. However, the argument misses the point, because the Agreement is (or would be in the absence of ss 1 and 149 of the 1925 Act) a tenancy for life, not because of the specific terms of, or circumstances described in, cl 6(c), but because it is treated as such by a well-established common law rule.

It is also suggested that s 149(6) does not apply to arrangements such as the Agreement which are determinable in circumstances other than the tenant's death—eg on the grounds set out in cl 6. I can see no reasons of principle for accepting that contention, and it appears to me that there are strong practical reasons for rejecting it. The common law rule that uncertain terms were treated as life tenancies applied, almost by definition, to arrangements which determined in other events, and it is hard, indeed impossible, to see why the rule should be limited to cases where an event automatically determines the term, as opposed to cases where an event entitles the landlord to serve notice to determine the term. In each case, the term is uncertain. At least one of the reasons the common law treated uncertain terms as tenancies for lives was, as I see it, to save arrangements which would otherwise be invalidated for technical reasons, and I find it hard to accept that the modern law requires the court to adopt a less benevolent approach to saving contractual arrangements [. . .]

It is strongly pressed by [counsel for Mexfield] that the conclusion that the Agreement gives rise to a valid tenancy for 90 years determinable on the tenant's death would be inconsistent with high modern authority. In particular, he said that such a conclusion would be contrary to the outcome in *Lace v Chantler*,[76] and inconsistent with clear dicta of Lord Greene MR in that case and of Lord Templeman in *Prudential*. I accept the factual basis for that argument, but do not agree with its suggested conclusion.

The fact is that it was not argued in either of those two cases that the arrangement involved would have created a life tenancy as a matter of common law, and that, following s 149(6), such an arrangement would now give rise to a 90-year term, determinable on the tenant's death (and [counsel for Ms Berrisford] was kind enough to point out that such an argument would not have assisted, and may even have harmed, the unsuccessful respondent's case

---

[76] [1944] KB 368.

in *Prudential*).[77] Some of the statements about the law by Lord Greene and Lord Templeman can now be seen to be extravagant or inaccurately wide, but it is only fair to them to repeat that this was, at least in part, because the tenancy for life argument was not raised before them.

Is Ms Berrisford accordingly entitled to retain possession?

For the reasons given, I accept [counsel for Ms Berrisford's] case that (i) the arrangement contained in the Agreement could only be determined in accordance with clauses 5 and 6, and not otherwise, (ii) such an arrangement cannot take effect as a tenancy in accordance with its terms, but (iii) by virtue of well-established common law rules and s 149(6), the arrangement is a tenancy for a term of 90 years determinable on the tenant's death by one month's notice from the landlord, and determinable in accordance with its terms, ie pursuant to clauses 5 and 6.

I indicated earlier in this judgment that this conclusion would apply irrespective of whether the purported tenancy created by the Agreement was simply for an indeterminate term or was a periodic tenancy with a fetter on the landlord's right to determine. There is no difficulty if the former is the right analysis. If the latter is correct, then there is a monthly tenancy which the landlord is unable to determine unless he can rely on one or more of the grounds in cl 6. In *Breams Property Investment co Ltd v Strougler*,[78] the court concluded that a periodic tenancy with a fetter on the landlord's right to determine for three years was valid. It seems to me that the term thereby created was equivalent to a fixed term of three years (subject to a restricted right of determination in the landlord and an unrestricted right of determination by the tenant) followed by a periodic tenancy.

Accordingly a periodic tenancy with an invalid fetter on the landlord's right to determine should be treated in the same way as a tenancy for a fixed, if indeterminate, term. That seems to me to be justified in principle, logical in theory, and it ensures the law in this area is the same for all types of tenancy, whether or not periodic in nature (which was, I think, part of the reasoning in *Prudential*). On that basis, even if the tenancy created by the Agreement was a monthly tenancy with an objectionable fetter, it seems to me that it would have been treated as a life estate under the old law (subject to the right to determine in accordance with the terms of the fetter), and so would now be a tenancy for 90 years.

Ms Berrisford is still alive, and it is common ground that she has not served notice under cl 5 and that Mexfield is not relying on cl 6. In those circumstances, it follows that Ms Berrisford retains her tenancy of the premises and that Mexfield is not entitled to possession.

[Lord Neuberger then considered the argument that Mexfield was in any case bound as a matter of contract law not to remove Ms Berrisford, stating that he inclined '*fairly strongly*' to accept it.]

Conclusion

In these circumstances, I would allow Ms Berrisford's appeal, and discharge the order made against her. It is only right to repeat that the Court of Appeal and Peter Smith J were bound by authority which made it impossible for them to reach the same conclusion as I have done on the points on which I would allow the appeal.

---

[77] [After all, in *Prudential Assurance*, it is likely to have been the case that Mr Nathan, the original tenant, had died by the time of the litigation (see *per* Lady Hale at [92]): a lease for Mr Nathan's life would therefore have been of little use to his successors in title, the respondents in that case.]

[78] [1948] 2 KB 1.

Lord Hope

[Lord Hope considered how Scottish law would deal with the facts of the case, noting that a lease is seen principally as a contract conferring only personal rights, and can have proprietary effect against third parties only if the requirements of the Leases Act 1449 are met. He also noted that, under the relevant Scottish housing legislation, it was very likely that a body such as Mexfield would be a registered social landlord and that an occupier such as Ms Berrisford would thus have the statutory protection of a secure tenancy. He also stated that there was no good reason why Ms Berrisford could not simply enforce her contract with Mexfield.]

At [81]

I also wonder whether the time has not now come for the legislative fetter which prevents mutual housing associations from granting protected or statutory tenancies in England and Wales to be removed, so that they are placed on the same footing as other providers of social housing as in Scotland. The reason that was given by the Minister of State in the Department of the Environment, the Earl of Caithness, for introducing an amendment to the Bill which became the Housing Act 1988 that provided that a fully mutual housing association cannot create an assured tenancy was that a statutory regime designed to regulate the relationship between landlord and tenant had little relevance in a situation "where, as is the nature of a co-operative, the interests of landlord and tenants as a whole are in effect indivisible.[79] That statement was repeated in the House of Commons by the Parliamentary Under Secretary of State, David Trippier, when the Lords amendment was approved.[80] The facts of this case suggest that, as least so far as Mexfield is concerned, that happy state of affairs no longer exists. The assumption on which that measure was put through Parliament seems now to rest on doubtful foundations, as financial pressures may cause the parties' interests to diverge to the detriment of the residential occupier. That is not something that this court can deal with. But I suggest that it is something that might be considered in any future programme for the reform of housing law.

Lady Hale

At [87]–[88]

Periodic tenancies obviously pose something of a puzzle if the law insists that the maximum term of any leasehold estate be certain. The rule was invented long before periodic tenancies were invented and it has always been a problem how the rule is to apply to them. In one sense the term is certain, as it comes to an end when the week, the month, the quarter or the year for which it has been granted comes to an end. But that is not the practical reality, as the law assumes a re-letting (or the extension of the term) at the end of each period, unless one or other of the parties gives notice to quit. So the actual maximum term is completely uncertain. But the theory is that, as long as each party is free to give that notice whenever they want, the legal maximum remains certain. Uncertainty is introduced if either party is forbidden to give that notice except in circumstances which may never arise. Then no-one knows how long the term may last and indeed it may last for ever.

---

[79] Hansard (HL Debates), 3 November 1988, vol 501, col 395.
[80] Hansard (HC Debates), 9 November 1988, vol 140, col 337.

These rules have an Alice in Wonderland quality which makes it unsurprising that distinguished judges have sometimes had difficulty with them [. . .]

At [93]–[96]

So we have now reached a position which is curiouser and curiouser. There is a rule against uncertainty which applies both to single terms of uncertain duration and to periodic tenancies with a curb on the power of either party to serve a notice to quit unless and until uncertain events occur. But this rule does not matter if the tenant is an individual, because the common law would have automatically turned the uncertain term into a tenancy for life, provided that the necessary formalities were complied with, before the Law of Property Act 1925. A tenancy for life was permissible at common law, although of course it was quite uncertain when the event would happen, but it was certain that it would. I suppose at the time of the hundred years' war there was uncertainty both as to the "when" and the "whether" it would ever end. Be that as it may, a tenancy for life is converted into a 90 year lease by the 1925 Act.

As it happens, in the particular agreement with which we are concerned, it is not difficult to conclude that the parties did in fact intend a lease for life determinable earlier by the tenant on one month's notice and by the landlords on the happening of certain specified events. So our conclusions are in fact reflecting the intentions of the parties. But it is not difficult to imagine circumstances in which the same analysis would apply but be very far from the intentions of the parties. And that analysis is not available where the tenant is a company or corporation. So there the court is unable to give effect to the undoubted intentions of the parties. Yet, as the court pointed out in *Midland Railway*,[81] it is always open to the parties to give effect to those intentions by granting a very long term of years, determinable earlier on the happening of the uncertain event. The law, it would seem, has no policy objection to such an arrangement, so it is difficult to see what policy objection it can have to upholding the arrangement to which the parties in fact came.

It is even more bizarre that, had the "tenancy for life" analysis not been available, the conclusion might have been, not that this was a contractual tenancy enforceable as such as between the original parties, but that it was a contractual licence, also enforceable as such between the original parties. This, as I understand it, is the difference between English and Scots law. I do not understand that it makes any difference to the result.

As will be apparent, I entirely agree with the reasoning and conclusions reached by Lord Neuberger on the first question: does Ms Berrisford have a subsisting tenancy? For that reason, I do not think it necessary to express an opinion on the alternative case in contract. But it seems to me obvious that the consequence of our having reached the conclusions which we have on the first issue is to make the reconsideration of the decision in *Prudential*, whether by this court or by Parliament, a matter of some urgency. As former Law Commissioner Stuart Bridge has argued:[82]

"If the parties to a periodic tenancy know where they stand, in the sense that the contract between them is sufficiently certain, then that should be enough. If a landlord, in this case a fully mutual housing association, decides that its tenants should be entitled to remain in possession unless and until they fall into arrears with their rent or break other provisions contained in the tenancy agreement, it is difficult to see what policy objectives are being furthered in denying the tenant the rights that the agreement seeks to create."

Quite so.

---

[81] *In re Midland Railway Co's Agreement* [1971] Ch 725.   [82] [2010] Conv 492, [497].

Lord Dyson

At [116]–[120]

At all events, as a result of [counsel for Ms Berrisford's] impressive and scholarly research (which was not placed before the Court of Appeal), it is clear that it is unnecessary to get rid of the uncertainty rule in this case. This is because before the enactment of the Law of Property Act 1925 ("the 1925 Act"), the tenancy purportedly created by the Agreement would have been treated as a tenancy for life, defeasible by determination on any of the grounds specified in clauses 5 and 6. Lord Neuberger has referred to some of the pre-1926 authorities at paras 37 to 39. The position is well summarised in the last edition of the standard work on land law before the 1925 legislation, *Joshua Williams' Law of Real Property*,[83] in these terms:

'Where land is given to a widow during her widowhood, or to a man until he shall become bankrupt, or for any other definite period of time of uncertain duration, a freehold estate is conferred, as in the case of a gift for life. Such estates *are regarded in law* as determinable life estates [. . .]' (Emphasis added).

Accordingly, a periodic tenancy determinable on an uncertain event was treated as a defeasible tenancy for life. In disputing this proposition, [counsel for Mexfield's] principal submission was that, before the enactment of the 1925 Act, the question whether a periodic tenancy determinable on an uncertain event was a defeasible tenancy for life was one of construction of the particular agreement. But, as Lord Neuberger explains, it is clear from the authorities that this is incorrect. It was a rule of the common law that such a tenancy was automatically treated as a tenancy for life. It had nothing to do with the intention of the parties.

The effect of s 149(6) of the 1925 Act was to convert such a tenancy into a term for 90 years, subject to earlier termination in accordance with its terms. It follows that the Agreement is such a tenancy and all the terms of cl 6 apply with full force and effect. Mexfield cannot terminate the Agreement by serving a notice to quit as if this were a simple monthly tenancy without more.

This is a just result which plainly accords with the intention of the parties. But it may legitimately be said that it is not satisfactory in the 21st century to have to adopt this chain of reasoning in order to arrive at such a result. It is highly technical. There should be no need to have to resort to such reasoning in order to arrive at the result which the parties intended. That is why the radical solution of doing away with the uncertainty rule altogether is so attractive. There is the further point that the s 149(6) route to the right result can only be followed where the purported tenant is an individual and not a corporate entity. To treat an individual and a corporate entity differently in this respect can only be explained on historical grounds. The explanation may lie in the realms of history, but that hardly provides a compelling justification for maintaining the distinction today.

To conclude, in my view the answer to this appeal lies in the law of landlord and tenant and the appeal must be allowed. I do not find it necessary to address the alternative arguments advanced by [counsel for Ms Berrisford]. I would, however, go so far as to say that, like Lord Neuberger (paras 57 to 62), I am strongly attracted by the submission that, if by reason of the uncertainty argument the Agreement did not create a tenancy, then it was enforceable as a contract according to its terms like any other contract.

---

[83] 23rd edn (1920, p 135).

In *Prudential Assurance*, Lord Browne-Wilkinson noted that the need for certainty of term may produce 'bizarre' or 'extraordinary' results. The facts of *Berrisford* form an almost perfect example of the apparent injustice to which the rule may lead. The basis on which Ms Berrisford sold her home and then entered into an agreement with Mexfield was that she would be secure in her occupation: that she could be removed only if one of the events set out in Clause 6 occurred. Mexfield's principal argument, successful in the front of Peter Smith J and the Court of Appeal, was that, notwithstanding the clear terms of Clause 6, Ms Berrisford could in fact be removed at the whim of Mexfield, provided that she was given one month's notice of Mexfield's intention not to renew her implied periodic tenancy.

It is no surprise, then, that the Supreme Court found a way to avoid that seemingly unjust result. It is important to note, first of all, that the Supreme Court's solution does *not* reform or remove the rule, applied in *Prudential Assurance*, that a lease involves exclusive possession of land for a limited period. The Supreme Court rather found that Ms Berrisford had a right to exclusive possession of her home for a maximum period of 90 years, with Mexfield having a power to end that right only on her death or if one of the events set out in Clause 6 occurred. To find that Ms Berrisford had such a right, the Supreme Court had to take two steps. First, her agreement with Mexfield, which seemingly gave her a right to exclusive possession for an uncertain term, was re-interpreted as giving her a right to exclusive possession for her life, determinable on the grounds set out in the agreement. This re-interpretation was the result of a common law principle that applied before the Law of Property Act 1925. Second, it was held that, as Ms Berrisford had a right to exclusive possession for her life, determinable on the grounds set out in the agreement, s 149(6) of the LPA 1925 could be applied to turn her right into a 90 year lease, again determinable on the grounds set out in the agreement. The Supreme Court's analysis can therefore be set out as follows:

Starting point: The parties' agreement gives Ms Berrisford a right to exclusive possession for an uncertain term, determinable on limited grounds.

Step 1: A common law principle transforms Ms Berrisford's right into a right to exclusive possession for her life, determinable on the limited grounds set out in the agreement.

Step 2: Section 149(6) of the LPA 1925 transforms Ms Berrisford's right into a lease for 90 years, determinable on her death as well as on the limited grounds set out in the agreement.

As Lord Templeman remarked in *Prudential Assurance*, it has always been a simple matter for well-advised parties to avoid the effects of the certainty of term rule: instead of a right to exclusive possession 'until the land is needed for road-widening', a party can be given such a right 'for 999 years, or until the land is needed for road-widening'. The solution adopted in *Berrisford* effectively allows for the same tactic to be applied, even if the parties did not think of it themselves. It is important to note, however, that the solution cannot work in cases where the purported lease is given to a company—in such cases, a right to exclusive possession 'for life' makes no sense, and therefore the common law rule, operating at Step 1 above, cannot apply. Following *Berrisford*, the case for some form of legislative intervention is very strong, as it is difficult to justify a position where the same agreement has a quite different effect depending on whether the tenant is a natural person or a company.

A further limit on the applicability of the *Berrisford* reasoning was developed in the following case, which also involved an agreement between an occupier and a housing co-operative.

Southward Housing Co-operative Ltd v Walker
[2016] EWHC 1615, [2016] Ch 443

Facts: A [the claimant housing co-operative] gave a notice to quit to B (and other occu-piers) as B was in arrears of rent. Unlike *Berrisford*, the case did not involve a mortgage rescue scheme in which B had been assured of a right to occupy the property for as long as he or she wished. Rather, it was a standard case of B moving into accommodation. The terms of the 'tenancy agreement' between A and B stated that it was a weekly tenancy and allowed A to give notice to quit (i.e. notice that the tenancy would not be renewed) on specific grounds, which included rent arrears. B argued that the agreement itself, like that in *Berrisford*, did not give a right to exclusive possession for a certain term, as it did not fix any maximum duration: the agreement could continue indefinitely if the grounds on which notice to quit could be given did not arise. B therefore argued that he had a lease for life, converted by statute into a 90-year lease, terminable on his death, and that the notice to quit was therefore irrelevant, as there was no weekly tenancy which had to be renewed. The 'tenancy agreement' did not contain any express forfeiture pro-visions that A could rely on to end such a 90-year lease.

Hildyard J accepted that, as in *Berrisford*, the agreement itself was not for a certain term. However, he found that the rule that such an agreement, before 1925, would have given rise to a lease for life did *not* apply, and distinguished the facts of the case from those of *Berrisford*.

At [67]–[95]

Does the uncertainty of term mean that a tenancy for life must have arisen by operation of law?

The question then is whether that conclusion [that the term is uncertain] has the inexorable effect that the Agreement would, prior to 1925, have been treated, not as a tenancy, but as a lease for life, so that post-1925, it is treated as a lease for 90 years pursuant to s 149(6) of the LPA 1925.

Two sub-questions arise: these are (a) whether it was the intention of the parties to create a lease for life and, if not (b) whether contrary intention of the parties is nevertheless negated by an overriding principle of law [. . .]

In the *Mexfield* case, all the justices of the Supreme Court were agreed that in the par-ticular circumstances of the case it was intended that the defendant should enjoy the prem-ises for life; that, to put that into more legal language, the parties did in fact intend a lease for life determinable earlier by the tenant on one month's notice and by the landlord on the happening of cetain specific events.

That meant that they did not have to consider the conundrum that arises if that is not the intention of the parties, and where, accordingly, the inexorable application of a rule that transmogrifies into a 90 year term an agreement that is incapable of constituting a tenancy (which is what Lord Neuberger acknowledged was the 'Carrolian' consequence)[84] defeats the intention of the parties.

[It was then found that it was clear on the facts of the case that A and B had not intended that B would enjoy the premises for life, as it was intended to be a standard weekly tenancy, with a provision for a notice to quit, whereas the agreement in the *Mexfield* case, part of a mortgage rescue scheme, had a right of re-entry, which is consistent with a fixed term rather than a periodic tenancy. The question therefore was whether the *Mexfield* approach meant that a 90-year lease arose despite the contrary intentions of A and B. It was noted

---

[84] [2012] 1 AC 955, [34]. [i.e. characteristic of Lewis Carroll, the author of *Alice in Wonderland*.]

that there is some support for that view in *Mexfield* itself, as e.g. Lord Dyson stated that, where an attempt was made to give B a periodic tenancy determinable on an uncertain event then:[85] '*It was a rule of the common law that such a tenancy was automatically treated as a tenancy for life. It had nothing to do with the intention of the parties.*']

[. . .] with diffidence and anxiety, I have eventually concluded that there is a solution which does give effect to the intention of the parties. The solution revolves around the difference between, on the one hand, accepting (as plainly one must) that the 'rule' can be applied in circumstances where the parties had no inkling or intention that it would, and, on the other hand, accepting that its application is mandatory even where the parties' intentions were to the contrary and their agreement contains fundamental terms that simply cannot be carried over into a 90 year lease [. . .]

I have concluded that the 'rule' does not depend for its application on the parties' intentions; but the judgments of the Supreme Court in the *Mexfield* case leave open the possibility that it may be disapplied where those intentions and fundamental aspects of their agreement would be confounded by it.

I am fortified in this conclusion by the consideration that the origin of the 'rule' must have been intended to save agreements that would otherwise fail, in accordance with the maxim *ut res magis valeat quam pereat*,[86] not to destroy the essence of their bargain and foist on them a long term relationship against their will and which one of them may not be able to terminate . . .

[The result therefore was that B had only a contractual licence against A, and no lease.]

Lastly in this context, I think it is permissible to take into account the following additional matters in support of my approach:

(i) All members of the Supreme Court appear to have been receptive to the analysis that, if an agreement could not take effect as a tenancy (for want of certainty of term), it could nevertheless subsist as a contractual licence taking effect between the parties according to its terms.[87]

(ii) All members of the Supreme Court recognised that, unless the insistence on certainty of term is ultimately abandoned, some such solution must be devised in the case of corporate tenants.[88]

(iii) All members of the Supreme Court concurred that the contractual licence would have the same effect as between the parties.[89]

(iv) Lord Hope was plainly puzzled why the solution of a contractual licence was not both obvious and sensible,[90] as well as being plainly the solution offered under Scottish law.

(v) That solution of a contractual licence may not have been contemplated when the 'rule' was devised: and not a single authority post-1925 was found in support of the inexorable application of this aspect of the 'rule'; and it seems odder still that pre-1925 authority should be treated as mandating the negation of an entirely workable agreement and its replacement with a different relationship which is not only not what the parties intended but is quite contrary to their intention and the structure of their underlying contract.

In short, I consider the solution of a contractual licence is not precluded by the *Mexfield* case, is open to this court, and should be adopted.

[85] [[2012] 1 AC 955, [117].]

[86] [i.e. it is better to interpret words (or decide on the legal effect of a transaction) in a way that gives some effect to those words (or that transaction) rather than to leave the words (or transaction) as wholly ineffective.]

[87] See especially *per* Lord Mance.

[88] See especially *per* Baroness Hale [2012] 1 AC 955, [94]–[95].

[89] Again, see [2012] 1 AC 955, [95].   [90] See [2012] 1 AC 955, [80].

The judgment in *Southward Housing* is an important one, as it shows the limits to the reasoning in *Berrisford*. In the context of a mortgage rescue scheme, where B has been assured of a home for life, a 90-year lease may be a sensible outcome; but it is clearly not the best solution in any case involving a right to exclusive possession for an uncertain term. Where, however, that solution is not adopted, and, as in *Southward Housing*, B is found to have only a contractual licence, that does have an important effect: not only will B's right then be incapable of binding a third party, it also means that B will not qualify for any statutory protection that is limited to those with leases.

The analysis of Hildyard J is also interesting, because, whilst it is directed only to cases where a lease for life (then converted into the statutory 90-year lease) is inconsistent with the parties' intentions, it may also cast some doubt on the 'rule' recognized in *Berrisford* itself. Certainly, some doubts can be expressed about the analysis of the Supreme Court.[91] Firstly, the effect of the common law rule applied at Step 1 has to be carefully defined. For example, the 1920 textbook[92] quoted by Lord Dyson[93] states that where land is given for a 'definite period of time of uncertain duration, a freehold estate is conferred, as in the case of a gift for life. Such estates are regarded in law as determinable life estates [. . .]'. It is important to distinguish a determinable freehold for life from a lease for life. Prior to the LPA 1925, it was possible, for example, for a testator to leave his land to B1 for B1's life, then to B2 and thus to give each of B1 and B2 a legal estate: B1's estate was known as a life estate, and B2's estate as a fee simple in remainder. B1's estate, however, was *not* a lease: it was one of the three forms of *freehold* estate that could exist at common law before 1926.[94] So, for example, B1 held his life estate without being in a landlord-tenant relationship; B1's life estate counted as part of his 'real property', whereas a lease held by B1 would count as part of his 'personal property'; and B1 was subject to liability for waste to B2.[95]

On this analysis, the common law rule operating at Step 1 thus did *not* convert a lease for an uncertain term into a lease for life; it rather converted it into a freehold life estate. This may cause two problems for the reasoning in *Berrisford*. Firstly, can that common law rule still operate even after 1926, given that the life estate no longer exists as a legal estate in land? Secondly, if the common law rule does operate, then can Step 2 apply? After all, s 149(6) of the LPA applies to leases, not to freehold life estates.

Commentators have also pointed out some practical difficulties with the result in *Berrisford*, as can be seen from the following extract.

Bright, 'The Uncertainty of Certainty in Leases', (2012) 128 LQR 337 at 339

Although in this case the lease for life reasoning worked to protect Ms Berrisford, the wider ramifications will not always be welcome, and some are positively alarming. A 90-year lease of a dwelling appears to come within s 166 of the Commonhold and Leasehold Reform Act 2002 which would mean that the tenant is not liable to make payment of rent unless notice has been

---

[91] See too Roche, 'Legal History in Court: Lessons from *Mexfield* and *Southward*' [2016] Conv 86.

[92] *Joshua Williams' Law of Real Property* (23rd edn, 1920) p 135. [93] [2012] 1 AC 955, [116].

[94] The other two being the fee simple and the fee tail.

[95] The concept of 'waste' is discussed in the chapter on successive interests, available with the online resources.

served in the prescribed statutory form. As a long lease it will need to be registered for legal tutle, the statutory implied repair covenants may not apply (Landlord and Tenant Act 1985, s 11) and there are doubts as to whether tenants of long residential leases can claim housing benefit.

Whatever one's view as to the effect or validity of the Supreme Court's reasoning in *Berrisford*, one can also ask if, rather than adopting a technical work-around to the certainty of term rule, it would be simpler and better to remove the rule itself. It must be emphasized that, as the Supreme Court was not asked by either party to overrule *Prudential Assurance*, it would have been inappropriate for it to do so. Nonetheless, it may seem odd that the law is left with a rule for which judges in the highest court in the land have twice been unable to find a persuasive justification. The following extracts consider if a rationale for the rule can be found.

McFarlane, *The Structure of Property Law* (2008, pp 677–8)

A Lease consists of a right to exclusive control of land for a limited period. So, if A gives B a right to exclusive control of land "until England win the football World Cup" that right does not count as a Lease. The problem is *not* that the parties will be unable to tell if the specified event has happened: if and when England win the football World Cup, they (and everyone else) will know about it. The problem is rather that it is impossible for A to know *if and when* he can regain his right to exclusive control of the land. And that uncertainty is simply incompatible with a Lease. A Lease arises where A retains his property right in the land and grants B a new property right. So, if A grants B a Lease, A does *not* lose his property right in the land. But if it were possible to have a Lease in which A does not know if and when he will again have a right to exclusive control of the land, A's property right will, in effect, be meaningless [. . .]

[In *Prudential Assurance*] Lord Browne-Wilkinson expressed frustration that the rationale for the rule was unclear, stating that "No one has produced any satisfactory rationale for the genesis of the rule" that "the maximum duration of a [Lease must be] ascertainable from the outset". However, the problem may lie with his Lordship's formulation of the rule. It is *not* the case that the maximum length of the Lease must be known at the outset: the important point is that A must be able to tell if and when he will be able to assert his right to exclusive control of the land. The rule therefore has a valid doctrinal purpose.

Williams, 'The Certainty of Term Requirement in Leases: Nothing Lasts Forever' [2015] CLJ 592

At 599–600

[An] aspect of medieval land law could provide an explanation for the requirement that a lease is for a certain term – an explanation which remains valid today. That is the nature of the rights which owners of land hold as owners of estates in land, rather than owners of the land itself. It is the system of estates in land which explains why a perpetual lease cannot be created [. . .]

While the fee simple estate has been described as the only perpetual estate known to the common law, this is incorrect. The fee simple always was, and remains in English law, an estate which can end. The common law doctrine of estates recognises no perpetual rights in land. At best the fee simple estate is potentially perpetual, a crucially important distinction.

Medieval and early-modern lawyers understood this point very well. An attempt to grant land 'forever' failed to convey a fee simple. A fee simple was a grant 'to X and his heirs'. If X died without heirs, or his line of heirs died at any point, the fee simple estate would end and the land escheat to the feudal lord, now more or less inevitably the Crown [. . .] Escheat for want of heirs was abolished by the Administration of Estates Act 1925, which instead provides that, if a person dies without any heir entitled to receive their estate, the Crown takes the property as *bona vacantia*. However, escheat does still arise, principally in two contexts. The first is insolvency. If an individual's trustee in bankruptcy or a company's liquidator exercises his statutory power to disclaim the land, the land will escheat. The second is the dissolution of a company. If an English company is dissolved, the company's property will pass to the Crown as *bona vacantia*. The Crown may disclaim the property, at which point escheat occurs. If a foreign company is dissolved, escheat occurs automatically. The Explanatory Notes to the Land Registration Act 2002 observe that 300–500 cases of escheat occur every year – a figure which remains accurate. The perpetual fee simple therefore remains unknown to the common law. As a consequence, the owner of land in fee simple cannot grant a perpetual right in land: *nemo dat quod non habet*.[96]

On each of these views, then, the certainty of term requirement has a valid doctrinal purpose: either to avoid undermining the right to exclusive possession of A, the party granting the lease; or as a result of the fact that, as A does not him- or herself have a perpetual right to exclusive possession of the land, he or she cannot then grant such a right to B. These are not, however, conclusive arguments against statutory reform of the requirement: Williams, for example, notes that simply abolishing the rule would be '*awkward*' as the rule '*has its foundations in wider principles of property law*', but that a reform '*recognising the fee simple as a genuinely perpetual estate in land*' would be sufficient, as then the *nemo dat* argument would disappear:[97] if A, as freehold owner, has a right to exclusive possession forever, A could then grant a potentially perpetual right of exlcusive possession to B.

It is therefore also important to consider if the rule has any benefits in terms of utility. Bright has noted that in particular cases, the limited period requirement may be justifiable on the grounds that it allows a party to escape an improvident long-term contract: in *Prudential Assurance*, for example, the parties intended a short-term arrangement, and set the rent accordingly, so it would be unjust to have such an agreement continue to bind their successors in title over 60 years later.[98] In *Berrisford*, in contrast, this effect of the rule was wholly unattractive: there would have been a clear injustice if Mexfield had been allowed to remove Ms Berrisford contrary to the terms of its agreement with her. One way to avoid that injustice would be to reform the rule that a lease must be for a limited period; but it must be noted that, as demonstrated by the decision of the Supreme Court in *Berrisford*, other solutions are possible. Indeed, as Lord Hope noted,[99] there is a strong

---

[96] [Nobody can give what he does not have—the argument is that, since A, the party granting the lease, does not have a right to exclusive possession forever, they cannot then grant such a right to B.]

[97] [2015] CLJ 592, 606. It is also stated at 607 that the current law of escheat is in any case in need for reform, as noted by Law Com No 271 (2001) [11.26]–[11.27].

[98] See Bright, 'Uncertainty in Leases – Is it a Vice?' (1993) 13 LS 38 and *Landlord and Tenant Law in Context* (2007) 73-4.

[99] [2011] UKSC 52, [81].

case that the legislature erred in denying statutory protection to tenants of fully mutual housing co-operatives. Had Parliament taken a different view, the approach of the House of Lords in *Prudential Assurance* would have caused no difficulty to Ms Berrisford, as the implied periodic tenancy arising from her payment of rent, and Mexfield's acceptance of that rent, would have been enough to give her statutory protection and therefore to limit the grounds on which Mexfield, or any successor in title to Mexfield, could have removed her from the property. It is worth noting that, in the *Southward Housing* case, B argued that the current statutory regime is discriminatory, and so contrary to B's human rights, as it denies the general statutory protection to members of housing co-operatives. That argument was rejected,[100] and one of the reasons given was that it is within Parliament's wide margin of discretion to give certain tenants more limited rights;[101] as a matter of policy, rather than legality, there is, however, an argument for extending the current statutory protection.[102]

2.8 EXCEPTIONS?

The discussion so far suggests that there is a relatively simple test for the content of a lease: does B have a right to exclusive possession of land for a limited period? In *Street v Mountford*, however, Lord Templeman set out a number of exceptions: situations in which B can have a right to exclusive possession without having a lease. We need to ask if those situations really do constitute exceptions to the basic rule.

Bruton v London and Quadrant Housing Trust
[1998] QB 834, CA[103]

Millett LJ

At 843

In *Street v Mountford* Lord Templeman gave only three examples of exceptional circumstances where the grant of exclusive possession does not create a tenancy. First, where the circumstances negative any intention to create legal relations at all. Secondly, where the possession of the grantee is referable to some other legal relationship such as vendor and purchaser or master and servant. Thirdly, where the grantor has no power to create a tenancy, as in the case of a requisitioning authority. As I pointed out in *Camden London Borough v Shortlife Community Housing*,[104] the first and third of these are not exceptions to a general rule. The relationship of landlord and tenant is a legal relationship. It cannot be brought into existence by an arrangement which is not intended to create legal relations at all or by a body which has no power to create it. The existence of these two categories is due to the fact that the creation of a tenancy requires the grant of a legal right to exclusive possession.

---

[100] [2016] Ch 443, [154]–[236]. See too *Watts v Stewart* [2017] 2 WLR 1107, discussed in section 2.8.
[101] [2016] Ch 443, [166].
[102] As noted e.g. by Lord Hope in *Berrisford v Mexfield* [2012] 1 AC 955, [81].
[103] See Chapter 20, section 4, for discussion of the facts of the case and the decision of the House of Lords.
[104] (1992) 25 HLR 330.

On the view of Millett LJ, which seems to be correct, we need to focus our attention on cases in which *'possession of* [B] *is referable to some other legal relationship such as vendor and purchaser or master and servant'*. In *Street v Mountford*,[105] Lord Templeman stated that: *'an occupier who enjoys exclusive possession is not necessarily a tenant. He may be owner in fee simple, a trespasser, a mortgagee in possession, an object of charity or a service occupier.'*

In the first three of Lord Templeman's examples we can explain the absence of a lease by simply pointing to the absence of a term: B may have exclusive possession, but he does not have it for a limited period.[106] The 'object of charity' exception may admit of two explanations. Firstly, it may be that, as in *Booker v Palmer* [107] (see section 2.2), A's charitable motive means that he does not intend to enter legal relations with B. This may well be the case, where, for example, B pays no rent. In that case, the absence of a lease is easy to explain.

Secondly, in *Gray v Taylor*,[108] Mrs Taylor occupied an almshouse under an agreement with the trustees of a charity. Sir John Vinelott stated:[109] *'A person who is selected as an almsperson becomes a beneficiary under the trusts of the charity and enjoys the privilege of occupation of rooms in the almshouses as beneficiary.'* As noted by Barr,[110] the analysis here seems to be that the occupier's rights come from her *status* as a 'beneficiary' of the charitable trust. The argument seems to be that the agreement between the parties, by itself, did not define Mrs Taylor's right to occupy; rather, that right flowed from, and depended on the continuation of, the charity's decision to regard her as a suitable recipient of its generosity. Equally, of course, this approach promotes a policy of ensuring that landlords acting with altruistic motives are not hampered by the statutory protection that may be available to B if he or she is found to have a lease. Certainly, in *Gray v Taylor*, Sir John Vinelott noted that it would be absurd if, due to that statutory protection, the charity was prevented from ending the occupation of a party who, for example, won the lottery. Similarly, in *Watts v Stewart*,[111] where the charity provided accommodation to 'poor single women of not less than 50 years of age', it was held that security of tenure for occupants would be inconsistent with the duties of the charity's trustees as it *'would be impossible to ensure that only qualifying persons occupied the almshouses'*.[112]

The final case, of a service occupier, can also be explained without needing to create an exception to the basic test for a lease. There is a general principle, not confined to land law, that an employee in possession of property in the course of his or her employment does not hold that possession in his or her own right, but instead holds it on behalf of on his or her employer.[113] That principle may now seem outdated and can certainly be attacked,[114] but, as long as it continues to exist, it ensures that a contractual agreement between an employer and an employee simply cannot give the employee a right to exclusive possession of property *if* that property is to be used by the employee in the course of his or her employment.

---

105 [1985] AC 809, [825].   106 See McFarlane, *The Structure of Property Law* (2008) p 670.

107 [1942] 2 All ER 674.   108 [1998] 4 All ER 17.   109 Ibid, p 21.

110 Barr, 'Charitable Lettings and their Legal Pitfalls' in *Modern Studies in Property Law* (ed Cooke, 2001) pp 247–9.

111 [2017] 2 WLR 1107 (CA).

112 [2017] 2 WLR 1107 (CA), [87]: it was held that B, the occupier, did not have exclusive possession of the property, and the Court of Appeal also rejected a human rights challenge, made on the basis that the lack of security of tenure discriminated against occupiers of almshouses as opposed to occupiers of other residential accommodation.

113 See *Parker v British Airways Board* [1984] QB 1004, [1017], *per* Donaldson LJ; Bridge, *Personal Property* (3rd edn, 2002) p 20.

114 See ibid, pp 20–1; McFarlane, *The Structure of Property Law* (2008) p 156.

2.9 SUMMARY

It seems that, despite the supposed 'exceptional categories' noted by Lord Templeman in *Street v Mountford*, B has a lease (in the sense of a property right in land) *if and only if* he or she has a right to exclusive possession of land for a limited period, given to him or her by A, a party who has the power to give B such a property right.

The main complications arise from two sources. Firstly, it is necessary to analyse the agreement between A and B to see what legal rights it creates. It may be that, when asking if B has a right to exclusive possession, an apparent contractual term can be disregarded if it is a 'pretence'—that is, if it is clear that A had no intention to enforce that term in practice. As we saw in section 2.4, the court's power to disregard such apparent terms is, on one view, doctrinally justified: it is simply an application of a general concept which, when properly understood, makes such terms invalid as a matter of contract law. On another view, the disregarding of such terms is not doctrinally justified, and can be justified, if at all, only from a utility perspective: it denies A an easy means of withholding the statutory protection available, in some circumstances, to parties with a lease.

The second complication occurs where B1 and B2, acting together, claim to have a lease. It is currently the law that B1 and B2 can only have a lease if they are *genuinely* joint tenants— that is, if the four unities of possession, interest, time, and title are all present. On one view, this restriction is doctrinally justified;[115] on another, more widespread, view it is not: it overlooks the possibility that B1 and B2, acting together, can acquire a lease as tenants in common and thus without the need to show unity of interest, time, or title.[116] Certainly, from the utility perspective, it is hard to find a convincing policy argument for the restriction.

As we have seen throughout this section, it is important to remember that the courts' approach to the content of a lease may be shaped by the fact that, if B has such a right, he or she may qualify (or have qualified) for significant statutory protection. On the summary given above, this utility concern may (perhaps) have been an influential factor in the development of the 'pretence' test. As we will see in Chapter 23, section 4 it may also have affected an important House of Lords' decision that has also had an impact on the definition of a lease: *Bruton v London & Quadrant Housing Trust*.[117]

3 THE *ACQUISITION* QUESTION

To show that he or she has a lease, B must show that he or she has *acquired* a right to exclusive possession of land for a limited period. In considering the *acquisition* question, it is vital to distinguish between *legal* leases and *equitable* leases.

3.1 LEGAL LEASES

As we saw in Chapter 5, section 4, there are, in general, two different ways in which B may acquire a legal property right. Firstly, and most commonly, B can acquire such a right through a dependent acquisition: by showing that A gave him or her the right; secondly, and more

---

[115] See Smith, *Plural Ownership* (2004) pp 24–6; McFarlane, *The Structure of Property Law* (2008) pp 714–15.
[116] See Sparkes (1989) 18 AALR 151.   [117] [2000] 1 AC 406.

rarely, B can acquire a legal property right by an independent acquisition—that is, simply by relying on his or her own conduct. For example, as noted in section 1.2.2, as well as in Chapter 9, section 3, if B takes possession of land, so that he or she has exclusive physical control of that land, B independently acquires a legal freehold. It is, however, very difficult to see how B could ever independently acquire a lease: firstly, a lease consists of a right to exclusive possession for a *limited period*—if B simply takes control of land, he or she is not asserting such a limited right; secondly, a lease depends on a relationship between A and B, as landlord and tenant—and it is hard to see how such a relationship can arise solely because of B's conduct.

Nonetheless, under the provisions of the Land Registration Act 2002 (LRA 2002), it is now possible for B to acquire a lease independently.[118] As noted in Chapter 9, section 5.3, and explored further in the online material that accompanies this book, if B can successfully show adverse possession of land subject to a registered lease, B can apply to be registered as the new holder of that lease. From a doctrinal point of view, this is a very strange result: B's possession of the land gives him or her a freehold, but he or she then acquires a lease by applying to the registrar. From the utility perspective, however, there may be something to be said for this result: it essentially represents a compromise solution to the difficult practical and theoretical questions raised by the adverse possession of land subject to a lease.

In any case, in looking at the acquisition of leases, we can concentrate on the case of dependent acquisition—that in which B claims that A has given B a lease.

3.1.1 Basic formality requirements

As we saw in Chapter 8, B's claim that A has given him or her a legal property right, such as a lease, may be affected by formality rules.

1. A contract to grant a lease, like a contract to grant a freehold, must, in general, satisfy the need for writing signed by both A and B, as required by s 2 of the Law of Property (Miscellaneous Provisions) Act 1989 (LP(MP)A 1989) (see Chapter 8, section 3).

2. A's grant of the lease to B must, in general, be made in a deed, as required by s 52 of the LPA 1925 (see Chapter 8, section 5).

3. Again, in general, the transaction will not be complete, and B will not acquire a legal lease, unless and until B is registered as the holder of that lease. That registration requirement is imposed by s 4 of the LRA 2002 in a case in which A does not hold a registered estate and s 27 of that Act in a case in which A does hold a registered estate (see Chapter 8, section 6).

It is important to note that exceptions are provided to each of these three rules. In some cases, of course, none of those exceptions applies.

In considering the exceptions, it is useful to distinguish between: (i) cases in which A gives B a new legal lease; and (ii) cases in which B1 transfers his or her existing legal lease to B2.

3.1.2 Where A attempts to give B a new legal lease

If A attempts to give B a new legal lease of more than seven years, the full set of formality requirements applies: in particular, B does not acquire that legal lease unless and until he or

---

[118] For the background to this change, see Law Com No 271 at [14.66]–[14.73].

she registers as its holder. As we will see in section 3.2, B's failure to register will not prevent B from acquiring an equitable lease—but there may be disadvantages to B in having only an equitable lease: in particular, an equitable lease can only count as an overriding interest if B is in actual occupation of the land; in contrast, a legal lease *always* counts as an overriding interest (see Chapter 16, section 4.3). Further, as we saw in Chapter 3, section 3.2.1, once B has registered as the holder of a legal estate, s 58 of the LRA 2002 operates to vest that right conclusively in B. So, unless and until the register is changed, B is secure in knowing that he or she has a legal lease. And, indeed, even if the register is rectified, B, if he or she has not acted fraudulently or carelessly, is very likely to qualify for an indemnity payment from the Land Registry.

There is an exceptional category of leases that, even if given for seven years or less, must be registered. The leases falling within this category are defined by ss 4(1)(d)–(f) and 27(2)(b)(ii)–(v) of the 2002 Act. One example consists of a lease taking effect in possession only after a gap of more than three months from the date of its grant by A to B.[119] In that particular case, it seems that the registration requirement is imposed as such a legal lease could otherwise cause a trap for C, a party acquiring a right after the lease has been granted to B, but before B has taken possession of the land.

It should also be noted that, if A expressly grants B an easement at the same time as granting B a lease, then B will need to register that easement in order to acquire a legal easement: that is the case even if the lease itself, as it is for seven years or less, does not require registration. As we noted in Chapter 8, section 6.4, this may cause a trap for B, and the Law Commission has suggested reforming the rules for the acquisition of legal easements as a result.[120]

If A attempts to grant B a non-exceptional lease of seven years or less, B can acquire a legal lease without needing to register his or her right. As we have seen, the general rule under s 52 of the LPA 1925 is that A must use a deed to grant B a legal lease. There is, however, an exception to the need for a deed, provided by s 54(2) of the 1925 Act.

Law of Property Act 1925, s 54(2)

Nothing in the foregoing provisions of this Part of this Act shall affect the creation by parol of leases taking effect in possession for a term not exceeding three years (whether or not the lessee is given power to extend the term) at the best rent which can reasonably be obtained without taking a fine.

If the requirements of s 54(2) are met, B can acquire a legal lease as a result of a purely oral grant from A: registration is not needed; nor a deed; nor even any writing.[121] The basic policy of the exception is clear: as a matter of convenience, parties should be free to enter relatively short-lived arrangements without having to express their intentions in a particular form.

---

[119] Other examples are a discontinuous lease (such as a time-share lease, in which B has a right to exclusive possession only for a limited part of each year) and leases that, under the provisions of the Housing Act 1985, would, in any case, require registration.

[120] Law Com CP No 227 (2016) [16.32].

[121] There is an argument that any easement that A grants to B as part of the lease would, however, need to be made in a deed, as s 54(2) contains an exception only for leases, and otherwise the general s 52 formality rule applies: for discussion see Chapter 8, section 5 and Law Com CP No 227 (2016) [16.17]–[16.20].

It is, however, important to note that the length of the lease is only *one* of the requirements of the exception. To acquire a legal lease without a deed, B needs to show that the lease:

- is for three years or less; *and*
- takes effect in possession; *and*
- is at the best rent reasonably obtainable without taking a fine.[122]

The third requirement will be satisfied if B is paying a reasonable market rent[123] rather than, for example, acquiring the lease by paying a one-off premium. This requirement may be seen as a means of protecting C, a party to whom A might later transfer A's estate in the land. The problem for C is that B's oral, but legal, lease may be hard to discover. Of course, in practice, B may well be in occupation of the land—but, under Sch 3, para 1 of the LRA 2002, B's legal lease counts as an overriding interest in its own right and so is immune from the lack of registration defence even if B is not in actual occupation of the land. The rent requirement in s 54(2) provides some protection for C: even if he or she is bound by B's oral lease, he or she will at least, receive a reasonable rent from B.

In the following case, the second of the three requirements was decisive.

Long v Tower Hamlets London Borough Council
[1998] Ch 197

Facts: Tower Hamlets LBC had a freehold of No 21 Turners Road, consisting of a ground-floor shop and a maisonette. It gave Mr Long permission to occupy the shop; Mr Long later decided to occupy the maisonette as well. As far as the shop was concerned, Mr Long, before moving in, had received a letter setting out the terms of occupation. The letter was sent in early September 1975 and stated that Mr Long's right of occupation would begin on 29 September. Mr Long indorsed and returned the letter on 8 September. At some point (claimed by Mr Long to be in 1977), Mr Long stopped paying rent. In 1995, Mr Long claimed that, because he had been occupying both the shop and maisonette, without Tower Hamlets' consent, for over twelve years, the doctrine of adverse possession extinguished Tower Hamlet LBC's freehold of that land (see Chapter 8 for a discussion of that doctrine). According to Sch 1, para 5, of the Limitation Act 1980, if Tower Hamlets LBC could show that Mr Long had occupied under a 'lease in writing', Mr Long's adverse possession claim would fail, because the twelve-year limitation period would have begun in 1984 and so would not yet have expired. But if Tower Hamlets could not show that Mr Long had a 'lease in writing', the twelve-year clock would have begun to count down from an earlier point (when Mr Long stopped paying rent) and so Mr Long's adverse possession claim could succeed. The case was therefore slightly unusual: the claim of a lease was made not by the occupier, but rather by the party granting the rights of occupation.

---

[122] For an argument that the 'best rent' requirement should be abolished, and that the 'takes effect in posssession' requirement should be modified so as to require only that a lease take effect in possession within three months of its grant, see Brown and Pawlowski, 'Re-thinking Section 54(2) of the Law of Property Act 1925' [2010] Conv 146.

[123] See *Fitzkriston LLP v Panayi* [2008] EWCA Civ 283, [23], *per* Rix LJ. There may thus be cases where the rent agreed by the parties is below market rent, and so s 54(2) does not apply: ibid, [27], *per* Rix LJ.

Tower Hamlets LBC applied for an order striking out Mr Long's adverse possession claim, on the basis that, because he had been given 'a lease in writing', the limitation period only began to run against Tower Hamlets LBC in 1984. James Munby QC, sitting as a deputy High Court judge, rejected that argument, holding that Mr Long had *not* been given a 'lease in writing'.

James Munby QC (sitting as a Deputy High Court judge)

At 205

At common law a lease could be granted in any way, even orally [. . .] Moreover, there was at common law no restraint upon the grant of a reversionary lease, that is, a lease to take effect in reversion on some future day, however distant, and conferring no right to take possession in the meantime. Such a lease [. . .] gave the lessee an immediate vested legal *interest* in the land, that interest being known as an interesse termini, though until the date when the lease was due to take effect this interest was vested in interest and not in possession. On the other hand, the lessee under a reversionary lease acquired no *estate* in the land until he had actually entered, that is, taken possession in accordance with the lease; until then all he had was an interesse termini [. . .]

At 216–17

In the first place, the words 'in possession,' when used as part of the phrase 'taking effect in possession for a term not exceeding three years,' in my judgment have their normal legal meaning. They connote an estate or interest in the land which is vested 'in possession' rather than merely vested 'in interest.' This reading is powerfully reinforced by the distinction drawn in section 205(1)(xxvii) of the Law of Property Act 1925 between a 'term of years taking effect in possession' and a 'term of years taking effect in reversion.' The words 'taking effect in possession' in section 54(2) are, in my judgment, used in the same sense in which those words are used in section 205(1)(xxvii) and thus, and this is the critical point, in distinction to the words 'taking effect in reversion.' This, as it seems to me, demonstrates that [. . .] reversionary leases were not intended to come within the ambit of section 54(2).

Moreover, there has been omitted from section 54(2) any express reference to the date of 'the making' of the lease. Thus, if [counsel for Tower Hamlets'] argument is correct, there is no limit expressed in section 54(2) to the period which may elapse before the lease 'tak[es] effect in possession,' the only requirement being that the lease, when eventually it does 'tak[e] effect in possession,' must be 'for a term not exceeding three years.'

As interpreted in *Long v Tower Hamlets LBC*, the requirement that the lease must 'take effect in possession' can also be seen as providing some protection for C: a lease under which B has no right to immediate possession may be particularly hard for C to discover.[124]

But whilst the decision must be correct as a matter of statutory interpretation, it reveals that the s 54(2) exception has only a limited practical impact.

[124] It should be noted, however, that a lease can 'take effect in possession' even if B does not immediately go into occupation; the question is whether B has an immediate *right* to exclusive possession.

Bright, 'Beware the Informal Lease: The (Very) Narrow Scope of s 54(2) Law of Property Act 1925' [1998] Conv 229, 232–3

Whilst the reasoning behind [*Long v Tower Hamlets*] is hard to fault, the practical implications of the decision are absurd. It is easy to state that, to be safe, all leases should be entered into by deed, but this is unrealistic. Another option is to say that where there is an informal lease, the term date should be stated to pre-date the date of the agreement (presumably it is the term commencement that indicates whether a lease is in possession). This again is an unrealistic option for in most situations the parties want a binding commitment prior to the commencement date. The absurdity of the subsection is revealed when we consider what the policy is underlying it. There are many reasons why formalities may be required in land transactions but underlying section 52 is the benefit it secures for the parties to the transaction (creating evidence, warning of legal effects, protecting against outside influences) and for the court (evidential). Given the advantages of formality in this context, why are short leases exempted? The answer in part is probably that many short leases are, in fact, entered into without legal advice and if a formality requirement were imposed many parties would remain in ignorance of it. In addition to non-compliance through ignorance there is likely to be a high level of non-compliance through fear of costs. Deeds are likely to involve instructing lawyers, which means expense and delay. The disadvantages of requiring a deed outweigh the advantages to be gained from requiring one. If these ideas explain why the law permits the creation of short leases by parol, the exemption should not be restricted to those taking effect immediately in possession. Instead, the exemption should apply to those leases that are most likely to be entered into without the benefit of legal advice, informally, and where the costs of a deed would discourage compliance. Looked at in this light, the exemption should apply to short leases which are to take effect in possession within a reasonable period, and perhaps twelve months would provide a sensible cut-off.

There is another form of short legal lease that can be acquired by B without a deed, or any writing. As we saw when considering *Prudential Assurance Ltd v London Residuary Body* in section 2.7, B's payment and A's acceptance of rent can give rise to an *implied periodic tenancy*. In such a case, the conduct of the parties *may* lead a court to imply, or assume, that A granted a lease to B; there is no need for any formal proof of that grant. It should be noted, however, that: '*The payment of rent gives rise to no presumption of a periodic tenancy. Rather, the parties' contractual intentions fall to be determined by looking objectively at all relevant circumstances.*'[125] So, for example, A's acceptance of rent is unlikely to give rise to an implied periodic tenancy if A and B are at the same time involved in negotiations for the grant a formal lease, as '*the obvious and almost overwhelming inference will be that the parties did not intend to enter into any intermediate contractual arrangement inconsistent with remaining parties to ongoing negotiations.*'[126]

In practice, B may occupy land for a long time under a succession of periodic tenancies (in *Prudential Assurance*, for example, the House of Lords held that the strip of land in question

---

[125] *Erimus Housing Ltd v Barclays Wealth Trustees (Jersey) Ltd* [2014] EWCA Civ 303 *per* Patten LJ at [23].

[126] Ibid. The case involved negotiations between A and B following the expiry of a business tenancy. If an implied periodic tenancy had been found, B would then have qualified for statutory protection under Part II of the Landlord and Tenant Act 1954, and this provided a further reason for the finding that A was unlikely to have intended to have granted such a periodic tenancy. See too *Cardiothoracic Institute v Shrewdcrest Ltd* [1986] 1 WLR 368.

had been occupied in that way for over sixty years). The maximum duration of any individual periodic tenancy is, however, a year. The length of the term depends on how B pays
rent: if B pays weekly, a weekly tenancy will be implied; if B pays monthly, a monthly tenancy
will result; and if the frequency is calculated by reference to a year (e.g. if B pays quarterly), B
will have a yearly periodic tenancy. To terminate the lease, either party needs to give notice
of an intention not to renew it at the end of the current period. A week's notice is needed in
the case of a weekly tenancy; a month's notice for a monthly tenancy; six months' notice is
required for a yearly tenancy.

Given that the maximum length of a periodic tenancy is a year and that B will necessarily
have a right to immediate possession, it may seem that any implied periodic tenancy will fall
within the s 54(2) exception. Because an implied periodic tenancy can arise even if B does
not pay a reasonable market rent, however, it seems that it provides an independent exception to the general rule that a legal interest in land can only be acquired where a deed is used.

The position can be summarized as in Table 19.1.

Table 19.1 Formality requirements for the creation of a new legal lease.

Type of legal lease	Deed required?	Registration required?
For more than seven years *or* in an exceptional category*	Yes	Yes
(i) Implied periodic tenancy or (ii) For three years or less, *and* taking effect in possession, *and* at a reasonable market rent	No	No
All other leases	Yes	No

* See Land Registration Act 2002, ss 4 and 27, for the exceptional categories (e.g. a lease taking effect in
possession more than three months from the time of the grant).

3.1.3 Where B1 attempts to transfer an existing legal lease to B2

Imagine that A has a legal estate in land and then grants B1 a legal lease. It is then possible for B1 to retain his or her lease and to grant B2 a new lease (a sublease): in such a case,
the formality requirements will apply in the way set out above. It is also possible for B1 to
transfer his or her lease to B2. In that case, the formality requirements apply in a slightly
different way:[127] firstly, if B1's lease is registered, B2 cannot acquire that right until he or she
registers as its new holder; secondly, if B1's lease is not registered (e.g. because it is a lease of
seven years or less), B1 *must* use a deed to transfer the lease to B2. That rule applies even if
B1 acquired his or her lease orally, by relying on the s 54(2) exception. The Court of Appeal
confirmed this in *Crago v Julian*.[128]

It is clear, as a matter of statutory interpretation, that the s 54(2) exception does *not* apply
to the transfer of an existing lease; it applies only to the creation of a new lease. Yet this can
cause problems in practice, because, if B1 has acquired his or her lease orally, he or she may
be unaware that the lease can only be transferred by using a deed. It is worth noting that,

---

[127] The terms of B1's lease may attempt to prevent B1 from granting a sublease to B2 or from transferring
his or her lease to B2. In such a case, the sublease or transfer does still occur (see *Old Grovebury Manor Farm
Ltd v W Seymour Plant Sales and Hire Ltd (No 2)* [1979] 1 WLR 1397), but B1's breach may give A a power to
forfeit the lease (see Chapter 21, section 6.4).

[128] [1992] 1 WLR 372.

when the provisons of the Renting Homes (Wales) Act 2016 are brought into force, different rules will apply in Wales: where B1 occupies a dwelling under a contract with A, whether that agreement is a lease or a licence, it will be possible for B1 to transfer the benefit of the contract to B2 without using a deed.[129] This is part of the Act's wider reforms of the law, which will be discussed in Chapter 20, section 5.

3.2 EQUITABLE LEASES

It was suggested in Chapter 6, section 1 that all equitable interests depend on A's being under a duty to B. Certainly, it seems that, to acquire an equitable lease, B needs to show that A is under a duty to grant B a lease. In Chapter 8, section 4.1 when considering *Walsh v Lonsdale*,[130] we saw that B can acquire an equitable lease when A comes under a *contractual* duty to grant B a lease.

Walsh v Lonsdale
(1882) LR 21 Ch D 9, CA

Facts: Lonsdale agreed to grant a lease of a mill to Walsh for seven years. Under the agreement, the rent was to be payable yearly in advance. No lease was granted, but Walsh moved in and started paying rent quarterly in arrears. Lonsdale, however, demanded payment in advance, in accordance with the agreement, and when Walsh failed to pay, Lonsdale levied distress (i.e. took possession of Walsh's goods on the premises and sold them to meet the rent due). Walsh argued that he was not under a duty to pay the rent yearly in advance, as the agreed lease had never been granted, and so he had only an implied periodic tenancy, arising at common law as a result of his payment, and Lonsdale's acceptance, of rent. Lonsdale argued that Walsh instead had an equitable lease, on terms mirroring those of the planned legal lease.

Jessel MR

At 14–15

There is an agreement for a lease under which possession has been given. Now since the Judicature Act the possession is held under the agreement. There are not two estates as there were formerly, one estate at common law by reason of the payment of the rent from year to year, and an estate in equity under the agreement. There is only one Court, and the equity rules prevail in it. The tenant holds under an agreement for a lease. He holds, therefore, under the same terms in equity as if a lease had been granted, it being a case in which both parties admit that relief is capable of being given by specific performance. That being so, he cannot complain of the exercise by the landlord of the same rights as the landlord would have had if a lease had been granted. On the other hand, he is protected in the same way as if a lease had been granted; he cannot be turned out by six months' notice as a tenant from year to year.

---

[129] Renting Homes (Wales) Act 2016, s 72(2). It is necessary under s 69(2) for the transfer to be signed or executed by each of the parties to it and, if the consent of the landlord is required, by the landlord too. Section 236 of the Act also makes provision for the use of electronic documents and signatures.
[130] (1882) 21 Ch D 9.

The context of the case lies in the merger of law and equity by the Judicature Acts 1873–75. The specific issue was the effect of the Acts on the position of a tenant who moves into possession and starts to pay rent in the absence of a formally granted lease. At common law, such facts gave rise to an implied periodic tenancy, as noted in section 3.1.2. If such a tenancy was present on the facts of the case, then Walsh was only liable for rent in arrears (as had been paid) and Lonsdale's distress for non-payment of rent in advance was illegal. In equity, it was already established that the effect of the maxim 'equity looks on as done that which ought to be done' was that the parties would be treated as though the lease had been granted,[131] with the effect that all of the terms of the parties' agreement were enforceable. Applying the Judicature Acts, the Court gave precedence to equity's analysis. The agreement for the grant of a legal lease created an equitable lease under which the parties were bound by the same terms as their intended grant.

As we saw in Chapter 8, section 3, A can only come under a *contractual* duty to grant a lease to B if the formality rule set out by s 2 of the Law of Property (Miscellaneous Provisions) Act 1989 has been satisfied. Further, B will only acquire an equitable lease if A's duty to grant a lease is capable of being enforced by an order of specific performance: see Chapter 8, section 4.1.

There may be situations in which A has not made a contractual promise to give B a lease but, instead, has simply tried and failed to make an immediate grant of a lease: for example, A may attempt to grant B a five-year lease, but fail to use a deed. In such a case, if B provided something in return for the failed grant (e.g. money), A will be regarded as under a duty to give B a lease and B can thus acquire an equitable lease.[132] Further, B may well be able to acquire an equitable lease if he or she can show that the doctrine of proprietary estoppel imposes a duty on A to grant B a lease.[133]

If B1 has an equitable lease, arising as a result of A being under a duty to grant B1 a lease, it should also be possible for B1 to transfer that equitable lease to B2. In such a case, the basic formality rule set out by s 53(1)(a) of the LPA 1925 will apply: the transfer must be made in writing signed by B1.

It is sometimes suggested that an equitable lease is 'as good as' a legal lease. Certainly, if B has an equitable lease, this will generally be enough to entitle him or her to any statutory protection available to a holder of a lease (see section 1.2.1).[134] Further, an equitable lease is capable of binding a third party who later acquires a right in relation to the land from A (see section 1.2.3). But certain advantages do come with a legal lease. Firstly, as we have noted, a legal lease, unlike an equitable lease, *necessarily* counts as an overriding interest and so C, a party later acquiring a right from A, will not be able to use the lack of registration defence against B's right.

Secondly, if B acquires a legal lease for value, then, under s 29 of the LRA 2002, B may him or herself be able to use the lack of registration defence against a pre-existing property

---

[131] *Parker v Taswell* (1858) 2 De G & J 559.   [132] See e.g. *Parker v Taswell* (1858) 2 De G & J 559.

[133] For example, it seems that B acquired such an equitable lease in *Lloyd v Dugdale* [2002] 2 P & CR 13. See further Bright and McFarlane, 'Proprietary Estoppel and Property Rights' [2005] CLJ 449. The problem for Mr Dugdale (B) was that, because he was in not in actual occupation of the land when A transferred his freehold to C, C had a defence to B's pre-existing equitable lease. B therefore tried to assert a new, direct right against C, arising as a result of a promise made by C when acquiring the freehold: this point of the case in was considered Chapter 7, section 3.3.1.

[134] See e.g. *R v Tower Hamlets, ex p van Goetz* [1999] 2 WLR 582.

right (such as a prior equitable lease created by A in favour of Z).[135] But if B has only an equitable lease, he or she cannot use that defence.

Thirdly, if B acquires a legal lease from A, B will also be able to rely on s 62 of the LPA 1925, which can imply the grant of additional rights by A (such as easements—see Chapter 22, section 3.2) into the creation of B's legal lease. But if B has only an equitable lease, s 62 cannot apply.

Finally, if B has a legal lease, it is then clear that the rest of the world is under a *prima facie* duty to B: as a result, for example, a stranger who interferes with B's enjoyment of the land will commit the tort of nuisance against B (see the discussion of *Hunter v Canary Wharf*[136] in section 1.2.2). If, however, B has only an equitable lease, it is far from clear that B has the same protection: B can assert a right against C, a party who later acquires a right from A; but, as discussed in Chapter 6, section 7, it is not clear that the rest of the world owes a duty to B not to interfere with the land.

3.3 METHODS BY WHICH A LEASE MAY END

In sections 3.1 and 3.2, we considered the methods by which a lease can come into being. We also need to consider the various ways in which a lease may end.

3.3.1 The effluxion of time

The simplest method by which a lease may end is the passage of time: if the term for which a lease has been granted comes to an end, the lease itself ends. So, if A granted B a 21 year lease in 1994, that lease will end in 2015. We saw in section 3.1.2 that, if B has a periodic tenancy, his right to exclusive possession will automatically be renewed at the end of each period, unless one of the parties gives sufficient notice of his or her intention not to renew. If no such notice is given, B can end up occupying A's land for a long time: in *Prudential Assurance*, for example, B's occupation, under a succession of yearly tenancies, had lasted over 60 years. It is important to note that, in such a case, B does not occupy under one, continuing lease—rather, B occupies under a succession of periodic tenancies. This technical point is important in ensuring that periodic tenancies are consistent with the need for a lease to be for a limited period: the maximum duration of each in a series of periodic tenancies is known in advance. The technical point was also important in the following case.

Hammersmith and Fulham LBC v Monk
[1991] UKHL 6, [1992] AC 478, HL

Facts: Mr Monk and Mrs Powell cohabited in a flat at 35 Nitron Street, South West London, under a joint weekly tenancy, given to them by Hammersmith and Fulham London Borough Council. As the landlord was thus a local authority, the grounds on

---

[135] Usually, B needs to register his or her own right if he or she wishes to rely on the lack of registration defence. But s 29(4) of the Land Registration Act 2002 means that B can rely on that defence if he or she has been *granted* a lease that cannot be registered (e.g. a non-exceptional lease of seven years or less). The term 'grant' is crucial, because it excludes a party with only an equitable lease: if B has only an equitable lease, he or she has not been granted a right; rather, A is under a duty to make such a grant.

[136] [1997] AC 665.

which it could recover possession of the flat were limited by statute. In 1988, the couple fell out and Mrs Powell left the flat. She consulted with the council who agreed to provide her with alternative accommodation, if she terminated the periodic tenancy of 35 Nitron Street. The terms of the tenancy allowed for termination with four week's notice. Without Mr Monk's knowledge or consent, Mrs Powell gave this notice to quit to the council, who then sought possession of 35 Nitron St against Mr Monk.

The council's argument was that Mr Monk had occupied under a succession of weekly periodic tenancies and each new tenancy arose only because each of Mr Monk and Mrs Powell had failed to give a notice to quit. When Mrs Powell gave such a notice, their joint periodic tenancy could not continue into a new period and so the tenancy, and the statutory protection it gave to Mr Monk, was now at an end. As a result, the council now had the choice of removing Mr Monk from the land. The first instance judge held that Mrs Powell's notice to quit could not end the joint tenancy, and so dismissed the council's claim for possession. The Court of Appeal allowed the council's appeal; the House of Lords agreed that Mrs Powell's notice to quit meant that the succession of joint weekly periodic tenancies, and with it Mr Monk's right to occupy the flat, was brought to an end. The council were therefore free to claim possession of the flat.

Lord Bridge

For a large part of this century there have been many categories of tenancy of property occupied for agricultural, residential and commercial purposes where the legislature has intervened to confer upon tenants extra-contractual rights entitling them to continue in occupation without the consent of the landlord, either after the expiry of a contractual lease for a fixed term or after notice to quit given by the landlord to determine a contractual periodic tenancy. It is primarily in relation to joint tenancies in these categories that the question whether or not notice to quit given by one of the joint tenants can determine the tenancy is of practical importance, particularly where, as in the instant case, the effect of the determination will be to deprive the other joint tenant of statutory protection. This may appear an untoward result and may consequently provoke a certain reluctance to hold that the law can permit one of two joint tenants unilaterally to deprive his co-tenant of 'rights' which both are equally entitled to enjoy. But the statutory consequences are in truth of no relevance to the question which your Lordships have to decide. That question is whether, at common law, a contractual periodic tenancy granted to two or more joint tenants is incapable of termination by a tenant's notice to quit unless it is served with the concurrence of all the joint tenants. That is the proposition which [Mr Monk] must establish in order to succeed.

As a matter of principle I see no reason why this question should receive any different answer in the context of the contractual relationship of landlord and tenant than that which it would receive in any other contractual context. If A and B contract with C on terms which are to continue in operation for one year in the first place and thereafter from year to year unless determined by notice at the end of the first or any subsequent year, neither A nor B has bound himself contractually for longer than one year. To hold that A could not determine the contract at the end of any year without the concurrence of B and vice versa would presuppose that each had assumed a potentially irrevocable contractual obligation for the duration of their joint lives, which, whatever the nature of the contractual obligations undertaken, would be such an improbable intention to impute to the parties that nothing less than the clearest express contractual language would suffice to manifest it. Hence, in any ordinary agreement for an initial term which is to continue for successive terms unless determined by notice, the obvious inference is that the agreement is intended to continue beyond the initial term only if and so long as all parties to the agreement are willing that it should do so. In a common law situation, where parties are free to contract as they wish and are bound only so far as they have agreed to be bound, this leads to the only sensible result [. . .]

[. . .] from the earliest times a yearly tenancy has been an estate which continued only so long as it was the will of both parties that it should continue, albeit that either party could only signify his unwillingness that the tenancy should continue beyond the end of any year by giving the appropriate advance notice to that effect. Applying this principle to the case of a yearly tenancy where either the lessor's or the lessee's interest is held jointly by two or more parties, logic seems to me to dictate the conclusion that the will of all the joint parties is necessary to the continuance of the interest [. . .]

[Lord Bridge then considered a number of previous decisions, including *Doe d. Aslin v Summersett*[137] finding at 487 that there was a 'formidable body of English authority' in support of the Court of Appeal's decision that Mrs Powell's notice to quit brought the succession of weekly tenancies to an end]

[. . .]

Finally, it is said [by Mr Monk] that all positive dealings with a joint tenancy require the concurrence of all joint tenants if they are to be effective. Thus, a single joint tenant cannot exercise a break clause in a lease, surrender the term, make a disclaimer, exercise an option to renew the term or apply for relief from forfeiture. All these positive acts which joint tenants must concur in performing are said to afford analogies with the service of notice to determine a periodic tenancy which is likewise a positive act. But this is to confuse the form with the substance. The action of giving notice to determine a periodic tenancy is in form positive; but both on authority and on the principle so aptly summed up in the pithy Scottish phrase 'tacit relocation' the substance of the matter is that it is by his omission to give notice of termination that each party signifies the necessary positive assent to the extension of the term for a further period.

Lord Browne-Wilkinson

My Lords, there are two instinctive reactions to this case which lead to diametrically opposite conclusions. The first is that the flat in question was the joint home of the appellant and Mrs. Powell: it therefore cannot be right that one of them unilaterally can join the landlords to put an end to the other's rights in the home. The second is that the appellant and Mrs. Powell undertook joint liabilities as tenants for the purpose of providing themselves with a joint home and that, once the desire to live together has ended, it is impossible to require that the one who quits the home should continue indefinitely to be liable for the discharge of the obligations to the landlord under the tenancy agreement.

These two instinctive reactions are mirrored in the legal analysis of the position. In certain cases a contract between two persons can, by itself, give rise to a property interest in one of them. The contract between a landlord and a tenant is a classic example. The contract of tenancy confers on the tenant a legal estate in the land: such legal estate gives rise to rights and duties incapable of being founded in contract alone. The revulsion against Mrs. Powell being able unilaterally to terminate the appellant's rights in his home is property based: the appellant's property rights in the home cannot be destroyed without his consent. The other reaction is contract based: Mrs. Powell cannot be held to a tenancy contract which is dependant for its continuance on the will of the tenant.

[. . .]

---

[137] (1830) 1 B. & Ad. 135.

In property law, a transfer of land to two or more persons jointly operates so as to make them, vis à vis the outside world, one single owner. "Although as between themselves joint tenants have separate rights, as against everyone else they are in the position of a single owner."[138] The law would have developed consistently with this principle if it had been held that where a periodic tenancy has been granted by or to a number of persons jointly, the relevant "will" to discontinue the tenancy has to be the will of all the joint lessors or joint lessees who together constitute *the* owner of the reversion or the term as the case may be.

[. . .] the law was in my judgment determined in the opposite sense by *Doe d. Aslin v. Summersett*.[139] The contractual, as opposed to the property, approach was adopted. Where there were joint lessors of a periodic tenancy, the continuing "will" had to be the will of all the lessors individually, not the conjoint will of all the lessors collectively [. . .]

It was submitted that this House should overrule *Summersett's* case. But, as my noble and learned friend, Lord Bridge of Harwich, has demonstrated, the decision was treated throughout the 19th century as laying down the law in relation to the rights of joint lessors. It is not suggested that the position of joint lessees can be different. Since 1925 the law as determined in *Summersett's* case has been applied to notices to quit given by one of several joint lessees. In my judgment no sufficient reason has been shown for changing the basic law which has been established for 160 years [. . .]

The decision of the House of Lords in *Monk*, like many of the cases we have examined in this chapter, can be considered both from the doctrinal and utility perspectives. As a matter of doctrine, the result seems to be correct: a periodic tenancy, like any lease, has to be renewed if it is to continue from one term to the next. And the renewal of a periodic tenancy, like the renewal of any contract, requires the consent of all the parties to that tenancy. When Mrs Powell removed her consent, then, the periodic tenancy ended, taking with it the statutory security of tenure it gave to Mr Monk. From a utility perspective, in contrast, the result may seem concerning: Mr Monk's security of tenure was lost without his consent. The Law Commission, for example, has proposed that it should be possible for one joint tenant, such as Mrs Powell, to give a notice to quit, and thus end her involvement with the tenancy, without ending the joint tenancy itself.[140] Indeed, as we noted in Chapter 4, section 4.2.2, the approach in *Monk* has been subjected to human rights challenges, questioning its compatibility with Art 8 and with Art 1 of the First Protocol of the European Convention on Human Rights.[141]

In *Sims v Dacorum BC*,[142] the Supreme Court considered such challenges. Mr and Mrs Sims had a joint weekly tenancy, which was protected under the Housing Act 1985 as a secure tenancy. As long as it continued, the grounds on which either tenant could be removed were limited by statute. When Mr and Mrs Sims separated, however, Mrs Sims served a notice to quit, and so, under *Monk*, the joint periodic tenancy, and with it Mr Sims's security of tenure, came to an end.

---

[138] *Megarry and Wade, The Law of Real Property*, 5th edn (1984) p 417.
[139] (1830) 1 B. & Ad. 135.
[140] Law Com No 297, 'Renting Homes: The Final Report' (Volume 1, 2006) paras 2.44–2.46, 4.9–4.12.
[141] See also *Harrow LBC v Qazi* [2004] 1 AC 983, discussed in Chapter 4, section 4.1.1; and Bright, 'Ending Tenancies by Notice to Quit: The Human Rights Challenge' (2004) 120 LQR 398.
[142] [2014] UKSC 63.

The Supreme Court found that the council's decision to evict Mr Sims was not a breach of Art 1 of the First Protocol. Mr Sim's 'possession' under that Article was his right under the joint tenancy, and his agreement with the council made clear that, if notice to quite was served by Mrs Sims, that right would end, and the council would then decide whether to allow him to remain. Nor was there a breach of Art 8. As a result of the Protection from Eviction Act 1977, the council could not evict Mr Sims without a court order and, following *Pinnock v Manchester City Council*[143] and in *Hounslow LBC v Powell*,[144] 'the court could not make such an order without permitting him to raise a claim that it would be disproportionate to evict him'.[145] That procedural protection ensured that any special personal circumstances relevant to Mr Sims could be considered, and so ensured that Mr Sims' Art 8 right was adequately protected even though the council had chosen to evict him.[146]

This solution implements the suggestion made in the previous edition of this book: whilst the basic rule in *Monk* gives a local authority the option of regaining possession after one joint tenant fails to renew a periodic tenancy, the local authority will have to bear Art 8 in mind when exercising its discretion as to whether to use that option.[147]

3.3.2 The exercise of a power to end a lease before its term expires

There are a number of situations in which a lease may end before the planned term has expired. Firstly, the terms of the lease may give one or both of the parties a power to terminate the lease early. Such a 'break clause' is common, for example, in a commercial lease. It may be wise for a tenant taking a 21 year lease of business premises to insist on a clause allowing him or her to terminate the lease after five years: the tenant can then take advantage of that clause if the business does not prove successful.

Secondly, and much more rarely, a change of circumstances may give a party the power to end the lease early, even if the terms of the contract do not expressly confer such a power. For example, in *National Carriers Ltd v Panalpina (Northern) Ltd*,[148] the House of Lords acknowledged, for the first time, that the doctrine of frustration can apply to a lease. So, if A gives B a lease of a warehouse, and both A and B know that B plans to use that warehouse for commercial storage, the closure of the only road giving access to the warehouse could, if continuing for a long enough period, lead to the parties' contract being frustrated.[149]

Similarly, in *Hussein v Mehlman*,[150] Stephen Sedley QC, sitting as an assistant recorder, held that, where A gave B a lease of a house, A's serious breaches of his duty to repair, rendering the house unfit to live in, interfered with the 'central purpose'[151] of the contract and

---

143 [2011] 2 AC 104.   144 [2011] 2 AC 186.
145 [2014] UKSC 63 *per* Lord Neuberger at [23].
146 In *McCann v UK* (2008) 47 EHRR 40, for example, the ECHR did find a breach of Art 8 in a case where the local authority took advantage of the rule in *Monk* to remove Mr McCann from his home. The problem, however, was that the court had no discretion to consider the proportionality of the possession order and that problem was later solved by *Powell* and *Pinnock*: see Chapter 4, section 4.2.1.
147 This also seems to have been the suggestion of Lord Walker in *Doherty v Birmingham CC* [2009] AC 367 at [121]–[123].
148 [1981] AC 675.
149 In the case itself, the contract was *not* frustrated: the road was closed only for twenty months of a ten-year lease.
150 [1992] 2 EGLR 87 (County Court).   151 Ibid, 91.

so allowed B to terminate the contract by moving out and ceasing to pay rent.[152] Of course, the general contractual rule applies, and so the tenant's power to terminate the lease early will arise only where the landlord's breach is so serious as to deprive the tenant of substantially the whole of the benefit which the contract was intended to secure for the tenant.[153] We will consider both *Panalpina* and *Hussein* again in section 5, when looking at the contractual aspects of a lease.

If the tenant, rather than the landlord, is in serious breach of his or her obligations under the lease, the landlord may have a power to bring the lease to an end. If the landlord exercises such as a power, this is said to be a 'forfeiture': the tenant loses the right to exclusive possession due to his or her serious breach of the terms of the lease. Given the often severe consequences of forfeiture, the courts have the power to protect a tenant by granting relief from forfeiture: this power was first developed by courts of equity, and is now regulated, in part, by statute.[154] We will consider forfeiture of leases in detail in Chapter 21, section 6.4. It is also worth noting that, even if a landlord does have the freedom to forfeit a lease, such a landlord may instead elect to keep the lease alive so as to continue to claim rent from the tenant. As the Court of Appeal confirmed in *Reichman v Beveridge*,[155] this course is open to the landlord even if the tenant has left the premises, and even if the landlord could reduce his losses by renting the premises to a different tenant. This is in part because of a long-standing rule that if the new tenant pays a lower rent, the landlord is *not* permitted to pursue the former tenant for this difference in rent: the landlord's decision to end the first lease also ends the first tenant's liability for any future rent. To this extent, it seems, the normal contractual liability rules do not apply between a landlord and a tenant.[156]

3.3.3 Where the lease is subsumed into a different legal estate

Firstly, if A has granted B a lease, it is possible for A and B to agree to B's surrender of the lease before its term expires. A surrender is a '*consensual transaction between landlord and tenant*'[157] and its effect is that '*the tenancy is absorbed by the landlord's reversion and is extinguished by operation of law*':[158] the lease thus ceases to exist as it is subsumed into A's estate in the land. An express surrender must be made by deed, even if the lease itself was initially created orally. Most surrenders occur by operation of law, however, and are therefore excepted from the need for a deed.[159] A surrender by operation of law requires both the tenant's re-delivery of possession of the land to the landlord, and the landlord's acceptance of such re-delivery.[160] It is also worth noting that, if A grants a lease to B, and B then grants a sublease

---

[152] That reasoning has since been confirmed by the Court of Appeal: see *Chartered Trust plc v Davies* [1997] 2 EGLR 83.

[153] The general contractual test is set out by Diplock LJ in *Hong Kong Fir v Kawasaki* [1962] 1 All ER 474, 489. For a case in which the landlord's breach was not sufficiently serious, see *Nynehead Developments Ltd v RH Fibreboard Containers Ltd* [1991] 1 EGLR 7. In such a case, the landlord is liable in damages to the tenant for the breach.

[154] See Law of Property Act 1925, s 146(1).

[155] [2006] EWCA Civ 1659. See too Chapter 21, section 6.

[156] The position is different in many other common law jurisdictions: see Bright, *Landlord and Tenant Law in Context* (2007) pp 508–11.

[157] *Per* Lord Scott in *Kay v Lambeth LBC; Leeds CC v Price* [2006] 2 AC 465, [141].

[158] *Per* Lord Millett in *Barrett v Morgan* [2000] 2 AC 264, [270].

[159] Law of Property Act 1925, s 52(2)(c) excepts surrenders by operation of law from the general deed requirement imposed by s 52.

[160] See further *per* Peter Gibson LJ in *Bellcourt Estates Ltd v Adesina* [2005] EWCA Civ 208, [29]–[31].

to C, the surrender by B to A of B's lease does not end C's sub-lease; rather, A then becomes C's landlord, as would be the case had B transferred his lease to A. This result is based on the basic principle that C's property right cannot be terminated without C's consent.[161]

Secondly, if A grants B a lease, and A's estate and B's lease are later acquired by the same party, it is possible for the lease to end by a merger: by being subsumed into A's estate. For example, in Chapter 7, section 3.3.1, we saw that in *Ashburn Anstalt v Arnold*,[162] Mr Arnold initially held a lease of the land; Arnold & Co then acquired a sub-lease. Cavendish Land Co Ltd later acquired the freehold subject to Mr Arnold's head-lease. Cavendish then also acquired both the head-lease and the sub-lease. The effect of this, as noted by Fox LJ in the Court of Appeal, was that '*the head-lease and the sub-lease merged into the freehold*'.[163] In that case, merger allowed Cavendish to achieve its aim of holding its freehold free from any leases. Similarly, if B has a very long lease and then, as in *James v UK*,[164] exercises his or her statutory right of enfranchisement, B will generally want to hold his or her freehold free from any leases. It is important to note, however, that merger is not automatic. If B has a lease from A, and then acquires A's estate, it may well be that B does *not* want merger to operate. For example, Bright notes that '*A tenant of a flat who, for example, acquires the freehold reversion to the block may want the lease to continue as an independent and saleable asset.*'[165] In such a case, courts of equity focussed on B's intention and therefore held that merger did not occur: that equitable approach is now preserved by the Law of Property Act 1925, s 185.

4 THE *DEFENCES* QUESTION

If B acquires a legal or equitable lease of A's land, his or her right will be prima facie binding on C, a third party later acquiring a right relating to that land from A. It may, however, be possible for C to have a defence to a pre-existing property right of B. In practice, the key defence is the lack of registration defence provided by the LRA 2002.

In considering the defence, we again need to distinguish between cases in which B has a legal lease and those in which B's lease is equitable.

4.1 LEGAL LEASES

To acquire a legal lease of more than seven years of registered land, B must register as the holder of that right (see section 3.1). In such a case, C clearly will not be able to rely on the lack of registration defence. B can, however, acquire a shorter legal lease without needing to register as the holder of that right. Even in such a case, it is still impossible for C to rely on the lack of registration defence, because Sch 3, para 1, of the LRA 2002 ensures that B's right counts as an overriding interest: that is the case even if B is not in actual occupation of the land. If A has an unregistered legal estate and grants B a legal lease, it may be the case that, when A transfers his or her estate to C, C will register that estate for the first time. In such a case, B's legal lease is again overriding, this time under Sch 1, para 1, of the 2002 Act.

---

[161] See *Mellor v Watkins* (1874) LR 9 QB 400, 405; and *Kay v Lambeth LBC; Leeds CC v Price* [2006] 2 AC 465, [141].
[162] [1989] Ch 1.   [163] [1989] Ch 1, 6.   [164] (1986) 8 EHRR 123: see Chapter 4, section 2.2.3.
[165] Bright, *Landlord and Tenant Law in Context* (2007) p 73.

4.2 EQUITABLE LEASES

Where B has an equitable lease of registered land, it is possible for B to protect that right by entering a notice on the register. The entry of a notice does not guarantee B's equitable right—but it does prevent C, when later acquiring a right, from using the lack of registration defence against B's right. If B fails to protect his or her equitable lease by entering a notice, that right will be vulnerable to the lack of registration defence *unless* B is in actual occupation of the land under Sch 3, para 2 of the LRA 2002 (where C registers a legal estate for the first time, Sch 1, para 2, of that Act has the same effect). But if B is *not* in actual occupation at the relevant time, his or her equitable lease does *not* count as an overriding interest.

The key point, therefore, is that, unlike a legal lease, an equitable lease, by itself, does not count as an overriding interest. This flows from the fact that Sch 3, para 1 (like Sch 1, para 1) protects only 'A leasehold estate in land granted for a term [. . .]'. As confirmed by the Court of Appeal in *City Permanent Building Society v Miller*,[166] a grant necessarily implies the acquisition of a *legal* property right: if B has an equitable lease, he or she has not been granted a lease by A; rather, A is instead under a duty to make such a grant.

5 THE CONTRACTUAL ASPECT OF A LEASE

In this chapter, we have been examining the lease *as a property right* and have therefore asked the three key questions relating to such rights: the *content*, *acquisition*, and *defences* questions. There are, however, other aspects to a lease. In Chapter 20, we will examine how a lease can confer *status*, by allowing B to qualify for important statutory protection. In addition, it is sometimes stated that, due to developments in the law occurring in the last thirty years or so, the lease has become more 'contractualized'. It is certainly true that, *as well as* functioning as a property right in land, a lease almost always has an important contractual aspect. As the following extract suggests, however, we have to be very careful when framing a debate about the nature of leases as a conflict between property, on one hand, and contract, on the other.

McFarlane, *The Structure of Property Law* (2008, pp 697–8)

It is often said that there is a tension between two different views of the Lease. On the first view, the Lease is seen as primarily a *property right*; on the second, it is seen as chiefly a *contractual right* [. . .]

However, this tension is an illusion. There is *no* conflict between property rights on the one hand and contractual rights on the other. The classification of a right as a property right depends on the content question: does B's right impose a *prima facie* duty on the rest of the world not to interfere with B's use of a thing? The classification of a right as a contractual right depends on the acquisition question: does B's right arise as a result of a promise which, because it was made in an agreement for which consideration was provided, binds A? It is therefore perfectly possible for B to have a right that is *both* (i) a property right; *and* (ii) a contractual right. An example occurs where A, by means of a sale, transfers his Ownership

---

[166] [1952] Ch 840.

of a bike to B. B acquires a property right; and that right arises as a result of the contractual bargain between A and B.

Indeed, in almost all cases where he has a Lease, B's right to exclusive control of land for a limited period is *both* (i) a property right; *and* (ii) a contractual right. It is a property right because it is a right, relating to a thing, that imposes a *prima facie* duty on the rest of the world. It is a contractual right as B acquires that right as a result of a promise made to B in return for which B provided consideration. In fact, B usually acquires a number of different contractual rights: (i) a right to exclusive control of the land for a limited period; (ii) the benefit of contractually agreed leasehold covenants (rights that can be enforced against parties later acquiring A's estate); and (iii) personal rights against A. All those rights are acquired in the same way; but their content differs.

This analysis does not mean that a Lease *must* arise as a result of a contract. It is possible for a Lease to arise purely by consent: A can exercise his power to grant B a Lease *without* coming under any contractual duties to B.[167] However, it does mean that it is misleading to say that there is a tension between the proprietary view of the Lease and the contractual view of the Lease. A Lease is simply a property right that can, and almost always does, arise through a contract. Indeed, when analysing the practical problems that are often said to depend on a choice between the 'proprietary' and 'contractual' views, that false opposition only obscures the solution to the problems.

So, what does it mean to say that the lease has been 'contractualized'? In a very controversial decision, the House of Lords has stated that the term 'lease' can be extended to cases in which A, even if he or she has no property right in land, makes a binding promise to give B exclusive possession of that land for a limited period. In such a case, B has a lease even though the core feature examined in this chapter, B's acquisition of a property right, is missing. We will examine this decision (*Bruton v London & Quadrant Housing Trust*) in Chapter 20, section 4.

In *Hammersmith and Fulham LBC v Monk*, which we examined in section 3.3.1, we saw that Lord Browne-Wilkinson contrasted the 'proprietary' and 'contractual' approaches to the question of whether a joint periodic tenancy can be ended by the choice of just one of the joint tenants not to renew the tenancy. His Lordship's view was that the proprietary approach would give a negative answer to that question, whilst the contractual approach favoured a positive response. As we saw, the answer given in the case was the positive one, and so the decision may thus seem to contribute to the 'contractualization' of the lease. We should be wary, however, of attaching too much weight to the result. For, as we noted in section 3.3.1, the crucial factor was that occupation of land under a periodic tenancy, even if it continues for a long time, occurs not under one continuous lease but rather under a succession of periodic tenancies. Each new periodic tenancy, as it is a new lease, must then require the consent of all the parties to it. The necessity of consent is not a feature exclusive to contracts: after all, the transfer of property from A to B also requires the consent of both parties.

---

[167] See *per* Millett LJ (dissenting) in *Ingram v IRC* [1997] 4 All ER 395, [421]–[422]: '*There is no doubt that a lease is property. It is a legal estate in land. It may be created by grant or attornment as well as by contract and need not contain any covenants at all.*' There was a successful appeal against the decision of the majority of the Court of Appeal ([2000]1 AC 293): Lord Hutton, at 310, expressly agreed with Millett LJ's analysis of the nature of a lease.

In other cases, the so-called 'contractualization' amounts not to a denial of the proprietary status of a lease, but rather to the recognition that, where A grants B a lease, the *purpose* of the parties' contract extends beyond the simple acquisition of a property right by B.

This point has been made by Bright,[168] who has argued that the key issue relates to the *characterization* of a contract granting B a lease. The question is whether B's acquisition of a property right should be seen as: (i) the *sole* aim of the parties' contract; or (ii) only one of the aims of the contract, or even as a means to a more important end (e.g. the provision of a home or business premises). In Bright's words, is the contract: (i) for possession only; or (ii) for possession 'plus'?[169]

The traditional view of a lease, it seems, favoured the former analysis. This affected the application to the lease of normal contractual principles and, as a result, had a number of important practical consequences. Firstly, it meant that judges were very reluctant to use the particular purpose for which a lease was acquired (e.g. to give B a home) as a reason to imply contractual terms into that lease. As noted in section 1.2.1, certain minimal duties are implied as a result of B's acquisition of a property right (e.g. A is under a duty not to interfere with B's 'quiet enjoyment' of the land), but the courts would not go beyond those duties by looking to the particular factual circumstances in which the lease was granted.

Secondly, it meant that the doctrine of frustration was not applied to leases: even if there was a radical change in circumstances, frustrating the particular purpose for which B acquired his or her lease, B would still have a property right and so, on the traditional view, the principal purpose of the contract would have been achieved.

Thirdly, and similarly, it meant that a significant breach by A of one of his or her continuing duties under the contract (e.g. to provide repairs) could never allow B to terminate the contract: after all, B would still have the principal benefit he or she had sought under the contract—a property right in the land.

Over time, the courts have recognized that, in many circumstances, it is unrealistic to view A and B's lease agreement as *solely* a means for B to acquire a property right in land. This has led to a reversal of each of the three consequences, as set out in the preceding paragraphs, of that former view. Firstly, in *Liverpool City Council v Irwin*,[170] the House of Lords recognized that, where A gave B a lease of a flat in a tower block, the obvious purpose of providing B with accommodation meant that, under normal contractual principles, terms could be implied allowing B to use other parts of the block (such as the lift and stairs) and imposing a duty on A to make reasonable efforts to keep those parts working and usable by B.

Secondly, we noted in section 3.3.2 that, in *National Carriers Ltd v Panalpina (Northern) Ltd*,[171] the House of Lords acknowledged that, where A gave B a lease of a warehouse for storage, the obvious commercial purpose of the contract meant that, under normal contractual principles, the closure of the only road giving access to the warehouse could, if continuing for a long enough period, lead to the parties' contract being frustrated.[172]

---

[168] See Bright, *Landlord and Tenant Law in Context* (2007) pp 30–3.   [169] Ibid, p 31.
[170] [1977] AC 239.   [171] [1981] AC 675.
[172] In the case itself, the contract was *not* frustrated: the road was closed only for twenty months of a ten-year lease.

Similarly, we also saw in section 3.3.2 that, in *Hussein v Mehlman*,[173] Stephen Sedley QC, sitting as an assistant recorder, held that, where A gave B a lease of a house, A's serious breaches of his duty to repair, rendering the house unfit to live in, interfered with the 'central purpose'[174] of the contract and so allowed B to terminate the contract by moving out and ceasing to pay rent.[175]

These developments have proceeded on the eminently reasonable basis that, in many situations, the acquisition of a property right in land, whilst fundamental, is not the *only* purpose that B has in mind when entering a lease agreement with A. As we will see in the next chapter, its effect in giving B a property right is only *one* of the lease's key features.

QUESTIONS

1. If A makes a contractual agreement to allow B to occupy land, why might B want to claim that the agreement gives him or her a lease?

2. In *Street v Mountford*, the House of Lords held that A's contractual agreement with B can give B a lease even if A clearly did not intend the agreement to have that effect. Can that aspect of the decision be defended, either from a doctrinal or policy perspective?

3. In *Antoniades v Villiers*, the House of Lords, in deciding that Mr Villiers and Miss Bridger had a joint right to exclusive possession, disregarded a term in an agreement signed by both Mr Villiers and Miss Bridger. Can that aspect of the decision be defended, either from a doctrinal or policy perspective?

4. In *AG Securities v Vaughan*, the House of Lords assumed that it is impossible for B1 and B2 to acquire a lease as tenants in common. Is that assumption correct?

5. Are there any genuine exceptions to the rule that if A gives B a right to exclusive possession of land for a limited period, B has a lease?

6. What is the effect of the Supreme Court's decision in *Berrisford v Mexfield* on the rule that a lease must be for a limited period?

 For guidance on how to answer these questions visit the online resources at www.oup.com/uk/mcfarlane4e/.

FURTHER READING

Bright, 'Avoiding Tenancy Legislation: Sham and Contracting Out Revisited' [2002] CLJ 146

Bright, '*Street v Mountford* Revisited' in *Landlord and Tenant Law: Past, Present and Future* (ed Bright, Oxford: Hart Publishing, 2006)

Bright, *Landlord and Tenant Law in Context* (Oxford: Hart Publishing, 2007), esp chs 1–3

---

173 [1992] 2 EGLR 87 (County Court).   174 Ibid, 91.
175 That reasoning has since been confirmed by the Court of Appeal: see *Chartered Trust plc v Davies* [1997] 2 EGLR 83.

Hill, 'Intention and the Creation of Proprietary Rights: Are Leases Different?'
    [1996] LS 200

McFarlane, *The Structure of Property Law* (Oxford: Hart Publishing, 2008, Part G1B)

Roche, 'Legal History in Court: Lessons from *Mexfield* and *Southward*' [2016] Conv 286

Sparkes, 'Co-Tenants, Joint Tenants and Tenants in Common' (1989) 18 AALR 151

Williams, 'The Certainty of Term Requirement in Leases: Nothing Lasts Forever' [2015]
    CLJ 592

20

REGULATING LEASES AND PROTECTING OCCUPIERS

CENTRAL ISSUES

1. In Chapter 19, we concentrated on a key feature of a lease: its ability to count as a property right. This can be referred to as the *property right-conferring* aspect of a lease. We also saw, in Chapter 19, section 5, that the conferral of a property right is not the *only* key feature of a lease: as now recognized by the courts, a contract giving B a lease can also be a means for B to achieve a further practical end, such as to have a home in which to live, or premises from which to run a business.

2. In Chapter 19, we also saw that the applicability of various forms of important statutory protection may be dependent on B showing that he or she has a lease. In this chapter, we will examine that statutory protection in more detail. Such protection can be important in a number of different contexts, such as, for example, if B has an agricultural or commercial lease. In this chapter, we will focus on the protection available to B where he or she occupies land as his or her home. The degree of statutory protection available to B depends on the identity of B's landlord: A. If A is a private individual, the statutory protection

available to B is now very slight; where A is a local authority, however, significant statutory protection is still available to B, in the form of a 'secure tenancy'.

3. In examining this statutory protection, we will see that a lease can give B *status*: the status of a party qualifying for statutory protection. This demonstrates a further key feature of a lease: its *status-conferring* aspect. It also raises a fundamental question: is it possible for an agreement between A and B to give B the status of a party with a lease *without* giving B a property right? A key recommendation of the Law Commission's most recent review of the area, which has been adopted by the Renting Homes (Wales) Act 2016, is that the statutory protection available to B, a party occupying land as a home and paying rent, should not depend on whether or not B has a property right in that land.

4. Having focussed on the *property right-conferring* aspect of a lease in Chapter 19, and its *status-conferring* aspect in this chapter, we will then move on, in Chapter 21, to examine its *relationship-creating* aspect. There, we

will see that the landlord–tenant relationship arising when A gives B a lease may impose duties and confer rights not only on A and B, but also on later parties stepping into the shoes of A or B, and thus entering into a landlord–tenant relationship. In Chapter 21, section 6.4, we will also see how the courts and statute have given B some protection against the risk of losing his or her lease due to a breach of one of his or her duties to A.

1 INTRODUCTION

In Chapter 19, we focussed on a particular aspect of the lease: its ability to confer a property right on B. In this chapter, we will also consider the *status-conferring* aspect of a lease—that is, its ability, in certain circumstances, to allow B to qualify for important statutory protection.

Bridge, 'Leases: Contract, Property and Status' in _Land Law: Issues, Debates, Policy_ (ed Tee, 2002, pp 98–9)

The lease straddles the worlds of contract and property. It is an estate the duration of which is determined by the agreement of the landlord and the tenant. It is also highly significant as a status, tenants enjoying rights and incurring obligations that are denied to others. The law of leases is extraordinarily complex, and the search for order out of the inherent chaos can at times seem an almost futile exercise. The student of land law [. . .] tends to concentrate on the 'general principles' affecting the leasehold relationship [. . .] It is inevitable that this emphasis on 'general principles' provides a view of the law of landlord and tenant which is some way removed from the practical realities of the leasehold relationship. One obvious divergence relates to security of tenure. It may be that according to the 'general principles', a lease can be terminated by notice, but there may be statutory restrictions on such termination, nor does it necessarily follow that recovery of possession ensues upon termination of the lease. The landlord and tenant practitioner must be aware that specific types of lease are dealt with by statute in very different ways, and that engrafted on to the 'general part' are principles which may or may not apply according to the specific kind of lease.

The 'general principles' referred to in the extract can be seen as the principles, set out in Chapter 19, that govern the *property right-conferring* aspect of a lease. If we analyse a lease as no more than a grant by A to B of a property right, giving B a right to exclusive possession of land (and thus ownership powers over land) for a limited period, then the positions of A and B seem clear. Each is free to pursue his or her own self-interest: B, by making use of the land during the period of the lease; A, by recovering possession of the land when the agreed period ends. If either party wants to control the actions of the other, the basic position is that he or she can only do so by convincing the other party to agree to that limit and thus making it a term of the parties' contractual agreement. As we will see in this chapter, there are many situations in which that simple model of a lease has been found wanting.

2 THE *STATUS-CONFERRING* ASPECT OF A LEASE: BACKGROUND

The first important challenge to the simple model of a lease set out above comes from Parliament: as noted by Bridge, statutory intervention means that, in many cases, we have to look beyond the *property right-conferring* aspect of a lease. Again, it is useful to refer back to the contrasting approaches that we noted in Chapter 1, section 5.2. From the perspective of *doctrine*, the simple model of a lease, with its emphasis on the parties' property rights and their freedom of contract, may seem perfectly adequate—but from the perspective of *utility*, Parliament has accepted that the simple model may fail to secure important policy goals.

In very broad terms, there are two general reasons why Parliament may have decided that A and B cannot simply be left to determine their respective rights: firstly, it may be that the use of land is sufficiently important that a particular party's individual wishes can be over-ridden; secondly, it may be that differences in the parties' relative bargaining positions mean that, absent statutory protection, one may be left at the mercy of the other. In particular, given the limited availability of land and the uniqueness of each individual plot of land (see Chapter 1, section 4), it may be that A holds too powerful an advantage when negotiating the terms of a lease with B: even if B finds the proposed terms unattractive, it may not be possible, in practice, for B to walk away and negotiate better terms elsewhere.

Of course, the particular policy goals that Parliament wishes to advance will vary according to the particular context in question. This means that, as Bridge notes in the extract above, B's position may vary according to the particular context in which he or she has acquired his or her lease.

For the purpose of considering the statutory regulation of leases, we can distinguish between four broad types of lease:

- agricultural leases;
- commercial leases;
- long-term residential leases;
- short-term residential leases.

In line with the approach taken in Part D of this book, our focus will be on the protection that may be available to B where he or she occupies land as his or her *home*.

In Chapter 24, section 2.2, we will see how the statutory protection applicable to long-term residential leases may be useful to B where, generally by having paid a large purchase price, he or she has acquired a long lease (e.g. 99 or 125 years) of a flat. The central problem for B, in such a case, is that B may reasonably regard himself or herself as 'the owner' of the flat: B may have made significant financial investments in the land, as well as establishing his or her home there. Yet as time passes, and the period remaining on the lease grows shorter, the prospect of B losing his or her right to exclusive possession of the land undermines B's position.[1] Of course, if we apply the simple doctrinal model set out above, in which A and B's positions are to be determined entirely by their property rights and the agreed terms of their contract, B's loss of the land at the end of the agreed period will be unavoidable. Nonetheless, as we will see in Chapter 24, section 2.2, Parliament has intervened on policy grounds to ensure that B is protected even at the end of his or her lease.

---

[1] 'B' here refers both to the party originally acquiring the lease and any of his or her successors in title.

A very similar form of intervention forms the background to *James v UK*,[2] a case that we considered in Chapter 4 (see especially section 2.2.3). That case concerned the effect of the Leasehold Reform Act 1967. That Act does not apply to flats, but it protects B where he or she holds a long lease, at a low rent, of a house. B is given a statutory power to 'enfranchise'—that is, to purchase A's freehold at a price set by a statutory formula.[3] The Duke of Westminster (who was obliged by the 1967 Act to sell a number of freeholds) claimed that the 1967 Act infringed his right, protected by Art 1 of the First Protocol of the European Convention on Human Rights, to the '*peaceful enjoyment of his possessions*'. Certainly, the Act departed from the simple model in which A and B's positions are to be determined entirely by their property rights and the agreed terms of their contract. Nonetheless, as we saw in Chapter 4, the Court found that the UK had *not* infringed the Duke's Art 1 right. Taking into the account the 'margin of appreciation' afforded to the UK (see Chapter 4, section 2.2.3), the Court recognized that the Act employed a proportionate means of pursuing a legitimate aim: to give effect to B's 'moral entitlement' to the ownership of the house and thus to remedy the 'social injustice' inherent in the precariousness of B's position.[4] Whilst dealing with a specific form of statutory intervention, applying only to long-term residential leases, the *James* case also reveals the tension inherent whenever Parliament intervenes to protect B at A's expense. In some cases, at least, it seems that wider policy goals can justify a departure from the simple model based on the parties' property rights and their freedom to contract.

In this chapter, our focus is on short-term residential leases. Around 37 per cent of all homes in England and Wales are occupied by tenants with such leases.[5] The protection available to such tenants may come from many different sources: for example, the criminal law prohibits certain forms of harassment by a landlord;[6] local authorities also have regulatory powers to ensure that certain minimum housing and public health standards are maintained.[7] In addition, in around one fifth of all short-term residential leases, A (the landlord) is a local authority.[8] This means that public law may also limit A's exercise of its property rights as landlord: in particular, as a public body, a local authority has a basic duty not to act inconsistently with B's rights under the ECHR. Many of the cases that we examined in Chapter 4, exploring the impact of Art 8 of the ECHR, concerned the position of residential occupiers of land owned by a local authority.

In addition, as we saw in Chapter 19, section 5, general contractual rules, when applied to leases, may provide B with some protection: for example, A's incentive to comply with his or her statutory repairing duty may be increased by the prospect of B, in the event of a serious breach by A, being able to terminate the lease and then move out and cease paying rent.[9]

Further, statutory regulation applying to all contracts will also apply to leases and thus provide some protection to B: for example, B may able to rely on the Consumer

---

[2] (1986) 8 EHRR 123.

[3] A power of enfranchisement (or instead to extend the length of the lease) was extended to a holder of a long residential lease of a flat only with the introduction of the Leasehold Reform Housing and Urban Development Act 1993: see Chapter 24, section 2.2.

[4] (1986) 8 EHRR 123, 47.   [5] See Wilcox et al (eds) *UK Housing Review 2017*, Table 17d.

[6] See the Protection from Eviction Act 1977.

[7] See the Environmental Protection Act 1990, esp ss 79–82.

[8] See Wilcox & Pawson (eds) *UK Housing Review 2017*, Table 17d.

[9] See *Hussein v Mehlman* [1997] 2 EGLR 87 (County Court), considered in Chapter 19, section 5.

Rights Act[10] to show that particular terms of the lease contract are unfair and hence not binding on B.[11]

Clearly, in this chapter, we cannot consider the full scope of the protection available to a short-term residential tenant. As noted in Chapter 1, section 2, our focus in this book is not on all of the legal rules that affect the use of land; rather, our primary concern is with property rights relating to land. In this context, it is with the statutory protection that is made available to B *because* B has a property right in the land: a lease.

In considering that protection, we can start by noting that there is a clear difference between short-term residential leases and their long-term equivalents. Generally, to acquire a long-term residential lease, B will pay a large purchase price and then a very low, often nominal, rent. In contrast, a short-term residential lease generally involves no such premium but, instead, a duty on B to pay regular, more significant sums as rent. Of course, some tenants opt for a short-term residential lease simply as a matter of convenience: they do not wish to make a long-term commitment to a particular property or area. But the absence of a purchase price may mean that many tenants acquire a short-term residential lease out of financial necessity rather than choice: such a tenant may well wish to establish a permanent home, but lack the money needed to acquire a freehold or long-term lease. As a result—in those cases, at least—there may be a particularly strong case for statutory intervention in favour of a tenant with a short-term residential lease. Certainly, as we saw in Chapter 19, the Rent Act 1977 gave significant protection to such a tenant: that was precisely why private landlords such as Mr Street (see Chapter 19, section 1.2.1) and Mr Antoniades (see Chapter 19, section 2.4) went to such lengths to try to deny B a lease. This was not because they wanted to deny B a property right—their concern was not with whether B would have a right capable of binding third parties; rather, it was because they wished to deny B the *status* that would come with a lease: that status would enable B to qualify for statutory protection.

In the following extract, Bridge develops the idea of the *status-conferring* aspect of a lease. He also explains how the statutory protection available to a short-term residential tenant has changed, very significantly, since the time of the Rent Act 1977.

Bridge, 'Leases: Contract, Property and Status' in *Land Law: Issues, Debates, Policy* (ed Tee, 2002, pp 105–8)

The lease as status

The status-conferring dimension of the landlord-tenant relationship is given little attention in modern land law courses. Yet [. . .] the leading cases have frequently been motivated by a desire on the part of the landlord to avoid legislative status and [. . .] there are many other cases where the courts have been faced with the interaction of the general principles of landlord and tenant law with specific statutory provisions that apply to certain kinds of lease. The landlord-tenant relationship does not exist within a vacuum, it exists within a factual

---

[10] The Act applies where one party to the contract is a 'trader' and the other a 'consumer'. Unlike the Unfair Contract Terms Act 1977 Sch 1, para 1(b), it contains no special exemption for leases. In its 13th Programme of Law Reform, the Law Commission has included a project on 'Unfair Terms in Residential Leasehold', noting the problem that only B, the party to the initial contract, can challenge the fairness of a term in the lease under the Consumer Rights Act 2015, as under s 62(5) of the Act, the fairness of the term depends on the circumstances at the time of the agreement, not on the circumstances at the time of an assignment from B to B2, the current tenant.

[11] Some core terms are not subject to the fairness test, if written in plain and intelligible language and prominent: e.g. the level of the agreed rent.

context, and the type of property let (a house, a flat, a farm, an office), for instance, will make considerable differences to the legal regime applicable. There is insufficient space here to do justice to the multifarious forms of statutory intervention in the landlord-tenant relationship. However, it may be useful to mention three particular areas in an attempt to show how the legal background has moved on, even since the days of *Street v Mountford*, to illustrate why it is that private sector residential landlords have changed their practices, and to compare the operation of principle in the residential sector of property with that in the commercial field.

Part 1 of the Housing Act 1988 came into force on 15 January 1989, less than four years after the decision in *Street v Mountford*. The Conservative government had taken the view that the decline in the private rented sector of residential property was attributable to the impact of rent control, and that any revival would require landlords to obtain a commercial return for their investment. The 1988 Act sought to phase out the Rent Acts by providing that tenancies granted after the legislation came into force would be taken out of the operation of the Acts altogether. Instead, a new regime of letting, known as the 'assured tenancy', would apply to them, pursuant to which landlords could charge whatever rent the tenant agreed to pay. The assured tenant was given statutory security and a limited form of succession on death was also enacted. Eight years later, by the Housing Act 1996, the statutory security of private sector tenants was dealt a further blow. As from 28 February 1997, any new tenancy was to take effect as an 'assured shorthold tenancy', unless the parties expressly agreed otherwise, under which the landlord can recover possession once any fixed term has expired by giving notice of a sufficient length. The legislative matrix is extremely convoluted, but the sum effect is clear. Since the enactment of the Housing Act 1988 there has been a highly significant diminution in the statutory rights of the tenant of residential property in the private sector. The spectre of the Rent Acts, which cast a long shadow over residential lettings, has been vanquished, and market forces are now allowed to prevail. Over the course of the last decade, private sector landlords have ceased to care whether they grant tenancies or licences.

[. . .] The public sector of housing has never been subjected to the regime of the Rent Acts, as it was for many years assumed that local authorities would act in the interests of their rate-paying tenants and not be influenced by unseemly market forces. Council tenants were therefore left to resort to public law remedies in cases where they fell into dispute with their local authority landlords over matters such as the negotiation of council rents. The systematic conferment of security of tenure on public sector tenants was initiated by Margaret Thatcher's first Conservative administration, contemporaneously with its highly publicised promotion of the tenant's right to buy the reversion of their landlord. Thus there arose, in the public sector, the status of 'secure tenant', conferring security of tenure, rights to exchange tenancies, and succession rights on death.

3 THE *STATUS-CONFERRING* ASPECT OF A LEASE: PRACTICE

The final part of the previous extract refers to the 'secure tenancy'. The secure tenancy is an excellent example of the status-conferring aspect of the lease. This statutory creation[12]

---

[12] Introduced by the Housing Act 1980. See now Housing Act 1985, s 79.

can arise where the landlord is a local authority[13] and its chief effect is to ensure that a court order is necessary to remove the tenant without his or her consent, and that such an order can only be made if the local authority can establish one or more of a limited set of 'grounds of possession'. A form of security of tenure is conferred, as those limited grounds do *not* include the expiry of the term of the lease. Moreover, even if one of the grounds for removal arises (e.g. because the tenant is in arrears of rent), a possession order can be granted only if it would be 'reasonable' to make such an order.[14] Indeed, even if one of the grounds for possession exists, and it would be reasonable to make the order, a court still has a wide discretion: as noted by Lord Neuberger in *Manchester City Council v Pinnock*[15] (discussed in Chapter 4), a court may instead '*refuse to make any order, it may adjourn the proceedings, it may make an outright possession order which takes effect on a specific day, or it may make a suspended possession order which will not take effect so long as, for instance, the tenant pays the rent or creates no nuisance.*'

A secure tenancy can arise only where B is an individual who '*occupies a dwelling-house as his only or principal home*'.[16] It is important to note that s 79(3) of that Act states that the secure tenancy rules also '*apply in relation to a licence to occupy a dwelling-house (whether or not granted for consideration) as they apply in relation to a tenancy*'. In *Westminster City Council v Clarke*,[17] which we examined in Chapter 19, section 2.3, however, the House of Lords explained that s 79(3) was intended to deal only with those cases in which, under the approach to the definition of a lease applying before *Street v Mountford*,[18] B could have a licence involving exclusive possession (see Chapter 19, section 1.1.1). In practice, then, the protection given to a secure tenant can apply only where B has a lease. That was precisely why, in *Westminster City Council v Clarke*, it was vital to decide if B had a right to exclusive possession of the land for a limited period. It could well be argued that the policy behind the secure tenancy (in particular, the need to allow B to be secure in his or her home) applies equally where B occupies as a licensee, lacking a right to exclusive possession. Crucially, however, it is only B's acquisition of a *lease* that gives B the statutory status of a secure tenant.

As Bridge noted, in the extract above, the status-conferring aspect of a lease can change over time, as Parliament adopts different views as to the level of protection that a particular type of tenant should enjoy. For example, prior to the introduction of the Housing Act 1988, private sector tenants had enjoyed security of tenure under the Rent Acts, which limited the grounds on which a landlord could regain possession of the land, and thus allowed a tenant to remain even after the expiry of the term of the lease. Due to the statutory changes introduced from 1988, things are now very different. If A is a private party and B (the tenant) is an individual, rather than a company, B's short-term lease may be an 'assured shorthold tenancy', *or* an 'assured tenancy'.[19] A has a choice as to which tenancy to give B: the default

---

[13] Housing Act 1985, s 80(1). Under that section, a secure tenancy can arise in other cases (e.g. where the landlord is a development corporation, or a housing action trust), but by far the most common case is where the landlord is a local authority.

[14] Housing Act 1985, s 84(2). Under that section, a possession order may also be made, in particular circumstances, if the court is satisfied that suitable alternative accommodation will be available to the tenant.

[15] [2011] 2 AC 104, [6].

[16] Where there is a joint tenancy, it will be a secure tenancy if each of B1 and B2 is an individual and '*at least one of them occupies the dwelling-house as his only or principal home*': Housing Act 1985, s 81.

[17] [1992] AC 288.   [18] [1985] AC 809.

[19] Of all dwellings in the United Kingdom, 19.4 per cent are occupied by tenants of private landlords: Wilcox et al (eds) *UK Housing Review 2017*, Table 17d.

position is that it will be an assured shorthold tenancy.[20] As noted by Bridge in the extract above, that form of lease is only very lightly regulated: certainly, B acquires no security of tenure. So, parties such as Mr Street or Mr Antoniades, who once went to such lengths to avoid granting a lease, are now perfectly content to grant B an assured shorthold tenancy. In fact, assured shorthold tenancies now dominate private sector lettings.

Whilst the secure tenancy remains the predominant form of local authority tenancy, statutory reform has led to the introduction of other forms, which confer less protection on the tenant. As we saw in Chapter 4, section 4.2.2, the 'demoted tenancy' (considered by the Supreme Court in *Manchester City Council v Pinnock*) was introduced by the Anti-social Behaviour Act 2003.[21] That Act gave a court the power to make a 'demotion order', turning a secure tenancy into a demoted tenancy. As Lord Neuberger stated in *Pinnock*,[22] a demotion order can be made only if: *'(a) the tenant (or someone living with him) has engaged, or has threatened to engage, in (i) "housing-related anti-social conduct"[23] or (ii) conduct which consists of or involves using the "premises for unlawful purposes",[24] and (b) it is reasonable to make the order.'* If a demotion order is made, *'the demotion results in much reduced rights of security of tenure for the tenant.'* The reduction in the security of tenure available to particular local authority tenants was the result of a Parliamentary desire to address the perceived problem of anti-social behaviour. Similarly, in Chapter 4, section 4.2.3, we also noted the existence of the 'introductory tenancy' (considered by the Supreme Court in *Leeds CC v Hall* and *Birmingham CC v Frisby*).[25] As Lord Hope noted in those appeals,[26] Parliament allowed local authorities to create such tenancies when wishing, in effect, to put a tenant on probation, the idea being that the introductory tenancy would mature into a secure tenancy (and thus confer security of tenure) only if the tenant behaved appropriately during the term of the introductory tenancy.

As we noted in Chapter 4, section 4.2.2, an important feature of demoted and introductory tenancies is that each allows for *mandatory* grounds of possession: the statutory framework sets out circumstances in which a judge is not given any discretion to refuse a possession order. This feature is also present when a local authority, acting to meet its duty to a homeless person, grants such person a non-secure tenancy under Part VII of the Housing Act 1996 (such a tenancy was considered by the Supreme Court in *Hounslow LBC v Powell*).[27] This explains why, in each of *Powell* and *Manchester City Council v Pinnock*, the Supreme Court considered whether the statutory framework could be interpreted in such a way as to afford sufficient protection for a tenant's right, under Art 8 of the European Convention of Human Rights, to respect for his or her home. In the case of a secure tenancy, such a question is more easily answered: even if a grounds on which possession can be sought arises, a judge still has the discretion to decide whether or not it would be 'reasonable' to grant a possession order, and to decide whether or not to postpone or suspend such an order, and that discretion can

---

[20] Before 1 October 2010, a tenancy with a rent of over £25,000 per year was excluded from the Housing Act regime, and so could not be an assured or an assured shorthold tenancy. As from 1 October 2010, that limit has been raised to £100,000: The Assured Tenancies (Amendment) (England) Order 2010 – SI 2010 No 908 (25 March 2010).

[21] That Act inserted provisions into the Housing Act 1996.   [22] [2011] 2 AC 104, [8].

[23] As defined in s 153A of the Housing Act 1996.

[24] As explained in s 153B of the Housing Act 1996.

[25] [2011] 2 AC 186. These appeals were heard along with *Hounslow LBC v Powell*. See too *Southend-on-Sea BC v Armour* [2014] HLR 23.

[26] Ibid, [15]–[19].

[27] [2011] 2 AC 186. Lord Hope discusses the nature of such tenancies at [11]–[14].

be exercised in such a way as to ensure Art 8 is not infringed.[28] Where Parliament has decided, however, that it is permissible for a local authority to grant a non-secure tenancy, it may be more difficult, as we saw in Chapter 4, section 4.2.2, to reconcile the framework set out by statute with the demands of Art 8.

The introduction of demoted and introductory tenancies thus provides a good example of how Parliament's policy to the status-conferring aspect of a lease may change over time. Indeed, in passing the Localism Act 2011, Parliament set out a new approach to the provision of public sector and social housing. The aim of Part 7 of the Act is to give local authorities and registered providers of social housing greater 'flexibility' and thus to reduce the statutory protection available to tenants.[29] For example, a local authority may be able to grant a new type of tenancy, known as a 'flexible tenancy'. Such a tenancy, whilst technically still a form of secure tenancy, will confer less statutory protection than the current, general form of secure tenancy: in particular, there will no longer be security of tenure, as a flexible tenancy will have a stated maximum duration, and the landlord will therefore be able to serve a notice and to claim possession of the land at the end of that period.[30] Many councils decided not to make use of the power to grant flexible tenancies,[31] but the Housing and Planning Act 2016 went further still, and aims to prevent local authorities granting new secure tenancies, on the basis that: *'continuing to offer social tenancies on a lifetime basis is not an efficient use of scarce social housing'.*[32]

There may be a number of reasons why Parliament's views as to the proper level of statutory protection for residential tenants may change over time. Firstly, it may be felt that giving significant protection to tenants can be counterproductive. As noted by Etherton MR:[33]

> The history of legislation in this jurisdiction concerning residential tenancies has involved a process of balancing and rebalancing of the respective interests of owners and occupiers of property [. . .] the Housing Act 1988 represented a key step in making it easier for landlords to obtain possession of their property from tenants. An important consideration underlying this change was that if the balance was weighted too heavily in favour of securing the protection of tenants, there would be a reduced incentive to rent properties and the available housing stock would be reduced.

In this way, the cost of protecting those in need of accommodation *and* fortunate enough to have found it already may be that others, also in need of accommodation, have more

---

[28] It is true that *Harrow LBC v Qazi* [2004] 1 AC 983 (see Chapter 4, section 4.1.1) concerned an Art 8 challenge in the context of a secure tenancy. This was because the secure tenancy was held by two joint tenants and, technically, it ended due to the choice of one of those joint tenants not to renew it. The local authority therefore did not need to rely on any of the grounds for possession set out in the Housing Act 1985. See further Chapter 19, section 3.3.

[29] The policy behind the changes is set out in, for example, the consultation paper issued by the Department for Communities and Local Government in November 2010 entitled 'Local Decisions: A Fairer Future for Local Housing'.

[30] In addition, the class of people with a statutory right to succeed to a secure tenancy has been reduced by s 160 of the Localism Act 2011.

[31] In 2014–15, only 8 per cent of social tenancies granted by local authorities were flexibile tenancies: see statement of Parliamentary Under-Secretary of State for Communities and Local Government to to the Public Bill Committee on the Housing and Planning Bill 2015–16: PBC Deb 10 Dec 2015 (morning), c 650.

[32] Statement of the Minister to the Public Bill Committee on the Housing and Planning Bill 2015–16: PBC Deb 10 Dec 2015 (morning), c 650.

[33] *Watts v Stewart* [2016] EWCA Civ 1247, [2017] 2 WLR 1107.

difficulty in finding a home. It may also be felt that security of tenure can, in certain cases, encourage anti-social conduct, if a tenant, or those occupying with a tenant, feel that they cannot be evicted no matter how they behave.

Secondly, there is a political question. Parliament's willingness to enforce a departure from the simple model of a lease (for example, by preventing A from regaining exclusive possession at the end of the agreed lease period) will depend on its view of the importance of the parties' property rights and their freedom to contract. Certainly, the political consensus from the mid-1990s or so has been broadly in favour of reduced state intervention and greater deregulation: as we will see in Chapter 27, that consensus has also shaped the degree of protection available to a mortgage borrower. Of course, it is possible that things may change in the future, as further 'rebalancing' occurs: the private rental market has grown in recent years,[34] with many people finding it impossible to buy a home, and there have been calls, for example, for forms of rent control to be re-introduced.[35]

4 THE *STATUS-CONFERRING* ASPECT OF A LEASE: ITS IMPACT ON THE DEFINITION OF THE LEASE

The status-conferring aspect of a lease gives rise to an important question: if particular statutes give B important protection *if and only if* B has a lease, will judges be tempted to widen (or narrow) the definition of a lease in order to ensure that B does (or does not) receive such protection? For example, we noted in section 3 above that the Rent Acts formerly gave significant protection to a tenant of a private landlord. In *Street v Mountford* (see Chapter 19, sections 1.2.1 and 2.1), Lord Templeman stated that: [36]

> I accept that the Rent Acts are irrelevant to the problem of determining the legal effect of the rights granted by the agreement. Like the professed intention of the parties, the Rent Acts cannot alter the effect of the agreement.

This strict view can be seen as favouring the 'doctrinal' approach, as opposed to the 'utility' approach (see Chapter 1, section 5.2): if Parliament has decided that statutory protection should be available only to those with a lease, the term 'lease' should be given its usual meaning. A contrasting approach would be to interpret the term 'lease' in a way which ensures that the statute succeeds in protecting those who, in the view of the court, deserve protection. The tension between these two approaches was apparent in Chapter 19, section 2.4, when we considered the courts' response to 'shams' or 'pretences' used by a landlord in an attempt to prevent a lease arising. It is also clear in the House of Lords's decision in *Bruton v London & Quadrant Housing Trust Ltd*,[37] and in commentators' response to that decision.

---

[34] Wilcox et al (eds) *UK Housing Review 2017*, Table 17d: from 13.6 per cent of all UK dwellings in 2007, to 19.4 per cent in 2015.

[35] For discussion, see e.g. Wilson, 'Private Rented Housing: The Rent Control Debate' (House of Commons Library Briefing Paper No 6760, 3 April 2017).

[36] [1985] AC 809, [819].   [37] [2000] 1 AC 406.

4.1 *BRUTON V LONDON & QUADRANT HOUSING TRUST*

To understand the background to *Bruton*, we first need to look at the reason why Mr Bruton wished to claim that he had a lease. It was provided by s 11 of the Landlord and Tenant Act 1985, which essentially[38] ensures that, where B has a lease, for less than seven years, of a dwelling, A is under the following duties:

Landlord and Tenant Act 1985, s 11

[. . .]

(a) to keep in repair the structure and exterior of the dwelling-house (including drains, gutters and external pipes);

(b) to keep in repair and proper working order the installations in the dwelling-house for the supply of water, gas and electricity and for sanitation (including basins, sinks, baths and sanitary conveniences, but not other fixtures, fittings and appliances for making use of the supply of water, gas or electricity), and

(c) to keep in repair and proper working order the installations in the dwelling-house for space heating and heating water.

The policy behind this statutory duty seems clear: if B has a short-term lease, it seems unreasonable for B to have to bear the cost of repairs that may ultimately benefit A when A regains exclusive possession of the land.[39] In addition, having rented a home in a particular condition, B may reasonably expect a certain basic level of maintenance and repair. In practice, it may be that B's need for accommodation and relatively weak bargaining position make it impossible to leave the matter to the parties' freedom to contract: hence the mandatory statutory duty. Those policy concerns would also seem to apply in a case in which B has a licence rather than a lease—it is difficult to see how B's acquisition of a property right makes him or her more deserving of the protection afforded by s 11. Nonetheless, the statute makes clear that the duty it imposes can only be implied into a *lease*. It is in this way that B's acquisition of a lease provides the *status* needed to qualify for the statutory protection.

Bruton v London & Quadrant Housing Trust Ltd
[1999] UKHL 26, [2000] 1 AC 406, HL

Facts: The London Borough of Lambeth ('the council') owned a block of flats, Oval House, in Brixton, London. It planned to demolish the block and build new flats, but there were delays to that project. In the meantime, the council gave the London & Quadrant Housing Trust, a charitable body that sought to provide accommodation to the homeless and those in need, a licence to use the flats for that purpose. It was clear that

---

[38] There are some exceptional situations in which the duty does not arise: see Landlord and Tenant Act 1985, s 14.

[39] As a result of s 166 of the Localism Act 2011, s 11 of the 1985 Act also applies to any future secure tenancies of seven years or longer; and any future assured tenancy for a fixed term of seven years or longer, granted by a registered provider of social housing, as long as it is not a shared ownership lease.

its agreement with the council gave the Trust only a licence: in particular, the council had no statutory power, in the circumstances, to give the Trust a lease. Mr Bruton was one of the parties housed by the Trust in Oval House. The agreement entered into by Mr Bruton and the Trust was described as a licence. It stated that:

The trust has the property on licence from [the council] who acquired the property for development [. . .] and pending this development, it is being used to provide temporary housing accommodation. It is offered to you on the condition that you will vacate upon receiving reasonable notice from the trust, which will not normally be less than four weeks. Mr Bruton claimed that his agreement with the Trust, in fact, gave him a lease; that the Trust was therefore under a statutory repairing duty, imposed by s 11 of the Landlord and Tenant Act 1985; and that the Trust had failed to perform that duty. The Trust argued that Mr Bruton could not have a lease: the Trust had no power to grant Mr Bruton a property right in the land because it had no such right itself (it had only a licence from the council). Judge James, sitting at Lambeth county court, found in favour of the Trust. The Court of Appeal dismissed Mr Bruton's appeal (Sir Brian Neill dissenting)—but the House of Lords found that Mr Bruton *did* have a lease and thus that the Trust was, therefore, under the statutory repairing duty.

Lord Hoffmann

[. . .]

Did this agreement create a 'lease' or 'tenancy' within the meaning of the Landlord and Tenant Act 1985 or any other legislation which refers to a lease or tenancy? The decision of this House in *Street v. Mountford*[40] is authority for the proposition that a 'lease' or 'tenancy' is a contractually binding agreement, not referable to any other relationship between the parties, by which one person gives another the right to exclusive occupation of land for a fixed or renewable period or periods of time, usually in return for a periodic payment in money. An agreement having these characteristics creates a relationship of landlord and tenant to which the common law or statute may then attach various incidents. The fact that the parties use language more appropriate to a different kind of agreement, such as a licence, is irrelevant if upon its true construction it has the identifying characteristics of a lease. The meaning of the agreement, for example, as to the extent of the possession which it grants, depends upon the intention of the parties, objectively ascertained by reference to the language and relevant background. The decision of your Lordships' House in *Westminster City Council v. Clarke*[41] is a good example of the importance of background in deciding whether the agreement grants exclusive possession or not. But the classification of the agreement as a lease does not depend upon any intention additional to that expressed in the choice of terms. It is simply a question of characterising the terms which the parties have agreed. This is a question of law.

In this case, it seems to me that the agreement, construed against the relevant background, plainly gave Mr. Bruton a right to exclusive possession. There is nothing to suggest that he was to share possession with the trust, the council or anyone else. The trust did not retain such control over the premises as was inconsistent with Mr. Bruton having exclusive possession as was the case in *Westminster City Council v. Clarke*. The only rights which it reserved were for itself and the council to enter at certain times and for limited purposes. As Lord Templeman said in *Street v. Mountford* such an express reservation 'only serves to emphasise the fact that the grantee is entitled to exclusive possession and is a tenant.'[42] Nor

---

[40] [1985] AC 809.   [41] [1992] AC 288.   [42] [1985] AC 809, [818].

was there any other relationship between the parties to which Mr. Bruton's exclusive possession could be referable.

[Counsel for the trust] submitted that there were 'special circumstances' in this case which enabled one to construe the agreement as a licence despite the presence of all the characteristics identified in *Street v. Mountford*. These circumstances were that the trust was a responsible landlord performing socially valuable functions, it had agreed with the council not to grant tenancies, Mr. Bruton had agreed that he was not to have a tenancy and the trust had no estate out of which it could grant one.

In my opinion none of these circumstances can make an agreement to grant exclusive possession something other than a tenancy. The character of the landlord is irrelevant because although the Rent Acts and other Landlord and Tenant Acts do make distinctions between different kinds of landlords, it is not by saying that what would be a tenancy if granted by one landlord will be something else if granted by another. The alleged breach of the trust's licence is irrelevant because there is no suggestion that the grant of a tenancy would have been ultra vires either the trust or the council [. . .] If it was a breach of a term of the licence from the council, that would have been because it was a tenancy. The licence could not have turned it into something else. Mr. Bruton's agreement is irrelevant because one cannot contract out of the statute. The trust's lack of title is also irrelevant, but I shall consider this point at a later stage. In *Family Housing Association v. Jones*,[43] where the facts were very similar to those in the present case, the Court of Appeal construed the 'licence' as a tenancy. Slade L.J. gave careful consideration to whether any exceptional ground existed for making an exception to the principle in *Street v. Mountford* and came to the conclusion that there was not. I respectfully agree. For these reasons I consider that the agreement between the trust and Mr. Bruton was a lease within the meaning of section 11 of the Landlord and Tenant Act 1985.

My Lords, in my opinion, that is the end of the matter. But the Court of Appeal did not stop at that point. In the leading majority judgment, Millett L.J. said that an agreement could not be a lease unless it had a further characteristic, namely that it created a legal estate in the land which 'binds the whole world.'[44] If, as in this case, the grantor had no legal estate, the agreement could not create one and therefore did not qualify as a lease. The only exception was the case in which the grantor was estopped from denying that he could not create a legal estate. In that case, a 'tenancy by estoppel' came into existence. But an estoppel depended upon the grantor having purported to grant a lease and in this case the trust had not done so. It had made it clear that it was only purporting to grant a licence.

My Lords, I hope that this summary does justice to the closely reasoned judgment of Millett L.J. But I fear that I must respectfully differ at three critical steps in the argument.

First, the term 'lease' or 'tenancy' describes a relationship between two parties who are designated landlord and tenant. It is not concerned with the question of whether the agreement creates an estate or other proprietary interest which may be binding upon third parties. A lease may, and usually does, create a proprietary interest called a leasehold estate or, technically, a 'term of years absolute.' This will depend upon whether the landlord had an interest out of which he could grant it. *Nemo dat quod non habet*.[45] But it is the fact that the agreement is a lease which creates the proprietary interest. It is putting the cart before the horse to say that whether the agreement is a lease depends upon whether it creates a proprietary interest [. . .]

Secondly, I think that Millett L.J. may have been misled by the ancient phrase 'tenancy by estoppel' into thinking that it described an agreement which would not otherwise be a lease

---

43 [1990] 1 WLR 779.   44 [1998] QB 834, [845].
45 [No one can give what he does not have.]

or tenancy but which was treated as being one by virtue of an estoppel. In fact, as the authorities show, it is not the estoppel which creates the tenancy, but the tenancy which creates the estoppel. The estoppel arises when one or other of the parties wants to deny one of the ordinary incidents or obligations of the tenancy on the ground that the landlord had no legal estate. The basis of the estoppel is that having entered into an agreement which constitutes a lease or tenancy, he cannot repudiate that incident or obligation [. . .] Thus it is the fact that the agreement between the parties constitutes a tenancy that gives rise to an estoppel and not the other way round. It therefore seems to me that the question of tenancy by estoppel does not arise in this case. The issue is simply whether the agreement is a tenancy. It is not whether either party is entitled to deny some obligation or incident of the tenancy on the ground that the trust had no title.

Thirdly, I cannot agree that there is no inconsistency between what the trust purported to do and its denial of the existence of a tenancy. This seems to me to fly in the face of *Street v. Mountford*. In my opinion, the trust plainly did purport to grant a tenancy. It entered into an agreement on terms which constituted a tenancy. It may have agreed with Mr. Bruton to say that it was not a tenancy. But the parties cannot contract out of the Rent Acts or other landlord and tenant statutes by such devices. Nor in my view can they be used by a landlord to avoid being estopped from denying that he entered into the agreement he actually made.

For these reasons I would allow the appeal and declare that Mr. Bruton was a tenant. I should add that I express no view on whether he was a secure tenant or on the rights of the council to recover possession of the flat.

Lord Hobhouse

I agree that this appeal should be allowed as proposed by my noble and learned friend Lord Hoffmann and for the reasons which he has given. I would add only this.

The claim made in the action seeks to enforce a contractual cause of action. The breach of contract alleged against the defendant housing trust is the failure to maintain and keep in repair the flat in which the plaintiff, Mr. Bruton is living. He relies upon a written agreement between himself and the housing trust dated 31 January 1989. The written agreement does not contain any undertaking by the housing trust to repair the flat. But Mr. Bruton alleges that the agreement creates a relationship of landlord and tenant between the housing trust and himself and that therefore an undertaking to repair by the housing trust is compulsorily implied by statute—section 11 of the Landlord and Tenant Act 1985.

Counsel for the housing trust accepted before your Lordships that a contractual relationship of landlord and tenant suffices to make the provisions of the Act applicable. The question therefore is whether the agreement creates such a relationship. The answer to this question is, in my judgment, determined by the decision in *Street v. Mountford*. The agreement was an agreement to give Mr. Bruton the exclusive possession of the flat for a period or periods of time in return for the periodic payment of money; the grant of exclusive possession was not referable to any other relationship between the parties. It follows that the relationship created was that of landlord and tenant and the provisions of the Act apply to the agreement. Mr. Bruton is entitled to succeed [. . .]

The Court of Appeal were influenced by the way in which the case for Mr. Bruton was argued before them. They understood that his case depended upon establishing a tenancy by estoppel. This was not a correct analysis. He needed to do no more than rely upon the written agreement he had with the housing trust and its legal effect. The only concept of estoppel which was possibly relevant was that which arises from the agreement [. . .] The present case does not depend upon the establishing of an estoppel nor does any problem arise from the fact that the housing trust did not have a legal estate. The case of Mr. Bruton depends upon his establishing that his agreement with the housing trust has the legal effect of creating a relationship of tenant and landlord between them. That is all. It does not depend upon his establishing a proprietary title good against all the world or against the council. It is not necessary for him to show that the council had conveyed a legal estate to the housing trust. I therefore cannot agree with the reasoning of the Court of Appeal and would allow this appeal.

The decision of the House of Lords in *Bruton* has proved to be controversial, to say the least. A number of different explanations of the decision have been put forward, and we will consider four here.

4.1.1 *Bruton*: The non-estate lease

Prior to the House of Lords decision in *Bruton*, it had been assumed that, to take advantage of the *status-conferring* aspect of a lease, B necessarily had to have a property right—but the House of Lords departed from that assumption. It was held that Mr Bruton's agreement with the Trust, *even if it did not give him a property right in the land*, could nonetheless give Mr Bruton the status of a tenant and therefore allow him to take advantage of s 11 of the Landlord and Tenant Act 1985: in other words, B may have a 'non-estate tenancy'.[46]

As Bright notes in the following extract, this suggests that there are two forms of lease: the standard proprietary lease; and a new, purely contractual, lease.

Bright, 'Leases, Exclusive Possession and Estates' (2000) 116 LQR 7, 8–9

Certain propositions emerge clearly from the speeches in the House of Lords:

1. Mr Bruton had a right to exclusive possession;
2. the relationship of landlord and tenant existed between Mr Bruton and the Housing Trust;
3. this relationship does not give a title good against all the world; and
4. the fact that the Housing Trust had no estate did not matter.

Cumulatively, these propositions illustrate an understanding about the essential nature of leases that was not shared by the Court of Appeal. Although both courts agree that exclusive possession is necessary in order for there to be a lease, there are contrasting views as to whether this is an absolute or relative concept. In the House of Lords, exclusive possession was found on the basis of the contractual agreement between Mr Bruton and the Housing Trust. The agreement gave Mr Bruton the right to exclusive possession: he did not have to share possession with anyone else, and the Housing Trust retained only limited rights over the premises. The Housing Trust's lack of title is not relevant. In contrast, Millett L.J. regarded exclusive possession as looking beyond the relationship between the two contracting parties. According to this view, exclusive possession, meaning possession to the exclusion of the whole world, is essential for a lease; if 'the grantor has no power to

---

[46] To use the term applied by Lord Scott when considering the *Bruton* tenancy in *Kay v Lambeth London Borough Council* [2006] 2 AC 465, [145]–[147]. We examined the human rights aspects of that case in Chapter 4.

exclude the true owner from possession, he has no power to grant a legal right to exclusive possession and his grant cannot take effect as a tenancy'.[47] This means that Mr Bruton could not have exclusive possession and, thus, he could not have a lease. If it is possible to have exclusive possession in the relational sense referred to in the House of Lords, the further question arises as to the nature of the resulting relationship. We are told that it is a relationship of landlord and tenant but not whether it is an "estate". Given that relativity of title is a fundamental aspect of English land law, it could be classified as an estate in this relative sense. This is hard to accept, however. For derivative title, at least, the principle of *nemo dat quod non habet*—no one can convey what he does not own—is also fundamental to English land law. The Housing Trust did not have an estate, and so could not grant an estate to Mr Bruton. Indeed, this is implied when Lord Hoffmann states that a 'lease may, and *usually does*, create a proprietary interest called a leasehold estate [. . .] This will depend upon whether the landlord had an interest out of which he could grant it' (emphasis added). If usually, then it must be that sometimes there can be a lease which is not an estate.

On this point, too, the Court of Appeal had differed. The premise in the Court of Appeal was that a lease is (always) a proprietary concept: 'A tenancy is a legal estate'.[48] There is much to be said for this view. Although there can be tenancies of sorts which do not confer estates, the tenancy at will and the tenancy by estoppel, these are generally treated as special cases and would not be described as 'leases' without qualification. Moreover, much previous case law proceeds on the assumption that all leases are estates in land, an assumption which has, on occasion, been made explicit: 'I myself find it impossible to conceive of a relationship of landlord and tenant that has not got that essential element of tenure in it, and that implies that the tenant holds of his landlord, and he can only do that if the landlord has a reversion. You cannot have a purely contractual tenure.'[49] More recently, Neuberger J. stated that "a lease involves not only a contract, but also an estate in land".[50] [. . .] It is, therefore, a surprise that both Lord Hoffmann and Lord Hobhouse of Woodborough state clearly in *Bruton*, with little discussion of the point, that, though usual, an estate in land is not an essential element of a lease. A lease, in the words of Lord Hoffmann 'describes a relationship between two parties who are designated landlord and tenant. It is not concerned with the question of whether the agreement creates an estate or other proprietary interest which may be binding upon third parties'.

If this is a correct reading of what Lord Hoffmann says and it is possible to have leases which are not estates, contractual rights of occupation will need to be classified as either proprietary leases giving an estate in land and enforceable against all third parties, or as contractual leases conferring exclusive possession and giving rights against all who interfere with possession other than those who can show a better right to possession, or as licences. There will be consequential issues to be addressed. Will 'contractual leases' count as leases for all statutory purposes? Can 'contractual leases' be created informally? It would appear so, as the formality requirements set out in the Law of Property Act 1925, ss 52 and 54, and the Law of Property (Miscellaneous Provisions) Act 1989, s 2, apply only to interests in land. The rules on certainty of term presumably apply to 'contractual leases'—otherwise the outcome in *Prudential Assurance Co. Ltd v. London Residuary Body*[51] would have been different and the agreement upheld as a contractual tenancy [. . .] What status will a 'contractual lease' have vis-à-vis third parties?

---

[47] [1998] QB 834, [845], *per* Millett LJ.
[48] Ibid.   [49] *Milmo v Carreras* [1946] KB 306, [310], *per* Lord Greene MR.
[50] *Re Friends Provident Life Office* [1999] 1 All ER (Comm.) 28, [36].
[51] [1992] 2 AC 386 [see Chapter 19, section 2.7].

4.1.2 *Bruton*: A tenancy by estoppel?

In the following extract, it is suggested that the House of Lords could have reached the conclusion in *Bruton* without relying on the concept of a 'non-estate lease': it could instead have used the well-established notion of a 'tenancy by estoppel'.

Routley, 'Tenancies and Estoppel: After *Bruton v London & Quadrant Housing Trust*' (2000) 63 MLR 424, 424–8

As generally understood, a tenancy by estoppel results where a person purports to grant a tenancy of land, but does not in fact have a sufficient interest in the land to create a tenancy: he is then estopped from denying that the relationship of landlord and tenant exists between him and the grantee [. . .] As between the parties it is as though they are actually landlord and tenant *even though in fact they are not.*

The authorities describe a tenancy by estoppel as a different creature from the more familiar estoppel by representation, as a development from the doctrine of estoppel by deed, but extended in the field of landlord and tenant to all grants whether merely written or oral. A tenancy by estoppel could be said to be the result of the operation of estoppel by grant. Unlike its cousin, estoppel by grant does not rely upon any express representation as to title: 'It is the product of a fundamental principle of the common law which precludes a grantor from disputing the validity of his own grant.'[52]

[. . .] Confusion between the doctrines of estoppel by representation and estoppel by grant gave rise to some of the difficulties in *Bruton* [. . .] Millett LJ [in the Court of Appeal] found that there is no estoppel 'unless the grantor's denial of title is inconsistent with his grant.'[53] There was no estoppel here, because there was no inconsistency between the nature of the alleged grant (a licence), and therefore there could not be any tenancy. The principles of estoppel and of *Street v Mountford* were irreconcilable:

'*Street v Mountford* rejects the professed intentions of the parties in favour of the true effect of the transaction. Estoppel by convention gives effect to the professed intentions of the parties. Any attempt to combine them produces a hopeless circularity.'[54]

I fear that Millett LJ may have been too bemused by the elegance of that conundrum to notice its flaws: it is an oversimplification to say that estoppel 'gives effect to the professed intentions of the parties'. While Millett LJ acknowledges the difference described above between estoppel by representation and by grant, he then applies the 'representation' test to the facts of the case before him, basing his conclusion of no estoppel on a finding of no misrepresentation.

The flaw in that reasoning is that this estoppel does not arise from a representation, but from the grant, and if one correctly concludes via *Street v Mountford* that the grant was in fact the grant of a tenancy, then the Trust's denial of title *is* inconsistent with that grant, and, despite the fact that both the Trust and [Mr Bruton] thought that a licence was being granted, a tenancy by estoppel arises [. . .]

The whole corpus of law relating to landlord and tenant derives from the status of landlord and tenant, from privity of estate, from the fact of ownership of a proprietary interest in land, not from the fact of having entered into an agreement which might or might not have created such a proprietary interest.

---

[52] *Per* Millett LJ in *Bruton* in the Court of Appeal: [1998] QB 834, [844].   [53] Ibid, 845.
[54] Ibid.

> An agreement in the form of a lease, but which does not create a proprietary interest, cannot be a lease. And the order of cart and horse is not as Lord Hoffmann would have it, but as it has always been.
>
> Which is precisely why the common law imposes an estoppel upon the man who purports to grant a lease by means of an agreement in the form of a lease which purports to create one: to prevent him from saying 'I did not have the interest out of which to create a lease, therefore I could not have granted one, therefore the grantee is not my tenant, and I am not bound by any obligations as landlord.' But it must never be overlooked that a 'tenancy by estoppel' is not a tenancy: not a proprietary interest.

Routley's argument is that the House of Lords in *Bruton* reached the correct result, but by the wrong route. Certainly, given the policy behind s 11 of the Landlord and Tenant Act 1985, it would seem unreasonable for the Trust to use its own lack of a property right as a means to escape a statutory repairing duty. Routley suggests that the unfairness comes from the fact that the Trust entered an agreement seemingly giving Mr Bruton exclusive possession of the land for a limited period: as a result, the Trust should have been prevented from denying that Mr Bruton had a lease. This form of estoppel thus has the same effect as the estoppel by representation (see Chapter 10, section 1): it does not, in fact, give B a lease, but it prevents A from denying that B has a lease. That reasoning could thus have been used to prevent the Trust denying its statutory repairing duty. Routley's argument is convincing—but, as he admits, it does not fit with the reasoning of the House of Lords.

4.1.3 *Bruton*: The role of relativity of title?

In *Kay v Lambeth LBC*, Lord Scott described the circumstances in *Bruton* as analogous to those arising if '*a person not the owner of land but in adverse possession of it were to grant a tenancy of the land to another. As between the grantor and grantee there would be a valid "non-estate" tenancy. But unless and until the adverse possession had continued for the requisite 12 years the tenancy would not bind the true owner of the land.*'[55] We have noted elsewhere that a licensee, if he or she in fact has possession of A's land, may thereby acquire a separate freehold title, even before the expiry of any limitation period in his or her favour.[56] It is then possible for the licensee to grant a lease, albeit one that cannot bind A, or those acquiring rights from A, who will be able to rely on A's pre-existing property right. This explanation of the decision in *Bruton* has been supported by Roberts,[57] who notes that, in the House of Lords, counsel for Mr Bruton did cite decisions to show that: '*Title in English law is founded on possession [...] Title is not absolute. It is relative only.*'[58]

As noted by Roberts, on this analysis, the crucial factual question is whether the Trust in *Bruton* did in fact possess the land in such a way as to acquire its own, independent freehold title.

---

[55] [2006] 2 AC 465 at [144],

[56] See, for example, the observation of Lord Upjohn in *National Provincial Bank v Ainsworth* [1965] AC 1175, 1232 discussed at, for example, Chapter 7, section 2.2.

[57] Roberts, 'The Bruton Tenancy: A Matter of Relativity' [2012] Conv 87.

[58] [2000] 1 AC 406 at [408] (argument of Lewison QC).

Roberts, 'The *Bruton* Tenancy: A Matter of Relativity' [2012] Conv 87

At 92

Looking at the problem from the perspective of the agreement between the Council and [the Trust] then clearly it was not the intention of the parties that [the Trust] should have possession of the block of flats. However, whatever may have been the position *de iure*, [the Trust] clearly had de facto possession; and the example of an adverse possessor suggests that it is possession *de facto*, not *de iure*, which gives standing to grant a lease. The squatter is not entitled to exercise possesion (at least *quoad* the title holder), but in practice does so, and can grant a lease; a licensee such as [the Trust] is not entitled to possession, but in practice exercises it; as [the Trusts's] possession is *precario*, its possessory title will not displace that of the freeholder; but why should this prevent it from granting a lease?

In principle, the argument from relativity of title provides a neat explanation of how a licensee such as the Trust may be able to grant a lease: it is that such a party does not merely have a licence but also has its own, independent freehold, acquired as a result of its possession of the land. Factually, however, the explanation depends on showing that the licensee in each case did indeed have such possession. This raises the question of whether the statutory rights of an occupier, such as Mr Bruton, ought to depend on the position of the other party to the agreement, such as the Trust. This point is explored by the next possible explanation of the decision in *Bruton*.

4.1.4 *Bruton*: An example of purposive statutory interpretation?

The key aspect of the House of Lords' reasoning in *Bruton* seems to be the separation of the *status-conferring* and *property right-conferring* aspects of the lease. The agreement between Mr Bruton and the Trust, whilst it could not give Mr Bruton a property right in the land, *did* give him the status needed to qualify for statutory protection. The validity of that approach can be seen as a question of statutory interpretation: when Parliament used the word 'lease' to define the scope of the repairing duty, did it intend that term to be confined to cases in which B has a property right in land?

This suggestion is pursued in the following extract.

McFarlane and Simpson, 'Tackling Avoidance' in Rationalizing Property, Equity and Trusts: Essays for Edward Burn (ed Getzler, 2002, pp 175–6)

[It may] be significant that Lord Hoffmann posed the question: 'Did this agreement create a 'lease' or 'tenancy' within the meaning of the Landlord and Tenant Act 1985 or any other legislation which refers to a lease or tenancy?'[59] and also that counsel for the housing trust, in the words of Lord Hobhouse, accepted that 'a contractual relationship of landlord and tenant suffices to make the provisions of the Act applicable.'[60] It can be argued that *Bruton* [. . .] does not involve a re-working of the general test for a lease but rather involves an attempt to further the presumed purpose of a legislative scheme by looking not for a lease

---

[59] [2000] 1 AC 406, [413].   [60] Ibid, 417.

in the technical sense of a legal right to exclusive possession but instead for a lease in the wider, non-juristic sense of an arrangement which confers practical control of property. The decision can thus be seen as based on an implicit assumption that the legislature's use of the concept of a tenancy to determine the bounds of particular protection for occupiers is simply a means to achieve an underlying purpose of giving such protection to those who, in practice, occupy property as one occupies a home. Provided such occupation exists, the precise legal rights enjoyed by the occupier are therefore not decisive in determining the application of the statute [. . .]

Hence, it may just be possible to justify the decision in *Bruton* by arguing that "lease" and "tenancy", when used in the Landlord and Tenant Act 1985, include an occupier under an agreement which only fails to confer a legal right to exclusive possession because of the grantor's lack of title. It could be said that the purpose of the legislation is to regulate the relationship between grantor and occupier, and the lack of title of the grantor, whilst it will prevent the occupier gaining rights against the true owner or those claiming through him, should not deny the occupier the protection of the Act: put simply, in such a situation the fact that the occupation agreement is technically unable to confer a lease in the full legal sense is not the fault of the occupier [. . .]

McFarlane and Simpson also explore whether this 'statutory interpretation' approach can be used to explain the 'pretence' concept applied by the House of Lords in *Antoniades v Villiers*.[61] As we saw in Chapter 19, section 2.4, there is a debate as to whether that concept provides a doctrinal justification for ignoring terms in the parties' contract that, if valid, would prevent B from acquiring a right to exclusive possession of the land. McFarlane and Simpson suggest that, in *Antoniades*, the House of Lords may have been motivated by an understandable desire to ensure that the statutory protection then provided by the Rent Acts should extend not only to parties with a legal right to exclusive possession, but also to parties, such as Mr Villiers and Miss Bridger, who, *in practice*, enjoyed exclusive control of a home in return for paying rent. As the authors go on to note in the following passage, however, this approach to statutory interpretation, whilst it may be able to explain the results in *Bruton* and *Antoniades*, seems to be inconsistent with the seminal decision of the House of Lords in *Street v Mountford*.[62]

McFarlane and Simpson, 'Tackling Avoidance' in *Rationalizing Property, Equity and Trusts: Essays for Edward Burn* (ed Getzler, 2002, p 177)

Lord Templeman's [speech in *Street v Mountford*] is founded on a rejection of the previously prevailing idea that the term 'tenancy' could be given an unorthodox meaning when used in the Rent Acts. A heresy had sprung up in the Court of Appeal which allowed an owner wishing to avoid the burdens of such legislation to do so provided he demonstrated an intention not to grant a lease. It seems clear that this heresy was motivated by sympathy towards such an owner, and a consequent willingness to narrow the application of the Rent Acts. Lord Templeman firmly emphasises that the orthodox, traditional definition of a lease as the

---

[61] [1990] 1 AC 417. See also Simpson, 'Sham and Purposive Statutory Construction' in *Sham Transactions* (eds Simpson and Stewart, 2013) ch 5, arguing that modern developments of the sham test can often best be understood as depending on purposive statutory interpretation.

[62] [1985] AC 809.

grant of exclusive possession is the true test to apply. This can be defended on the simple grounds that when Parliament selects a concept such as 'lease' or 'tenancy', with an established juridical meaning, to communicate with judges there is no reason to believe it intends an unorthodox meaning of that term to be applied. Therefore whilst the result in *Street* may be favourable to occupiers rather than owners, its methodology is avowedly neutral.

The authors of the extract go on to make the point that, if the terms 'lease' or 'tenancy' can be interpreted in a novel way when used in a statute, this will not necessarily lead to an *increase* in the availability of statutory protection. For example, a court could find that, because of the special duties imposed on A if B has a lease, the term should be given a particularly narrow definition. Indeed, as we noted in Chapter 19, section 2.1, it seems that the Court of Appeal adopted just such an approach in the period leading up to *Street v Mountford*. Even if it is agreed that a judge, when interpreting a statute, should try to advance its purpose, we have to ask *how* a judge should discern that purpose. After all, as noted above, it may seem that the policy underlying s 11 of the Landlord and Tenant Act 1985 should apply even if B's agreement with A has not given B a property right. But it is doubtful that a court can make that decision given that: (i) the statute expressly limits its scope to cases in which B has a 'lease'; and (ii) as noted by the authors of all the extracts in this section, the term 'lease' is generally understood as applying only where A's agreement with B gives B a property right in land.

The solution, of course, is for Parliament to make its policy clearer. One resolution would be for the statutory protection currently available to those with leases to be extended to parties with licences. The lease would then be left to play its role as a concept conferring a property right; it would not have to perform the further task of conferring the status needed to qualify for statutory protection. In fact, as we will see in the next section, the Law Commission has proposed just such a change, and it has been implemented in Wales.

5 THE *STATUS-CONFERRING* ASPECT OF A LEASE: REFORM?

There have long been calls for the reform of the statutory regulation of short-term residential leases. One of the central complaints has been that the law is too complex, with occupiers and landlords often unsure of their positions. Certainly, any protection that the law aims to provide for occupiers will be undermined if, in practice, those occupiers are unaware of their legal rights.[63]

In 2006, the Law Commission, following what it described as '*one of the largest consultation exercises [it had] ever undertaken*',[64] published its report on *Renting Homes*. The report considered the statutory protection available to short-term residential tenants and suggested significant changes, based on three objectives of '*simplification, increased comprehensibility, and flexibility*'.[65] It produced a very detailed draft Bill (the Rented Homes Bill) and stated

---

[63] For a good example of this problem, exploring occupiers' ignorance of the legal protection given to them by the Protection from Eviction Act 1977, see Cowan, 'Harassment and Unlawful Eviction in the Private Rented Sector – a Study of Law in(-)action' [2001] Conv 249.

[64] Law Commission Report No 297, *Renting Homes* (2006), [1.3].   [65] Ibid, [1.9].

that its proposals were based on '*two radical changes to the legislative approach to the regulation of rented housing*'. Those changes are set out in the extract below:

Law Commission Report No 297, *Renting Homes* (2006, [1.4]–[1.6])

First, we recommend the creation of a single social tenure. At present, local authorities can only let on secure tenancies; registered social landlords only on assured tenancies. Our recommendations are 'landlord-neutral'. They enable social housing providers, referred to in the Bill as 'community landlords', and those private sector landlords who so wish to rent on identical terms. This has long been sought by local authorities and registered social landlords. This offers the prize of vastly increased flexibility both to policy makers and landlords in the provision and management of social housing.

Secondly, we recommend a new 'consumer protection' approach which focuses on the contract between the landlord and the occupier (the contract-holder), incorporating consumer protection principles of fairness and transparency. Thus our recommended scheme does not depend on technical legal issues of whether or not there is a tenancy as opposed to a licence (as has usually been the case in the past). This ensures that both landlords and occupiers have a much clearer understanding of their rights and obligations.

The terms of the contract, underpinned by our statutory scheme, will be set out in model contracts that we anticipate will be free and easily downloadable. They will benefit landlords by explaining their rights and obligations, thus reducing the ignorance many landlords have about their responsibilities. They will benefit occupiers who will also have a clear statement of their rights and obligations, which sets out the basis on which they occupy accommodation, and the circumstances in which their rights to occupy may come to an end.

The aim of simplification would be achieved in a number of ways. Firstly, the current focus on the identity of the landlord, and, with it, the different statutory categories of lease (e.g. 'assured shorthold tenancy', 'assured tenancy', 'secure tenancy', etc.), would be removed. Secondly, and most importantly for our current purposes, the *status-conferring* aspect of a lease would be lost: to qualify for statutory protection, it would no longer be necessary for B to show that he or she has a lease. The new scheme would instead regulate 'occupation contracts'. There would be two forms of such contract: the 'standard contract', lightly regulated and offering no security of tenure (similar to the current assured shorthold tenancy), and the 'secure contract', more heavily regulated and providing security of tenure, to be used (like the current secure tenancy and assured tenancy) by local authorities or social landlords.

Law Commission Report No 297, *Renting Homes* (2006)

At [3.9]

A number of points about the definition of 'occupation contract' should be noted at the outset.

1. It is specifically provided that an occupation contract can be either a tenancy or a licence. This avoids historic complications whereby statutory schemes only applied where

premises were 'let'. This definition recognizes that the distinction between a lease/tenancy and a licence exists. This will often be important. For example, where a landlord sells their legal estate in a property to another, it is highly relevant whether that estate is subject to a lease or a licence. These issues continue to be determined by application of the current law. We also make explicit that, where an occupation contract is a tenancy, any land registration requirements must be satisfied.

2. The contract must be made between a landlord and an individual (the 'contract-holder'). The contract must confer the right to occupy premises as a home. Where the contract is made with two or more persons, at least one must be an individual. Contracts relating to the occupation of premises for purposes other than occupation as a home fall outside the scope of our scheme. In many situations, such agreements fall within the scope of other statutory schemes, for example business tenancies [. . .]

3. Despite the breadth of the definition, not all contracts which confer the right to occupy premises as a home fall within the scope of the Bill [. . .][66]

4. Most of the ancillary tests currently used to define the scope of statutory protection are removed. Thus, there is no requirement that the rent should be above or below a defined rent limit. Nor is there any requirement that the premises must be occupied as the 'only or principal home'.

5. Most importantly in the context of the social rented sector, there is no 'landlord condition'. Our emphasis on the principle of landlord neutrality means that the scheme will, for the first time, enable the creation of a single type of contract that can apply throughout the social rented sector, irrespective of the identity of the landlord.

6. Once created, an occupation contract continues in existence either until it is terminated in accordance with the provisions of the scheme, or unless the premises or the contract come within the scope of the exceptions listed in paragraph 3 of schedule 1[67] [. . .]

At [3.18]–[3.21]

In place of the current multiplicity of statutory statuses, the scheme provides for just two types of occupation contract: secure and standard.

Secure contracts

Secure contracts are modelled on secure tenancies which currently can only be created by local authorities. As with secure tenancies, secure contracts have a high degree of security of tenure protected by the Bill. They can be created only on a periodic basis. The reason for this is that in the context of the high security of tenure granted by the Bill for a secure contract, having a fixed term would not be useful [. . .] The idea of the secure contract is to provide a security gold standard for use in the social sector. To allow fixed term secure contracts would at best muddle the picture, and at worst, undercut that objective.

Standard contracts

Standard contracts are modelled on the current assured shorthold tenancy granted by private landlords. Although they have a low degree of security of tenure protected by statute,

---

[66] [One example of a type of contract not covered by the Bill occurs where B pays to *share* occupation of A's land with A.]

[67] [That is, if a change in circumstances means that the contract now falls into one of those types not covered by the Bill.]

there is nothing preventing landlords entering contracts which have a greater degree of security than the Bill requires. Often this happens because it is in the landlord's interest to do so, for example to minimize void letting periods. Standard contracts can be either fixed term or periodic.

In the case of standard contracts only, the Bill provides that a landlord is able to specify periods where, notwithstanding the existence of the contract, the premises cannot be used for occupation. The purpose of this provision is to enable, for example, universities to enter occupation contracts with their students for the whole academic year, but also enable them to regain possession during vacation periods when the accommodation is needed for conferences. It would be a disproportionate administrative burden for there to be separate contracts for each academic term or semester.

The Law Commission's proposals have not been enacted in England. Later statutory reform in the Westminster Parliament, for example in the Localism Act 2011 and the Housing and Planning Act 2016, has continued to organize statutory protection around the question of whether or not B has a lease, and so does not adopt the Law Commission's contract-centred approach. In Wales, however, the position is different. Using its devolved powers, the Welsh Assembly passed the Renting Homes (Wales) Act 2016, which the Law Commission helped to draw up. It implements what is, for our present purposes, the key aspect of the Law Commission's proposals: the decision to decouple statutory protection from the presence of a property right.

Renting Homes (Wales) Act 2016, s 7

Tenancies and licences that are occupation contracts

(1) A tenancy or licence is an occupation contract if

    (a) it is within subsection (2) or (3), and

    (b) rent or other consideration is payable under it.

(2) A tenancy or licence is within this subsection if—

    (a) it is made between a landlord and an individual, and

    (b) it confers on the individual the right to occupy a dwelling as a home.

(3) A tenancy or licence is within this subsection if—

    (a) it is made between the landlord and two or more persons at least one of whom is an individual, and

    (b) it confers on the individual (or, if there is more than one individual, on one or more of them) the right to occupy a dwelling as a home.

As then noted by s 7(4), there are exceptions to this general provision, in Sch 2 to the Act, for certain tenancies and licences. The Act then regulates the effects of occupation contracts, which are sub-divided, as proposed in the Law Commission's 2006 Report, into standard contracts and secure contracts. The distinction between a tenancy and a licence itself is not, however, critical in setting the scope of the statutory scheme. The thinking behind the decision to regulate occupation contracts, rather than only leases, is set out clearly in one of the Law Commission's earlier Consultation Papers.

Law Commission Consultation Paper No 162, *Renting Homes 1: Status and Security* (2002, [9.39]–[9.40])

We have thought very carefully about whether the lease-licence distinction should be retained as a means to determine which agreements should fall within our proposed scheme, and those which should fall outside. Considerable conceptual difficulties are caused by the distinction between exclusive occupation and exclusive possession. It is not readily understandable by the public at large.

As we have already argued, we regard the contract between the landlord and the occupier as central to the operation of our scheme. We see no reason why any distinction should be drawn between a contract which comprises a lease and a contract which comprises a licence. This distinction is essential where the proprietary consequences of the contract are concerned, and should remain so, but it should not affect the statutory regulation of the contract as between the contracting parties themselves.

The Renting Homes (Wales) Act 2016, when its full provisons are brought into force, will therefore mean that those occupying their home under a contract, whether they have a lease or a licence, will have either a 'standard contract' or a 'secure contract'. The former is based on the assured shorthold tenancy, and the latter on the secure tenancy. Model forms of the contracts will be produced, and any departure from those forms will need to be fair and transparent. As was proposed in the Law Commission's 2006 Report, the contracts will contain four classes of term: (i) key matters; (ii) fundamental terms; (iii) supplementary terms; and (iv) additional terms.[68] The Act introduces many other changes, designed to simplify and clarify the law, and, in many cases, to increase the rights of an occupier: it includes, for example, rules as to succession to occupation contracts following the death of the occupier,[69] and a provision to allow for a joint holder of a secure or standard contract to withdraw from that contract without terminating the contract between the landlord and other joint holder(s) of it,[70] thus dealing with the issue in *Hammersmith and Fulham LBC v Monk*.[71] The Act also seeks to address other common complaints about residential letting, including provisions, for example as to deposits paid by occupiers,[72] and as to the information that needs to be provided to an occupier.[73] Indeed, in December 2017, the Law Commission included in its 13th Programme of Law Reform a project on 'Residential Leasehold', which will address regulation of managing agents,[74] and a distinct project on 'Unfair Terms in Residential Leasehold'.

Certainly, one advantage of the approach adopted in Wales, if also adopted in England, would be the elimination of the current *status-conferring* aspect of the lease. In addition to its practical benefits, such a change could have an important conceptual effect: it would permit the courts to consider the doctrinal definition of the lease (as a property right in land), free from the concern that the same definition may also have to be used to advance the policy goals behind a particular statute.

---

[68] Ibid, [2.10].   [69] Sections 73–83.

[70] Sections 111–12 (secure contracts); ss 130–1 (standard contracts); s 52 (for the effect of withdrawal).

[71] [1992] 1 AC 478 (HL). See Chapter 19, section 3.3.1.   [72] Sections 43–7.

[73] Sections 31–41.

[74] As well as commonhold (see Chapter 24, section 3) and enfranchisement (see Chapter 24, section 2.2).

QUESTIONS

1. Why might Parliament intervene to give a tenant extra rights beyond those expressly agreed between that tenant and his or her landlord?

2. '*The distinction between a lease and a licence should only matter if a third party is involved: it should make no difference when considering the positions of A (the landlord/ licensor) and B (the tenant/licensee).*' Do you agree?

3. What is a 'tenancy by estoppel'? Should the House of Lords in *Bruton v London & Quadrant Housing Trust* have found that Mr Bruton had a tenancy by estoppel?

4. What is the wider significance of the Renting Homes (Wales) Act 2016 for the status-conferring aspects of a lease?

For guidance on how to answer these questions visit the online resources at www.oup.com/ uk/mcfarlane4e/.

FURTHER READING

Bridge, 'Leases: Contract, Property and Status' in *Land Law: Issues, Debates, Policy* (ed Tee, Devon: Willan, 2002)

Bright, *Landlord and Tenant Law in Context* (Oxford: Hart Publishing, 2007, chs 5 and 6)

Dixon, 'The Non-Proprietary Lease: The Rise of the Feudal Phoenix' [2000] CLJ 25

Law Commission Report No 297, *Renting Homes* (2006, especially Pts 1 and 2)

McFarlane and Simpson, 'Tackling Avoidance' in *Rationalizing Property, Equity & Trusts: Essays for Edward Burn* (ed Getzler, London: LexisNexis, 2002)

Pawlowski, 'The *Bruton* Tenancy: Clarity or More Confusion?' [2005] Conv 262

Roberts, 'The *Bruton* Tenancy: A Matter of Relativity' [2012] Conv 87

Skerratt-Williams, 'A Comparison of Residential Tenancies in England and Wales' (2016) 20 L & T Rev 137

21

LEASEHOLD COVENANTS

CENTRAL ISSUES

1. Both the positive and negative obligations of landlord and leaseholder have long been enforceable by the principle of privity of estate. The appropriate legal framework now differs according to whether the lease was granted before or after the enactment of the Landlord and Tenant (Covenants) Act 1995 on 1 January 1996.

2. *Pre-1996 leases:*

   • *The burden:* A leaseholder's covenants (provided that they touch and concern the lease) are enforceable against a purchaser of the lease by privity of estate. The burden of the landlord's covenants (provided that they relate to the subject matter of the lease) is enforceable against the purchaser of the freehold reversion by s 142 of the Law of Property Act 1925.

   • *The benefit:* The leaseholder's covenants and the landlord's covenants (both having reference to the subject matter of the lease) are enforceable by a purchaser of the freehold reversion and by a purchaser of the lease, respectively, under ss 141 and 142 of the 1925 Act.

   • *The contractual liability* of the original parties to the lease continues throughout the term of the lease.

3. *Post-1996 leases.*

   • *The benefit and burden* of the leaseholder's and landlord's covenants (provided that they are not expressed to be personal) are enforceable against and by purchasers of the lease and the freehold reversion under s 3 of the 1995 Act.

   • *The contractual liability* of the original leaseholder is automatically released upon his or her assignment of the lease under s 5 of the 1995 Act, and the original landlord may apply for a release from his or her liability upon his or her assignment of the freehold reversion under ss 6 and 8 of the Act.

4. A sub-lessee is not within the privity of estate relationship, but is obliged (inter alia) to observe the negative leaseholder covenants in the head lease under the doctrine in *Tulk v Moxhay* discussed in Chapter 23.

5. The primary remedy for breach of a leasehold covenant that has not been waived is for the landlord to exercise a right of re-entry to forfeit the lease.

6. The landlord may re-enter peacefully or by serving proceedings for possession.

7.. Before a landlord is able exercise a right of re-entry for breach of covenant (other than to pay rent), a notice must be served in accordance with s 146(1) of the 1925 Act.

8. A tenant (and subtenant or mortgagee) may apply for relief from forfeiture based upon a breach of either the covenant to pay rent or a breach of any other of the tenant's covenants.

1 INTRODUCTION

A lease will not only contain the grant of the leasehold term by the landlord to the tenant, but also covenants detailing the respective obligations of the landlord and the tenant. Certain covenants are implied, but, in a written lease, these covenants will be supplemented by often extensive and detailed covenants stipulating the tenant's obligations to the landlord and the landlord's, often more limited, obligations to the tenant. The landlord's covenants will include a covenant for quiet possession, and may also include obligations to repair and insure; a tenant's covenants will include a covenant to pay the rent and covenants governing his or her use of the premises, as well as covenants detailing the tenant's responsibilities for repair and maintenance, and to meet the cost of the landlord's obligations in this regard, by paying a management or service charge.

In this chapter, we will examine the mechanisms by which both negative and positive leasehold covenants bind, on the one hand, subsequent purchasers of the lease from the original tenant and, on the other, subsequent purchasers of the freehold reversion from the landlord. We will also consider the law governing the enforcement of leasehold covenants and, in particular, the process of forfeiture by which a landlord can bring the lease to an end for a failure by the tenant to perform the tenant's covenants.

The legal regulation of leasehold covenants is applicable to all leases that are capable of assignment. As we saw in Chapter 20, most short-term tenancy agreements of residential accommodation will contain a restriction on assignment of, or otherwise dealing with, the leasehold term. The most common types of lease in which the enforcement of leasehold covenants is important are in the commercial context or in the ownership of flats, where the long lease structure is employed. Indeed, in Chapter 24, we will see that the long lease is employed in the ownership of flats, precisely because it provides a mechanism whereby positive obligations can be enforced against subsequent flat owners. In the commercial context, a lease of business premises will usually be capable of assignment (unless it is for a very short term), although it is common for the tenant's ability to assign or otherwise dispose of his or her term to be qualified by the need to obtain the landlord's consent, which cannot be unreasonably refused. Many of the cases that we will be considering are set in the commercial context, perhaps because commercial landlords and tenants are more inclined to litigate. Our focus will, however, be on the residential long lease.

1.1 LEASEHOLD COVENANT TERMINOLOGY

Where a lease or a freehold reversion is assigned, it is necessary to determine whether or not the covenants given by the original tenant (TO) to the original landlord (LO) in the

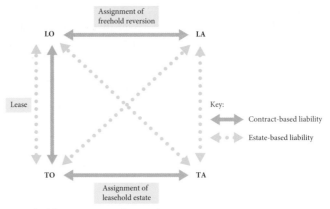

Figure 21.1 Leasehold covenant relationships

lease (the tenant's covenants) may be enforced by a purchaser of the freehold reversion (the landlord's assignee, or LA) against TO and any purchaser of the lease (the tenant's assignee, or TA). Likewise, it is also necessary to establish whether TO and TA can enforce against LA the covenants granted by LO to TO in the original lease (the landlord's covenants). This web of relationships can be depicted as shown in Figure 21.1.

The answer to these central questions on the enforceability of both the landlord's and tenant's covenant depends on when the lease was granted. This is because the law was amended and codified by the Landlord and Tenant (Covenants) Act 1995, but the amendments enacted apply only to those leases granted on or after 1 January 1996. There are, of course, many leases granted before 1 January 1996 that still have many years to run and which will continue to be governed by the old law. It is thus necessary to look at the law governing leases entered into before 1 January 1996 ('pre-1996 leases') and the law regulating leases entered into on or after 1 January 1996 ('post-1995 leases').

1.2 CONTRACT AND ESTATE-BASED LIABILITY

We saw in Chapter 19 that a lease has a dual personality: firstly, as a contract between the original parties; and secondly, as a proprietary interest in the form of a leasehold estate in the land, which may be transferred or left by will. Liability on the landlord's covenants and the tenant's covenants in the lease is based either upon the contractual relationship between LO and TO, or upon the leasehold estate that will vested in TA, upon his or her purchase of the lease, or the freehold reversion (subject to the lease), which likewise may be transferred by LO to LA. Where the parties fall within this leasehold relationship, we say that there is *privity of estate*.

Students of contract law will recognize that, between LO and TO, there is *privity of contract*, which is unaffected if and when LO and/or TO assign their interests to LA and TA, respectively. The lease contract continues between the original parties throughout the term of the lease.

Privity of estate exists between the current parties to the leasehold estate. It can thus vary during the leasehold term, depending on in whom the lease and the freehold reversion are vested. Initially, LO and TO are the parties to the leasehold estate. If LO assigns the freehold reversion, then privity of estate will exist between LA and TO: LO falls out of privity of estate because he or she no longer holds the freehold reversion. Likewise, if TO assigns his or her lease to TA, TA comes within privity of estate with the current holder of the freehold reversion, whether that is LO or LA, and TO is no longer within the privity of estate relationship.

The concept of privity of estate was developed many centuries ago, and continues to be central to the enforceability of leasehold covenants by and against the current parties to the lease. Where there is privity of estate, both the positive and negative leasehold covenants, which are so closely related to the leasehold estate that they form part of it, will be enforceable by and against the current parties to the leasehold estate.

Lord Templeman explains the interplay between the operation of privity of contract and estate in the following case.

City of London Corp v Fell
[1994] 1 AC 458, HL

Lord Templeman

At 464

The principle that the benefit and burden of covenants in a lease which touch and concern the land run with the term and with the reversion is necessary for the effective operation of the law of landlord and tenant. Common law, and statute following the common law, recognise two forms of legal estate in land, a fee simple absolute in possession and a term of years absolute: see section 1 of the Act of 1925. Common law, and statute following the common law, were faced with the problem of rendering effective the obligations under a lease which might endure for a period of 999 years or more beyond the control of any covenantor. The solution was to annex to the term and the reversion the benefit and burden of covenants which touch and concern the land. The covenants having been annexed, every legal owner of the term granted by the lease and every legal owner of the reversion from time to time holds his estate with the benefit of and subject to the covenants which touch and concern the land. The system of leasehold tenure requires that the obligations in the lease shall be enforceable throughout the term, whether those obligations are affirmative or negative. The owner of a reversion must be able to enforce the positive covenants to pay rent and keep in repair against an assignee who in turn must be able to enforce any positive covenants entered into by the original landlord. Common law retained the ancient rule that the burden of a covenant does not run with the land of the covenantor except in the case of a lease, but even that rule was radically modified by equity so far as negative covenants were concerned: see *Tulk v. Moxhay* (1848) 2 Ph. 774.

The effect of common law and statute on a lease is to create rights and obligations which are independent of the parallel rights and obligations of the original human covenantor who and whose heirs may fail or the parallel rights and obligations of a corporate covenantor which may be dissolved. Common law and statute achieve that effect by annexing those rights and obligations so far as they touch and concern the land to the term and to the reversion. Nourse L.J. neatly summarised the position when he said in an impeccable judgment [1993] Q.B. 589, 604:

> "The contractual obligations which touch and concern the land having become imprinted on the estate, the tenancy is capable of existence as a species of property independently of the contract."

The common law did not release the original tenant from liability for breaches of covenant committed after an assignment because of the sacred character of covenant in English law [. . .] This only means that the fortunate English landlord has two remedies after an assignment, namely his remedy against the assignee and his remedy against the original tenant. It does not follow that if the liability of the original tenant is released or otherwise disappears then the term granted by the lease will disappear or that the assignee will cease to be liable on the covenants.

As between landlord and assignee the landlord cannot enforce a covenant against the assignee because the assignee does not covenant. The landlord enforces against the assignee the provisions of a covenant entered into by the original tenant, being provisions which touch and concern the land, because those provisions are annexed by the lease to the term demised by the lease. The assignee is not liable for a breach of covenant committed after the assignee has himself in turn assigned the lease because once he has assigned over he has ceased to be the owner of the term to which the covenants are annexed.

2 THE ORIGINAL PARTIES (LO AND TO) AND CONTRACTUAL ENFORCEABILITY

2.1 PRE-1996 LAW

LO and TO remain contractually liable on their leasehold covenants throughout the term of the lease, even though they may have disposed of their respective interests, unless they have expressly agreed to limit their respective liabilities in their original covenants. Upon the assignment of the lease by TO to TA, the landlord might also insist that TA enter into a direct covenant with them creating an additional contractual link (and liability) between the landlord and TA.

This contractual liability can operate harshly particularly against TO, who, many years after he or she has assigned the lease, can find him or herself sued in respect of a breach of the tenant's covenants (usually a failure to pay the rent or service charge) committed by TA. For example, the current landlord will be tempted to rely on this contractual liability where TA is insolvent.[1] Although this liability is more often relied upon in commercial leases, where rentals reflect market levels, the principles are equally applicable to residential long leases.

Lord Nicholls explained the problems in the following case.

Hindcastle Ltd v Barbara Attenborough & Associates Ltd
[1997] AC 70, HL

Lord Nicholls

At 83

The insolvency may occur many years after the lease was granted, long after the original tenant parted with his interest in the lease. He paid the rent until he left, and then took on

---

[1] The economic downturn of the late 1980s and early 1990s resulted in a number of well-publicized and criticized cases in which original leaseholders were successfully held liable.

the responsibility of other premises. A person of modest means is understandably shocked when out of the blue he receives a rent demand from the landlord of the property he once leased. Unlike the landlord, he had no control over the identity of assignees down the line. He had no opportunity to reject them as financially unsound.

TO does have the benefit of an indemnity covenant for the performance of the tenant's covenant from TA, which will build up a chain of indemnity covenants following each assignment of the lease,[2] and also a restitutionary action for any damages that TO may have to pay as a result of the default of another (i.e. TA).[3] But these actions will be of little value where the defaulter is insolvent or the chain of indemnity covenants has been broken.[4]

In a series of decisions, the courts added further to TO's woes by confirming that his or her liability could be affected by a variation in the lease terms (e.g. an upward rent review), where that variation was made in pursuance of the terms of the lease.[5] A variation would not affect TO where it resulted from the separate agreement of the current parties to the lease, whether that variation resulted in a renewal or extension of the leasehold term,[6] or was to the terms upon which the lease was held.[7]

This contractual liability was the target of criticism by the Law Commission.

Law Commission Report No 174, Landlord and Tenant Law: Privity of Contract and Estate (1988, [3.1]–[3.3])

In Part III of the Working Paper, we identified the following criticisms of the present law:

(a) It is intrinsically unfair that anyone should bear burdens under a contract in respect of which they derive no benefit and over which they have no control: contractual obligations undertaken in a lease should only regulate relations between current owners with interests in the property.

(b) When demand is made under continuing liability of the original tenant it will often not only be unexpected, but beyond the means of the former tenant; there is no logical way in which a former tenant who does understand that there is a contingent liability can estimate the amount.

(c) A single lease can contain some covenants of which the burden automatically passes to an assignee, by privity of estate, and others of which the burden does not pass automatically. This contrast in a single document, which is not apparent from its wording is unsatisfactory [. . .]

---

[2] See Law of Property Act 1925, s 77(1)(c), and Land Registration Act 2002, Sch 12, para 20. The indemnity is implied into each assignment of the lease and so can build up a chain of indemnity covenants to pass liability down to the defaulting leaseholder. As to the operation of indemnity covenants, see Chapter 23, section 2.4.2.

[3] *Moule v Garrett* (1872) LR 7 EX 101.

[4] *RHP Ltd v Mirror Group Newspapers and Mirror Group Holdings* (1992) 65 P & CR 252.

[5] See *Centrovincial Estates plc v Bulk Storage Ltd* (1983) 46 P & CR 393, in which the leaseholder was liable for rent varied from £17,000 to £40,000 pursuant to a rent review clause contained in the original lease, and *Selous Street Properties Ltd v Oronel Fabrics Ltd* (1984) 270 EG 643, in which the rent review took into account unauthorized alterations that were subsequently approved by the landlord.

[6] *City of London Corp v Fell* [1994] 1 AC 458.

[7] *Friends Provident Life Office v British Railways Board* (1997) 73 P & CR 9.

(d) Many laymen do not realise that the original parties have a continuing liability and most leases do not make this clear on their face.

(e) Where a lease contains a rent review clause, the original tenant's liability, under privity of contract, normally extends to payment of the higher rents after revision. For this reason, privity of contract sometimes results in the original tenant having a greater liability then he understood he was assuming. While this may merely reflect the increase in value of the premises it can cast on a former tenant a burden resulting from an increased value from which he has derived no benefit.

(f) Landlords who are in practice the main beneficiaries of the privity of contract principle are unduly protected. They have the ability to enforce obligations undertaken by tenants by action against both the original tenant and the current tenant [. . .] This makes the principle one-sided, and unreasonably multiplies the remedies available to landlords.

(g) Original tenants against whom covenants are enforced after they have assigned the lease are not adequately protected, nor do they have adequate means of reimbursement. They are not released even if the tenant in possession agrees materially to vary the extent of liability, they are not entitled to notice of default and they have no right to take back possession of the property. Former tenants are therefore often deprived of the opportunity to limit their liability by taking prompt remedial action. Faced with demands that they must meet, they are often unable even to have recourse to the property to recoup any losses.

(h) The contingent liability which privity of contract imposes on an original tenant who has parted with his interest in the property can create difficulty in winding-up and distributing the estates of tenants who have died. The response to the Working Paper suggests that this difficulty is more theoretical than practical.

[. . .]

Against these criticisms we pointed out that continuing liability of the parties to leases is a matter of contract. They are free to vary the normal rule. This is sometimes done, but not frequently. Some feel that a heavy burden lies on those who propose any further restriction on freedom of contract, but others question whether there is any true freedom here because there is widely thought to be an inequality of bargaining power between landlords and tenants, favouring landlords.

These criticisms have, in part, been addressed by the Landlord and Tenant (Covenants) Act 1995. The reforms of the 1995 Act affecting pre-1996 leases address only the worst excesses of privity of contract. The original parties' liability under post-1995 leases is subject to more far-reaching reform, which is considered below.

Section 18 of the 1995 Act provides that TO's liability to pay an amount due under the lease will not be altered by a variation of the lease, which the landlord had an absolute right to refuse, made after the time at which he or she has disposed of his or her interest.

Section 17 of the 1995 Act provides that the current landlord, who wishes to recover a fixed sum from TO, must give notice of the amount that he or she is intending to recover within six months of the sum becoming due.[8] Where TO complies with this notice, he or

---

[8] Landlord and Tenant (Covenants) Act 1995, s 17. This notice must be in statutory form (see s 27) and is commonly referred to as a 'problem notice'.

she may claim an overriding lease to secure any sums that he or she has been required to pay. An overriding lease takes effect as a statutory lease interposed between the current landlord and the current defaulting leaseholder. As such, it will enable TO to enforce the tenant's covenants, for example, by claiming the rental due and seeking forfeiture if the rent is not paid.[9] Thus TO is at least given a warning of his or her potential contractual liability for fixed sums, and is provided with a mechanism to try to recover the sums that he or she has had to meet. His or her contractual liability for unliquidated sums, however, is undiminished.

2.2 POST-1995 LAW

2.2.1 Release of TO

Section 5 of the Landlord and Tenant (Covenants) Act 1995 releases TO from contractual liability once he or she has assigned his or her lease. It also confirms TA's release from estate-based liability should he or she, in turn, dispose of the leasehold estate.

Landlord and Tenant (Covenants) Act 1995, s 5

Tenant released from covenants on assignment of tenancy

(1) This section applies where a tenant assigns premises demised to him under a tenancy.

(2) If the tenant assigns the whole of the premises demised to him, he—

   (a) is released from the tenant covenants of the tenancy, and

   (b) ceases to be entitled to the benefit of the landlord covenants of the tenancy, as from the assignment.

A tenant's guarantor is also released from liability.[10] Where the tenant requires the consent of the landlord to assign the lease, however, a landlord may refuse his or her consent unless the tenant enters into an authorized guarantee agreement, under which the tenant guarantees the assignee's payment of the rent and performance of the other tenant's covenants.[11] A landlord's consent to assign is a common feature of commercial leases, but not of residential long leases.

2.2.2 Release of LO

LO can also be released from his or her contractual liability, although a release is not available from liabilities that are expressed to be personal to LO.[12] LO's release does not operate automatically upon assignment of the reversion, but must be requested by LO serving a notice on TO, within four weeks of the assignment of his or her reversion. The process is governed by s 8, which provides that, where TO refuses to grant a release, the county court may grant a release where it is reasonable to do so.

---

[9] Ibid, s 19.   [10] Ibid, ss 24 and 25.   [11] Ibid, s 16.
[12] *BHP Petroleum Great Britain Ltd v Chesterfield Properties Ltd* [2002] Ch 194: see section 3.2.2.

Landlord and Tenant (Covenants) Act 1995, s 6

Landlord may be released from covenants on assignment of reversion

(1) This section applies where a landlord assigns the reversion in premises of which he is the landlord under a tenancy.

(2) If the landlord assigns the reversion in the whole of the premises of which he is the landlord—

    (a) he may apply to be released from the landlord covenants of the tenancy in accordance with section 8; and

    (b) if he is so released from all of those covenants, he ceases to be entitled to the benefit of the tenant covenants of the tenancy as from the assignment.

The provisions of the 1995 Act cannot be excluded or varied: for instance, so as effectively to continue the contractual liability of a tenant or their guarantor.[13] But the House of Lords has held that a limitation of liability contained in the terms of the original covenant does not fall foul of this prohibition. In so doing, the Lords explained the purpose and effect of the Act's limitation of LO and TO's contractual liability.

London Diocesan Fund v Phithwa
[2005] 1 WLR 3956, HL

Facts: A lease provided that the original landlord (Avonridge Property Co Ltd) would not be liable for the payment of rent under the head lease after it assigned the reversion. After Avonridge assigned its leasehold reversion, the head lease was forfeited as a result of its assignee's failure to pay the rent under the head lease; the sub-lessees obtained relief from forfeiture, but had to pay the arrears of rent. They unsuccessfully claimed that the limitation of Avonridge's liability in the head lease was void under s 25 of the 1995 Act.

Lord Nicholls

At 14–21

These statutory provisions might readily be stultified if the parties to a lease could exclude their operation. In particular, the provision for automatic release of tenant covenants on assignment of a lease would be a weak instrument if it were open to a landlord to provide that the original tenant's contractual liability should continue for the whole term notwithstanding

---

[13] Landlord and Tenant (Covenants) Act 1995, s 25. A contractual obligation upon TO's gurantor to guarantee the liability of TA thus is void under s 25 unless they do so pursuant to an authorized guarantee agreement see *Good Harvest Partnership LLP v Centaur Services Ltd* [2010] EWHC 330 (Ch), [2010] Ch 426; *K/S Victoria St. v House of Fraser (Stores Management) Ltd* [2011] EWCA Civ 904, [2011] 2 P & CR 15; *Tindall Cobham 1 Ltd v Adda Hotels* [2014] EWCA Civ 1215. Likewise, a gurantor cannot take an assignment of the tenant's lease because by so doing they would assume liability for the tenant's covenants and thus frustrate their release from the tenant's covenants pursuant to ss 5 and 24, see *EMI Group Ltd v O&H Q1Ltd* [2016] Ch 529.

section 5. So the Act, in section 25, enacts a comprehensive anti-avoidance provision. Subsection (1) relevantly provides:

> "Any agreement relating to a tenancy is void to the extent that- (a) it would apart from this section have effect to exclude, modify or otherwise frustrate the operation of any provision of this Act, or (b) it provides for- (i) the termination or surrender of the tenancy, or (ii) the imposition on the tenant of any penalty, disability, or liability, in the event of the operation of any provision of this Act [. . .]"

The words in parenthesis in Avonridge's covenant in clause 6 of each sublease are an "agreement relating to a tenancy" within the meaning of this section: section 25(4). But does this agreement "frustrate the operation" of any provision of the Act? That is the key question.

The subtenants submit it does. The limited release provisions in sections 6 to 8 were intended to be the sole means whereby an original landlord could obtain a release from the landlord covenants when he assigned the reversion. The parenthetical words in clause 6 would frustrate that statutory purpose if they were allowed to have effect according to their tenor.

I am unable to agree. Where I part company with this submission is its statement of the statutory purpose. Sections 5 to 8 are relieving provisions. They are intended to benefit tenants, or landlords, as the case may be. That is their purpose. That is how they are meant to operate. These sections introduced a means, which cannot be ousted, whereby in certain circumstances, without the agreement of the other party, a tenant or landlord can be released from a liability he has assumed. The object of the legislation was that on lawful assignment of a tenancy or reversion, and irrespective of the terms of the tenancy, the tenant or the landlord should have an exit route from his future liabilities. This route should be available in accordance with the statutory provisions.

Thus the mischief at which the statute was aimed was the *absence* in practice of any such exit route. Consistently with this the legislation was not intended to close any *other* exit route already open to the parties: in particular, that by agreement their liability could be curtailed from the outset or later released or waived. The possibility that by agreement the parties may limit their liability in this way was not, it seems, perceived as having unfair consequences in practice, even though landlords normally have greater bargaining power than tenants. So there was no call for legislation to exclude the parties' capacity to make such an agreement, ending their liability in circumstances other than those provided in the Act.

Section 25 is of course to be interpreted generously, so as to ensure the operation of the Act is not frustrated, either directly or indirectly. But there is nothing in the language or scheme of the Act to suggest the statute was intended to exclude the parties' ability to limit liability under their covenants from the outset in whatever way they may agree. An agreed limitation of this nature does not impinge upon the operation of the statutory provisions.

[. . .] Whatever its form, an agreed limitation of liability does not impinge upon the operation of the statutory provisions because, as already noted, the statutory provisions are intended to operate to relieve tenants and landlords from a liability which would otherwise exist. They are not intended to impose a liability which otherwise would be absent. They are not intended to enlarge the liability either of a tenant or landlord. The Act does not compel a landlord to enter into a covenant with his tenant to pay the rent under a headlease. The Act does not compel this, even though it may be eminently reasonable that a landlord should do so. Nor do the statutory restrictions on the circumstances where a landlord can end his liability without his tenant's consent carry any implication that a tenant may not agree to end his landlord's liability in other circumstances. Such an implication would be inconsistent with the underlying scheme of these provisions.

This appraisal accords with the thrust of the Law Commission's report [. . .]

Nor do the events in this case exemplify a loophole in the Act Parliament cannot have intended. The risks involved were not obscure or concealed. They were evident on the face of the subleases. The sublessees were to pay up-front a capitalised rent for the whole term of the subleases. But clause 6 enabled Avonridge to shake off all its landlord obligations at will. Any competent conveyancer would, or should, have warned the sublessees of the risks, clearly and forcefully.

The decision does provide an escape route, particularly for landlords, who can use their bargaining power and superior knowledge of the law to limit their liability when negotiating the term of the lease. Not all of the Law Lords were happy to accept this possibility.

London Diocesan Fund v Phithwa
[2005] 1 WLR 3956, HL

Lord Walker (dissenting)

At 35

I am driven to the conclusion that although the general legislative purpose of the Act was to effect the release from liability of landlords and tenants on their assignment of their interests, subject to and in accordance with the provisions of the Act, section 25 is expressed in terms wide enough to interfere with the freedom of contract which was available to the parties in negotiating a tenancy before the coming into force of the Act. By restricting the parties' freedom of contract, the Act (in a case such as the present) does operate to make it more difficult for a landlord to escape liability on landlord covenants (within the meaning of the Act). I would accept the submission of Mr Wells, for the respondents, that that can be done only by the procedure laid down in section 8 of the Act. To that limited extent the Act does operate, as it seems to me, to shut off what my noble and learned friend, Lord Nicholls of Birkenhead, has described as "any other exit route" previously open to the parties.

3 ASSIGNEES (LA AND TA) AND ESTATE-BASED LIABILITY

3.1 PRE-1996 LAW

The benefit and burden of the landlord's covenants and the tenant's covenants have run with the freehold reversion and the leasehold estate since the sixteenth century. Statute has conferred upon LA the right to sue upon the tenant's covenant given to LO and has imposed upon LA the obligation to observe the landlord's covenant's given by LO in the original lease. The current statutory provisions are now found in ss 141 and 142 of the Law of Property Act 1925 (LPA 1925).[14]

3.1.1 The landlord's covenants

Law of Property Act 1925, s 142(1)

Obligation of lessor's covenants to run with reversion

(1) The obligation under a condition or of a covenant entered into by a lessor with reference to the subject-matter of the lease shall, if and as far as the lessor has power to bind the reversionary estate immediately expectant on the term granted by the lease, be annexed and incident to and shall go with that reversionary estate, or the several parts thereof, notwithstanding severance of that reversionary estate, and may be taken advantage of and enforced by the person in whom the term is from time to time vested by conveyance, devolution in law, or otherwise; and, if and as far as the lessor has power to bind the person from time to time entitled to that reversionary estate, the obligation aforesaid may be taken advantage of and enforced against any person so entitled.

Section 142 relates both to the benefit and to the burden of the landlord's covenants given by LO to TO, by imposing upon LA the obligation to perform these covenants and conferring upon TA the right to enforce these covenants. Thus TO can sue LA and TA can sue LO or LA, as appropriate (see Figure 21.2).

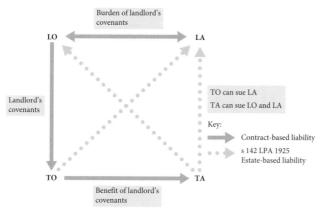

Figure 21.2 Law of Property Act 1925, s 142: benefit (who can sue) and burden (who can be sued) of landlord's covenants

---

[14] They were originally contained in the Grantee of Reversions Act 1540 and amended by the Conveyancing Acts of 1881 and 1911.

3.1.2 The tenant's covenants

Law of Property Act 1925, s 141

Rent and benefit of lessee's covenants to run with the reversion

(1) Rent reserved by a lease, and the benefit of every covenant or provision therein contained, having reference to the subject-matter thereof, and on the lessee's part to be observed or performed, and every condition of re-entry and other condition therein contained, shall be annexed and incident to and shall go with the reversionary estate in the land, or in any part thereof, immediately expectant on the term granted by the lease, notwithstanding severance of that reversionary estate, and without prejudice to any liability affecting a covenantor or his estate.

(2) Any such rent, covenant or provision shall be capable of being recovered, received, enforced, and taken advantage of, by the person from time to time entitled, subject to the term, to the income of the whole or any part, as the case may require, of the land leased.

Section 141 relates to the benefit of the tenant's covenants, and confers upon LA the right to sue for the rent and upon the other covenants given by TO to LO in the original lease. Thus, LA can sue TO (see Figure 21.3).

The missing link in the enforceability matrix is provided, not by statute, but by *Spencer's Case*,[15] which imposes upon TA the obligation to perform the tenant's covenants given by TO, including the covenant to pay rent.[16] Thus, LO and LA can sue TA (see Figure 21.4).

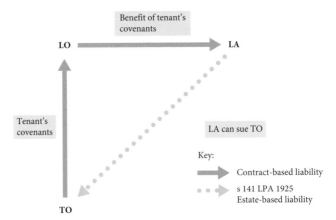

Figure 21.3 Law of Property Act, s 141: benefit of tenant's covenants (who can sue)

---

[15] (1583) 5 Co Rep 16a.
[16] The omission of this link from the statutory framework is a result of 'parliamentary fumbling': see Sparkes, *A New Landlord and Tenant* (2001) p 749–52.

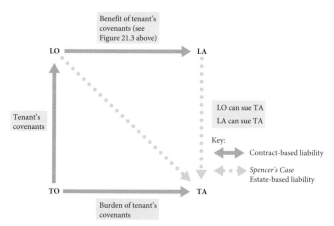

Figure 21.4 *Spencer's Case*: burden of tenant's covenants (who can be sued)

Spencer's Case
(1583) 5 Co Rep 16a

If lessee for years covenants to repair the houses during the term, it shall bind all others as a thing which is appurtenant, and goeth with the land in whose hands soever the term shall come, as well those who come to it by act in law, as by the act of the party, for all is one having regard to the lessor. And if the law should not be such, great prejudice might accrue to him; and reason requires, that they, who shall take benefit of such covenant when the lessor makes it with the lessee, should on the other side be bound by the like covenant when the lessee makes it with the lessor.

3.1.3 Covenants that touch and concern, or have reference to the subject matter of, the lease

Sections 141 and 142 relate to covenants that '*have reference to the subject matter of the lease*', whilst *Spencer's Case* refers to covenants that '*touch and concern the land*'. The expressions have identical meaning,[17] but that meaning has proved somewhat elusive.

Lord Oliver provides the clearest explanation in the following case.[18]

---

[17] See *Caern Motor Services Ltd v Texaco Ltd* [1994] 1 WLR 1249.
[18] And *Coronation Street Industrial Properties Ltd v Ignall Industries Ltd* [1989] 1 WLR 304. These cases concerned a surety's covenant, rather than leasehold covenants, but the test has been subsequently applied to leasehold covenants in *Caern Motor Services Ltd v Texeco Ltd* [1994] 1 WLR 1249 and *Cardwell v Walker* [2003] EWHC 3117.

P&A Swift Investments v Combined English Stores Group plc
[1989] AC 632, HL

Lord Oliver

At 642

In my opinion the question of whether a surety's covenant in a lease touches and concerns the land falls to be determined by the same test as that applicable to the tenant's covenant.

Formulations of definitive tests are always dangerous, but it seems to me that, without claiming to expound an exhaustive guide, the following provides a satisfactory working test for whether, in any given case, a covenant touches and concerns the land: (1) the covenant benefits only the reversioner for time being, and if separated from the reversion ceases to be of benefit to the covenantee; (2) the covenant affects the nature, quality, mode of user or value of the land of the reversioner; (3) the covenant is not expressed to be personal (that is to say neither being given only to a specific reversioner nor in respect of the obligations only of a specific tenant); (4) the fact that a covenant is to pay a sum of money will not prevent it from touching and concerning the land so long as the three foregoing conditions are satisfied and the covenant is connected with something to be done on to or in relation to the land.

There should be no difficulty in the common covenants found in the long leases of flats satisfying this test: covenants for quiet enjoyment; the payment of rent or service charge; for repair and insurance; or relating to the user of the flat or the common areas and facilities.

More difficult questions have tended to arise with commercial leases. Here, the application of test has led to '*arbitrary and inconsistent outcome(s)*'.[19] A surety's covenant runs with the land,[20] but a covenant to repay a deposit does not;[21] an option for a tenant to purchase the reversion does not touch and concern with the land,[22] but an option to renew the lease does;[23] a covenant to sell only the landlord's products is a covenant that touches and concerns the land,[24] but a non-competition covenant by a landlord does not.[25]

3.1.4 Equitable leases and assignments

A further qualification affects the running of the burden of the tenant's covenants to TA under *Spencer's Case*, although not the passing of the benefit and burden under ss 141 and 142 of the LPA 1925. *Spencer's Case* operates where the leaseholder's

---

[19] Gray and Gray, *Elements of Land Law* (5th edn, 2009), [4.5.52].

[20] See *Kumar v Dunning* [1989] QB 193 and *P&A Swift Investments v Combined English Stores Group plc* [1989] AC 632.

[21] *Hua Chiao Commercial Bank Ltd v Chiap Hua Industries Ltd* [1987] AC 99.

[22] *Woodall v Clifton* [1905] 2 Ch 257, [279].

[23] *Phillips v Mobil Oil Co Ltd* [1989] 1 WLR 888, [891], *per* Nicholls LJ, who excuses the anomaly only on established practice.

[24] *Caern Motor Services Ltd v Texeco Ltd* [1994] 1 WLR 1249 and *Cardwell v Walker* [2003] EWHC 3117.

[25] *Thomas v Hayward* (1869) LR 4 Ex 311.

covenants form part of leaseholder's legal estate in the land. Thus it has been held that the burden of the leaseholder's covenants will not pass to TA where the lease[26] or the assignment[27] to TA is equitable. This limitation has been described as '*anomalous and inconvenient*',[28] and various other approaches have been suggested.[29]

Boyer v Warbey
[1953] 1 QB 234, CA

Denning LJ

At 246

[. . .] since the fusion of law and equity [by the Judicature Act 1873], the position is different. The distinction between agreements under hand and agreements under seal has largely been obliterated. There is no valid reason nowadays why the doctrine of covenants running with the land—or with the reversion—should not apply equally to agreements under hand as to covenants under seal; and I think we should so hold.

This view, whilst attractive, rather stretches the effect of the Judicature Act 1871. A more satisfactory route to overcome the problem could be based upon finding a separate contractual nexus, or even legal periodic tenancy, between LO (or LA) and TA, from the fact of TA's possession and payment of rent, and LO (or LA's) acceptance of that rent by way of acknowledgment of TA's position as tenant.

LO or LA are not without redress: they can still exercise a right to forfeit the lease in the event of a breach of covenant (see section 6.4), or, where the covenant is negative, rely upon its enforceability as a restrictive covenant under the doctrine of *Tulk v Moxhay*.[30]

3.2 POST-1995 LEASES

3.2.1 The Landlord and Tenant (Covenants) Act 1995 framework of enforceability

The Landlord and Tenant (Covenants) Act 1995 provides a statutory framework for passing the benefit and burden of the landlord's and the tenant's covenants. TA is entitled to sue upon the landlord's covenants and is bound by the tenant's covenants by s 3(2), and LA becomes entitled to sue upon the tenant's covenants[31] and is bound by the landlord's covenants by s 3(3).

---

[26] *Purchase v Lichfield Brewery Co* [1915] 1 KB 184.   [27] *Cox v Bishop* (1857) 8 De GM & G 815.
[28] Gray and Gray *Elements of Land Law* (5th edn, 2009), [4.5.86].
[29] Smith, 'The Running of Covenants in Equitable Leases and Equitable Assignments of Legal Leases' [1978] CLJ 98.
[30] See Chapter 23, section 2.
[31] Landlord and Tenant (Covenants) Act 1995, s 4, provides that the landlord's right of re-entry will also pass.

Landlord and Tenant (Covenants) Act 1995, s 3

Transmission of benefit and burden of covenants

(1) The benefit and burden of all landlord and tenant covenants of a tenancy—

    (a) shall be annexed and incident to the whole, and to each and every part, of the premises demised by the tenancy and of the reversion in them, and

    (b) shall in accordance with this section pass on an assignment of the whole or any part of those premises or of the reversion in them.

(2) Where the assignment is by the tenant under the tenancy, then as from the assignment the assignee—

    (a) becomes bound by the tenant covenants of the tenancy except to the extent that—

        (i) immediately before the assignment they did not bind the assignor, or

        (ii) they fall to be complied with in relation to any demised premises not comprised in the assignment; and

    (b) becomes entitled to the benefit of the landlord covenants of the tenancy except to the extent that they fall to be complied with in relation to any such premises.

(3) Where the assignment is by the landlord under the tenancy, then as from the assignment the assignee—

    (a) becomes bound by the landlord covenants of the tenancy except to the extent that—

        (i) immediately before the assignment they did not bind the assignor, or

        (ii) they fall to be complied with in relation to any demised premises not comprised in the assignment; and

    (b) becomes entitled to the benefit of the tenant covenants of the tenancy except to the extent that they fall to be complied with in relation to any such premises.

[. . .]

(6) Nothing in this section shall operate—

    (a) in the case of a covenant which (in whatever terms) is expressed to be personal to any person, to make the covenant enforceable by or (as the case may be) against any other person; or

    (b) to make a covenant enforceable against any person if, apart from this section, it would not be enforceable against him by reason of its not having been registered under the Land Registration Act 2002 or the Land Charges Act 1972.

3.2.2 All but personal covenants

The 1995 Act also removes any distinction between legal and equitable leases, and between covenants that touch and concern the land, and those that do not. All that is required is that the covenant is contained (either expressly or impliedly) in a legal or equitable lease and that the covenant is not expressed to be personal to any particular person.[32]

Landlord and Tenant (Covenants) Act 1995, s 2

Covenants to which the Act applies

(1) This Act applies to a landlord covenant or a tenant covenant of a tenancy—

    (a) whether or not the covenant has reference to the subject matter of the tenancy, and

    (b) whether the covenant is express, implied or imposed by law[. . .]

Landlord and Tenant (Covenants) Act 1995, s 28(1)

Interpretation

"landlord covenant", in relation to a tenancy, means a covenant falling to be complied with by the landlord of premises demised by the tenancy;

[. . .]

"tenancy" means any lease or other tenancy and includes—

    (a) a sub-tenancy, and

    (b) an agreement for a tenancy, but does not include a mortgage term;

"tenant covenant", in relation to a tenancy, means a covenant falling to be complied with by the tenant of premises demised by the tenancy.

There is thus a shift in emphasis. There is no need to prove that a covenant touches and concerns the land: all covenants are transmissible, unless the parties specifically agree that they should not be so because they are expressed to be personal.[33]

BHP Petroleum Great Britain Ltd v Chesterfield Properties Ltd
[2002] 2 Ch 195, CA

Facts: Chesterfield had covenanted personally to carry out certain remedial works to premises leased by BHP. It then transferred its reversion to an associated company and served a notice under s 8, seeking a release from its contractual liability on the covenant, to which BHP did not respond. Chesterfield unsuccessfully claimed that it had been re-leased from its covenant when it was called upon to carry out repairs under the covenant.

---

[32] Although not in an unexercised option to grant a lease see *Ridgewood Properties Group Ltd v Valero Energy Ltd* [2013] EWHC 98.

[33] It seems extraordinary that a purely personal obligation can be transmissible because the parties do not expressly identify it as such: see Clarke and Kohler, *Property Law: Commentary and Material* (2005) p 647.

Jonathan Parker LJ

At 59–62

The crux, as we see it, is the definition of "landlord" in section 28(1) as meaning "the person *for the time being* entitled to the reversion expectant on the term of the tenancy". (My emphasis.) We find it impossible to read that definition as meaning only the original landlord [. . .] we consider that those words clearly connote the person who may from time to time be entitled to the reversion on the tenancy. It follows that, transposing that definition into the definition of the expression "landlord covenant", what one has is an obligation "falling to be complied with by [the person who may from time to time be entitled to the reversion on the tenancy]". An obligation which (that is to say, the burden of which) is personal to the original landlord is, by definition, not such an obligation, since it does not fall to be performed by the person who may from time to time be entitled to the reversion on the tenancy.

It follows that in our judgment Chesterfield's obligations in clause 12 of the agreement, being expressed to be personal to Chesterfield, are not "landlord covenants" within the meaning of the 1995 Act, and that the notice was accordingly ineffective to release Chesterfield from such obligations.

With respect to Mr Lewison, Chesterfield's argument on the 1995 Act issue seems to us to be based on the fallacy that there is a direct antithesis between a personal covenant (that is to say a covenant which is personal in the sense that the burden of it is expressed to be personal to the covenantor) on the one hand and a covenant which "touches and concerns", or which relates to, the land on the other. As Mr Barnes correctly submits, there is no such direct antithesis. A covenant which relates to the land may nevertheless be expressed to be personal to one or other or both of the parties to it. That is a matter for the contracting parties.

Nor can we see anything in the 1995 Act to fetter the freedom of contracting parties to place a contractual limit on the transmissibility of the benefit or burden of obligations under a tenancy. On the contrary, that no such fetter was intended by Parliament is clearly demonstrated, in our judgment, by section 3(6)(a) (quoted earlier).

The decision seems, on the face of it, correct, but it could lead to unfortunate consequences. In *BHP*, it was the landlord who was denied a release from contractual liability, but the same reasoning might equally be applied to the tenant's covenants. If a tenant's covenant is expressed to be personal, then TO will be unable to obtain a release from his or her contractual liability, unless he or she can negotiate an express release from his or her current landlord.[34]

Slessinger, 'Precedents Editor's notes' [2007] Conv 198, 199

If the argument stands up, the whole purpose of the 1995 Act is destroyed. The primary mischief at which it was aimed was the continuing liability of tenants despite assignment of the lease.

---

[34] Kenny [2007] Conv 1.

[Slessinger goes onto to suggest that, to avoid this result, the courts might be tempted to conclude] [. . .] that there are certain covenants which are essential to the lease and cannot be made personal. Unfortunately the covenant in the *BHP* case was, essentially, a landlord's repairing covenant, so it would be difficult to distinguish the decision on that basis. In any case, such a distinction runs the risk of reintroducing the concept of covenants which "touch and concern" the lease by the back door when this too was intended to be swept away by the 1995 Act.

A subtler version of the distinction would be for the courts to say that it is not for the parties to define what is a personal covenant merely by sticking a label on it (see, for example, the court's attitude to documents labelled "licences"). To be a personal obligation there must be some reason why this landlord or this tenant is peculiarly in a position to perform it.

The crux of the matter is the extent to which the 1995 Act provides a complete code or merely alters existing concepts of privity of contract and estate, as shaped by the parties' (or their draughtsmen's) expressed intentions.

This tension is also evident in the distinct views expressed by the majority and minority in *London Diocesan Fund v Phithwa*,[35] in respect of which Dixon makes the following observation.

Dixon, 'A Failure of Statutory Purpose or a Failure of Professional Advice?'
[2006] Conv 79

[. . .] a chance was missed, possibly deliberately, to establish the 1995 Act as a self contained scheme free from the dictates of privity of estate and privity of contract. So it seems that, after all, the 1995 Act is another example of piecemeal intervention in the landlord and tenant relationship and an intervention that can be sidestepped—in some circumstances—by careful draughtmanship.

4 THE CONTINUING LIABILITY FOR BREACHES OF COVENANT

An assignee's liability under privity of estate ends when he or she no longer holds the estate upon which enforceability depends.[36] Thus neither LA nor TA is liable for breaches of covenant that occur after they have disposed of their respective estates. They will also not be liable for breaches that occurred before they acquired their respective estates, unless those breaches are of a continuing nature.

This position is reflected by s 23 of the 1995 Act, as well as ss 5 and 6, which we have already considered.

---

[35] [2005] 1 WLR 3956.   [36] *Onslow v Corriw* (1817) 2 Madd 330.

Landlord and Tenant (Covenants) Act 1995, s 23

Effects of becoming subject to liability under, or entitled to benefit of, covenant etc.

(1) Where as a result of an assignment a person becomes, by virtue of this Act, bound by or entitled to the benefit of a covenant, he shall not by virtue of this Act have any liability or rights under the covenant in relation to any time falling before the assignment.

(2) Subsection (1) does not preclude any such rights being expressly assigned to the person in question.

(3) Where as a result of an assignment a person becomes, by virtue of this Act, entitled to a right of re-entry contained in a tenancy, that right shall be exercisable in relation to any breach of a covenant of the tenancy occurring before the assignment as in relation to one occurring thereafter, unless by reason of any waiver or release it was not so exercisable immediately before the assignment.

4.1 CONTINUING RIGHTS TO ENFORCE BREACHES OF COVENANT

Where a breach of covenant occurs before the lease, or freehold reversion, is assigned, the question is who may sue for that breach: is it the assignee (e.g. LA or TA, as appropriate), or does the right to sue remain with the assignor (e.g. LO or TO, as appropriate)? The answer again differs according to whether or not the lease is governed by the Landlord and Tenant (Covenants) Act 1995.

4.1.1 Pre-1996 law

A landlord is not able to sue in respect of a breach that has occurred after he or she has sold his or her reversion, because he or she has suffered no damage, nor can he or she take action in respect of a breach of the tenant's covenants that occurred before the assignment. The benefit of the right to sue passes to the landlord's assignee. This result flows from the interpretation of s 141 in the following case.

Re King
[1963] Ch 459, CA

Facts: Mr King had owned a factory, the lease of which required him to repair and insure, and to lay out any insurance moneys successfully claimed in reinstating, the factory. The factory was destroyed during the Second World War, but, after the war, the land was resumed by the government and a housing estate built. Mr King's estate sought directions as to whether it remained liable for breach of the covenant to repair, insure, and reinstate the factory.

UpJohn LJ

At 487

I turn, then, to a consideration of the meaning of section 141 and construe the language used in its ordinary and natural meaning, which seems to me quite plain and clear. To illustrate this, consider the case of a lease containing a covenant to build a house according to certain detailed specifications before a certain day. Let me suppose that after that certain day the then lessor assigns the benefit of the reversion to an assignee, and at the time of the assignment the lessee has failed to perform the covenant to build. Who can sue the lessee for breach of covenant? It seems to me clear that the assignee alone can sue. Upon the assignment the benefit of every covenant on the lessee's part to be observed and performed is annexed and incident to and goes with the reversionary estate. The benefit of that covenant to build, therefore, passed; as it had been broken, the right to sue also passed as part of the benefit of the covenant and, incidentally, also the right to re-enter, if that has not been waived. I protest against the argument that because a right to sue is itself a chose in action it, therefore, has become severed from, and independent of, the parent covenant; on the contrary it remains part of it. The right to sue on breach is merely one of the bundle of rights that are contained in the concept "benefit of every covenant." [. . .] Suppose the right to sue for breach of that covenant did not pass, and that right remained in the assignor, then the assignee would take the lease without the benefit of that covenant and he could never enforce it. So he has not got the benefit of every covenant contained in the lease and the words of the section are not satisfied. That cannot be right. The obligation to build being (as I have assumed) clearly defined by detailed specifications in the lease, it seems to me quite plain that the assignee could bring an action for specific performance compelling the lessee to perform his covenant to build. That is one of the rights which passed to him when the benefit of that covenant passed. The assignor has by the operation of section 141 assigned his right to the benefit of the covenant and so has lost his remedy against the lessee. Of course, the assignor and assignee can always agree that the benefit of the covenant shall not pass, in which case the assignor can still sue, if necessary, in the name of the assignee.

This view has been followed in *London & County (A&D) Ltd v Wilfred Sportsman Ltd*[37] in respect of the right to recover rent. Accordingly, under s 141 of the 1925 Act, the right to sue for arrears of rent due before the assignment will pass to the landlord's assignee and cannot be recovered by the assignor landlord.

This approach is to be contrasted with the interpretation of s 142, which preserves the rights of the tenant to continue to sue, after he or she has disposed of his or her leasehold term, in respect of a breach that occurred before the assignment.

City and Metropolitan Properties Ltd v Greycroft Ltd
[1987] 1 WLR 1085, HC

Facts: Greycroft was in serious breach of its covenant to repair premises leased by City. After abortive attempts to sell the property, City successfully took action against Greycroft to carry out the much-needed repairs. It was then able to sell its lease, but also sought damages against Greycroft for the damages that it had suffered in its earlier, but abortive, sale attempt.

Mowbray QC

At 1086

The landlord's first defence is that, when the tenant assigned the lease, all its rights passed to the assignee, including any right to damages such as are claimed under the pre-existing

---

[37] [1971] Ch 764 and, in so doing, has disapproved the pre-s 141 decision of *Flight v Bentley* (1835) 7 Sim 149.

specially indorsed writ, so the tenant has no cause of action left to support its claim. In my view that defence is not well founded. No authority was cited on the precise question whether a tenant who has assigned his lease can afterwards recover damages from the landlord for breaches of the landlord's covenants committed while the tenant held the lease. It is common ground, though, that a tenant (not the original lessee) who has assigned his lease again remains liable to the landlord for breaches of covenant which he committed while tenant [. . .] Both this liability and the benefit of the landlord's covenants run with the lease at common law by privity of estate under *Spencer's Case* (1583) 5 Co.Rep. 16 a: see *Smith's Leading Cases*, 13th ed. (1929), vol. 1, p. 51. There is a close analogy between the two. I take the view that, by this analogy, the landlord's liability to the tenant for existing breaches survives the assignment of the lease, in the same way as the tenant's liability to the landlord.

Mr. Moss argued for the landlord here that the tenant's rights against the landlord did not survive the assignment of the lease, because on the assignment section 142(1) of the Law of Property Act 1925 made a statutory transfer of the tenant's rights to the assignee of the lease [. . .]

He pointed out that the Court of Appeal has held section 141(1) to make a statutory transfer of the whole benefit of a tenant's covenant to an assignee of the reversion: *In re King, decd.* [1963] Ch. 459 and *London and County (A. & D.) Ltd. v. Wilfred Sportsman Ltd.* [1971] Ch. 764. He asked me to apply that principle by analogy to an assignment of the lease.

It is not possible to apply those decisions. They turned on words corresponding to the first part of section 142(1), "shall [. . .] be annexed and incident to and shall go with that reversionary estate." The middle passage of section 142(1) is quite different. [. . .] If the intention had been to effect a statutory transfer of the right to an assignee of the term, I should have expected words to have been used similar to those in section 141(1) and the beginning of section 142(1) itself.

4.1.2 Post-1995 law

The divergence evident in *Re King* and *Greycroft* is resolved by s 23 of the 1995 Act in favour of the *Greycroft* solution. The right to sue in respect of a breach committed before an assignment of the lease or the freehold reversion remains with the assignor, although the benefit of the right to sue may be expressly assigned to the purchaser.

5 SUB-LESSEES

Where a tenant grants a lease for a shorter term than he or she enjoys, even if it is only a day shorter, he or she grants a new estate that is called a 'sublease', or 'underlease'. The sub-lessee is bound by covenants in the sublease by way of privity of contract, but he or she is not within the privity of estate of the head lease and thus is not bound by, or able to enforce, the covenants in the head lease on this basis. A sub-lessee cannot, however, ignore the covenants in the head lease.

Firstly, a well-drafted sublease will include a covenant that the sub-lessee must observe and perform the covenants contained in the head lease. The head tenant, as landlord of the sublease, can thus enforce this covenant by way of privity of contract to ensure that the sub-lessee acts in a manner that does not place the head lease in jeopardy. A carefully drafted covenant to this effect may also confer the benefit of the sub-lessee's covenant upon the head landlord, who, although not within privity of contract, may be able to rely upon s 56 of the LPA 1925, or the Contracts (Rights of Third Parties) Act 1999, to enforce the covenant directly against the sub-lessee. An action based upon s 56 failed in *Amsprop Trading Ltd v Harris Distribution Ltd*[38] on the wording of the covenant, which was not expressed (as the section requires) as made with the head landlord. The Contracts (Rights of Third Parties) Act 1999 is less restrictive and could enable a head landlord to rely upon a covenant in the sublease where it is merely made for his or her benefit.[39]

Secondly, if the covenants in the head lease are not observed, the head landlord may forfeit the head lease. A forfeiture of the head lease will trigger the automatic extinction of the sublease, unless the sub-lessee successfully applies for relief from forfeiture. Relief will usually only be granted on condition that the sub-lessee remedies the breach.[40]

Thirdly, the restrictive covenants in the head lease have independent proprietary status and may be enforced in accordance with the principles that we will examine in Chapter 23. The head landlord may thus require the sub-lessee (or, indeed, any occupier of the land) to observe the restrictive covenants in the head lease under the doctrine of *Tulk v Moxhay*.[41] The requirement of land to be benefited by the covenant has traditionally been identified as the landlord's reversionary interest,[42] although Gardner and Mackenzie suggest an alternative rationale and, in so doing, controversially questions the whole exclusion of sub-lessees from privity of estate.

Gardner & Mackenzie, *An Introduction to Land Law* (2015, p 266)

This special application of the restrictive covenant rule involves a radical departure from the rules original thrust [. . .] the rule in its standard form makes obligations operate in rem if, *and because,* they protect the standard of amenity prevailing between neighbouring plots of (necessarily) physical land. By not conforming to that factual pattern, the special application therefore cannot rest on the same justification. It must have a basis of its own, on the lines that the distinction between assignee and sub-tenant [. . .] is unimportant: the protection of the landlord's reversionary interest requires the lease terms be effective against both. Contrary to the assumption made by the idea of privity of estate, that seems a very understandable position, resting on the idea that a tenant, on sub-leasing, should not be able to confer more (in the sense of an interest with fewer obligations to the landlord) then he himself has [. . .] and that idea makes as much sense for positive obligations as it does for negative ones. This lesson can best be absorbed, however, not by extending the standard rule to positive as well as negative covenants [. . .], but by attacking the fundamental problem—privity of estate—itself.

The 1995 Act confirms the operation of *Tulk v Moxhay* to post-1995 leases in s 3(5).

---

[38] [1997] 1 WLR 1025.
[39] See Contracts (Rights of Third Parties) Act 1999, s 1(b), and Chapter 23, section 3.3.3.
[40] See section 6.4.   [41] *Hemingway Securities Ltd v Dunraven Ltd (1996)* 71 P & CR 30.
[42] *Hall v Ewin* (1887) 37 Ch D 74.

Landlord and Tenant (Covenants) Act 1995, s 3(5)

Any landlord or tenant covenant of a tenancy which is restrictive of the user of land shall, as well as being capable of enforcement against an assignee, be capable of being enforced against any other person who is the owner or occupier of any demised premises to which the covenant relates, even though there is no express provision in the tenancy to that effect.

The subsection may be applied to enforce a restrictive covenant contained in the head lease against a sub-lessee but it may not be employed to allow a sub-lessee to enforce a covenant in the head lease against the head landlord.[43]

In a block of flats in which the flat leases are all granted subject to the same covenants, the principles of a building scheme may also be applied to create a letting scheme,[44] with the head lease covenants creating a local law for the development, binding upon and enforceable by all leaseholders within the block.[45] This local law might also encompass sub-lessees.[46]

6 REMEDIES FOR BREACH OF LEASEHOLD COVENANTS

In addition to the usual contractual remedies of common law damages, and the equitable discretionary remedies of specific performance and injunction, the breach of a tenant's covenant may lead to the forfeiture of the lease. Where the breach is a failure to pay rent, the landlord may decide to sue the tenant in debt for the rent as it becomes due for payment. Where the tenant has effectively abandoned the premises the landlord is not obliged to re-possess and re-let the premises to mitigate his or her loss.[47] There is also the possibility of recovering rent by seizing the tenant's goods, previously governed by the law of distress. In this section, we will concentrate on forfeiture, as the most common measure with which to compel performance of the tenant's covenants.

6.1 DAMAGES

Damages are recoverable, in accordance with usually contractual principles, either by a landlord or tenant, for the loss occasioned by a breach of a covenant.

A landlord's recovery of damages for breach by the tenant of a repairing obligation is, however, limited by statute. Firstly, s 18 of the Landlord and Tenant Act 1927 limits the amount recoverable to the loss in value to the landlord's reversion and provides that no damages are recoverable where the premises are demolished or the premises are so altered that the repairs are valueless.

Secondly, the landlord of a lease granted for more than seven years, and which has at least three years left to run, is precluded by the Leasehold Property (Repairs) Act 1938 from seeking

---

[43] *Oceanic Village Ltd v United Attractions Ltd* [2000] Ch 234 ('demised premises' refers to the land under the head lease and not the sublease).

[44] See Chapter 23, section 3.3.

[45] *Williams v Kiley (t/a CK Supermarkets Ltd) (No 1)* [2003] L & TR 20.

[46] See *Brunner v Greenslade* [1971] Ch 993.

[47] The landlord is suing for the rental due and not for contractual damages flowing from the breach of covenant see *Reichman v Beveridge* [2006] EWCA Civ 1659.

damages for breach of a tenant's repairing covenant, unless notice is served under s 146 of the LPA 1925, which is extracted and considered below. This notice must include a statement that the tenant may serve a counter-notice, which will have the effect of prohibiting any further proceedings without leave of the court. This latter provision has caused difficulties where the landlord carries out the repairs and seeks to recover the cost of doing so from the tenant,[48] although where the landlord does so pursuant to a suitably drafted 'self-help' clause in the lease, it has been held that his or her recovery falls outside the Act as an action for a debt.[49]

A tenant suffering damage as a result of a landlord's breach of a repairing covenant cannot simply refuse to pay the rent.[50] He or she may resort to self-help by arranging for the necessary repairs and recovering the cost from the landlord, either by direct action or by offsetting the cost against the rent.[51] This convenient route to redress may, however, be excluded by the clear terms of the lease.[52] We will consider the more far-reaching issues of ensuring effective and efficient management of flats later in Chapter 24.

6.2 SPECIFIC PERFORMANCE

It is now clear that, where damages are an inadequate remedy, there is inherent jurisdiction, and also statutory jurisdiction limited to residential leases, for the court to award specific performance of a landlord's repairing obligations.[53] Specific performance may also be ordered of a tenant's obligations, although this jurisdiction is likely to be only rarely exercised.[54] Forfeiture is likely to remain the more appropriate remedy against a tenant.

6.3 DISTRESS AND TAKING CONTROL OF THE TENANT'S GOODS

The ancient law of distress permits seizure and sale of the tenant's (and other person's) goods that are at the premises in order to pay arrears of rent. Distress has long been in the firing line of reformers given not only its antiquity and resulting complexity, but also the priority that it confers upon a landlord's claims over those of other creditors and its almost certain incompatibility with the Human Rights Act 1998 (HRA 1998). It thus has been abolished and replaced with an alternative process by the Tribunals, Courts and Enforcement Act 2007.

Part 3 of this statute abolishes the previous common law and statutory provisions, and enacts a new statutory code. In particular, distress for rent is abolished[55] and a new remedy termed 'commercial rent arrears recovery' is introduced.[56] As its name suggests, the remedy

---

[48] *SEDAC Investments Ltd v Tanner* [1982] 1 WLR 1342.

[49] See *Jervis v Harris* [1996] 1 ALL ER 303, overruling *Swallow Securities Ltd v Brand* (1981) 45 P & CR 328, noted at [1997] Conv 299.

[50] *Melville v Grapelodge Developments Ltd* (1978) 39 P & CR 179. It should also be noted that recovery may lie for breach of statutory duty under the Defective Premises Act 1972.

[51] *Lee Parker v Izzet* [1971] 1 WLR 1688; *British Anzani (Felixstowe) Ltd v International Marine Management (UK) Ltd* [1980] QB 137.

[52] *HSBC v Kloeckner* [1990] 2 QB 514, but see *Connaught Restaurants Ltd v Indoor Leisure Ltd* [1994] 1 WLR 501.

[53] See *Jeune v Queen's Cross Properties Ltd* [1974] Ch 97, and Landlord and Tenant Act 1985, ss 17 and 32.

[54] See *Rainbow Estates Ltd v Tokenhold Ltd* 1999] Ch 64, noted at [1998] Conv 495 and [1998] JBL 564. The Law Commission has recommended that this jurisdiction be afforded a statutory basis: see Law Commission Report No 238, *Responsibility for State and Condition of Property* (1996), [11.33]–[11.34].

[55] Tribunals, Courts and Enforcement Act 2007, s 71.   [56] See ibid, ss 72–80.

is unavailable to landlords of domestic premises, who entirely lose their right to seize goods to enforce rent arrears; they must rely on their right to sue for recovery of rent or rely upon forfeiture.

6.4 FORFEITURE

6.4.1 Introduction

Forfeiture is the process by which a landlord can extinguish a lease by exercising a right to re-enter the premises. A right of re-entry is invariably expressly granted[57] by the lease and it exists as a separate legal interest of the landlord.[58] An agreement for a lease will, however, imply (as a usual covenant) a right of re-entry, which the landlord can insist is included in the lease itself.[59]

A right of re-entry is generally expressed to be exercisable if the tenant fails to pay the rent, or if the tenant fails to observe or perform any of the other covenants contained in the lease. Occasionally, a right of re-entry may be triggered by some other specified event: for example, the tenant's bankruptcy, in the case of an individual tenant, or entry into one of the corporate insolvency regimes, where the tenant is a company.[60]

A common form of a right of re-entry is set out below.

Encyclopaedia of Forms and Precedents, Landlord and Tenant (Residential Tenancies) Vol 23(2) (2002, Form 9)

Recovery of possession

(1) The Landlord's rights under this clause arise if and whenever during this Term:

    (i) the rent, or any part of it, or any other sum reserved as rent by this lease, lawfully due from the Tenant is unpaid [14 days] after becoming due, whether formally demanded or not, or

    (ii) the Tenant breaches any covenant, condition or other term of this lease.

(2) If and whenever during the Term any of the above events occurs, the Landlord may bring an action to recover possession from the Tenant and re-enter the Property subject:

    (i) in the case of unpaid rent to the Tenant's right to relief on payment of the arrears and costs, and

    (ii) in the case of a breach of any obligation other than to pay rent, to his obligations to serve notice on the Tenant specifying the breach complained of, requiring its remedy if it is capable of remedy, and requiring the Tenant to pay compensation in any case, and to allow the Tenant a reasonable time to remedy a breach that is capable of remedy.

On the making of a court order for possession this tenancy shall cease absolutely, but without prejudice to any rights or remedies that may have accrued to the Landlord against the Tenant, or to the Tenant against the Landlord in respect of any breach of covenant or other term of this lease, including the breach in respect of which the re-entry is made.

---

[57] A right to re-enter for denying the landlord's title is implied.
[58] See Law of Property Act 1925, s 1(1)(e).
[59] *Chester v Buckingham Travel Ltd* [1981] 1 WLR 96.
[60] A right of re-entry on bankruptcy or insolvency is unlikely to be regarded as usual covenant: see ibid.

The law has taken a broad approach to what constitutes a right of re-entry. Thus, for example, a right of the landlord to serve notice to terminate the lease upon a breach by the tenant of his or her obligations under the lease has been interpreted as a right of re-entry.[61]

Forfeiture provides 'an essential management tool, particularly in relation to commercial and long residential leases',[62] but it can also be a heavy-handed response. It is possible for a tenant holding for a long term to lose his or her whole interest because of a comparatively minor breach. What is more, any derivative interest granted out of that lease—for example, a sublease or mortgage—will also be lost. Forfeiture should thus only be employed as a long-stop remedy.

Clarke, 'Property Law' (1992) 45(1) CLP 81, 104

Forfeiture displays the best and worst features of a self help remedy. When exercised extra-judicially it is a fast and effective remedy for breach, and it is sufficiently drastic in effect to deter breaches. In fact it has been so successful in this jurisdiction that it has developed at the expense of the doctrines of repudiatory breach and frustration. On the other hand, its bad features are, first, that it affects the interests of third parties, who may have had no knowledge of the breach and no means of preventing it, and secondly that its effects between the parties bears no relation to the effects of the breach: it can inflict loss on the tenant quite disproportionate to the blameworthiness of the breach, and it can produce a windfall profit for the landlord.

The draconian nature of forfeiture is tempered, firstly, by the law's attitude to the ease with which a landlord is deemed to have waived a right of re-entry (see section 6.4.3), secondly, by the procedural steps that must be followed (see sections 6.4.4 and 6.4.5), and lastly, by the court's jurisdiction to grant relief from forfeiture (see section 6.4.6). In addition, certain short-term residential leases cannot be forfeited and the forfeiture of residential long leases is subject to additional controls, which we will examine when looking more closely at such leases.[63]

In the following case, Lord Templeman explains how the law has tempered the operation of forfeiture.

Billson v Residential Apartments Ltd
[1992] 1 AC 494, HL

Lord Templeman

At 534

By the common law, when a tenant commits a breach of covenant and the lease contains a proviso for forfeiture, the landlord at his option may either waive the breach or determine the lease. In order to exercise his option to determine the lease the landlord must either re-enter the premises in conformity with the proviso or must issue and serve a writ claiming

---

[61] *Richard Clarke & Co Ltd v Widnall* [1976] 1 WLR 845 and Law of Property Act 1925, s 146(7).
[62] Gravells [2006] JBL 830.   [63] See Chapter 20 and Chapter 24, section 2.6.

possession. The bringing of an action to recover possession is equivalent to an entry for the forfeiture [. . .]

Before the intervention of Parliament, if a landlord forfeited by entering into possession or by issuing and serving a writ for possession, equity could relieve the tenant against forfeiture but only in cases under the general principles of equity whereby a party may be relieved from the consequences of fraud, accident or mistake or in cases where the breach of covenant entitling the landlord to forfeit was a breach of the covenant for payment of rent [. . .]

In 1881 Parliament interfered to supplement equity and to enable any tenant to be relieved from forfeiture. The need for such intervention was and is manifest because otherwise a tenant who had paid a large premium for a 999-year lease at a low rent could lose his asset by a breach of covenant which was remediable or which caused the landlord no damage. The forfeiture of any lease, however short, may unjustly enrich the landlord at the expense of the tenant. In creating a power to relieve against forfeiture for breach of covenant Parliament protected the landlord by conferring on the court a wide discretion to grant relief on terms or to refuse relief altogether. In practice this discretion is exercised with the object of ensuring that the landlord is not substantially prejudiced or damaged by the revival of the lease [. . .]

Section 146(1) prevents the landlord from enforcing a right of re-entry or forfeiture by action or otherwise so that the landlord cannot determine the lease by issuing and serving a writ or by re-entering the premises until the tenant has failed within a reasonable time to remedy the breach and make reasonable compensation. Section 146(2) enables the tenant to apply to the court for relief where the landlord "is proceeding, by action or otherwise" to enforce his right of re-entry or forfeiture. If the landlord "is proceeding" to determine the lease by issuing and serving a writ, the tenant may apply for relief after the writ has been served. If the landlord "is proceeding" to determine the lease by re-entering into possession, the tenant may apply for relief after the landlord has re-entered.

After considering the effect of forfeiture more closely, we will go on to examine each of these ways in which the law regulates its operation, before finally looking at the current proposals for reform in the light of the Law Commission's conclusion that the law governing forfeiture *'is complex, it lacks coherence, and it can lead to injustice'.*[64]

6.4.2 The effect of forfeiture

As Lord Templeman explains, where the tenant has breached a leasehold covenant, the landlord has a choice: he or she may either elect to ignore the breach, or he or she may exercise his or her right of re-entry and so trigger forfeiture. The lease will be brought to an end, but the landlord must then recover possession either by peacefully gaining entry to the premises, or by issuing and serving on the tenant proceedings for possession. It is the landlord's decision to re-enter, either peacefully or by court process, which forfeits the lease and not the court's order for possession.[65] From the time of the landlord's re-entry, the tenant is a trespasser and no longer liable to pay rent. Instead, the landlord may claim mesne profits—being damages for the tenant's use of the land—which is calculated according the current rental value of the land.

The Law Commission explains the artificiality of this process.

---

[64] Law Commission Report No 174, *Landlord and Tenant: Privity of Contract and Estate—Executive Summary* (2004).

[65] *Canas Property Co Ltd v KL Television Services Ltd* [1970] 2 QB 433.

Law Commission Report No 303, *Termination of Tenancies for Tenant Default* (2006, [1.9])

When a landlord commences court proceedings with a view to forfeiting the tenancy and recovering possession, a "constructive" re-entry takes place. This means, counter-intuitively, that the tenancy terminates not when the court makes an order to such effect, but on the date the proceedings are served on the tenant. This has several highly artificial consequences. First, the tenancy ends before there has been any opportunity for the parties to make representations to the court. Secondly, the tenant's obligations to pay the rent and observe the covenants are extinguished. Thirdly, the landlord's proceedings are not to terminate the tenancy (as forfeiture has technically already occurred) but are instead to recover possession of the premises. Fourthly, if the former tenant wishes the tenancy to continue, it is incumbent upon the tenant to bring a claim for "relief" in order retrospectively to revive the tenancy that has been forfeited.

We have described the lease as being extinguished by forfeiture, but until the proceedings for possession and, in particular, any claim for relief is decided, that is not quite accurate.[66]

Meadows v Clerical Medical & General Life Assurance Society
[1981] Ch 70, HC

Sir Robert Megarry VC

At 75

There are, of course, curiosities in the status of a forfeited lease which is the subject of an application for relief against forfeiture. Until the application has been decided, it will not be known whether the lease will remain forfeited or whether it will be restored as if it had never been forfeited [. . .] The tenancy has a trance-like existence pendente lite; none can assert with assurance whether it is alive or dead.

Bignall describes the unsatisfactory position of the parties during this 'twilight period'[67] between the service of the landlord's application for possession and the determination of the proceedings.

Bignell, 'Forfeiture: A Long Overdue Reform?' [2007] L&T Rev 140, 142

Such historic hangovers from the early days of forfeiture by physical re-entry mean the status of the occupier is now unclear during this time. Such a period may be a lengthy one. This is disadvantageous for landlords, tenants and those with derivative interests. Until matters are resolved one way or the other, the tenant is no longer bound by the covenants in the

---

[66] See also *Driscoll v Church Commissioners* [1957] Ch 70; *Ivory Gate Ltd v Spetale* (1999) 77 P & CR 141; *Maryland Estate v Joseph* [1991] 1 WLR 83; *Twinsectra Ltd v Hynes* [(1995) 71 P & CR 145.
[67] This expression was used by Lightman J in *GS Fashions Ltd v B&Q plc* [1995] 1 WLR 1088, [1093].

tenancy, including the obligation to pay rent, or to repair. If the tenant remains in possession , the landlord cannot rely on the covenants in the lease so as to make a claim for an interim injunction, or claim damages for dilapidation which have accrued during the "twilight period". There is no good reason for this and the practical consequences may be very serious for the landlord. By contrast, because the tenant has not elected to treat the lease as at an end, the tenant is entitled to seek an injunction to enforce the landlord's covenants, to pursue a claim for a new tenancy [. . .] and to collect rent from a sub-tenant.

Further in the event that the tenant remains in possession whilst court proceedings are conducted, the tenant becomes a trespasser whose continuing use and occupation of the premises simply entitle the landlord to recover mesne profits, or damages, from the date of actual or notional re-entry. Where the rent payable under the tenancy represents the fair market value of the property, the mesne profits will be payable at the same rate. If the fair market rental value is higher or lower than the rent, the mesne profits will be different. The quantification of this claim to damages may lead to another round of litigation, and will compound any financial hardship suffered by a landlord who has receive no income at all from the property whilst the forfeiture proceedings have run their course.

6.4.3 Waiver

Landlords cannot rely on a breach of covenant to forfeit the lease where he or she has waived his or her right of re-entry. A waiver of a right of re-entry will occur where the landlord, with knowledge of the breach of covenant, acts in some way that recognizes the continued existence of the lease.[68] The most common action is the demand or acceptance of the rent payable under the lease.[69]

The effect of waiver has been criticized as operating unfairly to landlords, bearing in mind that a tenant may avoid the harsh consequences of forfeiture by applying for relief.

Smith, *Property Law* (6th edn, 2009, p 408)

Three criticisms may be made of this rule. First, one must feel sympathy for the position of L [the landlord] who can claim neither rent nor mesne profits until the action is heard. Secondly, rent is usually accepted because of some mistake within L's offices: it is not as if a conscious decision has been made to keep the lease alive. Thirdly, and most damning, it does not matter that T [the tenant] is well aware that L has no intention of waiving the forfeiture.

Waiver is less of an issue where the breach is continuing in nature: the landlord can simply rely upon a subsequent breach. An example of a continuing breach is a breach of a covenant to repair,[70] or, as in the following case, a covenant that restricts the user of the premises.

---

[68] *Matthews v Smallwood* [1910] 1 Ch 777; *Central Estates (Belgravia) Ltd v Woolgar (No 2)* [1972] 1 WLR 1048; *Cornillie v Saha* (1996) 72 P & CR 147; *Greenwood Reversions Ltd v World Environment Foundations Ltd* [2008] EWCA Civ 47 [2008] HLR 31.

[69] The acceptance of rent due before the breach will not operate as a waiver.

[70] *Penton v Barnett* [1898] 1 QB 276.

Segal Securities Ltd v Thoseby
[1963] 1 QB 887, HC

Facts: Mrs Thoseby rented a maisonette under a 21-year lease for a rent of £300 a year, which was payable quarterly in advance. The lease contained a covenant that it should be used only as a residence for one household. After the death of her husband, Mrs Thoseby shared her accommodation with two other women, one of whom was a friend and the other, a paying guest. The landlord alleged that she had breached the user covenant and served the required statutory notice at the beginning of June. It demanded the rent that was payable in advance on the next quarter day at the end of June; its demand was expressed to be 'without prejudice' to any breaches. Mrs Thoseby, in the landlord's action for possession, unsuccessfully claimed that the landlord had waived the breach of the user covenant. The breach was continuing and, although the right to re-enter flowing from breaches occurring before the date of service of the notice had been waived, the demand for rent did not waive future breaches.

Sachs J

At 897

When one approaches the law relating to waiver of forfeiture, one comes upon a field—one might say a minefield—in which it is necessary to tread with diffidence and warily. That is to no small degree due to the number of points in that field that are of a highly technical nature, originating in the days before the court was able to give relief, if at all, with such freedom as it can nowadays.

[. . .] In this field of law, one point, however, is plain and was conceded by counsel for the landlord. The law as to the effect of the acceptance of rent "without prejudice" must be taken as that stated in a classic passage in the judgment of Parker J. in *Matthews v. Smallwood* [1910] 1 Ch 777 at 786 [. . .]:

> "It is also, I think, reasonably clear upon the cases that whether the act, coupled with the knowledge, constitutes a waiver is a question which the law decides, and therefore it is not open to a lessor who has knowledge of the breach to say 'I will treat the tenancy as existing, and I will receive the rent, or I will take advantage of my power as landlord to distrain; but I tell you that all I shall do will be without prejudice to my right to re-enter, which I intend to reserve.' That is a position which he is not entitled to take up. If, knowing of the breach, he does distrain, or does receive the rent, then by law he waives the breach, and nothing which he can say by way of protest against the law will avail him anything."

[. . .] It is thus a matter of law that once rent is accepted a waiver results [. . .] Where forfeiture is involved, in essence once the landlord has knowledge of a past breach, the law thus treats the rent as a piece of cake equivalent to the land out of which it derives: its nutritional qualities in the landlord's hands being unaffected by attaching to it the label "without prejudice," the law treats that attachment as having no effect.

Whether a demand for rent made without prejudice similarly operates as a waiver has, apparently, not been specifically decided [. . .] As both demand and acceptance respectively are in law merely different forms of a notification by a landlord of election not to avoid or forfeit the lease, to my mind no distinction can nowadays be drawn between them in relation to a question whether the label "without prejudice" affects their quality as an election [. . .]

One thus has to consider the position on the basis that this is a case where, according to the rule in *Penton v. Barnett*, [1898] 1 QB 276 there were a fresh series of breaches after July 6 of which the landlord is entitled, subject to any waiver, to take advantage without serving a further notice under section 146 of the Law of Property Act, 1925.

With that rule in mind, I now turn to the important and decisive question as to the circumstances in which a demand for or acceptance of rent payable in advance constitutes a waiver of breaches during the period covered by the rent demanded. Clearly it cannot be a waiver of future breaches of which the landlord has no advance knowledge: *Ellis v. Rowbotham* [1900] 1 QB 740 which relates to a default in payment of rent in advance, seems to illustrate this point, despite being an Apportionment Act case. Equally clearly, an acceptance of rent in advance does waive a once and for all—that is to say, a non-continuing—breach in the past: such a waiver applies both to the past and to the period covered by the rent.

As regards continuing breaches, it seems to me that, in the absence of express agreement, the acceptance of rent in advance can at highest only waive those breaches that are at the time of demand known to be continuing, and to waive them for such period as it is definitely known they will continue. When it is a question of estimating the chances as to whether the tenant's breach will continue, the position is, in my view, different, irrespective of whether those chances are high or low. The object of a covenant by which rent has to be paid in advance is to obtain a certain security for that payment: *Ellis v. Rowbotham* points to the nature and effect of that covenant. A landlord cannot, to my mind, lightly be deprived of the benefit of such rights: he cannot be put in the position of having to wait until the end of the period covered by the rent before demanding or accepting it merely because there are chances that the tenant may so break or continue in breach of covenant as to render himself liable to forfeiture.

6.4.4 Notice

The reason for requiring the landlord to give notice of a breach of covenant is explained in the following case.

Horsey Estate Ltd v Steiger

[1899] 2 QB 79, CA

Lord Russell

At 91

The object seems to be to require in the defined cases (1.) that a notice shall precede any proceeding to enforce a forfeiture, (2.) that the notice shall be such as to give the tenant precise information of what is alleged against him and what is demanded from him, and (3.) that a reasonable time shall after notice be allowed the tenant to act before an action is brought. The reason is clear: he ought to have the opportunity of considering whether he can admit the breach alleged; whether it is capable of remedy; whether he ought to offer any, and, if so, what, compensation; and, finally, if the case is one for relief, whether he ought or ought not promptly to apply for such relief. In short, the notice is intended to give to the person whose interest it is sought to forfeit the opportunity of considering his position before an action is brought against him.

When considering a landlord's obligation to warn the tenant of his or her intention to exercise his or her right of re-entry, we must distinguish between a re-entry based upon a tenant's failure to pay the rent and that based on a breach of another leasehold covenant.

Breach for non-payment of rent

Rent must be formally demanded before a right of re-entry can be exercised, unless, as is invariably the case, the right excludes the need for a formal demand.[71] The right of re-entry extracted at section 6.4.1 provides an example in clause (1)(i).

Breach of covenants other than to pay rent

Where a breach of another covenant in the lease is relied upon,[72] the landlord must serve a notice under s 146(1) of the LPA 1925. A notice that fails to comply with the subsection is void and the landlord will have to serve another notice before re-entering.

Law of Property Act 1925, s 146(1)

Restrictions on and relief against forfeiture of leases and underleases

(1) A right of re-entry or forfeiture under any proviso or stipulation in a lease for a breach of any covenant or condition in the lease shall not be enforceable, by action or otherwise, unless and until the lessor serves on the lessee a notice—

    (a) specifying the particular breach complained of; and

    (b) if the breach is capable of remedy, requiring the lessee to remedy the breach; and

    (c) in any case, requiring the lessee to make compensation in money for the breach; and the lessee fails, within a reasonable time thereafter, to remedy the breach, if it is capable of remedy, and to make reasonable compensation in money, to the satisfaction of the lessor, for the breach.

The purpose of the notice, as Lord Russell explains in his point (2) of the above extract, is not only to warn the tenant, but also to let them know what they must do to avoid forfeiture. The nature of the breach must thus be accurately and sufficiently stated.

Akici v LR Butlin Ltd
[2006] 1 WLR 201, CA

Facts: Mr Akici acquired a lease of commercial premises that contained a covenant '*not to charge assign* [. . .] *underlet or part with possession of a part of the demised premises* [. . .] *nor to share possession of the whole or any part of the* [. . .] *premises nor to part with possession of the whole of the* [. . .] *premises*'. Mr Akici operated a takeaway pizza business at the premises, through a company owned by another. Butlin, as landlord, served a

---

[71] Common Law Procedure Act 1852, s 210, also dispenses with the need for a formal demand where the rent is six months in arrears and there are insufficient goods at the premises to distrain for the arrears.

[72] Save for certain cases in which re-entry is based upon the tenant's bankruptcy: see Law of Property Act 1925, s 146(9) and (10).

s 146 notice, alleging '*assignment or alternatively subletting or alternatively parting with possession of the premises without the landlord's consent*'. The Court decided that Mr Akici was sharing (but had not parted with possession of) the premises with the company, although this breach of covenant had not been adequately identified in the s 146 notice.

Neuberger LJ

At 54–8

I accept the submission that the approach of the majority of the House of Lords in *Mannai* [*Investment Co Ltd v Eagle Star Life Assurance Co Ltd* [1997] AC 749] to contractual notices would apply to section [146] notices, despite Mr Butler's submission to the contrary. However, I have none the less come to the conclusion that Mr Lloyd's defence of the notice cannot stand. Even applying the *Mannai* case the notice has to comply with the requirements of section 146(1) of the 1925 Act, and if, as appears pretty plainly to be the case, it does not specify the right breach, then nothing in the *Mannai* case can save it.

Quite apart from this, if, on its true construction, the section 146 notice did not specify sharing possession as a breach complained of, it can be said with considerable force that it neither informed the recipient of the breach complained of, nor indicated to him whether, and if so how, he must remedy any breach. On the basis that there was a sharing of possession, a reasonable recipient of the section 146 notice would have been entitled to take the view that he need do nothing, because the lessors were only complaining about the presence of the company if there was a parting with possession (or assigning or underletting) by Mr Akici to it.

Accordingly, a reasonable recipient in this case (and it is the understanding of such a hypothetical person by reference to which the validity of the notice is to be assessed according to the *Mannai* case) could, to put it at its lowest, reasonably have taken the view that the lessors were not objecting to any sharing of possession, and consequently that no steps need to be taken, either with a view to remedying the breach or with a view to improving the prospects of obtaining relief from forfeiture [. . .]

It is [. . .] appropriate to mention the decision of the House of Lords in *Fox v Jolly* [1916] 1 AC 1, 23 where the last sentence of the speech of Lord Parmoor appears to me to encapsulate the proper approach to section 146 notices and, it may be said, to notices generally:

> "I think that the notice should be construed as a whole in a common-sense way, and that no lessee could have any reasonable doubt as to the particular breaches which are specified."

In this case I think it is impossible to say that no lessee would have been in any doubt but that the lessors were not contending that he was sharing possession of the premises.

It is not necessary for the landlord to specify compensation if he or she is not seeking compensation,[73] but it is the requirements of s 146(1)(b) of the 1925 Act that have proved problematic. Where the breach is capable of remedy, the notice must call for the breach to be remedied. It is only where the breach is incapable of remedy that the landlord's notice can

---

[73] *Rugby School (Governors) v Tannahill* [1935] 1 KB 87.

overlook s 146(1)(b). It is relatively easy for landlords to avoid the difficulty in distinguishing between those breaches that are capable of remedy and those that are not: they merely have to call for the breach to be remedy 'if it is capable of remedy'. Where a landlord has failed to use this convenient wording, it is vital to establish whether a particular breach is capable of remedy. As we will see, the question is also of significance when the court exercises its discretion to grant relief.

It could be argued that no breach can be remedied, in the sense that it is impossible to put the clock back to before the breach, but the courts have taken a wider approach by asking whether or not the harm occasioned by the breach can be remedied.

Savva v Hussein
(1997) 73 P & CR 150, CA

Facts: The lessees holding under a twelve-year lease of commercial premises in London carried out various alterations, including changing the sign and facia to the premises, without obtaining the prior consent of the landlords as they were required to do by the terms of the lease. In holding that the landlord's s 146 notice was invalid, the Court held that the breaches were capable of remedy.

Staughton LJ

At 154

[. . .] [T]he question is: whether the remedy referred to is the process of restoring the situation to what it would have been if the covenant had never been broken, or whether it is sufficient that the mischief resulting from a breach of the covenant can be removed. When something has been done without consent, it is not possible to restore the matter wholly to the situation which it was in before the breach. The moving finger writes and cannot be recalled. That is not to my mind what is meant by a remedy, it is a remedy if the mischief caused by the breach can be removed. In the case of a covenant not to make alterations without consent or not to display signs without consent, if there is a breach of that, the mischief can be removed by removing the signs or restoring the property to the state it was in before the alterations.

The courts have tended to draw a distinction between positive and negative covenants. A positive covenant is generally capable of remedy, whether it relates to a once-and-for-all breach or a continuing breach: for example, a failure to perform a covenant to repair is generally capable of being remedied by carrying out the necessary repairs.

Expert Clothing Service & Sales Ltd v Hillgate House Ltd
[1986] Ch 340, CA

Facts: Hillgate was granted a lease of premises, which it agreed to convert either into office space, or into a gym and health club. The conversion work was to be substantially completed by 28 September 1982—but, by this date, the work had not even started. The landlord served a s 146(1) notice on Hillgate, which claimed that its breach of covenant was incapable for remedy. The Court disagreed.

Slade LJ

At 351

In a case where the breach is "capable of remedy" within the meaning of the section, the principal object of the notice procedure provided for by section 146(1), as I read it, is to afford the lessee two opportunities before the lessor actually proceeds to enforce his right of re-entry, namely (1) the opportunity to remedy the breach within a reasonable time after service of the notice, and (2) the opportunity to apply to the court for relief from forfeiture. In a case where the breach is not "capable of remedy," there is clearly no point in affording the first of these two opportunities; the object of the notice procedure is thus simply to give the lessee the opportunity to apply for relief.

At 354

[After reviewing the authorities, Slade LJ continued] Mr. Neuberger, on behalf of the defendants, did not feel able to go so far as to support the view of MacKinnon J. that the breach of a positive covenant is *always* capable of remedy. He accepted, for example, that the breach of a covenant to insure might be incapable of remedy at a time when the premises had already been burnt down. Another example might be the breach of a positive covenant which in the event would be only capable of being fully performed, if at all, after the expiration of the relevant term.

Nevertheless, I would, for my part, accept Mr. Neuberger's submission that the breach of a positive covenant (whether it be a continuing breach or a once and for all breach) will ordinarily be capable of remedy. As Bristow J. pointed out in the course of argument, the concept of capability of remedy for the purpose of section 146 must surely be directed to the question whether the harm that has been done to the landlord by the relevant breach is for practicable purposes capable of being retrieved. In the ordinary case, the breach of a promise to do something by a certain time can for practical purposes be remedied by the thing being done, even out of time. For these reasons I reject the plaintiffs' argument that the breach of the covenant to reconstruct by 28 September 1982 was not capable of remedy *merely* because it was not a continuing breach [. . .]

In contrast with breaches of negative user covenants, the breach of a positive covenant to do something (such as to decorate or build) can ordinarily, for practical purposes, be remedied by the thing being actually done if a reasonable time for its performance (running from the service of the section 146 notice) is duly allowed by the landlord following such service and the tenant duly does it within such time [. . .]

In my judgment, on the remediability issue, the ultimate question for the court was this: if the section 146 notice had required the lessee to remedy the breach and the lessors had then allowed a reasonable time to elapse to enable the lessee fully to comply with the relevant covenant, would such compliance, coupled with the payment of any appropriate monetary compensation, have effectively remedied the harm which the lessors had suffered or were likely to suffer from the breach? If, but only if, the answer to this question was "No," would the failure of the section 146 notice to require remedy of the breach have been justifiable [. . .] In the present case, [. . .] for the reasons already stated, I think the answer to it must have been "Yes."

By contrast, it has been suggested that breach of a negative covenant is incapable of remedy. For example, MacKinnon J, at first instance in *Rugby School (Governors) v Tannahill*,[74]

---

[74] [1934] 1 KB 695, [701].

raised this possibility, although the Court of Appeal refused to indorse his view.[75] The Court did accept, however, that a covenant against an immoral or illegal user could be incapable of remedy where the breach carries a continuing stigma from which the premises cannot easily be cleansed. In *Tannahill*, the premises had been used for prostitution.[76] In the later case of *Scala House & District Property Co Ltd v Forbes*,[77] the Court of Appeal also decided that a once-and-for-all breach of a negative covenant against subletting, without the prior consent of the landlord, was incapable of remedy.

The Court of Appeal has subsequently backtracked from broad statements that negative covenants are incapable of remedy. In *Expert Clothing*, the decision in *Scala* was doubted and limited to covenants against subletting. This change in approach has gone hand in hand with an appreciation of the wider meaning of remedy explained in *Savva*, in which Aldous LJ also doubted the usefulness of distinguishing between positive and negative covenants.[78]

Neuberger LJ outlined the current approach in his dicta comments in the following case, in which he went so far as he was able, in the light of authority, to explain that all breaches of positive or negative covenants should be capable of remedy unless falling within the authority of *Scala* or the stigma cases.

Akici v LR Butlin Ltd
[2006] 1 WLR 201, CA

Neuberger LJ

At 64–75

In those circumstances it seems to me that the proper approach to the question of whether or not a breach is capable of remedy should be practical rather than technical. In a sense it could be said that any breach of covenant is, strictly speaking, incapable of remedy. Thus, where a lessee has covenanted to paint the exterior of demised premises every five years, his failure to paint during the fifth year is incapable of remedy, because painting in the sixth year is not the same as painting in the fifth year, an argument rejected in *Hoffmann v Fineberg* [1949] Ch 245, 253, cited with approval by this court in *Expert Clothing Service and Sales Ltd v Hillgate House Ltd* [1986] Ch 340, 351c-d. Equally it might be said that where a covenant to use premises only for residential purpose is breached by use as a doctor's consulting room, there is an irremediable breach because even stopping the use will not, as it were, result in the premises having been unused as a doctor's consulting room during the period of breach. Such arguments, as I see it, are unrealistically technical.

In principle I would have thought that the great majority of breaches of covenant should be capable of remedy, in the same way as repairing or most user covenant breaches. Even where stopping, or putting right, the breach may leave the lessors out of pocket for some

---

[75] [1935] 1 KB 87, [90], *per* Greer LJ.

[76] See also *Egerton v Esplanade Hotel, London Ltd* [1947] 2 All ER 88; *Central Estates (Belgravia) Ltd v Woolgar (No 2)* [1972] 1 WLR 1048; *British Petroleum Pension Trust Ltd v Behrendt* (1985) 52 P & CR 117. The court takes a less robust view where the breach against immoral user is indirect because the lessee acts promptly to end the immoral user committed by a sub-lessee see *Glass v Kencakes* [1966] 1 QB 611; *Patel v K&J Restaurants Ltd* [2010] EWCA Civ 1211. Other 'stigma' cases have related to: gambling (*Hoffman v Fineberg* [1949] Ch 245); pornography (*Dunraven Securities Ltd v Hollaway* [1982] 2 EGLR 47); and spying (*Van Haarlam v Kasner* (1992) 64 P & CR 214).

[77] [1974] QB 575.   [78] (1996) 73 P & CR 150, 157.

reason, it does not seem to me that there is any problem in concluding that the breach is remediable. That is because section 146(1) entitles the lessors to "compensation in money [. . .] for the breach" and, indeed, appears to distinguish between remedying the breach and paying such compensation.

On this basis I consider that it would follow, as a matter of both principle and practicality, that breaches of covenants involving parting with or sharing possession should be capable of remedy. One can see an argument, albeit that it strikes me as somewhat technical, for saying that the breach of covenant against assigning or subletting is incapable of remedy, because such a breach involves the creation or transfer of an interest in land, and a surrender or assignment back does not alter the fact that an interest in land has been created or transferred. Were the point free of authority, I would see much force in the contention that such an analysis is over-technical, and I would be attracted to the view that a surrender or assignment back could be a sufficient remedy, at least in most cases, for the purposes of section 146.

So far as the authorities are concerned it appears to me that, at least short of the House of Lords, there are two types of breach of covenant which are as a matter of principle incapable of remedy. The first is a covenant against subletting: that is the effect of the reasoning of this court in the *Scala House case* [1974] QB 575. At least part of the reasoning in the leading judgment of Russell LJ, at p 588, justifying that conclusion is defective, as was explained by O'Connor LJ in the *Expert Clothing case* [1986] Ch 340, 364e-f in a judgment with which Bristow J agreed (at p 365c). However, as O'Connor LJ also said, the *Scala House case* is a decision which is binding on this court. In terms of principle (which may not be a wholly safe touchstone in this field) this is, I think, based on the proposition that one cannot, as it were, uncreate an underlease. It therefore appears to me that it should very probably follow that the general assumption that an unlawful assignment also constitutes an irremediable breach is correct. (This would suggest that breach of a covenant against charging a lease is irremediable, which strikes me as arguably unsatisfactory; failure to comply with a covenant to give notice of a charge, a somewhat different breach, is remediable: see the *Expert Clothing case* at p 355d).

The other type of breach of covenant which is incapable of remedy is a breach involving illegal or immoral use: see *Rugby School (Governors) v Tannahill* [1935] 1 KB 87 and *British Petroleum Pension Trust Ltd v Behrendt* [1985] 2 EGLR 97. This has been justified on the basis of illegal or immoral user fixing the premises with some sort of irremovable "stigma", which results in the breach being incapable of remedy. Especially in the light of the provision for damages in section 146, it is not entirely easy to justify this, particularly as it does not appear to apply where the lessee himself does not know of the illegal or immoral user: see *Glass v Kencakes Ltd* [1966] 1 QB 611. However, in terms of policy there is force in the view that a lessee, who has used premises for an illegal or immoral purpose, should not be able to avoid the risk of forfeiture simply by ceasing that use on being given notice of it, particularly as relief from forfeiture would still be available. Another example, mentioned in the *Expert Clothing case* [1986] Ch 340, 355a, might be a breach of covenant to insure against damage by fire, where the property burns down before insurance can be effected.

In the *Expert Clothing case* itself the Court of Appeal held that a covenant to carry out substantial building works was capable of remedy at the time of the service of the section 146 notice, even though the work should have been completed by the date of service and had not even been started. Slade LJ said, at p 357, that breach of a positive covenant could "ordinarily, for practical purposes, be remedied by the thing being actually done". However, the notion that any breach of a negative covenant will be irremediable plainly cannot be right, as is demonstrable by considering an innocuous and innocent breach of a user covenant.

There are three types of classification of covenants. They are (a) positive and negative (relevant to the transmission of the burden of freehold covenants, equitable in origin),

(b) continuing and "once and for all" (relevant to waiver of forfeiture, with a common law origin), and (c) remediable and irremediable (relevant for section 146, and thus statutory in origin). These three types of classification are thus for different purposes and have different origins. Attempting to equate one class of one type with one class of a different type is therefore likely to be worse than unhelpful.

Any idea that negative covenants are by their nature irremediable has been put to rest by the decision of this court in *Savva v Hussein* (1996) 73 P & CR 150. In that case the breach of covenant consisted of carrying out alterations in breach of a covenant not to do so. After quoting the passage I have just cited from the *Expert Clothing case*, Aldous LJ said, at p 157, that he could "see no reason why similar reasoning should not apply to some negative covenants". He went on to quote with approval of a subsequent passage in Slade LJ's judgment [1986] Ch 340, 358:

> "if the section 146 notice had required the lessee to remedy the breach and the lessors had then allowed a reasonable time to elapse to enable the lessee fully to comply with the relevant covenant, would such compliance, coupled with the payment of any appropriate monetary compensation, have effectively remedied the harm which the lessors had suffered or were likely to suffer from the breach?"

As Aldous LJ, with whom Sir John May agreed, then went on to say 73 P & CR 150, 157: "It is only if the answer to that question is 'no' it can be said that the breach is not capable of being remedied."

In these circumstances it appears to me that, unless there is some binding authority, which either calls into question the conclusion or renders it impermissible, both the plain purpose of section 146(1) and the general principles laid down in two relatively recent decisions in this court, namely the *Expert Clothing* [1986] Ch 340 and *Savva* 73 P & CR 150 cases, point strongly to the conclusion that, at least in the absence of special circumstances, a breach of covenant against parting with possession or sharing possession, falling short of creating or transferring of legal interest, are breaches of covenant which are capable of remedy within the meaning of section 146.

The Supreme Court has been influenced by this change of approach in its views on the 'remediability' of a breach of covenant against committing a nuisance. Although the case concerned an eviction from a mobile home under the Mobile Homes Act 1983, based upon a failure to comply with a notice to remedy the breach, the court placed heavy reliance on s 146 jurisprudence.

Telchadder v Wickland (Holdings) Ltd
[2014] 1 WLR 4004, SC

Lord Carnworth

At 30–2

The breaches of negative covenants in the Rugby School, Savva and Akici cases had a continuing effect. They precipitated a state of affairs. The brothel stayed open until it was closed—and even then the continuing stigma precluded remediability. The sign stayed up until it was taken down; the alterations remained until they were removed. Possession remained shared until the sharing was discontinued. Mr Telchadder entered into negative covenants of analogous effect. He undertook, for example, not to erect a shed on the plot licensed to him. Had he done so, the breach would surely have been remediable by his dismantling it and paying any necessary compensation. But the nature of the covenant which he broke and of his breach of it was of a different order. The covenant was not to act so as to annoy or disturb other occupiers and the breach was to jump out at Miss Puncher while he was dressed in camouflage and thereby to startle her. Nothing could thereafter have been done to "unstartle" Miss Puncher. That is why the word does not exist. The incident had ended. It must have been highly unpleasant for her but there is unsurprisingly no evidence that she suffered other than transient distress. So its effects had ended too. Was that breach remediable and, if so, how?

In my view the answer is to be found by a practical inquiry whether and if so how (to adapt the words of Staughton LJ in the Savva case) the mischief resulting from Mr Telchadder's breach could be redressed. In relation to a breach of a covenant against anti-social behaviour, there is no escape from the conclusion that the inquiry requires a value judgment on the part, first, of the covenantee and, then, of the court in determining whether the requirements of section 146(1) of the 1925 Act, or, as the case may be, of the paragraph 4 term have been satisfied. Had Mr Telchadder not only jumped out at Miss Puncher but, for example, deliberately perpetrated a significant injury on her, Wickland might well have been entitled to conclude that the breach was irremediable; that there was therefore no need for it to serve a notice to remedy; that it should apply directly to the court under the paragraph 4 term; but that, as a prelude to doing so, it should notify Mr Telchadder of its proposed application and of its reasons for having concluded that the breach was irremediable and that therefore there was no need for it to serve a notice to remedy. Obviously there would have been a risk that the circuit judge would either have disagreed with Wickland about the irremediability of the breach or have declined to consider it reasonable for the agreement to be terminated. Nevertheless, by reference only to the simple facts postulated, Wickland might have contemplated that risk with equanimity.

But Mr Telchadder's breach was in no way of that gravity. To an inquiry whether, and if so how, the mischief resulting from it could be redressed, the practical response is to say: yes, of course it can be redressed by his committing no further breach of his covenant against anti-social behaviour for a reasonable time.

Once a valid notice has been served, the tenant must be given a reasonable time to remedy the breach, if it is capable of remedy, or to pay any compensation. A reasonable time will depend primarily on the nature of the breach and the time frame of the dispute, including the remaining residue of the lease.

Slade LJ explained the significance of allowing a reasonable time.

Expert Clothing Service & Sales Ltd v Hillgate House Ltd
[1986] Ch 340 CA

Slade LJ

At 358

An important purpose of the section 146 procedure is to give even tenants who have hitherto lacked the will or the means to comply with their obligations one last chance to summon up that will or find the necessary means before the landlord re-enters. In considering what "reasonable time" to allow the defendants, the plaintiffs, in serving their section 146 notice, would, in my opinion, have been entitled to take into account the fact that the defendants already had enjoyed 15 months in which to fulfil their contractual obligations to reconstruct and to subject the defendants to a correspondingly tight timetable running from the date of service of the notice, though, at the same time, always bearing in mind that the contractual obligation to reconstruct did not even arise until 29 June 1981, and that as at 8 October 1982 the defendants had been in actual breach of it for only some 10 days. However, I think they were not entitled to say, in effect: "We are not going to allow you any time at all to remedy the breach, because you have had so long to do the work already."

If the tenant does respond to the notice and remedies the breach, the landlord cannot forfeit the lease, even though the tenant's record in performing his or her leasehold obligations has been poor.[79]

Where the breach is incapable of remedy, the landlord must allow the tenant a short period before proceeding to forfeiting the lease; fourteen days is usually considered sufficient time for the tenant to prepare to accept his or her fate or plea for relief.[80]

6.4.5 Peaceful re-entry

The prospect of criminal liability under s 6 of the Criminal Law Act 1977, for forcible entry, or under the Protection from Eviction Act 1977, which prohibits the forfeiture of the lease of an occupied dwelling house other than by court order, discourages landlords from trying to enter peacefully, unless the premises are used for commercial purposes and they are empty. Despite these dangers, there was once an incentive for a landlord to try to re-enter peacefully, because it was believed that the tenant was then unable to apply to the court for relief from forfeiture under s 146(2) of the LPA 1925. The House of Lords held this belief to be erroneous in *Billson v Residential Apartments Ltd*,[81] a decision that we shall examine in more detail shortly. The decision also reflects a move away from self-help remedies, which have led to proposals for reform that we will examine below.

Gray and Gray, *Elements of Land Law* (5th edn, 2009, [4.4.25])

There is nowadays a widespread apprehension that, although forfeiture by actual re-entry remains lawful at common law, it is 'undesirable to encourage landlords to self-help'. The gathering perception can only be intensified by the statutory assimilation of the European Convention guarantee of the right to a 'fair and public hearing' [. . .] The clear trend of modern human rights jurisprudence is to castigate the resort to self-help remedies as 'inimical to a society in which the rule of law prevails'. It is highly unlikely that the landlord's remedy of peaceable re-entry without court order can survive much longer as a general feature of the English law of landlord and tenant.

---

[79] Law Commission Report No 302 *Termination of Tenancies for Tenant Default* (2006), [1.12.6].
[80] *Scala House & District Property Co Ltd v Forbes* [1974] QB 575, but see *Horsey Estates Ltd v Steiger* [1899] 2 QB 79.
[81] [1992] 1 AC 494.

6.4.6 Relief from forfeiture

The draconian nature of forfeiture is tempered by the tenant's ability to apply for relief from forfeiture. Relief operates to recharacterize forfeiture from a tool of expropriation of the tenant's term to a security for the tenant's performance of the covenants contained in the lease. The rules governing relief are, however, complicated by the interplay between the courts' original equitable jurisdiction to grant relief and subsequent statutory measures. Furthermore, we again see a distinction drawn between different types of breach: namely, a failure to pay rent and breaches of other covenants. There are also differences in the treatment of the original tenant's right to relief and the rights to relief of holders of derivative interests: for example, under-lessees and sub-lessees; mortgagees and chargees.

Relief for non-payment of rent

Equity has long granted relief from forfeiture for non-payment of rent upon payment of the arrears and any costs, provided that it is equitable to grant relief.[82] This jurisdiction is overlain by various statutory measures. The result is 'an intricate maze'[83] of absolute and discretionary rights that differ according to whether the application is made before or after possession is ordered or the landlord has re-entered (whether peacefully or otherwise), and depend upon whether proceedings are brought in the High or county courts.[84]

In the High Court, relief before trial is available under s 212 of the Common Law Procedure Act 1852, which confers an absolute right to relief, and the continuance of the original lease, where the tenant pays the rent arrears and costs before trial. Under s 210 of the 1852 Act, the tenant may also claim similar relief after the hearing, provided that the claim is made within six months of execution of the order for possession. Relief under the 1852 Act is rather bizarrely only available where the rent is at least six months in arrears and there are no goods on the premises that would satisfy a landlord's claim for distress.[85] It is also unavailable where the landlord has re-entered peacefully.

Where proceedings are brought in the county court, s 138(2) of the County Court Act 1984 confers an absolute right to relief where the tenant pays the arrears and costs at least five days before the hearing. Under s 138(3), the court must allow at least four weeks before an order for possession can be executed. This period may be extended.[86] Where the possession order has been executed or where the landlord has re-entered peacefully, the tenant may apply for relief from forfeiture provided that his or her application is made within six months of the date on which the landlord regained physical possession.[87]

Where statutory relief is unavailable, the court's equitable jurisdiction may assist. The manner in which the court will exercise its discretion under its equitable jurisdiction is explained in the following case. Similar considerations apply where the court is exercising its discretion to grant relief under it statutory jurisdiction.[88]

---

[82] *Howard v Fanshawe* [1895] 2 Ch 581, [588], *per* Stirling J; *Ladup Ltd v William & Glyns Bank plc* [1985] 1 WLR 851, [860], *per* Warner J. This jurisdiction is available for a failure to pay other charges, for example, a service charge, where those charges are expressed to be paid by way of rent: see *Escalus Properties Ltd v Robinson* [1996] QB 231.

[83] Luxton [1994] JBL 37.

[84] The county court has unlimited jurisdiction in forfeiture and relief proceedings.

[85] *Billson v Residential Apartments Ltd* [1992] 1 AC 494, [529], *per* Nicholls LJ.

[86] County Court Act 1984, s 138(4).

[87] Ibid, ss 138(9A) and 139(2). See *United Dominions Trust Ltd v Shellpoint Trustees Ltd* [1993] 4 All ER 310.

[88] *Howard v Fanshawe* [1895] 2 Ch 581 and *Lovelock v Margo* [1963] 2 QB 786.

Gill v Lewis
[1956] 2 QB 1, CA

Jenkins LJ

At 13

As to the conclusion of the whole matter, in my view, save in exceptional circumstances, the function of the court in exercising this equitable jurisdiction is to grant relief when all that is due for rent and cost has been paid up, and (in general) to disregard any other causes of complaint that the landlord may have against the tenant. The question is whether, provided all is paid up, the landlord will not have been fully compensated; and the view taken by the court is that is he gets the whole of his rent and costs, then he has got all he is entitled to so far as rent is concerned, and extraneous matters of breach of covenants, and so forth, are generally speaking irrelevant.

Exceptional circumstances may exist where the landlord has, not unreasonably, altered his or her position, or where a third party's interest would be affected.[89] The poor payment record of the tenant is irrelevant.

Where relief is granted after completion of forfeiture, whether by possession order or the landlord's peaceful re-entry, the lease will be restored and the landlord placed in the same position as if there had been no forfeiture.[90]

Relief from breach of other covenants

A tenant's right to relief, from a right of re-entry based upon a breach of the other covenants contained in the lease, is governed by s 146(2) of the LPA 1925.

Law of Property Act 1925, s 146(2)

Where a lessor is proceeding, by action or otherwise, to enforce such a right of re-entry or forfeiture, the lessee may, in the lessor's action, if any, or in any action brought by himself, apply to the court for relief; and the court may grant or refuse relief, as the court, having regard to the proceedings and conduct of the parties under the foregoing provisions of this section, and to all the other circumstances, thinks fit; and in case of relief may grant it on such terms, if any, as to costs, expenses, damages, compensation, penalty, or otherwise, including the granting of an injunction to restrain any like breach in the future, as the court, in the circumstances of each case, thinks fit.

The right to relief is available where the landlord has entered peacefully,[91] but not where the landlord has entered into possession pursuant to a court order. In the latter case, the tenant must apply for relief during the possession proceedings.

---

[89] See *Gill v Lewis* [1956] 2 QB 1, 9–10, *per* Jenkins LJ, referring to *Stanhope v Haworth* (1886) 3 TLR 34.

[90] *Bland v Ingrams Estates Ltd* [2001] EWCA Civ 1088, [13]–[15].

[91] In *Billson v Residential Apartments (No 2)* [1993] EGCS 155, the court warned that it may be more disposed to grant relief where landlords have entered peacefully without the sanction of a court order for possession.

Billson v Residential Apartments Ltd
[1992] 1 AC 494, HL

Facts: In breach of covenant, Residential Apartments had made substantial alterations to the property without the written permission of Billson as landlord. Billson served notice under s 146(1) and, fourteen days later, at 6 a.m., peaceably re-entered the premises before workmen of Residential Apartments retook possession four hours later. At the centre of the dispute was whether Residential Apartments could apply for relief under s 146(2) of the 1925 Act.

Lord Templeman

At 535

Mr. Reid submitted and referred to authority for the proposition that on the true construction of section 146(2) a tenant cannot apply for relief against forfeiture after the landlord has re-entered without obtaining a court order. Thereafter the landlord is no longer "proceeding" to enforce his rights; he has succeeded in enforcing them. The proposition is in my opinion historically unsound because the effect of issuing and serving a writ is precisely the same as the effect of re-entry; in each case the lease is determined. The landlord is entitled to remain in possession if he has re-entered and he is entitled to possession if he has issued and served a writ because the lease no longer exists. In each case the tenant seeks relief because the lease has been forfeited. The proposition is also inconsistent with the language of section 146(2). The tenant may apply for relief where the landlord is "proceeding, by action or otherwise" to enforce his rights. The tenant may apply for relief where the landlord is "proceeding" by action and also where the landlord is proceeding "otherwise" than by action. This can only mean that the tenant may apply for relief where the landlord is proceeding to forfeit by re-entry after the expiry of a section 146 notice. If re-entry bars relief, the right of the tenant to apply for relief where the landlord is proceeding otherwise than by action is substantially inoperative and the words "or otherwise" in section 146(2) have no application. In my opinion those words must have been included because Parliament intended that a tenant should be able to obtain relief against a landlord whether the landlord has asserted his rights by a writ or by re-entering. It is said that a tenant served with a section 146 notice could during and after the expiration of the notice apply for relief under section 146(2) but if he fails to do so he is at the mercy of the landlord who decides to re-enter and whose rights are therefore, it is said, quite unaffected by the provisions of section 146(2) designed to relieve tenants from the consequences of breach of covenant. In my opinion the ambiguous words "is proceeding" can mean "proceeds" and should not be construed so as to produce the result that a tenant served with a section 146 notice can only ensure that he will be able to apply for relief if he does so before he knows whether or not the landlord intends to proceed at all or whether, if the landlord decides to proceed, he will issue and serve a writ or will attempt to re-enter.

When a tenant receives a section 146 notice he will not know whether the landlord can be persuaded that there is no breach or persuaded to accept in due course that any breach has been remedied and that he has been offered adequate and satisfactory compensation or whether the landlord will seek to determine the lease by issuing and serving a writ or will seek to determine the lease by re-entering the premises. The tenant will not wish to institute proceedings seeking relief from forfeiture if those proceedings will be aggressive and hostile and may be premature and unnecessary. Parliament cannot have intended that if the landlord employs the civilised method of determining the lease by issuing and serving a writ, then the tenant will be entitled to apply for relief, but if the landlord employs the dubious and dangerous method of determining the lease by re-entering the premises, then the tenant will be debarred from applying for relief.

Mr. Reid concedes that re-entry can only avail the landlord if the entry is lawful. Re-entry is unlawful where the premises are occupied by the tenant but not unlawful where the premises are occupied by the tenant's goods. If the argument of the landlords is correct, section 146 provides a method by which a landlord can sneak up on a shop at night, break into the shop, and install new locks so that the tenant loses his lease and can only press his nose against the shop window being unable to obtain the assistance of the court because he has become a trespasser entitled to no rights and to no relief. The farce in the present case when the landlords occupied the premises for four hours should not be allowed to defeat the statutory rights of the tenants.

The right conferred by section 146(2) on a tenant to apply for relief against forfeiture may without violence to the language, be construed as a right to apply "where a lessor *proceeds*, by action or otherwise" to enforce a right of re-entry. So construed, section 146(2) enables the tenant to apply for relief whenever and however the landlord claims that the lease has been determined for breach of covenant. I have no doubt that this was the object and intention and is the effect of section 146.

[His Lordship considered past authorities, which suggested the contrary conclusion, but which he held had not decided the point in issue.]

My Lords, I accept that it is now settled law that a tenant cannot apply for relief after the landlord has recovered judgment for possession and has re-entered in reliance on that judgment. But I do not accept that any court has deprived or is entitled to deprive a tenant of any right to apply for relief if the landlord proceeds to forfeit otherwise than by an action instituted for that purpose [. . .]

The landlords or their advisers, perhaps incensed by the activities of the tenants in the present case, conceived and carried out a dawn raid which fortunately did not result in bloodshed. Since the decision of the Court of Appeal in the instant case there has been a proliferation of section 146 notices followed by pressure on tenants to surrender on terms favourable to the landlord. If this appeal were not allowed, the only safe advice for a tenant would be to issue proceedings for relief against forfeiture as soon as a section 146 notice is received at a time when the tenant cannot know whether relief will be necessary. A tenant ignorant of the development in the law pioneered by the landlords in the present case will be at the mercy of an aggressive landlord. The conclusions which I have reached will not entail these consequences and will not again involve Parliament in correcting judicial constructions of statute by further legislation.

The results of section 146 and the authorities are as follows. A tenant may apply for appropriate declarations and for relief from forfeiture under section 146(2) after the issue of a section 146 notice but he is not prejudiced if he does not do so. A tenant cannot apply for relief after a landlord has forfeited a lease by issuing and serving a writ, has recovered judgment and has entered into possession pursuant to that judgment. If the judgment is set aside or successfully appealed the tenant will be able to apply for relief in the landlord's action but the court in deciding whether to grant relief will take into account any consequences of the original order and repossession and the delay of the tenant. A tenant may apply for relief after a landlord has forfeited by re-entry without first obtaining a court order for that purpose but the court in deciding whether to grant relief will take into account all the circumstances, including delay, on the part of the tenant. Any past judicial observations which might suggest that a tenant is debarred from applying for relief after the landlord has re-entered without first obtaining a court order for that purpose are not to be so construed.

Given this interpretation of s 146(2) of the LPA 1925, it was unnecessary for the House of Lords to consider whether the subsection provided a complete statutory code or whether there was a residual equitable jurisdiction to grant relief to a tenant from a breach of covenant, other than to pay rent. The majority of the Court of Appeal in *Billson* had decided that s 146(2) was a complete statutory code. The question remains significant to the holder of a derivative interest seeking relief under s 146(4), which we will consider below.

The court's jurisdiction to grant relief is wide and unfettered.[92] All of the circumstances of the case are to be considered, but particularly significant are the gravity of the breach, the conduct of the parties, the question of whether or not the breach can be remedied, and the disparity between the loss caused to the landlord by the breach and the loss caused to the tenant should the lease be forfeited.[93] Relief will rarely be granted where the breach is intentional or cannot be remedied, unless the breach is trivial and the damage to the landlord's reversion insignificant or the potential windfall to the landlord is disproportionate to the damage occasioned by the breach.[94]

Relief and derivative interests

We have already noted that the forfeiture of a lease will also extinguish interests that are carved out of that lease: namely, underleases (of the whole of the lease premises), subleases (of part of the leased premises), mortgages, and charges. It is thus important that persons holding such interests are also able to claim relief. There is a confusing array of possibilities.

The primary jurisdiction is found in s 146(4) of the LPA 1925, which provides a right for under-lessees and sub-lessees, mortgagees and legal chargees,[95] to apply for relief against forfeiture based upon a breach of a covenant, both to pay rent and other covenants. Equitable chargees are excluded.[96]

Law of Property Act 1925, s 146(4)

Where a lessor is proceeding by action or otherwise to enforce a right of re-entry or forfeiture under any covenant, proviso, or stipulation in a lease, or for non-payment of rent, the court may, on application by any person claiming as under-lessee any estate or interest in the property comprised in the lease or any part thereof, either in the lessor's action (if any) or in any action brought by such person for that purpose, make an order vesting, for the whole term of the lease or any less term, the property comprised in the lease or any part thereof in any person entitled as under-lessee to any estate or interest in such property upon such conditions as to execution of any deed or other document, payment of rent, costs, expenses,

---

[92] *Rose v Hyman* [1912] AC 623, [631].

[93] See *Ropemaker Properties Ltd v Noonhaven Ltd* [1989] 2 EGLR 50, in which relief was granted, even though the breach was serious, because the financial loss to the tenants would be out of proportion to the loss suffered by the landlords.

[94] See *Central Estates (Belgravia) Ltd v Woolgar (No 2)* [1972] 1 WLR 1048, *Van Haarlam v Kasner* (1992) 64 P & CR 214, *Greenwood Reversions Ltd v World Environment Foundations Ltd* [2008] EWCA Civ 47, *Patel v K&J Restaurants Ltd* [2010] EWCA Civ 1211, *Magnic Ltd v UL-,Hassan* [2015] EWCa Civ 224 and *Freifeld v West Kensington Court Ltd* [2015] EWCA Civ 806.

[95] *Grand Junction Co Ltd v Bates* [1954] 2 QB 160.

[96] *Bland v Ingram's Estates Ltd (No 2)* [2002] Ch 177.

damages, compensation, giving security, or otherwise, as the court in the circumstances of each case may think fit, but in no case shall any such under-lessee be entitled to require a lease to be granted to him for any longer term than he had under his original sub-lease.

A successful application will result in the grant of a new lease held directly from the head landlord. Where relief is grant to a mortgagee, the expectation is that the new lease will be held on the same terms as the original lease. Where relief is grant to an under-lessee or sub-lessee, the new lease cannot exceed the length of the original term and where a sublease is in issue, the new sublease will also be limited to the relevant part of the premises.[97] If there is a difference in rental between the head and under/sublease, the higher rental will prevail.[98] The courts' discretion is exercised in a similar manner to relief granted under s 146(2), with an expectation that the breach will be remedied.[99] The court may also be circumspect in imposing upon the landlord a tenant that he or she has not chosen.

A derivative interest holder may also apply for relief from forfeiture based upon a breach of a covenant other than to pay rent under s 146(2), which we considered above.[100] The right is based upon the definition of 'lessee' found in s 146(5)(b).

Law of Property Act 1925, s 146(5)

(5) For the purposes of this section [. . .]

    (b) "Lessee" includes an original or derivative under-lessee, and the persons deriving title under a lessee; also a grantee under any such grant as aforesaid and the persons deriving title under him;

[. . .]

The difference between relief granted under s 146(2) and the general ground in s 146(4) is that, under s 146(2), the existing lease will continue, whilst under s 146(4), a new lease is granted.

Relief from the breach of a covenant to pay rent is also available to a the holder of a derivative interest under the provisions of the Common Law Procedure Act 1852 and the County Court Act 1984, considered above.

Where the court is persuaded to exercise its jurisdiction to grant relief, the expectation is that the breaches will be made good in respect of the affected premises.[101]

Despite these various statutory routes to relief, there are still gaps. It is thought that the approach adopted in *Billson* will also apply to applications for relief by the holders of derivative interests, whether under s 146(2) or (4). Accordingly, the right will be lost where the landlord has obtained possession pursuant to a court order, although not where the landlord has entered peacefully. This possibility presents a real danger to lenders who, not being in possession, may well be unaware of the head landlord's proceedings. Equitable chargees also fall through the safety net provided by s 146(2) and (4), and the Common Law Procedure Act 1852. Equitable chargees can rely upon the county court jurisdiction, or, alternatively, may insist that the tenant asserts his or her right to relief in order to protect the security.[102]

---

[97] *Cadogan v Dimovic* [1984] 1 WLR 609.   [98] *Ewart v Fryer* [1901] 1 Ch 499.
[99] *Hill v Griffin* [1987] 1 EGLR 81.   [100] *Escalus Properties Ltd v Robinson* [1996] QB 231.
[101] *Chatham Empire Theatres (1955) Ltd v Ultrans Ltd* [1961] 1 WLR 817.
[102] *Bland v Ingrams Estates Ltd* [2001] Ch 767.

These statutory gaps in the relief available to holders of derivative interests might be plugged if resort can be made to the courts' equitable jurisdiction. We have noted that the court has long exercised an equitable jurisdiction that provides relief from a breach of covenant to pay rent. The ability of the court to grant relief from forfeiture based upon breach of another covenant was doubted until the House of Lords decision in *Shiloh Spinners Ltd v Harding*.[103] But the House, whilst holding that such an inherent equitable jurisdiction did exist, indicated that the jurisdiction would not prevail where Parliament has made statutory provision covering the particular case. The question thus turns upon whether s 146 provides a complete statutory code. As we have already noted, the Lords in *Billson* did not provide an answer to this question.[104]

Rexhaven Ltd v Nurse[105] raises one further possibility for the derivative interest holder where the landlord has executed a possession order against the tenant—that is, to apply to have the possession order set aside on the basis that he or she has a good claim to relief, which he or she has been unable to present to the court, for example, because of his or her ignorance of the possession proceedings.

6.4.7 Reform

It should come as no surprise that there have long been calls for reform of the law governing forfeiture. The Law Commission first mooted reform in 1968,[106] although it was not until 1985 that its first report on the question was published.[107] Implementation of these proposals was delayed by other projects and developments—most notably, title registration, the HRA 1998, and changes to the civil procedure rules—but, in 2006, a further report was issued.[108]

The proposals are to replace the existing forfeiture schemes for non-payment of rent and breaches of other covenants with a single scheme for the termination of leases based upon any relevant default by the tenant. This scheme is outlined in the Executive Summary to the report.

Law Commission Report No 303, *Termination of Tenancies for Tenant Default: Executive Summary* (2006, [1.9]–[1.24])

Tenant default

The scheme introduces a new concept of "tenant default" to define the circumstances in which a landlord may seek to terminate the tenancy before the end of its term. In simple terms, tenant default is a breach by the tenant of a covenant or condition of the tenancy. There is no need for a forfeiture clause or right of re-entry to be included in a tenancy

---

[103] [1973] AC 691.

[104] The Court of Appeal in *Billson* had reluctantly concluded that s 146 was a complete code, *per* Lord Browne Wilkinson VC [1991] 3 WLR 264, 279. See also *Official Custodian for Charities v Parway Estates Development Ltd* [1984] 3 WLR 525. There is conflicting first instance authority to the contrary in *Abbey National Building Society v Maybeech* [1985] Ch 190, which was heard at the same time, but without reference to *Parway*.

[105] (1995) 28 HLR 241.   [106] Law Commission Working Paper No 16 (1968).

[107] Law Commission Report No 142, *Forfeiture of Tenancies* (1985).

[108] Law Commission Report No 303, *Termination of Tenancies for Tenant Default* (2006), following the favourable response to its Consultation Paper No 174 (2004).

agreement entered into post implementation, although the tenant should be given an "explanatory statement" explaining what can happen in the event of tenant default.

It is open to the parties to agree that the breach of one or more covenants will not comprise tenant default and so exclude or limit the application of the scheme. It is no longer possible for the landlord to "waive" the breach (either intentionally or inadvertently).

Tenant default notice

The scheme requires the landlord wishing to proceed to warn the tenant of the impending action by giving a written notice. The tenant default notice must set out the details of the breach, any remedial action required and the date by which it should be completed. The scheme limits the period after a tenant default during which a tenant can be served with a tenant default notice.

The tenant default notice must also be served on those who hold qualifying interests deriving out of the tenancy of which the landlord has knowledge (principally mortgagees and sub-tenants).

The primary purpose of the tenant default notice is to ensure that the tenant complies with the obligations under the tenancy. It can also provide a period for negotiation by the parties. For a minimum period of seven days, or until the date for remedy set out in the notice expires, the landlord cannot take any further steps in the process that might culminate in the termination of the tenancy.

Making a termination claim

If the service of a tenant default notice fails in its primary purpose, the landlord may make a termination claim. The claim is served on the tenant and on all qualifying interest holders who have previously been served with a tenant default notice.

The orders available to the court

Once the court is satisfied that the tenant default has occurred, it may make such order that it thinks appropriate and proportionate in all the circumstances. In arriving at this decision the court is required to take into account a number of considerations. These include the conduct of the landlord and the tenant, whether any action can be or has been taken to remedy the default and whether the deadline by which it was to be remedied was reasonable.

A termination order ends the tenancy and any interests deriving out of it on a date specified in the order.

A remedial order will set out what the tenant must do to remedy the default and the date by which it must be remedied. The order does not affect the continued existence of the tenancy. It stays the landlord's claim for a termination order for a period of three months from the day by which the tenant is required to have carried out the work. During that period the landlord can apply to lift the stay and proceed with the termination claim. On lifting the stay, the court may make any order available to it, including a termination order.

An order for sale requires that the tenancy is sold and the proceeds distributed. This may be appropriate where the tenancy has a significant capital value and a termination order would provide a disproportionate windfall to the landlord.

There are two orders that can only be sought by qualifying interest holders. The first is the transfer order. This requires the tenancy to be transferred to the applicant or a third party (for example, a tenants' management company). The second is the new tenancy order which grants the applicant a new tenancy of all or part of the demised premises [. . .]

Summary termination procedure

The scheme provides an alternative procedure under which the landlord can bring a tenancy to an end without applying to the court. It is intended for use in cases where the tenant would have no realistic prospect of resisting a termination order or where premises have been abandoned. The procedure cannot be used concurrently with the court-based procedure; the landlord must elect which route to take.

The procedure cannot be used where (1) someone is lawfully residing in the premises, (2) the unexpired term exceeds 25 years, or (3) the tenancy was granted for a term in excess of seven years and there are three or more years unexpired, and the default is breach of a repairing covenant.

The procedure is commenced by service of a summary termination notice and operates to bring the tenancy and all interests deriving out of it to an end one month after the notice is served. However, the tenant or any qualifying interest holder can resist the summary termination by applying to court to discharge the notice. This application suspends the termination of the tenancy until it has been decided. The landlord must rebut the presumption that the notice should be discharged by showing that, on a termination claim being made, the tenant would have no realistic prospect of persuading the court not to make a termination order and that there is no other reason why the matter should be disposed of by way of a hearing of a termination claim.

For six months after summary termination of a tenancy, the former tenant (or a former qualifying interest holder) can apply to court for a "post-termination order". This may be any order in connection with the tenancy that the court thinks appropriate and proportionate and includes the grant of a new tenancy to the applicant or the payment of compensation. However, the court cannot in any circumstances revive the terminated tenancy.

QUESTIONS

1. Explain what we mean by 'privity of estate'? Why does a sub-lessee fall outside the privity of estate matrix of the head lease and does this matter?

2. Why is the contractual liability of the original parties to a long lease unfair? How does the Landlord and Tenant (Covenants) Act 1995 address the problem? In any event, did this contractual liability present so much of a problem for long leases of flats?

3. Is it easier for the benefit and burden of a tenant's and landlord's covenants to pass in a post-1995 lease than in a pre-1996 lease?

4. The Landlord and Tenants (Covenants) Act 1995 abandons the concepts of a covenant 'touching and concerning', and 'having reference to the subject matter' of the lease. Is it sensible for it to do so?

5. How draconian a remedy is forfeiture?

6. Why does a 'twilight period' occur during the process of forfeiture?

7. Can a negative leasehold covenant be remedied?

8. Is there any role for equity's inherent jurisdiction to provide relief from forfeiture or does the statutory right to relief provided by s 146 of the Law of Property Act 1925 provide a complete code?

For guidance on how to answer these questions visit the online resources at www.oup.com/uk/mcfarlane4e/.

FURTHER READING

Bridge, 'Former Tenants, Future Liabilities and the Privity of Contract Principle' (1996) 55 CLJ 313

Clarke, 'Property Law' (1992) 45(1) CLP 81

Davey, 'Privity of Contract and Leases: Reform at Last' (1996) 59 MLR 78

Gravells, 'Forfeiture of Leases for Breach of Covenant' [2006] JBL 830

Law Commission Report No 174, *Landlord and Tenant Law: Privity of Contract and Estate* (1988)

Law Commission Report No 303, *Termination of Tenancies for Tenant Default* (2006)

Luxton, 'Waiver of Forfeiture: Time to Shake Away the Doctrine of Election' [1991] JBL 34

PART G

NEIGHBOURS AND NEIGHBOURHOODS

22 Easements 885

23 Freehold Covenants 957

24 Flat Ownership: Long Leases and Commonhold 1008

22

EASEMENTS

CENTRAL ISSUES

1. An easement is the proprietary right to enjoy limited use of the land of another, which may exist in both positive and negative form.

2. The defining characteristics of an easement are: (i) there must be a dominant and a servient tenement; (ii) each of the tenements must be in separate occupation; (iii) the easement must accommodate the dominant tenement; and (iv) the easement must be capable of being the subject matter of a grant.

3. Easements may be created by express, implied, or presumed grant.

4. An implied grant of an easement may arise: (i) by necessity; (ii) by common intention; (iii) under the rule in Wheeldon v Burrows;[1] or (iv) by the operation of s 62 of the Law of Property Act 1925.

5. A grant of an easement may be presumed by prescription as a result of long user as of right either at common law, or under the doctrine of lost modern grant or the Prescription Act 1832.

6. The status of easements as overriding interests presents a challenge to a complete register, which has been addressed by the Land Registration Act 2002.

7. An easement may be extinguished by common ownership of the dominant and servient land, by release, by abandonment, or by excessive user (in extreme cases).

1 INTRODUCTION

1.1 WHAT ARE EASEMENTS?

An easement is the right of a landowner to enjoy limited use of the land of another land-owner. There is thus a need for two pieces of land: the ***dominant*** land, to which the right is attached, and the ***servient*** land, over which the right is exercised and which must thus suffer

---

[1] (1879) 12 LR Ch D 31.

the burden of the right. In England and Wales, easements are very common. Land Registry figures reveal that 65 per cent of existing registered freehold titles and 24 per cent of existing registered leasehold titles are subject to an easement.[2]

Easements may be positive or negative in nature. A positive easement will allow the owner of the dominant land to use some facility upon the servient land. The most common positive easement is a right of way to use a path or road on the servient land. A negative easement is a right to receive something from the servient land: for example, a right to receive light or air flowing from the servient land. It is negative in nature because the dominant owner is not entitled to do anything over the servient land.

Easements are proprietary rights that exist for a defined estate.[3] They are thus capable of accruing to the benefit of purchasers of the dominant land and will bind purchasers of the servient land.[4] In this respect, they differ from licences, which, as mere gratuitous or contractual permissions, allow a person to use another's land without committing a trespass, but will only bind the parties personally.[5] We saw, in Chapters 5, 6, and 7 that the boundary between personal and proprietary rights is strictly patrolled and that only rights over the land of another that display certain characteristics are accepted as easements. Those that fail to display these characteristics may operate as licences.

We will confine our attention in this chapter to easements, but easements sit within a range of other limited rights over the land of another. There are a number of public rights that are not dependent on owning land: for example, we all have a right to use the public highways and many will gain access to their properties directly from a public road.[6] The utility companies enjoy 'way-leaves' granted by statute to run the services that they provide over land in order to supply mains gas, electricity, water, and sewage services.[7] Landowners may also claim the benefit of natural rights of support from neighbouring land and, where appropriate, the right to water flowing naturally in a river or stream. Profits à prendre are private rights to take the natural produce from another's land: for example, the right to fish or take game. Profits are very similar to easements, save that they do not have to be connected with the use of any dominant land, but may be held purely for the benefit of a particular individual. In our next chapter, we will be looking at restrictive covenants, which can operate negatively to regulate the user of land for the benefit of adjacent land. As such, they are similar to easements—particularly negative easements.

In this chapter, we will examine the defining characteristics of easements, before looking at how they operate as proprietary interests in terms of their mode of creation, their effect on third parties, and the manner in which they may be extinguished. Before we do so, however, we should note the underlying concerns that have shaped the law governing easements.

---

[2] See Law Commission Consultation Paper No 186, *Easements, Covenants and Profits à Prendre* (2008, Appendix A). This percentage is based upon statistics for the years 2003–4 and 2004–5.

[3] To exist at law, an easement must be held for a freehold or leasehold estate. An easement for life can only exist in equity.

[4] See section 4.   [5] See Chapter 7.

[6] The public also has rights of access to certain commons: see Law of Property Act 1925, s 193; the Countryside and Rights of Way Act 2000 now confers rights of public access to some areas of private land.

[7] For example, under the Water Industry Act 1991, Electricity Act 1989, Gas Act 1986, and Telecommunications Act 1984.

1.2 THE UTILITY BALANCE

Easements have a long history. They were known to medieval lawyers, but their essential characteristics remained rudimentary until the nineteenth century, when easements became increasingly prominent as a result of the agricultural and industrial revolutions that underpin much of our modern way of life.[8] It is no coincidence that it was in 1839 that Gale wrote an influential book on easements, which remains the leading text today.[9]

Gardner and Mackenzie explain the reason why the nineteenth century saw a growth in the importance of easements when, to maximize its economic utility, communally owned land was divided into smaller areas of individual ownership. These imperatives remain relevant today as the intensity of land use continues to grow.

Gardner & MacKenzie, *Introduction to Land Law* (2015, p 315)

The English law of easements thus developed most during the 19th century. During the first three quarters of that century, English agricultural land was being divided into sealed packets, in a process known as 'enclosure'. Previously, the land had been operated much more communally. Enclosure was born of a realisation that the old communal approach impeded the land's maximum exploitation. But easements were developed out of a realisation, in turn, that even greater exploitation was possible if one could have it both ways. At about the same period, too, intensive building was taking place, centred on the mills, factories and so on which were perceived as the most effective tools by which to exploit downstream resources. Maximum intensity was achieved by introducing easements to allow the collaborative use of neighbouring plots of land.

Care is needed, however. Cross-exploitation does harm as well as good for it erodes the benefits to be had from dividing land into sealed packets. The less *my* land becomes simply 'mine' because there are obligations such as easements affecting its use, the further I shall be from having the maximum opportunity and incentive to exploit it, by growing crops myself, or building houses, or whatever. So the establishment of easements needs to be restricted to the situations in which sealed packets does more good than harm. The law does this by rules that limit the forms of benefit that can be associated with easements, favouring those that are traditional, ordinary, agricultural, and as a matter of business rather than recreation, and its rule limiting easements to rights that do not deprive me of 'any reasonable use' of my land.

As Gardner and Mackenzie highlight, there is a need to balance the benefit of exploiting the dominant land against the burden placed upon the servient land. This balance is central in determining what characteristics a right must satisfy to qualify as an easement.

A further balance that must be struck is between the desirability of implying an easement to promote utility and the conveyancing problems that arise where such rights are difficult to trace. This question was in the minds of the architects of the Land Registration Act 2002 (LRA 2002) and we will consider their solution later in the chapter.[10]

---

[8] See Holdsworth, *Historical Introduction to the Land Law* (1927) p 265.
[9] Now in its 20th edition: see *Gale on Easements* (eds Gaunt and Morgan, 2016).
[10] See section 4.

2 THE *CONTENT* QUESTION

The leading case of *Re Ellenborough Park* summarizes the essential characteristics of an easement.

Re Ellenborough Park
[1956] Ch 131, CA

Facts: Ellenborough Park is a development of houses surrounding a park. Each house was sold together with the right to full enjoyment of the park. During the Second World War, the park was requisitioned and a dispute arose as to who was entitled to the resulting compensation. It was held that the house owners' right to use the park was an easement, because it satisfied the legal characteristics of an easement, and so they were entitled to share the compensation.

Evershed MR

At 163

For the purposes of the argument before us Mr Cross and Mr Goff were content to adopt, as correct, the four characteristics formulated in *Dr Cheshire's Modern Real Property* 7th ed pp456 et seq. They are (1) there must be a dominant tenement and a servient tenement: (2) an easement must "accommodate" the dominant tenement: (3) dominant and servient owners must be different persons, and (4) a right over land cannot amount to an easement, unless it is capable of forming the subject matter of a grant.

We will use these four characteristics as our guide to explore the characteristics of easements, although we will look at them in a slightly different order.

2.1 'THERE MUST BE A DOMINANT TENEMENT AND A SERVIENT TENEMENT'

There must be two pieces of land: the servient tenement, over which the right is exercised, and the dominant tenement, which benefits from the right.

2.1.1 Should we have easements in gross?

In some jurisdictions, it is possible for there to be only a servient tenement, over which the right is exercised by a person who is not required to be the owner of any land. The easement is then said to exist *in gross*. English law accepts the possibility that profits may exist in gross and statutory way-leaves confer what are, in effect, easements in gross. For example, service suppliers, such as the gas, electricity, water, and telephone infrastructure companies, enjoy way-leaves to run their pipes and wires over and under land to maintain the national supply of these services.

Sturley has argued that easements in gross should also be permitted in English law.[11] He believes that the requirement for a dominant tenement is '*without authority or*

---

[11] See also McClean, 'The Nature of an Easement' (1996) 5 West LR 32, 36–42.

justification',[12] and that the arguments against easements in gross, in terms of imposing a potentially excessive or unjustified burden on the servient tenement, can be overcome.

Sturley, 'Easements in Gross' (1980) 96 LQR 557

At 562

Though no justification is given against the rule against easements in gross in the cases which establish it, it may nevertheless be possible to justify it after the fact. Two possibilities, both of which are suggested by nineteenth century cases, should be considered. The first, which may be labelled the "surcharge argument," holds that an easement in gross, not being limited to the needs of the dominant tenement is likely to burden the servient tenement with excessive use. The second and somewhat more convincing, which may be labelled the "clogs on title argument," holds that an easement in gross is likely to be an unjustified incumbrance on the title of the servient tenement [. . .]

At 563

Certainly surcharge concerns are genuine, but they should not be overemphasised. Though not limited by reference to the dominant tenement, an easement in gross would still be limited by the terms of its grant [. . .] Possibilities of surcharge have long existed, both in profits and easements, but there have not been problems sufficient to justify the total prohibition of the interests. It seems the same should be true of easements in gross [. . .]

The clogs on title argument may be seen as an underlying rationale of *Keppel v Bailey* and *Hill v Tupper* where it was decided that novel rights cannot be annexed to land. The concern in both cases, however, is the type of right held rather than the means of holding it, and thus they properly relate to Cheshire's fourth characteristic of an easement, the subject matter of a grant. With respect to easements in gross the argument suggests not that anything is wrong with the right, per se, but that the owner in gross may be difficult to discover, thus making any right an unjustified clog on title when held in gross [. . .]

At 566

A solution, it seems, is to be found in the Land Charges Act [1972 or Land Registration Act 2002] scheme. If an easement in gross has to be registered, it is not very different from an appurtenant easement from the point of view of the clogs on title argument.

The Law Commission has considered whether, as a matter of policy, easements in gross should be permitted, but, whilst acknowledging the arguments made by Sturley, its view is that the requirement for a dominant tenement should not be relaxed.[13] To do so would also require a rethink of the fundamental need for an easement to accommodate the dominant tenement.[14]

---

[12] Sturley, 'Easements in Gross' (1980) 96 LQR 557, 568.
[13] Law Commission Consultation Paper No 186 (2008), [3.16].
[14] See also Lawson, 'Easements' in *Land Law: Issues, Debates, Policy* (ed Tee, 2002) p 71.

2.1.2 The need to identify the dominant tenement

The extent of the dominant land must be clearly established at the time that the easement is granted.

London & Blenheim Estates Ltd v Ladbroke Retail Parks Ltd
[1994] 1 WLR 31, CA

Facts: Leicestershire Co-op sold part of its land (the dominant land) to London & Blenheim, together with the right to park cars on land retained by the Co-op (the servient land). The agreement also included a provision that, in the event of London & Blenheim acquiring additional land, it should be entitled to give notice to the Co-op for that additional land (the alleged additional dominant land) to acquire similar parking rights. Before any notice was given, the servient land came into the ownership of Ladbrooke. London & Blenheim failed in its claim to a right to park for the benefit of the additional land that it had acquired, because, at the time that the servient land was sold by the Co-op, the alleged dominant land was not adequately identified.

Peter Gibson LJ

At 37

If one asks why the law should require that there should be a dominant tenement before there can be a grant, or a contract for the grant, of an easement sufficient to create an interest in land binding successors in title to the servient land, the answer would appear to lie in the policy against encumbering land with burdens of a uncertain extent. As was said by Fox LJ in *Ashburn Ansalt v Arnold* [1989] 1 Ch 26, "In matters relating to the title to land, certainty is of prime importance." A further related answer lies in the reluctance of the law to recognise new forms of burden on property conferring more than contractual rights. Thus in *Ackroyd v Smith* (1850) 10 CB 164, 188 Cresswell J., giving judgment of the judges of Common Pleas, after referring to the impossibility of a grant of a right of way in gross said "nor can the owner of the land render it subject to a new species of burden, so as to bind it in the hands of an assignee." "Incidents of a novel kind cannot be devised, and attached to property, at the fancy and caprice of any owner:" per Lord Brougham LC in *Keppel v Bailey* (1834) 2 Myl & K 517. A right intended as an easement and attached to a servient tenement before the dominant tenement is identified would in my view be an incident of a novel kind.

2.1.3 The rule in *Harris v Flower*[15]

A dominant owner, who acquires additional land adjacent to or close by the dominant land, may wish to use the easement that he or she enjoys for the benefit of that additional land. In general, he or she will be unable to do so without committing a trespass to the servient land. This prohibition is known as the 'rule in *Harris v Flower*', outlined by Romer LJ in the case of the same name as: '[I]f a right of way be granted for the enjoyment of Close A, the grantee because he owns or acquires Close B cannot use the way in substance for passing over the Close A to Close B [. . .]'[16]

---

[15] (1904) 74 LJ Ch 127.   [16] Ibid, 127.

Harris v Flower envisages the additional land being adjacent to the dominant land, so it is necessary to pass from the servient land to access the dominant land and then over the dominant land to access the additional land. Whilst it is perfectly acceptable for the dominant owner to use the right of way to access the dominant land, his or her use of the right of way will become unacceptable if he or she uses it to gain access to the additional land.

An alternative situation may arise where the additional land does not lie beyond the dominant land, but to the side, or close by: there is then no need for the dominant owner to pass over the dominant land to gain access to the additional land. This is what happened in *Das v Linden Mews*,[17] in which mews houses in London enjoyed a right of way along a privately owned street. Two of the owners acquired ground at the end of the street on which to park their cars. The owners of the street (the servient land) successful argued that the rule in *Harris v Flower* prohibited the house owners from exercising the right of way attached to their house to drive along the street to the land that they had acquired for parking. In *Gore v Naheed*,[18] however, the Court of Appeal drew no distinction between the approach to be adopted in the passing through and passing alongside scenarios.

The rationale for the rule lies in keeping within the terms of the easement, rather than excessive use of the servient land. The question is whether the dominant owner can establish that use of the right in respect of additional land is within the terms of the grant because it is merely ancillary to the use of the dominant land.

Peacock v Custins
[2002] 1 WLR 1815, CA

Facts: Peacock owned a field ('the red land', i.e. the dominant land), which was accessed by a right of way over land owned by Custins ('the yellow strip', i.e. the servient land). Peacock also owned another field adjacent to the dominant land ('the blue land'), but he failed to prove that he could use his right of way over the servient land once or twice a year to access the additional field.

Schiebsmann LJ

At 22

The law is clear at the extremes. To use the track for the sole purpose of accessing the blue land is outside the scope of the grant. However in some circumstances a person who uses the way to access the dominant land but then goes off the dominant land, for instance to picnic on the neighbouring land, is not going outside the scope of the grant.

At 25

Considering the position as a matter of principle, we would consider that the defendants are entitled to the declaration that they seek. In our judgment the authorities to which we have referred, and in particular *Harris v Flower* (1904) 74 LJ Ch 127, also confirm that, where a court is being asked to declare whether the right to use a way comprises a right to use it to facilitate the cultivation of land other than the dominant tenement, the court is not concerned with any comparison between the amount of use made or to be made of the servient

---

[17] [2002] EWCA Civ 590, [2003] 2 P & CR 4.   [18] [2017] EWCA Civ 639.

tenement and the amount of use made or that might lawfully be made within the scope of the grant. It is concerned with declaring the scope of the grant, having regard to its purposes and the identity of the dominant tenement. The authorities indicate that the burden on the owner of the servient tenement is not to be increased without his consent. But burden in this context does not refer to the number of journeys or the weight of the vehicles. Any use of the way is, in contemplation of law, a burden and one must ask whether the grantor agreed to the grantee making use of the way for that purpose [. . .]

At 27

It is in our judgment clear that the grantor did not authorise the use of the way for the purpose of cultivating the blue land. This cannot sensibly be described as ancillary to the cultivation of the red land. We therefore allow the appeal and declare that the claimants are not entitled to use the yellow strip for the purpose of obtaining access to the blue land in order to cultivate it.

It has to be remembered that the dominant owner is perfectly entitled to use the right in connection with his or her enjoyment of the dominant land, and it may be that he or she goes onto, or makes some use of, the additional land, which is merely ancillary to his or her use of the dominant land.

Whilst the cultivation of the 'blue land', or the use of the car park, was held not to be ancillary to the use of the dominant land in either *Peacock v Custins* or *Das v Linden Mews*, in *Massey v Boulden*,[19] the use of the additional land was considered ancillary.[20] The Masseys claimed a prescriptive easement over a village green to gain access to their house. Their house had been extended by the addition of two rooms from an adjoining property. They had used the access to their original house for the required prescription period, but they had acquired the additional rooms just short of that period. It was nevertheless held that their use of the two additional rooms was ancillary to their use of their original house and thus fell within the prescriptive easement.

The scope of the ancillary use exception is not easy to identify. The possible principles underlying ancillary use were explored in the following case, in which the court sought to reconcile the authorities by identifying that a use will be ancillary where the use is not 'in substance' for the benefit of non-dominant land, either because there is no benefit to the non-dominant land, or because any benefit is insubstantial.

Macepark (Whittlebury) Ltd v Sargeant (No 2)
[2003] 1 WLR 2284, HC

Facts: A hotel close to Silverstone race circuit was leased with the benefit of a right of way across adjoining land. A wood lay between the hotel and Silverstone. With the agreement of the owners of the wood, Macepark planned a short cut through the wood as a direct link to Silverstone. The hotel unsuccessfully claimed that the right of way could be used by hotel guests to drive from the hotel, and along the short cut through the wood, to Silverstone. The use of the right of way would not merely benefit the hotel as the dominant land, but would also substantially benefit the owners of the wood and

---

19 [2003] 1 WLR 1792.
20 See also *National Trust v White* [1987] 1 WLR 907 and *Gore v Naheed* [2017] EWCA Civ 639.

Silverstone (the non-dominant land). The owners of the wood could charge for the short cut over their land and Silverstone would benefit from an additional access route.

Gabriel Moss QC (sitting as a High Court judge)

At 35–8

The principle underlying the "ancillary" exception is not spelt out.

There seem to be at least two possibilities. One is that a use of the right of way to go on to non-dominant land can be ancillary where it is *insubstantial*, as in the case of going on to non-dominant land for a picnic, but cannot be ancillary if it is *substantial*, as where the access is used for going on to non-dominant land in order to cultivate another field or to store on the dominant land timber grown and felled on non-dominant land.

A second approach, which would often coincide with the first, would be that a use can be ancillary if it does not *benefit* the non-dominant land, ie does not *in effect extend the dominant land*. The picnic for example concerned a situation where the use of the right of access involved going on to non-dominant land but not benefiting it [. . .] By contrast, non-dominant land is benefited if the access is used to enable it or to facilitate it to be cultivated or logged.

A third approach would be to say that a use was ancillary if it were *either* insubstantial *or* not a benefit [. . .]

At 47–52

In accepting and applying the "ancillary" doctrine I must assume that the Court of Appeal in *Massey v Boulden* [2003] 1 WLR 1792 chose to follow the approach in *Peacock v Custins* [2002] 1 WLR 1815 rather than *Das v Linden Mews Ltd* [2002] 2 EGLR 76, since both cases are referred to in the judgment of Simon Brown LJ [2003] 1 WLR 1792, 1803, para 37. I must accept, therefore, that there is an "ancillary" doctrine.

The apparent clash with *Harris v Flower* (1904) 74 LJ Ch 127 is more difficult to resolve. The facts seem essentially similar. Moreover, there seems no doubt that in *Massey v Boulden* the access was used for the benefit of the non-dominant land as well as the dominant land. The only way, therefore, in which the Court of Appeal could have regarded the use of the access to benefit the non-dominant land as "ancillary" is if they regarded it as insubstantial: compare the use of the phrase "in substance" by Romer LJ in *Harris v Flower* at 132 and Morritt LJ in *Jobson v Record* [1998] 1 EGLR 113 at 114. The additional rooms which extended the dominant land appear to have been regarded as mere appendages to the dominant land, so that the use of the access could be seen as being *in substance* for the benefit of the dominant land and not in substance for the benefit of the non-dominant land.

If I have reconciled the apparently conflicting authorities on the question of ancillary use successfully, the result seems to be as follows. (1) There is a doctrine of "ancillary use". (2) It applies where the use of the access for the benefit of the non-dominant land in addition to the benefit of the dominant land is insubstantial, e g where it is used to reach rooms which are mere appendages to the dominant property. (3) It also applies where the use of the access to reach the dominant land and then go on to non-dominant land does not benefit the non-dominant land, e g where there is a picnic on the non-dominant land. (4) With regard to the question of what "benefits" the non-dominant land, where the access makes the use of the non-dominant land profitable, that access is being used to benefit the non-dominant land. For example, where the access, by an arrangement between the owner of the dominant land and the owner of the non-dominant land, is used to enable a profit to be made out of the use of the non-dominant land, there is a benefit to the non-dominant land.

Summary of the law

On the basis that I have accurately understood the current standing of the "ancillary" doctrine, the following propositions now seem to be correct. (1) An easement must be used for the benefit of the dominant land. (2) It must not "in substance" be used for the benefit of non-dominant land. (3) Under the "ancillary" doctrine, use is not "in substance" use for the benefit of the non-dominant land if (a) there is no benefit to the non-dominant land or if (b) the extent of the use for the benefit of the non-dominant land is insubstantial, ie it can still be said that in substance the access is used for the benefit of the dominant land and not for the benefit of both the dominant land and the non-dominant land. (d) "Benefit" in this context includes use of an access in such a way that a profit may be made out of the use of the non-dominant land, eg as a result of an arrangement with the owner of the dominant land.

The application of these principles can involve potentially difficult questions of fact and degree.

One significant factor, identified by the Court of Appeal in *Peacock v Custins* at para 24, is whether the benefit to the non-dominant land is likely to have its own "commercial value". It also seems from *Peacock v Custins* that it is not necessary to prove that separate value if it can be regarded as "self-evident".

The rule in *Harris v Flower* has been the subject of criticism.

Paton and Seabourne, 'Can't Get There From Here? Permissible Use of Easements After *Das*' [2003] Conv 127, 132

If the rule is to be justified purely on grounds of doctrinal "neatness", then it must be recognised that its application, and the concept of "bona fide" or "colourable" use of a right of way for a particular purpose, produces some odd doctrinal consequences. It introduces something like "guilt by intention" to the law of trespass in this area. Conduct which externally is wholly consistent with the lawful exercise of right of way to land A—for example, the tractors driving along the way in *Peacock v Custins*—is made unlawful by the presence of an *intention* to carry on through A to B, land in which the servient owner has no legal or practical interest.

Yet in such cases where the right of way serving A is the only means of access to A and B, the courts have noticeably stopped short of the logical conclusion that land B is thereby landlocked and effectively sterilised. In *Peacock v Custins*, Schiemann L.J. suggested that the owner of land A could still go from A to B, perhaps for a picnic. What he could presumably not do was use the right of way serving A with that ultimate purpose (going to B) in mind. In other words, excursions from A to B, for picnics or otherwise, must be spontaneous, the idea originating once the owner is safely ensconced in A, having used the way to get there first. If, however, the servient owner one day spies the owner driving along the way with his car packed full of hampers, then sees him picnicking on B later that day, a trespass will have been committed [. . .]

The implication of this [. . .] is not a logically inevitable analysis. If lands A and B are contiguous and in common ownership, one of the most elementary incidents of such ownership must be the owner's right to *move freely between the two*. He needs no externally granted "right" to do this. There is no reason why use of the right of way to go to B via A can not be seen as a two stage process: use of the right of way to get to A, followed by access from A to B along the owner's own land as an incident of his ownership of both.

[. . .] In cases other than "passing through" ones, the above argument is not possible, but nor is it necessary. If the *only* threatened use of additional land B is by the owner/occupier of the land A which has the benefit of the right, such use of B is either ancillary or necessarily connected to the use of A, and the use of B generates no risk of increased user of the way, it is difficult to see any justification for a further, prohibitive rule.

As Paton and Seabourne identify, the intention with which the dominant owner uses the access cannot be ignored. If the dominant owner intends to access the additional land, what might appear objectively lawful becomes unlawful. The Court of Appeal in *Giles v Tarry*[21] acknowledged that the intention with which the access is used is crucial when they held that a farmer had fallen foul of the rule where he used a right of way granted for the benefit of one field with the intention of driving his sheep through that field to graze in another pasture.

Paton and Seabourne instead advocate that the determining principle should be based upon the concept of excessive user of the servient land.[22]

Paton and Seabourne, 'Can't Get There From Here? Permissible Use of Easements After *Das*' [2003] Conv 127, 134

A Modified Rule: Excessive User

[. . .] As a controlling principle, excessive user is clearly related to the law of nuisance, in which the courts are more accustomed to balancing the competing activities, rights and convenience of neighbours, and giving some degree of latitude to worthwhile or productive uses of land. A court considering a claim of excessive user can have regard to the likely duration and nature of the proposed user, and the likelihood and severity of any actual or threatened damage, and can impose temporary or permanent conditions/restrictions on any relief granted.

The "rule in *Harris v Flower*", by contrast, originates in the strict construction of deeds and the conceptualisation of the law of easements around identifiable dominant and servient tenements. Ultimately, it is unnecessary. It can be qualified without collapsing the principle of appurtenance to an identified dominant tenement into "easements in gross". So long as the proposed additional activity bears *some* connection to the original dominant tenement, and does not generate excessive user or damage, the servient owner is protected. No further policy is served, or interest protected, by maintaining the strict rule for the sake of doctrinal purity.

2.1.4 Appurtenant to the dominant land or the dominant estate?

We have already noted that an easement may be granted for a freehold or leasehold term which will be co-extensive with the freeholder's or leaseholder's estate in the land. Orthodoxy has regarded easements as appurtenant to the grantee's estate in the dominant land rather than appurtenant to the land itself.[23] Thus, upon the early termination of a lease

---

[21] [2012] 2 P & CR 15.

[22] See section 5. The Law Commission prefer this approach see Consultation Paper No 186 (2008), [5.64]–[5.71].

[23] Although see the different views expressed by Cooke, 'The Genetics of Appurtenant Interests' in *Modern Studies in Property Law Vol 6* (ed Bright, Oxford: Hart Publishing, 2011) ch 10 and Lyall 'What are easements attached or appurtenant to' (2010) Conv 300.

of the dominant land, for instance by notice or forfeiture, an easement enjoyed by the holder of the lease would also cease. But this orthodoxy has been challenged in the following case:

Wall v Collins
[2007] Ch 390, CA

Facts: Adjoining semi detached houses were held on 999 year leases. The dominant land (House A) enjoyed the benefit of a right of way also for a term of 999 years along a passageway forming part of the servient land (House B). The freehold of House A was acquired by its leasehold owners so that their lease merged with the freehold reversion. The question arose whether their right to use the passageway also merged and was extinguished.

Carnworth LJ

At 14–16

As to the scope of the right granted in 1911, it is clear that Mr Hurst could neither grant the benefit, nor accept the burden, of a right in excess of his then 999-year interest in each property. To that extent the judge's conclusion that the right granted at that stage could not benefit or burden the freehold reversion, in which Mr Hurst had no interest, is clearly right [. . .]

That is not the same as saying that the right was "attached to" the leasehold interest. An easement must be appurtenant to a dominant tenement, but not necessarily to any particular interest for the time being [. . .] there is nothing to suggest that an easement for a term of years has to be attached to a leasehold interest of equivalent duration. All that matters is that the grantee has an interest at least co-extensive with the period of the easement [. . .]

It follows in my view that merger of the lease into a larger interest in the dominant tenement is not in itself fatal to the continued existence of the easement, for the period for which it was granted. The dominant tenement remains unchanged and there is no legal impediment to the continued enjoyment of the easement by the occupier for the time being of that tenement.

The decision is not thought to extend to situations where the dominant owner's lease is forfeited or disclaimed. However, as Carnworth LJ noted, the decision has its practical advantages upon merger. To bring practicality into line with orthodoxy the Law Commission has recommended that the decision be reverse by statute but that the dominant owner should be able to elect to retain the benefit of the easement upon merger or surrender.[24]

2.2 THE DOMINANT AND SERVIENT TENEMENTS MUST BE IN SEPARATE OWNERSHIP AND OCCUPATION

It is not possible to have an easement over your own land.[25] Any rights that are exercised over two adjoining pieces of land that you own are exercised as a result of your ownership.

---

[24] Law Commission, Law Com 327 (2011), [3.255].
[25] *Roe v Siddons* (1889) 22 QBD 224, 236; *Metropolitan Railway Co v Fowler* [1892] 1 QB 165; *Kilgour v Gaddes* [1904] 1 KB 457, [461].

Accordingly, where the dominant and servient land come into the same ownership and occupation, the easement is extinguished, although if the dominant land is sold off, an easement may once again be created by implied grant.[26] If the dominant and servient land come only into the same occupation—for example, because a tenant takes a lease of both pieces of land—the easement is suspended until the common occupation comes to an end.

The necessity for separate ownership of the dominant and servient land can be inconvenient when housing estates are developed, because developers will be unable to create easements between the plots whilst the plots remain in their common ownership. The Law Commission has, thus, recommended, in respect of registered titles, that it should be possible for an easement to exist where the dominant and servient land are owned by the same person but held under separate registered titles.[27]

2.3 AN EASEMENT MUST ACCOMMODATE THE DOMINANT LAND

The right must benefit the land, as opposed to an individual owner of the land, if it is to have the necessary proprietary character to qualify as an easement. The concept of the land being able to enjoy rights is somewhat strained when it is the use of the land by its occupier that derives any benefit. The import of the requirement thus relates to the benefit enjoyed by the owner for the time being of the land, rather than a personal advantage of a particular owner. The point has been explained in the following case.

Moody v Steggles
(1879) 12 Ch D 261

Fry J

At 266

It is said that the easement in question relates, not to the tenement, but to the business of the occupant of the tenement, and that therefore I cannot tie the easement to the house. It appears to me that that argument is of too refined a nature to prevail, and for this reason, that the house can only be used by an occupant, and that the occupant only uses the house for the business he pursues, therefore in some manner (direct or indirect) an easement is more or less connected with the mode in which the occupant of the house uses it.

A right that was held to confer only a personal advantage is found in the early case of *Hill v Tupper*.[28] As we saw in Chapter 5, section 1, a canal company leased land beside the canal to Mr Hill and granted him the exclusive right to put or use boats on the canal. Mr Tupper owned a pub situated beside the canal and, when he also rented out boats to be used on the canal, Mr Hill objected. The court held that his exclusive right to put boats on the canal was not an easement, but a personal advantage. In the following case, Evershed MR explained why.

---

[26] See the rule in *Wheeldon v Burrows*: section 3.2.
[27] Law Commission, Law Com 327 (2011), [4.44].   [28] (1863) 2 H & C 121.

Re Ellenborough Park
[1956] Ch 131, CA

Evershed MR

At 175

It is clear that what the plaintiff was trying to do was to set up, under the guise of an easement, a monopoly which had no normal connexion with the ordinary use of his land, but which was merely an independent business enterprise. So far from the right claimed subserving or accommodating the land, the land was but a convenient incident to the exercise of the right.

The question of accommodation was of central importance in *Re Ellenborough Park* when the Court decided that the right to use the communal gardens satisfied the test.

Re Ellenborough Park
[1956] Ch 131, CA

Evershed MR

At 173

Can it be said, then, of the right of full enjoyment of the park in question, which was granted by the conveyance of December 23, 1864, and which, for reasons already given, was, in our view, intended to be annexed to the property conveyed to Mr. Porter, that it accommodated and served that property? It is clear that the right did, in some degree, enhance the value of the property, and this consideration cannot be dismissed as wholly irrelevant. It is, of course, a point to be noted; but we agree with Mr. Cross's submission that it is in no way decisive of the problem; it is not sufficient to show that the right increased the value of the property conveyed, unless it is also shown that it was connected with the normal enjoyment of that property. It appears to us that the question whether or not this connexion exists is primarily one of fact, and depends largely on the nature of the alleged dominant tenement and the nature of the right granted. As to the former, it was in the contemplation of the parties to the conveyance of 1864 that the property conveyed should be used for residential and not commercial purposes [. . .] We have already stated that the purchasers of all the plots, which actually abutted on the park, were granted the right to enjoy the use of it, as were also the purchasers of some of the plots which, although not fronting upon the park, were only a short distance away from it. As to the nature of the right granted, the conveyance of 1864 shows that the park was to be kept and maintained as a pleasure ground or ornamental garden, and that it was contemplated that it should at all times be kept in good order and condition and well stocked with plants and shrubs; and the vendors covenanted that they would not at any time thereafter erect or permit to be erected any dwelling-house or other building (except a grotto, bower, summer-house, flower-stand, fountain, music-stand or other ornamental erection) within or on any part of the pleasure ground. On these facts Mr. Cross submitted that the requisite connexion between the right to use the park and the normal enjoyment of the houses which were built around it or near it had not been established. He likened the position to a right granted to the purchaser of a house to use the

Zoological Gardens free of charge or to attend Lord's Cricket Ground without payment. Such a right would undoubtedly, he said, increase the value of the property conveyed but could not run with it at law as an easement, because there was no sufficient nexus between the enjoyment of the right and the use of the house. It is probably true, we think, that in neither of Mr. Cross's illustrations would the supposed right constitute an easement, for it would be wholly extraneous to, and independent of, the use of a house as a house, namely, as a place in which the householder and his family live and make their home; and it is for this reason that the analogy which Mr. Cross sought to establish between his illustrations and the present case cannot, in our opinion, be supported. A much closer analogy, as it seems to us, is the case of a man selling the freehold of part of his house and granting to the purchaser, his heirs and assigns, the right, appurtenant to such part, to use the garden in common with the vendor and his assigns. In such a case, the test of connexion, or accommodation, would be amply satisfied; for just as the use of a garden undoubtedly enhances, and is connected with, the normal enjoyment of the house to which it belongs, so also would the right granted, in the case supposed, be closely connected with the use and enjoyment of the part of the premises sold. Such, we think, is in substance the position in the present case. The park became a communal garden for the benefit and enjoyment of those whose houses adjoined it or were in its close proximity. Its flower beds, lawns and walks were calculated to afford all the amenities which it is the purpose of the garden of a house to provide; and, apart from the fact that these amenities extended to a number of householders, instead of being confined to one (which on this aspect of the case is immaterial), we can see no difference in principle between Ellenborough Park and a garden in the ordinary signification of that word. It is the collective garden of the neighbouring houses, to whose use it was dedicated by the owners of the estate and as such amply satisfied, in our judgment, the requirement of connexion with the dominant tenements to which it is appurtenant. The result is not affected by the circumstance that the right to the park is in this case enjoyed by some few houses which are not immediately fronting on the park. The test for present purposes, no doubt, is that the park should constitute in a real and intelligible sense the garden (albeit the communal garden) of the houses to which its enjoyment is annexed. But we think that the test is satisfied as regards these few neighbouring, though not adjacent, houses. We think that the extension of the right of enjoyment to these few houses does not negative the presence of the necessary "nexus" between the subject-matter enjoyed and the premises to which the enjoyment is expressed to belong.

It is evident from Evershed's judgment that there must be some physical proximity between the servient and dominant tenements for the necessary benefit to arise, although it was no objection that some of the houses did not immediately border the park, but were a short distance away.

It is also clear that an increase in economic value of the dominant land, whilst influential, is not the sole yardstick. The issue is whether or not the normal enjoyment of the land is enhanced, which is a question of fact to be determined by considering both the nature of the dominant land and the right itself.[29] Thus, a right to use a communal garden will accommodate a residence, but is most unlikely to accommodate a factory or farm. Where the land is used for commercial purposes, the right may enhance the business conducted on the land. Thus, in the case of *Moody v Steggles*,[30] a right to erect a sign to announce and promote a public house on the dominant land was held to be an easement.

---

[29] Lawson (2002) p 73.   [30] (1879) 12 Ch D 261.

Although labelled a test of fact, there are value judgments to be made, taking into account current social conditions, technical advances, and accepted modes of use of property. In the past a question mark has been raised over whether rights of recreation and amusement can qualify as an easement. The Court of Appeal considered the question in *Re Ellenborough Park*, when it rejected the claim that the right to use the garden was a right of mere recreation and amusement. It did so as part of the fourth requirement that the right must be capable of being the subject matter of a grant, but, because the question relates to issues of benefit, it falls more appropriately within Cheshire's second condition.

Re Ellenborough Park
[1956] Ch 131, CA

Evershed MR

At 177–8

The third of the questions embraced in Dr. Cheshire's fourth condition rests primarily on a proposition stated in *Theobald's The Law of Land*, 2nd ed. (1929), at p. 263, where it is said that an easement "must be a right of utility and benefit and not one of mere recreation and amusement." It does not appear that a proposition in similar terms is stated by Gale.

[The Court considered the authorities quoted by Theobald in support being, *Mounsey v. Ismay*,[31] *Dyce v Lady James Hay*,[32] and *Dempster v Cleghorn*.[33]]

In any case, if the proposition be well-founded, we do not think that the right to use a garden of the character with which we are concerned in this case can be called one of mere recreation and amusement [. . .] No doubt a garden is a pleasure—on high authority, it is the purest of pleasures—but, in our judgment, it is not a right having no quality either of utility or benefit as those words should be understood. The right here in suit is, for reasons already given, one appurtenant to the surrounding houses as such, and constitutes a beneficial attribute of residence in a house as ordinarily understood. Its use for the purposes, not only of exercise and rest but also for such domestic purposes as were suggested in argument—for example, for taking out small children in perambulators or otherwise—is not fairly to be described as one of mere recreation or amusement, and is clearly beneficial to the premises to which it is attached [. . .] the right in suit is, in point of utility, fairly analogous to a right of way passing over fields to, say, the railway station, which would be none the less a good right, even though it provided a longer route to the objective. We think, therefore, that the statement [. . .] must at least be confined to exclusion of rights to indulge in such recreations as [. . .] horse racing or perhaps playing games, and has no application to the facts of the present case.

With the growth of residential developments which include leisure facilities such as swimming pool, tennis courts, and even golf courses, the question has grown in importance. In the following case the Court of Appeal has held that a right to use such recreational facilities can indeed be an easement. They emphasized the changing attitudes to the health benefits of sport and other outdoor activities as well as questioning previously expressed judicial opinion.

[31] (1865) 3 H & C 486.   [32] (1852) 1 Macq 305.   [33] (1813) 2 Dow 40.

Regency Villas Title Ltd v Diamond Resorts (Europe) Ltd
[2017] EWCA Civ 238

Facts: A timeshare development granted the owners of the villas within the development a right to use the Italianate gardens, swimming pool, putting and croquet lawn, 18-hole golf course, and squash and tennis courts forming part of the development, as well as to use the ground and basement floors of the main house which included a billiard room, television room, restaurant, bar, gym, and sauna. A question arose as to whether these rights were granted as easements or mere personal rights. The Court of Appeal held that the right to use the outdoor facilities were easements but the right to use the facilities within the main house failed to qualify largely because their use rested upon the use of chattels and services provided by the dominant owner.

Sir Geoffrey Vos Chancellor of the High Court

At 53–6

Before dealing with these 9 facilities in turn, we should, however, attempt to summarise the principles that are applicable to determining whether easements of this kind can exist under English law. It was established by *Ellenborough Park* that an easement can exist for the use of the park as a garden, including the right to walk over the pathways and (subject to necessary restrictions) the lawns, to rest on the seats or in other places provided, but not to trample at will all over the park, not to cut or pluck the flowers or shrubs, or to interfere in the laying out or upkeep of the park. That easement was not said to be a "mere recreation or amusement", because the right had the necessary quality of utility and benefit to the dwellings that were the dominant tenements.

Easements in the modern world must, of course, retain their essential legal qualities. But the views of society as to what is mere recreation or amusement may change, even if the exclusion of such rights were authoritative, which we rather doubt. Physical exercise is now regarded by most people in the United Kingdom as either an essential or at least a desirable part of their daily routines. It is not a mere recreation or amusement. Physical exercise can, moreover, in our modern lives, take many forms, whether it be walking, swimming or playing active games and sports. We cannot see how an easement could either in 1981 or in 2017 be ruled out solely on the grounds that the form of physical exercise it envisaged was a game or a sport rather than purely a walk in a garden. It is also noteworthy that profits à prendre (another incorporeal hereditament, but one that can exist without a dominant tenement) have commonly been held to exist in respect of the right to take game or fish, both of which activities are often (but obviously not solely) undertaken for recreation or sport.

In any event, in our judgment, Baron Martin's *dictum* in Mounsey v. Ismay *supra*, from which the exclusion of rights of "mere recreation or amusement" derived in 1865, was *obiter* as we have said, since the decision in that case was that there could be no easement to hold horse races in favour of the townspeople generally without the existence of a dominant tenement. What Baron Martin actually said that is relevant was as follows at page 498: "But, however this may be, we are of opinion that to bring the right within the term "easement" in the second section [of the Prescription Act 2&3 Wm. 4, c.71] it must be one analogous to a right of way which precedes it and a watercourse which follows it, and must be a right of utility and benefit, and not one of mere recreation and amusement". He was construing the Prescription Act, although that is not the central point.

In our view, the requirement that an easement must be a "right of utility and benefit" is the crucial requirement. The essence of an easement is to give the dominant tenement a benefit or a utility as such. Thus, an easement properly so called will improve the general utility of the dominant tenement. It may benefit the trade carried on upon the dominant tenement or the utility of living there. As the treatment of Dr Cheshire's 2nd and 4th conditions in *Ellenborough Park* demonstrated, they are inter-connected. As we have said, an easement should not in the modern world be held to be invalid on the ground that it was "mere recreation or amusement" because the form of physical exercise it envisaged was a game or a sport. To be clear, we do not regard Baron Martin's *dictum* as binding on this court, and we would decline to follow it insofar as it suggests that an easement cannot be held to exist in respect of a right to engage in recreational physical activities on servient land.

2.4 THE RIGHT MUST BE CAPABLE OF BEING THE SUBJECT MATTER OF A GRANT

Cheshire's fourth condition has been described as '*both obscure and unhelpful*'.[34] At one level, the condition is deceptively simple: as a legal interest in land, an easement must be capable of being granted by deed. There must be a grantor and grantee, who have the necessary capacity and who enjoy the necessary title to create the easement in question. If the grantor does not hold the appropriate title, the easement can only operate to estop the grantor denying the right as against the grantee.

In fact, the condition hides '*an inept shorthand*'[35] for a number of criteria, the common features of which operate to circumscribe the effect upon the servient land of those rights that qualify as easements. We will examine these criteria under four headings:[36]

1. the requirement for certainty in the scope of the grant;

2. the requirement that the right places no positive burden on the servient owner;

3. the limitations on new easements;

4. the 'ouster' principle, which prohibits rights that amount to a claim to exclusive or joint ownership.

2.4.1 Certainty in the scope of the grant

Certainty is a constant refrain of the law when defining parties' rights and obligations. It must be clear what the dominant owner is entitled to do, and what is the nature and extent of the burden to which the servient owner must submit. The call for certainty is particularly insistent when rights are proprietary and thus capable of binding third parties. In the case of easements, certainty can be elusive when there are a wide variety of rights that can operate over another's land. There is thus a '*heightened emphasis on rigorous definitional clarity*'.[37]

---

[34] McClean, 'The Nature of an Easement' (1966) 5 West LR 32, 61. The Court of Appeal in *Re Ellenborough Park* [1956] Ch 131, [164], described the fourth condition as 'not entirely clear'.

[35] Gardner & MacKenzie, *An Introduction to Land Law* 4th ed (2015) p 309.

[36] In *Re Ellenborough Park* [1956] Ch 131, [164], the Court of Appeal identified three criteria—prohibitions against: (i) vague and uncertain right; (ii) rights that are claims to joint user; and (iii) rights of mere recreation and amusement. We have examined (iii) in the context of Cheshire's second requirement of accommodation. Criteria (i) and (ii) relate to our criteria (1) and (4); our criteria (2) and (3) did not arise in the context of the case.

[37] Gray and Gray, *Elements of Land Law* (5th edn, 2009), [5.1.41]. See also the discussion of what can count as a property right in Chapter 5, section 5.

There is no right to an uninterrupted right to light or air; such a right can only operate through a defined channel.[38] Nor is there a right to a view[39] or to uninterrupted television reception,[40] although the Supreme Court has accepted the possibility of a positive easement to make a noise that would otherwise be a nuisance.[41] In *Re Ellenborough Park*, the Court of Appeal drew a distinction between the certainty of a right to use a communal garden attached to dominant residential land, and the uncertainty of a right to wander at will over a large and ill-defined area.[42]

Re Ellenborough Park
[1956] Ch 131, CA

Lord Evershed

At 179

As appears from what has been stated earlier, the right to the full enjoyment of Ellenborough Park, which was granted by the 1864 and other relevant conveyances, was, in substance, no more tha[n] a right to use the park as a garden in the way in which gardens are commonly used. In a sense, no doubt, such a right includes something of a jus spatiandi [a privilege to wander at will], inasmuch as it involves the principle of wandering at will round each part of the garden, except of course, such parts as comprise flower beds, or are laid out for some other purpose, which renders walking impossible or unsuitable. We doubt, nevertheless, whether the right to use and enjoy a garden in this manner can with accuracy be said to constitute a mere jus spatiandi. Wandering at large is of the essence of such a right and constitutes the main purpose for which it exists. A private garden, on the other hand, is an attribute of the ordinary enjoyment of the residence to which it is attached, and the right of wandering in it is but one method of enjoying it.

2.4.2 No positive burden on the servient owner

An easement does not require the servient owner to do anything: he or she merely has to allow the dominant owner to exercise his or her easement without interference. Furthermore, he or she is not required to keep the subject matter of the easement in repair so that the dominant owner can exercise his or her right. Thus, if the easement is a right of way or drainage, the servient owner is not required to keep the road or drains in good repair.[43] For the same reason, a right to the passage of water through pipes running through the servient land does not require a continuous supply of water; the right imposes only a negative obligation not to interrupt any supply that there is.[44]

There is one exception to this rule: namely, a prescriptive right to require a neighbour to maintain a boundary fence. The right stems from the ancient and anomalous obligation to

---

[38] *Harris v De Pinna* (1886) 33 Ch D 238, 250.   [39] Ibid, 262.
[40] *Hunter v Canary Wharf* [1997] AC 655, [699].
[41] *Coventry (t/a RDC Promotions) v Lawrence* [2014] AC 822.
[42] But see *Magrath v Parkside Hotels Ltd* [2011] EWHC 143 where an undefined right to fire escape was found sufficiently certain because it did not allow unrestricted access over the servient land and would be rarely exercised.
[43] *Duke of Westminster v Guild* [1985] QB 688.
[44] *Schwann v Cotton* [1916] 2 Ch 459; *Rance v Elvin* (1985) 50 P & CR 9 and re electricity supplies *Duffy v Lamb* (1998) 75 P & CR 364; *William Old International Ltd v Arya* [2009] EWHC 599.

maintain stock-proof fences to keep out a neighbour's cattle, a breach of which is a defence to cattle trespass.[45]

An obligation to repair may, however, arise as a result of some other source of liability. For example, an obligation to repair may arise by contract, whether as a result of an express or implied term.[46] Although a positive obligation to repair will not usually be enforceable against third parties, it may be enforceable in certain circumstances, which we will explore in the next chapter. Liability to repair may also arise in tort, whether under the torts of negligence or nuisance,[47] or as a result of obligations imposed upon occupiers by the Occupiers Liability Act 1984.

2.4.3 Limitations on new easements

It is said that the class of easements is never closed,[48] because developments in lifestyle call for the recognition of new forms of easement.[49] Nevertheless, the courts are cautious in recognizing unusual new forms of easement. There is a particular reluctance to accept new negative easements, as Lord Denning MR explained in the following extract. He also pointed out that the same protection may be achieved by taking a restrictive covenant from the servient owner.[50]

Phipps v Pears
[1965] 1 QB 76, CA

Facts: There were two adjoining detached houses. The wall of the most recently constructed house was very close to the adjoining house and it had not been rendered to make it weatherproof. The other house was demolished, leaving the wall of the remaining house exposed to the weather. Because this wall was not weatherproof, cracks appeared. The owner unsuccessfully claimed a right to protection from the weather against the owner of the house that had been demolished.[51]

Lord Denning MR

At 82

But a right to protection from the weather (if it exists) is entirely negative. It is a right to stop your neighbour pulling down his own house. Seeing that it is a negative easement, it must be looked at with caution. Because the law has been very chary of creating any new negative easements.

---

[45] *Jones v Price* [1965] 2 QB 618. [46] See *Liverpool City Council v Irwin* [1977] AC 239.
[47] See *Rees v Skerrett* [2001] 1 WLR 1541, in which a duty arose to take reasonable steps to weatherproof a wall after demolition of an adjoining wall; cf *Phipps v Pears* [1965] 1 QB 76.
[48] *Re Ellenborough Park* [1956] Ch 131, [140], *per* Dankwerts J.
[49] See Lord St Leonards' observations in *Dyce v Lady James Hay* (1852) 1 Macq 305, 312, that '*the category of servitudes must alter and expand with changes that take place in the circumstances of mankind*'.
[50] See Chapter 23. Dawson and Dunn advocate the formulation of a single means of creating negative property rights: see Dawson and Dunn, 'Negative Easements: A Crumb of Analysis' (1998) 18 LS 510.
[51] Following *Rees v Skerrett* [2001] 1 WLR 1541, he might have claimed a tortuous remedy requiring the owner to take reasonable steps to protect a neighbour's wall from foreseeable damage occasioned by the withdrawal of support or protection.

The reason underlying these instances is that if such an easement were to be permitted, it would unduly restrict your neighbour in his enjoyment of his own land. It would hamper legitimate development, see *Dalton v. Angus* (1881) 6 App Cas 740 at 824 *per* Lord Blackburn. Likewise here, if we were to stop a man pulling down his house, we would put a brake on desirable improvement. Every man is entitled to pull down his house if he likes. If it exposes your house to the weather, that is your misfortune. It is no wrong on his part [. . .] There is no such easement known to the law as an easement to be protected from the weather. The only way for an owner to protect himself is by getting a covenant from his neighbour that he will not pull down his house or cut down his trees. Such a covenant would be binding on him in contract: and it would be enforceable on any successor who took with notice of it.

2.4.4 The 'ouster' principle

An easement is a right to use the land of another for some limited purpose. It thus falls short of a claim to exclusive or joint possession or occupation. The Law Commission points out that this important distinction between easements and possessory rights is not easy to define.

Law Com No 327, *Easements, Covenants and Profits à Prendre* (2011, [3.191])

[. . .] an easement [. . .] is an interest in land, not an estate. If what the dominant owner can do on the servient land actually amounts to an ownership right [. . .] then it cannot be an easement. That much is clear. What is more difficult is to delineate precisely the point at which the dominant owner's rights can be said to be "too much" to be merely an interest in land.

The ouster principle has been developed to try and draw that distinction.

Copeland v Greenhalf
[1952] Ch 488, HC

Facts: A repairer of vehicles unsuccessfully claimed an easement by prescription (long user) over a strip of land belonging to Greenhalf. He had been using the strip of land for fifty years, as a place on which to store his customers' vehicles whilst awaiting repair or collection.

Upjohn J

At 498

I think that the right claimed goes wholly outside any normal idea of an easement, that is, the right of the owner or the occupier of a dominant tenement over a servient tenement. This claim (to which no closely related authority has been referred to me) really amounts

> to a claim to a joint user of the land by the defendant. Practically, the defendant is claiming the whole beneficial user of the strip of land on the south-east side of the track there; he can leave as many or as few lorries there as he likes for as long as he likes; he may enter on it by himself, his servants and agents to do repair work thereon. In my judgment, that is not a claim which can be established as an easement. It is virtually a claim to possession of the servient tenement, if necessary to the exclusion of the owner; or, at any rate, to a joint user, and no authority has been cited to me which would justify the conclusion that a right of this wide and undefined nature can be the proper subject-matter of an easement. It seems to me that to succeed, this claim must amount to a successful claim of possession by reason of long adverse possession. I say nothing, of course, as to the creation of such rights by deeds or by covenant; I am dealing solely with the question of a right arising by prescription.

It is to be noted that Upjohn J suggested that a claim to ownership by adverse possession might have been successful. Alternatively, if Copeland had been granted permission to use the land, he may have claimed a lease or an occupational licence. Upjohn J also suggested that the different considerations may apply if the parties had been able to demonstrate their intentions by an express grant, rather than where an easement is claimed by prescription—but this distinction has been doubted.[52]

Difficulties arise in clearly defining the scope of the ouster principle. To some extent, all easements oust the servient owner from some use of the servient land: for example, the grant of a right of way will prevent the servient owner from building on the road so as to obstruct free passage. In *Miller v Emcer Products*,[53] the Court of Appeal saw no objection to the grant of a right to use a lavatory, although the servient owner would be excluded from the lavatory whilst the dominant owner was using it. In *Re Ellenborough Park*,[54] the Court of Appeal was also not impressed by the suggestion that use of a communal garden was effectively a claim to joint ownership because it excluded the servient owner from any use of the garden.

The uncertainty over the scope of the ouster principle has centred in recent years over rights of storage and car parking. In principle, rights of storage were accepted in *AG for Southern Nigeria v John Holt & Co (Liverpool) Ltd*[55] and in *Wright v Macadam*,[56] and the right to park cars has been accepted in principle in a number of cases..[57]

Various tests have emerged to trigger the ouster principle. In earlier cases the test was said to be one of degree.

---

[52] Hill-Smith, 'Rights of Parking and the Ouster Principle After *Batchelor v Marlow*' [2007] Conv 223, 232. See also *Moncrieff v Jamieson* [2007] UKHL 42, [59], *per* Lord Scott.

[53] [1956] Ch 304, [316].   [54] [1958] Ch 131, [176].

[55] [1915] AC 599 (right to store materials and trade goods and produce).

[56] [1949] 2 KB 744 (right to store coal).

[57.] See *London and Blenheim Estates Ltd v Ladbroke Retail Parks Ltd* [1992] 1 WLR 1278, HC; [1994] 1 WLR 31, CA; *Hair v Gillman* (2000) 80 P & CR 108; *Bachelor v Marlow* [2001] EWCA Civ 1051, [2003] 1 WLR 764; *Central Midlands Estates Ltd v Leicester Dyers Ltd* [2003] 2 P & CR D1; *Saeed v Plustrade Ltd* [2001] EWCA Civ 2011, [2002] 2 P & CR 19; *Montrose Court Holdings Ltd v Shamash* [2006] All ER D 272, *Moncrieff v Jamieson* [2007] UKHL 42, [2007] 1 WLR 2620, and *de La Cuona v Big Apple Marketing Ltd* (unreported). The right to moor boats has also been accepted as an easement: see *P&S Platt Ltd v Crouch* [2003] EWCA Civ 1110, [2004] 1 P & CR 18.

London & Blenheim Estates Ltd v Ladbroke Retail Parks Ltd
[1992] 1 WLR 1278, HC

Judge Paul Baker QC

At 1288

The essential question is one of degree. If the right granted in relation to the area over which it is to be exercisable is such that it would leave the servient owner without any reasonable use of his land whether for parking or anything else, it could not be an easement, though it might be some larger or differing grant.

Thus, it is suggested that, if the area of storage or car parking is relatively small when compared with the area of the servient land, the ouster principle does not apply, because the servient owner is still able to make 'reasonable use' of the servient land. This reasonable use test was applied in *Batchelor v Marlow*[58] to reject an exclusive right to park on weekdays between the hours of 9.30 a.m. and 6.00 p.m when the Court of Appeal concluded that the servient owner's ownership was 'illusory.'[59] Subsequent cases have applied the test more leniently in deciding that servient owners have retained some benefit where they were able to build over the parking spaces[60] or could improve the visual impact by resurfacing the parking area.[61] Indeed, it is becoming increasingly apparent that the restrictive approach of *Batchelor* is unlikely to be followed both because of the commercial pressure to accept parking rights and the doubt cast on the reasonable use test by the House of Lords' dicta in the following Scottish case in which Lord Scott suggested that the test should be refocussed to consider whether or not the servient owner retains sufficient possession and control over the servient land subject to the right to park.[62]

Moncrieff v Jamieson
[2007] 1 WLR 2620, HL

Lord Scott

At 57

It has often been commented that *Wright v Macadam* was not cited to Upjohn J and the possible inconsistency between the two cases was addressed by Judge Paul Baker QC in *London & Blenheim Estates Ltd v Ladbroke Retail Parks Ltd* where a right of parking had been claimed. He commented, at p 1286, that the question whether the right to park that had been claimed was consistent with the nature of an easement was one of degree: "A small coal shed in a large property is one thing. The exclusive use of a large part of the

---

[58] [2001] EWCA Civ 1051, [2003] 1 WLR 764.   [59] Ibid at 18 *per* Tuckey LJ.
[60] *Kettel v Bloomfold Ltd* [2012] L & TR 30.
[61] *Virdi v Chana* [2008] EWHC 2901, *Begley v Taylor* [2014] EWHC 1180, and *De Law Cuona v Big Apple Marketing Ltd* (unreported).
[62] He was influenced by arguments made by Hill-Smith [2007] Conv 223.

alleged servient tenement is another." I think, with respect, that this attempt to reconcile the two authorities was addressing the wrong point. The servient land in relation to a servitude or easement is surely the land over which the servitude or easement is enjoyed, not the totality of the surrounding land of which the servient owner happens to be the owner. If there is an easement of way over a 100-yard roadway on a 1,000-acre estate, or an easement to use for storage a small shed on the estate access to which is gained via the 100-yard roadway, it would be fairly meaningless in relation to either easement to speak of the whole estate as the servient land. Would the right of way and the storage right fail to qualify as easements if the whole estate bar the actual land over which the roadway ran and on which the shed stood, with or without a narrow surrounding strip, were sold? How could it be open to the servient owner to destroy easements by such a stratagem? In my opinion such a stratagem would fail. It would fail because the servient land was never the whole estate but was the land over which the roadway ran and on which the shed stood. Provided the servient land was land of which the servient owner was in possession, the rights of way and of storage would continue, in my opinion, to qualify as easements [. . .]

At 59

In my respectful opinion the test formulated in the *London & Blenheim Estates case* and applied by the Court of Appeal in *Batchelor v Marlow* [2003] 1 WLR 764, a test that would reject the claim to an easement if its exercise would leave the servient owner with no "reasonable use" to which he could put the servient land, needs some qualification. It is impossible to assert that there would be no use that could be made by an owner of land over which he had granted parking rights. He could, for example, build above or under the parking area. He could place advertising hoardings on the walls. Other possible uses can be conjured up. And by what yardstick is it to be decided whether the residual uses of the servient land available to its owner are "reasonable" or sufficient to save his ownership from being "illusory"? It is not the uncertainty of the test that, in my opinion, is the main problem. It is the test itself. I do not see why a landowner should not grant rights of a servitudal character over his land to any extent that he wishes. The claim in *Batchelor v Marlow* for an easement to park cars was a prescriptive claim based on over 20 years of that use of the strip of land. There is no difference between the characteristics of an easement that can be acquired by grant and the characteristics of an easement that can be acquired by prescription. If an easement can be created by grant it can be acquired by prescription and I can think of no reason why, if an area of land can accommodate nine cars, the owner of the land should not grant an easement to park nine cars on the land. The servient owner would remain the owner of the land and in possession and control of it. The dominant owner would have the right to station up to nine cars there and, of course, to have access to his nine cars. How could it be said that the law would recognise an easement allowing the dominant owner to park five cars or six or seven or eight but not nine? I would, for my part, reject the test that asks whether the servient owner is left with any reasonable use of his land, and substitute for it a test which asks whether the servient owner retains possession and, subject to the reasonable exercise of the right in question, control of the servient land.

Lord Neuberger was rather more reserved in accepting this different test.

Moncrieff v Jamieson
[2007] 1 WLR 2620, HL

Lord Neuberger

At 143–4

I see considerable force in the views expressed by Lord Scott in paras 57 and 59 of his opinion, to the effect that a right can be an easement notwithstanding that the dominant owner effectively enjoys exclusive occupation, on the basis that the essential requirement is that the servient owner retains possession and control. If that were the right test, then it seems likely that *Batchelor v Marlow* was wrongly decided. However, unless it is necessary to decide the point to dispose of this appeal, I consider that it would be dangerous to try and identify what degree of ouster is required to disqualify a right from constituting a servitude or easement, given the very limited argument your Lordships have received on the topic.

Luther has argued that what matters is '*what the claimant could do by virtue of his easement not what the owner could not do*'.[63] Focussing either on the dominant or servient owner is rather like looking at different sides of the same coin, but Luther suggests that it is more straightforward to look at the issue from the point of the view of the claimant—that is, the potential dominant owner.

Luther, 'Easements and Exclusive Possession' (1996) 16 LS 51, 62

Surely to ask 'What the claimant can do?' (the certainty approach) is the same as to ask 'What can the servient owner *not* do? (the exclusion/substantial interference approach)? There is some substance in this argument, and certainly it is possible to imagine cases where it would be difficult to answer one question without answering the other. A line would have to be drawn in difficult cases. But against this it must be said that to look at the positive characteristics of a claimed right must in many cases be easier than to assess its negative impact on someone else's rights. This latter enquiry must involve a large number of external factors, not least as noted above the total size of the servient tenement, the characteristics of the owner and the uses to which he might wish to put his land. It might also involve uncertainty in the definition of rights.

The Law Commission believes that the ouster principle is not useful and recommends that a right should not be rejected as an easement merely because it prevents the servient owner from making any reasonable use of servient land.[64] Xu suggests that the courts have already effectively reached this position in relation to rights of parking but he points out that there are still issues to be resolved and cautions against a wholesale abolition of the ouster principle.

---

[63] Luther, 'Easements and Exclusive Possession' (1996) 16 LS 51, 59.
[64] Law Com 327 (2011) [3.207]–[3.209].

Xu, 'Easement of Car Parking: The Ouster Principle is Out but Problems may Aggravate' [2012] Conv 291, 301

The real problem then is to find a place for such exclusive parking right in the established framework of easement and property law [. . .] Perhaps the root of the problem lies in the fact that no dominant tenement owner of any other type of easement would have as much interest in the way the servient tenement is run [. . .]

Car-parking is such a drastically different right from any other easement. The established structure of English property law may be exposed to an incoming flood of these rights following the end of the ouster principle. We know very little about exclusive parking rights, other than they are being created in considerable quantity. We have few answers to the difficulties in relation to shared parking rights, other than perhaps neighbourly advices and common sense. It must bewilder any layperson that property lawyers can be so ignorant about such earthly things as parking spaces [. . .]

At 303

The ouster principle is highly useful and flexible tool in the hand of the court, allowing some intensive-use easements while denying others. Of course uncertainty is unavoidable with any flexible test [. . .] In the realm of car parking, the need for it is so prevalent and unstoppable that perhaps any sense of uncertainty is unacceptable. Hence the ouster principle should be abolished, either in substance or formally, in the context of car parking rights in recognition of the social demand and commercial reality.

On the other hand, the wholesale abolition of the principle in all contexts seems unnecessary, excessive and potentially damaging to too much of the established property law.

3 THE *ACQUISITION* QUESTION

We have already noted that easements lie in grant and there are three mechanisms by which that grant may arise: (i) by express grant; (ii) by implied grant; and (iii) by presumed grant as result of long user. Rights in the nature of easements may also arise by statute: for example, the Access to Neighbouring Land Act 1992 and the Party Walls Act 1996 both grant an owner a right to go onto neighbouring land in order to carry out certain repairs and building work.[65]

3.1 EXPRESS GRANT

Easements may be created by the methods examined in Chapter 8. A legal easement must be created by deed. Where a legal easement is created after 13 October 2003 over registered land, that deed must also be registered,[66] with the benefit of the easement being recorded in the property register of the dominant land and the burden of the easement being noted

---

[65] See Gratton, 'Proprietarian Conceptions of Statutory Access Rights' in *Modern Studies in Property Law Vol 2* (ed Cook, 2003) ch 18.
[66] Land Registration Act 2002, s 27.

in the charges register of the servient land.[67] A legal easement created by deed before that date may, but need not, be registered to bind a purchase—it will take effect as an overriding interest.[68] An equitable easement may be created in writing, by agreement, or by estoppel,[69] but will need to be registered to affect a purchaser.[70]

3.2 IMPLIED GRANT

An easement may be acquired by implied grant usually when land is subdivided into two or more parts, whether by sale or lease. There are four ways in which a grant may be implied:

- easements of necessity;
- intended easements;
- the rule in *Wheeldon v Burrows*;[71] and
- by the operation of s 62 of the Law of Property Act 1925 (LPA 1925).

The Law Commission has described these methods as providing a *'complex matrix of over-lapping rules'*,[72] which *'have developed in piecemeal and uncoordinated fashion'*.[73]

The underlying rationale for the first three of these rules lies in the principle that a seller or landlord should not be allowed to derogate from his or her grant: *'A grantor having given a thing with one hand, is not to take away the means of enjoying it with the other.'*[74] Thus a landowner who has disposed of part of his or her land for a particular purpose cannot use his or her retained land in such a way as to make the disposed portion unfit for its particular purpose.

The principle of non-derogation from grant is general in its application and may itself form the basis for an implied easement.[75] Hopkins explains the influence of non-derogation from grant upon the implied grant of easements.

Hopkins, *The Informal Acquisition of Rights in Land* (2000, p 205)

The rule of non-derogation from grant is seen as the basis for three specific rules enabling the acquisition of an easement [. . .] The general rule itself may give rise to the acquisition of easements. Therefore the question arises to what extent there is an overlap between the general and specific rules. It seems that there are three characteristics that separate the specific rules. First, each specific rule has its own requirements which are distinct, in some respects, from

---

[67] Where the servient land is unregistered, the dominant owner may enter a caution against first registration of the servient land to ensure that the relevant notice will be entered when the servient land is registered: see ibid, ss 15–21.

[68] Land Registration Act 2002, Sch 3 para 3.

[69] For an example of an easement by estoppel, see *Crabb v Arun District Council* [1976] Ch 179, discussed in Chapter 10.

[70] Because it is not an overriding interest, see Land Registration Act 2002, Sch 3 para 3.

[71] (1878) 12 Ch D 31.   [72] Law Commission Consultation Paper No 186 (2008), [4.109].

[73] Ibid, at [4.99].

[74] *Birmingham, Dudley and District Banking Co v Ross* (1887) 38 Ch D 295, 312, *per* Bowen LJ.

[75] See *Cable v Bryant* [1908] 1 Ch 259. The Law Commission proposal for the statutory implication of easements would exclude the general principle of non-derogation from grant as an independent ground: see Law Com 327 (2011), [3.45].

the general rule. Secondly, in each case the right claimed must fulfil the general characteristics of an easement. The specific rules are not the source of proprietary rights *sui generis*. In these respects the specific rules are more restrictive in their application than the general rule. However, thirdly it seems that the specific rules alone can create positive easements. The general rule may be limited to enabling the creation of negative easements. In addition to the three rules derived from non-derogation from grant, there is a fourth, related, rule enabling the acquisition of a legal easement by words implied into a conveyance by statute.

Even though the rationale for implied grant stems from the principle of non-derogation from grant, the basis for the rules is confused. They are said to be based upon the presumed intention of the parties and may indeed be excluded by a contrary intention, but in the background lurks the public policy of maximizing the effective use of land. Easements of necessity, in particular, reveal this confused interaction. The Law Commission recommends that utility should become the overt basis for implication, by replacing the separate rules with a single rule based upon what is 'necessary for the reasonable use of the land' at the time of the disposition, thus rooting implication in policy rather than intention.[76] Douglas has criticized this proposed change by suggesting that implied easements are derived from a single rule of intention with complexity arising from evidential difficulties rather than the rule itself. As a result he believes that reform is not necessary or helpful.

Douglas, 'Reforming Implied Easements' [2015] 131 LQR 251

What the 'tests' for implication are really doing is identifying relevant background information against which a deed should be read. They focus on factors such the physical layout of the land (was the land granted or retained completely inaccessible?), the past usage of the land (was there an apparent quasi-easement?) and the purpose of the grant (was the land granted, for instance, for a specific business purpose that required an easement?). Although the deed may be silent on the matter when it is read with one or more of these background factors, a reasonable grantee may conclude that the grantor did intend to grant or reserve an easement, but failed to express it. In other words, the law presently provides a single test for implication: did the grantor intend but fail to state, the grant or reservation of the easement? [. . .] If this analysis is correct the case for reform is a weak one. The Law Commission's first criticism, that the law is overly complex as it provides several separate tests for implication, cannot be sustained. The current law, as we have seen actually provides a single test of intention, not several separate tests. So far as complexities exist, it does not result from the law itself, but from evidential difficulties, as courts must engage in the difficult task of ascertaining the grantor's unexpressed intentions.

Before we examine the methods of implying an easement, we must consider two contrasting situations. Firstly, we will consider that in which the dominant land is sold or let and the new dominant owner or tenant claims an easement over the servient land retained by the seller or landlord. If an easement is implied, it will be by means of an implied grant. This is illustrated in Figure 22.1.

---

[76] Ibid. See also the statutory schemes for the implications of easements in Australia canvassed in Burns, 'Easements and Servitudes Created by Implied Grant, Implied Reservation or Prescription and Title-by-Registration Systems' in *Modern Studies in Property Law Vol 5* (ed Dixon, Oxford: Hart Publishing, 2009).

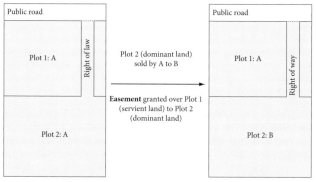

Figure 22.1 Easement by implied grant

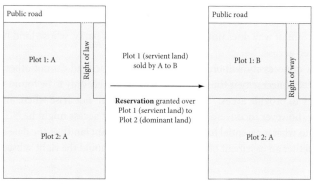

Figure 22.2 Easements by implied reservation

Secondly, we will consider that in which the servient land is sold or let and the seller or landlord claims an easement over the servient land for the benefit of the dominant land that he or she retains. If an easement is implied, it will be by means of an implied reservation. This is illustrated in Figure 22.2.

The law is more reluctant to imply a reservation than the grant of an easement. The seller or landlord is expected to take steps to protect the use of his or her retained dominant land. The possibility of an implied reservation only arises where easements are implied on the basis of necessity or intended use. Here, the implication looks to the future use of the land. The implied grant of an easement also may arise in these circumstances and, in addition, under the rule in *Wheeldon v Burrows* or s 62 of the LPA 1925, where the implied grant looks to the past use of the land.

The Law Commission has recommended that the distinction between the implication of easements and reservations should be abandoned.[77]

3.2.1 Easements of necessity

The requirements for implying an easement of necessity were explained in the following case.

---

[77] Ibid, [3.30].

Manjang v Drammeh
(1991) 61 P & CR 194, PC

Lord Oliver

At 197

There has to be found, first, a common owner of a legal estate in two plots of land. It has, secondly, to be established that access between one of those plots and the public highway can be obtained only over the other plot. Thirdly, there has to be found a disposition of one of the plots without any specific grant or reservation of a right of access. Given these conditions, it may be possible as a matter of construction of the relevant grant [. . .] to imply the reservation of an easement of necessity.

Easements of necessity are confined to situations in which land becomes landlocked when a common owner sells (or leases) part of his or her land. In this situation, it is clear that the burden of the right of way does not fall upon some third party, whose land happens to provide the required access.[78]

An easement of necessity will only be implied where the land cannot otherwise be used at all. A high degree of necessity is thus required, which is likely only to be found where a right of way is necessary to provide access.[79] Even then, a right will not arise where an alternative access is available, however inconvenient or impractical that access might be.[80] The scope of the right is limited to what is essential to the use of the dominant land[81] at the date of its disposal.[82] It is unclear whether an easement of necessity will cease should the right subsequently become unnecessary.[83]

The basis of easements of necessity lies in intention and not public policy.[84]

Nickerson v Barraclough
[1981] Ch 426, CA

Brightman LJ

At 440

In this court we have heard a great deal of argument about ways of necessity—what is their basis, how they can be acquired and whether they can be lost. With the utmost respect to

---

[78] Thus avoiding a claim that the third party's human rights had been infringed by an unjustified interference with his possessions under Art 1 of the First Protocol to the European Convention on Human Rights. See further Chapter 4.

[79] In *Walby v Walby* [2012] EWHC 3089 the court accepted that easement of necessity might extend to other easements. An essential right of support might be another candidate.

[80] *Union Lighterage Co v London Graving Dock Co* [1902] 2 Ch 577; *Manjang v Drammeh* (1990) 61 P & CR 194; *Titchmarsh v Royston Water Co Ltd* (1899) 81 LT 673; *J&O Operations Ltd v Kingston & St Andrew Corp* [2012] UKPC 7.

[81] For example, vehicular access will not be necessary where pedestrian access is adequate: see *MRA Engineering Ltd v Trimster* (1988) 50 P & CR 1.

[82] *Corporation of London v Riggs* (1880) 13 Ch D 798.

[83] See the conflicting authority in *Holmes v Goring* (1824) 2 Bing 76; *Donaldson v Smith* [2006] All ER (D) 293; *Proctor v Hodgson* (1855) 10 Exch 824; *Barkshire v Grubb* (1881) 18 Ch D 816; *Huckvale v Aegean Hotels Ltd* (1989) 58 P & CR 163.

[84] These comments are dicta, but have been subsequently approved by the Court of Appeal in *Adealon International Corp Pty Ltd v Merton LBC* [2007] EWCA Civ 362, [2007] 1 WLR 1898.

the Vice-Chancellor, I have come to the conclusion that the doctrine of way of necessity is not founded upon public policy at all but upon an implication from the circumstances. I accept that there are reported cases, and textbooks, in which public policy is suggested as a possible foundation of the doctrine, but such a suggestion is not, in my opinion, correct. It is well established that a way of necessity is never found to exist except in association with a grant of land: see *Proctor v. Hodgson* (1855) 10 Exch. 824, where it was held that land acquired by escheat got no way of necessity; and *Wilkes v. Greenway* (1890) 6 T.L.R. 449, where land acquired by prescription got no way of necessity. If a way of necessity were based upon public policy, I see no reason why land acquired by escheat or by prescription should be excluded. Furthermore, there would seem to be no particular reason to father the doctrine of way of necessity upon public policy when implication is such an obvious and convenient candidate for paternity. There is an Australian case, *North Sydney Printing Pty. Ltd. v. Sabemo Investment Corporation Pty. Ltd.* [1971] 2 N.S.W.L.R. 150, where that conclusion was reached. Furthermore, I cannot accept that public policy can play any part at all in the construction of an instrument; in construing a document the court is endeavouring to ascertain the expressed intention of the parties. Public policy may require the court to frustrate that intention where the contract is against public policy, but in my view public policy cannot help the court to ascertain what that intention was. So I reach the view that a way of necessity is not founded upon public policy; that considerations of public policy cannot influence the construction of the 1906 conveyance; and that this action is not concerned with a way of necessity strictly so called.

This view has limited the scope of easements of necessity in a number of respects. Most obviously, an easement of necessity will give way to a contrary intention, but the intention-based nature of the rule has other consequences. For example, easements of necessity will not arise where land has been acquired by adverse possession or compulsory purchase where there is no agreement from which to derive any intention. The need for common ownership of the dominant and servient land, and the static assessment of necessity at the date of severance of the land, also flow from the constraints of intention.

Several commentators have argued that public policy is a more attractive foundation for easements of necessity. They argue that any intention of the parties is purely fictional,[85] and suggest that the rational development of the doctrine has been compromised by the focus upon intention rather than utility.[86]

Bradbrook, 'Access to Landlocked Land: A Comparative Study of Legal Solutions' (1983–85) 10 Syd LR 39

At 56

[A] guaranteed access to landlocked land could most easily be achieved in common law jurisdictions if the courts were to recognise public policy as the basis of the easement of necessity. This change would remove the limitations on the scope of easements [. . .] for

---

[85] Simonton, 'Ways by Necessity' (1925) 25 Col LR 571. 576 and 601; Jackson (1981) 34 CLP 133, 152; Bodkin (1973) 89 LQR 87.

[86] Bradbrook, 'Access to Landlocked Land: A Comparative Study of Legal Solutions' (1983–85) 10 Syd LR 39, 44–6; Davis, 'Informal Acquisition and Loss of Rights in Land: What Justifies the Doctrines?' (2000) 20 LS 198, 219; Lawson (2002) p 81.

example, if it were based upon public policy rather than intention of the parties it would not be restricted to cases where the landlocking arose on a subdivision, and in appropriate cases could be granted through private land belonging to third parties. While this change would run contrary to the recent Court of Appeal decision in *Nickerson v Barraclough*, it would not be revolutionary as the earliest reported cases on the easement of necessity appear to have accepted public policy rather than intention as the basis of the easements [. . .] The change to the present basis of intention did not occur until the nineteenth century and appears to have been due to the jurist tendency by the courts at that time to treat all legal transactions as if they were based on contracts.

3.2.2 Intended easements

The circumstances when an easement may be implied on the basis of intention were explained in the following case.

Pwllbach Colliery Co Ltd v Woodman
[1915] AC 634

Lord Parker

At 646

[. . .] the cases in which an easement can be granted by implication may be classified under two heads. The first is where the implication arises because the right in question is necessary for the enjoyment of some other right expressly granted [. . .] Thus the right of drawing water from a spring necessarily involves the right of going to the spring for the purpose. The implication suggested in the present case does not fall under this principle; there is no express grant of any right to which the right claimed must be necessarily ancillary, [. . .] The second class of cases in which easements may impliedly be created depends not upon the terms of the grant itself, but upon the circumstances under which the grant was made. The law will readily imply the grant or reservation of such easements as may be necessary to give effect to the common intention of the parties to a grant of real property, with reference to the manner or purposes in and for which the land granted or some land retained by the grantor is to be used [. . .] But it is essential for this purpose that the parties should intend that the subject of the grant or the land retained by the grantor should be used in some definite and particular manner. It is not enough that the subject of the grant or the land retained should be intended to be used in a manner which may or may not involve this definite and particular use.

Lord Parker identifies two circumstances: the first, where the easement is necessary for the enjoyment of a right that is expressly granted; the second, where the easement is necessary to enable the dominant owner to use the land for the purpose for which it was sold or leased. An example of the first instance is given by Lord Parker in the above extract and an example of the second instance is found in *Wong v Beaumont Property Trust Ltd*.[87] Mr Wong leased

---

[87] [1965] 1 QB 173. See also *Davies v Bramwell* [2007] EWCA Civ 821 and *Donovan v Rana* [2014] 1 P & CR 23.

the basement of a building to use as a Chinese restaurant. The lease provided that the basement should be used for this purpose, and, furthermore, that Mr Wong should control and eliminate all smells, comply with the required health regulations, and should not cause any nuisance to the landlord or adjoining occupiers. It became clear that the existing ventilation system was inadequate and a larger flue was required, but his landlords objected. An easement was implied to enable Mr Wong to comply with his obligations under the lease. In this second situation, it is clear that the implication does not arise because the parties necessarily intended that an easement be granted: it was clear in *Wong* that the parties had not anticipated the need for the larger flue, but they had made clear the intended use of the premise in the terms of the lease and it is from this intention that the right was implied.

Nourse LJ in the following case explains the process of proof being, firstly, to establish on a balance of probabilities the nature of the intended user, and secondly, to prove that the easement claimed is necessary to give effect to that use. In *Wong*, the parties had clearly expressed their intended use, but as the following case shows, the requisite intention may be established on a balance of probabilities.

Stafford v Lee
(1993) 63 P & CR 172, CA

Facts: In 1955, an area of woodland that fronted on a private drive was conveyed to Mrs Lee's predecessor in title, but no right of way was expressly granted over the drive. Mrs Lee wanted to build a house on the woodland, and claimed a pedestrian and vehicular right of way over the drive, on the basis that it was the intention of the parties to the 1955 conveyance that a house be built upon the woodland.

Nourse LJ

At 175

There are therefore two hurdles which the grantee must surmount. He must establish a common intention as to some definite and particular user. Then he must show that the easements he claims are necessary to give effect to it. Notwithstanding the submissions of Miss Baker, for the defendants, to the contrary, I think that the second hurdle is no great obstacle to the plaintiffs in this case. The real question is whether they can surmount the first.

It is axiomatic that in construing any conveyance you must take into account the facts in reference to which it was made. But here, no extrinsic evidence having been adduced on either side, we can refer only to the 1955 deed [. . .] The defendants admitted in their defence that the 1955 deed did pass to Mrs Walker a right to use Marley Drive and that that right had passed to the plaintiffs. But they have at all times contended that the right was limited to use for all purposes necessary for the reasonable enjoyment of the land as woodland, being the manner of its enjoyment in 1955. Such a right is manifestly inadequate for the plaintiffs' purposes.

The first point to be made about the defendants' contention is that, although it may sometimes come to the same thing, the material question in a case of an intended easement is not how was the land enjoyed in 1955, but did the parties to the 1955 deed intend that it should be used in some definite and particular manner and, if so, what? [. . .] The requirement that the parties should have intended a definite and particular use for the land does not require that the intention be proved as a certainty. As always, it is enough that it is proved on the balance of probabilities. What help do we get from the 1955 deed in this regard? First, it is to be observed that Mrs. Walker's address, far from being in the neighbourhood, is stated to be in distant Sussex. Secondly, and far more significantly, there is the plan [. . .]

The significant, indeed the eye-catching, feature of the plan here is that it delineates, as the land conveyed, a plot adjoining and of comparable area to two other enclosures, each adjoining the other, which, from the legends they bear, are seen to be plots of land on which dwellings have already been constructed. In these circumstances and given, as the defendants accept, that some appurtenant right of way was intended over and along Marley Drive, what are the probabilities as to the intended use of the land? In my judgment, on the balance of probabilities, the parties can only have intended that it should be used for the construction of another dwelling to be used thereafter for residential purposes. I cannot see what other intention could reasonably be imputed to them. Having got to that point, I am satisfied that the easements claimed by the plaintiffs and declared in their favour by the judge are necessary, and are no more than are necessary, to give effect to the intention so established.

Lawson points out that there is a third situation in which an intended easement may be implied, which, although broadly based upon *Pwllbach*, is distinguishable from an easement of intended use.[88] This third category is derived from the following case, in which the Court indicated that a reservation[89] could be implied, based upon the parties' intention—although here it is the parties' intention as to creation of the right itself.

The case concerned an implied reservation, which is less readily implied then an easement—the rationale being that the grantor should avoid the risk of derogating from his or her grant by taking care to expressly reserve any rights that he or she wishes to enjoy. Jenkins LJ explains in the case that although a reservation will not generally be implied, there are exceptions: we have already considered easements of necessity; another exception is intended easements.

Re Webb's Lease
[1951] Ch 808, CA

Facts: Webb ran a butchers shop on the ground floor of a building that he leased in south London. He sublet the upper floors, on the external walls of which advertisements were displayed. For many years, the tenant of the upper floors raised no objection to these advertisements, but he then demanded payment for them to be retained.

Jenkins LJ

At 823

As to the law applicable to the case, it is not disputed that as a general rule a grantor, whether by conveyance or lease, of part of a hereditament in his ownership, cannot

---

88 Lawson (2002) p 83.

89 The case concerns a reservation, but there seems no reason why the grant of an easement should not also be implied under this third category, although there have been no such cases. Lawson (2002) p 85 explains that other grounds for the implication of the grant of an easement present more attractive options.

claim any easement over the part retained unless it is expressly reserved out of the grant [. . .] There are however, certain exceptions to the general rule. Two well-established exceptions relate to easements of necessity and mutual easements such as rights of support between adjacent buildings. But it is recognised in the authorities that these two specific exceptions do not exhaust the list which is indeed incapable of exhaustive statement, as the circumstances of any particular case may be such as to raise a necessary inference that the common intention of the parties must have been to reserve some easement to the grantor, or such as to preclude the grantee from denying the right consistently with good faith, and there appears to be no doubt that where circumstances such as these are clearly established the court will imply the appropriate reservation.

The question arises as to how the courts are to find this intention. In *Re Webb's Lease*, Jenkins LJ went on to state that the appropriate test was one of necessary inference, based upon proof by the landlord that the facts were not reasonably consistent with any other explanation—a test that Mr Webb failed to satisfy.[90]

Re Webb's Lease
[1951] Ch 808, CA

Jenkins LJ

At 828

The question is whether the circumstances of the case as proved in evidence are such as to raise a necessary inference that the common intention of the parties was to reserve to the landlord during the twenty-one years' term some, and if so what, rights in regard to the display of advertisements over the outer walls of the demised premises, or such as to preclude the tenant from denying the implied reservation to the landlord of some such rights consistently with good faith.

That question must be approached with the following principles in mind: (i) If the landlord intended to reserve any such rights over the demised premises it was his duty to reserve them expressly in the lease of August 11, 1949 (*Wheeldon v. Burrows*); (ii) The landlord having failed in this duty, the onus was upon him to establish the facts to prove, and prove clearly, that his case was an exception to the rule (*Aldridge v. Wright*); (iii) The mere fact that the tenant knew at the date of the lease of August 11, 1949, that the landlord was using the outer walls of the demised premises for the display of the advertisements in question did not suffice to absolve the landlord from his duty of expressly reserving any rights in respect of them he intended to claim, or to take the case out of the general rule [. . .]

Does this circumstance suffice to raise a necessary inference of an intention common to both parties at the date of the lease that the landlord should have reserved to him the right to maintain these advertisements throughout the twenty-one years' term thereby

---

[90] The test was also not satisfied in *Chaffe v Kingsley* (2000) 79 P & CR 404, but was met in *Peckham v Ellison* (2000) 79 P & CR 276 and *Collins v Collins* [2016] P&CR 6. The former decision has been criticized: see Fox [1999] Conv 353.

> granted? I cannot see that it does. The most that can be said is that the facts are consistent with such a common intention. But that will not do. The landlord must surely show at least that the facts are not reasonably consistent with any other explanation. Here he manifestly fails.

There is considerable uncertainty as to the interface between easements of necessity and of intention. They seem to overlap, but it is clear that intended easements may be applied to a wider range of rights.

Lawson advocates realigning the categories, with easements of intended use ('*Pwllbach* easements') encompassing and taking over from easements of necessity, and intended easements being confined to those based upon the parties' intention to create such rights ('*Re Webb's Lease* easements').

Lawson, 'Easements' in *Land Law: Issues, Debates and Policy* (ed Tee, 2002, p 85)

[. . .] there is a great deal of uncertainty about the precise relationship between easements of necessity and *Pwllbach easements*. In *Nickerson v Barrowclough* Megarry V-C seemed to regard them as 'two distinct but overlapping' ways in which easements might be implied on the basis of necessity. Both require the right to be strictly necessary for the use of the land concerned. The distinction is that for easements of necessity the right must be necessary in order for the land to be used in any manner at all, whereas for intended easements the right must be necessary in order for the land to be used in the particular manner intended by the parties.

The distinction between easements of necessity and the *Pwllbach* intended easements is frequently clouded by a judicial tendency to refer to both as easements of necessity. It may be that, in any event, it is a distinction without a difference. It is arguable that, as the courts are now prepared to imply a common intention to use the land in a specific way, they will be able to find such an intention whenever landlocked plot is conveyed—thus eclipsing the traditional easements of necessity. The precise limits of the situations in which the courts are prepared to find that there is an implied intention to use the land in a particular way have not yet been fully explored, however. It is suggested, for instance that a court will not be as inclined to find that a use was intended in the case of a reservation as it is in relation to a grant.

The view that the easement of necessity, at least in relation to implied grant, has been subsumed within the *Pwllbach* intended easement is very attractive. Both are driven by the policy that land should not become sterile but be used to its full potential. Though intention is relevant to both, neither requires proof that the parties actually intended the claimed easement. The *Pwllbach* easement could drop the misleading title of 'intended easements' and become a legitimate easement of necessity. The title 'intended easement' could, instead, be reserved for easements implied under *Re Webbs Lease*. These do not require the easement to be necessary for the land to be used and are therefore quite distinct.

3.2.3 The rule in *Wheeldon v Burrows*

The rule in *Wheeldon v Burrows* is stated by Thesiger LJ in the case of that name.

Wheeldon v Burrows
(1879) 12 LR Ch D 31

Thesiger LJ

At 49

[. . .] on the grant by the owner of a tenement or part of that tenement as it is then used and enjoyed, there will pass to the grantee all those continuous and apparent easements (by which, of course, I mean quasi easements) or, in other words, all those easements which are necessary for the reasonable enjoyment of the property granted, and which have been and are at the time of the grant used by the owner of the entirety for the benefit of the part granted.

The rule thus applies on the sale or lease of part of property when certain qualifying rights, enjoyed for the benefit of the part sold or leased (the dominant land) over the part retained (the servient land), will mature into easements. Prior to the sale or lease, such rights could not exist as easements, because of the common ownership of the dominant and servient land; they are thus referred to as 'quasi-easements'.

The rule is based upon the intention of the parties that the grantor should not derogate from his or her grant and thus gives way to a contrary intention. The rule only applies to the grant of easements, or where the sales of the dominant and servient land are simultaneous.[91] It does not operate to imply a reservation; indeed, this was the point at issue in *Wheeldon v Burrows*,[92] and is referred to as the 'second rule in *Wheeldon v Burrows*', found later in Thesiger LJ's judgment.

Wheeldon v Burrows
(1879) 12 LR Ch D 31

Thesiger LJ

At 58–9

These cases [. . .] support the propositions that in the case of a grant you may imply a grant of such continuous and apparent easements or such easements as are necessary to the reasonable enjoyment of the property conveyed, and have in fact been enjoyed during the unity of ownership, but that, with the exception which I referred to of easements of necessity, you cannot imply a similar reservation in favour of the grantor of land.

---

[91] *Schwann v Cotton* [1916] 2 Ch 120. See also *Donaldson v Smith* [2006] All ER (D) 293, [16], *per* Donaldson QC, measuring simultaneity in context to look not solely at chronological proximity, but also at the interconnection between the two transactions.

[92] Burrows was seeking a right to light from land owned by Wheeldon, after a hoarding was erected that blocked the light to Burrows' workshop. Burrows and Wheeldon had acquired their land from a common vendor, with Burrows purchasing his land after Wheeldon.. Any rights that Burrows wished to claim over Wheeldon's land would, thus, have to be reserved by their common vendor—but there had been no express reservation and thus Burrows' claim failed.

Only certain quasi-easements qualify to pass under the rule. They must be enjoyed at the time of the sale or lease, be 'continuous and apparent', and/or be reasonably necessary for the enjoyment of the property.

The first requirement is relatively straightforward. It imposes a timing constraint on the application of the rule that flows from the principle of non-derogation from grant.[93] It is the second and third requirements, and their interrelationship, that has led to the greatest uncertainty and debate.

The second requirement has its origins in the French Civil Code.[94] 'Continuous', in this context, does not mean that the right must be continuously exercised, but rather invokes the sense of permanence, so that the right might be exercised whenever necessary. 'Apparent' is the more significant part of the second requirement. Indeed, it has been suggested that *'continuousness is little more than a distraction'* and could be jettisoned.[95] For a right to be apparent, it should be discoverable from a reasonably careful physical inspection of the land. There must thus be some feature on the servient land—for example, a roadway or manhole cover—that signals the right to a purchaser.

Ward v Kirkland
[1967] Ch 194, HC

Facts: The Wards' cottage adjoined Kirkland's farm, which, at one time, had been owned by a common owner. The cottage was built so close to the farm's boundary that the only practical way for its walls to be maintained was to go onto the farm. The Wards and their predecessor in title had done so for some time before Kirkland objected.

Ungoed-Thomas J

At 225

Here, there certainly has been continuous user, in the sense that the right has in fact been used whenever the need arose. But the words "continuous and apparent" seem to be directed to there being on the servient tenement a feature which would be seen on inspection and which is neither transitory nor intermittent; for example, drains, paths, as contrasted with the bowsprits of ships overhanging a piece of land.

Here it is conceded that it was only possible or practicable for the occupiers of the cottage to maintain the boundary wall by going onto the defendant's property as claimed in this case. That would be obvious on an inspection of the properties. But there was no feature on the defendant's property designed or appropriated for such maintenance ... . It seems to me that in the absence of a continuous and apparent feature designed or appropriate for the exercise of the easement on the servient tenement, there is not a continuous and apparent easement within the requirements of Wheeldon v. Burrows in the case of alleged positive easements. I, therefore, come to the conclusion that the easement claimed was not created by implication of law.

---

[93] *Sovmots Investment Ltd v Secretary of State for the Environment* [1979] AC 144.
[94] Simpson, '*Wheeldon v Burrows* and the *Code Civile*' [1967] 83 LQR 240.
[95] Lawson (2002) p 88.

The third requirement calls for the right to be necessary for the reasonable enjoyment of the land and flows directly from the principle that the grantor should not derogate from his or her grant. 'Necessity', in this context, is significantly wider than the test demanded of easements of necessity, although the degree of necessity is unclear.

Thompson bemoans this uncertainty and advocates a test that merely calls for the right to be capable of being an easement by accommodating the dominant land.

Thompson, 'Paths and Pigs' [1995] Conv 239, 240–1

What appears to be necessary is that, to acquire an easement under *Wheeldon v. Burrows*, the right in question must do more than merely accommodate the dominant tenement but need not be an absolute necessity. Rather, it hovers somewhere in between, at some ill-defined point between the two. The difference between what is essential for the land to be used and what is necessary for its reasonable use is not an easy one to draw and, in consequence, it may, in the future, prove difficult to predict when a quasi-easement will be transformed into a full easement under the rule.

[. . .] [I]t would seem preferable that the second limb of *Wheeldon v. Burrows* should be interpreted to mean, in essence, that the right claimed accommodates the dominant tenement; the same requirement as exists when section 62 is in issue.

The uncertainty is illustrated by cases in which an alternative means of access is claimed to be reasonably necessary for the enjoyment of the land. An existing means of access will not be fatal to a claim under *Wheeldon v Burrows*, but it is evident that simply providing a more convenient access is unlikely to be enough:[96] the alternative access should offer some additional advantage.[97] The impact upon the servient land of the additional access should also be considered.[98]

A question that has dogged debate on *Wheeldon v Burrows* is whether the second and third requirements are synonymous, alternative, or cumulative. The authorities are not conclusive.[99] Douglas suggest that the 'question is misplaced … [because] the two elements of the "rule" are really just different types of evidence that a court must consider when trying to ascertain the unexpressed intention of the grantor'[100] nevertheless the case for a cumulative interpretation has strong advocates.[101]

---

[96] See *Goldberg v Edwards* [1950] Ch 247 and *Wheeler v Saunders* [1996] Ch 19.

[97] See *Borman v Griffith* [1930] 1 Ch 493, in which the alternative access was more suitable for the claimant's business as a poultry dealer, the other access being impassable to heavy vehicles at certain times of the year; *Millman v Ellis* (1995) 71 P & CR 158, 163, in which the right to use a lay-by to join a busy road was held to be reasonably necessary as '*a matter concerned with safety and possible injury to life and limb*'.

[98] Ferris, 'Problems Postponed: The Rule in *Wheeldon v Burrows* and *Wheeler v Saunders*' (1996) 3 Web JCLI.

[99] See *Hansford v Jargo* [1921] 1 Ch 322, 338, *per* Russel J; *Borman v Griffith* [1930] 1 Ch 493, 499, *per* Maugham J; *Ward v Kirkland* [1967] Ch 194, [224]–[225], *per* Ungoed Thomas J; *Savmots v Investments Ltd v Secretary of State for the Environment* [1979] AC 145, 169, *per* Lord Wilberforce, and 175, *per* Lord Edmund-Davies; *Squarrey v Harris Smith* (1981) 42 P & CR 118, 124, *per* Oliver LJ; *Wheeler v Saunders* [1996] Ch 19, 31, *per* Peter Gibson LJ.

[100] Douglas, 'Reforming Implied Easements' [2015] 131 LQR 251.

[101] See also Harpum, 'Easements and Centre Point: Old Problems Resolved in a Novel Setting' (1977) 41 Conv 415, 422, who points out that the two limbs of the rule have separate functions: one that facilitates discovery and the other derived from non-derogation from grant.

Gardner & MacKenzie, *An Introduction to Land Law* (2015, p323)

> [. . .] [T]he rule in *Wheeldon v Burrows* [. . .] actually generates an easement, by imputing an intention to confer it. And the existence of a continuous and apparent quasi-easement alone is an inadequate basis on which to do this. The imputation is acceptable only when the additional utilitarian argument for it is sufficiently powerful. The fact that I visibly did something in the past may contribute to the making of such an argument, by giving a prima facie indication that the alleged easement would be useful. But to complete the argument, the easement must be positively needed: as the law has it, 'necessary for the reasonable enjoyment' of the land transferred. Perhaps for this reason, although the relevant case law is in disarray, the majority of commentators agree that this third requirement is essential.

However, this debate is of less significance when we take into account the recent developments under the next route by which easements may be created.

3.2.4 Law of Property Act 1925, s 62

Law of Property Act 1925, s 62(1)[102]

> (1) A conveyance of land shall be deemed to include and shall by virtue of this Act operate to convey, with the land, all buildings, erections, fixtures, commons, hedges, ditches, fences, ways, waters, watercourses, liberties, privileges, easements, rights, and advantages whatsoever, appertaining or reputed to appertain to the land or any part thereof, or, at the time of conveyance, demised, occupied, or enjoyed with, or reputed or known as part or parcel of or appurtenant to the land or any part thereof.

Section 62(4) of the LPA 1925 provides that the '*section applies only if and as far as a contrary intention is not expressed in the conveyance*'.[103]

The section was conceived as a word-saving device by implying what is known as a 'general words clause' into conveyances of land, with the object of ensuring that, on a sale or other disposal, all rights and privileges appurtenant to the land at the time of the conveyance will pass without express mention.[104] It can only operate where there has been the creation or transfer of a legal right in a deed—that is, a conveyance.[105] Judicial interpretation of the section has, however, extended its operation: not only will the section pass existing easements, but it will also operate to upgrade a mere permission into a full-fledged legal easement. In effect, the informality of the original permission is cured by the formality of the subsequent conveyance, which is '*deemed to include and shall [. . .] operate to convey*'

---

[102] Replacing Conveyancing Act 1881, s 6.

[103] *Selby DC v Samuel Smith Old Brewery (Tadcaster) Ltd* (2000) 80 P & CR 466; *P&S Platt Ltd v Crouch* [2003] EWCA Civ 1110.

[104] Legal easements pass automatically, without express mention, and thus the primary focus was upon equitable and quasi-easements. It was conveyancing practice to include an express general words clause.

[105] In contrast to *Wheeldon v Burrows*, which may operate at the contractual stage: see *Borman v Griffith* [1930] 1 Ch 493.

the right. It is this aspect of the section that we must explore further, as a means of implied grant.[106]

Farwell J first held that this was the effect of what is now s 62 of the 1925 Act[107] in the following case.

International Tea Stores Co v Hobbs
[1903] 2 Ch 165

Facts: Hobbs was a blacksmith who let the shop adjoining his forge to the claimants and allowed them to use a private road, which formed part of the forge, to access the rear of the shop. The claimants subsequently bought the shop from Hobbs, who tried to prevent them from using the road. They successfully claimed that the privilege that they had enjoyed to use the road had become an easement by virtue of the implied general words. Farwell J rejected as immaterial the fact that the privilege was enjoyed merely by permission; it was only significant that they had used the road.

Farwell J

At 171

But, in my opinion, precariousness has nothing to do with this sort of case, where a privilege which is by its nature known to the law—namely, a right of way—has been in fact enjoyed [. . .] The real truth is that you do not consider the question of title to use, but the question of fact of user; you have to inquire whether the way has in fact been used, not under what title has it been used, although you must of course take into consideration all the circumstances of the case [. . .]

Farewell's views were indorsed by the Court of Appeal in the following case, in which the Court also set out the other characteristics of the rights that come within the section.

Wright v Macadam
[1949] 2 KB 744, CA

Facts: Wright was a weekly tenant of two rooms on the top floor of Macadam's house when Macadam gave her permission to use the coal shed at the bottom of the garden to store coal. Subsequently, Wright took a new tenancy of the two rooms, plus another room; the tenancy agreement contained no reference to the use of the coal shed, which Wright continued to use until Macadam asked her to pay for the privilege. Wright refused and successfully claimed that she had an easement to use the coal shed by virtue of s 62 of the 1925 Act.

---

[106] Section 62 is sometimes categorized as giving rise to an express grant because the right is read into the conveyance. It is perhaps more convenient to view the grant as implied, given that it does not need to be completed by registration: see Land Registration Act 2002, s 27(7).

[107] The provision was previously comprised in s 6 of the Convenyancing Act 1881.

Jenkins LJ

At 748

First, the section is not confined to rights which, as a matter of law, were so annexed or appurtenant to the property conveyed at the time of the conveyance as to make them actual legally enforceable rights. Thus, on the severance of a piece of land in common ownership, the quasi easements de facto enjoyed in respect of it by one part of the land over another will pass although, of course, as a matter of law, no man can have a right appendant or appurtenant to one part of his property exerciseable by him over the other part of his property. Secondly, the right, in order to pass, need not be one to which the owner or occupier for the time being of the land has had what may be described as a permanent title. A right enjoyed merely by permission is enough. The leading authority for that proposition is the case of *International Tea Stores Co. v. Hobbs* [. . .]

At 750

There is, therefore, ample authority for the proposition that a right in fact enjoyed with property will pass on a conveyance of the property by virtue of the grant to be read into it under s. 62, even although down to the date of the conveyance the right was exercised by permission only, and therefore was in that sense precarious.

The next proposition deducible from the cases is the one laid down in *Burrows v. Lang* [1912] 2 Ch 502, which has been referred to in some of the passages I have already read. It is that the right in question must be a right known to the law [. . .] It is necessary to keep clearly in mind the distinction between "precariousness" in the sense in which it is used in relation to quasi rights of that description, and precariousness of title as used in relation to a permissively exercised right. For the purposes of s. 62, it is only necessary that the right should be one capable of being granted at law, or, in other words, a right known to the law. If it is a right of that description it matters not, as the *International Tea Stores case* shows, that it has been in fact enjoyed by permission only. The reason for that is clear, for, on the assumption that the right is included or imported into the parcels of the conveyance by virtue of s. 62, the grant under the conveyance supplies what one may call the defect in title, and substitutes a new title based on the grant.

There is one other point to be mentioned. A further exception has been recognized in cases in which there could in the circumstances of the case have been no expectation that the enjoyment of the right could be other than temporary. [A]pplying the principles [. . .] to the present case one finds, I think, this. First of all, on the evidence the coal shed was used by Mrs. Wright by the permission of Mr. Macadam, but *International Tea Stores Co. v. Hobbs* shows that that does not prevent s. 62 from applying, because permissive as the right may have been it was in fact enjoyed.

Next, the right was, as I understand it, a right to use the coal shed in question for the purpose of storing such coal as might be required for the domestic purposes of the flat. In my judgment that is a right or easement which the law will clearly recognize, and it is a right or easement of a kind which could readily be included in a lease or conveyance by the insertion of appropriate words in the parcels. This, therefore, is not a case in which a title to a right unknown to the law is claimed by virtue of s. 62. Nor is it a case in which it can be said to have been in the contemplation of the parties that the enjoyment of the right should be purely temporary. No limit was set as to the time during which the coal shed could continue to be used. Mr. Macadam simply gave his permission; that permission was acted on; and the use of the coal shed in fact went on down to August 28, 1943, and thereafter down to 1947.

Therefore, applying to the facts of the present case the principles which seem to be deducible from the authorities, the conclusion to which I have come is that the right to use the
coal shed was at the date of the letting of August 28, 1943, a right enjoyed with the top floor
flat within the meaning of s. 62 of the Law of Property Act, 1925, with the result that (as no
contrary intention was expressed in the document) the right in question must be regarded as
having passed by virtue of that letting, just as it would have passed if it had been mentioned
in express terms in cl. 1, which sets out the subject-matter of the lease.

This '*metamorphosis from personal to property right*'[108] has been subject to criticism,[109] and
the Law Commission has recommended that this aspect of s 62 should be abrogated.[110]

Tee suggests the Court's reasoning in *Wright v Macadam* is faulty because the word 'right'
within the section is being used to encompass two different meanings. First, it is used in the
sense of a legal or equitable property right and secondly as 'the negative and precarious right
not to be sued in trespass before the permission is revoked';[111] for instance, Mrs Wright's
defence to an action for trespass for using the shed to store her coal. This second sense does
not constitute a property right and thus she maintains should not be construed as a privilege appurtenant to land within the meaning of s 62 and, therefore, should not benefit from
the 'uplift' effect ascribed to the section. However, Douglas disagrees.[112] He suggests that,
as a word saving provision reflecting conveyancing practice, the section was intended to
incorporate both formally created property rights 'appertaining … or appurtenant to the
land' and factual but extinct rights or informally conferred permissions that either were
'reputed … to appertain' or were 'occupied, or enjoyed with' the dominant land. The 'uplift'
effect of the section was thus intentional and he maintains entirely reasonable. Nevertheless,
he agrees that reform is justified given the dangers the section presents to parties who do not
appreciate its potential 'uplift' effect.

Douglas, How to Reform Section 62 of the Law of Property Act 1925'
[2015] Conv 13

Section 62 was drafted in broader terms, however, referring to both rights 'reputed' to
appertain, and 'occupied, or enjoyed with' the land. As we have seen, these words have
a wider meaning. They allow s.62 to be understood as an undertaking not just to transfer
existing easements, but to create new ones that reflect the past usage of the land. The
criticism of the s.62 uplift, that it results from a misconstruction of the words in the section,
cannot be maintained. The uplift is a consequence of an entirely reasonable interpretation
of the words in the section[. . .]When parties are aware of the operation of s.62, yet do not
exclude it from the conveyance, then the 'uplift' can be said to be an intended consequence.

---

[108] Tee, 'Metamorphoses and Section 62 of the Law of Property Act 1925' [1998] Conv 115, 115.
[109] See, for instance, judicial criticism in *Wright v Macadam* [1949] 2 KB 744, [755], *per* Tucker LJ; *Green
v Ashco Horticulturist Ltd* [1966] 1 WLR 889, [897], *per* Cross J; *Hair v Gillman* (2000) 80 P & CR 108, 116,
per Chadwick LJ; *Commission for the New Towns v Gallagher* [2002] EWHC 2668, (2003) 2 P & CR 24, [61],
per Neuberger J.
[110] Reform has been advocated by the Law Commission since 1971. Its most recent recommendation is
found in Law Com 327 (2011), [3.64].
[111] Tee, 'Metamorphoses and Section 62 of the Law of Property Act 1925' [1998] Conv 115 at 123.
[112] Douglas, 'How to reform Section 62 of the law of Property Act 1925 [2015] Conv 13.

Conversely, when parties are unaware of the section, it is not possible to say that any resulting easement is an intended outcome. This conclusion is significant as it demonstrates the potential of s.62 to impose an unconvenanted burden upon the grantor of the land. In this respect, therefore, the Law Commission's criticism of the s.62 uplift is justified, and it is a legitimate target of statutory reform.

Section 62 may thus operate to create an easement where the dominant and servient land are in common ownership, and the dominant land is sold or leased in circumstances under which an informal right has been enjoyed by the purchaser or tenant over the servient land retained by the seller or landlord. It cannot operate to create an implied reservation where the servient land is sold or leased.[113] In this respect, it looks similar to *Wheeldon v Burrows*, but there are distinctions:

- s 62 requires a conveyance by deed to create/transfer a legal estate, but *Wheeldon v Burrows* may operate upon the creation/transfer of an equitable interest;
- the nature of the rights that are capable of passing as easements under s 62 are wider than those that can pass under *Wheeldon v Burrows*.

It had also been thought that *Wheeldon v Burrows* and s 62 operated in different situations: *Wheeldon v Burrows* where there is common ownership and occupation of the dominant and servient land; and s 62 where there is diversity of occupation of the dominant and servient land. Perhaps the most usual scenario for the operation of s 62 was upon the renewal of a lease (as in *Wright v Macadam*) where the landlord is in occupation of the servient land and the tenant in occupation of the dominant land.[114] However, it seems as though this distinction is no longer correct.

Diversity of occupation

Section 62 of the LPA 1925 calls for the right to be appurtenant to the dominant land. This requirement led to a divergence of opinion. On one view the requirement called for diversity of occupation between the dominant and servient land since it was argued that where the dominant and servient land are in common ownership and occupation, the rights exercised over the servient land are exercised by virtue of the occupier's ownership of servient land and not by virtue of any right appurtenant to the dominant land. This was the approach adopted in *Long v Gowlett*[115] when Sargant J stated:

At 199

As it seems to me, in order that there may be a "privilege, easement or advantage" enjoyed with Whiteacre over Blackacre so as to pass under the statute, there must be

---

[113] *Kent v Kavanagh* [2006] EWCA Civ 162, [2007] Ch 1. An implied reservation may arise upon enfranchisement under Leasehold Reform Act 1967, ss 8 and 10.

[114] Other possible scenarios include when a privilege granted to a tenant is followed by their acquisition of the freehold reversion, see *International Tea Stores Co v Hobbs* [1903] 2 Ch 165; upon leasehold enfranchisement, see *Kent v Kavanagh*, ibid; or where a privilege has been granted to a purchaser who entered into occupation before the seller executed the formal conveyance of the land, see *Goldberg v Edwards* [1950] Ch 247, 256 and *Green v Ashco Horticulturist Ltd* [1966] 1 WLR 889, [898].

[115] [1923] 2 Ch 177.

something done on Blackacre not due to or comprehended within the general rights of an occupying owner of Blackacre, but of such a nature that it is attributable to a privilege, easement, right or advantage, however precarious, which arises out of the ownership or occupation of Whiteacre, altogether apart from the ownership or occupation of Blackacre. And it is difficult to see how, when there is a common ownership of both Whiteacre and Blackacre, there can be any such relationship between the two closes as (apart from the case of continuous and apparent easements or that of a way of necessity) would be necessary to create a "privilege, easement, right or advantage" within the words ..., of the statute. For this purpose it would seem that there must be some diversity of ownership or occupation of the two closes sufficient to refer the act or acts relied on not to mere occupying ownership, but to some advantage or privilege (however far short of a legal right) attaching to the owner or occupier of Whiteacre as such and de facto exercised over Blackacre.

Long v Gowlett was a controversial decision,[116] but was cited with approval by the House of Lords in *Sovmots Investment Ltd v Secretary of State for the Environment*[117] and followed in *Kent v Kavanagh*.[118] Nevertheless, uncertainty continued to rumble.[119] The following decision by the Court of Appeal has tried to settle the controversy by holding that diversity of occupation is not a requirement for an easement to be created under s 62 provided the right is 'continuous and apparent' in the sense that we have already explored in *Wheeldon v Burrows*.

Wood v Waddington
[2015] EWCA Civ 538

Facts: Mr Crook owned Manor Farm which was crossed by various tracks and bridleways. He sold Manor Farm in parts in 1998. One part was acquired by the Woods' predecessor in title, the Sharmans, who ran a horse livery stables, which was carried on and expanded by the Woods. Another part of Manor Farm over which some tracks and bridleway ran was sold to Mr Waddington. A dispute arose between the parties as to whether the Woods were entitled to use two tracks over land now owned by Mr Waddington.

Held: The Woods were entitled to use the tracks over Mr Waddington's land by virtue of the rights having passing under s 62 when Mr Crook sold the land to the Woods' predecessor in title. Although there was unity of occupation between the servient and dominant land by Mr Crook, the right to use to tracks and bridleway was continuous and apparent.

---

[116] Harpum, 'Easements and Centre Point: Old Problems Resolved in a Novel Setting' (1977) 41 Conv 415; Smith, 'Centre Point: Faulty Towers with Shaky Foundations' [1978] Conv 449; Harpum, '*Long v Gowlett*: A Strong Fortress' [1979] Conv 113.

[117] [1979] AC 144, [176], but see [42].   [118] [2007] Ch 1 at 43–7 *per* Chadwick LJ.

[119] See the Court of Appeal decisions in *P&S Platt Ltd v Crouch* [2003] EWCA Civ 1110, [2004] 1 P & CR 18, *Alford v Hannaford* [2011] EWCA Civ 1099; *Campbell v Banks* [2011] EWCA Civ 61 in which confusion with the rule in *Wheeldon v Burrows* continues. A further appeal on the issue is pending in *Wood v Waddington* [2014] EWHC 1358.

Lewison LJ

At [24]–[37]

The second way of putting the case was based on section 62 of the Law of Property Act 1925 [. . .]

Consideration of that section required the judge to make findings of fact about the way in which the claimed rights had been used in the period leading up to the transfer to Mr and Mrs Sharman. That was because section 62 only applies to advantages etc. "enjoyed with" the land at the time of conveyance although, as the judge rightly accepted, "the time of conveyance" includes a reasonable period before the conveyance. Before the transfers to Mr and Mrs Sharman on the one hand and Mr Waddington on the other all the relevant land had been occupied by Mr Crook. Accordingly there had been no "diversity of occupation". Diversity of occupation helps to distinguish between cases where a landowner is simply making use of the whole of this land as he pleases, and cases where a particular use can be discerned as being in the nature of an easement (or quasi-easement) enjoyed for the benefit of a particular part of the land. However, although the usual circumstances in which section 62 applies are cases where there has been diversity of occupation, the judge held at [131] that there was no absolute bar to the operation of section 62 even where there has been no diversity of occupation. He said:

"... a right, such as a right of way, can pass under section 62 even where there has been no diversity of occupation, provided always that the right was continuous and apparent."

In reaching that conclusion the judge referred to the decision of this court in *Alford v Hannaford [2011] EWCA Civ 1099* in which Patten LJ said:

"... where there has not been diversity of occupation prior to the sale, the generally held view is that s.62 can only operate to grant easements over the land retained by the vendor where the exercise of the relevant rights has been continuous and apparent in the sense described in *Wheeldon v Burrows* ."

Having considered how the concept of "continuous and apparent" easements had been deployed in the context of the rule in *Wheeldon v Burrows* the judge said at [132]:

"However, in that context, the phrase 'continuous and apparent' does not stand alone as it operates in conjunction with a requirement that the right claimed is necessary for the reasonable enjoyment of the land conveyed. This further requirement helps to identify the relationship of dominance and servience between the land conveyed and the land retained. Further, the phrase 'continuous and apparent' on its own has been considered to be lacking in clarity: see *Dalton v Angus (1881) 6 App Cas 740* at 821 per Lord Blackburn. If the phrase 'continuous and apparent' is to be used as a proxy for the statutory words 'enjoyed with', then (in the context of section 62) what must be apparent is that the advantage claimed is enjoyed with the land to be conveyed rather than enjoyed as part of the common ownership of both the land to be conveyed and the land to be retained."

The judge concluded at [133]:

"There is no absolute rule that a right of way cannot be claimed under section 62 where there has not been diversity of occupation before the relevant conveyance. The ultimate question is whether the advantage in question was, on the facts, "enjoyed with" the land conveyed. Those words require two things to be shown. The advantage must have been "enjoyed" in the period before the conveyance. Further, the advantage must have been enjoyed "with" the land conveyed so that, after the conveyance, it will be appurtenant to the land conveyed as the dominant tenement. For these purposes, a consideration of how the advantage was actually used and whether it was apparently for the benefit of the land conveyed and apparently a burden on the land retained will be of great importance." [. . .]

Mr Gaunt QC argued that the judge was right at [132] to say that it must be *apparent* that the enjoyment is for the benefit of the land conveyed; otherwise (unless there is diversity of occupation) there is no reliable way of distinguishing between an owner's right to use his land as he pleases and a continuous and apparent easement that will pass under section 62 . [. . .] In our case, he says, Mr Crook's use of the various tracks was simply a case of a land owner making use of the whole of his land as he pleased. However, the second sentence of the quoted extract is both immediately preceded and immediately followed by the express exclusion of cases in which there is a made road or a continuous and apparent easement. That is the context in which the second sentence must be read; and in my judgment it is not concerned with cases where there is a made road or other continuous and apparent easement.

What is important is the extent to which there are visible signs of a track or road. In *Bayley v Great Western Railway (1884) 26 Ch. D. 434* at [456] Fry LJ put the point of principle thus:

"... if one person owns both Whiteacre and Blackacre, and if there be a made and visible road over Whiteacre, and that has been used for the purpose of Blackacre in such a way that if two tenements belonged to several owners there would have been an easement in favour of Blackacre over Whiteacre, and the owner aliened Blackacre to a purchaser, retaining Whiteacre, then the grant of Blackacre either 'with all rights usually enjoyed with it' or 'with all rights appertaining to Blackacre,' or probably the mere grant of Blackacre itself without general words, carries a right of way over Whiteacre."

A "made" road, however, is not essential. In *Hansford v Jago [1921] Ch. 322* Russell J said:

"Now what is required in the case of a quasi-easement is the quality of being apparent. That quality may be arrived at in different ways, and, no doubt, the easiest case is that of a made-up road; it is most important, if not essential, that the road should be made up when it is sought to establish the apparency of a quasi-easement of way over an unenclosed piece of land. But when every other possible indication is present as here and they all point to a defined and enclosed strip having been set aside to provide an access to the rear of certain houses, I certainly decline to hold, unless compelled to do so by authority, that the absence of a made-up road prevented the establishment of an implied grant."

Russell J referred also to Donnelly v Adams [1905] 1 IR 154, a case in the Irish Court of Appeal in which Fitzgibbon LJ said:

"I admit that neither by express nor by implied grant can a vague or uncertain right be created. Every lawful way must be capable of identification; it must have a *terminus a quo*, and a *terminus ad quem*. But it is not essential to a way that there shall be a beaten track between its *termini*."

Both *Bayley v Great Western Railway* and *Hansford v Jago* were cited to Sargant J in *Long v Gowlett* ; and *Bayley v Great Western Railway* was mentioned expressly in his judgment ([1923] 2 Ch. 177,179). I do not consider that *Long v Gowlett* can be taken as having added an extra requirement to what those cases decided. I agree, therefore, with Patten LJ in *Alford v Hannaford* that in cases where there has been no diversity of occupation, all that is necessary to establish is that the exercise of the relevant rights has been continuous and apparent in the sense developed for the purposes of the rule in *Wheeldon v Burrows*.

It is common ground that, for the purposes of section 62, if a quasi-easement falls within the category of easements "enjoyed with" the land conveyed, there is no additional requirement that such an easement must be *necessary* for the reasonable enjoyment of the land: Watts v Kelson (1871) 6 Ch App 166. In this respect section 62 differs from and is broader than the rule in *Wheeldon v Burrows*. It is difficult to see how Mr and Mrs Wood could succeed under the rule in *Wheeldon v Burrows* if they fail under section 62. Since the rule in *Wheeldon v Burrows* is concerned with implication, while section 62 operates by way of express grant that is, perhaps, not surprising.

In order to reach a conclusion about the applicability of section 62 it is necessary to consider both the features observable on the ground at the date of the conveyances in 1998 and the use made of the claimed rights.

This decision is not without its problems. Simon Gardner questions the role of "continuous and apparent" in the unity of occupation situation particularly where the right claimed was originally conferred as a personal privilege.

Gardner, 'The Grant of an Easement under the Law of Property Act 1925 section 62' (2016) LQR 192 at 194

Another question is why this "continuous and apparent" requirement should apply to s.62's treatment of "unity of occupation" cases, but not "diversity of occupation" ones. Lewison L.J. does not answer this question. At first instance [. . .] Morgan J. appears to have seen the usage's being "continuous and apparent" as an indicator that the usage was, in s.62's words, "enjoyed with" Whiteacre—that is, that it appertained to Whiteacre, as opposed to being merely the personal practice of A, as common occupant of both Whiteacre and Blackacre—and as such was conveyed by the section with Whiteacre and turned into an easement. Seen thus, the "requirement" is logically not really a requirement at all; the key thing is that the usage was "enjoyed with" Whiteacre, as determined in this or any other way. And this of course reunites the section's treatment of "unity of occupation" cases with that of "diversity of occupation" cases. In both, there is the same demand for the usage to have been "enjoyed with" Whiteacre; and in both, that demand can be satisfied by reference to any aspect of the facts. Though apparently unsupported by previous authority, this position does at least follow the words of the section, which make no mention of a "continuous and apparent" test at all. On appeal, Lewison L.J. notes it, but dispatches the matter simply by asserting the requirement, as a requirement, but for "unity of occupation" cases alone, after all [. . .] At least one kind of usage that is not substantively qualified to become an easement, but yet does so via s.62, is a usage that was enjoyed not "with" that land (though in abstract terms it could have been), but on a personal basis by the land's previous occupant. This is clear from *Wright v Macadam* itself. Of course, the rule is controversial, in all probability misconceived. But so long as it prevails, we need to be able to say which usages that are not truly "enjoyed with" the conveyed land will nevertheless qualify to become easements under s.62. This is clearly going to be especially difficult in a "unity of occupation" case, for there, not only (*ex hypothesi*) does the common occupant in fact maintain the usage for his or her own benefit, but, in contrast to the "diversity of occupation" case, where one occupant necessarily uses the other's land, there is not even a superficial appearance to the contrary. Perhaps the requirement that the usage be "continuous and apparent" will distract attention from this difficulty, but in truth it ought not to.

The application of s 62 where there is unity of occupation means that there is very little continuing role for the rule in *Wheeldon v Burrows* which, as we have seen, requires an element of utility in additionally requiring the right to be reasonably necessary for the enjoyment of the dominant land. Gardner goes on to point out this limited difference between the operation of the two rules.

At 195

[. . .] the vision of s.62 that we are now to accept leaves the rule in *Wheeldon v Burrows* largely redundant. (Indeed, in retrospect, it did so only two years after the rule's first utterance, when s.62's predecessor, the Conveyancing Act 1881 s.6, was introduced.) Even if the idea of a quasi-easement is not identical with the sort of previous usage that will attract s.62, it seems to be wholly contained within the latter. With its "continuous and apparent" requirement in "unity of occupation" though not "diversity of occupation" cases, s.62 is less demanding than *Wheeldon v Burrows*, which maintains such a requirement in both contexts. And whereas *Wheeldon v Burrows* further requires that the new easement be "necessary to the reasonable enjoyment" of *B's* new interest, s.62 makes no such demand. All in all, then, there will normally be no advantage, indeed there will be disadvantage, to claimants in relying on the latter, so presumably they will not. The most obvious, perhaps the only, remaining application for *Wheeldon v Burrows* is to the case where there is no "conveyance", as required by s.62. It should therefore remain an active possibility where the transaction between A and B is one that takes effect in equity only, notably an estate contract or equitable lease. There is, of course, no reason of substance why the two contexts should attract different treatments in this way.

The two rules' divergence over the "necessary to the reasonable enjoyment" issue also merits a moment's attention for its own sake. As s.62 lacks such a requirement, the law's net position is that, in all "conveyance" cases, appropriate prior usage can yield an easement without more, other than satisfaction of the "continuous and apparent" requirement in a "unity of occupation" case. In contrast to what would have been the case had the net position comprised the rule in *Wheeldon v Burrows*, there is no demand that the claimant, B, should have any sort of need for the easement in question. For a rule generating an easement when the grantor does not even realise it, this is unsatisfactory.

The nature of the rights implied under s 62

A further distinction between *Wheeldon v Burrows* and s 62 flows from the nature of the rights that can pass under each rule. We have examined the need for rights under *Wheeldon v Burrows* to be continuous and apparent, and reasonably necessary for the enjoyment of the dominant land; there are no such limitations under s 62, which, accordingly, can apply to a wider range of rights.[120] In so doing, s 62 runs the danger of failing the utility test that underpins implied grant, although the discoverability of the right presents less of a problem.[121]

---

[120] There are a number of cases in which claims have failed under *Wheeldon v Burrows*, but succeeded under s 62: see *Goldberg v Edwards* [1950] Ch 247 and *Ward v Kirkland* [1967] Ch 194.

[121] Although others have argued that the right should be apparent: see Lawson (2002) p 93.

Gardner 'The Grant of an Easement under the Law of Property Act 1925 section 62' (2016) LQR 192

At 196

The most obvious justifications for recognising an easement as generated are the consent of the grantor, and utility. Grant under s.62 can be ascribed to the grantor's consent only to the extent that the grantor should anticipate its operation, which is quite an ask, given the latter's opacity; and that the grantor then fails to opt out, something which s.62(4) permits, but only by a contrary intention "expressed" in the conveyance, a stipulation which the present decision takes strictly [*Wood v Waddington*] [...] The degree of consent needed for the operation of s.62 is thus vestigial. This might be offset if its operation demanded a high degree of utility, but the lack of a "necessary to the reasonable enjoyment" requirement means that it in fact demands none at all [. . .] not even the degree that would be present if the previous user had genuinely to appertain, even though unnecessarily, to the land conveyed.

The easement-generating effect of s.62 has always been viewed by many as disquieting. After the present decision, which in various ways aggrandises the effect's scope, it is about as disquieting as it could possibly be. It is almost enough to attract one to the reform proposals of the Law Commission (*Making Land Work: Easements, Covenants and Profits à Prendre (2011), Law Com. No.327*), which, among other things, would entail the effect's abolition.

Nevertheless, to pass under s 62, the right must be capable of existing as an easement.

Phipps v Pears
[1965] 1 QB 76, CA

Lord Denning

At 84

A fine view, or an expanse open to the winds may be an advantage to a house, but it would not pass under section 62. Whereas a right to use a coal shed or to go along a passage would pass under section 62. The reason being that these last are rights known to the law, whereas the others are not. A right to protection from the weather is not a right known to the law. It does not therefore pass under section 62.

Rights that are capable of fulfilling the easement test, however, may not pass under s 62 where the particular permission given is personal to the individual, or merely temporary, or inherently precarious.[122]

Goldberg v Edwards
[1950] Ch 247, CA

Facts: Mrs Edwards owned a house and rented an annex to Goldberg, from which he ran a business. Prior to the formal entry into the lease, Mrs Edwards had let Goldberg into

---

[122] See also *Green v Ashco Horticulturist Ltd* [1966] 1 WLR 889.

possession, and had allowed him and his customers to pass through the house to get to the annex, although access could be obtained via an outside passage. She also gave him permission to put up an advertising sign, bell, and a letterbox for the business. The right for Goldberg to use the access through the house became an easement by the operation of s 62, but the other rights were limited to the period of Mrs Edward's ownership of the house and thus did not pass.

Evershed MR

At 255

[. . .] the finding of the Vice-Chancellor shows quite clearly, to my mind, that everything except the plaintiffs' right to come and go via this route [i.e. through the house] was expressly limited to such time as the landlord should occupy the house herself. In other words, it was a privilege which she herself allowed so long as she was there, because it did not interfere with her own affairs and business. It was clear that she was not making that privilege any part of the bargain between herself and the tenants of the annex. It is plain, in my view, that these rights, other than the plaintiffs' personal right of passage, were not within the language of s. 62 so as to be covered by the demise to them.

That leaves only the personal right. As I have indicated, my main difficulty has been in deciding whether that was similarly limited or limited in some other way so as not properly to be capable of being annexed to the subject-matter of the demise. Having regard to his judgment, I think that I am bound to regard the view of the judge as having been that, in contra-distinction to the other rights, it was intended to be something which the plaintiffs should enjoy qua lessees during the term of the demise, though it should not be enjoyed by their servants, workmen or any other persons with their authority.

[. . .] As I have held, though it is limited to the lessees themselves and does not extend to other persons, it would be capable of formulation and incorporation as a term of the lease, and it is, in my judgment, covered by s. 62. To that extent, therefore, but to that limited extent only, the plaintiffs are entitled to succeed [. . .]

I am anxious to guard myself from saying that rights, which were purely personal in the strict sense of that word, would necessarily in every case be covered by s. 62. I base myself on the view that the right here given, though limited to the lessees, was given to them qua lessees; and, as such, it seems to me, it is covered by the principle of *Wright v. Macadam* and by s. 62.

Gardner and MacKenzie[123] accuse the courts of displaying '*a degree of insouciance*' in monitoring the easement-like qualities of the rights that have been held to pass as easements under s 62. For example, we have already noted that *Wright v Macadam*[124] failed to consider whether rights storage ousted the servient owner, whilst the distinctions drawn in *Goldberg*[125] between rights conferred upon the tenant as a personal favour and as a lessee are not convincing.

3.3 PRESUMED GRANT: PRESCRIPTION

A grant of an easement may be presumed as a result of long user. Lord Hoffman explains the function and development of the law governing prescription in the following case, which

---

[123] Gardner & MacKenzie, *An Introduction to Land Law* (4th edn, 2015) p 327.
[124] [1949] 2 KB 744, CA.   [125] See also *Green v Ashco Horticulturist Ltd* [1966] 1 WLR 889.

concerned the registration of land as a village green by reason of the long user of the land for recreation by the inhabitants of the village.[126] The claim was for acquisition of a public right, but similar prescription principles apply to the acquisition of easements by private landowners.[127]

R v Oxfordshire CC, ex p Sunningwell Parish Council
[2000] 1 AC 335

Lord Hoffmann

At 349

English law [. . .] has never had a consistent theory of prescription. It did not treat long enjoyment as being a method of acquiring title. Instead, it approached the question from the other end by treating the lapse of time as either barring the remedy of the former owner or giving rise to a presumption that he had done some act which conferred a lawful title upon the person in de facto possession or enjoyment. Thus the medieval real actions for the recovery of seisin were subject to limitation by reference to various past events. In the time of Bracton the writ of right was limited by reference to the accession of Henry I (1100). The Statute of Merton 1235 (20 Hen. 3, c. 4) brought this date up to the accession of Henry II (1154) and the Statute of Westminster I 1275 (3 Edw. 1, c. 39) extended it to the accession of Richard I in 1189.

The judges used this date by analogy to fix the period of prescription for immemorial custom and the enjoyment of incorporeal hereditaments such as rights of way and other easements. In such cases, however, the period was being used for a different purpose. It was not to bar the remedy but to presume that enjoyment was pursuant to a right having a lawful origin. In the case of easements, this meant a presumption that there had been a grant before 1189 by the freehold owner.

As time went on, however, proof of lawful origin in this way became for practical purposes impossible. The evidence was not available. The judges filled the gap with another presumption. They instructed juries that if there was evidence of enjoyment for the period of living memory, they could presume that the right had existed since 1189. After the Limitation Act 1623 (21 Jac. 1, c. 16), which fixed a 20-year period of limitation for the possessory actions such as ejectment, the judges treated 20 years' enjoyment as by analogy giving rise to the presumption of enjoyment since 1189. But these presumptions arising from enjoyment for the period of living memory or for 20 years, though strong, were not conclusive. They could be rebutted by evidence that the right could not have existed in 1189; for example, because it was appurtenant to a building which had been erected since that date. In the case of easements, the resourcefulness of the judges overcame this obstacle by another presumption, this time of a lost modern grant. As Cockburn C.J. said in the course of an acerbic account of the history of the English law of prescription in *Bryant v. Foot* (1867) L.R. 2 Q.B. 161, 181:

> "Juries were first told that from user, during living memory, or even during 20 years, they might presume a lost grant or deed; next they were recommended to make such presumption;

---

[126] Attempts to prevent development by registering land as a town or village green, which depends also on user as of right, has led to a surge in cases, a number of which have reached our highest court see *R v Oxfordshire CC, ex p Sunningwell Parish Council* [2000] 1 AC 335, *R (Lewis) v Redcar & Cleveland BC* [2010] UKSC 11 and *R(Barkas) v North Yorkshire CC* [2014] 2 WLR 1360 overruling the earlier decision of *R (Beresford) v Sunderland CC* [2003] UKHL 60.

[127] Pratt suggests that it is time to distinguish between the acquisition of public and private rights by prescription in her case note on *Winterburn v Bennett*, see Pratt, [2106] Conv 414.

and lastly, as the final consummation of judicial legislation, it was held that a jury should be told, not only that they might, but also that they were bound to presume the existence of such a lost grant, although neither judge nor jury, nor any one else, had the shadow of a belief that any such instrument had ever really existed."

The result of these developments was that, leaving aside the cases in which (a) it was possible to show that the right could not have existed in 1189 and (b) the doctrine of lost modern grant could not be invoked, the period of 20 years' user was in practice sufficient to establish a prescriptive or customary right. It was not an answer simply to rely upon the improbability of immemorial user or lost modern grant. As Cockburn C.J. observed, the jury were instructed that if there was no evidence absolutely inconsistent with there having been immemorial user or a lost modern grant, they not merely could but should find the prescriptive right established. The emphasis was therefore shifted from the brute fact of the right or custom having existed in 1189 or there having been a lost grant (both of which were acknowledged to be fictions) to the quality of the 20-year user which would justify recognition of a prescriptive right or customary right. It became established that such user had to be, in the Latin phrase, nec vi, nec clam, nec precario: not by force, nor stealth, nor the licence of the owner. (For this requirement in the case of custom, see *Mills v. Colchester Corporation* (1867) L.R. 2 C.P. 476, 486.) The unifying element in these three vitiating circumstances was that each constituted a reason why it would not have been reasonable to expect the owner to resist the exercise of the right—in the first case, because rights should not be acquired by the use of force, in the second, because the owner would not have known of the user and in the third, because he had consented to the user, but for a limited period. So in *Dalton v. Angus & Co.* (1881) 6 App. Cas. 740, 773, Fry J. (advising the House of Lords) was able to rationalise the law of prescription as follows:

"the whole-law of prescription and the whole law which governs the presumption or infer-ence of a grant or covenant rest upon acquiescence. The courts and the judges have had recourse to various expedients for quieting the possession of persons in the exercise of rights which have not been resisted by the persons against whom they are exercised, but in all cases it appears to me that acquiescence and nothing else is the principle upon which these expedients rest."

In the case of easements, the legislature intervened to save the consciences of judges and juries by the Prescription Act 1832 (2 & 3 Will 4, c. 71), of which the short title was "An Act for shortening the Time of Prescription in certain cases." Section 2 (as amended by the Statute Law Revision (No. 2) Act 1888 (51 & 52 Vict. c. 57), section 1, Schedule and the Statute Law Revision Act 1890 (53 & 54 Vict. c. 33), section 1, Schedule 1) provided:

"No claim which may be lawfully made at the common law, by custom, prescription, or grant, to any way or other easement [. . .] when such way or other matter [. . .] shall have been actually enjoyed by any person claiming right thereto without interruption for the full period of 20 years, shall be defeated or destroyed by showing only that such way or other matter was first enjoyed at any time prior to such period of 20 years, but neverthe-less such claim may be defeated in any other way by which the same is now liable to be defeated [. . .]"

Thus in a claim under the Act, what mattered was the quality of enjoyment during the 20-year period. It had to be by a person "claiming right thereto" or, in the language of section 5 of the same Act (as amended by the Act of 1888), which dealt with the forms of pleadings, "as of right." In *Bright v. Walker* (1834) 1 C.M. & R. 211, 219, two years after the passing of the Act, Parke B. explained what these words meant. He said that the right must have been enjoyed "openly and in the manner that a person rightfully entitled would have used it" and not by stealth or by licence. In *Gardner v. Hodgson's Kingston Brewery Co. Ltd.* [1903] A.C. 229, 239, Lord Lindley said that the words "as of right" were intended "to have the same meaning as the older expression nec vi, nec clam, nec precario."

As Lord Hoffman explains, the user must be of a certain quality—that is, it must be open and exercised without force or the permission of the servient owner—and it must be established that this user has been exercised for one or more of the three prescription periods. Prescription at common law requires use from time immemorial, which means 1189; accordingly, a successful claim is most unlikely. Prescription by lost modern grant calls for proof of twenty years' user, which will lead to a presumption that a grant of the right had been made, but has now been lost. This presumption is strong and will not be rebutted by positive proof that no grant was made.[128] The Prescription Act 1832 operates by preventing a servient owner from contesting a claim at common law because the right could not have been exercised in 1189 where the claimant can prove user for the twenty years immediately preceding the commencement of proceedings in which the right is claimed. The Act also introduces a long prescription period, which operates positively to give rise to an absolute right on the expiry of the forty years' user.[129]

The Prescription Act 1832 has been much criticized as '*one of the worst drafted Acts on the Statute Book*'[130] and, as such, has not supplanted the fiction of lost modern grant. In particular, lost modern grant will operate whenever twenty years' uninterrupted user is established, even if that user was some time ago. In contrast to the Prescription Act 1832, the period of use does not have to continue up to the commencement of proceedings.

3.3.1 The basis of prescription

In Chapter 9, we saw that an adverse possessor may: (i) acquire a property right by taking possession of land; and (ii) later be able to rely on a limitation period that extinguishes the right of the paper owner to recover possession. Prescription operates in a different manner. Long user justifies a presumption or fiction that the servient owner has granted an easement. The presumption is founded upon the acquiescence of the servient owner in failing to prevent the dominant owner from exercising the claimed right.

---

[128] See *Tehidy Minerals Ltd v Norman* [1971] 2 QB 518, [543], *per* Buckley LJ; *Mills v Silver* [1991] Ch 271, [278], *per* Dillon LJ. The presumption will be rebutted by proof that the grant could not have been made because of the incapacity of the servient owner, although incapacity may not affect the 40-year prescription period under the Prescription Act 1832: see dicta of the Court of Appeal in *Housden v Conservators of Wimbledon and Putney Commons* [2008] EWCA Civ 200 [2008] 1 WLR 1172 noted at [2009] Conv 349. See also the recommendation of the Law Commission in Law Com 327 (2011), [3.168].

[129] The forty-year period must also expire immediately before the commencement of proceedings in which the right is claimed.

[130] Law Reform Committee, *Fourteenth Report: Acquisition of Easements and Profits by Prescription* (Cmnd 3100, 1966), [40].

Dalton v Angus & Co
(1881) 6 LR App Cas 740

Fry J

At 773

[I]n my opinion, the whole law of prescription and the whole law which governs the presumption or inference of a grant or covenant rests upon acquiescence. The Courts and the Judges have had recourse to various expedients for quieting the possession of persons in the exercise of rights which have not been resisted by the persons against whom they are exercised, but in all cases it appears to me that acquiescence and nothing else is the principle upon which these expedients rest. It becomes then of the highest importance to consider of what ingredients acquiescence consists. In many cases, as, for instance, in the case of that acquiescence which creates a right of way, it will be found to involve, 1st, the doing of some act by one man upon the land of another; 2ndly, the absence of right to do that act in the person doing it; 3rdly, the knowledge of the person affected by it that the act is done; 4thly, the power of the person affected by the act to prevent such act either by act on his part or by action in the Courts; and lastly, the abstinence by him from any such interference for such a length of time as renders it reasonable for the Courts to say that he shall not afterwards interfere to stop the act being done. In some other cases, as, for example, in the case of lights, some of these ingredients are wanting; but I cannot imagine any case of acquiescence in which there is not shewn to be in the servient owner: 1, a knowledge of the acts done; 2, a power in him to stop the acts or to sue in respect of them; and 3, an abstinence on his part from the exercise of such power. That such is the nature of acquiescence and that such is the ground upon which presumptions or inferences of grant or covenant may be made appears to me to be plain, both from reason, from maxim, and from the cases.

As regards the reason of the case, it is plain good sense to hold that a man who can stop an asserted right, or a continued user, and does not do so for a long time, may be told that he has lost his right by his delay and his negligence, and every presumption should therefore be made to quiet a possession thus acquired and enjoyed by the tacit consent of the sufferer. But there is no sense in binding a man by an enjoyment he cannot prevent, or quieting a possession which he could never disturb.

The fiction of a presumed grant raises the distinction that we made in Chapter 9 between *independent* and *dependent* acquisition. The fiction suggests that a prescriptive easement is acquired by dependent acquisition—that is, because a grant from A is presumed—rather than because of independent acquisition as a result of B's own unilateral conduct. McFarlane questions whether prescription really is a dependent grant.

McFarlane, *The Structure of Property Law* (2008, pp 864–5)

It is possible for B to acquire an Easement simply through the *consistent exercise, over a long period, of a right to use A's land*. This method of acquisition, referred to as *prescription*, looks very much like a form of independent acquisition:

1. B acquires the right through his own, independent conduct, without needing to show that A has exercised his power to give B an Easement.

2. Once B has behaved, for a long period, *as though* he has the right, it is no longer possible for A to deny B that right.

However, the courts do *not* currently treat prescription as an example of independent acquisition. Instead, when B acquires an Easement through long use, it is assumed that A, or a former owner of A's land, exercised his power to give B an Easement. Strictly speaking then, prescription is simply another type of implied grant. This approach seems puzzling: why should we rely on an (almost certainly incorrect) assumption that the claimed Easement was once granted by an owner of A's land to an owner of B's land? It would seem simpler to say that prescription is an example of an independent acquisition.

The idea that a grant of an easement by prescription is presumed has been the subject of much criticism. Indeed, it has been described as a 'revolting fiction'.[131]

Goymour provides a number of reasons why this approach is so misguided.

Goymour, 'Rights in Property and the Effluxion of Time' in *Modern Studies in Property Law Vol 4* (ed Cooke, 2007, p 182)

First, the notion of a presumed grant is so fictitious that it offends common sense and is furthermore inconsistent with the technical requirements for prescription. The idea that prescriptive rights rest in a grant conflicts with the condition that prescription must be nec precario [without permission]. Any indication that the owner had given permission for another person to enjoy the land, whether by grant of an easement or merely a licence, will prevent a prescriptive right from arising. For the doctrine to be internally inconsistent is unsatisfactory.

Secondly, in conjunction with the first point, the technical mechanism of presumed grant has led to an acceptance by many that the policy rationale for prescriptive rights is 'acquiescence' by the servant owner in the other party's long-established enjoyment. So long as there is a theory of grant, it follows logically that acquiescence is relevant. However, it is far from obvious that acquiescence is the policy rationale for prescription, for the following reasons. First, as is apparent in the previous point, the requirement that use must be nec precario introduces an element of adversity into the prescriptive claim that cannot easily be explained by acquiescence. Furthermore, it is often equally fictitious to assume acquiescence on the part of the servient owner as it is to presume a grant. Finally the assumption that acquiescence is the rationale for prescriptive rights fails to take account of the fundamental distinction between rights that arise by consensual grant and rights that arise otherwise, by operation of law. The policy that lies behind the recognition of expressly granted rights can be explained by the law's respect for the wishes of the legal actors when they are executed in legally recognised forms, for which acquiescence is relevant. However, once it is accepted that prescriptive easements arise not by grant but by operation of law, it no longer follows that the policy justification for their existence is acquiescence [. . .]

The third problem with time's masked effect is linked to the first two. Because the law has inappropriately tied itself to the mechanism of grant and the rationale of acquiescence, the questions that occupy the courts in prescription cases tended to concern whether or not the technicalities of a hypothetical conveyance are satisfied [. . .] This focus comes at the expense of a proper consideration of why and in what circumstances long use should, as a matter of policy, give rise to a prescriptive right.

---

[131] *Angus v Dalton* (1877) LR 3 QBD 85, 94, *per* Lush J.

Clarke and Kohler point out that, whilst the presumption of a grant may make some (if un-satisfactory) sense to support positive easements by long user, the presumed grant of nega-tive easements cannot be rationalized.

Clarke and Kohler, *Property Law* (2005, p 495)

There are two important points about negative easements. First, is the absence of an ease-ment, I do not have a right to receive these forces, but only a liberty to make use of them. Secondly, when I exercise my liberty to enjoy these forces, I do not infringe *any rights* of yours [. . .] In other words, from the outset I had the liberty to receive the forces and you had the liberty to obstruct them. So from the outset I had no need of your authorisation to 'use' the light, or air, or support etc for twenty years: I would automatically receive them un-less and until you exercised your liberty to interrupt them [. . .] It would be odd to infer from the fact that I have enjoyed uninterrupted receipt of these forces for twenty years that you positively promised not to interrupt them: this is a promise I had no need for, and you had no reason to give. A much more likely explanation is that you did nothing because you had no selfish reason to develop your land in a way that would interrupt my receipt of these forces.

A particular concern arises when a negative easement is claimed by prescription, because the right will arise even though there is no evidence of the user because the dominant owner has not made any positive use of the servient land. Lord Hope referred to this concern in the following case, in which the House of Lords canvassed (and rejected) possible redress (including the possibility of a new negative easement) against interference with television reception.

Hunter v Canary Wharf Ltd
[1997] AC 655, HL

Lord Hope

At 726

The presumption however is for freedom in the occupation and use of property. This pre-sumption affects the way in which an easement may be constituted. A restraint on the owners' freedom of property can only be effected by agreement, by express grant or—in the case of the easement of light—by way of an exception to the general rule by prescrip-tion. The prospective developer should be able to detect by inspection or by inquiry what restrictions, if any, are imposed by this branch of the law on his freedom to develop his prop-erty. He should be able to know, before he puts his building up, whether it will constitute an infringement.

   The presumption also affects the kinds of easement which the law will recognise. When the easements are negative in character—where they restrain the owners' freedom in the occupation and use of his property—they belong to certain well known categories. As they represent an anomaly in the law because they restrict the owners' freedom, the law takes care not to extend them beyond the categories which are well known to the law. It is one thing if what one is concerned with is a restriction which has been constituted by express grant or by agreement. Some elasticity in the recognised categories may be permitted in

> such a case, as the owner has agreed to restrict his own freedom. But it is another matter if what is being suggested is the acquisition of an easement by prescription. Where the easement is of a purely negative character, requiring no action to be taken by the other proprietor and effecting no change on the owner's property which might reveal its existence, it is important to keep to the recognised categories. A very strong case would require to be made out if they were to be extended.

Lord Hope refers to rights to light as a recognized negative easement that can be acquired by prescription. However, rights to light have caused problems where they have been asserted to impede development and, as a result, the Law Commission have recommended increased controls upon their acquisition by prescription and their subsequent enforcement.[132]

The acquisition by prescription of certain forms of positive easements may also raise problems. For instance, in *Coventry (t/a RDC Promotions) v Lawrence*,[133] where the acquisition of a right to noise by prescription was in issue, the Supreme Court noted that it was only where the noise constituted a nuisance that a servient owner could be said to have acquiesced by not taking preventative action. Furthermore, it may be difficult to establish both the parameters of a right to noise (in terms of its level and frequency) and when those parameters had been exceeded. The Supreme Court nevertheless accepted that these obstacles should not preclude the possibility of such an easement arising by prescription, although on the facts none had been established.

The three existing forms of prescription at common law, under lost modern grant, and under the Prescription Act 1832 have been described as '*anomalous and undesirable*',[134] and the consequences of their interrelationship as '*messy overlaps*'.[135] The Law Commission have recommended that these three forms of the prescription should be replaced and prescription should be based simply upon the passage of time, with a single prescription period of twenty years.[136]

3.3.2 User as of right

Given that the servient owner's acquiescence of the claimant's user underpins the prescription, the nature of that user is of central significance. The vital connection is explained in the following case.

Sturges v Bridgman
(1879) LR 11 Ch D 852

Thesiger LJ

At 863

Consent or acquiescence of the owner of the servient tenement lies at the root of prescription, and of the fiction of a lost grant, and hence the acts of user, which go to the proof of either

---

[132] Law Com No 356 (December 2014). [133] [2014] AC 822 *per* Lord Neuberger at [28]–[42].
[134] *Tehidy Minerals Ltd v Norman* [1971] 2 QB 518, [543], *per* Buckley LJ.
[135] Goymour, 'Rights in Property and the Effluxion of Time' in *Modern Studies in Property Law Vol 4* (ed Cooke, Oxford: Hart Publishing, 2007) p 185.
[136] Law Com 327 (2011) [3.123]. The civilian systems look to the Roman law concept of *usucapio*, by which rights may be acquired by the passing of time.

the one or the other, must be, in the language of the civil law, nec vi nec clam, nec precario; for a man cannot, as a general rule, be said to consent to or acquiesce in the acquisition by his neighbour of an easement through an enjoyment of which he has no knowledge, actual or constructive or which he contests and endeavours to interrupt or which he temporarily licenses.

The phrase that describes the required user is that the claimant's user must be 'as of right'—a phrase that is discussed by Riddall.

Riddall, 'A False Trail: The Meaning of "As Of Right" in the Public Law of Prescription' (1997) Conv 199, 201

Since for the user to be "as of right" it must be nec vi, without force; nec clam, without secrecy; and nec precarious, without permission, the meaning of the phrase becomes apparent. User "as of right" means that the user must be in the same fashion *as if* there was a legal right to use the way. As the matter was expressed by Parke B in *Bright v Walker* (1834) 1 CM&R 211, user is as of right if exercised "in the same manner that a person rightfully entitled would have used it". In the same *manner*, this is the crux of the matter. Since this is what "as of right" means; its meaning cannot have anything to do with whether users believe that they are entitled to use a path. A person can use a path in the same *manner* as if he had a right to use it nec clam, nec vi and nec precario without having any shred of belief that he has a legal right to do so.

The question has arisen as to whether user can be as of right where the prescriptive user defers to the servient owner's continued use of the land. This issue looks to reconciling competing uses of the land as Lord Hope observes.

R (Lewis) v Redcar & Cleveland Borough Council
[2010] 2 AC 70

Facts: Local inhabitants had used a council owned golf course for recreation but had not interrupted the golfers' play by stopping when the golfers were playing their shots. Upon an application for the registration of the golf course as a town green, it was held that the local inhabitant's user was as of right despite the deference they had showed to the servient owner's user.

Lord Hope

At 75–6

But once one accepts, as I would do, that the rights on either side can coexist after registration subject to give and take on both sides, the part that deference has to play in determining whether the local inhabitants indulged in lawful sports or pastimes as of right takes on an entirely different aspect. The question is whether the user by the public was of such amount and in such manner as would reasonably be regarded as being the assertion of a public right. Deference by the public to what the owner does on his land may be taken as an indication that the two uses can in practice coexist.

> Of course, the position may be that the two uses cannot sensibly coexist at all. But it would be wrong to assume, as the inspector did in this case, that deference to the owner's activities, even if it is as he put it overwhelming, is inconsistent with the assertion by the public to use of the land as of right for lawful sports and pastimes. It is simply attributable to an acceptance that where two or more rights coexist over the same land there may be occasions when they cannot practically be enjoyed simultaneously

We have seen that prescription looks to the intention of the servient owner rather than the prescriptive user as it is based upon a presumed grant by the servient owner. The competing uses and their possibly inconsistency should, thus, be viewed from the perspective of the servient owner. Lord Walker makes this point whilst characterizing the local inhabitant's use as mere civility and not deference to another's ownership. He does, however, also stress that the situation may differ where a private as opposed to a public right is being claimed.

Lord Walker

At 36–8

[. . .] I have no difficulty in accepting that Lord Hoffmann was absolutely right, in Sunningwell [2000] 1 AC 335, to say that the English theory of prescription is concerned with "how the matter would have appeared to the owner of the land" (or if there was an absentee owner, to a reasonable owner who was on the spot). But I have great difficulty in seeing how a reasonable owner would have concluded that the residents were not asserting a right to take recreation on the disputed land, simply because they normally showed civility (or, in the inspector's word, deference) towards members of the golf club who were out playing golf. It is not as if the residents took to their heels and vacated the land whenever they saw a golfer. They simply acted (as all the members of the court agree, in much the same terms) with courtesy and common sense. But courteous and sensible though they were (with occasional exceptions) the fact remains that they were regularly, in large numbers, crossing the fairways as well as walking on the rough, and often (it seems) failing to clear up after their dogs when they defecated. A reasonably alert owner of the land could not have failed to recognise that this user was the assertion of a right and would mature into an established right unless the owner took action to stop it (as the golf club tried to do, ineffectually, with the notices erected in 1998).

There is in my opinion a significant difference, on this point, between the acquisition of private and public rights. As between neighbours living in close proximity, what I have referred to as "body language" may be relevant. In a Canadian case of that sort, Henderson v Volk (1982) 35 OR (2d) 379, 384, Cory JA (delivering the judgment of the Court of Appeal of Ontario) observed:

> "It is different when a party seeks to establish a right-of-way for pedestrians over a sidewalk. In those circumstances the user sought to be established may not even be known to the owner of the servient tenement. In addition, the neighbourly acquiescence to its use during inclement weather or in times of emergency such as a last minute attempt to catch a bus, should not too readily be accepted as evidence of submission to the use. It is right and proper for the courts to proceed with caution before finding that title by prescription or by the doctrine of lost modern grant was established in a case such as this. It tends to subject a

> property owner to a burden without compensation. Its ready invocation may discourage acts
> of kindness and good neighbourliness; it may punish the kind and thoughtful and reward the
> aggressor."

> That is, if I may say so, obviously good sense. But I do not think it has any application to a
> situation, such as the court now faces, in which open land owned by a local authority is regu-
> larly used, for various different forms of recreation, by a large number of local residents. The
> inspector's assessment did in my opinion amount to an error of law. He misdirected himself
> as to the significance of perfectly natural behaviour by the local residents.

The Latin phrase *nec vi, nec clam, nec precario*, meaning 'without force, without secrecy, and without permission', is commonly used to describe user as of right and the Law Commission's definition of qualifying user continues to rely upon these requirements.[137] We, thus, need to explore a little more the implications of this phrase.

The use of force refers not only to physical force, but also to the exercise of the right despite protests by the servient owner.

Smith v Brudenell-Bruce
[2002] 2 P & CR 51, HC

Pumfrey J

At 12

> It seems to me a user ceases to be user "as of right" if the circumstances are such as to indi-
> cate to the dominant owner, or to a reasonable man with the dominant owner's knowledge
> of the circumstances, that the servient owner actually objects and continues to object and
> will back his objection either by physical obstruction or by legal action. A user is contentious
> when the servient owner is doing everything, consistent with his means and proportion-
> ately to the user, to contest and to endeavour to interrupt the user.

Thus, the breaking down of fences or breaking through locked gates will amount to force. But such overt behaviour is not always indicative. Ignoring prohibitory signs may amount to 'forceful' action as the following case demonstrates.[138]

Winterburn v Bennett
[2016] EWCA Civ 482

Facts: For over 20 years the Winterburns operated a fish and chip shop that was next door to a car park owned by Bennett's predecessor in title, the Conservative Club. The Winterburns' suppliers used the car park to unload and their customers also used the car park when coming to the shop. They carried on such use despite the fact that there were clearly visible signs prohibiting parking erected by the Conservative Club and in-deed claimed a right to do so by prescription.

---

[137] Ibid.   [138] *Betterment Properties (Weymouth) Ltd v Dorset CC* [2012] EWCA Civ 250.

Held: The Winterburns' use of the car park in the face of the signs was 'forceful' and thus could not qualify as prescriptive 'user as of right'.

David Richards LJ

At 40–1

In my judgment, there is no warrant in the authorities or in principle for requiring an owner of land to take these steps in order to prevent the wrongdoers from acquiring a legal right. In circumstances where the owner has made his position entirely clear through the erection of clearly visible signs, the unauthorised use of the land cannot be said to be "as of right". Protest against unauthorised use may, of course, take many forms and it may, as it has in a number of cases, take the form of writing letters of protest. But I reject the notion that it is necessary for the owner, having made his protest clear, to take further steps of confronting the wrongdoers known to him orally or in writing, still less to go to the expense and trouble of legal proceedings.

The situation which has arisen in the present case is commonplace. Many millions of people in this country own property. Most people do not seek confrontation, whether orally or in writing, and in many cases they may be concerned or even frightened of doing so. Most people do not have the means to bring legal proceedings. There is a social cost to confrontation and, unless absolutely necessary, the law of property should not require confrontation in order for people to retain and defend what is theirs. The erection and maintenance of an appropriate sign is a peaceful and inexpensive means of making clear that property is private and not to be used by others. I do not see why those who choose to ignore such signs should thereby be entitled to obtain legal rights over the land.

There has been some controversy over the circumstances in which an illegal user can qualify as user as of right. At first sight, it might seem inappropriate to condone any illegal user, but, until the prescription period has expired, the claimants user is inevitably illegal—in the sense that it is a trespass or nuisance. The House of Lords has settled the controversy by distinguishing between those illegal actions that the servient owner cannot legitimize and those actions that would cease to be illegal if the servient owner were to choose to permit their exercise. The Law Commission recommendations adopt this distinction.[139]

Bakewell Management Ltd v Brandwood
[2004] 2 AC 519, HL

Facts: The owners of several houses adjoining Newtown Common had driven over the common via a track to gain access to their homes. The common came into the ownership of Bakewell, which demanded payment for the house owners' continued use of the track. The owners successfully claimed a right of way over the track by prescription, although their user was illegal, being a breach of s 193(4) of the Law of Property Act 1925 (as amended).

---

[139] Law Com 327 (2011), [3.123].

Lord Scott

At 46–7

It is accepted, however, that a prescriptive right, or a right under the lost modern grant fiction, can be obtained by long use that throughout was illegal in the sense of being tortious. That is how prescription operates. Public policy does not prevent conduct illegal in that sense from leading to the acquisition of property rights. The decision in *Hanning's case* can only be justified on the footing that conduct illegal in a criminal sense is, for public policy purposes, different in kind from conduct illegal in a tortious sense. Why should that necessarily be so? Why, in particular, should it be so where the conduct in question is use of land that is not a criminal use of land against which the public law sets its face in all cases? It is criminal only because it is a user of land for which the landowner has given no "lawful authority". In that respect, the use of land made criminal by section 193(4) of the 1925 Act, or by section 34(1) of the 1988 Act, has much more in common with use of land that is illegal because it is tortious than with use of land that is illegal because it is criminal.

In my opinion, if an easement over land can be lawfully granted by the landowner the easement can be acquired either by prescription under section 2 of the 1832 Act or by the fiction of lost modern grant whether the use relied on is illegal in the criminal sense or merely in the tortious sense. I can see no valid reason of public policy to bar that acquisition.

The user must not be secret, in the sense that a reasonable person in the position of the servient owner should be able to discover that the right is being exercised. A servient owner cannot acquiesce unless he or she knows, or ought to have known, of the exercise of the right.

Union Lighterage Co v London Graving Dock Co
[1902] 2 Ch 557, CA

Facts: A dry dock was secured to an adjoining wharf by underground rods, which were not visible to the eye. The owner of the dock failed in his claim for an easement of support by prescription, because the Court decided that his user was not reasonably discoverable.

Romer LJ

At 570

Now, on principle, it appears to me that a prescriptive right to an easement over a man's land should only be acquired when the enjoyment has been open—that is to say, of such a character that an ordinary owner of the land, diligent in the protection of his interests, would have, or must be taken to have, a reasonable opportunity of becoming aware of that enjoyment. And I think on the balance of authority that this principle has been recognised as the law, and ought to be followed by us. In support of this statement I do not think it necessary to do more than refer to those parts, which deal with this point, of the speeches made by Lord Selborne and Lord Penzance in the House of Lords in *Dalton v. Angus* (1881) 6 App Cas 740, and I gather that their views as there expressed on this point were not dissented from by the other members of the House who took part in the hearing of that case, and, indeed, Lord Blackburn said at 827 that no prescriptive right "can be acquired where there is any concealment, and probably none where the enjoyment has not been open."

Although the right of support failed in *Union Lighterage*, it is clear that rights of support are not inherently secret, they may be evident from the way in which buildings are constructed.[140]

The permission of the servient owner to the claimant's exercise of the right will prevent prescription. It is important to distinguish permission from the servient owner's acquiescence, which underlies prescription. It is clear that toleration of user without objection does not constitute permission; some positive approval is needed.[141] The inter-relationship between acquiescence and user as of right is fundamental, as Meager explains in the following extract.

Meager, 'Prescription and User "As of Right": Ripe for Wholesale Reform?'
in *Modern Studies in Property Law Vol 6* (ed Bright, Oxford Hart: 2011, p 254)

> Notwithstanding the apparent importance of acquiescence and its role in establishing that user has been of right, it does not appear to be an added component of the as of right test. Its role is simply confined to a recognition that, in the face of user which is nec vi, nec clam, nec precario, it is necessary for the landowner to do something, to take some positive steps, to bring the user to an end; acquiescence, as a matter of fact, in the face of such user, will be determinative that user as of right is continuing.

Meager goes on to suggest that, even though the Law Commission's proposal that prescription be established solely by qualifying long user may suggest that acquiescence should no longer underpin prescription, 'it will be impossible to depart from the many judicial statements which recognise the central importance of acquiescence' and, in order to prove prescriptive use, to 'sever the link between acquiescence and user as of right.'[142]

The Supreme Court has cast some light on the interplay between permission and acquiescence in the following case in which a distinction is drawn between the expressions 'as of right' and 'by right'. In this case the user was permitted by statute, rather than the direct permission of the servient owner, but, nevertheless, was held to be 'by right' rather than 'as of right.'[143]

R (Barkas) v North Yorkshire CC
[2015] AC 195

Lord Neuberger at 14

[. . .]it is, I think, helpful to explain that the legal meaning of the expression "as of right" is, somewhat counterintuitively, almost the converse of "of right" or "by right". Thus, if a person uses privately owned land "of right" or "by right", the use will have been permitted

---

[140] *Dalton v Angus & Co* (1881) 6 LR App Cas 740, *per* Lord Selbourne at [798].

[141] See also *Mills v Silver* [1991] Ch 271 at [279]–[281]; *London Tara Hotel Ltd v Kensington Close Hotel Ltd* [2010] EWHC 2749.

[142] Meager, Prescription and User 'As of Right': Ripe for Wholesale Reform? in *Modern Studies in Property Law Vol 6* (ed Bright, Oxford: Hart Publishing, 2011) p 254.

[143] Thus, overruling the House of Lords's earlier decision in *R(Beresford) v Sunderland CC* [2004] 1 AC 889.

by the landowner—hence the use is rightful. However, if the use of such land is "as of right", it is without the permission of the landowner, and therefore is not "of right" or "by right", but is actually carried on as if it were by right—hence "as of right". The significance of the little word "as" is therefore crucial, and renders the expression "as of right" effectively the antithesis of "of right" or "by right" [. . .]

At 17

In relation to the acquisition of easements by prescription, the law is correctly stated in *Gale on Easements*, 19th ed (2012), para 4-115:

"The law draws a distinction between acquiescence by the owner on the one hand and licence or permission from the owner on the other hand. In some circumstances, the distinction may not matter but in the law of prescription, the distinction is fundamental. This is because user which is acquiesced in by the owner is 'as of right'; acquiescence is the foundation of prescription. However, user which is with the licence or permission of the owner is not 'as of right.' Permission involves some positive act or acts on the part of the owner, whereas passive toleration is all that is required for acquiescence."

The concept of acquiescence in this context was explained in the opinion delivered by Fry J (with which Lord Penzance expressed himself as being "in entire accord" at p 803), in *Dalton v Henry Angus & Co (1881) 6 App Cas 740*, 774, where he said:

"I cannot imagine any case of acquiescence in which there is not shown to be in the servient owner: 1, a knowledge of the acts done; 2, a power in him to stop the acts or to sue in respect of them; and 3, an abstinence on his part from the exercise of such power.".

At 28

Furthermore, the fact that the landowner knows that a trespasser is on the land and does nothing about it does not alter the legal status of the trespasser. As Fry J explained, acquiescence in the trespass, which in this area of law simply means passive toleration as is explained in *Gale on Easements* [. . .] does not stop it being trespass. This point was well made by Dillon LJ in *Mills v Silver [1991] Ch 271*, 279–280, where he pointed out that "there cannot be [a] principle of law" that "no prescriptive right can be acquired if the user ... has been tolerated without objection by the servient owner" as it would be "fundamentally inconsistent with the whole notion of acquisition of rights by prescription." Accordingly, as he added at p 281, "mere acquiescence in or tolerance of the user ... cannot prevent the user being user as of right for purposes of prescription."

Thus, if a trespass has continued for a number of years, then the fact that it has been acquiesced in (or passively tolerated or suffered) by the landowner will not prevent the landowner claiming that it has been and is unlawful, and seeking damages in respect of it (subject to the constraints of the Limitation Act 1980). For the same reason, if such a trespass has continued for 20 years and was otherwise as of right, it will be capable of giving rise to a prescriptive right. On the other hand, if the landowner has in some way actually communicated agreement to what would otherwise be a trespass, whether or not gratuitously, then he cannot claim it has been or is unlawful—at least until he lawfully withdraws his agreement to it. For the same reason, even if such an agreed arrangement had continued for 20 years, there can be no question of it giving rise to a prescriptive right because it would clearly have been precario, and therefore "by right".

3.3.3 User in fee simple

The presumption that a permanent grant has been made at some time in the past dictates that prescriptive user must be by, and against, a fee simple owner.[144] A lessee thus cannot acquire a prescriptive easement over adjoining land held either by his or her landlord or by anyone else.[145] This position has been criticized, for instance, by Lord Millett when sitting as a judge of the Final Court of Appeal in Hong Kong where the rule is particular significant as all land is leasehold. Indeed in *China Field* the Hong Kong Final Court of Appeal abandoned the rule.[146]

China Field Ltd v Appeal Tribunal (Buildings)
[2009] HKCU 1650

The [fee simple] rule is both counter intuitive and contrary to the policy of the law. It is counter intuitive because it is difficult to see why it should be impossible to presume a lost grant of an easement by or to a lessee for the term of his lease when such a grant may be made expressly [. . .] It is contrary to the policy of the law, for if the disturbance of long established de facto enjoyment of a right is contrary to legal policy, then this is equally the case whether the enjoyment is by or against a freeholder or leaseholder.

However, there are no proposals to follow suit in this jurisdiction. Law Commission has abandoned its proposals to extend the benefit of prescription to leaseholders because they wish to keep prescription within narrow confines.[147]

An owner of dominant land also is unable to claim prescription against servient land that is let, when the servient freehold owner cannot object to the use either because they did not know about it or because they were unable to take any action to stop it under the terms of their lease.[148] However, where the prescriptive user is initiated between freehold owners, the subsequent grant of a lease, either of the dominant or servient land, will not interrupt the prescription period.[149]

3.3.4 The function of prescription

Lord Hoffman in *Sunningwell*[150] noted that '[a]*ny legal system must have rules of prescription which prevent the disturbance of long-established de facto enjoyment*'. The Law Commission, in rejecting the abolition of prescription, has summarized the most important arguments for and against prescription.

---

[144] *Simmons v Dobson* [1991] 1 WLR 720; *Kilgour v Gaddes* [1904] 1 KB 457.
[145] The benefit of their prescriptive user accrues to the holder of the freehold.
[146] Noted at [2010] Conv 176.   [147] Law Com 327 (2011), [3.150].
[148] *Williams v Sandy Lane (Chester) Ltd* [2006] EWCA Civ 1738 and *Llewellyn v Lorey* [2011] EWCA Civ 37. See also Law Commission's proposals to codify this position in Law Com 327 (2011), [3.127].
[149] *Pugh v Savage* [1970] 2 QB 373.   [150] [2000] 1 AC 335, [349].

Law Commission, Law Com 327 *Easements, Covenants and Profits à Prendre* (2011)

At [3.75]–[3.76]

The arguments in favour of retention are that prescription has proved invaluable over the centuries as a way of regularising long use, bringing the legal position into line with practical reality. More specifically, it is valued as a way of ensuring the continuation of facilities that are essential to the use and marketability of land, and making good omissions in conveyancing.

However, the other side of the coin is that prescription penalises neighbourliness and generosity. A landowner who has made no objection to a neighbour's walking across his or her land may regard it as unfair if that tolerance eventually leads to the land being burdened with a legal easement.

4 EASEMENTS: THE *DEFENCES* QUESTION

We have already explored the aim of the LRA 2002 that the register '*should be a complete and accurate reflection of the state of the title of the land*'.[151] Easements presented a challenge to that goal, stemming from the fact that easements can arise by express, implied, and presumed grant, and that, under the Land Registration Act 1925 (LRA 1925), all easements potentially took effect as overriding interests.[152] Thus legal easements (whether arising by express, implied, or presumed grant) did not need to be entered on the register to bind a third party, although it was common practice for express easements to be so recorded. Somewhat controversially, equitable easements—arising, for example, from an agreement to create an easement—were also held to take effect as overriding interests, provided that they were openly enjoyed.[153]

The LRA 2002 has risen to the challenge by providing that:

- easements that are protected by registration will bind a purchaser;[154]

- easements created before the Act came into force on 13 October 2003, which are not protected by registration, but which are overriding interests, will continue to override;[155]

- an express easement created after 13 October 2003 must be registered if it is to take effect as a legal easement;[156]

- an equitable easement created after 13 October 2003 can no longer count as an overriding interest in its own right and so is vulnerable to the lack of registration defence (see Chapter 16, section 4.4);

- implied or presumed legal easements will only override if certain conditions are met—see Sch 3, paragraph 3 extracted below.

---

[151] Law Commission Report No 271, *Land Registration for the Twenty-First Century: A Conveyancing Revolution* (2001), [1.5]. See further Chapter 16.

[152] Land Registration Act 1925, s 70(1)a.

[153] *Celsteel Ltd v Alton House Holdings Ltd* [1985] 1 WLR 204, reversed in part on another point [1986] 1 WLR 512.

[154] Land Registration Act 2002, s 29(2)(a).   [155] Ibid, Sch 12, para 9.   [156] Ibid, s 27.

Implied easements arising by necessity, common intention, under *Wheeldon v Burrows*, or by the operation of s 62 of the LPA 1925, and presumed easements created by prescription present a particular problem to a system of title by registration.[157] If the grant or reservation of such an easement is implied into the grant or reservation of a legal estate in land, the implied easement will be a *legal* interest in land. Similarly, an easement arising by prescription is also a legal easement, of which there need be no documentary record. Such legal easements may be difficult to discover, because there is no express grant that can be lodged at the Land Registry.

The LRA 2002 seeks to overcome this problem by providing that implied and presumed legal easements will only override if they satisfy certain conditions that focus upon their discoverability.

Land Registration Act 2002, Sch 3, para 3

(1) A legal easement or profit a prendre, except for an easement, or a profit a prendre which is not registered under the Common Registration Act 1965 (c64) which at the time of the disposition—

    (a) is not within the actual knowledge of the person to whom the disposition is made, and

    (b) would not have been obvious on a reasonably careful inspection of the land over which the easement or profit is exerciseable.

(2) The exception in sub-paragraph (1) does not apply if the person entitled to the easement or profit proves that it has been exercised in the period of one year ending with the day of the disposition.

Thus, an implied or presumed legal easement created after 13 October 2003 will only bind a purchaser of the servient land if the purchaser knew, or should have known from a reasonably careful inspection of the servient land, of the easement, or the easement had been exercised by the dominant owner in the year preceding the sale. Those easements that fail to satisfy these conditions will vanish upon a disposal of the servient land, because they will not bind a registered purchaser for value.[158] A dominant owner claiming the benefit of an implied or presumed easement, however, may avoid this unhappy result by applying to have the easement registered.[159]

A disposal of the unregistered servient land, whether by way of transfer, a lease for more than seven years, or first mortgage, will now trigger first registration of that land.[160] Existing legal easements over that servient land (whether by express, implied, or presumed grant) will, on first registration, bind the purchaser as overriding interests.[161] Equitable easements will not, however, bind a purchaser of the servient land and the owner of the dominant land is well advised to lodge a caution against first registration of the servient land, so that they can assert their right against any purchaser.[162]

---

[157] See Burns (2008).

[158] Kenny, 'Vanishing Easements in Registered Land' [2003] Conv 304; Battersby, 'More Thoughts on Easements under the Land Registration Act 2002' [2005] Conv 195.

[159] Land Registration Rules 2003 (SI 2003/1417), r 74.   [160] Land Registration Act 2002, s 4.

[161] Ibid, Sch 1, para 3.   [162] Ibid, Part 2.

5 EXCESSIVE USER

Where a dominant owner exceeds the ambit of the right that he or she has been granted, the servient owner, or another dominant owner whose own rights are affected, may seek redress in nuisance for excessive user. That redress may include the grant of an injunction or an award of compensatory damages, or, in extreme cases, the extinguishment of the easement. In addition, a servient or another dominant owner may take self-help measures to stop the excessive user.

Whether or not a user is excessive will depend on the terms of the grant. Where the easement has been expressly granted, that will be determined by looking at the terms of the deed. Where the easement is implied or presumed, the courts will look at the use and the nature of the land at the time of the implied or presumed grant.[163] A mere increase in user will not be excessive; what is required is a radical change in the character of the user of the dominant land, which leads to a substantial increase in the burden that user places upon the servient land.

The Court of Appeal considered the question of excessive user in the following case.

McAdams Homes Ltd v Robinson
[2005] 1 P & CR 30, CA

Facts: The MacAdams built two homes on the site of an old bakery, which enjoyed a right of drainage over Robinson's land under *Wheeldon v Burrows*. Robinson successfully prevented McAdams from using the drain once the two houses were built, because the Court of Appeal found that McAdams' user was excessive, representing a substantial increase in the burden on the servient land.

Lord Neuberger

At 50–1

The authorities discussed above appear to me to indicate that that issue should have been determined by answering two questions. Those questions are:

i) whether the development of the dominant land, ie the site, represented a "radical change in the character" or a "change in the identity" of the site [. . .] as opposed to a mere change or intensification in the use of the site [. . .]

ii) whether the use of the site as redeveloped would result in a substantial increase or alteration in the burden on the servient land, ie the cottage [. . .]

In my opinion, the effect of the authorities in relation to the present case is that it would only be if the redevelopment of the site represented a radical change in its character and it would lead to a substantial increase in the burden, that the dominant owner's right to enjoy the easement of passage of water through the pipe would be suspended or lost.

At 55

The [. . .] potentially unsatisfactory feature of the approach I have suggested is that both questions could be said to involve an exercise which, in many circumstances, may have

---

[163] *British Railways Board v Glass* [1965] Ch 538.

a rather uncertain outcome. What may appear to be "a radical change in character" to one judge could easily appear differently to another judge; equally, one judge may consider a particular increase in the burden on the servient land to be "substantial", whereas another judge may not. It is, perhaps, inevitable that the questions have to be expressed in this rather generalised way, because each case will very much turn on its own facts, with regard to the particular easement, the position on the ground at the date of grant, the surrounding circumstances at the date of grant, and the nature and effect of the redevelopment that has subsequently taken place. What [the] cases [. . .] demonstrate is that, before a change of use or redevelopment can be sufficiently substantial for the servient owner to succeed on the first question, it really must involve something "radical". Similarly, before the servient owner can succeed on the second question, the cases show that the court must be satisfied that there has not merely been an increase (or change) in the enjoyment of the easement as a result of the changed character of the dominant land, but that there has been a real increase (or change) in the burden on the servient land.

6 EXTINGUISHMENT OF EASEMENTS

We have already seen that an easement will be extinguished, in the case of freehold land, where the dominant and servient land come into common ownership, and will be suspended, in the case of leasehold land, where the dominant and servient land come into common occupation.[164] We have also considered when an easement attached to a lease will be extinguished upon the termination of that lease.[165]

The dominant and servient owners may bring an easement to an end by express release and, more controversially, a release may also be implied as a result of abandonment.[166] Whereas partial abandonment of an easement as to part of the dominant land may be conceivable, it is not possible to abandon an easement limited by reference to a class of potential users entitled to exercise the easement.[167] An easement is abandoned if the dominant owner acts, or fails to act, with an intention to relinquish the right. The permanence of proprietary rights is demonstrated by the difficulty of proving that intention.[168] The fact of non-user does not raise any presumption of abandonment;[169] something more is required—particularly where the right by its nature is not continuously exercised.[170] For example, the alteration of the dominant land may demonstrate an intention to abandon where the right can no longer be exercised.[171]

McFarlane has suggested that abandonment is better viewed as an application of estoppel.

---

[164] See section 2.2.   [165] See section 2.1.4.

[166] Shorrock, 'Non-user of Easements' (1998) 4 Nott LJ 26.

[167] *Dwyer v Westminster CC* [2014] 2 P & CR 7.

[168] *Tehidy Minerals Ltd v Norman* [1971] 2 QB 528.

[169] The Law Commission has suggested that a presumption of abandonment should arise after twenty years—see Law Com 327 (2011), [3.230].

[170] *Amstrong v Shappard & Shroff* [1959] 2 QB 384; *Benn v Hardinge* (1993) 66 P & CR 246.

[171] *Ecclesiastical Commissioners for England v Kino* (1880) 14 Ch D 213; *Williams v Sandy Lane (Chester) Ltd* [2006] EWCA Civ 1738.

McFarlane, *The Structure of Property Law* (2008, p 873)

> However the concept of abandonment is very problematic. In general, a party with a property right does *not* have the power to simply give up that right: if he wishes to dispose of the right, he needs to transfer it to another. B [the dominant owner] can of course release an Easement; but only if a deed is used. Cases of so-called informal abandonment are hence better seen as examples of: (i) C [the servient owner] having a defence to B's Easement as a result of defensive estoppel; or C [the servient owner] relying on proprietary estoppel to show that B [the dominant owner] is under a duty to release his Easement.

An example of estoppel forming the basis for abandonment is found in *Lester v Woodgate*,[172] where the dominant owner's failure to object to the servient owner's actions in obstructing a right of way formed the basis for an estoppel by acquiescence upon which the servient owner had relied to his detriment such that it was unconscionable for the dominant owner (and his or her successors in title) to continue to assert his or her legal rights to use the right of way.

The Law Commission, meanwhile, has recommended that the jurisdiction of the Lands Chamber of the Upper Tribunal under s 84 of the LPA 1925, which we examine in the next chapter, should be extended to provide for the modification and discharge of easements.[173]

QUESTIONS

1. Do you think that a right to use a swimming pool could exist as an easement?

2. Why has the right to park caused such difficulty in being recognized as an easement?

3. What conceptual challenges do negative easements present?

4. An easement can be impliedly granted either by looking at the future use of the dominant land, or by looking at how the grantor has used the land in the past. In what circumstances can an easement be impliedly reserved?

5. Does it matter whether easements of necessity are based upon public policy or intention?

6. *Wheeldon v Burrows* and s 62 look deceptively similar, but how do they differ?

7. Should prescription be abolished?

8. In what circumstances will an implied or presumed easement vanish upon the sale of the servient land?

For guidance on how to answer these questions visit the online resources at www.oup.com/uk/mcfarlane4e/.

FURTHER READING

Burns, 'Easements and Servitudes Created by Implied Grant, Implied Reservation or Prescription and Title by Registration Systems' in *Modern Studies in Property Law Vol 5* (ed Dixon, Oxford: Hart Publishing, 2009)

---

[172] [2010] EWCA Civ 199.   [173] See Law Com 327 (2011) Part 7.

Burns, 'Prescriptive Easements in England and Legal Climate Change' [2007] Conv 133

Cooke, 'Re Ellenborough Park (1955) A Mere Recreation and Amusement' in *Landmark Cases in Land Law* (ed Gravels, Oxford: Hart Publishing, 2013) ch 3

Cowan, Fox O'Mahony, and Cobb, 'Third-Party Interests in the Use and Control of Land' in *Great Debates in Property Law* (Basingstoke: Palgrave Macmillan, 2012) ch 7

Douglas, 'Reforming Implied Easements' [2015] 115 LQR 251

Douglas, How to reform Section 62 of the Law of Property Act 1925 [2015] Conv 13

Goymour, 'Rights in Property and the Effluxion of Time' in *Modern Studies in Property Law Vol 4* (ed Cooke, Oxford: Hart Publishing, 2007)

Haley and McMurty, 'Identifying an Easement: Exclusive Use, De Facto Control and Judicial Constraints' (2007) 58 NILQ 490

Hill Smith, 'Rights of Parking and the Ouster Principle after *Batchelor v Marlow*' [2007] Conv 223

Lawson, 'Easements' in *Land Law: Issues, Debates, Policy* (ed Tee, Devon: Willan, 2002)

Luther, 'Easements and Exclusive Possession' (1996) 16 LS 51

Meager, 'Prescription and User "As of Right": Ripe for Wholesale Reform?' in *Modern Studies in Property Law Vol 6* (ed Bright, Oxford: Hart Publishing, 2011)

Paton and Seabourne, 'Can't Get There From Here? Permissible Use of Easements After *Das*' [2003] Conv 127

Shorrock, 'Non-user of Easements' (1995) 4 Nott LJ 26

Special Issue on Easements [2012] Conv 1–65

Sturley, 'Easements in Gross' (1980) 96 LQR 557

Tee, 'Metamorphoses and Section 62 of the Law of Property Act 1925' [1998] Conv 115

23

FREEHOLD COVENANTS

CENTRAL ISSUES

1. Restrictive covenants play an important role in controlling land use, supplementing and complementing public planning laws.

2. A covenant is an agreement by deed and, as such, generally only enforceable between the parties—but restrictive covenants can be enforced by and against subsequent owners of the land to which they relate.

3. A restrictive covenant must: (i) relate to land; (ii) be intended to be enforceable against subsequent owners of the land; (iii) be capable of benefiting adjacent land; and (iv) be negative in nature.

4. To be enforceable as an equitable proprietary interest, a restrictive covenant must be protected by appropriate registration.

5. The benefit of a restrictive covenant will run if it is: (i) expressly assigned; (ii) annexed to the land; or (iii) subject to a building scheme.

6. The breach of a restrictive covenant may result in an award of damages or the court may exercise its discretion to grant an injunction to restrain a breach or order action to 'cure' the breach.

7. The Lands Chamber of the Upper Tribunal has jurisdiction under s 84 of the Law of Property Act 1925 to modify or extinguish restrictive covenants.

8. The law governing covenants has long been regarded as unsatisfactory and has been subject to repeated proposals for reform which are likely to be shortly enacted.

1 INTRODUCTION

A covenant is an agreement entered into by deed and, as such, it binds the parties to the covenant. We saw in Chapter 21 how leasehold covenants may be enforced by and against a landlord's assignee of the freehold reversion and a tenant's assignee of the leasehold estate by privity of estate.[1] In this chapter, we will examine how certain

---

[1] See Goulding, 'Privity of Estate and the Enforcement of Real Covenants' (2007) 36 3 CLWR 193 for an interesting view that privity of estate, at one time, extended to covenants affecting the freehold estate and a comparative examination of the US position.

covenants relating to land between freehold owners can overcome the normal privity of contract rule, and can be enforced by and against third parties. For example, where neighbouring freeholders agree with each other that they will not build on their land without the consent of the other, the covenant will be of little value unless it can be enforced not only between the parties to this mutual covenant, but also any person who becomes an owner of either piece of land. Incidentally, the same principles may also be applied to enforce leasehold covenants against parties who are not within privity of estate: for example, subtenants.

1.1 THE ROLE OF LAND COVENANTS

The transformation of land covenants from mere personal contracts between landowners to proprietary obligations that affect subsequent owners of the land occurred during the nineteenth century, when the Chancery courts developed the rules that will be the subject of this chapter.

Gardner and McKenzie explain what prompted these developments.

Gardner & MacKenzie, *An Introduction to Land Law* (2015 p 339)

They date from the first half of the 19th century, a time of rapid growth of English towns. Many inhabitants were poor, but there was also an affluent urban middle class, which aspired to a high standard of living. The prevailing environment of slum housing, factories and so on was inimical to this: even if a middle class family's home was inwardly agreeable, stepping outside the front door could entail a quite different experience. Things could be improved, however, by creating enclaves of middle class housing, producing a more pleasant external as well as internal environment. The techniques by which this was done included the architectural (eg the terrace; and the square was an especially useful way of creating such an enclave especially if the rear rooms of the houses facing the squalor beyond, were made the servants quarters), and the horticultural (eg creating a pleasant garden in the middle of the square, a larger space than each individual house could command, and a place for socialising with persons similarly circumstanced).

But the trick would work only if it was possible to secure the enclave's integrity over time [. . .] This was a task for the law. Restrictive covenants are best understood as the new right in rem developed to perform it.

It was thus a desire to control land use that was the major driver at a time when there was little public health or planning control. Of course, there are now many legal controls over land ownership. Indeed, Gray and Gray[2] describe land ownership as being '*intrinsically delimited by social or community-orientated obligations of a positive nature*'. There are extensive public planning laws and building control regulations, so an owner cannot build on his or her land without the approval of the local planning authority, and only in a manner that accords with high safety and environmental standards. Cowan, Fox O'Mahony, and Cobb explain this interface and the values they reflect.

---

[2] See Gray and Gray, *Elements of Land Law* (5th edn, 2009) [1.5.54]–[1.5.57].

Cowan, Fox O'Mahony, and Cobb, *Great Debates in Property Law* (2012, pp 130–1)

We typically tend to think of controls over land use as being primarily public, administered (in the public interest) through planning law and environmental law. Yet private law (in the form of property law's easement and restrictive covenant, and tort's doctrine of nuisance) has also played its part in both the historical development of land use policies and in the matrix of controls that regulate the uses that contemporary private landowners can make of their land.

The idea that law places limits on the use of privately held land by an absolute owner raises important debates relating to popular conceptions of private ownership, on the one hand, and community ethics concerning land as a valued resource, on the other. Just how private is – or should be - ownership of land? [... .] The issue of third-party rights to control the use of privately owned land usually invokes quality of life and environmental considerations, whether on the part of the community at large (the so-called public interest), or one or more private individuals who own or occupy proximate land [... .] both public and private actions concerning land use are (explicitly or, in the case of private claims, sometimes implicitly) potentially informed by a broad range of ethical, aesthetic, ecological and socio-economic values concerning land use.

1.2 THE STRUCTURE AND TERMINOLOGY OF LAND COVENANTS

Before we go on to examine the detailed legal rules that achieve this regulation of land use and amenity, it is important that we understand the structure in which these rules operate and the terminology employed.

As illustrated in Figure 23.1, A (the owner of Plot A) may agree with his or her neighbour B (the owner of Plot B) that he or she will not build on Plot A without B's consent. Here, A has the *burden* of the covenant: his or her ability to build is restricted and he or she can be sued if he or she builds without consent. A is called the *covenantor*, while B is the *covenantee*. B has the *benefit* of the covenant: he or she can sue if A breaches the covenant.

As illustrated in Figure 23.2, if A sells Plot A, B will need to prove that the burden of A's covenant has passed with Plot A to the new owner. If B, in turn, sells Plot B, his or her purchaser will need to prove that the benefit of the covenant passes with Plot B to the new owner. These processes are referred to as the 'running of' the burden and the benefit.[3] We will use

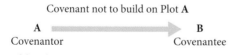

Covenant not to build on Plot **A**

| **A** | ⟶ | **B** |
| Covenantor | | Covenantee |

Figure 23.1 A restricted land covenant

---

[3] Gardner and Mackenzie have rightly pointed out that it is not the covenant that runs, but the owners of Plots A and B. The benefit and burden of the covenant is attached to the land itself, and thus goes nowhere; it is the owners that change: see Gardner & Mackenzie, *Introduction to Land Law* (4th edn, Oxford: Hart, 2015) pp 350–2.

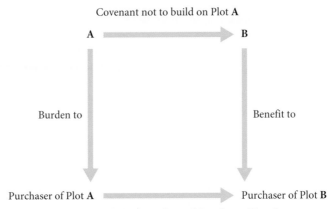

Figure 23.2 The transmission of the benefit and burden of land covenants

the expression 'dominant land' to refer to the land that has the benefit of the covenant and 'servient land' to refer to the land that is burdened.

Where the purchasers of Plots A and B acquire, whether by sale or gift, A and B's full freehold title, they are known as the *successors in title* to A and B, but if A leases Plot A and B mortgages Plot B, the new lessee and mortgagee are referred to as *persons deriving title* from A and B, respectively, because the interests that they acquire are carved out of A and B's freehold estates.

As illustrated in Figure 23.3, the structure becomes a little more complicated in the common situation in which A and B agree with each other that neither of them will build on their land without the consent of the other. Here, the covenants are mutual: A and B have both the benefit and the burden of the covenants; they are each both covenantor and covenantee. To work out, in a given scenario, whether we need to prove whether it is the benefit or the burden that has passed to the current owner of Plots A or B it is easier to ask whom we wish to sue (we need to prove that the burden has run) and then who wishes to sue (he or she must have the benefit of the covenant to do so).

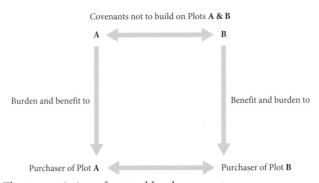

Figure 23.3 The transmission of mutual land covenants

2 THE BURDEN: WHO CAN BE SUED?

The burden of a covenant does not run at law,[4] so we must turn to the equitable principles initially formulated in the following leading case.[5]

Tulk v Moxhay
(1848) 2 Ph 774

Facts: In 1808, Tulk sold part of land that he owned in Leicester Square to Elms, who covenanted to Tulk that he would '*at all times thereafter at his own cost keep and maintain the piece of ground in sufficient and proper repair, and in an open state, uncovered with any buildings, in neat and ornamental order*'. This land came into the ownership of Moxhay, who had notice of the covenant that Elms had given to Tulk. When Moxhay made plans to develop the land, Tulk obtained an injunction to restrain him from doing so.

Lord Cottenham LC

At 777

That this Court has jurisdiction to enforce a contract between the owner of land and his neighbour purchasing part of it, that the latter shall either use or abstain from using the land purchased in a particular way, is what I never knew disputed. Here there is no question about the contract: the owner of certain houses in the square sells the land adjoining, with a covenant from the purchaser not to use it for any other purpose than as a square garden. And it is now contended, not that the vendee could violate that contract, but that he might sell the piece of land, and that the purchaser from him may violate it without this Court having any power to interfere. If that were so, it would be impossible for an owner of land to sell part of it without incurring the risk of rendering what he retains worthless. It is said that, the covenant being one which does not run with the land, this Court cannot enforce it; but the question is, not whether the covenant runs with the land, but whether a party shall be permitted to use the land in a manner inconsistent with the contract entered into by his vendor, and with notice of which he purchased. Of course, the price would be affected by the covenant, and nothing could be more inequitable than that the original purchaser should be able to sell the property the next day for a greater price, in consideration of the assignee being allowed to escape from the liability which he had himself undertaken.

That the question does not depend upon whether the covenant runs with the land is evident from this, that if there was a mere agreement and no covenant, this Court would enforce it against a party purchasing with notice of it; for if an equity is attached to the property by the owner, no one purchasing with notice of that equity can stand in a different situation from the party from whom he purchased.

Lord Cottenham's reasoning is primarily based on the fact that Moxhay acquired the land with knowledge of the promise that Elms had made to Tulk. On this reasoning, Tulk did

---

[4] *Austerberry v Oldham Corp* (1885) 29 Ch D 750, affirmed in *Rhone v Stephens* [1994] 2 AC 310.

[5] It appears that the principles first emerged in the earlier cases of *Whatman v Gibson* (1839) 2 My & K 517 and *Mann v Stephens* (1846) 15 Sim 377.

not assert a pre-existing equitable interest against Moxhay; rather, Tulk acquired a new, direct right as a result of Moxhay's conduct. But Lord Cottenham also hinted that the initial promise made by Elms to Tulk had proprietary characteristics. Certainly, as the doctrine developed during the latter half of the nineteenth century, the Chancery courts reinterpreted *Tulk v Moxhay* as a case in which Tulk *did* assert a pre-existing equitable interest, arising as a result of Elms' covenant with Tulk.[6]

In doing so, those courts also defined the characteristics of that equitable interest more clearly. The rules that they developed may be summarized as follows.

1. The burden of the covenant must not be personal, but must relate to, and be intended to run with, the land to which it relates.

2. There must be dominant land that is capable of benefiting from the covenant.

3. The covenant must be negative in nature.

These characteristics define the content of a land covenant, which, in common with any proprietary interest, must conform to the relevant creation and priority rules if it is to bind the parties and a subsequent purchaser.

2.1 THE COVENANT MUST RELATE TO LAND

The covenant must relate to the land and not to some personal obligation between the parties. A might agree to send B a dozen red roses on Valentine's Day, but whilst that might say something about A's personal attraction to B, it has nothing whatsoever to do with A's ownership of Plot A. The most common covenants that relate to land are concerned with the use of the land, or its repair or maintenance.[7] The parties must also intend that the covenant should affect them as owners of the land, rather than in a solely personal capacity, although such an intention is presumed.

Law of Property Act 1925, s 79(1)

(1) A covenant relating to any land of the covenantor or capable of being bound by him, shall, unless a contrary intention is expressed, be deemed to be made by the covenantor on behalf of himself his successors in title and the persons deriving title under him or them and subject as aforesaid, shall have effect as if such successors and other persons were expressed.

There have been several attempts to argue that s 79 of the Law of Property Act 1925 (LPA 1925) in itself enables the burden to run with the land, but these attempts have failed.[8]

---

6 See McFarlane, 'Tulk v Moxhay (1848)' in C Mitchell and P Mitchell (eds), *Landmark Cases in Equity* (Oxford: Hart Publishing, 2012) p 203.

7 Some covenants prohibiting competition have been held to be personal see *Morrells of Oxford Ltd v Oxford United Football Club Ltd* [2001] Ch 459, although restricting the user of land to prevent a particular commercial activity may not be see *Newton Abbott Co-operative Society v Williamson & Treadgold Ltd* [1952] 1 Ch 286.

8 *Re Royal Victoria Pavilion, Ramsgate* [1961] Ch 58; *Tophams Ltd v Earl of Sefton* [1967] 1 AC 50; *Rhone v Stephens* [1994] 2 AC 310; *Morrells of Oxford Ltd v Oxford United Football Club Ltd* [2001] Ch 459; but see Turano, 'Intention, Interpretation and the Mystery of Section 79 of the Law of Property Act 1925' [2000] Conv 377.

Section 79 is a word-saving device that makes it unnecessary to refer to 'successor in title' and 'persons deriving title' expressly in the covenant itself.

Robert Walker LJ explained (as dicta) its role in the following case, which concerned whether a covenant limiting competition was a personal covenant displaying a contrary intention for the purposes of s 79.

Morrells of Oxford Ltd v Oxford United Football Club Ltd
[2001] Ch 459, CA

Robert Walker LJ

At [40]

Section 79 is concerned with simplifying conveyancing by creating a rebuttable presumption that covenants relating to land of the covenantor are intended to be made on behalf of successors in title, rather than be intended as purely personal. That is a necessary condition, but not a sufficient condition, for making the burden of the covenants run with the land.

A little earlier in his judgment, he explained its effect.[9]

Morrells Oxford Ltd v Oxford United Football Club Ltd
[2001] Ch 459, CA

Robert Walker LJ

At [35]

My tentative view, therefore, coinciding, I think, with the judge's, is that section 79, where it applies, and subject always to any contrary intention, extends the number of persons whose acts or omissions are within the reach of the covenant in the sense of making equitable remedies available, provided that the other conditions for equity's intervention are satisfied. Where [. . .] section 79 applies, its normal effect is not to turn "A covenants with X that A will not build" into "A and B covenant with X that A will not build". Rather it is that "A (on behalf of himself and B) covenants with X that A (or, as the circumstances may require, B) will not build".

2.2 BENEFIT TO DOMINANT LAND

In a similar way to easements, there must be dominant land to which the benefit of the covenant is attached.[10] The benefit is attached to the covenantee's estate in the land[11] and, once he or she has disposed of that estate, he or she cannot enforce the covenant unless, as the

---

[9] See also Hurst, 'The Transmission of Restrictive Covenants' (1982) 2 LS 53, 75.
[10] Some earlier authorities had suggested otherwise: see *Catt v Tourle* (1869) LR 4 Ch 654 and *Luker v Dennis* (1877) 7 Ch D 227.
[11] A landlord's reversion is a sufficient estate for these purposes: see *Hall v Erwin* (1887) 37 Ch D 74.

original covenantee, he or she has a contractual right to do so. It is thus not possible for a covenant to exist in gross.

A common scenario arises where an owner of land sells part and requires the purchaser to enter into a covenant restricting what he or she can do with the purchased land, to maintain the amenity and value of the land that the seller retains.

London CC v Allen
[1914] 3 KB 642, CA

Facts: In order to obtain permission to form a street on part of his land, Mr Allen entered into a covenant with the London County Council that he would not build on the land at the end of the proposed street so that the new street could be extended. He then sold the land subject to the covenant to his wife, who built on the land. The London County Council tried to enforce the covenant against Mrs Allen, but was unsuccessful because it held no land that could benefit from the covenant.

Buckley LJ

At 654

The reasoning of Lord Cottenham's judgment in *Tulk v. Moxhay* is that if an owner of land sells part of it reserving the rest, and takes from his purchaser a covenant that the purchaser shall use or abstain from using the land purchased in a particular way, that covenant (being one for the protection of the land reserved) is enforceable against a sub-purchaser with notice. The reason given is that, if that were not so, it would be impossible for an owner of land to sell part of it without incurring the risk of rendering what he retains worthless. If the vendor has retained no land which can be protected by the restrictive covenant, the basis of the reasoning of the judgment is swept away. In *Haywood v. Brunswick Permanent Benefit Building Society* the Court of Appeal declined to extend the doctrine of *Tulk v. Moxhay* to covenants other than restrictive covenants. They rejected the doctrine that, inasmuch as the defendants took the land with notice of the covenants, they were bound in equity to perform them. That therefore is not the principle upon which the equitable doctrine rests. In the present case we are asked to extend the doctrine of *Tulk v. Moxhay* so as to affirm that a restrictive covenant can be enforced against a derivative owner taking with notice by a person who never has had or who does not retain any land to be protected by the restrictive covenant in question. In my opinion the doctrine does not extend to that case. The doctrine is that a covenant not running with the land, but being a negative covenant entered into by an owner of land with an adjoining owner, binds the land in equity and is enforceable against a derivative owner taking with notice. The doctrine ceases to be applicable when the person seeking to enforce the covenant against the derivative owner has no land to be protected by the negative covenant. The fact of notice is in that case irrelevant.

The particular equity recognized in *Tulk v. Moxhay* has been said to be analogous to an equitable charge upon land subsisting in the owner of the adjoining land, or to a negative easement enjoyed, not in gross, but by the adjoining land over the land to which the covenant relates. It arises from the possession by the covenantee of land enjoying the benefit of the negative covenant coupled with notice of the existence of the covenant. In *London and South Western Ry. Co. v. Gomm* Sir George Jessel says:

"The doctrine of *Tulk v. Moxhay*, rightly considered, appears to me to be either an extension in equity of the doctrine of Spencer's Case to another line of cases, or else an extension in equity of the doctrine of negative easements; such, for instance, as a right to the access of light, which prevents the owner of the servient tenement from building so as to obstruct the light. The covenant in *Tulk v. Moxhay* was affirmative in its terms, but was held by the Court to imply a negative. Where there is a negative covenant expressed or implied, as, for instance, not to build so as to obstruct a view, or not to use a piece of land otherwise than as a garden, the Court interferes on one or other of the above grounds. This is an equitable doctrine, establishing an exception to the rules of common law which did not treat such a covenant as running with the land, and it does not matter whether it proceeds on analogy to a covenant running with the land or on analogy to an easement."

The situation of the London County Council would not arise today, because statute has granted local authorities (and some other bodies) the ability to enforce covenants in the exercise of certain of their powers, although they hold no dominant land.[12]

2.2.1 Conservation covenants

A proposal to make an inroad into the need for dominant land lies in the Law Commission's recommendation to introduce conservation covenants as a tool to promote the conservation of the natural and built environment.[13] Although termed covenants, the proposal would establish a statutory regime, rather than a proprietary interest,[14] by which a landowner could enter into an agreement with a responsible body, for instance a charity, local authority, or other public body with conservations functions, which would impose positive or negative obligations upon the landowner for the time being. As such the obligation would exist in gross for the public good rather than be for the benefit of adjoining land with the responsible body charged with the enforcement of the obligation against both the original landowner and subsequent owners of the land. The crucial balance between imposing a new form of permanent burden on the land and flexibility to cater for changing circumstances, whilst acknowledging the public interest, is hoped to be achieved through locating monitoring and enforcement rights in a select group of public bodies and by providing routes by which the burden can be modified or discharged.[15] Similar schemes exist in other jurisdictions, including the USA, Canada, Australia, New Zealand, and Scotland, and have proved effective in advancing conservation objectives.

2.2.2 Identification of the dominant land

The dominant land needs to be identified with reasonable certainty, although general words, such as the references to the covenantee's retained land, will suffice and it is evident that the courts may look beyond the terms of the conveyance to the surrounding circumstances at the time of the creation of the covenant in order to ascertain the dominant land.[16]

---

[12] See (in the cases of local authorities) Housing Act 1985, s 609 considered in *Cantrell v Wycombe DC* [2008] EWCA Civ 866, and (in the case of local planning authorities) Town and Country Planning Act 1990, s 106.

[13] Law Commission, Law Com No 349.

[14] Pratt argues that conservations covenants should be afforded proprietary status see 'Conservation covenants: a proprietary analysis' [2014] Conv 328.

[15] See Reid, 'Conservation covenants' [2013] Conv 176 and Hodge, 'Conservation covenants: a policy perspective [2013] Conv 490.

[16] See also *Marten v Flight Refueling Ltd* [1962] 1 Ch 115.

Newton Abbott Co-operative Society v Williamson & Treadgold Ltd
[1952] Ch 286, HC

Facts: Mrs Mardon owned premises known as 'Devonia', on which she carried on business as an ironmonger. She also owned property across the street, which she sold, taking a covenant from the purchaser that he or she would not carry on business as an ironmonger. There was no indication in the covenant that it was taken for the benefit of Devonia. Some years later, the property subject to the covenant came into the ownership of Williamson & Treadgold, who began to sell items of ironmongery and hardware. The Co-op, as the present owner of Devonia and to which the benefit of the covenant had been assigned successfully, obtained an injunction restraining them from doing so.

Upjohn J

At 296

In my judgment, therefore, the problem which I have to consider is this: First, when Mrs. Mardon took the covenant in 1923, did she retain other lands capable of being benefited by the covenant? The answer is plainly yes. Secondly, was such land "ascertainable" or "certain" in this sense that the existence and situation of the land must be indicated in the conveyance or otherwise shown with reasonable certainty?

Apart from the fact that Mrs. Mardon is described as of Devonia, there is nothing in the conveyance of 1923 to define the land for the benefit of which the restrictive covenant was taken, and I do not think that carries one very far; but, for the reasons I have given, I am, in my judgment, entitled to look at the attendant circumstances to see if the land to be benefited is shown "otherwise" with reasonable certainty. That is a question of fact and, on the admitted facts, bearing in mind the close juxtaposition of Devonia and the defendants' premises, in my view the only reasonable inference to draw from the circumstances at the time of the conveyance of 1923 was that Mrs. Mardon took the covenant restrictive of the user of the defendants' premises for the benefit of her own business of ironmonger and of her property Devonia where at all material times she was carrying on that business, which last-mentioned fact must have been apparent to the purchasers in 1923.

The benefit of the covenant must also accommodate the dominant land of the covenantee, in the sense that it affects 'either the value of the land or the method of its occupation or enjoyment'.[17] In the *Newton Abbott Case*, the Co-op's counsel unsuccessfully argued that the covenant was a personal anti-competition covenant, which only benefited Mrs Mardon's business and not Devonia.

Newton Abbott Co-operative Society v Williamson & Treadgold Ltd
[1952] Ch 286, HC

Upjohn J

At 292

The second main question was whether the defendants are liable to have the covenant enforced against them. This was Mr. Bowles' main defence in this action and he says that the

---

[17] *Re Gadds Land Transfer* [1966] Ch 56, 66, *per* Buckley LJ.

restrictive covenant was not taken for the benefit of Devonia, and he puts his case in this way: [. . .] he says that in any event this was not taken for the benefit of any land, but was a covenant with Mrs. Mardon personally, solely for the benefit of her business [. . .] Mr. Bowles strongly urged that the covenant was taken solely to protect the goodwill of the business carried on at Devonia, that it had no reference to the land itself, and that it was not taken for the benefit of that land; in brief, that it was a covenant in gross incapable of assignment. He urged that taking such a covenant would benefit the business in that an enhanced price could be obtained for the business, but no such enhanced price would be obtained for the land. He relied on the fact that the covenant did not mention the vendors' assigns and that it was a covenant against competition. Further, he pointed out that when Leonard Soper Mardon assigned to the Bovey Tracey Cooperative Society, the benefit of the covenant was assigned in the deed which assigned the business and not in the lease of Devonia. If that be the right view, then he said there could be no right to enforce the covenant against the defendants because the mere fact that the defendants took with notice is not sufficient to bind their consciences in equity, and he relied on the two cases of *Formby v. Barker* and *London County Council v. Allen*. Those cases show, he submitted, and I agree with him, that in order to enforce a covenant such as this against an assign of the covenantor, you must show that the covenant created something analogous to an equitable easement, that is, you must find something in the nature of a dominant tenement for the benefit of which the covenant was taken and a servient tenement which was to be subject to that covenant. Here he says there was no dominant tenement; the covenant was taken not for the benefit of any land, but for the benefit of the business.

I do not accept this view of the transaction of 1923. In 1923 Mrs. Mardon was carrying on the business of an ironmonger at Devonia. No doubt the covenant was taken for the benefit of that business and to prevent competition therewith, but I see no reason to think, and there is nothing in the conveyance of 1923 which leads me to believe, that that was the sole object of taking the covenant. Mrs. Mardon may well have had it in mind that she might want ultimately to sell her land and the business and the benefit of the covenant in such manner as to annex the benefit of the covenant to Devonia for, by so doing, she would get an enhanced price for the totality of the assets which she was selling; a purchaser would surely pay more for a property which would enable him to sue in equity assigns of the defendants' premises taking with notice and to pass on that right, if he so desired, to his successors, than for a property which would only enable him to sue the original covenantor, for that is the result of the view urged on me by Mr. Bowles.

2.2.3 Establishing benefit

Accommodation will normally require reasonable proximity between the servient and dominant land, although it is conceivable that a comparatively large area can benefit where it forms an identifiable unit.[18] There tends to be a presumption of benefit unless such a conclusion just cannot be sustained.[19]

The approach is illustrated and explained in the following case.[20]

---

[18] See *Marten v Flight Refueling Ltd* [1962] Ch 115 and *Earl of Leicester v Wells-next-the-Sea UDC* [1973] Ch 110, but note the earlier case of *Re Ballard's Conveyance* [1937] Ch 473. Conveyancers usually circumvent any problem by providing for the severance of the covenant between those parts of a large estate that do benefit from the covenant and those parts that do not: see *Marquess of Zetland v Driver* [1939] Ch 1.

[19] It is for the party being sued, that is,. the covenantor or his or her successors in title, to prove the lack of benefit: see *Cryer v Scott Brothers (Sudbury) Ltd* (1988) 55 P & CR 183.

[20] See also *Marten v Flight Refuelling* [1962] Ch 115, 136, *per* Wilberforce J.

Wrotham Park Estate Co Ltd v Parkside Homes Ltd
[1974] 1 WLR 798, HC

Facts: Part of the Wrotham Estate was conveyed subject to a covenant that the land should only be developed in accordance with a layout plan approved by the estate company. Most of the land was developed in accordance with the covenant, but, when Parkside proposed to develop the remaining central area without obtaining prior approval, the estate company successfully took action on the covenant.

Brightman J

At 808

There can be obvious cases where a restrictive covenant clearly is, or clearly is not, of benefit to an estate. Between these two extremes there is inevitably an area where the benefit to the estate is a matter of personal opinion, where responsible and reasonable persons can have divergent views sincerely and reasonably held. In my judgment, in such cases, it is not for the court to pronounce which is the correct view. I think that the court can only decide whether a particular view is one which can reasonably be held.

If a restriction is bargained for at the time of sale with the intention of giving the vendor a protection which he desires for the land he retains, and the restriction is expressed to be imposed for the benefit of the estate so that both sides are apparently accepting that the restriction is of value to the retained land, I think that the validity of the restriction should be upheld so long as an estate owner may reasonably take the view that the restriction remains of value to his estate, and that the restriction should not be discarded merely because others may reasonably argue that the restriction is spent.

2.3 NEGATIVITY

The covenant in *Tulk v Moxhay* had both negative and positive aspects: firstly, it called for keeping the land in an open state, i.e. it should not be built upon; and secondly, it called for the maintenance and repair of the land, although it was the negative obligation against building that was enforced.[21] In the later cases of *Hayward v Brunswick Permanent Benefit Building Society*[22] and *London and South West Railway v Gomm*,[23] the court made clear that it would only enforce negative obligations. Negative obligations restrain the owner of the servient land from acting in some way, whilst a positive obligation requires owners to put their hands in their pockets to fund some activity: for example, to maintain the land or repair some building upon it.

There has been growing pressure to enforce positive land covenants, but the judiciary has firmly passed this particular buck to Parliament. In the following case, the House of Lords refused to overcome more than a century of orthodoxy.

---

21 In *Morland v Cook* (1868) LR 6 Eq 252 and *Cooke v Chilcott* (1876) 3 Ch D 694, positive obligations were enforced. See Bell, '*Tulk v Moxhay* Revisited' [1981] Conv 55; Griffiths, '*Tulk v Moxhay* Reclarified' [1983] Conv 29.

22 (1881) 8 QBD 403.   23 (1882) 20 Ch D 562.

Rhone v Stephens
[1994] 2 AC 310, HL

Facts: Walford House was divided into two dwellings—a house and a cottage—in such a way that one of the cottage bedrooms lay under the roof of the house. Upon the sale of the cottage, the owner of the house covenanted with the purchaser to keep the roof in repair. Some years later, when the roof had fallen into disrepair, the owner of the cottage unsuccessfully brought action against the then owner of the house: a successor in title to the original covenantor.

Lord Templeman

At 317

My Lords, equity supplements but does not contradict the common law. When freehold land is conveyed without restriction, the conveyance confers on the purchaser the right to do with the land as he pleases provided that he does not interfere with the rights of others or infringe statutory restrictions. The conveyance may however impose restrictions which, in favour of the covenantee, deprive the purchaser of some of the rights inherent in the ownership of unrestricted land. In *Tulk v. Moxhay* (1848) 2 Ph. 774, a purchaser of land covenanted that no buildings would be erected on Leicester Square. A subsequent purchaser of Leicester Square was restrained from building. The conveyance to the original purchaser deprived him and every subsequent purchaser taking with notice of the covenant of the right, otherwise part and parcel of the freehold, to develop the square by the construction of buildings. Equity does not contradict the common law by enforcing a restrictive covenant against a successor in title of the covenantor but prevents the successor from exercising a right which he never acquired. Equity did not allow the owner of Leicester Square to build because the owner never acquired the right to build without the consent of the persons (if any) from time to time entitled to the benefit of the covenant against building [. . .] Equity can thus prevent or punish the breach of a negative covenant which restricts the user of land or the exercise of other rights in connection with land. Restrictive covenants deprive an owner of a right which he could otherwise exercise. Equity cannot compel an owner to comply with a positive covenant entered into by his predecessors in title without flatly contradicting the common law rule that a person cannot be made liable upon a contract unless he was a party to it. Enforcement of a positive covenant lies in contract; a positive covenant compels an owner to exercise his rights. Enforcement of a negative covenant lies in property; a negative covenant deprives the owner of a right over property. As Lord Cottenham L.C. said in *Tulk v. Moxhay*, at p. 778: 'if an equity is attached to the property by the owner, no one purchasing with notice of that equity can stand in a different situation from the party from whom he purchased.'

Following *Tulk v. Moxhay* there was some suggestion that any covenant affecting land was enforceable in equity provided that the owner of the land had notice of the covenant prior to his purchase.

[His Lordship then considered the authorities: namely, the cases of *Morland v Cook*,[24] *Cooke v Chilcott*,[25] *Haywood v Brunswick Permanent Benefit Building Society*,[26] and *London and South Western Railway Co v Gomm*.[27]]

---

[24] (1868) LR 6 Eq 252. [25] (1876) 3 Ch D 694.
[26] (1881) 8 QBD 403. [27] (1882) 20 Ch D 562.

At 321

For over 100 years it has been clear and accepted law that equity will enforce negative covenants against freehold land but has no power to enforce positive covenants against successors in title of the land. To enforce a positive covenant would be to enforce a personal
obligation against a person who has not covenanted. To enforce negative covenants is only
to treat the land as subject to a restriction.

[His Lordship then referred to academic criticism of the rule and to recommendations by
the Law Commission to alter the law.]

In these circumstances your Lordships were invited to overrule the decision of the Court
of Appeal in the *Austerberry case*. To do so would destroy the distinction between law and
equity and to convert the rule of equity into a rule of notice. It is plain from the articles, reports
and papers to which we were referred that judicial legislation to overrule the *Austerberry
case* would create a number of difficulties, anomalies and uncertainties and affect the rights
and liabilities of people who have for over 100 years bought and sold land in the knowledge,
imparted at an elementary stage to every student of the law of real property, that positive
covenants, affecting freehold land are not directly enforceable except against the original
covenantor. Parliamentary legislation to deal with the decision in the *Austerberry case* would
require careful consideration of the consequences. Moreover, experience with leasehold
tenure where positive covenants are enforceable by virtue of privity of estate has demonstrated that social injustice can be caused by logic.

Lord Templeman argues that where land is burdened by a negative covenant, the purchaser
never receives the ability to act in breach of that covenant. Where the covenant is positive, however, he argues that the purchaser's title is burdened with an additional obligation that equity cannot order should be performed without contradicting the common law.
O'Connor explains the distinction:

O'Connor, 'Careful what you wish for: positive freehold covenants' [2011]
Conv 191

A restrictive covenant removes one or more use rights from the burdened owner's bundle
of use rights, making it inequitable for a purchaser with notice to assert a use right which
he or she did not acquire. Positive obligations to other landowners never formed part of the
bundle in the first place. They can only be added by contract, and they bind only those who
have agreed to undertaken them.

Gardner comments that Lord Templeman's reasoning is not convincing; rather, the decision
springs from an understandable reluctance to entertain judicial legislation.

Gardner, 'Two Maxims of Equity' (1995) 54 CLJ 60, 67

He appears to suppose that the common law, with its privity rule, "objects" to covenants
being enforced against purchaser, but is "content" for them to bind purchasers under nemo
dat, if some other system—equity—wants to make them do so.

But this analysis is surely chimerical. We simply do not know whether the common law "objects" to covenants being enforced against non-parties, either as such or by virtue of nemo dat; or whether it is "content" for this to happen; or whether indeed, it aches for it to happen. And the reason we do not know is, of course, that the common law cannot possess such states of mind or emotions. That is not quite to say that Lord Templeman's version of the proposition is unworkable, however. It can be made workable if the judges are prepared to make the attitude of the common law the subject of oracular pronouncement, as though it were a mystery of which they were the priests. This is in effect how Lord Templeman proceeds when he tells us that to make positive covenants binding on purchasers would "contradict", rather than "supplement", the common law. But when we understand that the proposition must operate, if at all, in this way, we cannot but find it a quite remarkably indeterminate and opaque tool of reasoning, outstripping in these respects even the established maxims. Its acceptability in the law must therefore be in extreme doubt.

In *Rhone v Stephens*, the considerations which resort to the proposition concealed were essentially as follows. Whilst it is widely felt that to provide for the running of positive covenants is desirable, the reform is an unsuitable one for judicial legislation, for two reasons. First it would need to be accompanied by a good deal of fine print, which could only be supplied by statute. Secondly, a judicial decision to enforce positive covenants would necessarily operate retrospectively, which would defeat the legitimate expectation of purchasers, advised on the basis of existing law, that they take free of such covenants.

The Law Commission has again looked at the question and we will be considering its proposals in section 5. In the meantime, there are a number of mechanisms that conveyancers use to try to enforce positive covenants.

2.4 INDIRECT ENFORCEMENT OF POSITIVE COVENANTS

The inability to directly enforce positive freehold covenants against subsequent purchasers of the servient land causes inconvenience and conveyancers have needed to be inventive. The need to enforce positive obligations is particularly acute where properties share facilities when provision needs to be made for their upkeep and repair. We have already seen, in Chapter 21, that the same problem does not affect positive leasehold covenants and, in the next chapter, we will examine the mechanisms employed to address the repair and maintenance of shared facilities in flat ownership. For now, we will consider the other devices that have been employed.

2.4.1 Mutual benefit and burden

The principle of mutual benefit and burden is encapsulated in the maxim that 'he who takes the benefit of a right must bear the burden upon which it is dependent'. If A enters into a positive covenant with B, the benefit and burden principle may sometimes impose a duty on C, a party later acquiring A's land, to perform that positive covenant. The principle is illustrated by the case of *Halsall v Brizell*,[28] in which purchasers of houses on an estate in Liverpool were granted a right to use the estate roads, the drains, the promenade, and the sea wall, subject to an obligation to contribute to the repair and upkeep of these facilities. When

---

[28] [1957] Ch 169.

Brizell, a successor in title to one of the original purchasers, questioned his contribution, the court held that he could not claim the benefit of the right to use these facilities without accepting the attendant obligation to pay for their upkeep.

In *Tito v Wadell (No 2)*,[29] Megarry V-C drew a distinction between *conditional benefits*, in which the benefit was conferred subject to a condition that a burden be accepted, and *independent obligations*, in which the right and obligation, although granted by the same instrument, were not interdependent. In the case of conditional benefits, the burden clearly passes, because the obligation is an intrinsic part of the right. In the case of independent obligations, Megarry V-C argued that the burden should also pass, under what he called the 'pure benefit and burden' principle, where the construction of the instrument demonstrated that a successor in title was not intended to take the benefit without also accepting the burden. In other words, although the initial grant was not conditional upon the burden, its subsequent assignment was. The principle of pure benefit and burden, taken to its logical conclusion, could have circumvented the common laws' prohibition on the burden of covenants passing, but the House of Lords has rejected the principle.

Rhone v Stephens
[1994] 2 AC 310, HL

Lord Templeman

At 322

Mr. Munby also sought to persuade your Lordships that the effect of the decision in the *Austerberry case* had been blunted by the 'pure principle of benefit and burden' distilled by Sir Robert Megarry V.-C. from the authorities in *Tito v. Waddell (No. 2)* [1977] 1 Ch. 106, 301 et seq. I am not prepared to recognise the 'pure principle' that any party deriving any benefit from a conveyance must accept any burden in the same conveyance. Sir Robert Megarry V.-C. relied on the decision of Upjohn J. in *Halsall v. Brizell* [1957] Ch. 169. In that case the defendant's predecessor in title had been granted the right to use the estate roads and sewers and had covenanted to pay a due proportion for the maintenance of these facilities. It was held that the defendant could not exercise the rights without paying his costs of ensuring that they could be exercised. Conditions can be attached to the exercise of a power in express terms or by implication. *Halsall v. Brizell* was just such a case and I have no difficulty in wholeheartedly agreeing with the decision. It does not follow that any condition can be rendered enforceable by attaching it to a right nor does it follow that every burden imposed by a conveyance may be enforced by depriving the covenantor's successor in title of every benefit which he enjoyed thereunder. The condition must be relevant to the exercise of the right. In *Halsall v. Brizell* there were reciprocal benefits and burdens enjoyed by the users of the roads and sewers. In the present case clause 2 of the 1960 conveyance imposes reciprocal benefits and burdens of support but clause 3 which imposed an obligation to repair the roof is an independent provision. In *Halsall v. Brizell* the defendant could, at least in theory, choose between enjoying the right and paying his proportion of the cost or alternatively giving up the right and saving his money.

---

[29] [1977] 1 Ch 106.

The Court of Appeal has subsequently formulated a two-stage test to establish whether a covenant falls within the mutual benefit and burden principle. The first stage looks to proof that the benefit is conferred conditionally upon performance of the burden; the second stage calls for the successor in title to have a choice as to whether he or she will accept the benefit and its attendant burden.

Thamesmead Town Ltd v Allotey
(2000) 79 P & CR 557, CA

Facts: A tenant on the Thamesmead Estate purchased the freehold reversion of his house under a right to buy. In the conveyance, he entered into a covenant to contribute to the upkeep of the roads, footpaths, sewers, and cables, as well as the landscaped and communal areas. The conveyance included a right for the purchaser to use the roads, footpaths, sewers, and cables, but no right to use the landscaped or communal areas. The tenant sold his house and his purchaser, Mr Allotey, questioned the amount of the service charge that he was required to pay. The Court held that he was not liable to pay that proportion of the charge which related to the costs of the landscaped and communal areas, because he had not been granted a right to use these facilities.

Peter Gibson LJ

At 564

The reasoning of Lord Templeman suggests that there are two requirements for the enforceability of a positive covenant against a successor in title to the covenantor. The first is that the condition of discharging the burden must be relevant to the exercise of the rights which enable the benefit to be obtained. In *Rhone v. Stephens* the mutual obligations of support was unrelated to, and independent of, the covenant to maintain the roof. The second is that the successors in title must have the opportunity to choose whether to take the benefit or having taken it to renounce it, even if only in theory, and thereby to escape the burden and that the successors in title can be deprived of the benefit if they fail to assume the burden. On both those grounds *Halsall v. Brizell* was distinguished. Although Lord Templeman expressed his wholehearted agreement with Upjohn J.'s decision, Lord Templeman's description of that decision was limited to the defendant being unable to exercise the rights to use the estate roads and to use the sewers without paying his costs of ensuring that they could be exercised. Nothing was expressly said about the cost of maintaining the sea wall or promenade and it is a little difficult to see how, consistently with Lord Templeman's reasoning and, in particular, the second requirement for the enforceability of a positive covenant, the cost of maintaining the sea wall would fall within the relevant principle [. . .]

Lord Templeman was plainly seeking to restrict, not enlarge, the scope of the exception from the rule that positive covenants affecting freehold land are not directly enforceable except against the original covenantor. Lord Templeman treated *Halsall v. Brizell* as a case where the right to use the estate roads and sewers was conditional on a payment of a due proportion of the maintenance expenses for those facilities. Whilst agreeing with the decision, Lord Templeman made clear that for a burden to be enforceable it must be relevant to the benefit. He said that simply to attach a right to a condition for payment would not render that condition enforceable. Similarly, it is not possible to enforce every burden in a convey-ance by depriving the covenantor's successors in title of every benefit which he enjoyed under the conveyance. There must be a correlation between the burden and the benefit which the successor has chosen to take. Lord Templeman plainly rejected the notion that taking a benefit under a conveyance was sufficient to make every burden of the conveyance enforceable. Further, there is no authority to suggest that any benefit obtained by a suc-cessor in title, once the property has been transferred to him, to enable the enforcement of a burden under the conveyance is sufficient, even if that benefit was not conferred as of right by the conveyance. In my judgment, it cannot be sufficient that the taking of an incidental benefit should enable the enforcement of a burden against a person who has not himself covenanted to undertake the particular burden.

In *Davies v Jones*[30] Sir Andrew Morritt C conveniently summarized these requirements:

(1) The benefit and burden must be conferred in or by the same transaction. In the case of benefits and burdens in relation to land it is almost inevitable that the transaction in ques-tion will be effected by one or more deeds or other documents.

(2) The receipt or enjoyment of the benefit must be relevant to the imposition of the burden in the sense that the former must be conditional on or reciprocal to the latter. Whether that requirement is satisfied is a question of construction of the deeds or other docu-ments where the question arises in the case of land or the terms of the transaction, if not reduced to writing, in other cases. In each case it will depend on the express terms of the transaction and any implications to be derived from them.

(3) The person on whom the burden is alleged to have been imposed must have or have had the opportunity of rejecting or disclaiming the benefit, not merely the right to receive the benefit.

The second requirement is approached as 'a matter of substance rather than form'[31] in that the benefit of the right does not have to be expressly conditional upon acceptance of the burden but a link needs to be drawn. The choice referred to in the third requirement may be more theoretical than real in that a purchaser may need the benefit of the rights conferred, for instance a right of way, and thus effectively has to accept the burden.

In *Thamesmead* the service charge could be apportioned between the facilities that the householders were entitled to use and those they were not, but in *Wilkinson v Kerdene Ltd*[32] it was impossible to do so. In these circumstances the Court of Appeal held that where the service charge could not be apportioned the burden of the whole service charge is recover-able provide 'it relates at least in part to the rights'[33] granted. Apportionment of expenses resulting in a positive burden is also in issue where the subsequent purchaser acquires part of the land to which the burden relates. In these circumstances the landowner will be re-quired to pay a fair and reasonable proportion of the expenses appropriate to their part of the land.[34]

---

[30] [2010] 1 P & CR 22 at [27].   [31] Per Patten LJ in *Elwood v Goodman* [2014] 2 WLR 967 at [28].
[32] [2013] EWCA Civ 44.   [33] At [32] *per* Patten LJ.
[34] *Per* Patten LJ in *Elwood v Goodman* [2014] 2 WLR 967 at [30].

2.4.2 Chain of indemnity covenants

It is common practice for conveyancers to build up a chain of personal covenants between successors in title of the covenantor, to try to ensure that contractual liability may be passed down from the original covenantor to the current owner of the servient land. If the current owner breaches a positive covenant, the covenantee can sue the original covenantor, who, in turn, can sue his or her direct successor in title on his or her personal covenant—and so on down the chain of covenants, until liability comes to rest upon culprit. The mechanism provides an unsatisfactory solution, both because the covenantee may only recover damages in respect of the breach, rather than an injunction, and because the chain may easily be broken by the disappearance or insolvency of one of the links.

2.4.3 Estate rentcharges

The expenses incurred in maintaining and repairing common facilities within an estate may be recoverable by imposing an estate 'rentcharge' on the land.[35] An estate rentcharge is a legal interest that requires the owner of the burdened land to pay a periodic sum, which may be recovered by exercising an attached right of re-entry.[36] That sum may be nominal, where the estate rentcharge is used as a device to enforce positive covenants, or may reflect the cost incurred by the holder of the rentcharge (i.e. the developer or manager, as owner of the estates' common parts) of *'meeting or contributing towards the cost of performance* [. . .] *of covenants for the provision of services, carrying out maintenance or repairs, effecting insurance or the making of any benefit'.*[37]

2.5 THE ACQUISITION AND PRIORITY OF RESTRICTIVE COVENANTS

2.5.1 Creation of covenants

Covenants are invariably expressly created by deed—usually in the conveyance, when part of land is sold off—and are made pursuant to the contract for the sale of that land.[38] Because restrictive covenants operate in equity rather than at law, however, it is theoretically possible for a restrictive covenant to be created by signed writing[39] or even through the operation of proprietary estoppel.[40]

2.5.2 The priority of covenants

The decision of Lord Cottenham in *Tulk v Moxhay* was based upon the unconscionability that would result if purchasers with notice of the covenant could then claim that they were not bound. Indeed, purchasers could be unjustly enriched if the land, freed from the burden covenant, were then to increase in value. As the doctrine developed, the courts came to

---

[35] Whilst new rent charges cannot generally be created following the Rentcharges Act 1977, estate rent charges are exempt from this prohibition: see Rentcharges Act 1977, ss 2(1), (2), and (3)(c).

[36] Bright, 'Estate Rentcharges and the Enforcement of Positive Obligations' [1988] Conv 99.

[37] Rentcharges Act 1977, s 2(4)(b) and (5).

[38] Theoretically, a covenant might be implied as a result of the usual contractual principles governing the implication of terms.

[39] See Law of Property Act 1925, s 53(1)(a).   [40] See Chapter 10.

recognize restrictive covenants as equitable proprietary interests, which would bind all save for a bona fide purchaser of the legal estate without notice of the covenant. This metamorphosis of restrictive covenants from personal obligation to proprietary status was a remarkable development. It is not surprising that the courts then had to work hard to keep the doctrine within clear definitional bounds, to maintain a balance between the amenity advantages of restrictive covenants and the danger of sterilizing land development by '*incidents of a novel kind* [. . .] *devised* [. . .] *at the fancy and caprice of any owner*'.[41]

The proprietary status of restrictive covenants is explained in the following case, in which the question before the court was whether a squatter took subject to restrictive covenants affecting the title that had been extinguished.

Re Nisbet & Potts Contract
[1906] 1 Ch 386, CA

Collins MR

At 402

It seems to me, therefore, that the principal question before us is whether or not Sir George Jessel was right in the view that he took in *London and South Western Ry. Co. v. Gomm*, that an obligation created by a restrictive covenant is in the nature of a negative easement, creating a paramount right in the person entitled to it over the land to which it relates. If that is so, then, in the present case, the squatter, by his squatting, simply acquired a right to land subject to this incident. Of course, the burden of that incident must pass to all persons who subsequently become assignees of the land, and the squatter is not entitled to hand it over freed from the obligation that was imposed on the person whose title he has ousted by his possession.

Now, is that the law or not? In the first place, I do not think there was anything inconsistent in the view taken by Sir George Jessel with the law as laid down in the leading case of *Tulk v. Moxhay*, though, no doubt, words are used there pointing to the equity arising out of the injustice which would accrue if a person who had acquired land at a reduced price by reason of its user being subject to a restriction were afterwards enabled to pass on that land to other persons freed from that restriction receiving in return, on that ground, an increased price. That element, no doubt, does enter into consideration, when one comes to inquire what is the position of a person who acquires for value the legal estate in land subject to a right that has previously been created in another person to restrict the user of that land. The right so created is an equitable right, and, therefore, it is one capable of being defeated in certain circumstances by a person who acquires the legal estate for value. The question thus arises whether, in the circumstances of the particular case, there is anything which would make it inequitable for that person to avail himself of his legal estate to defeat that equitable right. That, as Mr. Upjohn pointed out, is an inquiry which is inevitable in cases where you are dealing with equitable rights and legal estates. But that does not in the least prevent the right in question being what Sir George Jessel considered it to be, namely, a burden imposed upon the land, and passing with the land, subject, of course, to this, that it may be defeated by a purchaser for value without notice; but the burden is upon the person who takes the land to shew that he has acquired it under such conditions as to defeat the right as against him, namely, that he has acquired it for value and without notice.

---

[41] *Keppel v Bailey* (1834) 2 My & K 517, 535, *per* Lord Brougham.

McFarlane points out that this decision, so far as it relates to imposing a duty upon a squatter to observe a restrictive covenant affecting the paper owners title, is 'impossible to justify as a matter of doctrine' but is 'based on the needs of practical convenience'.[42]The value of restrictive covenants would be much diminished if their observance could be ignored by squatters acquiring an independent title to the servient land.

The priority of restrictive covenants created before 1925 continues to be regulated by notice, but restrictive covenants created after 1925 have been assimilated into the relevant registration regime. Where the servient land is registered, the covenant must be protected by the entry of a notice on the charges register.[43]

Where a positive covenant is enforceable against a subsequent owner of the land by the principle of mutual benefit and burden the obligation is personal and thus the covenant does not have to be registered.[44]

3   THE BENEFIT: WHO CAN SUE?

Those entitled to the benefit of a land covenant defines those who can take action on the covenant. There are three ways in which the benefit of a covenant can pass from the original covenantee to a new owner of the dominant land:

- by assignment, both at law and in equity;
- by annexation of the benefit of the covenant to the land, either by express words, implication, or by the operation of s 78 of the LPA 1925; or
- under a building scheme.

These three methods, particularly annexation, have been the subject of highly technical rules that have been described as providing '*one of the richest areas of fantasy in printed English*'.[45] The search has been to find both an intention that the benefit of the covenant should pass and also to identify, with a degree of certainty, the land to which the benefit is attached.

Wade explains the tensions that have resulted.

Wade, 'Covenants: "A Broad and Reasonable View" ' (1972) 31 CLJ 157, 162–5

After making much heavy weather over the transmission of the benefit, and so producing a body of law of notorious and unnecessary difficulty, the Chancery judges have now for twenty years been striving to relax their own rules. They have been working towards what might be called implied annexation, where there is no requirement of any formality but the decisive factor is the intention of the parties to the covenant, as inferred not only from its language but also from the surrounding facts at the time when it was made. The tendency is thus to assimilate the law of covenants to the law of easements, where no formalities are required for establishing the rights as appurtenant to the dominant tenement.

---

[42] McFarlane, *The Structure of Property Law* (Oxford: Hart, 2008) p 894.
[43] See Chapter 16; Land Registration Act 2002, ss 29, 32–4.
[44] *Elwood v Goodman* [2014] 2 WLR 967.
[45] Kenny, 'Conveyancer's Notebook' [2006] Conv 1, 2.

This policy is uncomfortable to conveyancers, who inhabit a world of paper and ink in which all important facts are expected to be clearly stated in documents of title [. . .]

Accordingly there may be said to be two opposing views: the "conveyancers' view," if it may be so called advocates compulsory formality; and the "judicial view" which at present indicates away from formality, and which at all times is concerned to temper the injustice which compulsory formality entails.

3.1 ASSIGNMENT

Like the benefit of any other contract, the benefit of a land covenant may be assigned. Thus the original covenantee may transfer both the land and the benefit of the covenant to a purchaser of the land by using express words of assignment, provided that the covenant relates to the land, in the sense that it is not personal to the covenantee. The benefit of the covenant will need to be expressly assigned on each disposal of the land to build up a continuous chain of assignments. The assignment may take effect at law where the original covenantee and his or her assignee hold a legal estate in the land, although that need not be the same legal estate.[46]

Assignment at law is, however, of limited value: only the original convenator can be sued, given that the burden does not run at law, and, because a covenant cannot be severed at law, a legal assignment will not assist where part of the dominant land is sold.

Assignment in equity, the requirements of which are found in the following case, overcomes these deficiencies and is frequently employed by conveyancers.

Miles v Easter
[1933] Ch 611, CA

Romer LJ

At 631

It is plain, however, from these and other cases, and notably that of *Renals v. Cowlishaw*, that if the restrictive covenant be taken not merely for some personal purpose or object of the vendor, but for the benefit of some other land of his in the sense that it would enable him to dispose of that land to greater advantage, the covenant, though not annexed to such land so as to run with any part of it, may be enforced against an assignee of the covenantor taking with notice, both by the covenantee and by persons to whom the benefit of such covenant has been assigned, subject however to certain conditions. In the first place, the "other land" must be land that is capable of being benefited by the covenant—otherwise it would be impossible to infer that the object of the covenant was to enable the vendor to dispose of his land to greater advantage. In the next place, this land must be "ascertainable" or "certain," to use the words of Romer and Scrutton L.JJ. respectively. For, although the Court will readily infer the intention to benefit the other land of the vendor where the existence and situation of such land are indicated in the conveyance or have been otherwise shown with reasonable certainty, it is impossible to do so from vague references in the conveyance or in other documents laid

---

[46] *Smith and Snipes Hall Farm Ltd v River Douglas Catchment Board* [1949] 2 KB 500.

before the Court as to the existence of other lands of the vendor, the extent and situation of which are undefined. In the third place, the covenant cannot be enforced by the covenantee against an assign of the purchaser after the covenantee has parted with the whole of his land.

3.2 ANNEXATION

Annexation is a once-and-for-all process by which the benefit of the covenant is glued to the land, so as to become part of the land and thus pass automatically upon a conveyance of the land. Two concerns need to be met to ensure annexation: firstly, there must be an intention that the benefit of the covenant should become part of the land; and secondly, it is necessary to determine the physical limits of the land to which the covenant is annexed—that is, what area is covered by the annexing glue? These questions are the flip side of the requirement for accommodation that we examined in section 2.2.

It is in the clarity of the evidence required to prove these two elements that the tension between the 'conveyancers' view' and the 'judicial view' is most evident. Conveyancers have looked to express words of annexation contained in the covenant and to clear evidence of the physical definition of the land in the conveyancing documents, whilst the courts have accepted a lower standard of evidence.

3.2.1 Express annexation

Express words of annexation can be demonstrated by contrasting the wording of the covenants in *Rogers v Hosegood*[47] and that in *Renals v Cowlishaw*.[48]

In *Rogers v Hosegood*, a covenant was made in the following terms.

'With the intent that the covenant might as far as possible bind the premises [. . .] conveyed and every part thereof, into whosoever hands the same might come, and might enure to the benefit of the mortgagees, their heirs and assigns and others claiming under them to all or any of their lands adjoining or near the premises.'

In *Renals v Cowlishaw*, the covenants merely stated that it was taken for '*the vendors, their heirs, executors, administrators and assigns*'.

Thus, in *Rogers v Hosegood*, it was clear that the covenant was to become part of the land, because it was made with the covenantee and his or her successors in title in their capacity as owners of adjoining land; in *Renals v Cowlishaw*, the absence of any reference to the covenantee's land was fatal.

The technicality of express annexation and its relationship with the passing of the burden is illustrated by the following judgment of Farwell J.

Marquess of Zetland v Driver
[1939] Ch 1, CA

Facts: A conveyance of a shop in Redcar made by the Marquess' estate contained a covenant by the purchaser not to commit any nuisance to the vendor or occupiers of any

---

[47] [1900] 2 Ch 388.   [48] (1878) 8 Ch D 125.

adjoining property in the neighbourhood. The covenant was expressed to be made for the benefit of such parts of the Marquess' estate as should remain unsold or be sold with the benefit of the covenant. An injunction was granted to restrain the use of the shop for the sale of fish and chips.

Farwell J

At 8

[. . .] [C]ovenants can only be validly imposed if they comply with certain conditions. Firstly, they must be negative covenants. No affirmative covenant requiring the expenditure of money or the doing of some act can ever be made to run with the land. Secondly, the covenant must be one that touches or concerns the land, by which is meant that it must be imposed for the benefit or to enhance the value of the land retained by the vendor or some part of it, and no such covenant can ever be imposed if the sale comprises the whole of the vendor's land. Further, the land retained by the vendor must be such as to be capable of being benefited by the covenant at the time when it is imposed. Thirdly, the land which is intended to be benefited must be so defined as to be easily ascertainable, and the fact that the covenant is imposed for the benefit of that particular land should be stated in the conveyance and the persons or the class of persons entitled to enforce it. The fact that the benefit of the covenant is not intended to pass to all persons into whose hands the unsold land may come is not objectionable so long as the class of persons intended to have the benefit of the covenant is clearly defined. Finally, it must be remembered that these covenants can only be enforced so long as the covenantee or his successor in title retains some part of the land for the benefit of which the covenant was imposed. Applying those conditions to the present case, the covenant sued upon appears to comply with them [. . .]

Under those circumstances, there does not appear to be any ground on which the appellant can properly be refused the relief which he seeks; but Bennett J. took the opposite view and held that the benefit of the covenant had not passed to the appellant. In coming to that conclusion he founded himself upon a decision of Clauson J. in *re Ballard's Conveyance*, which he considered to be exactly in point and binding upon him. In our judgment the learned judge was wrong in thinking that *In re Ballard's Conveyance* was an authority in this case. It is not necessary for us, and we do not propose, to express any opinion as to that decision beyond saying that it is clearly distinguishable from the present case, if only on the ground that in that case the covenant was expressed to run with the whole estate, whereas in the present case no such difficulty arises because the covenant is expressed to be for the benefit of the whole or any part or parts of the unsold settled property.

In the above extract, Farwell distinguished *Re Ballards Conveyance*,[49] in which annexation failed because the dominant land was so large that it was impossible to prove that the entire area benefited.[50] Whilst part of the land clearly could benefit, the court refused to sever the covenant so that the benefit could at least pass with that part. This unfortunate result was avoided in *Marquess of Zetland v Driver*, in which the covenant was expressed to be annexed to 'each and every part of the estate'.

Brightman LJ doubted the need for these words in the following case.

---

[49] [1937] Ch 473.   [50] The area was a 1,700-acre estate.

Federated Homes Ltd v Mill Lodge Properties Ltd
[1980] 1 WLR 594, CA

Brightman LJ

At 606

[. . .] [T]he idea of annexation of a covenant to the whole of the land but not to part of it is a difficult conception to grasp [. . .] I would have thought, if a covenant is, on a proper construction of a document, annexed to the land, prima facie it is annexed to every part thereof, unless the contrary clearly appears.

His views have subsequently been followed at first instance in *Small v Oliver & Saunders*.[51]

3.2.2 Statutory annexation

The technicalities of express annexation have been sidestepped by judicial recognition that s 78 of the LPA 1925 provides automatic annexation in respect of covenants entered into after 1925.[52]

Law of Property Act 1925, s 78

(1) A covenant relating to any land of the covenantee shall be deemed to be made with the covenantee and his successors in title and the persons deriving title under him or them, and shall have effect as if such successors and other persons were expressed.

For the purposes of this subsection in connection with covenants restrictive of the user of land 'successors in title' shall be deemed to include the owners and occupiers for the time being of the land of the covenantee intended to be benefited.

(2) This section applies to covenants made after the commencement of this Act, but the repeal of section fifty eight of the Conveyancing Act 1881 does not affect the operation of covenants to which that section applied.

The Court of Appeal considered the effect of this section in the following case.

Federated Home Ltd v Mill Lodge Properties Ltd
[1980] 1 WLR 594, CA

Facts: A vendor sold an area of land for development ('the blue land') to Mill Lodge, subject to a covenant restricting the density of development so as not to prejudice

---

[51] [2006] EWHC 1293, [29].

[52] Express annexation continues to be necessary under Conveyancing and Law of Property Act 1881, s 58, where the covenant is entered into before 1925: see *J Sainsbury plc v Enfield LBC* [1989] 1 WLR 590, *Southwark Roman Catholic Diocesan Corp v South London Church Fund and Southwark Diocesan Board of Finance* [2009] EWHC 3368 and *Seymour Road (Southampton) Ltd v Williams* [2010] EWHC 111.

development of the vendor's retained land under an existing planning permission. Subsequently, two further areas of land ('the red land' and 'the green land') were sold by the vendor and came into the ownership of Federated Homes. Mill Lodge threatened to breach the covenant and Federated Homes successfully sought an injunction claiming the benefit of the covenant. There was no express annexation conferring the benefit of the covenant upon the red and green land, although there was an express assignment of the benefit of the covenant in respect of the green land.

Brightman LJ

At 604

Mr. Price submitted that there were three possible views about section 78. One view, which he described as "the orthodox view" hitherto held, is that it is merely a statutory shorthand for reducing the length of legal documents. A second view, which was the one that Mr. Price was inclined to place in the forefront of his argument, is that the section only applies, or at any rate only achieves annexation, when the land intended to be benefited is signified in the document by express words or necessary implication as the intended beneficiary of the covenant. A third view is that the section applies if the covenant in fact touches and concerns the land of the covenantee, whether that be gleaned from the document itself or from evidence outside the document.

For myself, I reject the narrowest interpretation of section 78, the supposed orthodox view, which seems to me to fly in the face of the wording of the section. Before I express my reasons I will say that I do not find it necessary to choose between the second and third views because, in my opinion, this covenant relates to land of the covenantee on either interpretation of section 78. Clause 5 (iv) shows clearly that the covenant is for the protection of the retained land and that land is described in clause 2 as "any adjoining or adjacent property retained by the vendor." This formulation is sufficient for annexation purposes: see *Rogers v. Hosegood* [1900] 2 Ch. 388.

There is in my judgment no doubt that this covenant "related to the land of the covenantee," or, to use the old-fashioned expression, that it touched and concerned the land, even if Mr. Price is correct in his submission that the document must show an intention to benefit identified land. The result of such application is that one must read clause 5 (iv) as if it were written: "The purchaser hereby covenants with the vendor and its successors in title and the persons deriving title under it or them, including the owners and occupiers for the time being of the retained land, that in carrying out the development of the blue land the purchaser shall not build at a greater density than a total 300 dwellings so as not to reduce, etc." I leave out of consideration section 79 as unnecessary to be considered in this context, since Mill Lodge is the original covenantor.

The first point to notice about section 78 (1) is that the wording is significantly different from the wording of its predecessor section 58 (1) of the Conveyancing Act 1881. The distinction is underlined by section 78 (2), which applies section 78 (1) only to covenants made after the commencement of the Act. Section 58 (1) of the Act of 1881 did not include the covenantee's successors in title or persons deriving title under him or them, or the owner or occupiers for the time being of the land of the covenantee intended to be benefited. The section was confined, in relation to realty, to the covenantee, his heirs and assigns, words which suggest a more limited scope of operation than is found in section 78.

If, as the language of section 78 implies, a covenant relating to land which is restrictive of the user thereof is enforceable at the suit of (1) a successor in title of the covenantee, (2) a person deriving title under the covenantee or under his successors in title, and (3) the owner or occupier of the land intended to be benefited by the covenant, it must, in my view, follow that the covenant runs with the land, because ex hypothesi every successor in title to the land, every derivative proprietor of the land and every other owner and occupier has a right by statute to the covenant. In other words, if the condition precedent of section 78 is satisfied—that is to say, there exists a covenant which touches and concerns the land of the covenantee—that covenant runs with the land for the benefit of his successors in title, persons deriving title under him or them and other owners and occupiers.

The decision was controversial and has been criticized by those taking the traditional 'conveyancers' view'.[53] Two particular objections have been raised. The first, it is argued, is that this interpretation of s 78 is at odds with the interpretation given to its sister provision concerning the running of the burden found in s 79.[54] But the wording of the two sections is different, as Snape explains.

Snape, 'The Benefit and Burden of Covenants: now where are we?' (1994) 68 Nott LJ 68, 71

The crucial difference between the two sections is that, whilst section 78 [. . .] deems the covenant to be made "with the covenantee and his successors in title and the persons deriving title under him or them ", section 79 [. . .] deems the covenant to be made "on behalf of [the covenantor] and his successors in title and the persons deriving title under him or them". Whatever the precise scope of the word "deemed" is in each section, this difference in wording makes it clear that the benefit is, in principle, to pass to the covenant[ee]'s successors etc quite easily, whilst section 79 is intended, in the absence of contrary intention, to ensure that the burden remains firmly with the original covenantor.

The second objection is that, whilst s 79 expressly gives way to a contrary intention, s 78 does not. This objection is considered in the following case, in which the vendor of plots sold off from an estate imposed building restrictions, but provided that the benefit of these restrictions should not pass unless expressly assigned.

Roake v Chadha
[1984] 1 WLR 40, HC

Paul Baker QC

At 45

The *Federated Homes case* shows that section 78 of the Act of 1925 brings about annexation, and that the operation of the section cannot be excluded by a contrary intention. As I have indicated, he supports this last point by reference to section 79, which is expressed to

---

[53] Newsome, 'Universal Annexation' (1981) 97 LQR 32, (1982) 98 LQR 202; Snape, 'The Benefit and Burden of Covenants: Now Where Are We?' (1994) 3 Nott LJ 68; but see Hurst, 'The Transmission of Restrictive Covenants' (1982) 2 LS 53.

[54] See section 2.1.

operate "unless a contrary intention is expressed," a qualification which, as we have already noticed, is absent from section 78. Mr. Walter could not suggest any reason of policy why section 78 should be mandatory, unlike, for example, section 146 of the Act of 1925, which deals with restrictions on the right to forfeiture of leases and which, by an express provision "has effect notwithstanding any stipulation to the contrary."

I am thus far from satisfied that section 78 has the mandatory operation which Mr. Walter claimed for it. But if one accepts that it is not subject to a contrary intention, I do not consider that it has the effect of annexing the benefit of the covenant in each and every case irrespective of the other express terms of the covenant.

The true position as I see it is that even where a covenant is deemed to be made with successors in title as section 78 requires, one still has to construe the covenant as a whole to see whether the benefit of the covenant is annexed. Where one finds, as in the *Federated Homes case*, the covenant is not qualified in any way, annexation may be readily inferred; but where, as in the present case, it is expressly provided:

"this covenant shall not enure for the benefit of any owner or subsequent purchaser of any part of the vendor's Sudbury Court Estate at Wembley unless the benefit of this covenant shall be expressly assigned [. . .]"

One cannot just ignore these words. One may not be able to exclude the operation of the section in widening the range of the covenantees, but one has to consider the covenant as a whole to determine its true effect. When one does that, then it seems to me that the answer is plain and in my judgment the benefit was not annexed. That is giving full weight to both the statute in force and also what is already there in the covenant.

The Court of Appeal indorsed this view in the following case, by explaining that 'successors in title' is limited to those purchasers who are intended to benefit from the covenant and thus a contrary intention may exclude certain purchasers.[55]

Crest Nicholson Residential (South) Ltd v McAllister
[2004] 1 WLR 2409, CA

Chadwick LJ

At 2426–7

I respectfully agree, first, that it is impossible to identify any reason of policy why a covenantor should not, by express words, be entitled to limit the scope of the obligation which he is undertaking; nor why a covenantee should not be able to accept a covenant for his own benefit on terms that the benefit does not pass automatically to all those to whom he sells on parts of his retained land. As Brightman LJ pointed out, in the passage cited by Judge Paul Baker QC, a developer who is selling off land in lots might well want to retain the benefit of a building restriction under his own control. Where, as in *Roake v Chadha* and the present case, development land is sold off in plots without imposing a building scheme,

---

[55] A contrary intention has been found in the following cases *Margerison v Bates* [2008] EWHC 1211; *Norwich City College of Further and Higher Education v McQuillin* [2009] EWHC 1496; *Churchhill v Temple* [2010] EWHC 3369; but not in *89 Holland Park (Management) Ltd v Hicks* [2013] EWHC 391.

it seems to me very likely that the developer will wish to retain exclusive power to give or withhold consent to a modification or relaxation of a restriction on building which he imposes on each purchaser; unfettered by the need to obtain the consent of every subsequent purchaser to whom (after imposing the covenant) he has sold off other plots on the development land. I can see no reason why, if original covenantor and covenantee make clear their mutual intention in that respect, the legislature should wish to prevent effect being given to that intention.

Second, it is important to keep in mind that, for the purposes of its application to restrictive covenants-which is the context in which this question arises where neither of the parties to the dispute were, themselves, party to the instrument imposing the covenant or express assignees of the benefit of the covenant-section 78 of the 1925 Act defines "successors in title" as the owners and occupiers of the time being *of the land of the covenantee intended to be benefited.* In a case where the parties to the instrument make clear their intention that land retained by the covenantee at the time of the conveyance effected by the transfer is to have the benefit of the covenant only for so long as it continues to be in the ownership of the original covenantee, and not after it has been sold on by the original covenantee—unless the benefit of the covenant is expressly assigned to the new owner—*the land of the covenantee intended to be benefited* is identified by the instrument as (i) so much of the retained land as from time to time has not been sold off by the original covenantee and (ii) so much of the retained land as has been sold off with the benefit of an express assignment, but as not including (iii) so much of the land as has been sold off without the benefit of an express assignment. I agree with the judge in *Roake v Chadha* that, in such a case, it is possible to give full effect to the statute and to the terms of the covenant.

This approach to section 78 of the 1925 Act provides, as it seems to me, the answer to the question why, if the legislature did not intend to distinguish between the effect of section 78 (mandatory) and the effect of section 79 (subject to contrary intention), it did not include the words "unless a contrary intention is expressed" in the first of those sections. The answer is that it did not need to. The qualification "subject to contrary intention" is implicit in the definition of "successors in title" which appears in section 78(1); that is the effect of the words "the land of the covenantee intended to be benefited". If the terms in which the covenant is imposed show—as they did in *Marquess of Zetland v Driver* and in *Roake v Chadha*—that the land of the covenantee intended to be benefited does not include land which may subsequently be sold off by the original covenantee in circumstances where (at the time of that subsequent sale) there is no express assignment of the benefit of the covenant, then the owners and occupiers of the land sold off in those circumstances are not "owners and occupiers for the time being of the land of the covenantee intended to be benefited"; and so are not "successors in title" of the original covenantee for the purposes of section 78(1) in its application to covenants restrictive of the user of land. [. . .]

On a true analysis there is no difference in treatment in the two sections. There is a difference in the drafting technique used to achieve the same substantive result. That may well simply reflect the legislative history of the two sections. Section 78(1) of the 1925 Act re-enacted section 58 of the Conveyancing and Law of Property Act 1881 (44 & 45 Vict c 41) as applied by section 96(3) of the Law of Property Act 1922 and amended by section 3 of, and paragraph 11 of Schedule 3 to, the Law of Property (Amendment) Act 1924. Section 79 was a new provision, first introduced in the 1925 Act.

Statutory annexation may address the first evidential concern—namely, to demonstrate an intention that the benefit is to run to the covenantee's successors in title as owners of the dominant land—but it is still necessary to satisfy the second evidential requirement that the dominant land is adequately identified.[56]

Crest Nicholson Residential (South) Ltd v McAllister
[2004] 1 WLR 2409, CA

Facts: Crest intended to develop land that formerly comprised a number of different plots, originally sold off between 1926 and 1936, when they were made subject to similar covenants restricting their development and user. Some of the covenants contained express words of annexation, but others did not. Mrs McAllister, who lived in a house built on part of the plot sold off in 1936, opposed the development, claiming to be entitled to the benefit of the covenants. She was unsuccessful. Her land was insufficiently identified for the benefit to be expressly annexed or annexed via s 78.

Chadwick LJ

At 2421

The decision of this court in the *Federated Homes case* leaves open the question whether section 78 of the 1925 Act only effects annexation when the land intended to be benefited is described in the instrument itself (by express words or necessary implication, albeit that it may be necessary to have regard to evidence outside the document fully to identify that land) or whether it is enough that it can be shown, from evidence wholly outside the document, that the covenant does in fact touch and concern land of the covenantee which can be identified.

[The judge then referred to the cases of *Rogers v Hosegood* and *Marquess of Zetland v Driver.*]

At 2422–3

In its later decision in the *Federated Homes case* this court held that the provisions of section 78 of the 1925 Act had made it unnecessary to state, in the conveyance, that the covenant was to be enforceable by persons deriving title under the covenantee or under his successors in title and the owner or occupier of the land intended to be benefited, or that the covenant was to run with the land intended to be benefited; but there is nothing in that case which suggests that it is no longer necessary that the land which is intended to be benefited should be so defined that it is easily ascertainable. In my view, that requirement, identified in *Marquess of Zetland v Driver* remains a necessary condition for annexation.

There are, I think, good reasons for that requirement. A restrictive covenant affecting land will not be enforceable in equity against a purchaser who acquires a legal estate in that land for value without notice of the covenant. A restrictive covenant imposed in an instrument made after 1925 is registrable as a land charge under class D(ii): section 10(1) of the Land Charges Act 1925 and, now, section 2(5) of the Land Charges Act 1972. If the title is registered, protection is effected by entering notice of the restrictive covenant on the register: section 50 of the Land Registration Act 1925 and, now, section 11 of the Land Registration Act 2002. Where practicable the notice shall be by reference to the instrument by which the covenant is imposed and a copy or abstract of that instrument shall be filed at the registry: section

---

[56] See also *Mohammadzadeh v Joseph* [2006] EWHC 1040.

50(1) of the Land Registration Act 1925 and section 3(5) of the Land Charges Act 1972. It is obviously desirable that a purchaser of land burdened with a restrictive covenant should be able not only to ascertain, by inspection of the entries on the relevant register, that the land is so burdened, but also to ascertain the land for which the benefit of the covenant was taken-so that he can identify who can enforce the covenant. That latter object is achieved if the land which is intended to be benefited is defined in the instrument so as to be easily ascertainable. To require a purchaser of land burdened with a restrictive covenant, but where the land for the benefit of which the covenant was taken is not described in the instrument, to make inquiries as to what (if any) land the original covenantee retained at the time of the conveyance and what (if any) of that retained land the covenant did, or might have, "touched and concerned" would be oppressive. It must be kept in mind that (as in the present case) the time at which the enforceability of the covenant becomes an issue may be long after the date of the instrument by which it was imposed.

Section 78 is, thus, not a panacea for poor covenant drafting. The land to be benefited must be identified '*from a description, plan or other reference in the conveyance itself, but aided, if necessary, by external evidence to identify the land so described, depicted or otherwise referred to*'.[57] Even so, as Howell points out, identifying the land intended to be benefited can be problematic—particularly where time has elapsed and the original covenantee's land has been fragmented.

Howell, 'The Annexation of the Benefit of Covenants to Land' [2004] Conv 507, 513

The necessity of the benefited land to be sufficiently identified is the same whether the covenant is annexed by express words or by s78. The problem is that actually identifying the land on the ground which is to be benefited may be impossible and raise all the difficulties of enquiry which Chadwick LJ deplored. Simply stating as in *Rogers v Hosegood* that the land to be benefited "is nearby" and is all the land owned by X is surely no identification at all. In *Marquess of Zetland v Driver* the covenant imposed in 1928 was expressed for the benefit of land which was part of a settlement set up in 1871. The breach of the covenant was in 1938 and as it happened the whole of the land settled in 1871 was still intact in the hands of the tenant for life in possession, so identification of the land benefited was straightforward. It would be different where the covenants were imposed many years before and the land to be benefited had been sold in pieces [. . .]

There is no similar requirement in the law of easements that the land to be benefited be identified in the conveyance but there does not seem anything in the different natures of an easement and a restrictive covenant which justifies the difference in principle.

Drawing upon the easements analogy, arguments[58] have been put forward from time to time that the benefit of a covenant should pass under s 62 of the LPA 1925, which we considered

---

[57] *Crest Nicholson Residential (South) Ltd v McAllister* [2004] EWCA Civ 410, [45], *per* Chadwick LJ. See also *Stocks v Whitgift Homes Ltd* [2001] EWCA Civ 1732. Note the different evidence required to identify the dominant land where the burden and benefit pass: see section 2.2.

[58] See Hayton (1971) 87 LQR 539, 570, and Wade (1972) 31 CLJ 157, 175. The argument was raised in *Federated Homes Ltd v Mill Lodge Properties Ltd* [1980] 1 WLR 594 and in *Shropshire CC v Edwards* (1982) 46 P & CR 270, 279, but in each case, the courts have declined to consider the issue.

in the last chapter. In both *Roake v Chadha*[59] and *Kumar v Dunning*,[60] however, the courts were unimpressed by the analogy and declined to accept that a covenant that is not annexed to the land is a right appertaining to it.[61]

3.3 BUILDING SCHEME

Early in the development of restrictive covenants, the Chancery courts recognized that the enforcement of common covenants within a development merited special consideration.[62] Where a building scheme or scheme of development can be proved, equity supports the reciprocal enforcement of common covenants between all owners of the development, creating, in effect, a 'local law'.[63] A building scheme thus permits both the burden and the benefit of a covenant to pass to all owners for the time being within the scheme, but it is in the context of determining who can sue that building schemes are most often employed. The reason for this lies in the timing of sales.

3.3.1 The timing problem

Whilst the burden of a covenant can be imposed upon the sale of each plot within a development, the benefit is more difficult to pass once the first plots have been sold, because the dominant land shrinks. Thus, if we have a small development of ten plots, the benefit of covenants taken by the developer from the purchaser of Plot 1 may be annexed to the plots that the developer still owns (i.e. Plots 2–10). When Plot 2 is sold, the benefit of the covenants taken from the purchaser cannot be annexed to Plot 1, which, having been sold, does not form part of the developer's dominant land. By the time that the later plots are sold, the problem is magnified. Thus when Plot 9 is sold, the purchaser's covenants cannot be annexed to Plots 1–8; the benefit can only be annexed to the Plot 10. Once Plot 10 is sold, the developer retains no land capable of benefiting from the covenant, and thus neither the burden nor benefit of the covenants can pass.

3.3.2 A local law

Where a building scheme is found, timing is not an issue. All of the current owners of land within the scheme may sue (i.e. claim the benefit) and be sued (i.e. subject to the burden) on the common covenants, regardless of when the covenants were originally imposed upon their properties or when they acquired ownership.

The classic statement of the evidence required to prove a building scheme is found in Parker J's judgment in the following case.[64]

---

[59] [1984] 1 WLR 40, 46.   [60] [1989] QB 193, 198.

[61] In *Sugarman v Porter* [2006] EWHC 331, a similar argument was rejected based upon s 63 of the Law of Property Act 1925.

[62] There is evidence of mutually enforceable covenants as early the late 1830s: see *Lawrence v South County Freeholds Ltd* [1939] Ch 656, 675, *per* Simonds J; *Re Pinewood Estates* [1958] Ch 280, 286, *per* Wynn Parry J.

[63] See *Reid v Bickerstaff* [1909] 2 Ch 305, 319, *per* Coxens Hardy MR; *Re Dolphin's Conveyance* [1970] Ch 654, 662, *per* Stamp J.

[64] Approved on appeal at [1908] 2 Ch 665.

Elliston v Reacher
[1908] 2 Ch 374, HC

Parker J

At 384

[. . .] [I]t must be proved (1) that both the plaintiffs and defendants derive title under a common vendor; (2) that previously to selling the lands to which the plaintiffs and defendants are respectively entitled the vendor laid out his estate, or a defined portion thereof (including the lands purchased by the plaintiffs and defendants respectively), for sale in lots subject to restrictions intended to be imposed on all the lots, and which, though varying in details as to particular lots, are consistent and consistent only with some general scheme of development; (3) that these restrictions were intended by the common vendor to be and were for the benefit of all the lots intended to be sold, whether or not they were also intended to be and were for the benefit of other land retained by the vendor; and (4) that both the plaintiffs and the defendants, or their predecessors in title, purchased their lots from the common vendor upon the footing that the restrictions subject to which the purchases were made were to enure for the benefit of the other lots included in the general scheme whether or not they were also to enure for the benefit of other lands retained by the vendors. If these four points are established, I think that the plaintiffs, would in equity be entitled to enforce the restrictive covenants entered into by the defendants or their predecessors with the common vendor irrespective of the dates of the respective purchases.

Whilst these requirements will be met by many housing developments, in some cases, they have proved too prescriptive. As a result, the courts in recent decades have looked to the more general requirements articulated in the following case,[65] in which the Court of Appeal outlined two essential elements: first, that there must be a defined area of land subject to the scheme; and secondly, that there must be an intention that all owners of plots within that area are subject to, and have the benefit of, the covenants that are imposed on each plot.

Reid v Bickerstaff
[1909] 2 Ch 305, CA

Cozens Hardy MR

At 319

What are some of the essentials of a building scheme? In my opinion there must be a defined area within which the scheme is operative. Reciprocity is the foundation of the idea of a scheme. A purchaser of one parcel cannot be subject to an implied obligation to purchasers of an undefined and unknown area. He must know both the extent of his burden and the extent of his benefit. Not only must the area be defined, but the obligations to be imposed within that area must be defined. Those obligations need not be identical. For example, there may be houses of a certain value in one part and houses of a different value in another part. A building

---

[65] Decided only six months after *Elliston v Reacher*, and reflecting the earlier authorities of *Renals v Colishaw* (1878) 9 Ch D 125 and *Spicer v Martin* (1888) 14 App Cas 12. This relaxation is attributed to the cases of *Baxter v Four Oaks Properties Ltd* [1965] Ch 816 and *Re Dolphin's Conveyance* [1970] Ch 654.

scheme is not created by the mere fact that the owner of an estate sells it in lots and takes varying covenants from various purchasers. There must be notice to the various purchasers of what I may venture to call the local law imposed by the vendors upon a definite area.

Buckley LJ

At 322

There can be no building scheme unless two conditions are satisfied, namely, first, that defined lands constituting the estate to which the scheme relates shall be identified, and, secondly, that the nature and particulars of the scheme shall be sufficiently disclosed for the purchaser to have been informed that his restrictive covenants are imposed upon him for the benefit of other purchasers of plots within that defined estate with the reciprocal advantage that he shall as against such other purchasers be entitled to the benefit of such restrictive covenants as are in turn to be imposed upon them. Compliance with the first condition identifies the class of persons as between whom reciprocity of obligation is to exist. Compliance with the second discloses the nature of the obligations which are to be mutually enforceable. There must be as between the several purchasers' community of interest and reciprocity of obligation.

The first element, requiring the area of the building scheme to be ascertainable by any subsequent purchaser, reflects the concerns that we have already considered in the context of annexation. In the following case the Court of Appeal considered the evidential requirements to determine that area. Invariably these will be found in the conveyancing documentation.

Birdlip v Hunter
[2016] EWCA Civ 603 Lewison LJ

At [25]

One would have thought, a priori, that in the case of a scheme of mutual covenants designed to last potentially for ever, that that intention would be readily ascertainable without having to undertake laborious research in dusty archives searching for ephemera more than a century old. In almost all the cases to which we were referred where a scheme of mutual covenants was found to exist, the area of land to which the scheme applied was ascertainable from the terms of the conveyance and other transactional documents in question. Conversely where the conveyance or other transactional documents gave no indication of the land to which the scheme applied, no scheme was found.

At [30]–[32]

What was critical then, was that the document containing the covenants (and the map) could be identified from the conveyance [. . .] If the conveyance expressly refers to a plan, but the plan has been lost, the court may well infer that the lost plan sufficiently identified the land to which the scheme applied [. . .] The fact that there is no map or plan in the conveyance itself of the area to be affected is not necessarily fatal to the existence of a scheme of mutual covenants if the verbal description of the area to which it applies can be identified by extrinsic evidence. But this is no more than a reflection of the ordinary rules of evidence applicable to conveyances.

For example in *Re Dolphin's Conveynance*,[66] the court was able to identify the area by reference to a well-known verbal description.

The second element requires proof of intention that the covenants were imposed for the common benefit of all of the owners within the scheme.

Re Dolphin's Conveyance
[1970] Ch 654, HC

Facts: Robert Dolphin owned Selly Hill Estate in Birmingham. After his death, the bulk of the estate was sold off by nine conveyances: the first four were sold by his sisters, and the remaining five, by his nephew. All except the last were in identical form and contained covenants as to the type of house that could be built on each plot. The vendors further covenanted that they would impose similar covenants on the sale of other plots. The current owner of one of the plots wished to redevelop in breach of the covenants and requested a declaration on the enforceability of the covenants. The court decided that a building scheme had been created, although there was no common vendor and the estate had not been laid out into plots prior to its sale.

Stamp J

At 661

That it was the intention of the two Miss Dolphins, on the sale of the parcel comprised in Coleman's conveyance, that there should be imposed upon each and every part of the Selly Hill Estate the restrictions set out in the conveyance—precluding the erection of buildings other than dwelling houses having the characteristics specified in the restrictions—cannot be doubted. And each conveyance evidenced the same intention. Nor can it be doubted that each purchaser, when he executed his conveyance, was aware of that intention. The covenant by the vendor in each conveyance, to the effect that the same restrictions would be placed on all future purchasers and lessees, makes this clear. Furthermore, I would, unless constrained by authority to the contrary, conclude as a matter of construction of Coleman's conveyance, and of all the others, that the vendor was dealing with the Selly Hill Estate on the footing of imposing obligations for the common benefit, as well of himself, as of the several purchasers of that estate. It is trite law that if you find conveyances of the several parts of an estate all containing the same or similar restrictive covenants with the vendor, that is not enough to impute an intention on the part of that vendor that the restrictions should be for the common benefit of the vendor and of the several purchasers inter se: for it is at least as likely that he imposed them for the benefit of himself and of the unsold part of the estate alone. That is not this case. Here there is the covenant by the vendors that on a sale or lease of any other part of Selly Hill Estate

"it shall be sold or leased subject to the stipulations above mentioned numbered 1, 2, 3, 4, 5, 6, 7 and that the vendors their heirs or assigns will procure a covenant from each purchaser or lessee upon Selly Hill Estate to the effect of those seven stipulations."

---

[66] [1970] Ch 654. The area was referred to as 'Selly Hill Estate' which was determined by reference to evidence produced by the Town Clerk of Birmingham City Corporation that the area of the estate was well known, in the same sense that Richmond Park is well known. See also *Stocks v Whitgift Homes Ltd* [2001] EWCA Civ 1732.

> What was the point of it? For what possible reason does a vendor of part of an estate who has extracted restrictive covenants from a purchaser, covenant with that purchaser that the other parts of the estate, when sold, shall contain the same restrictions, unless it be with the intention that the purchaser with whom he covenants, as well as he himself, shall have the benefits of the restrictions when imposed? In view of these covenants by the vendor in the several conveyances, I cannot do otherwise than find that the covenants were imposed, not only for the benefit of the vendors or of the unsold part of their estate, but as well for the benefit of the several purchasers. As a matter of construction of the conveyances, I find that what was intended, as well by the vendors as the several purchasers, was to lay down what has been referred to as a local law for the estate for the common benefit of all the several purchasers of it. The purpose of the covenant by the vendors was to enable each purchaser to have, as against the other purchasers, in one way or another, the benefit of the restrictions to which he had made himself subject.

Stamp J points out that the fact that similar covenants are taken from purchasers of several plots within an estate is not enough, although it is not necessarily an objection that different covenants are imposed on different properties within the estate.[67] An express power reserved to one party to vary the covenants is not necessarily fatal but needs to be considered in the light of other evidence.[68] What is required is that the covenants were taken on the understanding (of which all purchasers were aware) that they should be for the benefit of all of the purchasers of plots within the estate, not only the vendor. This wider community of interest was proved in *Re Dolphin's Conveyance*, because the vendor covenanted with each purchaser that he would impose the same user restrictions on the sale of each plot.

Proof of the requisite intention is a question of fact. Early cases looked to a deed of mutual covenant entered into by all of the purchasers of plots—a convenient means where there are a limited number of plots all sold at the same time, but increasingly impractical where a large number of plots are sold over an extended period.[69] Deeds of mutual covenant are now rare and the necessary intention is more often found (as in *Re Dolphin's Conveyance*) from the terms of the conveyances themselves. Occasionally, an intention may be gleaned from the circumstances of the initial sales when the courts may well look to the stricter approach of *Elliston v Reacher*.[70] The distinction between these circumstances may help to account for the so-called 'relaxation' of building scheme requirements in more recent decisions.[71]

---

67 *Elliston v Reacher* [1908] 2 Ch 374, 387, *per* Parker J, [1908] 2 Ch 665, 672, *per* Coxens-Hardy MR.

68 *Birdlip v Hunter* [2016] EWCA Civ 603 at [40].

69 See *Baxter v Four Oaks Properties Ltd* [1965] Ch 816, 825.

70 See *Lund v Taylor* (1975) 31 P & CR 16; *Jamaica Mutual Life Assurance Society v Hillsborough Ltd* [1989] 1 WLR 1101; *Emile Elias & Co Ltd v Pine Groves Ltd* [1993] 1 WLR 305.

71 A point that he reiterated when elevated to the Court of Appeal in *Lund v Taylor* (1975) 31 P & CR 16, 177.

Re Dolphin's Conveyance
[1970] Ch 654, HC

Stamp J

At 662

As Cross J. pointed out in the course of the judgment in *Baxter v. Four Oaks Properties Ltd*, to which I have already referred, the intention that the several purchasers from a common vendor shall have the benefit of the restrictive covenants imposed on each of them, may be evidenced by the existence of a deed of mutual covenant to which all the several purchasers are to be parties. That common intention may also be evidenced by, or inferred from, the circumstances attending the sales: the existence of what has often been referred to in the authorities as a building scheme. I have been referred to a considerable number of author-ities where the court has had to consider whether there were, or were not, present in the particular case those facts from which a building scheme—and, therefore, the common intention to lay down a local law involving reciprocal rights and obligations between the several purchasers—could properly be inferred. In *Elliston v. Reacher* [1908] 2 Ch. 374, 384, Parker J. laid down the necessary concomitants of such a scheme.

What has been argued before me is that here there is neither a deed of mutual covenant nor a building scheme. In the latter connection, it is pointed out that there was not a common vendor, for the parcels were sold off, first by the Dolphins and then by Watts. Nor, prior to the sales, had the vendors laid out the estate, or a defined portion of it, for sale in lots. Therefore, so it is urged, there were not present the factors which, on the authority of *Elliston v. Reacher*, are necessary before one can find the existence of a building scheme.

In my judgment, these submissions are not well founded. To hold that only where you find the necessary concomitants of a building scheme or a deed of mutual covenant can you give effect to the common intention found in the conveyances themselves, would, in my judgment, be to ignore the wider principle on which the building scheme cases are founded and to fly in the face of other authority of which the clearest and most recent is *Baxter v. Four Oaks Properties Ltd*. The building scheme cases stem, as I understand the law, from the wider rule that if there be found the common intention and the common interest referred to by Cross J. at p. 825 in *Baxter v. Four Oaks Properties Ltd*. the court will give effect to it, and are but an extension and example of that rule.

The local law of a building scheme is a creature of equity founded not on contract, but on a community of interests. Megarry J observed, in *Brunner v Greenslade*,[72] that

'[t]he major theoretical difficulties based on the law of covenant seem to me to disappear where instead there is an equity created by circumstances which is independent of con-tractual obligation'.

He continued:

'[I]n the field of schemes of development, equity readily gives effect to the common inten-tion notwithstanding any technical difficulties involved. It may be, indeed, that this is one of those branches of equity which work best when explained least.'

---

[72] [1971] Ch 993, 10005. See also Parker J in *Elliston v Reacher* [1908] 2 Ch 374, 385.

It is a somewhat unusual equity. It may revive following the common ownership of plots within the scheme[73] and can apply with equal force where a lot within the scheme is subdivided into smaller units.[74]

3.3.3 Contractual solutions

Possible contractual solutions to the timing problem are provided by s 56 of the LPA 1925 and by s 1 of the Contracts (Rights of Third Parties) Act 1999.

Law of Property Act 1925, s 56(1)

(1) A person may take an immediate or other interest in land or other property, or the benefit of any condition, right of entry, covenant or agreement over or respecting land or other property, although he may not be named as a party to the conveyance or other instrument.

When a covenantor makes a promise to a covenantee, a third party who also benefits from that covenant may, in limited circumstances, be able to rely on s 56 of the 1925 Act to acquire a direct right against the covenantor. Thus, if a covenant is expressed to be made not only with the developer (as the owner of the rest of the development), but also with the owners for the time being of the plots already sold, those owners are entitled to claim the benefit of the covenant as named covenantees.[75]

A similar result is achieved by the Contract (Rights of Third Parties) Act 1999, which governs covenants entered into after 11 May 2000.

Contract (Rights of Third Parties) Act 1999, s1

(1) [. . .] a person, who is not a party to a contract (a "third party") may in his own right enforce a term of the contract if:
   (a) the contract expressly provides that he may, or
   (b) subject to subsection (2), the term purports to confer a benefit on him.

(2) Subsection (1)(b) does not apply if on a proper construction of the contract it appears that the parties did not intend the term to be enforceable by a third party.

(3) The third party must be expressly identified by name, as a member of a class or as answering a particular description but need not be in existence when the contract is entered into.

It is, therefore, clear that s 1 of the 1999 Act can also be used by a third party to acquire a direct right against a promisor. We saw there that the terms of s 1 of the 1999 Act open up possibilities beyond the circumstances catered for by s 56(1) of the LPA 1925. In particular, the covenant does not have to be made with the non-party: it is sufficient if it is made for his

---

[73] *Texaco Antilles v Kernochan* [1973] AC 609.   [74] *Brunner v Greenslade* [1971] Ch 993.
[75] These provisions also apply to restrictive covenants that do not form a building scheme.

or her benefit. Additionally, the non-party, whilst he or she must be identified by name or by a defined class, need not be in existence when the covenant is made. Thus a covenant could be made for the benefit of the future owners of the dominant land and come within the scope of s 1 of the 1999 Act, even though those owners (as a class) are not yet in existence when the covenant was made.

4 ENFORCEMENT, DISCHARGE, AND MODIFICATION OF COVENANTS

4.1 ENFORCEMENT

A restrictive covenant may be enforced by an award of damages or by the grant of an injunction, either prohibitory (to restrain a threatened or continuing breach) or mandatory (to require the covenantee to act to remedy a breach that has already occurred). Damages are available at law where action is against the original covenantor, and in equity, under Lord Cairns Act 1858, where a subsequent owner of the servient land has committed the breach. Injunctive relief is important because, in most cases, the owner of dominant land wishes to make sure that his or her neighbour does not act in breach of the covenant but the award of an injunction is discretionary and will not be granted where damages are an adequate remedy.

In the following case the Supreme Court reviewed the guidelines governing the court's discretion to grant damages rather than an injunction. In so doing they signalled a more restrictive approach to the grant of an injunction.

Coventry t/a RDC Promotions v Lawrence
[2014] AC 822, SC

Lord Neuberger

At [102]–[104]

The question which arises is what, if any, principles govern the exercise of the court's jurisdiction to award damages instead of an injunction. The case which is probably most frequently cited on the question is *Shelfer v City of London Electric Lighting Co [1895] 1 Ch 287*, but there has been a substantial number of cases in which judges have considered the issue, some before, and many others since. For present purposes, it is necessary to consider Shelfer and some of the subsequent cases, which were more fully reviewed by Mummery LJ in *Regan v Paul Properties DPF No 1 Ltd [2007] Ch 135*, paras 35–59.

In Shelfer the Court of Appeal upheld the trial judge's decision to grant an injunction to restrain noise and vibration ... .

A L Smith LJ said, at pp 322–323, in a frequently cited passage:

"a person by committing a wrongful act (whether it be a public company for public purposes or a private individual) is not thereby entitled to ask the court to sanction his doing so by purchasing his neighbour's rights, by assessing damages in that behalf, leaving his neighbour with the nuisance, or his lights dimmed, as the case may be. In such cases the well known rule is not to accede to the application, but to grant the injunction sought, for the plaintiff's legal right has been invaded, and he is prima facie entitled to an injunction. There are, however, cases in which this rule may be relaxed, and in which damages may be awarded in substitution ... In my opinion, it may be stated as a good working rule that— (1) If the injury to the plaintiff's legal rights is small, (2) And is one which is capable of being estimated in money, (3) And is one which can be adequately compensated by a small money payment, (4) And the case is one in which it would be oppressive to the defendant to grant an injunction:—then damages in substitution for an injunction may be given."

At 110

In more recent times, the Court of Appeal seems to have assumed ... the four tests suggested by A L Smith LJ are normally to be applied, so that, unless all four tests are satisfied, there was no jurisdiction to refuse an injunction.
[Lord Neuberger then reviewed the relevant authorities]

At 116–25

It seems to me that there are two problems about the current state of the authorities on this question of the proper approach for a court to adopt on the question whether to award damages instead of an injunction. The first is what at best might be described as a tension, and at worst as an inconsistency, between two sets of judicial dicta since Shelfer.... Observations in Slack, Miller, Kennaway, Regan, and Watson appear to support the notion that A L Smith LJ's approach in Shelfer is generally to be adopted and that it requires an exceptional case before damages should be awarded in lieu of an injunction, whereas the approach adopted in Colls, Kine, and Fishenden seems to support a more open-minded approach, taking into account the conduct of the parties. In Jaggard, the Court of Appeal did not need to address the question, as even on the stricter approach it upheld the trial judge's award of damages in lieu, although Millett LJ seems to have tried to reconcile the two approaches.

The second problem is the unsatisfactory way in which it seems that the public interest is to be taken into account when considering the issue whether to grant an injunction or award damages. The notion that it can be relevant where the damages are minimal, but not otherwise, as stated in Watson, seems very strange. Either the public interest is capable of being relevant to the issue or it is not. As part of this second problem, there is a question as to the extent to which it is relevant that the activity giving rise to the nuisance has the benefit of a planning permission.

So far as the first problem is concerned, the approach to be adopted by a judge when being asked to award damages instead of an injunction should, in my view, be much more flexible than that suggested in the recent cases of *Regan [2007] Ch 135* and *Watson [2009] 3 All ER 249*. It seems to me that (i) an almost mechanical application of A L Smith LJ's four tests, and (ii) an approach which involves damages being awarded only in "very exceptional circumstances", are each simply wrong in principle, and give rise to a serious risk of going wrong in practice ... .

The court's power to award damages in lieu of an injunction involves a classic exercise of discretion, which should not, as a matter of principle, be fettered, particularly in the very constrained way in which the Court of Appeal has suggested in Regan and Watson. And, as a matter of practical fairness, each case is likely to be so fact-sensitive that any firm guidance is likely to do more harm than good. On this aspect, I would adopt the observation of Millett LJ in *Jaggard [1995] 1 WLR 269*, 288 where he said:

"Reported cases are merely illustrations of circumstances in which particular judges have exercised their discretion, in some cases by granting an injunction, and in others by awarding damages instead. Since they are all cases on the exercise of a discretion, none of them is a binding authority on how the discretion should be exercised. The most that any of them can demonstrate is that in similar circumstances it would not be wrong to exercise the discretion in the same way. But it does not follow that it would be wrong to exercise it differently."

Having approved that statement, it is only right to acknowledge that this does not prevent the courts from laying down rules as to what factors can, and cannot, be taken into account by a judge when deciding whether to exercise his discretion to award damages in lieu. Indeed, it is appropriate to give as much guidance as possible so as to ensure that, while the discretion is not fettered, its manner of exercise is as predictable as possible. I would accept that the prima facie position is that an injunction should be granted, so the legal burden is on the defendant to show why it should not. And, subject to one possible point, I would cautiously (in the light of the fact that each case turns on its facts) approve the observations of Lord Macnaghten in *Colls [1904] AC 179*, 193, where he said:

"In some cases, of course, an injunction is necessary—if, for instance, the injury cannot fairly be compensated by money—if the defendant has acted in a high-handed manner—if he has endeavoured to steal a march upon the plaintiff or to evade the jurisdiction of the court. In all these cases an injunction is necessary, in order to do justice to the plaintiff and as a warning to others. But if there is really a question as to whether the obstruction is legal or not, and if the defendant has acted fairly and not in an unneighbourly spirit, I am disposed to think that the court ought to incline to damages rather than to an injunction. It is quite true that a man ought not to be compelled to part with his property against his will, or to have the value of his property diminished, without an Act of Parliament. On the other hand, the court ought to be very careful not to allow an action for the protection of ancient lights to be used as a means of extorting money."

The one possible doubt that I have about this observation relates to the suggestion in the antepenultimate sentence that the court "ought to incline to damages" in the event he describes. If, as I suspect, Lord Macnaghten was simply suggesting that, if there was no prejudice to a claimant other than the bare fact of an interference with her rights, and there was no other ground for granting an injunction, I agree with him. However, it is right to emphasise that, when a judge is called on to decide whether to award damages in lieu of an injunction, I do not think that there should be any inclination either way (subject to the legal burden discussed above): the outcome should depend on all the evidence and arguments. Further, the sentence should not be taken as suggesting that there could not be any other relevant factors: clearly there could be. (It is true that Colls, like a number of the cases on the issue of damages in lieu, was concerned with rights of light, but I do not see such cases as involving special rules when it comes to this issue. Shelfer itself was not a right to light case; nor were Jaggard and Watson. However, in many cases involving nuisance by noise, there may be more wide ranging issues and more possible forms of relief than in cases concerned with infringements of a right to light.)

Where does that leave A L Smith LJ's four tests? While the application of any such series of tests cannot be mechanical, I would adopt a modified version of the view expressed by Romer LJ in Fishenden 153 LT 128, 141. First, the application of the four tests must not be such as "to be a fetter on the exercise of the court's discretion". Secondly, it would, in the absence of additional relevant circumstances pointing the other way, normally be right to refuse an injunction if those four tests were satisfied. Thirdly, the fact that those tests are not all satisfied does not mean that an injunction should be granted.

As for the second problem, that of public interest, I find it hard to see how there could be any circumstances in which it arose and could not, as a matter of law, be a relevant factor.

Of course, it is very easy to think of circumstances in which it might arise but did not begin to justify the court refusing, or, as the case may be, deciding, to award an injunction if it was otherwise minded to do so … In some cases, the grant of planning permission for a particular activity (whether carried on at the claimant's, or the defendant's, premises) may provide strong support for the contention that the activity is of benefit to the public, which would be relevant to the question of whether or not to grant an injunction. Accordingly, the existence of a planning permission which expressly or inherently authorises carrying on an activity in such a way as to cause a nuisance by noise or the like, can be a factor in favour of refusing an injunction and compensating the claimant in damages. This factor would have real force in cases where it was clear that the planning authority had been reasonably and fairly influenced by the public benefit of the activity, and where the activity cannot be carried out without causing the nuisance complained of. However, even in such cases, the court would have to weigh up all the competing factors.

The grant of an injunction has been considered a natural remedy for breach of a restrictive covenant and there has been an expectation that injunctive relief will be available.[76] A mandatory injunction is less readily granted, even though, by refusing injunctive relief, the court will be authorizing an unlawful state of affairs.[77] The Supreme Court's guidance in *Coventry* would seem to herald a more restrictive approach to the grant of an injunction although the case concerned the remedy to be awarded for a nuisance rather than a breach of restrictive covenant. The decision whether or not to grant an injunction can raise tricky issues: on the one hand, the courts is reluctant to sanction effectively the breach of a legal obligation; on the other hand, the dominant owner may not actually suffer any real monetary damage, and, indeed, may try to use the breach to extract some payment from the servient owner.[78] The court needs to balance whether or not damages provide an adequate remedy to the dominant owner against whether the grant of an injunction would cause oppression to the servient owner.[79] Nevertheless, a mandatory injunction may be granted where the covenantor's conduct is particularly reprehensible, because, for example, the breach is in flagrant disregard of warnings.[80]

Timing can present problems for the dominant owner seeking an injunction. As we have seen, the law in this area is far from straightforward and the case may not be finally heard for some time.[81] The dominant owner can preserve the status quo by seeking an interlocutory injunction pending the full hearing, but he or she will have to give an undertaking that he or she will indemnify the servient owner if the case is lost. If the dominant owner fails to seek interlocutory relief, however, he or she runs the risk that the court will be less inclined to grant an injunction at the final hearing.[82]

---

[76] *Doherty v Allman* (1878) 3 App Cas 709.   [77] *Jaggard v Sawyer* [1995] 1 WLR 269.

[78] For example, in *Gafford v Graham* (1999) 77 P & CR 73, 83, the fact that Gafford tried to negotiate a release of the covenant was influential in the refusal of an injunction.

[79] See *Shepherd Homes Ltd v Sandham* [1971] Ch 340, in which the court refused to order a mandatory injunction to pull down a fence built in breach of covenant where the claimant had delayed in bringing the action and the defendant intended to apply for the discharge of the covenant. See also *Wrotham Park Estate Co Ltd v Parkside Homes Ltd* [1974] 1 WLR 798 and *Site Developments (Ferndown) Ltd v Barrett Homes Ltd* [2007] EWHC 415.

[80] See *Wakeham v Wood* (1982) 43 P & CR 40, but see *Wrotham Park Estate Co v Parkside Homes Ltd* [1974] 1 WLR 798.

[81] In *Gafford v Graham* (1999) 77 P & CR 73, the case was not finally heard at first instance until 1996, some seven years after the breaches. The appeal was heard in 1998.

[82] See *Shaw v Applegate* [1977] 1 WLR 970 and *Gafford v Graham* (1999) 77 P & CR 73, 82.

Damages, which are capable of monetary estimation, will be granted where the court declines to grant an injunction.[83] At common law, the measure of damages is guided by the loss suffered by the dominant owner.[84] Equitable damages under Lord Cairns Act 1858 may be awarded where the dominant owner continues to live with the effects of the breach: for example, where a user or building restriction is breached, even though there is little (if any) monetary loss to the value of the land. Damages in this case reflect the market cost to secure a release of the covenant.[85] The measure of damages both at common law and equity thus remains compensatory, rather than restitutionary.[86] Unfortunately the Supreme Court in *Coventry* declined to give further guidance on the measure of damages. Indeed the court acknowledged that they held different views.[87]

4.1.1 Defences

A servient owner may defend an action for breach of covenant on a number of grounds. We have already seen that the dominant owner must be able to claim the benefit of the covenant in order to sue upon it and that the servient owner must be bound by the covenant, both because it qualifies as a restrictive covenant and because it is protected by appropriate registration.

In addition, the servient owner may argue that his or her actions do not constitute a breach on a proper construction of the covenant, or because the dominant owner agreed to release the covenant. The action or inaction of the dominant owner may give rise to an implied release by way of estoppel where it would be unconscionable to allow the dominant owner to enforce the covenant. An estoppel may arise where the dominant owner is implicated in the breach,[88] or, as a result of his or her acquiescence, where he or she knows of the breach, but fails to take sufficiently prompt action.[89]

4.2 EXTINCTION AND MODIFICATION OF COVENANTS

The character of neighbourhoods change over time, so that the covenants imposed on a particular piece of land or estate may outlive their usefulness and impose a break on much-needed development. In addition to the limits on injunctive relief already considered, the court may, on rare occasions, be persuaded that a covenant should not be enforced because it has become obsolete.[90]

More significant is the jurisdiction of the Lands Chamber of the Upper Tribunal to discharge or modify a restrictive covenant conferred by s 84 of the LPA 1925. Nevertheless, the number of

---

[83] See *Coventry t/a RDC Promotions v Lawrence* [2014] AC 822.

[84] See *Surrey County Council v Bredero Homes Ltd* [1993] 1 WLR 1361.

[85] *Wrotham Park Estate Co Ltd v Parkside Home Ltd* [1974] 1 WLR 798; *Jaggard v Sawyer* [1995] 1 WLR 269; *Winter v Traditional & Contemporary Contracts* [2007] EWCA Civ 1088; *Gafford v Graham* (1999) 77 P & CR 73.

[86] This view has been criticized by restitution lawyers: see Birks (1993) 109 LQR 518; O'Dair [1993] 1 RLR 31. See also *AG for Hong Kong v Blake* [2001] 1 AC 268, 283.

[87] [2014] AC 822 at [132].   [88] *Sayers v Collyer* (1885) 28 Ch D 103.

[89] See *Gafford v Graham* (1998) 77 P & CR 73, 80.

[90] See *Duke of Bedford v British Museum Trustees* (1822) 2 My & K 552; *Sobey v Sainsbury* [1913] 2 Ch 513; *Chatsworth Estates Co v Fewell* [1931] 1 Ch 224; *AG for Hong Kong v Fairfax Ltd* [1997] 1 WLR 149.

cases is modest with the majority seeking the modification or discharge of covenants to permit further residential development.[91]

An application may be made by any person interested in the servient land in respect of any restrictive covenant whenever made for valuable consideration.[92] The application is publicized, to alert the owners of any dominant land in the neighbourhood who may wish to object and then can be joined as parties.[93]

Law of Property Act 1925, s 84(1)

The Upper Tribunal shall [. . .] have power from time to time, on the application of any person interested in any freehold land affected by any restriction arising under covenant or otherwise as to the user thereof or the building thereon, by order wholly or partially to discharge or modify any such restriction on being satisfied—

(a) that by reason of changes in the character of the property or the neighbourhood or other circumstances of the case which the Upper Tribunal may deem material, the restriction ought to be deemed obsolete; or

(aa) that (in a case falling within subsection 1A below) the continued existence thereof would impede some reasonable user of the land for public or private purposes or, as the case may be, would unless modified so impede such user; or

(b) that the persons of full age and capacity for the time being or from time to time entitled to the benefit of the restriction, whether in respect of estates in fee simple or any lesser estates or interests in the property to which the benefit of the restriction is annexed, have agreed, either expressly or by implication, by their acts or omissions, to the same being discharged or modified; or

(c) that the proposed discharge or modification will not injure the persons entitled to the benefit of the restriction; [. . .]

Discharge or modification on the grounds of consent in s 84(1)(b) does not usually raise any particular problems, so we will concentrate on the remaining grounds.

4.2.1 Ground (a): obsolescence

The yardstick of obsolescence is whether or not, in the light of changes to the servient land or the surrounding area, the restriction still achieves its *original* purpose.[94] An obsolete covenant may still retain some value to the dominant owner because it achieves another purpose that was not originally contemplated, but this is relevant only to grounds (aa) or (c).[95] The reasonableness of the servient owner's proposed use is also an issue for ground (aa) rather than ground (a).[96]

---

[91] See Sutton, 'On the brink of land obligations again' [2013] Conv 17.   [92] Ibid, s 84(7).

[93] Ibid, s 84(3).

[94] *Re Truman Hanbury Buxton & Co Ltd's Application* [1956] 1 QB 261. See *Re Quaffers Ltd* (1988) 56 P & CR 142, in which the covenants were obsolete as soon as they were imposed because of the motorway network that surrounded the land.

[95] *Re Kennet Properties Ltd's Application* (1996) 72 P & CR 353.

[96] *McMorris v Brown* [1999] 1 AC 142, 147.

4.2.2 Ground (aa): obstruction of reasonable user

This ground was added in 1970 to expand the Upper Tribunal's jurisdiction to balance public utility against the current benefits derived from the covenant, when the damage caused by its removal or modification can be compensated in money. The obstruction of reasonable user needs to be considered in the light of s 84(1A) and (1B) of the 1925 Act.

Law of Property Act 1925, s 84(1A) and (1B)

(1A) Subsection (1)(aa) above authorises the discharge or modification of a restriction by reference to its impeding some reasonable user of land in any case in which the Upper Tribunal is satisfied that the restriction, in impeding that user, either—

(a) does not secure to person entitled to the benefit of it any practical benefits of substantial value or advantage to them; or

(b) is contrary to the public interest;

and that money will be an adequate compensation for the loss or disadvantage (if any) which any such person will suffer from the discharge or modification.

(1B) In determining whether a case is one falling within subsection (1A) above, and in determining whether (in any such case or otherwise) a restriction ought to be discharged or modified, the Upper Tribunal shall take into account the development plan and any declared or ascertainable pattern for the grant or refusal of planning permissions in the relevant areas, as well as the period at which and context in which the restriction was created or imposed and any other material circumstances.

The Upper Tribunal must thus:

- consider the reasonableness of the proposed user;
- be satisfied either that the covenant no longer provides any practical benefit of substantial value or advantage to the dominant owner, or that the covenant is contrary to the public interest; and
- be satisfied that any damage that its removal or modification may cause can be adequately addressed by monetary compensation.

The reasonableness of the proposed user does not normally present a problem, thus attention is focussed upon the practical benefit or advantage.

In considering the value of the practical benefit, the Upper Tribunal looks not only to the original purpose of the covenant, but also to the present benefits which fall within the ambit of the covenant.[97] For example, surviving practical benefits might include retaining a property's value,[98] or preserving environmental advantages (including a view or privacy),[99] or the low density of a development even though the surrounding area is of a higher density.[100] In this respect, a higher burden of proof will be required to displace the

---

[97] *Stannard v Issa* [1987] AC 175; *Re Kennet Properties Ltd Application* (1996) 72 P & CR 353; *Sheppard v Turner* [2006] 2 P & CR 28.

[98] *Re Azfar's Application* (2002) 1 P & CR 215, *Duffield v Gandy* [2008] EWCA Civ 379.

[99] *Re Page's Application* (1996) 71 P & CR 440; *Re Azfar's Application* (2002) 1 P & CR 215.

[100] *Re Hydeshire Ltd's Application* (1994) 67 P & CR 93; *Re Snaith and Dolding's Application* (1995) 67 P & CR 93.

evident community interest of covenants under a building scheme.[101] The alternative filter of public interest is less commonly asserted. Here, it is not enough that proposed user is in the public interest; the covenant, by preventing that user, must be shown to be contrary to the public interest.[102] In determining the public interest, the Upper Tribunal is required by s 54(1B) to consider the planning policies applied in the area, as evidenced by the development plan and the pattern of planning decisions. The fact that planning permission for a development has been granted does not of itself mean that a covenant contrary to that permission is no longer enforceable or will be modified or discharged. Indeed Gray and Gray have observed that 'the Lands Tribunal in England has begun to function as a residual guarantor of a degree of environmental amenity which the individual citizen can no longer count on receiving at the hands of his or her local planning authority.'[103]

If the Upper Tribunal decides to discharge or modify the covenant, then it may order the servient owner to pay the dominant owner compensation either for any damage that the dominant owner has suffered, or to account for the increased value of the servient land now that it is freed for the restriction.[104]

4.2.3 Ground (b): no injury to the dominant owner

The last ground provides a long-stop test against vexatious objections and, as such, provides the most stringent test.[105] No compensation is payable to the dominant owner because no loss has been suffered. In determining whether or not the dominant owner's interest is injured, the courts are sympathetic to 'the thin end of the wedge' argument that whilst relaxing a covenant in the current situation may not be particularly injurious, it may be so because of its consequences for future applications and development.[106]

It is clear that '*restrictive covenants cannot be regarded as absolute and inviolable for all time*'.[107] Where a court exercises its discretion to award damages in lieu of an injunction, a clear breach of covenant is condoned and the dominant owner is forced to accept monetary compensation.[108] Likewise, where the Upper Tribunal is persuaded to discharge or modify a covenant, a dominant owner is powerless to prevent the unwanted development. But the rationale underlying the proprietary nature of covenants lies in the amenity that they afford. Where those continuing benefits can no longer be justified against wider social utility, a covenant's proprietary status is in jeopardy. There are human rights implications here, but there have been few serious challenges either to the exercise of the courts' discretion, or to s 84.[109] Any interference that there may be with the dominant owner's possessions is more than likely to be justified under the public interest balance upon which enforcement, modification, or discharge decisions are made.

---

[101] *Re Lee's Application* (1996) 72 P & CR 439; *Re Hussain's Application* [2016] UKUT 297.

[102] *Re Collins Application* (1974) 30 P & CR 527; *Re Azfar's Application* (2002) 1 P & CR 215 and but see *Re Lloyds and Lloyds Application* (1993) 66 P & CR 112.

[103] 'The future of real burdens in Scots law' (1999) 3(2) EdinLR 229 at 234. For an example see *George Wimpey Bristol Ltd v Gloucester Housing Association Ltd* [2011] UKUT 91.

[104] Law of Property Act 1925, s 84(1).

[105] *Re Kennet's Application* (1996) 72 P & CR 353; *McMorris v Brown* [1991] 1 AC 142.

[106] *McMorris v Brown* [1991] 1 AC 142, 151.

[107] Per Lord Bingham in *Jaggard v Sawyer* [1995] 1 WLR 296, 283.

[108] Mrs Jaggard complained of 'expropriation' of her property: see ibid, at 286.

[109] See *Scott v UK* (App No 10741/84); *Lawntown Ltd v Kamenzuli* [2007] EWCA Civ 949; *Site Developments (Ferndown) Ltd v Barrett Homes Ltd* [2007] EWHC 415.

The ability to sweep away unwanted burdens has played its part in lifting the rigidity of the 'conveyancer's view' of covenants to allow the judiciary to develop a more flexible attitude to those covenants that continue to serve their purpose.[110]

5 REFORM

There have long been calls for the reform of the law governing land covenants. The main defects identified are the need to provide for the running of the burden of positive covenants, the undue complexity of the rules governing the running of the benefit of covenants, the difficulty of identifying the dominant land to which the benefit of a covenant is attached, and the continuing contractual liability of the original parties to the covenant.[111]

The call for positive obligations to run is particularly acute where landowners enjoy common facilities and it is necessary to provide effective mechanisms for the use, maintenance, and repair of those facilities. In the next chapter, we will be examining the measures adopted to address this issue between flat-owners—through the use of leasehold covenants and the introduction of commonhold tenure—but there may still be instances when other positive obligations need to be enforced between adjoining freehold owners.

Reform recommendations have been put forward on a number of occasions.[112] The latest proposals are found in the Law Commission's Report, *Making Land Work, Easements, Covenants and Profits à Prendre*,[113] which look set to be enacted in the near future. The suggestion is to phase out restrictive covenants and introduce a new proprietary interest for both unregistered and registered land; the land obligation.

Law Commission, Law Com 327 (2011)

At [5.69]–[5.70]

We recommend that the owner of an estate in land shall be able to create positive and negative obligations that will be able to take effect (subject to the formal requirements for the creation of legal interests) as legal interests appurtenant to another estate in land, and therefore as registrable interests pursuant to the Land Registration Act 2002, provided that:

1. the benefit of the obligation touches and concerns the benefited land;

2. the obligation is either:

    a. an obligation not to do something on the burdened land;

---

[110] Gray and Gray, *Elements of Land Law* (5th edn, 2009), [3.4.84].

[111] Law Commission, Law Com 327 (2011), [5.4].

[112] See *Report of the Committee on Positive Covenants Affecting Land* (Cmnd 2710, 1965); Law Commission Report No 11, *Transfer of Land: Report on Restrictive Covenants* (1967); Law Commission Working Paper No 36, *Transfer of Land: Appurtenant Rights* (1971); Law Commission Report No 127, *Transfer of Land: The Law of Positive and Restrictive Covenants* (1984); Law Commission Report No 201, *Transfer of Land: Obsolete Restrictive Covenants* (1991). The history of these recommendations is summarized in the latest report Law Commission Consultation Paper 186 (2008), [7.1]–[7.8].

[113] Law Com 327 (2011), see Pts 5 and 6.

> b. an obligation to do something on the burdened land or on the boundary (or any struc-
>   ture or feature that is treated as marking or lying on the boundary) of the burdened and
>   benefited land; or
>
> c. an obligation to make a payment in return for the performance of an obligation of the
>   kind mentioned in paragraph (b); and
>
> 3. the obligation is not made between lessor and lessee and relating to the demised
>   premises.
>
> 5.70 We recommend that for the future, covenants made by the owner of an estate in land
> and that satisfy the conditions set out above shall take effect, not as promises and not in ac-
> cordance with the current law relating to restrictive covenants, but as legal interests in the
> burdened land, appurtenant to the benefited estate in land.

These recommendations provide a final acknowledgement that a covenant affecting land should be a *'genuine proprietary interests'* rather than a *'a peculiar species of personal contract'*.[114] A land obligation would give its holder a legal interest in land (rather than an equitable interest) with the benefit and burden of the obligation binding later parties acquiring all or any of the dominant land or servient land without the need either to rely on the rule in *Tulk v Moxhay* or to establish one of the three methods of passing the benefit of a covenant that we have examined.[115] The enforceability of land obligations would, thus, be brought into line with the enforceability of easements.

A land obligation could be either negative or positive, including a payment to support the expense of performing a reciprocal obligation; for instance to contribute to the repair costs of a shared facility. However, a land obligation must relate to land in the sense that it must 'touch and concern' the dominant land. It would be created by deed[116] and completed by registration.[117] Where land is registered, the benefit would be recorded in the property register of the dominant land and the burden in the charges register of the servient land. A plan would be required to identify the two pieces of land adequately. Where land is un-registered, it would only be possible for the burden to be registered as a land charge as there is no mechanism in the Land Charges Act 1972 to identify the dominant land.

The recommendation to introduce a new form of property right is a bold move. McFarlane has noted, in the context of the *Numerus Clausus Principle* which advocates a limited list of property rights that can bind third parties, that *'a strong case must be made before a new type of property right can be recognised, especially [. . .] to perform a positive act'*.[118] The Law Commission have tried to make that case and to reinforce the argument by providing certain limitation to protect third parties against onerous obligations. Those limitations are, first, measures that operate up-front to confine the new form of land obligation to coven-ants that touch and concern the dominant land and, secondly, measures to promote public

---

114 Wade, 'Covenants: A Broad and Reasonable View' (1972) 31 CLJ 157, 170.

115 It is contemplated, however, that certain third parties (e.g. those with short leases or a mortgagee who has not taken possession) will not be bound by a positive land obligation see Law Com 327, [6.98], [6.101]–[6.104], and [6.115].

116 It could not be created by implication see Law Com 327, [6.62].

117 An equitable land obligation could be created by the doctrine of anticipation (Chapter 8) see Law Com 327, [6.52].

118 McFarlane, 'The Numerus Clausus Principle and Covenants Relating to Land' in *Modern Studies in Property Law Vol 6* (ed Bright, Oxford: Hart Publishing, 2011) p 328.

knowledge of land obligations through registration. In addition the s 84 jurisdiction to discharge and modify land obligations would provide a final escape route.[119] The question is whether these controls are enough or whether home owners purchasing houses, for instance subject to payment of a service charge to support common facilities, will need more overt consumer protection of the type that flat owners enjoy—see Chapter 24. Not all are convinced of the prudence of the proposed land obligation.

O'Connor, 'Careful what you wish for: positive freehold covenants'
[2011] Conv 191, [206]

Like other limiting rules in the law of covenants, the *Austerberry* rule serves to balance competing interests: "freedom of contract" versus "freedom from transaction" or inter-generational equity [. . .]

Many jurisdictions have arrived at a decision point. They can abolish the *Austerberry* rule and allow the developers to impose positive covenants. Or they can provide for the imposition of positive obligations on current and future landowners by legislation [. . .]

To take the 'easy option' of abolishing the *Austerberry* rule would significantly expand the regulatory power of developers by allowing them to impose positive obligations as well as land use restrictions on present and future lot owners. [. . .]

Jurisdictions which have abolished the Austerberry rule have generally imposed minimal *ex ante* controls, since the law still assigns covenants to the realm of choice rather than choicelessness. Instead, the reforming jurisdictions have relied on ex post removal of covenants by judicial order. This approach provides much less protection for burdened owners and significantly higher transactions costs [. . .]

The 'easy option' of opening the door to positive covenants may turn out to be the hard option in the long run. One person's onerous obligations is another person's valuable property right, the barriers to *ex post* relief are formidable. In an era of human rights, the need to provide compensation for extinguishment of property rights will significantly limit the ability of future legislators to protect purchasers and to relieve against onerous covenants. This may explain the reluctance of legislators in many jurisdictions to act upon recommendations to abolish the *Austerberry* rule.

In addition, the route the Law Commission suggests to affect this reform has been subject to criticism. These criticisms stem from the complexities of trying to move covenants from personal obligations to proprietary interests.

Cash, Freehold Covenants and the Potential Flaws in the Law Commission's 2011 Reform Proposals [2017] Conv 212]

[. . .] the Commission appears to have been so seduced by the appeal of its unification scheme that it has ignored the essential differences between these interests. Easements and profits, being fundamentally proprietary rights, are capable of grant, whereas covenants, being essentially contracts, are not. Yet the draft Bill seeks to append covenants

---

[119] Sutton, 'On the brink of land obligations again' [2013] Conv 17.

directly to land as if they have an independent existence. It has also ignored the difference between positive and restrictive covenants. It is nonsense to speak of land being burdened by positive covenants, which require a person to perform them. An *estate* in land can be burdened, but not the land itself. The estate owner can perform the covenant, and to that extent the obligation will be proprietary. There simply was no need for the Law Commission to ignore the contractual character of covenants. It would have been perfectly acceptable, and much more natural, to start by treating the new interest as a covenant initially and, if the covenant was of the appropriate kind, allow the statute to convert it. In failing to do this, legislation of dubious validity has been drafted.

The Commission's decision to limit qualifying obligations to those that "touch and concern" the land to be benefited seems innocuous enough in principle. In a statutory scheme, however, there is no need to limit the character of qualifying obligations in this way, or indeed at all [. . .] Market forces will always, it is submitted, restrict the type of obligations that the parties will create. Those developing land are not inclined to impose frivolous obligations on landowners; if they did, values would be affected [. . .] The unfortunate effect of adding in the "touch and concern" precondition is that (i) the burden of reciprocal payments will not run, and (ii) neither will apportionment obligations, as these are also pure payment obligations and precisely the same arguments apply.

QUESTIONS

1. Given the scope of public planning legislation, is there a continuing place for restrictive covenants in controlling land use?

2. How have the characteristics of restrictive covenants developed since *Tulk v Moxhay*?

3. Should the burden of a positive covenant run with the land as a general principle?

4. Restrictive covenants have been described as an equitable extension of either privity of estate or negative easements. How helpful are these analogies?

5. How does the courts' interpretation of ss 78 and 79 of the Law of Property Act 1925 differ? Is the difference justified?

6. Why is it important to identify the land to be benefited from a restrictive covenant?

7. Have the courts relaxed their approach to the proof of a building scheme?

8. Can the courts' approach to the enforcement of restrictive covenants be described as the compulsory purchase of the benefit of the covenant?

 For guidance on how to answer these questions visit the online resources at www.oup.com/uk/mcfarlane4e/.

FURTHER READING

Cowan, Fox-O'Mahony & Cobb, 'Third-Party Interests in the Use and Control of Land' in *Great Debates in Property Law* (Basingstoke: Palgrave Macmillan, 2012) ch 7

Gardner, 'The Proprietary Effect of Contractual Obligations Under *Tulk v Moxhay* and *De Mattos v Gibson*' (1982) LQR 279

Gardner, 'Two Maxims of Equity' (1995) 54 CLJ 60

Gravells, 'Federated Homes Ltd v Mill Lodge Properties Ltd (1979) Annexation and Intention' in *Landmark Cases in Property Law* (ed Gravells, Oxford: Hart Publishing, 2013) ch 5

Hurst, 'The Transmission of Restrictive Covenants' (1982) 2 LS 53

Law Commission Report, *Making Land Work, Easements, Covenant and Profits à Prendre* Law Com 327 (2011)

McFarlane, 'The Numerous Clausus Principle and Covenants Relating to Land' in *Modern Studies in Property Law Vol 6* (ed Bright, Oxford: Hart Publishing, 2011) ch 15

O'Connor, Careful what you wish for: positive freehold covenants [2011] Conv 191

Snape, 'The Benefit and Burden of Covenants: now where are we?' (1994) 68 Nott LJ 68

Sutton, 'On the brink of land obligations again' [2013] Conv 17

Turano, 'Intention, Interpretation and the "Mystery" of Section 79 of the Law of Property Act 1925' [2000] Conv 377

24

FLAT OWNERSHIP: LONG LEASES AND COMMONHOLD

CENTRAL ISSUES

1. Communal living calls for the reciprocal enforcement of negative and positive rights and obligations between flat owners, and for mechanisms to facilitate the use, maintenance and repair of the common areas and facilities. To overcome the difficulty of enforcing positive obligations between freehold landowners, flat ownership has adopted the long lease.

2. The ownership of flats is achieved by granting the flat owner a long lease of his or her flat, with the freehold reversion being held either by an independent landlord or by a company owned collectively by the flat owners. The management and repair of the communal areas and facilities is conducted by the landlord, and funded by service charges paid by the flat owners.

3. The long lease structure of flat ownership has been open to abuse, particularly where an independent landlord holds the freehold, but legislative reform tries to address the worst abuses.

4. Long leaseholders may collectively enfranchise or obtain an extended lease, exercise a right to manage, or question the reasonableness of service charges, cure by variation a defective lease, and seek some protection from forfeiture.

5. The Commonhold and Leasehold Reform Act 2002 introduced commonhold to provide a new framework for flat ownership. The flat owners own the freehold of their flats and communally own the freehold of the common parts through a commonhold association, which is responsible for the management of the development funded through commonhold assessments paid by the flat owners. The relationship of the flat owners is governed by a commonhold community statement, which binds all flat owners within the commonhold.

1   INTRODUCTION

Owners of flats are the closest neighbours. They live one on top of each other, as well as side by side. The need to regulate the legal rights and obligations of flat owners within a block of flats is thus particularly significant. An acceptable living environment is important, and thus the user of individual flats and the block as a whole needs to be controlled: late night parties are occasional fun, but can be a nuisance if a nightly occurrence. Restrictive covenants (see Chapter 23) provide a convenient mechanism for control. It is also necessary for flat owners to enjoy limited rights over their neighbours' flats, as well as the common areas of the building (often referred to as the 'common', or 'communal' parts). Rights over the common parts will include rights of way to reach the flat, as well as rights of drainage and to services. There may be a right to use communal gardens, car parking space, and other common facilities. Rights over neighbouring flats will include rights of support for flats on the higher floors from the flats below and rights of protection for the flats on the lower floors from the flats above. The passage of services through the flats will also need to be accommodated. All of these rights can qualify as easements (see Chapter 22) attached to the dominant flats over the servient common parts or other flats over which the rights are exercised.

The missing link in this framework is the need for an effective mechanism for the maintenance and repair of the flat development. Here, there is a problem, because positive covenants (see Chapter 23) to repair or contribute to the costs of repair are not enforceable against subsequent freehold owners.

Clarke explains the problems.

Clarke, 'Occupying "Cheek by Jowl"' in *Land Law: Themes and Perspectives* (eds Bright and Dewar, 1998, p 383)

The common law was, however, unable to adequately cope with the demands of the horizontal division of property. In a simple example of a property on three floors with each floor comprising a flat or apartment with freehold title the person with title to the middle flat has only a freehold of a block of air space. The market value of such a title is dependent upon the support provided by the lower flat and the protection from the weather provided by the flat above. It is, therefore, essential that the freeholders of these flats are under an obligation to support, on the one hand, and maintain the roof, on the other. Indeed, there must be mutual enforceability of repairing obligations, with the middle flat-owner paying a fair proportion of the benefit by contributing to repair and maintenance. Such mutual enforceability is prevented by the common law principle that the burden of a freehold covenant does not run with the land. A subsequent owner cannot be forced to pay by virtue alone of title to the property.

Lawyers have tackled this problem by utilizing the lease, because, as we saw in Chapter 21, positive obligations can be made to run with the leasehold estate in land. Rather late in the day, Parliament has addressed the issue with the introduction of 'commonhold' under the

Commonhold and Leasehold Reform Act 2002. In so doing, it has followed the lead of other common law jurisdictions, which have enacted similar statutory solutions, known variously as 'strata',[1] or 'condominium' title.[2]

We should emphasize at the outset that we are concerned with long-term ownership solutions to multi-unit occupation of a building and not short-term tenancy agreements that provide the framework for mostly temporary living arrangements (whether of flats or houses).[3] Again, Clarke explains the context.

Clarke, 'Occupying "Cheek by Jowl"' in *Land Law: Themes and Perspectives* (eds Bright and Dewar, 1998, p 378)

The communal occupation with which this chapter is concerned [. . .] occurs whenever a person seeks to purchase a proprietary interest of significant value of part of a building which is realizable by sale or assignment and which gives an exclusive right to occupy a part only of that building. Typically for a long lease at a low rent, a substantial upfront payment of premium will be paid to a developer or property-owner. The new occupier is generally styled 'leaseholder' rather than tenant, for although the basic relationship may be the same as a tenant paying a market rent, the expectations are very different. The new resident has not only secured a home under a shared roof but has invested capital in part of the property by means of the price paid when the flat was purchased. Such a leaseholder expects the investment to be permanent and recouped by a sale of the property interest at any time of his choosing. However, the value of that property interest will be reduced if the legal arrangements with the other occupiers are inadequate and by the rights of the freeholder who retains an interest in the building as a whole if those rights are adverse to the leaseholder. The leaseholders will have collective self interest in issues of repair, maintenance and management of the buildings as a whole and a degree of united and coherent action is often appropriate.

In this chapter, we will initially consider the long lease framework that lawyers have developed for flat ownership, noting the remedial statutory measures that have been enacted to address the specific problems that this solution presents. We will then look at the essential features of commonhold as an alternative framework. This is a complex area of the law, although, given the increasing density of development and the prevalence of communal living, one that is vital to many homeowners. It is evident that flat owners understandably are often unclear of their respective rights and obligations and the legal structures employed.[4] We will not, however, be delving too deeply into this complexity, but will concentrate on offering an overview.

---

[1] Strata title was introduced in New South Wales, but has spread throughout Australasia and to other common law jurisdictions, for example, Singapore.

[2] Condominium title is found across North America.

[3] We cover short-term tenancy agreements in Chapter 20.

[4] See Cole and Robinson, 'Owners Yet Tenants: the Position of Leaseholders in Flats in England & Wales' (2000) 15 Housing Studies 595 and Blandy, Dixon & Dupuis, 'Theorising Power Relationships in Multi-owned Residential Developments: Unpacking the Bundle of Rights' (2006) 43 Urban Studies 2365.

Whilst we will concentrate on the ownership structures employed in flat ownership it should be remembered that blocks of flats and other communal developments do not exist in isolation from the neighbourhoods in which they are geographically located. Particularly in our larger cities, there has been a rise in gated communities in which bespoke communal facilities, such as car parking, recreational facilities and open spaces, are provided for flat owners within such developments. The secure access, which often accompanies these private developments, can be seen as isolating the development from the local communities: a feature that has attracted critical comment as explained in the following extract. Although these observations are framed in relation to commonhold they are equally applicable to gated communities held under a long lease structure.

Cowan, Fox-O'Mahony, and Cobb, *Great Debates in Property Law* (2012) p 134

Beyond the basics of maintaining communal areas in a block of flats, commonhold allows [. . .] the provision of a 'bespoke package of paid-for neighbourhood facilities and services [making] it possible for middle and higher-income people to move back into the city. The amenities bundled into the schemes by developers include secure access, uncongested parking and good quality, uncontested on-site facilities.' This can be viewed as the ultimate privitization of housing: what would been previously viewed as public neighbourhood amenities are re-created as private goods exclusive to the commonhold owners within the development, so enabling the residents of such a community to opt out of the public system [. . . .]

Lee and Webster have described the worldwide growth in gated communities as a 'general enclosure of the urban commons', with potential implications for the availability of amenities and neighbourhood goods on a social (rather than private) basis. This raises a new set of policy issues: while there are clearly benefits for those who buy in to this type of property ownership, there are also potentially negative spill-over effects for those outside, particularly if the concentration of wealth within the private community has an adverse impact on the viability of amenities in the public neighbourhood. Other risks of privately controlled neighbourhoods include spatial-social segregation and homogenization of neighbourhoods; .... .

2 LONG LEASES OF FLATS

Long leases are privately negotiated contracts, and, as such, they come in all shapes and sizes. Variety is the spice—and sometimes the bane—of life, and conveyancers spend long hours drafting and reading different forms of long leases. The common features are that they are originally granted for an extended term at a market price (commonly referred to as a 'premium'), but for a low annual rental (commonly referred to as a 'ground rent'). They are leases, but, in terms of the value of the interest that they confer, they are intended to replicate the timeless ownership of freehold. We are concentrating upon flat ownership, but occasionally houses may be held on long leases too. Long leases of houses are more common in some parts of the country, for instance in Manchester, largely as a result of the conveyancing techniques adopted by local developers. However, recently developers around the country have sold houses on long leases with ground rents that escalate so sharply that they soon become unmortgageable and cannot be sold. The Government has promised urgent action against this latest example of developer greed.

2.1 WHO IS THE LANDLORD?

The use of the long lease inevitably results in the division of estates in the land. There are the leases of the individual flats granted for terms varying from 99 to 999 years, which are held by the flat owners, and the freehold reversion on those leases, which, together with the freehold of the common parts, is held by the landlord.

Originally, the developer of the flats, as the freehold owner of the development, will grant the leases. The developer then has a choice in its sale of the development. It can sell the whole development without retaining any interest by selling the leases of the individual flats to purchasers for their market value, together with a share in a management company to which the developer transfers the freehold of the whole development, subject to the flat leases. Thus whilst the flat lessees own their own flats individually, they also communally own the freehold of the whole block, including the freehold of the common parts and the freehold reversion of the flat leases.

Alternatively, the developer can retain the freehold either directly or by transferring it to a company that it owns. The developer will choose this latter option where it wishes to retain the investment and income-producing opportunities that the freehold reversion represents. Given the common length of leasehold terms and relatively low ground rents, the capital value of the freehold reversion will be low at least until the leasehold term has run its course and falls to be renewed. However, an investment return can lie in the provision of management services or from further development of any of the physical areas (for instance the roof or open space) retained by the landlord.[5] Davey explains the position of the landlord and some of the problems associated with long leases that legislation has tried to address.

Davey, 'The Regulation of Long *Residential* Leases' in *Modern Studies in Property Law: Vol 3* (ed Cooke, 2005, p 206)

Thus in the case of long leases of flats where there is an unrelated freeholder, there is a stark contrast between the interest of the landlord and the leaseholder. For the latter the property is his home in which he will have staked a considerable investment for a long-term interest. But what does ownership of the freehold mean to the landlord, especially where the flat leases have a long period to run? Its capital value is low, reflecting the low ground rent, so why would anyone want to be a landlord in these circumstances? The answer lies in the management of services. In other words the freehold is a source of income and as such has an investment value. But this suggests of course that, for the business to be profitable, leaseholders must be paying through their service charge for more than the cost of the services to the landlord including his management expenses; this is the profit element. Some landlords also make a profit through placing insurance of the building with an insurer who pays commission to the landlord or by placing contracts for repairs and other services with associated companies.

---

[5] See for instance *Waites Ltd v Hambledon Court Ltd* [2014] EWHC 651 and *Kettel v Bloomfold Ltd* [2012] EWHC 1442.

Thus the leasehold structure of flat ownership was ripe for exploitation and so it proved to be the case. The problems are legion and were first officially identified in a *Report on the Management of Privately Owned Blocks of Flats* published in 1985. They include:

- Delay in dealing with repairs;
- The levying of excessive charges;
- A lack of consultation and provision of information;
- A lack of sinking or contingency funds for infrequent but expensive major schemes of repair and renovation;
- The different levels of interest exhibited by absentee investor leaseholders and occupational leaseholders.

Other legal problems identified included uncertainties over enforcement of obligations, the need for cheap and convenient resolution of disputes, the unresolved question of ownership and taxation of sinking funds and the means of remedying defective leases.

Many of the problems associated with long leasehold are not so significant where the flat owners own the freehold collectively. They are their own landlords, and their leases are merely a convenient device to ensure that both the negative and positive covenants in their leases are enforceable by, and against, all of the flat owners in the block.

2.2 THE LEASEHOLD TERM, AND RIGHTS TO ENFRANCHISEMENT AND EXTENSION

Common long leasehold terms for flat developments are 99 or 125 years, and for specialist gated communities, 200 years is a common term. In times gone past, even longer terms of 999 years were sometimes granted. Time nevertheless ticks away and, where the residue of the term nudges the fifty or sixty-year mark, the lease starts to be considered a wasting asset that is declining in value year by year, and which will ultimately become unmortgageable and unmarketable. The only way in which the long lease can replicate the infinity of freehold ownership is thus for the leaseholder to negotiate with the landlord either to acquire the freehold (usually collectively with the other flat owners) or to extend his or her lease.

Rights to collective enfranchisement and to obtain an extended term were granted to leasehold flat owners by the Leasehold Reform Housing and Urban Development Act 1993.[6] The rights were notoriously complex to exercise,[7] but have been relaxed somewhat by the Commonhold and Leasehold Reform Act 2002.[8] A flat owner may obtain at a market premium an extended lease for a period equal to the unexpired residue of the lease plus ninety years. The right of an individual flat owner to obtain a longer lease of his or her flat, although easier to achieve than enfranchisement, is of limited value on its own. It is of more value for all of the flat owners to acquire the freehold of the development and then to extend

---

[6] Enfranchisement of leasehold houses was earlier granted by the Leasehold Reform Act 1967.

[7] See Clarke, 'Leasehold Enfranchisement: Leasehold Reform, Housing and Urban Development Act 1993' [1994] Conv 223.

[8] For example, the right to enfranchise may be exercised by a simple majority, rather than a two-thirds majority, and there is no longer a residency condition: see Commonhold and Leasehold Reform Act 2002, ss 119 and 120.

their leases. Collective enfranchisement may be achieved through a right to enfranchise company, in which all the flat owners are given an opportunity to become members, and through which they can participate in the enfranchisement claim. The company is able to acquire the freehold on behalf of the flat owners so that, collectively, the flat owners become their own landlords, with the freedom to extend their leases and take over the management of the block.

Taking over the management can, however, be a mixed blessing, as Davey explains.

Davey, 'The Regulation of Long Residential Leases' in *Modern Studies in Property Law Vol 3* (ed Cooke, 2005, p 221)

[. . .] [O]n enfranchisement leaseholders may find that the management of a block of flats can be fraught, expensive and depressing business. They will become landlords of themselves and non-participating leaseholders as well as any non-long leaseholder tenants or commercial tenants, with all the responsibilities that entails. They will need to deal with contractors, comply with a host of regulatory requirements on health and safety employment etc. But this should not detract from the fact that leaseholders will now be in control and this often brings a high degree of satisfaction especially in smaller blocks. Furthermore the tribulations of management can be avoided to a considerable degree by the appointment of managing agents. However, this will not stop aggrieved leaseholders transferring their grievance from the freeholder to the new management company.

2.3 MAINTENANCE AND REPAIR

An effective machinery for the maintenance and repair of the block of flats is crucial. The most common structure is for the leaseholders of flats to be responsible for the repair and maintenance of the interior of their individual flats, and for the landlord to take on responsibility for the repair and maintenance of the structure (including the roof and foundations), plus the common parts and facilities. The landlord's costs are then recovered from the individual flat owners through a periodic service charge, which may be supplemented by contributions to a sinking fund to meet major replacement expenditure or unexpected costs.

Two main problems can emerge: firstly, the flat leases may provide an inadequate repair and maintenance framework, because the division of responsibility is unsatisfactory; and secondly, the service charge provisions and their performance may be inadequate, and may operate unfairly. The first problem calls for a variation of the leases, to provide a more satisfactory repairing and maintenance framework, and will be considered below. The second has been the source of particular complaint, as Davey outlines in the above extract.[9] It has proved a challenging nut to crack. One solution is found in the flat owners gaining control over the management of their block and in the regulation of service charge levels.

---

[9] These problems were first reviewed in a *Report on the Management of Privately Owned Flats* ('the Nugee Report') (1985).

2.3.1 The right to manage

The right of the flat owners to appoint a manager was first conferred by the Landlord and Tenant Act 1987, which was amended by the Housing Act 1996. This power is exercisable upon application by the flat owners to the First Tier Tribunal (Property Chamber) and rests upon proof of some fault by the landlord or his or her managers: for example, the levying of unreasonable charges, or a failure to comply with the Code of Practice approved under the Leasehold Reform Housing and Urban Development Act 1993.[10] This limited power, unfortunately, did not solve the problem: proof of fault was not always easy to establish. Thus a new right to manage was introduced by the Commonhold and Leasehold Reform Act 2002 without either having to establish fault or resorting to the tribunal where the exercise of the right is not disputed. This right to manage is implemented through the creation of a right to manage company formed by the flat owners.[11] This company, either directly or through managing agents, takes over the management duties and powers under the flat leases, without the flat owners having to enfranchise.

2.3.2 Levels of service charge

Excessive service charges have long been a source of complaint and have been the subject of regulation for all residential leases since 1972.[12] Control operates through ss 18–30 of the Landlord and Tenant Act 1985, and an extensive set of regulations. The controls relate to those variable charges that fall within the definition of 'service charge' being the variable sums payable by the tenants of dwellings for services, repairs, maintenance, improvements or insurance as well as the landlord's management costs. [13]

Service charges must be both reasonably incurred and must relate to works or services that are carried out to a reasonable standard.

Landlord and Tenant Act 1985, s 19

Limitation of service charges: reasonableness

(1) Relevant costs shall be taken into account in determining the amount of a service charge payable for a period—

   (a) only to the extent that they are reasonably incurred, and

   (b) where they are incurred on the provisions of services or the carrying out of works, only if the services or works are of a reasonable standard;and the amount payable shall be limited accordingly.

(2) Where a service charge is payable before the relevant costs are incurred, no greater amount than is reasonable is so payable, and after the relevant costs have been incurred any necessary adjustment shall be made by repayment, reduction or subsequent charges or otherwise.

---

[10] See s 87.   [11] Commonhold and Leasehold Reform Act 2002, s 21.

[12] See the Housing Finance Act 1971, which was amended by the Housing Act 1974 and the Housing Act 1980, before being consolidated in the Landlord and Tenant Act 1985, which itself has been subject to amendment by the Landlord and Tenant Act 1987, the Housing Act 1996, and the Commonhold and Leasehold Reform Act 2002.

[13] Landlord and Tenant Act 1985, s 18.

The First Tier Tribunal (Property Chamber) determines reasonableness on the application of either the landlord or the leaseholder, with each party bearing its own costs. The Tribunal can also determine on whom the liability falls under the terms of the lease.[14] The test of reasonableness looks to the actual cost, excluding any element of profit to the landlord, and does not extend to the cost of managing agents employed by the landlord where that managing agent is an alter ego of the landlord.[15]

The Landlord and Tenant Act 1985 contains other useful protections for flat owners, including provisions giving tenants the right to challenge insurance effected by the landlord,[16] requiring consultation with flat owners before carrying out certain works,[17] requirements for statements of accounts,[18] and controls over the manner in which demands for service charges are made.[19] Other legislative controls call for service charges to be held in trust fund accounts[20] and enable the flat owners to apply to have their leases varied to impose an obligation on the landlord to insure the common parts.[21]

Unfortunately, there remain some residential properties to which these controls over service charges do not apply. One of the most notorious examples is found in *Arnold v Britton*,[22] which concerned payments made by the long lessees of holiday chalets in a development on the Gower peninsula in Wales. These payments did not fall within the definition of a service charge for the purposes of the Landlord and Tenant Act 1985 and the Supreme Court decided that they could do nothing to overcome the contractual interpretation of the relevant leasehold covenant which would lead to the initial annual payment of £90 spiralling to over half of million pounds per annum by 2072.

2.4 COMMUNAL LIVING

Flat owners, as the closest neighbours, have to get along. The purpose of many of the negative user covenants in the flat leases is to provide a code of conduct for the flat development to maintain an acceptable, even attractive, living environment. The rules for the enforcement of leasehold covenants provide a route to legal redress where this code is breached, but there are a number of difficulties.

The enforcement of leasehold covenants is designed with a hierarchical structure in mind, thus landlord can sue leaseholder and vice versa. We have already seen that even enforcement against a subtenant falls outside the basic scheme and recourse to *Tulk v Moxhay* is required.[23] But problems of enforcement of user restrictions often lie between individual flat owners, presenting a need for horizontal control unless the landlord can be persuaded to become involved A lease may include what is known as a mutual enforceability clause, whereby the landlord agrees, subject to conditions as to costs etc, to enforce the covenants at the request of the tenant. Possible routes to horizontal enforcement may exist through proof of a building scheme, in which all of the flats are subject to common covenants, or

14 Landlord and Tenant Act 1985, s 27A.
15 *Finchbourne Ltd v Rodrigues* [1976] 3 All ER 581; cf *Embassy Court Residents Association v Lipman* (1984) 271 EG 545, in which the landlord's administration charges were recoverable, and *New Pinehurst Residents Association (Cambridge) v Silow* [1988] 1 EGLR 227 and *Skilleter v Charles* [1992] 13 EG 113, in which the manager was not the alter ego of the landlord.
16 Landlord and Tenant Act 1985, s 30A and Sch 1, para 9.   17 Ibid, ss 20 and 20ZA.
18 Ibid, ss 21, 21A, and 22.   19 Ibid, s 21B.
20 Landlord and Tenant Act 1987, ss 42; Commonhold and Leasehold Reform Act 2002, s 156.
21 Commonhold and Leasehold Reform Act 2002, s 162.
22 [2015] AC 1619 and see case note at [2016] Conv 70.   23 Chapter 23, section 5.

where individual flat owners can otherwise claim the benefit of the covenants.[24] Even so, adversarial court processes are ill equipped to resolve disputes between neighbours where continuing amicable relationships are so important.

2.5 VARIATION

The terms of a long lease are set in stone when it is first entered into. They are individually drafted documents, which vary from development to development, although all leases within a block should be in the same form to provide a coherent and common framework. If the leases are found to be defective, it can prove an insurmountable task to try to vary all of the leases. All of the flat owners, together with any lenders with mortgages secured against the leases, will need to agree and be involved in the process. Part IV of the Landlord and Tenant Act 1987 now provides statutory powers for the First Tier Tribunal (Property Chamber) to vary defective leases[25] and to vary other leases on broad discretionary grounds provided it is supported by 75 per cent of the flat owners and not opposed by more than 10 per cent.[26]

2.6 FORFEITURE

Leases of flats will contain a right for the landlord to forfeit and re-enter the flat in the event of the leaseholder failing to pay the rent or service charge, or failing to perform the other covenants contained in the lease. We have seen that a right of forfeiture can only be exercised following service of notice on the leaseholder and is subject to the courts' discretion to grant relief from forfeiture.[27] Nevertheless, it remains a draconian remedy, which marks a long leasehold estate out from the security offered by a freehold tenure, and which has been abused by landlords wishing to intimidate flat owners.[28]

A number of protections have been enacted to assist long leaseholders facing forfeiture for non-payment of rent or service charge: in particular, the amount of a disputed service charge must be determined by a court or the Tribunal,[29] and must exceed a prescribed amount or have been outstanding for a prescribed period.[30]

In respect of a breach of a covenant other than a covenant to pay rent the landlord cannot serve a notice under s 146(1) of the Law of Property Act 1925, or otherwise re-enter, unless the breach is admitted by the tenant or has been determined by a court or tribunal.[31] In addition, if the breach is of a repairing covenant, s 1 of the Leasehold Property (Repairs) Act 1938[32] provides that the s 146(1) notice must inform the leaseholder of his or her right to serve a counter-notice, and, upon service of a counter-notice, forfeiture cannot follow unless the court orders otherwise.[33] Leave will not be granted unless immediate repair is necessary, or unless the court considers it just and equitable.[34]

---

[24] Chapter 23, section 3.3.

[25] See Landlord and Tenant Act 1987, s 35. [26] Ibid, s 37. [27] See Chapter 21, section 6.4.

[28] See ODPM Consultation Paper, *Restrictions on the Use of Forfeiture for Long Residential Leases* (2002). Challenges have been mounted on human rights grounds with varying success, see *Di Palma v UK* (1986) 10 EHRR 149 and *Khursid Musafa & TarziBachi v Sweden* (2011) 52 EHRR 24.

[29] Housing Act 1996, s 81. [30] Commonhold and Leasehold Reform Act 2002, s 167.

[31] Commonhold and Leasehold Reform Act 2002, s 168.

[32] The Act applies to leases of more than seven years that have at least three years to run. See Smith, 'A Review of the Operation of the Leasehold Property (Repairs) Act 1938' [1986] Conv 85.

[33] Law of Property Act 1925, s 1(3). [34] Ibid, s 1(5), and *Sidnell v Wilson* [1966] 2 QB 67.

Many feel that these measures do not go far enough, and that forfeiture in the case of long leases is 'simply inappropriate' and should be abolished.[35]

3 COMMONHOLD

Commonhold has been described as '*a vital and necessary new form of land holding for the twenty-first century*'.[36] The Commonhold and Leasehold Reform Act 2002 introduced it to address the problems of flat ownership, although its application is not confined to flats, but can be used for the ownership of any residential or commercial development with shared facilities.

As its name suggests, commonhold is designed to facilitate communal living and working, by providing a structure for the ownership of individual units and the communal owner-ship, control, and management of common areas and facilities. It abandons the leasehold and instead provides a framework in which the freehold ownership of units, with communal areas and facilities, can be accommodated. As such, it does not introduce a new tenure or estate, but a new means of structuring freehold land ownership.[37]

3.1 THE STRUCTURE OF COMMONHOLD

A commonhold block of flats will be divided into individual freehold flats, held by each flat owner as a registered freehold proprietor, with the freehold of the common parts registered in the name of the commonhold association in which the flat owners are all members. As Van der Merwe and Smith point out, there are thus three elements to commonhold and a need to appreciate not only the property framework, but also company law, which governs the workings of the association.

Van Der Merwe and Smith, 'Commonhold—A Critical Appraisal' in *Modern Studies in Property Law Vol 3* (ed Cooke, 2003, p 229)

[. . .] [C]ommonhold is structured as a threefold unity combining ownership in a unit with collective rights with regard to the common parts and membership of the commonhold as-sociation [. . .] From the threefold unity embodied in commonhold, the institution straddles both the law of property and that of association.

The structure is similar to the leasehold structure, in which flat owners hold leases of their individual flats, and collectively own the freehold reversion on their leases and the freehold of the common parts through their ownership of shares in a management company. The essential distinction is that the commonhold owners are freeholders and not leaseholders. There is thus no inherent limitation on the length of their ownership and no danger of early

---

[35] See Davey, 'The Regulation of Long Residential Leases' in *Modern Studies in Property Law Vol 3* (ed Cooke, 2005) p 222. See Chapter 21, section 6.4, for the Law Commission's proposals for reform to forfeiture.
[36] Clarke, *Commonhold: The New Law* (2002) p 2.
[37] See Roberts, 'A New Property Term: But No Property in a Term!' [2002] Conv 341.

termination of their ownership through forfeiture. Nevertheless, commonhold has been described as a 'sub-species' of freehold that '*is better seen as a distinct form of land holding*'.[38]

All flat owners must be members of the commonhold association and, on the sale of a commonhold flat, the seller ceases to be a member, with his or her place being taken by the purchaser—that is, the new owner of the flat. Every member of the association is bound by the commonhold community statement, which contains rights and obligations, both positive and negative, to generate a 'local law' for the development. The statement plays the same role as the easements and covenants contained in a standard flat lease, as well as helping to define the relationship between the individual flat owners and the association as owner of the common parts. There will be familiar rights of support and protection, rights of way over, and to use, the common areas and facilities, and for drainage and the passage of services. There will also be obligations similar to the restrictive user covenants found in leases to maintain the ambience and character of the development, and positive obligations to repair individual flats, and to contribute to the cost of repairing and maintaining the common parts. The difference lies in the fact that these rights and obligations will be contained in a single document, rather than in the individual leases.

Wong explains the central significance of the commonhold association and the commonhold community statement, both of which must follow the form specified in the Commonhold and Leasehold Reform Act 2002 and its regulations.[39]

Wong, 'Potential Pitfalls in the Commonhold Community Statement and the Corporate Mechanisms of the Commonhold Association' [2006] Conv 14, 34

Under the commonhold concept, the CCS [commonhold community statement] and the CA [commonhold association] are the fundamental organs which provide the statutory and corporate frameworks for the running of the commonhold. Good management in a commonhold would depend on the quality of the execution of these two frameworks in achieving a balance between uniform protection and local flexibility as well as balance between the rule of the majority and protection of minority members.

3.2 CREATION OF COMMONHOLD

Consistent with the drive towards registration, a commonhold development may only exist where the land is (or is to be) registered. There are two routes by which a commonhold may be established: firstly, a new development may be set up as a commonhold development;[40] and secondly, an existing development may be converted from long leasehold to commonhold.[41]

The conversion of an existing development requires the agreement of all of the flat owners within the development where the leases have more than twenty-one years to run.[42] There is a statutory process for the extinction (and the payment of compensation) of shorter-term

---

[38] See Clarke (2002) pp 16–17.
[39] The commonhold association's constitutional documents are specified in Schs 1 and 2, and the commonhold community statement in Sch 2.
[40] Commonhold and Leasehold Reform Act 2002, s 7.   [41] Ibid, s 9.   [42] Ibid, s 3(1)(b).

leases and other interests.[43] Given this need for unanimity, it is unlikely that existing flat developments will be converted to commonhold. Commonhold is a more feasible option for new flat developments.

Where a new development is to be created as a commonhold, there are two stages to the process. Firstly, the developer will need to apply for its freehold estate to be registered as commonhold land, when it will need to submit to the Land Registry the commonhold association's constitutional documents, the commonhold community statement, any necessary consents (e.g. from an existing mortgagee), and the compliance certificate of the association's directors. Upon approval, the estate will be registered as commonhold land, although it is not yet operational as a commonhold community. The commonhold is only activated upon the registration of the first purchaser as the owner of his or her flat when the commonhold community statement comes into force and the commonhold association is registered as the proprietor of the common parts.[44]

3.3 COMMONHOLD LAND OWNERSHIP

Commonhold can only exist where there are at least two units: it is, after all, a form of communal land holding. The individual flats and the common parts are defined by the commonhold community statement, with the common parts defined in a negative fashion as those areas that are not comprised within the flat owners' individual titles.[45] The common parts may be further split between those areas over which all flat owners may exercise rights and those limited-use areas, the user of which may be confined to certain flat owners.[46] Any redefinition of these areas requires the agreement of those affected and the consequent amendment of the commonhold community statement.[47]

It is a fundamental principle that freehold is the only title that can exist within a commonhold development. Smith explains the consequences of what has been called the 'purity of commonhold'.[48]

Smith, 'The Purity of Commonholds' [2004] Conv 194

No conversion of an existing long leasehold development is possible unless 100 per cent of registered lessees, with terms over 21 years of the whole or part of the land, consents. It is not possible to get around this bar, and there is draconian provision for the clearance of all shorter leases of commonhold land. A second aspect of the purity principle is the restriction on the ability of the holder of a residential commonhold unit to grant leases of that unit. Intertwined with this is the issue of diversion by the commonhold association of assessments, on default of the unit holder, from lessees and sub-lessees of rented units.

The second aspect referred to by Smith compromises the fundamental principle of the free alienability of freeholds—but such is the strength of the purity principle that, although flat

---

[43] Ibid, ss 9(3)(f) and 10.   [44] Ibid, ss 7(3) and 8.

[45] Ibid, s 25. The importance of defining these areas is explained by Van der Merwe and Smith, 'Commonhold—A Critical Appraisal' in *Modern Studies in Property Law Vol 3* (ed Cooke, 2005) p 230.

[46] Commonhold and Leasehold Reform Act 2002, s 25(3).   [47] Ibid, ss 23, 24, and 30.

[48] Hansard, HC Vol 627, col 491 (16 October, 2001).

owners within a commonhold are free to sell, mortgage, and charge their flats, they are not able to grant a lease for a premium or for a term greater than seven years, nor are they able to dispose of part of their flat, other than by way of lease, without the consent of the commonhold association.[49]

The rationale behind the prohibition of longer leases is a determination to avoid replication of long-lease landholding within commonholds, as well as to discourage absentee landlords. The consequence, however, is to discourage the choice of commonhold altogether; for instance, it can inhibit affordable housing shared ownership schemes and Islamic mortgages.[50]

The commonhold association, as freeholder of the common parts, is able to dispose of these areas without the consent of the flat owners, but with one important limitation:[51] it cannot charge the common parts except by way of a legal mortgage that has the prior unanimous approval of the flat owners as its members.[52] This freedom seems remarkable, given the crucial importance of the common parts, but may be explained as an attempt to give the commonhold association some freedom of action in the event of possible insolvency.

3.4 THE COMMONHOLD ASSOCIATION

The commonhold association is central to the commonhold scheme. It is simply not possible to have a commonhold without a commonhold association to hold the common parts, and to be responsible for the management of, and the enforcement of rights and obligations within, the commonhold.

Originally, it was envisaged that the association would be a purpose-built association, but the government opted for adapting an existing corporate form—the company limited by guarantee, the members of which are the individual flat owners.[53] As such, the association has separate legal personality and limited liability. It is regulated through the Companies Act 2006, with obligations to hold annual general meetings, to file accounts, and to appoint corporate officers to run the association.[54] But the commonhold association is a distinct form of company limited by guarantee and the flat owners have no choice but to be members. Its constitutional documentation is central to the flat owners' relationship with the association, and must incorporate mandatory provisions to try to achieve a fair distribution of power.[55]

Wong, 'Potential Pitfalls in the Commonhold Community Statement and the Corporate Mechanisms of the Commonhold Association' [2006] Conv 14, 26

The CA [commonhold association] must adopt all the provisions in the model articles – alterations are only permitted for a few articles and any additions must be clearly labelled.

---

[49] Commonhold and Leasehold Reform Act 2002, ss 15, 17, 20, 21, and 22 A more flexible approach is permitted for non-residential units where there is no statutory prohibition on leases, although control may be imposed through the commonhold community statement: ibid, s 17(5).

[50] See Chapter 25, section 6.   [51] Commonhold and Leasehold Reform Act 2002, ss 27 and 28.

[52] Ibid, s 29.

[53] All unit holders must be members and no person who does not own a unit may be a member.

[54] Directors of the commonhold association may be either appointed by the flat owners from within their own number, or professionals appointed by the flat owners to run the association on their behalf.

[55] See Schs 1 and 2.

> These strict rules help to ensure that the democratic nature of the general meeting and director's meeting, which is of particular importance in the context of commonhold, since unit-holders are "captive members" of the particular CA of their building. One underlying threat to democracy is the abuse of the resolutions mechanisms by the developer through his membership or directorship in the CA.

The association operates through two organs: the board of directors and the flat owners in general meeting.

Each flat owner is entitled to single membership in the commonhold association and is entitled to cast a single vote. Co-owners of a flat are required to nominate one of their number to be the association member for their flat and, as such, entitled to vote.

The general meeting appoints the directors, who are responsible for the management of the commonhold through their duties to manage and to uphold compliance with the commonhold community statement. The directors need not be flat owners with an interest in the development. Thus professional property management may be achieved either by appointing professional managers as directors, or, alternatively, through the employment of professional managing agents by the directors.

The commonhold association as a corporate vehicle is governed by the rule of the majority. As such, fears have been expressed that a minority of flat owners may be subjected to the 'tyranny' of the majority in decisions that adversely affect their everyday lives within the commonhold community.[56] The vital question is thus whether the mandatory provisions of the association do achieve a fair balance. In particular, the power of the directors to appoint managing agents and to fix the level of commonhold assessment without the prior approval of the flat owners in general meeting has drawn criticism.[57]

The association may be wound up following the standard procedures contained in the Insolvency Act 1986.[58] The flat owners, as members of the association, may initiate winding up voluntarily where it is solvent: for example, should the flat owners wish to redevelop. A compulsory winding-up by court order may occur where the association is insolvent: for example, upon the petition of one or more of its unpaid creditors. In this latter event, the court has power to make a succession order transferring the common parts to a new commonhold association, which will take over the management of the commonhold, unless such an order is 'inappropriate'.[59] A succession order may well be inappropriate unless there is in place some mechanism to clear the debts of the insolvent association.[60] For example, the liquidator of an insolvent commonhold association may be able to pursue defaulting flat owners for any unpaid commonhold assessments, as well as raise further assessments from the flat owners to meet the debts of the association. Thus the limited liability of the flat owners as members of the association could be more fictional than real.[61] It is anticipated that the insolvency of a commonhold

---

[56] See Kenny [2003] Conv 1.

[57] See Wong, 'Potential Pitfalls in the Commonhold Community Statement and the Corporate Mechanisms of the Commonhold Association' [2006] Conv 14.

[58] Insolvency Act 1986, ss 122 and 124.   [59] Ibid, s 51.

[60] See Crabb, 'The Commonhold and Leasehold Reform Act 2002: A Company Law Perspective' (2004) 25 Comp Law 213.

[61] Ibid.

association will be an unlikely event, given that it can raise additional funds from the flat owners by levying further assessments, but the possibility exists, for instance where widespread damage has been caused by an event for which there is no or under insurance cover. This risk has proved of sufficient concern to discourage purchasers. Lenders have also been hesitant to accept security over commonholds because of uncertainty surrounding how their security would be affected should the commonhold association be wound up.

3.5 COMMONHOLD COMMUNITY STATEMENT

The commonhold community statement is a crucial document. It sets out '*details of how the community is to run*',[62] in terms of what the flat owners and the commonhold association, respectively, must do, are able to do, or cannot do.

Commonhold and Leasehold Reform Act 2002, s 31

(1) A commonhold community statement is a document which make provision in relation to specified land for—
   (a) the rights and duties of the commonhold association; and
   (b) the rights and duties of the unit-holders.
(2) A commonhold community statement must be in prescribed form.
(3) A commonhold community statement may—
   (a) impose a duty on the commonhold association;
   (b) impose a duty on a unit-holder;
   (c) make provision about the taking of decisions in connection with management of the commonhold or any other matter concerning it.

The 2002 Act and its attendant regulations detail what the statement must include by way of mandatory terms and what it may include in optional provisions. The draftsman is provided with a model as a starting point and guide in preparing the statement, which will be a unique document for each development.[63]

Wong explains the format and content of the statement.

Wong, 'Potential Pitfalls in the Commonhold Community Statement and the Corporate Mechanisms of the Commonhold Association' [2006] Conv 14, 19

The CCS [commonhold community statement] is the central property document stipulating the rights and duties of the CA [commonhold association] and the unit-holders. To promote uniform protection, the overall format of the CCS and the contents of its main body are prescribed in the model form in Sch.3 to the Regulations. Part 4 of the main body of the CCS

62 Clarke (2002) p 74.

63 Commonhold and Leasehold Reform Act 2002, Sch 3.

lays down the mandatory "rules" of the commonhold regarding general property rights and duties. These include duty to contribute to assessments and reserve funds (Part 4.2), duty to insure (Part 4.4), duty to maintain and repair (Part 4.5), as well as restrictions on use (Part 4.3), alteration (Part 4.6) and disposition (Part 4.7). In addition to these general provisions, more specific rules are needed to cater for the local needs of a given commonhold. This is achieved by Annex 4 where the developer can insert "local rules" to fine-tune the mandatory rules in Part 4, and by Annex 5 where "supplementary local rules" can be inserted to impose further restraints such as restrictions on keeping pets. In contrast to the mandatory "rules" which can never be amended, "local rules" and "supplementary local rules" can in general be amended by ordinary resolution, with a few exceptions requiring special resolution (and/or consent of the affected unit-holder). The combination of mandatory rules on general property rights and duties and self-prescriptive tailor-made local rules reflects the legislative intention of striking a balance between certainty of protection and local flexibility.

The balance between certainty and flexibility should vary according to the subject matter of the rights and duties. While an individualistic approach is suitable for certain subject matter such as restrictions on use and behaviour, other matters such as the duty to repair and maintain and the duty to insure would require a more prescriptive approach so as to achieve adequate protection for the unit-holders.

The statement is registered against all of the titles within the commonhold, being both the freehold titles to the individual flats and the common parts, and thus will bind the commonhold association and the individual flat owners. The mechanism by which subsequent flat owners are bound is found in s 16 of the 2002 Act.

Commonhold and Leasehold Reform Act 2002, s 16

Transfer: effect

(1) A right or duty conferred or imposed—

    (a) by a commonhold community statement, or

    (b) in accordance with section 20, shall affect a new unit-holder in the same way as it effected a former unit-holder.

(2) A former unit-holder shall not incur a liability or acquire a right—

    (a) under or by virtue of the commonhold community statement, or

    (b) by virtue of anything done in accordance with section 20.

(3) Subsection (2)—

    (a) shall not be capable of being disapplied or varied by agreement, and

    (b) is without prejudice to any liability or right incurred or acquired before the transfer takes effect.

Thus both the negative user and alienation provisions, and any positive obligations (including obligations to repair, maintain, insure, and to pay the service charge), are binding on purchasers acquiring a flat in the commonhold development.

3.6 THE MANAGEMENT OF COMMONHOLD

The commonhold community statement will set out the allocation of management responsibilities, and will usually provide that the flat owner will be responsible for the repair, maintenance, and insurance of the interior of his or her flat, while the commonhold association will be responsible for the repair, maintenance, and insurance of the common parts, including the structure of the building and the common facilities.

Commonhold and Leasehold Reform Act 2002, s 14

Use and maintenance [Commonhold Unit]

(1) A commonhold community statement must make provision regulating the use of commonhold units.

(2) A commonhold community statement must make provision imposing duties in respect of the insurance, repair and maintenance of each commonhold unit.

(3) A duty under subsection (2) may be imposed on the commonhold association or the unit-holder.

Commonhold and Leasehold Reform Act 2002, s 26

Use and maintenance [Common Parts]

A commonhold community statement must make provision—

(a) regulating the use of the common parts;

(b) requiring the commonhold association to insure the common parts;

(c) requiring the commonhold association to repair and maintain the common parts.

The cost of repairing, maintaining, and insuring the common parts will be recovered from flat owners by the commonhold association through commonhold assessment, which may be made up of three elements: first, the regular day-to-day expenses, which will be calculated according to prepared budgets made by the association; secondly, the levies to a reserve fund to budget over a period for the larger costs of occasional replacement and repair (for example, the painting of the block or the repair of the roof or lifts); and finally, emergency levies to recover unexpected expenditure. The reserve fund is held by the commonhold association and may be attached by certain unpaid judgment debtors of the association.[64]

---

[64] Ibid, s 39(4).

Commonhold and Leasehold Reform Act 2002, ss 38 & 39

Commonhold assessment

38 (1) A commonhold community statement must make provision—

    (a) requiring the directors of the commonhold association to make an annual estimate of the income required to be raised from unit-holders to meet the expenses of the association,

    (b) enabling the directors of the commonhold association to make estimates from time to time of income required to be raised from unit-holders in addition to the annual estimate,

    (c) specifying the percentage of any estimate made under paragraph (a) or (b) which is to be allocated to each unit,

    (d) requiring each unit-holder to make payments in respect of the percentage of any estimate which is allocated to his unit, and

    (e) requiring the directors of the commonhold association to serve notices on unit—holders specifying payments required to be made by them and the date on which each payment is due.

[...]

Reserve fund

39 (1) Regulations under section 32 may, in particular, require a commonhold community statement to make provision—

    (a) requiring the directors of the commonhold association to establish and maintain one or more funds to finance the repair and maintenance of common parts;

    (b) requiring the directors of the commonhold association to establish and maintain one or more funds to finance the repair and maintenance of commonhold units.

  (2) Where a commonhold community statement provides for the establishment and maintenance of a fund in accordance with subsection (1) it must also make provision—

    (a) requiring or enabling the directors of the commonhold association to set a levy from time to time,

    (b) specifying the percentage of any levy set under paragraph (a) which is to be allocated to each unit,

    (c) requiring each unit-holder to make payments in respect of the percentage of any levy set under paragraph (a) which is allocated to his unit, and

    (d) requiring the directors of the commonhold association to serve notices on unit-holders specifying payments required to be made by them and the date on which each payment is due.

Each flat owner must contribute the percentage of these costs that is allocated to his or her flat by the commonhold community statement.[65] The commonhold association has no

---

[65] There is no provision for the commonhold assessment to be 'split' between different types of use within a development to enable distinct service charge provisions for residential units, office space, and other commercial units.

special powers to recover unpaid service charges beyond the usual dispute resolution process to be considered shortly.

Proposals for the association to be given a right to secure unpaid assessments by charge were rejected by the government, which wished to avoid any suggestion that the freeholds within a commonhold scheme could be effectively forfeited by the process of charge and subsequent sale.[66] This has led to criticisms that the association has no effective means by which to ensure that the costs of management are met by all of the flat owners.[67] There is the danger that effective management will be compromised and that, to maintain the necessary flow of funds, compliant flat owners will have to pick up the shortfall.

The association is obliged to ensure that the flat owners observe the obligations imposed by the statement. As we have seen, these obligations are extensive and cover not only the payment of service charges, but also negative obligations relating to user of both individual flats and the common parts, as well as positive obligations regarding the repair and maintenance of individual flats. The 2002 Act does, however, recognize that living in a community requires give and take, so that it may not be to the overall benefit of that community for enforcement action to be taken against all breaches. The association is thus granted a right of inaction where it reasonably believes that doing nothing will promote harmonious relationships.

Commonhold and Leasehold Reform Act 2002, s 35

Duty to manage

(1) The Directors of a commonhold association shall exercise their powers so as to permit or facilitate so far as possible—

    (a) the exercise by a unit-holder of his rights, and

    (b) the enjoyment by each unit-holder of the freehold estate in his unit.

(2) The directors of a commonhold association shall, in particular, use any right, power or procedure conferred or created by virtue of section 37 for the purpose of preventing, remedying or curtailing a failure on the part of a unit-holder to comply with a requirement or duty imposed on him by virtue of the commonhold community statement or a provision of this Part.

(3) But in respect of a particular failure on the part of a unit-holder (the 'defaulter') the directors of a commonhold association—

    (a) need not take action if they reasonably think that inaction is in the best interest of establishing or maintaining harmonious relationships between all unit-holders, and that it will not cause any unit-holder (other than the defaulter) significant loss or significant disadvantage, and

    (b) shall have regard to the desirability of using arbitration, mediation or conciliation procedures (including referral to a scheme approved under section 42) instead of legal proceedings whenever possible.

---

[66] The association may enforce a judgment debt by way of charging order, but will rank behind other existing secured creditors: see Chapter 25, section 4.4.

[67] See Clarke (2002) p 143.

3.7 DISPUTE RESOLUTION

Traditional court processes are ill equipped to deal successfully with disputes between neighbours, in relation to whom the maintenance of a continuing working relationship is so important, and an economic and timely response is necessary. Although no distinct statutory dispute resolution system is introduced by the 2002 Act, it is envisaged that the court process will be used as a last resort or where decisive action is needed.[68]

Clarke explains the hope that disputes will be resolved through alternative means.

Clarke, *Commonhold: The New Law* (2002, p 151)

There is [. . .] no statutory system for the resolution of disputes. Instead of such a statutory system, the CLRA [Commonhold and Leasehold Reform Act] 2002 envisages a staged response. Although much will depend on regulations and rules to be introduced later, it is envisaged that the [. . .] CCS [commonhold community statement] will set out an internal complaints procedure which members must first adopt. The dispute resolution procedures then involve an inter-relationship of three approaches after any such internal procedures have been exhausted. There is specific provision for regulations to provide that a commonhold association shall be a member of an approved Ombudsman scheme. There is a general statutory duty on the directors of a commonhold association to have regard to the desirability of using arbitration, mediation or conciliation procedures (including referral under approved Ombudsman schemes), instead of legal proceedings. Finally, the courts will have an overriding jurisdiction.

4 CONCLUSION

Flat ownership presents a complex challenge to devise a legal framework that will effectively balance the freedom of individual ownership against the compromise necessary for communal living. There has been considerable legislative activity: firstly, to provide an effective framework for the enforcement of leasehold covenants; secondly, to try to overcome the considerable shortcomings of the long-lease system of flat ownership; and thirdly, to introduce an alternative form of communal land holding—the commonhold. Areas of reform are still outstanding, with the enforcement of freehold positive obligations through the land obligations likely to be enacted shortly.[69]

The question is whether commonhold provides an effective solution. Commentators expressed the hope that commonhold should be sufficiently attractive to sideline the long lease of flats, but that has not proved to be the case. Clarke, writing in 2002,[70] shortly after the passing of the Commonhold and Leasehold Reform Act, foretold a 'bright future' for commonhold—but only shortly after he doubted this prediction.

---

68 See Commonhold and Leasehold Reform Act 2002, Sch 3, s 35(3)(b) extracted above, and s 42.
69 See Chapter 23, section 5.
70 'The Enactment of Commonhold: Problems, Principles and Perspectives' [2002] Conv 349.

Clarke, 'Long Residential Leases: Future Directions' in Landlord and Tenant
Law: Past, Present and Future (ed Bright, 2006, p 181)

However Part I of the Commonhold and Leasehold Reform Act 2002, for all the assurances
that it was a fine piece of legislation, contains some fundamental flaws that will prevent its
widespread adoption for both large and mixed residential estates and developments. Indeed,
these inadequacies are proving so fundamental to the key players (developers and lenders)
that commonhold will possibly be consigned to the margins. There were, by 27 September
2005, only five commonholds registered a year after commonhold was brought into force,
and they all are small homogeneous developments.

[. . .] [I]f nothing is done, at best commonhold will be peripheral, at worst it will be largely
irrelevant, to the solution of developing homes for the future.

The number of commonhold developments are still counted in the tens rather than the hundreds. Compulsion seems the only answer, but not before the legislation is refined to overcome deficiencies, the most significant of which we have explored.[71]

Both the long lease and commonhold systems are complicated structures and neither can solve the friction that communal living can bring. The bottom line is that the distinction between commonhold and long leases, where a management company owns the freehold that the flat owners control are largely matters of legal detail. Commonhold may still win over the long lease held from an independent landlord, but, even here, enfranchisement and the right to manage has narrowed the score.

QUESTIONS

1. Why is it difficult to achieve the freehold ownership of flats?

2. How successful do you think the long leasehold system of flat ownership has been?

3. What are the current deficiencies in commonhold, as it has been enacted in the Commonhold and Leasehold Reform Act 2002?

4. Is there a pressing need for commonhold?

For guidance on how to answer these questions visit the online resources at www.oup.com/
uk/mcfarlane4e/.

FURTHER READING

Blandy, Dupuis and Dixon, *Multi-owned Housing: Law, Power and Practice* (Aldershot:
Ashgate, 2010)

Clarke, *Commonhold: The New Law* (Bristol: Jordans, 2002)

---

[71] See Clarke, 'The Enactment of Commonhold: Problems, Principles and Perspectives' [2002] Conv 349;
Davey, 'The Regulation of Long Residential Leases' in *Modern Studies in Property Law: Vol 3* (ed Cooke,
Oxford: Hart, 2005) ch 10; Van Der Merwe and Smith, 'Commonhold: A Critical Appraisal' in *Modern Studies
in Property Law: Vol 3* (ed Cooke, Oxford: Hart, 2005, ch 11); Wong, 'Potential Pitfalls in the Commonhold
Community Statement and the Corporate Mechanisms of the Commonhold Association' [2006] Conv 14.

Clarke, 'Long Residential Leases: Future Directions' in *Landlord and Tenant Law: Past, Present and Future* (ed Bright, Oxford: Hart Publishing, 2006) ch 9

Clarke, 'Occupying 'Cheek by Jowl': Property Issues Arising from Communal Living' in *Land Law: Themes and Perspectives* (eds Bright and Dewar, Oxford: OUP, 1998)

Clarke, 'The Enactment of Commonhold: Problems, Principles and Perspectives' [2002] Conv 349

Crabb, 'The Commonhold and Leasehold Reform Act 2002: A Company Law Perspective' (2004) 25 Comp Law 213

Davey, 'The Regulation of Long Residential Leases' in *Modern Studies in Property Law Vol 3* (ed Cooke, Oxford: Hart, Publishing 2005) ch 10

Smith, 'The Purity of Commonholds' [2004] Conv 194

Van Der Merwe and Smith, 'Commonhold—A Critical Appraisal' in *Modern Studies in Property Law Vol 3* (ed Cooke, Oxford: Hart Publishing, 2005) ch 11

Wong, 'Potential Pitfalls in the Commonhold Community Statement and the Corporate Mechanisms of the Commonhold Association' [2006] Conv 14

PART H

SECURITY RIGHTS

25 Security Interests in Land 1032
26 Lender's Rights and Remedies 1064
27 Protection of the Borrower 1116

25

SECURITY INTERESTS IN LAND

CENTRAL ISSUES

1. Securing the repayment of money may be achieved by the grant of a legal or equitable interest in land, giving the creditor a right of recourse. For example, such a right may allow a lender to sell a borrower's freehold or lease if the debtor fails to repay the creditor.

2. There are four types of security interest: the pledge, the lien, the mortgage, and the charge. A lien, mortgage, or charge may be created over land.

3. The legal charge by way of mortgage of land is a hybrid form of security, being, in form, a charge, but granting the lender the rights associated with a mortgage.

4. If the borrower has a legal estate or equitable interest in land, a creditor can acquire an equitable security interest by means of a mortgage or a charge.

5. The equity of redemption represents the borrower's interest under a traditional mortgage of property. It has been of central importance to equity's protection of borrowers, but its continued utility, in a case in which the lender is granted a legal charge, is questionable.

6. The provision of secured credit is fundamental to modern living and commercial life, and lawyers have proved adept at creating different forms of security to cater for a wide variety of circumstances.

1 INTRODUCTION

In this chapter, we are concerned with the use of land (or legal and equitable property rights relating to land) as security for the repayment of money by a borrower to a lender. The lender acquires security by *being granted* a distinct legal or equitable property right in the land. This gives the lender a number of rights to which it can resort if the borrower fails to repay the loan. Crucially, because it has a legal or equitable property right in the land, the lender may also be able to assert its security against third parties.

Sir Nicholas Browne Wilkinson VC accepted the following definition of security.

Bristol Airport plc v Powdrill
[1990] Ch 744, CA

Sir Nicolas Browne-Wilkinson VC

At 760

Security is created where a person ('the creditor') to whom an obligation is owed by another ('the debtor') by statute or contract, in addition to the personal promise of the debtor to discharge the obligation, obtains rights exercisable against some property in which the debtor has an interest in order to enforce the discharge of the debtor's obligation to the creditor.

There are, thus, two elements to a security transaction: firstly, the loan made by the lender to the borrower; and secondly, the creation of the proprietary interest by the borrower to the lender to secure the repayment of the loan. We commonly call that proprietary interest a 'mortgage', but, as we shall see, we need to be careful of our terminology when dealing with security interests. The loose use of terms can, and often has, caused confusion.

In this chapter, we will look first at why proprietary (or what are sometimes called 'real') security interests are so popular with lenders today; we will then explore the different types of proprietary security interest, before examining the development and particular nature of security interests over land. In Chapter 26, we will focus on the rights and powers conferred upon the lender to enforce its security over land. .Finally, in Chapter 27, we will turn our attention to the loan contract and the controls that the law has imposed to protect the borrower.

2   THE ROLE AND IMPORTANCE OF SECURITY

Lending in both the domestic and commercial spheres is prolific and an important indicator of economic conditions. Bank of England statistics revealed that at the end of March 2014 lending to UK non-financial businesses was £444 billion, of which £170 billion was lent to small and medium size business,[1] and the overall value of residential loans was £1,243 billion.[2]

In the domestic market, policies by all political parties since the mid-twentieth century have promoted home ownership, through the ready availability of mortgage finance, to reduce public expenditure on housing, and to enhance social and political stability.[3]

Oldham, 'Mortgages' in *Land Law: Issues, Debates Policy* (ed Tee, 2002, p 172)

[. . .] [P]roperty ownership effects a form of special inclusion or community bonding. The purchase of a house affiliates the mortgagor to a particular locality and to a particular social group. The purchaser acquires a sense of belonging not only to the neighbourhood in which

---

[1] Bank of England, Trends in Lending July 2014.
[2] Bank of England & FCA, MLAR Statistical Release June 2014.
[3] See also Gray and Gray, *Elements of Land Law* (5th edn, 2009), [6.1.3]–[6.1.5] for some of the social and political effects of mortgage finance.

the house is located, but also to a larger group of homeowners generally. Home ownership signals respectability, responsibility and, usually, also upward mobility. The particularly
English ideology surrounding home-ownership has had the result that non-homeowners
have become almost second-class citizens.

Most people aspire to the economic and social advantages that are associated with home
ownership, but they can only attain those advantages by borrowing from a financial institution. Instead of paying rent for their accommodation, they repay their mortgage by instalments, in the expectation that they will not only enjoy the use of their home, but also be able
to reap the benefits of an increase in its capital value as property prices increase—a bonus
that is unavailable to a tenant.

The availability of credit is also vital to business and the economy, particularly to promote
the growth of small and medium-sized businesses. Banks and other financial institutions
are more ready to lend, and offer less onerous terms, where the risks associated with non-
payment are reduced by the availability of security.

Oldham describes this economic significance.[4]

Oldham, 'Mortgages' in *Land Law: Issues, Debates Policy* (ed Tee, 2002, p 169)

In terms of function, mortgages constitute a key economic institution—the means by which
assets are mobilised, capital generated and productivity and the wider economy boosted.
The mortgage is a mechanism that transforms 'passive 'land value into active value in that
it allows the value of land to be released for other purposes while the freeholder or leaseholder is still able to enjoy the benefits of physical occupation or possession. It has even
been argued that the ability to mortgage land is the key to the fundamental distinction
between rich and poor countries. In poor countries, assets mobilisation is not possible because the capital invested in housing is incapable of being released because of inadequate
underlying structures of property ownership and of social, political and legal control.

Clarke and Kohler have summarized the functions of secured credit as five-fold. As argued in
the extract below, a security interest can give a lender: (i) a right of first recourse; (ii) priority;
and (iii) the opportunity for non-judicial enforcement of the borrower's duties. Security
interests can also serve: (iv) a hostage function; and (v) as a means of signalling the creditworthiness of the borrower, and allowing the lender to monitor and control the borrower's
behaviour.

Clarke and Kohler, *Property Law: Commentary and Materials* (2005, p 659)

18.1.2.1 Right of first recourse

First, security over an asset gives the security interest holder the right of first recourse to it.
If there is default in repayment, the secured creditor can sell the asset and obtain repayment
out of the proceeds of sale in priority to anyone else (except someone with a prior ranking

---

4 See also the Law Commission Consultation Paper No 176, *Company Security Interests* (2004), [1.16]–[1.18].

security interest over the same asset). Most importantly, this applies even if the debtor goes bankrupt. A secured creditor is largely unaffected by the bankruptcy or liquidation of its debtor: its power to sell is generally not restricted in any way. If there is a surplus left after it has done so, that goes into the general pool of assets to be divided among the unsecured creditors. So, in any bankruptcy or liquidation, unsecured creditors are paid just a fraction of what they are owed (almost invariable a tiny fraction) whereas secured creditors are paid in full (assuming the secured asset was worth more than the total indebtedness).

This is not only a good thing in itself, as far as the secure creditor is concerned. It also dramatically reduces the risk in lending. Provided the lender ensures that there is a sufficient margin between the value of the asset it accepts as security and the amount it lends, its return of capital is more or less guaranteed.

18.1.2.2 Attachment to the asset

Since security interests are property interests in the secured asset, they are attached to the asset, in the sense that the asset owner cannot sell the asset free from the security interest unless he either pays off the debt or obtains the lender's consent. If he does neither, the security interest will be fully enforceable against the buyer (subject to the [appropriate] enforceability rules). This does not make the buyer personally liable for the debt, but it does entitle the security interest holder to sell the asset and recoup the debt out of the proceeds, handing back to the buyer only whatever is left after that.

18.1.2.3 Non-judicial enforcement

The security interest holder's primary remedy [. . .] is to sell the secured asset, and in most cases to do so without first obtaining a court order, or going through any other formal procedure. It does not even have to sell by auction: the sale will be an ordinary private sale. This ability to enforce security by a simple self-help process is uncommon in other jurisdictions. It has considerable attraction to lenders. It means that the lender does not have to satisfy anyone in advance that default has justified enforcement [. . .], there is no public scrutiny of the conduct of the sale or the price obtained, and no time-consuming, costly court process to go through [. . .]

18.1.2.4 The hostage function

[. . .] Security acts as a hostage, providing an incentive to the borrower to comply with the loan agreement. If the lender takes security over an asset that the borrower values highly, fear of losing the asset will induce the borrower to go to greater lengths than it might otherwise have done to keep up the payments. When money is short, it will make these repayments before paying other debts, and it will hesitate before engaging in risky behaviour which might endanger its ability to repay [. . .] This helps to explain why lending money on the security of peoples' homes is such good business [. . .]

18.1.2.5 Signalling, monitoring and control

A debtor who offers a valued asset as security can be said to be signalling his confidence that he will be able to repay, thus lessening the need for the lender to engage in expensive checks on his creditworthiness. If the asset has a predictable market value which is greater than the proposed loan, the creditor has even less need to check creditworthiness [. . .]

> [. . .] [S]ecurity can also be used as a means of enabling the lender to monitor the behaviour of the borrower. The terms of a security interest over assets will usually require the borrower to maintain the value of the secured asset by keeping it in good state of repair, to insure it [. . .] and notify the lender of any event threatening the value of the secured asset or the ability of the borrower to repay. In this country bank loans to businesses are usually secured by security interests taken over all the assets of the business. This not only gives the lender access to comprehensive information about the running of the business, but also gives the lender the opportunity to exercise a significant level of control over decision-making, as well as enabling the lender to take early action to safeguard its interests.

It is easy, however, to be beguiled into overvaluing security interests, as opposed to the underlying debt that they secure. Clarke makes the following point.

Clarke, 'Security Interest in Property' in *Property Problems From Genes to Pension Funds* (ed Harris, 1997, p 122)

> [. . .] [T]he value to the mortgagee *of the mortgage* fluctuates depending on the likelihood of the mortgagor repaying the debt in full and in time with—paradoxically—the value of the mortgage decreasing as the likelihood of default decreases.

She also notes that '*security interests start to look distinctly marginal as property interests*'[5] when one recognizes that a security interest generally confers rights of recourse only if the debt is not repaid—an event that lies solely within the control of the borrower.

Nevertheless, the taking of security has considerable advantages for the lender, which may, in part, be passed onto the borrower (e.g. through lower interest rates), but if one party has a security interest, this is clearly disadvantageous to the borrower's other, unsecured creditors—particularly in the event of the borrower's insolvency. As a result, the probity and overall efficiency of secured credit has been questioned.[6]

Clarke and Kohler summarize some of these arguments.[7]

Clarke and Kohler, *Property Law: Commentary and Materials* (2005, p 661)

> Intuitively, it seems likely that it is, because it has been so pervasive in market economies for such a long time [. . .] But efficient for whom? It seems fairly obvious that it is efficient for the secured creditor, in that the risk of not recovering the loan in full is decreased. This should result in lenders charging a lower rate of interest for secured loans, which suggests

---

[5] Clarke, 'Security Interest in Property' in *Property Problems From Genes to Pension Funds* (ed Harris, 1997) p 123.

[6] See Finch (1992) 62 MLR 633 and Mokal (2002) 22 OJLS 686, who refer to the extensive US literature on this question, which considers the utility of security rights not only in relation to land, but also in relation to other rights held by a borrower or debtor. See also Getzler, 'The Role of Security Over Future and Circulating Capital: Evidence from the British Economy circa 1850–1920', *Company Charges: Spectrum and Beyond* (eds Getzler and Payne, 2006), ch 10.

[7] See also Clarke (1997) p 124.

that secured credit is more advantageous for borrowers as well. However, whilst the risk of not being repaid in full is decreased for the secured creditor, it is correspondingly increased for all the unsecured creditors of the same debtor, because the secured assets are removed from the pool of assets out of which they can be repaid. So at best, unsecured creditors will increase the rate of interest they charge the debtor by an amount corresponding to the discounted rate charged by the secured creditor and secured credit then becomes a "zero sum game". Even in such a case, the outcome is likely to be inefficient rather than neutral because setting up security arrangements is costly, so the debtor's total credit bill [. . .] will be greater in a world where secured credit is permitted than it would be in a world where it is prohibited. At worst—and this is rather more in line with what actually happens in the real world—some unsecured creditors will be unable to respond to the granting of secured credit by raising their interest rates (because they are involuntary creditors, or are not in a position to negotiate or re-negotiate the terms on which they extend credit). This benefits the debtor, but it does mean that the advantages to the debtor and the sophisticated and relatively affluent creditor are bought at the expense of the relatively poor and unsophisticated creditor [. . .]

However, there are other benefits that secured lending brings. We have already noted the monitoring and control functions that security enables the creditor to undertake can benefit everybody [. . .] Whether, these advantages outweigh the disadvantages remains a matter of debate.

The unsecured creditor is in a particularly vulnerable position where the secured asset represents all (or the mammoth share) of the debtor's wealth, because the creditor will be left with nothing (or little) against which he or she can seek recovery.

Clarke notes the impact of the secured creditor's privileged position on inhibiting the use and development of insolvency regimes.[8]

Clarke, 'Security Interest in Property' in *Property Problems From Genes to Pension Funds* (ed Harris, 1997, pp 122–3)

This virtual isolation of the secured creditor from the bankruptcy process has a profound effect on the development of bankruptcy law in this country in at least two respects. First, it has significantly hampered the development of a workable business rescue procedure [. . .] Even more significantly, but less often publicly acknowledged, the secured creditor's aloofness from the bankruptcy process has made bankruptcy virtually unusable for individuals whose only significant asset is a mortgaged house.

3   GENERAL FORMS OF SECURITY

Millett LJ identified the forms of security interest found in English law as follows.

---

[8] Since Clarke was writing, administration has been promoted as a collective corporate rescue regime, but one in which the secured creditor continues to play a pre-eminent role: see Enterprise Act 2002, amending Insolvency Act 1986, Sch BI.

Re Cosslett Contractors Ltd
[1998] Ch 495 CA

Millett LJ

At 508

There are only four kinds of consensual security known to English law: (i) pledge; (ii) contractual lien; (iii) equitable charge and (iv) mortgage. A pledge and a contractual lien both depend on the delivery of possession to the creditor. The difference between them is that in the case of a pledge the owner delivers possession to the creditor as security, whereas in the case of a lien the creditor retains possession of goods previously delivered to him for some other purpose. Neither a mortgage nor a charge depends on the delivery of possession. The difference between them is that a mortgage involves a transfer of legal or equitable ownership to the creditor, whereas an equitable charge does not.

In this extract, Millett LJ sets out the *general* forms of security right that can apply over property which we will consider in a little more detail in this section. In section 4, we will focus on the security interests that are important where land is concerned.

3.1 THE PLEDGE

The pledge is the most traditional form of security. It is dependent upon the borrower delivering possession or control of property to the lender. Ownership in the property is retained by the borrower and the lender obtains its own property right (a 'special interest' in the property), entitling it to sell if the loan is not repaid, accounting to the borrower for the proceeds of sale over and above that required to repay the loan.[9]

A pledge is found in a wide variety of situations, from pawn-broking, to international finance and trade. Its strength lies in the protection that it can afford the lender: by taking control of the property, the lender can assert its priority against the claims of other creditors. The disadvantage of a pledge lies in the fact that physical possession or control of the property must be delivered to the lender so that the borrower is deprived of the use of the property. Chattels, being moveable assets, lend themselves to the essential possessory nature of the pledge. Documents that constitute the title to goods, money, and other investments may also be pledged.[10] Given its immovable nature, land does not form the natural subject matter of a pledge—although the original forms of security over land tried to replicate the nature of a pledge.[11]

3.2 THE LIEN

As Millett LJ points out, a consensual lien operates as a legal form of security: for example, a borrower can agree with a lender that the lender has a right to retain possession of property until the borrower's outstanding debt is paid. In addition, the common law has also implies

---

9 *The Odessa* [1916] 1 AC 145; *Matthew v TH Sutton* [1949] 4 All ER 793.

10 For example, bills of lading, negotiable instruments such as cheques, promissory notes, treasury bills, and bills of exchange.

11 The name 'mortgage' is derived from the medieval word for pledge: the 'gage'.

liens into certain contracts: for example, a repairer of property is entitled to a lien to secure the costs of repair.[12]

An equitable lien needs to be distinguished from a consensual lien and a common law lien. It gives a lender an equitable property right, rather than a legal property right. The rules relating to the content and acquisition of an equitable lien therefore differ from those applying to a common law lien. As to its *content*, an equitable lien is in the nature of a charge: it does not require the lender to have possession. As to its *acquisition*, an equitable lien can only arise by operation of law, rather than as a result of the agreement of the parties.

The most significant equitable lien for our purposes arises upon the sale of land and is called the 'unpaid vendor's lien'. A vendor who has transferred his or her freehold or lease to the purchaser, but has not received the full purchase price, is entitled to claim an equitable lien (over the freehold or lease now held by the purchaser) to secure the unpaid portion. Likewise, a purchaser who has paid, or partly paid, the purchase price for land, but has not yet received the vendor's freehold or lease, may have a power (for example, because of a breach of the contract of sale by the vendor) to pull out of the contract and claim back any payment that he or she has made. In such a case, the purchaser has an equitable lien over the vendor's freehold or lease in order to secure the vendor's duty to repay that money.

3.3 THE MORTGAGE

Buckley LJ has described the form of a mortgage as follows.[13]

Swiss Bank Group v Lloyds Bank Ltd
[1982] AC 584, HL

Buckley LJ

At 594

The essence of any transaction by way of mortgage is that a debtor confers upon his creditor a proprietary interest in property of the debtor, or undertakes in a binding manner to do so, by the realisation or appropriation of which the creditor can procure the discharge of the debtor's liability to him, and that the proprietary interest is redeemable, or the obligation to create it is defeasible, in the event of the debtor discharging his liability. If there has been no legal transfer of a proprietary interest but merely a binding undertaking to confer such an interest, that obligation, if specifically enforceable, will confer a proprietary interest in the subject matter in equity. The obligation will be specifically enforceable if it is an obligation for the breach of which damages would be an inadequate remedy. A contract to mortgage property, real or personal, will, normally at least, be specifically enforceable, for a mere claim to damages or repayment is obviously less valuable than a security in the event of the debtor's insolvency. If it is specifically enforceable, the obligation to confer the proprietary interest will give rise to an equitable charge upon the subject matter by way of mortgage.

---

[12] Other common law liens include an innkeeper's (or hotelier's) and carrier's lien. Liens may also arise from the general usage of a particular trade or business: e.g. solicitors, factors, bankers, stockbrokers, and insurance brokers.

[13] Buckley misuses the term 'an equitable charge' in the last line of this extract. He should have referred to 'an equitable mortgage'.

A mortgage thus transfers the borrower's interest in the property to the lender, subject to an obligation on the lender to return that interest to the borrower once the debt is repaid—an obligation that confers upon the borrower what is known as 'a right to redeem'. The borrower's legal right to redeem is governed by the need for strict compliance with the repayment terms set out in the loan agreement. But equity will recognize the borrower's continuing equitable right to redeem even if he or she has failed to repay the loan in accordance with the contractual terms. This equitable right to redeem is of such import that it is recognized as giving the borrower an equitable property right: a right that is capable of binding third parties. In Chapter 6, section 1, it was suggested that equitable property rights depend on one party being under a duty to another; the equitable right to redeem is based on the lender's duty to transfer a mortgaged right back to the borrower if the underlying debt is repaid. Thus, although the mortgagee has the legal title to the property, a mortgage differs from an outright sale, because the lender's title is subject to the borrower's equity of redemption, the economic value of which is represented by the value of the property less the amount required to repay the lender. In this rather roundabout fashion, the security nature of the mortgage is achieved. We will have more to say about the borrower's equity of redemption in section 5.

The lender's inherent rights under a legal mortgage are defined, firstly, by their ownership of the legal title, which confers a right to possession, and secondly, by their right to apply to bar the borrower's equitable right to redeem, and thus extinguish the equity of redemption, by a process known as 'foreclosure'.

As Buckley LJ indicates, mortgages may take a legal or equitable form. A mortgage will be equitable where the borrower has only an equitable interest in the property and transfers that interest to the lender, or where the formalities used to create the mortgage fall short of the requirements to convey the legal title,[14] but nevertheless are recognized as an agreement to create a mortgage, and so give the lender an equitable property right under the doctrine of anticipation (see Chapter 8 and section 4.3).

3.4 THE CHARGE

Millett LJ, again in *Re Cosslett Contractors*, defined a charge as follows.

Re Cosslett Contractors Ltd
[1998] Ch 495, CA

Millett LJ

At 508

It is of the essence of a charge that a particular asset or class of assets is appropriated to the satisfaction of a debt or other obligation of the chargor or a third party, so that the chargee is entitled to look to the asset and its proceeds for the discharge of the liability. This right creates a transmissible interest in the asset. A mere right to retain possession of an asset and to make use of it for a particular purpose does not create such an interest and does not constitute a charge.

---

[14] See Chapter 6.

A charge creates a new proprietary interest that encumbers or burdens the borrower's own-ership of the property. In contrast to a mortgage, there is no transfer of an existing owner-ship interest. The charge entitles the lender to look to the charged property to satisfy the debt. In the absence of any express or implied powers contained in the charge, the lender does so by applying to court for an order for the sale of the property, or for the appointment of a receiver to apply the capital or income from the property (as appropriate) in repayment of the debt. Upon satisfaction of the debt, the charge is automatically discharged, because there is simply no continuing debt to be met out of the property. The charge resembles the Roman law *hypothec*; indeed, it is sometimes described as a 'hypothecation'.

The charge is a creature of equity, although the Law of Property Act 1925 (LPA 1925) also uses the term 'charge' to describe a special form of legal interest that can be used to give a lender a security right in land.[15] It is important to distinguish the equitable charge (which can apply even where land is not involved) from the legal charge created by the 1925 Act (which can apply only to land). An equitable charge may be taken over existing and future property, and may be *fixed* over specific property or taken in *floating* form over a changing fund of assets. For example, one of the most common forms of commercial security is the floating charge over all of the rights, whether present or future, of a company. The floating charge affects the assets for the time being owned by the company, yet permits the company to deal with those assets in the ordinary course of the company's business without the consent of the lender. A floating charge may be converted to a fixed charge, by a process known as 'crystallization', which will occur either where the company is unable to deal with its assets in the ordinary course of its business or an agreed event occurs. The categorization of fixed and floating charges has been the source of much litigation, but has been finally settled by the House of Lords, which identified the de-fining factor as the degree of control that the lender exercises over the charged asset.[16]

Re Spectrum Plus Ltd
[2005] 2 AC 680, HL

Lord Walker

At [138]–[139]

Under a fixed charge the assets charged as security are permanently appropriated to the payment of the sum charged, in such a way as to give the chargee a proprietary interest in the assets. So long as the charge remains unredeemed, the assets can be released from the charge only with the active concurrence of the chargee. The chargee may have good commercial reasons for agreeing to a partial release. [. . .] But under a fixed charge that will be a matter for the chargee to decide for itself.

Under a floating charge, by contrast, the chargee does not have the same power to control the security for its own benefit. The chargee has a proprietary interest, but its interest is in a *fund* of circulating capital, and unless and until the chargee intervenes (on crystallisation of the charge) it is for the trader, and not the bank, to decide how to run its business.

---

[15] See section 4.2.

[16] See also Worthington, 'Floating Charges: The Use and Abuse of Doctrinal Analysis' in *Company Charges: Spectrum and Beyond* (eds Getzler and Payne, 2006), ch 3. The analysis of the House of Lords in *Re Spectrum Plus* [2005] 2 AC 680, HL, essentially matches that of Worthington in *Proprietary Interests in Commercial Transactions* (1996) pp 78–86.

4 FORMS OF SECURITY OVER LAND: MORTGAGES AND CHARGES

The English mortgage has been described as 'a work of fiction' and 'a confusion of things'.[17] To understand that fiction, we must look to the development of the form of English mortgage, bearing in mind the general forms of security interest examined in section 3.

4.1 DEVELOPMENT OF MORTGAGES OF LAND

Mortgages have a long history, which was much influenced by the laws against usury that prohibited the charging of interest.[18]

Baker, *An Introduction to English Legal History* (4th edn, 2002, p 311)

From the earliest times, debtors have used property as security—or 'gage'—for loans of money. Whether the gage was a chattel or land, possession had to be handed over to the lender, to be returned on payment. In some early forms of gage no term was fixed: the gagee held the property until he was satisfied. Another early form, [. . .], was a lease of years to the gagee, the term being the period of the loan. If the gagee took the profits in reduction of the loan, this was known in early times as a living gage (*vivum vadium*) apparently because the property continued to work for the borrower; but if the lender took the principal as well as the profits, it was a dead gage ('mortgage') and the arrangement, though sinful as giving the lender a usurious return, was legally valid. By the fifteenth century, however, the name 'mortgage' has apparently come to be used for any arrangement whereby a loan was secured by a conveyance of real property[. . . .] Two new ways of effecting such a security were developed in the thirteenth century: either the mortgagor leased the land for years to the mortgagee, with a proviso that if the debt was not paid by a certain date the mortgagee would have the fee, or the mortgagor conveyed the fee to the mortgagee forthwith, on condition that he might re-enter (and regain the fee) if he paid by a certain date [. . .] In the seventeenth century a further alternative device came into almost universal use, the long term of years with clause for defeasance [. . .] and it later became a common practice under the common law forms of mortgage [. . .] to allow the mortgagor to remain in possession as a tenant at will or at sufferance of the mortgagee.

We can, thus, see that the lawyers of old utilized both the pledge and the mortgage as security devices, although it was the classic mortgage by conveyance or demise that prevailed. The 'fiction' referred to lies in the fact that, at common law, the *lender* was the owner of the property and so entitled to the incidents of ownership—in particular, possession—while the borrower held only a right to insist on reconveyance of the legal title upon repayment of the debt. This was despite the fact that, as the laws against usury relaxed and the charging of interest was permitted, the lender had no wish to take possession unless and until the borrower failed to repay the loan. Despite the position at common law, the borrower generally

---

[17] Watt, 'Mortgage Law as Legal Fiction' in *Modern Studies in Property Law Vol 3* (ed Cooke, 2007) pp 73 and 76.

[18] The laws against usury were not finally abolished until the Usury Laws Repeal Act 1854.

kept possession of the property and both parties saw him or her as its true owner. It was the borrower's equity of redemption that redressed the balance somewhat: equity's protection of the borrower's right to repay the debt and redeem the property resulted in the borrower (in effect) being regarded as the owner in equity, with the lender's legal title being held only by way of security.

The LPA 1925 introduced the current incarnation of the legal charge by way of mortgage. This special security interest, existing only in relation to land, allows a borrower with a freehold or lease to give the lender a legal interest by way of security *without* needing to transfer his or her freehold or lease to the lender. Unfortunately, however, the legal charge has not been able to escape the fiction that lies at the heart of the mortgage.

4.2 THE LEGAL CHARGE BY WAY OF MORTGAGE

The LPA 1925 contemplated only two methods of creating a legal mortgage: the mortgage by sub-demise, and the legal charge by way of mortgage. Section 85(1) and (2) provides as follows.[19]

Law of Property Act 1925, s 85(1) and (2)

Mode of mortgaging freeholds

1. A mortgage of an estate in fee simple shall only be capable of being effected at law either by a demise for a term of years absolute, subject to a provision for cesser on redemption, or by a charge by deed expressed to be by way of legal mortgage.

   Provided that a first mortgagee shall have the same right to the possession of documents as if his security included the fee simple.

2. Any purported conveyance of an estate in fee simple by way of mortgage made after the commencement of this Act shall (to the extent of the estate of the mortgagor) operate as a demise of the land to the mortgagee for a term of years absolute, without impeachment for waste, but subject to cesser on redemption, in manner following, namely:—

   (a) A first or only mortgagee shall take a term of three thousand years from the date of the mortgage;

   (b) A second or subsequent mortgagee shall take a term (commencing from the date of the mortgage) one day longer than the term vested in the first or other mortgagee whose security ranks immediately before that of such second or subsequent mortgagee;

   and, in this subsection, any such purported conveyance as aforesaid includes an absolute conveyance with a deed of defeasance and any other assurance which, but for this subsection, would operate in effect to vest the fee simple in a mortgagee subject to redemption.

The mortgage by sub-demise creates a proprietary estate in the lender, although, rather than a fee simple, it is a leasehold estate for 3,000 years. The mortgage by sub-demise has, however, fallen into disuse as the legal charge by way of mortgage has gained in popularity.

---

[19] Law of Property Act 1925, s 86, contains similar provisions governing the mode of mortgaging leaseholds.

The Land Registration Act 2002 (LRA 2002) reflects this trend by effectively rendering obsolete the mortgage by sub-demise.[20] A legal mortgage of unregistered land will trigger first registration[21] and, whatever the form of mortgage, s 51 provides that it will have effect as a charge by deed by way of mortgage.

Land Registration Act 2002, s 51

Effect of completion by registration

On completion of the relevant registration requirements, a charge created by means of a registrable disposition of a registered estate has effect, if it would not otherwise do so, as a charge by deed by way of legal mortgage.

Section 23 then provides that a registered owner is only capable of entering into a mortgage of a registered estate by way of charge.

Land Registration Act 2002, s 23

Owner's powers

1. Owner's powers in relation to a registered estate consist of—
   (a) power to make a disposition of any kind permitted by the general law in relation to an interest of that description, other than a mortgage by demise or sub-demise, and
   (b) power to charge the estate at law with the payment of money.

Thus, it is the legal charge by way of mortgage that provides the pre-eminent form of legal security interest over land. But the effect of the mortgage by sub-demise has not been laid to rest, because s 87(1) of the LPA 1925 provides as follows.

Law of Property Act 1925, s 87(1)

Charges by way of legal mortgage

1. Where a legal mortgage of land is created by a charge by deed expressed to be by way of legal mortgage, the mortgagee shall have the same protection, powers and remedies (including the right to take proceedings to obtain possession from the occupiers and the persons in receipt of rents and profits, or any of them) as if—
   (a) where the mortgage is a mortgage of an estate in fee simple, a mortgage term for three thousand years without impeachment of waste had been thereby created in favour of the mortgagee; and

---

[20] For an interesting, but unsuccessful, claim of an unregistrable mortgage by sub-demise, see *Roberts v Lawton* [2017] 1P&CR 3.

[21] Land Registration Act 2002, s 4(1)g.

> (b) where the mortgage is a mortgage of a term of years absolute, a sub-term less by one day than the term vested in the mortgagor had been thereby created in favour of the mortgagee.

The result is a hybrid security interest: the lender gains a legal charge (not a lease),[22] but enjoys the same protections, powers, and remedies as if it held a lease for a term of 3,000 years. Certainly, there is no transfer to the lender of the borrower's freehold or lease: the borrower retains that estate, but holds it subject to the lender's legal charge.

So the old fiction continues in a different, but just as complicated, form. The inappropriateness of this form has been highlighted by the Law Commission, which has long advocated reform by the adoption of a statutory form of security interest with defined rights and powers.

Law Commission Report No 204, *Land Mortgages* (1991, [2.14], [2.17]–[2.18], [3.1]–[3.2])

Removal of the distinction between mortgage and charge

A mortgage is conceptually different from a charge [. . .] However in English law the distinction is blurred and the terms are often used interchangeably, sometimes as if they were synonymous and sometimes as if one was a generic term including the other. The confusion is exacerbated by uncertainty over the correct classification of the mortgage by demise and the charge by way of legal mortgage. The mortgage by demise is technically a mortgage, in that it involves the grant of a substantial legal estate to the mortgagee. However, equitable restriction of the mortgagee's ownership-type rights has resulted in it acquiring a close resemblance to a charge. The charge by way of legal mortgage is in name and form a charge, but in substance it is the same as the mortgage by demise.
   [. . .]

Inappropriateness of form

The second root cause of the artificiality and complexity of mortgage law is the methods used to create security interest in land give rise to inappropriate relationships between the parties. This is particularly apparent in the mortgage by demise [. . .]

   The problem here is of central importance because it affects not only the mortgage by demise, but also the charge by way of legal mortgage which is treated by statute as if it were a mortgage by demise and the equitable mortgage of a legal estate which is treated in equity as if it were a legal mortgage, hence a mortgage by demise. The problem is that it creates a relationship of landlord and tenant between the parties. There is nothing unusual about using the leasehold relationship as an investment device: institutional lenders are probably more likely to use leases rather than mortgages as a means of financing property developments or investing in non-residential land. However, in the case of the mortgage by demise the leasehold relationship is the wrong way round: as tenant, the mortgagee has an inherent right to

---

[22] *Grand Junction Co Ltd v Bates* [1954] 2 QB 160, 166; *Weg Motors Ltd v Hales* [1962] Ch 49, 74; *Cumberland Court (Brighton) Ltd v Taylor* [1964] Ch 29, 36; *Regent Oil Co Ltd v JA Gregory (Hatch End) Ltd* [1966] Ch 402.

possession which would more appropriately lie with the mortgagor (subject to whatever restrictions may be necessary to protect and enforce the security). Similarly, it is necessary for the preservation of the security that the mortgagor should be under a duty more usually imposed by a landlord on a tenant, rather than a tenant on a landlord. Even if reversed, the landlord-tenant relationship is fundamentally different from that created by a mortgage: investors under a leased-based arrangement buy outright a share in the property, and the value of the share fluctuates in direct proportion to the value of the retained property; mortgagee-investors, on the other hand, have an interest in the property only for the temporary purpose of safeguarding the repayment of a loan or the value of the obligation secured. Historically the mortgage by demise was a useful device to bridge the gap between abolition of the mortgage by assignment and the general acceptance of the legal charge. Now that it has fulfilled that purpose, it seems an unnecessary impoverishment of the system to blur the distinction between the lease and mortgage by continuing to define one device in terms of the other.

[. . .]

Nature of the new mortgage

It is central to our proposal for the creation of a new kind of mortgage that the attributes of the mortgage should be expressly defined by statute, rather than defined by reference to pre-existing forms of mortgage or by analogy to any other legal relationship. It is therefore necessary to consider what interest in the mortgaged property a mortgagee ought to have under the new mortgage, whether formal or informal [. . .]

The guiding principle we have adopted in defining the nature of the new mortgage is that the only function of the mortgaged property is to provide security for the performance of the mortgagor's payment obligations. It follows from this that the nature and extent of the mortgagee's interest ought to be dictated by the need to preserve the value of the security and, where necessary, to enforce it.

4.3 EQUITABLE MORTGAGES AND EQUITABLE CHARGES OF LAND

The legal charge by way of mortgage now monopolizes the creation of legal security over land. In equity, there remains a number of ways in which an equitable security right can arise. To see the differences between legal and equitable security rights, we again need to focus on the *content* and *acquisition* questions (see Chapter 1, section 3).

4.3.1 Equitable charge of a legal estate: the *acquisition* question

A borrower with a legal estate in land may attempt to give a lender a legal charge by way of security—but to acquire such a legal interest, the lender needs to show that the borrower granted that right by means of a deed, and also that the lender has now registered its charge.[23] If those steps have not been taken, the lender may nonetheless acquire an *equitable* charge (under the doctrine of anticipation—see Chapter 8) by showing that the borrower is under a duty to grant the lender a legal charge. So, the lender will acquire an equitable charge

---

[23] See Chapter 8 for the general formality rules applying to the creation of a legal interest in land.

if the borrower has made a contractual promise to grant a legal charge.[24] In addition, even if the borrower has made no contractual promise, a court can impose a duty to grant a charge if, in return for the loan provided by the lender, the borrower has attempted to grant a legal charge, but has failed to do so (e.g. because of a failure to comply with formality rules).[25] In such cases, there can be said to have been an 'equitable charge' of the borrower's legal estate in the land.

Under this form of equitable security of a legal estate in land, the parties' relationship is treated in equity as if the agreement had been performed and a legal charge had been created. Thus, the lender is treated as if it had a legal charge by way of mortgage, with the benefit of the remedies and powers of a mortgage by sub-demise so far as they are consistent with the equitable nature of the lender's rights.[26]

To constitute this type of equitable charge of a legal estate, an agreement to create a legal mortgage must be valid. It should thus comply with the terms of s 2(1) of the Law of Property (Miscellaneous Provisions) Act 1989 (LP(MP)A 1989) (see Chapter 8, section 3). Prior to this enactment, it was common practice for lenders to take a deposit of the borrower's title deeds. This deposit of the deeds would create an equitable security: the loan supported by the act of deposit was interpreted both as evidence of the parties' agreement to create a legal charge, and as an act of part-performance to support the enforcement of that agreement. It is now clear that, given the formalities required under the LP(MP)A 1989, the practice of creating an equitable security by deposit is no longer possible.

United Bank of Kuwait plc v Sahib
[1997] Ch 107, CA

Peter Gibson LJ

At 137

I would emphasise the essential contractual foundation of the rule as demonstrated in the authorities. The deposit by way of security is treated both as prima facie evidence of a contract to mortgage, and as part performance of that contract [... .]

I accept that there need not be an express contract between the depositor of the title deeds and the person with whom they are deposited for an equitable mortgage to arise (subject to s 2). But I have already stated why it is clear from the authorities that the deposit is treated as rebuttable evidence of a contract to mortgage. Oral evidence is admissible to establish whether or not a deposit was intended to create a mortgage security [. . .],To allow inquiries of this sort after the 1989 Act in order to determine whether an equitable mortgage has been created and on what terms seems to me to be wholly inconsistent with the

---

[24] It seems that the lender should also acquire an equitable charge if the borrower is under a *non- contractual* duty to grant a legal charge: see Chapter 10, section 2. For example, in *Kinane v Mackie-Conteh* [2005] EWCA Civ 45, the Court of Appeal found that proprietary estoppel imposed a duty on the borrower to grant a legal charge. As a result, the lender acquired an equitable interest in the land— although the Court held that the lender's interest arose under a constructive trust, not by means of an equitable charge.

[25] *Bank of Scotland plc v Waugh* [2014] EWHC 2117 and *No 2* [2014] EWHC 2835 although the court incorrectly identified the charge as a legal charge by virtue of its registration.

[26] For example, an equitable chargee or mortgagee cannot sell the legal estate: Law of Property Act 1925, s 88(6) but see *Swift 1st Ltd v Colin* [2011] EWHC 2410 and *Skelwith (Leisure) Ltd v Armstrong* [2016] Ch 345.

philosophy of s 2, requiring as it does that the contract be made by a single document containing all the terms of the agreement if it is to be valid [. . .]

To the extent that part performance is an essential part of the rationale of the creation of an equitable mortgage by the deposit of title deeds, that too is inconsistent with the new philosophy of the 1989 Act. As the Law Commission said in its report (para 4.13):

'Inherent in the recommendation that contracts should be made in writing is the consequence that part performance would no longer have a role to play in contracts concerning land.'

In the present case, for the reasons already given, it seems to me clear that the deposit of title deeds takes effect as a contract to mortgage and as such falls within s 2.

The judge said [at first instance ...]:

'The recommendation [of the Law Commission] that contracts relating to land should be incorporated in a signed document which contains all the terms was, clearly, intended to promote certainty. There is no reason why certainty should be any less desirable in relation to arrangements for security over land than in relation to any other arrangements in respect of land. The present case itself illustrates the need to be able to identify the obligation which is to be secured. I do not find it surprising that Parliament decided to enact legislation which would be likely to have the effect of avoiding disputes on oral evidence as to the obligation which the parties intended to secure.'

I agree. Indeed, it seems to me that the whole of the judge's reasoning, to which I would pay tribute, on the s 2 point cannot be faulted. Like him, I am fortified by the support for the same conclusion given in *Emmet on Title* para 25.116. I therefore conclude that by reason of s 2, the mere deposit of title deeds by way of security cannot any longer create a mortgage or charge.

In Chapter 10 we examined how arrangements that fail to comply with s 2(1) may nevertheless continue to have effect through the doctrines of proprietary estoppel or constructive trusts. In *Sahib*, Peter Gibson LJ rejected the lender's arguments that it had acquired an equitable charge on the grounds of proprietary estoppel or a constructive trust—but in *Kinane v Mackie- Conteh*,[27] in which the lender advanced £50,000 in reliance upon the parties' understanding that the loan would be secured, a similar argument succeeded and the lender did acquire an equitable charge.[28]

It does seem correct that the lender should acquire an equitable charge if the borrower is under a *non-contractual* duty to grant a legal charge, however, in light of the House of Lords' decisions in *Cobbe v Yeoman's Row Management Ltd*[29] and *Thorner v Major*[30] the role of proprietary estoppel in the creation of equitable interests (particularly in the commercial context) must now be re-examined.

4.3.2 Equitable mortgage of an equitable estate: the *content* question

If the borrower has no legal estate in land, but only an equitable interest, then it is impossible for the lender to acquire a legal charge: the content of the borrower's property

---

[27] [2005] EWCA Civ 45, noted Dixon [2005] Conv 247 and McFarlane [2005] Conv 501.

[28] Although it has been suggested that estoppel is an inadequate replacement for part-performance: see Griffiths [2002] Conv 216.

[29] [2008] UKHL 55, [2008] 1 WLR 1752.   [30] [2009] UKHL 18, [2009] 1 WLR 776.

right prevents it. In such a case, any security interest acquired by the lender must take an equitable form. Such a right can arise by means of an equitable mortgage: if, for example, the borrower transfers his or her equitable interest to the lender. Such equitable mortgages are not as common as mortgages of the legal estate, but they may arise where a purchaser mortgages his or her equitable interest under a sale and purchase agreement of land, or where a beneficiary under a trust of land has mortgaged his or her interest. Where an equitable mortgage is created intentionally, it is created in the classic form by assigning the borrower's equitable interest to the lender, subject to the lender's covenant to reassign upon repayment of the loan.

4.3.3 Equitable charge: the *content* question

Finally a charge may be created in equity, whether over a legal estate or an equitable interest in the land, where the parties demonstrate an intention that the borrower's right is to make available, or appropriated, for the discharge of a debt or other obligation. That intention must be evinced in writing, but no particular form of words is required.[31] That intention may be construed from a failure to create a legal charge by way of mortgage: for example, consider a case in which a freehold or lease is held jointly by two co-owners under a trust of land.[32] One of the co-owners then purports to mortgage the legal estate by forging the other co-owner's signature. The purported legal charge by way of mortgage cannot be valid—but the lender will acquire an equitable security right, taking effect only against the equitable share of the co-owner who purported to grant the legal charge.[33] A similar result can apply where the other co-owner does consent to the legal charge, but does so as a result of undue influence or misrepresentation (see Chapter 27, section 3.3).

Under this form of equitable charge, the lender acquires an equitable property right due to the content of the borrower's duty to the lender: a duty to allow the lender to use the borrower's right to meet the debt, should the borrower fail to repay. This form of security right is *not* special to land: as we saw in section 3.4, it arises whenever a borrower comes under such a duty to a lender.

It must be remembered that this form of equitable charge is conceptually different from the equitable charge that we examined in section 4.3.1, when looking at equitable charge of the legal estate. Where there is such an equitable charge, the borrower is under a duty to grant the lender a legal interest: a legal charge. The lender can thus call for that right, and, with it, will acquire all of the powers and remedies associated with a legal charge. In the case of the equitable charge examined in this section, however, the lender enjoys none of these rights. Its implied rights are confined to a right to apply to court for an order for sale or the appointment of a receiver.

In the following extract, McFarlane emphasizes this distinction by giving different names to the form of equitable charge that we examined in section 4.3.1 and that which we have examined in this section. In the passage, a legal charge by way of mortgage is referred to as a 'charge'. The first type of equitable charge is then called an 'equitable charge' and the second a 'purely equitable charge'. This underlines the fact that, in the second case, the borrower is under no duty to give the lender a legal interest in land.

---

[31] See Law of Property Act 1925, s 53(1)a.   [32] See Chapters 13 and 14.
[33] See *Ahmed v Kendrick* [1988] 2 FLR 22; *First National Securities Ltd v Hegerty* [1985] QB 850; *Thames Guaranty Ltd v Campbell* [1985] QB 210.

McFarlane, *The Structure of Property Law* (2008, p 818)

It is important to distinguish between (i) an Equitable Charge; and (ii) a Purely Equitable Charge. First, an Equitable Charge, unlike a Purely Equitable Charge, can exist only in relation to land. Second, even where land is concerned, there is a difference between the two rights. An Equitable Charge arises where [the borrower] is under a duty to grant [the lender] a Charge. A Purely Equitable Charge arises where [the borrower] is under a duty to hold his Freehold or Lease as security for a duty owed to [the lender]. Third, formality rules can apply differently to each right:

Equitable Charge: Where [the borrower] has a Freehold or Lease, his power to come under a *contractual* duty to give [the lender] a Charge is regulated by s.2 of the 1989 Act [. . .] However, [the lender] can acquire an Equitable Charge in the absence of writing if [the borrower] is under a *non-contractual* duty to give [the lender] a Charge.

Purely Equitable Charge: Where [the borrower] has a Freehold or Lease, his power to make a contractual promise to hold his right as security is regulated by s.53(1)(a) of the LPA 1925. That rule requires only writing signed by A.

4.3.4 Equitable security rights in land: reform?

We have distinguished between three different ways in which a lender can acquire an equitable security interest in land. The Law Commission recommended the rationalization of this confusing multiplicity of forms.

Law Commission Report No 204, *Land Mortgages* (1991, [2.13])

Reduction in the number of types of security

Whilst this proliferation of types of security interest in land is historically explicable, we are satisfied that it no longer serves any useful purpose [. . .] The problem of equitable security in a legal estate is rather different. The principle underlying equitable mortgages of the legal estate is the rule in *Walsh v Lonsdale*, a general property law principle which applies to mortgages in precisely the same way as it applies to fee simples, leases and easements. Nevertheless, if the equitable charge is included it does mean that there are at least three, and possibly four, ways of taking informal security over the legal estate. Whilst there are small differences in the effect between these different types of equitable security, there is no apparent difference in function: none seems to fulfill a function that could not be fulfilled by any one of the others. The same can be said of the different ways of taking security over equitable interests in land: responses to the Working Paper confirmed that the differences in form and effect between equitable mortgages and equitable charges are regarded as no practical significance. Finally, there is the question of whether it remains necessary for the method of creating a security interest over an equitable interest to be different from the method for creating a security interest over a legal estate. In the Working Group we put forward the view that there was no reason in principle why the same type of security should not be used for both legal and equitable interests in land [. . .]

4.4 CHARGING ORDERS

A charging order provides a means by which a judgment creditor can enforce his or her judgment, by providing some of the advantages conferred by security. Charging orders are governed by the Charging Orders Act 1979. In theory, a judgment creditor can apply for a charging order over *any* property of the debtor; in practice, however, a judgment creditor is likely to ask for a charging order in relation to valuable, immovable property—the debtor's land.

Charging Orders Act 1979, s 1(1)

Charging orders

(1) Where, under a judgment or order of the High Court or [...] the county court, a person (the "debtor") is required to pay a sum of money to another person (the "creditor") then, for the purpose of enforcing that judgment or order, the appropriate court may make an order in accordance with the provisions of this Act imposing on any such property of the debtor as may be specified in the order a charge for securing the payment of any money due or to become due under the judgment or order.

The judgment creditor must thus apply to court for the grant of a charging order.[34] If a charging order is granted, a charge is created over the judgment debtor's interest in land as specified in the order to secure the payment of the judgment debt,[35] and should accordingly be registered to preserve its priority.[36] This charge has '*the like effect and shall be enforceable [. . .] in the same manner as an equitable charge created by the debtor under his hand*'.[37] The judgment creditor becomes a secured creditor and will be able to claim priority against unsecured creditors if the debtor becomes insolvent. The charging order may be enforced by application to court for an order for sale, or for the appointment of a receiver.

A judgment creditor thus must submit to the court's discretion at two points: firstly, when the court decides whether or not to make the order; and secondly, when the court decides whether or not the charging order should be enforced.

The court in exercising its initial discretion whether or not to grant a charging order must consider all of the circumstances of the case, including the personal circumstances of the debtor and whether any other creditor would be prejudiced by the order.[38] Where relevant circumstances subsequently come to light, the court may vary or discharge the charging order.[39]

---

[34] The making of the order is a two-stage process. Initially, the charging order nisi is granted usually ex parte. If the judgment debtor fails to meet the judgment as required by the order nisi, the charging order is made absolute.

[35] Including a beneficial interest held under a trust of land: see Charging Orders Act 1979, s 2(1)(a)(i).

[36] In respect of a registered estate by a notice, see Land Registration Act 2002, ss 32–4, or by a restriction where the judgment debtor's interest is a beneficial interest under a trust, see Land Registration Act 2002, s 42(1)(c) and (4). Where land is unregistered, a charging order against the judgment debtor's legal title is registrable as an order affecting land: see Land Charges Act 1972, s 6(1)(a); but where the judgment debtor holds a beneficial interest under a trust of unregistered land, there is no provision for registration.

[37] Charging Orders Act 1979, s 3(4).

[38] The charging order process has been criticized as deficient to draw out the relevant circumstances, see Capper, Conway and Glennon, 'From Obligation to Proprietary Interest: A Critique of the Charging Order System in England and Wales' in *Modern Studies in Property Law Vol 6* (ed Bright, Oxford: Hart Publishing, 2011) ch 4.

[39] The application can be made by the debtor or any other person with an interest in the property: see s 3(5).

Charging Orders Act 1979, s 1(5)

Charging orders

(5) In deciding whether to make a charging order the court shall consider all the circumstances of the case and, in particular, any evidence before it as to—

(a) the personal circumstances of the debtor, and

(b) whether any other creditor of the debtor would be likely to be unduly prejudiced by the making of the order.

A creditor, although not entitled to a charging order, can expect an order to be granted in its favour unless there are circumstances that would persuade a court that an order should not be made. For example, a charging order will not be granted if it is likely that the debtor will become bankrupt or go into liquidation; in such a case, a charging order would give the judgment debtor an undue advantage over other unsecured creditors.[40]

Where the judgment debtor's interest is an interest in his or her home, which he or she holds jointly with his or her spouse or partner, the court will also consider the position of that spouse or partner and any children. The situation may be complicated by the possibility that divorce proceedings are contemplated, or pending, in which the judgment debtor's spouse is entitled to claim ancillary relief. In these circumstances, there is a balance to be struck between the exercise of the court's family jurisdiction, in which the welfare of any children are a primary consideration, and the court's commercial jurisdiction, in which contracts must be honoured and judgment debts paid.

The Court of Appeal, in the following case, considered this a balancing exercise. After noting that where the application for a charging order is made before a spouse has started divorce proceedings there is no balance to be struck, as there is no competing claim to the judgment creditor's application, the Court of Appeal went onto to consider the proper approach where divorce proceedings had been started.

Harman v Glencross
[1986] Fam 81, CA

Balcombe LJ

At 99

2. Where the charging order nisi has been made after the wife's petition, then on the application for a charging order absolute the court should consider whether the circumstances are such that it is proper to make the charging order absolute, even before the wife's application for ancillary relief has been heard by the Family Division. There will, of course, be cases ... where the figures are such that even if the charging order is made absolute, and then the charge is realised by a sale of the house, the resultant proceeds of sale (including any balance of the husband's share after the judgment debt has been paid) will be clearly sufficient to provide adequate alternative accommodation for the wife and children.

---

[40] *Roberts Petroleum Ltd v Bernard Kenny Ltd* [1983] 2 AC 192; *Nationwide Building Society v Wright* [2010] Ch 318. After 1 October 2012, default on a judgment debt payable by instalments is unnecessary—ss1(7) and (8).

3. Unless it appears to the court hearing the application for the charging order absolute that the circumstances are so clear that it is proper to make the order there and then, the usual practice should be to transfer the application to the Family Division so that it may come on with the wife's application for ancillary relief, and one court can then be in a position to consider all the circumstances of the case. When considering the circumstances, the approach of the court should be to recall the statement of Sir Denys Buckley in the *Hegerty case* [1985] Q.B. 850, 866, that a judgment creditor is justified in expecting that a charging order over the husband's beneficial interest in the matrimonial home will be made in his favour. The court should first consider whether the value of the equity in the house is sufficient to enable the charging order to be made absolute and realised at once, … even though that may result in the wife and children being housed at a lower standard than they might reasonably have expected had only the husband's interests been taken into account against them. Failing that, the court should make only such order as may be necessary to protect the wife's right to occupy (with the children where appropriate) the matrimonial home. The normal course should then be to postpone the sale of the house for such period only as may be requisite to protect the right of occupation—a Mesher type of order—again bearing in mind that the court is holding the balance, not between the wife and the husband, but between the wife and the judgment creditor. If the judgment creditor asks, even in the alternative to his claim to an immediate order, for a Mesher type of order, then it seems to me that it would require exceptional circumstances before the court should make an order for the outright transfer of the husband's share in the house to the wife, thereby leaving nothing on which the judgment creditor's charging order can bite, even in the future. Finally, the court should consider whether there is any point in denying the judgment creditor his charging order, if the wife's rights of occupation could in any event be defeated by the judgment creditor making the husband bankrupt.

4. Once the charging order absolute has been made, it would normally require some special circumstances—e.g., where (as here) the wife had no proper opportunity to put her case before the court—for the court to set the charging order aside under section 3(5) of the Charging Orders Act 1979, and thereby deprive the judgment creditor of his vested right.

The Court of Appeal has subsequently considered this guidance in the following case where the facts were somewhat unusual. The husband was wealthy and his wife was awarded £12.5 million by way of ancillary relief. However, the only asset within the jurisdiction in addition to the matrimonial home was a house in Weybridge worth £600,000. The husband had previously tried to ensure that even this property was beyond the reach of his wife by transferring it to a friend who in turn transferred it to Mr Agrest. The transfer was set aside but Mr Agrest was awarded damages to cover his litigation costs. It was this judgement debt which he sought to enforce by obtaining a charging order against the house. In agreeing with the trial judge in rejecting his claim, Thorpe LJ explained how the court needed to consider the circumstances of each case in balancing the creditor's, the wife's, and children's interests.

Kremen v Agrest
[2013] 2 FLR 187 CA

At [29]–[37]

This court there [referring to *Harman v Glencross*] addressed the typical situation in which a judgment creditor sought to enforce a judgment obtained against the husband by a charging order designed to result in an order for sale against the wife remaining in occupation of the matrimonial home.

In such a paradigm case this court naturally stressed the strength of the entitlement of a bona fide creditor without other involvement in the marital dispute.

Mr Feehan QC submits that the judgments of Balcombe LJ and Fox LJ establish the principal that the just entitlement of the creditor is not to be denied save and in so far as some element of that entitlement has to be allocated to provide a roof for the wife to a minimum standard.

There is no clear statement to that effect within the judgments. I can see no rational reason to distinguish between the wife's bare needs whether for housing, lump sum or maintenance; particularly maintenance for children, for in assessing what is fair the court has to have first regard to the welfare of the children.

Now, in having due regard to all the circumstances of this case, the judge was bound to give considerable weight to the fact that the appellant sought a charging order over a property which the husband had purchased in the name of a company for his own occupation. The assets against which the wife might hope to enforce her substantial award were confined to her home, with an equity of approximately £640,000, and the property subject to the interim charge, with an equity of approximately £400,000. Together they put the enforceable value of the wife's award at about £1 million, approximately 8% of her due.

The dealings by which the husband's ownership of South Lodge had passed to the appellant were shadowy to say the least. Although Mostyn J was deeply suspicious, he had found [. . .] that the hard evidence did not permit the conclusion that the appellant had acted in collusion with the husband with the intention of defeating or diminishing the wife's financial claims [. . .] Additionally the comparative needs of the appellant and the wife were hardly commensurate. Whilst the wife needed every penny that she could get to meet her needs and the needs of the children the appellant is a significantly rich man seeking to extricate himself from a bad deal which he had chosen to strike with full knowledge of the risks that he ran and without any additional consideration to justify the risks.

All these cases are facts specific and in all the circumstances of this case the judge was, in my opinion, fully entitled to exercise his discretion as he did. Indeed I would go so far as to say that there was no other discretionary conclusion that he could reasonably have reached.

A creditor holding the benefit of a charging order cannot sell the charged property out of court. They must once again apply to the court to enforce the charging order by applying for an order for sale. Where the debtor's interest is an interest under a trust of land held in co-ownership with others, the creditor will need to apply for an order for sale under s 14 of the Trusts of Land and Appointment of Trustees Act 1996, when the court will be guided by the criteria found in s 15 when deciding whether or not to order sale. This jurisdiction has already been considered in Chapter 14. In *Close Invoice Finance Ltd v Pile*[41] the court indicated that similar considerations will also influence their discretion to order sale where the debtor is the sole owner of the charged property.

There has been an alarming increase in the use of charging orders in recent years as unsecured creditors have become more aggressive in the recovery of their debts.[42] This increase led to measures to curb their use in the recovery of smaller consumer debts.[43]

---

[41] [2008] EWHC 1580, [2009] 1 FLR 873.

[42] See Capper, Conway, and Glennon, 'From Obligation to Proprietary Interest: A Critique of the Charging Order System in England and Wales' in *Modern Studies in Property Law Vol 6* (ed Bright, Oxford: Hart Publishing, 2011) ch 4.

[43] Financial thresholds can be imposed—s 3A. See Charging Orders (Order for Sale: Financial Thresholds) Regs 2012.

5   EQUITY OF REDEMPTION

We have seen that, under a classic mortgage by conveyance or sub-demise, the borrower holds the equity of redemption—an equitable property right that represents the value of the land less the amount owed to the lender under the mortgage. We now need to examine this influential concept and, in particular, its continuing place (if any) in the modern law, given that the classic mortgage has essentially been replaced by the device of the legal charge by way of mortgage.

5.1   DEVELOPMENT OF THE EQUITY OF REDEMPTION

The exact time at which the equity of redemption was first recognized is difficult to trace, but what is clear is that it emerged as an equitable response of the Chancery courts to the harsh terms of the common law mortgage by conveyance. The form of the mortgage by conveyance transferred the borrower's entire estate in the land to the lender, subject only to a covenant by the lender to reconvey the land to the borrower upon the borrower re-paying the loan at the time and in the manner agreed. The agreement of the parties thus gave the borrower a contractual or legal right to redeem. If the borrower failed to repay as required, the lender was not obliged to perform the covenant to reconvey. The lender was instead entitled to retain the land as its legal owner, free from the covenant, and so the borrower lost (or forfeited) his or her land, even though it might be worth considerably more than the mortgage debt.

The common law rule was clear, but harsh, and from the seventeenth century, courts of equity were routinely coming to the aid of the borrower by allowing repayment after the legal date for redemption had passed and thus allowing the borrower to recover his or her land.[44] The means by which equity upheld the borrower's equitable right to re-deem is not entirely clear. The possibilities, as Watt explains, were an award of specific performance of the lender's covenant to reconvey, or the grant of relief to the borrower against forfeiture.

Watt, 'Mortgage Law as Legal Fiction' in *Modern Studies in Property Law Vol 4* (ed Cooke, 2007, p 81)

The next challenge is to identify the doctrines by which it was developed, for this will de-termine whether it is realistic to remove the fiction. There are two main candidates for the doctrinal source of equity's refusal to follow the law in the mortgage context. On the one hand, there is the equity's doctrinal commitment to relieve against penalties and closely related to it, the equitable doctrine of relief from forfeiture. On the other hand, there is equity's willingness to issue injunctions (decrees) requiring specific performance of the mortgagee's covenant to reconvey the mortgage land to the mortgagor. The two bases are compatible but distinct. The former is concerned to set aside the conveyance to the

---

[44] See *Emmanuel College v Evans* (1625) 1 Ch Rep 18. There is some earlier evidence, from the reign of Elizabeth I onwards, that Chancery would assist a borrower in certain circumstances, but it seems that as-sistance became routine from the early seventeenth century.

mortgagee, whereas the latter is concerned to enforce the reconveyance to the mortgagor. Both bases were united in permitting the mortgagor to bring a bill to redeem even though it was considered at law to breach the mortgagor's covenant to grant the mortgagee quiet enjoyment of the estate conveyed.

This right became known as the 'equitable right to redeem', which would only be lost if the Chancery courts could be persuaded that there was little or no hope of the borrower being able to repay. In such a case, the lender would be granted a decree of foreclosure. The equitable right to redeem came to be recognized as no mere personal right, but a proprietary right, which could itself be sold or mortgaged, representing, as it did, the borrower's equitable 'ownership' of the land.[45] What is more, to retain the essential security nature of the classic mortgage by conveyance, courts of equity were at pains to protect the borrower's equity of redemption. This aim was accomplished by the principle that there should be no 'clogs and fetters' on the equity of redemption. We will examine the continued significance of this principle in Chapter 27.

In the face of the borrower's equitable right to redeem, the legal date for redemption lost its import. It is now regarded as a merely nominal date and is often set to occur shortly after the mortgage is entered into. It is the equitable right to redeem upon which borrowers rely to insist upon their right to repay their mortgage and to clear their property of its mortgaged status.

The evolution of the equity of redemption provides an interesting insight into the emergence of equitable doctrine, and the relationship between the courts of common law and equity. It emerged at a time when a number of influential Lord Chancellors were shaping the Chancery jurisdiction from an ad hoc jurisdiction based upon individual petitions, to a coherent body of fundamental rules and principles.[46] Inevitably, at times, this set Chancery at odds with the position at common law. This was certainly the case with the development of the equity of redemption: it amounted to a '*barefaced disavowal of the legal form*'[47] of the mortgage by conveyance. But then the mortgage by conveyance was, itself, a mere form developed originally to overcome restrictions on charging interest imposed by the laws against usury. Thus it may well have been that the courts of common law were not wholly opposed to these developments, achieving as they did a degree of fairness to protect the vulnerable borrower. The emergence of the equity of redemption may also have been accommodated by judges, drawn largely from the nobility, to the threat presented by lenders to the forfeiture of their fellow noble landowners' estates.[48]

5.2 EQUITY OF REDEMPTION AND THE LEGAL CHARGE

The equity of redemption is a key component of the classic form of mortgage by conveyance. It thus retains its import in the equitable mortgage by conveyance (see section 4.3.2)—but what of the predominant form of legal mortgage: the legal charge?

---

[45] *Casborne v Scarfe* (1738) 1 Atk 603, 26 ER 377.
[46] Including, in particular, Lords Bacon, Nottingham, and Hardwick.
[47] Watt, 'Mortgage Law as Legal Fiction' in *Modern Studies in Property Law Vol 4* (ed Cooke, 2007) p 80.
[48] Sugarman and Warrington, 'Telling Stories: Rights and Wrongs of the Equity of Redemption' in *Property Problems: From Genes to Pension Funds* (ed Harris, 1997) p 207.

Under a legal charge, the borrower retains his or her freehold or lease, but his or her land is encumbered (or burdened) by the legal charge.[49] We have already seen that, as a result of s 87(1) of the LPA 1925, the lender enjoys the rights powers and remedies of a mortgagee by sub-demise, although the section does not actually confer a lease upon the lender. The lender's interest in the borrower's land is merely that of a legal charge. The problem is that the section does not clarify the borrower's position.

McHugh J made this observation, giving judgment in the following case (referring to the Torrens system registered charge under the Australian State of Victoria's equivalent legislation).

Figgins Holdings Pty Ltd v SEAA Enterprises Ltd
(1999) 196 CLR 245, High Court of Australia

McHugh J

At [65]

The great difficulty of the cases arises from the attempt by s81 [Transfer of Land Act 1958 (Vic)] to confer on the mortgagee the rights and remedies of a mortgage at common law when the nature of the Torrens system mortgage is fundamentally different from that of the common law mortgage. The difficulty is increased by the section's failure to define the liabilities of, and the consequences for, the mortgagor as a result of conferring these common law rights and remedies on the mortgagee.

Thus, for example, under a mortgage by conveyance or sub-demise, the lender has an immediate right to possession arising by virtue of the legal estate that is preserved by s 87(1). Under a classical mortgage by conveyance or sub-demise, the borrower's right to possession was cast as that of a mere tenant at will, occupying by the permission of the lender, but under a legal charge, the borrower retains the legal estate and thus equally has a right to possession by reason of that estate, subject only to the lender's ability to assert its own right to possession should it wish to do so.[50]

Likewise, whilst, under a classic mortgage by conveyance, the borrower needed to recover or redeem legal title to the land when the debt was repaid, under a legal charge, there is nothing to recover. There is a charge to remove, but the act of repayment extinguishes the charge. Once there is no debt, there can be no effective appropriation of property to its repayment to constitute the charge. The formality rules governing land call for documentary evidence of the discharge of a legal charge, either through a deed or a written receipt,[51] which, in the case of a registered charge, will also have to be recorded at the Land Registry. These documents also provide convenient evidence that the debt has been repaid.

Nield has questioned the utility of the equity of redemption as a distinct proprietary interest in cases in which the lender has a legal charge.

---

[49] But see *Horsham Properties Group Ltd v Clark* [2008] EWHC 2327, [22], in which Briggs J said '*whilst it is true that the mortgagor of registered land remains the registered proprietor* [. . .], *it is wrong in substance to describe the rights of such a mortgagor as tantamount to freehold ownership*'.

[50] *Figgins Holdings Pty Ltd v SEAA Enterprises Ltd* (1999) 196 CLR 245, High Court of Australia, at [82]–[83], [87]–[88].

[51] See Law of Property Act 1925, ss 52 and 115.

Nield, 'Charges, Possession and Human Rights: A Reappraisal of Section 87(1) Law of Property Act 1925' in *Modern Studies in Property Law: Vol 3* (ed Cooke, 2005, p 159)

Redemption in the sense of obtaining a reconveyance or cesser of the mortgaged estate is inconsistent with a legal charge for there is simply no transfer of the borrower's estate or the creation of demise by way of security. The borrower retains the legal estate, so there is neither any property of the borrower to redeem or recover from the lender nor any proviso for redemption from which relief can be granted. What is necessary is a continuing right to require the lender to accept repayment of the debt and effect a discharge, despite default in the borrower's repayment obligations. Thus whilst it is appropriate to speak of an equitable right to repay, or of discharge, it is questionable whether it is still accurate to refer to the borrower's equity of redemption in the sense of a distinct proprietary interest.

If the borrower's continued right to repay the debt and obtain a discharge represents a separate equitable interest which does not merge with his legal estate, it is appropriate to speak of a distinct equity of redemption. However, if the continuing right of the borrower to obtain a discharge upon repayment, regardless of default, is characterised as an incident of the borrower's estate then the use of the term equity of redemption, as distinct from an equitable right of repayment, is strained. The borrower continues to hold the legal and beneficial ownership of the mortgaged land, subject only to the burden of the charge, thus it could be argued that there is no room or need for a separate proprietary interest in the form of an equity of redemption.

Watt goes further and suggests that it is time to kill off the equity of redemption.

Watt, 'Mortgage Law as Legal Fiction' in *Modern Studies in Property Law Vol 4* (ed Cooke, 2007, p 87)

Parliament has killed off the mortgage by conveyance and reconveyance of a fee simple, yet the courts have so far failed to acknowledge that the notion of the equity of redemption should have died with it. They have failed to acknowledge that land subject to a registered charge is not 'redeemed' as was land conveyed under the classic form of mortgage rather the charge is simply discharged from the land upon repayment of the debt.

Killing the equity of redemption would breathe reality into the position of the parties under a legal charge and cement the legal charge as a pure security interest. It would also provide the opportunity to remove, or at least recast, a number of doctrines that were associated with redemption. These are the doctrines of consolidation, the entitlement of the lender to costs on redemption, and the clogs and fetters doctrine. We will examine this latter doctrine and its continued utility in Chapter 27.

Consolidation entitles a lender holding two or more mortgages over different pieces of land owned by the borrower to insist upon the redemption of all of these mortgages, should the borrower seek to repay any one of them. Consolidation thus gives the lender an equitable right, developed in response to the borrower's equitable right to redeem. If the borrower was seeking the indulgence of equity to redeem after the legal date for redemption, he or she was required to meet certain conditions: namely, to pay the costs of redemption, and to redeem all mortgages granted to the lender, if the lender so required. Consolidation is controversial and s 93 of the LPA 1925 excludes the right unless it is expressly preserved, which lenders usually insist it is. The Law Commission has recommended the abolition of consolidation.[52] The Australian courts have taken that step, by rejecting the lender's rights to redemption costs and to consolidate on the grounds that it is inconsistent with the concept of a charge.[53]

6 MODERN DEVELOPMENTS ON MORTGAGE FORMS

Changing social and economic trends means that there is always pressure to develop alternative means of unlocking the security potential of land. The domestic lending market has seen the development of Islamic mortgages, the emergence of shared-ownership schemes to assist low-income borrowers—particularly first-time buyers—mount the first step of the home-ownership ladder, and equity release schemes to enable the elderly to use the investment value of their home to fund their living expenses. Further, the onward march of the European single market has seen proposals to developing a European form of mortgage, or *Eurohypothec*.

6.1 ISLAMIC MORTGAGES OR HOME PURCHASE PLANS

Islam prohibits the charging of interest (*riba*).[54] Making a profit from trade is permitted, but the charging of interest is unacceptable, because it reduces the risk that is inherent in trade. Traders share the risk that market movements (whether up or down) may adversely affect them, but the charging of interest cushions only the lender against the risk that the borrower is unable to repay the loan.[55] The charging of interest, which is an inherent part of conventional mortgage lending, thus presents a problem to followers of Islam, particularly those who wish to purchase their own home. A number of financial institutions have thus developed mortgage products that are thought to comply with Islamic principles.[56]

There are three main products available to assist with the purchase of a house, as follows:

- The *murabaha* utilizes the concept of deferred purchase. The bank purchases the property from the seller, but then agrees to sell on to the borrower at a price that reflects the original price plus an agreed profit. The purchase price is then paid by the borrower by periodic payments over a fixed period of time. Title is usually transferred to the borrower immediately, with the outstanding purchase price being secured by a mortgage.

- The *ijarah* is based upon a lease. The lender purchases the property that the borrower wishes to buy and then leases it to the borrower for a fixed period. The lease is coupled with an agreement by the lender to sell the property to the borrower at the end of the term.[57] The rent is periodically assessed to reflect the capital value of the property, prevailing market rentals, and a contribution to the final resale price (being the

---

[52] Law Commission Report No 204 (1991), [6.44].
[53] *Greig v Watson* (1881) 7 VR 79; *Perry v Rolfe* [1848] VLR 297.
[54] *The Qur'an*, [30.39], [4.161], [3.130]–[3.132], and [2.275]–[2.281].
[55] See further Watt (2007) p 94.   [56] See Latif, 'Islamic Finance' (2006) 1 JIBFL 10.
[57] Technically, this is known as *ijarah wa iqtinah*.

original sale price minus the deposit already paid). Thus, at the end of the term, the borrower will have paid the lender the full purchase costs plus a return to the lender, by making the rental payments.

- The diminishing *musharakah* involves shared ownership. Again, the lender purchases the property and leases it to the borrower—but part of the monthly payment made by the borrower goes toward increasing his or her ownership share in the property, so that the rental element of the periodic payment diminishes as the borrower's ownership share increases.[57]

All of these methods utilize different vehicles, but, like a conventional mortgage, the borrower makes periodic payments to the lender to reflect repayment of the original capital cost, together with a financial return to the lender. There is continuing debate amongst Islamic scholars as to whether these schemes do, indeed, comply with Islamic principles, the payments being made by the borrower reflecting profit to the lender, rather than a genuine sharing of commercial risk. The diminishing *musharakah* is seen as the most in tune with sharia law.

6.2 LOW COST HOME OWNERSHIP

Property prices in many parts of the country are now so high that many cannot afford to buy a home, even with the aid of a mortgage, and the consequences of the financial crisis has reduced the availability of mortgage finance. One response of the government has been to develop schemes to help those with insufficient income to fund a purchase from their own resources and mortgage from a private sector lender. A myriad of different schemes are clustered around two legal models. First, in shared ownership or 'part-buy, part-rent' schemes a buyer purchases a share in a property—usually from a housing association—using mortgage finance and pays rent on the unpurchased share. Here, therefore, the mortgage is combined with rent and the purchaser is granted a 'shared ownership lease'. Secondly, in shared equity schemes a government-backed loan, combined with a loan from a house builder, is used to provide top-up finance to enable the purchase of a home. The top-up loans are secured as second charges on the property. Typically, the purchaser will pay no interest on the second charges for an initial number of years and will pay a low rate of interest thereafter. However, the amount repayable to discharge the loans is not necessarily based on repayment of the capital sum plus interest as is the case with commercial finance. Instead, the purchaser repays the loan as a proportionate percentage of the value of the property. Hence, for example a 25 per cent shared equity loan is repaid at 25 per cent of the value of the property at the time the debt is discharged. Under both models, as the buyer's financial situation permits he or she can increase his or her share of ownership until he or she fully owns the property—a process known as 'staircasing'.

Other forms of state assistance have, from time to time, tried to promote home ownership, for instance, through Government guarantees of repayment and savings incentives, as well as the notorious Right to Buy/Acquire which enables local authority and housing association tenants to purchase their home at a discounted price.[58]

---

58 See Housing Act 2004, Pt 6.

6.3 EQUITY RELEASE OR HOME REVERSION PLANS

As homeowners get on in years, they may find that they own a valuable home (having paid off their mortgage), but that they have little income. They could, of course, move and buy a less valuable home, invest the balance, and live off that investment income. But if they do not want to move, they may consider using the value of their home through an 'equity release', or 'home reversion', plan, to provide either a lump sum or a regular income (or both). These plans can take a number of forms, but the key features are that the homeowner grants either a mortgage or a share of the ownership of his or her home to the lender, in return for regular periodic payments or a lump sum, which can be invested in an annuity or other investment vehicle to provide a regular income.

6.3.1 Lifetime mortgage

The idea of a lifetime mortgage is that it is not repayable until the borrower dies. Some schemes also provide that the lender will share in any increase in value of the home. There are various ways in which interest can be paid under these schemes. It may be paid on the usual interest-only basis, but, if the borrower is already short of income and cannot meet regular interest payments, the interest may be 'rolled up' and added to the capital secured by the mortgage. In that case, the interest is only repayable when the borrower dies or sells his or her home. Alternatively, an annuity may be purchased with the advance and part of the income from the annuity used to meet the interest due.

6.3.2 Home reversion plans

Under a home reversion plan, the borrower sells all of, or a share in, the house to a specialist company, which thus benefits from any further increase in the value of the home. Where the whole house is sold, it is leased back to the borrower—usually only for a nominal rent—for a term that may be brought to an end when the borrower dies. The sale price for the house is less than its market value with vacant possession, to reflect the fact that the borrower remains in occupation.

These plans have proved controversial. They are often quite complicated in their terms, with technicalities that it can be challenging for an elderly borrower to understand. They also play on the desire of the borrower to stay in his or her own home.

6.4 THE EUROHYPOTHEC

The idea of developing a common form of mortgage for Europe was first mooted by the European Commission over forty years ago.[59] This idea has moved a little nearer reality, with the European Commission Green Paper on *Mortgage Credit in the European Union*,[60] which reports that serious consideration is being given to '*the feasibility and desirability*' of a Euromortgage. In response, a European Union research group has put forward proposals for a European mortgage, or *Eurohypothec*.[61] Their proposal is not to replace the numerous

---

[59] European Commission, *The Development of a European Capital Market* (1966) [153]–[158].

[60] (2005) [48].

[61] See <http://www.eurohypothec.com> and Mortgage Credit Foundation, *Mortgage Bulletin 21: Basic Guidelines for a Eurohypothec* (2005); Nassarre-Aznar, 'The Eurohypothec: A Common Mortgage for Europe' (2005) 69 Conv 32; Watt, 'The Eurohypothec and the English Mortgage' (2006) 13(2) MJECL 173.

security devices used in the member States, but to provide an alternative common form, to be governed by the laws of the country in which the land is situated, and which can operate alongside national forms. It will thus be vital that the national laws of the member States are able to accommodate the proposed Eurohypothec.

The form of proposed Eurohypothec is intended to be very flexible. The proposal is for a non-accessory form of charge, which, although it would secure repayment of a debt, may exist independently of that debt.[62] All existing forms of security in England are accessory to a debt. Once the debt is repaid, the borrower can insist that the security interest over his or her land is extinguished, thus, the notion that a security interest may continue to affect the borrower's land even though the debt has been repaid presents somewhat of a problem for English law.[63]

The gap between the loan and the Eurohypothec would be bridged by a security agreement, governed also by the law of the member State in which the land is situated. The security agreement would form a contract between the lender and borrower, and would provide for such matters as the terms upon which the Eurohypothec is held and enforced. It is envisaged that the Eurohypothec would be registered in a public registry and be capable of transfer to another lender provided the transfer was accompanied by a new security agreement to govern the relationship between the borrower and the new lender.

There are points of tension between the proposed Eurohypothec and English law.[64] For example, it is proposed that the borrower may hold the benefit of a Eurohypothec over his or her own land, but English law has always refused to accept such a proposition, because of the corollary impossibility of owing a duty to oneself. Furthermore, the priority provided by the LRA 2002 for overriding interests does not accord with the priority that is envisaged for a registered Eurohypothec. Even if these doctrinal issues could be overcome, the most significant stumbling block, both for English law and for the law of other member States, is likely to be compatibility of enforcement of the Eurohypothec with existing consumer protection—particularly over domestic property.[65]

The impetus for a Euromortgage comes from a belief that a common mortgage form would promote an integrated mortgage credit market across the European Union, enabling lenders to secure a number of loans, which could be made in different member States, against land assets that are held in more than one jurisdiction. Whether such developments are attractive to financial institutional remains to be seen but they do not appear advantages to many borrowers—particularly consumer borrowers.[66]

QUESTIONS

1. What is the difference between a 'mortgage' and a 'charge'? Why is the legal charge by way of mortgage described as a hybrid security?

2. In what circumstances may an equitable form of security interest be created?

3. What advantages would there be if the Law Commission's recommended changes to the form of land mortgages were enacted?

4. Do you agree that the concept of an equity of redemption has outlived its usefulness?

---

[62] Mortgage Credit Foundation (2005).

[63] Although Watt argues that this obstacle can be overcome: see 'The Eurohypothec and the English Mortgage' (2006) 13 MJECL 173, 185–8.

[64] Ibid, at 188–91.

[65] Ibid, at 191–2. We will explore this protection in Chapter 27.

[66] Ibid, at 179–81.

For guidance on how to answer these questions visit the online resources at www.oup.com/uk/mcfarlane4e/.

FURTHER READING

Clarke, 'Security Interests in Property' in *Property Problems: From Genes to Pension Funds* (ed Harris, London: Kluwer, 1997)

Law Commission Report No 204, *Land Mortgages* (1991)

Nield, 'Charges, Possession and Human Rights: A Reappraisal of Section 87(1) Law of Property Act 1925' in *Modern Studies in Property Law Vol 3* (ed Cooke, Oxford: Hart Publishing, 2005)

Oldham, 'Mortgages' in *Land Law: Issues, Debates, Policy* (ed Tee, Devon: Willan, 2002)

Sugarman and Warrington, 'Telling Stories: Rights and Wrongs of the Equity of Redemption' in *Property Problems: From Genes to Pension Funds* (ed Harris, London: Kluwer, 1997)

Watt, 'Mortgage Law as a Legal Fiction' in *Modern Studies in Property Law Vol 3* (ed Cooke, Oxford: Hart Publishing, 2007)

26

LENDER'S RIGHTS AND REMEDIES

CENTRAL ISSUES

1. A lender's rights and remedies arise from the nature of its security, the powers implied by the Law of Property Act 1925, and any express powers. The most important remedies are the right to take possession, the power to sell, and the power to appoint a receiver.

2. The lender has an immediate right to take possession, but this right is carefully controlled by equitable duties and, in the case of dwelling houses, procedural safeguards, legislation, and regulation.

3. Section 36 of the Administration of Justice Act 1970 enables the court to delay execution of a possession order of a dwelling house if the borrower is able to clear any sums due within a reasonable period either from income or from a sale of the house.

4. The lender's power of sale is implied by s 101(1)(i) of the 1925 Act and can only be exercised if the borrower has defaulted.

5. The lender is able to sell out of court, but is subject to twin equitable duties: to act in good faith and to take reasonable steps to obtain a proper market price.

6. A lender also has an implied power conferred by s 101(1)(iii) of the 1925 Act to appoint a receiver to collect the income from the property. This power is important in the commercial context, when a receiver may also be granted power to manage and sell the property.

1 INTRODUCTION

We now need to turn our attention to the whole point of the lender taking security—namely, the rights and remedies that security provides if the debt is not repaid. We will concentrate our attention on the most common security over the land: the legal charge by way of mortgage. The most attractive remedy for a lender is the power to sell the land and repay the debt from the sale proceeds—but to sell the land most advantageously, the lender will usually wish to sell with vacant possession. Thus, where the land is the borrower's home, the lender will need to evict the borrower and take possession as a prelude to sale. Where the lending is for commercial purposes and the legal charge is over premises that form part of the assets of the business, the lender may prefer to appoint a receiver. A receiver, who is usually a professional insolvency practitioner, has power to collect the income from the premises—for example, the rents from the property portfolio of a business—and to apply that income in the repayment of the debt. A receiver is also usually granted power to manage and sell the land, and any business conducted upon it.

At one time, the ability of a mortgagee to foreclose was an important right. Under a classic mortgage by conveyance, foreclosure operated by barring the borrower's equitable right to redeem to extinguish his or her equity of redemption, so that the lender became the full legal and equitable owner of the property. Under a legal charge by way of mortgage, statutory machinery is required to achieve the same result.[1] But the prospect that the lender could reap a windfall profit where the debt was considerably less than the value of the land led to careful regulation of foreclosure. The lender has to apply to court, which will, as a matter of course, give the borrower a generous time to clear the debt before confirming the foreclosure order.[2] The court also has power to order the sale of the property in preference to foreclosure.[3] Even if a foreclosure order is made, the court may be persuaded to set it aside in certain circumstances.[4]

Given the time, expense, and uncertainty of foreclosure, it is not surprising that it became unpopular and is now effectively obsolete.[5] In this chapter, we will thus concentrate on the right to take possession, and the powers of sale and appointment of a receiver.

1.1 SOURCE OF THE LENDER'S RIGHTS AND REMEDIES

1.1.1 The nature of the security

The lender's rights and remedies will be defined, initially, by the nature of the security itself. A classical mortgage by conveyance or sub-demise gave rise to a right to possession by reason of the legal estate that it conferred upon the lender, whether that was a freehold or a leasehold term. Foreclosure was also an inherent right of a mortgagee by conveyance or sub-demise. A charge, in contrast, gives no inherent right to possession or to foreclose: the chargee at common law must go to court to enforce the charge by obtaining a court order for sale or for the appointment by the court of a receiver. The legal charge by way of mortgage, however, whilst creating a security by way of charge, confers upon the legal chargee the rights and remedies enjoyed by a mortgagee by way of sub-demise for a term of 3,000 years. This is the import of s 87(1) of the Law of Property Act 1925 (LPA 1925).[6] The legal charge by way of mortgage, as a hybrid form of security, thus confers upon the legal chargee the rights and powers enjoyed by a legal mortgagee, including the right to take possession and to foreclose, although its proprietary form is merely a charge.

---

[1] See Law of Property Act 1925, ss 88(2) and 89(2).

[2] The process involves two stages: the grant of a foreclosure order nisi, requiring accounts to be drawn up detailing exactly what the borrower owes and giving him or her time to repay; and the foreclosure order absolute, which will be made if the borrower has failed to repay as directed.

[3] Law of Property Act 1925, s 91(2).

[4] See *Campbell v Holyland* (1877) 7 Ch D 166. See also the Hong Kong cases of *Hang Seng Bank v Mee Ching Development Ltd* [1970] HKLR 94 and *Frencher Ltd (in liq) v Bank of East Asia* [1995] 2 HKC 263.

[5] The Law Commission has recommended its abolition: Law Commission Report No 204, *Land Mortgages* (1991), [7.27]. In respect of shares and other financial collateral, the right of appropriate conferred by the Financial Collateral Arrangements (No 2) Regulations 2003 SI2003/3226 has revived an interest in foreclosure see *Cukurova Finance International Ltd v Alfa Telecom Turkey Ltd* [2009] UKPC 19, [2013] UKPC 2 and [2013] UKPC 20.

[6] See Chapter 25, section 4.2.

1.1.2 Powers implied by statute

Section 101 of the LPA 1925 provides another source of the lender's rights and remedies. The section implies into a mortgage made by deed a number of powers, the most important of which are the power to sell and the power to appoint a receiver without, in either case, having to obtain a court order.

Law of Property Act 1925, s 101(1)

Powers incident to estate or interest of mortgagee

(1) A mortgagee, where the mortgage is made by deed, shall by virtue of this Act, have the following powers, to the like extent as if they had been in the terms conferred by the mortgage deed, but not further (namely):

   (i) A power, when the mortgage money has become due, to sell, or to concur with any person in selling, the mortgaged property, or any part thereof, either subject to prior charges or not, and either together or in lots, by public auction or by private contract, subject to such conditions respecting title, or evidence of title, or other matter, as the mortgagee thinks fit, with power to vary any contract for sale, and to buy in at an auction, or to rescind any contract for sale, and to re-sell, without being answerable for any loss occasioned thereby;

   (ii) [. . .]

   (iii) A power, when the mortgage money has become due, to appoint a receiver of the income of the mortgaged property, or any part thereof; or, if the mortgaged property consists of an interest in income, or of a rentcharge or an annual or other periodic sum, a receiver of that property or any part thereof;

   [. . .]

A legal charge by way of mortgage, to create a legal interest, must be created by deed and registered; it will thus enjoy the powers implied by s 101. The powers are also implied into second or subsequent legal charges created by registered deed, although by reason of the rules of priority, a second chargee will only be able to sell subject to the first charge. Alternatively, a second chargee may decide that it is in its interests to take control of any sale of the property, which it can do by paying off the first charge and thus improving its priority position.

Whether or not an equitable mortgagee or chargee will enjoy the statutory powers under s 101 is considerably more complicated and turns on the acquisition and content questions relating to equitable security rights that we examined in section 4.3 of Chapter 25. First, the equitable mortgage or charge must be created by deed for s 101 to apply. Secondly, one must look to the property that is expressed to be subject to the security. In *Swift 1st Ltd v Colin*,[7] the High Court held that a purported legal charge over the whole of the borrower's interest in the property, which took effect only as an equitable charge because it was unregistered,[8] nevertheless conferred power under s 101 to sell both the legal and equitable estate.[9] By

---

[7] [2011] EWHC 2410 relying on *Re White Rose Cottage* [1965] Ch 940, but see critique in Evans, 'A Scrutiny of Powers of Sale Arising Under an Equitable Mortgage: A Case for Reining these in', [2015] Conv 123 and Lees, 'Powers of the Beneficiary of a Trust of a Charge' [2016] Conv 157.

[8] See Chapter 25, section 4.3.1.

[9] See LPA 1925, s 88. An unregistered assignment of a registered legal charge, which takes effect only as an equitable assignment of the legal charge, may nevertheless exercise the powers of the registered legal chargee

contrast, an equitable mortgage or a purely equitable charge of a borrower's equitable estate even if made by deed[10] should only entitle the equitable mortgagee or chargee to sell the estate that is the subject of the security.[11] Some further authority, for instance a power of attorney, would be required to sell the borrower's legal estate (if any) in the land.

1.1.3 Express powers

The implied powers of a legal chargee to take possession, to sell, to appoint a receiver, and of foreclose may be excluded, varied, or supplemented by the terms of the security itself.[12] Institutional lenders, like banks and building societies, pay their lawyers to draft a standard set of terms and conditions to be incorporated into their legal charges, which will invariably affect the operation of their implied powers and may grant additional express powers, such as a power to lease. It is thus always important to read the legal charge itself to see how the implied powers may have been altered and what additional express powers have been granted.

1.2 REGULATION OF THE LENDER'S RIGHTS AND REMEDIES

In Chapter 27, we will see how the borrower's position can be protected. The borrower is particularly vulnerable where the lender is exercising its rights and remedies—after all, he or she stands to lose his or her home or business.

Equity has long cast a watchful eye over the exercise of the lender's powers to ensure that they are employed only to facilitate recovery of the lender's debt, and then only with due probity and care. A modern expression of this duty is found in the following case.

Palk v Mortgage Service Funding plc
[1993] Ch 330, CA

Sir Donald Nicholls V–C

At 337–8

[. . .] [A] mortgagee can sit back and do nothing. He is not obliged to take steps to realise his security. But if he does take steps to exercise his rights over his security, common law and equity alike have set bounds to the extent to which he can look after himself and ignore the mortgagor's interests. In the exercise of his rights over his security the mortgagee must act fairly towards the mortgagor. His interest in the property has priority over the interest of the

---

by virtue of s 106 of the LPA 1925 as a person 'entitled to receive and give a receipt for the mortgage money', see *Shelwith (Leisure) Ltd v Armstrong* [2016] 2 WLR 144.

[10] See Chapter 25, sections 4.3.2 and 4.3.3.

[11] The LRA 2002 does not assist. An equitable mortgage or charge of an equitable estate is not capable of registration. Whilst an equitable charge of the registered estate is capable of registration, LRA 2002, ss 23–24 as interpreted in *Shelwith (Leisure) Ltd v Armstrong* [2016] 2 WLR 144, only empowers a registered chargee to exercise the powers *'permitted by the general law in relation to an interest of that description'*. It is not thought that such general powers encompass a power to deal with the legal estate—for further discussion see Lees, 'Powers of the bBeneficiary of a Trust of a Charge' [2016] Conv 157.

[12] See, in relation to the s 101 powers, s 101(3)–(4). As to the relationship between the expressed and implied powers, see *Horsham Properties Group Ltd v Clark* [2009] 1 WLR 1255.

mortgagor, and he is entitled to proceed on that footing. He can protect his own interest, but he is not entitled to conduct himself in a way which unfairly prejudices the mortgagor. If he takes possession he might prefer to do nothing and bide his time, waiting indefinitely for an improvement in the market, with the property empty meanwhile. That he cannot do. He is accountable for his actual receipts from the property. He is also accountable to the mortgagor for what he would have received but for his default. So he must take reasonable care to maximise his return from the property. He must also take reasonable care of the property. Similarly if he sells the property: he cannot sell hastily at a knock-down price sufficient to pay off his debt. The mortgagor also has an interest in the property and is under a personal liability for the shortfall. The mortgagee must keep that in mind. He must exercise reasonable care to sell only at the proper market value.

Parliament has also intervened through section 36 of the Administration of Justice Act 1970 (as amended) where the lender is seeking possession of a dwelling house by obtaining a court order for possession.[13] The county court has primary jurisdiction, which provides a more informal venue for such intimidating proceedings. More significantly, the court is given discretion to halt the progress of the proceedings to allow the borrower time to try to pay any arrears or remedy any other default.

Market regulation, through the Financial Services and Market Act 2000 (FSMA), also plays its part in trying to ensure that lenders treat borrowers in default fairly. We will consider the impact of this legislation in Chapter 27 (see section 2). In this chapter we will concentrate on how market regulation can affect how a lender exercises their right to possession and their most potent remedy of sale. Most legal charges, secured upon an individual borrower's home, are regulated under the FSMA, with rules in the Mortgage and Home Finance Conduct of Business Sourcebook (MCOB)[14] setting standards on the handling of arrears.

FSA Handbook, Arrears and Repossessions: Regulated Mortgage Contracts and Home Purchase Plans (MCOB 13)

MCOB 13.3 Dealing fairly with customers in arrears: policy and procedures

MCOB 13.3.1

(1) A firm must deal fairly with any customer who:

    a. has a payment shortfall on a regulated mortgage contract or home purchase plan;

    b. has a sale shortfall; or

    c. is otherwise in breach of a home purchase plan.

(2) A firm must put in place, and operate in accordance with, a written policy (agreed by its respective governing body) and procedures for complying with (1). Such policy and procedures must reflect the requirements of MCOB 13.3.2AR and MCOB 13.3.4AR.

---

[13] See section 2.5.   [14] Part of the Financial Conduct Authority (FCA) Handbook.

MCOB 13.3.2A

A firm must when dealing with any customer in payment difficulties:

(1) make reasonable efforts to reach an agreement with a customer over the method of re-paying any payment shortfall or sale shortfall, in the case of the former having regard to the desirability of agreeing with the customer an alternative to taking possession of the property;

(2) liaise, if the customer makes arrangements for this, with a third party source of advice regarding the payment shortfall or sale shortfall;

(3) allow a reasonable time over which the payment shortfall or sale shortfall should be re-paid, having particular regard to the need to establish, where feasible, a payment plan which is practical in terms of the circumstances of the customer;

(4) grant, unless it has good reason not to do so, a customer's request for a change to:

    a. the date on which the payment is due (providing it is within the same payment period); or

    b. the method by which payment is made;

and give the customer a written explanation of its reasons if it refuses the request;

(5) where no reasonable payment arrangement can be made, allow the customer to remain in possession for a reasonable period to effect a sale; and

(6) not repossess the property unless all other reasonable attempts to resolve the position have failed.

MCOB 13.3.3A

In complying with MCOB 13.3.2A a firm must give a customer a reasonable period of time to consider any proposals for dealing with the payment difficulties.

MCOB 13.3.4A

(1) a firm must consider whether, given the individual circumstances of the customer, it is appropriate to do one or more of the following in relation to the regulated mortgage con-tract or home purchase plan with the agreement of the customer:

    (a) extend its term; or

    (b) change its type; or

    (c) defer payment of interest due on the regulated mortgage contract or of sums due under the home purchase plan (including, in either case, on any sale shortfall); or

    (d) treat the payment shortfall as if it was part of the original amount provided (but a firm must not automatically capitalise a payment shortfall); or;

    (e) make use of any Government forbearance initiatives in which the firm chooses to participate.

(2) a firm must give customers adequate information to understand the implications of any proposed arrangement; one approach may be to provide information on the new terms in line with the annual statement provisions.

MCOB 13.3.4B

A firm must make customers aware of the existence of any applicable Government schemes to assist borrowers in payment difficulties in relation to regulated mortgage contracts.

Furthermore, terms governing enforcement in consumer mortgages may be subject to scrutiny as unfair terms under Consumer Rights Act 2015, which we will consider in Chapter 27 at section 4.1.3.

A Pre-action Protocol on Possession Actions based upon Mortgage Arrears has been introduced by the Civil Justice Council.[15] This protocol reflects MCOB 13 but affects all court sanctioned repossessions of dwelling houses whether or not regulated by FSMA. It operates by requiring scrutiny at court level to try and ensure that repossession proceedings are not issued before the lender has taken steps (where appropriate) to reschedule the borrower's indebtedness or otherwise resolve the borrower's repayment difficulties.[16]

The guiding principle in mortgages secured on a dwelling house is thus for lenders to try to agree with their defaulting borrowers a way of clearing arrears by rescheduling repayments, rather than resorting to immediate legal redress. At the time of the financial crisis the Government also introduced temporary measures to try and assist distressed borrowers.[17] These initiatives have led to a change in culture with mortgage repossession actions falling below predicted levels.[18]

'Wallace & Ford, Limiting Possessions? Managing Mortgage Arrears in a New Era' (2010) IJHP 133 [142]

Despite the initial continuation of 'pay and possess', by mid-summer 2008 a strong strategic shift in the management of mortgage arrears was underway towards an approach better characterised as 'managed forbearance'. One lender described previous forbearance policies as 'do nothing' and watch the arrears rise. In contrast, this fresh approach aimed first to support borrower to rehabilitate their accounts, but, second also ensure that if the situation remained unsustainable, there was a sound basis for possession. Lenders' priority, however, is to ensure that the debts are repaid and the mortgage serviced correctly, but several interviewees reiterated that there was now a *business case*, a commercial imperative to allow this recovery to take place in a range of ways over time, often by significant modification of the terms of the loan to support actions to avoid possession. Several lenders described the change in approach as a 'cultural shift'.

---

[15] Available online at <http://www.civiljusticecouncil.gov.uk>. The Protocol was implemented earlier than planned on 19 November 2008.

[16] Whitehouse, 'The mortgage arrears pre-action protocol: an opportunity missed' (2009) 72 MLR 793.

[17] Through a temporary relaxation of the criteria for entitlement to social security benefits, a Mortgage Rescue Scheme to facilitate sale and leaseback between borrowers and registered social landlords and a Mortgage Support Scheme to persuade lenders to show forbearance by offering a Government guarantee. The two latter schemes have ended.

[18] Ford and Wallace, *Uncharted Territory? Managing arrears and possessions*, (Shelter, 2009); Whitehouse, 'Longitudinal Analysis of the Mortgage Repossession Process 1995–2010: Stability, Regulation and Reform' in *Modern Studies in Property Law Vol 6* (ed Bright, Oxford: Hart, 2010) ch 7, A Wallace, "Feeling like I'm doing it on my own': Examining the Synchronicity between Policy Responses and the Circumstances and Experiences of Mortgage Borrowers in Arrears" (2012) 11 Social Policy and Society 117 and S Bright & L Whitehouse, *Information, Advice and Representation in Housing Possession Cases* (Universities of Oxford & Hull 2014). However, the FCA acknowledges that the forbearance story is mixed see FCA, *Mortgage lenders' arrears management and forbearance* TR14/3 (February 2014).

2 POSSESSION

2.1 THE STARTING POINT: AN IMMEDIATE RIGHT TO POSSESSION

A legal chargee of land is entitled to take possession of the charged property. This right arises because a legal chargee is entitled to the rights of a mortgagee by way of sub-demise who enjoys a right to immediate possession by reason of the leasehold term.[19] This right to possession is thus not inherently dependent upon default. The express terms of the mortgage may, and in the case of domestic mortgages will invariably, require default before the lender can seek possession. It might be argued that a lender exercising its right to possession pursuant to a consumer mortgage, for reasons other than to protect their security, is an unfair term under the Consumer Rights Act 2015.[20]

Harman J emphasized the immediate nature of the lender's right to possession in a number of decisions—most infamously, in the following case.[21]

Four-Maids Ltd v Dudley Marshall (Properties) Ltd
[1957] Ch 317, HC

Harman J

At 320

I repeat now, that the right of the mortgagee to possession in the absence of some contract has nothing to do with default on the part of the mortgagor. The mortgagee may go into possession before the ink is dry on the mortgage unless there is something in the contract, express or by implication, whereby he has contracted himself out of that right. He has the right because he has a legal term of years in the property or its statutory equivalent [. . . .] If there is a provision that, so long as certain payments are made, he will not go into possession, then he has contracted himself out of his rights. Apart from that, possession is a matter of course.

Even equity will not intervene, beyond granting a short adjournment to allow the borrower to redeem the whole loan. Arguments suggesting that there was such an equitable jurisdiction were soundly rejected in the following case.

Birmingham Citizens Permanent Building Society v Caunt
[1962] Ch 883, HC

Russell J

At 896

For the building society it was contended that the argument based on the equity of redemption and the tenor of the mortgage was novel and fundamentally unsound. Equity had always

---

[19] See Law of Property Act 1925, s 87(1). The right is unaffected by the grant of a subcharge: see *Credit and Mercantile plc v Marks* [2004] EWCA Civ 568, [2005] Ch 81.
[20] See *Aziz v Caixa d'Estalvis de Catalunya, Tarragona i Manresa* [2013] 3 CMLR 5.
[21] See also *Alliance Perpetual Building Society v Belrum Investments Ltd* [1957] 1 WLR 720; *Hughes v Waite* [1957] 1 WLR 713.

interfered with legal rights in order to ensure that the mortgage should not operate otherwise than as it was intended to operate—namely, as security for repayment of money. But there was no principle upon which equity had ever attempted or could ever rightly attempt to interfere with the security *as a security*, or to destroy or suspend or nullify any rights of the mortgagee which were part and parcel of that security. The whole purpose of equity was, by insisting that the transaction was a security for the repayment of money, thereby to shield the mortgagor from attempts in reliance on strict legal rights to turn it into something more. Equity was never and should never be in the hands of the judges a sword to attack any part of the security itself, and the right to possession was an important part of that security, more particularly in the association with the ability to give vacant possession on the exercise of the power of sale. These appear to me to be sound answers to an attempt to give reasons for the existence of a jurisdiction such as is suggested. I think there was and is no such jurisdiction.

This fundamental principle also leads to the conclusion that the existence of a counterclaim or equitable right of set-off—by which the borrower might be able to argue that, at the end of the day, he or she owes no money to the lender—does not detract from the lender's immediate right to possession.[22]

2.2 THE EQUITABLE DUTY TO ACCOUNT

Equity will not interfere with the lender's right to take possession, but it will control the exercise of that right. Where the property is let and the lender goes into possession by collecting the rents, it must apply the rent in the discharge of the debt. Furthermore, it is under a duty to account not only for the income received, but also the income that should have been received *but for* the lender's wilful default.[23]

Frisby has examined a mortgagee's duty to account following its application to receivers in *Medforth v Blake*.[24]

Frisby, 'Making a Silk Purse Out of a Pig's Ear: *Medforth v Blake & Ors'* (2000) 63 MLR 413, 416

Liability to account for wilful default is of ancient origin arising out of the account jurisdiction of the Courts of Equity. On a suit for redemption a Chancery Master took an account, whereby the mortgagee's principal, interest and costs were set against the amount received from the mortgaged property. Where the mortgagee had previously taken possession, this last item included not only what *had been* received but what *might have been* received but for his wilful default. Thus equity's traditional protective stance towards the mortgagor's equity of redemption was manifest by the imposition of 'almost penal liabilities.'

Whilst the basic principle of wilful default liability is easily stated, its content is less readily identifiable. Some cases ascribe liability to stated misconduct without further comment.

---

[22] See *Samuel Keller Holdings Ltd v Martins Bank Ltd* [1971] 1 WLR 43; *Mobil Oil Co Ltd v Rawlinson* (1982) 43 P & CR 221; *Citibank Trust Ltd v Ayivor* [1987] 1 WLR 1157; *National Westminster Bank plc v Skelton* [1993] 1 WLR 72; *Ashley Guarantee v Zacaria* [1993] 1 WLR 62.

[23] *White v City of London Brewery* (1889) 42 Ch D 237. For a consideration for 'wilful default', see Stannard (1979) Conv 345.

[24] [1999] 3 All ER 97, considered further at section 4.3.

These 'factual instances' of wilful default include refusal to accept tenants and the disadvantageous letting of property. Permitting a mortgagor to intercept 'profits' or failing to receive the purchase price on a sale of the mortgaged property similarly attracted liability. The courts showed varying degrees of strictness in this regard.

These illustrations of liability give little guidance as to whether wilful default requires deliberate, reckless or simply unthinking conduct, the brevity of the reports making it difficult to discern whether the penalised behaviour was collusive or careless[... .]

Other authorities treat wilful default as established by a particular degree of dereliction. In *ex parte Mure* Thurlow LC contemplated that involuntary conduct might suffice to ground liability, although on the facts the negligence was 'gross'. Later cases tend to support the proposition that the carelessness in question may be less than fraud but more than mere negligence. If gross negligence and ordinary diligence exact differing standards of conduct, which is to be preferred? It is not immediately obvious that any of the above cases is conclusively authoritative, especially since many judicial statements in this regard appear to be mere *dicta,* and Stannard concludes that 'wilful default' is purely a relative term, meaning no more than a failure to perform a duty.

Whilst the older authorities may be unclear as to the degree of default, more recent authorities tend to support the view that a mortgagee's conduct should be tested according to standards of reasonableness. This was the test applied to receivers in *Medforth v Blake*, which also finds expression in the passage from *Palk* extracted at section 1.2.

Whatever the exact standard may be, these duties are usually perceived as sufficiently onerous to deter a lender from taking possession, except for a short time as a prelude to sale. As we shall see, a lender can avoid personal liability where it appoints a receiver, which is often the preferred course of action where the lender anticipates taking possession for an extended period under a commercial mortgage, including a buy-to-let mortgage.

2.3 THE PURPOSE OF TAKING POSSESSION

In the following case, a house had been let to students whom the landlord wanted to evict—but he could not do so, because their tenancy was protected by legislation. The mortgage of the house prohibited letting without the consent of the bank, which the landlord had failed to obtain. The landlord was thus in breach of the mortgage, but the bank refused the landlord's request to exercise its right to take possession and evict the students. As an alternative ploy, the landlord arranged for his wife to take a transfer of the mortgage, so that she could exercise the right of the mortgagee to evict the students. The Court of Appeal refused to grant an order for possession, although the judges differed in their reasoning.

Quennell v Maltby
[1979] 1 WLR 318, CA

Lord Denning MR

At 322

So here in modern times equity can step in so as to prevent a mortgagee, or a transferee from him, from getting possession of a house contrary to the justice of the case. A mortgagee will be

> restrained from getting possession except when it is sought bona fide and reasonably for the purpose of enforcing the security and then only subject to such conditions as the court thinks fit to impose. When the bank itself or a building society lends the money, then it may well be right to allow the mortgagee to obtain possession when the borrower is in default. But so long as the interest is paid and there is nothing outstanding, equity has ample power to restrain any unjust use of the right to possession.

The other members of the Court of Appeal agreed with the result, but based their reasoning upon a narrower premise. Lord Templeman stated:[25] '*The estate, rights and powers of a mortgagee* [. . .] *are only vested in a mortgagee to protect his position as a mortgagee and to enable him to obtain repayment.*' Nevertheless, surprisingly it seems that enforcement may be justified as a means of putting pressure on the borrower to repay the debt even though there is little or no prospect of recovery.[26]

The width of Lord Denning's views was criticized at the time,[27] but has subsequently been cited with approval.[28] The decision does give expression to equity's underlying concern that lenders exercise their rights bona fide for the purpose of recovering the debt due to them and not for some other purpose. This requirement has been repeated by the Privy Council in *Downsview Nominees Ltd v First City Corporation Ltd*[29] and *Cukurova Finance International Ltd v Alfa Telecom Turkey Ltd*.[30]

2.4 PROCEDURAL SAFEGUARDS

A mortgagee's claim to possession is not required to be made by application to court, although most lenders will invariably seek a court order.[31] This is because those who take it upon themselves to evict occupiers from their property face criminal sanctions and this legislation applies to lenders as to anyone else. By s 6 of the Criminal Law Act 1977, it is an offence to use violence to gain possession of occupied premises. Invariably, therefore, lenders will seek court assistance to gain entry to premises that are occupied. It is only where premises are empty, or where the borrower voluntarily gives up possession, that the lender will risk entering otherwise than by executing an order for possession.

Taking possession of a borrower's home is a particularly sensitive issue. By s 1(3) of the Protection from Eviction Act 1977, it is an offence to harass an occupier of residential premises to 'persuade' him or her to give up occupation.[32] Mortgages regulated by the FSMA are subject to additional safeguards. We have already considered the regulatory pressures upon FSMA lenders to come to some arrangement with the borrower to clear any arrears and to only seek repossession as a last resort. The Pre-action Protocol on Repossessions based upon Mortgage Arrears reinforces these standards.[33]

---

[25] At 324. [26] *Co-operative Bank plc v Phillips* [2014] EWHC 2862.

[27] Smith [1979] Conv 266; Pearce [1979] CLJ 257.

[28] See *Albany Home Loans Ltd v Massey* (1997) 37 P & CR 509, 513, in which the court refused an order for possession against a husband when to do so would have been futile, because his wife, who was not bound by the mortgage, was entitled to remain in possession as a joint tenant.

[29] [1993] AC 295. [30] [2013] UKPC 2.

[31] In stark contrast to claims to possession by mortgagees when some domestic mortgages were regulated by the Consumer Credit Act 1974, see s 126.

[32] For an example of unacceptable harassment see *Roberts v Bank of Scotland* [2014] EWCA Civ 882 where the bank made 547 phone calls to press for payment.

[33] See section 1.2.

The interface between the lender's right to possession and these regulatory safeguards is problematic. We have seen that a failure to comply with the MCOB does not in invalidate the loan or the supporting mortgage.[34] The FCA may take disciplinary action against the lender or the borrower may complain to the FOS or seek damages for breach of statutory duty, but a court cannot resist an order for possession.[35] One would hope that the pre-action protocol would catch those occasions when the regulatory safeguards requiring forbearance have not been observed. A clearer solution would be to provide that the mortgage is unenforceable, save with leave of the court, if the regulatory standards have not been observed.[36]

2.5 DWELLING HOUSES AND S 36 OF THE ADMINISTRATION OF JUSTICE ACT 1970 (AS AMENDED)

The decision in *Caunt* (see section 2.1) led to a need to rethink the exercise of the lender's immediate right to possession in respect of residential property.[37] The result is s 36 of the Administration of Justice Act 1970.

Administration of Justice Act 1970, s 36

Additional powers of court in action by mortgagee for possession of dwelling-house

1. Where the mortgagee under a mortgage of land which consists of or includes a dwelling-house brings an action in which he claims possession of the mortgaged property, not being an action for foreclosure in which a claim for possession of the mortgaged property is also made, the court may exercise any of the powers conferred on it by subsection (2) below if it appears to the court that in the event of its exercising the power the mortgagor is likely to be able within a reasonable period to pay any sums due under the mortgage or to remedy a default consisting of a breach of any other obligation arising under or by virtue of the mortgage.

2. The court—
   (a) may adjourn the proceedings, or
   (b) on giving judgment, or making an order, for delivery of possession of the mortgaged property, or at any time before the execution of such judgment or order, may—
      (i) stay or suspend execution of the judgment or order, or
      (ii) postpone the date for delivery of possession, for such period or periods as the court thinks reasonable.

3. Any such adjournment, stay, suspension or postponement as is referred to in subsection (2) above may be made subject to such conditions with regard to payment by the mortgagor of any sum secured by the mortgage or the remedying of any default as the court thinks fit.

4. The court may from time to time vary or revoke any condition imposed by virtue of this section.

---

[34] See Chapter 27, section 2.1.

[35] *Thakker v Northern Rock plc* [2014] EWHC 2017. See also in the Irish context *Irish Life and Permanent plc v Dunne* [2015] IESC 46.

[36] This was the solution adopted by the Consumer Credit Act 1974 when certain mortgages fell within its regulatory oversight, see *Re London Scottish Finance Ltd (in Administration)* [2014] Bus LR 424.

[37] See the Payne Committee Report (Cmnd 3909, 1969); Haley, 'Mortgage Default: Possession, Relief and Judicial Discretion' (1997) 17 LS 483.

The section does not limit the lender's right to take possession, but it does control its exercise by conferring upon the court power to adjourn proceedings, or to stay or postpone execution of the order for possession. The court cannot give an indefinite period of suspension, but it can extend the stay upon the borrower making a further application.[38] The court will thus grant the order for possession, but may not allow the lender to ask the bailiff to execute the order. The motive is to allow the borrower time to repay the sums owing or at least any arrears. Unfortunately for such a significant jurisdiction, s 36 is not the most happily worded and has raised a number of problems of interpretation, as well as calls for reform.[39]

It should also be noted that the court enjoys an additional discretion to grant a time order under the Consumer Credit Act 1974 to extend the time for enforcement of the lender's right to possession,[40] and, in such circumstances, to amend and vary the mortgage terms as it see fit.[41] This jurisdiction appears available to mortgages regulated under the FSMA, whether by way of first or subsequent charge.[42]

2.5.1 'Dwelling-house'

Needless to say there have been questions over what constitutes a 'dwelling-house'. It does not matter if only part of the property is a dwelling, or that the dwelling house is not the borrower's home.[43] The protection is thus not restricted to the residential lending market, but can catch commercial lending where the security includes a dwelling house. The time for determining whether or not the security is over, or includes, a dwelling house is the time of the order for possession, rather than the time of the mortgage itself.[44]

2.5.2 Court proceedings for possession

The more difficult question is whether the court's jurisdiction is only available where the lender has applied for an order for possession. We have noted that the lender will invariably do so where the borrower is in residence, but what about when the borrower, for one reason or another, is not? Just such a situation arose in the following case, in which the Court of Appeal—taking a literal, rather than a purposive, approach to interpretation of s 36—held that it had no application where a lender was not seeking an order for possession.

Ropaigealach v Barclays Bank plc
[2000] QB 263, CA

Facts: The Ropaigealachs fell into mortgage arrears and their lender, Barclays, wrote to them, making a final demand for payment and warning them that their property would

---

[38] *Royal Trust Co of Canada v Markham* [1975] 1 WLR 1416, 1424.

[39] See Smith [1979] Conv 266; Haley, 'Mortgage Default: Possession, Relief and Judicial Discretion' (1997) 17 LS 483.

[40] CCA, ss 129 and 130.

[41] Ibid, s 136. See McMurtry, 'Consumer Credit Act Mortgages: Unfair Terms, Time Orders and Judicial Discretion' [2010] JBL 107.

[42] See Consumer Credit Act 1974, s 126 and FCA, Handbook PERG 4.17.2G.

[43] See *Bank of Scotland v Miller* [2001] EWCA Civ 344, [2002] QB 255, in which the property was a nightclub with an unoccupied flat above.

[44] Ibid.

be sold. The Ropaigealachs did not receive the letter, because they were not living at the property whilst it was being renovated, and did not hear of the sale until told by a neighbour. The Court declined to grant a declaration that Barclays was not entitled to take possession and sell without obtaining a court order.

Clarke LJ

At 283

It is true to say that neither this court in *Caunt's case* nor the Payne Committee was considering whether the court should have similar powers in cases in which the mortgagee chooses not to take proceedings for possession but simply takes possession or perhaps sells the property under his power of sale and the purchaser takes possession. In these circumstances I agree that it cannot readily be inferred that Parliament intended to give protection to mortgagors in such a case. It does however strike me as very curious that mortgagors should only have protection in the case where the mortgagee chooses to take legal proceedings and not in the case where he chooses simply to enter the property. As Alison Clarke put it in her illuminating article "Further implications of section 36 of the Administration of Justice Act 1970" in *The Conveyancer & Property Lawyer* (1983), p. 293, [. . .] it is anomalous and undesirable to protect mortgagors against eviction by court process yet leave them open to eviction by self-help.

The second case which seems to me to highlight the potential problems is the decision of this court in *National & Provincial Building Society v. Ahmed* [1995] 2 E.G.L.R. 127, where it was held that the mortgagor's equity of redemption is extinguished when the mortgagee, in the exercise of his power of sale, enters into a contract of sale of the mortgaged property [. . .]

In a Law Commission Working Paper No. 99 on *Land Mortgages* (1986), which was produced before the report and was expressly stated not to represent the final views of the Commission, the position was put thus with regard to the court's discretion under section 36, at p. 103, para. 3.69:

> "(b) The discretion is to delay or withhold the possession order only, not any other remedy. In practice this usually prevents enforcement, but in theory it is still open to the mortgagee to proceed to exercise its power of sale notwithstanding the court's refusal to make a possession order. Since such a sale terminates the mortgagor's interest in the property, the purchaser presumably would have no difficulty in obtaining a possession order against the mortgagor after completion."

In a written note sent to us after the conclusion of the hearing Miss Gloster says that the bank would not go so far as to submit that that view is correct. Miss Gloster correctly adds that this kind of issue does not to fall [sic] for determination on this appeal, and I express no view upon the solution to such problems, but such considerations do highlight the potential problems. Such problems would not arise (or would be much reduced) if it were held that the effect of section 36 were [. . .] to give the court the same power to inhibit the exercise by the mortgagee of its right to possession at common law whether it were exercised by simply entering possession or by doing so pursuant to an order of the court [. . .]

It seems to me that if a mortgagor needs that relief he needs it whether the mortgagee chooses to exercise his right of possession by entering into possession with or without an order of the court. Indeed he also needs it if instead of doing either the mortgagee sells the property to a purchaser leaving the purchaser to take possession.

> I recognise that Miss Gloster says that responsible mortgagees do not in practice take possession of property in which the mortgagor and his family are living without an order of the court, and I accept that that is so, but in my judgment the problem should be approached by reference to the legal rights of the mortgagee and to the legitimate interests of the mortgagor in the light of the purpose of the Act. In these circumstances, if it were possible to construe section 36 by affording mortgagors protection whether or not the mortgagee chose to obtain possession by self-help or legal action, I for my part would do so. I have however been persuaded that it is not possible.

Clarke LJ refers also to the situation in which a lender exercises its power of sale without having first obtained possession. In these circumstances, the sale will overreach the borrower's equity of redemption and pass an unencumbered title to the purchaser.[45] But if the property is occupied (e.g. by the borrower or his or her tenant), the suggestion made by Millett LJ in *National & Provincial Building Society v Ahmed*[46] is that s 36 will again come into play if the purchaser seeks an order for possession, although, given that the borrower's interests will have been overreached, it is difficult to see how he or she could resist a purchaser's application for possession. Indeed, this was the approach taken by the High Court in *Horsham Properties Group Ltd v Clark*.[47] If a purchaser can be found to purchase the property whilst the borrower is still in occupation, there is thus a worrying route by which s 36 can be avoided.

2.5.3 Who needs to be told of possession proceedings and who can apply under s 36?

Possession proceedings will be issued against the borrower(s), as mortgagor(s), who can apply for relief under s 36.[48] The Civil Procedure Rules now require the lender to send notice of possession proceedings to the property so that a tenant or other occupier should hopefully also be aware of the proceedings.[49]

Two common situations need to be considered further. First, a borrower as mortgagor may hold the dwelling house on trust for themselves and their spouse or partner as equitable co-owners, or that spouse or partner may have a statutory right of occupation. We considered how these situations may arise in Chapter 12. Such a spouse or partner may not be a party to the mortgage and possession proceedings may not be directly issued against them. However, where they do learn of the possession proceedings, he or she may apply to court to be joined as a party and seek the relief afforded by s 36.[50]

Secondly, is the position of a tenant of the borrower. Where the tenancy is authorized by the lender it will be binding upon him and the lender cannot obtain possession unless entitled to do so under the terms of the tenancy. Although, as we will see in section 4, he or she may appoint a receiver to collect the rental income or sell the property subject to the tenancy.

---

[45] Law of Property Act 1925, ss 88(1) and 89(1).

[46] [1995] 2 EGLR 127; *Duke v Robson* [1973] 1 WLR 267.   [47] [2009] 1WLR 1255.

[48] A purchaser from the borrower who takes subject to the mortgage may also apply AJA, s 39(1).

[49] Civil Procedure Rules Pt 55 Rule 10(2). See also s 56 Family law Act 1996 which requires a lender to serve notice of proceedings upon a spouse who has registered his or her statutory right of occupation.

[50] In the case of an equitable co-owner because they fall within the definition of a mortgagor under s 36 see *Cheval Bridging Finance Ltd v Bhasin* [2008] EWCA Civ 1613 and in the case a spouse with a statutory right of occupation see Family Law Act 1996, s 55(2).

Where the tenancy is unauthorized by the lender the tenancy is not binding on the lender and the unauthorized tenant may be evicted by the lender. The unauthorized tenant may not apply under s 36[51] but limited protection against immediate eviction is now available under Mortgage Repossession (Protection of Tenant etc) Act 2010.[52] An unauthorized tenant may apply, either on the application for the possession order or its execution, for a stay of delivery of possession for a period for two months in order to give a breathing space to find alternative accommodation. The court in exercising its discretion whether or not to accede to the tenant's application must have regard to his or her circumstances and whether or not there is an outstanding breach of the tenancy agreement. The court may also order the tenant to pay their rent directly to the lender.

2.5.4 The court's discretion

The court may exercise its jurisdiction where it is satisfied that the borrower is likely to be able, within a reasonable period, to pay any sums due under the mortgage or to remedy any other default.[53] The vast majority of cases are concerned with mortgage arrears, when the court is solely concerned with how and when the borrower is able to meet his or her financial commitments.[54]

What sums are due under the mortgage?

Initially, there is the question of what sums are due under the mortgage where an acceleration provision in the mortgage operates on default to trigger repayment of all sums secured under the mortgage, including the full capital value of the loan and any outstanding interest. In *Halifax Building Society v Clark*,[55] the court held that it was, indeed, the total of these sums that the borrower was required to clear. The purpose of s 36 was accordingly placed in jeopardy: if the borrower was already unable to meet his or her periodic repayments, he or she was hardly likely to be able to repay the whole loan.

Parliament was swift to react to restrict the meaning of 'sums due' to any arrears.

Administration of Justice Act 1973, s 8

1. Where by a mortgage of land which consists of or includes a dwelling-house, or by any agreement between the mortgagee under such a mortgage and the mortgagor, the mortgagor is entitled or is to be permitted to pay the principal sum secured by instalments or otherwise to defer payment of it in whole or in part, but provision is also made for earlier payment in the event of any default by the mortgagor or of a demand by the mortgagee or otherwise, then for purposes of section 36 of the Administration of Justice Act 1970

---

[51] *Britannia Building Society v Earl* [1990] 1 WLR 422, 430.

[52] See O'Neill, 'The Mortgage Repossession (Protection of Tenants etc) Act 2010—Sufficient protection for tenants?' [2011] Conv 380.

[53] For example, in the case of breach of a covenant against letting by removing the tenants: see *Britannia Building Society v Earl* [1990] 1 WLR 422, 430. It should be noted that the jurisdiction is available even though there has been no default see *Western Bank Ltd v Schindler* [1977] Ch 1.

[54] Compare Trusts of Land and Appointment of Trustees Act 1996, ss 14 and 15 (see Chapter 14, section 3), where a mortgagee is applying for the sale of co-owner's interest in land.

[55] [1973] Ch 307.

(under which a court has power to delay giving a mortgagee possession of the mortgaged property so as to allow the mortgagor a reasonable time to pay any sums due under the mortgage) a court may treat as due under the mortgage on account of the principal sum secured and of interest on it only such amounts as the mortgagor would have expected to be required to pay if there had been no such provision for earlier payment.

2. A court shall not exercise by virtue of subsection (1) above the powers conferred by section 36 of the Administration of Justice Act 1970 unless it appears to the court not only that the mortgagor is likely to be able within a reasonable period to pay any amounts regarded (in accordance with subsection (1) above) as due on account of the principal sum secured, together with the interest on those amounts, but also that he is likely to be able by the end of that period to pay any further amounts that he would have expected to be required to pay by then on account of that sum and of interest on it if there had been no such provision as is referred to in subsection (1) above for earlier payment.

Section 8 brought its own problems of interpretation, in the shape of what type of loan repayment scheme fell within its terms. Clearly, the standard repayment mortgage, whereby instalments of capital and interest are repaid over a fixed term, are covered.[56] The court has held that endowment mortgages are similarly included,[57] but mortgages repayable on demand, which are common to secure an overdraft facility granted to provide funds to the borrower's business, do not fall within s 8.[58]

What is a 'reasonable period'?

The significance of s 8 has diminished somewhat as a result of the interpretation that the courts have accorded to what is a 'reasonable period' in which repayment is to be made. It is clear that the Payne Committee and Parliament envisaged a relatively short period, of a year or two, to provide the borrower with relief, so that he or she could overcome a temporary financial setback, such as the loss of a job, or an illness. The Court of Appeal, in the light of the property slump of the early 1990s during which mortgage repossessions soared, adopted a different approach.

Cheltenham & Gloucester Building Society v Norgan
[1996] 1 WLR 343, CA

Facts: Mrs Norgan had borrowed £90,000, repayable by monthly instalments over twenty-two years, with the loan being secured upon her farmhouse. She fell into arrears, and the Cheltenham & Gloucester obtained a possession order, which was stayed on several occasions. The arrears remained substantial, and the Cheltenham & Gloucester applied again to execute the possession order.

---

[56] *Centrax Trustees v Ross* [1979] 2 All ER 952.

[57] *Bank of Scotland v Grimes* [1986] QB 1179. Under an endowment mortgage, the borrower's instalment payments meet only the interest payable. The borrower also pays periodic insurance premiums to maintain an endowment policy that, at the end of the mortgage term, will mature to produce a lump sum, which should be sufficient to repay the capital advanced.

[58] *Habib Bank Ltd v Tailor* [1982] 1 WLR 1218; *Rees Investment Ltd v Groves* [2002] 1 P & CR DG 9.

Waite LJ

At 353

In the present plight of the housing market possession cases play a major part in the case-load for the county courts. That is particularly true of the district judges, who deal with those cases in such numbers that they develop a "feel" for them and have achieved an excellent disposal record. It is not surprising that they have found it convenient to adopt a relatively short period of years as the rough rule of thumb which aids a just determination of the "reasonable period" for the purposes of section 36 of the Act of 1970 and section 8 of the Act of 1973. Nevertheless, although I would not go quite so far with Mr. Croally as to say it should be an "assumption," it does seem to me that the logic and spirit of the legislation require, especially in cases where the parties are proceeding under arrangements such as those reflected in the C.M.L. statement, that the court should take as its starting point the full term of the mortgage and pose at the outset the question: "Would it be possible for the mortgagor to maintain payment-off of the arrears by instalments over that period?"

I accept all the grounds urged on us by Mr. Waters for saying that the dicta relied on in *First Middlesbrough Trading and Mortgage Co. Ltd. v. Cunningham* (1974) 28 P. & C.R. 69 and *Western Bank Ltd. v. Schindler* [1977] Ch.1 were directed to situations different from the circumstances of this case and most other cases of its kind, but they nevertheless in my judgment provide confirmation of the view that such is the right approach. I would acknowledge, also, that this approach will be liable to demand a more detailed analysis of present figures and future projections than it may have been customary for the courts to undertake until now. There is likely to be a greater need to require of mortgagors that they should furnish the court with a detailed "budget" of the kind that has been supplied by the mortgagor in her affidavit in the present case. But analysis of such budgets is part of the expertise in which the district judges have already become adept in their family jurisdiction and I would not expect that to present too great a difficulty. There will be instances, too, in which preliminary adjudication will be necessary to determine, when calculating the amount of arrears and assessing the future instalments for their payment-off, which items are to be attributed to the mortgagor's current payment obligations and which to his ultimate liability on capital account. The present case has shown—through the disparity introduced by the disputed items—how problematic that may sometimes prove to be. They are nevertheless disputes that it will be essential to resolve—in this case and others where they arise—before the court can undertake an accurate estimate of the amount which the mortgagor would be required to meet if the arrears were to be made repayable over the full remainder of the mortgage term. There may also be cases, as Mr. Waters points out, in which it is less obvious than in this case that the mortgagee is adequately secured—and detailed evidence, if necessary by experts, may be required to see if and when the lender's security will become liable to be put at risk as a result of imposing postponement of payments in arrear. Problems such as these—which I suspect will arise only rarely in practice although they will undeniably be daunting when they do arise—should not however be allowed, in my judgment, to stand in the way of giving effect to the clearly intended scheme of the legislation.

There is another factor which, to my mind, weighs strongly in favour of adopting the full term of the mortgage as the starting point for calculating a "reasonable period" for payment of arrears. It is prompted by experience in this very case. The parties have been before the court with depressing frequency over the years on applications to enforce, or further to suspend, the warrant of possession, while Mrs. Norgan and her husband have struggled, sometimes with success and sometimes without, to meet whatever commitment was currently approved by the court. Cheltenham has (in exercise of its power to do so under the terms of the mortgage) added to its security the costs it has incurred in connection with all these attendances. One of the disputed items turns upon the question whether such costs fall to be allocated to capital or to interest account. What is not in dispute, however, is that one day, be it sooner or later, those costs will have to be borne by the mortgagor, and if the day comes when she decides—or is compelled by circumstances—to move to more readily affordable accommodation, her resources for rehousing will be correspondingly reduced. It is an experience which brings home the disadvantages which both lender and borrower are liable to suffer if frequent attendance before the court becomes necessary as a result of multiple applications under section 36 of the Act of 1970—to say nothing of the heavy inroads made upon court hearing time. One advantage of taking the period most favourable to the mortgagor at the outset is that, if his or her hopes of repayment prove to be ill-founded and the new instalments initially ordered as a condition of suspension are not maintained but themselves fall into arrear, the mortgagee can be heard with justice to say that the mortgagor has had his chance, and that the section 36 powers (although of course capable in theory of being exercised again and again) should not be employed repeatedly to compel a lending institution which has already suffered interruption of the regular flow of interest to which it was entitled under the express terms of the mortgage to accept assurances of future payment from a borrower in whom it has lost confidence.

Evans LJ

At 356

In conclusion, a practical summary of our judgments may be helpful in future cases. Drawing on the above and on the judgment of Waite L.J., the following considerations are likely to be relevant when a "reasonable period" has to be established for the purposes of section 36 of the Act of 1970. (a) How much can the borrower reasonably afford to pay, both now and in the future? (b) If the borrower has a temporary difficulty in meeting his obligations, how long is the difficulty likely to last? (c) What was the reason for the arrears which have accumulated? (d) How much remains of the original term? (e) What are relevant contractual terms, and what type of mortgage is it, i.e. when is the principal due to be repaid? (f) Is it a case where the court should exercise its power to disregard accelerated payment provisions (section 8 of the Act of 1973)? (g) Is it reasonable to expect the lender, in the circumstances of the particular case, to recoup the arrears of interest (1) over the whole of the original term, or (2) within a shorter period, or even (3) within a longer period, i.e. by extending the repayment period? Is it reasonable to expect the lender to capitalise the interest or not? (h) Are there any reasons affecting the security which should influence the length of the period for payment? In the light of the answers to the above, the court can proceed to exercise its overall discretion, taking account also of any further factors which may arise in the particular case.

Thus, the question to be considered by the court is whether, taking into account the whole of the term of the mortgage, it is likely that the borrower will be able to repay all that he or she owes the lender.[59] In coming to that decision, the court will need to consider the matters listed by Evans LJ, which, in turn, will require the parties to present to the court

---

[59] Although there is evidence that the courts in practice look to shorter periods, see Whitehouse, 'Longitudinal Analysis of the Mortgage Repossession Process 1995–2010: Stability, Regulation and Reform' in *Modern Studies in Property Law Vol 6* (ed Bright, Oxford: Hart, 2011) pp 163–4.

the necessary evidence, including detailed financial statements and projections of the borrower's likely income and outgoings, as well as evidence—for example, as to the spare equity in the property— which will enable the court to evaluate the exposure of the lender to a continuing risk of default. Another factor that may help a borrower is the possibility of state assistance to meet mortgage interest repayments. For example, Support for Mortgage Interest may provide some help, although such assistance is limited and not immediately available.[60] The Government have deliberately tried to restrict this support to encourage borrowers to seek private protection against the risk of a loss income by taking out mortgage payment protection insurance.[61]

These guidelines reflect those contained in the MCOB 13 and the Pre-action Protocol (see section 1.2); namely that the lender should try to agree a reasonable rescheduling of the borrower's debt repayments before seeking repossession. Thus it may well be that the feasibility of the borrower being able to repay within a reasonable period has already been explored. McMurtry has criticized this sidelining of s 36 as 'disappointing and limited',[62] although evidence suggests that the shift in lender's focus from 'pay and possess' to 'managed forbearance' already noted has led to a drop in mortgage possession actions.[63]

Bright and Whitehouse's empirical research of mortgage possession actions has also identified a number of factors which affect the optimal use of the court's discretion.

Bright and Whitehouse, 'Information, Advice & Representation in Housing Possession Cases' (Universities of Oxford and Hull, April 2014 at p 3)

Summary of Findings

Information about the Defendant's Circumstances

There is a lack of 'joined up thinking' within the legal process. This means that information about the defendant's circumstances, that may be important to the judge's decision about whether or not to order possession, may not be known to the judge [. . . .]

Importance of Defendant Participation in the Hearing

If the defendant participates in the possession process by filing a defence form and attending the hearing there is more likely to be an outcome beneficial to the defendant but participation rates are low [. . .]

Importance of Legal Advice and Representation

[. . .] advisers play a significant role in assisting occupiers. Frequently this leads to a more favourable outcome, perhaps by agreeing more realistic repayment terms with claimants.

---

[60] See Nield, 'Mortgage Market Review:Hardwired Commonsense' [2015] Consumer Law and Policy, on line 15 March 2015.

[61] Although there has been considerable concern expressed over the marketing of this insurance (see Chapter 27, section 2.2), and such insurance provides protection for the lender's and not the borrower's loss: see *Woolwich Building Society v Brown* [1996] CLC 625; *Banfield v Leeds Building Society* [2007] EWCA Civ 1369.

[62] McMurtry, 'Mortgage Default and Repossession: Procedure and Policy in the Post-*Norgan Era*' (2007) 58 NILQR 194 p 207.

[63] See section 1.2.

> Judges consider [advice] schemes to be valuable and yet the emergency legal advice offered [. . .] is not available in all courts, or for all users, when possession lists are heard. Few defendants receive any legal advice prior to the court hearing, and cuts in funding [. . .] will make it even harder to receive help before the hearing.

It should be noted that the court's approach to the interpretation of 'a reasonable period' is different where the borrower is proposing to clear his or her debt from a sale of property when the total amount owed to the lender will be repayable to discharge the mortgage. There must be some firm evidence that a sale is likely within the foreseeable future; a mere hope or an estate agent's optimistic projections are not enough.

Bristol & West Building Society v Ellis
(1997) 73 P & CR 158, CA

Facts: Mrs Ellis had fallen into mortgage arrears after her husband left her. She unsuccessfully applied for suspension of a warrant for possession, on the basis that she would sell the property in three–five years' time, when her children had finished their full-time education. In support of her application, she provided estate agents' opinions showing that the likely sale price for the property should be sufficient to discharge the mortgage.

Auld LJ

At 161

The prospect of settling the mortgage debt, including arrears of principal and/or interest, by sale of the property raises a number of questions on the reasonableness of any period which a court may consider allowing for the purpose.

The critical matters are, of course, the adequacy of the property as a security for the debt and the length of the period necessary to achieve a sale. There should be evidence, or at least some informal material (see *Cheltenham & Gloucester Building Society v. Grant* (1994) 26 H.L.R. 703), before the court of the likelihood of a sale the proceeds of which will discharge the debt and of the period within which such a sale is likely to be achieved. If the court is satisfied on both counts and that the necessary period for sale is reasonable, it should, if it decides to suspend the order for possession, identify the period in its order [. . .]

It all depends on the individual circumstances of each case, though the important factors in most are likely to be the extent to which the mortgage debt and arrears are secured by the value of the property and the effect of time on that security.

Where the property is already on the market and there is some indication of delay on the part of the mortgagor, it may be that a short period of suspension of only a few months would be reasonable [. . .] Where there is likely to be considerable delay in selling the property and/or its value is close to the total of the mortgage debt and arrears so that the mortgagee is at risk as to the adequacy of the security, immediate possession or only a short period of suspension may be reasonable. Where there has already been considerable delay in realising a sale of the property and/or the likely sale proceeds are unlikely to cover the mortgage debt and arrears or there is simply no sufficient evidence as to sale value, the normal order would be for immediate possession. See, e.g. *Abbey National Mortgages plc v. Rochelle Bernard* (July 4, 1995, C.A. unreported) and *National Provincial Bank v Lloyd* [1996] 1 All ER 630.

Mr Duggan submitted that, here, the material, formal or informal (see *Grant*) before the district judge and judge was insufficient to satisfy them that Mrs Ellis would or could sell the property within three to five years or that its sale proceeds when sold would be sufficient to discharge the mortgage debt and arrears. As to the time of sale, all that the district judge had was her statement in her affidavit that she anticipated selling within three to five years when her children completed their education. As to value, the evidence was not compelling: two estate agents' estimates of between £80,000 and £85,000 as against the redemption figure at the time of just over £77,000 plus costs. As a result of Mrs Ellis's payment of the lump sum ordered by the district judge and subsequent payments, the total figure of indebtedness is now about £70,000, including about £10,000 arrears of interest. Given the inevitable uncertainty as to the movement of property values over the next few years and the reserve with which the courts should approach estate agents' estimates of sale prices (see *Clothier*) no court could be sanguine about the adequacy, now or continuing over that period, of the property as a security for the mortgage debt and arrears. In my view, the evidence was simply insufficient to entitle the district judge to contemplate, behind the order he made, a likelihood that the house would or could be sold at a price sufficient to discharge Mrs Ellis's overall debt to Bristol & West within any reasonable period, and certainly not one of up to three to five years.

There may be a distinct marketing advantage in the borrower selling the property rather than the lender doing so after entering into possession: a home will often look more attractive to a purchaser if it is occupied, and the knowledge that a sale is being forced by a mortgagee can depress the price. A number of lenders provide some support to borrowers seeking to sell their homes to repay their mortgage debt through voluntary assisted sales schemes.[64]

However, a borrower may be slow to cooperate, with a lender wishing to gain possession to exercise its power of sale, either by obstructing effective marketing or the delivery of vacant possession on completion of the sale. A court will thus only rarely allow the borrower to remain in possession, by suspending execution of a possession order, whilst a lender arranges a sale and it is clear that such a jurisdiction will not be exercised if the lender objects.[65]

Subject to such conditions ... as the court thinks fit

Whilst the trigger for the court's discretion under s 36(1) is that the borrower can pay the sums due under the mortgage within a reasonable time, the court's discretion to impose conditions should it choose to delay proceedings or the grant of possession under s 36(3) is not so qualified.

---

[64] Nield, 'Mortgage Market Review: Hardwired Commonsense? (2015) Consumer Law and Policy on line 15 March 2015.
[65] *Cheltenham & Gloucester plc v Booker* ((1997) 73 P & CR 412).

Bank of Scotland plc v Zinda
[2012] 1 WLR 728 CA

Munby LJ

At [23]–[24]

First, there is the jurisdictional gateway created by the requirement on the mortgagor to demonstrate that he is (section 36(1)) "likely to be able within a reasonable period to pay" both (section 8(1)) the "amounts [he] would have expected to be required to pay if there had been no ... provision for earlier payment"—in other words, the arrears of the instalments due to date—and (section 8(2)) the "further amounts that he would have expected to be required to pay by then"—in other words, the future instalments accruing during the reasonable period. The power of suspension exercisable by the court under section 36 is *conditional* on its appearing to the court that in the event of the exercise of the power the mortgagor is likely to be able to pay the sums in question within a reasonable period. Absent such proof, the court has no jurisdiction to stay or suspend the order for possession.

Second, and assuming that the mortgagor surmounts the jurisdictional hurdle, the court is given a wide discretion under sections 36(2) & (3). In particular, section 36(3) permits the court, if it decides to stay or suspend a possession order, to attach such "conditions with regard to payment by the mortgagor of *any sum* secured by the mortgage" (emphasis added) as the court thinks fit. This power is not confined to the arrears of the instalments due to date or to the future instalments accruing during the reasonable period referred to in section 36(1). It extends to "any" sum secured by the mortgage, including, for example, the totality of the future instalments accruing due throughout the remaining life of the mortgage. Section 36(3), in contrast to both section 36(1) and section 36(2), contains no reference to the "reasonable period". The power to impose conditions is not qualified by reference to, nor is it confined to, the "reasonable period".

Mr Grant understandably placed much emphasis upon this last point. And in my judgment he was right to do so. Whereas the *existence* of the court's jurisdiction is focussed upon an examination of what is likely to happen before the end of the reasonable period referred to in section 36(1), the *exercise* of the jurisdiction, once established, is not so limited. The terms of section 36(3) make clear that in deciding what conditions (if any) to attach, the court can have regard to events occurring at any stage during the remaining life of the mortgage.

The conditions imposed required Mr Zindal to pay off the arrears by monthly instalments as well as pay the current instalments payable under his mortgage. A couple of years later the parties agreed that the arrears should be consolidated by being added to the capital of the loan, thus increasing the amount of the repayment instalments Mr Zindal was bound to pay.[66] This is not an unusual forbearance technique. Unfortunately, Mr Zindal once again fell into arrears and the bank sought to execute the suspended possession order. In granting the bank's request the court firmly rejected Mr Zinal's argument that the consolidation of the arrears had extinguished the possession order. In so doing the court made some valuable observations.

---

[66] The unilaterally consolidate arrears by the lender is far more problematic see the robust criticism of the practice in the Northern Ireland case of *Bank of Scotland v Rea, McGready & Laverty* [2014] NIMasters 11.

The first issue: the effect of the consolidation ...

At 28–9

The events of March 2008 involved the consolidation of the arrears with the outstanding capital, with the consequential substitution of a loan of £168,699·71 for the original loan of £133,000 and adjustment of the amount of the monthly instalment. [. . .] The effect of what was done in March 2008 may have been, as Mr Zinda puts it, to create a new contract discharging the previous contract, or to vary the existing contract, though in my judgment it was probably neither. Be that as it may, what is quite clear—and this is decisive for present purposes—is that there was no discharge either of the mortgage deed dated 3 March 2003 or of the security created by the mortgage deed. In that sense, the mortgage created in March 2003 survived unchanged by anything that happened in March 2008. Indeed it survives unchanged today. [. . .]

The second issue: the meaning and effect of the possession order [. . .]

At [35]–[40]

This takes me on to the second point. It is quite clear that the condition set out in para 2 of the possession order comprises two elements, imposing a double requirement on Mr Zinda. If he is to stave off eviction, if the possession order is to remain suspended, Mr Zinda has, as Jacob LJ pointed out, to do two things: (i) first, he must pay off the arrears of £11,046·50 by monthly instalments of £96·02; *and* (ii) second, he must "in addition" pay what are described as "the current instalments under the mortgage". Doing the one without the other will avail him nothing. So the fact that he complies with the first requirement, paying off the arrears as required, is not sufficient; he must also comply with the second requirement. It follows, as Jacob LJ observed, that the mere fact that the arrears may have been discharged in their entirety—as they were by reason of the consolidation in March 2008—is not enough if there is none the less a failure to comply with the second limb of the condition.

The central issue on this appeal therefore reduces itself to this: What, on the true construction of the order and in the events which have happened (including in particular the consolidation in March 2008), is the meaning and effect of the words requiring Mr Zinda to pay "in addition" what are described as "the current instalments under the mortgage"?

As to that there is, in my judgment, no real room for argument. [. . .] Four factors, as it seems to me, all point in the same direction. First, the words are quite general and are not limited, whether in time or otherwise. Unlike an order in the form referred to by District Judge Allen, the order contains no provision allowing for proleptic discharge. The order refers to "the current instalments", current here being used in contradistinction to the arrears. The "instalments under the mortgage" are, as a matter of fact and legal obligation, payable throughout the remaining life of the mortgage. So, as a matter of simple language, "the current instalments under the mortgage" means the future instalments payable "under the mortgage", that is, payable until such time as the mortgage has been redeemed. Second, there is, as I have already explained, nothing in the statutory scheme to confine the conditions that can be imposed under section 36(3) to or by reference to the "reasonable period". [. . .] Third, all that this limb of the condition requires Mr Zinda to do is to perform his existing contractual obligations, namely to pay the instalments when and in the amounts he has contracted for. Fourth, and in a sense flowing on from the previous points, given that the ambit of such a condition is not confined to the "reasonable period", and given that his contractual obligations extend to the end of the mortgage term, what rational basis can there be for asserting that the condition is by implication limited in time [. . .]? Mr Zinda complains that this result is unfair since, as he puts it, it is tantamount to an indefinite death sentence [. . .] The order does not vary the terms of the contract at all so far as Mr Zinda is concerned. And the fact that he remains under the sword of Damocles—rather than simply having been evicted for default in 2005—is merely the consequence of the contract he entered into with the bank (in which expression I include the consolidation), of his default and of his successful seeking of relief under the 1970 and 1973 Acts. Any "unfairness"—in truth, there is none—is of his own making, the consequence of his own repeated defaults.

Moreover, as Mr Grant points out, it is not as if Mr Zinda is left wholly unprotected to face whatever steps the bank may take to enforce the possession order however far away in the future: in principle he can apply under section 36(4) to vary or revoke any of the conditions; in principle he can seek an order suspending any warrant of possession; and if six years have elapsed since the possession order was made it cannot be enforced without the permission of the court.

2.5.5 Section 36 and court orders for sale under s 91

Section 91 of the LPA 1925 provides that a borrower may apply to the court for an order for sale.

Law of Property Act 1925, s 91

Sale of mortgaged property in action for redemption or foreclosure

1. Any person entitled to redeem mortgaged property may have a judgment or order for sale instead of for redemption in an action brought by him either for redemption alone or for sale alone, or for sale or redemption in the alternative.

2. In any action, whether for foreclosure, or for redemption, or for sale or for raising and payment in any manner of mortgage money, the court, on the request of the mortgagee, or any person interested either in the mortgage money or in the right of redemption, and, notwithstanding that—

   (a) any other person dissents; or

   (b) the mortgagee or any person so interested does not appear in the action;

   and without allowing any time for redemption or for payment of any mortgage money, may direct a sale of the mortgaged property, on such terms as it thinks fit, including the deposit in court of a reasonable sum fixed by the court to meet the expenses of sale and to secure performance of the terms

---

The jurisdiction provides an alternative option for a borrower who wishes to solve his or her debt repayment problems through sale, although its application is limited. Traditionally, the jurisdiction was exercised only where there was a surplus between the value of the property and the outstanding mortgage, when it was not unusual to give the borrower the conduct of the sale. In *Palk v Mortgage Services Funding plc*,[67] the court was persuaded to use s 91

---

[67] [1993] Ch 330.

to order sale on the application of the borrower where there was negative equity. The lender had wanted to delay sale until the market improved, and proposed, in the meantime, to take possession and let the property, applying the rental in partial discharge of the mortgage repayments—but this strategy would have resulted in mounting arrears. The Palks preferred an immediate sale to clear a good portion of their debt, leaving the balance unsecured.

The application of s 91 to instances in which there is negative equity can, however, be problematic: for example, where the borrower resorts to the jurisdiction as a delaying tactic or to try to gain control of the sale. Accordingly, the court will not usurp the lender's right to seek possession with a view to sale by suspending proceedings under s 36 to allow an application for sale under s 91.[68]

2.5.6 Right or remedy?

We have already noted that the lender enjoys a right to possession that is inherently independent of default. Section 36 is, however, an important jurisdiction that effectively controls the lender's right to possession of a dwelling house within a remedial context, and, as such, plays an important role. Nevertheless, as our survey of the jurisdiction has highlighted, its parameters are highly dependent on judicial interpretation, which has not always been able hold this social function firmly in its sights.

Haley, 'Mortgage Default: Possession, Relief and Judicial Discretion' (1997) 17 LS 483, 483

The history of this interventionist jurisdiction is, however, chequered. It has been marked by the uneasy interaction between the laissez faire attitude of the common law (which upheld the lender's contract and estate rights) and the more protective and tender treatment of the mortgagor in equity (which, in appropriate cases, sought to restrict the exercise of those rights). The jurisdiction is now in statutory form, but the tension between the commercial interests of the mortgagee and the need for the mortgagor to maintain a home persists. Although the court must attempt to achieve a balance between those competing claims, under the present legal regime this is, patently, not a simple task. The judicial stance must necessarily reflect individual circumstances and broader notions of public interest, social and economic policy and parliamentary purpose. Consequently, the granting of relief against possession, as well as being reactive to prevailing community norms, is susceptible to major swings in judicial attitude and statutory constructions.

The remedial context of the lender's right to possession is reinforced by the regulatory controls imposed by the FSMA through MCOB 13, as strengthened by the Pre-action Protocol. These measures are predicated on the policy that possession should be a measure of last resort with the consequence that it is increasingly difficult to justify the lender's inherent right to possession. The law should reflect the reality that possession is a remedy that should only be capable of exercise under the scrutiny of the court.[69]

---

[68] *Cheltenham & Gloucester plc v Krausz* [1997] 1 WLR 1558, CA.
[69] As the Law Commission has recommended: see Law Commission Report No 204 (1991) [6.16], [7.28]–[7.38].

2.6 HOME REPOSSESSION AND HUMAN RIGHTS

Section 36 may wrestle the exercise of a lender's right to possession within the court's control, but there are gaps in its application—most notably, where there is no need for the lender to apply to court for possession. Several commentators have raised the suggestion that the lender's right to possession conferred by s 87(1) of the LPA 1925 is incompatible with Art 8 (respect for the home).[70] The issue is of course one of horizontal application of the Convention standards between private parties but, given that the lender's right to possession is derived from statute, s 3 of the Human Rights Act 1998 requires this statutory right to be interpreted in a human rights compatible manner.[71] The question of compatibility is governed by the familiar justification formula namely; whether or not the interference with the borrower's home presented by repossession, is justified, because it is lawful and serves a legitimate aim, which is necessary within a democratic society to address a pressing social need, yet is also proportionate in its effect upon the individual victim.[72] This call for proportionality necessitates an adequate process by which to assess the impact of the measure upon the personal circumstances of the borrower.[73] The exercise of a right to possession of the home must, thus, satisfy both substantive and procedural human rights standards. The fact that a lender's right to possession can be asserted, albeit in unusual circumstances, outside the court process leads to a direct clash with these standards.

Nield, 'Charges, Possession and Human Rights: A Reappraisal of s 87(1) Law of Property Act 1925' in *Modern Studies in Property Law: Vol 3* (ed Cooke, 2005, p 173)

The Strasbourg jurisprudence recognises that a lender's right to possession to facilitate the repayment of secured debt is a proportionate and legitimate aim. In *Wood v UK* (1997) 24 EHRR CD 69 the European Court, when considering Article 1 Protocol 1, stated that:

[. . .] to the extent that the applicant is deprived of her possessions by repossession, the Commission considers that the deprivation is in the public interest, that is the public interest in ensuring the payment of contractual debts and is also in accordance with the rules provided by law.

And when considering Article 8:

In so far as the repossession constituted an interference with the applicant's home the Commission finds that this was in accordance with the terms of the loan and the domestic law and was necessary for the protection of the rights and freedoms of others, namely the lender.

Proportionality calls for an examination of the process by which a legitimate aim is achieved. So that, even though repossession to ensure the efficient repayment of debts is a legitimate aim, the means by which that repossession is obtained is a vital consideration under both

---

[70] See also Gray and Gray, *Elements of Land Law* (4th edn, 2005, [15.147]); Dixon, 'Sorry, We've Sold Your Home: Mortgagees and Their Possessory Rights' (1999) 58 CLJ 281; I Loveland, 'Peaceable Entry to Mortgaged Premises: Considering the Doctrine's Compatibility with the HRA 1998' [2014] Conv 381; and Nield & Hopkins, 'Human Rights and Mortgage Repossession: Beyond Property Law using Article 8' (2013) 33 LS 431.

[71] See Chapter 4, section 2.4.   [72] See Chapter 4, section 2.2.

[73] See *Manchester CC v Pinnock* [2010] UKSC 45 [2010] 3 WLR 1441; *Hounslow LBC v Powell* [2011] UKSC 8 [2011] 2 WLR 287.

Articles 1 and 8. The possibility that the lender may obtain possession without some form of judicial consideration over its exercise must tip the fair balance that lies at the heart of proportionality. [. . .] This concern with process operates despite the fact that Article 6 may not be engaged and provides the strongest argument that the right to possession conferred by subsection 87(1) is incompatible with the [Human Rights Act 1998] and thus should be amended.

However, even where a lender seeks a court order for possession, does s 36 of the Administration of Justice Act 1970 provide a human rights compliant process? The decision of the Supreme Court in *McDonald v McDonald*,[74] which we consider in Chapter 4, suggests that the judiciary are most reluctant to question a statutory scheme for repossession of a home enacted by Parliament and thus it is unlikely that they would find s 36 incompatible. Arguments to do so might conceivably be presented on the basis that s 36 is of some vintage and has been the subject of attempts at legislative reform.[75]

3 SALE

The power of the lender to sell the mortgaged property without having to go to court is a powerful remedy. The lender can control the sale and recover the debt from the proceeds of a sale, accounting to the borrower (or a second chargee, if there is a subsequent mortgage) for any balance received in excess of the debt. In the conduct of the sale, the lender does have to act in a way that pays due regard to the interests of the borrower (or subsequent chargee).

Before examining the duties that a lender owes when selling the mortgaged property, we need to consider the mechanics of the sale itself.

3.1 MECHANICS OF SALE

3.1.1 Source of the power

The power of the lender to sell will be conferred either by the express terms of the legal charge or from the implied power contained in s 101(1)(i) of the LPA 1925 (extracted in section 1.1.2).

Where the power is express, the terms of the power should stipulate how and when it may be exercised. It is common for an express power of sale to be exercisable on specified events of default: for example, if the borrower fails to make an agreed repayment of capital or interest, or otherwise breaches any other covenant contained in the legal charge, or upon the borrower becoming insolvent.

Where a lender under a legal charge is relying upon its implied statutory power, there are two stages to be considered. Firstly, the power must arise: s 101(1)(i) provides that the power of sale arises when the mortgage money is due, being the legal date for redemption under the mortgage,[76] or, where the mortgage is repayable by instalments, when an instalment payment falls due.[77] Secondly, the power, once arisen, must become exercisable,

---

[74] [2017] AC 273.

[75] For example Home Repossession Protection Bill 2009, which failed to progress for lack of parliamentary time.

[76] *Twentieth Century Banking Corp v Wilkinson* [1977] Ch 99.

[77] *Payne v Cardiff RDC* [1932] 1 KB 241.

which, in the case of the statutory power, is upon the events of default specified in s 103 of the 1925 Act although these events may be, and frequently are, varied by the express terms of the mortgage.

Law of Property Act 1925, s 103

Regulation of exercise of power of sale

A mortgagee shall not exercise the power of sale conferred by this Act unless and until—

(i)   Notice requiring payment of the mortgage money has been served on the mortgagor or one of two or more mortgagors, and default has been made in payment of the mortgage money, or of part thereof, for three months after such service; or

(ii) Some interest under the mortgage is in arrear and unpaid for two months after becoming due; or

(iii) There has been a breach of some provision contained in the mortgage deed or in this Act, or in an enactment replaced by this Act, and on the part of the mortgagor, or of some person concurring in making the mortgage, to be observed or performed, other than and besides a covenant for payment of the mortgage money or interest thereon.

The power of sale is thus exercisable only on default. In the case of a default in meeting a demand for full repayment, the borrower must be given notice and three months in which to comply with that notice; in the case of default in the payment of interest, no notice is required, but there must be at least two months' arrears.

In the case of a regulated mortgage, a longer process is contemplated. MCOB 13 (extracted at section1.2), governing FCA-regulated mortgages, calls for the borrower to be given notice of any arrears, and for the lender to take reasonable steps to try to arrange the rescheduling of the debt before contemplating possession and sale. Where the Pre-action Protocol is applicable because the lender is seeking possession prior to sale, the lender must also comply with the steps that it outlines.

Haley has pointed out that, in the case of a dwelling house, the impact of s 36 of the Administration of Justice Act 1970 will give the borrower more time in which to clear any arrears than is contemplated by s 103 of the LPA 1925,[78] and thus *'a long delay in the mortgagee's right to possession is by a side wind eroding the value of the statutory remedy'* of sale.[79] He observes that the separate control of the mortgagee's right to possession and its power of sale is artificial when the purpose of obtaining possession is to enable the lender to sell, and advocates reform to bring the remedies into line. Otherwise, a lender may be tempted to sell without obtaining possession.[80]

---

[78] Technically, the reverse could be the case where s 36 does not apply, although it is unlikely that a lender will act so precipitously.

[79] 'Mortgage Default: Possession, Relief and Judicial Discretion' (1997) 17 LS 483, 496.

[80] See *Ropaigealach v Barclays Bank plc* [2000] QB 263; *Horsham Properties Group Ltd v Clark* [2009] 1 WLR 1255.

3.1.2 Passing title

The mechanics of passing title by a mortgagee's sale is the subject of ss 88(1) (for mortgages over freeholds) and 89(1) (for mortgages over leaseholds) of the LPA 1925.

Law of Property Act 1925, s 88(1)

Realisation of freehold mortgages

1. Where an estate in fee simple has been mortgaged by the creation of a term of years absolute limited thereout or by a charge by way of legal mortgage and the mortgagee sells under his statutory or express power of sale—

   (a) the conveyance by him shall operate to vest in the purchaser the fee simple in the land conveyed subject to any legal mortgage having priority to the mortgage in right of which the sale is made and to any money thereby secured, and thereupon;

   (b) the mortgage term or the charge by way of legal mortgagee and any subsequent mortgage term or charges shall merge or be extinguished as respects the land conveyed; and such conveyance may, as respects the fee simple, be made in the name of the estate owner in whom it is vested.

The sale by the lender vests title in the purchaser by overreaching the borrower's equity of redemption, and any other interest over which the mortgage has priority, which vests instead in the proceeds of sale.[81] The mortgage itself and any subsequent charge are extinguished so far as they affect the land itself.

3.1.3 Application of proceeds of sale

By s 105 of the LPA 1925, the lender holds the proceeds of sale (after the discharge of any prior mortgages or encumbrances) in trust, to be applied in, firstly, the meeting the sale costs, and secondly, repaying the amount owing to it under the mortgage,[82] with any balance being payable to the borrower or a subsequent mortgagee (if any).[83]

Law of Property Act 1925, s 105

Application of proceeds of sale

The money which is received by the mortgagee, arising from the sale, after discharge of prior incumbrances to which the sale is not made subject, if any, or after payment into court under this Act of a sum to meet any prior incumbrance, shall be held by him in trust to be applied by him, first, in payment of all costs, charges, and expenses properly incurred by him

---

[81] See s 2(1)(iii) LPA 1925, extracted at Chapter 17, section 2.1; *Horsham Properties Group Ltd v Clark* [2009] 1 WLR 1255.

[82] In the case of a shortfall the lender has discretion to appropriate sums to either capital or interest see *West Bromwich Building Society v Crammer* [2002] EWHC 2618.

[83] *West London Commercial Bank v Reliance Permanent Building Society* (1885) 29 Ch D 954.

> as incident to the sale or any attempted sale, or otherwise; and secondly, in discharge of the mortgage money, interest, and costs, and other money, if any, due under the mortgage; and the residue of the money so received shall be paid to the person entitled to the mortgaged property, or authorised to give receipts for the proceeds of the sale thereof.

A purchaser is not concerned to check that an event of default has occurred and the power of sale is exercisable,[84] nor is the purchaser concerned to see that the lender applies the sale moneys as required by s 105. The receipt of the lender is a good discharge for the purchase money.[85] The purchaser must, however, check that the lender has a power of sale in the first place, either because the power is expressed in the legal charge, or because it is implied under s 101(1)(i). We will explore the position of the purchaser in more detail below.

3.1.4 Human rights and sale

We have noted that the lender's right to possession of a borrower's home may be incompatible with Art 8. A separate question is whether the lender's out of court power of sale (whether pursuant to an express or implied power) is an unjustified interference with a borrower's property rights under Art 1 Protocol 1 (Deprivation of Possessions). Briggs J in *Horsham Properties Group Ltd v Clark*[86] rejected this possibility. His primary ground was to reject the horizontal application of Art 1 Protocol 1 to a privately negotiated power of sale. He believed that an implied statutory power of sale also did not engage a horizontal application of Art 1 Protocol 1 because it '*serves to implement rather than override the private bargain between mortgagor and mortgagee*'.[87] Briggs J, in the following extract, went onto consider as obiter the human rights compatibility of the power of sale.

Horsham Properties Group Ltd v Clark
[2009] 1 WLR 1255 HC

Facts: The lender, through its receivers, had sold the property without obtaining possession and their purchasers wanted to repossess the property. The borrowers' interest had been overreached by the sale, so they had no legal right to remain and were trespassers.

Briggs J

At [44]–[45]

In my judgment, any deprivation of possession constituted by the exercise by a mortgagee of its powers under section 101 of the Law of Property Act after a relevant default by the mortgagor is justified in the public interest, and requires no case-by case exercise of a proportionality discretion by the court, for the following reasons. First, it reflects the bargain habitually drawn between mortgagors and mortgagees for nearly 200 years, in which the ability of a mortgagee to sell the property offered as security without having to go to court has been identified as a central and essential aspect of the security necessarily provided if

---

84 See LPA 1925, s 104, extracted at section 3.2.6. 85 Ibid, s 107(1).
86 [2009] 1 WLR 1255. 87 Ibid, [35].

substantial property base secured lending is to be available at affordable rates of interest. That it is in the public interest that property buyers and owners should be able to obtain lending for that purpose can hardly be open to doubt, even if the loan-to-value ratios at which it has recently become possible have now become a matter of controversy.

Secondly, I am bound by the decision of the Court of Appeal in *Ropaigealach* to conclude that there was no wider policy behind section 36 of the Administration of Justice Act 1970 than to put back what the courts had shortly before taken away, namely a discretion to stay or adjourn proceedings for possession, triggered only where the mortgagee considered it necessary or appropriate to go to court in the first place. The question whether a wider policy ought to be implemented wherever steps taken by a mortgagee to release its security is likely to lead to the obtaining of possession is a matter for Parliament, and upon which Parliament has yet [. . .] to form any view. It would be quite wrong for the courts in a vigorous and imaginative interpretation of the Human Rights Convention to make that policy, as it were, on the hoof.

There is no doubt that a lender's power of sale can be substantively justified in human rights terms. It is the very essence of a security that the lender can recover his or her debt from a realization of the borrower's property. Indeed the Strasbourg Court has held as much in *Wood v UK*[88] in relation to both a potential interference with Art 1 Protocol 1 and Art 8. However, what Briggs J overlooks are the procedural imperatives that we have seen form an important part of the justification process.[89] Indeed the decision sparked proposals, which have since fallen by the wayside, to require a lender to obtain a court order either when taking possession or effecting a sale of a home so as to afford the borrower the opportunity to access the courts' protection.[90]

3.2 DUTIES OF THE MORTGAGEE IN THE CONDUCT OF THE SALE

The lender has a direct interest in any sale, but so too does the borrower, because, as we have seen, he or she is entitled to any surplus sale proceeds. Even where the sale proceeds are insufficient to meet the sums owing to the lender, the borrower is still concerned, because he or she remains liable to meet the shortfall under the contractual covenant to repay. The balancing of the interests of both the lender and borrower is thus at the heart of the lender's duties upon the sale.

3.2.1 General principles

It has long been asserted that the lender is not a trustee of the power of sale, but the interests of the borrower cannot be ignored.[91] The lender cannot sell with the object of recovering only enough to repay the debt, because, in so doing, the borrower's interests are inevitably overlooked. Early decisions were somewhat ambiguous as to the scope of the lender's

---

[88] (1997) 24 EHRR CD 69, [70]–[71].   [89] See Chapter 4, section 2 and section 2.6.

[90] Ministry of Justice, *Mortgages: Power of Sale and Residential Property* CP55/09 (December 2009). These proposals would not apply where the borrower had voluntarily given up possession.

[91] See *Nash v Eads* (1880) 25 SJ 95, although a lender is a trustee of the proceeds of sale: Law of Property Act 1925, s 105.

duties: it was unclear whether they were limited to a requirement of good faith or whether a degree of care was also required. The law has developed to recognize both of these elements as interrelated strands of the duty that the lender owes the borrower in the conduct of the sale. The lender must, firstly, be able to demonstrate good faith, and secondly, that reasonable care has been taken in the conduct of the sale.

Cuckmere Brick Co v Mutual Finance
[1971] Ch 949, CA

Facts: The borrower owned land with planning permission to build a hundred flats. It subsequently obtained planning permission to build thirty-five houses. The lender became entitled to exercise its power of sale, which it did by putting the land up for auction. The auctioneers referred only to the planning permission for the houses when marketing the property. Although, the borrower pointed out this omission, the lender refused to postpone the sale and merely asked the auctioneers to mention the planning permission at the auction. The land was sold for £44,000 at the auction. The borrower claimed that a price nearer £75,000 could have been achieved if the planning permission for the flats had been properly advertised. They successfully brought an action for an account against the lender for the amount that should have been received from the sale.

Salmon LJ

At 965

It is well settled that a mortgagee is not a trustee of the power of sale for the mortgagor. Once the power has accrued, the mortgagee is entitled to exercise it for his own purposes whenever he chooses to do so. It matters not that the moment may be unpropitious and that by waiting a higher price could be obtained. He has the right to realise his security by turning it into money when he likes. Nor, in my view, is there anything to prevent a mortgagee from accepting the best bid he can get at an auction, even though the auction is badly attended and the bidding exceptionally low. Providing none of those adverse factors is due to any fault of the mortgagee, he can do as he likes. If the mortgagee's interests, as he sees them, conflict with those of the mortgagor, the mortgagee can give preference to his own interests, which of course he could not do were he a trustee of the power of sale for the mortgagor [. . .]

It is impossible to pretend that the state of the authorities on this branch of the law is entirely satisfactory. There are some dicta which suggest that unless a mortgagee acts in bad faith he is safe. His only obligation to the mortgagor is not to cheat him. There are other dicta which suggest that in addition to the duty of acting in good faith, the mortgagee is under a duty to take reasonable care to obtain whatever is the true market value of the mortgaged property at the moment he chooses to sell it: compare, for example, *Kennedy v. de Trafford* [1896] 1 Ch. 762; [1897] A.C. 180 with *Tomlin v. Luce* (1889) 43 Ch.D. 191, 194.

The proposition that the mortgagee owes both duties, in my judgment, represents the true view of the law. Approaching the matter first of all on principle, it is to be observed that if the sale yields a surplus over the amount owed under the mortgage, the mortgagee holds this surplus in trust for the mortgagor. If the sale shows a deficiency, the mortgagor has to make it good out of his own pocket. The mortgagor is vitally affected by the result of the sale but its preparation and conduct is left entirely in the hands of the mortgagee. The proximity between them could scarcely be closer. Surely they are "neighbours." Given that the power of sale is for the benefit of the mortgagee and that he is entitled to choose the moment to sell which suits him, it would be strange indeed if he were under no legal obligation to take reasonable care to obtain what I call the true market value at the date of the sale.

Salmon LJ's reference to 'neighbours' led subsequent judges to adopt a tortious interpretation for the basis of the lender's duties. But this approach has been discredited. The basis for the lender's duties arises in equity from the relationship of lender and borrower. As we have seen, the lender is under a duty to account to the borrower both for what he or she receives and for what he or she ought to receive.[92] It is from this obligation that the duty to exercise reasonable care in the conduct of the sale finds expression.[93]

Silven Properties Ltd v Royal Bank of Scotland plc
[2004] 1 WLR 997, CA

Lightman J

At [19]

When and if the mortgagee does exercise the power of sale, he comes under a duty in equity (and not tort) to the mortgagor (and all others interested in the equity of redemption) to take reasonable precautions to obtain "the fair" or "the true market" value of or the "proper price" for the mortgaged property at the date of the sale, and not (as the claimants submitted) the date of the decision to sell. If the period of time between the dates of the decision to sell and of the sale is short, there may be no difference in value between the two dates and indeed in many (if not most cases) this may be readily assumed. But where there is a period of delay, the difference in date could prove significant. The mortgagee is not entitled to act in a way which unfairly prejudices the mortgagor by selling hastily at a knock-down price sufficient to pay off his debt: *Palk v Mortgage Services Funding plc* [1993] Ch 330, 337–338, per Sir Donald Nicholls V-C. He must take proper care whether by fairly and properly exposing the property to the market or otherwise to obtain the best price reasonably obtainable at the date of sale. The remedy for breach of this equitable duty is not common law damages, but an order that the mortgagee account to the mortgagor and all others interested in the equity of redemption, not just for what he actually received, but for what he should have received: see *Standard Chartered Bank Ltd v Walker* [1982] 1 WLR 1410, 1416b.

3.2.2 To whom is the duty owed?

The equitable nature of the lender's duties dictates both the parties to whom the duty is owed and the available remedies. The lender does not owe a duty to those whom it is foreseeable

---

[92] See section 2.2.
[93] See also *Downsview Nominees Ltd v First City Corp* [1993] AC 295, 315, *per* Lord Templeman.

will suffer damage (being a tortious standard); its duty is relationship-based. It is owed to the borrower, a subsequent mortgagee, and any guarantor of the mortgage debt. The position is summarized in the following case.

Alpstream AG v PK Airfinance Sarl
[2015] EWCA Civ 1318

Christopher Clarke LJ

At [115]–[119]

A mortgagee who sells the mortgaged property owes a duty: (i) to act in good faith and for proper purposes; and (ii) to take reasonable care to obtain a proper price, to:

a) the mortgagor [. . .];

b) any subsequent mortgagee of the property i.e. one whose security ranks after that of the first mortgagee: *Tomlin v Luce [1889] 43 Ch. D. 191; Downsview Nominees Ltd v First City Corp Ltd [1993] A.C. 295* , 311F–H;

c) a co-mortgagor, i.e. someone who mortgages his property as security for an advance made to the mortgagor of other property for which advance the latter is primarily liable [. . .] *Gee v Liddell [1913] 2 Ch. 62* ; and

d) a guarantor of the mortgagor's debt: *Standard Chartered Bank v Walker [1982] 1 W.L.R. 1410* at 1415 E–G; *China and South Sea Bank Ltd v Tan [1990] 1 A.C. 536* at 544A, 545D; *Raja v Austin Gray (A Firm) [2002] EWCA Civ 1965* at [55].

All of the above are persons who have an interest in the equity of redemption. If the mortgaged property is sold too cheaply the mortgagor's interest in it is impaired. A subsequent mortgagee has an interest in the mortgaged property since it stands as security for him also. A co-mortgagor [. . .] has also been held to have an interest in the mortgaged property of the principal debtor [. . .] In Gee v Liddell he was said to have an "*interest in [and] a charge upon the estate of the principal debtor*". A guarantor has a contingent interest in the mortgaged property. On payment by him of the debtor's debt to the creditor/mortgagee the guarantor will be subrogated to the rights of the latter, including his security in the property. On that account he also has a recognised interest in the equity of redemption before payment has been made.

In Barclays Bank Plc v Kingston [2006] EWHC 533 at [17]–[20] Stanley Burnton J, as he then was, declined to follow Lightman J's decision in Burgess v Auger [1998] 2 B.C.L.C. 478 at 481h–482b, in which he had held that no equitable duty was owed to the guarantor until the latter had satisfied the creditor's claim. Stanley Burnton J regarded this as inconsistent (as it appears to me to be) with the decision of this court in *Skipton Building Society v Bratley [2001] Q.B. 261* at 269, which establishes that "*the creditor's failure to obtain the proper value of a security which he sells reduces pro tanto the amount for which the guarantor is liable*" [. . .] But a mortgagee does not owe a duty to a tenant at will of the mortgaged property: *Raja v Austin Gray (A Firm) [2002] EWCA Civ 1965* at [55]; or a beneficiary of a trust of which the mortgagor is a trustee: *Parker-Tweedale v Dunbar Bank Plc (No.1) [1991] Ch. 12*; or the holder of an option to take a tenancy of the property: *Meretz Investments NV v ACP Ltd [2007] Ch. 197* at 293; or an unsecured creditor of the mortgagor: Burgess v Auger [1998] 2 B.C.L.C. 478 at 481H–482B, none of whom have any interest in the equity of redemption.

From the above extract it is stated that the equitable duty is not owed to a beneficial owner. He or she is not directly interested in the equity of redemption after repayment of the mortgage. His or her position is protected in equity by his or her relationship to the trustees of the legal estate, whom he or she may sue (if appropriate) for breach of trust.

Parker-Tweedale v Dunbar Bank (No 1)
[1991] Ch 12, CA[94]

Facts: Mrs Parker-Tweedale held the legal estate in the family home on trust for her husband alone. When Mr Parker-Tweedale had a car accident, the Parker-Tweedales ran into financial difficulties and their marriage broke up. The bank exercised its power of sale and Mrs Parker Tweedale agreed the sale price of £575,000. A matter of weeks later, the purchaser sold the property for £700,000. Mr Parker-Tweedale unsuccessfully sought an order to set aside the sale.

Nourse LJ

At 18

This reference to "neighbours" has enabled the plaintiff to argue that the duty is owed to all those who are within the neighbourhood principle; i.e., to adapt the words of Lord Atkin, to all persons who are so closely and directly affected by the sale that the mortgagee ought reasonably to have them in contemplation as being so affected when he is directing his mind to the sale. Further support for the application of the neighbourhood principle in this context can be gained from the judgment of Lord Denning M.R. in *Standard Chartered Bank Ltd. v. Walker* [1982] 1 W.L.R. 1410, 1415, where it was held that the duty to take reasonable care to obtain a proper price was owed to a surety for the mortgage debt as well as to the mortgagor himself.

In my respectful opinion it is both unnecessary and confusing for the duties owed by a mortgagee to the mortgagor and the surety, if there is one, to be expressed in terms of the tort of negligence. The authorities which were considered in the careful judgments of this court in *Cuckmere Brick Co. Ltd. v. Mutual Finance Ltd.* [1971] Ch. 949 demonstrate that the duty owed by the mortgagee to the mortgagor was recognised by equity as arising out of the particular relationship between them [. . .] The duty owed to the surety arises in the same way. In *China and South Sea Bank Ltd. v. Tan Soon Gin (alias George Tan)* [1990] 1 A.C. 536, Lord Templeman, in delivering the judgment of the Privy Council, having pointed out that the surety in that case admitted that the moneys secured by the guarantee were due, continued at p. 543:

> "But the surety claims that the creditor owed the surety a duty to exercise the power of sale conferred by the mortgage and in that case the liability of the surety under the guarantee would either have been eliminated or very much reduced. The Court of Appeal [in Hong Kong] sought to find such a duty in the tort of negligence but the tort of negligence has not yet subsumed all torts and does not supplant the principles of equity or contradict contractual promises [. . .] Equity intervenes to protect a surety."

Once it is recognised that the duty owed by the mortgagee to the mortgagor arises out of the particular relationship between them, it is readily apparent that there is no warrant for

---

[94] Noted at [1990] Conv 431.

extending its scope so as to include a beneficiary or beneficiaries under a trust of which the mortgagor is the trustee. The correctness of that view was fully established in the clear and compelling argument of Mr. Lloyd, who drew particular attention to the rights and duties of the trustee to protect the trust property against dissipation or depreciation in value and the impracticabilities and potential rights of double recovery inherent in giving the beneficiary an additional right to sue the mortgagee, a right which is in any event unnecessary.

The only exception for which Mr. Lloyd allowed was the special case where the trustee has unreasonably refused to sue on behalf of the trust or has committed some other breach of his duties to the beneficiaries, e.g., by consenting to an improvident sale, which disables or disqualifies him from acting on behalf of the trust. In such a case the beneficiary is permitted to sue on behalf of the trust. This exception is established by a series of authorities, some of which were recently considered by the Privy Council in *Hayim v. Citibank N.A.* [1987] A.C. 730 [. . .] It is important to emphasise that when a beneficiary sues under the exception he does so in right of the trust and in the room of the trustee. He does not enforce a right reciprocal to some duty owed directly to him by the third party.

3.2.3 The primacy of the lender's own interests

Although the lender owes a duty of good faith and of reasonable care in the conduct of the sale, the primary purpose of the power of sale is to safeguard the lender's own objective of securing repayment of the debt. As Salmon LJ pointed out in *Cuckmere Brick Co v Mutual Finance*,[95] the lender may thus choose whether and in what manner to exercise the power. In particular, the lender may choose its time of sale. The lender does not have to gauge the most opportune time to sell, nor is the lender required to wait for the market to recover, or to press ahead with a sale if prices are showing signs of falling.

For example, in the following case, the lender was not liable, although the value of the security—in this case, shares—had fallen dramatically following the collapse of the guarantor's property empire. Lord Templeman delivered the opinion of the Privy Council.

China and South Seas Bank Ltd v Tan
[1990] 1 AC 536, PC

Lord Templeman

At 545

If the creditor chose to exercise his power of sale over the mortgaged security he must sell for the current market value but the creditor must decide in his own interest if and when he should sell. [. . .]

No creditor could carry on the business of lending if he could become liable to a mortgagor and to a surety or to either of them for a decline in value of mortgaged property, unless the creditor was personally responsible for the decline [. . .] The creditor was not under a duty to exercise his power of sale over the mortgaged securities at any particular time or at all.

---

[95] [1971] Ch 949, CA.

Similarly, a lender is not obliged to improve the mortgaged property to try to maximize the sale price. A lender that goes into possession is only obliged to take reasonable steps to ensure that the property does not deteriorate in value.

Silven Properties Ltd v Royal Bank of Scotland plc
[2004] 1 WLR 997, CA

Facts: The borrower alleged that the receiver appointed by the bank to sell the mortgaged property was under a duty to maximize its value by obtaining planning permission for the development and letting some of the properties that were vacant. The receiver had explored the possibility of obtaining planning permission for some of the properties and of letting the vacant properties, but had decided to proceed to their immediate sale. The Court dismissed the borrower's allegation.

Lightman J

At [16]–[18]

The mortgagee is entitled to sell the mortgaged property as it is. He is under no obligation to improve it or increase its value. There is no obligation to take any such pre-marketing steps to increase the value of the property as is suggested by the claimants. The claimants submitted that this principle could not stand with the decision of the Privy Council in *McHugh v Union Bank of Canada* [1913] AC 299. Lord Moulton in that case, at p 312, held that, if a mortgagee does proceed with a sale of property which is unsaleable as it stands, a duty of care may be imposed on him when taking the necessary steps to render the mortgaged property saleable. The mortgage in that case was of horses, which the mortgagee needed to drive to market if he was to sell them. The mortgagee was held to owe to the mortgagor a duty to take proper care of them whilst driving them to market. The duty imposed on the mortgagee was to take care to preserve, not increase, the value of the security. The decision accordingly affords no support for the claimant's case

The mortgagee is free (in his own interest as well as that of the mortgagor) to investigate whether and how he can "unlock" the potential for an increase in value of the property mortgaged (e g by an application for planning permission or the grant of a lease) and indeed (going further) he can proceed with such an application or grant. But he is likewise free at any time to halt his efforts and proceed instead immediately with a sale. By commencing on this path the mortgagee does not in any way preclude himself from calling a halt at will: he does not assume any such obligation of care to the mortgagor in respect of its continuance as the claimants contend. If however the mortgagee is to seek to charge to the mortgagor the costs of the exercise which he has undertaken of obtaining planning permission or a lessee, subject to any applicable terms of the mortgage, the mortgagee may only be entitled to do so if he acted reasonably in incurring those costs and fairly balanced the costs of the exercise against the potential benefits taking fully into account the possibility that he might at any moment "pull the plug" on these efforts and the consequences for the mortgagor if he did so.

If the mortgagor requires protection in any of these respects, whether by imposing further duties on the mortgagee or limitations on his rights and powers, he must insist upon them when the bargain is made and upon the inclusion of protective provisions in the mortgage. In the absence of such protective provisions, the mortgagee is entitled to rest on the terms of the mortgage and (save where statute otherwise requires) the court must give effect to

> them. The one method available to the mortgagor to prevent the mortgagee exercising the rights conferred upon him by the mortgage is to redeem the mortgage. If he redeems, there can be no need or justification for recourse by the mortgagee to the power of sale to achieve repayment of the debt due to him secured by the mortgage.

As Lightman LJ observes, if the borrower wishes to protect his or her position further, a higher duty must be negotiated when agreeing the mortgage terms with the lender.[96] It is more likely that the lender may try to limit its duties by the express terms of the mortgage. But the courts have been reluctant to construe a purported limitation of liability by the lender as cutting down its duties. For example, in *Bishop v Bonham*,[97] a provision that stated that the lender could exercise its powers *'as it thought fit'* was construed as a discretion that could only operate within the constraints of good faith and reasonable care imposed by equity.

Loi explains that a lender's duties only flow from a decision to exercise their power of sale and thus they owe no duty as to when to sell.

Loi, 'Mortgagees Exercising Power of Sale: Nonfeasance, Privilege, Trusteeship and Duty of Care [2010] JBL 576 [598]

> Mortgagees do not owe a duty of care in deciding whether and when to sell but come under a specific duty of care in effecting sale because the line falls neatly along the feasance/non-feasance divide which is fundamental to private law. Until the mortgagee acts and decides to sell the property concerned, he has done nothing and comes under no duty of care. The specific duty of a selling mortgagee to take care in effecting the sale is also explicable by analogy with a selling trustee, for they both owe similar duties of case and are subject to equity's "self-dealing" and "fair dealing" rules. The existing law is also justified because it gives effect to the bargain struck between mortgagee and mortgagor. It would make no commercial sense for equity to interfere and impose a novel general duty of care which entails fettering the mortgagee's freedom to decide whether and when to sell the mortgaged asset or obtain repayment. The mortgagee has bargained for that privilege.

3.2.4 Reasonable care in the conduct of the sale

The lender is required to exercise reasonable care in the conduct of the sale. Earlier decisions refer to a need for the lender to take reasonable care to obtain a proper, fair, or true market price, but it is misleading to interpret this test as requiring the lender to attain a given valuation figure.[98] Rather, the courts, in determining liability, look to the reasonableness of the steps that the lender has taken to market the property and, in the light of these steps, to assess the price obtained against a valuation band that allows for some margin of judgment. It is only once the lender has been found to be in breach of its duty of care that the courts need to determine the price that should have been obtained, so that the damages payable to the

---

[96] For example, MCOB13.6.1 provides that, where a lender takes possession under a mortgage regulated under the FS MA, the property should be marketed as soon as possible.

[97] [1988] 1 WLR 742.   [98] See *Corbett v Halifax Building Society* [2002] 1 WLR 964.

borrower may be measured. The courts' focus is thus upon such matters as how the property was advertised or otherwise brought to the market,[99] whether a sale by auction or private treaty was more appropriate,[100] how the offer or reserve price was set,[101] how negotiations were conducted, and how the decision on the final sale price was reached.[102] In all of these steps, the advice of a suitably qualified agent will be influential in meeting the required objective standard of conduct.

Michael v Miller
[2004] 2 EGLR 151, CA

Facts: Michael's farm was mortgaged to Miller. Following Michael's default, the farm was sold for £1.625m. Michael called for an account, claiming that the farm was worth considerably more. The judge at first instance decided that the farm was worth £1.75m, but that an acceptable valuation band lay between £1.6m and £1.9m. Michael appealed unsuccessfully.

Jonathan Parker LJ

At [132]–[141]

It is a matter for the mortgagee how that general duty is to be discharged in the circumstances of any given case. Subject to any restrictions in the mortgage deed, it is for the mortgagee to decide whether the sale should be by public auction or private treaty, just as it is for him to decide how the sale should be advertised and how long the property should be left on the market. Such decisions inevitably involve an exercise of informed judgment on the part of the mortgagee, in respect of which there can, almost by definition, be no absolute requirements. Thus (as the judge recognised at p.68F of his judgment) there is no absolute duty to advertise widely. As he correctly put it (at p.69A):

> "What is proper advertisement will depend on the circumstances of the case."

Similarly, in some cases the appropriate mode of sale may be sale by public auction (in the instant case, no one has suggested that); in others, for example where there is a falling market, it may not. Moreover, a mortgagee who receives an offer in advance of an auction may have to make a judgment as to whether to accept it or whether to proceed to the auction.

The need for the mortgagee to exercise informed judgment in exercising his power of sale in turn means that a prudent mortgagee will take advice, including (where appropriate) valuation advice, from a duly qualified agent.

I turn, then, to the position of a mortgagee's agent such as Mr Hextall, whose duties included the giving of valuation advice. In my judgment, just as, applying the *Bolam* principle, a valuer will not breach his duty of care if his valuation falls within an acceptable margin of error (see, e.g., *Merivale Moore* and the *Arab Bank case*), so a mortgagee will not breach his duty to the mortgagor if in the exercise of his power to sell the mortgaged property he exercises his judgment reasonably; and to the extent that that judgment involves assessing the market value of the mortgaged property the mortgagee will have acted reasonably

---

[99] For example, *Cuckmere Brick Co Ltd v Mutual Finance Ltd* [1971] Ch 494.

[100] For example, *Tse Kwong Lam v Wong Chit Sen* [1983] 1 WLR 1349; *Alpstream AG v PK Airfinance Sarl* [2015] EWCA Civ 1318.

[101] Ibid. [102] *Michael v Miller* [2002] EWCA Civ 282.

if his assessment falls within an acceptable margin of error [. . .] I accordingly reject Mr Jourdan's submission that as a matter of principle a 'bracket' approach is inappropriate in the context of the exercise of a mortgagee's power of sale. In so far as the exercise of the mortgagee's power of sale calls for the exercise of informed judgment by the mortgagee, whether as to market conditions, or as to market value, or as to some other matter affecting the sale, the use of a bracket—or a margin of error—must in my judgment be available to the court as a means of assessing whether the mortgagee has failed to exercise that judgment reasonably.

It seems to me that Mr Jourdan's submissions on the bracket issue confuse the issue of breach of duty with the measure of damages should breach of duty be established. As Lord Hoffmann said in *Saamco* at p.221F:

> "Before I come to the facts of the individual cases, I must notice an argument advanced by the defendants concerning the calculation of damages. They say that the damage falling within the scope of the duty should not be the loss which flows from the valuation having been in excess of the true value but should be limited to the excess over the highest valuation which would not have been negligent. This seems to me to confuse the standard of care with the question of the damage which falls within the scope of the duty. The valuer is not liable unless he is negligent. In deciding whether or not he has been negligent, the court must bear in mind that valuation is seldom an exact science and that within a band of figures valuers may differ without one of them being negligent. But once the valuer has been found to have been negligent, the loss for which he is responsible is that which has been caused by the valuation being wrong. For this purpose the court must form a view as to what a correct valuation would have been. This means the figure which it considers most likely that a reasonable valuer, using the information available at the relevant date, would have put forward as the amount which the property was most likely to fetch if sold upon the open market. While it is true that there would have been a range of figures which the reasonable valuer might have put forward, the figure most likely to have been put forward would have been the mean figure of that range. There is no basis for calculating damages upon the basis that it would have been a figure at one or other extreme of the range. Either of these would have been less likely than the mean [. . .]"

In the instant case the judge took the, to my mind, somewhat unsatisfactory course of deciding first what was the market value of the Estate at the relevant time (concluding that it was £1.75M) and then asking himself whether the respondents, through Mr Hextall, were negligent in achieving a price substantially less than that. The judge's approach might perhaps be appropriate in a case where the mortgagee accepts the first offer that he receives, without the property having been exposed to the market at all. In such a case, the likelihood is that the only evidence of 'market value' will be expert valuation evidence. But where, as in the instant case, the property has been exposed to the market and a number of genuine offers have been received, the more logical approach (to my mind) is to start by considering the steps which the mortgagee took to sell the property and then to consider whether, in all the circumstances, the mortgagee acted reasonably in accepting the purchaser's offer and contracting to sell the property at that price.

3.2.5 The duty of good faith

A lender must exercise the power of sale in good faith. The impact of this requirement is most obvious where the lender is selling to a connected party, when there is a conflict of interest, and where the lender's motive for selling is improper.

A mortgagee cannot sell to itself, or to a trustee or agent acting on its behalf. In the words of Lindley LJ in *Farrars v Farrars Ltd*,[103] '[a] *sale by a person to himself is no sale at all'*. The lender can sell to a company or other organization in which it is interested, or to a person with whom it is connected, but, if the lender does so, the court will scrutinize the lender's conduct to ensure that reasonable care has been taken.[104] Nevertheless, the court should not treat the lender as a special purchaser required to pay over the market price to establish their bona fides.[105] In the Hong Kong case of *Tse Kwong Lam v Wong Chit Sen*,[106] Lord Templeman, giving the opinion of the Privy Council, stated that '*the sale must be closely examined and a heavy onus lies on the mortgagee to show that in all respects he acted fairly to the borrower and used his best endeavours to obtain the best price reasonably obtainable for the mortgaged property'.*

The case itself provides a useful example. The respondent exercised his power of sale by putting the mortgaged property up for auction. The auction was only advertised very shortly before it was conducted and only limited details were provided. A reserve price was fixed, but without the guidance of a qualified valuer. At the auction, only one bid at the reserve price was made—by the respondent's wife, acting on behalf of a company owned by the respondent and his family. The Privy Council held that, although the respondent was free to sell to a company in which he was interested, he had failed to demonstrate that he had taken reasonable care in the conduct of the sale. An auction was not necessarily the most appropriate mode of sale. The mortgagee should have sought the advice of a suitably qualified expert both as to the mode of sale, and, if the property was to be auctioned, regarding the reserve price and appropriate marketing.

A lender's motives may also affect its bona fides. In *Quennell v Maltby*,[107] we saw that the right to take possession must not be exercised for an ulterior motive. Likewise, the power of sale must be exercised with a view to discharging the mortgage debt. In *Downsview Nominees Ltd v First City Corp Ltd*,[108] in which receivers were appointed purely to frustrate the exercise of a second mortgagee's powers, there was '*overwhelming evidence that the receivership of the second defendant was inspired by him for an improper purpose and carried on in bad faith, verging on fraud'*. Mixed motives will not, however, breach the mortgagee's duties, provided that one of those motives was to recover the debt.[109]

3.2.6 Remedies and the position of purchasers

What action can a borrower take if a lender is in breach of its duties? He or she may either seek an order setting aside the sale, or an order for an account requiring the lender to account for what ought to have been received to compensate the borrower for any shortfall in the purchase price for which the lender is responsible.

An order for an account will be the usual course where the lender has fallen short of the objective standard of care which has resulted in a shortfall in the price that ought to have been received if reasonable care had been exercised. If there is no shortfall, despite suggestions

---

[103] (1889) 40 Ch D 395, 409.

[104] *Mortgage Express v Mardner* [2004] EWCA Civ 1859; *Bradford & Bingley plc v Ross* [2005] EWCA Civ 394.

[105] *Alpstream AG v PK Airfinance Sarl* [2015] EWCA Civ 1318.   [106] [1983] 1 WLR 1349, 1355.

[107] [1979] 1 WLR 318.   [108] [1993] AC 295, 317.

[109] *Meretz Investment NV v ACP Ltd* [2007] EWCA Civ 303, [2008] Ch 244.

of a lack of care, the lender is not liable.[110] An order to set aside the sale will not be available where the lender has merely sold at an undervalue; there must be some impropriety. The court has discretion to set aside the sale and a court will not do so if there has been an unwarranted delay,[111] or if to do so would cause unnecessary hardship.[112] Furthermore, the position of the purchaser, against whom the sale is to be set aside, must also be considered.

Section 104 of the LPA 1925 provides some protection.

Law of Property Act 1925, s 104

Conveyance on sale

1. A mortgagee exercising the power of sale conferred by this Act shall have power, by deed, to convey the property sold, for such estate and interest therein as he is by this Act authorised to sell or convey or may be the subject of the mortgage, freed from all estates, interest, and rights to which the mortgage has priority, but subject to all estates, interests, and rights which have priority to the mortgage.

2. Where a conveyance is made in exercise of the power of sale conferred by this Act, or any enactment replaced by this Act, the title of the purchaser shall not be impeachable on the ground:

   (a) that no case had arisen to authorise the sale; or

   (b) that due notice was not given; or

   (c) where the mortgage is made after the commencement of this Act, that leave of the court when so required, was not obtained; or

   (d) whether the mortgage was made before or after such commencement, that the power was otherwise improperly or irregularly exercise;

   and a purchaser is not, either before or on conveyance concerned to see or inquire whether a case has arisen to authorise the sale, or due notice has been given, or the power is otherwise properly and regularly exercised; but any person damnified by an unauthorised or improper, or irregular exercise of the power shall have his remedy in damages against the person exercising the power.

The extent of this protection is limited. It relieves the purchaser from making enquiries as to whether an event of default has occurred to trigger the exercise of a power of sale, but does not protect the purchaser if he or she has actual notice of the impropriety:

Corbett v Halifax Building Society
[2003] 1 WLR 964, CA

Facts: Although it was contrary to his terms of employment, an employee of the Halifax purchased, though his uncle, a repossessed property from his employer at a sum that the court found to be an undervalue. The Halifax was unaware of its employee's participation in the sale. The borrowers unsuccessfully applied to set aside the sale.

---

[110] *Alpstream AG v PK Airfinance Sarl* [2015] EWCA Civ 1318.

[111] See *Tse Kwong Lam v Wong Chit Sen* [1983] 1 WLR 1349.

[112] *Corbett v Halifax Building Society* [2002] EWCA Civ 1849, [2003] 1 WLR 964.

Pumfrey J

At [25]–[26]

Between contract and completion, the position is described in *Lord Waring v London and Manchester Assurance Co Ltd* [1935] Ch 310, 318–319 where in a passage subsequently approved by the Court of Appeal in *Property and Bloodstock Ltd v Emerton* [1968] Ch 94, Crossman J said:

> "The only effect of the conveyance is to put the legal estate entirely in the purchaser: that follows from section 104, subsection (1), of the Law of Property Act 1925, which provides that a mortgagee shall have power to convey the legal estate; and the whole legal estate can be conveyed free from all estates, interests, and rights to which the mortgage has priority. Section 104, subsection (2), upon which also counsel for the plaintiff relied, does not seem to me to affect the question at all. Its purpose is simply to protect the purchaser and to make it unnecessary for him, pending completion and during investigation of title, to ascertain whether the power of sale has become exercisable. Of course, if the purchaser becomes aware, during that period, of any facts showing that the power of sale is not exercisable, or that there is some impropriety in the sale, then, in my judgment, he gets no good title on taking the conveyance. The result in the present case is, in my judgment, that the sale effected by the contract, assuming, for the moment, that there is no objection to it on any other ground, binds the plaintiff, and that it is too late after the sale for him to tender the mortgage money and become entitled to have the property reconveyed to him [. . .]"

It would seem to follow from this that a completed sale by a mortgagee is not liable to be set aside merely because it takes place at an undervalue. Impropriety is a prerequisite, and section 104(2) makes it clear that the purchaser is not protected if he has actual knowledge of the impropriety. But if the purchaser has no notice of the impropriety, then on the face of it he takes free. Thus, the completed sale by a mortgagee pursuant to his statutory power is vulnerable only if the purchaser has knowledge of, or participates in, an impropriety in the exercise of the power.

The Halifax was bona fide throughout; it was its employee, acting without its knowledge, who was acting improperly. Although the Halifax had sold at an undervalue, a mere undervalue was insufficient to set a sale aside; there had to have been impropriety.

Section 104 will also not assist a purchaser of unregistered land where the lender has no power of sale, for example, because the mortgage is invalid or contains no adequate power of sale, or because any power that there is has not arisen. The lender is acting beyond its powers and any sale is ultra vires.

Where the land is registered and the lender is selling under a registered charge, the provisions of s 52 of the Land Registration Act 2002 (LRA 2002) must be considered.

Land Registration Act 2002, s 52

Protection of disponees

1. Subject to any entry in the register to the contrary, the proprietor of a registered charge is to be taken to have, in relation to the property subject to the charge, the powers of disposition conferred by law on the owner of a legal mortgage.

2. Subsection (1) has effect only for the purpose of preventing the title of a disponee being questioned (and so does not affect the lawfulness of a disposition).

A purchaser may thus assume that a registered chargee enjoys all of the powers of a legal mortgagee unless a restriction is registered, giving notice that these powers have been restricted. As we have noted, the power of sale under s 101(1)(i) of the LPA 1925 must have arisen, because the mortgage money is due, before it can become exercisable. It is thought that the power of sale must have arisen before a purchaser can take advantage of the protection afforded by s 52 of the LRA 2002. The section provides protection to a purchaser where the sale is within the powers of the lender (i.e. intra vires), but is actionable by the borrower because the power has not yet become exercisable or is liable to be set aside (e.g. for impropriety). In these circumstances, there remains the possibility that a purchaser who is implicated in, or has knowledge of, a breach of the mortgagee's equitable duties may be liable as a constructive trustee on the basis of knowing receipt.[113]

4 APPOINTMENT OF A RECEIVER

The implied power to appoint a receiver of the mortgaged land when the mortgage money has become due is conferred by s 101(1)(iii) of the LPA 1925 into all mortgages created by deed, including a legal charge by way of mortgage. The appointment of a receiver provides an attractive option for a lender under a mortgage of commercial property, because a lender can avoid personal liability for wilful default or for breach of duty if the property is sold. The remedy is utilized in buy-to-let mortgages where a legal charge of land owned by a company is coupled with a floating charge over all of the assets and undertakings of a company when the lender may appoint either an administrative receiver or administrator to take over the effective running of the company in the event of its insolvency.[114]

4.1 FUNCTIONS AND POWERS OF A RECEIVER

Section 109 of the LPA 1925 provides that a receiver may be appointed or removed by written notice, whereupon the receiver is entitled to enter into possession of the property to preserve the security and to collect any income that may be applied, after payment of any costs and expenses including the receiver's remuneration, in the repayment of the interest due, with any balance being payable to the borrower or the person next entitled to the equity of redemption. A receiver may also be appointed pursuant to an express power conferred by the mortgage. A mortgage will also invariably grant express powers to a receiver to manage and sell the property. By appointing a receiver, a lender can thus indirectly enforce the legal charge.

Section 109 contains the implied terms that govern the appointment of a receiver under s 101(1)(iii) of the Act.

---

[113] See Chapter 17, section 6.3.2.

[114] A floating charge entered into prior to 15 September 2003 may contain an express right to appoint an administrative receiver over all of the assets and undertakings of the company. By s 72A of the Insolvency Act 2006, a lender is no longer entitled to appoint an administrative receiver, but may appoint an administrator. The distinction between an 'administrative receiver' and an 'administrator' is that an administrative receiver owes duties only to the secured lender and the borrower, whilst an administrator's duties extend to all of the creditors of the company, both secured and unsecured.

Law of Property Act 1925, s 109

Appointment, power, remuneration and duties of a receiver

1. A mortgagee entitled to appoint a receiver under the power in that behalf conferred by this Act shall not appoint a receiver until he has become entitled to exercise the power of sale conferred by this Act, but may then, by writing under his hand, appoint such person as he thinks fit to be receiver.

2. A receiver appointed under the powers conferred by this Act, or any enactment replaced by this Act, shall be deemed to be the agent of the mortgagor; and the mortgagor shall be solely responsible for the receiver's acts or defaults unless the mortgage deed otherwise provides.

3. The receiver shall have power to demand and recover all the income of which he is appointed receiver, by action, distress, or otherwise, in the name either of the mortgagor or of the mortgagee, to the full extent of the estate or interest which the mortgagor could dispose of, and to give effectual receipts accordingly for the same, and to exercise any powers which may have been delegated to him by the mortgagee pursuant to this Act.

4. A person paying money to the receiver shall not be concerned to inquire whether any case has happened to authorise the receiver to act.

5. The receiver may be removed, and a new receiver may be appointed, from time to time by the mortgagee by writing under his hand.

6. The receiver shall be entitled to retain out of any money received by him, for his remuneration, and in satisfaction of all costs, charges, and expenses incurred by him as receiver, a commission at such rate, not exceeding five per centum on the gross amount of all money received, as is specified in his appointment, and if no rate is so specified, then at the rate of five per centum on that gross amount, or at such other rate as the court thinks fit to allow, on application made by him for that purpose.

4.2 RECEIVER AS AGENT FOR THE BORROWER

A lender is able to avoid personal liability by appointing a receiver, because the receiver is expressed to be the agent of the borrower, although appointed by and taking directions from the lender. A receiver thus owes duties both to the lender and the borrower, creating a rather unusual triangular relationship. In effect, by entering into the legal charge, the borrower empowers the lender to appoint the receiver as the borrower's agent in applying the income from the property, and (where express power is granted) to sell and apply the proceeds of sale in the discharge of the mortgage debt.

Silven Properties Ltd v Royal Bank of Scotland plc
[2004] 1 WLR 997, CA

Lightman J

At [27]–[28]

The peculiar incidents of the agency are significant. In particular: (1) the agency is one where the principal, the mortgagor, has no say in the appointment or identity of the receiver and is not entitled to give any instructions to the receiver or to dismiss the receiver. In the words of Rigby LJ in *Gaskell v Gosling* [1896] 1 QB 669, 692: "For valuable consideration he has committed the management of his property to an attorney whose appointment he cannot interfere with"; (2) there is no contractual relationship or duty owed in tort by the receiver to the mortgagor: the relationship and duties owed by the receiver are equitable only: see *Medforth v Blake* [2000] Ch 86 and *Raja v Austin Gray* [2003] 1 EGLR 91; (3) the equitable duty is owed to the mortgagee as well as the mortgagor. The relationship created by the mortgage is tripartite involving the mortgagor, the mortgagee and the receiver; (4) the duty owed by the receiver (like the duty owed by a mortgagee) to the mortgagor is not owed to him individually but to him as one of the persons interested in the equity of redemption. The class character of the right is reflected in the class character of the relief to be granted in case of a breach of this duty. That relief is an order that the receiver account to the persons interested in the equity of redemption for what he would have held as receiver but for his default; (5) not merely does the receiver owe a duty of care to the mortgagee as well as the mortgagor, but his primary duty in exercising his powers of management is to try and bring about a situation in which the secured debt is repaid: see the *Medforth case* at p 86; and (6) the receiver is not managing the mortgagor's property for the benefit of the mortgagor, but the security, the property of the mortgagee, for the benefit of the mortgagee: see *In re B Johnson & Co (Builders) Ltd* [1955] Ch 634, 661, per Jenkins LJ cited with approval by Lord Templeman in *Downsview Nominees Ltd v First City Corpn Ltd* [1993] AC 295, 313b, and [1955] Ch 634, 646, per Evershed MR cited with approval by Sir Richard Scott V-C in the *Medforth case* [2000] Ch 86, 95h-96a. His powers of management are really ancillary to that duty: *Gomba Holdings UK Ltd v Homan* [1986] 1 WLR 1301, 1305, per Hoffmann J.

In the context of a relationship such at the present, which is no ordinary agency and is primarily a device to protect the mortgagee, general agency principles are of limited assistance in identifying the duties owed by the receiver to the mortgagor: see *Gomba Holdings UK Ltd v Homan* at 1305b-d (Hoffmann J) and *Gomba Holdings UK Ltd v Minories Finance Ltd* [1988] 1 WLR 1231, 1233d-h (Fox LJ). The core duty of the receiver to account to the mortgagor subsists, but (for example) the mortgagor has no unrestricted right of access to receivership documents. The mortgage confers upon the mortgagee a direct and indirect means of securing a sale in order to achieve repayment of his secured debt. The mortgagee can sell as mortgagee and the mortgagee can appoint a receiver who likewise can sell in the name of the mortgagor. Having regard to the fact that the receiver's primary duty is to bring about a situation where the secured debt is repaid, as a matter of principle the receiver must be entitled (like the mortgagee) to sell the property in the condition in which it is in the same way as the mortgagee can and in particular without awaiting or effecting any increase in value or improvement in the property [. . .]

In practice, a receiver, before accepting an appointment, will invariably require an indemnity from the lender against any personal liability that the receiver may incur. Nevertheless, the appointment of receiver is an attractive and popular power available to a lender where the lender anticipates that a sale may not immediately follow the taking of possession, or the property will need to be managed prior to sale: for example, because it is tenanted or is used for business purposes.

4.3 DUTIES OF A RECEIVER

In *Downsview Nominees v First City Corp*,[115] the Privy Council had decided that a receiver owed the similar equitable (not tortious) duties to act bona fide and with reasonable care in the conduct of any sale as a mortgagee. But a receiver's role is rather different from that of a mortgagee: a receiver is given powers to manage the property, including (where a floating charge is granted over the borrower's business assets) any business that may be conducted on the land. As a result, their position needs to be distinguished as Loi explains.

Loi, 'Receiver's Power of Sale and Duty of Care' [2010] Conv 369 [389]

Whenever a person sells assets which do not belong absolutely to him, he must take reasonable steps to obtain a proper price or the market price available. This rule is a general principle of property law which, like the nonfeasance rule, is fundamental to English private law. It is not restricted to mortgagees or receivers selling mortgaged assets; and applies to bailees, agents and trustees, as well as to liquidators and administrators, when disposing of assets in which bailors, principals, beneficiaries and insolvent companies have a proprietary interest. Justice and rationality require that like cases be treated alike. There is nothing to differentiate receivers from all these other categories of persons. This is the basis of receivers' duty to take reasonable steps to obtain a proper price in effecting a sale: the receivers are selling assets which do not belong entirely to them.

However, whilst the nonfeasance rule may explain the law in relation to mortgagees simpliciter, receivership requires a different explanation because of contextual differences. Receivers are not appointed to do nothing and they are not entitled to remain entirely passive. Upon appointment, receivers assume control and take possession of mortgaged assets to the exclusion of the mortgagor. By assuming control and taking possession of mortgaged assets which may encompass the mortgagor's business (or even substantially the whole undertaking of corporate mortgagors in the case of administrative receivers), receivers have actively assumed management thereof. Such receivers are akin to mortgagees in possession (rather than mortgagees simpliciter) and come under a similar duty to manage the mortgaged assets with due diligence. Like mortgagees in possession, such receivers can no longer claim to have done nothing, and can no longer rely on the nonfeasance rule to exclude duty.

Yet, receivers are generally not liable to mortgagors even if their decision whether or when to sell mortgaged assets were to cause loss to mortgagors. This is because although they owe mortgagors a *duty* to manage the mortgaged assets with reasonable care, the *standard* of care expected of them is calibrated against their *overriding duty* to the mortgagee to bring about repayment of the mortgagor's secured debt. Thus, the receivers' decision whether or when to sell will be reasonable and the receivers will not be liable to the mortgagor for breach of duty even if loss accrues to the mortgagor; *provided* the decision was reasonably necessitated by the purpose of bringing about repayment of the mortgaged debt. In this respect, mortgagors are not entitled to expect receivers to *delay* a sale and wait for the mortgaged assets to appreciate in value, since the mortgagee is entitled to be paid without further delay and without taking any speculative market risks. Neither are mortgagors entitled to expect receivers to *expedite* a sale merely because the mortgagors *speculate* that mortgaged

---

[115] [1993] AC 295. See also *Yorkshire Bank plc v Hall* [1999] 1 WLR 1713.

assets will depreciate in value. Furthermore, courts will not readily impugn as unreasonable a receiver's decision whether or when to sell, since that is a priori a business decision for the receiver, except in unusual circumstances.

However, there could be exceptional circumstances in which receivers will more likely be held to have breached their duty. Such circumstances will be rare and exceptionally clear-cut; for example, where receivers inexplicably fail to sell mortgaged perishable goods timeously before they deteriorate in quality and value. In such a case, the receivers' decision can hardly be said to have been reasonably necessitated by the overriding duty to obtain repayment for the mortgagee, will not be regarded as reasonable in the circumstances, and will likely amount to a breach of the receivers' duty of care to both mortgagee and mortgagor [. . .]

Beyond the aforementioned, there is no principle upon which receivers could be made generally liable to mortgagors for their decision whether or when to sell mortgaged assets. It remains to be said that just because mortgagors cannot in principle complain about the receiver's choice whether or when to sell, their position is not as dire as it may appear at first glance. By statute [section 91 LPA 1925], a mortgagor who takes the view that mortgaged assets should be sold without delay may apply to court, which has a judicial discretion whether to compel a sale. If a mortgagor does not wish to help himself by availing himself of the statutory remedy, it is difficult to see why others—such as a receiver—should be *required* to do anything more.

The following case demonstrates the duties of a receiver in managing the mortgaged property that Loi explains.

Medforth v Blake
[2000] Ch 86, CA

Facts: Medforth was a pig farmer. When he ran into financial difficulties, Blake was appointed a receiver and manager under the terms of charges secured over the business. In running the business, Blake incurred losses and Medforth successfully claimed that his failure to obtain discounts on bulk purchases of pig feed had contributed to those losses, for which he should be liable to account.

Sir Richard Scott VC

At 98

The *Cuckmere Brick case* test can impose liability on a mortgagee notwithstanding the absence of fraud or mala fides. It follows from the *Downsview Nominees case* and *Yorkshire Bank Plc. v. Hall* that a receiver/manager who sells but fails to take reasonable care to obtain a proper price may incur liability notwithstanding the absence of fraud or mala fides. Why should the approach be any different if what is under review is not the conduct of a sale but conduct in carrying on a business? If a receiver exercises this power, why does not a specific duty, corresponding to the duty to take reasonable steps to obtain a proper price, arise? If the business is being carried on by a mortgagee, the mortgagee will be liable, as a mortgagee in possession, for loss caused by his failure to do so with due diligence. Why should not the receiver/manager, who, as Lord Templeman held, owes the same specific duties as the mortgagee when selling, owe comparable specific duties when conducting the mortgaged business? It may be that the particularly onerous duties constructed by courts of equity for mortgagees in possession would not be appropriate to apply to a receiver. But, no duties at all save a duty of good faith? That does not seem to me to make commercial sense nor, more importantly, to correspond with the principles expressed in the bulk of the authorities. [. . .] In my judgment, in principle and on the authorities, the following propositions can be stated. (1) A receiver managing mortgaged property owes duties to the mortgagor and anyone else with an interest in the equity of redemption. (2) The duties include, but are not necessarily confined to, a duty of good faith. (3) The extent and scope of any duty additional to that of good faith will depend on the facts and circumstances of the particular case. (4) In exercising his powers of management the primary duty of the receiver is to try and bring about a situation in which interest on the secured debt can be paid and the debt itself repaid. (5) Subject to that primary duty, the receiver owes a duty to manage the property with due diligence. (6) Due diligence does not oblige the receiver to continue to carry on a business on the mortgaged premises previously carried on by the mortgagor. (7) If the receiver does carry on a business on the mortgaged premises, due diligence requires reasonable steps to be taken in order to try to do so profitably.

By contrast, in the following case, the unique features of a receiver's agency led the court to reject a receiver's duty to the borrower to present the property for sale in its most advantageous condition.

Silven Properties Ltd v Royal Bank of Scotland plc
[2004] 1 WLR 997, CA

Lightman J

At [29]

[. . .] [B]y accepting office as receivers of the claimant's properties the receivers assumed a fiduciary duty of care to the bank, the claimants and all (if any) others interested in the equity of redemption. This accords with the statement of principle to this effect of Lord Browne-Wilkinson in *Henderson v Merrett Syndicates Ltd* [1995] 2 AC 145, 205e-h relied on by the claimants. The appointment of the receivers as agents of the claimants having regard to the special character of the agency does not affect the scope or the content of the fiduciary duty. The scope or content of the duty must depend on and reflect the special nature of the relationship between the bank, the claimants and the receivers arising under the terms of the mortgages and the appointments of the receivers, and in particular the role of the receivers in securing repayment of the secured debt and the primacy of their obligations in this regard to the bank. These circumstances preclude the assumption by, or imposition on, the receivers of the obligation to take the pre-marketing steps for which the claimants contend in this action. Further no such obligation could arise in their case (any more than in the case of the bank) from the steps which they took to investigate and (for a period) to proceed with applications for planning permission. The receivers were at all times free (as was the bank) to halt those steps and exercise their right to proceed with an immediate sale of the mortgaged properties as they were.

5 A FINAL WORD ABOUT THE COVENANT TO REPAY

Possession, sale, and appointment of a receiver are all proprietary remedies flowing from the security created by the legal charge by way of mortgage, but it should not be forgotten that the borrower is under a personal contractual liability to repay the loan in accordance with the terms of the loan agreement. A term for repayment of the capital of the loan will be implied in the absence of an express term.[116] This liability is independent of the security and will remain where there is a shortfall after the lender or receiver has sold the property. Thus, where there is negative equity, a borrower may be sued by the lender for the balance that remains owing after the sale proceeds have been applied in repayment. In enforcing that judgment, the lender is in no better position than any other unsecured creditor and may be forced to make the borrower bankrupt.

In suing upon the personal covenant to repay, the lender must bear in mind the relevant limitation periods. The recovery of interest is statute-barred six years[117] after becoming due and the capital, as a debt payable by deed, cannot be recovered after twelve years from the date upon which it became due.[118] The exercise by the lender of its power of sale does not affect these periods.[119]

QUESTIONS

1. Is it satisfactory that the lender has an immediate right to possession, or do the existing qualifications to this right provide adequate safeguards?

2. Compare the different approaches to the width of the courts' discretion under s 36 of the Administration of Justice Act 1936 that were taken in *Cheltenham & Gloucester Building Society v Norgan* and *Bristol & West Building Society v Ellis*. Do you think that the courts' approach in both cases is consistent?

3. Why would a borrower wish to apply to court for an order for sale under s 91 of the Law of Property Act 1925? When is a court likely to be sympathetic to such an application?

4. A lender's duties, in exercise of its power of sale, arise in equity rather than in tort, but what consequences flow as a result?

5. In exercise of its power of sale, a lender has a duty to obtain a proper market price. What does this mean and what would you advise a lender to do in order to fulfil this duty?

6. In what circumstances could a borrower successfully apply to set aside a sale made by a lender?

7. Contrast the duties expected of a lender and a receiver that they may appoint.

For guidance on how to answer these questions visit the online resources at www.oup.com/uk/mcfarlane4e/.

---

[116] *West Bromwich Building Society v Wilkinson* [2005] 1 WLR 2303.

[117] Limitation Act 1980, s 20(5).

[118] Ibid, s 20(1), but see MCOB 13.6.1 and 13.6.2, which effectively reduce the period to six years where the mortgage is regulated.

[119] *West Bromwich Building Society v Wilkinson* [2005] 1 WLR 2303.

FURTHER READING

Bright and Whitehouse, 'Information, Advice and Representation in Housing Possession Cases' (Universities of Oxford and Hull 2014)

Dixon, 'Sorry We've Sold Your Home: Mortgagees and Their Possessory Rights' (1999) 58 CLJ 281

Frisby, 'Making a Silk Purse Out of a Pigs Ear: *Medforth v Blake*' (2000) 63 MLR 413

Haley, 'Mortgage Default: Possession, Relief and Judicial Discretion' (1997) 17 LS 483

Loi, 'Mortgagees Exercising Power of Sale: Nonfeasance, Privilege, Trusteeship and Duty of Care' [2010] JBL 576

Loi, 'Receiver's Power of Sale and Duty of Care' [2010] Conv 369

McMurtry, 'Mortgage Default and Repossession: Procedure and Policy in the Post-*Norgan* Era' (2007) 58 NILQR 194

Nield, 'Mortgage Market Review: Hardwired Commonsense?' [2015] Consumer Law and Policy, [2015] Consumer Law and Policy on line 15 March 2015

Wallace, ' "Feeling Like I'm Doing it on My Own": Examining the Synchronicity between Policy Responses and the Circumstances and Experiences of Mortgage Borrowers in Arrears' (2012) 11 Social Policy and Society 117

27

PROTECTION OF THE BORROWER

CENTRAL ISSUES

1. Protection of borrowers operates through a number of mechanisms. Regulation of the credit market seeks to ensure that lenders treat borrowers fairly. In addition, direct duties operate to try and protect borrowers against unfairness in the creation and operation of the mortgage transaction and substantive unfairness of the mortgage terms. The level of protection differs according to the nature of the borrower and the type of security transaction.

2. The home mortgage market is regulated through the Financial Services and Markets Act 2000 and the Consumer Credit Act 1974, following principles of decentred regulation to encourage responsible lending and responsible borrowing.

3. A mortgage may be set aside because of procedural unfairness. There are a number of doctrines that underpin procedural fairness, including duress, undue influence, misrepresentation, and unconscionable bargain. Undue influence has been employed to try to ensure the procedural fairness of collateral mortgages over the family home to secure a business loan.

4. The control of mortgage terms seeks to balance the freedom of the parties to contract against a concern that borrowers' financial situation makes them vulnerable to exploitation.

5. Equitable protection has been provided by controls against penalties, and oppressive and unconscionable terms, as well as by protection of the borrower's equity of redemption.

6. Statutory consumer protection now provides additional protection to domestic borrowers.

1 INTRODUCTION

In Chapter 26 we consider the protection afforded to a borrower where the lender enforces its rights and remedies under the mortgage itself. In this chapter, we will be concentrating on the general protections afforded to the borrower, who is often considered to be the more vulnerable party. In modern commercial lending, that is not always the case where the borrower is a profitable company, the liquidity of which is maintained with the assistance of an overdraft facility from its bankers, or which requires finance to fund the expansion of its flourishing business. Such companies can not only source the most competitive terms from financiers, but can also afford the services of lawyers and other advisers to ensure that their position is protected. Other companies may not be so fortunate if they are small and struggling to start a business, or to maintain profitability in a competitive marketplace. They may have few assets to offer as security and may be only able to obtain finance if their directors or shareholders are prepared to offer their personal assets as security.

In the domestic lending market, a distinction needs to be drawn between those who wish to use their earning power to buy a home, and the individual who is in financial difficulties and needs to raise money or consolidate his or her immediate liabilities. The former will be able to choose from a number of mainstream banks and building societies, which are prepared to offer competitive terms because the risk of default is low. The borrower's earnings will meet the instalment repayments and the loan, in any event, will be secured against a property. This type of borrower is only likely to be exposed either from an unanticipated rise in interest rates, or from an unforeseen decline in his or her earnings or the housing market. The borrower who is in urgent need of funds is the most vulnerable. These borrowers are also unlikely to have the luxury of choice or to have the strength of bargaining position to negotiate terms.

This diversity in types of borrower and the circumstances in which they require funds leads to a need to draw distinctions in the appropriate controls. Whitehouse has noted that mortgage law itself has changed little over the decades but has managed to accommodate changes in the socio-economic context in which it operates by looking to other methods of control.

Whitehouse, 'A Longitudinal Analysis of the Mortgage Repossession Process 1995–2010: Stability, Regulation and Reform' in *Modern Studies in Property Law Vol 6* (ed Bright, 2011, p 151)

The English law of mortgage is remarkable [. . .] Its stubborn retention of archaic terms and concepts operate in sharp contrast to the ever changing world of finance which it inhabits. Most impressive of all, however, is its capacity for stability in the face of fundamental shifts in the socio-economic context, to put the legal device of the mortgage to new uses without the need to alter its fundamental doctrinal characteristics. The stability apparent within the law of mortgage [. . .] derives from a concern to establish requirements as to formality and procedure, leaving much of substance of the mortgage relationship to be 'regulated' through more malleable processes such as contractual 'negotiation', 'discretion' and 'soft law.'

The measures that we will need to examine in this chapter fall into a number of categories. We will first consider the legal regulation of the home loan and consumer credit market, which has grown considerably in recent years. We will then consider the protection afforded to the borrower in the creation of the mortgage. We will briefly consider the common vitiating factors that may lead to the avoidance of a mortgage, before examining the application of undue influence to collateral mortgages of the family home to secure a business loan. Finally, controls over the terms of the mortgage itself must be considered. Here the traditional concern of equity to guard against oppressive or unconscionable terms has been supplemented in the consumer context with an array of statutory and regulatory controls.

2 MARKET REGULATION

Recent decades have seen significant changes in the domestic mortgage market and its regulation. Building societies, once the predominate source of home finance, were deregulated during the 1990s triggering a wave of building society demutualizations and mergers. In this process larger building societies converted to become banks. Other high street banks and lenders also entered into the lucrative home mortgage market. This increased competition saw a dramatic rise in the availability of credit to fund home ownership and other consumer expenditure, which suffered an equally dramatic decline with the global financial crisis of 2007/2008. The financial system has stabilized and confidence has returned with a resultant rise in both commercial and domestic lending and signs of economic and property market recovery. This stabilization was only achieved with considerable Government support of vulnerable banks and other measures to encourage lending. There has followed an intense period of financial regulatory reform, at both national and international levels, to reduce the risk of future financial instability.

In the context of the promotion of private home ownership, Whitehouse has noted the rise in regulation of mortgages through market forces.

Whitehouse, 'The Homeowner: Citizen or Consumer?' in *Land Law: Themes and Perspectives* (eds Bright and Dewar, 1998, p 189)

[. . .] [T]he promotion of home-ownership has allowed central government to replace direct state intervention with the regulation offered by the market system. The private contractual basis of mortgage finance makes it eminently suitable for regulation by the market. Because of the varied types of accommodation available within the owner-occupied sector and the wide range of mortgagees willing to offer different types of mortgage products, the state could reduce its intervention within the housing system and allow market forces to regulate the activities of mortgagors and mortgagees.

The justification for the reduction in direct state intervention within the housing system is based upon an 'idealistic' view of consumerism which extols the benefits of market forces as the guardians of choice, competition, and accountability. The shift in emphasis away from citizenship and towards consumerism may seem uncontroversial, particularly as the term consumer is often combined with concepts of 'rights', 'protection', and 'legislation'. The rhetoric of consumerism implies that, where the market fails to provide a sufficient degree of choice and accountability, the state will intervene, on the consumer's behalf, by implementing legislation which corrects the failings in the market. The 'protection' afforded to homeowners, therefore is claimed to derive from a combination of market regulation and direct legal intervention [. . .]

At the time that Whitehouse was writing, the market was largely self-regulated. The Council of Mortgage Lenders, the influential trade organization of lending institutions within the residential mortgage market, had a Statement of Practice to which its members were expected to adhere. The Consumer Credit Act 1974 (CCA)[1] regulated consumer credit under the auspices of the Office of Fair Trading (OFT) but its major focus is unsecured credit provided, for instance, by credit cards, hire purchase, and pay-day loans. It also regulated

---

[1] The CCA 1974 was subject to major amendment by the Consumer Credit Act 2006.

secured loans but only where the loan did not exceed £25,000—a limit that became increasingly irrelevant as property prices increased.

The picture has and is continuing to change with what has been termed a 'decentred regulatory approach'[2] to the mortgage market under the auspices of a single financial services regulator responsible for the conduct of mortgage business. Initially this was the Financial Services Authority (FSA), but is now the Financial Conduct Authority (FCA), under the Financial Services and Markets Act 2000 (FSMA).[3] The FCA shares primary responsibility for financial services regulation with the Prudential Conduct Authority (PRA). Under this twin peaks model of financial regulation, the FCA regulates the way in which financial service providers, including lenders, conduct their business and the PRA regulates the financial stability of banks under the auspices of the Bank of England.

The mortgage regulatory net of the FSMA was initially cast, from 31 October 2004, over first legal charges secured on the home. Home purchase plans[4] and home reversion plans,[5] followed from 6 April 2007 and, after considerable disquiet over the operation of sale and leaseback transactions, they too became subject to FSMA regulation in 2009. Responsibility for the regulation of consumer credit moved from the OFT to the FCA in 2014 and in 2016, as a result of the Mortgage Credit Directive,[6] all lending secured by a second or subsequent charge over a dwelling house as well as certain buy-to-let mortgages became subject to the FSMA.

The decentred regulatory approach of the FSMA moves away from traditional command and control rules to general principles (although backed up by codes of conduct) which provide overarching expectations of standards of conduct. How a lender meets those standards is for them to formulate within their business with the regulator monitoring compliance through persuasion in preference to coercion but with the ultimate power to take disciplinary proceedings against non-compliant mortgage providers. Alongside this de-centred approach to regulation, there has also been a shift in consumer redress from court adjudication to alternative dispute resolution through the Financial Ombudsman Service (FOS).

The standards of conduct expected within the mortgage market have been founded on the neo-liberal premise of rational and self-interested players. For instance, it is assumed that in credit markets lenders will make responsible lending decisions that minimize the risk of bad debts and that borrowers will choose credit terms best suited to their needs. Regulation seeks to promote this rational decision making by addressing possible market failure through the promotion of competitive market conditions in which informational and experiential inequalities are to be mitigated by borrowers receiving standardized information upon which they can make a responsible borrowing choice from a range of mortgage products offered within a competitive market. Meanwhile, lenders are expected to adhere to benchmarks of good practice including expectations that they will make responsible lending decisions.

---

[2] There is a considerable literature on the role and impact of this new approach to regulation: see Black, 'Decentring Regulation: Understanding the Role of Regulation and Self-regulation in the "Post-Regulatory" World' (2001) 54 CLP 103; Black, 'Tensions in The Regulatory State' (2007) PL 58; Baldwin, 'Is Better Regulation Smarter Regulation?' (2005) PL 485.

[3] Which was subject to major revision following the 2007/2008 financial crisis primarily by the Financial Services Act 2012 but see also Financial Services (Banking Reform) Act 2013.

[4] Being Islamic mortgages: see Chapter 25, section 6.1.

[5] Being, equity release schemes: see Chapter 25, section 6.3.

[6] 2014/ 17/ EU, see Mortgage Credit Directive Order 2015 SI 2015/910.

Ramsay, 'Consumer Law, Regulatory Capitalism and the "New Learning" in Regulation' (2006) 28 Sydney LR 9, 12–13

A decentred regulatory approach might include initiatives that aim to 'responsibilise' both the supply and demand side of consumer markets, such as the current reforms to consumer credit law in the UK and Europe that are based on the twin pillars of 'responsible lending' and 'responsible borrowing'. Corporate social responsibility normally may contribute to the responsibilisation of suppliers. Responsibilisation of consumers seeks to reconstruct the consumer as a regulatory subject, a project that is both innovative and complicated. Within the traditional market model, consumer sovereignty was the goal of consumer policy. However, there was little concern for how consumers exercised their sovereignty. By contrast, the new learning on regulation positions the consumer as an important regulatory subject perceived as crucial to achieving national goals such as greater competitiveness. The 'responsibilisation' of the consumer is being pursued in areas such as credit and financial services, where governments are investing heavily in such projects to ensure that individuals become responsible consumers through the use of information, the development of financial capability, and financial literacy programs. These programs often make heroic assumptions about the ability of consumers to use and process information on market choices and their ultimate results remain uncertain and difficult to measure.

The financial crisis exposed the weakness of the 'responsiblisation' agenda to which Ramsay refers and with it the viability of the neo-liberal premise to market regulation. On the one hand, irresponsible lending has been identified as one of the causes of the crisis.[7] Whilst on the other hand, there is a growing awareness of behavioural economic research which demonstrates that borrower decision making is far more nuanced than a rational choice based upon standardized information.[8] A comprehensive review of the mortgage market following the financial crisis has resulted in a reassessment of the responsibility dynamic with lenders expected to shoulder greater responsibility for lending decisions by assessing affordability and providing advice on the suitability of particular loan terms.[9]

2.1 FINANCIAL SERVICES AND MARKETS ACT 2000, AND REGULATED MORTGAGE CONTRACTS

The FSMA establishes the FCA as the regulatory authority for the conduct of financial services.[10] We will concentrate our attention on the FCA's role in the oversight of regulated mortgage contracts which became subject to the FSMA from 31 October 2004.

---

[7] See for instance FSA, The Turner Report: A regulatory response to the banking crisis (March 2009).

[8] FCA, *Journey to the FCA* (October 2012) at p 45 and FCA, *Applying Behavioural Economics at the Financial Conduct Authority* (April 2013).

[9] FSA, *Mortgage Market Review*, DP09/3 (October 2009); FSA, *Mortgage Market Review: Responsible Lending*, CP10/16 (July 2010); *Mortgage Market Review: Distribution & Disclosure*, CP10/28 (November 2010); FSA, *Mortgage Market Review: Arrears and Approved Persons* CP10/2 (January 2010); *Mortgage Market Review, Proposed Package of Reforms* CP11/31 (December 2011) resulting in a final policy statement see FSA, *Mortgage Market Review* PS12/16 (October 2012). See also Nield, 'Mortgage Market Review: Hard Wired Commonsense' [2015] Consumer Law and Policy, on line March 15 2015.

[10] S1A. Their remit also includes the regulation of insurance and investment services as well as unsecured credit.

Regulated mortgage contracts are the most prevalent form of domestic mortgage financing and their regulatory framework provides a model for the regulation of other forms of secured credit.

2.1.1 Regulated mortgage contracts

Regulated mortgage contracts are defined by the Financial Services and Markets Act 2000 (Regulated Activities) Order 2001.[11]

Financial Services and Markets Act 2000 (Regulated Activities) Order 2001, Art 61(3) (as amended)

(a) [. . .] a contract is a "regulated mortgage contract" if, at the time it is entered into, the following conditions are met—

 (i) the contract is one under which a person ("the lender") provides credit to an individual or to trustees ("the borrower");

 (ii) the contract provides for the obligation of the borrower to repay to be secured by a mortgage on land in the EEA;

 (iii) at least 40% of that land is used, or is intended to be used—

   (aa) in the case of credit provided to an individual, as or in connection with a dwelling; or

   (bb) in the case of credit provided to a trustee which is not an individual, as or in connection with a dwelling by an individual who is a beneficiary of the trust, or by a related person;

The FCA's remit thus covers most home loans that are secured by a legal charge over the borrower's home and accordingly FSMA regulation plays a significant role in the promotion of home ownership within overall housing policy.[12] Regulated mortgage contracts also include legal mortgages of second homes and may extend to loans made to small businesses, where the loan is secured by a charge over the business proprietor's home.[13] The reference to land held on trust and occupied by beneficiaries reflects the co-ownership structures that we considered in Chapter 12. The majority of buy-to-let mortgages fall outside FSMA regulation—only consumer buy-to-let mortgages are caught.[14]

2.1.2 The Financial Services and Markets Act 2000 regulatory framework

The FCA's strategic objective is to act in a manner that is compatible with the financial markets functioning well.[15] Within this remit, the FCA's operational objectives are threefold, namely to provide consumers with an appropriate degree of protection, to protect and

---

[11] SI 2001/544.

[12] See for instance Nield, 'Mortgage Market Review: Hardwire Commonsense?' [2015] Consumer Law and Policy, on line 15 March 2015.

[13] The business gross annual turnover must not exceed £1m.

[14] For the definition of a consumer buy-to-let mortgage see Mortgage Credit Directive Order 2015 SI 2015 No 0000, Art 4(2) and FCA, PS/11.

[15] S1B(2) FSMA.

enhance the integrity of the markets, and to promote effective competition in the interests of consumers.[16] In pursuing these objectives, the FCA's role reflects decentred regulation. The means by which the FCA is to achieve these objectives are also essential threefold: first through authorizing those entitled to conduct mortgage business, secondly by setting standards for the conduct of mortgage business, and lastly by seeking to ensure compliance with those standards.

Licensing

The FCA controls those who can conduct regulated mortgage business, for instance, banks and building societies as well as mortgage brokers. It does so by licensing.[17] An unauthorized mortgage provider is guilty of a criminal offence[18] and any mortgage they have entered into is unenforceable, [19] except to the extent that the court is satisfied that it is just and equitable to order enforcement.[20] In addition, an authorized mortgage provider who acts contrary to their permission to conduct regulated mortgage business may be in breach of statutory duty so as to trigger a claim for damages but they are not criminally liable nor is the enforceability of the mortgage affected.[21]

The FCA also exercises control over those with a significant role in an authorized mortgage provider's business; for instance, senior management who decide the substance of the mortgage provider's business and sales personnel who have direct contact with borrowers. The FCA's control is both positive, by approving such personnel as 'fit and proper persons',[22] and negative, by prohibiting certain persons from carry out regulated activities.[23] Where a borrower suffers loss as a result of a person acting without approval or in breach of a prohibition order, damages may be recovered pursuant to an action for breach of statutory duty.[24] In addition, a breach of a prohibition attracts criminal sanctions.[25]

Standard setting

Any permission to carry out regulated mortgage business is subject to the statements of principle, codes of practice, and rules that the FCA may make.[26] The principles, codes, and rules represent a three-tier strata of regulatory guidance. The statements of principle set out the overarching ethos governing the conduct of regulated mortgage business; the codes of practice provide guidance on the types of activity that, on the one hand, comply with and, on the other, breach the relevant principles; but it is the rules that set out the detailed regulations that govern the conduct of mortgage business itself. The principles, codes, and rules are contained in the FCA Handbook.[27]

In preparing the conduct of business rules, the FCA is required to consult with both the mortgage industry and with bodies representing the interests of borrowers, and to take account of the views of its practitioner and consumer panels.[28]

---

[16] Section 1B(3) and s 1C–1E.   [17] Ibid, s 19.   [18] Ibid, s 23.   [19] Ibid, s 19.
[20] See ibid, ss 26–28A. For example, *Helden v Strathmore Ltd* [2011] EWCA Civ 542.
[21] Ibid, s 20.   [22] Sections 59–59B.   [23] Sections 56–58.   [24] Section 71.
[25] Section 56. The enforceability of the mortgage is unaffected.   [26] Part IX A.
[27] See FCA Handbook, available online at <http://fshandbook.info/FS/html/FCA>.
[28] FSMA, s 1M–1R.

Compliance and redress

The FCA is under a duty to supervise compliance with expected standards of conduct and enjoys extensive monitoring and enforcement powers in order to do so.[29] Designated consumer bodies, such as the FOS, may initiate action themselves or prompt the FCA into action by making a complaint to which the FCA must respond.[30]

The expectation is that mortgage providers can be persuaded to meet the required standards of conduct. Nevertheless, the FCA is empowered to take disciplinary action for a breach of the principles, codes of conduct, or the rules, which may result in the imposition of a fine or in extremis the modification or withdrawal of FCA authorization.[31]

A borrower is expected first to try and resolve a complaint directly with his or her mortgage provider, with each firm required to have a complaints handling process.[32] The alternative dispute resolution services offered by the FOS provide a realistic and increasingly important route to redress for an aggrieved borrower. Finally, an individual borrower may recover damages by taking direct action for a breach of statutory duty where his or her lender has breached the rules although the enforceability of the mortgage itself is unaffected.[33] There is no individual redress for breach of the principles or codes of conduct. The Financial Services Compensation scheme underwrites damages where the mortgage provider or broker has become insolvent.[34] *Emptage v Financial Services Compensation Scheme Ltd*[35] provides an example. Ms Emptage was negligently advised to remortgage her English home on an interest only basis to buy a holiday home in Spain. When the Spanish property market crashed she was left without funds to repay the capital element of her mortgage. She successfully recovered full damages for breach of MCOB 4.7.2 as the mortgage sold was unsuitable for her needs.

2.1.3 The principles and the rules

The overarching rules by which mortgage business should be conducted are found in the PRIN rule book.[36] One, if not the most significant, principle is that mortgage providers should '*Pay due regard to the interests of its customers and treat them fairly*'.[37] This principle forms a central theme of the FCA's treating customers fairly programme, which has spawned its own set of outcomes and provides a target of FCA compliance action.[38] Other significant principles include requirements '*to pay due regard to the information needs of its clients, and communicate information to them in a way which is clear, fair and not misleading*',[39] and to

---

[29] Section 1M and Parts XI. See generally FCA, 'The FCA's Approach to Advancing its Objectives' (July 2013).

[30] Part XVIA.

[31] Part XIV. The FCA has taken enforcement action against several lenders for irresponsible lending and unfair treatment of customers in arrears see Kensington Mortgage Co Ltd (Final Notice: 12 April, 2010), J Cummings (Final Notice: 20 October, 2010) and DB UK Bank Ltd (Final Notice: 15 December, 2010).

[32] FCA Handbook, Dispute Resolution: Complaints (DISP).

[33] Ibid, s 150. This course of action is increasingly being utilized with varying degrees of success see, for example, the success for the mis-selling of payment protection insurance in *Figurasin v Central Capital Ltd* [2014] EWCA Civ 504 and *Saville v Central Capital Ltd* [2014] EWCA 337 but the unsuccessful attempts at recovery for the selling of interest rates swaps to business borrowers in *Green v Royal Bank of Scotland plc* [2013] EWCA Civ 1197 and *Nexis Property Ltd v Royal Bank of Scotland plc* [2013] EWHC 3167.

[34] Part XV.   [35] [2013] EWCA Civ 729.

[36] See <http://fshandbook.info/FS/html/FCA/PRIN>.   [37] FCA Handbook, PRIN6.

[38] See <http://www.fca.org.uk/firms/being-regulated/meeting-your-obligations/fair-treatment-of-customers>.

[39] FCA Handbook, Principle 7.

'take reasonable care to ensure the suitability of its advice and discretionary decisions for any customer who is entitled to rely upon its judgment'.[40]

The more detailed rules and guidance affecting mortgage providers, which are intended to give effect to the Principles, are found in the Mortgage and Home Finance Sourcebook (MCOB).[41] The interrelationship between the principles and the rules was described in *R (on the application of British Bankers Association) v FSA*[42] in the following terms:

Ouseley J

At 162

The Principles are best understood as the ever present substrata to which the specific rules are added. The Principles always have to be complied with. The specific rules do not supplant them and cannot be used to contradict them. They are but specific applications of them to the particular requirements they cover. The general notion that the specific rules can exhaust the application of the Principles is inappropriate. It cannot be an error of law for the Principles to augment specific rules.

The MCOB adopts a 'cradle to grave' approach, which governs the whole course of the borrower's relationship with his or her lender. There are rules governing the marketing of mortgage products[43] and the provision of information through all stages from the first visit of a potential borrower to a mortgage provider, through to the pre-application illustration of the available loan terms[44] and the mortgage offer itself,[45] with continuing requirements for information to be provided on the actual grant of the loan and periodically during the course of the mortgage term.[46] Further rules call upon the lender to lend responsibly in the light of a prospective borrower's ability to pay.[47] If the borrower should fall into arrears, there are rules that regulate how the mortgage provider should respond, which we considered in Chapter 26.[48]

The twin principles of responsible lending and responsible borrowing are enshrined within a lender's duty to provide information to the borrower in an intelligible and prescribed form, which is intended to enable borrowers to compare different mortgage products and make informed choices about which particular mortgage terms will best suit their circumstances. The most significant piece of information is the 'European Standardised Information Sheet' (ESIS).[49] This illustration must be in the prescribed form, to facilitate comparison between different mortgage products, which includes details of (inter alia) the type of mortgage, the overall cost of the mortgage, the monthly repayments, any arrangement fee, and any charges made for early repayment.[50] The rules also stipulate that any charges imposed—for example, in the event of default or early repayment—must not be excessive.[51] A borrower is also allowed a cooling off period to give time to consider their mortgage offer.

---

[40] FCA Handbook, Principle 9.

[41] See <http://fshandbook.info/FS/html/FCA/MCOB>.   [42] [2011] EWHC 999.

[43] FCA Handbook, MCOB 3A and 3B.   [44] FCA Handbook, MCOB 4, 4A, 5, and 5A.

[45] FCA Handbook, MCOB 6 and 6A.   [46] FCA Handbook, MCOB 7 and 7A.

[47] FCA Handbook, MCOB 11 and 11A.   [48] FCA Handbook, MCOB 13.

[49] ESIS replaces the Key Facts Illustrations pursuant to the MCD.

[50] FCA Handbook MCOB 5. MCOB 10 details how the annual percentage (APR) of interest is to be calculated.

[51] FCA Handbook MCOB 12.

This need for clear and consistent information is laudable, but the experience of the credit crunch has demonstrated its deficiencies in protecting borrowers.

Nield, 'Responsible Lending and Borrowing: Where to Low Cost Home Ownership?' (2010) 30 LS 610 (footnotes omitted)

Under the FSMA, the pre-application key facts illustration [. . .] has been described by the FSA as the 'cornerstone' of mortgage regulation. However, even before the credit crunch, there was evidence from both the FSA and Citizens Advice that suggested weakness in disclosure. Their research found that certain mortgagors, particularly within the sub-prime market, did not compare different mortgage products or even understand some of the fundamental features of mortgage borrowing and thus could not play their part as a rational consumer [. . .]

There is growing recognition that a mortgagor's decision to borrow may not be made on solely rational grounds but is a more complex process that is also influenced by factors that have inspired the development of behavioural economics. For instance, individuals can tend to be over optimistic and even when warned, for instance, that they may lose their house if they do not keep up their mortgage payments, do not believe that they will default and face repossession. Individuals' assessment of risk also may not be rational, with dramatic events which attract high media attention being overestimated as more likely to happen as against less vivid risks that excite only muted attention. Hyberbolic discounting suggests that a mortgagor's ability to value discounted mortgage rates, arrangements fees, pre-payment penalties and the like may not be rationally consistent over the time frames in which these charges operate [. . .]

The FSA Review notes that mortgagors' (as opposed to other consumers') decisions are subject to particular behaviours which can reduce mortgagors' caution and entice them into borrowing decisions which are not best suited to their interests. Mortgages can appear deceptively cheap products. Considerable sums are received for relatively small periodic repayments which, being repaid over an extended term, contribute to the apparent affordability of the borrowing.

Mortgagors are motivated to borrow by immediate want or need which will lead them to focus on the end result. In contrast to other financial products, the mortgage (like other credit) is not always seen as the product being bought and sold but as a means to an end. The focus is then on the asset purchased. In relation to first legal charges, this will often be the mortgagor's prospective home.

Thus, although the borrowers are provided with information, they may find it difficult to adequately assess the implications of that information to their particular circumstances and so fail to make responsible choices. The financial education of borrowers is a policy aim with the Consumer Financial Education Body (now known by the catchier title of The Money Advice Service) established by the Financial Services Act 2010.[52]

The limitations of information disclosure have to some extent been acknowledged by the changes to MCOB that have been made following the MMR which sees a shift to greater lender responsibility. MCOB 11 previously merely required lenders to take account of the borrower's ability to pay. In the heady days before the financial crisis lenders interpreted

---

[52] See s 3S FSMA.

this requirement to sanction high loan to value [of the security] ratios and to use higher and higher multiplies of borrowers' income to set lending ceilings. Additionally, they lent on an interest only basis without any account of borrowers' ability to repay the capital loan. The practice also grew of lending without checking the borrowers' ability to pay by verifying their income or considering their other liabilities. A far more detailed MCOB 11 and 11A now requires lenders to assess the affordability of their lending by checking the borrower's income and outgoings whilst lending on an interest only basis is curtailed by requiring lenders to assess affordability on an interest and capital repayment basis and to ensure the borrower will have the resources to repay the capital. In addition, MCOB 4.7A provides that most mortgage sales are made on an advice basis, which requires lenders to ensure that a particular mortgage is suitable for an individual borrower.[53] However, the consequent restriction in mortgage finance has excluded many from the housing market and left the aspiration of home ownership out of reach for numerous people.[54]

2.2 CONSUMER CREDIT ACT 1974 (CCA)

The CCA was passed following the recommendations of the Crowther Committee, which, in 1971, undertook a comprehensive review of consumer credit.[55] The Act brought the regulation of the different forms of credit available to individual consumers under one legislative umbrella.[56] The rapid growth and changing face of the consumer credit market in the following years led to a further review and the substantial amendment of the CCA in 2006.[57]

Mortgages were not the primary target of the CCA, because they were thought to present low consumer risk. Nevertheless, second (and other subsequent) mortgages and mortgages securing loans less than £25,000 were subject to the CCA—this latter ceiling was lifted in 2008. The regulatory importance of the CCA for secured loans has waned considerably. Firstly, legal charges were excluded from almost all of the CCA when they became subject to FSMA regulation in 2004, and the regulatory transfer to the FSMA of second charges and consumer buy-to-let mortgages followed in 2016. The most significant remnant of the CCA applicable to mortgages now regulated by the FSMA is the jurisdiction of the court to grant a time order, which we referred to in Chapter 26. We will thus merely provide an overview of the CCA regulatory regime, noting the similarities and distinctions with that of the FSMA.[58]

Within the CCA we also see regulation based upon neo-liberal principles of rational and responsible lending and borrowing within a competitive market in which possible market failures are sought to be addressed through licensing, to control the probity of lenders with access to the market, information disclosure, to assist borrower to make responsible borrowing decisions, and oversight of lenders' conduct by an independent regulator with disciplinary powers.

---

[53] See Nield, 'Mortgage Market Review: Hardwired Commonsense' [2015] Consumer Law and Policy, on line 15 March 2015.

[54] Ibid.   [55] Cmnd 4596, 1971.

[56] The CCA is primarily intended to protect individual borrowers but covers some business borrowing by sole traders and small partnerships: CCA ss 8 and 189.

[57] The Consumer Credit Act 2006 following a major review, see *Fair, Clear and Competitive: The Consumer Credit Market in the 21st Century* Cm 6040, 2003.

[58] For more detailed insight see E Lomnicka, 'The Future of Consumer Credit Regulation: A Chance to Rationalize Sanctions for Breaches of Financial Services Regulatory Regimes?' [2013] Comp Law 13.

CCA lenders are now subject to the FSMA licensing regime and must be licensed by the FCA in order to make a regulated consumer credit agreement.[59] An unlicensed lender, and a licensed lender who acts outside their permission, commits a criminal offence[60] and any CCA regulated mortgage they have entered into is unenforceable save by direction of the FCA.[61]

Conduct standards are set out in the separate consumer credit rule book of the FCA handbook.[62] Lenders are thus now subject to the general principles and rules already examined, including the general principle to treat their customers fairly.[63] Additional rules and guidance are set out in the CONC handbook and relate to such matters as advertising,[64] information disclosure,[65] responsible lending (including affordability assessments),[66] and default,[67] as well as particular rules and guidance for lending secured on land.[68]

In addition, credit governed by the CCA are subject to the statutory rules set out in the CCA.[69] These statutory rules are significantly more formalistic and prescriptive. There are defined forms and procedures with compliance prompted by the threat of unenforceability.[70] Furthermore, the obligation to supply copies of relevant documentation, both at the time of creation and during the currency of the credit,[71] and the process of enforcement in the event of default,[72] are also proscribed.

In addition, although CCA borrowers have access to the FOS, the courts have greater oversight of CCA lending both through their adjudication of compliance with the required processes and their statutory discretion to intervene on the grounds of unfairness. Accordingly complaints under the CCA tend to raise highly technical issues prompting adverse comment by Clarke LJ in *McGinn v Grangewood Securities*.[73] The consequences of a failure to comply with the CCA statutory rules are far-reaching.[74] In such event the credit agreement and any supporting security are deemed incorrectly executed, and cannot be enforced except by order of the court.[75] The court has wide discretion, in the light of the prejudice caused to the borrower and the culpability of the lender, whether or not to order enforcement and, if enforcement is ordered, to impose conditions and amend or vary the credit terms.[76]

A distinctive feature of the CCA is to empower the court to reopen consumer credit agreements. Initially the test to trigger this power was where the court found that the agreement 'grossly contravene[d] ordinary principles of fair dealing',[77] but the test proved notoriously difficult to satisfy[78] and was amended by the CCA 2006. The revised provisions, found in

---

[59] FSMA, ss 19 and 20.   [60] FSMA, s 23.   [61] FSMA, ss 26, 26A, 27, and 28A.

[62] See FCA Handbook CONC.   [63] See FCA Handbook PRIN particularly Principle 6.

[64] CONC 3.   [65] CONC 4.   [66] CONC 5.   [67] CONC 7.   [68] CONC 15.

[69] See generally CCA Parts V–VIII.   [70] CCA, ss 55, 60–64, and 105.

[71] CCA ss 55C, 58, 61A–64, 77–78A, and 107–111.   [72] See CCA Part VII, ss 76 and 126.

[73] [2002] EWCA Civ 522 at [1]s.

[74] See ss 55, 65, and 106. Strangely there is no sanction for breach of s 126, which prohibits the enforcement of a land mortgage other than by court order. See *Waterside Finance Ltd v Karim* [2013] 1 P & CR 21.

[75] CCA, s 127. See *London North Securities Ltd v Meadows* [2005] EWCA Civ 956, *Phoenix Recoveries (UK) Ltd v Kotecha* [2011] EWCA Civ 105, *Consolidated Finance Ltd v Collins* [2013] EWCA Civ 475, *Grace v Black Horse Ltd* [2014] EWCA Civ 1413, and *Re London Scottish Finance Ltd (in Administration)* [2014] Bus LR 424 where almost 1700 loans were affected. Prior to 6 April 2007 the loan and mortgage were void but human rights concerns led to discretionary enforceability, see *Wilson v First County Trust (No 2)* [2013] UKHL 40.

[76] Ibid, ss 127, 129, 135, and 136. See, for instance, *Carey v HSBC plc* [2009] EWHC 3417.

[77] CCA, ss 137–140.

[78] See *A Ketley Ltd v Scott* [1980] CCLR 37; *Davies v Direct Loans* [1986] 1 WLR 823; *Paragon Finance plc v Nash* [2002] 1 WLR 685.

ss 140A–C, look to the unfairness of the relationship between the creditor and debtor and allow the court to consider not only the terms of the agreement, but also the lender's behaviour and practices throughout the term of the mortgage. The redress that the court can order is also far-ranging and may extend to ordering the repayment of any sums paid by the debtor, the alteration of the terms of the loan, or the setting aside, either in whole or in part, of any duty imposed upon the borrower by the terms of the loan.[79]

Although s 140A–C did apply to second mortgages before the regulatory re-organization in 2016, s 140A(5) now excludes all regulated mortgage contracts from this measure of consumer protection. This exclusion is regretted. The jurisdiction had the potential to offer a powerful mechanism of direct borrower redress through judicial oversight. Its most significant use is in the case of *Plevin v Paragon Personal Finance Ltd*,[80] in which the non-disclosure of commission paid on the sale of payment protection insurance was held to be unfair.[81] Despite this important decision, the main problems associated with the mis-selling of payment protection insurance have been addressed by the regulatory authorities with lenders being required to pay out millions in compensation.[82]

2.3 FINANCIAL OMBUDSMAN SERVICE

The FOS is established under Part XVI of the FSMA 2000 as a body that is independent of the FCA, to provide an alternative means of resolving disputes.[83] The FOS may consider complaints made by borrowers and may call upon the lender to provide the requisite information to enable them to do so.[84] The FOS determines complaints on what it considers to be 'fair and reasonable' rather than being bound to apply the strict legal rules.[85] This ability has sparked concern that its exercise should not result in arbitrary and inconsistent decisions which 'operate according to the length of [the Ombudsman's] foot.'[86] This concern is to some extent addressed by the requirement for the FOS to make rules which are subject to FCA approval on the 'matters that are to be taken into account in determining whether an act or omission was fair and reasonable.'[87] In addition, the FOS may issue information and advice that does not require FCA approval.[88] For instance, it has issued advice and guidance on

---

[79] CCA, s 140B(1).

[80] [2017] 1 WLR 1249. See also *Verrin v Welcome Financial Services Ltd* [2017] ECC 7, *Nelmes v Nram Plc* [2016] EWCA Civ 941, *Swift Advances plc v Okokenu* [2015] CTLC 302, and *McMullon v Secure the Bridge Ltd* (unreported).

[81] This insurance purports to cover the risk of non-payment of unsecured loans and also mortgages (MPPI) if the borrower suffers a loss of income from ill-health or unemployment. It was commonly sold by an insurer associated with the lender at the same time as the loan often by the payment of a single substantial premium.

[82] See Competition Commissions Market Investigation into Payment Protection Insurance (January 2009) which led to certain policies being prohibited and the FSA's Policy Statement 10/12 (July 2010) on handling mis-selling complaints.

[83] See generally Morris and James, 'The Financial Ombudsman Service: A Brave New World in "Ombudsmanry"' [2002] PL 640; Ferran, 'Dispute Resolution Mechanisms in the UK Financial Sector' (2002) 21 CJQ 135.

[84] FSMA, s 231.

[85] Ibid, s 228 and *R (on the application of IFG Financial Services Ltd v FOS* [2005] EWHC 1153. See also *R (on the application of the British Bankers Association) v FSA* [2011] EWHC 999 for the inter-relation between the FSA principles, codes, and rules and the FOS jurisdiction.

[86] *FOS v Heather Moor & Edgecombe Ltd* [2008] EWCA Civ 643 at [79] *per* Rix LJ. The process is compliant with Art 6 of the European Convention on Human Rights see *Heather Moor & Edgecomb Ltd v UK* (2011) 53 EHRR SE18.

[87] FSMA Sch 17 para 8.   [88] Ibid, Sch 17 para 8.

their approach to mortgage arrears and hardship, early repayment charges, and mortgage under funding.[89] It is now also required to publish reports of its decisions.[90] As a backstop the rationality of FOS's decisions are subject to judicial review.

In resolving complaints the FOS may direct a mortgage provider to take such steps as the FOS considers 'just and appropriate' or make an award based upon what it considers to be 'fair',[91] with any compensation subject to a statutory cap of £150,000.[92] That award is binding upon the lender and enforceable as such in the same way as a court judgment. The borrower, however, may decline the FOS's award and continue to pursue his or her claim through the courts.[93]

The FOS provides a practical redress route for borrowers. It has the advantage of being free at the point of entry and, with speedier and less formal methods of working, more accessible to many borrowers.[94] The mis-selling of endowment mortgages and, more recently, payment protection insurance have been major sources of complaints to the FOS.[95]

3 CREATION OF THE MORTGAGE

Freedom of contract is a fundamental principle governing loan contracts as much as any other contract. We will see, in the next section, the legal controls over the parties' freedom to agree the substantive content of their loan terms and any mortgage taken to secure repayment of that loan. In this section, we are concerned with the process by which those terms are agreed. The focus here is with the quality of the parties' consent to contractual terms: in particular, the borrower's ability to enter freely into the loan without the lender abusing a dominant position.

We will concentrate in section 3.3 on the role that the doctrine of undue influence has played in collateral mortgages of the family home to secure a business loan. There are, however, other factors that can affect the procedural fairness of a loan, which we will briefly survey in section 3.1, before considering the conceptual basis that underlies these controls in section 3.2.

3.1 FACTORS GOVERNING PROCEDURAL FAIRNESS

The principal factors that may affect the procedural fairness of a mortgage will be familiar to any student of contract law and thus it is proposed to outline their essential features only briefly. The factors are:

- *non est factum*;
- duress;

---

[89] See FOS, Technical Notes at <http://www.financial-ombudsman.org.uk/publications/technical_ notes>.
[90] FSMA, s 230A. Its newsletter, published statistics and annual report provide further information.
[91] Ibid, s 29.   [92] *Bunney v Burns Andersen plc* [2007] EWHC 1240.
[93] But see *Binns v First Plus Financial groups plc* [2013] EWHC 2436, *Clarke v In Focus Asset Management & Tax Solutions Ltd* [2014] 1 WLR 2502.
[94] *R (on the application of Williams v FOS* [2008] EWHC 2142.
[95] Mortgage endowment complaints accounted for 63 per cent of complaints in 2005/06 and payment protection insurance accounted for 78 per cent of complaints in 2013/14; see FSO, *Annual Reviews* available online at <http://www.financial-ombudsman.org.uk>.

- undue influence;
- misrepresentation;
- unconscionable bargain.

Non est factum and duress find their roots in the common law, and, accordingly, render the contract void from the outset. Undue influence and unconscionable bargain are equitable doctrines that entitle the wronged party to elect to rescind the transaction. The court may also award equitable compensation or set aside a transaction on terms where full restitution is not possible, because, for example, some benefit has been received by the victim. The remedies for misrepresentation will depend upon the intention with which the misrepresentation is formulated, and may result in a claim to rescind the transaction or to damages, either in the tort of deceit, where the misrepresentation is fraudulent, or in negligence or under statute, where the misrepresentation is negligent or innocent.

3.1.1 *Non est factum*

Where a party has made a fundamental mistake as to the character and effect of the obligations imposed by the mortgage, he or she may plead *non est factum*, provided that the mistake was no fault of his or her own.[96] The doctrine does not require any proof of fraud or wrongdoing, because its basis lies in the absence of the victim's consent. It was originally applied where a party could not read, because he or she was blind or illiterate, but has since been extended to wider circumstances in which a party's lack of comprehension is due to other reasons (e.g. age, illness, limited education or understanding). Nevertheless, the doctrine has very limited application, because the victim must prove that he or she took due care in understanding the nature and effect of the mortgage, for example by asking for an explanation of its effect. A failure to read the mortgage is plainly insufficient.

3.1.2 Duress

A party may claim duress where he or she has been coerced or pressurized into a transaction. Originally, the coercion had to take the form of physical threats to the victim[97] or to his or her property,[98] but the doctrine has been expanded to admit more subtle means of pressure, including the illegitimate use of economic pressure: for example, threats to breach a contractual obligation.[99] The difficulty is to distinguish the use of sharp, but legitimate, negotiating tactics in the cut and thrust of commercial life from the illegitimate threats that may constitute economic duress.[100] Again, the rationale for intervention on the grounds of duress is that the victim has not freely consented to the transaction.

---

[96] See *Saunders v Anglia Building Society*, sub nom *Gallie v Lee* [1971] AC 1004.

[97] *Barton v Armstrong* [1976] AC 104.   [98] *Astley v Reynolds* (1731) 2 Str 915.

[99] See *Pao On v Lau Yiu Long* [1980] AC 614; *DSDN Subsea Ltd v Petroleum Geo-services ASA* [2000] BLR 530; *Huyton SA v Peter Cremer & Co* [1999] CLC 230; or, in the context of a mortgage, *Jones v Morgan* [2001] EWCA Civ 995.

[100] Economic duress is distinguishable from other forms of duress in that: firstly, it renders the contract voidable not void; and secondly, to be actionable, the duress must be the main reason that the victim acted as he or she did.

The Universe Sentinel
[1983] 1 AC 366, HL

Lord Scarman

At 400

There must be pressure, the practical effect of which is compulsion or absence of choice. Compulsion is variously described in the authorities as coercion or the vitiation of consent. The classic case of duress is, however, not the lack of will to submit but the victim's intentional submission arising from the realisation that there is no other practical choice open to him.

3.1.3 Undue influence

A comprehensive definition of undue influence is elusive.[101] Lord Clyde observed in *Royal Bank of Scotland plc v Etridge*[102] that '[i]*t is something which can be more easily recognised when found than exhaustively analysed in the abstract*'. At its core is the use of improper pressure or influence, which effectively deprives a party of his or her free and independent will. The victim may perfectly understand his or her actions, but, nevertheless, his or her judgment may have been overborne by the improper influence of another. In *Daniel v Drew*[103] Ward LJ gave the following guidance:

Ward LJ

At [36]

[. . .] in all cases of undue influence the critical question is whether or not the persuasion or the advice, in other words the influence, has invaded the free volition of the donor to accept or reject the persuasion or advice or withstand the influence. The donor may be led but she must not be driven and her will must be the offspring of her own volition, not a record of someone else's. There is no undue influence unless the donor if she were free and informed could say "This is not my wish but I must do it".

Undue influence takes one of two broad forms: firstly, actual undue influence arises where overt acts exert improper pressure in a similar manner to duress, to which the concept has been compared; secondly, undue influence may be presumed to exist from the relationship between two parties, where one has used his or her dominant position to exploit the weaker party. Certain types of relationship are accepted, in themselves, as giving rise to a presumption of undue influence without any further evidence that the trust inherent in these relationships has been abused. These relationships include solicitor and client, doctor and

---

[101] In *Allcard v Skinner* (1887) 36 Ch D 145, 183, Lindley LJ commented that '*no court had ever attempted to define undue influence*'.
[102] [2002] 2 AC 773, [92].   [103] [2005] EWCA Civ 507.

patient, religious leader and follower, parent and child. This list is not exhaustive and a presumption of undue influence may also arise where trust and confidence is established in the context of a particular relationship.

Lord Nicholls in *Etridge* sought to pin down the nature of this relational form of undue influence.

Royal Bank of Scotland plc v Etridge
[2002] 2 AC 773, HL

Lord Nicholls

At [10]–[11]

The law has long recognised the need to prevent abuse of influence in these "relationship" cases despite the absence of evidence of overt acts of persuasive conduct. The types of relationship, such as parent and child, in which this principle falls to be applied cannot be listed exhaustively. Relationships are infinitely various. Sir Guenter Treitel QC has rightly noted that the question is whether one party has reposed sufficient trust and confidence in the other, rather than whether the relationship between the parties belongs to a particular type: see Treitel, *The Law of Contract*, 10th ed (1999), pp 380–381. For example, the relation of banker and customer will not normally meet this criterion, but exceptionally it may: see *National Westminster Bank plc v Morgan* [1985] AC 686, 707–709.

Even this test is not comprehensive. The principle is not confined to cases of abuse of trust and confidence. It also includes, for instance, cases where a vulnerable person has been exploited. Indeed, there is no single touchstone for determining whether the principle is applicable. Several expressions have been used in an endeavour to encapsulate the essence: trust and confidence, reliance, dependence or vulnerability on the one hand and ascendancy, domination or control on the other. None of these descriptions is perfect. None is all embracing. Each has its proper place.

As a result of this relationship of trust and confidence between the parties, the dominant party is said to owe a special duty to deal fairly with the other—a duty that has been described as 'fiduciary'.[104]

Actual undue influence is actionable as a legal wrong.[105] The relational form of undue influence may give rise, in the light of the nature of the transaction that is being impugned, to a factual presumption of undue influence, which shifts the burden of proof to the dominant party to demonstrate that he or she dealt fairly with the weaker party, who was thus able to exercise his or her own judgment.

3.1.4 Misrepresentation

It is not uncommon for a party to try to persuade another party to contract by misrepresenting the facts surrounding the transaction. For example, in *Barclays Bank plc v*

---

[104] Ibid at [104], *per* Lord Hobhouse.   [105] *CIBC v Pitt* [1994] 1 AC 200.

O'Brien,[106] Mr O'Brien persuaded his wife to mortgage her interest in the family home to secure a loan made to his business by misrepresenting the amount of the debt that was secured by the mortgage. An actionable misrepresentation is a material misrepresentation of existing fact, rather than of opinion or future intention, which induces a party to enter into the contract. Misrepresentation is often linked with undue influence in the common scenario that occurred in *O'Brien*, which we will be examining in more detail in section 3.3. However, it is necessary to show that the misrepresentation caused the victim to enter into the impugned transaction, whereas proof of undue influence is by itself an equitable wrong upon which the transaction can be set aside. Proof that the victim would not have entered into the transaction if they had known the truth is not required.[107]

3.1.5 Unconsionable bargain

Equity will provide redress where one party has abused the strength of his or her relative position to impose unacceptable terms upon the other party, who is in a position of relative weakness or disadvantage. The doctrine seeks to protect the weak or disadvantaged from those who would use their superior position unscrupulously.

In the context of a security transaction, this principle may be established by proof that:

- the borrower is at a serious disadvantage because of some particular weakness or disability;
- the borrower has been unconscionably exploited by the lender because of that disadvantage; and
- a mortgage has resulted on terms that are oppressive.

The doctrine is based upon the relative strengths of the parties to the mortgage and the fact that the dominant party has acted reprehensibly in taking advantage of that imbalance. The weaker party must establish that he or she was in a position of special disadvantage vis-à-vis the dominant party, and that his or her vulnerability was evident to the dominant party, so that the court is able to infer that the resulting transaction was procured by the abuse of that superior position. The balance of proof then shifts to the dominant party to establish, if he or she can, that he or she did not take advantage of that superior position and that the resulting mortgage, although onerous, did not result from any abuse.[108] The relative positions of the parties, the conduct of their negotiations, the improper use of influence or power, and the lack of information or absence of real choice are all relevant factors. The focus is upon the procedural, rather than the substantive, nature of the transaction, although oppressive terms may provide evidence that demonstrates the unconscionability of the process.[109]

The Court of Appeal considered the operation of the doctrine in the following case.

---

[106] [1994] 1 AC 180. See also *Royal Bank of Scotland plc v Chandra* [2011] EWCA Civ 192.
[107] See for instance *Hewett v First Plus Financial Group plc* [2010] 2 P & CR 22.
[108] *Louth v Diprose* (1992) 175 CLR 621.   [109] *Hart v O'Connor* [1985] AC 1000, 1018.

Alec Lobb Garages Ltd v Total Oil (GB) Ltd
[1885] 1 WLR 173, CA

Lord Dhillon

At 182

The whole emphasis is on extortion, or undue advantage taken of weakness, an unconscientious use of the power arising out of the inequality of the parties' circumstances, and on unconscientious use of power which the Court might in certain circumstances be entitled to infer from a particular—and in these days notorious—relationship unless the contract is proved to have been in fact fair, just and reasonable. Nothing leads me to suppose that the course of the development of the law over the last 100 years has been such that the emphasis on unconscionable conduct or unconscientious use of power has gone and relief will now be granted in equity in a case such as the present if there has been unequal bargaining power, even if the stronger has not used his strength unconscionably. I agree with the judgment of Browne-Wilkinson J. in *Multiservice Bookbinding Ltd. v. Marden* (1979) Ch. 84 which sets out that to establish that a term is unfair and unconscionable it is not enough to show that it is, objectively, unreasonable [. . .] Inequality of bargaining power must anyhow be a relative concept. It is seldom in any negotiation that the bargaining powers of the parties are absolutely equal. Any individual wanting to borrow money from a bank, building society or other financial institution in order to pay his liabilities or buy some property he urgently wants to acquire will have virtually no bargaining power; he will have to take or leave the terms offered to him. [. . .]

The Courts would only interfere in exceptional cases where as a matter of common fairness it was not right that the strong should be allowed to push the weak to the wall. The concepts of unconscionable conduct and of the exercise by the stronger of coercive power are thus brought in [. . .]

There are close links between relational undue influence and unconscionable bargains, and the same facts can give rise to an action based upon both doctrines. Indeed, some have argued that undue influence should be subsumed within a wider doctrine of unconscionability.[110] The English courts have preferred the undue influence route, but in other jurisdictions, the courts have applied unconscionable bargains. For example, in the Australian case of *Commonwealth Bank of Australia Ltd v Amadio*,[111] the doctrine was employed to set aside a mortgage granted by elderly Italian immigrants, with little command of English or experience of business, to secure a loan to their son's business. They believed that the business was flourishing: a belief based upon their son's misrepresentations and the bank's practice of dishonouring only some of the son's cheques to create an appearance of solvency. They also believed that their liability was limited and they received no independent advice to cast a more realistic light on the transaction. In England, these facts would produce a clear claim of undue influence, but the case was pleaded and decided by the High Court of Australia on the grounds of unconscionable bargain—although the High Court criticized the pleadings and expressed a hope that such cases would, in future, be approached from the perspective of undue influence.[112]

---

110 Capper (1998) 14 LQR 479.   111 (1983) 151 CLR 447.
112 See ibid, at 464, *per* Mason J.

There remain distinctions between undue influence and unconscionable bargains. Undue influence focusses upon the quality of consent of the weaker party, which is called into question by the nature of the relationship between the parties, whereas unconscionable bargain concentrates its attention upon the conduct of the dominant party. It is the exploitation of the relative weakness of one party, which is derived from some social or transactional disability, which merits the court's intervention.

3.2 THE CONCEPTUAL UNDERPINNINGS

There has been considerable debate surrounding the conceptual basis of these various vitiating factors: in particular, duress, undue influence, and unconscionable bargains. The main features of this debate are twofold: firstly, whether they are claimant-based, looking to the impaired consent of the victim, or defendant-based, looking to the exploitative nature of the defendant's conduct; secondly, there have been growing calls to assimilate the three grounds by looking to the underlying unconscionability of the defendant's use of their relative power.

Birks and Chin[113] have advocated a claimant-sided approach to undue influence that leads to a distinction between undue influence and unconscionable bargains. Undue influence looks to the vulnerability of the claimant's consent as a result of his or her dependence on the defendant, whilst unconscionable bargains is concerned with the defendant's exploitation of the claimant's weakness. We have already noted that, despite the obviously reprehensible conduct of duress and actual undue influence, the traditional conceptual foundations of these doctrines have been found in the suspect nature of the victim's apparent consent. Birks and Chin point out that presumed undue influence does not depend upon any conscious wrongdoing on behalf of the defendant, and that the presumption of influence may be rebutted by proof that the claimant did exercise his or her free and independent will.

Others have rejected this approach and have refocussed the spotlight on the exploitative nature of the defendant's behaviour, thus drawing closer parallels with both duress and unconscionable bargains, which have resulted in calls for the assimilation of the three doctrines.[114] The common features of the doctrines have been identified as relational inequality (e.g. of bargaining power), transactional imbalance, and the defendant's unconscionable conduct, which, in the case of presumed undue influence, may be more passively imposed than overtly or intentionally exerted.[115] These features do not necessarily contribute equally, but rather form an evidentiary mix that combine in different measure according to the circumstances of the particular case.

Intriguing though these arguments are, the more practical policy imperatives that underpin the exercise of 'state-assisted rescission' of apparently binding obligations should

---

[113] Birks and Chin, 'On the Nature of Undue Influence' in *Good Faith and Fault in Contract Law* (eds Beatson and Friedman, 1995, ch 3). See also Birks, 'Undue Influence as Wrongful Exploitation' (2004) 120 LQR 34.

[114] Bigwood, 'Undue Influence: Impaired Consent or Wicked Exploitation' (1996) 16 OJLS 503; Chen-Wishart, 'The *O'Brien* Principle and Substantive Unfairness' (1997) 56 CLJ 60; Chen-Wishart, 'Undue Influence: Beyond Impaired Consent and Wrongdoing Towards a Relational Analysis' in *Mapping the Law* (eds Burrows and Rogers, 2006), ch 11; Capper, 'Undue Influence and Unconscionability: A Rationalisation' (1998) 114 LQR 479; Deveney and Chandler, 'Unconscionability and the Taxonomy of Undue Influence' [2007] JBL 541.

[115] See Capper (1998) and Chen-Wishart (1997).

not be overlooked.[116] This policy is particularly evident in the series of decisions on undue influence that have occupied the House of Lords, which seeks to balance the protection of the vulnerable surety against modern business lending practices. The House of Lords first expressed its opinion in *Barclays Bank plc v O'Brien*,[117] but some years later, developed and refined its views in *Royal Bank of Scotland plc v Etridge*.[118] These two decisions will dominate our consideration of the operation of undue influence in mortgage transactions.

3.3 UNDUE INFLUENCE AND MORTGAGES

Undue influence has been raised as a defence to enforcement proceedings where a collateral mortgage has been granted over the family home to secure a loan made for the benefit of the husband's business. The loan is made to the husband, as borrower, but the wife's participation to create the mortgage is required where she is a legal or beneficial joint owner of the family home. The danger is that the wife's consent to the mortgage is questionable, because, in the husband's desire to finance his business, he may have misrepresented the amount of the secured liability or the risks of enforcement, or have unduly influenced his wife to mortgage her interest.

The trend was noted in *O'Brien*.[119]

Barclays Bank plc v O'Brien
[1994] 1 AC 180, HL

Lord Browne-Wilkinson

At 188

The large number of cases of this type coming before the courts in recent years reflects the rapid changes in social attitudes and the distribution of wealth which have recently occurred. Wealth is now more widely spread. Moreover a high proportion of privately owned wealth is invested in the matrimonial home. Because of the recognition by society of the equality of the sexes, the majority of matrimonial homes are now in the joint names of both spouses. Therefore in order to raise finance for the business enterprises of one or other of the spouses, the jointly owned home has become a main source of security. The provision of such security requires the consent of both spouses.

In parallel with these financial developments, society's recognition of the equality of the sexes has led to a rejection of the concept that the wife is subservient to the husband in the management of the family's finances. A number of the authorities reflect an unwillingness in the court to perpetuate law based on this outmoded concept. Yet [. . .] although the concept of the ignorant wife leaving all financial decisions to the husband is outmoded, the practice does not yet coincide with the ideal. In a substantial proportion of marriages it is still the husband who has the business experience and the wife is willing to follow his advice without bringing a truly independent mind and will to bear on financial decisions. The number of

---

[116] Bigwood, 'Contracts by Unfair Advantage: From Exploitation to Transactional Neglect' (2005) 25 OJLS 65; Ferris; 'Why is the Law of Undue Influence So Hard to Understand and Apply?' in *Modern Studies in Property Law: Vol 4* (ed Cooke, 2007) ch 3.

[117] [1994] 1 AC 180.   [118] [2002] 2 AC 773.

[119] See also *Royal Bank of Scotland plc v Etridge*, ibid at 800–1, *per* Lord Nicholls.

recent cases in this field shows that in practice many wives are still subjected to, and yield to, undue influence by their husbands. Such wives can reasonably look to the law for some protection when their husbands have abused the trust and confidence reposed in them.

On the other hand, it is important to keep a sense of balance in approaching these cases. It is easy to allow sympathy for the wife who is threatened with the loss of her home at the suit of a rich bank to obscure an important public interest viz., the need to ensure that the wealth currently tied up in the matrimonial home does not become economically sterile. If the rights secured to wives by the law renders vulnerable loans granted on the security of matrimonial homes, institutions will be unwilling to accept such security, thereby reducing the flow of loan capital to business enterprises. It is therefore essential that a law designed to protect the vulnerable does not render the matrimonial home unacceptable as security to financial institutions.

The context is rather different from that commonly associated with undue influence where a donee has obtained a gift that the donor subsequently seeks to set aside, because his or her consent was obtained by undue influence. Here, it is the husband who, it is alleged, exerted undue influence to persuade his wife to grant a mortgage to the lender. There is no suggestion that the lender is guilty of undue influence, but, in *O'Brien*, the House of Lords decided that a lender who has actual or constructive notice of the risk of undue influence or misrepresentation by the husband will be bound by any right of the wife to set aside the mortgage against her interest in the home.

Barclays Bank plc v O'Brien
[1994] 1 AC 180, HL

Lord Browne-Wilkinson

At 191

But in surety cases the decisive question is whether the claimant wife can set aside the transaction, not against the wrongdoing husband, but against the creditor bank. Of course, if the wrongdoing husband is acting as agent for the creditor bank in obtaining the surety from the wife, the creditor will be fixed with the wrongdoing of its own agent and the surety contract can be set aside as against the creditor. Apart from this, if the creditor bank has notice, actual or constructive, of the undue influence exercised by the husband (and consequentially of the wife's equity to set aside the transaction) the creditor will take subject to that equity and the wife can set aside the transaction against the creditor (albeit a purchaser for value) as well as against the husband: see *Bainbrigge v. Browne* (1881) 18 Ch.D. 188 and *Bank of Credit and Commerce International S.A. v. Aboody* [1990] 1 Q.B. 923, 973. Similarly, in cases such as the present where the wife has been induced to enter into the transaction by the husband's misrepresentation, her equity to set aside the transaction will be enforceable against the creditor if either the husband was acting as the creditor's agent or the creditor had actual or constructive notice.

It is unlikely that the husband is an agent of the lender and so it is the application of the concept of notice that has attracted the greatest attention. This application of notice must be contrasted with the doctrine of notice that we have considered in relation to the priority of proprietary interests in Chapter 15. Instead, what is in issue is the notice of a party to the mortgage (i.e. the lender) to the possibility that the wife's consent to the mortgage may have been obtained by improper means.

The distinction was highlighted in *Royal Bank of Scotland plc v Etridge*.[120]

Royal Bank of Scotland plc v Etridge
[2002] 2 AC 773, HL

Lord Scott

At [144]

The doctrine of notice is a doctrine that relates primarily and traditionally to the priority of competing property rights. [. . .] Banks and other lenders who take charges from surety wives are certainly purchasers of property rights. But they acquire their rights by grant from the surety wives themselves. The issue between the banks and the surety wives is not one of priority of competing interests. The issue is whether or not the surety wife is to be bound by her apparent consent to the grant of the security to the bank. If contractual consent has been procured by undue influence or misrepresentation for which a party to the contract is responsible, the other party, the victim, is entitled, subject to the usual defences of change of position, affirmation, delay etc, to avoid the contract. But the case is much more difficult if the undue influence has been exerted or the misrepresentation has been made not by the party with whom the victim has contracted, but by a third party. It is, in general, the objective manifestation of contractual consent that is critical. Deficiencies in the quality of consent to a contract by a contracting party, brought about by undue influence or misrepresentation by a third party, do not, in general, allow the victim to avoid the contract. But if the other contracting party had had actual knowledge of the undue influence or misrepresentation the victim would not, in my opinion, be held to the contract (see *Commission for the New Towns v Cooper (Great Britain) Ltd* [1995] Ch 259, 277–280 and *Banco Exterior Internacional SA v Thomas* [1997] 1 WLR 221, 229). But what if there had been no actual knowledge of the third party's undue influence or misrepresentation but merely knowledge of facts or circumstances that, if investigated, might have led to actual knowledge? In what circumstances does the law expect a contracting party to inquire into the reasons why the other party is entering into the contract or to go behind the other party's apparent agreement, objectively ascertained, to enter into the contract? These are the questions that Lord Browne-Wilkinson had to answer in *O'Brien*. They are contractual questions, not questions relating to competing property interests [. . .]

At [146]–[148]

In particular, it must be recognised that in the "bank v surety wife" cases the constructive notice that is sought to be attributed to the bank is not constructive notice of any pre-existing prior right or prior equity of the wife. The husband's impropriety, whether undue influence or misrepresentation, in procuring his wife to enter into a suretyship transaction with the bank would not entitle her to set it aside unless the bank had had notice of the impropriety. It is notice of the husband's impropriety that the bank must have, not notice of any prior rights of the wife. It is the notice that the bank has of the impropriety that creates the wife's right to set aside the transaction. The wife does not have any prior right or prior equity.

---

[120] See also [38]–[43], *per* Lord Nicholls.

In a case where the financial arrangements with the bank had been negotiated by the husband, no part in the negotiations having been played by the wife, and where the arrangements required the wife to become surety for her husband's debts, the bank would, or should, have been aware of the vulnerability of the wife and of the risk that her agreement might be procured by undue influence or misrepresentation by the husband. In these circumstances the bank would be "put on inquiry", as Lord Browne-Wilkinson put it. But "on inquiry" about what? Not about the existence of undue influence, for how could any inquiry reasonably to be expected of a bank satisfy the bank that there was no undue influence? "On inquiry", in my opinion, as to whether the wife understood the nature and effect of the transaction she was entering into. This is not an "inquiry" in the traditional constructive notice sense. The bank would not have to carry out any investigation or to ask any questions about the reasons why the wife was agreeing to the transaction or about her relationship with her husband. The bank would not, unless it had notice of additional facts pointing to undue influence or misrepresentation, be on notice that undue influence or misrepresentation was to be presumed. It would simply be on notice of a risk of some such impropriety. What Lord Browne-Wilkinson had in mind was that the bank should be expected to take reasonable steps to satisfy itself that she understood the transaction she was entering into. If the bank did so, no longer could constructive notice of any impropriety by the husband in procuring his wife's consent be imputed to it. The original constructive notice would have been shed. If, on the other hand, a bank with notice of the risk of some such impropriety, failed to take the requisite reasonable steps, then, if it transpired that the wife's consent had been procured by the husband's undue influence or misrepresentation, constructive knowledge that that was so would be imputed to the bank and the wife would have the same remedies as she would have had if the bank had had actual knowledge of the impropriety.

Under Lord Browne-Wilkinson's scheme for the protection of vulnerable wives it is the bank's perception of the risk that the wife's consent may have been procured by the husband's misrepresentation or undue influence that is central. The risk must be viewed through the eyes of the bank. Some degree of risk can, usually, never be wholly eliminated. But it can be reduced to a point at which it becomes reasonable for the bank to rely on the apparent consent of the wife to enter into the transaction and to take no further steps to satisfy itself that she understood the transaction she was entering into.

To avoid notice of the risk that the wife's consent to the mortgage has not been freely given, the lender must take reasonable and adequate steps to satisfy itself that the wife understood the nature of the mortgage into which she was entering, and that she was doing so of her independent will.

Three distinct stages were identified in *Etridge* to determine whether or not a mortgage may be set aside on the ground of undue influence.

Royal Bank of Scotland plc v Etridge
[2002] 2 AC 773, HL

Lord Hobhouse

At 819

It can be expressed by answering three questions: (1) Has the wife proved what is necessary for the court to be satisfied that the transaction was affected by the undue influence of the husband? (2) Was the lender put on inquiry? (3) If so, did the lender take reasonable steps to satisfy itself that there was no undue influence? It will be appreciated that unless the first question is answered in favour of the wife neither of the later questions arise. The wife has no defence and is liable. It will likewise be appreciated that the second and third questions arise from the fact that the wife is seeking to use the undue influence of her husband as a defence against the lender and therefore has to show that the lender should be affected by the equity—that it is unconscionable that the lender should enforce the secured contractual right against her.

3.3.1 The first stage: proof of undue influence

The wife must prove that she was unduly influenced by her husband: if there is no undue influence, there is no basis upon which she can set aside the mortgage against her interest in the home. Undue influence may be established either by proof of facts that demonstrate actual undue influence (e.g. threats of physical violence or psychological pressure), which left the wife unable to exercise her own judgment, or by producing evidence that will enable the court to infer that the wife's entry into the mortgage was obtained by the undue influence that her husband was presumed to have exerted. It is for the wife to prove either actual or presumed undue influence; upon establishing facts that raise a presumption of undue influence, however, the burden of proof shifts to the dominant party (i.e. the husband or the bank) to demonstrate that, in fact, the wife's participation was an exercise of her independent will.

These alternative ways of proving undue influence were characterized in *BCCI v Aboody*[121] as 'Class 1 actual undue influence' and 'Class 2 presumed undue influence', which could be inferred either through proof of a Class 2A relationship, when certain limited types of relationship (see section 3.1.3) were themselves sufficient to found the presumption, or in Class 2B, upon proof that the particular relationship was one of trust and confidence. Although the House of Lords in *O'Brien* adopted this classification, in *Etridge*, the House observed that the classification had led to an overly formulaic approach that had obscured the evidentiary role of presumed undue influence. Instead, the Lords reiterated that proof of undue influence was a question of fact, and articulated in more detailed and stringent terms when undue influence would be proved.[122]

Royal Bank of Scotland plc v Etridge
[2002] 2 AC 773, HL

Lord Nicholls

At [13]–[14]

Whether a transaction was brought about by the exercise of undue influence is a question of fact. Here, as elsewhere, the general principle is that he who asserts a wrong has been committed must prove it. The burden of proving an allegation of undue influence rests upon the person who claims to have been wronged. This is the general rule. The evidence required to discharge the burden of proof depends on the nature of the alleged undue influence,

---

[121] [1991] 1 QB 923.   [122] See also [2002] 2 AC 773, [882], *per* Lord Hobhouse.

the personality of the parties, their relationship, the extent to which the transaction cannot readily be accounted for by the ordinary motives of ordinary persons in that relationship, and all the circumstances of the case.

Proof that the complainant placed trust and confidence in the other party in relation to the management of the complainant's financial affairs, coupled with a transaction which calls for explanation, will normally be sufficient, failing satisfactory evidence to the contrary, to discharge the burden of proof. On proof of these two matters the stage is set for the court to infer that, in the absence of a satisfactory explanation, the transaction can only have been procured by undue influence. In other words, proof of these two facts is prima facie evidence that the defendant abused the influence he acquired in the parties' relationship. He preferred his own interests. He did not behave fairly to the other. So the evidential burden then shifts to him. It is for him to produce evidence to counter the inference which otherwise should be drawn [. . .]

At [16]–[19]

Generations of equity lawyers have conventionally described this situation as one in which a presumption of undue influence arises. This use of the term "presumption" is descriptive of a shift in the evidential onus on a question of fact. When a plaintiff succeeds by this route he does so because he has succeeded in establishing a case of undue influence. The court has drawn appropriate inferences of fact upon a balanced consideration of the whole of the evidence at the end of a trial in which the burden of proof rested upon the plaintiff. The use, in the course of the trial, of the forensic tool of a shift in the evidential burden of proof should not be permitted to obscure the overall position. These cases are the equitable counterpart of common law cases where the principle of res ipsa loquitur is invoked. There is a rebuttable evidential presumption of undue influence.

The availability of this forensic tool in cases founded on abuse of influence arising from the parties' relationship has led to this type of case sometimes being labelled "presumed undue influence". This is by way of contrast with cases involving actual pressure or the like, which are labelled "actual undue influence": [. . .]

The evidential presumption discussed above is to be distinguished sharply from a different form of presumption which arises in some cases. The law has adopted a sternly protective attitude towards certain types of relationship in which one party acquires influence over another who is vulnerable and dependent and where, moreover, substantial gifts by the influenced or vulnerable person are not normally to be expected. Examples of relationships within this special class are parent and child, guardian and ward, trustee and beneficiary, solicitor and client, and medical adviser and patient. In these cases the law presumes, irrebuttably, that one party had influence over the other. The complainant need not prove he actually reposed trust and confidence in the other party. It is sufficient for him to prove the existence of the type of relationship.

It is now well established that husband and wife is not one of the relationships to which this latter principle applies.

Thus, a wife wishing to raise a presumption of undue influence will need to provide evidence to the court: firstly, that the relationship she enjoyed with her husband in respect of financial decisions was one in which she reposed trust and confidence, rather than exercised her own judgment; and secondly, that the nature of the mortgage itself leads to an inference that there was a risk that her husband persuaded her to enter into the mortgage by questionable means. The burden of proof will then shift to establish that the wife did, in fact, give her consent freely.

As we have already observed, a relationship of trust and confidence is easier to recognize than to define. Lord Scott in *Etridge* went so far as to suggest that, in the normal course, a husband and wife's relationship was one of trust and confidence, and what was required was proof that this inherent trust and confidence had been abused.

Royal Bank of Scotland plc v Etridge
[2002] 2 AC 773, HL

Lord Scott

At [159]–[160]

For my part, I would assume in every case in which a wife and husband are living together that there is a reciprocal trust and confidence between them. In the fairly common circumstance that the financial and business decisions of the family are primarily taken by the husband, I would assume that the wife would have trust and confidence in his ability to do so and would support his decisions. I would not expect evidence to be necessary to establish the existence of that trust and confidence. I would expect evidence to be necessary to demonstrate its absence. In cases where experience, probably bitter, had led a wife to doubt the wisdom of her husband's financial or business decisions, I still would not regard her willingness to support those decisions with her own assets as an indication that he had exerted undue influence over her to persuade her to do so. Rather I would regard her support as a natural and admirable consequence of the relationship of a mutually loyal married couple. The proposition that if a wife, who generally reposes trust and confidence in her husband, agrees to become surety to support his debts or his business enterprises a presumption of undue influence arises is one that I am unable to accept. To regard the husband in such a case as a presumed "wrongdoer" does not seem to me consistent with the relationship of trust and confidence that is a part of every healthy marriage.

There are, of course, cases where a husband does abuse that trust and confidence. He may do so by expressions of quite unjustified over-optimistic enthusiasm about the prospects of success of his business enterprises. He may do so by positive misrepresentation of his business intentions, or of the nature of the security he is asking his wife to grant his creditors, or of some other material matter. He may do so by subjecting her to excessive pressure, emotional blackmail or bullying in order to persuade her to sign. But none of these things should, in my opinion, be presumed merely from the fact of the relationship of general trust and confidence. More is needed before the stage is reached at which, in the absence of any other evidence, an inference of undue influence can properly be drawn or a presumption of the existence of undue influence can be said to arise.

Relevant factors in determining the strength of a spousal relationship of trust and confidence include: the relative ages, education, and experience of the husband and wife; as well as the nature of their relationship, including its length; their respective characters; and the roles that they have assumed in their joint lives. Cultural factors may also have a part of play where particular religious or social norms dictate that a wife plays a subservient role in financial matters.[123] Feminist legal scholars have highlighted the gender imbalance inherent in the spousal relationship and have dubbed the phenomenon 'sexual transmitted debt'.[124]

---

[123] See *Barclays Bank v Coleman* [2002] 2 AC 773.
[124] See Kaye, 'Equity's Treatment of Sexually Transmitted Debt' (1997) 5 Feminist LS 35.

The House of Lords have underlined that a relationship of trust and confidence may exist between cohabiting heterosexual and homosexual couples, as well as between husband and wife. Nevertheless, trust and confidence is not dependent on a sexual relationship, but may arise in other close relationships—for example, between other family members[125]—and may even exceptionally exist in relationships that are apparently commercial—for example, that between employer and employee.[126]

Proof of a relationship of trust and confidence is not in itself sufficient; the wife must also prove that her entry into the mortgage is not readily explicable as an exercise of her independent will. In *National Westminster Bank v Morgan*,[127] the House of Lords had initially called for proof of a transaction that was 'manifestly disadvantageous' to the wife because, for example, she did not benefit from the loan. The courts often inclined to the view that a collateral mortgage over the family home to secure a loan to the husband's business was manifestly disadvantageous, in that the wife was placing the residential security of the home at risk for no direct financial benefit. A flood of undue influence cases followed. The House of Lords in *Etridge* abandoned the manifest disadvantage label and reverted instead to the test laid down in *Allcard v Skinner*,[128] which looks to whether or not the transaction is explicable by the relationship of the parties or calls for some further explanation.[129] The House also observed that a collateral mortgage of the family home to secure a husband's business debts will often be explicable by the nature of the parties' relationship and will not require any further explanation.[130]

Royal Bank of Scotland plc v Etridge
[2002] 2 AC 773, HL

Lord Nicholls

At [30]–[33] and [36]

[. . .] I do not think that, in the ordinary course, a guarantee of the character I have mentioned is to be regarded as a transaction which, failing proof to the contrary, is explicable only on the basis that it has been procured by the exercise of undue influence by the husband. Wives frequently enter into such transactions. There are good and sufficient reasons why they are willing to do so, despite the risks involved for them and their families. They may be enthusiastic. They may not. They may be less optimistic than their husbands about the prospects of the husbands' businesses. They may be anxious, perhaps exceedingly so. But this is a far cry from saying that such transactions as a class are to be regarded as prima facie evidence of the exercise of undue influence by husbands.

I have emphasised the phrase "in the ordinary course". There will be cases where a wife's signature of a guarantee or a charge of her share in the matrimonial home does call for explanation.

---

[125] See *Abbey National Bank plc v Stringer* [2006] EWCA Civ 338.
[126] See *Credit Lyonnais v Burch* [1997] 1 All ER 144.   [127] [1985] AC 686.
[128] (1885) 26 Ch D 145.
[129] See *Chater v Mortgage Services Agency Number Two Ltd* [2003] EWCA Civ 490; *National Commercial Bank (Jamaica) Ltd v Hew* [2003] UKPC 51; *Maklin v Dowsett* [2004] EWCA Civ 904; *Turkey v Awadh* [2005] 2 FCR 7; *Abbey National v Stringer* [2006] EWCA Civ 338.
[130] Lord Hobhouse suggested that a mortgage to secure the unlimited debts of the husband's business called for an explanation: [2002] 2 AC 733, [112].

I add a cautionary note [. . .] It concerns the general approach to be adopted by a court when considering whether a wife's guarantee of her husband's bank overdraft was procured by her husband's undue influence. Undue influence has a connotation of impropriety. In the eye of the law, undue influence means that influence has been misused. Statements or conduct by a husband which do not pass beyond the bounds of what may be expected of a reasonable husband in the circumstances should not, without more, be castigated as undue influence. Similarly, when a husband is forecasting the future of his business, and expressing his hopes or fears, a degree of hyperbole may be only natural. Courts should not too readily treat such exaggerations as misstatements.

Inaccurate explanations of a proposed transaction are a different matter. So are cases where a husband, in whom a wife has reposed trust and confidence for the management of their financial affairs, prefers his interests to hers and makes a choice for both of them on that footing. Such a husband abuses the influence he has. He fails to discharge the obligation of candour and fairness he owes a wife who is looking to him to make the major financial decisions [. . .]

At the same time, the high degree of trust and confidence and emotional interdependence which normally characterises a marriage relationship provides scope for abuse. One party may take advantage of the other's vulnerability. Unhappily, such abuse does occur. Further, it is all too easy for a husband, anxious or even desperate for bank finance, to misstate the position in some particular or to mislead the wife, wittingly or unwittingly, in some other way. The law would be seriously defective if it did not recognise these realities.

In the latter part of the above extract Lord Nicholls refers to the need for 'candour and fairness' in a relationship of trust and confidence and the connotations of impropriety upon which undue influence is founded. He makes these observations in the context of the (mis-) statements that may be made to encourage the wife to act as surety but candour and fairness may equally call for openness by the husband, which requires disclosure of facts that would affect the wife's decision. For instance, in *Hewett v First Plus Financial Group plc*[131] a husband, who hid the fact that he was having an affair when persuading his wife to mortgage their family home to avoid his bankruptcy, was found to have unduly influenced his wife.

A presumption of undue influence may be rebutted by proof (provided by the husband or lender) that the wife did, in fact, enter into the mortgage of her own free and independent will. The most usual way of demonstrating that this is so, is to show that the wife decided to enter into the mortgage after receiving independent advice, thus breaking the influence that previously controlled her actions.[132] The courts have been at pains to point out, however, that independent advice is no assurance that the presumption is rebutted; that is a question of fact, in the light of all of the circumstances.[133]

The House of Lords in *Etridge* provided guidance to solicitors when called upon to advise a wife.[134] The solicitors must be suitably qualified, both in terms of their professional capability to provide advice and their impartiality. There must be no conflict with the interests of their other clients: for example, the husband or the lender. The advice must be given in an environment that is free from the husband's influence and at a time before the transaction that provides sufficient opportunity for the wife to consider the import of the advice before she decides whether or not to proceed. The advice itself must not only explain the terms of the mortgage, but must also explain the implications and consequences of the mortgage for

---

[131] [2010] 2 P & CR 22. See also *Royal Bank of Scotland plc v Chandra* [2010] 1 Lloyds Rep 677.
[132] See, for instance, *Pathania v Adedeji* [2010] EWHC 3085.
[133] *BCCI v Aboody* [1990] 1 QB 923, 971; *UBC Corporate Services Ltd v Williams* [2002] EWCA Civ 555.
[134] [2002] 2 AC 733, [64]–[69], *per* Lord Nicholls, and [169]–[170], *per* Lord Scott.

the wife—in particular, that she could lose her home or become bankrupt if the loan is not repaid. The more difficult issue is the extent to which the solicitor should weigh and advise on the risks of enforcement, in the light of the wife's liabilities under the mortgage. The solicitor can make observations on the legal extent of these liabilities, but may not be qualified, or may not have sufficient information, to provide guidance on the commercial risks of the business generating the projected profit to meet those liabilities. What is clear is that the solicitor should press home that '*the wife has a choice. The decision is hers and hers alone*'.[135]

3.3.2 The second stage: notice of the bank

We have already observed that a lender, although not itself guilty of undue influence, may become subject to a wife's equity to set aside a mortgage entered into as result of the husband's actual or presumed undue influence, where it has notice of the risk that a wife may not have exercised her own independent judgment.

The House of Lords in *O'Brien* had set a test of notice that required proof of a relationship carrying a heightened risk of equitable wrong (whether of duress, undue influence, or misrepresentation) and a transaction that was disadvantageous to the weaker party—a test that tended to converge with that of presumed undue influence under *O'Brien*. In *Etridge*, however, the Lords clearly differentiated the two stages. Whilst they expressed proof of presumed undue influence in more stringent terms, they set a simple and relatively low-level threshold of notice, which would be straightforward for lenders to identify. The *Etridge* test provides that a lender should be put on notice whenever a wife stood as a surety for her husband's debts. The difficulty is that it is not always easy to identify whether it is the husband's business or a family business in which the wife is also interested.

Royal Bank of Scotland plc v Etridge
[2002] 2 AC 773, HL

Lord Nicholls

At [48]–[49]

As to the type of transactions where a bank is put on inquiry, the case where a wife becomes surety for her husband's debts is, in this context, a straightforward case. The bank is put on inquiry. On the other side of the line is the case where money is being advanced, or has been advanced, to husband and wife jointly. In such a case the bank is not put on inquiry, unless the bank is aware the loan is being made for the husband's purposes, as distinct from their joint purposes. That was decided in *CIBC Mortgages plc v Pitt* [1994] 1 AC 200.

Less clear cut is the case where the wife becomes surety for the debts of a company whose shares are held by her and her husband. Her shareholding may be nominal, or she may have a minority shareholding or an equal shareholding with her husband. In my view the bank is put on inquiry in such cases, even when the wife is a director or secretary of the company. Such cases cannot be equated with joint loans. The shareholding interests, and the identity of the directors, are not a reliable guide to the identity of the persons who actually have the conduct of the company's business.

---

[135] Ibid, [65]. Solicitors were found negligent in *Burbank Securities Ltd v Wong* [2008] EWHC 552.

The House of Lords in *Etridge* set a similar low threshold where there is a risk of presumed undue influence between other parties, who enjoy a relationship of trust and confidence, and who enter into a mortgage that calls for an explanation. In these circumstances, a bank is 'put on inquiry' of the risk of presumed undue influence whenever the relationship between the surety and the debtor is non-commercial.[136] Clearly thus the bank must be aware that the wife is acting as a surety.[137]

A bank will, thus, not be put on inquiry where the loan is to the husband and wife (or other parties) as joint borrowers unless the bank is aware that the loan is solely for the use of just one of the parties.[138] Where the loan is made to a sole borrower the lender will be put on inquiry if they were aware that the loan was for the benefit of another with whom the borrower enjoyed a relationship of trust and confidence.[139]

3.3.3 The third stage: the steps that the bank should take

Where the bank has notice of the risk that the surety's consent may have been procured by undue influence, it is required to '*take reasonable steps to bring home to the individual guarantor the risks he is running by standing as surety*'.[140] In both *O'Brien* and *Etridge*, the House of Lords was at pains to outline what those steps should be. In *O'Brien*, Lord Brown-Wilkinson suggested that the bank should arrange a private interview with the wife to explain to her those risks and advise her to take independent advice. But this practice did not find favour with lenders; they were reluctant to take direct responsibility for advising the wife; instead, they preferred to look to solicitors to shoulder that task. As a result, the House of Lords in *Etridge* reformulated the steps that a lender should take, emphasizing that the situation should be examined from the point of view of the lender. Those steps are not directed at '*discovering whether the wife has been wronged by her husband*', but are '*concerned to minimise the risk that such a wrong may have been committed*'.[141]

Royal Bank of Scotland plc v Etridge
[2002] 2 AC 773, HL

Lord Nicholls

At [54]

The furthest a bank can be expected to go is to take reasonable steps to satisfy itself that the wife has had brought home to her, in a meaningful way, the practical implications of the proposed transaction. This does not wholly eliminate the risk of undue influence or misrepresentation. But it does mean that a wife enters into a transaction with her eyes open so far as the basic elements of the transaction are concerned

[. . .]

---

136 Ibid, [87], *per* Lord Nicholls.   137 *Mortgage Business plc v Green* [2013] EWHC 4243.
138 Ibid, [48] *per* Lord Nicholls. See also *CIBC v Pitt* [1994] 1 AC 200, *Chater v Mortgage Services Agency Number Two Ltd* [2003] EWCA Civ 490, *Mortgage Business Plc v Green* [2013] EWHC 424, *Bradley v Governor of Bank of Ireland* (unreported), and *O'Neill v Ulster Bank Ltd* [2016] BPIR 126.
139 See, for example, *Burbank Securities Ltd v Wong* [2008] EWHC 552.
140 156 *Royal Bank of Scotland plc v Etridge* [2002] 2 AC 773, [87], *per* Lord Nicholls.
141 Ibid, [41], *per* Lord Nicholls. See also [164]–[165], *per* Lord Scott.

At [79]

I now return to the steps a bank should take when it has been put on inquiry and for its protection is looking to the fact that the wife has been advised independently by a solicitor.

1. One of the unsatisfactory features in some of the cases is the late stage at which the wife first became involved in the transaction. In practice she had no opportunity to express a view on the identity of the solicitor who advised her. She did not even know that the purpose for which the solicitor was giving her advice was to enable him to send, on her behalf, the protective confirmation sought by the bank. Usually the solicitor acted for both husband and wife.

Since the bank is looking for its protection to legal advice given to the wife by a solicitor who, in this respect, is acting solely for her, I consider the bank should take steps to check directly with the wife the name of the solicitor she wishes to act for her. To this end, in future the bank should communicate directly with the wife, informing her that for its own protection it will require written confirmation from a solicitor, acting for her, to the effect that the solicitor has fully explained to her the nature of the documents and the practical implications they will have for her. She should be told that the purpose of this requirement is that thereafter she should not be able to dispute she is legally bound by the documents once she has signed them. She should be asked to nominate a solicitor whom she is willing to instruct to advise her, separately from her husband, and act for her in giving the necessary confirmation to the bank. She should be told that, if she wishes, the solicitor may be the same solicitor as is acting for her husband in the transaction. If a solicitor is already acting for the husband and the wife, she should be asked whether she would prefer that a different solicitor should act for her regarding the bank's requirement for confirmation from a solicitor.

The bank should not proceed with the transaction until it has received an appropriate response directly from the wife.

2. Representatives of the bank are likely to have a much better picture of the husband's financial affairs than the solicitor. If the bank is not willing to undertake the task of explanation itself, the bank must provide the solicitor with the financial information he needs for this purpose. Accordingly it should become routine practice for banks, if relying on confirmation from a solicitor for their protection, to send to the solicitor the necessary financial information. What is required must depend on the facts of the case. Ordinarily this will include information on the purpose for which the proposed new facility has been requested, the current amount of the husband's indebtedness, the amount of his current overdraft facility, and the amount and terms of any new facility. If the bank's request for security arose from a written application by the husband for a facility, a copy of the application should be sent to the solicitor. The bank will, of course, need first to obtain the consent of its customer to this circulation of confidential information. If this consent is not forthcoming the transaction will not be able to proceed.

3. Exceptionally there may be a case where the bank believes or suspects that the wife has been misled by her husband or is not entering into the transaction of her own free will. If such a case occurs the bank must inform the wife's solicitors of the facts giving rise to its belief or suspicion.

4. The bank should in every case obtain from the wife's solicitor a written confirmation to the effect mentioned above.

The focus of these steps is thus to ensure that the wife is legally represented and that the lender receives confirmation from the solicitor acting for her that she has received advice.[142] To ensure that the wife's solicitor is in a position to give meaningful advice, the lender must disclose relevant financial information and any information that gives rise to any particular suspicions that the wife may have been improperly influenced by her husband. Given that the situation is viewed from the position of the lender, the lender is not required to be privy to the advice that the wife actually receives; it merely needs to receive confirmation that she has received advice, even if that advice is inadequate. The wife's right of action in these circumstances is against her solicitor for his or her negligent advice; she cannot challenge the mortgage itself unless the lender actually learns that she did not received advice or that the advice was inadequate.[143]

A further difficult question is the independence of the wife's solicitor: can a solicitor who acts also for the bank and/or the husband provide adequate independent advice to the wife? Clearly, it is preferable that the wife receives advice from a solicitor who can take a wholly impartial view of the prudence of the mortgage, but to add the fees of another professional adviser may be unwarranted in a situation in which finances are already stretched. The House of Lords in *Etridge* addressed this issue in a pragmatic fashion by leaving it to the solicitor's professional judgment to decide if there was an unacceptable conflict of interest.

Royal Bank of Scotland plc v Etridge
[2002] 2 AC 773, HL

Lord Nicholls

At [74]

The advantages attendant upon the employment of a solicitor acting solely for the wife do not justify the additional expense this would involve for the husband. When accepting instructions to advise the wife the solicitor assumes responsibilities directly to her, both at law and professionally. These duties, and this is central to the reasoning on this point, are owed to the wife alone. In advising the wife the solicitor is acting for the wife alone. He is concerned only with her interests. I emphasise, therefore, that in every case the solicitor must consider carefully whether there is any conflict of duty or interest and, more widely, whether it would be in the best interests of the wife for him to accept instructions from her. If he decides to accept instructions, his assumption of legal and professional responsibilities to her ought, in the ordinary course of things, to provide sufficient assurance that he will give the requisite advice fully, carefully and conscientiously. Especially so, now that the nature of the advice called for has been clarified. If at any stage the solicitor becomes concerned that there is a real risk that other interests or duties may inhibit his advice to the wife he must cease to act for her.

These steps lay down straightforward practical guidance for the normal case, but where the lender is aware of particular circumstances that increase the risk of impropriety, it needs to take additional precautions: for example, by making sure that the wife is advised by a solicitor who is not also representing the husband.[144]

---

[142] *Lloyds TSB Bank plc v Holdgate* [2002] EWCA Civ 1543 [2003] HLR 25, *Bank of Scotland v Hill* [2002] EWCA Civ 1081, and *HSBC Plc v Brown* [2015] EWHC 359.

[143] *Per* Lord Scott at [175]. See for instance *Padden v Bevan Ashford* [2012] 1 WLR 1759.

[144] *Per* Lord Scott at [174].

4   CONTROL OF MORTGAGE TERMS

The underlying principle is freedom of contract: the parties should be free to determine the terms of their loan and any mortgage to secure its repayment. But throughout the history of money lending, there has been a recognition that *'necessitous men are not, truly speaking, free men'*[145] and thus borrowers may require a level of protection against the often stronger bargaining power of lenders. The focus of this protection has changed as social and economic conditions have altered the nature of borrowers and their borrowing.

In early times, the laws against usury initially prohibited, and then controlled, interest rates to protect the souls of all. We have seen that, under the traditional mortgage by conveyance, the Chancery courts from the seventeenth century onwards would protect the borrower's right to redeem, so that the mortgage took effect only by way of security. Borrowers during this period were often landowners who needed relatively short-term financial relief, but, with the growing impact of the Industrial Revolution, the expansion of the Empire, and the importance of trade, the nineteenth century saw a growth in commercial borrowers. More often than not, they were astute businessmen who were able to wield sufficient negotiating power to look after themselves. Accordingly, protection of the equity of redemption on mortgages taken out to finance business exploits became less of a priority.

We have also noted that equity would frustrate the exploitation of particularly vulnerable borrowers by setting aside unconscionable bargains. This equitable jurisdiction was originally intended to protect heirs mortgaging their prospective interests in their family's landed estates, but it developed into a general jurisdiction to protect all vulnerable borrowers. It has been employed to vary mortgage terms that are demonstrably oppressive or unconscionable—a contribution that remains of significance today where borrowing is not subject to statutory control.

In more recent times, it is the cash-strapped consumer who is more often in need of protection from institutional lenders. Government has come to his or her relief through legislation that, as we have already examined, operates initially through market regulation, but may also intervene to control particular mortgage terms.

In our survey of the legal control of mortgage terms, we will look first at the sources from which control can emanate. In consumer borrowing statutory consumer legislation provides the most effective and intrusive form of control, which operates against the backdrop of market regulation that we have already examined in section 2. In commercial borrowing the principles of freedom of contract generally stand firm. Residuary protection is derived from common law and equitable control mechanisms and, in the case of lending to small and medium size business, the probity of certain practices in commercial lending is attracting some attention from regulatory authorities, principally the FCA.[146] We will then turn to examine how these mechanisms operate to control different types of term that have been the primary targets, namely terms that inhibited redemption, terms that provide for some collateral advantage to the lender, and terms that determine the level or fluctuation of interest rates.

---

[145] *Vernon v Bethell* (1761) 2 Eden 113, *per* Lord Nottingham.

[146] See, for instance, the sale of interest rate hedging products at <http://www.fca.org.uk/consumers/financial-services-products/banking/interest-rate-hedging-products>, accessed 3 November 2014.

4.1 SOURCES OF CONTROL

4.1.1 The common law

Common law controls are few, but the restraint of trade doctrine has been pressed into service to control collateral advantages that require the borrower to purchase products solely from the lender. Nowadays, extensive competition laws and market regulation provide a more effective and comprehensive framework to promote a free market domestically, globally, and within the European context. Implied terms have provided some limited control over the power of lenders to vary interest rates but an appeal to control on public policy grounds has largely failed.

4.1.2 Equitable control

Equitable control of mortgage terms is derived from two sources.[147] First, equity's protection against unconscionable bargains has been applied to vary oppressive and unconscionable mortgage terms, where both substantive and procedural unconscionability is established, and now underpins equity's most effective intervention in commercial borrowing.

Secondly, using the clogs and fetters doctrine, equity has struck down terms that bar or inhibit the borrower's equitable right to redeem.

The origin of equity's jurisdiction was described by Lord Haldane in the following leading case.

G & K Kreglinger v New Patagonia Meat and Cold Storage Co Ltd
[1914] AC 25, HL

Lord Haldane

At 35

The reason for which a Court of Equity will set aside the legal title of a mortgagee and compel him to reconvey the land on being paid principal, interest, and costs is a very old one. It appears to owe its origin to the influence of the Church in the Courts of the early Chancellors. As early as the Council of Lateran in 1179, we find, according to Matthew Paris (*Historia Major*, 1684 ed. at pp. 114–115), that famous assembly of ecclesiastics condemning usurers and laying down that when a creditor had been paid his debt he should restore his pledge. It was therefore not surprising that the Court of Chancery should at an early date have begun to exercise jurisdiction in personam over mortgagees. This jurisdiction was merely a special application of a more general power to relieve against penalties and to mould them into mere securities[... .]

My Lords, this was the origin of the jurisdiction which we are now considering, and it is important to bear that origin in mind. For the end to accomplish which the jurisdiction has been evolved ought to govern and limit its exercise by equity judges. That end has always been to ascertain, by parol evidence if need be, the real nature and substance of the transaction, and if it turned out to be in truth one of mortgage simply, to place it on

---

[147] Bamford, 'Lord Macnaghten's Puzzle: The Mortgage of Real Property in English Law' [1996] CLP 207.

that footing. It was, in ordinary cases, only where there was conduct which the Court of Chancery regarded as unconscientious that it interfered with freedom of contract. The lending of money, on mortgage or otherwise, was looked on with suspicion, and the Court was on the alert to discover want of conscience in the terms imposed by lenders. But whatever else may have been the intention of those judges who laid the foundations of the modern doctrines with which we are concerned in this appeal, they certainly do not appear to have contemplated that their principle should develop consequences which would go far beyond the necessities of the case with which they were dealing and interfere with transactions which were not really of the nature of a mortgage, and which were free from objection on moral grounds. Moreover, the principle on which the Court of Chancery interfered with contracts of the class under consideration was not a rigid one. The equity judges looked, not at what was technically the form, but at what was really the substance of transactions, and confined the application of their rules to cases in which they thought that in its substance the transaction was oppressive [. . .] The principle was thus in early days limited in its application to the accomplishment of the end which was held to justify interference of equity with freedom of contract. It did not go further. As established it was expressed in three ways. The most general of these was that if the transaction was once found to be a mortgage, it must be treated as always remaining a mortgage and nothing but a mortgage. That the substance of the transaction must be looked to in applying this doctrine and that it did not apply to cases which were only apparently or technically within it but were in reality something more than cases of mortgage, *Howard v. Harris* (1683) 1 Vern 33 2 Ch Cas 147 and other authorities shew.

Equity's protection of the equitable right to redeem has been gradually eroded since its heyday, when any clog or fetter on the borrower's right to recover his or her property was struck down. It only continues to be of significance where a device bars the right to redeem. This remaining intervention has been the subject of criticism by both judges and commentators.[148] In *Jones v Morgan*,[149] the Master of the Rolls, Lord Phillips, suggested that '[the] *doctrine of a clog on the equity of redemption is* [. . .] *an appendix to our law which no longer serves a useful purpose and would be better excised*'. The Law Commission has made such a recommendation, but the doctrine continues to limp along, causing more problems than it solves.[150]

We should add one further equitable contribution to the regulation of mortgage terms: the prohibition on penalties. Equity will strike down a provision that provides for a payment to be made by a party in default because the charge imposed is out of all proportion to the lender's legitimate interest for instance in compensating them for their loss as opposed to punishing the defaulter for their breach.[151]

---

[148] See Devonshire, 'The Modern Application of the Rule Against Clogs in The Equity of Redemption' (1997) 5 APLJ 1; Thompson, 'Do We Really Need Clogs?' [2001] Conv 502; Duncan and Wilmott, 'Clogging the Equity of Redemption: An Outmoded Concept' (2002) 2 QUTLJJ 35; Berg, 'Clogs on the Equity of Redemption: Or Chaining an Unruly Dog' [2002] JBL 335; Devenney, 'A Pack of Unruly Dogs: Unconscionable Bargains, Lawful Act (Economic) Duress and Clogs on the Equity of Redemption' (2002) JBL 539; Watt, 'Mortgage Law as Fiction' in *Modern Studies in Property Law: Vol 4* (ed Cooke, Oxford: Hart Publishing, 2007, p 89).
[149] [2001] EWCA Civ 995, [72].
[150] Law Commission Report No 204, Land Mortgages (2001, Part VIII).
[151] *Makdessi v Cavendish Square Holdings BV: ParkingEye Ltd v Bevis* [2016] AC 1172.

4.1.3 Statutory consumer control

We have already noted the extensive regulation of the domestic credit market both through the FSMA and the CCA.[152] Inevitably, these regulatory controls impact upon mortgage terms.

Another source of protection arises from the treatment of borrowers as consumers and entitled to general consumer protection. This consumer protection is now to be found in the,Consumer Rights Act 2015 (CRA), which replaces the Unfair Terms in Consumer Contract Regulations.[153]

After some initial hesitation, it is clear that this general consumer legislation does apply to contracts affecting land, including mortgages.[154] They apply to individual borrowers, but not companies. Thus they may be used to control the fairness of terms and practices governing many non-commercial mortgages. An unfair term is not binding on the borrower and an individual borrower can challenge terms as unfair and thus of no effect.[155] Both the FCA and the Consumer Protection and Markets Authority (CMA) also acts at a regulatory level as consumer watchdogs by considering and taking action on complaints made both by consumer and consumer organizations, by investigating and providing guidance on potentially unfair terms and practices.[156] The CMA derives their authority from the CRA whilst the FCA has power to act both under the FSMA and the CRA. In relation to consumer credit, including mortgages, the FCA takes primary responsibility for control over unfair terms.[157] In accordance with the principles of decentred regulation we considered in section 2, both the CMA and the FCA try and educate and give guidance to lenders on the fairness of their standard terms and they have both issued regulatory guidance to this end.[158] Where the CMA or the FCA consider that a lender's particular terms are potentially unfair they will enter into a dialogue with that lender to persuade them to alter their terms and may ask the lender to enter into an undertaking to that end. It is only where these informal means fail that regulators will resort to judicial proceedings.[159]

The definition of an unfair term is found in ss 62–64 of the CRA.

Consumer Rights Act 2015

62 Requirement for contract terms and notices to be fair

(1) An unfair term of a consumer contract is not binding on the consumer.

(2) An unfair consumer notice is not binding on the consumer.

---

[152] See section 2.

[153] 1999 SI 1999/2083 and continues to apply to contracts entered into from 1 July 1995 to 30 September 2015. These statutory protections implement the Unfair Terms in Consumer Contracts Directive (93/13/EC). The Consumer Protection from Unfair Trading Regulations SI 2008/1277 apply to land sales but are not significant in relation to mortgage sales.

[154] *Newham LBC v Khatun* [2004] EWCA Civ 55, [2005] QB 37.   [155] CRA s 62(1).

[156] CRA, s 70. This role was exercised by the Office of Fair Trading before its abolition and the transfer of its regulatory responsibilities to the CMA.

[157] Although they co-ordinate with other consumer agencies, see CMA, Consumer Protection: Guidance on the CMA's approach to use of its consumer powers.

[158] See CMA,Unfair Contracts Terms Guidance CMA 37 (July 2015) and FCA UNFCOG Handbook.

[159] See CMA, Consumer Protection: Guidance on the CMA's approach to use of its consumer powers and the FCA, Enforcement Guide in the FCA Handbook.

(3) This does not prevent the consumer from relying on the term or notice if the consumer chooses to do so.

(4) A term is unfair if, contrary to the requirement of good faith, it causes a significant imbalance in the parties' rights and obligations under the contract to the detriment of the consumer.

(5) Whether a term is fair is to be determined—

    (a) taking into account the nature of the subject matter of the contract, and

    (b) by reference to all the circumstances existing when the term was agreed and to all of the other terms of the contract or of any other contract on which it depends.

63 Contract terms which may or must be regarded as unfair

(1) Part 1 of Schedule 2 contains an indicative and non-exhaustive list of terms of consumer contracts that may be regarded as unfair for the purposes of this Part.

(2) Part 1 of Schedule 2 is subject to Part 2 of that Schedule; but a term listed in Part 2 of that Schedule may nevertheless be assessed for fairness under section 62 unless section 64 or 73 applies to it.

64 Exclusion from assessment of fairness

(1) A term of a consumer contract may not be assessed for fairness under section 62 to the extent that—

    (a) it specifies the main subject matter of the contract, or

    (b) the assessment is of the appropriateness of the price payable under the contract by comparison with the goods, digital content or services supplied under it.

(2) Subsection (1) excludes a term from an assessment under section 62 only if it is transparent and prominent.

(3) A term is transparent for the purposes of this Part if it is expressed in plain and intelligible language and (in the case of a written term) is legible.

(4) A term is prominent for the purposes of this section if it is brought to the consumer's attention in such a way that an average consumer would be aware of the term.

(5) In subsection (4) *"average consumer"* means a consumer who is reasonably well-informed, observant and circumspect.

The CRA test of unfairness encompasses both a lack of good faith, and a significant imbalance in the rights and liabilities of the parties, which operates to the detriment of the borrower. Sch 2 of CRA illustrates the test by setting out a non-exhaustive 'grey list' of terms, which potentially may be regarded as unfair: for example, para (e) provides that a term '*requiring any consumer who fails to fulfill his obligation to pay a disproportionately high sum in compensation*' is potentially unfair. The grey list's focus is upon the substantive rights and obligations of the parties, but Lord Bingham, giving the leading judgment in *Director General of Fair Trading v First National Bank*, clearly contemplated that good faith also called for procedural fairness in how the loan is entered into.

Director General of Fair Trading v First National Bank plc
[2002] 1 AC 481, HL

Lord Bingham

At [17]

[Referring to the earlier form of the Regulations] [. . .] But the language used in expressing the test, so far as applicable in this case, is in my opinion clear and not reasonably capable of differing interpretations. A term falling within the scope of the regulations is unfair if it causes a significant imbalance in the parties' rights and obligations under the contract to the detriment of the consumer in a manner or to an extent which is contrary to the requirement of good faith. The requirement of significant imbalance is met if a term is so weighted in favour of the supplier as to tilt the parties' rights and obligations under the contract significantly in his favour. This may be by the granting to the supplier of a beneficial option or discretion or power, or by the imposing on the consumer of a disadvantageous burden or risk or duty. The illustrative terms set out in Schedule 3 to the regulations provide very good examples of terms which may be regarded as unfair; whether a given term is or is not to be so regarded depends on whether it causes a significant imbalance in the parties' rights and obligations under the contract. This involves looking at the contract as a whole. But the imbalance must be to the detriment of the consumer; a significant imbalance to the detriment of the supplier, assumed to be the stronger party, is not a mischief which the regulations seek to address. The requirement of good faith in this context is one of fair and open dealing. Openness requires that the terms should be expressed fully, clearly and legibly, containing no concealed pitfalls or traps. Appropriate prominence should be given to terms which might operate disadvantageously to the customer. Fair dealing requires that a supplier should not, whether deliberately or unconsciously, take advantage of the consumer's necessity, indigence, lack of experience, unfamiliarity with the subject matter of the contract, weak bargaining position or any other factor listed in or analogous to those listed in Schedule 2 of the regulations. Good faith in this context is not an artificial or technical concept; nor, since Lord Mansfield was its champion, is it a concept wholly unfamiliar to British lawyers. It looks to good standards of commercial morality and practice. Regulation 4(1) lays down a composite test, covering both the making and the substance of the contract, and must be applied bearing clearly in mind the objective which the regulations are designed to promote.

The focus of the requirement of fairness is generally upon standard terms and conditions, which are not individually negotiated by the lender and the borrower.[160] The European Court of Justice has provided some guidance on how this question should be approached in the following important case.

Aziz v Caixa d'Estalvis de Catalunya, Tarragona i Manresa (Catalunyacaixa)
[2013] 3 CMLR 5

Facts: Mr Aziz's mortgage specified a default rate of interest of 18.5 per cent and that the total amount of the loan would be immediately repayable in the event of default.

---

[160] CRA, s 62(5). See *UK Housing Alliance (North West) Ltd v Francis* [2010] EWCA Civ 117.

Mr Aziz fell behind in his mortgage repayments and in accordance with Spanish law his home was repossessed. Although Mr Aziz could challenge the fairness of a mortgage term before the court, he could not prevent the repossession of his home. Mr Aziz applied for declaratory relief that these terms were unfair under the Unfair Contract Terms Directive.

At [76]

In the light of the foregoing, the answer to the second question is that:
 Article 3(1) of Directive 93/13 must be interpreted as meaning that:

 — the concept of "significant imbalance", to the detriment of the consumer, must be as-sessed in the light of an analysis of the rules of national law applicable in the absence of any agreement between the parties, in order to determine whether, and if so to what extent, the contract places the consumer in a less favourable legal situation than that pro-vided for by the national law in force. To that end, an assessment of the legal situation of that consumer having regard to the means at his disposal, under national law, to prevent continued use of unfair terms, should also be carried out; and

 — in order to assess whether the imbalance arises "contrary to the requirement of good faith", it must be determined whether the seller or supplier, dealing fairly and equitably with the consumer, could reasonably assume that the consumer would have agreed to the term concerned in individual contract negotiations.

Article 3(3) of Directive 93/13 must be interpreted as meaning that the annex to which that provision refers contains only an indicative and non-exhaustive list of terms which may be regarded as unfair.

Terms concerning the main subject matter or the price payable of the contract are ex-cluded from the requirement for fairness, [161] It is suggested that the main subject matter of a mortgage should be restricted to the amount of the loan and the level of interest chargeable. The House of Lords, in *Director General of Fair Trading v First National Bank plc*, made clear that the interpretation of such excluded terms should be restrict-ively construed and, thus, did not extend to additional charges payable as a result of the borrower's default.

Director General of Fair Trading v First National Bank plc
[2002] 1 AC 481, HL

Lord Steyn

At [34]

Clause 8 of the contract, the only provision in dispute, is a default provision. It prescribes remedies which only become available to the lender upon the default of the consumer. For this reason the escape route of regulation 3(2) is not available to the bank. So far as the description of terms covered by regulation 3(2) as core terms is helpful at all, I would say that clause 8 of the contract is a subsidiary term. In any event, article 3(2) must be given a

---

[161] CRA s 64(1).

> restrictive interpretation. Unless that is done article 3(2)(a) will enable the main purpose of the scheme to be frustrated by endless formalistic arguments as to whether a provision is a definitional or an exclusionary provision. Similarly, article 3(2)(b) dealing with "the adequacy of the price of remuneration" must be given a restrictive interpretation. After all, in a broad sense all terms of the contract are in some way related to the price or remuneration. That is not what is intended. Even price escalation clauses have been treated by the Director as subject to the fairness provision [. . .] It would be a gaping hole in the system if such clauses were not subject to the fairness requirement.

The CRA moves away from reference to 'the core terms of the contract' which was the wording used in the regulations the CRA replaced. Instead the reference is to 'the main subject matter of the contract' or 'the appropriateness of the price payable'. This change seeks to address criticism resulting from the case of *OFT v Abbey National Plc*[162] in which the Supreme Court refused to consider the fairness of unauthorized overdraft charges because they decided it was part and parcel of the core terms.

The CRA also requires terms, including excluded terms, to be 'transparent and prominent' in the sense that they are expressed in plain and intelligible language[163] and are brought to the consumer's attention.[164] The terms must be capable of being understood by ordinary members of the public and not only lawyers or other experts. These requirements present a challenge where the subject matter is inherently complex. It is the comprehensibility of the result that was important. It was no excuse that a reasonable attempt to explain complex subject matter had been made, if a layman would still fail to grasp its meaning. The aim of comprehensibility is supported by prohibition on terms that a borrower has no real opportunity to consider before the mortgage is completed.[165]

The message is clear: lenders must make sure that their standard terms and conditions meet the standards of fairness required by the legislation, and illustrated by CMA and FCA guidance.[166] Furthermore, lenders must ensure that the import of those terms and conditions are brought home to the borrower, both because they can be understood by any layman, and also because there is a process that ensures that borrowers are given an opportunity to read and consider these terms before they are bound. The indications are that certain, but not all, lenders have received and understood that message.[167]

4.2 PARTICULAR MORTGAGE TERMS: REDEMPTION

At the heart of the clogs and fetters doctrine is the protection of the borrower's equity of redemption, and the attendant right of the borrower to repay the loan and redeem, or recover, the land free of the lender's mortgage. Any device that could prevent the borrower from exercising his or her right to redeem will be struck down. As we have noted, the clogs and fetters doctrine is of marginal significance and then only in the commercial context. Any

---

[162] [2010] 1 AC 696.   [163] CRA, s 64(2).   [164] CRA, s 64(2)–(4).

[165] See CCA, Sch 1, para 1(i).

[166] See generally Simmonds, 'Bankers' Documents and the Unfair Terms in Consumer Contracts Regulations 1999' (2002) 17 JIBL 205.

[167] The FSA's *Report on Fairness of Terms in Consumer Contracts* (2008, available online at <http://www.fsa.gov.uk>) found that some lenders, particularly smaller lenders, are unaware of the need to comply with CRA.

limitations upon consumer borrowers' rights to redeem will be addressed through market and statutory controls.

4.2.1 Options to purchase

The most common example of a device falling foul of this principle is the grant to the lender of an option to purchase the mortgaged property, although the courts have become increasingly frustrated with this assault on the parties' freedom to agree commercial terms.

Lord Halsbury expressed such sentiments in the following case.

Samuel v Jarrah Timber & Wood Paving Corporation Ltd
[1904] AC 323, HL

Lord Halsbury

At 323

A perfectly fair bargain made between two parties to it, each of whom was quite sensible of what they were doing, is not to be performed because at the same time a mortgage arrangement was made between them. If a day had intervened between the two parts of the arrangement, the part of the bargain which the appellant claims to be performed would have been perfectly good and capable of being enforced; but a line of authorities going back for more than a century has decided that such an arrangement as that which was here arrived at is contrary to a principle of equity, the sense or reason of which I am not able to appreciate, and very reluctantly I am compelled to acquiesce in the judgments appealed from.

Lord Halsbury refers to the fact that if a day had intervened between the mortgage and the option, the transactions would have been upheld.

The principle is not quite as easily avoided. It must be evident that the mortgage and the option are separate transactions in substance, and not merely in form.[168] For example, in *Jones v Morgan*,[169] an option granted some three years after the date of the original mortgage was struck down because the Court took the view that the option formed part of a variation of the original mortgage. It was of no matter that the Court also found that the option was neither an unconscionable bargain, nor extracted as a result of economic duress.[170]

Echoing the words of Lord Haldane in *Krelinger* (extract at section 4.1.2), the transaction must also be, in substance, a mortgage—an issue that was central to the following case.[171]

---

[168] See *Reeve v Lisle* [1902] AC 461; *Lewis v Frank Love* [1961] 1 WLR 261.

[169] [2001] EWCA Civ 995.

[170] Devenney, 'A Pack of Unruly Dogs: Unconscionable Bargain, Lawful Act (Economic) Duress and Clogs on the Equity of Redemption' [2002] JBL 539.

[171] See also *Brighton & Hove CC v Audus* [2009] EWHC 340.

Warnborough Ltd v Garmite Ltd
[2003] EWCA Civ 1544, CA

Facts: Warnborough sold land to Garmite, leaving the purchase money outstanding, but secured by a mortgage to Warnborough. At the same time, Garmite granted Warnborough an option to repurchase the land for the original sale price as a further protection against the risk that the purchase price would not be paid. The option was not a fetter on the equity of redemption, because the transaction was, in substance, a sale and purchase, not a mortgage.

Jonathan Parker LJ

At [72]–[73]

In the light of the authorities to which I have referred, it has to be accepted that the "unruly dog" is still alive (although one might perhaps reasonably expect its venerable age to inhibit it from straying too far or too often from its kennel); and that however desirable an append-ectomy might be thought to be, no such relieving operation has as yet been carried out. Indeed, Mr Teverson did not seek to contend otherwise.

That said, it is in my judgment glaringly clear from the authorities that the mere fact that, contemporaneously with the grant of a mortgage over his property, the mortgagor grants the mortgagee an option to purchase the property does no more than raise the question whether the rule against 'clogs' applies: it does not begin to answer that question. As has been said over and over again in the authorities, in order to answer that question the court has to look at the 'substance' of the transaction in question: in other words, to inquire as to the true nature of the bargain which the parties have made. To do that, the court examines all the circum-stances, with the assistance of oral evidence if necessary.

4.2.2 Postponement of the right to redeem

The postponement of the right to redeem is not, per se, an unacceptable clog on the equity of redemption. A postponement will be struck down if it renders the right to redeem illusory. For example, in *Fairclough v Swan Brewery Co*,[172] the right to redeem was held to be illusory where the borrower could not repay the loan until just six weeks prior to the expiry of the mortgaged leasehold term.

A postponement will also be struck down if it is oppressive or unconscionable; unreason-ableness is insufficient. This conclusion was reached in the following case, in a judgment that illustrates the courts' reluctance to interfere with the freedom of contract of commercial parties.

Knightsbridge Estates Trust Ltd v Byrne
[1939] Ch 441, CA

Facts: Knightsbridge mortgaged a number of freehold properties to secure a loan of £300,000, with interest payable at 6.5 per cent. In 1931, the company renegotiated the

---

[172] [1912] AC 565.

loan on more favourable terms. It was to be repayable by eighty half-yearly instalments (i.e. over forty years), with interest at 5.25 per cent, and the lender agreed not to call in the loan, provided that the borrower performed the loan terms. Interest rates fell further and Knightsbridge wished to repay the loan to obtain still more favourable terms.

Greene MR

At 453

The first argument was that the postponement of the contractual right to redeem for forty years was void in itself, in other words, that the making of such an agreement between mortgagor and mortgagee was prohibited by a rule of equity. It was not contended that a provision in a mortgage deed making the mortgage irredeemable for a period of years is necessarily void. The argument was that such a period must be a "reasonable" one, and it was said that the period in the present case was an unreasonable one by reason merely of its length. This argument was not the one accepted by the learned judge.

Now an argument such as this requires the closest scrutiny, for, if it is correct, it means that an agreement made between two competent parties, acting under expert advice and presumably knowing their own business best, is one which the law forbids them to make upon the ground that it is not "reasonable." If we were satisfied that the rule of equity was what it is said to be, we should be bound to give effect to it. But in the absence of compelling authority we are not prepared to say that such an agreement cannot lawfully be made. A decision to that effect would, in our view, involve an unjustified interference with the freedom of business men to enter into agreements best suited to their interests and would impose upon them a test of "reasonableness" laid down by the Courts without reference to the business realities of the case.

It is important to remember what those realities were. The respondents are a private company and do not enjoy the facilities for raising money by a public issue possessed by public companies. They were the owners of a large and valuable block of property, and so far as we know they had no other assets. The property was subject to a mortgage at a high rate of interest and this mortgage was liable to be called in at any time. In these circumstances the respondents were, when the negotiations began, desirous of obtaining for themselves two advantages: (1.) a reduction in the rate of interest, (2.) the right to repay the mortgage moneys by instalments spread over a long period of years. The desirability of obtaining these terms from a business point of view is manifest, and it is not to be assumed that these respondents were actuated by anything but pure considerations of business in seeking to obtain them. The sum involved was a very large one, and the length of the period over which the instalments were spread is to be considered with reference to this fact. In the circumstances it was the most natural thing in the world that the respondents should address themselves to a body desirous of obtaining a long term investment for its money. The resulting agreement was a commercial agreement between two important corporations experienced in such matters, and has none of the features of an oppressive bargain where the borrower is at the mercy of an unscrupulous lender. In transactions of this kind it is notorious that there is competition among the large insurance companies and other bodies having large funds to invest, and we are not prepared to view the agreement made as anything but a proper business transaction.

But it is said not only that the period of postponement must be a reasonable one, but that in judging the "reasonableness" of the period the considerations which we have mentioned cannot be regarded; that the Court is bound to judge "reasonableness" by a consideration of the terms of the mortgage deed itself and without regard to extraneous matters. In the absence of clear authority we emphatically decline to consider a question of "reasonableness" from a standpoint so unreal. To hold that the law is to tell business men what is reasonable in such circumstances and to refuse to take into account the business considerations involved, would bring the law into disrepute. Fortunately, we do not find ourselves forced to come to any such conclusion [. . .]

But in our opinion the proposition that a postponement of the contractual right of redemption is only permissible for a "reasonable" time is not well-founded. Such a postponement is not properly described as a clog on the equity of redemption, since it is concerned with the contractual right to redeem. It is indisputable that any provision which hampers redemption after the contractual date for redemption has passed will not be permitted. Further, it is undoubtedly true to say that a right of redemption is a necessary element in a mortgage transaction, and consequently that, where the contractual right of redemption is illusory, equity will grant relief by allowing redemption [. . .]

Moreover, equity may give relief against contractual terms in a mortgage transaction if they are oppressive or unconscionable, and in deciding whether or not a particular transaction falls within this category the length of time for which the contractual right to redeem is postponed may well be an important consideration. In the present case no question of this kind was or could have been raised.

But equity does not reform mortgage transactions because they are unreasonable. It is concerned to see two things—one that the essential requirements of a mortgage transaction are observed, and the other that oppressive or unconscionable terms are not enforced. Subject to this, it does not, in our opinion, interfere. The question therefore arises whether, in a case where the right of redemption is real and not illusory and there is nothing oppressive or unconscionable in the transaction, there is something in a postponement of the contractual right to redeem, such as we have in the present case, that is inconsistent with the essential requirements of a mortgage transaction? Apart from authority the answer to this question would, in our opinion, be clearly in the negative. Any other answer would place an unfortunate restriction on the liberty of contract of competent parties who are at arm's length—in the present case it would have operated to prevent the respondents obtaining financial terms which for obvious reasons they themselves considered to be most desirable.

4.2.3 Charges for early redemption

It is common practice for lenders to offer advantageous rates of interest to domestic borrowers who agree that they will not redeem for a fixed period. Lenders benefit from the certainty of receiving a known return on their investment for the fixed term. The price to be paid for these advantageous rates of interest is payment of an agreed sum should the borrower wish to redeem before the fixed period has expired. Such charges are a frequent cause of complaint by borrowers, although regulations under both the FSMA require such charges to be explained to the borrower, and to be calculated as a genuine pre-estimation of the lender's loss. A redemption charge that fails to do so also runs the risk of being unfair under the CRA,[173] or attracting regulatory redress if it does not comply with MCOB rules.[174] It is also conceivable that a redemption charge could be held to be an oppressive and unconscionable term or a penalty.

---

[173] *Falco Finance Ltd v Gough* [1999] CCLR 16; *Evans v Cherry Tree Finance Ltd* [2008] EWCA Civ 331.
[174] See MCOB 12.

4.3 PARTICULAR MORTGAGE TERMS: COLLATERAL ADVANTAGES

A collateral advantage is an added benefit that the lender negotiates as a condition of the mortgage. The most common examples are the tied and solus agreements that a brewery or petrol company requires of its retailers. These agreements are often associated with a mortgage, which, together, operate to require the borrower to purchase their supplies solely from the lender as a condition of the lender providing loan facilities to purchase, improve, or support the borrower's business. They thus occur most commonly in the commercial lending environment,[175] where regulation operates through equitable controls or the common law, and statutory controls on competition. A collateral advantage encountered in the domestic lending market will be subject to the regulatory controls of the FSMA, as well as the fairness test demanded by the CRA.[176]

4.3.1 Equitable controls

Historically, equity would strike down any collateral advantage. When the usury laws limited interest rates, a collateral advantage was considered an illegal means of avoiding these limits. With the abolition of the usury laws and the surge in economic activity of the nineteenth century, equity's abhorrence of collateral advantages waned. Initial relaxation was exemplified in the cases of *Biggs v Hodinott*[177] and *Bradley v Carritt*,[178] in which collateral advantages limited to the life of the mortgage were accepted. A collateral advantage that could extend beyond the life of the mortgage was seen as an unacceptable clog on the equity of redemption, because the borrower would not be able to redeem his or her property free of this burden.[179]

Further relaxation flowed from the following landmark decision.

G & K Kreglinger v New Patagonia Meat and Cold Storage Co Ltd
[1914] AC 25, HL

Facts: Kreglinger advanced the meat company funds that were secured by a floating charge. In addition to the loan, Kreglinger negotiated a right of pre-emption to purchase any sheepskins produced by the meat company over a five-year period, for the best market price, and to be paid a commission on any sheepskins that the meat company sold to third parties. The meat company redeemed the loan within the five-year option period and unsuccessfully claimed that it should be free of its obligations regarding the sale of the sheepskins.

Lord Haldane LC

At 37

The Legislature during a long period placed restrictions on the rate of interest which could legally be exacted. But equity went beyond the limits of the statutes which limited the

---

[175] Although see *Cityland and Property Holdings Ltd v Dabrah* [1968] Ch 166, in which a premium on the amount repayable over the amount lent was characterized as a collateral advantage.

[176] For instance, the way in which payment protection insurance was sold by lenders, or their associated companies, began to look suspiciously like a collateral advantage.

[177] [1898] 2 Ch 307.   [178] [1903] AC 25.   [179] *Noakes v Rice* [1902] AC 24.

interest, and was ready to interfere with any usurious stipulation in a mortgage. In so doing it was influenced by the public policy of the time. That policy has now changed, and the Acts which limited the rate of interest have been repealed. The result is that a collateral advantage may now be stipulated for by the mortgagee provided that he has not acted unfairly or oppressively, and provided that the bargain does not conflict with the third form of the principle. This is that a mortgage [. . .] cannot be made irredeemable, and that any stipulation which restricts or clogs the equity of redemption is void. It is obvious that the reason for the doctrine in this form is the same as that which gave rise to the other forms. It is simply an assertion in a different way of the principle that once a mortgage always a mortgage and nothing else.

My Lords, the rules I have stated have now been applied by Courts of Equity for nearly three centuries, and the books are full of illustrations of their application. But what I have pointed out shews that it is inconsistent with the objects for which they were established that these rules should crystallize into technical language so rigid that the letter can defeat the underlying spirit and purpose. Their application must correspond with the practical necessities of the time. The rule as to collateral advantages, for example, has been much modified by the repeal of the usury laws and by the recognition of modern varieties of commercial bargaining. In *Biggs v. Hoddinott* [1898] 2 Ch. 307 it was held that a brewer might stipulate in a mortgage made to him of an hotel that during the five years for which the loan was to continue the mortgagors would deal with him exclusively for malt liquor. In the seventeenth and eighteenth centuries a Court of Equity could hardly have so decided, and the judgment illustrates the elastic character of equity jurisdiction and the power of equity judges to mould the rules which they apply in accordance with the exigencies of the time. The decision proceeded on the ground that a mortgagee may stipulate for a collateral advantage at the time and as a term of the advance, provided, first, that no unfairness is shewn, and, secondly, that the right to redeem is not thereby clogged. It is no longer true that, as was said in *Jennings v. Ward* 2 Vern. 520, "a man shall not have interest for his money and a collateral advantage besides for the loan of it." Unless such a bargain is unconscionable it is now good. But none the less the other and wider principle remains unshaken, that it is the essence of a mortgage that in the eye of a Court of Equity it should be a mere security for money, and that no bargain can be validly made which will prevent the mortgagor from redeeming on payment of what is due, including principal, interest, and costs. He may stipulate that he will not pay off his debt, and so redeem the mortgage, for a fixed period. But whenever a right to redeem arises out of the doctrine of equity, he is precluded from fettering it. This principle has become an integral part of our system of jurisprudence and must be faithfully adhered to.

My Lords, the question in the present case is whether the right to redeem has been interfered with. And this must, for the reasons to which I have adverted in considering the history of the doctrine of equity, depend on the answer to a question which is primarily one of fact. What was the true character of the transaction? Did the appellants make a bargain such that the right to redeem was cut down, or did they simply stipulate for a collateral undertaking, outside and clear of the mortgage, which would give them an exclusive option of purchase of the sheepskins of the respondents? The question is in my opinion not whether the two contracts were made at the same moment and evidenced by the same instrument, but whether they were in substance a single and undivided contract or two distinct contracts. Putting aside for the moment considerations turning on the character of the floating charge, such an option no doubt affects the freedom of the respondents in carrying on their business even after the mortgage has been paid off. But so might other arrangements which would be plainly collateral, an agreement, for example, to take permanently into the firm a new partner as a condition of obtaining fresh capital in the form of a loan. The question is one not of form but of substance, and it can be answered in each case only by looking at all the circumstances, and not by mere reliance on some abstract principle, or upon the dicta which have fallen obiter from judges in other and different cases. Some, at least, of the authorities on the subject disclose an embarrassment which has, in my opinion, arisen from neglect to bear this in mind. In applying a principle the ambit and validity of which depend on confining it steadily to the end for which it was established, the analogies of previous instances where it has been applied are apt to be misleading. For each case forms a real precedent only in so far as it affirms a principle, the relevancy of which in other cases turns on the true character of the particular transaction, and to that extent on circumstances.

My Lords, if in the case before the House your Lordships arrive at the conclusion that the agreement for an option to purchase the respondents' sheepskins was not in substance a fetter on the exercise of their right to redeem, but was in the nature of a collateral bargain the entering into which was a preliminary and separable condition of the loan, the decided cases cease to present any great difficulty.

It is thus necessary to consider initially the substance of the transaction, and whether the advantage is part and parcel of the mortgage consideration or independent of it, despite being part of the parties' overall bargain—an enquiry that it is not always easy to conduct. If it forms part and parcel of the mortgage, one may then move on to consider whether the advantage is repugnant to the equitable grounds already identified.

4.3.2 Restraint of trade

The ability of the law to strike down terms in restraint of trade has a long history, dating at least from Elizabethan times. A party's freedom to contract must be balanced against the wide public interest of the freedom of all to trade. The doctrine has been pressed into service on a number of occasions to attack collateral advantages in mortgages—not always with success. The doctrine has no application to a collateral advantage in a mortgage used to acquire the borrower's business premises,[180] in which there is no restraint of an existing trade, but may be applied to a collateral advantage in a mortgage taken over business premises that a borrower already owns. In these circumstances, the question of whether an attendant collateral advantage is in restraint of trade looks to the reasonableness of the protection it affords. In *Esso Petroleum Co Ltd v Harpers Garage (Stourport) Ltd*,[181] a mortgage that postponed the borrower's right to redeem for twenty-one years, and a connected solus agreement that required the borrower to purchase all of its petroleum products from Esso for a similar period, were struck down as unreasonable restraints on trade. Similar agreements for shorter terms of five years or so have been upheld.[182]

The utility of the doctrine is overshadowed by the extensive competition laws that now govern commercial activity.[183]

---

[180] *Cleveland Petroleum Ltd v Dartstone Ltd* [1969] 1 WLR 116; *Alec Lobb (Garages) Ltd v Total Oil Great Britain Ltd* [1985] 1 WLR 173.
[181] [1968] AC 269.   [182] Ibid; *Texaco v Mulberry Filling Station* [1972] 1 WLR 814.
[183] Hopkins (1998) 49 NILQ 202.

4.4 PARTICULAR MORTGAGE TERMS: INTEREST RATES

The rate of interest and other costs associated with borrowing is, of course, of central importance to both the borrower and the lender.

4.4.1 Fluctuating and index-linked interest rates

Gray and Gray[184] have observed the surprising acceptance of the uncertainty inherent in the market norm of fluctuating or index-linked interest rates, which withstood attack on the basis of public policy in *Mutliservice Bookbinding Ltd v Marden*[185] (extracted at section 4.4.2), and has not been questioned as being oppressive or unconscionable. The CRA also accepts that an interest rate in a mortgage will not be unfair because it is fluctuating or index-linked, provided (in the case of a fluctuating rate) that the lender both abides by the terms of the loan contract[186] and gives notice to the borrower of any change and the borrower is able to redeem if he or she so wishes.[187] However, the FCA, in pursuance of the principle that borrowers should be treated fairly, is considering the fairness of changes to consumer mortgage contracts prompted, in part, by concerns surrounding the projected increase in interest rates from their historic low following the financial crisis.[188]

At common law the lender's discretion to alter a fluctuating interest rate is not unfettered. The Court of Appeal, in the conjoined appeals of *Paragon Finance plc v Nash* and *Paragon Finance plc v Staunton*,[189] accepted two grounds upon which a term should be implied to define the manner in which a discretion should be exercised. The first implies a term that rates will not be altered improperly, arbitrarily, or capriciously, and the second, that, in exercising a discretion, the lender will not do so unreasonably—in the sense that no lender acting reasonably would act similarly.[190]

Paragon Finance plc v Nash
[2002] 1 WLR 685, CA

Dyson LJ

At [30]–[32]

I cannot accept the submission of Mr Malek that the power given to the claimant by these loan agreements to set the interest rates from time to time is completely unfettered. If that were so, it would mean that the claimant would be completely free, in theory at least, to specify interest rates at the most exorbitant level. It is true that in the case of the Nash agreement clause 3.3 provides that the rate charged is that which applies to the category of business to which the claimant considers the mortgage belongs. That prevents the claimant from treating the Nashes differently from other borrowers in the same category. But it does not protect borrowers in that category from being treated in a capricious manner, or, for

---

[184] Gray and Gray, *Elements of Land Law* (5th edn, Oxford: OUP, 2009), [6.2.40].
[185] [1978] Ch 84.   [186] *Alexander v West Bromwich Mortgage Co Ltd* [2016] EWCA Civ 496.
[187] See CRA, Sch 2, para 2(b) and (d).
[188] FCA, Fairness in Changes to Mortgage Contracts (DP14/2).
[189] See also *Paragon Finance plc v Pender* [2005] EWCA Civ 760.
[190] See also *Bank of Scotland plc v Rea, McGeady, Laverty* [2014] NIMaster 11 where a unilateral decision by the lender to capitalize arrears was held to be 'Wednesday unreasonable.'

example, being subjected to very high rates of interest in order to force them into arrears with a view to obtaining possession of their properties.

The Stauntons do not even have the limited protection that is afforded by clause 3.3 of the Nash agreement. In the absence of an implied term, there would be nothing to prevent the claimant from raising the rate demanded of the Stauntons to exorbitant levels, or raising the rate to a level higher than that required of other similar borrowers for some improper purpose or capricious reason. An example of an improper purpose would be where the lender decided that the borrower was a nuisance (but had not been in breach of the terms of the agreement) and, wishing to get rid of him, raised the rate of interest to a level that it knew he could not afford to pay. An example of a capricious reason would be where the lender decided to raise the rate of interest because its manager did not like the colour of the borrower's hair.

It seems to me that the commercial considerations relied on by Mr Malek are not sufficient to exclude an implied term that the discretion to vary interest rates should not be exercised dishonestly, for an improper purpose, capriciously or arbitrarily. I shall come shortly to the question whether the discretion should also not be exercised unreasonably [. . .]

At [37]

I come, therefore, to the question whether the implied term should also extend to "unreasonably". The first difficulty is to define what one means by "unreasonably". Mr Bannister was at pains to emphasise that he was not saying that the rates of interest had to be reasonable rates in the sense of closely and consistently tracking LIBOR or the rates charged by the Halifax Building Society. He said that what he meant by the unreasonable exercise of the discretionary power to set the rate of interest was something very close to the capricious or arbitrary exercise of that power [. . .]

At [41]–[42]

So here, too, we find a somewhat reluctant extension of the implied term to include unreasonableness that is analogous to Wednesbury unreasonableness. I entirely accept that the scope of an implied term will depend on the circumstances of the particular contract. But I find the analogy of the *Gan Insurance case* [2001] EWCA Civ 1047 and the cases considered in the judgment of Mance LJ helpful. It is one thing to imply a term that a lender will not exercise his discretion in a way that no reasonable lender, acting reasonably, would do. It is unlikely that a lender who was acting in that way would not also be acting either dishonestly, for an improper purpose, capriciously or arbitrarily. It is quite another matter to imply a term that the lender would not impose unreasonable rates. It could be said that as soon as the difference between the claimant's standard rates and the Halifax rates started to exceed about two percentage points the claimant was charging unreasonable rates. From the defendant's point of view, that was undoubtedly true. But, from the claimant's point of view, it charged these rates because it was commercially necessary, and therefore reasonable, for it to do so.

I conclude therefore that there was an implied term of both agreements that the claimant would not set rates of interest unreasonably in the limited sense that I have described. Such an implied term is necessary in order to give effect to the reasonable expectations of the parties.

4.4.2 Excessive interest rates

The laws against usury set limits on the level of interest rates and, since their abolition, there have, from time to time, been monetary levels imposed upon interest rates for certain types of borrowing.[191] The modern thinking is against setting interest rate ceilings,[192] but to consider other mechanisms by which interest rates can be kept within acceptable bounds.

In the mortgage market, these mechanisms are to be found in the FSMA.[193] For example, the MCOB rules prohibit excessive charges and the charging of compound interest—a mechanism of capitilizing interest that can lead to a sharp increase in the amount of the debt.[194] In respect of the CRA, it should be noted that the interest rate will escape the requirement for fairness if it is a core term, although subsidiary provisions that deal with the calculation or variation of interest—for example, on default—will be caught.[195] Equity's jurisdiction over oppressive and unconscionable terms is also available, but presents a stricter test than the appropriate statutory controls.[196] Where these statutory controls do not apply, for instance in the commercial context, equity's control of oppressive and unconscionable terms provides a final, although rather fragile, safety net.

The test of an oppressive and unconscionable term is strict, looking not only at the substantive fairness of the terms themselves, but also at the procedural fairness with which they were agreed, when the financial expertise and bargaining position of the parties is of central concern.

Multiservice Bookbinding Ltd v Marden
[1979] Ch 84, HC

Facts: Multiservice borrowed £36,000 from Marden to fund the purchase of new premises. The loan could not be redeemed for ten years; interest was calculated at 2 per cent above the bank rate on the entire amount of the loan, regardless of capital repayments, with arrears of interest being compounded after twenty-one days. In addition, any repayments of capital and interest were linked to the Swiss franc to protect the lender against sterling exchange rate fluctuations. Sterling did, indeed, decline in value against the Swiss franc, leaving the amount payable by Multiservice when it tried to redeem in excess of £133,000. Mutliservice unsuccessfully claimed that these terms were oppressive and unconscionable.[197]

---

[191] See the Moneylenders Act 1900.

[192] See Department of Trade and Industry, *Fair, Clear and Competitive: The Consumer Credit Market in the 21st Century* (Cm 6040, 2003), [3.49]–[3.55]: the FCA have imposed an interest rate cap on payday and other high interest rate loans, see FCA PS14/16.

[193] For allegations of excessive interest contributing to an unfair relationship under ss 140A–C see *Barons Finance Ltd v Olubisi* (unreported 26 April 2010) where an interest rate of 3.5 per cent per month contributed to the unfairness of the relationship and *Chubb & Bruce v Dean* [2014] EWHC 1282.

[194] Compound interest is acceptable and common practice in commercial lending *The Maira* [1990] 1 AC 637; *Guardian Ocean Cargors Ltd v Banco Brasil SA (No 3)* [1992] 2 Lloyds Rep 193; *Westdeutsche Landesbank Girozentrale v Islington BC* [1996] AC 669.

[195] *Falco Finance Ltd v Gough* [1999] CCLR 16; *Director General of Fair Trading v First National Bank plc* [2001] UKHL 52.

[196] See *Cityland & Property (Holdings) Ltd v Dabrah* [1968] Ch 166.

[197] Multiservice also unsuccessfully claimed the indexation terms were contrary to public policy.

Browne-Wilkinson J

At 110

[. . .] in order to be freed from the necessity to comply with all the terms of the mortgage, the plaintiffs must show that the bargain, or some of its terms, was unfair and unconscionable: it is not enough to show that, in the eyes of the court, it was unreasonable. In my judgment a bargain cannot be unfair and unconscionable unless one of the parties to it has imposed the objectionable terms in a morally reprehensible manner, that is to say, in a way which affects his conscience.

The classic example of an unconscionable bargain is where advantage has been taken of a young, inexperienced or ignorant person to introduce a term which no sensible well-advised person or party would have accepted. But I do not think the categories of unconscionable bargains are limited: the court can and should intervene where a bargain has been procured by unfair means.

Mr. Nugee submitted that a borrower was, in the normal case, in an unequal bargaining position vis-à-vis the lender and that the care taken by the courts of equity to protect borrowers—to which Lord Parker referred in the passage I have quoted—was reflected in a general rule that, except in the case of two large equally powerful institutions, any unreasonable term would be "unconscionable" within Lord Parker's test. I cannot accept this. In my judgment there is no such special rule applicable to contracts of loan which requires one to treat a bargain as having been unfairly made even where it is demonstrated that no unfair advantage has been taken of the borrower. No decision illustrating Mr. Nugee's principle was cited. However, if, as in the *Cityland case* [1968] Ch. 166, there is an unusual or unreasonable stipulation the reason for which is not explained, it may well be that in the absence of any explanation, the court will assume that unfair advantage has been taken of the borrower. In considering all the facts, it will often be the case that the borrower's need for the money was far more pressing than the lenders need to lend: if this proves to be the case, then circumstances exist in which an unfair advantage could have been taken. It does not necessarily follow that what could have been done has been done: whether or not an unfair advantage has in fact been taken depends on the facts of each case.

Applying those principles to this case, first I do not think it is right to treat the "Swiss franc uplift" element in the capital-repayments as being in any sense a premium or collateral advantage. In my judgment a lender of money is entitled to insure that he is repaid the real value of his loan and if he introduces a term which so provides, he is not stipulating for anything beyond the repayment of principal [. . .] Secondly, considering the mortgage bargain as a whole, in my judgment there was no great inequality of bargaining power as between the plaintiffs and the defendant. The plaintiff company was a small but prosperous company in need of cash to enable it to expand: if it did not like the terms offered it could have refused them without being made insolvent or, as in the *Cityland case*, losing its home. The defendant had £40,000 to lend, but only, as he explained to the plaintiffs, if its real value was preserved. The defendant is not a professional moneylender and there is no evidence of any sharp practice of any kind by him. The borrowers were represented by independent solicitors of repute. Therefore the background does not give rise to any pre-supposition that the defendant took an unfair advantage of the plaintiffs [. . .] However, Mr. Nugee's other points amount to a formidable list and if it were relevant I would be of the view that the terms were unreasonable judged by the standards which the court would adopt if it had to settle the terms of a mortgage. In particular I consider that it was unreasonable both for the debt to be inflation proofed by reference to the Swiss franc and at the same time to provide for a rate of interest two per cent. above bank rate—a rate which reflects at least in part the unstable state of the pound sterling. On top of this interest on the whole sum advanced was to be paid throughout the term. The defendant made a hard bargain. But the test is not reasonableness. The parties made a bargain which the plaintiffs, who are businessmen, went into with their eyes open, with the benefit of independent advice, without any compelling necessity to accept a loan on these terms and without any sharp practice by the defendant. I cannot see that there was anything unfair or oppressive or morally reprehensible in such a bargain entered into in such circumstances.

4.4.3 Penalties and other onerous terms

In assessing the fairness of a consumer loan or the unconscionability of a commercial loan, it is significant to look not only at the interest rate, but also at the other terms of the agreement. Of particular import are terms that operate upon default and which may operate as a penalty, rather than a genuine and proportionate charge to safeguard the lender's legitimate interest,[198] or which may attract particular scrutiny under the MCOB rules, or against the test of fairness under the CRA.[199]

An increase in the rate of interest payable on arrears following default runs the risk of being a penalty, although a modest uplift in the interest rate payable on future interest payments following default may be acceptable, particularly in the commercial context.[200] A lower concessionary interest rate paid upon prompt payment is not generally regarded as a penalty,[201] although, in a consumer contract, it may still fall foul of the fairness test.

The case of *Falco Finance Ltd v Gough*[202] serves as an example. Mr Gough obtained a third mortgage over his home from Falco for £30,000 in the hope of clearing the arrears on his prior mortgages. The loan was repayable over a term of twenty-five years at a flat interest rate of 13.99 per cent, with an APR of 19.4 per cent. A concessionary rate of 8.99 per cent was, however, payable unless the mortgage went into arrears, when all future payments would not qualify for the discount. Mr Gough missed the first payment and thus the standard rate become immediately payable. The enforceability of these terms became an issue when Falco applied for possession. The court held that the disparity in the dual interest rate mechanism was unfair under the CRA.[203] The fact that interest was paid at a flat rate on the whole of the capital, irrespective of any amounts repaid, was also found to be unfair.

QUESTIONS

1. Compare the regulatory regimes established by the Financial Services and Markets Act 2000 and Consumer Credit Act 1974. Which regime do you think is most effective in protecting borrowers?

2. Does the alternative dispute resolution facility provided by the Financial Ombudsman Service provide sufficient and effective redress to consumer borrowers?

---

[198] See as an example in the leasehold context *Vivienne Westwood Ltd v Conduit Street Development Ltd* [2017] EWHC 350.

[199] *County Leasing Ltd v East* [2007] EWHC 2907.

[200] Although see *Lordsvale Finance Ltd v Bank of Zambia* [1996] QB 752, in which an interest uplift of 1 per cent on future interest payments to be made following default was held not to be a penalty in a commercial loan.

[201] *Wallingford v Mutual Society* (1880) 5 App Cas 685.   [202] [1999] CCLR 16.

[203] See CRA, Sch 2, para 1(e).

3. How does a wife prove that her husband has unduly influenced her and when will a bank be 'on notice' that a wife may have been unduly influenced by her husband?

4. In *Barclays Bank v O'Brien* and *Royal Bank of Scotland plc v Etridge*, the House of Lords tried to ensure that '*a law designed to protect the vulnerable does not render the matrimonial home unacceptable security to financial institutions*'. Has it succeeded?

5. What is the relationship between undue influence and unconscionable bargains? Would it be helpful to assimilate the two doctrines?

6. Does the clogs and fetters doctrine continue to have any utility?

7. When is a mortgage term 'unfair' within the meaning of the Consumer Rights Act 2015?

8. What legal controls can a borrower use to challenge the interest that he or she has agreed to pay the lender?

For guidance on how to answer these questions visit the online resources at www.oup.com/uk/mcfarlane4e/.

FURTHER READING

Bamford, 'Lord Macnaghten's Puzzle: The Mortgage of Real Property in English Law' [1996] CLP 207

Berg, 'Clogs on the Equity of Redemption: Or Chaining an Unruly Dog' [2002] JBL 335

Bigwood, 'Undue Influence: Impaired Consent or Wicked Exploitation' (1996) 16 OJLS 503

Birks and Chin, 'On the Nature of Undue Influence' in *Good Faith and Fault in Contract Law* (eds Beatson and Friedmann, Oxford: Clarendon Press, 1995, ch 3)

Devenney, 'A Pack of Unruly Dogs: Unconscionable Bargains, Lawful Act (Economic) Duress and Clogs on the Equity of Redemption' (2002) JBL 539

Deveney and Chandler, 'Unconscionability and the Taxonomy of Undue Influence' [2007] JBL 541

Nield, 'Borrower as Consumers: New Notions of Unconscionability for the Domestic Borrowers' in *Unconscionability in European Commercial Transactions: Protecting the Vulnerable* (eds Fox, Kenny, and Devenney, Cambridge: CUP, 2010) ch 10

Nield, 'Responsible Lending and Borrowing: Whereto Low Cost Home Ownership' (2010) 30 LS 610

Nield, 'Mortgage Market Review: Hardwired Commonsense?' [2015] Consumer Law and Policy Whitehouse, 'A Longitudinal Analysis of the Mortgage Repossession Process 1995–2010: Stability, Regulation and Reform' in *Modern Studies in Property Law Vol 6* (ed Bright, Oxford: Hart Publishing, 2011) ch 7

Whitehouse, 'The First Legal Mortgagor: A Consumer Without Adequate Protection' [2015] Consumer Law and Policy on line 15 March 2015

INDEX

A

Absolute title 297
Acquisition of rights
    see also **Adverse possession; Trusts of land**
    easements
        express grant 910–11
        implied grant 911–35
        prescriptive rights 935–51
    equitable mortgages 1046–8
    equitable rights and interests 188–9
        proprietary estoppel 359–415
    formalities
        central issues 258
        contracts 263–6
        creation and transfer 289–95
        e-conveyancing 304–6
        introduction 260–2
        overview 262–3
    freeholds 169
    impact of LRA 2002
        equitable interests 700
        legal estates and interests 698–700
    leases 169
        equitable leases 792–4
        legal leases 786–92
    legal estates 169
    legal rights and interests 169, 175–6
    proprietary estoppel 359–415
    registration of title under LRA 2002 70–6
    restrictive covenants 975–7
    shared homes
        central issues 454–5
        introduction 455–7
        trusts 457–94
    trusts 188–9
Adverse possession
    'adverse' defined 316–20
    based on relativity of title 313–14
    central issues 309
    conclusions 356–7
    criminalization of residential squatting
        Best litigation 349–52
        effect of criminalization 346–9
        overview 344–5
        statutory provisions 345–6
    effects
        registered land 334–44
        unregistered land 333–4
    effect of interruption 326–9
    human rights 352–6

impact of LRA 2002 699–700
introduction 310–11
justifications for conferring legal rights 311–12
key date for accrual of action 314–16
leases 357
'possession' defined
    acknowledgement starts time again 329–32
    essential requirements 320–1
    factual possession 321–2
    intention 322–4
    ordinary meaning 320
    rule in *Leigh v Jack* 325
possessory title 297
termination by claimant 326
Annexation of covenants
    express 979–81
    once-for-all process 979
    statutory provisions 981–8
Anticipation *see* **Doctrine of anticipation**
Appurtenant land 895–6
Assignments
    enforcement of leasehold covenants 878–80
        assignees—post-1995 847–51
        assignees—pre-1996 842–7
        original parties—post-1995 839–42
        original parties—pre-1996 836–9
    freehold covenants 978–9

B

Bad faith *see* **Fraud**
Bankruptcy
    applications for sale involving co-owners
        applications by creditors 553–62
        applications by trustees in bankruptcy 565–75
        introduction 549–51
        policy considerations 551–3
    charging orders 1050–4
    severance of joint tenancies 517, 521
Bare licences
    licensee's rights against strangers 210–11
    licensee's rights against third parties 210–11
    meaning 209
    revocation by licensor 209–10
Beneficiaries
    consultation by trustees 535
    occupation rights
        applications for sale 551
        overreaching 669–73
        trusts of land 535–9

Bona fide purchasers for value
doctrine of notice 535
human rights safeguards 109–10
limits on tracing 687
restrictive covenants against 976
without notice 64
Building schemes 988–95

C

Charges
see also **Land Charges; Mortgages**
defined 1040–1
equity of redemption
history and development 1055–6
legal charges 1056–9
Land Register 307
legal charges by way of mortgage 1043–6
mortgages distinguished 1045–6
priority 582–91
Charging orders 1050–4
Children
occupiers' rights 625–6
overriding interests 625–6
trustee applications 543
Co-habitation
see **Shared homes**
Collateral advantages
equitable controls 1161–3
meaning and scope 1161
restraint of trade 1163
Collateral contracts 272–5
Commonholds
central issues 1008
commonhold associations 1021–3
community statement 1023–4
creation 1019–20
dispute resolution 1028
legal structure 1018–19
management 1025–6
objectives 1018–19
purity of title 1020–1
Common intention constructive trusts
beneficial ownership of shared homes
critique of common intention 492–4
impact of *Stack v Dowden* 463–6
Jones v Kernott clarification 466–74
central issues 417
Pallant v Morgan constructive trust 447–8
presumed resulting trusts
distinguished 429–34
provision of loans 283
severance of joint tenancies 525–6
shared homes
central issues 454
introduction 455–7
joint tenancies 507, 509

severance issues 525–6
sole legal owners 475–7
type of constructive trust 436
Common law rules
relationship with equity 194–202
Compensation *see* **Damages and compensation**
Completion
e-conveyancing 306
effect 290–3
formal requirements 289–90
Consent
see also **Licences**
adverse possession 316–20
defence to priority claims
express consent 596
implied consent 596–602
prescriptive rights 942–9
Conspiracy *see* **Lawful act conspiracy**
Constructive trusts
beneficial ownership of shared homes
impact of *Stack v Dowden* 463–6
Jones v Kernott clarification 466–74
overview 463
common intention constructive trusts
central issues 417
home ownership 454–7
joint tenancies 507, 509
Pallant v Morgan constructive trust 447–8
presumed resulting trusts
distinguished 429–34
severance issues 525–6
sole legal owners 475–7
type of constructive trust 436
contractual licensee's rights against third
parties 229–31
institutional and remedial versions
distinguished 435–6
judicial definitions 434–5
Pallant v Morgan equity
difficulties of analysis 447–8
three requirements 443–6
unconscionability 446–7
practical difficulties with occupiers and
banks 17–19
proprietary estoppel compared 277–84
rationalization of common links 443–6
Rochefoucauld v Boustead doctrine
overview 437–8
three-party case 441–3
two-party case 438–41
search for rationalization 448
sole legal owners of shared homes
express and inferred agreement constructive
trusts 477–85
impact of *Stack v Dowden/Jones v
Kernott* 485–9
leading case of *Lloyds Bank plc v Rosset* 475–7

Consumer credit
  excessive interest rates 1165–8
  FSMA licensing regime 1127
  history and development 1126
  unfair relationships 1127–8
  unfair terms 1152–6
Contractual promises
  basis of proprietary estoppel 360–8
  completion
    effect 290–3
    formal requirements 289–90
  effect
    acquisition of equitable interest 286–7
    creation of third-party property rights 288–9
    estate contracts 287–8
    requirement of doctrine of
      anticipation 284–6
  formal requirements
    collateral contracts 272–5
    completion 289–90
    by correspondence 268
    effects of non-compliance 271–2
    exchange of contracts 268–9
    executed contracts 271–2
    legal and equitable rights and interests 263–6
    overview 262–3
    proprietary estoppel 277–84
    rectification 275–7
    signatures 269–71
    statutory provisions 263–6
  leases
    characterization of contract 801–4
    effects of lease 731–40
  licences
    licensee's rights against strangers 218–22
    licensee's rights against third parties 223–45
    licensee's rights against grantor 213–18
    meaning and scope 211–13
  mortgages 1114
  overriding interests 618
Conversion see Doctrine of anticipation
Co-ownership
  applications for sale
    applications by creditors 553–62
    applications by trustees in
      bankruptcy 565–75
    central issues 549
    impact of statutory changes 563–4
    introduction 549–51
    overlapping jurisdiction under
      FLA 1996 564–5
    policy considerations 551–3
  central issues 503
  introduction 503–4
  joint tenancies
    desirability of the beneficial joint
      tenancy 530–1

  factors determining type of ownership
    506–9
  severance 510–28
  survivorship 509–10
  tenancies in common distinguished 504–6
  overlap between the FLA 1996 and the TOLATA
    1996 545–8
  overreaching
    breach of trust 674–80
    effect 649–50
    interests capable of being
      overreached 652–61
    occupying beneficiaries 669–73
    possible future developments 682–5
    scope 651–2
    shared homes 680–2
    transactions with overreaching effect 662–9
  priority of rights and interests
    see also Overreaching
    central issues 648
    introduction 649
    where overreaching does not occur 688–91
  tenancies in common
    factors determining type of ownership 506–9
    joint tenancies distinguished 504–6
  termination 529–30
  trusts of land
    beneficiaries' rights 535–9
    court applications relating to trustee
      functions 540–5
    dominant feature of the regulation of
      co-ownership 531–3
    statutory scope 533
    trustees' powers 533–5
Courts
  applications for sale involving co-owners
    applications by creditors 553–62
    applications by trustees in
      bankruptcy 565–75
    impact of statutory changes 563–4
    overlapping jurisdiction under FLA
      1996 564–5
  charging orders 1050–4
  statutory control of mortgage repossession
    discretionary powers 1079–88
    'dwelling-houses' 1076
    jurisdiction 1076–8
    notice to lender 1078–9
    postponement of sale 1088–9
    social functions 1089
  trustee applications
    child welfare 543
    general principles 541–3
    impact of TOLATA 1996 543–5
    statutory provisions 540–1
Covenants see Freehold covenants; Leasehold
    covenants

Creation of legal rights and interests *see*
 Formalities
Creditors *see* **Insolvency**
Curtain principle 66–7, 77, 168, 613, 631, 641,
 683, 688

D

Damages and compensation
 adverse possession 352
 breach of freehold covenants 999
 breach of leasehold covenants 856–7
 importance of indemnities 722–3
 interference with protection of property
  (ECHR Art 1) 123–5
 rectification and indemnity of title register 306
 role of indemnity payments 65–6
Deeds
 easements 910–11
 formal requirements 293–5
 leases 787
Defences
 breach of freehold covenants 999
 easements
  registered land 951–2
  unregistered land 952
 impact of LRA 2002
  equitable interests 701
  legal estates and interests 700–1
 leases
  equitable leases 801
  legal leases 800
 priority of rights
  exceptions to basic rule 591–2
  express consent 596
  implied consent 596–602
  lapse of time 602–4
  legal and equitable property rights
   distinguished 604
 public authorities 104–5
 registration of title under LRA 2002 76–9
Delivery of deeds 294–5
Direct rights
 see also **Equitable rights and interests; Legal
  interests**
 fraud giving rise to new right 643–5
 licensee's rights against third parties
  bare licences 210–11
  contractual licences 223–31
  estoppel licences 248
  licences coupled with an interest 256
  possibility of new direct right 206–7
  statutory licences 252
Discrimination (Art 14)
 Convention text 111
 horizontal protection of the vulnerable 111–13
 overreaching 684

Dishonest assistance 685–6
Distress for rent 857–8
Doctrine of anticipation
 acquisition of equitable interest 286–7
 central issues 259
 constructive trusts 419
 effect of completion 290
 gifts 295
 need to comply with formalities 266
 proprietary estoppel 365
 registered land 295
 revocation of licences 235
 security interests 1040, 1046
 underlying requirement for contracts 284–6
Doctrine of conversion 654–5
Dominant tenements
 essential characteristics 888
 essential requirements
  accommodation by servient land 897–902
  land separate from servient tenement
   888–96
  separate ownership from servient
   tenement 896–7
  subject matter of grant 902–10
 excessive user 953–4
 freehold covenants
  equitable rules of enforcement 961–2
  particular requirements 962–3
Duress
 conceptual underpinnings 1135–6
 meaning and scope 1130–1
Dwelling houses 1075–89

E

Easements
 acquisition of rights
  express grant 910–11
  implied grant 911–35
  prescriptive rights 935–51
 central issues 885
 effect of adverse possession 334
 essential requirements
  accommodation of dominant land 897–902
  overview 888
  separate ownership of dominant and servient
   tenements 896–7
  separate pieces of land 888–96
  subject matter of grant 902–10
 excessive user 953–4
 extinguishment 954–5
 history and development 887
 introduction 885–6
 overriding interests 619–20, 637–8
 priority of rights
  registered land 951–2
  unregistered land 952

E-conveyancing
  formal requirements 304
  legal impact 304–6
  objectives 304
Enforcement *see* **Remedies**
Enfranchisement of long leases 1013–14
Environmental themes 4–5, 130
Equitable leases
  assignee's liability
    post-1995 law 848
    pre-1996 law 846–7
  defences 801
  formalities 792–4
Equitable mortgages
  acquisition of rights 1046–8
  equitable charges 1049–50
  equitable estates 1048–9
  reform proposals 1050
Equitable rights and interests
  see also **Equitable leases; Equitable mortgages;**
    Trusts of land
  acquisition of rights
    formalities 193–4
  beneficial ownership of shared homes
    impact of *Stack v Dowden* 463–6
    Jones v Kernott clarification 466–74
    overview 463
  central issues 179
  concept of equitable interest in land 184–5
  contents
    equitable interests 189–90
    limitations 191–3
    longer list of property rights 189
  contractual formalities 263–6
  development of equitable property
    rights 181–4
  doctrine of anticipation
    acquisition of equitable interest 286–7
    central issues 259
    constructive trusts 419
    effect of completion 290
    gifts 295
    need to comply with formalities 266
    proprietary estoppel 365
    registered land 295
    revocation of licences 235
    security interests 1040, 1046
    underlying requirement for contracts 284–6
  easements
    registered land 951–2
    unregistered land 952
  effect of contract
    acquisition of equitable interest 286–7
    estate contracts 287–8
  functions of equity 180–1
  impact of LRA 2002
    acquisition of rights 700

    content question 698
    defences 701
  overreaching
    breach of trust 674–80
    effect 649–50
    interests capable of being
      overreached 652–61
    occupying beneficiaries 669–73
    possible future developments 682–5
    scope 651–2
    shared homes 680–2
    transactions with overreaching effect 662–9
  overriding interests 618–19
  proprietary estoppel
    central issues 359
    essential requirements 369–95
    extent of duties owed 395–410
    priority of rights 410–15
    prospect of detriment 386–9
    reliance on assurances 382–6
    role of unconscionability 389–95
  trusts
    acquisition of dependant rights 188–9
    contents 185–8
Equity
  functions 180–1
  relationship with common law 194–202
Equity release 1061
Escrows 295
Estate contracts
  effect 287–8
  overriding interests 618
Estate rentcharges 975
Estates in land *see* **Legal estates**
Estoppel *see* **Proprietary estoppel**
Eurohypothec 1061–2
Exchange of contracts 268–9
Executed contracts 271–2
Execution of deeds 293–5
Express rights
  easements 910–11
  Rochefoucauld v Boustead doctrine 440–1
  trusts of land 420–1
Extinguishment of title *see* **Limitations**

F

Fair trial (Art 6)
  central issues 87
  protection of due process 109
Fee simple estates *see* **Freeholds**
Financial services regulation
  ombudsman 1128–9
  principles and rules 1123–6
  regulated mortgage contracts 1121
  statutory framework 1121–3
Finders' rights 46–56

Fixtures and fittings
  chattels 38–46
  meaning and scope 38–46
Flats
  central issues 1008
  commonholds
    commonhold associations 1021–3
    community statement 1023–4
    creation 1019–20
    dispute resolution 1028
    legal structure 1018–19
    management 1025–6
    objectives 1018
    purity of title 1020–1
  conclusions 1038–9
  introduction 1009–11
  long leases
    changes of landlord 1012–13
    enforcement of covenants 1016–17
    enfranchisement and extensions 1013–14
    forfeiture 1017–18
    maintenance and repair 1014–16
    variations 1017
Forfeiture of leases
  effects 860–2
  flat owners 1017–18
  introduction 858–60
  peaceful re-entry 873
  proposed reform 880–2
  requirement for notice of breach 864–73
  statutory relief
    derivative interests 878–80
    rent 874–5
  waiver 862–4
Formalities
  contractual promises
    collateral contracts 272–5
    by correspondence 268
    effects of non-compliance 271–2
    exchange of contracts 268–9
    executed contracts 271–2
    legal and equitable rights and interests 263–6
    overview 262–3
    proprietary estoppel 277–84
    rectification 275–7
    signatures 269–71
    statutory provisions 263–6
  creation and transfer of legal rights
    deeds 293–5
  introduction 260–2
  leases
    basic requirements 786
    registration of long leases 786–7
    subleases 791
  overview 262–3
  trusts of land 420
Franchises 296

Fraud
  constructive trusts 437–8, 442–3
  enforcement of pre-existing property rights
    registered land 641–5
Freedom from discrimination (Art 14)
  bankruptcy applications 573
  central issues 87
  Convention text 111
Freehold covenants
  acquisition and priority of restrictive
    covenants 975–7
  annexation
    express 979–81
    once-and-for-all process 979
    statutory provisions 981–8
  assignment of benefits 978–9
  the benefit—persons entitled to sue 977–8
  building schemes 988–95
  the burden—persons entitled to sue
    benefit to dominant land 963–8
    equitable rules of enforcement 961–2
    requirement for negativity 968–71
  central issues 957
  extinction and modification
    no injury to dominant owner 1002–3
    obsolescence 1000
    obstruction of reasonable user 1001–2
    statutory provisions 999–1000
  indirect enforcement of positive covenants
    chain of indemnity covenants 975
    estate rentcharges 975
    mutual benefit and burden 971–4
  introduction 957–8
  reform proposals 1003–6
  remedies for breach
    damages 999
    defences 999
    general principles 995
    injunctions 995–8
  role 958–9
  terminology 959–60
Freeholds
  see also Freehold covenants
  adverse possession 313–14
  commonhold developments 1020–1
  impact of LRA 2002 698–700
  legal estates
    contents 163–5
  prescriptive rights 950
  registration of title
    events giving rise to first registration 296
    grades of title 297
    registrable title 296

G
Good leasehold title 297

H

Home reversion plans 1061
Home rights *see* **Shared homes**
Human rights
  applications by creditors involving
    co-owners 562–3, 571–3
  central issues 87
  extinction and modification of covenants 1002
  fair trial (Art 6)
    central issues 87
    protection of due process 109
  freedom from discrimination (Art 14)
    bankruptcy applications 573
    central issues 87
    Convention text 111
  history and development of ECHR 88–9
  horizontal effect
    direct and indirect horizontality 107–8
    direct statutory horizontality 107
    intermediate horizontality 108–11
    much-debated issue 106–7
    prevention of discrimination (Art 14) 111–13
    the problem of balancing rights 113
    public liability horizontality 107
    remedial and procedural horizontality 107
  impact on proprietary rights 150–2
  incorporation of ECHR
    compatibility 91
    justification formula for qualified
      rights 92–101
    statutory interpretation 90–2
  jurisdiction under HRA 1998 89
  justified interferences
    in accordance with the law 92–3
    judicial deference 98–101
    legitimate aims 93
    margins of appreciation 93–6
    proportionality 96–8
  mortgagee sales 1094–5
  mortgage repossessions 1090–1
  overreaching 683–5
  privacy (Art 8)
    contractual licences 239–40
    Convention text 127
    implications of respect 129–31
    justified interferences 131–50
    meaning of 'home' 127–9
    repossession 130–1
  protection of local authority tenants 809
  protection of property (ECHR Art 1)
    adverse possession 352–6
    controls over possession 118–20
    Convention text 113–14
    deprivations 118
    fundamental dilemma 114
    interference with possessions 115–18

    justified interferences 120–7
    peaceful enjoyment 120
  public authorities
    defences 104–5
    vertical effect 101–6, 102–4
  retrospective application 99, 107

I

Implied rights
  defence based on consent 596–602
  easements
    extinguishment 954–5
    intended easements 916–20
    necessity 913–16
    overview 911–14
    rule in *Wheeldon v Burrows* 920–4
    statutory provisions 924–35
Injunctions 214–18, 995–8
Insolvency
  applications for sale involving
    co-owners 549–51
  applications involving co-owners
    applications by creditors 553–62
    applications by trustees in
      bankruptcy 565–75
    policy considerations 551–3
  charging orders 1050–4
  severance of joint tenancies 517, 521
Inspection of land
  overriding interests 620–2
Insurance principle 66–7, 82
Intention *see* **Common intention
  constructive trusts**
Interest rates
  excessive rates 1165–8
  fluctuating and index-linked rates 1164–5
Investigation of title
  effect of overreaching 650
  impact of LRA 2000 69, 695
  Law Reform Committee 21st Report 312
  mortgagee sales 1107
Islamic mortgages 1059–60

J

Joint tenancies
  central issues 503
  desirability of the beneficial joint
    tenancy 530–1
  factors determining type of ownership 506–9
  severance
    common intention constructive trusts 525–6
    by joint tenant operating on his or her
      share 518–22
    limitations of current rules 526–8
    by mutual agreement 522–4

Joint tenancies (*cont.*)
    overview 510–11
    statutory provisions 511–17
    through course of dealings 524–5
    through unlawful killing 525
  survivorship 509–10
  tenancies in common distinguished 504–6
Judicial review 105–6

K

Knowing receipt 685–6

L

Land
  as form of private property 25–30
  meaning and scope
    fixtures and fittings 38–46
    physical reach 30–8
    things found on or in land 46–56
  special features
    limited availability 10–11
    multiple simultaneous uses 8–9
    permanence 7–8
    social importance 9
    uniqueness 8
Land charges
  charging orders 1051
  easements 952
  estate contracts 288
  freehold covenants 986–7, 1004
  occupation rights 253
  overreaching 652
Land law
  impact of human rights 150–2
  importance 2–3
  practical difficulties with occupiers and banks
    alternative approaches 13–14
    comparisons of the alternative
      approaches 19–20
    doctrinal model 14–17
    essential dilemma 11–13
    general lessons to be drawn 22–3
    later developments and lessons 21–2
    utility model 17–19
  role of registration of title 61–2
  scope
    core topics 5
    key themes 4–5
    overview 3–4
  underlying questions 6–7
Lands Tribunal
  extinction and modification of covenants
    no injury to dominant owner 1002–3
    obsolescence 1000

    obstruction of reasonable user 1001–2
    statutory provisions 999–1000
Leasehold covenants *see* **also Leases**
  central issues 832–3
  flat owners 1016–17
  introduction 833
  privity of contract and estate
    assignees—post-1995 847–51
    assignees—pre-1996 842–7
    continuing liability for breaches 851–2
    continuing right to enforce breaches 852–4
    original parties—post-1995 839–42
    original parties—pre-1996 836–9
    overview 834–6
    subleases 854–6
  remedies for breach
    damages 856–7
    distress 857–8
    forfeiture 858–82
    overview 856
    specific performance 857
  terminology 833–4
Leases *see* **also Leasehold covenants**
  acquisition of rights
    equitable leases 792–4
    legal leases 786–92
  adverse possession 357
  central issues
    key features 728–9
    statutory protection 806–7
  contractual aspects 801–4
  defences
    equitable leases 801
    legal leases 800
  effects
    overview 731
    between parties 732–6
    against the rest of the world 736–40
    third parties acquiring freehold 740
  exclusive possession
    exceptions 783–4
    general position 746–9
    limited term 764–83
    multiple occupancies 759–63
    proprietary rights 763–4
    shams and pretences 749–59
    summary 785
  executed contracts 271–2
  flats
    changes of landlord 1012–13
    enforcement of covenants 1016–17
    enfranchisement and extensions 1013–14
    forfeiture 1017–18
    maintenance and repair 1014–16
    variations 1017
  impact of LRA 2002 698–700

importance and diversity 729–31
intention
    to create legal relations 745–6
    to grant lease 741–5
landlord tenant relationship 740
legal estates 167
notices on the register 612
priority of rights and interests 637
registration of title
    events giving rise to first registration 296–7
    grades of title 297
    registrable title 296
status-conferring effects of lease
    impact on definition of lease 815–26
    practical considerations 811–15
    proposed reforms 826–30
statutory protection
    history and development 808–11
    introduction 807
termination
    effluxion of time 794–8
    exercise of powers before expiry of
      term 798–9
    surrenders 799–800
Legal estates
see also **Legal rights and interests**
acquisition formalities
    central issues 258
    introduction 260–2
    overview 262–3
acquisition of rights 169
central issues 154–5
contents
    freeholds 165–7
    leases 167
effect of s 1(4) of the LPA 1925 173–5
formal requirements for creation or transfer
    deeds 293–5
impact of LRA 2002
    acquisition of rights 698–700
    defences 700–1
limit on types 167–8
registrable titles 296
relevance of underlying concept 160–3
Legal rights and interests
see also **Legal estates**
acquisition formalities
    central issues 258
    introduction 260–2
    overview 262–3
dependent and independent acquisition
    175–6
formal requirements for creation or transfer
    contracts 263–6
    deeds 293–5
justifications for adverse possession 311–12

numerus clausus principle 170–3
relevance of underlying concept 169–70
Licences
bare licences
    licensee's rights against strangers 210–11
    meaning 209
    revocation by grantor 209–10
central issues 204
contractual licences
    licensee's rights against grantor 213–18
    licensee's rights against strangers 218–22
    licensee's rights against third
      parties 223–45
    meaning and scope 211–13
coupled with an interest
    licensee's rights against grantor 254–5
    licensee's rights against strangers 255–6
    licensee's rights against third parties 256
    meaning 253–4
estoppel licences
    licensee's rights against grantor 246–7
    licensee's rights against strangers 247
    licensee's rights against third
      parties 248–50
    meaning 245–6
leases distinguished 740
meaning and scope 207–9
statutory licences
    licensee's rights against grantor 251–2
    licensee's rights against strangers 252
    licensee's rights against third parties 252–3
    meaning 250–1
Liens 1038–9
Lifetime mortgages 1060
Limitations
adverse possession
    acknowledgement starts time again 330
    'adverse' defined 316–20
    key date 314–16
    registered land 334, 336–44
    underlying principles 313–14
    unregistered land 333
prescriptive rights 935–8
'Lock-out' agreements 266

M

Margins of appreciation
    domestic approach 98–101
    justified interferences with human rights 93–6
Matrimonial homes *see* **Shared homes;**
    Spousal rights
Mirror principle 66–7, 615
Misrepresentation
    conceptual underpinnings 1135
    mortgages 1132–3

Mistake
  Law Commission Consultation Paper 2016 711–12
  rectification and indemnity of title register 306
  three-party cases 703–8
  two-party cases 702
  void and voidable transactions
        distinguished 708–11
Mortgagees
  collateral advantages
    equitable controls 1161–3
    meaning and scope 1161
    restraint of trade 1163
  remedies
    central issues 1064
    introduction 1064–5
    possession 1071–91
    receivers 1108–13
    sale 1091–108
    sources of rights and remedies 1065–7
    statutory regulation 1067–70
Mortgages
  charges distinguished 1045–6
  collateral advantages
    equitable controls 1161–3
    meaning and scope 1161
    restraint of trade 1163
  control of terms
    sources of control 1150–6
    underlying principles 1149
  defined 1039–40
  equity of redemption
    history and development 1055–6
    legal charges 1056–9
  factors governing procedural fairness
    conceptual underpinnings 1135–6
    duress 1130–1
    misrepresentation 1132–3
    non est factum 1130
    overview 1129–30
    unconscionability 1133–5
    undue influence 1131–2
  history and development
    legal charges by way of mortgage 1043–6
    mortgages over land 1042–3
  interest rates
    excessive rates 1165–8
    fluctuating and index-linked rates 1164–5
    penalties 1168
  lender's remedies
    central issues 1064
    contractual issues 1114
    introduction 1064–5
    possession 1071–91
    receivers 1108–13
    sale 1091–108
    sources of rights and remedies 1065–7
    statutory regulation 1067–70

modern forms
  equity release and home reversion plans 1061
  Eurohypothec 1061–2
  Islamic mortgages 1059–60
  state assistance 1060
mortgagor protection
  central issues 1116
  control of terms 1149–56
  introduction 1116–17
  market regulation 1117–26
  procedural fairness 1129–35
overreaching 653
practical difficulties with occupiers and banks
  general lessons to be learnt 22–3
registration of title
  charges registers 307
  events giving rise to first registration 297
regulated mortgage contracts 1121
role and importance 1033–7
undue influence
  notice to lender 1145–6
  proof 1140–5
  role in shared homes 1136–40
  steps the lender should take 1146–8
Mortgagors
  central issues 1116
  introduction 1116–17
  market regulation
    consumer credit 1126–8
    financial services regulation 1120–6
    history and development 1117–20
  restrictions on redemption
    options to purchase 1157–8
    postponement of right to redeem 1158–60

N

Necessary easements 913–16
Non est factum 1130
Notice
  forfeiture of leases 864–73
  severance of joint tenancies 511–17
  statutory control of mortgage
        repossession 1078–9
Notices on the register
  equitable leases 801
  nature and effect 611–12
  persons entitled to apply 613–14
  role 611
  scope 612–13
Numerus clausus principle 170–3

O

'Occupation contracts' 827–30
Occupiers' rights
  see also Licences; Possession

beneficiaries
  applications for sale 551
  overreaching 669–73
overlap between the FLA 1996 and the TOLATA
      1996 545–8
overriding interests
  actual occupation 616–20
  assessing occupation 627–37
  children 625–6
  failure to disclose property right 622–5
  inspection of land 620–2
  proxy occupiers 626–7
  statutory provisions 616–17
  timing 627
practical difficulties with occupiers and
      banks 22–3
statutory provisions 494–5
Options
  contractual formalities 266–8
  protection of mortgagors 1157–8
'Ouster' principle 905–10
Overreaching
  breach of trust 674–80
  co-ownership
    central issues 648
    introduction 649
  effect 649–50
  interests capable of being overreached 652–61
  occupying beneficiaries 669–73
  possible future developments 682–5
  priority of rights and interests 594–5
  scope 651–2
  shared homes 680–2
  transactions with overreaching effect 662–9
Overriding interests
  easements and profits 637–8, 951–2
  importance of indemnities 722–3
  lack of registration defence 593–4
  leases 801
  nature and effect 615–16
  occupiers' rights
    actual occupation 616–20
    assessing occupation 627–37
    children 625–6
    failure to disclose property right 622–5
    inspection of land 620–2
    proxy occupiers 626–7
    statutory provisions 616–17
    timing 627
  right to seek rectification 719–22
  short leases 637
  underlying rationale 717–18

P
Personal rights
  see also Licences

legal rights distinguished 205–7
real property rights distinguished 155–60
Pledges 1038
Positive freehold covenants
  chain of indemnity covenants 975
  estate rentcharges 975
  mutual benefit and burden 971–4
Possession
  see also Adverse possession; Occupiers' rights
  impact of human rights 150–2
  justified interferences under Art 8 142–50
    private landlords 142–50
    repossession generally 131
    social housing 132–42
  leases
    exceptions 783–4
    general position 746–9
    licences distinguished 740
    limited term 764–83
    multiple occupancies 759–63
    proprietary rights 763–4
    shams and pretences 749–59
    summary 785
  limits to rectification
    where C in possession 712–15
    where C not in possession 715–16
  mortgagee's remedy
    court powers 1075–89
    duty to account 1072–3
    express terms 1067
    human rights 1090–1
    immediate right to possession 1071–2
    procedural safeguards 1074–5
    rationale 1073–4
    security provisions 1065
    statutory provisions 1066–7
  protection of property (ECHR Art 1)
    controls over possession 118–20
    Convention text 113–14
    deprivations 118
    fundamental dilemma 114
    interference with possessions 115–18
    peaceful enjoyment 120
Possessory title 297
Pre-contract negotiations 374–82
Pre-existing property rights
  see also Equitable rights and interests; Legal
      interests
  licensee's rights against third parties
    bare licences 211
    contractual licences 231–45
    estoppel licences 248–50
    licences coupled with an interest 256
    statutory licences 252–3
  priority 591
  registered land
    central issues 607

Pre-existing property rights (*cont.*)
  conclusions 645–6
  easements and profits 637–8
  effect of registered disposition 610–11
  fraud 641–5
  introduction 608
  notices on the register 611–15
  overriding interests 616–38
  restrictions on owner's powers 638–41
  short leases 637
  starting point to priorities 608–10
Prescriptive rights
  advantages and disadvantages 950–1
  basis of prescription 938–42
  history and development 935–8
  reform proposals 951
  user as of right 942–9
  users in fee simple 950
Priority of rights and interests
  basic rule 580–1
  central issues 578–9
  conclusions 421
  co-ownership
    see also **Overreaching**
    central issues 648
    introduction 649
    where overreaching does not occur 688–91
  defences based on consent
    express consent 596
    implied consent 596–602
  easements
    registered land 951–2
    unregistered land 952
  effect of contract 288–9
  exceptions to basic rule 591–2
  impact of LRA 2002
    acquisition of rights 698–700
    central issues 693
    concluding remarks 724–5
    content question 698
    defences 700–1
    overview 697
    registration gap 701
  introduction and overview 579–80
  lapse of time
    registered land 603–4
    unregistered land 602–3
  legal and equitable property rights
    distinguished 604
  licensee's rights against third parties
    bare licences 210–11
    contractual licences 214–18
    estoppel licences 248–50
    licences coupled with an interest 256
    statutory licences 252–3
  overreaching 594–5
    breach of trust 674–80

  effect 649–50
  interests capable of being
    overreached 652–61
  occupying beneficiaries 669–73
  possible future developments 682–5
  scope 651–2
  shared homes 680–2
  transactions with overreaching effect 662–9
period between completion and registration
    of title
  impact of e-conveyancing 305
  vulnerability 298–304
proprietary estoppel
  introduction 410–11
  position after court order 411
  position before court order 411–15
registered land
  basic defence 592–4
  conclusions 645–6
  easements and profits 637–8
  effect of registered disposition 610–11
  exceptions to basic defence 593–4
  fraud 641–5
  introduction 608
  lapse of time 603–4
  notices on the register 611–15
  overriding interests 616–38
  restrictions on owner's powers 638–41
  short leases 637
  starting point to priorities 608–10
registration of title under LRA 2002 76–9
restrictive covenants 975–7
role of registration of title 62–3
timing questions
  charges 582–91
  independent acquired rights 591
  overview 581
unregistered land
  lapse of time 602–3
Privacy (Art 8)
  applications by creditors involving
    co-owners 562–3, 571–3
  contractual licences 239–40
  Convention text 127
  early treatment of land as private
    property 25–30
  implications of respect 129–31
  justified interferences 131–50
  meaning of 'home' 127–9
  mortgagee sales 1094–5
  mortgage repossessions 1090–1
  overreaching 683–5
  protection of local authority tenants 809
  repossession 130–1
Privity of contract and estate
  freehold covenants
    the benefit—persons entitled to sue 977–8

benefit to dominant land 963–8
building schemes 988–95
the burden—persons entitled to sue 961–2
requirement for negativity 968–71
leasehold covenants
assignees—post-1995 847–51
assignees—pre-1996 842–7
continuing liability for breaches 851–2
continuing right to enforce breaches 852–4
original parties—post-1995 839–42
original parties—pre-1996 836–9
overview 834–6
subleases 854–6
Procuring a breach of contract 223–4
Profits à prendre
overriding interests 637–8
registrable title 296
Property
effects of lease 736–40, 785–6
impact of human rights 150–2
protection of property (ECHR Art 1)
adverse possession 352–6
controls over possession 118–20
Convention text 113–14
deprivations 118
interference with possessions 115–18
justified interferences 120–7
peaceful enjoyment 120
role of covenants 958–9
Property registers 306–7
Proportionality
general principles 96–8
horizontal effect 106–7
justified interferences under Art 8
procedural safeguards 136–41
vulnerability 141–2
Proprietary estoppel
central issues 359
essential requirements
assurances in relation to land 370–82
overview 369–70
prospect of detriment 386–9
reliance on assurances 382–6
estoppel licences
licensee's rights against grantor 246–7
licensee's rights against strangers 247
licensee's rights against third parties 248–50
meaning 245–6
extent of duties owed 395–410
failure to comply with contractual
formalities 277–84
interests capable of being overreached 658–61
introduction and overview 360–8
leases 793
pre-contract negotiations 374–82
priority of rights
introduction 410–11

position after court order 411
position before court order 411–15
role of unconscionability 389–95
Proprietorship registers 307
Protection of property (ECHR Art 1)
adverse possession 352–6
controls over possession 118–20
Convention text 113–14
deprivations 118
extinction and modification of covenants 1002
fundamental dilemma 114
interference with possessions 115–18
justified interferences 120–7
overreaching 684–5
peaceful enjoyment 120
Public authorities
defences 104–5
interface with judicial review 105–6
vertical effect 102–4
Public-sector housing
importance of land 5
repossession and justified interferences under
Art 8 132–42
statutory controls 810
Puisne mortgages 652
Purchase money resulting trusts
judicial exposition 423–5
presumption of advancement 425–6
rebuttal of presumption
general principles 426–7
illegal transfers 427–9
scope 429–34

Q

Qualified title 297

R

Real property rights
central issues 154–5
personal rights distinguished 155–60, 205–7
relevance of underlying concept 160–3
Receivers
agent of borrower 1109–10
duties 1111–13
express appointment 1067
functions and powers 1108–9
mortgage provisions 1066–7
statutory provisions 1066–7
Rectification
failure to comply with contractual
formalities 275–7
false thinking about property 28
right to seek rectification as overriding
interest 719–22
title register 306

Rectification (*cont.*)
    impact of LRA 2002 716–17
    limits to rectification 712–16
    limits where persons in occupation 74–6
    meaning of 'mistake' 702–12
    overriding interests 619
    scope 702
Redemption of mortgages
  history and development 1055–6
  legal charges 1056–9
  protection of mortgagors
    early redemption charges 1160
    intervention of equity 1150–1
    options to purchase 1157–8
    postponement of right to redeem 1158–60
Re-entry *see* **Forfeiture of leases**
Registered land
  see also **Registration of title**
  adverse possession
    LRA 1925 334–6
    LRA 2002 336–44
  basis of overreaching 656–8
  easements 951–2
  impact of LRA 2002
    acquisition of rights 698–700
    central issues 693
    concluding remarks 724–5
    content question 698
    defences 700–1
    overview 697
    registration gap 701
  Law Commission—aims and rhetoric
    Consultation Paper 2016 695–7
    Report 2001 694–5
  licensee's rights against third parties
    contractual licences 238
    estoppel licences 249–50
  overriding interests
    concluding remarks 724–5
    importance of indemnities 722–3
    right to seek rectification 719–22
    underlying rationale 717–18
  priority of rights and interests
    basic defence 592–4
    central issues 607
    conclusions 645–6
    easements and profits 637–8
    effect of registered disposition 610–11
    exceptions to basic defence 593–4
    fraud 641–5
    introduction 608
    lapse of time 603–4
    notices on the register 611–15
    overriding interests 616–38
    restrictions on owner's powers 638–41
    short leases 637
    starting point to priorities 608–10

proprietary estoppel 412
rectification of title
  impact of LRA 2002 716–17
  limits to rectification 712–16
  meaning of 'mistake' 702–12
  scope 702
unregistered land distinguished 59–60
Registration of title
  see also **Registered land**
  alternative approaches 64–6
  basic underlying principles 66–7
  central issues 58–9
  effect 306
  events giving rise to first registration 296–7
  general aims 60–1
  grades of title 297
  impact of e-conveyancing 304–6
  importance 295
  judicial interpretation of rules
    looking outside LRA 1925 79–81
    looking outside LRA 2002 81–2
    revolution or adaptation 83–4
  leases 786–7
  legal charges by way of mortgage 1044–5
  LRA 2002
    acquisition of title 70–6
    aims of scheme 67–70
    defence against pre-existing rights 76–9
  purchaser protection 62–3
  rectification of register 306
  registers and title number 306–7
  registrable estates and interests 295–6
  registrable titles 296
  registration of title under LRA 2002
    judicial interpretation of rules 79–84
  role in land law 61–2
  role of indemnity payments 65–6
  subsequent dealings 297–8
  types of title 297
  vulnerable period between completion and
    registration 298–304
Relativity of title
  adverse possession 313–14
  leases 821, 823–4
Relief from forfeiture
  derivative interests 878–80
  other covenants 875–8
  rent 874–5
Remedies
  breaches of contractual licence 214–18
  breach of freehold covenants
    damages 999
    defences 999
    general principles 995
    injunctions 995–8
  breach of leasehold covenants
    damages 856–7

distress 857–8
forfeiture 858–82
overview 856
specific performance 857
defective mortgagee sales 1105–8
failure to comply with contractual formalities
proprietary estoppel 277–84
rectification 275–7
mortgagees
central issues 1064
introduction 1064–5
possession 1071–91
receivers 1108–13
sale 1091–108
sources of rights and remedies 1065–7
statutory regulation 1067–70
specific performance
breaches of contractual licence 214–18
Rent
assignee's liability 844
forfeiture of leases
relief from forfeiture 874–5
requirement for notice of breach 865
intention to grant lease 741–2
requirement for legal leases 788
Rentcharges 296
Repairs
flat owners
commonhold associations 1025
long leases 1014–16
forfeiture of leases 875–8
leases
Bruton case 816–19, 823–4
status-conferring effects of lease 811–30
statutory provisions 809
Restraint of trade
collateral advantages 1163
sources of control 1150
Restrictions on the register
importance 638–9
nature and effect 639–41
persons who may apply 641
Restrictive covenants
acquisition and priority 975–7
assignment of benefits 978–9
the benefit—persons entitled to sue 977–8
the burden—persons who can be sued
benefit to dominant land 963–8
equitable rules of enforcement 961–2
requirement for negativity 968–71
central issues 957
effect of adverse possession 334
effect on leases
equitable leases 846–7
subleases 854–6
notices on the register 612

role 958–9
terminology 959–60
Resulting trusts
alternative approaches 421–3
purchase money resulting trusts
judicial exposition 423–5
presumption of advancement 425–6
rebuttal of presumption 426–9
scope 429–34
sole legal owners of shared homes 489–92
Rights *in rem* 155–60

S
Sale of land
applications involving co-owners
applications by creditors 553–62
applications by trustees in bankruptcy 565–75
introduction 549–51
policy considerations 551–3
mortgagee's remedy
court powers 1075–89
express terms 1067
mortgagee's duties 1095–108
security provisions 1065
statutory provisions 1066–7
trustees
basis of overreaching 656
overreaching and breaches of trust 674–80
transactions with overreaching effect 662–9
Securities
central issues 1032
charging orders 1050–4
equitable mortgages
acquisition of rights 1046–8
equitable charges 1049–50
equitable estates 1048–9
reform proposals 1050
equity of redemption
history and development 1055–6
legal charges 1056–9
general forms
charges 1040–1
liens 1038–9
mortgages 1039–40
pledges 1038
history and development
legal charges by way of mortgage 1043–6
mortgages 1042–3
introduction 1032–3
modern forms
equity release and home reversion plans 1061
Eurohypothec 1061–2
Islamic mortgages 1059–60
state assistance 1060
role and importance 1033–7

Servient tenements
essential characteristics 888
essential requirements
accommodation of dominant land 897–902
land separate from dominant
tenement 888–96
separate ownership from dominant
tenement 896–7
subject matter of grant 902–10
excessive user 953–4
prescriptive rights
basis of prescription 938–42
Severance of joint tenancies
common intention constructive trusts 525–6
by joint tenant operating on his or her
share 518–22
limitations of current rules 526–8
by mutual agreement 522–4
overview 510–11
statutory provisions 511–17
through course of dealings 524–5
through unlawful killing 525
Shared homes
acquisition of rights
central issues 454–5
introduction 455–7
trusts 457–94
applications for sale involving
co-owners 564–5
co-ownership
central issues 503
desirability of the beneficial joint
tenancy 530–1
factors determining type of ownership
506–9
introduction 503–4
joint tenancies and tenancies in common
distinguished 504–6
overlap between the FLA 1996 and the
TOLATA 1996 545–8
severance 510–28
survivorship 509–10
termination 529–30
trusts of land 531–48
meaning of 'home' under Art 8 127–9
occupation rights
statutory provisions 494–5
overreaching 680–2
practical difficulties with occupiers and banks
general lessons to be learnt 22–3
reform proposals 494–5
trusts
beneficial ownership under constructive
trusts 463–74
critique of common intention 492–4
joint legal owners 461–3
overview 457–61

sole legal owners 475–92
undue influence
notice to lender 1145–6
proof 1140–5
role in shared homes 1136–40
steps the lender should take 1146–8
Shared ownership 1060
Sharia compliant mortgages 1059–60
Signatures
contracts 269–71
deeds 293–5
leases 787
trusts of land 420
Specific performance
breaches of contractual licence 214–18
breach of leasehold covenants 857
Spousal rights
overlap between the FLA 1996 and the TOLATA
1996 545–8
practical difficulties with occupiers and
banks 22–3
statutory licences 251–2
Squatting
Best litigation
evaluation 351–2
outcome 349–51
effect of criminalization 346–9
overview 344–5
statutory provisions 345–6
Statutory interpretation
duty under HRA 1998 90–2
horizontal effect 106–7
Statutory licences
licensee's rights against grantor 251–2
licensee's rights against strangers 252
licensee's rights against third parties 252–3
meaning and scope 740–1
Subleases
formalities 791
legal charges by way of mortgage 1044
privity of contract and estate 854–6
relief from forfeiture 878–80
Subrogation 590–1
Surrender of leases 799–800

T
Tenancies in common
central issues 503
factors determining type of ownership 506–9
joint tenancies distinguished 504–6
Termination of leases
effluxion of time 794–8
exercise of powers before expiry of term 798–9
surrenders 799–800
Third party rights *see* **Priority of interests**
Time limits *see* **Limitations**

Title
    see also **Registration of title**
    investigation of title
        effect of overreaching 650
        impact of LRA 2000 69, 695
        Law Reform Committee 21st Report 312
        mortgagee sales 1107
    mortgagee sales 1093
Torts 223–4
Tracing 687–8
Transfer of legal rights and interests
    e-conveyancing
        formal requirements 304
        legal impact 304–6
        objectives 304
    formal requirements
        contracts 263–6
        deeds 293–5
        e-conveyancing 304
    registration of dealings 297–8
Trustees
    alternative causes of action against
        breach of trust 685
        knowing receipt and dishonest
            assistance 685–6
        tracing 687–8
    applications to court
        child welfare 543
        general principles 541–3
        impact of TOLATA 1996 543–5
        statutory provisions 540–1
    powers of sale
        basis of overreaching 656
        overreaching and breaches of trust 674–80
        transactions with overreaching effect 662–9
Trusts
    equitable rights and interests
        acquisition of dependant rights 188–9
        contents 185–8
    shared homes
        beneficial ownership under constructive
            trusts 463–74
        critique of common intention 492–4
        joint legal owners 461–3
        overview 457–61
        sole legal owners 475–92
    vendor-purchaser trusts 286–7
Trusts of land
    adverse possession of registered land 336
    applications for sale involving co-owners
        applications by creditors 553–62
        applications by trustees in
            bankruptcy 565–75
        impact of statutory changes 563–4
        introduction 549–51
        overlapping jurisdiction under FLA 1996 564–5
        policy considerations 551–3

basis of overreaching 653
central issues 417–18
common intention constructive trusts
    central issues 417
    home ownership 454–7
    joint tenancies 507, 509
    Pallant v Morgan constructive trust 447–8
    presumed resulting trusts
        distinguished 429–34
    severance issues 525–6
    sole legal owners 475–7
    type of constructive trust 436
constructive trusts
    contractual licensee's rights against third
        parties 229–31
    five principal types 436–7
    institutional and remedial versions
        distinguished 435–6
    judicial definitions 434–5
    Pallant v Morgan equity 443–8
    proprietary estoppel compared 277–84
    Rochefoucauld doctrine to prevent
        fraud 437–44
    search for rationalization 448
co-ownership
    beneficiaries' rights 535–9
    court applications relating to trustee
        functions 540–5
    dominant feature of the regulation of
        co-ownership 531–3
    statutory scope 533
    termination 529–30
    trustees' powers 533–5
express trusts 420–1
    Rochefoucauld v Boustead doctrine 440–1
introduction 418–20
notices on the register 612
overlap between the FLA 1996 and the TOLATA
    1996 545–8
resulting trusts
    alternative approaches 421–3
    purchase money resulting trusts 423–34

U
Unconscionability
    constructive trusts
        judicial definitions 434–5
        Pallant v Morgan equity 446–7
        Rochefoucauld v Boustead doctrine 442–3
    knowing receipt and dishonest
        assistance 685–6
    mortgages
        control of terms 1157–8
        factors governing procedural fairness
            1133–5
    proprietary estoppel 389–95

Unconscionability (*cont.*)
  unfair mortgage terms
    collateral advantages 1161–3
    interest rates 1164–8
    redemption of mortgages 1157
    sources of control 1150–6
Undue influence
  conceptual underpinnings 1135–6
  mortgages
    meaning and scope 1131–2
  protection of mortgagors
    notice to lender 1145–6
    proof 1140–5
    role in shared homes 1136–40
    steps the lender should take 1146–8

Unjust enrichment 442
Unregistered land
  adverse possession 333–4
  easements 952
  priority of rights and interests
    lapse of time 602–3
  registered land distinguished 59–60

V

Vendor-purchaser trusts 286–7

W

Waiver of forfeiture 862–4